# PUBLIC PAPERS OF THE PRESIDENTS
## OF THE
## UNITED STATES

Published by the
Office of the Federal Register
National Archives and Records Administration

For sale by the
Superintendent of Documents
U.S. Government Printing Office
Washington, DC 20402

# Foreword

During the first six months of 1992, my administration moved forward on many fronts to advance a domestic and foreign policy agenda that would prepare the country for the 21st century, and take advantage of the historic opportunity that our victory in the Cold War presented for sustained peace and prosperity.

In January, in my State of the Union address, I laid out an economic plan that would have stimulated the economy by providing help for home buyers, tax relief for families, and critical incentives for investment. We proposed a comprehensive health care reform proposal and a GI Bill for children to provide choice in education. We initiated a moratorium on additional federal regulation, which ultimately saved the taxpayers an estimated $20–$30 billion, and granted waivers to permit innovative state welfare projects that encourage self-sufficiency.

In June, the Nation reacted with shock and dismay to the riots in Los Angeles. We sought to repair the short term damage with emergency funds to rebuild homes and small businesses. We also confronted the long-term problems of the inner cities through our Job Training 2000 proposal, our enterprise zone initiative to attract investment in urban areas, and our Weed and Seed program to eliminate crime and create an environment of opportunity.

In April, I proposed the FREEDOM Support Act, a package of proposals designed to help develop freedom and free markets in Russia and the other newly independent states of the former Soviet Union. In June, I met with Boris Yeltsin at the White House for the first ever U.S.-Russia Summit. We agreed on far-reaching new strategic arms reductions to eliminate the world's most dangerous weapons—heavy ICBMs and all other multiple warhead ICBMs. We concluded economic agreements that open new avenues to trade and investment in Russia. And we signed the Washington Charter, a formal statement of our mutual future together as democratic partners.

I travelled to Brazil to attend the United Nations Conference on Environment and Development to sign the Framework Convention on Climate Change.

We continued to maintain close ties with our Latin American allies and met in San Antonio, Texas to continue our dialogue to end the scourge of drug trafficking.

Finally, I began this six month period with a trip to Asia and the Pacific. The United States is readjusting its policies in Asia to reflect the end of the Cold War and a transformed security environment. Our economic relations with the Pacific region remain a central concern. To address this new reality, I pushed to open new markets and highlight the opportunities available to American business in that part of the world.

*George Bush*

# *Preface*

This book contains the papers and speeches of the 41st President of the United States that were issued by the Office of the Press Secretary during the period January 1–July 31, 1992. The material has been compiled and published by the Office of the Federal Register, National Archives and Records Administration.

The material is presented in chronological order, and the dates shown in the headings are the dates of the documents or events. In instances when the release date differs from the date of the document itself, that fact is shown in the textnote. Every effort has been made to ensure accuracy: Remarks are checked against a tape recording, and signed documents are checked against the original. Textnotes and cross references have been provided by the editors for purposes of identification or clarity. Speeches were delivered in Washington, DC, unless indicated. The times noted are local times. All materials that are printed full-text in the book have been indexed in the subject and name indexes, and listed in the document categories list.

The Public Papers of the Presidents series was begun in 1957 in response to a recommendation of the National Historical Publications Commission. An extensive compilation of messages and papers of the Presidents covering the period 1789 to 1897 was assembled by James D. Richardson and published under congressional authority between 1896 and 1899. Since then, various private compilations have been issued, but there was no uniform publication comparable to the Congressional Record or the United States Supreme Court Reports. Many Presidential papers could be found only in the form of mimeographed White House releases or as reported in the press. The Commission therefore recommended the establishment of an official series in which Presidential writings, addresses, and remarks of a public nature could be made available.

The Commission's recommendation was incorporated in regulations of the Administrative Committee of the Federal Register, issued under section 6 of the Federal Register Act (44 U.S.C. 1506), which may be found in title 1, part 10, of the Code of Federal Regulations.

A companion publication to the Public Papers series, the Weekly Compilation of Presidential Documents, was begun in 1965 to provide a broader range of Presidential materials on a more timely basis to meet the needs of the contemporary reader. Beginning with the administration of Jimmy Carter, the Public Papers series expanded its coverage to include all material as printed in the Weekly Compilation. That coverage provides a listing of the President's daily schedule and meetings, when announced, and other items of general interest issued by the Office of the Press Secretary. Also included are lists of the President's nominations submitted to the Senate, materials released by the Office of the Press Secretary that are not printed full-text in the book, acts approved by the President, and proclamations and Executive orders. This information appears in the appendixes at the end of the book.

Volumes covering the administrations of Presidents Hoover, Truman, Eisenhower, Kennedy, Johnson, Nixon, Ford, Carter, and Reagan are also available.

The Public Papers of the Presidents publication program is under the direction of Gwen H. Estep. The Chief Editor of this book was Karen Howard Ashlin.

White House liaison was provided by Marlin Fitzwater, Assistant to the President and Press Secretary. The frontispiece and photographs used in the portfolio were supplied by the White House Photo Office. The typography and design of the book were developed by the Government Printing Office under the direction of Robert W. Houk, Public Printer.

Martha L. Girard
*Director of the Federal Register*

Don W. Wilson
*Archivist of the United States*

# Contents

# Cabinet

Secretary of State............................................. James Addison Baker III

Secretary of the Treasury.............................. Nicholas F. Brady

Secretary of Defense....................................... Richard B. Cheney

Attorney General............................................. William P. Barr

Secretary of the Interior................................ Manuel Lujan, Jr.

Secretary of Agriculture ............................... Edward R. Madigan

Secretary of Commerce................................... Robert Adam Mosbacher
Barbara Hackman Franklin
(sworn in March 23)

Secretary of Labor.......................................... Lynn M. Martin

Secretary of Health and Human Services ... Louis W. Sullivan

Secretary of Housing and Urban
Development.................................................. Jack Kemp

Secretary of Transportation .......................... Samuel Knox Skinner
Andrew H. Card, Jr.
(sworn in March 11)

Secretary of Energy........................................ James D. Watkins

Secretary of Education .................................. Lamar Alexander

Secretary of Veterans Affairs........................ Edward J. Derwinski

Director of the Office of Management
and Budget.................................................... Richard G. Darman

United States Trade Representative............. Carla Anderson Hills

Administration of George Bush

1992–93

# Exchange With Reporters in Sydney, Australia
*January 1, 1992*

*The President.* I wish all the people of Australia, too, a very happy New Year.

### Australia-U.S. Relations

*Q.* Mr. President, do you think you will be able to get some kind of concession on wheat? The Australians are upset about that.

*The President.* I don't think it's a question of concession. What we do is tell them our problems, and they are very frank with us. That's how you can tell a good friend; that's how you can tell an ally, when they lay it right out on the table. They have some difficulties with what we call the EEP. I understand those. I hope they understand that legislation was not aimed at Australia. But if they don't, they will by the time I get through.

*Q.* No change, then?

*The President.* So what we're going to do is talk to them openly, as friends do with each other, and move this relationship forward, although it's pretty far forward now. It's strong.

You all are too young, except for one or two gray heads around here, but I remember the Battle of the Coral Sea. I wasn't quite in it. I was almost 18; I think the following month I went into the service. But the emotion that Americans with the memory have is the same as Australians with the memory have.

There's a guy had an American flag up, out on the point, and there was a neat story about him in today's paper. So I called him up this morning. I did not detect any hangover from New Year's Eve—[*laughter*]—being a doctor, he is. And I asked him to come over to the hotel, which he'll do, Dr. Marsden. I don't know the man. But I can tell you, I think I speak for all Americans when I say how wonderful it was to see the Stars and Stripes flying along the shore as we were here to celebrate New Year's.

And I say that, I cite it only as one manifestation of a friendship that I know exists. You drive along the street and see these guys tearing out of the pubs, offering up a Foster's, and wishing you well—you know it's real. So, that's what I'm going to concentrate on today.

### Trade Issues

*Q.* Mr. President, will there be no concessions then, sir, on foreign subsidies?

*The President.* We're not talking concessions; we're talking about eliminating differences where possible.

*Q.* Can't the Japanese tell you the same things then, if you tell the Australians, though, it's not possible?

*The President.* We're in—wait until we get to Japan, and we'll talk about that.

*Q.* Isn't there a little irony in that, sir?

### New Year's Resolutions

*Q.* Did you make any New Year's resolutions?

*The President.* New Year's resolution? Always for peace; certainly this year, with Americans hurting, our economy sluggish, for prosperity at home. I think of the people that don't have it so good back there. But I also am confident that they will. I believe that with what we're going to be proposing, plus what this economy will do anyway, it's going to be all right. But while people are hurting like that, I mean, my first resolution has to be for the well-being of the American people.

*Q.* Any personal New Year's resolutions?

*The President.* Oh, yes.

*Q.* More jogging, more——

*The President.* Well, a little speedier. I'm not going to increase it. Two miles; I want to do it a little faster so the secret branch, the Secret Service here in Australia, will report into their bosses a little more proficiency. I'd like to catch a few more fish, and I don't get a chance to do it here although this is a sportsman's paradise. Keep up with sports. Our family does it; I believe in it.

I'll tell you something. You're from here; I think these people know it. We are blessed with family, with kids that come home, and with the loyalty and strength that one gets when one is in public life from sons and a daughter. And so, I don't have to ask for any more there. But if I were, I would simply say, "Keep it strong, Lord, because we're going into a hell of a year over there." It's politics; it's politics from tomorrow on. And it isn't very pleasant.

*Q.* Welcome to Australia.

*Q.* What about getting reelected? Is that one of your resolutions?

*The President.* I'm very confident about that because we've got a lot to do. But I'm confident of it, and I'm confident that if I do my job right the American people will support me.

*President's Schedule*

*Q.* Will you play golf with Bob Hawke?

*The President.* Well, I think that's unfortunately been wiped out. I've got my sticks, but I don't think I'm going to get a chance to play. He's an avid golfer, an avid sportsman, but I'm not sure it's on the schedule. I don't think we'll be able to do that because this is the holiday. We're taking a rather restful day here today; go down to Canberra and have some fun there. But then I think it's work, work, work. So I'll have to save it. But I was looking forward to getting a little of that Australian money.

Well, we'll see you guys.

*Note: The President spoke at 8:20 a.m. while jogging through Scots College in Sydney, Australia, where he arrived on December 31, 1991. In his remarks, he referred to the U.S. Department of Agriculture Export Enhancement Program (EEP) and Robert Hawke, former Prime Minister of Australia.*

# Remarks at the Australian National Maritime Museum in Sydney
*January 1, 1992*

Thank you, Mr. Prime Minister. Well, it is a pleasure for Barbara and me to be here, and I will speak to her afterward about her frankness here. [*Laughter*] I'm sure I can work it out. We've been married 47 years, and I haven't been able to work it out yet, but I will try. [*Laughter*]

Now, Prime Minister, to you and Anita, thank you for your hospitality. To the Premier, Nick Greiner, and Kathryn, thank you for yours, sir. To Minister Fatin, the Minister for Arts and Tourism in the Territories, we are grateful to you for your leadership in this field.

I want to salute our own Ambassador, Mel Sembler, who came up from Canberra here, and Betty, who are with us; thank chairman Peter Doyle for his comments. I have to tell you, though, you can tell he's an avid sportsman, and he loves fishing. And inside he said to me, "The only time I see pictures of you, you are fishing. You

must love fishing." Please don't repeat that for the people back in the United States. I think sometimes they think the only thing I like to do is go fishing. [*Laughter*] But nevertheless, I'm sorry we missed the opportunity on this particular trip. But I love it.

And may I salute Dr. Fewster, the director who is going to, I understand, show us around; say to your Ambassador to the United States how proud we are that he is with us, Ambassador Michael Cook and his wife, Catriona. They have many, many friends in the United States, and they are doing a first-class job for your country in the United States. And then, of course, I want to salute Dr. Hewson and his wife, Carolyn, who came up to be with us today, too.

I am really thrilled to take part in this dedication, a gift from the people of the United States to the people of Australia, the U.S.A. Gallery of the Australian National

Maritime Museum. President Reagan announced this gift in 1988 in honor of Australia's bicentennial. And now as we dedicate the new gallery, we mark another bicentennial, the Prime Minister referred to it, and that is the 200th anniversary of the arrival of the first foreign trading ship in Sydney, an American vessel named for the City of Brotherly Love in our country, *Philadelphia.*

Never was a ship more aptly named. Brotherhood has linked the Australian and American people now for two centuries. And if anybody at home, if anyone in the States doubt it, I just wish they could have been with me and with Barbara when we came in from the airport or when we rode across to the bridge over here or wherever we have gone in this short period of time. You can just feel it. And I hope that they can feel that it is reciprocated because it certainly is. Our common ancestors endowed us with language and culture, the rule of law, a spirit of enterprise, and a passion for freedom that we still share today.

Australians and Americans have been together for many a maritime adventure, in peace and, yes, in war; in commerce and in sporting competition. And visitors to this gallery may see historical displays of the three Americans who were among the crew of Captain Cook's *Endeavor* on its voyage to Australia in 1770. Visitors will get a unique glimpse into life aboard a 19th-century trading ship. Other displays commemorate the common courage Australian and American naval forces showed half a century ago in the fateful battles of World War II.

Fraternal ties of culture and commerce between our two nations literally have never, ever been stronger. And I am proud that the United States and Australia are committed to open and robust world trade, trade that creates jobs and lifts the standards of living in both our countries.

And in this spirit and in this anniversary year, I am very honored to have been asked to take part in opening the U.S.A. Gallery of Australia's National Maritime Museum. Thank you. May God bless you all, and may you have a wonderful New Year. Thank you very, very much.

*Note: The President spoke at 12:25 p.m. at the dedication ceremony for the U.S.A. Gallery of the Australian National Maritime Museum. In his remarks, he referred to Australian Prime Minister Paul J. Keating and his wife, Anita; Nick Greiner, Premier of New South Wales, and his wife, Kathryn; Peter Doyle and Kevin Fewster, chairman and director of the museum; and Liberal Party leader John Hewson, head of the Federal Opposition Coalition.*

# Remarks During a Luncheon Cruise in Sydney Harbor, Australia
*January 1, 1992*

Mr. Premier, thank you, sir. I prepared rather extensive remarks I'd hoped to give, but the Premier said we're making short remarks here at lunch. So, I tore up this. I will forego these, but simply to say that Barbara and I first want to thank everyone involved for this extraordinary hospitality.

There is no way that I can tell you what it feels like to travel with so little hostility on the street. And I'm starting right at home, you know. [*Laughter*] I'm a man that knows every hand gesture you've ever seen—[*laughter*]—and I haven't learned a new one since I've been here, so something is terribly wrong. [*Laughter*] Because we just feel a genuine warmth from the people along the way, right from the airport into town. And then this morning I went running, and early birds, those that were sober enough to get up, were out there waving away. And so, it has been a really heartwarming experience for us to be back.

I will note that this relationship is of fundamental importance to the United States. I also know that there's some apprehension in this part of the world—here, then north to the ASEAN countries, maybe even in Japan, possibly in Korea—about the United States role in the world. And I understand that because people look at the evolution of change in the Soviet Union; they see the freedom of the Baltic States; they see the interest that we all had, and thank God for Australia's early support, steadfast support, in the war against Iraq; they see us working very hard to bring parties together in this Middle East, people that have never even spoken to each other. And they're saying to themselves, "I wonder if the U.S. cares? I wonder if the United States really wants to remain involved?"

They see us working on a trade agreement with Mexico in which Canada would participate. And some in commerce in this part of the world are understandably saying, "Where are we going to fit in? Does this mean we're going to have one trading bloc in Europe and one trading bloc in America, and then somebody else look to some different kind of trading bloc in Asia and Australia?" And the answer to that is no. And the only thing I want to say here, having been denied my full speech which would have taken 45 minutes, is—[*laughter*]—that we will be involved. We're going to stay totally involved in this part of the world.

That's the first point. And the second

point is, we know friends when we see them. And the longer I am in this job, the more important true friends are. And we have a couple of differences, and we'll talk about those in Canberra. We talked about them here today privately. But the differences are so overwhelmed by the common purpose and the genuine friendship that they're not even registering on the radar screen.

So, we are blessed. We Americans are blessed by having this long and tremendously important relationship with this wonderful country in which you all live. And we're grateful to you. We won't let you down. And we will stay involved right up until the very end of eternity because we know it's fundamentally in our own interests. And we hope like hell it's in yours.

But I just want to wish each and every one of you a wonderful new year. And yes, sir, Mr. Premier, you have started the year off in a glorious and grand way not just for the Bushes but for all of those Americans that are privileged to be with us here today. Thank you for your hospitality. And may God bless Australia. Thank you.

*Note: The President spoke at 2:16 p.m. aboard the "John Cadman III" in Sydney Harbor. In his remarks, he referred to Nick Greiner, Premier of New South Wales.*

## Remarks to the Australian Parliament in Canberra
*January 2, 1992*

Thank you, Mr. Speaker and Mr. President, Mr. Prime Minister, and the leader of the opposition, Mr. Leader, Members, and Senators. It is a deep and wonderful honor for me to be here, and I am very, very grateful for the honor of appearing before this House of the Australian Parliament. I know that the Members have gone to extraordinary lengths to arrange this special session. And I think the people in our country will appreciate this very, very much.

I want to offer special greetings and thanks to the members of the Australian-U.S.A. parliamentary group who have done

so much to deepen the friendship between our countries.

Let me just make an initial observation if I might. You have a wonderfully vigorous political climate. [*Laughter*] That has got to be the classic understatement of the year. [*Laughter*] And I see this rough and tumble that goes forth like this, and I thank God for the Presidential system at home. But nevertheless—[*laughter*]. Let me make this observation, though. I feel very fortunate to have known several of your Members from both sides of the aisle over the years. And amidst all the intensity and emotion brought forth in these Chambers, I've always been impressed by the united message that your leaders have sent to my country. Even when out of office or in the opposition, they have always placed Australia's interests ahead of personal interests. That says something very positive, very important about your great country.

That's certainly one reason that any visitor from the United States cannot help but feel a warm kinship with Australia. Both of our young nations were seen by explorers and pioneers and immigrants as destinations of freedom and opportunity. Our cultures reflect an extraordinary diversity, from British and Irish, to Italian and Polish, to Vietnamese and Cambodian.

This Parliament building displays an original copy of the Magna Carta, I'm told, one of only four such manuscripts to have survived to this day. The U.S. National Archives is home to another of those original manuscripts. I can think of no more powerful symbol of our shared commitments to the rights of the individual, to the rule of law, and to the government of consent, by consent of the people.

With our common ancestries and shared ideals, Americans and Australians also find other similarities. Each of our countries spans a continent rich in agricultural and mineral resources. Spectacular natural beauty abounds in fantastic variety in both our nations as well. To be frank, our people think big. And their biggest ideas are the ones we share: The belief in the indivisibility of human freedom and the willingness to struggle and sacrifice for the peace and security of other nations.

This year marks the 50th anniversary of the fateful Battle of the Coral Sea. We remember the courage and fighting skill of the Australian and American naval forces. Their valor spared Australia from invasion and stemmed the tide of totalitarianism.

In Korea and Vietnam, Australians and Americans again joined forces. Their sacrifices were not in vain. Korea is a democracy, setting a standard for free market development worldwide. Long-suffering Cambodia now has the hope of a durable peace and free elections. Even Vietnam is opening to the world, seeking reintegration with the dynamic market economies of the region.

In the Persian Gulf, we stood together against Saddam Hussein's aggression. Indeed, the first two coalition partners in a joint boarding exercise to enforce the United Nations resolutions were Australians from the H.M.A.S. *Darwin* and Americans from the U.S.S. *Brewerton*. During the war, the joint defense facilities here in Australia played an invaluable role in detecting launches of Iraqi Scud missiles. And today, two of the three navies represented in operations enforcing the embargo against Iraq are those of Australia and of the United States of America.

But even as we recall our struggles and successes, we must now look forward to the opportunity to shape our shared destiny.

First, we face together the challenge of economic opportunity and growth, creating jobs for our people and for their families. Second, we face new but no less exacting challenges to our security, the threats of regional conflicts and proliferation of the weapons of mass destruction. Third, we face the exciting task of fostering the remarkable momentum for democracy and freedom that swept the world these past few years. A strong America has been central to the triumph of free markets and free people. I am confident that the United States will continue to have the conviction and the capacity to be a force for good and that a new era of economic opportunity will unfold with enhanced opportunities for peace.

The coming era promises unparalleled potential for economic growth in the nations of the Pacific. In 1990, the Asia-Pacific region accounted for a total of $300 billion in two-way commerce with the United States, a total nearly one-third larger than America's volume of trade across the Atlantic. This region is the fastest growing market in the world. And still, there are voices on both sides of the Pacific calling for economic isolationism. And while for some nations, including Australia and the United States, these are tough, hard economic times, we both know protectionism is a fundamentally bankrupt notion. Make no mistake, America will continue to stand for open trade and open markets.

And trade means jobs; it means good jobs,

at home and abroad. And I'm sure it comes as no surprise that my highest priority as President of the United States is to promote economic growth and jobs for our people. That goal is fully consistent with economic growth and jobs for Australians. You and I know that open markets generate growth, that international trade is not simply a zero-sum game.

And you also know that the nations who share the rewards of a vibrant and growing international trading system must also share the responsibilities. Australia has stood as a true leader in efforts to achieve success in the Uruguay round of the GATT negotiations. And you brought great skill and energy in seeking deep cuts in trade-distorting agricultural subsidies. Progress on agriculture is the key to the success of the GATT talks. Your farmers are not alone in feeling the pain caused by the heavy subsidies of the European Community. Our wheat production dropped by almost 30 percent last year. But I'm also aware of the concern such United States trade programs as this Export Enhancement Program can cause Australian farmers.

Our EEP program has one and only one objective, and that is to force the EC to stop its avalanche of subsidized exports. And the fact is that the EC subsidizes over 10 times the amount of farm exports that we do. Moreover, our program seeks to minimize the effects on Australia and other nonsubsidizing nations. While I don't like having to use these remedies, I will safeguard the interests of American farmers. And without EEP, the European Community would absorb additional markets, forcing out those who can compete fairly, farmers in countries like Australia and the United States.

We both know, all of us know, that the real answer is what our two governments are doing, working hard for an historic new GATT arrangement that cuts back subsidies, especially for exports. That's why the U.S. is committed to working with GATT Director Dunkel's new text. We believe his draft moves us closer to finally concluding an agreement. While not perfect, it makes an important contribution, and the international trading system is too important to pass up this opportunity. I trust and hope

that Australia and other Pacific nations will join us to instill additional momentum in the Uruguay round negotiations when they resume later this month. This is the best comprehensive approach that we can offer to our hard-working farmers and ranchers.

We also see the potential for using regional organizations to expand and liberalize trade around the globe. We are especially encouraged by Australia's leadership in the APEC, in the Asia-Pacific Economic Cooperation process. The success of the November APEC ministerial in Seoul was proof that APEC is emerging as the economic forum in the Pacific and is increasingly fostering a sense of community around the Pacific Rim. North America—Mexico, the United States, and Canada—is part of this community. And so, let me just assure you, every one of you, both sides of this aisle, that the North America free trade agreement will not become an exclusive trading bloc. It will lower internal barriers without raising external barriers. Our growth will help stimulate yours, just as growth in Asia will spur our exports.

We also can do more bilaterally to expand trade. That's why I am proposing a United States-Australia trade and investment framework agreement, one way to enhance our already strong economic engagement. That's our agenda to expand exports and growth through reducing trade barriers, whether globally, regionally, or bilaterally.

Clearly, with the dramatic changes in the world we must adapt to new security realities as well. But let me simply pledge to you, our friends: No matter what changes may come about in the defense expenditures in the United States or in the nature of the threats to international peace, the U.S.-Australian alliance is fundamental to the stability of the Asia-Pacific region.

I understand that there is some concern in Asia about America's commitment given our imminent departure from Subic Bay in the Philippines. Let me put it plainly: I've served in Asia, personally, in time of war and in time of peace, and with changing times, our posture is going to change to suit different needs. But our role and our purpose as a Pacific power will remain constant. It is important that the people of Australia understand this. We intend to remain engaged no matter whatever the changing security arrangements of our time.

And yes, we've talked about it here today with the Prime Minister, with the leader of the opposition, with others. The cold war is over. But the threat of communism which for so many decades occupied our energies is now replaced by the instabilities of ethnic rivalries and regional conflicts. And yes, the Soviet Union, as we have known it, is history. It's a new era. But like Australia, the United States has fought three wars in Asia over the past 50 years. We know that our security is inextricably linked to stability across the Pacific, and we will not put that security and stability at risk. I can assure you that the United States intends to retain the appropriate military presence to protect its allies and to counter threats to peace.

Just recently in the Persian Gulf we witnessed that the dangerous combination of volatile regional conflicts and weapons of mass destruction requires our constant attention. And so, I salute Australia's leadership in stemming the threat of chemical, biological, and nuclear weapons. It's your children and the children of the entire world who will grow up in a safer world thanks to such efforts.

Australia and the United States are also working to end another long-standing and tragic regional conflict. Our combined initiatives in the United Nations have been major factors in the progress toward peace and free elections in Cambodia. Both of us have now reestablished official representation in Phnom Penh in order to move the peace process forward. Australia is making an additional contribution by sending a senior military officer to head the U.N. peacekeeping force in Cambodia. And I am proud of our collective efforts to end the nightmare in Cambodia and usher in a new era of hope and rebuilding.

And finally, American and Australian aspirations for the future are evident in our increasing cooperation on such matters as environmental protection, educational, and social issues. We can take pride in our Governments' joint actions toward conservation of the tropical forests, protecting endangered species, and promoting technologies for clean-burning coal.

Australia also plays a leading role in the international fight against illicit drugs. And I know I speak for millions of American parents in expressing thanks for your efforts to fight drug abuse, to fight drug trafficking.

I believe the next generations of Australians and Americans will grow even closer. I see no threat to that at all. And I foresee a steady expansion of travel and cultural exchanges in years to come. Australia's natural beauty, of which I've seen regrettably little this trip, is really sensational, a powerful magnet for American tourists. But more than this, it is the spirit of your country that earns Australia so much admiration in our country, in America, and indeed around the world. Your artists' contributions to film and dance and music have whetted our appetites for more and more things Australian. U.S. television carries Australian-rules football, and many Americans enjoy the rough and tumble of hard hitting with reckless abandon. We have something similar; we call it politics in the United States. [*Laughter*]

But I credit the clear air of Australia for its effect on one of the freshest minds now working in Washington. I'm speaking about our Secretary of Education, Lamar Alexander. In 1987, after completing 8 years as Governor of Tennessee, Lamar took his wife and children to spend half a year in this beautiful country. And now that he's joined my Cabinet as Secretary of Education, Lamar Alexander is working for revolutionary changes to improve our schools.

And this, too, is part of our program to make America competitive and strong and to help it grow. Secretary Alexander is promoting innovative ideas that he saw in practice right here in Australia, for instance the large measure of freedom that Australians have in choosing among private and religious or state-operated schools. And when we succeed with some of these reforms, we'll thank pathfinders such as Australians for their example.

Of course, we've always shared fraternal ties and a spirit of freedom ever since an American vessel named *Philadelphia* became the first trading ship to call at Sydney's Port Jackson in 1792. Almost a century later, Mark Twain visited Australia and spoke for all Americans when he said, "You have a spirit of independence here which cannot be overpraised."

And 50 years ago in the Coral Sea, Australians and Americans paid a high price for freedom, but they proved to the world that the future belongs to the brave and the bold. For the half century since, we have deepened our friendship, our economic interdependence, and our collaboration on mutual defense. And now, more clearly than ever, we can see a hopeful future for the farflung kinsmen of Australia and America and for all who share those fundamental ideals that we hold dear. We're prepared to work as partners in the next century to break new ground for freedom, cooperation, and economic progress.

For me, this has been a great honor. For Barbara and me, it has been a sheer pleasure to be with you all here for these short 2½ days. But this hospitality of the Australian people is indescribable. I couldn't possibly tell you how emotional I feel about it. So, let me simply say thank you again for the extraordinary honor of allowing me to address this distinguished Parliament. May your debates be lively and full of friendship and affection, as they once in a while are. And may God bless you all. And may the Lord smile on the kinship and friendship of Australia and the United States of America. Thank you very, very much.

*Note: The President spoke at 1:45 p.m. at Parliament House.*

# Remarks Announcing Funding for the Australian Center for American Studies in Canberra
*January 2, 1992*

Thank you, sir, for those kind words. And let me just say how pleased I am to be here helping to launch this Australian Center for American Studies. We share a lot in common. You touched on that, sir, culturally, historically, even linguistically. But differences do exist. And we can and should do much more to foster greater understanding.

There's much that we can learn from each other, education and the sciences, certainly in trade, economics. Study and exchange in these areas will not only benefit our two nations but enrich the lives of those involved and increase the productive capacities of the participants in our two countries' economies.

Mutual understanding is not only enriching but also is a vital prerequisite to peace and prosperity. The Fulbright program has brought about the exchange of thousands of Australians and Americans. And among the many distinguished alumni of that program are my host in Sydney yesterday, Nick Greiner, and U.S. Ambassador, our U.N. Ambassador, Tom Pickering, who received

his master's degree from Melborne University.

The benefits of educational interchange come in many, many ways. The late Gordon Samstag, an American artist who taught at the South Australia School of Fine Arts, endowed that school with a scholarship fund of $6 million to support Australian students studying abroad. And in 1988, former Prime Minister Bob Hawke helped to launch this Center for Australian Studies at the U.T., at the University of Texas at Austin, contributing $50,000 Australian dollars to the Center.

Today I'm pleased to announce that the U.S. Information Agency is similarly contributing $50,000 to the Australian Center for American Studies. I hope this center will lead to an expansion of American studies in Australia. More broadly, I have spoken today about our intention to host an education ministerial under APEC auspices. And our Secretary of Education will invite APEC education ministers to Washington next summer. And I'm very enthusiastic about this addition to APEC's agenda. It seems only right that it not all be about politics and war and peace. We're talking here about an educational agenda.

The challenge the future holds is to find new ways to increase mutual understanding. And I am confident that the Australian Center will open many new paths for Americans and Australians to deepen these ties, deepen our ties and help ensure prosperity for our citizens.

So, this is a good day, a happy day. And I know I speak for Barbara when I say that we are both proud to have a part in it.

And to those Australians here, let me just tell you what I told our joint meeting in

here. We've really had a good time here. And your hospitality has been absolutely fantastic. And I think it says something about how this center can prosper. People just get that feeling of mutual camaraderie, et cetera. That in itself, I think, will help in these troubled times.

So, thank you all very much for being a part of this.

*Note: The President spoke at 2:20 p.m. in Mural Hall at Parliament House. In his remarks, he referred to Nick Greiner, Premier of New South Wales.*

# The President's News Conference With Prime Minister Paul J. Keating of Australia in Canberra
*January 2, 1992*

*The Prime Minister.* Good day. Thank you for coming. And just before I invite the President to say a few words, just to outline, first of all, the structure of the press conference so we can operate smoothly, our program will be to take, first of all, some general remarks from the President first and then from me and then permit time for about seven or eight questions. And I hope we'll be able to take a roughly even amount from both the Australian and visiting press. I presume you are delineated here somewhere and that we can point to you.

In the interest of maintaining order, I'll nominate the questioner, who should state their name and organization that they represent before directing the question to either myself or to the President.

Could I now invite the President just to make some introductory remarks, and then I'll follow him.

*The President.* My remarks, Mr. Prime Minister, will be very brief. And I simply want to, once again, thank you, thank all of our official hosts, and thank the people of Australia for the warmth of the reception on this visit. We've enjoyed it. It's been a busy time. I hope that we've made progress on the issues where we may have differences. I should say "issue" because I think

there's only one area of difficulty, and we've talked about that very frankly with you, sir, with the opposition, with agricultural leaders. And I feel it's been very fruitful in terms of the U.S. on all of this.

But otherwise, I would simply say to you we're very pleased to be here, and thank you for your hospitality. And I'll be glad to take my share of the questions.

*The Prime Minister.* Mr. President, I thank you for those remarks and say what an honor it has been for me to represent the Government and people of Australia in welcoming you and Mrs. Bush to Australia and having you here. You've had a warm reception from the Australian public, which I think has been evident to everybody, and we've been most, most pleased about that.

And it is true, we've had broad discussions which I think have increased the bonds of friendship between our two countries and certainly given me as Prime Minister a chance, an opportunity to get to know the President and his views and to also make a couple of important, what we think are important points to him. And that was the importance that Australia places on having the United States engaged in a political and economic framework in the Asia-Pacific and the importance of having won the cold war, setting up an institutional framework of a Breton Woods style but in trade.

And we see this best being accommodated with the GATT, a successful conclusion of the GATT round, as a framework for the reentry of countries reentering the world economy for the first time in either half a century or most of a century.

So, on those very broad fronts we've had extensive discussions, as the President said. On the other issues, we've dealt with them in a working-like way. And he has very kindly met our farm representatives, and I think we have a reasonable understanding of our positions on those issues.

So, could I now invite questions.

### U.S. Export Enhancement Program

*Q.* My question is in relation to the EEP. I understand, following your discussions with the farmers, you've agreed to have some sort of consultative process operate in the future before decisions are made. How exactly do you envisage that consultative mechanism will work? And do you envisage that it will have the effect in future of stopping the areas that have in the past affected Australia?

*The President.* Well, we discussed having some consultative arrangement, and I suggested it would be very useful to the farm leaders if they'd come—they've been to the States, I think, several of them—they come again and consult on this EEP.

There were some factual differences presented at the meeting by our expert and by them. And so, I think we ought to just try to eliminate differences where possible. And I made very clear to them, and I'd like to say it once more, that the EEP legislation was not aimed at Australia. It was aimed to try to get the EC, who are subsidizing 10 times as much as the United States, to come into line and to get on board on a sound GATT agreement.

So, we'll see how that works out. But we didn't set up any procedures in any exact, you know, three-point program for eliminating differences that we might have. The answer, though, that they do agree with me on, and I'm sure the Prime Minister does, is to get a successful conclusion of the GATT round. And I told them that we are pledged

to that end. And I know they've tried. These farm leaders have traveled to Europe, and they've been to England and, I believe, France and Germany. And so, they are fully engaged, private sector.

I think now it's important, given the Dunkel report, that I as President and the Prime Minister as Prime Minister engage to the fullest to try to get the one answer to EEP that's going to make the most sense. And that is a successful conclusion to the GATT round on agriculture.

### Japan-U.S. Trade

*Q.* Mr. President, last weekend your Commerce Secretary, Bob Mosbacher, said that Japan was partly responsible for the recession in the United States. Was he reflecting official policy in saying that?

*The President.* Well, Mr. Mosbacher always reflects official views except when I disagree with him. [*Laughter*] And that is very, very seldom. And on this one I haven't heard his statement, so I would only want to see it in full context.

But look, we've got a tremendous imbalance with Japan, tremendous. And one of the reasons we're going there is to see if we can't find ways to sort that matter out. But we're enjoying sluggish times, and not enjoying them very much. And the Prime Minister has impressed on me that Australia is having difficult economic times. And the answer to all of this, whether it's in Japan-U.S. or Australia-U.S., is to get these economies going through expanded trade.

And so, I'd want to know in context what Bob said, but anytime you have an extraordinarily big trade imbalance, I think you would say that that would be contributing to a lack of economic growth. And so, if that's what he said, I certainly couldn't find a way to differ with him.

*Q.* Could I cheat a little and ask a very closely related double-hitter?

*The President.* Sure.

### Multilateral Trade Negotiations

*Q.* Mr. Bush, are you able to give a commitment, irrespective of what might happen in other sectors of the Uruguay round, the United States Government will accept nothing less in agricultural trade than has been proposed by Arthur Dunkel? And I was wondering if I could ask you, Mr. Keating, your report of how satisfied you are with Mr. Bush's response both to our EEP submissions and to our concerns that NAFTA could, under some circumstances, develop into an inward-looking trading bloc.

*The President.* Let me answer. We see some very positive elements in the Dunkel paper. I can't say—we certainly don't want to accept less, if that was your question, and there's some things there that we would like to see improved. But I do think that there's a lot of good work being done there. And we will be working closely with the Europeans to try to get agreement. And I'd leave it right there because I don't want to indicate that we think that we've gotten everything that the United States wants, nor do we think that the Cairns group has gotten everything the Cairns group wants out of the Dunkel paper. All we're saying is it's a good position from which to finalize the agricultural part of trade and the rest of it, too. We've got some difficulties with some parts. Agriculture, we see, has moved fairly well.

*The Prime Minister.* Could I add to that? I think that the thing which is most comforting to Australia—I think in answering the question, I'll make three points: The first is, it's a matter of great comfort to us that we have an internationalist as President of the United States, someone who has committed himself to an open trading system, multilateral trading system, that resisted protectionist pressures and is committed to seeing the GATT round successfully concluded. And as the President has said, there are elements of the GATT round that can't be—it's a package. Some parts all countries would be more satisfied with than others, but it is a package, and it's a package about round which we believe discussions can take place.

If there is a successful conclusion of the GATT round, many other things will change, and including in that would be, of course, mandatory windbacks under EEP which you asked me about. And the President has agreed this morning that we will have an information exchange on EEP; that is, at least we will know more about the

operation of EEP. And as well as that, we've asked him that where the U.S. is not engaged in sales in markets where the European Commission is engaged in sales, that is, in non-EC markets, would he examine those markets with a view to keeping the subsidization of EEP from them. He can't, obviously, at this point, give a clear commitment on the markets, but he has agreed to look and examine them. And we're very happy about that.

So on the general point, we believe the GATT offers the best opportunity on trade generally, that the Dunkel package is just that, a package, and if adopted would lead to significant improvements in the trade and agriculture, and including the impact on EEP.

*Q.* Mr. Bush, what do you see as the consequences if Europe does not buy into Dunkel's proposal?

*The President.* I see that it would be very, very bad if we don't get a successful conclusion to the GATT round. And we have not discussed here in Australia fallback positions. We are not prepared to give up on the successful conclusion of the GATT round. But without trying to predict disaster, I can simply say I think it would be a very bad thing because I think you'd see more protection, more selfishness in the trading system that would inevitably shrink markets and cost countries jobs. And so, we must go forward, and we must try to get a successful conclusion.

I feel more strongly about that since I've had the benefit of several long conversations with this Prime Minister. He's very knowledgeable on these international financial matters and also with the agricultural sector in this country. I really had my—I'm more highly attuned even than I was to the importance of getting this done. So, I don't want to worst-case it, but I can just say that it would be totally unsatisfactory to see that GATT round fail to come to a satisfactory conclusion.

*Trading Blocs*

*Q.* Any possibility, sir, of three world trading blocs, as the Prime Minister has discussed?

*The President.* Well, we don't want any

trading blocs that do not include Australia. And I went out of my way to say that as we're negotiating for a free trade agreement with Mexico and Canada, for example, I want our Australian friends to know that that would not be detrimental to our free trade with them.

And one of the things the Prime Minister and I discussed, and I'll clearly defer to him on this, is the fact that we don't want to see Asia and Australia kind of pushed aside into some separate bloc. So, you might have a European trading bloc; an American trading bloc, North, South, and Caribbean; and an Asian bloc. That is not the way you get more jobs. The way you do that is to have broad expanded trade between them. So, I don't want to predict and suggest that this would be an outcome, but it would be an outcome that we certainly would not find satisfactory.

*Cambodian Peace Plan*

*Q.* The United Nations appears to be dragging its feet a little bit on the Cambodian peace plan. There's no concrete plan in place, no budget being put forward. Have you been asked or do you intend to urge in the United Nations that more speed be taken on these matters? Certainly, Mr. Hun Sen, the Prime Minister of Cambodia, is extremely concerned about this matter.

*The President.* Well, I wasn't asked to accelerate anything on this visit. I was told by the Australian leadership of the importance of this. We feel that way. Secretary Baker, as you know, has been involved in it, and we strongly support this concept of the U.N. acting in this peacekeeping role. But I wasn't asked to take on a specific assignment in that regard. But it is important, with agreement having come this far, that it be followed up on now, that it not be allowed to fall apart.

*Domestic Politics and Trade Policy*

*Q.* Mr. President, Democratic leaders in Congress last week said the success or failure of your trade mission will depend on whether you obtain any major concessions from Japan. Do you agree, and at this point are you at all hopeful that you will be able to obtain any major concessions?

*The President.* Well, in the first place, I don't take much stock in what the Democratic leaders in the Congress say, setting up goals for a trip or knocking them down. I'm just not inclined to run the foreign policy of the United States in that regard. It's been happening for 3 years, and they're entitled to their opinion. But it won't influence how I conduct myself on this trip, and I certainly am not going to accept their standards for success or failure of a mission.

Having said all that, I want to see us get more jobs created in the United States eventually by concessions made or by positions taken in Japan. I think it is very important. And we need more access to their markets. We need to have more content in autos that are made in the United States, have U.S. content there, have a fair shot at it. But I don't think that I should let the agenda be set by some political challenge in an election year. That is not the way one conducts sound foreign policy.

I saw all kinds of crazy, "Well, if he doesn't get this or that, we're going to throw in the legislation." We know political posturing when we see it. And I know what's good policy. And it is to stay involved internationally, and it is to create more jobs at home, not by trying to protect and pull back into some isolationistic sphere but by expanding markets. And that is what this trip is about.

*Q.* Mr. President, if the Japanese are offered concessions that they consider inadequate, are you prepared——

*The President.* It's too hypothetical a question; let me just cut it off right there. I cannot go into hypothetical—we haven't even gotten to Japan yet. We're still in Australia, remember?

*The Economy*

*Q.* Mr. President, you referred earlier to the sluggishness of the U.S. economy. Do you feel the recent cut in discount rate to 3.5 percent is sufficient to stimulate your economy? And if you think extra measures are needed, when would you expect to announce these?

*The President.* No question that it will have a stimulatory effect. It takes a while for that to get through something as complex as the U.S. economy, but it has been very, very well received at home.

And I think that it is well-known at home that I plan additional stimulatory measures to be announced in the State of the Union Message which comes at the end of this month. And they will not be counterproductive; they will not be on-the-cheap politically, something that has a nice political ring to it but then would be counterproductive in terms of interest rates. But I do think that the U.S. economy could use a sound fiscal stimulation, and I will be proposing that kind of a program in our State of the Union Message.

But yes, this was very, very important.

*Free and Fair Trade*

*Q.* President Bush, doesn't this whole flap here in Australia about agriculture subsidies in the United States, which you indicated you were not in a position at this time to abolish, undermine your credibility, sir, when you get to Japan wearing the mantle of a free-trader asking for concessions there?

*The President.* No, because nobody's pure. We have differences with Australia on this; I won't unnecessarily bring them up in front of my very genial host here. But I had a chance to tell them of things that I'd like to see Australia do where we might feel there could be a little less protection. He was very clear and very forceful in telling me his.

I don't consider it a flap, incidentally, when you discuss an issue where you have differences. I think it's very important that the American people and the President understand how the agriculturalists in this country look at this Export Enhancement Program.

And so, I don't think it's contradictory at all. We've never said we're totally pure. We are working for freer and fairer trade. And certainly the Japanese should be working for freer and fairer trade. And if one country could hold up its hand and say, "We have never had any protection of any kind or subsidization of any kind," that country then should be—holier than thou—be able to make the point.

We are going there into Japan and asking for equity, fairness, fairplay. And so, I don't think a discussion, a healthy discussion of an

export program that is causing great concern in this country is either a flap or diminishes my credibility as I go into a market where we are getting real problems in terms of access.

*Q.* We, of course, welcome you, perhaps with the observation that it only took 25 years for the White House to find the map of where we live since the last time a President visited. Sir, following on from that question, isn't there just——

*The President.* I'm not sure I get that point. [*Laughter*]

*Q.* Twenty-five years since we last saw an American President here.

*The President.* Oh, President. I'm sorry, I misunderstood.

*Q.* Wondered if you lost the map, perhaps?

*The President.* Oh, I see, yes. [*Laughter*]

*Q.* Sir, following on from the last question, is there not just the faintest whiff of hypocrisy here that you are demanding of the Japanese that they lower their barriers so that you can sell more motor vehicles to them, yet you impose and extend the barriers on our meat and sugar in particular?

*The President.* No, I don't think so. We were extraordinarily helpful in opening the Japanese markets on meat. And indeed, the agricultural leaders that I met with today thanked me for that, similarly for citrus. So, besides that, I love coming to Australia. So, I take your point, but if somebody takes that as to be a matter of neglect, why, that's too bad because this relationship is very, very strong.

But I'm glad to be here now. I was glad to be here as Vice President, glad to be here earlier on as a private citizen, and undoubtedly will come back.

*Japan-U.S. Trade*

*Q.* Mr. President, President Miyazawa, in honor of your trip, a few days in advance of your trip anyway, is urging his automakers to buy more U.S. auto parts and encouraging consumers to buy more American cars. Do you consider that already a success for your mission, or do you think that the Japanese still need to do more?

*The President.* Well, I want to find out exactly what all this means, how it's going to be translated, but clearly, we welcome statements of that nature. I think that's very, very good, very heartening. But I have not had a chance to sit down with Mr. Miyazawa and talk about that in some detail.

*The Prime Minister.* Perhaps a couple more questions. One on this side.

### Consultation on Agricultural Subsidies

*Q.* President Bush, could you just clarify this mention of consultations for us? The farmers seemed very convinced you have given an undertaking to have consultations before subsidized sales. That doesn't seem to square with what you said earlier in this press conference. If that's not right, you haven't gone as far as that, how does your undertaking about consultations differ from those given by your predecessor?

*The President.* I'm not sure I understand; I don't know what they've said publicly. What they said is they, the farmers, would like to come over and consult. And I said, "Come on, let's go." This would be good, and I'd like to have some American farmers there, as well as Government officials. It wasn't tied in, as far as I know, to any specific pending action under the export program.

*Q.* And not in relation to any future action?

*The President.* Well, they asked that there be consultation on a whole array of things. But I think we're getting it mixed up a little bit with what the——

*The Prime Minister.* I think it's a mix-up between information——

*The President.* ——the Government and also with this private sector group. These farmers were there not as Government officials but wanting to come over and talk to our agricultural experts and to our farmers themselves about this whole program. And I said, "Come on, we would welcome you." But that was where that one was left. Now, the other one, I have not been able to make—I think the Prime Minister—let me put it this way, I subscribe to the way he phrased it.

### "JFK"

*Q.* A change of pace, if I may, sir. There's a new movie called "JFK," which has not

wafted its way down here yet, but it casts some aspersions on the findings of the Warren Commission's reports. And also it raises some questions about possibly the CIA's role in this. You're a past CIA Director. I wonder, knowing you possibly haven't seen the movie, are you concerned about movies like this which may trouble people who weren't even born at the time of John Kennedy's assassination?

*The President.* Well, I don't know much about the movie. I haven't seen it. And there's all kinds of conspiratorial theories floating around on everything. Elvis Presley is rumored to be alive and well someplace—[*laughter*]—and I can't say that somebody won't go out and make a movie about that. I have seen no evidence that gives me any reason to believe that the Warren Commission was wrong, none whatsoever. And so, if it's helpful to reassure the American people in this way by saying that, fine. But it wouldn't lead me to suggesting that Mr. Stone be censured or something of that nature.

*Q.* As a former CIA Director, did you ever go back and see the CIA's findings during that period to satisfy any of your curiosity?

*The President.* About this subject?

*Q.* Yes.

*The President.* No, I didn't have any curiosity because I believed that the Warren Commission, which acted—when was that finding? When was the Warren Commission finding? Was it——

*Q.* It was in '63 or '64.

*The President.* Which was about 12 years before I was out at the Agency. I saw no reason to question it, still see no reason to question it.

### U.S. Role in the Pacific

*Q.* President Bush, you said today that you promised again today to maintain a military presence in the region at an appropriate level. People in the region are not so sure. What does appropriate mean and, for instance, is the ANZUS treaty, in effect, dead?

*The President.* Well, the appropriate level of security depends on conditions at the time. What I was addressing myself to was the fact that some felt with the closing of Subic that we would withdraw and pull way back from any possible security commitments. And I think one has to know—I can't tell you what that means in terms of keeping our security interests alive here or keeping a military presence here. It depends on events. It depends obviously on deployments of various naval groups. But all I wanted to do was reassure the people of this area that we are not, because of the closing of Subic, we are not pulling back from future security considerations. We are a Pacific power, we think. We know we're a Pacific trading power. And we are going to stay involved with the security concerns of our friends.

I can't tell you exactly what that means in terms of troops, where they'll be; vessels, where they'll be. That depends on the situation that might exist at the time. We had a very different security deployment in the Middle East a year ago than we have today. And so, things can change dramatically.

But all I'm just doing is giving proper assurances that our military as well as our economic interests are still housed in the Pacific to a large degree.

*ANZUS*

*Q.* ——the ANZUS treaty with the countries of the region?

*The President.* Do I what?

*Q.* Do you still need the ANZUS treaty?

*The President.* Well, we still need the treaty that exists, that we refer to as ANZUS. As you know, there's been some difficulties with that that it's no point going into now, as much as this is the last question. But nevertheless, the concept of the ANZUS is very, very important to us.

*The Prime Minister.* Important to both of us here.

That will do it. Thank you, ladies and gentlemen. Thank you, Mr. President.

*The President.* Thank you very much. Thank you, Prime Minister.

*Domestic Politics and Trade Policy*

*Q.* Mr. President, you were talking with some glee about engaging the Democrats, knocking some Democratic heads. In the last 2 days you've said——

*The President.* ——in the last couple of days. That could change. That could change.

*Q.* The status——

*The President.* No, not totally. I think it's ridiculous to start throwing in special legislation just before a trip to kind of look like the macho trying to dictate the foreign policy of this country. It's crazy. But they have their own constituents, and I've got mine. But it's all good-spirited, and we'll do our thing, keep it on broad international principles, and then take my case to the American people.

And the American people do not want to go back into isolation, cutting off foreign markets. They want to expand them. And they remember, some of them are old enough to remember the thirties with decreasing world trade. And some of them are not old enough, but they've studied enough about it to know that protectionism begets shrunk markets and further unemployment. And so, I can understand it when a Congressman gets up and, "Well, if you don't get *x* commitment here in this district, why, I'll introduce legislation." That's fine. They don't have the responsibility for conducting the policy, and I do.

*Q.* Does Europe show signs of understanding that, though, Mr. Bush?

*The President.* They will before we're through.

*Note: The President's 115th news conference began at 2:50 p.m. in the Main Committee Room at Parliament House. In his remarks, he referred to Arthur Dunkel, Chairman of the Trade Negotiation Committee and Director General of the General Agreement on Tariffs and Trade, and Prime Minister Kiichi Miyazawa of Japan.*

## Remarks at a Dinner Hosted by Prime Minister Keating of Australia in Canberra
*January 2, 1992*

This is an impossible situation, following two such articulate, young, and vibrant leaders of this country. But first, let me simply say thank you to the Prime Minister for his hospitality and to all of you for making Barbara and me feel so very much at home.

It feels odd to hear myself referred to as the leader of the free world. I told Barbara, somebody in Sydney said I was the leader of the free world. She says, "Hurry up and get out of the bathroom; we're late. Run." [*Laughter*]

I won't try to put you in what we call double jeopardy. You heard me over there, here next door in this beautiful building. And I'm also reminded of two sayings. One in our Congress is, "The speech you don't give is the one that helps you get reelected." [*Laughter*] And I'm about to be running, I think, for President. And secondly, I love the one about the kid that went to church with his grandfather, and he said, "Granddad, what are all the flags along the side of the church for?" The grandfather said, "Well, that, son, is for those who died in service." And the kid said, "Oh, really? The 9 o'clock or the 11 o'clock service?" [*Laughter*] And I'm reminded that I went on for about 25 minutes today, so you don't need another full load.

I was reminded of something, though, today perhaps of some significance, international significance, that it is likely that I will be the last President of the United States who served in the World War II. And I heard very generous assessments by the Prime Minister and by the leader of the opposition about my service. And yes, I was shot down off the shores of Chichi-Jima. And I had only wished that I had met Dawn Fraser before because I tried to set the record for swimming away from the island. And if I'd known her I might have done a better job of it—[*laughter*]—and not been so scared.

But anyway, why, I think of the Coral Sea experience and what it means to the United States and, of course, what it means to Australia. And I think back to my own little history: I was 17, about to reach my 18th birthday a month later, when the Battle of the Coral Sea took place. And I think those of us in that vintage, and there are not many in the room I'm pleased to say, but those of us in that vintage will always remember that and therefore will always have this very special feeling about Australia.

But one of the things that interests me on this visit is hearing some educators talking about the need to be sure that the younger generations remember this, not necessarily the smoke and the gunfire and all of that, but the significance of these two great countries standing together. And this visit for us has simply reminded me, and then I think through me as President, the American people, of the importance of this relationship. It is clear. It is unambiguous. There is great friendship.

And yes, we have some differences. And we faced up to them. They thrust me into the arena with three of the biggest farmers I've ever seen in my life. [*Laughter*] I won't single them out, but when I shook hands with one I made the mistake of giving him that kind of political embrace when you put your hand on his arm; it's all muscle, sheer iron. And I said, "I'd better listen to what this guy has to say." [*Laughter*]

And so, it's been a good, frank visit. We haven't held back. We discussed our differences. But I think they have been overwhelmed by the common interests that the United States and Australia have.

So, it has been for us an enormous privilege. We'll never forget it on a personal basis. And I happen to believe that it will simply reinforce this feeling of friendship and alliance and strength that is indeed the relationship between Australia and the United States of America.

So, thank you from a grateful heart for a fantastic visit.

*Note: The President spoke at 9:32 p.m. in the House of Representatives Chamber at Parliament House. In his remarks, he re-ferred to Olympic gold medalist Dawn Fraser. A tape was not available for verification of the content of these remarks.*

## Remarks to Business and Community Leaders in Melbourne
*January 3, 1992*

Premier, thank you for that wonderfully warm introduction; and to all of the people of Victoria, this wonderful city, for the warmth of your reception. I'd like to salute the Deputy Premier, Jim Kennan, and his wife, Janet; Governor McCaughey and his wife, Jean; our Ambassador, Mel Sembler, and his wife, Betty. I'd like to single out and identify, for those of you who have not met him, our very able Secretary of Commerce who's traveling with me on this trip, Secretary Bob Mosbacher, over here; and thank our hosts for a wonderful day here, two of whom I think are also with us at this luncheon, Dick Warburton, who's president of the American Chamber of Commerce, and Brian Loton, the president of the Business Council of Australia.

Australia's national anthem speaks of a land abounding in nature's gifts, of beauty rich and rare. Well, Barbara and I feel richer for the rare privilege of being with you today. And Joan, tell your friend that the only button that I have my finger on these days is the one where I try to set the clock on my VCR. [*Laughter*] And I hope it always stays that way.

And I'm also glad to visit this country where much of your beautiful land is known as bush country. [*Laughter*] And now, if I can just get that description to apply to 50 States back home, all will be well. [*Laughter*]

Ten years ago this May, I first visited Australia to mark the 40th anniversary of the Battle of Coral Sea. And since then, we have toiled together to advance what I call the hard work of freedom. I'm here to talk of how Australia and America can use that work to help build a better world. And we will build it through liberty and opportunity and through trade that is both free and fair. And we will build it by using our common

culture and principles to promote prosperity at home and democracy abroad, especially the jobs and economic growth that is my highest priority.

This morning, Barbara and I visited the Australian War Memorial, where our alliance reminded me of General Patton's words: "Wars may be fought with weapons, but they are won by men." The memorial stirs the memory of heroes who stood with our troops in combat, heroes who fought together to defend our common ideals. And our task now is to join together to create a world where the force of law outlasts the use of force.

The successful end of the cold war brings the promise of a world of peace and dignity. Its triumph is inevitable, but only if democracies are resolute. Globally, Australia has encouraged this concept by supporting a more engaged United Nations. And regionally, you helped shape the framework for the Cambodian peace settlement agreed to by warring factions. And I assure you, here too, we, America, are your partners. We will not abandon the special responsibility we have to help further stability in this region.

More than 150 years ago, President Andrew Jackson appointed J.H. Williams as the first American consul here. Arriving from Boston, Williams was greeted by a newspaper article. "We welcome his arrival," read the Australian paper, "as a pledge of increasing intimacy between the two countries from which mutual advantages may be expected to flow." One hundred and fifty years ago.

In the Persian Gulf conflict, those advantages served the cause of peace. And you were quick to condemn the Iraqi invasion, to endorse economic sanctions, to send ships to participate in the multinational coalition. And I thank you also for sending medical teams and humanitarian relief to Kurds and Iraqis fleeing Saddam's oppression. On Iraq, it is my hope that the Iraqi people now will rid themselves of that brutal dictator, Saddam Hussein, so that our countries can start over with Iraq. You see, we have no argument with the people of Iraq or even with the military in Iraq. Our difference is with the bully, Saddam Hussein.

Australia has stood fast for principles of decency and peace. In 1984 you helped create the Australia Group, which today includes 22 member nations, each dedicated to preventing the use and spread of chemical and biological weapons. Australia believes that multilateral solutions can solve global problems. And so do I. Through two World Wars and other international conflicts, Americans have learned that they cannot divorce their destinies from the destinies of Europe and Asia.

History teaches that peace is indivisible; political isolationism doesn't work. As a new century beckons, we will use that lesson in support of peace and in hopes of preventing future wars. The Australian statesman Alfred Deakin once said, "Next to our own nation we place our kindred in America." He knew that we are all members of the world community. And so, we need to strengthen our already steadfast commitment to Asia and to the Pacific region, increasing democracy, free expression, and yes, free markets.

In 1990, the two-way trade between this region and the United States totaled $300 billion. And I say that we can, we must, and we will expand our ties of trade. In America, one-third of our growth between 1986 and 1990 flowed from merchandise exports. To increase that growth, which means more jobs, Australia and America need the cooperation that must be a cornerstone of the post-cold-war world. That cooperation will increase trade, open markets, and ensure jobs.

On the other hand, economic isolationism is a bankrupt notion. Protectionism, it closes markets, it ensures poverty, and it costs jobs. America cannot and must not go down that dead-end street, and we won't as long as I am President of the United States.

You know that America is enduring tough economic times, and I know that Australia is facing hard times as well. American companies exported $8.5 billion in merchandise to Australia in 1990, $200 million more than in 1989. And we both need the new jobs that increased exports provide. Competition has compelled American companies to produce better goods and services than ever before. And I have full confidence that on a level playing field our workers can compete with anybody, anywhere.

And speaking of success in a free and fair trade environment, I have with me a delegation of American business leaders, including some that do business very successfully right here in Australia. Their success is a tribute not only to their commitment to quality but also to the basic openness and fairness of Australia's markets.

I had an outstanding chance to visit today with businesses doing business right here in Victoria, some American, some others, but all doing business and pleading for more open and fair access to markets. The business delegation is with me to help our efforts to open markets and spur economic growth all around the Pacific Rim. We ask no more and no less than you do: A playing field where partners treat each other fairly.

And like us, you understand that free trade must be fair trade. I applaud your policies to foster greater openness and competitiveness in the economy, especially erasing most import quotas and cutting domestic subsidies and tariffs. And I commend your efforts to strengthen the international economic system, spurring a regional effort to promote freer trade by erasing trade barriers.

Now, none of this has come easily, but thanks to you, we have made steady progress. And I am grateful that several years ago Australia led the way to create Asia-Pacific Economic Cooperation, APEC, the premier economic forum in the Pacific. Since APEC's first ministerial meeting in Canberra 2 years ago, it has mobilized the support of all 15 participants to push for progress in the GATT Uruguay round.

And like the United States, other APEC members want to find ways to achieve sustainable growth, increase employment, and preserve the environment. And so do we. We want the jobs that stem from economic cooperation among Pacific Rim market economies, including the United States.

And just as we need your help, I want to pledge you our help. It is true that with so much in common, our two nations generally agree on goals. And let's face it, it is also true that occasionally we differ on means. I've heard a good deal about one: One difference is our use of this Export Enhancement Program, the EEP, it is known as, to counter the agriculture subsidies of the European Community.

And let me be clear, Australia is not the target of the program. As I said before the Parliament yesterday, the EEP has one and only one objective, to force the EC to stop its avalanche of subsidized exports. The EC subsidizes 10 times the exports as do we in the United States of America.

I know discussions on this issue are difficult and that Australia's position is based on the fact that Australian farmers are enduring hardship. I've learned that firsthand on this trip. I met with representatives of Australia's farmers just yesterday. And I heard firsthand their deep concerns, and I shared with them the depth of sentiment among America's farmers. Our farmers are hurting, too. I told them we weren't looking for sympathy, but I pointed out that our wheat production dropped by 30 percent last year.

Both of us want progress. Back in Washington, an Australian delegation recently visited our Department of Agriculture. We heard your perspective on the current world market situation and your appeal for sensitivity to Australian trade. Australian officials have expressed interest in holding followup talks early this year. That too is very encouraging.

Both our Governments are working hard on the real solution to this difficult problem. We can regain the momentum for progress by using what's called the Dunkel draft as a basis for achieving a successful conclusion to the GATT round of trade talks. It is essential, believe me, it is absolutely essential, not just for agriculture but for world trade, that those talks succeed and that we make real progress in a wide array of areas, but particularly on agriculture.

I have agreed to greater bilateral dialog on this and other economic issues. Let us show how the "Waltzing Matilda" can meet the "Texas Two-Step." It can be done. And we will seek understanding in the future as in the past. We can be proud of working together over the last five decades. And so, together let's build upon that record.

We must expand our bilateral relationship in new ways that help our people. We both breathe the same air. So last April, we agreed to pursue energy policies that will increase exports while preserving our environment.

We both believe in the importance of education. So we launched the Australian Center for American Studies. This new center will expand bilateral links by developing programs of value to business and education and the universities. We hope this center will cause future generations to say of America and Australia, in the words of the great hymn, "Blest be the ties that bind."

These ties are economic, military, social, and cultural. This trip I'm on is about broad principles that draw our two great nations together. It's about the security of the Pacific. And it's about our global partnership. And it's about our prospects for economic growth.

Our relationship rests upon the shared values of our people: love of family, faith in God, pride in country, desire to conquer the unknown. The first pictures of Neil Armstrong's adventure on the Moon were beamed from Australia's radio telescope at Parkes to a waiting world. Later, Apollo XV was named *Endeavor* after Captain Cook's ship, in the hope of many future endeavors between our two nations.

So this new year, 1992, let's look forward to our next century together. Let's do the hard work of freedom for ourselves and especially for our children. Let's help them meet the challenges of their time, as we've met ours: Building the peace, creating opportunity, increasing the benefit of God's bounty for all.

Thank you all very much, and may God bless the people of this great land, Australia.

*Note: The President spoke at 12:40 p.m. at*

*the World Congress Centre. In his remarks, he referred to Joan Kirner, Premier of Victoria.*

## The President's News Conference With Prime Minister Goh Chok Tong in Singapore
## *January 4, 1992*

*The Prime Minister.* Good morning, ladies and gentlemen. The President and I have had discussions on many wide-ranging topics. I will not go into details. I would invite the President to say a few words, and then you can ask the questions from there. Mr. President.

*The President.* Well, thank you, Mr. Prime Minister. And let me just say that it is an honor and a privilege to be the first American President to visit Singapore. I've been moved by your hospitality, the openness of our conversations, and indeed, by the welcome that Barbara and I have received here.

Today I met with President Wee and had two very positive sessions, make that three, with Prime Minister Goh because we just met with the business group that was here, his ministers, our businessmen, and the Prime Minister and myself. We focused on three areas: Expanded growth and opportunity, security engagement, and the development of democracy and freedom in the region.

On trade, I'm pleased to announce that we have agreed in principle to a bilateral investment agreement. This will build on the work we've begun under the trade and investment framework agreement or the TIFA that we concluded last October.

In the security area, the Prime Minister and I discussed America's continuing role in the area. Our security arrangements in this region will take a new form. The access agreement that we have with Singapore is an excellent example of the types of arrangements we would hope to develop to meet the challenges of the post-cold-war world. We've agreed in principle to look at headquartering an element of the 7th Fleet in Singapore, CTF–73. It's a logistics command for surface ships. And it's symbolic of our commitment to the region and the fact that we intend to stay as long as we are welcome.

Singapore increasingly illustrates the characteristics of a truly successful nation in the modern era and a well-educated electorate, increasingly free to make its political choices felt, with access to information to make informed choices. I recognize that democracy underlies prosperity, and I also recognize that no nation has a monopoly on defining how to put it into effect. But there are universal values of civil, political, human rights that we all can share.

And I'm proud of the progress Singapore and the U.S. have made together, proud of the friendship its people and leaders have shown over the past many years, and proud to know that we have a very bright and prosperous future together.

So, thank you. And now, Mr. Prime Minister, I'm delighted to follow your lead and take whatever questions come my way.

*The Prime Minister.* Will I be the chairman?

*The President.* Unless we want to appoint someone else to do it.

*The Prime Minister.* I'll do it.

### *Japan-U.S. Relations*

*Q.* Mr. President, there have been reports that East Asia nations want you to moderate your demands for trade liberalization by Japan, fearing that if you don't you may inflame anti-American sentiment and actually endanger U.S. security ties in the region. Have you heard such concerns, and are you worried about a possible backlash that already seems to be building in Japan?

*The President.* I don't think there's a backlash building. I've read certain reports that address themselves to the question you raise. It is not my intention to do anything other than to improve and foster a relationship with Japan that we view as very, very important. And I've been very encouraged by statements by Mr. Miyazawa and others in anticipation of this trip.

I might add, we're going there to talk about economic opportunity and jobs; there's no question about that. But we also have other broad areas to discuss. And I would say the security concerns that we talked about today with Prime Minister Goh will be high on the agenda. We'll talk about the world trading system. We'll talk about our need to work together, Japan and the United States, to help countries as they are emerging into the democratic world.

So, we're not going there in a kind of a aggressive mode, and I'm encouraged by the statements that I see coming out of Japan.

### Federal Budget

*Q.* Mr. President, you've been mentioning along on this trip how things are bad economically at home. And we understand now that you're prepared in your State of the Union to call for renegotiation of the budget agreement to pay for various tax breaks and antirecession measures, such as tax breaks for first-time homebuyers. Is that the case, sir? And do you think things have now gotten bad enough where it's time to renegotiate the budget agreement?

*The President.* I don't think the time has come, and nor will it come as long as I'm President, to try to do anything other than to hold the line on Federal spending. The American people are very, very clear that the Federal Government spends too much. And the only good thing about the budget agreement is that it does have overall caps on Federal spending. So, it is not my view that we need to break those spending caps.

*Q.* So, you're not considering in any way renegotiating the budget agreement?

*The President.* Well, I'm not thinking of renegotiating it in the sense of spending more money or getting out from under the only constraints, the only assurance that the American people have that the Federal Government isn't going to take more out of their pockets. And the budget agreement puts caps on spending, and I am for constraining the growth of Federal spending.

And it gets to deficits. And one way to be sure that you don't have a recovery, and I think we will have one, one way to be sure you don't is to indicate that you're going to send Government spending through the roof. And that would put long-term interest rates through the roof. And that would be bad for the whole world trading system, and it would be bad for the taxpayers in our country.

### Relocation of Command Task Force

*Q.* Mr. President, a question for both of you, please: Yesterday U.S. officials left the impression that the transfer of CTF–73 to Singapore was a done deal. Is it a done deal this morning?

*The Prime Minister.* Is it already a done deal?

*Q.* Yes. I mean did you sign on the transfer?

*The Prime Minister.* No. The President and I discussed the possibility of their transferring the Command Task Force from Subic Bay to Singapore. We have agreed in principle. We welcome the presence of America in terms of security in this area. And so long as the access of Singapore is within the memorandum of understanding which we have signed some time ago, the presence will be welcome. So, the details will be looked into by our Secretary of Ministry's departments.

*The President.* I'm referring to the Prime Minister here to orchestrate this, but go ahead.

### Myanmar and Vietnam

*Q.* There has been information that the United States is about to lift the trade embargo on Cambodia. Will the United States also consider similar moves to other Southeast Asian countries, especially Myanmar and Vietnam? Thank you.

*The President.* Well, we want to see more progress in Burma, Myanmar, before—I think it's a little premature to talk about that. Vietnam, similarly, the United States has a overriding, compelling desire to have total assurance that we know the fate of every American involved in the conflict with Vietnam. So, it is a little premature to answer in the affirmative regarding Vietnam here and way premature in terms of Burma, Myanmar.

### Trading Blocs

*Q.* Mr. President, the United States has consistently opposed the East Asia economic caucus proposed by Malaysia. What will it take to change your mind?

*The President.* Well, we've had an opportunity to discuss that here. We understand Singapore's position fully. What we want to do is be sure that we don't look like we are in favor of dividing the world up into mutually exclusive trading blocs. And thus, I took a lot of time in Australia and had an opportunity here to give our view to the Prime Minister and his colleagues on NAFTA, the North American free trade agreement, to make sure, to the best of my ability, that our friends in Asia understand that we are not trying to divide the world up into trading blocs.

Our view has been, possibly the answer better lies in using APEC, an expanded role for that, perhaps. So, we are listening in terms of the Singapore view on this one, but I think the overriding point is we don't want to do something that perhaps accidentally does that which Singapore doesn't want, what the United States doesn't want, and divide the world into mutually exclusive trading blocs.

### Myanmar

*Q.* Mr. President, there is a clear difference of view between the United States and ASEAN towards the approach to be taken towards Myanmar. Have you discussed this subject at all with the Prime Minister?

*The President.* This didn't come up today, and we'll have some more time if the Prime Minister wants to raise it. Our view is quite well-known.

### Asia-U.S. Trade

*Q.* Some Asian businessmen and some Asian politicians, too, have criticized American businessmen for not being aggressive enough. They say Americans complain so much about trade barriers, unfair trade practices, but they say that the old American can-do, the old American good salesman, for example, that's just not true any more. How do you feel about that? Is some of this criticism justified, and will you be talking to these businessmen who are with you?

*The President.* Well, perhaps some is, but I'll tell you something, we have a bunch of business leaders with us who represent not just their own companies and the successes that they've had, nor do they only represent those who have successfully dealt in Asia, but they also represent some of the largest trade organizations, Chamber of Commerce, NMA, National Manufacturers; the smaller business outfits, NFIB, the National Federation of Independent Business; and others, too, President's Export Council. We've had vigorous discussions, they have, and the Prime Minister made this possible, with the top commercial ministers here and others about just that point. The Prime Minister says to me, "Hey, come on over, but you've got to be aware of what the market's like here. You've got to do better."

And everybody in our country would say that. But we say, "Yes, we'll do better, and yes, we think there's opportunity, and let's work together to make these." But also we want access and cutting down of barriers so we can be here.

But I think there's some fairness to that in some areas. Singapore, it's been pretty vigorous, I think, in a two-way street.

Is that responsive?

*Q.* Yes. I was thinking about Korea. They've often criticized Americans, and the Japanese too, for not being aggressive enough.

*The President.* Yes. Well, I think most American businessmen would say we've got to do better in trying to adapt to foreign markets. So, that's part of it. The other part of it is, hey, we want full access to markets. And so, it's not mutually exclusive. But our message is: The more access we have, the more we can invest, the more that means, eventually means, for jobs in our country. So, I think it's a two-way street.

But our message is going to be listening to where we're not doing it right. These business people are smart. They'll take the message back to their colleagues through these vast organizations and say, "Here's what we need to do now to get smaller and other businesses doing better in the United

States by having investment and trade abroad." So, that's the approach we've been taking.

### U.S. Military Presence in the Pacific

*Q.* Mr. President, I'd like to ask you one question. Do you see any political reasons to keep the strong military presence of the U.S.A. in this part of the world after the breakup of the Soviet Union?

*The President.* We see less—because of the hostility that existed, cold war hostility—we see less imminent threat. But who knows in this changing world where the security threats will come to the freedom of small ASEAN countries, for example. And what we will do is preserve a certain security presence.

But I think it's fair to say that as the world has changed dramatically, as the cold war is over, the threat that existed between the Soviet Union and the United States is certainly way, way, way down. And I think our friends in Asia see it that way. But I think everyone recognizes that there can be untoward happenings. We saw one just a year ago in the Persian Gulf that required a mobility and a presence eventually in the Gulf by the United States.

So, we are not in a war frame of mind. We're in a peace frame of mind, but we're keeping our eyes open. And there are certain security considerations that ASEAN countries agree with us exists, and we'll just act accordingly.

*Q.* Mr. Prime Minister, if I could bring you back to an earlier question.

*The President.* He's got one for the Prime Minister. Then let me come over there, sir, if you would.

### Relocation of Command Task Force

*Q.* I'd like to bring you back to the earlier question about the bases here in Singapore since there had been this expectation of agreement and there now seems to be more to talk about. Do you have specific reservations about more American troops coming into this country?

And if I could, Mr. President, bring you back to an earlier question as well, which was the question about defense spending in the U.S. Even though you don't want to break the budget, are you now going to cut deeper into defense spending?

*The Prime Minister.* There was no reservation. What I said was, we have agreed in principle. Of course, the details are not available to us, and the details would have to be discussed between the two sides. And only when you know the details can we then sign an agreement. But this will be within the framework of the memorandum of understanding which we have with the United States. So in principle, I've told the President that there's no problem.

### U.S. Military Spending

*The President.* And my answer to that question is, we are examining all these questions right now. And if, given the changes in the world, there are ways we can save further on defense that has absorbed quite a few cuts, I'd like to be able to recommend that to the American people. But all that, we're working right now with the Secretary of Defense on these questions. But I would hope that the answer would be in the affirmative. But again, I'd like to have the available time left between now and when I finalize all of this to stay a little loose on it. But we're looking for saving taxpayers' money everyplace we can.

*Q.* Well, if I may, sir, Secretary Cheney says he and Dick Darman have already agreed on a figure.

*The President.* Well, I don't know that he said that. I haven't been told that he's agreed with Dick Darman. So, I'll let you know as soon as I hear, maybe.

### U.S. Military Presence in the Pacific

*Q.* Mr. President, a few minutes ago you mentioned the Gulf crisis. Is it one of the objectives of the United States in devising these new, more flexible regional security arrangements to ensure that, if there is in future some kind of regional crisis, that the United States and its friends and allies in this region can cooperate together more effectively to damp down or contain such a problem? And can you give us an idea of the kinds of crises you see emerging in the future?

*The President.* No, but I think the first answer to your question is, yes, I think there should be an ability to respond flexibly. And that is what any security arrangements would be about. They would be very sensitive to the desires, indeed, demands of any host country. But the point I'm trying to make is, as we move out of Subic because the Filipinos want us to, the Philippine Government wanted us to, that does not mean that we're withdrawing, pulling back, and saying we have no responsibilities to our friends in the area.

I'd rather not try to hypothecate as to what kinds of conflicts might emerge in the future. I gave you an ex post facto example of one that was very much on the minds of everybody from just a year ago. And that happens to be over in the Persian Gulf. And I might say I'm very grateful for Singapore's understanding of that; their willingness to, as they did, send medical teams to the area. But I just think it would not be productive to try to foresee a specific flare-up that would require the presence, the kind of presence I'm talking about. I just think that would be—I don't want any prophecy of that nature to be self-fulfilling. We're talking about a much more peaceful world today and an American security presence helping keep it more peaceful. So, I would just not like to go into the second part of your question.

Yes, Jessica [Jessica Lee, USA Today].

*Job Creation*

*Q.* Mr. President, you said that the focus of this trip now is jobs, jobs, jobs. When you were campaigning for President in 1988 you promised that you were going to try to create 30 million jobs. I'd like to know how many jobs you estimate you could create between now, let's say, and the fall to help people who are hurting right now in the United States, over the next 6 to 8 months?

*The President.* I don't know that there's any number that I could put on something of that nature. The question is to numbers of jobs. All I know is the world and certainly the United States, much of the world has gone through some sluggish, difficult economic times. And therefore, what we want to do is to do everything we can through this international trip, through things we can do at home to create jobs in this country. But I don't think I can set a exact number for you. Some of what we're going

to be doing is setting in motion, hopefully, machinery that will result in more American jobs. Just the discussions we had on investment here today could do that.

So, I can't help you on exact numbers, but I can say, yes, I am determined to do everything I can, internationally and domestically, to try to create more jobs. Our unemployment rates there are not satisfactory, 6.9 or whatever the last figure is. Some say, "Well, that's 3 or 4 points lower than the depth of the recession in '82." That doesn't matter to me, because I will repeat what I've said: "For the person out of work, the unemployment is 100 percent." So, we're going to just keep on trying.

*Budget Agreement*

*Q.* Back to the budget agreement, sir. Separate from the caps issue is the question of categories and the fact that, as it stands now, you cannot take savings from one category and put it in another. Are you ready to change that part of the agreement so that you could take savings from the defense and put it into domestic issues?

*The President.* Let me say, frankly, I'd like to put it into the pockets of the American taxpayer if I possibly could because I think that's what is needed. Maybe it would be nice to do something about the deficit, and maybe it would be nice to do certain things that can stimulate our economy, and that could call for alterations in the tax system. But I would just leave it right there because I think it is important that we have the overall restraining effect of the budget agreement.

Now, what that means in terms of juggling it around from one account to another, we have to wait and see what the recommendations are out of defense and other areas. Because as you know, if you do change, touch defense, why, that could require some kind of adjustment. But it's a little premature to go beyond that which I said in an interview that has triggered an awful lot of this interest on December 23d, and I don't intend to go beyond that.

But I will simply reiterate my determination not to do anything that is going to reverse the economy and make it worse.

And one thing that would make it worse is if I came out of here, talking about, okay, Katie, bar the door, let's let spending go back out through the roof and remove all the restraints on it. And I'm not going to do that. The American people still feel the deficit is too high. They still feel that they're taxed too much, and they're right.

So, one way to work in good faith with the American people is say I'm going to do my level-best to stand up against these crazy spending schemes that want to go further and make the deficit worse. And I'm not going to do that.

### U.S. Role in the Pacific

*Q.* There's been a lot of talk about how power in this region, particularly, in the future will not be military; it will be economic. And that there is a perception among Asian nations that the United States is a declining economic power and that you have put too much emphasis on this tour as a panacea to America's economic ills. How do you answer that?

*The President.* I answer it by referring to able leaders of ASEAN countries who tell me what it is they'd like to see us do to be more active in Asian markets. I answer it by saying we are a Pacific power, and we're going to stay involved in the Pacific. We have disproportionate responsibilities for security around the world. And I think the Prime Minister would probably agree with that, and we are going to keep those commitments. And I'd leave it on a very broad basis like that.

*Note: The President's 116th news conference began at 11:40 a.m. in the courtyard at Istana Palace. In the news conference, the following persons were referred to: Prime Minister Kiichi Miyazawa of Japan and Richard G. Darman, Director of the Office of Management and Budget.*

## Remarks and a Question-and-Answer Session With the Singapore Lecture Group
*January 4, 1992*

*The President.* Thank you, Mr. Minister. To Prime Minister Goh, Senior Minister Lee. I'm delighted to be here, and thank you, sir, for that very kind introduction. Let me take this opportunity to say a few words about these two gentlemen I've just referred to.

Minister Lee, a quarter of a century ago, you led this small island of cultural and ethnic diversity, of limited physical resources, to independence. And then, through your vision and your force of intellect and will, you forged Singapore's nationhood. You stood courageously in a life-and-death struggle against the Communists, and you prevailed. You led your nation and your region in the quest for peace and prosperity. It is my convinced view that future generations will honor the name of Lee Kuan Yew. And as you know well from your visits in my own home in Kennebunkport, Barbara's and mine, I am pleased to know you as a friend.

Prime Minister Goh, I salute you, sir, for your wisdom, for your vigor in carrying Singapore forward now on its path to the future. I am grateful for the wonderful talks we had this morning, and I pledge America's steadfast friendship as you lead Singapore in facing the challenges of the coming generation. And I'm also pleased that you, like many of your countrymen, came to the United States of America for part of your education. These too are ties that bind us together.

Now, on to the business at hand. It's an honor to deliver this lecture, following such leaders as Brian Mulroney and Helmut Schmidt and Ruud Lubbers, Bob Hawke, Mahathir bin Mohamad, and Valéry Giscard d'Estaing, and such distinguished thinkers as Henry Kissinger and Milton Friedman. Let me acknowledge Professor K.L. Sandhu, director, Institute of Southeast

Asian Studies; A.V. Liventals, the chairman, Mobil Oil Singapore; Lee Hee Seng, deputy chairman and board of trustees, ISEAS; and Dr. Richard Hu, chairman of the Monetary Authority of Singapore and the Finance Minister.

Let me also salute the members of the U.S.–ASEAN Business Council, with whom I just met, who are here with us in this auditorium today.

The addresses in this series reflect the changes in our world. Your first lecturers focused on the ideological and military struggle between socialism and democratic capitalism, and especially between the United States and what we used to call the Soviet Union.

Think of that phrase for just a moment, "what we used to call the Soviet Union." When citizens pulled down the hammer and sickle 10 days ago and hauled up a new tricolor of freedom over the Kremlin, the Soviet Union ceased to exist, and the prospect of a new world opened before us. That act culminated a decade of liberation, a time in which we witnessed the death throes of totalitarianism and the triumph of systems of government devoted to individual liberty, democratic pluralism, free markets, and international engagement.

As this struggle has drawn to a close, these lectures have shifted their focus from military confrontation to matters of economic cooperation. Our new world has little use for old ways of thinking about the roles and relations of nation-states. The cold war categories, North-South, East-West, capitalist-communist, no longer apply. The future simply belongs to nations that can remain on the cutting edge of innovation and information, nations that can develop the genius and harness the aspirations of their own people.

Individuals wield power as never before. An innovator, equipped with ideas and the freedom to turn them into inventions, can change the way we live and think. Governments that strive only to maintain a monopoly of power, rather than to strengthen the freedom of the individual, will fall by the wayside, swept away by the tides of innovation and entrepreneurship.

Liberating technologies—telephones, computers, facsimile machines, satellite dishes, and other devices that transmit news, information, and culture in ever greater volumes and at ever greater speeds—have disabled the weapons of tyranny. The old world of splintered regions and ideologies has begun to give way to a global village universally committed to the values of individual liberty, democracy, and free trade and universally opposed, I might add, to tyranny and aggression.

If we are to realize the opportunities of this new era, we must address three intertwined challenges: The new requirements of peace and security, the challenge of promoting democracy, and the challenge of generating greater economic growth and prosperity around the world.

Consider first the challenge of peace and security. The world has learned, through two World Wars and most recently, as Senior Minister Lee talked about, through Saddam Hussein's naked aggression, that the dogs of war can be unleashed anytime would-be aggressors doubt the commitment of the powerful to the security of the powerless.

As a nation that straddles two great oceans, a nation tempered by painful wartime experience, the United States remains committed to engagement in the Atlantic community and the Asia-Pacific region, and we are unalterably opposed to isolationism. That's my vow to you, as long as I am President of the United States of America.

A quarter century ago, many feared that free nations would fall like dominoes, remember the domino theory, fall like dominoes to the subversion of communism. Now, we can say with pride and a robust sense of irony that the totalitarian powers, the powers that fomented conflict the world over, have indeed become the dominoes of the 1990's.

This end to the cold war gives the United States an opportunity to restructure its military. Having said that, I want to assure you and all of our many friends in this part of the world that the closing of bases in the Philippines will not spell an end to American engagement. We will maintain a visible, credible presence in the Asia-Pacific region with our forward-deployed forces and through bilateral defense arrangements with nations of the region.

That is why I'm pleased to announce that this morning we've reached agreement with the Government of Singapore to explore in detail how we can transfer a naval logistics facility from Subic Bay in the Philippines to Singapore in the next year. We appreciate Singapore's far-sighted approach to the security requirements of a new era.

The United States does not maintain our security presence as some act of charity. Your security and your prosperity serve our interests because you can better help build a more stable, more prosperous world. An unstable Asia burdened with repression does not serve our interests, nor does an Asia mired in poverty and despair. We need you as free and productive as you can be, and we understand that our security presence can provide a foundation for our mutual prosperity and shared defense.

But we also need your support in addressing the new threats of this new era, regional conflicts, weapons proliferation. And so, I'm pleased that the ASEAN nations are working with us to craft new and flexible arrangements to ensure the common defense. Access agreements and increased ASEAN–U.S. dialog can help us work cooperatively to promote stability in the whole region. By working cooperatively, we better share the security responsibilities of the post-cold-war era.

Strong, credible security arrangements enabled us to meet the second challenge, the challenge of democracy, a challenge of shared interests and shared ideals. Again, ASEAN is helping to spread positive political change in ways that reflect the values, aspiration, and cultures of the nations in this region. ASEAN is trying to help the former Communist states in Indochina reintegrate themselves in a world that respects free markets and free people. Those efforts are starting to produce very hopeful results.

Just a few weeks ago American diplomats arrived in Phnom Penh for the first time in 16 years. We owe that breakthrough to years of effort by many nations. But the Cambodian peace accord signed by Secretary Baker in Paris last October could not have existed without the help and the cooperation of ASEAN. This historic agreement offers the very real hope of national reconciliation to the long-suffering people of Cambodia.

And additionally, when the Paris conference agreed on a peace settlement for Cambodia, my Government offered to remove our trade embargo as the United Nations advance mission began to implement the settlement. And today I am pleased to announce the lifting of that embargo. Working with others, we need to turn attention to the economic reconstruction of that deeply wounded land, and so its new political reconciliation has a home from which to grow.

We are now normalizing our ties with Laos and have begun to move with Vietnam along a path marked by implementation of the Paris accords, and for the sake of many, many American families, the satisfactory resolution of our concerns, our deep concerns about POW's and MIA's.

The key point is this: After being strong, determined, and patient, we finally can entertain realistic hopes of building lasting ties of interest and affection with Indochina. Organizations such as ASEAN which promote security, more open political systems, and open markets form the building blocks for what I've called the new world order.

This movement toward democracy leads us to the third challenge for the future, the challenge of economic growth and building a world of open and fair trade.

Everyone agrees that political rivalry and military adventurism threaten international stability. But no one should doubt that economic isolationism, protectionism, can be at least as threatening to world order. The protectionist wars of the twenties and the thirties deepened the Great Depression and set in motion conflicts that hastened the Second World War.

On the other hand, during the past half century, engagement and trade have produced unprecedented peace and prosperity here in Singapore, throughout free Asia, in Europe, and in the United States. This prosperity also has led naturally to democracy, a fact that illustrates the indivisible relationship between security, democracy, and individual liberty.

The United States will remain engaged economically, especially in this part of the world. The Asian-Pacific region has become the world's economic dynamo. Our trade with Singapore, it's increased tenfold during the past 16 years. We now export more to Singapore than to Italy or Spain, more to Indonesia than to the whole of Eastern Europe. The economies here continue to grow at an astonishing rate while enjoying impressive income equality and general prosperity.

The ASEAN countries, along with other nations in the region, helped initiate the Asia-Pacific Economic Cooperation process 2 years ago, APEC. APEC offers a powerful vehicle for sustaining free, market-based trade, for advancing the cause of regional and global trade liberalization, and for strengthening the cohesion and interdependence of the whole Asia-Pacific region.

Now this is important to us. Most of America's recent economic growth has come from export industries. Each billion dollars' worth of U.S. exports support many thousands of good American jobs.

A delegation of executives from major American businesses, from the automobile industry to computer and electronics firms, to food and energy companies, has joined me in order to express our national commitment to free and fair trade. Our executives will learn more about opportunities here, and they will also work to help other firms compete fairly throughout the world. With us today also are the American Ambassadors to the ASEAN countries. They will be returning to the United States soon to tell American businesses there about the opportunities that exist in ASEAN.

The United States is trying to establish an economic operating framework to facilitate and to encourage these ties. This past October we agreed to a new trade and investment framework agreement with Singapore. And I propose that we complement that agreement by negotiating a bilateral investment treaty. When combined with our global efforts through GATT and our regional initiatives through APEC, this comprehensive approach can enable us to meet the economic challenges of the post-cold-war era.

Americans believe in free and open trade. Nations can achieve astonishing levels of prosperity when they embrace the challenge of the marketplace. The General Agreement on Tariffs and Trade can play an especially crucial role in expanding freedom's economic frontiers. And that's why on each stop of this important trip I'm calling for urgent action on behalf of the international trading system. I am urging the world's trading nations to join with us in making GATT Director Dunkel's proposed draft agreement the basis for the successful conclusion of the Uruguay round.

While all of us have problems with portions of that draft, none of us can afford to let the progress it represents slip away into the past. Now is the moment for a strong collective response. And I particularly urge the dynamic trading nations of this region to help us to convince all GATT participants to build the momentum to achieve this agreement. A successful conclusion to this Uruguay round can prepare the way for even greater trade liberalization in years to come and greater prosperity for everyone.

GATT ensures that the world will continue moving toward broad economic integration and not toward trade blocs. I don't have to point out to an audience in Singapore, especially an informed audience like this, that there's a huge difference between a free trade zone, an oasis of free trade, and a trade bloc that attempts to hold the rest of the world at bay. We resolutely oppose efforts to create economic fortresses anywhere.

On the other hand, we wholeheartedly endorse free trade agreements. Let me be clear on something. Our North American free trade agreement will beckon all nations to make the best of the resources and opportunities that the United States, Canada, and Mexico have to offer. NAFTA, that North American free trade agreement, is not a threat to Asia. It would not encourage the division of the world into trading blocs. Instead, our increased growth can stimulate more trade with Asia. And we support efforts to build free trade agreements elsewhere, including among the ASEAN nations.

Consider your own experience. A regime of free trade has enabled Singapore to become one of the Four Tigers of Asia and one of the fastest developing nations on

Earth. When other nations' economies falter, you suffer. The worldwide economic slowdown has slowed your rate of economic growth this year, although most nations would be overjoyed to settle for 6-percent growth. I can speak for one. [*Laughter*] Singapore has one of the most open economies on Earth, and I appreciate Singapore's leadership on pressing for even greater market freedom around the world.

But we also need to consider the full import of economic development. An economy is the aggregate of work, ingenuity, and optimism of a nation. The term "economy" encompasses what millions of people do with their lives. And therefore, when we talk about strengthening economies, about growth, about opportunity, we mean much more than signing trade pacts. We mean building better lives for our people.

Americans understand that no nation will prosper long without a first-rate educational system. And I've encouraged Americans to mount a revolution in education. We call it the America 2000 education strategy. America 2000 challenges our citizens to set high standards for their schools. It encourages all Americans to join forces in creating world-class schools. And meanwhile, we will continue to strengthen our university system, we think the world's finest and the host today to over 200,000 students from Asia. Perhaps one may be a future Prime Minister. I am certain she'll be a good one. [*Laughter*] And our APEC educational partnership initiative is seeking to link these educational ties to our mutual economic interests.

Once we have given students basic skills, we must give them the freedom to make the most of the knowledge they have acquired. Tax cuts and deregulation in the 1980's helped unleash the greatest peacetime economic recovery in American history. And while in my country reducing the tax on capital gains is somewhat controversial politically, most of our competitors impose very low taxes on capital gains. Some, like Singapore, don't tax capital gains at all. We can learn from you. We can create a climate even more conducive to risk, to innovation, to the bold exploration of new technologies and ideas, and I'm confident we will.

Beyond that, the nations of the world want to enjoy the blessings of growth without destroying the environment. And we need to achieve environmental protection without denying developing nations the opportunity to develop. The United States has environmental expertise and state-of-the-art environmental technology. The Asian nations have environmental challenges.

I am pleased to announce today that AID, the U.S. Trade Development Program, the Overseas Private Insurance [Investment] Corporation, OPIC, and our Ex-Im Bank have developed a creative approach in partnership with this region to better address the challenge of balancing the environmental protection with development. We hope we can coordinate our effort with those of other developed nations through various types of support, including U.S. equipment and technology. This will be good, be good for Asia's environment, good for American jobs.

In conclusion, the nations committed to democracy and free markets have brought the world to a new era, one that promises unprecedented freedom from violence and deprivation. But this world will not simply happen. It will require hard work, tough negotiation, sacrifice, and the courage of our convictions. And if we cast our lot with the forces of enlightenment and freedom over the counsels of defeatism and ignorance, we will build a better world, a world bound by common interests and goals.

Like you, Americans desperately want a world at peace, one in which no blood must be shed for the ideals we all share. So, we will maintain a vigorous security presence in order to prevent despots and tyrants from undermining the triumphs of freedom and democracy.

Like you, Americans want to live in a world enriched and enlivened by international trade in goods, in ideas, in cultures, and in dreams for the future. We want the opportunity to compete aggressively in the international marketplace. And at the same time our consumers want access to the best goods and services that your economies have to offer. We want to live in a world made better by the genius and achievement of every culture. So, we will advance the prospects for more open trade.

And like you, Americans want a world united and enlightened by freedom and justice, by political pluralism, by the universal commitment to individual liberty and prosperity. So, we will stand fast by our principles and remain confident, strong, and vigilant.

Since 1784, when an American trading ship, the *Empress of China*, sailed for Canton from New York, the United States has tried to build strong ties of commerce with Asia. We remain committed to that vision. And together, the United States and its Asian-Pacific allies can indeed build a world filled with economic tigers, nations growing rapidly, pioneering new intellectual, commercial, and cultural terrain, spreading the blessings of free markets, democracy, and peace. My trip through Asia this week marks a new start. The next step is up to all of us.

Thank you again. And may God bless you, the people of Singapore, people of the United States of America. Thank you all very, very much.

*Q.* Ladies and gentlemen, we have a tight schedule, threaten to squeeze out the question-and-answer session. We have a very few questions that the President has offered to meet. So, can I ask the questioners to be brief, to the point. State your name, and get to the point quickly, please.

*Free and Fair Trade*

*Q.* Mr. President, the trend in closer economic interaction within region, with Europe forging a single market and the U.S., Canada, and Mexico moving towards a North American free trade area, will grow in momentum in the 1990's. How, in your opinion, can we ensure that these trends do not result in inward-looking economic blocs? How can APEC as a body promote greater economic openness and counter these inward-looking trends? Thank you.

*The President.* One, help us reach a successful conclusion to the GATT round. Therein lies the most important single step that can guarantee against trading blocs. Secondly, accept my word that nothing in the North American free trade agreement wants to contribute to dividing the world into trading blocs, into blocs that shut out

other people's goods. That is not what it's about. If we are successful in the NAFTA, that will increase markets for Asian goods in South America which has been an area that needs economic help.

So, the first answer is, help with GATT, successful conclusion of the Uruguay round. And the second answer is, please understand that NAFTA, and I can only speak for American participation therein, and I'm sure it's true of President Salinas of Mexico and of Brian Mulroney of Canada, have no intention of having that free trade between ourselves be a block to ASEAN goods. Stop worrying about it. That isn't going to happen.

If I could think of a third reason, I'd tell you. [*Laughter*] But those are the two I've got.

*U.S. Role in the Pacific*

*Q.* Mr. President, I believe that most countries in the Asia-Pacific region want to see the U.S. continue to play a major economic and security role in the western Pacific. But many are worried that Japan may become the leader in the economic competition, especially in trade and investments, in the Asia-Pacific region. Will the U.S. respond to this Japanese economic challenge and stay in the competition? However, if Japan eventually becomes the preeminent investor and trader in the region, will the U.S. remain engaged in the economies and the security of the region?

*The President.* Good question, and the answer is yes. Regardless of what happens, we are going to continue our cooperation in terms of security. That's a given. That's important. It's important, I think, to ASEAN. And I think it's very, very important to my country, to the United States of America.

I'm not as gloomy as the question implied in terms of Japan dominating ASEAN. I would be worried about it if I thought that we would all acquiesce, including Singapore, in a bloc to offset Canada or to offset a perceived trading bloc in Europe. Then I would be concerned about that. But I don't think that is going to be the reality because we are going to forcefully, with our best we can offer in terms of economics and investment and in two-way trade, stay involved in the area.

If you predicated it by saying, the world will divide into three blocs, do we have any concern about domination from an economic superpower, which is Japan, I'd say you could have some concerns there. But that's not what I see as the reality. And I hope that in some way this trip contributes to the idea that we want to avoid blocs that shut people out and we want to open markets that cause people to come in.

And so, that is the way I look at it right now. But we will stay engaged. I'm looking forward to the part of my trip that takes me to Japan. We have trade problems there. They're aware of it; we're going to talk to them. But it's not going to be exclusively on that. I'm interested, as you know, in creating jobs for Americans through fair trade, through access to markets, through matters of this nature. But we also have a wide array of other considerations that I will be discussing with the very able leaders of Japan. And it might well be that we will talk about the idea that we ought not to see this world divided up into regional blocs.

So, I'll do my best in that regard.

### Europe

*Q.* It was with some irony that I read recently in the observation of Li Peng, Chinese Prime Minister, China's Prime Minister, that in fact, with events surrounding the dissolution of the ex-Soviet empire, events in Yugoslavia, that in fact the single source of threat to your new world order is no longer security in Asia-Pacific but in fact Europe. Your comments, please.

*The President.* Mike, please elaborate. I didn't see the comment by Li Peng, and I need a little more of what he was talking about. Threat to Europe, in what sense?

*Q.* In the sense of the threat to the new world order that you referred to earlier, the theater of threat from a sort of geopolitical and military sense is no longer question marks over Asia-Pacific but more question marks over the European theater.

*The President.* Well, see, I wouldn't agree with the premise that in the past the concern wasn't about the Soviet Union, if that's what he was talking about. The major so-called "superpower confrontation" has been between the United States and the Soviet Union, Soviet Union with its satellites and the United States with its friends and allies. And now, with the dissolution of the Soviet Union, we see that this doesn't exist. That major cold war security threat, if we handle things properly with the emergence of the republics or this Commonwealth, should no longer concern us.

We're going to stay engaged with the republics. We're going to stay engaged with the Commonwealth, helping in every way we can these now-fledgling democracies as they emerge and strengthen their independence. We want to see that there isn't a security threat from that part of the world.

I may be missing what he's getting at, but I just think we have to guard against unpredictability, and thus the security presence will remain in Asia. It may be different than it's been in the past. The whole makeup of the U.S. defenses has been changing, as you know, but we are going to retain, because of unforeseen circumstances and with the welcome of our friends in this area, a security presence here.

So, if the distinguished leader of China was implying that wasn't necessary anymore, fine. That's a good—and I'm confident that China is not seeking external hegemony. There was a time when everybody was much, much more concerned about that. But we'll be here. We'll be around as a stabilizing, reassuring security presence where wanted.

By that, I can't say that we think the only threats to worldwide security might emerge in this area; we don't. But we've had a Pacific presence, and we're going to continue to have a Pacific presence.

Still not sure I got to the point, but anyway, that's the answer.

*Note: The President spoke at 12:50 p.m. at the Westin Stamford Hotel in Singapore. A portion of these remarks could not be verified because the tape was incomplete.*

## Remarks at a Breakfast With Korean and American Business Groups in Seoul
*January 6, 1992*

First, let me just thank our Korean business guests for taking time away from fantastically busy schedules to be with us today. I view this as an important meeting. I view this as a meeting where I undoubtedly will learn.

Secondly, I'd like to comment overall on our trip. A lot of this trip is about business and how we can do more, thus creating opportunities in the United States, job opportunities; and similarly, if you believe as we do, and I'm sure everyone here does, in free trade, job opportunities here in Korea.

But in saying that, I wanted to also emphasize that I am not neglecting, because of this emphasis, my sincere concerns about security considerations that bind us together, the cultural aspects, the scientific aspects that bind Korea and the United States together. So the trip's about a lot of things. But this breakfast, obviously and properly, the focus is on business.

We watch in admiration the success of the companies that you all represent around here. We have with us a distinguished group of American businessmen who have taken a lot of time from their own busy lives to go with me. And I wondered at the beginning how all of this would be received by our foreign hosts. But in Australia and Singapore and then just a preliminary feeling here, I think it's been a wonderful idea. And I think they've learned, and I hope you've learned from the interchange with these business leaders from the States. And they are not only representative of their companies, but many of them, as you know, are heads of our leading business groups, large and small. So, they'll go back and take back the message of how we further business opportunity.

I will say that I'm determined as President of the United States to fight the waves of protection that are almost inevitable when one's own economy is not doing well. But one way to make things do less well is to resort to protectionism. And I am not going to do that. But we're in an election year, and I'm sure some of you all wonder what the heck does this mean in terms of the U.S. commitment to free and fair, open trade. And I just want to assure you that we will remain committed. I think the American people want that in spite of the siren's call of protection.

I would like to urge that every business person here from the United States and Korea use whatever influence you have with your trading partners in Europe and elsewhere to get a successful conclusion of the GATT round. The one thing that I think is vitally important now, the thing that should most be targeted is the successful conclusion of that trading round. And it really is important.

And the last point I'll make is, I know that some look at the North American free trade agreement in Asia and wonder, is the United States—worried about perhaps the GATT round not finishing properly, successfully—planning on forming a trading bloc in North America and South America, that would spill on down past Mexico into South America?

Let me tell all of you here, our Korean friends, that we will not be trying to acquiesce in dividing up the world into trading blocs. And the NAFTA in our view, when successfully concluded, will open up markets for Korean businessmen in a more prosperous Central and South America. We're convinced in the United States, I am, and I think the businessmen here are, that a successful conclusion of that round means more jobs for Americans. But it also means broader trading markets for our friends in Asia.

And I've stated this to the leaders in Australia, to the leaders in Singapore, and I just wanted you to hear from me directly that we aren't having some fallback position of a North American trading bout that in any way would detrimentally affect the private business interests here in Korea. You're doing too much, you're moving out in exactly the way we respect.

And I am grateful, as I walked around the room, hearing about the American and the Korean partnerships and about the investments that some of your companies have made in the United States. That means jobs to us. It means opportunity for Americans. So we don't view that with alarm; we view that as something that is very, very good. And the only thing I'd like to ask is that all of us do our level-best after the successful conclusion of this GATT round to be sure that all the markets are open and free and fair. Trade is the goal. And I think that will ensure the prosperity of the people not only in my country but the people, the average man on the street in Korea.

So, thank you all very much for coming. And now, I came to listen. I talked too long already. But I want to hear what you all have, and please don't hold back. If there's some criticism or suggestions as to how the U.S. Government can do things better, I want you to let me know, because this is a good opportunity.

*Note: The President spoke at 8:17 a.m. at the Hotel Shilla.*

## The President's News Conference With President Roh Tae Woo of South Korea in Seoul
*January 6, 1992*

*President Roh.* Good morning, ladies and gentlemen. I am especially delighted to meet again with the journalists traveling with President Bush. Today I have had very useful talks with President Bush for more than one hour and a half. We have exchanged wide-ranging views about the ongoing changes in the world and the shifting situation in the Asia-Pacific region.

President Bush and I have earnestly discussed the roles of our two countries in promoting durable peace and security on the Korean Peninsula, as well as ways to advance our bilateral cooperation. We have also exchanged frank and candid views on how to strengthen the free international trade system and how to expand economic and trade ties between our two countries.

At the outset I expressed my deep appreciation for the outstanding leadership of President Bush in dismantling the cold war structure and in freeing all mankind from nuclear terror. I emphasized that the roles of our two countries in promoting lasting peace and prosperity in the Asia-Pacific region and the bilateral cooperation are growing even more important.

In the quest for those common goals, all nations in this region, including Korea, ought to fulfill their responsibilities commensurate with their capabilities. President Bush made clear that as a Pacific power the U.S. will continue to play a constructive role in promoting peace and common prosperity in this region.

I explained to him the initiatives and endeavors that we have put forth to ease tension and secure peace on the Korean Peninsula and the consequent progress in relations between South and North Korea. President Bush reaffirmed the principle that the problems of the Korean Peninsula should be settled directly by the South and North themselves and fully supported the accords that have recently been reached between the two areas of Korea.

President Bush and I jointly reaffirmed the unshakable position that North Korea must sign and ratify a nuclear safeguard agreement and that the recently initiated joint declaration for a nonnuclear peninsula must be put into force at the earliest possible date.

We discussed ways for the U.S. to regular expand contacts with North Korea in close consultation between our two countries, in tune with progress on the North Korean nuclear issue and in inter-Korean relations.

President Bush once again stressed that the U.S. security commitment to Korea remains unchanged and will continue to be honored. We agreed that our two nations should further strengthen bilateral ties in the diplomatic, security, economic, scientific, technological, and all other fields and further develop enduring partnership so that both will be able to prosper together in the Pacific era anticipated in the 21st century. Once again affirming that common prosperity must be sought through free trade, we pledged our two nations to closely cooperate to that end.

I emphasized that my government is taking positive approaches to all areas for helping to bring the Uruguay round of trade negotiations to a successful conclusion. As for negotiations in the agricultural sector, I explained that because of our peculiar situation it will be exceedingly difficult to fully open our market in the immediate future and asked for America's understanding and cooperation in resolving the issue.

I also stressed that our trade balance with the U.S. dipped into the red last year and explained our current economic realities, emphasizing that a healthier development of the Korean economy will be beneficial to America also.

President Bush and I agreed to have the Governments of both countries mutually support and promote Korean business activities in the U.S. and U.S. business activities in Korea. To that end, we agreed to initiate Korea-U.S. subcabinet economic consultations to develop ways to promote economic partnership between our two countries.

We also agreed on the need to further expand bilateral cooperation in the fields of science and technology, and thus a new science and technology agreement and a patent secrecy agreement were signed between our two countries this morning.

Ladies and gentlemen, let me ask you now to give President Bush, our guest of honor, an opportunity to speak.

*President Bush.* First, Mr. President, may I thank you for your hospitality. And of course, Barbara and I are very pleased to be in Korea again at this historic time.

We have had good, productive discussions with the President, with members of his Cabinet on security, economic, and political issues. And I reaffirmed the commitment of the United States to the security of Korea. And let there be no misunderstanding: The

United States will remain in Korea as long as there is a need and that we are welcome.

I told President Roh that he deserves tremendous credit for the progress that has been made toward reunification on the peninsula. His November 8th announcement set the standard for a nonnuclear peninsula which I fully endorse. While rapid progress is being made between the North and the South, I expressed my concern that the North fully implement its IAEA obligations under the Nuclear Non-Proliferation Treaty. And moreover, the North and South should implement the historic bilateral inspection arrangements under the joint nonnuclear declaration of December 31st, 1991. If North Korea fulfills its obligation and takes steps to implement the inspection agreements, then President Roh and I are prepared to forgo the Team Spirit exercise for this year.

On economic and trade issues, I stressed the need for Korean support to bring the Uruguay round to a successful conclusion, a subject he just addressed himself to. I congratulated the President on Korea's superb job of hosting the last APEC ministerial meeting, and we agreed to support and strengthen APEC which I believe is one of the keys to continued regional growth.

Bilaterally, I am pleased to announce that we have agreed to an economic action plan which will establish a framework to resolve bilateral trade and economic issues between us.

And on one final note, I think that the science and technology agreement that we signed today is a serious framework for concrete cooperation.

So, thank you again, Mr. President. I'm delighted to be here.

*South and North Korean Negotiations*

*Q.* South and North Korea have recently agreed on a South-North basic accord and the nuclear-free Korean Peninsula. But North Korea's sincerity in carrying out this accord is questioned. Therefore, with regard to the building of a structure for peace on the Korean Peninsula, what discussions have been taken at the summit meeting?

*President Roh.* There are a lot of worries

about North Korea's compliance with the nuclear inspection. And when South and North Korea agreed on the declaration of nuclear-free Korean Peninsula, the precondition was that North Korea will sign the nuclear safeguards treaty with the IAEA and submit its facilities to international inspection. And that has been promised by the North Korean side. And in my view, they will faithfully follow through with their commitment.

Now, if and when North Korea balks at these commitments, then I believe North Korea clearly understands what international sanctions are awaiting for their faults. And in light of North Korea's current situation and realities, I do not believe North Korea could forfeit their promises regarding these commitments.

And the United States and the Republic of Korea will continue our cooperation and our efforts to eliminate North Korea's nuclear weapons development, as well as to have North Korea abandon their nuclear reprocessing plants as well as the enrichment facilities to the extent they exist. And we will expect support and cooperation of the international society. And along with this support, I am quite certain that our efforts will succeed.

As far as South-North Korean summit talks, we did not go into any specifics, but President Bush has expressed his support of these talks to the extent that these talks will be conducive for the reduction of tension on the Korean Peninsula and for the long-term unification of the Korean people.

### Japan and the U.N. Security Council

*Q.* Mr. President, the U.S. has called for Japan to take a broader role on the world stage, to go beyond checkbook diplomacy. In line with that expectation, is the U.S. prepared to accept Japan's request for a seat on the permanent U.N. Security Council? And if not, why not?

*President Bush.* Japan is a very important country. They are an economic power to be respected and to be reckoned with. But your question relates to changing the Charter of the United Nations Security Council, something that is extraordinarily difficult to do. And in addition to Japan, there are other claimants to seats on what clearly

would have to be an expanded Security Council. So, we are in the position of hearing from, as the world has changed, from various friends, Japan being one of them, others in Europe being among them, as to their aspirations to be on the Security Council.

But before there could be any change in the Charter, there would have to be extensive consultation. It simply is not going to just happen. And so, we haven't tried to stand in the way of it, nor have we advocated Japan over other seriously interested people.

I think President Nixon back in '72 indicated a willingness to support Japan if the Charter ever came open for change. But my experience at the U.N. tells me changing the Charter is extraordinarily difficult. But we'll be open-minded, and we will be prepared to consult.

### Visit to Japan

*Q.* Mr. President, tomorrow you head for Japan, which has been characterized sort of as the Super Bowl of this Asian trip of yours. Politically, sir, what is the bottom line for you? What do you have to achieve in Japan and take home to the United States to make that a successful trip?

*President Bush.* I don't know, but the political opponents are already kind of raising the bar on the high jump. And we will be discussing in Japan economic issues, not exclusively economic. We're going to be talking about the very important security considerations that Japan has. Indeed, we've talked about them here in Korea. And so, I have no set list that must be achieved to declare this visit a success. I've heard very positive statements coming from a very respected leader, Mr. Miyazawa. And that is all very encouraging. Indeed, they've already taken some steps on the economic front, the monetary front, that I think are important in terms of lowering interest rates.

So, I just can't help you in what makes a success or what makes a failure. I can guarantee you political opponents, no matter what is achieved, will be saying, "Hey, you didn't jump quite high enough. You need to get over the bar. We've just raised it another foot." But that's politics. That's what's to be expected.

What is important is that we handle this relationship with a broad global sense; that we make progress on the economic front, the bilateral trade front; and that we make clear to the Japanese leaders that we are interested in their views on security and on a wide array of other topics.

So, I can't define for you exactly what makes a success or what doesn't. I am encouraged by the forthcoming statements, as I say, on the monetary policy as well as some that have been forthcoming in terms of the trade formula. But I just can't give it to you, Ellen [Ellen Warren, Knight-Ridder].

### North Korea

*Q.* The question was to President Roh, that North Korea has indicated that they will sign the nuclear safeguards treaty and submit to inspections. But the question was, will the United States and North Korean relations be upgraded later in the year once North Korea carries out these promises? And to President Bush, what would be the conditions on the part of the United States to upgrade U.S. relations with North Korea?

And again, back to President Bush, the United States is reportedly putting pressure on the Republic of Korea to open the markets, Korean markets, to U.S. products. But one thing we can point out is, we are recording already a $.7 billion trade deficit vis-a-vis United States. And at what point would these pressures be let off?

*President Roh.* The question was about North Korea's signing of the safeguards treaty and the inspections and whether U.S.-North Korean relations will improve upon these events. I have consistently maintained the position since my July 7th declaration of inter-Korean exchanges that North Korea should stop being the threat to international society, not only in this area but across the world. And they should come out to the open world and cooperate with the nations around the world.

And since North Korea has indicated that they will renounce the development of nuclear weapons, if North Korea's nuclear development ceases to be a threat to us and to the area and if South and North Korean

relations improve, we would not only not oppose U.S.-North Korean contacts upgraded, we would rather encourage the upgrading of contacts between North Korea and the United States.

And President Bush fully agreed with my recommendations and views, and he also indicated that as far as North Korea is concerned, the U.S. position is that United States will pursue in full consultation with the Republic of Korea, and Korea will never be passed up in the U.S. efforts to maintain contacts with North Korea. And we have confirmed our positions.

*President Bush.* May I say with admiration that this reporter has perfected the art of the follow-on question, getting one to you and two to me. It's a magnificent performance.

Let me try to remember mine. One of them was what conditions to upgrade. And I would just follow on to what President Roh Tae Woo said: Nuclear question; peaceful intentions; I would add some respect, in their case because of the miserable record, for individual rights, human rights, before there would be an upgrading with the United States. But let me just reassure the people here. We are not going to get out in front of the Korean Government here, and we are not going to permit North Korea to make an end run to start in talking to us about upgrading before these fundamental problems that President Roh has talked about have been solved.

### Free and Fair Trade

Mr. President, I have to finish the other; he had another one. Very well done. And the question, as I recall it, was when do you let up on the pressure about getting into the other guy's market because we have a central trade balance.

And the answer to that is, it's not a question of balance or imbalance. It's a question of fair trade. And we will continue to work with Korea where we think that trade is less than fair. Their businessmen pointed out to me some things this morning that they think we can do better in this.

But it's not a question of a trade figure. It's a question of access to markets. It's a question of fair treatment. And this thing we signed today is very good, copyright and patents; that's all very good.

So, just because there's a balance, that doesn't mean that either side should refrain from trying to get full and fair access to the other guy's market.

Thank you very much.

*Q.* ——to open the markets of Korea anytime soon. Are you satisfied with that, and how does that square with your promise to the American people you're going to open markets for jobs, jobs, jobs?

*President Bush.* Open markets where?

*Q.* For jobs, jobs, jobs.

*President Bush.* Yes. Are you talking about North Korea?

*Q.* No, I'm talking about what the President said. He said it's not anytime in the near future. Because of their austerity program here, you won't be able to open the markets.

*President Bush.* I don't think he said that. I don't think that's what he said. That's not what we've been talking about.

*Q.* Well, I think that's what the translation was.

*Q.* Have you even discussed rice, for example?

*President Bush.* We talked about that and the global—yes, absolutely, but in the global sense of let's get a satisfactory conclusion to the Uruguay round. I should have added that to that last guy's question, as a matter of fact. That is the key to a lot of what that last Korean questioner was asking about.

*North Korea*

*Q.* Mr. President, we understand North Korea——

*President Bush.* Hey, listen, it just ended here, the press conference. You weren't listening when the thing ended. You're still jet-lagged out.

*Q.* We understand North Korea said no to a dialog with the United States, that they've said no to the United States about——

*President Bush.* That's fine. Our policy is not going to shift. We're not going to start having dialog with North Korea. We're dealing as we have in the past, and progress is being made. We salute the President for that progress. And we're not about to take some end run around our staunch ally in order to accommodate Kim Il-song. And if he doesn't want it, so much the better. That just suits the heck out of us.

*Note: The President's 117th news conference began at 12:01 p.m. at the Blue House. President Roh spoke in Korean, and his remarks were translated by an interpreter. In the news conference, the following were referred to: President Kim Il-song of North Korea; the Agreement on Reconciliation, Non-Aggression, and Exchanges in Cooperation Between the South and the North, signed December 13, 1991; and the Joint Declaration for a Non-Nuclear Korean Peninsula, initialed December 31, 1991. A portion of this news conference could not be verified because the tape was incomplete.*

# Remarks at the American and Korean Chambers of Commerce Luncheon in Seoul
*January 6, 1992*

Well, thank you all very much, and good afternoon. And let me first say thank you to our master of ceremonies, my old friend and our very able Ambassador here, Don Gregg. Thank you for that introduction.

And I'd like to also acknowledge Minister Han Pong Su, the Minister of Trade, and of course our able Secretary of Commerce, Bob Mosbacher. He is heading up, as I think

everyone here knows, our delegation of top American business leaders as they come here to explore new opportunities for American goods and services, not just here but all around the world.

I also want to single out and thank our hosts, Don Myers of the AmCham and Kim Sang Ha of the Korean Chamber of Commerce, for bringing together some of the top business leaders from both countries this afternoon. This American Chamber of Commerce in Seoul is leading the way toward free and open trade throughout Asia. And it's playing what I am told is a vital role in expanding business ties between the United States and Korea, ties which are growing into a true economic partnership.

Let me begin by telling you why I'm here. As you might expect, with tough times at home in the United States, my highest priority is stimulating economic growth and jobs for Americans. And one way to get our economy growing is to increase trade between our two nations. Opening more markets here in Korea for quality American goods and services clearly means more exports and more good jobs in America. And as you all know, that also holds true for Korea as well.

And so, I've come to the capital of one of the world's leading economic success stories, success based on hard work, market orientation, and access to international capital and markets. Your 9-percent growth rate may seem mediocre to you compared to some previous years, but back home, I'd settle for that, like that. [*Laughter*]

With a generation, Korea has transformed itself from one of the world's poorest states into the world's 13th largest economy, on the cutting edge of high-tech growth. The generation that created that success knows that enduring security comes not through aggression but through hard work and effort by free people working through free markets. And if we are to secure the opportunities of the post-cold-war era, we must rise to the call of three daunting demands: The new requirements of peace and security, the challenge of fostering democracy, and the summons to generating greater economic growth and prosperity for the peoples of the world.

First, the challenge of ensuring peace and security. The world has learned that weakness tempts the warlike. We saw, with Saddam Hussein's naked aggression, that the misery of war results when tyrants doubt the commitment of the powerful to defend the security of the powerless. And that's why, as long as I'm President, the United States will remain absolutely opposed to isolationism. As a nation straddling two great oceans, the U.S. remains committed to engagement in both the Atlantic community and the emerging community of the Asia-Pacific region.

The emerging post-cold-war era that we face presents the United States with an opportunity to restructure its defenses. Now, I know there's been some concern about how we'll proceed with that complex and difficult task. But let me assure you and your Asia-Pacific neighbors that our restructuring, such as the closing of bases in Subic there in the Philippines, does not mean the end of American engagement in the Pacific area. We will remain a visible, credible security presence in the Asia-Pacific area with our forward-deployed forces and through bilateral defense arrangements with our friends.

And let me be clear, maintaining our security presence is not some kind of a charitable exercise. Your security and your economic growth are in our interests because together we will thrive in a stable, developing world. An unstable Asia does not serve our interests, and nor does a poverty-stricken or repression-ridden Asia. We need an Asia-Pacific region that is free and productive. And our security presence provides a foundation for mutual prosperity and for shared defense.

Strong, stable security arrangements enable us to meet the second challenge, and that is the call to democracy. The tyranny of totalitarianism is dead, and freedom is being born and reborn in nations from Latin America to Eastern Europe to Cambodia and to Mongolia. The Soviet Union as we've known it has vanished, and with it the delusions of communism.

The Republic of Korea has stood strong for democracy, particularly since the momentous events of 1987. This year, Korea will put this renewed faith in democratic institutions to the test in several elections. And I am confident that again this year the Korean people will demonstrate that freedom's way is the way of the future in Asia. Nations which build their prosperity on the freedom of their people know that there is no alternative.

This worldwide movement toward democracy leads us to the third challenge that's awaiting us, that of promoting economic growth and building a world of free and open markets.

Korea and the United States have a tremendous amount at stake in their economic relations. The U.S. is Korea's largest export market, and Korea is our sixth largest export market. The business executives with this wonderful team that we brought out with us today believe in building stronger economic ties with you. They stand ready to work side by side with Korean businessmen. And like you, they seek to build even more growth, opportunity, and stability for our two nations.

In building this world of free enterprise and economic growth, we know we have much to do. The United States is taking steps to boost our own competitiveness in foreign markets: Improving education, working to bring down our budget deficit, and enhancing productivity. We're working overtime to produce quality products at affordable prices, products that win in the marketplace.

And while Korea has made great progress in removing visible trade barriers to foreign business over the last 5 years, doing business in Korea is still more difficult than it should be for such a proud and successful country. Korea must address fundamental problems that stifle the ability of foreign firms to compete in your great country, problems like certain unjustified standards and regulations, or cumbersome customs procedures, delays in scheduled reductions of duties, and these financing restrictions.

Attitude towards imports must change. And while the notion of frugality isn't inherently bad, import restrictions hurt your own consumers and weaken the competitiveness of your firms. And while numerous restrictions in foreign trade have been lifted, such as certain performance requirements and sectoral restrictions, we look to Korea to remove all nontariff barriers to free trade.

Free trade has propelled Korea into a position of economic prominence and leadership. And because of this, Korea has a growing responsibility to lead in strengthening the whole world trade and financial system. The General Agreement on Tariffs and

Trade, GATT, can play an especially crucial role in expanding economic frontiers. On each stop of this trip, I've called for urgent action on behalf of the international trading system. And I am urging the world's trading nations to join with us in working towards a successful conclusion of that all-important Uruguay round with GATT Director Dunkel's proposed draft agreement, incidentally, as its basis.

And while every one of us has problems with some portions of that draft, none of us can afford to let the progress that it symbolizes slip through our fingers. The time has come for a strong collective response. A successful conclusion to the Uruguay round will pave the way for even greater trade liberalization in the coming years, with greater prosperity for absolutely everyone.

In order for Korea to build upon its own spectacular growth, it will need a more open financial system. I know that American businesses are particularly concerned with restrictions in the financial system here which prevent them from trading and investing in the Korean economy. But the bottom line is that broader access for foreign financial firms is in your best interest; it is in Korea's best interest because a more open economy will benefit Korean businesses and their customers.

But there's more to it than that. During the last 50 years, engagement and free trade have produced peace and prosperity. Here, in Korea it's been remarkable, throughout the Asia-Pacific region, in Europe, and indeed, in the United States. This prosperity has gone hand-in-hand with the growth of democracy, a fact that illustrates the indivisibility of security and political and economic liberty.

In the emerging post-cold-war era, economic engagement and expanded markets will ensure prosperity and stability for the people of the world. And that's why we've come here today. We want to build hope for a better life for our people. We want to create opportunity for all men and women. And we want to leave as our legacy peace for our children. And so, it is in that spirit of hopeful anticipation that I say thank you to all of you. What a remarkable, what a great job you have done. And yet what tremendous work lies ahead for us all.

May God bless your wonderful country. May God bless the relationship between our countries. And thank you for this opportunity to speak to such a distinguished group of business leaders. Thank you very, very much.

*Note: The President spoke at 1:24 p.m. at the Hotel Shilla.*

## Remarks to the Korean National Assembly in Seoul
*January 6, 1992*

Mr. Speaker, Mr. Secretary General, Assemblyman Park, and distinguished members of this National Assembly: Believe me, it is a great honor to return once more to this house, the symbolic center of Korean democracy. As the Speaker said, I first came to this chamber in February of 1989, just one month after taking office, and Barbara and I still recall the warm welcome we received then from the people of Korea. And here we are, celebrating our 47th wedding anniversary with all you young people. And you make us feel very much at home, and I'm grateful to each and every one of you. Thank you very much.

February of '89, that was nearly 3 years ago. In the short time since then, we have seen our world transformed. The epic cold war struggle between the forces of freedom and the Communist world came to an abrupt end; with God's mercy, a peaceful end. Gone is the Berlin Wall, the Warsaw Pact, not simply the Soviet empire but even the Soviet Union itself. Everywhere we see the new birth of democratic nations, a new world of freedom bright with the promise of peace and prosperity.

During my visits these last few days to Australia, to Singapore, and now to your wonderful country, Korea, I have stressed that this new world of freedom presents us with fresh and demanding challenges: Meeting new requirements for global security and stability, promoting democracy, and enhancing world economic growth and prosperity.

Korea, too, is a part, an important part, of this changing world. Indeed, you are at the center of these challenges. At home your country is developing its own democratic and free market traditions, and in the world

Korea is helping to shape a changing security and geopolitical landscape. Your influence in world affairs is enhanced by the fact that at long last Korea is assuming its place as a full member of the United Nations. Mr. Speaker, as President of a nation that fought under the U.N. flag to keep Korea free and to establish the conditions for growth and prosperity, we share your pride in what you have justifiably achieved.

Yes, change transforming our world, a revolution is on our hands. And yet, the cold war continues to cast its shadow over Korea. Just 25 miles north of this capital city, the Korean Peninsula is still cleaved by that DMZ, the ribbon of land that separates one people yearning to live in peace. Who can calculate the human cost: 10 million Koreans separated now from family members for 4 decades.

For 40 years, the people of Korea have prayed for an end to this unnatural division. For 40 years, you have kept alive the dream of one Korea. The winds of change are with us now. My friends, the day will inevitably come when this last wound of the cold war struggle will heal. Korea will be whole again. I am absolutely convinced of it.

For our part, I'll repeat what I said here 3 years ago: The American people share your goal of peaceful reunification on terms acceptable to the Korean people. This is clear. This is simple. This is our policy.

Recently, North and South made progress in easing tensions, in exploring opportunity for peace and understanding through direct talks at the prime ministerial level. This search has produced positive results: First, December's historic nonaggression agreement, and then, on the eve of this new year, an agreement to forever ban nuclear weapons from the Korean Peninsula. These positive developments come at a critical time of rising concern, at a time when North Korea's pursuit of nuclear arms stands as the single greatest source of danger to peace in all of northeast Asia.

This progress is a tribute to the policies of President Roh and the Government of this Republic. South Korea has systematically eliminated any possible action that could justify the North's pursuit of such deadly weapons. This Republic has rejected all weapons of mass destruction, and to give further meaning to this pledge, South Korea renounced all nuclear reprocessing and enrichment activities. On December 18th, President Roh announced that there were no nuclear weapons on South Korean soil. To any who doubted that declaration, South Korea, with the full support of the United States, has offered to open to inspection all of its civilian and military installations, including United States facilities.

At every point, South Korea's approach was open, sincere, and fair. Each good-faith action increased the call for the North to make a positive response. Today the prospects for real peace on this peninsula are brighter than at any point in the past four decades.

And yet, paper promises won't keep the peace. I call on North Korea to demonstrate its sincerity, to meet the obligations it undertook when it signed the Non-Proliferation Treaty 6 years ago. North Korea must implement in full all IAEA safeguards for its nuclear facilities without exception, and I might add, without delay. Moreover, North Korea, together with the Republic of Korea, should proceed to implement the inspection and verification portions of their unprecedented joint declaration on nonnuclearization, signed one week ago. Prompt action by the North will mark a new milestone on the path toward peace.

But let this be clear: The United States has and will support the security aspirations of its ally in the South in the cause of peace.

We are pleased that our September announcement about nuclear weapons helped lend momentum to the effort to make Korea safe from nuclear proliferation. And we've worked with others in the region to send a multilateral message to North Korea. And we've been willing to open our facilities to Korea to challenge North Korea to do the same.

We've also left no doubt that we'll back these overtures for peace with a demonstration of our military resolve. As you know, we've postponed our plan to reduce the number of American troops stationed here in Korea. Let there be no doubt: The people of this republic should know that the United States commitment to Korea's security remains steady and strong.

I renew that pledge as an ally, as President of a nation that shares your devotion to democracy and self-determination. Down through the decades, from Korea to Kuwait, from the American soldiers who gave their lives at Inchon, Pork Chop Hill, to the Korean forces who stood with us in Desert Storm, our two nations have upheld the international ideal that between nations and not just within them, common interests call for common action.

Today, in many quarters, that ideal is being questioned, even criticized. There are those who see the many changes in our world and say, "Well, our work is done." They urge us to declare victory, celebrate the collapse of our common enemy, and then come on home. They fail to recognize a fundamental fact: The cold war era changed our world forever. We did far more than hold a common enemy at bay. Together, we built a new world: A system of collective security to keep the peace, a system of free trade that fueled a generation of prosperity the likes of which the world has never seen, and a common commitment to political openness and liberty that now sustains a worldwide movement toward democracy.

The passing of the cold war must not mark the beginning of a new age of isolationism. The nations of the free world share more than a common history; they share a common destiny. There is no going back, only forward.

The developments of the past 40 years, the dramatic expansion of democracy, the geometric increase in global trade has created a system of common interests. To turn our backs now, to walk away after this great victory for freedom, or to retreat behind high trade walls into regional blocs would turn triumph to tragedy.

America is a Pacific nation. We will remain engaged in Asia, as we are in the other regions of the world. But just as the world itself stands on the threshold of a new era, so too we now enter a new era in U.S.-Korean relations. What began in the heat of the war as a military alliance has grown into a broader relationship, a partnership anchored in shared economic interests and common political ideals.

Korea's new role will, yes, mean new responsibilities, a new partnership based upon Korea's growing capabilities and increased ability to contribute to peace and prosperity in the Pacific and beyond.

The world now recognizes Korea as an economic powerhouse. We are pleased that over the past few years that we've narrowed our current account imbalance from about $9 billion to about $1 billion and that U.S. exports to Korea have increased at a pace of more than 7 percent over the last 2 years.

We must acknowledge the equally important strides that you have made in strengthening the institutions of democracy. Even in the 3 years since my last visit, the change is clear for all to see. With the encouragement of President Roh, this National Assembly now plays a greater role in Korean politics. I understand you have some very avid debates in this chamber. Well, join the club. That's what we do at home all the time. That's democracy in action.

In 1992 alone, South Korea will hold at least three elections at the local and national levels. Across the country, democracy is giving voice to new ideas and opinions, and since 1990 alone, 10 new daily newspapers and nearly 1,000 other new publications.

Free speech, free elections, private property: these are the cornerstones of the new world order, fundamental freedoms that secure peace and prosperity.

Consider your own history, a case study in contrasts between North and South. More than four decades ago, the South, with less land, fewer resources, and more people than in the North, set its course for free enterprise and free government. North Korea, well, they traveled a different path.

Blessed with rich resources and a stronger industrial base, the regime that ruled the North marched its people down the dead-end path of totalitarianism and international isolation. Its economy stalled. Its society suffocated. Its cohorts went their own way.

Today, the South is a dynamic participant in the community of democratic and market-oriented societies. The South is at peace, free, and prosperous, with an average annual income four times higher than in the North and a history of double-digit growth that has propelled it into the front ranks of the world's economies.

And now, you must build on your success. You must sustain the conditions that fueled your phenomenal growth. Korea did not raise the living standard of its people by closing itself off from the outside world. Today, Korea stands as America's seventh largest trading partner. With me on my trip are executives from some of America's leading companies, many with interests in expanding business with Korean companies and Korean consumers. America is not only your largest market, Korea's largest market, but a leading source of the technology and capital that helps fuel your economic growth. This nation owes much of its economic miracle to open markets abroad. Korea must see clearly that prosperity in the new century lies in open markets.

Trade is one activity where the interests of all nations intersect. Let me repeat here what I've said in Australia and in Singapore: At home in the United States, especially during tough economic times, my highest priority must be jobs and economic growth. But my allegiance to the American worker is not at odds with the interests of the Korean consumer. Trade is not a zero-sum game enriching some nations at the expense of the others. Growing trade provides the people of both our nations with higher standards of living and better lives.

Pressures for protectionism are building. We see it in my country with the new breed of economic isolationists who urge us to build barriers to expanding trade and opportunity. We see it here in Korea in a frugality campaign that's been used by too many to discourage imports. But wherever this impulse shows itself, we must fight back for trade that is free, fair, and open.

We must heed the lessons of history. For the first half of this century, great nations sought refuge in isolationism and in its economic accomplice, protectionism, and the world succumbed to the ravages of war, and think back, to depression. Since the Second World War, free nations large and small pursued a common course, forging alliances and fostering trade, and the world as a consequence has enjoyed an era of unprecedented peace and prosperity.

The history of this century is not lost on Korea. As a founding member of APEC, the forum for Asia-Pacific Economic Cooperation, you have worked with your economic partners in the region to bring down barriers to trade. But the key test, the key test now is before us in this Uruguay round. As an emerging economic power, Korea has shared greatly in the bounty of an open and growing world trading system. That reward carries with it profound responsibilities. Korea must now shoulder with other trading nations the burden of leadership on behalf of the multilateral trade regime.

As I mentioned before the business leaders of our two nations earlier today, I am urging at each stop of my trip that we use the Dunkel draft text as the basis for successfully concluding the GATT round of trade talks. Korea has the opportunity to help fight the forces of protectionism, to help tip the balance in favor of free and fair

trade policies that remain the world's one path to prosperity.

Our two nations share a history written in the blood of our people. The bonds forged in the cold war, at the brink of Korea's mortal danger, have grown stronger through the years. Forty years ago, the free world made your struggle their own struggle. Our forces fought here for a future free from tyranny. And you did far more than survive. In the shadow of the cold war, you showed what we can achieve so long as we are free.

For four long decades, Korea has stood at the frontier of freedom, vigilant, determined, never wavering in its commitment to the great cause of independence and liberty. So today, as we enter a new world, the world we fought for 40 years ago, Korea stands with us: a steadfast friend, ally, and partner; proud, prosperous, and free.

I salute you. I congratulate you. And may I thank you for this warm welcome. And may God bless the wonderful people of Korea. Thank you all very, very much.

*Note: The President spoke at 2:40 p.m. at the National Assembly Hall. In his remarks, he referred to Park Jyun Kyu, Speaker of the National Assembly; Park Sang Moon, Secretary General of the National Assembly; and Park Chung Soo, chairman of the Foreign Affairs and National Unification Committee.*

# Text of Remarks at Camp Casey in Yongsan, South Korea
*January 6, 1992*

I understand you've come to Yongsan from far and wide. It's a great privilege to meet with all of you today. Let me salute the proud men and women of the 2d Infantry Division. You are truly "second to none."

You serve at a time when Korea is reaching new world status, when we can build on the progress and the promise of a new year. More than a military alliance, our countries are moving toward a political, economic, and security partnership.

We stand here just a few miles from the DMZ, a relic of the cold war, tragically separating one people. History's verdict is in: On freedom's side stands one of the fastest developing countries in history. On the other side, a failed regime that produces only misery and want.

For more than 40 years, the United States commitment to the Republic of Korea's security has been firm and unwavering. Nothing will change that. Korea is where America made a clear commitment to liberty.

Korea is where we first stopped the spread of communism in Asia and fought to defend the international ideal of freedom.

In recognition of this republic's great achievements, we will gradually shift to a supporting role as the Korean military takes the lead in defense of their nation. But North Korea must know that we will resist any aggression and will keep our forces strong enough to do so for as long as the Korean people want our support.

Here at Camp Casey, you're a long way from home, and that's especially tough during the holiday season. With much of the world's attention on events in Eastern Europe, Moscow, and the Middle East, you may sometimes feel forgotten, just like Korean war veterans sometimes feel forgotten. So, I want you to hear this from the top. You have not been forgotten. The veterans of Korea won a mighty victory in the fight against communism. You honor them

with your presence here on the frontier of freedom. America never forgets those who serve. For the sake of the families of the 8,000 MIA's of the Korean war we will continue to seek the fullest possible accounting from North Korea.

You've got a tough assignment here. Our able Chairman of the Joint Chiefs of Staff, General Colin Powell, served here himself and was back for a visit in November. He agrees with me: Your professionalism, your courage, and your vigilance are the keys to our success here.

I will not forget this day. I am inspired and invigorated just looking at you. The time is coming when the Korean people will be united and free. Each one of you should be proud of your contribution to that inevitable triumph.

*Note: The text of this address was issued by the Office of the Press Secretary on January 6.*

# Remarks at a State Dinner Hosted by President Roh Tae Woo of South Korea in Seoul
*January 6, 1992*

Mr. President, Mrs. Roh, distinguished guests, tonight we have much to celebrate, first and foremost our solid alliance. Many think that our partnership was born that moment 40 years ago when we joined forces against aggression. But it dates back over a century. When your nation looked outward for diplomatic and commercial opportunity, it looked then first to the United States. Today, our alliance has grown into a political, economic, and security partnership. I assure you, our commitment will continue well into the 21st century.

As you said, Mr. President, during your visit to the White House, "Democracy in Korea is on course and is moving inexorably forward." Through hard work and commitment, the Republic of Korea has moved from a war-ravaged past to a prosperous present and an enviable future.

This republic's progress in resolving differences with your brothers in the North is

a great step in the journey toward the day when all of Korea is free. I admire your steadfastness and commitment to a peaceful resolution. The many successes of your *Nordpolitik* policy, your enhanced relations with Russia and China, your active dialog with North Korea, move us closer to that day. If North Korea can truly abandon not only its nuclear weapons program but its belligerence as well, that ribbon of land at the 38th parallel will no longer divide this nation.

Mr. President, we know each other well; I know you are a modest man. Your leadership of the Republic of Korea during this period of incredible change has earned you an honorable place in the wonderful history of this nation. You've knocked down trade barriers, opened markets, and your nation's economy has prospered. With each election your country holds, at least three this year, free ideas and opinions flourish. Under your leadership, at long last South Korea took its rightful place in the United Nations.

So, Mr. President, with many thanks for a visit that we will long cherish and long remember, I raise my glass and ask all of you to join me, a glass to peace and unification for Korea, to your leadership of the Republic of Korea, to peace and prosperity, to the wonderful people of this land that we treasure as true friends. To you, sir, Mrs. Roh. And thank you all for a magnificent time. To your health, sir.

*Note: The President spoke at 7:30 p.m. at the Blue House.*

## Remarks to Japanese and American Students in Kyoto, Japan
*January 7, 1992*

Thank you all very much. Why don't you all please be seated? [*Laughter*] Let me just say what a pleasure it is to be here with our very able Ambassador in Tokyo, Mike Armacost, who is doing a superb job. He's one of the great career Ambassadors of our service, and he's in a difficult and an important post, and he is doing an outstanding job. And I'm very pleased that he's here with us today.

I want to also say how pleased I am to be here with the former Prime Minister, Toshiki Kaifu. When he was Prime Minister and I was President, we worked very closely together on a lot of matters relating to world peace, better understanding between Japan and the United States. He was frank; he was straightforward; he was friendly to our great country. And I can tell you, I will never forget his many courtesies to me, and I will never forget what he did to strengthen the relationship between these two great countries, Japan and the United States. So Toshiki, thank you, sir, for all you've done.

And it's a great pleasure to have this first day of our trip to visit these ancient centers and shrines of really the Japanese soul and the Japanese nation, Kyoto and, later this afternoon, Kashihara in Nara Prefecture. But I come as a friend. I come with some ideas that we're going to be discussing with the Government in Tokyo starting tomorrow, and I also bring an open interest in learning a lot more about this great country.

I want to take note of the achievements of three mayors, Mayor Kumakura, Mayor Aoki, and Mayor Kudo, over here. These guys, they're from small towns in rural Japan, and these mayors have been instrumental in the establishment of branch campuses of American universities. And I really firmly believe, and you all are better equipped to speak to it than I, that these grassroots exchanges pay important benefits to both our countries. So, thank you very, very much, sir, all three of you, for what you're doing.

Let me just say to the students, this is kind of what we call in the trade a cameo appearance; you're in here and you're out of here in a hurry. But to the students of the Stanford Center, well, one or two here—[*laughter*]—and the Kyoto program students at Doshisha University—[*laughter*]—how many are there? When I click all these things off, it would be fun to see. University of Michigan, how many there? [*Applause*] All right. And how about the Aggies, Texas A&M? [*Applause*] Small but vocal contingent over here.

Incidentally, what the former Prime Minister was referring to is that each President, as you all know, Americans know, when he gets out of office, has a library, archive for the papers. And mine is going to be in my home State, but at Texas A&M. And I'm looking forward to that very, very much; not too soon. [*Laughter*]

Let me just click off, for some of the journalists with us today, some things that I know you all know. About 2,000 American students now attend undergraduate and graduate programs in Japan. Many more Japanese students take part in comparable programs back in the U.S. And more than

1,000 Americans now teach in Japanese schools. And I hope that we will continue to do everything that we can to promote greater and greater participation in these important exchanges in the years to come.

They open up, in my view, new intellectual and cultural horizons, and these experiences really, I think, turn an awful lot of participants into the great leaders of our country, and both countries I might say. Look at today's Prime Minister of Japan, Prime Minister Miyazawa. When he was a university student, some may not know this, he took part in the sixth Japan-America student conference at the University of Southern California.

I also want to single out once again Prime Minister Kaifu. Toshiki's first travel to the United States was through the U.S. Information Agency's International Visitors Program. And then as Minister of Education and later as Prime Minister, he made great efforts to promote educational and executive exchanges that really do foster understanding between our two countries. Another leader who recognized the value of exchanges was my friend the late Minister Abe, Foreign Minister of Japan, who passed away. But the Global Partnership Fund, which he was so instrumental in organizing, carries on his good work today in supporting these student exchanges.

So in all, they are an aspect of the major purpose of this visit to Japan, namely to open and expand opportunities for interchange between our countries. And I want the people of our countries to have a far better understanding of one another. We need more Americans who can speak Japanese and who understand the workings of the Japanese marketplace.

I want to increase access for American goods and services in these Japanese markets. Open markets, like student exchanges, yield a bounty for all who participate. They help each other better understand. Open markets lift the technical progress to new heights. And they raise everybody's standards and benefit consumers, as a matter of fact, through the expanse of the global marketplace.

I've been saying this as I've traveled on this trip through Asia, but I am strongly convinced—I'm sure there are some eco-nomic majors out here—I am strongly convinced that free and open commerce is not a zero-sum game. Free trade on a level playing field creates jobs and lifts standards in both of our countries. So, the challenge of global competition can be driving our efforts for educational reform.

I don't know whether it's caught up with you all here, but we have a nationwide program called America 2000, has people from both sides of the aisle, Democrats and Republicans, from Governors in all States, helped me set the six major educational goals. American educational leaders and experts look to Japan for some examples as to how we can improve our schools.

David Kearns, I don't know if that name rings a bell. He's our number two at the Department of Education. But he visited Japan many, many times to examine Japanese quality products, first when he was the chairman and chief executive officer of one of our great companies, Xerox. He came back with a lot of ideas that he's now trying to help us implement there at the Department. American education experts attach importance to the fact that Japanese parents, more than in our country, are active in the children's schools and demand better performance. So, we're trying to find ways to increase parental interest.

And if I might say a pleasant word of my bride of 47 years as of yesterday, newlyweds we are, I think what Barbara is trying to do in terms of getting kids and getting families to read to their kids and kids to read to one another and adult education all adds into this program which we call America 2000.

Next spring, actually, we're going to hold a meeting of the education ministers of the APEC, the Asia Pacific Economic Cooperation group. And it's going to bring together the total experiences of 15 member societies to raise our common educational standards and to draw the most from our precious resource, the imagination and the energy of our people.

So, student exchanges reach beyond the technical and the expert level. They enrich the individual spirit, and they nourish the cultures of communities and nations. So, we need them. And while we need them to promote efficiency in markets and institutions, we simply must not neglect exchanges in the humanities, in history, fine arts, philosophy, the study of religion, languages, and literature.

Octavio Paz, the 1990 Nobel laureate for literature, put it well when he wrote, "If human beings forget poetry, they will forget themselves." So, those of you all involved in the liberal arts, you have nothing to do but be proud of the work you're engaged in. And if you don't believe it, just ask old Octavio Paz, winner of the Nobel Prize. [*Laughter*]

But look, I do honor you, salute you for your spirit of scholarship and adventure. And if you get a little lonely from time to time, keep it in the big perspective. As I see it, with the crying need for better education, the crying need for peoples to understand each other better, you are doing something important just being here, just working, just understanding the culture of this great country. In my view, you're really doing something important.

I will simply conclude by this broad comment on my job opportunities, my own, that is. I can't think of a more exciting time in the history of this country, in the recent history of this country, to be President of the United States. Now, you go back to where things were just a couple of years ago as you look at Eastern Europe; you look at parties in the Middle East that weren't

even willing to talk to each other; you look at the Soviet Union that we lived in fear of when you all were two or three years younger. You wondered whether we were going to evolve into some kind of a nuclear holocaust, little kids going to bed scared in our country and in other countries all around the world. And that's changing, and it's changing for the better.

And so, it is a very exciting time to represent the only, I guess in terms of both military and economic, the only remaining, what they call superpower. But what we want to do is use our ingenuity and use our energies, well-represented by this group here today, to help people around the world; to assure the peace; to raise the standards of living of our own people by, as I said earlier on, opening markets and having our economy much more vibrant.

So, it's a wonderful time to be fighting these battles and accepting these challenges that will always be with whoever is President of the United States. This, as I say, is a cameo appearance; it's a quick drop-by. But looking around here, I can get a little sense of enthusiasm that occupies this crowd. And I really wanted to wish you a very, very happy new year. And may God bless you in your important work.

Thank you all very, very much.

*Note: The President spoke at 2:29 p.m. in the Cosmos Ballroom at the Miyako Hotel.*

# Remarks at the Opening of Toys-R-Us in Kashihara, Japan
*January 7, 1992*

Thank you all very, very much, all of you. And may I first thank Governor Kakimoto and Mayor Miura for their gracious hospitality and say to all of you that it really is, for Barbara and me, a deep honor to visit this ancient and venerable city of Kashihara right here in Japan. And may I thank Minister Watanabe for being here. His ministry did so much to change the great retail store law, and I am personally very grateful to him for taking the time to be with us today.

And Mr. Charles Lazarus, thank you, sir,

for your introduction. It's a pleasure being at your side and sharing your joy in the successful opening of Toys-R-Us. When our grandchildren heard about this trip to the Far East, they figured the highlight would be today, stopping at Toys-R-Us. And I'll just have to tell them I couldn't buy them anything because Barbara has cut my *kozukai*, my allowance, that is. [*Laughter*]

What we see here today is success for Japanese consumers as well as for ourselves in the effort to eliminate a major barrier in the Japanese distribution system. For years, American retailers have sought to compete in the Japanese market. And after all, Japan has the second largest economy in the world, and its consumers are increasingly demanding wider choices for themselves and their families, lower prices, and certainly uncompromising quality.

But American companies before weren't making any headway because the regulations, particularly the large retail store law, made opening new foreign retail stores virtually impossible. From the beginning of our administration we've had a key trade policy objective, and that was to break down the barriers to the sales of U.S. goods and services.

And in 1990, we launched the Structural Impediments Initiative, or what we call SII, those talks to remove the underlying economic barriers to trade and balance of payment adjustment and to promote open markets. SII has indeed enabled us to take aim at the rules that prevent our companies from competing in Japanese markets.

And when Japan changed its large store law, it lowered a key barrier to open trade. And Japanese consumers, your buyers here in this country, and our workers stand to reap the benefits. Japanese consumers will get stores with wider selections, more competitive prices, and quality goods from around the world. And U.S. companies will be able to operate businesses and sell their products in this huge and promising market.

And I think we're all here today because Toys-R-Us was ready to take up the challenge of SII, and it literally lived up to the old Japanese saying, "Three years on top of a stone." We have much to learn from the 3-year battle that Toys-R-Us waged to pry open the $6 billion Japanese toy market. After all, this is the first time that a large U.S. discount store has opened here, and it's blazed a trail. And now all kinds of companies can come on in, from toy stores to high-tech outlets.

And I hope that Toys-R-Us is but the first in a long line of American retailers to locate in this great country. Greater access is an exciting idea, and it will help create more jobs in America. And the opening of the Japanese retail market gives our manufac-turers, particularly the small manufacturers, a conduit into markets they otherwise couldn't have touched and brings the Japanese consumer a wide choice of world-class goods.

The relationship between the United States and Japan is one of the world's most vital economic relationships. Our two nations produce over 40 percent, 40 percent of the world's gross national product, and therefore, our actions, taken separately or together, affect many countries.

We've worked together in close cooperation, for instance, at the economic summit, in the G–7 framework, and in international financial institutions to promote global growth and shared prosperity, Japan and the U.S. working for those common goals.

But we still face many challenges. And each partner must realize that it benefits from free trade and open markets. Our economic relationship is not a zero-sum game for either side. And though we're pleased at the success so far, we're not satisfied with just reaching these piecemeal trade agreements. In the cause of free and open trade, we want agreements that produce permanent improvement in access and in U.S. sales to Japanese markets and permanent improvement in the lives of Japanese consumers.

And what makes me so happy here today is that we see here the beginning of a dynamic new economic relationship, one of greater balance. There is much that we can do for the world based on a forward-looking global partnership between two great nations, two powerful economies, and two resourceful, innovative peoples. And together we will go far.

Just two last points. I will do my level-best as President of the United States to preserve and strengthen the important relationship between Japan and my great country. It has a lot to do with world peace. It has a lot to do with world economic stability. It has a lot to do with two great economic and democratic countries working together, setting an example for other countries around the world. So, I want to say to the Minister and to the Prime Minister, I will do my part to keep this relationship on track.

And lastly, and this is the end, you'll be happy to know, I just want to thank all of the people in this wonderful city who have given Barbara Bush, over here, and me such a warm welcome. When we got off that helicopter here and came by those wonderfully warm, smiling faces, extending to us a warm, Japanese welcome, we felt very, very grateful and very emotional. And that said an awful lot about the friendship between Japan and the United States of America.

Thank you. And may God bless each and every one of you.

*Note: The President spoke at 4:10 p.m. In his remarks, he referred to Yoshiya Kakimoto, Governor of Nara; Taro Miura, Mayor of Kashihara; Michio Watanabe, Japanese Minister of Foreign Affairs; and Charles Lazarus, chairman and chief executive officer of Toys-R-Us. A tape was not available for verification of the content of these remarks.*

# Remarks With Prime Minister Kiichi Miyazawa of Japan to the Presidential Business Delegation in Tokyo
*January 8, 1992*

*The President.* Let me just say to those on the American side and this very distinguished delegation of American business people that are here, led by our able Secretary of Commerce, how pleased we are to be in Japan and, Mr. Prime Minister, how much we appreciate your hospitality.

Are we going to have a translation or do we——

*The Prime Minister.* Go ahead. I think we understand.

*The President.* And to the Japanese here, let me say how important we view this part of our trip. The trip is not simply about jobs and business. This is a terribly important part of it. But given the breadth of understanding of this Prime Minister, we've been able to talk about world security problems, about a global partnership, about the big picture. To guarantee that this big picture continues to unfold in a positive way, we must make dramatic progress on the business side. And indeed, Prime Minister Miyazawa and I have had a real opportunity now to begin once again our discussions of this.

But I would say to you, my friend, these are good people, our business people. They are people that not only represent individual American companies, but in a sense we've brought a delegation that is widely connected with chambers of commerce, Federation of Independent Business, the

heartbeat of our country in jobs in small business, independent business. And so, the head of the Independent Business Association is here, the National Association of Manufacturing. And in these discussions, your friends and colleagues are talking to our organizations as well as to these business executives and individuals in whom I have so much personal confidence.

But we're grateful to you. And I would just like to turn the floor over to you, sir, for any comments that you'd care to make.

*The Prime Minister.* Thank you, Mr. President. If I may, a few words.

Secretary Mosbacher, distinguished U.S. business executives, I hope you are having a productive meeting. It must be quite rare, even in the United States, for such an outstanding group of business executives to get together in one room, particularly from such a broad spectrum of industries ranging from potato chips to computer chips. [*Laughter*] I should be delighted if you take full advantage of this special occasion for the benefit of both economies.

President Bush and I are working hard to advance our bilateral relationship including its economic aspect, not only for the sake of our two countries but also for the rest of the world. In so doing, both the President and I have great expectations for the input from the private sectors.

Now, 18 people are enough to form 2

baseball teams. I hope you will be throwing balls of imaginative and creative ideas back and forth with the Trade Minister here today, as well as with Japanese business representatives tomorrow morning, so as to further utilize market-access opportunities here in Japan.

You are welcome. Thank you very much.

*The President.* May I correct an omission? Yesterday, far beyond the call of duty, Mr. Watanabe, the Minister, met with our people and came down and couldn't have been more hospitable to Mrs. Bush and me. And I'm very sorry I did not mention that in the beginning of my remarks.

We note these things. We Americans note these courtesies. And that one, I think, was wonderful. And your asking the former Prime Minister to come down there to greet us also was noted with great appreciation and got this visit off, I think, Mr. Watanabe, to a good start yesterday.

But now we've got to follow through. We've got to be specific. We've got to get to as much as we can, set tables, times— "Let's do it by then." And I think we can do it. I really believe that we can move this process forward. And it is in our interests; it is in your interests. And I like to think that because of the progress Japan has made and the enormous potential that we both have, that world leadership is at stake.

We've got something here with the world that's changing. These people have heard me give this speech, but I'll be very short. But Kiichi, when you look at where we were a year ago or 2 years ago in terms of world peace, your little kids in this country or kids in our country growing up worried about nuclear holocaust, and now we see a tremendous opportunity——

*The Prime Minister.* This is really a new wind in the world.

*The President.* It is. So, we've got to lead it. And we've got to work; we've got to iron out these differences between us so that we can go forward without tensions mounting and dividing up the world into trading blocs. And I am really excited about the potential. But here's a man that's demon-

strated his interest.

*The Prime Minister.* You have done a great deal to bring this new world of peace, really, after the Gulf thing.

*The President.* I might use this opportunity to say here in front of our leaders in Japan that there had been some rumors around that in the United States, that I have addressed myself to in the United States, of a disappointment on the part of me as President about Japan's part in Desert Storm. With the press here, let me just repeat what I've said at home: Japan stepped up and did what Japan was asked to do.

And I have been very grateful for that. And to the degree that anyone here might be asked about whether we were disappointed in Japan's role, the answer, as I've said back then, is no. Japan did what was asked of Japan. And Japan was there in several important ways, and they were not asked to send troops into Desert Storm. We understand, and we didn't ask for that. And so let me just take this opportunity to tell you that's not an irritant between us.

*The Prime Minister.* I, Mr. President, greatly appreciate your saying so. I think we did our utmost, and I do appreciate your saying that. There perhaps had some misunderstanding on your part, on our part, both sides of the Pacific. But I do appreciate your saying that.

*The President.* Yes. Well, there's none on mine, but there may have been on our side of the Pacific. There's a lot of misunderstanding over there. But I want you to know that because we thought you responded very positively. You shouldn't have a burden of people saying you didn't.

*The Prime Minister.* Should we get down to our discussions again?

*The President.* Okay. Thank you all.

*Note: The President spoke at 12:26 p.m. to Japanese and American business leaders meeting in Akasaka Palace. In his remarks, he referred to Michio Watanabe, Japanese Minister of Foreign Affairs.*

# Joint Statement by the President and Prime Minister Kiichi Miyazawa of Japan: A Strategy for World Growth
*January 8, 1992*

President Bush and Prime Minister Miyazawa today announced A Strategy for World Growth designed to strengthen the world economy.

The President and Prime Minister expressed concern that growth of the world economy in 1991 slowed to the lowest level in nearly a decade. They recognized that the outlook for growth of the world economy this year is weaker than previously expected. This situation could adversely affect the prospects for income and jobs, undermine the efforts of newly emerging democracies and the developing countries to implement sound market-oriented economic reforms, and raises the spectre of renewed protectionism.

The United States and Japan are the two largest countries in the world economy, together accounting for nearly 40 percent of total global production and more than 20 percent of world trade. The President and Prime Minister, aware of a special responsibility placed on their countries by their position, recognize that each country needs to pursue responsible economic policies that strengthen the international economy and global trading system. They have decided to undertake domestic policies to improve growth prospects, as a part of a cooperative effort which contributes to the attainment of sustainable growth with price stability and the promotion of global economic recovery.

Prime Minister Miyazawa, with these considerations in mind, stated that the Government of Japan will submit to the Diet the fiscal 1992 budget and the Fiscal Investment and Loan Program aimed at strengthening domestic demand by increased public investment through the central government and local governments, and contributing to

the world through its official development assistance (ODA) and other measures, despite tight fiscal conditions. Prime Minister Miyazawa stated that the Government of Japan will monitor the progress of the above measures so as to assure that the expected effects are realized. The recent decision by the Bank of Japan to reduce interest rates is also intended to maintain sustainable growth with price stability.

Toward the same end, President Bush also stated that he would be submitting to the Congress a comprehensive program to strengthen U.S. growth and competitiveness. The details of the program will be contained in the President's State of the Union message and his budget proposals for fiscal 1993 to be announced later this month. The President noted that the recent reduction in interest rates reflected the determination by the Federal Reserve to facilitate U.S. economic recovery and growth. The President also reaffirmed his commitment to achieve a substantial reduction of the U.S. budget deficit over the medium term.

The President and Prime Minister reviewed developments in financial markets and agreed that recent exchange rate movements were consistent with current economic developments. They expressed confidence that the above measures and developments will contribute to correction of external imbalances.

President Bush and Prime Minister Miyazawa expressed their continued support for ongoing economic policy coordination among G–7 countries as essential for achieving their common objectives as expressed in this statement. They stressed the importance of continued cooperative efforts and called on other industrial countries to join with them.

## Text of Remarks at the State Dinner Hosted by Prime Minister Kiichi Miyazawa of Japan in Tokyo
*January 8, 1992*

*Mrs. Bush.* Mr. Prime Minister and Mrs. Miyazawa, I rarely get to speak for George Bush. But tonight I know he would want me to thank you, on behalf of the members of his administration and the American businessmen who are here, for a wonderful visit and for a great friendship, in my part, for a lovely day, and I think for a wonderful day for all of you.

You know, I can't explain what happened to George because it never happened before. But I'm beginning to think it's the Ambassador's fault. [*Laughter*] He and George played the Emperor and the Crown Prince in tennis today, and they were badly beaten. And we Bushes aren't used to that. [*Laughter*] So, he felt much worse than I thought. [*Laughter*]

But General Scowcroft is going to speak for the President. And thank you very much for a wonderful visit.

*Mr. Scowcroft.* Ladies and gentlemen, it's my great honor on behalf of the President, and without his assured elegance, to deliver the remarks he was going to make. May I first, Mr. Prime Minister, on his behalf, thank you for your very kind words, your expressions of solidarity, hope, and friendship.

Prime Minister Miyazawa, Deputy Prime Minister Watanabe, distinguished ministers, distinguished former Prime Ministers, ladies and gentlemen. Mr. Prime Minister, it is already clear from our discussions that we share much in common. Most important, we both want stronger ties, better trade, and a closer friendship between our two countries.

Barbara and I are honored to be here. I am proud to join you in welcoming the season of the new year and to look ahead with honesty and understanding to the era of a new century.

Mr. Prime Minister, let me offer my very warmest congratulation on your election. I sincerely look forward to the work that lies together before us. As you remarked earlier this year, the United States and Japan share the same values and bear a heavy responsibility for world order. It is my conviction that the United States and Japan must move forward together as partners. We share a common vision for the post-cold-war world, a world knitted together by a global trading system with common rules making possible free and equitable competition.

Kiichi, I know our people share a love of baseball, so perhaps we should think of this new world in this spirit. You've called your country a team player, a description I would also apply to America. So let's compete in the arena of free and open trade. Open competition and close cooperation will make both our countries winners. Working together, no two nations can do more to realize a new era of peace and prosperity than Japan and the United States.

You once spoke of the need to create an economy for the benefit of mankind and to challenge the unknown. So now, let us join together. Let us forge a global partnership as we confront the challenges of the coming century. For the sake of our children, for the sake of their children, we must not let these opportunities slip through our fingers.

Mr. Prime Minister, I hear you are fond of the phrase "large trees with deep roots." Let us guard the growing tree of our friendship so that it may shelter all the generations to come.

To this friendship, I raise my glass.

*Note: The dinner was held in the Small Dining Room at the Prime Minister's residence in Tokyo. The President became ill at the dinner before the scheduled remarks, and he returned to the Akasaka Palace. Mrs. Bush spoke at 8:55 p.m. Gen. Brent Scowcroft, Assistant to the President for National Security Affairs, delivered the President's remarks.*

## Text of Remarks at the Japanese Welcoming Committee Luncheon in Tokyo
*January 9, 1992*

Thank you, Prime Minister Kaifu. Of course, I want to start my remarks by extending to all of you the President's apologies for not being present at lunch today. This meeting was to be a high point of his trip. I'm sure you all know as well of his great respect and warm feelings for former Prime Minister Kaifu. And it is with real regret that he was not able to be here at lunchtime today.

As Prime Minister Kaifu said, the President is fine. I talked to his doctor just an hour ago. The doctor is a former classmate of mine at college. I know him very well, so I can assure you the information is correct. The doctor has told the President in very strict terms to rest this morning. He will be resuming his schedule later today and, I'm sure, will express to all of you his deep regret at not being able to join you at this wonderful gathering.

Mr. Prime Minister, members of the Diet, distinguished guests, it is a deep honor to be here today. President Bush has asked me to make his remarks to you this afternoon. Although there have been minor grammatical changes in pronouns, this is the President's speech. These are his words.

We come to Japan at the culmination of a long and productive journey. Today we stand at a turning point in history. The cold war is over. The Soviet Union has vanished and with it the delusions of communism. Centuries-old enemies in the Middle East are tempering ancient hatreds in pursuit of peace. Freedom's phoenix is rising from the ashes of tyranny in nations from Latin America to Eastern Europe and from Cambodia to Mongolia.

Freedom's rebirth was painful, its triumphs inscribed in blood, its truce seared by the fires of war and sacrifice. This century has taught us two crucial lessons: First, that isolationism and protectionism lead to war and deprivation; and second, that political engagement and open trade lead to peace and prosperity.

These last few years we again learned of the power of ideas. Technologies that transmit ideas in the blink of an eye carry the human spirit over barricades and through barbed wire. They hurdle walls designed to hold back the truth. We live in a world transformed, shrunken by swift travel and instant communication, drawn closer by common interests and ambitions, propelled forward by people's imaginations and dreams.

As leaders of this transforming world, the United States and Japan must help build a new international order based on the rule of law, respect for human rights, and political and economic liberty. We must shape a world enriched by open trade and robust competition, a world that will create a better life for people of all nations.

The United States lies between two great oceans, the Atlantic and the Pacific. We are a nation of the Atlantic by birth, but our ties to the Asia-Pacific region deepen daily. Our two-way trade is now $310 billion annually, one-third larger than that with Europe. Our prosperity and yours are indivisible. American businesses cannot flourish in Asia unless the economies of Asia thrive and grow.

At the same time, Japan's growth needs American markets open and growing. Since 1975, the number of Americans of Asian origin has nearly quadrupled. What happens here is very important to us. And at the core of our continuing Asian engagement stands our alliance with Japan.

At each stop during his visit to the region, the President has stressed the challenges we must face, addressing the new security requirements of our transforming world, promoting democracy, and generating world economic growth and prosperity. Let me expand upon that by focusing on the special relationship that the United States enjoys with Japan. Rarely in history have two nations with such different and differing historic cultural roots developed such an extraordinary relationship. Our people are bound by shared security, by democracy, and by our deep economic ties.

There are those who doubt the future of this relationship. There are reasons for tension. Here in Japan you have a saying, "Some rain must fall to prepare the ground for building." We can all see that without progress we may be in for some rough weather. And I must be frank in saying that there are problems in our economic relationship. Speaking not only for the United States but for many developed countries, Japan's trade surplus is too high, and its market access too restricted.

President Bush has come to Japan as a friend, seeking solutions to these concerns, believing that the expansion of free and fair trade will do nothing but strengthen our relationship. We in the United States are confident about our capacity for partnership. Our areas of common interest are too important. Consider the four key areas of our joint relationship.

First, the U.S.-Japan security alliance. We enjoy a strong security bond with Japan. Japan's generous host-nation support for U.S. forces stationed here is an important demonstration of shared responsibilities. Let us make the most efficient use of our defense resources by building greater coordination of our military forces and by promoting the two-way flow of defense technology. Such cooperation enhances our security and builds even stronger political ties between us.

The Gulf crisis sparked spirited debate here about Japan's global role. That makes it all the more profound that no nation outside the Gulf region provided more generous financial support than did Japan. The American people and peace-loving people everywhere appreciate deeply your contribution, Japan's contribution, to the United Nations coalition in the Gulf.

Even before the Gulf war, but especially in its aftermath, Japan has continued to define its growing role in world affairs. An increasingly active, engaged, and responsible Japan is critical to a forward-looking post-cold-war community. That community will not exist unless its leading powers lead.

This brings us to the second area of our relationship, our foreign policy cooperation. We must fulfill the bright promise of our global partnership. Together, we produce 40 percent of the world's gross national product. We contribute together 40 percent of all bilateral aid. We have the ability to marshal unrivaled resources to build a better future if our foreign policies are well coordinated.

America has a responsibility here, but it is a responsibility we share with Japan. The upcoming conference on assistance to the nations of the former U.S.S.R., now the Commonwealth of Independent States, is a timely example of such foreign policy coordination.

The collapse of the Soviet Union has also spurred questions within Japan about the durability of U.S.-Japan alliance. For decades, this alliance has stood as the bulwark of American-Japanese international cooperation. It is today every bit the linchpin of regional stability and bilateral cooperation that wise men foresaw years ago.

The demise of the Soviet Union may confront us both with ominous dangers, but it also presents us an historic opportunity. The leadership Japan and other Asian nations can provide to help transform a once-totalitarian empire into market-oriented and democratic states helps guarantee the future peace and stability of our world.

Let me add that with the changes in the former Soviet Union, the United States sees no reason why Japan should not regain the Northern Territories. We share this goal, and in whatever way we can, we will help you attain it.

We cannot imagine meeting the foreign policy challenges of our time without Japan as a partner. That is why today Prime Minister Miyazawa and President Bush will issue a document called the Tokyo Declaration, setting out the basic principles and major challenges of our global partnership. By putting into words the fundamentals of the two great partners, we hope to guide the way through the turbulent waters ahead. We must be clear about our responsibilities and our requirements, for our renewed alliance will do much to define the shape of the post-cold-war world.

Third, we must deepen our understanding of each other. For all of our interaction politically and economically, our peoples know too little of the other's history, traditions, and language. We welcome the work of the Center for Global Partnership in expanding exchanges and interactions, intellectual, scientific, and cultural. Thanks to such programs, our two nations will have an ever-increasing number of people who have lived in each other's country, speak each other's language, and understand more fully how important we are to each other.

Although more than 200,000 Asian students now study in American colleges and universities, more Americans must immerse themselves in Asian societies and cultures.

As the exchange of free people and ideas flows between our nations and as the cold war ends in victory for our cause, our economic relations have taken center stage. This brings me to the fourth and most important point.

If we are to expand our economic ties, we must face up to the economic tensions that threaten our relations. We must reduce those tensions now by opening markets and by eliminating barriers to trade and investment. We are now each other's largest overseas trading partner. Japan will sell about $90 billion worth of goods and services to the United States this year. We will sell nearly $50 billion to Japan.

Our economies, the world's two largest and most technologically advanced, have become irreversibly intertwined. Closing markets and restricting trade have previously brought the world to the brink of economic disorder. Isolation and protectionism must remain the sleeping ghosts of the past, not the waking nightmares of the future. We must reject these failed notions in the sure knowledge that expanding markets mean expanding jobs and increasing prosperity for both our countries.

We must ensure a continued strong two-way economic relationship between Japan and the United States, with markets more open to new goods and services, manufacturers more open to new competitive ideas, the financial services industry competing on a fair basis, and an equitable flow of technology on both sides.

Our two countries share a special responsibility to strengthen the world economy. Yesterday the President and the Prime Minister announced a strategy for world growth which commits both our countries to domestic policies to stimulate growth. Expanded domestic demand in Japan translates into additional exports to Japan for American products and jobs at home. And we are seeking broad support for growth policies among other industrialized countries as well.

Many American businesses learned during the past decade that the old ways no longer work in our changing international marketplace. Our companies have cut costs, improved quality, and championed innovation. As a result, our products sell in markets everywhere they have access. And candidly, such access is still limited in Japan.

We must reduce the trade imbalance between us, not through managed trade, through gimmicks or artificial devices, but simply by gaining true and welcome access to your markets. We want to create fair opportunities for traders and investors, both buyers and sellers, by removing the barriers both seen and unseen to open and equitable trade.

American business doesn't need a handout and doesn't want one. Some say that perhaps it is time to help the United States out of a sense of pity or compassion. Let me tell you, we are looking for no such help. What the United States wants from Japan is for Japan to recognize its international economic responsibility for its own sake and for the sake of the global marketplace upon which Japan depends. When we express appreciation to those who seek to open Japanese markets, it is not because we need a handout but because we know an open Japan is good for us all.

Our companies simply expect the chance to compete fairly in markets around the world. Our Government remains committed to open markets, and we will further reduce our own trade barriers as our friends dismantle their own.

Our two countries have embarked on a unique experiment in economic independence called the Structural Impediments Initiative. In this effort, each side pinpoints the other's barriers to competitiveness, and each commits to reduce them. We both must reinvigorate this commitment to market access, whether for high quality American products or quality American services. The beneficiaries will be the workers and consumers on both sides of the Pacific.

Improving our economic relations includes further opening your markets. It means greater openness in many sectors of the Japanese economy still biased against outside investment. These practices hurt American companies, but they also hurt Japanese consumers.

Americans want the same things you want, a better quality of life for themselves and their families. Americans never say, "Please raise our prices." And I'll bet the Japanese don't either. Every worker is also a consumer, and economic competition brings them great choices and lower prices. In fact, the Toys-R-Us store that the President visited in Kyoto offers prices up to 30 percent lower than its Japanese competition. The stunning success of the consumers' response to its sister store north of Tokyo tells the same story. That's good for us, and it's good for you.

U.S. export business is stronger than ever. We sold more exports last year than ever before. We enjoy a trade surplus with Europe. About one-third of our economic growth between 1985 and 1990 was attributable to merchandise exports. To Japan, our manufactured exports are up 70 percent since 1987, a $20 billion increase that represents almost half a million jobs.

Still the overall trade deficit with Japan remains large. And I might add, its persistence is truly the exception among our trading partners. Let me say this: We have waited a long time, but now the time has come for equal access. Fairplay is in both our interests.

As you know, the United States and Japan also face the urgent challenge of leading the way to a successful conclusion of the Uruguay round. Because of the benefits we each derive from free trade, Japan and the United States bear a special responsibility for tackling the remaining difficult issues quickly and decisively. The success of the round depends on bold, farsighted leadership. We must lift our gaze to the glimmering horizon of broader prosperity and not worry over the stones in our immediate path.

Yes, all of us have problems with portions of the so-called Dunkel draft, but we cannot let the progress it represents slip through our fingers. If we allow that draft to be picked apart by special interests, who wins? Not our people, not yours, not the less developed nations. No one. The GATT round is the world's best hope for expanding trade for all countries.

Men and women from all walks of life and all parts of America constantly tell the President this: They believe very, very strongly in creating a level playing field for everyone. We want all our trading partners to give the United States companies the same kind of opportunities that their firms enjoy in the United States. That's not just free trade; that's fair trade. And it creates a basis for even greater freedom and greater prosperity for all.

Many of our Japanese friends argue that the United States must improve its competitiveness, and they're right. We recognize that some of our bilateral trade imbalance stems from causes other than restricted market access. One reason for Japan's competitiveness is because Japan has saved and invested at a rate double that of the United States. You have focused on applied research and development and new manufacturing technologies. Your companies have established fine quality control systems. You have developed a highly educated labor force and have taken the long view to develop markets abroad.

There is much for us to learn from you. We are taking steps to boost our competitiveness. We can and will increase our rate of savings and investment. We will continue to boost our manufacturing's excellence. We will reduce the budget deficit. To stimulate innovation, risk, and longer term business outlook, the President is pushing for investment incentives, R&D credits, and capital gains tax cuts. In America, cutting capital gains is politically extremely difficult. It would be easier if our politicians saw the positive effect on Japan's competitiveness due to low capital gains rates.

And America must raise its educational standards. Our America 2000 education strategy will fuel a revolution for better quality schools. This is another path to competitiveness. The education achievements of

Japan and others in the Asia-Pacific region inspire us. That is why President Bush has invited the countries of the Pacific Rim to send their education ministers to Washington for a conference this spring to seek new ways to cooperate and to learn from each other's accomplishments.

With the President today, traveling with him, is a delegation of America's top business leaders. They've come to explore new business opportunities in all the nations the President has visited. Every one of them can tell you that despite the fact that our economy is facing some new tough times right now, America still draws upon tremendous strengths. Our basic research is the best anywhere. We have many of the world's finest universities. American technology remains on the cutting edge in many advanced fields such as computers and biotechnology. Our society is energetic, creative, and talented. It has the added advantage of drawing upon the strengths and insights of many cultures, including Japan's.

The chief executive officers accompanying the President will also tell you that they care about American jobs. They care about American exports. Obviously, so does the President. We know that the Asian-Pacific market offers enormous potential to those American businesses that will accept the challenge of competition. That same competition has propelled Japan toward world leadership. Open markets around the world has provided Japan with economic prominence. Japan must now join the ranks of world leadership in strengthening free markets and freedom.

Finally, let me leave with you a message that the President wished to give directly to the people of Japan. And I quote:

The American people are your friends. Friendship must be built upon three pillars: fairness, trust, and respect. We expect nothing less, and we ask for nothing more. Today marks a turning point for us in many ways. Together, we face the next millennium, a new order for the ages, a new world of freedom and democracy. We stand as the world's powers with the future presenting us with a decision. The United States has made its choice against isolationism and in favor of engagement, against protectionism and for expanding trade. Today we bid Japan to do the same because engagement and open trade are in your best interest.

Together, let us shape a new and open world, a world of vigorous competition and dazzling innovation. Let us build a world of greater prosperity and peace than ever before, if not for the sake of ourselves, then for the sake of our children. This is the finest legacy that we could bequeath to them.

Thank you very much.

*Note: Secretary of the Treasury Nicholas F. Brady delivered the President's remarks at 12:45 p.m. at the Akasaka Prince Hotel.*

# Exchange With Reporters Prior to Discussions With Prime Minister Kiichi Miyazawa of Japan in Tokyo
*January 9, 1992*

*President's Health*

*Q.* Mr. President, what can you say to reassure people that you're all right, sir?

*The President.* Tell them to talk to my doctor. I feel pretty good. Coming back strong. I've got a 24-hour flu. But I feel pretty good. I had a fair sleep, slept this morning. Still mainly on fluids. But I think it was just one of those bounces that come along. But I'm feeling all right.

Try to pace it for this afternoon, go over a little business here with—and I apologize to the Prime Minister for such a shabby performance.

But you know one thing, Mr. Prime Minister, it was wonderful, the flowers and cards from your associates. It was very touching. And it is not that serious, but it was so sweet to do that.

*Q.* Are you back to normal, sir, or are you

still a little under the weather?

*The President.* Well, I don't think I'll go running this afternoon. But I'm, I'd say, close to back to normal. This is a 24-hour thing, and apparently I got it over the evening. But I really do feel pretty good, Rita [Rita Beamish, Associated Press]. Not as strong as I'd like to be, but strong enough to continue on now.

*Q.* Are you going to slow down the pace a little bit, sir?

*The President.* Nope.

*Q.* Why not?

*The President.* Well, because everybody gets the flu. Some of you guys have had it. You can't change your pace because of that. This is just a 24-hour bug. I've been very lucky, lucky, knock on wood, for the last 3 years, and I've been relatively spared of the flu. I've had a flu shot, so I hoped that that would guard against it. But all the signs—Burt Lee can tell you—but the heart and all, the EKG, all the things they do just to doublecheck are perfect, absolutely perfect.

*Trade With Japan*

*Q.* Sir, are you going to get the sweeping changes on trade that you wanted instead of the piecemeal changes that you talked about and said you didn't want?

*The President.* Well, we're going to talk about that today. But the Prime Minister has been extraordinarily cooperative, and we're going to have some good discussions. But I'd rather wait until we get a full package to be discussed. But put it this way, I don't want to put words in his mouth, but I'm quite encouraged. And as you know, from day one, even before we got here, Prime Minister Miyazawa's approach has been one that I've appreciated very, very much. The things he has said and now the way he is driving his team to do what I'm doing, driving our team to come to agreement.

So, did you want to add to that?

*The Prime Minister.* I'm so glad, Presi-

dent, that I think everything is all right. We will shortly announce our joint resolve this afternoon. And I'm glad the President is in such good shape that he can now enjoy the rest of his stay here, and he's having dinner this evening.

*President's Health*

*The President.* So anyway, why, it all worked out well. A little alarmed there. I felt so embarrassed.

*The Prime Minister.* No, no, that happens to everybody.

*The President.* I got a preview in the receiving line. And I turned to the Prime Minister, and I said, "Would you please excuse me?" And I rushed into the men's room there, and then I thought that had taken care of it. But back I came, and it happened, and oh, it was just the beginning.

*Q.* Are you going to tell him to take it easy on you today in the trade talks because you've been ill? [*Laughter*]

*Q.* Mr. President, did you see the TV pictures of what happened last night, sir?

*The President.* I'm not sure I want to, but I heard it was pretty dramatic.

*The Prime Minister.* I did.

*The President.* Did you see it?

*The Prime Minister.* Just normal, kind of, nothing out of the ordinary.

*Q.* When did you start feeling ill? Early in the day or earlier?

*The President.* Really sick, you mean? Well, late in the afternoon I had a little indication, then at the reception, and then, of course, at the dinner.

Thank you all.

*Q.* Feel better, sir. Feel better.

*The President.* Thanks a lot. I really do.

*Note: The exchange began at 1:38 p.m. prior to an expanded bilateral meeting at the Akasaka Palace. In his remarks, the President referred to Dr. Burton J. Lee III, Physician to the President.*

# The President's News Conference With Prime Minister Kiichi Miyazawa of Japan in Tokyo
*January 9, 1992*

*The President.* The Prime Minister has suggested I go first. So let me just say that we've had a highly productive and extremely enjoyable visit to Japan. Last night's coverage might not have looked like I was enjoying myself, but all in all it's been great. And for those who have been so nice to inquire, I really do feel almost back to the way I felt before I got hit by this flu.

But in any event, I want to first express my deepest appreciation to the Emperor and the Empress and to Prime Minister and Mrs. Miyazawa. I just can't imagine anything more hospitable than their kindnesses to us. We appreciate the warm and gracious welcome that they've extended to us, and I also want to thank the many other Japanese leaders and people that Barbara and I have met in the last few days for their kindnesses and for the wonderful cards and the flowers that came in when I had that little flu bug.

We feel we have a much better understanding of your great country, sir, and the great promise of what truly is a global partnership.

The substantive focus of my visit has been the three very productive sessions that I had with Prime Minister Miyazawa, an old and respected friend. As leaders of the two largest economies in the world with a wide range of security and political, as well as economic interest, we had an awful lot to talk about. And on the basis of these discussions, I can make three fundamental observations about U.S.-Japan relations.

First, our security alliance is sound. The U.S.-Japan security treaty remains the core of stability in East Asia, a region still beset with the uncertainties of a world in profound change. Japan's generous host-nation support agreement has helped ensure our continuing ability to retain a forward-deployed presence in Japan, a presence that is essential to American, Japanese, and regional interests.

Second, as we enter the post-cold-war era with its many challenges and opportunities, increased cooperation between the United States and Japan on global issues and regional problems is absolutely essential to achieve the foreign policy objectives of both countries. In this visit, we've dedicated ourselves to building a more prosperous and peaceful world. And for this purpose, the Prime Minister and I have stressed the common purposes of our global partnership, and we've set forth the principles for this partnership in a Tokyo Declaration.

And third, we made progress in our all-important economic relationship. Over the past few years we've worked with some success to open markets here so both our countries can benefit from increased trade, lower prices, better goods, and more jobs. And indeed, we've increased our exports to Japan some 70 percent since 1987 and cut our trade deficit with Japan by about 30 percent.

My administration has negotiated some 11 arrangements to increase our exports in specific sectors. This trip adds another significant but interim step to that progress, and, of course, we will keep pressing ahead and monitoring progress. I believe the U.S. Government and our business leaders have sent a strong message about the importance of fair access to markets.

The detail in the Action Plan, including the voluntary import proposals involving many billions of dollars and increased U.S. content for Japanese cars made in the United States, make it clear that the message has been received.

Our agreement on government computer procurement will open up additional opportunities in a large leading-edge industry for the United States. We've worked out specific commitments in other sectors representing increased opportunities for U.S. exports including auto parts, paper, and glass and resolved over 50 standards problems, this is the key, 50 standards problems that have impeded American businesses. And we've agreed to expand our Structural Impediments Initiative by adding new commitments that will help us follow up on this trip. And I'm pleased that we have worked out together the announcement from a day ago, a strategy for world growth. That one will be helpful to both economies.

I'm also particularly pleased that Japan and the U.S. could agree on a strong joint statement about the Dunkel draft for the Uruguay round negotiations. We're sending a joint message that I hope will build momentum to drive the GATT negotiations to a successful finish.

There is no doubt that we have much more work to do, abroad and at home, to increase U.S. exports and the jobs they create. Yet, we've made headway. There's no question about that. And I'm committed to accomplishing more in the future, using all available measures.

In conclusion, this visit has been a success. It has reaffirmed our vital political, security, and economic relationship. It has advanced our goal of leveling the playing field in U.S.-Japan competition, of further opening Japan's markets to our exports.

So, this progress translates into jobs and economic growth in America because I know the American worker can compete with anyone around the world if given a fair chance. And that's exactly what we intend to do. And the accomplishments I've mentioned here aim us directly in that direction. Thank you, Mr. Prime Minister.

*The Prime Minister.* Well, those of you who watched the television last evening must have been concerned very much. But as you can see, the President is very well today. And I think people around the world feel assured now. And I sincerely pray for his continued good health.

This is the first time in 8 years that we welcome the U.S. President here. And we had three meetings with him. We were able to have a very candid exchange of views. And I'm also very glad and satisfied that we have been able to strike very close personal relations.

As shown by the dismemberment of the Soviet Union at the end of last year, the world in the post-cold-war era doubtless are developing new moves and trends towards the building of peace and democracy. And in creating such historic developments, I should like to express once again my deep respect to President Bush for his outstand-ing foresight and leadership as shown in the START agreement as well as the nuclear disarmament proposal.

Japan and the United States have stead-fastly maintained freedom, democracy, and basic human rights, and market economies; together account for 40 percent of the global GNP, establishing unprecedented prosperity together. And I think it's important that we together work to further promote the building of the new world order, the new world. And it is important that the United States continues to exercise leadership. And Japan wishes to actively support those efforts by the United States. I believe that the meetings that I had with the President would mark a concrete first step towards the building of a Japan-U.S. global partnership.

I had a candid exchange of views on various trade and economic issues as well. And in addition to steadily implementing our economic policies as reflected in the joint statement issued yesterday, I believe we were able to engage in substantive discussions on various measures related to the automobiles and automotive parts and components, the central area of Japan-U.S. trade issue today.

Now, in view of the closeness of the economic ties between our two countries, frictions would be inevitable from time to time, and, of course, our agreement this time would not necessarily resolve all the problems. But I believe that the discussions I had with the President have been very useful, and I'm satisfied with the meetings.

Furthermore, on the basis of the discussions that I have had with the President this time, we have come up with the Tokyo Declaration and the attached document called the Action Plan. These documents are indeed very dramatic and epoch-making in that they spell out how our bilateral relations ought to be, bearing in mind the 21st century, and also spells out our responsibilities and roles that our two countries respectively should play and the issues we together ought to address. And we are determined to further strengthen global partnership between our two countries on visa fees and documents.

I believe it is quite unprecedented that

countries in terms of human history, countries with so strikingly different cultures and history have established a deep interdependence and cooperation. It is unprecedented that countries with such different cultural and historic backgrounds share the future together and together would work for the world. And I believe that we are attracting a lot of attention from around the world, and I intend to do my best, together with the President, to respond to these adaptations.

I should like to give the first opportunity to the Japanese press. And when asking a question, please state your name and affiliation and also to whom you are directing the question.

*Japan-U.S. Relations*

*Q.* First of all, I'm quite relieved to see you fit and well. My question is for President Bush. Before coming to Japan, Mr. President, you stated that there are two objectives to your visit. One is, this is a job-creating trip; you are going to increase jobs for the Americans. I think that was the first objective that you've stated. The second objective, and I think this was stated during the press conference in Singapore, you referred to the sense of dislike for the United States in Japan, and one of your objectives is to overcome such sentiment in Japan. In your statement just now you mentioned that you believe your visit has been successful for the first objective, that is, for growth. So, I should like to ask a question with regard to the second objective.

A U.S. high official said in Seoul, "Even if the political strength of Prime Minister Miyazawa is weak, there is the Liberal Democratic Party in Japan." That was a statement that came out on the 5th of this month, and then on the 6th—well, I think he was referring to remarks that were made by Prime Minister Miyazawa at the Ise Shrine that since Japan enjoyed favor of the United States after the war, it is time for Japan to return that friendship. And that high official said the United States is not seeking charity.

You've come with business leaders this time and I think the——

*The President.* What's the question?

*Q.* ——Japanese people feel that is somewhat strange. So, with regard to the second objective, I wonder if your visit this time really has been helpful in overcoming the sense of dislike for the United States.

*The President.* I'm embarrassed to say I didn't follow all the hypothesis. But I think I got the two points that you asked. One is jobs. I think we have created jobs. We get back there, and we'll have to see. We've got the growth agenda. We have entrance to certain markets, computers and other things. We've got auto parts; they'll be discussed with you later on by the people that have worked out the details. So, I think we can say this has been productive in that account.

In terms of—you only said dislike for U.S. in Japan. I have been troubled about anti-Japanese feeling in the United States and anti-U.S. feeling in Japan. And I think, because of the hospitality of Prime Minister Miyazawa, because of the schedule that had been worked out, because of the personal attention to us by Their Majesties the Emperor and Empress, and hopefully by the way our business people have moved out and talked to a lot of different folks, and Barbara's visit to the schools, I hope that that has helped in this second category that you properly ask about.

I think time will tell. But I'll tell you from our standpoint, I think that the signals going back to the United States of this kind of hospitality, this kind of genuine friendship, this kind of caring when I have a little tiny bout of flu sends a good signal. And sometimes we forget the big picture. And as I tried in my statement to say, this U.S.-Japan relationship is vital to world security and to many other things.

So, I hope the visit has helped in that second account, sir.

*The President's Health*

*Q.* Mr. President, people all around the world yesterday saw some very disturbing video of you collapsing in apparently very severe distress that many of us are not accustomed to when we see people with the flu. Can you describe what you were experiencing there? And also, can you say that your doctors have conclusively ruled out anything other than the flu, or will there be further tests?

*The President.* No further tests. Totally ruled out anything other than the 24-hour flu. I've had an EKG, perfectly normal. I've had blood pressure taken and probing around in all kinds of ways. And it's all going very well, indeed. And I got a call from Bill Webster today, former head of CIA. I didn't take it, but somebody passed it along, and he told me of exactly the same thing happening to him where he went in and totally collapsed.

So, this is the flu. I'm very fortunate that in all the years that I've been President, I don't think I've had much of it. And so, let me just take this question and then reassure the American people and others that have expressed so much interest that that's all there is to it. Nothing else to it.

And somebody asked me earlier, am I going to slow down my schedule? I don't think it has anything to do with speed or slowness of the schedule. One of the businessmen, who is young and aggressive and eager, this morning—a young guy on this trip—got it. I understand some of the journalists have had flu. And people in our country have had it, so why isn't the President entitled to 24 hours? [*Laughter*]

But really, I'm glad to get the question because they've done all the checking in the world. The heart is normal, the thyroid, or whatever is left of it, is going fine, and— [*laughter*]—I really have no hesitancy or worry at all.

*Q.* Are you at all concerned that now that you've had two quite, sort of public health episodes, that some of the Democratic political opponents who are a lot younger than you might make a subtle issue out of the fact that you're somewhat older and perhaps you, because of your hectic schedule——

*The President.* Do you think only old people get the flu, Rita [Rita Beamish, Associated Press]? Do you think only old people get the flu? I think Democrats get the flu from time to time. [*Laughter*] So, I wouldn't worry about that. I think it would backfire if somebody tried to make an issue. I've been blessed by a good, strong physical condition. I played tennis yesterday and then, wham, got hit with the flu. But that's perfectly normal. So, I don't think there's

any political downside.

I have always said that if I felt I couldn't do my job for some physical reason, I wouldn't run for President. But all signals are still go.

## Multilateral Trade Negotiations

*Q.* I've got a question for Mr. Miyazawa. I think you referred to giving impetus to the Uruguay round talks, to the Dunkel document. I wonder what sort of momentum you're talking about. What sort of momentum does Japan intend to add?

*The Prime Minister.* This document refers to this moment which could be a stimulus or whatever you call it. Now, at these final stages of the Uruguay round talks, the talks would be boiled down, and in this Dunkel text, which is not a final text, the issues have been clarified. So, the range of issues are becoming narrower. That is what we are referring to.

## '92 Presidential Election

*Q.* Mr. President, I read an interview, a transcript of an interview with Mrs. Bush in which she stated that if there should come a defeat in November for you, that she wouldn't be extremely disappointed at the possibility of doing some other things. I'm wondering, sir, are you mentally prepared for the possibility of not winning in November, and if you have given any thought to her view of doing something else other than going all over the world and living 18-hour days?

*The President.* The answer to your question is no and no. [*Laughter*] I think I'm going to win. I have not thought of any alternative. I believe I've been a good President. Everybody talks about "dogged by sagging polls"—any time the country is facing problems and people are hurting, the President must and should pay a certain price for that. But I'm also confident that our economy will recover, and I think that we'll have a strong case to take to the American people.

So literally, I've never thought about it. I don't think "defeat" when I'm fixing to go into a campaign, and I don't think of alternatives. So, it never has come up. Now, I won't give her equal time. I don't know what she's thinking about, but I literally have not thought about it at all. I believe I'm going to win.

### Japan-U.S. Trade

*Q.* I'd like to ask a question of Prime Minister Miyazawa. I wonder if you've been able to establish the results—it seems that this has been unilateral concessions made by Japan depending on how you look at it. And I wonder how the Japanese should read the results.

*The Prime Minister.* The issues to be resolved between Japan and the United States, of course, in resolving these problems, the good will and friendship between our two countries would be very important. But in the midst of such new and major changes in the world, I think it is very important that the United States, the world leader, remains firm and steady. And it would not be good for us for the United States to be encumbered with such difficulties and headaches. Now, in welcoming the President, we had engaged in a long period of preparations, and we've come up with these results. There are various issues which we've been thinking about for a long time and we hadn't acted on, problems of our own.

More specifically, there have been some actions we thought it would be better, specifically, to better the trade balance between Japan and the United States. So there were areas of betterment of the Japanese economic structure itself and also betterment of the Japan-U.S. trade balance as well. And I think as a result of the measures we have agreed on, we will be able to respond to both issues.

### Auto Industry

*Q.* American leaders since Nixon have been engaging in trade talks with Japan and emerging claiming great success, and nothing seems to change too much. Some of that, in a more specific sense, has been related to the American auto industry, relief from competition from Japan. And yet they continue to lose market share. Some Americans feel it's because of bloated salaries in Detroit, because of lack of responsiveness to consumers, and the fact or the claim that they make cars that are not competitive.

What's different from this round of trade talks than previous ones?

*The President.* Gene [Gene Gibbons, Reuters], let me simply say that when this is over I believe there are going to be some briefings from our experts to give you the specifics of what has been worked out on auto parts or access to the Japanese market with autos. And so, it's come a long way. There's some specificity here that I think will answer that question that I understand will be provided when this broader scale briefing is over.

So, I think when you look at the agreements, you're going to see that both sides have agreed to more in the way of auto parts, more in the way of autos coming into this country from the United States, and in a couple of other areas as well. So, I think there's some specificity to go with the hope in this case.

### Economic Growth Package

*Q.* Do you feel that the American auto industry has to do more to——

*The President.* Yes, I think we've got to do more as well, and not just on autos, in both the public and the private sector. One of the things that we haven't focused on here today is this economic growth agenda, and there the United States must do something. Japan is growing more than we are. So, they should say, "Well, hey, how about yourselves?" And we're saying: "We're going to submit a growth package. We're going to fight for it. We're going to try to get our interest rates down." And we've got to do a better job in all industries on building quality, improving competitiveness, knowledge and understanding of the Japanese market so we can be vigorous competitors based on more cultural understanding and background.

So, it isn't a one-way street. And I'm very unreluctant to say that right here.

### Japan-U.S. Relations

*Q.* In your press conference on New Year's Day, you said you were thinking of America as—[*at this point, the reporter spoke in Japanese*]—and my dictionary says it means "with a feeling of sympathy, a feeling of compassion." Why do you feel sympathy for America?

*The Prime Minister.* Well, you use the words "sympathy" or "compassion," and I would not claim that these are inaccurate. What I really tried to say was that we have to understand the other person's position. When you say "favored," and there is the antonym "disfavor," well, what I'm trying to say is that we have to try and understand the other's position. And it is with that in mind that I've tried to address these series of issues.

And at the very base of all that is the longstanding relations, friendship between our two countries. But for various reasons, U.S. society—and I might say I believe U.S. society is a great society, but there are homeless people; there is the problem of AIDS and so on. And for various reasons, education is not as high as in the past. And U.S. industries are not as competitive as in the past for various reasons.

Americans are pointing to these problems. And since Americans themselves are aware of these problems, I am convinced they will overcome these problems because I believe that United States is a great country. But until those problems are cured, those problems will continue to exist. And we have to understand the position of United States, and with that understanding we have to address the issues between our two countries because these problems appear in the form of trade imbalance between our two countries as well. So, it is with that sort of understanding I think we ought to approach the problems.

I wonder if there is a Japanese press reporter who wishes to ask a question. If not, then we'll move over to the foreign press.

### The Economy

*Q.* Since you are talking about your State of the Union in which you're going to propose some things that you hope from the U.S. side will help stimulate the economy, I imagine you might have heard something about that from some of the CEO's on this trip. Can you tell us if a payroll tax cut that would be an instant increase for businesses' bottom line and in individual taxpayers' pockets is on the short list of any possible tax changes under consideration?

*The President.* No, I can't tell you that because I'm not prepared to say what's on the short list of what we are considering. We will have a sound growth package that is sound enough that it will not adversely affect the long-term interest rates that will get to investment and job creation at home.

And that's what's needed in our economy right now. And I will be working with the Congress to try to get that done. I will try to avoid some of the ideas that I've seen out there that would shoot the interest rates right through the roof, would take too long to do anything, and would in the long run be counterproductive. But I just do not want to go into detailing what's on a possible short list, although we are narrowing down now to, just since I've been on this trip, to what our final proposal will include.

### Japan-U.S. Relations

*Q.* Mr. President, in your summit meeting yesterday, Mr. President, you have said now that the cold war is over, the Japan-U.S. relations are at a turning point or a crossroads. And I think instead of confrontation, what do you think we must do for cooperation?

A question for the Prime Minister. You mentioned that we were very much touched by the President's speech in Pearl Harbor. Now, bearing that in mind, I wonder how you would respond to the question raised by the President yesterday, Mr. Prime Minister?

*The President.* Well, I would say cooperation, the successful conclusion of the GATT round, although that's multilateral. I would say that Japan and the United States continue to be in such close touch that when it comes to helping other countries, be it in South America as democracy starts moving there or be it in Eastern Europe or, indeed, in the Commonwealth, that it's the U.S. and Japan that stay in very close touch on those things. I had a chance today, with Prime Minister Miyazawa, to take a *tour d'horizon* around the world.

I would also say that it includes cooperation in trading in Asia itself, outside of Japan. Neither he nor I want to see the world divided up into trading blocs. And so, as I was assuring him that the NAFTA, the North American free trade agreement which will affect Canada and Mexico, is not a trading bloc, I had an opportunity to glean from him that Japan would lose if, say, there was an Asian trading bloc. I think in terms of cooperation, as your question asked, we will cooperate to be sure that we don't inadvertently fall into trading blocs that will narrow trade rather than increase it.

But Japan is a respected world power, and we must cooperate. I've supported publicly the return of the Northern Islands to Japan. And there's an area where perhaps cooperation between the two parties can be helpful. We had long talks about Mr. Yeltsin's coming out and trying to bring democracy and free markets to Russia. And I think that there's an area where we can have cooperation.

So, as I look around the world, I believe cooperation is called for in almost every instance. I can't think of one where it's not. United Nations, working in the U.N. now with Japan on the Security Council for 2 years, close cooperation as we try to use international law to solve some of these problems as we did in the Gulf.

*The Prime Minister.* In the speech delivered by the President in Honolulu, he said he held no rancor against Japan or Germany. These former enemies have become best friends for democracy, is what basically he said. There are quite a few warships that are sunk in Pearl Harbor with the dead bodies of the soldiers and with veterans in front of him. So, I believe it was not easy for the President to say all those things. And that is why I was especially moved by the friendship shown by the President, the sense of trust expressed by the President.

Japan was able to grow this much, thanks to the continued support and help by the United States. This again we should not forget. And this friendship was at the very foundation of the meetings that I had with the President this time.

The President in Honolulu also mentioned that we must fight against or fight off isolationism and protectionism. And I think these words were uttered with Japan in mind. Now, in discussing economic issues this time, there was concern expressed that the entire world might fall into protectionism, and what can we do in order to prevent that? Trade imbalance has persisted for 20 years or so, and if nothing is done then one of the parties concerned may well fall into protectionism. So, something ought to be done about it.

*Q.* Both the President and the Prime Minister have very busy schedules, and I'd like to say they have to adjourn the meeting today. Thank you very much, President and Prime Minister.

*Note: The President's 118th news conference began at 2:50 p.m. at the Akasaka Palace. The Prime Minister spoke in Japanese, and his remarks were translated by an interpreter.*

## Remarks at a State Dinner Hosted by Emperor Akihito of Japan in Tokyo
*January 9, 1992*

Your Imperial Majesties and honored guests, on behalf of the American people, we wish to thank you for the warmth of this reception and for your tireless efforts in support of the relationship between our two great nations.

The United States and Japan today stand on the threshold of a new era of cooperation in which our nations seek to build a new world of freedom and democracy. The task before us is daunting, one which will require vision and courage. But it is one from which we cannot shrink. Too much depends on us.

As leaders of this new world, we face several challenges together, addressing the new security requirements of a changed world, promoting freedom and democracy, and generating world economic growth and prosperity.

Tonight, we celebrate the essence of this new world order and the opportunity to be true partners in its construction. We see how former enemies can become close allies and friends, real friends, each supporting, competing, growing, dreaming. Each understands that we must resolve our differences fairly and constructively.

Our people both believe in work, community, faith, and family. We know how democracy supports the cause of peace among nations. We realize that although half a world may separate us, great ties unite us, ties that are economic and military, moral, and intellectual.

Your Majesty, the name you have chosen for your reign can be translated as "achieving peace." That choice signifies your deep personal commitment to this noble aspiration and your resolve not to revisit the tragedies of the past. We are now closer to achieving the blessings of peace than we have been at any time in this century.

When the great Japanese novelist Kawabata received the Nobel Prize in literature, the citation praised him for "building a spiritual bridge spanning East and West." In this changing world where the walls that once divided whole nations from each other are crumbling, we all must become both bridges to and partners in a new world order.

In that spirit and with heartfelt thanks, Your Majesty, for your wonderful hospitality, I ask all of your guests to raise their glasses. To your health, sir, and to the bridge of friendship and common purpose uniting our countries, to those who built it and cross it still, and to the prosperity of our two great peoples.

*Note: The President spoke at 8:10 p.m. at the Imperial Palace.*

# Remarks and an Exchange With Reporters on Arrival From the Trip to Asian/Pacific Nations
*January 10, 1992*

*The President.* Let me first say that it is great to be home, and Barbara and I want to thank all those who made this important trip a success. Secretary Brady is with us here, Secretary Mosbacher, and then our first-ever Presidential delegation of business leaders. I want to thank also in addition to them our ambassadors, their dedicated staffs, and so many others. And I really want to offer my heartfelt thanks to countless people at home and abroad who so kindly offered prayers and good wishes when I had that very brief but dramatic bout with the flu.

Our mission was uniquely American. America is a world leader not just because of our military or economic might but because we've always held the conviction that we're part of something larger than ourselves. We now live in an entirely different economic world than a generation ago and in a completely different political and security environment than just a year ago. Foreign relations have never before been so important to our well-being at home. When we foster democracy abroad, when we strengthen our security engagements with our allies and friends, when we work to open markets and expand trade, we make a priceless investment in our own children's future.

The Tokyo meeting I concluded yesterday with Prime Minister Miyazawa caps a successful series of talks with four of America's most important friends in the Asia-Pacific region. With each of these countries, Australia, Singapore, Korea, and Japan, we're forging ever-stronger bonds of democratic values, of mutual security, and of economic growth through expanding trade. Each of four nations that I visited are robust democracies. With each we confirmed the necessity of providing nourishment for the blossoming of democracy throughout the region.

At each stop on our journey I reaffirmed

America's interest and fundamental commitment to Pacific security. We and our Pacific partners are determined to maintain strong defenses to protect our hard-won peace and stability during this new era and to provide a security umbrella under which political pluralism and market economies can flourish.

In each country on this mission we made progress on a top priority of this trip, renewing the strength of the American economy and generating world economic growth. Now, while I'm disappointed that the unemployment numbers went up in December here, our work over the last few days will help open markets for American companies and provide more jobs for our workers. Make no mistake about it, our progress this week will translate into progress on jobs and economic growth in America. The results will be clear and measurable.

Everywhere we've been I've sought urgent action on the successful conclusion to the Uruguay round of the GATT talks. The best achievement we can offer our farmers, our manufacturers, and indeed our service industries is a GATT breakthrough in unprecedented new accords for open trade.

With Australia, we reaffirmed our alliance and announced plans to conclude a new trade and investment framework agreement. With Singapore, we announced an agreement to conclude a new bilateral investment treaty as well. Everywhere I found support for strengthening APEC, that's the new Asia Pacific Economic Cooperation group, as it promotes trade and economic cooperation around the Pacific Rim. And I've carried our enthusiasm for our North America free trade agreement across the Pacific and shown how it, too, can add to everyone's prosperity by reducing the barriers to trade.

Our summit meeting in Tokyo was a turning point in our relationship with Japan. And it highlighted the progress we've made these last few years with that nation. Japan is our largest market for agricultural exports, our largest, now some $8 billion a year. Since 1987, the U.S. merchandise exports to Japan have increased more than 70 percent, and they now account for 64 percent of our total exports to Japan, up nearly 10 percent since 1985. We reinvigorated our commitment to the bilateral Structural Impediments Initiative talks, and we garnered new support for a successful conclusion to the GATT round.

A substantial portion of our trade deficit with Japan is in the auto sector. That is not going to change overnight. But here, too, we made significant progress, not only in terms of selling American cars and automobile parts in Japan but also in raising the percentage of American parts in Japanese-brand cars built in the United States by U.S. workers. Japanese automakers agreed over the next 3 years to increase their purchase of American-made parts from $9 billion to $19 billion.

Our summit meeting this week accelerated the opening of more Japanese markets to our exports. In addition to the Japanese car manufacturers, 23 companies in the Japanese electronics, automobile, and machinery industries announced plans to increase American imports into Japan by a total of $10 billion over the next 3 years. Some of this will be to the automakers, and taken together represents a welcome increase in exports made in the U.S.A.

This week we breached the wall that kept American exports of computer products and services out of the $3 billion Japanese Government market. Our agreement will expand Japanese public sector procurements of our quality computer goods and services. Our leading-edge computer industry employs millions of technologically savvy Americans, and we can expect dramatic gains in this market.

We made breakthroughs for access to Japan's huge markets for our glass and paper products, virtually untapped markets that are billions of dollars in size. We reaffirmed goals for our higher market shares for semiconductors and then resolved standards problems—these are the invisible barriers to free trade—in 49 different sectors of American industry, from processed foods and cosmetics to industrial equipment and machinery.

Anybody who thinks that Americans can't compete with the Japanese hasn't talked with these business executives who joined me in Japan, some of whom made the trip all the way. And they haven't seen the recent studies that show overall U.S. productivity is the highest in the world, far exceeding Japan's. We must work hard to keep that productivity growing. I know and these business leaders know that as long as the playing field is level, American workers can outcompete and outproduce anybody, anyplace, anytime.

Yes, we faced a turning point with Japan, and when the time came, we took a major step forward. But it was only a step, one in a long process to achieve markets as open as our own. We will build on these results. We will monitor the progress, and I will keep pressing for jobs and market access when Prime Minister Miyazawa comes to the United States, hopefully in a few months.

That ongoing effort includes the strategy for world growth which the Prime Minister and I developed and which we are coordinating with the other industrialized nations. America and Japan are the two largest economies in the world. Together we comprise 40 percent of the total world economy. And global growth is a top priority for both of us. Already our two countries have made deep progrowth cuts in interest rates. Japan cut their discount rate to 4.5 percent, and as you know, our Federal Reserve has just lowered interest rates a full percentage point, both of which are keys to stimulating long-term growth here and abroad.

But clearly, with December's unemployment figures, our economy is not growing fast enough. In my State of the Union Message later this month, I'll present to the American people my action plan to get it growing faster. And I am looking forward to spelling out our ambitious agenda for economic growth clearly and repeatedly to the American people in this vigorous and exciting political year. I am absolutely confident that the American people will join me in this vision for a new era of expanded markets, of peace, and prosperity.

So, thank you all very much, and thank you for being with us on that trip. I appreciate it enormously.

### Unemployment

*Q.* Does the unemployment increase

mean that the Federal Reserve System's interest rate cuts aren't working?

*The President.* No, I think it takes a while to work. But certainly the Federal Reserve cuts will work their way through, and they are very, very important to economic growth. But I think it is a little too soon to expect them to have taken hold and turned around the December unemployment figures.

### Japan-U.S. Trade

*Q.* Sir, what else can you do to put the pressure on Japan to open up its markets?

*The President.* Well, in the first place, we're going to monitor the agreements we've made, and then we'll see. I will resist protectionist legislation, however; I don't view that as pressure.

*Q.* Mr. President, why are you optimistic about the auto agreement, and the auto makers so pessimistic?

*The President.* Well, I think that we might have achieved more. I am proud of what we did achieve. And I think there is nobody suggesting anyone here is totally satisfied. What I am saying is, we made dramatic progress, and it will result in jobs for the American workers.

*Q.* Cuomo says it's inadequate.

*The President.* Well, he is entitled to his opinion. And I can't say that we've gotten everything we want, so maybe we're not very far apart. Who knows?

*Q.* What are the short-term——

*Q.* Why isn't the managed trade——

*The President.* Will you make up your mind? I'll go with either one of you. You're both wonderful people. Jim [Jim Miklaszewski, NBC News], go ahead. Men first, maybe. Whoops, Michel [Michel McQueen, Wall Street Journal], sorry about that. [*Laughter*]

### Results of President's Trip

*Q.* In the short term, was this trip a political bust for you personally?

*The President.* I don't think collapsing with the flu helped, but I think I can handle that one, Jim. I feel fine, my health is good, and I don't think it's a bust at all. And I'll be glad to debate any of the—eventually; maybe I'd better phrase this properly—be glad to take on those ideas that I hear that the way to handle this economy is through protection, shrinking world markets. That is the wrong answer. And I think we made progress. And so, I think it was a successful trip.

Yes, Michel, sorry.

### Free and Fair Trade

*Q.* Let me ask you, why isn't this managed trade, something you say you're very much against, when you're pressuring another government to force its companies to buy that which they would not otherwise buy?

*The President.* Well, I don't think we're forcing them to buy something that is noncompetitive, and I don't think we're forcing anybody to buy something that is inadequate. What we're trying to do is get free and fair access to markets, and indeed, as I mentioned, we broke down a lot of barriers. We changed the standards procedures over there to some degree. We still have a lot of work to do. So, I don't view that as managed trade where you set a number. I remember back when I was in China, the people would come over, and they'd say, "All right, we're going to buy *x*, and you're going to buy *y*." That's managed trade. That's not what we've done here at all. What we've done is expand markets and get more access for American workers to have their products go into the Japanese market and others.

### New Hampshire Primary

*Q.* Mr. President, with regard to New Hampshire, do you think you're in trouble there?

*The President.* No, I think I'm going to win in New Hampshire. And I think New Hampshire has some serious economic problems, and I can identify with the hurt of those people. I can't tell you how many times I've been in New Hampshire in the last, well, since I was Vice President and including being President. So, I have some feel for the hardship they're going through. And I think I can identify with it, and I think I can rally support for what I will be proposing. I know that they, if they have it in focus, would be supporting what I have been proposing. So, I think we'll do fine

there.

### Multilateral Trade Negotiations

*Q.* Mr. President, your own briefers and senior administration officials in Tokyo asked three times whether Japan was on board on the GATT negotiations. You refused to say that they were. Are they?

*The President.* Well, what do you mean by "on board" on them?

*Q.* My question is, does Japan support your position regarding the Dunkel letter?

*The President.* Well, I think they agree to use the Dunkel draft as a significant document from which to work. And they also agree we need to get that round solved. I think they've probably got problems with the Dunkel draft, and so do we. What we're trying to do is use that as the basis now for hammering out differences. I think that's about the way we left it with them.

Two more, and then I've got to go. This nice gentleman over here.

### China-U.S. Relations

*Q.* Did anything you heard from Mr. Miyazawa on his talks with Li Peng encourage you to respond in any way, or could you tell us what you heard?

*The President.* Talks with Li Peng on what?

*Q.* Mr. Miyazawa talked to you about his trip to China and his talks there. Did he tell you anything that caused you to respond or give you any message?

*The President.* I believe it was Watanabe, wasn't it, the Foreign Minister? No, he had a good trip to China. He talked a little to them about the problems that we're having with China. He gave me some suggestions in terms of the problem of the people that are held because of Tiananmen Square. But beyond that, I can't say much. There wasn't too much specific as it relates to the U.S.-China relations.

*Q.* Nothing to cause you to respond?

*The President.* Nothing at this juncture that cause us to respond. We will keep pressing for fair treatment of people there, and I will try to keep that important relationship on track also. It is a big one and very important.

One more, and then I've got to run.

*The Economy*

Q. Mr. President, don't the unemployment figures show you that the economy is in fact getting worse?

*The President.* No, I don't think that. But they are certainly unsatisfactory. And what they show is, we need growth. And we need to stimulate growth in a sound, fiscally sound way and not through some way that will set the economy back by shooting interest rates, long-term rates, up through the roof. And by that I mean things that are going to recklessly break this budget agreement. They show that the economy has been sluggish. They show that people are hurting. And they show that we need to get going now with a growth agenda that will do short-term that which it can do; a lot of the suggestions are more long-term. And I think they show that, I hope they show that wherever we can make progress on expanding markets abroad, we ought to do it. And that's one reason I'm satisfied that we have made real progress on this trip. I think it will help in that situation.

Thank you all very much.

*Note: The President spoke at 9:15 a.m. upon arrival at Andrews Air Force Base in Camp Springs, MD, from his trip to Asian/Pacific nations. In his remarks, he referred to Gov. Mario Cuomo of New York and Premier Li Peng of China.*

# Remarks to the President's Drug Advisory Council
*January 10, 1992*

Thank you all very much for that welcome, and thank you, Bill Moss, especially, and thank you for the job you did as Chairman in launching the Drug Advisory Council.

I'm delighted to be home. And you've got to admit, when I get the flu, I do it in a very dramatic—[*laughter*]—way. But it was so embarrassing. [*Laughter*] But I do feel well, a little bit jet-lagged. We just flew 12 straight hours from Tokyo. In fact, we got here before we took off, if you look at the international dateline. So, you will excuse me if I'm a little bit tired. But my health is good, and I am so grateful to so many across our wonderful country and then also in Japan who, I think, thinking I was a little more seriously sick than I was, expressed their concerns. And I just want to say thanks to everybody who did that.

I am delighted to be here. I did not want to go off to Camp David without stopping by this very, very important meeting. And I'm glad to be here with so many hard workers. I want to single out, of course, Bob Martinez, the former Governor of Florida, who is in charge of the fiercely committed fighters in our battle to lead America away from drugs. You heard from one of these earlier when David Kearns, representing Lamar Alexander—David, our outstanding executive there at the Department of Education. And in addition, we are very fortunate in a Government sense to have the leadership of Attorney General Bill Barr, who is working closely with Bob Martinez, with Lou Sullivan, our very able Secretary of HHS, intimately involved in all of this. And we are trying as a Government to meet this scourge head-on.

But I believe that the answer lies right here. I know it lies with the leadership from Jim Burke who is sitting here at my left. As many of you are aware, Jim's done an outstanding job unleashing the power of the media through this Partnership for a Drug-Free America. There is no way that Government itself could do what this individual has done in getting the message, antidrug message, out across this country. We are very, very grateful to him.

I also am sitting next to another tireless worker, very successful man, Alvah Chapman, who just took this on to organize this meeting, organize this crusade all across the country, providing all of us with the vision and leadership this whole coalition movement represents. So, my thanks to him.

I was told by Jim, coming in here, of the many successful efforts going in the communities represented here and then some that aren't even represented. And so, I want to thank all who have come from all across this land to explore this idea of community coalitions gathering momentum. And if you needed any inspiration—I didn't get to hear her; maybe she hadn't sung yet. But I've heard her many times. She's been our guest up at Camp David. If you need a little momentum-gathering, try Sandy Patti on for size because she is magnificent.

Well, let me just say, it is a pleasure to be back, and it was a great trip. Ten fascinating days in the Far East talking and listening and learning, working hard for the objectives that we all share of trying to get this country moving through expanding our exports markets, assuring our friends also that we are going to stay actively involved in the Pacific. You know, given all the changes in Eastern Europe and the hope that is about now because of people that had hated each other over the years, been ancient enemies, now talking in the Middle East, some in the Pacific area thought that we've just forgone our interests in that part of the world. So, I wanted to convince those leaders there that we will fulfill our security responsibilities to that critical area, and we will stay actively involved with that area, our largest trading partner incidentally.

But I came here today because I really believe that what you do is vitally important to the well-being of our country. And I wanted to just say this to you: Your Nation recognizes the critically important work of your community antidrug coalitions, and your Nation is very, very grateful to each and every one of you.

We are working hard, all of us, all of you, to blast the curse of drugs off the face of our map. Our antidrug effort is one of the highest priorities of any domestic initiative in the Federal Budget. In 1992, our budget proposal called for $11.7 billion for the drug war, an increase of 82 percent since the beginning of our administration and an 11-percent increase since the previous year, one of the largest in the entire overall budget.

In our war, you know the answer, and I understand and think I know the answer,

we are seeing results. I'm not sure the entire country understands this yet, Jim and Alvah, but I believe we are seeing results. For 1990, we exceeded our goal for reducing overall drug use. We'd hoped for a decrease of 10 percent between '88 and '90, and it fell by more than that. I believe the figure was 11 percent. Occasional cocaine use went down 29 percent when we'd set a goal—I think again, trying to just think positively, I think the goal we had set in our minds was 10 percent.

For 1991, figures show we've even more dramatically exceeded many of our goals, particularly in areas like adolescent cocaine use. You know and I know there's a problem. It's a horrible thing to think about, adolescent cocaine use. But it's out there, and it's tough. And we are making headway. We'd hoped to reduce that by 30 percent since 1988, and it's fallen more than 60 percent. So, what you're doing is working. What you're doing is having an effect and saving the lives of children.

But let's face it, much remains to be done. More than 12.5 million, 12.5 million Americans currently still use drugs; 1.9 million of them currently use cocaine. And adolescent drug use has fallen, but still more than 1.3 million of our kids currently abuse drugs.

We're also committed to toughening the drug laws. We devote more effort to fighting drugs than to any other single area of crime. But we cannot do it alone. We need Federal drug laws that are on the side of the people. We need a bipartisan effort to help law enforcement protect our present and ensure our children's future. As I said 2 years ago when we announced the drug strategy, with this drug problem we face the toughest challenge in decades. We face the challenge not as partisans but as a Nation.

As we've said time and time again, we cannot win the drug war through law enforcement alone. I'm convinced we can do better on law enforcement, and I salute those who are out there enforcing our laws. But we can't win it through law enforcement alone. We've got to have effective treatment programs, and we need national action.

More than 2 years ago we established this President's Drug Advisory Council. America was lucky, very, very fortunate to gain the wisdom and vision of these distinguished American leaders who share our goal of ridding this Nation of the devastation caused by illegal drugs. I want to give very special thanks today to our Council members who work tirelessly to mobilize the enormous power the private sector can wield in the war against drugs. Look at this head table, look around, look at the names of the people, the men and women who are serving, and you'll see we've got very busy, successful people giving of themselves to help others.

In addition, every one of you here today are frontline soldiers in our war. You lead this country's local efforts to reduce drug use in the workplace, schools, and neighborhoods. We've got a good program. I was briefed by Al Casey and others not so long ago, and Jim was up there, in Camp David on this drug-free workplace concept. And we're making headway. Still a ways to go, but a very fundamental and important part of our work.

You organize your communities into coalitions. The key to healing this Nation is found at the grassroots level, being what I call a Point of Light, holding your hand out to a neighbor. And this audience today certainly exemplifies in the finest sense the willingness of one American to reach out and help another.

As Americans hear your stories, they realize that there is an alternative to drugs, and its name is hope. They hear stories of people like Brad Gates, the sheriff in Orange County. So concerned was he about drug deaths that he created the "Drug Use is Life Abuse" program. With the business community, he launched a massive drug education effort targeted at area youth. And the program works because it changes people's attitudes, gets to the fundamental attitude change towards drugs.

And so does Tad Foote's. When he saw how drugs were destroying his community, he gathered top business leaders like Alvah Chapman and others, the busiest, the most successful, and they formed the Miami Coalition, a broad-based community organization. And it was dedicated to tackling every aspect of the drug program, divided it into eight task forces. They've convinced over one-third of all Miami businesses to adopt drug-free workplace policies and employee assistance programs, and they have closed down 1500 crack houses. Now, that is success, and that is due to the voluntary effort all the way.

The point is simple: No community, none at all, has to accept drug abuse. Americans don't have to live in fear. Drugs and so many other social problems can be driven from every community, if every community cares enough to reach out and try.

Americans deserve a lot of credit for their individual and collective efforts. But we still have much to do. There are casualties in this war. We live in an age when tens of thousands of drug-affected babies are born each year. Therein is the real tragedy. Hold in your arms one of those babies, and you just can't help but have a broken heart. We live in an age when one out of every 4,000 American teens dies by his own hand or at someone else's, and too often drugs play a part, a fundamental part, in these tragedies. We live in an age when the scourge of drugs has cheapened life and threatens to erode the moral fabric of this great Nation of ours.

Well, you've set an example, summed up by the antidrug banners created by citizens in Albuquerque that read, "It's easier to build a child than repair an adult." With that kind of tough-minded dedication, we will win. We will make a difference. Each and every one of you is making a difference, and may God bless you all for that.

Thank you very, very much. And thanks for that warm welcome.

*Note: The President spoke at 11:41 a.m. at the J.W. Marriott Hotel. In his remarks, he referred to Jim Burke, chairman of the Partnership for a Drug-Free America; Alvah Chapman, Chairman of the National Coalition Committee of the President's Drug Advisory Council; and Albert V. Casey, Council member.*

## Letter to Congressional Leaders on the Determination Not To Prohibit Fish Imports From Venezuela and Vanuatu
*January 10, 1992*

*Dear Mr. Speaker:* *(Dear Mr. President:)*

Pursuant to the provisions of subsection (b) of the Pelly Amendment to the Fishermen's Protective Act of 1967, as amended (22 U.S.C. 1978), I am reporting to you that the Secretary of Commerce reported to me that the countries of Venezuela and Vanuatu have been under a court-ordered embargo since March 26, 1991. No yellowfin tuna or products derived from yellowfin tuna harvested in the eastern tropical Pacific Ocean (ETP) by purse seine vessels of Venezuela and Vanuatu may be imported into the United States.

The Secretary's letter to me is deemed to be a certification for the purposes of subsection (a) of the Pelly Amendment. Subsection (a) requires that I consider and, at my discretion, order the prohibition of imports into the United States of fish and fish products from Venezuela and Vanuatu to the extent that such prohibition is consistent with the General Agreement on Tariffs and Trade. Subsection (b) requires me to report to the Congress within 60 days following certification on the actions taken pursuant to the certification; if all fish imports have not been prohibited, the report must state the reasons for doing so.

After thorough review, I have determined that, given that an embargo is currently in effect and given the negotiations toward an international dolphin conservation program in the ETP, sanctions will not be imposed at this time. Venezuela and Vanuatu will continue to be certified, and we will review their marine mammal incidental mortality under the Marine Mammal Protection Act if findings are requested for 1992. I will make further reports to you as developments warrant.

Sincerely,

GEORGE BUSH

*Note: Identical letters were sent to Thomas S. Foley, Speaker of the House of Representatives, and Dan Quayle, President of the Senate.*

## Letter to Congressional Leaders on the Determination Not To Prohibit Fish Imports From Certain Countries
*January 10, 1992*

*Dear Mr. Speaker:* *(Dear Mr. President:)*

Pursuant to the provisions of subsection (b) of the Pelly Amendment to the Fishermen's Protective Act of 1967, as amended (22 U.S.C. 1978), I am reporting to you that the Secretary of Commerce has reported to me that the countries of Costa Rica, France, Italy, Japan, and Panama have been under an embargo since May 24, 1991. No yellowfin tuna or products derived from yellowfin tuna harvested in the eastern tropical Pacific Ocean (ETP) by purse seine vessels of Mexico, Venezuela, or Vanuatu may be imported into the United States from these nations.

The Secretary's letter to me is deemed to be a certification for the purposes of subsection (a) of the Pelly Amendment. Subsection (a) requires that I consider and, at my discretion, order the prohibition of imports into the United States of fish and fish products from Costa Rica, France, Italy, Japan, and Panama, to the extent that such prohibition is consistent with the General Agreement on Tariffs and Trade. Subsection (b) requires me to report to the Congress within 60 days following certification on the actions taken pursuant to the certification; if fish and wildlife imports have not been prohibited, the report must state the reasons for the lack of a prohibition.

After thorough review, I have determined that, given that an embargo is currently in effect and given the negotiations towards an international dolphin conservation program in the ETP, sanctions will not be imposed against intermediary nations at this time. Costa Rica, France, Italy, Japan, and Panama will continue to be certified, and we will review their status as intermediary nations under the Marine Mammal Protection Act, if requested for 1992. I will make further reports to you as developments warrant.

Sincerely,

GEORGE BUSH

*Note: Identical letters were sent to Thomas S. Foley, Speaker of the House of Representatives, and Dan Quayle, President of the Senate.*

# Letter to Congressional Leaders Reporting on the National Emergency With Respect to Libya
*January 10, 1992*

*Dear Mr. Speaker: (Dear Mr. President:)*

I hereby report to the Congress on the developments since my last report of July 9, 1991, concerning the national emergency with respect to Libya that was declared in Executive Order No. 12543 of January 7, 1986. This report is submitted pursuant to section 401(c) of the National Emergencies Act, 50 U.S.C. 1641(c); section 204(c) of the International Emergency Economic Powers Act ("IEEPA"), 50 U.S.C. 1703(c); and section 505(c) of the International Security and Development Cooperation Act of 1985, 22 U.S.C. 2349aa–9(c).

1. Since my last report on July 9, 1991, the Libyan Sanctions Regulations (the "Regulations"), 31 C.F.R. Part 550, administered by the Office of Foreign Assets Control ("FAC") of the Department of the Treasury, have been amended. One amendment, published on August 5, 1991, 56 *Fed. Reg.* 37156, added the names of 12 companies to Appendix A of the Regulations, which contains a list of organizations determined to be within the definition of the term "Government of Libya" (Specially Designated Nationals of Libya). This amendment also added a new Appendix B, "Individuals Determined to be Specially Designated Nationals of Libya," containing the names of persons determined to be acting, or purporting to act, directly or indirectly on behalf of the Government of Libya. An amendment removing one name from Appendix B was published on December 20, 1991, 56 *Fed. Reg.* 65993. A further amendment of the Regulations, effective December 19, 1991, 56 *Fed. Reg.* 66334 (Dec. 20, 1991), with a correction published on January 7, 1992, 57 *Fed. Reg.* 525, revoked the authorization set forth in Section 550.514 that permitted transfers between two non-Libyan foreign banks located outside the United States to clear through accounts located in the United States when the money is being sent to or from the Government of Libya. This action was taken as a partial response to evidence of the Government of Libya's role in the bombing of Pan Am Flight 103. Copies of these amendments and correction are enclosed.

2. During the current 6-month period, FAC made numerous decisions with respect to applications for licenses to engage in transactions under the Regulations, issuing three new licenses and amending three previously issued licenses. The new licenses typically permit, for the benefit of U.S. persons, minor transactions of little or no economic benefit to Libya. The license amendments permit several U.S. firms with substantial pre-embargo investments in their Libyan oil concessions to renew standstill agreements preserving their interests despite nonperformance of concession agreements due to the U.S. sanctions.

3. Various enforcement actions mentioned in previous reports continue to be

pursued, and several new investigations of possibly significant violations of the Libyan sanctions were initiated. During the current reporting period, substantial monetary penalties were assessed against U.S. firms for engaging in prohibited transactions with Libya. In one such case, a penalty of $137,500 was collected from a major U.S. manufacturer, after an investigation developed evidence that it had exported services to Libya and engaged in contracts in support of projects in Libya.

Due to aggressive enforcement efforts and increased public awareness, FAC has received numerous voluntary disclosures from U.S. firms concerning their sanctions violations. Many of these reports were triggered by the recent amendment to the Regulations listing additional organizations and individuals determined to be Specially Designated Nationals ("SDNs") of Libya. For purposes of the Regulations, all dealings with the organizations and individuals listed will be considered dealings with the Government of Libya. All unlicensed transactions with these persons, or in property in which they have an interest, are prohibited. The initial listing of Libyan SDNs is not a static list and will be augmented from time to time as additional organizations or individuals owned or controlled by, or acting on behalf of, the Government of Libya are identified.

4. The expenses incurred by the Federal Government in the 6-month period from June 15, 1991, through December 14, 1991, that are directly attributable to the exercise of powers and authorities conferred by the declaration of the Libyan national emergency are estimated at $487,815. Personnel costs were largely centered in the Department of the Treasury (particularly in the Office of Foreign Assets Control, the Office of the General Counsel, and the U.S. Customs Service), the Department of State, and the Department of Commerce.

5. The policies and actions of the Government of Libya continue to pose an unusual and extraordinary threat to the national security and foreign policy of the United States. I shall continue to exercise the powers at my disposal to apply economic sanctions against Libya fully and effectively, as long as those measures are appropriate, and will continue to report periodically to the Congress on significant developments as required by law.

Sincerely,

GEORGE BUSH

*Note: Identical letters were sent to Thomas S. Foley, Speaker of the House of Representatives, and Dan Quayle, President of the Senate.*

# Remarks to the American Farm Bureau Federation in Kansas City, Missouri
*January 13, 1992*

Thank you, Dean Kleckner. It's a great pleasure to be up here with so many supporters of agriculture. First, let me single out Secretary Madigan, who is doing a superb job as our Secretary of Agriculture. A former Illinois Congressman, he knows the farm business inside out, and believe me, agriculture has a good friend in these GATT negotiations with Ed Madigan. I also salute my friend, the Governor of your host State, Governor Ashcroft is with us; plus two great Senators, Jack Danforth and Kit Bond; and then also Congressman Tom

Coleman. All three of these Senators plus this Governor are well-steeped in agriculture. They know the problems. They have been friends to agriculture. And farmers have voiced their support of all three of them plus the Governor over and over again.

I just had a chance just a few minutes ago to meet with the board, your board. It's good to see John White again. I spent the day with him in Chicago last month when I spoke to the Illinois Farm Bureau.

I won't lead you in the singing, but if you see Ed Madigan later on personally, you might want to wish him a happy birthday.

That great voice of rural America, Will Rogers, once observed, "A man in the country does his own thinking, but you get him into town and he will soon be thinking second-handed." Today I want to give you my firsthand report on my trip to Australia, Singapore, Korea, and Japan and to talk agriculture.

All of you know my real reason for going to Asia: prosperity, ours and theirs. That requires security; it requires stability, democracy, and certainly trade. Twenty-five percent of our farm product is exported, 25 percent. Free trade can give the American farmer new opportunities to save, invest, create, and dream.

The cold war has ended. What a miraculous year it's been. We stand on the verge of a new age of competition. Our ideals triumphed in the cold war, and the new wave of democracy represents nothing less than the political restructuring of the entire world. That was a tough fight, a long fight, but it was worth it.

Just one year ago today, one year ago, think back, we closed the American Embassy in Iraq, and American troops stood prepared to answer the call to duty, the call to liberate Kuwait from Iraqi oppression. That victory that ensued not only lifted the spirits of our Nation but clearly established the United States of America as the undisputed world leader, standing for what is right and decent, for democracy, for freedom against bullying and aggression. Go anywhere in the world, and you will see the respect in which we are held. Do not listen to those prophets of doom we hear every night, those frantic politicians who say we are a second-class power. We are the undisputed, respected leader of the world. We are the United States of America.

One wonderful dimension of this dramatic world change is that our children no longer have the same worries about nuclear war that their parents had just a few years ago. It was the leadership of the United States of America that brought this about. Now, make no mistake about it, now we must stay involved overseas to lead in economic restructuring for free and fair trade,

open markets all over the world.

Open markets are the key to our economic future, both for American agriculture and business. That fight is going to take time, and lots of people will want immediate results. This new world of opportunity isn't going to happen overnight. But I can tell you this: Empty-headed rhetoric won't get us there. Hard work, savvy, experienced negotiation, and confidence in ourselves will get us there, proud and strong. We won the cold war, and we will win the competitive wars. We will do it on the merits, and we're going to do it the American way, through grit, through determination, and through quality.

My trip to Asia was an important and successful step toward building that new world, not with just Japan but with the whole world. We reached dozens of new agreements on market openings, from computers to paper to glass to automotive products. In Japan alone our negotiators reached 49 standards agreements in nonautomotive industries and hammered out marketing opening agreements in a variety of industrial sectors. And that was just a start. Japanese Prime Minister Miyazawa has agreed to visit Washington later this year as a followup to the trip, and both sides have pledged to advance the cause of open, free, and fair trade.

Some political critics say that I shouldn't have taken the trip at all. They're wrong. I will continue to fight for American jobs everywhere. In these tough times, a President should do no less.

Some of these critics say that I wanted to promote managed trade. Wrong. I oppose managed trade. What I want to get is more fair access to the other guys' markets, and that's exactly what we got. Not everything we wanted, but we made progress. We cannot ask foreign markets to buy inferior goods, but we can insist that our quality goods must have fair access to overseas markets.

Our Asian allies understand that we don't want handouts or a home-field trade advantage. We just want a level playing field. Give us a fair shot, and American workers will outthink, outwork, and outproduce anyone in the world. American farmers—

and I saw this and heard it loud and clear on this trip—already do that.

Our farmers and ranchers thrive in the international marketplace despite the barriers that other governments throw in their way. As I said earlier, a full 25 percent of our agricultural production gets sold abroad. You don't complain; you get the job done.

Look, we all know that protectionism boils down to defeatism. If you don't trust your product, you try to keep others from sampling the competition. But if you trust your handiwork, you see foreign markets as a great opportunity.

And here's another point that I've made over the years: A capital gains tax cut would reduce the cost of capital and increase investment in business. Traveling in Asia, I was once again reminded of how we put ourselves at a competitive disadvantage with this high capital gains tax rate. Now more than ever, a capital gains tax cut will help our economy back on track. It will put more real value on America's farms and homes. It is good for everyone in our economy and especially for you, the American farmer. And I need your help to make the Congress understand this once and for all.

Consider the payoff. Every $1 billion of American agricultural exports means 25,000 American jobs. Farm exports should exceed $40 billion in 1992. In this time of trade deficits, that's a farm trade surplus of $17 billion, and 1 million good American jobs.

Now we hear it again, we hear some politicians want to set quotas, want to legislate balance of trade. Do you know who would get hurt the most by this? The American farmer.

Don Shawcroft knows what I'm talking about. Japan imports $1.7 billion in beef, and 53 percent of that beef comes from America. This helps cattle ranchers like Don, who runs a 600-head beef herd with his dad in Alamosa, Colorado.

Five hundred miles away lives Arlene Wessel, who produces farrow-to-finish hogs, dryland wheat, corn, on her family's farm near Huron, South Dakota. Arlene also knows how to keep America's standard of living number one in the world: not by building a fence around America but by convincing other countries to tear their

fences down. I want to give all farmers, the grain farmers, the rice farmers, those who grow the best produce in the world, a fair shot at selling their goods everywhere.

To achieve this, of course, will require diligence and patience. I recall an old Quaker farmer who would never take the name of the Lord in vain. Perhaps you have heard of him. But one day his mule, who was hitched to a hay wagon, wouldn't budge an inch. The farmer tried every bit of coaxing. No success. Finally, he reached the end of the rope. "Mule," he said, "I cannot beat thee or curse thee or abuse thee in any way. But mule, what thou doesn't know is that I can sell thee to an Episcopalian." [*Laughter*]

In that context, and as an Episcopalian, let me say a few words about export subsidies. Ultimately, they stifle growth, burden the taxpayer, cost consumers, and make industry less competitive. I also know that I must and will safeguard the interests of American farming. I will not let American agriculture disarm unilaterally.

Today, the trade practices of the European Community hurt American farmers. Our agricultural Export Enhancement Program, the EEP, is specifically designed to counter the EC's massive export subsidies. Without this effort, which is less than one-tenth the size, I might say, of the EC subsidy, American farmers would lose even greater market shares to the EC.

Yes, we want to end export subsidies; we must do that. But we will not do it until other nations do the same thing. I am not going to put our farmers at an unfair disadvantage. Sooner or later, the EC must stop hiding behind its own iron curtain of protectionism. Meanwhile, we will remain leaner, tougher, and more competitive.

The world's future progress and prosperity really depend upon free trade. I am working to conclude the Uruguay round of the GATT negotiations successfully. I especially appreciate, and I've told Dean Kleckner this, the Farm Bureau's steadfast support for free and fair trade. GATT will help the world move toward broader economic integration, not trading blocs.

Our administration will settle for nothing less than a GATT agreement that expands markets and increases opportunities for our exporters. We want free trade, and we want fair trade. And we want abundant trade. And GATT, believe me, really holds the key. I know the EC's behavior threatens progress, but I am optimistic there will be an agreement. And I will not be a part of an agreement unless it's a good agreement for America.

While my administration supports American business abroad, we're also doing our best to help at home. In that spirit, I recall something written about people who grow up close to the soil: "There's something about getting up at 5 o'clock, 5 a.m., feeding the stock and chickens and milking a couple of cows before breakfast that gives you a respect for the price of butter and eggs." That writer knew that when it comes to farming, Washington does not know best. American farmers do.

In 1990, I worked hard with the legislative leaders, two of whom are here today, in the Senate and one of whom is in the House, here today with us, to get congressional approval of a farm bill that is evenhanded and level-headed. That bill helped reduce interest rates, slash inflation, and increase flexibility for farmers to decide what to grow.

I've promoted firsthand thinking in farm policy from day one. We set out to reduce farm debt and increase farmers' independence, and there have been good results. Farmers' equity has grown $45 billion in 3 years. Meanwhile, agricultural sales, gross cash receipts, have risen $17 billion since I took office, to $168 billion. Again, real results.

We are committed to common sense in a wetlands policy. My direction to Vice President Quayle's Council on Competitiveness was to protect environmentally sensitive wetlands and protect the property rights of landowners. I've asked the board here to send in specific recommendations during this hearing period. Our new guidelines will distinguish between genuine wetlands, which deserve to be protected, and other kinds of land, including your farmlands.

Also, last month I signed a bill making nearly $1 billion in disaster relief available to producers for 1990 and '91 crop losses.

Put these initiatives together, and you get a farm policy that lets farmers do what they do best: farm and compete all over the world. Our policies reflect the values that we all cherish: self-reliance, generosity, family, community. They draw upon your strengths, your intelligence, diligence, determination, and faith.

Today we meet in a city that testifies to all these virtues. Kansas City has braved three major floods this century and risen to new greatness each time. Ninety-two years ago, the Convention Hall burned to the ground. Proud men and women rebuilt it in 90 days. "In Kansas City," someone explained, "we don't know what 'impossible' means." My friends, I am still convinced that in America we don't know what "impossible" means.

The American dream isn't an impossible dream. Don't listen to all those gloomsayers around this country saying that we are a nation in decline. We are, once again, the respected leader of the entire world. And working together, we are going to make the lot of every single American better.

Thank you very much. Thank you very, very much. And I am proud to lead an America that leads the world towards new freedom and prosperity. Thank you. And may God bless you all. Thank you.

*Note: The President spoke at 10:46 a.m. at the Municipal Auditorium. In his remarks, he referred to Dean Kleckner, national president of the American Farm Bureau Federation, and John White, Jr., president of the Illinois Farm Bureau.*

## Statement on the Death of Meade Alcorn
*January 13, 1992*

Barbara and I are deeply saddened by the death of our longtime family friend and leader of the Republican Party, Meade Alcorn. Meade was chairman of the Republican Party in the late 1950's and was an inspiration to all who were formulating political careers during the time of his leadership. He was a practitioner and a believer who gave the party ideals and strength through its national organization.

Meade was a personal friend of my father and our entire family. He gave us support and advice at many points in our lives. I spoke with his wonderful wife, Marcia, this afternoon to offer our sympathy and condolences. Barbara and I offer our prayers for Meade Alcorn.

## White House Statement on the President's Meeting With President Mario Soares of Portugal
*January 13, 1992*

The President met with Portuguese President Mario Soares for approximately a half hour in the Oval Office. President Soares is in town on a private visit during which he attended an exhibition at the National Gallery. The President expressed his strong desire to cooperate closely with Portugal as the EC President, an office which Portugal took over in January. The President stressed the importance of concluding the Uruguay round. The two Presidents discussed Asian developments and the former Soviet Union, as well as issues relevant to southern Africa. The President and President Soares reaffirmed our strong bilateral relationship and committed each side to continued cooperation.

## Remarks to the America 2000 Community Leadership Conference
*January 14, 1992*

Lamar, thank you so much and all of you. When I walked in here, Ed told me there's an electricity in that room, a real commitment. Well, you can feel it just coming here. And I want to thank all of you for being here, coming from all across our great country to participate in something that is fundamentally important to our future.

I want to thank Lamar, who has taken this leadership role, taken it across the country, taken it out there in the best nonpartisan spirit that one could possibly conceive, and making dramatic progress, I might add. He's too modest. He set out some of the examples, building his examples around those who are here and have taken leadership roles in the community. But he himself has been to countless numbers of States and gotten this program really rolling. And I think the country is grateful to him for that leadership.

And he's put together a first-class team over at the Department of Education, I might add. David Kearns, giving up a fantastically large corporate assignment, as Pete Silas and all of you know, to take on this key role simply because he is committed, as is Lamar, to helping the children of this country. And so we're fortunate to have this program in good hands.

I want to thank Ed Donley. I want to

thank Dick Lesher, the able head of this organization, day-to-day head of it; Bill Lurton and all in this organization here in Washington who are providing the leadership, the catalytic leadership, to mobilize these communities.

And as you know, Pete Silas, a very busy man, is sacrificing and giving an awful lot of time to the Chamber nationally, not just on this issue but on a wide array of issues. He and I just returned from what we both agree was a productive trip to Asia with one terrible downside: Neither of us can sleep. [*Laughter*]

I talked to him about it, and we've determined that it'll take a couple of more days, but I am very grateful to Pete for going all that way into these various capitals to take the American message across the world. It reminded us, that trip, that we're entering an unparalleled new century of the high-tech global, and I emphasize that word, marketplace.

It's going to be a tough, extraordinarily competitive world. And the key to success is going to be education. It's simple: Nations that take the responsibility to invest in the minds of their citizens, all their citizens, are going to move ahead. And nations that don't, even great nations, are going to be left behind.

And America 2000 will help us succeed in a new age of competition. It's going to liberate the best minds and brightest thinkers of this land and will teach us that learning is a lifelong endeavor. And we're in the midst of a revolution, a revolution to free us from the past and open every sort of thrilling new gate of opportunity in the future.

But I think everyone here knows at the community level that it is going to be a tough battle. Everyone knows that at present our schools will not pass the test of the 21st century. And who knows it best? Who know that best? Parents. Parents know it. Business community leaders know it. And our kids, I'm afraid our own kids know it.

But we also know how to meet this challenge, and that is by achieving these six national education goals that Lamar referred to. These are those goals:

By the end of this decade, our children will start school ready to learn. On the Fed-

eral side that means Head Start, but it means a lot more than that.

Our children will achieve at least a 90-percent high school graduation rate. It's an achievable goal.

Our children will demonstrate competence in five core subjects measured against world-class standards.

Our children will be first in the world in science and math.

Our adults will be literate and able to compete, therefore, in the work force.

And then the sixth, our schools will be disciplined, safe, and drug-free.

Those are the six education goals. They were set, as Lamar said, not in a partisan way but in a convening of the Governors at Charlottesville was the first step and then working together with partisanship aside to come up with these education goals which have been universally endorsed.

And I'm so pleased that you and the Chamber are committed to this crusade and that more than 600 individual chambers have pledged to make their communities America 2000 communities. The tie between this organization and the America 2000 program is a natural. America 2000 arises out of the understanding that educational excellence is everyone's business. Everyone must take part in creating a climate in which the schools and the communities of the future can flourish.

Our national goals, as I mentioned, were born out of a bipartisan conference of all our Governors, Democrats and Republicans, working not for parties but for the Nation. And let me say I'm sorry to have missed the Governor of Georgia, who was up here in just that spirit—Dick filling me in on his contribution to this organizational gathering. Now, with America 2000, every person of every party in this Nation can take part in what is a populist revolution.

America 2000, believe me, it is spreading like a prairie fire. Since April, 30 States and 1,000 communities have joined up, embracing our challenge to adopt and achieve these national goals, these national education goals.

But not everyone's ready for the future. As the train pulls out of the station, many Members of Congress have not yet climbed on board. The House has taken some important steps towards the American achievement tests. Its bill, I think you'd agree, shows some promise. But while Americans across this Nation are working to spark a revolution for the future, the Senate regrettably remains riveted on the past. Its bill, S. 2, is sponsored by Senator Kennedy, and it falls far short, tragically short, of any of our goals. And when the American people want transformation, we are being offered business-as-usual up there.

We want a half-billion dollars to create break-the-mold, new American schools. We want school choice to provide middle- and low-income families the same control over their children's education that wealthier people have, school choice. We want to give communities and teachers flexibility in spending $9 billion in Federal education money. And we want to give the Secretary of Education more discretion in sweeping away burdensome regulations. We want these exciting and essential innovations for the good of our country, and to all of this, regrettably, S. 2, the Kennedy bill, says no.

The train's gathering steam, and that bill is literally standing in the way. And we have to tell Congress of our priorities. We want school choice for parents. We want to return power to the local schools, not mandate everything from Washington but return that power to the local schools. We want American achievement tests. And they'll be fair; they can be voluntary. But we want those American achievement tests. We want new, and by new I'm talking revolutionarily new, American schools. We want America 2000 communities. And we want our kids to excel.

Americans do not want to live in the past. Things move too quickly, and we have to prepare ourselves for the future. Our schools must lead the way, not follow. We need schools for the 21st century, not museums to the failed experiments of the past. And you have to get this message to the people in your communities. You are the leaders. You can do it. You are in the process of doing just that.

America 2000 is a national partnership that requires the involvement of students, teachers, parents, principals, and certainly business and community leaders because

this battle for educational excellence will be won home by home, school by school, community by community all across our Nation. You can be a catalyst for change right in your own hometown.

When you return home from this landmark conference, first make sure your schools have adopted those six national goals. Make sure they raise standards for educational performance and hold schools and teachers accountable. That is the key word: accountability.

And second, encourage your employees to take an active role in their children's education, help them with their homework, read to them every day. Parents must pass on to their own kids the drive for educational excellence.

Third, reinforce the message to students that hard work today pays off for the future. Not only does this mean a good job for them, it means a good, strong future for our country.

And when you get home, you, your neighbors, and your friends really must send Congress a message: Start building tomorrow's schools today. Give parents the choice they want and children the education they deserve. And remind them that anyone who says they understand America must understand that we want the best schools for our children.

America 2000 restores the natural relationship between the family and the school. And as I look at the educational problems facing our country, that is a tremendously important relationship. It's been weakened. We've got to strengthen it. It closes the gap between the living room and the classroom. It invites everyone to help break the mold, to build schools for the future, and to lay the foundations for a new American century.

I can assure you, and Lamar has followed up beautifully on this, that every Department in our Government, Defense included, are on board in terms of this America 2000 program. I'm delighted that Pat Saiki, the head of the SBA, is here. She and her organization are enormously important in furthering the objectives of America 2000.

So, it's not just the Congress I'm appealing to. It is the administration that is now on board. It is this Chamber that is in a leadership role for the future. The entire Nation, if you look at it broadly, has really embraced America 2000. And now, we just need to get the message to the people up there on the Congress who work at the Hill and who have a lot to say about the funding that is necessary to see this program successfully concluded.

Not all of it depends, thank heavens, on Federal funding. You're where the action is, right at the community level. But we've got to get the message to 535 people who work down the street to think anew, to work with you in creating these brand-new, revolutionarily new schools. Together, I really believe that we're onto something here, that we will make our future proud and bright.

And so thank you all very, very much for your commitment, for your leadership role, for laying aside the politics to think of the future of the kids in this greatest, freest nation on the face of the Earth.

Thank you, and may God bless you all.

*Note: The President spoke at 8:55 a.m. at the U.S. Chamber of Commerce. In his remarks, he referred to Edward Donley, chairman, Center for Workforce Preparation and Quality Education; David T. Kearns, Deputy Secretary of Education; C.J. (Pete) Silas, chairman, Richard L. Lesher, president, and William H. Lurton, vice-chairman, U.S. Chamber of Commerce; and Gov. Zell Miller of Georgia.*

# Exchange With Reporters Prior to a Meeting With Earvin (Magic) Johnson
## *January 14, 1992*

### *Johnson's Role on AIDS Commission*

*Q.* Mr. President, what kind of contribution do you think Magic Johnson can make in the AIDS battle?

*The President.* Well, it is my view that he can make an enormous contribution. He already has when you read the interviews and the reaction that he's having on the young people of this country for this very honest, compassionate, and sensitive view he's taken. It makes an impression on you. And he'll make a contribution on the Commission.

I wrote him a letter, a personal letter, some time ago and said that I recognize there are all kinds of opportunities now to serve mankind and that I'd love to have him on this Commission but he should feel free to say no if there were other priorities. And if he accepted that there would be no pressure, not that you could pressure a guy this size anyway—*[laughter]*—but no pressure to do anything other than do what the umpire does: Call them as they see them. And he's doing that. And he's out on his own around this country.

I think it's a wonderful thing, and I think he's already having an effect on lifestyle, for one hand, and, on the other hand, this whole question of compassion and understanding for people that are afflicted by this. So, it's a two-way street as I see it. One is the education process, and the other is just because of who he is, his character. The way people look up to him in this country, he can probably make a better appeal for compassion and understanding for victims of this than any American. It's that simple.

### *AIDS Funding*

*Q.* Mr. President, have you committed in your new budget to spend more on AIDS treatment and research?

*The President.* In anticipation of getting that question, I will point out the fact that we are spending $4.25 billion total now. We are spending on research $1.8 billion, which is more than we do on cancer, more than we do on heart disease. And we will do the utmost possible.

I have been in close touch with the people at NIH, and I expect, Magic, you'll be if you haven't: Dr. Fauci and Dr. Broder and some out there. And we will try to get the maximum research funding level possible. They are not in the mode to tell me that the Federal Government has not come forward with a good level of funding. I mean, they've been quite positive about that. But if there's some place where you can put a little more money to get this problem solved, of course, we want to be sensitive to that.

*Johnson's Role on AIDS Commission*

*Q.* Mr. President, what sort of impression did Earvin's announcement have on you personally?

*The President.* Emotional. And of course, the Bush family are sports fans, and we've followed Magic. We've done it with great respect and admiration. But it's been not just that, not just a great athlete hit, but it's been the way he's handled it. It's been that that's had the real emotional effect. And people see this around the country. They really do. I'm not just saying it because I'm sitting next to this big guy; I'm just telling you that's the way they see it. They see it as here's a man that's got hit, and he's standing up and doing something about it and helping others. That's what this country's about.

*Q.* Did you have any hesitation yourself in joining this Commission?

*Mr. Johnson.* No. After I received President Bush's letter, I mean, first of all I felt honored, and I just wanted to learn a little bit about the Commission, what were my duties, what my responsibilities were before

I accepted. Once I found out what the Commission was all about, I was ready to jump in right away. You always want to help in any way you can, and this can only help the battle that I had already taken before that, my stand to try to help people.

*Q.* Do you have any suggestions for what the President might do to further help to fight AIDS?

*Mr. Johnson.* Well, the President and I are going to sit and talk.

*The President.* Talk about that.

*Mr. Johnson.* Maybe we'll let you know later. [*Laughter*]

*Presidential Campaign*

*Q.* Mr. President, what about the New Hampshire poll that showed a closer contest than before?

*The President.* I'm not going to talk about polls here today. I'll take care of that when the election rolls around. This is a nonpolitical event with a nonpolitical guy who's out there doing the Lord's work. So, I'd rather defer that until some more appropriate time. But thank you for inquiring.

*Note: The exchange began at 1:50 p.m. prior to a meeting in the Oval Office. In his remarks, the President referred to Anthony S. Fauci, Associate Director for AIDS Research, and Samuel Broder, Director of the National Cancer Institute, at the National Institutes of Health. Professional basketball player Earvin (Magic) Johnson was a member of the National Commission on AIDS.*

# Remarks on the Presentation of a Natural Gas Powered Van and an Exchange With Reporters
*January 14, 1992*

*The President.* Let me just make a couple of brief statements. Last April, as part of the national energy strategy, I signed an Executive order that established goals for greater energy efficiency in the Federal Government, and that included the use of alternative fuel vehicles in the Federal fleet.

This van, driven over here and delivered by Secretaries Lujan and Watkins and then the able head of the GSA, Mr. Austin, uses compressed natural gas. And yesterday GSA announced that this year it will purchase from U.S. automakers 3,125 alternative fuel vehicles for use in the Federal fleet. This program demonstrates our continuing commitment to implementing the national energy strategy, which promotes energy conservation and environmentally sound energy initiatives.

I am also pleased to announce that in our '93 budget, fiscal '93 budget, I will include $15 million for the Department of Energy to assist other Government Agencies in purchasing alternative fuel vehicles. This should allow us to purchase over 5,000 alternative fuel vehicles next year.

These actions will put us ahead of schedule for the purchases of alternative fuel vehicles as required by the Clean Air Act. And I was so pleased to learn about the delivery of this van over to the Department of the Interior that we used a slight Presidential prerogative and invite Secretary Lujan and Secretary Watkins and Administrator Austin to drive the van here for use in the White House fleet. So, we preempted one. But natural gas is a clean burning fuel. It's got a great future in this country, and here's but one more manifestation of that.

*Q.* You're going to drive it, Mr. President?

*The President.* What?

*Q.* Are you going to drive it?

*The President.* Yes, I've got my license. [*Laughter*]

*Q.* You haven't driven in years.

*The President.* It doesn't matter, I have my license. I would like you to be witness before I get in there.

*Mr. Skinner.* Looks good to me.

*President's Health*

*Q.* How come you can't sleep these nights?

*The President.* What?

*Q.* Jet lag?

*The President.* Doing fine, Helen [Helen Thomas, United Press International]. Please don't worry about that.

*Q.* I'm really worried.

*The President.* You wake up at night. I'll tell you, it's crazy.

*Q.* We're all worried.

*The President.* All right, here we go.

[*At this point, the President took the van for a test drive.*]

*Meeting With Earvin (Magic) Johnson*

*Q.* Mr. President, was Magic Johnson critical of your performance on AIDS?

*The President.* What?

*Q.* Was Magic Johnson critical of what you've done so far?

*The President.* Good, constructive suggestions, but very, very constructive. We had a very positive meeting. If he was, why, he didn't tell me that. But he left me some suggestions that we'll try to work on.

*Note: The exchange began at 2:35 p.m. on the South Lawn at the White House.*

# Letter to Congressional Leaders Reporting on Iraq's Compliance With United Nations Security Council Resolutions
*January 14, 1992*

*Dear Mr. Speaker: (Dear Mr. President:)*

Consistent with the Authorization for Use of Military Force Against Iraq Resolution (Public Law 102–1), and as part of my continuing effort to keep the Congress fully informed, I am again reporting on the status of efforts to obtain compliance by Iraq with the resolutions adopted by the U.N. Security Council.

Since I last reported on November 15, 1991, the International Atomic Energy Agency (IAEA) and the Special Commission created under U.N. Security Council Resolution 687 have continued to conduct inspections and other activities related to Iraqi weapons of mass destruction and ballistic missiles. Iraq has not impeded these efforts insofar as they concern sites and activities declared by Iraq and Iraq's participation in the destruction of identified chemical weapons. In the main, however, Iraq continues to be uncooperative and obstructive with respect to inspection of sites identified by the Special Commission and the IAEA (based on their own sources of information) as potentially involving clandestine, proscribed activities.

Since obtaining extensive and detailed documentation of Iraq's nuclear weapons program in September 1991, two additional inspections have been conducted of facilities judged to be directly associated with the testing and development of high-explosive components of the implosion system of a nuclear weapon, contrary to Iraq's explanation of their purpose. Iraq maintains that it conducted studies but had no program to develop nuclear weapons. This position is inconsistent with the documents obtained in September and the characteristics observed in subsequent visits to Iraqi facilities. These documents and facilities reveal a well-funded and broadly based nuclear weapons development program involving sophisticated facilities. Additional analysis and investigation in this area are required.

The Special Commission has continued to compile a detailed and comprehensive picture of Iraq's chemical and biological weapons program. From November 17 to November 30, 1991, the Special Commission conducted a chemical and biological weapons inspection and visited, at short notice, 13 sites designated by the Special Commission as potentially having chemical weapons or biological weapons. Initial reporting indicates no chemical or biological weapons activities at these sites. In addition, a Special Commission team visited Iraq in mid-November to discuss issues related to Iraq's destruction of identified chemical weapons and agents, with particular emphasis on safety issues. The Special Commission has made recommendations to Iraq regarding an Iraqi design for a mustard agent incinerator, the destruction of nerve agents caused by caustic hydrolysis, and the breaching and draining of munitions. It is estimated that destruction of such munitions can commence early in 1992.

Two ballistic missile inspections have been completed since my last report. To date, Special Commission inspection teams have supervised the destruction of 62 ballistic missiles, 18 fixed missile launch pads, 33 ballistic missile warheads, 127 missile storage support racks, substantial amounts of rocket fuel, an assembled 350mm supergun,

components of two 350 and two 1,000mm superguns, and one ton of supergun propellant. The United States believes, however, that Iraq continues to possess large numbers of undeclared ballistic missiles. Questions also remain about whether all aspects of Iraq's attempts to produce the Scud missile indigenously and to develop a more capable solid-propellant missile have been discovered.

The United States continues to assist the United Nations in its activities, including by conducting U–2 surveillance flights and providing intelligence. Although the Special Commission has received important monetary contributions from other nations, including Kuwait and Saudi Arabia, the shortage of funds readily available to the Special Commission has become acute, particularly because the Special Commission and the IAEA are now beginning to remove spent irradiated fuel from Iraq.

Since my last report, additional important progress has been made in implementing the Security Council resolution on compensating the victims of the unlawful invasion and occupation of Kuwait. The Governing Council of the U.N. Compensation Commission held its third formal session in Geneva, November 25–29, 1991, and continued to make rapid progress in establishing the framework for processing claims. The Governing Council adopted criteria for the remaining categories of claims of individuals, claims of corporations, and claims of governments and international organizations (including claims for environmental damage and natural resource depletion). In addition, the Governing Council set July 1, 1993, as the deadline for filing claims of individuals under $100,000, with expedited consideration to be given to claims filed by July 1, 1992. The Governing Council has scheduled meetings in January, March, and June 1992 to address additional issues concerning the compensation program.

In accordance with paragraph 20 of U.N. Security Council Resolution 687, the Sanctions Committee continues to receive notice of shipments of foodstuffs to Iraq. The Sanctions Committee continues to consider and, when appropriate, approve requests to send to Iraq materials and supplies for essential civilian needs. To date, Iraq has declined to use U.N. Security Council Resolutions 706 and 712 to sell $1.6 billion in oil to generate revenues for the purchase of foodstuffs for Iraqi citizens.

On November 24, 1991, the Secretary General's representative for the U.N. humanitarian program in Iraq entered into a Memorandum of Understanding with Iraq covering the period January 1, 1992, to June 30, 1992. This Understanding establishes the framework for U.N. humanitarian activities (primarily the provision of food, medical care, and shelter) in Iraq, which are conducted through centers staffed by U.N. and personnel not affiliated with governments. The Understanding contemplates the use of up to 500 U.N. armed guards to protect U.N. personnel, assets, and operations. On January 2, 1992, the Government of Turkey extended for 6 months the authority for U.S. Armed Forces to operate in Turkey in furtherance of Operation Provide Comfort.

Through the International Committee of the Red Cross (ICRC), the United States,

Kuwait, and our allies continue to press the Government of Iraq to comply with its obligations under Security Council resolutions to return all detained Kuwaiti and third-country nationals. Likewise, the United States and its allies continue to press the Government of Iraq to return to Kuwait all property and equipment removed from Kuwait by Iraq. Iraq continues not to cooperate fully on these issues and to resist unqualified ICRC access to detention facilities in Iraq.

I remain grateful for the support of the Congress for our efforts to achieve Iraq's full compliance with relevant U.N. Security Council resolutions, and I look forward to continued cooperation toward achieving our mutual objectives.

Sincerely,

GEORGE BUSH

*Note: Identical letters were sent to Thomas S. Foley, Speaker of the House of Representatives, and Robert C. Byrd, President pro tempore of the Senate.*

# Statement on the Death of WUSA–TV Sportscaster Glenn Brenner
*January 14, 1992*

Barbara and I are greatly saddened by the untimely death of Glenn Brenner, a man whose wit and ability has endeared him to so many Washingtonians. The suddenness of his death and the warmth of his personality leave all of us with a painful emptiness. Sometimes we think we know television personalities better than we

really do. But Glenn Brenner's life and his many friends demonstrate that the man we saw was real, a man who loved his work, his family, and the community he served. We will remember him for those qualities that made him so special. Barbara and I offer our prayers and sympathy to his family and friends.

# Appointment of Timothy J. McBride as an Assistant to the President for Management and Administration
*January 14, 1992*

The President today announced the appointment of Timothy J. McBride, currently Deputy Assistant to the President, to be an Assistant to the President for Management

and Administration.

Most recently Mr. McBride served as Deputy Assistant to the President and Executive Assistant to the Chief of Staff, October

1991 to December 1991. Prior to this Mr. McBride served as Assistant Secretary of Commerce for Trade Development, 1990–91; Special Assistant to the President, 1989–90; personal aide to the Vice President, 1985–89; Deputy Director of the Vice Presidential Advance Office, 1985; consultant to the Republican National Convention arrangements committee in Dallas, TX, 1984; and a small business management consultant in Coral Springs, FL, 1982–84.

Mr. McBride graduated from Eastern Michigan University (B.B.A., 1982). He was born October 10, 1958, and is a native of Michigan. Mr. McBride resides in Alexandria, VA.

## Appointment of Nicholas E. Calio as Assistant to the President for Legislative Affairs
*January 14, 1992*

The President today announced the appointment of Nicholas E. Calio, of Ohio, to be Assistant to the President for Legislative Affairs. He would succeed Frederick D. McClure.

Since 1991 Mr. Calio has served as vice president of the Duberstein Group, Inc., a Washington-based consulting firm. From 1989 to 1991, Mr. Calio served as Deputy Assistant to the President for Legislative Affairs. He served with the National Association of Wholesaler-Distributors as senior vice president for government relations and executive director of the wholesaler-distributor political action committee from 1984 to 1989. Mr. Calio served as litigation counsel for the Washington Legal Foundation, 1981–84; Of Counsel with the law firm of Santarelli & Bond, 1981–84; and as an associate with the law firm of Santarelli & Gimer, 1978–81.

Mr. Calio graduated from Ohio Wesleyan University (B.A., 1975) and Case Western Reserve University School of Law (J.D., 1978). He was born January 10, 1953, in Cleveland, OH. Mr. Calio is married to the former Lydia Keller, has three children, and resides in Washington, DC.

## Statement by Press Secretary Fitzwater on the Resignation of Richard J. Kerr as Deputy Director of Central Intelligence
*January 14, 1992*

President Bush accepted with regret today the resignation of Richard J. Kerr, who has served as Deputy Director of Central Intelligence since March 1989. Mr. Kerr will return to private life after serving 32 years as a professional intelligence officer. His resignation will become effective March 2, 1992.

Mr. Kerr has served the country and CIA with dedication and creativity for more than three decades. He played a critical role in the recent transition at CIA, serving with distinction as the Acting DCI, and he provided critical leadership at a time when CIA and the intelligence community were confronted with profound changes in the world. He was an important member of the intelligence team during Desert Shield and Desert Storm, for which he was awarded the Presidential Citizen's Medal. He also made an extraordinary contribution to the NSC Deputies Committee during his tenure as DDCI. The President has great respect for Dick and is grateful for his counsel and support throughout this administration.

## Excerpted Remarks With Community Leaders in Portsmouth, New Hampshire
*January 15, 1992*

*The President.* First, let me just say thanks to the Governor for providing this cold weather—[*laughter*]—but warm welcome. And I will make a couple of comments at the end, but I do want to do what Judd said, to listen.

I want to single out, of course, Senator Bob Smith, who came up on the plane with us, and Bill Zeliff, your able Congressman, who came with us. I don't think Warren is here, Warren Rudman. But Judd Gregg—and thank them for their support and being with us in this campaign. I also see Bonnie Newman over here, who is well-known to every businessperson in this State and who's been a great addition to our administration, now back in the private sector.

The only point I want to make at the beginning is, look, I have not just discovered New Hampshire. When a storm hits the seacoast here, it hits me. [*Laughter*] And I can give you some vivid examples of that. And we've been here over and over again, not only New Hampshire but 48 States. And I care. And I hope I understand, but I know I'll understand better after I hear the depth of concerns that the people in this group have to offer me.

So, I will listen, and I'll be glad to take any questions. I'll be glad to tell you what I think would help the economy of this State. And what helps the economy of the whole Nation clearly will help, so I'll give you a little preview of coming attractions for the State of the Union because we've got to do something there.

Incidentally, I omitted a former Senator sitting over here, Gordon Humphrey. And I'm just thrilled to have his leadership and his support involved. And if I start clicking it off and leaving out people sitting next to me—I'm already in trouble with Ruth. [*Laughter*] But I really am very pleased. I feel nothing but warmth here. I know I've got big problems, but we're going to take care of those by demonstrating what I feel in my heart and answering some of the outrageous allegations that we hear at this time

of year, every 4 years, from political opponents. But that's the way life is.

I've done my part for the economy. We've brought 300 press up here. [*Laughter*] My answer to you is, if you can take it, so can I. [*Laughter*] So go ahead. I don't know what the order is, but Judd, fire away.

*[At this point, remarks were made by participants.]*

*The President.* Let me just comment on these, and then I want to hear from as many people as possible. First, on Doug, one of the things this trip was about was trying to expand markets abroad. And I get hit by some saying this is managed trade. I am for free and fair trade, not managed trade. And what we did was go over there and get access, not everything I wanted, but get access to markets.

Doug mentioned high-tech. One of the things we did do, and we've been supported 100 percent by the computer industry, is get access to the Government computer industry. Forty percent of the computers in Japan are American; in the Government, .04 percent are. Now we've broken that barrier down.

We can help the Governor on his trade missions by this kind of initiative. And I am not going to stop trying to open these markets because somebody said I ought to stay home. We've got a global economy. And he put his hands on it when he talked about the high-tech factor. We are good in this area; we need to do better.

You mentioned financing and venture capital. Please help me and Bob Smith and Bill Zeliff and Warren Rudman get a capital gains tax cut. This is not a tax break for the rich; it is a creation of small jobs.

We are in a demagogic year. A lot of people that have discovered New Hampshire for the first time, they've never been to this State before, never heard of it, don't know the heartbeat of the State. I think I do. Went to school across the line here, have a house down the road here, can see it almost, what's left of it, when we landed at Pease—[*laughter*]—and come in here all the time. And I think I understand.

And I think that this State would prosper by getting the kind of capital gains reduction—and let me take the heat on whether it's a tax cut for the rich or not. But help me when I come out with this yet again in the State of the Union.

Deborah, you talked about "hope that the light at the end of the tunnel is not a train." I would remind you of another country-western song by the Nitty Gritty Dirt Band, "If you want to see a rainbow, you've got to stand a little rain." And New Hampshire has stood more than a little rain. It's had a flood of bad news. And again, I understand it, but I think the answer: less in the regulations.

We're trying to do better on regulations. I do believe that the Fed interest rates that are down now—and interest rates are at a wonderful level, I'd like to see them down further frankly, but at a wonderful level—will kick in and will stimulate investment. There is no other side to that coin. It will help. And it will help the real estate business.

Frankly, I think that the talks we've had with the regulators, so that the good loans are not marked up, is going to help. I hope it will. I think we have had some excesses of regulation. Yet some of the people running around this State are the very ones in their hearings that are trying to say that forbearance, they call it, forbearance is bad. By that they mean you need more regulation. We need less regulation. And I think the Vice President is trying very hard on this Competitive Council. We've got a better job to do there, but I just wanted you to know I think you're on to something on that.

And I won't comment on all the others, but in terms of bank funding and bank—the only good news out of all this dreary news in terms of the financial institutions is that the depositor, thank heavens, and again, I salute the Members of the Senate and Congress that are here today, has not lost a dime. The depositors haven't. But the financial institutions—I still feel good banks should make good loans. And as this interest rate goes down, I think, inevitably, that is

going to happen.

But real estate has been hurt. And I will have proposals in the State of the Union Message that I think will put value back, and capital gains is a part of this, in the asset people care about the most; that's their homes. Part of the fear that I think exists is because people wonder, "Hey, what's happened to my home, my house?"

Again, I might say that I haven't diverged one inch from my commitment to what I think are New Hampshire values; I know they're Bush family values, in terms of family and neighborhood and community and child care that can be done at the local level and all of this.

Last point, Dan, yes, I remember talks long ago here. And this helps me. I think I've known, look, this economy is in free-fall. I hope I've known it. Maybe I haven't conveyed it as well as I should have, but I do understand it. And your comments make that even clearer. But I do think that on high-tech, which does offer a partial and hopefully optimistic part of the answer to the problem, R&D, capital gains, a new education program that literally revolutionizes schools, but one of which's goals is proficiency in math and science for young people. Little longer range, incidentally, but it is absolutely fundamental to the innate well-being of a State like New Hampshire. And in the meantime, we can go forward with job training to take the work force you're talking about and try to equip them for jobs that will be there as this economy turns around.

I've got a couple of other specific things, the R&D that you mentioned and Doug mentioned also. Somebody mentioned mandated benefits. We are going to continue to fight against the mandated benefits, telling the communities that if they want, quote, Federal money, they've got to do it by some Federal formula. I think that has been a problem on health care containment and a lot of other things. So, I'll stop there, but R&D, we will continue to press for the R&D credits that I do think will have a big difference in creating the kind of job opportunities that you appropriately mentioned. There are many more. But again, these comments were helpful, and I welcome any more. Or comments.

*Q.* Would you like to comment on the depreciation or investment tax credits?

*The President.* Yes, I would, because we're getting to a funny season here politically where everybody's running around saying, what's going to have the most populist appeal? What is the thing that's going to help the most? There was a proposal made by one of Bob Smith's colleagues a while back, last fall, of a massive tax cut, and the long-term interest rates shot up the very next day. I will not go for a quick fix.

What we will be proposing and have proposed and have been stiffed by a Democratic Congress are things that would do what you're talking about. Capital gains is part of it; IRA's that affect the first-time homebuyers is another part of it; extension of the R&D tax credit is another part of it. And these are aimed at what you're talking about, real growth. And to those I would add an education and retraining program that is absolutely fundamental to be able to compete. I would add a necessity for this President and for Governors to do what we're trying to do, and that is to get access, fair access, to others' markets.

I would avoid the siren's call of protection that suggests the way for us to get strong is to put quotas on and to start managing trade. We'd be right back where we were in the Smoot-Hawley days of the thirties, and there are one or two other people around here that are old enough to remember what it was like when we shrunk the foreign markets.

So, I agree with what you say. I hope this is what we've been trying to do. And I know this is a political trip because the campaign has to pay for it, so give me more Congressmen like Senator Smith and Bill Zeliff and Gordon Humphrey and this Governor, and I believe we can get the kind of investment-oriented programs through the Congress. I am going to try again. And I would like to save one or two additions to what I've told you for the State of the Union, but I hope you'll agree that what we're proposing is not a quick political fix that will get you votes through a series of southern primaries after the New Hampshire primary, but something that will take

the Government role and use it in partnership with private industry and State governments to get this sick economy moving.

I don't want to try to be up here to assert blame; I'll take my share of it. But when you look at what we have tried to do in terms of growth incentives and the way we've been stiffed by a hostile Congress for pure political reasons, I need the help of the people in this State. That's one reason I'm just delighted to be here. But again, when it rains before you see that rainbow, the President has to take his share of the blame. And I'm here to do just exactly that. But we will stay involved internationally, and I will press for those kinds of sound investment—you mentioned depreciation schedules or ITC, that's sound.

And please stay tuned for the State of the Union.

[*At this point, remarks were made by a participant.*]

*The President.* That might well be, the double declining balance of the depreciation and some of these things taken out so that there could be an overall tax cut. It worked for a while, but I think now anything we do with the Tax Code should be to stimulate real investment, some degree real savings, because we're not saving enough as a nation and thus the banks don't have enough of the capital that they would have otherwise to loan out, and through education and R&D and all of this keep our technological edge. We've still got it, but we need to keep it and build it and strengthen it.

So, that's the approach we're going to be taking in terms of real investment. And I am going to resist, I don't care what it costs in terms of votes, some of these siren's calls that go out to simply take across-the-board tax cuts that have a good sound to them but do not do what you're talking about. The way to create jobs is through what you're talking about, and that's what I have tried to do. And I'm going to be more effective doing it in the future because I'm going to take my case right to the American people and say, "Look, here's what I've tried to do; now I need your help." New Hampshire's hurting, these other States are hurting. And this is the approach we're going to take. And I hope it makes sense.

*Q.* During the Persian Gulf war, one thing that I thought was very obvious was the fact that we had daily updates on where the war was going. People knew what was going on on a daily basis. It created a lot of interest, and it created a lot of support for what you were doing over there. In my lifetime, whenever I've watched the State of the Union Address I've agreed with a lot of things any administration has said, but as the weeks go on it loses some of its interest, some of its impact. I would suggest to you that during your State of the Union Address you tell the American public that once a week, for the next 4, 6, 8, 10 weeks, you're going to come on prime time and update us on the status of your proposals that you make in the State of the Union Address.

*The President.* It's an interesting suggestion. Here are the people you want to talk to about giving me the prime time out here because we're in an election year and you'll have every jackleg jumping up demanding equal time with some screwy scheme. [*Laughter*]

But I believe that you've got something. I have to keep it before the American people. I have not done a good job in getting people to understand we've had a growth agenda. I have proposed in three State of the Union Messages some of the various things I'm hearing around here we should do. And I don't believe there's a working guy in New Hampshire that understands that. That's my fault. We've got to do better on it, and I think you've got a pretty good idea.

I'd like to take the same kind of energy and leadership that we had in Desert Storm and use it to help the working men and women in the State of New Hampshire and across this country. There is one significant difference. When I moved 500,000 troops about 14 months ago, I didn't have to ask permission from a Democratically controlled Congress. When I said, a year ago to this very day, we may have to go into battle, and I don't like sending any mother's son into battle, or daughter either, but we did it. Didn't have to get permission. Didn't have to go to subcommittee chairmen that Bill Zeliff has to wrestle with, or Bob Smith,

every day to have a debate on what's going to happen the minute I finish this State of the Union. They've already prepared their response. We just did it.

I'm the Commander in Chief. I have the responsibility for the national security of this country. We led, and we lifted the American spirit. And now you see some of these magazines coming out with the revision of all that, trying to take it away from the American people. I talked to one of our leading generals about it yesterday, and he's just sick about that kind of revisionistic reporting. The American people know what they saw. They saw leadership. They took pride in their young men and women. And we can do the same thing domestically, I believe.

I'm not arguing about your suggestion. I'm simply arguing about the modalities because, one, political year; two, getting access to the airwaves for the kind of update is pretty complicated and quite expensive.

We will try very, very hard again. And I think I can be more effective, and I'm going to say, "Look, let's do it this way. Let's lay aside the politics. Let's do it this way." And then if they don't like it, fine. Keep hammering that away to the American people. So, I realize that we need a followup, but I just argue whether we can get that nice, crisp, clean air time that I'd like to have.

And it was available, in a sense, to our national purpose. Remember on Desert Storm, though, the criticism of the President, it goes with my job, didn't sell it, American people don't understand what we're doing, American people don't know, let's wait, let's wait, this man will get out, these sanctions will take care of it, body bags. It wasn't all as clear on the international front as it seemed after these young men and women did that job.

But we can do it here. And again, this meeting helps sensitize me to the fact that we must do it.

*Q.* You can't mention this, but I can, and I do recall there was some criticism. In fact, there were some people that openly opposed the idea of standing up to Saddam Hussein in Kuwait, and one of them is running for President in the Republican Party. [*Laughter*]

*Q.* As a corollary to Desert Storm, I'm not at all certain that you might not have been in a worse position than we are in trying to stimulate new business if you had to justify some of the actions with the OSHA's and the EPA's. And I think that one of the things that is very important is to put some type of a stop to the burgeoning and, in some cases, very much overrated types of bias that come out from someone that does not get elected.

*The President.* Dave mentioned that, and sometimes you're caught between a rock and a hard place. I think we've got a good environmental record. I think it's important we've got a good environmental record. But I think, in some cases, we should be erring on the side of jobs and employment.

And I look out on—I'll give you a problem out on the Northwest. All across the country we have a spotted owl problem. And yes, we want to see that little furry, feathery guy protected and all of that. But I don't want to see 40,000 loggers thrown out of work. And so, we have to work it out properly. Bill Zeliff and Bob were telling me that they've had good cooperation from Bill Reilly on some of these very difficult environmental matters.

I think of this State as, you know, good conservation. You've got a lot to conserve. You've got beauty. But we've got to find the proper balance between the excesses of the regulatory movement, which is the conservation movement, and the excesses on, the rape, pillage, and plunder on the business side.

The State has always been able to sort that out pretty well. So I take your criticism. And we will endeavor to bring home to the regional bureaucrats the need for the balance that—I think you're calling for balance in this. And I think we can do better there.

[*At this point, remarks were made by a participant.*]

*The President.* The national figures on manufacturing are not all discouraging even in rough economic times. What I think we were talking about here probably would have the most stimulative effect, short and long run, if you add R&D and education into it, of manufacturing. But the concept that we need a strong manufacturing base is very, very important. And I hope I can emphasize that.

You get into a political debate; you get into a political kind of pledging debate: Who is going to cut the taxes the most to get the most votes? I think I have to resist that. I have the responsibility now, accept the responsibility for good things and the bad things, and I have to propose what I think will create the most jobs and bring the economy back the quickest. And a strong manufacturing base is part of it.

But again, let me make this pitch to you all because I do think of New Hampshire as resisting from the left or from the extreme right the siren's call of protection. We are in a global economy now. You can't separate it out. It is exports that have saved the national economy to the degree it's even been saved, and it hasn't been saved, but I mean, put it this way, it would be a lot worse if we weren't exporting to these foreign countries.

And we can compete in a manufacturing way with these foreign countries if we get the proper access, fair access to markets, and if we protect our competitiveness through the kinds of taxing that we've heard here today that I think you probably favor. So, I'll try to keep that in focus as we go forward here.

[*At this point, remarks were made by a participant.*]

*The President.* What you ask for is, as I thought at the opening of your remarks, an opportunity to take some specifics and to take this New Hampshire view and be heard on it. And that is easily arranged. I mean, I'd be delighted to have set up at whatever level you want to take these specifics and make clear to the regulators, or higher if you want to go, as to what the mechanics are that are holding back this recovery.

So, I accept your offer, and we'll be glad to set it up. But be specific, bring the specifics because there is some feeling that some of these problems have been resolved. And to the degree that they are still out there, and it's something other than the judgment of the lending institution who got burned for loaning in ways they shouldn't have loaned before and are saying, "Hey, I've got to protect my stockholders," we can do something about it. If it's the judgment of a financial man, lending officer, then I don't know that the Government has a role. But if it's the Government regulator that's putting this dampener on the lending community in a small New Hampshire town, I'd like to have our people listen to that and try to be sensitive to it and try to change it. To some degree we've made progress, but obviously we haven't made enough.

[*At this point, remarks were made by a participant.*]

*The President.* And after you get through talking to us, and I hope that we can help as an administration, save a little time to talk to some of those who don't think we've got enough regulation on Congress and will hold up the name of a very good man for the OCC because they think he's been too lenient on regulation. And he gets stiffed in these Senate politics. Bob Smith knows this very well, indeed. We've got to sell the other side that you've got a point here, and you do have a point here.

I don't want to sound like an expert, because I've been out of meeting a payroll for a long time. When I was in the drilling business, if I went into loan on a drilling rig, I had to have a contract from a major oil company or some good credit, or they wouldn't loan me a dime. They wouldn't loan unless I had that to pay it out.

In the go-go years that followed, there got to be a lot of competition for loans for drilling platforms, and you didn't have to have a contract. And the lending institutions started making loans that they wouldn't have made in more normal times or more conservative times.

In real estate, you had to have a contract to pay out *x* percent of your building, if not the entire building. And then in the go-go days, through the S&L's and some degree the banks trying to compete, understandably so, thinking there will be no tomorrow, and the consumer and the loaners thinking the same thing, they made loans that now

are bad, shouldn't have made in the first place. We got carried away by the excesses.

Now, I know that from personal experience, not from some textbook, not from listening to some handler in the campaign just discovering New Hampshire. So, we have been recovering from some of the excesses. It is my point that in some of this regulation we've gone too far, that we've swung too far back. And the lender is saying to himself, "Wait a minute. I've been through all that once. Don't ask me to make the same mistake twice."

A lot of what you're talking about is psychological between the lender and the borrower. But to the degree the Government is being inhibiting, not for sound economic reason but just kind of reaction to the excesses of the past, we can help, and we should help. And we should try to lighten up on the regulations, and I know Judd feels that way at the State level.

So, I think something good can come of this, and we will set it up at whatever level you want.

*Q.* Thank you, Mr. President. We've got a very busy day planned for you, so I guess we've got to sort of wrap this up. I didn't know if you wanted to make any additional comments, or we can move on and say hello to some of the folks out there.

*The President.* Well, I'd rather say hello, but I—for busy people, working hard in a struggling economy, to take the time to come here has been extraordinarily helpful to me.

And I just want to end where I started. I don't know what I have to do to convince people here that I really care about this; I do. I probably have made mistakes in assessing the fact that the economy would recover. Last year at this time, 49 out of the 50 blue-chip economists thought that by now we'd be in recovery. They were wrong; I was wrong. Maybe one or two of you around the table would admit he or even she was wrong. Sorry, Bonnie. I don't know.

So, it's not a question of blame; I will accept that. But what I want to do is convince the people here, one, that I understand the problem—I think I do; two, that I need help in solving the problem, and that means support for the growth initiatives, some of which I've tried and failed on because of a stiff by a partisan Congress, and some of which we will try again, and add to that additional ones that I've been listening to around this table. So, we're going to go, and go forth in this State of the Union.

Then I also took on board this comment about needing to follow that up. And what we can get done in an election year, I don't know. But I'll conclude this way: Without having it sound like Mrs. Rose Scenario, this is New Hampshire. You've done a lot; you've accomplished a lot. And this State is going to pull out of this. This national economy is going to pull out of this. You look back in history of this country; it always has, and it will.

So, my message without, as I say, just being euphorically optimistic, is that in place there are some fundamentals that we haven't talked about today. Somebody ought to—the market's seeing them, incidentally. What are they? They are: Interest rates are down. Inflation, the cruelest tax of all, is down. Unfortunately, part of the reason is economic growth is so slow. But nevertheless, that is down. Inventories are in fair shape. And I think most people here understand that. We are making progress on access to foreign markets. The exports are vibrant.

Couple those with the bad news, and we all know what that is, of unemployment and, somebody put their finger on it, confidence, the confidence factor. I mean, we had national unemployment at 10.7 percent in about 1981 or 1982, and confidence was higher then than it is now. People were saying, "Hey, tomorrow is going to be better."

So, I don't want to be the cheerleader saying tomorrow is going to be better. I do think the economy is going to come out of it. But I need the help of sound-thinking people to resist the siren call of protection, to resist some of these quick political appeal taxing schemes that may get you a vote or two, but will do nothing to stimulate jobs, investment, and economic growth.

And so, I came here to ask for support in this very important field, as well as to listen to the heartbeat of this State that I do feel Barbara and I both know. Somebody mentioned her, and I am very proud of what she is doing, not just because she knows how to handle her husband when he throws up—[*laughter*]—but she is expressing something that I think the people of New Hampshire understand. And that is love of family, faith, determination, helping kids—taking an AIDS baby and holding it in her arms and say, "Hey, we need a little compassion and understanding on all this." And I have a very comfortable feeling that people here know that we do feel a part of this State.

In any event, that's what I'd say in conclusion. And thank you all very, very much. I've learned a lot.

*Note: The President spoke at 8:52 a.m. at the Pease Air National Guard Base. In his remarks, he referred to J. Bonnie Newman, former Assistant to the President for Management and Administration, and Ruth L. Griffin, member of the Governor's Council.*

# Remarks and a Question-and-Answer Session at a Town Hall Meeting in Exeter, New Hampshire
*January 15, 1992*

*The President.* I am very, very pleased to be back. Mike, how are you? This guy meets me at Pease every time I come in there. [*Laughter*] Exeter rose-grower.

Let me just say how really pleased I am to be here and to thank you for turning out. I want to make a couple of comments, and then it's mainly questions. Isn't it, Judd? First, I want to thank the Governor for being at my side. You know my and Barbara's affection for Governor Judd Gregg and for Hugh and Kay, old longtime friends who stay in touch and who have kept me informed of this State—both of them, both

Greggs—of the problems that we face in this State. And I'm not talking political; I'm talking about hardship for people that are hurting.

One of the things I'm pleased to be able to do here is to at least let the people of this State know that even though I am President and do have two or three other responsibilities, that when people are hurting, we care. We get the message there. We read the mail. We can understand. And I just wanted to get that out loud and clear because we're in a political year, and you hear a lot of people that have discovered New Hampshire for the first time running around trying to say something different. Of course, we care.

Secondly, I am very grateful not only to the Governor but to Senator Bob Smith, Senator Rudman, who couldn't be with us—Bob Smith here today—who are doing a superb job, and then your Congressman, another dear friend, a man I respect, Bill Zeliff. These are leaders in the Congress. And they talk about pledges and all of this. Let me tell you something. I took a pledge when I was sworn in, the oath of office, and what I need a pledge about is to get more Congressmen and Senators like Senator Smith and Gordon Humphrey, who was in the Senate and is supporting me, and your Congressman here, Bill Zeliff, and Warren Rudman. Then we would be able to control this Federal spending better. Then we would be able to see that we get these tax improvements that I've been asking for. So that's the pledge I want, is the pledge from the people to give us more. And you're going to have to use your influence out of the State because you've done pretty darn well in the State in the United States Congress.

So, that was one point I wanted to make. The other one is that people say, "Well, you're in trouble in New Hampshire." Well, that may be. But I'm here to listen. I'm here to take the questions. I'm here to say, hey, there's a lot to do in partnership, the Federal Government, the State government where you've got superb leadership, and the people themselves.

And of course, we care. And somebody gave me the analogy of a country-western song about a train, hoping they'd see the

light at the end of the tunnel is not a train coming through. And I trumped it with saying, well, remember the Nitty Gritty Dirt Band one, if you've got any country music people here, "If you're going to see a rainbow, you've got to stand a little rain."

Well, New Hampshire has stood more than its share of rain, job—hurting and the families wondering how they're going to make their ends meet. But there is going to be a rainbow out there. There's some fundamentals that are pretty darn good. And yet, we've got to do better.

And the last point I want to make is I hope that you will listen to the State of the Union Message. I have proposed, 3 straight years, growth agenda programs. Not some fancy quick fix that's going to have broad appeal in an election time, but things that would stimulate this economy. Now we're putting this all together again with new additions to it to take these proposals to the American people. And then what I hope we can do is rally the American people and get the economy moving by sound investment-oriented treatment of the Tax Code.

That is what's needed, and still hold the line on spending. One of the few benefits of that budget agreement was that we have caps on the excesses of Federal spending, those things that can be controlled. And I want to keep them there. I do not want to bust the one restraint that is on the spenders in the United States Congress.

So having said that, I hope you'll ask the questions. We'll have a good health program that I think will have appeal to the voters here because it's family; it keeps things close to the people themselves rather than having a lot of mandated benefits out of Washington.

And this is the last point. I'm just back from a rather spectacular trip to Asia. I say spectacular—you try getting the flu at a dinner. [*Laughter*] I have a feeling the people in New England, and certainly having been a neighbor of this State for so long, understand that even Presidents get the flu. I said over there, even Democrats get it from time to time. [*Laughter*] But you've got to admit I did it in a dramatic way.

Having said that, exports account for a

tremendous amount of the growth in this country. A lot of the jobs, I think it's estimated—I was talking to Bob and Bill coming over here—35,000 to 40,000 jobs in New Hampshire related to exports. So please don't buy this protection legislation that the Democrats and some others are putting out, this idea that we can shrink back inside. I want to put America first in the sense of the values, in the sense of getting this economy to be first, but not in the sense of some kind of protection legislation that is going to shrink markets and throw the working people of New Hampshire further out of work. Let's expand these markets.

Now, fire away. Shoot. Any questions, even if they're tough ones. I know we've got a few fans in here for someone else. Bring them up.

You're second. Got the first guy, and we'll be right over.

### The Economy

*Q.* Mr. President, first let me say the conditions in the country today, with our Government in deficit, most every State in the Union in deficit, and most every municipality in the country in deficit, never mind the households, what do we have to do—and I'm glad you brought a few—to get the Congressmen and the Senators in this country to realize when we have millions of people without jobs, homeless, without health care, and these fellows have the gall to vote themselves a raise, what can we do other than vote out every incumbent? I hate to see that, but I mean, what do we have to do to get the message across to these people in Washington?

*The President.* Well, I think this kind of meeting helps. Fortunately, you have congressional delegations, the ones I mentioned from this State, that understand that. They fight against the excesses of Congress.

One of the things that I proposed or seconded the motion on were these proposals that are there, and they're bipartisan, I might add, for Congress to reform itself in terms of proliferation of committees and needing reforms, Congress to adhere to the same laws that the American people have to adhere to. One of the comments that I've made after the Clarence Thomas hear-

ings was that that needed to be done. They ought not to exempt themselves from the laws you and I have to honor. And this congressional delegation understands that; these people here do. So, you've got to spill over and use your influence across the border, two ways I might add, Maine and Massachusetts, good places to start. So, try that one.

But no, you've got a good point. Look, I'm not up here to assign blame. I'll take my share of the blame. I don't take it for not caring or not understanding. I do. Barbara does. I hope we have projected the family concerns that we feel. We've tried to do that in this job. But I'm not here to blame.

But I am here to remind the voters up here that in two previous State of the Unions I have proposed growth initiatives that would have stimulated the economy. Now I'm going to do it again, and this time I'm going to look the American people in the eye, as I did in the past, and say, "All right, people are hurting more now. I've just come back from the State of New Hampshire, and a lot of people are out of work. And if you really care, pass this package. Then we can put it back into politics and debate it for the rest of this political year. But get something done that's going to get the people of this State and of this country back to work." That's the approach I'm going to take.

Now, we had one here, and then I'll come over there.

### AIDS

*Q.* We had a wonderful Surgeon General who led us in health care in the man of Dr. Chick Koop.

*The President.* Yes.

*Q.* Can he help us with some of our health problems in the future?

*The President.* Yes, he can. He's a good man. I think he wants to, too. I saw him the other day. And one of the things that Dr. Koop, who came into office and people said, "Well, this guy's a little conservative for the national agenda." He wasn't; very sensitive guy. One of the things that he has done— and this is a sensitive subject; it's on my mind again because yesterday I met with

Earvin "Magic" Johnson—is to project the idea that treating AIDS is a health problem. We are concerned about it. We care about it. When Barbara holds an AIDS baby in her arms, she's trying to express the compassion that both of us feel. When I go out to NIH and meet with those people that are afflicted with it—we have to do it on a health problem: Prevention, research and development, caring, making people understand this now is a national health problem.

And Magic, who's on that Commission, following in the footsteps of the education that Chick Koop has put forward to the beginning, is saying, "Look, lifestyle's important." He said, "I've made some mistakes." And he did. He made some big ones. But now I want to help, get this thing out for open debate, compassionate treatment as a disease, and see what we can do. Then use our office, the bully pulpit of the White House and Chick Koop and others, our new Surgeon General, to educate people. We've got to treat with the health aspect through prevention and research. I think he will have—we'd love to have him involved.

### Health Care

*Q.* On the national health plan, what do you have planned as a help for the 35 million people who don't have health insurance?

*The President.* The question in the back is a very important question. What are you going to do about the 35 million who don't have health insurance? What we've done so far is emphasizing prevention, emphasizing inoculations and this kind of thing. Now at the State of the Union, I will have what I think is the proper, if you'll permit me to hold back some of the details, but a comprehensive health care program that does not increase the Federal mandates but does bring protection to the numbers of people that are uninsured. Therein lies the big problem.

So, we will have a comprehensive—it's only 2 weeks away, so stay tuned, and I think it will be done with the values I think of as New Hampshire values in mind, without busting the budget. I ask you, when you hear all these people who have just discovered New Hampshire on the road map coming up here with these health plans, ask them what that is going to do to the people that pay the taxes, as well as those who need the health care.

So, I think we've got a good program, and I hope we can get the support from everybody in this room.

Yes, in the back in the middle.

*Q.* If I can just comment, I think we have time for about two more questions. We'd like to have everybody come up and have a chance to shake hands with the President.

*The President.* Anybody got a real controversial one or want to make a statement? I want some guy that really wants to be tough, some tough guy. Who is it? This guy in the middle? Yes. Who are you for, first, and then let's hear the question. [*Laughter*]

*Q.* I don't think you want to know.

*The President.* No, but really, they shouldn't be soft balls. Call it as you see it, and you'll get it back.

*Q.* I'm a registered Democrat.

*The President.* All right, sir.

### *Education*

*Q.* I haven't made up my mind yet. Four years ago you proclaimed yourself the education President.

*The President.* Yes.

*Q.* Well, I'm a student at the University of New Hampshire, and to the best of my knowledge New Hampshire is 51st out of 50 States. We're behind Puerto Rico as well, as far as State funding for education. And I just haven't seen very much evidence of your being the education President.

*The President.* The man asked a very important and very fair question. In the first place, Federal spending, and I can understand why you might not sense this, is up significantly in the Department of Education. As you know, Federal spending is 6 or 7 percent of the total education budget for the country. Educational spending, leave out Federal, is also up substantially.

Here's the good news: We do have a good program. I went to the 50 Governors. We put politics aside on this one, believe me. We've got the national education goals, six goals now. They were agreed by Democrats and Republicans alike. They are now encompassed in a program called America

2000, which is a national education strategy. It literally calls for revolutionizing the schools.

Yes, it requires some more Federal spending, but we're budgeting that. It requires much more participation of parents and of communities. I addressed a national Chamber meeting yesterday on it. Democrats, Republicans, liberals, conservatives coming together to say we've got to do it differently.

Please take a look at that program. It is sensible. I'm determined to keep it out of the political crosscurrent. I don't care about my personal label; I am committed to education. This program, under the able leadership of Lamar Alexander, is one of the things that is beginning to get to the American consciousness.

You and I might differ on this one; I still like the idea of parents being able to choose. When I came out of the military to the GI bill a thousand years ago nobody said, "Hey, you've got to go to school A or school B, university A or B, or high school extension program A, B, or C." The person could choose. And choice in the State of Minnesota, formerly run by a Democratic Governor, has resulted in educational excellence.

And so, one of the concepts of this is choice. Another one is doing better in math and science. Another is to continue the increases that we've already started on Head Start, ready to learn. Another one is, you're never too old to learn. Even I, and it's not just show business, have a little computer there, and I'm trying to learn it. I'm doing something, and I hope it's an example that you're never too old to learn, although I'm having a few difficulties with the cursor. [*Laughter*]

The thing that troubles me is I don't think that we've gotten that across. It is a good, sensible program. It's really just starting, but it holds the answer because we are not going to be as competitive in this world if we don't do better in math or science.

Another part of it is voluntary testing at the 4th, 8th, and high school level. And it's voluntary. But there's nothing wrong with testing. There's nothing wrong with standards so a school knows whether it's keeping up with other schools. We've gotten away

from that sense of discipline. Then I want the schools to be drug-free so a kid can go and learn in a safe environment.

So, those are some of the ingredients of our program called America 2000.

### War on Drugs

*Q.* Mr. President, it seems that as the economy gets worse and worse, that more and more people are turning to the sales of drugs and more and more people are using drugs as they see the economy toughen and their families suffering. What do you propose to do about this problem because it seems to keep getting worse?

*The President.* Let me repeat the question because I want to argue with the premise a little bit, not totally. The premise is, it seems to be getting worse on narcotics, drugs, amongst young people, and what do you propose to do about it?

We have a national drug strategy. We are making significant if not dramatic progress amongst young people, for example, in the use of cocaine, down by 10 percent. Where we're hurting as a society is the 35 and older, kind of the addicted crowd is not shaking it.

Education is a part of it. Treatment is a part of it. Interdiction, a much more successful interdiction effort, is a part of it. But the national drug strategy is working. And then there's another ingredient to this. It's the private partnership under the leadership of a guy named Jim Burke. We're spending $1 million—they are, not Government—$1 million a day with, I don't know whether you've seen them, with advertisements, pro bono advertisements trying to help educate children and parents that drugs are—you know, turn off of drugs.

We are making progress. We've made big progress in marijuana, made big progress in cocaine use. And yet, we've still got a long way to go. So, we'll keep fighting the problem, but I just want to give a little hope out there that these figures are fairly encouraging in terms of the age group that you asked about.

Last pitch is this on it: I still think that the people of New Hampshire, in spite of the economic problems and being out of work, still really epitomize for a lot of the rest of the country what Barbara and I talk about as family values. I worry about the decimation of the American family. Everything we do, like child care, we try to make it that the family has a choice, or education, that the family does.

Barbara is out there trying to get people—"Read to the kids." So, I do think that family involvement is vital to the success. The Federal Government cannot get this drug thing done by itself. We've got a program. We've got to keep the families together and the families involved in solving this. That isn't a vote-getter, and that isn't going to outpromise some Democrat halfway across the State. But it is something I feel very, very strongly about and will continue to try to help the American people understand.

You've got to read to your kids. You've got to hug them. You've got to lift them up and dust them off and put them back into the game. And if you don't do that, they drift off into some of this mire. In the inner city they need help on it, too.

[*At this point, County Commissioner Maureen Barrows presented a book on the history of Exeter to the President.*]

*The President.* Listen, I apologize, but we're really almost just getting started. This is not show business. I mean, when a guy asked a very good question on education it gave me a chance to say what I think, but also it shows what concerns people. So I hope you don't feel this—whoops, even the guy at the end of the table here feels that it's just some kind of a useless exercise.

But message: I care. We're trying. We need help. We have had and will continue to have, I think, sound and sensible programs.

And let's not forget this: It was one year ago that I had to make a very fateful decision that affected the lives of a lot of Americans. And we saw instantly the return of American pride. It doesn't matter about how you feel about when we should have gone to war, the country came together. I want to use that same kind of leadership to bring the country together now on the social problems that affect us and on getting this economy going and getting New Hampshire back to work. And I need your help.

Thank you very, very much.

*Note: The President spoke at 10:50 a.m. at the Exeter Town Hall. In his remarks, he referred to Michael Dagostino, a retired rose-grower in Exeter, and Hugh and Kay Gregg, parents of Gov. Judd Gregg.*

# Remarks to Davidson Interior Trim Employees in Dover, New Hampshire
*January 15, 1992*

First, let me just say thanks for the warmth of this reception. And your chairman is just back from a trip with me abroad, and the thing got a little caught up in some of the politics of the moment, which is hard to avoid. But the concept was: Look, this isn't any time to pull back; this is a time to try to expand American markets. I am not in favor of protection in the sense of pulling away from our export markets.

So, we went over there and tried to hammer away in getting our export market extended. And one of the things that saved us in the extraordinarily difficult times that, well, this State faces and the neighboring State of Maine, Massachusetts, and New England, and also some of the rest of the country, is our exports. So, one pitch I'd make is, no matter what your politics are, is please resist this siren's call, this wonderful call, "Well, we're going to protect." Because when you protect, you shrink the markets abroad, and you throw people at home out of work.

So that's the theme that I—take you up on your chance to say something. [*Laughter*] And the other thing, and I guess, is that

I expect it's difficult for somebody working in a plant here in New Hampshire to wonder, to know if the President really cares about what's happening in the economy. And I think I know this State. Went to school a thousand years ago across the border, and go up every summer of my life except 1944 to Maine, spending a fair amount of time, almost you can see it, practically, coming in on the plane. So when you get clobbered on the seacoast by a storm, I get clobbered on the seacoast by a storm. It goes further than that. When you get hurting because you worry whether you're going to have a job or you get thrown out, I do care about it. And I just wanted to say that.

What we're trying to do from the Federal level is to stimulate the economic growth of this country. And I hope you'll stay tuned at the State of the Union. I've made some proposals. I'm having difficulty, I think we all know, getting them through the Congress. But I'm going to try again, look the American people in the eye, and say, "Now look, here's what it's going to take to take a sick economy and make it a well economy."

Having said that, I'm convinced this economy is going to turn around. I've been wrong about how fast it would be, and I think a lot of other people, smarter than I, have been wrong about how fast it would be, the economists and all that. But we are the United States. We don't need to fear anything at all. We can turn this thing around, and we're going to do it.

And the last point is simply this, because I want to eat this chili before it gets cold—[*laughter*]—and some of you guys have got to go to work. But the last part of it is that a year ago, almost to the day—and maybe some of you all were involved; I know you were with your emotions, your hearts, and everything—but we, almost a year ago to this very minute, went into battle halfway around the world. And the country demonstrated something in support of the young men and women that fought there that we'd really lost since World War II. We came together, came together in anticipation, came together in war, and came together in victory. And it lifted the country up; the country came together.

Well, even though we're in an election year—and I'm a realist, I've been in politics one hell of a long time, if you'll excuse the expression—some things transcend the politics. One of them is that what I want to do, even though we're in an election year, is take the same spirit of leadership and the same spirit that affected this country then, can-do spirit, and say, "All right, now let's see if we can't do the same thing with our economy," through getting the incentives built back into the system or keeping the lid on the Federal spending or whatever it is.

And I just wanted you to know: One, I know you're hurting; two, I care about it; three, I've been wrong about how fast this recovery would take; but, four, I am determined to use the role as leader of the free world, leader of the United States, to make things better. And I think we'll have a window in here, even though it's political, right after the State of the Union to have something happen in terms of stimulating the growth of this economy.

So please, vote any way you want to—that's your right and privilege—and say what you feel, but please avoid the quick fix that might sound good. One of the charges: The President doesn't know where New Hampshire is. Look, I know where New Hampshire is, and I know the heartbeat of this State. And I know the people, and I care about them, and so does Barbara Bush.

You can argue with me on the politics or on what we might have done sooner, but I just wanted you to know we do care desperately. We have tried in the White House to project a certain commitment to family, which, if you look at your kids and you worry, as Bar and I do, about the decline of the American family, it is important. So when she hugs a baby that's sick with AIDS or when she reads to a child, what we're trying to do is say we think the parents of this country—leave out the politics for a minute—have to stay involved, whether it's on child care, and our child care gives the parents a choice, whether it's on health care, don't mandate it all, get a system. And we're going to be proposing a good program that keeps the strong families of this country strong.

I say I know this State; I do. I know it

enough to know that regardless of the politics, family is important. Pride in the country is important. And I want to try to do my job in such a way to identify with that and to lead this country.

Somebody reminded me of a country-western song over here at Pease. Incidentally, I want to see how the Federal Government can help in the economic redevelopment of that area. It's a tremendous asset. And yes, I'm having to cut back on defenses, and yes, thank God, your kids and my grandkids are growing up in a world where they don't need to worry quite as much about nuclear weapons. I mean, that's a very important thing. But with it comes some big problems for jobs. So, we want to help on the economic development.

This highway bill is going to help; it's going to help New Hampshire a lot. Small business moves we've made are going to help. The new visa center is going to help. So I want to try to do the best we can. Somebody says, "Hey, Bush is bragging about the highway bill helping New Hampshire." I've got to brag about something, and you're darn right I'm going to brag about the highway bill and all the jobs that go with it.

So, we'll keep slugging it out on that basis. In spite of the problems, I think this is probably the most challenging and, in a sense, rewarding time since, well, in this whole century, to be President of the United States. Who would have thought that the changes around the world that make the world more peaceful would have happened so fast and happened, thank God, on my watch? So, I'll take the hit for the bad stuff, and give me just a little bit of the credit for the fact that your kids and mine may have a chance for a more peaceful world.

But anyway, good luck to you. I didn't mean to—he invited me, so it's his—[*laughter*] Thanks, and bless you all. Thanks a lot.

[*At this point, Frank Biehl, manager of human resources, Davidson Interior Trim, presented a gift to the President.*]

Let me just say this: Your chairman was tough over there and took that case dramatically. You can compete. If we can get the markets open, you can sell. You workers are better than they are. The competence you see out there is better than the next guy.

I get criticized on this trip, saying Bush is trying to manage trade—all the liberal columnists on this one. Normally get hit from the other side saying protect. But this one is saying, "Well, he's now giving away his one commitment to free trade." It's not doing that at all. It is simply saying I am for free trade, but we need fair access to the other guy's market.

And that's what Bev was trying to do, and that's what I was trying to do. And we made some progress. Not as much as we wanted, but we're going to keep on. And for those that say, "Stay home," I know what they're getting at. They're thinking, "Well, the President is over there talking to Gorbachev or Yeltsin or Middle East. I wonder if he really knows that we're hurting in Dover, New Hampshire?" I've got to say to the people, yes, I know that. But the world is such you've got to stay involved. And it means jobs in Dover, New Hampshire, if we stay involved and do it effectively.

So we'll keep on trying. And now that's the second speech, and thanks for my sneakers. I'm glad to have them.

*Note: The President spoke at 12:48 p.m. In his remarks, he referred to Beverly F. Dolan, chairman of Textron, parent company of Davidson Interior Trim.*

## Remarks to Liberty Mutual Insurance Employees in Dover
*January 15, 1992*

Let me first thank, of course, Governor Gregg, who's heading up our campaign in this State. And let me also single out Senator Bob Smith—I don't know whether you all have been introduced—Senator Bob Smith over here, Congressman Bill Zeliff, both extraordinarily good friends, tremendous supporters for the values that you and I share; and then also a former Senator, Gordon Humphrey, who is also in my corner and working hard. And I'm so proud to have these leaders and others, Warren Rudman and others who couldn't be here today, at my side.

Somebody said, "Well, why do you want to go to Liberty?" And I was thinking back, coming over, the last time I was here in an earlier campaign effort, somebody in a parking lot ran over Governor Hugh Gregg's foot. [*Laughter*] And I wanted to come back and try to do better this time— [*laughter*]—and thank everybody here for this welcome, Mr. Laszewski, Mr. Countryman, and just say it is a pleasure to be back in this State.

Let me deny a vicious rumor that's circulating here. I have not come back to New Hampshire to personally renew my subscription to the Union Leader. [*Laughter*] I did come back to talk about jobs. But I wanted to start with something. I was just over at a cafeteria at Davidson, and this guy—I don't know what his politics were, really is indifferent—and he asked me what for some might be an easy question. And he said, "If you had to name one thing, what would your message be today; why are you here?" We were sitting with our sleeves rolled up at the table.

My thought process went this way: I think I know this State. I know I know the problems of this State. We live near this State. I went to school across the border, to Massachusetts, and have a feel for this New England where I grew up. I think I understand it. I understand the heartbeat; I understand the hardship. And I said to this guy, we've got all of these issues: health care, which I'll mention; we've got world

peace; we have economic stimulation to get the economy. One message: I want the people of this State to know that I care. I care very much about the people that are hurting in this State, and I am determined to turn this State around. And that is the message.

And I have not simply just discovered New Hampshire. You ask some of these characters running around there with these scatterbrained ideas and these quick fixes to something as tough as this economy, "When were you last in New Hampshire?" And you'll find they've never been here at all. They wouldn't know how to get here.

I know the heartbeat of this State. I know the values, the family values of this State. Barbara and I try to live those values in our lives as President and First Lady of this country. And I can identify with those who are hurting in this State. Please give me credit for that, and do not listen to these guys that want to take political opportunity, come up with a quick fix to something as complicated as this economy, and then be gone and never to return. I've been here, been here a lot. And I will return, as President, and when I get through being President, as neighbor. So, you've got my pledge on that one.

I know times are tough. This State has gone through hell, gone through an extraordinarily difficult time, coming off of a pinnacle, you might say, of low unemployment. Now you're at about the national level. And yes, people are hurting. And I am determined to turn it around.

I told some of them over there, there's a big difference, you know, people say to me, difference between domestic and foreign policy. "How could you lead the world"— and they gave me some credit for that in Desert Storm, that the American people still feel very, very strongly about—"how can you do that and then have such difficulties with this economy?" Well, let me tell you something. When I moved those forces I didn't have to ask Senator Kennedy or some liberal Democrat how, whether we were going to do it. We did it. I didn't have to ask some smart-aleck columnist who was saying, "Bush hasn't explained this to the American people." We did it.

The young men and women, the best fighting force we've ever had, stood up and lifted the spirits of this country. And now I want to take that same leadership, bring this country together after the State of the Union, and solve the domestic economic problems, and do it in a sound, sensible New Hampshire way. And that is why I'm here.

It's a weird year here. You've got crazy people running all over, thinking that the way to put this country back to work is to stop exports. In other words, they call it this, they call it protection. I'm going to protect an American job. Do not listen to the siren's call of protection if it comes out of the far right or the far left. What that means is shrinking jobs, getting into trade wars and retaliation.

What we're trying to do is to expand exports by making that playing field level and getting access to foreign markets. So, when someone says to me, some politician out of some State that never heard of New Hampshire before, comes up here and says, "The President ought not to worry about world peace or the global economy," I'm going to say, "Let me run my business the way I think is best." I am going to continue to work to open markets, to take this question of equal opportunity—that's all the American worker needs—equal opportunity in the global marketplace.

Those workers I saw at Davidson and you in this business are the most efficient there is, and you can compete with anybody. And don't try to do it by shrinking world markets and going into some siren call of protection that threw this country into a depression back in the thirties. I'm talking 25 percent unemployment back in those days. Let's not set the clock back. Let's continue to exercise world leadership. We are the United States of America. And I am not about to give up on world leadership.

And to those cynics out there, these political newcomers hitting this State for the first time, let me say this: I won't apologize one minute for the fact that your kids and my grandkids might just have an opportuni-

ty, because of the way we've conducted the foreign affairs of this country, to grow up in a world with a little less worry about nuclear war. There has been dramatic change. And I'll take the hit. I'll take my share of the blame for the economy, and I'll dish out plenty to Congress on that, I might add. [*Laughter*] But just give us a little credit for the fact that we now have a tremendous change in the world, old totalitarian systems now democracies, people in the south of our border now working for free markets. And that means more jobs for the people of New Hampshire.

And so, it isn't all gloom and doom. And what I want to do is this. We've had growth agendas. They've been stymied by a Democratic Congress. And you ask these guys that come, where were you when the President proposed a capital gains cut to stimulate jobs? Where were you when he proposed IRA's to help the first-time homebuyer? He's got a growth agenda.

They didn't do it. So now I'm going to take my message on the State of the Union to the American people, look them right in the eye and say, "All right, let's do this. Let's lay aside these election-year politics for about 2 weeks or 3, and let's pass this package." And it's going to have in it not quick fixes. It's going to resist some of the short-term quick political briefs. But it's going to have the stimulation of jobs and investment and savings to get this country moving again. And that's what we need.

We don't need a quick political promise out in a parking lot somewhere only to be forgotten when the southern tier of primaries roll around. We need sound economics, and this time I'm going to succeed because I believe I can get the American people for me, in spite of the fact that we've got some congressional leaders down there that are opposed every step of the way.

I might say, Bill Zeliff is up for election, all the Congressmen are; Bob Smith, not. But if we had more Senators like Bob Smith and Warren Rudman and Congressmen like Bill Zeliff, we would not be facing the spending out of control and the problem that we're having in stimulating the growth of this economy. So, my prayer for Christmas was give me a Republican Congress while you're at it, and then watch what we can do. [*Laughter*]

Let me just give you some standards if you do watch that State of the Union, what we need. A real growth package must stimulate investment that's needed to create jobs. We've got to encourage risk-taking. We've got to encourage business people to take risks.

The second one: It's got to stop the slide in real estate values. For most Americans, their home is a large part of what they own, a large part of their assets. And if those real estate values go down, people have lack of confidence in the economy. We've got to find things, and I'll make some proposals in the State of the Union, that's put underpinning under that and says to a person: The investment you made in your home is sacrosanct, and we want to keep that value so you and your kids will have that value for the rest of your lives.

Thirdly, it's got to give people the confidence that the costs of health care—and here's a specialty where your company has been absolutely superb, leading in the health care field—that the costs of health care, the costs of education, the costs of raising a family are affordable.

And then the last point: It's got to make America more competitive. And that leads you, of course, to a sensible and sound education program, and we've got a very good one in a program we call America 2000. And then I also think it's about time that the Congress get its house in order, that they live by the same laws that you and me and other Americans are asked to live by. And I'm going to be challenging them to do a little reorganization in Congress itself.

So I want to restore the faith of this country in the future. As I say, we lifted up the spirits of this country with your help. And some of you all probably served in the Storm. And don't let the revisionists, don't let these smart alecks that opposed it from day one come back a year later and try to take it away from you, the American people. It was a clear, solid victory. It reversed the Vietnam syndrome; it gave us pride. And now I want to take that same sense of leadership and, again, solve the problems that have been plaguing this Nation and the economy. I believe I can do

it.

We've got a lot of other programs out there: antidrugs, proeducation, anticrime legislation that's hung up. We need a good, new financial—we didn't get a chance to talk about this—but financial reform legislation that's going to modernize our banking system and make it far more competitive, which means more loans, more affordability for people that are borrowing. There's a wide, tremendous agenda. But the underlying theme here in this State is get this country back to work again.

And some guy over here at the first stop at Pease—and I'm interested in this economic development for Pease Air Force Base. You can take a hit that comes from the results of—actually, having to peel back at Pease is the fact that we're succeeding in terms of world peace and less defense spending and all of that. But there's hardship with it. So, I want to see the success of the economic development program at Pease, and I want to be a part of it. I understand the people around there. I know a lot of people around there. And we should help that area, and this gets close to it, help them in economic redevelopment.

The guy over there at Pease—a woman, actually—she said something about a country-western song about the train, a light at the end of the tunnel. I only hope it's not a train coming the other way. [*Laughter*] Well, I said to her, "Well, I'm a country music fan. I love it, always have." Doesn't fit the mold of some of the columnists, I might add, but nevertheless—[*laughter*]—of what they think I ought to fit in, but I love it. You should have been with me at the CMA awards at Nashville. But nevertheless, I said to them, you know, there's another one that the Nitty Ditty, Nitty City Great—[*laughter*]—that they did, and it says, "If you want to see a rainbow, you've got to stand a little rain." We've had a little rain. New Hampshire has had too much rain. A lot of families are hurting.

The answer—Barbara cares, and I care—the answer is we've got proposals that will help. They're not quick fixes; they're not things that are going to garner a political vote only to fall on your face a couple of weeks later. Stay tuned to the State of the

Union, and if you agree with me, spread the word.

Lastly, I need your help. I am here to ask for your vote. I will take, as I say, my share of the blame for things that have gotten off track in this country. But I understand. And I want to get them back on track. I'd like a little credit for the things that have gone right. I think of New Hampshire as a State that understands what we Bushes mean when we talk about family and faith and family values. I think people understand when Barbara hugs an AIDS baby or reads to a child. I think they understand what we're saying, and that is: Family is important.

Everything I do in legislation I ask our people, "Is this going to strengthen or is this going to diminish family?" Our child care bill, I fought back the mandated benefits from the liberals, and I fought it back because it would weaken the family's chance to take care of the child care situation in the way they think back. I want our school program to emphasize community and family. I worry about these families that are broken up, ache for them, worry about them and want to do what we can, Barbara and I, as leaders in this country, to help strengthen family.

And so I do understand New Hampshire because I have this wonderfully warm feeling that New Hampshire feels exactly the way we do on these questions of family values and faith. Somebody said to me, "We prayed for you over there." That was not just because I threw up on the Prime Minister of Japan, either. [*Laughter*] Where was he when I needed him? [*Laughter*] I said, let me tell you something. And I say this—I don't know whether any ministers from the

Episcopal Church are here; I hope so. But I said to him this: "You're on to something here. You cannot be President of the United States if you don't have faith." Remember Lincoln, going to his knees in times of trial in the Civil War and all that stuff. You can't be.

And we are blessed. So don't feel sorry for—don't cry for me, Argentina. We've got problems out there, and I am blessed by good health, strong health. Geez, you get the flu, and they make it into a Federal case. [*Laughter*] Anyway, that goes with the territory. I'm not asking for sympathy, I just wanted you to know that I never felt more up for the charge.

I wish I could tuck each one of you for 10 minutes into that car as you ride along and see the reception that Judd Gregg talked about that we're getting as I return to this State that I do understand. And it's been great. I'll go back to Washington all fired up for tomorrow and tackle the President or the Prime Minister of this or the Governor of that coming in. But I'll have this heartbeat, vigorous and strong, because of what I've sensed here today.

So now, listen, here's the final word: Vote for me. And listen, go listen politely. These guys, these executives, they've got to do their thing here and have fairplay for all. But don't vote for them. Vote for me, okay?

Thanks a lot.

*Note: The President spoke at 2:11 p.m. in the cafeteria of the Liberty Mutual Insurance Building. In his remarks, he referred to Robert L. Laszewski, executive vice president of group markets, and Gary L. Countryman, chairman of the board, Liberty Mutual Insurance Group.*

# Remarks to Cabletron Systems Employees in Rochester, New Hampshire
## *January 15, 1992*

You guys are fired up. Thank you very much. What is it about the water around this place? You guys just standing out here for 2 hours and being so darn nice. But

thanks for the welcome. I appreciate it. To Craig and Bob, let me phrase it this way: Who would have thought that I would be standing shoulder-to-shoulder with two guys who but a handful of years ago had a dream and who together, with some very able men and women I want to mention in just a minute, made this happen.

I mean, this is America, and it's strong, and it's wonderful. And I am all fired up and pleased with the reception here but, more important, pleased to see the quality of the work and the pride in the work. It just reinforces my view that we've got to resist this siren's call of protection and continue to send our quality goods wherever the market is, domestic or foreign. And I'm going to keep on trying to open these foreign markets to fairplay. And if we succeed in that, these goods are going to compete. They are quality goods. And I'll tell you, that's the strong lesson I'd take back to Washington, DC.

I had a chance to chat with some of you all's associates in there. And I will single out but two because I wrote down their names. But Dominique MacDonald and Frank McWilliams—I don't know whether you have to have a "Mc" to work in the quality end of this thing, but I don't think they were programmed by one of these machines out here—both of them telling me about how their fellow workers took pride in what they were doing. And then you hear Craig and Bob reflect this, too, the Tom Selleck and the Arnold Schwarzenegger of the high-tech world up here.

I was briefed on this visit by my longtime friend and the able Governor of this State, Judd Gregg, who I'm proud to say is running our campaign in this very important State, who's with us here. I'm also pleased that we have Bob Smith, one of the two great Senators from New Hampshire, and also Bill Zeliff, the Congressman here, and then Ed DuPont, the State Senate leader.

Let me just say this. I'm not up here to assign blame. Look, I know some people aren't doing as well here as the people at Cabletron. I'm sure people here have friends and family that they wonder whether they're going to have a job. So, I will accept my share of the responsibility as President of the United States. And I will state to you my determination to do everything I can to turn this economy around. But let me put it in stark political terms. If the growth initiatives that I have been pro-

posing for the last three State of the Union Messages had been supported by more people like Senator Smith and Congressman Zeliff and Senator Rudman, we would have this economy on the move.

We can stimulate the growth through sensible tax policy in this country, and that's what I will be proposing in the State of the Union once again. Then I'm going to look to the American people, including everybody here: Help me. Help me get a sensible program through this Congress that's still back in the dark ages of Government intervention, liberal spending, and more taxes. That's not what's needed.

I'm impressed with the spirit here, the creation of more jobs. And believe me, the rest of the State can succeed if we give them the proper support in Washington, DC, in terms of stimulation of the economy. I'm going to have to resist the siren's call, obviously, for protection. It's coming at me from the right, way out on the right, coming at me from the left. But you guys— I forget what the export figures are here. They're strong, 28 percent in something like 5 years. That's a tremendous growth. That means jobs. And it isn't just Cabletronics, other countries. And if we go back the protection route, why, we are simply going to dry up markets and invite retaliation from other countries.

I got criticized for this trip to Japan, not just for throwing up on the Prime Minister. [*Laughter*] You've got to admit when I get sick for 24 hours I do it with a certain flair, you know. [*Laughter*] But all that aside, some people—"Well, the President shouldn't do this, hat in hand." My eye. What I was doing was saying to these foreign leaders, look, give us a shot at these markets. We're not asking for protection. We're not asking for quotas like some of this silly Democrat legislation that I'm going to have to knock on its—knock down when I get back to Washington, DC. [*Laughter*] What we're asking for is access to the other guy's market.

And let me tell you something. I will bring the same kind of leadership, world leadership, we brought to Desert Storm to these economic questions around the world. We will expand our markets abroad. And I will not listen to the protectionists.

You did it the old-fashioned way: You took risks. You took pride. You built quality into what you're doing. And you can hold your heads up, and you can compete with anyone in the world. We've got to get that spirit going across the rest of this country. And I really believe we can do it. Yes, times are tough. And yes, unemployment is unacceptably high. But interest rates are down. Inflation is down, so you're not being wiped out by the cruelest tax of all. And we are poised now for a real recovery.

I will repeat it for the third time today, but the first visit was over at Pease, and I want to see how we can assist in the economic development of Pease. We can make something positive. We have to cut back because we're doing better in terms of world peace. And because the way our soldiers performed in Desert Storm has now led to a more peaceful world, we're able to cut back. That's something that's being demanded, and I think properly so. And we will have more to say about that in the State of the Union.

But I want to help and take something that is a difficult situation and turn it around and make it positive for the people of New Hampshire. And I believe we can do it. It's happened in other parts of the world. Waco, Texas, is a good place to look, and other places that had great big installations. They were turned to civilian use, and they made real progress. So, we want to go forward and help on that.

But we need to keep this spirit alive. And over there at Pease this woman said to me, also a country music fan like I am, and she said, "Well, do you remember the song about the light at the end of the tunnel," and the song goes, "I just hope it's not a train coming down through the tunnel." Well, good warning. But there is light at the end of the tunnel. And I told her my song that many of you have heard, "If you want to see a rainbow, you've got to stand a little rain."

New Hampshire stood a lot of rain. And there is going to be a rainbow, because we are America. We can compete. And I'll take this case in the State of the Union, and I'll spell out the incentives that I think are smart. I'm going to have to resist some of these instant fixes that takes this so-called Federal money—that's yours, incidentally, if you're paying taxes—and kind of spreads it around out there in some giveaway fashion that sounds good and has appeal but does not stimulate the economy. So, we're going to do what we can to have sound fiscal policy.

And as I say, I sure would like to have your help. Spill it over into Maine, or spill it over into Massachusetts, so we can get some more people in the Congress like those that are supporting me here and get the job done in Washington. I'm sick and tired of a Congress that thinks old thoughts and can do nothing but try to tear down the President of the United States. We need some changes in the Congress, and I'm going to fight for them.

We made some progress on our Japanese trip there. We got 49 nonauto standards, these are standards just for access to market, cleared up. That was good. We signed dozens of literal market-opening agreements in these four countries that I visited. And I think that the business leaders who spoke out and said, in the computer business, that we at least—we get them to keep the agreements, but that we'd broken into the Government computer market. Here's a figure. We sell 40 percent of computers used in Japan—are American because they're good—and Government, Japanese Government, .04 percent. And what we think we've done now, and the computer industry agrees, is to break into that market and insist on fairplay. No tariffs, no subsidies needed, just the ability to let you guys that know what you're doing compete. That was what this trip was about. And as I say, I'm going to stay engaged, stay engaged in this all the way.

We've got some other blessings in this country. You won't hear them in a primary. One thing, I'm a little tired of people telling me that I've just found New Hampshire. My God, I was growing up around here before some of you guys were born and certainly before some of these people that are now campaigning for President knew where New Hampshire was on a map. They've never been here before. They don't know the heartbeat of it. When a hurricane hits Portsmouth, it hits my house up there, not so far away from here. And when I was going to school, we used to compete into New Hampshire. And my daughter-in-law is from here.

And one thing that really—I will clean this up for this marvelous audience—burns me up, put it that way, is this charge that I don't care. And I can understand it. Some people think you get to live in the White House, and you're dealing with all kinds of world figures. But we do care.

At lunch this fellow asked me, he said, "If you could get one message over to the people in New Hampshire, what would it like to be?" And I thought that you can help me with the fiscal program or open up these markets or help us with crime or help us with our wonderful education program. But I said to him, "Listen, I guess the one message would be, both Barbara and I care. We think we understand your heartbeat. When somebody hurts, we think we know enough about family to identify with that. And we care." And then we can build from there in terms of where this country ought to go.

It was one year ago, one year ago that Desert Storm was fixin' to begin, as they say in another of my home States, Texas, one year ago. And you think back to the criticism—that goes with the job—from the media, the columnists, "The President hasn't prepared the American people." Look back at the very people, some of whom are running today for President, criticizing me for moving forces. Look back at them telling me what I could not do as Commander in Chief. And we did it. You and I and those brilliant young men and women did it. And we lifted the spirits of America.

I want to take that same leadership and lift the spirits of America in the economy. And we can do it if I can get some help in the United States Congress. That was the difference. They ask me what's the difference. Well, let me tell you guys. Let me tell you 250 mournful pundits what the difference was. I didn't have to go ask Senator Kennedy if I could declare war or go on and move these troops. I didn't have to. Listen, if I'd have listened to the leader of the United States Senate, George Mitchell,

Saddam Hussein would be in Saudi Arabia, and you'd be paying 20 bucks a gallon for gasoline. Now, try that one on for size.

I'm getting sick and tired, I am, every single night hearing one of these carping little liberal Democrats jumping all over my you-know-what. [*Laughter*] And I can't wait for this campaign. And if I decide to become a candidate for President of the United States—[*laughter*]—why, I'm going to come right back up here and ask for your help.

Look, there's a lot of problems out here, a lot of things wrong with our country. But there's an awful lot of things that are right about our country. Some people around here that may have been old enough to remember the conflict of the Vietnam war. There are some people around here that may have kids, parents—maybe in the 10th, 12th grade—who wonder, "Hey, is my kid going to have to go off and do combat in a superpower war?"; who go to bed at night saying their prayers, as most families do, wondering about the fear of nuclear war. That's been diminished. I'll take the blame for some things, but please give us a little bit of credit for the fact that your kids and my grandkids have a chance to grow up now in a world that's much more peaceful. And that is fundamental.

And the second thing I'd say is this: This ain't the easiest job in the world. But I didn't expect it would be. But I love it, every single minute, the challenge of trying to work for and hopefully improve the lot of the American people.

And the longer I'm in this job, the more important I think are the values that I think of as New Hampshire values, your family values, I hope they're mine, of family, involvement of parents in the lives of these kids, the need to do better in education, the need for all of us to come together at the community level or family level to knock out this scourge of drugs. And there's some good news on that in terms of the teenager use of cocaine. There's some good things happening out there.

But it's family and, yes, faith. Somebody reminded me of Abraham Lincoln's comments about, during the Civil War, praying. Of course, you feel that way. These are fundamental values. And we have tried to live them. We have tried to emulate them. We have tried to advocate them. Thank God, Barbara Bush is out there hugging those kids and teaching people to read and serving, as she should, as an example to a lot of people in this country of a caring person. No political agenda, she just gives a darn.

And so, I'll roll up my sleeves and get into the arena when they decide who they want to have as their nominee. But in the meantime, let me tell you this: I know how I got there. I know how I got this opportunity to serve as President of the United States. And I've tried to be a good President.

Now, things aren't so good in some parts of this country. And we do care about it. But I believe there is a rainbow out there. And I need your help to prove it. So, I would appreciate your support. But whatever you decide, keep up this work. This is the America's spirit, alive and well and flourishing. May God bless our great country. And don't ever apologize for it.

Thank you very much.

[*At this point, Cabletron Systems officers presented a jacket to the President.*]

All right. Thank you all very much. That's great. Thank you.

Thank you all very, very much. Good to be with you. I hope we can—how long have you been standing out there? An hour? Two? Oh, no! A thousand apologies. But really, it's been a great day for the spirit. And I meant what I said. I am terribly impressed. And please keep doing this. People are learning; people understand. We've got some problems, but you're showing we also got some wonderful answers. Thanks a lot.

*Note: The President spoke at 3:41 p.m. at Cabletron Systems, Inc. In his remarks, he referred to company officers Craig R. Benson, chairman of the board of directors, chief operating officer, and treasurer; S. Robert Levine, president and chief executive officer; Dominique R. MacDonald, sales trainer; and Frank McWilliams, test manager.*

# Remarks and a Question-and-Answer Session at a Rotary Club Dinner in Portsmouth, New Hampshire
## January 15, 1992

*The President.* Thank you all very much for that welcome back. Thank you, Cliff. Thanks to you and Bill and Don Reeves and so many others. Captain Mark, thank you, sir, for that lovely blessing. And you have a wonderful way here of making a person feel at home. I can't pronounce the name of the river; I've been crossing it for 66 years. But nevertheless—[*laughter*]—I would like to remind people that it's been many, many times they've gone across that river. And there's something about the air here. A hurricane that is designed to hit Portsmouth knocks the hell out of my house in Kennebunkport—[*laughter*]—and I would like to speak to the Rotarian meteorologist as soon as this is over.

But thanks for the warm welcome. Hugh Gregg asked me to deliver his speech to-night. [*Laughter*] For those of you who will remember 4 years ago, he delivered my speech 4 years ago. But you've heard once again the story of my last visit here, and you wondered, well, was it the broccoli that did it? And I appreciate Harry out here working it out, and it is great to see so many friendly and familiar faces, neighbors and friends that I've gotten to know over the years.

Captain Mark, you were very nice to mention Barbara Bush, who believes in your work very much, has taken a leadership role in that cause, that wonderful cause that she do the Lord's work. I'm very sorry that she's not here. And if you really want to make my day, please don't ask why she didn't come. Everybody is talking about, "Where's Barbara?" We miss her very, very much." I told her I didn't need her, I was not going to throw up. [*Laughter*]

You guys, you talk about—hey, look, it was the 24-hour flu. How many people here have had the flu? And I bet none of you have done it quite so dramatically. And I'd like a loan because it cost a lot to dryclean a suit over there in Japan. And the Prime Minister had a nice expensive one, used to have a nice expensive one. [*Laughter*] Sorry.

No, it's been a great day and an exciting day. One horrible disappointment, I was not able to stop by and see Evelyn Marconi at Geno's Coffee Shop. She is a longtime supporter of flag and country, and I'm sorry we missed her there. Glad that she's all decked out and here with us tonight. Bill, thank you again, sir, for arranging all this, and I'd say to you and the committee, on relatively short notice, given—I think you heard about it probably the day before Christmas. Then that period between then and New Year's, obviously, there's other pursuits. Then this thing has just been a wonderful, warm response here.

May I salute the Governor, of course, Judd Gregg, my campaign manager here, my friend of long standing, a quality Governor, a decent guy. I am so proud to have his support and the support, of course, of my dear friend Hugh Gregg as well.

I'm glad that Bob Smith is at my side. He came in and took over for another friend and supporter, Gordon Humphrey, who is with us tonight. He is doing a superb job for you all, for this great State. Regardless of party, he's in there strong for the principles you believe in, in the United States Senate. I'm glad he's here. And of course, Bill Zeliff, with whom I campaigned when he was first elected, doing a superb job in the Congress. So, you have a great delegation. I might also mention two other New Hampshirites not with us, both leaders, one in the Senate now, Warren Rudman, a strong supporter, and of course, my friend Governor John Sununu, who served this country with great distinction and this State with great distinction. So, I'm proud to have the support of these leaders.

I think you've got to hand it to Yoken's and the incomparable Harry MacLeod. Who would have held a reservation for 4 years? [*Laughter*] Hey, listen, I hope with this crowd I don't have to tell you that I haven't just today discovered New Hampshire. This is, Judd reminds me, the fourth time that I've had a meal at Yoken's. And that ain't discovery time. I mean, that's good eating time. And I know it when I see it, and I like it. And I'm glad to be back on the seacoast.

Cliff Taylor pointed it out, and he said, well, a lot has happened in those intervening 4 years between the time I stood you up and the time I got invited back. Let me just put it in a rather broad, ideological perspective. Our world was locked back then, less than 4 years ago, in an enormous struggle, in an ideological struggle, in what you might call a nuclear standoff between superpowers. And I think about the problems we face in this State, the problems we face in the Nation about the economy.

But let's not lose sight of our blessings. I happen to think that it's a good thing that my grandchildren and this little guy over here can grow up in a world with less fear of nuclear weapons. And I am very, very proud of my predecessors in this great office for President who have brought this about, and I'm proud of the record of our administration in help bringing about the changes that we enjoy in this world today. We have a lot to be grateful for. And world peace is one of them.

You know, 4 years ago the world was literally under siege. And today, look anywhere; look to our south; look over in Eastern Europe; look at the Commonwealth, meaning what used to be the Soviet Union, and you'll see that freedom is on the march. The Berlin Wall and the Warsaw Pact and the Soviet Union itself, all vanquished, not by force, not by force but by history's most powerful idea: the love of freedom.

Today, the cold war is over, and a great victory for this Nation, our principled United States of America, the Nation we cherish, and a triumph to people everywhere who look to us and will continue to look to us as the land of liberty, the land of the free. And believe me, everywhere you go in the world they see that it is only the United States that is the leader for freedom and democracy and market economies and, indeed, for peace.

I can't help but note on this evening that one year ago, one year ago today, our commitment to liberty, our commitment to international law was put to the test. Saddam Hussein, who never in my view felt that we would use force—I think he thought that the Vietnam syndrome was with us forever—he miscalculated twice. One, he didn't think we'd use force, and secondly, he felt if we did use force, he could have some kind of a standoff with the men and women of the U.S. military. And he was wrong on both counts. He mistook a voice of protest and a handful of editorials and a couple of speeches in the Congress for the United States lacking the will. And he was dead wrong. Aggression was set back, and our country came together with a pride that we hadn't had since the end of World War II. And I am very grateful for that.

I don't know a single American, regardless of party or philosophy, liberal or conservative, who doesn't in his heart of hearts or her heart of hearts celebrate the changes that have taken place and, really, the hope, the hope they bring to the entire world.

But I also know that it is very tough to focus on what's happening thousands of miles away when things are tough here at home, and when the company work force shut down. Bill and I were talking about this today, about the hardship for some of the families in this State. Something else, the fear that some have, some that have jobs, they lack the confidence they'll have them tomorrow; the worry that families have on the economic front. It's very hard when you have these concerns and these worries to take a look at the big picture and say, "Well, we ought to be very thankful for a world at peace." And I understand that.

Hard times have come to this State. A guy at a luncheon today—I sat next to some of the workers at one of the plants, and he asked me a question that you might expect would be an easy one. It wasn't; it was a tough one really. But he said, "If you could leave one message from your visits here in New Hampshire today, what would it be?" And I thought about it. Should I tell him it's for fighting crime, or should I tell him about world peace, or should I tell him

about our education program? And what I told him, and what I hope has happened today, is that I told him we care. We care. Privileged as I am to be President, Barbara and I are not isolated from the feelings of people in this State that are hurting. And that, I think, is an important message. Friends have to know, and I think it's important to the people that are hurting that their President knows and the President cares. And in this case the President is going to do something about it.

Now, we're getting back into the swing of the political season. And you're hearing a lot of people jumping all over me. I know where New Hampshire is. I know what the values of the families are in New Hampshire, and I hope we're practicing them in the White House as a family. I understand what joins the people of this State together.

And you're going to hear all kinds of cheap promises coming out of deep left field, past the running track, up against the fence in the left field, offering a quick fix to a troubled economy. And my appeal to you today is: Resist it. Do not listen to those that want to enlarge the deficit and in the name of that try to make this economy recover.

I have offered growth incentives, growth proposals for 3 straight years. Now we're going to take those, build on them, look into that lens, and tell the American people 2 weeks from now this is what it's going to take to get this economy going, how we're going to stimulate investment, how we are going to stimulate savings, how we are going to keep this Federal deficit under control as best we can, and how we can do it without this tax-and-spend philosophy you're hearing about every single day in this State.

I vowed I would come over here tonight and be calm, but I'll tell you something, I'm a little sick and tired of being the punching bag for a lot of lightweights around this country yelling at me day in and day out. And I'm sick of it. If they want a fight, they're going to have one. I mean it.

If they want to do something for the middle class, rich against poor and all that, pass the incentives that I'm talking about. It will get this country and this State back to work. That's my challenge to them, and that's going to be the challenge to the entire Nation. I'm going to try and work my heart out to do my level-best. And I hope I've dispelled with the idea that we don't care, because we certainly do.

You hear a lot about the talk of the domestic agenda. We've got a good one. We've got a child care bill, and it passed finally, that says hey, let the parents choose. Let's keep the families strong. Let's not mandate all these benefits from Washington, DC, whether it's a health program or a child care program. Let's strengthen the family by giving them the opportunity to decide what's the best way to deal with these kids.

We have a new education program, transcends party lines. We got together with the Democratic and Republican Governors; we adopted the strategy, six education goals, not to be dictated from Washington, six education goals. Starts from be ready to learn—that means Head Start, and that was one Washington can help—ends up with you're never too old to learn. That means old guys like me learning to use a computer, and some of you other old guys around here going over to the library maybe and reading a book. It wouldn't hurt any of us. [*Laughter*]

But it means you got math and science, volunteer tests to let your kids know how they're doing. It's a wonderful new program, and it revolutionizes the schools. And it does it without setting a lot of mandates from these subcommittee, tired subcommittee chairmen in Washington, DC, that haven't had a new thought in the 50 years they've been sitting there.

I'm getting a little tired of this. I hate to unload on you again. Last time. I heard two of the Democrats get up the other day and they said, "Heck with holding the line on the budget deficit. Forget about it. We're going to propose spending $50 billion more Federal money." If you haven't discovered it, that's your money. Comes right out of your pocket whether you're working or not around here. Federal money, $50 billion. Forget the one constraint we have and that is the caps on spending that are in that budget agreement, just forget it, and then we'll spend our way back to prosperity. That is not going to solve the economic

problems of this country.

What is? Carefully defined incentives to increase investment, to increase research and development, to build so we can be competitive in the educational field so that people can save, use some incentives to save, use incentives to build some strength under a person's home. A home is one's castle, and one of the reasons there's lack of confidence, families see the value of their homes going down. I saw mine blown away up here, but nevertheless—[*laughter*]. No, they see the values going down, and there are things we can do on that. And so, let's do what will help, not do what sounds good for garnering votes in a hotly contested primary on the Democratic side of the agenda.

Then there's another point. Sorry I came to this one because I will get wound up. I'm talking about protection. I'm talking about the siren's call from the extreme right and the extreme left in the political spectrum saying, "Look, people are hurting, and what we're going to do about it is go back to isolation and protection." You want a recipe for disaster? That is it. We will shrink this economy. We will throw 35,000 more people out of work in New Hampshire, and we will be cutting off our nose to spite our face.

The answer is to expand markets. And what our trip to Asia was about was not managing trade. You get a lot of egghead academicians writing, "This guy's deserted the free trade." That's not the case. All I'm saying is, look—and I saw it today in the workers I saw—we can compete with anyone, but we need fair access to the other guy's market. And I am not going to stay home and keep from fighting to open these markets. I'm going to keep on doing it until we are successful.

And for those that want us to pull back into some isolationism a la the 1930's, take a look at world history. You don't have to be a rocket scientist to see what that led to. The United States, as long as I am President, is going to stay involved and continue to lead around the world.

What I really want to do is try to take the leadership that I think and hope we demonstrated in Desert Storm, that lifted the spirits of this country and brought this country together unlike any time since the end of World War II, brought it together, and take that now and apply that to the domestic economy to get the support from the American people for incentives that will give us that vibrance and that feeling of optimism that we, the American people, pride ourselves on.

And I believe we can do it. And one of the reasons I do is I think there are some sound things in place now. Yes, there are some people hurting; unemployment is too high. Inflation is pretty good. Interest rates are down. Inventory is not bad. The market is saying, hey, things are going to be looking better. And I'm always one who likes to see the glass half full and not so pessimistic and half empty. And that's the way I am.

No, I've listened to what the people of this State have to say one way and another. And today it was an excellent visit back to this State that I believe I understand, whose heartbeat I feel. And I would just encourage you all to avoid the quick-fix bumper-sticker slogan that tells you there is some easy way. There isn't an easy way, but there is a sound, sensible, economic approach. And I believe that what I have suggested and will continue to work for is the answer.

You've got to stimulate investment to create jobs. You've got to stop that slide on real estate values so that you increase home sales. You've got to give Americans confidence that the cost of health care, providing for the kids' education, and raising a family are affordable. And I will be unveiling a national health care program, but believe me, it is not going to have a lot of mandates or turn to some foreign country for an example. We have the best quality health care in the world, and I don't want to diminish that. What I want to do is make it more affordable for everybody.

And then we've got to be able to compete. Whatever it is, whatever the fix is, it must make us more competitive in the global economy. And fifth and finally, and maybe the most important, you've got to control the most unproductive end of our society, and that is Government spending. We have got to keep the caps on and enforce them on wasteful Government spending. And I need more people like these Congressmen to help me do just exactly that.

And in conclusion, let me say this, just a couple of confessions to friends. And this will go to the Democrats who may have been smart enough to join Rotary, too. [*Laughter*] No, but I really mean this one from the heart in the sense that some things, at least the way I look at this—and again, I'm concerned in this country about the decline in family. And I don't want to be preachy or lecturing, but Barbara and I talk about this a great deal.

In the first place, I'm pretty proud of her. When she hugs a baby or teaches somebody to read, why she's saying something. But what I will continue to try to do as President is to look at the legislation and say, does this help or does this diminish family? The longer I'm in this job, and I say this to you as a friend, the more convinced I am, Cap, maybe you understand this, that family and faith are terribly important ingredients for being President of the United States. I believe it. I feel it very strongly.

Obviously, I believe in the separation of church and State, but I understand from having been tested by a little fire what Lincoln meant when he talked about spending some time on his knees. We are one Nation, under God. We are a strong, free Nation that believes in certain principles. Barbara and I have tried very hard to live up to those kinds of principles and those kinds of values.

Now I need your help to continue in that effort to help make things better for the people of New Hampshire and the people all the way across this State. And whether you vote for me or not, may I thank you for this unforgettably warm reception. I'll never, never forget it.

May God bless you all. Thank you very much.

*Q.* Mr. President, I know you're a little pressed for time, but we normally end with a couple of questions.

*The President.* Does that mean two?

*Q.* If I limit it to two.

*The President.* Sure.

*Q.* A couple of questions?

*The President.* Yes.

*Q.* We have a microphone set up somewhere up front here. Yes, right there. Step right up to the microphone, Bob.

*The Economy*

*Q.* Mr. President, welcome to the south-side of the Piscataqua River. This question, we are in a political year and a recession year. How can we get both parties together to solve the recession problem?

*The President.* In the State of the Union Message—frankly, it's tough. You put your finger on why. We're in a competitive polit-ical year, all kind of weird dances going on out there. And that's the way it always has been and probably always will be.

But I think the economic problems are serious enough, and I think the answers are clear enough, that what I will try to do as President is say in the State of the Union Message: Look, here's what I think it will take. Now, let's lay it aside for just long enough to pass a program. And then if you guys got one you think is better, come on we'll talk about that and debate it and ne-gotiate it. And if I've got some additions that I think would help but can't put into this first go-round and get done, why, we'll debate all that. We'll go back to our politi-cal posturing and yelling at each other and making outrageous claims about each other.

But the American people deserve that politics be put aside right after that State of the Union Message to get something done that's going to stimulate this economy and help the families in this country. And I'm going to try it. And I'll give it my level-best shot, and I hope you'll find that there will be some cooperation. Things can happen in the Congress if they make up their mind they want to move. I know Bob Smith will tell you that. And I know Warren would. And I know Bill Zeliff would tell you that.

So, this idea that you have to have end-less subcommittee hearings and have to defer and bow to some other committee that has jurisdiction, the American people are a little bit tired of that. They want con-gressional action, and I will do my level-best to see that they get it.

Who's got the last one?

*Q.* Mr. President, lower interest rates are great to get the economy going again. If I could refinance my home at 8 percent it would save me almost $300 a month. Unfor-tunately, like many New Hampshire home-owners our property values have dropped, and because of that banks won't approve our refinancing because we don't have the 20 percent equity that we need.

Now, as a country we've given loan guar-antees to Israel, Russia, and other countries around the world. What do you think about the possibility of giving loan guarantees to middle class Americans like myself so that banks could then approve our loans, we could refinance at a lower rate, and then put that mortgage money back into the economy at little or no cost to the Govern-ment?

*The President.* We have Government fi-nanced loans that I hope are of some help. I will be making proposals in this State of the Union, again, that I hope will do what you're talking about, put some value under the person's largest asset, and that is the home. And there are ways to do that. One of them is through the IRA system, for ex-ample. So, listen carefully and see if what I propose won't be a long step.

Whether we can do what you're asking or not, I've said I want to hold the line on spending and keep it within the caps. I'd have to, to be honest with you, know exact-ly what the total cost that would be if that was applied nationwide. I think we're talk-ing about jillions of dollars. But I think there are ways to put value under a per-son's major asset. And you're right, the de-cline and the pessimism has come because real estate has been so slow.

Now, if we're honest with each other, I think you'd admit and I certainly will, that some of the lenders in the real estate busi-ness, whether it's S&L's or banks, made loans that they might not ought to have made under more prudent, cautious times. And we got away from our standards. So, I think that there's plenty of blame to go around on all this, and one result of that has been some excesses in the regulatory field.

And some of the bankers and some of those savings and loan people are saying, "Wait a minute. These regulators come in and scare the heck out of me and my loans," and they pull back. So, we're trying to do a better job on the regulation front, not to be reckless, not to be accused of going back into some S&L crisis again but try to have reasonable balance. On the one hand protecting the financial institutions, seeing that they're safely and prudently run, and secondly, on protecting the rights or the well-being of the borrower, the guy that needs to do what you're talking about, to refinance or whatever it is.

So, we're making a little progress. I'm not satisfied we've gone far enough. But where I agree with you is, let's get some value under a man and woman's major asset. And that major asset is a person's home. You talk about strengthening the family, homeownership, that's one of the things we're working hard to get through instead of these massive Government projects, homeownership. That's a good way to strengthen it, and what you're suggesting makes a good deal of sense in terms of strengthening the family and in strengthening the assets.

So listen, that's two. I'm heading back to DC to see my dog and my wife. Thank you all very, very much.

[*At this point, Don Reeves presented a gift to the President.*]

*The President.* Thanks so much. May I make one correction here? First, thank you very much for this picture of the Harbor Light and Nubble Light, and that means a lot. And I, as you know, love this coastline. But I said, I was going home to see my dog and my wife. [*Laughter*] May I, with your permission, may I change the order. I just don't want to have any misunderstanding. [*Laughter*]

Thank you very, very much.

*Note: The President spoke at 7:37 p.m. at Yoken's Restaurant. In his remarks, he referred to Portsmouth Rotary Club president William Holt and members Clifford Taylor and Don Reeves; Capt. Mark Weaver of the Salvation Army, who led the dinner prayer; Harry MacLeod, owner of Yoken's Restaurant; Evelyn Marconi, owner of Geno's Coffee Shop; and former Senator Gordon Humphrey of New Hampshire. A tape was not available for verification of the content of these remarks.*

# Appointment of D. Cameron Findlay as Deputy Assistant to the President and Counselor to the Chief of Staff
*January 15, 1992*

The President today announced the appointment of D. Cameron Findlay, of Indiana, as Deputy Assistant to the President and Counselor to the Chief of Staff.

Since 1989, Mr. Findlay has served at the Department of Transportation, first as Special Assistant to the Secretary and then as Counselor to the Secretary. From 1988 to 1989, he was a law clerk to Associate Justice Antonin Scalia of the U.S. Supreme Court. From 1987 to 1988, Mr. Findlay served as a law clerk to Judge Stephen F. Williams of the U.S. Court of Appeals for the District of Columbia Circuit.

Mr. Findlay received a bachelor's degree from Northwestern University and a master's degree in philosophy, politics, and economics from Oxford University, which he attended as a Marshall scholar. He returned to the United States to study law at Harvard University, where he received his J.D. Mr. Findlay was born September 7, 1959, in Chicago, IL. He is married to a law school classmate, Amy S. Findlay, and they have one child. They reside in Alexandria, VA.

## Statement on the Anniversary of Operation Desert Storm
*January 16, 1992*

One year ago tonight I spoke to the American people at the moment an international coalition acting under United Nations authority went to war to end Saddam Hussein's brutal occupation of Kuwait. We can all take pride in the results of that effort: Kuwait is liberated, and the legitimate government restored; the fires set by Saddam's retreating army are extinguished; the flow of oil from the Gulf is secure from political and economic blackmail; much of Iraq's arsenal is destroyed, and what remains is now under international supervision; and the United Nations has been greatly strengthened.

The determination and strength demonstrated by the United States and its coalition partners has had lasting dividends throughout the region. A critical region of the world, vital to its economic well-being, is secure. Thanks in large part to our efforts, direct peace talks between Arabs and Israelis are underway for the first time, multilateral negotiations on regional arms control have begun, and America's hostages in Lebanon are home.

The coalition fought a limited war for a limited but vitally important purpose. It prevailed. Saddam's Iraq is weak and isolated, unable to impose its extremist policies on the region or the peace process. Nevertheless, the American people and I remain determined to keep the pressure on Saddam until a new leadership comes to power in Iraq. As was the case from the outset, our quarrel is not with the people of Iraq but with the dictator whose misrule has caused terrible suffering throughout the Middle East. We will maintain U.N. sanctions and keep Saddam's regime isolated, a pariah among nations. We will work to ensure adequate food and medicine reach the Iraqi people under international supervision, while denying Saddam the means to rebuild his weapons of mass destruction.

We salute the efforts of thousands of brave Iraqis who are resisting Saddam's rule, both inside and outside of Iraq. The United States reiterates its pledge to the Iraqi people and the Iraqi military that we stand ready to work with a new regime. A new leadership in Baghdad that accepts the U.N. resolutions and is ready to live at peace with its neighbors and its own people will find a partner in the United States, one willing to seek to lift economic sanctions and help restore Iraq to its rightful place in the family of nations.

## Remarks on Signing the Martin Luther King, Jr., Federal Holiday Proclamation in Atlanta, Georgia
*January 17, 1992*

Thank you for that warm welcome, and thank you, Mr. Hill. And let me just tell you, sir, how pleased I am to be a part of this program today. It's, of course, a pleasure to have flown down here and to be at the side of Coretta Scott King and all this wonderful King family, sitting here and here. It takes me back to a couple of other visits to this historic center that I've been privileged to make.

With me also today is one well-known to the Atlanta community, now well-known to the Nation, our Secretary of HHS, Dr. Lou Sullivan. He is doing a superb job for our Nation. And after he heard the successful, wonderful rendition of the Morehouse Glee Club, these guys that came and swept into Washington at the Kennedy Center Honors and carried the day in a magnificent national performance, after Lou heard them here today he now is claiming that he, too, was a member of the Morehouse Glee Club. [*Laughter*]

And when Maynard Jackson, the distinguished Mayor and my friend, heard them, he also claims to have been a member of the Morehouse Glee Club. It's the first time I've heard this. But nevertheless—[*laughter*]—I salute both of them, and both, one here in the city of Atlanta, one in Washington, and thus across the Nation, doing a wonderful job for our country.

Let me just say, flying down here with my dear friend Newt Gingrich, who is with us, a Member of the United States Congress, we talked about the center, and we talked about a lot of things of national interest. And then I said, "Well, Newt, how's it going in Georgia?" And he said, and I don't want to get him in trouble because this is a nonpartisan event, but he said, "Governor Miller is doing an outstanding job for this State." And Zell, I'm very pleased to see you here, sir.

And Reverend Roberts, I appreciate those words. I do believe that you can't hold this job if you don't look to God for guidance. I feel strongly about that, and I appreciate those kind words of guidance in your invocation.

It is for me an honor to stand here at this living memorial in Martin Luther King's hometown, steps from his birthplace and his pulpit, to talk about the promise of his life. We all know of his eloquence: the letter from the Birmingham jail, and then no one will ever forget the "I Have A Dream" speech. They moved us with their hope and love and with the abiding faith that Dr. King had in the American people. What you have done, Coretta, if I may, with this glorious living memorial, serves to remind us of the courage with which Martin Luther King overcame hatred and mistrust. It's too easy for us, almost a quarter of a century after his death, to forget the loneliness of that struggle.

Think of the early days of the movement when organizers of the Montgomery bus boycott called him to be their leader. In his book, "Stride Toward Freedom," he wrote of sitting alone at the kitchen table one night during the lonely time and saying aloud, "I've come to the point where I can't face it alone." But almost at once his fear and his uncertainty began to melt away. An inner voice, as he called it, an inner voice spoke to him, and it told him to continue to do what he knew to be right. And because he could express what he knew with such passion and such eloquence, the American people awakened to the promise of civil rights for all.

And today, thanks in large part to Martin Luther King, Jr.'s work, we have a battery of laws dedicated to a colorblind America. We have a renewed commitment from Government to enforce the basic rights of its citizens. And I'm proud that two significant civil rights bills have become law since I was President: the ADA, the Americans with Disability Act, and the civil rights bill of '91. Perhaps most marvelous of all, there's been a sea change, there's been a change in the hearts of many Americans who set aside old stereotypes and old prejudices to embrace the values that Dr. Martin Luther King, Jr. beseeched us to embrace, the values of tolerance and decency and mutual respect.

At the heart of these values, as Dr. King knew, is the family. And I am struck, Mrs. King, by how often in our conversations together you have stressed the importance of family life. Barbara and I feel it in our own lives. And think of the problems that afflict so many American communities today, homelessness and crime and drugs. Yet, these are not so much isolated problems as symptoms of one great problem, and that's the decline of the family. For far too many of our children pass through life without the goals larger than themselves, without a sense of their own worth or the worth of others, without the values that only the love of a parent or a grandparent can instill.

Yesterday, purely coincidentally, I met with the mayors who lead the National League of Cities. And some were from great big cities like Los Angeles; Trenton, New Jersey. Some were from hamlets and tiny cities, Plano, Texas, a city of 3,000; another one in North Carolina. And some were Democrats, and some were Republicans. But every single one of them agreed— they'd met before I met with them—that the urban problems stem in large part from the weakening of the family. And this problem, this terrible weakening of family, is not just somebody else's problem. It demands something from each of us.

Martin Luther King taught us that each of us is called to serve, regardless of personal circumstances. And each of us can serve. On the last night of his life, before that terrible day in Memphis, Dr. King told a story that I do think of often—visiting the Holy Land when he was a young man, with you, Coretta. Happened to travel the road from Jerusalem to Jericho, the same road where the Good Samaritan stopped, the Bible teaches, to help a stranger. The road was rocky and full of blind curves. And as he traveled, Dr. King realized that the reason others failed to stop to help the stranger was that they were afraid. Others had asked themselves, "If I stop to help this man, what will happen to me?" But the Good Samaritan asked himself, "If I don't stop to help this man, what will happen to him?" The joy of personal service is that it is open to all.

The other day I met with Magic Johnson in the Oval Office, and I was impressed with the way that he has now dedicated his life to others, not only to those with HIV but in educating those who are at risk. And he's been very honest, been very forthright about this tragic issue. He's out there right now teaching kids that lifestyle matters, lifestyle is important. He's admitting, "Well, I made some terrible mistakes." Now he wants to get the message out.

I want to help. I want to use the bully pulpit of the White House, continue to use it for that same purpose, to speak out for strong research, to help people better understand the disease, and to speak out for a change of behavior.

Anyone who visits AIDS clinics, incidentally, as Barbara and I have done, can't help but be struck by the dedication, the selfless dedication, and Lou knows what I'm talking about, Dr. Sullivan does, of the countless doctors and the nurses and the researchers and the volunteers who understand the human face of AIDS.

When Barbara holds an AIDS baby in her arms, she's trying to express that same message, a message of compassion and service. There are so many ways to serve. With her interest in literacy, she's tried to impress upon people the importance of reading to kids, broadening their horizons, expanding their young minds. And it's important to remember that one of the first goals of the civil rights movement was as basic as can be: quality education for all. We've made enormous progress, thanks in large part to Martin Luther King, in removing the legal barriers that blocked progress for minority Americans.

But let's face it. Regrettably, other kinds of barriers remain. For instance, the dream of quality education remains an unfulfilled promise for too many of our children. And now, our America 2000 education program will help lift up those kids who have been left behind.

I want to stop here also to salute two great leaders in American education, Dr. Keith of Morehouse and Dr. Cole of Spelman. With leaders like this, we are, in a sense, inspiring new generations. And I also want to salute and honor Dr. Gloster, who was previously the head of this great institution represented here today not only by Dr. Sullivan but by these magnificent young people.

Yes, too much prejudice, racism and anti-Semitism, and blind hatred still exist in our land. Martin preached something different, but they still exist in our land. And as President, I'm trying and all of us must try and must pledge to root out bigotry wherever we find it. Speak out in whatever community you are. Every day, Mrs. King, you and your colleagues here at this center train young people that the way to counter hatred and ignorance and prejudice is peacefully, with nonviolence, with compassion, with love and service to others.

That is the honorable, noble continuation of your husband's work. He taught us the difference one man can make in a country dedicated to the ideals of brotherhood. He saw an America that was like the welcome table the spiritual speaks of, where all Americans can eat and never be hungry, drink and never be thirsty. With your continuing commitment and help, we will meet these great challenges and make real the dream of Martin Luther King.

Thank you all very much. Now it is my honor for the United States of America to sign this proclamation. Thank you.

*Note: The President spoke at 10:29 a.m. in*

*Freedom Hall at the Dr. Martin Luther King, Jr. Center. In his remarks, he referred to Jesse Hill, Jr., chairman of the board, Dr. Martin Luther King, Jr. Center; Rev. Joseph L. Roberts, Jr., senior pastor, Ebenezer Baptist Church; Leroy Keith, Jr., and Hugh M.*

*Gloster, president and former president, Morehouse College; and Johnetta B. Cole, president, Spelman College. The proclamation is listed in Appendix E at the end of this volume.*

## Remarks Announcing the Job Training 2000 Initiative in Atlanta
*January 17, 1992*

Let me say it's been a joy to be back in Atlanta. I was privileged to be over at the Martin Luther King Center, pay fitting and appropriate tribute to that great leader, and now have an opportunity to be here.

I want to single out again, to those who weren't over there, Secretary Sullivan. Dr. Sullivan is the Secretary of HHS, the largest Department in the Federal Government, and doing a superb job. And for you kids, he's from Morehouse Medical right here and went to Morehouse. So, we've got an Atlanta man running this enormous part of the Federal Government and doing a superb job at it.

I was so pleased to have been greeted by the Mayor, who I don't think's here right now, and the Governor, both of whom gave me a warm welcome, one to Georgia and one to Atlanta. I want to salute the Private Industry Council of Atlanta members who have taken the time to be with us. Pleased to be joined by Alvin Darden, members of this effective CATALYST team, now on their coffee break. [*Laughter*]

I've come here to Morris Brown College in the center, the Atlanta University center, to see this wonderful work in progress and to announce a pioneering new approach to job training, a program that I call Job Training 2000. Programs like the CATALYST project highlight just how critical job training is to the American economy, to American competitiveness, and yes, to the American dream.

As a Nation, America's ability to prosper in the century coming up rests on our collective capacity to learn new skills and test the limits of our potential. On an individual level, what we learn defines who we are.

No one, young, old, or in between, can hope to reach their dreams without sharpening their skills and mastering the tools of thought. That's the idea behind our overall national education strategy, America 2000. And it's the impulse behind the initiative that I'm announcing today, Job Training 2000.

Job training must be more than merely make-work. It's got to suit the needs of the workplace and the marketplace. And the private sector will always bear primary responsibility for training the workers it needs to get the job done, the unions here taking a very active and critical role in all of this. But government at all levels can and must play a role, to use a word that's well-known, as catalysts in this process.

And we are. Right now, the Federal Government's commitment to worker training spans more than 60 programs, 7 Federal Agencies, resources totaling some $18 billion a year. Well, we've got to make certain that these funds are spent to maximum effect, and that's where Job Training 2000 comes in. It's the product of hard work of our Vice President and of Secretary of Labor Lynn Martin, of our Education Secretary, all these working together trying to express a commitment to this country's future.

Job Training 2000 rests on four cornerstones: First, the creation of a 21st-century training system. Job Training 2000 creates a one-stop shopping center for job training, coordinated by private industry councils all across the country. It will move us away from the heavy hand of bureaucratic overkill to a system that allows greater freedom for the private sector and local governments to shape programs that work. I've been asking that question, "Does this work?" And each person I've asked said, "This one works. It's effective."

Second, this program will help ease the transition from welfare to work, from dependence to independence. Under Job Training 2000, we'll dedicate more than $20 million to demonstration projects to place welfare recipients in permanent jobs. And then we'll enlist market forces to break the welfare dependency. A substantial portion of the money government saves as each new worker leaves welfare behind will be shared with the company that helped that person get a job.

And thirdly, this program will ease the transition from school to work. Job Training 2000 will encourage voluntary apprentice programs for high school students, combining quality education, on-the-job training, and mentoring. This approach will help these apprentices keep their options open to pursue their education or, alternatively, to enter the work force as they wish.

Fourth and finally, Job Training 2000 promotes lifelong learning. Job Training 2000 establishes lifetime training and education accounts, enabling the Federal Government to provide the average American tens of thousands of dollars' worth of education and training over the course of his lifetime. Job Training 2000 will create a kind of passport to continuing education, making it easier for people of all ages to receive grants and loans that they need to keep pace with the challenges of the 21st-century workplace. This program is our plan to capture the spirit of programs like the ones that I've been privileged to see today and bring that innovative Atlanta approach, if you will, to every American community.

Let me say to the young men and women that I've met today: Not long from now, these four walls will house the new Project CATALYST Center. But what you're building here is far more than a work of bricks and mortar or plaster or paint. This renovation is a symbol of the larger commitment of this community to generate opportunity for the people who call it home.

So once again, my congratulations on the future that you're building here, on the opportunity you're giving the young people here. And my thanks to the CATALYST team for showing me around this site. And thanks to all of you, whether you're in city government, State government, marketplace, business, labor unions, whatever, for the fine work you are doing, the example you're setting.

And now, back to work. [*Laughter*] Hammer time. Thank you all very much. Thank you all very, very much.

*Note: The President spoke at 11:52 a.m. at the Ventures in Community Improvement classroom on the campus of Morris Brown College. In his remarks, he referred to Alvin Darden, coordinator of Project CATALYST.*

# Nomination of William O. Studeman To Be Deputy Director of Central Intelligence
*January 17, 1992*

The President today announced his intention to nominate Vice Adm. William O. Studeman, USN, to be Deputy Director of Central Intelligence. He would succeed Richard J. Kerr.

Currently Vice Admiral Studeman serves as Director of the National Security Agency in Fort Meade, MD. Prior to this, he served as Director of Naval Intelligence, 1985–1988, and as Director of the Long Range Planning Group at the Department of the Navy, 1984–1985. In addition, Vice Admiral Studeman served as commanding officer of the Navy Operational Intelligence Center, 1982–1984, and executive assistant to the Vice Chief Naval Operations, 1981–1982.

Vice Admiral Studeman graduated from the University of the South (B.A., 1962); George Washington University (M.S., 1973); Naval War College (1973); and National

War College (1981). He was born January 16, 1940, in Brownsville, TX. Since 1962, Vice Admiral Studeman has served in the U.S. Navy. He is married, has three children, and resides in Fort Meade, MD.

# Remarks at a Head Start Center in Catonsville, Maryland
*January 21, 1992*

Maryanne Anderson, thank you so very much, not just you but everybody that has given us this very warm welcome. May I salute our Secretary of Education, who is with us. Were you introduced before I walked in here? Stand up, come on: Lamar Alexander, the Secretary of Education for the United States. Lou Sullivan, right here, is the Secretary of HHS. And most of you know him by his works, but Lou, I guess you were greeted.

And may I single out Congressman Helen Bentley, who flew over with us on Marine One. Here she is, over here. And I would be remiss if I didn't especially single out my friend, your Governor, Don Schaefer.

We have these national education goals, and then we have a group of Governors, nonpartisan, come together, all of them as a matter of fact, to endorse them. And to implement these goals we have a program that Lamar is working so hard on—Lou helping, I'm trying to help—called America 2000. And I think you and Maryland can take pride that your Governor was the first one on and has been an early advocate of goal one, or the whole program, first one on board, and secondly, a very early advocate of Head Start and this early learning concept. So I appreciate, Governor, your taking the time to come here in that spirit.

And I salute the parents without whom this program cannot work to its fulfillment, parents, parental involvement, and we saw that. And I salute the parents, not only here but out there, who are doing so much to get these kids ready to learn.

Last Friday, I had the privilege of visiting the living memorial to Dr. Martin Luther King in Atlanta, went down there with Coretta Scott King. And contemplating the legacy that Dr. King left for us all, I was struck once again by the immense impor-tance that he placed on quality education. He called it "the passport to a better life." And he was right.

We face a great challenge today in making America a country that will lead not only in the 1990's but in the 21st century, lead, the leadership in education. This mission involves many things. And next week when I deliver a State of the Union Message, you'll see that we've been doing some hard thinking about how to fulfill this uniquely American destiny. And one of the keys is to make sure that this generation of young Americans, like these young people here today, are prepared to lead.

And in a word, that demands educational excellence. As many of you know, we've launched a comprehensive strategy to radically transform, radically transform America's schools. And yes, we've set high goals. And the first goal is this, and I mentioned it earlier: By the year 2000, every American child must start school ready to learn.

Many children need a head start, and we're going to make sure they get it. Today I'm pleased to announce that we're taking a large step toward meeting that first crucial goal. In the budget that I'll submit later this month, I will ask Congress for a $600 million increase in Head Start, the largest increase ever. And we've fought for increases the last 3 years, but this one is the largest ever. It's the third straight one, as a matter of fact. Increasing funding for Head Start has been a priority with me, with Dr. Sullivan, with Secretary Alexander and others for a long, long time, certainly for the teachers, the dedicated teachers that we've seen here today.

And in 1989, just a little review here, we increased funding over 1988 levels, as well as in 1990 and then again in 1991. And these funds will allow every eligible 4-year-old child whose parents want them to participate to have the Head Start experience before starting school, every eligible 4-year-old. And when Congress approves my request, and I'm confident they will go along, we will have more than doubled the program's funding over the past 3 years.

Of course, in education as in other fields, Government is just one part of the larger solution. Real progress in America comes from strong families and communities, from committed individuals binding together in common purpose, whether it's a church congregation opening a day care center in its neighborhood or parents taking a little extra time to read to their children.

No Government program alone can guarantee that children start school ready to learn. No Government program can take the place of parents and of communities that nurture the children who otherwise might have been left far behind. But in Head Start we found a Government program that works, that works to strengthen communities and families for the future.

Time has proved that Head Start brings out the best in us. And last year, more than 800,000 Americans gave of themselves by volunteering in a Head Start program. That is an amazing figure. You can see it right here at the Emily Harris Head Start Program where the entire staff, including volunteers, make sure their young pupils get the skills that will stand them in good stead for the rest of their lives. They learn about getting along; they learn about sharing with others, about independence, about self-confidence.

Every parent here knows that Head Start is really more than education. It provides hot meals, ensures that children receive immunizations and access to needed social services, health and dental care. Dr. Sullivan, whose Department does such a splendid job in administering Head Start, knows from personal experience the importance of nurturing the body as well as mind.

And most of all, Head Start is about family. Head Start couldn't be the success it's been without the direct involvement of parents. Governing councils give parents the opportunity to set the program's direction. Head Start brings parents right into the classroom and into the learning process. And they attend child care workshops, and they learn how to prepare well-balanced meals. And all of these serve to reinvigorate those family values that are the true key to a happy, wholesome, and productive life.

Head Start works. It's not perfect. We're committed to making a good program better. Over the past 3 years we've made sure these increased funds best serve the needs of families. We've made family service centers part of Head Start to provide substance abuse counseling, job training for parents who need them. And we've encouraged every Head Start program to offer adult literacy classes for Head Start parents.

But our greatest challenge lies in ensuring that when children leave Head Start ready to learn, they enter an educational system where they can learn. We're helping with the head start; let's make sure that they cross the finish line too, prepared to be the leaders of the next century.

I really was very pleased to be here today. And I'm honored that I've had a chance to see firsthand the work that the teachers, the parents, the community is doing to support this worthwhile program. It is an example for the rest of our Nation. So, thank all of you.

And let me say in conclusion, thanks for the kids. I learned an awful lot about bathtub toys; about how to work the telephone—several of them know their own phone numbers; preparation to go to the dentist; and a lot of things that I'd forgotten. [*Laughter*] So, it's been a good day.

Thank you all very, very much.

*Note: The President spoke at 10:05 a.m. at the Emily Harris Head Start Center. In his remarks, he referred to Maryanne Anderson, Baltimore County Head Start director.*

# Statement by Press Secretary Fitzwater on the Death of Rose Bowen
## *January 21, 1992*

The President and Mrs. Bush extend their sympathies to former Secretary of Health and Human Services Otis Bowen upon the death of his wife, Rose. As a member of the Cabinet in the Reagan administration, Sec-retary and Mrs. Bowen became close friends of the Bush family. President Bush spoke with Secretary Bowen today to express his sympathies.

# Memorandum on Transportation of Humanitarian Assistance to the Former Soviet Union
## *January 21, 1992*

*Memorandum for the Secretary of Defense*

*Subject:* Transportation of Humanitarian Assistance to the Former Soviet Union

Pursuant to the laws of the United States, including section 109 of the "Dire Emergency Supplemental Appropriations and Transfers for Relief From the Effects of Natural Disasters, for Other Urgent Needs, and for Incremental Cost of 'Operation Desert Shield/Desert Storm' Act of 1992" (Public Law 102–229):

1. I designate as emergency requirements, pursuant to the terms of the Balanced Budget and Emergency Deficit Control Act of 1985, as amended, the full amount for which section 109 provides.

2. Effective upon satisfaction of applicable congressional notification requirements, I direct the Secretary of Defense to transfer funds under section 109 as it incorporates by reference section 301(b) of H.R. 3807 as passed the Senate on November 25, 1991.

3. The authorities and duties of the President under section 301 of H.R. 3807 as passed the Senate on November 25, 1991, and referred to in section 109 (except the designation of emergency relating to funding addressed in paragraph 1 and the direction addressed in paragraph 2) are hereby delegated to the Secretary of Defense.

You are directed to publish this memorandum in the *Federal Register*.

GEORGE BUSH

[*Filed with the Office of the Federal Register, 4:26 p.m., January 24, 1992*]

*Note: This memorandum was released by the Office of the Press Secretary on January 22.*

# The President's News Conference
## *January 22, 1992*

*Secretary of Transportation Nominee*

*The President.* Let me just say that I am nominating Andy Card, Andrew H. Card, Jr., to be the Secretary of Transportation. His distinguished career in government service at both the State and the national level give him the unique background for serving the Nation's transportation interests. He's a friend of many years who started his career as a legislator in the Massachusetts House of Representatives. I have valued that experience often in the last 3 years here in Washington.

As Deputy Chief of Staff, he has offered wise and loyal counsel on legislation, on management of Federal programs, and on intergovernmental relations. Scores of people from all walks of life know him as the White House manager who will listen to their concerns and get things done. That's true here. That's true on Capitol Hill.

And I also want to express my appreciation once again to Sam Skinner for his expert and dedicated stewardship over at that Department, culminating in the landmark Transportation Act. He was known over there for his foresight and innovation, and he's brought that same energy, distinctive energy, to the White House.

Our Nation's transportation system faces many important challenges in the years ahead. And a vast new highway system is taking shape under the Surface Transportation Act that was just signed into law. Whether it be in aviation, railroads, mass transit, shipping, or the Coast Guard, I know that Andy Card's leadership will be an important ingredient in providing the most effective transportation system possible.

I look forward to having him in this important position on the administration team, look forward to having him as a valued counselor and member of the President's Cabinet. And he will do a first-rate job at Transportation, just as his predecessor did.

Thank you very much. Andy, do you want equal time here?

*Mr. Card.* I'm honored and quite privileged to be part of the President's team, and I'm flattered that he would choose me to be part of his Cabinet. I look forward to working with the other members of the Cabinet, with the rest of the Bush administration, and I want to carry on the fine tradition that Secretary Skinner brought to the Department of Transportation.

Mr. President, I'm proud to be part of your team. Thank you.

*The President.* We're scooting over to the State Department for an event. But maybe I should take a question or two. I know you're all interested in this appointment.

### State of the Union Message

*Q.* Mr. President, are you going to go for a middle-income tax cut? And are you going to cut the Pentagon budget by $50 billion? And are you going to break the budget agreement?

*The President.* Helen [Helen Thomas, United Press International], you have 6 days to wait for answers to all those questions. So, I'm not going to now start taking specifics on the State of the Union. I'm confident that what we suggest will be widely received, well-received by the American people. I think we're transcending politics. So, I'm confident what I propose will have strong support from all elements on the Republican side——

*Q.* How about the conservatives?

*The President.* ——strong support there. And I think we're going to have a very good package. But we're going to eschew some of the pure political approaches. We're going to try to do something that will stimulate the economy and avoid these things that may have strong primary political appeal but would hurt the economy in the long run by shooting interest rates up. So, just stay tuned, and I'll give you all the answers to that one.

*Q.* Can I follow that on a nonspecific——

*The President.* Yes, you can.

*Q.* Do you agree with those who say, even from among your own party, that you really don't have a message that you've presented so far?

*The President.* No, I don't agree with them.

*Q.* Why not?

*The President.* But I think the State of the Union will give us a strong opportunity to get it across. Because we're in a political season, Ann [Ann Compton, ABC News]. And I point out what we've done in various areas, the benefits of a transportation bill, what we're doing in terms of a brand new education program. And it's pretty hard when you're out there getting hammered by the—the only way for the opposition to win in the political season is to tear down the President. The American people see that.

So, what I've got to do is get out and above all that by this State of the Union and then following up vigorously, which we will do.

*Japan-U.S. Trade Agreements*

*Q.* Mr. President, there's concerns from comments from Prime Minister Miyazawa and other industrialists in Tokyo that there may be some backsliding in Japan on agreements they made during your trip. What is your reaction?

*The President.* I was pleased with the correction or the comments coming out of Japan yesterday. I was not pleased with the statements that challenged the ability of American workers. I have full confidence in the American workers' competence, their ability. I do think that our products have to be competitive, and there's no question about that. But we've got the best workers in the world. So, when I saw a statement challenging that, I was upset.

But I was also pleased when I saw a reaffirmation of these goals that were established, and we'll have more to say on that, on a computer agreement that has had strong support, and I've seen very little coverage on that. It's a very good agreement. And the Japanese have every intention of fulfilling that agreement.

So, you know, I hope they don't judge American policy by some of the outrageous statements I've seen against them. And I won't judge Japanese policy by some of the outrageous statements I've seen against us. You need a steady hand here. You need to build on the progress we've made.

*Economic Growth Initiatives*

*Q.* Mr. President, you used much the same words that you used this morning, eschewing a political approach, avoiding something that would send interest rates shooting up——

*The President.* Right.

*Q.* ——earlier this, or last year, in saying you would oppose a broad, general tax cut. Can we construe from your comments today that you will oppose a middle class——

*The President.* You just have to wait and see. But I'll stay with what I've said here in terms of definition of our approach. And I think it will be well-received. And what it will do is to target growth of jobs in this economy. And I saw last year one program, I forget which it was, on the Democratic side that was just kind of a broadly—do

away with the constraints on spending. People are tired of all this Government spending. They want to see the caps on the spending held. That program would have done away with the caps, give everybody a tax cut. And interest rates shot up the very next day.

So, our proposal will try to avoid that kind of politically popular approach, but will focus on those things that will encourage jobs, investment, savings, whatever.

*Q.* Mr. President, you talked a few minutes ago about political opponents tearing apart the Presidency.

*The President.* The President.

*Q.* The President.

*The President.* To some degree the Presidency, the President.

*Q.* But Republican conservatives are tearing apart your economic advisers. They're saying they haven't been bold enough. There are reports that you're considering some kind of staff shakeup. First of all, have the proposals not been bold enough? Are you going to become more bold in that approach? And do you have a shakeup in the works?

*The President.* One, I feel confident that we'll have strong support in our party. There's some, one or two out on a real fringe running around up there, that might find it difficult to support me for political reasons. I mean, we all know we're in a political season. But I think the broad numbers of Republicans in the House and in the Senate will be supportive when they see what this package is.

What was the second part?

*White House Staff*

*Q.* Staff shakeup.

*The President.* Well, anytime you have a new Chief of Staff, I tell him, "Hey, take a look at the structure here; see what we can do to do a better job." We're moving into a very complicated and difficult year. And I have full confidence in the people around us, but whether there will be some structural changes that will facilitate one end or another of our responsibilities, let's wait and see.

### Aid to the Commonwealth of Independent States

*Q.* Mr. President, on the C.I.S. conference you're about to host, a number of European countries are complaining that the U.S. is not in a good position to lead this because this country lags behind the rest of the world in aid for the Soviet Union. The French, in particular, have been outspoken. Do you feel they have a point, and do you anticipate adding more to the U.S. contribution?

*The President.* Look, it's always been a hallmark of U.S. foreign policy, and I think of the heartbeat of this country, that if people are hurting, health reasons, famine, food reasons, that the United States is willing to help. So, I would anticipate our stepping up and trying to do as much as we possibly can. We have already made significant contributions. And I'm very proud that we have. That's the heartbeat of our country, trying to help people, home and abroad.

And so I would expect that we'll do some more. But what we're doing now over at State is making sure everybody understands what really has been done. And yes, I've seen some comments out of the EC, for example, that they've done more. I don't think it's a question of who's doing the most. It's a question of each country in there doing its best. And I'm very proud that there's such fine attendance for this coordinating conference here. And we will do our level-best to help.

We've got enormous problems here that need attention, but we're not going to change the view that when people are hurting the United States ought not to help. And we do have a big stake in this, in the success of the democracies in the Commonwealth. We've got an enormous stake.

And isn't it better to send some money to help people who are hungry or perhaps need medical attention than it is to be ever increasing your nuclear weapons, one against the other? We're living in an exciting age where this country has much less to fear from nuclear weapons. And I am very proud that we have made a real contribution to that.

So, we'll do what we can. But we have

and I think everyone around the world has restricted funds on all of this. So, I think we'll have a good answer over there.

*Q.* Do you feel Americans don't understand the need?

*The President.* No, I think Americans do understand the need, particularly, I hope, the way I've explained it here. And I think in Congress most people seem to. They understand we have a big stake in the peaceful, democratic evolution of the Commonwealth. I think it's an enormous stake. And whether it's popular politically or not, I mean, we've got to continue to conduct ourself as the United States of America and not knuckle under to every political charge from right or left. I mean, it's in a funny time now, as we all know. And I'm going to keep a steady hand on this and do our very best. And we've got a good program.

The last one.

*Q.* Mr. Burbulis, who's the Deputy Prime Minister, this morning in an op-ed piece in the Washington Post is asking for significantly more money, specifically 6 billion for a type of stabilization program and another 6 billion for food and medicine. What is your reaction to that?

*The President.* I've just given my answer to it here. I can't comment. One, I didn't see his comment. And secondly, we are in touch with the Soviet, the Russian leadership, the leadership of the republics at the highest level. And I'll take a look at what he says, but I can't comment on a story I haven't seen. But I gave the answers to what we want to try to do here.

### Economic Growth Initiatives

*Q.* You've promised a dramatic economic growth plan in your State of the Union, but the Democrats are already planning their own growth plan. The Democratic candidates have already planned a press conference the night of your speech. How likely do you think it is that you'll actually get cooperation from Congress?

*The President.* I think the American people want action. I think they'd like to think that even in an election year we can lay politics aside long enough to get something done to help the American people. And yes, the Democrats control both

Houses of the Congress. And I think the American people see that there's blame to be shared all around on all of this.

But I will make the strong view that, "Hey, this is a tough one, but let's try to get something done that's going to get this country back to work, that's going to create jobs." And we'll see. That's the approach I'll take. And I will resist and fight against things that won't do that, that will make the situation worse. And I'll fight very hard for things that I think will make it better.

And indeed, looking back over my shoulder, I just wish that the growth initiatives that I've been proposing for 3 years had been passed by the Congress. And so, I will now challenge the Congress and ask the American people's support for a sound package. It won't have everything I'd like to see get done, I'm sure, but I think in that spirit, maybe we can get something accomplished.

*Q.* You'll set a deadline, sir?'

*The President.* You wait now and see about this message.

*Note: The President's 119th news conference began at 8:40 a.m. in the Briefing Room at the White House. Gennadiy Burbulis was First Deputy Prime Minister of the Russian Federation.*

# Remarks at the International Conference on Humanitarian Assistance to the Former U.S.S.R.
## *January 22, 1992*

I would first start off by saying I got bawled out by the Secretary of State for being late. And my position is: I'm not late; you guys are early.

But I just want to give a warm welcome to the United States and to Washington, our Capital, to the many distinguished guests in this room today who include foreign ministers and senior officials from 47 countries, the United Nations, major international financial institutions, and other major international organizations.

We come together this morning as partners at a historic time, a turning point in our century and, I think, in modern history. Our mission is to respond together to the dramatic revolution that swept away Soviet communism and left in its place 12 new nations moving to establish their place in the world and struggling with the critical task of feeding, clothing, and housing their peoples this winter, this spring, and beyond.

Before you discuss these issues in depth over the next 2 days, I wanted to take a moment to reflect on the meaning of these events in the former Soviet Union for those of us in North America, in Europe, the Middle East, Africa, Latin America, Asia, the Pacific, in all corners of the globe.

For nearly 50 years, throughout most of the adult lives of almost everyone in this room, mankind endured a dangerous global conflict, the cold war. It divided continents and peoples and held all countries hostage to the possibility of nuclear annihilation. The free world rose up against that threat posed by Soviet expansionism in the decades after the Second World War. We spent hundreds of billions of dollars and sacrificed precious lives and national resources in that great struggle.

With the revolution in Eastern Europe in 1989 and in the Soviet Union in 1991, that mortal threat has withered. And with the dissolution of the Soviet Union itself just last month, we find ourselves at the entryway to a new world, a world of hope for a lasting peace and growing prosperity.

Led by a courageous President, Boris Yeltsin, reformers have come to power in the enormous Russian Federation. Ukraine has won independence, and the government of President Leonid Kravchuk holds out the promise of a new political and economic order. In Armenia, a former prisoner of conscience, President Ter-Petrosyan, has led an extraordinary national effort to transform his country's economic system and liberate its people from political oppression. And in Central Asia the same stories, as President Nazarbayev, President Akayev are leading the fight for reform there. A new day has dawned throughout the Commonwealth of Independent States, with hope for a fundamental transformation in the way people live and work and think.

As we begin a new year and chart our course for the rest of this decade, let us bring equal commitment to the challenge of helping to build and sustain democracy and economic freedom in the former U.S.S.R., just as we did to winning the cold war. Let us help the people throughout the Independent States to make the leap from communism to democracy, from command economies to free markets, from authoritarianism to liberty. And then let us pull together to win the peace in this post-cold-war era.

We should not underestimate the enormity of this challenge and the difficulty of unraveling economic dislocations resulting from over 70 years of Communist economics. Ultimate success or failure rests squarely with the efforts and wisdom of the peoples of Russia and the Ukraine and the Caucasus in Central Asia. The battle is really theirs to win. But they cannot win it alone. These 12 new countries will need the hard work, creativity, and good will of all of our countries from every continent.

And that is why we meet today, to assure that our commitment and assistance will be up to the task, well-conceived and efficiently executed. And we meet to demonstrate to the peoples in these new States that the international community cares about them and supports their hard struggle to build new societies on the ruins of communism.

So, let us join together to give these people a reason to hope. Let us commit ourselves this morning to work in full partnership as we proceed.

First, we must continue to act resolutely this winter, this spring, and then throughout 1992 to meet the critical emergency needs of these States, food and medical supplies and energy and shelter. The shortages now evident throughout the 12 States will not soon disappear and will require sustained attention, our sustained attention.

Second, we must also meet the challenge of promoting economic growth and development of new free-market institutions through a collective international effort to provide technical assistance. Our work will be critically important to help the new States construct banking and taxation systems, to provide a healthier environment, to promote the rule of law and, yes, nuclear safety.

In short, we must support those who are standing up for reform and freedom. We should stimulate concrete investments and expanded trade. President Boris Yeltsin's courageous economic reforms deserve our support, as do efforts in the other States to introduce economic change.

Our success or failure will hinge on our ability to work effectively together on this common cause. The challenge is too great for any one nation or group of nations. It is a global challenge requiring the efforts and commitment of nations from all over the world. And your presence here, a truly remarkable presence, is vivid testimony that this is and must be a global coalition. Nothing else can work.

As we come together during these 2 days and then certainly in the months ahead, let us do so constructively, in the spirit of partnership, avoiding sterile debates over which one of us has done the most or the least and which should lead our response to this historic challenge. All of us have a role and obligation to fulfill. And many of us have already undertaken concrete actions to help.

The European Community has shouldered a major and generous share of the burden. Its prompt actions over several years to provide humanitarian support were vitally important, and its commitment to a vigorous technical assistance program is far-reaching and most welcomed. Germany alone has assumed enormous responsibility in providing military housing and in channeling credits to the former U.S.S.R. and now to the Federation, to the Russian Federation. Other EC governments have made important contributions. The Atlantic alliance stands ready to help with the knowledge that the peoples of the former U.S.S.R. are moving toward the same values that have sustained NATO since its birth.

It is especially satisfying to see here today our friends from Central and Eastern Europe as the pioneers in discarding communism and embracing democracy. You are here as symbols of success. And though you still face problems yourselves, the world applauds your willingness to help freedom elsewhere.

The challenges before us require efforts not just from Europe but from other regions and countries as well. Japan has made important contributions, commitments and will be critical to this effort. And now other nations in the Far East and the Middle East and Latin America should commit their expertise, their resources to assure the success of reform.

And I can assure you today that the United States, which for so long has led the struggle to contain communism, is also contributing its share so that democracy is its permanent replacement. For over 40 years, we have led in the reconstruction and defense of the free world. And now that the torch of liberty has sparked freedom among our former adversaries, the greatest good of our long labor is at last visible.

The U.S. cannot and will not falter at the moment that these new States are struggling to embrace the very ideals that America was founded to foster and preserve. Accordingly, as a further U.S. contribution to this urgent worldwide effort, I am proposing that the Congress approve over $600 million for new technical assistance and humanitarian efforts. In addition to the assistance already announced, this will bring to over $5 billion the level of various forms of U.S. assistance to these people in their time of need.

In closing, I would like to reiterate the importance of seizing this moment to commit ourselves individually and collectively to an opportunity that may not come our way again in our lifetimes. The prospect that our former adversaries may become our friends and our partners, this is in the national interest of every country represented around this table and those countries that are not represented around this table.

By coordinating our efforts toward common goals, we have a chance to reshape the world for our children and for generations to come. And if we do not, we risk the reversal of the historic leap to freedom made by the Russian, Ukrainian, Armenian, and other peoples during these last months.

So, let us work together over the next 2 days to promote our national and collective security, continued global economic growth, and to do what is right for the ordinary people who yearn for a better, free life in these new Independent States.

Thank you all very, very much for being here. I know it is not easy to make the long trek. It is desperately important. Thank you for this opportunity to speak with you today. And may God bless the peoples of all the countries represented here and the peoples of these new, struggling Independent States. We have such confidence that we can succeed, all of us working together.

Thank you all very much.

*Note: The President spoke at 9 a.m. at the Department of State. In his remarks, he referred to President Nursultan Nazarbayev of Kazakhstan and President Askar Akayev of Kyrgyzstan.*

# Remarks to the Citizens Democracy Corps Conference
*January 22, 1992*

This is strictly a cameo appearance, a drop-by. I would ask these distinguished panelists to excuse the interruption and let you return to your regular program in just a few minutes. But I'm delighted to see Ambassador Hartman here, who served his

country with such distinction; most recent post, unless I missed one, was to what used to be the Soviet Union, and did a great job. Then, of course, Ambassador Polansky, the CDC's Executive Director.

In less than 2 years, this Corps, this Citizens Democracy Corps, has proved to be an idea ahead of its time. The first mission was to reach out to the newly independent nations of Eastern and Central Europe. And today, the CDC's mandate extends not only to the nations in the old Soviet bloc but to the Baltic States and then even to the former Soviet Union itself.

Let me also welcome a couple of others: Cooper Evans, that worked long and hard in this building after he served with such distinction in the Congress, a good friend of long standing; Diane Butterfield, who I know is doing a lot of efficient work with the staff, modestly standing over here. And I'm told, but I don't see him right here, that Max Kampelman was here. Was he, or not? Well, he's supposed to be here—[*laughter*]—and tell him he's got three demerits for not being here—[*laughter*]—because I was going to say something very—where is he? Hey, Max. Anytime they can put Max Kampelman in the back of the room in the shadows, there's something wrong with the way this thing is set up. But let me just say I'm grateful for his participation. And like Art Hartman and others here, he really worked hard for human rights and for peace and for all the values that all of us believe in so strongly. George Soros is here, the president of the Soros Fund management. My thanks to all of you, all of you, for coming to Washington to take part in an effort that really can, literally, shape the history.

You meet at a critical moment. Right now in the lands of the former Soviet Union, a new revolution is unfolding right before our very eyes. Millions of people have shed the dead weight of the Communist past to reclaim their heritage and their history, to revive the powerful hope all people share of living in freedom.

This moment of great hope is also a time of terrible hardship, tremendous hardship. Seventy years of the Soviet experience and the implosion of the socialist economy have taken their toll, the harsh winter, empty shelves fueling discontent and threatening democracy's great gains. The challenge now for the newly independent States of the old Soviet Union is to create a breathing space for free-market reform and democratic institutions to take root and grow.

Earlier this morning I went over to the State Department, meeting with representatives of over 47 nations. I think 40 of them are at the foreign minister level. They're all now focusing on the urgent question of humanitarian aid for the former Soviet Union. Look, our country has always helped when people need food or medical attention. We've always tried to do our level-best to help people in need around the world, and this should be no exception.

And today I proposed that Congress now approve an additional assistance, $600 million in technical assistance, in humanitarian aid to help the people of the Commonwealth of Independent States. At the urging of many in this room, we have stepped up, and we have tried to do our part with several billion dollars of food aid arrangements. We have a tremendous stake in the success of Russia and, indeed, of the other members of the CIS, of this Commonwealth of Independent States.

But I came here to make the point that obviously you all understand, and that is that Government to Government is only part of the overall equation. Bringing the former Soviet Republics into the community of free nations is a task that can never be accomplished by Government alone, particularly now, particularly with this experience that's taking place before our eyes. The move to market economy, the need to remake, totally remake the financial institutions, whatever it is, it cannot be done by Government alone.

So, we've got to build the human contacts that give free government its real meaning. The countless exchanges that take place every day among private individuals, they help; and between businesses and labor, terribly important; the academic exchanges or just contacts by our academicians making contacts with theirs, wherever that may be, terribly important.

All the groups and organizations that give life to a free society ought to be trying in one way or another to interact. And that's where each one of your organizations come in. That's why I proposed the Citizens Democracy Corps. As I said back in the spring of '90 when it was announced, the real strength of democracy is its citizens, the collective strength of individual Americans.

So, let me single out the work of one group here today as a proof of the kind of difference that all of you can make. It's a project called Dakota Cares, sponsored by the North Dakota Grain Growers Association. It started with one of the traditions of the American heartland, pitching in to help someone in need, and transported that idea to people in need thousands of miles away.

Right now, Dakota Cares is moving 100 tons of flour to the people of St. Petersburg, each bag stamped as a gift from the State of North Dakota. Its ability to move that flour across the country, across an ocean, and off the docks and into the homes of people who need it is testament to our spirit, to the American spirit at its very best.

That same spirit animates all the people gathered in this room because you do represent a cross section of American society, people with the expertise and the energy to help an old adversary make the transition to free markets and free government, people who show the world the true meaning of democracy in action. And I am very, very pleased to see so many American organizations, so many individuals so active in strengthening the forces of freedom and democracy.

Let me just say on the Government's part, we are going to stay involved. We're in a funny kind of tough year now in terms of priorities. But I must not and I will not neglect my responsibilities to do what I can do as the President of this great country in mobilizing others to do the good work of government, to help where governments can. I'm looking forward to seeing President Yeltsin, for example, when he comes here, talking about the problems that I'm sure many of you are talking about today. We will stay actively and fully involved.

Everyone is looking to the United States of America, to our leadership, since the crumbling of the Soviet Union, not just in how we treat with the Commonwealth but how we treat with other problems from the Middle East to South America to wherever in the world. So we've got to stay involved as a Government, and I just wanted you all to know that I will do my level-best to keep the Government-to-Government programs on the right footing. But the Government simply can't do it, can't do it all. We need your help, and we need your active involvement.

And it is an enormously exciting period. It's a time of trouble, a time of great grief and worry for the people over there, human suffering. But we've got to look at it like it's a time of great promise, not just for democracy and freedom and free markets in these things but for a whole new relationship between our country and these former—the one former adversary, parts of which we are trying to help now to the best of our ability.

So thank you very, very much for your concern and your interest. And believe me, you are engaged in something that is fundamental, fundamental to world peace. Thank you.

*Note: The President spoke at 11:17 a.m. in Room 450 of the Old Executive Office Building to the Conference on Private Sector Assistance to the Commonwealth of Independent States, sponsored by the Citizens Democracy Corps. In his remarks, he referred to Cooper Evans, member of the board of directors of Volunteers in Overseas Cooperative Assistance; Diane Butterfield, director of finance and administration for the CDC; and Max M. Kampelman, member of the board of the International Media Fund and member of the Executive Committee of the American Bar Association's Special Committee on the Central and Eastern European Law Initiative.*

## Teleconference Remarks to the March for Life Rally
*January 22, 1992*

I admire your conviction and dedication as you watch out for the most helpless members of our human family.

The most compelling legacy of this Nation is Jefferson's concept that all are created equal. It doesn't say "born equal." He says "created." From the moment the miracle of life occurs, human beings must cherish that life, must hold it in awe, must preserve, protect, and defend it. It's there in our Declaration of Independence that we are created equal and endowed with certain inalienable rights to life, to liberty, and to the pursuit of happiness.

I want to reaffirm my dedication and commitment to the simple recognition that all life is a precious gift, that each human being has intrinsic dignity and worth. We are making progress towards this recognition, and I will continue to oppose and fight back attempts by Congress to expand Federal funding for abortions.

Much remains to be done as we reflect upon the gift of life. So, let us redouble our efforts, both in public and private sector, to encourage alternatives such as adoption.

And on a personal note, I find the figures on the numbers of pregnancies that are terminated by abortion simply unconscionable.

So, thank you for what you're doing, for your heartfelt, selfless work. For 19 years you've been tirelessly committed to a righteous cause. And I am out there with you in spirit. And may God bless you all.

Thank you very much.

*Note: The President spoke at 12:13 p.m. from the Oval Office at the White House to rally participants gathered on The Mall.*

## Remarks at the Signing Ceremony for the Computer Trade Agreement With Japan
*January 22, 1992*

*The President.* First, let me welcome Foreign Minister Watanabe of Japan and Japan's able Ambassador to the United States, Ambassador Murata. And of course, well-known to all in this audience is our distinguished USTR, Ambassador Carla Hills.

I want to welcome the CSPP, the Computer Systems Policy Project member companies which are represented here by this distinguished group. And in particular, I want to acknowledge James Unruh from Unisys; Ronald Skates of Data General; Dick Iverson, the president of the American Electronics Association; and a special thanks to CSPP Chairman John Scully, who regrettably is not with us today.

And I'm proud to be here as we sign this path-breaking agreement for Japanese public sector procurement of American computers. It's just one of the highlights of our Asia trip. It illustrates the success that we had fighting for America, for American jobs, and for our own future, for America's future. This agreement also highlights why foreign relations have never been as important to our well-being at home than they are now. When we foster democracy abroad, when we strengthen our security engagements with our allies and friends, when we work to open markets and to expand trade, we make a priceless investment in our own children's future.

The promise contained in this agreement is great. For example, in one segment of the computer market, mainframes, foreign companies have 41 percent of the overall Japanese private sector market, but only .4 percent of the Japanese central government market. Ten years ago, Japan's markets were much more closed than they are now. And 10 years down the road, they'll be much more open than they are today as a result of constructive agreements like this one.

In Tokyo, we were determined to ensure that U.S. computer companies be allowed to compete fairly for the total Japanese government computer market, estimated as a $9 billion market. Since our own highly competitive electronics industry employs 2.4 million American workers, this would mean dramatic gains in exports and therefore in quality American jobs. So, we set as a top priority working with the Japanese Government to continue the process to open Japan's markets to free and fair trade.

Ambassador Hills and our negotiators worked with stunning speed, and I am tremendously proud of our team's steadfast commitment to open markets and fair competition. And as a result of their concerned effort and the hard work and cooperation of our Japanese friends, especially by my good friend Minister Watanabe here, this remarkable agreement will help propel our nations together into the next century of global marketplace.

High-tech trade benefits our consumers, strengthens our industries. And we have representatives from America's computer industry here today. They know how important our successful negotiations will be to their future, and they've said so publicly in commending this achievement.

We're entering an entirely different economic world than the one we grew up in, a new age of American competition in a fiercely challenging global marketplace. Agreements like these are only the first step; the next step will come as American businesses meet worldwide challenges. And they will succeed because as long as that playing field is level, American workers, I think, can outcompete and outproduce

anyone, anywhere, anytime. I know we all have that confidence in our workers.

In the State of the Union Address, I'm going to present my action plan to move our economy into the 21st century. It's an ambitious agenda for growth, and I'm absolutely confident that the American people will join me in this vision for a new era of expanded markets, growing opportunities, peace, and prosperity.

And overlooked to some degree is, with full cooperation from Japan's Prime Minister and their Foreign Minister, we signed a very important growth agenda with the Japanese. It has broad economic implications for the entire world. And again, sir, I thank you for your personal role in that.

We salute the hard work and determination between our two Governments that brought about this landmark agreement. More than 150 years ago, a British politician, Lord Macaulay, made an observation that could still guide us today. He said that free trade is "one of the greatest blessings which a government can confer on a people." And I think with the signing of today's agreement, Japan and the United States both give their people a gift for the future. This relationship between Japan and the United States is very, very important, and I plan to keep it with very, very high priority.

And now, Minister Watanabe, with thanks to you, sir, for taking time from your other busy schedule here, welcome, and we're just delighted to have you here.

*Note: The President spoke at 2:10 p.m. in the Roosevelt Room at the White House. Ambassador Ryohei Murata of Japan and U.S. Trade Representative Carla A. Hills signed the agreement.*

# Message to the Senate Transmitting the Spain-United States Legal Assistance Treaty
*January 22, 1992*

*To the Senate of the United States:*

With a view to receiving the advice and

consent of the Senate to ratification, I transmit herewith the Treaty on Mutual Legal

Assistance in Criminal Matters between the United States of America and the Kingdom of Spain, signed at Washington on November 20, 1990. I transmit also, for the information of the Senate, the Report of the Department of State with respect to the Treaty.

The Treaty is one of a series of modern mutual legal assistance treaties being negotiated by the United States in order to counter criminal activities more effectively. The Treaty should be an effective tool to assist in the prosecution of a wide variety of modern criminals, including members of drug cartels, "white collar criminals," and terrorists. The Treaty is self-executing.

The Treaty provides for a broad range of cooperation in criminal matters. Mutual assistance available under the Treaty includes: (1) the taking of testimony or statements of witnesses; (2) the provision of documents, records, and evidence; (3) the execution of requests for searches and seizures; (4) the serving of documents; and (5) the provision of assistance in proceedings relating to the forfeiture of the proceeds of crime and restitution to the victims of crime.

I recommend that the Senate give early and favorable consideration to the Treaty and give its advice and consent to ratification.

GEORGE BUSH

The White House,
January 22, 1992.

# Letter to Congressional Leaders Transmitting a Report on the U.S.-U.S.S.R. Standing Consultative Commission
*January 22, 1992*

*Dear Mr. Speaker: (Dear Mr. Chairman:)*

In accordance with section 38 of the Arms Control and Disarmament Act as amended by section 3(b) of the Arms Control and Disarmament Amendments Act of 1987 (22 U.S.C. 2578), attached is a classified report prepared by the United States Commissioner to the U.S.-U.S.S.R. Standing Consultative Commission (SCC) concerning the activities of the SCC during calendar year 1991. The report includes detailed information on all substantive issues raised by either party to the Treaty on the Limitation of Anti-Ballistic Missile Systems and the responses to the other party to those issues.

Sincerely,

GEORGE BUSH

*Note: Identical letters were sent to Thomas S. Foley, Speaker of the House of Representatives, and Claiborne Pell, chairman of the Senate Foreign Relations Committee.*

# Statement by Press Secretary Fitzwater Announcing the Drug Summit in San Antonio, Texas
*January 22, 1992*

The President, after consultations with other participating governments, is announcing today that the second regional drug summit will be held in San Antonio, TX, February 26 and 27. This meeting, 2 years after the Cartagena summit, represents another important milestone in the war on drugs. The purpose of this meeting will be to discuss and coordinate our expanding counternarcotics cooperation with the Presidents of Colombia, Bolivia, Peru, Venezuela, Ecuador, and Mexico.

## Remarks to the National Association of Wholesaler-Distributors
*January 23, 1992*

Thank you very much, and welcome to all of you. Thanks to Alan Kranowitz for all his fine work and, of course, to my friend Dirk VanDongen, over here. History, a little history, I understand that he's celebrating his 25th anniversary with the NAW this year. And I might say to those who haven't worked with him closely, as I have, that he does a superb job for sound economic principles, most of which affect the NAW but some of which don't. But he's in there for these solid principles day in and day out. And I am very grateful to him for that.

I want to welcome Jay Church and Jimmy Taylor, who just welcomed me. Thank our Chief of Staff, Sam Skinner, who's come into a tough job, taken the ball, running with it and doing a first-class job. I understand you also heard from Lou Sullivan, a great Secretary of HHS, and then, of course, the Chairman of the Joint Chiefs, Colin Powell. So I hope, through these two avenues and then Sam, you've gotten some feel in a little more detail as to what it is we're trying to do. I'm delighted to have this chance to speak to the certain key and most influential people of NAW.

The last time we got together I could hardly speak at all. [*Laughter*] I know it's good to leave them speechless, but I don't think the speaker is the one they have in mind. But look at it this way, I could have thrown up on the front row here and— [*laughter*]—you've got to admit when I get the flu it's really dramatic. I don't want to dwell on that subject, but one, it was embarrassing, and two, in 24 hours I just felt like a million bucks again. So, I have a funny feeling that a lot of people in this country maybe understood getting the flu. But nevertheless, that's history, and I'm just delighted to be here and see you all today.

You probably read a lot about it: We are working hard on a State of the Union Message for next week. I believe that people that think as you do will be pleased with the results. I'm going to use that occasion to continue to push for the things we stand

for, and that means jobs. It means a strong and growing economy and a marketplace that's free of needless interference. It means telling Congress that we've got to hold the line on Government spending. And yes, there's a lot of pressures for more and more Federal money. That means taxpayers' money, incidentally. I still understand that point. [*Laughter*] And yet I think it is my responsibility to recognize that the deficit is outrageously large and that we have got to say no from time to time to these fantastically good-sounding but horribly detrimental spending plans. And I plan to bring that point up. We have got to hold the line on spending.

You here at NAW have been a tremendous help through the years in working for a commonsense approach to the economy. In fact, I count on the NAW's expertise in more ways than you realize, having just asked Nick Calio, an alumnus, to return to help us work on Capitol Hill. Many of you may not have met him, but he was here and then went over to NAW and will be returning to head up a very important part of our White House organization.

Let's face it, this is an election year. And so you're going to hear all kinds of proposals out there promoting a lot of gimmicks. Given the fact this country is hurting, people are hurting, you're going to see a lot of quick fixes that will supposedly turn the economy around. I don't believe we need them. I think we've got to set commonsense goals, stick with them, and then, as I say, in the State of the Union Message I'll be making specific proposals as to how to help more rapidly achieve those goals.

Any plan that truly prepares our economy for the future has got to meet five tests. One, it must stimulate investment that's necessary to create jobs. Secondly, it's got to bolster the real estate values and increase home sales. One of the disturbing things in these slow times has been the diminution of a family's fundamental balance sheet that comes from the marking down of homes and real estate. And so we've got to bolster real estate values, increase home sales. That's number two. Number three, it must give Americans confidence that they will be able to afford the cost of raising a family. That means education; we've got some bold educational reforms. It means obtaining health care. And fourth, it must increase America's capacity to compete in a global economy. And finally, number five, it must control this wasteful Government spending and got to work to bringing this deficit down.

And taken all together, these tests, I think, will separate serious proposals from the quick-fix proposals, the gimmicks. Some of my critics say they want to create jobs, and then they call for raising taxes and imposing even more mandates, centrally controlled mandates to hamstring businesses with Government redtape. Or they say they want to make the U.S. economy competitive, and then they call for building a fence around the United States of America, the old-fashioned siren's call of protection.

These gimmicks are about politics. They are not about prosperity for the United States of America. And prosperity lies in opening markets, not closing them. And I'm pleased that recently, with our trip to Asia, we've been able to make progress in that regard without resorting to protectionism.

Yesterday, for example, we signed a path-breaking agreement ensuring the U.S. computer companies will be able to compete and compete fairly for the Japanese Government, not the private sector there. We're already selling—40 percent of computers into Japan's private sector are U.S. But .4 percent, to give you an example, .4 percent of the Government-bought computers are U.S. So, it can't be a question of quality. So, yesterday we signed this path-breaking agreement that ensures the U.S. computer companies will be allowed to compete fairly for Japanese Government, for the computer market of the Government. And that's what we should be doing, beating down the barriers to our exports.

I mentioned health care. We must and will be doing something about that. I think I'll have sound proposals. But you'll also hear a lot of loose talk in an election year about health care. And I'm going to discuss this issue in depth and quite positively in

my address next week. But we ought to be clear about a couple of health care principles at the start.

First, Government efforts to centrally manage or mandate benefits produce more problems than they solve. And secondly, we must forgo approaches to the problem that cost jobs. Now this is a time to concentrate on creating jobs, not driving small businesses out of business. And that means don't overburden the small businesses with a lot of Federal mandates.

I salute the NAW for its leadership in creating HEAL, the Health Care Early [Equity] Action League, a major coalition that promotes market-based solutions to the problems in our health care system. And I look forward to working with HEAL after I announce my health care plan.

As each of you knows, what American businesses want is a fair shake from our trading partners and certainly from the Government. And let them go head-on-head in a world marketplace, and I am absolutely convinced the American companies can outthink, outwork, outcompete anyone in the world. The companies and the workers, the work force, they can do just that. And I share your faith, your undiminished faith in American business because, like you, I understand the values that have made American business the model for the whole world: Hard work, creativity, and certainly a willingness to take risks, to believe in your dreams and then make good on them.

If we build on those values and if we use them as our guiding light, this economy is going to turn around. I am not a gloom-and-doom person about the American economy. We've been through an awful lot, but this economy will turn around, particularly if we take the approach to these economic issues that I've outlined here today. We're going to lead the world. We are the undisputed leader of the world. We ought not to forget that.

There are some people in this room that are young enough to have children, young children that is. [*Laughter*] And I don't happen to fit into that category about young children, but I've got grandchildren. Some of you all have got little kids. And there's something rather nice that they're going to school, coming home, going to sleep at night, and not worrying about a nuclear conflict erupting and engulfing the whole world.

We've got a lot to be grateful for in this country. We've got a lot of problems, but we're the leader of the world, and I intend to keep it just exactly that way. We're going to whip this economic problem we're facing. We are going to continue to lead the world. We are going to stay involved at home and certainly abroad, now and well into the next century.

So, don't let the continuous pounding of what's wrong with this country obscure your fundamental confidence, your fundamental conviction, which is mine, that we are the greatest, freest country on the face of the Earth, and we're going to prevail.

Thank you all very, very much.

*Note: The President spoke at 9:20 a.m. in Room 450 of the Old Executive Office Building. In his remarks, he referred to the following association officers: Dirk Van-Dongen, president; Jay Church, chairman of the board; Jimmy Taylor, chairman-elect; and Alan Kranowitz, vice president for government relations.*

# Remarks on the Presentation of the Senior Executive Service Awards
*January 23, 1992*

Connie, thank you. And at the outset of these remarks, let me just pay my respects to Connie Newman and say what a first-class job I know she's doing at OPM. And I know that you take a lot of pride in this event, since you rose through the ranks yourself, starting, as I understand it, if my history is correct, 30 years ago as a GS–3—[*laughter*]—I've still got you beat on the age now—[*laughter*]—GS–3 clerk-typist at Interior. And look at you now. And we are very, very proud of you.

I also want to welcome Ed Derwinski, Secretary Derwinski; Acting Secretary Busey; Secretary Stone; Pat Saiki, the Administrator at SBA; Director Sessions; and so many other distinguished guests. I think I see Admiral Truly out there.

I hear that when one of the recipients was told that the speaker today would be the most important man in Washington, he said, "I thought Joe Gibbs had already left for Minneapolis." [*Laughter*] We are caught up in a frenzy here. but that should not detract from the importance of this event.

And it is a privilege for me to be over here today to congratulate some extraordinary people, you might say unsung heroes. You don't always get at the head table, don't always have your name flashing out there in lights. You may be lucky on that one. [*Laughter*] But really extraordinary people.

Vince Lombardi, you remember, he gave some pretty good advice off the field as well as on. He put it this way; he said, "The quality of a person's life is in direct proportion to their commitment to excellence."

Well, today what we're doing is honoring the lives of great quality. I am told that only one percent of our SES can receive the Distinguished Executive Award. And that means that out of more than 3 million public servants, you few here today embody the very finest qualities of leadership, dedication, personal integrity, and public service.

I reminisce that when I was growing up, my parents, particularly my dad, instilled in me a tremendous respect for the duty and obligation of public service. And I know that you share my belief that Government service is a public trust, that the highest honor we can have is to serve our country and in so doing serve our countrymen.

Good government cannot work without you, committed men and women who devote yourselves to making certain that our Government truly serves the people. Look at the contributions that you've made in this past year alone. Some of you were instrumental in one way or another in Operation Desert Storm. You share in the triumph we won for freedom abroad and, of some noted significance, of unity at home.

Some devoted your efforts to stirring economic growth here at home, creating opportunity for businesses and farmers and workers. Others dedicated your career to establishing ties abroad, bringing security and jobs to the people of this country in the process. You worked on child nutrition programs, directed the census, planned water resource projects, managed scientific research, oversaw economic analysis, helped reform the Federal pay system, managed aeronautical research, formulated human rights programs, managed veterans care, led drug investigations. The list goes on and on. In other words, through putting into practice administration programs, you touched the daily lives and shaped the future of all Americans.

And so, I am proud to participate in this program. I wanted to extend my congratulations to all for living by the words of Abraham Lincoln, who said, "I do the very best I know how, the very best I can; and I mean to keep on doing so until the end." Your country is grateful. And we thank you for your service.

And now, Connie, let's get on with the main business at hand. Thank you, and congratulations to each and every one of you.

[*At this point, the awards were presented.*]

Thank you all very much, and to all of you, congratulations. This is special, and it sends a wonderful message about the quality of our public service across the whole country. So keep it up.

*Note: The President spoke at 10:35 a.m. in Room 450 of the Old Executive Office Building. In his remarks, he referred to James B. Busey IV, Acting Secretary of Transportation; William S. Sessions, Director of the Federal Bureau of Investigation; and Richard B. Truly, Administrator of the National Aeronautics and Space Administration.*

## Remarks on Environmental Policy
### *January 23, 1992*

*The President.* Let me just say that I've had an upbeat and very impressive briefing from Administrator Bill Reilly, from Secretary Watkins, and from Chairman Mike Deland on some of our ongoing efforts to protect America's precious environment. The budget that I will release next week I think demonstrates our continuing commitment to the environment in a way that is consistent with efforts to create economic growth and to preserve and create jobs.

In EPA's budget we're providing significant increases for Superfund; implementing the Clean Air Act; for enforcing our environmental laws, and that's critical; and protecting important resources like the Great Lakes, the Gulf of Mexico, and the Chesapeake Bay: a strong program. Our budget includes specific grants to help clean up the water in some of our major coastal cities: Boston and New York on the east coast; Los Angeles, San Diego, Seattle on the west coast; and then back to Baltimore on the east coast.

This budget is going to include $200 million, double the amount enacted last year, for pollution control in the border area— Bill's just back from there, I understand— along from California across to Texas.

Secretary Jim Watkins and I have tried hard making a major effort to clean up the Federal facilities at which his Department, the Department of Energy, has manufactured nuclear weapons materials. That's been going on now for 3 years. And next week's budget will reflect a major step forward in that commitment, a $1.1 billion increase, 25 percent above last year's level. The 5.5 billion that I'll put in my budget for cleaning up Federal facilities is more than triple the amount included in the '89 budget when Secretary Watkins and I arrived.

And finally, our budget is going to increase funding in our commitment to the program known as America the Beautiful, expanding and improving our national parks, our forests, our wildlife refuges, and our recreation land. The budget is going to increase the program to about $1.9 billion, more than double the amount devoted to parks and the outdoors in 1989.

Now, included in that amount is a major expansion, from 23 million to 60 million, for our partnership with the States for the creation of State parks. Now, this is an innovative partnership approach, one that leverages the Federal dollars to get the most for every dollar. And I think you'll see this as a wave of the future in terms of guaranteeing the precious environment that means so much to our country.

So, I really want to thank Bill Reilly, thank the Secretary, thank the Chairman, Michael Deland, for coming over and to say I look forward to working with them and the other members of the Cabinet to win support for this budget on Capitol Hill and for continuing to be responsible stewards of the environment. I think we've got a positive record. We've certainly got able, committed individuals, three of whom are with me right here, working this problem. And I think this preview of coming attractions on the budget will be good news for all of us who share our concern about America's environment.

So, I think Bill, as I understand the plan, is going to go in and take some questions in the press room on this expansion of this, what I've announced here today. And I think this will be well received.

### Domestic Initiatives

*Q.* Mr. President, in recent days you've been busy on many different fronts, education, trade, now the environment——

*The President.* Recent years, yes.

*Q.* Well, recent days also, sir, and recent years, but is this at all reflective of the, perhaps, concern about dropping polls? And are you concerned about falling polls?

*The President.* No. What I think it does is show a continuing interest in domestic affairs. I've cited some history here, what's been accomplished over 3 years. But we're in an election year, and you get all kinds of charges and countercharges. And I think people realize there's been this commitment. Some of this commitment to the domestic side has been overshadowed by the fantastic changes that have taken place around the world. But I think if you take a look at my schedules and my own use of personal time, you'll see that this isn't anything new, just a continued commitment. We've made great progress. And I keep getting reassured by Bill Reilly and by Mike Deland and in his field by Jim Watkins. But we're just going to keep on. And polls go up one day and down the next.

### Unemployment Benefits

*Q.* Mr. President, 5 months ago you vetoed one unemployment extension, and you blocked the second. Now we're told that you're going to back an extension on your extension. Isn't this an election-year conversion?

*The President.* What we did before is to guarantee that the extensions were within the Federal budget because, you see, I think the American people are also concerned about the Federal Government spending too much. And what I did was stand for a program that would alleviate the suffering and would get the checks to individuals, but did it inside the budget agreement. So, it wasn't a conversion; it was fighting for what was right, the taxpayer as well as those who were hurting. And we prevailed. We prevailed in both instances. But you stay tuned for the next chapter. It will be coming up.

### Disarmament

*Q.* How about the disarmament, Mr. President? Can you tell us anything about that?

*The President.* Maybe I'll have something to say about that in the State of the Union Message.

*Note: The President spoke at 11:17 a.m. in the Oval Office at the White House.*

## Remarks Honoring the Women's World Cup Soccer Champions
*January 23, 1992*

Well, a thousand apologies for keeping such a distinguished group waiting. And thank all of you for coming here to the White House. First, may I single out the Acting Secretary of Commerce, Rock Schnabel, down here, and John Keller, the Under Secretary for Travel and Tourism. Coach Dorrance, the coach is over here, the guiding light of the women's national soccer team, and congratulations.

J.B. Marine, the U.S. Youth Soccer Association champions, are they out there? Way back there. All right. Hold up your hands. Let's see you. How about the Potomac School Panthers; I want these champs to look you over and see the competition coming up. [*Laughter*] They're the Independent School League division champs. Georgetown Visitation's team, anybody here from them? Right back there. They are DC's Independent Schools League champs. The Special Olympics Virginia champs, right over here.

Let me just say that it's great to join you in honoring a group of women who reflect a favorite American pastime; it's known as winning. [*Laughter*] Leave it to an American team to win the first FIFA world championship—world championship, I emphasize. And leave it to an American women's team to win our first world soccer championship ever. And that is a marvelous accomplishment. And someone once said that "sport was the first great separator of the sexes." For the sake of the male ego, I hope the men start catching up. [*Laughter*]

I've done a little bit of research on this gang, and it may take a while to describe the terrific lineup. But I'm told of your exploits. Of Michelle Akers-Stahl—where's Michelle? Right down there—winner of the Golden Boot Award. That has all kind of connotations for those of us in politics—[*laughter*]—but having been a former soccer player, I imagine it says something about her excellence and her commitment. She scored the winning goal, showing what Hemingway so clearly described as "grace under pressure." And then there's Carla

Werden and Debbie Belkin and Lori Henry and Joy Biefeld—where are they now? There are some of them. They gave a new meaning to the term "U.S. defense." Next, "Crazy Legs"—[*laughter*]—I hope she owns up to it. Does she? There is such a person—[*laughter*]—"Crazy Legs" Karen Jennings on offense. Julie Foudy, right here, who was found studying biology before the winning game, frogs' legs and all that kind of thing, but what a game. And finally, here's to Tracey Bates. Where's Tracey? I think she's the real reason why Arnold Schwarzenegger said he couldn't make it today. The coach calls her the "tiny terminator."

But look, for each of you, winning this cup capped a long road of sweat and sacrifice and determination. First the qualifying tournament in Haiti, where I hear you ran circles around the competition, 49 goals in 5 games. Then you trekked to China for that grueling championship tournament. I was told that many of you weren't used to some of those more exotic Chinese delicacies that Barbara and I encountered when we lived there for a year and a half—[*laughter*]—duck feet, snakes, all of this kind of thing. These wise guys invented their own slogan, "Come to China; we take off weight." [*Laughter*]

But then for the matches in the championship, you took on tough opposition: Edging Sweden, 3 to 2; upsetting Germany—maybe you didn't think it was an upset; sportswriters played it as that—5 to 2. You beat the injuries; you beat the odds. And then on November 30th, you proved yourselves again, ousting Norway for the World Cup. No wonder Michelle Akers-Stahl said, "This team never gives up." You showed how America can outscore, outfight, and outcompete any nation we're up against.

That kind of spirit made you champions. The American spirit is proud, not arrogant, confident, determined, and victorious. I remember the day when America's athletic excellence was limited to perhaps baseball and football in the eyes of the world. Well, today, Americans are taking over everywhere from sumo to soccer. And as proof of just how far soccer has come in this country, the U.S. will proudly host the 1994 World Cup championship.

So, let me just say to today's champions, world champions: Your victory is an inspiration, no matter what sport. Your victory is an inspiration to all our athletes, male and female, young and old. And thank you for winning one for America. You've made us all very, very proud.

I get accused in my job of having perhaps too keen an interest in sports. Well, too bad. [*Laughter*] I think it does a lot for the real

spirit of this country. And certainly this team has made a contribution to the real spirit of this country. You've made us very, very proud. So, bless you all, and thanks for being with us today.

*Note: The President spoke at 2:42 p.m. in Room 450 of the Old Executive Office Building. In his remarks, he referred to Anson Dorrance, coach of the U.S. National Women's Soccer Team, and the Federation Internationale de Football Association (FIFA).*

# Remarks to the Young Astronaut Council and a Teleconference With the Crew of Space Shuttle *Discovery*
*January 24, 1992*

*The President.* Thank you all very much. Please be seated, and thanks for that warm welcome. The Vice President and I are just delighted to be with you. And of course, I might say I'm so proud of the leadership that the Vice President is giving in this all-out effort to support the space program, strengthen it, build on it. And this is a great day.

Let me say to Wendell Butler, the CEO of Young Astronauts, that we appreciate all your good work. I am also so proud that Dick Truly is here, Admiral Dick Truly, the first astronaut to serve as Administrator of NASA. All told, well, you've seen them, there are 23 veteran astronauts here today. And I'm told this is one of the largest gatherings of space explorers ever at the White House.

Our thoughts also are with seven other astronauts who right now are orbiting the Earth in a space shuttle mission. We're proud of all these men and women. They take risks; they do it with great courage, and they do it with great determination and dedication.

I'm also glad to see so many boys and girls here, from kindergarten through ninth, in this Young Astronauts program. And as President, I've set a goal that involves you young people, and my goal is for young

Americans like you who are in grade school right now to travel to Mars someday. New travels in space will give us answers to some of the things that children wonder about. I might add, many adults who contemplate our great universe wonder about these same things, too.

The other day I heard what one 5-year-old wonders about. One of my staff members asked his 5-year-old kid if we should build new spaceships and send people to the Moon again. And the kid said, "Yes, of course, we should." His father said, "Well, why? Why should we send them to the Moon?" He said, "That's easy," the kid said. "It's to see if there's any Martians there." [*Laughter*]

Well, we can chuckle about that, but the kid got it about right. As most of you young astronauts know, we've challenged America to go back to the Moon to stay, and then onward to Mars. And sending people back to the Moon for more experience in an environment different from ours is the first step on the journey to explore the gigantic rift valleys and mountains of Mars.

When we break through barriers of the unknown we not only help ourselves, we learn a lot more about ourselves. And when we reach our goal of sending men and women to Mars, we can find out the answer to that little 5-year-old's wondering about life on other planets. We can learn whether we can extract air and water from materials on Mars to sustain life. We can look for clues on Mars not only to teach us how the Earth developed but also about the wellspring of life itself.

And pushing forward into space already is helping us here and now. More and more, the new jobs for people of your parents' generation are being provided by our space programs. Revenues from American commercial space programs alone grew by 14 percent in 1991, and this year they're projected to grow by 20 percent. The commercial space business has grown so far and so fast that it now takes in about as much money each year as all the receipts at the movie theaters all over the United States. If this trend continues, the celestial stars will be getting more attention than the Hollywood stars, and that might be all right. [*Laughter*]

America now exports $1 billion a year in commercial space goods and services. Those exports alone translate into jobs for 20,000 Americans. Real progress is happening almost faster than we can imagine. Navigation satellites that helped guide our troops in Desert Storm just a year ago now help hikers and fishermen and surveyors and motorists find their way. Personal navigation receivers now help us manage our forests and wetlands, speed the shipment of goods on our own highways.

Ten years from now the older kids here will be finished with college, some of you maybe even finished with graduate school. And when that day comes, when you're ready to start careers and families, I hope many of you will be prepared to become the movers and shakers in our space program. It's up to your parents and grandparents and the Congressmen they elect to keep us on track for this promising future of space exploration and commercial space enterprises.

To stress how important this is, a few weeks from now I will formally direct the establishment of a new national space exploration office led by NASA and including scientific talent from our Defense and Energy Departments and other agencies as well. Space exploration should be and will

be a national effort. And I should again state that Dan Quayle's leadership as Chairman of the National Space Council has been absolutely vital to the renewed focus and momentum of our space programs.

When I send my annual budget up to Congress next week, it is going to mark the third straight year that I've called for a real increase in spending on our civil space program. And this includes full funding for Space Station *Freedom*, $2.25 billion, an increase of 11 percent. Space Station is back on track and on schedule. Last year we had an honest debate with those in the Congress who wanted to kill Space Station. We won because the American people agree that Space Station *Freedom* is not only a very valuable scientific program but it is essential to our destiny as a pioneering Nation, a pioneering Nation in space.

And I know many are concerned about the balance between science and exploration in our space program, and the budget that I will propose next week will not shortchange science. Space science will remain more than 23 percent of NASA's program, will increase by 10 percent over the current year. But America's destiny must include manned exploration. So my budget increases funding for technologies we need to send man beyond Earth's orbit. And that includes propulsion technologies, life support technologies, two new missions to complete the mapping of the Moon. And finally the budget will include a dramatic expansion of two exciting new programs: $250 million to triple funding for our new launch system, to develop a new family of rockets for the 21st century, and 80 million for the National Aerospace Plane which may one day enable direct flights from Earth to orbit.

For you to fulfill your dreams of space exploration when you become adults, we must make a new public investment in our space program now. And I'm asking Americans to make a farsighted commitment, one that looks dozens of years and millions of miles beyond the recession and the other things that tend to preoccupy us today.

And I'm challenging you young people, too: Start your preparations for tomorrow's new age of space exploration right now.

Keep that pledge you've made in joining the Young Astronauts Council. Make yourselves better and better students of math and science. Make the U.S.A. the leading country in the world in early education for math and science. Make your families proud. Make your teachers proud. Give your very best, and America will be better for it.

In doing this, you not only help our space program, you'll also help us meet one of the most demanding goals that I've set for our schools. It aims to involve parents more with our schools, to revolutionize our schools with higher standards and better performance by the start of the new century.

Among the goals of America 2000 is to make America the world leader in math and science education. If we want to reach the Moon and Mars, we've got to aim high. And if you share my aim of making America's students and teachers the best in the world and if you share my goal of sending American men and women to explore Mars and if you share my dream of discovering the unknown to make our lives better, you'll see it will require time and effort and study and money.

And it's going to take teamwork across the years. That includes parents, your parents and then my generation's. Most of all, for a long time to come, it will call for your own best efforts. And I applaud this Council for making a positive difference with America's children. The Council is committed to our America 2000 education goals and is playing a true leadership role in our observance of 1992 to celebrate exploration, not only as the 500th anniversary of Christopher Columbus' voyage but also as International Space Year.

Barbara and I are very proud to serve as honorary cochairmen of the Young Astronauts Council. And it's a pleasure to recognize three dedicated Americans who have been honored as 1992 Young Astronaut Teachers of the Year: Glenda Parker of Denver, North Carolina, right here; Arthur Perschino, Arthur, from Norwalk, Connecticut; and Karyn Sotero from right here in Washington, DC.

And now I understand that three young astronauts, Russell Frisby, Rachel Heck-

mann, and Conner Sabatino, have something they're going to give to me. See, this is a very nice ending to this thing. So, you guys come on up here.

[*At this point, the young people presented a gift to the President. Following the presentation and announcement of the NASA/Young Astronauts Council poster contest to commemorate International Space Year, the President began a teleconference with the "Discovery" crew.*]

*The President.* Are we on the air, I mean, way out there on the air? Colonel Grabe, can you hear me?

*Commander Grabe.* Yes, sir, Mr. President, we hear you loud and clear.

*The President.* What happened? Can you guys hear me up there all right?

*Commander Grabe.* We hear you loud and clear, Mr. President.

*The President.* Loud and clear. Well, let me just say to Commander Grabe and all the rest of you all, I'm here with a lot of the young astronauts and some of the older astronauts, as a matter of fact—[*laughter*]—four of the crews, here in the White House complex. And we just called up to wish you well. The Vice President is with me. Admiral Truly is with me. And we just want to get from you all how it's doing down there.

A lot of these kids want to get going and get out to Mars. Have you got any advice, first of all, for these young guys here, young kids, boys and girls?

*Commander Grabe.* Well, certainly, Mr. President. For any Young Astronauts that want to pursue a career as an astronaut, they ought to be emphasizing math and science in their studies and just doing as well as they can. It's a long, hard road to get there, and it takes a little luck along the way as well. But it's certainly worth the effort.

*The President.* We've been talking a little bit about the contribution that these journeys make to science. Can you tell us a little bit, in layman's terms, please, about the experiments that you all are conducting?

*Commander Grabe.* Let me turn that over to Bob Thagard. He's our payload commander here on my right.

*Commander Thagard.* Well, Mr. President, taking the experiments to orbit is an excellent way to do experiments in some areas of science, and it makes this whole journey well worthwhile. The two principal things or areas that come to mind are physiology, both plant and animal, and crystal growing and other material science experiments. And we have some 55 experiments, I think, in the IML complement. Most of those are working even as we speak. And it is our plan to do some more TV, some more explanation later on about some more details of that science.

*The President.* Well, that is very interesting. Now, if you guys have a couple more minutes, we don't want to detract you from all this experimentation, but it might be fun if one of these young astronauts, or maybe a couple, would like to—here comes my man. [*Laughter*] He's back. This guy just gave a great speech here. Tell them your name, and see if you've got a question for them.

*Q.* My name is Russell Frisby, and here's my question: What's it like in zero gravity?

*The President.* Did you get that? He wanted to know what it's like in zero gravity.

*Commander Grabe.* Yes, sir, we understood the question, what's it like in zero gravity. And I'll turn that over to Bill Readdy, who's on Bob's left.

*Astronaut Readdy.* It's great, just floating around and everything. And a lot of things it just makes a whole lot easier, besides from putting your pants on both legs at the same time. [*Laughter*] It's easy to translate back and forth. It makes it a whole lot easier to do a lot of the science because any particular orientation you choose works the same as any other.

*The President.* That makes it all very clear. [*Laughter*] Thank you.

Any other? Come on, you come up and ask one. This is a rare opportunity. Fire away.

*Q.* I wanted to know what was your favorite experiment you've taken up so far?

*Commander Grabe.* That sounds like a good question for Steve Oswald, our pilot, to answer. Steve's over here on Bill's left.

*Astronaut Oswald.* Actually, I guess I'm not sure that, being in the front of the bus, we're working the experiments all that hard. But we've got the I-90 camera aboard. And Bill and Ron and I have been having a great time taking those movies that you see on the big screen. And we're taking pictures right now for a movie that will be coming out here within a year or two.

*Q.* I would like to know, which one do you like better——

*Astronaut Oswald.* ——the camera up— [*inaudible*]—I can just show that to you, how big it is.

*Astronaut Readdy.* You're asking about what's great about zero G. Well, this camera on Earth probably weighs about, oh, 110, 120 pounds. Even a big moose like Os has trouble hefting it. But you can see you can quite easily do it with just fingers.

*Astronaut Oswald.* The camera probably weighs as much as Roberta, who's manipulating it right now, and you can see she has no trouble at all with it.

*The President.* That's great. Do you have one?

*Commander Grabe.* Mr. President, the one crew member——

*Q.* Which one do you like better, being in space or being on Earth?

*Commander Grabe.* I'd like to introduce our Canadian payload specialist, Roberta Bondar, who will be glad to answer that one.

*Dr. Bondar.* Actually, living both in space and on the Earth really makes you appreciate the good and the bad of both. I think right now we're enjoying very much the limited opportunity we've had so far with being up here. We've certainly enjoyed looking back at the Earth during our brief moments when we're not in the lab working the sciences. And we're really looking forward to our return to Earth to bring back all the scientific information and all the enthusiasm and experience that we've gained in this flight.

So, for all of us, I think right now we're just enjoying where we are, and we're going to be enjoying where we're going to be when we come back. And I think it's just great to have had this opportunity to be assigned with this great crew.

*The President.* Dr. Bondar, this is not a young astronaut, this is the President speaking now. But I just want to say how pleased we are that you, representing Canada, are a part, a fundamental part of this. I think it's a wonderful thing, and I think in a wonderful way it shows the strength of ties between our two great countries.

So, I understand the Prime Minister, my friend Brian Mulroney, called. Did he actually get through the other day?

*Dr. Bondar.* That was right about the time we were having our briefing just near launch time. And instead, I had a lovely telegram from him, and he wished us all well and Godspeed.

*The President.* Well, keep up the good work. Now, have you got time for one more question? We've got a real eager one right here. Front of the line. Here we go.

*Q.* I wonder how you feel in space.

*The President.* They're trying to decide here.

*Commander Grabe.* The question was, how do we feel in space?

*The President.* Yes.

*Commander Grabe.* Well, in space, it takes a little bit of time to get used to it. When you first get up, you might feel just the slightest bit queasy or so. But by about today—this is our third day in space—we're beginning to adapt pretty well. I think you can see we all feel pretty comfortable up here. So after you get over the initial adjustment, you can live in space quite well and do things that you do on Earth.

*The President.* I have a rather technical question. What happens if you get the flu in space? [*Laughter*]

*Commander Grabe.* Some of the older as-

tronauts—[*inaudible*]—anything that can give you the enthusiasm a kid has, has got to be a great experience. And I feel like I'm about 12.

*Q.* What planets have you seen?

*The President.* What planets have you seen?

*Commander Grabe.* Well, of course, we've got the world's greatest view of our world. But on some of our night passes we can see Saturn and Jupiter and Mars and Venus. It's really spectacular up here. Hope we can go to Mars here one of these days.

*The President.* Well, we're going to keep trying to get this program geared up to do just that. And maybe, just maybe, Colonel, one of these kids here today will be a part of that. Maybe sooner, maybe later. But I'll bet one of them will be a part of that mission.

But listen, I'm told we've got to run on. I've got a lot of eager questioners, but unfortunately, I guess we don't have the time. But we certainly want to wish you well. Your fellow astronauts are standing here quietly in the shadows, and I know that they are wishing you well for a successful conclusion of this productive journey.

You have our blessings and our support, and keep up the fine work. You're on the cutting edge, and you're setting a great example for the rest of our country, the rest of the world. Congratulations, and thanks for taking the time out.

*Note: The President spoke at 3 p.m. in Room 450 of the Old Executive Office Building.*

# Teleconference Remarks to the National Association of Home Builders
## *January 24, 1992*

*The President.* Thank you so much. And Mark, thank you for those very kind words. And I wish I were there in person, but from a distance, hello to Roger Glunt and Tommy Thompson and Martin Perlman and Kent Colton; Jay Buchert, your incoming president; and to all of you celebrating the

golden anniversary of the National Association of Home Builders.

I heard via the grapevine that we were promised a daytime fireworks display. So I will give this my very best shot, and after Mark's enthusiastic endorsement there, welcome there, I must say I've got a tough job to fulfill here.

First, though, Barbara and I wanted to remind you that we're doing our part for homebuilding and remodeling, thanks to a little rough weather back in Kennebunkport, Maine. So we want to be a part of this rebuilding. But there's been more than a little rough weather in your industry. I heard what you said there, Mark, and I've heard it for a long time. Back in December, I met with Mark and Kent at the White House. And to you members there, let me just say we talked about the tough times you've experienced. These men were both very articulate. We agreed on the need for strong action to get this economy moving again.

The housing industry has been hit hard. And you've been pinched by the credit crunch, hurt by first-time homebuyers forced by economic circumstances to defer their shot at the American dream and homeowners who have watched their equity erode.

On the credit front, we've been working hard to get the message out to lending institutions and the regulatory community that sound banks make sound loans. And I am also pleased to see interest rates down, lower than they've been since the late seventies.

There's a pent-up demand for new housing that promises a strong comeback, one that will bring homebuyers back into the market and have homebuilders working overtime. But no issue right now matters more than the state of our economy. Next Tuesday, I'm going to take my economic action plan to the American people in the State of the Union Message. And without tipping my hand today, I can say that some of the reforms that I want to see are geared specifically to get the housing market back on its feet.

I pledged as President that we'd see an increase of one million in the number of new American homeowners, and I'm proud to say we've reached that goal. And I'm convinced our housing initiatives will help even more Americans reach their dream.

One way we'll succeed is by breaking down the barriers to affordable housing. Jay and Roger served on my Advisory Commission on Regulatory Barriers. Many of the

recommendations in what the Commission called the NIMBY report, Not In My Backyard, have been built into the 1993 budget. I'll be calling for prompt action by the Congress because it's even more urgent we get these critical reforms through Congress now. So count on it. I'm going to hit the line again, push hard to turn solid proposals into policy. And I hope I can count on your strong support to help me get the job done.

As for the rest of my progrowth plan, you've got to stay tuned for Tuesday. But I can say right now, by way of a coming attraction, that any growth package worth the name should pass the following five tests: First, it must stimulate the investment necessary to create jobs. Second—and this points up the vital importance of your industry—it must bolster real estate values and increase home sales. And third, it must give Americans confidence that the costs of health care, providing for their kids' education, and raising a family will be affordable. And fourth, it must increase America's capacity to compete in the global economy. And then fifth and finally, it must control wasteful Government spending and bring the Federal deficit under control.

So, please listen, and please hear me out in the State of the Union. I will avoid, and I'll be frank about this one, the quick political fixes that cause the deficit to skyrocket and cause long-term interest rates to go right through the roof. I'm confident that we have a sound plan, the best plan, to get this economy growing again. And I am absolutely certain that we will get this economy turned around. I plan to do what Mark says: Take that same leadership we used in Desert Storm, bring this country together, and get the job done. And I am sure that once again it is your industry, it is the housing industry, that will lead the way to a strong and steady recovery.

So, good luck to you all. We've listened to your leaders. We appreciate the support from so many people there. And I am going to do my level-best to lead this country to a vigorous recovery.

Now, I guess I'd better stop there and be glad to take some questions. And thanks for your hospitality.

*Q.* Thank you, Mr. President. You are a

"take charge" kind of President, and you have been a tremendous asset to this country and the world. We, the homebuilders, support you continuously. Your remarks are excellent, and we are ready for you to take charge in this State of the Union. And we're going to go hand-in-hand down the path with you to try to get your programs implemented. We think it very, very important that housing leads this economy back to the great state that it was before. And we think that together we can do this.

The question I have, Mr. President, is: NAHB has suggested a number of proposals to stimulate housing-led economic recovery, including a tax credit and use of IRA's for first-time homebuyers and reinstatement of passive losses and capital gains tax. Is there any hope that any of these will be included in your State of the Union?

*The President.* Hey, listen, I will not be betraying any secrets to say that the answer to that question is a resounding affirmative. I hope you'll let me off the hook if I don't respond to each and every one of those points, but I think you're going to be happy with the message in that regard.

You have known, and I don't say this as targeting what I'm going to say, but you've known of my commitment to capital gains. I've been hit, as you know, for a capital gains tax cut as a tax cut for the rich. It isn't any such thing. And families benefit. I'm worried, Barbara's worried about the decline in the American family. One thing that strengthened it is owning their own home. One thing that puts some value under a person's home is a capital gains differential. And so I am committed on that one, and you can bet that that's going to be there.

The others, I think you'll be happy; I'd like to stop right there. But the reason I give you encouragement, without going into which I will accept and can propose and won't propose, is that these initiatives that you've talked about here, it's not a quick fix; it's not something that's going to just spread money around in a political year. They will stimulate investment. And that's what—there's a crying need for investment and savings in this country. And let me just say philosophically, I feel very comfortable with those initiatives that you

have outlined there. But you'll have to excuse me if I don't give away absolutely everything that's going to be in this message.

*Q.* Mr. President, you talked just a moment ago about the credit crunch, and we truly appreciate your personal work on behalf of the credit crunch and all of the work that has been done in that area.

In the meetings I've attended in the last couple of days here with all of the builders that have gathered, we're now confident that the economic stimulus package will contain provisions to let housing lead this economy forward.

I think the big concern here is: Will the credit be available for the builders to then build those homes? And the feedback we're getting from the builders here today, Mr. President, is that despite our combined efforts, you working hard, your administration working hard, and us working hard, the banks and examiners still aren't getting the message out according to the builders.

Is there anything that can be done more, Mr. President? Is there anything else we can do to get this message out? Our fear is that without it, we're not going to see an economic recovery. And as you said so well, sound banks should make sound loans now.

*The President.* I would welcome suggestions from you all after your meetings finish as to what in addition we might do.

Let me say this. First place, I think the regulators do have some responsibility. I think everyone would agree that we got into kind of a go-go period of excess over the past few years and some loans were made that should have been questioned at the time and that weren't. And we're paying an enormous price. I might say that I take some pride that not one single depositor has lost money, but it's taken an awful lot of money to bail out some questionable loans.

What I'm about to say, I am not suggesting that the Government does not have some obligation in our regulatory authorities for the soundness of the banking system and the S&L system. I frankly think that there has been an overreaction. And we have gotten the Treasury to bring into Baltimore the other day well in excess of 500 regulators and tell them that what we're looking for is balance. What we're looking for is certainly not to go down the path that we went down before but to stop impeding progress and kind of putting a damper on this concept that good banks should make good loans.

We have sent out bulletin after bulletin to the regulating community out there. I have convened meetings with the Chairman of the Fed, Bill Taylor; others from the various Agencies; the Office of Thrift Supervision, saying, let's find a reasoned approach.

Frankly, I think the pendulum has swung at times too far over in terms of dampening the enthusiasm that these lending institutions sometimes should have, and that they're almost afraid in some areas to make loans. So, I hope that the programs we have in effect of trying to work for the balance is good.

I'll be honest with you, we are encountering some resistance. The Office of the Comptroller head was held up, because they thought he was lightening up on the regulatory burden, by a couple of Senators who leaned over too far the other way in favor of labeling what we were doing as forbearance. In their view, that meant too little regulation. I've got to do a better job with Congress, getting them to understand that the excesses of regulation are bad.

On a fundamental point, I am firmly—I am of the conviction that the lower interest rates have things ready now for a good recovery. At some point those interest rates definitely will translate into a much better situation for the homebuyer, for the developer. And some of that hasn't taken place because of what you're talking about. I think banks have taken the difference now and tried to strengthen their balance sheets. They're getting stronger, and I think that's probably a good thing.

So, we will continue to struggle against this concept of overregulation. Some report to me arrogance on the part of some regulators, and we're trying very hard to sensitize these people. We will continue to work hard for a financial reform package that is long overdue. We've got to bring these banks and lending institutions, through a change in the law, back up now to 1992 and not have it back in the 1930's somewhere. We got stiffed by Congress on trying to get that banking reform bill through. And I'm going to try again on that one. I think that will help your industry very much.

And again, the third point, less regulation, banking reform, financial reform, and then, of course, this whole concept of interest rates and inflation being down, setting the base for a sound recovery for this country.

And I don't want to be accused of being too optimistic because there are still some very, very troubling signs around. But I believe that these things I've mentioned here will inevitably contribute to an upturn in this economy and an upturn in this industry that is absolutely essential. I believe that homebuilding will lead the recovery. It's not going to be a lagging industry. It will be a lead industry. I believe the ingredients are there. And I hope that the proposals I make in the State of the Union will guarantee, if I can get them through Congress, will guarantee the recovery will be right around the corner and not way down the road.

Thank you again. And if there's another one, fine. Otherwise, I'll let you go back to work. But send the suggestions; if you have specifics, send them along, Jay.

*Q.* Thank you, Mr. President, for taking time out of your busy schedule. Ladies and gentlemen, let's give the President of the United States a great thank you.

*The President.* Good luck to you all.

*Note: The President spoke at 3:34 p.m. via satellite from Room 459 of the Old Executive Office Building to the National Association of Home Builders annual convention and exposition in Las Vegas, NV. In his remarks, he referred to the following association officers: Mark E. Tipton, immediate past president; Roger Glunt, first vice president; Tommy Thompson, vice president and treasurer; Martin Perlman, a past president; Kent Colton, executive vice president; and Jay Buchert, president.*

## Letter to Congressional Leaders Transmitting a Report on International Action to Curtail Exports to Iraq
*January 24, 1992*

*Dear Mr. Chairman:*

Enclosed is the second semiannual report on the steps taken by other nations to curtail the export of goods, services, and technologies to Iraq which might contribute to, or enhance, Iraq's nuclear, biological, chemical, and ballistic missile capability. This report is submitted pursuant to section 586J(c) of the Foreign Operations, Export Financing, and Related Programs Appropriations Act, 1991 (Public Law 101–513).

Sincerely,

GEORGE BUSH

*Note: Identical letters were sent to Robert C. Byrd, chairman of the Senate Appropriations Committee; Claiborne Pell, chairman of the Senate Foreign Relations Committee; Jamie L. Whitten, chairman of the House Appropriations Committee; and Dante B. Fascell, chairman of the House Foreign Affairs Committee.*

## Statement by Press Secretary Fitzwater on the Appointment of W. Henson Moore as Deputy Chief of Staff to the President
*January 24, 1992*

The President intends to appoint W. Henson Moore, of Louisiana, as Deputy Chief of Staff to the President. Mr. Moore, 52, currently serves as Deputy Secretary of Energy, a position he has held since 1989. As Deputy Chief of Staff in the White House, Mr. Moore will assist Chief of Staff Samuel Skinner in directing the day-to-day operations of the White House staff.

Mr. Moore has served as a Member of the U.S. House of Representatives from the Sixth Congressional District in Louisiana, 1975–1987. He has served on the Energy and Commerce Committee, Ways and Means Committee, and the Budget Committee and has worked extensively in both energy and tax policy. Mr. Moore has also

been a partner with the law firm of Sutherland, Asbill and Brennan, an Atlanta/Washington-based firm, since January 1987. He was also a Republican candidate for U.S. Senate in 1986. Between 1987 and 1988, he also served as one of three American Commissioners of a Panama Canal Consultative Committee created by the Panama Canal Treaty.

Mr. Moore graduated from Louisiana State University (B.A., 1961; M.A., 1973) and Louisiana State University Law School (J.D., 1965). He served in the U.S. Army, 1965–1967. He was born October 4, 1939, in Lake Charles, LA. He is married to the former Carolyn Ann Cherry of Franklin, LA, and has three children.

## Appointment of Sherrie S. Rollins as Assistant to the President for Public Liaison and Intergovernmental Affairs
*January 24, 1992*

The President today announced his intention to appoint Sherrie S. Rollins to be Assistant to the President for Public Liaison

and Intergovernmental Affairs.

Since 1990, Ms. Rollins has served as director of news information for ABC News in New York. Prior to this, she was Assistant Secretary for Public Affairs at the Department of Housing and Urban Development, 1989–1990. She has also served as vice president of communications for the Oliver Carr Co. in Washington, DC, 1985–1989. Ms. Rollins was assistant press secretary for the 1984 Reagan-Bush campaign and director of media support for the 1984 and 1988

Republican National Conventions. In addition, she has served as executive director of the Business and Professional Association of Georgetown, 1981–1984.

Ms. Rollins graduated from the University of Virginia, receiving a bachelor of arts degree in communications. She was born June 11, 1958, in Roanoke, VA. She is married and resides in Alexandria, VA.

# Nomination of Fred T. Goldberg, Jr., To Be Assistant Secretary of the Treasury for Tax Policy
*January 24, 1992*

The President today announced his intention to nominate Fred T. Goldberg, Jr., of Missouri, to be an Assistant Secretary of the Treasury for Tax Policy. He would succeed Kenneth W. Gideon.

Since 1989 Mr. Goldberg has served as Commissioner of the Internal Revenue Service at the Department of the Treasury in Washington, DC. Prior to this, Mr. Goldberg served as a partner with the law firm of Skadden, Arps, Slate, Meagher & Flom,

1986–1989; Chief Counsel for the Internal Revenue Service, 1984–1986; and a partner with the law firm of Latham, Watkins & Hills, 1982–1984. From 1981 to 1982, Mr. Goldberg served as Assistant to the Commissioner of the Internal Revenue Service.

Mr. Goldberg graduated from Yale University (B.A., 1969; J.D., 1973). He was born October 15, 1947, in St. Louis, MO. Mr. Goldberg is married, has five children, and resides in Potomac, MD.

# Nomination of Shirley D. Peterson To Be Commissioner of Internal Revenue
*January 24, 1992*

The President today announced his intention to nominate Shirley D. Peterson, of Maryland, to be Commissioner of Internal Revenue, Department of the Treasury. She would succeed Fred T. Goldberg, Jr.

Currently Ms. Peterson serves as Assistant Attorney General for the Tax Division at the Department of Justice. From 1969 to 1989, she served as a partner with the law

firm of Steptoe & Johnson in Washington, DC.

Ms. Peterson graduated from Bryn Mawr College (A.B., 1963) and New York University School of Law (LL.B., 1967). She was born September 3, 1941, in Holly, CO. Ms. Peterson is married, has two children, and resides in Bethesda, MD.

# Remarks at the Annual Convention of the National Religious Broadcasters
*January 27, 1992*

Thank you for that wonderfully warm welcome. And to President Dave Clark, may I thank you, sir; Brandt Gustavson, the executive director. And let me salute your leadership of the NRB. I understand that former Secretary Dole was to be here; I don't know that she is. I know FCC Chairman Sykes is. And I see, of course, two good, respected friends, Jim Dobson and Billy Graham.

Ladies and gentlemen, this marks the fifth time that I've had the honor of addressing the annual convention of the National Religious Broadcasters. A year ago we met in the first week of a struggle to protect what is right and true. And I came before you to talk of what was not a Christian or Jewish war, not a Moslem war. It was a just war. And in the Persian Gulf we fought for good versus evil. It was that clear to me: right versus wrong, dignity against oppression. And America stood fast so that liberty could stand tall.

Today I want to thank you for helping America, as Christ ordained, to be "a light unto the world." Your support honored the finest soldiers, the finest sailors, marines, airmen, and coastguardsmen that any nation has ever known. And what they did in war, let us now do in peace. Just as our forces fought to defend all of what is best about America, we need you to help instill the traditional values that make life and liberty worth defending.

Let me begin with some good news for modern man. According to Gallup, the Gallup surveys, no society is more religious than the United States of America. Seven in ten Americans believe in life after death; 8 in 10, that God works miracles. Nine in ten Americans pray. And more than 90 percent believe in God, to which I say, thank God. I wish it were 100 percent.

Now, I know this is an election year. And I don't know about Damascus, but this primary season we're seeing a lot of conversions on the road to New Hampshire. [*Laughter*] But I don't want this to be a partisan speech, and I appreciated so much what David Clark said about values. I want to speak of the values that I know you all believe in, values which sustain America, values that are always in fashion.

The first value is not simply American but universal. And I refer to the sanctity of life. I will stand on the side of choosing life.

Next comes a value which gives each life meaning: the self-reliance central to the dignity of work. Go to the barrios of San Antonio or the suburbs of St. Paul, and there you will find people who ask for only what our forefathers had, the same opportunity which helped us brave independence, push back the wilderness, win two World Wars, and create the highest standard of living in the history of man. The Bible reminds us, "By thy works shall ye know them." What we must do is give working Americans that level playing field to keep us as rich in goods as we have been blessed in spirit.

Tomorrow I'm giving a speech. [*Laughter*] The State of the Union Address will detail how we can nurture creativity as old as 1776, harness it to the needs of a new American century. Remember, to this day the only footsteps on the Moon are American footsteps. The only flag on the Moon is the Stars and Stripes. The knowledge that put it there is stamped "Made in the U.S.A." Yes, the world looks to us to lead, and lead we will. Americans can outwork, outproduce, outcompete any nation in the world. And we must do all we can to further that end. And I will do my level-best. And I need your help.

The next value I speak of must be forever cast in stone. I speak of decency, the moral courage to say what is right and condemn what is wrong. And we need a Nation closer to "The Waltons" than "The Simpsons"— [*laughter*]—an America that rejects the incivility, the tide of incivility, and the tide of intolerance. We see this tide in the naked epithet and in the code words that play to our worst prejudices. We see it when

151

people ridicule religion and religious leaders, like the group which desecrated communion hosts on the steps of St. Patrick's Cathedral. We see this tide of incivility and intolerance in bigotry, in discrimination, and anti-Semitism.

Have they no decency? Have they no honor? Have they no respect for the rights of others? I will continue to speak out against these apostles of hate who poison our kids' minds and debase their souls. There is no place, whatever our views, there is no place in America for religious prejudice, for anti-Semitism, or racial prejudice.

This, then, brings me to a fourth value crucial to America: the belief in the family, the foundation of our strength. Take my kids, for example. Having helped put them through college, I remember receiving letters from them. Barbara does, too. And there would always be a P.S. at the bottom. It was those three words that said so much about the bond between parents at home and kids at school, "Please send money." [*Laughter*]

But this one is true. The other day I was visited by the leaders of the National League of Cities, mayors from big cities and small, liberal and conservative, Republican and Democrat. And they were unanimous in their view that the major underlying problem in our cities is the decline of the American family. And they are right; too often, family is under siege. Each one of us, parents, preachers, politicians, and teachers, must do our part to defend it. I do not want one single action that I take as President to weaken the American family. And I want to strengthen it in every way that I can. Every law that is passed should guard against weakening the family.

And that is why I insisted that the child care bill that I signed in 1990 allow parents, not bureaucrats, to decide how to care for their children. I refused to see the option of a religious-based child care restricted or eliminated.

Our national education strategy—we call it America 2000, and it is an exciting program—helps the family by enhancing parental involvement in education, insisting that choice include both private and public schools. I do not believe it is unconstitutional for schoolkids to have the same choice that I got under the GI bill or that college kids now get under the Pell grant or that ex-servicemen now get under the Montgomery bill.

Last week, I announced another policy to strengthen the family, expanding the preschool program to serve all those 4-year-olds who are eligible, the largest funding increase in the history of project Head Start. And when this is enacted, we will be much closer to achieving one of our six national educational goals, that every schoolchild should start school ready to learn.

And finally, families will stay together only if drugs do not drive them apart. Winning the war on drugs means waging war on crime. Now, we've made the commitment. And altogether, the new Federal budget that I'll introduce 2 days from now will increase spending to combat crime by $1.2 billion, to a total of almost $16 billion. Now that's nearly 60 percent higher than when I took office in 1989.

My new budget will provide a half a billion dollars for an initiative that we call "Weed and Seed." Not enthralled with the name, but listen to what it does. [*Laughter*] Today our very able Attorney General, Bill Barr, point man in this new operation, is spelling out all its details. But let me say this much right now. "Weed and Seed" works this way. First, we join Federal, State, and local forces to weed out the gang leaders, the violent criminals, the drug dealers who plague our neighborhoods. And when we break their deadly grip, we follow up with part two: We seed those neighborhoods with expanded educational opportunities, job training, health care, and other social services. But the key to the "seed" concept will be jobs-generating initiatives such as enterprise zones to give people who call these neighborhoods home something to hope for.

There is more to do to win the final victory in our war on drugs. We are making progress. We are winning. Over the past 4 years, marijuana, crack, and cocaine use has definitively declined. And what's more, today kids aged 9 to 12 are the most anti-drug group in America. The highest at-risk group remains 13- to 17-year-olds. But last year, for the first time, 13-year-olds mirrored the behavior of preteenagers.

Drugs affect a multitude of issues. They contribute to AIDS; they contribute to homelessness, shattering families and futures, hopes and dreams. And that's why, literally, we should thank God for the drug use decline. The drop in use doesn't just prove we were right in our assault on substance use, it shows how we can achieve drugs' unconditional surrender. We will triumph through tough enforcement and through education, increasing awareness of the damage drugs do.

And in that spirit, let us resolve to treat the victims of AIDS and drug abuse with compassion and caring. Let us redouble our efforts to help with treatment and with education. That will help eliminate the risks involved.

Over the last 4 years, more kids talked about drugs with their parents and teachers. Another reason for drug use decline has been America's print and electronic media, the major source of drug information and the primary influencer on drug use, especially among the young. Together, they have helped reawaken America's conscience which, in turn, inspires America's greatness.

Later today I will unveil our fourth national drug control strategy to build on these beginnings. It will say no to drugs. It will say yes to life. But it cannot just be done by the Government. To stop drug use will require caring and community, above all, abundant love.

Let me tell you, remind you, for some of you, tell you others a story. Once, a great First Lady, Pat Nixon, toured a medical center. And she stopped to embrace a little girl that was blinded by rubella. And for a few minutes, she talked to the girl and held her close. And then later, someone told her that the child was deaf as well as blind. And Pat answered that she had known that. "But she knows what love is," Mrs. Nixon said. "She can feel love."

America's love is conveyed in many ways: in what we oppose, injustice and tyranny; in what we support, the inalienable rights that include the freedom to think and dream and worship and, yes, vote as we please. To preserve our liberty, America once deposed a king, fought a great Civil War, and five times in this century sent Americans into major battle.

And yet, freedom is not ours alone; it is our most treasured export. If you doubt freedom's victory, look to the Persian Gulf. Look to the former Soviet Union, where those once oppressed crowd reopened churches and synagogues. Look to Eastern Europe, where Christmas carols warm the bright winter chill. It is written, "In the beginning was the Word." Here is the word for 1992: Today, the times are on the side of peace because the world, increasingly, is on the side of God.

I remember an early trip to the Soviet Union by our friend Billy Graham. He came back, and he reported that faith in God was very much alive in Russia. And some hardliners ridiculed him. Some even thought he shouldn't go. Today, we see that he clearly was right.

This brings me, then, to the ultimate value that sustains America and the values I have already cited: a belief in prayer. Obviously, no country can claim a special place in God's heart. Yet we are better as a people because He has a special place in ours.

I once asked one of my grandkids how he felt about prayer. And he said, "Just try getting through a math test without it." [*Laughter*] In Sunday school children learn that God is everywhere, but in public school they find that He's absent from class. And I continue to believe, as do the overwhelming majority of Americans, in the right to nondenominational voluntary school prayer.

The values I have spoken of remind us of the truth that comes on one's knees. And I believe with all my heart that one cannot have this job, cannot be America's President, without a belief in God, without a belief in prayer.

The poet Walt Whitman once asked what made America America, and he replied simply, "Its religion. Otherwise there is no real and permanent grandeur." Let that be our essence as a people and our message as a Nation.

Thank you for this occasion. And may God bless this most wondrous land on

Earth, the United States of America. Thank you very, very much.

*Note: The President spoke at 11:59 a.m. at the Sheraton Washington Hotel. In his remarks, he referred to James Dobson, clinical psychologist and president of Focus on the Family, and evangelist Billy Graham.*

## Appointment of Les T. Csorba as a Special Assistant to the President and Associate Director of Presidential Personnel for National Security Affairs
*January 27, 1992*

The President has announced his intention to appoint Les T. Csorba to be Special Assistant to the President and Associate Director of Presidential Personnel for National Security Affairs. He would succeed Jose E. Martinez.

Since 1989, Mr. Csorba has served as Acting Associate Director of Boards and Commissions in the Office of Presidential Personnel, the National Security Deputy Associate Director of Boards and Commissions, and Special Assistant in the Office of Special Placement and Administration in the Office of Presidential Personnel. In 1989, he served as deputy to the Special Assistant to the President for Public Liaison. In addition, he served on the transition staff in the Office of the President-Elect in 1988; on the national voter coalitions staff during George Bush for President, 1988; and as a member of the Bush/Quayle '88 National Youth Steering Committee, 1988.

The son of 1956 Hungarian refugees, Mr. Csorba is a naturalized United States citizen. Mr. Csorba graduated from the University of California, Davis (B.A., 1985). A Sunday school teacher at the First Baptist Church of Alexandria, he is married, has one child, and resides in Alexandria, VA.

## Remarks at a Drug Control Strategy Meeting
*January 27, 1992*

Thank you all very much. And let me single out those gentlemen with me: Governor Bob Martinez; Attorney General, Mr. Barr; Secretary Sullivan; and Secretary of Education Alexander. It's a pleasure to be with all of you, and I'm especially happy to welcome the Ambassadors of Bolivia, Colombia, Ecuador, Mexico, Peru, and Venezuela, neighbors with whom we're intensifying our cooperation in the fight against drugs. And ladies and gentlemen all, thank you.

I've been briefed on what kind of a prestigious audience, an important group we have here with us today. All of us are here today to give you an update on America's war against drug abuse.

First, let me say it is a real war. This isn't a headline writer's hype of some sort. The poison of drug abuse and the violence it breeds have left a trail of death and destruction in our cities. And anyone who lives in a big city knows of places close to home that look like war zones, with the neighborhoods burned and scarred, tyrannized by gangs, by drug gangs. Gang violence is claiming the lives of kids who get caught up in drugs, and the drug gangs' gun battles are even stealing the lives of innocent bystanders.

We haven't won this war yet, but I'm determined that we will. Everybody that is working the problem is determined that we will win this war. It is imperative that we put more resources into our fight. Accordingly, I'm asking the Congress for fiscal '93 to provide $12.7 billion to wage this war on drugs. If Congress approves my request, funding for the war against drugs will have increased by 93 percent to nearly double the level of just 3 years ago when I took office.

We start by taking our Federal dollars to the front lines. More than one-quarter of our proposed Federal budget for drug control, more money than ever before, will go to assist State and local government in their drug control programs. Treatment and prevention programs, working to reduce the demand for drugs, would receive over $4.1 billion in 1993. We will expand programs to help high-risk groups like adolescents and pregnant women. We'll increase emergency grants for drug-free schools and communities by 100 percent. And we'll increase by 15 percent the Federal funding for community partnership grants in the fight against drugs. Community partnership grants help good neighbors like the volunteers who brought about the demolition of more than 800 crack houses in Miami. And we're continuing the excellent HUD drug elimination program where we've increased annual funding from $8.2 million to 165 million since '89. This HUD program has helped such citizens as the men and women of Chicago's Cabrini-Green housing project in their efforts to get those drug gangs out of their buildings.

As President, I am determined that our Federal authorities offer all the support that they possibly can to the communities that make this full commitment. You have my word: I will demand an equal commitment from the Congress. No American, young or old or in-between, should have to live in fear.

We've made real progress in this fight against drug abuse, drug use. Between '88 and '91, current overall drug use dropped by 13 percent, while among adolescents drug use dropped by 27 percent. Cocaine use tells the same story. While current use of this deadly drug among the general population decreased by 35 percent, 35, among teenagers it dropped by 63 percent.

Now, think about that last one, that last statistic. Compared with 4 years ago, almost two-thirds fewer of our kids are falling for the temptation of cocaine. Our young

people are getting the message. Millions and millions more of our kids are listening to good advice and saving themselves from the lives of addiction and misery. Of course, one life sacrificed to the demons of drugs or drug abuse violence is one too many. Saving those lives has got to be everyone's mission, from Federal officials to county prosecutors and cops on the beat.

We cannot gain total victory without the strength and the resolve and the dedication of countless volunteers. Every time an individual parent or teacher or clergyman motivates a young person to say no to drug abuse, we as a nation move much closer to our goal. So let me say as clearly as I possibly can: Success in the drug war depends crucially on our churches and synagogues; our schools; our service clubs and young people's organizations; and most important, American families, strengthened by the virtues and bonds of love and honor and just plain strength. American families, that's the key.

Before I turn the program over to Governor Martinez, who's doing a superb job in this field, let me mention again something that we announced last week, namely that he and I will be meeting next month with the Presidents of Colombia, Bolivia, Peru, Venezuela, and Ecuador and Mexico. This will be the second regional drug summit. We must work more effectively than ever with these nations in fighting the spread of drugs. And I'll drive home the message that there are no half measures.

I will also convince those world leaders, leaders of those countries that we are tackling the demand side of the equation. I remember Cartagena, and I remember there was some doubt on the parts of those Presidents as to what we were doing at home on the demand side. I think now we have a good record with real progress to report to them. It makes a difference to how they can go about using their resources in their countries.

Now I'd like to turn the podium over to Bob Martinez and the other briefers who are working so hard to win this drug war. And I really do thank each of you for your commitment and for your effort. I will single out just one group here, the Partnership against drugs, where we have this marvelous media effort going on now. It's about $1 million a day being spent on pro bono advertising to get the message to the young people. And that is not Government; that is volunteers taking that message to the people of this country.

And there are so many wonderful stories of that nature, and I know many of the programs that work are represented by people right here. So I do thank you for your commitment and your effort, and let's continue this fight until we can say, each one of us, that we have conquered the scourge of drug abuse.

Thank you very much for letting me pop in.

*Note: The President spoke at 2:05 p.m. in Room 450 of the Old Executive Office Building. In his remarks, he referred to Bob Martinez, Director of the Office of National Drug Control Policy, and to the Partnership for a Drug-Free America.*

## Presidential Determination No. 92–11—Memorandum on Export-Import Bank Services for Latvia, Lithuania, and Estonia
*January 28, 1992*

*Memorandum for the Secretary of State*

*Subject:* Presidential Determination under Subsection 2(b)(2)(D)(i) of the Export-Import Bank Act of 1945, as Amended—Latvia, Lithuania, and Estonia

Pursuant to subsection 2(b)(2)(D)(i) of the Export-Import Bank Act of 1945, as amended (12 U.S.C. 635(b)(2)(D)(i)), I determine that it is in the national interest for the Export-Import Bank of the United States to guarantee, insure, extend credit, and participate in the extension of credit in connection with the purchase or lease of any product by, for use in, or for sale or lease to Latvia, Lithuania, and Estonia.

You are authorized and directed to report this determination to the Congress and to publish it in the *Federal Register.*

GEORGE BUSH

[*Filed with the Office of the Federal Register, 2:35 p.m., February 13, 1992*]

## Address Before a Joint Session of the Congress on the State of the Union
*January 28, 1992*

*Mr. Speaker and Mr. President, distinguished Members of Congress, honored guests, and fellow citizens:*

Thank you very much for that warm reception. You know, with the big buildup this address has had, I wanted to make sure it would be a big hit, but I couldn't convince Barbara to deliver it for me. [*Laughter*]

I see the Speaker and the Vice President are laughing. They saw what I did in Japan, and they're just happy they're sitting behind me. [*Laughter*]

I mean to speak tonight of big things, of big changes and the promises they hold, and of some big problems and how, together, we can solve them and move our country forward as the undisputed leader of the age.

We gather tonight at a dramatic and deeply promising time in our history and in the history of man on Earth. For in the past 12 months, the world has known changes of almost Biblical proportions. And even now, months after the failed coup that doomed a failed system, I'm not sure we've absorbed the full impact, the full import of what happened. But communism died this year.

Even as President, with the most fascinating possible vantage point, there were times when I was so busy managing progress and helping to lead change that I didn't always show the joy that was in my heart. But the biggest thing that has happened in the world in my life, in our lives, is this: By the grace of God, America won the cold war.

I mean to speak this evening of the changes that can take place in our country, now that we can stop making the sacrifices we had to make when we had an avowed enemy that was a superpower. Now we can look homeward even more and move to set right what needs to be set right.

I will speak of those things. But let me tell you something I've been thinking these past few months. It's a kind of rollcall of honor. For the cold war didn't end; it was won. And I think of those who won it, in places like Korea and Vietnam. And some of them didn't come back. Back then they were heroes, but this year they were victors.

The long rollcall, all the G.I. Joes and Janes, all the ones who fought faithfully for freedom, who hit the ground and sucked the dust and knew their share of horror. This may seem frivolous, and I don't mean it so, but it's moving to me how the world saw them. The world saw not only their special valor but their special style: their rambunctious, optimistic bravery, their do-or-die unity unhampered by class or race or region. What a group we've put forth, for generations now, from the ones who wrote "Kilroy was here" on the walls of the German stalags to those who left signs in the Iraqi desert that said, "I saw Elvis." What a group of kids we've sent out into the world.

And there's another to be singled out, though it may seem inelegant, and I mean a mass of people called the American taxpayer. No one ever thinks to thank the people who pay a country's bill or an alliance's bill. But for half a century now, the American people have shouldered the burden and paid taxes that were higher than they would have been to support a defense that was bigger than it would have been if impe-

rial communism had never existed. But it did; doesn't anymore. And here's a fact I wouldn't mind the world acknowledging: The American taxpayer bore the brunt of the burden and deserves a hunk of the glory.

So now, for the first time in 35 years, our strategic bombers stand down. No longer are they on 'round-the-clock alert. Tomorrow our children will go to school and study history and how plants grow. And they won't have, as my children did, air raid drills in which they crawl under their desks and cover their heads in case of nuclear war. My grandchildren don't have to do that and won't have the bad dreams children had once, in decades past. There are still threats. But the long, drawn-out dread is over.

A year ago tonight, I spoke to you at a moment of high peril. American forces had just unleashed Operation Desert Storm. And after 40 days in the desert skies and 4 days on the ground, the men and women of America's Armed Forces and our allies accomplished the goals that I declared and that you endorsed: We liberated Kuwait. Soon after, the Arab world and Israel sat down to talk seriously and comprehensively about peace, an historic first. And soon after that, at Christmas, the last American hostages came home. Our policies were vindicated.

Much good can come from the prudent use of power. And much good can come of this: A world once divided into two armed camps now recognizes one sole and preeminent power, the United States of America. And they regard this with no dread. For the world trusts us with power, and the world is right. They trust us to be fair and restrained. They trust us to be on the side of decency. They trust us to do what's right.

I use those words advisedly. A few days after the war began, I received a telegram from Joanne Speicher, the wife of the first pilot killed in the Gulf, Lieutenant Commander Scott Speicher. Even in her grief, she wanted me to know that some day when her children were old enough, she would tell them "that their father went away to war because it was the right thing to do." And she said it all: It was the right thing to do.

And we did it together. There were honest differences right here in this Chamber. But when the war began, you put partisanship aside, and we supported our troops. This is still a time for pride, but this is no time to boast. For problems face us, and we must stand together once again and solve them and not let our country down.

Two years ago, I began planning cuts in military spending that reflected the changes of the new era. But now, this year, with imperial communism gone, that process can be accelerated. Tonight I can tell you of dramatic changes in our strategic nuclear force. These are actions we are taking on our own because they are the right thing to do. After completing 20 planes for which we have begun procurement, we will shut down further production of the B–2 bombers. We will cancel the small ICBM program. We will cease production of new warheads for our sea-based ballistic missiles. We will stop all new production of the Peacekeeper missile. And we will not purchase any more advanced cruise missiles.

This weekend I will meet at Camp David with Boris Yeltsin of the Russian Federation. I've informed President Yeltsin that if the Commonwealth, the former Soviet Union, will eliminate all land-based multiple-warhead ballistic missiles, I will do the following: We will eliminate all Peacekeeper missiles. We will reduce the number of warheads on Minuteman missiles to one and reduce the number of warheads on our sea-based missiles by about one-third. And we will convert a substantial portion of our strategic bombers to primarily conventional use. President Yeltsin's early response has been very positive, and I expect our talks at Camp David to be fruitful.

I want you to know that for half a century, American Presidents have longed to make such decisions and say such words. But even in the midst of celebration, we must keep caution as a friend. For the world is still a dangerous place. Only the dead have seen the end of conflict. And though yesterday's challenges are behind us, tomorrow's are being born.

The Secretary of Defense recommended these cuts after consultation with the Joint Chiefs of Staff. And I make them with con-

fidence. But do not misunderstand me. The reductions I have approved will save us an additional $50 billion over the next 5 years. By 1997, we will have cut defense by 30 percent since I took office. These cuts are deep, and you must know my resolve: This deep, and no deeper. To do less would be insensible to progress, but to do more would be ignorant of history. We must not go back to the days of "the hollow army." We cannot repeat the mistakes made twice in this century when armistice was followed by recklessness and defense was purged as if the world were permanently safe.

I remind you this evening that I have asked for your support in funding a program to protect our country from limited nuclear missile attack. We must have this protection because too many people in too many countries have access to nuclear arms. And I urge you again to pass the Strategic Defense Initiative, SDI.

There are those who say that now we can turn away from the world, that we have no special role, no special place. But we are the United States of America, the leader of the West that has become the leader of the world. And as long as I am President, I will continue to lead in support of freedom everywhere, not out of arrogance, not out of altruism, but for the safety and security of our children. This is a fact: Strength in the pursuit of peace is no vice; isolationism in the pursuit of security is no virtue.

And now to our troubles at home. They're not all economic; the primary problem is our economy. There are some good signs. Inflation, that thief, is down. And interest rates are down. But unemployment is too high, some industries are in trouble, and growth is not what it should be. Let me tell you right from the start and right from the heart, I know we're in hard times. But I know something else: This will not stand.

In this Chamber, in this Chamber we can bring the same courage and sense of common purpose to the economy that we brought to Desert Storm. And we can defeat hard times together. I believe you'll help. One reason is that you're patriots, and you want the best for your country. And I believe that in your hearts you want to put partisanship aside and get the job done because it's the right thing to do.

The power of America rests in a stirring but simple idea, that people will do great things if only you set them free. Well, we're going to set the economy free. For if this age of miracles and wonders has taught us anything, it's that if we can change the world we can change America. We must encourage investment. We must make it easier for people to invest money and create new products, new industries, and new jobs. We must clear away the obstacles to growth: high taxes, high regulation, red-tape, and yes, wasteful Government spending.

None of this will happen with a snap of the fingers, but it will happen. And the test of a plan isn't whether it's called new or dazzling. The American people aren't impressed by gimmicks; they're smarter on this score than all of us in this room. The only test of a plan is: Is it sound, and will it work?

We must have a short-term plan to address our immediate needs and heat up the economy. And then we need a longer term plan to keep combustion going and to guarantee our place in the world economy. There are certain things that a President can do without Congress, and I'm going to do them.

I have, this evening, asked major Cabinet departments and Federal agencies to institute a 90-day moratorium on any new Federal regulations that could hinder growth. In those 90 days, major departments and agencies will carry out a top-to-bottom review of all regulations, old and new, to stop the ones that will hurt growth and speed up those that will help growth.

Further, for the untold number of hard-working, responsible American workers and business men and women who've been forced to go without needed bank loans, the banking credit crunch must end. I won't neglect my responsibility for sound regulations that serve the public good, but regulatory overkill must be stopped. And I've instructed our Government regulators to stop it.

I have directed Cabinet departments and Federal agencies to speed up progrowth expenditures as quickly as possible. This should put an extra $10 billion into the economy in the next 6 months. And our new transportation bill provides more than $150 billion for construction and maintenance projects that are vital to our growth and well-being. And that means jobs building roads, jobs building bridges, and jobs building railways.

And I have, this evening, directed the Secretary of the Treasury to change the Federal tax withholding tables. With this change, millions of Americans from whom the Government withholds more than necessary can now choose to have the Government withhold less from their paychecks. Something tells me a number of taxpayers may take us up on this one. This initiative could return about $25 billion back into our economy over the next 12 months, money people can use to help pay for clothing, college, or to get a new car. Finally, working with the Federal Reserve, we will continue to support monetary policy that keeps both interest rates and inflation down.

Now, these are the things I can do. And now, Members of Congress, let me tell you what you can do for your country. You must pass the other elements of my plan to meet our economic needs. Everyone knows that investment spurs recovery. I am proposing this evening a change in the alternative minimum tax and the creation of a new 15-percent investment tax allowance. This will encourage businesses to accelerate investment and bring people back to work.

Real estate has led our economy out of almost all the tough times we've ever had. Once building starts, carpenters and plumbers work; people buy homes and take out mortgages. My plan would modify the passive loss rule for active real estate developers. And it would make it easier for pension plans to purchase real estate. For those Americans who dream of buying a first home but who can't quite afford it, my plan would allow first-time homebuyers to withdraw savings from IRA's without penalty and provide a $5,000 tax credit for the first purchase of that home.

And finally, my immediate plan calls on Congress to give crucial help to people who own a home, to everyone who has a business or a farm or a single investment. This time, at this hour, I cannot take no for an answer. You must cut the capital gains tax on the people of our country. Never has an issue been more demagogued by its opponents. But the demagogs are wrong. They are wrong, and they know it. Sixty percent of the people who benefit from lower capital gains have incomes under $50,000. A cut in the capital gains tax increases jobs and helps just about everyone in our country. And so, I'm asking you to cut the capital gains tax to a maximum of 15.4 percent.

I'll tell you, those of you who say, "Oh, no, someone who's comfortable may benefit from that," you kind of remind me of the old definition of the Puritan who couldn't sleep at night, worrying that somehow, someone somewhere was out having a good time. [*Laughter*] The opponents of this measure and those who have authored various so-called soak-the-rich bills that are floating around this Chamber should be reminded of something: When they aim at the big guy, they usually hit the little guy. And maybe it's time that stopped.

This, then, is my short-term plan. Your part, Members of Congress, requires enactment of these commonsense proposals that will have a strong effect on the economy without breaking the budget agreement and without raising tax rates.

While my plan is being passed and kicking in, we've got to care for those in trouble today. I have provided for up to $4.4 billion in my budget to extend Federal unemployment benefits. And I ask for congressional action right away. And I thank the committee. [*Applause*] Well, at last.

Let's be frank. Let's be frank. Let me level with you. I know and you know that my plan is unveiled in a political season. [*Laughter*] I know and you know that everything I propose will be viewed by some in merely partisan terms. But I ask you to know what is in my heart. And my aim is to increase our Nation's good. I'm doing what I think is right, and I am proposing what I know will help.

I pride myself that I'm a prudent man, and I believe that patience is a virtue. But I understand that politics is, for some, a game and that sometimes the game is to stop all progress and then decry the lack of improvement. [*Laughter*] But let me tell you: Far more important than my political

future and far more important than yours is the well-being of our country. Members of this Chamber are practical people, and I know you won't resent some practical advice. When people put their party's fortunes, whatever the party, whatever side of this aisle, before the public good, they court defeat not only for their country but for themselves. And they will certainly deserve it.

I submit my plan tomorrow, and I'm asking you to pass it by March 20th. And I ask the American people to let you know they want this action by March 20th. From the day after that, if it must be, the battle is joined. And you know, when principle is at stake I relish a good, fair fight.

I said my plan has two parts, and it does. And it's the second part that is the heart of the matter. For it's not enough to get an immediate burst. We need long-term improvement in our economic position. We all know that the key to our economic future is to ensure that America continues as an economic leader of the world. We have that in our power. Here, then, is my long-term plan to guarantee our future.

First, trade: We will work to break down the walls that stop world trade. We will work to open markets everywhere. And in our major trade negotiations, I will continue pushing to eliminate tariffs and subsidies that damage America's farmers and workers. And we'll get more good American jobs within our own hemisphere through the North American free trade agreement and through the Enterprise for the Americas Initiative.

But changes are here, and more are coming. The workplace of the future will demand more highly skilled workers than ever, more people who are computer-literate, highly educated. We must be the world's leader in education. And we must revolutionize America's schools. My America 2000 strategy will help us reach that goal. My plan will give parents more choice, give teachers more flexibility, and help communities create new American schools. Thirty States across the Nation have established America 2000 programs. Hundreds of cities and towns have joined in. Now Congress must join this great movement: Pass my proposals for new American schools.

That was my second long-term proposal, and here's my third: We must make commonsense investments that will help us compete, long-term, in the marketplace. We must encourage research and development. My plan is to make the R&D tax credit permanent and to provide record levels of support, over $76 billion this year alone, for people who will explore the promise of emerging technologies.

Fourth, we must do something about crime and drugs. It is time for a major, renewed investment in fighting violent street crime. It saps our strength and hurts our faith in our society and in our future together. Surely a tired woman on her way to work at 6 in the morning on a subway deserves the right to get there safely. And surely it's true that everyone who changes his or her life because of crime, from those afraid to go out at night to those afraid to walk in the parks they pay for, surely these people have been denied a basic civil right. It is time to restore it. Congress, pass my comprehensive crime bill. It is tough on criminals and supportive of police, and it has been languishing in these hallowed halls for years now. Pass it. Help your country.

Fifth, I ask you tonight to fund our HOPE housing proposal and to pass my enterprise zone legislation which will get businesses into the inner city. We must empower the poor with the pride that comes from owning a home, getting a job, becoming a part of things. My plan would encourage real estate construction by extending tax incentives for mortgage revenue bonds and low-income housing. And I ask tonight for record expenditures for the program that helps children born into want move into excellence, Head Start.

Step six, we must reform our health care system. For this, too, bears on whether or not we can compete in the world. American health costs have been exploding. This year America will spend over $800 billion on health, and that is expected to grow to 1.6 trillion by the end of the decade. We simply cannot afford this. The cost of health care shows up not only in your family budget but in the price of everything we buy and everything we sell. When health coverage

for a fellow on an assembly line costs thousands of dollars, the cost goes into the products he makes, and you pay the bill.

We must make a choice. Now, some pretend we can have it both ways. They call it "play or pay," but that expensive approach is unstable. It will mean higher taxes, fewer jobs, and eventually a system under complete Government control.

Really, there are only two options. And we can move toward a nationalized system, a system which will restrict patient choice in picking a doctor and force the Government to ration services arbitrarily. And what we'll get is patients in long lines, indifferent service, and a huge new tax burden. Or we can reform our own private health care system, which still gives us, for all its flaws, the best quality health care in the world.

Well, let's build on our strengths. My plan provides insurance security for all Americans while preserving and increasing the idea of choice. We make basic health insurance affordable for all low-income people not now covered, and we do it by providing a health insurance tax credit of up to $3,750 for each low-income family. And the middle class gets help, too. And by reforming the health insurance market, my plan assures that Americans will have access to basic health insurance even if they change jobs or develop serious health problems. We must bring costs under control, preserve quality, preserve choice, and reduce the people's nagging daily worry about health insurance. My plan, the details of which I'll announce very shortly, does just that.

Seventh, we must get the Federal deficit under control. We now have, in law, enforceable spending caps and a requirement that we pay for the programs we create. There are those in Congress who would ease that discipline now. But I cannot let them do it, and I won't.

My plan would freeze all domestic discretionary budget authority, which means no more next year than this year. I will not tamper with Social Security, but I would put real caps on the growth of uncontrolled spending. And I would also freeze Federal domestic Government employment. And with the help of Congress, my plan will get rid of 246 programs that don't deserve Federal funding. Some of them have noble titles, but none of them is indispensable. We can get rid of each and every one of them.

You know, it's time we rediscovered a home truth the American people have never forgotten: This Government is too big and spends too much. And I call upon Congress to adopt a measure that will help put an end to the annual ritual of filling the budget with pork barrel appropriations. Every year, the press has a field day making fun of outrageous examples: a Lawrence Welk museum, research grants for Belgian endive. We all know how these things get into the budget, and maybe you need someone to help you say no. I know how to say it, and I know what I need to make it stick. Give me the same thing 43 Governors have, the line-item veto, and let me help you control spending.

We must put an end to unfinanced Federal Government mandates. These are the requirements Congress puts on our cities, counties, and States without supplying the money. If Congress passes a mandate, it should be forced to pay for it and balance the cost with savings elsewhere. After all, a mandate just increases someone else's burden, and that means higher taxes at the State and local level.

Step eight, Congress should enact the bold reform proposals that are still awaiting congressional action: bank reform, civil justice reform, tort reform, and my national energy strategy.

And finally, we must strengthen the family because it is the family that has the greatest bearing on our future. When Barbara holds an AIDS baby in her arms and reads to children, she's saying to every person in this country: Family matters.

And I am announcing tonight a new Commission on America's Urban Families. I've asked Missouri's Governor John Ashcroft to be Chairman, former Dallas Mayor Annette Strauss to be Cochair. You know, I had mayors, the leading mayors from the League of Cities, in the other day at the White House, and they told me something striking. They said that every one of them, Republican or Democrat, agreed on one thing, that the major cause of the problems of the cities is the dissolution of the family. They asked for this Commission, and they were right to ask because it's time to determine what we can do to keep families together, strong and sound.

There's one thing we can do right away: Ease the burden of rearing a child. I ask you tonight to raise the personal exemption by $500 per child for every family. For a family with four kids, that's an increase of $2,000. This is a good start in the right direction, and it's what we can afford.

It's time to allow families to deduct the interest they pay on student loans. I am asking you to do just that. And I'm asking you to allow people to use money from their IRA's to pay medical and education expenses, all without penalties.

And I'm asking for more. Ask American parents what they dislike about how things are going in our country, and chances are good that pretty soon they'll get to welfare. Americans are the most generous people on Earth. But we have to go back to the insight of Franklin Roosevelt who, when he spoke of what became the welfare program, warned that it must not become "a narcotic" and a "subtle destroyer" of the spirit. Welfare was never meant to be a lifestyle. It was never meant to be a habit. It was never supposed to be passed from generation to generation like a legacy. It's time to replace the assumptions of the welfare state and help reform the welfare system.

States throughout the country are beginning to operate with new assumptions that when able-bodied people receive Government assistance, they have responsibilities to the taxpayer: A responsibility to seek work, education, or job training; a responsibility to get their lives in order; a responsibility to hold their families together and refrain from having children out of wedlock; and a responsibility to obey the law. We are going to help this movement. Often, State reform requires waiving certain Federal regulations. I will act to make that process easier and quicker for every State that asks for our help.

I want to add, as we make these changes, we work together to improve this system, that our intention is not scapegoating or finger-pointing. If you read the papers and watch TV, you know there's been a rise these days in a certain kind of ugliness: racist comments, anti-Semitism, an increased sense of division. Really, this is not us. This is not who we are. And this is not acceptable.

And so, you have my plan for America. And I'm asking for big things, but I believe in my heart you'll do what's right.

You know, it's kind of an American tradition to show a certain skepticism toward our democratic institutions. I myself have sometimes thought the aging process could be delayed if it had to make its way through Congress. [*Laughter*] You will deliberate, and you will discuss, and that is fine. But, my friends, the people cannot wait. They need help now.

There's a mood among us. People are worried. There's been talk of decline. Someone even said our workers are lazy and uninspired. And I thought: Really? You go tell Neil Armstrong standing on the moon. Tell the men and women who put him there. Tell the American farmer who feeds his country and the world. Tell the men and women of Desert Storm.

Moods come and go, but greatness endures. Ours does. And maybe for a moment it's good to remember what, in the dailiness of our lives, we forget: We are still and ever the freest nation on Earth, the kindest nation on Earth, the strongest nation on Earth. And we have always risen to the occasion. And we are going to lift this Nation out of hard times inch by inch and day by day, and those who would stop us had better step aside. Because I look at hard times, and I make this vow: This will not stand.

And so, we move on together, a rising nation, the once and future miracle that is still, this night, the hope of the world. Thank you. God bless you, and God bless our beloved country. Thank you very, very much.

*Note: The President spoke at 9:07 p.m. in the House Chamber of the Capitol. The address was broadcast live on nationwide radio and television. The Executive order of March 12 establishing the National Commission on America's Urban Families is listed in Appendix E at the end of this volume.*

# Message on the Observance of National African-American (Black) History Month, February 1992
*January 29, 1992*

"When I found I had crossed that line, I looked at my hands to see if I was the same person. There was such a glory over everything." With these words, Harriet Tubman described her escape from slavery during the mid-19th century. The glory of which she spoke was nothing less than freedom— and the promise of better days to come.

Although African-American history begins long before the days of Harriet Tubman, who helped to lead thousands of her fellow Blacks out of slavery during the Civil War, it is filled with similar accounts of faith, courage, and triumph in the epic struggle for liberty and justice. This month, through special programs and activities across the country, we honor the many African Americans who have helped to uphold our Nation's declaration "that all men are created equal, that they are endowed by their Creator with certain unalienable Rights, that among these are Life, Liberty, and the pursuit of Happiness." Just as all Americans should study the words and deeds of our Founding Fathers, so should all Americans learn about the Black leaders who have helped to make the promise of freedom a reality.

The men and women whom we remember this month will long inspire others. In addition to honoring individuals such as Rosa Parks and other heroes of the civil rights movement, we also recall pioneers like George Washington Carver, who made important discoveries in agriculture, and Benjamin Banneker, who served as one of the architects of Washington, D.C., our Nation's Capital. We remember outstanding Black American artists, including legendary singers and musicians such as Marian Anderson, Charlie Parker, and Dizzy Gillespie. Others, we remember for their devoted service to our country: from military heroes such as the Tuskegee Airmen to remarkable international civil servants like Ralph Bunche. The stories of these individuals, together with many other accounts, make up the rich fabric of African-American history.

That history, of course, continues to unfold each day, and I am heartened to know that many parents and teachers will be using this occasion to challenge and to inspire young people. With the past as their guide, Black youth can make their future bright, as they weave their own strands in the rich tapestry of African-American history.

GEORGE BUSH

# Message to the Congress Transmitting the 1992 National Drug Control Strategy
*January 29, 1992*

*To the Congress of the United States:*

I am pleased to transmit today for the consideration of the Congress and the American people the 1992 National Drug Control Strategy, in accordance with section 1005 of the Anti-Drug Abuse Act of 1988 (Public Law 100–690; 21 U.S.C. 1504).

This is the Fourth National Drug Control Strategy, and it lays out a comprehensive plan for Federal drug control activities for Fiscal Year 1993 and beyond. The principal goal remains unchanged from the previous three strategies: to reduce the level of illegal drug use in America.

We are fighting a two-front war against drugs. The first front is against casual drug use, and I am pleased to report that significant progress is being made here, particularly among our Nation's youth. Casual drug use is still too high, however, and this Strategy rightly continues to stress efforts to reduce it. The second front, against hardcore drug use, poses a more difficult challenge. Progress here is slower. There are still too many neighborhoods, families, and individuals who suffer the consequences of drug use and drug-related crime. To address this problem, the Strategy proposes a variety of carefully targeted and intensified efforts. I urge the Congress to expedite their enactment.

The war on drugs is vital to our country's economy, international competitiveness, and security. Previous Strategies have enjoyed bipartisan political and funding support in the Congress. I ask for your continued support in this critical endeavor.

GEORGE BUSH

The White House,
January 29, 1992.

# Appointment of Daniel B. McGroarty as Special Assistant to the President and Deputy Director of Speechwriting
*January 29, 1992*

The President today announced the appointment of Daniel B. McGroarty as Special Assistant to the President and Deputy Director of Speechwriting.

Mr. McGroarty has served as speechwriter to the President since 1989 and Deputy

Director of Speechwriting since 1991. Prior to coming to the White House, he held the positions of senior speechwriter to Secretary of Defense Frank C. Carlucci III, speechwriter to Secretary of Defense Caspar W. Weinberger, and editorial writer at the Voice of America.

Mr. McGroarty graduated from Kenyon College (B.A., 1979) and is currently a Ph.D. candidate at Boston College. He was born August 23, 1957, in Cleveland, OH. He resides with his wife and two children in Annandale, VA.

## Memorandum on Regulatory Coordination
*January 28, 1992*

*Memorandum for the Secretary of the Treasury, the Chairman of the Board of Governors of the Federal Reserve System, the Chairman of the Securities and Exchange Commission, the Chairman of the Federal Deposit Insurance Corporation, the Chairman of the Commodity Futures Trading Commission*

*Subject:* Regulatory Coordination

As you know, the Congress has failed to enact important growth-oriented legislation that we have proposed. Although we will continue to work with the Congress to enact these proposals, we must also redouble our efforts to create jobs and achieve economic growth within existing statutory constraints.

For such efforts to succeed, we must prevent the fragmentation of policy-making and better coordinate existing programs within the executive branch. I recognize that you have already made considerable efforts to coordinate your activities, and ask only that you intensify these efforts over the next three months to ensure that we have done all that we can to eliminate unnecessary regulatory burdens.

I look forward to your reports on this important undertaking. Although the Congress has created the regulatory schemes within which we must operate, I am confident that, with your help, the executive branch can do much to create conditions conducive to a healthy and robust economy.

GEORGE BUSH

*Note: This memorandum was released by the Office of the Press Secretary on January 30.*

## Memorandum on Regulatory Coordination
*January 28, 1992*

*Memorandum for the Secretary of Transportation, the Secretary of Energy, the Chairman of the Interstate Commerce Commission, the Chairman of the Federal Maritime Commission*

*Subject:* Regulatory Coordination

As you know, the Congress has failed to enact important growth-oriented legislation that we have proposed. Although we will continue to work with the Congress to enact these proposals, we must also redouble our efforts to create jobs and achieve economic growth within existing statutory constraints.

For such efforts to succeed, we must prevent the fragmentation of policy-making and better coordinate existing programs within the executive branch. We have made great strides in this area, but more remains to be done. Because your agencies share responsibility for regulating the transportation sector of our economy, it is essential that you work together to streamline the regulatory process and ensure that the regulated community is not subject to duplicative or inconsistent regulation.

I hope that improved coordination will be one especially valuable outcome of the 90-day moratorium and review period described in the attached memorandum. I look forward to your reports on this important undertaking. Although the Congress has created the regulatory schemes within which we must operate, I am confident that, with your help, the executive branch can do much to create conditions conducive to a healthy and robust economy.

GEORGE BUSH

*Note: This memorandum was released by the Office of the Press Secretary on January 30.*

## Memorandum on Regulatory Coordination
*January 28, 1992*

*Memorandum for the Secretary of the Interior, the Secretary of Agriculture, the Secretary of Energy, the Administrator of the Environmental Protection Agency, the Chairman of the Federal Energy Regulatory Commission, the Chairman of the Nuclear Regulatory Commission*

*Subject:* Regulatory Coordination

As you know, the Congress has failed to enact important growth-oriented legislation that we have proposed. Although we will continue to work with the Congress to enact these proposals, we must also redouble our efforts to create jobs and achieve economic growth within existing statutory constraints.

For such efforts to succeed, we must prevent the fragmentation of policy-making and better coordinate existing programs within the executive branch. We have made great strides in this area, but more remains to be done. Your agencies share responsibility for promoting safe and efficient energy production while at the same time protecting the environment. It is therefore essential that you work together to streamline the regulatory process and ensure that the regulated community is not subject to duplicative or inconsistent regulation.

I hope that improved coordination will be one especially valuable outcome of the 90-day moratorium and review period described in the attached memorandum. I look forward to your reports on this important undertaking. Although the Congress has created the regulatory schemes within which we must operate, I am confident that, with your help, the executive branch can do much to create conditions conducive to a healthy and robust economy.

GEORGE BUSH

*Note: This memorandum was released by the Office of the Press Secretary on January 30.*

## Memorandum on Reducing the Burden of Government Regulation
*January 28, 1992*

*Memorandum for Certain Department and Agency Heads*

*Subject:* Reducing the Burden of Government Regulation

As you know, excessive regulation and red tape have imposed an enormous burden on our economy—a hidden tax on the average American household in the form of higher prices for goods and services. Just as Americans have the right to expect their government to spend tax dollars wisely, they have the right to expect cost-effective and minimally burdensome regulation. Although the Congress has thus far failed to pass most of the Administration's regulatory reform proposals, there is much the Administration can and should do on its own to reduce the burden of regulation.

A major part of this undertaking must be to weed out unnecessary and burdensome government regulations, which impose needless costs on consumers and substantially impede economic growth. We must be constantly vigilant to avoid unnecessary regulation and red tape.

We must also remember that even those regulatory programs that may have been justified when adopted often fail to keep pace with important innovations. New technologies and markets can quickly make existing rules obsolete. By the same token, existing regulations often impose unnecessary constraints on emerging technologies and markets that could not have been foreseen at the time the regulations were promulgated. Existing regulatory programs also need to be revised to take advantage of regulatory innovations, such as the flexible, market-based approaches to regulation that many of your agencies have developed over the past few years.

I am concerned that, because of the constant pressure to develop new programs, we are not doing nearly enough to review and revise existing programs. For that reason, I ask that each of your agencies set aside a 90-day period, beginning today, to evaluate existing regulations and programs and to identify and accelerate action on initiatives that will eliminate any unnecessary regulatory burden or otherwise promote economic growth. During this period, agency resources should, to the maximum extent possible, be devoted to these efforts. Specifically, I request that you take the following steps:

1. During the 90-day review period, your agency should work with the public, other interested agencies, the Office of Information and Regulatory Affairs, and the Council on Competitiveness to (i) identify each of your agency's regulations and programs that impose a substantial cost on the economy and (ii) determine whether each such regu-

lation or program adheres to the following standards:

(a) The expected benefits to society of any regulation should clearly outweigh the expected costs it imposes on society.

(b) Regulations should be fashioned to maximize net benefits to society.

(c) To the maximum extent possible, regulatory agencies should set performance standards instead of prescriptive command-and-control requirements, thereby allowing the regulated community to achieve regulatory goals at the lowest possible cost.

(d) Regulations should incorporate market mechanisms to the maximum extent possible.

(e) Regulations should provide clarity and certainty to the regulated community and should be designed to avoid needless litigation.

2. To the maximum extent permitted by law, and as soon as possible, your agency should propose administrative changes (including repeal, where appropriate) that will bring each regulation and program into conformity with the standards set forth above. As you implement these proposals, you should carefully order your agency's regulatory priorities to ensure that programs imposing the largest unnecessary burden are the first to be revised or eliminated.

3. You should designate, in consultation with the Council on Competitiveness, a senior official to serve as your agency's permanent regulatory oversight official. This person will be responsible for conducting the review, for implementing the resulting proposals, and for ensuring that future regulatory actions conform to the standards set forth in this memorandum and in applicable Executive orders.

4. To the maximum extent permitted by law, and subject to the exceptions listed below, your agency should refrain from issuing any proposed or final rule during the 90-day review period. This moratorium on new regulations will ensure that, to the maximum extent possible, agency resources are devoted to reducing the regulatory burden on the economy. Of course, you should not postpone any regulation that is subject to a statutory or judicial deadline

that falls during the review period. This moratorium does not apply to:

(a) regulations that you determine, after consultation with the working group of the Council on Competitiveness described below, will foster economic growth;

(b) regulations that respond to emergencies such as situations that pose an imminent danger to human health or safety;

(c) regulations that you determine, after consultation with the working group of the Council on Competitiveness described below, are essential to a criminal law enforcement function of the United States;

(d) regulations issued with respect to a military or foreign affairs function of the United States;

(e) regulations related solely to agency organization, management, or personnel; and

(f) formal regulations required by statute to be made on the record after opportunity for an agency hearing.

5. At the end of the review period, each agency should submit a written report to me. Each report should indicate the regulatory changes recommended or made during the review period and the potential savings to the economy of those changes, including an estimate of the number of jobs that will be created. It should also include a summary of any regulatory programs that are left unchanged and an explanation of how such programs are consistent with the regulatory standards set forth in paragraph 1 above.

The 90-day review, and the preparation of the reports described in paragraph 5 above, will be coordinated by a working group of the Council on Competitiveness, chaired by the Chairman of the Council of Economic Advisers and the Counsel to the President.

I look forward to your reports on this important undertaking. I am confident that, with your help, the executive branch can do much to create conditions conducive to a healthy and robust economy.

GEORGE BUSH

The Secretary of the Treasury, the Secretary of Defense, the Attorney General, the Secretary of the Interior, the Secretary of Agriculture, the Secretary of Commerce, the Secretary of Labor, the Secretary of Health and Human Services, the Secretary of Housing and Urban Development, the Secretary of Transportation, the Secretary of Energy, the Secretary of Education, the Chairman of the Interstate Commerce Commission, the Chairman of the Board of Governors of the Federal Reserve System, the Chairman of the Federal Trade Commission, the Chairperson of the Federal Deposit Insurance Corporation, the Chairman of the Securities and Exchange Commission, the Chairman of the Federal Communications Commission, the Chairman of the Federal Maritime Commission, the Chairman of the Equal Employment Opportunity Commission, the Administrator of the Environmental Protection Agency, the Chairman of the Nuclear Regulatory Commission, the Chairman of the Commodity Futures Trading Commission, the Chairman of the Federal Energy Regulatory Commission

*Note: This memorandum was released by the Office of the Press Secretary on January 30.*

# Remarks at the National Prayer Breakfast
*January 30, 1992*

Thank you, Senator Heflin, for such a lovely introduction. To Dan and Marilyn, the Vice President and Mrs. Quayle; to the members of my Cabinet here; to the Members of Congress, all, so many here in faith; to General Powell; especially to our host, Ted Stevens; to our dear friend Billy Graham; and to all gathered.

Let me first just say a special greeting to Prime Minister Ratu Mara of Fiji. This is not his first time here; I'm sure it won't be his last. But he's an inspiration to all of us that know him and consider him a friend, as I do. May I salute our other guests from overseas. And though sometimes you might feel like it, we don't consider you overseas, those who serve in the State legislatures, and we're glad you all are here. [*Laughter*]

Four principles, four ideas really, inspire America. And I think they're all here this morning reflected in one way or another: Freedom, family, and faith, that Dan Quayle talked about, and to that I would add fellowship. So many people brought together by a shared spirit, the simple joy of praying to God.

Slava, that was a tremendously moving story and one of the most dramatic moments in recent history. You referred to sound. If sound has anything to do with entry into heaven, I believe you can choose the fluffiest, most generous cloud in the firmament up there when you get there. [*Laughter*] And thank you for your inspiring message.

But I think you reminded us all of the powerful role that prayer has played in the unprecedented events of the past year. Since we last met, nations have been reshaped, and the lives have been restored throughout the land and throughout the entire world. And the force that unites them, as we've heard here today from the Vice President to General Powell, is faith in God. The link they share is prayer.

When I last stood here, as Colin reminded us, we were at war. Compelled by a deep need for God's wisdom, we began to pray. And we prayed for God's protection in what we undertook, for God's love to fill hearts, and for God's peace to be the moral North Star that guided us. Abraham Lincoln said, and we remember it, everyone in this room would remember it, "I've been driven many times to my knees by the overwhelming conviction that I have nowhere else to go." And in his example, we came together for a special National Day of Prayer. And Americans of every creed turned to our greatest power to bring us peace, "peace . . . which passeth all understanding." And at the end of the war, we prayed as one during our National Days of Thanksgiving.

Let us pray that as a people we will continue to bring the power of prayer to bear on all the challenges we confront. And let us pray that we will strengthen the values that this great land was founded on, that we will reverse any threat of moral decline, and that we will dedicate ourselves to the ethic of service, being what I call a Point of Light to someone else, someone in need.

In this work, we are not without inspiration. We need look no further than the handful of men who became heroes by their courage, their strength, and above all their faith—last of whom returned in December. I'm talking about our hostages. And in brutalizing conditions, as we've heard this morning, they prayed together daily in what they called the "church of the locked door." They unwove floor mats in order to make rosaries. These men, who every day lived the story of Job, treasured their first book, the Bible. When Terry Anderson was released, one of the first things he did was to thank strangers across the world who had prayed that he be set free. "Your prayers made a big difference," said this man who, imprisoned, had rediscovered the faith that sets and keeps men free.

There's another story from last year's news that tells of the transformation of faith. While it's a story familiar to all of you, it's intensely personal to Barbara and me and to others in this room. We lost a dear friend last March, Lee Atwater, a restless, fiercely driven, fun-loving good ol' boy from South Carolina who rode life as hard and fast as he could. But he also lived a kind of miracle because his illness reintroduced him to something he'd put aside, his own faith. And in his last months, he worked intensely to come to grips with his faith. And through reading the Bible and through prayer, he learned that, as he put it, "What was missing in society was what was missing in me, a little heart and a lot of brotherhood."

He was so right. Prayer has a place not only in the life of every American but also in the life of our Nation, for we are truly one Nation under God.

May God bless this very special gathering. For those of you who have come from overseas, for those of you from across our land, for those of you right here in the Nation's Capital, thank you for participating in this celebration of faith.

Thank you very much.

*Note: The President spoke at 9:10 a.m. at*

*the Washington Hilton Hotel. In his re-*
*marks, he referred to Senator Ted Stevens,*
*evangelist Billy Graham, Prime Minister*
*Kamisese Mara of Fiji, and National Sym-*
*phony Orchestra director Mstislav Rostropo-*
*vich.*

## Remarks to the Greater Philadelphia Chamber of Commerce
*January 30, 1992*

Thank you all very, very much for that welcome back. Please be seated, and thank you. Please be seated. I don't want to keep Boris Yeltsin waiting later on. [*Laughter*] Thank you, Joe. Senator Specter and Joan, laboring in the vineyards of the city council here, we're delighted to be with you. And coming up with us from Washington were two of our great Congressmen from this area, Larry Coughlin and Kurt Weldon, over here.

May I, too, salute the Mayor. I asked Joe earlier on how was it going, realizing that, as in Washington, things have been tough, and across the country in many ways. But I said, knowing a little bit about history in Philadelphia, I asked this question, "How's the Mayor doing?" And Joe and everybody else I've spoken to has said he's really hit the ground in a wonderful way, going forward, bringing out the best in this city. So, I want to salute Ed Rendell and his wife, Midge.

Joe Paquette, who introduced me, is the chairman of the Greater Philadelphia Chamber. That was a very enthusiastic presentation he made about how things were going. So much so that maybe he can make a little loan to those of us in Washington, DC, who cannot have quite that optimistic a report. [*Laughter*] But I like that can-do spirit of this chamber, and I'm grateful to Charlie, to Charlie Pizzi, and to Joe and all the rest of you that have put together this opportunity for me, all of you at the chamber.

And so, thank you very much. I am happy to be here in Philadelphia. As you can imagine, these last few weeks in Washington have been pretty high pressure, high pressure time for me, what with all the experts and the instant analysis and the columnists giving unsolicited advice. Thank goodness the Super Bowl is over. [*Laughter*]

I am very pleased to be here, particularly pleased to be here today because American businesses, as represented by this group gathered here, have a unique perspective on the tough times we've been going through recently. And as businessmen and businesswomen, you can separate the sensational from the sensible, the sweet-sounding quick fixes from real solutions. When it comes to America's economy, we can't accept empty symbols and slogans. We need to work together—that's what I like, what Joe was saying about the way the Mayor and you all are approaching it in this city—we've got to work together nationally and turn this economy around.

Tuesday night, I came before the American people to outline a program for doing just that. And we all know this is an election year. The air back in Washington has been thick with feel-good gimmicks that have nothing to do with true prosperity and everything to do with politics. We need to get down to business, literally. In the critical weeks ahead, common sense must replace partisanship. And I came here to ask for your help.

The plan that I put before Congress and the American people contained several action steps. And one of the most critical was this, to free up American businesses by clearing away the obstacles to growth: high taxes, overregulation, and Government deficits. And I've offered the only comprehensive plan that doesn't raise taxes, doesn't throw away the spending discipline now in place on the Congress, these spending caps, and doesn't cut defense beyond what's necessary for this country's security. But let me tell you the three words that really separate my plan from what I think of the rest of them: It will work. Those three: It will work.

Each of us has a role to play, so I am moving forward with steps I can take right now. You may remember I divided that State of the Union Message into steps I can take, short-term areas where we need legislation and then a longer term program. Right now, I have instructed every Cabinet Department to speed up progrowth expenditures. And we estimate that will be as much as $10 billion worth in the next 6 months. We don't have to go to Congress to get them to do that; we just accelerate the spending plans to try to give this economy an extra kick.

I directed the Secretary of the Treasury to change the Federal tax tables so that millions of Americans can choose to have the Government withhold less from their paychecks. Now, that's a large number. That could pump as much as $25 billion into the economy this year alone. That is money in the pockets of working men and women to help pay for clothing or to help save for college or to help buy a new car. And after all, it is their money. And there has been this schedule where really there has been overwithholding. And this I think will give, for those who elect to do it—if everyone elected to do it, it would be $25 billion, and I think that will give the economy a jolt.

I have asked Cabinet Departments and Federal Agencies to institute a 90-day moratorium on new Federal regulations that could hinder growth. We'll undertake a top-to-bottom review in the fields of energy, the environment, transportation, exports, financial services, and communications, among others. Here's the test: We will accelerate any regulations that encourage growth and the creation of jobs. And whenever possible, we will scrap those that tie the hands of business and impede growth. I know that I have regulatory responsibilities affecting safety in the workplace, for example, health, environmental protection. And I will not neglect those responsibilities.

But you know as well as anyone how Government, sometimes with the best of intentions, can hobble innovation and risk-taking, the lifeblood of a successful business. Government naturally tends to expand ever outward, its redtape oblivious to anything

standing in its path. It touches everyone. Every regulation that reduces efficiency slaps a hidden tax on the consumer as well. From the tab on a bag of groceries at the checkout line to the sticker price on the showroom floor, every American takes a hit when the Government overregulates.

American business men and women need this freedom to experiment, to compete without looking over their shoulders for Washington's approval. Small businesses and those just starting up feel the sting of overregulation most of all. Yet these businesses drive America forward. They create most of our new jobs. They reinvigorate our communities. They embody the power of the American dream. I make this pledge: We will set America's dreamers and doers free and put an end to this regulatory overkill.

In some of this area I will need the help of the Congress, and I promise I will take the message as strongly as I can to the Congress in this regard. Even now, an untold number of hard-working, responsible men and women go without needed bank loans for starting up a new business or for investing more in an existing one. We've got to ease the credit crunch and give these people a chance. That's why we've given the bank regulators more than 30 policy changes and clarifications to restore common sense and balance to the regulatory system.

I've mentioned this before, but in regulation, again, we have a responsibility. We don't want to go back to what is known as forbearance, where we neglect the soundness that is required. But there is regulatory overkill. The people are afraid, I think, in some instances in the financial community because of the excesses of regulation. And we're going to try very hard to achieve a better balance.

Now, I've mentioned some of the things that I can do, and there's a few more. But Tuesday night I told Congress, directly challenged it, told it directly what it must do. And I started with the obvious: No investment, no new jobs. Congress must reward investment and stop punishing success.

For 3 years now, I have asked the Congress to lower the capital gains tax. And for 3 years, that essential growth measure has been pilloried and parodied as a windfall for the rich. Now, you and I know that claim for what it is. It's nonsense. Sixty percent, sixty percent of the people who benefit from lower capital gains have incomes under $50,000. A windfall for the rich? By freeing up investment, a cut in the capital gains tax creates new jobs for those looking for work and better jobs for those who want to move up. A lower capital gains tax helps anyone who owns a small business or a farm, anyone who owns a home, anyone who has a single investment. We're talking about helping every working man and woman and every retired person in this country.

We don't have time now for any more of this demagoguery on this question. Let me remind you, in Japan the effective capital gains tax rate comes to about one percent. Germany doesn't tax long-term capital gains at all. To create jobs, to restore a vibrant economy for all Americans, Congress must lower the capital gains tax, and it must lower the capital gains tax now, 15.4 percent.

With a few simple steps, taken right now, Congress can help get the housing industry, builders, investors, buyers, and sellers, back on its feet. To those young families who want to buy their first home but can't quite afford it, I say this: We can help put your dream within reach, and we will. I have offered a plan to allow first-time homebuyers to withdraw savings from IRA's without penalty and to provide a $5,000 tax credit for the first purchase of a home.

I might say parenthetically that Senator Specter, your Senator, has been in the forefront of fighting for the change on how IRA's are treated. He understands what this can mean in terms of stimulating the economy and helping the homeowner.

I have asked Congress to mark the calendar. They must put this recovery plan in place by March 20. Yesterday, right after— the State of the Union was the night before, and yesterday morning I went up to the Congress. And I met with the leaders of both the House and the Senate up on Capitol Hill, and I urged them to meet this timetable. I set the deadline because of a simple fact: The American people want action. They deserve action. Our States are

working overtime; so are thousands of communities across the country. They're tightening their belts, aggressively facing the future. And every day, individual Americans are working hard to get this economy back on its feet, and it's time for Congress to do the same thing. It can be done in that timeframe.

What troubles me is if we let it drag on, it's going to get really caught up in the rough-and-tumble of 1992 national politics. People are crying out for help now, and the Congress can move. We've seen them do it on a wide array of legislative initiatives, and they can do it on these stimulative tax changes. So, I ask every Member of Congress—and please tell them the same thing—to set aside now partisanship for just 51 days and give this plan a chance. Get the plan; put it to work.

Immediate growth, as I mentioned at the outset, is just one part of the picture, one part of our program. We've got to look even further ahead to ensure that when the American economy regains its strength, and inevitably it will, it stays strong.

We start by opening markets to American goods. In our trade negotiations, we will continue to push for open trade, pulling down the barriers that stand in the way of international competition.

To guarantee that American goods and services are the world's finest, we must guarantee America's preeminence in another field, in the field of education. Our America 2000 strategy will revolutionize education in this country, will create new American schools, places where our kids will learn the lessons they need for a new century. And it will allow parents to choose their children's schools. Choice means competition, and you understand as well as anyone what comes from competition. Competition inspires innovation and creativity. It inspires excellence. And that's why we are going to push for our program; we're going to push for school choice.

As I look at education and the fact that we are not where we should be in world standing, it isn't a question of a change here and there. It isn't a question of adding to programs that have failed, programs mandated in Washington. It is a question, literally, of revolutionizing. And that's what we tried to do when we set the education goals, working with Republican and Democrat Governors. That's what we're trying to do with Lamar Alexander in the lead for us, our Secretary of Education, as we take this America 2000 program all across the country. We need your help. It is the best possible investment for the future of this country.

Now, we need a healthy America, and that means reforming health care. I think everyone would agree we cannot afford our present system. But we've reached a fork in the road. We can either go the way of greater Government mandates, leading inevitably to a state system of nationalized care, with the long lines and indifferent service that such a system creates. Or we can reform our private system, preserving the greatest possible patient choice, maintaining the quality of care which, for all its faults, is still the best in the entire world. That's the approach I outlined in a rather broad detail Tuesday night, and that's the approach that I will take when we announce the full detail of our plan next week.

We've proposed another reform, one that is crucial to creating jobs. America has become the most litigious society on Earth. Frivolous lawsuits are exhausting our ability to compete. If we were as good at rewarding success as we are at suing each other, we would be a century ahead of the rest of the world. Lawsuit madness gums everything up. Needed new products never reach the marketplace because of concerns over liability. In many areas, businesses are forced either to drive prices into the stratosphere or literally close shop.

My Competitiveness Council that's chaired by the Vice President, Vice President Quayle, has offered 50 concrete recommendations to restore sanity to our civil justice system. I've enacted some of these recommendations by Executive order. Others, however, require Congress to act. And with all respect, there are 62 lawyers in the United States Senate, a lot of lawyers up there on Capitol Hill. I realize that might present a problem, but it also presents an opportunity. And I'd like to see them move forward now with these

changes to cap some of these outrageous areas of unlimited liability. It's driving our small businesses right flat into the ground and costing American workers jobs.

And finally, I can use Congress' help in another all-important area. We must get the Federal deficit under control. Now, let's face the facts: The Government in Washington is too big, and it spends too much. I have proposed a freeze on all domestic discretionary budget authority as well as a freeze on Federal domestic Government employment. And I have asked Congress to get rid of 246 federally funded programs. Now, some of them have very noble titles. But in these times, none of them is indispensable, and I'm going to call on Congress to get rid of them. I think we're talking about something like $4 billion in this regard.

For too long, Congress has been violating an important principle of good government: Do no harm. It's been imposing its own habits on State and local governments, and the taxpayer ends up, as you may all know, by footing the bill. These unfinanced Federal Government mandates, as they're called, require the cities, require the States to provide new services or institute new programs, but the Congress doesn't provide the money to pay for them. That means the local governments must pass along Congress' wish list to the taxpayer in the form of higher taxes at the local level.

Now, the National Governors' Association, made up, obviously, of Republicans and Democrats, continually urge the Congress to stop these mandates which are killing innovation, killing savings at the State and local level. From now on, if Congress passes a mandate, it shouldn't pass the buck. Congress must pay for the mandates it imposes without heaping on new taxes.

I've spared you some of the detail. But taken together, these and other steps that I've outlined will, in my view, reinvigorate our economy, give it the boost that it needs now, and ensure that it continues to provide opportunity and create jobs for all who want to partake. That is the promise America makes to her citizens. They have a right to expect no less.

Almost two centuries ago, Philadelphia's

merchants gathered together at the city tavern to form this Chamber of Commerce. They looked out on a Nation almost limitless in possibility. A special kind of faith brought them here, that if they worked hard and worked together, their young country would allow them to fulfill their dreams.

America has changed dramatically in those 200 years. And yet, the essentials remain. The pessimists are wrong; the pessimists are wrong. We are going to pull out of these tough times. Inflation is down; inventories are down. The market has been expressing optimism in the future. Interest rates are down. This is no time for gloom and doom. It is time for action in Washington to restore confidence and get this economy moving again.

And here's where you come in. We need your help. You can affect the way Congress approaches this program that I have outlined in some detail. We need your help. And with your help, we'll get that action, and we will reaffirm our country's rightful place as the world's leader for this decade and for the next century.

Thank you all very, very much for this opportunity. Thank you.

*Note: The President spoke at 12:11 p.m. at the Wyndham Franklin Plaza Hotel in Philadelphia, PA. In his remarks, he referred to Joan Specter, Philadelphia city councilwoman, and Charles P. Pizzi, president of the Greater Philadelphia Chamber of Commerce.*

# Remarks During Discussions With Prime Minister Kiichi Miyazawa of Japan in New York City
*January 30, 1992*

*The President.* This gives me a chance, with our friends from the press here, to tell you how much I appreciated your hospitality.

*The Prime Minister.* Let me tell, Mr. President, to all the audience that we will deliver all we promised to you.

*The President.* I never doubted——

*The Prime Minister.* I make it very, very clear to the audience.

*The President.* I never doubted it.

*The Prime Minister.* There will be no misunderstanding about it.

*The President.* Let me make clear that that was never a doubt in my mind. And secondly, I'm very grateful for the many manifestations of friendship and hospitality. And you, yourself, just went out of your way on a very personal basis to be considerate to me.

*The Prime Minister.* Oh, yes.

*The President.* So, it's most appropriate that we see you when you first get off this airplane. But I don't want to take too much time.

*The Prime Minister.* This is very kind of you, very kind.

*The President.* They'll be leaving us very soon now—[*laughter*]—and we can talk.

[*At this point, another group of journalists entered the room.*]

*The President.* I might say, with the Japanese journalists here, that I had a chance to tell the Prime Minister when he arrived here how grateful the United States is for the progress that we made on this visit and how grateful I am personally to this Prime Minister and to everybody in Japan for their hospitality. The concern when I had that very, very brief illness, but the concern from the people there and the members of your Government, Members of the Diet, I will never forget it. It was very, very thoughtful. And I want to take this opportunity to thank the people of Japan because, on the business side and the personal side, we could not have been treated with more dignity and more care and more friendship.

*The Prime Minister.* I am very much honored to hear it from you, Mr. President. And the Japanese people were really delighted to have you and Mrs. Bush in Tokyo. And unfortunately, just a slight illness, but that perhaps brought you and Mrs. Bush closer to the Japanese mind, naturally.

This reminded me, when President Ford came to Japan and he was inspecting the parade, his pants were all too short. [*Laughter*] And it was on the TV, and that really made him very familiar to Japanese TV watchers.

*The President.* I remember that. And

please tell His Majesty how much we appreciate the hospitality for me.

*The Prime Minister.* I will, sir.

*The President.* But here you are, and thank you for what you said here. This got all out of proportion, and I think we're in good shape. And I mean it.

*Note: The President spoke at 6:50 p.m. at the Waldorf Astoria Hotel.*

# Remarks to the United Nations Security Council in New York City
*January 31, 1992*

Thank you, Mr. President, for your key role in convening this first-ever summit of the United Nations Security Council.

Fellow members and Mr. Secretary-General, congratulations to you, sir, as you take office at this time of tremendous challenge and opportunity. And for the United States, it's a high honor to participate, to speak at this history-making event.

We meet at a moment of new beginnings for this institution and, really, for every member nation. And for most of its history, the United Nations was caught in a cold-war crossfire. And I think back to my days here in the early seventies as a Permanent Representative, of the way then polemics displaced peacekeeping. And long before I came on the scene and long after I left, the U.N. was all too often paralyzed by cruel ideological divisions and the struggle to contain Soviet expansion. And today, all that's changed. And the collapse of imperial communism and the end of the cold war breathe new life into the United Nations.

It was just one year ago that the world saw this new, invigorated United Nations in action as this Council stood fast against aggression and stood for the sacred principles enshrined in the U.N. Charter. And now it's time to step forward again, make the internal reforms, accelerate the revitalization, accept the responsibilities necessary for a vigorous and effective United Nations. I want to assure the members of this Council and the Secretary-General, the United Nations can count on our full support in this

task.

Today, for these brief remarks, I'll talk not on the economic and social agenda so eloquently addressed by President Borja, but rather I'll mention the proliferation of mass destruction, regional conflicts, destabilizing renegade regimes that are on the horizon, terrorism, human rights. They all require our immediate attention.

The world also challenges us to strengthen and sustain positive change. And we must advance the momentous movement toward democracy and freedom—democratization, I believe Boutros-Ghali called this, our distinguished Secretary-General—and expand the circle of nations committed to human rights and the rule of law. It's an exciting opportunity for our United Nations, and we must not allow it to slip away.

Right now, across the globe, the U.N. is working night and day in the cause of peace. And never before in its four decades has the U.N.'s Blue Helmets and Blue Berets been so engaged in the noble work of peacekeeping, even to the extent of building the foundation for free elections. And never before has the United Nations been so ready and so compelled to step up to the task of peacemaking, both to resolve hot wars and to conduct that forward-looking mission known as preventive diplomacy.

We must be practical as well as principled as we seek to free people from the specter of conflict. We recognize every nation's obligation to invest in peace. As conflicts are resolved and violence subsides, then the institutions of free societies can take hold. And as they do, they become our strongest safeguards against aggression and tyranny.

Democracy, human rights, the rule of law, these are the building blocks of peace and freedom. And in the lives of millions of men and women around the world its import is simple. It can mean the difference between war and peace, healing and hatred, and where there is fear and despair, it really can mean hope.

We look to the Secretary-General to present to this Council his recommendations to ensure effective and efficient peacekeeping, peacemaking, and preventive diplomacy. And we look forward to exploring these ideas together.

We have witnessed change of enormous breadth and scope, all in but a few short years. A remarkable revolution has swept away the old regimes from Managua to Moscow. But everywhere, free government and the institutions that give it form will take time to flourish and mature.

Free elections give democracy a foothold, but true democracy means more than simply the rule of the majority. It means an irrevocable commitment to democratic principles. It means equal rights for minorities. And above all, it means the sanctity of even a single individual against the unjust power of the state.

The will of the majority must never degenerate into the whim of majority. This fundamental principle transcends all borders. Human dignity, the inalienable rights of man, these are not the possessions of the state. They're universal. In Asia, in Africa, in Europe, in the Americas, the United Nations must stand with those who seek greater freedom and democracy. And that is my deep belief; that is the belief of the American people. And it's the belief that breathes life into the great principle of the universal declaration of human rights.

Our changed world is a more hopeful world, indeed, but it is not absent those who would turn back the clock to the darker days of threats and bullying. And our world is still a dangerous world, rife with far too many terrible weapons.

In my first address here to the United Nations as President, I challenged the Soviet Union to eliminate chemical weapons and called on every nation to join us in this crusade, His Majesty King Hassan of Morocco making this point so well right here today. What greater cause for this great body: to make certain the world has seen the last of these terrible weapons. And so, let us vow to make this year the year all nations at long last join to ban this scourge.

There is much more to do regarding weapons of mass destruction. Just 3 days ago, in my State of the Union Message here, I announced the steps, far-reaching, unilateral steps, that we will take to reduce our nuclear arsenal. And these steps affect each element in our strategic triad, the land, the sea, and the air.

In addition to these unilateral steps, we are prepared to move forward on mutual arms reduction. I noted his constructive comments here today, and tomorrow, in my meeting with President Yeltsin, we will continue the search for common ground on this vitally important issue. He responded with some very serious proposals just the other day.

We welcome, the world welcomes statements by several of the new States that won independence after the collapse of the U.S.S.R. that they will abide by the Nuclear Non-Proliferation Treaty. And yet, realism requires us to remain vigilant in this time of transition.

The danger of proliferation remains. And again, let me single out the earlier remarks by the President of the French Republic, President Mitterrand, on this subject, the clarion call to do something about it. We must act together so that from this time forward, people involved in sophisticated weapons programs redirect their energies to peaceful endeavors.

We'll do more in cooperation with our allies to ensure that dangerous materials and technology don't fall into the hands of terrorists or others. And we will continue to work with these new States to ensure a strong commitment in word and deed to all global nonproliferation standards.

Today, the threat of global nuclear war is more distant than at any time in the nuclear era. Drawing down the old cold war arsenals will further ease that dread. But the specter of mass destruction remains all too real, especially as some nations continue to push to acquire weapons of mass destruction and the means to deliver them.

Our triumph in the Gulf is testament to the U.N.'s mission. Its security is a shared responsibility. Today, this institution spearheads a quarantine against the outlaw regime of Saddam Hussein. It is the strong belief of my country that we must keep sanctions in place and take the following steps to preserve our common security: We must continue to focus on Iraq's capability to build or maintain weapons of mass destruction. And we must make clear to the world and, most important, to the people of Iraq that no normalization is possible so long as Saddam Hussein remains there, remains in power.

As on all of the urgent issues I've mentioned today, progress comes from acting in concert, and we must deal resolutely with these renegade regimes, if necessary, by sanctions or stronger measures, to compel them to observe international standards of behavior. We will not be blind to the dangers we still face. Terrorists and their state sponsors must know there will be serious consequences if they violate international law.

Two weeks ago, this Council, in unity, sent a very strong message to Libya. And let me repeat today Resolution 731, passed unanimously by this body, by the Security Council, calls on Libya to comply fully with the requests of three states on this Council. And I would just like to use this meeting today to call on Libya to heed the call of the Security Council of the United Nations.

Last year in the Gulf, in concert, we responded to an attack on the sovereignty of one nation as an assault on the security of all. So, let us make it our mission to give this principle the greatest practical meaning in the conduct of nations.

Today, we stand at another crossroads. Perhaps the first time since that hopeful moment in San Francisco, we can look at our Charter as a living, breathing document. And yes, after so many years, it still may be in its infancy, requiring a careful and vigilant nurturing of its parents, but I believe in my heart that it is alive and well.

Our mission is to make it strong and sturdy through increased dedication and cooperation, and I know that we are up to the challenge. The nations represented here, like the larger community of the U.N. represented by so many Perm Reps here today, have it in their power to act for peace and freedom.

So, may God bless the United Nations as it pursues its noble goal. Thank you, Mr. President.

*Note: The President spoke at 12:18 p.m. in the Security Council Chamber at the United Nations. In his remarks, he referred to Prime Minister John Major of the United Kingdom, Acting President of the United Nations Security Council, and President Rodrigo Borja of Ecuador.*

# The President's News Conference With President Boris Yeltsin of Russia
*February 1, 1992*

*President Bush.* Today, for the first time, an American President and the democratically elected President of an independent Russia have met, and we did so not as adversaries but as friends. This historic meeting is yet another confirmation of the end of the cold war and the dawn of a new era. Russia and the United States are charting a new relationship. And it's based on trust; it's based on a commitment to economic and political freedom; it's based on a strong hope for true partnership. So, we agreed here that we're going to pull closer together economically and politically.

I invited President Yeltsin to come to the States for a state visit; he accepted. He, in turn, asked me to come to the Soviet Union, and I accepted. That will be later in the year. And he will be coming in the first half of the year, the date to be determined later on.

We agreed to cooperate in the safe handling of nuclear weapons, arms reductions, and a wide array of other subjects. So, from my standpoint and the standpoint of the United States, our first team here, we felt it was a very good visit. The only problem was, it was very short. But we'll have a chance to follow up at the state visit.

And Mr. President, the floor is yours. And welcome once again, even though you're heading off now down to the Hill to meet some of the Members of Congress.

*President Yeltsin.* Mr. President Bush, ladies and gentlemen, I am very grateful to my friend George for the words which he has just spoken, in terms of our meeting and aimed at Russia and towards me. I feel that the meeting was exceptionally positive, necessary, and historic.

We discussed a whole range of issues, as a matter of fact, those kinds of issues that have never been exposed and opened many, many years and many, many decades: issues of economic reform in Russia, as well as cooperation and assistance so that this reform not die on the vine, and issues having to do with the Commonwealth of Independent Nations, economic issues having to do with the military condition now, the condition of the military.

And on the initiative of President Bush and Russia also, we talked about reduction of strategic and tactical arsenals down to the minimal of, say, two and a half thousand warheads for either side. And in this issue we will now begin very specific and concrete negotiations, the issue of arms sales, of nonproliferation of nuclear weapons, issues of the so-called brain drain, and a whole series of others. Now maybe some very specific and personal issues, but I think having to do with a relationship which really has a great importance. I'm very satisfied that today one might say that there has been written and drawn a new line, and crossed out all of the things that have been associated with the cold war.

Today we are going to sign a statement or declaration on a new nature or character of the relationship between the United States of America and Russia. From now on we do not consider ourselves to be potential enemies as it had been previously in our military doctrine. This is the historic value of this meeting.

And another very important factor in our relationship, right away today it's already been pointed out, that in the future there will be full frankness, full openness, full honesty in our relationship both of us value very, very much.

Thank you so much.

*President Bush.* Now I'll be glad to take a few questions before the President has to leave.

### Nuclear Weapons

*Q.* Mr. Bush, Mr. Yeltsin seems to have gone a long way towards meeting you halfway on land-based MIRV's. Are you prepared to deal your half of the deck on sea-based missiles?

*President Bush.* He has gone a long way. We agreed that all these subjects would be discussed in more detail when Secretary Baker goes back to Moscow. I think he'll be there within the next 2 weeks. We didn't go into any agreements on categories or numbers, but we decided that we would let the experts talk about this in much more detail. But we saluted his very broad proposals.

*Q.* We see in the declaration that Russia and the United States do not regard each other as potential adversaries. Does it mean you followed Mr. Yeltsin's, President Yeltsin's example so that retargeting of American nuclear weapons are not targeted on Russian targets anymore?

*President Bush.* We agreed that all these matters will be discussed in Moscow. But certainly I agree with his objectives, and that is to turn former enemies not only into friends but allies. And it's that that we're starting down that road, and I'm quite optimistic about it. We both realize that there is some negotiation that has to take place in terms of the specifics.

*Q.* President Yeltsin, if both sides are now friends, then why not call for a total elimination of nuclear weapons?

*President Yeltsin.* The thing is that there are still adventurers, terrorists, and irre-

sponsible politicians in some countries of
the world against whom we have to have a
certain arsenal of nuclear weapons for restraining them.

*Q.* Have you discussed with the President
some sort of overall initiative which would
defend?

*President Yeltsin.* Yes, we did discuss this
issue of a global shield, if you would. We
consider that it's a very interesting topic,
and George Bush confirmed that, yes, this is
an exceptionally necessary topic. It would
be interesting to utilize these systems on a
mutual basis maybe even with the participation of some other nuclear-club countries,
nuclear countries. But this requires a very
careful, very detailed study at the level of
specialists.

*Q.* President Bush, your thoughts on
President Yeltsin's proposal for a global
shield. Is this something that—we're working together on this—is that something that
you would philosophically be inclined towards?

*President Bush.* It's something that we
talked about at lunch with Secretary
Cheney. As I said, we reached no decision
on these matters. The Soviet Union has a lot
of expertise in space, for example. Perhaps
one area of real cooperation can be in
future space adventure; another could be in
this area of defense. But we reached no
conclusion except to say that we felt it was
worth discussing it in much more detail.

*Russian Reforms*

*Q.* Mr. President, I'm going to ask you a
question. This morning you said that the
United States are willing to participate in
the process that is going on in Russia. What
parts of economic assistance were discussed
today, I mean assistance for economic
reform, rather?

*President Bush.* Well, largely, today President Yeltsin had a chance to expand on the
reforms he has undertaken. His finance
expert, Mr. Gaydar, is meeting right now
with our Secretary of the Treasury, and we
agreed that they would talk about the details of the reform. So, I would leave any
substance to hear from those two.

But there are many areas where we already are beginning to work with the
Soviet Union, not only in these private dele-

gations. We feel it would be very important
that they be full members in these international financial organizations. I pledged the
United States' full efforts in support for
early entry into the IMF and into the World
Bank. We expanded a little bit on the programs we already have working. In terms of
additional support for the Soviet Union, financial and food, Jim Baker had an opportunity to discuss to some degree the follow-
on from the conference that we had, the
cooperation conference that was held in
Washington last week.

We didn't get into too many specifics on
that, but I was very interested in hearing
from him about the reforms in place. And I
did, in a general sense, say that the United
States would like to assist in any way possible.

*Q.* President Yeltsin, in your opinion, do
you consider that you are getting sufficient
assistance from the United States, economic
assistance? You heard a lot about it today.

*President Yeltsin.* Well, I would somewhat differently approach this question.
After all, what's important here is not just
aid. We were looking at the question of
support for the reform, cooperation in a lot
of different areas, a lot of directions, accomplishing a whole series of programs in order
to be supportive of reform.

I didn't come here just to stretch out my
hand and ask for help, no. We're calling for
cooperation, cooperation for the whole
world. Because if the reform in Russia goes
under, that means there will be a cold war.
The cold war is going to turn into a hot
war. This is again going to be an arms race.
Again, this will be the same regime that we
have just recently rid ourselves. We cannot
allow this to happen because in this reform
the whole world community has to participate, not just the United States, and not just
some sort of financial help but political support, cooperation, and the accomplishment
of overall programs by everybody in order
to help.

Also, humanitarian aid, we have agreed
on this. From February 10th there will be a
massive assistance on the part of the United
States and others, and I'm very appreciative
to George Bush for this.

### Nuclear Technology

*Q.* You said that during the negotiations you were talking about nonproliferation of nuclear technology outside of the former Soviet Union. Is there a possibility of leaking of this technology?

*President Yeltsin.* Yes. First is the moving of tactical weapons out of Kazakhstan, Ukraine, and Byelorussia onto the territory of Russia. All of the tactical weapons have been taken out of Kazakhstan, from Byelorussia. We are now finishing up that process. And in the Ukraine we will be done on July 1.

Now, as far as strategic weapons, this is a more difficult question. But there will be a transport, first of all, to Russia of those MIRV's warheads onto the territory of Russia so that they can be eliminated or so they can be turned to fuel for power plants, atomic power plants, and peaceful purposes. That's the one direction.

Secondly, how to take that 2,000 nuclear specialists who were working many decades, what to do with them and how to give them jobs. I looked at this issue in Moscow and took the decision to help them in a social sense, in a big way, to give them material support and radically change up to 5,000 rubles per month to give them a pay raise so that they would not flee to the West. Secondly, today we agreed on a whole series of joint programs where the scientists will be brought in and so that they can participate and work. And there was a proposal by President Bush to create a center, a research center where they could work together fruitfully, and that will attract them.

### Negotiation Timetable

*Q.* I just wondered, did you all agree on any sort of timetable for your arms negotiations, for example, to be coinciding with President Yeltsin's visit in the springtime and your visit, I guess, to Moscow later in the year?

*President Bush.* We agreed that the very next step will be a much more detailed discussion of this matter when Secretary Baker goes, in but 2 weeks, back to Russia.

Do you want to add to that, Mr. President, Boris?

*Q.* Do you have a goal for finishing these negotiations?

*President Yeltsin.* Yes, namely, in 2 weeks this schedule will be prepared by Mr. Baker together with our representatives. They'll put it together.

*Q.* The whole thing will be done in 2 weeks?

*President Bush.* No, no, just the beginning of the negotiations——

*President Yeltsin.* No, no, no. The schedule will be put together, the schedule.

### Russian Reforms

*Q.* Mr. President, are you convinced that President Yeltsin is committed to democratic and economic reform? And do you believe he will succeed?

*President Bush.* I am convinced that he is totally committed to democratic reform. And I'm convinced that the problems he faces are enormous, but I am also convinced that he will succeed if he gets the proper support from around the world for these worthy objectives. And we are pledging him support from the United States, but I think he himself recognizes the problems they face are enormous.

He put into effect economic reforms. Before he did it, he told me. But much more important, he told the people of Russia he was going to do it. He told them it would not be easy. He told them what he was going to have to do in terms of raising prices, which is not a popular thing to do. And he's done that.

And I think it's very hard to predict how this will go. I would leave that for him to comment on. But I will say this, that the experts that give me advice feel that because of the way in which he handled it and the commitment that is so obvious to democratic reform, that it is going, in spite of hardship, better than they would have predicted.

So, there is no question that this President, President Yeltsin, is committed to democratic reform. He laid his life on the line on top of a tank to make that message loud and clear, and the whole world rejoiced in it when they saw his courage. He's applying that same courage, and I'm not saying that just because he's standing here, he's applying that same courage now to this concept of economic reform. One certainly cannot doubt his full commitment to this subject.

### Commonwealth of Independent States

*Q.* Would either of you care to tell us about the personal relationship you've developed?

*Q.* Is the federation, Commonwealth working the way you wanted it to work? And how long is it going to exist?

*President Yeltsin.* [*Inaudible*]

*Q.* No, the Commonwealth. How is it working, and how long do you think it's going to exist?

*President Yeltsin.* Today I explained to Mr. Bush about our relationship with the other States within our Commonwealth. Yes, we have difficulties, especially in terms of the armed forces issues. We're going to be discussing that on 14 February in Minsk, where all the heads of the independent States will gather.

There are difficulties. Nonetheless, after all, for every time we meet, and we meet once every month, there is each time a step forward. You can't forget that the Commonwealth is only 2 months old. This is still a baby in diapers. You've got to take care of it; you've got to handle it carefully so you don't drop it. That's why we're trying together, all of us, to sit and have a dialog. We have good relations with all the heads of states of all these countries; we do. I believe that this Commonwealth will be stronger and stronger.

*President Bush.* Marlin tells me we've got time but for one more question because President Yeltsin has an appointment with the leaders from Congress at the Russian Embassy, and so we really do have to go.

### Relationship With President Yeltsin

*Q.* I'm just wondering if you gentlemen would care to share the personal relationship that you've developed. You've worked closely, certainly, with Mr. Gorbachev.

*President Bush.* Well, it's well-known that I had a very close relationship with Mr. Gorbachev. It was built on respect. It became friendship. And I can only speak for myself, one half of the equation, but the visits that I have had with President Yeltsin before this have always been very pleasant. I think that we have a good understanding. I have a very warm feeling in my heart about what he has done and is trying to do. And I consider him my friend.

*President Yeltsin.* I consider that I was very lucky in life, both as a political person and just as a man, to have met George Bush. We have contacted each other, have been in contact, oh, now about 2 years at least. And even in the days when I was in the opposition, we used to meet. And then, even then, I already felt his wide-ranging talent, his mind, and his qualities as a person. I'm just tremendously impressed by his wisdom. I think he has incredible qualities not only as a political person but also as a person, as a really great political figure of the United States.

Today our relations have now been formed up as friends, and we talk quite frequently to each other. We call each other on the telephone. We say "Boris"; we say "George." And already this says a lot.

*President Bush.* That's the last question. I'm awful sorry; Marlin is really looking nervous. [*Laughter*] Thank you very much.

*Note: The President's 120th news conference began at 1:37 p.m. at Camp David, MD. President Yeltsin spoke in Russian, and his remarks were translated by an interpreter.*

## Remarks and a Question-and-Answer Session With the National Governors' Association
### *February 3, 1992*

*The President.* I hate to interrupt your former colleague and now mine, Bob Martinez. I heard a little of that, and I think there is some room for optimism. But I also think, as John said, well, we've got a long way to go.

I want to just make some opening comments about the overall policies I spoke about the other night. And then I understand we'll have a Q&A session which I hope will be statements and positions from you as well as inquiry of me. I've learned from these sessions. But let me just make some remarks on where we are in our overall economy.

I salute the members of the Cabinet that are here, but especially our visiting Governors. It seems that everyone in this country agrees on two things: First, that we need to get the economy moving, and second, that our people are up to the challenge of remaining number one in the world. I do not believe for a minute this is a country in decline. If you doubt it, go talk to any single world leader.

Last Tuesday, I really made a challenge to the Congress to pass what I feel is a commonsense growth package and do it by March 20th, and pass a long-term series of growth initiatives without delay. So, we had it divided short term and long term. The package relies on some commonsense objectives. It encourages investment. It protects the value of basic investments, like a home. And it does not raise Federal taxes. It does not increase the Federal deficit. And it doesn't employ short-term gimmicks that create long-term trouble.

Now, we all know the political process, particularly people sitting around this table. And you know that in an election year of this magnitude, bipartisan good will is in basic short supply. But we really cannot afford politics as usual. I think we have a realistic window here of opportunity, a chance to make real progress and to do it now. And maybe I'm a little optimistic on this one, but I do sense that Members on

both sides of the aisle on Capitol Hill want action now. I've watched it and listened to the debate in the last few days, and that's my feeling.

Inflation and long-term interest rates are at their lowest level in two decades. That's good in terms of the recovery that inevitably is going to ensue. And I think more and more we're beginning to hear people say this sluggish economy is turning around. And certainly the American people are ready for action.

John Kennedy once wrote, "Any system of government will work when everything is going well. It's the system that functions in the pinches that survives." Well, it's pinch time. And I have proposed a way in which all of us can rise to the occasion.

In the State of the Union Address, I outlined a short-term growth package that does take care of the essentials. And it encourages investment which allows us to expand businesses and create new ones. And I'm talking here mainly about creation of new small business. It strengthens the real estate industry which historically has led us out of recessions in troubled times. And it encourages risk-taking and investment by cutting the tax on long-term capital gains and by some other stimulative procedures. It also reforms Government. We're going after a bunch of pork barrel projects. It holds the line on spending while moving money out of unnecessary programs and into vital ones.

And here's what I think it means for you: A 13-percent increase in money available for highway funding; a 158-percent increase from last year in land and water conservation fund grants; record amounts for education, a 15-percent increase from last year; and a 27-percent increase in Head Start. These proposals will make every 4-year-old eligible for Head Start, every one.

I believe the budget puts the money where it does the most good. Now, some complain, clearly, that it doesn't do much. I am proud of what it does. It lays out a blueprint for growth. And some of the things it doesn't do deserve some credit. It does not violate the budget agreement which is the only constraint in existence on discretionary Federal spending. And it doesn't raise taxes. And I think the program will work. And so while you're here, my pitch would be to visit the congressional delegations and urge them to move by March 20th. I really believe that deadline should be met.

Just a word about the long-term proposals. If you think of this moment in history, after the cold war, right in the middle of the information revolution where we are, something becomes crystal clear: We've got to retool America to meet the challenges of a new age, and that's an age of international competition. Cold war policies just simply are not going to get the job done.

Now, businesses have begun retooling for competition in the world economy. State governments have adopted innovations that let them provide better services for less money. And I believe that it's time the Federal Government becomes part of that solution, too. So, let's start with one long-term goal that will make a huge difference in your lives. For years and years we in Washington have talked about cutting the deficit. And I really believe we must get that deficit under control. The Federal Government is too big, and it spends too much. And what that leads you to then is real budget discipline, and the long-term plan and the short-term plan provide that discipline. And I simply cannot let the Congress bust the spending caps that now exist.

I want the Congress to do what I believe you want, transcending party lines, and that is to stop showering the States with these mandates, unfunded mandates. For businesses or for States, mandated programs and benefits too often mean mandated deficits. And I've told Congress: If you pass mandates onto the States, pay for them. And don't do it by raising taxes on all the Americans, on the American people.

I want Congress to give me something that you have. I'm not naive about this, but I'd like to have that line-item veto. And I understand the Legislature's urge to please a constituent by putting something in the budget. I was there. I was a Member of a

Congress. And I also know that that practice of bending to the constituents' will on every project enrages taxpayers across the country, as well it should. So, I will keep repeating that a line-item veto lets a President or a Governor say something that's very hard to say, and that is, no.

I want the Congress to let the States apply their own resources to important social programs, apply their imaginations. And too often we have this one-size-fits-all blueprint that just doesn't fit outside of here, outside of this beltway. Jefferson called the States laboratories. We referred to that at the summit, educational summit. Well, it's time we let the States do this R&D, get going on innovation. And I want to give State and local governments greater flexibility in administering services. And that's why we propose a revised $14.6 billion block grant. And that grant will provide the States with needed flexibility to administer education and health and social services and the drug program, some of which I guess Bob Martinez was talking about.

I want to focus the Federal policy on crucial issues like welfare reform. And the key to that lies in one real simple word, and that is "responsibility." Now, many States are in the innovation business, beginning to reform welfare with that responsibility. And they believe that when healthy adults receive Government assistance, they have responsibilities to the American taxpayers who fund them: seeking work, education, job training. I see Tommy Thompson; I had a long talk with him not just about the experience in Wisconsin but about what other States are doing in these areas. And we support that innovation. Clearly, we have responsibility to those in the social safety net. And we have a responsibility to ensure that welfare is a temporary net, not a guaranteed lifestyle. So, we're going to do what we can to help reform the systems. That leads us to waivers. If you need a waiver of Federal regulations to reform, we'll get you a waiver as quickly as we can.

And I want the Federal Government at another point to redouble our efforts for the most fundamental building block of a home, a school, a neighborhood, a city, our Nation,

183

and I'm talking about the family. Several weeks ago—I mentioned this in making the State of the Union—a group came in from the National League of Cities, Democrats, Republicans, large cities, small cities, urging me to appoint this Commission on the Urban Family. The decline and disintegration of the family was at the very heart of the problems that they spelled out. And it was without exception; they agreed on this unanimously. And of course, I'm very grateful to Governor Ashcroft and the former mayor of Dallas, Annette Strauss, who agreed to lead this Commission.

I believe our plan looks at the fundamentals. It gives much-needed support to those raising families by increasing that personal exemption on the Federal income tax by $500 per child. I wish it could be more, but that's all that can fit into this budget that will not bust the ceilings. That's all we can afford right now. We give families a greater stake in health care and education. And it proposes IRA reforms and tax changes that help people pay for these basics.

A final issue, and one where you all have literally starred in an exemplary bipartisan manner, and that's education. The Governors have helped unleash a long-overdue and much-needed revolution in education. And I want to commend the works of Governor Romer and Governor Campbell on that report of the National Council on the Standards and Testing. The Senate has indicated unanimous support for the recommendations, and our new budget injects new funds for research, statistics, and assessment funding that would be used to help implement these recommendations. So now, we must take the work that we began together and take it further. And we must revolutionize these American schools. I don't know if Lamar has had a chance to bring you up to date, but clearly, I hope you will ask him where it stands if he hasn't.

I'd like to urge you to help me send this message to Congress to literally join in this revolutionary crusade for American education and to pass the strategy, pass the American 2000 strategy. We have got to give every child full and fair opportunity to learn. We believe educational choice is the way, the clear way to help do that. Choice serves as a cornerstone in our America 2000 program. Thirty States have already embraced America 2000. And we can ensure just around this table that every State joins the march, that every community becomes an America 2000 community, that every kid is prepared for the competitive world of the 21st century.

So, our education revolution, and I use the term "our" advisedly. Governor Nelson chided me last night because I said "my" educational program. I was taking that up to Congress because, very candidly, they have a different approach there. But I accept that because it is "our" educational program. And that revolution is ours. It started in Charlottesville more than 2 years ago. It shows what can be done when we lay down our partisan swords in service to a higher cause. And I hope that you all will serve as an example, an inspiration for all of us in Washington during the next 6 weeks.

In sum, I don't want a partisan fight over our education program or, indeed, over this growth package. And I really want us to do what's right. And my eyes are open in terms of the partisan political year. But again, we have this timeframe now in which we can lay aside our partisan ambitions and get something done for this country, both in the educational field and in terms of growth.

So I guess the bottom line is, I need your help. I'd like to ask for your help to talk to the Congress about these initiatives. And certainly I would solicit, earnestly solicit your help to see us move this country forward to try to revolutionize education for the generations coming.

Thank you all very much. In just a second we will be alone and able to hear a few suggestions or answer a few questions. Who's next?

*Governor Ashcroft.* Mr. President, let me just begin by thanking you for your firm and steadfast leadership in the world during this time of rapid change. We're grateful for your budget initiatives to stimulate economic growth. And your partnership with Governors is a significant one in Federal-State relations. Especially in a city that is covetous of power, we appreciate the fact that you think of us as partners. Especially we've appreciated the opportunity of working with you on national education goals, child care legislation, on increased funding for Head Start——

*Governor Romer.* Could I ask the press not to leave yet? Go ahead. I'm sorry.

*Governor Ashcroft.* ——for clean air legislation, the U.S.-Canada trade treaty, and national transportation legislation, all of those things. We're here today to say to you that we appreciate your cooperation and pledge our cooperation with you as we share this opportunity to bring America into the 21st century.

*Governor Romer.* Excuse me, we need a new format here. I come as a part of a nonpartisan organization, NGA. I'm the incoming chairman, and I think there are a lot of things that we need to discuss with the administration. And unfortunately, this format is not a good one; it's kind of structured. They're assigned questions.

*The President.* Ask me anything you want.

### Budget Proposals

*Governor Romer.* But I think that there are things that we do have a bipartisan program on, and there are some things that we honestly differ, Mr. President. And I, before the press left, wanted to say that on the main issue that is on your mind, and that is the economic recovery program and the budget, I think that there are some very strong feelings about that issue from Governors. And I think that we, hopefully, can arrive at a bipartisan answer to it. However, there are a couple of points that you made that I think have partisan implications, and I just frankly want to answer them before the press leaves the room.

It is in reference to your budget proposal. I also want to get gimmicks out of that budget. I don't think they're out yet. I think there's a $12 billion gimmick, which is an asterisk which is not yet identified as to where the money is going to come from. And I think there is a $28 billion gimmick in there in terms of accrual accounting, of anticipating things in the future.

Now, I want this to be settled, if we can, by honestly working through the options. But I honestly believe that we ought not pose this meeting with the Governors of

how can we as Governors help you go to Congress and convince them that your approach alone is the only approach. I think there are other approaches, and we ought to, as Governors, recognize that and to say together that we need to take these differences and work at them positively. I just hope that whatever solution we come by, that we do not, in the short-term solutions, dig ourselves holes where we do not have long-term economic growth available to us.

I just wanted to lay out that issue because it was an honest issue among some Democratic Governors that we want to communicate to you, that we're concerned about the budget that you've laid out. We're concerned that it does not provide the revenue to do what is anticipated there, and we're concerned that some of those may end up on our backs, particularly the $12 billion undesignated source.

*The President.* But if it doesn't provide the revenue, are you all suggesting a tax increase now at the Federal level?

*Governor Romer.* I think that the approach that many Democratic Governors are taking is the following: That we ought to take the peace dividend, whatever size it is, $50 billion to $100 billion over 5 years, and have it directed toward economic stimulation of the country. Secondly, that we ought to take the issue of tax fairness and adjust it between the middle class and those in the upper brackets as Congress and you may jointly decide. I'm worried about trying to take the peace dividend and to make the economic tax adjustments that you suggested with figures in the budget that I do not yet believe balance.

*The President.* Well, let me get to the defense budget. The Democratic Governor has taken a position that it ought to be a $100 billion defense cut? I have said to the Nation I think it ought to be $50 billion, and the Joint Chiefs of Staff think it ought to be $50 billion. And I have a responsibility for the national security and the foreign policy. And in my view, $50 billion, based on recommendations from the Joint Chiefs and from the Secretary of Defense, is right.

Now, are we saying—we're getting to specifics here. Do you want it to be $100 billion, and if so, what bases do you want to close? What areas do you want to shut down? What weapon systems do you want to knock off right now? Where do you want to lay off the people? We've got a program. We're testifying on it every day. Now, I'd like to know what your suggestion is specifically, while we have the press here.

*Governor Romer.* Let me answer it. The reason I got into this is that I recognized in your presentation—and before the press was to leave—was an identification of these Governors to go to Congress and argue for the budget message that you made. And I simply am trying to say there is an alternate point of view that ought to be put on the table. And that alternate point of view is, first of all, in the size of the military peace dividend——

*The President.* Right.

*Governor Romer.* ——there is a debate whether it's $50 billion or $100 billion. And I don't know the answer to that because I don't sit in the Halls of Congress. But I think that debate ought to go forward. Secondly, there is a debate as to whether or not the tax structure is fair, and that debate ought to go forward. And I think that the Governors ought to be able to participate in both parties in that debate and——

*The President.* Well, let's discuss it. What do you think we ought to do? What level do we have of defense spending? We're testifying every single day for the details of this program. But if you've met and you want to say something in front of the press, I ask you to be specific with me. I think that's the way we ought to approach it.

*Governor Romer.* Well, the specific that I'm really concerned about, about the budget, and I'll be detailed about it, is there's a $12 billion asterisk that I think hangs over the head of Governors because it may be State programs that are cut. There is accounting, accrual accounting of future receipts that concern me. There are implications of tax revenue loss in the IRA treatment in years ahead that may produce additional deficit. And in the course of the 2 days that I have been in town, I find that there is a considerable point of view, at least among some Democratic Governors, as to what that's going to mean in terms of how we settle on the economic recovery package.

Now, Mr. President, I'm frankly trying not to make this any more partisan. I'm just saying that I want to have an opportunity that we can come to the table, we as Governors on both parties, have this discussion in detail so that whatever this economic package is, it's going to fit with the States when we get it passed.

*The President.* I think you will recall, at the opening of my remarks, I invited that kind of suggestion. Now, inasmuch as you raised a couple of specifics, I think you're entitled to an answer. And I'd like Dick Darman, who has testified, to respond to those two points.

*Director Darman.* Thank you, Mr. President.

The accrual accounting point is really quite arcane. But for those who are aware of the issue to which the Governor referred, let me clarify a couple of things. First of all, the budget numbers that we published and the deficit numbers we published do not, do not include the effect of the accrual reforms. In other words, the number that is an unattractive number for fiscal year '92, which we published, $399.4 billion estimated deficit with our program, does not include the effect of the accrual accounting reform we recommend, point one. In other words, the premise is wrong.

Second, the accrual reforms which we proposed, we proposed in June of last year before the growth package. They are independently desirable. We were asked by the Congress to make a recommendation. We made that recommendation. The Congressional Budget Office was also asked. They made the same recommendation, that insurance programs should be subject to accrual accounting. The two different independent accounting organizations, outside CPA's, made the identical recommendation. And in fact, many States followed the same approach and are ahead of the Federal Government. Some have argued that had we had accrual accounting in the past, we would have seen the adverse effect of the S&L crisis in advance, and it would have taken the appropriate preventive action in advance.

So, I think that that point is not quite apt as a criticism. In fact, it's a useful reform we're recommending, but it is not used in the deficit numbers that we published at the lead of the budget.

On the IRA scoring issue, again I'm afraid there's a little bit of confusion. We actually scored the IRA proposal as losing money. But we nonetheless propose it because we think it has a favorable long-term effect on growth. There are some in Congress who have proposed IRA reforms which they score positively. We did not adopt those. We adopted and explicitly over 5 years showed revenue losses: small gain in the first 2 years, substantial decline in the 3d, 4th, and 5th year, with the declines increasing in exactly the manner you suggested, Governor Romer. But we did it above board, and we financed it.

On the point about the asterisk—sorry for going on so long, Mr. President, this is all rather arcane. This one is extremely technical. I believe what you're referring to shows up in fiscal year '94 and '95. And it's the only thing that I can think of that would qualify as related to the number you've mentioned.

What we have done is we have proposed a budget authority freeze, fiscal year '93 relative to '92, with every single program cut fully identified above board, with every program termination fully identified, and with all the increases identified. That's what the law asks us to do. That's all we have to do in the Federal appropriations process, one year.

For the outyears, we extended the budget authority freeze forward, '94, '5, '6, '7. The outlays that are associated with that you can't know at this stage; you don't know until the Congress has made the decisions on fiscal year '93. And you have to assume an outlay ratio. We did, but they've hit the cap. So, we made an allowance adjustment to make it consistent with the law on the outyears at the same time as we proposed to amend the caps to make it conform correctly.

But none of that has effect on the actual appropriations process. For the appropriations process for this year every single line, every project, every proposal is specified in detail. There is no magic asterisk.

Thank you, Mr. President.

*The President.* While the press is here, did the Democratic Governors meet, and is there any feeling that we shouldn't press to try to get something done by March 20th? Is there a spokesman on that point? Because what I would like to suggest, not that you have to sign every "t" and "i" but that we all urge Congress to move by that date. If that date isn't good, what date? Is there feeling on that one?

*Governor Richards.* I don't believe, Mr. President, that there was any question that the Democratic Governors as well as the Republican Governors are anxious to have Congress move expeditiously. There was no discussion of a magic date, but I suspect that the Congress is going to move very quickly, not only because we're going to urge them to do that because it's the right thing to do, but because we are very cognizant that it is an election year. It is time for Congress to get its budget proposals out there.

*The President.* That's good because I think most agree, people in the country agree that it can move. It moved very fast on, and properly so, on these extended benefits, and I think it can. And I just hope that that's an area that we can have common, make common ground here because it's important.

While the press are here, are there any other—Jim, yes.

### Medicaid and Welfare Waivers

*Governor Florio.* Mr. President, I'm authorized to ask a question that I think is on the minds of many of the Governors. As we try to put together our budget problems, there are two areas that sort of jump out that are extremely difficult for us to deal with: One is health care in general, Medicaid in particular, and the other is the welfare situation that you've talked about.

We are all trying to, in the best federalistic tradition, frame our own packages to be able to be cost-effective. And we are doing it, at least some of us are doing it, in ways that are not, policywise, universally applauded. It is tough. I was pleased to hear in your State of the Union Message the discussion about waivers, and today again I was very pleased.

I guess what I would urge, and I think I

urge it on behalf of everyone, is that the Departments, particularly Health and Human Services and of course OMB, which gray eminence always plays a particular role here, look at these waiver requests with the—I'm hesitant to use the word—the most liberal interpretation capable in order to let us put these programs into play in the way that we think our localities will be able to deal with them.

And then, and most importantly, expeditious. There has to be some review of these things quickly as opposed to—and I was talking with the Governor of Massachusetts who was lamenting the fact that it took a year for something that he has an interest in. So that if there's a way that you can, in accordance with what you've expressed already, communicate directly with some of your folks that this is a high priority, it would help us. I suspect it would help the Nation. And I just want to lay that out as a very important initiative that the administration can take.

*The President.* I think we've got agreement on that one. And I can assure you that's what we will be trying to do. I hope it doesn't require—we were just talking about this when I was talking to the Director before coming over here, as to whether legislative changes are essential in any of this waiving of authority and control. And I gather we can do a lot without that.

But Dick, do you want to address yourself to that one? Some of it, again, is technical.

*Director Darman.* Only to say, Mr. President, that this is one where I do think we are in complete agreement and are anxious to make sure that the waiver process moves more quickly and also that in applying it we're more flexible than we have been in the past, both of which I think have been subjects of legitimate complaint by the Governors. That is, that we've been too slow and that we've been too, if you'll pardon the word, illiberal. So, I would think under the President's direction you'll see a visible and discernible and prompt change on this subject.

*Governor Miller.* I'd just like to ask a more particular followup question, after the President, of the Office of Management and Budget, and that is: Can that be interpreted to go into the provider payment in which

the OMB had a contrary position that was more limiting on States just several months ago and that was worked out, a temporary compromise, I believe, with the Congress? Can we interpret, then, that with that type of philosophy that we will be able to utilize that in the future? And that's something that affects our budget of potentially $25 million; some other States, a couple of hundred million. And that's the type of interpretation, I think, that has caused us some concern.

*Director Darman.* Are you referring to the Medicaid agreements we reached—excuse me, Mr. President, may I?

*The President.* No, please.

*Director Darman.* The Medicaid agreement we reached at the tail end of the Congress and then legislated? We propose to honor that 100 percent, notwithstanding the interest in reforming the health system. And some have advocated going back at disproportionate share and other things and reopening that agreement. We propose to stick with that agreement, honor it, and live within it. It, I think, is a stable and mutually agreeable place to move forward, isn't it?

### Trade Initiatives

*The President.* Any others? Tommy.

*Governor Thompson.* Mr. President, let me compliment you on your leadership as trying to get through GATT and the NAFTA. If we're going to get our economy moving, it's got to be done with a lot of exports. I was wondering if you could give us an update as to how the GATT is proceeding as well as NAFTA, which is very important to States like Wisconsin and Texas. And I want to compliment you on your leadership in that regard.

*The President.* Well, NAFTA, as you know, is getting a little caught up in politics. We are not going to take a bad agreement to the Congress. We are going to push for a North American free trade agreement. I talked to the Prime Minister of Canada yesterday on it. I've been in touch with Salinas of Mexico, who's doing a superb job down there. And I told them we are not going to pull back one inch, politics or no politics.

This expands job opportunity for Americans. And the argument that it takes American jobs away is just not true. Just in recent history, the exports to Mexico have dramatically gone up, and that's very, very good for American jobs. So on that one, we're pressing forward. I'm going to try to set aside any political timetable on it but move it to completion.

We are being fought by the unions, strong. They are wrong. And those of us who believe in expanding markets and a more prosperous Mexico is good for the United States, whether it's their ability to do something about their environment, or whether it's their ability to buy more American goods, that's sensible trade policy. So, we're going to press for it. Whether we'll get it, Governor Thompson, in time or not, I don't know.

The GATT, which in a sense is broader because it gives us problems in Europe, is extraordinarily difficult. The major stumbling block is still agriculture. It is not the only stumbling block. I had a chance to visit with President Mitterrand up at the United Nations on Friday. We've agreed to talk again in a bilateral meeting on this subject. The Germans are involved, and they tell me they're trying to be helpful. But I don't want to misrepresent it to the Governors; we still have some big problems on bringing this one to conclusion.

And it is essential that it get done because if it doesn't get done, what we're going to do is see the world start dividing up into trading blocs. There's one out in Asia that makes some sense, the ASEAN bloc. But if you add to that Japan and try to make a Pacific trading bloc, that would not be good for free trade worldwide. I similarly went to great ends to tell them that the NAFTA, the free trade agreement, was not an effort on the part of this hemisphere to divide into a trading bloc. And I think I've made that point, I hope convincingly, to the EC and to Europe.

But it is important we get that deal done, and get it done so the Congress can approve it. We're not going to take a bad deal up there. It isn't simply agriculture: We've got intellectual property rights; we have market access; we have some other ingredients. But we've got good people working this problem. There's Ed Madigan here

today. He's handling the agriculture end and can expand on that. But Carla Hills, doing a superb job. It isn't easy right now because I think it's much more European politics than it is U.S. at this time. Because the common agricultural policy there is one of high subsidization.

And the last thing I'd say, for those who are doubtful about it or unclear, the best way to help countries that need help the most is through a successful conclusion of the GATT round. The Third World countries would benefit there more than any others.

But Ed, do you want to add a word to that? Because I know a lot of people around this table are vitally interested in the agricultural component of this.

*Secretary Madigan.* Mr. President, the Director General of GATT, Arthur Dunkel, has made a proposal for the solution to the round, and that proposal is regarded by the United States as being a very acceptable framework for bringing the negotiations to a close. And as you point out, the Europeans will not accept it. So, Mr. Dunkel has begun meeting unilaterally with the Europeans this week to see if he can work out something with them that he would then propose to the rest of us. We don't know the status of those talks at this point.

*The President.* Pete, Governor Wilson.

### Congressional Mandates and State Priorities

*Governor Wilson.* This is really coming back on Jim Florio's point. I think that there should not have been a Governor listening to your State of the Union who didn't cheer when you made the point that you did and that you repeated this morning about waivers. If there should be bipartisanship on anything, at least among the Governors, it's on that point. I can't think of a Governor here who has not at some point or another given voice to the complaint that we are being compelled to spend State tax money in accordance not with our own priorities but really with the agenda of the congressional committee chair. And it does distort priorities. It does distort our spending, not just at the State level, but I would suggest that most of the distortion is linked to Federal spending.

And so, I would say that we have reason to be not only grateful but also, as we seek the waivers, I think we're all well aware that the waiver is temporary relief. God knows we're grateful for it, and we are very grateful for the speedy action that you're bringing about. The real answer is that Congress passed these laws, and Congress should repeal them. And I think we ought to help one another. I think, frankly, that those of us who have complained so loud and long have an obligation to ourselves as well as to you, not only to Federal taxpayers but to those common constituents who are State taxpayers as well, to go up there and really start changing the laws. Now, that's going to be hard to do because committee chairmen enjoy the power of the purse. They love that generalized prescription.

But this may not be the perfect season in which to do it. But after your reelection, to venture a partisan comment, we ought to go up there, bipartisan, and say to these committee chairmen, "We've had enough. You are distorting the whole process."

*The President.* Would it be possible to get agreement amongst Democrat and Republican Governors as what legislative changes would be enacted, whether we could get together on that, whether the Governors' Association might get together and suggest legislative changes? Because if that came up there in a bipartisan way, I believe it would make a tremendous impact on Congress, far better than, say, the administration taking it up with the backing of some Governors.

*Governor Romer.* I think that there is the possibility for us to do some bipartisan work in that area, and I think it would be very helpful for us to sort that out. And Mr. President, I appreciate this conversation. This is what I was hoping that we could do, is to identify those things where we bipartisanly really can go together, but also to identify that there are some times and some places in an election year that we do have differences. And I appreciate your giving us the opportunity to raise these differences this morning. And the reason I did it in an abrupt way, I just did not want us to be in the posture of endorsing only the one economic approach which was in your State of the Union Message. There is more than one, and I appreciate you giving us the opportu-

nity to expound that this morning.

*The President.* All I was doing was appealing for an endorsement, not suggesting you endorse it. [*Laughter*] I've known you too long.

Who's next? Terry.

### Agricultural Trade

*Governor Branstad.* Mr. President, first of all, I want to thank you for your assistance in trying to open some markets for us. Something that was done a few years ago, opening the market for beef in Japan, is really making a difference in my State. And I heard David Gergen say recently that 80 percent of the new jobs created last year were as a result of exports. We can't afford to go into protectionism. We have to continue to fight for access to those markets. And I just want to encourage you to continue to lead that effort for access.

We're being discriminated against in the European Community because of the hormone issue, which is a false issue, doesn't have anything to do with health. And we need to continue that. And I know that's a stickler; that's an issue in the GATT negotiations. But I just want to encourage you to continue to take a strong stand on that. It's very important to us, especially in agriculture. Given an opportunity to compete in a fair playing field, we can compete in the world.

*The President.* You want to respond, Ed?

*Secretary Madigan.* I think, Mr. President, in the Dunkel text, the standards on sanitary and biosanitary issues have been well-regarded by the wheat producers in the United States because they would deal with that hormone issue in Europe. That's one of the things that all of our producers seem to like about the Dunkel text.

*The President.* Governor Sinner had his hand up.

### Energy Policy

*Governor Sinner.* In this whole area of trade I get very nervous about us putting ourselves in a continual vulnerable position on energy. I can see why other countries have the same feeling about food. You and I had a long talk about energy when you were Vice President, and you had been over to the Middle East. And I remember then that you shared my concerns that we sit here totally vulnerable to a Middle East tyranny. And I want the free trade. But I think when you get into the area of energy and food, we have to understand that the people of Europe have been hungry, and they aren't going to forget that. And we have been through a horrible war, $100 billion we spent, a couple hundred thousand people dead to protect our energy resources. I want to say that I think we have to be extremely careful and not euphemize free trade as though there weren't some other considerations because it is not magic. It's not in the Constitution. What we are bound to do here is protect the people's needs.

The second thing, you asked a while ago if any of us were for tax increases. And I don't speak for anybody but myself. But my children and your children and the children of all the people around here are going to pay one hell of a debt. And I, for one, say my answer to your question: Yes, I would favor that. I think it's time we go back and tax some of the wealthy people. I'm not super-wealthy, but what I pay in income taxes isn't very much, really, compared to what people in low-income brackets pay. I think you could tax the wealthy a lot more.

And the fact is if we continue into this sewer of debt, our children and the families that are suffering today, that's nothing compared to what the families of tomorrow will suffer. So, I just want you to know that I, for one, would stand and say yes, I do think we should raise them.

*The President.* My problem on that is that the percentage of the GDP, GNP taken by taxes is inching up and is too high. But anyway, we have a difference on that one.

I don't think we've got a difference on energy. One, you and I do agree, I think, that there is a risk in becoming ever more dependent on foreign oil in this country. And one of the reasons I strongly support the ANWR is because, one, I think it's environmentally compatible, and secondly, most importantly, I think that offers us a chance to at least turn around this increasing dependence on foreign oil. And I think it's about time that we make that case. For those of us, Democrat or Republican, who

believes in our national energy strategy as outlined, we ought to fight for it. So, I don't think we have a difference.

What I'm getting at, though, is I don't think that there's anything in these free trade agreements that is going to adversely affect development of domestic energy. I just don't believe that there's anything, if we've got a good NAFTA or we get a good GATT agreement, that either one of those would make us more dependent on foreign oil at all. I don't see the connection on that one. Maybe I've missed it. But I certainly don't want to see us become more dependent on it, and I don't think we have to.

*Governor Sinner.* [*Inaudible*]—that free trade will somehow or other obliterate the dangers that befall society if we become totally dependent on something called free trade in energy. That's the point I wanted to make.

*The President.* Yes, unfortunately we're becoming, because of failure to move forward with safe nuclear power, which I think we can do—we'll get a lively debate on that one around this table, I'm sure—or getting more technology going, I think we've got a problem on energy dependence. And I'd like to see it reverse. And that's what we've tried to do in our national energy strategy which we have not gotten through the Congress. Again, I'd make an appeal for you people that are interested in the energy side of things to take a look at it and support it where you can.

I see Jim over there, who's done a superb job on our overall energy requirements, trying to make us less dependent. I cannot certify that our program—and, Jim, correct me—will make us independent of foreign sources of all energy. It won't. But it will move us in the right direction. Is that about right?

*Secretary Watkins.* Yes, that's right, Mr. President. The bill stripped down will come to the floor this afternoon at 2 p.m. It will then go through a debating period and come up for a motion to proceed. Whether there's going to be a filibuster, I don't know. That should happen on Wednesday, but we should be underway on the debate. Unfortunately, it does take out the Arctic National Wildlife Refuge. It takes out the

CAFE standards which we we've been against all the way along. Nevertheless, the Arctic National Wildlife Refuge, as you mentioned properly, is part of the growth package. It is worth about 500,000 jobs over the next 10 years. It's worth about $200 billion in reduction of our trade deficit. Those monies always go offshore.

The movement of that particular refuge will not only be worth that 8.5 billion barrels but will also carry along, with the residue of the Prudhoe Bay will add another billion barrels. Now, that's good for the economy of the United States. And so that's why you include it as part of your growth package and encourage them to pass this bill, which is filled with natural gas expedition movements to the private sector, to industry, to business. It's good; it's clean. You've got a very balanced program there, and I'm hopeful that the 14 titles that remain, that we will see an expeditious address by the Congress.

And I hope that we can continue the fight for bringing back the Arctic National Wildlife Refuge as part of your growth package, if nothing else. You can't get it in the energy bill; keep it in the growth package. It is real growth.

We need revenues to find the alternatives to oil which is the very thing we're trying to do in getting alternative fuels. You have the most powerful alternative fuel package that's ever been put together in this country, to go in all directions. It will help many Governors around this table with the ethanols; the methanols; the electric car, the opportunity to drive those electric cars with the off-peak loads in our industrial plant today. We have plenty of electrical power for 120 million of those vehicles. We can get off this oil in our transportation sector.

And we still need the oil, our own oil. And so, we can move in the direction that stabilizes that increase in imports. And I think your bill not only does that, but your bill is a very powerful growth package for both jobs and revenue for the country.

*Low Income Home Energy Assistance Program*

*The President.* Governor Dean.

*Governor Dean.* We've been tossing around huge numbers. I want to talk about a much smaller number, just about $500 million. In your budget last year, you recommended the cutting of the low-income human assistance program. It's a small program. It's $1.5 billion this year. It's principally used in the northern States to help people get through the winter with fuel assistance. We had to put some State money up. Of course, we had to level-fund our State budget this year, so that meant we had to take the money from somewhere else.

In your budget this year, Mr. President, it's recommended that you cut the program again by 33 percent. And we could barely handle last year's cuts. I would ask that you might reconsider and possibly levelly fund that, which I think would be consistent with your own budget goals. It would mean a great deal particularly to those over 65, living alone, and who really depend on this program in the northern States for keeping themselves warm throughout the winter.

*The President.* Has anybody got available the figures on home heating oil price, say, 2 years ago compared to what it is now?

*Governor Dean.* Well, this year, Mr. President, you're correct. This year we were able to——

*The President.* It's less, isn't it now?

*Governor Dean.* It's much less now, and that's one of the reasons we were not hurt as badly by the cuts this year. But I don't expect the home heating oil price to go down another 33 percent next year. And also, of course, there are a great many, at least in Vermont, that heat with other fuels such as wood or natural gas, and the price has not dropped commensurately.

I'm not so much complaining about last year's cut, which we did deal with, but if we were to lose 33 percent of that program, small program though it is, we would be devastated.

*The President.* Dick, do you want to comment on it? I can't remember the exact numbers. Go ahead.

*Director Darman.* The Governors will perhaps remember, Mr. President—it's all a question of perspective, I suppose. The standard proposal for this program, which is known colloquially as LIHEAP, the standard proposal has been zero in the past from the administration. And this year, we're at a billion. So, we look at it as a billion more than some might have recommended and proposed, and you look at it as half a billion less.

The way the appropriations process works, as you know, these things are still subject to adjustment within the caps. And so if this goes up 500, something else has to go down 500. This is not one that we would, I think it's fair to say, fight and die over. We thought a billion was a lot more than zero. I can understand why you think it's less than 1.5 billion.

*Medicaid Waivers*

*Governor Romer.* I want to thank the President for his willingness to exchange these views with us on such a candid level. And I appreciate his welcome to the White House that he has consistently extended to us as Governors.

And even more importantly, I appreciate the fact that we've been able to work together in a true federalism partnership which has made it possible for us to be more productive.

Some of the questions today even reflected the way in which we've been able to work out differences. The one about the Medicaid settlement was a very serious problem to a number of us. We worked together through the months of October and November in a fashion which included they-said-it-couldn't-be-done type activity. And the Congress, because the President had worked so arduously with us toward reconciling those differences, agreed. And we were able to stabilize the situation which was highly volatile for our own budgets and for the Federal budgeting process as well.

So, Mr. President, thank you very much for your special welcome to us, and your kindness to us, your cooperation with us, and your willingness to exchange these views with us. We're deeply grateful to you.

*The President.* Listen, I enjoyed having you. I see John Sununu. I think those of you, as we tried to get through that Medicaid problem, you had an inside voice here. [*Laughter*] And I really think he deserves credit for the fact we were able to reach agreement that brought some relief and, I wouldn't say joy, but at least less concern to the Governors around the table. I'm very grateful to him and Dick also. But it required some skill up on the Hill, too, which he demonstrated.

But in any event, thank you all very much. And I appreciate the spirit of this visit, and look forward to doing this again. Thank you very much.

*Note: The President spoke at 11:15 a.m. in the East Room at the White House.*

# Exchange With Reporters Prior to Discussions With President Ronald Venetiaan of Suriname
*February 3, 1992*

*Japan-U.S. Relations*

*Q.* Any defense of American workers in response to what Mr. Miyazawa said?

*The President.* Just go by what Marlin Fitzwater told you guys when you asked the same question about 6 hours ago. [*Laughter*]

*Q.* Have you seen the——

*The President.* Strong support. I just heard what Marlin said, and I back it 100 percent. I also saw the correction by Mr. Miyazawa, I'm pleased to say. So, that was fine.

*Q.* Do you accept that, sir, as an apology?

*The President.* I accept it for what it was, a very clear statement from a good man, a man who has said clearly that they're going to live up to their commitments, and I support him for that. And we had a very good visit. So, you know, he's gone out of his way to make clear that he was not denouncing all American workers. And I strongly support them and continue to say so. We can compete with anybody in the world if we're given access. Marlin summed up our position very well.

*Note: The exchange began at 4:31 p.m. in* *the Oval Office. In his remarks, the President referred to Prime Minister Kiichi Miyazawa of Japan.*

## Statement by Press Secretary Fitzwater on the President's Meeting With President Ronald Venetiaan of Suriname
*February 3, 1992*

The President met today with President Ronald Venetiaan of the Republic of Suriname.

The President expressed his satisfaction at the success of Suriname's elections and orderly transition to democratic civilian government following the military coup in December of 1990. He stressed the United States deep commitment to fostering democratic civilian rule throughout the hemisphere and emphasized that President Venetiaan enjoys our full support for his efforts to strengthen democratic institutions, undertake economic reform, and curb narcotics trafficking.

The two Presidents discussed the Surinamese Government's plans for economic reform and adjustment. The President pointed out that effective action in this area will enhance Suriname's ability to stimulate private investment and trade, which are the key to long-term growth.

The two Presidents also discussed the threat to Suriname of increased narcotics trafficking, and the President pledged our support for Suriname's counternarcotics efforts.

President Venetiaan is making his first visit to the United States since his inauguration in September 1991. He entered office as a result of elections held in May 1991 with the participation of observers from the Organization of American States.

## Message to the Congress Transmitting a Report on United States Government Activities in the United Nations
*February 3, 1992*

*To the Congress of the United States:*

I am pleased to transmit herewith a report of the activities of the United States Government in the United Nations and its affiliated agencies during the calendar year 1990, the second year of my Administration. The report is required by the United Nations Participation Act (Public Law 264, 79th Congress; 22 U.S.C. 287b).

GEORGE BUSH

The White House,
February 3, 1992.

## Message to the Congress Transmitting the Report of the Federal Labor Relations Authority
*February 3, 1992*

*To the Congress of the United States:*

In accordance with section 701 of the Civil Service Reform Act of 1978 (Public Law 95–454; 5 U.S.C. 7104(e)), I have the pleasure of transmitting to you the Twelfth Annual Report of the Federal Labor Relations Authority for Fiscal Year 1990.

The report includes information on the cases heard and decisions rendered by the Federal Labor Relations Authority, the General Counsel of the Authority, and the Federal Service Impasses Panel.

GEORGE BUSH

The White House,
February 3, 1992.

## Remarks to the National Grocers Association in Orlando, Florida
*February 4, 1992*

Thank you for that warm welcome, and please be seated. And Tom, thank you for that wonderful introduction. Thanks also to Bill Confer, your chairman. And before we get started, I don't know where they are, but I'd like to recognize two outstanding Congressmen from this area, Bill McCollum and Cliff Stearns, and also a former Congressman who is actively involved with me, Bill Grant, of Florida. You have three of the best right here with you today.

And it's a great pleasure, and I really mean that, to be here with this enthusiastic group. I originally had planned to be at your dinner last night. But then I found out it was called the Asparagus Club Banquet. [*Laughter*] Thought I'd better not take a chance. And you know why, dangerously close. [*Laughter*] Okay, Barbara won the broccoli war. I said what I thought, and she got out and received all these broccoli growers. And sales shot up about 500 percent. [*Laughter*]

You all know, I think, of my love for sports. And this being an election year, my competitive juices are flowing more than ever. And so, today I'm making an announcement that many of you have been expecting for a long time. I'm officially declaring my entry into your best bagger contest. Just one question: Paper or plastic? [*Laughter*]

I'll always remember, and Tom referred to it, but from a personal standpoint I'll always remember that warm reception that you all, the NGA, gave me when I addressed that 1985 convention. It was in New Orleans. You gave me a good education about your industry then, and I remember it still. A typical NGA member is a family-run business. Many of you carry on legacies built through the vision and sacrifice of a grandmother or a grandfather. Just met one of your directors. She was a third generation in the grocery business, perhaps an immigrant to this country; some were. You work on the thinnest of profit margins. You challenge one another with bracing competition that clearly benefits our consumers like no others in the world. And today as always, your success as community grocers depends not just on the bottom line but on the old-fashioned virtues of being a good neighbor.

Since I last met you all in 1985, the world has changed. We've got a lot to be grateful for. We won the cold war. We led a coalition in the Gulf to crush Saddam Hussein's aggression in Kuwait. We've created a world with the prospects of unprecedented prosperity and peace. But we've also run into some hard times here. Our economy has slowed down. We must get it fired up again.

The professional pessimists tell us America has become weak and disabled, that our

195

economy has fallen and it can't get up. Well, that's just plain bunk. It's not true. And I'm going to tell you what we can do about it. Day by day and step by step, we're going to get ourselves moving, and we'll do it as Americans always have. We'll combine our common sense, our work ethic, and our determination with progrowth policies. With these, we'll carry the entire world into the next American century. You can bet on it.

You don't have to be some rocket scientist to understand how. You stick with the basics. And I proposed a commonsense comprehensive action plan last week in my State of the Union Address. It gets investment going, because you can't build new businesses and create new jobs without new investment. It strengthens the industries that historically have led us into recoveries, especially real estate and housing. It hacks away obstacles to growth. It cuts the Federal deficit by holding back spending. Government is far too big, and it spends too much. And I am going to keep it within its limits of this budget agreement that is in place right now.

Ask yourselves the question: How free are we, really, when the Government gobbles up 25 percent of our GNP? I'm demanding, I need your support, that Congress get serious about this. One thing, I've listed 246 programs that I want cut out this year, 246. Each one has a protector; each one has a noble title. None of them is essential to the well-being of the United States of America. And I want something else. I want that line-item veto so I can enforce real spending disciplines. Forty-three Governors have it.

We've got to get Washington back to common sense. To do that, I really mean this, I need your help. I know you can deliver. You know your neighbors; they know you. The grocery business grows when your neighborhood grows, when the Nation's economy grows. I've asked Congress to enact some laws that will create jobs by getting our economy growing again. And I've set a deadline, March 20th. I ask you to circle that Friday on your calendar. Remember this deadline. Congress needs to take a few simple steps to create good American jobs, now.

The Capitol Hill hearings on my program begin today. But I must say, too often when I send progrowth proposals to Congress, all the public hears is sloganeering about fairness. This twists a good concept into a weapon of envy and divisiveness, desire to divide America along class lines. I don't look at it that way. Here's what fairness means to me: It means if you want to work, you can get a job. It means if you have a good idea, you'll get a chance to test it, or if you build a business, you don't lose your earnings to excessive taxes or overregulation. That's what fairness means to me. Above all, the most important test of fairness for my plan is that it will work for all Americans. It will create jobs.

And now, here's what I want by March 20th. And I set that date because I do believe we have a window in which we get something done, even though this is going to be a very controversial and difficult national election year. Here's what I want: First, incentives to make productive investments. These involve a 15-percent investment tax allowance and needed changes to the alternative minimum tax. Now, these will encourage business to invest in equipment and become more productive. I just took a tour through the exhibits here, amazed by some of the technology. These proposals will stimulate that kind of investment and will help individuals invest in high technology or in whatever machinery is needed.

Second, we need incentives to build and to buy real estate: a change in the passive-loss rules for active real estate developers. We need penalty-free withdrawals from IRA's for first-time homebuyers and a $5,000 tax credit for the first purchase of a home. Housing economists predict that my plan will mean an extra 200,000 homes built and 415,000 new construction jobs to build them. Real estate and housing, with this stimulus, will lead our way into active recovery.

And third, incentives to succeed: Cut the capital gains tax. This tax hurts anyone who has made a sensible investment in a home, a business, or a farm. None of our key competitors taxes gains at high rates, world global competitors. Let's stop penalizing savings and investment. Let's stop punishing excellence. And yes, let's talk about fairness. Lower capital gains mean more investment, and more investment means more jobs. So, let's get that capital gains tax cut, now.

Three measures, three pieces of common sense, three things Congress should do by March 20th. I know that Congress will listen to you; you come right from the grassroots. And I'm counting on your help. In the meantime, I've initiated some reforms that will get the economy moving without having to wait for Congress to act. I've imposed a 90-day freeze on Federal regulations that could hinder economic growth. And during that period, all Departments and Agencies will review regulations, old and new, and when possible, stop the ones that will hurt growth and speed up those that will help growth.

I see from your convention schedule that you have a workshop entitled "The Regulators Are Back." No wonder. You can't get through a day without having to worry about what some regulator is going to do to you through some thoughtless regulation. Regulations may have stated aims as wholesome as Mom and the apple pie. But you know better than anyone that when regulators carry that regulation too far, there won't be any apple pie for Mom to buy.

I ran a council on deregulation for 8 years as Vice President. And I'm here to assure you, we've not lost the spirit of deregulation. I want you to be able to spend your time working on what you can do for your customers rather than fretting about what some regulator might do to you.

And I'm also fighting hard against this epidemic of lawsuits. The costs and the delays in our legal system are a hidden tax on every single American consumer, on every business transaction in America. And that's why I'm sending to Congress today a reform bill, the "Access to Justice Act of 1992." My reform proposal will give Americans cheaper and easier alternatives to trial. And my plan will halt needless lawsuits by making changes in the way some attorney's fees are awarded. Let's stop America's love affair with the lawsuit. If we're as good at rewarding success as we are at suing each other, we'd be way ahead of the rest of the world. I might say parenthetically, health

care costs would be an awful lot lower if we didn't have a lot of frivolous lawsuits going after these doctors for malpractice.

One of the great lessons of our times is this: Freedom and cooperation work; big Government doesn't. And after 70 years, the new leaders in Moscow recognize that total Government regulation produces only one thing: total failure. And now, the Russians—I had a fascinating visit with Boris Yeltsin up at Camp David on Saturday—the Russians want to try something different, like grocery stores with groceries on the shelves. [*Laughter*] This man's put into some tough reforms there. Got to stay with him. Got to help him make them work.

Isn't it ironic, at the exact moment the world is turning to our values of more economic freedom and competition, some in the United States Congress want to go just the opposite way. And here's an example of the trouble brewing in Congress: That's the so-called FDA enforcement bill. I'm sure those of you who sell your own private-label groceries aren't exactly thrilled by the prospect of more legal and accounting and paperwork burdens. But that's just what some in the Congress want to do. Well, let me tell you in no uncertain terms: The time for overregulation is over. And if they send me any more legislation with excessive regulation in it, I'm going to veto it and send it back. It's going right back up there.

Again, the Congress can help get the economy moving if it will just do the right thing. Last week one Member of Congress, a Democrat, said it might be smart politics for the Democrats to meet the deadline and pass my plan intact. I can't say what their motives may be, but I know one thing, my plan will help the American people. So let me take the heat. I know that my program will get the economy moving again. And again, urge the Congress to pass it intact by March 20th.

March 20 isn't a moment too soon to enact this short-term program. But we also must take a longer look, look to longer horizons. And I proposed a long-term plan in my State of the Union Address. Let me just give you a couple of the highlights here, some of the highlights.

First, let's create more American jobs by

opening up and expanding markets all over the world. A new GATT agreement, we're working hard to get one, will make the world trading system come to grips with the damaging tariffs and export subsidies in agriculture. And by tearing down economic barriers with Mexico and Canada, a new North American free trade agreement can lift us to new heights of prosperity. And make no mistake about this: A sound free trade agreement will mean more American jobs, not less, more American jobs.

Second, let free choice and free markets reform this health care system of ours. This week I'm going to ask for a new credit to help those without health insurance, employed or not, to buy such coverage. My plan will assure that both American workers and the unemployed will have access to basic health insurance even if they change jobs or develop serious health problems. We can't improve health care by threatening the health of job-intensive businesses. The last thing we want is for companies to cut costs by cutting workers. And I am wholeheartedly opposed, as I believe you are, to schemes that cost jobs by mandating benefits that an employer must pay.

And thirdly, let's strengthen the family, the cornerstone of the American dream. Let's ease the burden of child-rearing. The personal tax exemption has not kept up with inflation. I'm asking Congress, immediately, to increase the exemption for each child by $500. It's a significant move in the right direction, and for our kids' sake, we must do no less.

Look at my economic proposals and you will find straightforward, plain solutions to our problems. Some may complain that they lack the flash of an expensive new program or that they don't have quite the right political ring for this political year. But I'm not seeking spending for spending's sake. I don't want a fancy title on a bill that will shoot interest rates right up through the roof. I want results. My plan is sound, and it will work.

If you hear people in Congress gripe that they can't get the job done by March 20th, remind them we won the Gulf war in 44 days. Surely Congress can pass my urgent domestic program in 52 days. Remember, Congress can act with lightning speed when it wants to. So, accept no excuses. Accept no delays. And accept no substitutes.

Please don't leave this message behind when you leave this convention hall. Take it home to your families, to your customers, to your neighbors. From February 8th till February 17th, your Congressmen will be home for the President's Day recess. That's a great time for you to go to their hometown offices and tell them to meet the deadline and to pass this plan. With an effort like this, I know we'll get their attention, and we'll get America moving again.

Thank you very, very much for this reception. And may God bless the United States of America. Thank you.

*Note: The President spoke at 11:35 a.m. at the Orange County Convention/Civic Center. In his remarks, he referred to Tom Zaucha, president of the National Grocers Association.*

# Message to the Congress Transmitting Proposed Legislation on Access to Justice
*February 4, 1992*

*To the Congress of the United States:*

I am pleased to transmit today for your immediate consideration and enactment the "Access to Justice Act of 1992". The purpose of this proposal is to reduce the tremendous growth in civil litigation that has burdened the American court system and imposed high costs on our citizens, small businesses, industries, professionals, and government at all levels.

A thorough study of the current civil justice system has been conducted by a special working group, chaired by the Solicitor General, Kenneth W. Starr. The working group's recommendations, which were unanimously accepted by my Council on Competitiveness, are reflected in the bill. The legislation seeks to reduce wasteful and counterproductive litigation practices by encouraging voluntary dispute resolution, the improved use of litigation resources, and, where appropriate, modified, market-based fee arrangements. Additional reforms would permit the judicial system to operate more effectively.

The Access to Justice Act would accomplish reforms in significant areas of litigation:

- a prerequisite for Federal jurisdiction over certain types of lawsuits (the amount in controversy requirement) would be redefined to exclude vague, subjective claims;
- prevailing parties could be entitled to award of attorney's fees in certain lawsuits brought in Federal court;
- the Equal Access to Justice Act would be amended to clarify and limit litigation over the amount of attorney's fees;
- innovative "multi-door courthouses" would be established to encourage utilization of alternative dispute resolution mechanisms;

- award of reasonable attorney's fees in disputes involving the United States would be permitted in appropriate instances;
- prior notice would be required, subject to reasonable limits, as a prerequisite to bringing suit in any United States District Court;
- flexible assignment of district court judges would be authorized;
- immunity of State judicial officers would be clarified and protected;
- the Civil Rights of Institutionalized Persons Act would be amended to encourage resolution of claims administratively; and
- improvements in case management in Federal courts would be effected.

I believe this proposed legislation would greatly reduce the burden of excessive, needless litigation while protecting and enhancing every American's ability to vindicate legal rights through our legal system. I recommend prompt and favorable consideration of the enclosed bill.

GEORGE BUSH

The White House,
February 4, 1992.

# Presidential Determination No. 92–13—Memorandum on Emergency Funding for the Organization of American States Mission to Haiti
*February 4, 1992*

*Memorandum for the Secretary of State*

*Subject:* Emergency Funding for OAS Mission to Haiti

Pursuant to the authority vested in me by section 614(a)(1) of the Foreign Assistance Act of 1961, as amended, I hereby determine that it is important to the security interests of the United States to furnish assistance to the Organization of American States (OAS) for its activities in Haiti notwithstanding section 513 of the Foreign Operations, Export Financing, and Related Programs Appropriations Act, 1991 (Public Law 101–513) and any other provision of

law within the scope of section 614, and authorize the furnishing of up to $2 million of funds made available to carry out chapter 4 of part II of the Foreign Assistance Act of 1961 for that purpose.

You are authorized and directed to transmit this determination to the Speaker of the House of Representatives and the Chairman of the Committee on Foreign Relations of the Senate and to arrange for its publication in the *Federal Register*.

GEORGE BUSH

[*Filed with the Office of the Federal Register, 2:23 p.m., February 13, 1992*]

## Appointment of Antonio Benedi as Special Assistant to the President and Deputy Director of Presidential Appointments and Scheduling
*February 4, 1992*

The President has announced his intention to appoint Antonio Benedi to be Special Assistant to the President and Deputy Director of Presidential Appointments and Scheduling.

From 1989 to the present, Mr. Benedi has served as the Deputy Director of the Office of Presidential Appointments and Scheduling. Prior to this, he served as Coordinator and then Director of Special Projects and Initiatives in the Office of the Vice President, Office of Advance, 1985–89. He also served as Special Assistant to the Assistant Secretary for Elementary and Secondary Education at the Department of Education,

1983–85. Mr. Benedi was the Special Assistant to the Director of ACTION, the Federal domestic volunteer agency, 1981–83. In 1980, he worked on the National Reagan-Bush Campaign Committee.

Mr. Benedi graduated from George Mason University in Fairfax, VA, receiving a bachelor of arts degree in psychology. He was born August 5, 1955, in Havana, Cuba. He left Cuba in 1960 for Honduras and moved with his family to Virginia in 1962. He is married to the former Maria T. Fernandez, has two sons, Tony and Jamie, and resides in Springfield, VA.

## Appointment of Linda Eischeid Tarplin as Special Assistant to the President for Legislative Affairs for the Senate
*February 4, 1992*

The President announced the appointment of Linda Eischeid Tarplin to be Special Assistant to the President for Legislative Affairs for the Senate.

Since 1990 Mrs. Tarplin has served as Deputy Assistant Secretary for Legislation at the Department of Health and Human Services. Prior to this she was the Director of Policy, Planning and Legislation for the

Office of Human Development Services, 1989–90; Special Assistant to the Deputy Assistant Secretary for Legislation, 1986–89; and legislative assistant to Representative Bill Frenzel, 1985–86.

Mrs. Tarplin graduated from the University of Minnesota. She was born January 23, 1961, in Carroll, IA. She is married to Richard Tarplin and resides in Arlington, VA.

## Appointment of Leigh Ann Metzger as Deputy Assistant to the President for Public Liaison
*February 4, 1992*

The President today announced the appointment of Leigh Ann Metzger as Deputy

Assistant to the President for Public Liaison.

Since 1990 Ms. Metzger has served as

Special Assistant to the President for Public Liaison. Prior to this she was coalitions and organization director at the National Republican Congressional Committee and legislative director for Phyllis Schlafly's Eagle Forum in Washington, DC. In 1987, Ms. Metzger also served as the Director of the Pornography Commission Report Project, an effort designed to highlight the release of the Attorney General's Commission

report. Ms. Metzger has worked on Capitol Hill for then-freshman Congressman Patrick L. Swindall. In addition, she was the Atlanta office manager for the Georgia Reagan-Bush '84 campaign.

Ms. Metzger is a graduate of Samford University in Birmingham, AL, receiving a bachelor of arts degree in 1984. She was born in Decatur, GA, and currently resides in Alexandria, VA.

# Remarks to the Small Business Legislative Council
## *February 5, 1992*

Thank you all very much. And Phil, thank you for the welcome, the kind introduction. Bob Banister, congratulations on being named chairman-elect of the SBLC. John Satagaj, thanks for your hard work in putting this wonderfully successful meeting together. And greetings, also, to Ted Olsen and John Kemp, who has done wonderful work in helping small business implement the ADA, the Americans with Disabilities Act. It was great a minute ago—I don't see him this second—to see my friend, Josh Smith, the Chairman, sitting over here, of the President's Council on Minority Business, a successful businessman himself.

Today, what I wanted to do is to follow up on some of the things that I discussed in the State of the Union Address. I really do enjoy going up to the Hill to deliver the State of the Union. It's the only time all year that you can get so many politicians so polite and understanding for so long. [*Laughter*] It's a wonderful feeling.

As you know, we've had a hectic week, from the State of the Union Address to releasing the budget to meeting with Boris Yeltsin. During this Presidency, I think it's fair to point out that the cold war has drawn to an end. We led the coalition that shoved Saddam Hussein out of Kuwait. Peace talks between ancient enemies have begun in the Middle East. The Soviet Union has collapsed, and we've begun working with its successor States. The whole world has changed. And still, some people say, "Hey, is that all? What have you done for us

lately?" [*Laughter*] I'd say, no, but it's a good start, and we recognize that we've got many other things to be working on, as I've been trying to do.

And now that we can look past the burdens of the cold war, we can do what we do best: create, innovate, build, produce, and lead. This afternoon, I'm going to be signing the Economic Report to the President. And it will not only describe and explain the causes of our current economic difficulties, it will also explain why virtually all economic analysts expect this economy to improve. More importantly, it will explain why if Congress enacts my progrowth policies, the improvement in the economy will be quicker, stronger, and much more certain.

In the State of the Union, I presented a comprehensive action plan for our economy. Today I want to discuss what that means for you. Think of this as my "small business State of the Union." My plan starts with what I can do as President without any congressional action required. We've taken a whole series of actions—I won't mention them all—but a series of actions to stimulate investment and get the economy moving. These, as I say, don't need congressional approval.

A couple of initiatives have earned kudos from this crowd. First, I have ordered major Departments and Agencies to put a 90-day hold on implementing new regulations. Regulations ought to foster economic growth, not crush it. And we're going to make sure that the days of overregulation are over once and for all. So, we're going to take a fresh look at the rules and regulations Washington hurls your way. We'll get rid of those that do nothing more than destroy jobs and weigh down businesses. And in this, we will pick some that will speed up and foster growth and support jobs. We're going to emphasize those regulations.

But that's not all. We also declared war on nuisance lawsuits. Yesterday I announced the "Access to Justice Act of 1992." That bill will give Americans less expensive and easier alternatives to trial. Let them solve problems out of court. And we've got to stop America's long liaison with the lawsuit. If we were as good at rewarding success as we are at suing each other, this country would be a lot better off. And that goes for health care, too. With those outrageous, sky-high malpractice awards, we've got to get those under control, and we are going to try hard.

And now the American people know better than to think that anyone, including a President, can wave a magic wand and revive something as complicated as our economy. Congress needs to do its job. And that means—and we were talking with your leaders about this earlier—that they should pass the short-term compact economic growth package that I put before the Congress, and pass it by March 20th.

You know, we're all realistic that we're going into a political year. And I'm fairly realistic that we're going into a political year—[*laughter*]—but I would simply point out that we have time now. There's a period of time that we can lower that political controversy and get something done, a rifleshot approach to stimulate this economy. And that's where I'm going to need your help. So here we go.

The plan starts with the basics. It stimulates investment by improving the alternative minimum tax and creating a new 15-percent investment tax allowance. L.W. Locke of North Carolina, and I'm told he's in the audience today, understands. He appreciates these changes. He's delayed building a convenience store/gasoline station because he just can't do it under our present system. The investment tax allowance would let him buy fixtures and gas pumps and fuel storage tanks, a $1 million commit-

ment. So don't tell me—here's a practical example—don't tell me, or don't listen to the voices that say this plan is a gimmick. And don't try to tell that to L.W., either, because he's right out there trying to move forward with investment.

I also want to fire up the engine that traditionally pulls us out of tough times, and that's the real estate industry. My plan helps builders. Ask Jay Buchert, a Cincinnati homebuilder, also here with us today. He's thrown his support behind this plan. The National Association of Home Builders predicts that my bill will create at least 415,000 construction industry jobs and set off $20 billion in economic activity associated with homebuilding. Now, that's no gimmick. That is no gimmick. That means jobs, good, solid American jobs.

And I also want to reward everyone who believes in the American dream, trying to make it work. I want Congress to cut the long-term tax on capital gains. And I want it cut to a maximum rate of 15.4 percent. The world's fastest growing economies and our major competitors, including Germany and Japan, have one thing in common: They tax capital gains at much lower rates than we do. And in many cases, capital gains isn't taxed at all.

It's ironic. Many politicians who oppose the capital gains tax cut also complain that we're not competitive. Well, they can't have it both ways. And if they really want us to be competitive, then they'll slash the capital gains rate and do it now in this comprehensive short-term package. The capital gains rate cut will help families who own homes, help people who own farms, help business owners, and will help everyone who invests in our future by purchasing stock.

Now, you've heard some people claim that a capital gains cut serves only the rich. Well, maybe those people should get out of Washington and talk to people around our country. Retirees say they can't sell their homes because capital gains rates punish them too much. Business owners say they can't expand their businesses; capital gains rates punish their success. A man from Florida, a retiree who built his own business, invested, saved, put it perfectly: He worked hard for years, and now he can't afford to cash in on his success. He said, "We are being penalized for having foresight." Well, I'm tired of people getting slammed because they risked their money and effort and succeeded. And it's about time the Congress realizes we should reward these people, not turn them into targets of envy. And that, of course, creates jobs. More people that take risks and start businesses; that means jobs.

So, let's get to the heart of this thing. The people in this room, small businessmen, investors from the National Venture Capital Association, you understand the gritty fundamentals of business. And you are the real experts. Well, America really needs your help now. So, don't accept no for an answer anymore. I'll take the heat on whether it's a tax cut for the rich or not, but you make the case as to what it can do to stimulate jobs and new businesses in this country and demand that the Congress cut the capital gains rate now.

And I might remind you when you do this work, remember that there were majorities in both Houses of Congress for what I'm proposing right now not so many months ago. The field is there for fertile reaping. And I tell you, I really hope that you can get up and help us do this job.

I'd also like to ask you that you demand action on my short-term plan without delay. You know, when I hear someone complain that this short-term plan won't do much, I wonder myself: Hadn't any of these guys ever run a business? Do they appreciate the difficulties of getting a loan, finding an investor, purchasing what you need, filling out all that Government paperwork? It's about time somebody understands that you need just a few minutes to concentrate on the customer. That's what some of this is going to do.

You may have detected this, but I'm tired of the term "fairness" being corrupted by political demagogs. You want fairness? Here's something fair: My plan will work for all Americans, and it will create jobs. How's that for fairness?

Congress has the legislation. It has a March deadline, March 20th deadline. And I ask you to circle the date on the calendar. Much beyond that, politics takes over.

We've got a chance now to get something done. So while you're in Washington, visit those congressional delegations. Let them know that you want this package passed. You are at the center of this plan, and you create, small business, you create the vast majority of jobs in this country. And I am determined to support you to create more jobs. I believe it is in your power to help lift this country and help get it moving again. I really am confident that you will do just that. Since Members of Congress will be home on break next week, drop by their offices, let them know how you feel. Send this message: No more delays, no excuses, no substitutes. And don't delay. Decision day is 6 weeks from Friday.

I didn't mention all the ingredients, but that's the rifleshot, short-term, incentive-building, job-creating part of this package. Now, for the longer term, I've also proposed an ambitious long-term agenda to ensure that our economy will continue leading the world for decades to come.

And let me discuss a critical issue in that plan, health care. I know health care has become a problem for many of you and your employees. And tomorrow I'm going to be announcing in detail my comprehensive health care plan. And I know you'll like it. I believe you'll like it a lot. People today worry about health care, yes. It costs too much, great concern. It's tough to find good comprehensive coverage. And you can't make choices like you used to. And you can't count on coverage if you move and change jobs or fall victim to a debilitating condition or disease.

I believe our plan solves these problems. And my plan ensures that people can find health care, choose health care, afford health care, and keep health care. I know that everyone with a plan promises the same thing, and that's why you have to use your common sense in evaluating the various proposals. And when you get right down to it, there are two fundamental health care choices. We can adopt a system that's been a proven failure all over the world, nationalized health care. Or we can reform our present system, which has its faults, certainly, but which also provides the highest quality care on Earth. People come from all over the world to participate in our health care. And if you want the freedom to choose your own doctor, to hold the line on costs, and to improve access to health insurance coverage, push for my plan. Look it over carefully. We're going to need your support. It gives everyone, and I emphasize everyone, access to the world's best health care, and it doesn't exclude anybody. So, take a look at this and support us if you can.

And finally, I'd like your help on one other item. The Federal Government is too big, and it spends too much. And it's just that simple. Now, my budget holds the line on new spending. It does not violate the only protection the taxpayer has, that's the spending caps that are now in the law. These caps are the only protection the taxpayer has against more spending by Congress. And it pulls the trapdoor on a host of federally funded programs, all with noble titles—246 programs to be exact—that we simply do not need. And you shouldn't have to pay for them. And it's that simple. Each one has a protector, but I think the time has come, and the times demand that we take action on these.

And also, get Congress to give me an important weapon to control spending. This one may be a little difficult, but get them to give me that line-item veto and give me a shot at it. Forty-three Governors have it; give the President a shot.

We must stop imposing mandates on others without paying for those mandates. Too often mandates, these mandated benefits dictated out of some subcommittee, mean mandated deficits. And that just isn't right. It's not fair to the States. It's not fair to the localities and the communities. And it's got to stop.

The bottom line is we've got a lot of work to do. And we can't let anyone stall us this time. Americans can't wait to get this economy moving. We want to throw off cynicism and fear. We want to shake away the gloom and the doubt. And I am, frankly, very tired of the professional pessimists who don't have any fresh ideas for the future and who literally feast on bad times and hard feelings and who talk as if our best days have passed by. They just don't understand.

Wouldn't you hate to go through life thinking, "The only way I can get a step up the ladder is if somebody else is hurting"? They just ought to get out of the way, these gloom-sayers and these pessimists. We can start a new economic revolution in America, one that builds on our innate optimism, our ambition, our determination, our willing to take risks, and our pride. And we're going to do just that. And that revolution will start a lot sooner if 535 people in Washington meet by March 20th deadline that I've proposed up there.

So let them know in no uncertain terms: Business as usual won't get this job done; election year politics as usual won't do. Tell them we need action by March 20th. And with your help, I believe we can get it.

Thank you all very, very much. And may God bless the United States.

*Note: The President spoke at 10:38 a.m. at the J.W. Marriott Hotel. In his remarks, he referred to SBLC officers Phil Chisholm, chairman, John Satagaj, president, and Ted Olsen, treasurer; John Kemp, executive vice president of the United Cerebral Palsy Association; L.W. Locke of Eastern Petroleum Corp., in Enfield, NC; and Robert Buchert of American Heritage Construction and Development Corp., Cincinnati, OH.*

# Letter to Congressional Leaders on Beneficiary Trade Status for Estonia, Latvia, and Lithuania
*February 5, 1992*

*Dear Mr. Speaker:* (*Dear Mr. President:*)

I am writing to inform you of my intent to add Estonia, Latvia, and Lithuania to the list of beneficiary developing countries under the Generalized System of Preferences (GSP). The GSP program offers duty-free access to the U.S. market and is authorized by the Trade Act of 1974.

In extending nondiscriminatory, most-favored-nation treatment to Estonia, Latvia, and Lithuania, the Congress provided that I should take prompt action to grant GSP benefits to the Baltic States, provided they each satisfied the eligibility requirements. I have carefully considered the criteria identified in sections 501 and 502 of the Trade Act of 1974. In light of these criteria, and particularly the Baltic nations' ongoing political and economic reforms, I have determined that it is appropriate to extend GSP benefits to Estonia, Latvia, and Lithuania.

This notice is submitted in accordance with section 502(a)(1) of the Trade Act of 1974.

Sincerely,

GEORGE BUSH

*Note: Identical letters were sent to Thomas S. Foley, Speaker of the House of Representatives, and Dan Quayle, President of the Senate. The related proclamation is listed in Appendix E at the end of this volume.*

## Remarks to the Greater Cleveland Growth Association in Cleveland, Ohio
*February 6, 1992*

Thank you very much for that welcome back to Cleveland. And first let me thank Dick Pogue, the chairman of the Greater Cleveland Growth Association, and all who help make this wonderful forum possible. I'm pleased to be back here in Cleveland, the capital city of the north coast. Hello to Bob Horton, who I understand not only warmed up the crowd but made it very difficult for me to come on as the next speaker. I salute what he and so many other business leaders in this community have done and are doing.

You always get this feeling of cooperation between the business community and the government of Cleveland, the city government. I had that when I first came here and Mayor Ralph Perk was in office, and particularly did I get that feeling when George Voinovich came in as your mayor and energized this place to a fare-thee-well. And business pitched right in. And you have this wonderful community spirit that this organization really epitomizes, Dick. And I am grateful to be here. And so let me get on with just saying I'm very pleased to have been introduced by George Voinovich, the great Governor of this State now. And may I salute Mike DeWine, who is over here, the Lieutenant Governor.

We've got some other friends with us, too. I know that Bob Taft is out here, the secretary of state. Three distinguished Members of the United States Congress came with us, Ralph Regula, Mike Oxley, and Dave Hobson. And I'm sure I'll forget somebody, but nevertheless I see our State senate president, Stan Aronoff, sitting over here. So that takes care of it. We've got good representation from Ohio's government; we've got representation from the wonderful congressional delegation; and we have outstanding representation here from the medical community and, of course, from the business community at large.

Good things are happening here for the Cleveland Cavs. [*Laughter*] In fact, I told the Governor I was going to be speaking today about the number one health issue on every Clevelander's mind. He said, "Mr. President, Mark Price's left knee is just fine." [*Laughter*]

People who know northern Ohio know that this region's on the move. In addition to the world-renowned Cleveland Clinic, now the city's number one employer, northern Ohio is also home to some of the most innovative approaches to health care. COSE and Cleveland Health Quality Choice are pioneers. Communities across the country can follow your lead to create workable solutions to health care challenges. And I had a briefing in Washington from the leaders of these organizations, and that really is why I've chosen to come to Cleveland this morning to address the health care crisis in our country and lay out my four-point program for comprehensive health care reform.

Reform is urgent for more reasons than one. Right now, far too many Americans are uninsured, and those who are insured pay too much for health care. And we're going to do something about that.

The one thing this crisis isn't about, and I was reminded of this in my visit to the hospital just now, the one thing it is not about is the quality of care. American health care is first-rate. It is the best in the entire world. And right now, the vast majority of Americans have access to that health care system. But the cost has skyrocketed from $74 billion in 1970 to $800 billion today. And if we keep going at the same rate, that $800 billion will double to $1.6 trillion by the year 2000.

These numbers alone would make the case for reform. They tell us there's a connection we simply can't ignore between what we pay for health care and the long-term health of our economy. But cold statistics don't show us the worry that people feel, the all-too-familiar fear about what happens to their health care if they change jobs or, worse still, if they lose their jobs. And in these hard times, we simply cannot accept the fact that one in every seven Americans is uninsured.

There's a better way. And my plan puts the emphasis on expanding access while preserving the choice people now have over the type of health care coverage and health care they receive. My plan will give Americans a greater sense of security, help ease the fears that so many Americans have that changing jobs will cost them their health coverage. And the key here is portability, changing the system to ensure people that they will always have access to health insurance no matter where they work. And finally, my plan will cut costs. It helps us make health insurance more affordable, and more affordable means more accessible. My plan will preserve what works and reform what doesn't. Above all, it will ensure every American universal access to affordable health insurance.

We stand at a crossroads. We can move forward dramatically to reform our market-based system, or we can force ourselves to swallow a cure worse than the disease. Some people have scribbled out a prescription for disaster. They want to nationalize our health system, put the Government in control of the system: Well, you let Government control the prices, let Government ration the kind of health care people get, let Government tell people looking for care how much they'll get, what kind, and when.

Nationalized systems cover everyone. But keep in mind the drawbacks that come with a nationalized system: Long waiting lists for surgery, shortages of high-tech equipment responsible for so many of the miracles of modern medicine. Let me cite just one example for you. The Cleveland Clinic performs 10 coronary bypass surgeries a day, I'm told, high-tech, high quality surgery without any wait. But if you live in British Columbia, the wait for coronary bypass surgery is 6 months. It's no wonder so many people from abroad come to American hospitals for surgery.

When you nationalize health care, you push costs higher, far higher. Some studies estimate that nationalized health care would cost the average American family a huge new tax burden; for the Nation, a staggering $250 billion to $500 billion a year in new taxes. Such a massive tax increase is simply unacceptable, and the American people should not be asked to accept it. And for that price, you get the worst of both worlds: No one has an incentive to control costs, and everyone pays.

But there are other proposals out there that sound simple but are every bit as harmful. One's called "play or pay." Each employer must play, provide insurance for employees, or pay a payroll tax to finance Government health coverage. Business men and women tell me horror stories about health care costs spiraling out of control. Well, "play or pay" will leave a lot of small businesses, businesses struggling on the edge of survival right now, with a tough choice. They can cut workers' wages to pay for mandated health care; they can fire some workers to cover the workers they keep; or they can raise prices and pass along the cost to the consumer. Some studies put the cost in jobs lost under "play or pay" as high as half a million or more. Lower wages, lost jobs, higher costs: Any way you look at it, that's the wrong choice for America.

Step away from the rhetoric, strip it out of there, and "play or pay" just creates a back-door route to nationalized health care. And it encourages employers to stop offering benefits, throw the problem in the Government's lap, and dump millions of fully insured workers into a public plan like Medicaid. And because the new employer taxes in "play or pay" don't pay for the program, the American taxpayer will obviously foot the bill. And I am not about to let that happen. You won't hear this from the people pushing "play or pay." Ask them about the side effects of their proposal, and they'll say, "Take two aspirin, and call me after the election."

I don't believe people want to be shoveled into some new health care bureaucracy. They want good health. A large part of the answer is prevention. And every one of us can make changes in our behavior to reduce the risk of disease and illness. And pardon me for being just a little bit old-fashioned, but what we're talking about is behavior: drugs, alcohol abuse, risky sexual behavior. You know what I'm talking about. And there's nothing wrong discussing that, trying to do better in this field. Tomorrow, in San Diego, I'll focus in more detail on the ways prevention can help people live healthier lives and help keep our economy healthy, too.

But today I want to focus on the health care system, on this comprehensive, market-based reform plan I have. The fact is, we do not have to create a new Government bureaucracy to give Americans access to affordable, quality health care. We need a system that delivers, a system that works for America, a system that puts quality care within reach of every American family.

Our system should be built on choice, not central control. It should keep costs down and open up access. But above all, it should allow all Americans to rest secure when it comes to health care, to ease their worry that if they change jobs, if they or their kids develop serious health problems, they'll still

be able to count on the coverage they need. Now, my comprehensive four-point plan meets every one of these commonsense tests. And here's how it works.

Point one, we will make health care more accessible by making health insurance more affordable. For low-income individuals and families, I propose a health insurance credit, up to $3,750 a year to guarantee people, even people too poor to file taxes, the ability to purchase private health insurance. That will give these families a certificate or voucher, to be used strictly for health care, worth more than $300 a month. They can use it to buy into the plan their employers offer but they could never afford, or they can shop for whatever private plan suits them best. That's the American commitment to choice at its best.

For middle-income individuals and families, I propose a health insurance tax deduction of $3,750. American families with incomes under $80,000 will receive new help from either the credit or the tax deduction. Let me tell you what that means: new help to purchase health insurance for 95 million Americans. And once again, this insurance will be portable. People who change jobs would have insurance regardless of their health, and this is important, or regardless of their family's health. But best of all, my plan will bring health care coverage to almost 30 million uninsured Americans, security to people who for far too long have had to do without. That's the first point in this four-point plan, access.

Point two, we will cut the runaway costs of health care by making the system more efficient. Today, I'm asking you to learn a new acronym, HIN, health insurance networks. Insurance costs obey the law of large numbers. The larger the group being insured, the lower the cost per individual. Pooling lowers insurance costs and significantly cuts administrative costs. HIN's will provide incentives for small companies to do what Cleveland's COSE group has done when it brought 10,000 small businesses together to make a joint purchase of health care. The Nation should listen and follow.

Another way to drive costs down: Make everyone a better health care consumer. Right now, most people pay more attention to the price of toothpaste then the comparative costs of health care. People don't waste much time thinking about the costs of their care, but in the end we all pay the price. We need to follow the lead of initiatives like Cleveland Health Quality Choice, programs that give people shopping for health care a kind of blue book for medical costs. Innovations like these will help all of us keep the costs of quality health care as low as possible.

Point three, we will wring out waste and excess in the present system. We've targeted medical malpractice for reform. It is time to put an end to these astronomical, sky's-the-limit lawsuits. You shouldn't have to pay a lawyer when you go to the doctor. And our doctors, the most able and dedicated in the world, shouldn't be living in fear of these outrageous lawsuits. And high malpractice premiums mean higher doctors' bills, higher hospital costs, costs passed along not only to the patient but to every American taxpayer.

Now, I have challenged the health insurance industry to cut redtape, to share common forms, to simplify and speed up claims processing. And here's a challenge for the next 4 years: There is no reason almost all health insurance claims can't be processed electronically. That single step would eliminate a mountain of health care paperwork and pare back costs.

We've got to attack the excesses of mandated benefits. When States now order health insurers to cover 1,000 different types of treatment, something's gone wrong. Next thing they'll be covering manicures for Millie. [*Laughter*] It's gone too far. And I think everybody knows it. And we should challenge the States to do something about the excessive mandates that shoot these costs right up through the roof.

Fourth and finally, we will get the growth in Government health programs under control. Right now, Government health care programs can claim a dubious distinction: They are the fastest growing parts in the Federal budget. For those of you interested in history, go back and listen to what was said about these programs at their inception. Go back and hear the rhetoric on the floor of the United States Congress. And now compare that to what actually has hap-

pened in these costs. This year alone, this year alone, let me repeat that, Medicaid costs will increase by 38 percent. We will not, repeat, not cut benefits. We can make real savings simply by reducing this huge rate of increase. We must bring runaway costs under control. Smart, sensible efficiencies will help our reform plan pay for itself.

The Federal Government should also give States flexibility to design these new universal access programs for the poor, programs that will provide quality services to all their citizens. I've just met with Governor Voinovich and the rest of the Governors. Regardless of party, Democrat or Republican, it doesn't matter, they want flexibility. And we must give it to them. Right here in Ohio, your Governor has proposed health care reforms that will do for this State what we want to do on the Federal level. States should be able to use new Federal resources to design programs that work, not some one-size-fits-all solution imposed by Washington, DC.

Providing affordable care, efficient care, wringing out excess and waste, and controlling Federal growth. These four points will create the kind of market-based reform plan that will give Americans the kind of health care they want and deserve and put an end to the worry that keeps them awake at night.

Remember what people want. People want quality care, care they can afford, and care they can count on, care they can rely on. I keep coming back to what works for this country. Think about the challenges that we face as a Nation. Anyone who is concerned about competitiveness has to see controlling health care costs as key to a healthy economy. We've got to make certain our reform corrects our weaknesses without destroying our strengths. When we talk about health care, we're talking about matters of the most personal nature, in some cases literally life and death and decisions that go with it. We don't need to put Government between patients and their doctors. We don't need to create another wasteful Federal bureaucracy. As President I simply will not let that happen.

We need commonsense, comprehensive health care reform, and we need it now.

And my plan I really believe is the right plan, a plan that meets our obligation to all Americans by putting hope and health within their reach.

Cleveland has led the way. Your hospitals, COSE, citizens in this community are way out front for these principles. And it's most appropriate that I give this speech to the Nation on health care reform right here in this city that is leading the way.

Once again, my thanks for this warm Cleveland welcome. May God bless you all and the United States of America. Thank you very, very much.

*Note: The President spoke at 12:36 p.m. at the Stouffer Tower City Plaza Hotel. In his remarks, he referred to Robert B. Horton, chairman of British Petroleum, and Mark Price, a member of the Cleveland Cavaliers basketball team. He also referred to the association's Council of Small Enterprises (COSE).*

# Remarks to the Staff of the University Medical Center of Southern Nevada in Las Vegas, Nevada
*February 6, 1992*

Thank you all very much. And again, I apologize if we've kept this distinguished group, busy people, waiting. But we're delighted to be here. It's kind of a hit-and-run day. It started in Cleveland where I announced the fundamentals of a new national approach for health care which I intend to work very hard for. But I want to thank Dr. Brandness and single out the Governor of the State, who has been most hospitable to me since we've been here. Also Barbara Vucanovich, who is a Congressman here, a great friend of mine of long standing, and simply say that I'm very pleased to be here to thank all of you for this afternoon's tour.

You can't help but when you walk through these halls and see the incredible work and dedication of the people, as we saw both at the neonatal care and the burn care center, you can't help but count your blessings for those who are devoting their lives to helping others. When you see somebody treating babies like that, tiny preemies, or those ravaged by burns, it just, at least in my heart, evokes tremendous gratitude and admiration for what you do. So, I hope you know that people outside the medical profession are extraordinarily grateful to those who give of themselves as you all do.

I did release this comprehensive health care program earlier today. And let me just, without giving you the full load, summarize a little bit. I know you're used to extended debates about health care. You probably get a lot of requests for free advice on this subject and many others. But I think everyone understands, all of you do, something that politicians sometimes forget, and that is that America's medical system offers the best care in the world.

It's not simply that we start with the scientific and research end, with far more Nobel Prize winners in medicine than any other country, but it's just generally the quality of care. And when people from other countries seek the best possible care, you just have to look, where do they go? Well, they come to the United States of America.

And with all the problems and all the breathless press reports about health care, I think of the guy who got in a car accident. And when he got to the hospital, the doctor set his broken bones, examined him carefully, and assured him that he could go home the next day. The next day came, and the doctor rushed to the patient's room with a look of great anxiety and concern. "Is something wrong?" the patient said. The doctor replied, "I'm not sure. Just to be safe, I'd like you to stay another day. You see, I didn't know how badly you were injured until I read about your accident in the newspaper." *[Laughter]*

Well, there's a parallel here. Reports of

the demise of American medicine in my view are greatly exaggerated. I will repeat, American medicine is the best in the entire world. My comprehensive health care plan builds on the strengths, on these strengths of our medical care system. I will not endorse nor go with a nationalized—they used to say socialized medicine—a nationalized plan that will guarantee only long lines, indifferent service, and very high taxes.

And I've worked hard to come up with a plan that will work. And that's the plan that we are proposing. It addresses Americans' basic concerns about health care: that too many people don't have access to care, I think we could all agree on that; that it costs too much; and that you can't be sure of keeping coverage if you change your job or if you or someone in your family has an illness or an injury. This plan ensures that every worker, regardless of health status, can get health care coverage, can choose providers, can afford care, and can keep it.

Let me just outline the plan in brief for you. It's got four points. One, we make health care affordable by offering a health insurance tax credit, a voucher, to low-income individuals and families, and then a health insurance tax deduction to middle-income individuals and families. Poor people who pay no taxes at all are covered, and they'll get insurance for free. These measures will help 95 million Americans purchase the health insurance that they need.

Two, we improve the efficiency of our system by reforming the insurance system and developing what we call health insurance networks. You probably refer to it as pooling. These networks will improve efficiency, and they literally will help drive insurance costs down. We make consumers of health care better able to compare costs, keep competition in the health care system.

Three, we're going to work hard to wring out the waste and excess. And we start by putting a lid on these outrageous medical malpractice lawsuits. Over the past decade malpractice insurance, the premiums, have risen by an average of more than 15 percent per year. This national epidemic of lawsuits has persuaded some doctors to avoid such vital specialties as surgery or obstetrics. America's love for the lawsuit has

just got to stop. And we've got legislation up there trying to do something about it. And it really is important in cost control, as everyone here knows. It's very, very fundamentally important in how we pay for the whole program.

Fourth, we're going to get the growth of Federal health programs under control. This isn't easy politically, but we've got to do it. Medicaid went up 38 percent this year alone. And we'll encourage major innovation at the State and local levels, and we'll do this without cutting benefits. And I believe it can be done without raising taxes.

America has been blessed by the world's best doctors, the best hospitals. I heard today how this hospital had been able to battle down the costs, eliminating some of the deficit that has been around. We've got the finest training institutions in this country; really, we have the finest. And this plan will not undermine this base of quality and excellence. You don't need your hands bound by redtape either, and you don't need these stethoscopes replaced by Federal millstones.

Having been around hospitals and blessed by seeing loving care for our kids, I am absolutely convinced that the medical profession is dedicated to the concept of service. This debate must not diminish that, must not take that away from the medical community at all. And I think you need our support. Everyone has got to play a part. I'm prepared to play mine in building a healthier Nation.

Every hospital depends also, as we all know, not just on professionals but also on volunteers. And you know this better than anyone, all of you do. Hundreds of thousands of people across this country, in literally hundreds of thousands of groups and organizations give their time to make medical care accessible to others. And every community relies not just on professionals, not just on physicians but also on teachers, on counselors, on nurses, people giving of themselves to help others along the path to good health. Our Secretary of HHS, Dr. Lou Sullivan, has talked eloquently about the rule of character in health. He's mounted an effective campaign to encourage preventive care. He teaches people about good habits, decent behavior, promotes the cause of immunization.

Celebrities, including my friend Arnold Schwarzenegger, promote active, healthy lifestyles. I might say a word about him. He's head of our Commission on Fitness, and he's taken it very seriously. He's gone to 28 States, all pro bono, and taken a message out there that the young people of this country are responding to. So, lifestyle is important. And I don't know about you, but when Arnold says exercise, I exercise. [*Laughter*] The point I'm trying to make is that everyone has a role. And this plan really encourages people to work together.

And so, I just again want to thank the doctors across this country, using all of you as the audience here today, but others not just here but around the country, for the careers that you've embarked on and are ennobling, on the challenge that you've chosen. And I am determined to push for a health care plan that will work. I think

we've got it, and I think we can do it without diminishing and losing the wonder of individual initiative and excellence. That's the hallmark, that's the underpinning of this plan. And needless to say, I don't want to see this many influential people assembled without putting in a pitch for it. So, please help us if you can, if you agree with us.

And thank you for what's been a wonderful few minutes for me in a busy day, started in Cleveland where we went to a hospital in Cleveland and then talked about a little more detail about this plan, then here today, and to San Diego tomorrow, going in there this evening. But it's been a joyous day for me. And thank you for what you do in helping other people across this country. Thank you so much.

*Note: The President spoke at 5:25 p.m. at University Medical Center. In his remarks, he referred to Dr. David Brandness, chief executive officer of the center.*

## Remarks to the San Diego Rotary Club in San Diego, California
*February 7, 1992*

Thank you all very, very much for that welcome. And Governor Wilson, Pete, thank you for that introduction, for being at my side in so many battles that I think affect this country. May I also salute Secretary Lou Sullivan, our distinguished Secretary of HHS who is sitting here, who came with me today; the Surgeon General, Surgeon General Novello is here somewhere out in the audience, sitting right over here; and next to her, Bill Roper, who is the head of the CDC, the Center for Disease Control, in Atlanta; and Dr. James Mason, who is our Assistant Secretary of HHS for Public Health.

So, you are surrounded, literally surrounded by health experts, our very best. And they are awful good, and I'm proud to be working at their side as we come to grips with some of these problems facing our Nation in health care.

May I also salute the Members of Con-

gress who are here: Representative Duke Cunningham, over here; Duncan Hunter I believe is with us, too; Bill Lowery and Ron Packard, somewhere modestly in the crowd. We've got a wonderful representation from this broad area in Washington, DC.

And may I thank Craig Evanco, the president of this Rotary Club, for assembling such a distinguished group at an awkward time, I'm sure, for some. But in any event, I'm just delighted to be here. And let me salute all, ladies and gentlemen.

It's a pleasure to be in San Diego. I've always loved it, been here many, many times. This is where I set sail for overseas way back in 1944, and this is where I returned to from overseas. And ever since then I've been coming here a great deal. It's a truly American jewel. And thank you for the privilege of visiting this beautiful city on the Pacific once again.

I know that the eyes of the sailing enthusiasts are again on San Diego this year with the America's Cup competition. And if you run low on wind—[*laughter*]—no, we've got a surplus back in Washington, and we'd be glad to help out. [*Laughter*] But good luck on all of that.

Earlier today—and I apologize for keeping you all waiting by some 15 minutes, I'm afraid—but I visited a catalyst of caring, something that I'm sure everyone in this Rotary Club that believes in service is proud of, the Logan Heights Family Health Center, founded by one Laura Rodriguez, what we call a Point of Light, one of San Diego's true Points of Light. And I saw the families and the children and watched one little guy get immunized there. Later, I had a chance to talk with the parents and community leaders about how greater immunization can increase illness prevention.

This morning, like immunization, I will try to be brief, and also like immunization, I will try to keep the pain to a minimum. I was so moved by that warm response to just being here that I'm sorely tempted to give a flamboyant political speech here today. [*Laughter.*] But I'm going to resist that because I think we've got a lot to get done for the country in health care, and I want to talk to you about that subject and discuss how prevention can achieve a priceless gift, good health in America. So let me begin, then, with an equation: Good health equals a change in the health care system plus a change in the way we act.

This country has the best health care system in the world, the best. The quality of health care in America is unrivaled. You couldn't tell it from some of the political criticism, but it is unrivaled. So, that's not the problem. Rather, the problem is, first, that too many Americans are excluded, leaving one-seventh of our people without health insurance coverage. And second, millions of Americans fear losing access to coverage when they change jobs or develop illness. This is absolutely unacceptable for the United States of America, and it's got to stop. Finally, health care costs too much. And this year, listen to this number now, this year Americans will pay more than $800 billion for health care, one-tenth of all we spend. The health of our economy and the health of our Nation cannot afford it. We've got to do something about it. And now is the time to start.

Imagine: Let's say you're making do, just getting by in your current job that offers health care for your disabled child. Let's say you get offered a better job with a higher salary. You want to take it. You need to take it. But you can't take the chance that it won't cover your child. That is not the American way. I know we can do better, and my plan does. We've got to roll up our sleeves and meet this challenge head on.

Affordability, access, portability: These are the issues we've got to address. So yesterday in Cleveland, I announced a pioneering plan to do just that, to stabilize costs, ensure access, and free workers from the fear of losing coverage. My plan will preserve what works and reform what doesn't work. It consists of four points, and I ask you to support this plan and help me make the best system in the world even better.

First, our plan will make health insurance more accessible by making it more affordable for millions of low- to middle-income families. For low-income families, I want a health insurance credit of up to $3,750 a year to help them buy insurance; for middle-income, a tax deduction up to the same amount.

Second, we will cut health care costs by making it more efficient. Studies show that the larger the group being insured, the lower the cost per individual. So, we will create what we call health insurance networks that help companies band together and cut administrative costs.

And the third point will also lower costs. We must reform medical malpractice litigation. Today we have too many malpractice suits driving up costs for a doctor, a nurse, or a hospital stay. And I might say parenthetically, this malpractice suit is just a symptom of what's happening all across the business spectrum in this country and in the eleemosynary area, like in a Little League. We've got too darn many lawsuits out there, very candidly. A recent study found that, listen to this one, that in 1989 the cost of defensive medicine, just for physicians' expenditures, to be over $20 billion, or nearly 18 percent of their total costs.

I don't want to get into trouble with the Bar Association—[*laughter*]—but I once quoted to someone that line, "An apple a day keeps the doctor away." He says, "What works for lawyers?" [*Laughter*] But this is a very serious point, and here's what will work for America: Let's spend as much time building a better health system as we do wrestling with our legal system. We'd do better caring for each other if we stop solving problems by suing each other.

And that brings me to point four. We will cut the outrageous growth of Federal health programs. Listen carefully to what I've said: We will cut the growth of health programs like Medicare so that we can protect the benefits. Our reform program will cut costs, ensure choice, and give everyone, rich or poor, sick or healthy, access to health care.

And yet there are those who, like an old dog, refuse to learn new tricks. Instead of a better health care system, they demand a nationalized health system. Very candidly, you want to call it what it is, that means a socialized system. Let me tell you straight, I will not allow those people to give America a prescription for failure. I am going to fight against a nationalized, socialized medicine approach for this country.

Folks who want national health care are the same people who said that Tony Gwynn would never amount to much of a hitter. [*Laughter*] Now, they can't see the future. They think socialized medicine—everything provided by the Government, totally Government-controlled medical care—is just the ticket for health care in America. And what they're not saying is it's also the ticket for treatment waiting lines.

Anyone who's spent months checking the mail for that income tax refund, or tried to track down a missing Social Security check, or wasted a day in line at the department of motor vehicles is going to think long and hard before they let the Government play doctor. Some say nationalized health care would serve everyone. Sure it would, yes, just like a restaurant that serves bad food but in very generous proportions. [*Laughter*]

Look at countries where socialized medicine violates the number one rule of the medical profession, "Do no harm." They can tell you, nationalized health care is a nationalized disaster. And it's true, socialized medicine plans have increased exports to our country. But what are the exports? I'll tell you: Patients coming here for prompt surgery and the finest care in the world, doctors coming here for better working conditions.

As long as I am President, we are not—again, I want to repeat it—we are not going to go down the road of nationalized health care. And nor will we jump from the frying pan into the fire. I oppose the other Government-takeover plan. They call it "pay or play," where employers are forced either to accept a health insurance plan or pay a payroll tax and join the Government plan.

The "play or pay" choice costs jobs and money. And it reminds me of the guy with the gun in your back, who says, "Your money or your life." Jack Benny used to respond by saying, "I'm thinking. I'm thinking." [*Laughter*] Well, we'd better think long and hard about a "pay or play" plan that would make us pay and pay and pay and drive a lot of small businesses out of work, out of business in the first place. And I'm not going to let Congress try to cure America's health and care ailments by binding wounds in redtape.

I have proposed a plan that is sensible, and really it will work. And I ask you to help, too. One of the best ways is keeping people healthy, keeping them healthy. So, let me talk just a minute about how we must also change the way we act. And in this field I again salute Dr. Sullivan, our Secretary of HHS, who's been way out in front of the power curve on this concept. If you'll forgive me for altering an old saying, Pete used it a minute ago, "A pound of prevention is worth a ton of cure."

My good friend Lou, Dr. Sullivan, has said better control of fewer than 10 risk factors could prevent up to 70 percent of premature deaths, one-third of all cases of acute disability and two-thirds of all cases of long-lasting disability, and yes, many, many AIDS cases. If you exercise and eat right and don't smoke or abuse drugs and drink less and avoid risky sexual behavior, you'll live longer. And America will live better. Let's change the behavior that costs society tens of billions, this is no exaggeration, tens of billions of dollars in lost earnings and productivity, treatment related programs, accidents, and certainly crime. Maybe I am a little old-fashioned, but I believe personal responsibility has a lot to do with making America a better country.

And now, let's also act through another prevention measure, immunization. With health care costs stretched to the limit, we can't afford not to immunize our youngest children. And last June, Secretary Sullivan and I announced our administration's immunization initiative. And our goal was simple, to bring immunization to every American child. This effort pays huge dividends. Every $1 spent for immunization now for measles, mumps, and rubella saves an estimated $14 later on.

Consider two facts. Two years ago, measle cases soared to a high of 27,000. In 1989 to '90 alone, measles caused 130 deaths, 60 percent of which were children under 5 years of age. Because of our immunization initiative we now have a national blueprint to bring this needless and tragic story to a speedier end. But we're also working on immunization's equivalent of putting a man on the moon, the one-time, all-in-one vaccine that immunizes a child against all vaccine-preventable childhood diseases.

You know, since September of 1991 there's not been a single reported polio case in the Americas. Now, that's an extraordinary immunization accomplishment. But we've got to do better. And that's why we've more than tripled the dollars for Federal immunization efforts since I took office in 1988—'89, January—[*laughter*]—from $98 million to $297 million for 1992. And our work will only be complete when we eradicate these terrible diseases not only from our neighborhoods but from the world's as well.

Let me tell you a story about a family right here in San Diego. Michael and Barbara Baines had always watched closely over the health of their children. And last year they were preparing for the holidays, but they were not prepared for the news, their two littlest stricken by whooping cough. Thank God, 2½-year-old Kensington has now left the hospital, and little 18-month-old Colleen has stabilized. And as Michael and Barbara prayed, they asked

that other parents would not make the same mistake. And said Michael, "You can't fight something you can't see. You've got to have them immunized; give them as much protection as you can as early as you can."

It's because of families like the Baineses that I put forth this message: We need improved immunization. We also need earlier immunization not merely of school-age kids, where immunization approaches 100 percent, but of our smallest victims, where a year of wait can be a year too long. Kids need to be completely vaccinated in the first and second years of life. Yet immunization rates at 2 years of age are only 50 percent in many States and often as low as 10 percent in some of the inner cities. We have to change that, and I am determined that we will.

It won't be easy to immunize every child. And yet the Government will do its part. And the private sector needs to do its part as well. We need to help it try creative ideas like one-stop shopping for health care and escorted referral for express lane immunization at the clinics. And finally I ask each of you, mothers, fathers, spouses, friends: Call your health official or physician. Join groups which encourage childhood immunization. Please, please, make sure your child is immunized.

I have outlined today a reform program to make health care accessible and affordable. It's a program which rejects outright the dead end of Government-controlled, of socialized medicine, a program which will be good medicine for the American economy and the American people. And so, please help me take this message to the Congress: "He who has health has hope, and he who has hope has everything." I need your support. I need you to be involved. And let's bring quality health care to every American.

You know, when I was little, I read a quote by Saint Francis of Asissi. "Give me a child until he is 7," he wrote, "and you may have him afterward." Through a better system and better behavior, we can ensure that the future will have our children afterward, hoping, building, dreaming, as Americans always have and as Americans always will.

Thank you very, very much. And may God bless the United States of America. Thank you.

*Note: The President spoke at 10:20 a.m. at the Sheraton Harbor Island Hotel.*

# Statement by Press Secretary Fitzwater on the Appointment of Robert L. Gallucci as Senior Coordinator for the Office of the Deputy Secretary of State
*February 7, 1992*

The President has announced the appointment of Dr. Robert L. Gallucci as Senior Coordinator reporting to the Deputy Secretary of State, with responsibility for coordinating the Administration's cooperation with the States of the former Soviet Union to reduce the risk that their scientists and know-how would contribute to the proliferation of special weapons. For this purpose, he will also assist in the coordination of assistance to the Commonwealth of Independent States in the areas of conversion of the state-run defense establishment to peaceful or commercial enterprises, and humanitarian and educational needs. Dr. Gallucci will carry the personal rank of Ambassador.

In order to assume these new responsibilities, Dr. Gallucci has resigned his position as Deputy Executive Chairman of the U.N. Special Commission charged with the destruction or removal from Iraq of weapons of mass destruction and ballistic missiles. Ambassador Michael Newlin has been nominated to succeed Dr. Gallucci in that position.

# Statement on Signing the Emergency Unemployment Compensation Bill
*February 7, 1992*

Today I am pleased to sign into law H.R. 4095 to extend and increase the benefits available under the Emergency Unemployment Compensation program. These benefits are financed in a manner consistent with the discipline of the budget agreement and long-term economic growth.

The 13 additional weeks of unemployment benefits provided by this legislation means real help to unemployed workers and their families during these tough times. It means getting checks into the hands of men and women to help pay the mortgage or the grocery bill, make the car payment or meet the daily expense of raising a family—at the same time they're seeking new employment.

As Americans who watched my State of the Union Address last week might remem-

ber, I called for swift enactment of this legislation. The bill I am signing today demonstrates clearly that when the Congress wants to act expeditiously it can. When the Congress and the Administration work in common cause, we can accomplish great things.

The greatest challenge we have before us now is getting the economy moving again. I have offered an immediate action plan to the Congress. The best thing the Congress can do for the American people is pass this action plan—and pass it by March 20, the deadline I announced in the State of the Union.

Yes, it's a political year. But we are in a window of opportunity right now—we can put partisanship aside—we've got 42 more days. The American people deserve action now, and it's time for the Congress to enact the plan we have put forward.

GEORGE BUSH

The White House,

February 7, 1992.

*Note: H.R. 4095, approved February 7, was assigned Public Law No. 102–244.*

# Remarks on Receiving the Boy Scouts of America Report to the Nation
*February 10, 1992*

Let me just first welcome everybody here, those up here and everybody out in the audience. I am pleased to be here because the goals of the Boy Scouts and the concerns of the young of our Nation are very important to me, important to our administration, and most of all, fundamentally important to our whole country. I want to recognize Ronald Moranville, the deputy chief Scout executive, seated here, right here in the front; and those members of the administration who are with us, our Chief of Staff, Sam Skinner, the future Secretary of Transportation here, Andy Card, and others with us who are all very interested in this.

Since 1910 with President Taft, every President, I think Ben referred to this, but every President has received the Boy Scouts report to the Nation. And I am again proud to receive it this year. The Scout slogan is "Do a good turn daily." This report represents the great and heroic deeds done by our Nation's future, from feeding the hungry to helping kids stay drug-free. I listened to those five goals, and clearly we should all be working to achieve those goals.

Boy Scouts and Scout initiative have been

recognized as what we call daily Points of Light for serving others and making positive differences, for example, the members of Boy Scout Troop 4 of Ann Arbor, Michigan. These Scouts made community service central to their mission, providing companionship to our elderly, beautifying the grounds of the elderly homes, as well as working with the hungry and those afflicted by drugs.

So I just mentioned one example; there are many, many more that I could point to. I want to thank all of you for the good turns done by the Scouts throughout the United States; thank each of you, those who have been singled out for personal heroism. It sets a wonderful example to young and old alike.

So for me, this is a very nice interlude, and I'm just delighted to see you all back here. I remember that marvelous encampment in Virginia. I hope someday I'll get to come back. It's good to see you guys. Thanks for coming.

*Note: The President spoke at 11:55 a.m. in the Roosevelt Room at the White House. In his remarks, he referred to Ben H. Love, chief Scout executive.*

# Remarks to the Conference on Healthy Children Ready To Learn
*February 10, 1992*

*The President.* Thank you, Dr. Sullivan. And might I just say at the beginning of these brief remarks that I am very proud of Lou Sullivan and what he's doing as Secre-

tary of HHS. He's doing a superb job, and we all are grateful to him. And when Dr. Novello and Lou suggested I could be here, let me just say it's a pleasure to be here today to help launch this historic conference.

I particularly want to thank our Surgeon General, Antonia Novello. I see she brought most of her family with her. [*Laughter*] No, but let me just say this: As an observer with a pretty good observation post, she's inspired people all across the country with her example and her message. And she sums it up this way, she sums up the message better than anyone: "All children have a right to be healthy." Then she says, "We need to speak for those who cannot speak for themselves."

And that's why you've gathered here this week, and you've come to lead a great movement of parents and doctors and teachers and public programs and private enterprise, a movement destined to transform America. And here's our goal—what's that guy got going? [*Laughter*] I think it's wonderful these kids are here, I really do. Makes me feel right at home.

Here's our goal: By the year 2000, every American child will start school healthy and ready to learn. Our success will provide a lifetime of opportunity for our children. And it will guarantee the health and safety of our families and neighborhoods, and it will ensure that America remains the undisputed leader of the world. Now, I am proud that our administration is part of this movement. In this administration, families come first.

We're proud to join hands with people like Trish Solomon Thomas, who's come from New Mexico to be here this afternoon. A little history: She has two children, both of them with special health needs. And she perfectly expressed the spirit of our movement when she said, "I used to be shy, but I had to learn to stand up for my kids." And that's why we're here, to stand up for our kids. And we will not let them down.

Our movement draws its strength from Trish and the millions of parents like her. The title of this conference says it all, "Healthy Children Ready To Learn: The Critical Role of Parents." Now, parents are a child's first teachers, offering the love and spiritual nourishment that no Government program can ever hope to provide.

And if I can brag for just a minute here today, you may know of Barbara's work pro-

moting literacy. And I'm very proud of her. She wants to help parents understand just how important it is to read to their kids. And when parents read aloud to their young ones, they open their children to the joy of a larger world; they teach the self-assurance and curiosity that comes from learning. Barbara asked me to extend her best wishes. She's down on a learning program, an education program, right this minute in the State of Mississippi. [*Applause*] Don't know whether you're clapping because she's there or because she's interested in education, but neverthe-less——[*laughter*]

*Audience member.* Mississippi.

*The President.* Oh, a little Mississippi delegation here.

But anyway, our movement instills the habits of good health, wholesome nutrition, sound hygiene, and protective measures like early immunization. Parents know learning and health are two sides, really, of the same coin.

And again, parents, families, communities are the key. But Government can help, must help. Last June, for example, Dr. Sullivan and I, with able advice from Dr. Novello, took steps to ensure that no American child is at risk from deadly diseases like polio, diphtheria, and measles. And we launched an initiative to support childhood immunizations, especially immunizations for kids in the early years of life. Now, that's a crucial step toward meeting our goal. And I'm proud we've been able to help. Since 1988, we've more than tripled the dollars for Federal immunization efforts, from $98 million to $297 million for 1992.

On Friday, Dr. Sullivan and the Surgeon General and I, we were just talking about it outside, were out in San Diego, and we had the privilege of visiting Logan Heights Family Health Center to see firsthand the benefits of this initiative. We spoke with parents and community leaders, and every one of them stressed the importance of early immunization in preventing illness.

Logan Heights, one of many, I'm sure, but it's a perfect example of what can be done if concerned individuals set their minds to it. The center was founded by a wonderful woman named Laura Rodriguez, who's become one of our administration's what we call Points of Light, helping others, setting an example in the process. Laura saw a need, and with hard work and dedication, she rolled up her sleeves and did something about it. Logan Heights now serves 75,000 patients a year. So, I say thank God for people like Laura. She's an example for all of us. And there are many, many other examples right here in this room.

And for those kids who need a head start in preparing for school, we've made sure that they'll get it. In the last 3 years, we have almost doubled the funding for Head Start programs, and this year I have proposed the largest single increase in Head Start's history, $600 million. This year's increase will ensure that 157,000 more kids will be able to start school ready to learn.

Head Start brings children and parents into the classroom, into the learning process. Head Start works because parents take the lead. You may not know this, but volunteers in Head Start outnumber paid staff by eight to one. Head Start works because people care. And we're making sure it continues to work. If it's good for America's kids, it's good for America.

These are important steps. But there's more to do. And we must address the larger issues of American health care. And last week, I proposed a four-point plan to do just that. Every American family must have access to affordable, high-quality care.

I don't need to tell you that the American health care system has problems. The crisis has probably touched many of you right here in this room. Right now, more than 8 million children go without health insurance because skyrocketing costs have placed coverage beyond the reach of their parents. And even parents who are covered worry about losing their family's insurance if they move on to a different job or, worse still, lose the job they have. You shouldn't have to live with this kind of uncertainty. No American family should. And my proposal will put an end to that.

And yet, I think we should keep one thing in mind. It's important to remember: For all its problems the system, our health care system, still provides the best health care in the world. And that's why people from all over the world come here seeking better care. Most often they're trying to escape health care systems in which the government dictates how much care you'll get and what kind you'll get and when you'll get it. In America, that's unacceptable.

Our great challenge, then, is to keep what works in our system and then reform what doesn't work. We must maintain a maximum freedom of choice and the highest quality care. And at the same time, we must make sure that our children have access to health care their parents can afford, sick or healthy, rich or poor. That's what this four-point plan does, and let me just briefly spell it out for you.

First, to make health care more affordable and accessible, I want a $3,750 tax credit for low-income families to help them buy health insurance. For middle-income families, I've proposed a tax deduction for the same amount. Poor people, those who don't file taxes, would be covered under this plan.

Second, to cut costs, we will make health care more efficient. The math is simple; the larger the group being covered, the lower the cost per individual. So what we've done is this: We've proposed health insurance networks that bring companies together to cut administrative costs and make insurance affordable for working parents.

And third, we must cut out the waste and abuse. We can start with medical malpractice lawsuits that drive up the cost of care for everyone. A doctor pestered with frivolous litigation ends up passing his legal costs right along to you, the American people, and right along to the patient. And when you go to the doctor, I don't want you to have to pay a lawyer, too. Just pay the doctor.

And finally, we must slow the spiraling costs of Federal health programs. These costs are rising far beyond the rate of inflation, which only endangers important benefits while making less money available for other pressing needs.

There it is, a commonsense reform that will maintain high-quality care, cut costs, ensure maximum freedom of choice, and give every family, rich or poor, sick or healthy, access to health care. I know how important this is, particularly for parents who have children with special needs. And my plan will assure that you can change jobs without endangering the health insurance your child depends on. We're building on our system's strengths. And we're avoiding the pitfalls of nationalized care, the kind that people from all over the world come to America to escape.

All these approaches for meeting our goal of "Healthy Children Ready To Learn" must build on a basic truth: In this country families come first. Government programs that overtake the rightful role of families and communities, that deny them the freedom of choice or bind them up in redtape, are simply unacceptable. Our movement is about strengthening families.

And over the next few days I'm told you will continue a great national dialog, share information, explore new ideas, and then return to your communities to lead the good fight. Your commitment is an inspiration, and I thank you for inviting me by to get a feeling of it firsthand. And may God bless all of you.

And now this little guy, I've got to tell you, those in the back, when I walked in and was sitting here looking very serious waiting for the doctor to introduce me, this guy in the blue, he goes like this to me. [*Laughter*] And I had to tell him, "No, I have to stay up here." You know, I tried to communicate with him, but now I'm going to invite him to come up here and say hello to me.

But thank you all, and may God bless America. Thank you very, very much.

*Note: The President spoke at 2:07 p.m. at the Ramada Renaissance Hotel.*

## Memorandum on Payments to the United Nations
*February 10, 1992*

*Memorandum for the Secretary of State*

Subject: Delegation of Functions Related to Payment to the United Nations and Its Specialized Agencies of United States Assessments and Arrears

By the authority vested in me as President by the Constitution and the laws of the United States of America, including section 301 of title 3 of the United States Code and sections 102 and 162 of the Foreign Relations Authorization Act, Fiscal Years 1992 and 1993 (Public Law 102–138) (the Act), I hereby delegate to you the functions vested in me by sections 102(a)(3) and 162 (b) and (d) of the Act, relating to payment

to the United Nations and its specialized agencies of United States assessments and arrears. These functions may be further redelegated within the Department of State.

The functions delegated by this memorandum shall be exercised in coordination with the Director of the Office of Management and Budget and the Assistant to the President for National Security Affairs.

You are authorized and directed to publish this memorandum in the *Federal Register*.

GEORGE BUSH

[*Filed with the Office of the Federal Register, 4:26 p.m., February 12, 1992*]

## Memorandum on Social Security Card Changes
*February 10, 1992*

*Memorandum for the Secretary of Health and Human Services*

*Subject:* Delegation of Authority to Report to the Congress and to Publish in the *Federal Register* Proposed Changes in the Social Security Number Card

Section 205(c)(2)(F) of the Social Security Act (section 405(c)(2)(F) of title 42 of the United States Code) directs the Secretary of Health and Human Services to issue Social Security number cards to individuals who are assigned Social Security numbers.

By the authority vested in me as President by the Constitution and the laws of the United States of America, including section 274A(d)(3)(A) of the Immigration and Nationality Act (the "Act") (section 1324a(d)(3)(A) of title 8 of the United States Code) and section 301 of title 3 of the United States Code, and in order to provide for the delegation of certain functions under the Act, I hereby:

(1) Authorize you to prepare and transmit, to the Committee on the Judiciary and the Committee on Ways and Means of the House of Representatives and to the Committee on the Judiciary and the Committee on Finance of the Senate, a written report regarding the substance of any proposed change in Social Security number cards, to the extent required by section 274A(d)(3)(A) of the Act, and

(2) Authorize you to cause to have printed in the *Federal Register* the substance of any change in the Social Security number card so proposed and reported to the designated congressional committees, to the extent required by section 274A(d)(3)(A) of the Act.

The authority delegated by this memorandum may be further redelegated within the Department of Health and Human Services.

You are hereby authorized and directed to publish this memorandum in the *Federal Register.*

GEORGE BUSH

[*Filed with the Office of the Federal Register, 1:14 p.m., June 5, 1992*]

## Statement on the Death of Alex Haley
*February 10, 1992*

Barbara and I extend our heartfelt sympathies to the family of Alex Haley upon his passing. Alex Haley was an extraordinary individual and a literary giant who served his country for 20 years in the U.S. Coast Guard.

He went on to produce many works, including the "Autobiography of Malcolm X" and "Roots." "Roots" in particular has been woven into the cultural patchwork that is America. Haley's own roots, nourished in the small town values of Henning, Tennessee, were central to his writings and his life.

He taught us that every community needs to strengthen and renew itself. I am particularly grateful for the encouragement that he continued to provide to thousands of Americans who work to make their communities places where education is nourished. Alex Haley understood that it was important to know where you come from— so that you could set a course for where you want to go. He will be an inspiration for generations to come. His talent and spirit will be greatly missed.

## Statement by Press Secretary Fitzwater on the Export Enhancement Program
*February 10, 1992*

The President met on February 10 with his key advisers to review the U.S. Export Enhancement Program (EEP). Secretaries Brady and Madigan, Richard Darman, Chief of Staff Samuel Skinner, Michael Boskin, General Scowcroft, Roger Porter, Michael Moskow, Robert Zoellick, and Timothy Deal participated in the meeting.

EEP was established in 1985 to help U.S. agricultural producers meet subsidized competition in foreign markets.

The group reviewed the existing criteria for approval of EEP sales with particular reference to several outstanding applications from potential foreign purchasers. There was general agreement that in considering whether to approve specific EEP proposals U.S. agencies must weigh the nature of the competition in the foreign market (i.e. subsidized v. nonsubsidized competition), U.S. historic presence in the market, and the budgetary impact of such sales.

U.S. agencies will apply these and other criteria in deciding on the merits of existing and future EEP proposals.

## Nomination of Robert C. Frasure To Be United States Ambassador to Estonia
*February 10, 1992*

The President has announced his intention to nominate Robert C. Frasure, of West Virginia, a career member of the Senior Foreign Service, class of Counselor, to be Ambassador Extraordinary and Plenipotentiary of the United States of America to Estonia.

Currently Dr. Frasure serves as the Chargé d'Affaires at the U.S. Embassy in Tallinn, Estonia. Prior to this, Dr. Frasure served as the Africa Director of the National Security Council at the White House, 1990–1991; Deputy Chief of Mission at the U.S. Embassy in Addis Ababa, Ethiopia, 1988–1990; Political Counselor at the U.S. Embassy in Pretoria, South Africa, 1986–1988; and Political Officer at the U.S. Embassy in London, England, 1982–1986. From 1980 to 1982, he served in the Southern Africa Office of the State Department.

Dr. Frasure graduated from West Virginia University (B.A., 1964; M.A., 1965) and Duke University (Ph.D., 1971). He was born April 20, 1942, in Morgantown, WV. Dr. Frasure is married, has two children, and resides in Falls Church, VA.

## Nomination of Ints M. Silins To Be United States Ambassador to Latvia
*February 10, 1992*

The President has announced his intention to nominate Ints M. Silins, of Virginia, a career member of the Senior Foreign Service, class of Counselor, to be Ambassador Extraordinary and Plenipotentiary of the United States of America to Latvia.

Currently Mr. Silins serves as Chargé d'Affaires at the U.S. Embassy in Riga, Latvia. Prior to this, he served as U.S. consul general in Strasbourg, France, 1989–

1991; Deputy Director for Bilateral Political Relations for the Office of Soviet Affairs at the U.S. Department of State, 1987–1989; a fellow at the Center for International Affairs at Harvard University, 1986–1987; Counselor for Political Affairs at the U.S. Embassy in Stockholm, Sweden, 1983–1986; and Deputy Principal Officer for the U.S.

consulate general in Leningrad, U.S.S.R., 1981–1983.

Mr. Silins graduated from Princeton University (A.B., 1965). He was born March 25, 1942, in Riga, Latvia. Mr. Silins served in the U.S. Army Reserve, 1966–1972. He is married, has four children, and resides in Alexandria, VA.

# Nomination of Darryl Norman Johnson To Be United States Ambassador to Lithuania
*February 10, 1992*

The President has announced his intention to nominate Darryl Norman Johnson, of Washington, a career member of the Senior Foreign Service, class of Minister-Counselor, to be Ambassador Extraordinary and Plenipotentiary of the United States of America to Lithuania.

Currently Mr. Johnson serves as Chargé d'Affaires at the U.S. Embassy in Lithuania. Prior to this, Mr. Johnson served as Deputy Chief of Mission for the U.S. Embassy in Warsaw, Poland, 1988–1991; Political Counselor at the U.S. Embassy in Beijing, China,

1984–1987; Special Assistant to the Under Secretary for Political Affairs at the U.S. Department of State, 1982–1984; and as a Pearson fellow on the staff of Senator Claiborne Pell, 1981–1982. From 1979 to 1981, Mr. Johnson served as the Officer-in-Charge of the People's Republic of China Affairs at the U.S. Department of State.

Mr. Johnson graduated from the University of Washington (B.A., 1960). He was born June 7, 1938, in Chicago, IL. Mr. Johnson has three children and resides in Washington, DC.

# Presidential Determination No. 92–14—Memorandum on Redesignation of Ethiopia Under the Export-Import Bank Act
*February 10, 1992*

*Memorandum for the Secretary of State*

*Subject:* Determination under Section 2(b)(2) of the Export-Import Bank Act of 1945, as amended: Ethiopia

Pursuant to the authority vested in me by section 2(b)(2)(C) of the Export-Import Bank Act of 1945, as amended (the Act), 12 U.S.C. 635(b)(2)(C), I hereby determine that Ethiopia (designated "Socialist Ethiopia" in section 2(b)(2)(B)(ii) of the Act) has ceased to be a Marxist-Leninist country within the definition of such term in subparagraph

(B)(i) of such section.

You are directed to report this determination to the Congress and publish it in the *Federal Register.*

GEORGE BUSH

[*Filed with the Office of the Federal Register, 5:07 p.m., February 26, 1992*]

*Note: This memorandum was released by the Office of the Press Secretary on February 11.*

# Exchange With Reporters Prior to Discussions With Prime Minister Suleyman Demirel of Turkey
*February 11, 1992*

### Turkey-U.S. Relations

*The President.* I have been looking forward to this visit to set the right tone of this important U.S.-Turkish relationship. And I should tell you that we were just delighted, and we will work closely with you in every way. And we're pleased to see you here.

*The Prime Minister.* I do appreciate your invitation, Mr. President. I think we have something to talk about.

*The President.* We've got a lot to talk about. The U.S.-Turkish——

*Q.* Mr. President, are you plotting the demise of Saddam?

*The President.* The U.S.-Turkish relationship is a very, very important one.

*Q.* How much do you intend to discuss the situation in Iraq? Will that be a big focus of your talks?

*The President.* Well, we're going to have a lot of discussion on a wide array of subjects. I'd let the Prime Minister set the agenda, of course. But I will be reiterating how important the U.S.-Turkish relationship is, how much confidence we have in this Prime Minister, and how closely I personally want to work with him. And I think out of that then, we'll discuss a wide array of issues. But we've got so many issues to talk about that I don't know where we're going to begin.

### Presidential Primaries

*Q.* Mr. Bush, Buchanan started running a spot in New Hampshire yesterday saying that he cares more than you do. Do you think you've settled that issue?

*The President.* Why don't we just let the voters settle that one on next Tuesday and keep our sights set on what we've got to do here.

### Trade Negotiations and NATO

*Q.* Mr. President, there are people in Europe wondering if the American Government is linking the GATT issue to the troops level.

*The President.* The GATT to troops? No, there is no linkage at all. I will be telling the Prime Minister, and he'll probably say the same to me, that it is important that we get a GATT agreement. Secondly, without setting priorities, it is important that we retain a strong presence in NATO in Europe. And so, there is no linkage between them. The Vice President made that very clear.

And so I'm glad you raised that one because there's been some confusion about it, and this is important. I want a successful conclusion to this GATT round, and we're going to press hard to get that. And I want a strong U.S. commitment to NATO. And I think that's important to Turkey, and I think it's important to freedom around the world.

*Q.* You're not going to get GATT, are you?

*Q.* But is GATT a security issue?

*The President.* No.

*Q.* Not at all?

*The President.* No. They're separate. These two questions are separate. One relates to world trade, and it is very important we get a successful conclusion to the GATT round. And you have a whole question of security. And NATO is very important to the security of Europe, indeed. And I think what it projects is important to worldwide peace and stability.

*Q.* Well, isn't it time they took care of themselves?

*The President.* So there is no linkage. There is no linkage.

*Q.* Isn't it about time after 45 years? We have 150,000 troops there. Aren't 75,000 enough?

*The President.* We've set the proper level, and we're going to stay with the level that we have set. And so we're not going to be driven by people that now think there is no threat in the world and that the U.S. has no responsibility. We have a disproportionate responsibility for world peace. We are very grateful and lucky that we have come as far as we have in terms of world peace. And we are not going to let this be set by a lot of politicians. We're going to do what's right for the national security, whether it's good politics or bad.

And we've set an appropriate level. And I will be guided not by political challenge but by the Joint Chiefs of Staff and by the leaders of the military in Europe with whom we work in close cooperation, Manfred Woerner to many others. So that's the way it is, and that's the way it's going to be.

*Q.* But sir, some in Europe are saying that you use the Senators to——

*The President.* This isn't a press conference. I've got a lot to learn here from the Prime Minister.

*Q.* Did you use the Senators to give Europe any warning?

*The President.* On what?

*Q.* On the GATT issue, that the GATT has to be resolved?

*The President.* Absolutely not. There is no linkage. No, I'm glad you raised that one. That's the last question. I am glad you—there is no linkage. What some Senator says over there, that's his business. I'm selling what the policy of the United States Government is. And there is no linkage, and we will have a strong presence in NATO. Those are the two givens.

And that's it. Thank you very much, Helen [Helen Thomas, United Press International]. Thank you very much.

[*At this point, one group of journalists left the room, and another group entered.*]

*Turkey-U.S. Relations*

*The President.* May I say to the visiting journalists from Turkey what an honor and, really, privilege it is to have the Prime Minister here. I respect him. I watched his vic-tory with admiration. I have congratulated him on that. And I'm going to assure him today that the relationship between Turkey and the United States is vitally important to us—I think it's important to Turkey, too—and that I will give him my full, unqualified cooperation. He's a good man, and he's there. He's the Prime Minister of Turkey, and I'm going to be working as closely with him as I possibly can.

And welcome to the United States, those of you who are not based here.

*Q.* Mr. President, your guest was an opposition leader when you met him last in Istanbul. Now he's a Prime Minister. How does this signify the strength of Turkish democracy?

*The President.* It signifies pretty good strength. It also shows he's a pretty good prognosticator or predictor because he sat there in great confidence and told me without any arrogance, with confidence in his own ability, "I will be the next Prime Minister." And I reminded him of that a few minutes ago. And yes, sure enough, he was just correct.

But it says a lot about the viability of Turkish democracy because we work closely with the government in Turkey. I'm not knocking the previous government. I'm simply saying this good man has been elected, and he has my full cooperation and the cooperation of the United States Government. And that's U.S.-Turkish relationship at its best.

Thank you all very much.

*Note: The exchange began at 11:02 a.m. in the Oval Office at the White House. During the exchange, the President referred to Manfred Woerner, Secretary General of NATO.*

# Remarks at the Departure Ceremony for Prime Minister Suleyman Demirel of Turkey
*February 11, 1992*

*The President.* Mr. Prime Minister, it's been a great pleasure to meet with a man whose career embodies a devotion to democracy and human rights. And seven times the people of Turkey have sent you to serve as Prime Minister, an office that you've served often with daring, always with dignity. And you've been a great European statesman. And you remain a spokesman for change.

No wonder you said when we met last summer, "I'm going to be Prime Minister." And your devotion to your people has been returned by their confidence in you. And for me, it was a pleasure to welcome you back to the Oval Office that you first visited 37——

*The Prime Minister.* ——years ago.

*The President.* Thirty-seven or——

*The Prime Minister.* Yes, 37.

*The President.* Thirty-seven years ago when President Eisenhower was in that very special office.

Barbara and I will never forget our trip to Turkey last year. And I recall especially the magic of Istanbul, the minarets of the Blue Mosque, the splendor of the beautiful palace, the boats that graced the Straits of the Bosporus, the lights that lit up the Asian and European parts of the city, their skyline a lovely silhouette against the night. And I marveled at this country which spans two continents, just as the friendship between our countries spans two centuries.

Today, as the Prime Minister and I mapped our path toward the future, we spoke of friendship and how it nurtures the ties between our peoples. Perhaps Kemal Atatürk said it best: "Nations are bound more by sentiments than by treaties."

Turkey is indeed a friend, a partner of the United States. And it's also a model to others, especially those newly independent Republics of Central Asia. In a region of changing tides, it endures as a beacon of stability. And so, I repeat what I told the Prime Minister: The United States will support its friend in its territorial integrity, its sovereignty and stability, particularly in its war against terrorism.

And we're going to work together to fortify the enhanced partnership which both links and lifts our nations. The pillars included trade, diplomacy, NATO and CSCE membership, and a shared commitment to justice and human rights. And last year in the Gulf, in the Persian Gulf, we joined to face aggression and then faced aggression down. We're going to continue to work through the United Nations to see that all Iraqi citizens get the food and medicine they need and the peace and liberty they deserve in an Iraq free of Saddam's tyranny.

Today we spoke of a world reborn through the cold war's death, of the plight of the new Republics emerging from the old Soviet Union. Already, Turkey and the United States have joined hands to feed mouths, rushing goods through Project Hope to needy friends in the Caucasus and Central Asia. I wish to announce that our Governments will expand that cooperation in these new Republics. We will seek new ways to help our new friends secure their independence and move quickly and peacefully to establish ties with the West.

Mr. Prime Minister, you once said, "Every question will be answered; discussion will be open and free." And in that spirit, we spoke of Turkey's importance to Europe, and I applauded your Government's commitment to improve relations with Greece. The Prime Minister and I did talk about the Cyprus problem. We share the objective of early negotiated settlement which will be both just and lasting. And we agreed to give full support to the good offices mission of the United Nations Secretary-General and to work with the other parties toward an agreement.

In closing, we've agreed to stay in touch personally and officially at many levels of our Governments. And we leave with the faith that our talks have covered much ground, charted new horizons.

The road toward progress may at times be difficult. It need not be lonely. An old Turkish proverb reminds us, "A long journey is shortened by good companions." So Mr. Prime Minister, let us make that journey together, as we have before and as we will again. And may God bless the peoples of Turkey and the United States of America.

*Note: The President spoke at 1:30 p.m. on the South Lawn at the White House. In his remarks, he referred to Kemal Atatürk, founder and first President of the Republic of Turkey.*

# Remarks at the Multilateral Investment Fund Agreement Signing Ceremony
## February 11, 1992

Welcome, especially, excellencies. And may I single out President Iglesias of the IDB, thank him for being here; and of course, Secretary Brady, who has been so instrumental from the U.S. side in all of this.

Today marks another milestone along the path of mutual progress for the United States and its friends and neighbors. And we move another step closer to fulfilling the vision of a free, peaceful, and prospering Western Hemisphere.

As we sign the charter for the new Multilateral Investment Fund, we advance the far-sighted aims of Enterprise for the Americas Initiative. Our new fund is an exciting innovation. It will provide targeted support for Latin American countries as they transform lumbering, state-run industries into efficient private enterprises.

This fund assures our neighbors that together we share a stake in a better future and that we will stand by them and help them as they carry out some very difficult reforms. In a neighborhood of free and growing economies, investment helps everyone. Our effort today will lift the tide of hope and freedom, and it will free up new resources so that the men and women throughout the Americas can carry their dreams and achievements as far as their God-given talents will take them.

Make no mistake: The future growth of the United States economy depends on expanding mutual investment and trade with our neighbors in the Americas. Flourishing trade and investment throughout the hemisphere will create new jobs and raise the

quality of life for people in Syracuse and St. Louis as well as Sao Paolo and Santiago.

Right now, we earn $62 billion, one in every seven of our worldwide export dollars, from Latin America. Well over half of our foreign investment in developing countries goes to Latin America. And we're moving forward to create in this hemisphere a new free trade area of 360 million consumers and $6 trillion in annual output, the North American free trade area of Mexico, Canada, and the United States.

This commitment will endure because we're in this to stay. And I know the people of the United States. And I can assure you that we will say no to the gloomy spirits that want to make pessimism a self-fulfilling prophecy. We embrace a future founded upon freedom, opportunity, and growth.

Working Americans and those looking for work have common sense. And they know that when other countries develop their economies, that results in more sales for America's airplanes and computers and other capital goods. The world is buying U.S. products at a record pace. Over the past 5 years, nearly half of America's real economic growth has been in exports. During those same 5 years, U.S. exports to Latin America and the Caribbean increased by 12 percent annually, much faster than the exports to the rest of the world.

Exports will carry us to rewarding new destinations in our future. And remember what exports do right here at home. Every billion dollar increase in exports generates 20,000 new jobs in the United States. And so, the long and short of it is, the prophets of American decline simply don't grasp the facts.

The 21 countries represented here already have pledged more than $1.2 billion to this important fund for our future. The U.S. pledge alone is $500 million, one-third of the $1.5 billion goal; Japan pledging an equal amount. I urge the United States Congress to act without delay to provide the funds to fulfill our pledge. And I also urge Congress to support debt reduction under the broader Enterprise for the Americas Initiative which will provide further support for U.S. exports, investment, and jobs.

Let me salute all of the representatives of the nations participating in this promising new effort. I want to commend the Inter-American Development Bank, its president, Enrique Iglesias, who will administer the new fund. And I am confident, sir, that you will do an outstanding job with your new responsibility.

This is a moment not so much for us but for future generations, really. It's they who will benefit from what's beginning here today. And it is for them that we invest in a new age of discovery and opportunity from Hudson Bay to the Straits of Magellan.

And now I would like to invite all the signatories who are here today with us, those that have signed this agreement already, to come up here, and we can muster behind the two remaining, two final signatures.

But thank you all for being here and for your constructive work on this wonderful project. Thank you.

*Note: The President spoke at 2:33 p.m. in the Roosevelt Room at the White House. Following the President's remarks, Secretary of the Treasury Nicholas F. Brady and Enrique V. Iglesias, President of the Inter-American Development Bank, signed the agreement.*

# Remarks and an Exchange With Reporters at a Meeting With Republican Members of the House Ways and Means Committee
*February 11, 1992*

*The President.* Let me just open with some comments here, and then what I want to do is throw this meeting open to discussion. But first, thanks for coming down. I know that many of you were just on your way back to town. I appreciate your being here.

With the markup starting in your committee, in Ways and Means tomorrow, I just wanted to discuss the prospects for a true economic growth package. And as you all know—and I appreciate your support—I sent up a comprehensive 49-title bill to Congress the week before last. It included both a short-term and a long-term growth agenda. And last week, through our leader, Bob Michel, and our leader on Ways and Means, Bill Archer, we introduced H.R. 4200, a streamlined package of the seven short-term growth items with budgetary offsets. And I've asked the Congress to act on that short-term package by March 20th.

And that package is fully paid for without raising taxes. And I don't believe we have to raise tax rates, should raise tax rates. Instead we ought to cut wasteful Government spending, and that's what our plan does. And we shouldn't ask any American, particularly in these economic times, to give more of their money to a system that doesn't spend wisely. And I can't understand how people can talk about stimulating the economy and then raising taxes in the same breath, just totally counterproductive. Raising taxes is not the way to create jobs and to foster growth.

And so once we're alone here, I want to hear from you, Bill, and the other able members of your committee the state of play. But what the Congress must do is go forward on the seven concise growth measures that will get this country back to work, stimulate real estate, and do things that are totally productive and will lead this recovery.

So thank you all very much for coming down here. I appreciate it. Now we will have a chance to discuss these items.

*Economic Plan*

*Q.* Mr. President, would you accept half a loaf, four of these measures or five of these measures?

*The President.* Well, I want the whole loaf in this case, and I think the country does, too. We've been very pleased with the support from groups all across it. But I want to hear a little more from our able Members here, the leaders on the tax side for the Republicans, tax committee side, Ways and Means side, and hear what they have to suggest. But I'm grateful for their support on the floor. They've been magnificent. I hope we can get these goals accomplished.

*Q.* How do you feel going into this reelection campaign, Mr. President, with your announcement tomorrow?

*The President.* Hey look, Terry [Terrence Hunt, Associated Press], I want to get this economic growth package passed. What I really feel like is we want to try and help the country and get some people back to work here and stimulate this economy. And that's exactly what this proposal is about. And that's the best thing for all people involved in politics, no matter what side of the aisle they're on right now. Put America's interests first, and that's what I'm trying to do here. And then we'll have plenty of time for politics after that.

But I want to get this done by March 20th. And Congress can move if they want to. They moved fast on the unemployment compensation extension and with the strong support from everybody at this table. And I think they ought to move fast on this. There is no reason it can't be done by March 20th.

And these are narrow. And then if they want to add in a lot of tax increases or anything else, we'll debate it. And if we have additional suggestions, our long-term package, we'll get that debated. But we've got a short-term set of proposals that would be the best medicine for this economy, and they ought to move on it now. Give it a try, and then go into the political dance later on. And that's what I'm going to be urging. And again, we're grateful to our members on Ways and Means.

That's about it because we've got to get to work now.

*Health Care Reforms*

*Q.* Mr. President, are you going to offer any ideas on how to pay for your health program, sir?

*The President.* We've got some good ones on there. There's 38 pages of how to do that. So it takes a lot of reading to get through them all, but they're very good suggestions. But the main one I want to see is to get rid of all of these frivolous malpractice lawsuits. And you're talking about megabucks there. So there's a big one for starters.

Now, I've got to go.

*Q.* How will it pay for it, sir?

*The President.* How will it pay for it? Because you won't be putting—you'll be reducing health care costs by $20 billion to $40 billion, depending on whose estimates you believe. So it's a very——

*Q.* ——the bill now, right?

*The President.* No, not if you don't have to spend. It's a big saving. Here we go. Those costs are passed along, you see, to the system.

*Note: The President spoke at 3:25 p.m. in the Cabinet Room at the White House.*

# Message to the Congress Reporting on the National Emergency With Respect to Iraq
*February 11, 1992*

*To the Congress of the United States:*

I hereby report to the Congress on the developments since my last report of July 26, 1991, concerning the national emergency with respect to Iraq that was declared in Executive Order No. 12722 of August 2, 1990. This report is submitted pursuant to section 401(c) of the National Emergencies Act, 50 U.S.C. 1641(c), and section 204(c) of the International Emergency Economic Powers Act ("IEEPA"), 50 U.S.C. 1703(c).

Executive Order No. 12722 ordered the immediate blocking of all property and interests in property of the Government of Iraq (including the Central Bank of Iraq) then or thereafter located in the United States or within the possession or control of a U.S. person. In that order, I also prohibited the importation into the United States of goods and services of Iraqi origin, as well as the exportation of goods, services, and technology from the United States to Iraq. I prohibited travel-related transactions and transportation transactions to or from Iraq and the performance of any contract in support of any industrial, commercial, or governmental project in Iraq. U.S. persons were also prohibited from granting or extending credit or loans to the Government of Iraq.

The foregoing prohibitions (as well as the blocking of Government of Iraq property) were continued and augmented on August 9, 1990, by Executive Order No. 12724 that I issued in order to align the sanctions imposed by the United States with United Nations Security Council Resolution 661 of August 6, 1990.

1. Since my last report, important and rapid progress has been made in establishing the framework for processing U.S. and other nations' claims against Iraq for damages arising from its unlawful invasion and occupation of Kuwait. The Governing Council of the U.N. Compensation Commission has adopted criteria for various categories of claims, including small and large claims of individuals, claims of corporations, and claims of government and international organizations (including environmental damage and natural resource depletion claims). In addition, the Governing Council agreed to begin expedited consideration of claims of individuals for up to $100,000 as of July 1, 1992, and set July 1, 1993, as the deadline for filing this category of claims with the Commission.

In a claims census conducted by the Treasury Department's Office of Foreign Assets Control (FAC) during the first quarter of 1991 pursuant to section 575.605 of the Iraqi Sanctions Regulations, 31 CFR Part 575 ("ISR"), reports of claims from approximately 1,100 U.S. nationals were received. Included were claims for items such as personal property looted or destroyed in Kuwait, loans or other obligations on which Iraq has defaulted, and lost future business or concession rights. Inasmuch as these claims have not been submitted to a formal claims resolution body, much less adjudicated, their actual aggregate value is not known.

2. FAC has issued 199 specific licenses (51 since my last report) regarding transactions pertaining to Iraq or Iraqi assets. Specific licenses were issued for payment to U.S. or third-country creditors of Iraq, under certain narrowly defined circumstances, for pre-embargo import and export transactions. Additionally, licenses were issued for conducting procedural transactions such as the filing of legal actions and for legal representation. Pursuant to United Nations Security Council Resolutions 661, 666, and 687, specific licenses were also issued to authorize the exportation to Iraq of donated medicine, medical supplies, and food intended for humanitarian relief purposes.

To ensure compliance with the terms of the licenses that have been issued, stringent reporting requirements have been imposed that are closely monitored. Licensed accounts are regularly audited by FAC compliance personnel and by deputized auditors from other regulatory agencies. FAC compliance personnel have also worked closely with both State and Federal bank regulatory and law enforcement agencies in conducting special audits of Iraqi accounts subject to the ISR.

3. Various enforcement actions discussed in previous reports continue to be pursued, and additional investigations of possible violations of the Iraqi sanctions have been initiated. These are intended to deter future activities in violation of the sanctions. Additional civil penalty notices were issued during the reporting period for violations of the IEEPA and ISR with respect to attempted transactions involving Iraq, and substantial penalties were collected.

After investigation by FAC and the U.S. Customs Service, a Virginia corporation and its export director were convicted in U.S. District Court for conspiracy and violations of the ISR. Investigation revealed that the corporation and its export director continued to engage in activities that were in violation of the Executive orders and the ISR after August 2, 1990. The corporation and its export director performed contracts in support of a government industrial project in Iraq, and engaged in prohibited transactions relating to travel by a U.S. person to Iraq. After conviction, the corporation was fined $50,000 and the export director sentenced to 5 months' incarceration, 5 months' supervised work release, and 2 years of supervised release administered by the Department of Justice.

4. The various firms and individuals outside of Iraq in Saddam Hussein's procurement network continue to be investigated for possible inclusion in the FAC listing of individuals and organizations determined to be Specially Designated Nationals ("SDN's") of the Government of Iraq. In practice, an Iraqi SDN is a representative, agent, intermediary, or front (whether open or covert) of the Iraqi Government that is located outside of Iraq. Iraqi SDN's are Saddam Hussein's principal instruments for doing business in third countries, and doing business with them is the same as doing business with Saddam Hussein himself.

Since the Iraqi government tends to operate its international fronts as interlocking networks of third-world countries and key individuals, the SDN program is an impor-

tant tool in disrupting Saddam Hussein's nuclear, military, and technological acquisitions efforts. The impact is considerable: all assets with U.S. jurisdiction of parties found to be Iraqi SDN's are blocked; all economic transactions with SDN's by U.S. persons are prohibited; and the SDN individual or organization is exposed.

5. The expenses incurred by the Federal Government in the 6-month period from August 2, 1991, through February 1, 1992, that are directly attributable to the exercise of powers and authorities conferred by the declaration of a national emergency with respect to Iraq are estimated at $2,992,210, most of which represents wage and salary costs for Federal personnel. Personnel costs were largely centered in the Department of the Treasury (particularly in FAC, the U.S. Customs Service, the Office of the Assistant Secretary for Enforcement, the Office of the Assistant Secretary for International Affairs, and the Office of the General Counsel), the Department of State (particularly in the Bureau of Economic and Business Affairs and the Office of the Legal Adviser), and the Department of Commerce (particularly in the Bureau of Export Administration and the Office of the General Counsel).

6. The United States imposed economic sanctions on Iraq in response to Iraq's invasion and illegal occupation of Kuwait, a clear act of brutal aggression. The United States, together with the international community, is maintaining economic sanctions against Iraq because the Iraqi regime has failed to comply fully with binding United Nations Security Council resolutions calling for the elimination of Iraqi weapons of mass destruction, an end to the repression of the Iraqi civilian population, the release of Kuwaiti and other prisoners, and the return of Kuwaiti assets stolen during its illegal occupation of Kuwait. The U.N. sanctions remain in place; the United States will continue to enforce those sanctions.

The Saddam Hussein regime continues to violate basic human rights by repressing the Iraqi civilian population and depriving it of humanitarian assistance. The United Nations Security Council passed resolutions that permit Iraq to sell $1.6 billion of oil under U.N. auspices to fund the provision of food, medicine, and other humanitarian supplies to the people of Iraq. Under the U.N. resolutions, the equitable distribution within Iraq of this assistance would be supervised and monitored by the United Nations and other international organizations. The Iraqi regime has refused to accept these resolutions and has thereby continued to perpetuate the suffering of its civilian population.

The regime of Saddam Hussein continues to pose an unusual and extraordinary threat to the national security and foreign policy of the United States, as well as to regional peace and security. The United States will therefore continue to apply economic sanctions to deter Iraq from threatening peace and stability in the region, and I will continue to report periodically to the Congress on significant developments, pursuant to 50 U.S.C. 1703(c).

GEORGE BUSH

The White House,
February 11, 1992.

# Letter to Congressional Leaders Transmitting the Report on Iraq's Offensive Military Capability
*February 11, 1992*

*Dear Mr. Chairman:*

Under cover of this letter I am transmitting to the Senate and House Committees on Appropriations, the Senate Committee on Foreign Relations, and the House Committee on Foreign Affairs the report on Iraq's Offensive Military Capability required by section 586J(b) of the Foreign Operations Export Financing, and Related Programs Appropriations Act, 1991 (Public Law 101–513).

This interim assessment of Iraq's offensive military capability and its effect on the Middle East balance of power includes an assessment of Iraq's power projection capability, the prospects for another sustained conflict with Iran, joint Iraqi-Jordanian cooperation, the threat Iraq's arms transfer activities pose to U.S. allies in the Middle East, and the potential extension of Iraq's political-military influence into Africa and Latin America.

The report unfortunately cannot be produced in an unclassified form. I recommend to your attention, however, the January 22, 1992, testimony on Iraqi unconventional weapons capabilities by Robert Gates before the Senate Armed Services Committee.

Sincerely,

GEORGE BUSH

*Note: Identical letters were sent to Robert C. Byrd, chairman of the Senate Committee on Appropriations; Jamie L. Whitten, chairman of the House Committee on Appropriations; Claiborne Pell, chairman of the Senate Committee on Foreign Relations; and Dante B. Fascell, chairman of the House Committee on Foreign Affairs.*

# Appointment of Edward D. Murnane as Deputy Assistant to the President and Director of Presidential Advance
*February 11, 1992*

The President has announced his intention to appoint Edward D. Murnane to be Deputy Assistant to the President and Director of Presidential Advance. He would succeed Jake L. Parmer as Director of Presidential Advance.

Since 1989 Mr. Murnane has served as Regional Administrator for the Small Business Administration in Chicago, IL. Prior to this, he served as executive director of the George Bush for President campaign in Illinois, 1988; as public affairs director for the Regional Transportation Authority in Chicago, 1984–1988; and in a senior management position in the Reagan-Bush '84 reelection campaign. From 1976 to 1984, Mr. Murnane operated his own political and public relations consulting firm in Chicago. From 1971 to 1976, he served on the Washington, DC, staff of Congressman Philip M. Crane,

first as press secretary and later as administrative assistant and chief of staff. He has also served on the White House volunteer advance staff since 1981 and has assisted on many domestic and international trips for President Bush as President and Vice President, as well as President Reagan and Vice President Quayle.

Mr. Murnane graduated from Northern Illinois University in 1966 with a degree in journalism and political science. He was born on March 2, 1944, in Chicago, IL. He and his wife, Laurel, have three children and reside in Arlington Heights, IL.

# Statement by Press Secretary Fitzwater on the Phaseout of Ozone-Depleting Substances

*February 11, 1992*

President Bush today announced that the United States will unilaterally accelerate the phaseout of substances that deplete the Earth's ozone layer and called on other nations to agree to an accelerated phaseout schedule. Current U.S. production is already more than 40 percent below the levels allowed by the Montreal Protocol and more than 20 percent ahead of Europe's nonaerosol production phasedown.

Recent scientific findings indicate that emissions of these substances, major CFC's, halons, methyl chloroform, and carbon tetrachloride, are depleting the stratospheric ozone layer more quickly than previously had been believed. The President announced that, with limited exceptions for essential uses and for servicing certain existing equipment, all production of these substances in the United States will be eliminated by December 31, 1995. To accelerate progress in the near term, the President called upon U.S. producers to reduce production of these substances to 50 percent of 1986 levels by the end of this year.

Under the terms of the Clean Air Act of 1990, which President Bush signed into law in November of 1990, the administration has authority to accelerate the phaseout of

these substances without new legislation. The President also announced that the U.S. will re-examine the phaseout schedule of HCFC's, and will consider recent evidence suggesting the possible need to phase out methyl bromide.

The President noted that due in large part to the use of innovative, market-based mechanisms such as production fees and tradable allowances, the U.S. has already reduced CFC production 42 percent below 1986 levels, a reduction beyond that required by either the Clean Air Act or the amended Montreal Protocol. The President pointed out that the U.S. has been a leader in reducing CFC's, agreeing to a full phaseout of these gases in February 1989, enacting a fee on their production in November of 1989, legislating the full phaseout in November of 1990, and making the first contribution to a multilateral fund established to assist developing countries in phasing out CFC's.

The President called upon those nations which have not yet signed and ratified the Montreal Protocol to do so, and urged other nations to join the U.S. in accelerating the phaseout of CFC's and other ozone-depleting gases even faster than required by the Protocol.

# Remarks Announcing the Bush-Quayle Candidacies for Reelection

*February 12, 1992*

*The President.* Thank you all very much. And Barbara, thank you for those kind remarks. And may I salute our Vice President, Dan Quayle, just back from overseas, and Marilyn. And my respects to the members of our great Cabinet, and friends all. Thanks to all of you for this wonderful, warm reception.

I have an announcement to make. [*Laughter*] I want to continue serving as your President, 4 more years. So from this moment on, I'm a candidate for President of the United States, officially.

Let me tell you why I'm running. I came here to do important work, and I finish what I start. In 1980 I came to Washington as a part of a team. We started a revolution to free America from, you remember, the politics of malaise and to set sail toward America's destiny. Then in 1988, Dan Quayle and I began our own partnership built on the same principles.

My message then and my message now is simple: I believe Government is too big, and it costs too much. I believe in a strong defense for this country and good schools, safe streets, a Government really worthy of the people. I believe that parents, not Government, should make the important decisions about health, child care, and education. I believe in personal responsibility. I believe in opportunity for all. We should throw open wide the doors of possibility to anyone who has been locked out. And I believe in a piece of wisdom passed on by my favorite political philosopher, Barbara Bush: What happens in your house is more important than what happens in the White House.

You see, America's future doesn't take shape in small rooms with heavy, polished wooden desks. It takes place in homes, where parents read to their children, talk about responsibility, teach them values, show them how to love one another, respect one another, and work hard, and live good lives. We must encourage families to remain strong and whole. We must extend our hearts and hands to children who have no one to hold them or call them by their names. Our future rides on the important things, the big things: Family, home, school, church, community, and country.

We're gathered here because the American people wanted leadership, and we answered the call. We didn't do the easy things. We did the right things. From day one, I fought for strong and effective national defense. I stuck to my principles, and we kept strong, and we won the cold war. And we stayed strong, and that enabled us to win a battle called Desert Storm.

But we did far more than that. We liberated the entire world from old fears, fears of tense, endless confrontation, fears of nuclear holocaust. Now our children grow up freed from the looming specter of nuclear war.

But having won the cold war, we did more. We led nations away from ancient hatreds and toward a table of peace. And we did still more than that. We forged a new world order, an order shaped by the sweat and sacrifice of our families, the sweat and sacrifice of generation upon generation of American men and women.

Think of it: Two years ago, the Berlin Wall came tumbling down. And last year, the Soviet Union collapsed. Imperial communism became a four-letter word: D-E-A-D, dead. And today, because we stood firm, because we did the right things, America stands alone, the undisputed leader of the world. We put an end to the decades of cold war and reaped a springtime harvest of peace. The American people should be proud of what together we have achieved. Now, together, we will transform the arsenal of democracy into the engine of growth.

I understand the world. That's crucial. But that's not enough. I understand America. And I know that American workers are the most productive in the world, bar none. And I know, to succeed economically at home, we need to lead economically abroad. If you want to lead in the world, you've got to know the neighborhood. Economic leadership means markets for American products, jobs for American workers, and growing room for the American dream. The American people do not believe in isolationism because they believe in themselves. We Americans don't hide from a good test of our abilities. We rise to the challenge. And after all, our national bird is the eagle, not the ostrich.

In 1992, the American people will decide what kind of leadership they want. They'll decide which team has the character, the experience, and the toughness to make the important decisions. They could cast their lot with a lot of fresh faces who tout stale ideas. But they won't. Voters know the difference between a sound bite and sound policy.

Let's not kid ourselves. We're in a tough fight. But you know me: I don't seek unnecessary conflict, but when principle is at stake, I fight to win. And I am determined to win. And I will win. This will be a long campaign. That's all right. Our campaign will focus on the future, the only subject that counts. We'll fight hard. We'll fight fair. And we will win.

Abraham Lincoln, whose birth we celebrate today, once told fellow Republicans, "We will make converts day by day, and unless truth be a mockery and justice a hollow lie, we will be in the majority after a while. The battle of freedom is to be fought out on principle."

And so be it. That's the way it will be. For 3 years an entrenched opposition in Washington has clung to the old failed ways, not out of principle but out of sheer politics. They blocked our comprehensive efforts to fight crime and drugs. They refused to join the revolution in American education. They stalled our efforts to cut taxes and slash regulation and encourage economic growth. And then they complained that nothing got done.

This year we say: No more. To those who want to obstruct progress, we say: Get moving, or get out of the way. We've got an agenda.

*Audience members.* Four more years! Four more years! Four more years!

*The President.* We've got an agenda, and here's what we will do: Together, we'll get our economy up and running at full speed. We'll restore decency to the American way of life. We will silence the voices of hatred and gloom. And we will attack programs that lock people in bleak dependency as we work to reform our dismal welfare program. And we will, in the process, provide the best kind of a welfare system imaginable, good jobs for Americans able to work. And we will build the America of our dreams.

In my life, I've seen miracles, and I've learned that no dream is too big for the American heart. When I was a little boy, the world moved at an easy pace. Then came the Depression; then came a World War. And in the fires of battle, I learned freedom's painful price. And I've seen wondrous changes, new ideas and new technologies, tempered by the humanity that makes us what we are. Amid the swells of change, gentle fundamentals anchor us still. Decency, honor, hard work, caring: That's the America I know.

And I have been blessed in my life, blessed by Barbara and by a family that fills me with wonder and joy and love. And I'm blessed with so many friends, friends like you. And I have been especially blessed because I have been given the opportunity to serve as your President, the President of the United States.

The glory of this century is America. And history will call this the American century because we fought the battle of freedom, and we won. And history will tell of a second American century when we led the world to new heights of achievement and liberty. This is our legacy. This is our challenge. And this is our destiny. And together, we will win. I am certain of that.

Thank you very, very much. And may God bless you. May God bless each and every one of you and our great country, the United States of America. Thank you very, very much.

*Note: The President spoke at 10:10 a.m. at the J.W. Marriott Hotel.*

# Remarks to the State Legislature in Concord, New Hampshire
*February 12, 1992*

Mr. Speaker, thank you, sir, and Ellie. Delighted to be with you. And Mr. President, Ed Dupont, and Andrea; and Mr. Chief Justice; members of the executive council; and of course, my special friend Governor Gregg. I am just delighted to be back here. And I want to single out three visitors that have been introduced here just a minute ago, Senator Rudman, Governor Sununu, and Congressman Zeliff. I'm just delighted that they're back here with us today. And my respects to a former United States Senator who has gone straight, one of your own, Gordon Humphrey, back here now.

And ladies and gentlemen of the New Hampshire State Legislature, first, my thanks for that warm welcome back. I decided to come here today because I figured it's been a while since the people of New Hampshire have heard a political speech. [*Laughter*]

New Hampshire's legislature is really the living legacy of Lincoln's words, of, by, and for the people. I look out at all the remarkable men and women who balance the responsibilities of work and home with this public trust. What leads you to serve? It can't be the salary. That's not enough to cover two tickets to the Celtics games. But what sustains this State is a tradition as old as America itself, a commitment to self-government that stretches from Pittsburg to Pelham, from Claremont to Conway, to every corner of this State. New Hampshire looks to government as a last resort, not as the first answer to each and every problem. It doesn't see people's paychecks as potential revenue. Its rule is right: Limit government, not freedom.

This body governs itself the way we as citizens want to be governed, by the rules of common sense and fairplay. Up here, you manage to avoid being enlightened by liberal economists. New Hampshire lawmakers operate on the radical notion that a legislature should spend no more than it takes in. New Hampshire lawmakers guarantee every bill a public hearing and every bill a vote. It's time for the United States Congress to follow your lead.

Twelve years ago, under the national leadership of my friend and yours, my supporter, President Ronald Reagan, this State helped spark a new American revolution, a revolution that marked the end of a weary era and a new birth for freedom. Together we made America proud. Together we made America strong. Together we made America respected in the eyes of all the world.

We fought great battles. We stood fast against imperial communism, and we watched walls the world over come tumbling down. For 45 years, we fought in the trenches of the cold war, and we won. And let me tip my hat to every man and woman who ever served and to the American taxpayer, because communism didn't just fall. It was pushed.

Finally, just one year ago, we drew a line in the sand and helped defend a small nation and a grand ideal. We said international law would be upheld, and aggression would not stand. And with our coalition partners, we kicked Saddam Hussein out of Kuwait.

One thing more about Desert Storm. There are those who didn't support us then, and there are those who second-guess us now. Not New Hampshire. As Commander in Chief, let me thank this legislature for its resolution in support of Desert Storm. Half a world away, to the men and women who carried the battle, your support gave them the strength to succeed, knowing that the people were behind them. In those difficult days, when our troops laid it on the line, New Hampshire did not hesitate.

We did these things because we had the courage to lead. And because we led, America is free. America is safe. America is at peace.

Yes, dangers remain, dark corners of the world not yet blessed by freedom. No, our work in the world is not yet over. But the great struggles we've won, the great changes we've seen do more than open new worlds. They open new opportunities for us at home. And this we know: If we can change the world, we can change America. But for us to move forward, for us to lead the world, we've got to get America's economy moving again.

Last month, I spoke to the American people and spelled out my plan to pull this country out of recession and into recovery. I know all of you have heard plenty about plans that promise the Moon. But let me say to the citizens of New Hampshire, judge my plan by its first principle: Government is too big, and it spends too much.

We put a stop order on new Federal regulation. We've begun a 90-day review, 90 days to take a hard look at regulations that hurt more than they help. The day of over-regulation is just that, over.

We declared war on frivolous lawsuits. If this country rewarded success as easily as we slap on a lawsuit, our economy would be well on its way.

We've worked to control spending. I've called on Congress to eliminate, cut out altogether, 246 Federal programs. One thing would make it a little easier. Give me the tools, and I will finish the job. Give me that line-item veto, and watch what can be done.

I took action with the authority that I have as President, and then I challenged the Congress to act. I set out a two-plan part to ensure economic growth: an immediate action plan to spark recovery and then a long-term plan for the future.

The people of New Hampshire have a right to ask: We've been hit hard; too many of us have lost our jobs, even lost our homes; what will this plan do for us? Fair question.

First, my plan will bolster the real estate market. In New Hampshire and across the country, real estate will lead the way to economic recovery. My plan helps New Hampshire homebuyers. It provides a $5,000 tax credit to first-time buyers: $2,500 this year, $2,500 next. And it lets them draw on their IRA accounts to make that purchase, penalty-free. For the average New Hampshire family buying the average New Hampshire house, my plan means tax breaks worth 6 months of mortgage payments. For families all over this State, that's an American dream come true.

And what's good for the families who want to buy that first-time home is good for the people who build them. Nationwide, experts in the housing industry predict that my plan will create a boom in homebuilding. In this State alone, the plan will generate 1,000 new housing starts and pump $120 million into the State economy. And that then, best of all, will put more than 2,000 New Hampshire construction workers back on the job.

My plan will also help the pioneering high-tech firms that call New Hampshire home. Pass this plan and give companies an investment tax allowance, helping growing firms accelerate investment. Make the R&E tax, that tax credit, a permanent part of the Federal Tax Code. Pass my plan and get investment flowing again. Cut the capital gains rate to 15 percent. That is what is needed. Pass my plan and give American companies a competitive edge. No games. No gimmicks. Just a plan that works. Pass my plan and get New Hampshire moving again.

Now, that's a summary of my short-term part of it, the short-term action plan. For the long term, we've got work to do as well, steps we can take right now to guarantee progress and prosperity into the next American century. We get there by investing in the technologies of tomorrow—you're good at that here in New Hampshire—tomorrow, with Federal support of R&D at record levels; it will help. We need to share the results, get the great ideas generated by public funds out into the private sector, off the drawing board and onto store shelves. Our national technology initiative will do just that. And right now at M.I.T., the first regional meeting is underway.

We get to the future by letting the States do what they do best. Far too often, States have their hands tied by Washington. Congress passes a mandate, and they pass you the buck. You get stuck raising taxes. New Hampshire's constitution, I'm told, prevents this body from burdening communities with unfunded mandates. Well, if it's good enough for New Hampshire, why not for the rest of the country?

Look at the problems that plague us today, crime, drugs, the erosion of moral values. Trace each one to its root, its root causes, and you'll see one common factor, the decline of the American family. This country must reaffirm a simple truth: When the family comes first, America is first.

We get to the future by strengthening the family. Look at our approach, for example, to child care. Our opponents backed a scheme that would have created a brave new child care bureaucracy. We preserved choice, and we put parents first. My plan puts the family first, this new one, and provides an extra $500 exemption for every child.

And just last week I announced a comprehensive health care reform, reforms that will keep costs down and open up access to affordable health care for all Americans, providing new coverage to almost 30 million uninsured Americans. And we'll do it through choice, not through central control. We've got—and I think every American would admit this or claim it—we've the best quality health care in the world, the best. And the last thing the American people want is a system that puts the Government between you and your doctor. And we're not going to do that.

Every parent knows our children are our future. That's why our health plan focuses on the children, increasing support for immunization, the early prevention that gives each kid a healthy start. And that's why we are funding Head Start at an all-time high, and it's the reason we're asking more of our schools. We must challenge ourselves to revolutionize, to literally reinvent American education. New Hampshire has joined the nonpartisan America 2000 revolution. Governor, we're grateful to you for your leadership. And let common sense be our guide, and let common sense begin by letting parents choose which school is best for their child.

Finally, we meet America's destiny by expanding trade, opening new markets for American goods. I'm proud of the progress we've made, working to open markets from Asia to Europe to the Americas. Just this week, I signed a new investment accord, just yesterday, with the nations of Latin America. Last month, the agreement we reached with Japan will help computer companies right here in this State, help

them get into that government-owned—the government computer market in Japan. That's a solid record in 3 years' time, a good start that we'll make even better.

But free trade has come under attack these days. The drumbeat mounts for some new isolationism; this one, an economic retreat from reality. The simple truth is, protectionism isn't a prescription for prosperity. Boil away all the tough talk, all the swagger, and all the patriotic posturing, and protectionism amounts to nothing more than a smokescreen for a country that's running scared. And that's not the America you and I know.

The America we know is a country ready to take on the world and ready to rise to new levels, not run for cover. Our national symbol isn't the ostrich; it's the eagle. And that's the way it should be. Never in this Nation's long history has America turned its back on a challenge, and we are not going to start now. A proud America will never be protectionist. It will never be protectionist.

Bring it close to home, make no mistake about it, no State would be hurt more by economic isolationism than New Hampshire. Right now, New Hampshire businesses reap more than $1.2 billion a year from exports. Across this State, that's 35,000 jobs tied directly to foreign trade. And even in these hard times, New Hampshire's manufacturing exports increased 80 percent in the past 5 years alone.

It's an economic fact of life: If we close our markets, other countries will close theirs. And when the walls go up, who gets hurt? That's an easy one. You do. You get hurt. And I cannot, and I will not, let that happen to New Hampshire or to any of the rest of the States in this country. We are not going to have protectionism. We're going to compete, not cut and run. And let the world know, we're in this to win.

Two weeks ago, I urged the Congress to work with me to do the will of the American people. I laid out the action plan I've sketched, that I've outlined here, and yes, I set a deadline to help move the Congress along the way. Today, back in Washington, maybe at this very minute, the House Ways and Means Committee is at work; they started work this morning. And I challenge them once again to pass this short-term action plan, seven specific actions to stimulate, immediately stimulate the economy. They say they are taking up my plan, but they are not.

So I'll say again: Don't relabel my plan. Don't change it. Don't use it as a way to raise tax rates. Just pass this plan, and give the American people a chance to see whether it's going to work, as I'm confident it will. And look, later on—get this passed—later on we can all debate it, put it out there in the political arena, add to it, detract from it. We can all have a big, strong debate.

It must sound strange to the people in this chamber, strange for you legislators who meet for only 45 days a year to hear Congress complain that 52 days isn't enough time to get this done. They say the deadline is arbitrary. They say the deadline is too early. They say the deadline is unfair.

And I say: The deadline is March 20, and we're going to hold their feet to the fire. By March 20th, I want to be able to report to the American people that the liberation of America's economy has begun. I ask the

people in this chamber, I ask the good people of New Hampshire to give me your strong support and send a message to the Congress. Tell them the time has come to act.

Today is a special day for me, for Barbara, for my family as well. I think back across the years to the lesson I learned long ago, and I look ahead in wonder to what can be. And I know there is no higher honor than serving this great Nation.

I want to thank you. I want to thank you, New Hampshire, for this warm welcome. And may God bless this land we share. We have much to be grateful for in these troubled times, and I want to be your leader for 4 more years. Thank you very much, and may God bless the United States of America. Thank you.

*Note: The President spoke at 2:10 p.m. at the statehouse. In his remarks, he referred to Harold W. Burns, speaker of the New Hampshire House, and his wife, Ellie; Edward C. Dupont, Jr., president of the New Hampshire Senate, and his wife, Andrea; and David A. Brock, State chief justice.*

# Remarks to Law Enforcement Officers and Firefighters in Concord
*February 12, 1992*

Thanks for that welcome back. And Dick, thank you so very much, and may I salute you, sir; the Governor, of course. And we've got our officials here, Senator Rudman, Congressman Zeliff, and former Governor John Sununu. And I'm just delighted to be here.

Before I say anything else, I see some new faces in law enforcement here and firefighting. And I see some older faces in law enforcement and, sorry, firefighting here. [*Laughter*] But I just want to say that Barbara and I are grateful to those of you with whom we've interacted over the last 12 years in one way or another, mainly over on the eastern part of the State, over on the seacoast. So many of you have had these odd hours, and I'm sure we've inconven-

ienced your families, but we are very grateful to each and every one of you. And of course, we're grateful for your service to your State, and we're grateful for your line of service. I hope that our administration will stay with this position of backing the firefighters and backing those out in law enforcement all the way.

I want to just mention a couple of things today in terms of the changes in the world. I won't give you the full load on foreign policy or the changes that have happened. But you know, we're having some tough times here. And I think it's good that we sometimes keep things in full perspective.

We've seen an awful lot of change in the world in the last few years. We've seen communism crumble in Eastern Europe.

Many of you are young enough to have remembered when you climbed under the desks as schoolchildren for the antinuclear drills that we had in those days. And thank God that the world has changed enough so that your kids and my grandkids don't have quite as much to worry about on that front.

I, of course, was proud of the way New Hampshire responded, starting with the legislature's endorsement but really beginning with the service of the men and women from this State that served in Desert Storm. It was a superb operation. And there was a pride across this State, I'm sure, that still exists, pride in the way this country and this State came together in support of those young men and women. And they served us well, and they set a great example.

And you know, these are cynical days now because we're in this crazy political season. And it's a dance that we go through every 4 years. But I can tell you from a good deal of experience dealing with other countries that we are the envy of the world. And we are clearly the leader of the world. And as long as I'm President, I'm going to do my level-best to see that we remain the leader of the free world.

I do not want to make this a partisan political appearance. It's hard not to these days, but I don't want to do it. But I did make a pitch to the legislature today for support for an economic program that avoids the quick fixes, that would stimulate the economy, particularly the homebuying business and homebuilding business in this country. We've put forward some incentives, laserlike incentives that, in my view and in the view of most economists that have looked at it, would really stimulate that area of the economy that has normally led this country out of recession. I'm talking about the real estate business generally, and I'm talking about homebuying and homebuilding. And so, take a look at that. I hope that it's something that will have the broad support, transcending party, all across this country.

Actually, I've set a deadline for the United States Congress, saying, look, we can get this thing done. So I set a deadline in that State of the Union Message for March 20th. I said, "Let's move by then. We can do it." And we can do it. And then we can

have all of the political debate and the political arguments afterward. But let's pass these seven points. And I've been challenging the Congress today to do that, and I hope those of you that agree with me will weigh in, although our Members of Congress here are very well in tune with this and way out front in support of it. So, the deadline is March 20th, and we're going to go after them in every way possible.

We've all heard the saying, and you all have lived it, really, "Take a bite out of crime." Well, Congress got a little backwards; they took a bite out of our crime bill. What we're trying to do there is to pass a strong anticrime bill that will support the law enforcement officers of this country. There's one that does transcend party, and it should transcend ideology, liberal or conservative. It is just sound common sense. I hope that you all will take a look at it because it backs the police officers. It backs those that are out there in DEA or wherever else they are in this antinarcotics fight, and it puts in tough provisions. There are some 60 tough provisions that have been avoided by the Congress that need to be passed.

I know that some of these prosecutors want the bill that's before the Congress to be vetoed or not to be passed. I want to see a strong bill. We've still got a chance now with the new Congress to get a strong bill that will back you in your work. We do not need loopholes for violent criminals, and I will fight against that. And I will fight to toughen the law and have the law that's a little kinder and gentler to the victim of crime and a little less so to the criminal. And that's our philosophy, and we're going to work on it.

So, the last thing I would say to you all is that these are tough times, I know. But I will say this, that I am very privileged and proud to be the President of the United States. All these kids come up and, "Can I have a question?" "What is it?" "What's it like to be President?" And they ask this all the time. It's not an easy question to answer because it's a great big country, and we have enormous responsibilities around the world. But the more I think about that and the more I look at my own personal life and try to figure things out for the future, the more grateful I am for family and the more grateful I am for friends.

You might think when you got to be President that some other things would transcend all of this, but they don't. And I think of people in this room—and I won't embarrass anyone by singling them out— whether they're firefighters or whether they're police officers or in the State or local police or whether they're superintendents or whether they're bosses, like some

standing up here. But we Bushes count our blessings for friends. And we are very, very grateful to all of you for this warm reception, and we won't let you down. Thank you very, very much.

*Note: The President spoke at 2:52 p.m. at the Department of Safety in the James H. Hayes Building. In his remarks, he referred to Richard M. Flynn, commissioner, New Hampshire Department of Safety.*

# Remarks to U.S. FIRST in Manchester, New Hampshire
## *February 12, 1992*

Let me just say first, thanks to Dean Kamen, the brains behind this effort. There were a lot of support brains working with it, too. And a little education right here and I've done a little homework on all the work, the marvelous work that's been done here. And I wish I could be at the inaugural of the FIRST Encounters contest.

By creating this imaginative new partnership between industry and education you all are taking a first step, a big step forward in meeting our goal of making America the number one in science education. Math and science, that's the key to the future, to our being competitive.

And I want to thank the various officials that are with us: Dr. Schmitt, the president of RPI; Jerry Fisher, Baxter Health Care; Ray Price, the president of the Economic Club of New York; Richard Osborne, the president of U.S. FIRST, and Donald Reed, the chairman.

In the 21st century we're going to face a technology race the likes of which we've never seen. But competition makes us strong. And American workers in my view can outthink, outproduce, outcompete anybody, anywhere. And competition made us number one, and competition is going to keep us there. And it compels us to do our best. And it stimulates the desire to win.

How America does at the technology race finish line depends on how we prepare the next generation for the starting line. And to teach this new generation, our administra-

tion has put the Federal Government's scientific brainpower and labs to work, teaching high school students about real-life science. Our national technology initiative will create new partnership to move technology out of the labs and into the marketplace.

And this America 2000 that I'm so enthusiastic about, our national education approach, strategy, is revolutionizing, literally, our Nation's schools. And you add it all up, and new technology means new products and new jobs and new economic growth.

When I put forth as one of our six national education goals making America's students the first in science and math, I knew it was a tough challenge. But I knew that challenge would bring out the best in all of us, our teachers, our students, our industries, and our parents. And I'm sure the competition here in Manchester is going to be fierce, but I also know that, no matter who wins, no one is going to lose. And how you play the game is what matters here. And you learn about engineering, but you'll also experience the joy of learning.

And I talk about competition: It's going to be active here, and it's going to be active abroad. But let me just say to the young people: Please do not listen to the siren's call that says, we can't compete, and we've got to turn inward, and we have to resort to isolationism or protectionism. I am confident that the young people here today are going to be able to compete with anyone around the world at any time.

And so we're looking outward. We're looking for more exports and more proficiency in math and science. And I believe, thanks to Mr. Kamen and others who are committed here, we can get the job done.

Thank you, sir, for having me here today.

*Note: The President spoke at 5:45 p.m. at*

*the Technology Center, the headquarters of U.S. FIRST (For Inspiration and Recognition of Science and Technology). In his remarks, he referred to Dean L. Kamen, founder of U.S. FIRST, and Roland Schmitt, president of Rensselaer Polytechnic Institute. A tape was not available for verification of the content of these remarks.*

# Statement by Press Secretary Fitzwater on the National Technology Initiative
## February 12, 1992

The President today endorsed a February 12, 1992, conference at the Massachusetts Institute of Technology to launch the national technology initiative.

The President today in New Hampshire said, "Look to the long-term, and we've got work to do . . . steps we can take right now to guarantee progress and prosperity into the next American century. We get there by investing in the technologies of tomorrow . . . with Federal support of R&D at record levels . . . . We need to share the results, get the great ideas generated by public funds out into the private sector, off the drawing board and onto store shelves. Our national technology initiative will do just that. . . . at M.I.T., the first regional meeting is underway."

The conference is the first of a series of regional meetings intended to spur U.S. economic competitiveness by promoting a better understanding of the opportunities for industry to commercialize new technology advances. The program will highlight the Federal Government's investment in advanced technologies, much of which may

have commercial potential. It also will stress recent changes in Federal policies designed to foster private sector cooperation in commercializing technology.

Secretary of Energy James D. Watkins, Acting Commerce Secretary Rockwell A. Schnabel, Acting Transportation Secretary James B. Busey, and NASA Administrator Richard Truly described the joint initiative as a way to address one of the key challenges facing industry: the need to translate new technologies into marketplace goods and services. Encouraging closer cooperation among U.S. companies and better links with Federal laboratories is a central element of the initiative.

The M.I.T. conference and subsequent meetings around the country will provide an opportunity for a discussion among Government, industry, and universities and increase awareness of Federal science and technology programs that can benefit U.S. firms. In recent years, Congress and the Bush administration have taken steps to better enable the private sector to commercialize federally supported research.

# Statement on the Resignation of Richard H. Truly as Administrator of the National Aeronautics and Space Administration
## February 12, 1992

I have today regretfully accepted the resignation of Richard H. Truly as Administra-

tor of the National Aeronautics and Space Administration.

It was almost 3 years ago that I nominated Dick to become Administrator of NASA. As a result of his leadership, NASA is better prepared for the 1990's and beyond. He has established a balanced space program, and he has worked closely with the Vice President in developing our space exploration initiative that begins with Space Station *Freedom.*

Admiral Truly has now spent 37 years of dedicated public service with lasting and fundamental contributions to the Nation's space program. He has had many significant and historic milestones in his career, but one of the most notable was the way he took over NASA's Office of Space Flight soon after the *Challenger* tragedy. It was under Dick Truly's able leadership and steady hand that NASA was able to rebuild the space shuttle program and return it to safe operation in 1988.

The Nation owes Admiral Truly a great debt of gratitude, and Barbara joins me at this time in extending to Dick and his family our heartfelt thanks and the admiration and appreciation of our Nation.

Admiral Truly has agreed to remain with NASA until April 1, and the search for a new NASA Administrator has begun. Because of Dick's work, I am confident that we will continue to press forward with an aggressive and innovative civil space program.

# Letter Accepting the Resignation of Richard H. Truly as Administrator of the National Aeronautics and Space Administration
*February 12, 1992*

*Dear Dick:*

It is with deep regret that I accept your resignation from the position of Administrator of the National Aeronautics and Space Administration.

Almost three years ago, I nominated you to become Administrator of NASA. As a result of your leadership, NASA is better prepared for the 1990s and beyond. You have established a balanced NASA program including aeronautics, space science, manned Space Shuttle operations—including the upcoming addition of the *Endeavour*—and robotic space exploration. Working with the Vice President, you developed our Space Exploration Initiative that begins with Space Station Freedom.

Some of the significant and historic milestones in your career include piloting the second flight of the Space Shuttle in 1981 and commanding the first night launch and landing of the Shuttle in 1983. But one of the most notable was the way you took over NASA's Office of Space Flight soon after the *Challenger* tragedy. Under your leadership, NASA was able to rebuild the Space Shuttle program and return it to safe operation in 1988.

You have served in many important positions throughout your career and have received numerous awards. The Nation owes you a great debt of gratitude for your 37 years of dedicated public service and the significant contributions you have made to America's flight and aerospace achievements.

Barbara joins me in extending to you and your family our heartfelt thanks and the admiration and appreciation of our Nation.

Best wishes.

Sincerely,

GEORGE BUSH

---

*Dear Mr. President:*

It is with the deepest regret that I submit this letter of resignation as the Administrator of NASA. As we discussed when we met today, and because NASA is without a Deputy, I will remain until April 1.

This action will conclude almost 37 years of continuous military and government service for me. I have been unbelievably privileged to have had so many challenging assignments in aviation, space flight, military command and public administration over these years. In our nation's space business, I have enjoyed jobs in every corner of it; civilian and military, highly classified and open, flight and management.

In the last six years since I arrived to join the NASA leadership just after the *Challenger* tragedy, I have watched the talented men and women of this elite agency turn heartbreak and disarray into the impressive achievements and superb organization of today. With 20 safe and successful Shuttle flights in the last 40 months, scientific discoveries pouring in, *Space Station Freedom* on track, and our wind tunnels testing the airframes and spacecraft of tomorrow, they deserve to be very, very proud. With your support, their opportunities to inspire America's people and drive our country's

competitiveness are boundless. Their achievements result from working daily in a fishbowl world of difficult and exacting tasks, tough judgments and carefully balanced risks; not an endeavor which some would have you think has quick, brilliant and easy solutions.

I think that the job of leading these people is the best one in Washington, and I am proud to have had that privilege. Cody and I particularly want to thank you and Barbara for the personal times you have shared with us over the years.

Sincerely,

RICHARD H. TRULY

*Note: These letters were made available by the Office of the Press Secretary on February 13 but were not issued as White House press releases.*

# Memorandum on the Conventional Forces in Europe Treaty Implementation Act
## *February 13, 1992*

*Memorandum for the Secretary of State, the Secretary of Defense*

*Subject:* Delegation of Authority with Respect to the Conventional Forces in Europe Treaty Implementation Act

By virtue of the authority vested in me by the Constitution and laws of the United States of America, including section 301 of title 3 of the United States Code, I hereby delegate to the Secretary of Defense the functions vested in me by section 93(a) and section 94 of the Arms Export Control Act, as amended (the "Act"), and to the Secre-

tary of State the functions vested in me by section 93(f) of the Act. Consistent with section 2 of the Act, transfers of defense articles under section 93(a) shall be subject to the policy direction of the Secretary of State, including the determination of whether such transfers shall occur.

The Secretary of State is authorized and directed to publish this memorandum in the *Federal Register.*

GEORGE BUSH

*[Filed with the Office of the Federal Register, 3:23 p.m., February 25, 1992]*

## Message to Congress Transmitting a Report on Science and Engineering Indicators
*February 14, 1992*

*To The Congress of the United States:*

Pursuant to 42 U.S.C. 1863(j)(1), I am submitting to the Congress a report of the National Science Board entitled *Science & Engineering Indicators—1991*. This report is the 10th in a continuing series examining key aspects of the status of American science and engineering.

The importance of scientific and engineering research to the well-being of our Nation is widely recognized. Science and engineering play a vital role in maintaining our Nation's defense, improving its health, and increasing its economic productivity.

GEORGE BUSH

The White House,
February 14, 1992.

## Message to the Senate Transmitting the Antarctic Treaty Protocol on Environmental Protection
*February 14, 1992*

*To the Senate of the United States:*

I transmit herewith, for the advice and consent of the Senate to ratification, the Protocol on Environmental Protection to the Antarctic Treaty, with Annexes, which was done at Madrid October 4, 1991, and an additional Annex, done at Bonn October 17, 1991. I also transmit for the information of the Senate the report of the Department of State with respect to the Protocol.

The Protocol designates Antarctica as a natural reserve, devoted to peace and science, and provides for an indefinite ban on mineral resource activities there. It specifically prohibits all activities relating to Antarctic mineral resources, except for scientific research, with the proviso that this prohibition cannot be amended by less than unanimous agreement of the Antarctic Treaty Consultative Parties for at least 50 years after entry into force of the Protocol.

The Protocol requires Parties to protect Antarctic fauna and flora and imposes strict limitations on disposal of wastes in Antarctica and discharge of pollutants into Antarctic waters. It also requires application of environmental impact assessment procedures to activities undertaken in Antarctica, including nongovernmental activities, for which advance notice is required under the Antarctic Treaty. Parties are further required to provide for response to environmental emergencies, including the development of joint contingency plans.

Detailed mandatory rules for environmental protection pursuant to these requirements are incorporated in a system of annexes, forming an integral part of the Protocol. Specific annexes on environmental impact assessment, conservation of Antarctic fauna and flora, waste disposal and waste management, and the prevention of marine pollution were adopted with the Protocol. A fifth annex on area protection and management was adopted October 17, 1991, by the Antarctic Treaty Consultative Parties at the Sixteenth Antarctic Treaty Consultative Meeting. Provision is also made for additional annexes to be developed following entry into force of the Protocol. The Protocol establishes a Committee on Environmental Protection to provide advice and recommendations to the Antarctic Treaty Consultative Meetings on the implementation of the Protocol.

The Protocol incorporates provisions to ensure effective compliance with its requirements, including compulsory and binding procedures for settlement of disputes relating to mineral resource activities, environmental impact assessment and emergency response action, as well as over the detailed rules included in the annexes.

I believe the Protocol, with its Annexes, to be fully in the U.S. interest. Its provisions advance basic U.S. goals of protecting the environment of Antarctica, preserving the unique opportunities Antarctica offers for scientific research of global significance, and maintaining Antarctica as a zone of peace. Its conclusion represents an important step in strengthening the Antarctic

Treaty and the unique form of international cooperation it has fostered.

I recommend that the Senate give early and favorable consideration to the Protocol on Environmental Protection to the Antarctic Treaty, with Annexes, and give its advice and consent to ratification.

GEORGE BUSH

The White House,
February 14, 1992.

## The President's News Conference in Belcamp, Maryland
*February 14, 1992*

*The President.* Let me just make a quick statement here. Today many families all across America share the same hope of owning their own home. But hard times have put a hold on the dream. And to these young families I made a pledge, and that is that we will help you get your dream within reach.

And I submitted to Congress an action plan to help the economy, not hurt the taxpayer. And I sent this plan to the House and the Senate. Brought it along, great big thing here. It includes a $5,000 tax credit for first-time homebuyers and a tax break for middle-class families. It's all there.

And we do not need to raise taxes in order to get this economy moving again. We need to cut the taxes and cut spending. And I've asked Congress for nothing flashy, just common sense, good common sense. And as I told these people I've been working with, construction workers and would-be homebuyers, I want that $5,000 tax credit for first-time homebuyers and penalty-free withdrawals from IRA's for the purchase of a first home. I want a modification in the tax rules that currently discourage real estate investors; it's known as the passive loss rule. And furthermore, I want a cut in the capital gains tax to boost real estate values and heat up the housing market, especially with interest rates at such low levels.

And I told them that my plan will work. They're the experts here, but some representatives of the National Association of Home Builders are with us today also. And that organization, and I'll let them speak for themselves, but that organization estimates that if Congress passes my plan by March 20th, we will create 415,000 new construction industry jobs and generate $20 billion in new economic activity, these figures from the experts.

And so I would ask you to ask one expert right here standing with me here, John Colvin, and he tells me that if Congress passes my plan by March 20th, he expects to add an additional 90 homes to the 256 he already plans to sell and build in 1992. Now, that's 355 new homes here at Arborview, homes within reach of the middle-class buyers.

Two days after the State of the Union I sent a plan to Congress to get our economy moving this spring. Now, let me tell you what happened to the plan this week. Wednesday, the majority, the Democrats on the Ways and Means Committee in the House voted against my plan twice. And just yesterday in a closed meeting the Democrats surfaced a scheme that raises taxes and, more importantly for you, everyone here, I think, kills my plan to help these first-time homebuyers.

Many firms in the housing industry have reached the make-or-break point. And so I've set a deadline for the Congress to act, you heard it in the State of the Union, March 20th, 35 days from today. Make a note of that date.

But remember, anyone who wants to buy a home like this, under my plan, would get a $5,000 tax credit. And under the Democrats' current package, they would get zero. And I've asked these good people here today to tell Congress not to send me a package that I have to veto on carrying a tax increase. The Democrats refuse to pass my plan out of the committee, and instead they are considering a package that would raise these taxes. And because it's not paid for, it would trigger cuts in the Medicare benefits.

The American people, I really believe, want action. And they will not stand for this maneuver there in the committee. I'm hoping the whole House of Representatives—Helen will do a better job on this, and Wayne, our other Congressman with me here today—they need to pass this plan and to quit playing kind of partisan, election-year politics.

So I'm glad to take this opportunity to encourage the Congress to move. And on this bill, this rifleshot approach that we have, it can be done almost overnight. It literally—it is not that complicated. There are seven stimulative tax provisions in here, and it will get the job done. It will really move this economy.

And so, I hope that everybody, regardless of political affiliation, will weigh in with the Congress and help us get this done.

So that is it. And thank you all very, very much.

Everybody read this, and I'm going to give you a quiz now on this. [*Laughter*]

*Economic Plan*

*Q.* Mr. President, the Democrats say your March 20 plan is too front-end loaded for the rich.

*The President.* That doesn't look like it to me, a $5,000 tax credit for first-time homeowner. That doesn't seem to me to be helping the rich. It seems to me to be helping people own a home. It seems to me to be stimulating the housing business.

So that's the charge, I understand, but I wish they'd get out here and talk to some people that are working in these buildings and maybe talk to some that aspire to own a home. You know, there's plenty of time

for politics later on, after March 20th. We ought to pass this one. Ask the head of the Home Builders, Jay down here. I mean, this is their business, and they'll tell you that that alone will have an enormously stimulative effect.

So, I'm asking them to say, let's set aside the politics as usual, get this part done, and then I'll go to battle stations with them on how I think the rest of this program should be enacted. But it's too urgent now. The economy's getting ready to move. Interest rates are down. Inflation is down. Everything's not all gloomy. But what it needs is a stimulative push right now. And it's good for the homebuyer. It's good for the homebuilder. It's good for the community.

Each one of these jobs, I was told in here, each one of these houses stimulates a lot of other jobs, whether it's in landscaping business or finishing these units out or all kinds of things, highway construction, whatever it might be. So that's what I would say.

*Q.* Mr. President, what's wrong with a tax increase on the wealthy as part of that?

*The President.* We don't need any tax increases. What we need to do is stimulate the economy. And every time they aim at the wealthy, you hit these guys. That's just the way it works. And so why divide, kind of keep trying to divide America class against class? Why not get on with stimulating this economy so everybody's going to have a piece of a bigger pie? That's the way I look at it.

*Q.* Are you trying to compromise with them, though, Mr. President, to sit down and——

*The President.* I don't want to compromise. I want them to pass this, and then we'll get into a negotiation on this big baby here. And there's a lot of things in there that are very important. I'm all for the provision on the child care credit, for example. But what I think is most important to the country now is to stimulate the economy where it will begin to move forward on jobs.

This will restore confidence. One of the problems we've had in this economy is the lack of confidence. And a couple of guys standing over here near this truck said, "Well, I'm beginning to get a little better feel for it. This will give it a boost." And I really think that's the approach we ought to take. Get this done, and then let's have the debate wherever it may be, on taxing the rich or taxing somebody else.

Marlin predicted yesterday to you all, they're going to come out with a tax increase. It was 12 hours later that I read in the paper a great big bill that was going to do just exactly that. And so, I'm just going to keep urging and trying to get the support of the American people to go for this stimulative package. I really think that's what's needed.

*Q.* Mr. President, did you just say that you're open to negotiating a tax increase once——

*The President.* No. No. I'm glad you put that—I said I'm glad to be talking about this whole package later on, but not negotiating a tax increase. Thank you for letting me clear that up.

*Q.* But you appeared to leave the door open, sir.

*The President.* Well, let me close it right here: Wham! [*Laughter*] We don't need it.

Thank you. Thank you, Jim [Jim Miklaszewski, NBC News]. No, I'm glad he raised it because sometimes they think I'm a little less than clear in what I say.

*Q.* Do you agree with Marlin's characterization of the Democrats on the tax and Ways and Means Committee as weasels?

*The President.* Well, I thought—I can't remember exactly what he—I thought it was eloquent, but I don't want to agree with him until I go back and review exactly what he said.

*Q.* Are they weasels?

*Q.* Are you confirmed that a tax cut now will do long-term damage to the economy?

*The President.* No, I don't think so. I think this kind of stimulative effect, which is paid for under our plan, is a good thing to do. And I also think that if the economy does what I think it will when stimulated, it will just create more and more jobs, and that, of course, would mean more and more revenues.

### Robert Goodwin

*Q.* James Cheek sees a hostile environment following the dismissal of Robert Goodwin who heads your office, your initiative on black colleges and universities. Do you know why Robert Goodwin was fired?

*The President.* No, but I certainly have a lot of respect for Dr. Cheek and would like to talk to him about that. But I don't.

### New Hampshire Primary

*Q.* Mr. President, Pat Buchanan says your proposal is a cynical betrayal of the middle class.

*The President.* Well, I'd vowed to try to get through this election without responding to him, and I think I've got a good chance because the election is Tuesday up there. And I'm going to keep on doing that, keep my sights focused on what's going to help this economy, country; what's going to help, in this instance, stimulate the housing industry. And then I'll be prepared to engage. But this is too important. And I really mean it.

So, I've been able to absorb these shots in New Hampshire from all sides. It's not just him. They're all having a field day. But what I'm trying to do is get the country moving, and then I'll come out with my dukes up and ready to do battle. But this is too important to get it caught up in charge and countercharge; it really is.

And I'm a competitor, and I don't like being the javelin catcher. But I really believe this, I really believe that if we can somehow—if I can preserve the climate in which to get this done, that's the best politics, and I know it's the best approach for our country. So, I'm going to stay with this.

*Q.* How competitive are you going to be in New Hampshire, Mr. President?

*Mr. Fitzwater.* Final question, please.

*The President.* How what?

*Q.* How competitive will you be in New Hampshire? How will you do?

*The President.* Well, I think I've got a good chance to win. Is that what you mean? [*Laughter*]

*Q.* Well, how well do you think you'll do? Will Pat Buchanan get 42 percent of the vote?

*The President.* Oh, I'm going to stay out of the prediction business. A guy asked me the other day, he said, "What do you have to have to win?" I said, "Help me will you. What does it take to win the Super Bowl? I can't remember." The guy said "One point." Thank you very much, thank you very much. [*Laughter*]

*Note: The President's 121st news conference began at 2:35 p.m. at the Arborview at Riverside construction site, Belcamp, MD. In the news conference, the following persons were referred to: John Colvin, president of Questar Builders; Representatives Helen Delich Bentley and Wayne T. Gilchrest; Jay Buchert, president of the National Association of Home Builders; James E. Cheek, chairman of the President's Board of Advisors on Historically Black Colleges and Universities; and Robert K. Goodwin, executive director of the White House initiative on historically black colleges and universities. Following the news conference, the President returned to Washington, DC.*

# Nomination of George J. Terwilliger III To Be Deputy Attorney General
*February 14, 1992*

The President today announced his intention to nominate George J. Terwilliger III, of Vermont, to be Deputy Attorney General at the Department of Justice. He would succeed William Pelham Barr.

Currently Mr. Terwilliger serves as Principal Associate Deputy Attorney General at the U.S. Department of Justice in Washington, DC. Prior to this, he served as U.S. Attorney for the District of Vermont, 1986–1990; First Assistant U.S. Attorney for Vermont, 1986; and Assistant U.S. Attorney in Vermont, 1981–1986. From 1978 to 1981, Mr. Terwilliger served as Assistant U.S. Attorney for the District of Columbia.

Mr. Terwilliger graduated from Seton Hall University (B.A., 1973) and Antioch School of Law (J.D., 1978). He was born June 5, 1950, in New Brunswick, NJ. Mr. Terwilliger is married, has three children, and resides in Oakton, VA.

# Nomination of Marc Allen Baas To Be United States Ambassador to Ethiopia
*February 14, 1992*

The President today announced his intention to nominate Marc Allen Baas, of Florida, a career member of the Senior Foreign Service, class of Minister-Counselor, to be Ambassador Extraordinary and Plenipotentiary of the United States of America to Ethiopia. He would succeed Frederick L. Chapin.

Currently Mr. Baas serves as Chargé d'Affaires for the U.S. Embassy in Addis Ababa, Ethiopia. Prior to this, he served as Deputy Chief of Mission in the U.S. Embassy in Kinshasa, Zaire, 1987–1991; Deputy Chief of Mission at the U.S. Embassy in Lome, Togo, 1985–1987; and a student at the Naval War College in Newport, RI, 1984–1985. From 1980 to 1984, Mr. Baas served as Deputy Economic Counselor and Resource Officer at the U.S. Embassy in Tokyo, Japan.

Mr. Baas graduated from American University (B.A., 1970). He was born June 23, 1948, in Grand Rapids, MI. Mr. Baas served in the District of Columbia National Guard, 1970. He is married and resides in Washington, DC.

## Remarks at the Door-to-Door Kickoff Rally in Nashua, New Hampshire
*February 15, 1992*

*The President.* Thank you so much. And first, let me thank our great campaign manager, our leader up here, our chairman, Judd Gregg, the Governor of this State. What a job he's done. And from the neighboring State, Governor Bill Weld, doing a superb job for the principles we believe in, and also Paul Cellucci, my longtime friend who is a great Lieutenant Governor of Massachusetts, here with us today. Speaking of Governors, I'm proud to be with the former Governor of this State, John Sununu. And there's another former Governor who's helped me so much, Hugh Gregg, who's around here someplace. And also, may I thank Senator Warren Rudman, the great Senator from New Hampshire; Congressman Bill Zeliff with us today; the distinguished Members of Congress, my friends from Washington and other States that are with us, three of them here today; and then John Stabile, our finance chairman. We've got a first-class team, and I'm glad to see all of you as a part of it. Thank you.

Let me be very clear as to why I'm here. I want to lead this country for another 4 years. And I ask for your support.

*Audience members.* Four more years! Four more years! Four more years!

*The President.* Having watched this, sometimes close in and sometimes from afar, I really honestly believe that the people of New Hampshire are a little bit tired of all the negative advertisements and all the attack-dog tactics coming from the left and coming from the right. What they want to do is see progress for the State of New Hampshire, not listen to a lot of political carping.

I will continue with a positive campaign. I will continue to lead this country. And first, on the economy, I have sent a comprehensive plan to the United States Congress. And it was so heavy I asked Barbara if she would carry it. Here it is. Here it is. Everybody read it, and we're going to have a quiz afterward here. [*Laughter*]

The reason I held that up is this: Yester-

day, I'm told, New Hampshire voters were subjected to flat, outright lies about this plan. This plan includes many things, including deductions for student loans and, perhaps most important, a tax relief provision for families with children. It's there. It's in this bill. And I want the Congress to move on this just as soon as possible. And it must be done in this session of Congress. Keep the pressure on the Congress.

And in addition, in addition, I've broken out seven of my proposals that would have the greatest immediate effect on stimulating this economy. These should be the least controversial provisions. I've asked Congress to put politics aside now, take a look at each one of them, and to move now. Interest rates are low. Inflation is low. The gloom-and-doom candidates are wrong. The way to help the people in this State who desperately need help is to get Congress to set aside politics long enough to pass the seven incentives in this bill. And they ought to do it.

The key provisions—you know this State—the key provision, a $5,000 tax credit to help people buy their first home. And for New Hampshire this year, 1,000 new housing starts and 2,000 construction jobs if Congress will only get going and pass this bill.

And in these incentives there's also an investment tax allowance, stimulate the purchase of capital equipment; capital gains cut so that businesses can invest and hire more people. That's money to buy equipment, to upgrade the plants, to create new jobs now. And this plan can help New Hampshire homebuyers and homebuilders literally as early as this spring. And it can help business buy new equipment and hire more people as early as this spring.

Now, I've sent forward this solid action plan. But it can only help the people of New Hampshire now if the Congress moves now. And you know, the New Hampshire Legislature is in session, I'm told, 45 days a year. Now, I gave Congress a deadline, to

March 20th. That's 52 days to pass this little—52 days to pass this straightforward, commonsense, compact program. It is an action plan, nothing fancy. And I say give them that, give the people of this State this legislation, and you watch this economy move forward. And you watch the pain and suffering be relieved.

But Warren Rudman knows this, and Bill Zeliff, our great Congressman, knows this. Wednesday, the Ways and Means Committee's Democrats, every one of them, voted against this plan twice. And Thursday, in a closed meeting, they surfaced a scheme that, you guessed it, raises taxes and kills this plan for first-time homebuyers. And this campaign, you hear a lot about sending messages. Well, my request to the people of this State is, send the Congress a message: Pass this plan by March 20th. It can be done, and it must be done.

Lastly, you've probably heard around this State, from the left, from other places as well, the call for economic isolation. Some would build a protective wall around this country. And that's wrong. That's head in the sand. That's not the America that you and I know. That is an America running scared. And our vision is an America up and running strong, the leader of the free world. And they're not going to do it by pulling back.

I think the voters in New Hampshire are pretty smart. They know that there are 35,000 jobs here that depend on exports. And I will not let those candidates or this Congress put walls of protection around that are going to throw those people out of work in New Hampshire.

And so in just a handful of days, New Hampshire is going to decide what kind of leadership is right for the nineties. And that's what makes the decision here on Tuesday so important for our country. Voters here will decide which candidate has the experience and the leadership to do right for you and to do right for your kids. And ladies and gentlemen, I'm in a tough race, but I've been in tough races before. And the stakes are high, not just for me but for you and for this country. I need your help, and I am asking for your support.

You know, I've been around the track some, and these campaigns are rough, perhaps roughest on the voters. But this year the New Hampshire voters have been subjected to literally millions of dollars of negative attacks, the kind that tear people down, don't offer any solutions, but tear down the other guy. And I am confident, very confident, that the people of New Hampshire understand what this election is really about. It's not about who can trash another's candidacy in some 30-second spot. What it's about is the very serious business of electing a President of the United States of America. And it's about somebody that has the toughness and the experience to lead this country. I believe I am that man, and I want your support. Now let's go out and get to work.

Thank you, and may God bless the United States of America.

*Audience members.* Four more years! Four more years! Four more years!

*The President.* Thank you all very much. Now let's go out and do a little canvassing.

*Note: The President spoke at 10:10 a.m. at the Davidson Flight Service hangar at Nashua Airport.*

# Remarks at a Community Welcome in New Boston, New Hampshire
*February 15, 1992*

Thank you for that warm welcome to New Boston. I was talking to Darlene a minute ago, and we were reminiscing. And it does seem like old times. I've been here several times before. And let me just get right to the point. I came here to thank you, but I also came here to ask for your vote so I will be President of the United States for 4 more years.

Let me not only thank Darlene Goodin,

our chairman here, who is doing a superb job day in and day out, but also Governor Gregg, the Governor of this State, who is my campaign leader; Governor Weld, next-door neighbor down in Massachusetts, a new Governor doing a superb job for that State where I was born, I'll tell you. And may I salute former Governor John Sununu, my friend with us here today, and also Senator Humphrey. He served with distinction in Washington, and now he's serving in the senate here. He believes in a government close to the people. I salute him; delighted to have this support.

And I heard a little bit of music, and I want to thank the principal of this school, Rick Matthews, I believe he's here with us today, for arranging all of this and also thank Dr. Jamrog and the fifth and sixth graders who did that marvelous work with the band back there. Thank you all.

I want to talk to you briefly about the economy. But before that I want to know if Jeremy Forest is here. Jeremy, where are you? Right over there; right here in the front row. Now, you guys can't see him in the back, but let me tell you a little about this guy. Jeremy Forest is one of, I believe it's 11 junior high students from all across New England who has been put into this Initiative For Understanding Between American and Soviet Youth. This is an ambassador of good will to the new Commonwealth of Independent States in Russia over there. And we're delighted, I'm delighted he's here. I single him out because it is, I think, interesting to know.

And these Congressmen that are up here from Washington, these distinguished Representatives who are my dear friends, who you were introduced to earlier on, they know what I'm about to say is true. We have moved a long way. We have won the cold war. We have beaten down the aggressor in Kuwait, that was Mr. Saddam Hussein. And now guys like Jeremy can go over there and interact with the young people in the Commonwealth of Independent States, and we can talk about friendship instead of nuclear war. And I think that is a blessing for the United States of America.

Well, I'm glad to be here on a positive, upbeat note. And let me just say I think the people here might be getting just a little bit tired of all the negative campaigns, all the attack-dog advertisements coming at them from left and right. The people of New Hampshire are positive. They don't like always trying to tear down the other guy. And so, I'm going to continue to keep on a positive note.

I must say as a competitor, you know, I get kicked around too much. But that's all right. They're coming at me from deep left field and deep right field. And I've been out there to Fenway Park; I know what it's like. Stay the course. Stand up and say what you are for.

And let me tell you what I am for. I'm going to continue with a positive campaign. And first, on the economy, we've got to get this economy moving again. And I have sent a comprehensive plan to the United States Congress. Now, I asked John Sununu to carry it for me. Here it is. I won't ask everybody to read one. Look at the size of this thing. This is a comprehensive plan. It is now before the House; it is now before the Senate. It is a message that we need. We need this passed. And it is all here.

And yesterday, I'm told that we got shot at from a couple of quarters up here. People and the New Hampshire voters were subjected to flat, let me call them outright lies about this plan. This plan includes many things, including deductions for student loans. But the one I want to mention, perhaps most important to every family here, is a tax relief provision for families with children. We need it. We've got it paid for in that plan, and we ought to pass it.

And so, don't listen to those negative ads that say it's not there; it is. And I want this whole program passed by the end of this session of Congress. And I think if we had more people like Bill Zeliff and Warren Rudman and Bob Smith in the Congress, we could get it passed. But please keep the pressure on the United States Congress.

Then, in addition to this major overall plan, I've broken out seven of my proposals that would have the greatest immediate effect on stimulating the economy. And these are important in a State where real estate has been on its back, homebuilding has been sluggish if not almost imperceptible.

And here's what it does, here's the background. Interest rates are now low. Inflation is now low. The economy is poised for recovery. And the way to help the people in the State who desperately need help is to get Congress to set aside politics just long enough to pass this part of this plan, the incentives, the seven incentives in the plan.

Now, let me give you one key provision. Young people ought to be interested in this, a $5,000 tax credit to help people buy their first home. It would get the homebuilding industry moving. And it is here. The head of the National Home Builders was up here saying if there was any single proposal that would help turn homebuilding around, it is this proposal of the President of the United States. And in New Hampshire it would mean 1,000 new housing starts, 2,000 construction jobs.

I also have in this plan, we have in this plan an investment tax allowance. We have in it a much-needed capital gains tax cut so that businesses can hire more people, get more people put to work.

But here's the key point: This is not campaign rhetoric. What this thing is—let me just tell you, New Hampshire homebuyers and homebuilders can be on the move as early as this spring. And it can help business get new equipment, hire more people as early as this spring. This is a solid action plan. It can only help the people of New Hampshire now if Congress acts now. And you know your legislature, the State legislature, what, meets for 45 days a year? Well, I gave Congress a deadline of March 20th. That's 52 days to pass these seven little incentives that would really help this economy. There's nothing flashy here. All we need is action.

And we gave them the legislation. I've showed you the bill. And let me tell you what the Democrats back in Washington did just this week. On Wednesday, the Ways and Means Committee Democrats voted against this plan twice, and then Thursday, in a closed-session meeting, they surfaced a scheme that raises taxes. They say, tax the rich. That hits the little guy over and over again. And we do not need to raise taxes; we need to put incentives into this economy.

So my plea is, don't vote for some gimmick. Don't vote for some shadowy promise. Here's a plan that is before the Congress right now, and it can start moving this economy out of the doldrums faster than any other answer. So I ask for your support.

Now, lastly, you've probably heard the call around here for economic isolation. Some would build a wall around America. That's wrong-headed. That's head in the sand, not the America that you and I know. Theirs is an America, those that would do that, whether they're on the Democrat side or the Republican side, those who would say protection and isolation are running scared. America is not a country to run scared. We are the leader of the free world. We need to stay involved in international trade, not get protection going again in this country.

Let me tell you what this means to your neighbors in New Boston. Thirty-five thousand jobs in this State depend on exports, selling abroad. We start to put up walls of protection, other people do the same thing, and those 35,000 jobs go down the drain. We cannot go back to the failed days of isolation and protection. And as long as I'm President we will not go back. Our exports are moving, and they have helped the New Hampshire economy. And with our plan in effect, they'll help it even more. Help me fight against protection and isolation.

And so, on Tuesday New Hampshire is going to have a lot to say about who is the next President of the United States. You're going to be asked to make a serious vote. Who has the experience? Who has the demonstrated leadership to stand up and do right? And I believe that I am the person that has the leadership. I hope I demonstrated that when we kicked Saddam Hussein out of Kuwait. And he'd still have been there if you had listened to some of my opponents, still been there.

So, I know I'm in a tough race, but I've been in tough races before, many of you at my side in those battles. And the stakes are high not just for me, but they are high for our country. And I need your help. And I am up here to proudly say I want to be your President and to humbly say I ask for your support. Give me that support so we can get this country moving on the economic front and keep us the leader of the world on the international front.

I'm told that, Judd was telling me and others today, that we've been subjected here to a lot of negative advertisements. The voters have been subjected to millions of dollars of these negative attacks, the kind that just tear people down by name and turn people off, I think. But I am confident that the people of New Hampshire understand what this election is about. It's not about who can trash another person's candi-

dacy in some 30-second spot. It's about who can lead this country, who can continue to lead the free world. And what it's really about is setting a direction of this country for the next 4 years.

And again, I need your support to continue this job. Thank you all. And may God bless our great country, the United States of America. Thank you very much.

*Note: The President spoke at 11:58 a.m. at New Boston Central Elementary School.*

## Remarks and a Question-and-Answer Session in Goffstown, New Hampshire
*February 15, 1992*

*The President.* Thank you for that warm welcome back. Before we get started, let me just thank Dr. Conway, the superintendent, and to thank Ms. Colby, who is the assistant principal here, and Vivian Blondeau, the chairman of the school board, and say how pleased I am to be here and pleased that we have this opportunity to meet in this wonderful school.

What we are going to do today is just, in the 20 minutes allocated, take questions. So, I think the way to do it is just let me say one word: I'm up here to ask the support of the people of New Hampshire to be President of the United States for 4 more years.

And we've made a lot of progress in the world. The cold war is over. International imperial communism, the aggressive part that's reaching out and trying to do in others, that's finished; it's dead. Aggression has been pushed back and international law established by the international defeat, you might say, of Saddam Hussein when we kicked him out of Kuwait.

So, a lot of good things have happened. And we are clearly the leaders of the world. And I do not want to see us pull back into isolation in fear because the economy of this State and other States is hurting. And so, what I'm asking the American people to do is say please help me get through Congress the economic growth package that I

have sitting down there now. It would move the housing industry, the real estate industry, would lift the spirits of this State. So, we've got a plan. It isn't a campaign plan. It's enshrined, enrolled in two big pieces of legislation. And I need your help leaning on the United States Congress.

Let me thank the man who introduced me, who is our leader here, Governor Gregg of this State. I'm very fortunate to have him as my campaign chairman and delighted he's here and has just introduced me.

Now, with no further ado, I'd be glad to take any questions. Yes, sir.

*Banking Industry*

*Q.* Mr. President, my question is, the banking industry in this State is very, very, very tight. I would like to know, what can our Government do to relieve the rules and the pressures of the Fannie Mae, which is from a one-family to a four-family home, and to stop the foreclosures that are going on with people that should not have their home foreclosed on? And then also, in the business sector, relieve the pressures from the banks so they can loan us money so we can put people back to work? They will not loan money to any business. Thank you.

*The President.* Well, it's a very important question. And one thing we are trying to do is to relieve this credit crunch by doing a better job on regulation. We've called in all the regulators. We can't go back to forgiving bad practices; we're not going to do that. But they've gone too far the other way. And I think the best answer to freeing up credit is trying to get these regulators to go forward and take a hard look at the existing regulations, as we've done, and say, "Look, good banks should make good loans; don't discourage them."

Interest rates are down. We are poised, because of where interest rates are and inflation is, to make a real recovery in this country. And so, I'm optimistic that these banks will begin to start making loans. Their balance sheets are in much better shape nationally. The regulation load is being lightened, although I'm having a big fight with Congress on some of that right now in the Senate Banking Committee. And I think it's going to move in the right direction.

On Fannie Mae, it's tough because those are independent, and we can't snap our fingers and control them.

But credit crunch, it's hurt us. My appeal is to the good, sound institutions to make sound banking loans, and I think that's the kind you're talking about. I don't think anyone wants to go back to the excesses of the eighties in terms of savings and loan excess or financial excess. One thing that's cost us and has hurt the deficit is the money that the Government has had to put in to cover the depositors. One good thing is not one single depositor has lost money. And I'm determined to keep it that way. But I think this change in regulations is going to help. Thank you.

Who's over—yes?

*Capital Gains Tax*

*Q.* Welcome, President Bush, thank you. I'm a student of business right now, and I have a business question for you. You proposed a capital gains cut which, it seems to me, is going to benefit people who are investing in art, in jewelry, and other things, instead of an investment tax credit which would invest in business and make it more competitive and more productive. Why is that?

*The President.* We have proposed, maybe

you missed it, in our proposal we have before the Congress right now an investment tax allowance. The ITC, itself, what you call investment tax, is terribly expensive. I think the revenue loss estimates were something like $250 billion. So, we couldn't do that and fit it into our budget plan without a tax increase, which I would like to firmly avoid and I'm determined to avoid.

Investment tax allowance is what you might more appropriately call more rapid depreciation which will stimulate the kind of investment you're talking about. The capital gains cut, I am absolutely convinced, will stimulate jobs and stimulate investment, too. It worked under the Steiger amendment in 1978. I think it would have a very salutary effect. And it isn't what some of the opponents call it, a tax break for the rich. It's going to create jobs. It's going to create people taking more risks. So, look at how it worked in '78. And I think you'll find that this combination of these two things really will stimulate the economy.

And what's happened, I send this seven-point—they're all stimulatory tax provisions—say to the Congress, "Pass it by March 20th." They go in behind closed doors, beat it on a straight party-line vote, including this investment tax allowance, ITC type of thing, and come out and say, "Well, what we've got to do is redistribute the wealth by increasing taxes."

I do not think that's what the American people want, and I'm going to fight for this growth package. I'm not going to give up on it. I think we can make some headway in the Senate and in the House floor. But I'm not sure; we may not agree on a capital gains. You take a look at this ITA, this tax allowance, this stimulation; I think you'll find it's good.

Yes, sir?

*Federal Budget*

*Q.* Thank you for coming here. My question to you, I've heard your speech recently, is reducing the size of the Government. We've gotten so big and so out of control. Can you speak to us, Federal level, what can be done to lower the cost and the size of the Government?

*The President.* Lowering the cost of it, it's a good point. It is too big and takes too much out in the gross national product in taxes.

The only good thing about the budget agreement that was passed in 1990 is that it put caps on the Federal spending. It put caps on discretionary spending. Now, I hear some candidates running around here, around this State, saying they're going to freeze all spending. That sounds attractive, but I don't think that's fair to the senior citizen, for example. I don't think that he should be denied, he or she denied the cost of living increase, for example. So it's easy to say that. And I think we've got to control the growth of the entitlements, but I don't think the freeze is the answer.

I do believe that this proposal of holding the caps on Federal discretionary spending is important. And right now, you listen to the Congress, Democrat Congress, they're talking about getting rid of those caps or shifting the caps. The best protection for the taxpayer is to hold those caps on Federal spending. And I believe, I think we can be able to do that. That's the key.

Who's next? Way in the back, Father.

*Education*

*Q.* Thank you, Mr. President. First of all, I commend you on your courageous position regarding the life of the unborn in our country. As president of a college, I'd like to ask a question on higher education and ask if you'd comment, please, on your plans to help low- and middle-income families have access to colleges of their choice and particularly independent colleges in terms of Federal aid.

*The President.* Father, let me say this: I believe in school choice. We have an excellent education program. It is called America 2000. It is not Republican. It's not Democrat. It's not conservative. It's not liberal. It works to implement the six national education goals that were passed by the Governors, Democrat and Republican alike. One of the provisions of our America 2000 program is choice.

When I got out of college, I was a recipient of the GI bill. I fought for my country, and one of the things that veterans got way back then was a GI bill. And they didn't say what kind of school you could go to. They simply said, "Take your choice." I believe that choice is one of the best ways to increase the quality of education from all schools, and I'm going to continue to fight for it. And that, I think, gets to your question. That is the fundamental part of America 2000. It is a fundamental part of how we improve education.

And you do it through vouchers, but different private schools ought not to be denied. One of the allegations is, well, people will leave a bad school to go to a good school. Where that's happened, the bad schools have improved. Take a look at Rochester, New York, as a good example.

So, the answer to the question you're raising is choice. And back it up so that the parents will have the main say. I had the mayors, I mentioned this in the State of the Union, I had the mayors from the National League of Cities in. And they were Mayor Bradley of Los Angeles, great big, complex metropolitan area, a Democrat; a tiny town in North Carolina with a Republican mayor, 3,000. And they said, "The one thing that concerns us is that the fundamental cause of a lot of these problems is the demise of the family." And what we're trying to do there is strengthen the family. And choice, I think, is one of the best ways to go about it.

Way in the back. Yes, ma'am. We can hear you. Go ahead.

*Energy Policy*

*Q.* This is something I don't hear a lot about. I would like to know what plans are in the works for the further development of solar energy, particularly where it appears we may have a lot more sun than we know what to do with soon? [*Laughter*]

*The President.* I'm very proud of our administration for first having taken the lead on phasing out CFC's and then speeding it up when new scientific information came in. We moved very fast on that. And I believe that set a good example for other countries around the world, and I confidently expect that the EC and other countries will follow the lead of this country in phasing out these CFC's that do damage to the ozone layer.

Our energy program puts a good deal of

emphasis on alternate sources of energy, not simply solar, incidentally. It is all sources of energy other than hydrocarbons. And we are not going to be independent so that we can get rid of all burning hydrocarbons; that simply can't be done. It's unrealistic. I want to see this country less dependent on foreign oil. And if our energy program gets passed, it will do that, alternate sources, conservation, and certainly not neglecting the domestic side of the hydrocarbon industry. So, it's in our energy bill, and I think we can move relatively fast. But to say to the country, as I've heard some people up here do, we can solve all these problems by going to solar energy today, that simply is not technologically feasible. We just don't have the delivery system of that kind of energy source.

Also, and I know this one might be controversial, and I don't know where you come down on this one, but I also happen to believe that safe utilization of nuclear power is in our interests. It burns clean, and technology is good. I know you get a lively debate on it, but as I look at the energy requirements, we ought to do that.

### U.N. Conference on Environment

*Q.* I was wondering if you could let us know whether or not you're planning to attend the United Nations Conference on the Environment and Development?

*The President.* Her question was whether I plan to attend the United Nations conference which will be held in Brazil on the environment. We're talking about that right now. The problem is it comes at a time when we've got a relatively hot political year here. But the United States must lead, and I have not told President Collor of Brazil yet whether I can do it. I'm talking to other world leaders as to whether they're attending. Bill Reilly, who is doing a superb job as head of the EPA, is back; we're going to have a meeting with him next week.

So, the answer is, a decision has not been made on that. I just don't know. But whether I'm there or not, they're certainly going to have full cooperation and, I'd say, leadership from the United States. It's an important conference.

Way in the back.

### Student Loans

*Q.* Yes, Mr. President, I am an ex-student from the New England area, and I'm sure you know that probably a good portion of the schools in the United States are located in the East. As of this year I'm not able to deduct the interest on my student loans anymore. That really hurts because I owe about $25,000 for school. So where do you stand on that?

*The President.* I stand on asking your support for the bill that I referred to that's before the Ways and Means Committee right now, before the Senate Finance Committee, because it does permit the deduction of interest on student loans. And I think you're absolutely right; it should be done. So, we need your help getting it passed. But we've got that in this legislation. I hope we can succeed.

### The Economy

*Q.* Mr. President, in tough times what can Americans do by pulling their own bootstraps?

*The President.* Well, I think what Americans can do is what we've always done, work hard, et cetera. But I think the economy needs some assistance now, like a tax credit for the first-time homebuyer. I have proposed that, $5,000. The National Association of Home Builders tell us that that would really stimulate this economy and do it fast. So, I think what we must do in Government is to try to give incentive, but it cannot be Government make-work programs. It has to be freeing up this economy to do a better job for the citizens.

See, I'm not as discouraged as some people are. I know people have had a tough time in this State. But I've seen what we can do when we come together. I saw what we've done around the world in establishing our leadership. We're still the number one country in terms of our gross national product, by far. So, what we've got to do is jump-start this economy and then get the Government out of the way as much as possible and let this ingenuity that you're talking about come to the fore more.

So, let's not be so discouraged that we cannot see any hope out there. I know people are hurting, but you've got interest rates at an all-time low; you've got inflation down; the economy is poised to come back. And I'm saying, give me the support I need in the Congress to get this one package passed, and then this ingenuity you're talking about really can flourish. I think you've got it in perspective.

How about this guy right over here?

*Q.* May I have your autograph? [*Laughter*]

*The President.* Come on. The answer to that question is yes. Here you go. I signed that for you.

All right, who's got—right here in the front.

*Q.* Thank you.

*The President.* You're welcome. That's a tough question. [*Laughter*]

### Health Care

*Q.* Mr. President, can you please assure us that you will not push through a national health plan? We would like to keep health care private.

*The President.* I have a strong health proposal, health care plan. It's printed; it's out there. It does not nationalize health care. We've got a lot of criticism about our health care. We still have the best quality health care in the entire world, the best. Otherwise, why do people come here from other countries to get it? And you hear some of these people—somebody told them a few months ago, health care's an issue. So they'll come out trying to emulate some foreign plan.

We're not going to have that. We are going to have the kind of plan that I put forward that will keep the quality and still make health care affordable to all through insurance. And people say, "Well, poor guy doesn't have money to pay for the insurance." Then we have the voucher system, where he goes to a central location, name is on there, they have access to privately held, competitive insurance coverage. And that is the answer, not what you've asked about, this national health care plan. And you've got to take a look at the cost, too. And ours is much easier to pay for.

Now, I'm getting a signal that we have time—let's say two more. Then I've got a special treat for you. Way back here in the red shirt, yes, sir.

### Congressional Term Limitations

*Q.* My question is very simple, Mr. President, is: Understanding we have many career politicians in Congress, how do you feel about term limitations?

*The President.* I am in favor of term limitations. I'm in favor of that, and if it's good enough for the President it ought to be good enough for some of these Congressmen.

All right. Yes, sir, right here.

### Government Decentralization

*Q.* Mr. President, with the high degree of communications technology that exists today, when can we look forward to decentralizing the large, expensive Washington-based form of Government?

*The President.* I'm not sure. I wouldn't hold my breath on that one. [*Laughter*] I think your point is well-taken. There can be a more diffused Government, Government closer to the people through technology. Computer networks are doing that. I don't honestly see, though, that it is going to be so decentralized that one agency will be in one place and one agency in another place. With the kind of Government we have where the action of Congress is very, very important, I don't see a really diffused transfer of these departments around the country. It has certain appeal, but I don't want to be unrealistic. It ain't going to happen.

All right. Now, let me tell you, we've got a special treat here, a good friend of mine. And this man is doing an awful lot on fitness. Somebody mentions health care; one of the reasons you do it is you prevent bad health by keeping fit. And so let me introduce to you a supporter and a great friend of mine, Arnold Schwarzenegger.

Give them the fitness test.

*Mr. Schwarzenegger.* Thank you very much, Mr. President. Thank you.

*The President.* He's part of our health plan, see.

[*At this point, Mr. Schwarzenegger spoke.*]

*The President.* Thanks so much. I guess we're out of here. Good to see you all. Thanks for coming. Glad to see you. Thanks for taking the time.

*Note: The President spoke at 1:04 p.m. at Mountain View Middle School. Arnold Schwarzenegger was Chairman of the President's Council on Physical Fitness and Sports.*

## Remarks at the Bush-Quayle Campaign Welcome in Derry, New Hampshire
*February 15, 1992*

*The President.* It is great to be here. Thank you all very much. And Governor, first may I thank Governor Gregg and Kathy for their leadership and terrific support. I'm just delighted to have him as the head of this campaign in New Hampshire. We're very, very lucky. And may I salute Governor Jock McKernan of Maine and his marvelous wife, Congresswoman Olympia Snowe, who are with us tonight. He's doing a great job for that State. And then from Massachusetts, our new and great Governor, Bill Weld, and Paul Cellucci, first-class job as Lieutenant Governor.

And of course, the man so well-known not just for his leadership in New Hampshire but for his leadership, sound, sensible leadership in Washington, Warren Rudman. I'm just delighted to be at his side. And may I salute Congressman Bill Zeliff and thank him for his support. And also, Mayor Dowd, the mayor of this wonderful town, he and his wife doing a superb job in the political leadership. And you met the visiting friends, those Congressmen that were with me, Congressmen Regula and Hobson and Dick Shulze from Pennsylvania. They've had to move on.

But now, first of all, thanks to the parents, the students, and the staff of Pinkerton Academy for opening the gym for tonight's event. And thanks to the Shaw Brothers for sending a little music our way. And of course, my thanks to Arnold, Arnold Schwarzenegger. You know, he and I have been out on the campaign trail before several years ago, now again today. But he's working on a new film about Congress; he calls it "The Procrastinator." [*Laughter*] You know, I might just take a tip from "Kindergarten Cop." When Congress doesn't behave, take away their recess, and let's get something done for the country.

But thanks to all of you here for coming from four corners of the State of New Hampshire to Derry on this Saturday night. And we've come here for one reason: Together we are going to win an election on Tuesday.

*Audience members.* Four more years! Four more years! Four more years!

*The President.* And in about 9 months from now, with your help, we're going to win an election in November. Make no mistake about that.

We've got much to be proud of and many challenges still ahead of us. But the remarkable changes of these last 3 years have shown without a doubt the United States of America is the undisputed leader of the world. And from the fall of the Berlin Wall to the last gasp of imperial communism, from the four decades of the cold war to the 40 days of Desert Storm, America has led the way. And America has changed the world.

And now the change and the challenge, as it has before, it's come home. And time after time, we've lifted ourselves up. And time after time, we've asked more of ourselves, more of each other. And each time, America met the challenge. And this time, America will do it again.

Next Tuesday, New Hampshire makes its choice. You take part in this State's proud tradition as first in the Nation. And you know this is serious business. You understand the importance of your vote. You go to the polls not to send a signal, not to register a protest; you go to the polls to elect the President of the United States of America.

The first order of business in our country and in this election is the economy. And count on this: We are getting this economy moving again, and we will get New Hampshire back on the road to recovery. Three weeks ago I laid out a two-part plan to New Hampshire and to the Nation: a short-term to jump start our economy, long-term to keep us competitive and strong into the next century. And I want, and the country needs, both parts of this program enacted by the Congress this year. It is just that important.

My plan boosts investment, and it gives incentives to businesses to buy equipment and upgrade their plants and hire more workers. And it helps restore the value of real estate, gets the housing market going again, gives a $5,000 tax credit to first-time homebuyers. And our plan takes an ax to 246 Government programs because Government is too big and it spends too much. And I need Congress to pass it.

The Democrats have a different idea, as you saw coming out of the Ways and Means Committee the other day. But there's one thing my plan doesn't do: It won't raise taxes on the American families who are overtaxed as it is.

And you know what I think, my plan is just what the economy ordered. When it comes down to me and the other candidates, from the left or from the right, here's the only difference that counts: I have a plan, and they don't have a clue.

Everyone knows we've got to work fast——

*Audience members.* Four more years! Four more years! Four more years!

*The President.* Everyone knows we've got to work fast to get the economy on its feet, but some are pushing protectionism, escape from economic reality. And they say they're going to play defense, they're going to fight back. Sounds tough, until you think about it. It's not the schoolyard bully; it's the boy who wants to take his ball and go home and get off the playing field. America is not that kind of country. And our national symbol is not the ostrich; it's the eagle.

Never in this Nation's history, never in this Nation's long history has America turned its back on a challenge. To succeed economically at home, you've got to lead economically abroad. You see, I believe in the American worker. We'll go head to

head with anyone. The American worker can outthink, outproduce, outperform the competition anywhere, anytime.

*Audience members.* Four more years! Four more years! Four more years!

*The President.* These are the things that Tuesday is about, the course we set for our country and the future we build for our kids——

[*At this point, AIDS activists interrupted the President's remarks.*]

May I just make a comment because these people, understandably, are concerned about AIDS. But unfortunately, because of their tactics, they sometimes hurt their own cause. But let me just give you a figure here. It's a very serious problem. When I came into office the first year, an increase, we spent $2.3 billion; this year, $4.9 billion. We are going to whip that disease. We're doing everything we can. And we're going to keep on until we succeed.

Sure, this is a tough race——

*Audience members.* We want Bush! We want Bush! We want Bush!

*The President.* Sure, this is a tough race, but I've been in tough races before. And yes, the stakes are high, not just for me but for you and our country as well. And I know the voters of New Hampshire. And you've been subjected to a lot of this negative campaigning that Senator Rudman talked about. You've seen the ads, the kind that only tear people down and, I believe, turn people off. Well, I am confident that you understand that this election isn't about who can trash another's candidacy in a 30-second spot.

New Hampshire voters have even been told some flat-out lies about the plan I sent to Congress. Here it is. Here's the bill I sent to the United States Congress immediately after the State of the Union. And in it are provisions for student loans deductions and, perhaps most importantly, tax relief for America's families with children. It's in this plan. It's before the Congress. And it's all right here. It gives me another opportunity to say to the Congress: Pass this plan; pass the whole plan. We need action by Congress.

Next Tuesday matters because you don't

just choose a candidate, you choose a future. You set the course this country will follow for the next 5 years. And here's what I know about this country's future. No matter how tough times are now, America's best day always lies ahead. I believe that now. I believe it every day I live because that's the great glory of the United States of America.

And I felt it today from Nashua to New Boston. The people of New Hampshire, like citizens all across this country, are ready to move ahead, ready to move forward to meet a new American destiny. Everyone sees the need for change. Everyone feels the excitement. Everyone is impatient to begin. Everyone, that is, except the crowd that controls the Congress, the liberal Democrats who still control both Houses of the United States Congress.

So, you won't be surprised to hear what's happening to this action plan, the part to jump-start this economy. And here it is here, seven key points. The Democrats who control the Ways and Means Committee pulled a back-room stunt and tried to make

this plan disappear. Thank goodness I kept a copy.

I'm a patient man. I know Congress can't pass my plan overnight, and that's why I gave them 52 days. And I know they say the deadline is arbitrary; they say the deadline is too early; they say the deadline is unfair. You know what I say? The deadline is March 20th, and the American people want action.

I cannot get this job done without your help. And so, Tuesday my request is this: Send this President, who's done his very best, who's turned this world around, who's working for economic recovery all across our country, send this President back to Washington for 4 more years.

Thank you, New Hampshire, for your trust and your support. And may God bless the United States of America. Thank you very much.

*Note: The President spoke at 6:46 p.m. at Pinkerton Academy. A tape was not available for verification of the content of these remarks.*

# Remarks at a Breakfast in Nashua, New Hampshire
*February 16, 1992*

Rhona, I'm glad to see you here, our able chairman of our party, friend to all, and Alice. This takes me back a year or two, I'll tell you. And thank you all very much for being here. In addition to thanking Alice Record, I want to thank Harold Acres, our Nashua chairman, and Valerie Walsh, who is handling the volunteers; and say to Alice Record, with whom I go back a long time, Barbara and I do, we are just delighted and pleased to be here at this wonderful breakfast.

What you don't need, I think, on this Sunday morning is a long political speech, so you're not going to get one. I think that deserves a round of applause, too, after what this State has been through. [*Applause*] But I will just say a quick word about it because we're getting to a crossroads now, getting to a very important

point.

Really, you make serious choices here, and you don't elect the loudest or the biggest protester. I think you take these elections seriously. And New Hampshire has a record of being a pretty good predictor on who should be bearing the responsibilities for President of the United States. We're not in this for messages. We're in here to see who should be chosen to be President and accept the full responsibilities of that job.

I have tried to stay above the fray in terms of all the negative campaigning that this State has been subjected to, much of it aimed towards me. But I think, in spite of the problems that exist here, people want to get a little bit of a positive idea as to where this country is going and what we stand for. And so I've tried to keep it on a good plane. I don't think this election is about trashing the candidacy of somebody else in some 30-second spot.

The issue, the one that counts the most here, is the economy. And this year there are two different kinds of choices: one who can tell you what he's doing right now, and then we have others from both extremes, it seems to me, who just don't have a clue as to where this country should be going or what to do about the problems that exist.

I've spelled out a two-part plan. And it's not political rhetoric. I have a responsibility as President of the United States to send a plan to the Congress each year. And regrettably, for the last 2 years, they have not acted on things that would have stimulated the growth in the New Hampshire economy. But I'm trying again now with very comprehensive programs, one short-term, one comprehensive and longer-term, both of which should be passed by the Congress this year to help the people of this State.

Though you hear the carping and the complaining up here in the campaign, but I haven't seen what I think of as a sensible action plan, one that fits in under these budget caps, one that will stimulate immediately. You hear some things that sound attractive to people, and there's great division amongst the candidates as what they should be. But our plan, I believe, really would move the country forward. It includes the student loan deductions. It includes tax relief for America's families with children. It is a good plan, and it will work. And it will stay under these budget limits. We've got to control the growth of Federal spending. And you ought to ask everybody that has one of these things, what does it cost? Ours, I have to account for it. It is before the Congress now. It will not increase these awful deficits we're facing.

Another subject that's come up is the one of protectionism and isolationism. And you talk about a sorry, negative approach. Those candidates on both sides who are promoting isolationism and protectionism, that is a clear blueprint for failure in my view, based on considerable experience. We can't go that way. The truth of the matter is we're not going to succeed economically at home unless we lead economically abroad. So when you vote, you've got to understand the new world, the world after the cold war.

And I think I might say, parenthetically, we ought to look at the whole record when we decide to elect, who a President of the United States is. And I'll claim to be second to none in terms of working for world peace and making it better for these kids to grow up in a world free of nuclear war.

I do believe that housing and real estate are going to lead this economy, lead the recovery, lead us out of recession. And that's one reason we have a proposal that will create 1,000 new homes and more than 2,000 new construction jobs in New York—I mean in New Hampshire, starting this spring. I hope it will do some for New York, too. [*Laughter*] But Congress has got to pass it on time. And it will create 415,000 jobs nationwide; you had the head of the Home Builders up here the other day confirming this, nationwide; generate $20 billion in new economic activity. It's based on investment incentives in our plan, and they're going to help business grow, buy new equipment, and hire new workers.

Because of the economy, you haven't heard about the successes we're having in fighting drugs. You haven't heard about the comprehensive energy plan. You haven't heard enough about our America 2000 education plan that would actually rejuvenate and revolutionize American education. We've got to do better. But the debate here is, for understandable reasons, on the economy. We've got a good health care plan that I put forward in detail, not a campaign plan but one that's right up there at the Congress right now. And I hope you'll pay some attention to that one.

But as I listen to the debate, sometimes from close in, sometimes from afar, I just hear the old thinking of let the Government do it all; or an isolationistic trend I mentioned; or bigger Government; or don't worry about the cost, pass this national health plan that's going to cost $250 billion more. And we just can't do that.

I've spent a lot of my life in this region of the country, as many of you know, spent a lot of my time in this State. I haven't just discovered it. We are, in a sense, neighbors; certainly not strangers. So, I want to ask you something. I'd like to ask you now to help me persuade the Democratic leaders in the Congress to get moving on our action plan. We've got to move it through the Congress, and we've got to do it now. Frankly, if we had more people like Judd Gregg, when he was on the Ways and Means Committee, and Bill Zeliff, who is there now, and Warren Rudman and Bob Smith in the Congress, that thing would be moving through. If we had control of the Congress, it would be moving right on through.

So the election is more than campaign slogans. It's more than who can get the 30-second bite by criticizing the President the most. The election is who do you want to be President of the United States. And I believe that when it comes Tuesday, I will carry this State, I hope substantially. I believe I will go on to have another 4 years as President. But I need your help. Send them a strong message, if you want to send a message that is positive, that is upbeat, that expresses confidence that the United States is the number one country in the entire world. And we're going to make it even better.

Thank you all very much. And I'm so pleased to be with you.

*Note: The President spoke at 9:11 a.m. at Pennichuck Junior High School. In his remarks, he referred to Rhona Charbonneau, chairman of the New Hampshire Republican Party, and Alice Record, State legislator. A tape was not available for verification of the content of these remarks.*

# Remarks and a Question-and-Answer Session in Hollis, New Hampshire
*February 16, 1992*

*The President.* Thank you all very, very much. Thank you so much, all of you. It's great to be back. It is great to be back, really. Nice to see all of you. Okay, let's get going. But first let me say how pleased I am to have been introduced by a hometown boy here and, I think, one of the greatest leaders that New Hampshire has ever produced, Senator Warren Rudman. I am very proud to have his support. With us also, also overdressed for the occasion since we've just been in church, and I didn't see all of you there—[*laughter*]—Governor Gregg, our campaign leader here, Judd Gregg, and Kathy and *uno* kid, *dos* kids right here. Judd, good to see you.

And let me also thank Hugh Gregg, predecessor in the Governor's office, but who's been so active once again for me and to whom I'm always grateful. Bill Zeliff is here, the Congressman, although I don't see him right this minute. Where is he? Bill, you here? Right over there, doing a first-class job in the United States Congress.

And I want to thank Katy Wienslaw. I want to thank Denis Joy, the principal, for letting us use his great school, this great facility. And, of course, a friend of long standing who asked that I not mention her name, but heck with that, Shirley Cohen, and we go back a long, long time. There she is.

I was reminiscing with Shirley about days gone by, but here we are. And what I wanted to do now, other than urge you to vote for me on Tuesday, which I'm up here for, is to simply say that I want to be President for 4 more years. I believe in this country. I am not a pessimist about the future of this country. When you look around the world and you see these kids, I hope that my Presidency has made a difference. These kids are going to grow up in a world with a lot less fear of nuclear weapons. And I think we can all take pride in the foreign policy of this country and what we've accomplished.

We got those energies turned now to try to turn this economy around. We've got a good program. It's not a campaign plan. It is a bill, two comprehensive bills, put it that way, before the Congress right now that would get this economy moving, not some campaign pledge. So, I need your help to lean on the Congress, not on Bill Zeliff, not on Warren Rudman or Bob Smith because they're doing the right thing, but lean on those that control the Congress to say, "Let's leave the politics aside now and pass the President's plan by March 20th." Then we can all roll up our sleeves and fight on the political turf. But too many people up here are hurting to have politics as normal. So, my challenge to the Congress is: Move by March 20th, and give the people of this State and across this country what they need.

And now I'll be glad to take some questions. These guys have the mikes right here. Yes, shoot. I'll repeat it if they don't get the mike to you fast enough, but go ahead.

### War on Drugs

*Q.* Mr. President, if elected, what steps would you take towards drug prevention in the United States?

*The President.* Drug prevention? What steps if elected? Follow-on on the steps we're taking now. And there is some good news with our national drug strategy; it is working. The use by teenagers of cocaine is down by 11 percent in this country, and that's encouraging news. We're doing better on the interdiction of narcotics coming in here. The budget is up at about $11 billion for fighting the drug scourge.

One thing where you can help me, anybody here can help me, once again, is with the Congress because we have some strong anticrime legislation that would also help in the fight against drugs.

So, the answer to your program is, build on the national drug strategy that we already have in effect and that is working, both internationally and domestic. We've got to fight that scourge and whip it. And one of our national six education goals is schools and workplaces, but schools that are free of drugs. And again, support our America 2000 education program. It's good for this country.

Now, who's next? Here we are, right back there.

### Education Reform

*Q.* Maria Gray. I'm a second-grade school-

teacher. And on behalf of the teachers I work with and my students, thank you for all that you do; Mrs. Bush, for all that you do, for your reading incentive programs. And would you give an encouraging word to those people who may be thinking about teaching as a profession?

*The President.* I'd be glad to give that encouraging word, and God bless the teachers. We'll start with that. I was hoping I would get a question on education. I only have one of these with me. But we have a good program called America 2000, and it gives parents choice. It says we can do better in math and science, so we'll be more competitive around the world.

And incidentally, this one started as a result of what the Governors, Democrat and Republicans, did at Charlottesville. They came together, put these six education goals before the Nation. And now we've got a program called America 2000. Judd Gregg, as your Governor, is out front for that program. And again, it transcends politics. And it really says this: We've got some good buildings, maybe need some better ones; we've got bricks and mortar, but we must revolutionize our schools. And that means strengthening the teachers, giving choice to the parents. And it is a good, sound program, and I hope you all will take a look at it. Not much of it needs legislation. Most of it is being done at the community and the State level, thank heavens, or it would take a longer time to get it through.

But as to the teachers, plenty of encouragement here. We have great respect for those who give their lives to the young of this country.

Now, how about this section? Well, all right. Is that for me? Oh, how nice. Here let me—you got a question to go with it?

*Q.* This is from a Democrat. [*Laughter*]

*The President.* All right. That's great. Can I read your slogan? "Willing and still able." Right here. Okay. Thank you all. Thank you very much.

Now, who's got the next question? Right in the back. Yes, sir.

### Environmental Policy

*Q.* I'm from Brookfield, Connecticut. And

I wanted to ask you, will you support the environmentalists in Rio de Janeiro that want to reduce the use of fluorocarbons and eventually stop them in the United States?

*The President.* We've already been in the lead of that. There was some new ozone information available the other day. It was the United States of America that took an early step to eliminate these CFC's that cause this terrible problem. Faced with this new information just last week, we sped up the timetable for the elimination. And I confidently expect Europe and the other countries to follow our lead. And the gentleman's pointing to an important conference, a U.N. conference that's going to be held in Brazil in June. And the United States will be in a leadership role there, not simply on the ozone layer but on the forests and everything else.

We've got a good, sound environmental record. We cannot keep some of the extremes in the environmental movement happy because I believe that sound environment can go hand-in-hand with reasonable growth. And in some corners of this country, particularly in the Northwest, there's some problems there where as many as 40,000 people can be thrown out of work by the excess of the environmental protection. So, we've got to find the balance, but I think we've got a very good record. And you put your finger on an important conference that will have the leadership and support from the United States.

Yes, sir, right back here.

### Federal Budget Deficit

*Q.* I was just wondering what you could do in your second term to eliminate the budget deficit, and in 1996, when you leave office, if it would be possible to have a balanced budget.

*The President.* I don't think it will be balanced by 1996. I do think a lot depends on what happens in the congressional elections next year. As Senator Rudman knows, we have fought—he's been way out front on trying to get the Federal deficit under control and keep spending under control. And remember, Congress appropriates every single dollar and instructs us how to spend every single dollar.

We're going to keep what we call the caps on spending. That 1990 budget deal was very controversial because there was a tax increase in it. People forget, however, there was spending caps put on what they call discretionary spending. A lot of spending the President has no control over, for example, Social Security and Social Security increases. And I don't want to fool with Social Security. I think people are entitled to receive those checks and have them on schedule.

But we will fight to keep those caps on. I have in my proposal a program to eliminate about 250 programs, just get rid of them altogether, and that's $4 billion right there. And the answer, and I'll be taking this to the country in the fall, is send us more people to the Congress like Bill Zeliff here, Senators like Rudman and Smith. And then I believe we can get the Congress to spend less and to get on with getting the deficit down.

As I look at the schedule ahead, I cannot pledge that it will be in balance by then. And if anybody does, ask them to show you how they're going to do it, given the entitlement programs that are on the books and need to be there, Medicare, Medicaid, Social Security. We're not going to be able to eliminate those. Change the health care, put in our health care plan; I think that will help. Keep the caps on; I think that will help.

Yes, ma'am.

### Domestic Policy

*Q.* It's a privilege to be in the same company with you and Mrs. Bush. Can you tell me, what is your response to those in your constituency who feel that you are too willing to compromise, especially when you know you have our support? And I don't mean any disrespect.

*The President.* No, that's a good question because I've heard a lot of flailing around up here in New Hampshire. Let me say something about—I've been in politics quite a while, as you know. I don't remember a campaign ever with quite this much negative campaigning. Maybe it's because most of it's aimed my way, coming out of a jillion Democrats over on one side and then a little out of the other side of the Republican spectrum.

I don't think I've been willing to compromise too much. I have had to veto 23 pieces of legislation, and the veto has been upheld every single time. I'll give you an example. I favored getting unemployment benefits extended for people, but the Democrats wanted to go ahead and just extend the benefits, forget the deficit, this guy's question. I said, "Look, I want to extend the benefits, but we're going to do it within the budget caps. If we're going to extend those benefits, let's find some offsets so we don't add to the mortgage of the future of these kids." And so, we have fought back bad legislation through the veto to get something good.

I'll give you another piece, and this is, I hear a little voice coming out of right field on this one. I'm for human rights. I'm for civil rights. I'm against discrimination. I am for civil rights. I did not want a quota bill. And we fought against it. I don't believe that quotas is the answer. We fought against it, beat it down, and finally got a progressive, forward-looking civil rights bill that gives equal opportunity in the workplace without setting up quotas. And then I hear lonely voices running around New Hampshire saying I'm compromising too much. That's the only way you can lead when you don't control the Congress. And I'm going to keep on fighting for a United States that is free of discrimination, free of anti-Semitism, and free to move forward in the workplace without going to quotas. There's a good example for it.

Right on the end. She's been very patient here.

### President's Family

*Q.* Is it hard being a grandfather and a President at the same time?

*The President.* There's one of the toughest questions. You can see the seams on that one coming across at Fenway Park, you know; you can read every seam. It's a good question, though, because I'll tell you something, it isn't as easy as you might think. We have four of our grandchildren live there, and one of the parents, my son Marvin, doesn't like public life. He wants his kids to grow up without having the cameras, all these things on them when they come out

and play on the White House lawn. And when they shed a tear, he wants to wipe it away in private, you know, so everybody doesn't see them crying.

Barbara and I try very hard to be good grandparents, and we stay in touch. And she's on the phone a lot. But I think you can do both. I think you can keep your family together. Of course, I salute Barbara Bush for what she does in there, encouraging them all the time. But you know you asked a very good question because there's a lot of times when you just wish you could do what everybody else does. But I wouldn't trade it because I've got a job to do, got a mission to fulfill, and I'm going to finish that. But then, I don't fear the future because after all that, I think we'll be better grandparents.

Right here in the middle. Yes, sir.

### Defense Budget Cuts

*Q.* I've got a two-part question. With the tremendous cuts in the defense budget, whether it's you or the Democratic candidates, there are going to be a lot of people displaced from employment. It's just the natural thing. One, how do you deal with that? I don't disagree with the cuts, but I'm concerned that they go too quick.

Secondly, there are some of us who aren't in the beginning of our career but in the second half of our career. And retraining isn't a quick solution. And if you're in the last 10, 15 years of your career, it can be devastating. How do you deal with that?

*The President.* Well, you asked a very important question. First, on the defense cuts. I am very pleased that the way we have conducted the foreign policy of this country permits us now to make sound defense cuts. We have won the cold war. Imperial communism, that's aggressive communism, wants to take over a neighbor that's on the ropes, is out of business. We've got people talking about peace in the Middle East. And we have different security responsibilities.

I have proposed a budget that has $50 billion of defense cuts over the next 5 years. I ask you, though, to listen to this gentleman because we cannot make reckless cuts in our defense. Last year at this time I was faced with a terribly important decision: Do we send your sons and your daughters into combat halfway around the world on the ground? One of the reasons I made the decision the way I did is, I knew that when we made that decision, these young men and women would have the best possible equipment, the best possible support, the best logistics behind them, the fastest transport, and the best way to move them.

And we did it, and they performed with magnificence. And that was Desert Storm that sent a message all across the world: The credibility of the United States means something. You see, Saddam Hussein never believed we'd do it. He was thinking back to Vietnam. He was thinking back to mixed signals out of the White House—wouldn't quite dare do it.

And I'd say to those who remember Desert Storm, it wasn't quite as simple as it seems today. Go back and look at the debate a year ago about whether you commit the sons and daughters of New Hampshire to war. And I did it, took the full responsibility, and it worked out. But one of the reasons I made the decision with confidence was because of the levels of defense spending and knowing that we'd be able to move anyplace, go quicker, have the best equipment, and see them succeed. That still must be the hallmark of our defense.

And my defense budget has the support of General Powell. It has the support of the Joint Chiefs of Staff. It isn't a political document. You listen to the raging debate around here from the extreme right and the extreme left, and all of them say, "We don't need to keep up our defenses. We don't need to keep NATO strong. We can cut another $50 billion or $100 billion." And one of them was up as high as $150 billion. That is crazy. And they can do the campaign rhetoric, but I have the responsibility as the President of the United States to keep this country strong. And I'm going to do it.

Now, the second one is much more complicated. The Defense Department does have some retraining programs. They've got some investment programs for, say, a Pease Air Force Base or whatever may happen in other installations around here. But I am troubled because I have no easy answer to it, frankly, for the guy that's this far along in his career, maybe he has 10 more to go, maybe he's been an aeronautical engineer who was laid off because we're not going to be able to keep the same level of spending.

All I know is, obviously, for those who are out of work, we've got to keep the benefits going until they find work, and that's a given. But you're talking about higher levels. You're talking about something more sophisticated. So, I would say job training and have it as responsive as possible to the kind of changing technology that we've got. And that, of course, means adult education. It means things of this nature. But it is not an easy question, and I don't want to oversimplify it. It's a heartbreaking one, too, but we've got to cope with it.

Yes, right back there.

*Discrimination*

*Q.* What are you going to do about the Ku Klux Klan?

*The President.* Ku Klux Klan? Can it. Speak out against it. And if anybody raises the specter of the Ku Klux Klan, you speak out against that ugly hatred. We're not a country of hating. We're not a country of bigots. We're not a country where we discriminate against people because of their religion or because of their race.

And they need the help of every kid here. If you see some guy in your class make some joke about somebody that might be of a different color or of a different religion, just turn on them. That's not us. That's not the United States.

And so, what the President can do about it, when you need legislation, why, you work for that. But in this one it's broader than that. You just stand up and say, "Look, we're against that." That's always been the hallmark of our country, particularly something as vicious as the Ku Klux Klan. I don't think it's on the rise at all.

I'll tell you something, though, this is a serious point on economics. As people start working and get thrown out of work, sometimes they might turn on or resort to bigotry or discrimination if another guy has a job. And we've got to guard against that. We've got some differences with Japan in terms of trade, but we don't need to resort on bashing each other. We need to work, as I'm trying to do, to open the markets but not try to discriminate or make some ugly recollection of discrimination. And so, stand up against it every chance you get.

*Capital Gains Tax*

*Q.* Hi, President Bush. Joe Birch. I haven't talked to you in about 4 years. You probably don't remember me, but I gave you some pretty hard questions last time when you were——

*The President.* Go ahead.

*Q.* I told you then I was thinking about voting for Kemp because I wasn't sure how conservative you are and whether or not you're going to defend the conservative principles that I believe in. And you convinced me then, and I did vote for you. And I wanted to tell you that I'm pretty much in the same position right now, except that now I'm thinking of Buchanan. Okay, there's a couple of things I don't like about him, about his views, I should say. One thing is, I don't like the isolationism, and I don't like what I consider to be the trade war implications that I don't like. I'm with you on that.

*The President.* Protection, you mean?

*Q.* Yes. But the thing I have a problem with is—it's got to do with education, but not in the sense you think. I don't think you're educating the rest of the people in this country as to the need for promoting business interest. Because business, as you know, has a lot to do with jobs.

Now, the capital gains issue is an issue that you're getting creamed on, left, right, and center, and it hurts the rest of us Republicans in a sense. Let me finish what I'm going to say, please. The capital gains issue, we're getting creamed, as a Republican, every time we turn around. I'm a Republican, and I don't have a capital gains problem because I don't make any money; that's not my problem. But my 10-year-old son here understands it better than 95 percent of the Democrats. I told him, "Hey, look, 35 years ago a farmer could have bought a farm for $50,000, sold it for $500,000 now." I said, "When I was your age a candy bar was a nickel; it's 10 times that now." And he said to me, he says, "Yeah, a comic book

was a dime, and now it's a buck and a half, $2.50." So the farmer that made a $450,000 gain, he didn't even keep up with inflation, and yet the people are calling him the one percent of the rich in the country. And they're killing us on that issue because they're making it like the Republicans are taking care of the rich, and we don't give a damn about the working of the business.

So, Buchanan's coming across with this. And I'm right on the fence with a half-a-dozen other voters, and I want to hear what you've got to say.

*The President.* I don't know. I'm a little unclear whether you favor a capital gains reduction. I do, and I've been fighting for it for a long time. And the answer is, get me more people in the Congress that will support it. I can't do any more. I'm getting creamed by the liberals saying, "You want a tax cut for the rich." A capital gains reduction will encourage investment. It will put ground under a person's home or their farm.

And so, I don't know where you're at. I am for it, and I'm going to continue to fight for it. And getting it done is a lot different than political, you know.

*Q.* I'm with that position. I'm with that position 100 percent. And the idea that Germany has none and Japan has none, it's understood. But the people aren't—they don't understand it. When you say capital gains, they say you're trying to help the rich.

*The President.* I agree with that. And I need help from the people to make them understand it and to get the Congress to pass it. We've had those bills before the Congress for 3 years; ask Warren Rudman, ask Bill Zeliff. So, we need the help there.

It's one thing to make campaign rhetoric, and it's another thing to get your sleeves rolled up and trying to support the President in getting it done. And that's my point to the voters in New Hampshire. We're not electing the guy who can make the most money out there or can demonstrate the quickest wit. We need somebody that can lead for these things and get them accomplished. And that brings me to say, help me with the United States Congress. That's where the problem is on getting this economy turned around with our budget package right now, with capital gains, with other things like this homeowners tax credit.

You know, a family trying to buy a first home, our proposal says, $5,000 tax credit. Congress must pass that by March 20th. Now if you feel upset about it, roll up your sleeves and get on the horn to the Congress or go down there and talk to them. I think you can do it; you look tough. [*Laughter*]

All right. Right over here. Good to see you again.

*Education Reform*

*Q.* Four years ago you promised to be our education President. And the America 2000 is a great set of goals. But can you think of one thing you've actually done to move us toward that goal here in Hollis, New Hampshire?

*The President.* Yes, I've gotten my wife to demonstrate her concern by reading to the children. And if you think that's not important, you're wrong. Because I had the mayors from the National League of Cities come into the White House, and you know what their main concern was? Urban problems. The mayor of Los Angeles, no flaming Republican, I might add, and a good man, and then a mayor from a small North Carolina town, a Republican, all came together, and they said the biggest problem is the dissolution of the American family.

And Barbara's out there, and I'm trying to help as best I can, saying, "You've got to hold the family together. You've got to participate. You've got to read."

We have passed for the first time, gotten the country together on six major national education goals. That's never been done before. That would not dictate to Hollis. That wouldn't tell them what the curriculum has to be. But these are the six goals, and let me just recite them because I do think it's a very strong program. And I do think we're making progress on it.

We need to go forward now and have every kid ready to learn. That means more Head Start. I have increased the levels for Head Start exponentially. We have it now budgeted so that every 4-year-old will get Head Start. You may not think that's progress on education; I think it is superb progress on education.

I think the high school graduation rate should increase to at least 90 percent. And we're making headway on that one.

The third one, American students will be competent in core subjects. You'd have to ask the teachers how they're doing on that one, but I think it's one where we've got to make better progress; I'll concede that.

U.S. students will be first in the world in science and math. And we're moving on that direction, the highest level of research that this country has ever had. And I believe that will help us achieve that education goal.

Every American adult will be literate. I'm trying to show the way there by learning to work a computer. And that's not just show business; it is suggesting to the American people we must have adult literacy. And that can help in this question of transferability over here.

And then the last one, every school in America will be free and safe from drugs and crime. Made progress; not near enough.

So, I would argue that we're making headway, but I would certainly agree with you that we haven't made enough headway. But I'm going to keep on fighting because I believe this record is a good one on education. And it's far better than what I hear coming out of left field out there, saying, "Hey, the answer is for the Federal Government to set the curriculum and the Federal Government to come in and control these programs." That is not going to get to the educational excellence that these six goals demand.

Way in the middle.

*Education Funding*

*Q.* I am on the school board here for the Hollis/Brookline high school and junior high schools. We are a small town, and special ed costs right now are escalating all over, including in our small town. And we have to be concerned about the fact that although the costs are escalating, the Federal funding is going away. And it's hurting us because our tax bill is the only thing that's supporting it. Think about Federal funding sometime.

*The President.* I will. Federal funding, incidentally, for the Department of Education is up. It's up considerably from where I came into office. But you know what a problem is? A problem is that Congress still wants to quote, mandate, unquote, the benefits. Hollis may have a problem where, better have more adult education. Hollis may—which is the one you mentioned?

*Q.* Special ed.

*The President.* Special ed. Hollis may need more on special ed. It is my feeling that block grants should be used instead of these mandates out of some subcommittee in Washington, DC. And if you need more for special ed, it ought to be here in a block grant for the people of Hollis and the Governor of New Hampshire to decide, rather than some subcommittee chairman that's been there 30 years on the Democratic side in Washington.

So, we're going to fight for the block grant approach and continue to try to do it, and that, I believe, will answer some of this problem, not all.

Yes, right here. Yes, sir.

*The Economy*

*Q.* President Bush, with all due respect to your opposition on the Republican side, personally I like Pat Buchanan on television, and I like George Bush in the Oval Office. Just a question I have. I know you have a package before Congress now, but beyond that, however long it takes to get through, beyond that, what type of things are you doing or do you plan to do to try to help the economy with jobs? I'm a senior manager, and I'm facing laying off many people at the company that I work at.

*The President.* The investment bill we've got before the Congress I believe really will work. We fought—and I can understand Joe's frustration—we fought for some of these incentives, changes in the IRA's, capital gains, for 2 years and have just not gotten them through Congress. Now there's enough awareness there that I believe the package we have that includes those two things, also includes the first-time tax break for homeowners, plus several others—there's seven points in it—will help stimulate the economy immediately.

We have a family tax credit that's in the overall bill. It's a longer term; it has to be done by this year, but it's not in those seven

"incentivizations", you might say.

The National Home Builders came up here to New Hampshire the other day and announced how many jobs they think this would create, just the adoption of the homeowners credit would create, and then get real estate leading the way out of this recession. So, I think we've got a good, sound economic program, but Congress has the votes. And I've got to change the Congress.

And I understand there are a lot of people out there a lot more charismatic than I am, but a lot of them don't have to make the tough decisions either. Heck, if that were the case, Phil Donahue might be President of the United States if you needed somebody to be out there on television—*[laughter]*—or some of the others, reporters we've got around here who are very good in their field, but I'm not sure we want them for President.

So, I'll keep doing my best. You know, I'll say to these kids here—and this may sound a little gratuitous or silly, but it's not—you go back to think what your parents are telling you, and they're saying: Do your best. Try your hardest. Don't let the critics get you down if somebody disagrees with you in your class. Work your hardest for what you believe in. And that's what I'm trying to do. And I'm going to keep on trying to do it.

And I've had to make tough decisions. Good God, a year ago, I was. I thought about that in church today. It wasn't an easy decision to commit some of your neighbors here to war. But you've got to do your best, and you've got to take the shots that come your way and say, "Hey, that goes with the territory."

But I believe in this country. I believe that we are good and decent and honorable. I believe we are the leaders of the free world. I believe that our workers can compete with anybody. And now we've got to get the programs to free that up and get them going. So don't let the pessimists get you down. We are the United States of America, and we got something moving. And now we've got to get this through so the people in New Hampshire are lifted up. That's the way I approach it.

We can hear you. I'll repeat it.

### Health Care

*Q.* Can you tell us a little bit about the health insurance plan?

*The President.* The health insurance plan. And again, it's not a campaign plan; it is up there for congressional consideration. It is built on this basis, building on this basis: We have the best quality health care in the world, the best. If not, why would neighbors from far and wide come to this country for specialized, strong health care? So, I want to change it in the sense that I want everybody to have access, everybody, rich or poor, to have access to insurance. And our program is built on that.

A person that doesn't have a job or is impoverished gets this insurance, they get the insurance. Middle-income people, they get deductions to permit them to put less money in the Government and more to get the insurance with. It is built on access, and that will keep us from turning to a state-run system.

I hear a lot of campaign rhetoric in New Hampshire about let's have a nationalized plan. What they mean there is a plan where the Government makes all the decisions. And that is wrong. And our plan will cost about $100 billion. We've sent up page after page of how to pay for it. But one of the ways is to cut down on these frivolous lawsuits that compel our doctors to go to all kinds of duplication in their care. Too many lawsuits, and too much liability for these people.

So the answer is to keep what works and build on what works and make insurance available and have access to all. And that's where the program——

Which one of you two want to ask this, reluctantly, but go ahead.

### Abortion

*Q.* What do you have to say to the women of America who feel that they're being reduced to breeders by your antichoice stand?

*The President.* Being introduced to what? I didn't hear the question.

*Q.* Breeders by your antichoice stand.

*The President.* Breeders?

*Q.* Yes.

*The President.* I've never looked at love between a man and a woman as a breeding proposition. I recognize there are differences on this question, but I happen to favor life. And I am appalled at the numbers of abortions that are going on. They are exponentially rising, and it's a tragedy. Some people use it as a birth control device. So, I just have a difference, an honest difference of opinion on that one. I'm not going to change my views.

But I certainly think the way you phrase it—I don't think people should look at affection between a man and a woman as that kind of ugly thing. When you have a relationship, I hope it's based on something that has more affection. Maybe love, we ought to try that one on for size; maybe a little more education than we've had in trying to teach people that indiscriminate sex is not good. And we're having an awful lot of disease because of indiscriminate sex. And we have a lot of broken families, kids that nobody knows their name. And we've got to find ways to strengthen the family.

All these things I think we could agree on, whether we agree on that question or not, of whether you want abortion or whether you happen to favor life and adoption, as I do.

### Line-Item Veto

*Q.* Mr. President, could you comment on how you might motivate Congress to adopt the line-item veto? One of the concerns clearly is that the budget needs to be controlled, and that might be a message.

*The President.* Well, the question is, for those who didn't hear it here, how do you motivate the Congress to go for the line-item veto?

One, I strongly support it. Forty-three Governors have it. I don't think you've got it in New Hampshire, but 43 Governors across the State have it, across the country. And it gives the executives the chance to make the tough decision. So again it goes back to Joe's question: How do you get it done? And the only way I know to get it done is to keep advocating it and to get the kind of people in Washington that would support it.

And I'm going to keep on doing that because—I don't believe it would solve this guy's question, or lady's question, whoever asked it originally, about the balanced budget. I'm not suggesting that there are enough items you could hack out of there unilaterally to do that overnight. But it would make a tremendous job.

I'm all for Lawrence Welk. Lawrence Welk is a wonderful man—he used to be, or was, or wherever he is now, bless him. [*Laughter*] But we don't need $700,000 for a Lawrence Welk Museum when we've got tough times and people in New Hampshire are hurting. And there's the kind of thing that could be line-itemed out of the budget, and I think we need it. We really do need it.

Right over there in the middle. Yes, sir.

*Accessibility of the President*

*Q.* ——I was wondering if you ever considered meeting groups of people one-on-one—[*inaudible*]—with this problem of the different groups. I know you have a staff and can't do everything, but local people—[*inaudible*]—will help you win the election.

*The President.* Interesting suggestion. His point is, he said not a lot of people would want to have my job, but a lot of people would know exactly how to run it. I think that was the premise. But have you considered, he says, meeting one-on-one with individual people? And the Cabinet, he says, can do their job, but that may not be as representative as you get it down closer to the grassroots. Is that a fair repetition?

Not bad, not a bad question at all. Good observation. I do get a ton of mail. And people say, "Well, you don't understand the heartbreak out there." I really believe I do. I don't think you have to have an experience yourself to understand it. Do you want me to put this on a real personal basis for you? Barbara and I lost a child. Some people here haven't done that. I wouldn't suggest that if that experience hadn't come to your family, that you would be less concerned about a neighbor who went through that. We care about it. We are in touch. I read the mail. I hear a lot of cries from the heart from people—many, many ways. Friends reporting of neighbors out of work,

whatever it may be.

I don't know how to implement what you've suggested. We've done some homework since we've been privileged to live in the White House. When Abraham Lincoln was President he lived right on the second floor of the White House, and he had his bedroom down at one end of the hall, same place where Barbara and I have the bedroom now. And the people could come up and wander into the White House and say, "Hey, we want to see Abe," and give him their view. It was pretty good. I mean, it was a good system in a sense.

Now you've got some problems from that, most of them of a security nature. You've got a lot of nuts out there. You've got a lot of crazy people wandering around that you can't take a chance with.

Let me think about it. I don't know whether there's a better way to kind of just pluck a name out of the phone book or get some guy that was thrown out of work, for example, to come there as an individual with no staff and no preparation. Maybe there is because I'm not going to shoot it down as a lousy idea.

Go ahead.

*Q.* [*Inaudible*]

*The President.* I'll tell you how we do a lot of that is through the different groups that represent these people. But that's not maybe as good as what you're suggesting here. There may be a way we can do more of that. You go to these hospitals and talk to an AIDS family, or something, you get a better feel. And we do a fair amount of that. But maybe there's more. I mean, I think it's a good suggestion.

They tell me we've got to go, all nervous-looking people over here, because we're heading on. But listen, thank you very much. And may I ask you to vote for me on Tuesday. We need your support. Thank you very, very much.

*Note: The President spoke at 11:45 a.m. at Hollis/Brookline High School. In his remarks, he referred to Kathryn M. Wienslaw, cochairman of the Bush-Quayle campaign in New Hampshire.*

# Statement by Press Secretary Fitzwater on the President's Meeting With President Mircea Snegur of Moldova
*February 18, 1992*

The President and Moldovan President Mircea Snegur met for 20 minutes today in the Oval Office. It was the first meeting between the two leaders. The President reiterated U.S. recognition of Moldovan independence and the two Presidents agreed that the U.S. and Moldova will establish diplomatic relations and exchange Ambassadors in the near future. The President also expressed our commitment to continue U.S. humanitarian and technical assistance to Moldova.

# Statement on the New Hampshire Presidential Primary Victory
*February 18, 1992*

I am delighted tonight to have won the New Hampshire primary.

Mindful of New Hampshire's proud history in selecting Presidents, I am indebted to all those in the State who voted for me, and my special thanks go to our able campaign leaders and to the volunteers who worked so hard.

This election was far closer than many had predicted. I think the opponents on both sides reaped the harvest of discontent with the pace of New Hampshire's economy. I understand the message of dissatisfaction. My most immediate task has been to get Congress to enact some very sensible, sound proposals that will help get this Nation's economy going forward.

The message of tonight is that Americans are concerned about the future. I have the right answers, and I will take my case to the voters in the next 8½ months. The goal of my campaign is to win reelection in November. I will campaign vigorously in those States whose primaries lie ahead. I am confident of winning our party's nomination and the election.

I want to thank the voters of New Hampshire, as well as Governor Gregg, Senators Rudman and Smith, Congressman Zeliff, Hugh Gregg, Gordon Humphrey, and the rest of my leadership team.

Once again, I am pleased to have finished first in New Hampshire. Now, on to the South.

# Presidential Determination No. 92–15—Memorandum on Export-Import Bank Services for South Africa
*February 18, 1992*

*Memorandum for the Secretary of State*

*Subject:* Determination to Permit Export-Import Bank Financing for Exports to the Government of South Africa or Its Agencies

Pursuant to the authority vested in me by section 2(b)(9) of the Export-Import Bank Act of 1945, as amended (12 U.S.C. 635(b)(9)) (the "Act"), I hereby:

1) determine that significant progress toward the elimination of apartheid has been made in South Africa;

2) authorize and direct you to transmit to the Congress a statement describing and explaining this determination.

You are further authorized and directed to publish this memorandum in the *Federal Register*.

GEORGE BUSH

*[Filed with the Office of the Federal Register, 4:43 p.m., February 27, 1992]*

*Note: This memorandum was released by*  the Office of the Press Secretary on February 19.

## Presidential Determination No. 92–16—Memorandum on Assistance for Angola
*February 18, 1992*

*Memorandum for the Secretary of State*
*Subject:* Foreign Assistance for Angola

Pursuant to the authority vested in me by section 614(a)(1) of the Foreign Assistance Act of 1961, as amended, 22 U.S.C. 2364(a)(1), I hereby:

(1) determine that it is important to the security interests of the United States to furnish assistance described in paragraphs (2) and (3) below notwithstanding section 512 of the Foreign Operations, Export Financing, and Related Programs Appropriations Act, 1991 (Public Law 101–513); section 512 as applied to fiscal year 1992 pursuant to the Joint Resolution making continuing appropriations for fiscal year 1992, and for other purposes (Public Law 102–145); other acts making appropriations for foreign operations, export financing, and related programs for fiscal year 1992; and any other provision of law within the scope of section 614(a)(1);

(2) authorize the furnishing of up to $1.5 million of Economic Support Funds made available for fiscal year 1991 for support for democratization in Angola; and

(3) authorize the furnishing of up to $13 million from funds made available for the Development Fund for Africa for fiscal year 1992 for support for democratization in Angola and to address other pressing needs in Angola in the period until elections are completed.

You are hereby directed to transmit this determination to the Congress and to publish it in the *Federal Register.*

GEORGE BUSH

*[Filed with the Office of the Federal Register, 4:44 p.m., February 27, 1992]*

*Note: This memorandum was released by the Office of the Press Secretary on February 19.*

## Memorandum Delegating Authority to Report on the Rebuilding of Kuwait
*February 18, 1992*

*Memorandum for the Secretary of Commerce*

*Subject:* Delegation Reporting Obligations Pursuant to Section 606(f) of the Persian Gulf Conflict Supplemental Authorization and Personnel Benefits Act of 1991

By the authority vested in me as President by the Constitution and the laws of the United States of America, including section 301 of title 3 of the United States Code, I hereby delegate to you the functions vested in me by section 606(f) of the Persian Gulf Conflict Supplemental Authorization and Personnel Benefits Act of 1991 (Public Law 102–25, 105 Stat. 111) relating to periodic reports to the Congress with respect to contracting for the rebuilding of Kuwait.

The functions delegated by this memorandum shall be exercised in coordination with the Secretary of State, the Army Corps

of Engineers, and such other executive departments and agencies as you may deem
appropriate.

You are authorized and directed to publish this memorandum in the *Federal Register.*

GEORGE BUSH

[*Filed with the Office of the Federal Register, 2:43 p.m., February 28, 1992*]

*Note: This memorandum was released by
the Office of the Press Secretary on February 19.*

# Exchange With Reporters in Knoxville, Tennessee
*February 19, 1992*

*The President.* Well, I'm sure people
would like to ask questions about the election, so fire away.

*New Hampshire Primary Results*

*Q.* Mr. President, did you feel that the
voters in New Hampshire, with the message
of dissatisfaction, were expressing dissatisfaction with you? And what are you going
to change?

*The President.* Well, I'm not sure of that.
I think there was a lot of pounding on me,
five Democrats, one Republican, and a certain editorial policy up there that for 9
weeks did nothing but hit me, with no defense on my part. Some of these Congressmen with me today said, "Hey, since when
has an 18-point victory been considered
anything other than a landslide?"

Now, I'm not saying that I wouldn't have
liked to do better. But I'm satisfied with the
results. And now we're down here, and
we're going to take this guy on in every
single State. I'd have to do a little definition
of who it is because all I did was lay back
and get hammered by these Democrats and
to some degree by Pat. And so, it's a new
ball game, and we're coming out strong.

I must say that I feel good today. I
thought I might be a little down because of
the earliest reports that some of you all put
on the air and some of your interpretations.
Now, with an 18-point win, most people
say, "Hey, that's not bad." Try to sell some
guy over here that an 18-point victory in a
political race isn't anything other than a
good victory.

So, we're going to go forward now. The
other thing I've got to do, though, I do
think I have to do better, is get this message to the country and particularly these
southern States, if you want an election contest, about what we're trying to do to help
people that are hurting, what we're trying
to do in the Congress to enlist support to
get our sound proposals through and beat
back the Democratic proposals.

And the last point is, it's a little ironic
that the Democratic frontrunner, and could
well be the party standard bearer, opposes
what the Democrats in the House of Representatives are doing. I mean, they're out of
step with their own leader at this point. So,
there are mixed signals. But look, I've been
in tough fights before, Rita [Rita Beamish,
Associated Press], and I'm looking forward
to this one.

*Q.* Do you admire Tsongas, Mr. President?

*The President.* I'm not admiring him. He's
knocking my socks off, and so are the other
four, and so is the other candidate. But
we're in a new territory now. If you don't
believe me, ask these guys.

*Q.* Was this the result, in part, of waiting
for the State of the Union Address to outline what you wanted to do to help the
economy? Do you think you might have
done better in New Hampshire if you had
started fighting with the Democrats on
these issues last year, as some urged you to
do?

*The President.* Well, I don't know. That's
a good question, Brit [Brit Hume, ABC
News]. But it didn't lighten up after I did
have the State of the Union Message, and so
I didn't notice a change there. I noticed
them trying to be very critical of that. I

can't say no to that, but I don't know enough about it, how it would have worked the other way.

## The Economy

*Q.* Is this a sign that having a plan, however plausible, is simply not going to be enough this year, that you're going to have to have not a plan for a recovery but an actual recovery?

*The President.* Well, I think there's good signs about recovery. I mean, I kept pointing out the interest rates are down; inflation is down. Today, housing starts—I don't know if you've seen it—took a rather dramatic kick up. I think people feel that the economy is poised for recovery.

And let's remember, New Hampshire people were hurting. New Hampshire was disproportionately affected by recession. Now, you talk to the people in Tennessee and yes, some people here have problems, but generally the State is upbeat. They feel we can whip these problems.

And so, I've got to get this—what I really want to do is get something done in terms of stimulating the economy. That first-time homebuyers credit is very important, and the whole rest of our incentives, capital gains. It's interesting, again, to note that the Democratic frontrunner is talking about capital gains also.

So, we've got to do better getting it through Congress. And I'm going to just keep fighting. I'll tell you another thing I'm going to do. I'm not taking anything for granted. I'm going to stay out here across this country—I've been in tough fights before—roll up my sleeves and go after them.

## Presidential Primaries

*Q.* Are you going to emphasize your conservative credentials now?

*The President.* I think I've got them, and I think, yes, they're clearly there. And I think most people understand that. But we might have to define the opponent. I've been very kind and gentle. I'll still be kind, and I'm now debating how gentle to be——

*Q.* What do you think the people should know about Buchanan?

*The President.* ——because I'm a little bit tired—well, I'll give you an example. I'll

give you an example. This State of Tennessee had 6,700 reservists and guardsmen volunteer. One community of 1,000 had 18 people. This is the Volunteer State. People are still very proud of the fact that this—of Desert Storm. And there's a national pride there; there's a pride in having a strong America. That's my position: a strong America and having led a very triumphant and very important war over there. So, I'll be taking that message, along with the message of economic change, economic hope. Mine's not going to be a pessimistic message, and it's for certain things.

*Q.* Sir, was it a political mistake——

*The President.* I'll be with you in just one second. You're the next in line. Get this one, and then right there.

## Tax Cut

*Q.* Was it a political mistake to hold back on the $500 personal exemption increase, to put that in your long-term package? Whether it made economic sense or not, was it a political blunder?

*The President.* Well, I don't think it's a political blunder. It was grossly misinterpreted. The question was whether—the opposition was saying it wasn't in there at all. And I want that whole package passed, and I'd like it passed now. But what I have said, and said in the State of the Union, here's some short-term things; let's get those passed now. And here's the bigger package; let's pass that this year. But I don't think it's a blunder. I think there was gross misrepresentation.

Charles [Charles Bierbauer, CNN]. Randall [Randall Pinkston, CBS News], you're next in line right after him.

## Presidential Primaries

*Q.* Mr. President, you say you need to define Pat Buchanan. How do you define him?

*The President.* Well, we're debating that. You just tell the truth. You just tell the truth.

*Q.* What would that be?

*The President.* Well, I don't think Social Security ought to be voluntary. That's the Bush position.

*Q.* How does that define Pat Buchanan?

*The President.* Well, people go ask him what he thinks about it.

*Q.* Don't you risk having a divided party in the fall if you attack him hard?

*The President.* That's a danger, but he doesn't worry about that. I've been attacked hard. I think I've seen that in—but it's much better to stay on the positive plane. I'll point out what I'm for. I was for what Tennessee did in supporting Desert Storm. I am for protecting those on Social Security. And there's a wide array of things that we can point out that are positive. And then you all can make the interpretation.

That's the kind side. It might not be as gentle as just forgetting about it altogether. But I was a little sick and tired of getting pounded by five Democrats day-in and day-out, not responding, and similarly, by the Republican challenger whom I beat by 18 points. And I'm going to stay, you know, taking a positive message across the country.

*Mr. Fitzwater.* We're running a little bit behind, Mr. President.

### The Economy

*Q.* ——yesterday's results, Mr. President, do you believe that it is still possible to meet that March 20th deadline, or are all the bets off now, and Congress is just going to dig in and make sure that you don't get any kind of economic growth package?

*The President.* When their standard bearer, the guy up front, has the same program in terms of what he thinks needs to be done for the economy, really essentially a Republican program, I would think they'd take a look at that. The voters up there on their side seemed to give some endorsement to that economic plan that called for a capital gains reduction and stood out against this 25-cents-a-day tax cut that's going to raise everybody's taxes over the years.

And so, I'm not going to give up on trying to get the Congress to move. We're going to stay in there and fight to get the Congress to do what they should have done a long time ago. And I think people in this State know that the Democrats that control the Congress are out of step with the American people. So, I've got to get that message across a little more clearly.

One more, and then I've got to go.

*Q.* It sounds like you're endorsing the Tsongas economic plan.

*The President.* No, he's endorsed our plan.

### Presidential Primaries

*Q.* Do you think Buchanan will be finished after Super Tuesday?

*The President.* I'm not making any predictions. That's the kinder side; I'm going to stay out of that. I'm going to just focus on what I think is best for this country and proclaiming, hey, 58–40, a lot different than I heard some of you guys talking about earlier last evening when, I admit, I was a little tense. Little tense, John [John Cochran, NBC News], with a couple of reports I heard there. But now when the results are in, people across the country are saying, "You mean somebody is going to say that 58–40 is not a good victory?" And you've got a lot of talking heads out there that don't agree with that, but let's see how they try that one on in Tennessee. I think they're going to say that's pretty good.

*Q.* Are the gloves off, Mr. Bush?

*The President.* No, no, the gloves are still on. Gloves are still on. Gloves are still on.

*Q.* ——running against an incumbent President?

*The President.* Do you remember the Reagan-Ford race?

*Q.* And what did Ford do in November?

*The President.* No, don't worry about November.

*Note: The exchange began at 9:50 a.m. on the President's arrival at McGhee-Tyson Airfield.*

# Remarks at a Cooperative Research and Development Agreement Signing Ceremony in Oak Ridge, Tennessee
*February 19, 1992*

Thank you for that welcome. Well, thank you so much. What a beautiful day in Tennessee. Thank you all. Let me just first start off by recognizing two who have been introduced, two members of my Cabinet, both should be familiar to you all. First, the Secretary of Energy, Jim Watkins, who's doing an outstanding job not just in the field of energy but in education and so many other things, standing here next to me. And I heard that nice reception for the hometown kid—[*laughter*]—but we refer to him as the Secretary of Education, the distinguished former Governor Lamar Alexander. And you talk about a man who's doing a great job for his country.

I know that this is the district of a very distinguished Congresswoman, Marilyn Lloyd, who couldn't be with us. But I want to re-present three with whom I work very closely in the Congress, Congressmen Jimmy Quillen and Don Sundquist and Jimmy Duncan, who are also right down here on the end. And my thanks to Al Trivelpiece, the Director of Oak Ridge, and to Joe Coors, who's been introduced, of Coors structural ceramics. He just handed me a ceramic putter. [*Laughter*] And he said if this fails, and it will, I'll use it as a hammer. [*Laughter*] You know what that's all about.

But this agreement today is one that I hope to see repeated across the Nation. This agreement, that I'm going to witness, combines in one place the resources of Government with the energy and inventiveness of private enterprise. And you're pointing our country toward the next American century.

In the old era, now ending, many of America's best scientists were engaged in winning the cold war. Well, the new era will free up those priceless talents to concentrate on the technologies of tomorrow, improving productivity and guaranteeing our long-term prosperity. We will transform the arsenal of democracy into the engine of economic growth. It's going to take the right kind of investments, the kind we've been making for 3 years. And our future

economic competitiveness demands that we invest in an area in which we've always led the world, and I'm talking about something you all know a lot about, research and development.

Our challenge now is to put more of these incredible technologies to work for the America of this decade and beyond. We've been busy sweeping away the obstacles that inhibit the transfer of technology from the Government over to the private enterprise sector. Two years ago, I signed a bill that allows private industry to take advantage of Government research. And there are 675 public-private agreements that are active today, 675.

And today, we witness another one. Coors Ceramics Company and the Oak Ridge National Lab are going to attack one of the obstacles to wider use of durable, efficient, and lightweight ceramic parts: machining ceramics without destroying their desirable qualities. Oak Ridge's high temperature materials lab, a world-class advanced materials testing facility, will be working with American industry to take the world lead in making precision ceramic parts. Ceramic parts will be vital to the longer lasting and more efficient engines of the future. And we're in a race with other nations for this multibillion dollar market, and we will get there first with the best products, thanks to the hard work of people right here, the imagination of these scientists.

And let me make this clear to the rest of the country, something that you all know: Getting there first, in this regard, means jobs, American jobs. Now, Coors moved here 2 years ago precisely to take advantage of the expertise and high-tech facilities here at Oak Ridge. And that means 85 new jobs here because of this partnership. And this is just one of the 25 cooperative agreements at this lab alone.

One of the reasons I'm here is to help get the message out. Our national technology initiative, which Admiral Watkins is spearheading and helping us spearhead, is bringing Government officials together with private businesses to let them know what Government can offer in technology. We must move these developments out of the laboratory and into the marketplace and create more American jobs. And that's what this is about.

I'm very, very pleased to be here with you all today. So without further ado, I'll be pleased to witness the signing of the agreement. I believe that's going to take place. Here it is. Thank you all very much.

*Note: The President spoke at 10:52 a.m. at the Oak Ridge National Laboratory. Alvin Trivelpiece, Director of the Laboratory, and Joe Coors, Jr., president and chairman of Coors Ceramics Co., signed the agreement.*

## Remarks to Community and Business Leaders in Knoxville, Tennessee
*February 19, 1992*

Thank you for such a warm welcome back. And thank you, Senator Baker, my esteemed friend, for that overly generous introduction.

May I extend my greetings to another longtime friend, Mayor Victor Ashe, who is doing a great job here in this community, and to thank all of the other Knoxville community leaders here today. And I'm not sure that that description includes the marvelous music we've had, but my thanks to those from the Vols over here who provided some upbeat sounds. And I also want to single out with great pride two Cabinet members who are with me here today: First, our Secretary of Energy, Jim Watkins, doing a superb job, with us over here, Jim; and then, of course, one that you all know so well, Lamar Alexander, our Secretary of Education.

You may know that Lamar, as part of his mission to promote lifetime learning in keeping with one of our education goals, one is never too old to learn, convinced me to learn how to use a computer. It's really paid off. I can now make typographical errors twice as fast as I used to on the typewriter.

And may I also single out three Members of the Tennessee congressional delegation, Jimmy Duncan, Jimmy Quillen, and Don Sundquist, all three doing a fantastic job for us in Washington. And a very heartfelt thanks, quick thanks, to the people at the Knoxville Chamber of Commerce who helped pull this magnificent event together,

Larry Martin and Jack Hammontree and Susan Shay. And I'm pleased that John Waters of the TVA could join us here today.

I feel very much at home, and I'm delighted to be here. Tennessee is a State with a special significance for me. After all, it's the Volunteer State. And during Operation Desert Storm you proved it all over again. So let me take this opportunity, thinking back a year just almost from this minute, when the ground war started, let me take this opportunity to thank the 6,700 Tennessee reservists and National Guard who were called up for Desert Storm and who served this State and served this country with such distinction.

It's a pleasure to be here in Knoxville, for what you've done here is a model for the Nation. This city combines in one place the enthusiasm of cutting-edge research, the resources of Government, and then the energy, the dynamic energy of the private enterprise. You are pointing our country toward the next American century.

We stand today at what I think most people would agree is a pivot point in history, at the end of one era and the beginning of another. As imperial communism died and as the clouds of the cold war part, America stands alone, the undisputed leader of the world. The old era demanded great sacrifices of our country; we met them, each and every one of them. But the new era opens up to us limitless possibilities, fresh challenges of the kind that have always brought out the best in America.

For the short term, of course, our challenge is to fire up the economy. I've put together a two-part plan, starting with a short-term package, seven commonsense steps to spur investment and create jobs. With inflation down and interest rates lower than they've been in 20 years, our plan offers incentives to business to buy equipment, upgrade their plants, and start hiring again. It offers a real boost to the housing market, often at the forefront of economic recovery, with a $5,000 tax credit for first-time homebuyers.

I have asked the Congress to pass this plan by March 20th. You may have heard about other tax plans floated up on Capitol Hill. The House Democrats are offering 25 cents a day, literally, in income tax relief in exchange for cuts in Medicare, student loans, farm payments, and true to form, a large permanent tax increase. That plan will deepen the deficit by $30 billion and cost jobs as well. That is a lose-lose proposition if ever there was one. Here in Knoxville, let me again remind the United States Congress: We are a month and a day away from the deadline. Help your country. Put politics aside for just those 31 days that it takes. No more games. Pass our plan and get this economy moving again all across the country.

But then we must look forward, beyond the short-term into the next century. Believe it or not, looking forward has become a more radical notion than it sounds. For some quarters, we hear the dim voice of defeatism, that tin trumpet sounding retreat. We're told that our future lies in turning away from the world, pulling down the shades, and hoping that the rest of the world just goes away. Well, don't be fooled by the tough talk and the patriotic bluster. Protectionism comes from fear, fear that American workers can't compete, fear that American ingenuity is spent, fear that we must turn away from the world because we can no longer lead the world. That's not the future that I see for the United States of America. The America of the future must embrace challenges, not cut and run. It must put back the frontiers of knowledge and technology and use our great strengths of individual initiative and determination. If we do, the America of the future will com-

pete, and it will win.

This century has taught us many lessons. But above them all stands an overarching truth: If America is to succeed economically at home, we must lead economically abroad. Now, our leadership ensures markets for American products and jobs for American workers. And it gives us room to spread our wings and show the world what we can do. Let us never forget: Our national symbol is the eagle; it is not the ostrich.

Each generation of Americans makes an implicit compact with the generations that follow. We pledge that their opportunities will be greater than ours. Our generation will make good on that pledge but only if we continue to lead the world.

So for the last 3 years, my administration has been laying the foundation for America's continued leadership. We've approached this pivot point in history, this moment of unparalleled opportunity, with a positive strategy to build on the enduring strengths of the American people, our capacity for hard work, our cutting-edge technology, our willingness to take risks. To continue as the world's economic leader we must excel in two vital areas: education and technology. That's where our future lies. Our strategy must target both, and it does.

American science is the best in the world. We've got to make sure that the same is true of American science education. Tomorrow's marketplace will demand workers highly skilled in math and science. Tennesseans know the importance of that, and I thank you for lending me your Governor and U.T. president, Lamar Alexander. He's on the cutting edge. He's out front in trying to revolutionize the schools in this country. Through our America 2000 education strategy, we're getting that education message to the rest of the country.

Working with the Nation's Governors, Secretary Alexander and I set six ambitious education goals, done on a bipartisan basis, wasn't Republican, Democrat, liberal, conservative. The Governors came together under Lamar's leadership, and we came up with these goals. And one of the most important ones was this: By the year 2000, American students will be first in the world in math and science. The budget that I've recently submitted to Congress calls for more than $2 billion in math and science education programs. That's more than a 120-percent increase over the past 3 years for programs at the precollege level.

Just 2 years ago, when I was last here in your wonderful city, I mentioned that our Energy Secretary, Jim Watkins, had joined up with U.T. and Oak Ridge to start a new math and science academy for America's teachers. Once again, Tennessee set the pace for our country. To better train teachers, we plan to double the number of math and science instructors receiving federally assisted in-depth instruction in their field. This year, almost half the Nation's precollege math and science teachers will receive some federally funded training.

In the old era now ending, many of our best scientists helped America win the cold war. The new era will free up those priceless talents to transform the arsenal of democracy into the engine of economic growth. That is the mission, that is the challenge of the nineties.

It will take the right kind of investments, the kind we've been making for years, for 3 years. And these have been tough decisions. This year, I've asked for a freeze on discretionary domestic spending—got to do that for the overall budget—which means that any increases have to be the result of hard thinking about priorities. Well, we've done the hard thinking, and we've made a fundamental decision. Our future economic competitiveness demands that we invest today in one of our greatest strengths, research and development. And I've asked for a record investment in R&D, $76 billion next year alone.

Now, let me give you just a few examples of what this means. This year we're investing $803 million to assist private enterprise in the development of a high-performance computing system 1,000 times more powerful than today's computer. And such a system will forecast droughts and hurricanes, design better aircraft, unlock the riddle of the genome.

We're investing more than $1 billion for research in energy technologies to improve energy efficiency, nuclear fusion, clean coal technologies, and alternatives to petroleum. We're investing almost $1.5 billion in transportation R&D. To relieve our overburdened highways and airports, we're stimulating research in new transportation technologies such as intelligent vehicle-highway systems and high-speed rail. Some of you unintelligent drivers beware; you may be replaced.

We're increasing investment in biotechnology research for a total of more than $4 billion, so that we continue to lead the world in conquering disease and relieving world hunger. Now, this research can pay dividends undreamed of just a few years ago, not only in health care but in manufacturing, energy, and in environmental protection. One recent development: microorganisms that emit light signals when they encounter pollution in the environment.

And there's much more, substantial increases for the superconducting super collider, agricultural research, and the development of advanced materials. We will double the budget for the National Science Foundation, home to some of our most fantastic scientific and technological advances.

And for a generation, when Americans have looked to the future, they have looked to the stars. Well, we're intensifying our efforts to explore the Moon and the planets, a quest that not only lifts our spirits but brings tangible benefits in new technology and economic growth.

These incredible technologies can't just sit in the science books; they need to work for America. And so, we're moving them out of the laboratory and into the marketplace. We've been busy sweeping away the obstacles that block the transfer of technology from the Government to private enterprise. And just over, I think it was 2 years ago, I signed a bill that allows private industry to take competitive advantage of Government research.

There are 675 public-private agreements active today. In fact, I had a great morning. I just witnessed another one out at Oak Ridge this morning. The Coors Structural Ceramics Company and Oak Ridge will be perfecting a new ceramic material that's tougher than steel. In fact, Coors has decided to locate in this area to be near the scientists and facilities at Oak Ridge. And in doing that, Coors joins more than 20 other companies that have moved to your area for the same reason. And that's the bottom line of these agreements: jobs for Knoxville, jobs for America.

Our national technology initiative brings Government officials together with private businesses to let them know what Government can offer in new technology. This initiative will take advantage of the irreplaceable resources at our national labs, including Oak Ridge, to foster technological excellence.

But make no mistake, Government has no business setting what's known as an industrial policy, where you pick winners and losers and protect favorite industries from market forces, no business doing that. The lightning pace of today's economy is too quick. It's too vital for the deadening hand of the bureaucrat. We will continue to lead only if we give the marketplace full play. A competitive market cuts fat, it encourages efficiency, and it rewards innovation.

That's why for 3 years we've tried to encourage private venture capital. You know, America taxes capital gains at a rate higher than any of our world competitors. And yet the same pessimists who complain we can't compete still stand in the way of lower capital gains taxes. So, let's put an end to that self-defeating nonsense. Congress must lower that capital gains tax to create jobs, and the time to lower it is right now.

Finally, we've asked Congress to make the R&E tax credit a permanent part of the Tax Code. For private companies, this credit reduces the cost of research and development by as much as 20 percent.

American businesses must be able to plan for the future knowing those savings are secure.

Each one of these measures has world-shaping implications. There is a strategy for a competitive, vigorous America, and it springs from a vision of what our future should be. The great blessing of our country is that we Americans have the power to create our own future. We have that extraordinary opportunity, once again, to guarantee that when our children attend school, they receive the best education in the world and that when they leave school, they enter a growing economy with good jobs of their choosing. Let us never forget, the future we plan for today belongs to them.

I am fortunate, very, very fortunate to be President of the United States at an exciting time in our country's marvelous history. The world still looks to this great country for leadership. And we have so much to be grateful for, and I am proud to serve as your President.

May God bless you, and God bless the United States of America. Thank you very, very much.

*Note: The President spoke at 12:06 p.m. at the Knoxville Auditorium-Coliseum. In his remarks, he referred to former Senator Howard Baker; Jack Hammontree, president, Larry Martin, chairman, and Susan Shay, member of the board of directors, Knoxville Chamber of Commerce; and John B. Waters, member of the Board of Directors, Tennessee Valley Authority.*

# Remarks on the Observance of African-American History Month
## *February 19, 1992*

Welcome to the White House, and thank you all very, very much for coming. The finalists and the semifinalists of the McDonald's Black History Makers of Tomorrow are here, and I want to salute them right off hand, over here. Welcome to the White House. And next let me single out, as a fan, the representatives of the Negro League

Baseball Players Association, over here, very famous, all. Welcome.

And to Mr. Justice White and members of our Cabinet, Chairman Powell, and others, let me just say that I am honored to join you in celebrating African-American History Month. I'm especially proud to introduce two special guests that we're going to hear from in a minute, Maya Angelou and Shirley Caesar, right here.

Dr. Angelou, an author, editor, dancer, producer, now the Reynolds professor of American studies at Wake Forest University, she built a career exploring the promise of freedom. And her book "I Know Why the Caged Bird Sings" has thrilled readers and students by making the case for decency and courage and hope and determination.

And our other guest is, of course, one of America's greatest gospel singers. Grammy award-winning—brought some family along to celebrate, I see, but never mind, that's fine even in the White House, Shirley— Grammy award-winning Shirley Caesar has long lifted her voice to sing the bittersweet song of gospel. And her message, like the words of the well-known anthem, is "full of the faith that the dark past has taught us and the hope that the present has brought us."

African-American History Month lets us reflect on our past, its triumphs and its tragedies, and it bids us to celebrate and to remember. But while we may use this time to stop and take stock of race relations, we must guard against the trap of viewing black experience solely against the backdrop of race.

Too often the book of black history is defined only by the chapters, important though they may be, of slavery and emancipation and civil rights. African-American History Month puts on view a whole world of African-American experience, experience that has often pushed back the boundaries of race relations, but that is not always and only defined by them.

This month explores another chapter, Africans' roots explore new worlds. It celebrates the black pathfinders and trailblazers who pushed back the bounds of the unknown and expanded the boundaries of knowledge. Explorers like Pedro Niño, who followed the stars to a new world; pioneers like Guion Bluford, Jr., who parted the stars toward the unknown; or Arctic explorer Matthew Henson, who braved the edge of creation at the newfound North Pole.

And then, of course, we salute other black pioneers, pioneers whose compass was courage, whose map, moral vision. These are people like Dr. Martin Luther King, Jr., who realized "that the time is always ripe to do right." And we think of Alex Haley; a writer described him as a man who "turned loss into pride, history into heritage, and helped make black America a family again." I'll never forget "Roots." You'll never forget Alex Haley. And then we think of A. Philip Randolph, the labor leader who fought to desegregate the military. Jesse Owens, whose triumph humiliated Hitler, before the entire world, I might add. George Washington Carver, Rosa Parks, Dr. Charles Drew, Benjamin Banneker, the legacy of the Tuskegee airmen. We think of Mr. Justice, right here in the front row, our dear friend Clarence Thomas. And we think, of course, of Colin Powell.

These pioneers and many like them peered over the rim of the possible and dared to walk where others had only dreamed. We, too, stand at the edge of a frontier, the frontier of brotherhood, the frontier of a better tomorrow. It's up to us to see beyond old divides and set our sights on new common ground. And as we continue our efforts to create prosperity for all, we must also create new trust, a new tolerance, a new opportunity. And we will.

There is not, and there will never be, a place in America for hatred, for prejudice, for intolerance. And this is not America; this is not us. And let's push back the small crowds who preach hatred. Let's create room for the American dream, for a land where all God's children sing in the joyous songs of freedom. And so, that's our challenge. And I hope it will form the next chapter of our national history.

And so, thank you all very, very much. And now for what we all came to hear. First, I've introduced you to Dr. Angelou, but I believe, Shirley, you are the lead-off hitter. And these guys would know exactly what that means. So come on up, Shirley Caesar.

*Note: The President spoke at 5 p.m. in the East Room at the White House.*

# Message to the Senate Transmitting the Protocol Amending the Australia-U.S. Extradition Treaty
*February 19, 1992*

*To the Senate of the United States:*

With a view to receiving the advice and consent of the Senate to ratification, I transmit herewith the Protocol Amending the Treaty on Extradition between the United States of America and Australia, signed at Seoul on September 4, 1990. I also transmit for the information of the Senate the report of the Department of State with respect to the Protocol.

The Protocol supplements and amends the Treaty on Extradition between the United States of America and Australia, signed at Washington on May 14, 1974. It is designed to update and standardize the conditions and procedures for extradition between the United States and Australia. Most significant, it removes an outdated list of extraditable offenses from the 1974 Treaty and expands upon the dual criminality approach contained in that Treaty. The Protocol also provides a legal basis for temporarily surrendering prisoners to stand trial for crimes against the laws of the requesting State. The provisions in this Protocol follow generally the form and content of extradition treaties recently concluded by the United States.

This Protocol will make a significant contribution to international cooperation in law enforcement. I recommend that the Senate give early and favorable consideration to the Protocol and give its advice and consent to ratification.

GEORGE BUSH

The White House,
February 19, 1992.

# Message to the Congress Reporting Budget Rescissions and Deferrals
*February 19, 1992*

*To the Congress of the United States:*

In accordance with the Congressional Budget and Impoundment Control Act of 1974, I herewith report one rescission proposal, totaling $16.7 million, one revised deferral, and one new deferral of budget authority. Including the revised and the new deferrals, funds withheld in FY 1992 now total $5.6 billion.

The proposed rescission affects the Department of Housing and Urban Development. The deferrals affect the Agency for International Development and the Depart-ment of Agriculture.

The details of the proposed rescission and deferrals are contained in the attached report.

GEORGE BUSH

The White House,
February 19, 1992.

*Note: The attachment detailing the proposals was published in the Federal Register on February 26.*

## Statement by Press Secretary Fitzwater on Establishment of Diplomatic Relations With Azerbaijan, Tajikistan, Turkmenistan, and Uzbekistan
*February 19, 1992*

The President has decided that the United States will take immediate steps to establish diplomatic relations with Azerbaijan, Tajikistan, Turkmenistan, and Uzbekistan. The United States had recognized their independence on December 25, 1991. Following Secretary Baker's recent visit to these countries, the President believes U.S. interests will be best served by having diplomatic ties to their Governments. Secretary Baker conducted detailed discussions with the leaders of the four countries on the political, economic, and security principles of most importance to the United States. The depth, extent, and richness of U.S. relations with each of these countries will depend on their commitment to these principles.

With this step, and yesterday's establishment of diplomatic relations with Moldova, the United States now has diplomatic relations with 11 of the 12 former Soviet Republics. The United States does not intend or seek to isolate the people of Georgia, as Secretary Baker said in Moscow. But, at this time, the United States is not in a position to establish diplomatic relations with Georgia.

The United States will open embassies in these countries by March 15. In addition, the U.S. will support their membership in relevant international organizations, including the International Monetary Fund and World Bank.

## Statement by Press Secretary Fitzwater on the President's Meeting With President Frederick Chiluba of Zambia
*February 19, 1992*

The President and President Frederick Chiluba of Zambia met for approximately 30 minutes in the Oval Office. They had an excellent meeting, during which they discussed the political and economic developments in Zambia. The President congratulated President Chiluba on moving Zambia into a democratic era. President Bush was also supportive of President Chiluba's economic policies, particularly the privatization program.

## Exchange With Reporters Prior to Discussions With Prime Minister Carl Bildt of Sweden
*February 20, 1992*

*The President.* Well, look who's here. You're not going to need this, I don't think.

*Q.* Mr. President, why have you not condemned the latest Israeli invasion into Lebanon, sir?

*The President.* We're not going to take any questions at this photo opportunity. We're going to be discussing very important relations between Sweden and the United States and also get into a lot of multilateral questions. But that's it.

*Q.* Will that issue come up in your talks, sir?

*The President.* Any issues he wants to talk

about will be coming up.

*Q.* Do you think the invasion might hamper the current Mideast peace talks?

*The President.* You missed it. I'm not going to take any questions. Thanks.

*Q.* Thank you.

*[At this point, one group of journalists left the Oval Office, and a second group entered.]*

*Q.* Are relations with Sweden different since Carl Bildt took over?

*The President.* Put it this way: I don't think they could be much better. And we're very happy with the relations with Sweden. We view it, incidentally, as a very important bilateral relationship. And I have great respect for what this gentleman on my right is doing and what he has already accomplished. And he's already had a very good, thorough discussion with the Secretary of State, and now I look forward to having one with him. But I welcome Prime Minister Bildt here, and just to say he comes to a fertile territory because there's an awful lot of respect for what he's doing, right here in this Oval Office, the State Department, all across our Government.

*Q.* Do you really have time with Sweden after the setback in New Hampshire?

*The President.* Yes, I've got time for it.

*Q.* Shouldn't you put America first, to quote the famous——

*The President.* I'd like to think America is first. But that's the way I look at it. But I don't think any President would look at it differently. But we are going to stay engaged around the world. We've got a leadership role, and we're working closely with leaders from different countries. And clearly, Sweden is a very important country. I can learn a lot from him——

*Q.* What can you learn?

*The President.* ——about what's happening in Eastern Europe, for example, what's happening in the Baltics, what's happening in Europe itself. And I can tell him that we plan to stay engaged. And no domestic politics is going to dissuade us from that.

*Q.* What specific roles do you see Sweden——

*The President.* Listen guys, this isn't a press conference. This is what we call a photo op. But I just really wanted to say, with the Swedish journalists here, a warm welcome to this very able Prime Minister. We're just so pleased he's here.

Thank you all very much.

*Note: The exchange began at 11:03 a.m. in the Oval Office at the White House.*

# Remarks at the Departure Ceremony for Prime Minister Carl Bildt of Sweden
## February 20, 1992

Mr. Prime Minister, I am delighted to have welcomed you on your first official visit to Washington and to have shared very profitable, congenial talks.

Prime Minister Bildt comes here at a time when Europe is being transformed and when Sweden itself is beginning a new chapter in its history. As the Prime Minister remarked on his election night last September, the winds of political change blowing through Europe have finally reached Sweden.

Well, he understands well his nation's past. Just more than 100 years ago, his great-great-grandfather was Prime Minister. But even more, Prime Minister Bildt represents a rising generation of leadership for a people seeking a new role in Europe and a new birth of freedom and initiative in Swedish domestic policy.

We welcome Sweden's desire to play a more active part in the emerging global community. The Prime Minister is committed to democracy, to free markets. And I know that as active partners in the common endeavor to create a free, open, and prosperous world, the United States and Sweden will make a real difference.

Sweden and the U.S. share a deep and unswerving commitment to peace, and Sweden is a vital partner in our global nonproliferation efforts. A model peacekeeper, Sweden has shown its commitment to this function of collective security many times, with distinction, in the United Nations system. Sweden has taken a firm stand against terrorism, supporting our efforts to bring to justice those who sabotaged Pan Am Flight 103. And during the Gulf war, Sweden provided humanitarian and economic assistance.

Our partnership in the service of freedom and democracy is not a new one. Americans and Swedes share more than 350 years of friendship, dating back to 1638 when the Kingdom of Sweden established a colony along the Christina River in Delaware. American patriots of Swedish origin fought in our Revolutionary War and signed the Declaration of Independence. Sweden was one of the first nations to sign a treaty of friendship and commerce with a newly independent United States.

That legacy of partnership continues today on contemporary issues, for example, through the new investor visa arrangements our Government agreed upon today. And after today's talks I am confident that this friendship will continue to flourish.

Mr. Prime Minister, let me explain to you our sincere thanks for this new spirit of cooperation and friendship. It strengthens our relations. And your visit has clearly helped build the basis for a solid partnership as we face together the challenges that lie ahead.

Thank you for coming our way. And the best of luck to you, sir.

*Note: The President spoke at 1:19 p.m. on the South Lawn at the White House.*

# Statement by Press Secretary Fitzwater on Senate Action on Energy Legislation
*February 20, 1992*

Last night the Senate passed S. 2166, the National Energy Security Act of 1992, which marks a substantial milestone in implementing the President's national energy strategy issued one year ago today. This legislation will lead to the creation of hundreds of thousands of jobs and keep billions of dollars from flowing overseas for the purchase of foreign oil between now and the year 2010. The bill includes increased conservation, promotes the use of alternative fuels for motor vehicles, and permits greater use of natural gas. We are extremely pleased that the Senate passed the President's legislation, and we urge the House to also act soon on this vital administration program.

# Remarks to the American Legislative Exchange Council
*February 21, 1992*

Thank you for the welcome. May I thank Fred Noye and Sam Brunelli and all the others assembled here. This has become an annual ritual, one that I look forward to very, very much. I don't know whether Jack Kemp is here—he was going to be; been here. And Sam spoke. I have great confidence in both of them. But I really wanted just to come over and say a few words, express my greetings to all of you.

Thinking of ALEC, I wanted to talk here about how you get things done, the key to good government. And Americans, I think, sensible ones, know that the Federal Government simply cannot do everything and shouldn't even try. It could get the job done and then let everybody else do his or her job. At ALEC, you get things done. And I want to help you do what you do best, and that is to lead and to innovate.

So, we want to take $14.7 billion, maybe Sam talked to you about this, in Federal program funds and turn them over to the States as a block grant. And that way people who run the programs can do what works rather than following some distant bureaucrat's notion of what works. We tried it last year, didn't get it; we're trying it again this year. I hope we can make some headway, even though it is an election year.

Another one, welfare reform. Our system too often promotes dependency and not independence. And so we've asked the departments to go back and the agencies to go back and make it easier to obtain the waivers that are necessary to institute welfare reform. Workfare's a good example. Learnfare, like they're doing in Wisconsin, is a good example. And the States are innovating. It is their responsibility, and we are trying to give them the support through waivers. So I would suggest where you see hangups on it, let us know because we are trying to see that there is not bureaucratic opposition to moving forward with these flexible approaches that require waivers. These reforms create, actually, the most important ingredients for success, and that is personal power and personal responsibility.

We're getting more money to States for the important things, programs that work. We've increased spending on education, on Head Start, conservation fund grants, and I'm sure Sam mentioned this, transportation. And don't think for a minute that we measure progress simply in terms of dollars; we do not. We measure it by results, and we fund these programs because they work. Head Start helps us achieve our six educational goals. Kids starting school ready to learn—this year we funded it so that every 4-year-old will have that opportunity.

So, we're moving forward on what we feel works. Jack's program, that I'm supporting him on and have been trying to get through Congress, the HOPE program, H–O–P–E, enabling low-income families to own homes. And I like HOPE for a simple reason: It is a sensible program, and it makes good sense. And when you own a

home, I think we all understand, you own a piece of the community. And you have a dignity and a self-respect that simply cannot be equaled in any other way. You all look at the world differently. You have an interest in improving your assets, and you have an interest in safer, cleaner, better communities. And let me simply say, HOPE works.

This pork barrel spending—there was an amazing article on that in the paper today—doesn't, and we've asked Congress to eliminate, totally eliminate, 246 programs. All of them have noble titles. All of them have wonderful titles, and all of them have sponsors in Congress. But they are not needed. And we are in tough financial times, and so we're trying to get rid of 246 of them and put the money where it gets results.

And at the same time, we've asked Congress to take a few steps to bolster confidence in Government and to strengthen the economy. We need real tools to cut spending. And I want that line-item veto. We're going to keep on pressing for it. In signing statements, I have said that we'll refute, we just are not going to accept some of the language, and so far that's gone on through in the bills that I have signed. But we want a line-item veto, and again, I'm going to take the case to the people for this in the fall.

I want a balanced budget amendment. We couldn't do it overnight, obviously. But if we got it, it would discipline not just the executive branch, but it would discipline the United States Congress which appropriates every dime and tells us how to spend every single dime. We've got to cut the deficit without raising taxes, and if that takes an amendment, let's get the amendment and get the job done.

Secondly, I want Congress to stop passing these unfunded mandates. If there is one thing we hear the most about from States, from Governors or State reps or State senators, it is unfunded mandates. And a Federal mandate is a promise that's made up there on Capitol Hill and then paid for back on Main Street. But the subcommittee chairmen up there have not changed their thinking at all. One program after another is mandated, and thus a big burden placed on the States. And so we say to Congress: Stop passing the buck back. If you pass a mandate, pay for it, and don't go and raise taxes.

Third, I want to put a lid on nuisance lawsuits. You know, the law should foster progress, not hinder it. When fathers stop coaching Little League because they fear lawsuits, there's something wrong. And we've gone way too far. When doctors stop delivering babies because they fear lawsuits, something's wrong. And when people stop volunteering to help other people because they fear ambulance-chasing lawyers, something is wrong. And the madness must stop.

We have legislation up there in the Congress sitting dormant. And here's one where we can take the case to the American people in the fall. It transcends party lines. It transcends ideology, liberal, conservative. It just does not make sense to have so many of these lawsuits settled in such an outrageous fashion. So, we are going to take that case clearly and loudly to the American people this fall. The madness has got to stop.

We've drafted a model act to help people engage in voluntary service without fear of unfair suits. And I hope your States will use this model to draft your own tort reform laws. Alabama, as Perry was telling me and reminding me because I've known it, put together such a statute, got it passed in less than 4 months. Perry Hooper—where is he, he was here right a minute ago—right over here, sponsored the legislation, and we're very proud of what he's done. It's a model for other States, and it makes me redouble our efforts here to get something done on the Federal level.

I've asked Congress to act upon our "Access to Justice Act" which encourages people to seek alternatives to court. And it used to be a joke; you'd get upset and someone would say, "Don't make a Federal case out of it." Now the joke's on us, and we've got to turn that around. People still turn small squabbles into lawsuits, and they sit in courtrooms listening to lawyers bicker about problems that should have been solved some way, over a cup of coffee at home maybe.

The "Access to Justice Act," and I urge you to take a look at it, provides alternatives and puts an end to this madness. And I'd like to challenge you to pass your own "access to justice" reforms. Lead the way. And then I think that will send a powerful message to the United States Congress.

The Council on Competitiveness here, under the able leadership of Vice President Dan Quayle, has prepared two model State statutes which are outlined for you in the packets that I am told you were given today. Take it home, and think it over, and craft your own antilitigation laws. Wouldn't it be nice to create a law that results in fewer lawsuits?

And I don't like to have this many influential people gathered here without soliciting your support, for you to ask Congress to do its part to help the economy. We've got a good plan. It is good. There's a lot of special interests don't like parts of it, but it is a good, sound, stimulative plan. It will protect today's jobs, and it will create new jobs for tomorrow.

Congressional leadership also has a plan. And it will protect today's congressional seats, and it'll promise action tomorrow. So, we are locked in a real fight up there. We're short on numbers, but we've got the facts and we've got the merits on our side.

So I've given Congress a long-term plan, longer—I'd like to see it pass this year—to build the foundations for the next American century, an America that is healthy and well-educated and confident and free and better in research and technology, all of these things.

The health care plan, incidentally, that I came out with fits perfectly with yours. It improves our health care system, which provides the highest quality care on Earth. We've got health care problems, but one of them is not the quality of American health care. It is the best in the entire world.

And so, our program doesn't knock that aside to pass some mandated nationalized program. It gives everybody access to health insurance. And it lets people choose where to get treatment, which doctors they like. And when people make these choices, they feel more comfortable; they get treatments sooner, much sooner than under these nationalized programs. And our plan provides something better than socialized medicine's false promises: health care itself. So I urge you to take a look at this one. I think philosophically it will be right in tune with what we all believe.

My administration also understands that we've got to meet the challenges that lie over the horizon, the challenges of the 21st century. And our America 2000 education strategy encourages revolution, a new generation, literally, a new generation of American schools. It stresses excellence. It stresses accountability. It stresses involvement. It stresses choice. And choice closes the gap between the kitchen table and the teacher's desk. It gets families involved in education. And it gives parents power over their children's schooling. And I urge you to take a look at that program again. A lot of it does not have to be enacted in Federal legislation. A lot of it can be done simply through innovation at the State and certainly at the local level.

The family really, when you look at the problems, is the key to our future. The mayors of cities in the National League of Cities, their executive board came in to see me. I mentioned this in the State of the Union. And all of them—Mayor Bradley of Los Angeles, a great big city; the Republican Mayor of a small town in North Carolina of about 2,000; and in between, Mayor of Plano, Texas, and cities of that size—all came together, and they said, "The biggest worry we've got that clearly works against these problems in the cities is the decline of the American family."

And family is a key to our future. It's been said that the best Department of Health and Human Services is the family. And it is. And it's also been said that what happens in your house—this was a quote by the famous Silver Fox that lives with me over in the White House, Barbara Bush—it's also been said that what happens in your house—and this is the way she put it, and I think it's very relevant—is more important than what happens in the White House.

And it's true. It is very, very true. And so I've asked this Commission that these mayors suggest we set up, this Commission on Urban Families, to find family policies that work, to ferret out Federal legislation that works against the family, to suggest Federal legislation that might bring the family together and might make an errant parent more responsible. Our laws shouldn't encourage a single-parent household or fail to punish men who abandon their children and the mothers. They should promote whole and healthy families.

That's what the purpose of that Commission is. And then when we get its suggestions, I really want to share them with ALEC and other groups because I believe you'll find some real merit in what this Commission will come up with. I'm confident I know the direction they're going to take.

So, these are in the longer term proposal. But I've also submitted a short-term economic plan. And that provides two essentials for families in our Nation, jobs and security. And this plan—I've challenged the Congress to move on it by March 20—stimulates investment. It energizes the real estate industry, and it cuts taxes that inhibit growth. And I've asked Congress, as I say, to pass it by March 20th, 4 weeks from today.

Now, very candidly, we're caught up in a political season here. And I have not been happy with what's come out of the Ways and Means Committee so far. The Democratic leaders have come up with a sorry plan. They want higher taxes, and they want higher spending. And they hope to buy off the people with a tiny temporary tax cut. If you belong to an average family of four, their scheme will give you about a quarter a day. And even the tooth fairy pays more than that in there. [*Laughter*]

And we Americans, we want a large and expanding economy that offers new options and challenges and that holds the promise of job security and employment opportunity. And frankly, I think the country has a reason to join me in being tired of the games being played. For 3 straight years we've tried to get a capital gains tax reduction. It would stimulate jobs. And all the people that control Congress do is say, "Well, it's a tax sop for the rich. This is a break for the rich." It isn't. When the Steiger amendment was passed in '78, new businesses were created; new jobs were created. And it would have the same effect now.

And we're competing in this world. And Japan has a capital gains tax, an effective tax of about one percent; Germany, I think it's zero. And we're asked to compete then with two hands tied behind our back in this important world competitive market which we cannot turn our back on.

And so, we're going to keep fighting for these things that stimulate this economy and get it moving. It is my conviction that if our first-time homebuyer credit is passed, and if our incentive through rapid depreciation is passed, and if our capital gains cut is passed—these are three of our seven points in this short-time program—it would send a signal of confidence to this economy. You don't have to see the effect of it when tax time rolls around. It will give a stimulation of confidence to the small-business guy that might just say, "I'm going to take a chance. I'm going to open a business here."

And so, we really need help now trying to encourage the Congress to pass this program by March 20th. And out of the budget agreement of 1990, which had things in there I didn't like, there was one good thing in it. There were a couple of things that were pretty good. But there was one good thing in it: For the first time in history, we put caps, meaningful caps, on discretionary Federal spending. The critics forget that. Those caps are in place. They can work. Federal spending's up because you have S&L's, you've had bank problems, enormous problems outside of this. You've had the entitlements going up; they're outside of the caps. But the caps are the only protection the taxpayer has against the growth of discretionary Federal spending.

And now, as the election approaches, you hear a lot of talk by the Democrats, "We want to change it. We want to change the caps, knock down the walls." Please help me keep those caps in place. I will veto any attempt to change it, but we're going to need help to keep those caps in place, to protect the taxpayer as best we can until we can get some Members of Congress on both sides of the aisle to share the values that you certainly epitomize and advocate.

So we're in a fight here. And I am going to take this one all the way. After March 20th they say, "Well, what are you going to do?" I say, "Well, I don't know," because I'm not going to give up until March 20th on trying to get this sensible, short-term, stimulative program through the Congress. But I guarantee you, if we fail, the message is going to be loud and clear. And we'll put it in very clear focus so the voters next fall are going to be able to make their determination as to what should have been done and those who stood against it.

So again, I would solicit your help in the time that remains between now and March 20. Help us on the short-term program. Advocate the things you agree with us on on the longer term program, all the things I've mentioned on education and research and family credits. These things are very, very helpful for the future.

So, thank you for what you're doing. I'm glad you came by. I wish we had a little more time, but I'm heading off to the South. You guess why.

Thank you all very much.

*Note: The President spoke at 11:42 a.m. in Room 450 of the Old Executive Office Building. In his remarks, he referred to Fred Noye, chairman, and Sam Brunelli, executive director of the council, and Perry Hooper, a council member from Alabama.*

# Letter Accepting the Resignation of John E. Frohnmayer as Chairman of the National Endowment for the Arts
## February 21, 1992

*Dear John:*

I received your letter of resignation today and, with sincere thanks and appreciation for your service, I accept your resignation effective May 1.

I recall your coming to talk to me about

this on October 24. At that time you told me you wanted to step aside. I told you then that I certainly understood your reasons for desiring to return to private life.

Your job is one of the most difficult in government. You have worked hard for freedom of expression; and yet, at times, as you have ruled against certain grants that you felt were beyond the bounds of common decency, you have been criticized.

I thank you for the integrity and commitment that you have brought to the National Endowment for the Arts.

No two people can agree in every instance on every grant or indeed on what is good art; in fact some of the art funded by the NEA does not have my enthusiastic approval. I expect some did not have yours, but this should not obscure the overall work of the NEA nor your contribution to it.

I thank you and wish you and your family well for a very bright future.

Sincerely,

GEORGE BUSH

---

*Mr. President:*

Last October I told you of my desire to return to private life. Accordingly, I submit my resignation effective May 1, 1992.

I have appreciated the opportunity to serve you and the arts; you know how much your personal support has meant to me during these difficult times. You and your administration have accomplished a great deal and I'm sure the best is yet to come.

Sincerely,

JOHN E. FROHNMAYER

*Note: These letters were made available by the Office of the Press Secretary on February 21 but were not issued as White House press releases.*

# Nomination of Sigmund A. Rogich To Be United States Ambassador to Iceland
## February 21, 1992

The President today announced his intention to nominate Sigmund A. Rogich, of Nevada, to be Ambassador to the Republic of Iceland. He would succeed Charles E. Cobb, Jr.

Currently Mr. Rogich serves as an Assistant to the President for Public Events and Initiatives at the White House in Washington, DC. Prior to this, he founded and served as the president of R&R Advertising in Las Vegas and Reno, NV, and Salt Lake City, UT, 1973–89.

Mr. Rogich graduated from the University of Nevada-Reno (B.A., 1967). He was born May 17, 1944, in Iceland. Mr. Rogich has two children and resides in Washington, DC.

# Statement by Press Secretary Fitzwater on the Confirmation of Andrew H. Card, Jr., as Secretary of Transportation
## February 21, 1992

The President is delighted that the United States Senate unanimously voted to confirm Andrew Card to be Transportation Secretary. As Transportation Secretary, Andrew Card will be a leader in the administration's drive to create jobs, increase economic growth, and prepare America for a bright future.

I am sure that Transportation Secretary Card will ensure that America continues to travel safely home and abroad and that the Nation's transportation systems are ready to move into the 21st century.

## Remarks to the Southern Republican Leadership Conference in Charleston, South Carolina
*February 21, 1992*

*The President.* Thank you, thank you. It is great to be here in Charleston, I'll tell you. I'm delighted to be back in the South. And may I say to our Governor, my dear friend Carroll Campbell, we're grateful for your hospitality and even more for your leadership as one of the finest Governors in the entire country, a real leader, Carroll Campbell. And I might say how pleased I am that Governor Campbell will serve as our national cochairman of the campaign and once again as southern regional chairman. I couldn't be in better hands, and thank you very much.

May I thank the Citadel Bulldog Band over there for some fine music. I appreciate it very much. And this is a real star-studded event. And I want to salute the Governors here today, past and present. I know Governor Jim Martin's here from North Carolina. And Members of the United States Congress, I think four or five Congressmen with us here today, a couple of them with us right here: Congressman Ravenel, hometown boy, and others. And other distinguished guests. And may I say that an early supporter and friend of mine is running for the Senate here, Tommy Hartnett. And I want to see him elected to the United States Senate—former Member of Congress. And I also want to acknowledge key members of our political team: Rich Bond is with us, our new chairman, and Jeanie Austin, doing a superb job. And of course, the conference chairman Martha Edens' superb work here. Keep up the good work, and thank you very much, Martha.

And it's great to be here in South Carolina, host for the first time, but I'm sure not the last time, of this prestigious Southern Republican Leadership Conference. Four years ago, the South led our party to a great victory across the entire country. And this year, the South will lead us to victory in November 1992.

And just to be perfectly clear about it, I am confident of winning the Presidency for 4 more years. I come here fired up and confident. But I'll need your support. We have much to do these next few months because we have much to do these next few years. Together, we can finish what we've started and move this country forward.

Let me open with a true story from my own past about the old days, Midland, Texas, 1956, trying to organize—I hear Ernie Angelo over there—[*laughter*]—trying to organize a Republican Party. And this is the gospel truth. I was a precinct judge, a poll judge, polling judge at primary election time, the first time the Republican Party had ever held a primary in Midland County. And Barbara and I were there alternating at the polls, poll watchers. She and I voted Republican, and we represented two-thirds of the Republican vote that year, gospel truth. The only other guy that voted was a slightly inebriated Democrat. He thought he was voting in the—[*laughter*]—and you can go back and look up the records.

But some of you all are old enough to remember those days. And sometimes if you tried to register Republican, they'd tell you not to bother because there was no Republicans to vote for in the primary. Or times, out and out, there was intimidation, sometimes violence. And we went through a lot back then. And in fact, I'm sure many of you can share similar experiences.

And you say, well, why did we do it? Why did we build a Republican Party in the South when some said it was impossible? We did it because we wanted change, and we did it because we believed in some fundamental values: faith and family, responsibility and respect, community and of course country, the United States of America. And we did it because we saw the Government getting too big and getting into our pockets, into every corner of our lives. And we did it because we worried about our families and our schools and our neighborhoods. And we did it because our taxes always seem to go up at the same time America's problems got worse. And each of us in our own small way finally said, "Enough is enough."

We were upstarts and mavericks. And we challenged the status quo. We challenged the old, what was known as the courthouse crowd, the closed-door, one-party rule of the Democrats. And we did it because we knew Republican principles were right. And they fought us every step of the way. But we fought hard, and we fought fair. And we took our message, smaller Government, better Government, to the people of the Carolinas and Virginia and Mississippi and Florida and the rest of this great region of America.

And we started winning, at first a House seat here and a Senate race there. But our momentum grew. Momentum grew, and it grew. And we owe a great debt of gratitude to our standard bearer in those early days, those that were out front: Howard Baker, the late John Tower, the Bo Calloways and Bill Brocks, Drake Edens and Clark Reeds, and Bill Dickinson and John Paul Hammerschmidt and of course, the phenomenal favorite son of South Carolina, right behind me, Strom Thurmond. When I think back to one year ago almost to this very day, the tough decision that had to be made about committing your sons and daughters into a war, Strom Thurmond was of more support to me than any single Senator in the United States Senate. And we should be grateful for him.

Well, these leaders paved the way, and they inspired a generation of talent that transformed the Nation's political landscape. And I'm thinking now of another South Carolinian, a good man and a good friend, Lee Atwater. We miss him. We miss him still. And it was great to have Sally Atwater flying down with us this afternoon on Air Force One. Sally, we're so pleased to be with you.

Well, today the Republican Party is the

force for positive change in the New South, and I'm proud to have played a modest role in that success. Our message then and our message now is simple. Carroll said a lot of it. We believe Government is too big and spends too much. We believe in good schools and safe streets and a Government worthy of the people's respect. And so, we believe in less Government, low taxes. Surely we believe in a strong defense. And we believe that we put America first when we put America's families first.

And so, we believe that parents, not the Government, should make the big decisions. Parents, not Government, should choose their children's schools. Parents, not the Government, should decide the family's health care. And parents should choose who cares for their children, not some bureaucrat in Washington, DC, telling us how to do it. And yes, we believe it ought to be okay to have a voluntary prayer for children in the classroom, and I'm not going to change my view on that ever.

Those are our beliefs. And those are why we built a party in the South and why we continue, with your help, to build it today. Those beliefs don't change from one election to the next. They still guide each and every one of us each and every day.

And now we're at the beginning of a new era in the history of our country. The cold war is over, and America won. The Soviet Union, as we remember it, has collapsed, gone. Imperial communism is finished for good. American leadership changed the world. Republican leadership will change America.

I know we've got tough times, but I am totally confident about our future. But we've got a lot of work ahead of us. There are some things that are simply on the wrong track in our country. Take our courts, for example. When fathers stop coaching Little League because they're afraid of liability lawsuits, something is wrong. And when doctors stop delivering babies because they fear a malpractice lawsuit, something's wrong. Or when people stop volunteering to help each other because they fear ambulance-chasing lawyers, something is terribly wrong. These days a sharp lawyer would tell the Good Samaritan, "Keep on walking."

We've proposed reforms to our court system—they've got them sitting up there in the United States Senate now—to address the questions of frivolous lawsuits, and that's a good step. But the real answer for solving problems is to be more concerned with helping each other than suing each other.

And then I think about our Nation's health care system. Our health care system provides, and let's not forget this, the highest quality care anywhere in the world. But it's not perfect. We all know that. And too many people do not have access to health insurance. Too many people worry that they're going to lose their coverage if they change jobs or, worse still, if they lose their job. And anybody who's had even minor surgery knows that health care costs are going through the roof.

The answer is not to go down the road of socialized medicine with its long lines and faceless, impersonal service. If that's what we wanted, we'd put our doctors and nurses to work for the department of motor vehicles. Our plan, my approach, written out in detail, is to reform our health system, make insurance available to all, keep the quality high, the bureaucracy low, and preserve choice. And that is vital. And the last thing we want is the Government standing between you and your doctor.

And then there's the sorry welfare system. It's pretty obvious that the system now too often perpetuates dependency when it should promote independence, promote initiative. We need to encourage individual success through personal responsibility, the dignity of a job. And so, I've asked the departments and agencies to make it easier—and this is upon the advice of Jim Martin and Carroll Campbell and others—to make it easier for State and local government to reform the system, reform policies that promote broken families. We need to get people to work, go after the deadbeat fathers who run out on those little kids, or as they do in Wisconsin, to make recipients work or study and to keep families together.

But we all know what the number one issue on the minds of Americans is, and it is the economy. And it's people worried about their jobs, providing for their families, meeting the everyday challenges of paying the bills and providing a home and teaching the kids and putting aside for our retirement.

The American people, your neighbors, want this economy fired up again, and so do I. And in my State of the Union Address, I put forward a two-part plan. And the first part gets business growing again right now, instantly upgrading plant and equipment again, hiring workers again. It uses incentives like an investment tax allowance. And yes, it is clearly time for the Congress to wake up and cut that tax on capital gains.

And to get housing back on its feet, I put forth several commonsense proposals—they're sitting right there in House now—to get people buying and building homes. And perhaps the most easily understood proposal is a $5,000 tax credit for first-time homebuyers. With our plan, young people almost able to buy that first home could do it with the extra $5,000 in their pocket. And the plan we're fighting against in the Congress this very day gives them absolutely nothing, nothing to that first-time homebuyer.

You're worried about the Democrats' current plan. I don't want to say too much about it. It's a nice evening here, and I don't want to ruin it. Current plan, I say current because it seems to change just about every hour as they change it to garner in some votes from the special interests, to buy votes. And that's why it's really not a plan. It is simply a bad deal. It smacks of, and you've heard it before, class warfare. And listen to the tradeoff in their deal: 25 cents a day in temporary tax relief for 2 years, paid for, true to form for the Democrats, by a large permanent tax increase.

Now, some Democrats in the Senate have other ideas. They want to get a bidding war going. But to pay for that they'd have to hike tax rates for the middle class, people making $35,000, you know, people like teachers and factory workers and everyday Americans. And they won't tell you that about their sorry plan. But that's the estimate I've been given by our experts. Any economist will tell you the last thing our economy needs now is a tax increase by that Democratic Congress. And their plan adds almost $30 billion to this deficit. And the jobs it creates are more likely to be for more tax collectors.

I believe the American people have about had it with this tax-and-spend thinking. And we drew a line in the sand in the Persian Gulf and kept our word, and I'll draw another line in the sand right here today. If the Democrats send me this nonsense they're talking about now, I will send it right back. I will veto it the minute it hits my desk.

I sent them a plan, a good one. And that's what they ought to work on, not some phony partisan maneuver that they know won't fly. And I'll say it again to the Congress: Here's the deadline, March 20th. And if we act by then, we can see some results this spring. No more games, no more empty gestures, just pass this plan and get the economy going again, and then we can have all the political fights we want. But let's set it aside now and do something for the American people that are hurting out there.

I said the plan had two parts; you may remember that from the State of the Union. The second part is a long-term plan to keep this country competitive, keep us vigorous. And it's a road map for competing and leading America in this fast-changing world of the 21st century.

Our plan revolutionizes America's educational system. Our plan gets the billions of dollars' worth of cutting-edge Government research and development into the hands of our private sector businesses and the workers faster than ever before. And that helps us get a real return on your tax dollars, investment helping to create new jobs and products.

Our plan provides tax relief to strengthen the family. We raised the tax deduction for children by $500. Make no mistake, I want this plan passed in this session of Congress. Keep the heat on the Congress, and we can get that done.

But a central idea behind our approach is that to succeed economically at home, we have to lead economically abroad. Carroll touched on this very eloquently. What he means and what I mean is jobs right here in America by opening markets for our exports all over the world. And I'm going to fight hard in every foreign market to do just exactly that. We've made headway. We have made dramatic headway with this increase in exports, but we are going to do even better.

Some people wish the rest of the world would just go away. That is naive, and that is defeatist. They're saying that a level playing field isn't level enough, that American ingenuity, American know-how, and the American can-do spirit are simply a bunch of hackneyed phrases. I don't believe it. I don't believe that for one minute, and neither do you. America is not going to cut and run, ever. We're going to stay involved, and we are going to continue to lead the entire world.

Before I finish now, I have something to say about this primary campaign. Of course, this campaign is important, not just to me but to you and to our country. And for the sake of our country, we must not turn over the Nation's leadership to the Democrats. Republican leadership must continue.

For 8 years, Ronald Reagan, I was at his side, led this country. For the last 3 years, I've stood on our principles and against a Democratic Congress that would undermine them. And with the help of our Republican leadership on Capitol Hill, 25 times our principles were upheld, vetoes of bad legislation sustained.

And the next 5 years of American history are just too important to entrust to the inexperienced. I believe the American people want to hear about how we're going to address our country's challenges, how we can unite our people, create more opportunity and hope for all Americans. And I believe the American people want to hear solutions, not just a lot of name-calling and running this country down.

And frankly, I also believe that sometimes somebody's got to stand up and say what's right about the United States of America. And you can't hear it from this campaign going on out there. We are number one, and make no mistake about it, and we're going to stay that way.

And another thing, maybe this is just my personal prejudice talking, let's not listen to the gloom and doom from all those intense talking heads who are happy only when they say something negative. We are the United States of America, and we don't have to put up with all that.

*Audience members.* Four more years! Four more years! Four more years!

*The President.* Let me just say, you and I believe in America, and we are optimistic about its future. And we believe in our party. And I am tremendously fortunate to serve as your President at this most exciting time in our Nation's history. Barbara and I count our blessings every day for the good fortune that we have to live in that majestic White House and to do our level-best to serve the people of this great country.

These next primaries are critical. I need your help. I need your help to keep our party strong and united so that we can win this fall. And yes, we have much to do. But I guarantee you, we will get the job done. And yes, we have many challenges before us. I guarantee you, we will meet them, each and every one of them. And yes, there's an election in November. And I guarantee you this: We will win it. I want to be your President for another 4 years.

Thank you very much. Thank you very, very much. Now let's go out and beat the Democrats in the fall. And may God bless the United States of America. Thank you.

*Note: The President spoke at 4:40 p.m. at the Omni Hotel. In his remarks, he referred to Richard N. Brown, chairman, and Jeanie Austin, cochairman, Republican National Committee; Martha Edens, chairman, Southern Republican Leadership Conference; and Ernie Angelo, Republican national committeeman from Tennessee.*

# Radio Address to the Nation on the Economy
## February 22, 1992

Today I want to talk to you about getting our economy moving. I know there's a lot of debate about how to create jobs and build economic strength, but in the end it all boils down to common sense. To strengthen an economy, you encourage investment. You support industries that pull nations out of recessions. You encourage success.

In my State of the Union Address, I proposed a short-term economic plan that does these things. I challenged Congress to set aside partisan politics for just a few weeks and pass my plan by March 20.

Unfortunately, Democratic leaders refused to submit my plan for a quick, clean vote. They chose politics over duty. They huddled behind closed doors and played games with the Tax Code. They put out one plan one day, another plan the next. Finally, they settled on a scheme that makes no economic sense.

Their proposal won't help homebuyers. Their proposal will increase the deficit. It borrows $30 billion to pay for a tiny temporary tax cut. For each person in the average family of four, it hands out about a quarter a day, but only for 2 years. This turns out to be a very costly quarter. After the temporary cut expires, Americans would shoulder the burden of a huge permanent tax increase. In other words, these congressional leaders want to give you 2 years of pocket change in exchange for a lifetime of higher taxes. And that is a very bad deal for us and for our children who must pay the bill.

And now my plan: My plan will create jobs. The real estate incentives alone will generate 415,000 new jobs this year. My plan offers the hope of homeownership to first-time homebuyers. Some people have begun buying homes already, expecting Congress to pass a plan that encourages real estate investment, my plan. Congress shouldn't let those people down.

My plan will not increase the deficit. It makes some tough choices on Federal spending because I refuse to mortgage our children's future for short-term political gain. My plan will not raise tax rates. I want to raise the child deduction on Federal income taxes by $500, and I want Congress to pass this permanent, long-term, profamily tax cut this year.

Put the plans side by side, and here's the bottom line: My plan works; theirs doesn't.

So today, join me in telling Congress: Stop fooling around with our future. Tell them to pass my plan now. If politicians hem and haw and offer up excuses, remind them your job is more important than any politician's job. Our recovery will get a huge boost the moment Congress passes my plan. But I need your help.

Thank you. And may God bless you and the United States of America.

*Note: This address was recorded on February 21 in the Oval Office at the White House and was broadcast at 9 a.m. on February 22.*

## Remarks to the United States Chamber of Commerce National Action Rally
*February 24, 1992*

May I, at the outset of these remarks, thank the colonel and this wonderful Marine band. They are sensational. And I think I speak for all when we say we've enjoyed the music. Thank you.

And I want to salute your incoming chairman, Bill Lurton, and your president, Dick Lesher, so well-known to everyone and doing a superb job for the chamber, and of course, your outgoing chairman, my friend Pete Silas.

Let me tell you something, just a little word about Pete. Last week there was a newspaper report that more and more American business leaders are hailing this recent and somewhat controversial mission I took to Asia, they're hailing it as a success for opening markets, for creating more American jobs. But let me say this to all of you in the chamber, no one did more to make that mission a success than Pete Silas. He gave the trip the same leadership he's given this organization, a forceful and effective presentation, taking our case for open markets to Japan and Korea. And I am very, very grateful to him. And I can see why you entrusted your leadership to him. Pete, thank you very, very much for that leadership that makes us so proud.

Well, today we're noting an anniversary of sorts. One year ago, almost to the hour, our troops began punching through Iraqi lines to liberate Kuwait. We mobilized our strength and won that war with an all-volunteer force including tens of thousands of reservists. Many of you had to do without key personnel during the Reserve callup. Some of you answered the call yourselves. And as your Commander in Chief, I want to express deep thanks to our business men and women for playing a proud role in America's world leadership. I think it is fitting a year later to take note of those historic events.

But I came here now to ask support on another matter. I need your help to meet yet another challenge, renewing the freedom and strength of our economy.

Four weeks ago, I spoke to the Congress and the American people. In my State of the Union Message, I announced a set of urgent measures that I would take to unshackle our economy. And I asked Congress of the United States to do its part and to meet a deadline. Most important, I asked Congress to cut the high taxes on job creation and investment and to do this by March 20th. Well, my plan will get our economy moving again. And we need to liberate private enterprise from a Government that's grown too big and spends too much. And we need to do it without raising taxes.

In my State of the Union Address, I instituted a 90-day freeze on Federal regulations that affect economic growth, and I asked major departments and agencies to carry out an unprecedented top-to-bottom review of all existing and proposed regulations. Within those 90 days, we will accelerate new rules that promote business growth and, whenever possible, halt those that would impede growth. Already, we've seen results.

Today, for example, I am announcing major new ground rules for regulation of biotechnology. Bill Reilly, the EPA Administrator, I understand is with you all today. He'll have a major responsibility for making our new rules work to foster economic growth. This is a $4 billion industry. And it should grow to $50 billion by the end of the decade, if we let it. The rewards we will reap include new medicines and safer ways to clean up hazardous waste and a revolution in agriculture. The United States leads the world in biotechnology. And I intend, through sensible regulation and, in some instances, deregulation, to keep it just exactly that way.

We've taken new actions to ease the credit crunch. For example, for healthy banks, we've changed overly strict definitions of bank capital, creating more access to capital. We're cutting redtape for healthy banks and thrifts. In these tough real estate markets, we've issued commonsense, realistic valuation guidelines.

We're making it easier for small businesses to get capital from securities markets. We're increasing the maximum for small public offerings that get simplified handling by the SEC from $1.5 million, raising that to $5 million. We're cutting paperwork, and we're simplifying securities registration for small businesses. We've also cut the cost of compliance with the payroll tax system. We've cut paperwork and increased access for small business to electronic payment systems. Instead of heavy-handed enforcement, we're helping small firms meet their obligations.

The few steps that I've just outlined, I know they're technical, but these few steps will provide billions of dollars in additional capital to the Nation's economy. But we won't stop after 90 days. We'll turn up the heat against overregulation, rule by rule and industry by industry.

We'll take the case to Capitol Hill. For every unreasonable regulation we can't change through executive action, we will introduce reform legislation, and we will push the Congress to do its job and put an

end to overregulation. I want the regulators and the Congress to remember one thing: If it doesn't make sense, if it hurts the economy, don't do it.

One of my prime responsibilities as President is to open up world markets, that's what this trip was about, open up world markets, unlocking new opportunities for American workers and businesses. Free trade has come under attack these days, and that makes no sense whatsoever. Our exports are at record levels, guaranteeing millions of American jobs. With your help, we're going to open up the tremendous market opportunities of Mexico sooner, not later. With your help, we'll win global trade reforms for agriculture, services, and intellectual property.

By protecting our freedoms, by opening markets here and abroad, and by pushing the envelope of excellence, I want to improve the quality of life for every man, woman, and child in this country. And I mean everyone. Some politicians want to divide us, divide us into economic classes. They're keen on defining people as poor or rich or middle class. They don't bother to ask you how you see yourselves or what your aspirations are. The Capitol Hill liberals have already made up their minds where everyone fits in some politically correct caste system. Well, that's not the way I see America. I don't apply a means test to the American dream. I want to increase opportunity for everyone. That's what fairness means.

And once again, I could not have had better allies in my fight than the U.S. Chamber of Commerce. Chamber members share a sense of responsibility to your families and your firms and your communities and your Nation. You take your responsibilities personally, in your homes, among your families. You know it's not so important what happens in the White House, it's what happens in your house.

My administration's strategies for fighting drugs and improving our schools are sound because they join Government's efforts to the responsibilities of parents and families. We know we'll win the battle against drugs through the moral grounding that begins and ends in the family. We'll renew education by giving parents more freedom and responsibility to choose their children's schools, to get involved in their kids' education.

You carry these values into managing your business, the kind of values that say when the company's losing money, the boss doesn't take home a seven-figure bonus. Your companies get involved in the community because you're good neighbors. Big Government didn't make this country great. You did it. Our Nation's strength and generosity flow from private enterprise and voluntary initiative. It comes from seeing a problem, taking charge, getting involved, and not taking no for an answer.

The Partnership for a Drug-Free America is a brilliant example of this. This business group, many of you may participate in it, voluntarily produces a million dollars a day in pro bono advertising to warn our kids about drugs. And we're making progress in that front. I am very pleased that the drug use for these teenagers is substantially down.

Freely undertaken, corporate responsibility is one of the strongest fibers in our social fabric. So it's only natural that you should expect Government to serve the people responsibly, not to behave as an arrogant ruler. On this I faced a big fight. Time and again I fought to get Members of Congress to apply to themselves the same laws they impose on everyone else, laws on ethics, on equal pay, on civil rights for women and minorities. Each time, Congress drags its feet. They're slow learners up there on Capitol Hill, but you and I can make them learn. And that's just what we must do.

As you know, and here's where I need you, I've sent the Congress a short-term plan to get our economy moving, as well as a longer term program for economic growth. I've given Congress a deadline of March 20th to act on our most urgent needs, to pass this short-term plan. We need to lower those sky-high taxes on new jobs and investment, and that means that we must cut the tax on capital gains. And we ought to do it now.

We need changes in the alternative minimum tax and a 15-percent investment tax allowance to encourage businesses to buy equipment, upgrade their plants, and start

hiring again. We need new incentives to build and buy real estate, through changes in the passive loss rules for real estate developers. And we need a $5,000 tax credit for first-time homebuyers and penalty-free IRA withdrawals for first-time homebuyers. This is not all that controversial. I want to sign these reforms on March 20th. And I do need your help working with the United States Congress.

We all know that this is a political year. We know Congress hates to make real decisions in election years. But that's why I see this March 20th deadline as fair and realistic. It gives us a window in which to get this plan passed and put it into action, and most economists tell you it will stimulate immediately. And it still leaves everyone then more than 7 months for this traditional partisan politicking before election time.

Today is the 27th day, the halfway mark of my 52-day deadline for action on that economic growth plan. So, it is time for a midterm report card. The stark and sorry fact is Congress so far deserves an F; they deserve a failing grade.

The Ways and Means Democrats considered my plan for 2 hours, a hefty 2 hours. And then, on a straight party line vote, they said no to these seven progrowth proposals. They said no to first-time homebuyers. They said no to letting people keep more of their capital gains earnings. They said no to helping new businesses write off their investment. They said no to each one of these vital proposals to create jobs now and get this economy moving.

They said yes, though, to politics as usual. They went behind closed doors—you ask your people here in Washington—they went behind closed doors to design what they think is clever politics. Now the door is opening. And they have proposed a bill that raises taxes and, just as incredibly, breaks the budget agreement of a year ago. They not only want to take away your income, they want to dream up new ways to spend it, to take the restraints off Government spending. Take off those caps. Take off the brakes. Take off the spending controls that are so essential.

They want to saddle Americans with a permanent tax hike, all to pay for a temporary tax cut of 25 cents per person per day. What's worse, some of them have a bidding war in mind. To pay for that, they'd have to raise tax rates on people making more than $35,000 a year. Any economist will tell you that the last thing this economy needs is a tax increase.

The contrast between my economic growth plan and the Democrats' new tax-increase scheme could not be more plain. Our plan will cut taxes on investment and job creation for all investors, for all home-owners, for all entrepreneurs. And it will do it without increasing the deficit.

So, to the Congress at this halfway point before the deadline, I'll say it again: Pass my plan. Let's get America moving again.

Come March 20th, if the Democrats send me the message they're talking about now, I will send it right back. I will veto it and send it back. And I don't want to veto a bad bill; I want to sign a good bill. And Congress has a responsibility to give the American people a growth bill right now.

As Pete Silas knows, and a handful of you others old enough to remember, my path to office as a Chief Executive of the United States began in the world of small business. Fresh out of college, I joined a couple of partners and started a little business out in Midland, out in west Texas. It was there that I saw firsthand what the chamber does to translate business efforts into community achievements. As businessmen we knew freedom's benefits would be stronger if we joined hands to meet our responsibilities as citizens.

Those days, Government wasn't quite as big or rapacious. But even back then we learned that we had to work together to keep Government growth and interference with free enterprise in check. That's what I'm asking that we do today, to do it urgently. I have a solid plan to get America moving again and keep it strong for the long haul.

So when you go up to Capitol Hill, give your Congressmen and Senators a message from me: Get moving, or get out of the way. Let me tell you something, and I say this not out of flattery, but you, you men and women in this room, really can make a difference. There's never been a more urgent moment to win a victory for jobs for all Americans. We've won battles before, and we'll win this one, too. Together we can get our country moving swiftly and surely to a better future.

Thank you all for what you are doing. And may God bless the United States of America. Thank you.

*Note: The President spoke at 10:55 a.m. at DAR Constitution Hall.*

# Statement on Signing the Omnibus Insular Areas Act of 1992
*February 24, 1992*

It is with great pleasure that I sign into law H.R. 2927, the "Omnibus Insular Areas Act of 1992." This Act creates a new unit of the National Park System known as the Salt River Bay National Historical Park and Ecological Preserve.

By signing this bill into law today, we make a significant contribution to the commemoration of the 500th anniversary of Christopher Columbus' voyages to the New World. We also protect an environment that is important to all citizens of the United States.

Located on the island of St. Croix, U.S. Virgin Islands, this new park is important for several reasons:

— It is the only known site where, 500 years ago, members of a Columbus party set foot on what is now territory of the United States.

— It presents an outstanding opportunity to preserve and interpret Caribbean history and culture, including the impact of European exploration and settlement.

— It contains a wealth of natural features ranging from wooded hillsides and mangrove forests to tropical reefs and a biologically rich submarine canyon.

—It is a refuge for migratory birds and a vital nursery for many of the marine animals that inhabit the beautiful waters of St. Croix.

—It will be planned and managed in full partnership with the Government of the U.S. Virgin Islands.

It is indeed exciting to take this major step toward preserving the natural and cultural heritage of the Virgin Islands, a heritage that has meaning for all Americans. I want to thank all of those who played a part in fashioning this innovative partnership between the Federal Government and the Virgin Islands Government.

My action here today is but one example of my Administration's commitment to protect the environment and America's heritage. This is the sixth time I have signed legislation creating a new unit of the Na-

tional Park System. In the past 3 years, we have acquired 57,000 acres of environmentally sensitive and historically significant lands for the National Park System.

Finally, I note that H.R. 2927 authorizes new technical assistance for insular areas after major storms. To ensure that hazard mitigation measures truly reduce future loss of life and property, all projects must be cost-effective, cooperative ventures between the Federal Government and the insular areas. The Act will not change this policy, diminish any existing matching share requirements, or change procedures for Presidential disaster declarations.

GEORGE BUSH

The White House,
February 24, 1992.

*Note: H.R. 2927, approved February 24, was assigned Public Law No. 102–247.*

# Nomination of Edward Joseph Perkins To Be United States Representative to the United Nations
*February 24, 1992*

The President today announced his intention to nominate Edward Joseph Perkins, of the District of Columbia, to be the Representative of the United States of America to the United Nations, with the rank and status of Ambassador Extraordinary and Plenipotentiary, and the Representative of the United States of America in the Security Council of the United Nations. He would succeed Thomas R. Pickering.

Since 1989 Mr. Perkins has served as Director General of the Foreign Service and Director of Personnel at the U.S. Department of State in Washington, DC. Prior to this, Mr. Perkins served as U.S. Ambassador to the Republic of South Africa, 1986–1989; U.S. Ambassador to the Republic of Liberia,

1985–1986; and Director of the Office of West African Affairs in the Bureau of African Affairs at the U.S. Department of State, 1983–1985. From 1981 to 1983, Mr. Perkins served as Deputy Chief of Mission at the U.S. Embassy in Monrovia, Liberia. In addition, he served as Counselor for Political Affairs at the U.S. Embassy in Accra, Ghana, 1978–1981.

Mr. Perkins graduated from the University of Maryland (B.A., 1967) and the University of Southern California (M.P.A., 1972; D.P.A., 1978). He was born June 8, 1928, in Sterlington, LA. Mr. Perkins served in the U.S. Army and the U.S. Marine Corps. He is married, has two children, and resides in Washington, DC.

# Nomination of Thomas R. Pickering To Be United States Ambassador to India
*February 24, 1992*

The President today announced his intention to nominate Thomas R. Pickering, of New Jersey, to be Ambassador Extraordinary and Plenipotentiary of the United States of America to India. He would succeed William Clark, Jr.

Currently Ambassador Pickering serves as the U.S. Representative to the United Nations and the Representative of the United States of America to the Security Council of the United Nations. Prior to this, Ambassador Pickering served as U.S. Ambassador to several countries, including Israel, 1985–1988; El Salvador, 1983–1985; the Federal Republic of Nigeria, 1981–1983; and the Hashemite Kingdom of Jordan, 1974–1978. In addition, he served at the U.S. Department of State as Assistant Secretary of State for Oceans and International Environmental and Scientific Affairs, 1978–1981; Special Assistant to the Secretary of State and Executive Secretary, 1973–1974; and Deputy Director of the Bureau of Political-Military Affairs, 1969–1973.

Ambassador Pickering graduated from Bowdoin College (A.B., 1953); Fletcher School of Law and Diplomacy (M.A., 1954); and the University of Melbourne (Australia) (M.A., 1956). He was born November 5, 1931, in Orange, NJ. Ambassador Pickering served in the U.S. Navy, 1956–1959. He is married, has two children, and resides in New York, NY.

# Appointment of Gail R. Wilensky as Deputy Assistant to the President for Policy Development
*February 24, 1992*

The President today announced his intention to appoint Gail R. Wilensky, of the District of Columbia, as Deputy Assistant to the President for Policy Development.

Since 1990 Ms. Wilensky has served as Administrator of the Health Care Financing Administration, the Agency that administers the Medicare and Medicaid programs. Prior to this, she was the vice president of health affairs at Project HOPE, an international health foundation. She has taught economics and public policy at the University of Michigan and George Washington University and has held several appointments in the Public Health Service and at the Urban Institute.

Ms. Wilensky received an A.B. in psychology (1964), an M.A. in economics (1965), and a Ph.D. in economics (1968), all from the University of Michigan. She was born in Detroit, MI. She is married to Robert J. Wilensky, has two children, Peter and Sara, and currently resides in Washington, DC.

## Appointment of John A. Gaughan as Deputy Assistant to the President and Director of the White House Military Office
*February 24, 1992*

The President today announced the appointment of John A. Gaughan, of Maryland, to be Deputy Assistant to the President and Director of the White House Military Office. He will succeed LTG Richard G. Trefry, USA (Ret.).

Since 1989 Mr. Gaughan has served as Chief of Staff to the Secretary of Transportation. Prior to this, he served as the Administrator of the Maritime Administration from 1985 to 1989; as Deputy Assistant Secretary of Governmental Affairs, Department of Transportation, in 1985; as Director of the Office of External Affairs in the Maritime Administration in 1984; and as a congressional liaison officer for the Department of Transportation from 1981 to 1984. From 1970 to 1980, Mr. Gaughan served on active duty in the U.S. Coast Guard and held various positions including command of the Coast Guard Cutter *Point Martin.*

Mr. Gaughan graduated from the U.S. Coast Guard Academy with a bachelor of science in 1970 and from the University of Maryland School of Law in 1977. He was born March 29, 1947, in Washington, DC. He and his wife, Janelle, reside in Bethesda, MD.

## Statement by Press Secretary Fitzwater on the President's Meeting with President Alfredo Cristiani of El Salvador
*February 24, 1992*

President Bush held a half-hour private meeting today with President Alfredo Cristiani of El Salvador. President Bush congratulated President Cristiani for his great personal leadership and courage in bringing peace to his country. He also praised the progress President Cristiani has made toward implementing the peace agreements signed earlier this month in Mexico City and achieving true national reconciliation. The President gave his assurance that the United States would do everything possible to support full implementation of the peace accord and to help El Salvador consolidate democracy and peace and expand economic opportunity. In this regard, the President mentioned that the United States Government was working with other governments to assure international support for the national reconstruction of El Salvador. The President also promised to work with Congress on a bipartisan basis for continued United States assistance to El Salvador in the future, through both direct aid programs and debt reduction under the Enterprise for the Americas Initiative (EAI). United States assistance and international support will be vital to the continued success of the peace process and national reconciliation in El Salvador.

## Remarks at the Bush-Quayle Campaign Kickoff in Bethesda, Maryland
*February 24, 1992*

Thank you, Connie Morella. What a great Congressman you have in Connie Morella. She's doing a superb job. And thank you very much. Let me salute our State chairman, two words come to mind, strong and decent, Helen Bentley, Representative Helen Bentley, who's leading our campaign in this State. And another of our great delegation from Maryland who is not here, Wayne Gilchrest, he was unable to join us, but doing a great job for us in Congress. And greetings to your State Republican chairman, Joyce Terhes, and to Republican national committeeman Dick Taylor.

My thanks to the Maryland Bush-Quayle leadership who are here and to Howie Dennis for performing the master of ceremonies duties tonight, first-class job. I don't know where the Barons band is, but they are doing a great job. And thank you, Barons, right there. I'm very happy to see three who served us so well in Congress, Charles "Mac" Mathias and Larry Hogan, my classmate Gilbert Gude. And I notice several fine Republicans here seeking your votes for delegates to the national convention. Well, I'm pleased to have their support, and I'm sure they'll have yours come March 3d. We need to elect them as delegates to our convention.

I'm delighted to be back with Connie here in Montgomery County and especially on the home court of the victorious battling Barons.

A week from Tuesday, hard to believe, but that's the day, Marylanders are going to make a big decision. And I know what the outcome will be. Together on March 3d, we're going to take a giant step closer to a great victory on November 3d. This vote carries a special meaning for Maryland and America. We've come to an exciting moment in our country's history, a crossroads, a place where one era ends and another begins.

From the fall of the Berlin Wall to the last gasp of imperial communism, from the four decades of the cold war to the 40 days of Desert Storm, America has led the way. We won the cold war—history will show this—we won the cold war because we Americans never shirked responsibility. We had a job to do, and we did it. That's why today, as the cold war ends, America stands alone the undisputed leader of the world.

Now the challenge has come home, as it has before. Time after time, we lifted ourselves up, we asked more of ourselves, more

of each other. And each time, America met the challenge. And this time, America will do it again.

Our first order of business is to get this economy moving. I know how to do it, and so do you. It's just plain common sense.

A month ago, I sent the Congress an action plan to jump-start the economy. We start by encouraging investment, to create jobs. We cut taxes that punish success, discourage saving, and stunt the growth of business. We boost real estate values by making it easier for young families to buy their first home.

The bottom line is this: My plan will work because it puts Americans to work. And I ask for your support. According to housing experts, my incentives for the housing industry alone will create 415,000 jobs this year. That's what this plan will do.

But just as important is what it doesn't do. It doesn't increase the deficit. It doesn't cloud the real issues with feel-good political gimmicks. And it doesn't raise tax rates on the American people. Maybe that's why the opposition in Congress are digging in against the plan.

When I presented this plan, I gave Congress a deadline to pass it: March 20, 25 days from now. But instead of putting this plan to a quick, clean vote, the Democrats in Congress went behind locked doors with the special interests and patched together a deal of their own. It's a bad deal for the American people.

True to form for the Democrats in Congress, their scheme will raise tax rates on the American people, permanently. In fact, Senate Democrats want to jack up the rates of people making $35,000 a year. That's right, $35,000. I've said it before, when they say they're aiming at the big guy, they end up hitting everybody else. And we can't let them do that. In return for this massive tax increase, the Democrats offer a temporary tax cut, amounting to about a quarter a day. Twenty-five cents a day, even a tooth fairy can do a little better than that one. [*Laughter*] Then after 2 years, the 25-cent tax cut vanishes. But the tax increase stays forever.

Well, you don't have to be an economist to figure it out. The last thing the American people need right now is a tax increase. And to pay for their plan, the Democrats want to borrow $26 billion from our children, pass on an IOU in the form of an enormous increase in the deficit. Raising taxes and deepening the deficit: That's their idea of speeding up the economy.

If the Democrats really want to send me this kind of nonsense, I will veto it. The American people have had enough of that old game of tax and spend. To the Democrats on Capitol Hill, I'll say it again and again and again: Meet this deadline, pass this plan, and get this economy moving. Do something good for the American people.

That's an example of what this election is going to be about, a clash between two views of America. The differences couldn't be clearer. Our view, the Republican view, is based on a fundamental principle: Government is too big, and it spends too much. Believe it or not, some people still don't understand that. You'll see some of them over the next week asking for your vote. When they do, ask them a few questions. Their answers will tell you all you need to know about how they see America's future. Ask them who should choose a family's medical care, parents or the Government? I say the parents. The last thing we need is the Government——

I think this young lady has a question. It's about AIDS. Let me say this because it's a matter of real concern. Under our administration, spending to fight AIDS is way, way up. And it's going to continue to stay up until we beat that disease. It is way up. And it's going to stay up until we whip that disease. And right here in this area in the National Institutes of Health, they're doing a superb job fighting to find an answer to that dreaded disease. And we're going to keep on doing it.

The last thing we need is the Government standing between you and your doctor. I have a sound health plan that makes insurance available to all. And we need to pass it as soon as we possibly can.

Connie and Helen have championed child care. And ask them—but better still, let's ask the Democrats who should control a child's day care, parents or the Government? I say the parents, not some bureaucrat down there in Washington.

And ask the Democrats who should choose a child's school, the parents or the Government? And I say the parents must have the right to choose their children's school.

We Republicans have always understood the way to keep America first is to put America's families first. And those are just some of the issues we face. In 1992, the first election of the post-cold-war era, you'll decide what kind of medical care your family receives, what kind of schools your children will go to, what kind of jobs you'll have.

And it will be a tough fight. And I know that. And I don't go seeking unnecessary conflict. But when principle is at stake, I fight to win. And make no mistake about it: We are going to win the primary, and we are going to win the general election. And we win by setting the pace. We win by leading.

This American century has taught us many lessons. Above them all is this: When it comes to jobs and economic growth, if America is to succeed at home, it must lead abroad. This year, America is exporting more than ever before. And over the past 5 years, nearly half of America's real income growth has been in exports. And that means jobs for American workers, markets for American goods.

No one said it was easy. Leadership demands character and experience. But right now we hear that America has no business leading the world, that we should just lock the doors and pull down the blinds and hope the world goes away. Well, America is not that kind of country. Never before in this Nation's proud history have we turned our back on a challenge. And we are not going to start now by becoming an isolationistic country.

Americans don't cut and run; we compete. You see, I believe in the American worker. And let's not build walls. Let's open markets, let our workers go head-to-head. When they do, the world will see Americans can outthink, outproduce, and outperform anyone in the world, anywhere, anytime.

And so, in summary, let me just put it this way: I want you on March 3d to send a message to those doomsayers and the pessimists. They say our economy has fallen into an abyss. They say America is a weakened giant. I say, "Bunk." We are the United States of America, and we can compete with anybody. I've heard these doomsayers all my life; so have you. Think back a year ago, one year to this very day. While American men and women risked their lives halfway around the world, what did we hear from those professional pessimists? They spoke of defeat and humiliation. They spoke of a long and bloody war, another Vietnam, a quagmire. Well, they were wrong then,

and they are wrong now.

Here in this county, here in your home county and all across the country, Americans are ready to move, ready to face the challenge and meet a new American destiny. So, I ask you on March 3d to cast your ballots for George Bush. The fight for our future has just begun, and it will continue for 4 more years.

Thank you for your trust.

*Note: The President spoke at 6:18 p.m. at Bethesda-Chevy Chase High School.*

# Exchange With Reporters Aboard Air Force One
*February 25, 1992*

*The President.* Good morning, traveling squad.

### President Reagan

*Q.* What's this about President Reagan says you don't seem to stand for anything?

*The President.* I don't believe that.

*Q.* Are you going to have trouble in California?

*The President.* Well, we're taking it time by time. I think we'll be all right in California. It's a little early to be into that one. We've got some earlier hurdles which I feel good about.

*Q.* Do you expect Mr. Reagan to campaign for you actively?

*The President.* Well, I don't know. He's been very good about that, but I haven't even discussed it with him. It's way premature for that. But he's been quite supportive, as you know, already endorsed me enthusiastically.

*Q.* Are you disappointed at all that he won't be at the fundraiser?

*The President.* No. I've known him for a long time. I'm going to go see him, I think. I don't know if it's going to work out or not.

### The Economy

*Q.* Why do you think your poll numbers are so much lower in California than——

*The President.* I think the economy. I think they're hurting there. And I think

anytime a person has—as President, you take the heat on the economy. It's happening worldwide.

### Loan Guarantees for Israel

*Q.* Any reaction from the Israelis to Secretary Baker's——

*The President.* I haven't seen it this morning, saw some yesterday but hadn't seen anything new to add to that. I thought the Secretary expressed the policy of the U.S. Government very clearly, very forcefully, and very correctly.

### General Motors Plant Closings

*Q.* Any reaction to the shutdown of GM?

*The President.* No, only regret for the hardship that it causes families, but just keep plugging away to try to get this economy moving and stimulated. That's what's needed. So, I'll keep challenging the Congress to do just that.

### Iraq

*Q.* How about Iraq?

*Q.* ——your help to Iraq? What was behind that to help them get loans?

*The President.* I haven't read all the charges about Iraq. But as you may remember in history, there was a lot of support at a time for Iraq as a balance to a much more aggressive Iran under Khomeini. So that was a part of the policy of the Reagan administration, and I was very proud to support it.

### Loan Guarantees for Israel

*Q.* If Congress were to pass the loan guarantees without the settlements freeze, would you veto any such legislation?

*The President.* That's too hypothetical. We spelled out our policy, and there it is. And it's the proper policy. We haven't changed. That's been the policy of the U.S. Government for a long, long time.

*Q.* Is it politically risky for you to now take this position?

*The President.* It might be, but I'm not going to shift the foreign policy of this country because of political expediency. I can't do that and have any credibility worldwide. And we have credibility worldwide. Otherwise we wouldn't have been able to facilitate the peace talks in the first place. So, we just have certain policy positions, and they're sound.

### Presidential Primaries

*Q.* Do you expect to be making a lot more trips to California? How are you going to try and turn around your situation there?

*The President.* Just go about our game plan, which is to take our message out there. I understand there's two extraordinarily successful fundraisers in place out there, so that should say something. Maybe that will get people thinking positively.

*Q.* Mr. President, do you think you'll be able to win California, sir? Do you think you'll be able to win?

*The President.* Oh, sure. Yes.

*Q.* Oh, sure?

*The President.* Yes.

*Q.* Pretty confident?

*The President.* Yes, I am.

*Q.* Patrick Buchanan—fire Bush immediately—do you think he's getting a little personal in his attacks and his charges?

*The President.* I haven't seen that, John [John Cochran, NBC News]. I wouldn't worry too much about that.

*Q.* Those FBI——

*The President.* Yes. I think we're going to do all right down South. I feel good about

it. We've got good people working, and I think the people down there understand my message. And I think as people compare the two candidates, why, we'll be fine.

*Q.* Will you be mentioning Buchanan by name? Last week you said you were going to take the gloves off. Do you intend to do so, sir?

*The President.* Well, I'm still sorting all that out. You heard me last night. I'd rather define it on the issues. There are plenty of surrogates that are willing to make it more specific. I think that's a good way to leave it.

*Q.* Ads starting up in Georgia against Buchanan?

*The President.* I think that there will be ads that define the differences in position, yes. And I expect that people will understand that, after the ads from the Democrats in New Hampshire against me and from him against me. But I'll try to keep it on a high plane—together and go on and win.

*Q.* You seem kind of subdued today, Mr. President. Are you feeling okay?

*The President.* Yes, I feel good, Rita [Rita Beamish, Associated Press].

*Q.* How come you're so subdued? It's early.

*The President.* Do you remember Lesley Stahl [CBS News] asking when the Berlin Wall came down why I wasn't jumping with joy? I said, "We're taking care of this." It's a little early. We're going on a long trip, and it's kind of a calm but determined approach.

*Q.* Have you added any additional stops on this trip? We heard you might add some on the end, Saturday or Sunday, additional stops.

*The President.* I haven't heard it yet, but I might be the last to know. [*Laughter*]

*Q.* We probably would.

*The President.* Have a nice trip to California, everybody.

*Note: The exchange began at approximately 8:30 a.m. prior to the President's departure from Andrews Air Force Base in Camp Springs, MD, for San Francisco, CA.*

## Remarks at a Bush-Quayle Fundraising Luncheon in San Francisco, California
*February 25, 1992*

Thank you so much for that welcome back. Pete mentioned this was my 15th visit. But you have a wonderful way of making people feel at home in this State. Thank you very much. And may I just say from halfway across the world, or at least in the east coast, watching with wonder, what a superb job, fighting difficult conditions, your Governor is doing. It's an inspiration to all of us in politics, I'll tell you. And Gayle, our greetings to you.

May I thank the Skyline College Musicians over there and pay my respects to Eric Stratman, who got up and gave us that wonderful rendition of the Star-Spangled Banner. No pitch pipe, no nothing, just the beautiful music, and we were all so moved by that. And though he didn't confess to this, your bishop or our bishop—my bishop, put it that way, and Barbara's—he used to be our pastor in Washington, DC, before he was elevated to being bishop here in San Francisco. And Bill, thank you, sir, for being with us today and for those inspiring words.

And of course, let me single out the master of ceremonies. I've seen him in all kinds of roles in terms of dealing with world leaders. I've never seen him, I don't believe, as master of ceremonies. But George Shultz is one of the truly great public servants. And I'm delighted to see he and Obie again.

And I want to salute our former Cabinet member Bob Mosbacher; and Bobby Holt here is our national campaign finance chairman; Jim Dignan, the California State chair; Katie Boyd and Howard Leach, who have done a superb job on this overflow luncheon. And also, Gretchen is out here who graciously met us at the airport. Thank you for all the work on the luncheon. And to all the other national vice chairs—Alex Spanos and Don Bren and Craig Berkman and Flo Crichton of the finance team. And a special thanks to Mr. Yong Kim over here, and to my old friend, Johnny Tsu over there, who have done a great job on this. Thank you all.

To paraphrase John Kennedy, I'm touched by that warm response, but not half as touched as all of you have been.

Before I begin, let me just share and express my concern for all the Californians who, after seemingly endless years of drought, have been ravaged by record floods. I am pleased to announce that today, as I came out on Air Force One, I signed a declaration to provide that much-needed disaster relief to these flood victims. They're hurting, and the Federal Government ought to do its part.

I want to talk to you today about some of the challenges that we face, Pete mentioned some of them, about the decisions we're going to make in this election year that are going to really chart the course of this country's future for the next 5 years. And let me lay it out straight: What Government can do and what it can't do, and what I will do as President, and where I will need your help.

Start, if you will, with the number one issue on everybody's mind, and that is the economy, the Nation's economy. One month ago, as the Governor said, in my State of the Union I laid out a two-part economic plan: for the short term, a plan to get the economy moving as early as this spring, seven points to stimulate investment; and a longer-term plan to keep America competitive in the new century ahead. I asked the Democrats who control all the committees in the Congress, both Houses of the Congress, to act for the good of the country. And I gave Congress 52 days to pass the plan.

Since then, some Democrats have been wrestling with their consciences. It is too early to predict who will win. But instead of working on my plan, the House Democrats surfaced their own, a tiny tax cut across the board, written in invisible ink, in exchange for a huge tax increase chiseled into stone. Ask the people out there, your neighbors, is it really worth borrowing from our children to give families an extra 25 cents a day?

That two-bit tax cut would make even the tooth fairy blush. It is not good legislation.

When the cameras are on, the Democrats say all the right things, especially in a political year, talk about a blueprint for an economic recovery. But then the doors close, and the backroom brokering begins. And in the end, it is the same old Democratic deal, another "jobs bill," but this one for the tax collectors.

Now, if the Senate Democrats want to make their temporary tax cut permanent, and this is a fact, they would have to jack up the income tax rate for every American making more than $35,000. You heard that right, $35,000, for a plan that's supposed to help the middle class. And that's going to come as real news to a lot of factory workers and school teachers and everyday Americans that are just struggling to make ends meet. So they are going to tax the middle class for the same reason that Willie Sutton robbed the banks, because that's where the money is.

If you want to give American companies reason to expand, then give them what we are calling for, an investment tax allowance. Speed up the rates of depreciation. If you want to boost the sagging housing market and if you want to give American families a real shot at the American dream, then don't look to the liberal leadership in the Congress. Give first-time homebuyers what our plan does, a $5,000 tax credit toward that first home. Finally, let me just say to the Congress here: If you're serious about competitiveness, if you're serious about creating jobs, then cut the tax on capital gains. These points I've listed, and four more, will stimulate the economy right away.

Now, let's switch over to the defense side of the equation. I'm sure you're reading a great deal about defense cuts. For decades we faced a very dangerous enemy abroad. And we fought the Democrats, those liberal ones at home, who would have stripped this Nation of the strength that it needed to defend itself and to defend freedom. Republicans fought hard on both fronts. Pete Wilson was a leader in this fight when he was a United States Senator. And winning the defense battle on Capitol Hill, as George Shultz will tell you, helped us win the cold war. No one understood that better than my predecessor, Ronald Reagan. He understood it from day one and fought for a strong defense.

Now, given the changes in the world—and they're dramatic and they are wonderful in terms of the future of our kids—given the collapse of the Soviet Union, we know now we can reduce defense spending substantially. So I went to the Joint Chiefs and to Dick Cheney, and based on the recommendation of the Joint Chiefs and the Secretary of Defense, I've proposed a substantial but a sensible defense build-down, one that will recognize post-cold-war realities but still leave this country with the muscle that we need to meet whatever danger comes our way or help defend those whose freedom are at stake.

And we have a number of Federal programs aimed at helping defense industry workers as they seek new careers now because of our defense cuts. We're taking steps to ease the transition that many firms will face as they shift from defense-related work to the commercial economy. That's what this technology transfer initiative is all about that I've proposed, getting research done in Government labs out into the private economy. And in May we're going to bring that message to Cal Tech through our national technology initiative. And that's good news for the high-tech firms right here in the Silicon Valley and all across this State. Our approach is the sensible way to go, the right way to keep the economy sound, and our Nation safe.

But there are political problems. There are Democrats with a different plan in mind in the United States Congress. They want to use the end of the cold war to open a bidding war to see who can gut the Defense Department the fastest. One plan would cut defense by an additional $200 billion over 5 years. Nationwide, cuts on that scale would wipe out hundreds of thousands of jobs, say nothing about rendering us incapable of responding to aggression overseas.

You might think about that. Right now, $1 out of every $5 spent on defense is spent right here in California. Think of the shock waves that would touch off in the construction and electronics and aerospace industries and the aftershock for the real estate markets. Think of the workers, the welders to the engineers, thrown out of work and onto welfare. You can call it a double play, a Democratic double play, cripple our defenses and the same for the economy, all at the same time.

For the sake of national security—and I still view that as my most fundamental responsibility, the national security of this country; I think that is the prime responsibility of the President—for the sake of just plain economic common sense as well, and for the sake of California and the country, I ask you to draw the line and say no to those Democrats who want to recklessly cut the muscle out of the national defense of this country.

We can turn this economy around, provided we deal in economic reality. It all comes down to this: To succeed economically at home, we've got to lead economically abroad. There is no better case in point than this wonderful State of California, none. This State accounts for $1 in every $7 of American exports. In 1990 alone, two-way trade reached nearly $166 billion. For the past 5 years that's an average annual increase of 20 percent. And statewide, I think Pete would agree, it means something like three-quarters of a million, I believe the figure is 725,000 jobs, close to three-quarters of a million, tied into trade.

It is more true than ever before: America's future lies in open markets. It does not lie in this negative view of protection. But the people we are battling in the Congress today aren't about to let the fact intrude on the fantasy. Their prescription for the nineties is really to pull back—not all of them but some of them—to pull back and sound an economic retreat, and then to raise up trade barriers, all in the name of fair trade, but to raise up trade barriers, build new barricades to keep imports out, and take this country back to a dangerous pre-World War II isolationism. As long as I am President, that will not happen to the United States of America.

That's not the American way, certainly not the California way. We don't cut and run. We compete. And we work hard. And I've got a lot of faith in the American worker because our workers have a lot of faith in themselves. If we can do better and make more progress in clearing away the trade barriers and go head-to-head, the American worker will outthink and outperform and outproduce anybody, anyplace, anytime. It's that direction that we've got to take this country.

There's a new reality now in the way people live and work and look at Government. People really don't buy that old "big Government" rhetoric. The American people have seen enough of what we call social engineering. They know the limits of Government. They know that our greatness doesn't spring from Government. America's strengths are in her people, in our families, in our communities. Government can't raise your kids to know right from wrong. It can't legislate happy endings. Government isn't why people work hard, raise a family, save for retirement. And people know, as Government tries to do more and more, it delivers less and less.

And year after year, the main opposition on the Hill, the liberal Democrats who control the Congress, have pushed spending higher and higher. In 1993, the Federal Government will spend $1.5 trillion of taxpayers' money. People are entitled to ask, "Am I getting my 1.5 trillion's worth?"

We need to get back to the basics that Government is too big, and it spends too much. And that leads me to ask you to urge your Congress to give me the line-item veto—43 Governors have it—and give the President, the executive branch, a chance. We need for Government to do less but do better, to focus on what people want and deserve: safe streets, good schools, strong economy, and certainly a strong country.

Today we see the return of responsibility, an old idea that never really went out of style. People have had it with the no-fault lifestyle. In their private lives, they know actions have consequences. What they want is a Government whose policies and programs recognize that people are responsible for their actions and that Government is responsible to the people. Now, if you think about it, that's nothing more than a working definition of freedom.

Because we believe in responsibility, we believe in education reform, fundamental reform. We've laid out a strategy called America 2000, to literally revolutionize our schools. It's not Democrat; it's not Republican. It's not liberal; it's not conservative. It is American, supported by the 50 Governors to meet our six education goals.

We need to hold our kids and our teachers to a higher standard; that's part of it. And here's a radical notion: Let's test these kids at the 4th and the 8th and the 12th grade, see what we're doing, where we're doing it well, and where we need to do more work. Our schools need a good dose of competition with each other. Right now, kids are a captive audience. You give the parents a chance to choose their children's schools, and you'll see our schools start doing their homework. And the bad schools will be picked up by the competition. School choice is working where it's in effect, and it will work nationwide.

Because we believe in responsibility, we back legal reform. Here's the fact: America's become the land of the lawsuit. We've put forward a plan, it's up on the Hill, to cut down a number of frivolous lawsuits. They sap our economy. They strain our patience. When a father can't coach Little League because he's worried about getting sued, something's wrong. When your neighbor becomes a plaintiff, something's wrong. Our country would be a lot better off if we spent as much time helping each other as we do suing each other.

Because we believe in responsibility, we take a hard line on drugs and crime. Tomorrow I go to San Antonio, Barbara and I go down there, and will meet with five or six Latin American Presidents, working with them to sharpen our strategy to beat the scourge. Yes, we're waging a war to cut the supply lines that bring drugs into this country. Interdictions are at an all-time high. But we're battling on the demand side as well. We set a goal to drive down the current adolescent cocaine use by 30 percent. That was our national goal. And we've seen a dramatic 60-percent decrease. Now, that's good news. That's good news for families across this country.

But we all know that we can't begin to claim total victory yet. We must show that here, too, actions have consequences. And that's why we need stiffer sentences for these drug dealers, courts that punish criminals, not honest cops trying to do their job out there, and laws that make life tougher on the criminals than on the victims of crime.

Because we believe in responsibility, I believe as Pete does, we believe as your Governor does in welfare reform. People are willing to support benefits. They've always been willing to give a hand up. Americans care. But they want to see some connection between welfare and work. They want to see governments at every level work together to track down the dead-beat fathers, the ones who can't be bothered to pay child support. And I think most of all they want to see us break this cycle of dependency, a cycle of dependency that destroys dignity and says to a little guy when he's just starting up, "You really don't have much of a chance," passes down poverty from one generation to another. That's wrong. We're going to do something to change it.

Right here in California, Governor Wilson's got a plan that will encourage people on welfare to take work when they can find it; for pregnant teens or parents to stay in school, get the education they'll need to make a better future, a future where they won't need that next welfare check.

What can we do to help California? What can we in Washington do? Simple: We can start by getting our bureaucracy out of the way. And we'll do all we can, Pete, to remove those Federal regulations, to help you cut through that web of redtape to real reform.

These reforms—changes we make now to boost the economy and to transform our schools and our legal and our welfare systems—can really spark a revolution, a revolution to bring this country home to the bedrock beliefs that have made us great. And they are fundamental: Family and faith, responsibility and respect, community and country. Simple words, certain truths that hold a world of meaning, I still believe, for every single American.

Here's what I know about this country's future: No matter how tough times are now, no matter what trials we face, America's best day always lies ahead. I believed that when I was a little kid. I believe it now. I am totally confident about the recovery of this country. And I'll believe it every day I live because that, in essence, is the great glory of our wondrous country.

Thank you all, and may God bless the United States of America.

*Note: The President spoke at 1:13 p.m. at the Westin St. Francis Hotel. In his remarks, he referred to Gov. Pete Wilson's wife,* *Gayle; Rt. Rev. William E. Swing, Episcopal Bishop of California; George P. Shultz, former Secretary of the Treasury, and his wife, Obie; Katie Boyd, luncheon cochairman and California Bush-Quayle campaign vice chairman; Howard Leach, luncheon cochairman and regional campaign vice chairman, and his wife, Gretchen; and Yong Kim and Johnny Tsu, national campaign vice chairmen.*

# Statement by Press Secretary Fitzwater on General Motors Plant Closings
## February 25, 1992

The White House made no attempt whatsoever to influence General Motors' decision over which plants to close and which plants to keep open. The White House considers such matters to be internal corporate decisions.

The President is very much aware of the human costs associated with these tough economic times. This recent plant closing announcement underscores the critical importance of the Congress acting promptly on the President's economic growth package before the March 20 deadline set down in the President's State of the Union Address.

# Letter to Congressional Leaders Reporting on the Cyprus Conflict
## February 25, 1992

*Dear Mr. Speaker:  (Dear Mr. Chairman:)*

In accordance with Public Law 95–384 (22 U.S.C. 2373(c)), I am submitting to you this bimonthly report on progress toward a negotiated settlement of the Cyprus question. This report covers the second half of October and all of November and December 1991. During this period there was a pause in the Cyprus negotiating process, in large part associated with national elections in Turkey and the process of government formation that followed. However, during this period, important contacts between the U.N. Secretary General and the Greek and Turkish Governments and the leaders of the two Cypriot communities continued, as did contacts of U.S. representatives with all parties.

The U.N. Secretary General's report on his good offices mission of October 8 and U.N. Security Council Resolution 716 of October 12 (both attached to my last report to the Congress) were widely discussed in Cyprus, Greece, and Turkey. On November 30, 1991, the U.N. Secretary General issued his semiannual report on U.N. Operations in Cyprus covering the period from June 1, 1991, through November 30, 1991 (copy attached). This was a prelude to the renewal, on December 12, by the U.N. Security Council of the mandate of UNFICYP, the U.N. Force in Cyprus, for an additional 6 months to start on December 15. (There had been informal discussion of changing the method of financing UNFICYP, but no changes were made although it was agreed to consider again, during the current mandate period, moving toward assessed rather than voluntary contributions.)

On December 3 President Vassiliou of Cyprus visited New York to meet with outgoing U.N. Secretary General Perez de Cuellar to review the Cyprus negotiations. He also had an informal conversation with Secretary General Designate Boutros Ghali about how the settlement process might be moved forward in 1992. President Vassiliou also met in New York with the U.S. Special Cyprus Coordinator, Ambassador Nelson Ledsky, and with the U.S. Permanent Representative to the United Nations, Ambassador Thomas Pickering.

On December 12 I met with Prime Minister Mitsotakis of Greece, who was visiting Washington. We discussed Cyprus along with other matters of mutual interest. During our meeting and, in a public statement after the meeting, I assured Prime Minister Mitsotakis that Cyprus remains an important issue on the U.S. agenda. I told Prime Minister Mitsotakis that I would send U.S. Special Cyprus Coordinator Ledsky to the Eastern Mediterranean early in 1992.

On December 19 Secretary of State Baker met with Foreign Minister Hikmet Cetin of Turkey while both were attending the North Atlantic Council meeting in Brussels. Among other subjects they discussed Cyprus, and Secretary Baker told Mr. Cetin of our continued strong interest in the U.N. Cyprus settlement process.

Also on December 19 U.N. Secretary General Perez de Cuellar distributed to the Security Council his final report (copy attached) on his Cyprus "good offices" mission. Although the Secretary General expressed his disappointment that the Cyprus question had not been resolved during his 10-year tenure, he noted the progress that had been made and laid out the areas where work still needs to be done to narrow differences. He then asked the leaders of the two Cypriot communities and of Greece and Turkey to devote their full energies to pursuit of a solution of the Cyprus question.

On December 23 the U.N. Security Council President issued a statement on behalf of the Council (copy attached) that noted the progress already made through the efforts of the Secretary General, endorsed his December 19 report, reaffirmed the Council's position that a high-level international meeting chaired by the U.N. Secretary General and attended by the two Cypriot communities, Greece, and Turkey represented an effective mechanism for concluding an overall framework agreement, requested full cooperation of all parties in completing on an urgent basis the U.N. set of ideas on an overall framework agreement, and called on the new Secretary General to report on progress by April 1992.

At the end of December 1991 Ambassador Ledsky prepared for his new consultation mission to the Eastern Mediterranean. His mission began on January 7, 1992, and will be the initial item in my next bimonthly report.

Like U.N. Secretary General Perez de Cuellar, I am disappointed that circumstances did not allow the Cyprus issue to be resolved in 1991. I would like to take this opportunity to add my personal thanks to Secretary General Perez de Cuellar for his tireless efforts over many years and share with him the sentiment he expressed in the final line of his final report on Cyprus: ". . . the long overdue solution can be reached and the two communities can live together in Cyprus in harmony, security, and prosperity."

Sincerely,

GEORGE BUSH

*Note: Identical letters were sent to Thomas S. Foley, Speaker of the House of Representatives, and Claiborne Pell, chairman of the Senate Committee on Foreign Relations.*

## Letter to Congressional Leaders Transmitting a Report on International Agreements
*February 25, 1992*

*Dear Mr. Speaker:* (*Dear Mr. Chairman:*)
Pursuant to subsection (b) of the Case-Zablocki Act (1 U.S.C. section 112(b)), I transmit herewith a report prepared by the Department of State concerning international agreements.

Sincerely,

GEORGE BUSH

*Note: Identical letters were sent to Thomas S. Foley, Speaker of the House of Representatives, and Claiborne Pell, chairman of the Senate Committee on Foreign Relations.*

## Message to the Congress Transmitting the Report on Alaskan Mineral Resources
*February 25, 1992*

*To the Congress of the United States:*

I transmit herewith the 1991 Annual Report on Alaska's Mineral Resources, pursuant to section 1011 of the Alaska National Interest Lands Conservation Act (Public Law 96–487; 16 U.S.C. 3151). This report, containing pertinent public information relating to minerals in Alaska, as gathered by the U.S. Geological Survey, the Bureau of Mines, and other Federal agencies. This report is significant because of the importance of the mineral and energy resources of Alaska to the future well-being of the Nation.

GEORGE BUSH

The White House,
February 25, 1992.

## Remarks at a Bush-Quayle Fundraising Dinner in Los Angeles, California
*February 25, 1992*

Thank you all very, very much. And what a pleasure it is to be here with Pete Wilson, to be introduced by this man who is doing so much for the State. And thank you for heading our campaign and being at our side today. It is a pleasure to see you and Gayle. May I thank our master of ceremonies, Johnny Grant; say to the next team, Rabbi Greenbaum and Cheryl Ladd, who did a great job on the pledge without missing a beat; and Bobby Britt who did the national anthem. And thanks to everyone who has organized this extraordinary gathering. What did you do? Tell these folks that they had moved the Academy Awards to tonight, I think, when we look around back here. And I'm very grateful.

And let me just say it's also a great pleasure to see Don Bren, who is one of our national cochairmen, and Lod Cook, another one. And thanks to both of you for making this a highly successful event. Greetings also to Bobby Holt, who is our national finance chairman; former Secretary Bob Mosbacher, who did a superb job as our Secretary of Commerce, who is the chairman of our campaign; and all the other Bush-Quayle vice chairmen here tonight.

What an amazing crowd and what enthusiasm. And you all make me feel so young, especially Bob Hope. [*Laughter*] You know, Bob told you only half the story. That story he told was true about Desert Storm. He went over there, but what he forgot to tell you because of his modesty is, I got more reports back from Norm Schwarzkopf and from Powell and from all of them about the lift that gave to those kids, many of whom had been months sitting out in the desert. And we're very, very grateful to him.

And I'm touched, to paraphrase John Kennedy, I'm touched by your warm response, but not half as touched as all of you have been. This has been a big success.

Let me start tonight by sharing my concern for all the many southern Californians who have been ravaged by the record floods here. And I'm pleased to say that today, on Air Force One, I signed a declaration to provide much-needed disaster relief to flood victims. You're hurting, and we'll get you help. And the Governor promptly moved on that for the State.

I want to talk tonight about some of the challenges that we face, about the decisions that will make this election year, that really are going to chart this country's history for the next 5 years. And let me say it straight: What Government can do and what it can't do, and what I will do as President, and then where I'll need your help.

Let's start with the number one issue on everyone's mind, and that is the economy. One month ago, as Pete said, in that State of the Union, I laid out a two-part economic action plan: for the short term, a plan to get this economy moving as early as this spring, and then a longer term plan to keep America competitive in the next century. And I asked the Democrats who control the Congress to act for the good of the country, to lay politics aside. And I gave Congress those 52 days to pass my plan.

And since then, some Democrats have been wrestling with their consciences. It's still too early to predict who will win. But instead of working on my plan, the House Democrats surfaced their own. And true to form, it is a temporary tax cut in exchange for a permanent tax hike. And that tax cut works out to 25 cents per person. Sounds big in a package for the consumption in the

political arena, but that's what it makes, 25 cents per person. And to make it permanent the Democrats would have to jack up the income tax rate for every American making more than $35,000 a year, $35,000. For a plan that is supposed to help the middle class, that's going to come as real news to a lot of factory workers and schoolteachers and everyday Americans struggling to make ends meet.

So let's face it, the Democrats are going to tax the middle class for the same reason that Willie Sutton robbed banks, because that's where the money is. They say they're going to hit the rich, and they end up hitting the small guy.

Now, my economic plan is built on seven specific proposals to stimulate this tired economy. And if you want to give American companies a reason to expand, then give them—and this can be done in the remaining days—my investment tax allowance. Speed up depreciation. And if you really want to do something about boosting the sagging housing market and if you want to give American families a shot at the American dream, then give those first-time homebuyers what my plan does, a $5,000 tax credit toward that first home. Give those young families a chance.

And finally, let me say this to the Congress: If you are serious about competitiveness and if you are serious about creating the jobs, then cut the tax on capital gains and stimulate investment.

That's not the only fight I've got with the Capitol Hill crowd. Take a look at national defense. And it is important to remind ourselves that 365 days ago to this very minute we were starting that flanking movement around the Iraqi army in the sands. And a few months before that, nobody dreamed we'd be faced with that kind of aggression. For decades, we faced a dangerous enemy abroad. And we fought those at home who would have stripped this Nation of the strength that it needed to defend itself, those that always wanted to cut defense. Republicans fought hard on both fronts. And winning the defense battle on Capitol Hill helped us win the cold war. And no one understood that better than my predecessor, Ronald Reagan. He stood for a strong defense and stood up for our principles.

And now, with the collapse of the Soviet Union, imperial communism as we know it gone, we can reduce defense spending substantially. I sat down with the Joint Chiefs and Chairman Powell and the Secretary of Defense, and we worked out a sensible defense build-down. We're talking about $50 billion more cut, one that will recognize post-cold-war realities, but still leave this country with the muscle that we need to meet whatever danger comes our way.

I know that's a concern here in southern California, with its proud tradition of pushing the frontier in aerospace and producing weapon systems that redefined state-of-the-art. We have a number of Federal programs aimed now, as we cut down on defense spending, at helping those workers, those good workers, those defense industry workers as they seek new careers. And we're taking steps to ease the transition that many firms will face as they shift from defense-related work to the commercial economy. And that's what my technology transfer initiative is all about, getting research done in Government labs out into the private economy. And in May we're going to bring that message to Cal Tech through our national technology initiative. Our approach is the sensible way to go, the right way to keep the economy sound and at the same time keep our Nation strong and safe.

But there are Democrats with a very different plan in mind. And they want to use the end of the cold war to open a bidding war to see who can gut defense the fastest. And one scheme would cut defense by an additional $200 billion. And nationwide, cuts on that scale would wipe out hundreds of thousands of jobs, to say nothing about rendering us incapable of responding to aggression overseas.

Right now, $1 out of every $5 spent on defense is spent right here in California. And think of the shockwaves that reckless defense cuts would touch off in the construction and in the electronics and aerospace industries and the aftershock for the real estate markets. Think of the workers, the welders to the engineers, thrown out of work and onto welfare. For the sake of national security and for the sake of just plain economic common sense and for the sake of this State and the country, I ask you to draw the line and say no to those who want to recklessly gut the national defense of this country.

We can turn this economy around provided we deal in economic reality. And it all comes down to this: To succeed economically at home, we've got to lead economically abroad. And there's no better case in point than California. This State accounts for $1 in every $7 of American exports. In 1990 alone, two-way trade reached nearly $166 billion. Statewide, that means 725,000 jobs, close to three-quarters of a million jobs tied to trade.

And it's more true than ever before today that America's future lies in opening markets. But our opponents aren't about to let fact intrude on fantasy. Their prescription for the nineties is to sound an economic retreat and raise the trade barriers and build new barricades to keep imports out and take this country back to the dangerous pre-World War II isolationism. I am not going to let that happen as long as I am President of the United States. We are going to stay engaged and lead the world.

That is not the American way. We don't cut and run; we compete. And I'll put my faith in the American worker. So clear away the trade barriers, go head-to-head, and the American worker will outthink and outperform and outproduce anybody, anyplace, anytime.

People here want to know that increased trade doesn't mean a tradeoff when it comes to concerns about our environment. And earlier this afternoon we had a wonderful meeting. I announced the new initiative to ensure that the promise of free trade includes protection for the environment. And we're working with the Government of Mexico. And we will commit well over $1 billion in new resources over the next 3 years to protect drinking water, pay for cleanups, and enforce hazardous waste laws along the U.S.-Mexican border. And I can say to the people of this great State: Here's proof that we can sustain a strong economy and a sound environment.

Whether it's the environment, the economy, or any other issue, there's a new reality now in the way people live and work and look at Government. People don't really buy the old "big Government" rhetoric. They've seen enough social engineering. And they know America's greatness doesn't spring from Government. Our strengths are in our people, in our families, in our communities. And Government can't raise your kids to know right from wrong. It can't legislate happy endings. Government isn't why people work hard, raise a family, save for retirement.

Year after year, the folks who control the Congress have pushed spending higher and higher. In 1993, the Federal Government will spend $1.5 trillion of taxpayers' money. And people are entitled to ask, "Am I getting my $1.5 trillion's worth?" We need to get back to the basics. Government is too big, and it spends too much. So give me the line-item veto, and let the executive branch try to cut some of the fat out of the budget. Forty-three Governors have it, and 43 Governors do a good job utilizing it. We need for Government to do less but do better and to focus on what people want and deserve: safe streets, good schools, a strong economy, and a strong country.

And today we see the return of responsibility, an old idea that never really went out of style. People have had it with the no-fault lifestyle. In their private lives they know actions have consequences. And what they want is a Government whose policies and programs recognize that people are responsible for their actions and that Government is responsible to the people. And if you think about it, that's nothing more than a working definition of freedom.

Because we believe in responsibility, we believe in education reform. And we've laid out a strategy called America 2000. It literally revolutionizes our schools. Doing it the old way isn't good enough anymore. And we need to hold our kids and our teachers to a higher standard. And here's a radical notion, as our national education plan calls for: Let's test our kids to see where we're doing well and where we need more work. And our schools need a dose of competition with each other. Right now in public schools in Los Angeles and across the country, kids are a captive audience. Now, give parents a chance to choose their children's

schools, and you'll see our schools start doing their homework. School choice is right, and it is working in many States. School choice will work across this Nation.

And because we believe in responsibility, we back legal reform. Sorry to say this in "L.A. Law" country, but here's the plain fact: America has become the land of the lawsuit. And we put forward a plan to cut down the number of frivolous suits. They sap our economy, and they strain our patience. And when a father can't coach Little League because he's worried about getting sued, something's wrong. And when your neighbor becomes a plaintiff, something's wrong. Our country would be a lot better off if we spent as much time helping each other as we do suing each other. And so I will challenge the Congress again and again to do something about the reforms that we have pending up there on Capitol Hill right now.

Because we believe in responsibility, we take a hard line on crime and drugs. Tomorrow Barbara and I fly down to San Antonio, and there I'll meet with five Presidents of Latin American countries, Latin American leaders, work with them to sharpen our strategy to beat this scourge. And yes, we're waging a war to cut the supply lines that funnel drugs into the crack houses that plague good neighborhoods across L.A. County. Interception of drugs coming in is way, way up. But we're battling, also, on the demand side. And we set a goal to drive down current adolescent cocaine use by 30 percent. And we've seen a dramatic 60-percent decrease. Now, that's good news.

But we all know we can't claim victory yet. We must show that here, too, actions have consequences. And that's why we need stiffer sentences for drug dealers. We need courts that punish criminals, not honest cops out there trying to do their jobs. We need laws that make life tougher on the criminals than on the victims of crime. And we need to get that House of Representatives to pass my crime bill and pass it now.

Because we believe in responsibility, we believe in welfare reform. And people are willing to support benefits. Look, we care. We're Americans. We care about the other guy. But Americans want to see some connection between welfare and work. They want to see governments at every level work together to track down the deadbeat fathers, those who can't be bothered to pay child support. And they want to see us break the cycle of dependency that destroys dignity and passes down poverty from one generation to the next. That's wrong to do that, and we're going to do something to change it.

Right here in California, your able Governor Pete Wilson's got a plan that will encourage people on welfare to take work when they can find it; for pregnant teens or parents to stay in school, get the education they'll need to make a better future, a future where they won't need that next welfare check. And we support him. You say, what can we do to help California? Simple, we can start by getting Washington out of the way. And I'll tell you, we will do all that we can to remove the burdensome Federal regulations, to help you cut through the web of redtape to real reform.

The reforms I've spoken about tonight can spark a revolution to bring this country home to the bedrock beliefs that have made us great: Faith and family, responsibility and respect, community and country. Simple words, certain truths that hold a world of meaning for every American.

And I might say parenthetically, if I could be prideful in my comment, I am very, very proud of what Barbara does to demonstrate strength of family and the caring that we all feel in our hearts.

But here's what I know about this country's future: No matter how tough times are right now, no matter what trials we face, America's best day always lies ahead. And I believed that when I was a little boy. I believe it now. I believe it every day I live because that is the great glory of the United States of America.

Thank you all, and may God bless our great country.

*Note: The President spoke at 8:58 p.m. at the Century Plaza Hotel. A tape was not available for verification of the content of these remarks.*

# Exchange With Reporters Prior to Discussions With President Alberto Kenyo Fujimori of Peru in San Antonio, Texas
## *February 26, 1992*

*Drug Summit*

*Q.* Mr. President, what do you hope to accomplish at the drug summit, sir?

*President Bush.* Well, I think we've already—we're going to build on the first meeting, the Cartagena meeting, and we're going to get maximum cooperation. We're going to redouble our efforts on the demand side and on the supply side. So, it's the big picture with very able leaders from south of our border that continue to address themselves to this problem. And there's been marvelous cooperation between the countries.

*Q.* The Ecuadorean President said today that his country needs more U.S. dollars. What's your response to him, sir?

*President Bush.* Well, I'll be discussing it with him when I see him.

*Q.* President Fujimori, will cutbacks in U.S. aid hamper your drug-fighting efforts?

*President Fujimori.* From the supply side, we can, we think we can do a lot on this side, but also we need the better comprehension and coordination.

*President Bush.* And that's all the things we'll be talking about.

*Q.* Do you need more U.S. money?

*President Fujimori.* Also. [*Laughter*]

*President Bush.* Everybody does, including us.

*President Fujimori.* That's the answer they want? [*Laughter*]

*Q.* President Bush, do you believe this summit is going to be of any value?

*President Bush.* I think there's a lot of value. I think the first one was—President Fujimori was not at it, but I believe that it set the ground rules, it set some objectives. I think this one will do the same thing. We have a broader number of countries here; cooperation is good. And we've got to talk about how we can do more on the supply and certainly on the demand side, something that we in the United States are very concerned about also.

So, I view this as a very special opportunity to meet with leaders, men who are doing a good job in their countries and who are determined to whip this narcotics threat just as we are. So I'm looking forward to it.

*Note: The exchange began at 3 p.m. at the Marriott Rivercenter Hotel. A tape was not available for verification of the content of this exchange.*

# Exchange With Reporters Prior to Discussions With President César Gaviria of Colombia in San Antonio
## *February 26, 1992*

*[A question was asked and answered in Spanish.]*

*Q.* How about you, sir? Do you have anything to——

*The President.* Yes.

*Q.* Same thing?

*The President.* Yes, now that I understand what he is saying.

*Q.* You're improving your Spanish. *[Laughter]*

*The President.* I've got Stephanie over here. *[Laughter]* No, but I agree that it's positive, it will be positive. I will say this to the journalists from Colombia who are here: The respect that we have for what this President is doing and has already done is very, very high. And this is a multilateral meeting; we're meeting with other coun-

tries as well, building on the Cartagena summit, which was the first one. But I'm confident that we will come out with more determination to do better on the demand side, which is largely a United States problem, and to redouble our efforts for coordination on the supply side, drawing largely on the experience and the success of this President that's sitting next to me.

And so, we can't take any more questions because we only have a few minutes to talk here. We're glad you guys are here.

*Note: The exchange began at 3:40 p.m. at the Marriott Rivercenter Hotel. In his remarks, the President referred to Stephanie Van Reigersberg, Director of Language Services.*

# Exchange With Reporters Prior to Discussions With President Jaime Paz Zamora of Bolivia in San Antonio
## *February 26, 1992*

*Q.* Mr. President, what do you say to Members of Congress who say your drug war has been a failure?

*The President.* I tell them they don't know what they're talking about. That's what I say. The record is good.

*[At this point, one group of journalists left the room, and a second group entered.]*

*The President.* I might say with your

countrymen here that we are very respectful of the job you're doing and cooperation, not only in the antinarcotics field but in so many other areas. I'm just delighted to see you again.

*Q.* Mr. Bush, is the Government of the United States going to support the private industry helping other programs in Bolivia?

*The President.* Well, we think we need

319

every facet of our society helping, the Government, private, everybody getting involved to help as best we can. And it's a two-way street. I think Bolivia has been very cooperative with the United States. We've got a couple of sticking points here that we'll talk about. But I think generally speaking it's going quite well, and we salute the President for his efforts. He is a dedicated leader who is trying to whip a tough problem. And we know that, and we respect that. So he's welcome here, and we're glad to have the whole team with us.

Thank you all very much.

*Note: The exchange began at 5:05 p.m. at the Marriott Rivercenter Hotel. Part of this exchange could not be verified because the tape was incomplete.*

## Remarks at the State Dinner for Drug Summit Participants in San Antonio
*February 26, 1992*

Excellencies, ladies and gentlemen: Barbara and I are honored to have you join us here tonight. It is a particular pleasure to welcome to the United States our good friends and our neighbors from Mexico, Colombia, Peru, Ecuador, Bolivia, and Venezuela. I am delighted that we've gathered in my home State, Secretary Baker's home State of Texas, with our Governor here, the Mayor of this city here, in this gracious city of San Antonio. For centuries, San Antonio has stood as an important cultural crossroads of the Americas.

We meet at a time of great hope for all the people of the Americas. In almost every nation in the hemisphere, people enjoy self-government and respect for human rights. We're making steady progress to improve our people's quality of life through more open trade and investment, by creating more jobs. That's why I am committed more strongly than ever to completing the North American free trade agreement linking the economies of Mexico, Canada, and the United States. And building upon that, we will realize the vision I call the Enterprise for the Americas Initiative for robust trade and investment from the Arctic Ocean to the Straits of Magellan.

During our meetings this week in San Antonio, we will refine and intensify our common efforts against the menace of drugs. Each of our nations is making progress. Bolivia has successfully intensified its law enforcement efforts against cocaine traffickers. Peru has taken important steps to control airstrips used by traffickers to move cocaine to Colombia. Ecuador is moving against money launderers and traffickers on its territory. Colombia has jailed some of its most violent drug traffickers and is seizing record quantities of drugs. Venezuela is clamping down on those attempting to use its territory to ship drugs to Europe and America. Mexico has reduced cultivation of both opium poppies and marijuana by unprecedented amounts while seizing record amounts of cocaine through Operation Halcion.

For each of our nations, the battle against drugs is truly a war. The ultimate stakes are the same: the minds, bodies, and the souls of our young people, so many of whom have been hurt or destroyed by the violent world of the drug dealers. In the United States, we're stepping up treatment, prevention, and research programs, and we're toughening our prosecution and punishment of drug kingpins.

We're seeing results on the demand side as well. In the United States over the past 6 years, we've reduced the number of regular users of cocaine by two-thirds. Adolescent use of all types of illegal drugs is down. The number of high school seniors using illegal drugs is the lowest since we began measuring their drug use.

We must do more. Drug abuse and drug violence, particularly in our inner cities, threaten to destroy our children and everything else we hold dear. At risk is the civilization we share, our common inheritance, and our common future.

So, let us renew our resolve. Let us strengthen our commitment to guarantee all people drug-free communities. And as we work to advance the quality of life in our own hemisphere in so many ways, let us win a lasting victory in the war against drugs.

And once again, a warm welcome to San Antonio, Texas. And may God bless you and all the peoples of the Americas. And may I raise a glass in honor of our distinguished guests and the important mission that all of us share.

*Note: The President spoke at 8:01 p.m. at the Majestic Theater.*

# Nomination of Joseph Gerard Sullivan To Be United States Ambassador to Nicaragua
*February 26, 1992*

The President today announced his intention to nominate Joseph Gerard Sullivan, of Virginia, a career member of the Senior Foreign Service, class of Minister-Counselor, to be Ambassador Extraordinary and Plenipotentiary of the United States of America to the Republic of Nicaragua. He would succeed Harry W. Shlaudeman.

Mr. Sullivan has served as Deputy Assistant Secretary of State for Inter-American Affairs at the U.S. Department of State in Washington, DC, 1989–1991. Prior to this,

he served as Director of the Office of Central American Affairs at the U.S. Department of State, 1988–1989. Mr. Sullivan served at the U.S. Embassy in Tel Aviv, Israel, as Political Counselor, 1987–1988; and as a political officer, 1984–1987.

Mr. Sullivan graduated from Tufts University (B.A., 1966) and Georgetown University (M.A., 1969). He was born August 9, 1944, in Boston, MA. Mr. Sullivan resides in Oakton, VA.

# Presidential Determination No. 92–17—Memorandum on Counternarcotics Assistance for Mexico
*February 26, 1992*

*Memorandum for the Secretary of State, the Secretary of Defense*

*Subject*: Drawdown from Department of Defense Stocks for Counternarcotics Assistance for Mexico

Pursuant to the authority vested in me by section 506(a)(2) of the Foreign Assistance Act of 1961, as amended, 22 U.S.C. 2318(a)(2) (the "Act"), I hereby determine that it is in the national interest of the United States to draw down defense articles from the stocks of the Department of Defense and defense services of the Depart-

ment of Defense for the purpose of providing counternarcotics assistance to Mexico.

Therefore, I hereby direct the drawdown of up to $26 million of such defense articles from the stocks of the Department of Defense and defense services of the Department of Defense, for the purposes and under the authorities of Chapter 8 of Part I of the Act.

The Secretary of State is authorized and directed to report this determination to the Congress and to arrange for its publication in the *Federal Register.*

GEORGE BUSH

*Note: This memorandum was released by the Office of the Press Secretary on February 27.*

## Exchange With Reporters in San Antonio
*February 27, 1992*

*North American Free Trade Agreement*

*Q.* Mr. President, did you make any breakthroughs on free trade this morning?

*The President.* No. We had good discussions on that with the President of Mexico. And we just reassured him that we want an agreement, a good agreement as soon as possible. No politics, no nothing is going to stand in the way of our doing what is right and what is best for the American people.

And what's best is to get a fair trade—free trade agreement through as soon as possible.

*Q.* Do you think there will be one this year, Mr. President?

*The President.* Well, we're hoping so, yes.

*Note: The exchange began at 8:42 a.m. at the Marriott Rivercenter Hotel. A tape was not available for verification of the content of this exchange.*

## Text of Remarks at the Opening Session of the Drug Summit in San Antonio
*February 27, 1992*

It is a great honor and pleasure to call to order an historic meeting, in a historic city, in a historic State, my home State of Texas. We are all here to make this San Antonio drug summit as successful as the first summit called by President Barco 2 years ago in beautiful, heroic Cartagena. It is fitting to begin this meeting with a warm tribute to the great, visionary man who first brought us together on this issue, Virgilio Barco.

In Cartagena, as President Paz Zamora, who is also here today, will recall, we faced a daunting, unprecedented, some thought hopeless challenge: How to unite against the scourge of drugs, violence, and corruption that was undermining our democratic societies, our institutions, our economies, and our environment.

That meeting gave birth to a new alliance to strengthen our democracies by attacking the drug trafficking and consumption with greater resolve than ever before. Cartagena

was when we stopped the finger-pointing and committed ourselves to cooperation, when we recognized that drugs are an international plague caused by both consumer and supplier.

Two years later the situation has markedly improved. We are facing the challenge. We are united. We are resolute. We are prevailing. We are now seven, not four. We welcome to this group Mexico, Venezuela, and Ecuador, all of whom have shown firm leadership and courage in this struggle. Others in the Americas and Europe are with us, seeing the threat more clearly. Progress is being made. We have courageously faced those who would subvert our societies, break our laws, and kill thousands of innocents. Top traffickers are dead or jailed. Record levels of cocaine and other drugs have been seized. Cultivation has leveled off. Interdiction is up worldwide. We have cracked down on drug users. Consumption is declining as our people increasingly reject drugs, especially our youth. Our judicial institutions are stronger, better able to meet the challenge. Our efforts against money laundering, chemical diversion, and illegal arms exports are improving.

But we are here today because the job is not yet done. We have not yet won this fight. It is time to assess our accomplishments and our plans, to learn from the past and look to the future. Let me mention what seems to me to be some priority areas.

First and foremost, we must reduce demand. All else will fail if we do not do that. I know that task falls heaviest on the United States, and we have made a good beginning. Since I came to office, there has been a 35-percent decrease in current cocaine users, and 27 percent fewer young people are using drugs.

Second, we must continue the economic reform, economic assistance, debt, trade, and investment measures which are so important to our antinarcotics programs. The United States wants alternative development to succeed. I am sure Peruvian and Bolivian peasants will stop growing illegal coca if there is an alternative besides starvation. The stick of law enforcement must have a carrot, an offer of viable economic alternatives for poor peasants.

Third, we must continue and enhance our effectiveness in eradication, interdiction, and law enforcement that have been so critical to our success thus far. Just as demand reduction will lower supply, so also supply reduction will lessen demand. We have laid this out in the "Strategy for Action" that is part of our declaration. We must make it happen.

Fourth, we must look carefully and imaginatively at what might be called nonviolent law enforcement measures. We must strengthen and harmonize our laws on money laundering, arms, exports, chemical controls, asset seizure, and in other areas. It is here that the long arm of the law can fracture the power of the traffickers. The antiracketeering laws in the United States have proven to be one of the strongest measures we have developed in recent years.

Fifth, our judicial systems need our attention. Many of us have underway legal reforms so that we can handle criminal cases

faster, more securely, and more effectively. These are important and should proceed. We must also cooperate by sharing information about traffickers and their crimes so they can be brought to justice.

Sixth, our cooperation has developed in the past 2 years, and I welcome that. We need to keep in close touch so that we can coordinate strategy and understand each others' perspectives and needs. That makes the high-level follow-on meeting very important. It will be the first review of how our "Strategies for Action" are progressing. We also must enlist the cooperation of the Europeans and Asians. To do that we should send a delegation to those countries to talk to their leaders.

Seventh, heroin production is a worrisome problem which Mexico and Colombia are moving against with some success. This is a sign the traffickers believe the cocaine trade is declining. We cannot ignore this new threat, or we risk a surprise in the future.

Eighth, we must do a better job educating our press and our publics about our progress. In the United States, for example, we are seeing a downturn in demand that was purchased at great cost in money and effort. Another example is the story of the drop in cultivation in the Chapare in Bolivia.

Ninth, as we take up the struggle within our own countries with renewed vigor, we must bear in mind that our efforts transcend borders. We must respect sovereignty, or our cooperation will not be sustained. But as sovereign states, we can agree to cooperate against the traffickers who trample on the sovereignty. If we do not work together, the traffickers will destroy us separately.

Finally, one more note of great importance. Everything we do must conform to our democratic principles. None of us wants a drug-free dictatorship. We must protect the human and civil rights of our citizens. We are all committed to defending democracy and its principles as we defeat the scourge of drugs.

*Note: This text was issued by the Office of the Press Secretary. Virgilio Barco was former President of Colombia.*

# The President's News Conference With the Drug Summit Participants in San Antonio
## February 27, 1992

*President Bush.* As the President of the host country, I will give a brief statement, and then we will respond under the plan for responding to questions.

First, let me just say that it has been a privilege and a pleasure to welcome six strong democratic leaders to San Antonio: President Gaviria of Colombia, President Fujimori of Peru, President Paz Zamora of Bolivia, President Borja of Ecuador, President Salinas of Mexico, and then Foreign Minister Duran of Venezuela.

The United States is indeed fortunate to have these leaders as allies in a cooperative fight against drugs. And this cooperative venture is reflected as well in the cooperation that permeates our bilateral relationships, for example, the recent agreement between Peru and Bolivia on access to the sea, a wonderful agreement; growing rapport between Ecuador and Peru, another good sign.

Drug traffickers corrupt our young people. They bring violence to our democracies and destroy our hemisphere's natural environment. This is a new kind of transnational enemy, well-financed, ruthless, well-organized, and well-armed, a foe who respects no nation's sovereignty or borders. The struggle to defeat the narco-traffickers requires cooperation, commitment, and it will not be won overnight. But make no mistake, defeat the traffickers we will.

Two years ago at Cartagena we formed a regional alliance with Peru, Bolivia, and Colombia to confront the narco-trafficking cartels. Today three new allies joined us, Mexico, Ecuador, and Venezuela. In the past 2 years we've made significant progress. First and most importantly, today in the United States there are one million fewer cocaine users and two million fewer marijuana users today than in 1988. Drug use among our young people is down 25 percent, a very good sign for the future.

And second, the so-called kings of cocaine, the leaders of the Medellin cartel, are now in prison or in their graves. And also,

last year, 203 tons of cocaine were seized in Latin America, a dramatic increase. We've shown law enforcement can work in the drug fight.

Third, we are making progress in creating economic alternatives to the coca trade. Farmers who once grew coca in Bolivia are exporting pineapples and bananas. Peru's economy is beginning to grow again, and the Andean States will expand trade with the United States under this new Andean trade preference initiative that I signed into law last December. We will expand our economic development efforts so that people in the coca growing regions can earn a livelihood growing legal crops. And I hope the U.S. Congress will do its part by fully funding my Enterprise for the Americas Initiative.

Let me highlight the most important elements of this joint declaration that is about to be issued, if it hasn't already been passed out. One, drug control and strengthening the administration of justice, includes programs to interdict trafficker aircraft in the air and on the ground, to control essential chemicals and money laundering, and to increase judicial cooperation.

Number two, economic and financial areas, focuses on investment, trade, debt, alternative development, and for the first time, the environmental destruction that is caused by drug trafficking.

And three, prevention and demand reduction, a critical area, involves programs for prevention, treatment, and rehabilitation, scientific research and training.

We agree that the laws of all signatory countries will criminalize all activities that permit the laundering of drug money. And we will exchange more financial information to investigate and to prosecute money launderers and seize their illegal profits. We will negotiate agreements that allow our countries to share the assets that we seize from the drug traffickers. And finally, we will deny traffickers the chemicals they need to produce their deadly drugs. We will regulate sales of chemicals. We will press producing nations to adopt strong controls. And we will increase our own enforcement.

We call upon other nations in the Americas, in Europe, and in Asia, as well as international organizations and financial institutions, to cooperate and to participate. To continue our efforts, we're going to hold a high-level follow-on meeting annually to review progress and plan for the future.

The declaration of San Antonio, building on the declaration of Cartagena, establishes an aggressive agenda for the rest of the century. We believe it will be an important milestone in the struggle against drug use and drug trafficking. We believe it will contribute to democracy and economic stability in the Americas.

It's been a great pleasure to have these leaders here. And may I take this opportunity to thank our hosts in San Antonio, in the museum, in the theater, and all across this great city; the mayor and the other leaders of this community that have made all of us feel so at home in wonderful San Antonio.

And now I understand that Marlin has indicated, so I guess we just go. Chris [Chris Connell, Associated Press], do you want to go first, sir?

*Tax Legislation*

*Q.* Mr. President, while you attending the summit, the House voted down your recovery program, passed the Democrats' tax bill with Republican support. You've lost a third of the GOP votes in the first two primaries. How do you plan to resurrect your recovery plan, and how will you shore up your standing with American voters?

*President Bush.* Well, let's hope that the Senate is a little more—a little wiser than the House. The American people want stimulation to our economy. They're unhappy with the economy, and that affects all politicians. I have won all three efforts so far, Maine and New Hampshire and South Dakota, and I will win this nomination.

But this is an international drug meeting; it has very little to do with the primary system. But I think something that does have something to do with what we are able to do is the American economy. And I

would just ask the United States Senate now to correct the tax-and-spend policies of the House of Representatives that went in almost on straight party lines. It was a predictable, sad, sorry performance, when I said, "Let's set politics aside, go for these specific growth initiatives, and then get on with all of this politics later on." But the House decided not to do that, and so I will just go forward and urge the Senate to take better action. But I am not going to sign a bill like the one that came out of the House. It won't become law. I won't sign it. But secondly, the next hurdle is the Senate, and I don't believe the Senate will go for the same kind of legislation.

*War on Drugs*

*Q.* Mr. President, following up on the drug summit, you say that occasional drug use of cocaine is down by a million. Hardcore use hasn't changed at all, and drugs are still pouring into this country.

*President Bush.* I think the progress— we've said——

*Q.* If I can just say, how will this summit make any difference to that?

*President Bush.* Well, the summit will make a difference to that because we talked about, at lunch, the difference between the spirit of Cartagena and the spirit of San Antonio. One, we have more countries involved; secondly, there is a new optimism. A lot of the talk was about the progress made by Colombia in jailing some of these criminal elements. The spirit of cooperation in terms of judicial reform and in terms of the approaches that I mentioned in this declaration was outstanding.

You don't solve it overnight. When I say young people in this country are using drugs substantially less, down by 60 percent, that is very encouraging to every family in this country. But yes, problems still remain here, and the demand in this country has inflicted serious problems on the economies of the countries represented by these Presidents here.

So the purpose of this meeting is to maximize cooperation, and I think each leader— and they can speak to it themselves—will agree that that's exactly what happened as a result of our discussions here. Now we go on to the next challenge, and that is making more headway on interdiction, making more headway on reduction of demand.

Now, I believe from Ecuador, the second—he's plugged into a different star there.

*Andean Economic Development*

*Q.* Television Bolivia. This is a question for the President of the United States. We have the impression that the U.S. position is much more emphatic in the sense of interdiction than for alternative development. In the case of Bolivia and Peru, this is a very delicate subject. And the Peruvian position indicated that Peru produces 60 percent of the coca used for producing cocaine later, whereas the United States only invests 5 percent of the antidrug budget in programs for these countries, in this case, Peru. Why is it that the United States continues to insist so strongly on the case of interdiction, and it has to be the pressure of the Andean countries that attempt to balance this situation through alternative development?

*President Bush.* One of the themes that I heard here today was trade, the importance of trade. And one of the things we've tried to do in the United States is facilitate trade with these Andean countries. Therein lies a lot of the answer.

We did have a good discussion here about interdiction, and we did have a good discussion about alternative crops. And I think it is for us to assign our own budgetary priorities, but I'll tell you one thing that I learned out of this is the need to work more cooperatively in alternative cropping.

So I'll just leave it very generally there, but we are doing our level-best. And everybody knows that these are not easy financial times for the United States. Spending is up tremendously in terms of our efforts, and I think there's more we can do to be of assistance on alternative cropping. And we had some good suggestions here today from the leaders.

So we will do our level-best, and we will continue to listen to those who say the best answer to the economies down there and to giving hope to the peasants who are locked into the coca growing is expanded trade in other areas. And so, we'll keep trying.

*Mexico-U.S. Relations and NAFTA*

*Q.* Mr. President, I am from Mexico, from the Herald in Mexico.

*President Bush.* I know, but who do you want to ask the question to? I'm over my quota already, but go ahead.

*Q.* I wanted to ask this of the President of the United States and of the President of Mexico. Mr. President, don't you think that the certification statement made by the United States is a way of having intervention in another country, because nobody is carrying out certification of consumption in the U.S.? Secondly, what guarantee do we have that the sovereignty of Mexico will not be impinged upon in the fight against drugs, as in the case we had in—[*inaudible*]. And third, I would like to have your impressions of this morning's breakfast. How about the NAFTA and your commitment made last night to get NAFTA, to bring forward the North American free trade agreement and sending it on to Congress?

*President Bush.* Is the last question for me or for President Salinas?

*Q.* The question is for you and President Salinas.

*President Bush.* I just wanted to be sure.

The guarantee about our overstepping the bounds of the sovereignty of Mexico is twofold: One, I wouldn't permit that to happen; and secondly, Mexico has a very strong, respected President who would not permit that to happen. So there is no danger. The relationship between Mexico and the United States has never been better. And it is built on mutual respect and respect for each other's sovereignty.

What was the first part of your question? I'm sorry, I wrote down interdiction, but I'm not sure that——

*Q.* Certification that the United States carries out annually on the progress made, because nobody is doing the same thing to the United States.

*President Bush.* Well, we try to level with our partners here on the progress or lack of progress we're making in every area. We presented to the leaders here today a thorough presentation as to the progress that we're making on the demand. It is very important that these leaders know that we are trying on the demand side.

I don't know that it has a meat stamp of certification, but these figures will be looked at and reviewed by the United States Congress. And I would be open for any suggestions that President Salinas would make if he feels he needs more information. But the relationship is so cooperative now in this field that I haven't heard any requests for more certification from the United States.

In terms of the free trade agreement, I will simply say what I said this morning: We want it done. We are not going to be dissuaded by political pressures in the United States. I remain convinced that a good NAFTA agreement is in the interest of the worker and of everybody in my country. And I believe President Salinas is convinced it is in the interest of the Mexican people as well. And already the very negotiations that we're having are leading to agreements, such as our recent environmental agreement on the border. So there's nothing but cooperation here. There's some problems that remain in bringing this to conclusion, but we both agreed today that we would press our able negotiators to get this agreement closed as quickly as possible.

And to those in Mexico who listened to some of the peculiar reporting that flows across the border on politics, please let me reassure them that we will press for an agreement. If we get an agreement, we're not going to hang back because of some special interest that may be making a lot of noise as to whether this is in the interest of the United States or not. It is in the United States'. We won't take to the Congress a bad agreement. And when we get a good one, I'm confident that it will be ratified. So, we will push forward on that.

Now, please, Mr. President.

*President Salinas.* The responsibility of the fight against drugs in Mexico will be left exclusively in the hands of Mexicans. It is our responsibility. Therefore, there will be no hot pursuit and no other modality that will go against what I have just stated. We are going to strengthen and reinforce our fight against drugs because it is in our own interest. It is in the interest and for the benefit of all Mexicans to fight decisively, frankly, and openly drug traffickers because

they go against the health of our families. They affect the health of our families, of our relatives. And they also have the money to corrupt anywhere and in any country. Therefore, we are going to continue waging this war against drug traffickers.

And you have there the results and the evidence. Last year we increased seizure of cocaine, 50 tons of pure cocaine seized in one single year with an equivalent value, street value, of twice as much the total external debt of Mexico. And at the same time we had the highest rates of eradication, the highest levels of eradication in the world in 1990 and 1991 to destroy marijuana and poppy crops. We are going to strengthen this because even though a lot of progress has been made, we have to continue waging a war energetically.

And at the same time we are convinced in Mexico that no country on its own is going to defeat drug traffickers. Therefore international cooperation is ever more important. Since we're going to intensify our domestic action, we are also going to strengthen international cooperation with dialog, through communication, through the level of communication and dialog that was attained at this meeting.

And finally, on the free trade agreement, negotiations are going well, very well.

*President Bush.* I think we'll finish this, and then we'll try to get you in the next round, sir, if that's agreeable.

*Money Laundering*

*Q.* My question is, are any possibilities that the United States, within the framework of this agreement, will lift the bank reserve to investigate drug traffickers at the request of Latin American countries which may ask for that in order to investigate cases of money laundering?

*President Bush.* I'm embarrassed to say I don't quite know how to answer your question. We did have a good discussion of money laundering and pledged total cooperation. But beyond that, I'm just not sure of the technical aspects of that question.

*Q.* Within the strategies put forth at this meeting, did any initiative arise to lift that bank security act?

*President Bush.* There was no discussion

of that. There was a lot of discussion of maximizing cooperation on money laundering. But the technical part was not raised with me. Now, maybe it came up in the working groups.

*Andean Economic Development*

Q. I am from Peru, and my question is for President George Bush. The optimistic tone that you express when speaking of the reduction of consumption of various drugs in the U.S., up to 25 percent. Unfortunately I think that this is not shared by the producing countries, and they cannot say the same thing as far as results are concerned because there is a very wide gap.

While the United States invests billions of dollars on the drug war within the United States, it only devotes a small amount to Peru for alternative development to combat drugs, et cetera. How can you explain this, Mr. President? Can't you offer anything better now? Do you plan to do something in the future? If you have the security of being reelected, what will economic cooperation be like, and what assistance are you going to give to Peru and Bolivia who need help in alternative development?

*President Bush.* I think it's fair to say that the responsibility of the President of the United States first is the people in the United States. I mean, I don't want to be here under any false colors. We are spending a considerable amount of money. Drug spending overall, antinarcotic spending in one way or another, is up tremendously, I think, close to 100 percent, 60-some percent since I've been President. So, I would say I have to look at it that way. I hope it's not overly selfish.

We do have very strong aid programs and, hopefully, antinarcotics programs that are effective with Peru. We are dealing, and I think most people here that know our economy would tell you, at a time of rather sparse resources. We are operating at enormous deficits that concern the American people enormously. I mean, they are really concerned about the size of the deficit. So we don't have all the money to spend on all the programs that we think are worthwhile and that we would like to spend it on.

I am determined to do everything I can in terms of setting priorities to help Peru,

to help Bolivia with this alternate cropping and also with their own economies. And I think we've got a fairly, maybe some there wouldn't think generous, but a fairly generous allocation of funds in terms of our overall expenditures to these countries. And I expect that others wish there were more.

I've had a very frank discussion with the President of Peru, who was working hard and has made some wonderful financial changes in that country. Progress has been rather dramatic. And there's no question that he could use more funds, and we respect that. But I have to tell him, I have to set the priorities, and I have to say, this is what we think we can do right now. So that's the way I'd explain it.

Having said that, I don't want to end on a negative note because I think the general feeling at this meeting was one of great cooperation and understanding and frankness—say, "Lay it out there; what do you think you ought to have? You tell us whether we're cooperating with your judicial system." And they'd tell us. And that's the way it's got to be. It is a two-way street. And I think that, you can't put a price tag on it, but that was one of the things that I found the most productive out of this summit.

Does anybody want to ask anybody else a question, because this—I'll take this row, and then everybody else has to ask someone else a question. I thought each one was to get two. Go ahead. I don't want to censor the press, though. I've learned——[laughter]

*Venezuela-U.S. Relations*

Q. My question is for President Bush. Venezuela has been unfairly excluded from tariff benefits which have been granted to other countries. What specific economic measures is your Government planning to take to correct this?

*President Bush.* Well, we did not discuss today bilateral difficulties, for the most part. That subject was not raised by the Venezuelan Foreign Minister who was here. And I just can't give you an answer to it as to how we're going to treat it in the future.

Having said that, let me just simply express my determination to give full support to Venezuela. We think of Carlos Andrés Pérez, frankly, as one of the great democrats in this hemisphere, a man who has stood for democracy. And they are having some difficult economic times. And so in a very general sense I say I would like the United States to be as cooperative as possible with Venezuela. It is essential that this relationship, which I consider good, grow and be even better. But I want to keep it on a very general basis.

Now—oh, you've got one for—you're not from the foreign press corps. You don't look——

*Q.* We get two questions.

*President Bush.* Oh, you do? You're the second American? All right, we're working down this row. This gentleman, and then you're next, okay? Is that fair?

Where's Marlin to do all this? [*Laughter*]

*Peru*

*Q.* My question is for the President of Peru. Yesterday you, Mr. Fujimori, were very clear in indicating that U.S. aid in the fight against drugs, especially in Peru, has not been sufficient. Peru is not asking for money to solve its problem, but rather to solve the problem of drugs which affects the population of the entire world.

You said that you will not accept a timetable as long as there is no financing for that schedule. We cannot speak of objectives unless we speak of financing first. Are you satisfied with the results of the summit meeting? Are you satisfied with the figures? Are you willing to accept a schedule or a timetable?

*President Fujimori.* Precisely I have made comments to this effect regarding the drug traffic in Peru. And that is how—regarding financing for the reduction of this activity in Peru, there have been serious problems, perhaps not so much regarding the amounts which the U.S. Government has generously allocated to us but above all because of the long time it has taken and the cuts there have been for reasons set forth by congressional committees to the effect that there are violations of human rights in my country, according to them, or because of the activity of the armed forces.

Therefore, that long time that it has taken to make these disbursements has led

to the problems. Although these disbursements cannot cover all the areas of the fight against drug trafficking, when there is a reduction, when there are cutbacks, this generates even more problems.

Today we did not speak of timetables, specific schedules establishing dates and deadlines. But I think that in that sense there is agreement among all the countries and among the Presidents for this reduction in drug traffic to be carried out as soon as possible. But obviously, we all understand that this is related to the size of financial support in every sense and the tools that every country has within its sphere of problems. That is why this is the position reflected in the declaration which has been signed today.

Up to now there has been great emphasis made on the subject of interdiction, and this is one of the concerns for producing countries, above all for those which, like Peru, have a high number of farmers and peasants working in the drug traffic.

But today, too, similar emphasis has been placed on alternative development. International cooperation and specifically that of the United States and President Bush particularly, I think, is extremely important. Alternative development which will allow us to have the support of 250,000 farmer peasants as allies, not as enemies, and this will allow us to fight much more intensively.

The bilateral agreement that we have signed with the United States precisely points in that direction. And that agreement now stands, and fortunately, we have the full support of President Bush. And I am sure that along the path of such development we will be able to achieve important results.

*President Bush.* May I say to Marlin—desperately signing "two questions"—but four of the leaders have not had questions. So I would like to address questions, one each, to the remaining four leaders here. And then, since the departures are scheduled very tightly, we're going to have to conclude this press conference.

Local question to one of these four. Yes, do you have a question to the Colombian President?

## Colombia

*Q.* There is a very controversial issue that has been talked about very loudly during the San Antonio summit, and that is your government has been very lenient and has come up with treaties with the narco-traffickers. If they give themselves up, they get a very lenient sentence. What kind of example are you setting for these people that are involved in this business?

*President Gaviria.* You can be sure the men who have submitted to justice, which were the leaders of the Medellin cartel, are going to have stiff sentences. I mean, there are some worries in the media about the sentences they will get, but we have the commitment with the international community. We have a new judicial system. We have transformed the judicial system, fortified, and we have received a lot of judicial cooperation from many countries, including the United States. And we are building strong cases against the narco-traffickers, and we can be sure that these men will get sentences that are proportionate to the kind of criminal activity they developed before they were submitted to the Colombian judicial system.

*President Bush.* This is for one of the three remainders, please.

*Q.* Actually, it's to you, President Bush. The question I have to ask is, over the last——

*President Bush.* Well thank you, I'm not going to take any more questions. I just told you. You didn't understand it.

*Q.* Well, over the last few days——

*President Bush.* Yes, this lady over here. Yes, please. I'm very sorry. You're dealing with somebody who has made up his mind. And we're trying to be courteous to everybody here. Now, if you have a question for one of the other three, ask it. Otherwise, sit down.

*Q.* I'll be happy to ask it to one of the other three; I would like for you to answer it as well. I'll ask it of the President of Mexico.

*President Bush.* He's already had a question. Sorry.

*Q.* Well, he's only had one.

*President Bush.* Okay, you go ahead. We're not used to this, but anyway, go

ahead.

## Mexico

*Q.* Since the Harrison Narcotics Act was passed in the United States, God knows at the beginning of this century, and since the United States and Mexico have cooperated on drug interdiction efforts for countless times since then, I spent some time with narcotics agents over the last few days who made busts who tell us that they're tired. They don't believe the war on drugs can be won. They consider this summit a joke, and they consider the Presidents cooperating in this summit to be a joke as well. What do you tell your people in the trenches, the people that are fighting it every day, what do you give them as a morale booster to tell them it's not a joke?

*President Salinas.* The most important thing is not to have impunity, for those who are acting as drug traffickers to know that in Mexico we are going to punish them with all the energy as is provided for in our law; and also with the conviction that by punishing them we are protecting our families; and also by acknowledging and being very much aware of the risk they're involved, how much their lives are at stake. Our action is completely determined, and we will completely maintain it with full energy. This is a true war in times of peace that we have decided to win against drug traffickers.

## Bolivia

*Q.* I want to ask the President of Bolivia what are his impressions about the summit and what are they expecting for the country.

*President Paz Zamora.* What I take with me from this summit? I think that what part of the press felt that the summit might be before coming here, in the sense that from here we would have a multinational interventionist force going out, moving into our countries, impinging on our sovereignty, I think has been fully cast aside by fact, by what has happened here. And rather, what we find here is a fraternal multinational effort of cooperation among brethren to combat the same evil in a fully independent way, respecting our rights and respecting our revindications, both individual as well as national.

In that sense, I want to tell you that it's a summit meeting in which I was satisfied, for example, to hear the report that I needed to hear as far as reduction in consumption in the United States is concerned. It's a summit that has satisfied me in the sense that I have been able to statistically witness that there has been a reduction in the crops of excess coca leaf in the area, a decrease which, by the way, coincides with what Bolivia has been able to obtain in the last 2 years, which is precisely 12,000 hectares.

Moreover, I believe that in this summit, the ideas put forth in Cartagena are better defined. And today, we see more clearly how one thing is the cocaine-drug traffic duo, and the other is the coca leaf-farmer peasant duo, and we must never, ever confuse the two in our strategies.

And finally, one impression that I want to give you: As always, President Bush has impressed us with his profound understanding of the problem. At this summit, too, I believe we have included concrete, practical elements, mechanisms that did not exist at Cartagena. And we have specifically insisted on what investment should play, what role it should have, both public and private, but noting that here we are not trying to place a drain on the U.S. taxpayers' pocket. We want to tell U.S. businessmen and industrialized countries' businessmen that we can contribute to this fight by investing money in producing countries and investing and establishing alternative development thus for the farmer peasants. I think this is a very important step for this summit meeting.

And something specific to conclude: We have all taken on the commitment, along with President Bush, to make an international offensive, an offensive we will carry out in Europe, in Japan, in Canada. And we've appointed a special group that will travel to get in touch with all of these countries so that they will also become involved in the efforts of Cartagena, one, and San Antonio, two, so that our efforts are truly global.

*Peru*

*Q.* President Fujimori, you yesterday sug-

gested that you're concerned that the drug war may be headed towards a total failure, and also noted that since Cartagena, the amount of drugs, the supply of drugs, has not been diminished at all. As a result of the agreements reached today, are you at all confident or at all assured that the drug war may turn around towards victory? And do you believe in 2 years from now that the supply of drugs in the world will reduce, or do you think it will stay the same or even increase? Thank you. And if the President of Ecuador could comment, too, I'd appreciate it.

*President Fujimori.* Today's meeting has been characterized by the total honesty with which we have faced the various subjects. And thus, when we spoke about reduction, this was studied based on statistical charts, for example, the subject of demand and how that demand in the United States had been reduced significantly.

As far as supply is concerned, the production of coca leaf, as far as the amount of hectares is concerned, we see a reduction of approximately 5 percent to 8 percent from 1989 to 1991. Carrying out an even clearer analysis, this reduction is due basically to what has been obtained in Bolivia, 6,000 hectares. In other words, in Peru there has not been any reduction as far as the amount of hectares devoted to the cultivation of coca leaf. Therefore, if we speak honestly, this program has not been as successful in reducing the production of coca leaf.

Therefore, last year Peru presented a project which finally was turned into a bilateral agreement to carry this out in a different way. Unfortunately, the resources available are scarce. I have stated and I insist that this is a global problem. It involves not only the countries that produce the coca leaf, the commercializing countries, the consuming countries; it involves absolutely the whole world. And what our financing is devoted is not simply for Peru. Therefore, too, we must point out the need for more allocations. For example, in the case of Peru, I'm not talking about allocations for the Peruvian Government, no. This is an allocation for the struggle against drugs which would be applied in the battlefield which happens to be Peru. This is a global war. Part of that war is being waged in Peru.

Therefore, we require greater resources, which I am sure that the U.S. Government and also the governments of the international community will consider in its appropriate dimension. I insist and I repeat that we have had serious difficulties in this past year because we have had those cutbacks and those delays in the disbursements. We hope that such obstacles will not be repeated.

Likewise, we should say that on the supply side, Peru specifically, as the producer of 60 percent of coca leaf in the world and with the participation of 250,000 coca-producing farmer peasants are willing to change lifestyle. And they can do much more. Their contribution can be extremely noteworthy. And that is the potential that every government of the international community must take full advantage of.

Therefore, I was also concerned by the allocations made to the producing countries. I repeat, hopefully this can be improved. And it is also necessary, and I must say this also very honestly, for the good of the struggle against the drug war, that cases such as Peru's will not be slanted exclusively towards interdiction, that this will not be the bias, that we study the problem in an integral fashion, as we are doing it with aid from the United States, for example, in our air control, and at the same time development.

I have criticized the activities that have been carried out in the last 10 years because this reduction has not come about. In other words, what we want is more integral treatment, less police treatment. I think that this is basic. And I think that in that we are in full agreement as well.

*Ecuador*

*Q.* President Borja, yesterday your spokesman told us that you and Ecuador do not have sufficient resources from the United States to fight drugs. Since now there are no specific timetables as far as money is concerned, what do you take back to your country in concrete terms?

*President Borja.* I think that it should be made very clear that, fortunately, Ecua-

dor—I repeat, it should be made very clear that Ecuador is an underdeveloped country as far as drug trafficking is concerned. We do not have coca cultivation. We do not refine cocaine. Drugs are not part of our exports, nor is it part of our economy. But naturally, that does not excuse us from our responsibility of agreeing to efforts with other countries in fighting in a united way against this modern scourge of drug trafficking and drug consumption, behind which there is enormous economic power. It is a plague that goes beyond any national borders. And therefore, as a response, it must receive concerted bilateral and multilateral action for that struggle to be successful.

I have spoken to President Bush bilaterally with regard to the need to finance certain defensive actions, now that we have the time to do it, to keep my country from becoming a drug producer. Up to now, all our struggles against the drug traffic basically have been financed with Ecuadorean capital. But this financing is not sufficient. The task to be carried out is very large. In fact, people have spoken of a war on the drug traffic. That implies a multiplicity of battles that must be won in order to win the war. That requires a lot of money. It requires great efforts. That is why we are here.

As President Salinas was saying, we are here to defend the things necessary for our countries in this battle against drugs. We must concert our battle against the drug traffic. And that struggle must be the result of an international response to a crime of international nature.

*President Bush.* May I apologize for any violation of the Fitzwater ground rules. I wasn't able to control it quite the way I would like to. And I apologize to the fellow Presidents here because we had a little divergence there where it got a little out of the plan that we agreed upon. But I hope you understand. And I hope those journalists from abroad who were denied a question or two would understand, too.

Thank you very, very much.

*Note: The President's 122d news conference*

*began at 3 p.m. on the lawn of the McNay Art Museum. The other Presidents and for-* *eign journalists spoke in Spanish, and their remarks were translated by an interpreter.*

# Exchange With Reporters Following the News Conference in San Antonio
*February 27, 1992*

## Tax Legislation

*Q.* Do you think the tooth fairy is watching over that tax package?

*The President.* What? Something about a——

*Q.* Tooth fairy. Watched over the Democrats' tax package.

*Secretary Baker.* Taxes? State. Treasury is taxes. [*Laughter*]

*Q.* A great line, but never gotten it on the air. This is intense. [*Laughter*] But it's really unsatisfactory?

*The President.* Put me down as dissatisfied, yes. Terrible. It's so political and so disappointing to the American people, I think. But the Senate, there's still some hope there, I think. But it's better to keep trying, keep working, keep pressing for something that will help, not something that has a good political ring to it, necessarily.

*Q.* There's been no attempt by them at bipartisanship?

*The President.* I haven't sensed it at all. I think they voted in the very first minute to try to go politically one up. But I think the American people need some action.

## Drug Summit News Conference

*Q.* You like to answer questions?

*The President.* No, I don't like to. She made me. [*Laughter*] The Devil made me do it. The Devil made me do it. [*Laughter*]

*Q.* Are you thinking about visiting South America?

*The President.* I hope I can get down there again. I know I will sometime.

*Q.* ——visit Ecuador.

*The President.* I've been there. As V.P., I was down there. I've been to Colombia several times.

*Q.* ——apologize to him?

*The President.* I apologized for getting the whole thing messed up. I don't know what happened. I told them all—I mean, I'm afraid I know what happened. It wasn't very nice, but that's the way it is.

*Q.* Mr. President, was Mr. Fujimori too frank?

*The President.* I think you heard what he said in answer to his first question. Be sure you take a look at the text because it was very—quite supportive.

*Q.* I need a question, please. One question.

*The President.* I may not have the answer.

## War on Drugs

*Q.* Do you have proof about the narco-traffic leaders? Did President Gaviria have proof about——

*The President.* Proof?

*Q.* Yes, proof against the narco-traffic leaders.

*The President.* Oh, well, we will give full cooperation to the Government of Colombia to see that these people are brought to justice. And I think he feels he's getting the full cooperation. But it's very important. Intelligence exchange, exchange of information is something where the United States must work closely with this courageous President who is working very hard to bring tranquility to his country and working very hard to break up these narcotic rings. And we salute him for what he's done. And yes, the United States must provide whatever evidence we can to support his cases. And the whole judicial system in the United States, our Justice Department, must work cooperatively with the Government. And we are. I believe he's satisfied.

I really better run.

*Note: The exchange began at 3:50 p.m. on the lawn of the McNay Art Museum. A tape* was not available for verification of the content of this exchange.

## Declaration of San Antonio
*February 27, 1992*

SAN ANTONIO DRUG SUMMIT 1992

We, the Presidents of Bolivia, Colombia, Ecuador, Mexico, Peru, and the United States of America, and the Minister of Foreign Relations of Venezuela, met in San Antonio, Texas, on the 26th and 27th of February, one thousand nine hundred and ninety-two and issued the following

DECLARATION OF SAN ANTONIO

We recognize that the Cartagena Declaration, issued on February 15, 1990, by the Presidents of Bolivia, Colombia, Peru, and the United States of America, laid the foundation for the development of a comprehensive and multilateral strategy to address the problem of illegal drugs. Those of us who represent the countries that met in Cartagena strongly reaffirm the commitments assumed at that time. Meeting now as representatives of seven governments, we express our determination to move beyond the achievements of Cartagena, build upon the progress attained, and adapt international cooperation to the new challenges arising from worldwide changes in the drug problem.

We recognize that the overall problem of illegal drugs and related crimes represents a direct threat to the health and well-being of our peoples, to their economies, the national security of our countries, and to harmony in international relations. Drugs lead to violence and addiction, threaten democratic institutions, and waste economic and human resources that could be used for the benefit of our societies.

We applaud the progress achieved over the past two years in reducing cocaine production, in lowering demand, in reducing cultivation for illicit purposes, in carrying out alternative development programs, and in dismantling and disrupting transnational drug trafficking organizations and their financial support networks. The close cooperation among our governments and their political will have led to an encouraging increasing in drug seizures and in the effectiveness of law enforcement actions. Also as a result of this cooperation and political will, a number of the principal drug lords who were actively engaged in the drug trade two years ago are in prison in several countries. Alternative development programs have proven to be an effective strategy for replacing coca cultivation in producer countries.

Although we are encouraged by these achievements, we recognize that mutual cooperative efforts must be expanded and strengthened in all areas. We call on all sectors of society, notably the media, to increase their efforts in the anti-drug struggle. The role of the media is very important, and we urge them to intensify their valuable efforts. We undertake to promote, through the media, the values essential to a healthy society.

In addition to the cocaine problem, we recognize the need to remain alert to the expansion of the production, trafficking, and consumption of heroin, marijuana, and other drugs. We emphasize the need to exert greater control over substances used in the production of these drugs, and to broaden consultations on the eradication of these illegal crops.

We are convinced that our anti-drug efforts must be conducted on the basis of the principle of shared responsibility and in a balanced manner. It is essential to confront the drug problem through an integrated approach, addressing demand, cultivation for illicit purposes, production, trafficking, and illegal distribution networks, as well as related crimes, such as traffic in firearms and in essential and precursor chemicals, and money laundering. In addition, our governments will continue to perfect strategies that include alternative development, eradication, control and interdiction, the strengthening of judicial systems, and the prevention of illicit drug use.

We recognize the fundamental importance of strengthening judicial systems to ensure that effective institutions exist to bring criminals to justice. We assume responsibility for strengthening judicial cooperation among our countries to attain these objectives. We reaffirm our intention to carry out these efforts in full compliance with the international legal framework for the protection of human rights.

We reaffirm that cooperation among us must be carried out in accordance with our national laws, with full respect for the sovereignty and territorial integrity of our nations, and in strict observance of international law.

We recognize that the problem of illicit drugs is international. All countries directly or indirectly affected by the drug problem should take upon themselves clear responsibilities and actions in the anti-drug effort. We call on the countries of the region to strengthen national and international cooperative efforts and to participate actively in regional programs. We recognize that in the case of Peru, complicity between narco-trafficking and terrorism greatly complicates the anti-drug effort, threatens democratic institutions, and undermines the viability of the Peruvian economy.

We express our support for the anti-drug struggle being carried out by our sister nations of the Western Hemisphere, we call on them to increase their efforts, and we offer to strengthen our governments' cooperation with them through specific agreements they may wish to sign. We value and encourage regional unity in this effort.

We note with concern the opening and expansion of markets for illicit drugs, particularly cocaine, in Europe and Asia. We call upon the nations of those continents and on other member countries of the international community to strengthen, through bilateral or multilateral agreements, cooperation in the anti-drug effort in which the nations of the Western Hemisphere are engaged. To this end, we have agreed to form a high-level group with representatives designated by the signatory countries of this Declaration, to visit other countries of this Hemisphere, Europe, and Japan, with the purpose of inviting them to participate actively in the efforts and cooperative strategies described in this Declaration.

We reaffirm our solid commitment to the anti-drug efforts of international organizations, notably the United Nations and the Organization of American States. Inspired by the mandate of the Inter-American Commission on the Control of Drug Abuse, we express our full support for its programs.

We recognize the fundamental importance of strong economies and innovative economic initiatives to the successful conduct of the anti-drug effort. Further progress in the areas of trade and investment will be essential. We support the Enterprise for the Americas Initiative as a means of improving economic conditions in the Hemisphere, and we are encouraged by the progress the countries of the region have made in restructuring their economies.

We reaffirm the importance of alternative development in the anti-drug effort. We note that the victims of narco-trafficking in the region include those sectors of society that live in extreme poverty and that are attracted to illicit drug production and trafficking as a means of livelihood. We consider that if our efforts to reduce illegal drug trafficking are to be successful, it will be essential to offer legitimate options that generate employment and income.

We propose to achieve the objectives and goals defined above in this Declaration and in its attached Strategies for Action.

Recognizing the need to ensure cohesion and progress in our anti-drug efforts, our governments intend to hold a high-level meeting on an annual basis.

In order to broaden international anti-drug efforts still further, we invite additional countries or representatives of groups of countries to associate themselves with this Declaration.

Done at San Antonio, Texas, on this, the 27th day of February, 1992, in the English and Spanish languages.

*[At this point, the representatives of the seven nations signed the declaration.]*

## STRATEGIES FOR DRUG CONTROL AND THE STRENGTHENING OF THE ADMINISTRATION OF JUSTICE

The Countries intend to strengthen unilateral, bilateral, and multilateral enforcement efforts and strengthen judicial systems to attack illicit trafficking in narcotic drugs, psychotropic substances, and precursor and essential chemicals. The Countries are determined to combat drug trafficking organizations through the arrest, prosecution, sentencing, and imprisonment of their leaders, lieutenants, members, accomplices, and accessories through the seizure and forfeiture of their assets, pursuant to the Countries' respective domestic legal systems and laws in force. To attain these objectives, the Countries intend to carry out coordinated cooperative actions through their national institutions.

Enforcement efforts cannot be carried out without economic programs such as alternative development.

The Countries request financial support from the international community in order to obtain funds for alternative development programs in nations that require assistance.

### 1. Training Centers

The Countries intend to provide training for the personnel who are responsible for or support the counter-drug battle in the signatory Countries at national training centers already in existence in the region. Emphasis will be given to the specialties of each of these centers in which personnel from governments of the other Countries may be enrolled as appropriate, in accordance with their respective legal systems. The signatory Countries, other governments, and international organizations are encouraged to provide financial and technical support for this training.

### 2. Regional Information Sharing

The Countries intend to expand reciprocal information sharing concerning the activities of organizations, groups, and persons engaged in illicit drug trafficking. The Countries will establish channels of communication to ensure the rapid dissemination of information for purposes of effective enforcement. This information sharing will be consistent with the security procedures, laws, and regulations of each country.

### 3. Control of Sovereign Air Space

The Countries recognize that drug traffickers move illicit drugs via identified air corridors and without regard to international borders or national airspace. The Countries also recognize that monitoring of airspace is an important factor in the apprehension of aircraft and crews involved in illicit drug traffic.

The Countries recognize that there is a need to exchange timely information on potential drug traffickers in and around each country's sovereign air space.

The Countries also agree to exchange information on their experiences and to provide one another with technical assistance in detecting, monitoring, and controlling aerial drug trafficking, when such assistance is requested in accordance with the domestic laws of each country and international laws in force.

### 4. Aircraft, Airfield and Landing Strip Control

The Countries, recognizing that private and commercial aircraft are being utilized with increasing frequency in illicit trafficking of narcotic drugs and psychotropic substances, intend to establish and increase the necessary enforcement actions to prevent the utilization of such aircraft, pursuant to the domestic laws of each country and international regulations in force.

The Countries also intend, if necessary, to examine their domestic regulations pertaining to civil aviation in order to prevent the illicit use of aircraft and airports. They will also take the enforcement measures necessary to prevent the establishment of clandestine landing strips and eliminate those already in existence.

The Countries will cooperate closely with each other in providing mutual assistance when requested in order to investigate aircraft suspected of illicit drug trafficking. The Countries, pursuant to their domestic legal systems, also intend to seize and confiscate private aircraft when it has been proven that they have been used in the illicit traffic of narcotic drugs and psychotropic substances.

### 5. Maritime Control Actions

As called for in Article 17 of the 1988 United Nations Convention against Illicit Traffic in Narcotic Drugs and Psychotropic Substances, the Countries intend to strengthen cooperation to eliminate to the extent possible illicit trafficking by sea. To this end, they will endeavor to establish mechanisms to determine the most expeditious means to verify the registry and ownership of vessels suspected of illicit trafficking that are operating seaward of the territorial sea of any nation. The Countries further intend to punish illicit traffic in narcotic drugs and psychotropic substances by sea under their national laws.

### 6. Chemical Control Regimes

The Countries recognize that progress has been made in international efforts to eliminate the diversion of chemicals used in the illicit production of narcotic drugs and psychotropic substances. They specifically support the "Model Regulations to Control Chemical Precursors and Chemical Substances, Machines and Materials" of the Organization of American States, the chemical control measures adopted at the April 1991 International Drug Enforcement Conference (IDEC) meeting, and the recommendations in the Final Report of the Group of Seven Chemical Action Task Force, published in June 1991. The Countries call on all nations, and in particular, chemical exporting countries, to adopt the recommendations of the Group of Seven Chemical Action Task Force. They welcome the work of the above-mentioned Task Force and await with interest its report to the 1992 Economic Summit, in which it will make recommendations for the proper organization of worldwide control of those chemical products.

The Countries express their support for including ten additional chemicals in the United Nations Convention Against Illicit Traffic in Narcotic Drugs and Psychotropic Substances, as proposed by the United States on behalf of the Chemical Action Task Force in the U.S. notification to the Secretary General.

The Countries call on the International Narcotics Control Board to strengthen its actions aimed at controlling essential and precursor chemicals.

The Countries intend to investigate, in their respective countries, the legitimacy of significant commercial transactions in controlled chemical products. The Countries call on the chemical producing nations to establish an effective system for certification of end uses and end users.

The Countries will take appropriate legal action against companies violating chemical control regulations.

Studies will be conducted in the countries where narcotic drugs and psychotropic substances are produced in order to quantify the demand for chemicals for legitimate purposes in order to assist in the control of these products. The United States intends to provide financial and technical assistance for conducting the aforementioned studies and for setting up national data banks.

The Countries urge all nations and international organizations to cooperate effectively with programs aimed at strengthening border control in order to prevent the illegal entry of chemicals.

### 7. Port and Free Trade Zone Control

The Countries intend to implement measures to suppress illicit drug trafficking in free trade zones and ports, as called for in Article 18 of the 1988 United Nations Convention Against Illicit Traffic in Narcotic Drugs and Psychotropic Substances and in accordance with the recommendations of the Ninth International Drug Enforcement Conference. A group of experts may be required to conduct a specialized study in order to identify the ports and free trade zones and identify the vulnerable points in the ports and free trade zones in the region that could be utilized for illicit traffic in drugs and chemicals. This study and subsequent reviews will serve as the basis for adopting measures to prevent illicit traffic in drugs and controlled substances in ports and free trade zones.

### 8. Carrier Cooperation Agreement

The Countries are concerned about the difficulties inherent in the identification of suspicious shipments included in the great volume of legitimate commerce. In order to improve the effectiveness of border controls and also facilitate the transit of legitimate merchandise, the Countries intend to enlist the cooperation of air, land, and maritime transport companies. The Countries agree, in principle, to implement common standards and practices in order to include carriers in measure to improve anti-drug security.

## 9. Money Laundering

The 1988 United Nations Convention Against Illicit Traffic in Narcotic Drugs and Psychotropic Substances establishes a series of measures related to the control of financial assets to which the Countries intend to conform their domestic laws. The Countries support full implementation of this Convention, which requires, inter alia, the criminalization of all money laundering operations related to illicit drug traffic.

The Countries recognize and support the efforts of the Group of Seven Financial Action Task Force. The Countries call upon the Eleventh Meeting of senior-level OAS/ CICAD officials to approve the Model Regulations on Money Laundering related to illicit drug traffic.

The Countries intend to make recommendations regarding the following:

—The elements of a comprehensive financial enforcement and money laundering control program;

—Exchange of financial information among governments in accordance with bilateral understandings.

## 10. Strengthening the Administration of Justice

The Countries recognize and support efforts designed to improve their judicial systems, in those cases in which this may be necessary, in order to ensure the effectiveness of those systems in establishing the culpability and penalties applicable to traffickers in illicit drugs. They recognize the need for adequate protection for the persons responsible for administering justice in this area inasmuch as effective legal systems are essential for democracy and economic progress.

The Countries call on all nations to strengthen the United Nations Drug Control Program.

## 11. Strengthening Judicial Cooperation

The Countries support the provisions of the 1988 United Nations Convention Against Illicit Traffic in Narcotic Drugs and Psychotropic Substances related to increased cooperation and mutual legal assistance in the battle against illicit drug trafficking, money laundering, and investigations and proceedings involving seizure and forfeiture. The Countries must consider approval of the projects of the OAS Inter-American Judicial Committee on mutual legal assistance in criminal matters and on precautionary measures.

The Countries will encourage the expeditious exchange of information and evidence needed for legal proceedings involving illicit drug trafficking, pursuant to their domestic laws and bilateral and multilateral agreements.

## 12. Sharing of Assets and Property

The Countries shall seek to conclude bilateral or multilateral agreements on the sharing of property seized and forfeited in the struggle against drug trafficking in accordance with the laws in force and the practices in each country. The Countries also consider that asset sharing would encourage international cooperation among law enforcement officials, and that confiscated property would be a valuable source of funds and equipment for combatting drug production and trafficking and for preventing drug consumption and treating addicts.

## 13. Firearms Control

The Countries recommend that measures to control firearms, ammunition, and explosives be strengthened in order to avoid their diversion to drug traffickers. The Countries also call for an enhanced exchange of detailed and complete information regarding seized weapons in order to facilitate the identification and determination of origin of such weapons, as well as the prosecution of those responsible for their illegal export.

To this end, the United States intends to tighten its export controls and to cooperate with the Governments of the other Countries to verify the legitimacy of end users.

The Countries consider that close cooperation with the OAS/CICAD is essential in such firearms, ammunition, and explosives control efforts.

### 14. Other Cooperative Arrangements

The Countries recognize that cooperative operations have been a useful tool in the war against drug traffickers in the past. The Countries intend to continue and expand such cooperative measures through their national organizations responsible for the struggle against illegal drug trafficking.

### STRATEGIES IN THE ECONOMIC AND FINANCIAL AREAS

The Countries propose to strengthen unilateral, bilateral, and multilateral efforts aimed at improving economic conditions in the countries involved in the cycle of illegal drug production and trafficking. Extreme poverty and the growth of the drug problem are the main reasons that peasants become involved in illegal coca leaf production. The Countries reaffirm the principles in the Declaration of Cartagena, which accept that alternative economic development is an essential part of the comprehensive plan to reduce illegal trade in narcotic drugs and psychotropic substances. Alternative development cannot succeed in the absence of enforcement and interdiction efforts that effectively reduce this illegal drug trafficking.

The Countries recognize and approve of the structural changes that have taken place in the economies of the Andean countries and Mexico. These changes strengthen stability and increase prospects for economic growth. The Countries recognize that these reforms merit full support. Efforts to attract an increased flow of private investment will provide opportunities for sustained economic growth.

### 1. Economic Issues

The Countries recognize that the Enterprise for the Americas Initiative (EAI) with its three pillars—investment, trade, and debt—offers important means of improving economic conditions in the Hemisphere.

All of the Countries have signed bilateral trade and investment framework agreements with the United States. The Countries recognize that these agreements are important to encourage investment and trade liberalization, and they intend to move ahead with the three pillars of the EAI as follows:

#### a. Investment

The Countries recognize the critical importance of enacting laws and taking steps that encourage private investment and economic development. In this regard, the Countries have expressed their willingness to negotiate parallel bilateral agreements to protect intellectual property rights, as well as bilateral investment agreements, and others that promote trade liberalization. For this purpose, the Enterprise for the Americas Initiative includes trade and investment framework agreements.

The Countries express their satisfaction with the establishment of the Multilateral Investment Fund under the aegis of the Inter-American Development Bank. The Countries consider this Fund important to provide technical assistance and to encourage private investment.

The Countries note that the move towards a market economy in Latin America is a good vehicle for generating sustained economic growth, with benefits throughout society. They therefore view with interest experiences in privatizing services and industries that can serve to attract a significant flow of direct foreign investment. The initiation of operations by the Multilateral Investment Fund and technical assistance in support of privatization efforts will aid in the development of market economies. Some Andean countries plan to proceed with privatization programs and reforms of financial systems to the degree and depth possible in each country.

The Andean countries state that facilitating access to the 936 funds would have a catalytic effect in attracting private investment to that subregion.

The profound structural changes in the region make the active participation of financial entities in funding private projects more important than ever before. The Countries urge entities such as the International Finance Corporation (IFC) and the Inter-American Investment Corporation

(IIC) to continue working with the Andean region. The countries of the Andean region are pleased by Mexico's participation as a stockholder in the Andean Development Corporation (ADC), which is a suitable channel for development activity in the subregion, particularly for the private sector, within a framework of productive integration. These countries express their interest in also being able to count on active participation by the United States Government in the ADC. The United States takes note of that interest.

### b. Trade

The Countries express their satisfaction regarding enactment of the Andean Trade Preference Act which allows the countries of the Andean region to export a wide variety of products to the United States for a ten-year period without paying duties. Those eligible countries that wish to benefit from this law will take the required steps. The United States, furthermore, plans to implement the provisions of this law as rapidly as possible in order to extend its benefits to the countries determined to fulfill the criteria in the Law. The Andean countries also express their interest in having these preferences extended to Venezuela.

The Countries recognize that the proposed North American Free Trade Agreement will be an important step in the process of creating a hemispheric free trade agreement in accordance with the Enterprise for the Americas Initiative. The Countries stress the importance of continued economic integration and trade liberalization efforts.

### c. Debt

The Countries express their satisfaction with the progress achieved by some Andean countries and Mexico in renegotiating their debt with the private international banking system and intend, when appropriate, to continue to support reduction of this debt. The Countries point out that the economic reforms implemented by Bolivia have already made it possible for that country to benefit from the reduction of a large part of its bilateral debt with the United States under the auspices and in the spirit of the Enterprise for the Americas Initiative, which will make it possible to implement environmental projects in Bolivia. The Government of the United States will continue to take the necessary steps to obtain the legislative approval required for the debt categories that still do not have this authorization.

### 2. Alternative Development

The Countries acknowledge that the goals of the Cartagena Declaration regarding the substitution of other agricultural products for coca and other plants that feed the drug cycle, and the creation of new sources of licit income, have not yet been fully achieved. The Countries note that in a major new initiative, the United States—in consultation with Bolivia, Colombia, Ecuador and Peru—is engaged in a program to provide training and technical assistance in agricultural marketing that will stress participation by the private sector as well as assistance for animal and plant health. The Countries applaud this program and intend to facilitate its implementation to the maximum extent possible.

Notwithstanding assistance already pledged by the United States and the United Nations, the Countries recognize the need to establish a broad basis of funding for alternative development. For this reason, and given the worldwide range of illicit narcotics, the Countries intend to strive for increased participation of countries such as Japan and others as well as international financial agencies and institutions such as the World Bank, the Inter-American Development Bank the European Community, the OAS, the OECD and others. The Andean nations believe, and the United States takes note, that such actions should also include the establishment of a facility for alternative development in an international financial institution. The Countries are determined to enlist the support of the international community in their fight against drugs.

The Countries support the work of the OAS/CICAD Group of Experts charged with reviewing the alternative development approach and recommending ways to enhance it.

Under the alternative development program, the Countries recognize the importance of implementing short-term projects such as emergency food programs, food for work, and income and employment generation. The Countries recognize that these efforts must simultaneously accompany eradication efforts in order to reduce the economic impact on coca leaf producers. These short-term actions must be aimed at producing jobs and temporary income until such time as the alternative development projects are fully developed.

The Countries underscore the need for alternative development programs to be strengthened in coca leaf producing countries, or in those countries with areas that have potential for producing plants from which elements utilizable in the production of narcotics and psychotropic drugs can be extracted, so as to reduce the supply of raw material that feeds the narco-trafficking cycle. These programs will help farmers have different economic alternatives, which will allow them to move away from illegal coca production.

The Countries acknowledge the progress achieved in alternative development in Bolivia and the beginning of alternative development activities in Peru. In this context, the Countries note the bilateral agreements with the United States signed by Peru and by Bolivia to implement alternative economic development and drug control programs, as useful experiences applicable to other countries. These two most salient examples are summarized as follows:

## Bolivia

In Bolivia, with the firm support of the United States, efforts undertaken to develop other crops in coca producing zones, as well as in those areas from which people have been expelled, are having some success, starting with the production of genetic material with a proven biological viability, acceptable rate of return and a potential for export. Technical assistance and credit, as well as continued training of farmers, permits the achievement of a good level of technology transfer.

Actions taken in the infrastructure area have made it possible to improve the means of transporting agricultural products to consumer markets and processing them.

Aggressive marketing is slowly allowing the opening of internal markets to the first items of this production, in accordance with phytosanitary and quality control requirements. The support being given to the social dimension by providing infrastructure in the health and education sectors is making it possible to improve the quality of life of the rural population.

A new five-year project, which will start in early June of 1992, will provide continuity and strengthen key activities, such as marketing and private investment.

Multilateral cooperation through the United Nations Drug Control Program (UNDCP) has also assisted in the alternative development process, especially in basic sanitation, roads, energy and agroindustry.

Nevertheless, based on the above-mentioned Bolivian experiences it is recommended that:

1. Recognition be given to the fact that implementation of coca reduction policy has to be adapted to the pace of alternative development in order to reduce the gap between the loss of income and its replacement. It is evident that the success in alternative development will discourage farmers from growing coca.

2. Recognition be given to the importance of full and active participation by the farmers in alternative development processes.

3. Bilateral and multilateral cooperation in alternative development be considered with regard to its specificity. It should include comprehensive, multisectoral and long-term program guidance and should also be sufficiently flexible, broad and timely to be able to promote qualitative changes beyond the short term.

## Peru

In the case of Peru, progress can be summarized by the following points:

—The participation of the United States Government and Japan in the support group for the reentry of Peru into the international financial community. This allows the IDB and other bilateral donors to provide funds.

—The carrying out of massive food aid programs, promotion of a favorable eco-

341

nomic policy framework for the development of the private sector and the liberalization of two-way trade.

—The existence of projects, especially in the Upper Huallaga Valley where 14,000 farmers have received technical assistance in seed research, production, and marketing. The project provided credit and land titles and made it possible to resurface 1,200 kilometers of roads and to set up potable water systems, health posts and latrines.

—The massive support received by President Fujimori from the rural population in coca producing areas.

—Plans for 1992 that call for the resurfacing of the road linking the Upper Huallaga Valley to the coast, a program for recognizing and awarding property rights, and the participation of multinational firms interested in investing in alternative development projects.

—All this has been achieved in spite of insidious narco-trafficking, terrorism and the alliance between the two. Under the Agreement on Narcotics Control and Alternative Development signed on May 14, 1991, which includes aspects relating to interdiction and security, an autonomous Peruvian institution will be responsible for distributing the necessary resources. This institution and its U.S. counterpart will hold meetings to implement the shared strategy, immediately after the Presidential Summit in San Antonio.

—With respect to respect to human rights, the importance of conducting the anti-drug struggle within the framework of international standards is stressed.

—With respect to the citizens' commitment to the anti-drug effort, emphasis is placed on the need for them to have access to information and for efficient legal and administrative systems to exist.

—In order to have adequate farmer participation, consideration should be given, among other requirements, to:

(a) Creating the democratic tools that make it possible to involve the people directly in the decision-making process;

(b) Recognizing, awarding, and registering property rights;

(c) Concluding crop substitution agreements with farmers;

(d) Ensuring that eradication programs take into account the safeguarding of human health and preservation of the ecosystem;

(e) Fostering new economic opportunities, such as alternative development and crop substitution programs, that will help to dissuade growers from initiating or expanding illegal cultivation;

(f) Implementing reforestation programs in those areas where coca has been eradicated but where the land is not suitable for farming;

(g) Substantially facilitating access to business activity and to credit;

(h) Abolishing bureaucratic obstacles and mechanisms, particularly those that limit the production, marketing, and exportation of alternative goods;

(i) Promoting the participation of all countries interested in providing technical solutions and conducting specific alternative development projects with the peasants and/or their organizations.

### 3. The Environment

The Countries express their concern regarding the severe damage that coca cultivation and illegal processing of coca derivatives are causing to the environment of the Andean region. The slash-and-burn method employed by coca and opium poppy growers causes severe erosion of the soil, and indiscriminate disposal of the toxic chemicals used to produce coca derivatives is poisoning the rivers and the water table. These activities enrich a small group of traffickers and cause harm to thousands of people.

The United States Government notes that it is helping the Andean governments address the serious environmental problems caused by illegal coca and opium production. The United States is providing technical assistance and training under comprehensive environmental management programs that are important components of alternative development projects. The United States is providing assistance for watershed management, farm-level and community forestry, reforestation and environmental restoration, education on environmental problems, and environmental monitoring programs. These efforts are designed to prevent damage to—and to restore—the soil, water, and forest resources, thereby improving the quality of life and expanding opportunities for those who abandon, or never initiate, coca production in favor of alternative crops. The Countries agree that such technical assistance and training services must be designed to strengthen the capacity of Andean governments to protect their countries' natural environment.

The Countries agree to design and implement suitable programs to reduce the negative ecological impact of coca production and ensure that security, interdiction, and substitution activities take the protection of the ecosystem into account.

STRATEGIES FOR PREVENTION AND DEMAND REDUCTION

The Countries recognize that consumption of, and illicit traffic in, drugs and psychotropic substances are a comprehensive problem, and that it can therefore be resolved only if control, interdiction, and supply reduction measures are accompanied by vigorous and effective action in demand reduction.

It is also necessary for society, including its members who consume illegal drugs and those who are involved in illicit drug traffic or the cultivation of plants intended for conversion into illicit drugs, to be made aware of the harmful consequences of the production, traffic, and consumption of illicit drugs. It is imperative to provide warnings about the dangers of violence, crime, corruption, environmental damage, addiction, and the dissolution of society and the family resulting from the drug problem.

The Countries are convinced that raising awareness regarding the harmful impact of drug-related offenses will motivate society to develop a culture that rejects drug use and to support vigorously efforts to combat supply and demand. In order to support this awareness campaign, the Countries agree to assume the responsibility, either individually or jointly, to conduct long-term programs to inform the public through the appropriate mass media and other information resources.

The Countries also call on their respective private sectors to combine efforts to create a culture that rejects drugs.

In this regard, the Countries are aware that demand can be controlled and reduced and that the basis can be laid for increasing awareness by means of continuous, systematic actions that include:

*1. Prevention*

The Countries consider that prevention must be a priority aspect of national strategies to reduce the demand for drugs.

In order to prevent consumption of drugs and dissuade occasional users, the Countries must include in their national and drug control strategies comprehensive prevention programs that include, among other things:

*a. Education*

The Countries recognize that education is fundamental in the upbringing of the individual and the creation of positive values and attitudes toward life, and that the educational system at all levels and in all its forms is a suitable tool to reach most of the people. Consequently, the Countries undertake to engage in additional educational efforts for comprehensive prevention of drug use from pre-school through higher education, by means of scientific research, in order to create an attitude and a culture that rejects drugs and in which the family and the community play a fundamental role.

*b. Community Mobilization*

The Countries wish to emphasize the importance mobilizing all sectors of society against drugs as a fundamental part of national prevention efforts. This mobilization includes carrying out actions at the individual, family, and social levels by means of activities that include recreation, sports, and cultural events that make it possible to achieve a total rejection of drug consumption.

*2. Treatment and Rehabilitation*

In order for drug addicts to receive suitable assistance, the Countries consider that it is necessary to increase their capacity with regard to treatment and rehabilitation, in addition to improving the quality of services. The Countries consider that these programs must be designed not only to rehabilitate drug addicts but also to help them reenter society.

The Countries believe that treatment and rehabilitation are basic in reducing the consequences arising from drug use, including AIDS transmission, societal violence, and the destruction of the family and social structure.

### 3. Scientific Research

The Countries recognize that it is necessary to establish programs for basic and social research, including epidemiology, in their national strategies. Epidemiological programs must be conducted using a methodology that makes it possible to compare findings at the regional and international levels. These findings will also be useful in evaluating prevention programs. The Countries undertake to exchange information on drug abuse through a regional information network and to support initiatives to establish a data bank on this subject, especially within the framework of CICAD.

### 4. Training

The Countries undertake to cooperate by providing appropriate technical assistance for the education and training of human resources in these areas.

The Countries will also endeavor to consult with one another and exchange information on the prevention of illicit drug use, treatment, rehabilitation, and scientific research. In this regard, they agree to cooperate in order to determine the most effective ways to utilize the research findings in implementing the various programs.

### 5. National Councils

The Countries are convinced that the creation of national councils to coordinate efforts to develop strategies against illicit drugs has made an important contribution to the development of prevention, treatment, and rehabilitation programs in all the countries.

### 6. Follow-Up

The Countries undertake to engage in ongoing follow-up of the actions described above. To that end, they will assign responsibility to their national councils in line with OAS/CICAD programs.

*Note: The declaration was made available by the Office of the Press Secretary but was not issued as a White House press release.*

## Remarks at a Points of Light Recognition Ceremony for the San Antonio Spurs Drug-Free Youth Basketball League in San Antonio
### February 27, 1992

Let me thank David, David Robinson, for the introduction, what he does for you kids, what these other guys do for you guys; Mayor Nelson Wolf; and it's great to see all of you here. Gregg Popovich and Frank Martin, thanks for the great work you do for the league. I'm also glad to see some of the Spurs here and, of course, an old friend of mine, owner Red McCombs, and players. Thanks for letting Barbara and me take part in all of this.

I'm glad to see so many of the parents here today because the future of every community depends on the strong families. And that was the firm belief of our Founding Fathers, and it's just as true today.

And as for the San Antonio Spurs, well, I've often said that from now on in America, any definition of a successful life must include serving others. And we call helping others being one of a Thousand Points of Light. And it's great to see athletes who succeed off the court as well as on and are willing to help the young people in this country. They set a great example for all of us, and thank you, guys.

You know, many sports celebrities have volunteered their time and effort in the fight against drugs. But think of what could be accomplished if every basketball, baseball, football, soccer, hockey team, from major league to college, followed your example and became Points of Light in this struggle. And then, from San Antonio to Minneapolis, San Diego to Miami, a network of athletes would show our kids there is an alternative to drugs and crime. And think of what would be accomplished if leaders of every institution here committed themselves to helping the Spurs and other organizations solve social problems through voluntary service. San Antonio, the whole city, would become a community of light, something your Mayor over here is working for every single day.

And you kids are learning something more than just how to make a layup, although I saw some real pros out there doing that, put on a full-court press. You're learning about what really makes adults click, responsibility, conscience, and goals. And you're helping this wonderful community become a decent, drug-free, safe place to live. And by staying drug-free, and I just heard a group of these kids take the pledge in there, staying drug-free, you're helping the country set up a chance for everybody keeping away from the deadly grip of drugs.

We're seeing results. This year we've dramatically exceeded many of the goals that we'd hoped to reach, particularly in the area affecting kids like you. The national goal was to reduce casual drug use by 30 percent. It's actually fallen 63 percent. And that's something that we've all done together and something that everyone here, the adults who are working with these kids, should be particularly proud of.

And so, I came here today to meet with Latin American leaders for coordinating our nations' efforts to combat drugs. We are going to win that fight. We had a very good meeting with all these Presidents, who were thrilled to be in San Antonio.

We want to make life better for the kids in this country. And as a Nation, we have to celebrate the success stories. Showing the good that's being done inspires others to get out there and do good as well. And so, we're here to honor something special, your determination and your spirit. And you kids, and the 2,300 like you across this city, are learning very important lessons here: Staying drug-free can help you make your dreams come true.

Today, in order to highlight for others the good work that you are doing here, all of you, young and old, I recognize the San Antonio Spurs Drug-Free Youth Basketball League as our Nation's 705th daily Point of Light. You see, you prove that no community has to accept things as they are. Drugs and other problems can be driven from our backyards if leaders in every community are like these guys, if leaders in every community care enough to urge people to become Points of Light.

So congratulations to all of you who show us that it's better to build children than repair adults. Keep making those hoops against all odds. And may God bless each and every one of you.

And now I would like to ask Pop, Gregg Popovich, to come up here and let me present him with the symbol honoring his efforts, your efforts, the team's efforts as the 705th daily Point of Light for our whole country. You're going to set an example for many others in cities all across America.

Congratulations.

*Note: The President spoke at 5:02 p.m. at the West End Community Center. In his remarks, he referred to center David Robinson and assistant coach Gregg Popovich of the San Antonio Spurs and Frank Martin, director of the youth basketball league.*

# Statement on the Death of Former Senator S.I. Hayakawa
## February 27, 1992

Barbara and I are saddened to hear about the death of former Senator S. I. Hayakawa. Senator Hayakawa was a leading voice on behalf of the people of California and the Nation. His counsel was always sound and welcome, and his legacy will be well re-

membered.
  Barbara and I extend our sympathy to the
family and friends of Senator Hayakawa.

# Statement on House of Representatives Action on Tax Legislation
*February 27, 1992*

Democrats in the House of Representatives today took a turn down a familiar path; they voted to raise taxes. They voted against creating jobs and stimulating the economy. Instead of voting to provide greater opportunities for all Americans, they voted to saddle the economy with a $100 billion tax increase.

In my State of the Union Address I asked Congress to put politics aside and pass my economic growth plan by March 20th. It's a plan that will create jobs and put Americans back to work immediately.

Economists, Democrats and Republicans alike, agree that the Democrat package that passed today does not create jobs or stimulate the economy. The Democrat package gives typical Americans only about 25 cents a day for 2 years. But it increases taxes permanently. I believe a Congress that has consistently shown it spends too much of hardworking Americans' tax dollars should not be allowed to tax and spend any more.

I will not accept the Democrat tax increases. The American people would want me to veto this latest Democratic tax increase. And let there be no question, I will.

# Statement by Press Secretary Fitzwater on the President's Telephone Conversation With President Leonid Kravchuk of Ukraine
*February 27, 1992*

The President spoke by phone with President Kravchuk of Ukraine this morning for approximately 20 minutes. The two Presidents discussed the situation in Ukraine and Ukraine's international debt situation. President Kravchuk stated that Ukraine will meet its goal for withdrawing all tactical nuclear weapons from its territory. In addition, he emphasized Ukraine's intention to support ratification of the START and CFE treaties.

Both Presidents welcomed the excellent state of bilateral relations, and President Kravchuk accepted the President's invitation to make an official working visit to Washington on May 6.

# Statement by Press Secretary Fitzwater on the Confirmation of Barbara Franklin as Secretary of Commerce
*February 27, 1992*

The President is delighted that the United States Senate voted overwhelmingly to confirm Barbara Franklin as Secretary of Commerce. As Secretary of Commerce,
Barbara Franklin will be a leader in the administration's drive to create jobs, increase economic growth, and keep America at her competitive best in the global market

place.

Secretary of Commerce Franklin will work closely with Congress, business leaders, and organizations to ensure that the Nation's business and commerce needs are served in the most productive manner as we move into the 21st century.

# Nomination of Wayne A. Budd To Be Associate Attorney General
*February 27, 1992*

The President today announced his intention to nominate Wayne A. Budd, of Massachusetts, to be Associate Attorney General. He would succeed Francis Anthony Keating II.

Currently Mr. Budd serves as a U.S. Attorney for the District of Massachusetts in Boston, MA. From 1969 to 1989, he served with the law firm of Budd, Wiley & Richlin in Boston, MA, most recently as the senior partner.

Mr. Budd graduated from Boston College (B.A., 1963) and Wayne State University School of Law (J.D., 1967). He was born November 18, 1941, in Springfield, MA. He is married, has three children, and resides in Saugus, MA.

# Remarks at the Houston Livestock Show and Rodeo Dinner in Houston, Texas
*February 28, 1992*

Thank you very much, Don. Let me just say how pleased Barbara and I are to be back here. You have a wonderful way of making people feel at home, those involved in the Houston Livestock Show and Rodeo. Let me first salute last year's winners of the Scramble, of the Houston Calf Scramble, now celebrating its 50th year, and also the 1991 livestock and dairy judging contests. Congratulations on using your $800 certificate to help buy a heifer; what's more, to help pay for a year-long animal project.

To Tom Glazier and Bill Ruckelshaus and his wife, Jill, over here, and Judge Lindsay and our great new commissioner of agriculture, Rick Perry, and fellow Houstonians and Texans. As I say, it is a joy to be back here for a lot of reasons. It's a joy to be out of there; that's in Washington.

But first let me just thank Dick Graves. The first thing when we arrived here that was on our table was a beautiful book commemorating 60 years of the rodeo. And typical of him, his thoughtfulness, there it was awaiting us when we arrived. I want to thank him, and obviously thank him for these two very special commemorative belt buckles. In this tough political season I can't think of a more pleasant way to get belted. And once again, it is a pleasure to be with you.

I went to the first, I think, my first show when Bar and I just moved down here from Midland in 1960. And there we got the feeling of what was going on, seeing the whole community coming together to back these young would-be ranchers and farmers. And I've been back to the show many times.

The spirit of this show has obviously not changed since then or really since it started. Nor has the courage and the heroism of the cowboys, nor the titanic size of the cattle. Seven years ago, as I think Don mentioned, I first attended, a first for me, the Houston Calf Scramble banquet—steak and eggs was what I thought it was when I got going, "calf scramble"—*[laughter]*—but here we are once again 7 years later, and I see that Barbara and I are holding up the meal.

I want to tell you why we were a couple

of seconds late walking in here. We were presented a replica of this magnificent bronze that I understand you can see it from the freeway, Dan Gattis and Joe Ainsworth showing us a model of this. And I just can't wait to see the real thing, time and a half as big as the real horses and just a fabulous bronze. So if any of you haven't seen it, I expect most everyone here has, why, you're in for a treat. From what we've seen, it is really spectacular.

In 1988, I was the grand marshal of the rodeo parade. I would like everybody to know that; that was a great honor. It was only equalled by being the grand marshal a year before of the Daytona 500. I think I was going up, though, when I got to be the grand marshal of this one. And I just wish we were going to be able to be with you for one of the shows. But again, many, many thanks.

A couple of things pleased me. First, I liked the show's timing. Maybe I can pick up some tips on how to herd Congress my way. And if that doesn't work, there's always roping and tying. I'm looking forward to being back in this Astrodome, I might say, this summer very much. We're going to bring a lot of people with us, and I hope that's good for Houston. But I think they're in for a treat as well.

The reason I'm most glad to be with you, though, is a feeling that eclipses time and place. It's the feeling that we share as Americans, a feeling we share as Texans, and the feeling when you see the bluebonnets or spot the cattle grazing in the distance or see a landscape that causes a catch in the throat or a tear in the eye. Ours is a great State, and we don't like limits of any kind.

Ricky Clunn is one of the great bass fishermen. He's a Texan, young guy, and he's a very competitive fisherman. He talked about learning to fish wading in the creeks behind his dad; he in his underwear, wading in the creeks behind his father. And he said, as a fisherman he said, "It's great to grow up in a country with no limits." And I've always remembered that wonderful statement by this young kid who has gone on to be one of the champion fishermen in our country and a proud son of Texas.

We don't like limits of any kind. And we

know that sustained by the big things like family, home, school—and thank you, Reverend Payne—church, community, and country, we can remake a lot of our country in this image that I think of as Texas: generous, self-reliant, enterprising, proud, patriotic.

Here's a story that I think shows what I'm talking about here. It's a favorite of Phil Gramm's. Phil tells of a friend of his named Dickey Flatt who owns his own printing press, lives in Mexia, Texas, population of about, what, 7,000. And he's Phil's barometer of what is right and what is true. He says whether Dickey works 12 hours a day, 6 days a week, whether he's at church on Sunday or a Boy Scout meeting or the chamber of commerce, he can never quite get the blue ink off his fingers. So when a bill comes up in Congress, Phil asks, "Is it worth taking money out of the pocket of Dickey Flatt to spend on this program? And let me tell you, there are a lot of programs," he says, "that don't stand up to that test." And to that, I would simply say Amen. That's the kind of way I think we ought to look at some of the things that are going on in Washington.

Ask yourself or your neighbor: Wouldn't we all be better off if all of us, executive branch and the Congress, thought a little more about people like Dickey Flatt who is out there working his heart out? And wouldn't our lives be better, our Nation greater if, instead of Government, we put the individual first?

This guy Dickey Flatt is like a lot of Texans. We do believe in good schools and good streets. We believe in less Government and keeping taxes down. And we still believe, I think, in a strong defense.

I am very proud that since I've become President, the Berlin Wall has come down and the Soviet Union isn't anymore. Imperial communism, the aggressive communism that wanted to take over the world, doesn't exist anymore. And I think these young kids here today probably go to sleep at night without the fear of nuclear weapons and nuclear war that maybe their mothers and dads did, not so many years ago. So, we have a lot to be grateful for in terms of the changes that are taking place around the world.

Having said that, I have proposed substantial defense cuts based on the recommendation of the Joint Chiefs of Staff and of our very able Secretary of Defense. But people say to me, "What is the enemy?" And the enemy is unpredictability. The enemy is surprise. And I am determined as long as I am President to keep the muscle of our defense intact so that we can guarantee the national security for these young kids that are here today. And that's an awesome responsibility and one that I hope I can fulfill.

We believe that trapping people in dependency is wrong. There's an awful lot of people that need help. They need help from community, as our able judge knows, my friend Jon Lindsay. They need help from Government. And the Government should be compassioned and try to help. But when we have a system that assigns people, because of its inadequacy, to generation after generation of welfare, there's something wrong. And we're trying to change it, and we ought to change it because we need people to have a little more dignity and a little less dependence on a system that regrettably has let them down.

We believe that America is divinely blessed. I still feel this, and I still think that we ought to have voluntary prayer in our schools. I don't think anybody is hurt by that. And I think our Nation was weakened when that was removed from the classrooms of this country.

And so I've tried to highlight some of the values. You know, we had—I mentioned this in my State of the Union Message— several of the leading mayors, I think it was the executive committee from the National League of Cities, came to the White House. And they made a real impression on me— Mayor Tom Bradley of the sprawling city of Los Angeles and others from large cities; one Republican mayor from a tiny town in North Carolina; the Mayor of Plano, a woman from up in Plano, Texas—and all of them said, "We have met, and we believe that the major problems in the cities stem from the decline of the American family."

And so that night in the State of the Union Message, I appointed a commission to be headed by Governor Ashcroft and by Mayor Strauss, former Mayor Strauss, Annette Strauss of Dallas, to take a look at every single piece of legislation to see if in some devious way it weakens family and then to make proposals for legislation that can help keep our families together. The more I think about the problem, the more I think those mayors are right. And I hope as President we can demonstrate not only love for our own personal family but the fact that we think family is very, very important to the heartbeat and to the strength of our great country.

This is America. This is what we are and why we live. And these things are worth fighting for, as Texans have shown that from San Jacinto until just a year ago today, I believe it was, when that war in the Persian Gulf wrapped up with many volunteers, many reserves, many regulars coming from our great State in that war as they have in so many in the past.

There are also things which don't change from one year to the next in our neighborhoods, in our churches, in our families, and in ourselves. And I think these values show why the American way of life is the greatest way of all.

We're in some tough times now. I happen to think there's a little too much pessimism around because we are Americans, all of us here, we are Texans, and we're not going to be defeated. We're going to prevail as this economy comes back. And as we once—we will keep the position we have in the world as number one. I hear people talk about, 'Well, we want to be first." Well, we are first. You have to go to some foreign country, and there's never been more credibility or respect for the United States of America around the world than there is today.

So I think we've been a little too apologetic and a little too pessimistic in these tough economic times. And I hope I'm the one to lead us out of that pessimism into the kind of days that this State knows and knows well.

We are delighted to have been here today. And I might—listen, can I make one other family observation? I am very proud—Barbara's—I'm having difficulty living with her because this morning they named a school for her right here in—Barbara Bush School, and she's been on Cloud Nine since she got back. But I think she's doing a superb job in emulating and speaking for these values that I've talked with you a little bit about today.

I don't know why I've inflicted such a philosophical lecture on you at such an upbeat time as this. But maybe it's just because we feel we're among friends.

Thank you all very, very much.

*Note: The President spoke at 4:07 p.m. at the Sheraton Astrodome Hotel. In his re-* marks, *he referred to Don Jordan, master of ceremonies, Tom Glazier, vice president, Dick Graves, president, Dan A. Gattis, general manager, and Joseph T. Ainsworth, M.D., executive committee member, Houston Livestock Show and Rodeo; William D. Ruckelshaus, former Environmental Protection Agency Administrator, and his wife, Jill; Jon Lindsay, county judge, Harris County, TX; Senator Phil Gramm; and Claude Payne, rector of St. Martin's Episcopal Parish, Houston, TX, who gave the invocation.*

# Exchange With Reporters in Houston
## February 28, 1992

*Presidential Campaign*

*Q.* Mr. President, Marlin Fitzwater says Buchanan is a town bully.

*The President.* Hey, I don't want to take any questions. We're here talking rodeo.

*Q.* They're Fitzwater's words, not ours.

*The President.* I have great confidence in Marlin. [*Laughter*]

We've got to see the big guy here.

A little jackass coming up here. Get him over.

*Q.* I'm afraid to ask a question after that remark. [*Laughter*]

*The President.* That's right—[*laughter*]. I wasn't speaking about anybody in the traveling——

*Q.* Look out——

*The President.* Look out for that jackass there, guys—miniature mule, watch out for the miniature mule over here. These things can kick you.

*Q.* Are you getting tired of getting beat up by Pat Buchanan, Mr. President?

*The President.* No——

*Q.* [*Inaudible*]

*The President.* That's not what these guys thought.

*Q.* This is the symbol of the Democratic Party. [*Laughter*]

*Q.* Are you embracing this animal? [*Laughter*]

*Q.* ——gloves off, Mr. President?

*The President.* Well, some people are sug- gesting that, but I feel comfortable with where we are. I don't think a President should get down there in that level. I think just keep trying to do my job and try to say what I believe, as I did over here. And I was very pleased with the response here, incidentally. You can ask these guys——

*Q.* [*Inaudible*]

*The President.* Well, I feel comfortable with where we are.

*Q.* Do you think that voter discontent will remain so long as the economy——

*The President.* I think the economy has a lot to do with it. I think there's a little too much negative about it, but yes, I do think it will. I have to bear my share of responsibility. What I want to do is put the emphasis on the good things about this country and about the fact that things are beginning to move and about the fact that we've got some fine programs. But when you get into a campaign year, why, things are a little distorted.

The American people are a little tired of all the attack; I think they're a little tired of that. You know, five Democrats out there and then one other guy. So, I'm just trying to do my job and stay calm and say what I'm for and continue to lead this country. I think people——

*Q.* Are you resigned to losing the 20–30 percent in the primary?

*The President.* No, I'm resigned to winning the nomination and winning the Presidency. And I really feel very confident about both. I hope that confidence is justified, but I feel confident about it. And I can't be dissuaded by a lot of political attacks. I've just got to keep—you know, this drug summit yesterday happened to be important if you believe in the lives of our children, if you believe in trying to strengthen families by getting rid of some of this narcotics. So, I have to do certain things that the attackers don't have to do. One of them is be President. And I think I'll be there for another 4 or 5 years.

*Agriculture*

*Q.* Mr. President, in the campaign, agricultural issues haven't been at the fore——

*The President.* No. Part of that is because the early States haven't been as—[*applause*]—hey, wait a minute. Where's the response? Where's my response, hey. [*Applause*] Some of that I think is because Iowa normally is a battleground, and normally we get our ag policies out there. And I think that's one of the reasons you haven't heard quite as much about it, but a very important issue. But I think we've had good

agricultural programs.

One of the main things to do—and this gets into whether you get into the attack business in the primaries—what we're trying to do is conclude a Uruguay round of the GATT that will expand markets for agriculture and avoid some of the terrible Democratic policies of the past like agricultural boycotts. And I've been a President that understands that. And I think farmers, I hope they'll understand it. But I think the reason I gave you is why you're not hearing quite as much about ag issues.

*School Named for President*

*Q.* How many schools are named after you, Mr. President?

*The President.* One, and the vote was 3 to 2. [*Laughter*] But I won it, and the school is in Midland, Texas.

*Q.* So it's tied now.

*The President.* Yes, but she got a unanimous school board——

*Mrs. Bush.* Now, wait a minute.

*Note: The exchange began at 4:26 p.m. at the Houston Astrodome. A tape was not available for verification of the content of this exchange.*

# Presidential Determination No. 92–18—Memorandum on Certification for Major Narcotics Producing and Transit Countries
*February 28, 1992*

*Memorandum for the Secretary of State*

*Subject:* Certifications for Major Narcotics Producing and Transit Countries

By virtue of the authority vested in me by Section 481(h)(2)(A)(i) of the Foreign Assistance Act of 1961, as amended, 22 U.S.C. 2291(h)(2)(A)(i) ("the Act"), I hereby determine and certify that the following major narcotics producing and/or major narcotics transit countries/dependent territory have cooperated fully with the United States, or taken adequate steps on their own, to control narcotics production, trafficking and money laundering:

The Bahamas, Belize, Bolivia, Brazil,

China, Colombia, Ecuador, Guatemala, Hong Kong, India, Jamaica, Laos, Malaysia, Mexico, Morocco, Nigeria, Pakistan, Panama, Paraguay, Peru, Thailand, Venezuela.

By virtue of the authority vested in me by Section 481(h)(2)(A)(ii) of the Act, 22 U.S.C. 2291(h)(2)(A)(ii), I hereby determine that it is in the vital national interests of the United States to certify the following country:

Lebanon.

Information on this country as required under Section 481(h)(2)(D), 22 U.S.C. 2291(h)(2)(D), of the Act is enclosed.

I have determined that the following major producing and/or major transit countries do not meet the standards set forth in Section 481(h)(2)(A) of the Act, 22 U.S.C. 2291(h)(2)(A):

Afghanistan, Burma, Iran and Syria.

In making these determinations, I have considered the factors set forth in Section 481(h)(3) of the Act, 22 U.S.C. 2291(h)(3), based on the information contained in the International Narcotics Control Strategy Report of 1992. Because the performance of these countries varies, I have attached an explanatory statement in each case.

You are hereby directed to report this determination to the Congress immediately and to publish it in the *Federal Register*.

GEORGE BUSH

[*Filed with the Office of the Federal Register, 2:42 p.m., March 9, 1992*]

# Remarks to the Associated General Contractors of America in Dallas, Texas
*February 29, 1992*

Thank you all. Pleased be seated. And Marvin, thank you, sir, for your warm welcome, for your wonderful support, for being an outstanding leader of the AGC. And may I salute—although you are not officially in the lame duck status yet—[*laughter*]—several more months to go—may I also salute Robins Jackson over here, who will be your successor and I'm sure will do a good job as well. I am delighted to be here with Kirk Fordice, the new and outstanding Governor of the State of Mississippi, one of your own. He's served this outfit well as president. And let me also single out a man I've known for years, the Mayor of your host city, my old friend, a former Member of Congress, Steve Bartlett. What a job he is doing for this great city. Steve, where the heck is he? Right over here. And I'm proud to stand with you today, the men and women who work in construction in this great country. You are one gutsy group of Americans, and I believe the whole country knows it.

We mark an anniversary this week. One year ago, American and allied forces liberated Kuwait. In only 100 hours of ground combat, those troops achieved a magnificent victory. When we drew our line in the sand, I faced resistance from two corners. On one side was the latest wave of out-of-touch liberals who argued that we shouldn't fight for what was right. I also had to contend with another group of skeptics, folks who harbor a strange nostalgia for the 1930's, when America isolated itself from the world security challenges and from trade opportunities.

But standing steadfast with me were millions of commonsense Americans like yourselves, and right where you've been in good times and in bad. People in our construction trades have never, never, ever been confused about our national symbol. You know it's not the ostrich; it's the eagle. And I am grateful for your support. We agree on the big issues that shape our world and on the values, the values close to home. And I'm talking about jobs, about family, about peace, for ourselves and for, as Marvin said, for our kids.

Today, our top concern is getting the economy moving and growing again. And I couldn't have a better set of partners in this project than the Associated General Contractors of America. We've been together in earlier battles for this cause, and together we've won. And we've stuck to principles, and we've helped make this country strong. I'll always remember where you stood back in 1982, when times were as tough as they get. The economy then was still in a rather deep recession, reeling from the malaise days of the late seventies. Unemployment, you remember, in '82 was 10.7 percent. President Reagan and I knew that the only effective remedy wasn't more Government control; it was greater freedom. And you shared our long view of things, and you stood with us solidly.

In 1990, when the business cycle turned down, you stood with your President once again and helped me light a fire under the do-nothing Congress of the United States. And because you flexed your muscle, we got one good piece of economic legislation in 1991, one specially good piece: the $150 billion Surface Transportation Act. It took longer than we wanted, but we got the job done.

As you know, I've speeded up the flow of funds from this measure to modernize our bridges and highways. All across America, we're helping companies put people back to work. In fiscal '92 alone, Federal highway funding will support more than 900,000 jobs.

And I have good news for the American economy as we mark the first anniversary of the liberation of Kuwait. As President, I've placed a top priority on helping Kuwait recover from the ravages of that terrible war, from the environmental disaster, from so many things. And as Kuwait rebuilds, I'm pleased to report that American companies have won more than half of all the reconstruction contracts. In '91 and '92 alone, those contracts will pump an additional $5 billion into the American economy, and merchandise exports alone will create 60,000 new American jobs. Now, this good news proves that our long-range program to create jobs by pushing exports is working. In the past 5 years, exports have generated almost half of America's growth. And we're going to keep putting Americans to work by opening new markets for American goods around the world.

There's a lot more that we've got to do to build on our achievements. And in my State of the Union Message, I sent a comprehensive economic action plan to the Congress, and I set a deadline: March 20th. You and I know the major cause of the drag on our economy. It is that Government is too big and that it spends too much.

And that's why I was sorry to see what the Democrats in the House of Representatives did just this past Thursday. To play election-year politics as usual—let me step back. I urged the Congress in the State of the Union to put politics aside and to pass an incentive program, telling them I'll be glad to engage with them politically after the 20th of March and they should lay politics aside until then. I asked them to put politics aside as usual, but playing politics, they passed up a chance to stimulate the economy.

The plan they passed will raise the deficit, will raise taxes, will ruin the fledgling economic recovery, and worst of all, it will not create jobs. So let me right here, before the AGC, end any suspense: If that plan reaches my desk, I will veto it fast and send it back to the United States Congress.

On March 20th, I want to sign into law reforms to get our economy moving. I really think that's good. And we need to get business growing again right now, upgrading plant and equipment again, hiring workers again. We need incentives, incentives like an investment tax allowance. Consider how that would help Williams Brothers Construction Company, just for example. If my 15-percent investment tax allowance is passed by Congress, it will mean an additional $300,000 in working capital this year for this equipment-intensive contractor.

And yes, it is clearly time for Congress to cut that tax on job creation and investment. It is time to cut the tax on capital gains.

To get housing back on its feet, I've put forward what I think most people across this country see as commonsense proposals to get people buying and building homes. For instance—we talk about family—but for instance, I'm asking for a $5,000 tax credit for first-time homebuyers. The Democrats in the House offer these young people nothing. But with our plan, young people almost able to buy that first home could do it with the extra $5,000 in their pocket.

Just the other day I met with your industry partners, the National Association of Home Builders. Their economists predict that this year alone, this year alone, my plan would mean an extra 200,000 homes built and 415,000 new jobs in the home-building side of the construction business. Since you clear the tracts and pave the new streets and build the shopping and office centers that go with new neighborhoods, I know that growth in housing would be welcome on your side of the business, too.

Your powers of persuasion are legendary. You've got a lot of respect, power in the corridors of power. And so, I'm counting on you to get my message to the Congress: Pass this incentive plan, and meet the deadline. Tell your Members of Congress, March 20th is when the rubber meets the road. And March 20th is when the Congress has to make a choice: Put America back to work, or go with the old tax-and-spend politics as usual. I believe March 20th is the time to do something good for the American people. Please get that message to Congress.

While Congress chafes under that deadline, and while Senate Democrats now float tax plans that would end up raising tax rates for people who make $35,000 a year, I have taken actions on my own to get the economy moving. For example, we've begun an unprecedented, top-to-bottom reform of business regulation.

During the weeks since the State of the Union Address, we've changed key banking rules to ease the credit crunch. For healthy banks, we've changed overly strict definitions of bank capital, creating more access to capital. We've also cut redtape to make it easier for small businesses to get capital from the securities markets. And we've accomplished important reforms to the burdensome payroll tax system.

But that's not all. On January 28th, I instituted a 90-day freeze on new Federal regulations that could hinder economic growth. And we're also reviewing all existing rules, and we will propose legislation wherever needed to reform burdensome regulation. And let me tell you, we will take every action we can to stop regulations that hurt growth and speed up rules that will help get this economy growing. We are overregulated, and I need your help with Congress on that point as well.

Marvin and others have been in touch. And I know that the construction industry is hard-hit by Federal regulation. That's why we've acted to allow Federal contractors more flexibility in the use of less-skilled workers. We recently began implementing an important rule that allows such cost-

saving measures. Not only will the rule make it easier for construction firms to do business, it will also save taxpayers an estimated $600 million a year.

Many times there's a noble idea behind a regulation, but many times regulators go to unreasonable extremes. My message to Congress, and yes, to the regulators in the executive branch is this: Overregulation is just that, it's over. And let me say this: If there are exceptions—and some regulators have not gotten the word—tell your leadership, tell Marvin here, let us know. And I will do my level best to clear out any unfair obstacles to growth.

I'm also fighting hard against another epidemic that's stricken America, against the epidemic of lawsuits, 18 million last year alone. I think you got it but lest you didn't, 18 million last year alone. The costs and delays in our legal system are a hidden tax on every construction operator, on every consumer, on every business transaction in this country.

And it's not just the cost of doing business that's being affected. Frivolous lawsuits are tearing apart our social fabric in this country. Some of you probably coach Little League. You're aware, as well as I am, that all around this country fathers are quitting as Little League coaches because they're afraid of liability lawsuits. That's a sign that something's wrong. Or when people stop volunteering in their communities because they fear some ambulance-chasing lawyer, something is terribly wrong. And I've even heard that communities have had to cancel Fourth of July fireworks displays because they can't get liability insurance.

Well, I am determined to change that. And I've sent a reform bill to Congress to halt needless lawsuits and to give Americans easier alternatives for settling disputes. I see that you in the AGC have your own industry initiative to achieve more partnership and fewer lawsuits among contractors and subcontractors. And I applaud you for doing this. The real answer to solving problems is to be more concerned with helping each other than suing each other. And I want to fight for the reforms that will back up that principle. So, let's work together. Let's keep working together to break up

America's love affair with the lawsuit.

Since the first settlers came to our shores, Americans have been a restless people. We're forever on the move building, inventing, expanding, renewing. And I share that spirit, and I've never been more restless than now about the state of affairs in Washington. The rest of the world looks to us as a beacon—don't listen to the naysayers on this point—the rest of the world looks to us as a beacon, as the strongest, bravest, freest, most generous nation on Earth. But in our Nation's Capital, the tired old liberal leadership of Congress is mired in cynicism and defeatism.

For 3 years, I've wrestled with a Congress too often paralyzed, tangled up by a 30,000-person bureaucracy and a $1.5 billion budget, a Congress too caught up in protecting their special perks and privileges to perform the public's business. No wonder term limits for Congress are picking up support. And I agree. If we have term limits on the President, term limits for Congress is a good idea, too. And let's work for it.

The old ways have to change. People want change. Each one of you is a proven leader in a trade that wrote the book about getting top-quality projects done, and done within deadlines. So, I'm counting on you to make Congress learn how to meet a deadline.

My opponents have cornered the market for slick rhetoric. But when it comes to delivering results, I have a plan that will stimulate economic growth. And they don't.

I need your help. Help me get a message to Capitol Hill. Tell them what hard-hat America thinks about Congress and its politics-as-usual. Tell them the construction trades support this plan to get our economy moving. And tell them I'm dead serious about that deadline and that you're dead serious about the deadline. And tell them my plan sets down a solid foundation for lifting this country to new heights.

This convention hall holds very special memories for me. It was here in 1984 that Ronald Reagan and I accepted our party's nomination for a second term as President and Vice President of the United States. And I was very proud to serve with Ronald Reagan, and he's a man of vision and courage and achievement. And remember the recession of 1982? It was tough then. Remember the criticism? Remember the noise on Capitol Hill? Unemployment got up to 10.7 percent. But we stayed tough, kept the Congress from doing crazy things, renewed our commitment to keep this country moving forward for the long haul. We pulled out of the doldrums, and we kept moving America forward because we had your support and the support of millions like you who share our values.

And yes, times are tough now, but we will stick to principle. And we will again come through these sluggish economic times. This is no time for despair. This is time for determination. And this is time for action.

The American people are getting a little tired, frankly, of the gloom and doom they hear every single night on television. And I'm glad my frank wife, Barbara, is not here or she'd tell you what she thought about that. [*Laughter*]

Our side will prevail again. With your mind and your muscle, we'll prove the pessimists wrong again. People know we're in a battle for the future—about jobs; it's about family; it's about world peace; it's about the kind of legacy we're going to leave the young ones here today. And we will renew this country, and I guarantee you we will keep it strong. And we will build a better America.

Thank you. Good luck to each and every one of you. And may God bless the United States of America. Thank you very, very much.

*Note: The President spoke at 9:44 a.m. at the Dallas Convention Center. In his remarks, he referred to Marvin Black, president of the Associated General Contractors of America.*

## Remarks to the Georgia Republican Party in Atlanta, Georgia
*February 29, 1992*

*Audience members.* Four more years! Four more years! Four more years!

*The President.* Thank you, Alec. Thank you, Newt. And thank all of you. Let me single out our chairman, Alec Poitevint, and thank him for his leadership of this obviously activated, insurgent, and wonderful Georgia Republican Party. Get to Newt in a minute, but may I salute the members of the Georgia General Assembly that are here, my old friend Senator Mack Mattingly, who is sorely missed in the United States Senate, I might add.

And I understand that Savannah's Mayor is here, and I look forward to being with Susan Weiner tomorrow as well. And I thank our national committeewoman, Carolyn Meadows, and our Georgia campaign chairman, my old friend Fred Cooper, who is over here somewhere but doing a great job.

And as for Newt, there is no one quite like him. Let me simply say he is, as you know, clearly one of the very, very top leaders of the Republican Party nationally. And I am very grateful to him for the steadfast support and leadership that we get on Capitol Hill. Every single day that I work with him and with Bob Michel, I'm saying to myself: We have got to take the message to the people in the fall to get more Republicans in the Senate and get more Republicans in the House of Representatives. If you want change, that's the kind of change we need.

And my thanks to all of you for coming to Atlanta from all over, Macon to Marietta, from the four corners of this great State. This gathering marks a great triumph. You look around this room, and I think it's just clear how far we've come. It must be something about the Republican Party and red clay. [*Laughter*] In this State and all across the South, the Republican Party is here to stay. And that is what this meeting is about. And that's what the votes in this State are all about.

And with this rise comes a new generation of Georgia Republicans, the reformers, who are trying to teach Washington, DC, the wisdom of their ways. And I'm talking, of course, about Newt Gingrich and Mack, and about Bo Callaway and thinking back; thinking about Lou Sullivan now. And when we call the roll, let's not forget Pinpoint's favorite son, Supreme Court Justice of the United States Clarence Thomas. And I'm proud I named him to that Court.

Our party prospers here because the great strengths of the Republican Party are the great strengths of the South: bedrock belief in family and in faith, community and country; the virtues of hard work and humble worship; the willingness to sacrifice for country in times of war and to help others in times of peace. These are the beliefs that sustain us. It's our commitment to family, to jobs, to peace that inspires us. And all across America, these values are growing stronger, coming back by popular demand. And as a Nation, we've begun to see in these values a solution to so many of the crises that plague our cities and our schools and our streets.

People are coming home to the values that never left their hearts. We believe that parents, not the Government, should make the decisions that truly matter in life. Parents, not Government, should choose their children's schools. Parents, not Government, should choose who cares for their children. Parents know better than some bureaucrat in Washington, DC. And yes, we believe there's a place for voluntary prayer in our children's classroom.

And we believe America's first so long as we put family first. And these bedrock beliefs, they don't fade with age. They don't change from one election to the next. They are the home truths that call this Nation forward to greatness. And if America holds fast to these truths, we'll never lose our bearings.

Still, right now there's no denying it, in too many ways we're going down the wrong track. We've got to reform our legal system. The home of the free has become the land of the lawsuit. And we've got to end that. And that's why we sent up a bill to the Congress to stop these frivolous lawsuits. Nuisance suits sap our economy and tear its social fabric of our society. And when you're as likely to serve your neighbor a subpoena as a cup of coffee, something's gone wrong. And when doctors won't deliver babies and dads won't coach Little League for fear of lawsuits, something's wrong. America won't find its way out of this mess until we spend more time helping one another than we do suing one another. We need more people like Newt Gingrich in the Congress to support reform legislation in terms of these vicious and outrageous lawsuits.

We've got to reform this Nation's health care system. Right now, the quality of American health care is the best in the entire world, make no mistake about it. The problem is access. Too many Americans with families do not have health insurance coverage. And you know how even a short stay in the hospital can rip a hole right through the family's budget. Well, all Americans deserve quality health care and a sense of well-being. But socialized medicine is not the answer, and I will fight against those plans. We have a good, specific plan. And my plan focuses on opening up access to health insurance for all Americans, rich and poor. And if we wanted long lines and revolving-door health care, we'd put our doctors to work at the department of motor vehicles. The last thing we want is the Government playing doctor. And you listen to the campaign plans on the other side, and you'll know exactly what I mean. I will continue to fight for health care for all, and I will fight against those astronomically expensive schemes to socialize American health care.

We've got to reform our welfare system. People are willing to support benefits for families in need; of course they are. And yes, Americans care. We always have; we always will. But they want to see some connection between welfare and work. And they want to see government at every level work together to track down the deadbeat dads, the ones who can't be bothered to pay child support. And they want to see us break the cycle, that dreadful cycle of dependency that destroys dignity and passes down poverty from one generation to the next. Think about it. Think about a young child born into that. It's wrong. It's cruel. We've got to do something to change it.

A number one issue today, though, is the economy. I think we all know that. It's jobs. And that's what's keeping people up late at night, worrying about how they're going to pay the bills and put food on the table, care for their kids, and still manage to put away something for their own retirement. We've got to get this economy moving. And Americans want to work. They want the opportunity to earn more money. And that's why in my State of the Union Address, I laid out a two-part plan to spark economic recovery, to create jobs: a seven-point short-term plan to stimulate the economy as early as this spring and then a longer term plan to keep America growing tomorrow and into the next century.

And because I knew I couldn't wait for Congress to act, I set a deadline to help them along the way. And that's why I was sorry to see what the House Democrats did this past Thursday. Instead of working on my plan, liberal Democrats pushed through one of their own. And true to its form, it's a tiny temporary tax cut in exchange for a huge permanent tax hike. And to play election-year politics as usual, they passed up a chance to stimulate the economy. And the plan they passed will raise the deficit, raise taxes a whopping $100 billion, and ruin our economic recovery. And worst of all, it will not create jobs at all. And so, let me end the suspense. If that plan reaches my desk, I will veto it instantly and send it right back up to Capitol Hill.

And frankly, there's even greater danger here. If the liberal Democrats ever decide to make that two-bit tax cut permanent, they'd have to jack up—and I think Newt expressed this on the floor; certainly I've heard him speak about it—they'd have to jack up the tax rate for every American making more than $35,000 a year. You heard it right, $35,000, for a plan that's supposed to help the middle class. And that's going to come as real news to a lot of factory workers and hard-working schoolteachers, people you know, everyday Americans struggling to make ends meet.

Let's face it, when that tax-and-spend crowd talks about taking aim at the champagne-and-caviar set, it's middle America that always takes the hit. And the liberals are going to tax that middle class for the same reason that Willie Sutton robbed banks, because that's where the money is. So, do not listen to this silly campaign rhetoric out there. Ask any economist, and they'll tell you the quickest way to cut this recovery off at its knees is to raise taxes.

If they're serious about this recovery, Congress must pass my plan. My plan contains an investment tax allowance to create incentives for American businesses to buy new equipment and then hire more workers. To bolster sagging real estate markets, this plan will give the first-time homebuyer a $5,000 tax credit to help them with that down payment. For families here in the Atlanta area, that credit is worth 6 months' mortgage payments on the average Atlanta home.

And let me say to these opponents of mine: No one is fooled by your paying lip service to competitiveness and practicing class warfare. Quit punishing the people who create jobs, and pass my plan and cut the capital gains tax, cut it down so we can get America back to work.

My plan really, if you look at it, you'll see that it's shaped to meet the new economic realities, realities that have helped make Atlanta the South's great international city. And come 1996, Atlanta comes of age as America's very own Olympic city. And that's going to be just great. There's a popular saying: When I pass into the hereafter, I don't know if I'll be going up or down, but wherever I go, I'll change planes in Atlanta. [*Laughter*] They're going to see that one in 1996.

You know, Georgia's unemployment rate is low. But I'm sure Georgians know the actions we take now affect our economic health for the long term. We're working to expand trade. We're working to open markets all over the world to American products. That was my mission when I went to Asia. It's what our trade teams push for every time they sit down at the negotiating table. And if we want to ensure good jobs for the future, we've got to work for free trade now.

The truth is, if we want to succeed economically at home, we have got to lead economically abroad. Right here in Georgia, in the past 3 years, manufacturing exports have almost doubled. Today, an estimated 165,000 Georgia jobs are tied to trade.

So, get past all the tough talk out there, all the patriotic posturing about fighting back by shutting out foreign goods. If this country starts closing its markets, other countries will close theirs. And when that happened, who gets hurt? Easy, we do. Our economy does. The workers in the State of Georgia do.

But my opponents aren't about to let fact intrude on fantasy. They're peddling protectionism, a retreat from economic reality into a dangerous pre-World War II isolationism. Look closely, that's not the American flag they're waving; it's the white flag of surrender. And that's not the America you and I know. I will veto any protection legislation that comes to the White House from this protectionist Congress.

The bottom line is, we do not run, and we do not cut out; we compete. And never in this Nation's long history have we turned our backs on a challenge, and we're not going to start now. I put my faith in the American worker. Level the playing field, and the American worker will outthink, outproduce, outperform anyone, anywhere, anytime.

And I say let the world know we are in it to win. Don't listen to those talking heads out there, the folks who can't seem to feel good unless they've got something bad to say about our great country. If you think I feel strongly about this one, you ought to hear Barbara Bush, the Silver Fox, speak about it. [*Laughter.*] She wouldn't even let me listen to the TV news last night. There's a lot of gloom and doom out there.

America isn't a nation that gets ahead by tearing down others. Time after time, America's been called upon. And time after time, America has met the challenge. And this time America will do it again.

Think back to one year ago today, to the calm after Desert Storm. Ask any one of the proud sons and daughters of Georgia who became a liberator of Kuwait, and they'll tell you military strength is nothing without moral support right here at home.

I won't ever forget my visit during those difficult times to Fort Stewart, Georgia, the wives and parents that I talked to, the people who, their loved ones in harm's way, still told me this: America must do what is right. And their quiet courage and their patriotism said it all to me. It was an emotional time, I'll tell you. And never would this country tuck tail and let aggression stand. America would do what was right and good and just, and America would prevail.

And there were those who didn't support us then, and there are those who second-guess us now. But not the good people of Georgia. In those difficult days when our kids laid it all on the line, this State, its young men and women never wavered because, you see, Georgia kept the faith. And we're bringing that same spirit to the fight we face today.

From next Tuesday through the first Tuesday in November, we are going to take our message all across the country. You don't have to be a negative message. You don't have to always be saying something bad about somebody else. We've got lots to be proud of, lots to advocate, lots to be for.

So if you want to send a message to Washington, send this President back for 4 more years and send——

*Audience members.* Four more years! Four more years! Four more years!

*The President.* Send more good Georgia Republicans to Congress to help out this leader right here.

Let me close with just a couple of words right from the heart. Barbara and I are blessed. We are blessed to serve at this moment in time when so many of the old fears have been driven away, when so many new hopes stand within our reach. And since the day I took the oath of office, I made it my duty always to try to do what is right for this country. I have given it my best. I have done my level-best, and I'm not done yet.

And I ask the good people of Georgia— together we've got a lot to be proud of. I take particular pride that the young people in this country go to bed at night not worrying about nuclear holocaust. I think that's something good and something strong and says something wonderful about what's happened in the last few years. But my pitch to you, the leaders of this great State, is unashamedly this: Together we have made a great beginning; now, you give me 4 more years to finish the job.

Thank you all for this warm welcome. And may God bless the United States of America. And be sure to get to the polls next Tuesday. Many, many thanks.

*Audience member.* Amen. Georgia's Bush country.

*The President.* Thank you all very, very much.

*Note: The President spoke at 2:25 p.m. at the Marriott Marquis Hotel. In his remarks, he referred to former Representative Howard H. (Bo) Callaway.*

# Remarks at the Bush-Quayle Campaign Welcome in Savannah, Georgia
*March 1, 1992*

Thank you very much, Mayor. And may I be bold enough to say I think Savannah has a first-class new Mayor, and I'm glad to have her here at my side today. And thank you all for this warm welcome. It's great to see so many friends. Standing next to me over here is one of the great Governors across our country, Governor Carroll Campbell of South Carolina. And I am very much

indebted to him for his support. Alec Poitevint is the chairman of the party here, doing a first-class job. Fred Cooper is our statewide chairman for Bush-Quayle. And of course, Newt Gingrich, doing a superb job for this State and for our country in Washington, DC.

May I thank the band over there from Bradwell. And somewhere out here is Vidalia, right over there, thank them. And may I single out all the veterans of Desert Storm here today and to every one of you who have come down to the Riverfront to show your support. I'm glad to see all this activity. You'll notice I brought along my newest mode of transportation, "Riverboat One" right back here. [*Laughter*]

Well, we're here today because we believe on big issues and we believe that we're on the right side of these big issues, on the issues that shape the world and on the values that are close to home. I'm talking about jobs. I am talking about family. I am talking about world peace, for ourselves and for all of our kids. Jobs, family, and world peace.

And I believe all the people of Savannah and all the people of this great State believe that parents, not the Government, ought to make the decisions that matter in life. Parents, not Government, should choose the children's schools. And when it comes to child care, parents, not the Government, should choose who cares for the children. And I also think on this Sunday, and my views will never change on this, I believe there is a place for voluntary prayer in our children's classrooms. And I think, on this gorgeous family day, on this beautiful Sunday here in Savannah, I think we should put it this way: America is first as long as we put the family first.

Let me just say a word about the number one issue facing our country today: It's the economy; it's jobs. And that's what's keeping people up late at night, worrying about how they're going to pay the bills and put food on the table and care for their kids and still manage to put away something for their retirement. We've got to get this Nation's economy moving. That's why in that State of the Union Message I gave, I laid out a two-part plan to spark economic recovery, to create jobs: a seven-point short-term plan to stimulate the economy as early as this spring and then a longer term plan to keep America growing tomorrow and into the next century.

And because I know Congress tends to drag its feet, I set a deadline to help them along the way. But regrettably, the liberals that control the Congress had other ideas. Instead of passing my plan, they pushed

through one of their own. Here's what's in it: a tiny tax cut, 25 cents a day for every person, but in exchange for $100 billion in taxes. If you feel the way I do, tell the Congress, "Keep the change, and keep your hands off the taxpayer's wallet."

If the liberal Democrats decided to make their two-bit tax cut permanent, they'd have to jump up the tax rate for every American making more than $35,000 a year. You've heard that right, $35,000. Now, go tell that to some schoolteacher that's working her or his heart out for our kids. That is not fair, and I am not going to let it happen. They're going to tax the middle class for the same reason Willie Sutton robbed banks, because that's where the money is. And I'm not going to let them do that to you the taxpayers of Savannah. But listen, you saw that bill the other day, so let me make it very clear, with one of our great leaders standing next to me, if that tax-and-spend plan reaches my desk, I am going to send it right back. I will veto it fast; it will make your head spin. They want to raise the taxes, and I want get this country back to work.

And there's one critical part of our economic future that I want to talk to you about today, and that's really the kind of legacy we leave these young ones, our children. The world our kids call home will be far different than the world that we grew up in. The competition now comes from around the world, not just down the street. In that new world, there's a new economic reality. If we want to succeed economically at home, we've got to lead economically abroad.

And if this Nation needed any proof of what I just said, it's right here in Savannah. Statewide, Georgia's export business is booming, nearly $14 billion in 1991 for manufactured exports alone. Look around the Riverfront. More and more ships pass in and out of this harbor, saluting the Waving Girl. Today and every day this bustling hub of international trade puts jobs in your communities, money in your pockets, and dinner on your tables. Nearly 13 million tons of goods, billions of dollars in international trade, flow through your wonderful port. And in the port of Savannah alone, all that trade traffic adds up to 58,000 jobs for Georgia.

The world is at Savannah's doorstep. We've got to keep the door open, and I'm confident that we will. And that's why I've fought every day of my administration to open foreign markets and to guard against the siren's call of isolation and protection. Georgians are reaching out; they are not pulling back. Give you a little detail that I think is good for the rest of the country. Right here, we're creating additional opportunities for U.S. exports, companies like Savannah Foods and Fort Howard Paper and Union Camp—the V.P. is with us, Sid Nutting is with us here today. And their people are working hard to compete, and we're behind them all the way.

But the opponents are not about to let that fact intrude on fantasy. They are peddling protectionism; they are peddling a retreat from economic reality. Now, you cut through all the patriotic posturing, all the tough talk about fighting back by closing out foreign goods, and look closely: That is not the American flag they're waving; it is the white flag of surrender. And that is not the America that you and I know. We don't cut and run in this country; we compete. Never in this Nation's long history have we turned our back on challenge, and we are not about to start right now. So I put my faith in the American worker. I say: Level out that playing field, and the American worker will outthink, outproduce, outperform anyone, anywhere, anytime. And let me add this: America is in it to win.

Think back one year, one year ago today, to the calm after Desert Storm. Ask any one of the proud sons and daughters of Georgia who became a liberator of Kuwait, and they'll tell you: Military strength doesn't mean a thing without moral support right here at home. Georgia did its part and more. This port handled over 200,000 tons of cargo for Desert Storm. Nearly 10,000 sons and daughters of Georgia were called up through the Reserves and the National Guard, and thousands more answered the call from Fort Stewart or from Hunter Army Airfield.

And I'll never forget my visit to Fort Stewart during those difficult days, the wives and the parents that I talked to,

people with their loved one in harm's way, many of them gone for months. Their quiet courage said it all: Never would this country tuck tail and let aggression stand. America would do what was right and good and just. And America would prevail.

There were those who did not support us then, and there are those who second-guess us now. But not the good people of Georgia. In those difficult days, when our kids laid it all on the line, Georgia never wavered. Georgia kept its faith in freedom. Georgia said with me: Aggression will not stand. And I say thank you to the people of this great State.

And now we're locked in a political struggle, and I'm going to try to keep it above the fray. I've got to continue to be the President of this great country; honored to be that President. And I've been trying to keep things on a positive plane. But let me just say this to you: From next Tuesday through the first Tuesday in November, we're going to take our message all across this country. And my view is, if you want to send a message to Washington, send this President back for 4 more years, and send more good Georgia Republicans to the Congress.

People know that we're in a battle for the future. It's about jobs. It's about family. It's about world peace and about the kind of legacy we're going to leave our kids. And so, let some opponents sign the retreat, run from the new realities, seek refuge in a world of protectionism or high taxes or even bigger Government. That's not the future we want for our kids. And we believe in our country. And we believe we will move forward with open markets and low taxes and less Government, all focused on creating and preserving jobs. So we need your support.

Let me just close today with a few words from the heart. Barbara and I are blessed, blessed to serve this great Nation of ours at a moment in history when so many of the old fears have been driven away, when so many new hopes stand within our reach. Old fears: When I see these young kids, I think we're fortunate that they go to bed now worrying less about a nuclear holocaust than happened 5 or 10 years ago. We are blessed that we brought peace to this world. And because we've stood strong, we've beaten back aggression.

But since the day I took the oath of office, I've made it my duty to work for what's right for America. I go back, I guess we all do, to what our families say. I go back to what my mother says: Try your hardest. Do your best. Well, let me tell you something, I'm not done yet. I say to the good people of Georgia: Together we are going to make a great new beginning. I'm going to take this message to the United States Congress for change. Change that

Congress, and give the values that you believe in a real chance come November.

Thank you for this very warm welcome back. And may God bless the people of Georgia and the people of the United States of America. Let us count our blessings on this gorgeous day. Thank you, and God bless you all.

*Note: The President spoke at 1:20 p.m. at the Savannah Riverfront. In his remarks, he referred to Susan Weiner, Mayor of Savannah.*

## Message to the Congress Transmitting the Finland-United States Social Security Agreement
*March 2, 1992*

*To the Congress of the United States:*

Pursuant to section 233(e)(1) of the Social Security Act, as amended by the Social Security Amendments of 1977 (Public Law 95–216; 42 U.S.C. 433(e)(1)), I transmit herewith the Agreement between the United States of America and the Republic of Finland on Social Security, which consists of two separate instruments—a principal agreement and an administrative arrangement. The agreement was signed at Helsinki on June 3, 1991.

The United States-Finland agreement is similar in objective to the social security agreements already in force with Austria, Belgium, Canada, France, Germany, Italy, the Netherlands, Norway, Portugal, Spain, Sweden, Switzerland, and the United Kingdom. Such bilateral agreements provide for limited coordination between the United States and foreign social security systems to eliminate dual social security coverage and taxation, and to help prevent the loss of benefit protection that can occur when workers divide their careers between two countries.

I also transmit for the information of the Congress a report prepared by the Department of Health and Human Services, providing explanation of the key points of the agreement, along with a paragraph-by-paragraph explanation of the provisions of the principal agreement and the related administrative arrangement. In addition, as required by section 433(e)(1) of the Social Security Act, a report on the effect of the agreement on income and expenditures of the U.S. Social Security program and the number of individuals affected by the agreement is also enclosed. I note that the Department of State and the Department of Health and Human Services have recommended the agreement and related documents to me.

I commend the Agreement between the United States of America and the Republic of Finland on Social Security and related documents.

GEORGE BUSH

The White House,
March 2, 1992.

# Message to the House of Representatives Returning Without Approval the United States-China Act of 1991
*March 2, 1992*

*To the House of Representatives:*

I am returning herewith without my approval H.R. 2212, the "United States-China Act of 1991," which places additional conditions on renewal of China's most-favored-nation (MFN) trade status.

The sponsors of H.R. 2212 believe they can promote broad economic and foreign policy objectives in China by placing conditions on the renewal of China's MFN status. They expect that the Chinese will improve respect for human rights, cooperate in arms control, and drop barriers to trade, given a choice between losing MFN and addressing these concerns.

Let me state at the outset that my Administration shares the goals and objectives of H.R. 2212. Upholding the sanctity of human rights, controlling the spread of weapons of mass destruction, and free and fair trade are issues of vital concern. My objection lies strictly with the methods proposed to achieve these aims.

There is no doubt in my mind that if we present China's leaders with an ultimatum on MFN, the result will be weakened ties to the West and further repression. The end result will not be progress on human rights, arms control, or trade. Anyone familiar with recent Chinese history can attest that the most brutal and protracted periods of repression took place precisely when China turned inward, against the world.

Recent agreements by the Chinese to protect U.S. intellectual property rights, to abide by the Missile Technology Control Regime Guidelines, to accede to the Nuclear Non-Proliferation Treaty by April, and to discuss our human rights concerns—after years of stonewalling—are the clear achievements of my Administration's policy of comprehensive engagement.

We have the policy tools at hand to deal with our concerns effectively and with realistic chances for success. The Administration's comprehensive policy of engagement on several separate fronts invites China's leadership to act responsibly without leaving any doubts about the consequences of Chinese misdeeds. Our approach is one of targeting specific areas of concern with the appropriate policy instruments to produce the required results. H.R. 2212 would severely handicap U.S. business in China, penalizing American workers and eliminating jobs in this country. Conditional MFN status would severely damage the Western-oriented, modernizing elements in China, weaken Hong Kong, and strengthen opposition to democracy and economic reform.

We are making a difference in China by remaining engaged. Because the Congress has attached conditions to China's MFN renewal that will jeopardize this policy, I am returning H.R. 2212 to the House of Representatives without my approval. Such action is needed to protect the economic and foreign policy interests of the United States.

GEORGE BUSH

The White House,
March 2, 1992.

# Message to the Congress Transmitting the Annual Report on Hazardous Materials Transportation
*March 2, 1992*

*To the Congress of the United States:*

In accordance with the requirements of section 109(e) of the Hazardous Materials Transportation Act (Public Law 96–633; 49 U.S.C. 1808(e)), I transmit herewith the Annual Report on Hazardous Materials

Transportation for calendar year 1990.

GEORGE BUSH

The White House,
March 2, 1992.

## Statement on the Death of Albert Bel Fay
*March 2, 1992*

Barbara and I are greatly saddened by the death of Albert Bel Fay. Albert was a close personal friend, and we will miss him greatly.

He was a Texan through and through. He was a leader in building the Republican Party in Houston, starting in the early 1960's. Albert was a mentor who helped guide me in my early years in Texas politics, when getting Republicans elected was next to impossible. His service to the Republican Party has been invaluable.

Barbara and I send our deepest condolences and offer our prayers to his three children.

## Exchange With Reporters
*March 3, 1992*

*The President.* I just have a couple of brief statements here. But President Yeltsin, Boris Yeltsin of the Russian Federation, has accepted my invitation to pay a state visit to Washington, June 16th and 17th. I view this as an excellent opportunity to follow up on that historic February 1st meeting at Camp David. We're going to review progress on a wide range of issues including the ever-strengthening relationship between the two countries. We'll get into the nuclear and military questions and then the joint efforts in support of reform in Russia. It will give me yet another opportunity, this in a very formal visit, to pay my respects to Boris Yeltsin who is really doing a superb job there.

The other news, and I don't want to put too much on it, is I was very pleased that this morning at 8:30 a.m., the leading indicators came out and they rose substantially, or rose by .9 percent in January. And I think it's a little better than had been expected. So, it's nice to have some encouraging news. And then our advisers, economic advisers, are a little more optimistic on the housing front as well. So, there we are, and just wanted to get those announcements out.

*Taxes*

*Q.* Sir, do you feel that going along with taxes was the biggest mistake of your Presidency?

*The President.* Well, I don't know about the biggest, but yes, I—you see, I'm very disappointed with Congress. I thought this one compromise, and it was a compromise, would result in no more tax increases. I thought it would result in total control of domestic discretionary spending. And now we see Congress talking about raising taxes again. And some in Congress are talking about trying to break down the spending caps. And so, I'm disappointed. And given all of that, yes, a mistake.

*Q.* Is it a little late, Mr. President, to voice regret about this?

*Q.* Why the change of heart now? All through New Hampshire you defended the 1990 budget——

*The President.* Well, I explained why I did it. I don't know whether it was defending it.

*Q.* But Pat Buchanan kept saying all through New Hampshire, "Read my lips. Read my lips." And when you were campaigning up there you said, "I never signed that pledge that you wanted to——"

*The President.* Well, we're talking about two different things. But what I'm saying is, on this deal when you see Congress now going for more taxes, my whole view is that that one compromise probably wasn't worth it, although I'm going to still stay very firmly on these spending caps.

*Q.* Mr. President, though, the day before the primary, to say that you now regret having done this, isn't that a little bit late to do that, sir? And can it be seen as a little bit disingenuous?

*The President.* I don't know whether it's late or not, it's just the way I feel given what's going on on Capitol Hill. It's getting intense. As you know, the House passed a tax bill which I'll veto. And now, much to my consternation, you see the Senate going about the same old business. So, this just gangs up on you, plus the political flak out there.

*Economic Plan*

*Q.* With respect to your short-term growth package, many prominent economists, and including Federal Reserve Board Chairman Alan Greenspan, have said that given the economic realities it would be better not to tinker with the Tax Code at all, whether it's for tax incentives or for tax increases. How do you respond to that?

*The President.* I don't know that Greenspan was addressing himself to our growth package, but clearly a lot of economists are opposing what's happening in terms of these broad across-the-board handouts. And our incentive program, I think, would have instant stimulation on the economy, instant. And it would restore confidence very quickly. It's getting increasingly difficult, given the votes up there, and that's one of the reasons that I'm as frustrated as I am.

*Q.* If I may follow up, though. I think he was speaking in broad terms about any sort of short-term fiscal stimulus, whether it's your package or a Democrat's.

*The President.* Well, you'll have to ask Greenspan what he's speaking about. I think short-term stimulus, such as I men-

tioned, would stimulate the economy and would be very good for housing. I think housing would lead this recovery much quicker. You know my view on capital gains. So, ask him about his view, and I've just given you mine.

Yes? And I've got to get going.

*Federal Government Personnel Reductions*

*Q.* You've been saying that Government has grown too big, spends too much. Have you looked at your Agriculture Department where the numbers of employees has grown?

*The President.* Haven't had a chance to look at that lately, but I'll take a look at it. Is it getting—I mean, what we're doing is, total Government personnel, I believe you'll see, is down, a lot of that obviously coming from reductions in the Defense Department. But I haven't looked at the Ag Department.

*Presidential Primaries*

*Q.* How do you think you'll do today, sir?

*Q.* You say you were misled by the Democrats 2 years ago?

*The President.* Huh?

*Q.* How do you think you'll do in today's primaries?

*The President.* I think I'll win them. I think I'll win them.

*Taxes*

*Q.* Were you misled by the Democrats?

*The President.* Well, I had the distinct feeling that that one deal would be the one-time compromise. And as far as I'm concerned, it is. I'm going to veto their tax bill. So, we'll just leave it there. But I'd like to see them move forward on these incentives that we're talking about.

*Q.* Was it the biggest mistake, too, politically?

*The President.* Well, I don't know. I don't know. We'll see.

*Note: The exchange began at 9:53 a.m. on the South Lawn at the White House prior to the President's departure for Chicago, IL.*

## Remarks to the National Association of Evangelicals in Chicago, Illinois
*March 3, 1992*

Thank you for that welcome. And to Dr. Johnson, Dr. Billy Melvin, Don Argue, Dave Rambo, Bob Dugan, my sincere thanks, not just to you all, to everyone up here, but to all of you for that very warm welcome.

And I'd like to open, if I may, on a personal note, to thank you for the help that you've given me over the years. And I'm not really referring to the fine work that your team in Washington has been doing, although they've been of great help to our administration, advancing the values we share. Nor am I thinking only of the wonderful work you do in world relief and in helping people around this world, which is superb work. But my thanks are really more personal than that, and Barbara and I particularly want to thank you for your prayers.

As I said many times before, prayer always has been important in our lives. And without it, I really am convinced, more and more convinced, that no man or no woman who has the privilege of serving in the Presidency could carry out their duties without prayer. I think of Lincoln's famous remark, "I've been driven many times to my knees by the overwhelming conviction that I had nowhere else to go." The intercessory prayers that so many Americans make on behalf of the President of the United States, in this instance on behalf of me and also of my family, they inspire us, and they give us strength. And I just wanted you to know that, and Barbara and I are very, very grateful to you.

I am delighted to have this opportunity to speak to this most prestigious meeting, to speak with you today on the occasion of your 50th anniversary. Your theme: Forward in faith. And that says as much about your movement, much about what evangelicals have brought to America over its lifetime. Evangelicals point our country toward the future, and with the diligence and hard work and confidence that only a firm faith can provide. In so many crucial ways, your concerns are the concerns of your country-

men.

We agree on the big issues that shape the world and on the values, on the values so close to home. I'm talking about jobs, obviously; about family; about world peace, for ourselves and, I guess even more important, for our kids, for the generations coming along.

And we agree that we must speak out against racial bigotry and against anti-Semitism. And as I stressed in my State of the Union Address, it's especially critical in these days of economic difficulty to point out that racial bigotry and anti-Semitism simply have no place in America.

You want, as all Americans do, safe streets for your children. You want schools where your children can receive the finest possible education to prepare them for a life of industry and good citizenship and faith in God. And I believe that means that you are entitled to choose your children's schools.

You want a Government that understands the limited role that it must play in a Nation of free men and women; a Government that promotes economic growth and opportunity; a Government that spends your tax money for the common good, and for the common good alone.

And you want for yourselves and your country that most precious of gifts, peace on Earth. You understand that peace comes not from vacillation and weakness but from clarity of purpose and from strength. The last time a President came before you, I note that it is almost 8 years to the day, our country was nearing the climax of a titanic struggle, the cold war. President Reagan spoke to you then of what America must do to win this hard and bitter peace.

Like you, President Reagan and I understood that the cold war wasn't simply some mundane competition between rival world powers. It was a struggle for the mind of man. On one side was a system dedicated to denying the life of the spirit and celebrating the omnipotence of the state. On the other was a system founded on a profound truth, that our Creator has endowed his children with inalienable rights that no government can deny.

And now, 8 years later, we can say confidently, Americans won the cold war. We won it by standing for what's right. Tonight our children and grandchildren—and I take great joy in this—tonight our children and our grandchildren will go to their beds untroubled by the fears of nuclear holocaust that haunted two generations of Americans. In our prayers we asked for God's help. I know our family did, and I expect all of you did. We asked for God's help. And now in this shining outcome, in this magnificent triumph of good over evil, we should thank God. We should give thanks.

By the way, I notice from your Washington newsletter that recently even Time magazine called the old Soviet Union an evil empire. Now they tell us. [*Laughter*] I think you will recall only a few years ago when—many of you know this—about the time when Bill Graham went to the Soviet Union. And he came back and told a lot of people, told us of the people's hunger for religion. And some did not believe him then. Nobody here doubted that, but some across our country simply could not believe that. But now, no one doubts him. I know evangelicals understood this all along.

Our victory in the cold war came from the kind of work performed by people here in this room. Many of you, many of you bravely brought Bibles behind the Iron Curtain, sharing the Word of God with people who longed for it. And through your World Relief Corporation and other enterprises, you helped resettle thousands who were fleeing oppression. Many evangelicals risked their lives to bring theological training where such training was forbidden.

And now in the free countries of the former Communist bloc, your work continues to ensure that the vacuum left by communism's demise is filled by faith. You and I both know there is more to do in the cause of religious freedom, and you have my full support in that effort. Rest assured, our country, indeed the world, will be forever grateful for what you have done.

Americans are the most religious people on Earth. And we have always instinctively sensed that God's purpose was bound up with the cause of liberty. The Founders understood this. As Jefferson put it, "Can the liberties of a nation be thought secure when we have removed their only firm basis, a conviction in the minds of the people that these liberties are the gift of God?" That conviction is enshrined in our Declaration of Independence and in our Constitution. And it's no accident that in drafting our Bill of Rights, the Founders dedicated the first portion of our first amendment to religious liberty. We rightly emphasize the opening clause of that amendment, which forbids government from establishing religion. In fact, I believe the establishment clause has been a great boon to our country's religious life. One reason religion flourishes in America is that worship can never be controlled by the state.

But in recent times we have too often ignored the clause that follows, which forbids government from prohibiting the free exercise of religion. This myopia has in some places resulted in an aggressive campaign against religious belief itself. Some people seem to believe that freedom of religion requires government to keep our lives free from religion. Well, I believe they're just plain wrong. Our government was founded on faith. Government must never promote a religion, of course, but it is duty bound to promote religious liberty. And it must never put the believer at a disadvantage because of his belief. That is the challenge that our administration has undertaken. To be succinct, it is my conviction that children have a right to voluntary prayer in the public schools.

And we must hold the line on state intervention in other areas as well. Two years ago, for example, we were in a tough fight on Capitol Hill over child care legislation. But with the invaluable help of your group and of other pro-family organizations, we kept choice of child care out of the hands of the Government bureaucrats and kept it where it belongs, in the hands of the parents. And you remember the fight, but we were determined to help families get the kind of child care they want. And that included church-based care. And that's the way the law is now, and that's the way it should be.

And we will continue to fight for the parents' right to choose their children's schools. School choice is at the heart of America 2000, our strategy to literally revolutionize American education. All parents, rich or poor, must have the right to choose the kind of education their children will receive. And as I've said many times, that must include religious-based schools.

For many years Americans saw another disturbing trend. Judges legislating from the bench steadily expanded the power of government over the lives of ordinary Americans. Today, I am happy to report to you that that trend is over. Over the past 3 years I have appointed more than 160 judges who understand the limits of government and the rights of parents; judges who punish criminals, not honest cops out trying to do their jobs. And I am very proud of the two fine men who have taken their place on the Supreme Court since I've been President, Justice David Souter and Justice Clarence Thomas.

We must do everything in our power to preserve the institution that nurtures faith, the family. And I am firmly convinced that our greatest problems today, from drugs and welfare dependency to crime and moral breakdown, spring from the deterioration of the American family. And too often, overweening government has aided the tragedy.

Recently I announced a new Commission to isolate the causes of the family's decline. And I did that after meeting with Democratic mayors and Republican mayors from the National League of Cities, some from big cities, some from small, all saying what I've just said. The fundamental problem is the decline of the family, when you look at these urban problems. I think you'll agree that I found the right man to lead the Commission, your layman of the year last year, Governor John Ashcroft of the State of Missouri. John knows the importance that we place on strengthening the families. Families must come first in America.

We must always guard against laws that weaken the family, weaken traditional values. And at the same time, we can take positive steps to strengthen them. Here's an example that will begin to address the real costs of childrearing. I have asked Congress to increase the child tax exemption by $500 per child, and I want the Congress to do it now.

We're also waging war against the forces that would tear the family apart. In 1990 alone, our agents from the FBI and Customs and Postal Inspection Service won 245 convictions against the smut merchants who deal in child pornography. These creatures have been put on notice. There is no place in America for this horrifying exploitation of children.

Faith, family: these are the values that sustain the greatest Nation on Earth. And to these values we must add the infinitely precious value of life itself. Let me be clear: I support the right to life. Six times the Congress has sent me legislation permitting Federal funding of abortion, and six times I've told them no and vetoed these bills.

Now we've got another fight. The Democratic Congress has opened up yet another front in this battle. Tomorrow they will begin hearings on new legislation, and they call it the freedom of choice act. And it would impose on all 50 States an unprecedented regime of abortion on demand going well beyond even *Roe* versus *Wade*. It would block many State laws requiring that parents be told about abortions being performed on their young daughters, even though the Supreme Court has upheld such laws five times. It would override State laws restricting sex-selection abortions. And it would severely limit the States' ability to impose meaningful restrictions on abortions performed in the 8th or even the 9th month of pregnancy. This is not right. And it will not become law as long as I am President of the United States of America.

Lincoln once said, "My concern is not whether God is on our side, but whether we are on God's side." As President I have often spoken of service, not simply public service but personal service, one human being coming to the aid of another. And I'm always reminded of a phrase from the Book of Common Prayer: "Oh, God . . . whose service is freedom." We must be sustained by the confidence that in serving others, in promoting the values of faith and family and life, we serve Him as well. It is this confidence that will enable us to move our country forward in faith, and remember, one Nation under God.

Thank you, and may God bless you and your wonderful work. And thank you for having me with you.

*Note: The President spoke at 11:57 a.m. at the Hyatt Regency O'Hare Hotel. In his re-* *marks, he referred to association officers B. Edgar Johnson, president; Billy Melvin, executive director; Don Argue, first vice president; David Rambo, second director; and Robert Dugan, director of the office of public affairs in Washington, DC. The President also referred to evangelist Billy Graham.*

# Message to the Congress on the Determination Not To Prohibit Fish Imports From Certain Countries
## March 3, 1992

*To the Congress of the United States:*

Pursuant to the provisions of subsection (b) of the Pelly Amendment to the Fishermen's Protective Act of 1967, as amended (22 U.S.C. 1978(b)), I am reporting to you that the Secretary of Commerce reported to me that shipments of yellowfin tuna or products derived from yellowfin tuna harvested by Venezuela in the eastern tropical Pacific Ocean (ETP) have been prohibited from the countries of Costa Rica, France, and Italy since June 25, 1991.

The Secretary's letter to me is deemed to be a certification for the purposes of subsection (a) of the Pelly Amendment. Subsection (a) requires that I consider and, at my discretion, order the prohibition of imports into the United States of fish and fish products from Costa Rica, France, and Italy to the extent that such prohibition is consist-

ent with the General Agreement on Tariffs and Trade. Subsection (b) requires me to report to the Congress within 60 days following certification on the actions taken pursuant to the certification; if all fish imports have not been prohibited, the report must state the reasons for so doing.

After thorough review, I have determined that sanctions against Costa Rica, France, and Italy will not be imposed at this time while we continue to work toward an international dolphin conservation program in the ETP. Costa Rica, France, and Italy will continue to be certified. I will make further reports to you as developments warrant.

GEORGE BUSH

The White House,
March 3, 1992.

# Message to the Senate Transmitting the Spain-United States Second Supplementary Treaty on Extradition
## March 3, 1992

*To the Senate of the United States:*

With a view to receiving the advice and consent of the Senate to ratification, I transmit herewith the Second Supplementary Treaty on Extradition between the United States of America and the Kingdom of Spain, signed at Madrid on February 9, 1988. I also transmit for the information of

the Senate the report of the Department of State with respect to this Supplementary Treaty.

The Second Supplementary Treaty supplements and amends the Treaty on Extradition between the United States of America and Spain, signed at Madrid on May 29,

1970, as amended by the Supplementary Treaty on Extradition, signed at Madrid on January 25, 1975 and is designed to update and standardize the conditions and procedures for extradition between the United States and Spain. Most significant, it substitutes a dual criminality clause for a current list of extraditable offenses so that, *inter alia*, certain additional narcotics offenses will be covered by the Treaty. The Second Supplementary Treaty also provides a legal basis for temporarily surrendering prisoners to stand trial for crimes against the laws of the Requesting State.

This Supplementary Treaty further represents an important step in combatting terrorism by excluding from the scope of the political offense exception serious offenses typically committed by terrorists, e.g., murder; voluntary manslaughter; voluntary assault and battery inflicting serious bodily harm; kidnapping; abduction; hostage-taking; illegal detention; the illegal use of explosives, automatic weapons, and incendiary or destructive devices or substances; attempt or participation in such offenses, as well as conspiracy or illicit association to commit such offenses. It also excludes from the reach of the political offense exception a murder or other willful crime against the person of a Head of State or a member of the first family of a Contracting Party, as well as any offense for which both Contracting Parties have a multilateral treaty obligation to extradite the person or submit the case to prosecution.

The provisions in this Supplementary Treaty follow generally the form and content of extradition treaties recently concluded by the United States. Upon entry into force, it will supplement and amend the existing Extradition Treaty and Supplementary Extradition Treaty between the United States and Spain.

The Supplementary Treaty will make a significant contribution to international cooperation in law enforcement. I recommend that the Senate give early and favorable consideration to the Supplementary Treaty and give its advice and consent to ratification.

GEORGE BUSH

The White House,
March 3, 1992.

# Statement by Press Secretary Fitzwater on the President's Meeting With Prime Minister Filip Dimitrov of Bulgaria
*March 3, 1992*

The President met for approximately 30 minutes this afternoon with Bulgarian Prime Minister Filip Dimitrov. He welcomed the Prime Minister as the first popularly-elected Bulgarian leader ever to visit the United States and congratulated him on Bulgaria's national day of independence, celebrated today.

The President expressed admiration for the determination shown by President Zhelev and Prime Minister Dimitrov in advancing democracy and human rights, including minority rights, in Bulgaria and in pursuing a bold program of market economic reform. He expressed America's firm support for Bulgaria as it undertakes this difficult transformation and proposed that both countries work to promote foreign trade and investment, which can bring the capital, know-how, and new jobs Bulgaria needs.

The two leaders also discussed the situation in the Balkans. They reaffirmed their strong support for U.N. peacekeeping efforts in Yugoslavia and agreed that all countries should act with restraint so as to promote confidence and stability in the region.

## Statement on the Georgia Presidential Primary Victory
*March 3, 1992*

Thanks to the Republican voters of Georgia, we are another step closer to our goal of winning every primary and caucus. After the votes are counted in Maryland and Colorado, I'm confident our campaign will be seven-for-seven in this election season. We are well on our way to the nomination and look forward to taking the battle to the Democrats. Barbara and I deeply appreciate the support we received today for our message of jobs, family, and peace.

To those who have been with me in the past but did not vote for me today, I hear your concerns and understand your frustration with Washington. I am committed to regaining your support. To get the economy moving, I will continue pushing the Democratic majority in Congress to enact my growth initiatives by the March 20th deadline.

## Exchange With Reporters on the Presidential Primaries
*March 4, 1992*

*The President.* The communications czar has told me that we must be moving onward. And I can tell your lack of interest, or you would be going with us on to the Super Tuesday States. Why are you not there?

*Q.* Are you afraid of Buchanan?

*Q.* Do you think you'll consistently lose this 30-percent protest vote?

*The President.* We're doing well. We won everything, and we're going to keep on winning everything. Tough times out there, and I think people are beginning to understand that what counts is who wins these primaries. So I feel good about it, and I'm not going to keep raising the high bar. I'm just going to go one at a time and win them all and win the election in the fall.

So, I'm very grateful to the people that worked hard; they're working in a tough economic environment. I know that. But I'm very, very pleased.

*Q.* Do you feel good about repenting on taxes?

*The President.* Yes, very good about that.

*Q.* Do you accept the votes for Buchanan as votes against you?

*The President.* It seems to be that way, yes. I think that's a good way to analyze it. But that will turn around. The economy will turn around. We'll make some headway with Congress eventually, keep trying. And people will see that I'm the person to lead this country now, as I was in the past.

*Q.* ——margin in 30 percent?

*The President.* This is a high jump. I'm not going to raise the bar, nor lower it. Just leave it where it is.

*Note: The exchange began at 7:46 a.m. on the South Lawn at the White House prior to the President's departure for Tampa, FL.*

## Remarks at a Bush-Quayle Fundraising Luncheon in Tampa, Florida
*March 4, 1992*

Thank you, General. Thank you all very, very much. Thank you so much. I will have a word more to say about the introducer in just a minute. But thank you all so much for that warm welcome back. Well, I want to thank a lot of people, everybody in this audience. But I think of Alec Courtelis, our campaign's national finance cochairman;

Zach Zachariah, who has done a great job as our chairman here in this wonderful State. I don't think it's out of order to salute my Florida chairman, Jeb Bush. [*Laughter*] And of course, our Florida State chairman, Van Poole, a friend of long, long standing. Mike Bilirakis is not with us, the Congressman; but he and I and Evelyn, his wife, I think she is here, we were at the strawberry festival. I've eaten my second high-calorie dessert in 3 hours. But that was a wonderful occasion. And Senator Hawkins, Paula Hawkins, former Senator, is with us; and of course, Al Austin, who has been at my side in his most unselfish, productive way over and over again. Al, I'm very grateful to you, sir.

Now a quick word about the introducer, Tampa's favorite son, America's hero. Last year, when General Scowcroft—General Scowcroft, sorry; Brent will be thrilled—[*laughter*]—when General Schwarzkopf commanded the largest allied fighting force since World War II, he earned a lasting place of greatness in the history of our time. There is no question of that place in greatness. It is going to be there. The revisionists can look and figure and debate, but it was a clear, wonderful victory led by an outstanding soldier.

This general led a group of fighting men and women. He has told me, Colin Powell has told me about the merits of these young fighters. They included, incidentally, almost 8,000 Florida reservists and 1,500 Florida guardsmen and thousands more sailors and airmen from the bases around Florida; and of course, the mighty force of Tampa's own central command.

And I am so proud of General Schwarzkopf and all the men and women that he commanded. And they all said, all of us who looked at them say: With your sacrifice, with your courage, with your selfless service, you told the world that the United States of America will never tuck tail and let aggression stand. And you showed that we will do what is right and just, and in so doing we will prevail.

When you and those troops laid it all on the line, the people of this State never wavered. And for this, I want to express to all the people, heck with party, heck with political ideology, all of the people in this State, my profound thanks for this steadfast and loyal support in troubled times. Thank you, Florida, and thank you to the people of Florida. And thank you, most of all, General Schwarzkopf.

Now to the politics at hand. We had a good day yesterday. You may have trouble reading that, but we had a very good day yesterday. [*Laughter*] Somebody asked me, what does it take to win? And I say to them, I can't remember, what did it take to win the Super Bowl? Or maybe Steinbrenner, my friend George, will tell us what it takes for the Yanks to win: one run. But I went to the strawberry festival this morning and ate a piece of shortcake over there. Able to enjoy it right away. And once I completed it, it didn't have to be approved by Congress, so I just went ahead and ate it. [*Laughter*] That leads me to what I want to talk to you about today.

We've got a lot to do in these next few months because really we've got a lot to do in the next few years. And I am convinced that together, and I am so grateful for your support, that we can finish what we've started and move this country forward. And to do that, I need your support. Help me win the Presidency for 4 more years. And I ask for your support for the simplest of reasons: I think we believe in the same things, in the same values, the same important things. We know that taxes are too high because our Government is too big and it spends too much.

And we believe in a strong defense. And you listen to the proposals in Washington today. They all have these big, spendthrift political programs. And how are they going to take it? They're going to take it right out of the muscle of the defense of this country, and I am not going to permit that as President of the United States.

We believe in faith and family, responsibility and respect. We believe in community and, of course, country. And we believe there's a place for getting these values back. I happen to believe there's a place for voluntary prayer in our children's classrooms, and I'd like to see it back.

I'm firmly convinced of this, that we put America first when we put America's families first. So often today, politicians can do the easy thing, the popular thing. But it's the tough decisions that tell you something about character and principle. For I believe in things that don't change from one election to the next, things that guide each and every one of us each day of the year. And I believe in things that have led us to a new era in America's history, the important, fundamentally important things. I mentioned family but certainly world peace, certainly jobs.

The cold war is over. And if you want to count your blessings, there's one: The cold war is over, and America won, and the Soviet Union collapsed. The Soviet Union collapsed, and the imperial communism, the communism with outreach, is finished. It's dead all around the world. So, make no mistake about it.

As a result of this tremendous victory in Desert Storm, our credibility as a country has never ever been higher around the world. And it was our leadership that changed the world. And now what I want to do is see us come together, men and women of this great city, all across our country, come together and use that same spirit, that same leadership to change America.

We are changing it by setting right what is simply on the wrong track in our country. Take our courts, for example. When the rights of the criminal are more important than the rights of the victim, that's wrong. And I'm proud of our tough stand on crime, and I'm proud of our judicial appointments, judges who interpret and do not legislate from the Federal bench. And when fathers stop coaching Little League because they're afraid of liability lawsuits, that too is wrong. And so, we've proposed reforms to our court system to reduce the number of frivolous lawsuits. I don't want to get into any trouble with the bar association around here, but I once quoted to someone that line, "An apple a day keeps the doctor away." And he said, "Yeah, well, what works for lawyers?" [*Laughter*]

Legal reform will help our legal process work. But, you know the real answer for solving problems is to be more concerned with helping each other than suing each other. That seems to me a fundamental American principle.

Well look, we can't stop there. More than our court system needs reform, like our health care system. This is one of great concern to the people of Florida, not because it doesn't offer the world's best quality health care; it does. I think we'd all agree we are blessed by the best quality health care in the world. We must reform the system because too many people do not have access to insurance. And all Americans deserve quality health care and the sense of well-being that it brings. And too many people worry that they'll lose their insurance if they change jobs or, worse still, if they lose their job. And anybody who's had even minor surgery knows that health care costs are going right through the roof.

Well, you know the problem, but what's the solution? I can tell you what it's not first. It is not to go down the road of nationalized or socialized expensive programs that we hear from the Democratic side. All that means—you look at those other programs over there—all that means is long lines and impersonal service. Well, look, you can go down to the department of motor vehicles for that, you don't have to go change the medical system. [*Laughter*]

So, our approach: Make insurance available to all; keep the quality high, the bureaucracy low; and preserve choice for the patient. The last thing we want and need in this country is for the Government telling you who your doctor is going to be. Health care reform means improving the system, and that is what I'm attempting to do with this new comprehensive health care program that we have now.

There's another system where reform means changing the system, and I'm talking about the welfare system. Let's face it, too often that system perpetuates dependency instead of personal responsibility and the dignity of a job. Too often kids are born into yet another generation of despair; no hope, no dignity, simply another generation of welfare recipients. And we've got to change that. I've asked the Departments and Agencies to make it easier for the State and local governments to promote policies that protect and strengthen families. And we do that through what we call a much more flexible waiver system.

We need to help make families whole, help bring dignity back into their lives, and go after the deadbeat fathers who run out on their kids. That's what we need to be doing in reforming and strengthening the welfare system in this country.

We all know when it gets down to—certainly it's true now, Al and I were talking about it at lunch, and you can read it in these primary elections across the country—we all know that the number one issue on the minds of all Americans is the economy and jobs: people worried about providing for their families, meeting the everyday challenges of paying their bills, providing a home, teaching their kids, and setting aside for retirement. People are worried. Those that have a job, white-collar job perhaps, wonder whether they'll have it tomorrow.

The American people want this economy to work. They want it to create, preserve jobs. So in my State of the Union Address, I put forward a two-part plan. And the first part will get business stimulated right now. It would bring confidence back now, upgrading plant and equipment again, hiring workers again. And it uses incentives like the investment tax allowance, rapid depreciation. It calls for Congress to wake up and understand how the real world works and create jobs by cutting the tax on capital gains.

To get housing back on its feet, I unveiled several commonsense proposals to get people buying and building homes. And these proposals will create, in Florida alone, an estimated 26,500 additional housing starts and 51,000 new construction jobs. Perhaps the most easily understood proposal along those lines is a $5,000 tax credit for first-time homebuyers. And with our plan, young people almost able to buy that first home could do it with that extra $5,000 in their pockets. This is good. This is stimulative. This will work. This will restore confidence.

I hate to be critical at a wonderfully nonpartisan lunch like this. But a word about the Democrats' plan: It's a rip-off. I've studied it. I've considered it carefully. It's a rip-off. Listen to the deal: 25 cents a day in temporary tax relief for 2 years for individuals, paid for, typically, by a large permanent tax increase. And over in the Senate,

the bill the Democrats are working on is not much better than the one in the House. Its centerpiece is a huge tax increase. And the last thing our economy needs now is a $100 billion tax hike.

And we drew a line in the sand in the Persian Gulf and kept our word. And I'll draw another line in the sand right now. If the Democrats send me a monstrosity like the bill that passed through the House, I will send it right back, vetoing it the day that I get it. We are not going to let that happen to the taxpayer in this country.

And they ought to pass this plan, and pass it soon, to make our country more competitive. And here's the deadline: March 20th, the first day of spring. What a glorious day for some action out of the United States Congress. Just pass the plan, and get this economy moving again. That's my charge to them, and if they don't do it, then we'll have to see what happens after the 20th. But I'll tell you, I think the American people want to say, "Set politics aside for a minute; pass the President's plan." And then they and I can go to general quarters and fight each other all the way to the fall, playing politics. Right now, the American people need action that will stimulate this economy.

There's a broader gauge, the second part of the plan, roadmap to make America competitive in this fast-changing world of ours. Our plan revolutionizes the American education system, none too soon. We've got a brilliant program called America 2000. Doesn't fine-tune, it just revolutionizes the education system in this country. Broad support from the Democratic Governors, Republican Governors alike. I was reading that the average eighth-grader spends 4 times as much time watching TV as doing homework. And that is wrong. And we can help change that by making our education system demand responsibility and demand results.

Our plan will also get the billions of dollars' worth of Government R&D, research and development, more quickly into the hands of our private sector businesses and workers. That's the second part of this longer term plan: Get spectacular technological advances off the shelf and into the marketplace. We're turning to the Federal labs now and working partnerships with business to get that genius, that inventive genius in those labs, applied to U.S. commercial technology. Get those advances off the shelf and into the marketplace. And that's going to produce a real return on your tax dollars investment, helping to create new products, helping to create new jobs.

The plan provides tax relief to strengthen the family. We raise the tax deduction for children by $500. And make no mistake about it, I want all of this plan passed now. I want it passed as soon as possible.

Behind all of this is a very important decision for America. To succeed economically at home, we have to lead economically abroad. Some don't want us to lead. Some don't think we can compete. They want us to shut out the rest of the world. Well, those people could not be more wrong. Look over you shoulders to the thirties, to the days of protection and isolation and America first, in that sense. Look what happened to this country. Markets shrunk, and we ended up in the worst depression the world has seen, certainly in modern times.

They couldn't be more wrong. More than 200,000 workers in Florida owe their jobs to manufactured exports. Last year alone, more than $5 billion in exports went out through the Tampa customs district. The way to create jobs here isn't to cut and run. We're not going to do that, ever. The way to create jobs is by opening markets, opening markets for exports everywhere in the world. And I'm going to fight hard in every foreign market to do that, and I'm going to resist—I don't care about the politics—I am going to resist the siren's call for protection. It is not good for America. We are the leaders of the world, not in retreat.

And I'm going to fight hard, lastly, in every primary, not for my sake but for America's. I believe fundamentally we're an optimistic people. We saw it after Desert Storm. We saw the country come together, and we were lifted up. And now we're subjected to some tough economic times, and there's some icing on that cake with a lot of gloom and doom over and over again coming out of the political process itself. I believe the American people want to hear about how we're going to address our country's challenges. They want to hear solutions, not just a lot of name-calling and running this country down.

And I might say parenthetically, again without any regard to the primaries, I think we've got to come together as a country to resist the politics of ugliness and hate, racial bigotry and discrimination. We've got to stand against that wherever we are.

So the bottom line is, I need your help. I need your help to keep our party strong, keep it united so we can win this fall. And yes, there are many challenges before us, and I guarantee you we're going to meet them. We are the United States of America. We're going to come out of these rough economic times. We are going to continue to lead the world. And I, as President, am going to continue to see that our national security is second to none around the world.

We're going to meet these challenges, meet them all across the State of Florida from the Panhandle down to the Florida Keys. And yes, there's an important election next week, and then there's another one in November. And I say this, I hope without arrogance: I am confident I am going to win this nomination. And I am confident I am going to win this election because I believe that the values I've touched on here today are the fundamental values of the American people. And I will do my level-best. I will continue to try my hardest in tough times, and I will continue to lead the greatest, freest Nation on the face of the Earth. But I need your support on Tuesday, and I'll need it again in November.

Thank you all, and may God bless our great country.

*Note: The President spoke at 1:30 p.m. at the Omni Westshore Hotel. In his remarks, he referred to Zach Zachariah, Bush-Quayle financial cochairman for Florida; Jeb Bush, Bush-Quayle chairman for Florida; Van Poole, Florida Republican Party chairman; and Al Austin, chairman of the luncheon.*

## Remarks at the Bush-Quayle South Florida Rally in Hialeah, Florida
*March 4, 1992*

*The President.* Thank you very, very much. What a wonderful turnout. Thank you. Thank you, Jeb. And may I first salute your great Congresswoman, Ileana Ros-Lehtinen, doing a superb job in Washington, DC; Mayor Julio Martinez, also working at this important local level. And it's great to be back in south Florida. I believe I am the first President to visit Hialeah, but I am sure proud to be here. I want to mention three other State leaders who can't be with us today, Senator Casas and Representatives Garcia and Rojas. They'd planned on being here; they were called to Tallahassee for action in the legislature. And I just pay them my respects because they, too, are serving you all very, very well.

I wish we had a little more time here today. It would be great to have a Cafe Cubano at Chico Two's, but time won't permit it. And may I thank the people from south Miami here who are providing us with this cheering. And right over here, there they are, Hialeah.

I'm going to keep this speech short. When you've got to face the voters, you can't afford to give a 4-hour stemwinder, Castro-style. So I'll keep it shorter. Let me get right to the point of this visit. I want to be your President for 4 more years. We can and we will win elections up and down the line, in Congress, in the statehouses, and in local communities, for people that share our values, who are working for jobs, family, peace. And together, we can win a great victory on primary day and then another one on November 3d, 1992.

You see, I think we agree on the big issues that shape the world, on the values that guide us at home. And I'm speaking of world peace, the importance of family, the need to create and sustain good jobs in a productive society.

We have big plans for this year. Here's what we need to accomplish together. First, we are going to get that economy growing and thriving. Help me with the Congress. And with Ileana's help, I will try to keep rolling back a Government that's too big

and spending too much. We'll try to keep working on that one, Ileana. And we're holding Congress' feet to the fire, to meet this March 20th deadline for tax cuts to create jobs and incentives to get the housing market back on its feet.

Right now, the tired old liberal leadership in the Congress is moving in the wrong direction. You know, the House passed a bill that would raise taxes $100 billion, and if it comes to my desk, I am going to veto it so fast it'll make your head swim.

And let me say also, we've got to break this stranglehold of government monopoly on the schools. You see, we say don't let the bureaucrats decide. Let the parents decide. Let the parents choose where the children go to school, and let them have the freedom to choose among private and parochial schools as well as public schools.

Another point, and Jeb touched on it, we've got to take back our neighborhoods from the thugs and the drug dealers. Part of the answer is a tough crime bill in Washington, DC. Give me your support to get that passed. Our bill gives new protection to women and children, those that are victimized by sex criminals. It stops endless appeals. And for the worst kind of crimes, it provides the death penalty for the cop-killers and those narcotic kings. I support our police, and I think we need to show more compassion for the victims of crime and be a little tougher on the criminals.

And let me shift a little bit, to a little bit to do with foreign affairs. I am looking forward to the day when democracy has triumphed and the Castro dictatorship nearby is no more. And let me say to those people outside who are concerned about their country: I want to see democracy restored to Haiti, and we will continue to work for the return of President Aristide.

I want to honor the Cuban brave human-rights activists and its martyrs for freedom and those who died resisting the dictatorship of Castro. And I'm looking forward to being the first President of the United States to set foot on the free soil of post-

Castro Cuba.

*Audience members.* Four more years! Four more years! Four more years!

*The President.* Let's look at the real situation in the world. Look around the world. Fidel Castro is now hopelessly isolated. And let me be very clear about this: We cannot and we will not have a normal dialog with Cuba as long as that dictatorship remains in power. And we do not and we will not help Castro police that prison state. We're going to keep heavy pressure on the outlaw regime, and we are going to strictly maintain our embargo.

Now let me say, as I look at this situation as your President, Castro is showing signs of desperation. Over the past year, he has intensified his persecution of people who attempt free expression, of people who try to form independent organizations. And the secret police have carried out more arrests. The Government-controlled mobs are increasing their violence against brave individuals who stand up for the basic rights and liberties that we take for granted in this country. And so, Castro is trying to crush the Cuban spirit and the Cuban society in a manner like Stalin.

The world has run out of patience with Fidel Castro. Let me give you a profound example of what I have just said. Yesterday, at the Human Rights Commission in the United Nations in Geneva, they voted for the strongest action ever against Castro's human rights abuses. And listen to this one: A new democracy, a brandnew democracy, joined the world's condemnation of Castro's crimes, and that democratic was Russia. Imagine the change: Russia condemning Fidel Castro. And the vote of that important Commission was overwhelming. The ex-Communist states of Bulgaria and Hungary and Czechoslovakia cosponsored that anti-Castro resolution. But not a single Latin American country voted to defend Castro. It's changing. It's changing all around the world. And this man is isolated in his dictatorship.

But let me say this more positively. Let me say this more positively: When Castro falls, and inevitably he will, we are going to be instantly prepared to renew our friendship and then help instantly in the rebuilding of a free and democratic Cuba. And I'm

talking about a lot of trade.

And while I'm on that subject, let me mention in a broad sense that the people I am running against for President of the United States, or who are running against me, do not share this vision of free and fair trade. They want to barricade our borders against job-creating trade. And they're the same kind of people that said to Columbus, "The Earth is flat, don't go." And as for me, I'm going to keep working to increase the flow of foreign trade and investment which is the lifeblood of modern Miami. We will not go back to the sorry, sad, pessimistic days of protectionism. We're not going to do that as long as I am President.

My son Jeb told me that there were many people right here in the Guards and in the Reserve and in the regulars that served in Desert Storm. And they served with great patriotism. And let me say to them: You did a first-class job.

And now you're seeing in this political year many people that are saying, cut the heart out of defense. Cut it all up. Cut it away. Don't have a defense. Let me tell you something. I am going to keep this country strong and ready for the challenges ahead, whatever they may be. Yes, we can make cutbacks. Because these people fought so well, our credibility is high, communism is on the run, democracy is going forward. We can make cuts in defense. But true to form, the liberals want to cut it to the bone. And we must not let that happen. I am for prudent cuts. We have suggested some. They're on the recommendation of the Joint Chiefs and of Colin Powell and of Dick Cheney. But I am not going to permit these people to gut defense so they can run off and spend your money in a reckless way.

When I think of Hialeah, I think of patriotism and service to country. And the Florida reservists and guardsmen answered that call for Desert Storm, and airmen and sailors from Florida's bases, and of course, the soldiers of General Schwarzkopf, central command all responded. And I am so proud of those of you here who served. And with your service and with your courage you said, "Never will we tuck our tail and let aggression stand." And we fought. And we won. And you that served deserve the credit.

And there were those who didn't support us then, and there are those who second-guess us now. But not the good people of Hialeah, not the people of Florida. And when our kids laid it on the line, you never wavered. And for this, I want to thank the people of this great State.

And every 4 years we have this political dance. And now we are in the battle for the future of the United States of America. And we are determined to leave our kids the best legacy possible. We want to lead the world in good jobs with productive work. We want to remain a powerful force, the single world leader for world peace and freedom. And we're fighting to protect our most basic institution, the one that means so much to the people of Hialeah, and I'm talking about the family.

And on primary day and in November,

you are going to have the future of this country in your hands. And you can prove your faith in self-government. You can prove that this epitomizes success in America, people that come here halfway around the world and then make a success of their lives. You can prove your success, and we can prove the pessimists wrong. So stand up and vote for what you believe in. Show Florida your strength. Show America the power that you represent. And give me 4 more years as President of the United States of America.

*Audience members.* Four more years! Four more years! Four more years!

*The President.* Thank you all. Thank you all, and may God bless the greatest country on the face of the Earth. Thank you very much.

*Note: The President spoke at 6:08 p.m. at Milander Park Stadium.*

## Remarks at a Bush-Quayle Fundraising Dinner in Miami, Florida
*March 4, 1992*

Thank you all. Please be seated. And Zach, Dr. Zachariah, thank you, sir, for that wonderful introduction, for all you do, and I am very, very grateful to you. I want to thank Father Murphy for his thoughtful invocation; the national finance chairman, you met Bobby Holt; but the national finance cochairman, my old friend Alec Courtelis; and another good longtime friend, Jack Laughery; to our campaign manager in Florida, no nepotism involved, I just chose the best, Jeb Bush. And may I salute one who gives us so much support, gives me so much support in Washington, Congresswoman Ileana Ros-Lehtinen. Where is she? Right here. And State senator Lincoln Diaz-Balart who we just met over here. Thank you, sir. And Van Poole, our State chairman, where's Van? He's right down here somewhere at the end. I salute him. And, of course, our Dade County chairman, our masterful master of ceremonies, Armando Codina. Thank you, Armando.

It is a pleasure to be here tonight. And we have much to do these next few months because we've much to do in these next few years. Together we can finish what we've started, and we can move this country forward. And to do that, I need your support. Help me win the Presidency for 4 more years. I ask your support for the simplest reason: We believe in the same things, jobs, family, peace, the fundamentally important things. And Zach, thank you for your very kind words about my grasp of and leadership in the field of foreign affairs.

We know that taxes are too high in this country because the Government is too big and it spends too much. And we believe in a strong defense. We believe in family and faith, responsibility and respect, community and country. And we know that we put America first when we put America's families first. The National League of Cities' mayors came to me, and they said the major problem in the cities is the dissolution, the diminution of the American family. And we've got to do something about that.

So often today's politicians do the easy thing, the popular thing. But it's the tough decisions that tell you something important about character and principle. For I believe in things that don't change from one election to the next, things that guide each one of us every single day of the year.

During my Presidency I've been blessed to take part in a new era in America's history. And let's face it, my friends, the cold war is over, and America won. And we are the leader of the entire world. And the Soviet Union collapsed, and imperial communism is dead.

Last week marked a special birthday, the battle of Grito de Baire in Cuba's war of independence. We support independence. We want freedom and prosperity for the Cuban people and an end to Castro's totalitarian regime. But look around the world. Castro has become an outcast even among the dictators. And his beaches are not borders, they're the confines of freedom. For years, the Cuban community—and I salute Jorge Mas and so many others here tonight—the Cuban community has energized Miami. And someday freedom-loving people will change that island for the better, just like America has changed the world. It's going to happen. You can bet on it. It is inevitable.

And now tonight, I want to talk about how Republican leadership is changing America. We're changing it by setting right what is simply on the wrong track in our country.

Take our courts, for example. There's something wrong when the rights of the criminal are more important than the rights of the victim. And I am proud of our tough stand on crime, although if Congress passed my crime bill, we could be doing a lot better. We could be a lot tougher. And I'm proud of our judicial appointments, judges who interpret and do not legislate from the Federal bench.

And there are other things that are wrong. When kids can't say a voluntary prayer in school or when fathers stop coaching Little League because they're afraid of liability suits, that too is wrong, and the same when people stop volunteering to

help each other because they fear ambulance-chasers. This isn't the America we want. This isn't the way it's supposed to be, all these lawsuits out there. These days a sharp lawyer would tell the Good Samaritan, "Keep on walking." I want to change that, so I've proposed reforms to our system to reduce the number of frivolous lawsuits.

Now, I don't want to get in trouble with the Bar Association, but I once quoted to someone that line, "An apple a day keeps the doctor away." And he said, "What works for lawyers?" [*Laughter*] Legal reform will help our legal process work. But, you know, the real answer for solving problems is to be more concerned with helping each other than suing each other. We're going to try to correct that from this legal reform bill I have before the Congress.

Can't stop there though, not until we reform our health care system. Not because it doesn't offer the world's highest quality of health care; it does. I think everybody would agree on that. But we've got to reform it because too many people simply don't have access to health insurance. Too many people worry that they'll lose their insurance if they change jobs, or, worse still, if they lose their job. And anybody who's had even minor surgery knows that health care costs are going through the roof.

What's the solution? Not to go down the road of socialized medicine. All that means is long lines and impersonal service. And as I said at lunch, we can get that, long lines, impersonal service, at the department of motor vehicles. [*Laughter*] My idea, and we've got a good plan to do this, is to make insurance available to all, rich and poor alike, availability, keep the quality high, the bureaucracy low, and preserve choice. The last thing we want is the Government assigning you a doctor.

And I want you to know I'd written this before I knew there were going to be 200 doctors here tonight. [*Laughter*] But since I have your attention, I have an ache in my shoulder and a small headache, and I'd like to know what to do about it. [*Laughter*]

Health care reform means improving the system. And there's another area where reform means changing the system. And

I'm talking about welfare. Let's face it: Too often welfare encourages dependency instead of personal responsibility and the dignity of a job. And so we've asked all the Departments and Agencies to make it easier through the waiver process for State and local government to reform policies and help broken families. We need to help make families whole, help bring dignity back into their lives. And yes, that means going after the deadbeat fathers who run out on their children and leave some struggling mother to take care of the responsibility.

There are so many issues out here. But this leads me, then, to the number one issue on the minds of all Americans: the economy, jobs. People out of jobs are looking for jobs, people who have jobs are worried they might lose it tomorrow, worried about their jobs, providing for their families, meeting the challenges of paying the bills, buying a home, setting aside for retirement.

The American people want this economy to grow, to create and preserve jobs. So in January, some of you may remember it in the State of the Union, I unveiled a two-part plan. The first part gets business moving again, upgrading plant and equipment, hiring workers again. It uses incentives like an investment tax allowance that speeds up the depreciation, calls for Congress to wake up and understand how jobs are created and to cut the tax on capital gains which will create a lot of new small business jobs.

Housing and real estate have led us out of recessions in slow times before. So to get housing back on its feet I unveiled several commonsense proposals to get people buying and building homes. These proposals will create in Florida alone an estimated 26,500 additional housing starts and 51,000 new construction jobs. Now, perhaps the most easily understood proposal is a $5,000 tax credit for first-time homebuyers, that young family together that needs just a little more to own their first home. People almost able to buy that first home could do it with that extra $5,000 in their pocket.

Two hundred and three years ago on this very date the United States Congress met for the first time, this very date 203 years ago. I wonder what they would think today

about the House Democrats' so-called plan. Here's the deal: 25 cents a day in temporary tax relief for 2 years, paid for, typical of them, by a large permanent tax increase. Now, over in the Senate, the bill the Democrats are working on is not much better than the one that's in the House. And its centerpiece is a huge tax increase. The last thing our economy needs now is a $100 billion tax hike, and they are not going to get it.

Zach alluded to this, we drew a line in the sand in the Persian Gulf, and we kept our word. So I'll draw another line in the sand right now. If the Democrats send me nonsense like the bill passed through the House, I will send it right back. I will veto it the minute it hits my desk. We are not going to inflict this on the American people. Instead of their crazy political maneuvers, Congress ought to pass my plan to make America more competitive. Here's the deadline: March 20th, the first day of spring. Here's the challenge: Give American workers a spring break. No more games. No more empty gestures. Just pass my plan, and get this economy moving.

Some question the need to act now. Well, let me repeat the story of a little boy who asked why his friend's grandmother read the Bible so much. "I'm not sure," said his friend, "but I think it's because she's cramming for her finals." Urgency counts in any world. And so I'm asking Congress to also pass the second part of my plan this year. It's a roadmap to make us competitive.

Our plan revolutionizes America's education system. I was reading that the average eighth grader spends 4 times as much of his time watching TV as doing homework. TV should not be America's babysitter. We can change that by making our schools accountable and demand excellence. Our plan will get the billions of dollars of Government research and development more quickly to private sector businesses and workers. Good education, and then use our know-how to move our technology from the Government labs out into the competitive world.

We have a commitment to children and strong families, and our plan provides tax relief to strengthen the family. We want to raise the tax deduction for children by

$500. Make no mistake, I want this entire plan passed this year. I want it passed now.

Behind all of this is an idea vital to America: To succeed economically at home, we have to lead economically abroad. Zach put his finger on the importance of America's leadership around the world. Some don't want us to lead. They think we ought to just shut out the rest of the world. And they're dead wrong. More than 200,000 jobs in Florida stem from manufactured exports. And last year, more than $13 billion in exports went out through the Miami customs district.

You know that the way to create jobs is not to cut and run, not to pull back in some isolationistic sphere of protection; rather to open markets for our exports everywhere in the world. And I am going to fight hard in every foreign market to do just that. It is exports that have saved us in these rough times, and it is exports that will lead us into the most prosperous decade that lies ahead. And it's working. Our overall trade imbalance is down. Look at the figures. In 1988 the trade deficit stood at $119 billion. Today it's dropped to $66 billion, a 44-percent drop in that relatively short period of time.

Now, I believe the American people want to hear about how we're going to address all these challenges, our country's challenges. And they want to hear solutions, not just a lot of tearing this country down and telling America how bad everything is. We have an awful lot to be grateful for in this country. They want to hear about the solutions that will keep inflation low, get our confidence high, protect the savings of our elderly. Solutions that will win the war on drugs, and we are making great headway. And I salute Miami's heroic efforts in this battle against narcotics. We are winning. Witness the massive seizure of drugs in south Florida over the past several months. Witness the fact that drug use amongst teenagers is down by 60 percent in the last couple of years.

We've got a lot to do in this country, and a lot to do. But I am absolutely confident that we will get the job done. And I'm going to fight hard in the Florida primary for these people, fight for what is right and good. I saw, in the 8 years my friend Ronald Reagan led America, how leadership matters. Last year, as Zach mentioned, we saw America stand tall again in the Persian Gulf. And I believe the next 5 years are just too important to entrust to the inexperienced. So I ask for your help to keep our party strong, united so that we can win this fall.

And yes, we have many challenges before us. But when haven't we? We're America. We're on the move. We're a country of change. And I guarantee you, we will meet every single challenge, each and every one of them, and meet them from the great Panhandle to the tip of the Florida Keys.

And yes, there's an important primary next Tuesday, and then there's another election in November. And I guarantee you, I have never felt more confident about winning the primary and winning the general election. I've got to be a little careful; my mother's living up the coast here in Florida, so I've got to be careful. But I think I've been a good President, and I want to be your President for another 4 years. And I will give you my level-best and work my heart out for the greatest, freest country on the face of the Earth.

Thank you, and may God bless America. Thank you all very, very much. What a great evening and a great day in Florida.

*Note: The President spoke at 8:30 p.m. in the East Hall of the Radisson Mart Plaza Hotel. In his remarks, he referred to Zach Zachariah, Bush-Quayle financial cochairman for Florida, and Van Poole, Florida Republican Party chairman. A tape was not available for verification of the content of these remarks.*

## Remarks to the Home Builders Association of Greater Columbia in Columbia, South Carolina
*March 5, 1992*

Thank you very, very much, Carroll. Thank you all so much. What a nice welcome back to South Carolina. Thank you very, very much. It's great to be here. To Richard Sendler, congratulations on you and Carolyn's 26th wedding anniversary. The man knows timing. Timing is everything in life. And Governor Campbell, my dear friend Carroll, thank you for that generous introduction. We are grateful for your hospitality, for your leadership as one of America's greatest Governors.

Carroll mentioned the Governors' conference where we set these national education goals, a first. Wasn't just Republican Governors, wasn't just Democrats, all coming together to set national education goals that led to a program that will revolutionize our education. What he didn't tell you is he and only two or three others, maybe it was three, were the true leaders in designing this brandnew approach to revolutionizing education in America and bringing us into a competitive scheme for the next century. We are going to again be the leaders in education, and your Governor has been in the forefront of that change. And I am very, very proud that Carroll Campbell will serve as the national cochairman of my campaign, and once again, he's handling a lot of duties as the southern regional chairman.

Good morning to the other members on the dais here, Chuck Newman, Mike McMichael, and Dottie Lafitte-Woolston. America still remembers your strength, the strength and resilience shown by South Carolina during Hurricane Hugo. I promise not to be quite that windy today. [*Laughter*] It's great to be back in this State where political victory is in the air. And then it'll be on to the fall where already there's a battle shaping up. Both sides will go on the offensive and all out. And in the end, there will only be one winner. And I don't know if it'll be the Gamecocks or the Tigers, but you can bet there's a battle. [*Laughter*]

We were riding in from the airport here, I saw a guy with a Tigers T-shirt on. So I picked up the loudspeaker from the car there and said, "Go Clemson!" Carroll said, "Say Gamecocks! Say Gamecocks!" [*Laughter*] And so never forgets the politics.

And I'm going to ask everybody what today I ask of you: Help me—what we've started—help me move our country forward. Help me win the Presidency for 4 more years. And I ask your support for the simplest reason. I believe we believe in the same things: jobs, family, peace, world peace, the important things. And we know that taxes are too high because our Government is too big and spends too much. And we believe in faith and family, responsibility and respect, community and country, a strong defense and a strong economy. And we know that we put America first when we put America's families first.

So often politicians do the easy things, the popular things. But it is the tough things that tell you something about character and honor and leadership. Anyone can demagog, but the Presidents must make decisions. And so, let me tell you what has guided me as I've tried to do for America what is right and true.

I learned, and I expect we all did, I learned a great deal when I was young from the greatest teachers I ever had, and that was my parents. And at church and in dinner and in political talks with my mom and my dad, I learned that life means nothing without fidelity to principles. It's what I believed as a Navy pilot in World War II, as a businessman, and now as your President. It's why, for example, I've vetoed 26 bills, standing up against the Democratic Congress. And I'm proud to say not one single one of them was overridden. Sometimes you have to make the tough call.

Some of them were popular, but all, in my view, were ill-advised. And the Presidency is not a popularity contest. I think you elect a President to say what America needs to hear, even when it's not what people want to hear. In the campaign you hear all kinds of quick fixes, all kinds of political rhetoric, but a President must make decisions and lead.

And Carroll Campbell knows exactly what I'm talking about. And so does that great favorite son of South Carolina, Strom Thurmond. Like me, they believe in these eternal truths that don't change. And so did another South Carolinian, a good man from Columbia, Lee Atwater, my dear friend.

All of us know how values guide each of us every day of every year. It's true in your families; it's true in mine. It's these things that have helped bring America to a new world, a new era in our history. Carroll touched on it.

We've got a lot to be grateful for. The cold war is over, and America won. The Soviet Union collapsed, and imperial communism is a four-letter word, D-E-A-D, dead. I salute my predecessor, Ronald Reagan. American leadership changed the world. Republican leadership will change America.

We believe that parents, not the Government, should make the decisions that matter in life. Parents, not Government, should choose their children's schools. I believe in school choice. And parents, not the Government, should choose who cares for their children. Parents know better than some bureaucrat in Washington, DC, and that's why we fought for a child care bill that has choice as its fundamental practice. And yes, I still believe that there is a place for voluntary prayer in our children's classrooms. And when things aren't right, we've got to change them.

We've got to reform America's health care system. And right now the quality, the quality of American health care, is the best in the entire world, bar none. And the problem? The problem is access to care. Too many Americans, many with families, do not have health insurance coverage. And you know how even a short stay in the hospital can rip a hole right through a family's budget.

But socialized medicine is not the answer. If we wanted long lines and revolving-door health care, we'd put doctors to work down at the department of motor vehicles. You can go there every single day and get those long lines and revolving people coming in and out of there. Nationalized health care

would be a national disaster, it really would. And the last thing we want is the Government playing doctor. We've got to reform, and so our program says make insurance accessible to all, rich and poor alike. And that's the program that we need to bring health care to those who don't have it adequately now in our country.

And we've got to reform our country's legal system. The home of the free has become the land of the lawsuit. When you're as likely to serve your neighbor a subpoena as a cup of coffee, something is wrong. Medical malpractice suits, they've become an epidemic worse than many of the diseases. And we've got to turn this mess around, and we need to spend more time helping one another than suing one another. And that's why we've sent up there to the Capitol Hill a reform bill, a major reform bill to curtail needless lawsuits and give people easier ways to solve disputes out of court. Your industry depends on partnership. And if you'll join hands with me to pass legal reform, we can get this country moving in the right direction.

And we've got to reform our welfare system, make a connection between welfare and work. And yes, we're a compassionate country. We care. Americans care. And they will support welfare for families in need. But Americans want to see government at every level work together to track down the deadbeat dads, the ones who can't be bothered to pay child support. They want to see us somehow break this cycle, this pessimistic cycle of dependency that destroys dignity and passes down poverty from one generation to another generation and then to another generation. That's wrong. That's cruel. And we're working to change it right now. We're encouraging the States to innovate with workfare, with plans that help people break welfare dependency and begin learning, begin learning work skills.

This brings me, then, to what I'm sure we would all agree is the number one issue: the economy and how we change it. We must help people worried about providing for their families, meeting the challenges of paying the bills and providing a home and setting aside for retirement.

So, let me take a page from Richard Sendler's book and tell it like it is. My program will put America back to work. My State of the Union Message put forth a two-part plan that will get our economy running the way Richard Petty likes to move. My plan says: U.S. economy, start your engines. And when we carry out this plan, it's going to carry our competitive American workers and businesses all the way to the victory lane.

The first part of the plan, some of you are familiar with it, aims to get business growing right now. I want an investment tax allowance, speed up depreciation. I want Congress to quit punishing people who create jobs, and thus, I want to see a cut on the capital gains tax and get this country back to work.

And then there's the proposal that can help get the housing market going again. I'm feeling better about it, but it needs this: a $5,000 tax credit for first-time homebuyers, money that will help people buy a first home. And here's what that credit, that $5,000 credit will mean to South Carolina: 3,400 housing starts, 6,600 jobs. And if Congress passes my plan, the National Association of Home Builders predicts 415,000 new construction industry jobs and $20 billion, $20 billion in new economy activity across America.

My plan will help people like the Greater Columbia Home Builders sell and build homes. And for the family looking to buy that first home, that $5,000 credit means 8 months of mortgage payments on the average South Carolina home. I wish Congress, if they don't do anything else, I wish they would lay aside the politics of tax-and-spend and give that one break to the American economy and watch homebuilding lead out of this slow economic time.

Sadly, the liberal crowd that controls Congress doesn't seem to understand the things that matter to you: your home, your business, taking care of your kids. And otherwise last week's House Democrats wouldn't have passed a bill which reminds me of the old joke: It'll make builders sleep like babies. They'll wake up every hour and cry. [*Laughter*]

Listen to the deal: 25 cents a day in temporary tax relief for 2 years, paid for by a large permanent tax increase. Over in the Senate, the bill the Democrats are working on is not much better than the one in the House. And its centerpiece is, yes, you guessed it, a huge tax increase. And the last thing our economy needs now is a $100 billion tax hike.

We drew a line in the sand in the Persian Gulf, and we kept our words. And I'm going to draw another line in the sand right now. If the Democrats send me a monstrosity like the House bill, I will veto that bill the minute it hits my desk and send it right back to those people on Capitol Hill.

Our plan has two parts. And I also call on Congress to pass the second part of our economic plan, now. I stressed this in the State of the Union: short-term, quick, done by March 20th; and a longer term, but I want it passed now, things like education reform, support for enhanced research and development so we'll be competitive in the years ahead, a $500 tax deduction to strengthen the family for each child.

We must make America more competitive in the 21st century, helping us lead economically abroad so that we can succeed economically at home. And some, of course, don't want us to lead. They want to build a fence around America. Tell that to South Carolina. Here are an estimated 125,000 trade-related jobs. And by closing our borders as my opponents would, we'd put those people out of work. And the U.S. trying to build prosperity by turning its back on the world is like your trying to build prosperity without hammers and nails. Call it protectionism or isolationism, both mean surrender. And look closely. That is not the American flag they're waving; it's the white flag of surrender. And that is not the America that you or I know. We are going to stay engaged. We are going to sell abroad.

And of course, the playing field has to be level. Fair trade is the priority. My fight to open trade markets is paying off for America's farmers and manufacturers. Our overall trade imbalance is down. Still got a ways to go. Still need more access to foreign markets. But look at these figures. In 1988, the trade deficit stood at $119 billion. Today, it's dropped to $66 billion, a 44-percent drop. And I will continue to fight hard to open up markets for our exports all around the world. And that's the way to fight for South Carolina jobs and for South Carolina families.

Recently, Barbara and I saw a movie based on a book in South Carolina. I'm sure many of you saw it, "The Prince of Tides," where the author writes, "the southern way of the spirit." The southern way of the spirit, to me, the southern spirit is optimistic. It is confident. It is so clearly patriotic. And you never run this country down. You don't believe in the politics of hate, either. And I think you'd agree that sometimes it's important to talk a little about what is right in America, and there is plenty to talk about.

Let's talk for just a minute about the bravest and best young men and women in America, the volunteer guardsmen and reservists, the volunteer soldiers, sailors, and airmen who answered the call in Desert Storm. South Carolina's young men and women answered that call by the thousands. Their service told America and the world: Never will America tuck tail and let aggression stand. And we'll do what's right and good. And when we do so, we will prevail.

Now, of course, there were those who didn't support us then, and there are those who second-guess us now. But not you. When our kids laid it all on the line, those brave young men and women laid it all on the line, the people of South Carolina never wavered. And again, I want to thank South Carolinians for showing America at its best. The country came together in victory. And that spirit of optimism, that can-do spirit, must be our spirit as we lead this country out of the economic doldrums and into a prosperity, the likes of which we never would have seen.

And now in our fight to change America, we still have much to do. But I am absolutely confident we'll get the job done. And yes, we have challenges before us. But I guarantee you we'll meet them head on, each and every one. And yes, there's a big election here on Saturday. And I don't like to see this many people gathered together without mentioning it. [*Laughter*] And there's another one in November. And I don't want to come across as arrogant, but I believe I'm going to win. I believe I'm going to win the election on Saturday. I believe I'm going to win the election in the fall.

And I ask for your support to help keep our party strong and united. I want to be your President for 4 more years. I will try my level-best to continue to lead this country with honor, with decency, with respect for the principles that all of us hold dear.

Barbara and I are very, very privileged, and we know it. Every single day we live in that White House, we know that we are amongst the most privileged in the world to be able to serve in this way. I'm going to continue to try my hardest. I'm going to continue to do my level-best for the people of this country. I ask for your support.

Thank you, and may God bless the greatest country on the face of the Earth. Thank you very much.

[*At this point, Richard Sendler presented the President with an oversized hammer.*]

Thank you all very, very much. I'll take this and flee and bring it to bear next week on the Congress. Thanks a lot.

*Note: The President spoke at 10:37 a.m. at the South Carolina State Fair Grounds. In his remarks, he referred to Richard Sendler, president of the South Carolina Home Builders Association; Charles Newman, first vice president of the Home Builders Association of Greater Columbia; Mike McMichael, president of the Home Builders Association of South Carolina; and Dottie Lafitte-Woolston, BUILD-PAC trustee.*

## Remarks on Departure From Columbia, South Carolina
*March 5, 1992*

Hey, listen, let me just ask you now to go out and be sure to vote on Saturday and send the rest of the Super Tuesday States a strong message. I want to be your President for 4 more years, so give me that vote. And thanks for your fantastic support, and don't let all the doomsayers get you down. I love this South Carolina optimism, the South Carolina pride, the South Carolina patriotism.

So thanks for this warm welcome. Now we're off to Tennessee, Oklahoma, Mississippi, Louisiana, and then we're going to get back for a great big Super Tuesday. But show them what we can do on Saturday. And thank you for this great Governor at my side. Thank you all.

*Note: The President spoke at 1:10 p.m. at Columbia Metropolitan Airport. In his remarks, he referred to Gov. Carroll Campbell.*

## Remarks to Federal Express Employees in Memphis, Tennessee
*March 5, 1992*

Thank you so very much. Thank you so much for that enthusiastic welcome. And thank you to my friend Howard Baker, one of the great leaders in the United States Senate in all of its history. Thank you for the introduction, Howard. And may I salute Congressman Don Sundquist, who has been at my side in the political wars, a good friend, a great Congressman. And I'm delighted to be here at Federal Express, 1990 Malcolm Baldrige Quality Award winner, a national winner.

My staff told me they weren't sure they could fit this stop in our schedule. But when I said it was a "Fred said," I knew we had to do it and fast. Fred, thank you. You know, Fred Smith has always been very, very generous. And Fred, it's good to know that if Air Force One ever has a problem, I can always ride in the jump seat. And I hope I don't forget the cookies. And you know what that means.

The people of Memphis, indeed, all Americans, face a momentous decision this year. And I would never presume to tell you how to vote; it must be between you and your conscience: Which Elvis should be on the postage stamp? I noticed the sign.

And really, it is a delight to be in this State because the people of Tennessee believe in big things, and we agree on the values that are closest to our hearts. And I'm talking about job security. I'm talking about family. I'm talking about world peace for us and our children and for our families for generations to come.

I'm here today because the people in Memphis, as well as people at Federal Express, embody the values that have made America number one in the world. And I know that with leaders like you, America will stay number one. Don't listen to the gloom-and-doom pessimists on that evening news every night. You don't shrink from a challenge, whether in the marketplace or in the world at large. Think back to a year ago. Think back to Operation Desert Storm. America faced a great challenge then, and Tennessee met it proudly. More than 6,000 Tennesseans served their country as reservists or members of the National Guard. And Fed Ex flew more missions than any other single civilian carrier. And believe me, that is not a contribution that America will ever forget. Thank you all very much and all of you that helped make that possible.

What makes this city, this State, and this company so successful? It's not hard to figure out. Look closely at what happens right here at Federal Express. You seek out new technologies; you make them work. You see job training not as a one-shot deal but as an ongoing process. And you set high standards, constantly asking more of yourselves and your coworkers, and you're satisfied with nothing short of excellence. Innovation, that's what being competitive is all about.

The key to success, to our success as a Nation is competitiveness. And for some, that word, competitiveness, is just this year's political buzzword. Here in Memphis it's a reality. Competitiveness is your key to leadership. And companies like this one here, Fed Ex, understand a central truth about America: If we are to succeed economically at home, we must lead economically abroad. And that's what you are doing.

And here at Fed Ex that's just common sense. More than 1.5 million packages pass through here everyday en route to all parts of the globe. And Memphis, therefore, is already America's distribution center, and now you're becoming the world's. And that means economic opportunity, and it means jobs for the American people.

You know, in this political year, this political year some people can't seem to understand that. They see the challenges of a global economy, and they say, "Let's draw the blinds; bolt the doors. Maybe the world will go away." And they push protectionism, an ugly word that really means surrender. Don't be fooled by the tough talk and the patriotic political bluster out there. Protectionism comes from fear, fear that Americans can't compete, fear that Americans have no ideas and no foresight, fear that America can no longer lead. And let those skeptics come to Memphis, Tennessee, and let them come to Federal Express and see what it really is about. And maybe then they'll understand what you and I already know: Americans here and across our country can outthink, outperform, outproduce anybody in the world.

Never in this country's history have Americans turned their back on a challenge. And we don't run and hide. We compete. As long as I am President, we will continue to compete, and we will continue to compete. I don't believe in protectionism, and I don't believe in isolationism.

Yes, we've got a lot of work to do to keep America on top. And of course, you know and I know that our biggest challenge, my first priority, is to get this economy moving, to create and preserve American jobs. And in my State of the Union Address in January, I laid out a two-part plan for the economic recovery. First, a short-term plan to strengthen the economy right now. And then, second, a longer term plan to keep America growing strong for years to come. And my plan gets business moving again, hiring again. It gets the housing market back on its feet with a $5,000 tax credit for that first-time homebuyer. Give those young families a chance to own their own home, commonsense proposals to get people buying homes and then building homes.

Fortunately, Congress can't tie my hands on everything. I've been able to take some steps on my own. For example, I put a 90-day freeze on new Government regulations so that all major Cabinet Departments and Agencies can conduct a top-to-bottom review. And I've given them some advice: Wherever possible, they must speed up any regulations that encourage economic growth and scrap regulations that restrict economic growth in this country.

Overregulation robs the inventiveness and risk-taking the economy needs to grow. And you all understand that better than anybody. For the first year, Fed Ex ran its business with 32 small planes. Any further expansion was inhibited by air cargo regulations. And deregulation allowed Fed Ex to buy more planes, larger planes for transport. And literally, Federal Express took off when the regulatory burden was lifted from their backs. And so, we're going to energize our economy nationally the same way. The days of overregulation are just that, they are over.

And also there's another thing on the minds of the people in this great area, and that means reforming our legal system. When parents won't coach Little League for fear of being slapped with a liability lawsuit and doctors stop delivering babies for fear of a malpractice suit, there is something wrong. And that's why I've sent a bill to the Congress, supported by Don Sundquist, to stop the frivolous lawsuits that drain our wallets and tear apart our society. And here's the bottom line: America won't find its way out of this mess until we spend more time helping each other than we do suing each other.

We've got to also reform our health care system. Anyone who's had even a checkup knows that medical costs are going right through the roof. And I believe all Americans deserve quality health care. However, too many families go without health care coverage. And our plan focuses on opening up access to health care to all Americans, rich or poor. And some want to take us down the road of nationalized health care, and I think you and I both know that nationalized health care where Government makes all the decisions would be a national disaster. And so I say to the Congress, the Congress of the United States: The American people need your help, and now is not the time for the Government to play doctor. Give us an improved health care program for this country.

I'd like them to do it now. But see, I know Congress can be a little slow doing things. [Laughter] That's like the guy that takes an hour and a half to watch "60 Minutes." [Laughter] So I gave them a deadline, March 20th, to enact this short-term plan. And unfortunately for the American people, the Democrats, the liberals that control the Congress, had other ideas. Last week they passed a plan of their own. And here's what it does: In exchange for a two-bit tax cut, literally about 25 cents a day per taxpayer, they will raise another $100 billion in taxes. And they call that $100 billion new revenues. And I have another word for it: your money. [Laughter]

No matter how the the Democrats try to dress it up, any economist can tell you the last thing we need right now is a $100 bil-

lion tax hike. So if the Democrats in Congress want to send that bill to me, I've got a message for them: I will veto it, absolutely, positively, overnight.

No, the American people have had enough of the old tax-and-spend, and they want to get our economy back on track. And every day each one of you hears Federal Express airplanes flying overhead. To some people that might sound like noise, but it is music to my ears. It is the sound of an economy on the move, an economy that is worldwide. It is the sound of American ingenuity taking off.

Since I took office, it has been my responsibility to work for what is right for America. And I often go back, I expect we all do as families—and I wish Barbara Bush were with me to see this marvelous crowd today—we often go back to the simple ideal that in our case, that my parents taught me: Try your hardest. Be honest. Do your best. And let me tell you something: I'm not finished yet. I want your support for 4 more years to finish this job. And I say to the people of Tennessee, together we're going to make a change, a change that for once Congress will believe in you and give you values you believe in, give those values a real chance to work.

Thank you for your hard work. Thank you all for this enthusiastic welcome and your continued support. And may God bless the greatest, freest country on the face of the Earth, the United States of America. Thank you so much.

*Note: The President spoke at 2:35 p.m. at Memphis International Airport. In his remarks, he referred to Frederick W. Smith, chairman and chief executive officer of Federal Express.*

# Statement on Signing the Reclamation States Emergency Drought Relief Act of 1991
*March 5, 1992*

Today I am signing into law H.R. 355, the "Reclamation States Emergency Drought Relief Act of 1991." This bill provides, for a

period of 10 years, general authority for the Secretary of the Interior to take action in the Western States to protect and preserve fish and wildlife habitat and assist farmers and urban dwellers in overcoming drought conditions. In addition, the bill provides permanent authority for the Secretary to prepare drought contingency plans in consultation with States, Indian tribes, and other entities for the prevention or mitigation of the adverse effects of drought conditions.

As I sign this bill, some areas in our Western States, notably in California, are facing their 6th consecutive year of drought conditions. The authorities granted by this bill will allow the Federal Government greater flexibility in utilizing the facilities of the Federal reclamation program and the resources of the Department of the Interior to assist the States and other non-Federal entities fighting the ravages of drought. This bill allows us to be the good neighbors that we should be in time of common need. It is in the American tradition that neighbor helps neighbor in times of burden. We will not stand by and see either our local economies and jobs literally "dried up" by drought or our valuable refuges and wetlands parched by lack of water.

We are fortunate that, in the last few weeks, the water supply situation in California has improved. So I am pleased to announce that today Secretary Lujan will make available additional allocations of more than 1 million acre feet of water. This will enable us to deliver project water to agriculture in the Central Valley—without sacrificing *any* allocations provided for other uses. This is only a first step—but a very positive one for California agriculture. I have asked Secretary Lujan to continue to assess the water supply situation and to keep me informed of any opportunity to provide additional Federal water where it is needed.

I note, however, that section 204(a) purports to require that the Secretary of the Interior submit certain drought contingency plans to the Congress, together with the Secretary's recommendations for legislation. The Constitution grants to the President the power to recommend to the Congress such measures as he judges necessary and expedient. Thus, provisions such as the one contained in this bill have been treated as advisory and not mandatory. I will therefore interpret section 204(a) accordingly.

Section 204(b), which purports to allow the Secretary of the Interior to approve certain drought contingency plans only at the request of the Governor of the affected State, could be construed to permit the exercise of Executive power by Governors, who are not appointed pursuant to the Appointments Clause of the Constitution. In order to avoid constitutional questions that might otherwise arise, I will interpret the role of Governors under this provision to be an advisory one.

I also note that the Department of Agriculture conducts drought contingency planning and administers drought assistance programs in agricultural areas. New planning and technical assistance activities initiated by the Department of the Interior will of course be coordinated with the Department of Agriculture and other affected departments and agencies.

GEORGE BUSH

The White House,
March 5, 1992.

*Note: H.R. 355, approved March 5, was assigned Public Law No. 102–250.*

# Statement by Press Secretary Fitzwater on the Kissimmee Basin Restoration Project
*March 5, 1992*

The President is pleased to announce that the Federal Government has reached in principle agreement with the State of Florida to restore a major portion of the lower Kissimmee Basin. The project envisioned would restore 66 miles of river and 29,000 acres of wetlands. It will help benefit over 300 species and create jobs in the process. We are prepared to agree to a plan which will implement this project in partnership with the State, with many of the costs shared fifty-fifty. Tomorrow, Assistant Sec-

retary of the Army Nancy P. Dorn will meet with Governor Chiles to iron out the details. But we are ready to move forward with a project that is good for Florida's environment and good for its economy, too.

# Nomination of I. Lewis Libby, Jr., To Be Deputy Under Secretary of Defense for Policy
*March 5, 1992*

The President today announced his intention to nominate I. Lewis Libby, Jr., of the District of Columbia, to be Deputy Under Secretary of Defense for Policy. This is a new position.

Currently Mr. Libby serves as Principal Deputy Under Secretary for Strategy and Resources at the U.S. Department of Defense in Washington, DC. Prior to this Mr. Libby served as a partner with the law firm of Dickstein, Shapiro & Morin in Washing-

ton, DC, 1985–1989. In addition, he served at the U.S. Department of State as Director of Special Projects at the Bureau of East Asian & Pacific Affairs, 1982–1985, and on the Policy Planning Staff in the Office of the Secretary, 1981–1982.

Mr. Libby graduated from Yale College (B.A., 1972) and Columbia University School of Law (J.D., 1975). He was born August 22, 1950, in New Haven, CT. Mr. Libby is married and resides in Washington, DC.

# Remarks at a Bush-Quayle Rally in Oklahoma City, Oklahoma
*March 6, 1992*

*The President.* Thank you, Senator Nickles, for that kind introduction. May I salute our State chairman, Clinton Key, and finance chairman, Ed Lawson. And I'm pleased to share this stage this morning with some of this State's finest: State Representative Larry Ferguson, Mayor Norick of Oklahoma City, Mayor Randal Shannon of Edmond, and Commissioners Watts and Bob Anthony. Welcome to all of them and, last but not least, Treasurer Claudette Henry. And I also want to express my deep appreciation to your hometown Congressman, Mickey Edwards, who couldn't be here today because he's back in Washington participating in the budget debate and helping me hold the line on Federal spending.

And may I also salute two friends of long standing, Ed and Thelma Gaylord. This square is a fitting tribute to Thelma, and I

think we're all very grateful to them. And finally, let me note what a great host Terry Johnson has been today. And a special thanks to George Wesley, who we just heard doing a superb job singing the national anthem. But most of all, thanks to every one of you who got up at all hours this morning to come to Edmond, from Elk City to Enid and towns all across Oklahoma, to show your support. And a special welcome to all the students here from Oklahoma Christian. One question. One question, just one question: Is it too late to audition for the spring sing?

Well, let's talk about our country. We are in a battle for our future, and I am determined that America should leave young people like you the best possible legacy. And we want America to lead the world in good jobs with productive work. And we want to remain a force for world peace and freedom. And we are fighting—and we will continue to—to protect our most basic institution, which is the family. And that's why this year of decision is so important for America.

In next Tuesday's primary election and November's general election, you will hold this future of this country, your future, in your own hands. And I'm asking you to get out to vote and create a resounding mandate for transforming America. Let's nominate and elect men and women who share our values. We've got much more to do to get America on the right track. So, I'm asking you for 4 more years as your President of this great country.

*Audience members.* Four more years! Four more years! Four more years!

*The President.* This country was built on faith, family, and freedom, and we must renew those sources of our strength. And we must allow common sense to prevail.

For example, in our welfare system, restore the connection between welfare and work. Americans are not cold-hearted. We're a caring people. Americans support welfare and families in need. But we want to see government at every level work together to track down the deadbeat fathers, the ones who can't be bothered to pay their child support. And most important, we've got to break the cycle of dependency that destroys dignity and passes down poverty from one generation to the next. That's wrong. That's cruel. And we're working to change it. The way we're doing that is to encourage States to innovate with workfare and plans that help people break that dependency, begin learning work skills. Let's help those families.

And we will continue to fight for the parents' right to choose their children's schools, school choice. We've got a great education program, and school choice is at the heart of America 2000, our strategy to literally revolutionize American education.

Today, March 6th, is a World Day of Prayer. And I think it says something that the World Day of Prayer is observed a lot more frequently here in this community than it is in Washington, DC. You know there's something wrong when our kids cannot participate in voluntary prayer in the classrooms across this country. The Senate and the House, and they need it, I'll admit, open their sessions every day with prayer. Why can't we have a voluntary prayer in the classroom?

And let me be clear: Parents, parents, not some bureaucrat in Washington, DC, knows what is best for the kids. And that's why we worked hard to win a child care bill that provides parents the right to choose who provides the care. We know America is first as long as we put the family first.

Now, back to Congress, regrettably. For 3 years I've had to fight the liberal leadership of the Congress, one party having controlled that Congress for most of the last 50 years. And I will continue to stand for principle no matter how daunting the odds. We have fought; we've put judges on the bench who know their rule is to interpret the law, not to legislate from the Federal bench. And I'm going to keep on doing that.

And let me be clear to those here and those that are not here but might be listening: I will use the veto when I have to, to stand for principle, to stand up for family values. Sometimes even my friends said I was flirting with defeat by casting a veto instead of cutting out a deal. But we've never lost a veto fight, and I will never hesitate to use the veto when principle is at stake.

And so, here we go again. The liberal leadership of the Congress is once again on a collision course with my veto. You remember when I asked Congress to pass tax cuts and incentives to really stimulate this economy, to get it moving, to get real estate up and running, to reward risk takers who create good jobs. It's time to quit punishing people who create jobs. We ought to cut the tax on the capital gains.

But as Don Nickles knows because he's fighting against them every day, instead of passing my plan, the big spenders who control the Congress had other ideas, and they pushed through one of their own. And here's what's in it for you: a tiny temporary tax cut, 25 cents, a quarter a day for each man, woman, and child. And here's the catch: You can keep that quarter in exchange for $100 billion in new taxes. The Democrats call that new revenue, and I call it your money. And we are not going to let that happen.

If you feel the way I do, write your Congress, and then tell him to keep the change and keep your hands off of the taxpayers' wallets. Unless I haven't been clear. If they send me the bill, anything like the one that came out of the House, I'm going to veto it faster than an Oklahoma twister and send it right back.

And remember, I have set a deadline to the Congress: March 20th. And I have said to the Congress: Pass our plan, get our economy moving, set the politics aside for just a minute—and then we can fight about it politically from now on—and do something for the American people.

You've probably got some Will Rogers students around here, but I know Will Rogers once said it was better to have termites in your house than the legislature in session. [*Laughter*] But this time there's no way around it. Congress has got work, its work to do to get this country moving.

And I know full well how difficult times have been in the past few years in this State for the people in the oil and gas business, for example. And our domestic oil and gas industry is important to our national economy. It's important; it is vital to our national security. And all of us share an interest in a national energy strategy that will keep America strong and keep us competitive. And it's a commonsense plan, ours is, that will help both consumers and producers. Congress has been slow to act on our energy strategy, but finally it's beginning to move. And so, I'd like to ask all of the people of Oklahoma to join me and Don Nickles and Mickey and help us put the heat on Congress to get our energy initiatives in place.

Without getting too technical, I also want action on an issue absolutely vital to Oklahoma energy producers. This is technical, but it's important. The alternative minimum tax as applied to the energy industry is hurting our economy and helping no one. It is unfair to the independent producers. And it's costing us jobs. And Don Nickles understands this problem, and he's been in the lead to get it solved. And so, let me assure you, I will work with Don to get the Congress to reform this tax provision and restore fair treatment to our energy producers. It is in the national security interest of the United States to do this.

I am not going to sit around waiting for the congressional leadership to help the economy, though. Our administration has been reviewing what we can do under existing laws to help. And in the natural gas industry—help that get moving again as well. And so, today we're going to announce several new actions that will eliminate some of the regulatory barriers that have hampered the gas industry. And these actions will provide significant relief to industry, but they are no substitute for prompt action by Congress to pass my energy legislation.

We're going to fight as we must, and we will win. And in the world today, if we want to succeed economically right here at home, we've got to lead economically abroad. Each day, more and more American jobs are tied to trade, to international trade. And that's the case here in Oklahoma. In the past 4 years, Oklahoma's exports have jumped by 75 percent.

And today, 75,000 Oklahoma jobs are tied to trade. And remember, every billion dollars more in manufactured exports means 20,000 new jobs here. And each extra billion dollars in agricultural exports means thousands more jobs on Oklahoma ranches and farms and in the Oklahoma agribusiness.

And so, some of my opponents are out there peddling protectionism, a retreat from economic reality. And you cut through all the patriotic posturing and the political promising and all the tough talk about fighting back by shutting out foreign goods. Well, look closely. That is not the American flag they are waving; it is the white flag of surrender. And we must not have it. That is not the America that you and I know. We don't cut and run; we compete. And never in this Nation's long history have we turned our backs on a challenge. And we are not going to let them start doing it to us now.

I put my faith in the American worker. Level the playing field, and the American worker will outthink, outproduce, and outperform anyone, anywhere, anytime. So, let's back those workers with free and fair trade.

We're strong. We're strong because we value faith, family, and freedom. We are the world's greatest power because whenever our values are threatened, we fight to defend them. And we need to keep our defenses strong. In my State of the Union Message, I proposed far-reaching but still responsible cuts to bring our Armed Forces into line with the new realities of the world. These cuts were based on recommendations from the Joint Chiefs of Staff, from Colin Powell, from Secretary Cheney, all who have performed superbly. But now the liberals, true to form, want to put down this scalpel on that kind of cut and pick up a meat ax. And I am not going to let that happen. We are going to keep America strong. And you can count on it.

You see, as President, and I'm sure all of you all know this, I have a constitutional responsibility for the national security of this country. And as long as I am President, I guarantee you we will have defenses strong enough to meet our responsibilities. We were ready last year, and an unforeseen situation arose when Iraq's brutal dictator invaded Kuwait. And we will be ready when we face the next crisis. Do not let them cut the heart out of our defenses.

We must let the world know this: Whatever the challenge, America will stay strong. We are in it to win. And make no mistake about this, don't listen to these politicians on the other side who tell you we're in decline. You travel anywhere around the world, and you will find we are the undisputed, respected leader of the free world. And we're going to stay that way.

Think back to a year ago, the calm after Desert Storm. Ask any one of the proud sons and daughters of this great State of Oklahoma, ask any of the young people from this campus who became liberators of Kuwait. And they'll tell you military strength doesn't mean a thing without moral support right here at home. And let me say America is proud of the Oklahoma 45th, the 45th Brigade, and proud of the decision this week to keep that brigade in service.

Of course, there are those who didn't support us then; I can understand that. There are those who second-guess us now. But not here, not in Oklahoma. When I drew that line in the sand, you stood with me. And never would this country tuck tail and let aggression stand. And America did what was right and just and good, and America prevailed.

And we're bringing that same spirit to the fight that we face today. And so, let my opponents go out there and tell us everything that's wrong about our country. Let them try to win by tearing down our great fabric. My opponents sound the retreat, run from realities, seek refuge in a world of protectionism and high taxes and big Government. Let them drone on about what's wrong in America. We know what is right about the United States of America.

Once again, I'm proud to be on this campus. And let me close with just a couple of words right from the heart. In the first place, I think my wife is a fantastic First Lady of the United States. But we are blessed. She and I are blessed to serve this great Nation of ours at a moment when so many of the old fears have been driven away, when so many new hopes stand within our reach. And since the day I took the oath of office, I made it my duty always to try to do what is right for this country. And I've given it my level-best. And I am not done yet.

You and I have more work ahead before we've finished our mission. And it's a battle for our future. It's about jobs for your future. It's about the family. It is about world peace.

And together, I think we've made a great beginning to renew the miracle of American enterprise and to strengthen our values of family, faith, and freedom. And I am counting on Oklahomans, you young people especially, to reject the ugly politics of hate that's rearing its head again: anti-Semitism, bigotry. They have no place in the United States of America.

And now we're approaching an hour of decision next week. Don't wait until November. I'm asking you to vote on Tuesday in the Republican primary. Give me your vote in this important election next Tuesday, and help me win 4 more years to lead the fight for the values we share.

Thank you, and may God bless the United States of America, the freest and fairest and strongest country on the face of the Earth.

Thank you very, very much.

*Note: The President spoke at 9:13 a.m. at Oklahoma Christian University. In his re-* *marks, he referred to Edward L. Gaylord, president of Oklahoma Publishing Co., and his wife, Thelma; and J. Terry Johnson, president of Oklahoma Christian University of Science and Arts.*

## Remarks at Louisiana State University in Baton Rouge, Louisiana
*March 6, 1992*

Thank you very much. So pleased to be introduced by your Congressman and my chairman, Richard Baker, doing a great job up there in Washington. And I want to salute two other great Congressmen, Bob Livingston and Jim McCrery. What a job they're doing for the people of Louisiana. And we brought back to Louisiana with us another of Louisiana's sons, Jim McCrery, and secretary of state Fox McKeithen right here, whose dad used to be Governor, and also Henson Moore, my Deputy Chief of Staff, who represented Baton Rouge in the Congress. He now serves as our Deputy Chief of Staff there in the White House. And Chancellor Davis, thank you, sir, for letting us come to this beautiful campus, and thank all of you for the warm welcome.

Let me just say, when I saw the Tiger descending, it is great to be back in Tiger territory. And let me be very clear why I am here: Four more years. That's what we want. And I'm so pleased to see two that were in the White House not so long ago, Coach Brown and Shaquille, the "Shaq Attack" O'Neal. Shaq didn't think I'd come down for his birthday, did he? [*Laughter*] Right?

And I wonder if I have any Deke fraternity brothers out here. As I was driving— now, wait just a minute—as I was driving past the fraternity house, I heard him shouting: Four more years! And that's brotherhood for you, I thought. And then, Barbara said what they were really saying was: Four more beers! [*Laughter*] I think my fraternity, I think the Dekes get a bad rap. Some would compare to them to "Animal House," you know. They ought to take a look at what happens up on Capitol Hill.

Let me just comment about what we're doing. We're in a battle for our future. I'm determined that America should leave young people like you the best possible legacy. We want America to lead the world in good jobs with productive work. And we want to remain a force for world peace and freedom. And we are fighting to protect our most basic institution, the American family.

And that's why, really, I would say to all of you, no matter who you are for in this process, that's why this year of decision is so important for our country. In next Tuesday's primary election and November's general election, you will hold the future of this country, your future, in your hands. And I'm asking you to get out the vote and create a resounding mandate for transforming America. Let us nominate men and women, and elect men and women, who share our fundamental values. And we've got much more to do to get America on the right track. And so, I'm asking you for 4 more years as your President to finish the job.

Somehow I think Louisianians understand this, but this country was built on faith and family and freedom. And we must renew those sources of our strength. And we must allow common sense to prevail.

For example, in our welfare system, restore the connection between welfare and work. Americans aren't cold hearted. We are a caring people, and we support help for those families in need. But we want to see government at every level work together, for example, to track down the deadbeat fathers, the ones who cannot be bothered to pay child support. But more important, we've got to break the cycle of dependency that destroys dignity and passes down poverty from one generation to the next. That's wrong. That's cruel. And we've got to keep working to change it. And so we're encouraging States to innovate with workfare and with plans that help people break welfare dependency and begin learning and work skills.

So anyway, we're going to continue to fight for the parents' rights. We're going to fight for the parents' rights to choose their children's schools, school choice. We've got a great education program to help revolutionize the schools. School choice is at the heart of America 2000, our strategy to literally revolutionize American education.

And let's get our priorities right. There's something wrong. Our kids cannot participate in voluntary prayer in the classroom, and we need to change that. I will admit that they need it, but both the House of Representatives and the Senate open their sessions with a prayer. And Congress needs it, I will admit, but I think it ought to be true for voluntary prayer in the classrooms.

Parents, not some bureaucrat in Washington, really know what is best for their children. And that's why I worked to win a child care bill that provides parents the right to choose who provides the care. We know America is first as long as we put the family first. So everything I do is going to be shaped at strengthening the American family.

As Bob and Jim and Richard know, for 3 years I've had to fight the liberal leadership of the Congress. And I will continue to stand for principle no matter how daunting the odds. We've fought, and we've put judges, for example, on the Federal bench who know their rule is to interpret the law, not to legislate from the Federal bench. And I'll use the veto when I have to, to stand for principle, to stand up for these values. Sometimes even my friends said I was flirting with defeat by casting a veto instead of cutting a deal. But we've never lost a veto fight, and I'll never hesitate to use the veto when principle is at stake. That's the only way we can change the direction of the Congress.

The liberal leadership of the Congress is once again on a collision course with my veto. You remember I asked the Congress to pass tax cuts and incentives to get this stagnant economy moving, to get real estate up and running, to reward those that go out and take the risks, the risk-takers who create good jobs. And it's time to quit punishing people who create jobs. And so I say cut the tax on capital gains and start a lot of new businesses.

But instead of passing my plan, the spenders who control the Congress had other ideas. And they pushed through one of their own. And here's what's in it for people who work for a living: a tiny temporary tax cut, 25 cents a day, a quarter a day for each man, woman, and child in America. But here's the catch. You can keep that quarter in exchange for $100 billion in new taxes. Now, they call that new revenue. I call it your money.

And if you feel the way I do, tell the Congress to keep the change and keep their hands off the taxpayers' wallets. And just so I am clear with the Congress on this, let me say right here in Louisiana, but beamed to Washington, DC: If the liberals send me their scheme, I'll send it back the minute it reaches my desk. I will veto it. I will slam dunk it faster than L.S.U. can say "cha-ching."

Remember, I've set a deadline, March 20th. And I've said to the Congress: Pass our plan. Get our economy moving. Do something now for the American people. And let me say this: It's tough this time of year, right before a primary election, but let's set the politics aside long enough to take these few selective steps to stimulate the economy, and then we can put the politics in place for the fall. But let's stimulate the American economy and get people back to work.

But we will fight. I like a good fight. And we will fight as we must, and we will win. And in the world today, if we want to succeed economically at home—we must—we have got to lead economically abroad. Each day, more and more American jobs are tied to trade. Remember this one: Every billion dollars more in manufactured exports means 20,000 new jobs, and each extra billion dollars in agricultural exports means thousands more jobs on Louisiana farms and in Louisiana agribusiness.

But my opponents are peddling protectionism, a retreat from economic reality. And you can cut through all the patriotic posturing, all the tough talk about fighting back and bashing somebody by shutting out foreign goods, but look closely. That's not the American flag they are waving; it is the white flag of surrender. And that is not the America that you and I know. And clearly, when you look around the world, it is not the way of the future for young Americans. America doesn't cut and run. We compete. And never in our long history have we turned our backs on a challenge, and we simply are not going to start that now.

I put my faith in your talent to compete: Level the playing field, and Americans will outthink, outproduce, and outperform anyone, anywhere, anytime.

As I said earlier, we're strong because we value faith, family, and freedom. We're the world's greatest power, the world's greatest power because whenever our values are threatened, we fight to defend them. We need to keep our defenses strong. In my State of the Union Message, I proposed some far-reaching but still very responsible cuts to bring our Armed Forces into line with the new realities of the world. I based my recommendations to Congress on the unanimous opinion of the Joint Chiefs of Staff; of their able Chairman, Colin Powell; of our Defense Secretary. And we sent this program up that will keep our defense strong but still make cuts in defense; because of what's happened around the world, we can do that. But the liberals, true to form, want to put down the scalpel and pick up a meat ax. We cannot let that happen. We must keep America strong. I'll do that, and you can count on it. Who knows where the next threat comes from?

For those of you studying government, you know this: As President, I have a constitutional responsibility for the national security of this country. And as long as I am President of the United States, I guarantee you we are going to have defenses strong enough to meet our responsibilities. We were ready when Iraq's brutal dictator invaded Kuwait, and we will be ready when we face the next crisis. We must not cut into the muscle of our defense.

We must let the world know this: Whatever the challenge—and we're facing some right now if you look around the world—whatever the challenge, America will stay strong. America is in it to win.

Think back to just about one year ago today, the calm after Desert Storm. Ask any one of the proud sons and daughters of Louisiana, more than 250 from right here at L.S.U., ask any one of those young people from this campus who became the liberators of Kuwait, and they'll tell you: Military strength doesn't mean a thing without the moral support right here at home.

And yes, there are some revisionists out there trying to rewrite history now. And of course, there were those who didn't support us back then. There are those who second-guess us now. But not here, not across this State of Louisiana. When I drew that line in the sand, you stood with me. And never would this country tuck tail and let aggression stand. America did what was right and good and just, and we prevailed. And we are today the envy of the world, people looking to us to defend freedom and democracy wherever it may be.

And now we've got to bring that same victorious spirit, that same "America together" spirit to fight the problems we face today. And so let my opponents sound retreat, run from the new realities, seek refuge in a world of protectionism, high taxes, big Government. Let them drone on about what's wrong in America. We know what is right about this country.

The spirit of Desert Storm brought us together, Americans of every color and creed. And I'm asking you young people to do all you can to keep this country united, make it a land of harmony for years to come. And that means right now, every one of us, I don't care, South, North, East, or West, every one of us must stand up and say no to the politics of prejudice and hate and anti-Semitism and bigotry. They have no place in America.

Let me close with just a few words from the heart. Barbara and I are blessed, we are blessed to—and I might say I think the First Lady is doing a first-class job, if that's all right. No, but I know she feels this way, and I do. We are blessed to serve this great

Nation of ours at a moment when so many of the old fears have been driven away, when so many new hopes stand within our reach. Every day, and this is the gospel truth, we still say our prayers. But every day I thank God that young people like you will be able to follow your dreams without the nightmare of nuclear holocaust hanging over us as it did just a few years ago. And since the day I took the oath of office, I made it my duty to try, to try hard always to do what is right for this country. And I've given it my level-best, and I am not done yet.

You and I have more work ahead before we've finished our mission. It's a battle for our future. It's about jobs for your future. It's about the family. It's about world peace. Together, I believe we have made a great beginning to renew the miracle of the American enterprise and to strengthen our values of family and faith and freedom. Now we're approaching an hour of decision. Now it gets into the political trenches, next week. So don't wait until November, I'm asking you to vote in Tuesday on the Republican primary. And give me your vote in this important election next Tuesday. Help me win 4 more years to lead the fight for the values we share.

Thank you, and may God bless the United States of America, the freest, the fairest, the most decent country on the face of the Earth. Thank you all.

*Note: The President spoke at 12:55 p.m. in Pete Maravich Arena. In his remarks, he referred to William E. Davis, chancellor of the university, and head coach Dale Brown and center Shaquille O'Neal of the L.S.U. Tigers basketball team.*

## Remarks at a Bush-Quayle Rally in Jackson, Mississippi
*March 6, 1992*

Thank you all. Thank you, Governor. And may I pay my respects to Governor Fordice, thank him for that introduction, and tell him how glad I am to be working with him to help solve the many problems of our Nation. And it's great to be with you, Kirk, and of course with the First Lady, Pat. You both are off to a wonderful start for this State. And to the Lieutenant Governor, Lieutenant Governor Briggs, and to Mayor Charles Evers, it's an honor to share the stage. And then I see some of our Mississippi Bush-Quayle team, my dear friend Clarke Reed and Evelyn McPhail and Ann Wilson. And thank you, Reverend Felder, for the invocation; to Anna McDonald for her beautiful singing; Jerry Clower, who had you all in stitches, doing a great emceeing job. And may I thank the Mississippi Valley State band and also Pearl High School. Thank you all for the great music.

I know of the interest in agriculture here, and I have an announcement of interest to Mississippians. I will nominate Jim Huff of Taylorsville to join my administration in Washington as head of the Rural Electrification Administration. His farming, his ranching, his manufacturing, and Government experience make him the perfect choice to lead the REA. Insured loans and loan guarantees have helped provide service to 600,000 customers in Mississippi, so it is fitting that a native son of Mississippi takes on this important job.

Now, about the business at hand, it's refreshing to be here. And it's always refreshing to get away from Washington. I share your pride in your new Governor, Kirk Fordice. You see, he's a commonsense leader who shares our values and visions for America's future. And these values, if you do your history, these values have changed the world. And we need them now to change America.

We're in a battle for our future. We're determined to leave our kids the best possible legacy. And we want America to lead the world in good jobs with productive work. And we want to remain a force for world peace and freedom. And we're fighting to protect our most basic institution, the American family. And that's why this year of decision is so important for America. And that's why next Tuesday's election, the primary election, and then the November general election are vital to our future. And I'm asking you to get out the vote and create a resounding mandate for transforming America. Let's nominate and elect men and women who share our values. We've got much more to do to get America on the right track. And so I'm asking you for 4 more years as President of the United States.

This country was built on faith and family and freedom, and we must renew those sources of our strength. We must allow common sense to prevail in our welfare system, restore the connection between welfare and work. Americans aren't cold-hearted; we're a caring people. We support those families that need help. But we want to see government at every level work together to track down those deadbeat dads, the ones who can't be bothered to pay the child support. And we've got to break the cycle of dependency that destroys dignity and passes down poverty from one generation to the next. That's wrong. It is cruel. And we've got to work together, coming together to change it. We're encouraging States—full cooperation from the Governor—to innovate with workfare, with plans that help people break that dependency and begin learning work skills.

And we will continue also in another front to fight for parents' right to choose their schools, school choice. School choice is at the heart of America 2000, our strategy to literally revolutionize American education. And my wife, Barbara, recently joined Governor Fordice and your lovely First Lady, Pat, in the town of Winona to kick off Mississippi 2000, your own State's commitment to fundamental reform. We're going to stay the course and help every single kid in America have the best possible education. That means you.

Today, March 6th, is a World Day of Prayer. And I think it's quite a commentary on things that the World Day of Prayer is observed a lot more fervently in Mississippi and in our State of Texas than it is in Washington, DC. And speaking of Washington,

the House there and the Senate both open their daily sessions with a prayer. But there's something wrong when our kids cannot participate in voluntary prayer in the classrooms of the United States of America. And we need to change that.

You see, parents, not some bureaucrat in Washington, know what is best for their children. And that's why I worked to win a child care bill, a good one, that provides parents the rights to choose who provides the care. And we know America is first as long as we put the family first.

For 3 years I've had to fight the liberal leadership of Congress. And I'm going to continue to stand for the principle, no matter how daunting the odds. We fought, and we put judges on the bench who know the rule is to interpret the law, not to legislate from the Federal bench. I'm delighted that David Souter and Clarence Thomas are now members of the Supreme Court.

And also another point: I'll use the veto when I have to, to stand for principle, to stand up for family values. And sometimes even my friends said I was flirting with defeat by casting a veto instead of cutting a deal. But we've never lost a veto fight, and I will never hesitate to use the veto when principle is at stake.

Now, I'm sure you all have been reading in the papers, once again the liberal leadership of the Congress is on a collision course with my veto. You remember I asked Congress to pass tax cuts and incentives, investment incentives to get this economy moving again, and that means pass a new investment tax allowance. To get real estate up and running, that means pass incentives like a $5,000 tax credit for those first-time homebuyers, those young marrieds that want to buy their home for the first time. It means rewarding risk to those who create jobs, and that means cut the tax on capital gains so we can get more businesses going.

But instead of passing my plan, the big spenders who control the United States Congress had other ideas. They pushed through one of their own. And here's what's in it for you: a tiny temporary tax cut, 25 cents, a quarter a day for each man, woman, and child in America. And here's the catch: You can keep that quarter in

exchange for $100 billion in new taxes. Now, the Democrats call that new revenue. And I call it your money. If you feel the way I do, tell the Congress, "Keep the change, and keep your hands off the taxpayers' wallets."

Now, right here in Mississippi, you don't take storm warnings lightly. Hurricanes and tornadoes, nothing to trifle with. Well, Congress better not mistake my veto warning. The storm flags are flying. And if the liberals send me that tax bill, I'll send it back faster than a Mississippi whirlwind. And I will veto it the very day that I receive it.

And let me say to the Congressmen that might be listening up there in Washington: Remember, I've set a deadline, March 20th. And I've said to you all: Pass our plan. Get our economy moving. Do something for the American people. Set politics aside and stimulate this economy so the men and women of Mississippi and across our country will have more jobs.

I like a good fight. And we'll fight if we must, and we will win. And we'll keep to our course of leadership in the world economy, and that's absolutely a must if we're going to succeed economically at home. Trade with our neighbors, trade with the world is vital. It is absolutely essential here in Mississippi.

A couple of months ago, I visited Peavey Electronics in Meridian. And they told me 40 percent of their sales are exports. Across the State, 45,000 jobs now depend on exports. And remember, every billion dollars more in manufactured exports means 20,000 new jobs, and each extra billion dollars in agricultural exports means thousands more jobs on Mississippi farms and in Mississippi agribusiness.

But my opponents are peddling protectionism, a retreat from economic reality. And you cut through all the campaign statements and the patriotic posturing and all the tough talk about fighting back by shutting out foreign goods. Look closely. That is not the American flag they're waving; it is the white flag of surrender. And that is not the America that you and I know. We do not cut and run; we compete. Never in this Nation's long history have we turned our backs on a challenge, and we are not going to start doing that now.

And I put my faith in the American worker. Level the playing field, and the American worker will outthink, outproduce, and outperform anyone, anywhere, anytime. And you know what Dizzy Dean said, "It ain't bragging if you can back it up."

No, we're America. We're in the State of Mississippi. And because we're strong, because we value faith and family and freedom, we're the world's greatest power. Because whenever our values are threatened, we fight to defend them. We need to keep our defenses strong. In my State of the Union Message, I proposed far-reaching but still responsible cuts to bring our Armed Forces into line with the new realities of the world. But the liberals, true to form, want to put down the scalpel and pick up a meat ax, and we cannot let that happen to the defenses of this country. I will keep America strong, and you can count on it.

As President, I have a constitutional responsibility for the national security of this country. And as long as I am President, I guarantee you we will have defenses strong enough to meet our responsibilities. We were ready when Iraq's brutal dictator invaded Kuwait, and we will be ready when we face the next crisis; make no mistake about it. We must let the world know this: Whatever the challenge, America will stay strong. We are the undisputed, trusted leader of the world. And as President, I will keep it that way.

Think back a year ago, think back just a year ago to the calm after Desert Storm. Ask any one of the proud sons and daughters of Mississippi who became the liberators of Kuwait, and they will tell you military strength doesn't mean a thing without moral support right here at home.

And yes, we all know there were those who didn't support us then. There are those who second-guess us now. But not here, not in the State of Mississippi. And when I drew that line in the sand, you stood with me. And never would this country tuck tail and let aggression stand. America did what was right and good and just, and America prevailed.

And we're bringing that same spirit to the fight we face today. I want you to join me. Bring that same Desert Storm spirit to solving these problems at home, and let our opponents sound the retreat, run from the realities, seek refuge in a world of protectionism and high taxes and big Government. And let them drone on about what's wrong in America. We know what is right about our country.

And that brings me to another point, and I want to say it right here in front of the capitol of this great State: Desert Storm brought us together, Americans of every color and creed. And I am counting on the good people of this State and all across our country, the other 49 States, to build on that harmony. And let's stand up and reject the ugly politics of hatred that is rearing its head again. Racism and anti-Semitism and bigotry have no place in the United States of America.

Let me close with just a couple of words from the heart. Barbara and I are blessed. Let me say parenthetically—it's a little husbandly pride—I happen to think this First Lady is doing a pretty fine job for the United States of America and for these kids here. But we view it this way: We're blessed to serve this great Nation of ours at a moment when so many of the old fears have been driven away, when so many new hopes stand within our reach. Maybe you do the same thing, but every day, every day I thank God that our young people will be able to follow their dreams without the nightmare of nuclear holocaust hanging over us as it did just a few years ago. And

since the day I took the oath of office I made it my duty always to try to do my best, try to do what is right for this country. I've given it my level-best, and I am not done yet.

And you and I have more work ahead before we've finished our mission. It's a battle for our future: It's about jobs; it is about family; it is about world peace, the kind of legacy we will leave these young kids sitting here in front of me today. Together, we've made a great beginning to renew the miracle of American enterprise and to strengthen those fundamental values of family, faith, and freedom. And now we're approaching an hour of decision, next week. Don't wait until November. I'm asking you to vote on Tuesday in the Republican primary. Give me your vote in this important election next Tuesday. Help me win 4 more years to lead the fight for the values we share.

Thank you, and may God bless the United States of America. Thank you very, very much.

*Note: The President spoke at 4:52 p.m. at the State Capitol Building. In his remarks, he referred to Clarke Reed, State chairman for the Bush-Quayle campaign; Evelyn McPhail, chairman of the Republican Party of Mississippi; Ann Wilson, Republican national committeewoman; and Rev. Bert Felder, senior minister of Galloway Memorial United Methodist Church, Jackson, MS.*

# Message to the Congress Transmitting the Report of the White House Conference on Library and Information Services
*March 6, 1992*

*To the Congress of the United States:*

I am pleased to transmit to you the Summary Report of the 1991 White House Conference on Library and Information Services and my recommendations on its contents as mandated by the Congress in Public Law 100–382, section 4.

The world has changed dramatically since the last White House Conference on Library and Information Services. The thirst

for freedom has swept aside the acceptance of tyranny. New and amazing technologies have made ideas accessible to everyone. Books, faxes, computer disks, and television and news broadcasts have ended the reign of ignorance and helped create a whole new world of enterprise, competition and, with it, intellectual growth.

Library and information services are vital because they help ensure a free citizenry and a democratic society. It was appropriate that the 1991 Conference addressed three major themes of great concern to our own society: literacy, productivity, and democracy. These three issues are now more important than ever as we work to raise our Nation's educational level, to make the American work force preeminent in the world, and to serve as an example to the rest of the world regarding the benefits of a democratic society. We live in exciting times with our world changing daily. Not only are we on the verge of revolutions in educational practice and workplace improvements, but technology is helping to change the very way in which we learn and work. Library and information services are at the center of this change with new sophisticated technologies that not only improve the quality of information but actually make it more accessible to the people who need it. It was the realization that library and information services are in a period of rapid change that prompted the establishment of the 1991 White House Conference on Library and Information Services.

Participants at the White House Conference considered the themes of literacy, productivity, and democracy, and how library and information services can contribute significantly to the achievement of those goals. The 984 delegates to the Conference included librarians, information specialists, and community leaders. They represented all the States and territories and the Federal library community. Prior to the Conference, there had been innumerable pre-Conference forums involving more than 100,000 Americans. These meetings produced 2,500 initial proposals regarding library and information services. The Conference delegates deliberated on 95 consolidated proposals before making their final recommendations. I wish to commend the National Commission on Libraries and Information Science for its key role in making the Conference a success. The recommendations, thoughtfully considered by the delegates to the Conference, are intended to help frame national library and information service policies for the 1990s.

## The Importance of Library and Information Services

Library and information services have always played a significant role in our society. From colonial times forward, our libraries have acquired, preserved, and disseminated information to Americans. Today libraries and information services are expanding their roles and, with the advent of new technology, changing the ways in which we use and share information. As we move toward the new century, we should acknowledge the contributions that libraries have made and will continue to make in the years ahead.

A particular strength of our libraries and information services is that they are locally controlled. Whether in the public or private sector, these services are best maintained at the local level where they can be most responsive to citizens and where they can adapt to new local needs. Likewise, the States have a long tradition of fostering the development and expansion of library services to all citizens. In combination, both local and State governments are the primary supporters of our Nation's libraries and information services. The Federal role in library and information services has been one of encouraging and leveraging State and local support to expand the availability of library services to all Americans.

### Literacy

The quest for the future begins with literacy. Literacy is a goal that we must make every effort to achieve. It has been estimated that 23 million adult Americans are functionally illiterate, lacking skills beyond the fourth-grade level, with another 35 million semiliterate, lacking skills beyond the eighth-grade level. The effects of illiteracy in this Nation are staggering as people find themselves shut out of opportunities and as our governments struggle to find ways to assist these disadvantaged individuals.

My Administration is committed to improving education for all Americans. With broad bipartisan support, we are moving rapidly to implement strategies to achieve our six National Education Goals. These

Goals, developed cooperatively with the Nation's Governors, address critical education issues ranging from ensuring our children start school ready to learn and attaining a 90 percent high school graduation rate, to being first in the world in math and science, demonstrating competency in core subject areas, and ensuring safe, disciplined, and drug-free schools. Goal five states that by the year 2000, "Every adult in America will be literate and will possess the skills necessary to compete in a global economy and exercise the rights and responsibilities of citizenship." As we pursue education reform across America, one of our emphases must be on a literate America. To that end, I have consistently worked for an increase in Federal efforts for literacy programs. Our national education strategy, AMERICA 2000, is designed to help achieve all of the goals, and libraries, serving as community centers, can therefore play a major role in helping communities and schools across the country reach the goals.

The Conference recommendations include several statements that also address the literacy issue. I would urge the Members of Congress to review these suggestions carefully and to consider them in any future deliberations regarding literacy and library and information services.

### Productivity

Today's workplace demands a new definition of the term productivity. Rather than a traditional perspective that measures the production of items, we must recognize that we now live in an Information Age. In today's Information Age, many of our workers are knowledge workers who create and use information in totally new environments and in totally new ways. What we must do is to ensure that these workers achieve maximum productivity in their efforts.

The White House Conference recommendations regarding productivity are varied and far-reaching. Of perhaps greatest significance is the support shown for a national network for information sharing. The recent passage of the High-Performance Computing Act of 1991 responds directly to this recommendation and is a major step in the direction of increased productivity for American workers. Other recommendations address copyright statutes and business information centers, both of which would have a positive impact upon the efforts of American business and employees.

My Administration is committed to the full employment and increased productivity of the American work force. We can, and we must, become the most skilled work force in the world if we are to remain preeminent in today's global economy. Throughout the Federal Government, efforts are being made to bring to Americans the kinds of resources that they need to improve their on-the-job effectiveness. For example, within the Department of Education, an information resource for teachers, parents, and communities is being developed. To be known as SMARTLine, this data base will contain the best of education research and practice. This resource will be available locally—through schools and community libraries—to educators and parents who want to improve classroom instruction methods and to raise the education levels of our children.

### Democracy

An informed populace is a great guarantee that our democratic way of life will continue and flourish. Recent events have shown us that people in other countries are struggling to emulate what we have known for the past two centuries. The free flow of information in countries all over the world and especially in Eastern Europe has played a strategic role in releasing people from the bondage of ignorance.

Library and information services provide an infrastructure by which we can obtain information and can contribute to our democratic way of life. In our country, there are more than 30,000 public, academic, and special libraries, and there are an estimated 74,000 school libraries and media centers. These library and information centers are the links between our citizens and the information that they need. These libraries provide the kind of ongoing education that each man, woman, and child will need in order to remain a fully productive and fully participating citizen.

The 1991 White House Conference on Library and Information Services has generated many worthwhile recommendations. Clearly these ideas illustrate not only the changing role of libraries, but also the revolutionary changes affecting our own society. As our culture changes, so must the institutions that serve it. The Conference Report makes it clear that library and information services are changing rapidly in response to an increasingly complex and global society. As we strive for a more literate citizenry,

increased productivity, and stronger democracy, we must make certain that our libraries and information services will be there to assist us as we lead the revolution for education reform. As I stated in my speech at the White House Conference, "Libraries and information services stand at the center of this revolution."

GEORGE BUSH

The White House,
March 6, 1992.

## Nomination of James B. Huff, Sr., To Be Rural Electrification Administrator
*March 6, 1992*

The President today announced his intention to nominate James B. Huff, Sr., of Mississippi, to be Administrator of the Rural Electrification Administration, Department of Agriculture, for a term of 10 years. He would succeed Gary C. Byrne.

Currently Mr. Huff serves as State Director of the Farmers Home Administration for the U.S. Department of Agriculture in

Jackson, MS. From 1957 to 1989, Mr. Huff was director of operations for the Masonite Corp. in Laurel, MS.

Mr. Huff graduated from Mississippi State University (B.S., 1954). He was born August 4, 1932, in Jones County, MS. He is married, has two children, and resides in Taylorsville, MS.

## Exchange With Reporters in Pensacola, Florida
*March 7, 1992*

*The President.* That is amazing. He said, and this man's entitled to his opinion, that we set the course record for going down there and back, 2 miles.

*Q.* Do you believe it? [*Laughter*]

*Q.* They tell that to all the Commanders in Chief.

*The President.* Do you believe I'm going to win the primaries?

*Arms Shipments in Persian Gulf*

*Q.* Are you worried about the Scuds, sir?

*The President.* Scuds? Yes. But the man who ought to be worried about it is Saddam Hussein.

*Q.* Have you ordered boarding of those ships, of the Marine ships, sir?

*Q.* Are you contemplating some options?

*The President.* We're always contemplating options, yes.

Can you turn those cameras around because I want to take my shirt off, privacy. How many are honoring this?

*Q.* Everybody.

*The President.* Promise? No reporting on the body? [*Laughter*]

*Q.* Is it okay if we hoot a little bit?

*The President.* Yes, you can go like that. But no, I'm serious. Otherwise, I'll do it. Come on, Larry [Larry Downing, Newsweek], promise. Word of honor.

*Presidential Primaries*

*Q.* How are you going to do in the primaries, Mr. President?

*The President.* We're going to win them all and then keep on going and winning every one of them. All across the national campaign, I'm going to conduct myself with a certain amount of dignity and making very clear I'm not a candidate of hatred and trying to appeal broadly to this country.

When I look at the Democrats' side, I give them credit for working hard and doing their number out there, and I'm not about to intervene in the primaries. But I've got to tell you, I feel confident about winning in the fall. And I feel good about today and Tuesday. And so, it's not been easy out here, as you know, but we're going very well, indeed, making clear I understand the problems of this country. We've got good answers for it. And when we get into the fall campaign I'm ready to put my values, my programs on the line against some of these other things I hear out there.

Today is a nonpolitical day in terms of the visit itself, but I'll be talking about the defense of this country and the need to keep strong and the need to guard against any contingency. Sorry, but when I listen to the debate on the other side, I don't hear that concern for the national security. I am the President. I have a constitutional responsibility to keep this country strong, and I'm going to do it. So it's those issues, though, you see, are not in focus at all; they're not even being discussed.

So, we'll wait until the fall. But you caught me on a good day. I really feel pretty good. Marlin feels good. Marlin feels very good today.

*Q.* Why do you feel you can afford not to campaign tomorrow or Monday?

*The President.* Well, I think we're in good shape. I think we're in very good shape in the primary States. I don't know how you all felt, but I've felt that the response we've been having is very enthusiastic. The crowds have been superb, and so I'm just coming at it from a position of real confidence. But not enough confidence that I

didn't get on the phone this morning and talk to the Governor of South Carolina, the Senator from South Carolina, both of whom reiterated their confidence. Talked to our campaign manager in Florida, my boy Jeb. Talked to our son George who was campaigning in Mississippi yesterday and been going, crisscrossing Texas. And all of them are very upbeat. So, the voters will decide this on Tuesday and somewhat today.

*Q.* Mr. President, do you think the voters are getting the message from you, though it's thinly veiled, against Buchanan, that he is insensitive to——

*The President.* The message there I get is what George Bush stands for. And I've tried to stand for this every day of my Presidency. And I hope our Presidency has been one of decency, a sense of honor, a sense of fairplay, and I'm just going to continue to emphasize these themes.

I mean, I think Americans like a political battle, but I think they expect their President to express some of these fundamental values. And when I speak out against hatred, bigotry, anti-Semitism, racism, it's not aimed at anybody; it's aimed at values that this country really has, whatever side of the aisle you're on. And so, it's something that I just feel I must do. And it just didn't start with this campaign, if you'll go back and look at my speeches over the last few years.

So, it's really appealing to the better nature of the American people, and the American people are well-intentioned on these matters of fairplay. And so, I'll keep speaking out on it.

*Q.* How long do you think Buchanan will stick it out?

*The President.* Have no idea.

We'll see you guys. Thank you for the run.

*Note: The exchange began at 7 a.m. at Pensacola Naval Air Station. A tape was not available for verification of the content of this exchange.*

# Statement on the Death of Menachem Begin of Israel and an Exchange With Reporters
*March 9, 1992*

*The President.* We're going to have just a little statement here. Thanks for helping with the logistics here. But what I want to do now is to send our most sincere condolences to the people of Israel and to the family of Menachem Begin, former Prime Minister. His historic role in the peace conference, peace process, will never be forgotten; particular emphasis, of course, will always be on his historic and I would say very courageous and foresighted role at Camp David. And now people are talking peace, but people will remember Menachem Begin as the man that made a significant, courageous breakthrough, just as they will remember Sadat for the same thing. So, we send our most sincere condolences to the people there.

## Middle East Peace Process

*Q.* How do you think the peace talks are going now?

*The President.* Well, it's hard to tell. They're talking, though. A year ago nobody would have thought that possible. And it's very important that they keep talking. And that's what our whole policy is about; that's a lot of what post-Desert Storm was about. And I think there's a real chance just as long as people keep talking at the peace table.

## Arms Shipments in Persian Gulf

*Q.* What's the latest, sir, on this Korean ship that——

*The President.* I have no recent information. I talked to General Scowcroft this morning, but nothing to say publicly on that.

## Loan Guarantees for Israel

*Q.* Do you think Israel will drop its press for the loan guarantees?

*The President.* I have no idea.

*Q.* Do you wish they would agree to——

*The President.* We're perfectly prepared to, in accordance with U.S. policy, to go forward.

## Presidential Primaries

*Q.* Why do you think Pat Buchanan would stay in——

*The President.* Look, I——

*Q.* ——even when it's numerically impossible for him to take the nomination?

*The President.* I haven't been trying to analyze that up until now, and I don't think I'll start now, if you'll excuse me. We're waging a pretty good campaign. It's high-level. It's keeping my sights on the major issues. A lot of them, such as world peace, seem to be obscured by the hue and cry of the campaign trail. But that's still a very important issue and——

*Q.* You're not going to attack anybody?

*The President.* Not now, Helen [Helen Thomas, United Press International]. I might get on your case if you—[*laughter*]—no, I would never—well, it doesn't matter. [*Laughter*]

## Health Care Reform

*Q.* The Democrats are saying that your health plan is simply a theory that you're not getting, any way that it's paid for. How do you respond to those charges?

*The President.* I'd say that that's crazy. They haven't looked at it. What most of them want to do is have a nationalized health care. And that would result in far less quality health care. We have a plan that makes insurance accessible to all; that's the key to it. And there's 30 pages of how it's being paid for. I'm surprised to hear—not surprised really because I think most of them are committed to plans that have failed in other places.

*Q.* Basically, how does it get paid for?

*The President.* It gets paid for through a lot of things. I'll tell you one main way it gets paid for is by cutting down on these frivolous malpractice suits. Somebody estimated that would be $40 billion. And we're having great difficulty getting it through the trial lawyers' lobby on Capitol Hill. The American people want action on this kind of proposal so——

*Q.* This is going to take care of 90 million people without health care?

*The President.* It will take care of $40 billion. No, our plan takes care of the 90 million by giving—90 million? Come on, that's too high a figure.

*Q.* That's what they're saying.

*The President.* No, no. That's way high. It will take care of it through giving everybody access to health care.

### Presidential Primaries

*Q.* Mr. President, the Democrats are now down to three. You've got two or three on your side. How do you feel about how it's shaping up?

*The President.* Let the process work. I thought Saturday was fantastic, and I think we'll have a good day tomorrow. Just keep your sights set on the ball; don't get irritated, be pleasant. I've been through the other side of that drill over a period of years, so I don't intend to react. Act, not react.

*Q.* So you're changing your modus operandi?

*The President.* Well, I have over the last 3 or 4 years, yes. [*Laughter*] My modus operandi is to be pleasant with you people when you ask me irritating questions. And that isn't always easy. But I think you'll have to give me good marks for having done that, and I don't plan changing now.

*Q.* Well, you say you're willing to do anything you have to do to win.

*The President.* But I think being pleasant is the way to do it and keeping your sights set on the major issues facing this country, challenging the Congress to move.

And incidentally, I get credit for a full press conference here because I was only going to make one statement. Making the 231st since I've been President. Ready

access.

*Q.* But you haven't had any lately.

*The President.* No, I know it. Ask Marlin why.

*Q.* Mr. President, Michael Dukakis didn't respond, and look what happened to him.

*The President.* Well, look at the results of the election so far. Anytime you beat somebody by 40 points, that used to be considered a landslide. Now we've changed the—I don't know what different ground rules are being used, but I think it's fair in my own defense to say 40 points, 40-point victory over the nearest competitor is a pretty good size win. I will settle for that in the fall over the Democratic candidate.

*Q.* Buchanan is hoping to upset you in Michigan, Mr. President, a week from now.

*Q.* Is Pat Buchanan upsetting your agenda, Mr. President?

*The President.* No way. What?

*Q.* Michigan is where Buchanan wants to beat you.

*Q.* Is Pat Buchanan upsetting your agenda?

*The President.* We've spelled out our agenda over the last 3 years. What we want to do is get this country's economy moving and preserve and strengthen world peace. And I think we'll do it, plus better education, fighting against crime by trying to get some reasonable crime bill passed, winning the fight against drugs where we've made a good start. There are so many issues, but they're all obscured by the noise of the campaign. But that will be in focus in the fall; you watch.

*Note: The President spoke at 7:58 a.m. on the South Lawn at the White House. A tape was not available for verification of the content of this exchange.*

# Remarks to the National League of Cities
## *March 9, 1992*

Thank you very much. Glenda, thank you so much for that kind introduction, and to all of you. And may I salute the Members of Congress that have been with us here. Let

me say good morning to them, and please do what's right up on Capitol Hill. My greetings to all the special guests here at the head table; to Don Borut and Wallace

Stickney, who is with us.

Let me just say that I'm very pleased to join you today. I enjoyed, Glenda referred to it, I enjoyed speaking to you over the television hookup in December. It's much better face to face. And I hear that you have had a very energetic, very well attended series of meetings. And I salute your leadership, present leadership; and then, of course, an old former colleague of mine, or put it this way, a still young but former colleague of mine in the House of Representatives who will be your leader—what, starting next November, is it—Don Fraser.

In January, as Glenda said, I had a follow-up meeting with 10 of your members. And like your organization as a whole, they represented a broad cross section of urban America's leadership: Republicans and Democrats, liberals, conservatives, officials from large and small and midsize cities.

And of course, we're all concerned, all of us here, about the big issues, jobs and family and world peace. And even so, I was struck at this meeting by the unanimity of the message that your members wanted to deliver. It can't be repeated often enough in Washington or any State capitol or any city hall. Your message was simply this: The enormous problems facing cities today, from infant mortality to high dropout rates to runaway crime, are partly, at least, symptoms of one larger problem, the deterioration of the American family.

Now, I understand the breadth of the issues that you deal with daily, poverty to potholes to property taxes. And in addressing myself to this one subject, I don't want you to think that we are less concerned about these enormous problems you face every day. But this morning, I would like to discuss that same serious issue that you all raised with me, the family. The restoration of the American family is at the heart of much of what we have done these last 3 years. Leaving aside for a moment the enormous costs, the wasted human resources or the billions spent to repair the damage of broken homes, family breakdown ultimately endangers our position in a world increasingly driven by economic competition.

Certainly, the integrity of family is critical on its own merit. As Barbara Bush, my favorite philosopher, says, "What goes on at the White House is not nearly as important as what goes on in your house." And there's a lot of truth in that. But particularly at a time when our efforts must focus on economic growth, the family's disintegration endangers, for all of us, our ability to create and to preserve jobs, and to create an economy open to participation by all our citizens.

So we must start with a clear-eyed look at what is really happening to the family in American communities today, not just in poor urban neighborhoods but all across America. And then we've got to look inside ourselves, to establish the principles that will shape our approach. And then we must act.

The urgency is clear. We all know the statistics, perhaps you know them better than most Americans, the dreary drumbeat that tells of family breakdown. Today, one out of every four American children is born out of wedlock; in some areas the illegitimacy rate tops 80 percent. A quarter of our children grow up in households headed by a single parent. More than 2 million are called latch-key kids, who come home from school each afternoon to an empty house. And a large number of our children grow up without the love of parents at all, with nobody knowing their name.

We know from experience the consequences of family decline. Neglected children are more susceptible to the lure of crime and drugs; they're more likely to have poor health, drop out of school early, more likely to lead a life without hope. Each of you is in a position to know the human costs that these statistics can only dimly sketch. You know, as I do, that for every blip on a chart or dot on a graph, there is a human story to tell, and too often the story is a tragedy.

About 10 days ago, I was in Bexar County, Texas, in San Antonio, meeting with Latin American leaders to intensify our war on drugs. And while there, I saw a front-page story in the San Antonio Light. A cabdriver had been murdered last September, another act of random, selfless violence, and his murderer had just been found guilty. But what was truly horrifying, what would horrify any American, was this: The murderer was a 12-year-old boy. And as the deputies took the boy from the courtroom, according to the newspaper story, they had trouble fitting him with shackles and handcuffs, so slender were his wrists. This youngster was 4 feet tall, not yet a teenager but now a convicted murderer.

The drumbeat continues: two teenagers shot dead in a New York public school, an LSD ring busted up in an affluent northern Virginia suburb, or the harrowing stories of runaway kids and the horrors that befall them.

I know that almost all of you could tell stories equally distressing, stories from your neighborhoods and your cities where the unthinkable has become the commonplace. I am sure that many of you here took office with high confidence in the power to solve these problems, only to discover, sooner rather than later, I suspect, that they were far more stubborn than we could imagine. Let's not forget that the trials our citizens face each and every day were generations in the making. We can't expect change overnight. But make no mistake: Change will come because change simply must come.

Let's face it. We can only change things if we work in common purpose. We must call a cease-fire in the war of words that too often consumes us. Casting blame brings no solutions, nor will questioning each other's motives. We have got to focus every ounce of our energy to turn back this assault upon the American family and act as one Nation to defend and strengthen it. As public servants, we must never forget that the best department of HHS, of health and human services, is, indeed, the family. In restoring the family, we restore to coming generations the values, the sense of right and wrong, the will and confidence to succeed that only a family can provide a child. And in doing this, we will reinvigorate our cities and our communities as well.

We needn't look far for principles to guide us. There are old home truths: Rely on what works; discard what doesn't. Never be afraid to innovate. Remember that Government closest to the people responds best to the needs of the people. And let's not forget this as a guiding principle: If people

are to be responsible, they must be given responsibility.

The Government's first duty is like that of the physician: Do no harm. But the fact is, with the best of intentions, many past Government policies have worked against the institution of the family, undermined young people's desire to marry and stay married, to provide for their children, to plan for their future. As a practical matter, doing no harm means in part that we ensure parents retain the authority to make the big decisions for their families. This doesn't absolve parents of responsibility; it's just the opposite.

For example, even if we're able to reform our education system—and I am determined that the Federal Government assist all of you in every way in revolutionizing the education system—but even if we are, parents must still read to their children. The point is that Government harms the family when it restricts its autonomy or usurps the authority of responsible parents.

Let me give you another example. Those of us in Government can never plausibly claim to fight for families if we insist that Government, not parents, must choose who cares for their children. So 2 years ago our administration waged a fight in Congress over this very issue, and we won. We kept choice of child care out of the hands of Government and put it where it belongs, in the hands of parents.

And now we're engaged in a similar fight over whether parents should have the right to choose their children's schools. We know the benefits of competition; it is the linchpin of American prosperity. And competition among schools will be the linchpin of educational excellence, too. From Minnesota to Milwaukee to east Harlem, school choice works.

But you see, it's important for other reasons: It restores authority and responsibility to parents. Just as it makes our schools accountable, it also makes parents accountable for the decisions they make. Not only in child care and school choice but in other areas as well, a key to healing the American family will be restoring parental authority and accountability.

Another example, the initiative that we

call HOPE, H–O–P–E. It took more than a year to get that program through Congress and another year to get even partial funding for it. But HOPE will be crucial to our success by offering low-income families a greater opportunity to own their own homes. HOPE is based on a simple principle: To survive, people need the intangible values of dignity and self-respect. Government can't provide those, but homeownership can, an education can, a job can, and being part of a family can.

The Federal Government has a positive role in preserving the family, and we welcome that role. It's guided the decisions that we make every single day. Since 1989, for example, we have more than doubled the funding for the program that I bet everybody in this room supports, Head Start, a program that brings children and parents into the classroom, strengthens family ties, and reinforces parental responsibility. For the first time in the program's history, we can support now Head Start for all eligible 4-year-old children whose parents choose to have them participate.

There are many other examples. We've increased the earned income tax credit for low-income families. And since '89, we've increased the funding for WIC, the supplementary food program for women, infants, and children, by 47 percent to $2.8 billion next year. We've increased other nutritional programs by similar percentages. And this year Federal support for childhood immunization grants will top $340 million, an increase of 18 percent over last year's level. So all told, funding for children's programs, from nutrition and education to foster care and child immunization, has increased 66 percent since we took office.

But look, we will never measure, and I think you all would be the first to agree with this, we would never measure our compassion simply in dollars spent. We will measure it by results. The test will be the health and happiness of our children and, most important of all, the sense of well-being and self-reliance instilled by our families. Our administration has targeted funding to programs that efficiently fulfill Government's role in supporting families and keeping them together, programs that work for the family.

Yet, at the same time, we must face another fact. Government can sometimes be a burden as well as a boon. Over the past 40 years, the child tax exemption has lagged far behind the soaring costs of childrearing. And I have asked Congress to increase the exemption by $500 per child. For a family with four children, that's an increase of $2,000. And it's a crucial first step toward redressing the imbalance, and it's what we can afford to do right now.

And now I come to perhaps the most crucial matter of all, one that concerns you all. We must reform our Nation's welfare system. Americans are the most generous people on Earth, but they want to see and they are entitled to see some relationship between welfare and work. Welfare must never be what Franklin Delano Roosevelt warned it might become, "a subtle destroyer of the spirit." It is not meant to be a way of life or a family legacy passed from one generation to the next. Welfare can eat away at the ties that bind a family together.

And State and local governments are undertaking the brave work of reform: Learnfare in Wisconsin; REACH, Realizing Economic Achievement in New Jersey; Washington State's FIP, Family Independence Program. These are all demonstration projects that we support. And my administration is committed to reform, and we are acting now on waivers, to loosen up on waivers, to waive unnecessary redtape that impedes reform.

There's no hidden agenda here. This administration, the mayors, the State leaders who press for drastic reform of welfare aren't modern-day Scrooges chiseling one more dime out of some poor family. Democrat or Republican, California, New Jersey, Federal or State: In our heart of hearts, we really believe reforming the welfare system is the best way to serve people. Break this sorry cycle of despair. Give people real hope. And we're going to keep on trying to do just that because every single American deserves to believe in the American dream.

Today, with family as the center, I've highlighted the role of government, both positive and negative, because we're men and women of government. But let's never forget the work of private Americans dedicating themselves to the voluntary service of others, who create an environment where families can flourish. Each is a Point of Light, offering service with no thought of reward, though the reward will be reaped by every single American.

And let me be very clear. When I talk about Points of Light, they are not a substitute for the good that government can do, but it's more this: We will simply not solve our most pressing problems without the dedication of those Points of Light, of those volunteers. And I urge all of you, when you return to your cities, to do all in your power to encourage these caring men and women, to make yours a community of light.

In my State of the Union Address, I announced that we would soon institute a commission on America's urban families. Your executive board or directors or whatever group it was—I've never been sure with whom I was dealing, but they were all big shots, believe me—[*laughter*]—came together. And their work will be one result of my meeting in January with some of your leaders.

And I have asked Governor Ashcroft of Missouri, a caring man, Annette Strauss, the former Mayor of Dallas, a very able woman who also cares deeply, to lead the commission and fulfill its mandate: To identify those government programs, at all levels, that weaken or strengthen urban families;

to analyze ways to improve private efforts to strengthen families; and to recommend new policies to help families in our cities.

I am convinced that we can correct our mistakes, that we can learn from our failures and build on our successes. I do not exaggerate when I say that the future of America depends on our efforts. The family is the irreducible unit of comfort and love. And from families radiate neighborhoods, from neighborhoods come towns and cities, and their health determines the health of our country, for better or for worse. And like you, I am committed to making our health whole and to ensuring that our cities, as Theodore Parker said, "remain the fireplaces of America, radiating warmth and light against the darkness."

Thank you all very much for giving me this opportunity to visit with you today. And may God bless our great country. Thank you so much.

*Note: The President spoke at 11:36 a.m. at the Washington Hilton Hotel. In his remarks, he referred to Glenda E. Hood and Donald J. Borut, president and executive director of the National League of Cities; and Wallace E. Stickney, Director of the Federal Emergency Management Agency. The Executive order of March 12 establishing the National Commission on America's Urban Families is listed in Appendix E at the end of this volume.*

# Letter to Congressional Leaders on Nuclear Cooperation With EURATOM
## March 9, 1992

*Dear Mr. Speaker: (Dear Mr. President:)*

The United States has been engaged in nuclear cooperation with the European Community for many years. This cooperation was initiated under agreements that were concluded over 3 decades ago between the United States and the European Atomic Energy Community (EURATOM) and that extend until December 31, 1995. Since the inception of this cooperation, the Community has adhered to all its obliga-

tions under those agreements.

The Nuclear Non-Proliferation Act of 1978 amended the Atomic Energy Act of 1954 to establish new nuclear export criteria, including a requirement that the United States has the right to consent to the reprocessing of fuel exported from the United States. Our present agreements for cooperation with EURATOM do not contain such a right. To avoid disrupting cooperation with EURATOM, a proviso was included in the law to enable continued cooperation until March 10, 1980, if EURATOM agreed to negotiations concerning our cooperation agreements. EURATOM agreed in 1978 to such negotiations.

The law also provides that nuclear cooperation with EURATOM can be extended on an annual basis after March 10, 1980, upon determination by the President that failure to cooperate would be seriously prejudicial to the achievement of U.S. non-proliferation objectives or otherwise jeopardize the common defense and security and after notification to the Congress. President Carter made such a determination 12 years ago and signed Executive Order No. 12193, permitting nuclear cooperation with EURATOM to continue until March 10, 1981. President Reagan made such determinations in 1981, 1982, 1983, 1984, 1985, 1986, 1987, and 1988, and signed Executive Orders Nos. 12295, 12351, 12409, 12463, 12506, 12554, 12587, and 12629, permitting nuclear cooperation to continue through March 10, 1989. I made such determinations in 1989, 1990, and 1991, and signed Executive Orders Nos. 12670, 12706, and 12753, permitting nuclear cooperation to continue through March 10, 1992.

In addition to numerous informal contacts, the United States has engaged in frequent talks with EURATOM regarding the renegotiation of the U.S.-EURATOM agreements for cooperation. Talks were conducted in November 1978, September 1979, April 1980, January 1982, November 1983, March 1984, May, September, and November 1985, April and July 1986, September 1987, September and November 1988, July and December 1989, February, April, October, and December 1990, and September 1991. Further talks are anticipated this year.

I believe it is essential that cooperation between the United States and the Community continue and, likewise, that we work closely with our allies to counter the threat of proliferation of nuclear explosives. Not only would a disruption of nuclear cooperation with EURATOM eliminate any chance of progress in our talks with that organization related to our agreements, it would also cause serious problems in our overall relationships. Accordingly, I have determined that failure to continue peaceful nuclear cooperation with EURATOM would be seriously prejudicial to the achievement of U.S. non-proliferation objectives and would jeopardize the common defense and security of the United States. I therefore intend to sign an Executive order to extend the waiver of the application of the relevant export criterion of the Nuclear Non-Proliferation Act for an additional 12 months from March 10, 1992.

Sincerely,

GEORGE BUSH

*Note: Identical letters were sent to Thomas S. Foley, Speaker of the House of Representatives, and Dan Quayle, President of the Senate. The Executive order is listed in Appendix E at the end of this volume.*

# Remarks at a Meeting With Republican Congressional Leaders and an Exchange With Reporters
*March 10, 1992*

*The President.* May I thank everybody for coming down here. And I want to thank the Republican Members of both the Senate and House.

There are two very important legislative matters on the schedule for this week that I want to discuss with you all and get your advice. First, I appreciate your leadership on both of them, but it looks to us like the Senate is once again poised to follow the lead of their House colleagues and raise taxes again. And the centerpiece of both these bills is a huge tax increase that will kill job creation, particularly by small businesses. And so, there has got to be no mistake about this: Raising taxes on the American people, given the situation, is simply not acceptable. And I'm going to veto that tax increase bill as soon as it's sent to me.

It's hard to believe that they're trying to not only raise the taxes but eliminate one of the best, perhaps the only real fiscal discipline tool that we have, and I'm talking about the caps that came out of the '90 agreement. And they're talking now about getting rid of that, and that latest end-run on controlling Government spending is also destined to be sent right back once it hits this desk in there. I mean, I cannot accept busting the caps on discretionary domestic spending. And I am very grateful for your support, and I look forward to talking about these matters and many others in just a few minutes.

*Presidential Primaries and Aid to Former Soviet Union*

*Q.* How do you think you're going to do on Super Tuesday? And is President Nixon correct in saying that you are only giving a penny-ante support to Russia?

*The President.* Well, on the Super Tuesday, let's just wait. We don't have long to wait for the answer on that one, so I'm going to try to stay out of the prediction business. And I've done it relatively successfully so far, staying out of the prediction business. I was just thanking Senator Thurmond for his wonderful support and leadership that made South Carolina so successful. Phil Gramm here, who's been campaigning like mad, tells me he thinks we'll do well in Texas. I was happy, very happy, with the Georgia results, and I thank Newt here. I'll leave out people because a lot have been working hard, but I think we'll do all right. I think we'll do well.

And secondly, I will be talking to the leadership about how we can be as support-

ive as possible of Boris Yeltsin. I don't think President Nixon and I have any difference on this. I talked to him yesterday. There are certain fiscal, financial constraints on what we can do, but we have a huge stake in the success of democracy in Russia and in the other C.I.S. countries. And so, we will be working in every way possible to support the forces of democracy. Certainly, we've done a lot in terms of supporting the people that are afflicted by starvation, real hunger, and similarly, on medicine.

So there's a lot of taxpayer money going into this already; most, a lot of it, in terms of guarantees for agricultural products, which are emergency requirements. And we will do what's right, and I'm looking forward to going over this with Mr. Yeltsin when he's here.

*Q.* Well, do you think his criticism is valid? His seemed to be very personal.

*The President.* Well, I didn't read it as criticism, Helen [Helen Thomas, United Press International], because I talked with the man. And I learned to go to the source; I did it before I even saw the story in the paper. But I also had seen his paper itself, and I didn't take it as personally critical. And I think he would reiterate that it wasn't. So, I think it's just useless to react to all these press stories that try to interpret these remarks of a very constructive paper by Richard Nixon. You know, he's got very good ideas on this subject, and we're in very close touch on it.

*Note: The President spoke at 9:35 a.m. in the Cabinet Room at the White House. In his remarks he referred to Representative Newt Gingrich. A tape was not available for verification of the content of these remarks.*

## Message to the Congress Reporting Budget Rescissions
*March 10, 1992*

*To the Congress of the United States:*

In accordance with the Congressional Budget and Impoundment Control Act of 1974, I herewith report 30 rescission proposals, totaling $2.1 billion in budgetary resources.

The proposed rescissions affect the Departments of Commerce, Defense, Health and Human Services, Housing and Urban Development, the Interior, and Transporta-

tion. The details of these rescission proposals are contained in the attached report.

GEORGE BUSH

The White House,
March 10, 1992.

*Note: The attachment detailing the proposed rescissions was published in the Federal Register on April 1.*

## Nomination of Gregori Lebedev To Be Inspector General of the Department of Defense
*March 10, 1992*

The President today announced his intention to nominate Gregori Lebedev, of Virginia, to be Inspector General at the U.S. Department of Defense. He would succeed Susan J. Crawford.

Currently Mr. Lebedev serves as president of the consulting firm of New American Ventures Group, Ltd., in Washington, DC. Prior to this, he served as a senior partner and member of the U.S. executive committee of the Hay Group in Washington, DC, 1978–1991; Assistant Inspector

General for Foreign Assistance at the Department of State, 1976–1977; and Deputy Assistant Secretary of State for Security and Consular Affairs, 1975–1976. In addition, he served as Deputy Special Assistant to the President at the White House, 1973–1975.

Mr. Lebedev graduated from the University of South Dakota (B.A., 1966; J.D., 1969). He was born April 1, 1943, in New Brunswick, NJ. Mr. Lebedev is married and resides in Washington, DC.

## Remarks at the United Negro College Fund Dinner
*March 10, 1992*

Well, welcome. Barbara and I are just thrilled to welcome all of you to the White House. And this will be short because I remember Billy Graham's famous story he tells at the crusade about the speaker that went on and on. The guy sitting next to him picked up the gavel, threw it at the speaker, missed, hit the woman next to him. And the woman said, "Hit me again; I can still hear him." [*Laughter*] We're not here for all of this. Also, you'll forgive me if I'm a little nervous; it's a big election night out

there. So, if you see these little slips of paper coming in, forgive me.

Now, first let me thank Bill Gray and Andrea. And I've tried it both ways, of being on the opposite side from this guy when he was in the Congress and being on the same side with him now that he's running the United Negro College Fund. And I like it better this way. He was tough, strong, and able.

To those of you who have benefited the United Negro College Fund and you don't know Bill Gray, you've got a wonderful leader. You've got a man of principle, a man of faith. And we are very fortunate to have him. I say "we" because I consider myself a part of this family, and so does Barbara.

I will say a word about Walter Annenberg in a minute because he has a very special role in all of this. I want to salute members of the Cabinet that are here: Dick Cheney, Lou Sullivan, Jack Kemp, and our newest member, the Secretary of Transportation, Andy Card. And I also want to thank Joe Williams, the outgoing chairman, for what he's done for this organization. And unless it smacks of a little too much family, I'd like to single out the incoming chairman, my brother John. I think having the United Negro College Fund to a dinner in the White House is perhaps long overdue. And my arm is just twisted out of the sockets, but now it's back and all is well.

Let me just mention some good news for the UNCF. Together, a goal was set for Campaign 2000 of $250 million. And to get this campaign off to a fast start—and now I get to Walter Annenberg, who does so much for so many—the Annenberg foundation made a $50 million challenge grant. And since the kickoff, donations large and small have poured in. And I'm delighted to note this evening that we're about halfway there, $125 million raised so far.

I look around this room, and I see so many from corporate America, Points of Light all, who were asked day in and day out to support worthy causes, who respond overwhelmingly but have come through for the United Negro College Fund in a profound and wonderful way. And many of America's most successful corporations and business leaders are in this room with us tonight.

I've known many of you for more years than many of us care to count. And let me say to all of you what I've said to many in private conversations: Barbara and I really believe in the United Negro College Fund, and we want to help in any way we can. And that goes for two that aren't with us tonight: the Secretary of Education, Lamar Alexander, and his able assistant, so well-known to many here, David Kearns, who is the Deputy at the Department of Education. They believe in this. They want to support it. And so, we've got a good team who believe in the work here.

The guiding mission of the fund has not changed since the days when Barbara and I first came to the cause in '47, under the leadership then of a guy named Bill Trent that some of you may know, now living in retirement in Greenville, North Carolina, I believe. But when so many despair about a bleak future, this organization gives tomorrow's great minds room to grow. And when so many repeat the all-too-familiar litany of crime and drugs and violence that does concern us all, the UNCF answers with education and opportunity and freedom for all.

So let me say tonight, may the noble aims of this organization guide this Nation always. And once again, may I thank all of you for your support and for joining us here this special evening. And now may I ask Bill Gray, the only other and the final speaker, to come up and just say a word in his defense.

Thank you all very, very much.

*Note: The President spoke at 7:30 p.m. on the State Floor at the White House. In his remarks, he referred to William H. Gray III, president and chief executive officer of the United Negro College Fund; publisher Walter H. Annenberg, president of the M.L. Annenberg Foundation; and William J. Trent, Jr., the first executive director of the fund. A tape was not available for verification of the content of these remarks.*

## Statement on Presidential Primary Victories
*March 10, 1992*

To the voters who gave us their overwhelming support today, Barbara and I say thank you. We are especially grateful to those who have given so much of their time and energy to our cause. Because of your efforts, we are winners again tonight.

As a party and a Nation, let us turn our attention to our future. We must focus on the complex task of job creation in this country. Congress must act on my economic stimulus plan. We need action on housing, crime, health care, education, and a host of other issues. The voters of eight States have declared their support for my proposals on behalf of jobs, family, and peace. I pledge to them my best efforts to focus the Presidency on these challenges and to provide a more secure future for all Americans.

## Remarks at the Swearing-In Ceremony for Andrew H. Card, Jr., as Secretary of Transportation
*March 11, 1992*

Thank you, Admiral, and all of you. And I feel just as excited as you do about this occasion. May I thank Reverend Keller for those stirring words, as well as the Coast Guard band and the Hine Junior High chorus. And I'm pleased that so many members of the Cabinet and the Congress and the White House staff could be with us this morning. We have a nice contingent from Massachusetts led by our Lieutenant Governor, whom I don't see this minute but who is with us, over here, Paul Cellucci, and our State treasurer up there, Joe Malone; longtime friends of Andy Card's.

A special welcome to the former Secretaries who are with us; I've seen Sam Skinner and Alan Boyd, perhaps others. But it's just a great pleasure to have you all here. I know that Sam, now Chief of Staff, who served this Department—oh, I see Bill Coleman sitting over here. Who am I missing? Let's get the former Secretaries out there. Well, I think we got it, Alan and Bill and Sam Skinner.

And as I say, I know that Sam shares my great pride for Andy Card and this wonderful family of his on this very special day. And since this is a real family affair, I think I could speak for all of us when I singled out Tabetha for singing the national anthem so beautifully. That was first-class work.

And to those of you who know our new Secretary, you know he doesn't seek the spotlight. And I promised I'd keep the pomp and circumstance to a minimum, but Andy, I should warn you, it will be necessary to spend the next few minutes saying some nice things about you. Andy is one of this town's best kept secrets, one of the best liked, most well-respected members of the team. You know the saying, "Nice guys finish last"? Well, Leo Durocher never met Andy Card. [*Laughter*]

And this newest member of my Cabinet can claim a distinguished career in public service at both the national and State level. He served three tours in the White House, five terms in the Mass House of Representatives, with 6 years as a member of the house leadership there.

Transportation was one of the issues Andy gave great attention to during his time in the State legislature. Before he came to public service, he was trained and worked as a design engineer. He was talking about multimodalism or intermodalism long before it was fashionable. In fact, my first meetings with him were usually intermodal campaign experiences. [*Laughter*] He would pick me up at Logan Airport—I'm not going to criticize his car, it was a Chevy Chevette—[*laughter*]—and drive me

415

around the State. One paper called him the "commuter's friend." Well, the commuter's friend has found an apt home at the Department of Transportation. And I am just totally confident that his service will prove as loyal as our friendship, as our enduring friendship.

I know Andy to be a proven leader and a talented manager, experienced, efficient, energetic, a public servant of the first order, and above all, a man who gets things done. And that's important. For this job it's not enough to know your way around inside the beltway, at DOT, or working with the people who built the beltway.

So, you've got a good leader. And Andy takes his new position at a very critical time. This Department bears primary responsibility for putting the landmark Surface Transportation Act of 1991 into action, the act that Sam, his predecessor, worked so hard on. This act is creating jobs today, jobs to upgrade our Nation's highway system, jobs to provide for mass transit and meet this country's transportation needs.

And when I signed the new Surface Act last December, it made available some $11 billion to the States. And we directed this Department and urged the States to put those dollars to work right away. In the nearly 3 months since I signed the act, we've delivered 20 percent more highway money than during the same period a year ago.

DOT continues to play a pivotal role helping the airline industry adapt to the changes brought on by deregulation, changes which are producing economic benefits through more efficient service. DOT also has been a faithful supporter of our military and their own transportation needs. And with your energy and ability, Andy, I know that this Department will continue to ensure that the United States remains a world leader in providing safe and efficient transportation.

To meet each of these challenges, and they are big, Andy will be able to call on a really dedicated team of transportation officials in the Department. And to each and every one of you who serve over there, we are grateful to you. You exemplify the very, very best in public service. And I want to salute you along with your new Secretary.

And now, with all of that said, it is with great pleasure that I turn the podium over to Mr. Justice Thomas for the swearing-in of our new Secretary of Transportation, Andrew H. Card, Jr. Thank you.

*Note: The President spoke at 9:04 a.m. at the National Air and Space Museum. In his remarks, he referred to Admiral James B. Busey IV, Deputy Secretary of Transportation, and Tabetha Card Mueller, daughter of Secretary Card. Supreme Court Justice Clarence Thomas administered the oath of office.*

# The President's News Conference
## March 11, 1992

*The President.* Good morning. And first, on the politics, I think yesterday was a great day, and I am extremely grateful to the many people who worked so hard in these various States. We've been victorious in 15 States, and I'll continue to seek the endorsement of the party in every primary.

I've tried to let the people of this country know that we will turn this country around, and our great Nation should be a world-class leader in every category of economic and social activity. We need jobs for every-

one, medical care that is available to everyone. We need to build an education system that prepares kids for the competitive challenges of tomorrow. We need housing that is affordable and plentiful. We need safer neighborhoods and job security. We need to compete internationally for world markets and increase our exports. And there are many problems and opportunities that face the Presidency.

And the voters of these eight States have given me their support. I think they feel I have the experience and leadership to take America in new directions, to reach out for the complex solutions that we must undertake.

As we renew ourselves at home, we simply cannot relinquish our leadership abroad, either. The world is a vastly changed place from even a year ago. Democracy is won, the cold war is over, and now we have an opportunity to secure peace. We cannot let this opportunity pass. And Americans must not heed the lone trumpets of retreat. We must successfully meet every challenge, domestic or foreign.

And one of these important challenges is space. And our civil space program has had remarkable technological success over the last 30 years. America's taken great pride in the achievements of astronauts and our space scientists. And now the genius of that program must focus on new initiatives for the nineties. We intend to deploy a space station by the end of this decade. We must develop a new launch system that augments the space shuttle, a new system that can carry payloads which will give America superiority and flexibility in commercial as well as in scientific fields.

And I want to acknowledge the work of Admiral Dick Truly in providing valued leadership in the space program as an astronaut and as the Administrator of NASA. He deserves great credit for so many of the successes of our space efforts. And as we consider new directions in space, I intend to nominate Daniel S. Goldin, the senior vice president of TRW, Inc., to head NASA. He's a leader; Dan is a leader in America's aerospace industry and a man of extraordinary energy and vitality. And working with the Vice President as Chairman of the Space Council, Dan Goldin will ensure America's leadership in space as we enter the 21st century.

Thank you very much. Now, I have a meeting with some Members of Congress here in a little bit. But I'd be delighted to take some questions. Helen [Helen Thomas, United Press International].

### Defense Budget

*Q.* Mr. President, what do you say to critics in your own party who say you stand for nothing and that you really have no basic goals leading us toward the 21st century? And also, in your opening statement, you seem to be affirming a Pentagon report that we should be a military superpower, the superpower in the world, world-class. Did I misinterpret?

*The President.* Well, to the critics I say, please listen to the statement I just gave and to the many initiatives we've taken. And I don't think there are that many critics in our own party.

*Q.* A lot of protest votes.

*The President.* Well, yes, and I think a lot of that stems from the economy. I'm absolutely certain of that. And I believe those people will be with me in the fall. I'll conduct myself in a way that they will be with me in the fall.

In terms of defense, yes, I feel a keen responsibility to keep this country strong. I have made recommendations to cut defense. Those recommendations came to me from Colin Powell and the Joint Chiefs, the Secretary of Defense. And now what you're seeing is a lot of political promising on Capitol Hill, and to pay for it, they want to cut into the muscle of defense. And I'm not going to do that. I have an obligation for the national security of this country, and I'm going to fulfill it by having a strong defense.

So I don't know what you're referring to out of the Pentagon, but that is my view. And I'm sure it is shared by the Secretary of Defense.

### Presidential Primaries

*Q.* Mr. President?

*The President.* Yes, Terry [Terence Hunt, Associated Press].

*Q.* Many Republicans are calling on Pat Buchanan to get out of the race, saying that he's delivered his message and that all he's doing now is weakening you. Do you think that Mr. Buchanan is hurting you, and if you had your druthers, would you rather see him out of the race?

*The President.* I guess anybody that runs for office would rather have no opposition. I mean, you don't have to be a TRW rocket scientist to gather that one in. And I've tried to avoid entanglement there, taking my case to the voters. And it's been very,

very strong, and I'm very happy with it. So I would just let each person on both sides sort out their own fate.

*Q.* What's the point of him staying in any longer?

*The President.* You're asking the wrong guy.

*Federal Government Size*

*Q.* Mr. President, both you and the Vice President have interpreted the votes for your opponent as being a sign that people out there feel that the Government is too big; as you said, that it costs too much, that it overregulates and overtaxes, all circumstances which either have developed or persisted under your 3 years in office. Why are those interpretations reasons to vote for you again?

*The President.* Because I think we've got good programs to do something about it. I think the Government is too big and does spend too much. And we have sent up budgets that would constrain the growth of spending, and we're having difficulty with the Congress, again, on that question. So we've got to stand for that, and I think we've got to make clear to the American people that we're trying to do something about it.

*Taxes*

*Q.* Well, now, sir, that you have indicated you feel that the budget deal and the breaking of the tax pledge that went with it was a mistake, are you prepared now to renew that pledge for the rest of your administration?

*The President.* Let me say this: The whole thing, given the way it's worked out now, is a mistake. But the thing that is good about that budget agreement is the spending caps. And right now, we are seeing Congress trying to remove the only constraint on domestic spending that exists, domestic discretionary spending, and that's the spending caps. So I want to fight to keep those in place.

*Q.* What about taxes, sir?

*The President.* Well, I don't want to raise taxes. I'm going to veto this tax bill.

*Q.* Mr. President, if I can revisit——

*The President.* You've got too many. This would be the worst time to raise taxes. No

time is good, but this would be the worst. Yes?

*Q.* Is the pledge on again?

*The President.* I'll leave it sit right there. I'm going to veto this tax bill. Yes?

*U.S. Defense Role*

*Q.* If I can revisit Helen Thomas's question, a planning paper leaked out from the Pentagon last week which implied that in the future the United States should be the world policeman rather than place our emphasis on collective security. Do you share the Pentagon's feeling about——

*The President.* If this was an official Pentagon position, I expect the Secretary of Defense would come talk to the President about it. So please do not put too much emphasis on leaked reports, particularly ones that I haven't seen, because I can't comment on it. I just don't know; I'm sorry. I even missed the story on it.

*Q.* What is your own philosophy, sir? Do you feel we should be moving more toward collective security, or should the United States bear most of the burden for policing the world?

*The President.* Well, I think the United States has a burden to bear. But we have worked effectively through multilateral organizations. The clearest example of that is what happened in the Gulf war. You see the United Nations trying to stay involved in the resolution of the Yugoslavian question. We have peacekeeping set up in Cambodia and other places that relieves some of the unilateral burden from the United States.

But we are the leaders, and we must continue to lead. We must continue to stay engaged. So, it isn't a clear-cut choice of either-or. For people that challenge our leadership around the world, they simply do not understand how the world looks to us for leadership. Now, that does not preclude working closely with multilateral organizations.

*Iraq*

*Q.* The Deputy Prime Minister of Iraq is at the U.N. today asking to ease the sanctions. Is there any room for compromise?

*The President.* I would just simply stay with the views that have been so clearly expressed in a unanimous fashion by the Security Council itself. And there will be no compromise on the part of the United States with full compliance with the U.N. resolutions. Iraq is concealing, and they've got to stop doing that.

*Q.* In an electoral year, sir, how far are you going to go to have them comply with the resolutions? You are going through an election. Are you ready to have an attack against Iraq to demonstrate——

*The President.* Let's simply say I'd like to see them comply with the resolutions. It is in their clear interest to comply with the resolutions. And if they don't comply with the resolutions, then we'll contemplate all alternatives.

*Taxes*

*Q.* Mr. President, back on taxes for a minute. In one of the interviews before the Georgia primary, where you talked about your view that the budget deal was a mistake, you also said that you thought a surtax on millionaires might be the only way to get the capital gains tax cut that you want. Is that something you'd consider? Is there any room——

*The President.* No, I'm against that.

*Q.* You're against the surtax in any circumstances?

*The President.* Yes.

Susan [Susan Spencer, CBS News], and then John [John Cochran, NBC News].

*Q.* Why?

*The President.* Because I don't want to raise taxes.

*Q.* Even on millionaires?

*The President.* I don't want to raise taxes.

*Q.* Now I'll get to my question.

*The President.* You've already had it. You've got now what they call a followup.

*Q.* That was her question.

*The President.* No, no. Now, wait a minute.

*Q.* I yield my followup.

*Q.* Thank you.

*The President.* You can have her—wait a minute. You've assigned your followup to her? Okay. So you have a question and a followup?

*Q.* No, I don't. Well, I might.

*The President.* Go on, Susan.

*Assistance to Former Soviet Union*

*Q.* Thank you. President Nixon was fairly scathing in a memo that's been circulated, referring to the U.S. response in the crisis in the Soviet Union as "pathetically inadequate." He also implied that a truly courageous leader would go before the American public and explain why, even when foreign aid is so unpopular, we have to pursue this more vigorously than we are. Do you have any plans to do that?

*The President.* Well, I think the American people know of my commitment to U.S. leadership around the world. In the first place, I read that Nixon paper, and I didn't consider it scathing. But there's a good opportunity to ask him about it because he'll be in town tonight. I'll be attending a dinner there. And maybe there will be a chance for him to clarify what he means by all of this. I stay in close touch with President Nixon; I have great respect for his views on foreign policy. And when I look at the six points or whatever it was in that letter, I think we're in very close agreement.

Now, where we might have a difference is, we're living in a time of constrained resources. There isn't a lot of money around. We are spending too much as it already is. So to do the things I would really like to do, I don't have a blank check for all of that. And so, in that area there may be a slight difference, but I think the question should be addressed to President Nixon because fundamentally we're in agreement on how we ought to approach Russia and the other independent countries there.

*Q.* The next item to come up is likely to be a request for about a billion dollars for the United States to support the ruble. Will you go to Congress and ask for that money?

*The President.* Well, we're talking now about a stabilization fund.

*Q.* Will you support that?

*The President.* I will wait to make a prudent decision based on the recommendation of top advisers. But Treasury is considering it. The Secretary of State is considering it. This isn't a decision you just sit and click your fingers on. But we're talking to the Soviets about this, or the Russians about this, I should say. Boris Yeltsin will be coming here, and they know there are certain things that they have to do before the international community will put the monies in there that they would like to have in a stabilization fund.

So all this is evolving. But in principle, do I think it's a good idea? Yes.

*Presidential Primaries*

*Q.* You said last week you'd be willing to bury the hatchet with Pat Buchanan. How far would you be willing to go? If he gets out of the race long before the California primary, doesn't divide the party, which is already divided out there, would you be willing to sit down, discuss issues with him? Would you be willing to give him his 15 minutes at the Republican Convention with a speech?

*The President.* Why don't we just wait and see how all that evolves, John? He has said today he wants to stay in there. That's his choice. And I'm clearly staying in there. And I think we're doing pretty well. I think there's a little more recognition now that this challenge is sending the President a message, and I feel very good about where things stand. I think I've detected a slight change in the way it's being presented to the public, too.

So we'll just keep on and let him make these decisions. I really have tried very hard not to engage. Even a reply to your question would be more engagement than I want to go forward with.

*British Election*

*Q.* If you won't talk about Pat Buchanan, let me ask you about another election, the British election. There was a time when policymakers in this country worried when there was a Labor Prime Minister in power. Hasn't that changed over the years? Now we've had the end of the cold war, nuclear disarmament isn't the big issue. Does it really matter that much to the fate of the United States who's in power in Britain?

*The President.* I expect the worst thing an American President could do would be to try to intervene in an election in another country. Having said all that, the respect I have for the Prime Minister knows no

bounds. John Major is a superb leader, and I work very, very closely with him, through very difficult times, I might add. But I think it would be most inappropriate if I got into picking winners and losers in a British election or a French election or German election or any other. And I don't—I've got to be careful how I word things.

You know, it's different, if I might just put your question, very sound question, in a political context. It's easy for a candidate to go out and give an opinion on all that, but it's not so easy for a President. I have certain responsibilities as President. I am watching this evolution over there with great interest. I think it's perfectly appropriate to express my respect for John Major, but I don't want to go beyond that by looking like we're trying to shape a foreign election, whether it's here or whether it's anyplace.

*Q.* But isn't it true the Labor Party's platform, its foreign policy platform, is no longer antithetical to your foreign policy?

*The President.* I have to study before I can tell.

*The Economy and Presidential Primaries*

*Q.* Mr. President, if the economy does turn around, do you believe that that protest vote of roughly 30 percent will automatically disappear and people will——

*The President.* I believe it's going to come home anyway, Judy [Judy Wiessler, Houston Chronicle]. I don't know whether any of you heard my Florida campaign manager on television the other night with "Larry King Live." And this man is very able, this Florida campaign manager, my son Jeb. He was superb. And he pointed out that he saw some exit polls that said some of the Democratic primary voters were going to vote for me in the fall. Now, my boy is never wrong on a statistic like that.

And I would just point out that we're reading a lot about the other side, but let's take a look at some of the ones going into the Democratic election. We're going to do well, and I really believe they'll come home to roost. And we want them. I'm trying to conduct myself in such a way as to say, look, I understand your feeling on this issue or that, but we need your support, and we want you. And P.S., take a look at the alternatives over there. That's not even in focus yet. That's not even in focus yet, what the general election's going to be like, because we don't know who's there yet. But it's going to be fun, I'll tell you.

Yes, Ellen [Ellen Warren, Knight-Ridder Newspapers].

*Q.* Mr. President, you seem to be brushing off this 30-to-40-percent consistent voting for Pat Buchanan as a frustration with the economy. Sir, doesn't the buck stop here? Don't you take any responsibility—and your predecessor, Ronald Reagan—for the state of the economy, sir?

*The President.* Absolutely.

*Q.* Well, so why should people vote for you if it's your fault?

*The President.* Because they know I'm trying to change it, and they know that I've been a good leader. And they're going to be talking about leadership, not campaign promises. And it isn't easy. And I think when we get through defining clearly my objectives for this country, it will all come out when we get into the general election that these people will be voting for me. But when a family's hurting and they want to send a message, they don't want to go over and vote in the Democratic side because they see them as much worse. What do they do? They come and vote and try to express themselves in the manner they have. I really believe that that's the situation.

Back of the room.

*Q.* What's to prevent them from saying, sir, well, the President himself says it's his fault and the Republican Party's fault; I'm going to go the other way?

*The President.* Oh, you see, I only gave you half the equation. Everybody can accept blame. The Congress can accept its share of the blame. All of us seem to live and die by polls these days, but if I might be able to quote one, look at the ones that blame the Congress much more than the President. And please get that out there because I need the help. I'll be spelling that out.

Helen, in the back? Yes, sir, over here.

*Q.* Mr. President, you said you didn't want to talk specifically about Patrick Buchanan, but your surrogates have called him everything from a fascist to racist to possibly anti-Semitic. Do you endorse what your surrogates are saying? Do you want to rein them in? And what do you think Mr. Buchanan wants if he can't win the nomination?

*The President.* I don't know the answer to the second part and probably wouldn't respond if I did. I think most fair-minded viewers would feel that I've come under attack from my opponent, so I'm delighted when people defend me.

Helen. I mean Sarah [Sarah McClendon, McClendon News Service].

*Q.* I was talking about the attacks——

*The President.* Yes, excuse me. Go ahead, yes. Please, help me.

*Q.* I was talking about the attacks your surrogates were making on Mr. Buchanan, not to the defense of yourself. Do you endorse the attacks they're making on Mr. Buchanan?

*The President.* I endorse the strong defenders I have out there and am very pleased that they're out there getting the message out loud and clear.

Yes, Jess [Jessie Stearns, Stearns News Bureau].

*Economic Plan*

*Q.* Mr. President, some of your advisers have pressed you to fight Congress with everything you have, and if Congress won't pass a growth package that you want to sign by March 20th, that you should take the bull by the horns and do everything you can: start vetoing line items in their budget, index capital gains by regulation, go and have the Beck decision enforced, all these kinds of things. Have you decided to do any of that?

*The President.* No, I haven't decided it. I do think that in the fall the case is going to be taken to the American people regarding Congress. But I think at this juncture people are less anxious to hear their President blaming somebody than they are seeing him try to get something done. And so that will guide me. But I can't be under unilateral fire and not at least help put the congressional part of this into perspective. But I think people—look, Ellen asked me, do I accept my share of responsibility? Sure.

But I want to be sure Congress accepts its, and see what we can do.

What I've been trying to do is get a stimulative economic package through, lay the broad politics aside, and just take seven simple points that most economists think would turn around confidence and stimulate the economy. And I'm going to keep working on that. I'm going to have to veto a broad kind of handout, tax-and-spend bill, and then I'm still going to keep trying to get it through. And then later on, we'll have all the debate out there as to the responsibility of Congress or changing Congress which, of course, I feel very strongly about. But I think the people are less interested in hearing somebody going around blaming somebody, even though they're getting a lot of that from the Democratic side, than they are on, now, what are you going to do about it? How are you going to help us? How are you going to get this economy moving? And we've got good programs to do just that.

### Presidential Advisers

*Q.* And that's where the advisers, if I may, sir, that's what the advisers, your advisers, tell us they're telling——

*The President.* Well, I've got to read the papers before I know what the advisers are doing.

*Q.* They're asking that you define your Presidency. That's what they keep saying. And you seem to be saying that people want you to define the Presidency. So, what do you think that means at this point?

*The President.* You know one of the things I like least about this job is commenting on what advisers say, handlers say in campaigns. They're normally referred to as handlers in the campaign season and advisers—has a nicer tone—in the noncampaign season. And I read all the time about some anonymous source who is known to feel strongly about the very questions you asked about, Jess. I read about ideas that I'm considering I haven't even heard of yet. I don't know. What I'd say to the American people is, please ask for a name to be placed next to the source so I can get mad at the guy who's doing this.

It's strange out there. It's strange. No, really, I wish people would, in the White House or elsewhere, say, "My name is Joe Jones; I think the President needs to do this," or "I'm Sally Smith, and I think he ought to consider these three options." Instead of that, I pick up the paper every day and read some insider known to be close to the President or a person high up in the party not currently with the White House but having served there a long time, and it's confusing to me. And I think the American people don't like it. I don't think they like it very much. I'd like to see some sources put next to—yes?

### Free Trade and Job Creation

*Q.* Mr. President, you have often said that you were going to get more jobs, bring back jobs. And it's——

*The President.* Sarah——

*Q.* ——the figures have shown that the jobs have——

*The President.* We have another San Antonio incident.

*Q.* ——gone overseas. So with the jobs having gone overseas and we've lost our manufacturing base, and a poll of many of these highfalutin, very big firms say they are not going to build another plant in the United States when they can go to Mexico and pay a dollar an hour and not have to bother with environmental regulations and safety regulations. So, how are you going to get these jobs increased?

*The President.* Because we're going to pass the NAFTA; the North American free trade agreement is going to increase jobs dramatically. And the more exports you have, the more domestic jobs you have.

Now, some labor unions disagree with that. Some politicians disagree with that. Some are sounding the siren's call of protection: Pull back and don't engage in foreign trade. And I disapprove of that. I'm going to keep fighting for open markets, more access to the markets of others, conclusion of the GATT round, a conclusion of the North American free trade agreement. And that's what I'll keep doing, and that will create jobs. It's exports that have saved this economy as it goes through these tough times, and it is exports that will lead an extraordinary growth in the future.

*Q.* Can't we put a limit on the technology

that we have taken overseas?

*The President.* No, we're not going to limit. We're going to encourage. I'd like to see our cooperation with Russia, for example, result in a modernization over there. It will open up vast new markets for the United States. The potential is limitless. So we can't look inward like we did in the thirties where we threw the whole world into depression by a failed policy of isolation and pure protection. I'm not going to do that.

### House Bank Controversy

*Q.* Mr. President, the Vice President has called the check bouncing scandal at the House bank a good reason for term limitations, for Democrats, presumably. Do you feel he's right on that issue and should there be full disclosure of all of the Members who have——

*The President.* I'm strongly for term limitations. And secondly, I think there should be full disclosure. I hate to recite history here, but when I was in the Congress way back in the sixties with a group of newly elected Congressmen in what we called the 90th Club then, 90th Congress, I kind of took the lead in urging full disclosure of assets and liabilities. I did not endear myself to some of my colleagues, but I think that full disclosure of that, of one's own personal finances, is important. I think full disclosure of something of this nature is important, too, on a financial disclosure of that nature. So I agree that it's the way to go, and I think, inevitably, it will happen.

### Economic Plan

*Q.* One more on the economy, sir, if I could. The Democrats, even though their program includes a tax increase, the Senate package, say that it includes elements of all seven components of your economic revitalization program. Since, as you've said, the priority here is the economy and not politics, why not attempt to compromise instead of threatening to veto or rejecting it out of hand?

*The President.* Because I think they're so locked into a tax increase, that I was asked about earlier, that it would be very hard to get that done now. We've tried. Our leaders up in the Congress have tried very hard

to get the focus on these investment incentives. And I'm afraid I'm going to have to just end up vetoing the tax-and-spend bill. And I'm not giving up hope, though, on going forward then and saying, let's try this, let's try to get this through, but not do it in a way that is totally unacceptable.

*Q.* But you said——

*The President.* Ann [Ann Devroy, Washington Post], you had your hand up. Do you still have a question?

*Q.* Yes, Mr. President, I do.

*The President.* What is it?

### 1990 Budget Agreement

*Q.* When you said last week that you regretted the decision on the budget deal, was that budget deal a policy mistake or a political mistake?

*The President.* Total mistake. Policy, political, everything else.

*Q.* What was wrong with the policy?

*The President.* Policy, because it simply did not do what I thought, hoped it would do: control this, get this economy moving. There were some good things about it. So I can't say, shouldn't say, total mistake. But the spending caps was good; getting the spending caps was good. Keeping the Government going as opposed to shutting down for whatever number of days it would have taken, that was good. But when you have to weigh a decision in retrospect, have the benefit of hindsight, I would say both policy and politically, I think we can all agree that it has drawn a lot of fire.

Last question.

### RNC Chairman

*Q.* Mr. Buchanan. Revisit him one more time. He——

*The President.* I'll give you another question because I don't want to take any—go ahead, try it.

*Q.* He said as a condition for him coming back that he would have to get rid of Rich Bond as chairman of the campaign committee, or the Republican National Committee. Do you care if Buchanan himself comes back to roost?

*The President.* Do I what?

*Q.* Do you care if Buchanan himself comes back to roost?

*The President.* Listen, I want everybody. I want everybody to vote for me. But Rich Bond has my full confidence. He's doing a superb job up at the Republican National Committee. So that's the way I'd answer it.

All right, this is the last one.

### Interest Rates

*Q.* On the economy——

*The President.* Got any other subject?

*Q.* In your economic plan, the Fed can affect short-term interest rates, but it seems to be that long-term interest rates may be impeding growth. Do you think it's time for the Treasury and the Fed to come up with a strategy on pushing long-term interest rates down?

*The President.* Well, I don't. I am much more concerned about stimulating the economy today than I am about the long-term rates. They are manageable at this juncture. What would exacerbate the long-term rate problem would be to pass the Democratic tax legislation, for example, or some of the spending bills I've seen up there.

One thing that would shoot the long-term rates through the roof, and I'll guarantee you this, would be to get rid of the firewall or get rid of the spending caps that were a part of the 1990 budget agreement. In my view, that would send a totally counterproductive signal to the markets. In fact, when a very able Senator proposed kind of a tax plan that looked like the deficit would be exacerbated, the long-term shot up just on the proposal.

So, I think now the answer is to keep working with the Fed. I think what the Fed has done is good. If you were to ask me the question, would I like to see interest rates still lower, I would, I would, real rates. But I think the main worry now is not the long-term rate problem or certainly inflation. It is economic growth and stimulation.

I really do have to go because I don't want to—do I have time for one more?

*Mr. Fitzwater.* Okay.

*The President.* All right. I really have an 11 a.m. Yes.

### Campaign Travel

*Q.* Mr. President, it appears whenever you leave the White House and hit the campaign trail, your approval ratings seem to drop.

*The President.* So now stay here, huh?

*Q.* I'm wondering if you now think the answer is to stay here more and campaign out there less.

*The President.* I've not seen a correlation, actually. But no, I don't feel that. But you know, I can understand the debate that has gone on: Should the President be out campaigning, or should he be here? And what I tried to do is achieve a reasonable balance. If you don't go to these States—you had an enormously important election day yesterday where we did very, very well, very well. And if I had not, if I'd have showed disdain by not even showing up in these States, I think that could have been counterproductive.

On the other hand, I recognize that I have responsibilities that no other candidate has for leading this country and for being the President. And there are plenty of problems to face here and plenty of initiatives to take that could keep you here the whole time. So, what we did is try to achieve a balance. I think we're going to go to Michigan for one day, part of a day. And we have a primary coming up there. But I think the way the vote is working out, the overwhelming endorsement in terms of these delegations and everything, I think that you'll be seeing me here a lot, but not to the exclusion of going out.

Another side about going out: You do get to talk to people. You do get to hear first-hand about the problems the country faces. So I think the answer is: Achieve a proper balance. I hope I'm doing that. And I'm going to keep on trying to do it because it is very important that when you're elected President, you be President. But I also determined that I'm the best one to lead the next 4 years, and so you've got to do some of the politics. And that's how we've reached the formula that we use.

I've got to go. Pat [Patrick McGrath, Fox Television]?

### RNC Chairman

*Q.* Prime-time address after March 20th? You used to stand up for Al Haig when you were head of the Republican National Committee; you used to stand up to Al Haig and say you didn't work for the President and you didn't go along with a lot of what Richard Nixon wanted you to do. Rich Bond now is favoring your candidacy, calling Pat Buchanan, accusing him of race-baiting. Is that fair?

*Q.* Could you do this at the mike, sir?

*Q.* We can't hear you.

*The President.* Well, good, because I'm not going to answer it. [*Laughter*] I think the President is seen to be the titular head of the party. It's always been that way. And just like I support incumbent Senators and Congressmen, I think it would be appropriate that the national committee support the President. And I supported—what?

*Q.* You stood up to Al Haig. Al Haig asked you to do things at the RNC that you didn't want to do.

*The President.* That's quite different than endorsing the President. I worked very hard for President Nixon when he was President, as chairman of the national committee.

*Note: The President's 123d news conference began at 10:34 a.m. in the Briefing Room at the White House. A tape was not available for verification of the content of this news conference.*

# Remarks to the American Society of Association Executives
## March 11, 1992

Chairman Fondren, fellow Texan, thank you for that introduction. May I salute President Taylor and all the award winners here today. I heard a story about how when Lyndon Baines Johnson moved from the House to the Senate, Jake Pickle and Gene Fondren, then Texas State legislators, flipped a coin to decide who'd run for office and go to Washington. Well, Congressman Pickle's been calling for a rematch ever since. [*Laughter*] And this organization is very fortunate to have as its chairman a man of this strength and a man of this conviction.

Robert Frost once wrote that an idea is a feat of association. Well, association is an idea as old as the American dream itself. Actually, de Tocqueville 150 years ago, more than that, had much to say about you. He said, "At the head of some new undertaking in the United States you will be sure to find an association." Well, since that time, associations have played a vital role in our country's progress, and they continue that mission today, defining new frontiers and exploring new territory.

Before I spoke, President Taylor handed out the Associations Advance America Awards to salute those who've found a way to help, to be, in fact, Points of Light. We hear too often about what's wrong in America. Well, this is what's right about America, and I salute you for what you are doing to help your communities. And again, I single out the awardees here who have starred in all of this.

Of course, it's an election year. Independent of the current preoccupation with the hype and spin of the campaigns, there will remain the issues, the big things, the core concerns of every American that transcend political party or philosophical ideology: jobs, family, peace. They hold us together as a society. They are more than issues we bring to the next election; they are the legacy we must give to the next generation.

And really, that's what I want to talk to you about today, not just the issues but our mood as a Nation and how we must act now if we're to change America for the better. Today, weighing most heavily in the hearts and on the minds of Americans is the state of our economy: jobs, preserving jobs, creating jobs. You in this room know best, virtually every industry and every profession in America. I don't have to tell you that people are worried about the future.

Frankly, we've had tough economic times before, with higher unemployment but less national alarm. There's something different about today's times, something that touches a nerve. It strikes at the heart of what drives this country forward, our very confidence. It challenges our belief in ourselves.

Let me give it to you straight: Unemployment is, what, 7.3 percent, about 9 million people out of a total work force of 126 million. During the 1982 recession, 10 years ago, unemployment hit almost 11 percent, a level not experienced since the Great Depression. So we ask ourselves, why is confidence today lower than at the depth of the 1982 recession? I've heard a lot of theories. Some say those TV analysts are the problem, rejoicing in bad news. Others say, "Well, it's the politicians." I myself have noted that in a political year candidates often shower the voters with a message so bleak and hopeless, and at the same time they promise the rainbow if they're elected. That steady drizzle on the people's shoulders can wear away confidence and can wash away hope. So, it's easy to suppose that the constant drumbeat about what's wrong in America is a self-fulfilling prophecy.

There may be some truth to that. But I think there are other reasons for our country's mood. People are feeling the way they do because America's got some real problems. They're serious, stubborn, national problems. But I think it would be unfair and certainly untrue to suggest to the American people that we can't overcome these problems, to imply that the United States of America is a country in decline. So today I want to talk about what we must do to meet the economic challenge that is before us, how we can build economic vitality into our communities, how we must ensure that our children see a future that is an improvement over the present.

Sometimes it helps to take some of these enormous issues and bring them down to the personal level. So, when I talk about America's economic problems, this is what I mean: They are the worries of parents who have worked all their lives to get their kids through college, and those kids can't find work. They are found in discouraged families who can't afford to pay off anything but the interest on their credit cards month after month after month. They are the doubts of young people who believe that times will never be as good for them as

they were for their parents. Now, these are the things that dim our hope and drain our confidence.

American workers can see that technology and competition are changing the workplace faster than ever before. They can feel the heat, both at home and abroad. They know American industry is being challenged to keep up or step aside. I'm going to talk further about that later in the week out in Detroit, Michigan. We live in a competitive world, and people worry about our ability to compete.

American homeowners—that's almost 70 million people—worry that the biggest asset they will ever have, their home, will lose its worth because real estate values have declined. The same is true of any business, of association, or charitable organization that owns property; they're concerned, too.

Finally, as I discussed earlier this week with the League of Cities—and this one is fundamental—the deterioration of the American family is very, very serious, a root problem with tremendous ramifications for our economic well-being as a Nation.

These are the problems, but the picture is not all gloom and doom. America, we're now the only superpower in the world. Millions of immigrants still look to us as the land of opportunity because we are. We're the undisputed leader of the world that has a propensity for much more peace. And our economy is poised for recovery. Inflation is down; interest rates, low. Inventories are low; exports, at record highs. But this recovery will come sooner and stronger only if we in Government can come together and act now.

In January, as most of you know, I sent a message to the Congress, a plan of action. I felt it was a straightforward set of initiatives based upon tried and true economic realities. I proposed incentives for business to buy equipment, upgrade their plants, and start hiring again. I proposed a shot in the arm to get the housing industry back on its feet, lead us into economic recovery this spring. I proposed a cut on the capital gains.

And then I offered a broader plan of action to keep us strong and economically vigorous in the years ahead. And that included, as some of you all may remember, education reform, we call it America 2000, to bring the skills of our future workers up to a standard of excellence. It included a clampdown on excessive regulations that hurt our competitiveness and reform of our legal system, so that Americans can spend more time innovating and less time litigating. And I proposed record Federal support, research and development support, to keep our Nation on the cutting edge of new technologies, new incentives for business investment. I proposed a forward-looking trade policy that demands foreign markets open up to high-quality American goods and services. And I reiterated our determination to hold the line on Government spending and oppose new taxes.

Well, big issues, big challenges. This is the plan I proposed, and I set a deadline for the Congress to act. And while the Congress didn't have a comprehensive plan of its own, it didn't like the notion of a deadline. Instead, with great and earnest deliberation, the Congress fixated on how much more to tax the American people. And they would hike taxes by $100 billion. And that plan, in my view, destroys jobs, whereas the plan, the incentives I've outlined here create jobs. The last thing that this economy needs now is a massive tax increase. Any economist worth his salt will tell you that. But this is not new. Congress refuses routinely to take action to stimulate the economy, but insists on these job-destroying increases in taxes.

Everyone knows that Government is too big and spends too much. Everyone knows that. And there's something else everyone knows, too: Too often Congress spends the money of its customer, the taxpayer, the wrong way, inefficiently, ineffectively, without accountability, and frankly, without compassion. So again, I would like to call on the Congress to pass my plan by March 20 for the good of this economy and the good of the American people. Now, I realize this all may sound like simply an election year blast at the Congress controlled by the opposition party. But it is not. We really need a new way of looking at things.

And I have made proposals to bring back responsibility and accountability to a system answerable to no one but itself. They are based on some fundamental principles: Rely on what works. And when possible, decentralize. Institute choice to force competition into the system. Give people more power to make the big decisions in their lives. Make the system accountable. And understand the new realities of America's global position, that we must become more competitive. We are not going to retreat into the failed policies of uninvolvement, disengagement, isolation, protectionism. We cannot do that. That would shrink markets and throw people out of work in this country. Staying involved, then, is the fundamental answer on international trade. These are the important ways to reform and change our country.

Chairman Fondren once said that "Leadership requires forthrightness. Hidden agendas rarely, if ever, lead to progress and very often succeed in spoiling the brew." Well, I've never been very good at hiding an agenda, and I'm not about to try to start that now.

The agenda has really been to create jobs, protect the family, and promote world peace. Too many times I run up against a stone wall, a partisan guard more determined to take sides than to move the country forward. So, March 20th will be an important date. And if the Congress enacts my action plan on the economy by then, the real beneficiaries will be the American people. If the Congress cannot act, or if it sends to me a bill that it knows today that I cannot and will not sign, I will take this case to the American people and say: The problem is the Congress. Send a new Congress to Washington next November. But before that, I want to see us move something forward. I want to see us get something done.

And it's tough in an election year. I know that; I'm involved right up to my neck, just recovering from eight of these darn things yesterday. So, I'm not being unrealistic, but I think we still have time to set aside the politics and try to pass something that most economists agree—I think all economists agree—would stimulate this economy and get this country back to work again. In the meantime, I will act on my own in the interests of the American people.

I drew a line in the sand, Gene referred to it, a little over a year ago in the Gulf. When you look back, that wasn't an easy decision. But we kept our word, and we liberated a tiny country. And in the process, we sent the world, the whole world, a message. And the message was: Aggression will not stand. And that message is clearly understood. And because that message is so clearly understood, we have a newfound credibility all around, all around the world. Travel abroad, and find out that we are the United States, second to none.

And so now, in a figurative stance, I've drawn a line in the sand again, right here in our own backyard. And I will keep my word again, and if we all do our part, we can ensure that our economy and our country get back on the right track.

In the meantime, keep up the wonderful work that these associations do. Government can do a lot. I know I've got to do it better. I know that Congress has to do its work better. But it can never replace that thing that de Tocqueville found so amazing about this country, association, the propensity of one American to help another.

And when I talk about Points of Light, sometimes my critics say, "Well, he's simply forgoing his responsibility. He's simply trying to lay off on the back of private citizens the responsibility of a Government." That's the farthest thing from my mind when I commend you and thank you for being Points of Light. Government can help. Government must help. Government must reach out a hand to those that are hurting. But it is the Points of Lights, it is the private sector, it is the associations that are going to make a difference in the lives of the men and women and, especially, the children of this country.

So, may God bless you for your work. And thank you for letting me come back.

*Note: The President spoke at 1:10 p.m. at the Washington Convention Center. In his remarks, he referred to Gene Fondren and R. William Taylor, chairman and president of the American Society of Association Executives.*

## Remarks at the Richard Nixon Library Dinner
### March 11, 1992

Mr. President, thank you, sir, for that wonderfully warm introduction. I, like I think everybody across our country, was once again so impressed when we saw what you did today in outlining foreign policy objectives of this country. And it's a wonderful privilege for me to be introduced by you.

If you will excuse me a little reminiscence, why, in '64, I ran with a spectacular lack of success for the United States Senate. In 1966, I started off to run for the Congress in Houston, Harris County. And it was then Richard Nixon, former Vice President, President-to-be, who came down there to kick off my little campaign. And I thought I was right on top of the world. And what he did in endorsing and supporting me and many others like me that year resulted in our picking up some 49 seats, I think it was,

in the Congress and propelling me into a life that has been full and fascinating, sometimes frustrating but always rewarding. And I am very, very grateful to him then; I was grateful to him when I served while he was President, while I was head of the Republican National Committee. And I value his advice today. I get it. I appreciate it. And I'm very grateful to him for his continued leadership in this area that is so vital to the United States of America. So, Mr. President, my sincere thanks. And it's a great privilege to be here tonight.

And of course, I want to thank our friend, all of our friend, Jim Schlesinger, for his leadership on this; and Walter and Lee Annenberg for their fantastic support; of course, Julie and David Eisenhower over there. I agree with everything Jim Schlesinger said about Julie, first-class and wonderful. To Gavin and Ninetta Herbert and our friend George Argyros from California; John Taylor; Brian, over here; distinguished guests all; ladies and gentlemen. It is a pleasure to be here among friends and to renew old ties.

A writer once said of Richard Nixon, his life "somehow was central to the experience of being an American in the second half of this century." I am proud tonight to salute a President who made a difference, not because he wished it but because he willed it.

As our 37th President, he placed crime and drugs on the national agenda; he created a pioneering cancer initiative; he ended the draft; and he created the EPA. And we've been fighting over the spotted owl ever since he created the EPA. But nevertheless—[*laughter*].

As I said when his library opened, Richard Nixon will be remembered for another reason: dedicating his life to the noblest cause offered any President, the cause of peace among nations. A cause told in his books, now nine of them, each written out in longhand on those famous yellow pages, yellow legal pads.

So, I could not be more pleased, and I know I speak for Barbara on this, both of us, to be here this evening. And I'm pleased to be able to speak before this gathering devoted to exploring "America's Role in the Emerging World." The subject could not be more timely. The auspices couldn't be more appropriate. The Richard Nixon Library, and I was privileged to be there at the opening, stands as a monument to a President and to an administration devoted to an active, thoughtful, and above all, realistic approach to the world.

The challenge faced by President Nixon could hardly have been more daunting: How to maintain domestic support for a foreign policy mandated by a growing Soviet threat at a time that an overburdened America was fighting an unpopular war in Vietnam. What emerged, the policies of detente and the doctrine that bears the name of the 37th President, provided a balance between confrontation and cooperation. President Nixon managed this and more, extricating us from a war, negotiating the first comprehensive U.S.-Soviet arms control

agreement, opening up relations with China, mediating disengagement pacts in the Middle East, all while preserving a consensus at home favoring continued engagement in world affairs.

To be sure, today's challenge is fundamentally different. Yet I think we'd all agree it does bear some resemblance. Once again we've got to find a way to square the responsibilities of world leadership with the requirements of domestic renewal. What we must do is find a way to maintain popular support for an active foreign policy and a strong defense in the absence of an overriding single external threat to our Nation's security and in the face of severe budgetary problems. In this post-cold-war world, ours is the wonderful, yet no less real or difficult challenge, really, of coping with success.

This challenge is by no means unprecedented. Think back to the era after World War I or the years in the immediate wake of World War II. In both instances, the American people were anxious to bring their victorious troops home, to focus their energies on making the American dream a reality.

Perhaps more instructive, though, are the differences between our reactions following this century's two great wars. After World War I, the United States retreated behind its oceans. We refused to support the League of Nations. We allowed our military forces to shrink and grow obsolete. We helped international trade plummet, the victim of beggar-thy-neighbor protectionism. And we stood by and watched as Germany's struggling democracy, the Weimar Republic, failed under the weight of reparations, protectionism, and depression and gave way to the horror that we all know as the Third Reich.

Likewise, our initial reaction to victory in World War II showed little learning. But galvanized by an emerging Communist threat spearheaded by an imperialist Soviet Union, the United States acted. NATO, the IMF, the World Bank, the Marshall plan, these and other institutions prove that Americans grasped the nature of the challenge and the need to respond. Our military was modernized, free trade nourished, U.S. support for former adversaries Germany and Japan made generous. It was fitting that Dean Acheson titled his memoirs "Present at the Creation" for these years were truly creative.

The result, as they say, is history. We kept the peace. We won the cold war. Democracy is on the march. Now, for the third time this century, we've emerged on the winning side of a war, the cold war, involving the great powers. And so, the question before us is the same: We have won the war, but are we prepared to secure the peace?

That is the challenge that we must face. Yet already, there are voices across the political spectrum calling, in some cases shouting, for America to "come home, gut defense, spend the peace dividend, shut out foreign goods, slash foreign aid."

You all know the slogans. You all know the so-called solutions, protectionism, isolationism. But now we have the obligation, the responsibility to our children to reject the false answers of isolation and protection, to heed history's lessons. Turning our back on the world is simply no answer; I don't care how difficult our economic problems are at home. To the contrary, the futures of the United States and the world are inextricably linked.

Just why this is so could not be more clear. Yesterday we saw conflict, and today, yes, the world is a safer place. Yes, the Soviet Union—aggressive, looking outward—that we feared is no longer. But the successor Republics are still struggling to establish themselves as democracies, still struggling to make the transition to capitalism. We invested so much to win the cold war. We must invest what is necessary to win the peace. If we fail, we will create new and profound problems for our security and that of Europe and Asia. If we succeed, we strengthen democracy, we build new market economies, and in the process we create huge new markets for America. We must support reform, not only in Russia but throughout the former Soviet Union and Eastern Europe.

As a former President, Richard Nixon is a prolific author. As President, he wrote a chapter that previewed the new world order. Today we are building on RN's roots planted in Tel Aviv and Cairo and Moscow

and Beijing. Look at the lands of the former Soviet Union, reaching out toward Western ways. Look at the fledgling democracies here in our own hemisphere. You talk about an exciting story, look what's happening south of the Rio Grande, all moving towards democracy except one. Look at Cambodia and its neighbors in Southeast Asia, yearning for an end to decades of violence, or at the historic peace process in the Middle East, one that holds out the hope of reconciling Israel and her Arab neighbors. Long way to go, but they're talking. Look at a U.N. that may at long last be in a position to fulfill the vision of its founders. Look at Africa, the changes in South Africa. Look at the exciting changes in Angola or what happened in Zambia. The success of each depends on U.S. support and leadership.

Look, too, at the threats that know no boundaries, these insidious threats like drugs and terrorism and disease and pollution and above all, the one that concerns me perhaps the most, the spread of weapons of mass destruction and the means to deliver them. They, too, will yield only to an America that is vigilant and that is strong.

In the Nixon Library in Yorba Linda—I hope all of you have seen it; if you haven't, you ought to do that—there's a world leaders room, a room of giants who provided such leadership, Churchill and Chou En-Lai and Charles de Gaulle. President Nixon not only knew the greatest statesmen of the 20th century, he became one of them; like them, judged by disasters averted and dreams achieved.

A former aide once told of how President Nixon asked about a foreign policy speech. The aide shook his head. "Frankly," he said, "it's not going to set the world on fire." President Nixon shook his head. "That's the whole object of our foreign policy," he said almost to himself, "not to set the world on fire." [*Laughter*]

Yes, carrying out a leadership role in determining the course of the emerging world is going to cost money. But like any insurance policy, the premium is modest compared to the potential cost of living in a warring and hostile world. Many in Congress today, perhaps for understandable reasons, domestic policy considerations, are calling for a peace dividend. They would have us slash defense spending far below the reduced levels that we have calculated would be prudent. This must be resisted. The United States must remain ready and able to keep the peace; a well-trained, well-equipped military cannot simply be created overnight if and when the need arises. Anyone who has ever gone to war knows that peace is its own dividend.

Those who would have us do less ignore the intimate interrelationship between overseas developments and those here at home. If we had not resisted aggression in the Gulf a year ago, if we had not liberated Kuwait and defeated Iraq's invading army, we would now be facing the economic consequences not of a mild recession but of a deep depression brought on by Saddam Hussein's control over the majority of the world's oil. And I am absolutely certain—I expect we could get a good lively debate in this room of enormously intellectual people—but I am absolutely certain in my mind that if we had not moved against Saddam, he would be in Saudi Arabia today. The coalition would have fallen apart. He would be in Saudi Arabia, and we would be facing agony like we've never faced before in the history of our country.

It is a pipedream to believe that we can somehow insulate our society or our economy or our lives from the world beyond our borders. This is not meant to suggest that we should not do more here at home. Of course we should. But foreign policy, too, is a powerful determinant of the quality of life here at home.

Isolationism is not the only temptation we need to avoid. Protectionism is another siren song which will be difficult to resist. There are, indeed, many examples of unfair trade practices where U.S. firms get shut out of foreign government markets owing to trade barriers of one sort or another or owing to foreign government subsidies. But the way to bring down barriers abroad is not to raise them at home. In trade wars there are no winners, only losers.

Export growth is a proven economic engine. We estimate every billion dollars in manufactured exports creates 20,000 jobs for Americans. And we should have no

doubts about the ability of our workers and farmers to thrive in a competitive world. Our goal must be to increase, not restrict, trade. Opting out, be it under the banner of protection or isolation, is nothing more than a recipe for weakness and, ultimately, for disaster. And that's why I am so determined to do all I can to successfully conclude the Uruguay round, GATT, and to get a fair trade agreement with Mexico, the North American free trade agreement with Mexico and Canada. It is important to us; it creates jobs in the United States.

Now, if I can choose a theme for you to take away from what I have to say tonight, it is this: There is no distinction between how we fare abroad and how we live at home. Foreign and domestic policy are but two sides of the same coin. True, we will not be able to lead abroad if we are not united and strong at home. But it is no less true that we will be unable to build the society we seek here at home in a world where military and economic warfare is the norm.

Ladies and gentlemen, the responsibility for supporting an active foreign policy is one for every American. But this task, in some ways, falls especially upon those in this room tonight. We are entering a world that promises to be more rather than less complicated. I thought when we were facing an imperial Soviet communism that that was the most complicated of times. I don't see it that way; more rather than less difficult to lead in this world. And again you have a special responsibility to help show the way, all of you.

Mr. President, there have been literally millions of words written about you. As President Reagan said, some even have been true. But let me close with words that you used 33 years ago in the kitchen in Moscow in that famous meeting with Khrushchev, former Premier Khrushchev.

You describe the scene memorably in your last book, "Seize the Moment." When Khrushchev bragged that "Your grandchildren will live under communism," you responded that his grandchildren would live in freedom. He was wrong, but at the time you weren't sure you were right. Today, we know you were, just as you were right in helping build a safer, more peaceful world.

As we look toward the future, the only thing that is certain is that it will bring a new world. Our task, our opportunity is to make it orderly, to build a new world order of peace, democracy, and prosperity. Let's dedicate ourselves to making the most of this precious opportunity, of this privilege.

Thank you all very much. Mr. President, thank you, sir. It's a joy being with you. And may God bless the United States.

*Note: The President spoke at 9:35 p.m. at*

*the Four Seasons Hotel. In his remarks, he referred to James Schlesinger, chairman of the conference on "America's Role in the Emerging World" sponsored by the Richard Nixon Library & Birthplace; Walter H. Annenberg, Gavin Herbert, and George Argyros, members of the library's board of directors; Mr. Annenberg's wife, Lee; Mr. Herbert's wife, Ninetta; John H. Taylor, director of the library; and Brian Crozier, British biographer of Charles de Gaulle. A tape was not available for verification of the content of these remarks.*

# Remarks Prior to Discussions With King Hussein of Jordan
*March 12, 1992*

*Q.* Mr. President, may we ask King Hussein whose side he's on in the latest confrontation with Iraq?

*The President.* We agreed that we weren't going to take any questions, just because we want to get into the business side. I just want to say here, though, I will say this, that I am just delighted to see His Majesty again. For years we've had strong relations with Jordan. We know there were difficulties. He is my friend, and I welcome him back here.

And I might point out in a positive way that Jordan has taken a very courageous and forthright position on the peace talks,

recognizing we should talk for peace. And now we want to develop more on that and talk more about that. So, we're looking to the future. And I'm very pleased he's here. And I hope that will—it didn't exactly answer your question, but we're not going to take questions. And I just want to make sure that people know across this country how pleased I am to see His Majesty again.

Thank you all very much.

*Note: The President spoke at 11:05 a.m. in the Oval Office at the White House. A tape was not available for verification of the content of these remarks.*

# Statement by Press Secretary Fitzwater on the President's Meeting With King Hussein of Jordan
*March 12, 1992*

The President and King Hussein met for approximately one hour in the Oval Office. Also attending the meeting were Secretary Baker, General Scowcroft, and Jordanian Prime Minister Bin Shakir. Following the meeting, the President and the King, and their respective staffs, had a working lunch in the Residence.

There was considerable discussion of the peace process. The President stressed the

importance of all parties continuing to participate in the Madrid process. The two agreed to continue to consult closely, both about ways to solve remaining procedural issues affecting both the bilateral and multilateral talks and on how best to advance the peace process more generally.

On the question of Iraq, the two leaders agreed on the importance of full Iraqi compliance with all Security Council resolutions. King Hussein said that Jordan would continue to do its part. President Bush and King Hussein also agreed that the United States and Jordan would continue to consult closely on questions relating to Iraq and the Gulf war aftermath.

King Hussein also raised the matter of Jordan's economic situation, which has been made more difficult by the more than 300,000 men, women, and children who have entered Jordan from the Gulf. The President told the King that the United States would continue to do what it could to help Jordan, both directly and via international financial institutions.

# Remarks to Recipients of the Presidential Awards for Excellence in Science and Mathematics Teaching
*March 12, 1992*

Welcome to the chilly Rose Garden. I don't know whose idea this was, but— [*laughter*]. In any event, we are just delighted to have you all here. And it's great to see Lynn Martin, our Secretary of Labor; Dr. Massey; Dr. Wong; and most of all, let me welcome 108 very special men and women chosen from over one-quarter of a million secondary teachers in their fields. And congratulations to all of you in receiving this Nation's highest honor for math and science teachers.

As teachers, you know firsthand what the spirit of innovation has brought to this country, though we're not always ready for change. Sometimes I think that if Edison were to invent the light bulb today, newspapers would headline the story "Candle Industry Threatened." [*Laughter*] The one I like best, though, is one Lyndon Johnson used to tell about. Pointing down to the Potomac, he said, "If I walked across the Potomac, the press would say 'LBJ can't swim.'" [*Laughter*]

You have shown the kind of excellence that will help this country meet the ambitious goals that we've set for our Nation in this America 2000 education strategy, goals worthy of the talent you have and of the potential of these wonderful young kids that you teach. We know we've got to be competitive in math and science in a changing world. Our economic health, our economic strength, our survival, depend on how we educate ourselves to face the challenges of the next century. We've called on our kids to be number one in the world in your subjects by the turn of the century. And it's teachers like you who will help us reach our goal, set an example, and help America to excel.

As you know, we're helping to develop world-class standards for national assessment in five core areas, including math and science. And we've set a deadline for the first phase of the American Achievement Test, the start of the 1993–94 school year.

All told, we have requested more than $2 billion in Federal spending on math and science education for next year's budget. And if my math is correct—and with this crowd it better be—[*laughter*]—$768 million of that is for pre-college. That's an increase of 123 percent in the last 3 years.

But I believe that the single most important thing we in the Federal Government can do is to simply help you do your jobs. For instance, also in next year's budget, I have proposed an expanded program of federally assisted training for math and science teachers, in part using Federal labs, Federal laboratories and Federal personnel. Innovations like this will help us create a world-class corps of teachers.

We also want to bring new technology into the classroom, so that kids can interact with astronauts and explorers and scientists; so rural schools can have access to state-of-the-art resources; and so all American kids can be exposed to the cutting edge technologies and ideas that will shape their future.

The Federal Government can do a lot. We can do an awful lot, but we cannot do it all. Real excellence demands commitment from everyone in every community as we work to create a new generation of American schools. And together, we are literally going to reinvent the American school community by community, neighborhood by neighborhood, all across this country. You're showing us the way. You're leading. You're showing how we can break the mold, take our bearings by what works. And you're here today because you're not afraid to reach for excellence. And that's why I salute you all.

I salute winners like Julie Csongor, of Philadelphia—where's Julie? Somewhere, right there—who fled the persecution of her native Hungary, unable to speak English. And now she gives of herself to a generation of American kids. And listen to this; she says, "I have my cake in my classroom every day. This award is the icing." Welcome and congratulations. Well, I salute you, and I envy you. And you share in our kids' sheer joy of learning, of making something work, of understanding the world.

Think of the scientist or engineer who will one day discover the cure for cancer or who will use technology to push back the frontiers of space, maybe wipe out hunger. Today that man or woman is a student, maybe in your classroom. A kid who will catch a spark from you, a spark that will change his life, change her world. That's your gift. A teacher affects a lifetime.

I'm proud to be with you all here today because you demonstrate what it will take to make our students the best in the world. You encourage students by giving them direct hands-on experience. You foster curiosity not just in your students but also in

their parents and in your colleagues. You still have the joy of discovery, the excitement of optimism. And you still ask questions and try new ways. Above all, you believe in your students and in the future of this country. And that is the spirit we all need.

We all know the real rewards of teaching aren't their certificates that you received here, but they are something much more important. Sir Thomas More described it in the play "A Man For All Seasons." At one point, he suggests to a young man that he would make a fine teacher. "And if I was," the boy asks, "well, who would know about it?" And Sir Thomas replies, "You, your pupils, your friends, God; not a bad public, that."

Well, thank you all so much for what you do for the young people of this country. Thank you for your excellence. And on behalf of a very grateful country, let me just extend my personal thanks also. Keep up the good work and the good works. And may God bless you all. And now get out of this cold so you can thaw out. Thank you all for being here.

*Note: The President spoke at 2:33 p.m. in the Rose Garden at the White House. In his remarks, he referred to Dr. Walter E. Massey, Director of the National Science Foundation; Dr. Eugene Wong, Associate Director for Physical Science and Engineering in the Office of Science and Technology Policy in the Executive Office of the President; and Julie Csongor, a geometry and calculus teacher at St. Maria Goretti High School in Philadelphia, PA.*

# Remarks to the National Conference of State Legislatures
*March 12, 1992*

Let me salute those who preceded me. I guess Dick—has Dick Cheney been over here yet? And Sam Skinner, our Chief of Staff. And then the piece de resistance, our fabulous Secretary of HHS, Lou Sullivan, who is, I mean that, he's just doing a superb job for the country. But I'm pleased to be

here. I remember last year being unable to show up. I think it was the aftermath of the storm, of Desert Storm. But I'm glad to be here, glad to see Bud Burke and Bill Pound and Bob Connor and Terry Anderson, just greeting us. And last year, I think I owe you an apology for that.

That Desert Storm, I think, was a triumph for our country. And I still believe that it holds an enduring lesson for how we in Government can get things done. It's different, but there's some lessons that apply. We saw a challenge; we met it with resolve. The subject, as you will recall, was debated vigorously. And our duty as Americans—I think the country came together, seeing that our duty demanded nothing less than the action. But when the time came to act, partisanship was laid aside, and we put an end to the squabbling. And the job got done, and Kuwait was liberated.

Incidentally, it is my judgment that that action, and I salute the people that participated in it, really restored credibility to the United States all around the world. I see it every single day that I interact with these foreign leaders.

So now I don't have to tell you all who are on the firing lines in your various States that we face a great challenge again today. We're in tough economic times. We owe it to our country to do all in our power to get the economy moving. I am not gloomy about that, incidentally. Retail sales figures today were good. We've got some fundamentals that are getting in place, such as interest rates and inflation, that could be the forerunners of a very good recovery. But we've got to do something. So I take this getting the economy moving very seriously.

I don't believe there's any one single magic wand that can be waved to accelerate recovery. But I also know that by taking just a few commonsense steps and taking them now, we can stimulate investment, help struggling businesses back to their feet, and put Americans to work.

And what will happen if we can do what I'm about to suggest to you, I think you're going to see a rapid restoration of confidence. One of the great problems we have in this country today is, even though unemployment, for example, is statistically far lower than it was 10 years ago in the recession of '82, the confidence isn't there. And I think that what I'm about to suggest would restore confidence if they saw that these things were going to be put into effect.

To free up investment capital, we've asked for a new investment tax credit. It's a tax allowance, really. And what it does is speed up depreciation on the front end and would encourage, therefore, the purchase of new capital equipment, which obviously means jobs. I still favor, strongly favor, a cut in the capital gains tax. I think that would create jobs. And I also think that would restore confidence. We remember that both Houses had a majority for that, Democrats and Republicans supporting it a couple of years ago. We could never get it to a vote.

On the housing industry, and I'm sure many are familiar with this one, we've asked for a $5,000 tax credit and that would be for the first-time homebuyers, and penalty-free withdrawals from IRA's for the first-time homebuyers. The homebuilders have enormously high estimates as to what the credit itself would do for the homebuying business. So I think these would have a stimulative effect.

When I submitted this plan to the Congress, I asked them, as you remember, to put aside the partisanship and try to get some action, pass it in 52 days. We set a deadline, March 20th. And so now we're back in the political wars, and they're fixing to send me a package that I simply cannot and will not sign. And there is a massive increase in taxes on that package. And I fully believe that a tax increase here would be a disaster for the economy. I think it would hurt our future competitiveness.

And I think that Congress—I don't think they will, but they ought not to doubt my resolve on this particular veto because if they send that tax-and-spend plan down here, I have to veto it, send it back. And then possibly in the Senate we can get action because some of the—I know we've got a bipartisan group here—but some of the Democrat incentives are very close to what we're suggesting here. And if we can narrow this package down and just go for the incentives, then when we get into all this campaign stuff, we can debate whether you need a middle-income tax or a tax break on the rich or a tax increase on the rich or whatever it is. So, I'm going to keep trying very hard to keep the focus on these incentives.

I know that you feel, and I know I feel, that people are tired of the business-as-usual

435

from Washington. And I know it's burdening some of your State capitols, too. In that area, business-as-usual, I'm talking about these unfunded mandates.

Every time I meet with the Governors or legislators, they say, "Please help us keep Congress from inflicting mandates on us. Give us the flexibility. We might have a better answer in Mobile than they do in Moline, so let us try it our way." And I understand what happens when an unfunded mandate drops in on you from Washington. You've got to find the money if you want to participate in it to pay for somebody else's wish list, either by cutting out programs that you have on the books that you feel might be better or raising taxes at the local level. In other words, Washington takes the credit, and you end up taking the heat.

And this message has been drilled home to me over and over again. And I think these mandates are irresponsible, and they cut right to the heart of the Federal system. So I've told the Congress if they pass a mandate, they just simply cannot pass the buck. They've got to pay for it without a tax increase.

Then there's one other front in our fight to restore federalism. More than a year ago—and I know you all have been helpful working with us on this, and we're very grateful—we proposed a $15 billion block grant for the States because I believe that States are the laboratories of democracy. And you need and your constituents need the flexibility and the freedom to experiment, the freedom and flexibility that this grant would permit.

And the conference has been invaluable,

your conference, in helping get this proposal in shape. We introduced it last year, but we're going to be introducing to Congress soon, again. And I call on them to give it swift consideration.

The key, we all know this, is working together: Republicans and Democrats, the Federal and State governments, the legislative and executive branches. And I would be the first to confess that I understand the pressures of an election year. But we know what we can do in those moments when we can set partisanship aside. And I think that's what the American people are calling out for right now. And we must not let them down.

So, again, my thanks to you all for your support, for those of you who are supporting this block grant concept, helping us fend off more and more mandates from the Congress, and those who are with us in the idea that what we need for this economy now is something that will in a laserlike way stimulate an economy that is really ready to move and really ready to recover.

I really do thank you. And I hope this hasn't been too inconvenient, off and on again on the schedule. But I'm off early in the morning. And I just looked forward to having a chance to at least drop in and say hello. So thank you all very, very much.

*Note: The President spoke at 5:12 p.m. in Room 450 of the Old Executive Office Building. In his remarks, he referred to the following officers of the National Conference of State Legislatures: Paul (Bud) Burke, president; Robert Connor, vice president; William Pound, executive director; and Terry C. Anderson, staff chairman.*

# Message on the Observance of St. Patrick's Day
*March 12, 1992*

It gives me great pleasure to send greetings to all those who are celebrating St. Patrick's Day.

When we reflect on the extraordinary life and lasting influence of St. Patrick, it is easy to understand why the observance of this

day has become a cherished annual tradition, in the Emerald Isle and wherever the sons and daughters of Erin have made their home.

Although St. Patrick originally came to Ireland as a captive of pirates and spent six years in slavery before his daring escape by sea, he later returned and became one of the greatest figures in the history of the Celtic peoples. The man who once described himself as "the least of all the faithful" bravely made his way back to Ireland to bring Christianity to the island's inhabitants. Through St. Patrick's influence, the Celtic people added to their ancient history and culture a new and even richer legacy of spiritual faith and human values.

Today, the Irish heritage is as grand as the many stories and legends that have been inspired by the life of St. Patrick. That is why, on March 17th, we not only remember a beloved saint but also celebrate the many contributions that Irish Americans have made to this country, through their unique traditions and folklore and through their many accomplishments in civic and political life. These have been evident from the earliest days of our Republic, when nine men of Irish origin joined in signing the Declaration of Independence. This is a fitting time to salute them and all who have followed them in carrying forward the hard work of freedom.

Barbara joins me in wishing all Irish Americans, actual and honorary, a very happy St. Patrick's Day. God bless you.

GEORGE BUSH

# Statement on Signing the Torture Victim Protection Act of 1991
*March 12, 1992*

Today I am signing into law H.R. 2092, the "Torture Victim Protection Act of 1991," because of my strong and continuing commitment to advancing respect for and protection of human rights throughout the world. The United States must continue its vigorous efforts to bring the practice of torture and other gross abuses of human rights to an end wherever they occur.

I regret that the legislation proposed by the Administration to implement the United Nations Convention Against Torture and Other Cruel, Inhuman or Degrading Treatment or Punishment has not yet been enacted. This proposed implementing legislation would provide a tougher and more effective response to the problem, putting in place for torturers the same international "extradite or prosecute" regime we have for terrorists. The Senate gave its advice and consent to the Torture Convention on October 27, 1990, but the United States cannot proceed to become a party until the necessary implementing legislation is in place. I again call upon the Congress to take prompt action to approve the Torture Convention implementing legislation.

I note that H.R. 2092 does not help to implement the Torture Convention and does present a number of potential problems about which the Administration has expressed concern in the past. This legislation concerns acts of torture and extrajudicial killing committed overseas by foreign individuals. With rare exceptions, the victims of these acts will be foreign citizens. There is thus a danger that U.S. courts may become embroiled in difficult and sensitive disputes in other countries, and possibly ill-founded or politically motivated suits, which have nothing to do with the United States and which offer little prospect of successful recovery.

Such potential abuse of this statute undoubtedly would give rise to serious frictions in international relations and would also be a waste of our own limited and already overburdened judicial resources. As I have noted in connection with my own Civil Justice Reform Initiative, there is too much litigation at present even by Americans against Americans. The expansion of litigation by aliens against aliens is a matter that must be approached with prudence and restraint. It is to be hoped that U.S. courts will be able to avoid these dangers by sound construction of the statute and the wise application of relevant legal procedures and principles.

These potential dangers, however, do not concern the fundamental goals that this legislation seeks to advance. In this new era, in which countries throughout the world are turning to democratic institutions and the rule of law, we must maintain and strengthen our commitment to ensuring that human rights are respected everywhere. I again call upon the Congress to make a real contribution to the fight against torture by enacting the implementing legislation for the Torture Convention so that we can finally ratify that important treaty.

Finally, I must note that I am signing the bill based on my understanding that the Act does not permit suits for alleged human rights violations in the context of United States military operations abroad or law enforcement actions. Because the Act permits suits based only on actions "under actual or apparent authority, or color of law, of any foreign nation," I do not believe it is the Congress' intent that H.R. 2092 should apply to United States Armed Forces or law enforcement operations, which are always carried out under the authority of United States law.

GEORGE BUSH

The White House,
March 12, 1992.

*Note: H.R. 2092, approved March 12, was assigned Public Law No. 102–256.*

## Nomination of Vicki Ann O'Meara To Be an Assistant Attorney General
*March 12, 1992*

The President today announced his intention to nominate Vicki Ann O'Meara, of Illinois, to be an Assistant Attorney General for Land and Natural Resources at the U.S. Department of Justice. She would succeed Richard Burleson Stewart.

Since 1988, Ms. O'Meara has served as a partner with the law firm of Jones, Day, Reavis & Pogue in Chicago, IL. Prior to this, she served as Deputy General Counsel for Litigation and Regional Operations at the U.S. Environmental Protection Agency in Washington, DC, 1987–1988; and as a Special Assistant to the White House Counsel, 1986–1987.

Ms. O'Meara graduated from Cornell University (B.A., 1979); Northwestern University Law School (J.D. 1982); and George Washington University (M.A., 1987). She was born May 13, 1957, in Minneapolis, MN. Ms. O'Meara served in the U.S. Army, 1982–1986. She has one child and resides in Evanston, IL.

## Statement by Press Secretary Fitzwater on the President's Telephone Conversation With Prime Minister Suleyman Demirel of Turkey
*March 12, 1992*

The President spoke with Prime Minister Demirel of Turkey today on the escalating crisis between Armenia and Azerbaijan. The President is concerned about the situation in Nagorno-Karabakh and calls on the parties to declare an immediate cease-fire so that they can attempt to resolve their differences peacefully.

The involvement of the CSCE in the crisis in Nagorno-Karabakh reflects the deep concern of the international community about the violence that threatens to scar this region for generations to come. The parties must not seek to gain a temporary military advantage during a time of great uncertainty and heightened tensions. We call on them to exercise restraint even in the face of apparent provocation. The bloodshed must end.

The United States joins Turkey, Russia, and other countries in calling for an immediate cease-fire and for Armenia and Azerbaijan to cooperate with the CSCE to put a peaceful end to this growing tragedy.

## Remarks on Arrival in Battle Creek, Michigan
*March 13, 1992*

Thank you for the warm welcome on a cold, cold day. And I am delighted to be here, very pleased to be back in this State at the side of our great friend and Governor, John Engler, longtime supporter. And thank you very, very much for this welcome on this cold day.

My request is to go to those polls on Tuesday and give me 4 more years to lead this country out of this problem and keep our number one leadership in the world. We are the best. And now we've got to bring this economy in Michigan around and continue to lead the whole world.

Thank you all very, very much.

*Note: The President spoke at 9 a.m. at W.K. Kellogg Regional Airport. A tape was not available for verification of the content of these remarks.*

## Remarks to Stryker Corporation Employees in Kalamazoo, Michigan
*March 13, 1992*

Thank you, John Brown, for those kind words and that warm welcome. And may I just say to you how inspirational my little tour through this plant has been for me, seeing not only the spirit of this wonderful work force but getting to kick the tires on some of the most advanced technology in the health care field and to begin to understand it better. And so, I would like to take this opportunity to thank each of the people along the line that were so hospitable, welcoming me and our associates here today.

May I single out the Mayor who is graciously here today, Mayor Beverly Moore, and thank her for being here; and thank John, of course, and David Simpson and Si Johnson, Harry Carmitchel for the tour. And I'm pleased to, of course, be with my old friend John Engler, the Governor of this great State, and another man doing a fine job, and that's Congressman Fred Upton, all here with us today. And may I salute also the CEO council, who I understand has been introduced. And I said, "Who do I thank for the music?" And they said, "Don't, it's played on tape." So, nevertheless, here I am.

But really what we wanted to do was to come here today and salute an outstanding group of competitors in one of our leading-edge industries. Stryker is celebrated across the Nation and around the world for the quality of your work and the excellence of the management, the way it's handled. You're leaders in an innovative industry that makes our country proud.

And so let me offer a personal note. I'm a grandfather, yes, and time after time in recent years I've seen modern medical devices work miracles for other grandparents. I've seen grandparents who had been hobbled for years with arthritis. Now they're running and playing again, and those miracles are results of advances that your industry has made with these artificial joints.

I'm proud of how you at Stryker have gone abroad and captured new markets, John referred to this, but you've captured new markets for these high-quality American products. Exports as a portion of your sales, as the Governor mentioned, have risen steadily. They now account for almost one-third of your total sales. You have increased numbers of customers in Canada and Mexico and Europe, and you are the number one seller, I am told, the number one seller of artificial hips in Japan. Don't tell me the American worker can't compete with the Japanese.

And the bottom line is this industry is growing and creating good jobs for Americans because you give as good as you get. The health care technology industry, which is made up mostly of smaller companies like Stryker, invests an average of 6.3 percent of revenues in R&D, in research and development. That is nearly double, nearly double the national manufacturing average.

Your industry alone provides our great country with a favorable balance of foreign trade of almost $3 billion. You're solid proof that when that playing field is level, when you have access to the other guy's market, American workers can outthink, outperform, and outproduce anyone, anyplace in the world.

Some people simply don't get it. They see the challenges of the global economy and they say, "Let's draw the blinds, bolt the doors; maybe the whole world will go away." They push protectionism, which really means surrendering, surrendering our growth and surrendering our excellence.

The defeatists may carp, but over time they're going to become irrelevant. The future belongs to those who have the will to compete. And for my part, I will continue working with you to open up new markets wherever they are, Mexico, South America, all around the globe.

I'm also working urgently for a climate more favorable for prosperity at home. I know that people are hurting out there. People that have jobs are worried about them. But later today I'm going to be talking to the Economic Club there at Detroit, and I'll go into greater detail about an economic growth plan that I've challenged Congress to pass by March 20th, one week from now. We need new incentives; we need new incentives to get this economy moving. And I'm talking about an investment tax allowance. It sounds complicated, but what that means is speeding up depreciation on new equipment so people can go out and buy new capital items for their plants.

We need to get real estate up and running, and that means Congress should pass my $5,000 tax credit for those first-time homebuyers, the young family that wants to buy a home. Five thousand dollars would help, and it would stimulate the homebuilding industry. And they ought to pass that. That's not a political thing. It's something that will help the economy right now.

We need to reward the risktakers, those who create new jobs. And I still feel the way to create new jobs is to cut the tax on capital gains and stimulate new investment. And you're seeing this. We're competing with Japan; Japan taxes capital gains at 1 percent. Germany, I believe, is zero. And we're up there in the stratosphere. It's simply not right to people out there thinking, "How do I start a new business?"

I'd like to spend the rest of this brief time here today talking about another battle, and that's the battle against excessive regulation. A level playing field, I mentioned, outside the United States, that's fine; that's well and good. But you'll never reach it if you have to run yourselves to exhaustion right here at home on an uphill treadmill of overzealous regulators.

In my State of the Union, we put on a 90-day freeze on all proposed and existing Federal regulations, the ones that can affect economic growth. As much as possible, we're now speeding up rules that will help growth and halting rules that would harm the economy, set back this fragile economy.

I'm very concerned about the health technology business, the well-being of that business. Our whole future, as I look at it and what it's going to take to move briskly into the next century, is the high innovative tech industries like yours. The Commerce Department recently reported that America's health technology industry is the strongest in the entire world, but that if current political and economic trends continue, it would slip behind European and Asian competitors by the end of this decade. And need I say what one of those negative trends is? That is Government regulation.

Overregulation here in the United States can give foreign corporations an advantage over American firms. It also can drive U.S. businesses to move factories and jobs overseas. Recently, because of heavy regulation, the number of approvals of new medical devices has dropped dramatically.

Let me assure you: I am determined to roll back the tide of overregulation. After the 90-day freeze, I'm going to introduce what legislation it takes to change this, reform legislation to correct unreasonable rules we can't change simply through Executive action. And I will have to go to that Congress and challenge them to undo some of this regulatory knot that they've tied across the American economy. And I'll fight those liberals in the Congress who try to impose new and unreasonable burdens on America's livelihood. You know, if Congress sends me any more legislation with excessive regulation in it, I am going to have to veto it, and I will veto it as soon as it hits my desk. We need to free up businesses like this, not tie their hands anymore.

As long as I'm the President, I'm going to work to cut needless redtape. We've got to get the lifesaving drugs and devices to those who need them. Regulation of the healing arts and health technologies have got to respond to patients' needs and must be based on sound science, not on ideological politics or scare tactics.

And we need to heal something else, a legal system that is emptying our wallets and tearing our society apart. That's why I'd love to have your support for proposals to reform the liability system and the civil justice system. You know how the epidemic of lawsuits has become, neighbor suing neighbor, guys coaching Little League afraid to coach because of a lawsuit being filed at them: "You don't put the kid at first base, I'm going to sue you." I mean, it's not right; it's not fair. And we've overdone it, saying nothing of doctors who are pulling back because of malpractice suits filed against them. I want to be the President of a country where people spend more time helping each other than they do suing each other.

And the very last point: Our economy is going to be strong as long as it's free. That's the lesson that I've taken away from this, that I'll be taking away from this plant here at Stryker. You have learned that in the markets at home and around the world. It's a principle that we've got to redouble the efforts in fighting for. In my go-rounds with Congress and as Chief Executive of the Departments and Agencies that regulate American business, I'm going to try to do just that.

Let me say in conclusion, it's a joy to be here, not just simply a joy to be outside of what we call the beltway, Washington, DC. It really is. And when I come to a place like this and I see what you all are doing, I have a reaffirmation in my heart that this country is still the freest, the greatest, the fairest country on the face of the Earth.

We are the leader of the free world. We are the leader. Your kids and my grandkids don't go to bed today worrying as much as they used to about nuclear weapons. They have a feeling that we've done something big, and we've done it by leading, standing up to aggression and leading the world. And now let's take that same talent, bring it to bear on this economy, get it moving again, and reestablish our economy as the number one in the world.

Thank you all very, very much. Thank you.

*Note: The President spoke at 10:24 a.m. in the medical division of Stryker Corp. In his remarks, he referred to the following corporation officers: John W. Brown, chairman, president, and chief executive officer; David J. Simpson, vice president and chief financial officer; Stephen (Si) Johnson, executive vice president; and Harry E. Carmitchel, president of the medical division.*

## Remarks to the Economic Club of Detroit in Detroit, Michigan
*March 13, 1992*

*The President.* Thank you for that warm Michigan welcome. Governor Engler, my friend, thank you, sir, for that kind introduction, and my congratulations to you for trying to bring fiscal sanity to this wonderful State. And it's a great pleasure to be met by your Texas wife, Michelle, who's with us today. And also it's a great pleasure to see another old friend, a great leader of the State of Michigan, Lieutenant Governor Connie Binsfeld, who was out there at the airport, too. Thank you for being there. Mike Guido, the Mayor, is with us; I salute him. And one last thank-you to Jerry Warren, a former banker and now the miracle worker that can produce such a fantastic crowd on such short notice. Now, Jerry, if you want to go into the banking business again—[*laughter*]—there may be an opening in Washington, DC, on Capitol Hill. I think this guy could do it.

It's a pleasure to be back before this outstanding group. Four short days from now, Michigan faces a choice, and you'll make a decision that will really shape the way this country copes with the big issues, the issues that shape the world and the values close to home. And I am talking about jobs. I'm talking about family. And I'm talking about world peace for ourselves and also for our children.

Right now, the most important issue facing Michigan and this country is clearly the economy. It's my number one priority, jobs. Manufacturing—you know it perhaps better than most—has been the greatest generator of good jobs in American history. Take a look at the auto industry. I'm speaking not simply about the jobs created in the industry itself but the thousands upon thousands of jobs in supplier and spinoff businesses. Manufacturing is and always will be a basic strength of this country's economy. No nation will ever lead the world without a strong manufacturing base.

Fifty years ago, this great State of Michigan earned the proud title of Arsenal of Democracy. Industries centered here had no peers and practically no competitors anywhere on the planet. And yes, today things are different. Michigan's manufacturers are not just competing with a few outgunned adversaries. They are up against tough, hard-nosed competitors in practically every developed country. Today, the new reality is simply this: If we want to succeed economically at home, we have got to compete economically abroad.

All we seem to hear on the news is gloom and doom. But let's not overlook some of the fundamentals that prove that we are poised, not there yet, but poised for a national recovery. Interest rates are lower now than at any point in the past 10 years. The prime rate is now 6.5 percent. Inflation, most would agree, is under control. Monthly retail sales are up 1.3 percent in February, on top of a 2.1-percent rise in January. And then you know the story on housing starts; they're up 5.5 percent since December.

And for all our troubles, America is still the world's dominant economy, the one market other countries want to crack, the economy producing goods in demand in every country, every corner of the world.

Right now, nationwide, we're in the midst of a record export boom, one that's driven the trade deficit down 35 percent in the past year alone. And American exports have doubled, doubled since 1985. Not only do we export more than any other country, but we've been gaining ground, not losing it to our competitors. And I fully realize this has not always been true for our auto industry, but these are fundamentals that we can build on, the raw material, if you will, to manufacture the solid, strong recovery that I am confident we will see.

It looks different here in Detroit. Michigan's been through some extraordinarily tough times. And there's no sense pretending that things are better than they are. But there's also no sense underestimating our strengths and exaggerating our weaknesses. The simple fact is, we face a future with both challenges and opportunities.

In the past years, the United States has

helped bring about change that has reshaped our world for the better. We're the country that won the cold war, that drew a line on the sand and drove a dictator out of Kuwait. And we are the country that made sacrifices for freedom in four corners of the world. And because we did, right here at home our children are less fearful of the threat of nuclear war, and they sleep much more safely.

And yes, American leadership has changed the world, and now what I want to do is use that same leadership to change America. I don't think there's anyone in this room who doesn't believe that the key to America's economic future is our ability to lead, to succeed in the world economically as we have politically. And that's what my economic plan is all about.

Back in January, 45 days ago, I sent Congress a specific short-term action plan to stimulate this economy, to spark a recovery as early as this spring, a recovery that would increase auto sales and create jobs. And when I sent that plan to Capitol Hill, I set a deadline: one short week from now, March 20th, almost 2 months from the day I challenged the Congress.

And you know the story. Congress barely gave my plan a glance before they got busy on their own agenda: 90 billion dollar tax increase that will threaten our recovery and cost us jobs. Any economist worth his salt will tell you the last thing this economy needs is a massive tax increase. And you can count on this: If the Democrats send me that plan, they can get ready for a veto the minute it hits my desk. I am not going to accept it.

I believe that my plan—I'm convinced of it, and I've talked to lots of business people and lots of economists—I am convinced my plan will make America more competitive. It includes seven things that we've got to accomplish to ensure a strong market for America and for the automotive industry.

We've got to reduce Government spending and draw the line against new taxes. Deficit spending dries up sources of savings the private sector must have to invest, to grow, and to create new jobs. And there's only one protection the taxpayer has against uncontrolled, what we call discretionary spending in Washington: those spending caps that we got enacted a year and a half ago. That's the only protection the taxpayer has.

And guess what? You're right. The Congress wants to get rid of those spending caps now and go back to the days of unchecked spending. And I am not going to let that happen. We've got enough votes to sustain a veto to see that that does not happen to the American taxpayer.

We've got to put an end to excessive Government regulation. Our companies can't compete if the Government chokes them off in redtape. And we've got to stop counterproductive regulations that cripple your freedom of action and cost this country jobs. So I've ordered a 90-day review of all new regulations with this aim in mind: Whatever contributes to economic growth goes forward, and whatever stifles growth gets scrapped.

We're at midpoint in that review. But even now, you can see results. The sheer volume of new rules and regulations is down to 25 a week, from 6 times that amount just a year ago. That's progress. Already we've announced regulatory relief to benefit sectors of our economy from biotech to energy. And we're looking now for creative new ways to use regulations to clean up our environment, using market forces where possible.

Times have changed since the day nearly two decades ago when CAFE standards came into existence. And we now know that CAFE can cost a lot of jobs and even lives on the highway. And right now, through my Department of Transportation, I've been working with the auto industry and the UAW to fight irresponsible legislation. And I will not sign CAFE legislation that will destroy the auto industry and cost American jobs.

We will take several regulatory steps affecting the auto industry in the near future. There is one that I want to announce today. For some time, the EPA has been considering a requirement to order that all new cars be equipped with these onboard canisters to catch and contain fumes coming from the gas pump. As a result of our regulatory review, we have decided against such a rule. The Department of Transportation determined that onboard canisters pose a real risk to safety, a risk we simply cannot impose on American drivers.

If we want to make America more competitive, we've got to move forward on civil justice reform as well. Too many businesses can't start up or keep going because too many lawyers and too many lawsuits get in the way, 18 million lawsuits every year alone. Right here in Detroit, there are business men and women ready to expand, ready to hire new workers, stopped cold by the fear of litigation. All told, when you add in indirect expenses, lawsuits cost this economy $300 billion a year. And it's time for reform, time to replace the explosion of mindless litigation with a little common sense.

I have called on the Congress to pass reform in this area. It's a crime when you have people that don't dare coach Little League baseball because they're afraid they're going to get sued or doctors unwilling to deliver babies because they're afraid they're going to get some malicious malpractice suit filed against them.

I know the business people here would agree with this one, but we've got to keep our Nation on the cutting edge of new technologies. That's why I've proposed record Federal funding for R&D, research and development. It's why we back initiatives like one I signed at the White House last October to create a battery consortium to pioneer a new generation of electric cars. And in the global competition, it's going to come down to this: The best way to master new markets is to make them.

And if we want to be more competitive, we have got to encourage investment. That's why I've called on Congress to pass my investment tax allowance, speed up the front-end depreciation so people can buy capital equipment and write it off faster. And additionally, Congress ought to cut the tax on capital gains so we can compete with foreign interest. But political demagogs call that a tax break for the rich. Let me tell you something, you know what it is in Japan and Germany? Zero percent and one percent. And we're up there in the stratosphere somewhere.

We have got to provide our children, in addition, with a 21st-century education,

today. And we won't have a first-class economy with second-rate schools. To have the best economy, you have to have the best educated work force. And that's the idea behind our wonderful program known as America 2000, America 2000 strategy, our plan to revolutionize, to literally reinvent America's schools.

And finally, we've got to work to open markets around the world to American goods. Earlier this year, some of the people here today went with me to Japan. And we all took a little grief, a little flak in the press for that trip. But the fact is, that trip laid down a marker. The business community is beginning to understand this. It signaled to our trade partners that I am very serious about free and fair trade. Level the playing field, and American workers and American business can compete with anyone. And we'll keep pushing to open markets that for too long have been closed to quality American goods.

We've already seen a payoff: new markets for America in Japan's computer, glass, and paper market, all as a direct result of that trip. And American access to the Japanese Government mainframe computer market alone could mean an additional $5.5 billion in computer sales.

And we've seen positive steps in the automotive industry as well; not everything we want, but we've seen positive steps. Japan's auto industry intends to purchase an additional $10 billion worth of U.S. auto parts by 1994. And the benefits won't simply flow to the Big Three. Detroit Center Tool reports that its sales in Japan will jump 500 percent this year alone to $30 million.

And that trip was the beginning of an important process that we are going to continue, opening markets around the world. And that also means, in my view, a successful conclusion to the Uruguay round, GATT round. It's absolutely essential that we open markets, reduce these barriers.

So far today, I've talked about my plan, my plan to get the economy growing again and to get this country ready for the challenges of a new century. So let me repeat, here's what I'll do, and give it to you straight: I will veto mandates that pass the buck to business and hurt competitiveness.

I will veto job-destroying tax increases and fight for job-creating incentives. And I will fight to open markets around the world to American products. And I will fight against the forces of isolationism who want us to turn our back and run away from the future.

That's some of what I can do. And here's what you in the business community must do. But if we're going to work together to make America more competitive, you've got to continue your commitment to train and retrain your workers, give them the skills they'll need to cope with a changing workplace. And to help workers adjust to new economic conditions, Government can help, too. For example, last week a Department of Labor task force was here with the representatives of the UAW and GM on just that issue. Also, you've got to continue to build on recent progress that has labor and management working as allies, not adversaries. No company can compete when it is a war within itself. And you've got to fight for foreign markets, make the commitment for the long haul.

I, a long time ago—and I hate to bring it up in a room of successful business people, like the one that's here today—but was in a business, started the small business. And I think I know what it's like. I do know what it's like to sweat to make a payroll, to run risks, to succeed, and to overcome setbacks, too. And we all know how to measure performance. Performance is measured by performance improved: people back at work, assembly lines up and running, putting out a superior product, and bringing in a profit.

I want to close today, before taking a couple of questions here, by saying I know when I decided to come here I was going to a great city—been here many times; I've been privileged to be your guest at the Economic Club several times—going to a State that's experienced hard times. But I came here for that very reason: to look you in the eye, and to tell you what we are going to do to turn this economy around. And I have too much respect for the people in this room, too much respect for the men and women who work the assembly lines, to expect you to settle for anything short of the truth.

And yes, we're in an election year. We're in a highly partisan, shrill, not overly pleasant election year. And when the rhetoric heats up, it gets tough separating the fact from the fiction. Well, I can tell you this: All the quick-fix schemes in the world will not get us where we want to go. Some of them have wonderful political appeal, but they're not going to get us where we want to go. And the plan that I've laid out today will help America take on the toughest competition and win.

And so, let's not wring our hands, try to run away from a challenge. We've never done that. Let's do what America always does when challenge comes our way: Let's change America for the better. If we can install ourselves through action and principle as the undisputed leader of the free world, a leader with newfound credibility around the world, we can do the same thing here at home.

So I ask you to join me in this challenge. Join me in supporting these objectives I have spelled out, and we can and will change America and help the lives of every single American worker and business person in this country.

Thank you very much. And may God bless our wonderful country. Thank you.

*Governor Engler.* Thank you very much, Mr. President, for that wonderful address and that economic plan for our country. And now we have some specific questions that have been submitted by members of the Detroit Economic Club and some special guests. The first one actually—I'm sure that Chris McAllister from J.R. King Elementary School, who says "grade six" at the bottom of the card, is not a member but may be a guest here today. And he asks a question that's on the minds of a lot of people: President Bush, why did you choose a Texas plant over Willow Run?

*The President.* Let me take that question very seriously because—and I am reluctant to make it this definitive. I was told today, I hadn't seen it because I don't read too much of what Senator Riegle says, but— [*laughter*]—I was told today—I'm very serious about this because this a challenge to my integrity as President of the United States, and when it gets on that basis I take it seriously. And I was told by the Governor and I was told by a Congressman that I was accused by that Senator of intervening in the GM process, the private sector process. And I'm standing here to tell you with everything I can muster that I made no such intervention. And I take it as a direct attack on my character to have a United States Senator say that. It is a bald-faced lie. And Bob Stempel is right when he said it is.

That sixth grader is on to something. [*Laughter*]

*Governor Engler.* The UAW, AFL-CIO is actively working against your reelection. With times as tough as they are right now, what chance do you see of winning the rank-and-file worker in a State like Michigan?

*The President.* Well, I saw the UAW seems to be supporting Jerry Brown. That may not be accurate; I don't know. Look, one, there's time for politics; two, there's time for trying to lead this country. These are good people. Their families are hurting. Some have a job today, not sure they'll have it tomorrow. And so my answer to them is, I want to change this economy.

And I tried to spell out here today, and I hope some of them heard it, a program, a seven-point incentive program plus a broader program that will, indeed, get this economy moving now and stimulate it, and then we'll also be sure that we are competitive into the future.

So I would like to address myself—I know that the unions early on decided they were going to support somebody else for President. But for me, this transcends a political endorsement or political opposition. We have got to get the economy moving. There's a lot of families that are hurting out there, and I think what I've proposed here today is the answer.

*Governor Engler.* As a businessman running a 60-employee family company, I must run a tight ship in order to survive in a difficult economy. What can be done to see that our Federal Government begins now to reduce America's $2 trillion debt so we can enjoy a prosperous economy in the coming years? That's from David Keller, and related to that is another card that has a question: What is the status of the line-item veto?

*The President.* The debt is an enormous

worry. And for those who live and die by polls, really for the first time, the deficit and debt is about number one, I believe it is number one in the polls. I'll give you an example of what we're trying to do with it. One, I'm going to try to keep the caps on discretionary domestic spending. Government is too big, and it spends too much.

And right now I'm in a big fight in the Congress. The 1990 budget agreement did place caps on all discretionary spending. It did not touch the part of the budget that's growing the fastest, the entitlements, but it did put a cap on domestic spending. And now the Democrats in Congress—not all of them, thank heavens—are trying to remove the caps. They're saying this: "We can take defense cuts now." And I've proposed $50 billion, and some of them are saying, "Oh, we can do more. We'll take $150 billion." And that would cut right into the muscle of our defense and make us unable to respond to any eventuality around the world. But they're trying now to say, we're going to take that defense spending and spend it, defense money and spending it.

And I'm saying no, we're going to keep up what they call the firewalls, the different—the caps on defense and the caps on other domestic spending. And when we cut defense by the $50 billion I recommend, we will use that to reduce the Federal deficit.

And I'm in a whale of a fight in the Congress to do just that. And that is small compared to the overall size of the deficit, but it is a beginning. And again, I need your help because we are outnumbered in a fight like this. It is too easy in an election year to promise some new Government spending program. And I have got to fight it. I have got to keep the caps on, and I've got to apply the reductions in defense spending to this deficit to show the American people that we are concerned and we don't want to continue mortgaging the future of our young people.

*Governor Engler.* We have time for about three more questions according to the watch I was given. So President Bush—this is sort of like the old "Ask George Bush" program that I remember from the Vice President's days—President Bush, do you have any plans for changing antitrust laws to enable a closer relationship between Government, business, and labor?

*The President.* There's a review going on, and I don't know how it's going to come out. We have tried to lighten up on this concept that was overly restrictive on antitrust, where businesses couldn't even talk to each other for fear of antitrust attacks on them when they were trying to improve things generally in the community, for example.

I can't give you a definitive answer as to how that comes out. I do think we've got a ways to go before we can certify that the antitrust laws are not excessively burdensome. They are excessively burdensome. And I think by still protecting against monopoly and against conspiracies so prices go up, there's a way that we can go to lighten up on antitrust and to be sure that these laws do not set us back from competition abroad.

You know and I know that many people in foreign competition target industries. They get together. They have what you call financial centralized planning. We don't do that in this country, but I think we've leaned too far the other way when it comes to the tightness of antitrust. So we're taking a hard look on it, and I hope we can still protect against monopolistic practice and still lighten up so that we can be much more competitive around the world.

*Governor Engler.* Fearing the loss of jobs, big labor opposes the proposed free trade agreement with Mexico. Why do you feel the agreement will be beneficial to the United States?

*The President.* In the first place, I am absolutely convinced, absolutely convinced that in passing the NAFTA, the free trade agreement with Mexico, we call it the North American free trade agreement, it will create more jobs. I'm convinced that it's good for the environment. I believe a more prosperous Mexico, and there's going to be prosperity on both sides if we can get the proper kind of agreement, will be able to address itself to these environmental problems. I believe a more prosperous Mexico will be an even better market for U.S. goods.

And so, I do not accept the wisdom of some that says that a free trade agreement is going to result simply in an export of jobs. It is not going to do that. And I believe that we ought to keep pressing for it. I don't care what the politics of it are; I think it is best.

And I want to do exactly the same thing this NAFTA, this North American free trade agreement—I want to do exactly the same thing with the successful conclusion of the Uruguay round. And Michigan has a lot of agriculture. And I believe that if we are successful, we will be opening up all kinds of markets abroad for agriculture. I think we can do better in property rights.

And so we have two major initiatives in international trade. One is the NAFTA, which is mainly with Mexico and Canada, of course, and then I want to follow it with opening trade south of there. And secondly is the Uruguay round.

And the other point I want to make on this hemisphere is this. We look at the changes that have taken place in the former Soviet Union. And we look at the changes that are taking place in Africa, for example, South Africa and Zambia. But sometimes we don't look into our own front yard, the exciting markets of Latin America. And there, take a look at what's happened: Military dictatorships have given away to democracies. Communist regimes, a la Nicaragua, have given away to democracies. And there's only one holdout against democracy in this hemisphere really, except for the problems in Haiti. It's Cuba. It is Cuba. And democracy is on the move.

And what I want to do is help find ways to strengthen those economies so they can be not only perfecting their democracies but be better markets for American goods and services. And it is an exciting message down there. We are doing a first-class job on working with these Latin American, South American countries. And we ought not to neglect it.

And while saying neglect, let me add this point—too long an answer to a very simple question—but it has been suggested that I turn my attention away from national security matters and foreign affairs. I don't think a President should do that. I think it's important to find the right balance between doing something for the domestic economy but recognizing that it's only the United States of America that can lead this free world. And I am not going to neglect my responsibilities overseas, but I darn sure am going to pay as much attention as it requires to get this economy moving.

*Governor Engler.* This is another question from a youngster, Calvin Paines, I believe the name is, from J.R. King School in Detroit: Will there be jobs for black children in the future?

*The President.* I hope there will, and I think there will. And one of the reasons I'm so excited about America 2000, in which many of the business people I see sitting in this room are already assisting, is that our education program will result in just that kind of opportunity.

I met with some people from the National League of Cities, and one of the things that concerned this—this is a little addition to this guy's question—they told me, the mayors from big cities, small cities, Democrats, Republicans, liberal, conservative, "The thing that concerns us the most about the urban problems is the decline in the American family."

We have appointed a Commission led by Governor Ashcroft and former Mayor Strauss of Dallas to figure out what we can do, what legislation is diminishing the family. And underlying it all is the need for more education. And so I would say to this sixth grader, I think you've got a whale of an opportunity.

And let me say this also: I have been disturbed by kind of an ugliness out there. When things get tough, one person loses his job to another, people are uncertain about the future. They've lost confidence in the country, maybe in the President, certainly in the Congress, I think, too. But nevertheless, when that happens, somehow an ugliness crops up. And let me say this, let's leave this politics aside: Bigotry and discrimination and anti-Semitism have absolutely no place in America. And I'm going to continue to stand up for that principle.

*Governor Engler.* I have in my hands the last question. I was going to ask this one first, but it's unsigned. It starts out, Governor John Engler has done a heroic job—[*laughter*]—and it goes on. It could stop there but, no, Governor John Engler's done a heroic job working to stimulate growth in Michigan's economy by sponsoring the cut and cap plan for property tax relief. What can be done at the Federal level that would have similar impact to Michigan's cut and cap? And that will be the last question, Mr. President.

*The President.* Well, give me another one because I think I answered it, I hope I answered it, in my remarks. And so it's not fair to take you over that turf again, so I'll take one more.

I believe the best thing we can do is to incentivize this economy. Control the Government spending as best one can; that means sometimes vetoing legislation. Lighten up on the regulatory front; and then, in a longer vein, more, better education. And I think that's the answer to this economy.

But give me one more because that's not fair. Maybe it's not.

*Governor Engler.* I just like the question a lot. [*Laughter*] We'll get to one more here.

*The President.* What about the one that says Engler's screwing it up, we're not going to——[*laughter*].

*Governor Engler.* Passed over that one right away. [*Laughter*]

We'll end on a political question here. Assuming you will be nominated, overall, do you think Pat Buchanan's campaign efforts will hurt the Republican Party chances in November?

*The President.* My answer to that question is no. I am going to continue to try to run what I hope has been a high-level campaign. And I'm going to try to keep focusing on the issues. I'll say this, because it's not easy to find a balance in a competitive election year between how much time you devote to the campaign trail, how much time you spend in the Oval Office trying to help people and trying to solve the problems of this country.

Last week on Super Tuesday, we had eight States. And I felt I should at least make an appearance in each of the eight States so it didn't look like I was taking something for granted, turning my back on the people whose votes were very, very important in those States. And so I went to one, and I think some drew the conclusion from that, that was a little frenetic.

Super Tuesday was very, very good to me. And we will now have our primary here and in Illinois on Tuesday. I think that we've found the right balance. I think in terms of a primary challenge, the thing I must do is not get after the opponent. Let him chart his course, make up his decision on what to do. And let me now spend much more time—Super Tuesday out of the way; Michigan and Illinois by Tuesday—in trying to get these things done that I have outlined here.

And then we're going to be interacting overseas. Of course, Yeltsin's coming here; Helmut Kohl, I think, will be here next weekend. And there's a lot of things of this nature that I must attend to.

And so I can't fault somebody for challenging me. I feel very, very confident about winning this primary. But I think now I've got the proper balance as to how much—and it wouldn't help a bit to try to assess for you the opposition. That's what the elections are about.

But I know these are nonpolitical gatherings, but if you're Republican, please vote for me on Tuesday.

Thank you very much.

*Note: The President spoke at 12:50 p.m. in the Grand Manor Ballroom at Fairlane Manor. In his remarks, he referred to Jerry Warren, president of the Economic Club of Detroit, and Robert C. Stempel, president and chief operating officer of General Motors Corp.*

# Exchange With Reporters Aboard Air Force One
## *March 16, 1992*

*Iraq*

*Q.* Mr. President, exactly what is your approach towards Iraq at this point? There are constant stories about desires to take action, to put carriers—[*inaudible*]. Where do you stand now?

*The President.* We stand that we are just insisting in every way we can that Iraq comply with the United Nations resolutions. And I'm not discussing options. All options are open. And we're consulting our allies, as we have in various phases of the Iraq situation. So I wouldn't read too much into the movement of a carrier, inasmuch as we have carrier elements up in the Gulf from time to time. But on the other hand, I think it's fair to say we are determined that they follow through on what they said they'd do; serious business here. And the United Nations is saying firm—our Ambassador up there put it very well. And so we're watching and hoping they will fully comply.

*Q.* Does that mean that action is not imminent? That you are willing to give them time?

*The President.* I just would leave it where I stated it, Charles [Charles Bierbauer, Cable News Network].

*Q.* What did you think about Tariq 'Aziz's appearance at the United Nations? Did he seem to be foot-dragging?

*The President.* Yes, bobbing and weaving.

*House Bank Controversy*

*Q.* How much do you think this check scandal's going to hurt the House? Do you think people should vote based on whether or not a Member bounced a bunch of checks?

*The President.* No, I think you've got to look at the whole situation. But people are outraged by it. And I think each individual case has to be viewed as to its content. But I'm waiting and watching it unfold. I think it's an institutional thing. I think people are very concerned, but I'm not jumping on any individual. I mean, I think everyone has his own case, his or her own case to make to their constituents or to the people.

*Q.* Will you support Congressman Gingrich's call for a special prosecutor?

*The President.* Well, I haven't even talked to our attorneys about that.

*Illinois and Michigan Primaries*

*Q.* What do you look for in Michigan and Illinois?

*The President.* Victory.

*Q.* What kind of victory? How big?

*The President.* No, no, no. Never try to say how high the high bar should be on these primaries. I haven't done it. I've been very pleased. They seem to be getting better and better. But I'm just—keep working to try to, one, get the message out on the primaries, but two, try to address myself to the problems facing this country. And I am doing that. And I'm just going to keep on doing that.

*Q.* Are you going to offer any goodies to the people of Illinois and Wisconsin today, any Federal aid, Federal——

*The President.* Well, got a good program for them in terms of this economy. I just hope that they can use their influence with a recalcitrant Senate and House.

Well, welcome aboard. It's just a pleasure having you fellows here. It's a little long trip, but it will be a good one.

*Presidential Medal of Freedom*

*Q.* An early one tomorrow, too.

*The President.* What?

*Q.* An early one tomorrow.

*The President.* Look, I'm very much looking forward to that tomorrow. I have a very high regard for Sam Walton and what he's done and the way in which he's done it. And so to me, that one, I know some will say it's political. It is purely nonpolitical. It is to honor a great American. And that one I'm glad you asked about because I really feel viscerally and emotionally connected with tomorrow's visit.

*Q.* Don't you give them a speech there tomorrow?

*The President.* Down there?

*Q.* Yes.

*The President.* Well, I don't know. It depends on what they work out on the actual presentation.

*Legislative Action*

*Q.* What are your plans for March 20th, sir?

*The President.* I just hope the Congress does what I've asked. And it's not impossible. But it's—they're coming along with a great big tax increase. And I just—this one, I think, Tsongas is on to something. He says this is purely political. I think he's right about that, what the Senate and House appear to be doing.

*Q.* Would you look to veto one of those bills, or veto that bill this week?

*The President.* Oh yes, definitely will veto if it comes down close to what they did in the House.

*Q.* Do you think you'll get it this week though, sir?

*The President.* I don't know. I just don't know. Nobody seemed too sure of it when I left this morning.

I better get going.

*Q.* You don't really expect them to do it, do you?

*The President.* Don't expect it, but it would be nice, though, if they'd do something for the American people instead of raising taxes and spending the money.

*Note: The exchange took place in the morning while the President was en route from Washington, DC, to Milwaukee, WI.*

# Remarks to Steeltech Employees in Milwaukee, Wisconsin
*March 16, 1992*

Well, this is an exciting day. And Janet, thank you for the introduction. And of course, to the Guerrero family who greeted us here, some of them milling around with cameras, the boss up here, many, many thanks for this warm welcome to this exciting venture. And David, let me just say, from what I've seen, you have an awful lot to be proud of, not just in things, not just in what's happening but in the people that make up this organization of yours. Good morning also to Chuck Wallace. And it's good to, obviously great to be back with two dear friends of mine, Governor Tommy Thompson and Senator Bob Kasten, each in his own way doing a superb job for our country. May I also salute Mayor Norquist, modestly standing on the side, and thank him for attending today. Thank you, sir. And with him, the county executive is with us today, Mr. Schultz. Thank you, sir, for being with us. And I was looking because back out of the limelight is one of America's great heroes, a winner of the Congressional Medal of Honor, Gary Wetzel, but he's—he was there, but anyway—here he is right over here. Proud to have him with us today.

You know, Tommy—to me, Governor Thompson is fond of saying there are only two seasons in Wisconsin, winter and road construction. So I guess I'm glad to say that spring is just around the corner.

And I am proud to be with you today. And I want the media here to carry your message into every living room in this Nation because we're waging a battle today in America, a battle for jobs and for our economic future. And Steeltech is the kind of success story that points the way to victory. It was a dream that its supporters refuse to call impossible, a dream of startup, minority-owned firm, but committed to excellence. And Steeltech grew out of extraordinary bipartisan public-private cooperation, combining government action with economic initiative and the strong support of the community. And that is essential.

Governor Thompson on the State level, a great believer; Mayor Norquist, I'm told, on the city level, a great believer; and then Jack Kemp, our Secretary of HUD, who helped win a HUD grant; Pat Saiki, back in Washington, who is head of the SBA, and she helped qualify this company as a small disadvantaged business concern, that gave it another kick.

And I've heard about the private sector's involvement from Fred Luber, especially about Roger Peirce and the great folks at Super Steel who have held out a hand of hospitality. So, what I've glimpsed, what I've just seen, seen the periscope of, really, is a precedent-setting teamwork that brought about what I'm told, and I believe this is true, David, is the largest manufacturing minority business enterprise in the

Nation's history.

One of the most impressive things about Steeltech, and I referred to this earlier, is its vision of its workers. David Guerrero and Jan Crosby and others go to the hardest hit parts of minority communities here for their recruits. And some have been imprisoned; some are longtime unemployed. And I like what David says about these new beginnings. Here's his quote: "Forget about the past. Look to the future." And after intensive training with partner schools, these men and women become part of the high-quality, self-confident, drug-free Steeltech team.

And what a great team it is. Let me mention just a couple: players like Chester Gandy, who learned to weld at 47; Larry Holliman, who was honored by Mayor Norquist for perfect attendance; and father and son workers Gilbert Buenrostro II and III, two of them starting a family tradition. And they're all part of this Steeltech team that last year produced $1.8 million in sales and that this year expects to top $10 million. Remarkable, and it's not even the second anniversary of this firm yet.

And soon, you're going to move into what David described to me as a neighborhood factory, your new state-of-the-art plant with the largest automated E-coat painting line in the United States. And there you'll help contribute to the national defense of this country, working with Gene Goodson of Oshkosh, making high-quality steel components for the PLS, the new military cargo truck. And we're proud to have you working for America under a Federal Government contract. And I am proud, very proud, to be here to salute each and every one of you.

You should know, I hope you know that I'm trying very hard to fight for a better economic climate not just for people here but all across our country. And you've heard me talk about the economic growth plan that I've asked Congress to pass by March 20th. That's this coming Friday. And the plan offers new incentives to stimulate the economy in certain ways, incentives like an investment tax allowance that will help these kinds of dynamic companies to expand, speed up the depreciation rate so business can invest and get that payback sooner. It's critical to get congressional approval immediately.

Let me just mention today another battle for the health of the economy. And I don't know how badly you've been impacted by it, David, but I'm talking about the struggle against excessive regulation. American workers have shown to foreign competitors that given a level playing field, given equal rules, we can outthink, outperform, outproduce anyone, anytime, and anyplace. Well, a level playing field outside the United States is well and good, but you'll never reach it if you have to run yourselves to exhaustion here at home on a treadmill of overzealous regulation. Yes, we all have obligations for the safety, for example, of workers in the workplace. But we can't be overzealous; we can't go too far.

And so, in my recent State of the Union Message, I instituted a 90-day freeze on proposed and existing Federal regs that would hinder economic growth. And now we're speeding up rules that help growth and halting rules that would harm the economy. Overregulation here in the U.S. can give foreign corporations an advantage over us. And it can also drive businesses to move their factories overseas. And let me assure you, we are going to continue this fight until we roll back all of the overregulation.

During and after this 90-day freeze, our administration is going to do everything it can to roll this tide back and then to go forward with reform legislation. Some of it to win the battle against excessive regulations requires legislation itself. And we're going to fight against those in Congress who try to impose new and unacceptable regulatory burdens on Americans' livelihood. And

if Congress sends me any legislation with excessive regulation in it, I will have to veto it and send it back. We simply cannot tie the hands of our workers, tie the hands of our businesses.

And so, I'm tremendously impressed, in summary, by just what I've seen here today, by you. And as I travel across the country now I've got a wonderful story to take with me. And I will tell other Americans about a place where people still believe in hope, where they work together for their neighbors, where they succeed. And I'll tell the story of Steeltech, and I'll end by saying these men and women prove that the American dream can still come true. I just wish each and every one of you that might not be intimately familiar with this firm could have heard the spirit of the workers that I was privileged to talk to, albeit briefly, when I first came into this plant.

So thank you, David. And thank all of you for what you're doing in this wonderful, I would say, experience; let me call it instead a success story. I will take this message out and bring it home to America: We can succeed. We will succeed. And we will get this economy moving dynamically in the future.

Thank you all very, very much.

*Note: The President spoke at 11:05 a.m. at Steeltech Manufacturing, Inc. In his remarks, he referred to Steeltech officers G. David Guerrero, president and chief executive officer, Charles L. Wallace, chairman of the board, and Janet E. Crosby, human resources manager; Super Steel Products Corp. officers Fred G. Luber, chairman and chief executive officer, and Roger D. Peirce, president and chief operating officer; and R. Eugene Goodson, chief executive officer of Oshkosh Truck Corp.*

# Remarks at a Bush-Quayle Fundraising Luncheon in Milwaukee
*March 16, 1992*

Thank you, Governor Thompson, and thank all of you for that warm welcome. Sue Ann, it is such a treat to see you again. May I second the motion on Bob Kasten; it

is absolutely essential that he be reelected. And I'm glad to be here with him today.

And earlier this morning, we were out at a very dynamic steel company. And I want to thank Fred Luber for his sponsorship and leadership in seeing this minority business out there have a real shot at the American dream. But with us out there was Lieutenant Governor Scott McCallum and his wife, Laurie, both with us here today. I salute them. And may I single out former Secretary of Commerce Bob Mosbacher, who is now a cochairman of our campaign, sitting down here. And Bobby Holt's with us somewhere, our national finance chairman. And I am very, very grateful to both of them. And Bob did a superb job for commerce in this country. Thank you, Mr. Mosbacher.

And I could not possibly come back to Wisconsin without saluting my longtime friend—picked me up, dusted me off in the dark ages when we were really down and been at my side ever since, same for Tommy—and I'm talking about John MacIver, our Bush-Quayle chairman over here. And again, our thanks to Fred Luber for cochairing this and his wife, Ann; and also for Wisconsin's chairman, David Opitz; and Mike Grebe over here, a longtime friend and now our national committeeman. You have a wonderful team.

Someone asked me what I think of the challenger who has no leadership experience whatsoever but thinks he's qualified to assume high office. Frankly, I think Phil Garner will do a fine job with the Brewers, outstanding. [*Laughter*] And it is good to get out of Washington. And I'll tell you, what's going on on Capitol Hill right now gives new meaning to the phrase, "The check's in the mail." [*Laughter*]

You know, too many people in Washington are fixated on the next election, and too few are focused on the next generation. And we are in a battle for our future. And we want America to lead the world in good jobs with productive work. And we want to and we will remain a force for world peace and freedom. And we're for fighting to protect our most basic institution, the family.

That's why this year of decision is so vital for America. And that's why April's primary election and November's general election are vital to our future. I'm asking you to get out to vote and create a resounding mandate to transform America. Let's nominate and elect men and women who share our values. We've got more to do to get Amer-

ica on the right track. And so I am asking you today for 4 more years as President of the United States of America.

America was built on faith, family, and freedom. And these form the foundation of our great country. And we must now renew those sources of our strength. We must allow common sense to prevail, for example, in our welfare system, forge a new connection between welfare and work. And as I've said, I am encouraging States to seek waivers to reform the Nation's welfare programs. And today, standing right here, Governor Thompson is submitting such a waiver request, and I look forward to receiving it.

You're on the right track right here in Wisconsin with learnfare, Bob referred to this, with workfare, and the proposed Parental Responsibility Act. Those are just a few of the reasons why more and more people are beginning to say, "Watch Wisconsin because Wisconsin works."

The people of the country, like the people of the State, are not stingy. Americans are a caring people. If somebody else is hurting, we feel it. And we support welfare for families in need. But Americans want to see government at every level, for example, work together to track down the deadbeat dads, the ones who can't be bothered to pay child support. And they want to see us break this cycle, this ugly and deplorable cycle of dependency that destroys dignity and then passes down poverty from one generation to the next. It's wrong. It's cruel. And we're working to change it. And we're encouraging States to follow Governor Thompson's lead, to follow Wisconsin's lead, with plans that help people break welfare dependency and begin learning work skills.

And we will continue to fight for the parents' right to choose their children's schools. School choice is at the heart of our wonderfully exciting America 2000, our strategy to revolutionize, literally revolutionize, American education.

And Wisconsin knows what I mean. Think of the groundbreaking efforts of Polly Williams, whom I talked to from Air Force One this morning. This State pioneered the frontier of school choice, because, as

Tommy said, the Governor said, "It was the right thing to do." And I'm grateful to say it looks like your State supreme court would agree. And there are those who find change difficult. And some say, "Slow down." And we say to them, "Get out of the way." Choice works in Wisconsin, and we're going to take this crusade to every State in the Union.

Incidentally and perhaps parenthetically, here's another choice I deeply support. I really believe, because I talk about family and faith, I really believe our children have the right to choose voluntary prayer in school. And I'd like to see something done about it.

Parents, not some bureaucrat in Washington, know what is best for the kids. And that's why I worked to win this child care bill, with Bob Kasten's support, a bill that gives parents the right to choose who provides the care. And we know America is first as long as we put the family first.

And for 3 years I've had to struggle fighting the liberal leadership of the Congress on these issues. And I'm going to continue to stand and fight for principle even when Congress stands in the way. And thank God again for Bob Kasten and his cohorts on our side in the Senate.

We've put judges on the bench, on the Federal bench, who know their role is to interpret the law, not legislate from the Federal bench. And I will use the veto when I have to—another point—to stand for principle, to stand up for family values. And if I had the kind of line-item power that your Governor has, I would prove once and for all, that the pen is mightier than the sword. As it is, even my friends have said that at times I was courting defeat by casting a veto out there instead of compromising. But we've never lost a veto fight. And I'll never hesitate to use it when principle is at stake.

You remember, I asked Congress to pass tax cuts and incentives to get the economy moving, to get real estate up and running, to reward the risktakers who create good jobs. And one reason Wisconsin has weathered the recession better than most of the other States is that Wisconsin kept the cut on capital gains and Wisconsin business taxes are among the lowest in the Nation.

And Wisconsin works, and it's time Washington woke up to why. And I am again calling on the Congress to cut the tax on capital gains. It is a job creator, not a break for the rich.

But instead of passing my plan, the big spenders that control the Congress had other ideas. And here they are: In the House of Representatives, a temporary cut for more people, tax cut; in the Senate, a permanent cut for less people. How much? Twenty-five cents a day, a quarter a day for each man, woman, and child in America. Fine, but what's the catch? Ninety billion dollars in new permanent taxes. And the Democrats call that, as Bob knows, new revenue. And I call it your money.

And remember, we set a deadline, March 20th, and that's just 4 days away. And I said to Congress, "Pass our plan. Help get our economy moving. Do something good and right now for the American people." And we'll fight, and we'll win. We may have to veto—I will veto the tax bills if they come out of the House and Senate anything like they are today. Make no mistake about it.

And we're going to keep to our leadership course in the world economy. Because if we want to succeed economically at home, and Tommy touched on this one, we've got to lead economically abroad. Trade with our neighbors, trade with the world is important here in Wisconsin. And this State exports $15.4 billion in manufactured goods in a single year, that's billion dollars. And almost 200,000, I believe the figure is, Wisconsin jobs—somewhere in there—depend on exports, direct and indirect.

But my opponents are peddling protectionism, a retreat from economic reality. You cut through all the patriotic posturing and all the tough talk about "fighting back" by closing shop, and look closely. That is not the American flag they're waving. It is the white flag of surrender. And that's not the America that you and I know. America does not cut and run, and we compete. And never in this Nation's long history have we turned our backs on a challenge, and we simply are not going to start that now.

I put my faith in the American worker. I mentioned this out there at the steel plant:

Level the playing field and our worker, the American worker, will outthink, outproduce, and outperform anyone, anywhere, anytime. So we've got to let the world know this: Whatever the challenge, America will meet it. We are in it to win.

Think back. Think back to just about a year ago, to the calm after Desert Storm. And ask any one of the proud sons and daughters of Wisconsin who became liberators of Kuwait, and they'll tell you that military strength doesn't mean a thing without moral support right here at home.

And yes, there were some who didn't support us then, and there are those who second-guess us now. But not here, not in Wisconsin. When I drew that line in the sand, you stood with me. And never would this country tuck tail and let aggression stand. And America did what was good and just, and we did what was right.

And there are those who act as if America's work in the world is over—"Come back; come home." And to them I say: We will never neglect America's vital national interests. And as far as our national defense goes, I am going to continue to keep this country strong so that our worldwide credibility, now at an all-time high, will help us strengthen democracy, freedom, and peace around the entire world. Look around the world. It is only our country, it is only the United States of America that can lead the world. And as long as I am President, I am going to stay engaged and do just exactly that.

Let my opponents, both sides, sound the retreat, run from the new realities, seek refuge in a world of protectionism or high taxes or big Government. And let the analysts on the tube tick off everything that's wrong in America. We know what's right. And let me say, too, I am counting on the good people of Wisconsin to reject the ugly politics of hate that is rearing its head. Racism, anti-Semitism, and bigotry have no place in the United States of America. And we must continue to stand for that principle.

Let me close by saying that, in the first place, I'm very proud of our First Lady. She's not here, but I can say it with great pride in what Barbara Bush has done, raising the standards for literacy in this country and just being a wonderfully decent family person. And I know this sounds maybe a little too prideful, but I think she's been a superb First Lady. And we are very blessed, if you will, blessed to serve this great Nation of ours at a moment when so many of the old fears have been driven away and when so many new opportunities stand within our reach. Since the day I took the oath of office I made it my responsibility, my duty to try to do what is right for this wonderful country that's been so good to us. I've given it my level-best, and I'm not done yet. I am not finished.

You and I have much more work before we've finished our mission. It's a battle for our future: It's about jobs; its about family; it's about something big, world peace, the kind of legacy we're going to leave our kids. Together, we've made a great beginning. I take great pride that the young people in this country go to sleep today without quite the fear of nuclear war that perhaps their parents had not so many years ago. We want to renew the miracle of American enterprise. We want to strengthen the underpinnings of our society, the values of family and faith and freedom.

And now we're approaching an hour of decision—and next month, right here in this State. Don't wait until November. I'm asking you to vote on April 7th in the Republican primary. Give me your vote in this important election next month. Help me win 4 more years to lead the fight for these fundamental values we share.

Thank you all so very, very much. And may God bless the United States of America. Thank you.

*Note: The President spoke at 12:18 p.m. at the Pfister Hotel. In his remarks, he referred to Sue Ann Thompson, wife of Gov. Tommy Thompson; John K. MacIver, chairman, and Fred G. Luber, finance cochairman, Wisconsin Bush-Quayle campaign; David W. Opitz, Wisconsin Republican Party chairman; Phil Garner, manager of the Milwaukee Brewers baseball team; and State legislator Polly Williams.*

## Remarks to the Polish National Alliance in Chicago, Illinois
*March 16, 1992*

Well, thank you, Ed Moskal, very, very much, and all of you for this welcome. May I salute our great Governor, Jim Edgar, with me here today. I think I heard you greet him. My respects to Ed Dykla, to the bishop, to Father Phillips, and of course to one of your own, a great friend of ours who has helped so much in this administration, as he did in Congress; I'm talking about Secretary Ed Derwinski, known to all of you here. And may I pay my respects to Poland's consul general, Michal Grocholski, who is here behind us. Delighted to have you here, sir. And again, thank you for that warm Chicago welcome.

Somebody suggested that this visit has something to do with a primary election. True, I'm working to win that election. But if anyone thinks we've got political head-aches here, they're nothing compared with the problems that free Poland is facing today, particularly Lech Walesa is facing. We have two major parties here in this country. But look at all the parties he has to contend with, close to 20, 20 at the last count. Even the Polish Beer Drinkers' Party—[*laughter*]—true, they've split into two factions. Now, I know you follow Poland, but I don't know whether it's the light beer faction or whatever it is.

But I salute their President. I salute him for what he's doing. And he stood there when things weren't free, and there he is now, leading that country. And I really want to pay my respects here, surrounded by his many friends and admirers.

Whenever I come here, I remember other occasions that I've had to get together with the community. Back in 1988 at the wake for Al Mazewski, who was head of this marvelous alliance, I remember that well. At the inaugural celebration for my dear friend over here, Ed Moskal, I remember that one well, upbeat, enthusiastic. And then, of course, at a very beautiful special service, a Sunday Mass at St. Hyacinth's Church, which reminded me of a church that I visited outside Warsaw not so many months ago. But at St. Hyacinth's I had the privilege to join with many of you in prayers for peace and freedom and to lay a wreath at the memorial for the martyr of Solidarity, Father Popieluszko.

How our prayers have been answered in those short years. It is unbelievable. Since '88, the whole world has been transformed. And that change really, if you look at your history, began in Poland. Poland overthrew that cruel tyranny that Stalin imposed after Yalta. Now imperial communism, the communism that always wanted to take over someone else, is dead. The Soviet Union has ceased to exist. The threat of nuclear war has diminished dramatically. These are the blessings that millions of us have worked and prayed to attain.

For decades we faced a mortal danger. The Communists fought to dominate the world. The Soviet Union threatened the very existence of free Europe and the United States, too, with its massive armies and its nuclear arsenals. The Communists persecuted believers and demolished the houses of worship. They imprisoned the Cardinal, Cardinal Wyszynski, and murdered Father Popieluszko.

But all the while, believers, believers kept on believing: Stubborn believers, who suffered every sort of torment in prisons and labor camps; patient believers, who thought they'd never live to see the answer to their prayers; simple believers, who grasped little of geopolitical facts and circumstances and theories but knew they held the power to change their world in their folded hands. Inspired by heroic leaders like Lech Walesa and Pope John Paul, good people on both sides of the Iron Curtain worked as though everything depended on themselves, and they prayed as though everything depended on God.

And I remember how moving it was in 1987 when I, as Vice President, I stood with now-President Walesa on the balcony of Father Popieluszko's church that I'm sure many of you have visited in Warsaw, flashing the victory sign to thousands of supporters below; that when the Communists were still in power, I stood at his side, and we both did that. And once again, the church was central to the Polish people's yearning for freedom.

And then when I had the privilege in 1989 as President to stand with Lech Walesa and thousands of those freedom-loving Poles at the Gdansk Shipyard, when I saw the faith and courage of those people, you just knew, I knew in my heart what you've known for a long time as true believers, that freedom would prevail.

Even in the darkest days, we stood steadfast for Poland's right to be free. We kept the alliances strong. We gave humanitarian aid to Solidarity when it was needed the most. Today, as Ed mentioned, we continue to give assistance, helping Poland build a stable democracy, a prospering economy. In addition to the substantial financial aid, I understand the 1,000th cargo container of American humanitarian supplies was just sent on its way to Poland. And it's a wonderful thing. And I've just written Poland's President to offer further help in bringing more American investment to Poland.

Just as important has been the voluntary help from the church, from organized labor, from the Polish-American community. History will honor the role of Polonia, the worldwide Polish community, for giving birth to a new age of freedom. And to symbolize this, this year we will fulfill the dying wish of Mr. Paderewski and send his remains for burial in the sacred soil of a free Poland.

And yes, the world is safer and freer now, but we must not forget those who still have not won full freedom. I think especially of those brave people of those Republics of a disintegrating Yugoslavia who are seeking to establish their sovereign independence. As we told our European allies last week, we are giving positive consideration to the recognition of Slovenia and Croatia. We're also considering the most appropriate ways to meet the desire for peaceful transition to independence on the part of the other republics.

Our leadership for freedom must continue. You know that. No one knows better; no one knows that better than Polish-Americans. No one knows better the rewards of staying strong and engaged in the world.

No one knows better than you the tragic harm that can come from weakness and isolation. We are going to keep working together. We're going to secure the peace and win new prosperity for Poland and all the free world.

So we've got to continue changing the world, and we must redouble our efforts to change America for the better. We've got to get this economy moving and create good jobs and strengthen our families and put limits on big Government. When I think of family values, I think of the times that I've been in the Polish-American community. And it's family that gives the communities their strength. And we must hope that that can be extended all across the United States of America. In essence, we are going to keep working together. We're going to secure the peace and win new prosperity. And we're going to keep on doing everything we can to create good jobs, to strengthen the families, as I say, and put limits on the big Government.

Let me close with a fable about liberal social planners that reminds me of Lech Walesa's down-to-earth humor. It's a story Russians used to tell during the last days of communism. A farmer's chickens were dying. So for help he went to the Communist Party hack who was the local agricultural commissar. And the commissar said, "Give them aspirin." And over the next few days, 50 chickens dropped dead. The commissar then said, "Give them penicillin." And in a few days, 100 more chickens died. So the commissar advised castor oil. After the castor oil therapy, the farmer went to the commissar and announced that all the remaining chickens had died. "What a pity. What a pity," the commissar said. "I had so many other ideas I wanted to try." [*Laughter*]

Well let me tell you this: As long as I am President, American families will not be guinea pigs for social planners. And we are going to keep family, dignity, work, and responsibility first, and we are going to make this country better. And this country was built on family, faith, and freedom, and we must renew those sources of our strength.

As Barbara and I count our many blessings, and we have a lot to be grateful for, we know that we can count on Polish-Americans to move this country forward to new glories.

And let me say this: When the economy is tough, and it has been, some suggest we turn inward. Some suggest that we forget what's going on across the oceans. As long as I am President of the United States, recognizing that it is only the United States of America, it's only our country that can lead for freedom and democracy, I will stay involved. I am not going to pull back into some fortress America. We are not going to forget our responsibilities to lead around the world.

And Poland deserves our support, and as long as I am President, they will have it. And I want to end by thanking every person in this room because not one single person here ever gave up hope for this glorious time that we see: a free Poland moving to strengthen its democracy, strengthen its hold on freedom.

Thank you for what you've done. You set a great example for the rest of the country. Many, many thanks. God bless America.

*Note: The President spoke at 3:35 p.m. at the headquarters of the Polish National Alliance. In his remarks, he referred to Edward J. Moskal and Aloysius Mazewski, president and former president of the alliance; Edward Dykla, president of the Polish Roman Catholic Union of America; Bishop Joseph Zawistowski of the Polish National Church; Reverend Frank Phillips, pastor of St. John Cantius Church in Chicago; and Stefan Cardinal Wyszynski, former Primate of Poland.*

# Remarks at a Bush-Quayle Fundraising Dinner in Chicago
## March 16, 1992

Thank you very much, Jim Edgar. And Brenda, thank you for being here. And may I say how very lucky I am to have Jim Edgar heading my campaign here in this so important State. He's doing a superb job as your Governor, and I'm lucky to have him as our chairman.

And there are a lot of Members of Congress here, I think. Bob Dornan, I'm very pleased that Congressman Dornan could be here, winning the long-distance award. Bob Mosbacher, our former Secretary of Commerce, was to be here. I haven't seen him, but he's doing a superb job as the cochairman of our national campaign. You met Bobby Holt, who is our national finance chairman. And let me quickly thank Andrea Parish for her beautiful rendition of "The Star-Spangled Banner" and my old friend, my dear friend Henry Hyde for participating in the program and the invocation, great Illinois Congressman. And of course, Pat Ryan, who just outdid himself, bossing everybody around and raising all this money. What a superb job he's done putting together this event. Thank you very, very much.

And let me also salute one that Pat singled out, my good friend Rich Williamson. Believe me, Illinois needs this man in the United States Senate. And so please vote for him. And I noticed the fitting hand you gave Bob Michel, and I want to salute him as our leader in the House and the other Republican Members of the Illinois congressional delegation with us today. And a special thanks to our Bush-Quayle finance chairman, Bill Cellini, from downstate; and Jim Kenny—Bill, I see the Cellini family is here—and of course, another old friend, a regional chairman, Bill Ylvisaker here. I am very, very grateful to all of these people.

And as a bit of a name dropper, I too would like to salute the Chicago Bears who are with us tonight and say how very pleased I am they're here. And I often say when I'm away from Washington, I worry that I've left Congress "Home Alone." [*Laughter*] Well, Barbara and I got a kick out of meeting Macaulay Culkin there who is with us tonight. Where are you, Macaulay? Here he is, this guy; he's wonderful.

And thanks for being with us. That's it. I recognize him. He goes like that.

But anyway, it's a great evening, and it's great to be back in Chicago. And I might point out with great pride that I've imported my own Illinois army to Washington. And you've heard their names, but the Secretary of Agriculture, Ed Madigan, doing a superb job trying to bring this GATT round to a successful conclusion; Ed Derwinski, working well in the Veterans Administration and helping us through all the great ethnic communities of Illinois. Ed's the Secretary of Veterans Affairs. And of course, you know and I know Lynn Martin so well, former Congresswoman, now Secretary of Labor, and also doing a great job. And when I was looking to hire a Chief of Staff, once again we turned to Illinois, and Sam Skinner rose to the challenge. And I think he's doing an outstanding job, and I'm glad he's here.

Someone once wrote that "Chicago does not lie there, waiting for things to happen. Chicago moves, making things happen." This year, the people of Chicago and the people of this great State are going to make things happen again. The choices we make will affect not only the next election, they will really affect the next generation as well. We are now in a battle for our future. We want America to lead the world in good jobs with productive work. We want to remain a force for world peace and freedom. And we're fighting to protect our most basic institution, and that is the American family.

That's why this year of decision is so important for America. That's why tomorrow's primary election and November's general election are vital to our future. I'm asking you to get out the vote and create a resounding mandate to literally transform America. Let's nominate and elect men and women who share our values. We've got more to do to get America on the right track. We've got more to do. So I'm asking you for 4 more years as your President to get this job done.

America was built on family and faith and freedom. These form the foundation of our great country. And we must now renew those sources of our strength. We must, for example, allow common sense to prevail in our welfare system. We've got to forge a new connection between welfare and work. When Chicago, the "City That Works," finds that 17 percent of its population dependent on welfare, something's wrong.

Americans aren't cold-hearted. We're a caring people. Americans support welfare for families in need. But Americans want to see government at every level work together to track down the deadbeat dads, the ones who can't be bothered to pay child support. They want to see us break this cycle of dependency that destroys dignity and passes down poverty from one generation to the next. That's wrong. That's cruel. And I'll tell you this: We are working hard to change it. My administration will continue to encourage the States to innovate with plans that help people break welfare dependency and begin learning work skills.

Here's another way that we can fight for the family: We can give parents the right to choose their children's schools. Our students learn and grow by competing in school, and our schools will improve by competing for students. School choice is one of the things at the heart of America 2000; that's our new education strategy to literally revolutionize American education.

You hear a lot of people on the other side in these campaigns complaining and talking about what they're going to do. We have an outstanding program right now to revolutionize education in this country. And it's based on this: We believe that parents, not some bureaucrat in Washington, know what is best for their children. That's why we also worked in the same vein to win a child care bill that gives parents the right to choose who provides the care. We know America is first as long as we put the family first.

For 3 years I've had to fight—Bob Michel knows this, and Henry and the others here, John Porter—we've had to fight the liberal leadership of Congress on these issues. And I will continue to stand and fight for principle even when Congress stands in the way. And I will use the veto when I have to, to stand for principle, to stand up for these family values. As it is, some say, some of my friends have said that at times I was courting defeat by casting a veto instead of cutting a deal. But we've never lost a veto fight. And I will never hesitate to use the power of the pen when principle is at stake.

One more thing, and it's important: I am going to continue to put judges on the bench who know that their role is to interpret, to interpret the law, not legislate from the Federal bench. And we are making dramatic moves in that direction.

You remember I've asked Congress to pass tax cuts and incentives to get the economy moving, back in the State of the Union Message, to get real estate up and running, to reward the risk-takers who create jobs. It's about time Congress does what it should have done long ago, get more American jobs by cutting the tax on capital gains.

But instead of passing my plan, the big spenders that control the Congress have other ideas. In the House, a temporary tax cut for more people. In the Senate, a permanent cut for less people. How much? Twenty-five cents, a quarter a day for each man, woman, and child. And you say, "What's the catch?" A permanent tax increase of $90 billion. Temporary cut, 25 cents a day, and a permanent increase of $90 billion. The Democrats call that new revenue. I call it your money. If the liberal leadership sends me their scheme, I am going to veto it the minute it hits my desk. And there's going to be no fooling around, compromising with that.

Remember, I set a deadline, March 20th. That's just 4 days away. This deadline was set back in January, moons ago. Four days away, and I said to Congress, "Pass our plan. Do something that will really move this economy. Get it moving. Do something now for the American people."

Well, we'll fight, and we will win. And we'll keep to our course of leadership in the world economy because if we want to succeed economically at home, we have got to lead economically abroad. I spoke about this in December when I visited the Merc over here, the Mercantile Exchange. And those folks are out there on the front line, on the frontier of the global marketplace, and they know what I mean. So do your exporters in this great State. Illinois exports about $35 billion a year in manufactured goods. Over 400,000 Illinois jobs depend on exports. Think of it: This is the city that gave the world Sears and Wrigley and Motorola and

McDonald's hamburgers. That's free markets. That's free trade. That's my idea of how America competes and how America succeeds.

But what are we hearing now, because economic times are hard? We hear the opponents peddling protectionism, a retreat from economic reality. You cut through all the patriotic posturing, all the tough talk about fighting back by closing shop, and look closely. That is not the American flag they're waving. It's the white flag of surrender. And that is not the America that you and I know. We do not cut and run; we compete. Never in this Nation's long history have we turned our backs on a challenge, and we simply are not going to start doing that now.

I put my faith in the American worker. And I'm not about to sell our workers short. So what we're trying to do is open more markets, level the playing field. And you watch, the American worker will outthink, outproduce, outperform anyone, anywhere, anytime. The answer is not protection. It is more competition.

We must let the world know this: Whatever the challenge, America will meet it because we are in it to win. Think back, if you will, to a year ago, to the calm after Desert Storm. Ask any one of the proud sons and daughters of Illinois who became liberators of Kuwait, and they'll tell you military strength doesn't mean a thing without moral support right here at home.

Yes, I understand it, there were some who didn't support us then. There are those who second-guess us now. But not here, not in this State. When I drew that line in the sand, you stood with me. Never would this country tuck tail and let aggression stand. And we did what was good, and we did what was just, and we did what was right.

There are those who act as if America's work in the world is over now. To them I say this: We will never neglect America's vital national interests. We are never going to pull back. And as far as our national defense goes, I will continue to keep this country strong. Our worldwide credibility— ask anyone here that's traveled abroad—our worldwide credibility is now at an all-time high. And it will help us strengthen democracy, freedom, and peace around the world. And only the United States of America can lead the world. And as long as I am President I will stay involved and do just exactly that. We are not going to pull back.

So, let these opponents sound the retreat and run away from the new realities and seek refuge in a world of protectionism or gut our defense so we couldn't guarantee anybody security. Let them talk about the high taxes and provide us with more big Government. Let those analysts on TV tick off everything that's wrong in America. And I think it's time that somebody stood up and said what is right about this great country. And that's what I plan to do right now, on into the end of the year.

And one more thing: I'm counting on the good people of Illinois to reject the ugly politics of hate that is rearing its head lately. Remember, America is great because America is good. And racism and anti-Semitism and bigotry have no place in the United States of America at all, a campaign or in life, any other way. And we ought to denounce it for what it is.

Now let me just close by just saying that Barbara and I are blessed. We talk about it. I don't know that she will be pleasant to live with after that warm ovation you gave here—[*laughter*]—but I do think it's deserved. I think she's doing a first-class job out there for the—[*applause*]. But we talk about this, just as other families talk about things. And we are very, very blessed, blessed to serve this wonderful country of ours at a time when so many of the old fears have been driven away, when so many new opportunities stand within our reach.

And since the day I took the oath of office, I made it my duty always to try to do what's right for the country. I've given it my level-best, and I'm not done yet. I'm not

finished. You and I have much more work ahead before we've finished our mission. I think we've done a lot. I think it's a wonderful thing that little Andrea there or our "Home Alone" guy might go to sleep at night with not having the fear about nuclear weapons that the generation before them had. I think that's a wonderful thing. And I'm proud to have had a little part in that.

But there's so much more to do. And what it is, is a battle for our future, and it is about jobs and family and peace and the kind of legacy we're going to leave our kids or our grandkids. And I am absolutely convinced of this, believing in the goodness of our country, believing that this economy that's been so troublesome is fixin' to turn and move, I am convinced that together we can renew the miracle of American enterprise. We can strengthen our values, the underlying values of our family, faith, and freedom.

And now we're approaching an hour of decision tomorrow. And please don't wait until November. I'm asking you to vote on March 17th in the Republican primary. And give me your vote in this important election tomorrow. And help me win the greatest opportunity an American can have, 4 more years to fight, to lead the fight for the value we share.

And thank you, and may God bless the United States of America. Thank you very, very much. Thank you all.

*Note: The President spoke at 8:10 p.m. at the Hyatt Regency Chicago Hotel. In his remarks, he referred to Brenda Edgar, wife of Gov. Jim Edgar; Patrick G. Ryan, dinner chairman; James Kenny, Illinois Bush-Quayle campaign cochairman; and Representative John Porter.*

# Letter to Congressional Leaders on Iraq's Compliance With United Nations Security Council Resolutions
*March 16, 1992*

*Dear Mr. Speaker: (Dear Mr. President:)*
Consistent with the Authorization for Use

of Military Force Against Iraq Resolution (Public Law 102–1), and as part of my continuing effort to keep the Congress fully informed, I am again reporting on the status of efforts to obtain compliance by Iraq with the resolutions adopted by the U.N. Security Council.

Since I last reported on January 14, 1992, Iraq has continued its noncompliance with the relevant Security Council resolutions. As a result, United Nations Special Commission (UNSCOM) Chairman Rolf Ekeus was dispatched by the Secretary General of the United Nations to Iraq, where he met Iraqi Minister of State Sahaf, Foreign Minister Hussein, and Deputy Prime Minister Aziz. Iraqi cooperation has not improved. The U.N. Security Council released a statement on February 28 demanding Iraq's appearance in the Council no later than the week of March 9, 1992. Iraq has agreed and has sent a delegation to New York.

Nevertheless, the International Atomic Energy Agency (IAEA) and UNSCOM have continued to conduct inspections and other activities related to Iraqi weapons of mass destruction and ballistic missiles. Two nuclear inspections have been conducted since my last report. With the help of the German Government, UNSCOM/IAEA inspectors uncovered equipment in Iraq sufficient to support thousands of production centrifuges for enriching uranium.

The first chemical weapons destruction team is now in Iraq and has begun exploding Iraqi chemical-filled rockets. It is estimated that destruction will take approximately 18 months. In an example of Iraqi noncompliance, members of a chemical weapons inspection team recently were jostled at the entrance of their Baghdad hotel and pinned against the wall by a group of demonstrators as a larger group trapped the rest of the team on its bus for over 20 minutes. The Iraqi police simply observed.

The most recent example of Iraqi noncompliance came in the one ballistic missile inspection completed since my last report. This team was to begin the destruction of UNSCOM-designated Iraqi facilities and equipment used in the production of ballistic missiles. Because Iraq refused to comply, the team was withdrawn on February 29, 1992, pending the visit of a high-level Iraqi mission to the United Nations Security Council.

The Special Commission reported Iraq's noncompliance to the U.N. Security Council on February 28, 1992. Despite UNSCOM's observation of the destruction of 62 missiles and other equipment months ago, the United States believes that Iraq still possesses large numbers of undeclared ballistic missiles.

The United States continues to assist the United Nations in its activities, through U–2 surveillance flights, the provision of intelligence, and expert inspectors. The shortage of readily available funds to UNSCOM remains critical, in spite of our additional infusion of $2 million last month. The United Nations and the United States have agreed on the transfer of a $10 million U.S. arrearage payment to UNSCOM, pending completion of the funds' reprogramming.

Since my last report, there has been additional progress in implementing the resolution of the Security Council concerning compensation of the victims of the unlawful invasion and occupation of Kuwait. The Governing Council of the United Nations Compensation Commission held its fourth formal session in Geneva January 20–24, 1992, and continued to make progress in establishing the framework for processing claims. The Governing Council adopted ceiling amounts for compensation of nonmonetary losses for mental pain and anguish on the part of persons who, for example, were held hostage or forced into hiding, received serious personal injury, or suffered the death of an immediate family member. The Governing Council also considered additional guidance on compensation for business losses. Meanwhile, the Department of State has begun collecting from U.S. individuals claims under $100,000, in preparation for filing them with the United Nations Compensation Commission by July 1, 1992, for expedited processing. The Governing Council has scheduled meetings in March and June to address further issues concerning the compensation program.

In accordance with paragraph 20 of Resolution 687, the Sanctions Committee continues to receive notice of shipments of foodstuffs to Iraq. From March to December 1991, 5.4 million metric tons of foodstuffs were notified. The Sanctions Committee also continues to consider and, when appropriate, approve requests to send to Iraq materials and supplies for essential civilian needs. Iraq to date has refused, however, to utilize the opportunity under Resolutions 706 and 712 to sell $1.6 billion in oil for use in purchasing foodstuffs, medicines, materials, and supplies for essential civilian needs of its civilian population. Saddam bears full responsibility for the resulting suffering in Iraq.

Attention to possible illegal exports to Iraq has been focused on company names compiled during inspections in Iraq. We have received from UNSCOM a preliminary list of U.S. company names whose equipment has been seen in Iraq by U.N. inspectors. We provided this list, on a confidential basis, to investigative agencies and appropriate congressional committees.

Through the International Committee of the Red Cross (ICRC), the United States, Kuwait, and our allies continue to press the Government of Iraq to comply with its obligations under Security Council resolutions to return all detained Kuwaiti and third-country nationals. Likewise, the United

States and its allies continue to press the Government of Iraq to return to Kuwait all property and equipment removed from Kuwait by Iraq. Iraq continues to resist full cooperation on these issues and to resist unqualified ICRC access to detention facilities in Iraq.

As I stated in previous reports, in concert with our Coalition partners, we will continue to monitor carefully the treatment of Iraq's citizens, and together we remain prepared to take appropriate steps if the situation requires. To this end, we will continue to maintain an appropriate level of forces in the region for as long as required by the situation in Iraq.

I remain grateful for the support of the Congress for these efforts, and I look forward to continued cooperation toward achieving our mutual objectives.

Sincerely,

GEORGE BUSH

*Note: Identical letters were sent to Thomas S. Foley, Speaker of the House of Representatives, and Robert C. Byrd, President pro tempore of the Senate.*

# Nomination of Betty Jo Nelsen To Be an Assistant Secretary of Agriculture
*March 16, 1992*

The President today announced his intention to nominate Betty Jo Nelsen, of Wisconsin, to be an Assistant Secretary of Agriculture for Food and Consumer Services and a member of the Board of Directors of the Commodity Credit Corporation. She would succeed Catherine Ann Bertini.

Currently Ms. Nelsen serves as Administrator of the Food and Nutrition Service at the U.S. Department of Agriculture in Washington, DC. Prior to this, she served as

a State representative for the Wisconsin Assembly, 1979–1990; chairman of the Republican assembly campaign committee, 1987–1988; and area coordinator for the Milwaukee voluntary action center involvement corps, 1976–1978.

Ms. Nelsen graduated from Massachusetts State College (B.S., 1957). She was born October 11, 1935, in Boston, MA. Ms. Nelsen is married, has three children, and resides in Arlington, VA.

## Remarks on Presenting the Presidential Medal of Freedom to Samuel M. Walton in Bentonville, Arkansas
*March 17, 1992*

Thank you all. Mr. Sam, now, you sit down. And thank you, David. Good morning to all. And it is a true pleasure to be in America's heartland. And it is most appropriate that I should come to Arkansas to participate in this ceremony.

First, I will apologize to every single person with whom our advance squad, security people, communications people have come into contact—[*laughter*]—because I know your lives—but we pledge to those who have made these wonderful arrangements that we will leave right on schedule. [*Laughter*] And we will leave with a heart full of gratitude to all who handled, on very short notice, the arrangements that go with a visit of this nature.

You know, I got a letter last year from a young eighth grader, John Quinton Bagley, in Nashville, Arkansas. And he wrote, "You and Mrs. Bush could stay with me and my family. We do not have many reporters." [*Laughter*] Smart kids in Arkansas. No wonder I feel so at home here.

But first, of course, my respects to Sam Walton and to Helen Walton, one of God's truly special people. And also, my respects to Bud Walton. Also to the one you've just heard from, ahead of David Glass, John Paul Hammerschmidt. This, I think he and I figured, was my fifth district—not to the State but just to his part of it, his congressional district, first one as President. And I must say, I have been so pleased and so has Barbara as we rode in from Fayetteville and were warmly received by the people who just seemed glad to see the President of the United States. But in any event, you just have this wonderful way of making someone feel at home.

And also I salute David Pryor. And this is trivia that I'm sure no one is interested in, but I'll tell it to you anyway. He and John Paul and I were all elected to the Congress on the same day many moons ago, November 1966. And I am very pleased that both David, of course, and John Paul are here to join us as we fittingly honor Mr. Walton. In addition, I brought along our own grandson Sam. I wanted him to meet another Sam. He's standing over here, ripped off my Wal-Mart hat. But there he is, so—[*laughter*].

But anyway, we come here to honor a man who shows that through hard work and vision and treating people right, many good things can happen.

This visit is not about Sam Walton's wealth. He has earned his money, and that's his business. He's been generous with his fortune, and that is in the great tradition of America's commitment to this concept that I call a Thousand Points of Light.

It's not about money. It's not even about philanthropy. This visit is about what is fundamentally good and right about our country. And it's about determination. It's about leadership. It's about decency. His Nation honors him today as the outstanding example of American initiative and achievement. And at the same time, we take note that as he became more and more successful he never turned his back on his roots. His success never altered his lifestyle, a lifestyle that kept him close to his family, his friends, and his community.

I read somewhere that at one time Mr. Sam thought he wanted to be President of the United States. I have two thoughts on that one: One, I'm glad he's not running this year. [*Laughter*] And two, I've said he's a smart guy; not running proves it. [*Laughter*]

His story is known to everyone here, but let me just mention for the Nation a few of the highlights, if I might. After college at the University of Missouri, Sam Walton began a career in retailing. He started as a trainee for the J.C. Penney Company in Des Moines, Iowa. And after a stint in the Army during World War II, it was on to Newport, Arkansas, with a Ben Franklin store back in 1945. And over the years, he became the largest franchisee of Ben Franklin variety stores, operating 15 of them under the name of Walton's Five and Dime.

You see—you know this, but many around the country might not—you see, he had hit upon a combination that was to form the basis of the strategy of today's Wal-Mart Stores, smalltown markets for name-brand merchandise sold at a discount. When the folks at Ben Franklin's Chicago headquarters didn't jump at the vision that Mr. Sam put before them, he decided to go his own way. And that was back in 1962 when he started with one Wal-Mart store in Rogers, Arkansas, just 6 miles from here.

And I did hear a story about the opening of his second Wal-Mart over in Harrison, John Paul's hometown. [*Laughter*] Obviously you've heard it, but I'm going to repeat it. For those of you in Washington, I will repeat it. The way my esteemed friend David Glass tells it, Sam had watermelons for sale on the sidewalk; he offered donkey rides in the parking lot. The only problem was the heat, 110 degrees, 110. Well, the watermelons popped, and the watermelon juice was everywhere. The donkeys did what donkeys do in a situation like that, tracking the stuff all over the place. And according to David, who had a nice successful business of his own, Sam's turned into the worst looking store he'd ever seen. Dave went so far as to suggest to Sam that he ought to find some other line of work. [*Laughter*]

Now more people work for Sam's company than live in Tulsa, Oklahoma, 380,000 at the last count. This includes the man with that sound career advice, David Glass. [*Laughter*]

You know, some always think I see the glass as half full or maybe that I'm always emphasizing good news. Well, maybe that's right. But I think it's important that all Americans understand that some things are going very, very well in the United States of America. And one of those things is Wal-Mart. And who would have thought that when Sam Walton bought that first Ben Franklin store that his little venture would grow into a top-rated stock on Wall Street, racking up $44 billion in sales last year. Wal-Mart is the largest and the most profitable retailer in America, now with over 1,700 stores, enhancing the lives of millions.

And to Sam, or Mr. Sam, as he is known throughout his company, people don't just punch a time clock and draw a paycheck. As the people here know, his employees are known as associates. And no wonder they all think of him as a partner. When he's asked about the secret of his success, he credits his people. And he says, "The attitude of our employees, our associates, is that things are different in our company, and they deserve the credit." And it's not hard to see why they believe in the company. And it's just plain easy to see why they believe in its unpretentious leader.

There are also the quiet things about Sam Walton, the things beyond the bottom line, if you will. There's nothing corny about calling them what they are: They're good deeds. They are the relief funds set up when tragedy strikes an associate's family; scholarships in every community where there's a Wal-Mart store; benefactor of the University of the Ozarks in Clarksville; the Walton National Literacy Center in Bolivar over in Missouri; education grants for South American students to study in America and then return so they can better help their own countries.

These are the things that enhance the spirit of the community. And yes, of course Mr. Sam's a great businessman. But along with making a good profit, he helps make good citizens of his people by encouraging them to help one another.

And when you ask about Sam Walton, much of what you hear is from friends of many years. Some are wonderful stories that tell you something important about Sam's energy and competitive spirit; like George Billingsley, who used to fly with Mr. Sam in the early days. They'd be in a little Piper Cub heading out to check out one of his stores, and Mr. Sam would decide to check out the competition as well. He'd fly low over a Sears or a K-Mart, you see, tip one wing, and make a wide-eyed George count the cars in the parking lot, scaring him half to death in the process. [*Laughter*]

I could go on and on about his love of the outdoors. Bud took me into the illustrious quail room just a few minutes ago before we came in here: Talk about his sharp eye for quail, his love for riding around with his gone-but-not-forgotten closest adviser, his dog Roy, in that old red pickup truck, or perhaps his legendary driving record. [*Laughter*] Since 1988 things have gone better; he's had a white pickup, but I hear the driving is about the same. [*Laughter*]

I could also talk about his love of family, such a mainstay of his life. You talk about Helen Walton who, as Senator Pryor told me on the way down, is the soul of Wal-Mart. Her love of the arts inspires so many. Her faith, her deep faith in God, comes shining through.

The story of Sam Walton is an illustration of the American dream. His success is our success, America's success. And when Sam's grandchildren read about what makes America great, they'll read about people who have grand ideas and great dreams, resourceful people who make imagination come alive with accomplishment. And they'll read about adventurous people who have the drive, ambition, and talent to take big risks and to achieve great things; people who bring prosperity to their community and to their country. Sam's grandkids, like my own little guy over here, his down here, will read about people like Sam Walton.

And sir, you are generous and genuine, tireless and tenacious. You took risks and helped our country grow vigorous and strong. You brought out the best in people.

You and Helen have honored the important things in life: friendship, faith, and family. And at a time when young Americans look for role models, those are noble virtues. And your life is going to help them appreciate that ours is the freest, most blessed country on the face of the Earth. I salute you, sir, for your vision, and I am proud to give you your Nation's highest civilian honor.

And now, may I ask you all to be seated as we honor a man who loves his country, who loves his family, given far more than he's gotten.

And now if Major Cancilla of the United States Army will read the citation, I will present to Sam Walton the Medal of Freedom.

*Note: The President spoke at 11:08 a.m. at Wal-Mart Headquarters. In his remarks, he referred to Helen Walton, Mr. Walton's wife; James L. (Bud) Walton, Mr. Walton's brother and cofounder of Wal-Mart; David Glass, president and chief executive officer of Wal-Mart Stores, Inc.; Representative John Paul Hammerschmidt; Senator David Pryor; George Billingsley, Bentonville businessman and longtime friend of the Walton family; and Maj. Russell J. Cancilla, Army Aide to the President.*

# Remarks at a St. Patrick's Day Ceremony and an Exchange With Reporters
*March 17, 1992*

*The President.* May I just say to Minister Andrews how delighted I am to be here. I missed the traditional lunch on Capitol Hill, a lunch of genuine friendship between not only the parties here, but normally Ireland is so well-represented, as they were today. And as I think everyone knows, I was down in Arkansas for a Medal of Freedom ceremony. But may I say to our friends from Ireland, particularly the Minister, how sorry I am to miss the luncheon but how pleased I am to receive you here.

It gives me an opportunity to express, once again, the feeling I have and the feel-

ing the American people have about the Irish-American relationship. It is strong. It is good. And it is very, very important to us. And this ceremonial occasion gives me a chance to extend through the Minister to the people in Ireland our respects, our love, and our affection on this very special day.

So Mr. Minister, I'm glad you came our way, sir. And I'm delighted to have had this short visit.

[*At this point, Foreign Minister David Andrews of Ireland spoke and presented the President with a crystal bowl filled with*

*Irish shamrocks.*]

*The President.* Thank you very, very much.

*Q.* Mr. President, will the luck of the Irish be with Pat Buchanan on this day?

*Foreign Minister Andrews.* Yes and no, he asked me to say.

*The President.* I've got to put a little shamrock in here.

*Foreign Minister Andrews.* Did you want to say something in response?

*The President.* No.

### House Bank Controversy

*Q.* How about Secretary Cheney, Martin, and Madigan bouncing checks, Mr. President?

*The President.* No, I have no comment on all that. I just got home and am looking about it. I heard that Secretary Cheney, as would be expected, did an outstanding job. I haven't seen the testimony, but needless to say I have great confidence in him, total confidence in his integrity. And I just haven't heard anything about any of the others.

What I've decided to do is let this matter unfold. It's a matter of considerable agony for good people on the Hill. And let's get the facts out, and then I think the American people are very smart. They will be able to make a determination as to what was wrongdoing and who were simply victims of a system that obviously has failed everybody. And so we'll just wait and see how that works out. But I have no further comment on that subject at all, so spare yourselves the agony of asking because I simply will not take any more questions on it on this marvelous St. Patrick's Day.

*Foreign Minister Andrews.* Irish journalist here.

*The President.* Sure.

### Northern Ireland

*Q.* Mr. President, what role can the United States play in bringing forward the progress for peace in Northern Ireland?

*The President.* Well, I'm not sure. I think heretofore we've tried to be a catalytic role, tried to support, as the Minister generally said, certain funds. But we've got to be in close touch with the Government. But it is not a problem that we ourselves can work

out. It is a problem that because of the many Americans of Irish heritage we are vitally interested in and because of Ireland's own substantial role in the EC that we're vitally interested in, and as Ireland-U.S. relations that we're vitally interested in. But we simply are not in a position to dictate a solution, to in any way be the sole arbiter of this difficult situation. But I've told the Minister we would like to help in any way he deems possible. But again, it isn't easy, as he and I both know.

### Loan Guarantees for Israel

*Q.* Mr. President, the Israeli loan guarantees, are they dead?

*The President.* What did you say?

*Q.* The Israeli loan guarantees, are they dead now?

*The President.* Well, I don't think they're dead. We have always wanted to go forward with loan guarantees. Our administration has been in the forefront of bringing and encouraging people to go home to Israel, whether it be from the Soviet Union or Ethiopia. We have a longstanding policy that feels that settlements are counterproductive to peace. This is not a new policy. This is a longstanding policy. And I am determined to see that that policy not be altered.

However, if there's room within that policy to do what we'd like to do, which is to support the people coming home, why, we'd like to do that. But settlements are counterproductive to peace, and everybody knows that. So we'll just have to wait and see. I have made my position very, very clear to the Congress, and Secretary Baker has done the same thing. And we have close historic relations with Israel, and they will always be that way. But we have a difference now, it appears, in terms of these settlements. But I have said over and over again that we want to help, we want to help in a humanitarian way, but that we simply are not going to shift and change the foreign policy of this country.

Yes, Brit [Brit Hume, ABC News]? And then I've got to go because I don't want to be rude to our guests. I want to say hello to our other friends here.

*Q.* What is your view, sir, of the compromise that was discussed yesterday on the Hill that's been offered there? I understand you're about to meet with Senator Leahy.

*The President.* Well, I'm not sure which one you're talking about.

*Q.* Well, do you have something to say to Senator Leahy that might——

*The President.* No, I'm listening. They asked for a meeting with me, and I'm very glad to have a meeting with him. Secretary Baker has had many meetings with Senator Leahy. I talked to him over the weekend, and I look forward to the meeting. But we'll see what it is that he has on his mind. But our policy is very, very clear, Brit, and I just hope everybody understands that. It's not that we're shifting ground. And it's not that we are being—in my view, I don't think we're being difficult. We're being consistent.

Yes? Then I've got to go. I really do.

*House Bank Controversy*

*Q.* Why are you confident that you yourself did not bounce any checks? Were you able to go through your own records during your time?

*The President.* Well, I'll tell you, I went through whatever I've got. I was in Congress 1967 to 1970. You were about 4 at the time. And I can't find checks back that long; most people in America don't save them. I did find a ledger sheet that shows I have positive balances at the beginning—for 4 years, my own bookkeeping—have positive balances at beginning of every month, at the end. And I take great pride in the fact I don't bounce checks. But heavens knows, with the way the operation went up there, whether there's anything to it or not. I don't believe so. I'd like to be able to say I didn't do it. But I just don't know yet.

*Q.* Do you sympathize though with some Members of Congress who say the same things you did? They don't bounce checks either; they didn't bounce checks——

*The President.* Yes, I do. I——

*Q.* ——and then they found out that they did.

*The President.* Yes, I can understand it. If, in other words, somebody writes a check and then he puts a stop order on it, and they go ahead and cash the check, and he's overdrawn—absolutely. Of course, I sympathize with that. And I think there's a major institutional problem. The bank's been closed now. But I'll have more to say about that when the facts are out there. But I will, in the meantime, grunge through every file I can find stored away in little cubbyholes here or in Houston, Texas, and try to find checks from 1967 to 1970. And I challenge everybody out here to try to do the same thing so his conscience or hers will be clear when they're asking these questions. And all you young ones can't go back that far. But for us, please, all my vintage, go back and see if you can find those checks from 25 years ago.

*Q.* Does that mean there's some question in your mind then, sir, that——

*The President.* What?

*Q.* Does that suggest there's some question in your mind whether you did bounce a check?

*The President.* No, I have no question, but when I hear the fact that checks were stopped and then they went ahead and didn't stop them, why, who knows? But I don't think I ever did that. I really do feel very—my conscience is very clear on this. And I hope I can satisfy this understandable inquiry to go back that far.

*Presidential Primaries*

*Q.* What about Pat Buchanan, sir? When and how do you make peace with him, or does he have to talk to you?

*The President.* Well, I just keep my sights on these elections. And I think we'll do well today. It's a little early to tell. But what I've got to do is lead this country and then, in the meantime, take care of these primaries that crop up every Tuesday. And so far I'm very, very pleased with the results. And I'm going to keep plodding ahead and not criticize the opponent, just keep shooting for victory.

And I hope that we achieve that today in Michigan. I hope I achieve that today in Illinois. I felt good when I was in those two States, but it's a strange year. So we're taking nothing for granted. And yet, I cannot be out there campaigning. I was in each State one day. And I can't spend any more time doing that because I have responsibilities here and duties here, one of which is most pleasurable today, I might add, that I'm determined to fulfill.

*Q.* Can you and Pat make peace after all that's gone on?

*The President.* Well, I have a—I think so, yes; I really do.

*Q.* If Buchanan loses, should he get out?

*The President.* Let's go down and say hello.

*Note: The President spoke at 4:13 p.m. in the Rose Garden at the White House.*

# Message to the Congress Transmitting the Poland-United States Nuclear Energy Cooperation Agreement
## March 17, 1992

*To the Congress of the United States:*

I am pleased to transmit to the Congress, pursuant to sections 123 b. and 123 d. of the Atomic Energy Act of 1954, as amended (42 U.S.C. 2153(b), (d)), the text of a proposed Agreement for Cooperation Between the United States of America and the Republic of Poland Concerning Peaceful Uses of Nuclear Energy with accompanying annex and agreed minute. I am also pleased to transmit my written approval, authorization, and determination concerning the agreement, and the memorandum of the Director of the United States Arms Control and Disarmament Agency with the Nuclear Proliferation Assessment Statement concerning the agreement. The joint memorandum submitted to me by the Secretary of State and the Secretary of Energy, which includes a summary of the provisions of the agreement and various other attachments, including agency views, is also enclosed.

The proposed agreement with the Republic of Poland has been negotiated in accordance with the Atomic Energy Act of 1954, as amended by the Nuclear Non-Proliferation Act of 1978 and as otherwise amended. In my judgment, the proposed agreement meets all statutory requirements and will advance the non-proliferation and other foreign policy interests of the United States. It provides a comprehensive framework for peaceful nuclear cooperation between the United States and Poland under appropriate conditions and controls reflecting our strong common commitment to nuclear non-proliferation goals.

Poland has consistently supported international efforts to prevent the spread of nuclear weapons. It was an original signatory of the Non-Proliferation Treaty (NPT) and has strongly supported the Treaty. It is committed to implementing a responsible nuclear export policy, and declared in January 1978 that it intended to apply a full-scope safeguards nuclear export requirement. Poland supports the work of the NPT Exporters ("Zangger") Committee and adheres to the Nuclear Supplier Guidelines. It is a member of the International Atomic Energy Agency (IAEA) and has played a positive role in the Agency's safeguards and technical cooperation activities. It has also cooperated with the United States and other like-minded members in working to prevent the politicization of the Agency. Poland is a party to the Convention on the Physical Protection of Nuclear Material.

I believe that peaceful nuclear cooperation with Poland under the proposed agreement will be fully consistent with, and supportive of, our policy of responding positively and constructively to the process of democratization and economic reform in Eastern Europe. Cooperation under the agreement will also provide opportunities for U.S. business on terms that fully protect vital U.S. national security interests.

I have considered the views and recommendations of the interested agencies in reviewing the proposed agreement and have determined that its performance will promote, and will not constitute an unreasonable risk to, the common defense and security. Accordingly, I have approved the agreement and authorized its execution and urge that the Congress give it favorable consideration.

Because this agreement meets all applicable requirements of the Atomic Energy Act, as amended, for agreements for peaceful nuclear cooperation, I am transmitting it to the Congress without exempting it from any requirement contained in section 123 a. of that Act. This transmission shall constitute a submittal for purposes of both sections 123 b. and 123 d. of the Atomic Energy Act. The Administration is prepared to begin immediately the consultations with the Senate Foreign Relations and House Foreign Affairs Committees as provided in section 123 b. Upon completion of the 30-day continuous session period provided for in section 123 b., the 60-day continuous session period provided for in section 123 d. shall commence.

GEORGE BUSH

The White House,
March 17, 1992.

# Statement on the Illinois and Michigan Presidential Primary Victories
*March 17, 1992*

Tonight the people of Illinois and Michigan have added their voices to the Nation's call for congressional action on our plan to get this economy moving. The March 20th deadline is Friday. To the Democrats on Capitol Hill, I say it again: Pass my plan to get the economy growing and Americans working. Do something good for the American people.

We must reinvent our schools, transform welfare and health care. We need housing that is affordable and plentiful. We need safer neighborhoods and job security. We need to compete internationally for world markets.

The voters of Michigan and Illinois have endorsed my approach to change in America. They have pushed the delegate count to a level where my nomination is virtually assured. As the nominee of the Republican Party, I will seek the support of everyone who believes that we can change America as we changed the world.

Barbara and I thank the voters of Michigan and Illinois for placing their confidence in me. We appreciate the hard work of Governor Edgar in Illinois and Governor Engler in Michigan in making this win possible.

# Statement on Air Pollution Regulatory Relief
*March 18, 1992*

I am today announcing a series of steps that will help clean up air pollution in this country and, at the same time, will promote jobs by reducing regulatory costs to automobile companies and other major transportation industries.

One of these steps, our "cash for clunkers" program, will allow States and industries to buy old, high-polluting cars, take them off the road, and use the resulting pollutant reductions to satisfy Federal clean air standards. This is just one example of the innovative, market-based approaches to pollution reduction that have been pioneered by our Environmental Protection Agency. The result is a cleaner, healthier environment and a more competitive economy.

These and other regulatory changes being announced today should provide major benefits to the economy.

# Memorandum on the Federal Savings Bond Campaign
*March 18, 1992*

*Memorandum for the Heads of
Departments and Agencies*

As a Nation we need to promote thrift, increase personal savings, save to educate our children, and reduce the cost of Government financing. By supporting the Savings Bonds program, we help meet these needs. The 1992 Federal Savings Bond Campaign will soon begin. It has my full support.

In 1991, 32 percent of Federal employees and members of the Armed Services purchased Savings Bonds through payroll allotments. This year, I hope to see that participation increase significantly.

To this end I challenge you to charge your managers to accept and achieve the following goals in 1992:

1. To increase your department's/agency's participation level by 10 percent; and

2. To raise your department's/agency's participation rate from its current level to a minimum level of 40 percent; and

3. To have 20 percent of current bond buyers increase their allotments.

These goals are achievable. Currently, many departments and agencies have already achieved what I am asking of you.

I have appointed Manuel Lujan, Jr., Secretary of the Interior, to chair the 1992 Federal Savings Bond Campaign. Please appoint one of your top officers as your Vice Chair to work with Secretary Lujan and his team.

Your personal commitment will insure the success of this Campaign. I look forward to receiving your Campaign results.

GEORGE BUSH

# Statement by Press Secretary Fitzwater on the President's Telephone Conversation With President F.W. de Klerk of South Africa
*March 18, 1992*

The President telephoned President F.W. de Klerk of South Africa today to congratulate him on his victory in Tuesday's referendum. The two Presidents discussed the continuation of the negotiating process in the light of the results of the referendum. President Bush reiterated the United States support for the reform process now underway in South Africa.

# Appointment of Joshua B. Bolten as Deputy Assistant to the President and Director of the Office of Legislative Affairs
*March 18, 1992*

The President today announced his intention to appoint Joshua B. Bolten, of the District of Columbia, to be Deputy Assistant to the President and Director of the Office of Legislative Affairs. He would succeed Stephen T. Hart, who will be joining the Department of Transportation as a Deputy As- sistant Secretary for Industry Liaison.

Since 1989, Mr. Bolten has served as General Counsel at the Office of the U.S. Trade Representative. Previously he served as international trade counsel to the U.S. Senate Committee on Finance. In 1984–85, prior to joining the finance committee, Mr.

Bolten was in private practice in international trade law with the Washington, DC, office of O'Melveny & Myers. From 1981 to 1984, he worked in the Office of the Legal Adviser at the Department of State, providing legal counsel primarily to the Bureau of Inter-American Affairs. He also served as executive assistant to the Director, Kissinger Commission on Central America.

During 1980–81, Mr. Bolten served as a law clerk at the U.S. District Court in San Francisco.

Mr. Bolten received his undergraduate degree in 1976 from Princeton University. He graduated in 1980 from Stanford Law School, where he was an editor of the Stanford Law Review.

## Appointment of Kim Fogal McKernan as Special Assistant to the President for Legislative Affairs
*March 18, 1992*

The President today announced his intention to appoint Kim Fogal McKernan, of Pennsylvania, to be Special Assistant to the President for Legislative Affairs (House). She would succeed Frances M. Norris.

Since October 1990, Ms. McKernan has served as executive assistant to the Deputy Secretary of Defense. Prior to this assignment, she served as Principal Deputy Assistant Secretary of Defense for Force Management and Personnel. Ms. McKernan came to the Pentagon as part of Secretary Cheney's transition team in March 1989. She was then appointed assistant to the Secretary of Defense for political and intergovernmental affairs. Prior to her appointment at the Pentagon, Ms. McKernan served as associate director in the House Republican whip and House Republican conference organizations. From 1985 to 1987, she was the administrative assistant to Congressman Beau Boulter (R–TX). She began her career in the U.S. House of Representatives with Congressman Robert S. Walker (R–PA) in 1979, where she served as senior legislative assistant.

Ms. McKernan graduated from Shippensburg University (B.S., 1978). She and her husband, Robert T. McKernan, reside in Washington, DC.

## Statement on Signing the Morris K. Udall Scholarship and Excellence in National Environmental and Native American Public Policy Act of 1992
*March 19, 1992*

Today I am pleased to sign into law S. 2184, the "Morris K. Udall Scholarship and Excellence in National Environmental and Native American Public Policy Act of 1992."

S. 2184 is a tribute to Mo Udall's long and admirable service to the Nation. He was a thoughtful and creative Member of Congress for 30 years. I respect him greatly and count him among my friends. This bill honors Mo by creating a foundation that will support programs involving the environment and issues related to Native Americans and Alaska Natives.

Regrettably, I must note a serious deficiency in the bill. S. 2184 purports to set qualifications, including requirements as to political party affiliation, for the trustees who will administer the foundation created by the bill. Under the Appointments Clause of the Constitution, article II, section 2, clause 2, congressional participation in such appointments may be exercised only through the Senate's advice and consent with respect to Presidential nominees. Accordingly, I will treat these provisions as precatory.

One other point deserves mention. S. 2184 purports to "repeal" S. 1176, passed in the last session of the Congress and presented to me in December. Because the bill came to me during an adjournment of the Congress and I withheld my signature, S. 1176 never became law. Therefore, the section of S. 2184 purporting to repeal S. 1176 can have no effect.

GEORGE BUSH

The White House,
March 19, 1992.

*Note: S. 2184, approved March 19, was assigned Public Law No. 102–259.*

# Statement by Press Secretary Fitzwater on the President's Meeting With Prime Minister Begum Khaleda Zia of Bangladesh
*March 19, 1992*

The President and Prime Minister Zia of Bangladesh met for approximately one hour in the Oval Office and the Cabinet Room.

The President reaffirmed our strong commitment to strengthening democracy and promoting economic development in Bangladesh. The two leaders recalled Bangladesh's contribution to the successful fight against Iraqi aggression. The President said we will continue to provide economic assistance and food aid to Bangladesh.

The President and Prime Minister Zia also deplored the actions of the Government of Myanmar (Burma) that have led to the massive recent influx of Burmese refugees into Bangladesh. The President announced that the United States will provide $3 million in funding from the Emergency Refugee and Migration Assistance Funds to help Bangladesh with the refugees.

# Statement by Press Secretary Fitzwater on the President's Telephone Conversation With President Boris Yeltsin of Russia
*March 19, 1992*

The President spoke with Russian President Boris Yeltsin for nearly one-half hour this morning. The two leaders discussed developments in Russia and the reform effort launched by President Yeltsin. The President expressed strong U.S. support for Russia's application for membership in the International Monetary Fund and for the reform effort in general. They also exchanged views on the situation in Nagorno-Karabakh and agreed that both Russia and the U.S. would work toward a peaceful resolution of that conflict.

## Appointment of Robert Anthony Snow as Deputy Assistant to the President for Media Affairs
*March 19, 1992*

The President today announced the appointment of Robert Anthony Snow as Deputy Assistant to the President for Media Affairs.

Since 1991, Mr. Snow has served as Deputy Assistant to the President for Communications and Director of Speechwriting. Prior to this, Mr. Snow served as editorial page editor of the Washington Times. The page received numerous local, regional, and national awards. Mr. Snow also served as deputy editorial page editor of the Detroit News, 1984–87; as editorial page editor of the Daily Press in Newport News, VA, 1982–84; and as an editorial writer for the Virginia Pilot, 1981–82. Mr. Snow began his journalism career as an editorial writer at the Greensboro Record in Greensboro, NC, in 1979.

Mr. Snow graduated from Davidson College in Davidson, NC, in 1977, receiving a bachelor of arts degree in philosophy. He was born in Berea, KY. He and his wife, Jill Snow, live in Alexandria, VA.

## Presidential Determination No. 92–19—Memorandum on Emergency Assistance for Cambodian and Burmese Refugees
*March 16, 1992*

*Memorandum for the Secretary of State*

*Subject:* Determination Pursuant to Section 2(c)(1) of the Migration and Refugee Assistance Act of 1962, as Amended

Pursuant to section 2(c)(1) of the Migration and Refugee Assistance Act of 1962, as amended, 22 U.S.C. 2601(c)(1), I hereby determine that it is important to the national interest that $18,000,000 be made available from the U.S. Emergency Refugee and Migration Assistance Fund (the Fund) to meet the unexpected and urgent refugee and migration needs of Cambodians and Burmese. Of this amount up to $15,000,000 will be used to support the repatriation of Cambodian refugees and displaced persons; $3,000,000 will be contributed to assist Burmese refugees. These funds may be contributed on a multilateral or bilateral basis as appropriate to international organizations, private voluntary organizations, and other governmental and nongovernmental humanitarian organizations.

You are authorized and directed to inform the appropriate committees of the Congress of this determination and the obligation of funds under this authority and to publish this memorandum in the *Federal Register*.

GEORGE BUSH

[*Filed with the Office of the Federal Register, 2:53 p.m., April 2, 1992*]

*Note: This memorandum was released by the Office of the Press Secretary on March 20.*

# Remarks Congratulating the Undefeated National Collegiate Athletic Association Division I Football Teams
*March 20, 1992*

Mr. Speaker, and distinguished Members of the Congress, Senate and House. We've got some other guests here, too, and let me single them out. The members of those championship teams from Jabbo Kenner Youth Football League, where are those guys? Over here, all right, there they are, looking good. Emiliano Salinas is here with us. Where is he? This man is the son of the President of Mexico, one of our strongest, staunchest allies. Emiliano, welcome, welcome. And did we get Wilson High School? Wilson, here they are back here, another championship ball team. And may I especially single out Coach James and Coach Erickson, who have the respect of anybody interested in sports in this country. It's great to have both of you here, Dennis, Don. And also to the players, the staffs, the friends, and the football fans here and across the country, Barbara and I just wanted to welcome you here to 1600 Pennsylvania Avenue.

For exactly 200 years this has been the people's house, and today we welcome the people's choice, the Hurricanes and the Huskies, two great teams, both national champions. And some thought I should take the ball and go outside and try to settle this thing right now. [*Laughter*] No, no, my black-and-white shirt is at the cleaners. We're not going to do that. I don't need this. I've got enough problems without getting in the middle of you guys.

Let me begin with what we have in common. You guys play football, and in an election year I sometimes feel like a football. But it's then that I recall what you did this year. Flanked by you household names, maybe I should be around getting autographs because this is a star-studded occasion.

First alphabetically—and I don't want to get into trouble—comes Miami, number one in the Associated Press. Two years ago we met to celebrate a national title. Today we salute the Nation's current longest home winning streak, 45 games, and the longest regular season winning streak; 4 national titles in the past 9 years including 1991; only the third undefeated team in Miami history.

And what memories you've given us. Of a college known as Quarterback U, Gino Toretta, take a bow. Where is the man? All right. Leon Searcy's not here, but I wanted to single him out. He's an offensive tackle, for those amateurs around here, who wears a 17EEE shoe; they call them battleships. [*Laughter*] And this year we are retiring the U.S.S. *Missouri*, and I think we ought to commission him instead. [*Laughter*] But I'm sorry he's not with us.

Next we come to Kevin Williams. Kevin promised Brent Musburger that he'd return a punt for a touchdown, and sure enough, he did it. And dealing with politicians, it's always a pleasure to meet a man of his word.

And defensive end Rusty Medearis is not with us. The Sack Man, the Hurricane receivers, the Ruthless Posse, all, they'd feel right at home in Washington. And this brings me to Carlos Huerta, called the Ice Man. Carlos, where is he? Right here. All right. Ask the children he helps, in addition to the sick he comforts, and they call him simply the nice man.

And finally, Coach Erickson, who spurned "Miami Vice" for virtue: Witness the drills that are so self-disciplined that one player said, "The games are easy. They're a cinch compared to our practices."

Out west then we'll shift. No game was easy for the opponents of the '91's other co-champion in the USA Today-CNN poll, the amazing Washington Huskies. And in a way you foretold the success of that other Washington team, the Redskins, halfway across the world, making Don James' 17th season as Huskie coach his finest. His fourth Rose Bowl victory; the Huskies' first undefeated and untied club since 1915; a team which made each opponent, yes, bow down to Washington.

And in one sense, you remind me of the

way we were. Thirty-eight years ago Don James graduated from Miami. Applying equal time, Dennis Erickson hails from Washington. And it's today, though, that we're here to focus on, on how the Purple and Gold turned opponents black and blue. And I think of the Purple Haze of Dave Hoffman and Lincoln Kennedy, nicknamed the "Oval Office." Now, where are these two guys? I've got to see them. I can see why. And at 6' 7" and 325 pounds, the Pentagon would be more like it. [*Laughter*] Incidentally, I want to salute your dad, a career Navy man who served in the Gulf.

And then there's Outland Trophy and Lombardi Trophy winner, all-American, Heisman Trophy finalist, Steve Emtman. Steve. You've got them all hiding in the back here. [*Laughter*] All right. Welcome to the White House.

And Mario Bailey. Mario, where are you? Right here next to me: 4 years, Rose Bowl heroics, six school records including receiving yards and touchdowns. And Washington's quarterback who made 1991 an "Ode to Billy Joe." Passing to the 3 Smurfs, throwing a school record 22 touchdowns, Billy Joe Hobert became the second straight Huskie sophomore quarterback to be named the Rose Bowl's most valued player.

And so today I salute the only two division I college football teams to finish undefeated and untied in the same season since 1976. Teams which showed, as quarterback Joe Kapp once said, "The greatest game in America is called opportunity. Football is a great expression of it."

The American political system has a playoff to decide a winner. It's called an election, Presidential election this year. And as of now the NCAA does not. And yet, in the truest sense, each of you are winners: undefeated, untied, unbowed.

And so, Barbara and I wanted to welcome you here to extend our most sincere congratulations not just for winning but for the example you and especially these two coaches set for the rest of the country, to our country, the greatest, freest land on the face of the Earth. Welcome to the White House. Congratulations. And may God bless all of you.

*Note: The President spoke at 1:40 p.m. in the East Room at the White House. In his remarks, he referred to University of Washington football coach Don James, University of Miami football coach Dennis Erickson, ABC sportscaster Brent Musburger, and former Minnesota Vikings quarterback Joe Kapp.*

# Message to the House of Representatives Returning Without Approval the Tax Fairness and Economic Growth Acceleration Act of 1992
*March 20, 1992*

*To the House of Representatives:*

I am returning herewith without my approval H.R. 4210, the "Tax Fairness and Economic Growth Acceleration Act of 1992." In my State of the Union Message, I proposed a responsible, balanced economic growth program. I challenged the Congress to pass incentives for growth by March 20. The Congress failed to meet that challenge. The Congress' response, H.R. 4210, is a formula for economic stagnation, not economic expansion.

My Administration's economic growth program would create jobs, generate long-term economic growth, and promote health, education, savings, and home ownership. My plan would encourage investment and enhance real estate values—without tax increases.

Tax increases would undermine the emerging recovery and act as a barrier to long-term growth. I call on the Congress to pass the seven commonsense measures that I asked for by this date, without tax increases, and to join me in pursuing a long-term agenda for growth.

I am disappointed that after 52 days the Congress has produced partisan, flawed legislation. Rather than work in a constructive manner to strengthen the economy and to create jobs, congressional leaders chose the path of partisanship. H.R. 4210 would jeopardize the recovery. It would not create jobs. It would not create incentives for long-term investment and growth, it does not contain a tax credit for first-time homebuyers, and it contains wholly inappropriate special interest provisions.

H.R. 4210 would increase taxes by more than $100 billion. More than two-thirds of all taxpayers facing tax increases as a result of this bill would be owners of small businesses and entrepreneurs. Small businesses are the primary source of new job creation.

H.R. 4210 would raise income tax rates substantially for some individuals, in some cases increasing marginal rates by more than 30 percent.

This is the wrong time to raise taxes, to increase the deficit, or to send a message of fiscal irresponsibility to financial markets.

I am therefore returning H.R. 4210, and I ask the Congress again to pass my economic growth program, without raising taxes.

GEORGE BUSH

The White House,
March 20, 1992.

# Remarks to Republican Members of Congress and Presidential Appointees
*March 20, 1992*

Welcome to the White House. Fifty-two days ago in my State of the Union Address, I asked Congress to act on my agenda for economic growth. And I asked for immediate action by March 20th on a series of proposals to help rekindle the economic recovery. And I asked the Democratic leadership to put partisanship aside, pledging to do the same, in order to enact seven sensible steps to increase investment, strengthen the value of American homes, and create jobs. Well, March 20th has arrived, and no recovery bill of any kind has come to the White House as of now.

This morning the congressional conferees finished work on a tax bill. It would increase taxes and harm the economy. And so, today I am doing three things. First, I have just signed the veto message to stop the Democrats' tax increase. And second, I am taking several additional steps on my own to help the recovery with or without action by Congress. And third, while the Democratic leadership in Congress is in disarray, I am proposing action on the real challenges facing America, on my long-term plans to help America compete in the global economy of the future.

Now is the time for real, significant change. And I am disappointed in Congress. In fairness, some Democrats did not want to put a tax increase in the bill. And I salute them for courageously standing up against more taxes. But politics prevailed. A slim majority passed the bill in the face of a certain veto. But they aren't blocking my economic recovery plan because they're afraid it won't work; they're blocking it because they're afraid it will work.

I do not take this step lightly. No President has vetoed a major tax bill since Harry Truman did it in 1948. But I submitted an economic growth plan to Congress for a reason: to promote a recovery in which every American has an interest. The package I proposed was carefully tailored. It was paid for without raising taxes. It was designed to encourage and strengthen the positive economic signs we're beginning to see: home sales and housing starts up as interest rates stay down; retail sales improving; 164,000 new jobs last month alone.

In response, the Democratic Congress has returned to form. It's produced a bill that will not strengthen the economy; it will weaken it. It's produced a bill that will not stimulate growth; it will stifle it. As if by reflex, the Democrats in Congress could not resist their natural impulse to raise taxes. But I assure you of this: I simply will not let them do it.

So, moments ago I signed the veto message for the Democrats' tax increase because raising taxes will not help create jobs. And the bill is not yet here, but the conference report tells me all I need to know. And when the bill is sent down tonight, this signed message will be waiting for it, and my veto will go back to the Hill the minute the bill arrives. And needless to say, I will not send it back via the House post office. [*Laughter*] The message is clear: My veto, and a block of votes ready to sustain it, stands ready to stop any tax increase on the American people.

With that clear, I ask the Democratic leadership to put aside once and for all the idea of a tax increase. And I ask the Congress again: Pass the seven commonsense measures that I have proposed to help the economy now. Do so without raising taxes, and I'll sign it. And then let's get on to the long-term agenda. But stop holding the American economy hostage in a partisan game.

Passing a tax increase is bad enough, but here's what really troubles me. The irresponsibility of Congress on this plan, it's a part of a pattern. It reflects a more serious problem, a deeper, systemic problem that is gnawing at the strength of our Nation. It is no wonder that Americans are angry. Today, looking at the accumulated evidence of several years, it must be said: Our congressional system is broken.

We have a long tradition in this country of pulling together when national need demands that we do so. And over the years, many accomplishments, large and small, have been truly bipartisan. But Congress today is different. It's more partisan. Its campaigns are financed by special interests. It's grown out of control. It's lost the ability to police itself. And perhaps most importantly, it is no longer accountable to individual American citizens and voters. And this must change.

One party has controlled the House of Representatives for almost four decades. Staff has become institutionalized. In 1950, there were about 2,000 personal staff in Congress. Today, there are almost 12,000

staff for Members of Congress themselves and almost 40,000 if you include the entire legislative branch. The number of committees and subcommittees has quadrupled.

And for this, we get a Congress incapable of passing the simple plan that I presented almost 2 months ago, a Congress controlled by the Democratic caucus which cannot manage a tiny bank or a tiny post office.

In the 1990 elections, special interest political action committees, PAC's, gave almost $117 million to incumbent Congressmen and Senators. Only about $15 million were donated to challengers. With this eight-to-one spending advantage, obvious voter discontent was buried in a wave of PAC-financed television advertising. And so, nearly every incumbent won.

The time has come for change because when the system is broken, you do have to fix it. And I have proposed to eliminate the PAC's which are poisoning our system. The time has come to eliminate these political action committees in their entirety.

I propose also to increase accountability. I'm ordering several steps to implement promptly the Supreme Court's *Beck* decision. No worker should be forced to have money taken out of his or her paycheck to fund politicians that he or she disagrees with. We should apply to Congress the same laws, from employment practices to civil rights to the Freedom of Information Act, which it imposes on everyone else.

And I believe the time has come to limit the terms of Congressmen. The terms of Presidents are limited. It's time for the terms of Congressmen to be limited.

The bottom line is that we all need a new Congress, one that can and will work with me for constructive change. And in the meantime, I will take additional actions on my own with every legal means at my disposal to keep the economy moving up. And I will do so in spite of the hopelessly tangled congressional web of PAC's, perks, privileges, partnership, and paralysis. There is, of course, a serious limit on what a President can do without Congress. But I am determined to do all I can to effect change.

First, I want to underline a fundamental point: Government is too big, and it spends too much. I have already proposed to freeze domestic discretionary spending in Federal employment next year. And I've also proposed to curb the growth of mandatory programs without touching Social Security. Mandatory spending, spending on programs that need no annual congressional action to keep growing, consumes almost two-thirds of the entire Federal budget. Over the next decade, this spending, if left unchecked, will grow by $2 trillion more than is needed for inflation and new beneficiaries. Currently, most of these programs grow automatically without congressional review or even a chance for a Presidential veto.

My proposal, which is before Congress now, would permit these programs to grow for inflation and new beneficiaries and, where necessary, some amount above that. But we need some ceiling to keep their growth within reasonable bounds. Uncontrollable spending is a major cause of the Federal deficit that I'm working to contain, and it must be addressed.

Today I am sending to Capitol Hill the first of a series of additional measures to cut Federal spending now, this year. I have also directed all Agency heads to look for further areas where spending cuts can be made now. The line-item rescissions identified so far, in total, will cancel out about $4 billion in unnecessary spending: funds for local parking garages, $100,000 for asparagus yield declines, mink research, prickly pear research. The examples would be funny if the effect weren't so serious. And this kind of wasteful spending destroys public confidence in the integrity of the Government. And Americans have every right to be outraged and disgusted. It's their money.

I will work with the Republicans in the House to bring these items to a vote individually. Forcing the Democratic leadership to allow line-by-line votes on items of pork will bring us a step closer to the accountability and the power that 43 Governors have, the line-item veto.

Some argue that the President already has that authority, the line-item veto authority, but our able Attorney General, in whom I have full confidence, and my trusted White House Counsel, backed up by legal opinions from most of the legal schol-

ars, feel that I do not have that line-item veto authority. And this opinion was shared by the Attorney General in the previous administration.

I ask the American people, then, to demand that a President be given line-item veto authority legislatively or, if necessary, by changing the Constitution. The line-item veto is essential, and I need it now.

Secondly, I've directed the Vice President to step up the assault on unnecessary regulation and paperwork. Let me give you a progress report that he gave to me, and he's doing a superb job on this. Though some in Congress oppose regulatory relief, I've already taken specific steps to remove the regulatory roadblocks to growth. We've implemented plans to promote biotechnology, to lower construction costs, help small business, ease the credit crunch, help clean up the air, reduce costs in transportation, and cut through the morass of regulation and agriculture.

And today, we're launching a new public-private partnership to promote research and development by bringing the good ideas from our Federal labs into the marketplace. Over the coming months, we will be announcing many more such steps to chop away at needless regulation and paperwork wherever we can. Too much regulation smothers innovation, eliminates jobs, and makes America less competitive.

I realize that these are only modest steps, but they reflect a fundamental attitude. And if the Democratic leadership that runs the status quo Congress will not help us change America, we have to change it without them. And if the Democratic leadership that runs the status quo Congress will not help us reform Government, we must reform it without them.

You see, change is nothing to fear. For more than two centuries, America has been a force for change. Our restlessness is legendary. Our energy is boundless. Because of this, today America, even given our economic problems, is the most productive Nation on the face of the Earth, with the highest standard of living. We have only one-twentieth of the world's population. But we produce one-fourth of the world's output, twice that of Japan, 4 times that of

Germany.

Today America's credibility and prestige in the world, not to mention our strength, have never been greater. But we didn't get where we are by standing still. We got where we are by always striving to do better. And that's why the current paralysis of the Congress, controlled over and over again by that liberal Democratic majority, is so troubling. It's caused too many Americans, at the exact moment of triumph for American values around the world, to lose confidence.

Americans are understandably worried about their future, not only about the economy right now, although that is a key problem, but about the economic competition of the future, about the central question that lies at the heart of the American dream: Will our children have a better life than we do?

Make no mistake: We will compete and win in the global economy. In the last 10 years we've become more productive. Our exports have more than doubled. Manufacturing productivity has increased. And we are capturing new markets around the world from Europe to Africa to Latin America. But in order to keep succeeding in this global economic competition we've got to change America in five key ways. We need a strategy that is confident, forward-looking, future-oriented, and we need to be willing to change.

First, we must expand markets for American products. So, I will continue to pursue a GATT agreement to open markets further. I will push for a North American free trade agreement to unlock the potential of markets in Mexico and Canada. And I will work for bilateral agreements to knock down barriers to American exports.

To win these markets we must guarantee that America will lead the world in knowledge, in new ideas, in making products of the highest quality. And that requires specific investments today. I've proposed to invest more in basic R&D, research and development, and in key technologies like high-performance computing, new and advanced materials in biotechnology. Congress should approve these investments. And not only the Government must invest more in the future. To maintain our edge by increasing private sector investment, Congress should pass the capital gains tax cut and make the R&D tax credit permanent.

And second, we must prepare our work force to compete, through better education, better training. And I've proposed a set of dramatic reforms in education called America 2000 and a new approach to job training, Job Training 2000. The idea of America 2000 is simple, to revolutionize American education. And that means creating new kinds of schools with new technology and new ways of learning. It means measuring progress and holding schools accountable for their performance. And it means giving all families, including low- and middle-income families, choice in picking their children's schools.

We've put the resources behind our efforts. Although budget dollars are very tight, education is so important to me that I've increased funding, funding for education, by 42 percent just since 1989 and gave it the biggest increase this year. I put in place a new program to help train teachers in math and science and increased funding for math and science education by over 69 percent. But more money alone won't do it. We need reform.

And thirdly, we must reform health care. America has provided the best quality health care in the entire world. But we are plagued by two problems: Too many Americans are not covered by health insurance, and health care costs too much. And I have proposed a comprehensive plan to make health care more affordable, more available, more sensible. It guarantees access for affordable health care, affordable health insurance for all Americans. Congress should pass it, and that will help our competitiveness all around the world.

Fourth, we've got to fix our legal system. America is drowning in a sea of litigation. Too many lawsuits means higher prices for consumers and reduced competitiveness for all America. It is estimated that fear of medical practice alone generates up to about $20 billion per year in increased health costs. This must change. In some cases we should require the loser to pay the winner's legal fees, and that would stop some of these frivolous lawsuits. You know the problem. When parents won't coach Little League teams, when obstetricians won't deliver babies, and when community pools are closed in the summertime, all because of the fear of liability, we know that something is wrong. And now is the time for Congress to pass my legislation to fix it.

And fifth, we must tackle each of these challenges without higher taxes or more Government spending. America doesn't need bigger Government; it needs better Government. On every one of these issues the Democrats in Congress are standing in the way of reform. They've cut my budgets for R&D and investing in the future and then voted instead for pork.

They've stripped choice and accountability out of the education bill. They are working on a Government takeover as a solution to our health care program, to be financed by a massive tax increase. And the special interests have made them afraid of legal reform. Well, it is time for Congress to either lead, to follow, or simply get out of the way.

On every one of these challenges there are two very different ways of looking at the world, one is reformist and the other protects the status quo. And that difference is driven by values. The special interests and the foot-draggers do not believe in the kind of change that we seek, change which respects markets more than Government dictates, which recognizes fundamental American values and the difference between right and wrong, which rewards excellence and punishes wrong-doing.

They do not believe that actions should have consequences. Well, one set of actions should have consequences. The failure of Congress to move on our program of change means only one thing: It is time for a new Congress. Give others a chance to control the United States Congress. You give me the right lawmakers, and I'll give you the right laws.

Over the coming weeks I'll be speaking more about these changes, and I'll be laying out further specific plans that I have for each. And I ask the American people to compare those plans to the response of the Democratic-led status quo Congress and the do-nothing caucus that has dominated that Democratic Party for too long.

Patrick Henry said, "I like the dreams of the future better than the history of the past." Well, Patrick Henry was right. Imagine the irony, as the world is beating a path to freedom's door, if we, ourselves, were to turn back now. If we carry the change forward, we can have a nation of productive workers and competitive companies, of healthy and secure communities, of schools that are the best in the entire world. And America can remain a nation whose exuberant confidence and commitment to freedom are admired worldwide.

I am ready to build such an America. Because if we can change the world, we can change America.

Thank you all. And may God bless the United States of America. Thank you very much.

*Note: The President spoke at 4:04 p.m. in the East Room at the White House.*

# Statement on Signing Legislation Waiving Printing Requirements for the Tax Bill
*March 20, 1992*

Today I approve H.J. Res. 446, which waives the printing requirements of sections 106 and 107 of Title 1 of the United States Code with respect to H.R. 4210. I do so to avoid any confusion as to my ability to act on any form of that legislation present-ed to me after certification by the Committee on House Administration of the House of Representatives that the form is a true enrollment. In signing the resolution, I express no view as to whether it is necessary to waive the provisions of Title 1 before I exercise my prerogatives under Article I, section 7 of the Constitution where the Congress has presented to me any form of bill it considers to be a true enrollment.

GEORGE BUSH

The White House, March 20, 1992.

*Note: H.J. Res. 446, approved March 20, was assigned Public Law No. 102–260.*

# Statement by Press Secretary Fitzwater on the Russia-United States Commission on Prisoners of War and Missing in Action
*March 20, 1992*

The United States and Russia have established a joint commission to investigate unresolved cases of prisoners of war and missing in action dating from the Second World War, including the Korean and Vietnam conflicts. The creation of this commission underscores the commitment of both the United States and Russia to work together in a spirit of friendship to uncover the fate of missing servicemen on both sides. This effort symbolizes the determination of the administration to resolve outstanding issues from the cold war period and is another step in developing our new cooperative relationship with Russia.

Former Ambassador to the Soviet Union Malcolm Toon has been designated the President's representative and Chairman of the U.S. delegation to this commission. The commission also will include Senators John Kerry and Robert Smith and Congressmen Pete Peterson and John Miller. The Russian delegation will be chaired by Gen. Dmitri Volkogonov, a senior adviser to President Yeltsin. The first meeting of the joint commission will be held March 26–28 in Moscow.

# Nomination of Bruno Victor Manno To Be an Assistant Secretary of Education
*March 20, 1992*

The President today announced his intention to nominate Bruno Victor Manno, of Ohio, to be an Assistant Secretary of Education for Policy and Planning. He would succeed Charles E. M. Kolb.

Currently Dr. Manno serves as Acting Assistant Secretary for Policy and Planning at the U.S. Department of Education. Prior to this, Dr. Manno served at the Department of Education in the Office of Educational Research and Improvement as Deputy Assistant Secretary for Policy and Planning; Acting Assistant Secretary and Chief of Staff; and as Director of Planning.

Dr. Manno graduated from the University of Dayton (B.A., 1970; M.A., 1972) and Boston College (Ph.D., 1975). He was born May 2, 1947, in Cleveland, OH. He is married and resides in Washington, DC.

# Nomination of David Spears Addington To Be General Counsel of the Department of Defense
*March 20, 1992*

The President today announced his intention to nominate David Spears Addington, of Virginia, to be General Counsel of the Department of Defense. He would succeed Terrence O'Donnell.

Currently Mr. Addington serves as Special Assistant to the Secretary and the Deputy Secretary of Defense. Prior to this, he served as Deputy Assistant to the President for Legislative Affairs at the White House, 1988–1989, and as a Special Assist-

ant to the President for Legislative Affairs, 1987–1988. From 1986 to 1987, he served as the Republican Chief Counsel of the Committee on Foreign Affairs of the House of Representatives.

Mr. Addington graduated from Georgetown University (B.A., 1978) and Duke University (J.D., 1981). He was born January 22, 1957, in Washington, DC. Mr. Addington resides in Arlington, VA.

# Nomination of Duane Acker To Be an Assistant Secretary of Agriculture
*March 20, 1992*

The President today announced his intention to nominate Duane Acker, of Virginia, to be an Assistant Secretary of Agriculture for Science and Education. He would succeed Charles E. Hess.

Currently Dr. Acker serves as Administrator of the Foreign Agricultural Service and Administrator for International Cooperation and Development at the U.S. Department of Agriculture. Prior to this, he served as Assistant to the Administrator for Food and

Agriculture at the U.S. Agency for International Development in Washington, DC. From 1975 to 1986, Dr. Acker served as president of Kansas State University.

Dr. Acker graduated from Iowa State University (B.S., 1952; M.S., 1953) and Oklahoma State University (Ph.D., 1957). He was born March 13, 1931, in Atlantic, IA. Dr. Acker is married, has two children, and resides in Arlington, VA.

# The President's News Conference With Chancellor Helmut Kohl of Germany
*March 22, 1992*

*The President.* Chancellor Kohl and I had a very productive discussion on a wide range of the issues that face us in the new era; among them, the American role in Europe, support for the democratic revolutions in Russia and Eastern Europe, and world trade talks.

We agreed that NATO remains the bedrock of European peace and there is no

substitute for our Atlantic link, anchored by a strong American military presence in Europe which the Chancellor and I both agreed must be maintained.

In our review of the Uruguay round negotiations, the Chancellor and I reaffirmed our determination to reach an early agreement that expands the world trading system. This would be a victory for U.S.-

European partnership in promoting free trade, spurring economic growth, and creating jobs in the U.S., Germany, and all developing countries.

We also discussed how we can best support democracy in the East. We agreed that as Russia and other new democracies adopt reform programs, we and the rest of the G–7 countries should take the lead in expanding financial support through the international financial institutions.

Our talks have shown that the Atlantic partnership is as vital and healthy as ever. And I'm especially pleased to see the United States and Germany are working as closely now as we did during the period of German unification.

And finally, on a very personal side, Barbara and I were just delighted to have this time together with Chancellor Kohl, with his wife, and it was also a great pleasure to have their son up there at Camp David. It was a good visit.

Mr. Chancellor, the floor is yours, sir.

*The Chancellor.* Mr. President, Mrs. Bush, ladies and gentlemen, I would like to take up where you left off, Mr. President, and thank you and Mrs. Bush for the very warm hospitality with which you received my wife, my son, and the members of my delegation at Camp David. It was a very, very friendly meeting, a very personal meeting, a very nice coda for these discussions on problems of interest to both of us and which will be of interest for the very near future.

One of these issues which we consider to be a very important one was the issue of GATT. Obviously, I did not come here as an official negotiator but as a member or as a representative of an EC member country. I explained our position on this question once again. The negotiations obviously are being weighed by the EC Commission, and the EC Commission enjoys the full confidence of the EC member countries.

President Bush and I are in agreement that it is of paramount importance for world economy to come to a successful conclusion of the GATT negotiations now. And we are in agreement that we have to prevent at all costs a fallback into a policy of protectionism. We know that it is, particularly at this juncture, a very important

thing that we maintain free world trade, that this is very important for a good development of the world economy. And this is, indeed, one of the main reasons why we intend to strengthen GATT.

And we are also, both of us, very well-aware of the fact that the successful conclusion of the GATT round is also of paramount importance for the countries of the Third World. And this is why we want to put all our efforts into these negotiations in the coming weeks and why we want to come to a successful conclusion of the GATT round at the very latest by the end of April.

In our talks, we talked, obviously, also about the preparations leading up to the world economic summit meeting in Munich in July. And the President supported me in the endeavor that these talks should focus more intensively on informal talks and that we should give room to the discussions on global issues that are of interest to all of us.

Very important issues for the summit meeting in Munich will be, first of all, the world economic developments. We want this summit to strengthen the trust and confidence in all countries in the world economy.

Another important subject for Munich will be the situation in the Commonwealth of Independent States and in the countries of Central and Eastern Europe. We will talk in Munich particularly about an overall package of so-called "help for self-help" where we want to draw up a sort of framework for cooperation of the West with the C.I.S.

And a third very important subject which we talked about is the improvement of cooperation of Western industrialized countries with the countries of the Third World now after the end of the cold war.

Another important subject we talked about in view of the very dramatic changes in the successor republics of the former Soviet Union and the Commonwealth of Independent States was the overall situation there, but also the relief activities that our two countries have already initiated. We just initiated the second of these assistance activities, and it is the second of the kind. But obviously, we cannot go on doing this kind of thing indefinitely.

What is important now is to give them a sort of a solid program of help or self-help where we focus on individual areas, where we focus, for example, on agriculture, on improvement of infrastructure, on the improvement of transport and communication links, and where we also concentrate on improving, for example, the safety standards of nuclear power plants in the former Soviet Union.

These were just some of the subjects that we dealt with during our very long and intensive discussions during these past 2 days. But I would like to mention the most important subject at the end of my remarks here: that once again, during these 2 days, it became apparent that the United States of America and reunified Germany are linked by very strong bonds of friendship and partnership. No matter what will happen in the world, this friendship, this partnership is of existential importance for us Germans. In future, too, freedom and security of Europe and also, therefore, of Germany can be safeguarded by this transatlantic alliance, which is why I would like to underline here in Washington, in the White House, that for us it is a matter of course that this includes also a substantial presence of American troops in Europe.

But it is our joint desire that our relationship will be deepened and widened beyond the mere scope of security and military issues, that we come to even closer relations in the cultural field, in the scientific field, in research and development, which is why I'm very pleased to be able to announce—and we have agreed on this—that this year we will inaugurate a German-American Academy of Sciences. This has never existed, to my knowledge, in the United States of America, and we have never had this sort of link with the United States before or with any other country across the Atlantic, for that matter. I think that an instrument such as this one is of utmost importance, particularly for the young generation, for fostering a mutual understanding of each other. And I would now like to issue an invitation to all our American friends to participate as guests in the German cultural festival that will take place here soon and to understand this as a sign of sympathy and

friendship with the American people.

Mr. President, allow me to thank you once again for these days where you once again demonstrated your friendship to us, which made it possible to meet in this very warm and hospitable atmosphere.

*The President.* Now, we'll take questions, and it would be nice to alternate between the Chancellor and me. And so, can we start off in a spirit of hospitality for a question for the Chancellor? Helen [Helen Thomas, United Press International].

*Multilateral Trade Negotiations*

*Q.* Yes, for both of you. It is well-known that you both want a GATT agreement. Was anything done? Were any ideas presented to make the breakthrough?

*The Chancellor.* Obviously, we talked about where we are already in agreement and where we still have some questions to solve before we can reach agreement. When I get back to Bonn, I will call on my European colleagues, and I will call also Jacques Delors, as representative of the EC Commission. And once again, I will give a full report of these 2 days of talks, and we will once again try to find out where there is further room for negotiations in order to come, then, at the end to a compromise.

And obviously, we're not going to talk about the content of these negotiations because this is, after all, what negotiations are about. You first of all negotiate, and then you come to some form of content.

*Q.* Do you have solid reason for your optimism?

*The Chancellor.* Obviously when we talk about compromise, it means that both sides have to move.

*Presidential Campaign*

*Q.* Mr. President, in this room on Friday you spoke a great deal about change and spoke of yourself as a person who wants to press for change. You have been President and Vice President for 11 years now; before that you had a long record as a Washington insider. This being the case, how can you convincingly present yourself as a candidate of change?

*The President.* I thought I spelled out the other day exactly what I mean by change:

far better system of education, vast improvement in many domestic problems, including the economy. I made suggestions that I have made before, and I'll keep making them to try to get the economy moving. And so, I do represent that, and I would like to get more cooperation to make the changes possible. But I will be prepared to take my case to the people in the fall about the future.

*Iraq*

*Q.* Mr. President, did you and the Chancellor have an opportunity to discuss what to do with, and to, Saddam Hussein?

*The President.* No, we didn't. We discussed about the fact that the United Nations resolutions must be implemented in their entirety. But I don't think it went beyond that. I thanked the Chancellor for their support back during the war; I thanked him for his total understanding and his cooperation. But we did not go into any details about what steps might next be taken. Is that——

*The Chancellor.* Yes.

*United Nations Environmental Conference*

*Q.* Both of you did not mention the summit in Brazil on the environment. Did you talk about it, and did you bridge any differences which might have existed?

*The Chancellor.* Yes, we talked about this subject, too. Obviously, my time here was limited, so I didn't mention all the subjects we raised during these 2 days of talks. We agreed that we would—obviously also with other governments—but first of all we would, namely the Government of the Federal Republic of Germany and the Government of the United States of America, work very closely together in preparing this conference.

We know how important this conference is for many, many countries in the world. And obviously, this importance is increased by the fact that this conference takes place only a few days or weeks before the G–7 summit meeting in Munich. And we all know, I think, about the difficulty of having to reconcile here the expectations of the countries of the Third World and, on the other hand, the determined effort of the industrialized countries to indeed come

here to program proposals that will preserve what is important for all of us, namely Creation.

*[A question was asked in German, and a translation was not provided.]*

*The Chancellor.* There are no differences. There are certain areas where we have to exchange views and deepen our knowledge about each other's position a little more, but we are in agreement.

*South Africa*

*Q.* To both gentlemen. I know among your many responsibilities you both followed what happened in South Africa this week. I wonder if either country has any plans to help South Africa further now? And are you confident that foreign investments will be protected?

*The President.* Let me just say we did talk about South Africa a little bit. I think we both are very pleased at the changes that have taken place there. I didn't tell Chancellor Kohl this, but I did call Mr. de Klerk the day after the election to salute him for his courageous leadership. And all I can think of is that we want to move forward bilaterally, the United States and South Africa, just as fast as we can.

There are some technicalities remaining, but our relationships have improved dramatically. And they will improve more under his leadership. The job isn't finished, but he has made a courageous start. So, we talked about it, and I think we both agreed the progress is dramatic.

Do you want to add?

*The Chancellor.* I would like to underline here what the President just said. I think many people have not quite fully understood what a wise political course President de Klerk steered here and how courageous he was at the same time and how much he risked. And I think if we think back to only 5 years ago, then it becomes apparent what a substantial step forward this is. And he deserves every support we can give him. And we are in agreement that we want to give him this support, each in his own way.

And at our next summit meeting in Lisbon, among the member countries of the EC, we will certainly discuss this subject very thoroughly. Let me say that a failure of de Klerk at the ballot box would have been indeed a catastrophe.

### Nuclear Weapons

[*The following question was asked in German.*]

*Q.* The question related to the dispute between Ukraine and Russia as regards the nuclear weapons and other weapons and the distribution of them.

*The Chancellor.* This indeed is one of the most pressing issues that we have to deal with in our contacts with the Commonwealth of Independent States because obviously a number of these republics have an enormous amount, an enormous arsenal of weapons, both nuclear and conventional. And I should also mention chemical weapons, which unfortunately are fairly often forgotten but which also can be used to devastating effect. And I think that it must be now in our joint interests to come to some form of settlement here of this issue. Russia and the Ukraine have to come to some form of arrangement between each other so that we achieve a lasting and durable safe situation for all of us.

And I would like to say here for the Federal Government, without wanting to create the impression that we want to interfere into the internal affairs or infringe on the sovereignty of any state, that this subject will indeed play a role when we discuss aid to these former Soviet republics, the republics which now form the C.I.S., and that we will think of that when we discuss "help for self-help."

*The President.* May I only add one thing on that, that I did talk to President Kravchuk of Ukraine yesterday. And he, knowing I was going to meet with Chancellor Kohl, asked me to assure the Chancellor that he was going to do everything he could to satisfy the requirements of the whole world on this question of safe disposal of nuclear weapons.

John [John Cochran, NBC News]?

### Presidential Campaign

*Q.* A question to both of you about foreign policy during an American political year. Mr. President, your interest in foreign policy has almost become a political alba-

tross around your neck. If, for example, there were to be a GATT agreement, would you use that to say, "Listen, this will prevent a worldwide depression, a worldwide trade war; it shows that foreign policy is important"? Would you be able to use this as a campaign issue?

And are you concerned about the level of debate among Democratic candidates when they talk about foreign policy? Do you think it's being ignored so far?

And Chancellor Kohl, are you concerned about the level of debate and the quality of debate so far in this election year? Mr. Bush's Republican challenger, for example, has shown isolationist trends. Does that concern you?

*The President.* May I start? Well, in the first place, John, that's a very broad question. I am convinced that foreign policy and world peace is going to be a major issue in the fall. I was asked the question here about change. I think all America rejoices in the fact that Germany is unified. I think they rejoice in the fact that our children go to sleep at night with a little less fear of nuclear weapons. You talk about change, this is significant. I think they rejoice in the fact that Eastern Europe is free and democratic. And I think they rejoice in the fact, if they think about it, that there is significant change in the Middle East, where people that were never willing to talk before are talking. This is significant change, and it is in the interest of the United States.

Now, it has not been on the front burner. But clearly, anybody aspiring to the Presidency is going to have to discuss these matters of world peace, national security, and the domestic policy as well.

So, I think you raise an interesting question, and I think the American people would agree that that subject of foreign policy and of world peace and of change that has happened in the last 3 years and, indeed, over the last 12 years has been significant. It's been dramatic; the world has dramatically changed for the better. And if we're going to be talking about problems in one area or another, we're going to be talking about them worldwide.

So, I think the debate has not been joined on that. I think it isn't in focus. To some degree, I can understand it. When people are hurting at home, the Chancellor and I talked about this, most of the concentration is on the domestic economy. But any Presidential debate is going to be about change in foreign policy as well as domestic. And we are very proud of the changes that have taken place around the world because of what we've done, what other Presidents before me have done in keeping this country strong, restoring credibility to the United States.

So, I think it is an issue. And ironically, the Chancellor and I did discuss it in very generic terms, in the sense of what were going to be the issues in the fall. And I told him I thought foreign policy was going to be one. Is that——

*Multilateral Trade Negotiations*

*Q.* Also, will the GATT agreement help you?

*The President.* Well, the GATT agreement will help the world. And clearly it will help the United States, and clearly it will help agricultural America. And it will help the Third World. Far better than aid programs is open trade. And so, it will help everybody.

But it shouldn't be viewed in a partisan mode. I know we still have some isolationists, some protectionists that don't want to go forward with these international agreements. They are wrong. It is in the interest of our country to conclude the GATT agreement. It is in the interest of our country to conclude a North American free trade agreement. You talk about change, there's something dramatic.

So, these things are in our interest, and I will keep pressing for them, good politics or not. They are in the best interest of the United States.

Chancellor?

*The Chancellor.* George, I would like to add a comment to your response to this question which I consider to be of utmost importance for us in Germany and in Europe as a whole. Obviously, in an election campaign there are a lot of issues that loom large, and a lot of them being domestic issues. And I certainly don't want to interfere into your internal affairs or into the election campaign. But if an American

asked my opinion on this, I would give him the following answer: I would tell him that a destiny of peoples is being decided on the foreign policy front and that each people that does not understand and follow this lesson of history, that it will have to pay very dearly for this.

And for a people such as the American people, that whether it wants it or not has this role, this decisive role in world politics to play and will have to play this role, this is even more valid. Had President George Bush not proved to be such a strong leader over these past years, obviously these dramatic changes would not have taken place in the world.

It is true that he was not the only one to bring about these changes; there were many others who influenced events. But he played a decisive role. I would just like to illustrate this by giving you a small example: When I was here 3 years ago and we gave a press conference here in the White House, one of the main topics on the agenda was the followup to Lance. Now, if you ask anybody what is Lance, what is the followup to Lance, they probably wouldn't be able to answer because the world has changed so dramatically. What we're talking about now are Russia, the Ukraine, building up democracy, promoting market economy there, building up free political systems in these countries.

We invested enormous sums of money in the past in the arms race, in building up huge arms arsenals, in trying to meet the Communist challenge everywhere. And now we are making a huge investment in peace, in freedom. There is no longer any Communist dictatorship in Europe. And I don't think that you have to be a prophet to be able to say that in the foreseeable future there won't be any Communist dictatorship in the world anymore. And I think that this is a fantastic fact.

*The President.* I think we have time, Marlin says, for one over here, sir, and then Frank [Frank Murray, Washington Times], and that's it.

*Nuclear Weapons*

*Q.* Mr. President, may I come back to that nuclear problem in the Soviet Union, or ex-Soviet Union? What can you tell us about ongoing productions of nuclear weapons in the former Soviet Union, and why are they doing that?

*The President.* Why are they not starting to get rid of them?

*Q.* They are producing.

*The President.* I can't answer that question for you, but I can say that they as recently as yesterday reiterated, the Ukrainians anyway, their conviction to get rid of nuclear weapons. They're having a dispute, as you know, or had one inside there with the Russians as to how to go about that. But I am confident that they are on the right track, that we are going to see substantial reductions.

And so, it's moving in the right direction, I can't answer your question on why they are producing any at all, unless it would be under the question of modernization. But we have numbers we're working towards. And indeed, in terms of destruction of tactical nukes and all, why, I think it's generally moving in the right direction. We still have to be sure that it's done safely, that it's done in accordance with the safest possible procedures. But I can't answer your question specifically, but I can say on a broader sense it's moving in the right direction.

Yes, Frank. This is the last one.

### Economic and Tax Legislation

*Q.* Mr. President, you discussed here today the need for compromise to win a GATT agreement. And yet, your Chief of Staff today said that on the major domestic issue right now, the taxes and economic legislation, that there will be no compromise. He referred to Senator Bentsen and Mr. Rostenkowski as being out of touch with reality. And I'm wondering how, with that kind of rhetoric and no compromise, you expect to achieve a settlement? Could you tell us what you're going to do about that?

*The President.* Just keep pressing for what's right. And I'm confident that at some point the pressure from the country will compel those that have resisted us to move forward in the right direction.

But I think most people in this country know that I held out my hand to this Congress in an effort to compromise. I've said that, worked with them in the past, pre-

pared to work with them in the future. But there are certain principles that I can't give in on. And I would also say that we're moving into this election year, and I think most people recognize that there's going to be a lot more political posturing out there. I'm President. I've got to try to keep moving the country forward. And I'm going to do that. And most of my time now will be spent in doing exactly that, with Super Tuesday and the high concentration of primaries behind us.

But I'm perfectly prepared to work with the Congress. But we've got to be realistic about politics. And I might add that far better than doing something bad to this economy is doing nothing at all. The best thing would be to do something that would stimulate investment. But if that can't happen then the next choice would be do nothing, and the worst choice would be to pass a tax-and-spend bill. So, we're coming into a political year when each side is going to be expressing its own political positions. And that might mean that we don't move things forward as fast as I would like. But I'm going to keep on trying.

*Q.* Does that mean that you subscribe to the premise of no compromise on taxes? And how long does that——

*The President.* Well, I think they will, at some point in here, will give up on trying to raise taxes on people. But in terms of sitting and talking about what we can do to move investment incentives forward, which does have to do with taxation, I think we ought to try to get something moving on that front.

So, it's in that area—I didn't hear the comments; I was busily engaged in a very fruitful and constructive discussion with the Chancellor, so I was spared the agony of listening to these talking shows that come on every Saturday and Sunday. [*Laughter*] So I didn't hear it, so I just can't comment on the byplay. I can tell you that I'm going to continue to take my case to the people for change, for change.

*Q.* Will you not extend your no-taxes pledge, and how far——

*The President.* I thought I expressed it pretty clearly here, just standing here in this room; it seems like ages ago, but it was only 48 hours ago.

Now, the Chancellor has to take a plane. He's got to be at work in the morning. What time is it back there in Germany? Eleven o'clock or something like that. So, we better let him go.

Thank you, Helmut.

*Note: The President's 124th news conference began at 4:15 p.m. in the East Room at the White House. The Chancellor spoke in German, and his remarks were translated by an interpreter. In his remarks, the Chancellor referred to NATO's Lance short-range nuclear missile.*

# Message on the Observance of the Iranian New Year
## March 16, 1992

I am delighted to extend greetings to all Iranian Americans as you celebrate Nowruz, the Iranian New Year.

This occasion provides a welcome opportunity to recognize the many outstanding contributions that Iranian immigrants and their descendants have made to the United States. Through your unique customs and traditions, you have greatly enriched American culture, while at the same time giving your fellow citizens a deeper understanding of your ancestral homeland. Through your myriad achievements in academia and in the workplace and through your increasing participation in government, you have also demonstrated your belief in freedom and in

equal opportunity for all—ideals that make this Nation's diversity a source of strength and pride.

On this occasion, as you gather with family and friends to forgive old grievances and to celebrate the arrival of spring, you fill your communities with a sense of reconciliation and renewal. What better way to begin a new year.

Barbara joins me in wishing you a memorable celebration.

GEORGE BUSH

*Note: This message was released by the Office of the Press Secretary on March 23.*

# Memorandum Delegating Authority Regarding Weapons Destruction in the Former Soviet Union
## March 20, 1992

*Memorandum for the Secretary of State, the Secretary of Defense, the Director of the Office of Management and Budget*

*Subject:* Delegation of Responsibilities under Public Law 102–229

By the authority vested in me by the Constitution and the laws of the United States of America, including section 301 of title 3 of the United States Code, I hereby delegate:

1. to the Secretary of State the authority and duty vested in the President under section 211(b) of H.R. 3807 as passed the Senate on November 25, 1991, and referred

to in section 108 of the Dire Emergency Supplemental Appropriations and Transfers for Relief From the Effects of Natural Disasters, for Other Urgent Needs, and for Incremental Cost of 'Operation Desert Shield/Desert Storm' Act of 1992 (Public Law 102–229) (the Act); and

2. to the Secretary of Defense the authorities and duties vested in the President under sections 212, 221, 231, and 232 of H.R. 3807 as passed the Senate on November 25, 1991, and referred to in section 108 of the Act.

The Secretary of Defense shall not exercise authority delegated by paragraph 2 hereof with respect to any former Soviet republic unless the Secretary of State has exercised the authority and performed the duty delegated by paragraph 1 hereof with respect to that former Soviet republic. The Secretary of Defense shall not obligate funds in the exercise of authority delegated by paragraph 2 hereof unless the Director of the Office of Management and Budget has made the determination required by section 221(e) of H.R. 3807 as passed the Senate on November 25, 1991, and referred

to in section 108 of the Act.

The Secretary of State is directed to publish this memorandum in the *Federal Register.*

GEORGE BUSH

[*Filed with the Office of the Federal Register, 3:10 p.m., April 2, 1992*]

*Note: This memorandum was released by the Office of the Press Secretary on March 23.*

# Remarks at the Swearing-In Ceremony for Barbara H. Franklin as Secretary of Commerce
*March 23, 1992*

May I thank Ambassador Schnabel for presiding here, but much more important, for the job he has done in an interim period. It's not easy. And he's done an outstanding job. And this gives me an opportunity also to thank those who work for this wonderful Department, the Department of Commerce. We're grateful to each and every one of you. Justice O'Connor and Senator Danforth, thank you for your participation in this ceremony. I thought Eli, Eli Barnes, the guy that gave the Pledge of Allegiance, did a first-class job, too. And Master Gunnery Sergeant Ryan, an old friend, thank you for leading us in the anthem. My respects to the marines here.

Then to our various Cabinet members with us today, it's most appropriate that you join your fellow Cabinet member at this special occasion. May I salute the former Secretary of Commerce Elliot Richardson. I know Pete Peterson was to be here, but I don't think he was able to make it. But Secretary Richardson is with us. And then we have other Cabinet secretaries, Bill Brock and Frank Carlucci and Jim Lynn and Margaret Heckler, all with us today. Members of Congress too numerous to acknowledge, but all vitally interested in Barbara's success as Secretary of Commerce.

And of course, a special salute to the one we honor today, Barbara Franklin, who is

about to become the current Secretary of one of our Government's great Agencies.

For me, today is sentimental. I remember a couple of months ago I was telling an aide that I had decided to nominate Barbara to this difficult post. And he replied, "Don't you think she's got enough to do already?", referring to Barbara Bush. [*Laughter*] But that brings me to the one, the Barbara that we are here to celebrate and to honor, the newest member of my Cabinet, a woman who claims a long and distinguished career in both public and private service.

Barbara's been a member of the Product Safety Commission, a member of the Advisory Committee for Trade Policy Negotiations, president and CEO of her own consulting firm, and also director of seven of America's most successful largest corporations. And always she's been a woman of courage, integrity, vision, and found plenty of time for service to her country.

And let it never be said that someone from Yale doesn't recognize talent from Harvard when he sees it. Hard to do. But her talent was spotted a lot earlier than that. Here's what her high school yearbook in Lancaster—this may prove embarrassing to her, but here's what her high school yearbook in Lancaster, Pennsylvania, said: "Versatile Barb is seen in all departments of Hempfield High School." But then it goes on: "A-student, honor society member, tennis team captain, high school cheerleader, student council president." And now, today, she is leading for a growing and prosperous American economy.

And may I salute her husband, Wally Barnes, who has been an outstanding success in business. When she needs consultation about free enterprise, she doesn't have far to go.

And let me repeat what she said in January upon accepting the Commerce post. She remarked that she would be "very proud to be an advocate for American business and jobs, manufacturing, service, every kind of business in this country. American business is the envy of the world."

Well, now that I have the benefit of her considerable talents, I am the envy of her former colleagues in American business. And I say that because she is energetic and experienced, extremely smart. And she can help us compete in the new world economy and create a new American century.

She knows how we must write new pages in the story of business and jobs, the story of American excellence. And I speak of the Pittsburgh mechanic, the Seattle computer specialist, the Des Moines mother who also holds down a job. And their tale is as old as the cotton gin and as young as magnetic tape. Work is noble in itself. No one has a right to look down at any American.

And Barbara Franklin of course, likes to lift things up. And some of you may know that in addition to her other talent she's an accomplished weight lifter. Arnold Schwarzenegger, eat your heart out. [*Laughter*] Now it's her time to lift people: people whose jobs and income depend on commerce and trade. And she won't help them through protectionism and isolationism either. Instead, she will be an evangelist for a strong economy, driven by competition, fueled by growth. And she will help protect jobs against those who would cost jobs by curtailing trade, by curbing trade.

I've known Barbara now for two decades, dating back to the early seventies. And at that time, she was at the White House in the early seventies, I was up at the United Nations. And we agree the way to create jobs is not to build a wall around America but to persuade other nations to tear their walls down. And I want a world of open markets, open competition, open hearts, open minds. And so does Barbara Franklin. And her record of dedication and integrity has transformed my admiration into confidence and my friendship into trust.

And at a time when competition in a global economy is changing the way we live, my friend takes her post to help change the way we lead. I know she will be able to count on a very able team of Commerce officials. She has big shoes to fill, coming in to take over from Secretary Robert Mosbacher, but she can do the job.

And to each and every one of you, again, who serve with her and who have helped her from the very first day she came over here in transition and now as Secretary, my profound thanks to you, not just for that but for the way you take the message of American business across this country and around the world.

In that spirit, it is with great pleasure that I turn the proceedings over to Justice O'Connor for the swearing-in of a woman who will help our economy thrive, our new Secretary of Commerce, Barbara Hackman Franklin. Thank you very much.

*Note: The President spoke at 9:36 a.m. at the Department of Commerce. In his remarks, he referred to Deputy Secretary of Commerce Rockwell A. Schnabel and former Secretary of Commerce Peter G. Peterson. Supreme Court Justice Sandra Day O'Connor administered the oath of office.*

## Letter to Congressional Leaders Transmitting the Report on Foreign Intelligence Activities in the United States
*March 23, 1992*

*Dear Mr. Chairman:*

Enclosed is the classified 1991 "Leahy-Huddleston Report" on the official representation in the United States of foreign governments that engage in intelligence activities within the United States that are harmful to our national security. The report is submitted in compliance with section 601(b) of the Intelligence Authorization Act for fiscal year 1985 (Public Law 98–618; 22 U.S.C. 254c–1(b)).

The report is based on information provided by the Department of State. The Department of State is prepared to respond to any questions that you may have.

Sincerely,

GEORGE BUSH

*Note: Identical letters were sent to David L. Boren, chairman of the Senate Select Committee on Intelligence; Dave McCurdy, chairman of the House Permanent Select Committee on Intelligence; Claiborne Pell, chairman of the Senate Committee on Foreign Relations; and Dante B. Fascell, chairman of the House Committee on Foreign Affairs.*

## Statement on the Strategic Defense Initiative
*March 23, 1992*

Today marks the ninth anniversary of the beginning of the Strategic Defense Initiative. The men and women of the SDI program have accomplished a great deal. They have proven repeatedly that we can intercept warheads in space. They have made great advances in smaller, cheaper, more sophisticated interceptors. In short, they have pushed back the frontiers of science and engineering.

Moreover, the events of the past several years have proven the critical importance of missile defenses. Last year in the Gulf war, our Patriot system defended our troops and allies from Saddam Hussein's Scud missiles. Today, the Russians join us in recognizing the value of missile defenses and have expressed interest in a global ballistic missile defense system. With the development of the GPALS missile defense system, the United States will be able to confront successfully the growing dangers of instability and missile proliferation.

With the passage of the Missile Defense Act in 1991, the Congress joined the administration commitment to fielding ballistic missile defenses. With continuing support from Congress we can achieve our goal and remove the threat of limited ballistic missile strikes for the American people and our friends and allies.

## Statement on the Death of Friedrich August von Hayek
*March 23, 1992*

Barbara and I are saddened by the death of Friedrich August von Hayek. I presented him the Presidential Medal of Freedom in 1991 because he was one of the great thinkers of our age who explored the promise and contours of liberty.

493

Professor von Hayek revolutionized the world's intellectual and political life. Future generations will read and benefit from his works.

## Statement by Press Secretary Fitzwater on the President's Telephone Conversation With President Boris Yeltsin of Russia
*March 23, 1992*

The President and President Yeltsin spoke for 20 minutes today. The President called to brief President Yeltsin on his meetings with Chancellor Kohl and said both the U.S. and Germany agreed on the need to support Russia's courageous economic reforms and would work with their G–7 partners to promote strong international support for the reforms. The President reaffirmed U.S. commitment to continued humanitarian and technical assistance efforts.

President Yeltsin briefed the President on the results of the C.I.S. heads of state meeting in Kiev, particularly on military and nuclear issues. He also reported C.I.S. willingness to actively work for a peaceful resolution of the conflict in Nagorno-Karabakh.

## Nomination of Thomas P. Kerester To Be Chief Counsel for Advocacy at the Small Business Administration
*March 23, 1992*

The President today announced his intention to nominate Thomas P. Kerester, of Virginia, to be Chief Counsel for Advocacy at the Small Business Administration. He would succeed Frank S. Swain.

Since 1985 Mr. Kerester has served as executive director of the Tax Executives Institute, Inc., in Washington, DC. Prior to this, he served as principal with the firm of Coopers & Lybrand in Washington, DC, 1974–85.

Mr. Kerester graduated from Ohio State University (B.S., 1951; J.D., 1953). He was born April 12, 1929, in Youngstown, OH. Mr. Kerester served in the U.S. Air Force, 1955–57, and the U.S. Air Force Reserves, 1957–66. He is married, has two children, and resides in Alexandria, VA.

## Remarks to the National American Wholesale Grocers Association
*March 24, 1992*

Boyd, thank you very much for the good news and for the introduction. And let me just say I am very pleased to be here. And I want to salute your leaders: first, Boyd, who did the honors here; Bill Eacho, who's with me; Richard Niemann; and T.C. Godwin. And also, before I get going here, I want to single out a former Cabinet member, Agricultural Secretary Jack Block, who's doing an outstanding job for the common interest so well represented here today.

And I am here to follow up on what I said Friday, but mainly to ask you to help me change this country, to make it stronger and make it better. And as Boyd so generously said, we have changed the world. We've won a great victory for world peace and freedom. And as President, believe me, I will stay fully engaged with the world. We have won the cold war. And I salute previous Presidents for their role in keeping our defenses strong; my predecessor, Ronald Reagan, for his foresight in doing what he could to bring about the collapse of international communism.

But now is no time to pull back from engagement in international affairs. So now let's put to work the same leadership that we used to change the world to change America. And let me tell you what that means: We'll leave a legacy of productive jobs for our citizens, with strong families secure in a more peaceful world.

And I have a strategy to renew America and to keep our country strong in the next century. I proposed a plan to stimulate the economy without raising taxes and without increasing the Federal deficit, action to strengthen real estate, action to help young families buy that first home now. Get it done now. And I asked for action to create good jobs. One of those actions was to cut the tax on capital gains. It's not a break for the rich. It is a job-creation incentive.

But the majority in Congress simply couldn't break their tax-and-spend habits. And I asked for action to stimulate this economy, not stifle it. And I asked for a jobs bill. And they passed a bill to increase income taxes by $100 billion. And they turned their backs on that first-time home-buyer by failing to enact this $5,000 tax credit. They watered down the investment tax allowance that we had, an allowance that would have sped up depreciation and encouraged people to buy new capital equipment, given them incentives to do that. They stifled other reforms to help businesses modernize and compete. And then they tinkered with the capital gains tax. But if their plan were adopted, that tax would still be among the highest in the developed world.

You people know this, but a lot of Americans don't. Japan and Germany tax capital gains at zero and at one percent. They don't even have—in essence don't have taxes on capital gains in one country and tax it at one percent in another. And we're to compete with all that in this highly competitive world.

And yes, I was disappointed in the Congress. But frankly, I was not surprised. And so last Friday that tax bill came down, and I

vetoed the tax increase. And that veto is going to be sustained. But not just to carp, then I announced actions that I would take on my own to do what I could to get the fat out of the Government, to cut the redtape that chokes our competitive spirit, and to get this country up to speed for the long haul.

You and I have business experience. We know what the tax increase would really do. About 80 percent of the revenue increase resulting from the higher rates would come from, you guessed it, small businesses. More than a million small businesses would be affected, many of them crippled by that Democratic-leadership tax increase. Thousands of family-run grocery and convenience stores are in this category. Small family farms also could face financial ruin from such a tax increase.

The bill I've just vetoed tried to raise the marginal rate for small family businesses and farms by about 18 percent. Now, just think about the impact of this on your own businesses. The grocery business, wholesale and retail, is fiercely competitive. I know you're being nice to the guy next to you here today, but when you go home, why, we'll understand if you go at each other. And why is it so competitive? You operate on the thinnest of profit margins; for wholesalers it's often less than a penny on the dollar. And if you had to face a big increase in the bracket where you pay most of your taxes, how would you cope? You'd feel pressure to cut back on the quality of your service. Competition would press you to hold out as long as possible before passing costs along to your customers. So you might have to eliminate jobs. Eventually everyone in the business would have to pass the costs along, and that would fuel inflation.

Those are simple facts of life for people trying to make a living. But even as millions of American families were huddling over their kitchen tables to work on their tax returns, the liberal Congress tried to raise their taxes by $100 billion.

Last Friday, as I say, I vetoed their massive tax increase. And I sent Congress my first line-item rescissions, cutting $3.6 billion in unneeded wasteful spending. These rescissions will serve notice to Congress that the days of wasteful spending are over. And it is a step symbolic of the power that 43 Governors have, the line-item veto. Incidentally, at their recent national meeting, the Nation's Governors, Democrat and Republican, went on record calling for line-item veto authority for the President. And I need that authority.

I'm also fighting for economic growth through actions that don't need to be passed by the Congress. Some things I need Congress to do; other things we can do without. Take a look at Government regulation. Day by day, rule by rule, and industry by industry, we are winning battles against overregulation. We're winning victories for common sense and freedom.

Just last Thursday, for example, our administration announced reforms on nutrition labeling for meat and poultry. Our reforms will keep our food supply every bit as safe, and I have responsibility for that, but we will reduce the burden and expense of regulation on American consumers and on our hard-working food producers and grocers. If Congress sends me any legislation that would overregulate economy, I'm going to veto it as soon as it reaches my desk.

Now, if we Americans are going to hone our skills and really compete in the years ahead, we've got a lot more to do. And I want to have us keep our sights on the next American century. And when I think of America in the year 2000, I think of five strategic concerns mentioned in my address to the Nation last Friday.

First, we must change and renew our schools. We must become a Nation of students, educating ourselves throughout our lifetimes in the best system of schools, colleges, and universities in the entire world. And this is going to take revolutionary change. Most of our States and hundreds of local communities are committed to change. They have joined me already in a crusade that we call America 2000, an exciting program to revolutionize education.

Business-as-usual is not going to help us reach our national education goals. We need to get behind world-class standards, new curriculum frameworks, break-the-mold schools, voluntary national testing. And a centerpiece of our plan is the belief that schools will do their best when parents enjoy real freedom and real responsibility to choose their children's schools, public, private, and religious. School choice for parents is an idea whose time has come.

Second, we need to make our excellent health care system more affordable and more available to Americans. We've got the highest quality health care in the entire world, but everyone should have access to it. And we all know the problems: Too many people don't have health insurance, and health care costs are going right through the roof. And we also know that the answer doesn't lie in costly and coercive plans like the scheme to make employers "play or pay." And the answer certainly isn't these nationalized, these socialized medicine plans. Nationalized health care would be a national disaster.

The way I propose that we help our society deal with this is based on markets and choice. Just as in education, vouchers are a key part of my strategy for giving Americans a fairer and more affordable health care system. And our answer is to change our health care system for the better, not ruin it. And we're going to keep fighting for this sensible plan.

Third—and I know you're going to agree with this one—we need fundamental legal reform to stop the epidemic of lawsuits. You all know the litany. You hear it in your communities. You hear it in your businesses. Things are so out of hand that some parents refuse to coach Little League for fear of liability lawsuits. Some doctors won't deliver babies anymore because of malpractice suits. Well, just imagine what we could achieve if we spent as much time helping each other as we do suing each other.

And the costs of litigation and liability on small business are absolutely staggering, horrendous. You know, in 1989 there were 18 million lawsuits filed in America, 18 million. And that's why I've again asked Congress to pass my civil justice reform bill which will help people resolve problems through means other than the courtroom. And it will help put a stop to frivolous lawsuits and reduce the drag on our economy caused by excessive litigation. And I need your help. I need your help with the Congress to pass this sensible approach.

And fourth, we must reform Government in line with one of America's most important founding principles: strict limits on the size and power of Government. With a Federal Government that gobbles up a quarter of GNP, we can't really say we're as free as we should be. One quarter of all we produce as a Nation, as a people, goes to pay for the central Government. Now, that's just not right. And right now, the system is not accountable, effective, efficient, or even compassionate. And we need Government that knows its limits. But more important, we need a Government that works.

We have got to fix a congressional system that's gone out of control. Congress, as an institution controlled by one party, the Democrats, for most of the past four decades, desperately needs reform. And I'm going to have more to say, constructively, about reforming Congress in not so many days from now, at a later date. But we can start by compelling Congress to be governed by the laws that they impose on people like you, such as civil rights law, wage and hour laws, fair labor standards. We must totally eliminate the special interest PAC's that give unfair advantage to incumbents in Congress and say yes to the people's call for term limits on Congress. My term is limited; the President's term is limited. And I believe theirs should be now if we want true reform.

Fifth, we must work to expand our markets. Of all the legacies that I want to help create as your President, few could be more important than open and fair trade opportunities for our manufacturers and our service industries and also for our farmers and our food industries. Food and agriculture trade is the critical problem of world trade. The European Community spends more than 10 times, 10 times as much as we do on agricultural export subsidies. This cannot and must not go on.

And I made that point in a very vigorous way to a very receptive Chancellor Kohl of Germany when he visited Camp David last weekend. His leadership will be vital if we are to break the deadlock in GATT and concluding the Uruguay round successfully. And I know from my talks that he wants to see a successful conclusion to the Uruguay round. So let me assure you, we'll be working as hard as possible the next few weeks to make a breakthrough in GATT. But as we see it, if there's no fair deal for agriculture, there simply cannot be a good GATT agreement. Agriculture is the key to getting this worked out.

And I'm also working to open up the exciting market opportunities in Mexico. With nearly 100 million people next door, Mexico is already one of our best customers. And they'll buy a lot more American goods as soon as these negotiations are concluded. It is one of our fastest growing markets anywhere in the world. And the bottom line is: A good agreement with Mexico means more U.S. jobs.

Last year, our exports around the world reached record levels. So the more trade barriers we can knock down the better. On a level playing field, I am absolutely convinced that Americans can outproduce, outperform anyone, anytime, anywhere. I have that kind of confidence in the American worker.

On each of these challenges, there are two roads to take: One is reform; the other protects the status quo. You and I are gathered on Capitol Hill today because we share a common purpose. We're here in the neighborhood of a Congress that fails to heed calls for reform, that so far has failed to pass a simple but effective plan to help create jobs and build confidence. We're not simply going to complain about the Congress; we're going to try to change it.

And there are hundreds of you here, hometown business leaders, who are the backbone of your community. And just after this speech, I understand that all of you are headed up the Hill to visit your Senators and Representatives. I hope you'll pass along my warmest thanks to those who have stood with us and urge all Members of Congress to support our long-term economic growth package, the five points I mentioned here today. It is just that important.

This will be, for me, my final campaign. And I plan to fight as never before. I have had the privilege of being your President at the great turning point when freedom prevailed over imperial communism, when the

497

Berlin Wall came down, when Iraq's aggression was defeated, ancient enemies talking peace in the Middle East, when democracy really got on the move in this, our own hemisphere. We are helping solidify a legacy of peace. But I cannot rest and you cannot rest until we help this country win another legacy: productive jobs for our citizens, with strong families secure in a more peaceful world. Working together, we changed the world. And now we can change America.

Thank you all very, very much. And may God bless you in your important work.

*Note: The President spoke at 11:04 a.m. at the Hyatt Regency Hotel. In his remarks, he referred to Boyd L. George, chairman of the board of governors, and John R. Block, president, National American Wholesale Grocers Association; William C. Eacho III, chairman of the board of directors, International Foodservice Distributors Association; Richard Niemann, vice chairman of the board of directors, Food Marketing Institute; and T.C. Godwin, Jr., chairman of the board, National Association of Convenience Stores.*

# Message to the Congress on Environmental Goals
## March 24, 1992

*To the Congress of the United States:*

In 1991 two events set the stage for a new era in history: the West won the Cold War and the United States led a U.N. coalition to roll back aggression in the Middle East. Both watershed events demonstrated the power of sustained international cooperation in pursuit of just and moral causes. They underscored the need for U.S. leadership in a complex, interdependent world.

Historic changes are also occurring in the relationship between humanity and the environment. We increasingly recognize that environmental improvement promotes peace and prosperity, while environmental degradation can cause political conflict and economic stagnation. We see that environmental protection requires international commitment and strategic American leadership in yet another just and moral cause.

*Merging Economic and Environmental Goals*

As I often have stated, we can have both economic growth and a cleaner, safer environment. Indeed, the two can be mutually supportive. Sound policies provide both.

My environmental strategy seeks to merge economic and environmental goals. For example, boosting two engines of economic growth—technological change and international trade—can also provide benefits for the environment. Likewise, regula-

tory approaches that emphasize economic efficiency can help lower the costs of securing greater environmental quality. The following examples are illustrative:

*Investments in Technology:* My Administration has invested aggressively in key areas of research and development that will boost productivity and economic performance. Several technologies heralded primarily for their benefit to economic growth and competitiveness, such as advanced materials, high performance computing, electric batteries, and biotechnology, also have valuable environmental applications. Increasing investments in basic environmental research will enable policymakers to devise more informed, effective, and efficient policies.

*International Trade:* In negotiations on the General Agreement on Tariffs and Trade (GATT), the United States calls on other nations to reduce farm subsidies, which harm competitive farm exports and contribute to environmental degradation. In parallel with negotiations toward a North American Free Trade Agreement (NAFTA), the United States and Mexico are expanding environmental cooperation. A free trade agreement would lead to stronger growth in both countries and provide increased financial resources for environmental protection.

*Economically Efficient Regulations:* Our Clean Air Act initiatives spur utility energy efficiency through innovative tradable sulfur emission allowances and an overall cap on emissions. Restraining electricity demand cuts emissions of carbon dioxide and acid rain precursors, lowers energy bills for homeowners and businesses, and limits the need for new powerplant construction.

*The Global Environment and Development*

Robust economic growth is needed to meet the needs and aspirations of the world's peoples. At the same time, the nations of the world must ensure that economic development does not place untenable burdens on the Earth's environment.

My Administration has been working with business leaders, environmentalists, scientists, and the governments of other countries to develop more effective, efficient, and comprehensive approaches to global economic and environmental issues. Preparations for the United Nations Conference on Environment and Development (UNCED or Earth Summit), which convenes this June in Rio de Janeiro, Brazil, have accelerated this process.

My priorities for this historic conference are as follows:

- Sign a satisfactory global framework convention on climate change;
- Agree on initial steps leading to a global framework convention on the conservation and management of all the world's forests;
- Improve U.N. environmental and developmental agencies as well as the Global Environment Facility (GEF), which provides financial assistance to developing nations in meeting the costs of gaining global environmental benefits;
- Launch an action program to conserve biodiversity and, if possible, sign a satisfactory global framework convention on biodiversity;
- Agree on a strategy and expand efforts to improve the condition of oceans and seas; and
- Adopt a strategy and initiatives to promote technology cooperation in a free market context.

*Climate Change:* On behalf of the United States, I hope to sign by June 1992 a global framework convention that will commit as many nations as possible to the timely development of comprehensive national climate action plans. Such plans would commit nations to a process of continuous improvement, addressing sources and reservoirs of all greenhouse gases as well as adaptation measures. Parties to the convention would compare their action programs on a regular basis and revise them as necessary.

By producing specific, comprehensive environmental commitments that fit each nation's particular circumstances, this approach is preferable on environmental and economic grounds to the carbon-dioxide-only proposals that others have espoused. The United States will continue to restrain or reduce its net carbon dioxide emissions by improving energy efficiency, developing cleaner energy sources, and planting billions of trees in this decade. But an exclusive focus on targets and timetables for carbon dioxide emissions is inadequate to address the complex dynamics of climate change.

*Forests and Biodiversity:* The nations of the world need to do a better job of studying and conserving the diversity of life on Earth. Nations also need to work together to improve the management and protection of all the world's forests. For these reasons, I am renewing my call for a global framework convention on the management and conservation of forests and restating the U.S. hope that UNCED will be the occasion for making progress toward such a convention. I am also hopeful that a convention on the conservation of biodiversity may be signed at UNCED.

*Institutional Reform and Funding:* Member nations need to coordinate U.N. structures and make them more efficient and effective in meeting UNCED goals. A related priority is to continue development of the World Bank's Global Environment Facility (GEF). The GEF should become the principal vehicle for assisting developing nations with the incremental costs of gaining global environmental benefits under new international agreements.

*Oceans:* Coastal and estuarine areas include some of the most diverse and productive ecosystems on Earth. Increasing population and development are stressing these areas, particularly in nations that lack effective programs to protect and manage marine resources. The United States urges UNCED parties to adopt a set of principles and an action plan to address such issues as the status of living marine resources, coastal zone management, ocean monitoring, and land-based sources of marine pollution.

*Technology:* The UNCED participants should adopt a strategy and initiatives to promote market-based environmental technology cooperation with developing nations. In some cases, the transfer of environmentally preferable technologies results from official foreign assistance. However, in the vast majority of cases it occurs as the result of private sector activities such as direct foreign investment, joint ventures, licensing, exports, and professional training. Thus the role of governments and international institutions should be to foster the market conditions that accelerate private sector activity in the growing global market for environmental goods and services.

### The Domestic Environment

In the midst of increased attention to global environmental issues, the United States in the last 3 years has enacted and begun to implement sweeping environmental reforms. We will continue to take action predicated on sound science and efficient solutions. State and local governments, businesses, community groups, and individual citizens must also play a part.

A number of items on the environmental agenda, including reauthorization of the Clean Water Act, the Resource Conservation and Recovery Act, and the Endangered Species Act, require a thorough, judicious review with an eye toward the long term. Wherever possible, such legislation should encourage economically sensible, market-based mechanisms. Quick-fix actions will not be in the best interest of the environment or of our economy.

The Congress should make a significant contribution to economic growth and the environment by taking the following steps during this session:

- Enact balanced national energy legisla-

tion, providing equal measures of new conservation and production;
- As requested in my budget, provide increased funds to a number of key environmental and natural resources programs; and
- Establish a U.S. Department of the Environment.

*National Energy Legislation:* In the year that has passed since I proposed a National Energy Strategy (NES) providing equal measures of new energy conservation and production, the Administration has moved to implement more than 90 NES initiatives that do not require legislative action. The Congress has followed through by increasing funding for an array of research and development initiatives. Now, in addition to these measures, the Congress needs to complete action on comprehensive national energy legislation.

*Environmental and Natural Resources Budget:* Within the context of initiatives to tighten Federal budget discipline, my proposed budget for fiscal 1993 reflects my continuing belief that we should increase national investments in key environmental and natural resources programs. Among my priorities are the following:

- $1.85 billion (a 17-percent increase over fiscal 1992) for the America the Beautiful program, including acquisition of key park, forest, refuge, and other public lands; my program to encourage public participation in the planting of one billion trees per year; a partnership with the States to create state parks and recreation facilities; and projects to improve environmental infrastructure and recreational opportunities on the public lands;
- A record $5.5 billion (a 26-percent increase over fiscal 1992) for the cleanup of Department of Energy facilities involved in nuclear weapons manufacture;
- $201 million (almost double the fiscal 1992 level) for U.S.-Mexico border region cleanup, consistent with the Environmental Action Plan I presented to the Congress last year in support of the proposed North American Free Trade Agreement;

• Almost $1 billion for energy research and development, including over $350 million for conservation research and development (more than double the fiscal 1989 level) and $162.4 million (a 47-percent increase over fiscal 1992) for transportation programs such as development of electric automotive batteries and the purchase of 5,000 alternative-fuel vehicles;

• $812 million (a 35-percent increase over fiscal 1992) for wetlands research, acquisition, restoration, and enhancement, achieving a 175-percent increase over fiscal 1989 levels;

• For the second year in a row, $340 million for accelerated construction of sewage treatment facilities in six coastal cities that currently have inadequate treatment facilities;

• $7 million (a 46-percent increase over fiscal 1992) for the designation and management of National Marine Sanctuaries;

• $229 million (a 22-percent increase over fiscal 1992) for implementation of the 1990 Clean Air Act;

• $1.75 billion (an 8-percent increase over fiscal 1992) for cleanup of Superfund toxic waste sites; and

• $1.37 billion (a 24-percent increase over fiscal 1992) for further expansion of the world's largest global climate change research program.

*U.S. Department of the Environment:* Considering the scope and importance of responsibilities conferred upon the Environmental Protection Agency (EPA), I announced my support in 1990 for legislative efforts to elevate EPA to Cabinet status. The Congressional leadership has responded with controversial, extraneous amendments and parliamentary delays. This legislation should not be held hostage any longer. Once again, I call on the Congress to elevate EPA to Cabinet status and make it the U.S. Department of the Environment.

### A National Commitment

There is a growing commitment from all segments of society to improve the environment. A key element of my environmental strategy is encouraging private companies and organizations to work with each other and with government to deliver conservation benefits that go far beyond what government acting alone could provide.

In July 1991 I named leaders of business, environmental, recreational, educational, and philanthropic organizations to serve as members of the President's Commission on Environmental Quality (PCEQ). I have challenged this Commission to develop and implement an action agenda to improve the environment through voluntary private sector activities that meet the test of economic efficiency.

I also established a Presidential medal for environment and conservation achievement and had the honor of presenting medals to an outstanding group of Americans last October. This program rewards private initiative in service to the environment in a manner equivalent to long-standing Presidential recognition of excellence in the arts, humanities, sciences, and world affairs.

We have encouraged additional private sector initiatives through such groundbreaking efforts as the "Green Lights" energy efficiency project, the "33–50" toxic emission reduction program, the U.S. Advanced Battery Consortium to support development of electric vehicles, and land management partnerships between conservation groups and the Departments of Defense, Agriculture, and the Interior.

### Freedom's Full Meaning

As more people around the world join the democratic family and reach for their God-given rights and aspirations, we Americans who have led the way for over 200 years will continue to bear a responsibility to give freedom its full meaning, including freedom from want and freedom from an unsafe environment.

The Cold War was a stark test of the global community's faith in these ideals. We passed that test.

The deadlock in negotiations for improved international trade rules is another challenge to the principles that have drawn the world closer together in the last half century. We must not fail that test.

These struggles for national security and economic growth are now joined by environmental concerns such as deforestation and potential climate change, which also have profound long-term implications. The year ahead will test our ability to redefine the relationship between humanity and the environment—and in so doing, to secure a greater peace and prosperity for generations to come. We must not fail that test.

GEORGE BUSH

The White House,
March 24, 1992.

## Statement by Press Secretary Fitzwater on the Open Skies Treaty
*March 24, 1992*

Today the United States, along with Canada and 22 European nations, signed the Treaty on Open Skies in Helsinki, Finland.

In May of 1989, at a time when the immense changes seen in Europe over the past 3 years were just beginning, President Bush proposed that the nations of the North Atlantic Treaty Organization (NATO) and the former Warsaw Pact agree to open their territories to frequent overflights by observation aircraft from the other side. The United States believes that the greater transparency in military activities brought about by such an agreement will help reduce the chances of military confrontation and build confidence in the peaceful intentions of the participating States.

The Open Skies Treaty is the most wide-ranging international confidence-building regime ever developed, covering the entire territory of North America and nearly all of Europe and the former Soviet Union. Its arrangements for observation flights using photographic, radar, and infrared sensors and its provisions for sharing among participants the information gathered are innovative means to help promote openness and stability in Europe in these uncertain times. Open Skies could also serve as a basis for similar arrangements in other regions of the world where there is a need to build confidence.

The treaty establishes an Open Skies Consultative Commission. In early April it will convene in Vienna, Austria, to complete work on outstanding technical and cost issues regarding treaty implementation. The treaty will be submitted to the United States Senate for its advice and consent to ratification once this work is finished to the satisfaction of all participants.

## Statement by Press Secretary Fitzwater on Diplomatic Relations With the Republic of Georgia
*March 24, 1992*

The President has decided that the United States will take immediate steps to establish diplomatic relations with Georgia. The United States had recognized Georgian independence on December 25, 1991. In recent weeks, the new Georgian Government has taken steps to restore civilian rule, begin a dialog on national reconciliation, and committed itself to holding parliamentary elections this year. On the basis of these actions and following communications between the leader of the Georgian State Council, Eduard Shevardnadze, and Secretary of State James Baker on the political, economic, and security principles of most importance to the United States, the President believes that U.S. interests will be best served by having diplomatic ties with the Georgian Government. The depth, extent, and richness of U.S. relations with Georgia will depend on the Georgian Government's commitment to these principles.

With this action, the United States now has diplomatic relations with all 12 of the new States of the former Soviet Union.

The United States will open an Embassy in Tbilisi as soon as possible. In addition, the United States will support Georgia's membership in relevant international organizations, including the International Monetary Fund and World Bank.

# Statement on the Connecticut Presidential Primary Victory
*March 24, 1992*

I want to thank the voters of Connecticut who made it clear today: The answer is less Government spending, not more taxes. As I announced on March 20, the line-item spending cuts I am sending to Congress will eliminate some unneeded weapons systems made in Connecticut. Cutting spending is a tough call, especially in a State where the economy is hurting. In spite of this, we won an impressive victory today from people who understand that being President of the United States sometimes means making difficult decisions.

# Remarks and an Exchange With Reporters Prior to a Meeting With Republican Congressional Leaders
*March 25, 1992*

*The President.* Let me just say I want to thank you all, Republican Members of the House and the Senate, for coming in here; and first, to thank you all for your help last week in trying to stop the tax increase bill. And it was a heroic effort, but we were outnumbered. They passed the bill, only narrowly, and I vetoed it. And thanks to you all, we have the votes now to sustain that veto. And I just would urge that we go the extra mile to have a strong show of support against this tax-and-spend legislation.

So the other point I want to mention is there is an effort, as we all know, to knock down the firewalls, in other words, to remove the spending caps. And I am convinced the American people think that we are spending too much. One safeguard we've got, thanks to many people around this table, are those caps. We just must keep those in place, the one discipline that helps you in your fight against excessive spending there.

So, I want to win that vote for controlling spending. If we can't do that, again, the only power I have to stand up against the excessive spending is the veto. And you all should know, I've told some, told the leadership personally that that certainly would be—and my intention would be to veto that kind of removal of the lid on spending. So we're going to keep doing it. I appreciate the support for the rescission approach. And we are going to make a change in attitude. This isn't just kind of a posturing for politics. I think the American people want to see significant change in the spending patterns and habits. You all have been magnificent in your leadership, and I just would urge you now as we go down to the crunch period here to do all you can to sustain this veto and to see that they don't take those caps off.

So thank you very much, and we can talk a little bit more about it as we go along here.

*Federal Budget*

*Q.* Mr. President, since you're talking to us, I wonder if I could ask you how, sir, you can——

*The President.* I was really talking to these guys.

*Q.* ——how you can boast of your economic plan's not increasing the deficit when your budget, sir, would result in the largest deficit in history?

*The President.* Well, I think I can boast of it because if we can get done what we want to do, we will begin to really put some checks on this deficit. There are some difficult things in my approach. For the first time, we're trying to control the growth, not cut but control the growth of these mandated spending programs. And that isn't easy, but it's a very important addition to the debate. And I'd like to see it done. So the program speaks for itself. And if we had more people like those around this table, we'd be able to make progress. It's just that clear.

*Connecticut Primary*

*Q.* Mr. President, are you disappointed by the rather sizable protest vote in your native State yesterday?

*The President.* No, I was very glad about the size of the win. You know, if I would win a general election by 65 to 20, or whatever it was, I would salute that as a magnificent victory. And I am very pleased the way it's going and grateful to many here that have been out on the stump helping with it.

*Q.* Are you pleased with how the Democratic race is shaping up?

*The President.* Let them sort out their business. Let them sort their business out. They don't need me to tell them who they

ought to vote for over there, but I see nothing to be unhappy about.

Thank you all very much.

*Cooperation With Congress*

*Q.* Mr. President, why have you refused to negotiate with the Democrats at all on your economic program?

*The President.* Listen, the American people know that from day one I held out my hand in trying to get something done. And now the time has come to take the case to the American people. The hand is still out there. But it's not going to be out there on the tax-and-spend plan. And that ought to be very, very clear. And if that's not clear now, it'll sure be clear when the debate really gets public out there in this election process. It goes on and on and on.

But that's the answer to it, and I don't think there's a single American that feels I haven't at least tried with the Congress. These people have tried. And every time they turn around, they have something jammed down their throat by majorities that simply are also aware of politics and want to put into play things that would not help this economy. We're trying to help it. We're trying to stimulate it. We're trying to increase investment. And we're not interested in more taxes, and we're not interested in ever-increasing levels of Federal spending. And that's the case that's getting in focus now.

Thank you all very much.

*Note: The exchange began at 10:08 a.m. in the Cabinet Room at the White House.*

# Remarks on Signing the Greek Independence Day Proclamation
## *March 25, 1992*

Welcome to the Rose Garden on this beautiful day. We're so pleased to have you all here. Thank you for the welcome for His Eminence and me. It's a pleasure to welcome you, many of you, most of you, back to the White House.

First, may I pay my most sincere respects to Archbishop Iakovos, a true spiritual

leader for whom we have enormous respect. And I'm just delighted that he's here with us today. And I want to thank our Cabinet Minister Ed Derwinski, who is so well-known in Greece, and Ambassador Zacharakis, who is here. And also our congressional contingent: Mike Bilirakis, over here; George Gekas was to be here, but he may have been kept away by work. And of course, Senator Arlen Specter is with us today. I would like to welcome Mr. Angelopoulos from Athens, who presented me this commemorative medal in the Oval Office just a minute ago. We are delighted you are here, sir.

This Greek-American—this Greek Independence Day—I say Greek-American day because Americans of Greek heritage celebrate it—it's a wonderful day for the Greek-American community and for all of us who cherish freedom. Greece can never be just another country to the United States. And the U.S. and Greece are the firmest of friends, the strongest of allies. And I might take this opportunity to salute Prime Minister Mitsotakis, with whom I have a very cordial relationship, most cooperative relationship. I talked to him just the other day on the phone.

We are committed to maintaining the close cooperation that has developed with his government, and we will continue to serve as a catalyst in the U.N. Secretary-General's effort to negotiate a fair and a permanent settlement to the Cyprus issue. In our view, there is one Cyprus, and we are going to continue to heal the division that scars this lovely island. Now, we have consistently made clear our view that the time has come to settle this question, and I am going to continue to give it my personal attention. We're also sensitive to Greek concerns about the breakup of Yugoslavia. And I've been in touch again, I mentioned, with my dear friend Prime Minister Mitsotakis about this highly sensitive issue. And as his Government works towards a solution to this, it can be assured of our support.

Neither Greece nor America is a stranger to the struggle for freedom. And as allies in NATO we've worked in common cause to preserve the peace. Today we remember that our ideals and values have been preserved at high cost, the valor and sacrifice of our nations' finest young men and women. Greek heritage is, in so many respects, American heritage. And I'm deeply moved to realize how important it is to interpret for future generations the significance of our independence days. We must not forget, and we cannot let our children

forget, lest the struggle be repeated. And so we celebrate these anniversaries of freedom, and we tell the old stories in order to preserve that which we value so highly.

This morning I want to commend the Greek-American community for the way you've preserved your traditions. The Greek-American culture continues to provide a model for greatness. I can cite many examples, but I want to particularly commend the value that this wonderful community places on family and on tradition. Through your commitment to strong families, those great traditions have endured, and your culture has thrived in this new land. These values, the ones that we pass along from one generation to the next, are the greatest of all legacies. But these are not just a comfortable luxury. They are a vital part of the social capital that a nation must possess if it's to be great, but more significantly, if it's to be good.

Today as we join with you to commemorate the 171st anniversary of Greek independence, we also celebrate Archbishop Iakovos' 33d year as Archbishop of the Americas. As His Eminence was at the forefront of the march for civil rights, now the Greek-American family is at the forefront in the modeling for today's generation those enduring personal and family values that are the necessary underpinning for continued democracy and freedom.

I still remember Archbishop Iakovos' benediction at our convention in 1988, and he prayed in a nonpartisan way, I want to say. But he prayed that we would, and here was the words, "Carry, renew, and redefine the legacy and mandate to keep this Nation under God in an unending quest for unity, justice, moral integrity, and spiritual alertness and readiness." On this Greek Independence Day, let that be the prayer and the challenge to us all.

And now it is my real pleasure to put pen to paper and proclaim Greek Independence Day: A National Day of Celebration of Greek and American Democracy.

*Note: The President spoke at 11:18 a.m. in the Rose Garden at the White House. In his remarks, he referred to Christos Zacharakis,*

*Greek Ambassador to the United States, and Panayiopis Angelopoulos, Greek industrial-* *ist. The proclamation is listed in Appendix E at the end of this volume.*

## Statement on House of Representatives Action To Sustain the Tax Bill Veto
*March 25, 1992*

I am pleased that the House of Representatives has voted to sustain my veto of the Democratic tax increase. This 215–211 vote indicates broad support for my position in both parties. We don't need a tax increase. We do need an economic growth package that will spur savings and investments in this country and create new jobs. I am hopeful that the many Democrats who gave us majority strength on the veto vote might join us on proposals to speed the economic recovery.

## Statements by Press Secretary Fitzwater on the President's Physical Examination
*March 26, 1992*

The President is in great shape. He completed a routine physical examination today at Bethesda Naval Hospital and is in excellent health. The President's examination lasted approximately 4 hours. The physical was conducted under the direction of Dr. Burton Lee, the President's personal physician. "The President remains in excellent health," Dr. Lee said. "He will continue his normal busy work schedule and physical activity."

Ophthalmologists continue to test the President for the raised pressure in his left eye, but his condition remains stable and there is no evidence of any development of glaucoma signs or symptoms. No treatment is indicated at the present time.

Among his test results are: chest x-ray, normal; x-rays of hips and neck, mild degenerative osteoarthritis; electrocardiogram (EKG), normal; urinalysis, no abnormalities;

normal urologic exam; blood tests completely normal including cholesterol, triglyceride, and lipoprotein levels; and dermatology, no significant problem or change. There is no evidence of any heart disease. His thyroid function remains completely normal, on Synthroid .15 milligrams a day.

[*Later in the day, Press Secretary Fitzwater issued the following additional statement on the President's physical examination.*]

The President's physical checkup this morning showed no evidence of skin cancer. However, the doctors did "freeze" with liquid nitrogen four very minute keratoses on the President's face. These will appear as small dark spots on the President's face and will disappear within a few days. The President has had keratoses removed on previous occasions over the years.

## Remarks to the Coalition for the Restoration of the Black Family and Society
*March 26, 1992*

Welcome, everybody. Please be seated now and relax here. First, let me just say how pleased I am—and I know you'll be, to hear from Lamar Alexander—but pleased I am that he's here. And you talk about something important for our Nation: What he is doing in working for a program that I'll just touch on today but that I think about every single day, our program America 2000, this chance to revolutionize, literally revolutionize American schools to give these kids a break, make them competitive in the future, it's just wonderful. So I know you're going to enjoy hearing from this former Governor who is now working so hard as a Cabinet member to do something for the kids and also, I might say for the teachers, those of you who teach. And so he's here, and you'll be hearing from him.

This, for me, is a very wonderful occasion. I'm looking forward to it. It's not just that I passed my physical a few minutes ago with flying colors. But you know, you always wonder about those things, you know, when you go out to get all this probing and checking, et cetera. But in any event, I feel blessed in that sense.

And let me just—a few serious comments. I have tried as President to preserve and strengthen three significant legacies: world peace, productive jobs for all here in this country, and then strong families. And when it comes to family, I think maybe Barbara said it the best. She said, "What goes on at the White House is not nearly as important as what goes on in your house." And what she was saying was emphasizing the importance of family, the importance of parents reading to kids, families staying together in these troubled times.

And I don't have to remind this group of committed leaders of the disturbing trends that we are bucking. You're fighting them in your neighborhoods, in your churches, and in your communities every single day, with broken hearts. And your hearts have already been stirred by the forces that threaten the American family and society.

And so let me put it this way: In too many cases, if our Government had set out determined to destroy the family, it couldn't have done greater damage than some of what we see today. Too often these programs, well-intentioned, welfare programs for example, which were meant to provide for temporary support, have undermined responsibility. They've robbed people of control of their lives, destroyed their dignity, in some cases—and we've tried hard to change this—encouraged people, man and wife, to live apart because they might just get a little bit more to put in their pockets.

We've got to do better. I know we've got a lot of reverends here, and I know I'm preaching to the choir—[*laughter*]—but let me just say this: No group is more aware of the necessity for character-based solutions in communitywide efforts than this coalition. And I want to assure you of our commitment to those same guiding principles, the principles that you try to inculcate into your parishes, into your schools, into your neighborhoods. No one cares more about it than we do. And I just want you to know we are committed. And I want to assure you of my confidence in this partnership, my support for your leadership out there, as I say, on the front lines of the battle for our Nation's families.

I have appointed a commission. You sometimes hear, "Oh, there he goes, one more commission." The mayors came to see me from the League of Cities, large cities like Los Angeles, small cities like a small community out in North Carolina, Plano, Texas, a wide variety of mayors. And they said, "The one thing that we think really gets to the fundamentals of the deterioration in the cities is the deterioration of the American family." So we put together this Commission to take a hard look at how do you strengthen the family, what legislation do you take away that may be dividing families, what legislation can we encourage to help the families and those that are trying to educate their kids and keep things together. And that Commission I look forward to hearing from. The Chairman of it is Governor Ashcroft out there in Missouri. Mayor Strauss, Annette Strauss, former Mayor of Dallas, is Cochair. And we've got a good Commission who share your views on family. I think the Commission will help a lot.

We've got to create new incentives for excellence. And Lamar will talk to you about that as how it fits into our education program. One incentive: school choice. We have to give all parents, not just the wealthy, the power to choose. And the schools that aren't chosen, as Lamar will explain, then improve themselves. There's a great record of that. And so we need your help there, the power to choose which schools serve the kids the best. And that means public; it means private; it means religious. And I don't believe that's against the Constitution.

We have shown that when we work together we can get the job done. And I want to thank everybody here that helped on the nomination of Clarence Thomas to the Supreme Court. He will be an outstanding Justice.

I know you can't do it alone, and I can't do it alone. But I want you to know I am going to continue to do what I can to bring down the walls of intolerance and prejudice in this country. I spoke out about it, will continue to speak out about it. I got a great joy in standing on the steps of the Mississippi capitol and saying in front of, whatever it was, 5,000–10,000 people, that there is no place for anti-Semitism or for racial bigotry or prejudice in this country. It is not regional. This is a national thing. And there's just as much tolerance or intolerance in States in the North or South or East or West. This is a national problem. And we've got to do what we can to make things better, to make things a little less ugly.

When economic conditions are tough, then we find people resorting to prejudice. We find neighbor looking at neighbor suspiciously. And we've got to try to change this. And so I will—I just wanted you all to know not only am I aware of the problem, but I want to do my level-best to be a constructive influence for change.

One thing that's vital to the family is a strong economy. And we're working to improve it. And I need your help on another issue, an issue that points out the urgent need for economic revival and Government reform.

Last week the Congress tried to put through a massive tax increase, the kind that would have stopped, in my view, stopped our economic recovery that's starting dead in the tracks. And I told Congress I'd veto that bill, and I did it. And yesterday the House leadership, Democrats, tried to override my veto. You may not have seen much on this, but what was meant to be a show of strength simply put a spotlight on disarray up there. Not only did the Democrats fail to muster enough votes to override that veto, but they failed to sustain the simple majority that passed the bill last Friday in the first place. And that is almost unheard of. I'm told this is the third time that's happened this century, first time since 1972, twice in the last 60 years. So I want to thank those Members of Congress from both parties who had the courage of their convictions to say no to more taxes on the American family.

That is a beginning. It is not enough. And if Congress really wants to help get this economy moving now, now that we've gotten this underbrush out of the way, to help me create jobs and revive hope, then I say pass this incentive plan that I have up there and to put America back to work.

We know we can't wait for Congress to see the light. And so, beginning today, I've asked a couple of Congressmen, Senator McCain of Arizona, Congressman Harris Fawell of Illinois, to formally introduce our request for rescissions. There are 68 Federal projects that we don't need. They are not related to jobs, and we simply cannot ask the taxpayers, given the needs that you all are aware of, to pay for things that aren't necessary in these troubled times.

So under the rules, what I've proposed now gives Congress 25 days to act, to uphold the cuts that we want to make, or they have to then stand up in broad daylight in front of you, their constituents, to go ahead with a vote, up or down, on spending that we simply don't need. We may see Congress resort to a lot of political gimmickry to get away from having to cast such a vote in the sunlight, but I think we owe it to the American family and everyone who works hard and struggles to make ends meet to hold the line on spending that is unnecessary. And we're going to keep doing that.

Also this week, the leaders who control Capitol Hill did something else: They began a new effort to remove the spending caps. That's the only protection the taxpayer has, the only defense he has against the excesses of Government spending, these enormous deficits that add to the mortgage on the future of my grandchildren and your children—you're all younger. [*Laughter*] So the Democratic leadership wants to kill those caps so Congress can then go ahead and spend more. And we simply cannot let that happen.

What we're seeing today is the beginning of a battle between those who want to change things up there and those who want to stick with the status quo. And I say, let the status quo people be warned: We are going to be making these changes, taking the case to the American people.

You see, I am very confident about this country. I know we've been through an awful lot. But America will be restored not just through Government, not Government meddling, empty slogans, symbolic gestures, but by strong, clear voices of reason and then consistent acts of responsibility. And we are going to be restored not by outsiders coming in with a better idea but by people who are passionate about, and this is where you all fit in, passionate about reclaiming your streets, rescuing the kids from the forces that literally would destroy them. And we will be restored. We've got to see our drug program succeed. We've got to see Lamar's program and mine, America 2000, be a success. And there's the challenge.

I thank you for what you've done, teachers, pastors, neighbors, friends. We are not about to give up on the United States. And you know, we've got a lot of blessings out there. Your kids and mine go to sleep at night with a little less fear of nuclear war. That's good. That's a good thing. Now, let's take what we did to change the world and use it working with you all to constructively change America.

Thank you very, very much for what you're doing. Good luck.

*Note: The President spoke at 3:11 p.m. in Room 450 of the Old Executive Office Building.*

# Nomination of Karl A. Erb To Be an Associate Director of the Office of Science and Technology Policy
*March 26, 1992*

The President today announced his intention to nominate Karl A. Erb, of Virginia, to be an Associate Director of the Office of Science and Technology Policy. He would succeed William D. Phillips.

Currently Dr. Erb serves as Acting Associate Director of Physical Sciences and Engineering in the Office of Science and Technology Policy, Executive Office of the President. Prior to this he served as Assistant Director of Physical Sciences and Engineering in the Office of Science and Technology Policy, 1989–91. In addition, Dr. Erb served with the National Science Foundation as Deputy Director of the Physics Division, 1991–present, and Program Director of Nuclear Physics, 1986–91.

Dr. Erb graduated from New York University (B.A., 1965) and the University of Michigan (M.S., 1966; Ph.D., 1970). He was born June 30, 1942, in Chicago, IL. Dr. Erb is married, has two children, and resides in Arlington, VA.

## Remarks to the Medal-Winning Teams of the National Science Olympiad
*March 27, 1992*

Everybody please be seated, and welcome, welcome. Well, I'm glad our previous meeting didn't run late, or I'd have had to bring a note from Barbara. [*Laughter*] But it is so great to see all of you and to be here with two of our very, very best: Secretary Watkins, Secretary of Energy, also has this compelling and overriding interest in things educational; and also Lamar Alexander, our Secretary of Education, who is leading from that Department for what we call America 2000, that I'll touch on in a minute. I'd like to greet the two up here also, Mr. Cairns and Mr. Putz, our leaders, your leaders, and thank them for their vision and for all they're doing. Their successful State competition has really inspired the Olympiad program. And most of all, though, let me welcome all of you, the very special young men and women here representing the 10,000 schools and the 1.5 million students who take part in the special Olympiad. Congratulations on your victory in America's olympics of the mind.

I know a lot of you are not only looking back with pride on last year's victory, but you're looking ahead to May 16th at Auburn, especially the teams from Grandville and Jenison Junior Highs. And you should be up for awards in the juggling event, too, because the way you can be in Washington with me today and then home in Michigan at your State olympics competition tomorrow is pretty good.

I am tremendously impressed by all of the students and, of course, all the teachers and by the incredible scope of activities in which you participate. You're really like decathlon athletes, good at so many varied skills like problem solving and test taking, device building.

I've looked over some of the things you've had to do to win in the Olympiad, and I'd never be able to build a musical instrument out of nonmusical materials or identify the age of reptiles. Mesozoic, I'm told is the correct one there for you amateur paleontologists. That's also around the time that dinosaurs started eating broccoli, your history books will tell you. [*Laughter*] I don't want to get off of this subject, but did you notice the other day they said broccoli is good for your health? I've felt it was a medicine all along. [*Laughter*]

So anyway, you've worked all year to get where you are, competing in 32 individual and team events in subjects like biology and chemistry, physics, Earth science, and computers.

You know, I might just be able to compete after all. Last year, at the urging, the insistence of Secretary Alexander, who is a very persistent fellow, I started to learn how to work a computer. And it's taken me a while, but a couple of months ago I wrote my first program. I called it "Michelangelo." [*Laughter*] And I wonder—I'm never quite sure what ever happened to it. [*Laughter*]

No, but seriously, you know, Lamar makes the point that nobody is too old to learn. And so he said, "You've got to do something." So I know I could learn from everybody in this room about it, but I'm really enjoying it, sending out memos and trying to master what you all know so much about. You're more than smart, and you're more than hard-working teams, I've heard. You're the best ambassadors that this country has. You show who we can be and what we can do if we just put our minds and our great American genius to work. And I am proud to honor you today because your Nation is proud to claim you, proud to recognize your achievement.

You've shown the kind of excellence that will help us meet the ambitious goals that we've set for our Nation in this America 2000 education strategy that I mentioned. We know we've got to be competitive all across the board, but we especially have to be competitive in math and science in this changing world. Our economic health, our economic survival depend on how we educate ourselves to face the challenges out there. We've called on our kids to be number one in the world in math and science by the turn of the century. And you are visible proof that we can do it.

I'm sure you've heard the results of the most recent science study of American students. And those scores simply reinforce the fact that science must be made a priority. We're serious about science and math. We've requested over $2 billion in Federal spending on math and science education in next year's budget. If my math is correct, and with this crowd out here it had better be, that's an increase of 123 percent in the last 3 years.

We also want to bring new technology into the classroom so kids can interact with astronauts and explorers and scientists, so rural schools can have access to state-of-the-art resources, and so all American kids can be exposed to the cutting-edge technologies and ideas that will shape their future.

Each one of you has learned for yourselves the true meaning of math and science. Before the numbers and the charts and tables, there is the question and the quest. And we've got to harness that same spirit of innovation, that same sense of discovery to reinvent American education, to turn our backs on the status quo, break the mold, and build a new generation of American schools. We've got to create new incentives for excellence like school choice, by giving parents the power to choose which schools serve their children best, public, private, religious.

And if we're really serious about excellence in education, we've got to recognize that renaissance begins with revolution. Real excellence demands commitment, not just from government but from everyone in every community, as we move this Nation towards achieving those six national education goals. It demands talented men and women giving their time to become tutors, mentors, and classroom assistants. I call them Points of Light. It demands businesses, churches and synagogues, civic groups forming partnerships to support local schools, working together towards what we call America 2000 communities, places where education doesn't just happen in the classroom, places where education means lifelong learning. Together, we really will reinvent the American school, community by community, neighborhood by neighborhood, all across the United States.

The Science Olympiad program shows us the way, lights the way. It brings together 3,000 volunteers, teachers, parents, business people, each one working to strengthen excellence in his or her own community. Folks like the neighbors of Pierce School, who ran car washes, sold candy, collected contributions to raise $12,000 so their team could go to the nationals. I hear even the fourth graders in the nearby Exton School raised $10, and when you're trying to get by on an allowance, $10 is a small fortune.

And you're all here today because of volunteers like these across this country. And you're here because you're not afraid to reach out for excellence. And that's why I was determined to come over here to salute you. We think of the scientist who one day will discover the cure for cancer, find the formula to guarantee against AIDS, or use technology to wipe out hunger. And we realize that today that man or woman is a student in a science class somewhere. Maybe it's a kid who will catch a spark from this program, a spark that will change his life, her life, and in the process literally change the world. The Science Olympiad has that kind of power.

So, congratulations on your achievements, on bringing to academic competition the pride and enthusiasm usually known in sports contests, and on making learning exciting. So good luck in everything you do. And when one of you kids can prove who started the Michelangelo virus, just remember: My name is Dana Carvey. [*Laughter*].

Now, thank you all for coming.

*Note: The President spoke at 12:50 p.m. in Room 450 of the Old Executive Office Building. In his remarks, he referred to John Cairns, science supervisor, Delaware Department of Public Instruction; Gerard J. Putz, science consultant, Macomb Intermediate School District, Macomb County, MI; and comedian Dana Carvey.*

## Statement by Press Secretary Fitzwater on Trade With the Former Soviet Union
*March 27, 1992*

The remarkable changes occurring in Russia and the other new States of the former Soviet Union offer the United States Government and the private sector unique opportunities to expand trade with these countries, especially in high-technology areas that have not before been readily available to us.

The administration's policy is to actively seek opportunities to acquire goods, services, and technologies from the new republics that benefit our economic and other security interests and to encourage private business to expand their search for new opportunities. We are particularly interested in access to new technologies that can be acquired economically. To facilitate this process we are moving to eliminate restrictions that prevented normal trade during the cold war. We are therefore announcing today several steps to promote greater levels of trade with these countries consistent with our firm support for democratic and market economic reforms.

First, the administration will promote a greater exchange of technology between our countries in an area once closed by both sides. Specifically:

- We will authorize the procurement by the Department of Defense of the Russian Topaz space power unit that will give us access to new technology at a significantly lower cost than if we were to try to develop it ourselves.
- We will also authorize the purchase by the Department of Defense of four Hall thrusters which have possible applications for efficient orbital transfers of satellites, and we have approved a license application for a private U.S. firm to proceed towards the purchase of these devices.
- We will authorize a purchase of plutonium-238 from Russia, an isotope of plutonium not used in nuclear explosives. This purchase will allow us to meet NASA schedules for needed space power supplies economically and without the need to restart a nuclear reactor to do so.

Second, we are also working to remove remaining barriers to commercial imports of nonmilitary items involving the private sector. In those few instances where import licenses may be required, we will review such licenses expeditiously.

Third, I would also note that the United States and our allies have reduced COCOM controls by over two-thirds and will continue to work to ensure that we maintain only those controls on high-technology trade that are needed to protect our most vital security interests. In that regard, the American business community should be assured that export licenses for civilian transactions will be processed expeditiously.

These transactions clearly signal our desire to normalize trade with the new States.

Additional details are available in a separate fact sheet.

## Nomination of Roman Popadiuk To Be United States Ambassador to Ukraine
*March 27, 1992*

The President today announced his nomination of Roman Popadiuk, of New York, a career member of the Foreign Service, to be Ambassador to Ukraine.

In January 1989, the President appointed Mr. Popadiuk to be Deputy Assistant to the

President and Deputy Press Secretary for Foreign Affairs, a position he holds to date. In President Reagan's administration, Mr. Popadiuk served as an Assistant Press Secretary from July 1986 until March 1988, when he became Special Assistant to the President and Deputy Press Secretary for Foreign Affairs. In October of that year, the President appointed him a Deputy Assistant.

Mr. Popadiuk has been a career Foreign Service officer since 1981. He served in Mexico City from 1982 to 1984, where he did consular and political work and was special assistant to the Ambassador. From 1984 to 1986, he had a tour with the Department of State and the National Security Council.

Prior to joining the Foreign Service, he was an adjunct lecturer in political science at Brooklyn College in New York City. Mr. Popadiuk was awarded the Meritorious Honor Award in 1987 and the Superior Honor Award in 1992 by the U.S. Department of State. In 1991, Mr. Popadiuk received the "Ukrainian of the Year" annual achievement award from the Ukrainian Institute of America, Inc.

Mr. Popadiuk was born in Austria on May 30, 1950. He graduated from Hunter College (B.A., 1973) and City University of New York (Ph.D., 1980). He is married to the former Judith Ann Fedkiw. They have four children and reside in Bethesda, MD.

# Radio Address to the Nation on Domestic Reforms
*March 28, 1992*

*Good morning.*

Many have called the 20th century the American Century. The question before us today is about the next century, looking just a few years ahead.

Let me tell you a story that will help shape that century, a story you probably haven't heard about. It's about a battle between those who want to change things and those who want to protect the status quo. And in this battle those who support change are telling those who want to stand pat: Lead, follow, or get out of the way.

Wednesday, those words were heard loud and clear. I'm talking about how the Democratic Congress couldn't muster a two-thirds majority—incredibly, couldn't even get a majority—to override my veto of the liberals' latest tax increase. This story you haven't heard about is also unheard of. Only twice before in the last 60 years has the House failed to muster a simple majority to override a veto.

Congressional liberals suffered this defeat for a simple reason: Americans measure progress in people helped, not dollars spent. And that's why I'm going to continue the fight to keep a lid on Federal spending. It's also why I asked Senator McCain of Arizona and Congressman Harris Fawell of Illinois to formally introduce legislation to endorse the 68 rescissions I announced last week to cut nearly $4 billion in waste from a bloated Federal budget.

Unlike liberal Democrats, given our big deficit, I don't think the Federal Government can afford to fund prickly pear research or study asparagus yield declines. Those who reject these pork barrel projects will stand with me and the American taxpayer. Those who support them will have to explain in November why the public interest has been denied.

If enough Members demand it, Congress must vote on each of these bills, yes or no, up or down. I'm going to work with those who want the Congress to be accountable and fight those who will try to block our initiatives through parliamentary gimmicks. I know that Government is too big and spends too much. And now let's see where Congress stands. Stay tuned, keep listening. We'll find out who really wants to cut spending and who just wants to keep the pork.

In a world more driven by economic competition than ever before, the challenge I am referring to is crucial to our future. I mean reform of the American Government.

During the last decade, one institution after another has looked within itself, decided on improvements, and acted to fix its problems and reflect its principles. Our task now is to bring that process of reform to the United States Government. All of us know Government's problem: Too often it is not accountable, not effective, not efficient. It's not even compassionate. Only by changing it can we protect America's general interest against selfish special interests.

My rescissions will help knock out one part of the special interest problem at work in Congress today, but the changes I want are even bigger. I want to end the PAC contributions which are corrupting our system. I want to place term limits on Congress, and I want to lead the American people in making changes that will make the 21st century another American century.

One challenge is to make our people educated, literate, and motivated to keep learning. And that's why I'm trying to reform our education system from top to bottom.

Our people must have a sense of well-being about their health and that of their children and families. My health care reform plan will guarantee them access to the finest health care system in the world and make that care affordable.

And next, help me return our civil justice system to its original purpose: dispense justice with civility. Eighteen million lawsuits a year are choking us, costing individuals and businesses billions, a tremendous drag on our morale as well as our economy.

And in the next century, as we look at the likely economic competition as well as the likely opportunities, they will be beyond our borders. That means we must open up more foreign markets to sell our goods and our services and to sustain and create jobs for our people.

Reform of Government, education, health care, our legal system, opening markets abroad: addressing these issues is fundamental to America's future. Already America has changed the world. Today I'm asking you to help me change America. If Congress won't change, we'll have to change the Congress. The battle has been joined, and it's your future that we're fighting for.

Thank you for your support. And may God bless the United States of America.

*Note: This address was recorded at 10:30 a.m. on March 27 in the Oval Office at the White House for broadcast after 9 a.m. on March 28.*

# Remarks to State Attorneys General
*March 30, 1992*

Well, may I salute Ken Eikenberry and Jeff Amestoy and all the State attorney generals, and salute also—whoops, there he is down there—our own Bill Barr, who I think is doing an outstanding job. And I know he's working closely with everybody in this room.

Bill has his forces moving out on several fronts, from tort reform to relief of prison overcrowding. We've also started what we call the "Weed and Seed" initiative, our plan to get the roots, rip them out, of the inner-city violence, and then plant seeds of hope with more educational opportunity, with more job training, with a new approach to health care. And then we are going to keep hammering away on the need for enterprise zones. This plan joins Federal, State, and local forces to go after and to take back our hardest hit neighborhoods. They're crucial missions, and I am determined to see them achieved and let nothing stand in the way.

The efforts of the Justice Department help shape the kind of legacy that we leave for future generations. And our children must inherit a society that is safe, is sane and just. And I've also spoken of other meaningful legacies like jobs and a world at peace and certainly strong families. The American heritage which I describe is one where children can sit on their porch without the fear of getting caught in an ugly crossfire, where decent people don't have to hide behind locked doors while gangs roam the streets, where the message is clear: When it comes to the law, if you're going to take liberties, you're going to lose your own; you're going to pay.

We cannot pass this legacy onto our children tomorrow unless we start going after tough crime legislation today. And for 3 years running, we have called on the Congress to pass a tough crime bill. We've pushed hard. Many of you have been at our side in trying to get something done. I want a bill that won't tie the hands of the honest cops in trying to get their jobs done, one that shows less sympathy for the criminals and certainly more for the victims of crime. And most of all, I want to get a crime bill that I can sign.

But law and order mean more than just safe streets and bigger prisons. Reforming the system also means going after public corruption in our cities and our States, the rot that eats away at our institutions and at our trust. Over the past 3 years, this administration has moved aggressively to hunt down corruption and stop it dead in its tracks.

For the record, in '89 and '90 alone the Department secured over 2,200 convictions, 2,200, in public corruption cases. Judges, legislators, and law enforcement officials, part-time crooks, full-time fakes: Nobody is immune. And this kind of crime does society real harm because these swindlers aren't satisfied merely with making crime pay; they stick the taxpayer with the tab. And millions and millions of hard-earned tax dollars are disappearing from public treasuries every single year and showing up in corruption's back pocket. And this is money that could be building roads or balancing budgets. I am preaching to the choir on this subject because you all are out there on the cutting edge, on the front line all the time, trying to do something about the problem.

But the problem is greater than a few individuals who stopped caring. The problem is a system that has stopped working. And the old bureaucratic system of big Government has ground to a halt. And it's not accountable; it is not effective; and it is not efficient. It's not even compassionate.

And the chronic problems we see today are sad proof that the old approaches are producing new failures.

So in this election year, it's understandable, I'm sure, that we hear a lot of talk about change. You all have been fighting for change. I think I have. And yes, the time has come for change, far-reaching, fundamental reform. That's the kind of change that this country needs in the fighting-crime field; not just in fighting crime, incidentally, and not just in Government but all across the board.

And that's why I've—proposing school choice reform—just finished almost an hour meeting with our Secretary of Education on that one—so that choices about education can be made from the kitchen table, not from the halls of bureaucracy. Where it's been tried, it has been effective in improving the schools that are not chosen as well as those that are.

And I've proposed a health care reform to improve access for those who need it the most.

Legal reform, we need your help on. We've got good proposals up there on Capitol Hill. Our legal reform is shaped so that Americans can start solving their problems face to face instead of lawyer to lawyer. I'm amazed at the number, the great increase in lawsuits that is really putting a damper on so many aspects in our society.

The kind of change that I'm describing is hard. It has its enemies, and the battle lines have been drawn: the allies of change versus the defenders of the status quo. So, I want to make it very clear which side I'm on; I know which side many of you are on.

So, let the cynics say that this is only a fight for the next election. We know it's a battle for the next generation. And I'm very glad you all are here. And what we'll do is go over here, and I'd love to have suggestions from you as to how we might be doing our job better down here. And of course, I'd be glad to take questions. If they're technical, I'll kick them off to perhaps the most able Attorney General a guy could hope to have with him.

Thank you all very much.

*Note: The President spoke at 10:36 a.m. in*

*the Roosevelt Room at the White House. In his remarks, he referred to Kenneth O. Eikenberry, attorney general of Washington,*

*and Jeffrey L. Amestoy, attorney general of Vermont.*


# Exchange With Reporters Prior to Discussions With President George Vassiliou of Cyprus
*March 30, 1992*

### Cyprus

*Q.* President Vassiliou, are you going to ask the United States to pressure Mr. Denktash to make some progress?

*President Vassiliou.* Well, I am grateful to the President for his support for a solution of the Cyprus problem, and I'm sure that the fact that he's meeting here, with him in an election campaign period, is the best proof of his interest. And I'm grateful.

*President Bush.* I am interested, and I just hope we can help. Our Ambassador's been wonderful and tried, a Special Ambassador, but now he's going on to greater pursuits. But we can't let him get too far away because he's very interested in all of that. No, but we'll talk about it, and I think your visit up there in New York probably is very important. I hope the new Secretary-General is energized. He told me he wants to be.

*President Vassiliou.* He's very interested. He wants to do it, and he needs your support.

*President Bush.* Well, you can——

*Q.* Mr. Denktash said he would like to meet you someplace.

*President Vassiliou.* Meetings are always easy to arrange; what is important is to have willingness to solve the problem.

### Aid to Former Soviet Union

*Q.* Mr. President, sir, are you going to send your Soviet aid package up to the Hill tomorrow?

*President Bush.* Listen, I can't tell you that right now. But we've been working on one for a long, long time, as you know. As I indicated Sunday, we'll have something to say on that very soon. I can't say about tomorrow, any package going up.

I don't think people know how long it takes. This is the Soviet—we've been working on this for 6 months, and we get a lot of people telling us, well, you've got to—I mean, it's very complicated when you're trying to get the whole world to come together on it.

[*At this point, one group of reporters left the room, and another group came in.*]

### Cyprus

*Q.* Mr. President, is Turkey to blame for the current impasse in the Cyprus talks?

*President Bush.* We're going to have a good talk about Cyprus. Anytime I see my friend, the very able President here, we have good, fruitful discussions. And I'm anxious for him to bring me up to date not only as to how things were at home when he left but how his talks in the United Nations went. As you know, the United States has felt that the United Nations has had and will continue to have a key role in all of this. So secondly, I hope the President knows that we have tried, with various interested parties, to be helpful. Sometimes you think you take a step forward, and you end up sliding back a little bit.

*President Vassiliou.* Yes.

*President Bush.* And I want to see what we can do to be sure that now, at this critical time, we don't take a step backwards. But I'm available. The United States is interested in trying to help solve this problem, and I need to hear from President Vassiliou what he thinks now I should be doing as President. We're going to stay right involved with him. It is very important.

*Q.* Mr. President, how much can one expect in this election year in the United States?

*President Bush.* The election will have no adverse effect on our efforts, either in terms of my commitment of time, whatever is necessary for me to commit. If that's what it takes, I'll make such a commitment right here.

Secondly, there is no political division on this. The American people are not off in 25 different camps like we are on a lot of other issues. We want to see if we can be helpful to the solution of this problem. So there's nothing in the political arena that would keep an administration at this election time from staying involved and trying to be constructive on a policy question.

*Q.* Mr. President, do you expect that the problems possibly could be solved this year?

*President Bush.* Listen, I thought it was possible to solve last year, and we tried, as you remember. I paid a visit to Greece, a visit to Turkey, and there was where we thought we might have helped take a step forward. But we'll keep working on it, and again I'm interested in hearing what the President has to say about this.

*Q.* Mr. President, how do you address the Greek—[*inaudible*]—on the Macedonian issue?

*President Bush.* Carefully. [*Laughter*]

Thank you all, and welcome.

*Note: The exchange began at 4 p.m. in the Oval Office at the White House. Rauf Denktash was the leader of the Turkish community in Cyprus, and Ambassador Nelson Ledsky was U.S. Special Cyprus Coordinator.*

## Statement by Deputy Press Secretary Smith on the President's Meeting With President George Vassiliou of Cyprus
*March 30, 1992*

The President met today with President George Vassiliou of Cyprus. The two leaders discussed the current status of the United Nations-led effort to negotiate a fair and permanent settlement to the Cyprus dispute. The President pledged continued U.S. support for the U.N. process and discussed with President Vassiliou ways in which the parties might work to generate greater progress in the talks in the coming months.

## Remarks at a Meeting With Health Care Representatives
*March 31, 1992*

One, we want change; everybody knows we need it. We want more accessibility; everyone knows we need that. Two, we want to retain the quality of health care that has singled out the United States. And under our plan I believe we not only retain the quality, but we will be able to provide the access. And you're right, market—let that work on this. And let's not turn to a socialized medicine scheme that sounds good and that's going to cost the taxpayers an arm and a leg. So, we'll keep on it.

But I want to just find out in a little more detail what more we should be doing here because we are very grateful to HEAL for this support. And when you see a coalition of this magnitude working for this common end, it gives me great confidence we can get something done. That's the main thing: Help those people that need help, and do it in a sensible and sound way.

So, we'll see how we go.

*Note: The President spoke at 11:17 a.m. in the Roosevelt Room at the White House. In his remarks, he referred to the Health Care Equity Action League (HEAL).*

## Message to the Congress Reporting on the National Emergency With Respect to Export Controls
*March 31, 1992*

*To the Congress of the United States:*

1. On September 30, 1990, in Executive Order No. 12730, I declared a national emergency under the International Emergency Economic Powers Act ("IEEPA") (50 U.S.C. 1701, *et seq.*) to deal with the threat to the national security and foreign policy of the United States caused by the lapse of the Export Administration Act of 1979, as amended (50 U.S.C. App. 2401, *et seq.*), and the system of controls maintained under that Act. In that order I continued in effect, to the extent permitted by law, the provisions of the Export Administration Act of 1979, as amended, the Export Administration Regulations (15 C.F.R. 768, *et seq.* (1991)), and the delegations of authority set forth in Executive Order No. 12002 of July 7, 1977, Executive Order No. 12214 of May 2, 1980, and Executive Order No. 12131 of May 4, 1979, as amended by Executive Order No. 12551 of February 21, 1986.

2. I issued Executive Order No. 12730 pursuant to the authority vested in me as President by the Constitution and laws of the United States, including IEEPA, the National Emergencies Act ("NEA") (50 U.S.C. 1601, *et seq.*), and section 301 of title 3 of the United States Code. At that time, I also submitted a report to the Congress pursuant to section 204(b) of IEEPA (50 U.S.C 1703(b)). Section 204 of IEEPA requires follow-up reports, with respect to actions or changes, to be submitted every 6 months. Additionally, section 401(c) of the NEA requires that the President, within 90 days after the end of each 6-month period following a declaration of a national emergency, report to the Congress on the total expenditures directly attributable to that declaration. This report, covering the 6-month period from October 1, 1991, to March 31, 1992, is submitted in compliance with these requirements.

3. Since the issuance of Executive Order No. 12730, the Department of Commerce has continued to administer the system of export controls, including antiboycott provi-sions, contained in the Export Administration Regulations. In administering these controls, the Department has acted under a policy of conforming actions under Executive Order No. 12730 to those required under the Export Administration Act, insofar as appropriate.

4. Since my last report to the Congress, there have been several significant developments in the area of export controls:

—In light of the ongoing changes occurring in Eastern Europe and the former Soviet Union, the Department of Commerce has been working with officials of Bulgaria, Czechoslovakia, Hungary, Poland, and republics of the former Soviet Union to implement and strengthen their export control systems, including pre-license inspections and post-shipment verifications. We are also engaged in activities with these countries to assist in the prevention of proliferation of weapons of mass destruction and corresponding technology. These developments will allow for enhanced and much-needed trade in high technology items and other commodities in the region, while helping to prevent unauthorized shipments or uses of such items.

—In my last report I noted that, following negotiations with our Coordinating Committee (COCOM) partners that produced a streamlined Core List of truly strategic items subject to multilateral national security controls, the Department of Commerce implemented a new Commerce Control List (CCL), effective September 1, 1991 (56 F.R. 42824, August 29, 1991). During the current reporting period, the Department issued a conforming regulation, effective January 7, 1992, to bring the CCL into line with special country- and commodity-based controls. In this action, foreign policy provisions in the Export Administration Regulations (EAR) were revised to adjust and expand controls on Iran and Syria. Controls affecting countries designated by the Secretary of State as supporting international terrorism were also revised, with Iraq added and Yemen deleted from the list. Additionally, the transfer from the Department of State to the Department of Commerce of licensing jurisdiction over certain civil aircraft inertial navigation equipment was implemented (57 F.R. 4553, February 6, 1992).

—Our efforts to address the threat to the national security and foreign policy interests of the United States posed by the spread of weapons of mass destruction and missile delivery systems remain ongoing. In this vein, we continue to work with our major trading partners to strengthen export controls over goods, technology, and other forms of assistance that can contribute to the spread of nuclear, chemical, and biological weapons and missile systems:

• The United States has been working with its partners in the 22-nation Australia Group (AG) to harmonize export controls related to the proliferation of chemical and biological weapons (CBW). At the December 1991 meeting, the participants agreed to control the export of certain biological organisms and CBW-related equipment. The list considered for possible adoption by the AG in this effort is nearly identical to the draft submitted by the United States.

• Additionally, the 27-nation Nuclear Suppliers Group, in which the United States participates, is expected formally to establish a multilateral regime to control nuclear-related, dual-use items along the lines of the nuclear referral list currently administered by the Department of Commerce.

• In the area of supercomputers, we have agreed on a supercomputer safeguard regime with Japan and will be negotiating with our European trading partners to expand this regime. Supercomputer exports involve sensitive national security and foreign policy interests such as cryptology, strategic defense, and submarine warfare; the multilateral safeguard regime is therefore intended to establish uniform and effective international policies and procedures to protect supercomputers from unauthorized end-uses and end-users.

• Developments in the Missile Technology Control Regime (MTCR) include revision of the MTCR control list or "Annex," and the inclusion of missiles capable of delivering all weapons of mass destruction within the scope of the MTCR, not just those capable of delivering nuclear weapons, which were originally designated as the focus of the regime.

—In response to commitments made by the People's Republic of China (PRC) to adhere to the MTCR nonproliferation guidelines, on February 21, 1992, the Department of State announced my decision to remove special missile sanctions imposed upon the PRC for the activities of Chinese entities involved in missile technology proliferation. As a result, certain sanctions, including restrictions on the export of high-performance computers, are being removed. Other controls affecting the PRC, such as those implemented following Tiananmen Square, remain in place.

—Finally, our enforcement efforts have continued unabated:

• During this 6-month reporting period, record civil penalties, totalling in excess of $3.5 million, were assessed in export control enforcement cases. The companies against which the penalties were imposed include the Digital Equipment Corporation; Ecosphere International; Everex Systems, Inc., and its subsidiary Everex Systems (Far East); and Kobe Argentina, the Argentine subsidiary of a U.S. company that was involved in the first case in which both export control and antiboycott violations were alleged.

• On December 19, 1991, special agents from the Department of Commerce's Bureau of Export Administration arrested a French businessman in New York on charges of diverting two shipments of aviation oil valued at over $2 million to Cuba. A German company and two of its executives were also indicted in connection with the diversion scheme. In addition, an American company and two of its executives were indicted and charged with falsifying

519

shipping documents, having knowledge of the diversion, and failing to report the diversion to authorities.

• On February 18, 1992, the Department of Commerce charged L.A. Gear, Inc., an athletic footwear manufacturer, with 46 violations of the antiboycott provisions of the Export Administration Act and Regulations. The Department alleged that, in July 1987 and January 1990, the company complied with boycott requests from a Middle Eastern customer, resulting in antiboycott violations including knowingly agreeing to refuse to do business with other persons in response to a boycott-based requirement, furnishing prohibited boycott-related information, and failure to report receipt of boycott-related requests.

5. The expenses incurred by the Federal Government in the 6-month period from October 1, 1991, to March 31, 1992, that are directly attributable to the exercise of authorities conferred by the declaration of a national emergency with respect to export controls were largely centered in the Department of Commerce, Bureau of Export Administration. Expenditures by the Department of Commerce are anticipated to be $20,254,000, most of which represents wage and salary costs for Federal personnel.

6. The unrestricted access of foreign parties to U.S. goods, technology, and technical data, and the existence of certain boycott practices of foreign nations, in light of the expiration of the Export Administration Act of 1979, continue to constitute an unusual and extraordinary threat to the national security, foreign policy, and economy of the United States. I shall continue to exercise the powers at my disposal to retain the export control system, including the antiboycott provisions, and will continue to report periodically to the Congress.

GEORGE BUSH

The White House,
March 31, 1992.

# Message to the Congress Transmitting Occupational Safety and Health Reports
*March 31, 1992*

*To the Congress of the United States:*

In accordance with section 26 of the Occupational Safety and Health Act of 1970 (Public Law 91–596; 29 U.S.C. 675), I transmit herewith the 1989 annual reports on activities of the Department of Labor, the Department of Health and Human Services, and the Occupational Safety and Health Review Commission.

GEORGE BUSH

The White House,
March 31, 1992.

# Nomination of Thomas C. Richards To Be Federal Aviation Administrator
*March 31, 1992*

The President today announced his intention to nominate Thomas C. Richards, of Texas, to be Administrator of the Federal Aviation Administration. He would succeed James B. Busey IV.

Since retiring from the Air Force in 1990, General Richards has served as a corporate consultant in Bryan, TX. In June 1990, General Richards was appointed by President Bush to serve as a member of the Commission on Aviation Safety and Security. Prior to this, General Richards, a four-star general in the U.S. Air Force, served as Deputy Commander in Chief for the Headquarters of the U.S. European Command in West Germany, 1986–1990. He was Commander of Air University, Maxwell Air Force Base in Montgomery, AL; Vice Commander of the 8th Air Force, 1984–1985; Commander of Keesler Technical Training Center in Biloxi, MS, 1982–1984; Chairman of the U.S.

Air Force Recruiting Service, Randolph Air Force Base, TX, 1981–1982; and Commandant of Cadets of the U.S. Air Force Academy in Colorado Springs, CO, 1978–1981.

General Richards graduated from Virginia Polytechnic Institute (B.S., 1956) and Shippensburg State College (M.A., 1973). He served in the U.S. Air Force, 1956–1990. General Richards was born February 13, 1930, in San Diego, CA. He is married, has three children, and resides in Bryan, TX.

# Nomination of Wade F. Horn To Be a Deputy Director of the Office of National Drug Control Policy
*March 31, 1992*

The President today announced his intention to nominate Wade F. Horn, of Maryland, to be Deputy Director for Demand Reduction for the Office of National Drug Control Policy. He would succeed Herbert D. Kleber.

Dr. Horn is currently Commissioner of the Administration for Children, Youth and Families and Chief of the Children's Bureau at the Department of Health and Human Services in Washington, DC. He has also served as a member of the National Commission on Children. From 1988 to 1989, he was a member of the Presidential transition team in the office of the President-elect; and a member of the health care advisory/research group for George Bush for President campaign, 1987–1988. From 1986 to 1989, he served in various capacities: director of outpatient psychological services for

the department of psychiatry at the Children's Hospital National Medical Center; vice chairperson for the department of pediatric psychology at the Children's Hospital National Medical Center; and an associate professor of psychiatry and behavioral sciences and of child health and development at the George Washington University School of Medicine. He has also served as assistant professor of the department of psychology at Michigan State University, 1982–1986; and associate director of Michigan State University's psychological clinic and director of the pediatric psychology specialty clinic, 1984–1986.

Dr. Horn graduated from the American University (B.A., 1975) and Southern Illinois University (M.A., 1978; Ph.D., 1981). He was born December 3, 1954, in Coral Gables, FL. He is married, has two children, and resides in Gaithersburg, MD.

# Message to the Congress on Trade With Hungary and Czechoslovakia
*March 31, 1992*

*To the Congress of the United States:*

In June 1991 I determined and reported to the Congress that Hungary continues to meet the emigration criteria of the Jackson-

Vanik amendment to, and section 409 of, the Trade Act of 1974 (19 U.S.C. 2432 and 2439). In October 1991 I determined and reported to the Congress that Czechoslovakia also meets the emigration criteria contained in title IV of the Trade Act of 1974. These determinations allowed for the continuation of most favored nation (MFN) status for Hungary and Czechoslovakia without the requirement of an annual waiver.

As required by law, I am submitting an updated formal report to the Congress concerning emigration laws and policies of the Republic of Hungary and the Czech and Slovak Federal Republic. You will find that the report indicates continued Hungarian and Czechoslovak compliance with U.S. and international standards in the areas of emigration and human rights policy.

The Administration is taking steps to exercise the authority provided me in section 2 of Public Law 102–182 to terminate the application of title IV of the Trade Act of 1974 to Czechoslovakia and Hungary.

GEORGE BUSH

The White House,
March 31, 1992.

*Note: This message was released by the Office of the Press Secretary on April 1.*

# The President's News Conference on Aid to the States of the Former Soviet Union
*April 1, 1992*

*The President.* I have a statement that is a little longer than the normal, but let me just say that I have just met with the congressional leadership to request their bipartisan backing for a new, comprehensive, and integrated program to support the struggle of freedom underway in Russia, Ukraine, and the other new States that have replaced the Soviet Union.

The revolution in these States is a defining moment in history with profound consequences for America's own national interests. The stakes are as high for us now as any that we have faced in this century. And our adversary for 45 years, the one nation that posed a worldwide threat to freedom and peace, is now seeking to join the community of democratic nations. A victory for democracy and freedom in the former U.S.S.R. creates the possibility of a new world of peace for our children and grandchildren. But if this democratic revolution is defeated, it could plunge us into a world more dangerous in some respects than the dark years of the cold war.

America must meet this challenge, joining with those who stood beside us in the battle against imperial communism: Germany, the United Kingdom, Japan, France, Canada, Italy, and other allies. Together we won the cold war, and today we must win the peace.

This effort will require new resources from the industrial democracies, but nothing like the price we would pay if democracy and reform failed in Russia and Ukraine and Byelarus and Armenia and the States of Central Asia. It will require the commitment of a united America, strengthened by a consensus that transcends even the heated partisanship of a Presidential election campaign. And today I call upon Congress, Republicans and Democrats alike, and the American people to stand behind this united effort.

Our national effort must be part of a global effort. I've been in contact with Chancellor Kohl, Prime Minister Major, President Mitterrand, other key allies to discuss our plans and to assure them of the high priority I place on the success of this endeavor. To this end, I would like to announce today a plan to support democracy in the States of the former Soviet Union.

This is a complex set of issues which took months to sort out, working within the administration, working with our major allies and with the leaders of the new independent States of the former Soviet Union. A number of things had to come together to make sure we got it right.

Let me give you a little bit of the history.

I asked Secretary Baker to outline our fundamental approach in his December 12th speech at Princeton. I spoke again on the need to embrace Russia and the other new States of the former Soviet Union in my January 22d speech at the Washington conference to coordinate the humanitarian assistance. On February 1st, Boris Yeltsin and I discussed these issues at Camp David. And that same day, Secretary Brady met with Boris Yeltsin's key economic adviser, Yegor Gaydar, to discuss how we could support Russian reforms. A week later, Jim Baker followed up during his meeting with Kozyrev, Foreign Minister Kozyrev, and Boris Yeltsin in Moscow. And just yesterday, the IMF reached tentative agreement with Russia on its market reform program. After weeks of intensive consultations in the G–7, Chancellor Kohl, currently serving as Chairman of the G–7, has announced today G–7 support for an IMF program for Russia.

The program that I'm announcing today builds on this progress and includes three major components. First, the United States has been working with its Western allies and the international financial institutions on an unprecedented multilateral program to support reform in the newly independent States. The success of this program will depend upon their commitment to reform and their willingness to work with the international community.

Russia is exhibiting that commitment. And I'm announcing today that the U.S. is prepared to join in a substantial multilateral financial assistance package in support of Russia's reforms. We're working to develop, with our allies and the IMF, a $6 billion currency stabilization fund to help maintain confidence in the Russian ruble. The U.S. will also join in a multilateral effort to marshal roughly $18 billion in financial support in 1992 to assist Russian efforts to stabilize and restructure their economy. We've been working with the Russian Government for 3 months to help it develop an economic reform plan to permit the major industrialized countries to provide support. We will work to complete action on this approximately $24 billion package by the end of April. And I pledge the full cooperation of the United States in this effort.

Secondly, the United States will also act to broaden its own capacity to extend assistance to the new States. I'm transmitting to Congress a comprehensive bill, the "FREEDOM Support Act," to mobilize the executive branch, the Congress, and indeed, our private sector around a comprehensive and integrated package of support for the new States. Now, this package will:

Authorize a U.S. quota increase of $12 billion for the IMF, which is critical to supporting Russia and the other new States. The IMF and World Bank will be the primary source of funding for the major financial assistance needs of the new governments. The U.S. quota increase for the IMF was specifically assumed in the budget agreement and does not require a budget outlay;

Support my existing authority to work with the G–7 and the IMF to put together the stabilization program for Russia and support possible subsequent programs for other States of the former Soviet Union as they embarked on landmark reforms, including up to $3 billion for stabilization funds.

It would also repeal restrictive cold war legislation so that American business can compete on an even footing in these new markets. And I'm determined that American business be given the chance to invest and trade with the new States. And to that end, I've also directed that the United States negotiate trade and bilateral investment and tax treaties with these countries just as soon as possible. Significant new trade relationships can create jobs right here in this country.

The package will broaden the use of $500 million appropriated by Congress last year to encompass not only the safe dismantling and destruction of nuclear weapons but also the broader goals of nuclear plant safety, demilitarization, and defense conversion.

It will also establish a major people-to-people program between the United States and the States of the former Soviet Union to create the type of lasting personal bonds among our peoples and Russian understanding of democratic institutions so critical to long-term peace. This effort will complement our existing programs to bring hundreds of businessmen to the United States from the Commonwealth and then send hundreds of Peace Corps volunteers to the new States.

In sending this authorization legislation to Congress, I call upon the Congress to act concurrently to provide the appropriations necessary to make these authorizations a reality.

Third, in addition to the 3.75 billion already extended by the U.S. since January 1991, I'm announcing today 1.1 billion in new Commodity Credit Corporation credit guarantees for the purchase of American agricultural products. Six hundred million of that will go for U.S. sales to Russia and an additional 500 million for U.S. sales to the Ukraine and other States.

Now, let me close on a personal note. I think every day about the challenge of securing a peaceful future for the American people. And I believe very strongly that President Yeltsin's reform program holds the greatest hope for the future of the Russian people and for the security of the American people as we define a new relationship with that great country. President Yeltsin has taken some very courageous steps for democracy and free markets. And I am convinced that it is in our own national interest to support him strongly.

For more than 45 years, the highest responsibility of nine American Presidents, Democrats and Republicans, was to wage and win the cold war. It was my privilege to work with Ronald Reagan on these broad programs and now to lead the American people in winning the peace by embracing the people so recently freed from tyranny to welcome them into the community of democratic nations.

I know there are those who say we should pull back, concentrate our energies, our interests, and our resources on our pressing domestic problems. And they are very important. But I ask them to think of the consequences here at home of peace in the world. We've got to act now. And if we turn away, if we do not do what we can to help democracy succeed in the lands of the old Soviet Union, our failure to act will carry a far higher price. And if we face up to the challenge, matching the courage of President Yeltsin, of Ukrainian President Kravchuk, of Armenian President Ter-Pe-

trosyan, many other future generations of Americans will thank us for having had the foresight and the conviction to stand up for democracy and work for peace in this decade and into the next century.

That's the end of this statement. I'll be glad to take just a handful of questions, and then Jim Baker and Secretary Brady—I think Secretary Baker will go into more detail on the legislation, and Secretary Brady and others will be available. I think Ed Madigan will talk to you about the agricultural sect of it.

Terry [Terence Hunt, Associated Press]?

*Q.* Mr. President, you mentioned several figures in your statement. Overall, what's the cost of this to taxpayers, and where's the money going to come from?

*The President.* Most of it will come from the IFI's, from the international financial institutions. About a fifth of the total is assigned to the—about a fifth of it, 20 percent of it, is our share. And there's not a lot of new money. It's our feeling and the feeling of the partners that we ought to go use these international financial organizations who were set up to do this very job. Now, we have a significant commitment to these organizations. But that's the fact as to how this breaks out.

*Q.* Was there any kind of figure that you could provide? You say there's not much new money. What——

*The President.* I'll let Jim Baker give you the details on it, but yes, we can. There is some new money in it. There's some new credits in it, you know, agricultural credits. But let him give you the details on what's going to be in the bill. It's not a tremendous amount of money. Our commitment is very, very substantial.

Yes, Helen [Helen Thomas, United Press International].

*Q.* Mr. President, not in the either-or sense, you've acknowledged the pressing domestic problems. What are you going to do to help the American people, the financially strapped States, the decaying cities? Is there a post-cold-war Marshall plan for America in view of its problems? And why do we have to have 150,000 troops in Europe when the enemy has disappeared from the screen?

*The President.* We are working on programs that will help the cities, including trying to get through a significant block grant that would help, including a crime bill, including a brand-new revolutionary approach to education that, longer run, is terribly significant. And yes, it is very important we do these things.

But my point to the American people is we have a major stake in the success of democracy in Russia and in these other States. And the cost of risking doing nothing, the cost of doing nothing could be exorbitant, could far transcend the money that we have spent in the past. And I just don't want to risk that.

In terms of the troops, it is important that the United States stay involved in guaranteeing against any unforeseen action. We saw the need to be involved a year ago in Desert Storm. And if we had listened to the critics that would have suggested that we disarm and unilaterally pull back, we would be in terrible shape today. And we're not in terrible shape today. We have a vital stake in European security. Our allies and ourselves agree that the United States should remain there with troops, and we will stay there with troops.

*Q.* Mr. President, if the risks are so great, the stakes so high, why did you wait until 3 months into an election year to outline this program and begin the push for it, especially when, as you say, there's little new money involved?

*The President.* Because—we haven't waited. If you listen to what I said earlier, we spelled out our determination to do this in December. We have been working with our allies constructively to bring about agreement on this international financial institution approach. That was hammered out this weekend by Secretary Brady's people overseas. The formulation of the bill has just been completed. And we've just gotten agreement from—this morning I talked to Kravchuk and to Yeltsin, once again, both of them on this. I might say that they both sounded quite enthusiastic about it.

A lot of work has been going into it. And rather than kind of posturing out there, we wanted to have a sound program that will have strong international support. And that is exactly, thanks to the cooperation of the allies, what we have. So this isn't any Johnny-come-lately thing, and this isn't driven by election year pressures. It's what's right for the United States.

And I must say, without committing anybody to anything, that the reception from the joint leadership seemed quite positive, Brit [Brit Hume, ABC News]. I was very pleased, but we'll let them speak for themselves, but most of them saying we should be doing this.

*Q.* Well, sir, whether you are posturing or not, have you not waited a while before beginning this sales pitch——

*The President.* I don't know that——

*Q.* ——in the knowledge that you were going to have to do something along these lines?

*The President.* I said something about it in January. Jim Baker mentioned it in December. I've been talking about it. The question, though, is not a lot of political rhetoric; the question is getting something done that's positive. And when you're dealing with a whole bunch of allies and you're dealing with many new countries, you want to be sure that you do it in a sensible way. And the fact that it's coming out now is because we now have, with great cooperation from the allies, working with them, come up with this approach that we think makes sense. And it's not something that's new.

*Q.* Sir, the reason there is this skepticism is, back when Pat Buchanan was beating you about the head in New Hampshire, you weren't out there in New Hampshire, you weren't in New Hampshire saying, "We've got to help Boris Yeltsin. We've got to help Kravchuk." You weren't talking about that at all. You weren't preparing American public opinion. Today Bill Clinton's out there talking about his plan for Russia and the republics. That's why it looks a little weird.

*The President.* Well, that I've explained to you, John [John Cochran, NBC News], that there's a great deal of diplomacy. I remember when one of the people that used to sit proudly in this room accused me of not being emotional about Germany, about trying to get a reunited Germany when the wall came down. I said—what I was saying to myself: Much less interested in emotion, much more interested in getting something positively done; use the power of the Presidency of the United States to see if you can't have that be accomplished in a very peaceful way.

And we have been doing the diplomacy that is necessary to come forward with a program that I hope will have the support of the American people, that I am proud to take to the American people, even though some people are going to be saying, "Well, you shouldn't be doing this in an election year." You've got to be, you know—along the lines of Helen's question, people will be suggesting that. But I'm going to fight for this because I believe in it.

Yeah, and then I'm getting out of here.

*Q.* Our recent poll showed that 55 percent of the public thinks that foreign aid should, in fact, be cut, and another 40 percent thinks that it shouldn't be increased at all. How are you going to persuade the public that this, in fact, is worthwhile when they look around and see roads deteriorating and schools in trouble and so forth?

*The President.* Simply make the case that to do nothing would be irresponsible, that the United States must continue to lead, and that we have an enormous stake, personal stake, for every American in the success of these democracies, and to risk their failure by doing nothing is very short-sighted. And so that's the case I'm going to make.

And I will also be saying we have a lot of blessings in this country, and one of them today is peace. Your kids and mine don't go to sleep at night as worried about nuclear weapons as some of the preceding generations here. And I want to be sure that I can certify to the American people I've done everything I can as President to see that

that continues, that democracies are strengthened, that freedom is on the march and continues to stay on the march. And this approach we're taking is the way to do what we can to guarantee that.

*Q.* Well, then to flip the question around a little bit, what do you say to those who are also going to say that this really isn't that much, that in fact Germany has already contributed $45 billion to this effort, and that compared to what we could do we aren't doing enough, if so much in fact is at stake?

*The President.* I will say that I think it is enough and that it's what we ought to do right now and fight like heck for what we believe in here. And I think it is. And I must say I was very pleased with the response by President Yeltsin, the response by President Kravchuk this morning. And I would cite that as evidence of their enthusiasm for what we're doing.

But I guess you're right, some people will attack you for doing too much, and some for not doing enough. I think this is right. I believe Congress will give it the proper support. And I want the American people to support it because I know that it is in the best interest of world peace. And the failure of world peace has a staggering price tag on it that I don't want to even contemplate. So I'll continue to work for this.

Now, let me turn it over to Jim.

*Note: The President's 125th news conference began at 11:04 a.m. in the Briefing Room at the White House. Following the President's remarks, the news conference continued with Secretary of State James A. Baker III, Secretary of the Treasury Nicholas F. Brady, and Secretary of Agriculture Edward A. Madigan.*

## Message to the Senate Transmitting the Nigeria-United States Legal Assistance Treaty
*April 1, 1992*

*To the Senate of the United States:*

With a view to receiving the advice and consent of the Senate to ratification, I transmit herewith the Treaty between the Government of the United States of America and the Federal Republic of Nigeria on Mutual Legal Assistance in Criminal Matters, signed at Washington on September 13, 1989. I transmit also, for the information of the Senate, the report of the Department of State with respect to the treaty.

The treaty is one of a series of modern mutual legal assistance treaties being negotiated by the United States in order to counter criminal activities more effectively. The treaty should be an effective tool to assist in the prosecution of a wide variety of modern criminals, including members of drug cartels, "white collar criminals," and terrorists. The treaty is self-executing.

The treaty provides for a broad range of cooperation in criminal matters. Mutual assistance available under the treaty includes: (1) the taking of testimony or statements of witnesses; (2) the provision of documents, records, and evidence; (3) the execution of requests for searches and seizures; (4) the serving of documents; and (5) the provision of assistance in proceedings relating to the forfeiture of the proceeds of crime, restitution to the victims of crime, and the collection of fines imposed as a sentence in a criminal prosecution.

I recommend that the Senate give early and favorable consideration to the treaty and give its advice and consent to ratification.

GEORGE BUSH

The White House,
April 1, 1992.

## Statement on Signing a Resolution Making Continuing Appropriations for the Fiscal Year 1992
*April 1, 1992*

I have today approved H.J. Res. 456. This resolution provides funding for economic and democratic development assistance to the republics of the former Soviet Union, funding for the remainder of fiscal year 1992 for certain international agencies, and emergency funding for loans to U.S. small businesses that have been adversely affected by natural disasters. The resolution also provides $270 million to finance special United Nations peacekeeping activities in Cambodia, El Salvador, Yugoslavia, and other countries.

GEORGE BUSH

The White House,
April 1, 1992.

*Note: H.J. Res. 456, approved April 1, was assigned Public Law No. 102–266.*

## Statement by Press Secretary Fitzwater on Organizational Changes in the Intelligence Community
*April 1, 1992*

The President has approved major program and organization changes in the intelligence community. This action results from a comprehensive review of the intelligence requirements and a critical assessment of intelligence capabilities needed, and not needed, to meet the new requirements.

Looking to the demands of a changing world over the next 15 years, the President approved a new formulation of policy requirements for intelligence support that adds emphasis in a number of areas and decreases it in others. As a result of these shifts, the President approved significant reallocations of resources in the FY 1993–1997 national foreign intelligence program. DCI [Director of Central Intelligence] Gates will present these changes to Congress in the next few days. In addition, DCI Gates will continue to assess intelligence resources with an eye toward greater efficiencies and additional reallocations.

The President also approved major changes in the structure and management of the intelligence community including:

—abolition of the intelligence community staff, establishment of a DCI community management staff headed by an Executive Director for Intelligence Community Affairs, and measures to strengthen community management of resources and requirements;

—improved coordination and management of intelligence collection activities and major disciplines;

—strengthening the National Intelligence Council and the national intelligence officers;

—initiatives to enhance support to the military, including establishment of an Assistant Deputy Director for Operations/Military Affairs in CIA and an Office of Military Affairs in CIA, and increased resources to enhance intelligence community support to military contingencies.

These measures together represent a significant reconfiguration of the intelligence community affecting structure, process, programs, and management.

## Remarks at the Departure Ceremony for Prime Minister Felipe González of Spain
*April 2, 1992*

President González, it's been an honor to meet with you again and a special pleasure to celebrate this anniversary of the greatest mission ever undertaken beneath the royal banner of Spain, Christopher Columbus' voyage of discovery.

Now, we've had a very good conversation today. I thanked President González for his leadership on so many questions, questions involving this hemisphere, questions involving our quest for a successful trade agreement. We thanked him and the rest of the Government of Spain and His Majesty for their foresight in hosting that historic

Madrid conference that brought factions together, parties together that had never sat down and talked in the same room before. History will remember that as very farsighted on the part of Spain.

And so it's been a good visit. I told the Prime Minister coming out here that I just wish we had had more time because, in my view, the relations between Spain and the United States have never been better. And we turn to him for advice on many issues. We turn to him with respect for his leadership on many issues.

And so it's been a very friendly visit, an

upbeat visit. And I'll let him speak for himself, but I think in terms of the big issues, the big problems facing the world, that President González and I, Spain and the United States, see eye to eye on almost every single question.

And so thank you, sir, for coming. And I hope you have a pleasant trip back, and I hope that our paths cross soon again.

*Note: The President spoke at 1:25 p.m. on the South Lawn at the White House. The Prime Minister was also President of the Government of Spain.*

## Statement on Antitrust Enforcement Policy
*April 2, 1992*

I am pleased to announce today a unified antitrust enforcement policy for mergers and acquisitions, by the Department of Justice and the Federal Trade Commission.

This new enforcement policy is an important part of the administration's ongoing efforts to improve the competitiveness of American business and to provide jobs for our people. A common policy will provide the business community with greater certainty about the standards to be applied in enforcing the antitrust laws. And where stiff international competition already exists, the new guidelines will make it easier for American companies to achieve the economic clout to compete effectively in the global marketplace.

I commend Attorney General Bill Barr and FTC Chairman Janet Steiger for this important contribution to American competitiveness.

## Message to the Senate Transmitting the 1985 Partial Revision of the Radio Regulations
*April 2, 1992*

*To the Senate of the United States:*

With a view to receiving the advice and consent of the Senate to ratification, I transmit herewith the Partial Revision of the Radio Regulations (Geneva, 1979), signed on behalf of the United States at Geneva on September 15, 1985, and the United States reservation and statements as contained in the Final Protocol. I transmit also, for the information of the Senate, the report of the Department of State with respect to the 1985 Partial Revision.

The 1985 Revision constitutes a partial revision of the Radio Regulations (Geneva, 1979), to which the United States is a party. The primary purpose of the revision is to incorporate into the Radio Regulations the decisions of the Regional Administrative Radio Conference for the Planning of the Broadcasting-Satellite Service in Region 2 (essentially the Western Hemisphere). The Broadcasting-Satellite Service is a radiocommunication service in which signals transmitted or retransmitted by satellites are intended for direct reception by the general public. The Partial Revision is broadly consistent with the proposals of and positions taken by the United States at the First Session of the World Administrative Radio Conference on the use of the Geostationary-Satellite Orbit and the Planning of Space Services Utilizing It (ORB–85).

At the time of signature, the United States submitted a reservation concerning technical matters included in the Revision; a statement in response to statements by Indonesia, Colombia, and Ecuador concerning claims of sovereign rights of segments of the geostationary-satellite orbit; and a statement in response to Cuba's characterization of Radio Marti as "the use . . . by the Government of the United States, of the radio spectrum as a means of aggression . . ." The specific reservation and statements, with reasons, are given in the report of the Department of State.

The 1985 Partial Revision of the Radio Regulations entered into force on October 30, 1986, for governments which, by that date, had notified the Secretary General of the International Telecommunication Union of their approval thereof.

I believe the United States should become a party to the Partial Revision, which will facilitate the development of a broadcasting-satellite service in the United States. It is my hope that the Senate will take early action on this matter and give its advice and consent to ratification.

GEORGE BUSH

The White House,
April 2, 1992.

# Message to the Senate Transmitting the 1988 Partial Revision of the Radio Regulations
*April 2, 1992*

*To the Senate of the United States:*

With a view to receiving the advice and consent of the Senate to ratification, I transmit herewith the 1988 Partial Revision of the Radio Regulations (Geneva, 1979), signed on behalf of the United States at Geneva on October 6, 1988, and the United States statement as contained in the Final Protocol. I transmit also, for the information of the Senate, the report of the Department of State with respect to the 1988 Partial Revision.

The 1988 Revision constitutes a partial revision of the Radio Regulations, to which the United States is a party. The primary purpose of this revision is to update the existing Regulations to guarantee for all countries equitable access to the geostationary-satellite orbit and the frequency bands allocated to space services. The revised Regulations are consistent with the proposals of and positions taken by the United States at the Second Session of the World Administrative Radio Conference on the Use of the Geostationary-Satellite Orbit and the Planning of the Space Services Utilizing

It (ORB–88).

At the time of signature, the United States joined 20 countries in submitting a statement in response to a statement by Colombia and Ecuador concerning claims of sovereign rights over segments of the geostationary-satellite orbit. The specific statement, with reasons, is given in the report of the Department of State.

The 1988 Partial Revision entered into force on March 16, 1990, for governments which, by that date, had notified the Secretary General of the International Telecommunication Union of their approval thereof.

I believe the United States should become a party to the 1988 Partial Revision, which provides new means and greater flexibility in securing access to the geostationary-satellite orbit and the frequency spectrum allocated to space services. It is my hope that the Senate will take early action on this matter and give its advice and consent to ratification.

GEORGE BUSH

The White House,
April 2, 1992.

# Nomination of Lauralee M. Peters To Be United States Ambassador to Sierra Leone
*April 2, 1992*

The President today announced his intention to nominate Lauralee M. Peters, of Virginia, to be Ambassador to the Republic of Sierra Leone. She would succeed Johnny Young.

Currently Ms. Peters serves as a member of the Senior Seminar of the Foreign Service Institute in Washington, DC. Prior to this, she served at the U.S. Department of State as Deputy Assistant Secretary of State for Personnel at the Bureau of Personnel, 1989–91; Personnel Counselor in the Office of Foreign Service Career Development and Assignments Bureau of Personnel, 1988–89; and Director of the Office of Monetary Affairs in the Bureau of Economic and Business Affairs, 1984–86. From 1986 to 1988, Ms. Peters served as Economic Counselor for the U.S. Embassy in Islamabad, Pakistan.

Ms. Peters graduated from the University of Kansas (B.A., 1964). She was born January 28, 1943, in Monroe, NC. Ms. Peters is married, has four children, and resides in McLean, VA.

# Nomination of Joan M. McEntee To Be an Under Secretary of Commerce
*April 2, 1992*

The President today announced his intention to nominate Joan M. McEntee, of New York, to be Under Secretary of Commerce for Export Administration. She would succeed Dennis Edward Kloske.

Currently Ms. McEntee serves as Acting Under Secretary of the Bureau of Export Administration at the U.S. Commerce Department. Prior to this, she served as Deputy Under Secretary for Export Administration, 1989–91; and Deputy Under Secretary for Trade Development at the International Trade Administration, U.S. Department of Commerce, 1988–89.

Ms. McEntee graduated from Marymount College (B.A., 1969) and the American University (M.A., 1972; J.D., 1981). She was born June 3, 1948, in New York, NY. Ms. McEntee is married, has one child, and resides in Washington, DC.

# Nomination of Marvin H. Kosters To Be Commissioner of Labor Statistics
*April 2, 1992*

The President today announced his intention to nominate Marvin H. Kosters, of Virginia, to be Commissioner of Labor Statistics at the U.S. Department of Labor, for a term of 4 years. He would succeed Janet L. Norwood.

Dr. Kosters has served at the American Enterprise Institute as a resident scholar and director for economic policy studies, 1987–present; director of the Center for the Study of Government Regulation, 1976–86; and a resident scholar, 1974. Prior to this, he served in the Office of the Assistant to the President for Economic Affairs at the White House, 1974–75; and as an Associate Director for Economic Policy at the U.S.

Cost of Living Council, 1971–1974.

Dr. Kosters graduated from Calvin College (B.A., 1960) and the University of Chicago (Ph.D., 1966). He was born August 4, 1933, in Corsica, SD. Dr. Kosters served in the U.S. Army, 1953–1955. He is married, has three children, and resides in Arlington, VA.

## Remarks to the Federalist Society of Philadelphia in Philadelphia, Pennsylvania
*April 3, 1992*

May I start by thanking Ms. Aikens for her hospitality, and the hospitality of all those to whom so much history is entrusted here. And what a superb job they do in preserving this lovely, lovely historic place. We're grateful, grateful to you that you are permitting us to have this event here today. May I thank Brian Guthrie, the president of the Federalist Society of Philadelphia, for his introduction, for hosting this. I see Joe Cicippio.

I want to say that Old Congress Hall is home to great ideas and great debate. In this very room, pivotal and profound discussions occurred, setting in motion a grand experiment in man's ability to chart his own future. The vision of the Founding Fathers may be hard for us to fully comprehend. But if you really think about it, their goals were not much different than ours. They wanted their new country to prosper, and they knew intuitively that the road to prosperity was freedom. They believed in the fundamentals, in the inherent strength of family, faith, and they were determined to preserve them. They wanted the citizens of our young Nation to live in peace, safe and secure from threats at home and abroad. It took a revolution to achieve their vision, and it is our duty to preserve it.

They say when British General Cornwallis surrendered to Washington at Yorktown in 1781, his troops marched to the tune "The World Turned Upside Down." It was a profoundly simple recognition that an old world order was ending and a new one beginning.

Now, more than 200 years later, we are again in the midst of great change. Democracy and freedom once again have turned the world upside down. America once again championed a great worldwide movement. We stood firm for our principles through some very difficult times. We did indeed change the world. Now, as you may have heard me say, if we could change the world, we can change America.

Henry Luce called the 20th century the American Century. In a world more driven by economic competition than ever before, we must now meet five great challenges to ensure that the next century is also the American century.

First, our children must develop good character, must develop values so they can be educated adults, literate, drug-free, motivated to make learning a lifelong pursuit. We must dramatically change our education system, literally revolutionize it. Our America 2000 education initiative means top-to-bottom educational reform.

Second, our people must have a sense of well-being about their physical health. And our health care proposal guarantees access to the finest health care system in the world and keeps that care affordable for all our citizens.

Next, our civil justice system: it must do what it was designed to do, dispense justice for all. Eighteen million lawsuits a year are choking us, costing us billions of dollars, and putting a tremendous drag on our civility and our economy. If Congress passes my "Access to Justice Act," this, too, can change.

And in the next century, economic competition, as well as economic opportunity, will come from beyond our borders. That's why we have aggressive progrowth trade policy. It demands more open foreign markets for quality American goods and services to sustain and create American jobs.

Finally, if we're to change America we must change the way Government works. That's what I will address today. G.K. Chesterton said, "We cannot discuss reform without reference to form." This has been amply demonstrated in just the last decade as one institution after another has been challenged, forced to take a hard look within itself, make needed improvements, and act to make the institution live up to its principles. That is the process called reform.

To ensure their competitive edge, businesses launch reforms that are geared to quality. Then, by measuring performance, they improve performance. Often it's not flashy, the return to old values and standards like "built to last a lifetime," or "service with a smile." Competition works. The proof? Today, look around this great country: American products are quantifiably better than just a few years ago.

Reform has improved performance in our military. In the face of tighter budgets we've cut the fat; we've gotten leaner and smarter. And Desert Storm proved it. The drive for excellence has influenced almost every other institution, from State and local government to trade associations and unions.

Yet, the Federal Government is a glaring holdout. It resists reform and protects a failed status quo, even in the face of an unambiguous need for change. I'm not talking here about barber shops or perks or calligraphers or parking spaces. It's about the governmental process, its potential to help or hinder the public good. It is about big things, important things, major changes to make Government more responsive. It's about the changes that are sweeping the rest of the country but are not being made in Washington.

The most recent proof that we have a major problem was the inability of Congress to rise to the challenge of helping our economy. Instead it reverted to form, trying to raise taxes, increase Government spending. If it cannot address a straightforward short-term proposal to stimulate the economy, how can it possibly deal with the more complex issues like the badly needed reforms of education, health care, legal systems. I would still like to see Congress put politics aside and give me an up-and-down vote on the seven incentives to stimulate this economy that I have pending before the Congress right now. But if we are to reform education and health care and our legal system and if we are to reduce red-tape and regulation, make our country competitive, get this horrendous deficit down, we must reform the congressional process itself. We've got to make it responsive to our country's real needs.

The growth of big Government has diminished the role of Congress from policy making to program making. Promulgating and protecting more programs sets in motion a perpetual cycle of congressional support for more unnecessary spending, creating bigger and even less responsive bureaucracies. Then, by servicing the needs of program recipients, congressional staffs help to ensure Members' reelection and a continuation of business as usual. Beyond that, Congress routinely exempts itself from the laws that it imposes on the rest of the Nation, laws like the landmark Civil Rights Act of 1964.

Prophetically, the Founding Fathers warned us about these dangers. Federalist Paper 57 asserts that—and I've just been given this beautiful volume by your president—asserts that elected officials "can make no law which will not have its full operation on themselves and their friends" and then it goes on, "as well as on the great mass of the society." Federalist Paper 52 argued that permanent majorities are dangerously undemocratic. James Madison would be appalled to hear that 98 percent of the Congressmen who seek reelection are, in fact, reelected; that one party, the Democrats, has controlled the House of Representatives for 56 out of the last 60 years.

And that means self-perpetuating staffs. It means a bureaucracy, an inbred bureaucracy, beholden to only one set of leaders. The bank and the post office scandals that have outraged the American people are the results of one-party control: one party's lack of supervision, lack of new blood, lack of change. There isn't the competition to make these institutions in the Congress more efficient.

One-party rule is a big part of the problem but certainly by no means all of it. We've had divided Government before, sometimes during periods of great crisis. And each time we have worked together in good faith to meet those challenges.

The larger issue is the systemic problem of Congress: the sticky web of 284 congressional committees and subcommittees, the almost 40,000 legislative branch employees and staff, $2.5 billion of taxpayer financing, overlaid with a $117 million in a reelection war chest for incumbents in these special-interest campaign contributions. None of this promotes reform and change. Rather, it aggressively protects the status quo.

Conscientious Members of Congress understand this. And that's why the Republican leader in the House, Bob Michel, has proposed congressional reform legislation. There's some good ideas there, great ideas for improving Congress and its procedures, like legislative calendar process reform, reduction in the number of congressional staff, reduction of the number of congressional committees.

There are good people in Congress, many on both sides of the aisle, and two of them are up here with me today. I think of your own Arlen Specter, who came up with us, and we talked about these reforms. Talk to him; he enthusiastically supports changing our congressional system because he believes in changing the status quo. Larry Coughlin, who's leaving the Congress—no special ax to grind—had a very good suggestion coming up here about changing the numbers on the rules committee so the minority programs would at least have a chance to be voted on from time to time in the United States Congress.

There's a lot of ideas, good ones, from Democrats and Republicans alike. And then talk to retiring Members, other retiring Members, many of them dedicated people like Warren Rudman of New Hampshire. I'm sure you heard what he had to say. Talk to him, and you'll hear this frustration. And when asked about the prospect of endless budget deficits, he issued this indictment of the system: "The fact is that we are unable, institutionally, to do what has to be done. We are literally not watching the fiddler fiddle when Rome burns; we are watching the entire orchestra."

Now, Senator Rudman knows the biggest threat to future job creation is deficit spending, and the current congressional structure is not capable of addressing that threat. He knows that Americans are generous, generous people willing to do what's necessary to make this country better. But there's a mismatch between their willingness to help and their skepticism about the United States Congress. They just don't trust Congress to use their hard-earned tax dollars wisely.

Today, Government is a $1.5 trillion enterprise. But people in Washington frequently forget that the taxpayer is the original investor, customer, shareholder, board member all rolled into one. And when folks in Government forget that, they issue nettlesome regulations. Now, those regulations increase the cost of doing business, but worse, they don't really solve the problems they were designed to solve.

The executive branch is involved. As President, I'm going to keep trying to change the regulatory process. But I will need, because of the legislation, I will need help of Congress.

When Government forgets who is really the boss, the American taxpayer, it becomes insulated, and it becomes unresponsive. But unresponsive Government doesn't just happen. Congress creates these giant, centralized bureaucracies, then lays down the mandates, funds the programs. And then it is the Congress that protects them or investigates them or micromanages them and ultimately perpetuates them. Programs that have outlived their function rarely outlive their funding. With a congressional subcommittee as godparent, some chairman there as the godparent, they become stepchildren of one of the committees of the Congress.

Some 107 different congressional committees and subcommittees claim some degree of oversight responsibility for the Department of Defense. Seventy-four compete for jurisdiction over the war on drugs, 74 separate entities. Just this week, after being reported from one committee in the House, our energy bill, one to make us more energy-efficient, energy-independent, was referred to no less than eight additional

House committees. It should be no surprise that it takes so long to get anything done.

Another example: When the Secretary of Agriculture and his top staff have to testify in 14 hearings in one day, think of the time and resources that takes. Think of the thousands of hours spent by the executive branch to fulfill the thousands of congressional demands for testimony and Government reports. Here's a man sitting right here that used to have to deal with this, Ken Cribb, and he knows what I'm talking about.

Democratic Senator David Boren, committed to reform, summed it up by saying, "No one doubts that the Congress is in trouble as an institution." And that's why I support, as President, his efforts, Senator Boren's efforts, to trim the overgrown thicket of committees and subcommittees which now paralyzes the Congress.

Congress has legitimate oversight responsibilities. We know that. I respect that. We all know it. And I know that the Federal Government cannot be run like IBM or the local convenience store. But we can improve its performance, and we must. What merely hampered us in the past could well paralyze us in the future.

Our ability to compete demands that we make these reforms not just of Congress, not just of the Congress but of the Federal bureaucracy, the executive branch bureaucracy as well. And it means emphasizing the building blocks of a more responsive Government by relying on what works: Choice, it works; competition works; decentralization. But let me be clear, we cannot reform the executive branch without first reforming the Congress. Taken together, the following actions will help make Government work for the people.

First, the Congress must govern itself by the laws that it imposes on others—no more special treatment—like age, race, sex, and disability discrimination laws. Congress should submit to the laws that it imposes on the executive branch, like the conflict of interest laws or the independent counsel law. And I will propose legislation to end such special treatment for Congress next week. And further, I will veto any future legislation that extends such special treatment to the Congress.

Second, Congress should reform its operation and procedures. I support the Boren-Domenici bill. It's a reform bill in the Senate. And over on the House side, Lee Hamilton, a Democrat, and Bill Gradison, a Republican, have that bill in the House which sets up a bipartisan group to evaluate congressional operations and make recommendations. It's a good beginning. But real reform, like that contained in the Michel bill, I think is essential right now. Change is still on the back burner. The American people have got to turn up the heat.

Third, sweeping campaign finance reform. Full disclosure of assets, liabilities, and compensation is a key element of real reform. Now, let me be subjective a minute. I am not required to disclose my income tax returns. And in a sense, I guess I feel like every other American, that it is an invasion of my privacy. But for 12 years I have made public in full detail those tax returns. And I believe that all people aspiring to the office I now hold should do exactly that. On Congress, perhaps Congress doesn't need to go that far. But they should make their existing disclosure rules much more thorough, much more rigorous. The way to solve a lot of the problem is to have the constituent know as much as possible. So I favor that kind of disclosure. Now, beyond that, we must totally eliminate the special-interest political action committees and then put limits on so-called leadership PAC's.

Now, I've proposed ways to increase the legitimate role of our political parties, reduce the influence of the special interests, and decrease the time candidates and incumbents spend fundraising. And let me say it straight out: Federal funding, now pending, Federal funding of congressional elections would only make the problem worse. Real campaign finance reform is stalled on Capitol Hill. But the time for action is long past, and we must clean up our election system.

The fourth one, spending reform: I have already proposed to freeze domestic discretionary spending and Federal nondefense employment next year. And I've proposed 2-year budgets. And I have proposed, as well, to curb the growth of mandatory programs without touching the Social Security System.

Now, if mandatory spending were allowed to grow for inflation and eligible population only, we could save about $2 trillion over the next decade. That's where the big expense is. The American people should demand that Congress pass the same measure that 43 Governors have, the line-item veto. And they should demand a balanced budget amendment to the Constitution. Obviously, given the financial problems we're facing, budgetary problems, a balanced budget requirement would have to be phased in. But such an amendment is needed now. It will discipline the executive branch; it will discipline the legislative branch.

In the absence of those important measures, I will continue to use whatever means are legally at my disposal, including what I called for just a few days ago, use of the line-item rescission to protect the taxpayer from the spending excesses of the Congress. And I will continue to vigorously oppose any attempt by the Congress to dismantle the only defense that the taxpayer has against congressional overspending. And I'm talking obviously about the budget caps, the caps that were implemented in the 1990 act.

Fifth, regulatory reform: We put a 90-day moratorium on new Government regulations. We are revising and eliminating regulations that impede our ability to compete, and we are accelerating regulations that enhance our competitive edge. Now, since I announced the moratorium on January 28th, the growth of burdensome regulations has already been reversed. And as our review continues we will announce further steps to reduce the burden of unnecessary regulations. But it cannot be done alone; I can't do it alone. Congress, in passing legislation, must be committed to cutting down the regulatory burden as well.

Sixth, we must limit congressional terms. We must address the Congress of the future. The cycle of virtually guaranteed reelection, particularly in the House of Representatives, through the built-in advantages of incumbency have got to be broken. And our Founding Fathers never considered elected Government service to be a career.

And I believe Senators should be limited to two terms and Representatives limited to six terms. As President my terms are limited; the same rule should apply to Members of the Congress. Our first concern should be the country, not the lifetime political career.

Now, this brings me to my final point. Certainly, governing today is far more complex and time-consuming. We have to give that; that's the fact. But not so many years ago, representing the people back home was a part-time Washington job. Somehow Members managed to finish their work and adjourn just before the hot, humid Washington, DC, summers. Air conditioning changed all this. [*Laughter*] And now, thanks to modern technology, Congress sits almost all year round. Many Members of the House and Senate are now permanent Washingtonians. And we do not need a career Congress. We need a citizen Congress. To borrow a line from former Senate Majority Leader Howard Baker, "They ought to be living in America and visiting Washington." I think Senator Baker was right in a serious way. He knew that the overwhelming majority of State legislatures are able to do their work each year in sessions lasting less than 6 months, some of them very short; some of them are about 3 months every 2 years.

With a streamlined committee structure, a leaner staff, Members' time organized around legislation rather than reelection, and better discipline on how they spend money, Congress could return to what the Founders envisioned as a Government truly close to the people. And I suggest that in the future, Congress and the administration work together to achieve a legislative schedule that allows Members to spend more continuous time at home so that they can truly stay in touch with the people.

Change is sweeping America, just as it is sweeping the world. It's exciting what's happening. As in the first days of our new Nation, we must change an unresponsive Government. The reforms that I've outlined today can help renew our faith in Government, confidence in Government. We cannot stop with congressional process. We must reform the Federal bureaucracy as well, as I am going to have more to say on that in the near future. But today, our mission is to begin restoring the principles of our Founding Fathers and guaranteeing for our children a new American century.

The choice is clear. On one side stand the defenders of the status quo; on the other, the forces of change. And we must make the choice worthy of the men who met here in this room and began the world's only permanent revolution. And now that we've changed the world—we have—we must make the choice to change America.

Thank you all very, very much. And may God bless the United States.

*Note: The President spoke at 10:28 a.m. in Congress Hall at Independence National Historical Park. In his remarks, he referred to Martha Aikens, Superintendent of the park; former hostage Joseph Cicippio; and T. Kenneth Cribb, Jr., former Assistant Counselor to the President and former member of the Council of the Administrative Conference of the United States.*

## Message to the Congress Transmitting the FREEDOM Support Act Proposed Legislation
*April 3, 1992*

*To the Congress of the United States:*

I am pleased to transmit a legislative proposal entitled the "Freedom for Russia and Emerging Eurasian Democracies and Open Markets Support Act of 1992" (the FREEDOM Support Act of 1992). Also transmitted is a section-by-section analysis of the proposed legislation.

I am sending this proposal to the Congress now for one urgent reason: With the collapse of the Soviet Union, we face unprecedented historical opportunity to help freedom flourish in the new, independent states that have replaced the old Soviet Union. The success of democracy and open markets in these states is one of our highest foreign policy priorities. It can help ensure our security for years to come. And the growth of political and economic freedom in these states can also provide markets for our investors and businesses and great opportunities for friendship between our peoples.

While this is an election year, this is an issue that transcends any election. I have consulted with the congressional leadership and have heard the expressions of support from both sides of the aisle for active American leadership. I urge all Members of Congress to set aside partisan and parochial interests.

Just as Democrats and Republicans united together for over 40 years to advance the cause of freedom during the Cold War, now we need to unite together to win the peace, a democratic peace built on the solid foundations of political and economic freedom in Russia and the other independent states.

This proposal gives me the tools I need to work with the international community to help secure the post-Cold War peace. It provides a flexible framework to cope with the fast-changing and unpredictable events transforming Russia, Ukraine, Armenia, and the other states. This proposal will allow us to:

- Mobilize fully the executive branch, the Congress, and the private sector to support democracy and free markets in Russia and the other independent states of the former Soviet Union;
- Address comprehensively the military, political, and economic opportunities created by the collapse of the Soviet Union, targeting our efforts and sharing responsibilities with others in the international community; and
- Remove decisively the Cold War legislative restrictions that hamstring the Government in providing assistance and impede American companies and businesses from competing fairly in developing trade and investment with the new independent states.

Passage of this proposal will enable the United States to maintain its leadership role as we seek to integrate Russia and the other new independent states into the democratic family of nations. Without the tools this proposal provides, our policy of collective engagement will be constrained, our leadership jeopardized.

This proposal has 10 key elements:

*First*, this proposal provides the necessary flexibility for the United States to extend emergency humanitarian assistance to Russia and the other new independent states.

Emergency humanitarian assistance will help the peoples of the former Soviet Union to avoid disaster and to reduce the danger of a grave humanitarian emergency next winter. In this endeavor, the United States will not go it alone but will continue to work closely with the international community, a process we initiated at the Washington Coordinating Conference in January and will continue in the months ahead in regular conferences with our allies. By dividing our labors and sharing our responsibilities, we will maximize the effects of our efforts and minimize the costs.

*Second*, this proposal will make it easier for us to work with the Russians and others in dealing with issues of nuclear power safety and demilitarization. This proposal broadens the authority for Department of Defense monies appropriated last fall for weapons destruction and humanitarian transportation to make these funds, as well as foreign military financing funds, available for nonproliferation efforts, nuclear power safety, and demilitarization and defense conversion.

*Third*, technical assistance can help the Russians and others to help themselves as they build free markets. Seventy years of totalitarianism and command economics prevented the knowledge of free markets from taking a firm hold in the lands of Russia and Eurasia. By providing know-how, we can help the peoples and governments of the new independent states to build their own free market systems open to our trade and investment. It will also allow agencies authorized to conduct activities in Eastern Europe under the "Support for East European Democracy (SEED) Act of 1989" to

conduct comparable but separate activities in the independent states of the former Soviet Union. Through organizations such as a Eurasia Foundation, we will be able to support a wide range of technical assistance efforts.

*Fourth*, this proposal will allow us to significantly expand our technical assistance programs that facilitate democratization in the new states, including our expanding rule of law program. It will authorize support for programs such as "America Houses." It also provides support for expanded military-to-military programs with Russia and the other new independent states to cultivate a proper role for the military in a democratic society.

*Fifth*, this proposal provides a clear expression of bipartisan support to continue to extend Commodity Credit Corporation credit guarantees to Russia and the other new independent states in light of the progress they are making toward free markets. As they overcome their financial difficulties, we should take into account their commitment to economic freedom in providing credit guarantees that will help feed their peoples while helping American farmers.

*Sixth*, for American business, this proposal expands authority for credit and investment guarantee programs such as those conducted by the Overseas Private Investment Corporation (OPIC) and the Export-Import Bank. It will allow us to waive statutory ceilings on credit guarantee programs of the Export-Import Bank Act and other agencies that applied to the Soviet Union and the restrictions of the Johnson Debt Default Act on private lending. In this way, it will expand U.S. exports to and investment in Russia and the other new independent states.

*Seventh*, this bill will facilitate the development of the private sector in the former Soviet Union. This bill removes Cold War impediments while promoting outside investment and enhanced trade. It will also allow waiver of restrictions on imports from the independent states of the former Soviet Union beyond those applied to other friendly countries. It will support efforts to further ease Coordinating Committee

(COCOM) restrictions on high technology. The bill will also allow the establishment of Enterprise Funds and a capital increase for the International Financial Corporation.

*Eighth,* this proposal will allow the United States to work multilaterally with other nations and the international financial institutions toward macroeconomic stabilization. At the end of World War II, the United States stood alone in helping the nations of Western Europe recover from the devastation of the war. Now, after the Cold War, we have the institutions in place—the International Monetary Fund (IMF) and the World Bank—that can play a leading role in supporting economic reform in Russia and Eurasia.

Therefore, this proposal endorses an increase in the IMF quota for the United States. This will help position the IMF to support fully a program of macroeconomic stabilization. I request the Congress to pass both the authorization and appropriations necessary for this purpose.

*Ninth,* this proposal endorses a significant U.S. contribution to a multilateral currency stabilization fund. Working with the international financial institutions and the other members of the G–7, we are putting together a stabilization fund that will support economic reform in Russia and the other independent states.

*Tenth,* this proposal provides for an expanded American presence in Russia and the other new independent states, facilitating both government-to-government relations and opportunities for American business. Through organizations such as the Peace Corps and the Citizens Democracy Corps, we will be able to put a large number of American advisors on the ground in the former Soviet Union.

In sending this authorization legislation to the Congress, I also request concurrent action to provide the appropriations necessary to make these authorizations a reality. In order to support fully multilateral efforts at macroeconomic stabilization, I urge the Congress to move quickly to fulfill the commitment of the United States to the IMF quota increase. And I urge prompt enactment of the appropriations requests for the former Soviet Union contained in the Fiscal Years 1992 and 1993 Budget requests presently before the Congress.

I call upon the Congress to show the American people that in our democratic system, both parties can set aside their political differences to meet this historic challenge and to join together to do what is right.

On this occasion, there should be only one interest that drives us forward: America's national interest.

GEORGE BUSH

The White House,
April 3, 1992.

# Presidential Determination No. 92–20—Memorandum on Trade With Armenia, Belarus, Kyrgyzstan, and Russia
*April 3, 1992*

*Memorandum for the Secretary of State*

*Subject:* Determination under Section 402(c)(2)(A) of the Trade Act of 1974, as amended—Armenia, Belarus, Kyrgyzstan, and Russia

Pursuant to section 402(c)(2)(A) of the Trade Act of 1974 (19 U.S.C. 2432(c)(2)(A)), as amended, (the "Act"), I determine that a waiver by Executive order of the application of subsections (a) and (b) of section 402 of the Act with respect to Armenia, Belarus, Kyrgyzstan, and Russia will substantially promote the objectives of section 402.

You are authorized and directed to publish this determination in the *Federal Register.*

GEORGE BUSH

[*Filed with the Office of the Federal Register, 2:50 p.m., April 15, 1992*]

*Note: The Executive orders of April 6 on Armenia and April 16 on Belarus, Kyrgyz-* *stan, and Russia are listed in Appendix E at the end of this volume.*

## Message to the Congress on Trade With Armenia, Belarus, Kyrgyzstan, and Russia
*April 3, 1992*

*To the Congress of the United States:*

Pursuant to subsection 402(c)(2)(A) of the Trade Act of 1974 (the "Act") (19 U.S.C. 2432(c)(2)(A)), I have determined that a waiver of the application of subsections (a) and (b) of section 402 with respect to Armenia, Belarus, Kyrgyzstan, and Russia will substantially promote the objectives of section 402. A copy of that determination is enclosed. I have also received assurances with respect to the emigration practices of Armenia, Belarus, Kyrgyzstan, and Russia required by subsection 402(c)(2)(B) of the Act. This letter constitutes the report to the Congress required by subsection 402(c)(2).

Pursuant to subsection 402(c)(2), I shall waive by Executive order the application of subsections (a) and (b) of section 402 of the Act with respect to Armenia, Belarus, Kyrgyzstan, and Russia.

GEORGE BUSH

The White House,
April 3, 1992.

*Note: The Executive orders of April 6 on Armenia and April 16 on Belarus, Kyrgyzstan, and Russia are listed in Appendix E at the end of this volume.*

## Statement by Deputy Press Secretary Smith on the President's Telephone Conversation With President Václav Havel of Czechoslovakia
*April 3, 1992*

The President spoke by telephone for 15 minutes this morning with Czechoslovak President Václav Havel, who had just returned from a state visit to Russia. They concurred on the critical need to galvanize international support for President Yeltsin and the Government of the Russian Federation.

Specifically, they agreed that the success of the Russian Government's landmark economic reform program was vitally important for peace and stability in Europe. Pointing to the package of economic measures he announced on April 1, the President assured President Havel of the firm U.S. resolve to assist the Russian Government and other reform-minded States in the former U.S.S.R.

## Radio Address to the Nation on Governmental Reform
*April 4, 1992*

American democracy was launched from great ideas which grew out of great debate.

Our Founding Fathers believed in the fundamentals: faith, family, and freedom. And they were determined to build prosperity. More than 200 years later, by holding firmly to our principles, America has changed the world.

Henry Luce called the 20th century the American Century. If we are to ensure that the next century is also the American century, we must meet five great challenges: education reform, legal reform, health care reform, international competitiveness and market expansion, and Governmental reform.

The latest unemployment figures were released Friday. They held steady at 7.3 percent. But unemployment is still too high. Too many Americans are out of work. To get this economy rolling again, faster and stronger, Congress should have passed our economic action plan. But they reverted to form, tried to raise taxes and increase Government spending. We can no longer afford this kind of business-as-usual. We need to reform Congress. And that is my focus today.

G.K. Chesterton said, "We cannot discuss reform without reference to form." In the face of overwhelming evidence that change is necessary, Congress has kept reform on the back burner. It is up to us to turn up the heat. If we are to improve education, health care, our legal system, if we are to reduce redtape and regulation, if we are to make our country competitive and get this horrendous deficit down, we must reform the congressional process itself.

It is true that one-party rule in Congress is a big part of the problem. But the larger issue is a systemic problem: the 284 congressional committees and subcommittees, the almost 40,000 legislative branch employees and staff, the $2.5 billion of taxpayer financing, overlaid with $117 million reelection war chest and special interest campaign contributions for incumbents. Such a system cannot promote reform and change; instead, it aggressively protects the status quo.

I know that the Federal Government cannot be run just like IBM or the local convenience store. But Government today is a $1.5 trillion enterprise, and programs that have outlived their function have not outlived their funding. We can and we must improve Government's responsiveness. What merely hampered us in the past will gridlock us in the future. Our ability to compete demands that Congress enact the reforms I have proposed. The set of actions I have proposed, when taken together, will help make Government respond to the people; Government for the people, as our founders envisioned.

First, Congress should govern itself by the laws it imposes on everyone else. No more special treatment.

Second, Congress should reform its operations and procedures.

Third, we must make sweeping campaign finance reforms.

Fourth, we need to change how Congress spends the people's money.

Fifth, we must revise and eliminate Government regulations that impede our ability to compete, and we must accelerate regulations that enhance our competitive edge.

Sixth, we must limit congressional terms. The cycle of virtually guaranteed reelection through the built-in advantages of incumbency must be broken.

And finally, the Congress of the future should be a citizen Congress, not a career Congress.

These reforms, taken together, can renew our faith in Government, restore the principles of our founders, and help guarantee for our children a new American century.

The choice is clear: On the one side stand the defenders of the status quo; on the other, the forces of change. And now that we've changed the world, we must make the choice to change America.

Thank you, and may God bless the United States of America.

*Note: This address was recorded at 8:04 a.m. on April 3 in the Oval Office at the White House for broadcast after 9 a.m. on April 4.*

## Statement on the Death of Stan Scott
*April 6, 1992*

Stan Scott was a close, personal friend. Barbara and I will miss him greatly. He was a man who dedicated his life to service of family, country, and the betterment of his fellow man.

Stan was universally admired. He was equally at home in the worlds of government, business, sports, and education. He used his friendships to improve the quality of life of all Americans. In particular, his lifelong commitment to the United Negro College Fund helped improve education for generations of Afro-American men and women.

Those who knew Stan felt a part of his extended family. To his wife, Bettye, and three children, Stan, Susan, and Kenneth, I send my deepest condolences and prayers.

## Statement on the Death of Samuel M. Walton
*April 6, 1992*

Barbara and I are deeply saddened by the death of our friend Sam Walton. It was my honor and privilege to award Sam with the Presidential Medal of Freedom just a month ago. Sam Walton was an American original who embodied the entrepreneurial spirit and epitomized the American dream. His commitment to family and selfless giving to others is an example to us all. Sam Walton will be greatly missed, and our prayers and sincere condolences go out to his wife, Helen, the other members of the Walton family, and the entire Wal-Mart community.

## Statement by Deputy Press Secretary Smith on the Peruvian Government Crisis
*April 6, 1992*

The President was very disappointed to learn of the action taken by President Fujimori in suspending the Peruvian Constitution and dissolving the Congress and the judiciary. This is a regrettable step backwards for the cause of democracy in the hemisphere. We will be consulting with other countries in the hemisphere and are currently reviewing our assistance programs to Peru. We urge a rapid return to constitutional rule.

## Appointment of Cecile B. Kremer as Deputy Assistant to the President and Director of the Office of Public Liaison
*April 6, 1992*

The President today announced the appointment of Cecile B. Kremer as Deputy Assistant to the President and Director of the Office of Public Liaison.

Since January 1989, Ms. Kremer has been Assistant to the Vice President and Director of the Office of Scheduling. In April of 1991, she assumed the additional duties of Director of the Office of Public Liaison. Prior to this, Ms. Kremer was director of scheduling and advance for Vice President-elect Quayle and from August to November 1988 served as the Bush-Quayle '88 deputy tour director for Senator Quayle. From 1985 to 1988, Ms. Kremer served as Deputy Assistant Secretary for Public Liaison at the U.S. Department of the Treasury. From 1981 until 1985, she was a staff assistant to President Reagan, serving as an advance representative in the Office of Presidential Advance.

Ms. Kremer is a graduate of the University of Maryland. She is married to Gene Goldenberg, has one son, Joshua, and resides in Chevy Chase, MD.

# Appointment of Bobbie Greene Kilberg as Deputy Assistant to the President and Director of the Office of Intergovernmental Affairs
*April 6, 1992*

The President today announced the appointment of Bobbie Greene Kilberg as Deputy Assistant to the President and Director of the Office of Intergovernmental Affairs at the White House.

Since January 1989, Mrs. Kilberg has served as Deputy Assistant to the President for Public Liaison. In 1988, Mrs. Kilberg served as special projects coordinator for the Bush campaign at the Republican National Convention. In 1987, she was the Republican State senate candidate for the 32d District of Virginia. From 1982 to 1983, Mrs. Kilberg was general counsel and vice president of the Roosevelt Center for American Policy Studies. She also served as Associate Counsel to President Ford, 1975–77; and as vice president for academic affairs at Mount Vernon College, 1973–75. Mrs. Kilberg was an associate in the Washington, DC, law firm of Arnold & Porter, 1971–73. Upon graduation from law school in 1969, she was selected as a White House fellow and served on the White House Domestic Council policy staff in that capacity from 1969 to 1971.

Mrs. Kilberg received a bachelor of arts degree in political science from Vassar College (magna cum laude and Phi Beta Kappa), a master of arts degree in public affairs and government from Columbia University (university fellow), and a law degree from Yale University. She resides in McLean, VA, with her husband, Bill, and their five children.

# Remarks at the Presentation Ceremony for the National Teacher of the Year Award
*April 7, 1992*

Thank you, Lamar, and welcome, everybody, to the Rose Garden. In addition to our outstanding Secretary Lamar Alexander, we have with us Gordon Ambach of the Council of Chief State School Officers; Superintendent Schiller and Michael Emlaw from Michigan; the kids here from Jefferson Junior High and St. Rita's School; and of course, the folks that I just had the pleasure of meeting in the Oval Office, Tom, Diane, and Malcolm Fleming and Diane's mother, Josephine Rosinski. Why don't you all just stand up so they can officially welcome you. Thank you.

Well, we're all here today to salute and thank the thousands of outstanding men and women who educate this Nation's children. There's no calling greater than a teacher's because there is nothing more precious than what they touch: the minds of our youth. The Talmud says teachers are our protectors, and that's true. By teaching our kids what we've learned and by teaching them to dream, teachers protect the treasures of our past and the promise of our future.

Today I want to share a story about a Detroit kid brought up by his grandparents, Gordon and Carrie Bell Starks. He struggled in school, was labeled a slow learner, and when he dropped out of high school, he couldn't read or write or spell. He didn't think that mattered, but one day it did. His faith became tremendously important to him. And he wanted to read the Bible, but he couldn't, didn't know how. From that moment, he thought about what it would really mean to take charge of his life. And that moment changed his life. And 5 years later, after he dropped out, he enrolled in night school to learn how to read his Bible and earn his high school diploma. He went on to Bible college while working as a minister to kids like himself in northwest Detroit. And here he found he had the power to touch and to change lives.

He decided to become a teacher and worked with forgotten kids at a State institution for juvenile offenders. And there's an old saying, "Whoever would be a teacher of men, let him begin by teaching himself before teaching others, and let him set an example before teaching by word." And that's exactly what the young man of this story did. And we're here today to honor him as the 1992 Teacher of the Year, Thomas Fleming.

He's a hero, a man of great strength, of courage and great heart. And for the last 20 years, as lead teacher in the Washtenaw County Juvenile Detention Program, he's taught history, government, and also geography to kids in the 12-to-16 age bracket. But he teaches much, much more. To kids who've had hope drained out of them by a vicious cycle of abuse, neglect, failure, drugs, crime, he gives life training. And here's what he says to them, "Knowledge is power. The more you know, the more you're worth." In these throwaway kids he installs pride.

Tom doesn't want the moon for his kids;

he wants something more important, a future. And in his classroom it will be a future forged out of new personal responsibility, enthusiasm, and learning, and yes, hope.

Some of his kids have gone on to respected civic and religious positions. One even rebuilt Tom's original youth club as a ministry of his own. And one of his kids, "Saturday Night Live" comedian A. Whitney Brown, is here with us today. Whitney, please stand up, and welcome. And I'm glad you didn't bring Dana Carvey. [*Laughter*]

No, but this guy spoke for many of Tom's kids when, more than 20 years after being taught in his classroom, he dedicated his book, "The Big Picture," to Tom and to his colleague Anne Klein, who is also here today. And he called them "two teachers who made a difference."

Well, I have a feeling this crystal apple over here isn't as important to Tom as his other rewards: seeing the first spark of light in a kid's eye or even just having a kid who never before had been able to read ask him for a book from the public library. But the apple does symbolize the respect with which Tom's country views him. And the apple reminds us of Tom's message: Education is important because every life can be redeemed, every life counts.

Whether you're concerned about the big issues that shape our world or about the values close to home, education is a fundamental part of the three precious legacies Americans take to heart: strong families, good jobs, a world at peace. Every day on the most intense and personal level, Tom Fleming sees the heart of the problems we face: the breakdown of families, the loss of traditional values, the lure of crime and substance abuse, the dead end of unemployment, and hopelessness. But he knows that good teachers will help us find a solution. For with every student you teach, you shape a future and you touch a lifetime.

But teachers cannot exist in isolation. Our tremendous respect for them and our utter conviction that education is the key to our country's future led us to develop America 2000, a revolutionary blueprint for educational reform. It will lead us to achieve our six national education goals, adopted, as you may remember, more than 2 years ago in an extraordinary nonpartisan Federal-State partnership by the Nation's Governors and by this administration. And let me remind you just briefly of these six goals which will propel this Nation forward into excellence:

By the year 2000 our children will start school ready to learn. America's students will achieve at least a 90-percent high school graduation rate. They will demonstrate competence in five core subjects measured against world-class standards. And by the year 2000 our children will be the first in science and math. Our adults will be literate and able to compete in the work force. And sixth, finally, our schools will be safe, disciplined, and drug-free.

We'll achieve these goals by advancing four transforming ideas at the heart of America 2000:

First, flexibility for teachers and principals, freedom from the web of Federal regulations that impose a one-size-fits-all solution to our schools;

Second, a generation of new American schools. Teachers are critical to this exciting break-the-mold experiment in what education can be;

Third, world-class standards and voluntary national exams. Again, teachers are leading the way in defining standards, creating curriculum frameworks, developing exams to help us raise our sights and measure our performance;

And fourth and finally, parental choice of schools, public, private, religious.

Now, our plan is innovative. It is exciting. It is uniting this country. And it will work. Changing our schools is too important to wait or to waste a generation. And that's why education is one of the five urgent reform challenges that I've been talking about. We know we've got to be competitive in a changing world. We can't go on sending our children into the working world undereducated and ill-equipped and expect the business community to spend billions teaching new workers what they should have learned in school. Status quo schools simply will not carry us into the next century.

We set our goals for the year 2000 because we know our economic health, our economic survival depend on how we educate ourselves to face the challenges a new century will bring. Tom and the thousands of men and women like him will help us meet those challenges.

Teachers know that real excellence demands commitment from everyone in every community as we work to create communities where learning can happen. It demands that talented men and women give time to become tutors and mentors. It demands that businesses, churches and synagogues, and civic groups join together to support local schools. It demands that every citizen help his community develop a plan of action based on America 2000 and help the Nation reach these national education goals. Together, we literally will reinvent the American school, community by community, neighborhood by neighborhood, all across this country. And at the heart of this shining new school will be, as always, the teacher.

Last week at the Oscars, George Lucas, filmmaker, might have captured it best when he thanked the teachers of his childhood. And he said, "All of us are teachers, teachers with very loud voices. But we will never match the power of the teacher who is able to whisper in a student's ear."

And so, Tom, on behalf of all Americans who have had the rare and priceless privilege of having a fine teacher whisper in their ear, congratulations. You teach the one lesson that matters the most. There's no distinction between who you are and what you do. You've woven the values of your life into your work. And thank you, sir. And may God bless you.

And now I have something special for you. This apple is the traditional symbol of teaching, and crystal represents the clarity of vision and commitment that the great teachers possess. And so, on behalf of a grateful Nation, an admiring Nation, with great pride in you, sir, congratulations. Now, may I hand you this apple.

*Note: The President spoke at 11:22 a.m. in the Rose Garden at the White House. In his remarks, he referred to Robert Schiller, superintendent of public instruction for the*

Michigan Department of Education, and
Michael O. Emlaw, superintendent of

Washtenaw Intermediate School District,
MI.

## Remarks to the American Business Conference
*April 7, 1992*

Thank you, Jim, very, very much. Thank you all, and I'm just delighted to be back with you. And Jim Jones, thank you, sir, for the introduction, for your leadership not just of this wonderful organization but of the exchange and for everything else you do for this economy.

Some people think I've been traveling a little too much so today, as an example of my new policy, no trips further than one block away from the White House. [*Laughter*]

It is a pleasure to be with you. I'm delighted to have been accompanied by Barbara Franklin, who many of you saw coming in, I think, our new Secretary of Commerce in whom I have great confidence, Barbara. And she and I both agree that she has large shoes to fill over there at Commerce with one of your originators, one of your founders, my dear, close friend Bob Mosbacher, sitting in the back, back here. What a job he did for his country as Secretary.

But let me just say it is always a pleasure to speak with the members of the ABC, the American Business Conference, because it's a pleasure to speak with the best, people that get things done. And I'd like to talk to you today about the future, the future of our country generally, and more particularly, the future of our country's business environment. In fact, we cannot separate the two. The America of the 21st century—Jim talked about some of the aspects of this, what ABC's about, its ability to make peace in the world, but to foster strong families, to create rewarding jobs—will be shaped today, in large part, by how hospitable we make America for business.

We can learn from your achievement. The key to the success of any high-growth company is the wise deployment of resources. The successful company channels labor and investment into those areas with the potential for the greatest expansion, for the highest return. And you take the risk; you reap the reward; everyone, meanwhile, benefits from the wealth you create. And that, in brief, is the genius of entrepreneurial capitalism, a system that has made America the envy of the world.

For 200 years our prosperity has sprung from our ability to innovate, to create, to change as the world changes. But America's world leadership is not automatic; it's not a birthright. We must continue to earn it day by day, quarter by quarter, year by year. And the world now is changing at a pace that no one could have dreamed of just a generation ago. And America, which has led the world's transformation, simply must change with it.

Over the last several years, deadweights have begun to slow the engine of growth, inefficiencies a competitive economy simply cannot tolerate. And today I want to discuss five areas of reform, five critical ways in which America must change if we are to continue to lead the world. You understand the urgency, for each of these problems presents itself to American companies not as an abstraction but in the most immediate way, as a cost of doing business, a cost you can't control, an expenditure with no possible return.

When our legal system becomes incapable of resolving disputes in a timely and civil manner, business loses the incentive to innovate and take risks. Secondly, when health care costs escalate, business picks up much of the tab. When Government imposes barriers to trade, business pays the price in opportunities lost. When our children leave school without rudimentary skills, business bears the burden in lowered productivity. And when Government freezes in gridlock, business can no longer plan rationally for the future.

Let me begin with the crying need to

reform our country's civil justice system. Every American has heard stories of bizarre or frivolous lawsuits. But most of you have lived with them, tales that could have been torn from the pages of Kafka. Consider one example related by one of your members, Roger Coleman, president of Rykoff-Sexton, a food manufacturer and distributor.

After record earnings in 1989, Mr. Coleman publicly expressed his confidence that 1990 would be even better. And when earnings fell short, his hopeful statement became the cause of a shareholder class-action lawsuit. First, in a meeting with plaintiffs' contingency-fee lawyers, at which the merits of the case were never even discussed, the issue, says Mr. Coleman, was "the depths of our pockets." And next came the nightmare of discovery, endlessly expensive and invasive. The company's managers, instead of managing, spent their time preparing for depositions. The lawsuit, he says, "brought everything to a stop." In the end, rather than permit the total exhaustion of company resources, Mr. Coleman decided to settle. And the tab for this exercise in futility, $8.7 million. And as he says, "That's over $8.7 million that was diverted from new investments in jobs and facilities."

The scenario is repeated daily throughout American business. And it is not repeated, let me stress, among our world competitors. Only the United States has seen the number of lawyers double over a 20-year period. And only the United States spends more than $80 billion annually in direct litigation costs, perhaps 4 times that in indirect costs. According to a recent survey, 40 percent of companies that had been the target of product liability suits have discontinued certain types of product research.

We must remove this ball and chain from our ability to produce, our ability to compete worldwide. And my Competitiveness Council, led by the Vice President, has offered 50 recommendations for legal reform. They would limit discovery to reasonable proportions, discourage some frivolous suits through a "loser pay" rule, and offer alternative means of resolving disputes.

This broad legal reform will not be easy. Just look at the fight that we've had on product liability reform. We introduced a reform bill in 1990 and again in 1991. And

the Senate opposition, the majority in the Senate refused to bring it to a vote. And in the House it's stuck in two committees. The special interests are lining up against legal reform, and we could certainly use your help in moving it forward. We must reform the legal system of this country.

If we are successful, the effects will be far-reaching, extending into another area critically in need of change. Medical malpractice premiums almost doubled in the second half of the eighties. Doctors are practicing defensive medicine, ordering an estimated $20 billion a year in unnecessary tests and procedures to protect against frivolous lawsuits.

The trends in health care costs are simply unsustainable. From less than 6 percent 30 years ago, total health care expenditures are today about 13 percent of GDP. Some midrange estimates put that figure at 30 percent by the year 2030. That's 30 cents of every dollar of national income spent on health care. Right now, according to one Federal study, American corporations already spend more on health care each year than they earn in aftertax profits.

We must reform the system, but we face a crossroad. Some have advocated nationalized care; others propose the so-called "pay or play" approach, which I am convinced is merely a step on the road to nationalized care. Neither is acceptable. Neither will preserve the quality of our country's health care, which remains the best in the entire world. And I will not let that high quality be taken away from the American people through some scheme of Government control.

Nationalized care means rationed care. Its promise of cost containment is a mirage. "Pay or play" would dump still more mandates on business. For employers, a 9-percent payroll tax would mean a 34-percent increase in health insurance costs. And that money has got to come from somewhere. And for a company unable to pass along the added costs through higher prices, that means decreased investment; it means lower wages; it means fewer jobs.

There is an alternative, a good one. And my proposed health care reform will build on the strengths of the existing system, preserving the quality of American care. We will increase consumer choice. And through transferable credits, we will assure access to basic health insurance for the uninsured and control costs through market incentives. And we will not have to raise taxes in the process, raise taxes on the employers.

I've targeted a third area for attention, like the others, absolutely critical to our success in the coming decades. You understand that for America to succeed economically at home we must succeed economically abroad. The fastest growing companies among your group, the ones creating the greatest number of jobs here at home, are those with far-reaching involvement in foreign markets.

I am committed to opening markets to American goods and services, removing the Government-imposed barriers that act as a hidden tax on American business. Each market shut off by protection is a lost opportunity to sell your products. A successful conclusion to the current Uruguay round of trade negotiations, for instance, could increase world output by $5 trillion over the next decade. More than $1 trillion of that boom will go to the United States, creating a higher standard of living and, yes, more jobs for Americans.

And then, even closer to home, an area where Bob Mosbacher did so much and now Barbara Franklin has taken up the cause: exports to Mexico. They have more than doubled over the last years, creating more than 300,000 American jobs. Now, our North American free trade agreement, Mexico, Canada, and the U.S., will lock in and even multiply these gains, creating a $6 trillion market for American products in Canada, Mexico, and the U.S.A.

As world trade expands, the need for a sophisticated, well-educated work force will intensify. And yet the fact is grim and undeniable, and Jim referred to this one in introducing me, our current educational system is unable to produce the workers the highly competitive world market demands.

Our educational failures have hit American employees hard. English is now the language of international business, and yet only 20 percent of 17-year-olds can write a simple two-paragraph letter applying for a job. The situation in geography, math, sci-

ence is equally dire. Too many businesses are forced to pay twice for the education of prospective employees, once through taxes that support our schools and again through job training to remedy the failures of those schools in educating our young.

Communities have begun taking matters into their own hands, with local businesses often acting as catalysts. ABC's Vital Link, which works with local schools to establish learning incentives for students, is a perfect example of the community-based efforts that our children need.

And still, there is much for the Government to do. This year seven different Federal agencies will spend $18 billion on a patchwork of 60 mandated vocational training programs. Is it any wonder that so many Americans who seek training don't know how to get it? Now, working with State and local governments, we've got a new program: our Job Training 2000 initiative, we call it. And that will bring coherence to these programs and try to offer "one-stop shopping" to aspiring workers. Job Training 2000 perfectly complements the revolution now taking place in American education as a whole.

And through this, I hope you've heard of it, our America 2000 initiative, we will reinvent, literally reinvent our schools. Your chairman, Jim Jones, is a leader in what we call the New American Schools Development Corporation. It's a private group created at my request to launch an entire generation of break-the-mold new American schools.

This revolution is essential to creating a world-class work force. Now to do that, we need to set world-class standards for students and create a system of voluntary national tests to measure their progress. We've got to redouble our efforts to rid our schools of drugs and violence, to cleanse America of this scourge that wastes so many young lives. And we must make schools more accountable by forcing them to compete. And that means giving parents the opportunity to choose their children's schools, public, private, or religious.

I am convinced that each of these major reforms, restoring sanity to our legal system, ensuring quality health care for all, expanding world trade, reinventing American education, is essential to this country's productivity. But each faces powerful opposition from special interests who profit from the status quo. And so, I've targeted a final reform, no less important than the others. If America is to change, our Government must change.

And last week in Philadelphia I presented seven specific programs, proposals really, to deal with the paralysis that grips the Congress. And the results of this gridlock are dismally plain. Congress was incapable even of passing a short-term stimulative economic growth package. But they must understand I am going to continue to fight for measures essential to economic growth, and that includes something you know something about, a lot about, including a cut in the tax on capital gains.

And you have sitting here today a leader that knows something about the success of a capital gains cut, Jim Jones. Because if my memory serves me correctly, it was the Jones-Stieger initiative in '78 that showed what can happen in the way of new investment, entrepreneurship, when a capital gains tax cut was enacted.

The American people, and I can understand this, are rightly fed up with business as usual, a deficit that is a fiscal and a moral outrage, a permanent governing class oblivious to the national interest, and hundreds of self-perpetuating programs that don't even aid the people they were designed to help. Now, I refuse to believe that this is the legacy we'll leave our kids. But it will be if we don't reform. I'm talking here about perks. I'm talking about the gymnasium. I'm talking about fundamental reform of the United States Congress.

The reforms that I've outlined here today are grounded in basic principles, a way of looking at the world. As Jefferson said, "The pillars of our prosperity are the most thriving when left most free to individual enterprise." In practice, that means Government must trust the wisdom of the markets more than the whims of the bureaucrats. The freely made decisions of business men and women must take precedence over the engineering schemes of Government. And all of our institutions, from the Congress to the local school board, must be accountable to those that they serve.

Over the last decade, America has changed the world. Given what's happening out there in this election year, we sometimes fail to count our blessings. There have been fundamental changes in this world, changes for world peace. And today we are blessed with those changes, and we are also blessed with the opportunity now to change America. With these principles that I've outlined here as our guide, I am absolutely convinced we will meet the challenges and exploit the opportunities of the world that is now being born.

Thank you all very much for what you do. And may God bless our country. Thank you all.

*Note: The President spoke at 2:11 p.m. at the Willard Hotel. In his remarks, he referred to James R. Jones, chairman of the American Business Conference and chairman of the American Stock Exchange.*

# Message to the Congress on the Release of Funds for Peacekeeping Purposes in El Salvador
*April 7, 1992*

*To the Congress of the United States:*

Section 531 of the Foreign Operations, Export Financing, and Related Programs Appropriations Act, 1991 (Public Law 101–513), provides that amounts in the Demobilization and Transition Fund established for peacekeeping purposes by that Act shall be made available for obligation and expenditure only upon notification by the President to the Congress that the Government of El Salvador and representatives of the Farabundo Marti Liberation Front (FMLN) have reached a permanent settlement of the conflict, including a final agreement on a cease-fire. On January 16, 1992, the Government of El Salvador and the FMLN signed such an agreement, bringing an end to the civil conflict.

Consistent with section 531, I hereby provide notification that the Government of El Salvador and representatives of the FMLN have reached a permanent settlement of the conflict, including a final agreement on a cease-fire.

This notification allows the amounts in the Demobilization and Transition Fund

(Fund) to be made available for obligation and expenditure. The Secretary of State will have responsibility for administering the Fund.

It is extremely important for the United States to support the implementation of this historic peace agreement, and I look forward to your continued cooperation toward achieving our mutual objectives in this endeavor.

GEORGE BUSH

The White House,
April 7, 1992.

# Message to the Congress Reporting on Economic Sanctions Against Haiti
*April 7, 1992*

*To the Congress of the United States:*

1. On October 4, 1991, in Executive Order No. 12775, I declared a national emergency to deal with the threat to the national security, foreign policy, and economy of the United States caused by events that had occurred in Haiti to disrupt the legitimate exercise of power by the democratically elected government of that country (56 FR 50641). In that order, I ordered the immediate blocking of all property and interests in property of the Government of Haiti (including the Banque de la Republique d'Haiti) then or thereafter located in the United States or within the possession or control of a U.S. person, including its overseas branches. I also prohibited any direct or indirect payments or transfers to the *de facto* regime in Haiti of funds or other financial or investment assets or credits by any U.S. person or any entity organized under the laws of Haiti and owned or controlled by a U.S. person.

Subsequently, on October 28, 1991, I issued Executive Order No. 12779 adding trade sanctions against Haiti to the sanctions imposed on October 4 (56 FR 55975). Under this order, I prohibited exportation from the United States of goods, technology, and services, and importation into the United States of Haitian-origin goods and

services, after November 5, 1991, with certain limited exceptions. The order exempts trade in publications and other informational materials from the import, export, and payment prohibitions and permits the exportation to Haiti of donations to relieve human suffering as well as commercial sales of five food commodities: rice, beans, sugar, wheat flour, and cooking oil. In order to permit the return to the United States of goods being prepared for U.S. customers by Haiti's substantial "assembly sector," the order also permitted, through December 5, 1991, the importation into the United States of goods assembled or processed in Haiti that contained parts or materials previously exported to Haiti from the United States.

2. The declaration of the national emergency on October 4, 1991, was made pursuant to the authority vested in me as President by the Constitution and laws of the United States, including the International Emergency Economic Powers Act (50 U.S.C. 1701, *et seq.*), the National Emergencies Act (50 U.S.C. 1601, *et seq.*), and section 301 of title 3 of the United States Code. I reported the emergency declaration to the Congress on October 4, 1991, pursuant to section 204(b) of the International Emergency Economic Powers Act (50 U.S.C. 1703(b)). The additional sanctions set

forth in my order of October 28 were imposed pursuant to the authority vested in me by the Constitution and laws of the United States, including the statutes cited above, and implement in the United States Resolution MRE/RES. 2/91, adopted by the Ad Hoc Meeting of Ministers of Foreign Affairs of the Organization of American States ("OAS") on October 8, 1991, which called on Member States to impose a trade embargo on Haiti and to freeze Government of Haiti assets. The present report is submitted pursuant to 50 U.S.C. 1641(c) and 1703(c) and discusses Administration actions and expenses directly related to the national emergency with respect to Haiti declared in Executive Order No. 12775, as implemented pursuant to that order and Executive Order No. 12779.

3. On March 31, 1992, the Office of Foreign Assets Control of the Department of the Treasury ("FAC"), after consultation with other Federal agencies, issued the Haitian Transactions Regulations, 31 C.F.R. Part 580 (57 FR 10820, March 31, 1992), to implement the prohibitions set forth in Executive Orders Nos. 12775 and 12779.

Prior to the issuance of the final regulations, FAC issued a number of general licenses to address urgent situations requiring an interpretation of U.S. sanctions policy in advance of the final regulations. These general licenses provided agency policy regarding the articles (baggage, personal effects, etc.) that could be exported or imported by travellers to and from Haiti; the treatment of amounts owed to the *de facto* regime by U.S. persons for certain telecommunications services; the movement of diplomatic pouches; the obligation of banks and other financial institutions with respect to Government of Haiti funds in their possession or control; authorization of commercial shipments to Haiti of medicines and medical supplies; and the circumstances under which certain exportations to, or importations from, the "assembly sector" in Haiti would be permitted. These general licenses have been incorporated into the Haitian Transactions Regulations.

4. The ouster of Jean-Bertrand Aristide, the democratically elected President of Haiti, in an illegal coup by elements of the Haitian military on September 30, 1991, was immediately repudiated and vigorously condemned by the OAS. The convening on September 30 of an emergency meeting of the OAS Permanent Council to address this crisis reflected an important first use of a mechanism approved at the 1991 OAS General Assembly in Santiago, Chile, requiring the OAS to respond to a sudden or irregular interruption of the functioning of a democratic government anywhere in the Western Hemisphere. As an OAS Member State, the United States has participated actively in OAS diplomatic efforts to restore democracy in Haiti and has supported fully the OAS resolutions adopted in response to the crisis, including Resolution MRE/RES. 2/91.

5. In these initial months of the Haitian sanctions program, FAC has made extensive use of its authority to specifically license transactions with respect to Haiti in an effort to mitigate the effects of the sanctions on the legitimate Government of Haiti and on U.S. firms having established relationships with Haiti's "assembly sector," and to ensure the availability of necessary medicines and medical supplies and the undisrupted flow of humanitarian donations to Haiti's poor. For example, specific licenses have been issued (1) permitting expenditures from blocked assets for the operations of the legitimate Government of Haiti, (2) permitting U.S. firms wishing to terminate assembly operations in Haiti to return equipment, machinery, and parts and materials inventories to the United States and, beginning February 5, 1992, permitting firms wishing to resume assembly operations in Haiti to do so provided the prohibition on payments to the *de facto* regime is complied with, and (3) permitting the continued material support of U.S. and international religious, charitable, public health, and other humanitarian organizations and projects operating in Haiti.

6. Since the issuance of Executive Order No. 12779, FAC has worked closely with the U.S. Customs Service to ensure both that prohibited imports and exports (including those in which the Government of Haiti has an interest) are identified and interdicted and that permitted imports and exports move to their intended destination without undue delay. Violations and suspected viola-

tions of the embargo are being investigated, and appropriate enforcement actions will be taken.

7. The expenses incurred by the Federal Government in the 6-month period from October 4, 1991, through April 3, 1992, that are directly attributable to the authorities conferred by the declaration of a national emergency with respect to Haiti are estimated at $323,000, most of which represent wage and salary costs for Federal personnel. Personnel costs were largely centered in the Department of the Treasury (particularly in FAC, the U.S. Customs Service, and the Office of the General Counsel), the Department of State, the Department of Commerce, and the Federal Reserve Bank of New York.

8. The assault on Haiti's democracy repre-

sented by the military's forced exile of President Aristide continues to pose an unusual and extraordinary threat to the national security, foreign policy, and economy of the United States. The United States remains committed to a multilateral resolution of this crisis through its actions implementing the resolutions of the OAS with respect to Haiti. I shall continue to exercise the powers at my disposal to apply economic sanctions against Haiti as long as these measures are appropriate, and will continue to report periodically to the Congress on significant developments pursuant to 50 U.S.C. 1703(c).

GEORGE BUSH

The White House,
April 7, 1992.

# Message to the Congress Reporting on Panamanian Government Assets Held by the United States
*April 7, 1992*

*To the Congress of the United States:*

1. I hereby report to the Congress on developments since the last Presidential report on October 3, 1991, concerning the continued blocking of Panamanian government assets. This report is submitted pursuant to section 207(d) of the International Emergency Economic Powers Act, 50 U.S.C. 1706(d).

2. On April 5, 1990, I issued Executive Order No. 12710, terminating the national emergency declared on April 8, 1988, with respect to Panama. While this order terminated the sanctions imposed pursuant to that declaration, the blocking of Panamanian government assets in the United States was continued in order to permit completion of the orderly unblocking and transfer of funds that I directed on December 20, 1989, and to foster the resolution of claims of U.S. creditors involving Panama, pursuant to 50 U.S.C. 1706(a). The termination of the national emergency did not affect the continuation of compliance audits and enforcement actions with respect to activities taking place during the sanctions period,

pursuant to 50 U.S.C. 1622(a).

3. The Office of Foreign Assets Control of the Department of the Treasury ("FAC") has released to the control of the Government of Panama approximately $134 million of the approximately $137.3 million that remained blocked at the time of my last report. The amount released represents blocked financial accounts that the Government of Panama requested be unblocked.

Of the approximately $6.1 million remaining blocked at this time (which includes approximately $2.8 million in interest credited to the accounts since my last report), some $5.5 million is held in escrow by the Federal Reserve Bank of New York at the request of the Government of Panama. Additionally, approximately $600,000 is held in commercial bank accounts for which the Government of Panama has not requested unblocking. A small residual in blocked reserve accounts established under section 565.509 of the Panamanian Transactions Regulations, 31 CFR 565.509, remains on the books of U.S. firms pending the final reconciliation of accounting records involving claims and counterclaims between the firms and the Government of Panama.

4. I will continue to report periodically to the Congress on the exercise of authorities to prohibit transactions involving property in which the Government of Panama has an interest, pursuant to 50 U.S.C. 1706(d).

GEORGE BUSH

The White House,
April 7, 1992.

# Statement on United States Recognition of the Former Yugoslav Republics
*April 7, 1992*

The United States recognizes Bosnia-Hercegovina, Croatia, and Slovenia as sovereign and independent states and will begin immediate consultations to establish full diplomatic relations. The United States accepts the pre-crisis Republic borders as the legitimate international borders of Bosnia-Hercegovina, Croatia, and Slovenia.

We take this step because we are satisfied that these states meet the requisite criteria for recognition. We acknowledge the peaceful and democratic expression of the will of citizens of these states for sovereignty.

We will continue to work intensively with the European Community and its member states to resolve expeditiously the outstanding issues between Greece and the Republic of Macedonia, thus enabling the U.S. to recognize formally the independence of that Republic as well. The United States will also discuss with the Governments of Serbia and Montenegro their interest in remaining in a common state known as Yugoslavia.

In light of our decisions on recognition, the U.S. will lift economic sanctions from Bosnia-Hercegovina, Croatia, Macedonia, and Slovenia. Sanctions were applied to Yugoslavia on December 6, 1991. We will lift sanctions against Serbia and Montenegro contingent on Belgrade's lifting the economic blockades directed against Bosnia-Hercegovina and Macedonia. The U.N. arms embargo remains in effect.

It has been U.S. policy throughout the Yugoslav crisis to accept any resolution arrived at peacefully, democratically, and by negotiation. The United States strongly supports the U.N. peacekeeping plan, as worked out by Cyrus Vance, and the full deployment of the U.N. peacekeeping force. We continue to support the EC Peace Conference as the indispensable forum for the parties to reach a peaceful settlement of their dispute and to establish the basis for future relations. U.S. recognition is without prejudice to any future association Yugoslav successor states might agree to establish.

The United States views the demonstrated commitment of the emerging states to respect borders and to protect all Yugoslav nationalities as an essential element in establishing full diplomatic relations. Equally, we view such a commitment by Serbia and Montenegro as essential to proceed in discussions on their future status.

The deployment of the U.N. peacekeeping force, the continuation of the EC Peace Conference, and the process of international recognition offer all of the former Yugoslav Republics an historic opportunity to reject decisively the tragic violence which has marked this crisis. Continued commitment to peaceful dialog should lead toward reconciliation, toward integration within Europe, and toward cordial and productive relations with the United States. The United States will continue to work to achieve these goals.

## Statement by Deputy Press Secretary Smith on the President's Meeting With President Francesco Cossiga of Italy
*April 7, 1992*

Italian President Cossiga today called on President Bush to bid farewell in anticipation of the end of Cossiga's 7-year Presidential term in July. He and President Bush discussed a range of bilateral and international issues. President Cossiga also shared his perspectives on the just-completed Ital-

ian elections. Among the other topics discussed were GATT, the Atlantic alliance, and Yugoslavia. Both Presidents reaffirmed their commitment to the closest possible cooperation between Italy and the United States and to ensuring the vitality of the transatlantic partnership.

## Nomination of William Dean Hansen To Be Chief Financial Officer at the Department of Education
*April 7, 1992*

The President today announced his intention to nominate William Dean Hansen, of Idaho, to be Chief Financial Officer at the Department of Education. He would succeed John Theodore Sanders.

Currently Mr. Hansen serves as Acting Assistant Secretary for Management and Budget at the U.S. Department of Education in Washington, DC. Prior to this, he served at the U.S. Department of Education as: Acting Assistant Secretary for Legislation and Congressional Affairs, 1991; Acting Deputy Under Secretary for Planning, Budget, and Evaluation, 1990–91; Deputy Assistant Secretary for Legislation and Con-

gressional Affairs, 1989–90; senior research associate in the Office of the Secretary, 1989; and Deputy Assistant Secretary for Elementary and Secondary Education, 1988. He was Executive Assistant for Legislative Affairs in the Office of Legislation, 1984–88; and a legislative assistant in the Office of Legislation and Public Affairs, 1981–84.

Mr. Hansen graduated from George Mason University (B.S., 1988). He was born May 13, 1959, in Pocatello, ID. Mr. Hansen is married, has four children, and resides in Arlington, VA.

## Statement on Presidential Primary Victories
*April 7, 1992*

Today's results are another endorsement of our proposals for fundamental reform. While the Democrats offer only confusion, we are earning a mandate to change America as we changed the world.

This is the message I will continue to take to the American people. We must have

schools where students can learn. We must restore reason to our legal system. Quality health care should be available to all. A productive America must be free to compete in world markets. And finally, a Congress frozen in gridlock must be made to work.

# Exchange With Reporters While Viewing the Cherry Blossoms at the Tidal Basin
## *April 8, 1992*

*The President.* Look, we're out here to enjoy the flowers, thank you very much. We don't discuss those kinds of things anyway.

*Q.* Good morning.

*Mrs. Bush.* Good morning.

*The President.* Good morning, everybody. Bright and early. Wait until the sun comes up.

*Q.* And then you'll tell us about that satellite and Arafat?

*The President.* The satellite.

*Q.* Are you going to buy our breakfast? I know a good bagel factory.

*The President.* Enjoy. Careful, careful, don't fall in.

*Q.* Don't fall down.

*The President.* This is beautiful. Isn't this beautiful? It's a little early. We're trying to avoid holding people up in the traffic.

*Q.* Did you see that Tsongas is back in the race?

*The President.* We're not commenting on the Democratic—all three of them are Democrats.

*Q.* What do you think about your latest——

*The President.* Outstanding. Excellent.

*Q.* Mr. President, you could see the colors better in the daytime.

*The President.* I know it, but you get——

*Q.* Brilliant.

*The President.* It will be daylight at 6:20 a.m., but we just wanted to get out here before we held up too much traffic. As I speak the sun is starting to rise somewhere.

*Q.* You think you're going to be running against Clinton?

*The President.* I don't know. I'm not going to comment on the Democratic side. I've got a good record of not doing that so far, and I'm going to stay with it.

*Q.* Well, he's the candidate for change.

*The President.* He's running against me. I'm not running against anybody right now. Let's see what they come up with.

*Q.* Is this your favorite monument?

*The President.* Helen [Helen Thomas, United Press International].

*Q.* You got me up this morning; I've got to work. Last time I came here was 3 a.m. in the morning with Nixon.

*Q.* You see things have gotten better. You don't have to come out quite so early.

*Q.* Oh, yes. In '71.

*The President.* How did he do in the primary? [*Laughter*]

*Q.* It was a Vietnam protest.

*Term Limitations*

*The President.* Helen, this might interest you. This might interest you all. Here's Thomas Jefferson's belief in term limitations.

*Q.* My favorite.

*The President.* This one. This is Jefferson's appeal for term limits. Read carefully, Helen.

*Q.* ——not an advocate.

*The President.* "Frequent changes . . . laws and institutions must go hand-in-hand with the progress of the human mind. As that becomes more developed, more enlightened, as new discoveries are made, new truth discovered, and matters of opinions change . . . change is certain . . . institutions must advance also to keep pace with times." If I've ever heard an eloquent plea for term limits, that's it.

*Q.* Doesn't sound like that to me.

*The President.* It does to me. "We might as well require men to wear—[*inaudible*]"—in other words, things have to change. Congress must change.

*Q.* I don't think Bob Michel would like that.

*The President.* Well, I think he probably would. But I really think this is a very important statement here. Let's see what he says over here.

*Q.* You're misinterpreting Jefferson.

*The President.* No, I'm not.

*Q.* You ought to send this statement to Peru.

*The President.* Perot?

*Q.* Peru.

*The President.* Oh, sorry, I heard you.

*Q.* Perot, right? Is he on your mind?

*The President.* No, I think he's on yours.

*Q.* Not at all.

*The President.* This is a lovely memorial.

*Q.* Do you care one way or the other if Perot gets in it, Mr. President?

*The President.* No.

*Q.* Tell Strom Thurmond about it. How many terms has he had?

*Q.* Do you have a favorite memorial?

*Mrs. Bush.* This may well be it. It's a nice one.

*The President.* This one is?

*Q.* You can see this from your balcony.

## U.S. Supreme Court

*Q.* Maybe he's talking about liberal interpretation of the Constitution vis-a-vis the U.S. Supreme Court and its need to interpret law in light of ever-changing circumstances?

*The President.* That's exactly what the Supreme Court does. They interpret the Constitution. They do not legislate from the Bench. One of the things I'm most proud of is my appointments to the Supreme Court. And it's a good court, and it does not legislate from the Bench as much as in the past. And that's good. And maybe that's what he's talking about. But I don't see that in that particular message there. What I think he's talking about there is change, and we are trying to get some change.

*Q.* What did you think of the march on Sunday?

*The President.* The march?

*Q.* Yes, the march.

*The President.* I think Jefferson would have approved of that. Everybody has a right to petition his Government, or her Government, Helen; his in the generic sense.

*Q.* But where does it fall on your ears?

*The President.* Everybody has that right.

## President's Schedule

*Q.* Mr. President, we've noticed that you've been taking some leisurely weekends. Is this, taking the advice of your doctor, as much of a vacation as you're going to——

*The President.* Well, I think probably yes. I don't think we're going to be able to get a 2-week vacation, nor do I feel need of that, although I was delighted when the doctor recommended it. Took a little pressure off so we could get a good long weekend. But I feel good. I think the health is strong. This weekend was good, and I got a lot of rest up there.

So, I think that I'm more apt to do that than I am to try to get a week off in a row, something like that.

## Legislative Agenda

*Q.* Are you anxious to return to full-fledged campaigning?

*The President.* Not particularly. Full-term governing, trying to move this Congress to do things that I've been trying to get done. For example, an education program that will change education and change it for the better; an anticrime bill that will give support to the people in the cities, the people in the rural areas that need it. So there's a lot of things we're still trying to get done with Congress. This period gives me time to concentrate on that. I'll keep going.

I'd like to see this legislation passed that will put some limits on liability. If there was ever anything people unanimously want in this country, it's to do something about the frivolous lawsuits, those that are just running up the cost of everything and frivolously driving people out of public service, out of helping their neighbor, out of medical practice. And yet it sits there in a Congress unwilling to even take it up for a vote.

So, there's plenty of things to be doing without having to concentrate on the primaries at this point or the elections at this point. And I'm trying very hard to do just exactly that.

Now, we're going to go up and see the sun come up and watch the——

*Q.* You're not even sending health financing up?

*The President.* We've got a wonderful health——

*Q.* Your health care program stands in limbo.

*The President.* Well, then blame the Congress because we've got the best health care plan there is. And it does not socialize medicine in this country. It preserves the quality of care. It gives health care access to all, and it does it without reducing the quality of American education. And I just hope the Congress will move on it instead of sitting there and griping for the status quo.

And that's it. When I'm talking about change, that's what I'm talking about, a whole array of issues. And I think the American people understand it, and I think as the campaign gets in focus in the fall they'll understand it more clearly. So this is what it is. It isn't about who's been President for 3 years, it's the question of who has the program for change that really will help this country. And it's about time the Congress moves on some of these items. And I've listed three or four here, and there's plenty more.

So, that's what we'll be talking about. I do have a period in here where I don't have to concentrate on the primaries, and that's good. Nor will I comment on the primaries on the Democratic side. They don't need me getting in fine-tuning it. I hear what they say about me. There will be plenty of time to respond, do it in a civil way and not take questions on who's up or who's down in New York or anything like that.

*Q.* Well, you were kind of scared of Buchanan's threat, weren't you? Weren't you a little bit frightened about Buchanan?

*The President.* No.

### President's Staff

*Q.* What do you think about the criticism of your Chief of Staff, Sam Skinner, and this alleged disarray?

*The President.* I think it's ridiculous. You know and I know that there's periodic stories of this nature. I've seen it in every single administration, Democrat and Republican. I discount it. I think we've got an outstanding staff. We've got good coordination between the campaign and the staff. And there's a hiatus in here, as I mentioned, where we can be sure the cooperation is the best. So it's coming along, and I don't——

*Q.* Is Marlin quitting?

*The President.* There's one of the most ridiculous——

*Mrs. Bush.* What?

*The President.* She said, "Is Marlin quitting?" That is so absurd. It's just absolutely absurd. And you know it. But you have to

ask the question because somebody beat you to a story that's untrue. [*Laughter*] So you have to ask it, but it's silly. It's silly.

*Q.* The best defense is offense. I could campaign——

*The President.* Exactly. You're darn right you can.

*Mrs. Bush.* You can't see in our bedroom window; that's good news.

*The President.* You can see George sleeping over there. See, on the far right window. That's my son George; that's our son George's room. And when he got the word that the Texas Rangers won 4 to nothing at 5:45 a.m., he went back to sleep for another hour and refused to come out to see the cherry blossoms. That's my boy for you.

*Q.* A chip off the old block. [*Laughter*]

### President's Opening Day Pitch

*The President.* Yes, rooting for his ball team. There's a beautiful view there. And I've gotten so many compliments on that first pitch, I'm surprised you don't ask about that. A lot of people—I thought there would be some criticism. They could visualize the left-handed hitter standing there and the pitcher on the first pitch saying, outside and away, do not bring it in over the strike zone, and bring it in a little slower than normal because he's looking for the heat. And so, as one reporter pointed out, you give him the chill or the freeze.

And it was wonderful because it was a great comparison with my grandson who had to get out there and arrogantly throw it right over the middle of the plate fast. So, I've been surprised at the reaction from the people. It's very understanding on that pitch.

*Q.* That's why you want to run for reelection, so you can throw out the first ball, right?

*The President.* Well, I think the American people seem to be sensitive. They see what the man is trying to do, keep it outside on the opening left-handed hitter. [*Laughter*] You notice how the third baseman came in on the very first pitch of the leadoff hitter. He was in for the bunt. Now, with my pitch, nobody could have bunted that thing. [*Laughter*]

*Q.* You're the ultimate outsider.

### Tidal Basin Visit

*The President.* I think we can go without fouling up the traffic there.

*Q.* Breakfast in the mess. We do know a good bagel factory.

*Q.* How's the Kennebunkport house?

*Mrs. Bush.* We're going to see in a couple of weeks.

*Q.* Habitable?

*Mrs. Bush.* Yes, we'll be up there Easter. No furniture, though.

*The President.* Valdez [David Valdez, President's Photographer], can you create a original "Valdez" out of this? A man of your ability ought to be able to make a real creation. I'll send this to my mother. This "Valdez" will live in history.

*Q.* Are these the campaign photos?

*The President.* No.

*Mrs. Bush.* Oh, you bet. [*Laughter*]

*The President.* This is an annual event for us. It's very nice.

*Mrs. Bush.* Next year we're going to go at 5 a.m.

*Q.* How long have you been doing this?

*The President.* Maybe three, I don't remember exactly.

*Q.* Not as Vice President?

*The President.* Well, we didn't have to worry about you in the daytime then. [*Laughter*] This is pretty.

*Mrs. Bush.* Beautiful.

*Q.* You're not saying that Vice President Quayle has an easier life than you?

*The President.* No. I'm just saying it's a little different between what you can do as President and what you can do as Vice President.

### Term Limitations

*Q.* If you're so much for term limitations, why don't you seek one term?

*The President.* Because we're limited to two terms. I think that's about right for a President. I didn't always feel that way either.

*Q.* Really? What caused your conversion?

*The President.* I think that's the kind of change that Thomas Jefferson is talking about. That's what caused it.

*Q.* I didn't read the same thing in his words. [*Laughter*]

*The President.* I did. Let's go. I think we better head on back before the traffic starts hitting the bridge.

### Tidal Basin Visit

*Q.* Walk. We have to run.

*The President.* No, you're right here.

Here, Ranger, get in. They want you, I know. I know everyone wants you in the picture.

*Mrs. Bush.* Sit down, Millie.

*The President.* Big guys in the middle. Here, Ranger; here, boy. Sit, sit. Good boy. Stay, stay.

*Q.* What perks are you giving up, Mr. President?

*The President.* He's like Helen Thomas. You tell him to do something, he doesn't write it—[*inaudible*].

Thank you all very much.

*Q.* Giving up any perks?

*The President.* Ranger, come here, boy. Sic her! [*Laughter*]

*Q.* That's all right. Ranger's okay.

*Q.* Any comment on the GAO report, Mr. President?

*The President.* Randall [Randall Pinkston, CBS News], nice to see you there.

You've got to admit the timing was perfect on this, right? It's so beautiful. It really is.

*Q.* Did you know it was going to be a perfect day?

*The President.* Well, we talked about either today or tomorrow. Here's the way the decisionmaking process works: Barbara got home at about 11 p.m., so I made the command decision to go either this morning or tomorrow morning. So we went this morning.

*Q.* The later the better.

*The President.* No, we wanted to do it so we wouldn't foul up traffic. But it's great to do. I thought she might be a little tired, but she wasn't, so off we go. We wake up at 5 a.m. every morning. Got that? It's true.

*Q.* I believe it.

*The President.* It's true. So it's routine. Good to see you all. Got to go to work.

*Note: The exchange began at 5:55 a.m. during a walk from the White House to the Jefferson Memorial and back. In his re-*

*marks, the President referred to Ross Perot, businessman and prospective Presidential* candidate.

## Remarks Congratulating United States Olympic Athletes
*April 8, 1992*

Well, please be seated. Mr. Vice President and Marilyn—I've been jealous of them ever since they got to go to see a little bit of Albertville, not as much as they would have liked, but we were just delighted they could represent our country, albeit briefly, at this marvelous event.

And may I salute an old friend, Bill Hybl, from Colorado, who is the president of the U.S. Olympic Committee and who stepped into a difficult job and has done a superb job for our athletes and for our country. I see next to him Oss Day, who was also on our delegation that represented us over there. Welcome, sir. And may I just salute all that are here today, fellow Americans, and most of all, the very special athletes who did our country so proud. And a special hello to another athlete in his own right, a former coach of Notre Dame's Fighting Irish, who has just come, as Dizzy Dean would say, from "commemertating" on the NCAA basketball tournament, Digger Phelps.

Now, a parenthetical note and one of great importance and, I think, benefit to our country. Today we're announcing that Digger Phelps will be a Special Assistant to the Director at the Office of National Drug Control Policy. Next to Digger is Governor Bob Martinez, who is doing a superb job heading up that Office. And now, Digger will be at his side, the side of the Attorney General Bill Barr. And he's joining our efforts to take back the streets from crime and drugs, working on our new "Weed and Seed" program, which is terribly important to every community in our country. Digger, welcome, officially, and please stand up.

Well, I'm so glad to see all of you here helping salute the Olympians. And let me say that it's an honor to have this team here, though I almost didn't recognize you all without the interruptions for commercials. [*Laughter*]

The Olympics—sorry about that one—[*laughter*]—the Olympics have been described as "going for the gold." Well, whether you took home a gold, silver, bronze, or simply just gave it your best, in my book and the book of your countrymen, you're all winners, indeed, heroes. And I think that's true for all Americans, look at it that way.

A book once proclaimed, "Let us now praise famous men." The 1992 Winter Olympics praised famous women. And did they do it well? I speak of champions like Kristi Yamaguchi over here, of Fremont, California. And I know Kristi's got her own cereal now, but we know she's the real Special K. [*Laughter*]

With us today, of course, is a champion whose specialty is speed skating. Bonnie Blair was supported in her early days by her hometown Champaign, Illinois, fire department. Now, after becoming the first American woman to take a gold medal in two straight Olympics, she's set the speed skating world on fire. Congratulations.

So did Cathy, Cathy Turner of Rochester, whose story even Ripley would disbelieve. A briefly retired speed skater, Cathy gave up her job as a nightclub singer to return to her sport and win the gold in short track, a silver in the relay event. And I congratulate her. Well done, well done. That brings me to other members of what's been called the Golden Girls, people like Donna Weinbrecht of New Milford, New Jersey, winning the first-ever gold medal in moguls skiing, or Juneau's Hilary Lindh, winning the silver in the women's downhill, the first Alaskan athlete to win an Olympic medal. Hilary, you've made Alaska almost forget about the Iditarod. Where are you?

I think, too, of Diann Roffe, Nancy Kerrigan, Amy Peterson, Darcie Dohnal, and

Nikki Ziegelmeyer, each of them winning bronze or silver. And also three-time Olympian Bonny Warner, who has now traded the luge for her new career as an airplane pilot. Bonny, you made the entire Olympics friendly skies for America. Now, where is Bonny? Way up high. There she is.

And then, members of the men's hockey team, of course, have now all spread out, returned to a variety of careers. And I know they'll be as successful as they were at Albertville, fourth in the Winter Games, best since the Miracle Team of '80, 1980. Team U.S.A. was led by Ray LeBlanc from Fitchburg, Mass., who did a superb job in goal. As an expert at taking a lot of shots, I know exactly how he felt. [*Laughter*] We can all learn from him. No wonder they call Ray "America's choice," just as Nelson Carmichael, winning a bronze in moguls freestyle skiing, is the choice of his hometown, Steamboat Springs, Colorado.

Then, Paul Wylie, a figure skater from Somerville, Mass., who won a silver medal when some said he was over the hill at age 27. Don't worry, Paul. Barbara and I know you'll get used to it. [*Laughter*] Had to rope her in on it. At the end of this year's games, Paul Wylie received the Olympic Spirit Award.

Let me add, that spirit owes much to this year's demonstration sport competitors, the men's curling team of Bud and Tim Somerville and Bill and Mike Strum, Jeff Hamilton in speed skiing, and Lane Spina and Sharon Petzold in freestyle ballet skiing, all here someplace. Hold up your hands now so we can get a little idea. There they are. Welcome, welcome.

But in the broad and in the truest sense, all of you here today mirror America's Olympic spirit: the work ethic, the desire to give of yourself and of your heart, the love of victory and, above all, competition. Each quality makes the Olympics great. Each, in turn, makes our country great.

In 1954, Dwight Eisenhower called the Olympics the means and methods by which some understanding of fairplay and justice can be developed among nations. Here is what we call it: human beings vying peacefully, athletes asking more of themselves, excellence, achievement, the boundless energy of the human spirit.

Each of you showed how the Olympics race can ennoble the human race, that cooperation and competition can produce a better world. And you led the way to America's best showing in the Winter Games since 1980, 11 medals, the most we've won on foreign soil.

And you pointed the way to Lillehammer in 1994. And you gave the world a taste of what we'll do when America holds the Summer Olympics in Atlanta in July of 1996. White House to the world: I can't wait. And I know all Americans agree with me.

More than two millennia ago, a Greek statesman asked, "Which would you rather be, a victor in the Olympic Games or the announcer of the victor?" Today I am privileged to be the announcer of you victors, Americans who showed what we mean by competition, decency, self-reliance, self-discipline, proving that the Olympics, like America, are truly number one.

For that I thank you, for coming to the White House. We just welcome you once again. And may God bless you all, and the Nation that you made so proud, the United States of America. Thank you, and welcome.

*Note: The President spoke at 2:47 p.m. on the South Lawn at the White House.*

## Message to the Congress Transmitting the Report of the National Endowment for Democracy
*April 8, 1992*

*To the Congress of the United States:*

Pursuant to the provisions of section 504(h) of Public Law 98–164, as amended (22 U.S.C. 4413(i)), I transmit herewith the Eighth Annual Report of the National Endowment for Democracy, which covers fiscal year 1991.

GEORGE BUSH

The White House,
April 8, 1992.

## Message to the Congress Reporting a Budget Rescission
*April 8, 1992*

*To the Congress of the United States:*

In accordance with the Congressional Budget and Impoundment Control Act of 1974, I herewith report one rescission proposal, totaling $145 thousand in budgetary resources.

The proposed rescission affects the Department of Energy. The details of this rescission proposal are contained in the attached report.

GEORGE BUSH

The White House,
April 8, 1992.

*Note: The attachment detailing the proposed rescission was published in the Federal Register on April 15.*

## Statement on Reforming Federal Regulation of Natural Gas Pipelines
*April 8, 1992*

I am pleased to announce comprehensive action taken today by the Federal Energy Regulatory Commission to reform Federal regulation of natural gas pipelines. The entire natural gas industry plays a critical role in the economic and environmental health of our Nation.

These reforms are part of the administration's national energy strategy as well as our continuing efforts to remove unnecessary regulatory barriers to jobs and economic growth. They also build upon prior reforms, such as the key legislation I signed in 1989 abolishing price controls on producers of natural gas.

By reforming Federal regulation of the pipelines that transport natural gas, FERC's so-called restructuring rule continues this trend away from heavy-handed Government regulation. Like the decontrol legislation I signed in 1989, FERC's action today will help to create a competitive, nationwide gas market, a market that will provide ample supplies of clean-burning natural gas for heating homes, running factories, and powering cars and trucks.

I commend Chairman Martin Allday and his colleagues on the Commission for their success in bringing reform to this vital American industry.

I call upon Congress, particularly the House of Representatives, to help us continue this reform effort by quickly enacting my national energy strategy legislation.

## Nomination of Kenton Wesley Keith To Be United States Ambassador to Qatar
*April 8, 1992*

The President today announced his intention to nominate Kenton Wesley Keith, of Missouri, to be Ambassador to the State of Qatar. He would succeed Mark Gregory Hambley.

Since 1988 Mr. Keith has served as the Public Affairs Counselor at the U.S. Embassy in Cairo, Egypt. Prior to this, he served as a Senior Cultural Affairs Officer at the U.S. Embassy in Paris, France, 1985–88; Deputy Director of Near East and South Asia Area Office for the U.S. Information Agency in Washington, DC, 1983–85; and Deputy Public Affairs Officer at the U.S. Embassy in Brasilia, Brazil, 1980–83. From 1977 to 1980, he served as Special Assistant to the Deputy Director of the U.S. Information Agency.

Mr. Keith received a bachelor of arts degree from the University of Kansas. He was born November 12, 1939, in Kansas City, MO. Mr. Keith served in the U.S. Navy for 4 years. He is married, has two children, and resides in Cairo, Egypt.

## Nomination of Donald K. Petterson To Be United States Ambassador to Sudan
*April 8, 1992*

The President today announced his intention to nominate Donald K. Petterson, of California, to be Ambassador to the Republic of the Sudan. He would succeed James Richard Cheek.

Currently Ambassador Petterson is studying at the Foreign Service Institute in Arlington, VA. Prior to this, Ambassador Petterson has served as Chargé d'Affaires at the U.S. Embassy in Harare, Zimbabwe, 1990–91; Director of the Liberia Task Force at the U.S. Department of State, 1990; and as Acting Deputy Assistant Secretary of State for the Bureau of African Affairs, 1990. He served as the U.S. Ambassador to Tanzania, 1986–89; and the U.S. Ambassador to Somalia, 1978–82.

Ambassador Petterson graduated from the University of California at Santa Barbara (B.A., 1956; M.A., 1960). He was born November 17, 1930, in Huntington Park, CA. Ambassador Petterson served in the U.S. Navy, 1948–52. He is married, has four children, and resides in Washington, DC.

## Nomination of Hume Alexander Horan To Be United States Ambassador to Cote d'Ivoire
*April 8, 1992*

The President today announced his intention to nominate Hume Alexander Horan, of the District of Columbia, to be Ambassador to the Republic of Cote d'Ivoire. He would succeed Kenneth L. Brown.

Currently Mr. Horan serves as the president of the American Foreign Service Association in Washington, DC. From 1989 to 1991, he served as Special Assistant to the Director General of the Foreign Service at the U.S. Department of State. Mr. Horan has served as the U.S. Ambassador to Saudi Arabia, 1987–88; Sudan, 1983–86; Equatorial Guinea, 1980–82; and Cameroon, 1980–

83.

Mr. Horan graduated from Harvard College (A.B., 1958) and Harvard University (A.M., 1963). He was born August 13, 1934, in Washington, DC. Mr. Horan served in the U.S. Army, 1954–56. He is married, has three children, and resides in Washington, DC.

## Appointment of Richard F. Phelps as Special Assistant to the Director of the Office of National Drug Control Policy
*April 8, 1992*

The President today announced the appointment of Richard F. "Digger" Phelps as Special Assistant to Gov. Bob Martinez, Director of the Office of National Drug Control Policy (ONDCP). In his role as Special Assistant, Mr. Phelps will serve as liaison between ONDCP and the Department of Justice in coordinating the newly expanded Operation "Weed and Seed" program, a Presidential initiative focusing on violent crime and neighborhood revitalization. This is a newly created position.

For 20 years Mr. Phelps headed the University of Notre Dame basketball program. Prior to joining Notre Dame, Mr. Phelps was head basketball coach at Fordham University for one year. He also served as an assistant coach at Rider College and the University of Pennsylvania. He has coauthored two books, "A Coach's World" and "Digger Phelps and Notre Dame Basketball," and most recently served as a commentator for CBS Sports. He serves on the Board of Directors of the Commission on National and Community Service; the U.S. Postal Service Citizen Stamp Advisory Committee; the Logan Protective Service Board for the Mentally Retarded and Developmentally Disabled of South Bend, IN; and as a volunteer with the Special Olympics.

Mr. Phelps graduated from Rider College in 1963 and was awarded an honorary doctorate of the arts degree by his alma mater in 1981. He was born July 4, 1941, in Beacon, NY. He is married, has three children, and resides in South Bend, IN.

## Nomination of Daniel A. Sumner To Be an Assistant Secretary of Agriculture
*April 8, 1992*

The President today announced his intention to nominate Daniel A. Sumner, of North Carolina, to be an Assistant Secretary of Agriculture for Economics and a member of the Board of Directors of the Commodity Credit Corporation, succeeding Bruce L. Gardner. Upon appointment as Assistant Secretary of Agriculture, he will be appointed a member of the Board of Directors of the Rural Telephone Bank.

Currently Dr. Sumner serves as Acting Assistant Secretary for Economics and Deputy Assistant Secretary for Economics at the U.S. Department of Agriculture in Washington, DC. Prior to this, he served as a professor of agricultural economics in the department of economics and business at North Carolina State University, 1979–90.

Dr. Sumner graduated from California State Polytechnic University (B.S., 1971); Michigan State University (M.A., 1973); and the University of Chicago (M.A., 1977; Ph.D., 1978). He was born December 5, 1950, in Fairfield, CA. Dr. Sumner has two children and resides in Alexandria, VA.

## Nomination of Christian R. Holmes IV To Be an Assistant Administrator of the Environmental Protection Agency
*April 8, 1992*

The President today announced his intention to nominate Christian R. Holmes IV, of California, to be Assistant Administrator for Administration and Resource Management at the Environmental Protection Agency, succeeding Charlie L. Grizzle; and Chief Financial Officer for the Environmental Protection Agency, a new position.

Currently Mr. Holmes serves as Acting Assistant Administrator in the Office of Administration and Resource Management at the Environmental Protection Agency in Washington, DC. Prior to this, Mr. Holmes served as Deputy Assistant Administrator for Federal Facilities Enforcement, 1990–91. From 1989 to 1990, Mr. Holmes served as Principal Deputy Assistant Administrator in the Office of Solid Waste and Emergency Response at the Environmental Protection Agency in Washington, DC.

Mr. Holmes graduated from Wesleyan University (B.A., 1968). He was born February 1, 1946, in Syracuse, NY. Mr. Holmes served in the U.S. Army Reserve, 1968–74. He is married, has two children, and resides in Washington, DC.

## Remarks to the American Society of Newspaper Editors
*April 9, 1992*

*The President.* Thank you, Dave. And may I start by thanking the members of the board and say to all the members of ASNE I'm grateful for this return engagement, glad to participate in an annual event that Washington looks forward to, this annual conference.

Even in the age of VCR's and CNN, people who want to understand the times we live in still, as Dave indicated in that sweet and short introduction, turn to the printed word.

And today I want to share some serious observations with you on events around the world. Look around the world today. Think of the page-one stories of the past few years and our victory in the cold war, the collapse of imperial communism, the liberation of Kuwait. Think of the great revolutions of '89 that brought down the Berlin Wall and broke the chains of communism and brought a new world of freedom to Eastern Europe. And think of the role this Nation played in every one of these great triumphs, the sacrifices we made, the sense of mission that carried us through.

Each day brings new changes, new realities, new hopes, new horizons. In the past 6 months alone we've recognized 18, in 6 months, 18 brandnew nations. The bulk of those nations, of course, are born of one momentous event, the collapse of Soviet communism.

And today I want to talk to you all about the most important foreign policy opportunity of our time, an opportunity that will affect the security and the future of every American, young and old, throughout this entire decade. The democratic revolutions underway in Russia, in Armenia, Ukraine, and the other new nations of the old Soviet empire represent the best hope for real peace in my lifetime.

Shortly after taking office, I outlined a new American strategy in response to the changes underway in the Soviet Union and East and Central Europe. It was to move beyond containment, to encourage reform, to always support freedom for the captive nations of the East. And now, after dramatic revolutions in Poland and Hungary and Czechoslovakia, revolutions that spread then to Romania and Bulgaria and even Albania; after the unification of Germany in NATO; after the demise of the one power, the U.S.S.R., that threatened our way of life, that mission has been fulfilled. The cold war is over. The specter of nuclear armageddon has receded, and Soviet communism has collapsed. And in its wake we find ourselves on the threshold of a new world of opportunity and peace.

But with the passing of the cold war, a new order has yet to take its place. The opportunities, tremendous; they're great. But so, too, are the dangers. And so, we stand at history's hinge point. A new world beckons while the ghost of history stands in the shadows.

I want to outline today a new mission for American policy toward Russia and the other new nations of the old U.S.S.R. It's a mission that can advance our economic and security interests while upholding the primacy of American values, values which, as Lincoln said, are the "last, best hope of Earth."

Americans have always responded best when a new frontier beckoned. And I believe that the next frontier for us, and for the generation that follows, is to secure a democratic peace in Europe and the former U.S.S.R. that will ensure a lasting peace for the United States of America.

The democratic peace must be founded on twin pillars of political and economic freedom. The success of reform in Russia and Ukraine, Armenia and Kazakhstan, Byelarus and the Baltics will be the single best guarantee of our security, our prosperity, and our values.

After the long cold war, this much is clear: Democrats in the Kremlin can assure our security in a way nuclear missiles never could. Much of my administration's foreign policy has been dedicated to winning the cold war peacefully. And the next 4 years must be dedicated to building a democratic peace, not simply for those of us who lived through the cold war and won it but for generations to come.

From the first moments of the cold war, our mission was containment, to use the combined resources of the West to check the expansion, the expansionist aims of the Soviet empire. It's been my policy as President to move beyond containment, to use the power of America and the West to end the cold war with freedom's victory. And today, we have reached a turning point. We

have defeated imperial communism.

We've not yet won the victory for democracy, though. This democratic peace will not be easily won. The weight of history, 74 years of Communist misrule in the former U.S.S.R., tells us that democracy and economic freedom will be years in the building. America must, therefore, resolve that our commitment be equally firm and lasting. With this commitment, we have the chance to build a very different world, a world built on the common values of political and economic freedom between Russia and America, between East and West and at long last, a peace built on mutual trust, not on mutual terror.

And today, we find ourselves in an almost unimaginable world where democrats, not Communists, hold power in Moscow and Kiev and Yerevan; a new world where a new breed of leaders, Boris Yeltsin, Levon Ter-Petrosyan, Leonid Kravchuk, Askar Akayev, among others, are pushing forward to reform.

They seek to replace the rule of force with the rule of law. And they seek, for the first time in their countries' histories, not to impose rule in the name of the people but to build governments of, by, and for the people. And they seek a future of free and open markets where economic rights rest in the hands of individuals, not on the whims of the central planners. They seek partnerships. They seek alliances with us. And they also seek an end to competition and conflict. Our values are their values. And in this time of transition, they are reaching out to us. They seek our help. And if we're to act, we must see clearly what is at stake.

Forty years ago, Americans had the vision and the good sense to help defeated enemies back to their feet as democracies. Well, what a wise investment that proved to be. Those we helped became close allies and major trading partners. Our choice today, just as clear: With our help, Russia, Ukraine, other new States can become democratic friends and partners. And let me say here, they will have our help.

What difference can this make for America, you might ask. We can put behind us, for good, the nuclear confrontation that has held our very civilization hostage for over four decades. The threat of a major ground war in Western Europe has disappeared with the demise of the Warsaw Pact. A democratic Russia is the best guarantee against a renewed danger of competition and the threat of nuclear rivalry.

The failure of the democratic experiment could bring a dark future, a return to authoritarianism or a descent into anarchy. In either case, the outcome would threaten our peace, our prosperity, and our security for years to come. But we should focus not on the dangers of failure but on the dividends of success.

First, we can reap a genuine peace dividend this year and then year after year, in the form of permanently reduced defense budgets. Already we've proposed $50 billion worth of defense spending reductions between now and 1997. Now, that cut comes on top of savings totaling $267 billion, more than a quarter of a trillion dollars in projected defense expenditures since the fall of the Berlin Wall. Make no mistake: I am not going to make reckless defense cuts that impair our own fundamental national security.

Second, working with our Russian partners and our allies, we can create a new international landscape, a landscape where emerging threats are contained and undone, where we work in concert to confront common threats to our environment, where terrorists find no safe haven, and where genuine coalitions of like-minded countries respond to dangers and opportunities together.

And finally, third, the triumph of free governments and free markets in the old Soviet Union will mean extensive opportunities for global trade and economic growth. A democratic Russia, one dedicated to free market economies, will provide an impetus for a major increase in global trade and investment. The people of the former Soviet Union are well-schooled and highly skilled. They seek for their families the same better future each of us wishes for our own. And together, they form a potentially vast market that crosses 11 time zones and comprises nearly 300 million people.

No economist can pinpoint the value of trade opportunities we hope to have. It's impossible to compute, but the potential for prosperity is great. Increased trade means vast new markets for American goods, new opportunities for American entrepreneurs, new jobs for American workers. And I'm committed to giving American business every possible opportunity to compete fairly and equally in these new markets.

For example, last week I asked the Congress to repeal the Stevenson and Byrd amendments that limit Export-Import Bank's ability to help promote American exports to the former U.S.S.R. And I'm pleased that Congress has acted. I'm also seeking to conclude trade, bilateral investment, and tax treaties with each of the new Commonwealth States. The first agreement between the U.S. and Armenia was signed last week, and we expect a lot more to follow.

Russian democracy is in America's interest. It's also in keeping with this Nation's guiding ideals. Across the boundaries of language and culture, across the cold war chasm of mistrust, we feel the pull of common values. And in the ordeal of long-suffering peoples of the Soviet empire, we see glimpses of this Nation's past. In their hopes and dreams, we see our own.

This is an article of the American creed: Freedom is not the special preserve of one nation; it is the birthright of men and women everywhere. And we have always dreamed of the day democracy and freedom will triumph in every corner of the world, in every captive nation and closed society. And this may never happen in our lifetime, but it can happen now for the millions of people who for so long suffered under that totalitarian Soviet rule.

Some may say this view of the future is a little unrealistic. Let me remind you that three of our leading partners in helping democracy succeed in Russia are none other than Germany, Japan, and Italy. And if we can now bring Russia into the community of free nations who share American ideals, we will have redeemed hope in a century that has known so much suffering. It is not inevitable, as de Tocqueville wrote, that America and Russia were destined to struggle for global supremacy. De Tocqueville only knew a despotic Russia, but we see and can help secure a democratic Russia.

One of America's greatest achievements in this century has been our leadership of a remarkable community of nations, the free world. This community is democratic; it is stable; it's prosperous, cooperative; it is independent. In America all of us are the better for that. And we have strong allies. We have enormous trade, and we are safer as a result of our commitment to this free world. And now, we must expand this most successful of communities to include our former adversaries.

Now, this is good for America. A world that trades with us brings greater prosperity. A world that shares our values strengthens the peace. This is the world that lies out there before us. This is the world that can be achieved if we have the vision to reach for it. And this is the peace that we must not lose.

And this is what we're doing right now to win this peace. Strategically, we're moving with the Russians to reach historic nuclear reductions. We've urged speedy ratification of START and CFE. And we're working with all the new States to prevent the spread of weapons of mass destruction. We are offering our help in safety, in nuclear weapons safety, in security, and yes, in the dismantlement. And we're engaged in an intensive program of military-to-military exchanges to strengthen the ties between our two militaries, indeed, to build unprecedented defense cooperation, cooperation that would have simply been unthinkable a few short months ago.

Politically, we're reaching out so America and American values will be well represented in these new lands. We are the only country with embassies in all of the former republics. We're planning to bring American houses and American expertise to the former U.S.S.R., to send hundreds of Peace Corps volunteers to help create small businesses, to launch major exchanges of students, professionals, and scientists, so that our people can establish the bonds so important to permanent peace.

Economically, working with the European Community and many other countries, we organized a global coalition to provide urgently needed emergency food and medical supplies this past winter. And now we will send Americans to help promote improvements in food distribution, energy, defense conversion, and democratization.

I have sent Congress the "FREEDOM Support Act," a comprehensive and integrated legislative package that will provide new opportunities to support freedom and repeal all cold-war legislation. In its key features this bill asks Congress to meet my request for $620 million to fund technical assistance projects in the former U.S.S.R. It urges Congress to increase the U.S. quota in the IMF, International Monetary Fund, by $12 billion. And I pledge to work with the Congress on a bipartisan basis to pass this act. And I want to sign this bill into law before my June summit with President Yeltsin here in Washington, DC.

Just as the rewards of this new world will belong to no one nation, so too the burden does not fall to America alone. Together with our allies, we've developed a $24 billion package of financial assistance. Its aim: to provide urgently needed support for President Yeltsin's reforms.

And ours is a policy of collective engagement and shared responsibility. Working with the G-7, the IMF, and the World Bank, we are seeking to help promote the economic transformation so central to an enduring democratic peace. Forty-five years after their founding, the Bretton Woods institutions we created after World War II are now serving their original purpose. By working with others we're sharing the burden responsibly and acting in the best interests of the American taxpayer.

I know that broad public support will be critical to our effort to get this program passed. And so, let me say something to those who say, "Yes, the people of Russia, and all across the old Soviet empire, are struggling; yes, we want to see them succeed, to join the democratic community. But what about us? What about the challenges and demands we must meet right here in America? Isn't it time we took care of our own?" And to them I would say this: Peace and prosperity are in the interest of every American, each one of us alive today and all the generations that will follow. As a Nation, we spent more than $4 trillion to wage and win the cold war. Compared to such monumental sacrifice, the costs of promoting democracy will be a fraction and the consequences for our peace and prosperity beyond measure. America must take the lead in creating this new world of peace.

Three times this century, America has been called on to help construct a lasting peace in Europe. Seventy-five years ago this month, the United States entered World War I to tip the balance against aggression. And yet, with the battle won, America withdrew across the ocean, and the "war to end all wars" produced a peace that did not last even a generation. Indeed, by the time I was born in 1924, the peace was already unraveling. Germany's economic chaos soon led to what, to Fascist dictatorship. The seeds of another, more terrible war were sown.

And still, the isolationist impulse remained strong. Years later, as the Nazis began their march across the Continent, I can still remember the editorials here in the United States talking about "Europe's war," as if America could close itself off, as if we could isolate ourselves from the world beyond our shores. As a consequence, you know the answer, we fought the most costly war in the history of man, a war that claimed the lives of countless millions. At war's end, once again we saw the prospect of a new world on the horizon. But the great victory over fascism quickly gave way to the grim reality of a new Communist threat.

We are fortunate that our postwar leaders, Democrats and Republicans alike, did not forget the lessons of the past in building the peace of the next four decades. They shaped a coalition that kept America engaged, that kept the peace through the long twilight struggle against Soviet communism. And they taught the lesson that we simply must heed today, that the noblest mission of the victor is to turn an enemy into a friend.

And now America faces a third opportunity to provide the kind of lasting peace that for so long eluded us. At this defining moment, I know where I stand. I stand for American engagement in support of a democratic peace, a peace that can secure for the next generation a world free from war, free from conflict.

After a half-century of fear and mistrust, America, Russia, and the new nations of the former U.S.S.R. must become partners in peace. After a half-century of cold war and harsh words, we must speak and act on common values. After a half-century of armed and uneasy peace, we must move forward toward a new world of freedom, cooperation, reconciliation, and hope.

Thank you all very much for inviting me here today. And may God bless the free peoples of the former Soviet empire, and may God bless the United States of America. Thank you very, very much.

*[At this point, the President answered questions from audience members.]*

*Persian Gulf*

Q. *[Inaudible]*

The President. *[Inaudible]*—of the Gulf area. At that time not only the United States but the United States and many of the Gulf countries, the GCC countries, felt that the major threat to stability in the Gulf was from Iran. We did not want an Iran that would take over Iraq and then inexorably move south. So, there was a real logic for that.

Shelby [C. Shelby Coffey III, Los Angeles Times], I'm not going to, by my silence, acquiesce in all the charges that the question included, but some of this was true. We did some business with Iraq, but I just don't want to sign off on each one of the allegations that some of these stories have contained. But this was our policy.

And then we saw what Saddam Hussein did after this war ended. We tried to bring him into the family of nations through commerce, and we failed. And when he reached out to crush a neighboring country, we mobilized the best and most effective coalition, I think, that's been seen in modern times. And the objective was to set back aggression.

The U.N. resolutions never called for the elimination of Saddam Hussein. It never called for taking the battle into downtown Baghdad. And we have a lot of revisionists who opposed me on the war now saying, "How come you didn't go into downtown Baghdad and find Saddam Hussein and do him in?" We put together a coalition. We worked effectively with the coalition to fulfill the aims of the United Nations resolutions. And we fulfilled those aims. We set back aggression. And as any one of our respected military leaders will tell you, we have all but removed the threat of Saddam Hussein to his neighbors.

Now, we are still concerned about him. There's no question about that. And I am very much concerned, as he goes north of the 36th parallel the other day with airplanes, as to what that means to the safety of the Kurds. I am concerned about the Shiites in the south and to the southeast. I was also concerned when I saw an Iranian incursion of the Iraq borders to go after those Shiites. We can't condone that, as much as we detest the regime of Saddam Hussein.

So we will—do I have regrets, was your question? I guess if I had 90–90 hindsight and any action that we might have taken beforehand would guarantee that Saddam Hussein did not move down into Kuwait, which he did, I'd certainly rethink our position. But I can't certify that by not helping Iraq in the modest way we did, that that would have guaranteed that he would stay within his confines, the confines of his own border. And I can't say to you what would have happened in terms of Iran's aggression.

We are dealing with the facts as they came down the pike. And one of them was that he committed an aggression that mobilized the whole world against him. And he is going to remain isolated as long as I am President. He is going to live by those U.N. resolutions, and we are going to see that he complies with each and every one of them, including the most dangerous area of all, the one where he is doing things he ought not to be doing in terms of missiles and in terms of a nuclear capability.

So we're not going to lighten up on it. I think—oh, there's one other point since you've given me such a wonderful opening, Shelby. I read that General Norm Schwarzkopf wanted to keep going after I stopped the war. I will tell you unequivocally that that is simply totally untrue.

I sat in the Oval Office that fateful day—when you remember the turkey shoot along the highway going north—and Colin Powell came to me, our respected Chairman of the

Joint Chiefs, and said, "Mr. President, it's our considered opinion that the war is over. We have achieved our objectives, and we should stop." And I said, "Do our commanders in the field feel that way?" And he said, "Yes." And I said, "Well, let's doublecheck," something to that effect. He walked over to my desk—I was sitting on this end near the Stewart picture in the Oval Office—picked up the secure phone, dialed a number, and talked to Norm Schwarzkopf out in the desert and said, "What do you think? The President has asked me to doublecheck. We have achieved our objectives. We ought to stop." We agreed that we would stop at, I think it was midnight that night, 100 hours after the battle began.

And now we're caught up in a real peculiar election year. And you hear all kinds of people, some of whom supported what I did, many of whom oppose it, now going after this administration and our military for stopping too soon. I don't think that's right. Am I happy Saddam Hussein is still there? Absolutely not. Am I determined he's going to live with these resolutions? Absolutely. But we did the right thing. We did the honorable thing. And I have absolutely no regrets about that part of it at all.

*Presidential Campaign*

*Q.* Mr. President, as you know, another Texan is thinking about running for President in 1992. He'll be joining us tomorrow morning. As a matter of fact——

*The President.* Are you speaking about Lloyd Bentsen? [*Laughter*]

*Q.* Let's say two other Texans.

*The President.* Oh, I see.

*Q.* Some might even think that Ross Perot sounds a little more Texan than you do. My question would be, why do you think he's been as successful as he has in the early going in gaining support? What impact do you think he might have in the general election, particularly his possible ability to carry the State of Texas? And finally, do you feel part of his appeal is based on his ability to connect with the average American who wants to lift himself economically? Is he better able to do that than you are?

*The President.* You know, I'm going to

give you another question because I am not
going to do something now I've assiduously
avoided all during the primary, going after
anybody else, or quantify it in any way, that
might run or is running. And I'm going to
stay with that ground rule right now. When
the battle is joined and the conventions are
over and the nominees are out there, I will
happily answer your question for you. But
let him, Ross, make his determination. Let
him do what the rest of us do, take our case
to the American people. Let him enjoy the
same scrutiny that I've had for, what, 12
years at this relatively high level of Government, Vice President and President.

But there's no point in me trying to
define his candidacy nor the candidacy of
the Democrats that are left in the race on
the other side. What I'm trying to do,
having gone into some of these primaries
and emerged, I think, as the nominee of
our party, is to lead this country, to talk
about these serious issues.

You know, they say to me, as they say,
"How can you be the candidate of change?
You've been in Washington all this time." I
say we're the ones that are trying to change
things, whether it's education, whether it's
tort reform, whether it's in matters of this
nature that have to do with life and death
and peace and war.

And so I'm going to keep on doing that
now. And then, when the battle is joined
and we get past the convention stage, I'll
have plenty of comment to help you along
in assessing the opposition. But I really am
going to stay out of it now. And this isn't a
new position. Just because I'm standing
before a lot of editors, I think these traveling White House press will tell you that's
the way it's been.

So, if you want another one that I can
answer, shoot.

### Abortion

*Q.* Let me ask one other one then, Mr.
President. Abortion certainly continues to
be one of the hottest issues not only in the
United States but in the Republican Party.
Is it your preference that the GOP platform
in 1992 stay silent on that issue, come out
flatly against abortion, or support those
abortion rights activists who are inside the
GOP?

*The President.* My position has not
changed. I am pro-life. And I'm going to
stay with that position. In terms of the platform, we have a platform committee that's
going to debate that. You mentioned inside
the Republican Party, take a look at the
State of Pennsylvania. This isn't an issue
that divides just Republicans; this is an issue
that divides Democrats as well, if you look
at the laws in the books and the position of
the Governor of that State and other States
as well.

So each of us should say what we feel,
fight for our views, and then we've got a
party platform process that will resolve
that.

### Multilateral Trade Negotiations

*Q.* Mr. President, you have attended
three economic summits since taking office
in which a very high priority was assigned
to a new world trade agreement under
GATT. Each time these deadlines have
been broken; on Easter I think we're going
to have another deadline broken. And you
just spoke about a world in which we would
trade with the Soviet Union or the former
Soviet Union. How can the Soviet Union
really survive unless we get a world trade
agreement?

*The President.* Well, I think they could
survive, but they would survive much less
well. And we are going to keep on working
for a successful conclusion of this Uruguay
round of GATT. The major stumbling block
has been agriculture. And we cannot have a
satisfactory conclusion to the GATT round
unless agriculture is addressed. That has
been a particularly difficult problem for
France and a particularly difficult problem
for Germany.

And we, as you know from following this,
have said we will work with the Dunkel
text. This is highly technical, but it spells
out some broad ground rules on agriculture.
And we still have some problems other than
agriculture.

I am told that the EC leader, Delors, now
feels that we are very, very close on agriculture. He's coming here soon with Cavaco
Silva of Portugal, and we're going to be
sitting down in one of each—we have meetings twice a year. I will then be talking to

him—I won't be doing the negotiating—but with our top negotiators and try to hammer out that agreement.

We still have some other problems, property rights and, you know, trademarks and all this kind of thing. But I am more optimistic now. I asked Brent the other day, my trusted and able National Security Adviser, where do each of these deadlines that you referred to come from? They keep coming. Well, we'd have a deadline, and you're right, somebody throws up a deadline and says we've got to meet it by February, we've got to do it by June. I don't know where the deadline comes from. But I do know that it is in the interest of the free world, say nothing of the now-freeing world, the Soviet Union, the former Soviet Union, that we achieve this agreement.

And one last point on the trade agreement. Far better, far better than a foreign aid program for the emerging democracies of the Third World, Africa particularly, is a trade agreement. Far better than aid is trade. And so we will keep on playing, I think, a very constructive role to achieve a conclusion of this.

And parenthetically, we are going to work for the North American free trade agreement. You know, we're in a political year, some of you may know, and we're getting shot at by various predictable organizations on the Mexican agreement. The Mexican agreement, in my view, will create jobs in the United States, will help the environment. A country that's doing better economically can do a lot more for its environment than one that is kept down on the ropes because we don't have fair and free trade.

So we're going to work to that end to get a Mexican agreement along with the Uruguay round. And yes, all of that will benefit the emerging republics that I've been talking about here today. But I'm not despairing about it. The point is, if we come to some new deadline, we're going to keep on pushing. But right now, it looks like we may have a better chance than we've had in the last years of negotiation.

*Q.* Your office says one more question.
*The President.* Do they? Okay.

## Foreign Aid and Trade

*Q.* Mr. President, oddly enough part of your reply there dealt with my question. You've given a good vision of our obligations to help redeem the emergent nations of the former Soviet empire. But I wonder if anyone's paying much attention to our obligations to the truly hungry, starving nations of the world. Patrick Buchanan wants to do away with all foreign aid as part of his, I guess, Judeo-Christian tradition platform, forgetting the admonition that we bear one another's burdens. Our foreign aid appropriation has been about $18 billion a year. Almost half went to Middle East countries. And our spending seems to me to be a disgraceful pittance in relation to the hunger and the deprivation of the really deprived nations of the Third World. I wonder if you think we should spend more to help the countries that have no influence, like Somalia and Ethiopia and even Haiti, closer, where there are millions of children with swollen stomachs crying for aid still. Do you think we are spending enough for actual food and aid for the hungry countries of the Earth?

*The President.* Not included in the figures you gave are other activities, such as the Peace Corps, such as some agricultural programs; and such is clearly the most important—the benefit of trade that you referred to in the first part.

Let me tell you something, it is going to be impossible to get anything through the Congress this year, in terms of foreign aid, beyond what we have suggested. We would be unrealistic to think that there might be more. I'm not suggesting, though, that the answer is to spend more money on it. I think the trade initiative is important. I think the position that our administration has taken in debt forgiveness has been tremendously important to many of these emerging democracies in Africa and, indeed, in this hemisphere.

Look at the basket case that was Argentina just a while back. And working with us, they are now on the move. They've come in, they've taken a very constructive approach to their economy. They are in the debt forgiveness. We've worked out a deal, they have, with the private financial institutions just very recently to lower their debt burden. The Enterprise for the Americas Initiative and the Brady plan are meaningful. And the impoverished people in that country and in other countries in our hemisphere are beginning to get a little break here.

So we're in a realistic time. I will continue to push for the trade agreements. I will continue to do what I can in these debt-reduction initiatives. And we'll continue to support foreign aid. And I think everybody here who writes, understands that that is not necessarily a popular position in an election year or any other time.

But we are dealing also with a time when we must address ourselves, and are trying so to do, to our own problems at home. And we are operating at enormous deficits in a sluggish economy, it isn't easy. And yet I want to not end here because we can take a couple more.

But I'm a little more optimistic on the economy. And I was very pleased today when the Fed lowered its rates by another quarter. That was instantly pretty well received in the market. Far be it for me to mention what levels markets should be at; I learned that long ago by mistake, saying something that triggered—I don't remember how it worked—triggered a market reaction. But I think the lowering of the rate by the Fed is a good thing, and I hope that it will guarantee that this fledgling recovery that we're seeing will now be a little more robust.

*Q.* Mr. President, over here, sir.

*The President.* Got you.

### Federal Budget

*Q.* The Government's going in the hole about a billion dollars a day right now. And what reason can you give the American people for voting for 4 more years of the same kind of deficit spending?

*The President.* I certainly don't want them to vote for 4 more years of deficit spending. And I would like to get some changes in the United States Congress to guarantee against that. I would like to see them enact our budget that takes a major step towards the containment of an area that is the main area that's causing the deficit, and that is the entitlement area. And

what are we proposing? We're proposing that the entitlements not grow beyond inflation and population growth. That in itself will save literally billions, billions, many billions of dollars.

So we've got to go forward with a sensible budget approach. Right now I'm battling against a Congress that wants to knock off the one guarantee that the American taxpayer has on spending, and that is the caps out of the nefarious 1990 budget agreement, the caps on discretionary spending. We're getting into an election year so we're trying to hold the line on those caps. And I'm determined to do it, and I think we will prevail.

But what I'll be doing is taking my case to the American people and say, yes, we've had some tough things. We've had banking problems that have cost the taxpayer enormously. We've had savings and loan problems that have cost the taxpayers enormously as we protect every single depositor. But we've got to try to exert some fiscal discipline on the system. And I'll be ready for the debate that will follow come fall because I think we're on the right track with what I've just told you here.

Dave says I'm out of here. We'll do one more, and then I'm gone.

*Q.* It's your staff, Mr. President, who says you're out of here. You can stay as long as you want.

*The President.* I don't want to be in trouble with them. [*Laughter*] Let's see what we've got here.

### Presidential Campaign

*Q.* Mr. President, as you've astutely noted for us today, we are in an election year.

*The President.* Thank you. [*Laughter*]

*Q.* And in 7 months, much to the chagrin of this group, many Americans will be deciding their vote on the basis of television advertising. In 1988, many voters, most of us, were bombarded with what we would probably consider very negative television advertising that attacked the reputation of your opponent and seemed to pander to some of the fears of our society. I guess my question to you as you look into this election year, do you plan to direct, encourage, or discourage your consultants from pursuing a similar negative ad campaign in 1992?

*The President.* Well, you asked me at a time when this is in the heightened attention of the American people, isn't it? I look across at the Democratic primary, and anything that happened in 1988 is pale in comparison to what's going on there. We've tried to have most of ours positive.

You may recall an ad we ran in Michigan that triggered the famous line I used at the Gridiron Club, "*Ich bin ein* Mercedes owner." [*Laughter*] But that is a negative ad. Now, I don't know whether you consider that a turnoff or not, but just by the genesis of that ad came about that the opponent in this case was talking about protection and jobs and American jobs and American workers and all of this, and he was driving a Mercedes. Nobody was pointing it out. A lot of editors here—and I don't remember a brutal revelation of this terribly important fact. So we brought it out.

Now, I don't know if you consider that—I don't want to get into a debate since you might clearly win it—[*laughter*]—but is that a negative ad or is that fair in the way—everybody now that puts on the television at least have a thing—and the newspapers, too—here's why the ad was fair or unfair. I can't remember what they said about that one. I think when you define a person on issues, that's very, very important. I think some would consider it negative. But just seriously on that one. Then I can maybe answer your question a little better.

*Q.* I think what it does is set the tone. I guess people maybe care whether the opponent drives a Mercedes. But I guess we get into discussions of other character issues. I think that's really where the——

*The President.* Well, as I've said, I would like to see it on the issues and not on some of the sleaze questions. I've said that before, and I'll keep repeating that. I know that we will try hard, but I also know that this is about the ugliest political year I've ever seen already. And I don't know what it's going to hold, but I will try to keep my head up and try to do my job as President, and try to do it with a certain sense of decency and honor.

But we've seen it start off that way in the early primaries, and then something else evolved for reasons I'm not quite sure I fully understand. But I don't want to make you a firm statement because I don't know what's negative and what's not these days. If it's just ripping down somebody's character or tearing them apart, I don't want to do that. If it's factual and brings out something that hasn't been brought out, I think that's fair. And so we have to just use your judgment, I guess is the answer to that one.

Well, I guess I really do have to go. but thank you all very, very much. I appreciate it.

*Note: The President spoke at 1:53 p.m. at the J.W. Marriott Hotel. In his remarks, he referred to David Lawrence, Jr., president of the society.*

# Exchange With Reporters Prior to Discussions With President Violeta Chamorro of Nicaragua
*April 9, 1992*

*President Chamorro.* It's a wonderful visit. It always is, but I think we feel even more united now than ever.

*President Bush.* Well, I think so.

*President Chamorro.* We always come to the United States feeling at home, just as we are awaiting your visit in Nicaragua.

*President Bush.* We weren't sure our Assistant Secretary, Bernie Aronson, was going to make it. He was down in Peru. He can tell us. He can tell us, yes. He's coming over. He's going to wait for these cameras.

*Manuel Noriega Verdict*

*Q.* Mr. President, your reaction to the Noriega verdict?

*President Bush.* Noriega was convicted, I think, on 8 out of 10 counts. Well, I think it's a major victory against the drug lords. We're going to continue the fight against drugs in every way possible. But I think it's significant that he was accorded a free and fair trial, and he was found guilty. And I hope it sends a lesson to drug lords here and around the world that they'll pay a price if they continue to poison the lives of our kids in this country or anywhere else. And so, in my view, the case was a solid case. And I've not commented on it since it began in the court, but now that he has been convicted I think it's proper to say that justice has been served.

*Q.* Was it worth invading Panama to get this verdict?

*President Bush.* It was certainly worth bringing him to justice. It's certainly always worth it when you protect the lives of American citizens. And when a part of the result of that is democracy in a country, it makes it doubly worth it. But yes, I'm glad he's out.

*Q.* Are you sorry things are not better for the Panamanians these days?

*President Bush.* I wish things were better for the Americans, for the Panamanians, for the Nicaraguans, and for everybody. But we're going to continue to work to see that that is true.

*Q.* Mr. President, are you surprised by the verdict, given the fact that it almost ended in a mistrial?

*President Bush.* No, because I've felt that from what I understood that the case was very solid. But I think it's a good thing, and I think the main thing is it sends a message to the drug lords that they are going to be brought to justice. And I salute those countries that are waging a good fight against narcotics in their countries, and many in this hemisphere are doing just exactly that.

*British Elections*

*Q.* Mr. President, have you heard from John Major?

*President Bush.* No, I haven't. Any exit polls here? They don't start—we talked to the——

*Mr. Scowcroft.* They don't cast anything about exit polls until the polls close, which is 5 p.m. our time.

*President Bush.* Ten p.m. their time, yes. They stay open late over there. Big British election, as you know.

Okay, you guys, you're out of here.

*Note: The exchange began at 3:13 p.m. in the Oval Office at the White House. President Chamorro spoke in Spanish, and her remarks were translated by an interpreter.*

# Statement by Deputy Press Secretary Smith on the President's Meeting With President Violeta Chamorro of Nicaragua
*April 9, 1992*

The President met this afternoon with President Violeta Chamorro of Nicaragua. President Bush congratulated her on the success of her economic reform program and her efforts to bring all Nicaraguans together in national reconciliation. The President reiterated his full support for President Chamorro's efforts to strengthen democracy in her country.

President Chamorro thanked the President for the generous assistance to her country from the United States, including substantial debt relief. She indicated that Nicaragua is committed to a strong economic stabilization program that will set the stage for economic growth. She also outlined her plans for reforming the police and resolving the problems surrounding property rights in her country.

## Statement on Reform of the Drug Approval Process
*April 9, 1992*

I am pleased to announce that, as part of the administration's ongoing efforts to reduce unnecessary regulatory burdens, the Food and Drug Administration is today implementing important reforms to the drug approval process.

The reforms announced today could ultimately save millions of lives by giving patients, including those suffering from such debilitating diseases as cancer, AIDS, and Alzheimer's, earlier access to promising new drugs. The reforms will also make American pharmaceutical companies more competitive by allowing them to cut years off the drug development process.

These are the first steps toward achieving the administration's goal of reducing by about 40 percent the average amount of time it takes to bring new drugs to market.

Today's announcement is the outgrowth of an initiative I began in 1988 as Chairman of President Reagan's Task Force on Regulatory Relief. I commend the Council on Competitiveness and the Department of Health and Human Services for bringing this initiative to fruition.

## Letter to Congressional Leaders Transmitting the Report on Soviet Noncompliance With Arms Control Agreements
*April 9, 1992*

*Dear Mr. Speaker: (Dear Mr. President:)*

Enclosed are classified and unclassified copies of the annual Report on Soviet Noncompliance with Arms Control Agreements.

Last year the Soviet Union ended and we have every reason to hope that this will lead to a new era of compliance with arms control agreements. The report I am forwarding covers actions taken in 1991 by the former Soviet Union, not the newly independent states which have succeeded it. We have already seen an improvement in the willingness of these new governments to adhere to arms control obligations.

For our part, the United States will continue to expect scrupulous compliance with all arms control obligations. Such compliance is especially important as we build new and better relations and as conventional and nuclear forces are dismantled.

Sincerely,

GEORGE BUSH

*Note: Identical letters were sent to Thomas S. Foley, Speaker of the House of Representatives, and Dan Quayle, President of the Senate.*

## Message to the Congress Transmitting the Report on Federal Advisory Committees
*April 9, 1992*

*To the Congress of the United States:*

In accordance with the requirements of section 6(c) of the Federal Advisory Committee Act, as amended (Public Law 92–463; 5 U.S.C. App. 2, sec. 6(c)), I hereby transmit the Twentieth Annual Report on Federal Advisory Committees for fiscal year 1991.

GEORGE BUSH

The White House,
April 9, 1992.

# Message to the Congress Transmitting Proposed Legislation on Accountability in Government
*April 9, 1992*

*To the Congress of the United States:*

I am pleased to transmit today for your immediate consideration and enactment the "Accountability in Government Act of 1992."

The legislation would extend to the Congress and the White House the relevant portions of five laws that apply to the private sector. The laws in question are the Fair Labor Standards Act of 1938 (minimum wage law), the Civil Rights Act of 1964, the Age Discrimination in Employment Act of 1967, the Rehabilitation Act of 1973, and the damages remedy created by the Civil Rights Act of 1991. The proposal also makes available the remedies currently available to other employees for violations of these laws, rather than special remedial schemes based entirely or in large part on internal congressional grievance mechanisms.

The legislation would also extend to the analogous portions of Congress five laws that presently apply to various portions of the executive branch. The laws in question are Title VI of the Ethics in Government Act, conflicts of interest laws, the Hatch Act, the Freedom of Information Act, and the Privacy Act. The scope of this proposal has been carefully tailored to take into account the unique characteristics of the Congress and its Members. Moreover, none of the provisions of this legislation except those implicating criminal penalties calls for executive branch enforcement. Rather, all are to be enforced either by private suit, entities within the General Accounting Office (an instrumentality of the legislative branch), or both. This legislation therefore does not present the constitutional separation-of-powers questions that might be presented by general executive branch administration of laws applied to the legislative branch.

I urge the Congress to give this legislation prompt and favorable consideration.

GEORGE BUSH

The White House,
April 9, 1992.

# Nomination of Jerome H. Powell To Be an Under Secretary of the Treasury
*April 9, 1992*

The President today announced his intention to nominate Jerome H. Powell, of New York, to be an Under Secretary of the Treasury. He would succeed Robert R. Glauber.

Currently Mr. Powell serves as Assistant Secretary of the Treasury for Domestic Finance at the U.S. Department of the Treasury in Washington, DC. Prior to this, he served as senior vice president with Dillon, Read & Company, Inc., 1984–90; and as an attorney with the firm of Werbel & McMillen, 1983–84; and as an attorney with the firm of Davis Polk & Wardwell, 1981–83.

Mr. Powell graduated from Princeton University (B.A., 1975) and Georgetown University Law Center (J.D., 1979). He was born February 4, 1953, in Washington, DC. Mr. Powell is married, has two children, and resides in Chevy Chase, MD.

# Nomination of Timothy E. Flanigan To Be an Assistant Attorney General
## *April 9, 1992*

The President today announced his intention to nominate Timothy E. Flanigan, of Virginia, to be an Assistant Attorney General in the Office of Legal Counsel. He would succeed J. Michael Luttig.

Currently Mr. Flanigan serves as Acting Assistant Attorney General in the Office of Legal Counsel at the Department of Justice. Prior to this, he served as Principal Deputy Assistant Attorney General in the Office of Legal Counsel at the Department of Justice,

1990–91. He served with the law firm of Milbank, Tweed, Hadley & McCloy in Washington, DC, 1988–90; and the law firm of Shearman & Sterling, 1986–88.

Mr. Flanigan graduated from Brigham Young University (B.A., 1976) and the University of Virginia (J.D., 1981). He was born May 16, 1953, in Fort Belvoir, VA. Mr. Flanigan is married, has 12 children, and resides in Great Falls, VA.

# Nomination of John Cunningham Dugan To Be an Assistant Secretary of the Treasury
## *April 9, 1992*

The President today announced his intention to nominate John Cunningham Dugan, of the District of Columbia, to be an Assistant Secretary of the Treasury for Domestic Finance. He would succeed Jerome H. Powell.

Currently Mr. Dugan serves as Deputy Assistant Secretary for Financial Institutions at the U.S. Department of Treasury in Washington, DC. From 1987 to 1989, Mr.

Dugan served as Minority General Counsel to the Senate Committee on Banking, Housing, and Urban Affairs.

Mr. Dugan graduated from the University of Michigan (B.A., 1977) and Harvard Law School (J.D., 1981). He was born June 3, 1955, in Washington, DC. Mr. Dugan is married, has one child, and resides in Washington, DC.

# Exchange With Reporters Prior to a Meeting on Welfare Reform
## *April 10, 1992*

*Welfare Reform*

*The President.* Photo opportunity here on welfare reform. We're delighted to have the Governor here—the leadership that he displays in reform and welfare. And we are glad that this administration is also taking a leadership role and making it easier, Tommy, for States like yours to innovate and help people get off the dependency of welfare. And we respect you for what you're doing, and I'm glad that this action

we're taking will facilitate the implementation of your plan. It'll be a good example for the rest of the country. We can all learn from that; all the States can learn from it. So we're glad you're here.

*Q.* Do you expect to have a Federal plan, Mr. President, changes?

*The President.* Well, I think the main thing here which we're doing at this juncture is to facilitate innovation by the States. In a sense, they're laboratories, but they're also on the firing line. This Governor has been way out front in innovation with Learnfare, Workfare, encouraging education to break the cycle of dependency. So we will have more to say on the Federal role later, but the thing for the moment is, speed up the relief that's necessary so these States can put into effect the kind of programs they think will work. These States aren't all the same. Welfare problems in Milwaukee are quite different than those in Juneau, Alaska, for example, or in California someplace. So this is a good step, and I'm very proud of Governor Thompson for his leadership.

*Q.* The Wisconsin plan penalizes women who have more than one child out of wedlock. Is that the kind of concept, Mr. President, that you would support?

*The President.* I'm very interested in the innovation of the Wisconsin plan. I want to see how it works. The Governor can defend or criticize any aspect of his own plan he wants. The Federal role is to encourage these Governors to do exactly what this Governor has done.

*Q.* But do you endorse that? Is that why you're giving——

*The President.* I'm not going into it point by point. I'm sure I have great confidence in him. If he thinks it's smart, that would be very persuasive with me. I can't say I know every detail of his plan.

*British Elections*

*Q.* Were you pleased with Mr. Major's victory?

*The President.* It was substantial, and it was wonderful. And I'll have more to say to you all later about that. I plan to meet with you a little more formally in something other than a photo op.

*Q.* Any parallel——

*The President.* So get your questions ready. [*Laughter*]

*Q.* Today?

*Q.* Before you leave? Is that when we're going to have something?

*The President.* No. We'll do something, I think, in the press room.

*Q.* What time?

*The President.* Well, we're working on that now. We have a lot to discuss.

*Note: The exchange began at 9:40 a.m. in the Oval Office at the White House, prior to a meeting with Secretary of Health and Human Services Louis W. Sullivan and Gov. Tommy Thompson of Wisconsin.*

# Statement on Wisconsin Welfare Reform
*April 10, 1992*

Last week in Philadelphia, I called for sweeping reform of how Government works. Nowhere is this need more apparent than in our Nation's welfare system. Our current system allows welfare to be a way of life. We must try new ways to get welfare to yield to work.

In our Federal system, States often act as laboratories for innovation. Welfare reform is an example. I am renewing my call to States to come forward with reforms which, like Wisconsin's, replace the assumptions of our current welfare system. We need to explore new incentives for welfare recipients to work and act responsibly in the best interest of their families. That is what underlies Wisconsin's "Parental and Family Responsibility Project."

I am committed to facilitating welfare reform by accelerating the approval process for every State with a worthy proposal that asks our help. Today, I am pleased to make good on my promise. Wisconsin's "Parental and Family Responsibility Project" has been approved 4 weeks after it was submitted.

Wisconsin is at the forefront of the welfare reform movement. Governor Tommy Thompson is a leader in the process of reform that will make welfare work.

# The President's News Conference
## *April 10, 1992*

*The President.* We were able to take several steps this week towards my efforts to address the challenges facing this country, towards the kind of fundamental reform that the people of America want and deserve.

Last Friday I spoke in Philadelphia about critical reforms that will help get the Government reformed and moving. And last night I transmitted to Congress the "Accountability in Government Act of 1992," legislation that would extend to the Congress and the White House relevant portions of laws that now apply to the private sector. And it will also extend to appropriate portions of Congress certain laws that presently apply only to the executive branch.

This morning I met with Secretary Sullivan of HHS and Wisconsin's Governor Tommy Thompson. Twenty-four days ago, Governor Thompson requested a Federal waiver to go forward with genuine welfare reform. And today, I granted the waiver relief that will allow Wisconsin to move ahead on its bold new strategy to reform that State's welfare system.

Along with reform of the Government, I'll continue to push for the changes necessary to fight for American jobs at home by expanding markets abroad, to better educate our children, fighting for America 2000, to reform a legal system that is drowning us in a sea of litigation, and to provide all Americans with access to quality health care. As you know, yesterday the Vice President announced regulatory reforms to speed up the availability of new drugs for long-term illnesses such as cancer and AIDS and Alzheimer's.

Also yesterday I was very pleased to see the Fed's action in lowering the key short-term interest rate by a quarter of a point. And I applauded the action of the Fed, and I believe the economy has been improving and that this action should help that improvement along.

This has also been a very busy week on the international front. My speech yesterday described our commitment to a democratic peace in the new nations of the old Soviet Union. Along with our allies, we are committed to assisting the C.I.S. States during this time of transition. And we're pleased with the bipartisan support that we have been receiving for our plan. Let me say to the American people: Peace and prosperity are in the interest of every American, and democracy inside the Kremlin is the best way to assure our security in the decades to come.

I talked this morning with President Kravchuk of Ukraine. And we discussed a number of issues that I had focused on in yesterday's speech, and I reiterated our support for Ukraine's efforts towards economic reform and building a lasting democracy. He told me that he had had good talks as recently as today with President Yeltsin as it related to the nuclear question and the fleet question and other questions we've been reading about.

I just now concluded a meeting with Prime Minister Čalfa of Czechoslovakia, had an opportunity to assure him that what we are trying to do in the C.I.S. in no way diminishes our interest in Eastern Europe and in Czechoslovakia particularly.

Also yesterday, Manuel Noriega was found guilty of drug trafficking. The Operation Just Cause enabled justice to be served, American lives were protected, and it helped Panama set out on a new democratic course. Panama is on the mend with encouraging economic growth rates, a reduction in drug-trafficking, and a new commitment to democracy.

In Great Britain, John Major won a parliamentary election. I spoke with him earlier today, not so long ago, and I look forward to a continued close working relationship with a good friend and ally. John Major has been a key partner in our efforts to encourage democratic reform in the former Soviet Union and to ensure global economic growth. I congratulate him on a sterling win. And I will be seeing him and the other G-7 leaders in Munich in July.

Finally, we welcome signs of progress in Afghanistan. The U.N. Secretary-General, Boutros-Ghali, has announced an impartial transition that will lead to an interim government. We've long supported a political settlement in Afghanistan, and we view this negotiating process as a result of our sustained support to end more than a decade of war by securing Afghans' self-determination.

So we've had a busy week. It's been a good week. Progress, I think, has been made on both the domestic and the foreign front. And I might say that I do not want to just add to this—that on the foreign front we had a good visit yesterday with President Violeta Chamorro of Nicaragua. And I've had talks this week with Carlos Andrés Pérez of Venezuela, seeing what we can do, working together, to address ourselves to other problems in this hemisphere.

So now, on with the questions and, Helen [Helen Thomas, United Press International].

*Health Care*

*Q.* Mr. President, you got a wake-up call from some 36 million people several months ago who are deprived of health insurance. Now we understand that you have ruled out any comprehensive health care legislation this year because of the congressional session ending and the fact that you don't want to make any mistakes and you have not presented a way to finance it. What does this say about your leadership and your really caring about these people?

*The President.* It says we are on the right track. The question, if you couldn't hear it, relates to health insurance. We've got a good health insurance proposal. We are putting the finishing touches to it. And if I had reason to believe it would sail through this contentious Congress, I'd like to see it done.

The problem we've got is, you have two other plans out there. One is, in my view, for pure nationalized health care, which I will strongly oppose, and the other is this so-called "pay or play" that would break what remains in the bank. And so we've got to work this through the system. But in the meantime, we have a proposal that I think is a very good one. It will retain the quality of U.S. health care, but it will not nationalize or socialize the medical system in this country. And we have proposals before the Congress in my budget right now that would contain the growth of some of the expenses of Medicare and Medicaid. So we'll see how that goes as it's considered by the Congress.

But if you're asking me, do I believe a health care program, given the political nature of this year, can get through this year, I'd have to agree with many of the Democratic leaders that it's unlikely.

*Q.* I'm asking you why you have not pinpointed a way to finance it.

*The President.* I think we have pinpointed it. And I would refer you to the OMB Director. One of the ways to do it would be to help by $20 billion by passing our reform of liability. And everybody knows the liability claims are extravagant, and it raised the cost exponentially. And so we've got to do something about that. And I also know that our budget calls for capping the growth, adding for population and new people, of the mandated spending. Therein lies a lot of the financing. So it's up there, not entirely, I'll admit that, but quite a bit of it.

*Social Security*

*Q.* Mr. President, the House has passed a Social Security bill that would double the amount of income recipients could earn before their benefits are cut back. It's estimated that this will cost about $7 billion over 5 years. Some Republicans think that this is a pandering to voters. What's your view of this bill, and would you sign it?

*The President.* We've long favored an increase in the Social Security earnings test. And we proposed, Dick Darman reminded me, a modest increase in the budget that I submitted to the Congress in January. That proposal also, though, did meet the terms of the Budget Enforcement Act.

Unfortunately, the House action violates the Budget Act and does increase the deficit. So the matter is not settled yet in Congress. The House has one approach, the Senate another. And we are going to be working to increase the earnings test while also protecting the integrity of the Social Security Trust Fund and avoiding a massive increase in the deficit. And so we are committed to the higher earnings test, but we are also committed to trying to hold the line on the deficit. So we've got to see, Terry [Terence Hunt, Associated Press], what comes out of the negotiations between House and Senate on this, working for those two ends.

*Q.* Well, the Senate bill would do away with the earnings test entirely. So that goes a lot further than the House——

*The President.* A lot further.

*Q.* Yes. So if you have to choose between those two——

*The President.* So we'll have to see what we can do, and then I'll make up my mind. But we'll be presenting our views with these two premises in mind. We'll just have to see how it works.

### Domestic Policy Goals

*Q.* Mr. President, in a second term, what single domestic policy goal would you most want to achieve?

*The President.* Single goal? Oh, there are several goals, and I've been spelling them all out. I think education reform certainly would be right up at the top of that, achieving our goals for education by the year 2000. Because that would render us much more competitive internationally, which gets you over into the economic side of things, and it will lift a lot of kids out of this impoverished area, the impoverished state they're in, give them an opportunity at the American dream.

It is awfully hard to single out one area, however. I'd like to be also in the same mode of trying to be sure this economy keeps moving and keeps strong, and you can't do that if we continue to add to the deficit. We're spending too much, and Government's too big. So we're going to try to do something about that. But if you had to single out one, education covers so many of these fields; and our goals, to achieve those goals, cover more because I'm talking about—one of them is being ready to learn, and that's Head Start. Another one is a place where you can learn; that means drug-free schools. So when I talk about education, I'm talking about all of these things.

*Q.* You've now articulated or begun to articulate a kind of a welter of programs to achieve various reforms. Which of those do you most want?

*The President.* Education, I think would be it.

*Q.* Well, I'm talking about the newer ones you've begun to lay out in the last week.

*The President.* Well, I've been talking about a bunch of them, but there are so many of them. You know, I'm for all of them. I'm for reform in the Congress. I'm for reform of the crime—I'd like to get our crime bill through, which would help enormously with civil tranquility. It's hard to separate them out.

One of the other goals is international trade. That means opening other markets and concluding successfully the NAFTA agreement and the GATT round. I cannot single them out for you or put numbers on each one. They're all very, very important.

Reform of the Congress, reform of the system, I think it's time to take a real hard look. And I'm for term limitations, for example. I'd like to see Congress much more responsive. People say, "Hey, how come the Presidency is limited and nobody else, none of the terms of the Congress?" Well, let's take a look at that.

### Peru

*Q.* Mr. President, just how concerned are you by developments in Peru, and would you favor some outside pressure to try to restore democracy?

*The President.* The answer is, very concerned. And yes, I'd favor some outside pressure. And we are looking with interest to the OAS meeting that's coming up next week. I've been talking to leaders. I mentioned Carlos Andrés Pérez, and I did not mention Carlos Menem of Argentina to whom I talked at length yesterday on this very question.

We cannot sit by without registering our strong disapproval about the aborting of democracy in Peru. And so we want it restored. And yes, outside pressure will be mobilized in the OAS, plus maybe a follow-on mission from the OAS would be a clear and productive step.

*Q.* Sir, would you consider sanctions, then, as one form?

*The President.* As I say, we're going to be talking to others about that. But yes, we considered sanctions in our efforts to try to restore democracy to Haiti when their process was frustrated, and certainly we'd consider.

## Media Coverage

*Q.* Sir, we understand that you're unhappy with some of the news coverage you're getting. You're unhappy about the stories about George W. Bush contacting White House aides, Mr. Skinner and others, and urging them perhaps to do a better job, to be more coordinated. We also understand, however, that you're unhappy yourself with the support you're getting. You're unhappy with the stories about the disarray, but isn't there some disarray? We understand you're complaining about disarray yourself.

*The President.* No. And I'm not unhappy about stories that are true. I read one today about my son George that isn't true. And so I'm glad to have that out there. It simply is not true. To suggest that Jim Baker and I were working to get George up here for a week is ridiculous. When George comes here, of course he goes to the campaign and talks to people here. But this isn't some manifestation of dissatisfaction. And if I were dissatisfied, you'd know about it loud and clear. I'm happy about it, and I know that many have to make a living by making these inside stories—inside, day-in, who's up, who's down, who's winning, who's losing. And it's ridiculous.

But the trouble is, nobody cares about it out around the country, although we thrive on it inside the beltway. But John [John Cochran, NBC News], you've asked about it. If you'd tell me the name of the author and which story you're referring to, I'll tell you whether it's true or not. If, by chance, you're talking about one that was on the front page of the New York Times today, regrettably, it was not true.

*Q.* Can I just follow up on that?

*The President.* You can follow it.

*Q.* Are you saying that Jim Baker is entirely happy with the way your campaign's being run?

*The President.* I have no idea whether he's entirely happy. What I'm saying is the allegations in that story are not true.

Next question.

*Q.* You haven't discussed this? The two of you never discussed this?

*The President.* Next question.

*Q.* I don't want to step on my colleague's——

*The President.* He's finished. [*Laughter*] Not forever, but just for this followup. Not John.

*Q.* I may be finished, too.

*The President.* Yes.

## Welfare Reform

*Q.* Why, sir, why has it taken 3 years for you to get interested in welfare reform or at least to make it a priority? I had not heard you speak of welfare reform until——

*The President.* We probably should have been speaking of it sooner. I think we've been encouraging the States to come forward with their programs. But it is a matter that's come to a head. It's a matter where I've become convinced that speeding up the waiver process is very important. These waivers, this waiver was received from Wisconsin 24 days ago. And it's now been approved in record time.

*Q.* Is that your idea of leadership, though, to simply say the States should go ahead and do their thing?

*The President.* My idea of leadership is to, yes, to have the States be the laboratories for innovation. And you see, there's where I differ with some up in the Congress who think the only way to do it is to have the Federal Government put mandates on the States. I am not in favor of mandates. I'm in favor of encouraging the States to innovate, to be creative, whether it's in education, whether it's in welfare reform. And that has been our philosophy since I've been President, and I believe it was President Reagan's philosophy. But do we need to do more in encouraging this kind of innovation in welfare? Yes, and I'll be doing more about it.

*Q.* Could you answer the concern about the Wisconsin plan that by eliminating the increase in benefits when women have more children, that in fact this might encourage abortions?

*The President.* I haven't heard that allegation about the Wisconsin plan. My—saying is to let them try it. The Wisconsin Legislature has passed a plan. Let them try it and see if it works to strengthen families and to break the cycle of dependency on welfare. And we sit here in Washington, DC, some with the view that we've got all the answers back here, particularly in the Congress. And that's not true. So I support the Governor in his, and the legislature there, Democrat and Republican, in their efforts to reform their welfare system.

*Presidential Campaign*

*Q.* Mr. President, 47 Members of the House have decided to retire, about 8 Senators, including your friend in New Hampshire, Warren Rudman, who said Washington has become a place increasingly partisan where fundamental issues are not being addressed. Many of the things that you talked about in your answer to Brit's [Brit Hume, ABC News] questions are goals of the first administration that aren't going to get through Congress. My question to you is, why do you want to be President again? And what possibility do you see of changing the gridlock that is in Washington today?

*The President.* I'm very optimistic about change now. Why do I want to be President again? I want to enhance world peace and democracy around the world. And I want to improve the lives of people here at home through making our cities safer by doing better in the fight against crime, by a better education program. And I am optimistic about getting it through once I take my case in the fall to the American people.

Susan [Susan Spencer, CBS News] asked about now—obviously elections bring forward issues, put them right out there on the front burner for much more lively debate than even between the Executive and the Congress during off years. And so I think people want change. They recognize that one party has controlled the Congress most of the last 55 years; one body of Congress for, I think, the last 52, whatever it is. And they want fundamental change. And I think I know the direction that they want to see things change.

So I am optimistic. I'm not discouraged when the Congress is going through this trauma up there. I think we can then say, "Now look, give us a shot. Bring some of our legislation up for a vote."

Brit asked me about reform, liability reform. You go to any community in this country and ask the doctors or the Little League people or people in the community, "What's bothering you?" And they'll tell you, "These outrageous lawsuits." And I haven't been able to get the liability reform legislation even considered. So I'm going to take my case to the American people, and let the Democratic nominee say whether he's for it or not. And if he's for it, that'll help encourage the Congress, Democrat or Republican. But right now it's locked in a trial lawyers benefit program up there, and we can't get anything done. That's the good thing about the election year. And that's one of the changes I want to see that will make life better for people. And that's another reason I'd like to be here. There's plenty of reasons.

*Education*

*Q.* If I could follow up. You wanted to be the education President. That was one of your campaign themes in your first election.

*The President.* Yes.

*Q.* That hasn't happened. In many cases throughout the last 3 years, you've offered the argument, "Give our program a shot." That hasn't happened. What can you do differently in 4 more years?

*The President.* Get more Republicans in there and more sensible Democrats that will vote for what we want. And I'll beg to differ with you, a lot has happened in education. For the first time we have national education goals, arrived at in a bipartisan or nonpartisan fashion. That is good. That is progress. And we're making progress out in the communities where we don't need legislation. I will differ with you on your question. There are 43 States that have become America 2000 States, where they embrace not only the goals of our program but have started implementing it where you don't need legislation from Washington to do it. Now that is progress in education. And we're going to keep on until we get a much better educated populace.

*Q.* Does that mean you feel you have to work around Congress now?

*The President.* It means I've got to get some changes in Congress. That's why I'm talking about change. But, for the people that aren't in the Congress, we're making some real progress under Democratic Governors, Republican Governors, communities. Take a look at what is happening out there, and please don't judge it all just by the turmoil in Washington on the Hill.

*Q.* Mr. President, I'm sure you know the computer term "garbage in, garbage out." You have suggested more testing of America's schoolchildren, testing the product coming out. Would you, like Governor Clinton, support testing the teaching force?

*The President.* I don't know anything about that one, but I'd certainly be open to consider it. Governor Clinton has supported the America 2000 objectives. Testing teachers isn't a part of it, but——

*Q.* Well, it was in Arkansas, sir. It was in an education bill in Arkansas.

*The President.* I didn't realize that.

*Q.* And you might see that as something——

*The President.* Well, I'll take a look at it. I'll talk to Lamar Alexander, our Secretary of Education. It's not one of our six education goals worked out in a bipartisan fashion with the Governors, but we'll take a look.

### Media Coverage

*Q.* Mr. President, I know you had some comments about what your son might or might not have done, but there are many people who are very loyal to you in this White House who feel that you're not getting the best break in organization and structure and that there's a lot of planning going on and not a whole lot of action. I wonder if you feel that way——

*The President.* No.

*Q.* ——and why there is such a communication gap that they are worried for you.

*The President.* I don't know who they are. If you sometimes would write a story and put a name next to the source, it would help me answer a question like that. But most of the time, Frank [Frank Murray, Washington Times], what I see is that the stories say "a high-ranking Washington official," "an insider in the administration," "a man known to be loyal to President Bush who doesn't do this or that." And you can't help me answer some of the charges that John asked about or that you've asked about.

But my answer is, if I were unhappy

about it, you'd know about it. I think our new team is doing a good job. But every day, I pick up the paper and read it, telling the American people how they think I feel about something. I wish you could help me with putting a name next to the sources in a few more of your stories. I don't want to go into this at every press conference, but you ask me to respond to questions, and yet you don't help me by telling me where it's coming from. So look, I am not unhappy about all of this.

Please believe me, what I get upset about is when I read something that I know factually is not true. That troubles me a little bit.

### Presidential Campaign

*Q.* The Democratic race is settling down now and you mentioned Governor Clinton a few moments ago. At this point, what's your assessment of him?

*The President.* I'm not going to assess it for you.

*Q.* Is he going to be as easy——

*The President.* Give you another question, and I'll tell you what: I am not going to comment until I get ready on the opposition—the independents, the Republican, or the Democrats—until the nominating process is entirely over.

I think you'll have to concede I've been reasonably good about that so far. I got a question at the newspaper editors yesterday, and I said, "Please take another question because I am not going to start doing that now, which I just don't feel comfortable doing." I've spelled out here what we're trying to do. I'm very pleased about some of the progress we're making, and to go off and start kind of assessing polls or talking about some opponent, we'll have plenty of time for that.

### Abuse of Privileges

*Q.* Mr. President, on March 20th you made some serious charges about the failings of Congress, and you said that congressional perks are "part of the hopelessly tangled web up there on Capitol Hill." Could you give us some examples of what you feel are the perks that are being abused, and will you tell us what perks that you have and your staff have that you're willing to eliminate?

*The President.* I think that they're addressing that very well indeed, and I don't see any need to single any out. You saw Dick Darman's testimony. We'll take a hard look at the executive branch. Congress is doing that with theirs. So I think it's moving in the right direction.

### Budget Deficit

*Q.* But Mr. President, over the past 11 years, with you as Vice President and now President, the Federal budget deficit has nearly quadrupled.

*The President.* Yes.

*Q.* How much of that is your responsibility?

*The President.* I don't know how to evaluate that. It is difficult. You've had things like the savings and loan problem, the banking problem, and it's very hard to assign, quantify out the blame on these matters.

### Presidential Campaign

*Q.* Mr. President, you may not be talking about Bill Clinton, but Bill Clinton is talking about you.

*The President.* Yes.

*Q.* And in particular, people in the Clinton camp, including Mrs. Clinton, have charged that it's the Republican Party who has engineered the charges on some of the character questions. Do you think there is any truth to that assertion?

*The President.* I hope not. I think not, and I have made specific instructions in writing to our people to stay out of the sleaze business.

*Q.* Mr. President, do you think these so-called character issues are fair game in a Presidential race?

*The President.* I'd like to stay on the hard issues and not on the kind of issues you're talking about.

### U.N. Conference on Environment

*Q.* Mr. President, have you made a decision yet as to whether to go to Rio to the Earth summit? And if not, what will it take? What are you waiting for?

*The President.* No, I've made no decision. We are talking about it. I'm giving a lot of attention in various Departments of our Government, here in the White House and other places as well—talking up in New York and I've talked to some world leaders about it, including Collor of Brazil. But no decision has been made.

*Q.* Wouldn't it be difficult for you, having sold yourself as an environmental President, not to go meet with so many other world leaders who are trying to gather?

*The President.* I think it could work out either way. I'm sure if I went there, there would be some differences. We've got a good, sound environmental record. The United States has done an awful lot to fight against pollution, and I would be proud to take that record, not just of what we've done but of previous administrations, to Rio or anywhere else. But what I want to do is see if we can't hammer out consensus so you have a meeting that's viewed as positive instead of a major harangue down there.

### The Economy

*Q.* Mr. President, you were talking earlier about things that are bothering people. But when we talk to those people about what's bothering them, they tend to talk about the economy of late. Now, it was one of your campaign promises that there would be 30 million new jobs in the next 8 years. In the current recession we've lost 2 million. So when do you envision being able to deliver on that promise of yours? When do you anticipate real economic recovery?

*The President.* Well, you know, I made a mistake last year, and I don't want to repeat it. Last year at this time, I think it was 49 out of the 50 leading economists felt that the economy would be in rather robust recovery by the third quarter. It started up and then leveled off. And I told the American people I thought that's what would happen. But now I'm not going to go into that again because I just am uncertain.

I can tell you that most economists are now feeling that we're in recovery and that it's going to be reasonably good. Not knowing exactly what percentages it's going to be, it's very hard to lay it down against job creation right now.

*Q.* Do you regret having made this promise to create 30 million new jobs?

*The President.* I regret the fact the economy has been so sluggish and so slow.

### Interest Rates

*Q.* Mr. President, you've mentioned about the economy, and you said that you applauded the interest rate reduction by the Federal Reserve this week. In view of the large 0.5 percent increase in inflation during March, do you think that future interest rate declines should be left to the marketplace to create or the Federal Reserve? Or is there still room to do more?

*The President.* Well, there might be room to do more. You've got to take a look at that CPI figure. The PPI figure was pretty good yesterday, or in the last couple of days, the Producer Price Index. It was constrained and showed that inflation is under control. So I wouldn't take one statistic and try to urge the Fed on one course or another. But I think the Fed having dropped this rate a quarter, it was well received in the markets. I think it will be well received across the country. And let's see, and then I'm sure that Chairman Greenspan will be sensitive to further action if that's what's required.

*Q.* But to follow on that, would you be urging banks to reduce their prime lending rates or pass on the rates to the consumers?

*The President.* You remember me and the credit cards? The lower the rates, the better. The lower the rates, the more it stimulates business and activity and thus jobs. But that's a matter for the marketplace, it seems to me.

### Education

*Q.* Mr. President, you've suggested that education is your top goal as President. And yet, your own Secretary of Education has suggested this week that there really is not much difference between your proposals on education and those of the Democratic heir apparent——

*The President.* Careful.

*Q.*——Mr. Clinton. And my question is, how could it be different? What can you offer that the Democrats cannot offer on education?

*The President.* Well, I'm offering something quite different than what the Con-

gress is willing to do. And if, indeed, Governor Clinton and I are close on that and the nominating process disgorges him as the nominee, why, then we'll have common ground to take to the American people, so much the better. And all Democrats that agree with us on this ought to start working on the Congress to get them to come forward with the funding for our new schools approach and whatever else it is. In the meantime, to his credit, Arkansas has joined the America 2000 program, and they're moving forward.

I'll have to say, Bill Clinton, early on, was a part of the Governors' inside circle that helped us adopt the national education goals, goals that proudly happened, that I might say I take great pride in having seen enacted since I've been President.

But look, if there are areas of agreement, we ought not to be restless about that. We ought to say, "Good, let's get on with it." And let's get this program through the United States Congress and have it implemented by the people.

### Environmental Policy

*Q.* Mr. President, in following Ann's [Ann McDaniel, Newsweek] question about the environment——

*The President.* I've lost it here. Yes, Karen [Karen Hosler, Baltimore Sun].

*Q.* Well, we all lose it from time to time.

*The President.* True.

*Q.* The environment—the Clean Air Act is considered one of your primary achievements in the domestic front of your first term, but it's something that we don't hear you talking about. You rarely talk about the environment at all. When you talk about your reform agenda and so forth, we don't hear the word "environment." I'm wondering, do you feel that you've done enough in this area, or are there no new challenges that you want to put before the voters this fall, or is this just not as important an issue because people are worried about the economy and the cost of jobs and so forth?

*The President.* I think you're on to—the last point is a valid point. I think what has dominated the debate so far in the election process has been the economy. In fact, it's almost the only thing that has been discussed up until very, very recently. The reason for that is when the American people are hurting, when they are discouraged, when the economy is slow, people should address themselves to that.

We have a good environmental record, and I'll be proud to take it to the American people, and we'll see where we go. We've got some very difficult environmental problems that we're facing right now. I think of the problems facing the work force in the Northwest over the spotted owl. This isn't easy. I think of what's happening with the salmon question out in the western areas, and there are some very important environmental questions. But I am determined to see that our environmental record results in protection of our national resources as we tried to do in the offshore drilling, have done in the offshore drilling area, things of that nature, and still not throw people out of work.

Every time I say that, I see some of the fringe groups in the environmental movement say I don't quite get it. Well, they don't quite get it if they are not concerned about the working man and the working woman in this country. And I will continue to try to achieve that balance.

*Q.* Mr. President, how can——

*The President.* Please, Sarah [Sarah McClendon, McClendon News Service]. You're third. You're third.

### Federal Budget

*Q.* With respect to unemployment and jobs, a few days ago your Labor Secretary said that you are in favor of extending unemployment benefits. However, she did not explain how you would finance this, nor did she attend the hearing yesterday on that issue. Could you explain why, if you're committed to extending jobless benefits, you have no financing mechanism and why no one from the administration attended——

*The President.* No, I can't. I can't explain that, but I know that Dick Darman is working with the Congress and others around here. I think it's been put off now until after the recess. But we will be addressing it in a timely fashion.

*Q.* And also, there does seem to be a pattern here with respect to some of your proposals, whether it's health care reform,

or even a few moments ago when you mentioned Social Security earnings limits. You do say you're in favor of these goals as well as extending unemployment benefits, but you've never committed yourself to one specific financing mechanism. Why is that?

*The President.* I think if you look at our budget proposal, as I said, it went up there with that in it, and the financing is included in the overall budget. So I just would respectfully disagree with you.

*Q.* Mr. President, a question——

*The President.* Take a look at the budget agreement and see if I'm not correct. I mean, the budget that we submitted.

### Iraq

*Q.* Let's switch to foreign policy, sir. What, if anything, does the administration——

*The President.* Foreign policy?

*Q.* Yes, sir. What, if anything, does the administration plan to do to put Iraq on notice, to warn it or take more stringent actions about the movement of those antiaircraft missiles, the renewed flying of combat missions, and the attacks on the Kurds?

*The President.* We are particularly concerned about Iraq's flying missions above the 36th parallel. We have made clear to Iraq that we will be carefully monitoring these flights, both above and below the 36th parallel. We take a very dim view of the deployment of any missiles.

But the bottom line is compliance not just with the U.N. resolution but with the ceasefire provisions. Iraq knows that we would take a very, very dim view of blatant violations of those. And so without going into it in much more detail, I will say that I notice that they are now participating in the dismantlement of one of their suspected nuclear facilities, something they said they'd never do. And I think that was brought about by firmness on the part of the United Nations people, Mr. Ekeus and others, and certainly on firmness on the part of the United States. I don't want to go beyond that.

*Q.* To follow up, sir, after all these months since the war, have you come to the conclusion that your nemesis, Saddam

Hussein, is definitely there to stay?

*The President.* No, I've not come to that conclusion at all.

*Q.* Why?

*The President.* Because I just don't think that a totalitarian of that nature, a man that brutalizes his own people, a man that is continuing to cause them hardship and that is an outcast in that part of the world, can survive. Take a look at Eastern Europe. Take a look at other dictators. They just have a way of not being around forever. And I think that this will be the case here.

### National Security and Federal Budget

*Q.* How can you talk about progress being made here today when we have a $400 billion deficit and a $1 trillion debt and you're spending so much money around the world on the CIA, selling arms around the world and doing covert action and not even giving any accounting to the Congress of how many billions they spend. How come you let them still do that, and how do you let the Defense Department put all these contracts overseas that take our jobs overseas and our technology so that we can't have jobs over here? That's the reason why we're in such a terrible economic situation, isn't it?

*The President.* Isn't what?

*Q.* The reason why you're spending billions of dollars with the CIA all around the world selling arms and doing other things that they don't account for, that we don't know about, secret moves that stir trouble in the world. And why do you let the Defense Department put these billions and billions of dollars of contracts overseas with firms over there rather than here? How can you expect to get jobs back here if you continue to do that? And why do you talk of progress when you're still doing something like that with all the debt we have?

*The President.* Well, Sarah, I don't blame the CIA for the economy. Maybe that's the simplest way to answer your question.

*Q.* You don't, but other people do.

*The President.* Well, we'll have to debate that with the Democrats in the fall, then, because I don't——

*Q.* No, I'm not talking about that. But why do you justify this when people in this country are hungry and need clothes and need food and children go hungry every night—spending those billions of dollars overseas? Do we need to do that? I don't believe we do, do we?

*The President.* Well, we've made a proposal to reduce defense spending by $50 billion. And that's a significant reduction. And I am determined to keep—may I please finish, Sarah? And I am determined to keep the national security of this country foremost in mind. Who can tell what's going to happen? We've made tremendous progress toward world peace. We've made tremendous progress toward reducing tensions. We are the undisputed leader of the world. And we've got to bear the responsibilities that go with that.

But we are not spending money in a profligate way. I don't think it hurts to try to help guarantee against instability by helping the C.I.S., for example, Russia, Ukraine and other countries. I think that is in the interest of the United States of America. And, of course, we've got to try to help at home. And spending at home is at an all-time high. And you say $1 trillion, yes, that concerns me very much. Thank God we have a $5 trillion economy, or we'd really be in the soup.

### Welfare Reform

*Q.* Mr. President, you've always prided yourself on your opposition to bigotry. But as you may know, some who work in the welfare field and some Democrats on the Hill have charged that you're bringing up this issue in an election year in order to play to racial divisions in the public. How do you respond to that?

*The President.* On which issue is that?

*Q.* The welfare issue.

*The President.* I don't think there's any validity to that charge at all. All you have to do is look at the hopelessness of people that have been, you know, third generation welfare people and say we've got to help these people. It's a matter of compassion, not anger. It's a matter of trying to help. And I think what we did today here with the Governor of Wisconsin, I hope it's just a manifestation of that.

I haven't heard that ugly charge, but I don't know of anybody who is suggesting that the welfare system is just great. If the charge is that anyone who wants to change the welfare system is a bigot, I would totally reject that. It's just not right.

*Q.* If I could follow up, sir, if you are so concerned with this issue, why haven't you been closely involved with it for the last 3 years?

*The President.* Well, that was a good question. And I think the politics drives some things. I think we've tried to move forward in terms of helping people in these cities. I don't think we've done absolutely nothing. But now we're moving forward at the request of this first State for a waiver to speed it up. And 24 days is pretty good.

My philosophy has always been to have flexibility at the State and local level. And so we've been encouraging that for a long, long time.

*Q.* What do you mean when you say politics drives some of those things?

*The President.* Well, I think, a lot of the issues we're talking about—some were asking about the environment, some were asking about these other issues. They get much more clearly in focus every 4 years, and then you go ahead and try to follow through and do something about them.

### Caterpillar Labor Dispute

*Q.* Mr. President, the Caterpillar Company is trying to replace striking workers. How do you feel about the issue of replacing strikers?

*The President.* Well, I feel that I'm in favor of collective bargaining. I think everybody must live within the law, and if they are permitted to do things under the law, they should feel that they're able to go ahead under the law. I believe that this matter should be resolved between labor and business, and I see no reason at this juncture to have the Federal Government in the big middle of this.

*Q.* So it's okay if Caterpillar decides to hire strikers, then you feel that's all right?

*The President.* I think labor should do what's legal, and I think management should do what people think are legal here—what is legal, not what they think is legal but what is legal. And I just feel that free collective bargaining under the law is the proper approach, not intervention by the Federal Government the minute a strike takes place. I don't think it's good for labor, and I don't think it's good for business.

### Congressional Investigation of White House Expenses

*Q.* Mr. President, when you came to Congress back in the sixties, you came out for full disclosure of financial information. You have often told us that you try to stand for high ethical standards——

*The President.* A little louder, Jessica [Jessica Lee, USA Today], I can't——

*Q.* You've often told us that you try to stand for high ethical standards in public service, and you came out for full disclosure of financial information when you first came to Washington to represent Houston. I wonder if you would now say that you are for full disclosure of the financial information on what it takes to run the White House, to run the Presidency, to do your job as President, to travel around on Air Force One, and to provide for the ceremonial, political and other functions of the Presidency as you conduct them here?

*The President.* I do favor full disclosure. Next week I'll be disclosing once again my full income tax returns. As I'll tell you next week, I think that's a little bit of an imposition on an American citizen's privacy; but I think this is the 12th year that I will have done that, assets and liabilities spelled out, full disclosure. And yes, you're correct. I took a leadership role in the 90th Congress, as just a freshman there, for more disclosure. And I believe that's what elected people should do. I think at the Presidential level it's got to be even fuller, challengers and incumbents. And I think we need full disclosure.

Now, in terms of Congress' investigation, I hope that we have fully cooperated with the various committees of inquiry on disclosing the costs of running the White House. This is the people's house. It is a magnificent house. I don't know how many people, hundreds of thousands of people, go through this house every year. It's almost like a museum. And much of what goes on there is to show the people their house in a good and sensible way.

However, those matters are looked at in full detail as our budget goes up from various different Departments that it takes to run this place. Some of it can be security, various security accounts. Some of it can be the Park Service's accounts. And don't ask me to say all of the accounts under this complicated congressional system that look at it.

But I have asked our people to go to the various committees that have jurisdiction and to cooperate fully. And that's what we're trying to do, Jessie. And we're going to keep on trying to do that.

*Q.* If I may followup with a specific incident, Mr. President. In the budget that you submitted in January or February, the statement is that White House travel, your travel, cost the taxpayers $29,000 last year. Now, Mr. President, with all the trips that you go on——

*The President.* Twenty-nine thousand dollars an hour, isn't it?

*Q.* No, no.

*The President.* Oh, Jess, you're wrong. I think the Air Force One costs $25,000 an hour.

*Q.* That was Air Force One. But——

*The President.* I think when the Congress appropriated the money for it, I think it was estimated to be $41,000 an hour. Now it's being operated at—for some reason, don't ask me to explain it—at $25,000 an hour, which is a tremendous amount of money. So it's not a year, it's an hour.

*Q.* But what your budget said is that you spent $29,000 on Presidential travel last year. It didn't deal with Air Force One. There's a category——

*The President.* But now——

*Q.* There's a category that talked about your travel. And that's what it said, and that they give you $100,000 to spend, and you only spent $29,000. Can you explain that?

*The President.* No, I just can't possibly explain that.

*Q.* Do you think that that figure is correct?

*The President.* We'll try to get the information for you because we're trying to disclose—and we'll do it to the Congress——

*Q.* Yes.

*Q.* It sounds unlikely.

*The President.* Yes, it sounds very unlikely when it costs $25,000 an hour, that it only costs $25,000 a year, $29,000 in a year.

*Q.* And the Congress has asked that question, and they have been unable to get——

*The President.* Well, the Congress will be satisfied.

*Q.* ——the satisfactory response. Are you going to tell them what it costs, what your travel last year costs? That's the question.

*The President.* We're going to answer every question they have to the best of our ability, and I think we're going to continue. You know, a lot of the cost of Air Force One and my travel was considered at the time these new airplanes were ordered. And I hope that we have prudently lived within whatever it was that was budgeted to encompass that travel. And we're going to keep on trying.

One thing I think that would be a shame is if we got into talks about gardeners and perks and calligraphers and lost sight of the need for real congressional reform, fundamental reform of the institution that has led to the scandals that we've seen all over the newspapers. So we will address ourselves to this disclosure; some of it, it seems to me to be coming up by Congress that seems a little defensive about the problems on Capitol Hill. But as head of the executive branch, we should cooperate with the committees of Congress, and I have instructed our people to do just that.

But as I end this press conference, I would make this nonobjective note, take this note: It seems to me very funny that, all of a sudden, faced with the outrage of the American people, not on cars, not on how much a hamburger costs in the Senate restaurant but on fundamental problems with an institution that was manifested in so many ways recently, the Congress now starts saying, "Well, what's it cost, how many calligraphers do you have making out cards for a state dinner in the White House?"

And we want to respond to these questions, but I want to keep the focus where fundamentally it belongs, on the need for genuine reform, reform that is necessary because of the laxity of one party control of the House of Representatives for, what, 48 out of the last 52 years. And that's the thing that concerns the American people. They are very concerned about it. And we have made suggestions, and I've mentioned some of them today, that Congress ought to live by the same laws they make you and me live by. And we've put forward legislation to do that. I happen to think the time has come for term limitations as well. I'd like to see changes along the lines suggested by Senator Boren, a Democrat, Congressman Lee Hamilton, a Democrat, in the procedures of the Senate and the House. I'd like to see that taken care of.

And so we're talking about fundamental change and reform that is clearly needed. And some up there—not all the Congressmen, because I think some are addressing themselves seriously to reform—and some are saying, "We'll get them. They're talking about the trip I took to some Timbuktu on a jet; let's go find out how many calligraphers there, or guys mowing the grass at the White House." And we'll try to respond as fully as we can. But let's keep the sights set on what is fundamentally—needs reform

and change. The institution needs fundamental change and reform up there.

Now, with no further ado and with the regret at having to not answer every question—come on—I really do have to go.

Judy [Judy Smith, Deputy Press Secretary], now let me say this if you'll turn off all cameras and turn off the CNN, you guys. In my view, Marlin—who will return in great spirits, I might add—[*laughter*]—on Monday and who, as we all know, has my full confidence—has had a stand-in for a couple of weeks. And in my view, Judy, to whom you have not been altogether kind, although she does not complain, has done a superb job, and I thank her. And if I don't do what she tells me now, which is to get out of here, I'm in serious trouble. Thank you all. And, Judy, thank you. Thank you.

*Note: The President's 126th news conference began at 2:38 p.m. in the Rose Garden at the White House. In his remarks, he referred to Rolf Ekeus, executive chairman of the United Nations Special Commission on Iraq.*

# Nomination of Edward Ernest Kubasiewicz To Be an Assistant Commissioner of Patents and Trademarks
*April 10, 1992*

The President today announced his intention to nominate Edward Ernest Kubasiewicz, of Virginia, to be an Assistant Commissioner of Patents and Trademarks, Department of Commerce. He would succeed James Edward Denny.

Since 1985, Mr. Kubasiewicz has served as Group Director of the U.S. Patent and Trademark Office at the U.S. Department of Commerce in Washington, DC. Prior to

this, he served as Patents Programs Administrator for the U.S. Patent and Trademark Office in Washington, DC, 1983–85.

Mr. Kubasiewicz graduated from the University of Detroit (B.S.E.E., 1961) and the Washington College of Law (J.D., 1967). He was born October 14, 1936, in Hamtramck, MI. Mr. Kubasiewicz served in the U.S. Army Reserves, 1962–69. He is married, has two children, and resides in Alexandria, VA.

## Nomination of Stephen Greene To Be Deputy Administrator of the Drug Enforcement Administration
*April 10, 1992*

The President today announced his intention to nominate Stephen Greene, of Maryland, to be Deputy Administrator of Drug Enforcement, Department of Justice. He would succeed Thomas C. Kelly.

Currently Mr. Greene serves as Acting Deputy Administrator at the Drug Enforcement Administration in Arlington, VA. Prior to this, he served at the Drug Enforcement Administration as: Assistant Administrator for Operations, 1990–91;

Deputy Assistant Administrator for Operations, 1989–90; and Deputy Assistant Administrator for International Programs, 1987–89.

Mr. Greene graduated from the University of Maryland (B.S., 1982). He was born January 5, 1943, in Plattsburg, NY. From 1966 to 1968, Mr. Greene served in the U.S. Marine Corps. He is married and resides in Annapolis, MD.

## Radio Address to the Nation on Welfare Reform
*April 11, 1992*

The American people have always been a people constantly searching for improvement, impatient for change when things need changing. Last week I spoke about the need for a change here in Washington, for Government reform, especially congressional reform. Today I want to focus on reforming our welfare system, especially on our Government's role in that reform process.

After years of trying to help those who are in need, we have found that too often our assistance does not help people out of poverty; it traps them there. It's not that people stopped caring; it's that the system stopped working. We want a welfare system that breaks the cycle of dependency before dignity is destroyed and before poverty becomes a family legacy. But today we must face this fact: Our system has failed.

I have repeatedly called for the forging of Federal-State partnerships that would make welfare reform a powerful, effective reality. Yesterday, at my direction, the Federal Government waived outdated rules to allow Wisconsin to try a new kind of welfare reform. The Wisconsin plan replaces some of the old assumptions of the welfare state and recognizes the importance of personal responsibility, self-respect, independence, and self-sufficiency.

In my State of the Union Address, I made a commitment to make it quicker and easier for States with welfare reform ideas to get the Federal waivers they need. By approving Wisconsin's waivers 24 days after we received their request, that commitment now has the force of action. I want to commend Wisconsin Governor Tommy Thompson, and I want to challenge other States to propose their own reforms.

We must balance America's generous heart with our responsibility to the taxpayers who underwrite governmental assistance. Our assistance should in no way encourage dependency or undermine our Nation's economic competitiveness. We pay twice for those who make welfare a way of life: once for the initial benefits, but even more because the Nation loses their contribution to the Nation's economic well-being.

Those who receive Government assistance have certain responsibilities: the responsibility to seek work or get education and training that will help them get a job, and the responsibility to get their lives in order. That means establishing lifestyles that will enable them to fulfill their potential, not destroy it.

We have responsibilities, too. We must structure our welfare programs so that they reverse policies which lock in a lifestyle of dependency and subtly destroy self-esteem. We must encourage family formation and family stability. Too often our welfare programs have encouraged exactly the opposite.

We must incorporate incentives for recipients to stay in school. For instance, in Wisconsin, teen parents are required by the Learnfare program to stay in school to obtain full benefits. They recognize that in many respects opportunity is equated with education. And I'll have more to say about the urgent need for educational reform next week as we mark the first anniversary of the crusade that I call America 2000.

My approach to welfare reform should not only open the doors of opportunity for our citizens who are on public assistance but also prepare them to walk proudly and competently through those doors. Our goal is to build a system of welfare that will encourage self-respect, build strength of character, and develop to the fullest each individual's potential for a productive, meaningful life.

Thank you for listening. And may God bless the United States of America.

*Note: This address was recorded at 8:15 a.m. on April 10 in the Oval Office at the White House for broadcast after 9 a.m. on April 11.*

## Remarks on Signing the Executive Order on Employee Rights Concerning Union Dues
*April 13, 1992*

Please be seated. And may I just say that we are delighted to see all of you here on this crisp, cool day in the Rose Garden. Before I begin, I'd like to recognize two members of the Cabinet here: Secretary Lynn Martin over here, Secretary of Labor, and then Attorney General Bill Barr, sitting over here in the front. I also want to single out two Congressmen with us today, Bob Walker and Tom DeLay, thank them for being here; Mr. James Stephens, the Chairman of the National Labor Relations Board. And also a very special welcome to Harry Beck and his wife, Karan. And fresh from parting the Red Sea yet again on TV last night—[*laughter*]—our old friend Charlton Heston. And I'll have more to say about him in a minute. But thank you for coming all this way.

Today happens to be a very special anniversary. Two hundred and forty-nine years ago today, Thomas Jefferson was born. And there is a renewed spirit of Jeffersonian reform sweeping through this Nation today. It is therefore a fitting occasion for putting into effect new reforms that will protect Americans' fundamental rights against political abuse by special interest groups.

For brilliance, for courage, for passion in the cause of freedom and democracy, no one has ever surpassed Thomas Jefferson. He eloquently stated a principle of fundamental fairness in 1779 when he declared, "To compel a man to furnish contributions of money for the propagation of opinions which he disbelieves and abhors is sinful and tyrannical."

Now, not long ago in Philadelphia, I spoke of the wisdom of the Founders on the subject of Government reform. It is this Jeffersonian insight that we reaffirm today with reforms to strengthen the political rights of American workers.

In the Executive order I will sign in just a few minutes, I am directing that companies performing Federal contract work must inform their employees in the clearest possible terms of their legal rights as affirmed in the Supreme Court's landmark *Beck* decision. This placard displayed here today represents the exact words of the notice that will be placed in workplaces around the Nation. And while this order will directly affect American workers employed by Federal contractors, I want to emphasize that the principles affirmed by the *Beck* decision are precious to all Americans.

The *Beck* decision is one of a series of cases protecting American workers from being compelled against their will to pay union or agency dues in excess of what is actually used for collective bargaining purposes and contract administration. Full implementation of this principle will guarantee that no American will have his job or livelihood threatened for refusing to contribute to political activities against his will. The Executive order that I sign today will make it easier for employees of Federal contractors to understand and then exercise their political rights.

The Secretary of Labor is separately proposing a rule clarifying and then bringing up to date requirements for labor organizations to account for how workers' dues are spent. This rule aims to foster union democracy, and it also will have the effect of helping employees protect their *Beck* rights.

The trial court in the *Beck* case found, for instance, that in plaintiff Beck's workplace, Harry Beck's workplace, 79 percent of the compulsory dues collected went to purposes unrelated to collective bargaining and contract administration. Our new rule will assist union members in discovering how their dues are being spent. And perhaps most important of all, I expect the NLRB, the National Labor Relations Board, to carry out its responsibilities to enforce the principles of the *Beck* decision.

One of America's most intrepid fighters for individual rights is Charlton Heston. He's been a member of four different labor organizations and, like my predecessor, President Reagan, a president of the Screen Actors Guild. He's given much of himself to put collective bargaining rights into practice. And he's been equally committed to seeing that no company or organization may infringe a worker's individual freedom of conscience. And we are very honored,

sir, that you came here today, traveled all across the country as a crusader for individual rights. You are most welcome.

Our new actions to protect individual liberties are important efforts in a larger crusade that I'm waging to reform our system of politics in Government. Institutions of public life, whether the Government, corporations, or unions, should be accountable to their constituents to produce results and then respond to their needs. Working Americans should have the right to decide whether contributing to political parties or candidates, at odds with their beliefs, fulfill that principle and represent the institutional responsibility that we rightfully expect.

In pursuit of the very same principles, accountability and responsibility, I am asking Congress to enact a sweeping reform of campaign financing. And I'm fighting to eliminate, not restrict but eliminate the special interest PAC's, which will stop the millions of dollars in administrative subsidies that corporations and labor organizations now are allowed to channel into their own PAC's.

Time and time again over our constitutional history, protecting universal rights has demanded the lonely courage of individual citizens standing up against powerful organized interests. And I'm especially honored that we have here today such an individual. It took this man 12 years of patient effort to carry his case to vindication in the highest Court of the land. And it is his crusade that brings us together today. So, Harry Beck, thank you, sir, for all that you have done. And I am proud to have you stand with me as I sign this Executive order. Welcome, and well done.

*Note: The President spoke at 11 a.m. in the Rose Garden at the White House. The Executive order is listed in Appendix E at the end of this volume.*

## Statement by Press Secretary Fitzwater on the President's Meeting With Prime Minister Jan Olszewski of Poland
*April 13, 1992*

The President met for approximately 45 minutes this afternoon with Prime Minister Jan Olszewski of Poland, who is in the United States on a private visit. The President reaffirmed his strong support for the pioneering transformation to democracy and a free market economy in Poland, whose success is all the more important in light of the revolutionary changes farther East.

The two leaders discussed economic and political developments in Poland as well as the larger European security situation. Prime Minister Olszewski outlined his government's economic policies and its commitment to working with the IMF on an agreed reform program. He thanked the President for U.S. support and discussed ways the U.S. could be helpful during the present difficult economic situation in Poland, particularly through encouraging greater trade and investment.

In that context, the Prime Minister welcomed the President's offer, made in a recent letter to President Walesa, to send a mission of U.S. business leaders to Poland with the aim of facilitating some of the many U.S. private investment projects now under negotiation. The President has asked former Deputy Secretary of State John Whitehead to lead the mission and to select a long-term U.S. adviser who would remain in Warsaw to follow up on the mission's recommendations and assist U.S. enterprises in their efforts to find joint venture partners and other investment opportunities.

## Remarks to Giddings & Lewis Employees and Local Chambers of Commerce in Fraser, Michigan
*April 14, 1992*

Thank you very much. And Governor Engler, thank you; I'm proud to be introduced by our great Governor here. I want to salute our Secretary of Labor, Lynn Martin. You met her when she came in. She is doing a lot, an awful lot in terms of job retraining, in terms of hope and opportunity for America's workers. I want to thank the CEO of Giddings & Lewis, Bill Fife here, who greeted us and has given us a short tour. Thanks to some of the workers here in this wonderful plant and then to Barbara Hollett and Linda Walling and Geary Maiuri and James Williams, Warren and to all the others from the six chambers of commerce. May I thank you for being here. I just want you to know I'm delighted to be with you today.

I'm sorry that Barbara Bush is not here. She's out in the State of Oregon today. But I take great pride in the fact that she's doing her part. I see these kids here trying to hit a blow for literacy in this country. And she asked me to extend her very best wishes.

Now, I want to talk to you today about the things that we really must do together, Government and business, public servants, private citizens, to leave our children a legacy worthy of this great country of ours. You see, I am not one who is so pessimistic about America. We are the leaders of the world, the undisputed leaders of the world, and now we've got great things to do here at home. I think that we've got to agree on what that legacy is going to be. Clearly, we want a world at peace. People say to the American people, "Well, how are things going?" And I take great pride in the fact that, see these little kids here, they won't go to sleep at night worrying about nuclear warfare the way the generations preceding had done. We want a world at peace. We want strong, wholesome families, and we want an economy that provides rewarding jobs for all.

More than any country on Earth, America has afforded each generation the opportunity to leave such a legacy. Today, we have that opportunity once again. The world is changing at a pace undreamed of a generation ago. And now America, which has led the world's transformation, must change as well. This afternoon I want to discuss five areas which I believe are overdue for reform, five key ways in which America must change if we are to honor coming generations with the legacy that they deserve.

As business men and women and as Giddings & Lewis employees, you understand the urgency. For each of these five problems presents itself to you not as some abstraction but in the most immediate way, as a cost, a cost of doing business. Too often these costs are beyond your control, drawing resources away from your primary goals of expanding your companies and creating good jobs for your communities.

When our legal system, and the Governor touched on this, becomes incapable of resolving disputes in a civil and timely manner, business loses the incentive to innovate, loses the incentive to take risks. And when health care costs escalate, business picks up much of the tab. And when Government imposes barriers to trade, business pays the cost in lost markets. And then when our kids, our children, leave school without rudimentary skills, business bears in the lost productivity. And when Government freezes in gridlock, business can no longer plan rationally for the future.

So, let me start with Washington, and again, the Governor referred to that: If America is going to change, the Government must change. Ten days ago I presented seven specific proposals to cure the paralysis that grips the United States Congress. My proposals range from an elimination of these special-interest political action committees, these PAC's, elimination, not reduction but elimination; extends to a line-item veto, which will allow us at last to get a handle on this deficit that is mortgaging the future of these children here today. And I think it's high time that we limited

the number of terms that Members of Congress may serve.

My aim is simple: We must create a flexible Government, responsive to the common good. And I have tried, I have tried over the past 3 years to invest my administration with this sort of flexibility. Now, let me give you a few examples of special concern right here to Macomb County.

A reformed Government knows its limits, refusing to impose undue burdens on business and consumers alike. For that reason, I've made it clear to Congress: This is no time to legislate an increase in the CAFE standards that would cost Americans jobs in the automotive industry. And I will not accept such legislation.

A reformed Government encourages innovation. Last October, by way of example, my administration joined with the Big Three, the automobile companies, to develop a new generation of batteries. And our goal: To make American car companies first in the world in producing competitive, electric cars by the year 2000.

A reformed Government finds flexible means to reach its goals. Our approach to the 1990 Clean Air Act, which requires deep reductions in air pollution, is a good example. To help communities and industries meet the objectives of that act, we've initiated a "cash for clunkers" program, allowing States and companies to buy the high-polluting old cars, get them off the road, and use the reduction in pollution to satisfy our clean air standards.

Flexibility, accountability, a willingness to innovate, Americans have a right to expect each of these from their Government and particularly from the United States Congress. Yet instead we get business-as-usual. I'll give you another example, dealing with a second area urgently in need of reform, the Nation's legal system. Our country—and this isn't true just of business, this is true of neighborhoods, true of towns and city government—our country is swamped in frivolous lawsuits. We tried to make a good start at reform in 1990 when I introduced a bill to reform product liability laws. Congress wouldn't budge. So we reintroduced the reform again in 1991. And the Senate Democrats refuse even to bring that bill to a vote. In the House it's stuck in two, that's right, two separate committees.

This inaction is inexcusable. America, regrettably, has become the most litigious society on Earth, and American companies pay the price, not only in dollars wasted but in lower productivity and a business environment hostile even to ordinary competitive practices. According to a recent survey, 40 percent of companies that had been the target of product liability suits have discontinued certain types of product research.

None of our competitors is afflicted with this lawsuit madness. We must remove this ball and chain from our ability to compete worldwide. And our Competitiveness Council, led by the Vice President, has offered 50 recommendations for legal reform, including reasonable limits to the discovery process, alternative means of resolving disputes, and a "loser pay" rule that would discourage the frivolous lawsuits. I urge you to urge the Congress to help stop this lawsuit madness.

We must help each other more and sue each other less. I'll give you an example. A lot of the people here in this plant, I'm sure, have kids in Little League. Some of you may coach Little League, like I did a thousand years ago. And some people are refusing to coach Little League because they're afraid of some frivolous lawsuit; doctors, afraid of delivering babies because of a frivolous lawsuit. We really have to change this litigious society into a more gentle and a more friendly society.

Our comprehensive legal reform will be far-reaching, extending then into a third area critically in need of change, our Nation's health system. Everybody here, I'm sure, is concerned about the health care system. The litigation explosion has hit Michigan's health care hard. Every year your physicians and hospitals pay almost $500 million for medical liability coverage, $500 million. For the patient, that translates into an extra $300 added on to the average hospital bill.

The trends are simply unsustainable. Some estimates say that by 2030, the year 2030, that's only, what, 38 years away, we will spend 30 cents of every dollar of national income on health care. Again, much of the burden falls on business. Right now,

American corporations spend more on health care each year than they earn in after-tax profits. Now, we've got to stop this drain on our productivity.

My proposed health care reform will build on our system's assets, especially in preserving the quality of care. We've still got the world's finest quality health care. We will reform the private insurance market and increase consumer choice. Through transferable tax credits we will bring coverage to those who are uninsured and control costs through market incentives. And we will avoid the pitfalls of what I would see as a nationalized care, with the rationing and the long waiting lines and the mediocre quality that comes with it. Health care reform must hew to this principle: Government has no business dictating what kind of health care you want to choose, dictating what kind of health care you receive.

I target then a fourth area for attention, like the others, absolutely critical for our success in the coming decades. With its global reach, this great company, Giddings & Lewis, exemplifies an indisputable truth about our future: If America is to succeed economically at home, we must succeed economically abroad. And in the postwar period, trade-related jobs have grown three times faster than the overall job creation. Exports have accounted for 70 percent of our economy's growth over the past 3 years. We will build on this success by continuing to open foreign markets to American goods and services, including the world's second largest market economy, Japan. And since I took office, our exports to Japan have grown 10 times faster than our imports from Japan, and our manufactured products are leading this expansion. That boom has already created an additional 200,000 jobs here at home.

And that's why we made this now-famous trip to Japan. I heard some criticism of that trip, but let's get the facts straight about what we accomplished. Of special interest to many of you, for example, was the pledge by private Japanese companies to increase the purchase of U.S.-made auto parts from $9 billion to $19 billion by 1994. And we didn't stop there. As a result of our trip, we've opened up Japan's $4 billion glass market, its $9 billion public-sector computer market, and its $27 billion paper market, offering American business enormous opportunities to sell American goods; and that, of course, means to create American jobs. And if we are to take advantage of the opportunities, we must stay abroad.

We must have a world-class work force. And yet the grim fact is undeniable: Our current education system is unable to produce the workers the highly competitive world market demands. The only solution left to us is radical change. That means we must literally reinvent American education. And on Thursday, I'm going to discuss the progress we've made in the year since we launched our America 2000 education initiative, a revolutionary movement that challenges every community to create what we call break-the-mold schools. We know how to do it. We set world-class standards for students. We redouble our efforts to rid our schools of drugs and violence, to cleanse Americans of this scourge that wastes so many young lives. And we make schools more accountable by forcing them to compete. And that means letting parents choose their children's schools, public, private, or religious. We must have that kind of choice to bring real competition into the classroom.

And we need to take the same bold approach to job training, to provide Americans with the skills that this age of intense international competition demands. And I have developed such an approach, working with the Secretary here, and when Congress returns from recess, we will submit the "Job Training 2000 Act."

Our current job training system is merely—it's kind of a crazy quilt of good intentions. Over the years Congress has put in place scores of training programs, but they are uncoordinated, sometimes redundant, and too often unaccountable. This year, seven different Federal Agencies will administer some 60 training programs at a cost of $18 billion.

And with this jumble, is it any wonder that an 18-year-old, fresh from high school, doesn't know where to go for career guidance; or that an unemployed older worker, eager to learn a new trade, is confused about how to find training; or that a young parent on welfare, in search of a rewarding job, can't find advice on which trade school to attend or which career to pursue? Unscrupulous operators, these fly-by-night trade schools prey on this confusion, and they take advantage of the system's lack of accountability. And they recruit the naive or somebody that's so desperate even though they know it's bad, they're willing to take a chance, signing them up for thousands of dollars in grants or loans, offer a few weeks training, and then leave the people burdened with debt.

A truly competitive America can't afford this waste of talent and energy. And it's not fair to the American worker. Job Training 2000 will disentangle that knot of Federal programs and make them serve the people who need them. And here are the key elements of this plan. First, it will create one-stop shopping for vocational training in every community. Second, it will certify programs so that they meet the needs of the local labor markets. And third, it will offer vouchers so aspiring workers can choose the training they want.

Along with Job Training 2000, I'm going to submit to Congress an important new initiative. It's called the "Youth Apprenticeship Act of 1992." Apprenticeship is one of the surest routes into the world of work, and we need to make it more widely available to our young people. And at the same time, we've got to encourage them to complete a sound high school education that prepares them for a lifetime of learning. The act accomplishes both these goals, making it easier for kids in the 11th and 12th grades to combine on-the-job training with their regular studies at school. And when they graduate from school, they will have not only a certificate that attests to their job skills but a diploma that represents a substantial and varied education.

Now, to get that "Apprenticeship Act" up and running, we will be offering demonstration grants to six States, California, Iowa, Maine, Oregon, Wisconsin, and right here in Michigan, as well as a series of local areas. We owe our young people, we owe every American who seeks to climb the ladder of economic advantage the finest job, the finest job training system the world can produce, and I mean to see that they get it.

Therefore I want to challenge the United States Congress to pass both of these initiatives, Job Training 2000 and the "Youth Apprenticeship Act," this session, before the Congress adjourns for the year. But as you know, I'm the first to admit that I can't always count on Congress to act, no matter how great the urgency. For real education reform I enlisted the help of the Nation's Governors. You may remember this a couple of years ago, we got together at Charlottesville, Virginia. So far 43 Governors have responded by enrolling their States in this program we call America 2000.

And now I ask their help again. I call on the Governors here today, all of the Governors around the country, to initiate Job Training 2000 strategies in their own States; several are already hard at work. And I ask every Governor to bring together labor and business leaders with local officials to consolidate their own job training programs. And wherever possible, my administration will grant waivers to accelerate these efforts. And we will provide incentive grants to help them get started.

Each of the reforms that I've outlined here today—making Government accountable and flexible, restoring sanity to our legal system, ensuring quality health care for all, expanding world trade, and reinventing American education and job training for tomorrow's work force—each shares a single goal, to ensure that America remains the undisputed leader of the world, the freest, most prosperous and competitive Nation on Earth.

And each of these reforms grows from a fundamental, uniquely American principle. Thomas Jefferson said it best: "The pillars of our prosperity are the most thriving when left most free to individual enterprise." And in practice that means Government must trust the wisdom of markets more than the whims of bureaucrats. And the freely made

decisions of the people must take precedence over the engineering schemes of Government. And all our institutions, from Congress to the local trade school, must be accountable to those that they serve.

Over the last decade, America has changed the world. Today, we're blessed with the opportunity to change America. I couldn't help thinking about that sentence, "Over the last decade, America has changed the world," as I was walking along the line here and reading the computer screen in English and then in what the man running the screen told me was Russian. I had to take his word for that. But here was a shipment going off, a machine going off to Russia. We have a tremendous opportunity, and I intend to see that we continue to lead the world. And in so doing, we will be offering enormous job opportunities, expanded job markets for the American worker. We cannot pull back. We cannot withdraw into some sphere of isolation.

And so, as your President, I take great pride in the fact we've helped change the world. And now I can tell you we are going to make these changes at home that will enable us to remain the undisputed, the undisputed, admired leader of this changing world in which we live.

Thank you all very much. And may God bless each and every one of you and your families. And may God bless the United States of America. Thank you very, very much.

*Note: The President spoke at 2:50 p.m. at the Giddings & Lewis, Inc., plant. In his remarks, he referred to William Fife, Jr., chairman and chief executive officer, Giddings & Lewis; Barbara Hollett, executive director, Metro East Chamber of Commerce; Linda Walling, director, Sterling Heights Chamber of Commerce; Gary Maiuri, chairman, Central Macomb County Chamber of Commerce; and James Williams, chairman, Warren, Center Line, and Sterling Heights Chamber of Commerce.*

## Remarks at a Bush-Quayle Fundraising Dinner in Dearborn, Michigan
*April 14, 1992*

Thank you very, very much. And John Engler, thank you, sir, Governor, for that kind introduction. John Engler and I have been side by side in politics for a long time, and I'll tell you, I am mighty proud of the job he is doing as Governor of this great State. You're lucky, and you ought to know it. I might salute your lovely wife, Michelle. He had to go to Texas to find her, but here she is, and we're all for her, too.

And let me thank Mike Timmis for the thoughtful invocation and Randy Agley for the superb job as master of ceremonies and for so many other things as well. Also, of course, our special thanks to our esteemed friend Max Fisher, whom we heard from tonight, always at my side, always with sound counsel and advice, a great friend of every Republican and a great leader of this State and, indeed, of our country. Max, thank you, sir.

And of course, if you want to get the job done, get Heinz Prechter involved; he'll twist the arm right out of your socket. But he did a first-class job. And I also want to thank Dave Doyle and Chuck Yob and Tim Leuliette. And let me also acknowledge Bob Mosbacher, our former Secretary of Commerce, now one of the great leaders of our campaign; Bobby Holt, the national finance chairman, whom you met; and Michigan natives Spence Abraham, who used to be the State party chairman, now doing a superb job for the NRCC in Washington, and then our special friend Bob Teeter, who is calling a lot of the shots at our campaign. We've got a great team, and I'm grateful to each and every one of them, all here tonight.

And there's two others I was privileged to sit between, Andrea Fischer and Yosef Chafari. These are the two leading ticket sellers. And I had a fairly relaxed evening, sitting between these two leading ticket sellers. They're trying to sell me tickets to the next event. [*Laughter*] But I'm telling you, this thing was put together in quite a short period of time, relatively short period of time, and we are very, very grateful. I un-derstand that there's even an overflow room. And after we finish these remarks, I want to go in there.

I will repeat for the benefit of the people in the overflow room: You are safe. By that, I'm referring to a joke that Billy Graham used to tell about the speaker that went on and on and on. And finally, the chairman picked up the gavel, heaved it at the speaker, missed him, and hit the woman in the front row. And she said, "Hit me again; I can still hear him." [*Laughter*] So, to the people in the overflow room, you are safe.

Let me say that it's a pleasure to visit the Detroit area. On our final approach on Air Force One, we had to climb a little higher over Tiger Stadium. Cecil Fielder's turn at bat, at the batting cage there, and we wanted to be out of his range. [*Laughter*]

Let me thank all of you who had contributed so generously to this reelection campaign. With help like yours and the efforts of millions of people like you at the grassroots level, our team is going to win 4 more years to lead this country. I'm absolutely confident of that.

And as John said, we have been trying since 1989, working for reform and change. And I've often had to buck a Congress that, frankly, is resistant to change. But now, this year, in the election year, we can put it in focus, the things we've been trying to get done, and let the American people say whether they want change or not.

We must accelerate reform, reforms to strengthen the bulwark of our Nation's character, and I mean the American family. A major mayors group came into my office, and the thing that they say is the most common problem in the great urban areas of America is the dissolution of the American family. And we've got to find ways to strengthen it.

We've got to find reforms to preserve half a century's hard-won gains for world freedom and peace, reforms to provide Americans with first-rate jobs in this whole new global, the new world economy. And that's why it's so important that you're here tonight. We have much to do if we're to prepare our Nation to compete in this exciting new century ahead.

None of us can do it alone. But together we are up to any challenge that lies ahead. And frankly, I'm a little sick and tired of some of the gloomy news out there every single night, telling us what's wrong with the United States of America. There's a lot right about it, and I'm going to take that message to the American people.

But your support is key if we're truly going to change this country. And it's key if we're to revolutionize our schools, make health care accessible and affordable. It's key to the frivolous court cases that drain our economy; reform the way our Government works, especially up there on Capitol Hill. And finally, your support is key if we're to open markets the world over for American goods and services, to sustain and to create jobs for Americans, jobs right here in Michigan.

Each one of you tonight is making a difference on these five important challenges because they're all part of my mission as President of the United States. And with your support, I aim to complete that mission. We've got to get this job done.

Take education, for example. Our America 2000 education strategy thrives on local initiatives. Polly Williams in Milwaukee and Patrick Rooney in Indianapolis have captured national attention for their new programs to give inner-city parents what wealthier families have right now, a real choice for schools for their children.

And right here in Detroit there's an exciting new effort in the inner city, Cornerstone Schools. And one of the leaders is Eddie Edwards, a Protestant pastor in the black community, whom I have been pleased to recognize as one of our daily Points of Light for our Nation. A key partner with the Reverend Edwards in this project is Archbishop Maida of the Catholic Church. And they've won generous support from business leaders as they break down barriers and reinvent, literally reinvent excellent schools for children who need them most. And they didn't wait for bureaucrats in Washington, DC, to mandate them or to give them direction. They rejected business-as-usual. And I salute them for reform. And our America 2000 education strategy will change America by encouraging that kind of innovation.

And meanwhile, grassroots Republicans in the Michigan Legislature are working with our great Governor on Michigan 2000, this State's plan to give parents more freedom and responsibility in their children's education. And there's a powerful reform spirit in Michigan to ease the strictures of teacher tenure and certification, to establish solid core curricula, and to measure results, and to give individual principals new incentives to innovate through charter schools and school empowerment.

I can assure you, the Republican reformers in Michigan's Legislature are light years ahead of the liberal Democratic leadership in the United States Congress. And I can't wait to elect a new Congress that will work for true reform of our Nation's schools. And I might add, a centerpiece for our strategy for reform is choice for parents for public, private, and religious schools. And then you watch the schools that are not chosen bring themselves up through competition. Parental choice is an important key to our reform program.

You know, Michigan is also a leader in making quality health care available and affordable to absolutely everyone. And Michigan soon hopes to become the first State in the Nation to enroll its entire Medicaid caseload, one million people, in managed care. Managed care improves quality while cutting costs. And it's an important part of our national health care reform package. We have the best quality health care in the entire world here in the United States, but too many people lack basic health insurance coverage. And the Capitol Hill liberals' ideas of health care are expensive and coercive.

And some Democratic leaders promote a plan they call "play or pay." It's a mandated benefit scheme whose costs would be virtually unmanageable. And then there's another favorite Democratic plan: It's to make the Federal Government the monopoly provider of national health insurance. And if you think socialized medicine is a good idea, ask a Canadian for a second opinion. Because central planners ration their health care, Canadians often must wait weeks or months for treatments readily available to Americans.

And like my agenda for literally revolutionizing our schools, my health care reform package emphasizes consumer choice. It promotes private sector competition. It promotes innovation. Transferable credits and tax deductions would enable virtually every American to purchase basic health insurance. We would change the law to assure that no one is denied coverage for a preexisting condition or because of a job change. And in many cases, providing basic health insurance will help us drive down costs. And right now, for instance, poor people who lack insurance often go to emergency rooms for nonemergency treatment. Well, with health insurance, these kind of cases would be handled in family doctors' offices more effectively and for much less cost. New efficiencies such as this would enable us to reform our health care system without having to raise taxes on the overtaxed American people.

Another institution that we've been trying to change—and now that we've taken the case to the American people maybe we'll have a chance to get it changed—one that's ripe for reform, is our legal system. We have become the most litigious society on Earth. We have 3 times as many lawyers per capita as Great Britain, 5 times as many as France. And I'm often asked, if an apple a day keeps the doctor away, what works for lawyers? [*Laughter*] Litigation costs, liability insurance costs, and other costs associated with litigation or the avoidance of litigation are estimated to run as high as $300 billion a year. And that is an indirect tax on every business transaction in America, and it siphons off more than 2.5 percent of our gross national product. And that's 5 times as high as the average in other nations.

And it's high time, then, we spent more time reaching out our hand and helping each other and less time suing each other. And that is why I have asked the Congress to pass my "Access to Justice Act," a reform bill to encourage people to resolve problems out of court and to crack down on frivolous lawsuits by making losers in certain cases, not all, but in certain cases, pay more court costs. And it's time for action to stop the epidemic of lawsuits. And we need some changes in Congress to get an up-or-down vote on this important reform program.

And now, if we're to reform education and health care and our legal system and if we're to reduce redtape and regulation and get our horrendous Federal deficit down, we must reform the United States Congress. And our congressional system is simply not working. And over the years we've all seen the symptoms: gridlock on important legislation; unconscionable delays on nominations; failure to modernize our banking laws, to reform our system, financial system; failure to strengthen our anticrime laws that would support the police, have a little more compassion for the victims of crime and a little less for the criminals themselves; failure to pass fair and simple proposals to stimulate our economy. I still have seven laserlike proposals that would stimulate the economy without increasing this deficit.

Major reforms are in order. And it's time for the Congress to govern itself by the laws it imposes on others. And I am going to fight to make them now pass laws that will put them under the same laws that you and I have to live by, laws they've exempted themselves from. No more special treatment. And it's time for sweeping reform of campaign financing, time to eliminate the special interest PAC's. It's time for real spending reform; time for the President to have what 43 Governors have, the line-item veto. And I'm going to take that case to the American people this fall.

And it's time to make Congress a citizen assembly, not a club for careerists. And it's time to limit the terms of Congress. My term is limited to two terms, and I want to serve both of them—[*laughter*]—but nevertheless, it's limited to two terms, and I don't see that it would hurt to have Congress limited to six terms for a Member of the House and two terms for a Senator. I think it would be good. I think it would keep Government more active and vital and closer to the people.

In my second and final term as President, I want to lead America in adopting each of these historic reforms, these changes. I'm also working to lead America to new success in the global economy. We're working to open markets to American products, to create new jobs for the great American worker. And if we succeed with the current round of world trade talks, the GATT talks, world output could increase by $5 trillion over the next decade, and more than $1 trillion of that boom will go to the United States of America. Now, this applies no less to Michigan than to the rest of the Nation. With the open markets and the level playing field that I'm fighting to achieve, I am confident that American workers can outperform, outproduce, outcompete anyone, anywhere in the world.

I was commenting to John Engler as we flew in here this afternoon that Detroit will always be a special place for me. It was here 12 years ago that Ronald Reagan and I accepted our nomination for President and Vice President. And it was here that Ronald Reagan reminded us of Tom Paine's revolutionary words: "We have it in our power to begin the world over again."

Think how much we have accomplished since then. Think of our blessings. With God's help and with hard work to support our convictions, we've helped change the world. We've helped the peoples of Eastern Europe and the old Soviet empire peacefully throw off the yoke of communism. And today we're aiding their transition to free markets, helping them reduce their nuclear arsenals. And we stood up against dictators and exporters of totalitarian revolution in Latin America, and we've helped democracy take root in nearly every country of our hemisphere.

When a ruthless tyrant overran Kuwait and threatened to engulf the Middle East in its worst conflagration, we protected the people of Israel and Turkey and Saudi Arabia. And we organized an unprecedented world coalition, and we liberated Kuwait from the aggressor. And in the process we accomplished a breakthrough sought by every President from Truman to Reagan. We brought Arab neighbors face to face with Israel for the first time at the peace table.

And we won the cold war and we stopped Saddam's aggression because, 12 years ago, we renewed our faith in our values and we strengthened our defenses. The United States is now the undisputed leader of the entire world. And we will keep ourselves strong. And we will stay engaged in world politics. This is no time to pull back and to retreat and to be afraid of the changes in the world. In world security and in world markets, we will remain engaged.

And we have a mission together to carry on the American dream for new generations. And with your help and with grassroots action, we can win a mandate to lead this country for 4 more years. And we can keep our country open to the contributions of immigrants, of trade, of ideas. And we can work together and win our plans to reform our schools, our health care system, our very system of Government. And we can assure that when we reach the new century, America still will be the strongest, the bravest, the freest Nation on the face of the Earth.

Thank you all. And may God bless each and every one of you and our great country, the United States of America. Thank you very much.

*Note: The President spoke at 7:55 p.m. at the Ritz-Carlton Hotel. In his remarks, he referred to Max Fisher, Bush-Quayle '92 honorary dinner chairman; Heinz Prechter, national finance cochairman; Dave Doyle, Michigan Republican Party chairman; Chuck Yob, Michigan Republican national committeeman; Tim Leuliette, Bush-Quayle Michigan finance chairman; and Robert Teeter, Bush-Quayle campaign chairman.*

## Remarks Congratulating the National Collegiate Athletic Association Men's and Women's Basketball Champions
*April 15, 1992*

Well, we're just delighted to have you all here in the Rose Garden. And may I salute our basketball-playing, basketball-loving Vice President. We didn't ask him about the Indiana game, but—[*laughter*]. And may I welcome Coach Mike Krzyzewski, Coach K we call him, the Blue Devils players and staff. And of course, Coach Tara VanDerveer over here, the Cardinal and all the members; and single out our Cabinet mate, mine, Carla Hills, who's here. She was on Stanford's tennis team. Little short for basketball but—[*laughter*]—plenty tough in trade negotiations. So, we're glad she's here. And then of course, a new addition to our administration who is working in the antidrug program, this new and, I think, very exciting "Weed and Seed" program, Digger Phelps, who some of you may remember. Digger, welcome back.

And also we have here, and I saw some of you all signing autographs and meeting them, the champions from H.D. Woodson and from Forestville High Schools. Where are you guys? All right, there they go. These guys all look forward to the visits of the champions to the Rose Garden. But we have the Boys and Girls Clubs of Washington. Now, where are you all? Well, maybe we don't have them—there they are. There are some of the guys there. Good to see you.

Well, last year Duke was here, and then Stanford in 1990. We have to stop meeting like this. [*Laughter*] People are getting concerned that there's a monopoly going out here in our country. But thank you for joining us to celebrate, once more, that championship season.

A sports figure noted for malapropisms once said of a losing streak, "Those games were beyond my apprehension." [*Laughter*] Well, today we've got two teams whose winning streak tested the comprehension of basketball fans everywhere. Take, for example, Stanford University, again the NCAA women's champions. This year the Cardinal won 30 games and their fourth straight

PAC–10 title. Then they upset Virginia and then beat Western Kentucky to win the championship. No wonder Tara and I are becoming old friends. She may be the best court strategist since Perry Mason. [*Laughter*]

Now, consider first, as evidence, Stanford's all-everything center, Val Whiting. Now, where's Val? Way down on the—there she is. And some of you may not know this, she's studying to be a doctor. She scored 28 points in the Cardinal's thrilling semifinal victory, grabbed 13 rebounds in the final, made the All-Tournament Team.

Her teammate Molly Goodenbour, over here, number 4, right there, majoring in psychology, and why not? [*Laughter*] All season she made opponents shake their heads. Her "Molly rules" helped set an NCAA tourney record for the most 3-point field goals, with 18, and a single-game record for the most 3-point field goals with 6. There's always enthusiasm here in Washington for someone with a good three-point program—[*laughter*]—especially in an election year.

Now, this season Academic Third Team All-American Chris MacMurdo scored points on the court and in the classroom, setting a great example. I want to note Ann Adkins, the only senior on the team; Christy Hedgpeth, excelling outside; and Rachel Hemmer, the PAC–10 Freshman of the Year, prevailing under the boards. Then there's Kelly Dougherty, right here, always at her best in March; and walk-on Kate Paye, way down at the end; and Anita Kaplan, in the middle, perhaps Stanford's top reserve; and Angela Taylor, way, way down there someplace, Angela. I won't say what kind of reputation Angela has for her skills on defense, but they want to talk to her, Cheney does—[*laughter*]—over at the Pentagon.

This brings me to today's other guests. As my predecessor might have said, "There you go again." [*Laughter*] A year ago I said you showed that nice guys can finish first.

This season you struck again: Atlantic Coast Conference record, 14–2, the overall record, 34–2, champions of the ACC regular season and tournament; then, the first team since UCLA in 1973 and first ACC team to win back-to-back NCAA titles. Duke and I have something in common. Both of us like the word "repeat." [*Laughter*]

Here's what we'll recall about their 1992 "stairway to heaven." First, one Christian that the lions would be afraid to take on. [*Laughter*] Listen to this box score: a record 23d tournament game, the first player ever to start in four straight Final Fours. His perfect game against Kentucky, including that amazing last-second shot that everybody that watched TV will remember all the rest of their lives. We salute Christian Laettner, a true Player of the Year. Welcome back.

And then of course, we'll remember Bobby Hurley's wizardry on the court. You know, to Bobby, basketball is a family affair. His dad coached him in high school. He guarded his brother in this year's regional semifinals. And this year Bobby made America Duke's family. Think of how he became Duke's career assist leader and NCAA Final Four MVP; or Bobby's amazing record in NCAA tournament play, 17–1. It's players like Bobby who helped Coach K, a graduate of West Point, do to opponents on the court which General Schwarzkopf did to his on the field of battle. Welcome back, Bobby.

Finally there are other players who helped the Blue Devils slam-dunk the opponents: Brian Davis, of nearby Capitol Heights, Maryland, he didn't have far to go; Grant Hill, another near-in guy from Reston, Virginia, who threw the pass against Kentucky; Thomas Hill, Duke's superb second-leading scorer; Ron Burt and Marty Clark, who grew up with six basketball-playing sisters. Marty, sounds like a typical weekend with my grandkids around this place. [*Laughter*] And all the Devils who helped Coach K, Duke's Special K, make basketball history.

This year, Duke became only the fourth school to gain its third straight NCAA championship game. Stanford's in the same league, three straight appearances in the Final Four. There's a word for that: consistency. And there's another word for that:

excellence. They are words which embody you as student athletes.

Both of these champions—and this is a very important point for the kids from the high schools here and the Boys and Girls Clubs here today—both of these champions have high academic standards. Each recruits aggressively, but honestly because neither bends the rules, because both play within the rules. A prediction: You players will make an even greater difference after graduation than before.

A Chinese scholar once wrote of "the great end of learning." Well, learning is a great end with either a book or basketball. That's why over the past decade more than 90 percent of Duke and Stanford players got their diplomas, rivaling the general graduation rates of their outstanding institutions.

Already, you've been missionaries for educational excellence. You've shown how a nation that is physically fit and educationally fit is fit to take on the world. So today, I ask you to carry that zeal to our educational systems at all levels, to your careers, and to the dream we call America. You stand here as examples of how will and heart can stir the human spirit.

So again, I am delighted to be out here. The Vice President's delighted to be with me to congratulate as fans, to thank you for showing how education is our most enduring legacy, vital to all that we are and all we can become.

So good luck. And may God bless you all. And now here's the drill. Last year we had a shoot-out by these, and another substitute team was here last year but—[*laughter*]. So after you all have a chance to visit a little bit and say hello, I'm going to invite the players down, and we will have a shoot-out, a White House shoot-out to see who wins our little trophy this year. The trophy is very modest, but we need these guys back. And we welcome the Cardinal to the White House court for a very, very brief appearance down there.

Now, thank you all very much.

*Note: The President spoke at 10:19 a.m. in the Rose Garden at the White House.*

## Message on the Observance of Passover
*April 15, 1992*

Beginning on the evening of April 17, Jews around the Nation and throughout the world will observe Passover, the traditional celebration of the Israelites' Exodus from Egypt. In the Jewish calendar, this holiday is also known as the Feast of the Unleavened Bread and the Festival of Spring. During Passover, a people who have all too often known oppression and persecution will reaffirm their faith in the Divine Judge, who brought them out of Egypt and delivered them from slavery. Passover is, in the words of the kiddush which Jews recite as they drink each of the four cups of Passover wine, "a time of freedom." This Passover comes at an especially precious moment in Jewish history. Since Jewish families and friends last gathered around the seder table a year ago, we have all rejoiced at the modern exodus of Jews from Ethiopia and the former Soviet Union to Israel. We have also triumphed in the repeal of United Nations General Assembly Resolution 3379, that infamous declaration, which wrongly equated Zionism with racism. We celebrat-

ed together the defeat of Iraqi aggression, a modern day threat to Israel and the entire Middle East. Finally, we began a process that for the first time in history brought together Israel and all of her neighbors to make peace.

The most well known portion of the Passover Hagaddah is the "Ma Nish'tana"—the four questions asked by the youngest child in the family about why this night is different from all others. This year the answers are especially vivid. Today, more people live in freedom than ever before. In the last few years, we have witnessed the liberation of millions of people from the political and ideological oppression under which they lived. As we stand united today in freedom, we have an unprecedented opportunity to move forward toward our goal of a more humane and peaceful world.

Barbara and I extend our best wishes to members of the Jewish community for a joyous Passover.

GEORGE BUSH

## Statement by Press Secretary Fitzwater on the President's Federal Income Tax Return
*April 15, 1992*

The President and Mrs. Bush paid $204,841 in Federal income taxes in 1991.

They donated $789,176 in income (minus taxes) from "Millie's Book" to the Barbara Bush Literary Foundation. The total royalty income (including taxes paid) was $889,176, bringing their adjusted gross income to $1,324,456.

In addition to the President's salary of $200,000, the Bushes reported $197,047 in income from their blind trust, $1,151 in interest income, and $1,359 from other sources. A net long-term capital gain of $49,669 was reported from the blind trust, less a short-term capital loss carryover from the prior year of $8,822. The blind trust is

managed by Bessemer Trust Co., N.A., New York City.

The President and Mrs. Bush made total charitable contributions in 1991 of $818,803. Of this amount, $818,126 was given by them individually to 48 charities and $677 was given to charities through the blind trust. Because Federal tax law allows a deduction of up to 50 percent of adjusted gross income, their charitable deduction was limited to $662,228. This produced a contribution carryover of $156,575, which will be available for use in their 1992 tax return. A list of the 48 charities is included in the tax return.

The President's and Mrs. Bush's tax

return has been reviewed by the Office of Government Ethics and will be filed in the Philadelphia Regional Office of the Internal Revenue Service.

# Nomination of G. Kim Wincup To Be an Assistant Secretary of the Air Force
*April 15, 1992*

The President today announced his intention to nominate G. Kim Wincup, of Maryland, to be an Assistant Secretary of the Air Force for Acquisition, Research, and Development. He would succeed John J. Welch, Jr.

Since 1989, Mr. Wincup has served as Assistant Secretary of the Army for Manpower and Reserve Affairs at the U.S. Department of Defense. From 1984 to 1989, he served as staff director of the House Armed Services Committee in Washington, DC.

Mr. Wincup graduated from DePauw University (B.A., 1966) and the University of Illinois (J.D., 1969). He was born September 6, 1944, in St. Louis, MO. Mr. Wincup served in the U.S. Air Force, 1970–73. He is married, has three children, and resides in Bethesda, MD.

# Nomination of James P. Covey To Be an Assistant Secretary of State
*April 15, 1992*

The President today announced his intention to nominate James P. Covey, of the District of Columbia, to be Assistant Secretary of State for South Asian Affairs. This is a new position.

Since 1989, Mr. Covey has served as Principal Deputy Assistant Secretary for Near Eastern and South Asian Affairs at the U.S. Department of State in Washington, DC. Prior to this, he served as Deputy Chief of Mission at the U.S. Embassy in Cairo, Egypt, 1986–89; as Special Assistant to the President and Senior Director for Near Eastern and South Asian Affairs for the National Security Council in Washington, DC, 1985–86; as Deputy Executive Secretary at the U.S. Department of State, 1983–85; and as Deputy Principal Officer at the U.S. Consulate General in Jerusalem, Israel, 1980–83.

Mr. Covey graduated from St. Lawrence University (B.A., 1965). He was born March 7, 1944, in Middletown, CT. Mr. Covey served in the U.S. Army, 1965–69. He is married, has children, and resides in Washington, DC.

# Statement by Press Secretary Fitzwater on Restrictions on Air Traffic To or From Libya
*April 15, 1992*

The President has signed an Executive order taking effect at 11:59 p.m. today to implement U.N. Security Council Resolution 748 by imposing additional sanctions on Libya. The Executive order bars any aircraft from landing in, taking off from, or overflying the United States as part of or a continuation of a flight to or from Libya. This prohibition covers legs or continuations of flights as well as direct flights. The Secretary of the Treasury, in consultation with the Secretary of Transportation and other Cabinet and senior administration officials, has primary responsibility for implementing this new ban.

This prohibition is in addition to the comprehensive embargo on U.S. exports to and imports from Libya adopted pursuant to Executive Order No. 12543, January 7, 1986. Taken together with the preexisting embargo, today's Executive order puts the United States in full compliance with U.N. Security Council Resolution 748.

*Note: The Executive order is listed in Appendix E at the end of this volume.*

# Letter to Congressional Leaders Reporting on Restrictions on Air Traffic To or From Libya
*April 16, 1992*

*Dear Mr. Speaker: (Dear Mr. President:)*

I have issued an Executive order (copy enclosed) entitled "Barring Overflight, Takeoff, and Landing of Aircraft Flying to or from Libya," pursuant to my authority under the Constitution and the laws of the United States of America, including the International Emergency Economic Powers Act, as amended (50 U.S.C. 1701, *et seq.*), the National Emergencies Act (50 U.S.C. 1601, *et seq.*), section 1114 of the Federal Aviation Act of 1958, as amended (49 U.S.C. App. 1514), section 5 of the United Nations Participation Act of 1945, as amended (22 U.S.C. 287c), and section 301 of title 3 of the United States Code. I am taking this action in implementation of United Nations Security Council Resolution No. 748 of March 31, 1992, and in order to take additional steps pursuant to the national emergency declared in Executive Order No. 12543 of January 7, 1986, in consequence of Libya's refusal to hand over the two men indicted in the explosion of Pan Am Flight 103 over Lockerbie, Scotland, and Libya's continued support for international terrorism. This report is being provided pursuant to section 401(b) of the National Emergencies Act (50 U.S.C. 1641(b)).

Security Council Resolution No. 748 imposes mandatory, multilateral sanctions by member states against Libya, effective April 15, 1992, if certain conditions are not met. Because the United States already maintains a comprehensive embargo against Libya pursuant to Executive Orders Nos. 12543 and 12544, implemented in the Libyan Sanctions Regulations, 31 C.F.R. Part 550, the only provision in Resolution No. 748 requiring implementation in the United States is that containing restrictions on aircraft en route to or from Libya. The Executive order provides that no aircraft may "take off from, land in, or overfly the United States, if the aircraft, as part of the same flight or as a continuation of that flight, is destined to land in or has taken off from the territory of Libya."

U.S. sanctions already cover other measures called for in Resolution No. 748, including its prohibitions on the supply of aircraft and aircraft components; the engineering or maintenance servicing of Libyan aircraft or aircraft components; the certification of airworthiness for Libyan aircraft; the insuring of, or payment of new insurance claims relating to Libyan aircraft; the provision of arms and related materials; the granting of licensing arrangements for the manufacture, maintenance, or production of, or maintenance technology for, arms and related material; and the furnishing of military advisory services. Resolution No. 748 also calls on governments to reduce the number and level of Libyan diplomats in their territory; prevent the operation of Libyan Arab Airlines offices; and deny entry to or expel Libyan nationals who have been denied entry to or expelled from other countries for involvement in terrorist activities.

I have sent the enclosed order fully implementing Resolution No. 748 to the *Federal Register* for publication.

Sincerely,

GEORGE BUSH

*Note: Identical letters were sent to Thomas*

*S. Foley, Speaker of the House of Representatives, and Dan Quayle, President of the Senate. The Executive order is listed in Appendix E at the end of this volume.*

# Remarks to the Lehigh Valley 2000 Community in Allentown, Pennsylvania
*April 16, 1992*

My fellow president, thank you very, very much. [*Laughter*] This is a nonpolitical appearance, if there is any such thing in a strange political year. But let me just say this: I'm very glad that Hilda is not running for President this year. [*Laughter*] And thank you for your introduction.

And may I congratulate all six of these guys that spelled out the six educational goals, reminding us of what our national goals are. And I asked one of them if he was nervous. He shook me off, said no. I don't believe him, but—[*laughter*]—they did a first-class job, all of them, every one of them.

And may I pay my respects to our very able Secretary of Education, Lamar Alexander, former Governor, now challenging this country with America 2000 and doing a superb job for all the American people; and at my side in the United States Congress, caring deeply about education, telling me over and over again about the changes and the wonder that's taking place right here in the valley, Don Ritter, your Congressman. He's doing a first-class job in Washington.

May I salute Mayors Daddona and Smith, the Mayor of Allentown and the Mayor of Bethlehem, and of course, pay my respect to Ed Donley, a driving force behind Lehigh Valley 2000 and cochair of Pennsylvania 2000. And my respect also to she who led us in the pledge, Ann Snyder, the valedictorian of the class of '92. Ann, thank you; our guests who did such a great job with the goals; Mike Meilinger, the principal, and I thank him for calling this special assembly today and getting a lot of you out of class. You ought to be grateful to him. My special thanks to the parents and the teachers and the staff. Thanks also to all the folks

here from Allentown and Easton and Bethlehem, the leading lights of Lehigh Valley. Last but not least, let me say hello to the students of Dieruff High, with special thanks to the band. It was first-class music. Thank you all very, very much.

I don't know who is in charge of signs around this place, but they did a first-class job, all through the building and everyplace else. And it's astonishing to be here with the class of '92 as a graduate of the class of '42. I realize the world I thought of as new, for you, well, it's history. But look now at the world you'll soon call your own, at the pace of change that we've come to expect. Each day we see history played out in the headlines, literally. Old empires expire; new worlds are born. In the past 6 months alone, 6 months, we've seen the birth of 18 new nations. Who knows how many there will be by the time you take your big geography final a few weeks from now.

But the challenges we face, the sheer complexity of our world, cannot obscure the basic values that guide this Nation. Times change; but truths, fundamental truths, endure. I'm talking about the big issues that shape our world, about the values close to home. Everything I've tried to do and done to preserve and advance three precious legacies: strong families, good jobs, and a world at peace. These are my goals. They should be all of ours. Securing those legacies has been my mission as President, and it's going to be my mission today and every day as long as I am President of the United States.

You know, right now here in Allentown and across America, the number one concern is the economy. Turning this economy around, creating jobs is the mission that

609

matters most. Listen to what people say about the economy. Get beneath the cold statistics; get down to the real heart of this issue. People want to know whether they can keep the job they've got and whether they're on track for a better one. For their kids, for each one of the students here today, parents have got grander visions, great hopes: Not just a job, a career; work that means more than simply making ends meet; work that gives real meaning to your life.

People have a right to ask, "What is Government's role in all of this?" No, we can't legislate the American dream. But Government can serve as a catalyst for change, clearing away the obstacles to economic growth and the unnecessary costs of doing business, expanding the opportunities for aggressive businesses, for enterprising individuals to create new jobs, training and educating our children, giving you the tools of thought you'll need to compete in this new, exciting world economy.

The fate of America's economic future rests on five key reforms:

Free and fair trade, our ability to break down barriers, open new markets to American goods;

Our future rests on legal reform, on ending the explosion of litigation that strains our patience and saps our economy. We're suing each other too much. We ought to be helping each other more;

On health care reform, opening up access to all Americans, controlling the runaway cost of health care without sacrificing choice and without sacrificing the best quality health care in the entire world;

And then on Government reform, because only if we reverse a generation of creeping bureaucracy and only if we restore limits to Government can we restore public trust;

Finally, the reason I've come here to the valley today: Our future depends on education reform, on our ability to revolutionize, literally reinvent our schools, to take that revolution beyond the four walls of the classroom, transform our attitudes and ideas, the way we think about education.

And I wish every adult and every kid could have been with me a few minutes ago as some of the leaders, business and education leaders assembled, civic leaders, to tell me about this exciting change taking place right here in Lehigh Valley.

Education, it represents a perfect community of interest between the individual and society, between one generation and the next, between the proud history we must pass on and the path-breaking future we must create. And in terms of America's economic future, education is nothing less than a matter of economic survival. It's just this simple: Better schools mean better jobs.

You've seen the news stories. You've heard the statistics. Anyone who worries about slack productivity or a bad balance of trade ought to be alarmed about the test scores. Millions of students work hard; millions of dedicated teachers, doing their very best; and still, in one test after another, America's children score at or near the bottom ranks of international achievement. We don't need another test to tell us something is wrong with the state of American education. For the sake of every student here today, we've got to shake off any sense of complacency; we've got to shake up the status quo.

Now, in a sense, I'm preaching to the choir because here in Lehigh Valley that's a lesson you learned long ago, years ago. But you didn't wait for word from Washington, DC. You didn't stand back and watch another generation of kids get less education than they deserved. This community took a direct interest in what was going on in the classroom. This community came together. This community took action.

I took office determined to put the power of the Presidency behind change. More than 2 years ago, we took a strong first step. Working together with the Nation's Governors, Democrat and Republican alike, we set six ambitious goals for the year 2000. It never had been done before. Every American child must start school ready to learn. We must raise the high school graduation rate to 90 percent. We must put in place a system of world-class standards and tests to measure students' progress. We must be first in the world in math and science. By the year 2000, every American adult must be literate, and every American school must be free of drugs, free from the violence that today too often follows our kids into the classroom. Let me sum up the six goals this way: Together, by the year 2000, we must create the best schools in the world for our children.

Let me share a story that our Secretary, Lamar, told me about a little girl, a fourth grader named Ariane Williams. At the kick-off for New Orleans 2000 down in Louisiana, she stood up, and here's what she said, "These goals are not just the President's goals. They're not just the Governor's goals. They are the Nation's goals." That little girl got the message, and so do you here in this valley. Goals define the mission. They tell us where we want to go, not how to get there.

That's why, as I was reminded at this meeting I told you about, nearly one year ago today, I mapped out a strategy I call America 2000, a plan to revolutionize American education. Then I heard the progress that had been made before that even began, to break the mold and, for the sake of our children, put an end to business-as-usual. Two days from now, we're going to mark the first anniversary of America 2000. Let me share with you today a kind of report card, if you will, on what we've accomplished. In one year's time, we've seen America 2000 literally catch fire all across this country. Already, 43 States and more than 1,000 communities, from Grand Junction, Colorado, to Lewiston, Maine, have joined the America 2000 crusade. Everywhere, people like you are working to break down the barriers between the classroom and the community, to spark a grassroots revolution to reinvent, not just rework but to literally reinvent the American school. But you know that story because, once again, Lehigh Valley has led the way.

I want to share with you an old African proverb that's the motto of Minnesota 2000, "It takes an entire village to educate one child." And that is what it takes because education doesn't just happen in the classroom. It doesn't start at 8:20 each morning and end at 5 of 3. All of us lead busy lives, but we must never be too busy to read to our kids. And if I might ad lib something in here, I am very, very proud of Barbara Bush for setting an example about how families ought to stay together and how families

ought to read to their kids. Parents ought to read to their kids.

And we must never be too busy to teach them right from wrong, to take an interest in the things that they worry about and wonder at, and to listen, really listen to what they say. We owe it to our children and to ourselves to see that we live in communities that care about education, communities where learning can happen.

You've got every right to ask, "What can Washington do to help?" Well, here's one way we can. Today, I want to announce a new legislative initiative that I call the "lifetime education and training account," a package of grants and line of credit worth $25,000 to every eligible American to further their education or acquire new job skills to make the most of their abilities. I've said before if we want to compete in the 21st century, we've got to become a Nation of students. To do that, we've got to take a new approach to the old notions of student aid. Think of the working mother, balancing her responsibility for her family and her job against her own hopes for the future. She'd take one college course at a time, but she doesn't qualify right now for the grant or loan that would help pay tuition. Our "lifetime education and training account" would help her get back into the classroom. Here's the message for the students here today and for their parents: Education doesn't end with graduation; learning has got to be a lifelong pursuit.

I came to Lehigh, to one of the first communities to join the America 2000 crusade, to set the agenda for the second year of America 2000. Our next step forward depends on our success in building a consensus for change around four core ideas, four ways to build on what we've begun, to transform the Federal Government into a catalyst for real education reform. First, if we're serious about reaching our goals, we must set world-class standards in five core subjects and establish a series of voluntary American achievement tests to measure our children's progress.

Second, we've got to grant States and local school districts relief from Federal rules and regulations that limit their ability to improve educational achievement and do nothing to help us meet our national education goals. And parenthetically, I'm told by the leaders I met with today that the Governor of this State has granted such regulatory flexibility and regulatory relief to this community effort here. Our teachers and our principals deserve flexibility, freedom to use their frontline experience on what works best in their schools to meet these national goals. Has anyone asked the teachers here today, "How can we ask you to teach and then tie your hands?"

Third, we've got to launch a wide-open effort to create thousands of new American schools, starting with at least one in every congressional district all across the United States. Right here in Lehigh Valley, you're hard at work on your plan to make this community home to its own new American school. I heard the exciting proposals on that today. These break-the-mold schools won't conform to any one blueprint. Some may make a quantum leap forward into tomorrow's technologies. Others might seek to reach the future by restoring older traditions, the discipline and disciplines of an earlier era. Each one of these schools would be a living example of how we can reinvent American education. All we need now from Congress is the seed money to help people like you translate ideas into action.

Fourth, we must create an incentive to improve education by promoting school choice. For far too long, we've shielded our schools from competition, allowed the system a damaging monopoly power over students. Well, just as monopolies are bad for the economy, they're bad for our kids. Every parent should have the power to choose which school is best for his child, public, private, or religious.

Look at our colleges; look at America's colleges; look at the students. Our university system is the envy of the world. Each year, we make over $20 billion in Federal grants and loans directly to students, one of every two students enrolled in college right now, to use at the university of their choice. No one asks whether they enroll at Penn State or Pennsylvania University or Villanova or Lehigh or Lafayette. It's time we make the same choice available to all parents from the moment their children go to school. Whether it's the public school on your street or the one across town, whether it's private, parochial, yeshiva, or Bible school, let parents, not the Government, make that choice.

And let's be clear. If we deny parents school choice, if we deny that choice, let's recognize who's hurt worst by the status quo. It's not the well-to-do. It's not the rich guy. It's not the upper-middle class. It's not any one of us who ever went house-hunting with a map of the good school districts. Deny people school choice, and the ones you hurt most are the middle class and lower and especially the poor.

That's why choice is catching on in some of the hardest hit neighborhoods in this Nation. Talk to parents that are spearheading the school choice crusade, people like now-famous Polly Williams in Milwaukee. They'll tell you how the lack of choice left them powerless to force change and how a public school bureaucracy turned students into statistics and parents into pawns. Look at Milwaukee today, pioneering school choice, giving poor parents control and poor children a sense of pride. Look at the schools closer to home, East Harlem, where teachers put their names on waiting lists to get a chance to teach in a choice school. They can't wait to stand in front of a classroom of children who want to be there, who want to learn.

Choice works, and here's why. When our students are a captive audience, our schools have no incentive to improve. Say what you want about reforming our schools, if you're for change, you are for school choice. These four ideas are generating interest and enthusiasm among Governors and mayors, Democrats, Republicans, liberals, conservatives; among business leaders, Ed Donley right here and the Allentown-Lehigh County Chamber of Commerce to the Fortune 500; among teachers and students and parents and principals, everyone at every level who understands the need for change.

Everyone, that is, except the leaders of the United States Congress. At a moment when the consensus for change seems to be reaching critical mass, on Capitol Hill you can watch the last stand of the status quo. Forces there are waging a last-ditch effort to put the brakes on change, to preserve the business-as-usual approach that brought us the present crisis in education. The mindset up on Capitol Hill reminds me of a letter I got the other day from an elementary school student, a little girl named Haruka Abe. "I like," she says, "when my teacher reads my class some books because everybody gets sleepy." [*Laughter*] Well, it reminds me of Capitol Hill and the way they're approaching change. Take a look at the bill that's now winding its way through the Congress, the tired old ideas, tried and failed, that it wants to substitute for the four path-breaking ideas I mentioned a moment ago.

As part of America 2000, we asked Congress for authority to help develop world-class standards and American achievement tests, tools that would help us measure our students' progress, help families understand where their kids might stand, and assess the return we're getting for our education dollars. And the status quo crowd up there on Capitol Hill said "slow down" to testing and standards. I asked Congress for funds for this new American schools. Congress said no, no to even funding one percent, 535 of 50,000 new American schools that this Nation needs. They want to funnel more Federal dollars into these existing mandated business-as-usual State bureaucracies, the very same bureaucracies that put us where we are today. And we asked the Congress for flexibility for teachers, flexibility for principals. And Congress said, "No, let's stick to the status quo." And finally, we asked the Congress to fund pilot programs to promote school choice, programs to help poor families in six American cities. And Congress said no to school choice.

So today, let me just serve notice on the lobby, on the education lobby and their friends back on Capitol Hill: One year ago, I asked you to join with me in a revolution, a revolution to be part of America 2000. The time has come to get on board or get out of the way and stay behind. No more business as usual. Congress can drag its feet, but it cannot stop change.

Lehigh Valley is living proof of the words of the great Abraham Lincoln, "Revolutions do not go backward." There's a time early in every revolution when the status quo looks steady and strong and the forces that challenge it weak and without effect. And there's the moment when the forces of change carry the day; the bankruptcy of the status quo stands revealed, and the whole hollow house of cards collapses.

The revolution in American education is already underway. In Lehigh Valley and in communities all across America, the old ways are being pushed aside. They're being abandoned; new ideas, advanced. This revolution will triumph for the simplest and the strongest of reasons, because American parents want the best for their children and also because there isn't a single child anywhere in the United States of America who doesn't deserve the best education possible.

From our schools to our courts, from our hospitals to the halls of Government, from the neighborhoods outside our door to the realities of the new world economy, the need for reform won't wait. The only acceptable response is the American response. We must rekindle a revolution, a revolution to bring change to the country that's changed the world. The American people have made their choice. The American people want change. And you here in Lehigh Valley can proudly say, "We are out front for fundamental, constructive change."

Thank you all for this wonderful day of learning, this warm welcome. Any may God bless the United States of America. Thank you very much.

*Note: The President spoke at 12:35 p.m. at Dieruff High School. In his remarks, he referred to Hilda Rivas, the school's senior class president.*

## Nomination of Roger A. McGuire To Be United States Ambassador to Guinea-Bissau
*April 16, 1992*

The President today announced his intention to nominate Roger A. McGuire, of Ohio, a career member of the Senior Foreign Service, class of Counselor, to be Ambassador Extraordinary and Plenipotentiary of the United States of America to the Republic of Guinea-Bissau. He would succeed William H. Jacobsen, Jr.

Currently Mr. McGuire serves as Principal Officer at the American Consulate in Porto Alegre, Brazil. Prior to this, he served as Chargé d'Affaires at the American Embassy in Windhoek, Namibia, 1990; Director of the U.S. Liaison Office in Windhoek, Namibia, 1989–90; and Deputy Examiner of the Board of Examiners of the Foreign Service, 1988–90. In addition, he served as Deputy Director of the Office of West African Affairs at the U.S. Department of State, 1986–88; and Political Officer at the American Embassy in Lusaka, Zambia, 1983–86.

Mr. McGuire graduated from Beloit College (B.A., 1965) and the University of Wisconsin (M.A., 1967). He was born July 1, 1943, in Troy, OH. Mr. McGuire is married, has two children, and resides in Brazil.

## Radio Address to the Nation on Job Training 2000
*April 18, 1992*

This past week I spent some time in the town of Fraser, Michigan. I met with workers at a major machine tool factory and talked with them and local business leaders about a program I call Job Training 2000. Thursday, I was in Allentown, Pennsylvania, in the Lehigh Valley, one of the first communities to take up our America 2000 crusade to revolutionize this Nation's schools.

In Michigan and in Pennsylvania, I announced specific proposals, legislative initiatives aimed at helping people with two of the real building blocks of opportunity: advancing their education and sharpening their job skills. If acted on by Congress, these initiatives will make a real impact on the way people live, not just in Fraser and in Allentown but all across America.

Let me start with a concept I call the "lifetime education and training account," a package of grants and a line of credit worth $25,000 to every eligible American to use to further their education or acquire new job skills to make the most of their abilities. It's a new way of thinking about an old idea known as student aid. And it's based on this simple fact: Education does not end with graduation.

How will this lifetime education account help real families? Think of a single mother struggling to balance her responsibility for her family and for her job against her own hopes for the future. Her dream is to set aside one night a week and take one college course at a time. But money's tight, and under present Federal rules as a part-time student she doesn't qualify for the grant or loan that would help pay tuition. That just doesn't make sense. Here's a woman willing to work hard to better herself, stopped short by a program that works against her. With our lifetime line of credit, all that would change. The woman would be able to go to school, bring that distant dream another day closer. When Government can help people help themselves, that's the kind of Government we need.

And the other proposal I announced was a new apprenticeship initiative, a companion program to our Job Training 2000. To see what kind of difference this initiative can make, take that same family, the working mother I mentioned earlier, this time with a 17-year-old son, a senior in high school. He's made the decision that it's time for him to enter the working world, to help out by bringing home a paycheck. Right now, he faces a tough choice, juggling school and a job. He's trying to do both, and both are suffering. He doesn't want to close the door on college, but he's feeling pressure to drop out.

Our "Youth Apprentice Act" can help that young man stay in school, keep his job, and keep his options open. It will let him sit down with his school and his employer, put together a course of study and a job schedule that will keep him on track for graduation. And later on, if that young man wants to change careers or go to college, he's got a skill certificate to show future employers and a diploma that really means something.

Each one of these initiatives begins with the same question: What can Government do to open the doors of opportunity to every American? As the President, I've made it my mission to preserve and advance three legacies close to all our hearts: a world at peace, an economy with good jobs, a Nation of strong families. The initiatives I've talked about today can help Americans make those legacies their own.

Thank you for listening today. And as so many of you celebrate Passover or prepare for Easter Sunday, may God bless the United States of America.

*Note: This address was recorded at 8 a.m. on April 16 in the Cabinet Room at the White House for broadcast after 9 a.m. on April 18.*

# Statement on Actions to Support Democracy in Cuba
## *April 18, 1992*

I am strongly committed to actions that will bring rapid, peaceful, democratic change to Cuba. My administration has pursued an effective policy of economic and political isolation of the Castro regime. We urge all democratic governments to join us. No nation should help bankroll this dictatorship. Aid to the Castro regime will prolong Castro's hold on Cuba and prolong the misery and suffering of the Cuban people.

Today we are closer than ever to our goal of returning freedom to Cuba. The Russian Government has announced that economic relations with Cuba will be on a hard currency basis. Also, Russia is withdrawing the former Soviet brigade and announced that as of January 1, 1992, it was ending all subsidies to Cuba. Castro is on his own. Cuba has lost a source of economic and military aid that has totaled as much as $5 billion annually in some years. Cuban trade with the new Independent States amounts to a mere fraction of its trade with the former Soviet Union.

For the first time, the Russian Republic voted with countries from Latin America, Africa, and Asia to condemn Cuba's human rights abuses at the United Nations Human Rights Commission meeting in Geneva. Our Latin American allies rejected Cuban requests to purchase oil at less than fair market prices and have called for a democratic opening in Cuba. My administration will support free trade arrangements that benefit our sister democracies but will not accept loopholes that aid the Castro regime. The benefits of these agreements are for governments committed to freedom and democracy.

The "Cuban Democracy Act of 1992" seeks to build on the strong prodemocracy policy of my administration. I applaud such efforts and endorse the objectives of this legislation to isolate Cuba until democratic change comes to that embattled island.

I believe in and I am committed to work with the Congress this session to pass a stronger, more effective "Cuban Democracy Act," which tightens the embargo and closes any unintentional loopholes that could benefit the Castro regime while preserving the proper constitutional prerogatives of the Congress and the President.

However, as currently written, the "Cuban Democracy Act" could, without intending to do so, weaken the embargo. It could result in the transfer of millions of dollars to the Castro regime from earnings on telecommunication services between the United States and Cuba. Current regulations allow balanced and even improved phone services but restrict hard currency transfers to Cuba.

Additionally, we should continue to license donations of food and medicines to nongovernmental organizations in Cuba for the benefit of the Cuban people. But we cannot permit either the sale of medicines or the donation of food to the Castro regime itself. To do so, as the bill proposes, could directly aid the security forces of the Castro dictatorship and could contribute to the building of a biotechnology industry.

Finally, consistent with my proposal of 3 years ago, the legislation should strengthen the provision providing for civil penalty authority for the Department of the Treasury

as a weapon against embargo violators.

With the appropriate changes, I expect to be able to sign this legislation. I intend to work with the Congress to pass a strong "Cuban Democracy Act" this year.

In this spirit, I am today instructing the Treasury Department to restrict further shipping to Cuba by issuing regulations that will prohibit entry into U.S. ports of vessels that are engaged in trade with Cuba. Additionally, I am instructing Treasury to begin the process of issuing licenses to permit shipment of humanitarian package mail on the Miami/Havana air charter services. This measure will further limit Cuba's hard currency earnings.

My administration will continue to press governments around the world on the need to isolate economically the Castro regime. Together we will bring to Cuba a new era of freedom and democracy.

## Remarks at the Opening Ceremony of the AmeriFlora '92 Exposition in Columbus, Ohio
*April 20, 1992*

Well, Bob, thank you very much. Barbara and I are just delighted to be here and, of course, delighted to be with our admired and respected friend Bob Hope. May I salute our Governor, George Voinovich; the Lieutenant Governor, Mike DeWine; Senator Glenn; Mayor Lashutka of Columbus; Dorothy and Bob Teater; Dick and Pam Frank; and of course, the one you heard from earlier, Mr. John Wolfe and his wife, Ann, John having done so much for this city.

And thank you all for the privilege of attending this marvelous AmeriFlora '92, America's celebration of discovery. It's great to be back in Columbus, this wonderful city, where my dad was born and grew up.

First, I appreciate the brevity of the Bob Hope introduction. [*Laughter*] Bob was telling me about Columbus' discovery of America; we were talking a little history. He was saying that one result of Columbus' voyage was the trade that first introduced broccoli

to the Europeans. They've been our friends ever since, anyway. [*Laughter*] They remain friends, for more than ever we believe in the same ideals like liberty, free trade, and democracy. We know ours is one world, an interdependent world.

The American spirit enriches the human spirit, brave, unafraid, and above all, free. That spirit, the spirit of discovery, forged America, for Christopher Columbus believed the mariner must, in his words, "probe the secrets of the world." So, the son of a Genoese weaver took that first step in a trek that ultimately produced the United States of America.

In saluting his quincentennial, we salute how freedom's ship has sailed to every corner of the Earth. We Americans celebrate discovery because we're never satisfied, because we are ever romancing the next horizon. That is why this beautiful sculpture here in front of us reminds us of the sails of the *Niña*, *Pinta*, and the *Santa Maria*, and why, too, a full-size replica of the *Santa Maria* graces the Scioto River.

Here in the largest city in the world bearing the explorer's name, we honor Columbus for the same reason as people in Peoria or Prague. We believe that the individual can make a difference and that human dignity can, indeed, change the world. Most of all, we know that dignity stems from values like hard work and self-reliance and faith. In 1492, those values sustained Columbus' voyage. In 1992, they must sustain our voyage to do right and thus achieve good.

Today, our world is smaller, faster than in Columbus' time, our fates at home linked to those abroad. Yet we need to keep these values in our hearts and in our minds. Columbus sought a new world. The values I refer to can help create a new world order.

Already, we see the outlines of a new world economy. Over the next week I'm going to be talking about this economy and how it can grow in the decades ahead. We need, as President Nixon once said, "an open world, open cities, open hearts, open minds." Only then can we not merely trade with other nations but profit from other nations, profit economically, intellectually, culturally, and spiritually.

In Columbus' day, commerce meant gold and trinkets. In our day, commerce means the exchange of goods and ideas that foster free markets, free governments, and ultimately, freedom itself. And that is why America must always be ready to compete by investing more in research and development, investing more in new technology, investing more in education. We're Americans. Performance is our name. So, as we concede what's changed in the world, let's prove what has not changed: America can still outwork and outproduce and outcompete any nation anywhere.

I thought of our country yesterday as Barbara and I attended our little church, little Easter service there in a little tiny church in Maine. As I looked around our church, we gave thanks for all that has truly blessed America. Now, it is my pleasure to introduce someone who has blessed my life, the life of the Bush family. For 2 years she has been your honorary patron of this marvelous fair, honorary patron of AmeriFlora. She's sure been around the world, continuing Columbus' grand tradition. You might remember how Columbus arrived in America and his luggage wound up in China. [*Laughter*] But anyway, for 47 years, she's been my wife. Ladies and gentlemen, your honorary chairman, my wife, our First Lady, Barbara Bush.

*Note: The President spoke at 11:05 a.m. In his remarks, he referred to Dorothy Teater, Franklin County commissioner, and her husband, Robert; Richard M. Franks, chairman of the AmeriFlora '92 management committee, and his wife, Pamela; and John F. Wolfe, chairman of the board of trustees of AmeriFlora '92, and his wife, Ann.*

# Nomination of Dennis P. Barrett To Be United States Ambassador to Madagascar
*April 20, 1992*

The President today announced his intention to nominate Dennis P. Barrett, of Washington, to be Ambassador to the Democratic Republic of Madagascar. He would succeed Howard K. Walker.

Since 1988, Mr. Barrett has served as Mission Director with the U.S. Agency for International Development in Pretoria, South Africa. Prior to this, he served with the U.S. Department of State with the Agency for International Development in the Bureau for Africa, 1988; Asia Liaison for the Bureau of External Affairs, 1984–87; and Office Director for East Asian Affairs, 1982–84.

Mr. Barrett graduated from the University of Portland (B.A., 1959) and the University of Southern California (M.P.A., 1966). He was born July 21, 1936, in St. Paul, MN. Mr. Barrett is married, has two children, and resides in Pretoria, South Africa.

## Nomination of William Lacy Swing To Be United States Ambassador to Nigeria
*April 20, 1992*

The President today announced his intention to nominate William Lacy Swing, of North Carolina, a career member of the Senior Foreign Service, class of Career Minister, to be Ambassador Extraordinary and Plenipotentiary of the United States of America to the Federal Republic of Nigeria. He would succeed Lannon Walker.

Since 1989, Ambassador Swing has served as U.S. Ambassador to the Republic of South Africa. Prior to this, he served at the U.S. Department of State as Deputy Assistant Secretary of State for Personnel, 1987–89,

and as Director of the Office of Foreign Service Career Development and Assignments, 1985–87. In addition, Ambassador Swing has served as U.S. Ambassador to the Republic of Liberia, 1981–85, and the People's Republic of the Congo, 1979–81.

Ambassador Swing graduated from Catawba College (B.A., 1956) and Yale University (M. Div., 1960). He was born September 11, 1934, in Lexington, NC. Ambassador Swing has one child and resides in Pretoria, South Africa.

## Nomination of Linda Gillespie Stuntz To Be Deputy Secretary of Energy
*April 20, 1992*

The President today announced his intention to nominate Linda Gillespie Stuntz, of Virginia, to be Deputy Secretary of Energy. She would succeed W. Henson Moore.

Currently Ms. Stuntz serves as Acting Deputy Secretary and Acting Assistant Secretary for Domestic and International Energy Policy at the U.S. Department of Energy. Ms. Stuntz has served with the U.S. Department of Energy as Deputy Under

Secretary for Policy, Planning, and Analysis, 1989–92, and as Acting Assistant Secretary for Fossil Energy, 1991.

Ms. Stuntz graduated from Wittenberg University (A.B., 1976) and Harvard Law School (J.D., 1979). She was born September 11, 1954, in Bellefontaine, OH. Ms. Stuntz is married, has two children, and resides in Alexandria, VA.

## Remarks Prior to a Meeting With Business Leaders
*April 21, 1992*

I am very pleased to welcome to the White House this morning 16 senior American business leaders to discuss how the American private sector can help to meet the most important foreign policy challenge that faces us, the transformation of the new

States in the former U.S.S.R. from command to market economies and from authoritarian to democratic governments. We are determined to expand the volume of our trade and investment with them. And I would like to announce today a series of measures to meet these important objectives.

First, I have asked that current negotiations with all the new States on trade, bilateral investment, and tax treaties be expedited and completed as soon as possible. These agreements will provide greater access for our companies, and they will lay a new foundation for our future commercial relationships.

Second, I have also asked OPIC, the Overseas Private Investment Corporation, and the Ex-Im Bank, the Export-Import Bank, to negotiate new agreements and expand their operations in the former U.S.S.R., another critical step so that American firms can compete equally and fairly for a share of the new markets there.

And third, I would like to reiterate my call to the Congress in a spirit of bipartisanship to pass, in time for my summit meeting with President Yeltsin in June, the "FREE-DOM Support Act," the landmark legislation that I announced on April 1st. We hope the business leaders here today and the larger American business community will support this bill which will lift cold war restrictions on trade and investment.

And finally, I have requested that our Secretary of Commerce, Barbara Franklin, create new business development committees with Russia, Ukraine, and other countries to eliminate the barriers that currently discourage trade with them.

All these issues will be high on my agenda when I meet with Presidents Kravchuk and Yeltsin. And I'm absolutely committed to giving American companies every opportunity to compete in these markets. The American private sector should seize this opportunity to do business with these countries. It's a vast and rich market, and expanding our business ties will benefit the American people.

Increased trade means new markets for American goods, greater opportunities for American investors, and more jobs for American workers. The U.S. increased its exports of manufactured goods to the U.S.S.R. by nearly 40 percent in 1991. We should aim to do even better this year and the next.

This is a defining moment in this century. And indeed, the private sector's role is absolutely critical. The need for capital, advanced technology, and human expertise in these countries during this decade and into the next century will be far too great for governments alone to meet. A great economic transformation to liberate the peoples of the former Soviet Union and benefit our own people will only occur if our private firms invest and trade to show them the way.

I thank those business leaders that are with us here today, many of them already involved in trying to do business in the C.I.S. countries. And I pledge my commitment to this partnership with the American private sector. And now we will go inside and discuss in detail the agenda that I've just outlined. Thank you all very much for being here.

*Note: The President spoke at 9:33 a.m. in the Rose Garden at the White House.*

# Remarks to the Young Presidents' Organization
*April 21, 1992*

Thank you all. Please be seated. I am delighted to be here, and it's delightful to have this distinguished group of executives here. I want to single out Doug Glant, the international president of YPO, and thank him for honcho-ing this outfit and getting everybody together. Some of you look a little old to be YPO's, but nevertheless— [*laughter*]—far be it from me to be throwing darts in this way.

But I'd like to briefly talk about some of the issues of concern, certainly of concern to this group but I think of concern to all Americans, but with particular emphasis for the business community. Your creativity and the know-how that I think of when I think of YPO really are the fuel that creates this country's wealth and provides rewarding and fulfilling jobs for our communities. And the role of Government in free enterprise is to allow this creativity to flourish. And that means growth.

I know we've had a very difficult time here, a far longer slowdown, indeed recession in some corners, than we would have liked. But for the past 3 years we have been trying to promote sensible policies that will help expand businesses and help create jobs. And we're going to continue to fight for a growth agenda. I had to veto some tax legislation recently, but we were pressing at the same time for seven bullet-point pieces of legislation that would have stimulated the economy. I am still hopeful that we can get some of them through this Congress, and I'll mention a couple of them in a minute.

We face a decision here in the White House now on another subject, and that's the participation in the U.N. Conference on the Environment and Development in Rio. The attendance of the U.S. President at the Rio conference would add a major political impetus to that undertaking; there's no question about that at all. The world looks to us for leadership in this field. But it could also commit the United States to a course of action that could dramatically impede long-term economic growth in this country. I am committed to international cooperation to preserve the world's environment. I want to be very clear on that. And that's why I would like to go to the conference. But I am not going to go to the Rio conference and make a bad deal or be a party to a bad deal. I am not going to sign an agreement that does not protect the environment and the economy of this country.

And this is a very important decision. It's an important decision for our environment, and it's a very important decision for our economy. And to play politics with the Rio conference severely undercuts the U.S. position as we try now to assure a world view that will protect the environment and the economy. Negotiations are going on right now to try to accomplish both before I make a decision as to whether or not I will go to Rio. We are going to consider intensely this matter in the days ahead. And I'm

going to let you know soon, let the country know soon of our final decision on my attendance in Rio.

Here at home last week, we had some more heartening news about the United States economy. All around the world, consumers and companies buy American goods and services in ever-greater amounts, despite the sluggish performance of some of their own economies. U.S. exports—I look around this room and I see many who are participating in this—U.S. exports are experiencing a surge, rising 7 percent in February to a one-month record high of almost $38 billion. And once again, I think in a good sense, American exports, manufacturing exports, are leading the way.

This good news underscores a fundamental truth about our own competitiveness: If we're to succeed economically at home, we must succeed economically abroad. And the evidence is indisputable. Open markets and free trade mean new jobs for American workers and certainly growth for American companies. Over the past four decades, trade-related jobs in our country have grown 3 times faster than overall American job creation.

We must build on this astounding success. And already, over the past 4 years, our exports to Mexico have more than doubled, creating more than 300,000 export-related jobs here at home. And I remember attending a YPO meeting in Mexico about 12 years ago, maybe 14 I think it was, when we were really way behind the power curve in terms of doing business with that country. And they were way behind the power curve in terms of a political situation that would permit the kind of vigorous business that I've just talked about here.

But what we're trying to do now is take that improvement and lock in the gains with what is known as the NAFTA, the North American free trade agreement. With Canada and Mexico, the North American free trade agreement will establish one of the world's largest trading areas, a $6 trillion market from the Yukon to Yucatan. And that's going to mean hundreds of thousands of new jobs for U.S. workers. Those that are fighting me or fighting us on this concept are saying it will cost jobs. We are

absolutely convinced that a successful conclusion to that trade agreement will create
jobs, and I mean good jobs.

Tomorrow, on another field, I'm going to
be meeting with Jacques Delors, the President of the EC Commission. And with him
will be President Cavaco Silva, an old
friend, President of the European Council.
He is the Prime Minister of Portugal, as you
know. And we're going to be discussing the
Uruguay round of the GATT, the world
trade negotiations that are so essential to
expanding trade for everybody.

Over the next decade, a successful conclusion of that Uruguay round could pump
$5 trillion into the global economy. And the
U.S. share of this growth would top $1 tril-
lion. And no one should doubt our resolve
to preserve and expand the worldwide
regime of open trade. GATT must be preserved for this reason: American workers
and American companies deserve the jobs
and opportunities that those open markets
offer.

I think these negotiations are going to be
tough. They are going to be difficult. But
we're approaching them, as we have earlier
negotiations, with a positive spirit. We will
do our part, but the United States must not
be asked to bear the entire burden of compromise when it comes to hammering out a
successful conclusion to this GATT round.

There's still much we can do to make
America more competitive. And one of our
serious economic problems right now—and
I won't tell you too much about this, lest
you tell me about it—that is the cost of
capital. And it's too high. We know that.
And that's why we're going to continue to
fight for a cut in the capital gains rate, capital gains tax rate. A high cap-gains rate
discourages investment and thus business
expansion and thus job creation. And it is
very clear to most business people that this
would be a helpful thing.

Ironically, 2 years ago, in both Houses we
had a majority for reducing the capital
gains tax. And it was beaten down purely
by the political leadership in the United
States Senate, keeping us from giving this
incentive to American businesses, large and
small. I am continuing to fight for this.
Some call it a tax break for the rich. I never
believed that in the first place, and I don't

believe it now. And we're going to keep
fighting to get that stimulative cut in capital
gains.

None of our industrial competitors, major
industrial competitors, tax capital gains at
rates comparable to ours. Germany, as some
of you know, Germany doesn't tax them at
all. And in Japan, an entrepreneur who sells
the company that he's built from scratch
pays a tax of one percent. And we are supposed to compete with those vigorous
economies with a much higher capital gains
rate.

And yet, the very people who complain
about America's ability to compete block
our effort, every effort to lower the capital
gains tax. A lower rate will benefit virtually
everyone in America, not only those who
run a business but anyone who owns a
house or share of stock, seeks a better job.
It will help a lot in the agricultural area of
this great country of ours, too. So, it's time
to stop punishing the pursuit of excellence.
And it's time, I think, to cut the tax on
capital gains.

We're also working to lighten up the regulatory burden that Washington imposes on
every American business. Last January we
announced a 90-day moratorium on Federal
regulations. Wherever possible, we blocked
those regulations that discourage growth
and we're accelerating those that encourage
growth. So far, the preliminary estimates
show that we've saved American business
$10 billion to $20 billion in regulatory costs.

When new legislation is passed, clearly
new regulations are required. I'm thinking
of the civil rights legislation that I'm very
proud of, the Americans for the Disabilities
Act. And yes, it imposed a burden on some,
but it was overdue. It's sound legislation. It
encourages people to get into the mainstream. And yet, there's been some cost
with that one. We renegotiated the Clean
Air Act, and that was long overdue. And I
think it's good. We tried to use market
forces, incidentally, in letting people meet
the clean air standards, but nevertheless,
that imposed a regulatory burden.

So, now we're trying to move forward
and fulfill our responsibilities for safety and
all of that but eliminate this movement towards overregulation. And as I say, these

621

preliminary estimates have been pretty encouraging in terms of the savings in regulatory costs. I'm going to soon be making an announcement about our battle against these excessive regulations, but for now I simply want to say the days of overregulation are just that, they are over. And we are going to stay in there to be sure that independent agencies, whatever they are, people, whoever come in with these excessive regulations are going to have them blocked, if at all possible.

We're pursuing comprehensive reforms in other areas that directly relate to America's long-term competitiveness. We've proposed, for example, market-based health care reform to control the skyrocketing costs and to bring coverage to the uninsured. I do not want to see us lose the quality of health care that we have in this country by going to the "pay or play" plan that's going to break a lot of small businesses, or even worse, to the so-called nationalized plans that have many of our neighbors sending their people over here for care. We are not going to go to that centralized or socialized approach to medicine. And the proposals that we have made, that give people access to insurance and show much greater flexibility in the insurance pool, I believe is the answer to this health care problem.

In another way, another field, through our America 2000 initiative, we are intensifying our efforts to literally revolutionize, reinvent American education. It isn't good enough anymore to simply throw more money at the mandated programs that have failed the young people of this country. And we're not going to do that. And we've gotten the Governors together, set six national education goals, very sensible goals, no partisanship involved in that coming together of the Governors, and now we're moving forward, trying to get this program underway.

Some legislation is required. Fortunately, a lot of legislation is not required, and we can go right to the communities to reinvent the American school. And it's a good program, and I urge you to take a hard look at it because I know that you know that we are going to have to do a better job of education, particularly in math and science,

if we're going to be competitive in the year 2000. I think we've got a good program, and I strongly urge you to give it your support.

Another area that I know is of concern to people here—it is to me—and that is the area of legal reform. We have introduced important steps to reform our legal system, to put an end to the frivolous lawsuits that mire so many businesses and individuals and community activities in a bottomless swamp of litigation. We've got to sue each other less and start helping each other more. And I will continue to fight to get this Congress, hostile Congress in this area, I might say, to at least give an up-or-down vote on reform of the liability system. We haven't even been able to get that. We haven't even been able to get it out of committee, blocked by powerful lobbies up there.

So, here's an area where I know your interests are at stake and an area where I would earnestly solicit your support because we must start capping some of these outrageous settlements that run the cost of business right off the chart, run doctors out of business, and say to Little League coaches, "Hey, you better not take a chance by coaching the Little League or this guy over on third base is going to sue you." And so, we're going to fight this one. But again, it's an area where we need your help.

And the last point is this: The fact is that none of these pressing social problems are going to be solved without the voluntary involvement of individuals and communities. And when I think of YPO and the success that this epitomizes, this organization epitomizes, I think of a thousand Points of Light, and I think of people who, in spite of spending an awful lot of time building and creating jobs for people, they find time to do something in the communities. From the very first day of this administration, we have called on every American to be a Point of Light, to bring hope to the helpless and to help the homeless and to love and care for those who are in need. And it is working. And it isn't a Government program; it is simply encouraging the sense of voluntarism that is in everybody.

Right here in your own organizations are

plenty of examples of what I'm talking about. Gay Mayer, who works with a drug rehabilitation program in his area, has helped more than 100 young adults recover from the ravages of drug abuse to lead productive lives. What one individual has been able to do just by giving of himself. Joe Lobozzo, who spends his Wednesday nights counseling children of alcoholics.

I would like today to challenge all of you to join these men in a movement that is literally transforming our country. It is much more effective than having a mandated specialized program coming out of some subcommittee in the United States House of Representatives. And it is working. It is the best in ourselves. And I urge you to really, really pitch in.

First, I ask you to make your company a Point of Light by personally devoting as much time as you possibly can to community service, encouraging the employees to do the same. This whole concept of mentoring, where businesses reach out and help in this Education 2000 program, is really working around the country. Secondly, you can encourage other leaders to make voluntary service part of their missions as well. And finally, you can work among your vast memberships to help America itself become a Nation with Communities of Light, the concept where an entire community comes together figuring how to solve its own enormous social problems.

I spoke earlier with some of your leaders, Doug and others, and I know that there is support among your members to assume this leadership role. And I know Doug has asked David Weaver, an old friend, to work with each of you to decide how you can all best respond to this challenge.

I am convinced the results will be profound. And urging this, we're not trying to escape the responsibility of the Federal Government. It's something entirely different. It's the concept that Thoreau noticed years ago about the propensity of one American to help another. And we're simply trying to revitalize this, especially in these days of scarce resources and failed centralized mandates.

So, we've got a lot at stake here, including the legacy that we leave our children. We all want a world at peace; strong, wholesome families; rewarding jobs for all who seek them.

You know, in these days, you hear and I hear mostly about the problems. We've got a lot to be grateful for in this country. Our kids, grandkids in some cases, go to bed at night with far less fear of nuclear war. The world has changed dramatically in the last 3 years, unprecedented changes that nobody would have believed possible.

In the Middle East, ancient enemies are at least talking about peace. South of our border you see the emergence of democracies that none of us would have predicted just 3 or 4 years ago, the solidifying of the democratic way. And you see countries coming to grips with their economic problems. Argentina comes to mind; Mexico, a sterling example of this dramatic change that is taking place around the world.

I spent this morning talking to a group of business people on working with them on what we can do to help democracy along in the C.I.S., the Commonwealth of these Independent States over there, led by Russia and then the Ukraine, with Kravchuk coming here next month and Yeltsin the next. And so, there's an awful lot of change in this world that is good and strong and positive.

And now what we've got to do is take these ideas, and maybe some that you have that I haven't mentioned, bring them to bear on the economic problems so we can regain the growth that is absolutely essential if the United States is going to continue to be the leader in these very important areas.

But you've caught me on an upbeat day, a day that I am confident about the United States leadership. It is only—I might tell you this, and some of you can confirm this from your trips abroad—it is only our country that the others look to now as the undisputed leader of the entire world. So, we've got to fulfill those responsibilities while still trying to do what we can to assist those that are hurting right here at home. And I am confident with your help, with your continued imaginative leadership, that we can do just exactly that.

So, thank you very, very much for coming to the White House. I didn't intend to give you this much of a lecture, but I'm just—I don't normally have such a high-talented, captive audience. Thank you all very, very much.

*Note: The President spoke at 2:04 p.m. in Room 450 of the Old Executive Office Building.*

## Statement on Earth Day
*April 22, 1992*

Earth Day, April 22, is an opportunity to rededicate ourselves to leaving a better quality of life for future generations. But I believe we must make every day Earth Day. A clean environment requires action from both Government and citizens. I believe that we can have both economic growth and a cleaner, safer environment. Sound policies do not force us to choose between the two.

In just 3 years, this administration has:

- Proposed, negotiated, and signed into law a new Clean Air Act that will cut sulfur dioxide emissions in half, reduce toxic air emissions by 90 percent, and clean up smog in cities across America;
- Established a moratorium until at least the next century on oil and gas drilling off the coasts of California, south Florida, Washington, Oregon, and New England;
- Led the world by proposing to phase out CFC's and other ozone-depleting substances by the end of 1995, and taken legislative action to put the U.S. 42 percent ahead of the internationally required phaseout schedule;
- Proposed to add over $1 billion in new lands to America's parks, forests, wildlife refuges, and recreation lands;
- Won international agreements to prevent hazardous waste from being illegally dumped in developing countries, to ban ivory imports, to ban large-scale driftnet fishing, and to protect Antarctica;
- Increased funding sharply for implementing and enforcing environmental laws (including a 53-percent increase in EPA's operating budget), for Super-

fund, for cleaning up Federal facilities, for protecting wetlands habitat, and for parks and recreation;
- Signed an Executive order requiring Federal Agencies, which generate 20 percent of the Nation's solid waste, to recycle paper, plastic, metals, glass, used oil, lead acid batteries, and tires;
- Made polluters pay the cost of cleanup. The Justice Department and EPA have collected more fines and penalties in the first 3 years of this administration than during the previous 18-year history of the EPA.

But our work is not finished. I have called on Congress to take the following actions this year:

- Enact balanced national energy legislation providing for increased energy conservation and environmentally responsible energy production, transmission, and use;
- Establish a U.S. Department of the Environment; and
- Increase budgets for environmental and natural resource programs, as requested in my budget. Last year, Congress cut my budget requests for Superfund and for America the Beautiful, which includes funding for parks, forests, wildlife refuges, outdoor recreation, and our program to plant one billion trees a year across the country.

These measures would build upon our recent progress and provide continuing momentum to achieve what Americans want in the months and years ahead, environmental improvement and economic growth.

# Remarks at the Departure Ceremony for European Community Leaders Anibal Cavaco Silva and Jacques Delors
*April 22, 1992*

Mr. Prime Minister, this year my country celebrates the Iberian spirit of discovery. Half a millennium ago, Portugal and Spain helped chart a course towards a new world. Five hundred years later, European unity guides the way towards a new world order. Those early pioneers believed their mission was to probe the secrets of the world. Now we must explore the frontiers of common interest and common ground. The next horizon: a strengthened partnership between the United States and the European Community.

Prime Minister Cavaco Silva, EC President Delors, and I and our top officials have discussed areas where we may deepen cooperation: peace efforts in the Middle East, coordination of aid to Central and Eastern Europe, the struggle of the emergent C.I.S. and international assistance, the agenda of next month's EC conference in Lisbon. We also talked about Yugoslavia, where, tragically, old hatreds are opening new wounds. The U.S.-EC partnership is working tirelessly to create conditions for a lasting democratic peace.

No topic on our agenda is more crucial than the Uruguay round of trade negotiations. We are committed to achieving an early agreement, one that will spur economic growth not just in America but in Europe and all around the world. It will create jobs not just for our generation but for generations to come. For Americans, agreement will mean more than free trade abroad; it will mean for Americans good jobs here at home and a better standard of living at home.

We had an extensive exchange of views on the outstanding issues, and some new ideas on how to conclude this Uruguay round were advanced by both sides. We are convinced, absolutely convinced, that the EC leaders are committed to an early agreement. And I hope they know that I am committed to such an early conclusion. We agreed to continue this process. We had some serious discussions, and the process will go on.

Forty-one years ago almost to the day, the countries of Europe began their quest for unity. Over the ruins of war they laid a blueprint for peace and began building the foundations for economic and political cooperation. They sought unity not out of convenience but out of conviction, a vision of economic interdependence that would inflate the costs of war and expand the dividends of peace. The wisdom of their actions has brought us today to a new Europe where peace has paid off.

Now, this new Europe has now joined its strength with the United States to support the spread of political and economic freedom in the lands only recently liberated from Soviet communism. Those that we helped four decades ago are now able to shoulder a larger part of these new challenges.

Jean Monnet, the grandfather of European unity, once asked: "If you are in a dark tunnel and see a small light at the end, should you turn your back on that light and go back into darkness, or should you continue walking toward it even though you know it's far away?" Five hundred years ago, a European mariner followed the light of his imagination to illuminate a new world. For almost 50 years, the West carried freedom's torch to protect the free world. Today, we stand at the shores of a new world order where diverse nations are drawn together in common cause to achieve the universal aspirations of mankind: peace and security, freedom and prosperity. A strong and united Europe offers the best hope for this united purpose and the best alliance for the United States.

I salute our two distinguished guests today, and now would like to ask Prime Minister Cavaco Silva to say a word.

*Note: The President spoke at 1:33 p.m. on the South Lawn at the White House. In his remarks, he referred to French diplomat Jean Monnet, a founder of the European*

*Community. Prime Minister Anibal Cavaco Silva of Portugal was President of the Euro-* *pean Council, and Jacques Delors was President of the European Commission.*

## Remarks Congratulating the 1992 Super Bowl Champion Washington Redskins
*April 22, 1992*

Please be seated, and welcome to the Rose Garden. May I first salute, of course, Joe Gibbs and Charlie Casserly, and the players, the coaches, the official family, and the friends of the Redskins. Welcome to the White House at last. We're delighted to have you here.

And you can imagine how much I've looked forward to the event. Today we honor the flagship franchise of the NFL since 1937, a team which this year earned the best mark in club history, 17 and 2. We're proud to salute the 1992 Super Bowl champions.

I think first of all of Mark Rypien: nearly 3,600 passing yards in the regular season, two touchdowns, the MVP award in the Super Bowl. Someone mentioned to me that Mark was born in Canada. It looks like the U.S.-Canada Free Trade Agreement is paying off already, at least from our standpoint. [*Laughter*]

And often Mark threw to the beloved number 81. And when the NFL decided last month to scrap instant replay, I thought I heard a big cheer go up. Barbara said, "What was that?" I said, "I'm not sure. Sounds like Art Monk." An instant replay cost him one touchdown in the Super Bowl, but not 60 others and a glorious career. And all Washington is proud of a future Hall-of-Famer.

Now, this brings me to the other members of the Super Bowl champions. Perhaps the NFL's best offensive line, the "Hogs," allowing a club record low, nine sacks. Next, with Art, members of the "Posse," wide receivers Ricky Sanders and Gary Clark. We salute, too, running backs like Gerald Riggs and Earnest Byner; Chip Lohmiller—Cole Porter must have seen the future when he wrote, "I get a kick out of you." [*Laughter*] And plus, of course, an-

other future Hall-of-Famer, Joe Gibbs, now with three Super Bowl victories, second only to Chuck Noll. Let's hear it for the coach. [*Applause*]

And yet, it's the "National Defense" that would make even the Pentagon proud. That great defense that still has Jim Kelly ducking tacklers in his sleep—Jim, nothing personal, the Skins k.o.'d opponents all year. Think of linemen like Fred Stokes and Jumpy Geathers, Tim Johnson; or linebackers Andre Collins and Wilbur Marshall, 11 tackles against Buffalo; or the secondary, featuring A.J. Johnson and all-pro speed demon Darrell Green. And each showed why coach Richie Pettibon said, "It's a case of the whole being even better than the parts."

Go to Bethesda or Anacostia, travel to Alexandria or Falls Church, and they'll talk about this team molded by Joe and Charlie. They'll talk, too, about things other than the won-and-lost record, impressive though that is. Things like Mark's support for the Cystic Fibrosis Foundation, Art Monk's and Earnest Byner's work on behalf of the Food for Families Program at Thanksgiving, Darrell Green's youth foundation, or the Joe Gibbs Youth for Tomorrow Home.

These things explain a lot. They explain why the Skins have become a barometer of whether Monday is good or bad for Washingtonians. And they're also an economic barometer. And I was glad, for example, to learn that whenever the Redskins have won the Super Bowl, the U.S. economy has improved that year. [*Laughter*] Other teams get covered in the sports section; this crowd gets covered in the "Wall Street Week." Whether it's Wall Street or Main Street, though, America loves the Redskins.

And so, I just want to welcome you all here. We're proud to have you here, your friends, your wives, dates, and whoever else. And so now let's get on to what's important, a little chow. But let me tell you that we've got a triathlon event out here. We have the horseshoe pit rigged up, and if I might spell out the ground rules here: Women and men welcome, just the players and their dates and friends, however, because we've got a time thing. And he who gets or she who gets the most ringers out of 10 tosses wins a fantastic prize. On the putting green, he or she who gets the lowest nine-hole score wins yet another fantastic prize. And then we move to the third

event—you can do this in any order you want, but try to do it before dinner—and the last one is the basketball, 10 shots from the foul line, another fantastic prize. So you don't have to go, and this isn't mandatory, but I want to stand around and laugh. [*Laughter*]

Thank you very much.

*Note: The President spoke at 6:02 p.m. in the Rose Garden at the White House. In his remarks, he referred to Chuck Noll, former head coach of the Pittsburgh Steelers.*

# Appointment of Walter H. Kansteiner III as Special Assistant to the President and Deputy Press Secretary for Foreign Affairs
*April 22, 1992*

The President today announced the appointment of Walter H. Kansteiner III, of Illinois, to be Special Assistant to the President and Deputy Press Secretary for Foreign Affairs.

Mr. Kansteiner is currently Director for African Affairs at the National Security Council, 1991-present. Mr. Kansteiner was a member of the State Department's policy planning staff from May 1989 to June 1991. He is a former vice president of W.H. Kan-

steiner, Inc., in Chicago, IL. He is the author of "South Africa: Revolution or Reconciliation" (1988).

Mr. Kansteiner graduated from Washington & Lee University (B.A., 1977), the School of International Service at American University (M.A., 1981), and Virginia Theology Seminary (M.T.S., 1985). He was born November 11, 1955, in Evanston, IL. Mr. Kansteiner is married, has two children, and resides in Lincoln, VA.

# Nomination of James D. Jameson To Be an Assistant Secretary of Commerce
*April 22, 1992*

The President today announced his intention to nominate James D. Jameson, of California, to be an Assistant Secretary of Commerce for Trade Development. He would succeed Timothy John McBride. Upon confirmation, he will be designated a member of the Board of Directors of the Overseas Private Investment Corporation.

Since 1975, Mr. Jameson has served as president and owner of LIDCO, Inc., in Brawley, CA. He has also served as chair-

man of the board of Glenair International, Ltd., in Mansfield, England, 1975-present, and international director and controlling shareholder of Glenair, Inc., in Glendale, CA.

Mr. Jameson graduated from Stanford University (B.A., 1971; M.B.A., 1974). He was born May 26, 1949, in Glendale, CA. Mr. Jameson is married, has two children, and resides in Rancho Santa Fe, CA.

## Remarks to the United States Academic Decathlon Winners
*April 23, 1992*

Welcome all. And first, may I greet our distinguished number two over at the Energy Department, David Kearns, coming down here from a fantastic leadership role in American business to help us in this important America 2000 education program. So I'm delighted he's with us here today.

I want to salute the president and the board of directors of the U.S. Academic Decathlon, all of them; thank particularly all of the corporate sponsors who make so much of this possible; and also single out Danny Ramirez, Chris Roorda, and Greg Rudnick, standing up here with me today; salute the coaches and the friends. And most of all, a warm Rose Garden welcome to our newest American champs, newest American heroes if you will, the 1992 Academic Decathlon champs, the team from J. Frank Dobie High in, yes, you guessed it, Houston, Texas. Now, where are they? Stand up. And they've got a good front-row seat, too. Thank you, guys, and welcome. It's a great feat for my hometown, the highest score, I'm told, in the history of the competition. And I'm very proud to welcome you all here. I hear that you wore "Rose Garden or Bust" pins. They work. And I'm wondering if you have an extra one for the fall. [*Laughter*]

Congratulations also to our silver and bronze medalists from Mountain View High in Mesa, Arizona, Whitney Young Magnet High in Chicago; our regional winners from New Jersey, Alabama, Ohio, Nebraska, and California; our small school winner from Wisconsin; and our 10 individual student scholarship winners, 9 from our top 3 winning schools, and then Mit Robertson here from Tupelo, Mississippi. Welcome all.

I want to send special good-luck wishes to those who will represent us at the International Decathlon in a couple of weeks, the Academic Decathlon, that is. And since you're the star decathletes, tell me who is going to win at Barcelona, Dan or Dave? [*Laughter*]

You've all done something remarkable. And this year's contest began with 30,000, more than 30,000 students at 3,500 schools coast to coast. And now it's just you. And not only did you work all year to conquer environmental science in a range of 10 categories, you also survived the blizzard of 25,000 pieces of test paper out in Boise. And I was impressed by your Habitat Earth Super Quiz questions like this one: "In a molecule of methane, the carbon atom is at the center of what?" For you out there in the press—[*laughter*]—the answer is "a tetrahedron with four S-P-3 bonds." Did you get that one down? I'll be glad to repeat the question. Got it? Never mind.

That was easy—not! Actually, pretty tough. But I know a category I could enter: computers. I was just in there with Secretary Kearns talking about it. I've been learning how to work one because one of our education goals is that nobody is too old to learn. I wrote my first program a while ago. I'm not sure what happened to it. It was called "Michelangelo." [*Laughter*]

Now, you kids here today represent every team member from across the country. And I want to tell you and them what all of you have done for America. You've shown that great things can be achieved by commitment, perseverance, hard work, and yes, teamwork. And I salute you, and I envy you. And you've found the sheer joy of learning, beginning to understand the world.

One day a scientist will discover the cure for cancer, the cure for AIDS. Other people will find new ways to feed the hungry. And there will be writers whose wisdom will touch lives. And right now, those men and women are kids in our classrooms or maybe even sitting right here in the Rose Garden.

Remember, study hard, and one day one of you might grow up to be President. But let's face it, even then you'll never make as much money as your dog. [*Laughter*] Millie, who normally comes to events like this, but she used to just roll over on the grass, and now all she rolls over is her money market account with—in the street.

But look, you've shown your peers that it

is as exciting to root for an academic team as an athletic one. And that's a point I wanted to make for our entire country. You've shown that it takes skill, stamina, and intensity to achieve in the classroom as well as in the stadium. And you've given them a priceless gift—your peers—the belief in their ability to reach out and shape their own lives.

There is a new century coming, one with absolutely unlimited horizons. And we must make sure all our children enter this new world equipped with the skills that will let them dream dreams and know they can make them come true.

One of the things that impresses me most about this decathlon is that each team is made up of A, B, and C students. And there's a great lesson there. What matters is simply that each kid be the best that he or she can be. As George Patton said, "If a man has done his best, what else is there?" We don't want the moon for our kids. We want something more important, a future.

And so one year ago, I unveiled America 2000, our long-range strategy to achieve our six national education goals. And it's a challenge posed to each of us in communities throughout America to literally reinvent American education. It urges us to reach deep within ourselves to find answers so that our kids can reach for the stars.

Changing our attitudes about education is too important to wait or waste a generation. To be competitive in this changing world, we must realize that we succeed economically at home; if we're to do that, we must lead economically abroad. Open markets, free trade, they mean jobs for American workers and economic growth for American companies. But we must be prepared to compete, ready to take advantage of these high-tech opportunities in the global marketplace. We know our economic health, our economic survival depend on how we educate ourselves to face the challenges of a new century. So we've set these six education goals to reach by the year 2000, when today's third and fourth graders will be taking part in this event, this Academic Decathlon, by then.

And you all know these goals. One of them, the first one: Our kids will start school ready to learn. That's more than

Head Start; Head Start's a part of that. Our high school graduation rate must be 90 percent. The third one: Our students will be achieving world-class standards. And then fourth: We'll be first in the world in science and math, a particularly important one. And then the fifth one: Every adult will be literate; no one is too old to learn. And sixth: Every American school must be safe, must be disciplined, must be drug-free, in other words, an environment where people can learn.

You will help us meet those challenges. Real excellence demands commitment from everyone as we create a new generation of American schools that demands more of the same choices of schools, public, private, or religious, for middle class and poor Americans that wealthier families already have. Give them a chance to choose.

It demands new creative partnership among parents, teachers, businesses, and kids like the community involvement that encourages this decathlon and the local and national corporate partnerships that fund it. And by the way, I want to give a special note to the corporate sponsors with us today, whose leadership and vision make this decathlon possible. This bond really, I referred to it earlier, but this bond between industry and the individual is the keystone of the American spirit. The country needs to follow this decathlon's example in all these areas because for our future every citizen must now help every community develop a plan of action.

Already 43 States and over 1,000 communities across this country have answered the call and have joined America 2000. This isn't Democrat or Republican or liberal or conservative. It is literally a move to revolutionize education. And together we are reinventing American education, neighborhood by neighborhood, community by community all across this country. And at the heart of it are you students, you kids, a new kind of campus hero with the good values you learn from disciplined determination, from a sharp mind that is not wasted on drugs, and from the confidence and pride that comes from proving yourselves. And you will help this America 2000 dream come true.

For a great example of this we don't have to look further than a woman who is not with us today, DC's Rhondee Johnson, a junior at Benjamin Banneker High who just won the National Academic Decathlon's Kristen Caperton Award for Inspiration and Courage. She takes her school responsibilities so seriously that she's helping her team at a track meet right now instead of joining us. And we all hope she wins the blue ribbon, but she's certainly winning it in life with her example. Rhondee's lived with the tragedy of violence. When her aunt was killed, her four children came to live with Rhondee's family, making 8-year-old Rhondee the oldest of nine kids in a single-parent household. She takes on a parent's duties, and she still manages a 4.0 average. She is an inspiration, accepting responsibilities and challenges and still striving to excel.

She and all of you give a 1990's example of how Abraham Lincoln defined his own life when he said, "I do the very best I know how, the very best I can; and I mean to keep on doing so until the end." I am proud of the message all of you winning decathletes send, that personal dedication, effort, and teamwork lead to success.

And when one of you bright young people solves the problem of who created "Michelangelo," just remember, my name is Dana Carvey.

Thank you all very much for coming. Congratulations, and may God bless you all.

*Note: The President spoke at 11:18 a.m. in the Rose Garden at the White House. In his remarks, he referred to Deputy Secretary of Education David T. Kearns; winning team captains Daniel Bruno Ramirez, Christine L. Roorda, and Gregory Rudnick; and comedian Dana Carvey.*

# Remarks at the Signing Ceremony for the Paper Market Access Agreement With Japan
*April 23, 1992*

*The President.* May I thank Ambassador Kuriyama for being here with us today, Japan's Ambassador to the United States, and also Mike Moskow up here. Everybody knows him, and we're grateful to him for his participation in all of this.

Today does mark a milestone for both the United States and Japan, a ceremony representing another step toward our two countries becoming equal partners in trade. The agreement I sign today is an important, positive development stemming from our January trip to Japan.

And I am pleased that since January, American companies have begun to enjoy a more positive atmosphere for doing business in Japan. The broader commitment which Prime Minister Miyazawa and I made during my visit was the Tokyo Declaration, and an important part that was the Global Partnership Plan of Action, an agreement to strengthen trade between our two countries, all part of our efforts to make the

relationship between us a true partnership. This is a very important relationship. And that all will ensure that U.S. firms have the same degree of access to the Japanese market that Japanese firms enjoy in the United States.

The Paper Market Access Agreement will increase opportunities and sales for foreign firms exporting paper products into Japan. And hereafter, the Government of Japan will encourage its paper distributors, converters, printers, and major corporate users to increase imports of competitive foreign paper products. That official encouragement will open the way for America's paper industry to export its products into Japan's $27 billion market.

Today's action is good for all concerned: good for the Japanese consumer, good for American industry, and good for the American worker. And it is also an important step forward in our large global trading system. As William McKinley said back in 1897,

"Good trade ensures good will." And the partnership between the United States of America and Japan ensures that the hallmark of the new globalization of trade will be world-class quality, competitive pricing, and of course, excellent service.

This alliance also recognizes that interactive partnerships like this one strengthen each of us and fire up the engine of economic growth. At the same time, it strengthens the relationship between us and makes the world a better, friendlier place for our children and our grandchildren.

So I am delighted to be here. And I welcome all of you from industry and from the diplomatic corridors. And let me just say in conclusion, I view this relationship between the U.S. and Japan as very, very important. And I will do my level-best as President of the United States to keep it on a stable, forward-looking basis. It is essential, and it is in our best interest that it remain strong.

So, Mr. Ambassador, you are entitled to equal time, or should we—why don't you go ahead, and then——

*Ambassador Kuriyama.* Well, thank you very much, Mr. President.

*The President.* Thank you for being with us, sir.

[*At this point, Ambassador Kuriyama spoke.*]

*The President.* Thank you, sir, very much. Now I will witness, if you all do the signing.

*Note: The President spoke at 11:49 a.m. in the Roosevelt Room at the White House. Ambassador Takakazu Kuriyama of Japan and Deputy U.S. Trade Representative Michael H. Moskow signed the agreement.*

# Remarks at the Unveiling Ceremony for the White House Commemorative Stamp
*April 23, 1992*

Thank you, Mike, very much, and greetings to all of you. May I greet Edward Horgan and Kenneth Hunter, Associate Postmasters General; Mike, thank you, sir, for the introduction and those remarks; old friend George Haley here, the Chairman of the Postal Rate Commission.

And welcome to Peerce Farm, or as we call it nowadays, the White House. George Washington selected this site for the President's house more than 200 years ago amid apple orchards owned by a colonial farmer named Peerce. Being a surveyor by trade, Washington knew what he was doing. Abigail Adams, the first lady to live here, wrote, "This is a beautiful spot. And the more I view it, the more I am delighted with it."

It was Thomas Jefferson who suggested a national competition to design the President's house. Washington himself chose the design of the winner, James Hoban, an Irish immigrant then living in Charleston. Hoban's plan won out over grander designs, some of which included vast central courts, rotundas, and—here's an intriguing idea—a draped throne for the President. [*Laughter*] His design was plainer than the others, more befitting the house of a democratic leader, but it was still stately and dignified, as Washington wanted.

Incidentally, when he won the contest, Hoban began another Capital tradition. He promptly leaked the news to his hometown papers in Charleston. And after many revisions to the original design and after some unfortunate redecorating by British troops in 1814, the President's house assumed the graceful form that we celebrate today.

And 1992 marks the 200th anniversary of this magnificent building. The cornerstone was laid in October of 1792, just a few yards from here, though the stone itself, I'm told by the historians and the custodians, has never been found. You'll notice we're restoring the exterior stone walls of the Residence as part of the anniversary, a celebration that includes commemorative books and museum exhibitions and symposiums. The far side of the house has been stripped down and painted. And I'm told again by the historians that this is the first time that the building has been taken down to its original stone.

The celebration also includes a commemorative postage stamp, which is what brings us here this afternoon. And I thank everyone who worked so hard to make this stamp possible, particularly the former Postmaster General Anthony Frank, who authorized it; Jack Ruther, who we just met, who did the superb design. And I hope the stamp serves as a reminder to every American that this place is truly the people's house.

One of the things I enjoy the most is taking our foreign visitors over here when the tours are on. And I'll never forget the reaction when I introduced a monarch to the visiting tourists coming through here. And one of the kids started yelling, "It's a real live king, Dad. It's a real live king." [*Laughter*] And it was a good experience

for the real live king to see how the people consider this properly their house.

One of the great blessings of the Presidency, obviously, is to live within the walls of this house, to roam its hallways, to absorb its history, and to be reminded at every turn of the noble men who have lived here and of their families. But a President can never, obviously, be more than a caretaker or a tenant in this house, for the White House belongs, as it has for 200 years, to every American.

And we are very grateful, Barbara and I both. And we pray that God continues to bless this house as He blesses the United States of America. Thank you all very much for coming. And now, Mike, do the honors.

[*At this point the stamp was unveiled.*]

That concludes our brief ceremony, but thank you all very much for coming.

*Note: The President spoke at 3:30 p.m. in the Rose Garden at the White House. In his remarks, he referred to Acting Postmaster General Michael S. Coughlin.*

# Remarks to the Forum of the Americas
*April 23, 1992*

Please be seated. And David, thank you, sir. And thank you for your really vital work in rallying the private sector and congressional support for the North American free trade agreement, for the Enterprise for the Americas Initiative. And let me say to his many friends here that David's personal involvement has been a major factor in the success we've enjoyed so far with both of these significant initiatives. And I also want to pay my respects to another old friend, Ambassador George Landau of the Americas Society, and Antonio Del Valle of the Business Council of Latin America, and Tom d'Aquino of the Business Council on National Issues. And I am grateful for all your leadership.

I understand also—and I can't see too well out here with these bright lights—that somewhere out there sits an old friend, a former colleague at the United Nations who

went on to greater heights than being an ambassador there, an old friend, Javier Perez de Cuellar, is with us. And I am just delighted that he could be here. And I just wish I could see him. Javier? There he is.

And may I particularly welcome all of our guests from south of the Rio Grande, leaders from both the public and the private sectors. I see several ambassadors here and many others that are in the Government sector but so many from the private sector. And we salute you for your leadership. And let me just say this: Public or private, from the United States, we are glad to be your partners.

And I can't think, really, of a more important moment than now to convene again this Forum of the Americas. Over the last 3 years, we've seen our world literally transformed: the Berlin Wall torn down and

Germany peacefully unified, the people of Eastern Europe and the Soviet Union liberated from communism, and South Africa's historic vote to reject apartheid. And we've seen Arab neighbors negotiating for the first time face to face with Israel, and a worldwide coalition under the banner of the United Nations stand up and turn back Iraqi aggression against Kuwait. And there's been a profound change with meaning for every man, woman, and child on the face of the Earth. And we have drastically reduced—and this is one I take great pleasure in having been a small part of—we have drastically reduced the threat of nuclear war.

And just today, the United States took steps to facilitate trade in high technology goods, an initiative made possible by the changed strategic environment and the peaceful rebirth of freedom in the formerly Communist lands. We relaxed trade restrictions on exports that served us well during the cold war era but are no longer necessary in our new world. And our actions today will eliminate requirements for thousands of export licenses, including many that affected computers, one of our strongest export earners. Trade covered today by today's deregulation amounts to about $2.5 billion.

Here in our own hemisphere, the Americas have launched an era of far-reaching and hopeful change. We've made history, all of us. We're well on our way to creating something mankind has never seen, a hemisphere wholly free and democratic, with prosperity flowing from open trade.

From Mexico City to Buenos Aires, that vision is becoming a reality. For the first time in many years, more private capital is flowing into the Americas for new investments than is flowing out. In country after country, the hyperinflation that literally devastated the region's economies, particularly its poor, has been halted. In nearly every nation, real growth has returned. A growing number of nations are taking advantage of the Brady plan, an important initiative of our administration designed to reduce the debt burden on our neighbors and set the stage for the renewal of growth. Barriers to trade and investment are coming down. Go to the financial centers of the world, and you'll get the same message: One of the most exciting regions for investment is Latin America.

Alongside this economic revolution, we have witnessed and played a vital role to shape a political revolution just as powerful. Two years after we initiated Operation Just Cause, Panama has replaced the repression of the Noriega era with freedom and democracy. In El Salvador, after 12 years of civil war, our consistent efforts have brought peace. In Nicaragua, we succeeded in our goal of restoring peace and democracy through free elections. And throughout Central America, civilian presidents hold office, and the principle of consent of the governed is now firmly established. And in South America, Chile and Paraguay have rejoined the community of democracies.

This peaceful revolution throughout the Americas did not happen by accident. It is the work of a new generation of courageous and committed democratic leaders with whom we have worked closely in pursuit of common goals, those leaders supported by this dynamic private sector that is so beautifully represented here tonight.

The new spirit was demonstrated in June of last year, when the OAS General Assembly passed a resolution designed to strengthen the international response to threats to democracy. Consolidating this revolution will not be easy; we understand that. Millions of people in our hemisphere are still mired in poverty and political alienation. Recent events in Haiti, Venezuela, and Peru remind us that democracy is still fragile and faces continued dangers. In all our nations, powerful special interests cling to old ideas and privileges, promote protectionism. They resist expanded trade.

For the diehards, for Castro's totalitarian regime, for those in the hemisphere who would turn the clock back to military dictatorship, for the stubborn holdouts for economic isolation, I want to make one point clear: Hundreds of millions of Latin Americans share a faith in human freedom and opportunity. And I stand with them. And as long as I am President of this great country, the United States will devote its energies to the true and lasting liberation of the people of the Western Hemisphere.

Sharing the democratic spirit makes a difference on every issue we care about. Democracy's rebirth led Argentina and Brazil to join hands to halt the spread of nuclear arms. Democracy energized Brazil to slow deforestation of the Amazon rain forest. Democracy gave Argentina the will to stop the Condor ballistic missile program financed by Libya and Iraq. Colombia's democracy is leading the fight against the drug trade and working to restore its economic vitality. The restored democracy in Panama has passed tough new laws to combat money laundering, and it's working to renew its importance as an East-West trade corridor.

Make no mistake: Political and economic freedom are linked; they are inseparable. And just as people have a God-given right to choose who will govern them, they also must be free to make their own economic choices. When we lift barriers to economic freedom within and among our countries, we unleash powerful forces of growth and creativity.

Before I leave office I want manufacturers in Cleveland to enjoy virtually the same access to markets in Monterrey as they now have in Minneapolis. And with new technologies, creators of services in Denver may be able to tap markets in Santiago as readily as those in Chicago. I'll work to assure that Government protection and excessive regulation don't stand in their way. To do this, we'll have to overcome the stunted vision of some special interests. And I am determined that we can and will do exactly that.

I've made it a top priority to conclude a free trade agreement designed to remove all tariffs on trade between the United States, Canada, and Mexico. This agreement will build on our historic free trade agreement with Canada. The success of the agreement with Canada demonstrates how free trade can benefit all concerned.

We cannot achieve this breakthrough by equivocating between the status quo protectionists and the movement for freedom and change. Some suggest that we can hide in a cocoon of protection and pretend still to benefit from the fresh air of competition. Well, if there's ever an audience that understands this, you and I know that is simply wrong-headed. Our economic future must not depend on those who pay lip service to free trade but full service to powerful special interests. We cannot have it both ways.

In our own War for Independence, those who took this kind of stand were known as the "summer soldiers." And they wanted the glory of the revolution without showing the gumption to stand for freedom even in tough times. Our stand is clear; my stand is clear: Open trade is vital to this country, to the United States, and every bit as vital as domestic reforms to renew our system of education, health care, Government, and administration of justice.

A free trade area comprising the United States, Mexico, and Canada would be the largest market in the entire world: 360 million consumers in a $6 trillion, $6 trillion economy. Mexico—and I salute its President, its business people here tonight—Mexico is among the fastest growing national markets for U.S. exports today. And over the last 3 years alone, American merchandise exports to Mexico have increased by two-thirds, two-thirds. Our exports of autos, auto parts, telecommunications equipment to Mexico have doubled. And while members of this audience may be aware of this, I doubt it is widely known in the United States that two-thirds of all imports into Mexico come from the United States.

It's not just the border States that profit from this growth. During my Presidency, 45 of our 50 States have increased their exports to Mexico. Our top 10 exporters to Mexico today include Michigan, Illinois, New York, Louisiana, Pennsylvania, Florida, and Ohio, as well as Texas, California, and Arizona, those border States.

Trade with Mexico already supports hundreds of thousands of U.S. jobs. And just as an example: Thousands of good jobs in Warren, Ohio, and Rochester, New York, depend on sister plants in Mexico to keep their products competitive. A North American free trade agreement would create thousands more. It would create competitive efficiencies and economies of scale that will help American companies compete in world markets.

Free trade with Canada and Mexico will make all of us winners in economic endeavor, but our relationship goes well beyond trade. We share borders that span the continent. We're linked by centuries-old ties of family and culture. I share a warm friendship with Prime Minister Brian Mulroney of Canada, whom I consult frequently. I count President Carlos Salinas also as a dear friend. And he and I have been promoting the "spirit of Houston" ever since our summit meeting just after both of us were elected in 1988. And both President Salinas and Prime Minister Mulroney are bold and imaginative leaders, and I am committed to working with them to forge enduring friendship among our countries based on open trade, cooperation, and mutual respect.

Now, you may have heard some suggest that politics will dictate delaying the North American free trade agreement until after the election. Well, let me say this: These voices are not speaking for me. The time of opportunity is now. I have instructed our negotiators to accelerate their work. I believe we can conclude a sound, sensible deal before the election. I want to sign a good agreement as soon as it is ready. And there will be no delay because of American politics.

Now, to other friends here let me say this: The North American free trade agreement is only a beginning. Our Enterprise for the Americas Initiative already has made noteworthy progress to open markets, expand investment flows, reduce official debt, and strengthen the environment throughout the hemisphere.

The Enterprise for the Americas Initiative reflects a revolution in thinking. Through this initiative, the United States is not seeking to impose our ideas on our neighbors. Rather, our program is designed to empower them to succeed with free market economic reforms they've chosen on their own, ideas developed in Latin America for Latin Americans.

The courageous Latin American leaders who are reforming their economies and breaking down barriers to trade and investment need our support. And they are the true liberators of our era. True success will mean opening up statist systems formerly rigged to protect wealthy elites and closed to working people and the poor. Free market reforms will banish burdensome

regulations that now prevent the urban poor from starting new businesses or *campesinos* from gaining access to credit and title to their land. Economic reform must also include honest government. Corruption is the enemy of both growth and democracy. New investment will flow only where the rule of law is secure, the courts are fair, and bidding processes are open to all.

To support reformers, to realize the hopeful new vision in Latin America, the United States Congress must meet its responsibility. I asked Congress to take long overdue action, to invest $310 million in this fiscal year under the Enterprise for the Americas Initiative. With this, we could write off more than $1 billion in the hemisphere's official debts and generate millions of dollars to preserve the environment. But regrettably, Congress has refused to approve any funds for this purpose. Congress apparently doesn't believe in return on investment, but I do. And our truckers and railroad people do. And our auto and electronics makers do, as do our environmental engineers and many, many more.

I have helped persuade our allies in Europe and Japan to contribute nearly two-thirds of a $1.5 billion fund to help Latin American reformers. This fund, administered by the Inter-American Development Bank, would help people privatize old state enterprises at the grass roots, with job retraining and small business loans. But Congress has refused to vote a penny for the U.S. share. I will keep on fighting for these vital programs of the Enterprise for the Americas Initiative until Congress demonstrates the vision and fortitude to provide the support they deserve. And if we can invest in the transformation of Eastern Europe and the old Soviet Union, and we must do so, then we can and must invest in the efforts of our closest neighbors on their peaceful road to true liberation and prosperity.

The United States' economic destiny is linked to Latin America's. No army of protectionists can change that. When Latin America suffered its debt crisis of the early eighties, 1980's, we suffered through a corresponding drop in trade. We did. If you don't believe me, ask Caterpillar workers from Illinois or employees from Cessna in Kansas. Ask them if they suffered when our best customers in Latin America were in crisis.

With the rise of democracy and economic reform, U.S. exports to Latin America have surged by nearly one-third in just 2 years, from $49 billion in 1989 to $63 billion in 1991. This is a much faster rate of growth than for our exports to Asia or Europe. It points to the fact that a stable, prosperous Latin America is a natural market for United States goods and services. Strengthening our neighbors' economies will result in more exports and more good jobs for people in the United States.

When any of us speak with our friends outside the Western Hemisphere, we need to assure them as clearly as possible there is nothing exclusionary in our vision of open trade and economic integration in our hemisphere. Our aim is simply to lower barriers to economic freedom within and among the nations of the Western Hemisphere, not, I repeat, not to create any barriers between ourselves and the nations of Africa, Europe, and Asia. All of our aims are consistent with the global policies of GATT.

And I would just like to commend the superb leadership of Arthur Dunkel, GATT's Director General, who spoke to you earlier today. And I want to assure you I urgently want to open up global markets through success with the Uruguay round. We all, all of us from whatever country in the Western Hemisphere, have a stake, a big stake, in a successful conclusion of the Uruguay round of the GATT.

And if the equivocators and the protectionists and the pleaders for the special interests want to debate this, bring them on. I will take the case for increased trade to the people in every corner of the United States of America. And I will make this abundantly clear: Free trade means more exports, more investment, more choices, more jobs for Americans. Our great country is the number one exporter in the world, over $422 billion last year. Imagine that, $422 billion. And we intend to pursue trade policies to keep that growth up now and in the future. And we will knock down barriers

wherever we find them to open markets, for instance, for our computer software, movies, books, and pharmaceuticals. We will fight hard against protectionism both at home and abroad.

And five centuries ago, a man of courage and vision set sail from Europe searching for new trade routes and opportunities. And he defied the timid counsel of those who said the Earth was flat. Christopher Columbus' voyage to the Americas transformed human history. Columbus was an entrepreneur, and the risk he took 500 years ago continues to pay off abundantly today. And today, we still have to combat the flat-Earth mentality, the mind-set that urges us to barricade our borders against competition, to shut off the free exchange of food and machinery and skills and ideas.

But the future does not belong to the status quo. It is the legacy of people like yourselves, people with far-sighted vision and then a spirit of enterprise. The future awaiting the Americas is a time of rediscovery, a time for empowering the poor through new investment, trade, and growth, a time for cultural renewal. Our efforts and the efforts of millions of citizens of the Americas can achieve new gains for honest, democratic, limited government. And together, we can usher in a new order of peace, a new time of prosperity, both animated by personal freedom.

Thank you all very much for what you are doing to strengthen free trade in this hemisphere. And let me say again how grateful I am to David and the other leaders of this wonderful organization for vitalizing and getting that private sector involved in all of these decisions. It is an absolutely essential ingredient if we are going to succeed in a course that is mutually beneficial.

Now, I heard you were having broccoli for dinner, so I'm out of here. Many, many thanks. And may God bless you all.

*Note: The President spoke at 8 p.m. at the Sheraton-Washington Hotel. In his remarks, he referred to David Rockefeller, chairman of the Americas Society.*

## Nomination of Richard Goodwin Capen, Jr., To Be United States Ambassador to Spain
*April 23, 1992*

The President today announced his intention to nominate Richard Goodwin Capen, Jr., of Florida, to be Ambassador to Spain. He would succeed Joseph Zappala.

Currently Mr. Capen serves as a consultant for Knight-Ridder, Inc. Prior to this, he served as vice chairman and director for Knight-Ridder, Inc., in Miami, FL, 1989–91; as director of Knight-Ridder, Inc., 1987–91;

and as chairman and publisher of the Miami Herald, 1983–89. From 1979 to 1982, Mr. Capen served as senior vice president for operations of Knight-Ridder, Inc.

Mr. Capen graduated from Columbia College (B.A., 1956). He was born July 16, 1934, in Hartford, CT. Mr. Capen served in the U.S. Navy, 1956–59. He is married, has three children, and resides in Miami, FL.

## Nomination of Clarence H. Albright, Jr., To Be General Counsel of the Department of Housing and Urban Development
*April 23, 1992*

The President today announced his intention to nominate Clarence H. Albright, Jr., of Virginia, to be General Counsel of the Department of Housing and Urban Development. He would succeed Francis Anthony Keating II.

Since 1990, Mr. Albright has served as Principal Deputy General Counsel in the Office of the General Counsel at the U.S. Department of Housing and Urban Development in Washington, DC, and as Deputy General Counsel, 1989–90. Prior to this, he

served as Deputy Associate Attorney General at the Department of Justice, 1988–89, and senior special assistant to the Assistant Attorney General at the U.S. Department of Justice, 1987–88.

Mr. Albright graduated from Presbyterian College in South Carolina (B.A., 1974) and George Mason University School of Law (J.D., 1980). He was born January 2, 1950, in Rock Hill, SC. Mr. Albright resides in Alexandria, VA.

## Remarks at the Presentation Ceremony for the National Crime Victims' Rights Awards
*April 24, 1992*

Please be seated, and welcome. Welcome to the Rose Garden on this beautiful Friday. We're here to commemorate National Crime Victims' Rights Week. I first salute the Attorney General, who is doing a superb job for our country in the whole area of law enforcement, Bill Barr, standing here. May I also single out Director Sessions, the head of the FBI, with us today. Bill, welcome, sir.

And to others, may I just say that the people seated in this garden are representatives of one of this country's strongest traits, compassion. And this compassion is the driving force behind the improvements that are balancing the scales of justice, strengthening the rights of the crime victims. For far too long, the agonizing experiences each victim must endure have been overlooked. The seldom-realized truth is that the crime is just the beginning of a process that will last months, if not years or lifetimes.

The award winners we honor today realize this fact. They've set out to improve, protect, and strengthen the rights of crime victims. As Attorney General Barr will explain shortly, each and every one of them is a hero worthy of saluting in this war on crime. But before the Attorney General begins the presentations, I would like to take this opportunity to reinforce our administration's commitment to the rights of crime victims. This administration, in particular the Department of Justice, has fought hard to make strides on behalf of the victims in the courtroom.

In 1991, we gained a landmark Supreme Court decision for crime victims in the case known as *Payne* versus *Tennessee*, a case which authorizes, against a constitutional challenge, the admission of victim impact evidence during the sentencing phase of capital cases. In the *Payne* versus *Tennessee* case, the Supreme Court recognized that the jury should be allowed to know the tragic impact that homicide crimes have on a survivor. In this case, the jury was allowed to know not only about the murderer's brutality toward his victims, but toward the survivors. The jury was allowed to know the pain and suffering caused 3-year-old Nicholas, the survivor of homicide victims, who missed his mother, Charisse, and his 2-year-old sister, Lacie. This decision rings of plain common sense, and it rings of fundamental fairness: A jury should know the victim, as well as the defendant.

I want to continue to see strides made in the courtroom. I've said it once, and let me just say it again: None of us should rest until all of our laws duly reflect the sympathy we should have for victims of crime. A key part of our program to make our cities safe again has been the appointment of judges who interpret the law and do not legislate from the bench. And that is exactly what I have done in naming these people to the bench.

This is a step in the right direction. And as we continue down the path of equal justice for accusers and the accused alike, we've encountered an uphill climb, frankly, one that is making our work more difficult and slowing the pace of progress considerably. As you know, that hill that I'm talking

about is Capitol Hill with all of its special interest groups.

Here is just one typical example of what we are up against. In 1990, the Congress created 11 new circuit and 74 new district judgeships to help us wage the war on crime. And yet, two and a half weeks ago, special interest groups managed to postpone a vote on my nominee to the 11th Circuit Court of Appeals, Ed Carnes. Ed Carnes' nomination has been before the Senate since January 27th. He has first-rate credentials, strong support through his home State of Alabama. In addition, no Senator has yet indicated opposition. However, some interest groups, not the Senate but the interest groups, oppose his nomination. Their reason? As a prosecutor, Ed Carnes has actively campaigned against procedural technicalities designed to prevent imposition of the death penalty. Their course of action? To obtain a one-month postponement on the vote. And the justification? The nomination needed—you've heard it before—"further study."

Personally, I do not understand the priorities of those special interest groups. Why so little concern for the victims and so much for criminals? It is my hope that the Democratic leadership of the Senate agrees with this. And if so, they will not allow Mr. Carnes' nomination to be held hostage any longer and will vote on it immediately as scheduled upon their return. It is also my hope that they will resist future efforts to play politics with the courts and will not yield to any more requests for delay on this or other judicial nominations. [*Applause*] I see one person agrees. Those of you here today play an important role in stopping this practice by special interest groups. You must make your voices heard. Let Congress know that these interest groups do not speak for you. Believe me, it will make a real difference if you check in on this point.

I am proud of what this administration has accomplished on behalf of crime victims and their survivors. But I am even more proud of this Nation's compassionate citizens who identified a fault in the system and then, through citizen action, set out to correct it.

I thank you for your dedication, for your

hard work, and applaud your successes. And I will now turn the meeting over to Attorney General Barr, asking him to do the honors. And may God bless you all. Thank you.

*Note: The President spoke at 10:02 a.m. in the Rose Garden at the White House. Following the President's remarks, Attorney General William P. Barr presented the awards to eight individuals for exemplary service on behalf of crime victims and their families and for achievements in defending the rights of crime victims.*

# Remarks Prior to a Briefing on Banking and Finance Regulatory Reform
*April 24, 1992*

I announced in the State of the Union Message a 90-day regulatory moratorium, and today another step is being taken to reduce the regulatory burdens. The 90-day moratorium has been a tremendous success. And I applaud the good work by the Council on Competitiveness, headed by Vice President Quayle.

As you know, excessive regulations add billions of dollars of costs to the American economy each year. We've got to do something about these costs. And during the moratorium we've made more than 70 deregulatory changes that will save tens of billions of dollars for American consumers and taxpayers. Many of these changes will also help create jobs for American workers.

We will have more announcements next week, and I'll have more to say on this subject on Wednesday. Today's announcement concerns financial service regulations, and we're announcing a package of banking initiatives designed to streamline financial regulation. Our new regulatory uniformity policy will reduce or eliminate unnecessary compliance costs by financial service institutions. We're also announcing measures to strengthen financial health and to reduce unnecessary regulatory barriers to new lending. These reforms will increase access to capital for individuals and businesses, thereby contributing to economic growth.

The Deputy Secretary of the Treasury, John Robson, and Boyden Gray, our General Counsel, and Michael Boskin will provide you with all the details.

Thank you very much.

*Note: The President spoke at 11:55 a.m. in the Briefing Room at the White House.*

# Teleconference Remarks to the National Association of Hispanic Journalists
*April 24, 1992*

*The President.* Thank you very much, Monica. And first, let me thank your President, Don Flores, for this opportunity to speak with you. May I salute the hundreds of Hispanic women and men who inform and enliven our great country through the press and through the broadcast media. I look forward to answering your questions.

A top priority of my Presidency is to consolidate the peaceful revolution that's taken place in Latin America over the past decade, the movement towards democracy and free markets. And yesterday I heard a solid endorsement of those goals in a meeting with hundreds of business and civic leaders and government leaders from around our hemisphere. Democratic neighbors are peaceful neighbors. Experience teaches us that. And I am determined to keep working to promote and protect democracy in Latin America.

Recently, we've been working closely with our partners in the hemisphere to defend democracy under attack in Venezuela, Haiti, and Peru. In Cuba we envision a new birth of freedom and democracy, and that day cannot be far off. I expect one day soon, after the inevitable fall of the Castro dictatorship, to be the first President of the United States to visit the free soil of Cuba.

Also vital is liberating the markets of the Western Hemisphere. I want to create a North American free trade area to increase the levels of trade, investment, and jobs in Mexico, Canada, and the United States of America. And I am thankful for the support from the Hispanic community that helped us win our great victory for fast track authority.

Some politicians don't share our views on the value of free trade. They want to address this issue from both sides of their mouths, and they suggest that we can hide in a cocoon of protection and still benefit from the fresh air of competition. Well, that is simply not possible. And you can pander to the protectionists, or you can promote free trade; you cannot have it both ways. I will fight to tear down economic barriers with Mexico and throughout the hemisphere, and I'll oppose any special interest that tries to stand in our way.

And one other thing: We must not let election year politics delay for one minute our getting a good free trade agreement and getting it approved. The North American free trade agreement will increase our trade with Mexico and create thousands more jobs right here in the United States of America. And I'll keep working with my good friend President Carlos Salinas, who is a bold and imaginative leader. Already, in just 3 years, I believe we've made U.S.-Mexican relations the best that they have ever been in history. And we're going to keep working to forge a new relationship between our nations, based on free trade, open markets, and mutual respect. And we will not stop with Mexico. My Enterprise for the Americas Initiative will encourage open trade and job-creating investment from Alaska to Argentina.

The interests we share do not end with free trade. I'm committed to action on a full range of key reforms, and I want to mention just two of urgent interest to the Hispanic community. On health care, I have put forward a comprehensive plan to open to all Americans access, access to quality health care. And I'm also proud of my administration as part of the public-private initiative called "Growing Up Hispanic" to improve the quality of health in your communities. And on the vital matter of education, Hispanic support for America 2000 has been steady and strong. And I want to see every American family win the right to choose which school is best for their children, public, private, and religious.

But even the most ambitious reform effort here at home must go hand-in-hand with economic growth through open trade. And I've asked Congress repeatedly for funds to assist the brave reformers who are now leading many of the Latin American nations. But Congress has done nothing. We must not stand for this lack of foresight. And if we can aid the transformation of the former Soviet Union—and in my view, we must do that—we can and we must also help our closest neighbors who are trying to consolidate their own revolution for freedom and prosperity.

And there are many, many other issues. But let me just say to you today before taking your questions, as I think of the Hispanic community in this country, I think of family. I think of family values. And Barbara and I are, I hope you know by now, dedicated to that concept. And every piece of legislation that comes my way, we're looking at it to see that it does nothing but strengthen the American family. That's one of the reasons I feel so strongly about choice that I just mentioned for education. We must strengthen the family values. And I will do my level-best to do just that.

And now on to the questions. Fire away. And thank you so much for letting me drop in on you.

### Statehood for Puerto Rico

*Q.* Why did your pro-statehood for Puerto Rico effort fail in Congress last year? What will you do about it if reelected?

*The President.* I have remained strongly in favor of pro-statehood. And the first step on that is a referendum. And we are having great difficulty getting that approved by the United States Congress, the part that has to be approved by Congress.

As you know, there's great divisions. It's divided in Puerto Rico by those who favor statehood, those who favor commonwealth, and then a tiny group of those who favor independence. That group has heretofore been considered one of the most radical groups.

My choice is for statehood. But I also say that the matter should be left up to the people of Puerto Rico. And so we will continue to push in a reluctant Congress to get them to come along and support Bob Lagomarsino's approach, to support a referendum that will make the determination. And then we'd have to follow on with whatever is required after that.

But I have not changed my position. And I wish, Monica, I could tell you that this is the only area where I'm having difficulty with the Congress, but it's not. But I haven't lessened my intentions at all in favor of statehood for Puerto Rico.

I know you could get in a lively debate right out there at your meeting. But I think it's best. I think it's right. And I believe it's in the best interest of all Americans, all the people in the United States right now, citizens herein. So, we'll keep trying.

### Federal Court Appointments

*Q.* Judges appointed by you and Ronald Reagan are more and more limiting access to fair treatment of U.S. Hispanics in such areas as voting rights, employment, housing, and education. If reelected, would you change your emphasis on conservative philosophy and appoint more persons to the bench who understand the realities of inequality faced by poor people of color?

*The President.* I think that people that I've appointed to the bench, both the district bench, the circuit bench, and the Supreme Court, understand that. But I don't want people to legislate from the bench. Now if the person that asked this question feels that we need judges that are going to set social policy from the bench, then we just have a philosophical difference. I have

appointed people that care. And I have appointed people that I think are compassionate. And I have appointed people that I am confident will interpret the Constitution and not legislate from the bench. So I do not plead guilty to the charges in that question at all.

I think the way that you better the lot of all people is to have them have equal access, fair access to the law. And the people that I've appointed certainly agree with that concept. So we'll continue to do this. We've got some fine Hispanic appointments, and others, to the various levels of the Federal bench. But I am not going to change my view that what we need are people that know the Constitution and interpret it and do not go into a bunch of social legislation from the Federal bench. That is not what is required, in my view, of an independent judiciary.

### Freedom of the Press

*Q.* Many people feel the first amendment was violated with severe press restrictions imposed during the war. In subsequent conflicts will your administration continue with the limitations imposed on the media during Desert Storm, or will we be allowed to do our jobs?

*The President.* Well, you're allowed to do your job. After Desert Storm a review was taken. I do not believe that the constitutional rights of the press were violated in Desert Storm. And if you remember, one journalist who didn't play by the rules was kidnaped and taken prisoner, and we spent a great deal of time and an awful lot of anxiety in trying to help get that person released from jail because he didn't follow the guidelines of the military. And when you're in a war, every correspondent should not have the freedom to go anyplace they want at any time. And that example proved it.

But I do think you're on to something because I think as each incident of this nature takes place—and let's hope there won't be another one for a long time—we ought to review it. We ought to see if there's ways that we can guarantee more access for journalists to the front lines or more access of journalists to the briefers or whatever it is. So, I don't think rights were violated. I do think we can learn from the desert war pooling experience and from the Desert Storm coverage and see if we can't do a better job on access for journalists.

*Q.* President Bush, on behalf of the National Association of Hispanic Journalists, we thank you for your time today.

*The President.* Monica, thank you very, very much. And good luck to you out there. I am one who, as you may know from my own family, is doubly blessed in a sense because of having three Hispanic-American grandchildren. And so, I hope I've been sensitive to your needs and to the things that bring you together. But I can guarantee you this, I'm going to keep on trying.

And when I think about patriotism and service to country, I know what I'm talking about when I say Hispanics have been in the forefront of that. And when I think about family values, I know what I'm talking about when I say the Hispanic-American families epitomize, more than most, the family values that Barbara and I, at least, hold so dear.

So I'll keep on trying, trying to do my best. And I might say in conclusion—you don't need to hear me twice now—but I might say in conclusion that the economic news is a little better. And as that turns around, and I'm confident it will, I think we'll see this country coming together; I think we'll see a return to a little more optimism. And certainly, I will keep dedicated and rededicating our administration to fairplay for our Hispanic-American citizens.

So thank you, and thanks for letting me drop in. And good luck to each and every one of you. Thank you.

*Note: The President spoke at 2:34 p.m. via satellite from Room 459 of the Old Executive Office Building to the National Association of Hispanic Journalists meeting in Albuquerque, NM. In his remarks, he referred to Monica Armenta, moderator of the teleconference.*

# Radio Address to the Nation on Trade Reform
*April 25, 1992*

A lot of the reports we Americans hear on TV or the radio seem to follow the maxim "Good news is no news." Well, today I'm going to break a few rules and talk about some good news. The story is jobs, jobs created and jobs sustained because of our ability to sell our product and services abroad.

Last week, we received the latest from the economic front. All around the world, more and more people are buying American. Our exports shot up 7 percent in February to a one-month record high of almost $38 billion, closing the deficit gap by 16 percent. If there's any moral to this story, it's a reminder that if Americans want to succeed economically at home, we've got to lead economically abroad. In the past couple of weeks, I've been talking to groups around the country and to leaders from around the world. The message is simple:

Expanding free trade abroad means expanding opportunity at home.

America's trade story is good news, not just for our coastal States and port towns but all across America. Here's a sampling: Colorado, about 90,000 jobs supported by trade; about 90,000 in Iowa; Arizona, 120,000 jobs; Tennessee, 150,000 jobs. America's manufacturing exports are more competitive than 10 years ago, our labor more productive. The Chicken Little hysterics of an America under siege may make better copy, but they leave out one little fact: The United States is the leading exporter in the world, bar none.

I don't mean to discount the competition. Our competitors are tough. More and more, America competes in an international marketplace where standing still means falling behind. Some want us to respond to these challenges as if they were a bad dream, just hide under the covers and hope it goes away. They may be talking tough, but they're really running scared. The problem is, they're running the wrong way. The answer isn't to build up our barriers; it's to get other countries to tear down theirs.

Two days ago, I met with the heads of Europe's Common Market. And we talked long and hard about how to bring the Uruguay round of GATT, the world trade negotiations, to a successful conclusion. Such an agreement could pump $5 trillion into the global economy over the next 10 years. The U.S. share would top $1 trillion. That's hundreds of thousands of new American jobs.

I don't plan to stop there. We're also negotiating an historic free trade agreement with Mexico and Canada. Listen to these facts: During my Presidency, 45 out of our 50 States have increased their exports with Mexico. Already over the 4 years, exports to Mexico have more than doubled, creating hundreds of thousands of jobs here at home. Clearly, with a successful agreement, we'd export more than ever before, increasing trade with Mexico by $10 billion and creating over 360,000 American jobs. And that's why a North American free trade agree-

ment is in our interest, because it means more jobs right here.

Just this week, the United States took steps to facilitate trade in high-technology goods, an initiative made possible by the rebirth of freedom in formerly Communist lands. We relaxed trade restrictions that served us well during the cold war but no longer serve their purpose. We will eliminate requirements for thousands of export licenses, including many that affected computers, one of our strongest export earners. Trade covered by this deregulation amounts to about $2.5 billion.

The choice is simple. We can either promote protectionism or promote free trade. To my reckoning, no one ever beat the competition by cringing behind a trade barrier. You see, I have faith in free trade because I have faith in the American worker. When trade is free and fair, Americans can beat the competition fair and square.

Thank you for listening. And may God bless the United States of America.

*Note: This address was recorded at 7:56 a.m. on April 24 in the Oval Office at the White House for broadcast after 9 a.m. on April 25.*

# Remarks on Legislative Goals and an Exchange With Reporters
*April 27, 1992*

*The President.* With Congress coming back tomorrow, I want to just emphasize those things that I hope we can accomplish in the next couple of months by actively seeking areas of consensus. What I'm about to list does not include everything I'd like to see done, but some main areas.

First, while the economy is recovering, we still need an economic boost to ensure the strength and length of this rise in economic activity. The growth package that I sent to Congress in my State of the Union is still before Congress, and it contains key elements of a plan to create jobs and stimulate investment and growth. And I ask the Congress to continue consideration of these proposals.

Secondly, there's the energy bill, an energy bill that will further our national energy needs and goals. The Senate produced a good bipartisan bill, and the bipartisan process appears to be breaking down in the House. That should not be allowed to happen. A comprehensive energy strategy is long overdue, and we need bills that make sense, not a veto.

The third is health care reform. Comprehensive reform is made up of many elements, and I believe there is relative consensus on some of the elements. And I'd like to act quickly in those areas where we can achieve consensus. There are 30 million people in this country without adequate health care insurance, and we must offer them the benefits of our health care system.

The fourth one is education. Our kids must be able to compete to get jobs, to create jobs, to participate in the global economy. And we must help spur fundamental reform by encouraging this new American schools concept, flexibility, world-class standards, and parental choice, including private, public, and parochial schools. A business-as-usual education bill simply will not take us where we need to go.

And finally, as I've repeatedly called for in the past, I'd like to see this constitutional amendment requiring a balanced budget. The Democratic leadership is changing their view on the issue, and I think there's a feeling they may be willing to help us move an amendment forward. So now is the time to pass that balanced budget amendment.

So, those are the five I'd like to see passed just as soon as possible by Congress. And then, of course, we'll be pushing for other legislative goals as well, liability reform and things like that.

*Fundraising Ethics*

*Q.* Mr. President, what do you think of allegations that some of your supporters are intimidating and coercing their employees to kick into Republican——

*The President.* I don't like that at all.

*Q.* ——fundraising?

*The President.* I disapprove of——

*Q.* Have you ever heard of it? I mean, have you ever seen it?

*The President.* Seen it?

*Q.* Yes, in action, in any of your fundraising?

*The President.* No, I've never seen that. No. And I've read some allegations that concern me very much because there ought not, there should not be coercion in fundraising. It's outrageous. And I pride myself on a good, clean record in this regard.

*Downing of U.S. Aircraft in Peru*

*Q.* Mr. President, is there anything new on the Peru incident?

*The President.* Nothing new on it. There's still some uncertainty. But to his credit,

President Fujimori did the right thing in expressing regrets and apologies. But there's still some uncertainties exactly what happened. The plane was marked. It was clearly on a predictable course. But we still don't know all the answers to it.

*Q.* Are you afraid of Ross Perot?

*World Economic Growth*

*Q.* Would you like to see Japan and Germany do more to stimulate world economic growth?

*The President.* Well, I'd like to see everybody involved in economic growth. And I'll be prepared to talk about that further to Helmut Kohl. I've discussed it. As you know, we had an economic growth deal with Japan on our trip. One of the things we both agreed on was a growth agenda. So I think all countries want that, but each one has to find his own way achieving economic growth. I'm hopeful that we are on the path. They have every reason to have been critical of us in the past. But I don't think the way to do it is to criticize the Chancellor of Germany, which I'm not about to do, nor the Prime Minister of Japan, Mr. Miyazawa. I think we all want growth. And the question is how to achieve it.

*Health Care*

*Q.* What are the areas of health care where you think there is consensus? Is it just insurance?

*The President.* Well, I think there's some talk now about accessibility to insurance, which would be good. I'd love to see a move forward on our malpractice legislation, legislation to put some caps on these outrageous liability claims. We're suing each other too much, and we ought to be taking care of each other more. So I think there's some areas like that where we can do some good.

Thank you.

*Note: The President spoke at 10:05 a.m. on the South Lawn at the White House prior to his departure for Miami, FL.*

## Remarks at the Florida International University Commencement Ceremony in Miami Beach, Florida
*April 27, 1992*

Thank you all very much. Thank you, Dr. Maidique, for that wonderful citation, those very kind words. May I salute Elsie Augenblick for the alma mater, Sister Flood for that very moving invocation, Provost Mau for opening the ceremony and presiding over this madhouse. I'm pleased to be here with so many leaders of the State, State legislators, members of the Florida Legislature, so many distinguished leaders in the Miami community. I want to salute Chairman Alvah Chapman, who does so much for this community, and the other members of the board of trustees; Regent Alec Courtelis; your own Congresswoman, or one of the Congresswomen from this area, Ileana Ros-Lehtinen, who came down with us. Today she's not known as a Congresswoman; she's known as a graduate of F.I.U. And we're very proud of that. I told Ileana coming down on the plane that the real reason that I'm here today, Andy Garcia made me an offer I couldn't refuse. [*Laughter*]

May I also salute my fellow honorees: Celia Cruz, "Queen of the Latin American Music," "Doctor of Salsa." [*Laughter*] She's captured the soul of a culture in her music. She asked me where Barbara was. I said Barbara is up there trying to get an agent for our rich dog. But I know that if she were here—she's a great Celia admirer—she would give her a *grande abraso* like the rest of us do. Celia, congratulations.

And to our other honoree, a longtime friend, respected friend, Abe Foxman. You heard it in the citation, but he is a lifelong fighter for fairplay and equity. His voice is strong against racism and against anti-Semitism. And all of us in public life can take an example from the man you honor here today. He's a great fighter for human rights and dignity. Abe, congratulations.

And may I salute honorees Bell and Weiser and Rosenberg and your teachers Smith and Jones. Very good going for both of them. They disappeared over here somewhere. But I loved those citations because it says so much about the commitment of our teachers to helping kids all across this country. And may I, too, salute the F.I.U. faculty, the students, the families. Thank you, Panthers, all, for this wonderful welcome to this coliseum.

I know today's commencement is one of the hottest tickets in town. President Maidique told me about one graduate, Yanira Bermudez, who needed a dozen tickets for family members who came all the way from Canada. You can't imagine how pleased I am to receive this degree, knowing, therefore, that I'd be guaranteed a seat at this tremendous turnout. [*Laughter*] It is spectacular.

And I really am, I mean this, I'm very honored to be a part of this special occasion. Today's ceremony marks more than a graduation. This commencement is a coming of age. Twenty years ago, Miami didn't have a public university. Today, under the leadership of President Maidique, Florida International is not simply a fixture in the intellectual and economic life of this thriving city; it is one of the 50 largest universities in the United States of America, and a quality one at that. I can tell you this: They won't be asking, "F.I. who?" anymore. Never again. You've come a long way from those early days 20 years ago, holding class in the air traffic control tower out at Tamiami Airport. And the progress that you've made stands as testimony to the power of a dream and also of your determination to make that dream real.

Let me speak for a moment about the secret of your success. Florida International has blazed its own path. Many of your students are a little older, a little more experienced. You're a little more likely to combine work and study, family life with college life. And because of that, you're a little less likely to treat your university years as some ivory tower exercise and more an extension of the everyday world around you. All of those factors keep this university close to the community it serves. And all of those factors make F.I.U. a force in shaping south Florida's fortunes in the new century ahead.

Even now, each day brings new changes, new nations, new realities, new hopes, new horizons. And it's not so much technology and science that we marvel at but the startling pace of political change. The democratic renaissance in Central and Eastern Europe, the blossoming of democracy here in our precious hemisphere, the end of the cold war, and the collapse of imperial communism, all would be unimaginable in a world where America turned inward, away from the challenges of a new world.

The changes in the world beyond our shores have real impact right here at home. In the new world you'll call your own, your children won't wake to the nuclear nightmare that played in the corners of your mind. We have made real, dramatic progress toward eliminating the threat of nuclear weapons and in turning our old adversary in the Soviet Union into new partners of peace. And I take great pride that U.S. leadership helped make that dramatic change possible.

But change brings new challenges. We've put an end to a long era of military confrontation and entered a new age of economic competition. And yes, dictators have given way to democracy, and yet, clearly, dangers still remain. Here in Miami, I know the great gains for democracy we've seen in the world have a bittersweet edge. Each triumph for freedom, each victory for the people from Moscow to Managua calls attention to the one island where communism continues to hold sway. And I cannot pretend to imagine the anguish that so many of you or your parents or your other family members must have felt at a cruel choice, the cruel choice between the land of your birth and the love of freedom. I share the dreams that you have for a democratic Cuba.

I have thought a great deal about this and anguished about it. And I am absolutely convinced that that day will come. And with the collapse of Soviet communism, Cuba now stands isolated and alone, and we continue to keep the pressure on to tighten the trade embargo, to champion the cause of human rights. The fact that dictators cling to power is a fact that will soon become a footnote. We are witnessing the collapse of the Communist idea, the demise of the crippling concept of the all-powerful state.

There are many reasons for this collapse. But in the end, one fact alone explains what we see today. Its advocates saw the triumph of communism written in the laws of history, and they failed to see the love of freedom written in the human heart. I know there's a Spanish saying about the Castro regime that is true in any language: *En las noventas, se revienta.* I guarantee you, freedom will come to Cuba. Make no mistake about it. And none of you professors give me a grade on my accent, either.

But the change we see doesn't stop at America's doorstep. Here at home we've got to ask: How can we open the doors of opportunity for every American? Our challenge, our new American destiny is to give the American dream room to grow. And to make that destiny our own, we must advance American ideals, help communism's old captive nations take their place among the world's democracies. We must advance America's economic interests, meet the competitive challenge of a new world economy.

Here in Miami, we see this new American economy in microcosm. This city is the hub, the economic gateway to the Americas. Here's the figure: Forty-five percent, nearly half, of all U.S. trade with Latin America passes through the Miami area. And that translates into 35,000 jobs in the Miami area alone tied to trade. And here's what that means for the graduates that are here today. Your standard of living, your opportunities, your future are certain to be influenced by the world beyond our shores.

Now, I know that there are some who see a different future, people who want to sound retreat, run from the new realities, seek refuge in a dream world of economic isolationism or protectionism. Those voices have nothing to say to this Nation. There is no turning back. There is no hiding from the new reality. We have no choice but to compete. The new reality of our new world economy is simply this: To succeed economically at home, we must lead economically abroad.

And finally, if we want to make a new American destiny our own, we've got to bridge the gap between the American people and the Government that's meant to serve it. I know there's a discontent. Travel around the country; you can't help but feel it, a deepening cynicism about the way things work or fail to work in Washington, a doubt about one person's ability to change, really change the system. To them, Government has grown more distant. Too often, the Government we get is not accountable. It is not effective. It is not efficient. And regrettably, it's not compassionate.

It's not that people are apathetic. It's that people are angry with Government. Many of you recycle empty cans and plastic bottles because when it comes to the environment, you believe that one individual's actions can make a difference. But when it comes to self-government, cynicism kicks in, and too many people have come to doubt the power of a single vote.

This didn't happen just overnight. It's the legacy of a theory of government grown too used to promising what government will do for the people. And this theory fails to see that people don't want government to make their decisions for them; they want government that gives them the freedom to choose. And they want a Government that spends within its means in the way families do. And they want welfare programs that provide opportunity, not the dead-end street of dependency. And they want to be free to choose the school that is best for their children, public, private, or religious.

And that message is getting through. Because in spite of the cynicism, we see positive signs, a new ethic of responsibility alive in America. The days of the no-fault lifestyle are coming to an end. We see it all around us: individuals taking responsibility, individuals taking action. In their private lives, people know actions have consequences. And what they want from government are policies and programs that hold people responsible for their actions. And that government is responsible to the people. And if you think about it, that's nothing more than a working definition of the word "democracy."

We've got to bring the ethic of responsibility back into government. And when we do, we'll see the sense of public trust return to politics. And we'll see a Government that reflects the real values of this great Nation, proud, confident, caring, and strong. That's my mission as President. It's our challenge as a Nation. And the way we do it is through reform.

I've already mentioned one of the areas where we need urgent action: expanding trade, to open new markets the world over to American goods. Beyond trade, there are four other key issues that together form the core of our reform agenda.

We've got to fight for legal reform to end the explosion of litigation that strains our patience and saps our economy. America would be better off it we spent less time suing each other and more time helping one another.

And we've got to reform this country's health care system, open up access to all Americans, and control the runaway cost without sacrificing the quality education that separates us from every other country in the world: choice and quality.

We've sparked a revolution in American education, community by community, to help our children get the world-class education that our new world demands. And I know the need for education dollars is great, and that's why at the Federal level we've increased our education budget by 41 percent since I took office. And I saw those stickers out there, and believe me, I came prepared with those statistics, 41 percent increase.

And finally, we've got to push forward on Government reform because only if we reverse a generation of creeping bureaucracy, only if we restore limits to Government, can we restore public trust.

Each reform is essential. And I've called on Congress to take action in each of these areas—legislation on Capitol Hill right now in most of it. Each reform will succeed so long as we draw on the strengths that got each of you here in this room today. As a society, as a Nation, we stand to gain from your skills and your training, your insight and your energy. But the most precious resource of all is this: It's that sense of optimism, your optimism. And there is still plenty of optimism in the American character.

Let me take someone many of you will know, a senior named Sylvia Daniels. She took her first class at F.I.U. 15 years ago, and she graduates today at the age of 77. And I've saved the best for last: This summer, Sylvia, they tell me, starts graduate classes in Cambridge, England. Good luck. And Sylvia, if you're looking for a new challenge to take on until school starts, there's always the national windsurfing championship. Good luck. [*Laughter*]

We see the power of optimism in Jose Marrero, who today becomes the first in his family to graduate from college. And he's done it at the age of 19. And we see it in Michael Yelovich. Ten years ago, at the age of 15, Michael was paralyzed, the result of an accidental shooting. And Michael's mother wrote me at the White House about that difficult time when, in her words, "Life to Michael and the rest of our family seemed unbearable." Michael's battled back against the odds and the obstacles to get here today. And his mother wrote that "When he graduates, the whole world should know." And it seems to her now that the whole world does know. And what a great story that is.

And so, when I hear that in America you can't get ahead, I say, "Tell that one to Michael Yelovich. Try that one on." And when I hear that in America our kids are in crisis, I say, "Tell that to Jose Marrero."

And when I hear that in America our best days are behind us, I say, "Tell that to Sylvia Daniels." Here's what I know: America's best days always lie ahead. In the next century, as in this one, America will be the strongest, the bravest, the freest Nation on the face of the Earth.

As President, I have made it my mission to preserve and advance three legacies close to all our hearts: a world at peace; an economy with good jobs, real opportunity for all Americans; a Nation of strong families, sturdy values of character and culture. To make this destiny our own, we've got to be part of a larger movement. As parents, as citizens, as members of the communities we call home, we must rekindle a revolution to bring change to the country that, indeed, has changed the world.

Thank you, once again, for this warm welcome and this high honor and for inviting me to share this special day with you and your families. And may God bless the United States of America. Thank you very, very much.

*Note: The President spoke at 2:50 p.m. at the Miami Beach Convention Center. In his remarks, he referred to Andy Garcia, actor and F.I.U. alumnus; Robert Bell, Sherwood M. (Woody) Weiser, and Mark B. Rosenberg, F.I.U. Distinguished Service Award recipients; Mary Ann Smith, Broward County Teacher of the Year; and Angel Stanford Jones, Dade County Teacher of the Year.*

## Statement by Press Secretary Fitzwater on Syria's Lifting of Restrictions on Syrian Jews
*April 27, 1992*

We are pleased to have obtained official confirmation from the Syrian Government on Saturday of the lifting of restrictions on travel and disposition of property for the Syrian Jewish community.

The Syrian Government has now informed us that, in the aftermath of President Assad's recent meeting with the leaders of Syria's Jewish community, all members of the Syrian Jewish community will be

accorded the same rights as those enjoyed by all other Syrian citizens. We have been told that Syrian Jews will be allowed to travel abroad as families, on business, and for vacations. Further, the Syrian Government has removed difficulties encountered by its Jewish citizens with regard to the sale and purchase of property. The Syrian Government has also released the Soued brothers, who had been imprisoned for violating

Syrian travel laws.

We welcome these decisions by President Assad and his Government. This administration has maintained a productive dialog with Syria's leadership on a number of important issues, including the peace process. The subject of Syrian Jewry has constituted an integral part of this dialog and has been raised by both President Bush and Secretary Baker with President Assad and other senior Syrian officials. We look forward to the full implementation of these decisions affecting Syrian Jews.

# Statement by Press Secretary Fitzwater on the Beer Market Access Agreement With Canada
*April 27, 1992*

The President welcomes the agreement in principle reached Saturday between the U.S. Trade Representative and Canadian officials to resolve longstanding bilateral differences over access for American beer to the Canadian market. The agreement is an indication of the importance of our bilateral trading relationship and the willingness of the U.S. and Canada to work cooperatively to resolve trade differences.

# Nomination of William Clark, Jr., To Be an Assistant Secretary of State
*April 27, 1992*

The President today announced his intention to nominate William Clark, Jr., of the District of Columbia, a member of the Senior Foreign Service, class of Career Minister, to be an Assistant Secretary of State for East Asian and Pacific Affairs. He would succeed Richard H. Solomon.

Since 1989, Ambassador Clark has served as United States Ambassador to India. Prior to this, he served as Principal Deputy Assistant Secretary of State for Asian and Pacific Affairs at the U.S. Department of State, 1987–89; and as Deputy Assistant Secretary of State for East Asian and Pacific Affairs, 1986–87. In addition, Ambassador Clark served as Chargé d'Affaires at the U.S. Embassy in Cairo, Egypt, 1986, and as Deputy Chief of Mission, 1985–86.

Ambassador Clark graduated from San Jose State College (B.A., 1954). He was born October 12, 1930, in Oakland, CA. Ambassador Clark served in the U.S. Navy, 1949–53. He is married, has one child, and resides in Washington, DC.

# Remarks at a Bush-Quayle Fundraising Dinner in Charlotte, North Carolina
*April 27, 1992*

Thank you so much for the warm welcome. Thank you, Jim Martin, Dottie—and Jim, for those kind words and for heading up our effort in this great and important State. Dr. Ford, thank you for your lovely words of invocation. Let me single out the Bravo Singers, did a superb job of harmony there on the anthem. And the Lees-McRae

College Clodhoppers out there, the cloggers, first-class from what I could see. I only saw one end of it down there, but it looked pretty good.

And my respects to your neighbor to the south, the incomparable, outstanding Senator Strom Thurmond. My heavens, what a great joy it is to have him and work with him in the United States Senate. He is a superb leader. And he's very proud of the Cat Band of Lexington, South Carolina, that's with us tonight.

And may I salute the three Congressmen introduced, Congressmen McMillan and Taylor and Ballenger, and thank them for being with us. Thank our finance team that's done so much for me already, Bobby Holt, our national chairman, and Jack Laughery, our regional—he's got five States, and he's twisting arms in every single one of them, doing a first-class job. And Mayo, thank you, sir, for leading the pack here. May I also thank Bob Bradshaw, our dinner chairman; salute an old friend, colleague— he and I were elected to Congress on the same day—Jim Gardner, now the Lieutenant Governor, with big plans ahead for him.

And Mayor Vinroot, you lead a wonderful city indeed. You know, coming into Charlotte is no longer a small-city experience. I can't believe your airport is now the eighth busiest in the country. The old saw used to be that you had to go through Atlanta to get to heaven; now they say it is much more fun to go through Charlotte. [*Laughter*]

But it's wonderful to see so many friends here. And Jim Martin and I have a lot in common. We both have to deal with a house full of Democrats. We don't need his Ph.D. to realize that that's bad chemistry. You know, I listened very carefully to what Jesse said, outstanding Senator Jesse Helms, and heard what he had to say about the spending habits of the Congress and then coupled that with what Strom had to say. And there's very little left for me. But they hit the main points. It is the Congress that appropriates every dime. It is the Congress that tells the Executive how to spend every dime.

People say they think that Jim Martin— back to him—will have a hard time making the transition from politics to medicine. I don't think so at all. I'll bet it won't take him any time at all before he's out playing golf on Wednesday afternoons. [*Laughter*]

There's a good reason for Charlotte to be a proud city. I especially admire the way you support two concerns that are very close to my heart: education, that Jim touched on, and service to others. Your Foundation for the Carolinas shows the priority you place on these community efforts. And yes, this is National Volunteer Week. And I'm reminded that Charlotte is the home to some remarkable, what we call Points of Light, including the Cities in Schools volunteers, Charlotte Habitat for Humanity, and the employees of the Duke Power Company that go out and do so much to help others get educated.

But now let me thank each of you who contribute so generously to this reelection campaign. This support is important for the future of our country. Let me say it right up front: I want to be your President for 4 more years, and I believe I'm going to be.

I know that many here are understandably concerned about the economy. That is my number one concern as well. But this month we had some heartening news about the United States economy, almost across the board, incidentally. It's turning around; it's beginning to move again. The leading indicator has been trade. U.S. exports are surging, rising 7 percent in February to a record one-month high of almost $38 billion. And once again, American manufacturing exports are leading the way.

The evidence is indisputable: Open markets and free trade mean new hires and new buyers, jobs for American workers from sales of American goods and services. Jobs in the trade sector have grown 3 times faster than overall American job creation. This good news underscores a fundamental truth about our own competitiveness: If we're to succeed economically at home, we must lead economically abroad.

There's still much more that we've got to do to make America more competitive. The Congress could get this recovery moving quicker and stronger if we would pass the economic package that Strom mentioned, the package that I sent up to Congress in January. One of our problems right now is the cost of capital; it is too high. But it's a problem we can do something about. A high capital gains tax rate deters investment, thus business expansion, and thus job creation. None of our major industrial competitors tax capital gains at rates that are comparable to ours. Germany doesn't tax them at all, zero. And in Japan, a businessman, entrepreneur who sells the company that he's built from scratch pays a tax of one percent. These are America's toughest competitors. But we disadvantage our own workers and then ask them to beat the competition. That's just plain dumb.

Yet, the very people who every year complain about America's ability to compete are the same people who every year block our efforts to lower the cost of capital. Once and for all they need to get the message: It is time to cut the tax on capital gains. And it is time that Congress gives us this investment tax allowance that we also put forward as one of our seven investment points. We need that, and we need that one now. And I wish, Strom, that the Congress would get moving on that.

For us to compete we also must lighten up the regulatory burden that Washington imposes on every American business. Just last January we placed a 90-day moratorium on Federal regulations. Wherever possible, we've blocked those regulations that impede growth and accelerated those that encourage growth. So far, we've saved American consumers and businesses many billions in regulatory costs. Wednesday, we'll announce our next step in our battle against these excessive regulations. But for now I simply want to say the days of over-regulation are just that, they are over. And we must all work to keep it that way.

I've talked often about the need for reform and the need for change. And I've acted, made specific and far-reaching proposals. I've called for reform of our education system, our health care system, our courts, and our election campaigns. I have fought for free and fair trade to sustain and create good jobs. These are five key issues at the forefront of the national agenda. Beyond that, right down the line, from crime that Strom talks about, in a field in which he's been such a leader, all the way to the Congress itself, our administration

has proposed fundamental changes to help us solve pressing national problems.

We've had some successes in our efforts to change things, but more often than not Congress stands in the way. They are supported by an army of special interests. Neither are interested in change. They stand squarely behind the status quo. They may be powerful. They may be influential. They may be very well-connected. But let me tell you this: They are absolutely wrong in their approach to the economy of the United States of America.

Let me tell you why. It used to be that a doctor's first concern was the care of the patient, not the chance of a malpractice suit. Lawsuit mania, you know what I'm talking about: Obstetricians not delivering babies, parents literally being driven away from coaching Little League, volunteers not helping the elderly, all because of the fear of lawsuits. That is wrong. That is not the America we want. People should spend more time helping each other and a little less time suing each other.

And you can help me by calling on the Congress to pass our "Access to Justice Act." It is languishing on Capitol Hill, blocked by special interest groups getting rich off these outrageous settlements. Our legal system is complicated. And people's rights certainly must be protected. But the system desperately needs reform, and no lawyers lobby should stand in the way. And we must fight to put some limits on these liability claims.

It used to be that we were confident that when we sent our kids to school they would get a first-class education, learn how to read and write, understand something about the world. We believed in building character, so education included teaching values and responsibility, simple right from wrong. We believed parents shared this responsibility for education. Parents are a child's first teachers, and the home is a child's first school. I believe that's still the way it ought to be.

But educational achievement has been stagnant for years. And now we thank our lucky stars that our child's school isn't the one where they find a gun in someone's locker or drug dealing out there in the playground, for heaven's sakes. And our teachers, they often double as counselors, mentors, social workers, and surrogate parents all rolled up into one. God bless our teachers for the work they do. They deserve our best effort, they deserve our best effort to make the system better.

And right here, Charlotte and the State of North Carolina are leading the way. We've set national goals, six national goals in a bipartisan fashion, and a strategy to achieve them. In every State in the Nation and over 1,200 communities across the country, our America 2000 reforms are gaining steam with innovation, these break-the-mold schools, world-class standards, voluntary national testing, more flexibility for teachers and principals. And whether it's among public schools or private or religious, all parents, rich or poor, deserve the right to choose their children's schools. And I challenge Congress to pass legislation to that end.

It's a giant undertaking to create the best schools in the world for our kids, to literally, in a country this big, to revolutionize the Nation's education system. But we are going to do it, with or without permission from the powerful NEA union or the United States Congress.

Charlotte is very fortunate. You've got a great Congressman in Alex McMillan. He's an expert on another urgent reform issue, health care. It used to be that going to the hospital didn't conjure up images of financial ruin. And while our health care still is the finest quality care in the world, too many people don't qualify for health insurance, or they simply cannot afford it. And the cost of even minor surgery has gone sky-high, right out through the roof. Many poor people would prefer going to a family doctor but end up waiting for hours in hospital emergency rooms for routine medical attention. This, too, is wrong, and it's got to change.

Our health care proposal is comprehensive. It makes health insurance accessible and affordable for all Americans without destroying the finest quality health care in the world. We must not go the way of these nationalized health care plans with long lines, impersonal service, and fewer options for consumers. If that's what we wanted,

we'd put health care under the department of motor vehicles, and we'd all stand in line all day long. We don't need another big bureaucracy.

Look what happened to Medicaid. It started as a $1 billion program, $1 billion. It is now $150 billion and growing at a rate of 17 percent a year, 38 percent last year alone. Yes, there are those whose first resort is a big new Government program with all the self-perpetuating features of the old big Government programs. But make no mistake, nationalized health care would be a national disaster. And I will fight any nationalized or socialized medicine plans for the United States of America.

In these and so many areas that demand our reform, our Government can play a pivotal and positive role in addressing many of our Nation's most critical problems. One half of my adult life, my own, has been in the private sector, and one half in government service. And I've seen this country change, sometimes for the better, sometimes for the worse. And you need to know what needs change. Change for change sake is meaningless and empty. It takes more than happy talk, more than lip service to reform or get service to special interest.

But that's what the Democrats are still offering if you look at these mandated programs they're proposing day in and day out. Our party stands for change. But the national Democratic Party will always revert to form, solve a problem by creating a program; more power to the bureaucracy, less to the individual. They do not understand that people are yearning for a return to responsibility and accountability, values that refuse to go out of style.

That is why major reforms of our Government are absolutely essential. The American people know that as Government tries to do more and more, it delivers less and less. Next year, the Federal Government will spend $1.5 trillion of your money. There is just no question about it: The Federal Government is too big and spends too much. So, we should start with real spending reform. It's time for the President—and I will not parrot Strom—to have what 43 Governors have, that line-item veto.

Next, I've sent up legislation to end the

Photographic
Portfolio

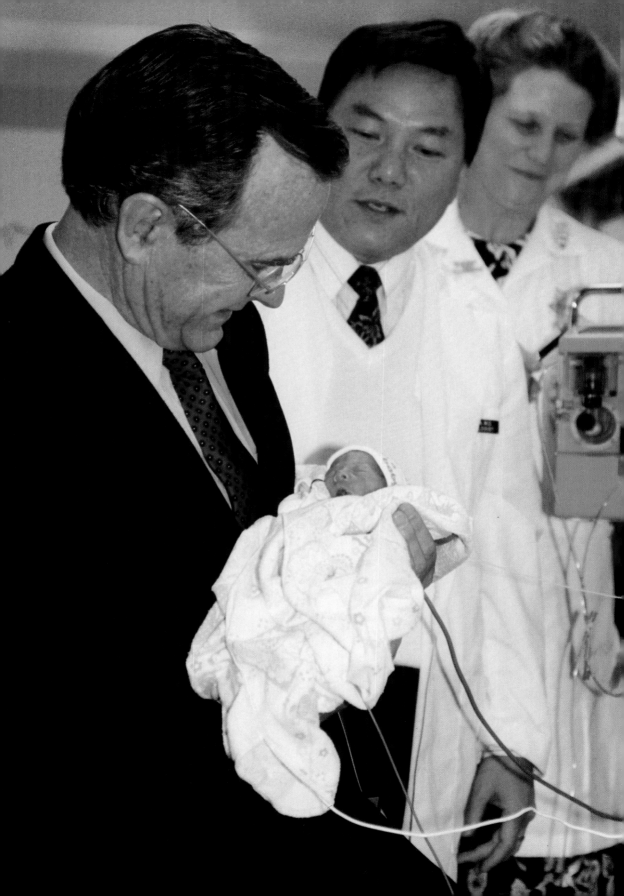

*Overleaf:* Working in the Oval Office, February 21. *Left:* Touring the University Medical Center of Southern Nevada in Las Vegas, February 6. *Right:* Conferring with Secretary of State James A. Baker III at the drug summit in San Antonio, TX, February 27. *Below:* At the ground-breaking ceremony for the Korean War Veterans Memorial on The Mall, June 14.

**Left:** At Mount Paran Christian School in Marietta, GA, May 27. **Below:** With economic summit leaders in Munich, Germany, July 6. **Right:** With President Boris Yeltsin of Russia on the South Lawn, June 16.

*Left:* Addressing the Greater Cleveland Growth Association in Cleveland, OH, February 6. *Below left:* Announcing the Bush-Quayle reelection candidacies at the J.W. Marriott Hotel, February 12. *Right:* Opening the new Oriole Park at Camden Yards with son George W. Bush and grandson George P. Bush in Baltimore, MD, April 6. *Below:* Touring the riot-damaged area in south central Los Angeles, CA, May 7. *Overleaf:* On the Senate steps following meetings with congressional leaders, January 29.

special treatment for Congress. It is time for the Congress to govern itself by the laws that it imposes on others. The laws that you and I have to abide by, the Congress ought to abide by. And it's time for sweeping reform of campaign financing, but let's not do it by making the taxpayer fund all these congressional elections. It's bad enough to have them put it in for the President's race. Finally, it's time to make Congress a citizen assembly, not a club for career politicians. And so, I think the time has come to limit the terms of Members of Congress. I favor six terms for a Member of the House and two for a Senator that precisely has limited terms—the Presidency has it limited. You might say, then, why should not the Congress?

These last few years have seen our world turned absolutely upside down. Think how much we have accomplished. We think of our problems, but think of our blessings for a minute. With God's help and with hard work to support the convictions we have, we've helped change the world. We literally have changed the world. We've helped the peoples of Eastern Europe and the old Soviet empire peacefully throw off the yoke of communism. Now we're helping their transition to free markets and helping them reduce their nuclear arsenals.

And if you ask me what gives you the most pride or pleasure out of having been President, I take great pride that it was the leadership of the United States that has diminished for our children the threat of nuclear war. We stood up against dictators and exporters of totalitarian revolution in Latin America; we've helped make democracy take root in nearly every country of our own hemisphere. Look south of the Rio Grande.

When a ruthless tyrant overran Kuwait and threatened to engulf the entire Middle East in its worst conflagration, we protected the people of Israel and Turkey and Saudi Arabia. And we organized an unprecedented world coalition, and we liberated Kuwait from the aggressor. In the process, we accomplished a breakthrough sought by every President from Truman to Reagan: We brought Arab neighbors face to face with Israel for the first time at the peace table. This is big. And this is historic. And we can all take pride in this as Americans.

We won the cold war and we stopped Saddam's aggression because 12 years ago we renewed our faith in our values and, as Strom pointed out again, we strengthened our defenses. And now, if any of you have traveled around the world I believe you'd agree with this one, the United States is the undisputed leader of the entire world. This is no time to pull back. This is no time to retreat, no time to be afraid of the changes in the world. We will keep ourselves strong. And in world markets, security, and politics, we are going to stay engaged, and we are going to continue to lead the entire world.

And so, in sum, we have a mission together to carry on the American dream for new generations. With your help we can win a mandate to lead this country for 4 more years. We can keep our country a champion of ideas and opportunity and justice. We can reform our schools and our courts and our health care system, our very system of government. And we can assure that when we reach the new century, America will still be the strongest, the bravest, and the freest Nation on the face of the Earth.

Thank you all. And may God bless each and every one of you. And may God bless our great country, the United States of America. Thank you very much.

*Note: The President spoke at 8:05 p.m. at the Adam's Mark Hotel. In his remarks, he referred to Gov. James Martin of North Carolina and his wife, Dorothy; Leighton Ford, president of Leighton Ford Ministries; and Mayo Boddie, a dinner fundraiser.*

## Remarks at Bush-Quayle Campaign Headquarters
*April 28, 1992*

*The President.* Good to see all of you.

*Audience members.* Four more years! Four more years! Four more years!

*The President.* Thank you so much. I've just had a wonderful tour of the headquarters. And now for the best part, to thank the volunteers who have done so much already. And we haven't really begun to fight yet. And this is good. I am grateful to each and every one of you. I had a chance to thank many on the professional staff here, but I just would never be able to adequately thank you who do so much in the way of volunteering. So I wanted to start with that.

Bob referred to the fact—Bob Teeter, who is doing a superb job—referred to the fact that if things go about the way we expect tonight, we'll have that magic number of 1105, and that is a very good one. I know it seemed like forever, but it's been a long, long election year. What I've decided to do is to concentrate on leading this country, to concentrate on bringing about the same kind of change domestically that we brought about in foreign affairs.

You know, when I look back to when I started and became President back in January of 1989, one of the great concerns that the young people of this country had was about nuclear war. I think because of the leadership that our administration has been able to bring to this area of foreign affairs, because we stood up against aggression when a lot of our critics in the Congress would not have us do so, we set an example. We proved that the United States is the only true leader of the entire world, and in the process, we bought significant change.

We're trying to implement and fulfill that promise of change in what used to be the Soviet Union. In the Middle East, ancient enemies are talking for the first time in history. And that is something very, very significant and very important. We look south of our own border and we see dramatic moves for democracy and freedom. We look all around the world, and you see things moving much, much better. These are big things when you're talking about war and peace and saying to a whole generation of Americans you don't have near as much to worry about because of the fear of nuclear weapons. That's big, and that's important, and we did it. Now what we want to do is to take that leadership that you all have been a part of, take that leadership and bring it to bear on the key domestic problems in this country.

This is an important election. We're talking about who is going to lead this country for 4 more years and who is going to be President. This isn't some kind of a charge and countercharge event. We're talking about significant change. And some of the cynics say, "Well, you've been President. What about it?" And I'm saying, "Well, let me tell you about it."

We have the best, most innovative education program that's ever been designed to raise the education standards in this country. And I'll be saying to the American people: Give us that kind of change. We've got it; it's out there; it's spelled out. And now help us, help us in the election. Help us with the Congress to bring to these kids what they need, quality education that's going to make the United States competitive into the next generation. So we're going to fight for that one.

I believe that we sue each other too much and aren't kind enough to each other. And so we are fighting for liability reform. So you let the status quo people say that we've been standing still. We have programs up there 3 years in a row to do something about limiting the liability that says to a Little League coach, "You know, you had better not coach because somebody is going to sue you," or to an obstetrician, "You had better not deliver this baby because you've got to be worried about some outrageous lawsuit." We are the party of change. I am the leader that's trying to change it. And with your help and the help of the American people, we're going to get that change brought to the American political scene. So that's another one.

The same thing is true in health care. We

are trying to change the health care system. Not by socializing medicine, like these nationalized plans would have you do, that some of the Democrats support. Not by these "pay or play" plans that would break every small business in the country but by our plan that makes insurance coverage available to every American, rich or poor alike. Some pay, obviously, but those at the lower end of the spectrum don't. We are going to revolutionize and change our health care system, but we need the support now of the American people. We've got to keep the high quality of American care, but make access available to all. That's what we're trying to do on our health care program.

We're talking also about Government reform. I've got an old-fashioned idea. I think Congress ought to live by the same laws that they make us live by. And so we need to reform the Congress itself or our whole method of Government. I happen to think that term limitations are good. They've got them on the President. Why shouldn't they be on the Congress of the United States? I happen to think that a President ought to have the same thing that 43 Governors have, a line-item veto. Let's take that one to the American people and see how it would work. I'm glad to hear the Democrats now getting on board for a balanced budget amendment, something I've been talking for, a change I've been trying to bring about for the last 3 years. So we've got these wonderful changes that we are working for. And now, all we need to do is change the Congress so we can get these changes through to benefit the American people.

The last of these five points relates to free and fair trade. We are not going to pull back into some isolationistic sphere or some protectionist sphere because of some outrageous promises by Democratic Congressmen that, if you only pull back, we can protect American jobs. I want to increase American jobs. And that's why I'm fighting hard for a successful conclusion of the GATT round, and that's why I want that North American free trade agreement with Mexico. It will create new jobs and expand our markets abroad. And we ought to be looking with optimism to the future instead of pulling back in some pessimistic scared mode. We're the United States of America. We are the undisputed leader of the free world, and we ought not to retreat. We ought to go forward. And give me 4 more years and give me a few changes in that Congress, and you watch us move this country forward.

*Audience members.* Four more years! Four more years! Four more years!

*The President.* Let me tell you this. This enthusiasm makes me want to change our game plan, but I don't think I will. The game plan is simply—might get killed by Teeter and Malek and Mosbacher, all of whom are doing a great job—but our game plan is this: Run this country; spell out these priorities; get these programs up to the Hill and try again to reach out and get these things passed to benefit the American people.

But the other part of it is, I have not been attacking any opponent. I hope you know that. I haven't done it. We've had able surrogates trying to put these people into proper perspective, but I have not been engaged in that. [*Laughter*] I have not been engaged in that because I believe it is important to be President of the United States. But let me tell you something. This enthusiasm here today gets my adrenaline flowing. I can't wait to get the proper signal at the proper time to get into that arena, not in a negative sense but to point out the positive things I've talked about today, to take on these opponents head on, whoever they prove to be, after the Republican Convention, because I am convinced that our values, our emphasis on family values is something that's stronger, not weaker, today than it was before. I think we need to perform for the American people, and I have suggestions as to how we can strengthen the American family. That's one example.

There are many other questions of values that I think our constituency is just as strong as it's ever been. I believe that when the campaign rolls around and we get the gloves off and we get into the arena with these people, we can conduct ourselves with a certain sense of honor, a certain sense of decency, a certain compassion, and a certain caring. But I'll be damned if I'm going to roll over for a lot of these outrageous charges that are coming out of the opposition day-in and day-out. We don't have to take that. So, since the air conditioning man didn't make it today, I will now finish my speech.

*Audience member.* He's a Democrat.

*The President.* He's a Democrat. That's all right; maybe he is. [*Laughter*]

But listen, really, let me end where I began. I've been in politics a long time. I figured it out the other day because this one actually has some political significance: Half of my adult life has been in public life and half of it in the private sector. I think that's a pretty good mix, so you don't lose track of what the fundamental problems are in this country or how to go about solving them. But I have always felt that there is no way, even for a President, to adequately express his appreciation for what you do.

In a few days, Barbara Bush—who I happen to think is doing a superb job as First Lady of the United States—she'll be coming over here to say thanks. I don't know whether George minded his manners the way he should have; he was in here. Somebody told me he went on for about 15 minutes, but nevertheless, I hope he said thank you. All of our kids who are in this ugliness of this campaign, they are very, very grateful. And there is no way to say thanks. So you keep up the work. I will keep up the work. We are going to win, and I think we're going to win big, come November.

Thank you very, very much. Thank you.

*Note: The President spoke at 1:44 p.m. In his remarks, he referred to Bush-Quayle '92 officers Robert Teeter, campaign chairman, Fred Malek, campaign manager, and Robert Mosbacher, general chairman, and to his son George W. Bush.*

## Statement on Signing the Act Approving the Location of the George Mason Memorial
*April 28, 1992*

Today I have signed into law H.J. Res. 402, which approves the location of a memorial to George Mason in the District of Columbia and its environs. Pursuant to the Commemorative Works Act, 40 U.S.C. 1001, *et seq.*, the Congress authorized the establishment of this memorial in 1990 (Public Law 101–358, 104 Stat. 419, August 10, 1990). On October 10, 1991, and again on April 22, 1992, the Secretary of the Interior notified the Congress of his determination that the memorial should be located in Area I, the central monumental core of the District of Columbia. It is my understanding that, upon enactment of this joint resolution, a memorial to George Mason may be established in Area I without further legislation.

GEORGE BUSH

The White House,
April 28, 1992.

*Note: H.J. Res. 402, approved April 28, was assigned Public Law No. 102–277.*

# Message to the Congress Transmitting Proposed Legislation on Job Training 2000
*April 28, 1992*

*To the Congress of the United States:*

I am pleased to transmit today for your immediate consideration and enactment the "Job Training 2000 Act." This legislation would reform the Federal vocational training system to meet the Nation's work force needs into the 21st century by establishing: (1) a network of local skill centers to serve as a common point of entry to vocational training; (2) a certification system to ensure that only high quality vocational training programs receive Federal funds; and (3) a voucher system for vocational training to enhance participant choice.

Currently, a myriad of programs administered by a number of Federal agencies offer vocational education and job training at a cost of billions of dollars each year. This investment in the federally supported education and training system should provide opportunities to acquire the vital skills to succeed in a changing economy. Unfortunately, the current reality is that services are disjointed, and administration is inefficient. Few individuals—especially young, low-income, unskilled people—are able to obtain crucial information on the quality of training programs and the job opportunities and skill requirements in the fields for which training is available.

The Job Training 2000 Act transforms this maze of programs into a vocational training system responsive to the needs of individuals, business, and the national economy.

Four key principles underlie the Job Training 2000 Act. First, the proposal is designed to simplify and coordinate services for individuals seeking vocational training or information relating to such training. Second, it would decentralize decision-making and create a flexible service delivery structure for public programs that reflects local labor market conditions. Third, it would ensure high standards of quality and accountability for federally funded vocational training programs. Fourth, it would encourage greater and more effective private sector involvement in the vocational training programs.

The Job Training 2000 initiative would be coordinated through the Private Industry Councils (PICs) formed under the Job Training Partnership Act (JTPA). PICs are the public/private governing boards that oversee local job training programs in nearly 650 JTPA service delivery areas. A majority of PIC members are private sector representatives. Other members are from educational agencies, labor, community-based organizations, the public Employment Service, and economic development agencies.

Under the Job Training 2000 Act, the benefits of business community input, now available only to JTPA, would enhance other Federal vocational training programs. PICs would form the "management core" of the Job Training 2000 system and would oversee skill centers, certify (in conjunction with State agencies) federally funded vocational training programs, and manage the vocational training voucher system. Under this system, PICs would be accountable to Governors for their activities, who in turn would report on performance to a Federal Vocational Training Council.

The skill centers would be established under this Act as a one-stop entry point to provide workers and employers with easy access to information about vocational training, labor markets, and other services available throughout the community. The skill centers would be designated by the local PICs after consultations within the local community. These centers would replace the dozens of entry points now in each community. Centers would present a coherent menu of options and services to individuals seeking assistance: assessment of skill levels and service needs, information on occupations and earnings, career counseling and planning, employability development, information on federally funded vocational training programs, and referrals to agencies and programs providing a wide range of services.

The skill centers would enter into written agreements regarding their operation with participating Federal vocational training programs. The programs would agree to provide certain core services only through the skill centers and would transfer sufficient resources to the skill centers to provide such services. These provisions would ensure improved client access, minimize duplication, and enhance the effectiveness of vocational training programs.

The Job Training 2000 Act also would establish a certification system for Federal vocational training that is based on performance. To be eligible to receive Federal vocational training funds, a program would have to provide effective training as measured by outcomes, including job placement, retention, and earnings. The PIC, in conjunction with the designated State agency, would certify programs that meet these standards. This system would increase the availability of information to clients regarding the performance of vocational training programs and ensure that Federal funds are only used for quality programs.

For the most part, vocational training provided under JTPA, the Carl D. Perkins Vocational Education Act (postsecondary only), and the Food Stamp Employment and Training program would be provided through a voucher system. The voucher system would be operated under a local agreement between the PIC and covered programs. The system would provide participants with the opportunity to choose from among certified service providers. The vouchers would also contain financial incentives for successful training outcomes. By promoting choice and competition among service providers, the establishment of this system would enhance the quality of vocational training.

This legislation provides an important opportunity to improve services to youths and adults needing to raise their skills for the labor market by focusing on the "consumer's" needs rather than preserving outmoded and disjointed traditional approaches. Enactment of this legislation would make significant contributions to the country's competitiveness by enhancing the opportunities available to our current and future workers and increasing the skills and productivity of our work force.

I urge the Congress to give this legislation prompt and favorable consideration.

GEORGE BUSH

The White House,
April 28, 1992.

# Message to the Congress Transmitting the Report of the Federal Council on the Aging
*April 28, 1992*

*To the Congress of the United States:*

In accordance with section 204(f) of the Older Americans Act of 1965, as amended (42 U.S.C. 3015(f)), I hereby transmit the Annual Report for 1991 of the Federal Council on the Aging. The report reflects the Council's views in its role of examining programs serving older Americans.

GEORGE BUSH

The White House,
April 28, 1992.

# Message to the Congress Transmitting the Report of the National Endowment for the Humanities
*April 28, 1992*

*To the Congress of the United States:*

In accordance with the provisions of the National Foundation on the Arts and Humanities Act of 1965, as amended (20 U.S.C. 959(b)), I am pleased to transmit herewith the 25th Annual Report of the National En-dowment for the Humanities for fiscal year 1991.

GEORGE BUSH

The White House,
April 28, 1992.

# Letter to Congressional Leaders Transmitting a Report on Nuclear Weapons Matters
*April 28, 1992*

*Dear Mr. Chairman:*

Enclosed, pursuant to section 3142 of the National Defense Authorization Act for Fiscal Years 1992 and 1993 (Public Law 102–190; 105 Stat. 1581), is a Report on Nuclear Weapons Matters. The report is un-classified, with a classified appendix.

Sincerely,

GEORGE BUSH

*Note: Identical letters were sent to Les Aspin, chairman of the House Armed Services Committee, and Sam Nunn, chairman of the Senate Armed Services Committee.*

# Statement by Press Secretary Fitzwater on the President's Meeting With First Deputy Prime Minister Yegor Gaydar of Russia
*April 28, 1992*

The President met for approximately 20 minutes this afternoon in the Oval Office with the First Deputy Prime Minister of Russia, Yegor Gaydar, who was in Washington to attend the annual meeting of the International Monetary Fund (IMF). The discussion focused mainly on the reform process in Russia. The President congratulated Mr. Gaydar on the outcome of the recent sessions of the Congress of People's Deputies and expressed the United States support for President Yeltsin and his program of reforms. The President stressed the importance of creating a favorable climate in Russia for private investment which will be vital to the success of the reform program. He also stated that it was important that Russia reach an agreement with the IMF on a standby program in order to activate the aid program that he had announced on April 1.

## Statement by Press Secretary Fitzwater on the President's Meeting With President Turgut Özal of Turkey
*April 28, 1992*

The President met with President Turgut Özal of Turkey today for 30 minutes in the Oval Office. The discussions included a number of regional issues, including the situation in Cyprus, Iraq, the Central Asian Republics, and the conflict in Bosnia. The President continues to urge all parties, Serb, Croat, and Muslim, to lay down their arms and negotiate their future in peace. President Bush and President Özal called on the leadership in Belgrade and Zagreb to work actively with the Izetbegovic government in Sarajevo to end the violence in Bosnia.

*Note: The statement referred to President Alija Izetbegovic of Bosnia.*

## Remarks at the Annual Republican Congressional Fundraising Dinner
*April 28, 1992*

Thank you all very much. Thank you, Guy, and thank you, Howard Baker, and thank all of you that made this dinner such a success. Thank you very, very much.

Let me just say that that is good news. And I'm very grateful to so many for this victory. And it's wonderful to be officially over the top. But I want to start by thanking both Dan Quayle and Marilyn, who have done such a wonderful job out on the campaign trail. And next, I thank all of those who have helped in so many ways, volunteering their time, their efforts. Barbara and I want to thank you and all those across the country who participated in this primary process to make these 1,105 delegates possible. Thank you all very much, wherever you may be.

I know to all it seems the way it does to Barbara and me: This has been a long election process. And we're only halfway through the journey, halfway to the goal. But there's some things I want to say. First, I have learned a lot in this campaign. I know better than I did the depth of the cares and concerns of those who chose to support us and of those who didn't. And lately I've been thinking of what we have in common, all of us who took part on the Republican side in this contest.

We all believe in America called America. We all believe the family is at the center of society and should be at the center of our thoughts as we make, in Washington, decisions that affect it. And the fact is, parties, like people, have tendencies. And we Republicans have believed in and protected some very important things.

We believe that Government has a place, but it also has limits on what it can and should do. Government can't solve everything. In fact, you always have to make sure Government doesn't start problems. We believe taxes should be small, not big. We believe those who pay them have rights, and those who benefit from them have responsibilities.

We believe that whatever the circumstances, cold war, hot war, relative calm, or a new age of peace and freedom, whatever the hand history deals you, there is one key to a safer, more peaceful world. And that is an American defense structure second to none. History has taught us that lesson, and Republicans always remember.

We believe in common sense. When something's broke, you fix it. Tonight so many of you came here to help me put an end to the obstruction and abuses of the Democratic majority in the Congress of the United States. When Ronald Reagan had a Republican majority in the Senate, led by Howard Baker, our great chairman, he made Reaganism a policy. He got a lot of his programs through. And my administration has put forth good ideas. We have a great Cabinet, new solutions. Then we've seen them killed by the Democratic majority up there on "Heartbreak Hill," or worse, have seen a Democratic leadership that refuses to let the Congress even vote on the ideas that the voters back in 1988 overwhelmingly endorsed.

You know, the other day someone asked me how I could be for change. I said, "Look, let me put it this way. I'm not out here trying to assign blame. We're all in this together. We must work together." But I told him, "Change the Congress, and I will get the job done." It is that clear. We need a majority of Republicans in the House and the Senate. And that is one important thing that this election year is all about. And as I survey the scene and listen to the American people, this could well be the year. It really could well be the year we get control of both Houses of Congress.

Finally, we Republicans believe in the old wisdom, the enduring values, the enduring social values that we live by as we build a great Nation: Religious faith, honesty, personal responsibility, hard work, and merit. Styles come and go, fads and fashions fade, but the old enduring values never go out of style. I really believe that. I believe that a President with the right ideas, the right intentions, the right beliefs can get them through the right kind of Congress. We're here tonight because we agree on the big issues, on the issues that shape the world, and on the values close to home.

As President, I have made it my mission to preserve and protect three legacies close to all our hearts: a world at peace, and we have a great record to take to the American people on this; an economy with good jobs, real opportunity for all Americans, and things are looking much better for the economy now; and we must preserve a Nation of strong families, communities where every child has someone he can count on, someone who calls him by his name. I am very proud of Barbara Bush and of her loving concern for the children of this country.

History has taken a turn in the past few years and given us a wonderful opportunity. If we apply our good beliefs, our sensible, heartfelt beliefs to this great opportunity, then we can say that we will make a contribution to our country, a contribution to our children's lives, and a contribution to history. The stakes are just that high.

One more thing: I intend to win this thing. I intend to win it, and with your help we will win it big come November.

Thank you all. And may God bless the United States of America.

*Note: The President spoke at 7:52 p.m. at the Washington Convention Center. In his remarks, he referred to Representative Guy Vander Jagt, chairman of the National Republican Senatorial Committee, who introduced the President, and former Senator Howard Baker, dinner chairman.*

# Remarks at the Arrival Ceremony for President Richard von Weizsäcker of Germany
*April 29, 1992*

President and Mrs. von Weizsäcker, Minister and Mrs. Genscher, distinguished members of the German delegation, on behalf of the American people, let me warmly welcome you to the United States and to Washington on this beautiful spring day. Barbara and I hope you have a productive and an enjoyable visit, and we're especially happy that you'll spend a few days in our hometown of Houston, Texas.

Mr. President, your presence doubly honors us. Not only is this your first state visit here, but I'm told that it is your first state visit to any country since the triumphant reunification one and a half years ago. Your presence here is testimony to the enduring ties that exist between our lands and our people. The German-American relationship has grown even stronger through cold-war and post-cold-war cooperation, drawing our two peoples even more closely together.

You come at a pivotal time for our two countries and, indeed, the entire world. Forty-five years ago at an equally pivotal time, some in the United States said that we should turn inward, turn our backs on our defeated adversaries. And we did not. Instead we committed ourselves to democracy's success, helping Europe, helping Germany and its fledgling democracy. What a wise decision that was, committing ourselves to a continuing global role and making an investment in German democracy. And today we see the fruits of that decision, united Germany, a model of democracy for the whole world and certainly a reliable friend and partner for the United States of America.

Today, Germany and the U.S. face a similar decision as the peoples of Russia and the other new States seek to follow the countries of Central and Eastern Europe in building democracy and free markets. Germany and America in partnership are committed to supporting those who are struggling with the legacy of a defeated Communist system, and making an investment in their democratic future. Those who would ask why this is the right course need only look at a united Germany, once our adversary, now our close friend, now our partner in leadership.

Mr. President, 3 years ago I accompanied Chancellor Kohl on a visit to your beautiful Rhineland city of Mainz. And there I spoke of how together we could build a Europe whole and free, at peace with itself. Because lasting security comes not from tanks, troops, or barbed wire; it is built on shared values and agreements that link free people. I believed that in Mainz, and I believe it just as firmly today.

United Germany is a key partner for the United States in promoting democracy and economic reform in Eastern Europe and the former Soviet Union. You are our partner in building a more united and cooperative Europe. And in that spirit, we strongly welcome German involvement in global affairs. Strong German-American cooperation is fully compatible with development of a more unified Europe, a goal that the United States has consistently supported over the years, just as unequivocally as we supported a united Germany.

As our world looks ahead to the coming century, I want to state this point as clearly as I can: The United States is firmly committed to remaining a world leader. We will play an active role in securing peace, security, and prosperity in Europe and in our transatlantic community. We must work together to overcome differences, to drive down barriers to free and fair trade, to achieve in the GATT negotiations agreements that will secure for all nations a new prosperity.

Mr. President, you, sir, have played a vital role in this. You've made it your task to help reconcile former adversaries, to overcome the antagonisms of the past, and to heal the wounds of division and strife. In a time of upheaval and rapid change, you've provided your countrymen with firm, moral leadership. And you've helped them come to terms with the twin catastrophes of dictatorship and division that befell Germany this century. And now, the German nation is at peace with itself, steadfastly committed to democracy and human rights.

Mr. President, Germany and the United States are guided by the words of your great national anthem: "May our path by peace be lighted." And as we walk down that path of peace together, may God bless our two great nations and the lasting friendship that unites the people of Germany and the United States of America.

Thank you.

*Note: The President spoke at 10:12 a.m. on the South Lawn at the White House. In his remarks, he referred to German Vice Chancellor and Foreign Minister Hans-Dietrich Genscher.*

# Remarks on Regulatory Reform
*April 29, 1992*

Well, a warm welcome to the White House for all of you. And first, I want to salute the three generals in the war for regulatory reform: our Vice President, Dan Quayle, Boyden Gray, and Dr. Michael Boskin. We also have here some frontline troops actively engaged in this process, members of the administration and Cabinet: Andy Card and Barbara Franklin and Jim Watkins and Lynn Martin and Dick Darman, Pat Saiki, Bill Reilly, and many others out here that are working for these kinds of changes. I also appreciate your efforts for fundamental reform of Government regulation. That's what brings us here today.

Regulation imposes what we see as a hidden tax on all Americans. This reform is one of the top priorities that I stressed in my State of the Union Message, and it's a vital element of our national reform agenda.

Two hundred years ago our Founding Fathers championed a whole new way of thinking about man's relationship to government by unleashing forces of social and economic freedom. They made the United States a haven for the poor and the oppressed, indeed, a land of opportunity. Our system did not promise material well-being, but it guaranteed personal freedom. In just one century's time, millions of poor people came here from every corner of the Old World. And because America empowered them to use their God-given talents to the fullest, people who came to our shores with nothing but faith and imagination made us the strongest and freest Nation on Earth.

Since the thirties, when a great economic shock hit the world, Government has often turned to projects of social engineering. And too often, in my opinion, Government embraced the notion that human actions, human choices could be organized to good effect only through bureaucratic blueprints. This posed a challenge to our precious heritage of limited government and the rule of law. It veered us away from the tradition of the accountability of citizen legislators.

When Congress shirks the responsibility for leadership, it tends to embrace many premises of the command economy. For example, when Congress passes laws mandating Americans to dance to the tune of arbitrary social and economic goals, it leaves the details of this choreography to the bureaucracy. This is not right. The bureaucracy is not accountable in the same way a legislature should be or a President should be.

Over the years, many Americans have felt the growing burden of regulation's tax in disguise. And we learned some hard lessons. We learned that lonely keepers of the flame of economic reform, men like the late Friedrich von Hayek, were right. The era of bureaucracy and regulation produced one example after another validating von Hayek's observation: Rule by bureaucracy undermines the true rule of law and runs headlong into the iron law of unintended consequences.

Let me tell you what this means in the real world. Take a common concern about safety. Inflexible safety rules can undermine safety in unforeseen ways: If Government mandates make ladders more and more costly to consumers, just for example, more people will turn to cheaper substitutes. They'll climb on chairs or step stools which are far less safe. Of course, regulators creating such a rule would not intend to make people less safe, but that's just how it works in practice. That's what we mean by unintended consequences.

Consider another example, this time with environmental rules. Command-and-control environmental rules actually can harm the environment. Regulations under the old Clean Air Act, for example, required new power plants to install scrubbers to clean up air pollution. Not only did this increase the cost of electricity, but it also generated scrubber sludge to be disposed of in landfills. Now we have a much better, market-based program which provides companies more options in how they reduce pollution, for example through our innovative emissions trading program or through increased use of cleaner burning natural gas.

I could go on all day with examples of inflexible rules that impose hidden taxes and costs on society. I could cite any number of abstract rules in collision with how things actually work: How highway fatalities can increase and American auto workers can lose jobs when Congress tries to legislate the fuel efficiency of cars; how a regulation system, plump with noble intentions, can keep life-saving drugs and medical devices from patients who need them. And let me add a personally gratifying note. The speed-up of approval for new "breakthrough" drugs for AIDS and for cancer and other life-threatening diseases is the culmination of the work that I was active in, that I helped begin almost 10 years ago.

Reforming regulation is a huge and time-consuming task. Presiding over the Task Force on Regulation during the eighties was, for example, one of the most important assignments that President Reagan gave me when I was Vice President. I've given a similar assignment to Vice President Dan Quayle and my Council on Competitiveness, and I am very grateful for his leadership and for the work of the Council.

Today regulation is facing a heightened public concern and a growing public impatience. Many times this manifests itself in the phrase, "Get the Government off our backs." More and more people are sending Washington an unmistakable message: Overregulation costs jobs. And thanks to this rising sentiment, we are able to accelerate needed reforms.

In my State of the Union Address, I lit a fire under our regulatory reformers, gave them 90 days to produce dramatic results. Today marks the 91st day, and let me report our reformers have come through with flying colors.

From biotechnology to banking to energy, we've made achievements that will lower costs and increase choices for American consumers. We've carried out reforms that will create and preserve good jobs for Americans and help us stay competitive in the world. We estimate that the reforms we've set in motion just since January 28th will save consumers about $15 billion to $20 billion a year. That's a savings of $225 to $300 per year for the average American

family. And this is just a down payment on savings to come.

Every Agency that I asked to participate has responded with action. Some Agencies already have accomplished important reforms, and all Agencies have completed a reform agenda which they will carry out in the months ahead.

To help us move forward with our reform agenda, today I am ordering a 120-day extension of the moratorium on new regulations. I am directing the Competitiveness Council to take the lead in implementing these reforms. Our objective must be to stop new rules that hurt growth while speeding up new rules to help our economy. During the next 120 days I expect many more gains for freedom and common sense.

I'll ask the United States Congress to do its part. I'll be working with regulatory reformers in every Federal Agency to propose new legislation where needed to eliminate unreasonable regulatory burdens that are now mandated by statute. And Congress also should pass legislation that has been pending for 3 years to reauthorize the Paperwork Reduction Act. And further, I'm putting Congress on notice: I will veto any bill that attempts to put excessive new burdens of regulation on the backs of our families, our consumers, our workers, and our businesses. There will be no, and I repeat, no return to business-as-usual.

Let me be very clear about our aims: We cannot and will not abolish all regulation. I have responsibilities as Chief Executive to enforce sound regulations for the health and safety of the American people, and I'll keep that trust. The best way to keep that trust is through a fundamental reform of our system of regulation. This is more than a 3-month or even a 3-year effort. This is more than an exercise in adjusting or fine-tuning the system. The economy is beginning to recover now. To ensure that recovery continues and is strengthened, to ensure that we can create new jobs, we must continue our course of regulatory reform.

Our campaign for regulatory reform meshes with our efforts for Government reform, like our proposal to limit the terms of Congressmen and make them more accountable. It fits also with our crusade for reform of the civil justice system, against the tyranny of these nuisance lawsuits that mock our time-honored traditions of justice. It goes hand in hand with our efforts to reform American education by allowing parents, not governments, to choose their children's schools. In short, there's a common purpose linking all of our efforts to renew the spirit and practice of limited government.

So let's take heart, and let's get to work. We can see the future, and it is a freer future. There is no doubt in my mind: The day is coming when we will put the final wrecking ball to the discredited system of the social engineers. We will restore this country. We will build it back, sturdy in the radical faith in freedom that is the legacy of our Founding Fathers.

Now I'm going to have the honor and privilege of signing the memorandum extending the regulatory moratorium. Thank you all very much.

*Note: The President spoke at 2 p.m. in the Rose Garden at the White House.*

# Memorandum on Implementing Regulatory Reforms
*April 29, 1992*

*Memorandum for Certain Department and Agency Heads*

*Subject:* Implementing Regulatory Reforms

On January 28, 1992, I issued a memorandum asking each of you to set aside a 90-day period to conduct a review of existing regulations and programs and to accelerate initiatives that will create jobs and stimulate economic growth.

Your response thus far has been excellent. Together, we have already implemented numerous reforms that will ultimately reduce the prices American consumers and businesses pay for energy and transportation, increase the amount of credit available for business expansion and homes, cut red tape for emerging industries such as biotechnology, and reduce many other regulatory barriers to job creation and economic growth.

But much remains to be done. Within the next few days, each of you will be submitting a report outlining additional proposals to eliminate or revise unnecessary, and unnecessarily burdensome, regulations. Every agency has identified a number of reforms that can be accomplished without new legislation. We must make every effort to implement as quickly as possible those proposals that will create jobs and enhance economic growth without endangering public health or safety.

Accordingly, I ask that each of your agencies set aside the next 120 days for this purpose. To that end, I request that, to the maximum extent possible, you adhere to the following specific guidelines:

1. Reforms that do not require public comment should be implemented as quickly as possible, but no later than June 1, 1992. Reforms that have already been noticed for public comment should be issued in final form as quickly as possible, but no later than August 1, 1992.

2. Other reforms requiring public comment should be noticed for comment as soon as possible—but no later than June 15, 1992—with a view to issuing final rules no later than August 27, 1992.

3. On September 1, 1992, each agency should submit an additional report to me. This report should summarize all the pro-growth reforms implemented since January 28. It should also estimate the potential cost savings or other benefits to the economy created by these pro-growth reforms, including an estimate of the expected net increase in jobs.

4. To ensure that adequate agency resources are devoted to the reform effort, your agency should continue, during this 120-day period, to adhere to the moratorium as described in my January 28 memorandum. I emphasize, as I did then,

that this moratorium does not apply to certain limited categories of regulations, including those that respond to situations posing an imminent danger to human health or safety.

5. Your agency should also continue to adhere to the substantive standards detailed in my January 28 memorandum with respect to all programs and regulations. And, to the extent it does not duplicate existing regulatory review processes, you should submit to me, in advance, a complete regulatory impact analysis of each major rule proposed to be issued during this period. This will help ensure that these regulations achieve their objectives at the least cost to American consumers and workers.

In implementing your reforms and in preparing the reports described in paragraph 3, you and your agency's regulatory oversight official should continue coordinating with the Competitiveness Council's Working Group on Regulatory Reform.

GEORGE BUSH

*The Secretary of the Treasury, the Secretary of Defense, the Attorney General, the Secretary of the Interior, the Secretary of Agriculture, the Secretary of Commerce, the Secretary of Labor, the Secretary of Health and Human Services, the Secretary of Housing and Urban Development, the Secretary of Transportation, the Secretary of Energy, the Secretary of Education, the Chairman of the Interstate Commerce Commission, the Chairman of the Board of Governors of the Federal Reserve System, the Chairman of the Federal Trade Commission, the Chairperson of the Federal Deposit Insurance Corporation, the Chairman of the Securities and Exchange Commission, the Chairman of the Federal Communications Commission, the Chairman of the Federal Maritime Commission, the Chairman of the Equal Employment Opportunity Commission, the Administrator of the Environmental Protection Agency, the Chairman of the Nuclear Regulatory Commission, the Chairman of the Commodity Futures Trading Commission, the Chairman of the Federal Energy Regulatory Commission.*

# Memorandum on Benefits and Costs of Legislative Proposals
*April 29, 1992*

*Memorandum for the Heads of Departments and Agencies*

*Subject:* Benefits and Costs of Legislative Proposals

I am today directing the establishment of procedures by which the likely benefits and costs to the American public of legislative proposals are disclosed, to the public and to the Congress, before enactment. These procedures will permit the full and fair evaluation of these benefits and costs, both direct and indirect, as part of the legislative process.

The rational and efficient balancing of the benefits and costs of proposed Federal legislation can be hindered by a lack of key information. Enactment of legislation without consideration of this information may result in costly and inefficient requirements

that show the rate of growth of jobs and incomes for the American people. Identifying the benefits and costs of proposed regulatory and other Federal legislation and their indirect effects is a crucial first step in assuring strong economic performance.

I therefore direct the Director of the Office of Management and Budget to ensure that quantified estimates of the likely benefits and costs of legislative proposals are provided on a timely basis to the Congress. This shall be undertaken as part of the legislative coordination and clearance process established by OMB, and shall be consistent with the policies stated in existing Executive orders.

Where appropriate, these estimates should include assessments of the effect of the proposed legislation on:

1. The expected benefits and costs for the

U.S. economy (including, for example, the impact on consumers, firms, and State and local governments);

2. U.S. employment, inflation, international competitiveness, and economic growth (measured, for example, by gross domestic product); and

3. Outlays and revenues by the Federal government as compared to outlays and revenues for the same activity in the current fiscal year.

Departments and agencies should prepare these estimates in a timely manner for significant elements of legislative proposals under active consideration by the Congress, or to be proposed by a department or agency, that have substantial impact upon the public, and should provide the Office of Management and Budget with such proposed estimates as may be requested by the Director. The Director of the Office of Management and Budget shall, in consultation with the Chairman of the Council of Economic Advisers, provide technical guidance to agencies on the methodology for preparing high quality and accurate estimates.

GEORGE BUSH

# Letter to Congressional Leaders Transmitting the Report of the On-Site Inspection Agency
*April 29, 1992*

*Dear Mr. Chairman:*

Pursuant to section 64 of the Arms Control and Disarmament Act, as amended (22 U.S.C. 2595b–1(a)), I hereby transmit the enclosed report on the activities of the On-Site Inspection Agency of the Department of Defense.

Sincerely,

GEORGE BUSH

*Note: Identical letters were sent to Sam Nunn, chairman of the Senate Committee on Armed Services; Les Aspin, chairman of the House Committee on Armed Services; Claiborne Pell, chairman of the Senate Committee on Foreign Relations; and Dante B. Fascell, chairman of the House Committee on Foreign Affairs.*

# Remarks at the State Dinner for President Richard von Weizsäcker of Germany
*April 29, 1992*

President and Mrs. von Weizsäcker, Barbara and I are just delighted, we are honored to welcome you here as the first President of a united Federal Republic of Germany. You are known the world over as a man who embodies the values that have made Germany's unity and democracy a source of hope to the world. President von Weizsäcker, throughout an era of division you constantly stood for unity, the unity of the German people, the unity of Europeans, East and West, and the unity and brotherhood, before God, of all mankind.

We are also honored that Foreign Minister Genscher, who just announced that he is stepping down from the position he's held with such distinction for 18 years, is with us, together with Mrs. Genscher. Hans-Dietrich, now, where is he? I'm looking, looking, looking. Over here. [*Laughter*] Hans-Dietrich, thank you, sir, for your fantastic service, for your friendship, and for all you have done for our common good. We are delighted that you are with us.

To all our German friends, let me say that we rejoiced with you a year and a half ago as Germany was united once more in peace and freedom. At midnight, the exact moment when two countries became one, Berlin's liberty bell pealed triumphantly. And we were proud to share in the glory of that moment since the bell, a replica of our own Liberty Bell, was a gift from the American people offered in friendship and support.

Mr. President, those half million people crowded around the Reichstag that night will always remember the words that you proclaimed as the bell rang, and here it is: "We want to serve world peace in a united Europe." Americans thrilled with you at that moment, we really did. And German unification, which for so long seemed so far away, so distant, was but one of the German miracles we've seen in our lifetimes.

There is, of course, Germany's legendary economic miracle. But I'm thinking of something else, your country's moral revival, of the patience and spirit of reconciliation that it took to create a climate of cooperation in a Europe burdened with bitterness.

Just as Germany has transcended and triumphed over its past, so has the German-American relationship shed the burdens that were history's legacy. United Germany, champion of a more united Europe, now stands as our partner in leadership. Together, we have achieved our common goal of a Germany united in peace and freedom. But our partnership did not end with that. To the contrary, now that we are free of the dangers and divisions of Europe's cold war confrontation, the German-American partnership has really just begun.

The world around us has changed almost beyond recognition. And we cannot know precisely where these revolutionary changes will take us. But this we do know: Our principles have not changed, for they have been proven right. And we are confident, for our shared values and unity of purpose have guided us through our past and will continue to guide us in our future.

Barbara and I speak proudly for this country when we call on everyone here to celebrate the promise our relationship holds. It's a relationship that this city, led by the Kennedy Center, whose Mr. Jim Wolfensohn is with us tonight, is commemorating with an unprecedented salute to 300 years of German culture, a festival under our joint patronage.

Now, in that spirit of cultural excellence, we have a present for you. There's a slogan in America, and it's particularly appropriate during a political year: If you want a friend, get a dog. [*Laughter*] And so in the spirit of enduring friendship, we'll give you the translation, the German translation. And I will now read it to you:

[*At this point, President Bush read the German title of the translation of "Millie's Book as Dictated to Barbara Bush" which he presented to President von Weizsäcker.*]

And may I suggest that we all raise our glasses: To unity, to freedom, to the new Germany. And to the long life and good health of our honored friend, President von Weizsäcker, and his wife, Mrs. von Weizsäcker. To your health, sir, and to the great friendship between Germany and the United States.

*Note: The President spoke at 8:30 p.m. in the State Dining Room at the White House.*

# Statement on the Verdict in the Los Angeles Police Trial
## *April 30, 1992*

Yesterday's verdict in the Los Angeles police case has left us all with a deep sense of personal frustration and anguish. Yet it is important that we respect the law and the legal processes that have been brought to bear in this case. Today Los Angeles faces the aftermath of a terrible night of violence in which several people have lost their lives. Yet out of this rage we must find tolerance for each other and adherence to the rule of law that protects the lives and property of everyone. I call upon all citizens to be calm and to abide by the law as the legal process in this case continues. The civil rights of all Americans demand this respect.

I am meeting this morning with the Attorney General of the United States to consider this matter. We will work with Governor Wilson, Mayor Bradley, and others to ensure that all appropriate steps will be taken to maintain law and order and to ensure that the legal process proceeds with due deliberation.

# Remarks on Civil Disturbances in Los Angeles, California
*April 30, 1992*

A tragic series of events have occurred in Los Angeles that include frustration over a verdict, the wanton destruction of property, and the senseless death of several citizens in the last few hours. I urge all Americans to approach this situation with calm, with tolerance, and with the respect for the rights of all individuals under the Constitution.

The United States Department of Justice will continue its criminal investigation of the police violence case in Los Angeles to ensure that the civil rights laws of our Nation are fully and equally applied. The Department of Justice has been monitoring this case since its inception, and as is customary in these kinds of situations, the Justice Department moved last night to accelerate the investigation that it started several months ago.

I have just met with the Attorney General of the United States to consider the Federal Government's legal course at this point and to review any other forms of assistance that we should provide the State of California and the city of Los Angeles. I also discussed these matters this morning with Governor Wilson and Mayor Tom Bradley and with other senior members of my administration. We are concerned about any question of excessive police violence, and we are equally concerned about excessive public violence.

The murder and destruction in the streets of Los Angeles last night and today must be stopped. Lootings, beatings, and random violence against innocent victims must be condemned. Society cannot tolerate this kind of behavior.

There are some principles of law and of behavior that should be repeated in these circumstances. First, we must maintain a respect for our legal system and a demand for law and order. Second, we have a right to expect a police force that protects our citizens and behaves in a responsible manner. Third, in the American conscience there is no room for bigotry and racism. And fourth, we have responsibilities as citizens of this democracy.

I want everyone to know that the Federal Government will continue to pursue its legal responsibilities in this case.

Thank you very much.

*Note: The President spoke at 12:05 p.m. in the Briefing Room at the White House.*

# Message to the Congress Transmitting the District of Columbia Budget and Supplemental Appropriations Request
*April 30, 1992*

*To the Congress of the United States:*
In accordance with the District of Columbia Self-Government and Governmental Reorganization Act, I am transmitting the Dis-

trict of Columbia Government's 1993 budget request and 1992 budget supplemental request.

The District of Columbia Government has submitted two alternative 1993 budget requests. The *first alternative* is for $3,311 million in 1993 and includes a Federal payment of $656 million, the amount authorized and requested by the D.C. Mayor and City Council. The *second alternative* is for $3,286 million and includes a Federal payment of $631 million, which is the amount contained in the 1993 Federal budget. My transmittal of this District budget, as re-

quired by law, does not represent an endorsement of the contents.

As the Congress considers the District's 1993 budget, I urge continuation of the policy enacted in the District's appropriations laws for fiscal years 1989–1992 of prohibiting the use of both Federal and local funds for abortions, except when the life of the mother would be endangered if the fetus were carried to term.

GEORGE BUSH

The White House,
April 30, 1992.

## Statement by Press Secretary Fitzwater on the President's Meeting With President Richard von Weizsäcker of Germany
*April 30, 1992*

The President met for approximately one hour with President Richard von Weizsäcker of Germany, who is in the U.S. on a state visit. The discussion focused on the nature of the new partnership between the U.S. and united Germany. The President stressed our intention to maintain a strong presence in Europe, along with the importance of NATO and the North Atlantic Co-

operation Council. He also reiterated our support for reforms and controlling nuclear weapons in Russia and the other republics. President Bush said it was important to reach an agreement on GATT soon and that he looked forward to addressing these and other issues at the upcoming G–7 meeting in Munich.

## Nomination of Robert L. Barry To Be United States Ambassador to Indonesia
*April 30, 1992*

The President today announced his intention to nominate Robert L. Barry, of New Hampshire, a career member of the Senior Foreign Service, Class of Career Minister, to be Ambassador to the Republic of Indonesia. He would succeed John Cameron Monjo.

Since 1989, Ambassador Barry has served as Special Adviser for East European Assistance to the Deputy Secretary of State. Prior to this, he served as Deputy Director of the

Voice of America at the U.S. Information Agency, 1987–89; and as the U.S. Representative to the Conference on Disarmament in Europe, 1985–87.

Ambassador Barry graduated from Dartmouth College (B.A., 1956) and Columbia University (M.A., 1962). He was born August 28, 1934, in Pittsburgh, PA. Ambassador Barry served in the U.S. Navy, 1957–60. He is married, has two children, and resides in Washington, DC.

## Remarks to the Ohio Association of Broadcasters in Columbus, Ohio
*April 30, 1992*

Thank you, Fred, very much; all of you, Gene and Dale and Tom, for the greeting out here. Good afternoon. I'm pleased to be back for my third appearance before— something about the Ohio Broadcasters.

I have a few remarks to make on a subject, but before that I want to comment just on the events that are concerning our country, building a little on comments I made earlier in a statement to the Nation about the news out of Los Angeles.

No one watching the television coverage of the violence yesterday afternoon and evening could have any reaction other than revulsion and pain. Mob brutality, the total loss of respect for human life was sickeningly sad. The frustration all of us felt seeing helpless victims pulled from vehicles and assaulted, it was hard not to turn our eyes away. But we must not turn our eyes away. We must keep on working to create a climate of understanding and tolerance and condemn a climate of bigotry and fear.

Last night was tragic for our country. It was tragic for the city of Los Angeles, for the people of east L.A. But there were small acts in all of this ugliness that give us hope: The citizens who ignored the mob, those who helped get the battered victims out of the area. There were people who spent the night in the churches. Many were seeking guidance in the wake of the unfolding chaos in the streets, praying that man's gentler instincts be revealed in the hearts of people driven by hate.

You say, "What can we do?" Well, before leaving Washington I spoke to Governor Wilson; I spoke to Mayor Tom Bradley; I spoke to Ben Hooks and some others on this problem. I also gave this statement to the Nation regarding our plans at the Federal Government level regarding the court case. We have instigated an investigation under civil rights protection. We will do what we can from the Federal Government to help those small business people that have been just wiped out by wanton destruction. I will keep telling the country that we must stand up against lawlessness and crime wherever

it takes place. Regrettably, what is happening in the city or did happen last night was purely criminal. It was outrageous, what happened. We are all sickened by what we saw.

On the larger issues, I've thought a lot about this. And say what you want, but it is important at a time like this to really talk about some old-fashioned values like respect for the others' rights, respect for property rights; manifest that respect in our actions as well as our words. We must make a compact with each other that we will not tolerate racism and bigotry and anti-Semitism and hate of any kind, anywhere, any time; not over the dinner table, not in the board room, not in the playground, nowhere.

We must condemn violence. I make no apology for the rule of law or the requirement to live by it. And yes, in some places in America there is, regrettably, a cycle of poverty and despair. But if the system perpetuates this cycle, then we've got to change the system. We simply cannot condone violence as a way of changing the system.

So we ought to change. We ought to try hard, change the status quo. We've got to do it peacefully, and we've got to do it thoughtfully. I am very hopeful that calm can be restored to this very important part of our country and that good will will prevail over the hatred that we've seen in the streets in the last few hours.

I am now switching off to what I came here to talk to you all about. Let me just first say a word about this city and about the great man who gave his name to this city. Columbus dared to explore far beyond the horizons of his continent, and he discovered a new world. You talk about the vision thing, well, he had it.

Speaking of vision, we wouldn't be attending the broadcasters convention had it not been for the daring of scientific prodigies like DeForest and Marconi. We should keep in mind just how new this thing called broadcasting is. The same year that my dad was born right here in Columbus, Ohio, just a few blocks away on East Broad Street, Marconi invented radio. It either makes me very old or makes radio very young; I can't figure out which that is. [*Laughter*] But I'm sure there are many here who can remember when the first TV broadcast went on the air. I can remember the first TV set I had, a great big square-looking box with a little tiny yellow-colored window. It was made by Hoffman. I don't think it proved to be too successful because I don't think they're making TV sets anymore. But it wasn't that long ago.

Telecommunications is still in its infancy. I think that it's taking big steps now. As you look over the horizon at the future of this country in technology, the steps are going to be enormous. There's something bright and new in human history.

In addition to all this new technology, I think we can look at a whole other area and talk about the worldwide spread of freedom and democracy. Around the globe, nations are joining a movement in which the United States is the great pioneer. We are, never forget it, the unsurpassed leader. And for those who will have you believe that this country is in a state of decline, travel abroad and see the respect with which this country is held.

We've got to protect our freedoms. We've got to trust people with their freedoms. These form the core of our crusade to make this country stronger. A free economy will be a strong economy, and it will create more good jobs. We'll keep society healthy if we keep our family first, put family first. And by keeping our defenses strong, we're going to keep the peace.

I'm working hard to open world markets. Open trade will create more and better jobs for this country. It offers our consumers lower prices and more choices. Expanding trade is one of five programs for this country's future that I view as really top priorities.

We're working as well to revolutionize— this is the second one—to revolutionize, literally to reinvent our schools. Parents are leading the way. In community after community, they are standing up to the bureaucratic establishment; they're asserting their rights in their children's education. I salute Governor Voinovich, whose wife is with us

here today, for the lead that Ohio is taking in achieving the goals of America 2000, our literally revolutionary education program.

We're working for fundamental reform of Government, including a balanced budget amendment. Now it has strong support on both sides of the aisle. Clearly, it has to be phased in. But there's a change in the country; people are saying we've got to do better. I support strongly term limits to make Congress much more accountable. I think the time has come for that. I also believe, and have submitted suggestions to the Congress for this rather revolutionary idea, that Congress ought to live by the laws that it passes, laws that affect others. It is no longer right to be separate.

The next category is, we are working to help the innovations and efficiencies of free market make quality health care available to all. I do not want to see us go to what they call a nationalized system or what some refer to as socialized medicine. We want to retain the quality of our health care, but we've got to give access to all, make insurance accessible to all. So we need to do that.

Then the last point I want to make is, we are fighting the explosion of nuisance lawsuits. Let's spend more time helping each other and less time suing each other. And that means we need to put some limits on these outrageous liability claims.

I might add that we are fighting hard to get the burdens of unreasonable Government regulation off the backs of the people. Regulation really imposes a hidden tax on every man, woman, and child in this country. In the State of the Union Address some 92 days ago, I lit a fire under our own administration's efforts for fundamental reform of Government regulation. This week we completed that 90-day moratorium that I ordered on new regulations. In just those 90 days we have completed or set in motion reforms that will save America $15 billion to $20 billion a year. And yesterday I ordered a 120-day extension on that moratorium, and I'm expecting many more achievements for freedom and for common sense.

Fundamental reform of regulation cannot be achieved overnight, and it's going to take a lot of tough, imaginative, patient effort. But I am totally committed to reforming regulation because the cost of inaction would be much more than we could bear. Think of some of the burdens and the contradictions that we already face.

Here in Columbus the city government has projected that over the next decade its cost of compliance with Federal environmental regulations alone will be $1.6 billion. And that's $856 per household per year. Now, this is for a community whose entire city budget last year was $591 million. The share of the city's budget to meet these regulations stands to increase from 10 percent to 23 percent. Right now, Columbus is one of the most attractive places in the country for people to work and live. But I can't say things will stay that way if the cost of meeting Government mandates keeps going right out through the roof.

In Juneau, Alaska, a local charity, the St. Vincent de Paul Society, wanted to build an addition to its shelter for the homeless, also requiring more parking space. Unfortunately, the building project was delayed for a whole year because bureaucrats declared the site a wetland. Now, get this: The shelter is in the middle of town surrounded by concrete, dry concrete, I think, on a city block that includes two car dealerships, a plumbing store, and a storage business. There is something wrong with this picture. Obviously somebody in this episode was all wet, but it wasn't the real estate for the homeless shelter. I cite this as just the kind of example that we must fight against at the Federal level, that the local level must fight against, too.

Back here in Ohio, an unreasonable Federal regulation almost forced the closing of this health plan in Dayton that we call the Dayton Area Health Plan. George Voinovich called this to my attention, an innovative managed-care program designed to offer high quality care to some 43,000 Medicaid recipients in Dayton. Governor Voinovich and the Lieutenant Governor, Mike DeWine, who I did not introduce but who is with us here today, led the effort to change this inequity. Just this week I signed legislation granting an exemption for this Ohio reform initiative. I have confidence in the new ideas that Ohioans are developing

on their own, and without the mandates from the know-it-alls in these subcommittees back in Washington, DC, or in our own bureaucracy. We don't do much for Americans' health when we put HMO's like the one in Dayton on the critical list.

It's stories like these that remind us what a visionary Alexis de Tocqueville was. A century and a half ago, a century and a half ago he warned that if Americans were not careful, Government would, and here's the quote, "cover the surface of society with a network of small, complicated rules, minute and uniform, through which the most original minds and the most energetic characters cannot penetrate." This is de Tocqueville, coming over and taking a look at our society back then. I don't know what would happen to him if he took a look at it today.

We've heard the warning. We're fighting back. Our reform efforts are breathing new life into America's ability to compete, to innovate, and to create jobs. Every Federal agency that I asked to participate has responded with action to ease the burden of unnecessary regulation. From biotechnology to energy, to the banking field, and yes, to broadcasting and telecommunications, we are taking the shackles off of American enterprise.

Let me take this occasion to salute the FCC, Federal Communications Commission, for its actions to relax needless restrictions on ownership of radio stations. The FCC also has taken action to allow competition among international satellite companies. Now, this will help reduce prices that Americans now pay on more than a billion telephone calls every year to other countries. These are very welcome reforms. Al Sikes, who is our Chairman, the FCC Chairman, believes in free markets, and he believes in innovation. It's clear to me that that is the right direction.

Looking forward, one can't help but see that new telecommunications technologies will revolutionize science, education, and the way we do business. They will be an important boon to families. The day is coming when mothers and fathers will be able to spend more time at home with their children even as they make ever more productive contributions to our economy. The

673

predictions for doing work at home in a productive way are absolutely outstanding, amazing. I think you're going to see a whole new area build up for productivity.

In the same spirit as regulatory reform is privatization, facilities now run by government to be owned and operated by competitive enterprises, and thus serve the public more fairly and more efficiently. Today before I came out here to Columbus, I signed an Executive order that will give State and local governments more freedom to sell or lease their infrastructure to the private sector if they choose to do so. We hear complaints that America's infrastructure is crumbling and that States aren't putting enough money into expanding or repairing it. At the same time, many private companies want to invest in these projects. So our Executive order will remove impediments to competitive enterprises buying infrastructure assets; that means bridges or roads or housing and sewage treatment plants.

This initiative could generate billions of dollars in new investment and millions of new jobs. American business has the funds to invest in infrastructure and has the funds to expand it. Through today's actions we will help more people enjoy cheaper and better waste water treatment service by letting businesses with real market incentives do the job. We'll help low-income tenants buy their own housing. The dignity that comes with homeownership is a wonderful thing for our country. We're promoting competition that could dramatically reduce the cost of urban mass transit. The money that States will receive for selling these facilities will be used to build even more new needed infrastructure or to lower the States' debts or to cut your taxes.

Privatizing state enterprises is one of the great hopes for economic growth and rebirth from Mexico City to Moscow. Take a look at what's happened south of our border under the courageous President of Mexico, Carlos Salinas. Look at the many formerly government-owned entities that he has turned over to much more efficient operation in the private sector. There is an example from what Mexico is doing for us right here in the United States.

Same thing is true in Moscow. As I sit down with the leaders from the new Commonwealth of Independent States, and I'll be meeting very soon with Kravchuk and shortly after that with Boris Yeltsin, we are encouraging them to move to the very kinds of privatization that I'm talking about here. I think you're going to find that they're doing it, and it's going to be highly successful. It offers them great hopes for recovery out of the economic morass that they're in right now.

So this idea presents many chances for positive change, change abroad and change right here in our own country. And they're opportunities, frankly, that we simply cannot afford to overlook. And of one thing I am certain: The status quo, the old thinkers are not going to yield on this without a fight. The special interest crowd will not like the agenda that I've outlined for you today. They think that Government ought to own more, not less. They think that Government ought to mandate more, not less.

When I meet with the Governors, and I've done that quite a few times since I've been President, all across party lines, all across ideological lines of conservative and liberal comes the cry from the Governors, "Do not burden us with mandates coming out of some old-thinking subcommittee in the Capitol Hill of Washington, DC." We are determined to try to facilitate what the Governors want by giving them flexibility and saddling them with far fewer mandates. Washington hasn't changed much since you all have been there. It is swarming with noisy lobbyists for the old interests who want this highly centralized Federal Government and people who have never met a regulation that they didn't really like.

This is springtime, and a young man's thoughts turn, as does his radio dial, to baseball. So I thought I'd leave you with a favorite story. I don't know whether all these Yogi Berra stories are true or not; you know, "Pair 'em up in threes," and things like that. [*Laughter*] In Yogi's hometown of St. Louis, the local people organized a celebration in his honor at the old Sportsman's Park. Yogi quavered with emotion as he stepped up to speak. "First," he said, "from the bottom of my heart let me thank all the people who have made this day necessary."

[*Laughter*]

I think the point of the story is this: The freedom-loving people of this country, people of ingenuity and enterprise, people in leading-edge industries like your own, are not merely making renewal of limited Government possible; they're making it necessary. They're making it inevitable. Technological advance is accelerating so rapidly that the old guard can only hope in vain to keep up. We'll make intrusive and gluttonous Government a thing of the past. We've reached a turning point. And we're on the verge of watershed reforms to make Government stop stifling people who want to use their freedoms, their own freedoms, to create and to produce and to serve.

The day is coming when enterprisers and innovators like yourselves will lead us into these exciting new horizons. The day is coming when dreams not yet imagined will come true. I am confident about the years ahead. I know we've had difficult times, but I don't believe for one single minute that the United States of America is in decline. The future is tremendously exciting. And if we handle the technological change with the innovative manner I've outlined here today, I believe we can usher in all kinds of new eras of prosperity for the working man and woman in this country.

Again, I'm confident of the years ahead. The big thing is to keep this Nation a champion of ideas and of opportunity and, with that first subject in mind, of justice. We can reform our schools and our courts and our health system, our very system of Government. And we can assure that when we reach the new century America will still be the strongest, the bravest, and the freest Nation on the face of the Earth.

It's good to be back with you. And thank you all very, very much.

*Note: The President spoke at 3:12 p.m. at the Hyatt on Capitol Square. In his remarks, he referred to Anthony (Fred) Cusimano, association vice president and general manager; Gene D'Angelo, president and general manager, WBNS–AM/FM/TV; Dale Bring, association executive vice president; Thomas S. Stewart, vice president and general manager, WBNS–AM/FM; and Benjamin L. Hooks, executive director, National Association for the Advancement of Colored People.*

# Remarks at a Bush-Quayle Fundraising Dinner in Columbus
*April 30, 1992*

Thank you, George, and thank all of you. It's a great honor to be introduced by Governor Voinovich, a man I've known for a long, long time and with whom I've worked for a long, long time. And thanks for that introduction, and to Janet, my respects. Barbara sends her love. And let me say what a great job the Pickerington High School Tiger Band has done with us tonight. Thank you all very much once again; appreciate it very, very much. And thank you, Rabbi Huber, for the invocation. Mr. Stokes, thank you for leading us in the pledge. And may I salute Columbus' mayor, Greg Lashutka; and my old friend with whom I've worked in Washington, now doing a great job here, and who I want to see back in Washington, the Lieutenant Governor, Mike DeWine.

Mike, delighted to see you; Fran, to you let me just say Barbara is looking forward very much to being at your house in the next few days, and so I'm glad to see you here.

And may I salute Bob Bennett, our State chairman, doing a superb job in that great Ohio organizational way. With me tonight is our national finance chairman for Bush-Quayle, Bobby Holt, from west Texas, and I want to thank him and our regional chairman, Dick Freeland; our Bush-Quayle State chairman and dinner chairman, Tim Timken, another old friend from whom we heard tonight. He is always out on the firing line doing a superb job for the President, but also for the party of Ohio. Nobody has done more, and I'm very, very grateful to him. And may I thank fundraiser extraordinaire Vinny Gupta, and I'd be remiss if I also didn't thank the Indian community. And also I don't know who is looking after the hospitals in Ohio tonight, but I feel very safe here tonight. [*Laughter*]

And Jim Rhodes, the man who fought the lonely battle in favor of the caribou up in Alaska, is here with us tonight. What a job he did serving this State. Jim, delighted to see you. What I'm referring to about those caribou, Jim was very far-sighted, recognizing that this country ought not to become more and more dependent on foreign oil and pointing out that a pipeline would not bring environmental disaster to Alaska. And he was absolutely right. He's been proven right. So you have a clairvoyant in your midst as well as an ex-Governor. Jim, I'm glad to see you.

Now, I was here just a week ago for the opening of AmeriFlora, and I want to congratulate Columbus. I see Mr. Wolfe sitting here, and he had some help on this. I know he's been in the forefront of it all, John, but what a job Columbus has done on this major international event.

I was here to commemorate a voyage 500 years old; made me think of the Democrats. They aren't impressed with such antiquity. Most of their ideas are older than that. [*Laughter*] While the Democrats build their agenda, literally, if you look at it, on timeworn policies, we have built the Republican agenda on timeless legacies, three underpinnings: good jobs, strong families, and George dwelled on this one a little, world peace.

Yes, it is campaign season. I've seen these seasons come and go. I've watched sound bites compete with sound policy, the battles of the bumperstickers and the war of words. But I believe democracy is more than that. During one political season in Great Britain, here's what Margaret Thatcher said: "We were told that our campaign wasn't sufficiently slick. We regard that as a compliment." You see, I believe that elections are about more than winning people's votes; they're about winning the trust of the American people. And that's what I will try to do again come November.

I've watched candidates try to convince people that the sky is falling just so they can promise the moon. But our national symbol is not Chicken Little; it is the American eagle. Our national spirit isn't self-doubt; it is self-confidence, self-reliance. What is the American dream? It's a dream that we struggled to make come true.

Now, I know this, and we all know it, and we all feel it in our hearts: There are places in America where people are caught up in a tragic cycle of despair and poverty. But the answer to a system that perpetuates such a cycle is change, peaceful and thoughtful change. Tonight I call on every American to show restraint and to respect people's rights and property.

The violence that we saw last night wrenched our hearts. We saw it there in east L.A., and it must not be repeated. It was ugly, mob brutality, selfish attack, mob brutality, the ugliest kind. And TV cameras didn't capture it all by any means. According to Los Angeles fire officials, between the hours of midnight and 3 a.m., they were called to respond to an average of three new fires every minute. But worse, there were firemen, public servants, unheralded firemen risking their lives fighting arson, who were assaulted themselves, sometimes with gunfire, even with axes.

We must condemn violence. We must make no apology for the rule of law or the requirement to live by it. At the same time, we must not tolerate racism, bigotry, anti-Semitism, or hate of any kind, anywhere. Not over the dinner table, not in the board room, not on the playground, nowhere in America. We must stand together on that. When we're in troubled times, and these are, we must work to make the dream of such a society, just society, real for our children. I believe in my heart, I really believe that we can do just exactly that.

As President, I pledge to this Nation I will do what I can to heal the wounds. I will see that the law's enforced. When it comes under the responsibility of the President, yes, I'll do that. Society deserves that sense of order. But I will do my level-best to heal the wounds and to bring people together in the aftermath of the ugliness that we witnessed last night. A President should do no less.

Now, think of what we've accomplished, building on what George said, around the world. It is indeed inspiring. Years ago when we thought about the Soviet Union and Eastern Europe, we dreamed of free people with freer markets and fewer bombs, and then we all worked to make that come true. I take great pride that it was American leadership that has diminished for our children the threat of nuclear war. No longer do they go to bed at night worrying about whether we're going to be caught up in a nuclear holocaust. That is big; that is important, significant change for the whole world. I am proud to have been a part of it.

For our neighbors in South America, we envisioned peace and democracy. Now we are on the threshold of an entirely free and democratic hemisphere. When the Iraqi nightmare threatened to engulf the Middle East, America protected the people of Israel and Turkey and Saudi Arabia and helped liberate that small country of Kuwait. In the process we turned what had been the mirage of 44 years into an oasis of hope. We brought Arab neighbors, in something that is truly historic, face to face with Israel for the first time, for the first step towards peace.

There were those that said that the defeat of communism, the liberation of the oppressed, the triumph of democracy, that all these things were nothing but a dream. They were right. It was an American dream.

America helped create a world of freer people and freer markets. That has brought greater prosperity, but it's also brought greater competition. There's good news: All around the world more and more people are buying American. Our exports shot up 7 percent in February to a record high of almost $38 billion. That's bad news for this Chicken Little mentality, but that's good news for America. It sums up words that will help chart a new American destiny: If we are to succeed economically at home, we have to lead economically abroad. We are not going to pull back into some isolationistic or protectionist mood as long as I am President of the United States.

You see, by expanding trade with other countries, we expand opportunity within our own. And sure, the competition's tough; we know that. But the answer isn't to build up trade barriers; it's to get other countries to tear down theirs. Last week I met with the heads of Europe's Common Market, Mr. Cavaco Silva and Mr. Delors, to talk about the world trade negotiations. If these negotiations succeed, an agreement could pump $5 trillion into the global economy over the next 10 years, with the U.S. share topping $1 trillion.

We're also working on our southern trade front with negotiations on what we call NAFTA, the North American free trade agreement, an agreement that would increase trade with Mexico by billions of dollars and create good American jobs right here in the State of Ohio. This agreement isn't about good politics; it's about good policy and good American jobs. And I have faith in open trade because I have faith in the American worker. And when trade is free and fair, the American worker can beat the competition fair and square, outwork, outhustle any worker anywhere in the world.

Fair competition, though, doesn't just mean playing by the same rules, it means competing with the same tools. I'm talking about the cost of capital. Tough competition from Germany, no capital gains tax there; Japan, an entrepreneur who sells the company he's built from scratch pays a tax of one percent. A low capital gains tax rate encourages investment, and that means new jobs.

When I listen to our critics rail against capital gains and then turn around and complain about foreign competition, it makes me think of someone who would price eggs at $100 a carton and then complains that no one wants to make omelets. A lower capital gains rate wouldn't just benefit someone who runs a business, it would help people who own homes or farms or simply seek better jobs. It's time to quit playing politics with this issue and cut the capital gains tax. And I will keep pushing the Congress to do just that.

While they're at it, I'd like to see them pass my first-time homebuyers credit—it would stimulate the housing market—and our investment tax allowance that would stimulate investment in our productive machinery in this country. We're going to

677

keep on trying to get that through Congress in spite of this election year.

If America is to remain truly competitive, we've got to stop regulating our businesses out of business. Washington really doesn't understand the deadly process that can turn redtape into pink slips. And here in Columbus, the city government—the Mayor knows this—they have projected that over the next decade the cost of complying with Federal environmental regulations alone would be $1.6 billion. That's for a community whose entire city budget last year, Greg, was what, $591 million?

It's time to put a stop to costly, counterproductive regulations. In January I announced a 90-day moratorium in that State of the Union Message—that was what, 92 days ago—moratorium on Federal regulation. We blocked regulations that hurt growth and speeded up regulations that help growth, and our efforts have paid off. Just since January the reforms we've set in motion will save consumers $15 billion to $20 billion a year. That is a saving of $225 to $300 a year for the average American household, and that is just the beginning. It is not being done to put worker safety at risk or the environment at risk. Wednesday, I ordered a 120-day extension of the moratorium on new regulation. And I put Congress on notice, telling them that I will veto any bill that attempts to put excessive new burdens of regulation on the backs of our families, our consumers, our workers, and our businesses. There will be no return to business-as-usual in the field of regulation.

I know there's been a lot of talk about change in this election year. Most of it has been just talk. But that's not good enough if we're going to build a truly better America. I've called for reform. More importantly, I've acted with far-reaching proposals for reform, and George generously referred to one of them: education, also in health care, in our courts, and in our campaigns. We've won our battles, but we've not yet won the war. Too often, in too many ways, Congress and an army of special interests have stood in the way of change. They're not interested in reform. They stand squarely behind the status quo. They may be powerful. They may be influential, too. They may be well-connected. But let me tell you this: They

are wrong. They are not going to stand in the way of bringing the kind of change that American people want.

First, our legal system: Volunteers—and everyone has a horror story on this—volunteers are afraid to volunteer, doctors are afraid to deliver babies, parents afraid to coach Little League, all because of the fear of lawsuits. And that's wrong. People should spend more time helping each other and less time suing each other. That's why we've introduced proposals to reform our legal system. And sure, the system's complicated, and yes, people's rights must be protected. But the system needs reform, and we are not going to let any powerful lobby stand in the way. This is going to the American people to be decided in November if I can't get action by the Congress this summer.

Second, in education, our America 2000 reforms are gaining steam, break-the-mold schools, national standards and testing, community by community. And whether it's among public schools or private schools or religious, parents deserve the right to choose their children's schools. It's a giant undertaking to change the Nation's education system, but we are going to do it with or without a note of approval from the NEA or the Congress. Fortunately, much of our America 2000 program can be decided by the people in the communities. This is happening with Ohio 2000.

Third, health care: No one should have to go broke just to get better. That's wrong, and it's got to change. While our health care is still the finest quality in the world, too many people can't qualify for health insurance or simply cannot afford it. Some say the answer is what they call nationalized health care. Ask the Canadian waiting months for critical surgery; ask him what he thinks of that idea. Our health care proposal is comprehensive. It opens access. It lowers cost. But it does not and will not lower the quality of American hospital care. National health care is a prescription for national disaster. We cannot let that happen, but we will fight to pass the new program that I favor.

In these and so many areas that demand reform, our Government can play a positive role. I figured this out the other day, as we get into the campaign: One half of my adult life has been spent in the private sector, working for a living, and one half in the government. I think I'm working for a living, but it's different, believe me. One half in the private sector, one half in government, and I've seen this country change, sometimes for the better, and yes, sometimes for the worse. You need to know what needs to be changed. Change, as I said, for change's sake, that's meaningless. It takes more than happy talk, more than lip service to reform and then full service to special interests.

The Democratic Party, I am convinced, will always revert to form, attacking problems by creating programs. They don't understand that people want a return to some old-fashioned values like responsibility, accountability. When it comes to Government, the American people know as Government tries to do more and more, it ends up, regrettably, delivering less and less. And next year the Federal Government will spend $1.5 trillion. There's just no question about it: The Federal Government is too big, and it spends too much. We must get control of the deficit, and that is going to take some tough medicine for the American people and for everybody. But it is essential for the children of this country.

In conclusion let me say this: Major reforms are in order. So the fourth reform of this reform agenda is about Government. First, it's time—I really believe this one, and I served in the United States Congress—for the Congress to govern itself by the same laws that it imposes on others. They must abide by the same laws that you and I do. And yes, it is time for sweeping campaign reform. But real reform is not saddling the taxpayer with the cost of congressional campaigns. It's time for real spending reform, time for the President to have what 43 Governors have. Give me that line-item veto, and see if we can't save a little money for the hard-working American taxpayer.

And the President's term is limited, and I think it's time to limit the terms for Members of the United States Congress. It will keep them closer to home. So I favor six 2-year terms for the Congress and two 6-year terms for the Senate. And I really believe it would keep Government more active, more vital, and closer to the people.

Thomas Jefferson knew, and here was the quote, "The people are the only sure reliance of our liberty." The people are the only sure reliance of our liberty. That's why you're here today. You're not among the cynics because, you know, I think you still feel you can make a difference. Think of a littered park; you clean it up one piece at a time. Then think of our Government; we can reform it, one vote at a time. And it makes a difference. I've been trying for 3 years to effect fundamental change in these fields, whether it's tort reform or education reform or whatever. And I'm going to keep on trying.

You might ask, "But why should we care?" It's the age of cynicism. Because this Government, just like a public park, isn't just something we inherited from our parents. It's something we borrow from our children.

And I know this country, as you do. America's got a heart of gold. We've got a will of steel. It's honest, and it's generous, and it's good. With your help, it's about to become even better.

Thank you all very much. And on this troubled night, may God bless the United States of America. Thank you very, very much.

*Note: The President spoke at 8:10 p.m. in the Lausche Building at the Ohio State Fairgrounds. In his remarks, he referred to Rabbi Gary Huber of Bath Tikvah Temple and Dewey Stokes, president of the National Fraternal Order of Police.*

## Remarks at the Great American Workout
*May 1, 1992*

Welcome, all, to the White House. And let me tell you how much I appreciate this wonderful display of fitness, something so important to our country. May I start off by saluting Secretary Sullivan, who I don't see, who's going to be with us in a minute; Chairman Schwarzenegger, of course. Where's Lou? Over here, suited up. [*Laughter*] And thank Barbara Mandrell and members of the President's Council on Physical Fitness and the National Fitness Leaders Association; and of course, Milton Berle and Bob Saget; Mary Lou Retton, an old friend; Peter Vidmar; Chris Evert; Lauri Single, National Fitness Director of the Year; and on and on it goes.

Welcome to the White House and to an event which kicks off National Fitness Month. That's the third Great American Workout. It's a special pleasure to be introduced by a friend, a man who embodies this event, the Chairman of the President's Council on Physical Fitness, Arnold Schwarzenegger, who literally has done a superb job, going to every single State in the Nation on his own to take this message of fitness to everybody. We're very grateful to him.

As I told Arnold earlier, I am sorry to have to cut short my participation in this great event. I hope you can understand; I am going to be getting, at 7:15 a.m., an update on the situation that troubles the whole country, the situation in Los Angeles, meeting with the Attorney General and the head of the FBI. Then we'll be meeting with some of our outstanding civil rights leaders to discuss our common commitment to justice, civil tranquility, and the rule of law.

But before I go, let me just say a few words about this important issue of fitness. Arnold, as I mentioned, or didn't, maybe, but yesterday he visited the 50th State out there in Ohio as Chairman. And he's spreading the word that each of us has a stake, a serious stake in making exercise a part of America's fitness and fitness a part of each American day.

When we see these workout stations, which I was privileged to participate in last year, you can understand it more clearly. Even a special workout to honor true heroes has been set up, and those are representatives of the Special Olympics. We welcome them back to the White House again. They set a great example for kids around this country.

Part of his message is that we need balanced and nutritional diet. And we've got to avoid tobacco and drug use, avoid excessive alcohol use. And fitness really can enrich the human mind and body by lowering stress and blood pressure and cholesterol.

We also have to act on another front by putting new emphasis on quality physical education in our schools. Arnold has pointed out to me that only one State, Illinois, gives daily physical education for K through 12. And that's the only State giving it, thus, the priority that it really deserves. Now, we've got to change that. So let's make it 50, just as our Chairman has done by going to 50 States.

A man with us, a special man, knows all about fitness. He knows that an American that is physically and mentally fit is fit to take on the world. And at 83—sorry about that, Milton—[*laughter*]—Milton Berle still rides his stationary bike, he does a lot of walking, he punches a heavy bag, and he maintains a healthy diet. So no wonder he's just been named a special adviser to Arnold. I welcome his leadership, showing that nobody, put it this way, is too old to stay fit.

So to Milton and to Arnold and all of you, my thanks for what you've done. Thanks for showing the Nation what fitness means. And I hope you enjoy the Great American Workout. I arranged for the weather here. [*Laughter*] And I know you'll enjoy the program which follows on the main stage, starring the famous and wonderfully generous Harlem Globetrotters. We welcome them. We have a basketball court down there. And I got a lot of laughs when I threw the basketball with Duke the other day. But the difference is these guys are funny on purpose. [*Laughter*]

So thank you all. And Arnold, once more, my heartfelt thanks for what you're doing in leading this country to new levels of fitness. Now I must leave, but Barbara's going to join in, so she will demonstrate the Bush family commitment to work out, every station, 20 minutes at each one.

*Note: The President spoke at 7:04 a.m. on the South Lawn at the White House.*

## Remarks at the Points of Light Awards Ceremony
*May 1, 1992*

Please be seated. Well, thank you, and welcome to the East Room. Barbara and I are very proud to be here with such an impressive group. And may I single out our truly special guest, Michael Jackson. I haven't seen so much excitement around here since Gorbachev came for the first time. Today we also want to extend a particularly warm welcome to members of our Cabinet, Dr. Lou Sullivan, Secretary Martin, and to the judges of this year's award: our ACTION Director, Jane Kenny; Rabbi Naiman of the Council of Jewish Organizations; our distinguished Surgeon General, Dr. Antonia Novello; James Renier, chairman and CEO of Honeywell; and thanks to Anita Baker and Frances Hesselbein who couldn't, regrettably, be with us today.

My special thanks to the Points of Light Foundation and to ACTION for their help with these awards. And welcome, also, to the board members of the Commission on National and Community Service. And the warmest welcome to you all who make up the very heartbeat of our country, our volunteers. And a special welcome to our guest presenter today, a friend, our unparalleled Olympic golden girl, Florence Griffith Joyner. Thank you for being with us.

Flo-Jo is here, and she's in reasonably good shape, but where's your husband who's trying out for—Al, right here, sitting down here. Got to give the man equal time. But we're delighted he's here. Flo-Jo wants everyone to work out, and she's targeted lazy Americans. [*Laughter*] I don't know why you're laughing, all of you, but anyway I guess with all this PC talk we should call them exertionally challenged. And she is going to wipe out couch potatoes, and I'm going to get her started on broccoli.

I am here today to talk about something that's really very personally important to me and Barbara. You all know I love music, Anita's always been a favorite. And I especially love country music because it gets to the heart of the basic decency and compassion and heartbreak of people who are proud to call themselves Americans. Well, Randy Travis has a line in one of his songs, called "Points of Light" incidentally, that's like a spotlight on an answer for us. And he sings, "There are dreamers who are making dreams come true, giving hope to those without. Isn't that what this land's all about." I'm sure most of you have heard that song. But those are profound words.

And you see, for all the good that Government can do, and it can do some good, to solve our country's social problems, we need people. We need every individual to respond to the problems right around them. And when each American is no longer willing to accept that someone on their street or someone in their town is homeless or jobless or friendless, then that's when we will truly renew America, when everybody understands that they're going to help their neighbor.

We already have shining heroes in this quest, and I call them Points of Light, as you know; I think everyone does now. And that's the name of Randy's song. And there are Americans in towns and cities just like yours across the land discovering that service to others is a rich source of meaning in life. And I honor these men and women and children for showing the better angel of their nature by volunteering to help others. They sum up the great and generous land that we have. They see the genius of this land and ordinary people doing extraordinary things.

Day in and day out, these Americans wage our war for human life and dignity. And they don't say, "This is why I can't help." They say, "This is why I can." And they say, "Maybe I don't have money, but I have time," and "Maybe I can't help someone build a house, but I'm a good listener; I care." And we celebrate that spirit. Whoever you are, you have something to share. For Americans are the greatest natural resource of this, the greatest Nation on Earth. And I am proud to be here for this very special, very important event.

We come together today at the culmination of National Volunteer Week, honoring the millions of Americans who transform communities across the country through voluntary service. In particular, for the 11th year, we recognize with these awards the inspirational example of people who meet a simple three-part test. One, they looked around. Two, they saw a need. And three, they filled it.

What a cross section of wonderful Americans are represented here today among these 21 winners of the 1992 President's annual Points of Light award. There are individuals like my seatmate—all but one— at the luncheon, 17-year-old Robert Zamora who created the Getting Busy Teen Club as an alternative to gangs in east Los Angeles. And there are businesses like IBM which gives its employees encouragement and time off to volunteer, and 90,000 of them do.

And our winners represent neighborhoods, places of worship, every kind of group across this broad and good land. They and all the others like them are shaping a Nation whose goodness grows out of the small acts of consequence made by many people.

America's pioneer days are not behind us. And we still have frontiers left to cross, the thrill of adventure yet to discover, an American renaissance yet to speak. I believe there are five core elements of the new America which are reflected in the award categories. And let me just share with you how some of our award winners are drawing us closer to each goal.

First, I believe every community must have excellent schools and a culture that fosters lifelong learning. Well, Kentucky's Berea College students saw a critical need right around them in the Appalachia, and so they volunteered as mentors and tutors to tutor grade school kids all the way up through adults struggling to overcome illiteracy. It started with the young, worked right on through those illiterate adults who needed help.

Second, every community must be a decent, drug-free, and safe place to live. Well, 1,800 members of the Emmanuel Reformed Church saw the need around them, joined with their city of Paramount, California, and started tackling the crises that threatened their neighborhood, like gangs and illiteracy and crime.

A third one: Every American community must offer quality health care for all. Well, 24 labor unions out in Omaha saw the need of families whose children were hospitalized for transplant operations. So, these unions joined together to buy a building, and then more than 500 skilled union volunteers renovated it to house these families.

The fourth example: Every American community must offer its members the hope of good jobs with a future. Well, Urban Miyares can tell you firsthand about this need. A Vietnam vet who became blind, he found there were no business counseling services available to people like him, and he received training and now volunteers to provide job counseling to people with disabilities.

And the fifth one: Every American community must be a place with a commitment to children, youth developing good character and values, and strong families. A Pennsylvania group called Magic Mix saw the needs of two generations and brought latchkey kids and at-risk students together with residents of local nursing homes who tutor, teach, and befriend them.

With role models like these, I am confident that together we can shape our future, not through our fears but through our dreams. And yes, we're going to continue to work for legislation to make this a safer America, fairer America, a better educated America, a more efficient America. But the most important legacy of all is one that each person in this great country can help create, the legacy of a more caring America.

Now, look closely at our world. People say the problem is crack or crimes or babies having babies. Those are only symptoms. The problem is a moral emptiness. And if, as President, I had the power to give just one thing to this Nation, it would be the return of an inner moral compass, nurtured by the family and valued by society. This compass would guide us to value every life. It would show us that each life lost to despair really devalues us all. And it would remind us that caring and conscience are what make us human.

So, let's make this National Volunteer Week an extraordinary moment in our Nation, our communal commitment to a true American renewal. And I urge each of you to step forward, to take this country's future in your own hands and become a Point of Light. And I ask leaders of businesses, places of worship, schools, neighborhoods, other organizations to lead their members toward the bright goal of service.

Wherever people from all walks of life work together and claim their community's problem is their own, they create communities of light to guide this Nation's path. As you cross this land, I'd ask you to remember some special words. Recently, Barbara and I had the magnificent honor of meeting Mother Teresa again. Her very life speaks only of service to others. And I was touched by her words. She said, "It is not how much we do, but how much love we put into it." May Americans continue to put love into all our works.

Bar joins me in saying congratulations to you and the millions more like you across America for what you do. You are an example for the rest of this country. And may God continue to bless this wonderful Nation in these troubled times.

And now, Barbara and I will present the awards, and I will ask Flo-Jo to come up here to do the honors and read the citations. Florence, all yours.

[*At this point the awards were presented.*]

Let me just say I want to now turn to the last item on the program, and I want to give special thanks to Michael Jackson for being here to help honor all of you today. Michael's work with disadvantaged young people and those with disabilities reflect his profound commitment to children. And I am delighted to recognize him as a Points of Light ambassador.

Michael, we wish you well, sir, as you bring light into children's lives, something you feel so strongly about as part of the Points of Light movement. And now, I want to put you on the spot. If you'd like to say a few words, the floor is yours, and we welcome you.

*Note: The President spoke at 1:25 p.m. in the East Room at the White House. In his remarks, he referred to entertainers Michael Jackson and Anita Baker; Frances Hesselbein, president and chief executive officer, Peter F. Drucker Foundation for Nonprofit Management; and U.S. Olympic gold medalists Florence Griffith Joyner and Al Joyner.*

# Nomination of Adrian A. Basora To Be United States Ambassador to Czechoslovakia
*May 1, 1992*

The President today announced his intention to nominate Adrian A. Basora, of New Hampshire, a career member of the Senior Foreign Service, class of Minister-Counselor, to be Ambassador to the Czech and Slovak Federal Republic. He would succeed Shirley Temple Black.

Currently Mr. Basora serves as a senior research associate at the Center for the Study of Foreign Affairs of the Foreign Service Institute in Arlington, VA. Prior to this, he served as Director of European and

Soviet Affairs for the National Security Council in Washington, DC, 1989–91; and as Deputy Chief of Mission at the U.S. Embassy in Madrid, Spain, 1986–89. From 1983 to 1986, he served as a Political Counselor at the U.S. Embassy in Paris, France.

Mr. Basora graduated from Fordham University (A.B., 1960) and Princeton University (M.P.A., 1962). He was born July 18, 1938, in New York, NY. Mr. Basora is married, has one child, and resides in Washington, DC.

## Statement by Press Secretary Fitzwater on Relaxation of Restrictions on Exports to Hungary
*May 1, 1992*

We welcome the decision by the Coordinating Committee of Multilateral Export Controls (COCOM) to remove Hungary from the list of proscribed destinations, effective today. COCOM's action is part of the ongoing efforts to liberalize COCOM controls in light of our dramatically changed world.

Hungary is the first country ever to be removed from the COCOM list. This is a tribute to Hungary's democratic transition and its adoption of safeguards on the use or transfer of controlled technologies. The U.S. cooperated closely with Hungary in the design and implementation of its export control safeguard system. As a consequence of COCOM's decision, Hungary will have access to more sophisticated levels of Western technology that are important to its economic modernization. U.S. exporters will benefit from the relaxation of these licensing restrictions on exports to Hungary.

## Appointment of Clayton S. Fong To Be Deputy Assistant to the President for Public Liaison
*May 1, 1992*

The President announced the appointment of Clayton S. Fong as Deputy Assistant to the President for Public Liaison. He will succeed Sichan Siv.

Since June 1991, Mr. Fong has served as Deputy Director of the Office of Consumer Affairs at the Department of Health and Human Services. Prior to this, Mr. Fong served as a Deputy Associate Director of Presidential Personnel at the White House, 1989–91. In 1984, he served as California Governor George Deukmejian's liaison to the Asian communities statewide, and subsequently served as deputy appointments secretary. Mr. Fong also served as the northern California field director of the California Republican Party, January to December 1984; director of the Bay Area child health network, 1983–84; and research fellow and legislative liaison at the Institute of Health Policy Studies, 1982–83.

Mr. Fong graduated from the University of California, Berkeley, in 1982. He was born May 18, 1959, in San Francisco, CA. Mr. Fong is married to Nancy Lem Fong and lives in Silver Spring, MD.

# Address to the Nation on the Civil Disturbances in Los Angeles, California
## *May 1, 1992*

Tonight I want to talk to you about violence in our cities and justice for our citizens, two big issues that have collided on the streets of Los Angeles. First, an update on where matters stand in Los Angeles.

Fifteen minutes ago I talked to California's Governor Pete Wilson and Los Angeles Mayor Tom Bradley. They told me that last night was better than the night before; today, calmer than yesterday. But there were still incidents of random terror and lawlessness this afternoon.

In the wake of the first night's violence, I spoke directly to both Governor Wilson and Mayor Bradley to assess the situation and to offer assistance. There are two very different issues at hand. One is the urgent need to restore order. What followed Wednesday's jury verdict in the Rodney King case was a tragic series of events for the city of Los Angeles: Nearly 4,000 fires, staggering property damage, hundreds of injuries, and the senseless deaths of over 30 people.

To restore order right now, there are 3,000 National Guardsmen on duty in the city of Los Angeles. Another 2,200 stand ready to provide immediate support. To supplement this effort I've taken several additional actions. First, this morning I've ordered the Justice Department to dispatch 1,000 Federal riot-trained law enforcement officials to help restore order in Los Angeles beginning tonight. These officials include FBI SWAT teams, special riot control units of the U.S. Marshals Service, the Border Patrol, and other Federal law enforcement agencies. Second, another 1,000 Federal law enforcement officials are on standby alert, should they be needed. Third, early today I directed 3,000 members of the 7th Infantry and 1,500 marines to stand by at El Toro Air Station, California. Tonight, at the request of the Governor and the Mayor, I have committed these troops to help restore order. I'm also federalizing the National Guard, and I'm instructing General Colin Powell to place all those troops under a central command.

What we saw last night and the night before in Los Angeles is not about civil rights. It's not about the great cause of equality that all Americans must uphold. It's not a message of protest. It's been the brutality of a mob, pure and simple. And let me assure you: I will use whatever force is necessary to restore order. What is going on in L.A. must and will stop. As your President I guarantee you this violence will end.

Now let's talk about the beating of Rodney King, because beyond the urgent need to restore order is the second issue, the question of justice: Whether Rodney King's Federal civil rights were violated. What you saw and what I saw on the TV video was revolting. I felt anger. I felt pain. I thought: How can I explain this to my grandchildren?

Civil rights leaders and just plain citizens fearful of and sometimes victimized by police brutality were deeply hurt. And I know good and decent policemen who were equally appalled.

I spoke this morning to many leaders of the civil rights community. And they saw the video, as we all did. For 14 months they waited patiently, hopefully. They waited for the system to work. And when the verdict came in, they felt betrayed. Viewed from outside the trial, it was hard to understand how the verdict could possibly square with the video. Those civil rights leaders with whom I met were stunned. And so was I, and so was Barbara, and so were my kids.

But the verdict Wednesday was not the end of the process. The Department of Justice had started its own investigation immediately after the Rodney King incident and was monitoring the State investigation and trial. And so let me tell you what actions we are taking on the Federal level to ensure that justice is served.

Within one hour of the verdict, I directed the Justice Department to move into high gear on its own independent criminal investigation into the case. And next, on Thursday, five Federal prosecutors were on their way to Los Angeles. Our Justice Department has consistently demonstrated its ability to investigate fully a matter like this.

Since 1988, the Justice Department has successfully prosecuted over 100 law enforcement officials for excessive violence. I am confident that in this case, the Department of Justice will act as it should. Federal grand jury action is underway today in Los Angeles. Subpoenas are being issued. Evidence is being reviewed. The Federal effort in this case will be expeditious, and it will be fair. It will not be driven by mob violence but by respect for due process and the rule of law.

We owe it to all Americans who put their faith in the law to see that justice is served. But as we move forward on this or any other case, we must remember the fundamental tenet of our legal system. Every American, whether accused or accuser, is entitled to protection of his or her rights.

In this highly controversial court case, a verdict was handed down by a California jury. To Americans of all races who were shocked by the verdict, let me say this: You must understand that our system of justice provides for the peaceful, orderly means of addressing this frustration. We must respect the process of law whether or not we agree with the outcome: There's a difference between frustration with the law and direct assaults upon our legal system.

In a civilized society, there can be no excuse, no excuse for the murder, arson, theft, and vandalism that have terrorized the law-abiding citizens of Los Angeles. Mayor Bradley, just a few minutes ago, mentioned to me his particular concern, among others, regarding the safety of the Korean community. My heart goes out to them and all others who have suffered losses.

The wanton destruction of life and property is not a legitimate expression of outrage with injustice. It is itself injustice. And no rationalization, no matter how heartfelt, no matter how eloquent, can make it otherwise.

Television has become a medium that often brings us together. But its vivid display of Rodney King's beating shocked us. The America it has shown us on our screens these last 48 hours has appalled us. None of

this is what we wish to think of as American. It's as if we were looking in a mirror that distorted our better selves and turned us ugly. We cannot let that happen. We cannot do that to ourselves.

We've seen images in the last 48 hours that we will never forget. Some were horrifying almost beyond belief. But there were other acts, small but significant acts in all this ugliness that give us hope. I'm one who respects our police. They keep the peace. They face danger every day. They help kids. They don't make a lot of money, but they care about their communities and their country. Thousands of police officers and firefighters are risking their lives right now on the streets of L.A., and they deserve our support. Then there are the people who have spent each night not in the streets but in the churches of Los Angeles, praying that man's gentler instincts be revealed in the hearts of people driven by hate. And finally, there were the citizens who showed great personal responsibility, who ignored the mob, who at great personal danger helped the victims of violence, regardless of race.

Among the many stories I've seen and heard about these past few days, one sticks in my mind, the story of one savagely beaten white truck driver, alive tonight because four strangers, four black strangers, came to his aid. Two were men who had been watching television and saw the beating as it was happening, and came out into the street to help; another was a woman on her way home from work; and the fourth, a young man whose name we may never know. The injured driver was able to get behind the wheel of his truck and tried to drive away. But his eyes were swollen shut. The woman asked him if he could see. He answered, "No." She said, "Well, then I will be your eyes." Together, those four people braved the mob and drove that truck driver to the hospital. He's alive today only because they stepped in to help.

It is for every one of them that we must rebuild the community of Los Angeles, for these four people and the others like them who in the midst of this nightmare acted with simple human decency.

We must understand that no one in Los

Angeles or any other city has rendered a verdict on America. If we are to remain the most vibrant and hopeful Nation on Earth we must allow our diversity to bring us together, not drive us apart. This must be the rallying cry of good and decent people.

For their sake, for all our sakes, we must build a future where, in every city across this country, empty rage gives way to hope, where poverty and despair give way to opportunity. After peace is restored to Los Angeles, we must then turn again to the underlying causes of such tragic events. We must keep on working to create a climate of understanding and tolerance, a climate that refuses to accept racism, bigotry, anti-Semitism, and hate of any kind, anytime, anywhere.

Tonight, I ask all Americans to lend their hearts, their voices, and their prayers to the healing of hatred. As President, I took an oath to preserve, protect, and defend the Constitution, an oath that requires every President to establish justice and ensure domestic tranquility. That duty is foremost in my mind tonight.

Let me say to the people saddened by the spectacle of the past few days, to the good people of Los Angeles, caught at the center of this senseless suffering: The violence will end. Justice will be served. Hope will return.

Thank you, and may God bless the United States of America.

*Note: The President spoke at 9:03 p.m. from the Oval Office at the White House. The address was broadcast live on nationwide radio and television. The proclamation and Executive order on law and order in Los Angeles are listed in Appendix E at the end of this volume.*

# Exchange With Reporters Prior to a Meeting With Cabinet Members
*May 4, 1992*

*Federal Aid to Cities*

*Q.* Mr. President, what hopes do you have for any long-range help for urban areas like Los Angeles?

*The President.* We have some very good proposals out on the table right now, proposals that clearly have come of age. But we're going to be talking about that today and tomorrow. Today we're probably going to think more about what we can do immediately in the aftermath of this violence. And then tomorrow, we'll put it in a little longer term perspective.

But I'm very pleased that it's calmed down out there. And we will do everything we can to support the people out there, to make things tranquil, and then to help get to the core of the problems.

*Q.* Do you intend to visit any of the damage sites?

*The President.* We're talking now about the schedule. It will probably change from what had been planned. As you know, I planned a trip out there for some time, so it fits in very nicely. And we had a briefing this morning from the Attorney General, who's here, Deputy Secretary of Defense, and Dave Jeremiah about the Federal presence on the ground and the state of play on the ground. And now we're going to be talking with our top people here as to how our various Cabinet Departments can assist. And then we'll have people going out there, and by Thursday a schedule will be worked out where I will be able to meet with the key participants in this recovery and those who also have responsibility for the long run.

*Q.* Are you saying, Mr. President, you have no idea what the core of this problem is?

*The President.* No, I'm not—didn't say that at all, Helen [Helen Thomas, United Press International]. I don't know how you could conclude that from what I just said. We have some very good ideas that we have out there that would have been extraordinarily helpful if they'd been put into effect. We think homeownership is a very good concept, and we've been fighting for it for a long time. So it's not that we have no idea whatsoever. I don't imagine how you could have concluded that from what I just said.

*Q.* You said you were going to look into the core of it.

*The President.* Well, we don't think we know all the answers. And I think you learn from every incident. As history shows, that after each one of these uprising, these things that have happened, people have taken a look to see what they could do to help. And certainly we're willing to do that.

I feel obligated to do that. And it's not like we have no idea whatsoever. If people had listened to some of our Cabinet Departments up on the Hill, we might be a little further along.

*Q.* How soon would you hope to see U.S. troops out of Los Angeles?

*The President.* I want to go to work here. Thank you very much.

*Note: The exchange began at 9:15 a.m. in the Cabinet Room at the White House. In his remarks, the President referred to D.E. Jeremiah, Vice Chairman of the Joint Chiefs of Staff.*

# Remarks at the Unveiling Ceremony for the Portrait of House Republican Leader Robert Michel
*May 4, 1992*

Thank you all very much. This is a wonderful occasion, and we need more like it. And may I salute the Chaplain of the House, Jim Ford, thank him for the invocation. I thought he was giving a speech out there, but it was a fine invocation; delighted to see him.

Of course, being with Bob Dole and Tom Foley and Dan Rostenkowski in this friendly, wonderful setting is very, very special. And we're here to honor our beloved Republican leader. I am glad to be here. Whenever you hear about somebody being done in oil in this town, you can't be sure that that means painting or boiling. [*Laughter*] But today it means honoring.

And I will confess it took me a while to convince Bob that it's an honor to be framed in Washington and hung in the Capitol. [*Laughter*] But before the portrait is hung, Bob wanted to make sure it would do what the Speaker talked about, play in Peoria. Well, it will, in Peoria and the Nation. And the reason is very simple, and I think you all have heard it here today from his friends, all of whom I have great respect for. To know you, Bob Michel, is to respect you.

And for 36 years Bob Michel has, indeed, embodied what is best in American politics

and best about the traditions of the House of Representatives. And I speak of honesty and fairplay and character and integrity, all the qualities that Dan and Bob Dole and Tom Foley mentioned. A willingness to govern, to work things out, to fight his opponents tooth and nail during the day and yet remain a good friend, someone they can talk to during the evenings.

And Bob Michel has stood up for fiscal sanity. I think he's done a lot to help our economy. He's helped keep our military strong. And it's true that he can be a fierce partisan. After all, that goes with the American psyche; that's the way we are. And Bob has been a true American. He won two Bronze Stars for his service in World War II; then in serving his district, our party, and most of all, the future well-being of our country.

I haven't seen this portrait over here, Corinne, but I'm sure it's going to depict what we admire in your husband: a man of conscience, a man whose word is good, a man who means what he says, says what he means, a man that one fellow Illinoisan would have loved very much. Remember Lincoln's words, "The noblest work of God is an honest man." And you've been all of that, Bob, and more. And ask anyone who is your colleague, which means anyone who is your friend.

And now it is my pleasure to introduce Corinne, Bob's lovely wife, for the unveiling of this official portrait. And I can tell you I'm sure glad to be a part of this program,

this wonderful program of warmth here today.

*Note: The President spoke at 5 p.m. in Statuary Hall at the Capitol.*

# Nomination of Arthur J. Rothkopf To Be Deputy Secretary of Transportation
## *May 4, 1992*

The President today announced his intention to nominate Arthur J. Rothkopf, of the District of Columbia, to be Deputy Secretary of Transportation. He would succeed James Buchanan Busey IV.

Currently Mr. Rothkopf serves as General Counsel at the U.S. Department of Transportation. Prior to this, he served as a partner with the law firm of Hogan & Hartson in Washington, DC, 1969–91, and as an as-

sociate, 1967–69. In addition, Mr. Rothkopf has served as Associate Tax Legislative Counsel with the U.S. Department of the Treasury, 1963–66.

Mr. Rothkopf graduated from Lafayette College (B.A., 1955) and Harvard Law School (LL.B., 1958). He was born May 24, 1935, in New York, NY. Mr. Rothkopf is married, has two children, and resides in Washington, DC.

# Nomination of Michael James Toohey To Be an Assistant Secretary of Transportation
## *May 4, 1992*

The President today announced his intention to nominate Michael James Toohey, of Virginia, to be an Assistant Secretary of Transportation for Governmental Affairs. He would succeed Galen Joseph Reser.

Since 1989, Mr. Toohey has served as senior Washington representative for Ashland Oil, Inc. Prior to this, he served as staff director for the Republican staff of the Committee on Public Works and Transportation at the U.S. House of Representatives in Washington, DC, 1983–89; as staff director for the Republican staff of the Committee on Merchant Marine and Fisheries at

the U.S. House of Representatives, 1981–83; and as a senior Republican professional staff member at the Committee on Public Works and Transportation for the U.S. House of Representatives, 1978–81.

Mr. Toohey graduated from the University of California at Berkeley, School of Forestry and Conservation (B.S., 1971). He was born February 1, 1949, in Helena, MT. Mr. Toohey served in the U.S. Army Corps of Engineers, 1971–75. He is married, has three children, and resides in Great Falls, VA.

# Appointment of John C. Harper as Chairman of the Advisory Council on Historic Preservation
*May 4, 1992*

The President has announced his intention to appoint the Reverend John C. Harper to be Chairman of the Advisory Council on Historic Preservation. He would succeed John F. W. Rogers.

Since 1963, Dr. Harper has served as rector of St. John's Episcopal Church, Lafayette Square, Washington, DC. He currently serves on the Decatur House Council, previously served on the Woodrow Wilson House Council, and is an ex officio member of the National Trust for Historic Preservation. He has also been active in the ongoing restoration of St. John's Church and its parish house, Ashburton House, both of which are listed on the National Historic Register.

Born in Winthrop, MA, Dr. Harper graduated from Harvard University (A.B., 1946), Episcopal Theological School (B.D., 1953), George Washington University (D.D., 1966), and Nashotah House (D.C.L., 1983). He is married, has three children, and lives in Washington, DC.

# Remarks at a Cinco de Mayo Celebration
*May 5, 1992*

If I might be informal, Gus, thank you very much for the warm introduction and the warm welcome. And I just can't tell you how pleased I am to be in this beautiful place. There are many familiar faces out there, so many Members of both Chambers from Mexico. We salute you, and we welcome you all. I had a chance to greet the Members a second ago. Members of the Mexican-American business community, we're very pleased to have you all here. I see Senator Gramm and Representatives Kolbe and Gilman and Tallon, all here to salute this show of force and show of friendship for the delegates from south of the Rio Grande. The interparliamentary union, the Mexican-American interparliamentary relationship, is a good one. I can tell some of you older members of this delegation that I was a member of that interparliamentary action back in 1968 and 1969 and 1970. So I welcome you all once again.

I was pleased earlier to see Jose Niño and Raul Yzaguirre, two American leaders who do so much for strong relations between Mexico and the United States. And, of course, I want to take this opportunity to congratulate President Carlos Salinas for preserving this remarkable historical landmark and for creating the institute to strengthen the ties of friendship between our two nations.

Relations between the United States and Mexico are tremendously important to both our countries. It's exciting to note, and I would note and I'd say with some pride, that relations between Mexico and the United States have never been better than they are now. And I take great pride in that, as I say, but I commend especially Carlos Salinas for the role that he's played in strengthening this special friendship that benefits both our peoples. The Mexican President has done an awful lot to hold out his hand to us, to emphasize the importance to Mexico of the U.S.-Mexican relationship. And he's done a wonderful job.

I want to thank all of you for letting me share this special day, a day made even more meaningful because 1992 marks 500 years of Hispanic heritage in this hemisphere. And this heritage is a wonderful, rich tapestry that our kids, Barbara, and I were lucky enough to first experience during our west Texas years. I remember our Cinco de Mayo festivities out there, exploring the ties between our countries, ties of family, friendship, and faith. So, my exposure to Cinco de Mayo started in the year 1949 out in west Texas, and it's been a part of us ever since.

The Bushes are very lucky to be able to keep that celebration alive. Our daughter-in-law, as some of you know, was from Mexico, now an American citizen, and we take great pride in that. Three of our grandchildren are Hispanic-American, and they bring the wonder of this dual heritage into our family. I have only one complaint with them. All four of them, my daughter-in-law and the three grandchildren, none of them has been able to teach their grandfather to speak Spanish. [*Laughter*] When things calm down a little, maybe I can make a little more headway.

I remember being so proud when Noelle, our granddaughter, and her mariachi group sang at Barbara's First Ladies luncheon during our inauguration. I heard the mariachi group upstairs, and I'm kind of glad that there wasn't a comparison between Noelle's mariachi group and this group of wonderful musicians that enlivened the festivities here. But I was delighted to hear the music today.

We all know the facts of Cinco de Mayo, that long-ago May 5th when General Zaragoza and his outnumbered troops stood up to the empire of Napoleon III. Stirring facts, but what's most important is the spirit of that day, the spirit of those few poorly-armed men who turned the battle into a glorious symbol. Cinco de Mayo is a symbol of the struggle for self-determination against astounding odds, and it's the symbol of a brave people's unbeatable determination to fight for their own destiny. It's a day like the downing of the Berlin Wall, the vote against apartheid, the defeat of Iraq's aggression: events that transform our world and the way we see each other. It's also of course, a national holiday, a day of pride in Mexican culture, a day of pride in Mexican heritage.

The Los Angeles Unified School District sponsors an annual Cinco de Mayo essay contest, and I just want to share with you a couple of the quotes. A senior high school student wrote that this day, and here's the quote, "instilled within me pride and appreciation for the beauty of my people and the richness of my roots." And a middle school student wrote, "The real significance of Cinco de Mayo is the pride Mexicans everywhere have in their heritage."

And that's a glorious thing to celebrate. And when I think of the Hispanic community in our country, the first words to come to mind are faith, family, and freedom. These values have been interwoven into the strong, bright fabric of the Hispanic tradition for generations, and they're also the very values that this Nation was founded on.

Cinco de Mayo shows that we all have debts to our ancestors who took risks and made sacrifices for us, whether on the battlefield or out in the farm field. And we must honor these men and women who ached to pass on a richer life, a freer life, a better life, who sacrificed all they had in order to guarantee opportunity, freedom, and hope for their children and their children's children. One essay winner in this Los Angeles contest wrote, "Celebrating the deeds of our ancestors helps us keep in touch with our history and reminds us of past suffering and hardship that brought about the comfort we have today." Cinco de Mayo, it does not belong solely to another land; it's a celebration of ideals that know no border. And today we rejoice at the men and women who came to this country from across the world, brought their finest strengths, their rich culture, their proudest tradition, and fit them into the vibrant mosaic that is America.

We must also look toward the future to prepare the legacy we will leave our children. I believe of all the gifts that we could give them, the three most important are jobs, family, and peace. And the America we will leave to our country will be a better land and a more just land if we make progress here on five key areas. I'm thinking of our health care system, our legal system, our education system, our system of Government, and of course, we must expand world trade. These are the keys to thriving in the future.

And so much depends upon trade. Mexico and the United States share a great deal. President Salinas, as I say, is a dear friend. He also is a bold and imaginative leader, and the deep and enduring relationship we're forging between our countries is based on cooperation, mutual respect, and open trade. And I will fight to tear down economic barriers with Mexico.

I notice the portrait of Juarez watching us. And seeing him reminds me of that great fresco I saw upstairs, "The Liberators of the American Continent." For those who haven't seen it, it's a symbol of the friendship and union that we share. It shows the great leaders of our lands and a picture of North America and Latin America shaking hands. This idealized portrait shows what we're going to achieve in trade because I am absolutely committed—put the politics aside—I am absolutely committed to signing a sound North American free trade agreement just as soon as possible. The time of opportunity is now. I've told our negotiators to accelerate their work. I believe we can conclude a sound and sensible deal before this United States election, and I will sign it just as soon as it's ready.

A great lesson of our age is that trade and enterprise can build jobs and certainly can preserve freedom. NAFTA, the North American free trade agreement, will be the key to higher standards of living for the peoples of our continent. I hope it helps, and I'm sure it will, the standard of living in Mexico. I know it will do the same for the United States. And then I believe the benefits will flow south where it will open the door for other such free trade agreements. It will liberate our markets, and it will increase trade, investment, and jobs, yes, jobs, in Mexico, in Canada, and right here in the United States of America.

I must say, as I look over here I have a little guilt complex because I see Bernie Aronson who is working so very hard and in such effectiveness to bring forth a trade agreement, and he's done a wonderful job in our relationship. Bernie, I should have mentioned you earlier, but I'm just delighted you're here.

But as he knows and all of us, I think, know, a free trade market made up of these three nations, Mexico, Canada, and the United States, would be the stuff of dreams, one of the largest markets in the world, 360 million consumers in a $6 trillion economy.

Now, Mexico is among the fastest growing national markets for U.S. exports, and they've increased by two-thirds just over the past 3 years. And our exports of auto parts and telecommunications equipment have doubled. Imagine what will happen under a free trade agreement. It will create thousands more jobs on both sides of the border. And all of us will be winners. And in that spirit of vital cooperation, I know that we will grow together.

But all communities within the United States need to pause right now in the wake of tragic events in Los Angeles. We must rethink and reaffirm the bonds that knit all nationalities together. The violence brought much suffering to the Los Angeles Hispanic community. And I am certain that many of you, as did I, shared in their pain. And even as my heart, too, goes out to them, I found in the midst of the devastation there were signs of promise, neighbor helping neighbor, regardless of race or cultural background. Converging in Los Angeles were three fundamental issues of a civilized society: justice, order, and tolerance. And these must remain our goals as we mend the wounds of Los Angeles. From New York to San Antonio to San Jose, we must redouble our efforts to build on our strengths, the same strengths of character that are at the heart of the Hispanic community here in the United States and in Mexico as well.

My friends, I look forward to spending future Cinco de Mayo days with you. I loved the music, as I said. I can't wait to hear it again. And thank you very much, Gus, for including me in this wonderful day. And here's something my 8-year-old grandson, Jebby, did teach me: *Vaya con Dios.*

Thank you very, very much.

*Note: The President spoke at 2:17 p.m. at the Mexican Cultural Institute. In his remarks, he referred to Ambassador Gustavo Petricioli of Mexico; Jose Niño, president of the U.S.-Hispanic Chamber of Commerce; Raul Yzaguirre, president of the National Council of La Raza; and Bernard W. Aronson, Assistant Secretary of State for Inter-American Affairs.*

# Nomination of Reginald Bartholomew To Be United States Permanent Representative on the Council of the North Atlantic Treaty Organization
*May 5, 1992*

The President today announced his intention to nominate Reginald Bartholomew, of the District of Columbia, a career member of the Senior Foreign Service, class of Career Minister, to be the United States Permanent Representative on the Council of the North Atlantic Treaty Organization, with the rank of Ambassador. He would succeed William H. Taft IV.

Since 1989, Mr. Bartholomew has served as Under Secretary of State for Coordinating Security Assistance Programs. Prior to this, he served as U.S. Ambassador to Spain, 1986–89; and U.S. Ambassador to Lebanon, 1983–86. Mr. Bartholomew has served as U.S. Special Negotiator for United States-Greek Defense and Economic Cooperation Negotiations, 1982–83; and Special Cyprus Coordinator at the Bureau of International Organization Affairs at the U.S. Department of State, 1981–82.

Mr. Bartholomew graduated from Dartmouth College (B.A., 1958) and the University of Chicago (M.A., 1960). He was born February 17, 1936, in Portland, ME. Mr. Bartholomew is married, has four children, and resides in Washington, DC.

# Nomination of Peter Barry Teeley To Be United States Ambassador to Canada
*May 5, 1992*

The President today announced his intention to nominate Peter Barry Teeley, of Virginia, to be Ambassador Extraordinary and Plenipotentiary of the United States of America to Canada. He would succeed Edward N. Ney.

Since 1985, Mr. Teeley has served as president with the consulting firm of Teeley & Associates in Washington, DC. Prior to this, he served as Assistant to the Vice President and Press Secretary, 1980–85; and as communications director and press secretary at the Republican National Committee, 1977–79. In 1976, Mr. Teeley served as press secretary to the President Ford Committee. Mr. Teeley served as press secretary to Senator Jacob Javits (R–NY), 1974–77; and as press secretary to Assistant Minority Leader, Senator Robert P. Griffin (R–MI).

Mr. Teeley graduated from Wayne State University (B.A., 1965). He was born January 12, 1940, in Barrow, England. Mr. Teeley is married, has four children, and resides in Alexandria, VA.

# The President's News Conference With President Leonid Kravchuk of Ukraine
*May 6, 1992*

*President Bush.* Mr. President and distinguished members of the Ukrainian delegation, on behalf of the people of the United States it's been my honor to welcome you on the first official visit by a freely elected President of independent Ukraine. May I also acknowledge Senators Pell and Lugar, who are with us today. Congressmen

Broomfield and Leach were supposed to be; they are missing in action. But nevertheless, welcome to the Senators. All of us join in celebrating the renaissance of freedom and independence for the great and ancient nation of Ukraine.

A few blocks from here stands an imposing monument erected by an act of the United States Congress approved by President Eisenhower. It's a statue of Taras Shevchenko, the poet and prophet of a free Ukrainian nation. And inscribed on the monument is this verse composed by Shevchenko more than a century ago:

Our soul shall never perish. Freedom knows no dying. And the greedy cannot harvest fields where seas are lying; cannot bind the living spirit, nor the living word; cannot smirch the sacred glory of the Almighty Lord.

Mr. President, when we welcome Ukraine's new independence we honor generations of women and men who kept a flame of hope alive through years of darkness. And free people must never forget the suffering Ukraine endured under the totalitarian yoke. We must remember the victims of Stalin's forced famine, the Harvest of Sorrow. We must remember the religious believers who endured persecution for their faith. We must remember the thousands who faced punishment in the gulag because they spoke out for cultural, political, or economic reform.

Now the darkness is lifted. Ukraine has entered a season of hope and rebirth. The Ukrainian people reclaimed their independence on December 1, 1991. And I am proud that the United States was among the first in welcoming that vote, in recognizing Ukrainian independence, and in establishing diplomatic relations. We also were one of the first to establish an Embassy in Kiev, soon to be led by a Ukrainian-American, Ambassador-designate Roman Popadiuk.

In our intensive and successful talks today the President and I, President Kravchuk and I agreed that the United States and Ukraine should be not just friends but partners. Ukraine's future security is important for the United States and for stability in Europe. We welcome President Kravchuk's assurance that Ukraine will remove all nuclear weapons from its territory and join the Non-Proliferation Treaty as a non-nuclear-weapons state. We have pledged to assist Ukraine in the accounting and control of its nuclear reaction materials, to establish a science and technology center in the Ukraine, and to explore additional assistance for weapons destruction.

We also are committed to Ukraine's future economic prosperity in a free market system. The United States will continue its program of technical assistance, including advice in establishing a new Ukrainian currency. We will extend $110 million in Commodity Credit Corporation guarantees to permit sales of American agricultural commodities to Ukraine. Opening up markets and expanding trade are essential to our new partnership. A robust exchange of goods and services, of ideas and technologies will create better jobs and enhance the quality of life for people in both of our countries.

The agreement we've just signed on trade and the opening of our new OPIC, Overseas Private Investment Corporation, program are an excellent beginning. This week I plan to waive the Jackson-Vanik amendment, and as soon as possible I hope to confer most-favored-nation status on Ukraine.

And finally, we hope to assure the closest possible political and cultural ties between independent Ukraine and the United States. We will continue to consult on our vision of a democratic peace in Europe. Our new Peace Corps program, established by another agreement that was just signed here, will bring volunteers to help develop small businesses and build personal links between our two peoples.

Mr. President, Ukraine is the birthplace or ancestral home of more than a million American citizens. They enliven and enrich this country with their creative talent and with their passion for freedom. Decade after decade, Americans of Ukrainian heritage have kept alive in this country the cause of Ukraine's freedom and independence. And this historic day is a tribute to them as well as to their kinsmen in Ukraine. We know Ukrainians face many challenges in the years ahead, during your historic transition to free enterprise and democracy.

And let me assure you, the United States will stand beside a democratic Ukraine.

And again, thank you, Mr. President. May God bless you and the people of your wonderful country. We're delighted that you came our way.

*President Kravchuk.* Mr. President, ladies and gentleman, friends, the official part of my first visit to the United States as the President of Ukraine is coming to an end. In this respect, I would like to sincerely and frankly say that the meetings with the President of the United States, the talks we had, the air of openness and the friendly nature of the talks and mutual understanding of the position and interests of our two states surpassed the limits of official ceremonies.

As you know, we have already had an opportunity of meeting President Bush and many officials of his administration, both in Kiev and Washington. No doubt such contacts always get appropriate and well-justified international coverage and attract public interest and that of the media. Most important, in my view, is our gradual progress from general political statements to the bilateral state-to-state relations filled with visible content.

We are very pleased to mention that yesterday in Washington, DC, we inaugurated the Ukrainian Embassy in the United States, headed by our first Ambassador, Mr. Oleh Bilorus, who's present here. We believe that we will soon welcome the Ambassador of the United States, Mr. Popadiuk, in Kiev.

For us, the opening of our own Embassy in your great country is an event of great historic and political significance. This is another step towards a true state independence of Ukraine. We will next have to solve the problems related to the establishment of consular and other respected offices of Ukraine in your country. These institutions should give a substantial impetus to further development of our cooperation in the areas that present mutual interest.

Today the President of the United States and myself and the Government officials authorized by us signed a number of important bilateral agreements, such as the agreement on trade, promotion of investment, implementation of the U.S. Peace Corps program in Ukraine, on the environmental protection, and some other documents. Our experts agreed on further cooperation, and I believe in the nearest future Ukraine and the United States could sign some new agreements, among them the agreements on the sea shipping, the lifting of dual taxation, preservation of and protection of religious national cultural monuments on the territories of both countries, and cooperation and facilitating programs of assistance.

But the most important issue now is to ensure that the signed agreements be implemented. I hope that the spirit of mutual understanding, openness, and trust which gradually turns into a characteristic feature of the Ukraine and American relations at the official level would be transferred into the relationships between the peoples of our two countries.

The entire experience of creating new international ties after the collapse of totalitarianism and the end of the long cold war period shows that the major issue now is to establish effective cooperation in the interests of universal, peaceful future, and to ensure such international conditions which would allow to find an optimal compromise of state, national, and general human interests.

That is why I'm deeply convinced that the development of friendly and equal relations between our two states, Ukraine and the United States of America, corresponds to their innate national interests. We are ready to further develop and deepen our fruitful bilateral dialog.

Ukraine is a young state, and it will have to go along a very difficult road. But we are totally convinced, including the experience of the United States, that we will go along that road if we would abide by the general human values.

With all my heart, I would like to wish peace, happiness, accord, and further prosperity to the great American people and every American home.

*President Bush.* I think the President has agreed to take a few questions, and I'll be glad to do the same.

*President's Visit to Los Angeles*

*Q.* Mr. President, I'd like to ask you about another subject. Your spokesman says that you're not going to Los Angeles today with any kind of new blueprint for the cities. Where does that leave matters for these hard-pressed urban areas, given that Congress has largely ignored your proposals and many people believe that you haven't fought very hard for them anyway?

*President Bush.* I have fought hard for them, and we have some excellent proposals. But what I want to do is go out there and see that we are doing everything we can to assist in the recovery. That will also be accompanied by my keen interest in seeing where we go from here. I'll have more to say about that. We have some excellent ideas. I am very interested in what is underway there from getting reports. Both the Mayor and Peter Ueberroth and the Governor feel things are moving in the right direction.

So we want to be sure that we have supplemented the overall effort for civil tranquility. I do think that that's in better shape, and I think the Federal Government responded very, very well. I'm pleased that both Mayor Bradley and the Governor felt that way. Then we've got to begin the healing process, and we also have to find answers that will guarantee tranquility in these cities. I come back to my emphasis that was brought home to me loud and clear by Mayor Bradley himself when he talked about, we must find ways to strengthen the family, he and other mayors having come in before this happened. So we have some good new ideas. I will try to bring those forth to the American people after I've had a chance to look at the scene there.

Anybody that would like to ask President Kravchuk a question?

*Q.* I'd like to ask you one.

*President Bush.* All right, go ahead, Helen [Helen Thomas, United Press International], and then you've got one for——

### Urban Policy Assessment

*Q.* Mr. President, both you and Marlin Fitzwater have blamed Great Society programs for what's happened in our country. But your critics say that through the benign neglect of the Reagan-Bush years, we are becoming what the Kerner Commission prophesied, which is a nation—two nations,

white and black, separate but unequal. What do you say to that?

*President Bush.* I say that we're not trying to assign blame. There's no point emphasizing programs that haven't worked, however. We want new programs. We want new ideas. We've put forward some, and we may have others to put forward. But there's no point trying to convince the American people that programs that have not worked is the answer to this problem. It isn't. I don't believe in—what I'm trying to do is heal and bring the people together. And I will go forward with ideas that have not been tried, emphasizing that it is far more important to give people a piece of the action than it is to have the Federal Government simply dump largesse on them.

We've tried it the other way. Now this gives us an opportunity, an excellent opportunity, to try some new ideas, and that's all. It's not a question of assigning blame. It's a question of a realistic assessment: Have we, as a country, done everything we can to help those people that have been left behind? I am not satisfied. We need to do more, and we are trying to do more.

So I told my Cabinet today that I think this offers us an excellent opportunity not to assign blame but to try to come out with ideas that can offer hope and upward mobility to people that have been bypassed. That's exactly what I'll be trying to do, and that's what I think we've been trying to do. We've got to get it in better focus, and we need some action.

But this isn't any time for blame. This a time to heal. It——

*Q.* You're not saying that Medicare or Head Start or vocational rehabilitation, Federal aid to education at all levels, and all the other laws that were implemented in the Great Society era didn't work?

*President Bush.* Not all of them, no. But I'm saying we can do better, and I think we should try. We ought to offer—here we are talking to Ukraine who's moving to privatization, moving to market economies, and I'd like to be sure we've done everything we can to give people a part of the real action in the private sector. Let's just see if we can't do a better job in terms of ownership for some of these people that have been passed by and assigned in the past to these endless construction projects that all seem to fall apart. There's a better way to do it, is all I'm saying, and that's what we want to try to do.

*Ukrainian Nuclear Weapons*

*Q.* For President Kravchuk. My name is Susan Cornwall with Reuters. I have two questions for you. The first is, you said this morning that all tactical nuclear weapons would leave the Ukraine by July. But some Russian officials in Moscow said today that all of the tactical nuclear weapons had already left the Ukraine. Could you clarify please, and tell us, have they all, indeed, left the Ukraine? The second question is, when do you think you might sign a protocol to the START Treaty? Thank you.

*President Kravchuk.* By the time of the statements that we would terminate the removal of the tactical weapons, because of lack of respective control, we have moved out about 50 percent of all the tactical weapons. On the 16th of April, President Yeltsin and I signed an agreement which formed the joint commission which is now verifying the process of removal of tactical weapons from Ukraine. As soon as the document was signed and the verification control groups were created, the removal was resumed. It is going on according to the schedule which we have, and we will move all of the tactical weapons by the 1st of July. This is where Ukraine stands. The weapons were not taken yet.

As to the START Treaty, we have discussed many details with Secretary of State James Baker. Our Minister for Foreign Relations and Mr. Baker had lengthy consultations. We prepared a letter signed by the President of Ukraine, and the letter clarifies all the aspects which are acceptable both by the United States and Ukraine. And as soon as the protocol is signed, the Ukraine would ratify the START Treaty and would fulfill all the commitments stipulated in that treaty.

*Ukraine-U.S. Relations*

*Q.* Would you estimate the relationship of partnerships between the Ukraine and such a developed country as the United States—

What can we do to help?

*President Kravchuk.* We have done lots today by the simple fact that we have signed very important documents which open up our relationship on an interstate level. As to the everyday practice, we had a very interesting meeting with the Secretary of Commerce and will meet other secretaries. We brought a delegation of businessmen who met and will continue meeting their counterparts in the United States. We would create mechanisms and working groups that might help implement what we have agreed upon already, and I think we would continue to go in that direction.

I think those actions would be beneficial for both the United States and the Ukraine. I would like to emphasize again that Ukraine is not asking for anything. Ukraine would like to have some credits to create new technologies and to transfer to a market economy as soon as possible, a free economy. We are not asking for credits to eat them up as food products; we've got other intentions.

*Urban Policy Assessment*

*Q.* Sir, you say you're not interested in the politics of blame nor assigning blame. In fact, starting this Monday you blamed Congress for not passing some of your domestic programs for the inner cities. Marlin Fitzwater attacked the Great Society. Vice President Quayle yesterday also attacked Lyndon Johnson's programs. A year ago in Michigan you said that the Great Society programs actually exacerbated racial animosity. You actually used the words "racial animosity." We still are unable to get a specific list out of the White House as to which programs have done this.

*President Bush.* John [John Cochran, NBC News], I think this is an inappropriate time to try to divide. I think it's a very appropriate time to rethink whether we've done it just exactly right in the past, whether it's the Great Society or all the way up to our administration. I cannot certify to the American people that we have tried the new ideas that might make urban America better, might give a better opportunity for everybody.

So there is no point trying to go into your

question, answering the specifics, trying to assign blame. I don't think that's what the country needs right now. I think it needs to come together. If I have my fights with Congress on getting some proposals through, some of which I have been proposing for 3 years, that's another matter. But this isn't the time to go out and try to divide the country. This is the time to bring it together.

Now, we've started on that. We started to bring it together by doing everything we could to assist the local law enforcement people because the American people are outraged by the violence. Secondly, we started to bring it together by providing every asset we could to the local people out there, the Mayor and Peter Ueberroth and the localities, to have the Federal Government assist, whether it's Department of Labor, whether it's HUD, whether it's HHS. We've got a good program moving forward right now to do that. Then I owe it to the American people to say, here's what I think is the longer range answer; can help right now if we can get some of these things through and if I can convince the American people that this is what we ought to do. And I'll have some proposals to that effect.

But I say I don't want to assign blame; I don't. If I said a year ago that these programs weren't working, perhaps I have been vindicated. But there's no point in going into that. Nobody in the United States political system can certify today that every program we've had has worked just perfectly; it hasn't. So there's no point going back on it. The point is, try to take this as an opportunity and bring the country together and then move it forward. That's exactly what I'm going to do, and I'm not going to go trying to help you get into what's worked and what hasn't. I will present that to the United States Congress in the future, as I have in the past.

*Q.* Mr. President, so much of the problems in California and the inner cities have been addressed in economic terms about enterprise zones, about homeownership. But how do you, sir, begin to address the social problems, the antipathy between not only blacks and whites but blacks, whites, Koreans, Hispanics? How do you attack it from the social, not the financial, side?

*President Bush.* Some of it's rhetorical. Some of it is trying to build on what we've started by this Family Commission. I remember when Tom Bradley, the Mayor of Los Angeles, came to see me before the outbreak there. He joined a lot of other mayors in telling me that the number one concern that the mayors have—all of them had it, Republican, Democrat, liberal, conservative—was the dissolution and the decline of the American family. We've got to find ways to help strengthen the family. One of them is through the education program; one of them through neighborhood activities; one of them is through the kind of private sector involvement that we've been talking about through our Points of Light and that Peter Ueberroth is now trying to bring to bear on the solution to the problem.

So that's the approach we'll be taking. But I'm very anxious to hear, before I make final decisions, from the local people as to what they think. One of the things that I mentioned in my speech to the Nation was the concern I felt and the concern that Mayor Bradley felt about the attacks on the Korean community. These people were peaceful people, and they were all assaulted. We've got to do something about it. I don't have an easy answer to it, but you put your finger on something that I think we have to find answer to. And somehow in the field of strengthening the family and in the field of ownership and in the field of the dignity that comes with having a piece of the action lies the answer.

*Q.* Have those questions, sir, been neglected simply by dealing with it from other aspects, from financial——

*President Bush.* I can't say that they haven't. Anytime you see problems, we've got to figure out that we haven't done all we can to have them solved if they're still out there.

*Ukrainian Security*

*Q.* President Kravchuk, you said a moment ago you didn't ask for anything in the economic. Can you tell us if you asked for anything from the U.S. security field vis-a-vis Russia? And second, on the protocol, is the protocol pretty much in place, or is there some detail where even some dis-agreement is still to be resolved?

*President Kravchuk.* We do not have seri-ous differences. We had some misinterpre-tation of the text during the translation period, but we have agreed upon those minor details. And the protocol is ready to be signed.

There is a problem of security for Ukraine because Ukraine is a large Europe-an country with a population of 53 million, with a powerful nuclear arsenal. And we initiated to annihilate those weapons. We think that this policy is correct in its con-cept, and we would not change that policy. But some of our neighbors, especially the great neighbors such as Russia, have politi-cal forces which would like to make territo-rial claims as to Ukraine. That certainly worries us. It worries the people in the Ukraine. We would do anything in our power to solve possible conflicts with Russia.

These problems will exist because the empire crumbled, and people have differ-ent interests. We would continue to pro-claim our request for the international com-munity to find a necessary forum to express its viewpoint as to the Ukrainian stand on the elimination of nuclear weapons and also provide some guarantees for the national security of Ukraine in case there is a possi-ble threat.

### Crimea

*Q.* Do you fear losing Crimea to your powerful neighbors?

*President Kravchuk.* The thing is the Crimea, from the legal point of view, is the 1954 act was totally legitimate. They acted according to the legal norms and standards which were in effect at that time in our huge country. You can't reverse the law be-cause if we start to reconsider the 18th-century rules, we can come to a total ab-surdity. So we think that the problem was solved in 1954 correctly according to law. The situation in the Crimea would have been totally normal. There is a multination-al population there; nobody is deprived of their rights. But there are some forces from the outside that stimulate and instigate sep-aratist moods. They also finance those moods and, in a way, egg on those moods

from the part of Russia.

Let us take the example of the Vice President of Russia, Mr. Rutskoy, who stepped on the Crimean soil and made a first statement that Crimea is Russian. He hugged the barrel of a huge gun and said, "Can we lose Crimea with that type of weapon? No." He's not a man in the street but a Vice President of Russia. Such state-ments are very dangerous. They are politi-cally ungrounded. And the people in the Ukraine can hardly understand the type of statements. People in Ukraine and Russia used to live in peace, and they want to live in peace. They want to associate. They want to have contacts in science and culture. We have many common problems dating back into history. But we should not use power play and political play and lead a situation toward danger.

### Nuclear Power Plants

*Q.* Sir, did you raise the issue of Cherno-byl at all? And did you seek any sort of help from the United States for safety of nuclear power plants? And President Bush, are you concerned about safety of nuclear power plants in the former Soviet Union?

*President Kravchuk.* We have shut down the Chernobyl power plant after the acci-dent that people had near Leningrad, at the power station over there. We have shut down the reactors in Chernobyl, and we can see that we cannot resume their func-tions. A lot of money and a lot of effort would be required. We will need about a year to resume their activities. Our Parlia-ment decided that the Chernobyl power station should be shut down by 1993. And we decided we should not resume the work of the reactors.

The most important thing for us is how to neutralize the ruined fourth power unit. We do not have any scientific solution of the problem yet. We have not addressed the President of the United States definitely about this problem. We think that the people in many countries, including our kin brothers here in the United States who are providing help to us. But we think that the liquidation are consequences of the Cherno-byl tragedy if that is possible at all. And the taking of the station out of the commission is a very, very difficult financial, technical problem. As to other nuclear power plants in Ukraine, they are based on a totally different principle. They do not present any threat similar to the Chernobyl power plants. The Leningrad station is similar to what we have in Chernobyl.

*President Bush.* My answer to your question would be, yes, of course, we'd be concerned about safety. And I would like to offer cooperation on the part of our side as to our technologically competent people in every way possible, cooperating with whoever needs our help. We think we've got good, safe systems here, and we'd like to be of assistance to others. But any time you have systems that have caused trouble, we must all be concerned in this world.

### Urban Policy Assessment

*Q.* Mr. President, you and your predecessor, Ronald Reagan, came to office 12 years ago under an economic system that promised a rising tide would lift all boats. During both of your terms in office we had the longest postwar, or peacetime recovery and economic expansion in history, and yet, the conditions that produced the riots in Los Angeles still existed. Are you now, as part of your effort to look at whether everything has worked, reassessing your economic programs and the role of the Federal Government in proving help to the cities, States, and social classes of the country?

*President Bush.* Yes, I think we ought to look at everything. I'm not satisfied. And I think we ought to look at everything, and we ought to move forward on these three tracks: One, the question of restoration of law, American citizens should not be asked to put up with wanton looting and pillaging; secondly, short-term answers to assist the city and the State in the cleanup and in the restoration of things in Los Angeles; and then, three, proposals that would really assist in rebuilding and in harmonizing in this country.

That's the way I'm going to approach it, and I'll look at what we've done and what we've tried to do, what others have done, but not with the question of blaming. I really don't think that's what's wanted. If we point out differences, if I point out a program that I think has failed, it's not to

blame. It is simply to say I'm not satisfied with the tensions that I see and want to try to do something about it.

*Q.* If I may ask about a specific, sir, to follow up, revenue-sharing, a program started by a Republican President, was also ended by your predecessor. A lot of people who have been studying the Los Angeles riots say that may have—the cities may be overburdened now; that because of the new federalism, the shifting of programs to the cities who may not have been able to provide. Is that a specific area, Federal aid to the cities, that you're willing to reconsider?

*President Bush.* If I can find some revenue to share. We are operating at unacceptably high levels of deficit, and everyone knows that. What I think we also need to do is consider that a vigorous economy, with job creation as its goal or as its hallmark, is the best poverty program. So we've proposed instead, as you know, a rather substantial block grant. We've not gotten that through, but we'll try again. It's very close to revenue-sharing, as a matter of fact. It's no strings attached, and it is something that we think is a good approach. But I think we should look at all of this.

*Q.* In the past when faced with a budget crisis, you and your predecessor called for a budget summit. Do you foresee anything like that in the area of urban problems, given the fact that enterprise legislation and things along that line have been proposed and reproposed in the past without success?

*President Bush.* I think there's enough focus on this now that if we come forward with a good, sound program, I would like to think we'd have a good opportunity to encourage the Congress and to get it passed by Congress. I don't know that we need another commission or another study group, anything of that nature.

*Q.* But as far as the leadership in both the House and the Senate, a bipartisan group getting together to try to form a consensus on this.

*President Bush.* I'd like to think that we could get it. We'd have to get a consensus if we're going to get it through. And so we'd have to do whatever is required to get the proposals, some of which I have made, the new ones I'll make, to get it through the Congress. Yes, I'll have to do that.

*Q.* Not a summit?

*President Bush.* Well, what's a summit? Everything's a summit, I guess, these days. But I don't know how you define that. But we'd certainly want a—we need to get cooperation on both sides of the aisle to get something done for America.

### START Treaty

*Q.* Mr. President, could I follow up on what Mr. President Kravchuk said about the START Treaty? He said the protocol was ready to be signed by Ukraine. But of course, you have a complicated situation where you have several countries involved, Russia, Byelarus, and Kazakhstan. How close are you to being able to work something that is mutually acceptable so you can go forward with the Senate?

*President Bush.* I think we've made progress, as the President said here today. And Jim and the Foreign Minister worked out the details this morning. So this one is in pretty good shape. But we have work to do with others, and it's not complete. And I would think that Jim might be going soon to try to hammer out some of the differences that exist with the countries that you mentioned.

*Q.* Would you expect that while President Kravchuk is here he would sign this protocol, or is not something you can sign now?

*President Bush.* I'd defer to the President. I just don't know whether there's any plan to be signed on it. But the agreement, the letters, the language has been worked out. I doubt it will be signed on this visit. But the language is; we sat there in the Oval Office, and I think the President would agree that we agreed on it. Correct?

*President Kravchuk.* Yes. [*Laughter*]

*President Bush.* Yes.

### Legislation on Social Programs

*Q.* Mr. President, have you personally lobbied Democratic Members of Congress on enterprise zones and on the HOPE program?

*President Bush.* Yes, and I'll continue to, but let me come forward with a package now. And I don't know how you quantify it, but I think you'll note that that's been part of our proposal for a long, long time. And when I look at the devastation and look at some of the hopelessness, not just in this particular area but others, it seems to me that the time has come to try something different.

I thought I heard the Congresswoman from the area say that the time has come for enterprise zones. Well, that's a very interesting development and an interesting shift, if true. But again, you don't get something done by saying, we were with A, B, or C before when we were trying to get these programs through. What we do say is, you mentioned enterprise zones, I think enterprise zones make a good deal of sense; to bring business into the area and get jobs, you've got to get some tax breaks in the area, get the jobs moving in the area, get the production in the area. We haven't really tried that at the Federal level, and I'd like to see it tried. And without assigning blame for failures in the past, I think that this is an idea whose time has come. And so we will try again. And I have tried, and I'll keep trying.

*Q.* To follow up on that, you say that you will try to get your proposals through. When we talked to Democrats on the Hill, they say that you're not willing to compromise, that you want it your way or you don't want it at all. Have the L.A. riots provided maybe the tone for a compromise?

*President Bush.* I don't know that the L.A. riots—but I think I'm the guy that's held out my hands to the United States Congress, saying let's try. But I'm not going to suggest that that means doing it somebody else's way all the time. But I think the time has come when the American people want action. They don't want any more rhetoric, and they say, "Let's try something new. Let's try something that will really help. Let's have order. Let's not condone the violence, but out of this, let's see if we can't find better answers." And you mentioned enterprise zones, I happen to think it's a better answer. And I think it's almost unarguable. But——

*Q.* Mr. President, to follow up on that. The Democrats say, in fact, the enterprise zones was in the growth package, but you vetoed it. And secondly, on the homeownership program, the HOPE program, as you mentioned several times, that was approved, but the funding was cut by 60 percent. And we're told that Jack Kemp asked you to veto the bill so you could get full funding but that you didn't because the bill also had full funding for the space station. So my question is, will you shift your priorities perhaps away from things like the space station and more towards the homeownership, as your Secretary asked you?

*President Bush.* I don't think he suggested we move it away from the space station. But my view is, here's an opportunity. I'm glad they're saying that they support this. And I hope we can do it in a way that is acceptable to us because I have to also keep in mind the overall economy of this country. The bill I vetoed was not vetoed on space stations or on HOPE; it was vetoed on a wide range of broad matters that would have burdened the taxpayer in this country. But let's hope that with this new interest in finding new answers, that we can get done these programs that I'm talking about. Yes, I'd like to think we can do that.

Last one. No, not again, Terry [Terence Hunt, Associated Press]. [*Laughter*] Well, last one. Go ahead.

### Federal Law Enforcement Role in Los Angeles

*Q.* How long are you going to keep the Army and the Marine Corps on duty in Los Angeles?

*President Bush.* Well, it won't be much longer, and I will be very much interested in getting recommendations on that from the Mayor and from the Governor. As you know, we've federalized the Guard at the request of the Governor and the request of the Mayor. They are there. The law enforcement officials and the civilian officials there have felt that their presence inhibited further rioting. I'm convinced in my mind that the fact that we moved as quickly as we did in federalizing them had a very quieting effect.

But we'll start moving out. We've moved out some of the Federal law enforcement people already. I think that's been reduced by about a half, maybe more by now, Terry,

the FBI people, the Customs people, Border Patrol people, and all of those who were in the law enforcement end of the Federal Government. But in terms of the Army and the Marines and the National Guard, I will be talking about that, I'm sure, tonight with our task force when I get out there.

*Q.* The benefit of hindsight, do you wish that you had put them on duty Thursday night or Wednesday night, rather than waiting until Friday?

*President Bush.* No, I still believe that you ought to work closely with the local officials. I think they are the ones that activate the Guard, and that's the way it should be. I don't think the President should call up and insist on something like that. So I have confidence in their judgment, and I think they did the right thing. And similarly, federalizing, a President can do that, but it is far better to do it when you have the full request and full cooperation of the local officials and of the Governor. And that's exactly what we did in very timely fashion. So I don't have any regrets on that.

*Q.* Will you be seeing Mr. Gates?

*President Bush.* Gates? I don't know. I don't know. I don't know.

### Legislation on Social Programs

*Q.* When you say "new proposals," do you mean the ones you've already submitted?

*President Bush.* John, I'll tell you about that when I get ready to. I'll announce the program when I'm ready, not sooner; not an answer to one question or another. But when I'm ready to do it, I will. I'm going to follow it just the way I've told you, do it without recrimination, without trying to blame anybody, in an effort to try to move this country forward.

*Q.* Are you sorry the White House has looked divisive the last couple of days?

*President Bush.* I don't feel it has. I don't feel it has.

*Note: The President's 127th news conference began at 12:47 p.m. in the East Room at the White House. President Kravchuk spoke in Ukrainian, and his remarks were translated by an interpreter. In his remarks, President Bush referred to Peter Ueberroth, chairman of the Rebuild L.A. Committee, and Daryl F. Gates, chief of police for the city of Los Angeles. The news conference followed a ceremony in which President Bush and President Kravchuk signed the Agreement on Trade Relations Between the United States and Ukraine; the United States-Ukraine Overseas Private Investment Corporation Agreement; and the Agreement Establishing a Peace Corps Program Between the United States and Ukraine.*

## Joint Declaration With President Leonid Kravchuk of Ukraine
*May 6, 1992*

### DECLARATION ON U.S.-UKRAINIAN RELATIONS AND THE BUILDING OF A DEMOCRATIC PARTNERSHIP

Today's talks mark a historic step in the development of relations between our two great nations. For the first time, an American President has met with the freely-elected President of a sovereign Ukraine. The Ukrainian people are now building their own state, one whose independence and commitment to democracy can make a vital contribution to the creation of a new Europe truly whole and free. The United States places special importance on the consolidation of Ukraine's democracy and independence. Toward this end, we are agreed that we must work together as friends and partners for the mutual benefit of both our peoples, and in the interests of international peace and stability.

Politically, we will strive to protect and promote the values that bind us together in the democratic community of nations, including free and fair elections, freedom of emigration, the rule of law, and respect for human rights, including the rights of all minorities, regardless of their nationalities and beliefs. The United States takes special note of Ukraine's commitment to establish its independence in full accordance with these principles, and its efforts to build a just and stable society where fundamental freedoms of all peoples are guaranteed.

Economically, we will work to advance the values of economic freedom without which democracy and prosperity cannot flourish. Ukraine will accelerate efforts to move toward a market economy through appropriate macroeconomic stabilization policies and structural/microeconomic reforms to promote recovery, market development, and growth. The U.S., through its technical assistance programs in areas like defense conversion and food distribution, will help Ukraine in these efforts and encourage the international community to do likewise. Together, we will take steps to promote free trade, investment, and economic cooperation between our two countries and peoples, as well as within the world economy at large. A critical feature of this cooperation will be a special effort by Ukraine to lower barriers to trade and investment in order to allow greater access for American firms. Ukraine and the United States will establish joint business development committees to achieve this objective and build a foundation for expanded commerce. We have concluded a trade agreement which will confer Most Favored Nation tariff treatment on Ukraine, and an OPIC agreement to make available investment insurance for American firms investing in Ukraine. We have also agreed to expedite negotiations on bilateral investment and tax treaties that will further promote private trade and investment, as well as on cooperation in shipping and civil aviation.

In the area of security, the United States and Ukraine will cooperate to promote a democratic peace across Europe. We are agreed that international security can no longer be achieved through the efforts of individual states to acquire ever increasing amounts of weaponry. Rather, security must be based on reduced levels of armaments among all nations, and on a multilateral commitment to uphold shared principles, especially democracy, the inviolability of borders and territorial integrity, and peace-

703

ful resolution of disputes. Working together in multilateral institutions like CSCE and the North Atlantic Cooperation Council will be an important means of promoting these goals and values throughout the new Europe. Also important will be the development of a regular bilateral dialogue on questions of peace and security that would address questions of common interest. We will use bilateral military and defense contacts to provide advice and assistance in the development of civil-military institutions.

As a matter of special urgency and concern, we also will work actively to prevent the proliferation of weapons of mass destruction and associated technologies. In this regard, the United States applauds Ukraine's leadership, manifested in its agreement to ratify and implement the START and CFE treaties, and its commitment to renounce nuclear weapons and join the Non-Proliferation Treaty as a non-nuclear weapons state at the earliest possible time. Consistent with these commitments, Ukraine reaffirms its decision to complete the removal of all tactical nuclear weapons from its territory by July 1, 1992, and all remaining nuclear weapons in accordance with her relevant agreements and during the seven-year period of time as provided by the START Treaty and in the context of the statement of the Verhovna Rada on the nuclear status of Ukraine. The United States

will assist Ukraine in these efforts by utilizing a portion of the $400 million appropriated by the U.S. Congress. The U.S. will also allocate part of this $400 million for the establishment of an International Science and Technology Center in Ukraine. This Center will help former weapons scientists and engineers in developing long-term civilian career opportunities that will strengthen Ukraine's scientific research and development capacity. In addition, the United States will continue its support of Ukrainian and international efforts aimed at minimizing the tragic aftermath of the Chernobyl catastrophe.

By agreeing to cooperate to advance these common political, economic, and security interests, the United States and independent Ukraine have laid the foundation for a strong and special partnership. For while relations between our governments may be new, the ties that connect our peoples are deep and long standing. We will seek to broaden these contacts through expanded people-to-people exchange programs such as the Peace Corps agreement we have signed to provide Ukraine with assistance in small business development and other areas, such as education. Working together and with others who share our principles, we will expand this partnership in pursuit of an enduring, democratic peace that can fulfill the aspirations of our two nations and the entire world.

# Teleconference Remarks to the American Newspaper Publishers Association
*May 6, 1992*

*The President.* Thank you, Bob, and thank all of you for that warm welcome. And I'd like to say hello to Cathy Black there, the ANPA CEO and president. I want to congratulate your incoming chairman, an old friend, Frank Bennack, who takes the gavel for the ANPA and the new NAA. And it's good to be with all of you again, this time via satellite.

Please excuse the slight delay here. I've just come from a longer than expected

press conference with President Kravchuk of Ukraine. And incidentally, that was an important meeting we had, and I think it went very well indeed. The relationship between the United States and Ukraine is a developing one, and it is a very important one. And I will be seeing him again in a couple of hours. But that's why I was a little late here.

Before taking your questions, let me just give you a brief update on events in Los

Angeles. As I think back today to when I spoke with the American people last Friday evening, I think of the oath that I took as President, the Constitution's charge to ensure domestic tranquility. This I know: We cannot and can never condone violence because without peace there can be no hope.

All of us are grateful that our actions have brought calm to Los Angeles. The kids are back in school; city buses are running; the curfew is lifted. After last week's shock and spectacle, we take heart at the willpower of the people of Los Angeles to join hands and hearts to mend their community.

Let me focus for a minute on what we're doing at the Federal level, working in cooperation with the Governor and the Mayor to help in the rebuilding. Through my Presidential disaster declaration, FEMA, the Federal Emergency Management Agency, will make assistance available to individuals and families and the city and county of Los Angeles. We've got a preliminary estimate of this assistance, and the preliminary estimate is approximately $300 million.

Now, we will make grants directly to people hit the hardest by the violence, personal grants up to $11,500 to meet urgent needs like food, clothing, and medicine. These grants will also help with temporary housing, money to provide shelter for up to 18 months for families who have lost their homes or money for repairs to minimally damaged homes. And we're also helping with crisis counseling and disaster unemployment assistance for those who are now without jobs as a result of the disaster.

A disaster field office is already up and running in Los Angeles. And FEMA's 800 assistance number is ready to receive calls in English, Spanish, Chinese, Thai, Korean, and Laotian. In addition, FEMA will assist State and local governments to repair and restore public utilities, like water and electricity, essential to everyday life. This is a cooperation program, a program of cooperation with State and Federal and local governments.

Beyond these emergency grants, we will provide low-interest Small Business Administration disaster loans up to $500,000 for business losses that exceed insurance coverage and up to $100,000 to homeowners and renters for damage not covered by insurance. Preliminary estimates indicate that roughly $300 million in loans will be made in the Los Angeles area.

Finally, the Department of Agriculture has arranged for delivery of over 2,000 cases of rice cereal, over 2,000 cases of infant formula, nearly 250 cases of nonfat dry milk, and continues to assess emergency food needs in the city of Los Angeles. So all told, Federal aid to speed the recovery process in Los Angeles is estimated at approximately $600 million.

Now tonight, I'll be traveling to California to get a firsthand look at the situation in Los Angeles. There I'll be meeting with members of the community to discuss how we can continue the work of building a future of hope, understanding, and tolerance, a future where there's no room for hatred. That's a story I know every one of us wants to see in print.

Let me say this about the desire that all Americans share to see that what happened in Los Angeles never happens again: We all want to solve the problems. This is no time to play the blame game. It is time for honest talk. And the fact is, in the past decades spending is up, the number of programs are up, and yet, let's face it, that has not solved many of the fundamental problems that plague our cities. We need an honest, open national discussion about family, about values, about public policy, and about race. That's the only way forward. And that's what I intend to do in the days ahead.

I'll never forget when Mayor Bradley of Los Angeles came with some other mayors to see me a few months ago. And he pointed out, as did all of them—small city mayors, big city mayors—that the decline in the family, the dissolution of the American family is at the core of the problems the cities face. And we've got to find ways to strengthen the American family. Barbara does it by encouraging parents to read to their kids, and we're trying to do it through our own education program and through revising the welfare system that in the past has encouraged families to live apart.

But the family is important in all of this. And I might add, lastly, so is the private sector. Peter Ueberroth talked to me in very optimistic tones the other day of how the private sector can now get involved in some of these areas in job-creating ways that will offer them hope for the future, not just a repair mechanism but real hope for the future.

So, I approach this with optimism. I know we've got to do better. The whole country has to do better. And I'm looking forward to going out there and then making some recommendations to the country about what we should do.

But anyway, thank you all very much for letting me be a part of your 106th convention. And now I'll be delighted to take some questions, Bob.

*Q.* All right. Thank you, Mr. President. There is a podium with a microphone here from which questions can be asked.

*Women's Issues*

*Q.* Mr. President, last night seven women who know each other only through this convention, for the most part—and we're from all over the country, ranged in age from 21 to over 70—had dinner together. During the course of the evening we found that we agreed almost 100 percent on the problems that are facing not just professional women but all women in this country over the next few years. I'd like to give you those problems.

The first one was physical violence, just the garden variety of crime that we see, random crime resulting from the rage in this country. The second was sexual violence, including rape, sexual harassment, and job discrimination particularly. The third is financial violence, including things like not only just getting along in our struggling economy and making ends meet but things that are gender-specific like years of pay discrimination and the fact that more women are supporting families alone and living longer than men in a time when services are declining and expenses are going up. And finally, the abortion issue and the question of whether women will, in private consultation with their God, have the right to choose how to manage their own body or whether our U.S. Government is going to tell us that.

Mr. President, we'd like to know what your agenda is for dealing with these issues facing American women.

*The President.* I think we've got a good agenda for dealing with these problems. First, on physical violence, and secondly, on rape and job discrimination, there are strong laws on the book. We're trying to make them even stronger by passing a meaningful crime bill that will, in my view, inhibit crime. I've had difficulty with that, but we're going to keep on trying to get such legislation through the United States Congress.

And I think you're absolutely correct in the underlying point that this kind of violence must end. I am not overly happy with some of the violence I see in the public media, and I've spoken out against that. I saw a film the other day, and I'll spare you its name, a rather prominent new one that almost glorified the use of narcotics, cocaine in this instance. And we have tried very hard, working with some of the media people to eliminate that. There's a great private sector effort going on under the leadership of Jim Burke to try to use the media to speak out against the narcotics and against the underlying things that lead to the kind of violence that both you and I decry.

Financial violence: The answer is to get this economy going. I'm a little more optimistic about that one right now. I believe that most people feel that the economy is starting to move. I was wrong last year. I thought the economy was starting in a recovery about this time and that by the end of August the recovery would be, if not robust, pretty steady; and it wasn't. And I think 49 of the 50 blue-chip indicating economists, who are leading economists, felt the same way.

But I think the answer to financial violence is equal opportunity. And I hope that the recovery—and it would have been stimulated, I think, if we could have passed these very laserlike growth initiatives that I have proposed and am still proposing. I hope that will take care of a lot of the financial violence that we've suffered through as a result of longer than normal recession.

On abortion, you and I just have different

views on that one, and I am appalled at the numbers of abortions. I know that others view it very, very differently. I have confidence in the court system and, of course, as President will uphold the Constitution of the United States. But when I see a 13-year-old—some of the groups are fighting legislation that would say to a 13-year-old, you've got to notify your parents; they're challenging that law in Pennsylvania. I'm sorry, I just disagree with it.

And I think that contributes to a weakening of the family, too. So, I have a difference. I come down on the side of the sanctity of life, and others look at it quite differently. But the matter is in the courts, and then we'll see what happens. I don't know how broad the Supreme Court decision will be, but at some point it will go back out to the States again.

*Urban Aid*

*Q.* The New York Times today asserts in its lead editorial that spending on direct aid for cities has fallen by more than 60 percent, after adjusting for inflation, since 1981. First, how will you explain that statistic to the people of Los Angeles whom you will soon be visiting? And second, if many of them have, in fact, suffered dramatic declines in economic opportunity in the last decade, they will, of course, want to know if recent events have convinced you to reconsider your strategies on Federal aid to cities.

*The President.* Well, first place, I'd like to look at the New York Times editorial. I have asked the Director of OMB to give me the amounts by which Federal spending has increased, and it's increased dramatically. We may be being judged by whether you should put money into these hopeless projects of bricks and mortar that we saw rot in St. Louis, for example, and deny everybody dignity.

If you can pick out a program like that one and say spending is down, you're correct. What we've tried to do is bring it to bear in different ways. We've tried for block grants that leave the individual communities to have a better shot. But overall, I can certify to you that spending is up. So, I'd have to see exactly what it is that the New York Times is talking about.

What was the second part of your ques-

tion? Is she gone?

*Q.* She's back. [*Laughter*] The second part was, many of the people in L.A. have, in fact, suffered dramatic declines in economic opportunity in the last decade. They will, of course, want to know if recent events have convinced you to reconsider your strategies on Federal aid to cities.

*The President.* I think we should certainly reconsider the status quo in terms of Federal aid to cities. And that's one of the things we've been trying to do by offering people HOPE, Home Ownership for People Everywhere, for offering them enterprise zones that would actually bring businesses into the communities. You see, I don't think this is a time for blame, as I said in my remarks. I think it is a time to rethink and to try some new ideas as to how we cope with the problems of the cities. I think we would all agree that it hasn't worked. It hasn't worked in the last 10 years; it hasn't worked in the last 30. And so we've got to do what we can.

All the time I have to bear in mind, however, because of my concern about the Federal deficit that's appalling, exactly how many dollars can be brought to bear in the community. And this is one of the reasons I like what Peter Ueberroth is talking—what we've tried to be talking about in terms of Points of Light, people, neighbors helping neighbors, in terms of block grants and fewer mandated programs.

One of the places that I may have a difference with the New York Times editorial page, and there may be others, relates to the concept of mandated programs. You see, every Governor, every Governor comes to Washington and says, "Do not mandate any more programs. Please do not pass programs that tell me as Governor or my mayors as mayors how they have to spend the money." So, we have a proposal for a substantial block grant that has been pending in the United States Congress, and maybe that time has come to think new thoughts and to try that one.

So I would tell them: Look, I'm not happy with the status quo, and clearly you're not happy with the status quo, so let's try some new ideas. Let's try some change. And this isn't any time for demagoguery or blame.

In my view, it's a time to go out and sensibly and sensitively survey the situation, do what I have suggested here, which is to bring the Federal resources to bear on the problem, and then say: Look, let's turn over a new leaf, and let's see what will heal. And all the time remembering that we cannot condone lawlessness and violence. And so we can separate that out. I will do what the Federal Government can do to support the local police, to support the mayors, to support the Governors in their requests for support for keeping the peace. So, that's one.

And then the other: What do you do about the problems? How do you bring hope where there has been hopelessness? And I think my challenge now is to find a package of answers that will at least give these people that you're talking about a shot at something new. And I am not pessimistic about it. I really believe that in our country sometimes out of despair or out of gloom comes real opportunity. That's the way I'm going to approach it, with no rancor in my heart, and do what we can to help.

And I must tell you, I am very pleased at the reaction from both the Governor and the Mayor about the Federal response. It is not easy when you want the Federal Government to be a partner, but you don't want it to dominate. I think we've handled it right in terms of putting down the violence. And I hope we're handling it right in terms of compassionate help to people that desperately need it.

*Q.* Mr. President, if we have time for one more question——

### Welfare Reform

*Q.* My question is, you have indicated that there are some basic flaws with our current welfare system, and that they are related to the crisis in Los Angeles. What are your specific ideas for welfare reform, and how will they relate to that crisis?

*The President.* The best answer on welfare reform is to give the States the flexibility through the waiver process to innovate. And that's exactly what we've done now with the State of Wisconsin. We have invited other States to send in requests for waivers so that we can let them innovate.

In the Wisconsin program, for example, there was Learnfare, there was Workfare, as a part of their reform program. Some were upset because in the program it suggests that if you curtail payments after so many children that that would be cruel. Others are saying that that'll be a disincentive for families that are going to just be on welfare and be there for decades. But let's see it work. This was passed by the Wisconsin Legislature. Let's see it work.

So, the Federal role predominantly is to provide the flexibility to the States that are required. But underlying my own philosophy is this concept of work incentive, learning incentive. And I'd like to see us really go forward on this program because therein, I think, lies the answer. I do not think that you're going to design one-size-fits-all welfare legislation out of Washington, DC. We've got to get past this view. And it's tough in an election year when you hear all the promises of these grand designs, which means just more Federal spending. I'm sorry, but I don't think the highly centralized Federal answers work, and I don't think that they need the support of people that are hurting, in the future.

So, this one on welfare, we're trying this diffused, decentralized approach, underpinning it as the kind of philosophy I've outlined for you. But I think it'll be well-received by the American people, and I wish those in Wisconsin who are starting with this waiver the greatest success with their approach.

*Q.* Mr. President, we thank you very much for taking time out of your schedule to join us, and we wish you well on your trip to Los Angeles.

*The President.* Thank you, Bob. Thank you very much.

*Note: The President spoke at 1:50 p.m. via satellite from Room 459 of the Old Executive Office Building to the American Newspaper Publishers Association convention in New York City. In his remarks, he referred to Robert F. Erburu, association chairman; Peter Ueberroth, chairman of the Rebuild L.A. Committee; and Jim Burke, chairman of the Partnership for a Drug-Free America.*

## Exchange With Reporters Prior to Discussions With President Rafael Callejas of Honduras
*May 6, 1992*

*Legislation on Social Programs*

*Q.* Mr. President, do you think your feelings about the blame game have been misinterpreted?

*The President.* I hope not. I've made it very clear. you heard me speak on it. I hope it's clear.

*Q.* Your remarks on Monday and your spokesman's remarks?

*The President.* My remarks on Monday about what?

*Q.* Blaming Congress for not passing your programs.

*The President.* Well, I'd like to get them passed. But I really don't think this is the time for blame; I think this is a time to move forward. And I think what Marlin said got grossly misinterpreted.

So I don't want to discuss it anymore. I've got a distinguished visitor and a good friend here. The man is doing a first-class job down there, and we've got some business to talk about.

*Q.* You're not taking him to the woodshed—Marlin?

*The President.* Absolutely not.

*Q.* Do you think that Clinton's playing politics——

*The President.* Helen [Helen Thomas, United Press International], you're out of here. Come on. We've got to go to work.

*Note: The exchange began at 3:15 p.m. in the Oval Office at the White House.*

## Statement by Deputy Press Secretary Smith on the President's Meeting With President Rafael Callejas of Honduras
*May 6, 1992*

The President met this afternoon with President Rafael Callejas of Honduras. The President congratulated him on the success of his 2-year-old economic reform program. He praised President Callejas' efforts to reduce tariffs, thereby opening Honduras' markets and increasing its trade. The President thanked President Callejas for his efforts to strengthen democracy and economic integration in the region.

President Callejas expressed his apprecia-tion to the President for the generous assistance to his country from the United States, including substantial debt relief. He indicated that he remains committed to the market-oriented economic reforms that have begun to spur economic growth in Honduras. He thanked the President for his firm support for liberalized trade in agricultural products in the ongoing GATT trade negotiations.

## Message to the Congress Transmitting the Report of the Corporation for Public Broadcasting
*May 6, 1992*

*To the Congress of the United States:*

In accordance with the Communications Act of 1934, as amended (47 U.S.C. 396(i)), I transmit herewith the Annual Report of the Corporation for Public Broadcasting for Fiscal Year 1991 and the Inventory of the

Federal Funds Distributed to Public Telecommunications Entities by Federal Departments and Agencies: Fiscal Year 1991.

GEORGE BUSH

The White House,
May 6, 1992.

# Letter to Congressional Leaders Reporting on the Cyprus Conflict
*May 6, 1992*

*Dear Mr. Speaker:* *(Dear Mr. Chairman:)*

In accordance with Public Law 95–384
(22 U.S.C. 2373(c)), I am submitting to you
this bimonthly report on progress toward a
negotiated settlement of the Cyprus question. This report covers January and February and, for the sake of continuity, the first
10 days of March 1992.

As reported in my last letter to you on
this subject, we were in contact with the
U.N. Cyprus negotiators at the end of 1991
in preparation for the installation on January 1 of the new U.N. Secretary General,
Mr. Boutros Ghali. On January 3, the first
full U.N. workday in 1992, the U.S. Special
Cyprus Coordinator, Nelson Ledsky, consulted in New York with the new Secretary
General on how to proceed during Ambassador Ledsky's projected trip to Ankara, Nicosia, and Athens.

Ambassador Ledsky was in the Eastern
Mediterranean from January 7 through January 17, and during that time he received
assurances from Prime Minister Demirel of
Turkey, the leadership of the two Cypriot
communities, and Prime Minister Mitsotakis
of Greece that the parties were committed
to proceed with the U.N.-sponsored settlement process, taking up where it had left
off in the late summer of 1991.

By the end of January, the U.N. negotiators had themselves returned to the area
and began their first round of consultations
in 1992 with the Governments of Greece
and Turkey and the leadership of the two
Cypriot communities. This round ended
without progress when, due to the illness of
Turkish Cypriot Leader Rauf Denktash, the
Turkish Cypriots were unable to address
substantively the issues contained in the
Secretary General's "set of ideas" for a
Cyprus settlement. Disappointed by this

lack of progress, the Secretary General's negotiators returned to New York on February 7.

On February 10, I discussed the Cyprus
issue with Prime Minister Demirel during
his official visit to Washington. He repeated
his assurances that Turkey wanted a Cyprus
settlement and would work cooperatively in
support of the U.N. Secretary General's
good-offices mission in an effort to obtain
such a solution. He gave similar assurances
directly to Secretary General Boutros Ghali
3 days later in New York.

The Secretary General's Cyprus negotiators returned to Ankara on February 17.
After meeting with representatives of the
Government of Turkey, they expressed concern that Turkey appeared to be placing
conditions on the continuation of the negotiation along lines put forward earlier by
the Turkish Cypriots. Moreover, these conditions seemed to go beyond the mandate
conferred on the Secretary General by the
U.N. Security Council as reaffirmed in U.N.
Security Council Resolutions 649 (1990) and
716 (1991).

On March 3, Under Secretary of State
Arnold Kanter met with Prime Minister
Demirel in Ankara. During their discussions
of Cyprus, Under Secretary Kanter reiterated the desire of the United States for the
success of the U.N. Secretary General's efforts to resolve peacefully, fairly, and permanently the Cyprus problem. Under Secretary Kanter had assured Greek Foreign
Minister Samaras of the same commitment
in Athens on February 29. Prime Minister
Demirel told Under Secretary Kanter that
he understood the U.S. position and that
any impression that Turkey had reversed
itself on the Secretary General's good-offices mission was a result of a misunder-

standing by the U.N. negotiators of Turkey's position.

On March 10, at the meeting of the North Atlantic Cooperation Council in Brussels, Secretary of State Baker met separately with Foreign Minister Cetin of Turkey and Foreign Minister Samaras of Greece. He received assurances that Greece and Turkey are committed to support the Secretary General's Cyprus good-offices mission. Having received these assurances, Ambassador Ledsky travelled to the Eastern Mediterranean once again on March 17 to discuss with the parties in greater detail the U.N. Secretary General's "set of ideas" for a Cyprus settlement.

I continue to believe that the Secretary General's efforts provide the only peaceful means of reaching a permanent settlement of the Cyprus issue. Further, I believe that the Secretary General's "set of ideas" can and should be an appropriate basis for moving forward. It is my hope that the next few months will see progress in this worthwhile effort.

Sincerely,

GEORGE BUSH

*Note: Identical letters were sent to Thomas S. Foley, Speaker of the House of Representatives, and Claiborne Pell, chairman of the Senate Committee on Foreign Relations.*

# Presidential Determination No. 92–25—Memorandum on Trade With Certain Former Soviet Republics
*May 6, 1992*

*Memorandum for the Secretary of State*

*Subject:* Determination under Section 402(c)(2)(A) of the Trade Act of 1974, as amended—Azerbaijan, Georgia, Kazakhstan, Moldova, Ukraine, and Uzbekistan

Pursuant to section 402(c)(2)(A) of the Trade Act of 1974, as amended (the "Act") (19 U.S.C. 2432(c)(2)(A)), I determine that a waiver by Executive order of the application of subsections (a) and (b) of section 402 of the Act with respect to Azerbaijan, Geor-

gia, Kazakhstan, Moldova, Ukraine, and Uzbekistan will substantially promote the objectives of section 402.

You are authorized and directed to publish this determination in the *Federal Register.*

GEORGE BUSH

[*Filed with the Office of the Federal Register, 11:07 a.m., May 22, 1992*]

*Note: The Executive order of June 3 is listed in Appendix E at the end of this volume.*

# Message to the Congress on Trade With Certain Former Soviet Republics
*May 6, 1992*

*To the Congress of the United States:*

Pursuant to section 402(c)(2)(A) of the Trade Act of 1974, as amended (the "Act") (19 U.S.C. 2432(c)(2)(A)), I have determined that a waiver of the application of subsections (a) and (b) of section 402 with respect to Azerbaijan, Georgia, Kazakhstan, Mol-

dova, Ukraine, and Uzbekistan will substantially promote the objectives of section 402. A copy of that determination is enclosed. I have also received assurances with respect to the emigration practices of Azerbaijan, Georgia, Kazakhstan, Moldova, Ukraine, and Uzbekistan required by section

402(c)(2)(B) of the Act. This message constitutes the report to the Congress required by section 402(c)(2).

Pursuant to section 402(c)(2), I shall waive by Executive order the application of subsections (a) and (b) of section 402 of the Act with respect to Azerbaijan, Georgia, Kazakhstan, Moldova, Ukraine, and Uzbekis-tan.

GEORGE BUSH

The White House,
May 6, 1992.

*Note: The Executive order of June 3 is listed in Appendix E at the end of this volume.*

# Nomination of Robert E. Gribbin III To Be United States Ambassador to the Central African Republic
*May 6, 1992*

The President today announced his intention to nominate Robert E. Gribbin III, of Alabama, a career member of the Senior Foreign Service, class of Counselor, to be Ambassador of the United States to the Central African Republic. He would succeed Daniel Howard Simpson.

Currently Mr. Gribbin is a participant in the Senior Seminar at the U.S. Department of State. Prior to this, he served as Deputy Chief of Mission at the U.S. Embassy in Kampala, Uganda, 1988–91; Deputy Director of the Office of East African Affairs at the U.S. Department of State, 1985–88; and a Congressional Fellow for Representative Stephen Solarz, 1984–85. From 1981 to 1984, Mr. Gribbin served as a Principal Officer in the United States Consulate in Mombasa, Kenya.

Mr. Gribbin graduated from the University of the South (B.A., 1968) and School of Advanced International Studies (M.A., 1973). He was born February 5, 1946, in Durham, NC. Mr. Gribbin is married, has two children, and resides in Springfield, VA.

# Nomination of Peter Jon deVos To Be United States Ambassador to Tanzania
*May 6, 1992*

The President today announced his intention to nominate Peter Jon deVos, of Florida, a career member of the Senior Foreign Service, class of Minister-Counselor, to be Ambassador of the United States to the United Republic of Tanzania. He would succeed Edmund DeJarnette, Jr.

Currently Ambassador deVos serves as the U.S. Ambassador to the Republic of Liberia. Prior to this, he served as Principal Deputy Assistant Secretary of State at the Bureau of Oceans and International Environmental and Scientific Affairs, 1989–90; and as Deputy Assistant Secretary of State for Science and Technology, 1987–89. In addition, Ambassador deVos has served as the U.S. Ambassador to the People's Republic of Mozambique, 1983–87; and as the U.S. Ambassador to the Republic of Guinea-Bissau and the Republic of Cape Verde, 1980–83.

Ambassador deVos graduated from Princeton University (B.A., 1960) and Johns Hopkins University (M.A., 1962). He was born December 24, 1938, in San Diego, CA. Ambassador deVos is married and resides in Cabin John, MD.

## Remarks on Arrival in Los Angeles, California
*May 6, 1992*

Well, I'm very pleased to be here in Los Angeles and thankful to see that calm has returned to the city; glad to receive that report just now from the Mayor, members of the city council, and from the Governor. As I think back today to what I said last Friday, I do think of the oath that I took when I entered the office, the Constitution's charge to every President to "insure domestic Tranquility." This I know: We can never condone violence, because without peace there certainly can be no hope. We cannot begin to move forward, could not begin to rebuild until the violence had stopped and the order restored. We've met the first mission, and I salute those who have participated in it. And now, the good people of south central L.A. are free to come out from behind those closed doors to begin the difficult but extremely important process of rebuilding the city.

Tomorrow I'll be meeting with community leaders, with some citizens, to see and speak with the people who have firsthand knowledge of last week's tragic events. I will assure them, as I can assure all the citizens of Los Angeles: The Federal Government is committed to help this city, help this city rebuild.

Let me focus just for a moment on the actions that we're taking at the Federal level to help. Through my Presidential disaster declaration, FEMA, that's the Federal Emergency Management Agency, will make an estimated $300 million in assistance available to individuals and families in the city and county of Los Angeles. It will make grants directly to people hit hardest by the violence, personal grants up to $11,500 to meet urgent needs like food and clothing and medicine. Now, these grants will also help with temporary housing, money for repair to homes with minimal damage, and to provide shelter for those families who lost their homes. We're also helping with crisis counseling and disaster unemployment assistance for those who are now without jobs as a result of the disaster.

A disaster field office is already up and running, and FEMA's 800 assistance number is ready right now to receive calls in a wide array of languages: English, Spanish, Chinese, Thai, Korean, Vietnamese, and Laotian. In addition, FEMA will assist the public sector in repairing and restoring public utilities like water and electricity that are absolutely essential to everyday life.

Beyond these emergency grants, we will provide SBA loans, disaster loans they're called, up to $500,000 for physical damage and lost inventory. Homeowners and renters are also eligible for assistance under SBA for programs up to $100,000 for damage and losses. Preliminary estimates indicate that roughly $300 million in loans will be made in this area.

All told, aid to speed the recovery process could total approximately $600 million. This assistance will help get boarded-up and burned-out businesses open again, up and running. It will help people clean up the streets, help the individuals and families who lost their home and all their belongings to cope with this most personal of tragedies.

Finally, the Department of Agriculture has arranged for delivery of over 2,000 cases of rice cereal, over 2,000 cases of infant formula, nearly 250 cases of nonfat dry milk, and continues to assess the emergency food needs.

This is a good beginning. The urgent need for assistance must not obscure the magnitude of the larger challenge that we face. Beyond these short-term actions, we must bring hope and opportunity to our inner cities. The aim must not simply be to recreate what we had but to build something better in its place. There must be no return to the status quo. Too often in the past, we've measured our compassion the wrong way, by budgets and bureaucracies instead of how many poor people have permanently escaped poverty. So this must end. And there's no question, the Federal Government has a terribly important, a fundamental role in ending poverty and despair in our cities. But the time really has come to try a new way. So we need to let poor families take back control of their lives by making our commitment to end poverty and despair greater than ever before.

So this time, we've got to make certain to put the Government on the side of opportunity, on the side of human dignity, on the side of hope. Anything less would really be a disservice to the people of Los Angeles who need our help. Anything less would be unworthy of our great country.

In 5 short days, Los Angeles has made great strides, and the number of people who deserve thanks runs up into the tens of thousands: The firefighters, the police officers who worked hours on end. There's this enormous corps of volunteers, I'm told, the churches, the churchgoers, those out in the communities organizing. The many people known and unknown who came to the aid of people that were hurt, people in need, who stepped forward to stop the violence, to save a life.

Let me say something, something I promised myself I'd say the moment we got here, say this to every one of the people who reached out across the barriers of color and put their own safety at risk to help others: Thank God for what you did. You did more than simply save a life. You gave a Nation great cause for hope. And you proved amidst the hate and the horror that this is still the City of the Angels.

I salute the local officials. I'm very grateful to the Mayor and the others who are here to greet me, from the city council to our Governor. I've listed what the Federal Government can do, but we recognize this is a team effort. I understand that on the ground already is a fantastic volunteer operation, one to stimulate the volunteer sector, and we salute those who are working in that way, too.

So it's a pleasure to be here. I know I will learn a lot from what I see. And I salute those, all of them standing right here with me, incidentally, who have worked tirelessly night and day to restore order and to return the city to a city of hope. Thank you all very, very much.

*Note: The President spoke at 8:50 p.m. at Los Angeles International Airport.*

# Remarks at Mount Zion Missionary Baptist Church in Los Angeles
*May 7, 1992*

Thank you, Reverend Hill. Let me just say to his parishioners and to his fellow members of the clergy that we Bushes have great respect for your pastor, respect for what he stands for, respect for his leadership, and respect for his emphasis on family values.

I listened to the prayers with wonder, admiration. I think we got a pretty good start, don't you, with Miss Elmore singing, but I heard what His Eminence Cardinal Mahoney said about racial tension. We must address that. What Bishop McMurray and Dr. Billy Ingram said about healing, we've got to address that; what Dr. Massey said about the importance of the church. And as you look at the chaos and turmoil in this country, not just in the wake of the riots of Los Angeles but all the problems we face in the country, the problems we face internationally, I keep coming back in my own thinking to the importance of the church, the importance of our faith. Then Reverend Massey talked about this is no time for blame, and he's right about that. This is not a time for blame, and I am not here in the mode of politics. I am not here in the mode of partisanship. I am not here in the mode of blame. I'm here to learn from the community and at this moment to tell you of the values that I strongly believe in.

When Reverend Hill and other national leaders came last Friday to the White House, I reminded the group of what Mayor Tom Bradley and other mayors, urban mayors, rural mayors, had to tell me not so many months ago. They told me of their concerns for their cities, their municipalities. But they came together on one key point: They told me that their major concern about the problems in the cities was the decline of the American family, the fact that the family is weaker today. I think that we have simply got to find ways to help strengthen the American family. This church does that for the immediate family; all of your churches do that for the families of your parishioners. But we've got to broaden it out.

This church brings the generations, grandparents, great-grandparents, and grandkids, here to work within this church—that strengthens the American family—and to give the kids not only indoctrination into faith and into the teachings of the Lord, but the church helps kids understand the larger family. We are one Nation under God. We must remember that. We must advocate that. We must continue to state that we are one Nation under God.

And we are our brother's keeper, not to keep him back, not to keep him down, but to keep him well and to keep him safe and to give him a shot at the American dream. Family values, that means respect for one another, and it does mean honor thy mother and thy father.

I talked to Barbara this morning and told her a little bit—I didn't know it fully—about what Reverend E.V. Hill had in store for all of us today, but particularly for me. He had failed to point out that he had the distinguished leaders of various denominations here and that I would be flanked behind me by people who are active pastors in the wonderful churches of this area. And she told me, she said, "You've got your nerve. You've got a lot of nerve to stand up in front of all those people and tell them what you think about values." But I'm going to try anyway. [*Laughter*]

I do want to single out Reverend Jones and Mrs. Jones for what they do, reaching across the States, bringing help to others. That's family. That's God's family. Family values means the church must continue to teach the kids right from wrong.

I was over at a supermarket, and the guy with tears in his eyes was telling me, "One of my own employees came in and took stuff out of this store." He couldn't understand it. We've got to teach right from

wrong. Government cannot do that. We can try, those of us in public life, to set reasonably good examples of family and faith. But the values have to be taught, and the church has a tremendously important role on that.

I think that when Barbara reads to kids that she is emphasizing not just the importance of education that we all believe in, so many of you working with children, but she's emphasizing the importance of the role of grandparents; even more, the importance of love.

To struggle against hard times, to overcome the devastation of poverty, of racism, or of riots, we need our family. We need our own family. We need our church family. And we must find ways to strengthen America as a family. Back to what the Cardinal said, we are embarrassed by interracial violence and prejudice. We're ashamed. We should take nothing but sorrow out of all of that and do our level-best to see that it's eliminated from the American dream. A family that respects the law, a family that can lift others up.

We need a family that is truly committed to faith, for again, we are one Nation under God; a family that says "I'm my brother's keeper." But it's here, it was here in the ugliest moments of the rioting, the brother's keeper aspect. I saw it in a police station just now. God bless the honest policemen that are defending the families of the neighborhood, all of them. But the message they got to me this morning was a little different than the one that I see in that first 2 minutes on the evening news. This was a message of forgiving and healing, how neighbors had called in and said, "Here's where you can go and pick up some looted goods," or brought them to the police station so that they could be returned to their owners. We don't hear enough of that kind of family action or that kind of fellowship.

Another pastor, Reverend Bennie Newton, laid his life on the line for his brother. He saw a man literally beaten into the ground, and he waded through the fray, and he laid his body on top of the victim until the beating stopped. And here's what he said. He said, "My heart was crying." But the bottom line is, he saved that man's life. He was his brother's keeper. These are the stories that I think America needs to know about. We saw the violence. We've seen the hatred. And we've got to heal, to see the love.

Los Angeles is going to recover. This is a great city. And I have pledged to the Governor, to the Mayor the full support of the Federal Government. And if I might take one mention of personal pride here to say that I'm very pleased the way these Departments in the Federal Government have responded. Not to preempt, not to get credit, again, not to assign blame but to supplement the work in the communities, the work of the Mayor, the work of the council, and the work of the Governor. And I'm proud that Lou Sullivan, our Secretary of HHS, and Jack Kemp, our Secretary of HUD, are here today. And many others wanted to be with me, but somebody had to mind the store back there.

Now Los Angeles will recover. I believe it is well on its way to recovery, thanks to what the local government and the State government and this Federal presence are doing. And as Los Angeles comes back to its glory, all of us must ask ourselves: What can we do to help? This is no time to outline Federal programs. This is a National Day of Prayer. This is a day to give our thanks. But we will do what we can to help and to assist and to lead in this reconciliation. To truly help, we've got to understand the agony of the depressed. You can't solve the problem if you don't feel its heartbeat. You've got to understand the hopelessness of those who literally have had no opportunity.

Trucks bringing food and bricks and mortar are rolling into Los Angeles. And this city will be rebuilt. And I am confident that new opportunities will arise. But all across this Nation, we've got to renew our fight to strengthen the American family. It isn't a burnt-out area in Los Angeles; it isn't

California. It is the entire country. That's where everyone in this room, everyone in this hallowed sanctuary comes in. We've got to find ways to do that. We've got to fight against discrimination. We've got to continue to speak out against bigotry. We've got to fight for justice and equality. And on this National Day of Prayer it is fitting that we pray to God to help us.

Abraham Lincoln was right, you can't do it alone. If we asked him what he did in times of turmoil—you think of the problems he faced—he said, "I spent a lot of my time on my knees." We have to understand that that faith is still terribly important to leaders, terribly important to citizens that lead these communities.

So I pray to God that He will give us the strength and the wisdom to bring the family together, the American family. Barbara and I pray that our personal family and your personal families will be engulfed in God's love and that every kid will have someone who knows his name and really cares about him.

One little 4-year-old girl, maybe you heard the story, Ryan Bennett, prayed special prayers as she saw her neighborhood riddled with bullets, her candy store destroyed. And Ryan said, "I asked God if He could make it so it's not dark anymore." Let this Nation vow to help that it won't be dark.

*Note: The President spoke at 9:10 a.m. In his remarks, he referred to Edward V. Hill, pastor of Mount Zion Missionary Baptist Church; Robert W. McMurray, bishop of the 16th episcopal district of the Apostolic Church; Billy Ingram, pastor of Maranatha Church; Floyd Massey, pastor of Macedonia Baptist Church; and Larry Jones, president of Feed the Children International in Oklahoma City, OK, and his wife, Frances.*

# Remarks in a Roundtable Discussion With Leaders of the African-American Community in Los Angeles
*May 7, 1992*

*Rev. Edward V. Hill.* May I give the ground rules, please. The persons who are seated in this assembly have been selected, a cross from young people to business people to leaders. The President wanted to meet just a few. He will not have an opportunity to hear a long question, but if you can make short your statement, the President of the United States would like to hear you.

Mr. President, we are honored again to have you.

*The President.* Reverend Hill, let me—I would never, ever correct E.V. Hill, especially in his own church in its centennial year, but rather than questions, and I will be glad to answer them, what I really would like to get is the heartbeat of the community, hear from you all as to what you think can best help, where matters stand.

It's hard on a short visit to get all this. I will assure you, and I hope that Pete, sitting here, and Tom Bradley would agree, that we have tried to bring Federal resources to bear in a timely fashion. It's been done pretty low-key in the sense that the Federal officers out here have been not seeking a limelight. But under David Kearns they've put together a good task force. And I've been very gratified that the leaders, both from city council and the Mayor's office, as well as the Governor's office, feel the Federal Government is responding, whether it's from FEMA or whether it's from Jack Kemp's HUD or whether it's from Lou Sullivan's HHS or the Department of Education. Leading the fray was Pat Saiki, out here very early for the SBA, small business loans.

So I don't want to go into all these programs, although I'd be glad to have our experts respond to any questions on them at all. But what I'd like to do is, first, to say thank you; second, to let you know that justice will prevail, that we will follow through with my responsibilities under the law, and the Department of Justice is fol-lowing through on the justice side of the equation to examine, to see if civil rights of anybody have been violated, King or anybody, Rodney King or anyone else, that there be fairplay and equity there.

But having said all that, let me tell you something, and you know it better than I. There is no way, really, I guess, that the President can come here in an every-4-year situation and not have it be accused by some of being political. I don't want it to be political. I want to get by this. We've got plenty of time later on in the year for the politics. I want to hear from you, just all the bark off as to what you think we can do, and please speak frankly about it.

If your comments have a political ring it will not offend because, as I say, it's a hard year to stay out of it. But we're here to help, and we're here to learn. And that's it.

[*A participant spoke on local oversight of funding allocations.*]

*The President.* That's a good opening comment.

[*A participant requested assistance to re-build his small business.*]

*The President.* May I make a comment on that, Reverend?

*Reverend Hill.* Yes.

*The President.* Because there are a lot of others like you, and you're not here as a special pleader. The Federal Government can in a situation like this be of real assist-ance. It is largely through SBA, but perhaps other facilities, Agencies can help, too.

Clearly this is one, this type of experience is one where the Federal Government has resources available, pumping them in now. I outlined the programs last night. I won't go through them here, although Pat Saiki is here now. And to others like you whose life has gone up in smoke, we can get assist-ance, no strings attached to it, largely through SBA but not only SBA.

And so we can get, in your case obvious-ly, somebody in touch with you. But others like you, the Small Business Administration and other Federal Agencies can help. I know that Pete or Tom Bradley can speak for the city. But this is clearly one where we have the resources.

*[A participant spoke on local investment in the rebuilding effort.]*

*The President.* Let me comment on that one. I strongly agree with that concept, and we will, again, push for the concept at the Federal level. But I am told by city officials that you are absolutely correct, that where ownership has been involved, there has been much more respect for property. And certainly this concept of ownership in the community, the businesses, is something I strongly endorse. And we will find ways to implement that at the Federal level, I promise you.

*[A participant spoke on assistance for community child development programs. Another participant spoke on the dissemination of information about available assistance.]*

*The President.* The things we're trying to work out for the Federal Government is that kind of, like a what you call a one-stop-shopping approach. And David Kearns, who is our number two in the Department of Education—some may remember him through his work with the Urban League and others when he was the chairman of Xerox, a very large company, but a great manager—is working that problem right now. And it would include not just the kind of services that this lady talked about, but all of it, including what the private sector can do to help. I know Peter Ueberroth's getting involved in that, and we have a national office on that. But I think that the plea here is a very good one for letting people know what's out there.

*[A participant spoke on the destruction of community organization facilities.]*

*The President.* May I ask you a question before you sit down? And it may be an impossible one to answer. But here's 100 Black Men, a respected organization that has no enemies. Why would someone target—no matter what the rage, why would somebody target that building?

We've seen this gentleman—what's your name again?

*Participant.* Dereke.

*The President.* Yes, Dereke. He was telling me this morning, he was the one I was referring to about who saw one of his own employees taking stuff out of the store. We went around and talked about the ownership and the different facilities there. One was a dentist's office. The dentist and his wife stood out there with a dog trying to keep people from coming in and taking—where is he—Dr. Faulkner right here. An amazing story. But why? Maybe that one is messed up because it was next door to a supermarket where people can go and get food. But why the 100 Black Men, why would somebody destroy that building? Can you——

*Participant.* The only thing that I think that it might have had—the city was leasing the building. It might have had the city emblem up there, I don't know. But I want to just conclude with the fact that the Young Black Scholars, a model program that is really being modeled by the State now with senate bill 1114, and it also reflects the Education 2000 vision that you are really pushing forward.

*[A participant spoke on job training. Another participant spoke on Federal aid for infrastructure improvements and employment of arrested rioters in cleanup efforts.]*

*The President.* Thank you, sir.

*[A participant spoke on minority business opportunity. Another participant asked about small business loans for rebuilding churches.]*

*The President.* I think the answer would be yes, but do you know the answer to that, Pat, whether SBA can apply to the reconstruction of churches?

*Administrator Saiki.* We'll look into it, Mr. President.

*The President.* She doesn't know offhand, but it ought to and we ought—there's a place, if we need change, there's something we ought to change.

*[A participant spoke on youth programs targeted at gang members. Another participant spoke on comprehensive, prevention-*

oriented aid and mentoring programs. *Other participants spoke on welfare reform, job discrimination, educational development programs, and family involvement in education. Another participant asked about the processing time for SBA loans.*]

*The President.* No, we have given instructions to Pat Saiki, who is here, to speed this process up. Now, I hope we're successful.

We will keep on it to see that we are. You might ask her just on this one specific—right behind you—because that is the underlying as to what we're trying to do here, and it is very, very important in the reconstruction.

*Note: The discussion began at 9:30 a.m. at Mount Zion Missionary Baptist Church.*

# Remarks in a Roundtable Discussion With Leaders of the Korean Community in Los Angeles
## May 7, 1992

*The President.* Are you going to say something, or do you want me to go ahead? Let me just say thank you to the community leaders assembled here. And let me single out Mr. Lee for his hospitality not just to us today, to Secretary Sullivan, the Governor, Senator Seymour, Secretary Kemp, Pat Saiki of SBA, but to so many.

This place has become not just a command center in times of turmoil, turmoil that every American regrets. This President, I'll tell you, my heart aches for those who have lost their jobs. But this community is strong. I wish all you guys would walk with me—maybe you've been there and seen the volunteers in the next building. It's unbelievable, 200 out there this very day, 200 to be trained; 180 of the 200, I'm told, are CPA's willing to pitch in to help do what's necessary to reconstruct.

I look at this in a very broad sense, not only in terms of families that were hurt but in terms of international. I think most people here will concede and rejoice in the fact that we have good relations with Korea, something I take great pride in, incidentally.

I think people in Korea share the same hurt that all of us do when they look and see this community of enterprising individuals that David reminds us came here, what, some 25 years ago, some more recently; got in, grabbed a piece of the American dream, and built something. To see it shattered is not the American way. And I will do everything I can to show our friends

abroad as well as here that it's not the American way. And with that in mind, it means I want to help. It means the Federal Government is prepared to help in every way we possibly can.

I want to go back to the volunteer concept that I mentioned a minute ago. That is also part of the American way. I'm sure it's part of the Korean way as well. But when you see one American reaching out to another in times of hardship, that is one of the things I think is very precious about our society. And the spirit of those volunteers out there, it's amazing. One of them actually hit me up for a little donation. [*Laughter*] I might say I understood perfectly, and in a modest way was able to contribute to this volunteer sector.

Let me just go into a couple of problems. This has been a command center. I understand that some in the community were unhappy by the location of the disaster relief center. And by early next week, that unhappiness should give way because we are going to have a new, acceptable location to serve the needs of the community. And I understand that not having forms in Korean is a problem, and now there's efforts going on to be sure that those forms are printed in a way that can be understood in Korean so they can be understood by those small family operators that have suffered because of these uncontrolled forces.

We also realize that translators are a problem, and we are working to provide

719

translators to help with disaster relief. And of course, once again I salute the community, because the community is doing some of that. I just noticed that in here in a volunteer sense. There is no way I can tell you how much I respect what Radio Korea has done. I happen to be sitting next to its boss. But I will simply say we applaud Radio Korea for the support that has constantly been given to the Korean community, the pride that this station reflects when it brings to others what the Korean-American community stands for. It is wonderful, and we're grateful to you, sir. And I think you've acted as a lifeline in a sense in this tragic situation. A couple of people told me that as I was walking in.

Two immediate concerns, and then I want to hear from you the priorities. I want to be sure that while I'm here I don't overlook a priority. Two immediate concerns are: What will the Government do to bring about a speedy economic recovery, and what can we do to ease the awful racial tension? I spoke about it in a church today, Reverend E.V. Hill's church. I think all Americans have to be concerned about both those points.

I want you to know that the situation in L.A. is on the minds of all Americans. It is not a local situation. What's happened here is not something that we saw for an ugly moment that'll be forgotten. We've got to continue to strive for racial harmony and for the elimination of discrimination wherever it occurs in this country. And I am thankful, of course, that the streets are safer, with kids back in school, and that businesses are reopening. But now we need to concentrate on a major rebuilding effort.

I have signed, as I'm sure you all know, a declaration, a disaster declaration, having directed FEMA, the Federal Emergency Management Agency, and Mrs. Saiki and the Small Business Administration that she so ably heads to provide immediate assistance to the victimized parties. Pat can answer your questions, can give you much more of the detail there. But it is a very important Agency at this time.

FEMA is providing grants for personal needs such as food and clothing and medicine, for minor home damage, and unemployment assistance to those who are now without jobs. Even though they have their own businesses, some are without work because those businesses were destroyed. We have an 800 assistance number that will also receive calls in six languages. The Korean community took it on the chin the most, I think, but others are hurting, too. So we, the Federal Government, and Governor Wilson, and the Mayor are trying to respond as best we can to all the hurt out there. The SBA is also making disaster loans available for business losses, for home damage. Those loans could total over $300 million. All told, the Federal aid to Los Angeles and the surrounding areas here could run in the range of about $600 million.

Again, I am delighted to have this opportunity to come here. And I just hope you will tell those who are hurt that, one, we care, and two, we are trying our level-best to heal those wounds, to get people back on their feet again. Because when I think of what this country needs, it's more small businesses, it's more entrepreneurs, people that will come here and take a risk and hopefully earn their share of what we think of as the American dream.

I know that this American dream is still real. I'm sure to a businessman, a wife and a husband, for example, whose business has been closed and brutalized and ruined, he might wonder: Well, what's it all about? What does this mean? We have got, you and I—maybe you all can do it best—is convince those people that are hurting that the American dream is for real. And you will rebuild, and we'll be a part of helping you.

So that's what I wanted to say. And David, I'd love to hear from members of the community and what you think we might do to assist. But we care very, very much. And as I say, I want to be the President to take the signal out around, back to Korea itself, and say: Look, people got hurt in my country, good people, good citizens. But we're going to make them whole, and we're going to give them some hope.

So now, I don't know what the schedule is——

*Participant.* Open for questions and comments.

*The President.* Fire away.

[*A participant requested that aid for*

*Korean-American victims go beyond standard disaster relief guidelines. Another participant spoke on cooperation among ethnic groups in the rebuilding effort.*]

*The President.* Thank you for your statement.

[*A participant asked about the location of the FEMA office in Koreatown and the creation of enterprise zones.*]

*The President.* Let me answer the first one by saying I'm not sure. I know we are pledged to move it. I'm looking around for somebody to tell me what has been decided. But I know there's been unhappiness with the first. I have this statement saying we will change it. But you're saying, in this very building?

*Participant.* Not actually. Next building. Next one across the street.

*The President.* Well, let me record that and tell our FEMA people who is——

*Presidential Aide.* Sir, we're going to be working with you to identify a suitable location. It is too premature to know exactly where it could be, but we want to work closely.

*The President.* But they're asking that it could be right across the street. Well, let's see what we can do to consider it, if that's the general feeling. I don't know if everybody feels that way.

*Participant.* That way we could communicate through radio. We have to mobilize people, mobilize volunteers, and we'd like to be close to the radio station. We would like to——

*The President.* We're trying to. Incidentally, on one-stop shopping—slightly different point—we've got a lot of Federal Agencies out here, and we want to have it as simple as possible. And that's why we have David Kearns and—out here, who are trying to coordinate the Federal effort. But thank you for the comment.

On the second one, I wish I could tell you the answer. We are going to urge the Congress to move right away on a legislation. And believe me, it will certainly include the Korean community. This is a concept that I've heard about all day long today. It's something we've been advocating for a long, long time. We're now talking about

the enterprise zones. That concept I think is an idea whose time has come. I'm seeing support publicly just in the last few days from people who have not supported it. I have said this is not a time for blame in terms of getting legislation going. But I can tell you, we feel much more optimistic, and we will be pushing hard to get it done. And the Korean-American community is obviously going to have a piece of the action.

[*A participant suggested scholarship assistance for victims' family members, an SBA hotline, and waiver of documentation requirements for SBA loans.*]

*The President.* Well, on waiving the requirements, I understand that some of the records are just going up in smoke, and therefore it's hard to have them.

*Participant.* That's right.

*The President.* Fortunately, we do have and would have access to the income tax returns. So, there will be a way to verify a lot of the claims. So, we hope we can get around this rigid requirement on that one.

The SBA, I don't know on the hotline. I'll let Pat speak. We will have, I think it is six offices to not only respond for SBA but put this in what we call a one-stop shopping approach where you have programs from HUD, you've got programs from HHS, you have programs from various different Agencies that can assist different parts of all of this.

On the third one, we believe that our approach to education is a good one, America 2000. And on scholarships, I don't know. Are you talking about a new scholarship program?

*Participant.* The individuals who have suffered the damage, the parents, the Korean-American parents may be unable to pay for the education of their children. So can you set aside some fundings for their children?

*The President.* Let me think about that one. I think we've got to be a little aware of the fact that there's a big demand for scholarship support all across the country. But whether it can be done on a set-aside basis, I just don't know how the law reads. But let me take a look.

[*A participant requested assistance for*

*living expenses.*]

*The President.* Thank you. Thank you, David. On the food assistance, there are substantial amounts of food coming in through our Department of Agriculture. I hope that's arranged so it's fitting for the requirements that it will be distributed here.

[*A participant spoke on Korean-American participation in government and in the rebuilding process.*]

*The President.* Good counsel. Thank you.

[*A participant spoke on the magnitude of the losses, unfavorable media coverage, and the speed of the Federal response.*]

*The President.* Let me comment on that, if I might. I don't know how anybody who has not been through what you've been through can say they understand. I don't know that. I believe that the Federal Government response is fast. I'm told by Mayor Bradley, I'm told by the Governor that it's fast. It may not seem fast to somebody that is hurting——

*Participant.* No, sir.

*The President.* ——but it is fast. Pat Saiki was out here the very day it happened and has already started. So we will keep trying, and I just wanted you to know.

I don't know about the demonstration last night. I know there were some nice political shots fired at me which I didn't appreciate particularly, but I understand also that it comes from people wanting to get something done. And that you were mistreated there, I feel very, very badly about that because you shouldn't have been. You were expressing your rights as an American.

I don't know. You say the media mistreated you. I will certainly apologize for that. I have no control over it. And you know our system, to know that we have no control over it. But I guess what I'm trying to say is we do care, and we will try very, very hard to help.

And when you get to be President, you do identify with people's suffering. Today it's here. And yesterday it was another place somewhere in the country, unrelated to riots. Tomorrow it will be something else. That's just the way our country is. But I will try to be as responsive as I possibly can. And I know it must feel a thousand miles away, Washington and all the forms to fill out. But these comments you have made I think sensitize all of us to the need to do our level-best and to move as fast as possible. So it's not in vain. We'll keep trying.

[*A participant spoke on efforts to resolve racial tension.*]

*The President.* That's a very important statement, Dr. Yang. Let me say this, that we had a very interesting meeting with some mayors here. One of them was the Mayor of Ingleside. The Mayor of Ingleside told us that he had led that community, church leaders, ethnic group leaders, whatever, long before the riots started. He'd had meetings with Korean business people or civic leaders or church leaders, meeting with black leaders, Afro-America leaders, and then the elected officials in the community.

You see, I am convinced that when you live close in—your second point is right on target—that it is going to have to be the local communities. The Federal Government can set a tone: no discrimination, rule out bigotry, hatred, and all of that. But to practice it, it's going to have to be done by getting across these lines and by leaders—and you and I are saying the same thing—with the churches in the lead, city governments being responsive, to get across these cultural boundaries.

And I salute you for what you've done. I was in E.V. Hill's church this morning. There were some Korean pastors there. And my emphasis was one on the essentiality of strengthening the American family. In your community, it is my perception that you have strong family values. I think you are blessed with the strength in family values. You've got to share with whoever is open-minded enough to listen. And religious leaders, I think, can do a lot. I'm not trying to avoid responsibility from the Federal Government, but I really think it's something that can't be legislated. This is something that really has to happen, come from the heart, and has to happen through what I think you're obviously trying to do in your church. And yes, it is longer range. But we can't give up on it.

And it is not just the Korean community or the black community; there are others who feel the same sense of anguish and hurt. We haven't talked about Hispanics here. But I think your point is very valid.

[*A participant asked about law enforcement measures after the departure of National Guard units.*]

*The President.* May I ask you one? I don't want to sound defensive, but why do you assume that I'm only concerned about Beverly Hills?

[*The participant cited media coverage of Los Angeles.*]

*The President.* No, that's why I asked the question, because that obviously is something local and I hadn't seen it. But the answer clearly is local law enforcement. There's no other answer. There's no Federal police force in this country, and there will not be as long as I am President. We don't need that. But we do need to guarantee the rights of citizens to be protected under the law by the local police. The State police have some role in this. Federal crime is violated, the Feds have some role in it.

What's happening now is we're just trying to guarantee everybody's civil rights under the civil rights statute. But in terms of the guy that gets beat up at a gas station, that clearly has to be a renewed effort by the local authorities to guarantee the safety of the life and limb of American citizens. The law has got to be totally colorblind in that regard, and people have to, local police have to do their level-best.

*Participant.* But they never did ask for us——

*The President.* They must do it. They must do it.

[*A participant requested the names of Federal relief staff members and stressed the need for bilingual staff.*]

*The President.* We're having a meeting tonight with people like David Kearns who is out here, who came here to set up the— you're talking about Federal response.

*Participant.* Right, the Federal response.

*The President.* And out of that, we will have the names of the people who are going to be staffing these regional centers.

That's the level at which the action will be taking place. So I hope we'll get this to the community and get that response to you as quickly as possible.

[*A participant spoke on Korean-American participation at decision-making levels of government.*]

*The President.* I appreciated what my Andover colleague said. We have at least tried to have a better record in terms of numbers of Asian-American appointees, and we'll keep working on that. Do not make the mistake of thinking that the Federal Government is going to wave a wand and solve these problems. You say you don't have any elected representative. I've heard some real talent here today. I've heard some very able and articulate voices. And I don't know how much participation these voices have tried to have in the local political process.

But you don't need a civics lecture from me when we're talking about how you help in a community that's been ravaged, but to really have the clout and to really effect the change on matters we're talking about here today, I think it calls for participation in the political process, not to give up on it, not to think Washington can dictate to the local. So maybe there's some good activity in that regard; but if there's not, I strongly would urge that kind of participation.

*Participant.* I'm primarily concerned about the appointing positions in both local and in Federal Government.

*The President.* That's not where the power is. The power with the people, with people that are elected, whether they're low—that's the only point I'm making.

*Participant.* We were simply saying we've been trying, and we'll work with you, and we need your support.

*The President.* Yes. That I agree with. No, there's no problem with that.

[*A participant spoke on Korean-American participation in government.*]

*The President.* No, I think that's a very good point, and I think that's where I think the action is. Whether it's elected or appointed, I think that kind of community decision-making level is what's required at this juncture. I'm not arguing against Federal appointments, but I'm saying that this is where——

*Participant.* Mr. President, I want you to know that the leadership by election is very unfeasible because only people who—persons of the Korean population, the whole general election area, how could you think that we expect someone to be elected by the Caucasian, white Caucasian. So appointing a position is the one that we can work with very closely as a part of our education, as a part of channel to work with the Federal Government and local government.

*The President.* I think that's important, but please do not give up on the local level, whether it's appointment to the—what Ueberroth is doing, whether it's representation on committees that will come out of how the Federal aid is coordinated or what the Governor does. That's all I'm saying, is I really think—and don't give up on the idea that if you only have got a certain percent, that means nobody else will vote for you.

I mean, I was listening. The concept of can we stay here, I have got to help on that. Everybody in the community has got to help to say: Look, this is a setback, this is a serious setback. And I think I maybe have more of a responsibility on this point to make clear to the American people that you're welcome and that this is an aberration. This isn't the American dream. So I'll try to assist in that as best I can. I did mention this in my speech to the—the heartbreak of the—and I got some messages back on that.

[*A participant asked what role Korean-American community organizations could play in the rebuilding and relief efforts.*]

*The President.* What you're doing. What I saw when I walked in here is profound. I mean, this isn't some passing fantasy when you see all those volunteers out there doing something that in some ways people might just hang back and say, where are the Government people to do this? These people are reaching out into the community, trying to find what the problem is, what the location of the disaster is, and then trying to reach out to the agencies to take care of those specific cases.

I would certainly continue that kind of effort. What these gentlemen were talking about is participating in the committees that inevitably are formed from the distribution of Federal or State assistance. I think that is very important. And I think what you project, how you project the problems—here are people that have come here very recently, settled in with the work ethic, the family ethic, clearly not just because the pastors are here but a sense of faith, and convey to the community that that is not dead in spite of the setback.

Now, that's asking a lot until there are some remedial action taken, but I sense, when I've come here, a certain determination. And I think you've got to project that. If you project the defeatism, that we've been defeated, we've been beaten, then I think that is real bad. That's what you asked, what you can do for the community. Again, I've tried to outline here what the Federal Government and other government entities can do for the community. I think they go hand in hand.

[*A participant asked about the terms of the SBA loans.*]

*The President.* Let me turn to my able assistant, Pat Saiki, who can answer the specifics on that, because I can't.

*Note: The President spoke at 2:05 p.m. at the Radio Korea broadcast studio. In his remarks, he referred to Peter Ueberroth, chairman of the Rebuild L.A. Committee.*

# Nomination of William T. Pryce To Be United States Ambassador to Honduras
*May 7, 1992*

The President today announced his intention to nominate William T. Pryce of Pennsylvania to be Ambassador to the Republic of Honduras. He would succeed Cresencio S. Arcos.

Since 1989 Mr. Pryce has served as Special Assistant to the President for National Security Affairs and Senior Director for Latin America and the Caribbean at the National Security Council. Before coming to the NSC, Mr. Pryce served as Deputy U.S. Permanent Representative to the Organization of American States in Washington, DC. He served as Deputy Chief of Mission at the U.S. Embassy in Panama from 1982 to 1986. Prior to that, he was Deputy Chief of Mission at the U.S. Embassy in Bolivia and Counselor for Political Affairs at the U.S. Embassy in Mexico City. Mr. Pryce joined the Foreign Service in 1958 after serving in the U.S. Navy from 1954 to 1958. During most of his career, he has specialized in Latin American and Eastern European affairs. His early assignments included Mexico City, Moscow, and Panama, as well as service in the Department as Assistant to the Under Secretary of State for Economic Affairs. After serving as Chief of the political section in the U.S. Embassy in Guatemala City, Mr. Pryce was assigned in 1974 as Chief of Soviet Programs for the State Department's Bureau of Educational and Cultural Affairs. He attended the National War College in 1976 prior to serving as executive assistant to Ambassador at Large Ellsworth Bunker.

Mr. Pryce was born in San Diego, CA, and grew up in Ebensburg, PA. He graduated from Wesleyan University and the Fletcher School of Law and Diplomacy. He is married to Joan MacClurg Pryce and has three children.

# Nomination of Teresita Currie Schaffer To Be United States Ambassador to Sri Lanka and Maldives
*May 7, 1992*

The President today announced his intention to nominate Teresita Currie Schaffer, of New York, a career member of the Senior Foreign Service, class of Minister-Counselor, to be Ambassador to the Democratic Socialist Republic of Sri Lanka and to serve concurrently and without additional compensation as Ambassador to the Republic of Maldives. She would succeed Marion V. Creekmore, Jr.

Since 1989, Ms. Schaffer has served as Deputy Assistant Secretary for Near Eastern and South Asian Affairs at the U.S. Department of State. Prior to this, she served at the Department of State as Director of the Office of Egyptian Affairs, 1987–89; Director of the Office of International Trade, 1982–84; and as Chief of the Division of General Commercial Policy, Office of International Trade, 1980–82.

Ms. Schaffer graduated from Bryn Mawr College (B.A., 1966). She was born September 28, 1945, in Washington, DC. Ms. Schaffer is married, has two children, and resides in Washington, DC.

## Nomination of David C. Fields To Be United States Ambassador to the Marshall Islands
*May 7, 1992*

The President today announced his intention to nominate David C. Fields, of California, a career member of the Senior Foreign Service, class of Minister-Counselor, to be Ambassador to the Republic of the Marshall Islands. He would succeed William Bodde, Jr.

Since 1990, Ambassador Fields has served as Director of the Office of Foreign Missions at the U.S. Department of State in Washington, DC. Prior to this, he served as U.S. Ambassador to the Central African Republic, 1986–89; Deputy Assistant Secretary for Security at the Department of State, 1984–86; and as Administrative Counselor at the American Embassy in London, England, 1980–84.

Ambassador Fields graduated from Armstrong College (B.A., 1960). He was born January 13, 1937, in San Pedro, CA. Ambassador Fields served in the U.S. Army, 1955–57. He is married, has two children, and resides in Vienna, VA.

## Nomination of William Henry Gerald FitzGerald To Be United States Ambassador to Ireland
*May 7, 1992*

The President today announced his intention to nominate William Henry Gerald FitzGerald, of the District of Columbia, to be Ambassador to Ireland. He would succeed Richard Anthony Moore.

Since 1959, Mr. FitzGerald has served as president of the FitzGerald Corp. in Washington, DC. In addition, he serves as vice chairman of the African Development Foundation; and as chairman of the Atlantic Council of the United States Foundation. Mr. FitzGerald founded and was chairman of the board of the North American Housing Corp., 1972–89.

Mr. FitzGerald graduated from the U.S. Naval Academy (B.S., 1931). He was born December 23, 1909, in Boston, MA. Mr. FitzGerald served in the U.S. Navy, 1941–48. He is married, has two children, and resides in Washington, DC.

## Nomination of Princeton Nathan Lyman To Be United States Ambassador to South Africa
*May 7, 1992*

The President today announced his intention to nominate Princeton Nathan Lyman, of Maryland, a career member of the Senior Foreign Service, class of Career Minister, to be Ambassador to the Republic of South Africa. He would succeed William Lacy Swing.

Since 1989, Dr. Lyman has served as Director of the Bureau for Refugee Programs at the U.S. Department of State. Prior to this, he served as Ambassador to the Federal Republic of Nigeria, 1986–89; Deputy Assistant Secretary of State for African Affairs at the Department of State, 1981–86; and as Director of the Office of Inter-African Affairs at the Department of State, 1980–81.

Dr. Lyman graduated from the University of California (A.B., 1957); Harvard University (M.A., 1959; Ph.D., 1961). He was born November 20, 1935, in San Francisco, CA. Dr. Lyman is married, has three children, and resides in Chevy Chase, MD.

# Remarks to Firefighters and Law Enforcement Personnel in Los Angeles
*May 8, 1992*

Let me just say I'm very pleased that the Governor's with us and Senator Seymour's with us. And really, what we did is to want to come over here and, one, see where some of the action stemmed from, but mainly to thank the firefighters and the patrolmen for a heroic job well done.

You know, at a time like this you think of your faith, and you remember that the Bible talked about, "Blessed are the peacemakers." Well, I must say, when I think of the firefighters and the highway patrol, I think of what you have done, and, frankly, do all the time in keeping the peace and restoring the peace. You certainly have the gratitude, you may not know it, but you have the gratitude of people all across this country.

I wanted to just recite a fact or two that you all know but the rest of the country might not. There were almost 6,000 fires responded to, nearly 12,000 arrests, thousands of buildings saved along with untold lives. That, I would say, is just one of the legacies of your work. And there was another one: You showed that people that would wantonly destroy, wantonly terrorize, wantonly kill their fellow citizens were not going to prevail. What you did took a good deal of courage, whether it was the patrol, whether it was the firefighters. I salute you for that, the country salutes you for that. And I think your very presence restored a sense of civility to an otherwise outrageous situation.

Yesterday, I was privileged to go to a memorial service—it was National Day of Prayer—at Reverend E.V. Hill's church. When I mentioned those who worked to restore the law, the police, et cetera, why, it broke out in spontaneous applause. People are very grateful in the neighborhoods for all that you have done.

I heard a lot of stories, anecdotes about what went on. They told me about Rich Perez, the lone gunman, the only armed officer guarding L.A.'s traffic control center. And these rioters came in and tried to break down the doors. Somehow, he managed to convince the rioters that they had met their match, and they turned away. And the traffic control system was safe and sound, and a legend was born.

I've just come from the hospital, from seeing one of your own, one of the firefighters' own, Scott Miller. You talk about courage and you talk about the way his fellow firefighters helped him, it's a great lesson for our whole country. Incidentally, he's a courageous man. They told me that what had happened to him was serious. But they also told me, the doctor, that because of his spirit, the same spirit so many of you exemplified, that he's going to make it. He's fighting hard, and his wife was there and his kids—his kids weren't, but they were together as a family. I'll tell you, the doctors and nurses are rallying around, and he's getting the best possible care.

But here was another example of an innocent guy going out to help others, taking a shot from some hoodlum going by in a car. And we just cannot condone that sense of violence, that kind of violence, anywhere in this country for whatever reason. There's no explaining it. There's no rationalizing it. And I will try to take that message to the country day in and day out.

There was Captain Kaemmerer, a captain of a fire company which doused flames at an ammunition shop in the face of gunfire. Here's a guy going into what you might call a hostile environment anyway, firefighting captain, and fighting that.

We all know the case of the LAPD's Michael Strawberry, Darryl's brother. Darryl said, "Michael was my rock." Well, that's fine. And the LAPD have many, many such rocks, people doing a job and doing it well. And you were rocks, saving buildings and saving lives. These pictures that I was handed, I mean, I'll tell you, they make a profound impression on—I'm sure they make an impression on firefighters, but they make a profound impression on the layman to think about battling something this powerful and doing it with the heroism and the dedication you do.

So, really, what I wanted to do is drop in here, trying to do it just as President of the United States, trying to leave the politics back there somewhere on the Potomac and come out here to see what I could see with my eyes and to give my heartfelt thanks to those—in this instance, highway patrolmen, firefighters—who have done so much for their country.

So that's my message, and it's a profound one in a sense that today and yesterday it was the riots in Los Angeles, tomorrow it'll be something else. And over the last years it's always been the same, the dedication, the selfless dedication. I don't want to think any of you guys would say you're overpaid, but you're doing something for your fellow man, and that in itself means an awful lot to your country.

So thank you, and may God bless you.

*Note: The President spoke at 7:51 a.m. at Fire Station No. 26.*

## Remarks to Military and Law Enforcement Personnel in Los Angeles
*May 8, 1992*

Thank you all. Thank you very, very much, and I'm just delighted to be here. I first would salute all that participated in keeping the peace, guaranteeing the peace, fighting against those who wanted to break the peace. And the events of the past 10 days, not just for the people in Los Angeles but people in the rest of the country, have been packed with emotion, raw and intense.

And in my time out here I've heard the shouts of anger and heard some whispered prayers yesterday in a lovely ecumenical church service. We've seen utter devastation, all of you have that have looked around the streets at all. We've seen the beginnings of restoration. And we've seen the worst that human beings can do, and then we've seen some of the very best.

So, I really wanted to come over here and thank all of you, the LAPD, the members of the military, the Guard and the regulars, both Marine—[*applause*]. And I think what this particular group and others that I just met with, the highway patrolmen, firefighters, are saying to the country is that we stand to defend decency and honor; we stand to defend and protect the honest men and women in this country. And that's the message that I think has gone out. And you did what's right, and you did what's demanded of you.

And yesterday in this little church service I mentioned, I mentioned the police officers particularly, singled them out, and the place broke into spontaneous applause for those officers that are out there bringing civil tranquility to this country. And I salute—[*applause*]. And then I want to single out and salute also the Federal law enforcement officers who worked side by side with many of you who were on the streets. The special agents from the FBI, the Bureau of Prisons people, the marshals, the Border Patrol, all were out there assisting the police in stopping the terrible violence and the looting. And of course, again, the local police officials, the LAPD, the officers on the beat who have the toughest job in the world. And I came, really, just to thank each and every one of you who worked around the clock to restore order.

I might say, I've just come from the hospital where I saw a young firefighter who was wantonly shot in the head. He's driving his fire truck, hook and ladder truck, to put out a fire, and some hoodlum comes alongside and shoots him. He's fighting right this minute for his very life. But it makes me grateful as a citizen of this country that you have courageous people like that willing to undergo the trauma that he is facing right now. So we can all maybe say a prayer for Scott and just hope that he makes it.

The men and women of the Armed Forces were out minding your own business when the call came. But I really believe this: that when it became clear—and I've talked to the Governor who's with me here today about it, talked to the Mayor of this city—but when it became clear that not only the Guard but the regulars were willing to respond and would be there, I think the very fact that the military was here, prepared to do what was necessary, served as an enormously inhibiting factor from those hoodlums that wanted to disrupt the civil tranquility of Los Angeles, indeed, of our country.

So, once again, I salute you for that. And even more fundamentally, I salute all of you who serve in uniform of the military for the United States of America. You have our pro-found thanks and gratitude.

I will do my level-best as President to work to help solve the problems in the communities. I pledge that. I'm going to go back to Washington; have more to say about that next week. But I'll tell you this: I will remain the President who strongly supports the law enforcement community in this country and who strongly supports our military. Without you, we would not enjoy the peace and tranquility that a lot of the rest of the country is enjoying right now. So thank you very much to each and every one of you who participated in any way in helping this great city of Los Angeles.

And the last point is this: I went around to a lot of the communities. And I have a genuine feeling in my heart that Los Angeles is going to bounce right on back and be this great city that it's always been.

So may God bless everybody here from Los Angeles, and my profound thanks to the rest of you. God bless you all. Thank you so very, very much.

*Note: The President spoke at 8:22 a.m. at the Los Angeles Coliseum. In his remarks, he referred to Scott Miller, a Los Angeles firefighter who was injured during the disturbances.*

# Remarks to Community Leaders in Los Angeles
*May 8, 1992*

I would get off to a bad start if I didn't say what I think everybody else is feeling, and I want to just congratulate Larisse for that marvelous rendition of "The Star-Spangled Banner."

And may I first thank all of you for being here today. I think they were introduced at the very beginning, but I want to single out two members of my Cabinet, Secretary Lou Sullivan of HHS and Secretary Jack Kemp from Housing and Urban Development who are here with me. We've really had a good tour. I want to salute Senator Seymour, Governor Wilson, who's been at my side, both of them, as we've made this tour through the city. Pat Saiki of SBA, the Ad-ministrator of the Small Business Administration, came out early, and she is on the ground and doing a first-class job. And of course, I would like to also salute Mayor Tom Bradley who has been so extraordinarily helpful on this visit. And I'm not going to forget the inspirational leader of the Challenger, Lou Dantzler.

I would also say to the city officials that I can just imagine, given what you all have been through, the headache that this visit has caused. And I promise you we plan to leave right on schedule so things can get back to normal. But I want to thank everybody involved in facilitating this visit that came, I'm sure, at a very complicated time for the city. The Governor, the Mayor, the police, the L.A. community, everyone has been just fantastic.

And let me say I am truly heartened by the speed with which the millions of dollars of Federal relief have reached the city, from FEMA grants to the small business loans to urgent food aid. And I salute David Kearns and others who came here to coordinate, not to dictate, not to try to dominate but to coordinate with the city and local officials. And I'm very pleased to see that there is smooth coordination, everyone pulling together on the Federal, State, and local level.

It was important, I feel, that as President, I come here to Los Angeles. The community has been the site of a terrible tragedy, not just for you who were impacted the most but for our entire country. And everyone around the world feels this trauma, everyone who looks to us as a model of freedom and justice.

And that's why I want to say just a few things about my visit, to speak to you about what I've seen in this city and, most importantly, as I said at a marvelous ecumenical church service yesterday at Mount Zion, we are one people, we are one family, we are one Nation under God. And so I want to speak about our course as a Nation.

I can hardly imagine—I try, but I can hardly imagine the fear and the anger that people must feel to terrorize one another and burn each other's property. But I saw remarkable signs of hope right next to the tragic signs of hatred. This marvelous institution, this boys and girls club, stands unscarred, facing a burned-out block. And its leader is this wonderful man next to me, Lou Dantzler. And he started it on the back of an old pickup truck with a group of kids that wanted to get off the street. And its existence proves the power of our better selves. And let's never forget it, and let's count our blessings.

Now let me personalize it a little bit and tell you why clubs like this matter. A story about a little kid, Rudy Campbell. I saw him on television. He looked about 8 years old. His father was murdered a few years back, and I didn't see his mother. Rudy is raised by his 22-year-old sister who has five kids of her own. And he lives in South Cen-

tral. Think about what he has already been through. Now he says he fears that things will only get "badder and badder and badder." And it breaks your heart. Our children deserve better than that.

I talked a week ago about the law and the pursuit of justice. And today I want to talk about what went wrong in L.A. and the underlying causes of the root problems. It can all be debated, and it should be, but not to assign blame. Casting blame gets us absolutely nowhere. Honest talk and principled action can move us forward. And that's what we've got to do for Rudy; that's what we've got to do for our children, these kids right here.

This tragedy seemed to come suddenly, but I think we would all agree it's been many years in the making. I know it will take time to put things right. I could have said "put things right again," but that would miss a point I want to make: Things weren't right before a week ago Wednesday. Things aren't right in too many cities across our country. And we must not return to the status quo, not here, not in any city where the system perpetuates failure and hatred and poverty and despair.

Most Americans now recognize some unpleasant realities. Let me just spend a minute on those. For many years we've tried many different programs. All of them, let's understand this, had noble intentions to meet the need of adequate housing or education or health care. Much of it went to construct what has been known as the safety net, a compassionate safety net to provide security and stability for people in need. Many other programs and policies aimed at stemming the tide of urban violence and drugs and crime and social decay. And we have spent huge sums of money. Some estimates are as high as $3 trillion over 25 years. And even in the last decade Federal spending went up for these kinds of efforts, everything from child care to welfare to health care has been the subject of some commission or report or study.

But where this path has taken us, I think we would all agree, is not really where we wanted to go. Put away the studies and just look around. For anyone who cares about our young people, it is painful that in 1960 the percentage of births to unwed mothers was 5 percent, and now it is 27 percent. It's hard to read about a young black man dying when the odds are almost one out of two that he was murdered. Kids used to carry their lunches to school, and the parents that I've talked to know that today some kids carry guns. I'm afraid some of you kids, you know that, too. Everyone knows that drug and alcohol abuse are serious problems almost everywhere.

In the wake of the L.A. riots, in the wake of a lost generation of inner city lives, can any one of us argue that we have solved the problems of poverty and racism and crime? And the answer clearly is no. Some programs, ones like Head Start or Aid to the Elderly, have shown some time-tested, positive results. All programs were well-intentioned; I understand that very, very well. Many simply have not worked. Our welfare system does not get people off of welfare, it keeps people trapped there. The statistics are sobering. The reality is sobering. The sum and substance is this: The cities are in serious trouble, and too many of our citizens are in trouble. And it doesn't really have to be this way.

Government has an absolute responsibility to solve this problem, these problems. I'm talking about all levels of government. And I've taken a hard look at what the Government can do and how it can help communities with concerns that really matter: how people can own property, own their own home, start a business, create jobs, and ensure that people, not Government, make the big decisions that affect the health and the education and the care of one's own family.

Think of the way that the world looks right now to the single mother on welfare. Government provides you just enough cash for the bare necessities. Government tells you where you can live, where your kids go to school. And when you're sick, Government tells you what kind of care you get and when. And if you find a job, the Government cuts the welfare benefits. And if you save, if you manage to put a little money away, maybe towards a home or to help your kid get through college, the Government says, hey, welfare fraud. Every one of those things happen with the system that

we have in place right now. And then we wonder: Why can't folks on welfare take control of their lives? Where's their sense of responsibility?

Well, if we had set out to devise a system that would perpetuate dependency, a system that would strip away dignity and personal responsibility, I guess we could hardly have done better than the system that exists today. Every American knows that it is time for a fresh approach, a radical change in the way we look at welfare and the inner city economy.

Every hour of meetings yesterday—and they were, for me, very emotional, very moving—confirmed why I believe in the plan that we have proposed for urban America. I kept hearing words like ownership, independence, dignity, enterprise, a lot of time from people who have never had a shot at dignity or enterprise or ownership. And it reinforced my belief that we must start with a set of principles and policies that foster personal responsibility, that refocus entitlement programs to serve those who are most needy, and increase the effectiveness of Government service through competition and true choice.

I believe in keeping power closer to the people, using States as laboratories for innovation. We cannot figure it all out back in Washington, DC, in some subcommittee or in the White House. And I believe in policies that encourage entrepreneurship, increase investment, create jobs. And these form the heart of the agenda for economic opportunity that I want to mention here.

Families can't thrive, children can't learn, jobs can't flourish in a climate of fear, however. And so first is our responsibility to preserve the domestic order. And a civilized society cannot tackle any of the really tough problems in the midst of chaos. And you know and I know it's just that simple. Violence and brutality destroy order, destroy the rule of law. And violence must never be rationalized. Violence must always be condemned.

We can reclaim our crime-ravaged neighborhoods through a new initiative that we call "Weed and Seed." And today I'm announcing a $19 million "Weed and Seed" operation for the city of Los Angeles to weed out the drug dealers and career criminals and then seed those neighborhoods with expanded educational, employment, and social services.

With safe and secure neighborhoods, we can spark an economic revival in urban America. And so, the second part of the agenda is to ask Congress to take action on enterprise zones, create these zones with a zero capital gains rate for entrepreneurs and investors who locate businesses and create jobs right here in America's inner cities.

And yes, I recognize that at the same time, we must help States bring innovation to the welfare systems. And at the Federal level, we've got to reform our own AFDC rules, stop penalizing people who want to work and save. These are the people who are mustering the individual initiative to get off welfare. And we've got to pledge ourselves to, at the Federal level, change the rules that keep them from doing just that.

Three: Safe, drug-free schools are places where our children can learn, but that's not enough. We've got to revolutionize our schools through community action, through competition, through innovation, through choice, principles at the heart of the strategy that we call America 2000. We must give children, these kids, these kids right here, the same opportunity as kids out in the suburbs.

And the fourth point: We must promote new hope through homeownership. People want a real stake, a real stake in their community, something of value that they can pass along to their kids. And that's what this HOPE initiative does. It turns public housing tenants into homeowners.

Now, these are just the highlight of an action agenda to bring hope and opportunity back to our inner cities. We have other ideas to try as well. Many in this room have innovative ideas they're trying right now. My first order of business upon my return to Washington will be to build a bipartisan effort in support of immediate action on this agenda. And I know some will say, "Well, you've proposed all this before." And that's true, they're right. And I'm proposing it again because, really, we must try something new. We've got to try something new.

It does not take a social scientist to know that we must think differently. We've tried the old ways of thinking. And now, as Lincoln says, "It is time to think anew."

And our approach is really a radical break from the policies of the past. It's new. Yes, it's new because it's never been tried before. And for the sake of the people of South Central, and the people in America's inner cities everywhere, I will work with the Congress to act now on this common-sense agenda.

You've been through an awful lot. You've been through an awful lot. And when I saw the verdict in the King case, my reaction was the same as yours; I told the Nation that. But I remain confident in our system of justice. And when I saw the violence and rage erupt in your streets, my reaction was the same as yours. We all knew we had to restore order. And when I saw and read about the heroic acts of firefighters and police or the selfless acts of so many citizens, my reaction was one of relief, one of hope for the future.

This morning I stopped by the hospital, Cedar, to see a young fireman who had been wantonly shot in the head as he was driving a fire truck to go out and put out fires that were ravaging somebody's neighborhood, maybe yours. The man's fighting for his life. And I think when we all go home we ought to pray for him.

Even in the very short time that I've been out here, I could sense that the real anguish in south central L.A. is a parent's concern about the kids, neighbors' concerns about the kids. And people are worried sick about the children. All must agree that whatever we do must be about the children. These kids are our future. And our actions in the wake of the tragedy are for them, not just here in Los Angeles. This is showcased now because of what you've been through, but it's all across the country.

And so far in these remarks I've mentioned what Government can do. And now let me talk just a little about what society must do. And yes, we have tried hard, spent a lot of money and haven't solved the problems. And some critics say that we are a morally, spiritually, and intellectually bankrupt nation. I don't believe that for one single minute. And, yes, we have problems. We have tough problems to solve. But we remain the freest and the fairest and the most just and the most decent country on the face of the entire Earth. And we now— I know that we have the drive and the gumption to prevail over these problems we face.

Tom Bradley, your Mayor, was among a group of mayors who came to see me last January. He and I may differ on how we approach one Federal program or another. But I've repeated often what he and others said to me that day. They said that the most important problem facing our cities is the dissolution, the decline of the American family. And they're absolutely right. He was right; a mayor from a tiny town in North Carolina, he was right. The decline of the family is something we must be concerned about. And history tells us that society cannot succeed without some fundamental building blocks in place.

The state of our Nation is the state of our communities. And good communities are safe and decent. And the young people are cared for, and they're instilled with character and values and good habits for life. Good communities have good schools. And they provide opportunity and hope, rooted in the dignity of work and reward for achievement.

And that's why guaranteeing a hopeful future for the children of our cities is about a lot more than rebuilding burned-out buildings. It's about the love right here under this roof. It's about building a new American community. It's about rebuilding bonds between individuals and among ethnic groups and among races. And we must not let our diversity destroy us. It is central, you see, it is central to our strength as a Nation. Our ability to live and work together has really made America the inspiration to the entire world.

Across this country tens of thousands of groups, hundreds of thousands of individuals who have never been involved before, who will never be paid one single nickel for their efforts, must become partners in solving our most serious social problems. The people right here in this room know exactly what I'm talking about. An officer in the LAPD who's a board chairman right here, I believe, in this organization, giving of his time, he knows what I'm talking about. Government alone cannot create the scale and energy needed to transform the lives of the people in need.

And I look around this auditorium and I am preaching to the choir because you're the ones that have your sleeves rolled up in your churches and in your communities, trying to help the other guy. In my conversations with the leaders of L.A.'s many communities, I heard over and over again that L.A. has many of the answers within itself.

I see our friend Bill Milliken here. He lives halfway across the country. There are four of his Cities in School programs, helping children learn here. And many members of a group called 100 Black Men, an inspirational group; for those not familiar with it, they mentor to the kids, the boys in South Central.

Now, if instead of 4, there were 25 Cities in School programs, and instead of 100, 10,000 black men working with boys, and so on with the hundreds of people in groups that work with the kids, there is no question that what happened last week wouldn't have been as bad. And so it only makes sense that a large part of our challenge is to dramatically expand in community after community the scale of what we already know works.

The phrase that I've repeated a lot and perhaps more than any other is worth repeating: From now on in America, any definition of a successful life must include serving others. And when we look to restoring a decent and hopeful future for our children, I mean this about every community:

First, every group and institution in America, schools, businesses, churches, certainly, must do its part. We must praise what works and share what works.

Secondly, all leaders, all leaders, must mobilize and inspire their people to take action.

Third, community centers must link those that care with those that are crying out for help.

Fourth, with respect, the media needs to show from time to time what's working, needs to cover what is working. And that way would help us share, that would really help us share and repeat these successes many times over.

And finally, this one perhaps a little technical, but we've got to change our liability laws that frighten people away from helping others. We ought to care for each other more and sue each other less.

But there's something else. There's something else that society must cultivate that Government cannot possibly provide, something we can't legislate, something we can't establish by Government order. And I'm talking about the moral sense that must guide us all. I guess the simplest way to put it is, I'm talking about knowing right from wrong and then trying to do what's right.

Let me come back again to the little boy I spoke about earlier, Rudy Campbell. Remember, "badder, badder, badder"? There's a lesson he learned that survived the horror and the hate. And in the midst of all the chaos, in the midst of so much that's gone wrong, he knows what's right. When he was asked about the violence, here's what he said: "They should know what's right and wrong. Because when I was 4, that's what I learned."

Now, that has got to give us hope. May God bless the person who cared enough to teach that little guy right from wrong. But it's up to us to guarantee that all the millions of kids like him grow up in a better America.

And I believe we are right about family. We're right about freedom and free enterprise. And we're right with respect to the clergymen here and the church men and church women here. We are right about faith. And most of all, we are right about America's future.

You see, I fervently believe that we have the strength and the spirit in our Government, you can see it here today in our communities and in ourselves, to transform America into the Nation that we have dreamed of for generations.

May God bless each and every one of you in your work. And thank you very, very much.

*Note: The President spoke at 9:18 a.m. at the Challenger Boys and Girls Club. In his remarks, he referred to William E. Milliken, president of Cities in Schools, Inc.*

# Nomination of Alexander Fletcher Watson To Be United States Ambassador to Brazil
*May 8, 1992*

The President today announced his intention to nominate Alexander Fletcher Watson, of Massachusetts, a career member of the Senior Foreign Service, class of Career Minister, to be Ambassador to the Federative Republic of Brazil. He would succeed Richard Huntington Melton.

Since 1989 Mr. Watson has served as Deputy Representative to the United Nations. Prior to this, he served as the U.S. Ambassador to the Republic of Peru, 1986–

89; and Deputy Chief of Mission at the U.S. Embassy in Brasilia, Brazil, 1984–86. From 1981 to 1984, Mr. Watson served as Deputy Chief of Mission at the U.S. Embassy in Bogota, Colombia.

Mr. Watson graduated from Harvard College (A.B., 1961) and University of Wisconsin (M.A., 1969). He was born August 8, 1939, in Boston, MA. Mr. Watson is married, has two children, and resides in New York, NY.

## Nomination of William Graham Walker To Be United States Ambassador to Argentina
*May 8, 1992*

The President today announced his intention to nominate William Graham Walker, of Maryland, a career member of the Senior Foreign Service, class of Minister-Counselor, to be Ambassador to Argentina. He would succeed Terence A. Todman.

Ambassador Walker served as the U.S. Ambassador to El Salvador, 1988–92. Prior to this, he served at the Department of State as a Deputy Assistant Secretary in the Office of Inter-American Affairs 1985–88;

Deputy Chief of Mission at the U.S. Embassy in La Paz, Bolivia, 1982–84; and as Deputy Chief of Mission at the U.S. Embassy in Tegucigalpa, Honduras, 1980–82.

Ambassador Walker graduated from the University of California at Los Angeles (B.A., 1960). He was born June 1, 1935, in Kearney, NJ. Ambassador Walker is married, has four children, and resides in Rockville, MD.

## Radio Address to the Nation on the President's Visit to Los Angeles, California
*May 9, 1992*

Less than 24 hours ago, I returned from Los Angeles. And today I'd like to use this opportunity to report in on what I saw and what I heard.

By now, each one of us has seen images of hate and horror we won't soon forget. But what I saw during my time in Los Angeles, even in the hardest hit parts of south central L.A., should give us all cause for hope. Everywhere, the people I talked with told me about the acts of individual heroism, about the extraordinary courage of ordinary people. Some braved the gangs of looters to form bucket brigades to put out fires when the fire trucks couldn't get through. Some stood against the angry mobs, reached across the barrier of color to save lives. Many of these aren't the stories you'll see on the first 2 minutes of the nightly news, but they are the stories that tell us the power of simple human decency.

I went to L.A. to meet with community leaders, to get firsthand information as to how best the Federal Government could speed the recovery. Part of it is to provide, as we're doing now, Federal funds to help shopowners get their businesses open again, funds to help the people who lost jobs when the places they worked were burned out.

But beyond this immediate emergency assistance, I set out a broader agenda, a means of bringing hope and opportunity to our inner cities.

First, we've got to preserve order, keep the peace, because families can't thrive, children can't learn, jobs can't flourish in a climate of fear.

Second, we must spark an economic revival in urban America. And that means establishing enterprise zones in our cities and reform of our welfare system to help people with individual initiative work and save.

Third, we've got to revolutionize American education. That's why we've built our America 2000 strategy around innovations like choice, competition, and community action. Children in our inner cities deserve the same opportunities that kids in our suburbs have.

Four, we must promote new hope through homeownership. And that's the aim behind my HOPE initiative, to give the least advantaged among us a stake in their neighborhood by turning public housing tenants into homeowners.

At every turn during my time in Los Angeles, I heard people talking about the principles that guide these initiatives: personal responsibility, opportunity, ownership, independence, dignity.

I can already hear some of the critics out there. They'll say, "Well, you've proposed all this before." That's true. They're right. But now it's time to act on these proposals, time to try something new. My first order of business now that I am back in Washington is to build a bipartisan effort in support of immediate action on this agenda.

So far I have spoken about what Government can do. Now let me talk about what society must do, because Government alone cannot create the scale and energy needed to transform the lives of people in need. All over America, people have already found the answers for themselves, and they're taking action to make things better. You can find them everywhere, even in south central L.A. I met a man there named Lou Dantzler, a bear of a man who runs the Challengers Boys and Girls Club. He started it out in the back of an old pickup truck

with a group of kids who wanted to get off the streets. And today, across from a burned-out block in south central L.A., the Boys and Girls Club stands unscarred. No, it wasn't a miracle that the building was left standing. The real miracle is what goes on inside. It's a place kids can go to get the concern and the love they need, a place where people care.

That's why guaranteeing a hopeful future for the children of our cities is about a lot more than rebuilding burned-out buildings. It's about building a new American community.

This I know: We have the strength and spirit in our Government, in our communities, and in ourselves to transform America into the Nation we have dreamed of for generations.

Thank you for listening. And may God bless the United States of America.

*Note: The President spoke at 9:03 a.m. from the Oval Office at the White House. The address was broadcast live on nationwide radio.*

## Message to the Senate Returning Without Approval the Congressional Campaign Spending Limit and Election Reform Act of 1992
*May 9, 1992*

*To the Senate of the United States:*

I am returning herewith without my approval S. 3, the "Congressional Campaign Spending Limit and Election Reform Act of 1992." The current campaign finance system is seriously flawed. For 3 years I have called on the Congress to overhaul our campaign finance system in order to reduce the influence of special interests, to restore the influence of individuals and political parties, and to reduce the unfair advantages of incumbency. S. 3 would not accomplish any of these objectives. In addition to perpetuating the corrupting influence of special interests and the imbalance between challengers and incumbents, S. 3 would limit political speech protected by the First Amendment and inevitably lead to a raid

on the Treasury to pay for the Act's elaborate scheme of public subsidies.

In 1989, I proposed comprehensive campaign finance reform legislation to reduce the influence of special interests and the powers of incumbency. My proposal would abolish political action committees (PACs) subsidized by corporations, unions, and trade associations. It would protect statutorily the political rights of American workers, implementing the Supreme Court's decision in *Communications Workers* v. *Beck*. It would curtail leadership PACs. It would virtually prohibit the practice of bundling. It would require the full disclosure of *all* soft money expenditures by political parties and by corporations and unions. It would restrict the taxpayer-financed franking privileges enjoyed by incumbents. It would prevent incumbents from amassing campaign war chests from excess campaign funds from previous elections.

These are all significant reforms, and I am encouraged that S. 3 includes a few of them, albeit with some differences. If the Congress is serious about enacting campaign finance reform, it should pass legislation along the lines I proposed in 1989, and I will sign it immediately. However, I cannot accept legislation, like S. 3, that contains spending limits or public subsidies, or fails to eliminate special interest PACs.

Further, as I have previously stated, I am opposed to different rules for the House and Senate on matters of ethics and election reform. In several key respects, S. 3 contains separate rules for House and Senate candidates, with no apparent justification other than political expediency.

S. 3 no longer contains the provision that the Senate passed last year abolishing all PACs. Although that provision was overbroad in banning issue-oriented PACs unconnected to special interests, S. 3 would not eliminate any PACs. Instead, the Act provides only a reduced limit on individual PAC contributions to Senate candidates and no change in the status quo in the House. Moreover, the limit on aggregate PAC contributions to House candidates to one-third of the spending limit, $200,000, is not likely to diminish the heavy reliance of Members on PAC contributions. The average amount a Member of Congress raised from PACs in the last election cycle was $209,000.

The spending limits for both House and Senate candidates will most likely hurt challengers more than incumbents, especially because S. 3 does little to reduce the advantages of incumbency. Inexplicably, there is no parallel House provision to the sensible Senate provision restricting the use of the frank in an election year. In the last election cycle, the amount incumbent House Members spent on franked mail was three times the total amount spent by all House challengers. The system of public benefits, designed to induce candidates to agree to abide by the spending limits, is unlikely in many cases to overcome the inherent favors of incumbency.

S. 3 contains several unconstitutional provisions, although none more serious than the aggregate spending limits. In *Buckley* v. *Valeo*, the Supreme Court ruled that to be constitutional, spending limits must be voluntary. There is nothing "voluntary" about the spending limits in this Act. The penalties in S. 3 for candidates who choose not to abide by the spending limits or to accept Treasury funds are punitive—unlike the Presidential campaign system—as well as costly to the taxpayer. For example, if a nonparticipating House candidate spends just one dollar over 80 percent of the spending limit, the participating candidate may spend without limit and receive unlimited Federal matching funds. The subsidies provided for in S. 3 could amount to well over 100 million dollars every election cycle, yet the Act is silent on how these generous Government subsidies would be financed. It seems inevitable that they would be paid for by the American taxpayer. I understand why Members of Congress would be reluctant to ask taxpayers directly to subsidize their reelection campaigns, but given the significant costs of S. 3, its failure to address the funding question is irresponsible.

Our Nation needs campaign finance laws that place the interests of individual citizens and political parties above special interests, and that provide a level playing field between challengers and incumbents. What we do not need is a taxpayer-financed incumbent protection plan. For these reasons, I am vetoing S. 3.

GEORGE BUSH

The White House,
May 9, 1992.

## Remarks on Maternal and Infant Health Care
*May 11, 1992*

Thank you, Lou, thank you, Secretary Sullivan, and welcome, everyone. Let me just pay a special thanks to Senator Dale Bumpers and to Congressman Tom Bliley, who have been spearheading many of our prenatal and immunization initiatives on Capitol Hill. They are true leaders for this cause, and we're delighted to see you all here today. Also to Jim Mason, our Assistant Secretary for Health; Bill Roper from Atlanta, doing a superb job as our Director at CDC. And a warm welcome to representatives of the Advertising Council and to all the very special mothers and children who are with us today.

Yesterday, on Mother's Day, millions of Americans took time to appreciate the miracle of motherhood. We thank the mothers who brought us into this world, who taught us our first lessons about life and love and character. Today, we're taking some vital steps to help American mothers, their children, and their families. We're announcing improved standards and a new action plan for immunization. We're beginning a public service ad campaign to promote an innovative prenatal care program called Healthy Start, the program Dr. Sullivan referred to.

Every year in America thousands of babies are delivered at dangerously low birth weights, and too many of these babies die or suffer chronic illness as a result. Thousands of our young children suffer crippling effects each year from measles and other communicable childhood diseases, and some even die. But the saddest fact of all is this: Most of this death and disease is easily preventable through immunization and through better prenatal care. To the extent they are preventable, they too often reflect bad health choices stemming from ignorance of good health behavior or absence of a defined sense of personal responsibility by the parents.

All of our maternal and child health programs are being improved, integrated, and developed to promote the principles of innovation, of community involvement, and personal responsibility. We are using new and creative approaches to bringing high-risk women into care. To attack this problem we are mobilizing the Nation's best ideas and resources. The hallmarks of our plan can be summed up in two words: immunization and action.

Last June I stood here in the Rose Garden with the Secretary to call for a stronger immunization effort. We sent out teams to six areas of our country to determine how we could do it better. We learned lessons that we're now applying nationwide. I was pleased to be a part of the visit to San Diego in February and happy that representatives of all six communities that we looked at are here with us today.

Today we're announcing a new action plan to get our children vaccinated when it makes the greatest difference, before the age of two. The plan requires more effective coordination to promote vaccination among the various Federal Agencies that serve children. We're helping States and localities with their own immunization plans. And our administration's budget for immunization continues to respond to the need. For fiscal '93, we're seeking an increase to $349 million. We're also announcing new standards for pediatric immunization, the work of an expert panel representing many private and public sector organizations. They're going to help clinics improve their method to provide vaccination to kids who need them the most.

I salute the leaders again of the Advertising Council for all the volunteer time and talent that you have organized for the cause of infant mortality. I know that public service ad campaigns such as this work. Think of the success of other Ad Council campaigns for kicking the smoking habit, for seatbelt use, for screening for cancer. All such efforts help people show greater responsibility in their own behavior.

Now, I've often thought that the same sort of diligent use of marketing science and communications talents could help motivate Americans to address other problems involving personal responsibility, for instance, in keeping families together, encouraging responsible sexual behavior, and other matters of personal and family well-being. So I'm confident that the Ad Council's new campaign will have strong and positive results.

The Council's messages will emphasize that the health of pregnant women and their unborn babies is a matter of concern to every member of a civilized society. When an expectant mother is financially needy or without a husband or a family to support her, it is all the more urgent for good neighbors to show that they care. The Ad Council's first message, therefore, targets the general public. It calls on all of us for action. The theme that you'll soon be hearing on television is this: We must not accept high rates of infant deaths because this is America.

The second announcement will impress upon men the importance of their role. Whether a man is an unborn child's father or another family member or friend, there is much he can and should do to help an expectant mother. We cannot understate male responsibility.

The third announcement will tell women that proper care begins long before the baby is born. Consider this: Babies born after a pregnancy with no prenatal care are four times more likely to die than those whose mothers received care beginning in the first trimester. The full series assures pregnant women in need that they are not alone. Care is available, and good neighbors are being mobilized to help.

The Healthy Start approach represents what we should be doing to solve our social problems: local solutions, local control, local accountability. The first 15 Healthy Start communities were chosen from a long list of applicants. I understand that representatives of many of these communities from around the Nation are here today, and thank you all for your good work.

We're not weighing down these community initiatives with burdensome Federal mandates and command-and-control regulations. We're seeking to empower neighborhood volunteers in local governments to invent effective new ways to help save babies' lives and keep babies and their mothers strong and healthy.

Healthy Start successes will come from people who see neighbors in need and ask, "What can I do to help?" And they follow through on their generous impulses. And they keep noticing and helping more people. I'm talking about people like Minnie Thomas in Oakland, California. An energetic grandmother, she was helping drug abusers when she learned there was no facility for drug abusers who became pregnant. So she opened her own facility called Solid Foundation. And 47 kids have been born to mothers at Solid Foundation, and not one suffered from low birth weight.

Here in Washington, Tawana Fortune-Jones is the woman with the Mom Van, and she knocks on doors in neighborhoods where infant mortality is high. She's enlisted the cooperation of doctors and clinics to establish a Healthy Start Pregnancy Register. She drives the Mom Van, and each morning at 7 a.m. she begins picking up women and taking them to doctors' offices. Afterwards she takes them home, and then she shuttles another group in the afternoon. She's a friend to women who have no other friends, and she's saved and bettered the lives of hundreds of babies. And she's here with us today. Tawana, where are you now? Right over here. Tawana, good neighbors are the heroes of our cities, and you're the model of a good neighbor. Thank you for what you do.

Unbelievable as it may seem, the innovations of Healthy Start ran into resistance up in Congress where they are still too much wedded to the old bureaucratic ways of doing things. I'm optimistic, though. I believe our approach for empowering people with new ideas is the way of the future. Our crusade for preventive health care for infants and expectant mothers will move a step further when we reform this—overall reform of the health insurance system. I've proposed making every American able to afford a basic health insurance plan of his choice, using credits or vouchers. And through the market system, we would provide needy Americans better health care than they now receive.

These two efforts represent a new way of solving our problems in infant mortality and immunization. Our guiding principle is to reach out: Reach out to young parents, make sure they know what they need to do, and then help them to do it; reach out to community organizations; reach out to the private sector; and reach across the artificial lines in our Government so that any program that touches young children and their parents will become an opportunity point for better health.

We have new kinds of problems, and so we've got to think in new ways. We need to think about all the opportunities that we have to draw in young families who may be left out today, to help them, to inform them. We need to enlist them and enlist our communities to work together to help them. All the community organizations

have a tremendous role to play. It's already worked in our six demonstration immunization cities, and I am confident that it's going to work in Healthy Start and in more immunization communities all around this great country.

Thank you all for your leadership. Again, my respects to the two Members of Congress here. Thank the doctors here, and thank all of you working in the communities to make life just a little better for the kids and for the families out there. Thank you all for coming.

*Note: The President spoke at 11:16 a.m. in the Rose Garden at the White House.*

# Statement by Press Secretary Fitzwater on the President's Meeting With Foreign Minister Roland Dumas of France
*May 11, 1992*

President Bush and French Foreign Minister Roland Dumas discussed a number of bilateral and regional issues during a 20-minute Oval Office meeting. Minister Dumas said that the development of increased unity within the European Community must be accompanied by efforts to re-

inforce ties between Europe and the United States. The President welcomed the desire to strengthen transatlantic ties, which the United States shares completely. The President also noted the need to conclude the Uruguay round trade negotiations.

# Remarks in a Roundtable Discussion With the Weed and Seed Revitalization Committee and Community Leaders in Philadelphia, Pennsylvania
*May 11, 1992*

*Mr. Michael Baylson.* Mr. President, good afternoon. We are honored to welcome you to our "Weed and Seed" neighborhood to meet with the members of the Weed and Seed Neighborhood Revitalization Committee and other community residents.

We want to tell you about some of the innovative programs in Philadelphia. For example, the Violent Traffickers Project, with whom you just met a few minutes ago, has been active in this neighborhood,

making substantial progress arresting the larger drug-trafficking gangs. Also, last week a Federal grand jury returned indictments against 72 defendants, allegedly members of the Cali cartel, their customers, or other major Philadelphia drug dealers, for dumping drugs into this community.

Mr. President, welcome to our "Weed and Seed" area.

*The President.* Michael, thank you. What I really want to do is listen to people in the community and from the city. I salute Michael for the job he's doing as U.S. attorney; thank the commissioner for being at my side through this tour. I expect you're going to miss him, but I think you're looking forward to his arrival to his new, enormous challenge.

Let me just say, I don't know if you've met Governor Martinez and Digger Phelps. Governor Martinez runs our National Drug Control program. And Digger, whom you all know by reputation, I'm sure, who understands a lot about the inner cities, he's got a key role in our "Weed and Seed" program. We believe in this program. I know that Members of Congress who are with us here, including Senator Specter and these House Members, agree. And we want to see it be successful. But I came here to listen, and I really appreciate you all taking the time to tell me what's on your minds and what you think would be best for the community and then see what we can do.

*Mr. Baylson.* Thank you, Mr. President. I'd like Commissioner Williams to just say a few words first, and then he'll be followed by Sister Carol, who is seated to your left.

*Commissioner Willie Williams.* Thank you very much, Mike. Mr. President, this area that we're in right now, at some time not in the too distant past, was probably one of the worst drug-dealing areas in the city of Philadelphia. You literally could not have walked through the schoolyard or driven even your car up there without being harassed by drug dealers. We had strong cooperation from the citizens. They simply asked us to "Please do whatever you can. We will work with you. We will stand behind you in trying to rid the area of some very, very structured and organized drug gangs."

We went about it through a combination of traditional policing methods, using city police, using State, Federal assistance, using the community's support, and starting out with the Violent Traffickers Project, I think. Within a 2-year period, we locked up at least 150 to 200 people. Ninety-eight percent of them pled guilty; the other 2 percent were found guilty in court. As I said, we were running 100 percent conviction rate. We snatched entire structured, organized gangs out of the neighborhood.

The next piece that we're now involved with is what we now call the "Weed and Seed," where law enforcement has come in and, to some degree, weeded out the very difficult people. It is now up to the city, State, and Federal agencies and the communities working together to reclaim their own neighborhoods for themselves, working together. That's where we're at right now, and Sister Carol and others here are all part of this collective effort from community, from government, from law enforcement, and from other various volunteers.

*The President.* Thank you, Commissioner.

[*A participant spoke on community revitalization funding and enterprise zones.*]

*The President.* Well, I hope we can do something on this enterprise zones. I will try to keep it out of the partisan politics.

Ironically, Sister, maybe not so ironically, but at every level in Los Angeles, in the community, community groups wanted that; they felt that that would draw jobs into the community. So I think it's a new idea in that it's never been tried at the Federal level. Literally green-line these areas and have a, say, zero capital gains so you can attract businesses. So we're going to try, and I'm glad that you all support that.

[*A participant presented documentation on the problems of obtaining mortgage insurance and ensuring residents' input on funding decisions.*]

*The President.* I have one question on the—do we have time to ask one question on the red-lining and stuff? Is that a Federal law or a State law or a city—what is it?

*Participant.* From what I know it's in the State legislature here. And we met with six banks; we put a housing group together. The banks say they're ready to lend money for low-income housing and for mortgages, but then the insurance companies, who were sitting at the same table, tell us that they will not approve mortgages in any community where there's a 10 percent vacancy in the block. And all that does is create the whole block to go. We can't lock these blocks and bring them back.

What we need is, we need HUD and we

need the Pennsylvania Housing Authority to come to meetings and work with us to try to look at the numbers of houses in these blocks and either rehabilitate property or tear it down and make a garden out of it for the property next to it, so we can move on and start to tie some of these neighborhoods together again.

*The President.* Thanks.

[*A participant presented a T-shirt to the President.*]

*The President.* That's very nice. Thank you very much. And good luck, Miriam. Thank you.

[*A participant questioned combating the multimillion-dollar drug-trafficking business with limited funds.*]

*The President.* Well, I'm not sure that funds is the entire answer. I just came from a project that the commissioner could describe where they have these satellite precincts where the police officers get the confidence of people in the neighborhood and are highly successful in discouraging drugs from being in that area. I don't think it was as much spending as it was community involvement on the part, in this instance, of law enforcement.

Our Federal law enforcement, obviously, should be in support of the locals and support of State law enforcement. I don't think anyone wants to see a Federal police force. Now, we do have Federal Agencies that we can talk about; I mean DEA and the FBI and all that are involved when Federal laws are being broken. But it's a combination, it seems to me.

[*The participant said that "Weed and Seed" funding was insufficient.*]

*The President.* One, you can't do it with "Weed and Seed" money alone. That's one thing. Two, we are going to the Congress to increase the "Weed and Seed" funds, and I think we'll be successful. But it's got to be that along with these other programs, I think most people would agree, because I don't think the "Seed" money itself will do it.

I'll tell you, one of the key concepts is this concept of trying to attract businesses to the community. The sister spoke about enterprise zones, and of course, that would help because it would give people a break. One of the things that is happening out in Los Angeles right now is a major push to bring private businesses in by Peter Ueberroth. I don't know if you're read about his approach, but it's one the commissioner will be running into out there. And I must say, the guy's very optimistic about being able to do that. Of course, that, in the final analysis, is the key, a job in the private sector.

So we're going to push for the enterprise zones that will make it more attractive for companies to come in and locate in this area. Give people a tax break so—it's wasted—if you don't have any businesses, you're not losing revenue, there's just nothing happening there.

So we think that this approach, coupled with the homeownership concept on our public housing and urban development program is a very good start on the part of the Federal Government. And so I hope—and "Weed and Seed," that's the third element of it, with more funding.

[*A participant expressed appreciation for Federal support of local law enforcement programs.*]

*The President.* Thank you.

[*A participant spoke on the need for youth-oriented programs.*]

*The President.* Thank you very much.

[*A participant requested additional funding for programs to benefit children.*]

*The President.* Thank you very much.

[*A participant emphasized the importance of helping children.*]

*The President.* Thank you, Felicia. Beautifully said.

[*Another participant reiterated the importance of helping children.*]

*The President.* Thank you, Tomasita.

May I ask a question? I don't know who could answer it. But I mentioned in the State of the Union Address a visit I had from the mayors, including Tom Bradley out in L.A. and a lot of smalltown mayors, you know, women, men, Republican, Democrat, liberal, conservative. They came to me, and they said, "The number one problem we see in the problem with the city is the demise of the American family." Can somebody make suggestions? Of course, you know, we think that what Ms. Melendez is doing, and other educators, is a big, important part of how you overcome that. But if anyone has suggestions—and I'm not sure it's a government thing—but has suggestions as to how you strengthen or turn around the decline in the family, it would be extraordinarily helpful.

We've appointed a Commission, and I hope it's not just one more study effort that gets filed and gathers dust. I'm just quoting what these mayors told me. And I mentioned it out there in Los Angeles, and several of the churches say, "Well, you know, when you have a decline in the family, the church has to fill in a lot more." And then there was a very active boys club.

But I just wonder if there's anything legislatively that's keeping the family apart, making it easier or better off if they live apart rather than together. We're looking at the laws from that end, but I'd welcome any comments. It's a very complex subject, but it is—John, maybe?

[*A participant spoke on the importance of strong families. Another participant spoke on the need to change attitudes and increase self-esteem in at-risk communities.*]

*The President.* Thank you very much. I think the answer is to try some new ideas. What we're doing we will all concede is not enough. Some programs, certainly community programs, are an example for everybody. I mean, they work. And what we've heard today is something new—or what I heard. It may not be new to Philadelphia, but it's new to a lot of the country in terms of the "Weed" part of it.

So I think the answer to your question is, we've got to try these new approaches that hopefully will not only encourage community service, like the "Seed"-ing part of the "Weed and Seed," but also bring jobs into the community from which you can then have more normal family lives. But that

would be a very easy answer to a very complicated question.

[*The participant said that attitudes throughout the Nation must be changed.*]

*The President.* Great.

[*A participant stressed the need for more funds to support community leaders and local programs, and questioned the value of tax breaks for the poor.*]

*The President.* Let me clarify one thing. Maybe you misunderstood part of what I said. I wasn't talking about tax breaks for a guy who doesn't have a job. What the enterprise zones does is talk about tax breaks for people that are willing to set up a business in an area so that it will be like a magnet, hopefully drawing jobs in there, even though the area may not be as attractive a part of the city or something like that.

So that was the only point I wanted to add here because I think it really will work. But we're trying hard to get it done anyway, see if it works.

*Mr. Baylson.* Mr. President, I'd like to thank you very much. The people around this table have worked very hard to put together our "Weed and Seed" application. And I have told them that if the enterprise zone bill passes, there will be more funds for "Weed and Seed" activities in this or the next fiscal year. And we pledge that we're going to do our damnedest to make a difference in this neighborhood.

*The President.* I think you obviously already are. But I'm most impressed with the community spirit, because what they're saying is, "How can we help some more?"

*Mr. Baylson.* Right.

*The President.* Thank you very much, very much.

*Note: The exchange began at 5:10 p.m. in the gymnasium at St. Boniface Church. In his remarks, the President referred to Willie Williams, Philadelphia police commissioner, and Peter Ueberroth, chairman of the Rebuild L.A. Committee.*

## Remarks at a Bush-Quayle Fundraising Dinner in Philadelphia
*May 11, 1992*

Thank you all. And Peter, thank you very much for that wonderfully warm introduction and for making me feel so welcome. I loved walking out through that crowd because it gave me a chance to see so many people who have been so supportive over the years, and I am very, very grateful to you. Barbara and I count our blessings, even in complicated times, and I am very privileged to serve as President of the United States. Believe me, I'll never forget how I got there. It was good, strong, loyal friends out in the precincts and at dinners like this over the years, and I am very grateful to all of you.

May I thank Reverend Gambet for his invocation; it was a unique invocation, and I kind of went along with the last part and could learn from the first part, but—[*laughter*]—and Malcolm Evans for the national anthem. I missed the Pledge of Allegiance crowd. I hear they were absolutely fantastic, and some of them are back there, but thank you very much for a unique joint Pledge of Allegiance. And I want to thank Peter and David here for making this dinner happen. Of course, Senator Specter, I'm just very pleased to have been with him today in what for, I think, both of us was a very moving tour through some of the less privileged, some of the impacted parts of this great city. Larry Coughlin is with us, who is our Bush-Quayle cochairman; Congressmen Weldon and Ridge and Ritter, all good people. We've got a great Republican delegation from Pennsylvania, I might add, in the United States Congress.

I was delighted to see Barbara Hafer earlier on. And, of course, Governor Mike Castle, an old friend who's done a great job in a neighboring State with us tonight. And I'd be remiss if I didn't single out Elsie Hillman, heading the campaign effort here in the Keystone State, and thank Dexter and then, of course, our team of Bobby Holt, Wally Ganzi. And then again, I'll single out Dexter, who gets the star seat. He gets to sit next to Elsie, and that means he sold more tickets than anybody else. So

that's terrific. And, of course, Charlie, Charlie Kopp, he is a fundraising czar. He is our finance chairman, a great friend, and a loyal, loyal supporter. And he is very successful—so successful that he didn't have to go to our dog Millie for a single dime. [*Laughter*] You may have seen our income tax returns, and you can tell who earns the money in the family. Millie is not a "fat cat," but nevertheless has done a great job as our dog. [*Laughter*]

I am pleased to be here. And I want to share with you just some observations. This is a year where you're hearing a lot of talk about change. And I would be the first to concede that we must make significant change in this country. I hear a lot of talk about it coming out of the political arena, but we've been trying to effect constructive change.

I came back from a very moving visit to Los Angeles; we got back Friday evening. And let me just give you a short report of what I saw and what I heard. Each one of us saw the images of hate and horror. That was all around you, images that we won't soon forget. But what I saw during my time in Los Angeles, even in the hardest hit parts of south central L.A., should give us some cause for hope. Everywhere, the people I talked with told about acts of individual heroism, about the extraordinary courage of just plain ordinary people. And some braved the gang of looters to form these bucket brigades to put out fires when the firetrucks couldn't get through. And then some stood up in the face of angry mobs and reached across the barrier of color to save lives of their fellow men and women. And many of these aren't the stories that you'll see on the nightly news. But believe me, they are the stories that tell us the power of simple human decency.

What it tells me is that the time has come to set the old, worn-out ideas aside. And the time has come, in the words of Abraham Lincoln, "to think anew and to act anew." And we start with the principles at the heart of this great Republican Party, principles that tell us something very obvious, and that is that we ought to keep the power close to the people, that we've got to strengthen families.

I'll never forget when Tom Bradley, the Mayor of Los Angeles, and others came to see me, large-city mayors, small-city mayors, Republicans, Democrats, liberals and conservatives joined, their National League of Cities. And they came and they said the one thing that united them in terms that they all agreed on was that the fundamental problem that the decline of the American family is causing in the cities. The prime cause of much of the unrest, the problems of crime, whatever, comes from the dissolution of the American family.

And we think we've got to find ways to strengthen that, instill character and values in our young people; that we must encourage entrepreneurship, ownership, increase investment, and create jobs. Now, these aims have got to form the heart of our agenda for economic opportunity, an agenda that can literally restore hope, can't solve the problem overnight but restore hope to our inner cities. And they define what we must do.

First, and let's be very clear on this one, we have got to preserve order. We've got to keep the peace because families can't thrive, children can't live, and jobs can't flourish in a climate of fear. And I support the police. I saw the commissioner here today, had a great—I see Governor Martinez, the head of our drug effort, here with him. He and I were together with the Senator and others. And I told the commissioner and told the people out here, "We support your efforts." They put themselves in harm's way to save all of us. And we must start by standing strongly for order and keeping the peace.

Now, those thoughts were foremost in my mind from the first hours of the violence in Los Angeles. A civilized society simply cannot tackle any of the really tough problems in the midst of chaos. It's just that simple. Violence and brutality destroy order. They destroy the rule of law. They must never be rationalized. And it must be condemned, violence, whenever you find it; we must condemn it as a society.

When I was out in Los Angeles, I called a

woman that had been a member of our little church in Houston, Texas, St. Martin's Parish. I'd got a message to call her. I called her, and she told me a tragic story of her brother and her son. They had gotten a call from a neighbor, a minority, a member of a minority group, and they'd climbed on their motorcycle and driven down to see this person. On the way, their motorcycle was surrounded by a gang. The motorcycle was upended. Her son was beaten. Somebody put a gun up to this kid's head, pulled the trigger, and it didn't go off. Her brother, not so lucky. He was beaten, and they put a gun up to his head, and he was killed right on the spot. This didn't have anything to do with Rodney King. This didn't have anything to do with anything other than wanton violence. We simply cannot be asked to condone that in our society. And so we're going to stand for——[*applause*]

In Los Angeles, I announced an addition to a program that's already at work here in Philadelphia, an exciting program that we saw today, an initiative that I call "Weed and Seed." The idea is to weed out the gang leaders and drug dealers and career criminals and then seed the community with expanded employment, educational, and social services. So we're going to push for that. I'm going to push and try to see that we can do more for the American people with this innovative new program.

Secondly, we must spark an economic revival in urban America. The best answer to poverty is a job with dignity in the private sector, and that means establishing what we call enterprise zones in our inner cities. It means reforming our welfare system, putting an end to the pervasive disincentives that encourage welfare and discourage work. So, enterprise zones and reform of welfare.

Thirdly, we've got to revolutionize American education. I might add, parenthetically, that I wish Barbara was here to see what you're doing with this show of support for literacy. Mr. Notebaert, wherever he may be, I would like to make this contribution. I'm not trying to sell this. [*Laughter*] This is "Millie's Book," and we want to donate this here as a contribution from the breadwinner in the Bush family. So please, we want the record to show we brought a book in.

Now, we have a good education program. It burns me up when I hear some of the old thinkers, the pass-the-mandated-Federal-program thinkers, criticize. We have a program called America 2000. It's an innovative strategy, and it has things in it like choice. You can choose your colleges; why not choose your schools and thus make them more competitive?

Competition, community action, all of these things are a part of it. Children in our inner cities deserve the same opportunities that kids in the suburbs have, and that's what a lot of that program is about. That means we've got to break the power of the establishment, the education establishment. And whether it's public or private or religious, parents, not the government, should be free to choose their children's schools. I am going to fight for that concept.

Then another ingredient of our urban policy, and one I've been trying to get through for a long time, is homeownership. And I've never understood how anyone could be content with the present system, to take pride in the warehousing of the poor. The aim behind our HOPE initiative is to give poor families a stake, give them a stake in their communities, to give them something of value they can pass along to their kids, by turning public housing tenants into homeowners. And we are going to fight for that principle.

At every turn during my time in L.A., I heard people talking about the principles that guide these initiatives. And these weren't big shots; these were community leaders. These were people that were out there on the front line trying to help the kids. Personal responsibility, that was one; opportunity; ownership; independence; and then, of course, with great pride, dignity. And you know the sound of those words. We all do. It really adds up to the American dream.

And we all know what the critics will say, and you've heard it. They'll say, "Well, you've proposed all this before, Mr. President." And the answer: It's true. That's right. But now it is time to act on these proposals because this time they know we are right. We are right, and we want to get it passed through the Congress. Tomorrow

I'll be meeting with the leaders to try to get it done. It's no longer good enough to try the old ones. Let's try these new ideas and see if they can't help some of the kids that we saw today here in Philadelphia.

My first order of business is, then, to build a bipartisan effort in support of immediate action on this agenda. We won't settle for business-as-usual, measuring what we achieve by the size of the bureaucracy we build or the number of mandated programs we can send down to these communities who are crying out for flexibility. This time, we've got to put our principles to work and take the case for change directly to the American people.

What's going on in urban America is just one part, though, of a larger issue because the need for reform doesn't end simply with our inner cities. It starts with the revolution in American education that I mentioned. America 2000, we call it. It starts with that. When you get down to what we've got to do really to be competitive in the future, to offer kids an opportunity, it is education. And it includes our aggressive action, also, to break down barriers to free trade. Opening markets to American goods the world over has got to be a part of it. In each case, we've taken aim at the status quo, and we've set our sights on change. That's why I'm fighting hard for a GATT agreement. That's why we have proposed and are working with Mexico's able President, Carlos Salinas, to try to get a North American free trade agreement. It will mean more jobs for the United States, more jobs for Mexico, and a Mexico much better able to do what it must do with its environment and do what it must do in controlling its own borders.

America needs legal reform to put an end to these outrageous court awards that sap our economy and strain our civility. We've gotten to a point where doctors won't deliver babies, where fathers are afraid to coach Little League, all because of the fear of some frivolous lawsuit. That won't change until people spend less time suing each other and more time helping each other. And we've got to change the laws in Washington. We must and we will reform the legal system.

Now, we need health care reform and to open up access to affordable health care for all Americans. I was talking to Charlie about this a little earlier here. It used to be that going to the hospital didn't conjure up visions of financial suicide. Today, the cost of even minor surgery has gone right out through the roof. More than 30 million Americans have no health care coverage at all.

We can change that. And we can do it better than some of these nationalized programs that we're hearing about from the opposition. We have a comprehensive health care reform plan that will help us keep the quality health care. Make no mistake about it, people are still pouring into the United States for specialized care because they know we have the best quality health care in the entire world. So we want to keep the quality health care that makes us first in the world and at the same time open up access to all Americans.

Contrary to what the big Government folks say, we can do it without putting the Government in charge of everybody's health care. If you want to stand in line, you can go to the department of motor vehicles. You don't need to go for a nationalized health care program. Let's face it, national health care, in my view, literally would be a costly national disaster, and I am not going to let that happen. We are going to fight for our plan of reform that gives access to insurance to the poor and the middle-income people alike. That's what we need, and that's what I believe we'll be able to get when we take this case to the American people.

So far, I've spoken a little bit about what Government can do. So let me conclude by speaking about what society absolutely must do. Because there's something society must cultivate that Government cannot provide, something we can't legislate, something that we can't make happen by Government order. I'm talking about the moral sense that guides us all. In the simplest of terms— you want to get it to fundamentals—I'm talking about knowing right from wrong and then doing what's right.

You go back to Los Angeles for a minute. Time and again the people I met with there put their finger on one root cause for the

turmoil we see, and that, of course, back to the point, the dissolution of the family. And they're right. They're absolutely right. And ask yourself: What's the determining fact right now for whether a child has hope, stays in school, stays away from drugs? It is not Government spending. It's not the number of SBA loans or HUD grants. It's whether a child lives in a loving home with a mother and a father.

Barbara Bush was absolutely right when she said, "What happens in the White House doesn't matter half as much as what happens in your house." We have tried, both of us, augmented by tons of grandchildren, et cetera, to put the emphasis on American family, put that emphasis first.

That's why I keep coming back to the Good Samaritans that we have called and will continue to call Points of Light: Everybody here devoting some time to helping someone else in the community. The people who help the poor, the elderly, kids in trouble, and never ask a nickel in return. Government alone simply cannot create the scale and the energy needed to transform the lives of people in need. Let the cynics scoff about it, but we know these volunteers are the lifeblood of the American spirit.

And I wish you could have been with me today because you heard it: Community action. People overburdened with financial problems but finding time to help the guy next door. It was a wonderful thing we saw right here in some of the most impoverished areas of Philadelphia. It was a community spirit. Government has a role, but it never can supplant the propensity of one American to help another. So we've got to find ways to help in that concept and help encourage it.

I believe there is a great future in store because I believe that all of these principles will be coming into focus now. I believe we're right about family. I think we're right about freedom and free enterprise, and I think we're right about faith. Most of all, I think we are right about America's future.

You know, we've been through a very tough time. There's been a sluggish economy with recession in many parts of the country. I have a feeling this thing is beginning to move a little bit, and it's long overdue. I hope like heck I'm right this time, but I really do feel that it's beginning to move. And with that there will be a return of this innate feeling of American optimism. And when it happens, let's all vow that we will save time to help the other guy, to do what we can to be Points of Light.

We've got the strength. We've got the spirit in our Government. We've got it. You can sense it even in the ravaged communities of Los Angeles. We've got it in ourselves to transform America into the Nation we've dreamed of for generations. So don't listen to those doomsayers. Don't listen to those top 20 seconds that tell you everything that's wrong with the United States of America. We are the freest and the fairest and the best country on the face of the Earth. And we are going to get the job done.

We have nothing to be apologetic for. We've got big problems. But the message, I think, is if we can try this new approach, I believe we can solve them and offer hope to those little kids we saw with their eyes bulging as we came by there today into these little community centers.

Thank you all very much for your support. Save a little energy for the campaign in the fall. I'm going to need you. But I believe we're going to win this election. Thank you very, very much.

*Note:. The President spoke at 7:40 p.m. in the Grand Ballroom at the Hotel Atop the Bellevue. In his remarks, he referred to Peter Terpeluk, Jr., and David Girard-di-Carlo, dinner cochairmen; Representative Lawrence Coughlin, Bush-Quayle Pennsylvania cochairman; Barbara Hafer, Pennsylvania auditor-general; Elsie Hillman, Bush-Quayle Pennsylvania chairman; Dexter Baker, Bush-Quayle regional cochairman; Bobby Holt and Wally Ganzi, Bush-Quayle national finance cochairmen; Charlie Kopp, Bush-Quayle Pennsylvania finance chairman; Willie Williams, Philadelphia police commissioner; Bob Martinez, Director of the Office of National Drug Control Policy; and Edmond Notebaert, president and chief executive officer, Children's Hospital of Philadelphia.*

## Statement on Urban Aid Initiatives
*May 12, 1992*

Today I am discussing with Congress a strategy to bring hope and opportunity to distressed communities. Our action is based on bedrock American values: personal responsibility, work, and family. We must end the cycle of dependency and give all Americans a place at the table of economic opportunity.

Clearly, the time has come to set aside old ideas and try something new. We in Government have a responsibility to act now to guarantee a hopeful future for the children of this Nation, a future where people are safe, neighborhoods can flourish, children can learn, and jobs can be created.

All Americans share the common goals of equal opportunity, advancement, and upward mobility. But the American dream is hindered by too many obstacles: unsafe cities, slow economic growth, an out-of-date education system, and dependency-creating Government programs.

We must start with policies that refocus programs to serve those who are most needy and increase the effectiveness of Government services through innovation, competition, and choice. Our approach is a radical break with the policies of the past. But as Abraham Lincoln once said, "It is time to think and act anew."

My action plan consists of six core components:

(1) "Weed and Seed": Our families cannot thrive and jobs cannot flourish in a climate of lawlessness and fear. Our "Weed and Seed" initiative to combat crime wins back our inner cities by weeding out gang leaders, drug dealers, and career criminals and seeding communities with expanded employment, educational, and social services.

(2) HOPE: When people lack jobs, opportunity, or ownership of property, they have little or no stake in their communities. Our HOPE (Homeownership and Opportunity for People Everywhere) initiative fosters a sense of community pride by offering inner-city residents a chance for homeownership and management of public housing.

(3) Enterprise Zones: We must spark an economic revival in urban America to create jobs and opportunity. Our enterprise zones initiative encourages businesses to re-enter our inner cities by creating tax credits, expanding capital investment, and bringing regulatory relief to some of the Nation's most economically depressed areas.

(4) Education Reform: It is time to reform and improve American education. Our education reform strategy, America 2000, envisions an America in which all parents have the choice of the best schools available, public, private, or parochial.

(5) Welfare Reform: While no one disputes that government has an obligation to provide a safety net to those in need, there is too much emphasis on programs that penalize ambition, promote alienation, and destroy individual dignity. We must encourage family formation and allow individuals to fulfill their potential for a productive, meaningful life.

(6) Youth Jobs—Youth Apprenticeships and Job Training 2000: The health of our cities and our economy depend on a skilled work force and facilitating the transition of students from school to work. Prompt enactment of our proposals can help provide job opportunities and training this summer.

# Remarks on Urban Aid Initiatives and an Exchange With Reporters
*May 12, 1992*

*The President.* I will be talking to the leadership in a few minutes, and we will be proposing these initiatives, all of them designed to increase personal responsibility, offer hope to these communities. And it's a good program.

I think most are familiar with "Weed and Seed," to weed out the criminals and then seed the neighborhoods. We talked about this up in Philadelphia yesterday and in Los Angeles last week, and I think there's strong support for this program.

HOPE is a homeownership program. And we believe that owning the home is the best way to strengthen the family and to give the community stability.

On enterprise zones, that almost is universally accepted now. It's a proposal that will bring businesses, act like a magnet to bring businesses into these communities. We are going to increase the attractiveness of this proposal that we've had up there. But in any event, it's going to be—I think it will be accepted by the Congress. We're going to push hard for it, as we will for the others.

I think most are familiar in the country now with our America 2000, but again, we believe that educational choice will help. This is a little longer range proposal, but it fits in. Without education, we are not going to restore hope to our cities.

Welfare reform is important. We're going to go forward not just with waivers that encourage work- and learning-fare, but we're going to try to broaden out the amount of monies that a family can keep before they have to go off of welfare. I believe the limit now is $1,000, and I think we're talking now about $10,000, which would say to a person, if you save anything, you're not going to be thrown off of welfare right away.

Then on a youth job program, we have a program of $683 million, I believe it is. But with our apprentice program and our job opportunity program that I've announced and that we talked about down there in terms of job training, we want to go forward with some new legislation on that.

All of these are designed to restore hope and to bring some cohesion to these communities and offer these young people some opportunities. So I will be taking this to the leadership; in the spirit of working together, I hope we can get it done.

*Q.* Is there anything new, and does it require——

*The President.* These are all new. Most of these—well, "Weed and Seed" is in operation now a little bit. There are some model grants right now. Philadelphia is working on one. But all of these need to be tried. They're all new in a way, yes.

*Q.* New monies?

*The President.* Yes. Well, we'll be asking for some.

*Q.* Price tag, please?

*The President.* On what?

*Q.* On this whole program, on your agenda.

*The President.* I don't know that I can give you the price tag on the whole program. I've written down some numbers. On the "Weed and Seed," for example, with going up from the model demonstrations of nine to, I believe, half a billion dollars, that's new.

*Q.* That's the same figure, though, that was announced in February, the $500 million.

*The President.* We haven't gotten it yet. It's new. It has not been enacted. This has not been done. A proposal that hasn't been tried is new. We need to try these new ideas; that's the figure.

*Q.* And where——

*Q.* Sir, did I understand you to say you were going to give the families going off of welfare $10,000?

*The President.* No. I think what it is now is that if you save more than $1,000, you're off of welfare. We're talking about making it $10,000 so people can at least save a little bit of money while they're on welfare. HOPE, $1 billion in '93, that's what we're asking for.

Enterprise zones, it's hard to put a price on that because we are trying to make it more attractive in terms of how the tax structure will treat these investors. But there's no price tag on that one. It is a very, very important part of it.

Education, you know the numbers there, I think. We're not asking for anything different than we've proposed on that one.

Welfare reform, I've told you the difference there.

And on youth jobs there's, I think it's 683 for the summer, and now we're going up for new authorization on youth apprenticeship and Job Training 2000.

*Q.* Mr. President, where would this money come from? The Democrats say that if you're serious about this program, that you would agree to either a tax increase or reducing even further the Pentagon budget.

*The President.* I don't think the American people need to pay more taxes right now. I think this is a good program. It is coming from within the budget. Some of it, as I say, is asked for new authority in fiscal '93, but the idea that you have to raise taxes at this time when the economy is just starting to recover, I'm sorry, I will not support that.

*Q.* But then where would the money come from specifically?

*The President.* You will have to ask Dick Darman to tell you because it's all in the very complicated budget proposal.

*Q.* Would you give us a little more detail about that welfare, going off of welfare?

*The President.* Well, you know, I think——

*Q.* You think people can save up to $10,000 before they go off of welfare?

*The President.* No, I just think that that's a good thing for them to be able to do. That's not going to get them off of welfare. What's going to get them off of welfare is jobs, and that's what all this is designed to do, is to create jobs in the private sector. Now there are summer job programs, but we are trying to work to bring hope to the cities.

You know, it's very interesting to me that the community workers in both Los Angeles and Philadelphia, heavily impacted areas, are saying now is the time to try enterprise zones. We think they'll act like a magnet to bring private business into these areas of despair, and it ought to be tried. It is new, and it has not been tried at the Federal level.

*Q.* Did it take riots to do all this for all of you?

*The President.* No, because as you know and have been pointing out to me, some of these things have been proposed before. But we're going to now fight for them to get them passed. I'm going in there in a couple of minutes in the spirit of coopera- tion, holding out my hand to Congress and saying, "Look, let's not try to get credit; let's try to get something done for this country. Get it back to work, help these cities." And I think this is a good program, and the fact that some of these ideas have been proposed before and have not been enacted does not mean that they're not new. They are new.

### Race Relations

*Q.* Mr. President, how are you going to address the racial divisions and racial mis- understandings in this country?

*The President.* Speak out against it as I've been doing and continue to. And I think that's the best thing a President can do, speak out against bigotry and racial hatred. I believe I've been doing that over and over again, and I'll keep doing it.

### U.N. Conference on Environment

*Q.* The Secretary-General of the U.N. Is here today. Have you decided to go to Rio? Are you going to tell him that you're going to Rio?

*The President.* Stay tuned. We'll talk about that when I see him.

### Cooperation With Congress

*Q.* Sir, will you be listening to the Demo- cratic proposals as well? I know some match, but——

*The President.* Yes, some match. And cer- tainly what we want to do is find common ground and move this country forward. And I think we've got to do that, Helen [Helen Thomas, United Press International].

### HOPE

*Q.* Can you give us a little more detail on number two?

*The President.* Homeownership?

*Q.* Yes.

*The President.* Well, it's just simply a question of encouraging people to own their own homes instead of building more projects. You know, some accuse us of pull- ing back on housing funds. That is not cor- rect. Now, we don't believe that building these projects is the answer. We want to see the money going into tenant management and homeownership.

Thank you all very much. We've got to get ready for the meeting.

### Philadelphia and Los Angeles

*Q.* How did you like Philadelphia? Pretty bad, huh?

*The President.* Interesting, though. Golly, I like the spirit of the people. But yes, the last part was more desolate than the first part. But the first part showed that the police getting involved like that made a tre- mendous difference on the drug fight. The message was very, very encouraging and upbeat. We would go out into these satellite precinct stations, and it was wonderful.

Incidentally, in here I have not talked about the things we have done in terms of dollars for Los Angeles up to now, some $600 million-plus, not counting the law en- forcement part of that. So there's a substan- tial amount of money going into L.A. that I——

*Q.* Do you think, though, that the riots are going to at least make it more possible for these programs to be accepted?

*The President.* I hope so. I think so. Yes, I do, because I think people are saying we've got to do something new. And I hear that from both sides of the aisle, so we'll see.

### Cooperation With Congress

*Q.* Are you willing to meet the Demo- crats halfway, sir, compromise?

*The President.* I don't know what that means. I'm willing to try to get some new programs going, and these are the ones I'm going to push. So I don't know what half- way is on a proposal like that.

*Q.* Is this a new, new you?

*The President.* No, same me. [*Laughter*] Actually, it's not a bad way to do it.

*Q.* You like being conciliatory, don't you?

*The President.* I've always been that way, Helen; you've known that for years.

*Note: The President spoke at 9:35 a.m. in the Oval Office at the White House, prior to a meeting with congressional leaders. Part of this exchange could not be verified because the tape was incomplete.*

## Remarks and an Exchange With Reporters Prior to Discussions With United Nations Secretary-General Boutros Boutros-Ghali
*May 12, 1992*

*The President.* Let me just say first how delighted I am to see the Secretary-General again, and also perhaps the world's most renowned international environmentalist, Mr. Maurice Strong, whom I've known for many, many years.

I want to take this opportunity to say that I will be going to Rio, to the important meeting there. I think that we have a big stake. I take great pride in the fact that, in many ways, the U.S. has been a leader for environmental matters. I'm convinced that we can have jobs and economic growth as well as sound economic environmental practice. I will be taking the U.S. message to Rio to that end. And I'm very pleased that it's been worked out. And I called the President of Brazil a few minutes ago, Fernando Collor, who is most interested in this. But I'm grateful to both of you. And we have lots to talk about, but I did want to get that message out.

*Q.* How long will you stay? Will you go for the whole meeting?

*The President.* Well, no, I couldn't possibly do that. We have an election on in the United States this year and plus some other pressing problems.

*Q.* Are you involved?

*The President.* No, it's a very complicated—and I explained that to Brazil's President, my dear friend, and I think he understands it. But we haven't actually picked a date. We can talk, I guess, if there's one that seems better than others. But I won't be able to stay long. We'll have representation there, good, high-level, strong representation, but I'm very pleased that it's been worked out so that I can be a part of this important meeting.

*Q.* Mr. President, after your meeting with congressional leaders, are you encouraged that compromises can be found quickly?

*The President.* Well, I was talking to Marlin about it, and I understand that the spirit that was in that room, a spirit of "let's

get something done," was reflected in the statements afterwards. And let's hope that we can move forward.

Now, I don't want to take any more questions in here because we've got a lot to talk about with the U.N. Secretary-General.

But let me just say before we close off those machines, in my view he came into the United Nations at a very difficult time, but also perhaps the most challenging time in its history as it begins to fulfill its mission in not just the social and economic side that Maurice Strong's been so active in but in the political side. I'm talking about peacekeeping, peacemaking. And he is off to a fantastic start, and I want to work with him to see where the United States can be as cooperative as possible with the United Nations. They're doing a lot of things that benefit mankind in both the economic and social council, all those agenda items, and now in this very important peacekeeping, beginning to fulfill the dream of the founders, and that's very, very important.

*Q.* Does that mean you're going to give them some more money?

*The President.* Well, I don't know, Sarah [Sarah McClendon, McClendon News Service]. You've got a price tag on everything. I'm going to tell him we don't have all the money we'd like.

*Q.* Is the accord watered down so much that they say it's so filled with ambiguities now that——

*The President.* Oh, I don't think so. They've got a broad agenda for this Conference, and people have been focusing on one part of it. But we've got lots to talk about down there.

Thank you all very much.

*Note: The President spoke at 11:35 a.m. in the Oval Office. In his remarks, he referred to Maurice Strong, Secretary General of the U.N. Conference on Environment and Development.*

## Statement on Attending the United Nations Conference on Environment and Development in Rio de Janeiro, Brazil
*May 12, 1992*

I have just informed President Collor of Brazil, U.N. Secretary-General Boutros-Ghali, and Maurice Strong, Secretary General of the U.N. Conference on Environment and Development (UNCED), that I will attend the Rio Conference in early June. Today's environmental problems are global, and every nation must help in solving them.

As the U.S. has demonstrated over more than two decades, protecting the environment and encouraging economic growth can go hand in hand. In fact, it is our conviction that they must go hand in hand. In the early 1980's, we phased out leaded gasoline. Other countries are now looking to follow suit. We phased out aerosol propellants as early as 1978, and this year we announced that we will phase out all CFC's by the end of 1995. In the last 3 years, we have worked to extend that record, signing a new Clean Air Act and an Oil Pollution Act, placing a moratorium on oil and gas drilling in areas off our coasts, investing in our national parks, launching a program to plant a billion trees a year, and enforcing our environmental laws to make the polluter pay.

Abroad, the U.S. has worked hard to promote responsible environmental policies through our bilateral aid programs and through the World Bank and the U.N. system. I believe our decades-long experience in developing and implementing economically sound policies can help others in improving the environment.

In Rio, world leaders will have before them a number of documents. One of those documents will be a framework convention on climate change which was concluded successfully this past weekend. We are pleased with the outcome, and I congratulate the negotiators for joining together in taking this historic step. This framework convention would not impede economic growth and our ability to create new jobs.

Climate change is only one subject to be addressed at Rio. It is vitally important that progress be made as well in protecting our oceans and living marine resources, in promoting openness and public participation in environmental decision-making, in promoting sound management and protection of the world's forests and biodiversity, and many other areas.

I look forward to discussing how all nations, working together, can ensure that we hand over to our children and grandchildren a healthy and safe planet.

## Statement by Press Secretary Fitzwater on the President's Meeting with United Nations Secretary-General Boutros Boutros-Ghali
*May 12, 1992*

The President met with United Nations Secretary-General Boutros Boutros-Ghali today for an hour and a half. The President informed the Secretary-General of his decision to attend the United Nations Conference on Environment and Development (UNCED) in Rio de Janeiro in June. The President stated his strong support for U.N. peacekeeping operations worldwide. The two leaders reviewed the situation in Bosnia, Cyprus, Somalia, and in other regions.

The President and the Secretary-General also agreed on the importance of complete Iraqi compliance with all relevant United Nations Security Council resolutions, particularly those concerning the elimination of weapons of mass destruction. They reaffirmed that Libya must comply with U.N. Security Council resolutions as well.

## Remarks at a Ceremony Honoring Small Business Administration Award Winners
*May 12, 1992*

Please be seated, and welcome. On perhaps the most beautiful day we've had here in the Rose Garden, I want to welcome all of you. Single out our Secretary of the Treasury, standing up here with me; Boyden Gray, my Counsel; and of course, Pat Saiki, the SBA Administrator, who's back from a very good mission, well-executed mission to a very troubling scene in Los Angeles. Pat runs the SBA, and she was with me out there in L.A. as we surveyed what can be done to help the city, and she's moving out on that. Let me also welcome our new Chief Counsel for Advocacy, Tom Kerester, right over here. Welcome, sir. And also single out Shirley Peterson, the Commissioner at IRS. Shirley? And next to her is the Deputy Secretary of the Treasury, John Robson. Welcome, sir.

It's hard on this Small Business Day not to think of the thousands of small business people who suffered damage out there in Los Angeles. And my commitment to them is this: We are working to get whatever disaster assistance the Federal Government can provide into their hands in record time. They have suffered enough. And I'm trying to make sure that frustration with redtape and bureaucratic stumbling doesn't add to their troubles. I know the SBA has been out there in the forefront of this effort working with our task force that we put together under the able leadership of David Kearns and Al DelliBovi.

As you know, today I called the congressional leaders of both parties to the White House. And I'm pleased with the early results of our efforts to forge a bipartisan basis and from which to support the opportunity agenda for America's inner cities. It's a promising start, and we will push ahead.

We're here today because it is Small Business Week. And we have with us from all 50 States and beyond the Small Business Persons of the Year. Welcome to the White House, America's ultimate mom-and-pop operation. [*Laughter*]

I computed this a while back, and I've spent 50 percent of my adult life in the private sector and 50 percent in Government. And I started in small business out there in west Texas. And I thus know something of what you all go through in starting something from scratch, working with it night and day, and then hoping that you succeed. Success goes to those who work hard, refuse to give up, and learn from their mistakes. Pat was telling me of the remarkable record of the winners that we have here with us today.

I also know what it's like to cope with regulation and paperwork from the Government. And sometimes the bureaucracy makes things needlessly complicated. We're supposed to serve the taxpayers in the same way the business has to serve its customers. So making things needlessly complex in Government is not only wrong, it is bad for business.

And so today, we're going to do something about that. To honor these outstanding business people, we're going to do something outstanding for small businesses across the country. Every business man and woman sitting here can tell you how burdensome it is to comply with IRS payroll tax rules. And if they can't tell you, it's because they're probably paying somebody else to cope with all the headaches for them. But today the IRS is implementing faster, cheaper, and simpler ways for businesses, large and small, to deal with the payroll tax system.

This week, the IRS will issue a proposed rule to reduce the complicated deposit schedule. Large companies will be able to make payroll tax deposits on a fixed day of the week. Moreover, as many as 75 percent of all businesses will make payments just once a month. Now, these simplifications will significantly reduce the cost, confusion, and complexity of the payroll tax system.

We're also moving forward to eliminate all the duplicate W–2 forms and other payroll tax information that employers have been required to supply. We're working to set up a single wage-reporting system so that separate forms don't have to be sent to the IRS and then the Departments of Labor and Social Security, and State and local governments.

In June, an experimental program in Georgia, South Carolina, and Florida will let employers make tax payments electronically, without even leaving their office. And no more paper coupons to file or standing in line at the bank. Small business learned long ago that computers could do more work in less time for less cost. And it's time we, therefore, bring the Government out of the horse-and-buggy era, into the information age, and stop having business do the Government's paperwork. [*Applause*] I felt that would go over reasonably well here.

The IRS may not be—with all respect, Commissioner—the most popular agency in town. But look, they're working hard now not to be the most infuriating agency in town. And we have a new, able leader and some very able people dedicated to that end. Last month, the IRS Center in Ogden, Utah, won our award, the President's Award for Quality, which goes to the Government office that provides excellent public service in a cost-effective manner. It is this new kind of attitude in Government service that must be brought to every Federal bureaucracy: putting people first, treating taxpayers as customers.

Now, there's a man who knows what I'm talking about. The small business winners here know, also, what I'm talking about. James Fleming, where is he now? Right here, sir. James Fleming started his metal component business in his basement, and he turned it into a $15 million international business. Jim's designed everything from medical equipment used in hip replacements to an assembly line for Jiffy Pop popcorn. And Richard Stewart, Mr. Stewart, right here, turned a part-time hobby selling natural spices into America's largest supplier of bulk herbs, spices, gourmet coffee, and tea to the natural foods industry.

And then there's Amelia McCoy. Amelia?

Right here, sitting here. Her business began, I'm told, as an act of love, making hair ribbons for her granddaughters. And now the hairbows that her company sells are handmade by 450 people in rural Oklahoma who work at home and generate $5 million in sales. And for that, Amelia is this year's Small Business Person of the Year. Maybe you should stand up so everybody can see you.

Since I announced our new moratorium on new regulations in January, our administration has worked to reduce the burden Government places on the businesses of this country. And we've also looked at existing regulations, like the ones I spoke of today, to see now we could help the economy by eliminating or by simplifying regulations that impede economic growth for no good reason. And I'm sure Amelia would rather be tying a red ribbon for her granddaughter than spending all day untying redtape. So maybe this will help out.

Every business dollar that goes into complying with some Government mandate is a dollar that won't be spent hiring new workers. Two-thirds or more of the new jobs in this country, two-thirds, are created by small business. And you are the heart and soul of what makes this economy work and what makes the American dream possible for your employees and for their families.

I will do my level-best, working with the officials I've introduced here today and others, to keep Government under control and out of your way so you can go out and do what you do best, create jobs, create goods and services for the American people.

So, thank you all for being here. Again, my congratulations to the winner. And may God bless our great country on this beautiful day. Thank you so much.

*Note: The President spoke at 3:05 p.m. in the Rose Garden at the White House. In his remarks, he referred to David T. Kearns, Deputy Secretary of Education, and Alfred A. DelliBovi, Deputy Secretary of Housing and Urban Development.*

## Message to the Senate Transmitting 1987 Partial Revision of the Radio Regulations
### May 12, 1992

*To the Senate of the United States:*

With a view to receiving the advice and consent of the Senate to ratification, I transmit herewith the Partial Revision of the Radio Regulations (Geneva, 1979) signed on behalf of the United States at Geneva on October 17, 1987, and the United States reservations and statement as contained in the Final Protocol. I transmit also, for the information of the Senate, the report of the Department of State with respect to the 1987 Partial Revision.

The 1987 Revision constitutes a partial revision of the Radio Regulations (Geneva 1979), to which the United States is a party. The primary purpose of the present revision is to update the existing regulations pertaining to the mobile radio services to take into account technical advances and the rapid growth of these services, and to implement the Global Maritime Distress and Safety System. The revised regulations, with the two exceptions noted below, are consistent with the positions taken by the United States at the 1987 World Administrative Radio Conference for the Mobile Services.

At the time of signature, the United States submitted two reservations and responded to a statement submitted by Cuba directed at U.S. use of radio frequencies in Guantanamo. The specific reservations and statement are addressed in the report of the Department of State.

Most of the Partial Revision of the Radio Regulations entered into force October 3, 1989, for governments that, by that date, had notified the Secretary General of the International Telecommunication Union of their approval thereof; provisions specifically related to the maritime mobile service in the high frequency bands entered into force on July 1, 1991.

I believe that the United States should, subject to the reservations mentioned above, become a party to the 1987 Partial Revision, which has the potential to improve mobile radio-communications worldwide. It is my hope that the Senate will take early action on this matter and give its advice and consent to ratification.

GEORGE BUSH

The White House,
May 12, 1992.

## Statement by Press Secretary Fitzwater on Proposed Extension of the Emergency Unemployment Compensation Program
### May 12, 1992

The President and the congressional Republican leadership jointly announced a proposal to extend the Emergency Unemployment Compensation Program from the current expiration date of July 4, 1992, to March 6, 1993. Senate Republican leader Bob Dole, Senator Bob Packwood, and House Republican leader Bob Michel joined the President in announcing the extension.

The proposal would continue the payment of a total of 46 weeks of benefits (which includes 20 weeks of extended bene-

fits in high unemployment States) and 39 weeks of benefits (which includes 13 weeks of extended benefits in all other States) until January 2, 1993. Thereafter, these extended benefits would be paid for 10 weeks and 7 weeks until March 1, 1993. Total costs of the new benefits are estimated to be $2.5 billion. These costs would be fully paid for by offsets contained in the President's 1993 budget.

Further, the proposal directs that Advisory Council on Unemployment Compensation to study and make recommendations on permanent unemployment compensation reforms by February 1, 1993.

As previously announced, workers who are unemployed as a result of the disturbances in Los Angeles and who may not qualify for standard unemployment benefits will be receiving unemployment benefits through the Disaster Unemployment Assistance Program.

The President stated, "I urge the Congress to join us in setting aside partisan politics and moving expeditiously to pass this extension so that unemployed workers will know they can count on these benefits as the economy begins to recover."

## Statement by Press Secretary Fitzwater on the President's Meeting With Prime Minister Patrick Manning of Trinidad and Tobago
*May 12, 1992*

The President met this afternoon with Prime Minister Patrick Manning of Trinidad and Tobago. The President congratulated him on his plans to further liberalize Trinidad and Tobago's economy by removing import restrictions and promoting privatization. He praised Prime Minister Manning's coordinated counternarcotics strategy and thanked him for his quick action in addressing the drug problem. The Prime Minister expressed his appreciation to the President for the support of the United States and reaffirmed his commitment to economic reforms and a strong counternarcotics effort.

## Nomination of Marilyn McAfee To Be United States Ambassador to Guatemala
*May 12, 1992*

The President today announced his intention to nominate Marilyn McAfee, of Florida, a career member of the Senior Foreign Service, class of Minister-Counselor, to be Ambassador to the Republic of Guatemala. She would succeed Thomas F. Stroock.

Since 1989, Ms. McAfee has served as Deputy Chief of Mission at the U.S. Embassy in La Paz, Bolivia. Prior to this, she served as Counselor of Public Affairs at the U.S. Embassy in Santiago, Chile, 1986–89; and in Caracas, Venezuela, 1983–86.

Ms. McAfee graduated from the University of Pennsylvania (B.A., 1961) and Johns Hopkins University (M.A.T., 1962). She was born January 23, 1940, in Portsmouth, NH. Ms. McAfee resides in Jacksonville, FL.

## Nomination of Robert F. Goodwin To Be United States Ambassador to New Zealand and Western Samoa
*May 12, 1992*

The President today announced his intention to nominate Robert F. Goodwin, of Maryland, to be Ambassador to New Zealand and to serve concurrently and without additional compensation as Ambassador to Western Samoa. He would succeed Della M.

Newman.

From 1977 to 1991, Mr. Goodwin served as staff vice president and director of governmental affairs at the Meredith Corp. in Washington, DC. In addition, he has served as a U.S. Commissioner on the International Joint Commission, United States and Canada, 1990 to present.

Mr. Goodwin graduated from Northwestern University (B.S., 1958). He was born August 11, 1936, in Des Moines, IA. Mr. Goodwin served in the U.S. Air Force Reserves, 1959–65. He is married, has three children, and resides in Bethesda, MD.

# Nomination of David J. Dunford To Be United States Ambassador to Oman
## May 12, 1992

The President today announced his intention to nominate David J. Dunford, of Arizona, to be Ambassador Extraordinary and Plenipotentiary of the United States of America to the Sultanate of Oman. He would succeed Richard Wood Boehm.

Since 1988, Mr. Dunford has served as Deputy Chief of Mission at the U.S. Embassy in Riyadh, Saudi Arabia. Prior to this, he served as Office Director of the Office of Egyptian Affairs at the Bureau of Near East and South Asian Affairs at the Department of State, 1984–87.

Mr. Dunford graduated from the Massachusetts Institute of Technology (B.S., 1964) and Stanford University (M.A., 1965; M.A., 1976). He was born February 24, 1943, in Glen Ridge, NJ. Mr. Dunford is married, has two children, and resides in Tucson, AZ.

# Remarks at the Arrival Ceremony for President Patricio Aylwin of Chile
## May 13, 1992

Friends of Chile and the United States and ladies and gentlemen. President Aylwin, I'm honored to welcome you to the White House, an opportunity not only to exchange views but to return that wonderfully warm hospitality that I received in Chile.

Mr. President, you once described Chile's success in this way: "The reflection of a mature country that knows what it wants and is able to achieve it by means of the democratic process."

Well, that maturity has been hard won; Americans shared your pain during some dark days in Chile when democracy was a fading dream and peace a faded hope. But it has been won. Today, your government serves its people and serves as a model to others. The same may be said of your leadership. Since taking office, you have revived Chilean democracy. In 1913, Teddy Roosevelt visited Chile and spoke of a "democratic experiment on a far vaster scale than has ever been attempted anywhere else in the world." Next month, your people will salute that experiment through Chile's first local elections in 20 years.

And democracy has also spurred your economy. Chile has married a free people with free markets, a union that has resulted in faster economic growth than any other economy in Latin America over the last decade. A successful conclusion to the Uruguay round of GATT will enhance that trend. Already, your trade barriers are falling, your exports rising. As a member of the Cairns Group, you've led the way against agricultural subsidies and protectionism. The United States and Chile are two of the world's foremost proponents of free trade, and we look forward to working with you to expand bilateral and global trade as rapidly as possible.

I applaud your achievements, and so did the Inter-American Development Bank, turning first to Chile to implement its investment policy support program. Under our Enterprise for the Americas Initiative, Chile was first to have a portion of its official debt to the United States forgiven because we want democracy to succeed. Not only do our people share what your government called the "community of ideas, of feelings and needs," we share this land. We share more than the New World; we share a responsibility to keep our world new. So, last February, under the Enterprise for the Americas Initiative, we signed an agreement helping Chile create an environmental project fund with money which would have otherwise serviced debt.

And we will continue to address bilateral economic concerns under our 1990 trade and investment framework agreement. Our challenge now is to build on those beginnings and show why Bernardo O'Higgins, Chile's great champion of freedom, wrote, "The Americans are giving great hope to philosophers and patriots alike."

Today, Chile gives hope to an entire hemisphere. With market-oriented reforms, you've led by example. In international relations, you're leading through integrity. Other nations count on Chilean leadership

in the Organization of American States, in the United Nations, and then in the community of nations. Your people are working for peace and freedom in Kuwait, El Salvador, Guatemala, and Cambodia. You joined your neighbors to defend democracy, first at last year's OAS General Assembly, then most recently in Haiti, Peru, and Venezuela.

There's a poem called Machado's "Caminante." There's one line that stands out, and here it is: "Traveler, there is no road, you make a road in traveling." Mr. President, I believe Chile is that traveler, traveling the road of history, a history made one step at a time. Chile offers an eloquent rebuke to those enemies of democracy on the extremes of left or right who try to mislead and confuse the people. Chile shows how liberty can not only shape a nation of great promise but ensure its people a legacy of promises kept.

So, traveling together, Mr. President, we will keep our promises, and we will make ours a road to a better tomorrow. We are honored to welcome you to Washington as our guest, one of this hemisphere's truly great leaders. Welcome, sir.

*Note: The President spoke at 10:13 a.m. on the South Lawn at the White House. In his remarks, he referred to the Cairns Group, a 13-nation group supporting agricultural trade liberalization and free market policies in the Uruguay round of multilateral trade negotiations.*

# Remarks to the Health Care and Business Community in Baltimore, Maryland
*May 13, 1992*

Thank you, Dr. Heyssel, for that introduction. I understand that you'll be retiring in a few weeks as CEO of Johns Hopkins Health System, after 20 years of building bridges with this marvelous community. I got briefed on this, and I'm told that you'll leave a great legacy, that new outpatient clinic which bears your name and opens for business on Monday, a well-deserved tribute

to a great man.

We also have with us today my top adviser on health and our head of HHS, Dr. Lou Sullivan; where's Lou? Right over behind me—who you met earlier on. But I just want to say what a joy it is to have him at my side as we try to come up with better answers for America's health care. He's doing a superb job there. And I want to single out also another that has been at my side all day and is an awful lot of the time, that I have great respect for, and that's Governor Schaefer, the Governor of your State, who is with us here today. We also have several members of the legislature, the city council from Baltimore. I'm glad to see Mr. Winters, an old friend who's CEO of the Prudential. And he's been to the White House to discuss the future of our Nation's health care with me. And then of course, Barbara Hill, you'll get around her for about 5 minutes, and you're semi-exhausted. The energy and the enthusiasm that she brings to this health plan is simply contagious. I have a much better feeling what it's all about just by being around Barbara Hill. Thank you very much for a great day.

I don't know whether it's appropriate or not to be discussing medical care here at Dunbar, the home of the Dunbar Poets, but nevertheless, to all at Dunbar, my sincere thanks. And with their unbeaten streak, maybe Pete Pompey should become my adviser on health care as well as on fitness. [*Laughter*]

But I was interested to hear about the school's cooperative health studies with Johns Hopkins, which is not only on a summit in Baltimore but is at the summit of medical excellence for our whole country. It's terrific that nearly 20 percent of Dunbar's student body is involved in this health studies program, 20 percent. And I also want to recognize another institution that calls Dunbar home, Sojourner-Douglass College, for its strong commitment to the Baltimore community.

Before sharing with you a few observations on health care, let me just touch on an issue that I know is of concern to all Americans, everyone concerned about conditions particularly in America's inner cities, with special reference in these remarks to Los Angeles. In addition to FEMA, the emergency management, and to SBA, the Small Business Administration's assistance, the Federal Home Loan Bank System is going to make available $600 million to finance the rebuilding of housing and businesses in Los Angeles. These loans, made through the Community Investment Programs, are good news for the people who lost homes and

jobs as well as the owners who lost businesses due to the unrest out there. It's one way that we can underscore the fact that we are serious about helping Los Angeles recover. I think the Nation is focusing on how well all levels of government come to bear on helping in the recovery and the re-stimulation of the community there in Los Angeles.

Beyond our urgent emergency aid, we have got to take action to bring hope and opportunity to Los Angeles. But it's not just Los Angeles, it is to all American cities. Yesterday we had a good meeting with the congressional leaders, Republican and Democrat. We outlined, or I did, a six-point plan for a new America: Our "Weed and Seed" crime initiative, weed out the criminals, seed the neighborhoods so that you can have hope and opportunity there. Our HOPE initiative, it's a homeownership, housing initiative. I think enterprise zones we've heard a lot of talk about, but when we were out in California, the community leaders all urged that we try this concept of enterprise zones to attract like a magnet, draw business and opportunity into the communities. Fourth, and a little longer run answer, is education reform. I'm kind of preaching to the choir right here in Dunbar on that one because there's an awful lot of innovation going on in Baltimore in the schools and in Maryland generally. But education reform is essential. Welfare reform, I think, is essential. And then, of course, a strong jobs program for city youth across the country.

So these are the ingredients or the tools that we are going to try to work with. I'd like to use this opportunity to report to the American people that yesterday's meeting put partisanship aside, and I am very hopeful that we can get something done for this country. I am pleased with the early reaction, as I say, but now the thing is to follow up and push ahead.

Now, to the reason that's brought us all together. I really had a wonderful experience here spending some time four blocks over in the East Baltimore Medical Center. It is a terrific example for the rest of the country. And the rest of the country can follow this example. It's based on a special kind of public-private partnership, and the kind that we've been advocating, in this case among Johns Hopkins, the Pru, the Prudential Insurance Company, the State of Maryland, and the Federal Government. It's that broad a partnership.

This problem-solving partnership advances what's known as coordinated care, the future of health care in this country. Thanks to this partnership, this is the largest, the largest and fastest growing HMO in Maryland. It was there, 8 years ago, that Hopkins helped pioneer the concept of a Medicaid HMO. And it's great to see EBMC's success because it proves what I strongly believe, that we can meet the challenge of controlling health care costs while providing the finest quality service. When I think of Johns Hopkins, I think of the quality of medical care, the quality of research, and we must not adopt a plan that diminishes the quality of American health care. So I congratulate you. For while this HMO saves members, employers and government money, health care stays first-rate, and it's a great example.

The key to this center's success, especially for Medicaid patients, is that coordinated health care makes creative approaches possible. It provides quality care at lower cost with an emphasis on, and we saw it right there, prevention. It's just plain common sense. We're better off keeping people healthy rather than treating them after they're sick.

Just Monday, Lou Sullivan and I met with some leaders on our effort to improve infant health and immunization. There's nothing that makes the case for coordinated care like seeing these healthy kids. Preventive medicine improves the quality of life for patients and certainly saves a lot of unnecessary expenditures. Coordinated care can work for all Americans. But it's especially important for Medicaid recipients. It ensures they get care when they need it, where they need it, and that they get it in a cost-effective way. EBMC proves this is a viable alternative to the opposite of coordinated care, that fee-for-service system.

It also means better care for a kid who steps on a rusty nail out on Orleans Street. Before belonging to a coordinated care center, he would have gone to Hopkins emergency room. They'd be seeing him for the first time so they wouldn't know his background; they wouldn't know if he'd had a tetanus shot or if he were allergic to, say, penicillin. They'd have to spend that time and money doing unnecessary tests, maybe double treatment. But now when he shows up at his center's urgent care unit, they just check his history and treat him faster and at a fraction of the cost.

I am excited to see so many pieces of this comprehensive health reform program that we are promoting already successfully at work right here at EBMC. I introduced a plan February 6 to address the twin challenges of expanding access and of containing cost, while building on the strengths of this present health care system. I was determined to treat the root causes of our problems, not just the symptoms. Above all, our plan is inspired by the words of physician Frederick Banting, "You must begin with an ideal and end with an ideal."

In the greatest, most technologically advanced Nation on the face of the Earth, there is no reason that one of seven Americans has no health insurance. And what we must do is clear. We must guarantee every American access, access to affordable health insurance.

Let's face it. We are in a peculiar year, in an election year, when all kinds of crazy things happen out there. And it seems like everyone's got a prescription for health care. And yes, people want quality care they can afford and rely on. But we don't need to put the Government between the patients and their doctors. And we don't need to build a whole new Federal bureaucracy. We need commonsense, comprehensive health care reform, and we need to start on it right now.

Sure, the other approaches can sound great, but you've got to look at what you really get. National health insurance, believe me, means more taxes, long lines, long waiting lists, and here's a matter of great concern to people that are in this area of excellence, lower quality care. Their idea for cost control is flat out what you call price fixing, an idea we know just simply will not work. Look at Medicare, which adopts set prices for many seniors' health services. But Medicare inflation far out-stripped private health care inflation in the seventies and the eighties, and it is still growing at 12 percent. The national rate of inflation, thank heavens, is far below 12 percent, and cost containment is not its strong suit. Price fixing by Congress has never worked before, and in my view, it simply will not work.

The so-called—we were talking about this coming in over in the car—the so-called "play or pay" approach, in my view, is equally unsound. Even many proponents admit that it will melt down into national health insurance within a few years. It does nothing to address the cost problem, where patients don't know or care how much health plans cost, nothing except to once again try to fix the prices. It's a package full of empty promises. Our comprehensive reform plan is based on these commonsense principles: Competition, consumer choice, quality, I come back to that, and efficiency.

Now while most people in this country are provided the highest quality health care in the world, millions of others are unin-sured. And those are the ones we've got to worry about. They are the ones that must be covered. And we must make people aware of the costs and varying quality of care, so they'll be better consumers. But there will always be a limit to how cost-sensitive we can make people. When a kid falls off a bike or cracks his head, not many parents question the cost of a CAT scan or an MRI; their kid's health is too precious to bargain over.

So the competitive answer must be to group our consumers together. We must combine small employers, who often pay the bills, and individuals into large, educat-ed, informed purchasing groups that can drive efficiencies back into the health care system. These health insurance networks are going to pool, what we call pooling. They will pool consumer information. They will pool risk, and they will pool purchasing power to make the system more responsive to the demands of the consumer. Our plan will dramatically reform our market-based system. It will ensure that quality care is within reach of every American family, and it will preserve choice. It will keep costs down, and we believe that it will keep

access up.

First, the plan will cut the runaway costs of health care by making the system more efficient. We'll call for innovative approach-es like the one we see here in east Balti-more. Secondly, it will wring out waste and excess. Third, it will control Federal growth, since health care is the fastest growing part of the Federal budget. And fourth, my plan will make health care more accessible by making it more affordable. We'll provide up to $3,750 in health insur-ance credit or deductions for low- and middle-income families—they have to use that to purchase insurance—and guarantee access to insurance for all low-income Americans. These credits, combined with market reforms, will bring health insurance to approximately 30 million now uninsured Americans.

Maryland is already getting on board this voucher approach with bipartisan legisla-tion. The Maryland State House, I'm told, has outlined a standard health package to cover all low-income Marylanders through tax credits. The proposal to implement this tax credit plan passed the house a few weeks ago and is being reviewed in the legislature this year. Under my plan, this type of low-income credit would be avail-able in all States, and Maryland would have the ability and financial help it needs to make this reform into a living reality.

I've proposed the most comprehensive health care package out there. And now is the time to challenge the Congress and to see if it's interested in this kind of real reform. Ours is a plan that will fundamen-tally restructure, and this is the point, re-structure health care in America.

There are steps we can and must take right now. Part of our plan entails signifi-cant reform of the insurance markets, for which there is a strong bipartisan support. Senator Bentsen, Chairman Dan Rosten-kowski of the Ways and Means Committee, Senate Republicans, the House Republican task force all support very similar reforms that with certain changes, some modifica-tion, can and should be passed immediately. Congress must begin to move now. Even if all they do this year is just pass our insur-ance market reform, we'll at least get a start on changing the system. These reforms will go a long way toward curing the inequities in cost and coverage under existing health insurance practices.

There's another bipartisan reform package out there. It was proposed by Senator Pat Moynihan and Senator Dave Durenberger, and that is in most respects consistent, it is, with my plan and would promote much greater use of coordinated care in Medicaid. East Baltimore knows that this works. We must make it easier for the rest of the country to follow your pioneering road to better health care. In fact, as part of our plan for comprehensive reform, I want to make coordinated care the norm, not the exception, for Medicaid. We must work together now to pass these reforms that will provide literally millions of Americans with affordable health coverage for the first time and then get a leg up on that comprehensive reform.

Our plan does everything the Government can and should do to ensure the quality of life of each citizen of this great land. It doesn't promise the Moon. It does something more important: It really guarantees, it promises the future. Reform is never easy, but in health care I think, wherever you're coming from, I think everybody would agree health care reform is a must. And we will deliver what we say we can, competition, competition-driven, market-based reform, and we'll deliver it proudly.

This is kind of a second unveiling of our overall program, but it seemed most appropriate to bring out these specifics here in Baltimore, an area where you've had so much innovation, so much excellence, so much success. So I just want you to know we're serious about this. We are going to continue to push for it, and we must get started right now.

I have learned a lot today, and I am very grateful to those who have shown me what is going on in this exceptional health care facility. I've always had great respect for what is going on in Johns Hopkins, this institution of excellence in every category.

So as I conclude, let me say, I am not pessimistic about our ability to help those people who need help in terms of health care. We can get the job done. I will now be trying to work with our hands extended in a nonpartisan or in a bipartisan mode to see if we can't make things a little better for the people, some of whom I saw here today.

Thank you all very much for listening. And may God bless the United States.

*Note: The President spoke at 3:30 p.m. at Paul Laurence Dunbar High School. In his remarks, he referred to Dr. Robert M. Heyssel, president, Johns Hopkins Health System; Robert C. Winter, chairman and chief executive officer, the Prudential Insurance Co.; Barbara Hill, president, Prudential Health Care Plan of the Mid-Atlantic; and Pete Pompey, athletic director and basketball coach at Dunbar High School.*

# Message to the Congress Transmitting Proposed Legislation on Youth Apprenticeship
*May 13, 1992*

*To the Congress of the United States:*

I am pleased to transmit herewith for your immediate consideration the "National Youth Apprenticeship Act of 1992." Also transmitted is a section-by-section analysis.

This legislation would establish a national framework for implementing comprehensive youth apprenticeship programs. These programs would be a high-quality learning alternative for preparing young people to be valuable and productive members of the 21st century work force. Although this framework has been designed to be comprehensive and national in scope, it is also flexible enough to allow States to customize the model to economic, demographic, and other local conditions.

I am proposing this legislation in order to

promote a comprehensive approach for helping our youth make the transition from school to the workplace and strive to reach high levels of academic achievement. The lack of such an approach is one very important reason that a significant proportion of American youth do not possess the necessary skills to meet employer requirements for entry level positions.

There is widespread agreement that the time has come to strengthen the connection between the academic subjects taught in our schools and the demands of the modern, high-technology workplace. Work-based learning models have proven to be effective approaches for preparing youth at the secondary school level.

Under my proposal, a student could enter a youth apprenticeship program in the 11th or 12th grade. Before reaching these grades, students would receive career and academic guidance to prepare them for entry into youth apprenticeship programs. Particular programs may end with graduation from high school or continue for up to an additional 2 years of postsecondary education. In addition to the high school diploma, all youth apprentices would earn a certificate of competency and qualify for a postsecondary program, a registered apprenticeship program, or employment.

A youth apprentice would receive academic instruction, job training, and work experience. The program is intended to attract and develop high-quality, motivated students. Standards of academic achievement, consistent with voluntary, national standards, will apply to all academic instruction, including the required instruction in the core subjects of English, mathematics, science, history, and geography. Students also would be expected to demonstrate mastery of job skills.

My proposal provides for vigorous involvement at the Federal, State, and local levels to ensure the success of the program. It also requires that employers, schools, students, and parents promise to work together to achieve the program goals. Enactment of my proposal will result in national standards applicable to all youth apprenticeship programs. Thus, upon completion of the program, the youth apprentice will have a portable credential that will be recognized wherever the individuals may go to seek employment or pursue further education and training.

I believe that the time has come for a national, comprehensive approach to work-based learning. The bill I am proposing would establish a formal process in which business, labor, and education would form partnerships to motivate the Nation's young people to stay in school and become productive citizens. It will provide American youth the opportunity to gain marketable and portable skills while establishing a relationship with a prospective employer.

I urge the Congress to give swift and favorable consideration to the National Youth Apprenticeship Act of 1992.

GEORGE BUSH

The White House,
May 13, 1992.

# Nomination of Joseph Charles Wilson IV To Be United States Ambassador to Gabon and Sao Tome and Principe
*May 13, 1992*

The President today announced his intention to nominate Joseph Charles Wilson IV, of California, a career member of the Senior Foreign Service, class of Counselor, to be Ambassador to the Gabonese Republic and to serve concurrently without compensation as Ambassador to the Democratic Republic of Sao Tome and Principe. He would succeed Keith Leveret Wauchope.

Currently Mr. Wilson serves as a member of the senior seminar at the Foreign Service Institute. From 1988 to 1991, he served as Deputy Chief of Mission at the U.S. Embassy in Baghdad, Iraq, and as Deputy Chief of

Mission at the U.S. Embassy in Brazzaville, Congo, 1986–88.

Mr. Wilson graduated from the University of California at Santa Barbara (B.A., 1971).

He was born November 6, 1949, in Bridgeport, CT. Mr. Wilson is married, has two children, and resides in Washington, DC.

# Nomination of John F. Daffron, Jr., To Be a Member of the Board of Directors of the State Justice Institute
*May 13, 1992*

The President today announced his intention to nominate John F. Daffron, Jr., of Virginia, to be a member of the Board of Directors of the State Justice Institute for a term expiring September 17, 1994. This is a reappointment.

Since 1982, Judge Daffron has served as a circuit court judge for the 12th judicial circuit of Virginia. Prior to this, he was a general district court judge, 1973–81, and a U.S. magistrate, 1970–73.

Judge Daffron graduated from the University of Richmond (B.A., 1961; LL.B., 1964). He was born January 25, 1939, in Richmond, VA. Judge Daffron is married, has four children, and resides in Chester, VA.

# Statement by Press Secretary Fitzwater on the President's Meeting With President Patricio Aylwin of Chile
*May 13, 1992*

In their discussions today, President Bush and President Aylwin stressed their joint commitment to free trade throughout the hemisphere as envisioned in the President's Enterprise for the Americas Initiative. President Aylwin told the President that the long-term vision of the EAI is very important to Latin America and described it as the first chance for a genuine partnership between Latin America and the United States based on free trade.

As a result of these discussions and in recognition of Chile's economic achievements, the President decided today that the United States intends to negotiate a comprehensive free trade agreement with Chile upon completion of the North American free trade agreement, and he intends to send notification to the Congress, pursuant to fast track procedures, at that time.

United States exports to Chile increased to $1.582 billion in 1991, including products such as mining machinery, computers, and telecommunications equipment.

Chile was the first in Latin America to receive bilateral debt reduction and an investment sector loan under the Enterprise for the Americas Initiative. By moving forward on free trade, Chile will be the first nation in South America to participate in the trade benefits of EAI.

The two Presidents also took note of the challenges to democratic processes in Haiti, Peru, and Venezuela and reaffirmed their strong commitment to support and defend democracy in the hemisphere through the OAS.

## Remarks at the State Dinner for President Patricio Aylwin of Chile
*May 13, 1992*

Ladies and gentlemen, President Aylwin and Mrs. Aylwin, Barbara and I are just delighted to welcome you both to the White House and to try to return the warm reception that you gave to me, sir, and to our daughter when we had the honor of visiting you in Chile.

Among my memories of my visit to your country was a lunch that we shared at that lovely home of yours in Santiago. And I still recall with pride and delight that you took in your children and your grandchildren. We did a little arithmetic yesterday, and between us, we have 10 children and 23 grandchildren. Perhaps we could arrange for a soccer game out on the South Lawn. [*Laughter*]

It has been said, Mr. President, that the greatest glory of a free-born people is to transmit that freedom to their children. Your country's bright future lies in the hands and hearts of a free-born people, determined to see their children born free, passing liberty from mother to daughter, father to son.

Today I was reminded how your father, an esteemed Supreme Court Justice, passed his love of law and liberty to his son, you, yourself a revered legal scholar. I thought of how more than 60 years ago our Louis Brandeis observed that the final end of the state was to make men free to develop their faculties. And he added that "Those who love freedom know liberty to be the secret of happiness and courage to be the secret of liberty."

Justice Brandeis could find no better example of courage in pursuit of liberty than the Chilean people and their leader. Today, Chileans are "free to develop their faculties" to the fullest, having at last inherited the political and economic rights their parents worked to achieve. They've also assumed liberty's responsibilities, the knowledge that freedom taken for granted can

become freedom taken away. Chile continues the hard work of freedom, defending democracy in Venezuela and Haiti and Peru, promoting peace in Central America and in the Middle East.

Mr. President, I know that Chile will continue to export its material goods. I know also it will export its dreams, the courage, hope, the imagination of free markets and free peoples. Chile teaches others that political differences never excuse indifference to the law and that social needs are better met by the invisible hand of the free market than by the iron fist of regulatory control and bureaucracy.

President Aylwin and I share a vision of free trade for all the hemisphere. The United States is now negotiating a free trade agreement with Mexico and Canada as a first step toward that goal. And as a result of our discussions today and in recognition of Chile's economic accomplishments and achievements, I want to announce that the United States intends to negotiate a comprehensive free trade agreement with Chile upon the conclusion of the North American free trade agreement. And I intend to send notification to the Congress in accord with the fast track procedures at that time.

Thirty years ago, President Eisenhower spoke to your people saying, "We in the Western Hemisphere are still young nations still growing, still experimenting." And I really believe that's still true today because democracy is young as our children, as all the children of the world.

Mr. President, may I propose a toast to you. And may I suggest we rise and lift our glasses: To you, Mr. President, to Mrs. Aylwin, to Chile, and to the bonds of friendship between our two people.

*Note: The President spoke at 8:13 p.m. in the State Dining Room at the White House.*

## Remarks to the Take Pride in America Volunteers
*May 14, 1992*

Let me first salute Derrick Crandall, who had a lot to do with this event and who does so much for the great outdoors, not just here but all across—whoops, look at this gigantic thing—[*laughter*]—all across the country. But I really wanted to thank the volunteers from the Recreation Coalition, members of the Recreation Roundtable for the good work you do for public lands all across our wonderful country. And I was pleased earlier to see the former Governor, Mike Hayden, Assistant Secretary for Fish, Wildlife and Parks; my old friend, John Turner, son of Wyoming here, Director of our Fish and Wildlife Service; Jim Ridenour, the Director of the National Park Service; and Bob Stanton, who's the Parks Director of the National Capital Region; and then all the other parks and officials here with us today. A very special greeting to Pervis—where did he go? You can't miss him. But there he is way back there—who does so much with the Bullets, but does so much to help the kids. And a special hello to all of you.

Let me just tell some of you kids that 70 million Americans enjoy fishing every year. And I understand that some of you were out on the river, I hope you were, trying out this sport. Of course, I didn't show up too well on the casting, but that's an important part of it and a fun part of it out there. But we have this Pathway to Fishing program that I think is a very good one.

Many of you from the Recreation Coalition were with Barbara and me when we visited some of this country's greatest fishing holes, camping sites, and hiking trails as well. We were out at Mount Rushmore, Glacier National Park, the Grand Tetons. And I hope every kid here gets a chance one day to see some of those great spots in the West. We have many other beautiful parklands across the country.

But we've got to remember that the great outdoors—and one of the things that's symbolic about this event is that the great outdoors isn't miles away and unreachable, it's close to home. And here we are in this great park right here in Anacostia. So whether you're from right here in DC or from Spirit Lake, Iowa, the great outdoors is yours for the asking, and each of you is a coowner. As coowners you've got to preserve our great parklands, keep them clean.

Since the beginning of our administration, we've added over $1 billion to help our national parks, forests, wildlife refuges, and other public lands. In this effort to preserve our environment, public-private partnerships are so important, and they help us all do our part. Practically every day, people sit and fish on the river dock just behind me, one funded by what Derrick talked about, that Wallop-Breaux Trust Fund, a program that was started in 1984 to bring together the efforts of both the fishing and the boating industries. I think he was quite generous about that, but I did have a small role in its creation and am prouder still that this year we're providing more than $240 million for this fund to aid the fishing and boating improvements. Last year we had a fight; Congress, I think, wanted to cut the Wallop-Breaux in the appropriations process. But we just can't let that happen.

Then there's our Scenic Byways program, a 6-year effort to improve some of our Nation's most traveled highways, not just the highways that you've got all across the country but roads that wind through the hearts of our cities. And we call them ribbons of green, the roads America loves. Here in Washington, our Scenic Byways program beautifies roads like the George Washington Parkway and Rock Creek Parkway. We're also helping to support the creation of greenways, those combinations of bicycles and hiking paths that are springing up throughout our cities and countrysides.

Then there are programs like the one that this banner celebrates, Take Pride in America, a program that generates tens of millions of volunteer hours each year from communities all across the country, people coming together to preserve the parks and public lands within their communities, picking up litter, planting trees, and building playgrounds for these kids.

Right now one of our public land initiatives is receiving favorable attention in Congress, the America the Beautiful Passport. This replaces that old wallet card style with a passport that would include such things as park information, helpful phone numbers, motor decal, and many, many more things. And the best part, sales proceeds could generate up to $30 million in additional revenue which would then go to fund other recreation and wildlife projects.

So as we enter summertime, and I know the kids here are counting the days until school gets out, we'll see more kids enjoy the benefits of this cleanup project today. We'll see them running off to this park, playing around on the new playground, casting the fishing lines the way John and Tom and other fishing experts taught them and shooting a few hoops the way Pervis told them to do, and learning from him and learning from the volunteers how important it is for one citizen to help another.

It's not just a kid's life, though, I'm talking about. The outdoors is a perfect playground for the entire family and this country's greatest natural resource. This summer can also be a time for lots of families, for whole communities to come together.

We all saw what happened out there in Los Angeles a couple of weeks ago, a community that was divided and torn apart and then turning on itself in despair. Already the communities within that south central L.A. are coming together. They're rebuilding; they're renewing. They're leaving the war zones behind to embrace the heart of what makes Los Angeles such a special place.

Beyond our urgent emergency aid, we've got to take action to bring hope and opportunity to Los Angeles. I don't want to go into a lot of detail here, but I met with the leaders of both sides of the aisle. We're trying to get nonpartisan or bipartisan approaches to solve the problems. We've put out a six-point program that included a "Weed and Seed," weed out the drugs, seed the neighborhoods with hope; our home-ownership initiative; enterprise zones that bring businesses into these communities that are hard hit, these cities; education reform; welfare reform; and then a strong jobs program. These six points, we're going to keep pressing for them, and I think they'll bring immediate relief to some of our cities. And I think it's a wonderful thing, if we're successful in them, to what it can mean for the lives of some of the kids right here today.

So, we've got to come together. We've got to rebuild the hearts of our Nation's cities, and we've got to renew that spirit of community. So I am just delighted to be here, very appreciative, once again, of the volunteers, those who live by that feeling one American must help another, hold out the helping hand to another. And the volunteers do it, and the result of that is cleaner and better parks, more and more hope and opportunity for the young people.

So thank you very, very much for what you're doing. It's a pleasure to be out here. I have only one regret, and that is that I can't stay out here all afternoon to do a little better in the fishing-casting tournament out there and to get to see you kids enjoy this lovely park. Thank you all very much for being with us. And again, my thanks to all the volunteers.

*Note: The President spoke at 1:22 p.m. in Anacostia Park. In his remarks, he referred to Derrick Crandall, president of the American Recreation Coalition; Pervis Ellison, Washington Bullets basketball player; and Thomas Bedell, president of Berkeley, Inc.*

# Message to the Congress Reporting on the National Emergency With Respect to Iran
*May 14, 1992*

*To the Congress of the United States:*

I hereby report to the Congress on developments since the last Presidential report on November 13, 1991, concerning the national emergency with respect to Iran that was declared in Executive Order No. 12170 of November 14, 1979, and matters relating to Executive Order No. 12613 of October 29, 1987. This report is submitted pursuant to section 204(c) of the International Emergency Economic Powers Act, 50 U.S.C. 1703(c), and section 505(c) of the International Security and Development Cooperation Act of 1985, 22 U.S.C. 2349aa–9(c). This report covers events through March 31, 1992. My last report dated November 13, 1991, covered events through September 30, 1991.

1. The Iranian Transactions Regulations ("ITRs"), 31 CFR Part 560, were amended on December 3, 1991, to further interpret the documentary requirements for obtaining a license to import Iranian-origin carpets from third countries, and to permit the importation of certain household and personal effects by persons arriving in the United States. A copy of these amendments is attached to this report. Except for minor clerical changes, the Iranian Assets Control Regulations ("IACRs"), 31 CFR Part 535, have not been amended since my last report.

2. The Office of Foreign Assets Control ("FAC") of the Department of the Treasury continues to process applications for import licenses under the ITRs. However, the December 3, 1991, amendments to the ITRs have resulted in a substantial reduction in the number of license applications received relating to the importation of nonfungible Iranian-origin goods, principally carpets, claimed to have been located outside of Iran prior to the imposition of the embargo. Those amendments have also made specific licenses unnecessary for most Iranian-origin goods permitted entry as duty-free household goods and personal effects by persons returning to the United States.

During the reporting period, the Customs Service has continued to effect numerous seizures of Iranian-origin merchandise, mostly carpets, for violation of the import prohibitions of the ITRs. FAC and Customs Service investigations of these violations have resulted in forfeiture actions and the imposition of civil monetary penalties. Numerous additional forfeiture and civil penalty actions are under review.

FAC worked closely with the Customs Service during the reporting period to further develop procedures to expeditiously dispose of cases involving the seizure of noncommercial importations of nonfungible Iranian goods by certain first-time importers. The opportunity for immediate re-exportation of such goods, under Customs supervision and upon payment of a mitigated forfeiture amount, has been made available in a greater number of cases to reduce the total cost of the violation to those importers.

3. The Iran-United States Claims Tribunal ("the Tribunal"), established at The Hague pursuant to the Algiers Accords, continues to make progress in arbitrating the claims before it. Since my last report, the Tribunal has rendered 7 awards, for a total of 528 awards. Of that total, 357 have been awards in favor of American claimants: 217 of these were awards on agreed terms, authorizing and approving payment of settlements negotiated by the parties, and 140 were decisions adjudicated on the merits. The Tribunal has issued 34 decisions dismissing claims on the merits and 80 decisions dismissing claims for jurisdictional reasons. Of the 57 remaining awards, 3 approved the withdrawal of cases and 54 were in favor of Iranian claimants. As of March 31, 1992, payments on awards to successful American claimants from the Security Account held by the NV Settlement Bank stood at $2,045,284,993.99.

As of March 31, 1992, the Security Account has fallen below the required balance of $500 million 34 times. Iran has periodically replenished the account, as required by the Algiers Accords, by transferring funds from the separate account held by the NV Settlement Bank in which interest on the Security Account is deposited. The last transfer of interest occurred on November 27, 1991, and resulted in a transfer of $26.6 million from the interest account to the Security Account. The aggregate amount that has been transferred from the interest account to the Security Account is $859,472,986.47. As noted in my last report, Iran has also replenished the Security Account with the proceeds from the sale of Iranian-origin oil imported into the United States, pursuant to transactions licensed on a case-by-case basis by FAC.

The Security Account was also increased on December 3, 1991, by an $18 million payment from the United States that was a part of the settlement of case B/1 (Claim 4). This payment brought the balance of the Security Account up to the required $500 million for the first time since June 1990. As of March 31, 1992, the total amount in the Security Account was $500,334,516.76, and the total amount in the interest account was $8,332,610.75.

4. The Tribunal continues to make progress in the arbitration of claims of U.S. nationals for $250,000.00 or more. Since the last report, six large claims have been decided, including two claims that were settled by the parties. Approximately 85 percent of the nonbank claims have now been disposed of through adjudication, settlement, or voluntary withdrawal, leaving 89 such claims on the docket. The largest of the large claims, the progress of which has been slowed by their complexity, are finally being resolved, sometimes with sizable damage awards to the U.S. claimant. Since September 30, 1991, U.S. claimants have been awarded over $4 million by the Tribunal.

5. As anticipated by the May 13, 1990, agreement settling the claims of U.S. nationals against Iran for less than $250,000.00 the Foreign Claims Settlement Commission ("FCSC") has begun its review of 3,112 claims. The FCSC has issued decisions in 460 claims, for total awards of over $8 million. The FCSC expects to complete its adjudication of the remaining claims by September 1993.

6. In coordination with concerned Government agencies, the Department of State continues to present United States Government claims against Iran, as well as responses by the United States Government to claims brought against it by Iran. Since the last report, the United States Government has settled one case with Iran, resulting in a payment to Iran of $278,000,000. As noted above, $18 million of this payment was deposited into the Security Account for replenishment purposes. The Department of State also represented the United States before the Tribunal in a case filed by an Iranian national.

7. As anticipated in my last report, after a final determination that there were no longer any bank syndicates pursuing claims against Dollar Account No. 1 at the Federal Reserve Bank of New York, appropriate steps were taken to close the account. On February 19, 1992, the remaining balance in the dollar account, $134,128.56, was transferred to Bank Markazi. On March 12, 1992, the United States and Iran filed a joint submission to the Tribunal requesting termination of Case No. A/15 (I:G), the case brought by Iran involving the syndicate claims.

8. The situation reviewed above continues to implicate important diplomatic, financial, and legal interests of the United States and its nationals, and presents an unusual challenge to the national security and foreign policy of the United States. The IACRs issued pursuant to Executive Order No. 12170 continue to play an important role in structuring our relationship with Iran and in enabling the United States to implement properly the Algiers Accords. Similarly, the ITRs issued pursuant to Executive Order No. 12613 continue to advance important objectives in combatting international terrorism. I shall continue to exercise the powers at my disposal to deal with these problems and will continue to report periodically to the Congress on significant developments.

GEORGE BUSH

The White House,
May 14, 1992.

## Message to the Congress Transmitting Proposed Legislation on Lifelong Learning
*May 14, 1992*

*To the Congress of the United States:*

I am pleased to transmit today for your immediate consideration and enactment the "Lifelong Learning Act of 1992." Also transmitted is a section-by-section analysis.

This legislation would provide to all Americans, including working men and women and the unemployed, access to grant and loan help throughout their lives that is not now available. This additional help would make it possible for more Americans to further their education and increase their job skills and productivity.

Enactment of this legislation would help move America forward in achieving National Education Goal Five: "Every adult American will be literate and will possess the knowledge and skills necessary to compete in a global economy and exercise the rights and responsibilities of citizenship."

This legislation would:

- *Extend eligibility for Pell Grants and the three Guaranteed Student Loan (GSL) programs to students studying less than half-time.* Providing grant and loan assistance to individuals taking as little as one course at a time offers American men and women the flexibility they need to improve their employment skills while recognizing their commitments to jobs and families. This program would extend loan eligibility to individuals who are enrolled in non-degree granting education and training programs and who are taking only one course at a time. These individuals have a legitimate need for skill enhancement and training that is not being met under existing loan programs. For example, a working mother in a low-wage job could receive financial assistance for courses that would qualify her for better paying, high-skilled jobs.
- *Extend new opportunities for education and training to all U.S. citizens.* Additional student loan eligibility would be available for full- or part-time

students. The Student Loan Marketing Association (Sallie Mae) would be authorized to originate up to $25,000 in loans, in addition to current GSL loan limits, through the Lifelong Learning Line of Credit for those borrowers who want the option of repaying loans on a basis tied to their actual income. The concept of basing student loan repayment on a borrower's future earnings has long been attractive to the Administration and to many in the Congress. However, a program of this type presents unique and complex design issues that demand careful analysis and structuring. This Act would call upon Sallie Mae, a leader in student loan administration, to offer $100 million per year in loans and to work with the Secretary of Education to devise actuarially and fiscally sound loan options that would be widely available.

- *Explore the use of high-quality education and training programs offered by non-school based providers.* The Secretaries of Education and Labor would be authorized to develop regulations under which students attending programs offered by nontraditional types of providers could be eligible for the Lifelong Learning Line of Credit. Community-based organizations, public or private agencies, and private employers are some examples of the types of providers that might participate. These providers could participate only if the high quality of the programs could be ensured and if these funds do not replace funds already being spent for this training.

I believe that all Americans should have an opportunity to pursue education and training throughout their lives. I look forward to working with the Congress on this legislation and welcome your recommendations on how this legislation can best secure this opportunity for all Americans.

I urge the Congress to give the Lifelong

Learning Act of 1992 prompt and favorable consideration.

GEORGE BUSH

The White House
May 14, 1992.

## Nomination of Donald Herman Alexander To Be United States Ambassador to The Netherlands
*May 14, 1992*

The President today announced his intention to nominate Donald Herman Alexander, of Missouri, to be Ambassador to the Kingdom of The Netherlands. He would succeed C. Howard Williams, Jr.

Since 1987, Mr. Alexander has served as president of the private investment firm of Don H. Alexander & Associates, Inc., in Kansas City, MO. Prior to this, he served as president of Perkins Industries, Inc., 1982–87, and as executive vice president of the Commerce Bank of Kansas City, 1966–82.

Mr. Alexander graduated from Washburn University (B.B.A., 1962). He was born July 11, 1938, in Amsterdam, The Netherlands. Mr. Alexander has three children and resides in Kansas City, MO.

## Remarks at the Law Enforcement Officers Memorial Ceremony
*May 15, 1992*

Thank you, Cyndi, very much. Thank you all. Cyndi, thank you. And may I salute our Attorney General who is doing an outstanding job for law enforcement, Bill Barr; the Members of Congress who are with us today; Adolph South; an old friend, Dewey Stokes; John Walsh; Suzie Sawyer; Barbara Dodge; Dave Derevere.

Ten years ago the FOP auxiliary began this nationally recognized service for law enforcement officers who gave their lives in the line of duty, and I salute you from the bottom of my heart. It is an honor to be with all of you to mark a day that celebrates America's finest.

Police work has been described as a thankless job. Well, I am here to say thank you on behalf of each American. We need you. We depend on you, and we cannot do without you. Yours is the priceless task of upholding good against evil. All of us saw sickening sights in Los Angeles of criminals breaking windows and burning buildings and looting businesses. But even worse was the looting of something harder to replace than merchandise, the stealing of something

precious, stealing hope, promise, the future. This we cannot allow.

You know better than anyone, it is not just a privilege to support our law enforcement officers. Standing in Mount Zion Church right in the heart of south central L.A. just a few days ago, I spoke out there in support of law enforcement, and the place erupted into spontaneous applause. The people were applauding, those most severely affected—but those were the ones that were doing this—were most severely affected by the rioting and by the looting, and they were supporting the police officers. And that's the way it should be.

So, today I pledge this to you, to that thin blue line that separates good people from the worst instincts of our society, I pledge my continuing and full support. We must show less compassion for the criminal and more for the victims of crime. That is why we reauthorized the 1984 Victims of Crime Act and boosted its annual crime victims compensation assistance fund to $150 million. These dollars did not come from the taxpayers but from the criminals' fines and penalties. After all, crime should not pay; the criminals themselves should. And my administration has also acted to punish the hardened criminals, career criminals, under the Federal Armed Career Criminal Act. No seasoned criminal should walk free because we didn't take the law and our law enforcement officers seriously.

We have proposed $15 billion for anticrime policies for fiscal year 1993, and that is up 59 percent in 4 years. We started Project Triggerlock and already thousands of gun-toting criminals have been charged, with a conviction rate of nearly 90 percent. And yet progress made is not mission accomplished. And so today I again call on the Congress to get with it and to pass our crime legislation. Let us back up our law enforcement officials with laws that are fair, that are fast, and that are final.

For more than 3 years I've asked Congress to pass a comprehensive crime package based on three simple principles: If criminals commit crimes, they will be caught; if caught, they will be tried; and if convicted, they will be punished. We need a crime bill which strengthens, not weakens, your ability to uphold our laws. And so I again appeal to the United States Congress: Send me a tough crime bill, one that will not weaken current law, one like the "Crime Control Act of 1992," and I will sign it right away.

Let me take this opportunity to salute organizations like COPS, that Concerns of Police Survivors, who provide aid when it is most needed. COPS was founded in 1984 to have survivors help other survivors, and today they help 5,000 families nationwide as Good Samaritans to those who have lost a loved one.

Another Good Samaritan can be found right up here on our stage today. I'm talking about John Walsh, host of television's "America's Most Wanted." Last Friday, the show celebrated its 200th capture of a fugitive of the law. Sadly, John knows firsthand about the horrors that crime can inflict upon parents and families and communities. His little boy, Adam, was abducted and murdered, and the killer has never been

found. John could have shut himself off from the world. Instead he started "America's Most Wanted," a show that helps law enforcement officers bring criminals to justice. John, we salute both what you are and what you do. Thank you. Thank you very, very much.

Let me close on a personal note. Some have called the Presidency the world's toughest job. Well, I think they're wrong. I believe police officers have the toughest job. Police work is not 9 to 5; it's full time. It is danger. It is fear. It is not knowing whether you will end your shift going home in a car or to the emergency room in an ambulance. It's populated by people willing to risk their lives to save ours, people who are part social worker and part soldier. It's a job that I sum up in two words: American hero.

Every day of every year you risk your lives so that Americans can proceed with theirs. You truly show what the Bible meant, "Greater love hath no man than this, that a man lay down his life for his friends." I still have with me this badge. This is the badge of a fallen police officer, a New York cop that many of you all knew, Eddie Byrne. I keep it right there in my desk in the Oval Office. It's there every single day to remind me of this Nation's debt to those who serve. I will never forget, nor will our Nation.

Thank you for what you do for our country. May God bless each and every one of you officers, and especially may God bless those families who have lost loved ones as those loved ones served our great Nation. Thank you all very, very much.

*Note: The President spoke at 10:15 a.m. at the Sylvan Theater. In his remarks, he referred to Cyndi Calendar, auxiliary president, Fraternal Order of Police; Adolph South, chaplain, National Fraternal Order of Police; Dewey Stokes, president, Grand Lodge Fraternal Order of Police; Suzie Sawyer, founder, and Barbara Dodge, president, Concerns of Police Survivors; and Dave Derevere, International Police Chaplains.*

# Letter to Congressional Leaders Reporting on Iraq's Compliance With United Nations Security Council Resolutions
## *May 15, 1992*

*Dear Mr. Speaker: (Dear Mr. President:)*

Consistent with the Authorization for Use of Military Force Against Iraq Resolution (Public Law 102–1), and as part of my continuing effort to keep the Congress fully informed, I am again reporting on the status of efforts to obtain compliance by Iraq with the resolutions adopted by the U.N. Security Council.

Since the events described in my report of March 16, 1992, the U.N. Security Council has rejected Iraq's contention that it was in compliance with the relevant Security Council resolutions. On March 19, 1992, Rolf Ekeus, Chairman of the United Nations Special Commission (UNSCOM), created pursuant to Resolution 687, received from Iraq additional declarations of weapons of mass destruction, which it claimed to have destroyed the previous summer. The declarations included 89 al Hussein (extended-range SCUD) missiles and warheads, 4 Soviet launchers, 4 Iraqi launchers and test and firing vehicles, 45 chemical warheads for the al Husseins and chemical bombs. In addition to expressing its willingness to accept Security Council Resolutions 707 and 715, Iraq said that it was prepared to comply fully with UNSCOM's demands to destroy ballistic missile equipment and provide a "comprehensive, complete, and final" dossier regarding its weapons of mass destruction programs. This full disclosure, which Iraq promised to deliver in early April, has not yet been received.

The International Atomic Energy Agency (IAEA) and UNSCOM have continued to conduct inspections and other activities related to Iraqi weapons of mass destruction and ballistic missiles. Most important, the destruction of nuclear weapons, missiles, and chemical weapons has begun. During the 11th nuclear inspection from April 8 to 15, the destruction of the Al Atheer nuclear weapons production facility began. Five buildings and 29 pieces of equipment were destroyed. During the 12th nuclear inspection, which is scheduled for May 26 to June 4, 1992, three remaining buildings, including the laboratories at Hatteen, are to be destroyed. During future inspections, the IAEA will designate other Iraqi nuclear facilities for destruction.

The first chemical weapons destruction team visited Iraq from February 21 to March 24, 1992. The team supervised the destruction of 463 122-millimeter rockets at the Khamissiyah storage site. Of the destroyed rockets, some were filled with sarin, a nerve agent; others were partially filled with the same agent, while some were empty.

From March 21 to 29, 1992, the ninth missile team began the process of verifying Iraq's most recent declaration. The team saw 86 al Hussein missiles (all but 3 of those recently declared by Iraq), verified the launchers described in Iraq's most recent declarations, and monitored the destruction of dual-use missile production equipment. The 10th ballistic missile team, from April 13 to 21, returned to solid propellant missile facilities to finish destroying dual-use ballistic missile production equipment.

The United States continues to assist the United Nations in its activities through U–2 surveillance flights, the provision of intelligence, and expert inspectors. Nonetheless, the shortage of readily available funds to UNSCOM remains critical. In my last report, I noted that the United Nations and the United States had agreed on the transfer of a $10 million U.S. arrearage payment to UNSCOM, pending completion of the funds' reprogramming. That reprogramming has been completed, and the funds have been provided.

Since my last report, there has been additional progress at the U.N. Compensation Commission in preparing for the processing of claims from individuals, corporations, other entities, and governments who suffered direct loss or damage as a result of Iraq's unlawful invasion and occupation of Kuwait. The Governing Council of the Commission held its fifth session in Geneva from March 16 to 20, 1992, and has scheduled meetings in June, September, November, and December. At its March session, the Council reviewed draft rules of procedure for the processing of claims, approving all but one part, which it expects to approve at its next session. The Council also reviewed the forms for individual claims above $100,000 and for corporate claims; discussed the "embargo loss" issue and claims by members of the allied coalition forces; and instructed the Secretariat to continue its work on locating blocked Iraqi oil deposits and to study extension of the deadline for filing environmental or public health claims. The Executive Secretary reported that shortages of financing continued to delay important activities. Meanwhile, the Department of State continues to collect and review U.S. individuals' claims for amounts under $100,000 in preparation for filing with the U.N. Compensation Commission by July 1 for expedited processing.

In accordance with paragraph 20 of Resolution 687, the Sanctions Committee continues to receive notice of shipments of foodstuffs to Iraq. From January to April 22, 1992, 2.22 million metric tons of foodstuffs were notified. The Sanctions Committee also continues to consider and, when appropriate, approve requests to send to Iraq materials and supplies for essential civilian needs. Iraq to date has refused, however, to utilize the opportunity under Resolutions 706 and 712 to sell $1.6 billion in oil, most of the proceeds from which could be used by Iraq to purchase foodstuffs, medicines, materials, and supplies for essential civilian needs of its civilian population. The Iraqi authorities bear full responsibility for any

suffering in Iraq that results from their refusal to implement Resolutions 706 and 712.

Through the International Committee of the Red Cross (ICRC), the United States, Kuwait, and our allies continue to press the Government of Iraq to comply with its obligations under Security Council resolutions to return all detained Kuwaiti and third-country nationals. Likewise, the United States and its allies continue to press the Government of Iraq to return to Kuwait all property and equipment removed from Kuwait by Iraq. Iraq continues to resist full cooperation on these issues and to resist unqualified ICRC access to detention facilities in Iraq.

Mindful of the finding of the U.N. Security Council in Resolution 688 that Iraq's repression of its civilian population threatens international peace and security in the region, in concert with our Coalition partners, we will continue to monitor carefully the treatment of Iraq's citizens, and together we remain prepared to take appropriate steps if the situation requires. To this end, we will continue to maintain an appropriate level of forces in the region for as long as required by the situation in Iraq.

I remain grateful for the support of the Congress for these efforts, and I look forward to continued cooperation toward achieving our mutual objectives.

Sincerely,

GEORGE BUSH

*Note: Identical letters were sent to Thomas S. Foley, Speaker of the House of Representatives, and Robert C. Byrd, President pro tempore of the Senate.*

# White House Statement on the Establishment of the Inter-American Institute for Global Change Research
## May 15, 1992

The President today announced that the United States has joined 10 other countries of the Americas in signing an agreement that will formally establish an Inter-American Institute for Global Change Research.

The Institute will bring together the resources and capabilities needed to address important issues of global change in the Western Hemisphere.

The agreement was signed this week by

D. Allan Bromley, Assistant to the President for Science and Technology, at a meeting hosted by President Lacalle of Uruguay in Montevideo.

The President first announced the concept of a network of regional institutes to study global change in his closing remarks to the White House Conference on Science and Economics Research Related to Global Change, which was convened by the President in April 1990. Since then, the United States has actively developed this concept and promoted the establishment of the first of these institutes which will be located in the Western Hemisphere. The United States will continue to work with senior representatives in the areas involved to establish institutes in the European/African region and in the Western Pacific region.

This agreement reflects the President's commitment to global stewardship and his desire to promote responsible environmental policies. It is consistent with his conviction that major decisions on the environment should be based on a sound, informed understanding of the scientific issues involved.

# Remarks at a Bush-Quayle Fundraising Luncheon in Pittsburgh, Pennsylvania
*May 15, 1992*

Thank you very much, and thanks to all of you. Elsie, you are fantastic. Thank you for that introduction. Let me quickly thank the Scouts, those that did the Pledge of Allegiance. May I thank also Susan, who did the anthem. It's tough to get up there, not a note, and sing "The Star-Spangled Banner." I thought she was great. Great treat to see Mr. Fred Rogers, who did the invocation. We Bush family are his fans.

May I salute, of course—oops, he's gone— Senator Specter, who flew up with us and whose reelection is very, very important not just to Pennsylvania but to this country. I am all-out for him, and I'm glad that he's doing as well as he is. But I strongly ask your support for him come the fall.

The Congressmen with us today are all outstanding: Rick Santorum is your own; Tom Ridge and Bill Clinger and Larry Coughlin. And let me just say as one who does not have the numbers on Capitol Hill I'd like, it is a joy to work with these Members of Congress. They are supportive. They are innovative. And they are outstanding.

I also wanted to single Bobby Holt out. Many of you know him; he's a Texan. But he was our national finance chairman, and he's done very, very well for us, thanks to you and many other groups like this around the country. Also, of course, an old friend is our event cochairman, Pete Love. We go back a long, long time. And Chuck Corry, I was delighted to have your support, and thank you. They give you great credit for this, you should know, behind your back, all good.

And to Dr. Murray, the president of Duquesne, my thanks for letting us be here. I am a doctor from Duquesne, I believe, some years ago, and I'm very proud of that. And Pastor Neal, thank you very much.

In sum, I am glad to be here. We've had a chance to shake a few hands out here, and somebody said, "Well, you're the President. Doesn't that seem a little onerous?" I said, "No. At least you get to look in people's eyes and thank them for what they're doing." Because sometimes in this line of work I'm in, that doesn't come so easy.

I just want to share with you some objectives. But I know there's been an awful lot of talk this year about change. But talk is very cheap; the tickets were not, I understand. [*Laughter*] But let me start with a promise: In terms of objectives, the time for talk nationally is over, and the time for change is now.

I saw that firsthand out in Los Angeles. I came back one week ago, a week ago I believe today, and I want to begin today by sharing a little bit what I saw, what I heard, and try to describe what I felt. Each one of us saw the images of hate, and we saw the horror, images that we can't possibly forget soon. But what I saw in Los Angeles, even in the hardest hit parts of south central L.A., the most heavily impacted area, should give us all cause for hope.

Everywhere, the people I met told me about acts of individual heroism, about ordinary people doing extraordinary things. Some braved the gangs of looters to form these bucket brigades and putting out the fires when the firetrucks couldn't get through. Some of them stood up to the angry mobs right out across the color lines to help a child or save a life. These stories may not make the headlines, but they sure make you proud, proud to be an American. I came away reinforced by the spirit of this community that had been devastated by their trial.

The founder of our party knew something about courage and change. He knew when the questions of the "stormy present" had outlived the "dogmas of the quiet past." Some still prefer the comfortable dogmas of quieter times. But you know and I know that the time has come for change. Without pointing fingers, we need to ask ourselves, is the present system meeting our goals? I believe that we all know that it is not. It is time, therefore, as Lincoln put it, "to think anew and act anew."

As Republicans, we all agree that we've got to rebuild our house on the rock of Republican faith, Republican principles. Those principles tell us that we must keep power where it belongs, and that's close to the American people. That was the lesson I got out of the riot-torn South Central: Keep the answers as close to the people as possible. Clearly we've got to strengthen the American families, somehow instill character and values in our young people, and that we must encourage entrepreneurship, ownership, risk-taking. We've got to increase investment, and that will create jobs.

The challenges that we face go deeper than the recent crisis in Los Angeles, of course. Beyond our emergency aid, we've got to bring hope and opportunity not only to that area but to all American cities as well. That was the message that I gave to the congressional leaders, Democrats and Republicans alike, when I called them down to the White House this past Tuesday. For your information, it was a good meeting. There was a good spirit of bipartisanship at that meeting. I laid out there a game plan, a six-point plan for a new America. Let me just run it by you, see what you think of it.

First, and this has to come first, we have to preserve order. We have to keep the peace because families cannot thrive and children cannot learn and jobs cannot flourish in a combat zone. So that is square one.

I was thinking about this in the first hours of that Los Angeles violence. People cannot tackle tough problems if they're too busy dodging bullets. It's just that simple. Violence and brutality destroy order, and they destroy the rule of law. That kind of violence should not be condoned. It should not be explained. It cannot be excused, and it must be condemned.

The fellow in Los Angeles named Reverend E.V. Hill, black pastor in a church at Mount Zion, and in the Mount Zion Church in south central Los Angeles, right in the heart of the riot zone, I stood up there, and there were 200 pastors behind me, and the church was full, large church. It was on the National Day of Prayer, Thursday. I mentioned support for the police, saying essentially what I've just said to you all, and the whole church erupted in applause.

And that is the spirit behind one of these initiatives that we've put forward. It's a leadership called "Weed and Seed." First, you've got to weed out the gang leaders, the drug dealers, the career criminals, and then you've got to seed the community with expanded employment and educational and social services. In walking distance from this very spot we are starting a "Weed and Seed" program in the Hill district. This is new, and it is tough. It's going to help people take back the streets and take back the neighborhoods and take back control of their lives.

The second one: We've got to rebuild the community, with investment this time, with investment and with opportunity, with hope. That means enterprise zones for our inner cities, and it also means a lot of private sector activity. The enterprise zones, if we work it properly through the tax committees, will serve as magnets for investment. Then you have the private side: Peter Ueberroth has taken on a big assignment out there. And he is confident that he can get a lot of businesses to set up suppliers in the troubled areas, real jobs in real businesses.

The third objective: We must reform the welfare system. We've got to replace the handout with a hand up. We've got to replace the perverse disincentives that penalize families for working, for saving, and worse, penalize some families for staying together. If we talk about the family being a problem in urban America, we ought to find ways to keep the family together. A review and a revision of the welfare system is the answer.

The fourth one: We've got to have a strong jobs program for city youth. We need to teach kids how to run a drugstore, not how to run a drug ring. That means things like our apprenticeship initiative and our Job Training 2000 program.

The fifth of the six: We've got to revolutionize, and I mean revolutionize, American education. We have a strategy. It's called America 2000. That strategy offers choice. It offers competition. It offers community action. Children in our inner cities deserve the same opportunities that kids in our suburbs have. The special interests can just step aside on this one. Whether it's the public or private or religious, parents, not the government, have the right to choose their children's schools. It works at the higher level; it will work at the lower level in the education system.

And sixth, the last of these six points I gave to the leaders: We must promote new hope through homeownership. I've never understood how anyone could be content with the present system, to take pride in warehousing the poor. Our HOPE initiatives gives poor families a stake in their communities, something they can pass on to their children. The bottom line: HOPE can turn housing into homes. We start with tenant management, ownership there, people in those areas, tenant management, and then move it right into owning one's own home. It's a good concept, and we've been proposing it now for, I think, 3 years.

But it's a time to try this new idea.

At every turn during this trip to L.A., I heard people—it's surprising, really—at all levels of the community talking about the principles that guide, underpin these initiatives: Personal responsibility, opportunity, ownership, independence, and dignity. There wasn't a single community leader, not one, that told me, well, we ought to keep doing it the way we've been doing it; all we ought to do is just add money to existing programs. I didn't hear that from one single person. These ideas I've put out are new. Some have been proposed before, but we've got to try them. You know the sound of those words about the American dream. Well, they're the heart and soul, these ideas, of the American dream.

Now, we all know what the critics will say. They'll come right back, "Well, you've proposed all this before." And that's true, but these ideas have not been tried, I repeat. Now is the time for a bipartisan approach. I think the American people are a little tired with this endless politics out there. I don't think you've caught me yet—that may change in the fall—criticizing any opponent, our own party or the other side. But I think far more important than criticizing, particularly at this time, is to try to get something done for the American people. And that's why I want these six points enacted.

Bipartisan support—I want to go back to that—for immediate action on this agenda has begun. As I say, I salute the Speaker and others. We had a good meeting with all the congressional leadership on Tuesday. But we must not settle for business-as-usual. That's the word that I gave to them, Republican and Democrat alike.

But what's going on in urban America is just one part of a larger issue because the need for reform doesn't end where the suburb begins. Our revolution in education is not just about helping inner-city students. It's about helping all our students, from kindergarten to college. Reform means aggressive action to break down barriers to free trade, to create new markets, cracking open new markets to American goods the world over. We went through a flurry during the early months of this year, flirting with protectionism. That's not the way to get the job done for the American worker or the American consumer. We've taken aim at the status quo in all of these things, and we've set our sights out there on pushing through the changes that we've been proposing.

I'll tell you another area, and I expect many of you here would agree: We need legal reform. We need to put an end to those outrageous court awards that strain our civility and sap our economy. Literally—if you traveled with me, you'd hear it over and over again—we've gotten to a point where doctors won't deliver babies, cost of insurance skyrocketing, where fathers are afraid to coach Little League, all because of the fear of some frivolous lawsuit. Americans need to spend less time suing each other and more time helping each other. We need to change the product liability laws and the tort reform laws. We must reform our legal system, and no lobby should stand in the way.

So far I've mentioned just some things that Government can do. Let me conclude this way. Government alone cannot solve our problems. We need health care reform to open up access to affordable health care for all Americans. It used to be you didn't have to go broke just to get better. And today, more than 30 million Americans have no health care coverage at all. We can and we must change that. We've put forward a comprehensive health care reform plan—again, change—a reform plan that will keep America first in the world in high quality health care. At the same time it would open up access, give access to all Americans regardless of their income status, making it more affordable by what is known in the insurance field as pooling. Contrary to what the big Government folks say, we can do it without nationalizing or socializing our health care system. That path would instantly diminish the quality of our health care, and we've got the best in the entire world.

So national health care would be a disaster. And as long as I am President, I simply cannot let a national health care plan become law. I'm going to keep working for the kind of health care reform to bring access to the poor through the insurance process. And I believe that will work.

I've mentioned what Government can do, but again, Government cannot solve all the problems. We may be able to make good laws, but it's never been able to make men good. That doesn't come from Big Brother. It comes from your family. It comes from your mother and your father. And I'm talking about the moral sense that must guide us all. In the simplest terms, I am talking about knowing what's wrong and doing what's right.

And go back to Los Angeles for a minute. Time and again the people I met there put their finger on one root cause for the turmoil we see, the declining influence of the American family. And they are right. They are absolutely right. Ask yourself: What keeps a kid in school, away from drugs, and off the street? It's not Government spending. It's not the number of SBA loans or HUD grants. It's whether a child lives in a home where they are loved and cared for and kept on the right path. Barbara Bush was right: What happens in the White House doesn't matter half as much as what happens in your house. As so we must find ways to strengthen the American family. I believe it, and I've made it my mission as President to put the American family first.

That's why I keep coming back to the Good Samaritans that I call Points of Light: Those who help the other guy; the people who help the poor and the elderly, kids in trouble, kids without families. They never ask a nickel. Government alone cannot create the scale and energy needed to transform the lives of people in need. So let the cynics scoff. Let the central planners scoff about it. We know these volunteers are the lifeblood of the American spirit. And it's not just in suburban Pittsburgh, outside of Washington, or Houston, Texas. It was right there, alive and vibrant, in south central L.A., a Point of Light, one American helping another, somebody lifting up a kid, somebody calling a kid by his name.

I believe in our party because I believe in our fundamental principles. We are right about family. We are right about freedom. We are right about free enterprise. And certainly, I believe, we are right about faith. And most of all, we are right about America's future.

I really believe—we're in times of pessimism out there. You don't have to listen to 20 seconds on the evening news to find out everything's wrong with this country. Out there in Los Angeles, when I said if some of these guys would just report some of the things that are positive that are happening in the community, it would inspire others. And the place out there broke into standing applause because they knew what I was talking about.

No, we have the strength and the spirit. I believe we have it in Government. I know we've got it in our communities. And I think each of us has it in himself or herself, in ourselves, to transform America into the Nation that we've dreamed of for generations.

I am not pessimistic about the United States of America. We are not a country in decline. Do not listen to the pessimists and the politicians that want to capitalize on somebody else's misfortune. We are turning this economy around. It's beginning to move. This Points of Light, this concept is valid. We're pushing with a new bipartisan spirit in the Congress. And we have a lot to be grateful for.

Thank you all very much for your support. And may God bless our country.

*Note: The President spoke at 1:20 p.m. in the Union Building at Duquesne University. In his remarks, he referred to Elsie Hillman, Bush-Quayle Pennsylvania chairman; Susan Giver, Allegheny County Young Republicans chairwoman; Fred Rogers, creator of public television children's programs; Charles A. Corry, chairman of USX Corp.; and Elsie Neal, Methodist minister.*

# Remarks at a Benefit for the United Negro College Fund in Houston, Texas
*May 15, 1992*

Thank you all, and please be seated. Bill, thank you very much. Bill Gray, as you may know, was in the leadership in the House of Representatives, one of the most popular and one of the most important and one of the most effective Members of Congress. He left that to head the United Negro College Fund. We have great respect for him, and I am delighted to have been introduced by him. And I just wanted all my fellow Houstonians to know how highly we regard him and what he is doing for this commitment to the UNCF.

I want to thank, too, Sandy McCormick, an old friend, and Warren Moon, an admired friend who everyone in Houston respects for their leadership on this drive. I want to single out, of course, Lee Trevino and Arnold Palmer. I had the pleasure of flying down here today from Pittsburgh with Winnie Palmer, and she said, "Well, I'm glad Arnold is not with us. He'd be trying to fly Air Force One." [*Laughter*] But it is really a pleasure to be here. And,

of course, Doug Sanders is an old friend; he and Scotty do so much for others. And I'm just proud once again to be at his side, and grateful to him.

I won't keep you, but let me just add a little to what Bill said about the United Negro College Fund. A mind is a terrible thing to waste. This organization is doing an outstanding job for higher education in this country, offering kids opportunity that might not have had another shot at the American dream.

Bill didn't give you the details, but let me just say that I think it was in 1947, maybe '8, that a man named Bill Trent came to New Haven when I was in school there. He got me interested in the United Negro College Fund, and I have remained interested in that. My brother John is now, what, chairman of the board nationally. And we know that it is worthwhile. And so we are very grateful to all of you who have pitched in and made this great expansion of their program possible. It's an outstanding outfit.

Now in conclusion, let me just say to Doug, I'm glad to be back at his side, proud to have seen a little bit of the activities here this evening, and only sorry that I didn't get a chance to tee it up and show the new Mr. Smooth form. I'm back. [*Laughter*] They can criticize me for hitting a golf ball, but I'm not going to stop, believe me. I love it.

So, good luck to each and every one of you participants.

*Note: The President spoke at 7:35 p.m. at the Doug Sanders Celebrity Dinner, a benefit for the United Negro College Fund (UNCF) at the Greenspoint Club. In his remarks, he referred to William H. Gray, UNCF president; Sandy McCormick, cochair of the UNCF campaign in Houston; Warren Moon, quarterback for the Houston Oilers; golfers Doug Sanders, Lee Trevino, and Arnold Palmer; Mr. Sanders' wife, Scotty, and Mr. Palmer's wife, Winnie.*

# Remarks at the Southern Methodist University Commencement Ceremony in Dallas, Texas
## May 16, 1992

Thank you, Dr. Pye, for the introduction, for the invitation, and I'm just delighted to be here. Let me also thank Reverend Finnin for the invocation. And of course, I was charmed as everybody around here is by the wonderful music of the S.M.U. Symphony Orchestra. I just heard the anthem, but I'm told they're good on everything. And may I salute Ray Hunt, your distinguished chairman. You know, when things were tough for S.M.U. a few years back, this great Mustang led your wonderful university back, working with Dr. Pye and so many others, led it back to its undisputed place of integrity and excellence. And we all owe him a debt of gratitude.

It's good to be back in Texas. I'm honored by this degree, even if I haven't put in all those long hours hitting the books at "Charlie's." [*Laughter*] I was supposed to say the library, but I learned a little about the senior class.

Let me tell you about a graduation at Yale University. They invited the bishop. And the bishop spoke, and he went, "Y is for youth," 25 minutes. "A is for altruism"; that one lasted about 32 minutes. "L, loyalty," another 45 minutes; "E" was excellence, 25 minutes. By the time the guy finished there was a handful of students left; one was in prayer. And the bishop went over to him, and he said, "Thank you, son. I noticed you, a faithful lad, are praying to God." He said, "Yes, I am thanking God I did not go to Southern Methodist University." [*Laughter*]

I will try to accommodate you. I know following this there's presentation of degrees. And I also want to single out Drs. Kay and Pelikan for their work and just am proud to be on the platform with them.

I know this is an exciting day for you and your parents, the close of one important chapter in your lives and the beginning—a way to look at it is the beginning of many, many more. Right after my own commencement, Barbara and I lit out for Odessa in our 1947 Studebaker to try our hands out there in the oil fields of west Texas. I had many reasons for coming west, but the advice from one family friend tipped the balance. "What you need to do is head out to Texas," he told me. "That's the place for ambitious young people these days."

Now, this was a few years, just a handful of years after World War II, what seems like a lifetime ago. My friend's advice was some of the best that I've ever had. I believe what he said then still holds true, not only for Texas but for all of America. Members of your graduation class hail from as far away, I'm told, as Czechoslovakia, as near as University Park, and then all the points in between. But for each of you, America is the place where ambition, energy, enthusiasm, and hard work are still rewarded;

where young people can still feel confidence in their dreams. And I'm a little tired of the pessimism in this country.

So many of us in that class of, way back then, 1948 had been through the war; we'd lost friends and loved ones. But even so, the opportunities America offered on that commencement day seemed limitless. I think many of you wonder whether that holds true for you. This morning I want to make the case that today's America is still a rising Nation, that the country you're inheriting offers those same limitless opportunities that it held for Barbara and for me and for your parents and for your grandparents.

We all are working to preserve for ourselves and the generations to come three precious legacies: Rewarding jobs for all who seek them, strong families, and a world at peace. Tomorrow, up at Notre Dame, I will discuss the things we can do to strengthen our families, the American family. Then next week, at Annapolis at the Naval Academy, I'm going to explore the great issues of war and peace. I might say parenthetically, I think we can all take some pride in the fact that the young kids in the country today go to bed at night without that awful fear of nuclear weapons that some of us had. That is progress. That's something dramatic, and that's something important.

But now let me just focus on the first of those legacies, the economic future. I'm making the case that America's best days lie before us, and I realize that I might not be taking the fashionable view. Much of the conventional wisdom these days portrays America in decline, and its energy dissipated, its possibilities exhausted, a country overrun by economic predators abroad and crippled by the insurmountable problems at home.

These declinists, as they are called, will hate to hear it, but they're saying nothing new. You flip through those history books here in the library, and you'll hear the gloomy predictions sounding again and again. As our western frontier filled up in the late 19th century, even that great American booster Walt Whitman worried that soon his country might, here's the quote, "prove the most tremendous failure in history." A few years later the American

Century dawned. In the 1930's, the declinists told us the Great Depression had made capitalism outmoded. Our victory in World War II put an end to that talk. In the 1950's, the Soviets launched the first satellite and the pessimists said America had lost the space race, 12 years before Neil Armstrong, an American, walked on the moon. Still more recently, while many of you were still in grade school, some of our national leaders spoke of an era of limits and malaise, right before Americans began the longest peacetime economic expansion in the history of our country.

So the pessimists were wrong. Pessimists always are when they talk about America. The optimists have the safer bet, but there's a difference between optimism and smug self-satisfaction. Americans should never be satisfied with the way things are. "I'm an idealist," said Woodrow Wilson. "That's how I know I'm an American." We still dream big dreams and hold the highest hopes. Our restlessness, our refusal to settle for anything less, is what propels us to make those dreams real.

There's something particularly ironic about the pessimism we're seeing today, for it comes at a moment of triumph that few countries in history have been privileged to enjoy. Over the past year we have seen the collapse of a seemingly implacable adversary, an empire deeply hostile to all that Americans cherish. We've seen emerge from that totalitarian darkness a host of new nations, each struggling with a free and democratic future, each looking to us, each turning to America for leadership.

In light of this, pessimism isn't just ungracious; it's also inaccurate. The fact is America is more than the world's sole military superpower, though it is that. It's more than the world's political leader, though it is that, too. It is also the greatest economic power the world has ever seen, a country uniquely able to provide each of you unparalleled opportunity. It is certain to remain so if we refuse to settle for anything less.

First, we must see our own situation clearly. That means debunking a few myths, for myths harm our ability to distinguish our real problems from false ones. Perhaps you've heard that the American worker is unproductive. In slow economic times people look for scapegoats. You've heard the American worker is unproductive. Well, this is a myth. The American worker is the most productive in the industrial world, 30 percent more productive than his Japanese counterpart. That's why, with one-twentieth of the world's population, we produce one-fourth of the world's goods and services.

Maybe you've heard that the American worker is unskilled. This audience here, about to enter the work force, puts the lie to that claim. In fact, more than one out of every four American workers has a college degree; another 20 percent have 1 to 3 years of college education. In Japan, only one-third of the population goes on to higher education.

Maybe you've heard that our standard of living, the average American's ability to buy goods and services, has fallen behind. Again, not true. Measured in purchasing power, our standard of living is far above other industrialized nations.

Here's another myth, that America has fallen behind in science and technology and innovation. Maybe the pessimists should come right here to the campus, come to S.M.U., talk to the grad students who will be working on the superconducting super collider next fall. Or they could ask those companies from Switzerland, Germany, Japan, Korea, and the list goes on, who open research labs in the U.S. simply to be close to the American scene.

"If not science," say the pessimists, "then how about industry?" You might have heard that American industry is on the decline, and they're wrong again. Manufacturing has grown faster than the rest of our economy. In fact, in the last decade, American manufacturing grew faster than the rest of the world combined. From one industry to another, the United States is more progressive and more efficient then its major trading partners in mining, oil and gas drilling, utilities, transportation, communications, agriculture, forestry, fisheries, construction, scientific instruments, and paper and glass products, all kinds of different products, textiles, you name it. The list, too, goes on, but I don't want to overdo it.

I don't recite these statistics so we can all pat ourselves on the back. I just want to make a point: America is a strong nation, getting stronger, and we can learn from our success. But those pessimists ignore the lessons of America's leadership. Instead, they push protection, and they push isolation, a strategy based on the misguided fear that America can't rise to the challenges of a global economy. The danger is that for all our undeniable strengths, fear of the future could prove to be a self-fulfilling prophecy. If America turned inward and insulated itself in a cocoon of defeatism, the result would be stagnation, fewer jobs with a lower pay, and a diminished standard of living for all.

Our astounding economic success is increasingly dependent on a basic fact: If we are to be prosperous at home, we must lead economically abroad. And in a word, that means trade. America is the world's leading exporter, $422 billion worth last year alone. And over the past 5 years, our merchandise exports have grown almost 90 percent, supporting more than 7 million jobs.

The defeatists, well, they pretend that trade is zero-sum game, where one partner's gain must be offset by another's loss. But once again they're wrong, demonstrably wrong, and I refuse to squander the gains of the last generation and the hopes of coming generations in this crabbed misreading of America's place in the world. For 3 years our administration has pursued a policy of open and free trade because it does create jobs and opportunity for Americans. Right now, with the support of the people of Texas, we are on the verge of concluding an historic North American free trade agreement which will create a $6 trillion free trade area from the Yukon to the Yucatan.

Is our policy optimistic? Well yes, I plead guilty to being an optimist about this country's ability to compete. And do not misunderstand; we've got difficulties ahead. We must now deal with a few alarming trends that endanger our world leadership and threaten your future.

I have challenged the Congress to join me in a reform agenda based on the same first principles that underlie our prosperity. Our economic success wasn't hatched in some committee room on Capitol Hill or around a conference table in the White House. It was determined on the shop floor, in the board room, in the research lab, where free men and women weighed the options, took the risks, and made their own decisions. America is the most prosperous Nation in history because it also is the freest. That same commitment to limited Government, to personal freedom, and to personal responsibility must shape the reforms that we urgently need to undertake.

A radical transformation of our education system, for example, is long overdue. And that means we must allow communities the freedom to create their own break-the-mold schools, giving maximum flexibility to teachers and principals. The G.I. bill says: Here's some money; go to the college of your choice. And now I believe the time has come for parents to have the freedom to choose their children's schools at all levels, public, private, or religious.

In the same way, my plan to reform our health care system makes health care more affordable and accessible while preserving the all-important benefit of consumer choice.

I have proposed comprehensive steps to restore sanity to our legal system. The explosion in litigation threatens our economic well-being and, worse, weakens the ethic of personal responsibility that lies at the heart of our national character. America would be a better country if we sued each other less and reached out to help each other more.

And yes, for those of us in Washington, it is high time to get our own house in order. The Federal Government must start living within its means. And to discipline both the executive branch and the Congress, I have long favored a balanced budget amendment. We will get it, and we need it now. And it's a good thing for our country.

Finally, Y–A–L–E, S–M–U—[*laughter*]—finally, as our country moves forward into the next century, we must resolve that no one is left behind. The riots in L.A. reminded us that we have much more work to do in our own neighborhoods. The American dream takes root in families whole and caring, in neighborhoods safe and secure, and in schools unsullied by drugs and violence. Every American deserves the opportunity to pursue this dream, unhindered by

the ugliness of racism or anti-Semitism or the benign neglect of a Government bureaucracy. We are past the time for casting blame or making excuses for despair in our inner cities. But we've got to ask ourselves this: Are the old ways, the old assumptions still good enough? I believe the time has come to try the untried, to build a new approach on the principles of dignity and personal initiative and opportunity.

Last week I presented to congressional leaders, in a very harmonious session at the White House, a six-point plan for a new America:

First, our "Weed and Seed" anticrime initiative. Weed out the criminals and then seed the neighborhoods with hope;

Second, our HOPE initiative to turn public housing into private homes. Homeownership, I think, is the key when it comes to dignity and stronger families;

Third, enterprise zones. Change the tax system so that it will serve as a magnet to bring jobs and investment to the inner city, jobs with dignity;

Then fourth, education reform, touched on that, but offer every child the chance at a world-class education;

Fifth, welfare reform, to replace the handout with the hand up;

And sixth, expanded job training for the young people of our cities.

When I visited L.A., and a very moving trip it was for me, I came away with a deepened sense of hope for America and her people. We all saw those horrifying acts of violence. But let me tell you another story from L.A. In the heat and chaos of the riots, a pastor named Bennie Newton saw a man being beaten to the ground. And despite the threats and the blows, Reverend Newton walked into the fray and draped his body over the bloody man until the beating stopped. "My heart was crying," said the pastor. He saved the man's life.

America is a nation of Bennie Newtons. You'll find him in every city, in every town, in every union hall, boy's club, Scout troop. You'll find a lot right here at S.M.U., with your proud tradition of serving others. Few of us, of course, are ever called to take the risks that Reverend Newton did. But every day we face the question posed in the New

Testament: "If anyone has the world's goods and sees his brother in need, yet closes his heart against him, how does God's love abide in him?"

On countless small occasions, each of us is called to open our hearts; each of us is called to lead, to take responsibility, to show the power of faith in action. I have spoken today of our economic future, about free enterprise, personal liberty. But the freedoms we cherish mean nothing unless they're infused with the old virtues, the time-honored values: honor, honesty, thrift, faith, self-discipline, service to others.

I do not pretend to know the shape of the next century. The genius of a free people defies prediction. Certainly Barbara and I, when we loaded up that Studebaker for the trip to Odessa so long ago, could never have imagined the technological marvels that our grandchildren now take for granted, fax machines and VCR's, for example, not to mention the most amazing invention of 1992, the supermarket scanner. [*Laughter*] But I do know this: the next century will be your century. If you believe in freedom and if you hold fast to your values and if you remain faithful to our role in the world, it is sure to be yet another American century.

Thank you again. May God bless the graduating class at S.M.U., and the United States of America. Thank you very, very much.

*Note: The President spoke at 10:33 a.m. at Moody Coliseum. In his remarks, he referred to A. Kenneth Pye, president, William M. Finnin, chaplain, and Ray Hunt, chairman of the board of trustees, Southern Methodist University; and honorary degree recipients Herma Hill Kay, dean of the Boalton School of Law, University of California, Berkeley, and Jarsoav Pelikan, Sterling professor of history and religious studies, Yale University.*

# Remarks at the University of Notre Dame Commencement Ceremony in South Bend, Indiana
## May 17, 1992

Thank you, Father Malloy. It is really wonderful to be back here at Notre Dame. Whenever I visit the campus or meet a group of Notre Dame alumni, I feel this sense of family, and at Notre Dame that truly means more than just words. I think it's at the very core of what this institution is all about. And with this honorary degree that I am so very proud to have, I am proud to become a Domer. Thank you for the honor. Thank you for the privilege.

I want to salute all of the honorary degree recipients. A pleasure to be among such distinguished educators and public servants. I want to single out again Father Malloy, whose graciousness means a lot to me. A special greeting to the man we all respect so much, Chile's President Aylwin, who has done so much for democracy not just in Chile but in our whole hemisphere. We're grateful to you, sir. And another old friend I'm proud to share this dais with. He

doesn't vote with me much. I don't vote with him much. But we're good friends and have been for a long time, and I respect him, Pat Moynihan. Pat, glad to be with you. May I pay my respects to the outstanding faculty of Notre Dame. They put up with a lot and have done a great job, I'll tell you. To our distinguished provost, don't worry, sir, there's a provost opening in a junior college just outside of Nome, Alaska. And I'm sure you'll qualify. [*Laughter*] But thank you for your warm introduction to me, thank you.

Now to the graduates. For you graduates, these have been 4 long years. But I first want to say, I want to congratulate—I don't know where they are, but the class of 1992. And I want to pay a special tribute to the family, to the parents, the family members, and the friends. At today's ceremony are a group of second generation Domers; 25 percent of the graduating seniors have a parent who attended Notre Dame. For you graduates, these have been 4 long, tough years. Now comes the hardest part, sitting through the commencement speech. [*Laughter*] But Billy Graham put it very well when he told, after a speaker had gone on a long time, a man sitting over here where Pat is picked up the gavel, heaved it at the guy that was speaking, missed him, clipped a lady in the front row who said, "Hit me again. I can still hear him." [*Laughter*]

Let me first say I'm not here in the mode of politics. I'm here to tell you the values that I strongly believe in. Those values can be summarized by the three major legacies that I certainly want to leave behind for my grandchildren, hopefully, for yours: jobs, both for today's workers who are actively seeking work and for graduates entering the work force; strong families, to sustain us as individuals, to nurture and encourage our children, and to preserve our Nation's character and culture; and peace, peace around the world, on our streets, and in our schools as well.

Yesterday I spoke down at Southern Methodist where I focused on the economy and ability to generate jobs. Next week it will be the Naval Academy, when I focus on our hope for a more peaceful world.

Freedom has swept around the world— you heard Chile's President paying homage to that—from the snows of Siberia to the sands of the Gulf. Because we and our allies stood strong and principled, our children and our grandchildren now sleep in a world less threatened by nuclear war. That is dramatic change, and it's something good that we can take great pride in.

Now we must concentrate on change here in America as well, in ways no less dramatic or important. We're taking a fresh look at Government and how we solve national problems. In Lincoln's words, we must think anew, act anew.

Preparing young men and women for lives of leadership, service, and meaning: Each is part of this fantastic Notre Dame tradition, a tradition that has generated a host of inspiring stories. I was particularly moved when I heard about Frank O'Malley's role in saving the bricks of your administration building. Most of you know the

story. The masonry was deteriorating, and some thought the time had come to replace it. Instead, Professor O'Malley reminded all who would listen, "These bricks contain the blood of everyone who helped to build Notre Dame."

Today, that 150-year heritage is fully yours, too. But your preparation began long before you walked in the shadow of the dome. Your parents instilled in you character and a moral bearing. They sacrificed so that you could experience the Notre Dame education, an education that's rooted in timeless faith and in a tradition of excellence, and in the process inculcating into each of you the worth of serving others. I hope each of you has also made a commitment to helping others and attacking some of the major problems facing American society; become a mentor, a community organizer, a Point of Light.

At the heart of the problems facing our country stands an institution under siege. That institution is the American family. Whatever form our most pressing problems may take, ultimately, all are related to the disintegration of the family.

Let us look objectively at a few brief and sad facts. In comparison with other countries, the Census Bureau found that the United States has the highest divorce rate, the highest number of children involved in divorce, the highest teenage pregnancy rates, the highest abortion rates, the highest percentage of children living in a single-parent household, and the highest percentage of violent deaths among our precious young. These are not the kind of records that we want to have as a great country.

In Philadelphia the other day, in the inner city in what they call the Hill area, I talked to a barber there, Mr. Buice, who is one of the leaders of the community there. I said, "Do these kids come from broken families?" He said, "Sir, it's a question of babies having babies," tears coming into his eyes. We've got to do something about this. And unless we successfully reverse the breakdown of the American family, our Nation is going to remain at risk.

Senator Moynihan, way back, way back, early in 1965, you gave us fair warning. You predicted with astonishing accuracy the terrible trends that would result from the breakdown of the family. And today, with respect, sir, you continue to sound the alarm. The Senator and I agree: If America is to solve her social problems, we must, first of all, restore our families.

In addressing the problems associated with family breakdown, nothing is more critical than equipping each succeeding generation with a sound moral compass. As Notre Dame has expanded it has never lost sight of its profound spiritual mission. Indeed, this institution takes seriously its role in building the character of our young people and the strength of our families, for those are the leading indicators of our future as a culture. When we instill faith in our youth, faith in themselves, faith in God, we give them a solid foundation on which to build their future.

As Pope John XXIII said, "The family is the first essential cell of human society." The family is the primary and most critical institution in America's communities.

In January—I'll never forget this meeting—I met with some mayors from America's League of Cities, including Mayor Tom Bradley of Los Angeles. They came together, smalltown Republican mayor from North Carolina, middle-size city mayors, large-city mayors, and they told me of their concerns for their cities, their municipalities. But most of all, the mayors came together on one key point, and they were unanimous: Their major concern about the problems in the cities, in their view, the people on the front line, was the decline in the American family. One result of that meeting is this Commission on America's Urban Families. And I hope it comes up with some good, positive, constructive answers.

It is clear that we all know that putting America's families back on track is essential to putting our country back on track. You may ask how we can proceed when we don't all agree on the causes of the problem or the remedies. I believe that one place to begin is by supporting Pope John Paul II's most recent encyclical calling for a new social climate of moral accountability in which to raise our children. Leadership in that task can and should be led by the Nation's churches; kids need to learn faith to

help them understand the larger family. And we are one Nation under God. We must remember that, and we must teach that.

Starting today, as you go from this fine institution to face the challenges of your adult life, the decisions you make will have one of two effects: Either you will add to the problems of family breakdown, or you will help rebuild the American family. You see, I am absolutely convinced that today's crisis will have to be addressed by millions of Americans at the personal, individual level for governmental programs to be effective. The Federal Government, of course, must do everything it can do, but the point is Government alone is simply not enough.

In my view, Government can, and we must, provide parental choice of the best schools for our children, whether public, private, or religious. The GI bill says here's some money; go to the college of your choice. Choice should apply to all levels of education. Parents must read to their children and instill a love of learning. Government can, and we must, fight crime. But fathers and mothers must teach discipline and instill those values in their children. Government can, and we must, foster American competitiveness. But parents must teach their children the dignity of work and instill a work ethic in the kids.

And to paraphrase that fantastic philosopher, Barbara Bush—[*laughter*]—what you teach at your house is more important than what happens at the White House. And she is absolutely correct on that.

All of us realize that merely knowing what's right is not enough. We must then do what's right. Today I'm asking you to carefully consider the personal decisions that you'll make about marriage and about how you will raise your children. Ultimately, your decisions about right and wrong, about loyalty and integrity, and yes, even self-sacrifice, will determine the quality of all the other decisions that you'll make. And as you think about these decisions, remember: It is in families that children learn the keys to personal economic success and self-discipline and personal responsibility. It is in families that children learn that moral restraint gives us true freedom. It is from their families that they learn honesty and self-respect and compassion and self-confidence.

And you would do well to consider the simple but profound words of Notre Dame's own Father Hesburgh when he said, "The most important thing a father can do for his children is to love their mother." Think how this vitally important commitment from fathers to mothers would radically transform for the better both the lives of thousands of our Nation's hurting children and their struggling mothers as well.

In many respects, I feel here at Notre Dame that I'm preaching to the choir because here at Notre Dame, you have benefited from the legions of great men and women of conviction and faith. Here, there is a tradition of passion for addressing the staggering needs of the day. Notre Dame's Alumni Association is the prototype for other universities in sponsoring service projects and working toward the restoration of faith and the family in America.

In fact, at this very moment, the Notre Dame alumni group out there in Los Angeles is in the midst of a massive food and distribution project to assist residents affected by the violence in south central L.A. When that food is distributed and the riot-torn areas are rebuilt, I hope that the alumni group and thousands of others who are helping will stay involved in this and other urban areas. Government alone cannot do what needs to be done by itself. People who care must help.

And since becoming President I have had an opportunity to see a groundswell of Americans who are working, and working hard, to restore our Nation's faith and heal the wounds that have undermined our Nation's families. These Americans are devoted to rebuilding, restoring America from the ground up, family by family, home by home, community by community.

I was impressed to learn that more than two-thirds of Notre Dame's students participate in community service, two-thirds, ranging from working with the handicapped children at Logan Center to assisting former prisoners at Dismas House. Fully 10 percent of your graduates plan to go into social service careers. And to paraphrase Pope John Paul II, the ultimate test of your greatness is the way you treat every human being, but especially the weakest and the most defenseless ones.

Let me challenge all of you to find a place to serve in some capacity, definitely as models but also as mentors. Remember each of us has a contribution that only we can make. And let me remind you as you assume the mantles of tomorrow's leadership that children tend to shape their dreams in the images that they have seen. Show how a good education prepares one for a full, productive life. Show what it means to be a person of strong principle and integrity. Demonstrate how concerned individuals, by working in partnership, can transform our communities and Nation.

Lastly, in a society that can sometimes be cold and impersonal, bring warmth and welcome. In a fragmented society, be a force for healing. In a society cut off from moral and spiritual roots, cultivate grace and truth. In the face of the uncertainties of the future, affirm your purpose and realize your promise. Together, we can lift our Nation's spirit. Together we can give our material, political, and economic accomplishments a larger, more noble purpose, to build God's kingdom here on Earth.

There is no surer way to build our Nation's future than with the mortar and the bricks of moral values and strong families. If you will add your blood to the bricks, the future will echo, then as now, "Never bet against Notre Dame or against the United States of America."

Thank you all, and good luck to this class of 1992 and to the entire Notre Dame family. And may God Bless our great country. Thank you very much.

*Note: The President spoke at 3:03 p.m. in the Joyce Athletic and Convocation Center. In his remarks, he referred to University of Notre Dame officials Edward A. Malloy, president; Timothy O'Meara, provost; Theodore M. Hesburgh, former president; and Frank O'Malley, former professor of English. A tape was not available for verification of the content of these remarks.*

## Remarks to the National Association of Home Builders
*May 18, 1992*

Thank you very much for that welcome, and welcome to the South Lawn of the White House. May I salute the national directors, the homebuilders, and the many, many friends that are here. I also want to single out two members of our Cabinet, Secretary Brady and then one you know so well because you've dealt with him a lot, Secretary Jack Kemp, who's out there doing an awful lot in the housing field.

Welcome to the people's house. Some of you may know this is like a museum, well over a million people going through every year. I don't know how many are going through right this minute, but I'm sure they're going to think we're having a yard sale out here when they see all of this stuff. [*Laughter*]

But we're here to mark a special birthday. I heard a little earlier from the leadership about this 50th anniversary of the Home Builders. I want to salute a special team of them, the leaders, with whom I just met in the Rose Garden. First, of course, Jay Buchert, who has done an outstanding job for this organization, outstanding, and then Roger Glunt and Tommy Thompson and Jim Irvine and Mark Tipton, Bob Bannister, and of course, Kent Colton. I want to thank you at the beginning of these brief remarks for your support. Even more, we Bushes are grateful for the friendships we have of those in the Home Builders.

Millie was a little disappointed. She thought she was going to get a new dog house here. We came and checked it out this morning. [*Laughter*]

But I do believe that Barbara and our kids believe in these same values that you all have: community, country, respect, responsibility, family, jobs, peace. We know we put America first when we put America's families first, and for 50 years, that's what the Home Builders have been doing. You're helping people fulfill the American dream and enlarge the American pie. When the Home Builders were founded, the NAHB, almost one-half of the Nation lived in substandard housing, and only four in ten

owned their own homes. Today, more than 70 million new homes and apartment units later, two in three households own their own home. That is dramatic progress, but we're not done yet.

For that, I salute you. Once again, you're helping our economy work so that America can get back to work. And yes, we have had some tough times in this country. But consider this: 264,000 housing starts in the first 3 months of this year; a 2-percent GDP growth in the first quarter, more that a quarter of that resulting from residential construction. The old adage is coming true: As housing goes, so goes the economy.

Your industry employs more than 6 million Americans. More and more, they're helping other Americans turn recession into recovery. I speak here as a participant, not a bystander. From my Texas business days I know what it means to meet a payroll and try to balance a budget and help people put food on the table. Like you, I know that strong housing can help a strong economy. I know how that helps Americans worrying about providing for their families, meeting the challenges of paying their bills, buying that home, and setting aside for retirement.

That's why, in my State of the Union Message, I announced a program for economic growth. I called for penalty-free withdrawal from IRA's for the purchase of a first home; changes in the passive-loss tax rules to spur the real estate and housing development; an extension of mortgage revenue bonds and the low-income housing tax credit. An i yes, I called for a job-generating cut in the tax on capital gains. Here's the one I feel would really also help this economy and help it fast, a proposal that we've made and that I'm proud of, a $5,000 tax credit for first-time homebuyers. We need this credit to keep the housing market on the mend, helping people like you sell and build homes. And here's why: $5,000 could pay 7 months of mortgage payments on the average American home. According to your own figures, these housing initiatives would mean 415,000 new construction industry jobs and $20 billion in new economic activity. This is just one more way that your slogan, "Housing equals jobs," can be realized. I challenged the Congress again today to pass these growth initiatives.

Parenthetically speaking, to discipline both the executive branch and the legislative branch, we need to get moving on that balanced budget amendment. I really believe the time for that has come.

Some in Congress haven't gotten the message yet. But I believe, and I think Jack and Nick Brady would agree with me, the time is right for some of these new ideas, ideas that we've been proposing but that haven't been tried. I think the American people want to see us take some action and get something new done. So I'm optimistic that we can move forward now in the Congress in a way that we haven't been able to in the past.

This year, the Home Builders ran an ad in the Washington Post. And the headline was marvelous, if you haven't seen it. The headline read: "Earth to Congress: Enough is enough." I don't believe anybody could have said it any better than that.

Well, you've heard the definition of a contractor: A gambler who never gets to shuffle, cut, or deal. [*Laughter*] We have to make it easier to deal, sell, hire, invest. So we're going to continue to sound that message that sound banks should make sound loans. The bankers should also work with the borrowers experiencing temporary difficulties from the remnants of the recession.

For our part, we have been working with the Federal Reserve to keep these interest rates low, and we've been fighting for commonsense regulation, not overregulation, of banks and thrifts. And we are going to keep on that fight. We have made over 30 specific regulatory policy changes, many, frankly, with the help from your leadership, to enhance the ability of banks and thrifts to raise new capital, to make new loans, and then to work with troubled borrowers. Nick Brady, Treasury Secretary, and I are going to work to be sure that these measures are carried out.

Next, we're going to push hard for the HOPE initiative, requesting $1 billion in funding for fiscal '93 and a key part of our plan for a new America to bring opportunity to our inner cities. Now, Jack Kemp knows how HOPE can give poor families a stake in their communities. And his message is beginning to get through up there in the United States Congress. Bottom line: HOPE will turn housing into homes.

HOPE is only one part, actually, of our six-point plan for a new America which will use opportunity, not bureaucracy, to combat poverty and inequality. And the plan also includes our "Weed and Seed" initiative, it's an anticrime initiative; enterprise zones; education reform; welfare reform; and also a strong jobs program for city youth. This plan makes a promising start. We are going to do our level-best to get it passed.

And yes, I will continue to push for what we mentioned a minute ago, regulatory reform, because I want Government to help, not hurt, the ability of private enterprise to expand and to create jobs. So I've extended for another 120 days the blanket moratorium on Federal regulation. Jay puts it this way, your president: "Let builders build." I know he agrees that we need policies that also let buyers buy, and that's what part of this is all about.

I wish everyone understood this concept. On the other hand, you know what it takes; it takes more than bricks and lumber and mortar to build a home. It takes heart. It takes skill. And it takes dreams. You know that owning a home helps America, makes it better, more caring. You show this in your Homes Across America program, where NAHB members build and renovate homes for the needy. So far I am told that this program has housed more than 600 families, and with us today is one of them, Gerald and Angela Williams and their four children, sitting right over here in the front row, Murria, Charlease, Gerald, and Latoya.

They moved into their new home in Jacksonville on Mothers' Day. And the Williams' home was built by the builders of the Jacksonville association of the NAHB and Habitat for Humanity. I salute them and also salute those who made it possible and also salute the Williams family.

You show how the dream of homeownership keeps the American dream alive. And that dream seemed elusive half a century ago, but you right here, all of you, have aided it and nurtured it as a parent does a child. And for that, we are all very, very grateful to you.

We salute you on behalf of each American. On this special anniversary, for those who have done so much, we say thank you from a grateful country. May God bless you all. And may God bless the United States of America.

Thank you all very, very much.

*Note: The President spoke at 11:12 a.m. on the South Lawn at the White House. In his remarks, he referred to association officers Jay Buchert, president; Roger Glunt, first vice president; Tommy Thompson, vice president and treasurer; Jim Irvine, vice president and secretary; Mark E. Tipton, immediate past president; Robert D Bannister, senior staff vice president; and Kent Colton, executive vice president.*

# Appointment of John A. Cline as Special Assistant to the President for Intergovernmental Affairs
*May 18, 1992*

The President today announced the appointment of John A. Cline as Special Assistant to the President for Intergovernmental Affairs.

Since January 1991, Mr. Cline has served as Director of the Office of Congressional Affairs at the Department of Transportation. Prior to this, Mr. Cline served as the Associate Administrator for Budget and Policy at the Federal Transit Administration, an agency of the Department of Transportation, 1989–91. Mr. Cline also served on the Secretary of Transportation's team to formulate a national transportation policy, which the President announced in March 1990. Prior to this, Mr. Cline served as vice president for management and labor relations for National Transit Services, Inc., a Chicago-based national transportation management firm.

Mr. Cline graduated from Northern Illinois University in 1981. He was born November 25, 1959, in Chicago, IL. Mr. Cline lives in Arlington, VA, with his wife, Krista L. Edwards, and their infant daughter.

# Nomination of Gregory F. Chapados To Be an Assistant Secretary of Commerce
*May 18, 1992*

The President today announced his intention to nominate Gregory F. Chapados, of Alaska, to be Assistant Secretary of Commerce for Communications and Information. He would succeed Janice Obuchowski.

Since 1986, Mr. Chapados has served as chief of staff to Senator Ted Stevens (R-AK) in Washington, DC. Prior to this, he served as a legislative assistant to Senator Stevens, 1983–86.

Mr. Chapados graduated from Harvard College (B.A., 1979) and Harvard Law School (J.D., 1983). He was born May 8, 1957, in Fairbanks, AK. Mr. Chapados resides in Washington, DC.

## Remarks at the Departure Ceremony for President Nursultan Nazarbayev of Kazakhstan
*May 19, 1992*

Well, Mr. President, distinguished members of the Kazakhstan delegation, it's been a great pleasure to welcome you to the White House on this historic occasion, the first-ever visit of the head of state of an independent Kazakhstan. I have never been to your country, but Secretary Baker has. And he has spoken to me about the tremendous potential of a nation rich in resources, a nation stretching from the steppes of Russia to the Tien Shan in the south, 4 times the size of Texas.

Mr. President, our meeting today marks the beginning of a new relationship, a relationship made possible by the end of the long era of East-West conflict that we called the cold war. With the passing of that bitter conflict, we enter into a new era of hope for a more democratic and free order in Eastern Europe and in Central Asia.

Under your leadership, sir, Kazakhstan is pursuing a course true to these aims. Our meetings today confirm the many interests that we share. The U.S. supports your independence. We believe its security, Kazakhstan's security, is important for stability in Europe and in Asia. We welcome President Nazarbayev's commitment that Kazakhstan will join the Non-Proliferation Treaty as a non-nuclear-weapons state and that it will adhere to the START Treaty. We'll continue to work toward a signing of the new START protocol by Kazakhstan, Ukraine, Byelarus, Russia, and the United States in the very near future.

I want to take this occasion to underline our pledge to maintain regular, high-level communication with the Kazakh Government on political and security issues, and that means exploring the possibility of cooperative programs in nuclear nonproliferation and beginning contacts between the armed forces of our two nations.

Beyond our common security interest, the U.S. is committed to helping Kazakhstan make the transition from the old Socialist command economy to the free market. We continue to aim at a tax treaty

between our nations. Today we took very positive steps toward increased trade with the signing of agreements on trade, bilateral investment, and the Overseas Private Investment Corporation.

The surest way, though, to increase trade remains for American firms to have the opportunity to compete fairly in Kazakhstan. I am pleased that the Kazakh Government has this week signed a landmark agreement with Chevron Corporation to open the Tengiz oil fields.

In order to expand trade, I've asked for our able Secretary of Commerce, Barbara Franklin, to form a business development committee to work with your Government to increase contacts between private Kazakh and American firms. We will continue to provide humanitarian assistance, including much needed food and medical aid. The U.S. also stands ready with technical assistance on a range of issues, from food distribution to speeding the conversion of defense sector industry to civilian economy.

But Government assistance is just one part of an outpouring of American support. As President, I am pleased to see the active efforts on behalf of private citizens to provide aid to your new nation, volunteer organizations like Project Hope and Mercy Corps, to the city of Waukesha, Wisconsin, which has sent 40,000 pounds of food, medical supplies, and clothing to its Kazakh sister city.

Like all of the former republics of the Soviet empire, Kazakhstan faces challenges that go beyond the need to build a strong, competitive economy. After more than 70 years of Communist rule, Kazakhstan and its Commonwealth neighbors are engaged in the difficult task of nation-building. At issue are the first questions of government and society: respect for the rule of law; the role of political parties, of free press and independent media; the freedom of association; and the freedom of the individual.

On behalf of all Americans, I pledge the support of the United States of America as

Kazakhstan seeks a future that is peaceful, prosperous, and free.

Once again, Mr. President, it has been a special privilege to welcome you to Washington, to welcome you to the White House. And may God bless your great country.

*Note: The President spoke at 1:17 p.m. in the Rose Garden at the White House. The*

*remarks followed a ceremony in which President Bush and President Nazarbayev signed the Agreement on Trade Relations Between the United States and Kazakhstan, the Bilateral Investment Treaty Between the United States and Kazakhstan, and the United States-Kazakhstan Overseas Private Investment Corporation Agreement.*

# Joint Declaration With President Nursultan Nazarbayev of Kazakhstan
## May 19, 1992

### DECLARATION ON U.S.-KAZAKHSTAN RELATIONS

At the conclusion of this important meeting, we—the President of the United States and the President of the Republic of Kazakhstan—have resolved to develop friendly, cooperative relations between our countries and peoples, and to work together to strengthen international peace and stability.

Kazakhstan and the United States favor an early ratification and implementation of the START Treaty as an important guarantor of maintaining global stability. Reaffirming its commitment to peace and security, Kazakhstan shall, at the earliest possible time, accede to the Treaty on the Non-proliferation of Nuclear Weapons as a non-nuclear state, while preserving the right of control over the non-use and reductions of the nuclear weapons temporarily deployed on its territory. Kazakhstan guarantees to carry out the elimination of all types of nuclear weapons, including strategic offensive arms, within the seven-year period provided for in the START Treaty. The United States welcomes these steps and shall take necessary measures to assist Kazakhstan in this matter. Kazakhstan and the United States agree on the need to establish effective national control over non-proliferation of the weapons of mass destruction and associated technologies to third countries.

The United States and Kazakhstan will work to strengthen international security on the basis of lower and more stable levels of armaments among all nations. We commit

to uphold shared international principles, especially democracy, respect for borders and territorial integrity, and peaceful resolution of disputes. Together we will promote respect for international law and the principles enshrined in the Helsinki Final Act, the Charter of Paris, other important documents of the Conference on Security and Cooperation in Europe, and the United Nations Charter. The United States welcomes Kazakhstan's efforts to establish equal and mutually beneficial relations with Russia and the states of Central Asia as well as with other states in accordance with these principles. Toward this end, the United States welcomes Kazakhstan's membership in multilateral institutions like the United Nations, the Conference on Security and Cooperation in Europe, the North Atlantic Cooperation Council, the International Monetary Fund and the World Bank, and its commitment to values and accepted norms of behavior in the world. We agree that our countries should maintain a regular bilateral dialogue on questions of peace and stability that are of interest to both states.

We believe that the basis for the development of a lasting partnership between our states must be a shared commitment to promote the values of democracy, free markets, and world peace. In this regard, the United States supports Kazakhstan's commitment to pursue far-reaching political and economic reform. The United States welcomes Kazakhstan's desire to build its independence in full accordance with the principles of a free and democratic society, including free elections, pluralism and tolerance, freedom of emigration, the rule of law, and respect for human rights, including equal rights for all individuals belonging to ethnic or religious minorities. The United States Government, in cooperation with the American private sector, will make available programs designed to help Kazakhstan establish the institutions, ideas, and practices that form the foundation of democracy.

Kazakhstan will seek to accelerate its efforts to move toward a market economy through a plan for macroeconomic stabilization and structural/microeconomic reform that will promote economic recovery, market development, and growth. This plan will be developed in cooperation with the International Monetary Fund and other international financial institutions. The United States will support such a plan and will encourage others to do so as well. In particular, the United States will provide Kazakhstan with access to technical assistance programs to assist its efforts to develop a market economy.

Kazakhstan and the United States will work actively to promote free trade, investment, and economic cooperation between our countries. The United States and Ka-

zakhstan have signed three economic agreements that constitute the basic framework of our economic relationship. They will promote economic ties between the two states and will further economic development. We have concluded a trade agreement that will confer Most Favored Nation tariff treatment on Kazakhstan, an OPIC agreement to make available investment insurance for American firms investing in Kazakhstan, and a Bilateral Investment Treaty. We have also agreed to expedite negotiations on a tax treaty, and to develop our cooperation in the area of scientific research and environmental protection. A critical feature of our cooperation will be an effort by Kazakhstan to lower barriers to trade and investment to allow greater access for American and foreign firms, especially in sectors such as oil and natural gas, mining, agriculture, manufacturing, and food processing.

By agreeing to work jointly to advance these common interests, we have taken an important step in the development of a strong, lasting friendship between Kazakhstan and the United States. Through expanded cooperation between our governments, and expanded contacts between our peoples, we seek to build an enduring relationship that will enhance the freedom and well-being of our nations and the world.

# Remarks to the National Retail Federation
*May 19, 1992*

*The President.* Let me first salute Lamar Alexander; most of you know who he is, our Secretary for Education. But as we're trying to literally revolutionize American education, give kids a real break, give them a shot at excellence, why, I can't tell you how grateful I am to have him as Secretary. He's doing a superb job.

Tracy, president, thank you for having me here. And to Joseph Antonini, I salute him, our chairman. And thank you all very much for coming.

I gather Pat Saiki has been here, right, or has she?

*Ms. Tracy Mullins.* She spoke to us this

morning.

*The President.* Yes. I want to say about Pat, when this problem broke out there in Los Angeles, she took that SBA and really rose to the occasion. I think she's really trying to help in that field. And of course, what they're doing, SBA, across the board, I hope, is beneficial in many ways to all business people in this country.

But as you know, these riots out there left a large number of retail operators and a lot of small businesses devastated. What happened in the Korean community, where it was particularly concentrated, was just horrible and, of course, all communities. But

Pat did respond very swiftly. The SBA and then also FEMA, the Federal Emergency Management Agency, have made massive resources available. The Federal Home Loan Bank is going to offer an additional $600 million to finance the rebuilding of homes and businesses there. Then we have a special task force to cut the redtape and to make sure that these businesses get the help that they deserve in record time.

So I wanted to just give you a report on that. I think the Federal Government has responded promptly to the troubles out there. The Governor and the Mayor have both thanked us for what we've done, not only in this side but also in the law enforcement side by bringing to bear some of the U.S. Army, the 7th Infantry, and the Marines at a time when it was very dicey. So I hope that our response has been proper. But now we've got to go beyond this tragedy and renew our commitment to bring hope and to bring opportunity not just to Los Angeles but to every city.

Last week, we went to the Congress with six action-oriented items. Again I had a chance to repeat that; we had the Democratic leaders and the Republican leaders into the White House today. And the six points: The first one was a "Weed and Seed" anticrime initiative, where you weed out the criminal elements and then seed the neighborhoods with investments and jobs that hopefully will bring opportunity to the communities.

The housing initiative is known as HOPE, that's Homeownership for People Everywhere. We get hit, saying, "Hey, we ought to try some new ideas." We said, "This is a new idea. It really hasn't been tried." It's a proposal we've had out there. But I happen to feel that dignity comes with owning your own home an awful lot of the time. So we're going to press, and I think Congress now will be much more receptive to that.

Education reform Lamar will talk about. But in terms of meeting medium and longer range objectives, therein lies the answer. These kids have got to be educated. They have got to understand that gang warfare is no substitute for jobs. So we're putting an awful lot of stake on trying to get through now the education program that I'm sure Lamar will describe to you.

Welfare reform, you've got to be careful that you put it forward in a very constructive way, and that, again, is what we're trying to do. I read the case of the family the other day where a little girl had managed to save a pittance, her mother being on welfare, and the welfare law was such that she couldn't save anything beyond $1,000. That seems to me to be counterproductive. So we're trying to make reforms there, as well as permit the States to try new things through what we call the waiver process: give waivers to the States from the existing guidelines and let them try innovative answers, whether it's learnfare or workfare or whatever it is. So this one is important. Again, it transcends just Los Angeles, but it's a national thing.

Strong job training programs for young people is a very good one. And we've got Job Training 2000, which is like a one-stop shopping for all the Federal Agencies to come together and help on that one.

Then the enterprise zones approach. I was amazed, but in everyplace I went, both there in South Central, in the Korean community, and then in Pittsburgh and in Philadelphia, there's an idea which really has unanimous support now. So I am very hopeful that this enterprise zones concept that passed the Congress, not in the form we wanted but that passed the Congress, will be enacted into law. It will bring private capital and jobs to the neighborhoods. It will act like a magnet, giving businesses a break to locate in these tough areas. And obviously, if it didn't work and wasn't productive, they wouldn't stay. But at least it's an idea that needs to be tried.

Now, on your business, I know the retailers have not had it easy. You've been through some tough times, as have many other sectors of the economy. I think there are reasons to be encouraged overall. In the first quarter of this year, retail sales were up by, I'm told, a strong 3 percent. And I want to tell you that we are going to try to do everything we can from here to ensure that the growth continues.

It's odd, I just saw some new surveys, and the American people still feel the economy is getting worse, even though most economists now and most business people are saying, "Hey, it's beginning to move." I think you'll see some growth figures that confirm that. But there's a confidence problem out there that I'm sure adversely affects some of your interests, some of your business. I think that can turn around now, and I think it will turn around.

We are going to try not to oversell where the economy stands but at least try to gun down some of this pessimism you get on the top of every news broadcast across this country. I mean, when a statistic comes out that's favorable, somebody finds a bad one to offset it with or trying to put a bad spin on it. But I believe things are beginning to move. And I think most people in the country feel that way. I hope that that is immediately felt in the retail business.

In Washington, clearly, we've got to get our own house in order. We have proposals before the Congress now that really would help with the Federal deficit. We are not going to get the deficit down until we cap the growth of—you don't have to cut—but cap the growth of the mandatory programs. There's no other way to do it. We've done fairly well by capping the discretionary programs. But we've got to get discipline back.

That leaves me to ask for your support for an idea that I've long been for, advocated it in campaign after campaign, but that we may have a chance to get through Congress now, and that is the balanced budget amendment. It will have to be phased in. It can't be done overnight. But it can be phased in. And I really think it would discipline not just the Congress but any executive branch, ours or subsequent executive branches. I would like to ask your support on that because that's beginning to churn around in the Congress right now.

Secondly, we are going to continue to go after redtape, reduce Federal redtape. It acts as a straitjacket. I was in business once, that was way back in the fifties and sixties, and I remember the pain it was to have to go to several Agencies to get permits to go out and do our business. So we are trying to simplify all that now, recognizing that every dollar you spend conforming to some Government mandate is a dollar that you could spend in some way making sales to your customers more efficiently or reducing costs or whatever.

As you may know, we have a moratorium now on new Federal regulations. It has been successful, and now we've renewed it. We're speeding up those regulations that encourage growth. Wherever possible, we are actually canceling regulations that needlessly burden business. I have certain responsibilities for safety, for the environment, but I am convinced that up until now we've not found, Government hasn't found, the proper balance. We are really working at this problem, and I hope that we can prove to you that the days of overregulation are just exactly that, that they are over. But if you get examples from your businesses where that is not true, please call them to our attention, and let us try to help with this bureaucracy out there where we have to fight to hold the line against the excesses of regulation.

The IRS, just by way of example here, at our direction has issued new rules to simplify the payroll tax system. Those new rules are really going to reduce, significantly, I might say, the payroll costs of businesses. We're launching an experimental program that will let employers make tax payments electronically. And there is no reason why you should waste time and money doing paperwork for the U.S. Government.

I also understand how crucial trade is to the growth of your area; this is a whole other point. In fact, I believe it is crucial for every American. Our economic success at home depends on our economic success abroad. We can no longer pull back in isolation or into protectionism. We simply can't do it. There are some bad politics in it. Maybe there are some good politics. I know there's good common sense in this approach I've outlined.

I really appreciate what you all have done on behalf of the North American free trade agreement. And I am convinced that it is in the interest of the American worker to get that agreement passed. When we get it, and I am confident we will, we're going to have created a $6.5 trillion market with the North America free trade agreement, $6.5 trillion market, one of the largest of the world.

Also on the GATT round, we're moving forward there. It's difficult, the hangups, I won't burden you with all the details, but I'm telling you it's like pulling teeth getting the GATT round completed. But a successful GATT agreement could pump more than $5 trillion into the global economy over 10 years. Our share of that promises to top $1 trillion. That means, obviously, more and more better jobs for Americans. I think it means better service for your customers, too, and I think it means better prospects to make your businesses grow. I think the consumer is helped here by prices being reasonable and more competitive.

Now, I am committed to both the NAFTA and GATT round conclusions. And some call this trade policy optimistic, and in a sense, I think they're right because I am optimistic about this country. I refuse to be one of the pessimists when it comes to where we stand in terms of the future. The creativity and the energy and the enthusiasm of the members of this organization are just the best possible rebuttal to the pessimists.

So with your help I think we can demonstrate, as we're coming out of this slow, infinitesimal growth period, that we've got plenty to be grateful for and that there's plenty of opportunity out there. The retailers have been in the lead for many sensible fiscal proposals up there on Capitol Hill, and this is a good opportunity just to say thank you from the bottom of a very, very grateful heart.

Thank you for being with us today. And now I will turn the program either to the chairman or to the other president, depending how we want to do all of this.

*Note: The President spoke at 3:03 p.m. in Room 450 of the Old Executive Office Building. In his remarks, he referred to federation officers Tracy Mullins, president, and Joseph Antonini, chairman.*

## Message to the Senate Transmitting the North Pacific Fish Conservation Convention
*May 19, 1992*

*To the Senate of the United States:*

With a view to receiving the advice and consent of the Senate to ratification, I transmit herewith the Convention for the Conservation of Anadromous Stocks in the North Pacific Ocean, with Annex, which was signed by the United States of America on February 11, 1992, in Moscow. I transmit also, for the information of the Senate, the report of the Department of State with respect to the Convention.

This Convention establishes a new organization, the North Pacific Anadromous Fish Commission (NPAFC), which will contribute significantly to the conservation of anadromous fishery resources and ecologically related species in the high seas area of the North Pacific Ocean. The Commission will serve as an effective forum for closer international coordination of North Pacific fishery enforcement activities on the high seas.

Canada, Japan, the Russian Federation, and the United States cooperated in the development of the Convention, which will enter into force following ratification, acceptance, or approval by all four of these signatory States. It is anticipated that the Convention will enter into force before the end of 1992 or by early 1993. It is important that the United States and the other concerned States ratify the Convention quickly so that we may operate under its beneficial framework as soon as possible.

I recommend that the Senate give early and favorable consideration to the Convention and give its advice and consent to ratification.

GEORGE BUSH

The White House,
May 19, 1992.

## Memorandum Delegating Authority To Report on China
*May 19, 1992*

*Memorandum for the Secretary of State, the Secretary of Defense, the Secretary of Commerce, the United States Trade Representative, the Director of the United States Arms Control and Disarmament Agency*

*Subject:* Delegation of Authority with Respect to Reports Concerning China Weapons Proliferation, Human Rights, and Trade Practices

By virtue of the authority vested in me by the Constitution and laws of the United States of America, including section 301 of title 3 of the United States Code, I hereby delegate to the Secretary of State the functions vested in me by section 303 and section 324 of the Foreign Relations Authorization Act, Fiscal Years 1992 and 1993 (Public Law 102–138). These functions shall be exercised in consultation with the Secretary of Defense, the Secretary of Commerce, the Director of the United States Arms Control and Disarmament Agency, the United States Trade Representative (with respect to the functions described in section 303), and other appropriate departments and agencies.

The functions delegated herein may be redelegated as appropriate.

The Secretary of State is authorized and directed to publish this memorandum in the *Federal Register.*

GEORGE BUSH

*[Filed with the Office of the Federal Register, 3:42 p.m., May 26, 1992]*

## Letter of Condolence to Lawrence Welk, Jr.
*May 19, 1992*

*Dear Larry,*

Barbara and I send to you and all your family our most sincere condolences. Your great and admired Dad set a wonderful, wholesome example for this Country. His personal story inspired us all and his music had broad appeal. Lawrence Welk was truly a great American.

Please convey our deepest sympathy and special prayers to all in your family.

Sincerely,

GEORGE BUSH

*Note: This letter follows the text as released by the Office of the Press Secretary.*

## Nomination of William Arthur Rugh To Be United States Ambassador to the United Arab Emirates
*May 19, 1992*

The President today announced his intention to nominate William Arthur Rugh, of Maryland, a career member of the Senior Foreign Service, class of Career Minister, to be Ambassador to the United Arab Emirates. He would succeed Edward S. Walker, Jr.

Since 1989, Ambassador Rugh has served as Director of the Near East and South Asia Bureau at the U.S. Information Agency. Prior to this he served as Ambassador to the Yemen Arab Republic, 1984–87, and as Deputy Chief of Mission in Damascus, Syria, 1981–84. He also served in a number of other positions in Cairo, Jidda, and Riyadh.

Ambassador Rugh graduated from Oberlin College (B.A., 1958); Johns Hopkins University School of Advanced International Studies (M.A., 1961); and Columbia University (Ph.D., 1964). He was born May 10, 1936, in New York, NY. Ambassador Rugh is married, has three children, and resides in Maryland.

# The President's News Conference With Prime Minister Brian Mulroney of Canada
*May 20, 1992*

*The President.* I'm just delighted to have had this visit with Prime Minister Mulroney of Canada, welcoming him back to the White House.

I think we covered an awful lot of ground in a short time. And just a couple of observations: I know that many are focusing on our trade issues, in particular on trade disputes. Well, that's natural. We've got this enormous, this immense trade that goes on between our two countries. And our bilateral trade has increased by $30 billion since the inception of the Free Trade Agreement in 1989 and now stands at a volume of nearly $200 billion. I believe that this trade is of enormous benefit to the two economies and demonstrates vividly the value of that Free Trade Agreement. And because of the large trade between the U.S. and Canada, there are bound to be some bumps in the road.

We have existing mechanisms for dispute settlement. We are using them, including the FTA itself. And as a consequence, I can report that we're making progress in overcoming some of our recent problems. I told the Prime Minister, who forcefully presented Canada's case, that I would work with our administration to see that these disputes receive proper high-level consideration before they go to some form of action. I think this will help. But in any event, we discussed frankly the problems.

We also talked about a wide range of international issues, including the coming summit, including the G–7. So we had a very good conversation. And in the Bush view, our administration view, this relationship between Canada and the United States is very, very important to the people of the United States of America.

So, welcome back, sir.

*The Prime Minister.* Thank you, Mr. President.

As the President said, we had a very farreaching discussion on a lot of subjects. I'd be happy to take whatever questions are appropriate.

But I tried to focus on what our priority problem is at this point in time, and it's trade. And for some time, Canadians have been troubled and angered by the attitude adopted by some people in Washington on major trade issues. Rather than move quickly to resolve or prevent irritants, the tendency was to retaliate against Canadian products by threatening to impose demonstrably unfair penalties on Canadian imports. These actions create uncertainty for investors and exporters and undermine the fundamental intent of the Free Trade Agreement.

The President has called me a number of times over the last few weeks, conscious of some of these difficulties that have arisen in a very complex and important trading relationship. We agreed at this meeting today to follow up on it. So we had a very constructive review of these issues.

We both intend to raise the level of commitment to resolve and to reduce disputes, to give a higher level of attention in order to manage the relationship and these issues. The President and I are going to work personally to that end. We both recognize that healthy trade between us is vital to recovery. We are the United States' best customer by far, and the United States is ours. We can help each other in terms of economic recovery by reducing the temperature and getting rid of a lot of these irritants, rather than allow them to fester and grow to important status.

For example, Canada's merchandise trade surplus was $3.1 billion in the first quarter, as announced this morning, the largest surplus since the second quarter of 1990, and for the first quarter, Canada's exports to the United States are up 8.8 percent from last year. As the President has pointed out, even in a difficult recessionary period, the growth in trade between Canada and the United States is up very impressively. That means jobs in the United States and jobs in Canada, and we have to keep that going.

It was a very instructive and helpful meeting, and I thank the President and his advisers and counselors and Cabinet ministers for that.

*Canada-U.S. Trade*

*Q.* Who are these mysterious "some people"? Are you suggesting that the President himself may not know who in his administration, in your view, is discriminating against Canadian trade?

*The Prime Minister.* I've already indicated, and you know full well, that a lot of the action is initiated by industry, by interest groups, by lobbying interests in isolation from some of the fundamental objectives of the Free Trade Agreement. And in some cases, as dispute mechanisms have pointed out, they may or may not have validity. Sometimes the United States wins; sometimes we win.

What concerns me is not that. That's normal. What concerns me are demonstrably unfair matters being initiated and allowed to grow and fester when they should have been dismissed because the object of the Free Trade Agreement was to make it a model for the rest of the world or certainly a model for this hemisphere. And anything that vitiates that undermines the effectiveness of what is a very valid and helpful instrument for both of us. That's what I was talking about.

*Q.* Mr. President, do you agree that we have not been fair?

*The President.* I agree that when you have a trading situation that's as broad and as big as we have, there are bound to be some disputes. What we've agreed today is to be sure that we engage early on at

proper levels to see that some of those disputes can be avoided. Some may not. Some may have to go to arbitration or to be adjudicated in legal manners. But I think we can do a better job of trying to avoid disputes. And that's what the spirit of these conversations were all about.

*Q.* Is the trade agreement jeopardized by this dispute?

*The President.* No. From our standpoint, we've got this agreement. I've cited for you the figures of advanced trade as taken place under the agreement. But what we've got to iron out are the differences, and they are overwhelmed by the common ground.

If you're referring to the NAFTA, I don't believe so. I think we just had a report on our side from our very able Ambassador, Carla Hills, who filled us in, and I detected no pessimism at all from her.

*The Prime Minister.* Helen [Helen Thomas, United Press International], from our point of view on that, we were very encouraged by the undertaking given today by the President to elevate the degree of attention that this trading relationship will receive in Washington by the administration. Oftentimes things get out of hand, but they tend to get less out of hand if the President is keeping an eye on it himself. That's what the President is going to work through his administration to make sure that they don't grow into the problems that they've become.

*Q.* What about Murphy Brown?

[*At this point, a question was asked in French and answered by the Prime Minister in French.*]

*Q.* Do you think Murphy Brown is a bad role model, sir?

*North American Free Trade Agreement*

*Q.* Mr. President, will you be personally involved in the North American free trade agreement negotiations and talk to the Prime Minister about any barriers to completing those talks?

*The President.* Oh, sure. But I'm not going to be the negotiator. We've got a very able, experienced team that knows far more about the detail than I know, and they have my full confidence. But I have such a relationship with the President of Mexico and the Prime Minister of Canada that they feel free to call me on these matters, and I feel free to call them. If we are needed to finalize these agreements, clearly, all of us want to be involved, all three of us.

### *Canada-U.S. Trade*

*Q.* Prime Minister, do you feel you've received the kind of assurances that will allow you to tell Canadians they will no longer be subject to the kind of action you yourself described as harassment?

*The Prime Minister.* Well, we'll have to see. But I also mentioned at that time, as you'll remember, that I was satisfied that President Bush was a free trader and a fair trader. I've consistently mentioned that. I believe that the kinds of harassment that we've seen must stop. I think that the President understands that. He understands my concerns and has indicated that at the highest level he plans to work with Secretary Baker and Carla and Brent and others to make sure that this is conducted in such a way that it is brought to a halt, not to preclude valid cases from coming forward on both sides, not to prevent that but to make sure that things that ought not to go forward, don't.

### *"Murphy Brown" Television Show*

*Q.* Let's get it over with, sir—Murphy Brown. [*Laughter*]

*Q.* ——Vice President Quayle's criticism of Murphy Brown, and also his statement that a lack of family values led to the L.A. riots?

*The President.* Everybody give me a Murphy Brown question. I've got one answer right here for you. [*Laughter*] What's your Murphy Brown question?

*Q.* What's your answer?

*The President.* What's the question? You're getting four different questions.

*Q.* Do you agree that she's not a good role model?

*Q.* Can a TV sitcom really influence a legitimate——

*The President.* All right, are you ready for the answer?

*Q.* Yes.

*The President.* All right, this is the last Murphy Brown question.

*Q.* Maybe.

*The President.* This is the last Murphy Brown answer, put it that way. [*Laughter*]

No, I believe that children should have the benefit of being born into families where the mother and a father will give them love and care and attention all their lives. I spoke on this family point in Notre Dame the other day. I've talked to Barbara about it a lot, and we both feel strongly that that is the best environment in which to raise kids. It's not always possible, but that's the best environment. I think it results in giving a kid the best shot at the American dream, incidentally. It's a certain discipline, a certain affection. One of the things that concerns me deeply is the fact that there are an awful lot of broken families. So that's really the kind of guidance I would place on that. I'm not going to get into the details of a very popular television show.

*Q.* You're contradicting your Press Secretary.

### *Urban Aid Initiatives*

*Q.* Mr. President, the Senate has almost doubled the amount of emergency funds in the supplemental for American cities. Is that acceptable to you?

*The President.* Which was it?

*Q.* The Senate has virtually doubled the amount of money in the emergency supplemental for Los Angeles and other cities. Is that acceptable to you? And also, sir, have you ruled out anything in terms of financing the programs that you're talking about, particularly taxes?

*The President.* We will be meeting this afternoon. I've appointed the Chief of Staff, who is already engaged with the leadership. I believe the meeting is going to be this afternoon with the leadership. I'm not familiar with what the Senate has done. There was one version of the bill that is unacceptable to us.

But here's my view on what we ought to do: There are some things that we agree on with Congress, have nothing to do with how you pay for it, but there are some things that are well within the budget agreement that can be done and where both Congress and the executive branch has shown an interest. It is my view that we ought to focus on those. "Weed and Seed" is one; enterprise zones is another. My pitch to the leaders is, look, you've got your priorities over here, and we've got ours. But let's do something that will help the people not just in Los Angeles but people that need jobs in the inner cities.

I'm still feeling that we have an opportunity to get it done that way. I can't comment on the Senate bill, except to say the one I saw yesterday, Kennedy-Hatch, is not acceptable to the administration, and we made that clear to the leaders. But let's get the common ground and try to do something to help people. Then we can have the debate and the votes and the countervotes as to whose plan, Senate plan, House plan, administration plan. I still think we can get it done that way.

*Q.* What about taxes, sir? Have you ruled out taxes?

### Thailand

*Q.* Can you comment, please, on the situation in Thailand? Some people are comparing this to Tiananmen Square. As far as I know you haven't mentioned it yet. What is——

*The President.* Well, we're very concerned about the instability in Thailand, very concerned about the violence that we've seen there, and we've made this position known to the Thais. In fact, our Ambassador had a meeting just yesterday with the Prime Minister on this. So let's hope that it calms down there.

*Q.* [*Inaudible*]—says that you are personally involved in helping to get loan guarantees for the—[*inaudible*]. Were you, sir? And were you at the time aware of——

*The Prime Minister.* I'll be happy to take these domestic questions at——

*Q.* Murphy Brown was more important, sir?

*The Prime Minister.* I didn't take Murphy Brown. Let me ask a question: Who is Murphy Brown? [*Laughter*]

I'll be happy to answer it later, Joe [Joe Schlesinger, Canadian Broadcasting Corporation].

### "Murphy Brown" Television Show

*Q.* Was it a mistake for Murphy Brown to portray an unwed mother in that show?

*The President.* I told you. You must have missed what I said, Pat [Patrick McGrath, Fox News]. I said I've just taken the last Murphy Brown question and tried to put it in a serious context that I hope the American people can understand. That's it.

Next for the Prime Minister here. We want fairplay here.

[*At this point, a question was asked in French and answered by the Prime Minister in French.*]

### President's Approval Rating

*Q.* Sir, I was just wondering, based on your own experience, have you been able to give the President any personal advice on how to handle this plummet in the polls that he's experienced recently?

*The Prime Minister.* Jim [Jim Miklaszewski, NBC News], I remember a time when President Reagan was here. And there was a front-page story in the New York Times in August of 1987 that said, "President Reagan's popularity has just plummeted to 59 percent." Right then I knew the difference between Canada and the United States; it's language. The word "plummet" does not mean the same in Canada as it does in the United States. So from where I'm sitting in the polls, I'm seeking advice, not giving any. [*Laughter*]

### Family Values

*Q.* Mr. President, do you agree with the Vice President that a lack of family values helped lead to these riots in Los Angeles? And do you think the California welfare reforms could ameliorate this?

*The President.* I think we'd have a much more stable environment everywhere in our country if we had more families, put it this way, if the kids had the advantages of two-parent households. It's not always easy. It's not always possible. But I really believe that is stabilizing. I think the decline in the family as this country's known it over the years is a discouraging factor, and I think it offers kids much less hope. I believe that if we had more stable families with a loving mother and father, and fathers taking their responsibility more seriously, that it would add to stability in the community, yes.

## Abortion

*Q.* Mr. President, the heart of the question seems to be whether or not there should be an abortion if you don't have a father. Can you specifically address——

*The President.* No, my position on abortion is well-known.

*Q.* But the two are in conflict here because the producer of the show says, "Well, then, you should ensure the right to abortion." Can you specifically address the main question?

*The President.* I'm not going to get—I don't know that much about the show. I've told you, I don't want to answer any more questions about it. I just tried to put it in terms of—John [John Cochran, CBS News] was asking about my view on stability of the family, I think. But I just can't go into the details.

*Q.* In this case, she chose to have a child and chose not to have an abortion. Do you applaud that?

*The President.* Well, as you know, I don't favor abortion. And I think that opting for life is the better path.

*Q.* Mr. President——

*The President.* Prime Minister, got one for him?

## Canada-U.S. Trade

*Q.* Any progress this morning on softwood lumber?

*The Prime Minister.* I indicated to the President that while we were encouraged by the reduction from 14.5 to 6.51, we still feel that this is a very unfair penalty on softwood exports from Canada that really do a lot of good for the United States. In fact, all that penalty is doing at the border is adding $1,000 or $2,000 to the cost of an average house in the United States, which is why the Governors in the Pacific Northwest are opposed to it. So what we're going to do is take this, under the Free Trade Agreement, under chapter 19, for resolution under the dispute settlement mechanism. I believe that Canada has a strong case and hopefully will win.

## Spotted Owl Habitat Protection

*Q.* President Bush, on the domestic side of the lumber supply issue, do you think that Secretary Lujan's alternative owl plan will help to reduce the shortage of lumber and to keep prices down?

*The President.* I think one thing it will do is see that fewer people are thrown out of work. And that I think is very important to many, many thousands of families in the Northwest. And what effect that particular decision is going to have overall on price, I just can't say. Whether it increases supply enough that the price will go down or not, I just don't—I haven't seen an economic analysis of that particular decision.

*Q.* Mr. President, what is your——

*The President.* We need—it's his turn, the Prime Minister's turn.

*The Prime Minister.* Okay, Hilary [Hilary MacKenzie, MacLean's Magazine]

## Canada-U.S. Trade

*Q.* Prime Minister, behind the trade dispute, is there a fundamental problem that Americans don't understand Canadian sensitivities on the trade issues?

*The Prime Minister.* No, I don't think that. I think the answer is the one that the President and I have referred to, that what it needs is an upgrading within the administration. In regard to the care and concern of—look, this is the most important trading partnership. A lot of Americans think their best trading partner is Japan. Wrong. Others think it's Europe. Wrong again. It's Canada. And the beauty of the trading relationship with Canada, unlike many others that the United States has, is that this $200 billion a year at the end of the year is in rough balance. The Americans are not carrying a big deficit to speak of in their trade with Canada. This kind of very valuable relationship has to be nurtured and looked after and admired for what it is. Otherwise, it could go the wrong way.

So it has nothing to do with Canadian sensitivities. It has a lot to do with upgrading this on the American side so that the American administration and people understand the importance of them not only to us but to them, and to use this as a model for trading agreements elsewhere in the world. I think it could be mutually beneficial.

*The President.* Marlin has signaled that we have time for one question each, if that's agreeable, Mr. Prime Minister.

*Q.* Mr. President, are you worried about Ross Perot?

*Q.* Mr. President. can you tell me if you believe that Canada has been harassed by decisions on trade cases brought by senior advisers, including the man who is now your deputy campaign manager?

*The President.* I believe that we ought to look at the whole picture. And I believe that that enormous trading relationship has been marred by a very few number of disputes. And I can understand it when people feel very strongly on a deal, whether it's lumber or whether it's autos or whatever else it is that's contentious. I'm inclined to look at the whole picture and see it relatively free of dispute.

But when there is a dispute, I can understand the passions being very high. We've got to try to avoid the disputes before they take place, and when they do take place, each side has every right to take it to adjudication.

So I'm not going to try to characterize it, but when the Prime Minister feels strongly about something like that and tells me of his strong feeling, clearly I want to do what I can, working with our bureaucracy, see that any feeling of harassment is eliminated. We'll work to eliminate these, get rid of the disputes before they happen. But then, if they have to happen because we have diverse interests, we'll try to peacefully and harmoniously settle them.

So that's the way—I can understand the passions on issues on both sides of the border. But I believe that we can, with this spirit that the Prime Minister has outlined here, minimize the chance for future disputes arising, and that's what I think is coming out of this meeting.

So when he presents me with strong feeling, the view of Canada on some very contentious issue, I don't take offense; I say, "Hey, let's try to work it out." And similarly, I expect that when we go forward with something we feel very strongly about, and there are recent cases there, the Prime Minister says, "Well, let's see whether we can't resolve that." Sometimes they have difficulties in Canada. They have provincial governments; they have central government, and we try to be understanding of that.

So I don't want to be standing here next to a good friend of the United States of America and a good free trader in some contentious mode. The meeting, albeit Brian Mulroney presents his case very forcefully—but I would simply say the meeting, as far as I'm concerned, some of it is let's find ways to avoid the disputes before they get to the point where one side or another feels harassment.

*The Prime Minister.* David [David Halton, Canadian Broadcasting Corporation], final question.

*Q.* Was there any discussion, sir, of the argument being made by some U.S. Senators that softwood lumber shouldn't even be allowed to go to a panel because it's exempted under the original FTA ruling?

*The Prime Minister.* No, we didn't get into the details of it, David, beyond what the President and I have indicated. But given the fact that we think that 6.51 is still unacceptable, we're going to take it to a chapter 19. And as I say, on behalf of the softwood industry in Canada, we think we've got a strong case and a good case, and that's what the dispute settlement mechanism is for. And we think that we can carry it successfully.

Thank you very much.

*The President.* Thank you all very much. Thank you, Helen. It's a wonderful meeting. Thank you.

*Note: The President's 128th news conference began at 1:34 p.m. on the South Lawn at the White House. Several questions referred to remarks by the Vice President concerning the CBS television comedy series "Murphy Brown," in which the title character, who was divorced, had a baby.*

## Statement on the 90th Anniversary of Cuban Independence
*May 20, 1992*

I would like to mark this day, the 90th anniversary of Cuban independence, by sharing my vision for a free and democratic Cuba. Just as the struggle for Cuban independence was hard fought, so too is the struggle of the Cuban people today to gain their freedom. The Castro dictatorship cannot and will not survive the wave of democracy that has swept over the world, and I believe the Cuban people are closer than ever to winning that freedom. On this Cuban Independence Day, I want to reiterate my firm solidarity with the Cuban people as they strive to bring peaceful, democratic change to their country.

Independence Day is the occasion to pay homage to the great heroes and freedom fighters of the past. But as we honor them, I also want to salute all those in Cuba who are placing themselves at personal risk by calling for peaceful change. We particularly want to express our admiration for the ever-growing number of Cuban men and women who are courageously speaking out against Castro's abuses of human rights and his denial of the Cuban people's most basic civil liberties.

We are working hard to ensure that those Cubans striving for human rights and civil freedoms have the broadest possible international recognition and support. I am pleased that the United Nations will be naming a special rapporteur to investigate and report on the human rights situation in Cuba. We will continue to help get the truth to the Cuban people through a free flow of information. Today, I reaffirm my commitment to oppose Castro at every turn and not to pursue normal relations until his dictatorship is done.

Castro's vision of the future is to cling to a failed past. His determination to keep Cuba an antidemocratic Communist state dooms the Cuban people to a predetermined fate. He tells them that their only choice is between "socialism or death." And he dismisses the basic rights of people, the rights to free speech and free association, as the "garbage" of democracy.

I reject Castro's vision of doom as I believe the Cuban people do. I see Cuba's future as one of hope and expectation. I believe that Cubans will enjoy a peaceful and democratic future, one in which they will be able to elect the leaders of their choice. My vision is one in which Cubans have open access to the newspapers, television, and radio; will be able to travel and study wherever they like; and will find jobs in a prosperous Cuba, resulting in better lives for their children and their grandchildren.

And I want the Cuban people to know that my administration and the American people will be prepared to help in a transition to a stable and free Cuba. Our elected officials, our businessmen, many of our ordinary citizens, and especially the members of our hard working and prosperous Cuban-American community are willing and able to help rebuild Cuba by lending their know-how to repair the shattered Cuban economy.

So on this historic occasion, I look forward to a new day of Cuban independence when decisions about their future are made through free and fair elections that reflect tolerance and respect for the views of each individual. This will be the foundation for building a new and better Cuba, a free Cuba.

# Message to the Congress Reporting on the National Emergency With Respect to Chemical and Biological Weapons Proliferation
*May 20, 1992*

*To the Congress of the United States:*

On November 16, 1990, in light of the dangers of the proliferation of chemical and biological weapons, I issued Executive Order No. 12735 and declared a national emergency under the International Emergency Economic Powers Act (50 U.S.C. 1701, *et seq.*).

The proliferation of chemical and biological weapons continues to pose an unusual and extraordinary threat to the national security and foreign policy of the United States.

Section 204 of the International Emergency Economic Powers Act and section 401(c) of the National Emergencies Act contain periodic reporting requirements regarding activities taken and money spent pursuant to an emergency declaration. The following report is made pursuant to these provisions.

The three export control regulations issued under the Enhanced Proliferation Control Initiative are fully in force and have been used to control the export of items with potential use in chemical or biological weapons or their delivery systems.

Over the last 6 months, the United States has continued to address actively the problem of the proliferation and use of chemical and biological weapons in its international diplomatic efforts.

The membership of the Australia Group of countries cooperating against chemical and biological weapons proliferation grew from 20 to 22 members when Finland and Sweden were welcomed into the Group in December 1991.

At the same December 1991 Australia Group meeting, all member countries confirmed that they had implemented or were implementing export controls on all 50 identified chemical weapons precursors. Almost all Australia Group members agreed at the meeting to impose controls on a common list of dual-use chemical equipment. In the first major Australia Group involvement in biological weapons nonproliferation, the December meeting also produced a draft list of biological organisms, toxins, and equipment to consider for export controls. This list was further refined by an Australia Group experts' meeting in March 1992, the first intersessional meeting held by the Australia Group, and will be considered for adoption by the June 1992 Australia Group plenary.

Encouraging progress can also be reported in the steps taken by countries outside the Australia Group, including several Eastern European countries and Argentina, to establish effective chemical and biological export controls comparable to those observed by Australia Group members.

Finally, the March 31, 1992, report regarding expenditures under the declaration of a national emergency to deal with the lapse of the Export Administration Act in Executive Order No. 12730 also includes measures related to the Enhanced Proliferation Control Initiative. Pursuant to section 401(c) of the National Emergencies Act, there were no additional expenses directly attributable to the exercise of authorities conferred by the declaration of the national emergency.

GEORGE BUSH

The White House,
May 20, 1992.

# Presidential Determination No. 92–26—Memorandum on Trade With Albania
*May 20, 1992*

*Memorandum for the Secretary of State*

*Subject:* Determination Under Section 402(c)(2)(A) of the Trade Act of 1974, as Amended—Albania

Pursuant to section 402(c)(2)(A) of the Trade Act of 1974, as amended (the "Act") (19 U.S.C. 2432(c)(2)(A)), I determine that a waiver by Executive order of the application of subsections (a) and (b) of section 402 of the Act with respect to Albania will substantially promote the objectives of section 402.

You are authorized and directed to publish this determination in the *Federal Register*.

GEORGE BUSH

[*Filed with the Office of the Federal Register, 2:45 p.m., October 26, 1992*]

*Note: The Executive order of June 3 is listed in Appendix E at the end of this volume.*

# Message to the Congress on Trade With Albania
*May 20, 1992*

*To the Congress of the United States:*

Pursuant to section 402(c)(2)(A) of the Trade Act of 1974, as amended (the "Act") (19 U.S.C. 2432(c)(2)(A)), I have determined that a waiver of the application of subsections (a) and (b) of section 402 with respect to Albania will substantially promote the objectives of section 402. A copy of that determination is enclosed. I have also received assurances with respect to the emigration practices of Albania required by section 402(c)(2)(B) of the Act. This message constitutes the report to the Congress re-

quired by section 402(c)(2).

Pursuant to section 402(c)(2), I shall waive by Executive order the application of subsections (a) and (b) of section 402 of the Act with respect to Albania.

GEORGE BUSH

The White House,
May 20, 1992.

*Note: The Executive order of June 3 is listed in Appendix E at the end of this volume.*

# Nomination of James E. Gilleran To Be Comptroller of the Currency
*May 21, 1992*

The President today announced his intention to nominate James E. Gilleran, of California, to be Comptroller of the Currency, Department of the Treasury, for a term of 5 years. He would succeed Robert Logan Clarke.

Since 1989, Mr. Gilleran has served as superintendent of the California State Bank-

ing Department in San Francisco, CA. Prior to this, he served as president of the Commonwealth Group, 1987–89; managing partner with Peat Marwick in San Francisco, CA, 1969–87; and as partner-in-charge of the banking industry group of Peat Marwick in Los Angeles, CA, 1958–69.

Mr. Gilleran graduated from Pace University (B.B.A., 1955). He was born May 1, 1933, in Ellenville, NY. Mr. Gilleran served in the U.S. Army, 1955–57. He is married, has two children, and resides in San Francisco, CA.

# Remarks at a Bush-Quayle Fundraising Luncheon in Cleveland, Ohio
*May 21, 1992*

Thank you all. Please be seated, and thanks for that welcome. George Voinovich gave our administration a lot of credit for these things that he clicked off today, and he talked about the blast furnace. You should have seen the letter that he sent to me, blasting us to get the blast furnace going. [*Laughter*] He's a hands-on Governor, just as he was a hands-on Mayor of this great city. And he is one of our very, very best across the whole country, and you all are awful lucky, in case you didn't know it. And that goes for Janet, too.

I, too, want to thank the Fairview High School Band and Virgil Brown; Jim Petro for leading us in the pledge. May I single out one who is with me today that some of you know personally, but who is doing a superb job fighting now to get some legislation that he and I believe in, legislation that's been lingering before the Congress for 3 years, through the Congress. I'm talking about our able Secretary of HUD, Jack Kemp, over here, Jack.

And may I wish Mike DeWine the very, very best. We need him in the Senate. We've got to get control of the United States Senate. And also, Art Modell, thank you, sir. I'll never forget a marvelous event out at Art's house when I was running for this job, and he's been a good supporter and an outstanding citizen of Cleveland. And of course, Tim Timken has been at my side for a long, long time, and I'm very proud of the job he does on the national level as well as working for the Bush-Quayle effort here in this State. Bob Taft is with us, the secretary of state, another longtime friend, also doing a superb job for all of you.

Bob Bennett, when I think back to my days of being national chairman, chairman of the Republican Party, there were some who just were ornaments. Some didn't hit a lick. And Bob Bennett is an outstanding, active, hands-on chairman of the Republican Party in this State; and that's why I believe we will get control of the State House of Representatives. And may I, too, thank Stan Aronoff and Martha Moore and single out Bobby Holt, our national finance chairman, and Dick Freeland, our regional Bush-Quayle finance chairman.

I am very, very pleased to be here. I will be out of here in time for you all to go back to work, suit up, and then watch the Cavs and the Bulls play at 8 p.m. tonight. So my priorities are correct.

Let me start by saying I think we have an awful lot to be grateful for as a Nation. These are troubled times, times of discontent. It isn't just America, if you look around the world, incidentally. Take a look at Germany. Take a look at France. Take a look at what was happening in England before their election. There seems to be a turmoil, an antipolitical mode.

But I think as George pointed out, we have a lot to be grateful for. We have effected, helped effect, worldwide change. Democracy is on the move. There's turmoil in Eastern Europe, but it's moving in the right direction. Totalitarianism is dead. South of our own border you're seeing, through our Enterprise for the Americas Initiative and through the Brady plan, you're seeing a whole resurgence of private sector activity and the democratic march in our own hemisphere.

The main point I would make is that our kids can go to sleep at night in this country with far less fear of nuclear war. That is significant change. That is worldwide change. And we had a hand in bringing it about, everybody that supported the strong defense of the United States.

So as we move into this election year, we're moving in there with something we can really be proud of to take to the American people. The spirit of Desert Storm is not dead in this country. The country came together after we were the ones that stood up to aggression, formed a coalition, and said to the rest of the world: One country, a big bully of a country, is not going to take over another. And that has given us the standing around the world that I think is unprecedented, certainly in recent times.

Now, what we're trying to do domestically is to take that move for change and bring it to bear on our problems right here at home. It's been put in focus by the troubles out in Los Angeles. We have a program that ties in and fits nicely to solving the problems in not only Los Angeles but the problems that are plaguing our cities. And indeed, many of the answers spill over into rural America as well. What I wanted to do is just point out where we stand in terms of trying to change things productively here at home.

The first thing I would say is we have to support our law enforcement people. We do; our administration does it in many, many ways. We have a program now that is called "Weed and Seed": Weed out the criminals, and then seed these neighborhoods with hope and with opportunity. But we must not move away and try to explain away the gang members and the terrorists in our cities.

I was pleased to see some of Cleveland's finest out here, police officers, because I like to be able to tell these men who are giving themselves for all of us that we back them up as they go into harm's way, trying to bring order and civility to the neighborhoods that need it the most. We must support our police. You know, I made that comment in the Mount Zion Baptist Church right in the heart of south central L.A. And I felt strongly about it, and I was flanked by 200 pastors from the various Baptist churches, the area's churches that were in the most heavily impacted area. The church came out in spontaneous applause. The people in the neighborhood know that they are the ones that are being ravaged by the gangs and the criminals and the criminal elements.

The next point, though, is not just "weed," it's not just law enforcement, law and order; it is also seeding the area with hope and with opportunity. This program we have, antidrug, profamily, proinvestment, is a good one. So we start with our first incentive: Fund our "Weed and Seed" program. The second one: We've got to rebuild community. And again, I salute Jack Kemp. He's been out on the firing line for this for the 3 years that our administration has been in office.

Enterprise zones: There is an idea whose time has come. And every place Jack and I went in the neighborhood, whether it was Hispanic, whether it was the Korean neighborhood, whether it was in the largely Afro-American neighborhoods, those community leaders were saying, "Give us enterprise zones. Change the tax structure so that this place can serve as a magnet to bring jobs with dignity into the private sector." That idea is here now; it's on the table right this minute in the Congress. And the Congress ought to pass it, and pass it fast.

And along with it is another concept: Homeownership. Isn't it far better, isn't it far better for the dignity and strength of a family to have a person own a home or have a tenant-managed project than it is to go to some desolate brick-and-mortar that has no heart, no soul, and falls apart because nobody cares? Homeownership is an idea whose time has come. And we've challenged the Congress again: Get moving and give us more to take to the American people in terms of homeownership. That's the third one.

The fourth one: Welfare reform. Some say, "Well, when you talk about welfare reform, you're injecting race into the situation." That isn't what we're talking about at all. Did you know that if a family—I saw a case the other day of a little girl, saved a little money in a welfare family, got past $1,000, and she was penalized. "Oh, you can't. Your family is on welfare. You can't do that." We've got to reform the welfare system, not only to make it so there's workfare and learnfare and give the States a chance to innovate but to change the rules so people are not punished for saving. It's not a racist thing. It isn't a black versus white or Hispanic versus anybody else; it's what's fair and right. We've got to give some dignity to the family. And the way to do it is to reform the welfare system, and we're going to keep on trying.

Number four: Job training. We've got a good new job training approach. Frankly, there's an awful lot of Government Agencies involved in servicing communities, as George Voinovich knows. He's working hard to help us streamline this. But we have a Job Training 2000 program that calls for one-stop shopping, so a person that doesn't quite know how to filter his way around through all this big bureaucracy of ours can go and take his tiny little problem to the one-stop office and try to get some job training that really is effective. And Job Training 2000 is a good, new program, and I believe that it needs to have the support of the American people. And we are going to keep working not only legislatively but administratively to bring more jobs and opportunity through job training to the various communities.

Then, the last point of these six is the question of education. It's a little longer run. Our education program won't solve the problems of the cities overnight. But if you take a look at what we really have to do in this country, we literally have to revolutionize education. And we've got a great Secretary of Education in Lamar Alexander. He's ably assisted by a former businessman that many of the people in this room know, David Kearns. He was the former chief executive of Xerox, who gave up his wonderful business challenge and perhaps retirement to come in as the number two guy in the Department of Education.

What we've done is design a program called America 2000. It literally revolutionizes the education system in this country. It emphasizes things like choice. We find that when parents have a choice of where their kids go to school, not only do they get a much better shot at what they want, but the schools that are not chosen improve themselves. So our administration stands firmly for parental choice, for private and public and religious schools alike. And we ought to get that done right now for the American people.

These are some specific points that we're working for, and right now I've challenged the Congress in this manner. I've said to them: Look, I know we have political differences. I'm a realist about the election, and I know that the closer and closer we get to the election, it isn't going to be easy. You're not going to want to see me get one leg up. And I'm going to continue to fight for the things we believe. But let's take the things we agree on now. Homeownership is one; enterprise zones is one. In fact, that passed the United States House of Representatives, wrapped up in a great big tax increase bill that, of course, I wasn't going to sign. But nevertheless, we have several of these programs that will help America right now.

Rather than play the political game—I've had two meetings with the leadership, both Republican and Democrat, and I said, look, let's agree on several of these points and pass it and show the American people that we can move forward instead of standing around there playing politics as usual. I will repeat that: Let's pass what we can, and pass it now.

Now if you think of these points I have outlined, there are themes to all this: Personal responsibility, opportunity, ownership, independence, dignity, empowerment. And that all adds up to the American dream. And we are not going to give up on the American dream, and we recognize that there's—overlying these issues are enormously big issues. And one of them is we've got to stop mortgaging our kids' future.

And the way to go about doing that—and there's another idea whose time has come— finally we are getting bipartisan consideration of the balanced budget amendment, something I've been talking about for 12 years. And it's time to pass it. We've got to phase it in, but pass it. And that will discipline not just the Congress but the executive branch as well. And it's really moving now. So if you have any influence at all on either side of the aisle, make your case. Because it's timely, and it's an idea whose time has come.

And the other one which I consider a great big issue that fits into the idea of fiscal sanity is this: Forty-three Governors can take a pen, and they can ax out something that they consider is irrelevant in terms of spending or excessive in terms of spending. So I say and ask for support from the American people on this one: You give me the line-item veto this fall, and let's see if we can't do a better job cutting the spending that is ruining America's fiscal standing.

And the third issue of that nature, a balanced budget amendment, line-item veto, is legal reform. We've got to help each other more and sue each other less. And the way to do it is for tort reform.

And the last point I want to make today has nothing to do with "Murphy Brown." [*Laughter*] But it does have to do with something that George Voinovich mentioned. I'm talking about family values. And I'm going to continue to talk about that.

I've talked with Jack about this, Jack Kemp. And I had a meeting with the National League of Cities—I mentioned this in the State of the Union—key mayors, Tom Bradley of Los Angeles, a Republican mayor from a tiny town in North Carolina, and all size city mayors from in between, one from Plano, Texas. And they came to me, and they said, "We've been thinking what we can do about the cities. And we think that the single most important problem is the demise, the dissolution, the decline of the American family." And I just can't tell you what an impact that made on me. They weren't saying, "Send us all this money." Of course they'd like to have that. But they addressed themselves to the decline of the American family, and they asked me to appoint an urban commission, a commission on the American family, which as you may recall I did, announcing John Ashcroft of Missouri and Mrs. Strauss, the former Mayor of Dallas, to be the Cochairs of that committee.

We have got to find ways to strengthen the American family. And that's why I ask you to give sincere consideration and support to those six objectives that I spelled out above. Because each one of them, in some way or another, strengthens and does not diminish the American family.

I feel very strongly about it. I know that there are those who are deprived, who are born into almost hopeless situations. But there are all kinds of ways that we can help. You can lift up the kid that starts off with a tremendous advantage through what we call Points of Light activities. You can look at every single piece of legislation to see that it doesn't encourage husband and wife to live apart. You can do what you can in the whole field of education.

But all of us as Americans must address ourselves to the idea that we must find ways to strengthen the American families. Because Barbara Bush is right: What happens in your house is much more important than what happens in the White House.

So here's our agenda. I think it's a good one. I think it is an optimistic one. I think it is an encouraging one. And I will be proud to be taking this case to the American people in the fall. But as I conclude today, my appeal to the American people would be, please, help us now with the United States Congress, and move this hope and opportunity agenda through the United States Congress. We need your help. We need the help of the people. And now is the time.

Thank you all, and God bless you. And thank you for your support.

*Note: The President spoke at 12:25 p.m. in the Grand Ballroom of the Stouffer Tower City Plaza Hotel. In his remarks, he referred to George Voinovich, Governor of Ohio, and his wife, Janet; Virgil Brown, Jr., who gave the invocation; Art Modell, Cleveland Browns football team owner; Tim Timken, luncheon chairman; Stan Aronoff, Ohio State Senate president; and Martha Moore, Ohio Republican Party vice chairman.*

## Remarks at the Ohio Freedom Day Celebration in Parma, Ohio
*May 21, 1992*

Thank you so much. Thank you, Governor Voinovich. I think the people in Parma probably understand this, but let me just say it: You've got a great Governor of this State, and I'm proud to be with him. May I salute two members of my Cabinet, the President's Cabinet, with me here today: Secretary Jack Kemp, who runs HUD, doing a great job; he's out there working to help through enterprise zones and home-ownership, doing a great job there. And then another one whom you all know very well, most of you do, a man who has introduced me to much of ethnic America, Secretary Ed Derwinski, the Secretary of the Veterans Administration.

I want to thank Mayor Ries, who greeted me earlier, Parma's Mayor, welcoming me to this wonderful community. Another old friend, Ralph Perk, we go back a long, long time, Ralph, to when he was Mayor of the city of Cleveland. And of course, Mike DeWine, who I want to see in the United States Senate, now the Lieutenant Governor of this State.

Let me thank all of you for this Freedom Medal. I was pointing out to Ralph something he had already seen. But I love these signs, all of them hand-done, but "Freedom Is America's Name" and "Let Freedom Ring." What says it better than that? I don't know. It is fantastic. I think it is very fitting that George Voinovich, your Governor, has proclaimed this Freedom Day. And Americans like yourselves, not just here but all across the country, gave us the strength, the determination, the will to topple the Berlin Wall and to work for the freedom of Eastern Europe and for the rest of what used to be the Soviet Union.

You never gave up. You never, ever gave up. You said your prayers; you said them over and over again, praying for your friends and your families that were left halfway around the world, but you never, ever gave up. And I've been in public life for some time; half my life in public life, half in private. And one thing I've seen, wherever, is the faith that the Americans, different

nationalities, had in the fact that their countries, their people would be free. You never gave up, and I congratulate you for that.

Today we hear so much gloom and doom about what's wrong with the United States of America. But we can all take pride that we brought about the fall of the Iron Curtain, the death of imperial communism, and we prevented the cataclysm of the third world war because freedom-loving people in America and in Europe persevered and won the cold war definitively. And we should take great pride in that.

It's risky to go into any particular country in this homogenous group, I'll tell you, but a group joined together because of freedom, but with many ethnic backgrounds. But the great leader of the Ukrainian Catholic Church, Cardinal Slipyj, endured years of pain in prison, and we'll never forget his role. We'll never forget Hungary's noble symbol of courage, the late Cardinal Mindszenty. Both of these men died in lonely exile. But they inspired others, not just in Hungary but others, to persevere. And they inspired others to literally change the world. And now both are hailed openly as heroes in their native land, just as they are honored here in America. The church, faith had a lot to do about the success of the United States in standing up against communism and working and prevailing for freedom.

This day, Freedom Day, we also honor heroes of the nineties, statesmen like Havel and Walesa and Landsbergis. And we marvel at how our world has changed. You know, during the eighties, Havel and Lech Walesa spent time in prison for the crime of speaking up for freedom. That was the crime, to speak up for freedom. And it was scarcely more than one year ago that Landsbergis of Lithuania took his stand, armed with only the truth and the spirit of patriotism against the Red army forces who were gunning down innocent citizens in Lithuania. So, we won't forget that.

And this day honors the work of half a century of our GI's and of our allies who kept NATO strong; the radio broadcasters who pierced the Iron Curtain with words of hope and truth. I remember when Lech Walesa came to the United States. He wanted to go to Radio Free Europe so he could meet and look into the eyes of the voice that he had heard speaking up for freedom when that was the only hope the people of Poland had, a wonderful story about our Nation's perseverance.

We think of world leaders whose deeds were as powerful as their words: Margaret Thatcher and Helmut Kohl, my predecessor Ronald Reagan, who had so much to do with keeping our sights set on the fall of communism, and of the families—we think of them—in the East and the West who prayed together, and parents who taught their children right from wrong. The physical and moral strength of these people transcended and destroyed the Iron Curtain.

And I believe that moral strength will prevail, even where violence and oppression hold forth, as in the states of the former Yugoslavia. We now recognize the full sovereignty of Slovenia and Croatia and Bosnia, and we stand in solidarity with their people. Let me make this clear: We will not recognize the annexation of territories by force. Aggression cannot be rewarded. But we must stay involved, trying to find a peaceful answer to the whole question of Yugoslavia.

So, as George said, we do stand on the threshold of a new world, a world of peace and opportunity. And I really see this as the opportunity of a century. And it's amazing to learn about some of the efforts that have already begun, think tanks and fax machines that are networking to foster democracy and free enterprise in the Baltic republics, in Ukraine and Russia, throughout Eastern Europe.

Governor Voinovich tells me the growth of telephone traffic between Ohio and Ukraine is absolutely phenomenal. New phone links are helping families restore these old bonds and helping new business ventures get going. People from Kiev and Vilnius now travel here without having to fear that they left home for the last time.

Government is doing its part. Two weeks ago I had a wonderful meeting, for those particularly interested in Ukraine, a won-

derful meeting with Kravchuk, President Kravchuk, welcoming him to the White House and then taking him up—we flew in a helicopter up to Camp David, pointing out the different rural communities in agricultural America and urban America.

I think we made real progress working with President Kravchuk on reducing the threat of nuclear war. We announced our pledge to establish the science and technology center in Ukraine. We signed agreements that are going to foster trade and investment with Ukraine. And I've taken action to grant most-favored-nation status for Ukraine as soon as possible. And again, for the Ukrainian-Americans present, I am very, very proud that one of the men closest to me in the White House, Roman Popadiuk, will be sworn in next week as the first American Ambassador to Ukraine.

We've got to keep working on this. Just last week, a couple of days ago actually, I had an equally good meeting with the President of Kazakhstan, President Nazarbayev. And like Kravchuk, Nazarbayev pledged to join the Non-Proliferation Treaty as a non-nuclear-weapon state. And he pledged to remove all the nuclear weapons within the 7-year period of the START agreement.

And in a few more weeks, the President of Russia, a gigantic new country, President Yeltsin coming to the United States, and we are going to meet together in Washington to chart a new partnership with Russia for the future. And it is a wonderful thing to be talking about business and freedom instead of talking about nuclear arms and the worry that our kids used to have in this country about the nuclear threat.

We're eager to develop strengths and strengthen our ties with Byelarus and Moldova and Armenia and all the nations that have won independence from Soviet rule. And working with them and our allies we want to establish a democratic peace, a lasting peace that is built on trust, a peace that is built on shared values, not simply the absence of war.

And so to finish this job, I need your help. We've done much to support the new nations of the Commonwealth, C.I.S. And there are other initiatives that will help these nations along the road to democracy and freedom. For Russia, largely for Russia but also for the Ukraine and others, we have the "FREEDOM Support Act" which I've sent up to the Congress, which will provide new opportunities for American business. It's going to clear away a lot of that cold war legislation, get rid of that, that now inhibits trade and investment with Ukraine and the other nations of the old Soviet empire. It provides new authority to continue food assistance totaling $110 million in food guarantees for the purchase of American ag products. And Congress should act now.

We've got problems at home, but we must not miss this historic opportunity to guarantee the peace for these kids here and to guarantee the freedom for those across the ocean. So join with me in asking Congress not to disappoint our children and to support us as we try to pass the "FREEDOM Support Act." And if we meet these responsibilities today, a generation from now people might be speaking about a "Ukrainian miracle" or a "Baltic miracle," much as we marvel at the recovery of Western Europe just a few years ago, ravaged by the Second World War. They came back strong. And everyone calls it the "miracle of Western Europe." Now we want the same things for these new republics. And with your support, we can get it.

I know that it is still Easter season in your church. And to close, I want to tell a story about Easter this year, not in Ukraine but in Russia. Many of you will recall the big military parades that the Soviets used to have there in Red Square, always with a huge portrait of Lenin as the backdrop, on the wall of the State Historical Museum. Well, this year at Easter, there was no portrait of Lenin. Instead, a massive icon towered over Red Square, an icon of the Resurrection, and atop it, the words *Christos Voskrese,* Christ is risen.

And the way I look at it is this: This really is a season of resurrection throughout the once-captive nations of Europe. And it is a wonderful time to be alive to see these days, to enjoy the freedom that God has given us in the freest, most wonderful Nation on the face of the Earth, the United States of America. May God bless each and every one of you.

And may I say, as the President of the United States, I will keep working for freedom around the world. And with your support, I know we will be successful in seeing these European and former Soviet republics become free and whole, with the people enjoying a life they never would have dreamed of.

Thank you, and may God bless the United States of America. Thank you.

*Note: The President spoke at 1:53 p.m. in the auditorium at St. Josephat's Cathedral.*

# Remarks at a Bush-Quayle Fundraising Picnic in Westchester, New York
*May 21, 1992*

Thank you all very much. It is a pleasure to be here, and I'm delighted. Lou, thank you, sir, for that introduction. Please be seated out there. And be seated up here. [*Laughter*] Sorry about that. No, but I'm delighted to be here. I'm sorry that Barbara Bush is not here. She was here just a couple of weeks ago at another event.

But it's a thrill to be back in my hometown, near it, one of my many hometowns. I just had a chance to drive up across the line into Greenwich to see my almost-91-year-old mother. So in a way, it is a homecoming. And it really is when you look out here and see so many friends, so many people that worked way back in the political wars and have given me this extraordinary opportunity to be President of the United States in these wonderfully exciting, challenging, yes, but wonderfully exciting times for our country.

And I am pleased—I want to thank Lou, I

want to thank Ginny, his wife; both of them so nervous they can hardly speak about the future grandchild that's appearing any minute now. I want to thank the Young Artists' Philharmonic for bringing us a little class into this hangar. Real good. Thank you all very, very much. And salute several old friends: John Rowland, who we miss in the Congress, and I expect you miss him as Governor of this State, but nevertheless—and Bobby Holt and my old friend Brian Gaffney and Betsy and Spike Heminway and Dick Foley and Bob Macauley and Leon Hirsh, Jack Neafsey, and fellow Republicans, including our very special Secretary of HUD, Jack Kemp, who is doing a superb job, trying to get this Congress to move.

And a special thanks to my old friends. They were with us in the convention and 4 years ago. I am a fan of theirs. They came down from Bangor, Maine, to be here, heading right on down to Atlantic City. But let's hear it once more for the Oak Ridge Boys. They say an awful lot about this great country of ours.

Now, not for a long one. Billy Graham tells this marvelous story about the speaker that went on and on and on. Somebody sitting over about where Jack was picked up the gavel, heaved it at him, missed the speaker, and hit a lady in the front row. And she said, "Hit me again. I can still hear him." [*Laughter*] I want to keep this one brief because it is a lovely and an informal evening. But let me just make a few comments.

In the first place, I do think we've got a lot to be grateful for in this country. I think we have many, many blessings. And I see these kids here, and I am very proud that our administration has had some hand in seeing that these kids don't go to sleep every night worried about nuclear war. We have changed the world, and we've changed it for the better.

I just came from a very emotional meeting—Freedom Day, it is, out in Cleveland, Ohio—came from a very emotional meeting with what used to be called the captive nations people: Ukrainians and Hungarians and so many others, Poles, Eastern Europeans of all kinds, and then those now republics, represented by the republics of the Soviet Union, former Soviet Union. And again we ought to keep that in sight as we count our blessings. The United States, because we stayed strong—and I salute my predecessor Ronald Reagan for this one—because we stayed strong and determined, those nations are no longer captive nations. They are free nations. And democracy is on the move all across the world.

So just as we have brought these changes, with a lot of help I will concede, but we brought these changes to the world, we've got to change things at home. And that is exactly what we have been trying to do for the last 3 years. Some successes, not enough. We've got to change the world. And let me just tell you, as Jack and I went out to Los Angeles and looked at it, what we feel needs to be done in the way of change. And it's not just to take care of that city that went through the horrible times. It's not just that, because the ideas I'll mention to you real quick are ideas that would resonate for other cities, other communities across this country. And all of them are built on the principles: personal responsibility, opportunity, ownership, independence, dignity, empowerment, the family. And it all adds up to the American dream.

And here's what we're talking about: We have a great program that we're trying to get the Congress to help us with now called "Weed and Seed." It backs our wonderful law enforcement people. It weeds out the criminals and goes after the drug dealers. And then it seeds the neighborhoods with hope and opportunity. We need to get that through the United States Congress, and I believe we can.

The next one is enterprise zones, something that we've been championing for 3 years, Jack on the cutting edge, and effectively so, I might add. And what that says is, better than some make-work program, let's change the tax structure so you can draw like a magnet into the inner cities some businesses who are going to take a chance, who are going to take a gamble. And it's going to make it worth their while through the tax changes so they will then offer jobs with dignity in the private sector to those that have been bypassed as far as the American dream goes. We need enterprise zones now, and I'd like to have your support with the Congress.

Another one is, we must reform the welfare system. And people say, "Oh well, wait a minute, is that some kind of code word." It is not. What we're doing is offering waivers to these States so they can try. Wisconsin came in, they've got a program called Learnfare to take welfare dependency people and give them an opportunity to learn; similarly, Workfare programs. We have got to innovate in this country. And then there's a much more compassionate side of welfare reform. A kid saved the other day a little over $1,000. And the welfare people came to get the family and said, "Your daughter here has saved a little over $1,000. You can't do that on welfare; that violates the rules." We're trying to change that so families can save a little money and work their way out or get themselves an education. So we've got to reform the welfare system. And the time has come. And the people that will benefit the most are those who have been on welfare hopelessly without any chance at the American dream. Help us change it.

We've got a wonderful job training program, Job Training 2000. We're going to coordinate the services to the people that need it the most. And again, we're going to push through, our able Secretary of Labor Lynn Martin and others, to get this Job Training 2000 enacted.

A fifth one is homeownership. You see, we believe that if a person owns the home, it is far better. They take a pride in it. A dignity comes back. It strengthens the family, and it is a far better approach than these failed housing projects that strip families of their dignity. And so we're pushing hard for homeownership. And again, we're going to try to get the Congress to help us in every way possible. Give that opportunity to American families.

And the last one—and it is vitally important and it doesn't have quite the short-term implications—we must reform our education system. And we are talking about a new program. David Kearns, that's so well-known in this part to many people, was very instrumental in it and so is Lamar Alexander, our Secretary. We're literally talking about revolutionizing American

education, brandnew schools in each State, not new necessarily in bricks and mortar but new concepts. Trying that and saying, "The old system hasn't worked; let's change it." For example, let's give parents a choice of where they want to send their schools, religious or private, whatever it is. Give them a choice and watch our educational system improve.

So these are some of the initiatives we're pushing. And then overlying that, we have some other fundamental ones. Every time I see young people I'm saying to myself, we've got to do something to keep from mortgaging their future. And we've proposed capping the growth of these mandatory programs. We are now fighting for a balanced budget amendment. And we need your help to get that one through the Congress. It will discipline our branch of Government, and it'll discipline the United States Congress. And the balanced budget amendment will be phased in, and it'll save the future generations if we can get it passed.

Two other points you'll be hearing more about as we engage in the fall—and I will be encouraging people to send more Republican Congressmen down there to Washington, both in the Senate and the House. One of them is the line-item veto. You give me that line-item veto that these 43 Governors have, and watch us get that spending under control. And the last one, we've got to reform our legal system. We've got to sue each other less and help each other more. And we have proposals to do just exactly that. That's the tip of the iceberg.

There's a domestic agenda for you. And we're going to take the case to the American people. And Lou is right: The American economy has begun to move. A recent poll that I saw and analyzed here just a few days ago, 70 percent of the American people think the economy is getting worse. They are wrong. It is beginning to turn. And when it does, the fortunes of the Republican Party and those people that share the values I've spelled out here are going to rise, and they're going to rise precipitously. We are going to win the election in the fall. We are going to get more people in the United States Congress that believe and think as you and I do. And thank you for your help in making that possible.

Thank you all, and may God bless you.

*Note: The President spoke at 6:07 p.m. in Hangar 26 at the Westchester County Regional Airport. In his remarks, he referred to Louis Bantle, Bush-Quayle Connecticut finance chairman; Bobby Holt, Bush-Quayle national finance chairman; Brian Gaffney, Bush-Quayle Connecticut cochairman; Betsy Heminway, Bush-Quayle Connecticut cochairman, and her husband, Spike; Dick Foley, chairman of the Connecticut Republican Party; and Bob Macauley, Leon Hirsh, and Jack Neafsey, event cochairmen.*

# Letter to Congressional Leaders Transmitting Proposed Legislation on New Mexico Public Lands Wilderness Designation
*May 22, 1992*

*Dear Mr. Speaker: (Dear Mr. President:)*

I am pleased to submit for congressional consideration and passage the "New Mexico Public Lands Wilderness Act".

The Federal Land Policy and Management Act of 1976 (FLPMA), (43 U.S.C. 1701, *et seq.*), directs the Secretary of the Interior to review the wilderness potential of the public lands.

The review of the areas identified in New Mexico began immediately after the enactment of FLPMA and has now been completed. Approximately 908,000 acres of public lands in 50 areas in New Mexico met the minimum wilderness criteria and were designated as wilderness study areas (WSAs). These WSAs were studied and analyzed during the review process and the results documented in six environmental impact statements and one instant study area report.

Based on the studies and reviews of the WSAs, the Secretary of the Interior recommends that all or part of 23 of the WSAs, totaling 487,186 acres of public lands, be designated as part of the National Wilderness Preservation System. From these 23 WSAs, the Secretary proposes to designate 22 wilderness areas by consolidating two WSAs into one wilderness area.

I concur with the Secretary of the Interior's recommendations and am pleased to recommend designation of the 22 areas (totaling 487,186 acres) identified in the enclosed draft legislation as additions to the National Wilderness Preservation System.

The proposed additions represent the diversity of wilderness values in the State of New Mexico. These range from the relatively undisturbed and expansive stretch of the Chihuahuan Desert in the West Potrillo Mountains, to the canyons of the Gila and Chama Rivers, to the rocky peaks of the Organ Mountains, Big Hatchet Mountains, and the Sierra Ladrones. These areas span a wide variety of New Mexico landforms, ecosystems, and other natural systems and features. Their inclusion in the wilderness system will improve the geographic distribution of wilderness areas in New Mexico, and will complement existing areas of congressionally designated wilderness. They will provide new and outstanding opportunities for solitude and unconfined recreation.

The enclosed draft legislation provides that designation as wilderness shall not constitute a reservation of water or water rights for wilderness purposes. This is consistent with the fact that the Congress did not establish a Federal reserved water right for wilderness purposes. The Administration has established the policy that, where it is necessary to obtain water rights for wilderness purposes in a specific wilderness area, water rights would be sought from the State by filing under State water laws. Furthermore, it is the policy of the Administration that the designation of wilderness areas should not interfere with the use of water rights, State water administration, or the use of a State's interstate water allocation.

The draft legislation also provides for access to wilderness areas by Indian people for traditional cultural and religious purposes. Access by the general public may be limited in order to protect the privacy of religious cultural activities taking place in specific wilderness areas. In addition, to the fullest extent practicable, the Department of the Interior will coordinate with the Department of Defense to minimize the impact of any overflights during these religious cultural activities.

I further concur with the Secretary of the Interior that all or part of 39 of the WSAs encompassing 420,400 acres are not suitable for preservation as wilderness and should be released for multi-use management.

Also enclosed are a letter and report from the Secretary of the Interior concerning the WSAs discussed above and a section-by-section analysis of the draft legislation. I urge the Congress to act expeditiously and favorably on the proposed legislation so that the natural resources of these WSAs in New Mexico may be protected and preserved.

Sincerely,

GEORGE BUSH

*Note: Identical letters were sent to Thomas S. Foley, Speaker of the House of Representatives, and Dan Quayle, President of the Senate.*

# White House Statement on Haitian Migrants
*May 24, 1992*

President Bush has issued an Executive order which will permit the U.S. Coast Guard to begin returning Haitians picked up at sea directly to Haiti. This action follows a large surge in Haitian boat people seeking to enter the United States and is necessary to protect the lives of the Haitians, whose boats are not equipped for the 600-mile sea journey.

The large number of Haitian migrants has led to a dangerous and unmanageable situation. Both the temporary processing facility at the U.S. Naval Base, Guantanamo and the Coast Guard cutters on patrol are filled to capacity. The President's action will also allow continued orderly processing of more than 12,000 Haitians presently at Guantanamo.

Through broadcasts on the Voice of America and public statements in the Haitian media, we continue to urge Haitians not to attempt the dangerous sea journey to the United States. Last week alone, 18 Haitians perished when their vessel capsized off the Cuban coast.

Under current circumstances, the safety of Haitians is best assured by remaining in their country. We urge any Haitians who fear persecution to avail themselves of our refugee processing service at our Embassy in Port-au-Prince. The Embassy has been processing refugee claims since February. We utilize this special procedure in only four countries in the world. We are prepared to increase the American Embassy staff in Haiti for refugee processing if necessary.

The United States Coast Guard has picked up over 34,000 since the coup in Haiti last September 30. Senior U.S. officials are seeking the assistance of other countries and the United Nations to help deal with the plight of Haitian boat people, and we will continue our intensive efforts to find alternative solutions to avoid further tragedies on the high seas.

The President has also directed an intensification of our ongoing humanitarian assistance efforts in Haiti. Our current programs total $47 million and provide food for over 600,000 Haitians and health care services which reach nearly 2 million. We hope other nations will also increase their humanitarian assistance as called for in the resolution on Haiti passed by the OAS foreign ministers on May 17.

*Note: The Executive order is listed in Appendix E at the end of this volume.*

## Radio Address to the Nation on Memorial Day
*May 25, 1992*

For many, Memorial Day signals summer's arrival. Families will pull out the picnic baskets and charcoal grills and head for the beach or the park. But more importantly, Memorial Day is one of our Nation's most solemn observances.

On this sacred day, we honor those Americans who died fighting for freedom. We pause to remember, to think about the meaning of the loss of brave men and women who did not return from the battle. And in cemeteries all across this great land, people will place flags or lay bouquets on quiet graves "where valor proudly sleeps."

On this day, we must tell the stories of those who fought and died in freedom's cause. We must tell their stories because those who've lost loved ones need to know that a grateful Nation will always remember. We must tell their stories so that our children and grandchildren will understand what our lives might have been like had it not been for their sacrifice. The thousands of us who fought alongside brave friends who fell will never hear "Taps" played without remembering them, nor will their families and friends.

So, let us remember the cause for which these Americans fought and the freedom and peace bought with their life's blood, and let us pass along to a new generation the awesome accounts of honor and courage. On Wednesday at the Naval Academy's commencement, I will talk about how the great victory of freedom in the world is a vindication of the American ideal. And I will remind those graduates that democracy is not our creation; it is our inheritance.

These reminders are important, for as someone said, "Memory performs the impossible for man, holds together past and present." So then, we who are left must nurture the sacred memories of those who paid the ultimate price. And we must let their sacrifices give meaning and purpose to our Nation's future. Because they fought, we have freedoms many all too often take for granted. And because of their sacrifice, our children can sleep soundly without the threat of nuclear war hanging over their heads.

May God bless the families of all whom we honor. And may God bless the United States of America.

*Note: This address was recorded at 8:05 a.m. on May 21 in the Cabinet Room at the White House for broadcast after 9 a.m. on May 25.*

## Presidential Determination No. 92–27—Memorandum Certifying Ethiopia for United States Assistance
*May 26, 1992*

*Memorandum for the Secretary of State*

*Subject:* Determination and Certification Under Section 8 of the Horn of Africa Recovery and Food Security Act: Ethiopia

Pursuant to the authority vested in me by section 8 of the Horn of Africa Recovery and Food Security Act (Public Law 102–274; 106 Stat. 115), I hereby determine and certify that the Government of Ethiopia:

(1) has begun to implement peace agreements and national reconciliation agreements;

(2) has demonstrated a commitment to human rights within the meaning of sections 116 and 502B of the Foreign Assistance Act of 1961;

(3) has manifested a commitment to democracy, has established a timetable for free and fair elections, and has agreed to implement the results of those elections; and

(4) has agreed to distribute developmental assistance on the basis of need without regard to political affiliation, geographic location, or the ethnic, tribal, or religious identity of the recipient.

You are authorized and directed to report this determination and certification to the Congress and to publish it in the *Federal Register.*

GEORGE BUSH

[*Filed with the Office of the Federal Register, 11:54 a.m., June 10, 1992*]

*Note: This memorandum was released by the Office of the Press Secretary on May 27.*

## Presidential Determination No. 92–28—Memorandum on Arms Exports to the Comoros
*May 26, 1992*

*Memorandum for the Secretary of State*

*Subject:* Eligibility of the Comoros to be Furnished Defense Articles and Services Under the Foreign Assistance Act and the Arms Export Control Act

Pursuant to the authority vested in me by section 503(a) of the Foreign Assistance Act of 1961, as amended (22 U.S.C. 2311(a)), and section 3(a)(1) of the Arms Export Control Act (22 U.S.C. 2753(a)(1)), I hereby find and determine that the furnishing of defense articles and services to the Government of the Comoros will strengthen the security of the United States and promote world peace.

You are authorized and directed to report this determination to the Congress and to publish it in the *Federal Register.*

GEORGE BUSH

[*Filed with the Office of the Federal Register, 11:55 a.m., June 10, 1992*]

*Note: This memorandum was released by the Office of the Press Secretary on May 27.*

## Remarks at the United States Naval Academy Commencement Ceremony in Annapolis, Maryland
*May 27, 1992*

Thank you, Mr. Secretary, and thank all of you. Thank you, Larry Garrett. Please be seated. And may I salute our great CNO, Admiral Kelso, who's with us today, and our Superintendent, Admiral Lynch, the several Members of the United States Congress that are here today. I want to single out the Navy band, thank the Academy band; and Captain Bill Hines, the Senior Chaplain; and Midshipmen First Class Joe Lienert and Melissa Miceli for leading us in the national anthem. Officers, members of the faculty, friends, parents, the brigade, and of course, the class of 1992. As I said that, the sun came out. [*Laughter*] Now, thank you for this warm welcome. Let me add a special salute to an honorary classmate of the class of '92, Midshipman Rob Boehning, a model of courage to his classmates.

Now, the real reason I came here today: I just wanted to salute the class that finally captured the Army mules. And to show you that I took Larry Garrett's remarks to heart, I will now tell you my favorite Billy Graham story about the guy, the graduation speaker, goes on and on and on. A guy sitting over here picks up the gavel, heaves it at him, misses, hits a woman in the front row. And she said, "Hit me again. I can still hear him." [*Laughter*] Look what you're in for. [*Laughter*] No, they're double-spaced.

As President, I've made it my mission to

preserve three legacies of concern to all Americans. I spoke a few days ago at Southern Methodist University about the new economic realities, about the promising job opportunities that we're going to have in the next century. At Notre Dame, my focus was the family because the first lessons in faith and character are learned at home. But today I want to speak about the great mission you've taken up as your own: preserving freedom, keeping the peace.

You take up your watch at a watershed moment, as old orders give way to new. Just think of the changes, the remarkable changes that have taken place since you first came to Annapolis 4 years ago, for plebe summer way back in 1988. That was a different era, another world, literally. Europe was a continent divided, East from West. From Central America to the Horn of Africa to Afghanistan and Southeast Asia, the U.S. faced Soviet expansionism. Today, all that has changed. Today, the "dominoes" fall in democracy's direction. Today, the Wall, the Warsaw Pact, the Soviet empire, even the Soviet Union itself, all are gone, swept away by the most powerful idea known to man: the undeniable desire of every individual to be free.

We must recognize these events for what they were: a vindication of our ideals, a testament to faith, but also a victory for the men and women who fought for freedom. Because this triumph didn't just happen. Imperial communism didn't just fall. It was pushed.

Your generation will be the first to enjoy the fruits of that victory. Today, the threat of a lightning strike across the fields of Europe has vanished with the Warsaw Pact. The threat of nuclear war is more distant than at any time in the past four decades. As Commander in Chief, I think back often to the day I did what so many of my predecessors must have longed to do, to give the order for many of our nuclear forces to stand down from alert. Last week in Lisbon, we reached agreement with four of the new nations of the old Soviet empire, Russia, Ukraine, Kazakhstan, and Byelarus, to make good on the great promise of the START Treaty that we signed just a year ago.

The end of the cold war, it means new opportunities for global prosperity. Free market reform is now sweeping away the dead hand of state socialism. Capitalism is recognized the world over as the engine of prosperity and social progress. And nations are reorganizing themselves to unleash the limitless potential of the individual.

Governments can help foster free enterprise, or they can put obstacles in its path. There is no question what course we must take. The United States will remain a forceful advocate for free trade. But the promise of new prosperity must not blind us to the new challenges of new economic realities. Nations that lack the confidence to compete will be tempted to seek refuge behind the walls of protectionism. We must fight the protectionist impulse here at home, and we must work with our partners for trade that is free, fair, and open.

Beyond this economic challenge, we must see clearly the dangers that remain. And yes, since the day you came to Annapolis, we have made great gains for freedom. But we have not yet entered an era of perpetual peace.

Some see the great triumph I mentioned a moment ago not simply as cause for celebration but as proof that America's work in the world is finished, is done. The fact is, never in the long history of man has the world been a benign place. It will take hard efforts to make and keep it a better place, and there is no substitute in this effort for America's strength and sense of purpose. When other nations look to the United States, they see a nation that combines economic and military might with a moral force that's born of its founding ideals.

Even in our new world, as old threats recede, new ones emerge. With the end of the East-West standoff, ideology has given way to ethnicity as a key factor for conflict. Ancient hatreds, ethnic rivalries frozen in time, threaten to revive themselves and to re-ignite. We see it now in the war-ravaged Balkans, in tensions within and among some of the new nations of the old Soviet empire. For all the overwhelmingly hopeful aspects of the new nationalism we see in the world, for all the proud history and heritage we see reclaimed, for all the captive nations now free, we must guard against those who would turn the noble impulse of nationalism to negative ends.

We will face new challenges in the realm of diplomacy. Where in the past we've relied almost entirely on established, formal alliances, the future may require us to turn more often to coalitions built to respond to the needs of the moment. Where in the past, international organizations like the U.N., the United Nations, had been paralyzed by cold war conflict, we will see a future where they can now be a force for peace. Where in the past, many times the heaviest burdens of leadership fell to our Nation, we will now see more efforts made to seek consensus and concerted action.

The United States will never rely on other nations to defend its interests, but we can and will seek to act in concert with the community of nations to defend common interests and ideals. We saw a glimpse of that future in the Persian Gulf. Such a world puts a premium on nations certain of their interests, faithful to their ideals, and on leaders ready to act.

We will face new challenges that take us beyond containment to a key role in helping forge a democratic peace. In the weeks ahead, Congress will be considering what we call the "FREEDOM Support Act," to promote democratic reform in Russia and the other Commonwealth States. For all the pressure to focus our energies on needs here at home, and for all that we must do and will do to open new opportunities to every American here at home, we cannot fail in this critical mission.

When we think of the world you and your children will inherit, no single factor will shape their future more than this: whether the lands of the old Soviet empire move forward into democracy or slide back into anarchy or authoritarianism. The outcome of this great transition will affect everything from the amount of resources Government must devote to defense instead of domestic needs to a future for our children free from fear.

And yes, the aid that I have requested from the Congress is significant, but it is also a tiny fraction of the $4 trillion that this Nation spent to wage and win the cold war. We owe it to those who began the task as well as those who will come up afterward to finish the great work that we have begun.

But if we hope to remain free and at peace in the world, a world that still holds dangers, we must maintain defenses adequate to the task. This defense rests on four key elements.

First, we must maintain a strong strategic deterrent. And yes, our nuclear forces can and will be smaller in the future. But even in the aftermath of the cold war, Russia retains its nuclear arsenal. We learned in Desert Storm about the progress that Iraq had made toward building nuclear weapons of its own. We must heed the lessons learned in the Gulf war, when a single Scud missile took the lives of more Americans than any other combat action in that war. We cannot count on deterrence to stop a madman with missiles. We must deploy a defense against ballistic missile attack.

Second, security means forward deployment. From the 40 years of cold war to the 40 days of Desert Storm, forward deployed forces have contributed to the world's stability and helped America keep danger far from its shores. Even in our new world, with the tremendous political transformation we've worked to bring about, the fundamental facts of geopolitics don't change. Forward deployed forces—I'm talking about ground forces, and I am talking the United States Navy—will keep America safe in the century ahead as they have in the century now coming to a close.

Third, the nature of the challenges we are likely to face will put a premium on rapid response. We live in a day when clear and present dangers are few, when new threats can emerge with little or no warning. Throughout history, our ability to project power has helped us keep the peace, and if need be, to win the war. And this I pledge as Commander in Chief: America's forces will continue to be the best trained, the best equipped, and most battle-ready forces anywhere in the entire world. We owe it to the generations coming up.

Fourth, even as we reduce our Armed Forces, we must retain the capability to reconstitute sufficient forces to meet the future threats that we may face. As we make significant cuts in our defense procurement, we've got to keep in mind that production lines for planes and tanks and ships cannot be turned on and off like water from a faucet. We've got to keep our technological edge, keep our R&D focused on the next generation of weapons that you'll need to succeed.

In conclusion, I just want to turn now to a final challenge, one that begins with a hard-won truth that shines through this century's great conflicts: America is safest at home when we stand as a force for stability in the world. In many respects, reaffirming this truth in our new world may be the greatest challenge of all because the history of this century reveals in the American character a desire to see in every hard-won victory a sign that America's work in the world is done. Such an urge is not unusual in democracies. It's a trait found in nations more interested in the quiet joys of home than in the glories of conquest abroad. But it can be devastating in a world that still holds dangers for our interests and ideals.

Winston Churchill made this point the theme of the last volume in his epic history of World War II. He called it, "How the great democracies triumphed and so were able to resume the follies which had so nearly cost them their life." Once more, our challenge is to avoid the folly that Churchill warned of, to remain engaged in the world as a force for peace. We will do it with your help, through the leadership you provide.

Today, John Paul Jones would say, "The measure of a ship is not its guns but its courageous men and women." Your courage, your integrity, your ability to lead, these are the qualities on which our Nation's security depends.

More than once this century, America has proved its mettle. More than once, we've come late to conflict and turned back mortal threats to freedom. But as a Nation, we have yet to prove that we can lead when there is no enemy on the doorstep. We have proved and proved again we can win the war. Now we must wage the peace.

Once again, to this wonderful graduating class, I wish you well. I wish you Godspeed. And thank you all for this warm welcome. May I thank the families that have labored in sweat to provide this wonderful day for these wonderful midshipmen, now to be ensigns or lieutenants. Welcome, congratulations to the class of 1992. And may God bless the United States of America, the freest, greatest country on the face of the Earth. Thank you very much.

*Note: The President spoke at 10:45 a.m. at the Navy/Marine Corps Memorial Stadium. In his remarks, he referred to Lawrence Garrett III, Secretary of the Navy; Rear Admiral Thomas C. Lynch, Superintendent of the U.S. Naval Academy; and Midshipman 1st Class Robert Boehning, an honorary graduate.*

# Remarks in a Roundtable Discussion With the Mount Paran Christian School Community in Marietta, Georgia
*May 27, 1992*

*The President.* Thank you, Dr. Walker, and all of you for taking your time. But what I wanted to do is just say a couple of brief remarks and then listen to you.

Tomorrow there's a report coming out on the schools. It's an NAEP report. I think it will be announced by the Education Department. And it's got some troubling statistics in it, conclusions in it about kids: too much television; not enough reading, parents reading to the kids, kids doing reading.

And I just wish Barbara were here because she spends a great deal of her life encouraging families to read together and teachers and kids to read together. But this report is going to say that we've got a long way to go.

Having said that, I am told that this school sets a pretty darn good example for the rest of the State, community, and Nation really in terms of parental involvement, which we think is absolutely fundamental, and also in terms of teacher-kid relationship. So what I want to do is to hear from you as to how you think it's working.

We think in America 2000 we have a good, strong education program. It puts emphasis on school choice. When I got out of the Navy a jillion years ago—it's on my mind because I was at the Naval Academy graduation today; did not go there, but when I got out of the service we had the GI bill. You could choose whether you wanted to go to whatever school. Similarly, in some of the grant programs for higher education you can choose. We think choosing public, private, religious schools makes all schools better. Competition never hurt anything. And we think it is a good way to go. So choice is a part of our America 2000 program. And then part of it is simply, in a revolutionary way, redesigning American education. But not dictating from Washington: Say here's a community; you come up with what you think is best for your community. Here's an urban area, and you all decide what you think is best.

And so this is our approach, and we've got a great Secretary of Education, Lamar Alexander. Dr. Roger Porter, over here, is with me in the White House, is an expert on not only what we're trying to do but I think on American education. So if you ask me questions I can't answer later on in the question-and-answer period, I'll just simply turn to Roger.

But I'm told that it works for you, that you're getting good results. And I'd like to know from all of you, board members, students, whether that conclusion is correct, and if so, why.

Jim—I met your headmaster down there. I don't know whether we have an order here, but maybe he's a good one to start it off.

*[A participant said that competition is good for education, as demonstrated in Japan.]*

*The President.* This is the point, ironically, that Benno Schmidt, who just left my university, Yale, yesterday to work with developing brand new schools, revolutionary schools, made on one of the television shows this morning, the point that choice breeds competition, and competition leads to excellence in the schools that are chosen.

And then those that aren't, I am told by education officials in Minnesota and elsewhere, upgrade themselves.

How do you feel about all of this? Not on just this subject, but any. What do you want to share with us about your educational experience?

*[A participant said that competition and parental involvement are key elements.]*

*The President.* Is there a special way in which you involve parents, or is it kind of an enhanced PTA way of doing it? Again, I think one of the things that this report tomorrow that Lamar Alexander will be announcing said is that we just have got to find new ways to get parents and kids involved. We're talking here about mainly, I think, Roger, out of the public schools, this report is based on findings; but parent involvement with kids, homework, reading, particularly reading. This relates largely to reading, this report that will be out. And we're just not performing as a Nation.

But do you all have very active parent participation at the school, or is it just encouraging parents at home to do more with the kids. Who can pitch in on that one?

*[A participant described parental involvement in the classroom and teacher involvement with the family. Another participant discussed parents' purchases of school equipment.]*

*The President.* Some schools in the public school system really do strive for that. It doesn't have quite the same feeling, but they have much more active parental relationships than others. And I'm told that those make a tremendous difference.

Who else?

*[A participant said that teachers send home parent information packets regularly. Another participant said that teaching moral values in schools was important.]*

*The President.* And I keep saying this, but I'll repeat it to you all. I said it in the State of the Union. When the mayors from these National League of Cities came to see me, some from gigantic cities—Los Angeles, Tom Bradley was one of them—to small, almost towns, to medium-sized cities like—I think of Plano, Texas, which is fairly small—

and united, Republican, Democrat, liberal, conservative, about the root cause of much of our urban decline was the diminution of the family, the decline of the American family.

And yes, we get criticized for raising it, but we're going to keep on talking about that and trying to encourage family participation. We've got this family commission, this commission on the family, and they will be reporting in a few months, looking at legislation to see if there's anything in the legislation that encourages through financial incentive a husband and wife to live apart, for example. We can't have that anymore. They're going to be looking at all kinds of things to come in with recommendations as to how to turn around this decline in the American family, the falling apart of the family structure. And I will keep on talking about it, and I think it's something that the American people are sensitive to and want to find ways to help.

And so we'll keep trying. And when Barbara goes out and hugs a kid and talks about reading to children, I think this is the way you strengthen families. If a kid comes home from school, no matter how impoverished the neighborhood, and picks up a book and sits with the kid and they read back and forth, that helps. And there's no question about it. And it might not be as sophisticated as some of our critics would like to have it, but it's fundamental. And it's good, I think. And so, when I sit there in the diplomatic entrance of the White House in what, okay, is somewhat show-biz reading to kids, it's supposed to send a signal that this is a good thing to do.

What were you going to say?

[*A participant asked if the role of schools would evolve in response to increased family instability.*]

*The President.* One of the national goals is to have learning take place in a safe and sound environment. I think a lot of schools are way out in front; I assume this is one of them in terms of no drugs, for example, in terms of getting the place safe. I expect you don't have a day-to-day gun problem in this school. Regrettably, other schools do. And so, one of the six national goals is to have a safe and sound place for people to live.

So I do see evolution towards that end. I am not pessimistic about all this. Unfortunately, in terms of our national education bill, we got socked in the House of Representatives by people that wanted to do it the old way, the way that has failed. That does not want choice, for example, and that wants to have it all mandated out of some subcommittee in Washington. We don't need that. I think the country has seen that doesn't work. So, with our new American schools concept for example, we're saying to communities: You figure it out. Marietta, Georgia, might have somewhat different requirements than downtown Chicago.

And so this is the approach we're taking. And I do see a favorable evolution towards these ideas, but I'm not sure, given the recalcitrance in Congress today, that it's going to happen overnight. We're going to keep pushing because I think the six goals, you know, are sound: Math and science. And you know, nobody's too old to learn; it gets into your whole feeling of adult education. Tests, volunteer, but nevertheless standards so a parent can tell how his or her kid adds up to others across the country. These are good. Knowledge in the key five subjects, that's another one of the goals.

So I think the education goals that were set by Governors, including Georgia's, in a very constructive role a few years ago are valid and sound. And what we're saying is give the communities and private schools, public schools, religious schools the flexibility from Washington to achieve these national goals. And I think it's sensible. And I think we got a long way to go before everyone in the country's behind this, but I think it's evolving in an evolutionary way.

[*A participant said that parents, rather than outside sources such as television, must set moral guidelines for children.*]

*The President.* Let me just amplify what you've said here because I think that's great. You mentioned television. This report that's being issued tomorrow will say that the American students spend little time reading for pleasure or as part of their schoolwork, rarely visit the library, and watch television on average more than 3 hours a day. It will also go on to scientifically state that those that watch it 2 hours or less do better. And 2 hours is a lot of TV, but I mean, that is a conclusion of the report. Now, who turns the set off? Probably the parents or some counselor saying, "Look, here's what happens to you if you don't," or whoever gives out the homework. Those are things that I think are vital.

[*A participant asked about tax breaks for private school tuition and said that parental involvement is a key to student success.*]

*The President.* That's a good point. I think we do have to face the fact that some parents can't afford tuition, but they can afford to have an environment that encourages the kind of values we're talking about. We've got to strive to that.

[*A participant said that parents should be involved in their children's education and schools should not have to fulfill the role of parents.*]

*The President.* I think it's a very good point, and that's why parental involvement in public schools is very, very important. And where it is so hopeless, where it is so disrupted, you do have schools, programs like Cities in Schools run by a guy named Bill Milliken, where they actually have to go in some of the really tough city areas and get city officials who almost adopt a kid. That kid isn't in school, go to the house and find out why the child wasn't there. Was the single parent on drugs, and if so, how does society help give that kid a chance? The theory being every kid, no matter what situation, has to have somebody who knows his name and cares about him.

And that is something that I don't think is a problem here, quite obviously, but it is a problem in some schools. And I think we hope that in this encouragement of family involvement, it will take some of that burden away. But where it still remains, we have got to find ways to have every kid have a mentor, every kid have someone who cares about them, lifts them up, brushes them off when he gets hurt, sends him off to school.

[*A participant said that teachers' involvement in students' lives is important.*]

*The President.* I think that's true. Yet I think we have to say, and I expect the teachers here would say, that there are teachers in the public schools that do give the kids that. So I know you know that, but it's a very valid point, Brian, that you're making.

I think of the guy that just was in to see me the other day. I don't know if any of you saw the movie "Stand and Deliver," Jaime Escalante teaching calculus to these kids. I was out and watched him in school. He was a super guy. But here he is teaching kids that are disadvantaged. They come to him with no special privilege. They're largely Hispanic. Some of them have a poor grasp of English when they come there, and yet he is such a teacher that he just makes it come alive. And it is very exciting to watch him and to listen to him and to be inspired by him. And so I guess what I'm saying is we need more Jaime Escalante in all schools. And yet, I'm not arguing your point.

[*A participant said that home, school, and church need to work together.*]

*Participant.* Mr. President, we'd like to have you here for the rest of the afternoon. But your people are giving me signals and you signals.

*The President.* So, thank you all for giving me your time. I'm just sorry I talked so much and didn't give everybody a chance. Thank you.

*Note: The President spoke at 5:14 p.m. in a classroom at the Mount Paran Christian School. In his remarks, he referred to Paul L. Walker, senior pastor, Mount Paran Church of God; Roger B. Porter, Assistant to the President for Economic and Domestic Policy; Benno C. Schmidt, president of Yale University; James R. Heyman, headmaster, Mount Paran Christian School; and William E. Milliken, president of Cities in Schools, Inc.*

## Remarks and a Question-and-Answer Session With the Mount Paran Christian School Community in Marietta
*May 27, 1992*

*The President.* May I simply start off by thanking you, sir, Pastor Rice. And Dr. Walker, of course, Dr. Heyman, Principal Susan King. And I understand there's a little overflow in the sanctuary; we'll greet them wherever they may be. And thank you for this warm welcome to this wonderful, wonderfully warm school environment. I know a little poster action went on over Memorial Day, and I see the tip of the iceberg. But thank you for the welcome.

I would like to say to Pastor Rice, we are trying. We are trying, because we are committed to making American education the best in the world. And it's not there yet. We're not close to that yet, so we've got to keep on trying. I left the two great Bush family experts on education behind, regrettably. Barbara Bush, I think, is doing a superb job encouraging people to read to their kids, and that is fundamental. And we have an author in the family, our dog Millie. [*Laughter*] You may have read my tax returns, and you can tell who the breadwinner is in that family. The dog made 5 times as much as the President of the United States. [*Laughter*] I might point out that all of that money that Millie made in her book goes to Barbara's foundation on literacy, which I hope will benefit children across this country. I'm sure it will.

Our America 2000 education crusade is not built on finding the answers in Washington, DC. It is built on encouraging a revolutionary approach to education, and that is where local communities put forward excellence. We believe that's right. We believe in parental choice. We believe that people should be free to choose public, private, religious schools. And our whole system, our whole approach to education is built on a concept of choice and actually revolution, not tinkering at the edges but revolutionizing American education at the public school level. You see, we've got the best college education in the world. When Yale's president announced his departure from Yale yesterday to go into some concepts similar to what we're talking about nationally, he pointed out that at the college level, choice makes State schools better and makes private schools better. The same thing will be true if this concept catches on nationally.

Another point that we want to make is that one of the reasons I wanted to come here is to point up for the rest of the country what excellent teachers mean and what parental involvement in kids' education mean. I'm told by Dr. Walker and your able principal that parents are involved and that they care and that they read to the kids and that they see that the homework is done. So I would salute this school for some way inculcating into the parent this concept of what they do is vital to American education.

The teachers, I'm told, here are excellent. I would recognize that your system here encourages that interaction between the kids and the teachers, not just in the classroom but by bringing in the parents for what some would call PTA activities or whatever. So I salute you for that, and I think you're setting a good example for other countries as well.

Some parents are out there checking homework and turning off the TV. Well, that's a good thing because tomorrow there will be a new study announced by our Department of Education. And I might say I have great confidence in our Secretary of Education, Lamar Alexander. But this is the NAEP, the National Assessment of Education Progress. It's coming out with conclusions that will not be a surprise to the teachers, the officials, the administration, and the parents in this school.

But the point explains that American students across the board spend too little time reading for pleasure or as part of their school work, that they rarely visit the library, and that they watch television on average more than 3 hours a day. Now, I think that these conclusions in this report will resonate around the country, and people are going to begin to say, "Wait a minute, let's try it a different way. Maybe let's try it the Mount Paran way where we're going to have less of that and a little more homework emphasis."

But in any event, I came here to take a few questions and hopefully to get an answer or two. My dad, who was in politics many years ago, always liked the guy that got up at the forum like this and said, "For your information, I'd like to ask this question." [*Laughter*] Well, I could use a little information, so don't be concerned if your question sounds a little bit like a lecture. So with no further ado, other than to once again say thank you from this grateful heart, I'd like to take your questions.

The last point I will make, and I promise it's the last: From the minute I walked in here I get the distinct feeling that this place has a real sense of what we call family values. I think that sets a good example for the rest of the country as well.

So, who's first?

*Vouchers for Private Schools*

*Q.* Mr. President, in an effort to improve the quality of education in America, do you support any Government funding of private education?

*The President.* Yes, I do believe that our system which calls for vouchers for private, public, or religious schools is the way to go. And I think it, incidentally, I think that will improve the school that is not chosen. That comes under what we call a concept of school choice, and I think that it will help those schools that are left behind. I think Minnesota will tell you that that's what happens when a school is chosen.

I might point out as one who benefited from the GI bill a thousand years ago when I got out of the Navy in nineteen-forty— what the heck was it—[*laughter*]—1945, they said, "Here's the GI bill. You can choose where you want to go. You can choose a private school. You can choose a State school." And no great damage was done to the Constitution. I think that same principle will inure to the benefit of the schools that are chosen and those that aren't. So yes, I do support that concept. Therein I have a big difference with the Court.

You guys right in the middle, go ahead. You've got a question? Scoot right up here. While you're coming up, let's see.

*Advice to Youth*

*Q.* What can a fifth grader do to help keep our country free and the greatest country in the world?

*The President.* What kind of what?

*Q.* What can a fifth grader do to keep——

*The President.* A fifth grader? A fifth grader can study. I know you're not going to like the answer too much. [*Laughter*] A fifth grader can watch less than the national average of kids watching television. You can learn. You can listen to those around you who are helping you with your value structure, and I think you then find that through your studies and through your environment, you have the values that will help keep this country strong.

I am an old-fashioned kind of guy. I think it's good when the people are patriotic and salute the flag and stand for the Pledge of Allegiance and say we are "one Nation under God." I think a fifth grader learns those things and shares them with her schoolmates, and then it's a part of your life as you get older. You'll be standing for something; you believe in something, something good.

What's your friend got? Are you a friend of hers?

*Q.* Yes.

*The President.* Are you?

*Balanced Budget Amendment*

*Q.* Yes. I have a question. If God can run the world on 10 percent, why can't Government run the country on 30 percent? [*Laughter*]

*The President.* That's a good question. You're talking about tithing? [*Laughter*] Well, that's a good question, and the answer is it's slightly more complicated than the question. [*Laughter*] But you know, there are some people—I assume that that's a pitch for 10 percent in taxes, but there are some that frankly can't afford it. I think under our system others manage to pitch in to help those who literally can't afford to pay a dime.

But I take your point. I think there's a

point behind the question, and that is that we've got to get our spending of our Government under control. Frankly, I think one way to do that is to now pass the balanced budget amendment to the Constitution. The liberals don't like it. The liberals do not like it, and they keep throwing up what I call the Washington Monument syndrome. That means if you have to cut somewhere, they'll point out, well, the first thing you've got to do is take down the Washington Monument or go after programs that everybody likes. That isn't what happens to get a balanced budget.

What we need to do without getting too technical here is to control the growth of the mandatory programs. You don't have to cut them, but you have to control the growth of that part of the budget that's running out of control. I believe we can do it. I think a balanced budget amendment would discipline the Congress, and I think it would discipline the executive branch. It's an idea I've been for for a long, long time. I believe it's going to pass the Congress now. The people are not listening to these sophisticated arguments. They're saying, "Do not saddle these young kids with more and more debt." And so we're going to try it.

The guys in the back of the bus are getting not equal opportunity on these questions. So you might have to just come up to the front, or just if you put your hand up and you've got a loud voice, we'll try some back there. Go ahead.

## Vouchers for Private Schools

*Q.* Mr. President, when if ever can private school and Christian school parents ever expect to see some type of tax credit?

*The President.* Well, I think what—we're frankly having a little difficulty getting this idea of vouchers, which is essentially a credit, through the Congress. But we're going to keep on because it is part of our America 2000 program. I think there's less resistance to it. But I'll be honest with you; I just don't know the answer as to when it's going to happen. I think our administration with our six education goals and our America 2000 program are on the right track in this regard. I'm going to keep pushing for it because I think it makes good sense.

Anyway, yes, ma'am, way in the back.

## School Choice

*Q.* [*Inaudible*]

*The President.* Where it's been tried, choice has been tried, I think the record shows that the school that is not chosen improves itself. That's the point that Benno Schmidt—I made this to a group earlier on—who's leaving Yale University—I still think it's a great university, not just because I went there—but nevertheless, he's leaving to go into what I would call a model school program. His point was that choice makes those schools, private schools in higher education better, and the State schools are better as well because of the competition.

So I don't look at it as a program that should diminish the quality of education in our very important public school system. We think the competition will enhance the—especially if we can strive to achieve our six education goals.

So, that's the answer I would give you.

## President's Domestic Agenda

*Q.* What will you do after you win your election?

*The President.* After I win? Well, you mean the very first thing? [*Laughter*] Take a little time off. [*Laughter*] No, but what I'll do is—and I think I'll win; I really think so. It's funny out there right now. But there is so much we need to do in the country, and this is one of the prime things, better education. I feel strongly about it.

You know—what grade are you in? Fifth grader. Well, it wasn't long ago that every fifth grader in this country went to bed from time to time very much concerned about what? Nuclear war. Now, thank God, because of my predecessor I think gets credit; other Presidents get credit; I hope I'll get a little; we've helped change the world. The changes are dramatic. There no longer is a Communist monolithic enemy. You don't probably worry about it. You don't have drills where you have to hide under your desk, wondering what would happen if there was a nuclear war. We've got a lot of blessings. We can thank our God for the blessings, the changes toward world peace.

So that's been some good that's happened. You don't hear much good these days, but that's something very good. What I'd like to do now is to take that energy and that emphasis that helped bring about that kind of change, after, you say after I'm elected, and then try to move forward in the field of anticrime; move forward in the field of education; move forward in the field of health reform—not to put in a socialized medicine program but to—where everyone has access to insurance through pooling and through various ways of doing it. I'd like to work for a society where we love each other more and sue each other less, and that means putting some caps on these liability claims.

But there is so much to do as President. There are so many things to work on and so much to do. But those are just some of the priorities that I would try to work very hard on if I'm lucky enough to win.

### Religion in Public Schools

*Q.* Can there be Bible in public schools?
*The President.* The answer to that is, I don't think so. I still favor voluntary prayer in the public schools. I believe in that, and I think there will be. [*Inaudible*]—in the Constitution. But prayer in school on a voluntary basis, I simply can't understand why it's not permitted. In the Senate, and heaven knows they need it—[*laughter*]—but in the Senate and in the House, they open with prayer every single day, and nobody complains about that.

So my position is well-known, and I say this.

Way up in the balcony. Yes, sir. You. I can hear you.

### Abortion

*Q.* I want to thank President Bush on behalf of the—[*applause*]. I'd like to know if you have any plans to eliminate abortion?
*The President.* Well, yes, because we're—well, of course, this is a matter that is enshrined in law. My position is, as you say, is publicly stated. And I think the matter now is in the courts. And I do, I worry very much about the mounting numbers of abortions. One of the cases before the Supreme Court now relates to whether a parent should be notified if a child, 13-year-old kid,

for example, is going to have an abortion. I feel, of course, a parent should be involved. But that matter is being adjudicated in the courts right now.

But my position is clear. I think it's correct. And there's room for a lively debate out there; you get plenty of argument on it. But I come down on the—err, if you're going to err, err on the side of life. And that's the way I feel.

### Local Control of Education

*Q.* Mr. President, as an educator for 21 years, what can you do to help us to eliminate the enormous amount of paperwork involved in education so that we who want to be good and positive role models for kids can get on about that business?
*The President.* Well, you touched a real nerve because we have now just redoubled our efforts to cut down on the regulatory burden, not just paperwork, which is enormous and where we've got to do better, but on a lot of excessive Government regulation that stifles many small businesses, for example.

I know educators feel that they are swamped when you're dealing with Government funds on paperwork. But one of our approaches is to get away from these mandated programs where some subcommittee chairman, some old curmudgeon that might have been there forever, has some idea about the way it used to work 40 years ago and insists on saying, if you want Federal money—happens to be your money—but if you want Federal money, you've got to follow these certain guidelines and fill out 23 reports.

Our whole approach on America 2000 is to let the decisions be made at the local level. And some schools might say, "We want 8 hours a day;" another might say "6 days a week"; another might say "11 months a year"; another might say, "Let's try the other way; back off and have less school time, more required homework." But let the American people decide that in their communities, as close to home as possible. That will take care of the problem you asked.

What's this guy, what have you got?

## Family Values

*Q.* President Bush, where do you stand on the issue of the traditional family unit?

*The President.* The traditional family? Well, I guess everybody looks at his or her own experience. Barbara Bush and I have been blessed with growing up in what you might call a traditional family, a family where a mother and dad are there, and they give love to a child. So I am, I guess, what you call a family values man.

But where you don't have that, where a kid, a little child comes into the world and doesn't have the father—the father may have run away, not even there to know the name of the child—somehow we then have to help that little kid. I told it earlier, every kid ought to have somebody that knows his name. It should be the parent, should be two parents. If not two parents, it ought to be one parent. If it can't be that, there's got to be a mentor. There's got to be somebody who cares, somebody who loves that child.

And on traditional family values where you can have the welfare system so it does not encourage a husband and wife to live apart. We've got to change it. We've got to make it so these kinds of traditional values have a chance to work in this troubled society of ours.

So I'm not ashamed about talking about family values and traditions of that nature. We'll keep on doing it, and I think it's beginning to resonate. Because as I told Dr. Walker and some others earlier, when the mayors of these cities, a lot of cities, came to see me, including Mayor Bradley of now-troubled Los Angeles, they said, "The thing that concerns us most about trouble in the cities, the most single cause is the decline or defamation of the American family." We've got to find ways to strengthen it.

## Haitian Migrants

*Q.* Good evening, President Bush. My question is a little different from what we have been talking about this evening, about family values and education. It has to do with the fact that, as we educate our daughter here at Mount Paran, one of the things we try to do as parents is to try to also educate our daughter in light of what is going on in the world in terms of what she's being taught.

My question has to do with the Haitian refugee situation. Earlier this week the Government announced a policy of repatriating Haitians back to Haiti. On the surface, Mr. President, that policy seems to run contrary to what America has stood for over the past couple hundred years, in that Americans opened their arms to all ethnic groups and different classes who sought to free themselves here in America from oppression in their homeland. Could you please explain why a policy was warranted to repatriate those Haitians?

*The President.* Absolutely. And it's a very good question. The answer is this: Yes, the Statue of Liberty still stands, and we still open our arms to people that are politically oppressed. We cannot and, as long as the laws are on the book, I will not, because I've sworn to uphold the Constitution, open the doors to economic refugees all over the world. We can't do that.

We're having a border crossing coming in from Mexico in unprecedented numbers. We're trying to, not to be mean about it, but we're trying to say, "Listen, we've got to live by the laws of this land."

It is my understanding that the vast majority of the refugees—and they're being screened; they're now going to be screened at the Embassy; they were being screened at Guantanamo—are economic refugees. There was one guy that was thrown out twice and vowed as he left the Coast Guard cutter the second time, "I'll be back in a week." There are merchants in Haiti today advertising almost like bounty, "Pay us $500 and you can climb into my unsafe boat and set out across the ocean," knowing that out of compassion the United States Coast Guard would save them.

We have to control our own immigration policy. We've got to do it with compassion. We've got to do it under the law, though. So what I'm saying to you is, we are not repatriating willfully people that are fleeing political oppression. Part of our policy on Haiti, and we're taking a leadership role in the OAS, is to return Mr. Aristide, who was democratically elected, to Haiti. We want him back there. And if we don't do that—I would say this, add this peripherally—if we don't do that, that sends a bad signal to those who might be plotting coups in other parts of our hemisphere, which, thank God, is almost totally democratic today.

So our policy is, I think, the right policy. I think we do have to control—some accuse it, incidentally, of being a racist policy. I would vehemently deny, that is not the case, because these people have every right to be screened. We've accompanied this program now, so we will not be faced with the numbers of leaky boats, with giving additional food aid to Haiti. We will continue with our sanction program, and we will continue to try to get Mr. Aristide returned.

Frankly, the numbers as of yesterday were down of the people fleeing. I still worry about it because some will get by and some will die on the sea because they are being—it's like a magnet to them, these advertisements that "we'll get you to Guantanamo" or "we'll get you to Florida." We're bound by our laws to screen people properly, to protect people's rights. But we are not bound to have an open policy where everybody in economic deprivation around the world can come to the United States. I don't think that should be our policy, and it's not.

So I worry about it. I worry about the appearance of it to some. But I'm glad you raised it because it's the first chance I've had since the new order to fully explain it. I am convinced that the people in Haiti are not being physically oppressed. We've got all kinds of ways to monitor that situation there. A returnee, for example, a guy that's taken from Guantanamo and sent back, I would not want on my conscience that that person having fled oppression, anyone that was fleeing oppression, would be victimized upon return.

So I think I can say to you they're not being oppressed. Political refugees, where they're caught up in this political turmoil, are being screened and have been admitted and will continue to be admitted to the United States under our laws. But under the other part of our laws, economic refugees will have to come in under the quotas designated under the law.

So there it is.

## North American Free Trade Agreement

*Q.* Mr. President, I'm an eighth grader, and my dad is concerned that American jobs will be going to Mexico and South America as a result of the American free trade policy. Will this happen?

*The President.* Well, I think your dad, with all respect, and don't tell him this, is wrong. I happen to believe that a fair trade agreement will result in more American jobs. I happen to think—we're talking here about compassion and economics—I happen to think that if the free trade agreement helps Mexico, as well as helping the United States, it's a good thing.

I don't believe in protection. I believe in fair trade. I believe the NAFTA, the North American free trade agreement, will result in better jobs and more jobs for the United States of America. If we're successful in this NAFTA agreement that your dad asked about and Canada stays in the deal, which I'm sure they will, we're talking about a $5 trillion market. And this is enormous. And that means prosperity for lots of families.

So please tell your father that we are not talking about exporting American jobs. We're talking about creating new American jobs. If in the process we create a more prosperous Mexico that can do more about its environment, can do more about its standard of living, so much the better. Mexico has a wonderful new President, Carlos Salinas, and he has done wonders with Mexico. I believe that this fair trade agreement not only is in his interest, but what I've got to look after, is it the interests of the United States of America. I am absolutely convinced that it is, because free trade is far better than turning inward to some kind of protection.

I wish I had it on the tip of my tongue the numbers of jobs in Georgia that depend on American exports. It is enormous. And we ought to keep opening, knocking down barriers, like our GATT agreement and getting a successful conclusion to the Uruguay round, knocking down barriers to American trade that will come with the North American free trade agreement.

So I am a free but fair trader. I think protection shrinks markets, and I think our policy will increase jobs and markets.

Listen, thank you all very, very much.

*Note: The President spoke at 5:46 p.m. in the school gymnasium. In his remarks, he referred to Pastor Darrell Rice, chairman,* *Mount Paran Christian School Board, who acted as moderator for the session. A tape was not available for verification of the content of these remarks.*

# Statement by Press Secretary Fitzwater on House of Representatives Action on Energy Legislation
*May 27, 1992*

The President is pleased that the House of Representatives, in passing H.R. 776, today made progress toward adopting a sound national energy strategy.

This legislation implements several key elements of the national energy strategy the President presented to Congress in 1991. It promotes energy efficiency and increases the use of renewable and alternative energy while providing much needed alternative minimum tax relief for independent oil and gas producers. This bill would also foster competition in wholesale electricity markets, reform the regulation of natural gas pipelines, and streamline the nuclear powerplant licensing process.

Although pleased with the progress, the President noted that the House bill needlessly locks up some of America's best prospects for domestic oil and natural gas production and restricts State prorationing authority, thereby interfering with the ability of States to properly regulate production of their own gas resources. While there is much work to be done, the President believes this bill forms a welcome bipartisan basis for moving to conference.

# Appointment of Eric D.K. Melby as Special Assistant to the President for National Security Affairs
*May 27, 1992*

The President today announced the appointment of Eric D.K. Melby as Special Assistant to the President for National Security Affairs and Senior Director for International Economic Affairs on the National Security Council staff.

Mr. Melby has served as Director for International Economic Affairs on the NSC staff since September 1987. Prior to joining the NSC staff, he served as Special Assistant to the Under Secretary of State for Economic Affairs (1985–87) and with the International Energy Agency in Paris (1980–85). He has also worked for the Agency for International Development and was a Peace Corps volunteer in the Philippines.

Mr. Melby received his B.A. from Haverford College and his M.A. and Ph.D. from the School of Advanced International Studies of the Johns Hopkins University. He is married to Pamela Tripp Melby and has two daughters, Alexandra and Sarah.

## Remarks at a Bush-Quayle Fundraising Dinner in Atlanta, Georgia
*May 27, 1992*

Thank you all so very much. And Jim, thank you for sharing this highly successful dinner. I'm deeply appreciative. Thank you also for the introduction. May I thank Kathleen Bertram, who rendered the national anthem with such beauty and such feeling. Thank you very much. To Dr. Tomlinson, thank you, sir, for the invocation. A Congressman from here, but I believe from this particular district, Newt Gingrich, is up—the House is in session tonight, but Marianne, his wife, is with us. And I welcome her and pay my respects to our deputy leader up there, Newt Gingrich.

May I salute Bobby Holt, who is our national Bush-Quayle finance chairman, a fellow Texan, and he's done a superb job in getting us this far along the way. Also Fred Cooper, who is our Bush-Quayle State chairman, political chairman, and did a superb job working with so many of you in the primary. We had a fantastic turnout in a year that some were quite critical of, and I was very, very pleased for the result of that. And next to him, of course, a guy that deserves an awful lot of the credit for that, our State chairman, Alec Poitevint. He did a marvelous job. And he's doing a great job for the party. May I also thank Krishna Srinivasa for his wonderful work. He has energized, along with some of the other leaders here, the Indian-American community, great loyal Americans, and doing a superb job. And thank you very, very much.

Someone once described the people of Atlanta as "pressing forward, grasping the future, shaping something strong and good, and yet acknowledging and taking pride in heritage." Well, I believe that certainly does apply to Atlanta. But I also believe it applies to the American people. And I frankly think the American people are a little bit sick and tired of this 90 seconds of gloom and doom every night on the top of the television news.

Things are moving forward in this country. The economy is moving forward. The regrettable part is that a recent survey I saw said that 70 percent of the American

people don't understand that, don't believe that yet. But it is moving stronger. And the new feeling of confidence, the figures of confidence out today I think send a wonderful signal to all of America.

So we're beginning to see things changing after a long, dreary period of recession and economic gloom. And I think that's good because I think of our country as what I said a minute ago, something strong and good. We are not a declining America. And that's the message I'm going to be taking to the country this fall.

I might also add that we've got a lot to be grateful for in terms of international affairs. Look at what's happened in Eastern Europe. Look at the decline and fall, the collapse of international communism. Look at the fact that ancient enemies are talking to each other for the first time in history in the Middle East. Look to our south and see a hemisphere that is almost totally democratic. And look at these little kids and say they go to bed at night without the fear of nuclear war that their older brothers and their parents did. And that is something good and something we can be very, very grateful for as Americans.

And so I would say, tipping my hat to my predecessor and to other Presidents: Yes, we have changed the world. And we did it because people like the people of Georgia stood behind us in terms of a strong defense and recognizing that the national security of this country was absolutely essential. We've helped change the world, changed it dramatically, and now we're working to change America. That's what I wanted to talk to you about tonight.

We are working for free trade. I just came from a wonderful Christian school out here, private school, and they asked me the question about the free trade agreement. The kid read the question and said, "Well, my dad thinks that we're talking about sending jobs overseas or sending jobs to Mexico." I said, "Well, tell your dad he got it wrong." He's got it backwards. What we're trying to do is create more American jobs through free trade and fair trade. That is the policy of this administration. And that is what Georgians understand because you have thousands of jobs that depend on American exports. We are not going to go protectionist in this country. I might say parenthetically, I want a successful conclusion to this NAFTA, this North American free trade agreement. I want a successful conclusion to the GATT round, the Uruguay round of GATT. And we're fighting to get both of those concluded, and that is in the interest of the American workers as well.

We're fighting for health care reform. I'm not talking about nationalized health care. I'm not talking about socialized medicine where the great quality of American health care is diminished because of Government interference. I am talking about a health care plan that, through changing the way insurance works, pooling of insurance, gives access to those who have no insurance at all and yet keeps the quality of American health care at the top of the heap. And that's exactly what our health care proposal will do. I believe it's going to work.

We're challenging the old thinkers in the United States Congress to help us, to the degree the Federal Government is involved, reform our education system. I think the time has come for parental choice in schools. It works at the college level, and it can work at the lower levels as well. Parental choice: Revolutionize American education, not by having some subcommittee in Washington mandate benefits but by literally keeping the Government out of the way and keeping control next to the American people, as close as possible. Our whole America 2000 education program is based on that concept, that local communities and families know better what to do about educating their kids than a bureaucracy in Washington, DC. And we need your help to get that one through the Congress.

I'm a little remiss; I might add this when I'm talking about education reform: You've got a great man running for the United States Senate in Paul Coverdell. You get him up there and six or seven more like him and give us control of that Senate, and these new ideas are going to get a chance. They are going to get tried.

I think the time has come for legal reform. We're suing each other too much and caring for each other too little. And we need to get some caps on some of these outrageous liability claims, malpractice claims. It is too much. The lawsuits are going out of sight. I want to see that changed, and I think we ought to get that done.

We did a little history, looking up for these remarks, and 200 years ago to this very day Jefferson put it this way, Thomas Jefferson: "The natural progress of things is for liberty to yield and government to gain ground." Two hundred years ago. And I'm now saying it is time to draw the line. And the philosophy that draws us together does exactly that. It keeps the empowerment with the people. It keeps choice with the people.

The need for change was brought tragically to focus in Los Angeles, in the Los Angeles crisis. And we moved in fast. I am very proud of the way the Federal bureaucracy moved on that one, with FEMA out there and SBA and all the loans and health and food. All these considerations were taken care of fast, including federalizing the National Guard and putting the 7th Army and some of the Marines out there to keep the peace. We cannot condone that kind of reckless, terroristic behavior, no matter how bad the conditions in any city in America. So we moved to restore order, and we now have a six-point plan for change, dramatic change.

Some of these critics, some of these liberal doctrinaire thinkers in Washington say, well, there's nothing new about these ideas. And I'll say they're all new because they haven't been tried by a Congress that has its head in the sand. Here's what we're talking about, our urban agenda:

"Weed and Seed," a brand new program to weed out the criminal elements and seed the communities with hope and opportunity and education.

The second one, enterprise zones. Everyplace I went in Los Angeles, people were saying, whatever walk of life, not just the business community but those that are working with the kids in the communities, enterprise zones is an idea whose time has come. What we're talking about is changing the tax structure so businesses can take a chance and locate in these underprivileged areas, drawing jobs like a magnet to the inner city. We believe it ought to be tried. And we believe the best answer to poverty is a job with dignity in the private sector, not some Government program.

The third one—we've been working on it for a long time, rebuffed sometimes by Congress, but I'm determined to keep fighting for it—homeownership. Isn't it better to have housing managed by the tenants, and for people then to go on to own their own homes, than it is to grow up in some project with no dignity and no hope of grabbing that piece of the American dream which is represented by owning your own home? We are for homeownership, and we're going to keep fighting for that one.

The fourth one is welfare reform. And there's some cynics out there. Some of the great editorialists will say anytime I talk about welfare reform, I'm playing a race card. That is not true. The people that are hurt the worst, those that are impoverished the most, are some in our minority communities. And what we're trying to do is change it, to offer learning, to offer workfare as opposed to the indignity that comes with the status quo.

A little girl saved over $1,000—her family being on welfare—and the system was so tough and so much of a penalty that they came along and tried to say that her mother could no longer get welfare because she'd managed to squirrel away a little over $1,000 to save for her education. We've got to reform the welfare system so it encourages people to save money, it encourages families to stay together. And it isn't race. It is what is right and decent for America. And I'm going to keep fighting for that one.

The next one is Job Training 2000, a one-stop shopping program that I announced right here in Atlanta, Georgia. It's a good program for job training. It brings in all the areas of the Government that have something to do with it, and there are quite a few. One person that needs job training can go to this one outlet and get advantage of what's available in the field of job training. It's a good new program, and I think we have a good chance to get that fully en-

acted.

And then the last one, which is a little longer range because it takes a while to get it implemented, is the program I mentioned in the beginning, America 2000, this revolutionary approach to how we educate our kids in the United States of America.

I've asked the Congress—when I came back from Los Angeles I said, look, can't we do this: Can't we lay partisanship aside; can't we just put it off the radar screen for long enough to enact these six programs or something like them? Can't we do it without having to make a statement and raise taxes, or go out and add to the Government spending that is already breaking the back of this country? And I'm hopeful still that the answer will be yes. I can't guarantee it, but I'm going to keep on fighting for these principles.

If you look to the core of these proposals, they are themes that all of us can agree on, no matter what side of the aisle you're on. Responsibility, opportunity, ownership, independence, dignity, empowerment: These aren't partisan values. These aren't liberal or conservative. These are plain, solid American values, and we have a duty to make them real for those who have not yet grasped the American dream.

We're not going to be able to spend our way out of these problems. We've tried that for too long. And we've got to remember these are not Government dollars. These are taxpayers' dollars. And when it comes to the deficit, horrendous as it is, let's remember who foots the bills, our children and our grandchildren. The time has now come to enact something that I've favored for a long, long time, and I am talking about a balanced budget amendment to the Constitution of the United States.

You're already having people tell you why it can't be done. And I am telling you it will work. Obviously, it has to be phased in. It will discipline the executive branch, but it will darn sure discipline the branch of Government that spends and appropriates every single dime, and that is the United States Congress. We have to do that.

And while we're talking about Government reform, another thing I'll be taking to the American people this fall is the case to give me what 43 Governors have, the line-item veto. Let's see if we can't cut some of this pork out of the Federal budget.

We've got a lot of cynics that are saying, "You haven't tried to do anything about it." And I said, look, take a look at the budget that's up in Congress right now that puts a cap on the growth of mandatory spending. A President does not have control over the mandatory spending programs. They're already there, and they don't have to be changed each year. They just go right out of sight. I am suggesting that we put a cap, not cut them but put a cap on the growth of those spending programs, and that will reduce the deficit enormously. And we're going to fight for that principle, painful though it may be in certain quarters.

Now, so far I've talked to you about what Government can do. But Government are not going to solve the problems all by ourselves. It cannot get done. And you might ask yourself, well, what keeps a kid in school? What keeps a kid off the streets? What keeps a kid off of drugs? And it isn't the Government. It is the family. I am very concerned about the decline of the American family. And I am determined, through exhortation and sometimes through legislation, to find ways to strengthen, not weaken, the American family. We have to do it, and I believe we can.

Barbara Bush is right—not all the time, but she's right on this—[*laughter*]—when she says what happens in your house is more important than what happens in the White House. And the longer I am your President, the more convinced I am that that is a sound and solid message for all of the American people.

And we're going to try. We're going to try to strengthen family through welfare reform. We're going to try to get the fathers, the deadbeat fathers who run away and bear no responsibility to the mother left to raise the children, to do what they're supposed to do.

Let the cynics who want to design some mandated program out of Washington; we, Barbara and I, will continue to encourage to get parents to read to their children. There's a new report coming out tomorrow out of the Department of Education that's going to be a little worrisome to this country. It's going to show that we're simply not doing enough in terms of reading to these kids or requiring that the kids learn to read in schools. The kids are watching over 3 hours of television a day and reading less than five pages a day. That is wrong. And you can't legislate, but we've got to keep talking out and saying the way to do this and help these kids is to have strong family values. And one of them is that the parents ought to read to their kids and take an interest in them in the schools.

You'll notice I haven't mentioned my opponents tonight, not one of them. And I'm just getting warmed up on you, though, about the message because, you see, I believe that these values that I spelled out here tonight are sound. I believe the programs that I've talked about here tonight are new. And as I say, we have changed the world, and now we've got to bring this kind of change to the United States of America.

And I can't wait for the fray in the fall. As for now, I'm trying to run this country, and I'm trying to get things done for the American people. But lest you think I've lost the fire, I'm ready. I am ready to take this case to the American people. Let them keep punching out there for another 2 months. But after the convention, with you at my side, we are going to win this election, and we're going to win it going away. America is a rising Nation, not a declining Nation. Don't listen to the pessimists trying to get my job. They don't know what they're talking about.

God bless you all, and many, many thanks.

*Note: The President spoke at 7:18 p.m. in the Grand Ballroom at the Stouffer Waverly Hotel. In his remarks, he referred to Jim Edenfield, dinner chairman and Bush-Quayle '92 Georgia finance chairman; Edward Tomlinson, senior minister, Northside Methodist Church; Alec Poitevint II, Georgia Republican Party chairman; and Krishna Srinivasa, event cochairman and member of the board of governors of the Georgia Republican Foundation.*

## Statement on Signing the Child Abuse, Domestic Violence, Adoption and Family Services Act of 1992
*May 28, 1992*

Today I have signed into law S. 838, the "Child Abuse, Domestic Violence, Adoption and Family Services Act of 1992." The Administration strongly supports reauthorization of the programs covered by this Act.

A child's physical and mental well-being is a crucial element in the achievement of his or her potential. Unfortunately, over one million children per year suffer because they do not receive adequate care and support. Reauthorization of the programs in this Act will help prevent child maltreatment and provide assistance to children in need.

The Act, however, contains an objectionable provision—a requirement that the Ad-

visory Board on Child Abuse and Neglect recommend changes in Federal law to implement a national policy on child abuse prevention. I must view this provision as advisory rather than mandatory, in order to avoid conflict with my exclusive authority under the Constitution to decide whether and when the executive branch should propose legislation.

GEORGE BUSH

The White House,
May 28, 1992.

*Note: S. 838, approved May 28, was assigned Public Law No. 102–295.*

## Statement on Denying Use of United States Ports to Vessels Trading With Haiti
*May 28, 1992*

I have today directed the Secretary of the Treasury and the Secretary of Transportation to deny the use of American ports to ships that violate the trade embargo against Haiti. This action is being taken in support of the resolution adopted by the Organization of American States on May 17, which calls on OAS member states to deny port facilities to vessels trading with Haiti in disregard of the OAS embargo.

The United States remains committed unequivocally to the restoration of democratic government in Haiti. We will continue working in close concert with our OAS allies toward a negotiated settlement of the political crisis that began with the overthrow of President Jean-Bertrand Aristide last September 30. In addition to today's action, and in accordance with the recent OAS resolution, we are examining other steps to tighten sanctions against the illegal regime in Port-au-Prince.

Our actions are directed at those in Haiti who are opposing a return to democracy,

not at the Haitian poor. We are continuing to provide substantial, direct humanitarian assistance to the people of Haiti and are working to intensify those efforts. Our current programs total $47 million and provide food for over 600,000 Haitians and health care services that reach nearly 2 million. While tightening the embargo, we will continue to encourage others to ship food staples and other humanitarian items to those in need. The action that I have directed will not affect vessels carrying permitted items.

We are expanding opportunities for Haitians who fear persecution in their homeland to apply for admission to the United States as refugees with our Embassy in Port-au-Prince. The Embassy has been receiving such applications since early February, and all persons who believe they may be qualified are urged to avail themselves of our expanded refugee operation in Haiti. I have asked the Department of State to ensure that Embassy personnel will also be available outside Port-au-Prince to assist applicants in other parts of the country in pursuing their claims.

# Statement by Press Secretary Fitzwater on Humanitarian Assistance to Refugees in Yugoslavia and the Caucasus
*May 28, 1992*

The United States will contribute $9 million for humanitarian assistance to refugees and displaced people in the former Yugoslavia and $4 million for humanitarian assistance to victims of conflicts in the Caucasus region of the former Soviet Union. This includes the new Republics of Armenia, Azerbaijan, and Georgia.

The situation in the Yugoslav former republics has created the largest movement of persons in Europe since the end of World War II. The total number of refugees and displaced persons in Yugoslavia, according to United Nations High Commissioner for Refugees (UNHCR), has now reached 1.3 million. Over 480,000 persons, mostly Slavic Muslims, have fled Bosnia and this number is growing daily. Six million dollars of this contribution will go to the UNHCR in support of its programs to assist refugees and displaced persons, especially those in Bosnia and Croatia. Three million dollars will go to the International Committee of the Red Cross (ICRC) in support of its efforts to aid the victims of the terrible conflict now raging.

This $9 million contribution is in addition to earlier contributions this year of $7 million. The United States also launched an emergency airlift of food and other relief assistance to aid war victims in Bosnia-Hercegovina. Five planes flew into Sarajevo carrying blankets, food, and medical supplies.

The United States contribution for victims of conflicts in the Caucasus will be given to the ICRC in support of its humanitarian aid to war victims, refugees, and other vulnerable groups, especially in Armenia and Azerbaijan. Over the past 2 years, the Caucasus has experienced an increase in ethnic strife leading to armed conflicts in the Nagorno-Karabakh region of Azerbaijan and in the South Ossetian area of Georgia.

# Nomination of Anthony Cecil Eden Quainton To Be an Assistant Secretary of State
*May 28, 1992*

The President today announced his intention to nominate Anthony Cecil Eden Quainton, of the District of Columbia, a career member of the Senior Foreign Service, class of Career Minister, to be Assistant Secretary of State for Diplomatic Security. He would succeed Sheldon J. Krys.

Since 1989, Ambassador Quainton has served as U.S. Ambassador to the Republic of Peru. Prior to this, he served as Deputy Inspector General of the Department of State, 1987–89; U.S. Ambassador to the State of Kuwait, 1984–87; and as U.S. Ambassador to the Republic of Nicaragua, 1982–84. Ambassador Quainton has also served as Director of the Office for Combatting Terrorism at the Department of State, 1978–81.

Ambassador Quainton graduated from Princeton University (B.A., 1955) and Oxford University (B.Litt., 1958). He was born April 4, 1934, in Seattle, WA. Ambassador Quainton is married, has three children, and resides in Washington, DC.

## Nomination of Henry Lee Clarke To Be United States Ambassador to Uzbekistan
*May 28, 1992*

The President today announced his intention to nominate Henry Lee Clarke, of California, a career member of the Senior Foreign Service, class of Minister-Counselor, to be Ambassador of the United States of America to the Republic of Uzbekistan.

Since 1989, Mr. Clarke has served as Economic Counselor of the American Embassy in Tel Aviv, Israel. Prior to this, he served as Deputy Chief of Mission at the American Embassy in Bucharest, Romania, 1985–89; and Economic Counselor at the American Embassy in Moscow, U.S.S.R., 1982–85.

From 1980 to 1981, Mr. Clarke served as Officer-in-Charge of Trade and Industrial Policy in the Office of European Regional Political-Economic Affairs for the U.S. Department of State.

Mr. Clarke graduated from Dartmouth College (A.B., 1962) and Harvard University (M.P.A., 1967). He was born November 15, 1941, in Fort Benning, GA. Mr. Clarke served in the U.S. Army, 1962–65. He is married, has two children, and resides in Turlock, CA.

## Nomination of Edward Hurwitz To Be United States Ambassador to Kyrgyzstan
*May 28, 1992*

The President today announced his intention to nominate Edward Hurwitz, of the District of Columbia, a career member of the Senior Foreign Service, class of Minister-Counselor, to be Ambassador of the United States of America to the Republic of Kyrgyzstan.

Currently Mr. Hurwitz serves as Deputy Examiner of the Board of Examiners for the Foreign Service in Washington, DC. Prior to this, he served as Director of the Office of Analysis for the U.S.S.R. and Eastern Europe at the Department of State, 1988–91; Counsel General at the American Consulate in Leningrad, U.S.S.R., 1986–88; and Chargé d'Affaires at the American Embassy in Kabul, Afghanistan, 1983–86.

Mr. Hurwitz graduated from Cornell University (A.B., 1952). He was born March 21, 1931, in New York, NY. Mr. Hurwitz served in the U.S. Army, 1953–55. He is married, has two children, and resides in Washington, DC.

## Nomination of Donald Burnham Ensenat To Be United States Ambassador to Brunei
*May 28, 1992*

The President today announced his intention to nominate Donald Burnham Ensenat, of Louisiana, to be Ambassador of the United States of America to Brunei Darussalam. He would succeed Christopher H. Phillips.

Since 1989, Mr. Ensenat has served as managing director of the law firm of Hoffman, Sutterfield, Ensenat & Bankston, APLC in New Orleans, LA. Prior to this, Mr. Ensenat served with Camp, Carmouche, et al. as managing director, 1985–

88; director, 1983–88; and as an associate, 1980–82.

Mr. Ensenat graduated from Yale University (B.A., 1968) and Tulane University School of Law (J.D., 1973). He was born February 4, 1946, in New Orleans, LA. Mr. Ensenat served in the U.S. Army, 1968–74. He is married, has two children, and resides in New Orleans, LA.

# Remarks to the American Legion in Phoenix, Arizona
*May 28, 1992*

May I thank our great Senator John McCain for that introduction and single out our Governor, Fife Symington. Greetings to all the commanders on the dais, Tony Valenzuela, Don Silva, Don Gentry. Thanks to our master of ceremonies, Joe Abodeely. And it's great, of course, to see Everett Alvarez here. And I'd also like to take this opportunity to thank Bob Stump, the Congressman from Arizona, the ranking Republican on the House Veterans Affairs Committee. He has worked hard up on Capitol Hill for the veterans of this country. I'm very sorry he couldn't be with us today, but I have great respect for his work.

It's not normal that I'm standing up here with three—maybe you're used to it in this great State of Arizona—but three winners of the Congressional Medal of Honor standing here. It really says something. I salute all of them.

And I'd like to think in some cross-sectional way that people out here in this audience and standing behind me represent, at least for today, more than 26 million veterans. It's great to be back here. An old saying goes, "Save the best for last." Well, today we're saving the best for first: The first campaign coalition to be announced for our campaign, Barry Goldwater, its honorary chairman, John McCain and Everett Alvarez, its national chairmen, and that is the Bush-Quayle '92 National Veterans Coalition. They're going to be good and strong, and I'm glad to have their support.

Now, I hope you know why I insisted the veterans be first to be unveiled. You know how service has preserved the values that make and keep us strong. John touched on that in that wonderfully generous introduction. You know how veterans have given of themselves and often of their lives in places whose names we all know, from the Argonne, Normandy, Da Nang, and of course, most recently, in the Persian Gulf. Think of our kids and our grandkids. They have inherited your bequest of faith in the country, in family, in democracy, in God. They can never repay the veterans, all of you, for what you've done for freedom.

From the time the torch of liberty was first lit in America, veterans have shed their blood to make sure that it would never go out. And that's what this campaign must be about, what we've got to fight for, enlist our hearts and minds for: to ensure people choice for the schools, for example; for society, pluralism; for God's children, the freedom to go about their lives, their daily lives, free of fear.

Freedom can let us vote as we want and pray as we choose. Freedom can ensure the legacies for our kids of family, peace, and jobs. Above all, freedom can secure what we fought for, Guadalcanal or Inchon or Hue City or Kuwait City: a world where liberty's tide is coming in. It's running in, just as tyranny's tide is running out.

I renew my pledge today in this opening to do all that's humanly possible to account for our comrades that are missing from the past wars. As long as I am President we will never forget those POW's and MIA's.

Another pledge: As we move to a post-cold-war defense force, we cannot forget to take care of our military and civilian men and women who worked and fought so hard to ensure that freedom and democracy would prevail. For them, we will continue to work together to make sure that American veterans receive quality health care that is second to none.

Now, there is a benefit to the end of the cold war, and that is that there will be substantial defense savings made possible in this new environment. However, it is my conviction that this transition must be managed in a rational manner. First, we've got to achieve an orderly reduction in our forces. We're talking about 25 percent over the next 5 years. That is substantial.

But as John McCain can tell you, there are people in the Congress that want to take everything out of defense and out of the national security and shift it over to some mandated program from Washington. Some have called for far deeper cuts than we have, and I reject this approach. As I told the graduating midshipmen down in Annapolis yesterday, never in the history of man has the world been a benign place. There is no substitute for America's strength, and no substitute for our sense of purpose. I am not going to let the Congress gut the muscle of our defense.

Next, Secretary Cheney and I are mindful of our obligation to treat defense and uniform employees and their communities fairly. Our plan already includes spending more than $7.1 billion to address defense transition over the next 2 years. And today I'm proposing a number of additional programs, including new GI bill benefits and an expansion of job training, employment, and other educational opportunities. We're going to dedicate more than one billion additional dollars through 1996 on these vital defense transition activities. Whether they're working as teachers in an elementary school or as environmental engineers, I am committed to ensuring that the vast talents of these former defense personnel can be put to productive use in private life.

With us today are talented and capable men and women who believe in this new world of freedom. No one needs to tell them about the inhumanity of war. Instead, they know that only a strong America can preserve the humanity of peace. I am proud of these men and proud that they have agreed to help me. And I thank you for your support. I hope to be worthy of your prayers.

Thirty years ago, Douglas MacArthur put it well. Returning to the plain up at West Point, he gave a speech to the cadets. "The soldier," he told them, "above all other people, prays for peace, for he must bear the deepest wounds and scars of war."

You've all been soldiers in the crusade of freedom, and this year I ask you to reenlist and help keep America what Lincoln called "the last best hope of Earth." For 200 years our veterans have fought for what is right and what is good, and I ask you to help me defend those values. And I thank you from the bottom of my heart.

I am very happy that the young kids now go to sleep every night without the fear, that constant fear of nuclear war that the generations before them had. I think that's a significant and a major accomplishment. And Barbara and I have—I was going to say 10—I think it's 12 grandchildren.

I take great pride in that fact, that in some way perhaps my Presidency was a part of all of that. But that is there. Now we've got to keep this movement towards freedom and towards peace around the world going forward. We've got to do it. With your help, I'm confident we can do it for the next 4 years.

Many, many thanks to all of you.

*Note: The President spoke at 4:55 p.m. at the American Legion Luke Greenway Post. In his remarks, he referred to Arizona State commanders Tony Valenzuela, American Legion, Don Silva, Veterans of Foreign Wars, and Don Gentry, Disabled American Veterans.*

# Remarks at a Fundraising Dinner for Senator John McCain in Phoenix
*May 28, 1992*

Thank you all very, very much for that welcome. May I pay my tribute to Jim Click. He's been a staunch supporter of the Republican cause for a long, long time, and I'm very grateful to see him again and grateful for that introduction. Of course, I'm proud to be at the side of John McCain and his wife, Cindy. I want to salute two from our Cabinet: Secretary Lynn Martin, our Secretary of Labor over here, who's doing a superb job, job training and a wide array of other issues; and then our irrepressible Secretary of HUD, who is going with me as we head back out to Los Angeles, but a man who is doing a superb job in this concept of homeownership, giving people a part of the action, Jack Kemp, our Secretary of HUD. And may I salute Governor Fife Symington and Ann; and of course, a special warm *abraso* for Barry and Susan Goldwater; and our chairman, Jerry Davis; Pastor Jackson, whom I've been privileged to be with before; Everett Alvarez, who today was announced as one of our cochairmen of our veterans effort, a great American.

Brenda High, appropriately named for the way she did that "Star-Spangled Banner." It was outstanding. You can't help but be stirred when you hear a rendition like that of our great national anthem. And thanks to the—where is the band? I can't see them, but I understand you've got a great Chaparral High School band over here. Thank you for your music. And thanks to Shannon Marketic, Miss U.S.A., for the pledge. And out with us in the audience, a guy I visited with earlier on, a true Point of Light, Kevin Johnson of the Phoenix Suns, and all he does for the young people out here. And then another old friend who I had a chance to greet earlier on, Joe Bugel of the Cardinals, a great guy and a great sportsman. And I'm proud to see him.

So it's a pleasure to be back, and I'm sorry Barbara's not here. And I will apologize; they told me that broccoli is on the menu, and I'm out of here as soon as I finish speaking. [*Laughter*] But seriously, we do have to head back out to Los Angeles, be sure we're following up the way we should there.

But I'm glad to have this opportunity to express my appreciation to our Senator, and I say "ours" because Barbara and I feel like he's just part of us, Senator John McCain, for his help in fighting against that pork barrel spending back in Washington and for his leadership and support for the line-item veto. He is a man of principle. John, your leadership has been absolutely invaluable. And when I see it I say to myself, if only we had control of the United States Senate. On budget, on taxes, on health care, on the needs of older Americans, John McCain's efforts mean so much to me and so much to our country. They, of course, mean an awful lot to the great State of Arizona and to all Americans. You are lucky, indeed, to have him in the Senate, and we must have him back come fall.

And of course, special tribute to Senator Barry Goldwater for his half-century of principled, and I use that word advisedly, principled service to our great country. What a record of achievement. What an example. What an accomplishment. Fifty years in public service, and underlying it all, character and integrity totally intact. I am proud to be his friend. I am grateful for his support. There have been some tough times in my political life, and one of them was 4 years ago. Barry came up there, suited up, got on a long flight and flew up to New Hampshire and bailed me out. I'll never, ever forget it. Not out of jail, but out of some political hot water up there. [*Laughter*]

How about this backdrop? I like it very much, not only as a great art work, but coming from a city where Congress spends so much money, it's always good to see something in black ink. [*Laughter*]

It was Barry who put it this way, "Those who do not have courage want complicated answers." Well, Republicans are courageous people, and our solutions to America's problems are simple and effective, not complicated out of a maze of redtape. While the Democrats put their faith in adding new bricks to the old bureaucratic programs, and they try to do it every single day up there in the Congress, we Republicans are focusing on leaving our children and grandchildren three fundamental legacies that are integral to their own future: Strong families to sustain individuals, to nurture and encourage children, and to preserve our Nation's character and our culture; and then, number two, peace, in our schools, on our streets, and yes, all around the world; and then, third one, jobs, both for those who are seeking work and for graduates entering the work force.

I might add, at long last our national economy is beginning to move. It's recovering, and consumer confidence, you might have seen it yesterday, is starting back up, is returning.

These legacies, all of them don't always translate into sound bites, but they are definitely sound policy. Senator Barry Goldwater and Senator John McCain have both been at the forefront in helping to establish these legacies and in building a sound Republican policy, policy that sees problems as something more than excuses for new centralized, mandated programs. This is the message I will be taking to the American people in the fall, and this is the message that is going to win for us not only the White House but control of the Congress. You watch and see, now.

What we are trying to do is to offer innovation and change. American industries lead the world in growth and efficiency. America is the world's leading exporter, producing $422 billion worth last year alone, $422 billion. Over the past 5 years, our exports have supported 7 million jobs. These are impressive accomplishments, a record of economic growth and international competitiveness to make any country proud.

Instead of excuses, we're offering education. More than one of four American workers has a college degree; another 20 percent have at least a year of college. Through this program we've got, the break-the-mold school program, and parental choice and choice for public, private, or religious schools for their children, I might add, our America 2000 initiative for education: it is new; it is revolutionary, and it doesn't mandate it from Washington. It says let the communities, let the States, let the families have a say in deciding what kind of education is best for our own children.

And yes, we are opening more and more doors of opportunity for Americans. And now we must address ways that we can strengthen our national spirit and return to the bedrock principles, faith, family, that made our Nation great. I would hate to be taking a case to the American people in the fall that was predicated on everything being bad, that the only way you can win is if the country's going to hell in a handbasket. We are America, and we are moving forward. And by fall we are going to show them that the positive message of change is the message of hope for the American people.

John McCain and I have the responsibility to provide the leadership that we need, the country needs, to get back to sound principles upon which our Nation was founded, principles that helped make us the world's leading Nation and principles that gave us a standard of living that is the envy of the entire world.

The cynics say that social conditions are too bad to turn around. And the skeptics say that faith and ideals are puny and inconsequential when put up against the problems that we face as a Nation. Well, I think they're wrong. I believe, along with Calvin Coolidge, "there is no force so democratic as the force of an ideal." I believe that the forces of character, of compassion, and goodness will ultimately triumph over the forces that can only tear down and destroy.

Tonight, as soon as we finish here, I'm going to be going back to Los Angeles to check on the progress of Federal aid efforts out there and to expand on my ideas for an urban agenda, an agenda of hope and opportunity in all our cities. I might say I am very proud of the rapid response of our Federal Agencies to that crisis out there: the Army, the Marines, there to restore law and order; the SBA and HUD and Labor and FEMA and Agriculture and HHS and others, too. They responded fast. We did it in a coordinated way, and all of them did very, very well.

But I am less proud of the fact that the Congress has not moved on our program to bring instant hope to the cities, not just Los Angeles but the cities all across our country, on enterprise zones or on the other proposals that we've made that would instantly bring hope to the cities. I challenge the Congress right here and now: Please take action. Let's set the partisanship aside for just long enough to get something done to help people in this country.

So let the others out there take their message of pessimism. They say that America's best days are behind us. The truth is that our Nation stands at a pinnacle of achievement that is unmatched. We are the unquestioned leader of the free world, which now includes more countries than ever before. All those new democracies are looking to America, to the United States of America, for leadership.

Yes, there is much left to be done in our own country. But many of the changes that we are pushing are stuck up there on Capitol Hill. There was no one who wants to work cooperatively with Congress any more than I do. And from my very first State of the Union Address I held out my hand and said, "The people didn't send us here to bicker; let's try to get something done."

I don't think there's anyone, I might say, who has been a better friend up there on Capitol Hill than John McCain because he understands these principles. He advocates them, articulates them. We bent over backwards to try to get the liberals who control the Congress to support our efforts to reform, reform programs that simply are not working anymore. We've tried to change things that aren't working. Now the time has come to change the control of the United States Congress itself and watch this country move forward.

There is a mood for change. There was talk in all of them. The Nation needs an infusion of fresh, new Republican Congressmen and Senators who will be statesmen, like Barry Goldwater, like John McCain, leaders willing to try out new ideas. We unveiled this plan for the cities, and some

cynics out there on the Democratic side are saying, "These aren't new. You proposed them before." They are new because they have not been tried. We need people who will put the best interest of the Nation first and foremost.

There are other problems that Government alone cannot reverse. At the top of the list is action to restore the American family. Simply put, our children cannot dream the American dream when they are living a nightmare. Look at a few brief and sad facts. In comparison with other industrialized countries, the Census Bureau found that the United States has the highest divorce rate, the highest number of children involved in divorce, the highest teenage pregnancy rates, the highest abortion rates, the highest percentage of children living in a single-parent household, the highest percentage of violent deaths among our precious young. These are not the kinds of records that we want to have as a great country.

Our Federal Government, of course, we have responsibilities. As President, I've got responsibilities in all of this. We must do more. We must do what we can. The American people must do those things that Government cannot do. Government can and must provide school choice, but parents must read to their kids and instill a love for learning. Government can and must fight crime, but fathers and mothers must teach discipline and instill values in their children. Government can and must foster American competitiveness, but parents must teach the kids the dignity of work.

To paraphrase that great philosopher of the silver hair, Barbara Bush—[*laughter*]—what you teach at your house is more important than what happens at the White House. And she is absolutely right about that.

So we're a country that has a lot of problems, big problems. But I am absolutely convinced we can solve them. We have laid the groundwork, and we've developed sound plans. We can transform America into the Nation we all want her to be.

It hasn't been much fun in the political arena lately. We've been hammered out there a little bit. Somebody said that builds character. I said, I'm a little long on character and looking forward to a change.

But let me tell you this. I am quietly confident about the election this fall. In sum, I am absolutely convinced as this economy moves back, as we sort out where everybody stands on these highly complex issues, when the country assesses the fact that we are at peace and that our children go to bed at night with less fear of nuclear war—and that is a major accomplishment of which I am very proud to have been a part—and it's when we get in focus the agenda, see who wants to pass this agenda of hope and opportunity and who wants to stifle it, when we take forward the values that you and I believe in to the American people again this fall on family and faith, I am absolutely convinced we're going to win

this election. We are going to win it. We're going to transform our problems into challenging opportunities to realize the American dream.

Thank you for your fantastic support for our great Senator. May God bless you, and may God bless the United States of America, the freest and greatest country on the face of the Earth. Thank you very, very much.

*Note: The President spoke at 6:23 p.m. at the Phoenix Civic Plaza. In his remarks, he referred to Jim Click, Bush-Quayle Arizona finance chairman; Gerald Davis, chairman, Arizona Republican Party; and Richard Jackson, pastor, North Phoenix Baptist Church.*

## Remarks at a Disaster Application Center in Los Angeles, California
*May 29, 1992*

*The President.* Let me just say, if you can hear this, why, I want to thank Ava. Where's Ava? Ava, get over here; we're talking about you guys, you and Maurice.

*Ms. Hagen.* Oh, are we in trouble?

*The President.* No, we're talking about good things about both of you and about Pat Saiki here, the head of SBA. I have been very pleased to learn and to be reinformed, actually, that the SBA has moved faster in trying to help people in this instance than at any time in its productive history. I congratulate not only the leadership of SBA but the volunteers and those that have come in, professionals from all across the country, to help.

FEMA has been responding very fast. And the thing that has impressed me as I've gone along here is, I do see a sense of coordination. Before I leave, I expect some will tell me we need to improve things in some way, but I've been very pleased that the Federal Government, which sometimes can be very insensitive, has moved fast in this regard.

It's nice to be sitting next to somebody that might share my view at least on that point because it is so important that you get

back on your feet. The only other point I'd make, Pat and Ava and Maurice, is the spirit of some of the people I've talked to, like that last lady, who have had a rough go, I mean, a really rough go. She still retains that faith that she's going to make it somehow, and that's pretty good. I don't know if that's typical of the people who have been afflicted so adversely or not, but it's a wonderful thing to hear somebody say, "With God's help, I'm going to make it." So what we've got to try to do is help, like in your case and those who are really trying to make it.

So that's the message I'll take away. We will keep trying very hard to assist. And I'm very grateful to Pat Saiki here, who is sensitive to these requirements.

*Ms. Hagen.* We just want to thank everybody for their help, sensitivity, and the rapidity in which they responded.

*The President.* Yes. How is the feeling in the communities in terms of future tranquility, peace? I mean, is there a determination there that this won't happen again and all that kind of——

*Q.* There is a determination now to rebuild and get started once again. And everyone is—[*inaudible*]. We have sat here the last 2 days and have shared more with each other about our businesses—[*inaudible*].

*Q.* [*Inaudible*]

*The President.* That is wonderful. Yes, you know, the approach was to try to coordinate it. We've got all these different Agencies, and I think there are now 10 of these—I thought it was 7; it's up to 10 now—of these centers. The Federal Government can be so complex because there are so many different Agencies, and we're trying to get it in what is called this one-stop shopping mode, yes, one-stop shopping mode. If it just continues like that, I think we can move faster.

*Q.* [*Inaudible*]

*The President.* Well, best of luck to you, to you all. And I'm impressed with the fact that some of these people that come in to help, to help fill out the forms, are from all across the country, Atlanta or Puerto Rico

even, Niagara, yes, Texas. Putting in a plug for the Texans down here. [*Laughter*] No, but it's good. It's a good thing.

*Q.* One more group to meet down there.

*The President.* There's one more stop down there? All right. Good luck to you now in your business. Lots of luck, sir.

*Mr. Robertson.* Sent a T-shirt to you.

*The President.* Did you? Wait a minute, you gave me a T-shirt, I'll give you my—here, take that, souvenir. If she makes you put on a tie, why, you can wear that. Okay.

*Ms. Hagen.* Thank you very much.

*The President.* Well, good luck. I'll get out of here.

*Note: The President spoke at 10:35 a.m. at Harvard Recreation Center. In his remarks, he referred to Harvard Disaster Application Center managers Ava Hagen, Federal Emergency Management Agency, and Maurice Robertson, California Department of Social Services.*

# Exchange With Reporters Prior to a Meeting With State and Local Officials in Los Angeles
*May 29, 1992*

*Q.* Sir, why do you think you're running third in recent California polls?

*The President.* Hey, John [John Cochran, NBC News], we're not taking any questions today.

*Q.* No?

*The President.* This is a nonpolitical visit. I've heard some very encouraging news about Federal cooperation and working with the State, localities, private sector. And I'm out here to try to follow up on a visit to see if we can be of further help to the people in this area. So, I prefer to keep it on that basis and thus will not be able to help you, as I wasn't able to help you yesterday—[*laughter*]—different setting. Thank you very much.

*Q.* ——about politics, sir? When are you going to start defining the——

*The President.* After our convention, I think we'll start working on that.

*Q.* After the convention?

*Q.* Are you deliberately waiting, sir?

*The President.* I'm not going to take any questions. You didn't hear what I said in the beginning. I want to find out from these people how the effort is going, Federal, State, local, to help people that have been hurt. And that's what this is about. And if I get diverted talking about these other subjects, it isn't going to help anybody. So, let's try to keep it on that basis. Thank you very much.

*Q.* Do you think the drive for the urban agenda is losing steam in Congress, though?

*Q.* Mr. President, are you optimistic about Mr. Ueberroth's Rebuild L.A.? Are you optimistic about what he——

*The President.* Anything he tackles, he can get done. That's the way I look at it.

*Note: The exchange began at 11:08 a.m. in*

*the Grecian Room at the Biltmore Hotel. In his remarks, the President referred to Peter*

*Ueberroth, chairman of the Rebuild L.A. Committee.*

## Remarks to Town Hall of California in Los Angeles
*May 29, 1992*

Thank you, Lod, for that very warm and very generous introduction and welcome back to Los Angeles. May I greet our Mayor, Tom Bradley, Governor Pete Wilson, and single out two of your former Governors, one sitting on the left and the other on the right of mine, read nothing into that politically—*[laughter]*—George Deukmejian and Pat Brown. It's a great pleasure to see both of them. And may I single out Pat Saiki, our head of SBA; and our fine Secretary of HUD, Jack Kemp, who is trying to do an awful lot to help over here, Jack, a fellow Californian. And to Adrienne and the others who are officials here with Town Hall, thank you for giving me access to what I am told is one of the most prestigious forums in all of California.

This morning I was over in South Central talking with some of the people that are trying to restore that neighborhood, put it back together. We have a long way to go. But let me say this: I was really struck by the progress that's already been made in bringing this great city back. And I was struck by the spirit of those individuals that were there, not as spear carriers from some TV shot, but were there actually filling out the loans. And these were people that had been devastated by what happened, and there they were with faith in God and with the spirit that they could make it back. I wish everybody could have seen that.

Now, this remarkable effort has brought together Federal, State, and local officials, and most importantly, thousands of volunteers, churches, and neighborhood groups. I think we've seen enough of the horrible images over and over. And my plea is, how about some of the wonderful things going on? Yes, Los Angeles will come back. And with all due respect, I hope the media will tell this heartening story loud and clear and give it as much attention as the looters and rioters received just a few weeks ago.

As you may know, at the outset of the riots I pledged to do whatever was necessary to restore order. And I ordered the federalization, after consultation with Tom Bradley and Pete Wilson, of the National Guard and dispatched several thousand Federal law enforcement officials to L.A. We also had several thousand troops stand by for any emergency, 7th Army and the Marines. And I've been pleased to hear that that swift response did a great deal to stabilize, help stabilize I should say because the LAPD and others were out there helping as well, certainly the sheriff's department, help stabilize an explosive situation.

We were also able to get disaster relief to Los Angeles in record time. Seven relief centers opened in the first week after the rioting, three more a few days later. We have now 10. Housing assistance checks were being mailed to applicants within 3 days. And the SBA, and I would again credit Pat Saiki, with us today, was able to approve loans in weeks instead of months. Within 3 weeks the first checks were cut, and that is a record for this kind of disaster assistance. Our response was massive; it was quick. And to my team, led by David Kearns and Al DelliBovi, and to all the people who made it work, my thanks for a job very well done.

I am proud of what the Federal Government was able to do, but there should be no misunderstanding: Federal assistance offers no reward for rioting. This help has been directed to the victims, not to the perpetrators of the violence. To the criminals who subjected this city to 3 days of terror and hate, the message has got to be unequivocal: Lawlessness cannot be explained away. It will not be excused. And it must be punished.

In the starkest possible terms, this tragedy made clear the great unfinished business that we face as a Nation. We've got to strike a new course. We'll rebuild our cities. And we can, but only if we learn the lessons of what happened here. Now, what are the lessons? Some people tell us that the hopelessness in urban America is a simple matter of economics, of jobs. Others say, no, the answer lies in tougher law enforcement, safer streets. This is a false choice, really.

Of course, the best antipoverty program is a job. A job provides more than money; it teaches dignity and self-reliance, the first rungs of the economic ladder. And more than that, it gives them hope. But jobs don't get created in a wake of a crime wave. The first lesson of L.A., then, is a simple one. The primary duty of government is to protect the safety of lives and property. There can be no opportunity, no hope in a community where decent citizens are held hostage to gangs of criminals.

I know perhaps more acutely than anybody here that this is a campaign year. And every time someone mentions crime or law and order the accusations fly about "playing the race card." Let me just say, stop right there. There is nothing racist, there is nothing divisive about protecting decent people from crime. Some say it's playing politics. Well, they're wrong. Playgrounds overrun by gangs, senior citizens locked behind triple-bolted doors, or mothers shot through open kitchen windows: this isn't the America we want. Making neighborhoods safe isn't politics; it's just plain, simple decency. And it's the right thing to do.

That fact points to the second lesson of Los Angeles. Other people say that our urban problems are only about money, taxpayer money, your money. They tell us the solution lies in ever-higher Government spending. Well, this, I think, is another false choice, more Federal money versus less, as if the problems of our inner cities are simply the result of a lack of Federal funds. They're not. And let's be clear about this: Over the last 25 years, we have spent the staggering sum of $3.2 trillion on our social welfare system. And the fact is, in hopes of eliminating poverty, we spent more money in the eighties than we did in the seventies, more in the seventies than in the sixties. For all of the good intentions, decay and despair have only seeped deeper and deeper into our inner cities. But the trage-

dy is not about wasted money; it's about wasted lives.

The fact points to this second lesson, then, of Los Angeles: For those left behind, the system itself is broken. We won't fix it with a simple increase in Federal funds. You don't pump more gas into a car that doesn't run. You lift the hood up, roll up your sleeves, and get to work. We need to overhaul the engine. So we start with the most basic question: How has the system failed? What went wrong? The American dream is based on the belief that if you get a good education, find a job, work hard, raise a family, save for the future, you will prosper. Our free economy, in which the important decisions are made by the people themselves, makes this possible.

But decent people in the inner cities, particularly those with low incomes, labor under an entirely different set of rules, some laid down by the lawless, others laid down by government. As the bureaucratic power of government has grown in the inner cities, the power of the residents there to shape their own lives, to make important decisions, has steadily gone down, steadily declined. The system operates on an unspoken premise that Americans who live in depressed neighborhoods are simply incapable of making the decisions that other Americans make every single day. And it assumes they're unable to take advantage of the same opportunities that Americans have always used to better their lives. And worst of all, worst of all, it presumes they don't even want to. That's wrong. That's not compassion; it's condescension. It is paternalism. And there's no room for that in America.

Think how the system works for families in the inner cities. They find their choices and opportunities restricted at every turn——

*Audience member.* Mr. President, Mr. President——

*The President.* Can I finish, and then I'll be glad to hear from you. Okay, thank you.

*Audience member.* Mr. President, Mr. President, from Paul J. Myer. Paul J. Myer, your best buddy. This is for you.

*The President.* Thank you, sir. An unusual way to deliver the mail, but I'll be glad to

849

receive it. I know Paul J. Myer. Thank you very much.

*Audience member.* I apologize for——

*The President.* No, that's all right. No, no problem.

*Audience member.* I apologize for ruining the party.

*The President.* No, no, you're not ruining anything.

*Audience member.* But it's an important message. I have waited 7 years to get you that message. I am from the community, okay. I have received the benefit of a message that you gave to Mr. Paul J. Myer, or gave for him, 11 years ago, an idea which revolved around a concept called "Realize Your Full Potential."

*The President.* Yes.

*Audience member.* And I emerged from the community a very successful business-man——

*Audience members.* No, stop. No, no——

*Audience member.* And I think everybody in the community needs these benefits of these bigger ideas, concepts, and precepts. And ladies and gentlemen, please forgive me, but that just had to be said today. Thank you very much.

*Audience members.* Sit down, sit down.

*The President.* Okay. Now, wait a minute; it's all right. I know the man he's talking about. But now, let me start where I was, if that's okay. I'll finish.

Here's my point. And he makes a good point—struggled, worked to get out of what I think I've been describing as some hopelessness there. But if you live in a public housing situation, the government now forbids you from owning your apartment, making it a private home, building equity. If you want to give your kids a decent education, the government tells you where to send them to school, even if crack dealers have taken over the playground. If you save to send your kids to college, you're accused of welfare fraud. If you marry someone with a full-time job, you're penalized with a loss of income. If you're still ambitious and try to open a business, to create jobs in your neighborhood, you face an informal red line. Government regulation and capital are already too expensive for our entrepreneurs in the inner city. Add the extra expenses there of job training and security, plus the

reluctance of investors to bring capital and credit into your neighborhood. No wonder the system doesn't work; no wonder it breeds irresponsibility and despair. It rejects a fundamental principle of a free society: People will act responsibly if they are given responsibility. And it is also true, people won't act responsibly if they are denied responsibility.

So this third lesson, then, is the simplest of all. If we have the courage to act, we can fix this system. But we have got to start right now. We have the right principles, and we've developed a straightforward plan, a plan for a new America. First, it makes government services, especially law enforcement, more responsive. Second, it returns the decision-making power to individuals and communities and gives them a stake in their own future. Now, why will it work? Because it takes what works for the rest of America and brings it into the inner cities. And that is long overdue.

In the wake of the riots, I met with the congressional leaders of both parties at the White House, and I presented them with the new American plan. And we talked; I think we found common ground. We agreed that the need for action was urgent. That was 3 weeks ago. Since then, nothing has happened on Capitol Hill. I just met with your able Mayor and your Governor and Peter Ueberroth. I told them I still believe and I certainly still hope that Congress can put partisanship aside, in what I would concede is an extraordinarily difficult election year, and pass this plan now and not pass something that they know I cannot sign. And that means doing something important now for people who need help now. And it means making this Nation a Nation of opportunity for all our people.

Let me briefly touch on our plan. First, we must attack crime with everything we've got. And I urge Congress once again to pass our comprehensive crime bill. The bill goes back to the fundamentals: If you commit a crime, you are going to be caught. If you're caught, you're going to be convicted. And if you're convicted, you'll go to jail. To redouble our war on crime, we have launched an initiative that I think is taking hold nationwide called "Weed and

Seed." With increased Federal resources, we can weed out the criminals from inner cities and then seed those areas with a concentration of social services so that crime can no longer take root.

Second, we must streamline the jumble of Federal job training programs. Our Job Training 2000 initiative offers essentially what I saw today in these headquarters out here, these 10. I went to one of them, a one-stop shopping system for those who want training, but can't get it now. For example, talking with Pete Wilson earlier today, I let him know of a new $12 million Labor Department effort targeted to rebuild L.A.'s employment base.

Third point, as Jack Kemp has said so often, we must turn the red line around our cities into a green line, to cut the costs of opening an inner-city business and create jobs. And that's what this concept of enterprise zones are all about. Now, I know that Tom Bradley agrees with me on that. I thank him for his strong support. Pete Wilson, the same; he agrees about that concept. I thank him for his support. Peter Ueberroth, who is trying to mobilize the private sector and get new businesses to take a shot at investing in the inner city, agrees with me on that point. He is supporting this concept. And as you know, I've asked Congress to cut the capital gains tax on all Americans. And in America's inner cities, where the need is most urgent, we ought to cut it to zero, eliminate it entirely. And that is how you bring real jobs to the inner city. And here's an open invitation to the mayors of America's cities and a challenge to the Congress. I want every American city with a deserving neighborhood, neighborhoods with high crime and high unemployment, to become an enterprise zone. And I urge the mayors, take your case to Congress, and we will support you all the way.

Fourth principle, and this is a valid one, is to extend the principle of private property into the inner city. And that means homeownership. Our HOPE initiative will offer residents the chance to turn public housing into private homes. Ownership gives people a stake in their neighborhoods. It instills pride and a sense of responsibility for what happens next door and down the block.

Fifth, welfare reform to strip away the penalties for people that want to work, who want to save, who want to start a family. Any genuine reform must meet three tests: It must encourage individual responsibility; it must tie welfare to work; and it must promote and sustain stable family life. Our welfare system is a travesty, and I am determined to help these Governors and help everyone change it.

Sixth, and I think we'd all agree on this one, education reform. Every American child deserves a shot at a world-class education. And that means developing innovative schools free of drugs and violence. And it means community support for high standards and educational excellence. And it means that whether a family lives in the inner city or lives out in the suburbs, parent should be able to choose their children's schools.

Now, each of these steps that I've outlined will work to restore a sense of self-sufficiency, of personal dignity to inner-city residents. Today I've talked about the need to overhaul our obsolete bureaucratic system, about the fact that the system robs the poor as well as the taxpayer, about the need for justice and order on our streets. But I also believe that there are deeper issues at work here, ones that transcend the present moment.

Now, let's be honest. The problems we face cannot be solved simply by adjusting economic outputs and inputs. Human beings respond to more than tax codes and bureaucratic rules. We are motivated first and foremost by values, by a sense of what is right and what is wrong. If we are to take values seriously, and we must, we should summon the courage to be frank about them. The word "values" is not relative. Values deal in absolutes. They separate right from wrong, virtue from vice.

Laws and budgets are not enough. We need a moral and, yes, a spiritual revival in our Nation so that families unite, fathers love mothers, stay together in spite of pain and hard times because they love their children and look forward to another generation growing up tall and confident in the warmth of God's love. That woman I saw today, whose beauty parlor had been ransacked or burned, said, "I am going to make it. With God's help, I am going to make it." That was a powerful message, and I think people are craving all around this world for that kind of spiritual, inner strength.

The Federal Government cannot teach values, but it can create an environment where they take root and grow. In every neighborhood in America, there are wellsprings of traditional values. And when I was last here in your great city, I had the privilege of meeting with the kids at the Challengers Boys and Girls Club. For those who haven't seen it, I expect there are other examples, Tom, around your city like it, but those who haven't seen this one, you really ought to check it out. The club was founded by a remarkable man, a man who flew back with us yesterday from Washington, being back there to share his experience with people in DC, his name, Lou Dantzler.

Now, Lou works day and night, day and night, to give these kids the values and habits that they have to succeed. And in the gym where I spoke there were huge handprinted signs covering the walls. And the signs said: "Preparation is the key to success." "Always have a positive attitude." "Education plus hard work plus discipline equals achievement." And in this sophisticated age, I suppose some people might find these old home truths a little on the corny side. But I don't, and I'm sure that Lou Dantzler's kids don't either. They've learned something that Americans across the generations have learned: Traditional values bring hope in place of despair; they hold the power to transform a neighborhood, a city, and indeed, a human life.

And this is a time of great change for our country. Change sometimes seems to threaten the most valuable legacies that we hope to leave our children: good jobs, strong families, a Nation at peace. Changes breed uncertainty and, yes, skepticism. And I understand that. But I also understand this: The skeptics won't do the work that needs to be done. People like Lou Dantzler will. He and every American like him are what make America a rising Nation, a country buoyed by the hopes and determination of people who refuse to settle for the status quo. Their faith is the best antidote to pessimism, the surest proof that the best days of America, the greatest and freest Nation on the face of the Earth, still lie before us.

Thank you all very, very much. It's a pleasure to be with you.

*Note: The President spoke at 12:10 p.m. in the Biltmore Bowl at the Biltmore Hotel. In his remarks, he referred to Lodwrick M. Cook, chairman and chief executive officer, ARCO; and Adrienne Medawar, president, Town Hall of California.*

# Remarks and a Question-and-Answer Session With the Sheriff's Youth Athletic League in Los Angeles
*May 29, 1992*

*The President.* Hey, you Dodgers, good to see you all. Sheriff Block, may I salute. Did you all meet the Governor of this State? Some of you have probably seen him. Where is Governor Wilson? There he is, right there.

Let me tell you all something. I've known Sheriff Block for a long time, long time, and probably before some of you all were born. But I have great respect for him. And after today, as I've seen the dimension of this program that helps so many kids, I've got a lot of different feelings now. The respect level is still there, but I didn't realize the extent of what he started, what, way back in 1972 when the first program started. I think it's a wonderful thing, and it's a great example for other communities all across our wonderful country.

I understand that not only do you get training, physical training, keep up an interest in sports, which is fundamental, but that you also are getting the concept from your deputies, from the deputies here and from your mentors and those who are giving of their time, that it is important to stay away from the drug scene. I was given this pin here, and I just think you all ought to listen carefully to what these deputies and what these supporters of this program tell you. I wish you well.

Somebody just asked me a question over here from the press that travels with us. A lot of these guys come with the President of the United States wherever you go just to report on what's happening. One of them said to me, "Well, what have you learned today?" And I told him, well, I think I've learned a lot about human nature. I've learned a lot about guys that are working hard out there on the law enforcement side, the sheriff's department, then taken their time to help kids, to lift them up and help them.

I don't know how each of you guys feel, but I'll tell you, I have a sense of gratitude in my heart for those who were really helping you in sports or in reading or in staying away from narcotics or whatever it is. I think we all owe them a vote of thanks not just for what's happening in this county but for others like them all across the country. We call it, incidentally, Points of Light, a thousand Points of Light, one person helping another. That's one of the things I've seen today, is this spirit of this wonderful outfit where people are reaching out.

I also got a little feeling over in the boxing arena about the competitive nature of some of you guys, and that's good. Competitive sports is very, very important. The kind of sportsmanship you learn as well as athletic ability, that's good.

I hope you learn a sense of family here, and I think you do from talking to the sheriff and talking to the others. They're talking to you of the importance of parents and family values and doing things the way your parents want them done, and that's good. So I've learned a little more about that dimension.

I've learned about the kindness of people that you work with. I bet once in a while when you get in trouble you may wonder if they're too kind, but I think I sensed here a, really, feeling of loving and caring for you guys. I think that is very important. So I saw that and felt it in my own heart a lot

more than before I walked in here.

I don't know what else to say about what I've learned, except it's made a big impression on me. And it is far better to get this sense of pride that each of you guys feel than it is to be out there drifting around with nobody caring and not really having identified what you want to do, not feeling wanted. The beautiful thing about this place is the minute you walk in, you feel welcome. You feel you're free to do your best, feel free from any pressures that might exist outside the walls of this place.

So, Sheriff Block, to you and everybody in this wonderful institution, I support you. I salute you, and especially to those adults that give their time to lift these kids up and give them a chance. It's a wonderful, wonderful thing.

Now, what I thought I'd do, and we don't have too long because we've got to go off to another meeting, but I thought if anybody—maybe we've got time for maybe two or three questions—because when I go to schools: "What's it like to be President?", all that kind of stuff; "How's Barbara?" Any questions? Let me take four questions. Anybody got one? Right there, first one. What's you name first?

*Q.* My name is Nancy.

*The President.* Nancy, shoot.

*"Murphy Brown" Television Show*

*Q.* What do you think about Murphy Brown? [*Laughter*]

*The President.* Good question, good question. Well, you know, I've got to make a confession. I haven't seen it. [*Laughter*] But here's my position on that: The values that you get here are good, sound values. And you know, I think what the Vice President was talking about was this concept of parents loving these kids and all of that. So I haven't really seen the program, but I do know that in terms of the values that you learn here, what we call family values, whether it's taught by family or whether it's inculcated into you by these people, your teachers and all, that's a good thing.

I don't know whether you feel closer to your parents when you go home or not, but if you do, you will have learned an awful lot from this place. So that's about the way I would answer it.

How about this guy?

*Los Angeles*

*Q.* How do you feel about L.A., about being out here?

*The President.* How do I feel out here? Well, tell me your name.

*Q.* David.

*The President.* David, here's the way I feel about it. I've got mixed emotions about it. I feel a sense of hope. I feel a sense of wonder at the way these guys help you, your coach. Who's your coach here? Do you have a coach, one coach, or who teaches you in here, any one person?

*Q.* I guess.

*The President.* Well, is it a woman or a man?

*Q.* A man.

*The President.* See, that guy, he's helping you. I think to myself, now, here's a guy, he could be doing anything he wanted probably outside here, but he's giving of his time to help you. So I have a sense of gratitude about that. I sometimes have a sense of the problems because the sheriff told me of some of the problems that are faced in the neighborhoods here of drugs and crime. So it's a mixed feeling being here.

But I'll tell you one thing. I'm leaving here with a sense of hope that this city is going to make it, and it's because of kids like you. You're learning good values, and you're doing good stuff. That's the kind of mixed feelings I get.

Over on this side.

*Q.* How do you feel about the L.A. riots?

*The President.* Very good question. The question is, "How do you feel about the L.A. riots?"

Well, you know, you don't feel it as close when you don't live in the neighborhood, but when you see it you feel a sense of, this is bad. This is a terrible thing when somebody will destroy someone else's property, break up somebody else's business, wantonly threaten somebody else's life. You feel that right away. And I automatically feel we've got to support our law enforcement community. They are working for you. In a sense, they're working for me and for everybody across this country, keeping order.

Then you say when you see it, "I wonder why all this is happening?" Then you get to some causes, some underlying causes, and you say, hey, institutions like this one is trying to help there. They're trying to teach kids, instead of a bad value of going in and doing something bad to somebody else, a good value of caring for the next. So the riots made a lot of people in our country think about both. How do we enforce the law, and then how do we encourage these wonderful volunteer programs like this not just here, not just in L.A., but in other cities across the country?

So it's a mixed feeling, I think, is the way I'd put it.

How about this guy?

*Sports*

*Q.* What is your favorite sport?

*The President.* Favorite sport?

*Q.* Yes.

*The President.* Let's see. I'd say baseball. Any of you guys play soccer? Soccer? Anybody play that? Not many, so few. I used to play that in school. I played basketball in school. I played baseball. And I'll tell you something—this may not be interesting to you because I see a lot of Dodgers suits, and I don't see many Angels. But our son has a team called the Texas Rangers. That's my boy George, and I'm very proud of him. He's the boss of that team, and they are in first place. I say that with all respect to the California Angels.

So I like baseball very much. I like to go to the games. I got to know some of the players, like Nolan Ryan—why, you talk about a great athlete.

*Native Americans*

*Q.* What kind of things are being done about the American Indian?

*The President.* David? Well, I think that we ought to give plenty of help to those people, and I think we are. I think education is terribly important on the reservation. I think we can do better on it, although I think we've got some good educational programs. Such a broad question that it's pretty hard to answer. I think everybody's entitled to their rights, that's how I'd answer it.

What's your name?

## "Weed and Seed" Program

*Q.* [*Inaudible*]

*The President.* About the riot thing? Kind of like I told him. I think you've got to have respect for the law. I don't think, no matter how much some guy's hurting, that he ought to take the law in his own hands and violate somebody else's property, somebody else's right, somebody else's house, somebody else's business.

Then you have to have programs. We've got a program, and it's got a funny name to it. It's called "Weed and Seed." The sheriff knows what I'm talking about. That's a Federal program. It comes out of Washington. But it's going to have ramifications for a lot of communities. The concept is to weed out the criminal elements and then to seed the neighborhoods with hope. This program does exactly that, seed the neighborhoods with hope.

Two more. Okay, you got it. I saw this guy. He must be tired because he showed me how he was working out.

## The Presidency

*Q.* Do you think it's fun to be a President when people give you a hard time? [*Laughter*]

*The President.* That's a good question. In case they didn't hear it, the question is, "Do you think it's fun to be President when people are giving you a hard time?" [*Laughter*] That's a good question. It's fun to be President. It's a challenge to be President. It's a great big job, and you kind of feel, well, I'm going to try to help people, or I'm going to try to keep the world at peace. And you meet interesting people and all that—the big problems across the country.

But I'll tell you this about the part that you asked about, about when people give you a hard time. You've got to learn something. When you lose something in sports, I learned this lesson from being President, when you lose something in sports, you can't get all upset about it. If somebody criticizes you because you do something that they don't like or something, you just try to do better. You can't let it get you down. So there are easy times, and there are difficult times. It's in your life, and it's in my life as President of the United States.

So I think what I'd say is, I like my job, and I'm working hard in my job. And I'm doing my best in my job. But if you get a little criticism, you get a little grief out there, don't let it get you down. Just do better. Just do better.

Yes, last one, this guy.

*Audience members.* Awwwwww!

*The President.* Well, hey, listen, I said 4, and it's been 40. Go on now.

## Los Angeles

*Q.* How do you feel about the troubles in L.A.?

*The President.* About what?

*Q.* The troubles in L.A.

*The President.* That's a pretty good question, and I got close to answering it. The guy wants to know, what are you going to do about the troubles in L.A.? Well, what we've done to start with is to bring a lot of Federal programs in to help, starting loan programs to help people get their businesses back, starting emergency programs to help people reconstruct their houses where they've been done grief. This "Weed and Seed" program is a good thing.

But the main thing we're trying to do is pass what we call, this is complicated, enterprise zones to bring businesses, through tax breaks, right into the south central L.A. area or other areas where there hasn't been many jobs. That's the answer for guys a little older than you, to create a climate where businesses will come near here, right near here to open up. So that's a big objective we have that would help in the cities.

Hey, you had one. We can't—I really have got to get out. There was one, the guy was a real insistent guy right here. Here it is, because the sheriff says I've got to get out of here. I know he feels that way. This guy here, he's been very patient. Yes, you, the guy up here, Karate Man, and who—another one was here. Right up here. That's the final one. Yes, go ahead.

## President's Life in the White House

*Q.* What is your life like?

*The President.* My life, my life like? The same as—this may be difficult for you to understand—pretty much the same as what a lot of people are. We've got 5 kids, and we've got 12 grandchildren, one of them—how old are you? Nine. I'm not sure we've got a 9-year-old; I think we do. [*Laughter*]

I get a kick when they come into the White House. Have you seen pictures of the White House? The President has to work there all the time. Sometimes when it's quiet, the door opens up. And my grandchildren, a couple of them will come running in, or a dog will come, one of my dogs, Millie or Ranger, will come in there. And you feel just like I did when I was a kid with the family, you know.

Some of it's personal like that, and then some of it very serious, when world leaders and presidents and kings and mayors and governors come to see you. So it's a mixture. But it's not that different in how we actually live our lives with Barbara and I over there in the White House. We try to stay in touch a little and try to keep our family going, get on the phone and call the kids that live in Texas and Florida and all around the country. Even though it's very formal and very complicated at times, you still have the feeling these are the values.

You know, when things are tough—my mother told me when I was a little guy, younger than you, "Do your best. Try your hardest." That advice is good for a kid, and it's good for a President of the United States.

Now, we've got two more.

### Rodney King Verdict

*Q.* How do you feel about the Rodney King verdict?

*The President.* The question was, how do I feel about the Rodney King verdict? As I told the Nation, what I saw I didn't like. I am also very confident that our law, our system of law in the final analysis is fair. I'm convinced that justice is done under our system of law. So I didn't like the pictures, but I also feel that everybody's entitled, no matter what you see, to a fair hearing, a fair trial. So those are—what did you feel? I'm just curious.

*Audience member.* They were wrong to beat him up.

*The President.* Yes, it's wrong to beat up people. I think that's a good point. I said that, you know, when I made a speech to the country on that point. It's a good point.

### Presidential Campaign

*Q.* How do you feel about running for President again?

*The President.* Good question to end on. [*Laughter*] You've got to admit, you guys have to admit there have been no politics in this up until now. And she said, "How do you feel about running for President again?" I will only answer it that I've got a lot of work left to do, and I'm going to try to do what I said over here to this guy: Do my best; try my hardest. I think things are getting better for some in this country, but nobody can relax until you try to help everybody.

So in some ways it's tough. You're going a lot. In some ways there's a lot of controversy; like this guy said, what if you're getting grief out there. But it's important, and I believe in this country, and I think our best days are ahead. I look around this room, and I am more confident than ever that the best days of our country lie ahead because you're a great part of our future.

Good luck to each and every one of you. Thanks a lot.

*Note: The President spoke at 5:30 p.m. at the Lynwood Youth Athletic Center. In his remarks, he referred to Sherman Block, Los Angeles County sheriff. Prior to his remarks, the President attended a briefing on league activities and toured the center. A tape was not available for verification of the content of these remarks.*

# Remarks at the Asian-Pacific American Heritage Dinner in Los Angeles
*May 29, 1992*

Thank you, Governor. And listen, it is a joy to be here. In a sense, it feels like a reunion. It's good to be here with Senator Seymour, who you met earlier, John Seymour, doing a superb job in Washington. I'm very proud of Pat Saiki, who came out with us yesterday, the Administrator of the SBA. Let me just say this, SBA moved faster in this situation than in any other situation of this kind across the country. And Pat, thank you for your leadership in that regard.

May I salute my old friend Johnny Tsu here. We go back a long time. Susan Allan, Matt Fong, one of our most senior elected officials, Inder Singh, Elizabeth Szu, and let me acknowledge this marvelous choir and the fantastic band. I'll tell you, that was a great combo. You guys ought to go on the road for "The Star-Spangled Banner." Thank you all very, very much. First class. Then, of course, the honorees, the eight that you have selected tonight, the men and women we honor tonight, and all of you. And what a moving welcome from the 442d Battalion, not only the most highly decorated unit but also a dramatic, inspiring personal story. I'm proud to be with you all to honor the Asian-Pacific Heritage Month.

On days like this, America celebrates our exuberant diversity. The genius of this land is how we take the bright, varied pieces that immigrants bring with them from all over the world and together create the proud, strong mosaic that is America. One passion unites everyone who comes to these shores: the yearning to reach for a piece of the American dream. Millions of people, your parents, or their parents, maybe even some of you, yourselves, chose to come here, to the land where we make our dreams come true.

I think of Quang Trinh, a young Vietnamese "boat person," kissing the ground when he arrived and calling America "Freedom Country." Asian-Pacific Americans came here seeking freedom. You came here wanting to work for it, determined to accept only the success you could carve out with your own discipline, sacrifice, and of course, tireless quest for excellence.

When we were privileged, Barbara and I, were privileged to represent this country in China, Barbara and I felt strongly that everyone could learn from the Asian culture with its emphasis on hard work and family. Like you, we should all strive for the success that comes not from luck and shortcuts but from education and merit. Like you, we should live by an inner moral compass that stresses not entitlement but personal responsibility. In your homes each generation grows guided by values proven by the test of time. Children revere their parents, their parents' parents, and the wisdom of morality which they embody. In the words of a Chinese proverb, "One generation plants the trees, another gets the shade."

In this land, Asian-Americans have created your own success and become full participants in the American dream. Through this proud determination, you've contributed to the strength of this entire Nation. Think of the legacies of so many who have enriched our lives, and this is but a handful, an honor roll of men and women like I.M. Pei; Yo Yo Ma, who performed so beautifully in the White House just a few nights ago; Seiji Ozawa; recently we all marveled at Kristi Yamaguchi; Michael Chang; Nobel Prize winners Leo Esaki and Yuan Lee; public servants like the late Spark Matsunaga, a dear friend; Hiram Fong; Danny Inouye; Patsy Mink; S.I. Hayakawa; Ambassador Julia Chang Bloch. Then of course, I take special pride in our Federal Agency heads Pat Saiki, Elaine Chao, Wendy Gramm; men of courage like Ellison Onizuka; and Taylor Wang and Damon Kanuha, who gave their lives for their country in the Gulf war.

You have contributed more than inspiration. We need look no further than your commitment to the entrepreneurial spirit to see how you've helped our country and helped our economy. You've built dreams.

You've also built jobs. You've opened up opportunities for all Americans by bolstering economic growth.

We look to job-creation leaders like those that we honor: Maryles Casto, David Lee, Bob Nakasone. I told Bob that I'm sorry Barbara's not out here because if he ever runs for anything, Barbara Bush will be his campaign manager. I'll guarantee you that, another great admirer. But another old friend over here, Jhoon Rhee; Ram Thukkaram; Ted Ngoy; Jang Lee, another man who I saw in action the other day in Koreatown; and the late John Fang, represented here tonight by his wife, Florence, another friend of mine.

Like these, the Asian-Americans' proud hold on the American dream seems secure. I still believe that today, even after this terrible tragedy that part of the Asian-American community suffered. I went through Koreatown, and I saw how a community that had been building its roots and reaching out for its dreams for 25 years could be reduced overnight to ashes, over 1,600 stores burned or ransacked in the rampage. I talked with victims like Helen Lim, who said that with each statistic America must realize that "It's a life, a human being is suffering."

One person told me how teenager Edward Song Lee said to his dad that "the Korean community needs my help," and then went out unarmed to protect his neighborhood, only to be killed in the crossfire. I heard of devastation that spread through Chinatown, Japantown, Vietnamese and Cambodian neighborhoods in Long Beach. I was heartsick to see how low humanity can sink. But on the same streets, on the same streets, I also saw how high humanity can rise.

Americans everywhere condemned the violence and the looting. Victimized neighbors, black, Hispanic, Asian-American, came together to renounce darkness and embrace healing. The buildings were destroyed but, you could feel it, not the spirit, not the spirit. The community will rebuild not just to make things the way they were but to make things better.

You've drawn on your inner strength for courage and hope. Thousands of you marched together to reclaim your streets.

And even as cinders smoldered, volunteers started cleaning and family storeowners started rebuilding. You have years of your lives' work invested in your communities and thousands of years of heritage to guide you. For those not in the devastated areas, you have support from the Asian-American community all across this country. And even after all that's happened, you still take to heart in the old Korean saying, "After sorrow, joy."

The Federal Government will help. We're trying hard to help. I wanted to come back here 3 weeks later to see what we are doing to help. I'm proud of our Federal Agencies. Pat Saiki here came out the day after the riots and worked tirelessly to expedite relief, especially for small-business owners who are the heart of your community. We will help, and we'll be here for you until the sprouts of a new spring of hope can be seen on Vermont Avenue.

America has embarked on a new chapter, a chapter of healing. Your Asian-American community shows how to begin. You came to this country to earn your share of the American dream, and you won't let this tragedy shatter it for you. You remind this Nation that the Asian-American values, freedom, family, self-determination, and opportunity, are the treasures of this land and the goals of our people.

In Asia I learned a lot. And I learned that the phoenix is one of the four sacred creatures in Chinese tradition. It can become for this country the symbol of our healing, for the phoenix is a bird reborn triumphantly from its own ashes. Shopowners in Los Angeles are resurrecting their physical lives right now. Together, let's do the same work for our spirit.

I wanted to be here today not just to speak to those whose close-in community had been victimized but to other Asian-American leaders from California and some from across this country. I have great respect, as I said at the beginning, for the values that unite you all, and I would say, unite us. I really wanted to come here and say thank you for this broad community's proud and very positive contribution to this land today and in the future.

May God bless each and every one of you

and this wonderful land that we call home, the greatest, the freest country on the face of the Earth, the United States of America. Thank you all very much for letting me come.

*Note: The President spoke at 6:40 p.m. at the Hyatt Regency at Broadway Plaza. In his remarks, he referred to John Tsu, president, Asian American Political Education*

*Foundation; Susan Allan, chairman, Pan American Chamber of Commerce; Matt Fong, member, California State Board of Equalization; Inder Singh, president, National Federation of Indian Americans; and Elizabeth Szu, coordinator, Asian/Pacific Islander American Coalition. A tape was not available for verification of the content of these remarks.*

# Nomination of Robert L. Gallucci To Be an Assistant Secretary of State
## *May 29, 1992*

The President today announced his intention to nominate Robert L. Gallucci, of Virginia, to be an Assistant Secretary of State for Politico-Military Affairs. He would succeed Richard A. Clarke.

Currently Dr. Gallucci serves as a Senior Coordinator for the Deputy Secretary at the Department of State in Washington, DC. Prior to this, he served as Deputy Executive Chairman for the United Nations Special Commission, 1991–92; professor at the National War College in Washington, DC, 1988–91; and Deputy Director-General

of the Multinational Force and Observers in Rome, Italy, 1984–88. Dr. Gallucci served at the Department of State as Office Director for the Office of Politico-Military Affairs, 1983–84; and the Office of Near Eastern and South Asian Affairs, 1982–83.

Dr. Gallucci graduated from the State University of New York at Stony Brook (B.A., 1967) and Brandeis University (M.A. and Ph.D., 1973). He was born February 11, 1946, in Brooklyn, NY. Dr. Gallucci is married, has two children, and resides in Arlington, VA.

# Nomination of Joseph Monroe Segars To Be United States Ambassador to Cape Verde
## *May 29, 1992*

The President today announced his intention to nominate Joseph Monroe Segars, of Pennsylvania, a career member of the Senior Foreign Service, class of Counselor, to be Ambassador of the United States of America to the Republic of Cape Verde. He would succeed Francis Terry McNamara.

Currently Mr. Segars serves as a member of the Senior Seminar of the Foreign Service Institute at the Department of State. Prior to this, he served as a career counselor in the Senior Officer Division, Department of State Office of Personnel, 1989–91;

Deputy Chief of Mission at the U.S. Embassy in Dar Es Salaam, Tanzania, 1986–89; and as Consul General of the U.S. Embassy in Lagos, Nigeria, 1983–86. From 1981 to 1983, Mr. Segars served as desk officer for Zimbabwe, Lesotho, and Swaziland in the Office of Southern African Affairs at the Department of State.

Mr. Segars graduated from the University of Pennsylvania (B.S., 1961). He was born January 6, 1938, in Hartsville, SC. Mr. Segars is married, has one child, and resides in Washington, DC.

## Remarks and a Question-and-Answer Session With the Agricultural Community in Fresno, California
*May 30, 1992*

*The President.* First, let me just thank Lee Simpson, the boys that I met. We had a chance to look at one method of growing. He was fair enough to tell me that others approach these things in different ways. But I must say, I've learned a lot. And it was most enjoyable, all too brief. But it wasn't just watching the computer in there; it was seeing him and his love of the soil and his boys and all the things that we talk about when we think of values when it comes to farm families. So they had a nice, neat way of making me feel at home here.

I want to thank the Governor for being with us and our very able Senator John Seymour. I mean, I'm not here on a political mission, but let me just say to you who are involved in agriculture, it is nice to have somebody in the Senate who understands the real problems facing us and then can bring that knowledge of agriculture down to the White House to be sure we are sensitive.

I had a chance earlier on with—I'm accompanied by the woman that many of you know, Ann Veneman. I thought it would be better coming to a bunch of experts in agriculture to have some brains with me. Mine are good for some things, and I think I have a feel for what we need to do in agriculture. But I certainly don't stand here as any expert. So I brought Ann in case some of you might have technical questions or where we stand on some specific initiative or other.

On the broad agricultural concepts, let me simply say I believe it's absolutely essential that we have free and fair trade. We will continue to seek access to foreign markets. We've made some progress in beef and citrus and some things into Japan. There are some big crops that are excluded; we've got to keep pushing. I want to see a successful conclusion to what's known as the GATT, the Uruguay round of GATT. And the hangup, as everybody in this room knows, the main one has been agriculture. We've made some progress working with the Europeans. And they themselves have reorganized their common agricultural policy, something that is just going to reduce the levels of subsidies.

But I just want you to know we're committed. I think I've a little better feel now for some of the problems that certain growers of certain commodities face in selling, for example, to Mexico. With Mexico I want an agreement, but I want it to be fair. I'm a great fan of Carlos Salinas, the President of Mexico. He's done a superb job. And it's not just in working towards free and fair trade; it's the fact that we're in very good sync with the Mexicans in terms of major foreign policy objectives. So I salute him. But he knows and I know that we cannot take to the Congress, and I will not, an agreement that is not based on free and fair trade. Our agricultural shipments to Mexico have increased threefold over the last few years. That's good, but we still have some problems on both sides. He has some problems with us.

On the GATT, Ann gives her expertise to this a lot. We had a meeting the other day with Mr. Andriessen from the EC. I'm told by our very able negotiator, Carla Hills, that we made some progress there, but again, I can't predict for you when either of these will be done.

The last point I'll make, and then I'll sit on my little stool and take any questions that come my way and maybe deflect a few off of here. But I feel that the United States economy is beginning to improve. California's had some very difficult times. Lot of defense problems here, as we've been able, given the demise of international communism, to properly cut back on defense. I would say to you in this very patriotic part of the State, I am not going to permit the Congress to cut into the muscle of our defense. We are able to make reductions. But now, especially in a political year with all the promises resonating out there, everybody wants to take $10 billion here or $20 billion there and spread it on some program, and we can't do that.

I am the President, and I have responsibility for our basic national security interests. The world is much safer. This little Redskin fan goes to bed at night with less fear of nuclear weapons than his older brothers or maybe his mother and dad did, and that's a wonderful accomplishment. But I can tell you, and General Scowcroft, who's with me here today, my very able National Security Adviser, could tell you it isn't that safe a world.

So we're trying to solidify the progress for democracy and freedom that has been made. It is major heavy lifting, but we are the only ones who can do it. The United States, we are the undisputed leader of the free world that's moving down the path to democracy. So I cite that because I cannot get in the promise business of taking $10 billion or $20 billion more from every defense account, and I'm not going to do it.

In any event, I do feel the U.S. economy's recovering—you saw the growth figures yesterday—and with it will surge back the optimism that belongs to the United States of America. It's been a tough go for people, and I know that. But we are a rising Nation, not a declining Nation.

Now, with no further ado, who wants the first question? I'm told that some of you have some real broad interest in areas that might not be specifically on agriculture; so much the better. That's fine with me. Yes, sir.

### Legal Services Corporation

*Q.* I'm an orange grower. We in the valley here, I'm in California, have a problem with an outfit called CRLA, California Rural Legal Assistance. These are the folks who seem to us to be creating answers to which there are no questions. Harassment, I believe, is one of the words. Your predecessor told us that he was going to do something about it, and I'd sure like to hear that you would take a shot at defunding the organization. I think they're out of hand.

*The President.* Well, let me first ask if it's a State or a local—are you talking about the Legal Services overall?

*Q.* Yes.

*The President.* Well, I don't know that we're going to defund it. What we're trying

to do is to get it, through competent and sensible appointees, get it confined so it doesn't go off into the political arena, trying to make a lot of political statements and affecting legislation. That's not what Legal Services, if that is what we're talking about, is supposed to be doing. I think we still have some appointees not confirmed, but I can assure you we are not going to put any loose cannons rolling around on that deck. I hope there's been changes, but I gather we've got some work to do.

### The Economy

*Q.* As you know, everybody's concerned about the economy, and I was wondering if you would sign this dollar bill, showing me that you would promise to try to make this dollar bill worth just as much or more as it is in 4 years from now.

*The President.* Yes, let me tell you something about the dollar. Let me tell you, one way to take that dollar and make it shrink is to let inflation get out of control. The cruelest tax of all is inflation. You don't see it, but you feel it. And the dollars shrink. They don't buy as much.

One of the bright spots in an otherwise gloomy economy over the last year has been that inflation is down. I want to have economic policies enacted that will stimulate economic growth. But that's got to be done without making that dollar bill shrink, and I think we can do it. Right now, interest rates are down; inflation is down. That makes us poised for the best kind of economic recovery. I'm just saying that we've got to be sure it stays down because that's the way you make this dollar come back.

When I come back 4 years from now, I think I'll be in this line of work then—[*laughter*]—it would shrink if we don't get control, try to keep control—we've got a long way to go—of spending. One of the things we're pushing for now, an idea whose time has come, that I've been for for many years is what's called a balanced budget amendment to the Constitution. It disciplines the executive branch, and it darned sure disciplines a Congress that has been very, very reluctant to do anything on the spending side.

So those are just a couple of thoughts

about how we're going to keep that dollar the same size, maybe make it buy more.

### Environmental Policy

*Q.* We've been working on a thing with the Federal Clean Air Act. And in that act of 1990, it addresses a thing called fugitive dust, referred to as PM10, particulate size. In that regulation it addresses where—it's going after farmland that makes dust, a tractor that's out there farming. And to try to control that dust, the EPA has certain deadline dates, '94, '97 and 2001, in which growers are going to have to develop control strategies to stop that dust from going in the air. That has been based on, in the Federal Clean Air Act, with research that was done that was inaccurate, totally wrong. And now we have these implementation things called a PM10 plan that every State has to submit an air agency. And yet they're not realizing, we've pointed it out, that they need to look at better science because it's very difficult to regulate dust on a tractor. Yet they're asking us for control measures that are very much—right now, there's not valid research. The USDA and EPA are hoping now to fund some money so we can do some valid research.

*The President.* I'm not an expert on that. Ann, do you want to just comment on his specific, and then I'll give you an answer on a broader sense. Let me give you the broader answer first.

You may have read about the Rio conference on the environment. I have withheld commitment to go there because it seemed to me that what we had to do before committing to go is to work out sound environmental policy, sound as far as the United States goes, and we are the leader because of our science and technology in international environment. So we had to work out sound environmental policy. But I also wanted an underpinning of sound economic policy. And we cannot permit the extremes in the environmental movement to shut down the United States on science that may not be as perfected as we in the United States should have it.

So I don't know the specific, I'll be honest with you, that you're talking about, that provision of the Clean Air Act. But my general philosophy is to have a good, sound

environmental practice. I think we do. I think we've got something to be really proud of and to take to Rio, but also to say to them, these countries, we cannot accept standards that are not based on the soundest of science, and we cannot shut down the lives of many Americans because of going to an extreme on the environment. So that's my philosophy, and that's what we're trying to do.

Now, on this one for those of you who are environmentalists or follow Rio, I think we're coming out all right on that. A lot of the world leaders have told me they think that our fighting for that balance has been a very good thing, and we've staved off setting such rigid standards that nobody can meet. When the United States makes a commitment, it has to keep it. And we do that. Our word is pretty good, and it should be. But we can't do it and throw an awful lot of people out of work, especially when it's not based on sound science.

Can you make a specific comment on the gentleman's, do you know?

*Deputy Secretary Veneman.* Well, I certainly am familiar with this issue. It's been in USDA. We are attempting to help to fund the science necessary to address this problem, and I think we are committed to continuing in that effort.

*Q.* I appreciate that very much, Mr. President and Ann Veneman, on that because we think that that needs to be looked at very, very strongly before we continue to put industry out of business because of unsound science, because somebody didn't do their job right. And I thank you very much.

*The President.* Well, we're trying. I know they're going to want to raise the question that might get me in trouble, but I know, for example, on endangered species you've got some major California problems. They're national problems. We are trying to get balance and use of science and also have those hallmarks of the policy, but also the fact that a family's got to work for a living. So that one is one that has to be filtered into any agreements we're making.

### Wetlands

*Q.* I was pleased to see that we have a wetlands preserve program just starting up, with California being one of the pilot States. I think that that offers a way to restore wetlands and, at the same time, make a workable relationship with farming. One thing I would like to see is in the following programs, should Congress support your budget proposal, is a wider definition of the crop and land that is allowable in it. Within California much of the land that would qualify——

*The President.* To be a wet?

*Q.* Right, exactly.

*The President.* We've had examples of that. The first gentleman was telling me about it, and we have—I consider myself a sound and hopefully sensible environmental President. But again, I think in terms of wetlands, the manual and definition, it's gotten a little ahead of where it should be in terms of a definition of a wetland.

So we're trying hard. I just had a meeting earlier, and one of the rice growers told me about a program that they are working closely on where it really does help create wetlands. And the bird hunters and all these people who are very interested in the flyways are very happy about it. So I think there's room for innovation. I think we ought to stay with our objective and no net loss of wetlands, but we don't want to over-define what a wetland is.

That's what I've tried to do, and again, I've taken a few shots as being too much on the growth side of that. But I don't think that's a fair shot because I think what happens during some periods, some of the bureaucrats in our regulatory agencies started defining the wetland problem in a way that really overdefines it. There was not a legitimate wetland we were trying to preserve. So we're working it. And I appreciate your suggestion.

### Domestic Agenda

*Q.* I think most people are wondering that during your first 4 years in the Presidency I think that your main objective has been to center on the foreign affairs with the fall of international communism. With Ross Perot coming out saying that you need to address the situations with the homeless and with the deficit and all these other sort of domestic affairs, if you are reelected, assuming you are, will you be focusing your attention on the domestic affairs and not so much on the military and communism, the fall of communism, and China and Russia and all these other areas such as the Baltics?

*The President.* The President's responsibilities are multifaceted. One of them is the national security of the United States. It is in this field that the President really has primacy, and I'm not going to neglect that. I'm not going to neglect it because of political criticism. Having said that, it is absolutely essential that our domestic program, which is sound, be brought before a Congress that will think some new ideas.

The Congress today, in my view, thinks old ideas. We've got some problems. How are we going to help the city of Los Angeles? I think an enterprise zone that greenlines the area and cuts the capital gains rate to zero will do more to bring jobs into the hopeless areas of Los Angeles than doubling the spending on some Government programs. I have had that proposal up there for years. I've had it up there for years, and it has been blocked by, for the most part, by a hostile Congress.

So I will not plead guilty to having neglected the domestic agenda. What we've got to do is get the facts out there that there is a good one that's based on empowerment. It is based on keeping Government close to the people. It's based on less regulation rather than more. It's based on giving people a part of the action. And that goes into all kinds of subjects. It also is based on fiscal sanity.

I argue for a balanced budget amendment. It will discipline the executive branch, and it will darned sure discipline the Congress. Now it's beginning to happen. The good thing about this 4-year election dance is, it does get to focus, it brings people's focus on these major problems. I think we have a rare opportunity now to pass some of the things that would help guarantee the future of that little girl's dollar bill.

I'd like to see a line-item veto for the President. Forty-three Governors have it, and it works. Somebody said, "You don't have a domestic program." Here's a good one. Try it on for size. And they say, "Well, that's not a new idea." As far as I'm concerned it's new until it's been tried. We ought to keep pushing until we get it. That gets the President then all interacting with the people running for Congress, and it gets you in there. If you believe that last point, for example, get your Congressman to say what he'll do when he goes there.

So I think we've got a good program. I'll give you one more, and then I'll stop filibustering. Education, we have a program called America 2000. It literally revolutionizes education. It creates 535 new American schools where the community and the families get involved in saying, "Here's what we think will work in Fresno. I don't care so much what's going to work in Austin, Texas," and create these new schools. We send the bill up to the Congress, and what do they do in education? They just add money to programs that have failed. We've got a good domestic agenda, and there is a significant flagship of that domestic agenda.

So what I've got to do is, one, make clear to the American people we've got it; and, two, take my case in the fall when I get into that political arena that I'm trying to stay out of at least until after our convention and say, all right, send me some Members of Congress that agree with this. Don't send people up there that come home and talk tough on law and order and crime and then go back and vote some other way.

I listened to some ads of people running to try to get into the United States Senate, and these happen to be on the Democratic side, all of them talking tough on law and order. We've got a tough crime bill that is sitting in the United States Congress because the very same people that are advertising today in California refuse to vote for it.

The good thing about an election year is, we can make that case clearly and say, look, send us some people, if you happen to think we're right, a little tougher on the criminal and little less tough on the victim of crime. Vote for them. Get our program going.

So I think we've got a good domestic agenda. I do not plead guilty to neglecting it. I think out of the 4-year process here we'll have time to get it in focus.

But look, I know that there's this feeling that we're living in a benign world now because of this magnificent victory over communism. But believe me, if you look at the Soviet Union and you see what's happening in some of the Republics, and if you look at the problems south of our border, although the hemisphere's going—the President can't neglect that. I can't shift entirely away from that responsibility.

But I take your point. I think I've got to do a better job explaining to the people. Send me Members of Congress that will vote for these kinds of initiatives. If you want to do it the old way, get them to go in and vote for the status quo. But I think people want change now. I think we can take that message of hope out there.

*Wristwatch Presentation*

*Q.* Last week you gave your watch away to Ensign Sam Wagener. You may not have realized it, but he was from Fresno. And so the Fresno Chamber of Commerce and the California Bowl Committee would like to present you with an official California Bowl watch, as a matter of fact, an official California Raisins Bowl watch.

*The President.* I'm a two-watch man again, but I'm telling you that I came out way ahead on the trade. That midshipman came out—he gave me—he did all right. He didn't have anything when he started. So he got my watch. But I didn't know he was from here. I'm very grateful. This is beautiful, and thank you. I accept with pleasure.

*Water Management Legislation*

*Q.* I'd first like to start off by thanking you and your administration for trying to add a little bit of sanity to the application of Environmental and Endangered Species Act by putting in people and jobs and the economy as part of the equation.

As you know, we are in the fight of our life here in the Central Valley of California over irrigated agriculture and the operations of Central Valley Project. Sir, Governor Wilson has shown historic and courageous leadership recently in announcing that there is a California solution to the Central Valley Project. Senator Seymour, likewise, has lead a courageous fight in the Senate to put aside some of the criticisms we have from some of the Democratic Senators from New Jersey who think they know how to manage water from Washington, DC, for what we do here in the Central Valley.

In the last 2 days there has been some—many call it negotiations—and discussions on the House side, unfortunately controlled by many of our Democratic colleagues who are no better for us than some of those liberal folks in the Senate.

I would like to say, sir, that if there is any doubt from the administration as to who they should look for, for whether or not these bills, as they go forward, are accepted by the leadership in California, you should please look toward Senator Seymour and Governor Wilson. I know they're going to be many mixed signals out there. But we will welcome the administration's overview and dedication to the fact that we have to balance environmental with jobs, economic, and people issues as we move forward for a solution to Central Valley water issues.

*The President.* The Seymour approach is far—and I'll put some names on it for you—the Seymour approach is far better, far better than Miller-Bradley. And yes, we're trying to—I don't want to be flirting around leaving any doubt. Miller-Bradley is unacceptable, unacceptable and I wouldn't sign it. We are now discussing it. We were talking about it coming up here on the plane as to how to move forward with implementation of a more sensible approach. So I appreciate your comments. It helps me understand the fervor of the feeling out here. But I'm not just saying this politically. We are not going to accept Mr. Miller's approach, seconded by Bradley.

*Multilateral Trade Negotiations*

*Q.* Mr. President, I'm a dairyman and a diversified farmer here in Fresno County. I want to thank you and your administration for pushing so hard for the successful conclusion of GATT as well as NAFTA. We thank you for hanging tough in agriculture, not giving in to the EC, the demands they have made upon us.

The concern that we have is on NAFTA, that recently the Canadians have said that they will not give up on their dairy quotas, that their dairy quotas are not negotiable. If we go ahead and negotiate a treaty where

we have to give up our Section 22 and the Canadians give up none of their dairy quotas, we're put at a tremendous disadvantage. Our plea to you, sir, is hang tough on that deal.

We do want a free trade agreement. I believe that the future of American agriculture depends on international trade. But we do want an agreement that we can live with and that is fair to everybody, and hopefully, that we can hang on tough. But if they don't give, well, we don't want to give. We don't want to be put at a disadvantage.

*The President.* Let me comment. The gentleman makes a very good point. It's not simply Canada on dairies; it is EC on bananas, for example. And I might say the Canadian pitch on this one relates to the unity of Canada itself. They're worried that if they don't continue to protect dairies, that that gives the Quebec people kind of a shot with a lot of concentrated dairies there, pulling away from what used to be called the Meech Lake Accords, which is technical, but that was the effort by our friend, and he is a friend, Brian Mulroney, to hold Canada together.

But on your point, the difficulty that we have with the Canadian request or the request from some of our smaller friends in the Caribbean is, once you start down the road of exception, exception, exception, you get farther away rather than closer to an agreement.

So we've got problems. I talked earlier about the rice problem as it affects Japan. I mean, there's an enormous market there. When I deal with the Prime Minister, the various Prime Ministers of Japan, the push always is, "Please understand we've got enormously complex political problems on rice in the Diet, in our political legislature."

So we say, well, yes, but we can't have a successful conclusion if everybody excepts what is precious to him or her or whatever it is. So I think your point is very, very valid. And there are ways in these agreements to phase things in so people aren't hectored and harassed and thrown out of business at the outset. But the principle that you've outlined is one I believe is underlying, and I've instructed our negotiators accordingly, underlying our negotiations on

NAFTA and the GATT.

Ann, do you want to add to that? I appreciate your comments on it.

### Agricultural Chemicals

*Q.* I'm glad to hear that you are America's environmental President because I think in this room today are America's first environmentalists. Farmers should be and are good environmentalists. We do not want to do anything that would poison the ground or poison our families. But I'm concerned about the deluge of regulation in the last decade, especially in regard to the use of farm chemicals.

I'm concerned especially about the minor-use chemicals that the chemical companies no longer wish to register. California grows over 250 different crops. Some of these crops are considered to be minor-use crops for some of the chemicals that we use. I'm concerned about the loss of those chemicals not because they are inherently bad but because the economics of the use really prohibits the chemical company from reregistering its chemicals for each of these minor-use crops.

Then we also have a problem with a major-use chemical, and that is methylbromide. As a nurseryman, we have a protocol in California whereby we cannot sell trees without following that protocol. It involves killing organisms within the soil, parasites that would eat the roots of the plants that we sell. Because of the strong phytosanitary regulations of the USDA and the California Department of Food and Agriculture, we are able to ship trees around the world. If we lose methylbromide, we will not only have the problem of not being able to ship around the world because we will have an inferior product, but we will have a problem within shipping in California because we can't meet the regulations. What can we do as good environmentalists but also as good business people to stem this regulatory tide?

*The President.* Let me say on that methylbromide, I'm certainly no expert on it. But I'll give you the philosophy again behind it. Decisions should be based on sound science. It is my understanding that the science is less than perfected as it relates to this chemical. It seems to me that the way to approach this problem is to be sure that the science is sound.

I would have to say, if the science proved that it was detrimental to the environment, I as President would be facing a significant problem because you cannot neglect the environmental destruction to our economy or to our country. So I think the answer is to try to move forward more fast on the science itself, as well as the alternate scientific work that's taking place.

Now, Ann knows a great deal more about this than I. Can you add something to that?

*Deputy Secretary Veneman.* Mr. President, I think that you're exactly right. We have to have the scientific evidence on these issues. We've certainly been trying in the USDA to work with EPA on the particular problems that face farmers as we deal with these chemical issues, and we'll try to continue to do that. Methylbromide does need additional science, and we'll participate in that to the extent that we can.

### Energy Policy

*The President.* And I agree. I mean, I think farmers are not only environmentalists but conservationists. I think that's very, very important. I think we have to do it.

Incidentally, I would like to make a pitch for our energy bill that passed the Congress the other day, which does have some good, sound conservation in it, but also it balances out the need for this country to grow. I don't want to shift the subject away from your question, but in all these fields—and this gets back to this young man's question—in all these fields there's a question of philosophy on a lot of this stuff.

On our energy approach, we're trying to keep growth going through more energy sources and through conservation. Some would have you just do nothing on the former part of it, and I'm in a big fight, although it's not in this bill, on the ANWR, the Alaskan Wildlife Refuge. I am absolutely convinced that you can have prudent development, as we did in Prudhoe Bay, of that. And yet I'm in a big row with the environmentalists because they say, "Well, you say you're for the environment; how come you're for ANWR?" I'm saying ANWR can be developed without decimating the environment or the species there, in this case caribou or whatever else it is.

So I just cite this because it is something in my job that you have to keep balancing, just as this guy's question was how do you balance the national security from domestic. Here's one: How do you balance domestic growth, families need to make a living, our hopefully becoming less dependent on foreign oil for a lot of reasons, and balance that with the environmental needs? And you've raised a more specific question. We've just got to keep that ethic going, and I think we can. I think we can do better on it.

Getting thrown out of here?

*Q.* Sir, we could sit here and talk all day long and probably all week long. We just appreciate so much your coming to Fresno and listening to our concerns. We wish you the best of luck in the near future.

*The President.* Let me say—thank you, Lee, very much. Let me just make this observation that you can't help but feel when you're here. We're talking about agriculture; we're talking about chemicals; we're talking about wetlands; we're talking about economic growth; we're talking about national security. These are all big issues. But I wish that Barbara Bush had been out here, the Silver Fox we call her, because I think she would sense the feeling of community and of family that we sensed when we lived in a climate not unlike this in west Texas for 12 years and long before I got wrapped up in the political world. These issues are terribly important.

But when we talk about family, you feel it when you walk into his house or his place of business and feel it just looking around this room. You get that sense this is something that is very important. And when those mayors came to me, long before the trouble in Los Angeles, and said, "The largest single concern we have about the decline in the cities, the biggest problem is the decline in the American family, the falling apart of the family."

So when Barbara hugs a child or we read to kids, it is trying as best we can to show the importance of family and the importance of the values that stem from family. I make that not as a pitch but just as a statement, because the Presidency is about issues. It's about doing your best. It's about national security, but it is also about understanding the strength of this country. And I've gotten a good lesson in that here today.

Thank you.

*Note: The President spoke at 10:58 a.m. at the Simpson Vineyards. In his remarks, he referred to Lee Simpson, owner of the vineyards, and Frans Andriessen, Vice President of the European Community Commission.*

# Remarks at the Miracles in the Sky Air Show in Fresno
*May 30, 1992*

I can hear you. We had a good look at the crowd there. And I want to salute Lonnie and Heidi English and I wish everybody there in the support of the Valley Children's Hospital all the best.

And I wish each of you could see this magnificent Air Force One piloted by Colonel Danny Barr. It's a marvelous airplane, and I think it represents our country very well as we go not just here but overseas as well.

I wish you well. This air show that will benefit the Valley Children's Hospital is just a wonderful thing. I salute you. I salute you all at TV 30 for their civic—I don't know how to say it, but the civic responsibility, you might say, of supporting this wonderful charity. But also you're bringing people a lot of happiness there.

So, good luck to each and every one of you. Again, to Lonnie and to Heidi who thought of this in the first place, well done. Well done. My only regret is I don't get down to see some of those shiny things we flew over.

*Note: The President spoke at 12:28 p.m. at the Madera Municipal Airport. In his remarks, he referred to Lonnie English and his wife, Heidi, members of the board of* *directors of the Miracles in the Sky Air Show. A tape was not available for verification of the content of these remarks.*

# Letter to Congressional Leaders on the National Emergency With Respect to Yugoslavia
*May 30, 1992*

*Dear Mr. Speaker:* (*Dear Mr. President:*)

Pursuant to section 204(b) of the International Emergency Economic Powers Act, 50 U.S.C. 1703(b), and section 301 of the National Emergencies Act, 50 U.S.C. 1631, I hereby report that I have exercised my statutory authority in order to declare a national emergency to respond to the threat to the national security created by the actions and policies of the Governments of Serbia and Montenegro, acting under the name of the Socialist Federal Republic of Yugoslavia or the Federal Republic of Yugoslavia, and to issue an Executive order that blocks all property including bank deposits of the Governments of Serbia and Montenegro, as well as property in the name of the Government of the Socialist Federal Republic of Yugoslavia or the Government of the Federal Republic of Yugoslavia, in the United States or in the control of U.S. persons including their overseas branches.

The Secretary of the Treasury is authorized to issue regulations implementing these prohibitions.

I am enclosing a copy of the Executive order that I have issued.

I have authorized these measures in response to the actions and policies of the Governments of Serbia and Montenegro, acting under the name of the Socialist Federal Republic of Yugoslavia or the Federal Republic of Yugoslavia, in their involvement in and support for groups attempting to seize territory in Croatia and Bosnia-Hercegovina by force and violence utilizing, in part, the forces of the so-called Yugoslav National Army. The grave events in Serbia and Montenegro constitute an unusual and extraordinary threat to the national security, foreign policy, and economy of the United States. The measures that I have taken today express our outrage at the actions of the Serbian and Montenegrin Governments and will prevent those governments from drawing on monies and properties within U.S. control.

Sincerely,

GEORGE BUSH

*Note: Identical letters were sent to Thomas S. Foley, Speaker of the House of Representatives, and Dan Quayle, President of the Senate. The Executive order is listed in Appendix E at the end of this volume.*

# Remarks at a Texas Victory '92 Fundraising Dinner in Dallas, Texas
*May 30, 1992*

Thank you for that wonderfully warm introduction, Senator, and I am just delighted to be at your side. I won't rave about Phil Gramm; we know what kind of Senator we have. But as I listen to him on the floor of the Senate from time to time, as I see him in action up there, I am absolutely convinced that with his leadership now of this Senate campaign committee which is taking him all across the country, and then given what I'm about to tell you how I see this country moving, I really believe with his leadership we have an opportunity to get control back of the United States Senate and to move this country forward. And he's doing a superb job for our State.

Dr. Criswell, it is very nice to see you again, sir. Last time I saw him was in his own church, and it was a moving experience for me. I am delighted that he is with us tonight. When you want to get somebody that knows how to sing "The Star-Spangled Banner," sign up an Aggie. And Fred McClure did it once again. As you may know, Fred was one of the top people in the White House, running all of our relationship with Congress, and did a superb job there. And now he's back here in business in Dallas. I want to thank the Rangerettes from Kilgore for their dance performance. I want to thank Rob Mosbacher who's heading this program, Victory '92; and of course, Dan Cooke who's just done a superb job on this dinner. A great success, and thank you to both of you. Then my State chairman for the Bush-Quayle campaign, Jim Oberwetter. He's beginning to peak a little early. He's out on that television all the time, but he's saying smart and sensible things. It saves me from doing something that I look forward to doing, but I'm not going to do it now, and that is get after these opponents. But I'm going to wait a little bit, and I'll tell you why in a minute. I'm grateful to Jim. I'm grateful to Barbara Patton, our cochairman; she's here from Houston. And of course, to salute Kay Bailey Hutchison, an old friend; Rick Perry, our commissioner; and then our State chairman, Fred Meyer, who continues to do a great, great job.

So welcome to all, and thank you for being here. Phil put it right: These are not easy times. They're not easy. But in my view, we have a great deal to be grateful for as a Nation. Phil touched on some of it. When you look at big things having happened, take a look around the world, the very fact that these little kids here, sitting over here, go to bed at night and do not have the fear of nuclear war that kids a generation before, is something significant. And we helped bring that about. I happen to think that a foremost responsibility of any President is the national security of this country. You don't read one single word

about it in all this gloom-and-doom television we're getting in this country, not one.

There have been significant changes. Ancient enemies are talking to each other in the Middle East, something that nobody dreamed could happen. Democracy's on the move south of the border. Almost every single country where there used to be military dictatorships, there are democratic regimes. South Africa's on the move; the states of the former Soviet Union, struggling to become democratic; Eastern Europe, free; the Baltics, free. So there's a great deal of gratitude that I have in my heart for the changes that are taking place in the world. It is only the United States of America that can lead and effect this change. And I am going to remain involved in bringing about more change for peace for the whole world.

Now, I hear the revisionists talking about Kuwait. If I'd have listened, as Phil said, to some of the critics on the Democratic Party up there, Saddam Hussein would be sitting in Saudi Arabia, and we'd be paying $10 a gallon for gasoline. And that's the fact. We ought not to let somebody revise history because they were wrong on the Persian Gulf war.

So we've changed the world with a lot of help. I salute my predecessor that I met with yesterday, Ronald Reagan, a steadfast contribution—"that wall will come down," and thank God, it did. So we've got a lot to be grateful for. We have helped change the world.

Here's now what we're doing to help change this country. Phil touched on some of it. We have a strong domestic agenda. It is significant, and it is in keeping with the principles that unite everybody here tonight: empowerment, government close to the people, trying to hold the rein on the ever-increasing Federal Government, and getting the action right back where it belongs, right here in the towns and cities around Dallas, Texas.

We're working hard for free trade. Some want us to retreat and pull back. Agricultural trade with Mexico is 3 times higher than it was just a few years ago, and we haven't even gotten the free trade agreement. I am going to continue to work for a job-creating free trade agreement with Mexico and a successful conclusion of the Uruguay round to the GATT. You watch, when we get that done, a level playing field, the creation of American jobs in this country. We're not pulling back. We're the United States. We're moving forward.

I would hate to take my case to the people in the fall that the only way I could win is if everything was bad, capitalizing on the gloom and doom and on the dreariness of the recession and of the slow growth that we've been in for the last couple of years. It has been bad. Families have been hurt, and they've been hurt bad. But this economy is beginning to move, and each inch of the way it starts up, the Democratic Party is panicking, because the only way they can win is if things are going to hell in this country. I wouldn't want that. I think we're much more positive than that, and the economy is moving. As it begins to go forward we have good answers.

We need health care reform. We need to keep the quality of health care we've got, and we have to make health insurance—give it access to all, rich and poor alike have a chance to have insurance. But what we don't need to do is put a socialized medicine or a nationalized medicine program in that will diminish the quality of the health care in this country. We have a good plan to take to the American people, and they'll see it loud and clear in the fall. It will be there.

Education: As I look at what we need to give those kids a break and to be competitive in the world, it gets right back to my passion for a change in education. We've got a good program. We've sent it to the United States Congress, and what did they do? They threw out this whole innovative approach that we call America 2000 and simply added more of your taxpayers' money to the programs that have failed. I want to take this case for education reform to the American people in the fall, and I'm confident we have a winner. We are right to fundamentally reform education in this country.

I might say I strongly favor parental choice in schools. It works at the college level, and it can work at the lower school levels. Where it's been tried, it's benefited

not just the chosen schools, but because of the old American theory of competition, it's benefited those that weren't chosen. They get their act together. So school choice and America 2000 is a positive program. But we have got to get more people elected to the Congress that don't want to do it the old-fashioned way.

Legal reform: Phil and I have been trying for at least 3 years to reform the legal system. The bottom line is simply this: We sue each other too much and care for each other too little. We're trying to change that. The political opposition—and don't take my word for it, ask Phil—the political opposition is so afraid to offend a powerful lobby they won't even let our liability reform proposals or malpractice reform proposals be voted on. We've got to change the Congress and get people there who will do what the people want done.

I am worried about these deficits and leaving these kids with a greater legacy of debt, and we've tried to do something about it. I'll give you a four-point program if you want one, and I'll be proud to take this one to the American people this fall:

One, you've got to cap the growth of mandatory spending, all these programs that a President never gets a shot at, that are just locked into the law. You can permit them to grow; they can grow at the rate of inflation plus population, and then that's it. And that in itself will have billions, literally $2 trillion of savings over the next 5 or 10 years. We've got to do that.

The second point is we've got to pass some of the things that we've got up in the Congress for stimulating economic growth. The biggest one is a reduction in the capital gains tax. It will encourage entrepreneurship.

The third one is an idea that the Texas Republican Party and many in this room have been in the forefront for for many, many years, but I believe its time has come, unless it gets blocked by the leadership, the Democratic Party in the House and Senate who are now nervously conniving to find out how to block it. I'm talking about a balanced budget amendment to the Constitution that will discipline the executive branch and discipline the Congress. The votes are there. It obviously has to be phased in, but it can work. And I'll be glad to make the tough decisions that go with it.

Then the fourth point: Give me what 43 Governors have now—and this one, the case I'm taking to the American people— you give me that line-item veto that 43 Governors have, and let's see what we can do.

We're talking about change—people in the cities, horribly brought to our attention because of what happened in Los Angeles. And we moved immediately and forcefully because I didn't have to ask the Congress what to do. We mobilized SBA and FEMA and Agriculture Department and HHS and all. We put in seven central locations in the areas, in South Central, the burned areas. We brought what we could without having one piece of legislation, the Federal Government to help these people. I was there yesterday and saw it, and it was very, very moving.

Now, I've said to the Congress, and again, Phil is in the lead on this, "We want to do something better now. These programs haven't worked. We want people to have jobs with dignity." The time has come, and I heard this in the Boys Clubs, I heard it in the churches in South Central, the time has come to pass enterprise zones to draw the businesses like a magnet into the inner city through getting rid of the capital gains tax in those green-lined areas.

Let me tell you this: The Mayor of Los Angeles wants it. The council of Los Angeles wants it. The Congressmen give a lot of lip service to it. Peter Ueberroth tells me that it will make his job a lot easier as he's trying to bring businesses in there. And yet, it's hung up because some of the leadership is afraid to give the President or to give the Republicans in Congress a victory. I want to get that clearly in focus for the American people. This isn't time just to have some broad, general thesis; this is something that will really help. We've got to get it done. We may have a chance, still, to get that passed—I hope we will, Phil—in the next few weeks.

We've got other programs that I think will help. We've got a good one for crime: "Weed and Seed," it's called; weed out the criminals, because I don't believe that this

is the time to go soft on those who commit crime. We need a tough crime bill, and we need this "Weed and Seed" program.

I was amazed out there in California, listening to some of the television commercials for the people running now out there in their primaries or running for the United States Senate, Democrats who come back to Washington and vote against our tough crime bill, out there on those 30-second spots: "I'm going to be tough on law and order." We have a good crime bill up there. It's tougher on the criminals, and it's kinder to the victims of crime. And it has been frustrated. As Phil said, he said 1,079 days; it seems like 3 million years. But we're going to keep fighting until we can get done what our police officers deserve and what the neighborhoods of this country are crying out for.

Welfare reform: You've got to be careful on that, because some say you're playing a race card. Who gets hurt the most by a system that's failed? Those who can afford it the least, and I want to reform the welfare system. A little girl saved about $1,200, and they came to her and said, "Well, you can't do that. Your mother's on welfare, and the law says you can't accumulate over $1,000." We've got to change it. We've got to structure it so it does not discriminate against saving but encourages the saving and encourages work and encourages learning. We are going to reform that welfare system. If I can't get it done before the fall, I'm taking that case to the American people, loud and clear.

Homeownership: Isn't it far better to have a Federal program that encourages owning homes than going into these tenements that strip you of your dignity? Of course it is. We've got a good program for that, and I'm hoping we can get that through the Congress, Job Training 2000, a forward-looking job training program.

Now, there are six incentives that would help the cities immediately. Dallas would be a beneficiary as well as Los Angeles or Houston or wherever else it might be.

Now, on those six points I've asked the Congress to put partisanship aside. I said, "Look, the American people really want something done." It's not just the cities, as a matter of fact. I think the whole country wants something done. If you look at the core of these proposals, there are themes that all of us can agree on, once again: Responsibility, opportunity, ownership, independence, dignity, empowerment. These are not partisan values. They are fundamental American values, and we have a duty to make them real.

Now, so far I've talked about what the Government can do. But as I finish here, let me just say the more I am in this wonderfully challenging job—and again, I'm very grateful to the people around this room because I see many, many that go back to my earliest days in Texas politics—but the longer I am in this job, the more convinced I am that Government alone simply cannot solve these problems. It can't be done.

You might say, "What keeps a kid in school? What keeps a kid away from drugs? What keeps a kid out of the gangs?" It's not Government. It is family. Barbara Bush said it right: What happens in your house is far more important than what happens in the White House. We have got to find ways to strengthen the American family, and we must find ways to see that not one piece of legislation passes that diminishes the American family.

I've been in politics a long, long time. I computed it the other day. Half of my adult life since I got out of the Navy and went to school and then moved out to Odessa in the spring of 1948, half of my adult life has been in public life, and exactly half has been in the private sector. We have been blessed, both Barbara and I have been blessed, by the challenges and the joy that we've had in all kinds of fascinating assignments.

The more I think of our country, I'd say this: We have been through tough times. The country's been through tough times.

That's changing. Things are beginning to move. We are not a pessimistic Nation. We are a rising Nation, and we are full of promise for the future. I have vowed, as we try to get something done with Congress before the shift goes entirely into politics in this every-4-year dance that we're all engaged in, that I will not attack any single opponent. I haven't done it since it started. Five people in the Democratic side, one on the Republican side, bolstered by the press that love a good fight. I am not going to do it. I am going to concentrate on trying to lead this country. I'm going to concentrate on trying to build and get something done.

But I want each and every one of you to know that I am ready for the battle that lies ahead. I have never felt more confident of a victory, and I have never felt more fired up about taking our sound message of values and opportunity to the American people in the fall.

So let all these other balloons go up. Let everybody else have their day in the sun. Our day is going to prevail because we are right on the issues, because we are compassionate and caring about the American people, and because our fundamental values, our fundamental values of faith and family is what this country is all about.

Thank you all for what you're doing, and may God bless the United States of America. Thank you.

*Note: The President spoke at 7:37 p.m. at the Grand Kempinski Hotel. In his remarks, he referred to Dr. W.A. Criswell, pastor, First Baptist Church of Dallas; Fred McClure, managing director, First Southwest Co.; Robert A. Mosbacher, Jr., chairman, Texas Victory '92; Kay Bailey Hutchison, Texas State treasurer; and Rick Perry, Texas commissioner of agriculture.*

# Remarks to Goddard Space Flight Center Employees in Greenbelt, Maryland
*June 1, 1992*

Thank you very, very much. Thank you for this welcome to Goddard. And Dan Goldin, thank you, sir, for the introduction, the leadership you're giving the Agency. With me is Bill Reilly. We've been talking today about the upcoming summit in Brazil, the environmental meeting down there. And this visit is very timely for both of us, I think, seeing what magnificent contribution Goddard makes to a better understanding of our planet. I want to salute Mike Deland, who was with us up at Camp David a little bit ago. He runs our Council on Environmental Quality. He's at my side in the White House, a sound environmentalist. Dr. Klineberg, I listened, I had the applause meter on when you walked in, and either they're scared of you or you're doing something right. [*Laughter*] I don't know which it is, but it was most impressive. And thanks for your hospitality. May I salute Brian Dailey, out here, of the Space Council. And I'd like to thank Dr. Fisk, who helped us in the tour.

Now, you know that it's been a month, and in just over a month on the job, Dan Goldin supervised the recovery of a satellite on *Endeavor*'s maiden voyage; he won a vote, a very important vote, to save the space station on the floor of the House; and he launched his own cultural revolution at NASA. And I'd say the new NASA is off to a flying start. And I am very grateful to him for taking on this terribly important assignment heading up NASA.

Twenty years ago this month, 20 years ago, the leaders of the world gathered in Sweden to talk about the human environment. The Stockholm Declaration that they adopted had a simple conclusion, that through fuller knowledge and wiser action we can achieve for ourselves and our posterity a better life in an environment more in keeping with human needs and hopes. Much has been accomplished since those early days of environmentalism, and much has been learned.

We've learned that only market-oriented economies and democratic systems provide the accountability needed to protect against environmental degradation. The coating of soot that the world found when the curtain of secrecy was pulled back from Eastern Europe was but one visible demonstration of that.

We've learned that the economy can grow even while pollution is reduced. Since 1973, our GDP has grown by more than 50 percent. And yet air quality has gotten better: Emissions of carbon monoxide and smog-forming ozone, sulfur dioxide, and particulate matter are all down by more than 20 percent. And water quality has gotten better: We've achieved an 80 percent reduction in suspended solids from industrial and sewage treatment plants.

We've learned that technology, spurred by the right incentives, can provide help to the environment that no amount of regulation of old technology could have achieved. Technological progress can cut pollution rather than increase it. And at the same time, the efficiency gained is good for profits.

And we've learned that market-based mechanisms and flexibility, aimed at ambitious objectives and backed up by rigorous enforcement, can help us solve environmental problems at less cost than command-and-control regulation.

We've learned about a new generation of environmental problems that are global in scope and that will require international cooperation to solve. This week, and I referred to this earlier, over 100 heads of state will gather in Rio de Janeiro, and it will be time to apply those lessons. And what better place to discuss our plans for taking on the problems of the international environment than here at Goddard.

I thought as I was on this little tour, which was all too quick but nevertheless gave me a little feel about the magnificent work that the wonderful employees of Goddard do, I thought wouldn't it be a wonderful thing if these 100 or more heads of state could actually walk through the laboratories here and get a practical feeling for what it is you are doing, to see how they can better monitor the changes that they talk about or that they get from their environmental ministers. It's a wonderful thing. And I think it's very timely that I've had this opportunity, and I look forward to sharing it with those people down in Rio.

It is science developed here that has given the world a new window from which to see its environment. A spacecraft managed by Goddard provided humanity with its first image of Earth from space. It was your scientists, Goddard's scientists, who developed the upper atmosphere research satellite launched last year, which is providing us new insight about the content of the ozone layer. And the lion's share of the science that the world is using to understand our climate comes from a program with its heart and soul right here, the Global Change Research Program, built around the Mission to Planet Earth that Goddard is developing.

When we go to Rio, the U.S. will go proudly as the world's leader, not just in environmental research but in environmental action. The United States was the first nation to recognize the danger of CFC emissions by eliminating aerosol propellants, which we did in 1978. Other nations are now following suit using the aerosol phaseout as credit to meet the terms of the Montreal Protocol. We are 42 percent ahead of the schedule required by that agreement. And earlier this year, on the basis of science developed by NASA, we unilaterally decided to speed up our timetable for phasing out CFC's to the end of 1995. We were the first nation, back in 1975, to adopt catalytic converters to reduce those emissions from our cars and trucks. In 1982, we began phasing out lead from American gasoline, and now ambient levels of lead in our air have been cut by 95 percent. Other nations are only now taking these two steps.

I came to this office committed to extend America's record of environmental leadership. And I've worked to do so in a way that is compatible with economic growth because this balance is absolutely essential and because these are twin goals, not mutually

exclusive objectives. You see, those who met 20 years ago at Stockholm and called for this UNCED, this summit, explicitly called for the discussion at Rio to be about both environment and development. And they knew even back then that the two were inextricably linked. Only a growing economy can generate the resources and the will to manage natural assets for the longer term and the common good. But only assets which are so managed can support the growth on which so much human hope is hinged. By definition, for development to be successful in the long term, it has got to be sustainable. And so, I invite comparison of the record that we as a country and as an administration have built. It is aggressive. It is comprehensive. And it is ambitious, but carefully balanced. What we've done in this administration reflects the new environmentalism, more sophisticated in its approach, that harnesses the power of the marketplace in the service of the environment. Let me give you some examples.

The 1990 Clean Air Act, which I proposed and signed into law, is the most ambitious air pollution legislation anywhere on Earth. It will cut acid rain, smog, toxic chemical emissions. And yet it will do so with innovations the whole world is watching. We have a trading system for sulfur dioxide reductions, have a new generation of cleaner fuels and cleaner cars, a massive—and to date successful—voluntary air toxics reduction program.

Our national parks are under stress from millions of visitors. And so, just in the last 4 years, we've added over a million and half acres to America's parks, forests, wildlife refuges, and to other public land. We've created 57 new wildlife refuges and restored or protected more than a half a million acres a year of important wetlands. And at the same time, we've streamlined the permitting process so that projects which don't hurt wetlands aren't slowed down. And we've made sure to respect people's private property rights.

We've placed a moratorium on oil and gas drilling along the most environmentally sensitive areas of our coasts, signed new laws to protect against oilspills, to end below-cost timber sales in America's largest rain forest, the Tongass, and to promote environmental education. We've backed our laws up with strict enforcement to make the polluters pay. And the results have been record contributions to cleanups from businesses.

And we have attended to the international environment with new agreements to stop the irresponsible export of toxic wastes, to ban trade in ivory and thereby stop the extinction of elephants due to poaching, and to use debt forgiveness to protect the environment through the debt-for-nature swaps.

In short, our country, America, retains its place at the forefront of international environmental accomplishment. Our laws have served as a model for environmental laws the world over. America's environmental accomplishments have not come by mistake; they are the result of sustained investment. Today, the United States spends about 2 percent of its gross domestic product, over $100 billion a year, on pollution control. In comparison to other nations, that's among the very, very highest in the world.

Americans have always believed that actions speak louder than words. And simple wisdom has guided our approach to the questions on the table at Rio. We will sign a good agreement on climate change. It is based on the idea that every nation should prepare an action strategy as we in the United States have done. We first laid our plan on the table in February 1991 with specific policy proposals and specific calculations concerning how much greenhouse gas emissions would be reduced. When the science on CFC's changed, we added new measures, and we again laid our plan on the table. We showed that our policies would reduce projected year 2000 greenhouse gas emissions by 125 million to 200 million tons, or by 7 to 11 percent. No other nation except The Netherlands has laid out such a specific plan of action. And that's why we insisted that the focus be on results, not on rhetoric. It may not have been widely reported in the press, but in area after area, the United States laid down specific proposals and worked for their adoption: Forests, oceans, living marine resources, public par-

ticipation, financing. Let me be clear: Our commitment to action did not begin and will not end with Rio.

So, when I travel down there next week, to Brazil, I will bring with me several proposals to extend the commitment of the world community into the future. Let me outline for you my four-point plan of cooperation:

First, I will propose a major new initiative to protect and enhance the world's forests. I mentioned lessons learned about cost effectiveness. Well, halting the loss of the Earth's forests is one of the most cost-effective steps that we can take to cut carbon dioxide emissions. Forests also filter the air and water. They provide products from timber and fuelwood to pharmaceuticals and foodstuffs. They are home to more than half the world's species. At the Houston G–7 summit 2 years ago, I proposed a global forest convention. At UNCED, we should get agreement on the principles leading up to that. But I propose today to move ahead faster. At Rio, I will ask the other industrialized countries to join me in doubling worldwide forest assistance with a goal of halting the loss of the world's forests by the end of the decade. As a down payment, the U.S. will increase its bilateral forest assistance by $150 million next year. The plan is to encourage partnerships between recipient countries who could propose new projects and investor countries who, in effect, could bid to support the most effective proposals for sequestering $CO_2$ or preserving biodiversity.

Second, with respect to climate, the signing of a convention that calls for action plans is simply a first step. We must implement them. So I will join in proposing a prompt start to adoption of climate action plans. Of course, as new and better science becomes available on climate change, we will adjust that action plan accordingly. The solution to climate change must include the developing countries. While today they account for about a quarter of the world's emissions, by the year 2025 they will contribute over half. So we must have their participation, and we will fund country studies to get them started. These countries will need new technologies if they are to enjoy green growth. And America can provide them. So, my budget includes an investment of almost $1 billion in developing new energy-efficient technologies. Hundreds of American businessmen will be traveling to Rio to make the case for our technology. But this effort must continue.

So then the third part of our plan is to support a program, a board program of technology cooperation. In particular, we're going to create a Technology Cooperation Corps to identify the green technology, those green technological needs of countries around the world, and then to knock down the barriers to making it available.

The fourth point of my program for a cleaner future is a continued program of research and understanding. This year we are requesting over $1.4 billion for the Global Change Research Program. That's more than the amount spent on climate research by the rest of the world put together. With Dan Goldin's leadership here at NASA, we will push for a program that provides results faster, cheaper, and better. At Rio, I will propose to make the data from our climate change program available and affordable for scientists and researchers all around the world. As part of this effort, we will distribute at that Conference, at UNCED, thousands of copies of computer disks with data on greenhouse effects, and we will open this year a Global Change Research Information Office.

These four steps—a dramatic program to protect and to enhance forests; quick action on climate change; cooperation in deploying cleaner, more efficient technology; and then an ongoing program to develop and share sound science—can help us seize that opportunity long after those speeches in Rio

have been given and the Conference is over.

Two decades ago, when they gathered at Stockholm, the leaders of the world could not possibly have foreseen the tumultuous events of the intervening two decades. Then they worried about nuclear war as a chief environmental threat. They couldn't have known that today the specter of nuclear war, with its unthinkable destruction, would be calmed as never before in our postwar history. They could not possibly have envisioned that, with the fall of statism and communism, those who would come to Rio would have the chance to launch a new generation of clean growth guided by the wisdom of free peoples and fueled by the power of free markets. They could never have known how far we've have come in 20 years. Now it is for us to imagine how much further we can go. And what better place to make that point than standing before these people that are dedicated to demonstrating to the rest of the world how much farther we can go.

I am grateful to each and every one of you who gives of himself or herself to further the science and thus to improve and keep something very, very special, the environmental quality of our entire world. Thank you for what you do. And may God bless our great country. Thank you.

*Note: The President spoke at 2:44 p.m. in the auditorium in Building 8. In his remarks, he referred to John M. Klineberg, Director, Goddard Space Flight Center; Brian D. Dailey, Executive Secretary-Designate, National Space Council; and Lennard A. Fisk, Associate Administrator for Space Science and Applications, NASA.*

# Nomination of Alison Podell Rosenberg To Be an Assistant Administrator of the Agency for International Development
*June 1, 1992*

The President today announced his intention to nominate Alison Podell Rosenberg, of Virginia, to be an Assistant Administrator of the Agency for International Development, U.S. International Development Cooperation Agency, for the Bureau of Africa. She would succeed Scott M. Spangler.

Since 1988, Ms. Rosenberg has served as Deputy Assistant Secretary of State for Economic Policy and Assistance for the Bureau of African Affairs at the Department of State. Prior to this, she served as Director of

African Affairs for National Security Council staff, 1987–88, and Associate Assistant Administrator and Director in the Office of Policy Development and Program Review at the Agency for International Development, 1985–87.

Ms. Rosenberg graduated from Smith College (B.A., 1967). She was born September 5, 1945, in Miami, FL. Ms. Rosenberg is married, has one child, and resides in McLean, VA.

# Nomination of Walter B. McCormick, Jr., To Be General Counsel of the Department of Transportation
*June 1, 1992*

The President today announced his intention to nominate Walter B. McCormick, Jr., of Missouri, to be General Counsel of the Department of Transportation. He would succeed Arthur J. Rothkopf.

Currently Mr. McCormick serves as Republican chief counsel and staff director of the U.S. Senate Committee on Commerce, Science, and Transportation in Washington, DC. Prior to this he served as a legislative

assistant to Senator John C. Danforth in Washington, DC.

Mr. McCormick graduated from the University of Missouri School of Journalism (B.J., 1976) and the University of Missouri School of Law (J.D., 1979). He was born February 8, 1954, in Kansas City, MO. Mr. McCormick is married, has one child, and resides in Alexandria, VA.

# Remarks at the Health Care Equity Action League Briefing
*June 2, 1992*

Please be seated, and thank you very much for coming. And Dirk, thank you, sir, and Pam, the cochairs of HEAL. I am delighted to have an opportunity to speak to you briefly here. And then our experts come on and you'll learn—I wouldn't say more than you want to know about this, but you'll be hearing from our very best in a few minutes, people that have shaped our approach to health care.

We are grateful for your support. I'll tell

you, the strong support of this organization for our health care reform plan is absolutely essential to getting something done for the people in this country. I can't overemphasize the importance of your contacts on the Hill today, of your organizing of the local coalitions. Both of these efforts are going to be determining factors in steering health care reform in the right direction.

We're at a crossroads, literally, at a crossroads on the issue of health care reform.

The real debate concerns the direction that health care reform is going to take. I don't think there's any argument in the country that health care reform is not needed. Nobody's taking that tack. The question is, will we preserve our public-private health care system through comprehensive reforms or are we going to substitute a plan that is Government-dictated, Government-mandated, Government-controlled? That's the bottom line. We have to spell out as clearly for the American public as we possibly can: The decision is as simple and as pivotal as that.

We have to make it clear to Americans that other proposals like the national health care, expanded Medicare, Americare, and "play or pay" are fundamentally Government-controlled. Some are a little more obvious about it than others, but ultimately each ends up controlled by a Government bureaucracy.

Let me also assure you that I share your specific concerns. Individual entrepreneurs need help in order to compete with the conglomerates; I understand that. You need a tax deduction for 100 percent of health insurance premiums, and you need market clout. As small business owners you also need rescuing from cherry picking by these insurers, and you need help in shopping smart, and you need a way to avoid costly frivolous coverage. Our plan provides comprehensive reform, and that's going to benefit, we compute, more than 95 million Americans.

We have two bills on the Hill already. These are nonpolitical; that is, the liberals agree with us in principle; that makes them nonpolitical. [*Laughter*] That being the case, I say Congress ought to act according to principle and pass this legislation for the good of the country. Where we agree, we must act. With your help up on the Hill, Congress will pass the bills immediately.

Under our plan, health insurers would have to cover all employers requesting coverage, and that coverage would be guaranteed. It would be renewable, and it would have no restrictions for preexisting medical conditions. It would also be portable, allowing workers to change jobs without fear of not being picked up by their new employer's plan. We would establish networks that would help small businesses purchase insurance and manage their premium costs. Our coordinated care provisions would reverse the upward spiral of health care costs, too.

Our plan also addresses something that we must do something about, and I'm talking about the malpractice costs, costs from excessive insurance paperwork, and also administrative costs. We address the special needs of urban and rural areas by providing for clinics and disease prevention activities.

In addition, we think consumers need better information in order to make better decisions. So we propose information booklets that will allow consumers to compare costs and then compare the quality of care provided by hospitals and other health care plans. These are things that I think that we all can whole-heartedly endorse and fully intend to implement.

But no discussion of health care reform is complete without emphasizing the necessity for personal responsibility for health promotion and then again for disease prevention. Tomorrow, Secretary Lou Sullivan, along with Prevention magazine, will announce the results of a survey on the health-related behavior of Americans. The prevention index tracks our national progress in avoiding special specific health-related risk behavior. We need your help in spreading the word that avoiding 10 common risk factors could prevent between 40 and 70 percent of all premature deaths, one-third of all cases of acute disability, and two-thirds of all cases of chronic disability. Individual action, that's what is needed around the Nation, at the level of personal health behavior.

At the same time, up here, right back to Washington, congressional action is needed to ensure that world-class health care continues to be directed by consumer choice and by free-market factors.

There's a crying need to change things. But I feel compelled to uphold the quality of American health care. We must not, in our desire to see change, diminish the quality of American health care. Our plan, I think, upholds the quality. Very candidly, I think the major two competing plans would tend to diminish the quality of American health care. We've seen it happen in some of these nationalized programs abroad, and I think the same thing would happen here. So we must not go for a program that is going to diminish the quality of American medical care.

So again, Dirk and Pam, thank you. We are very grateful for your leadership and helping to make all this happen. And to each and every one of you, my most sincere thanks. I really believe we can get something done, and I say that, recognizing that this is a weird year. [*Laughter*] This is what they call one of the weird ones out there. But when you have a commonsense idea, when you have something that is backed by the sound and sensible people like yourselves, we've got to find a way to make it

happen. So I pledge you my full support. My driving interest behind this really can be brought to bear in the Congress in ways that our pros here in the front row think necessary. So I am with you and very, very grateful to you.

Now, on for your real session where you're going to learn a lot more about it. Thank you all very much for coming.

*Note: The President spoke at 2:09 p.m. in Room 450 of the Old Executive Office Building. In his remarks, he referred to Dirk Vander Dongen, chairman, and Pam Bailey, executive director, Health Care Equity Action League.*

# Remarks Prior to a Meeting With Republican Congressional Leaders
## June 2, 1992

*The President.* I really appreciate everybody coming down. And we've got several key issues, but one that I am most interested in getting through is this balanced budget amendment. I think it is critical, and I think it's an idea whose time has come. It's an idea that the American people strongly support. One of the things I want to follow up on with you all now is how we do that. I know we've got problems in the Senate that are different than the House, but we've got to get it done for the American people. I'm very pleased with the way our troops are moving out on it, but that's one of the things on my mind for this meeting.

So let's pass a balanced budget amendment; discipline the Congress as well as the executive branch and everything else.

We've got to get it done.

*Q.* A lot of economists don't agree with you, like 400.

*The President.* Well, the people, the American people agree with me, and that's what matters. So we ought to get it done and not worry about those who don't. It's out there, and we've got ideas up there before the Congress right now that would accomplish this, too.

*Q.* What do you hear from the primaries?

*The President.* I haven't heard anything much there, Helen [Helen Thomas, United Press International].

*Note: The President spoke at 3:37 p.m. in the Cabinet Room at the White House. A tape was not available for verification of the content of these remarks.*

# Statement on the Conclusion of the Presidential Primary Season
## June 2, 1992

When the votes are counted tonight, millions of American voters will have participated in primaries, caucuses, and conventions from New Hampshire to California. This is a uniquely important election year for our country, and I commend every

American, Republican, Democrat, or independent, who has made their voice heard by attending a caucus, casting a ballot, or signing a petition.

As November approaches, I believe there will be two questions foremost in the minds of American voters: Who has the best ideas for America? Who do you trust to lead this country? With an unbroken string of primary victories behind us, I will continue to present my credentials and ideas to the American people.

To our supporters, Barbara and I say thank you for your confidence and trust. Tonight we extend a hand to every Republican. To all Americans who share our values and commitment to building a better America, we invite you to join us. Together this November, we can break the Washington lawmaking gridlock and set a new course for the next American century.

# Message to the Congress Transmitting the Report of the Saint Lawrence Seaway Development Corporation
*June 2, 1992*

*To the Congress of the United States:*

I transmit herewith the Saint Lawrence Seaway Development Corporation's Annual Report for fiscal year 1991. This report has been prepared in accordance with section 10 of the Saint Lawrence Seaway Act of May 13, 1954 (33 U.S.C. 989(a)), and covers the period October 1, 1990, through September 30, 1991.

GEORGE BUSH

The White House,
June 2, 1992.

# Message to the Senate Transmitting the Czechoslovakia-United States Investment Treaty
*June 2, 1992*

*To the Senate of the United States:*

With a view to receiving the advice and consent of the Senate to ratification, I transmit herewith the Treaty Between the United States of America and the Czech and Slovak Federal Republic Concerning the Reciprocal Encouragement and Protection of Investment, with Protocol and three related exchanges of letters, signed at Washington on October 22, 1991. I transmit also, for the information of the Senate, the report of the Department of State with respect to this treaty.

The treaty is an integral part of my initiative to strengthen economic relations with Central and East European countries. The treaty is designed to aid the growth of the private sector in the Czech and Slovak Federal Republic by protecting and thereby encouraging U.S. private investment. The treaty is fully consistent with U.S. policy toward international investment. A specific tenet, reflected in this treaty, is that U.S. investment abroad and foreign investment in the United States should receive fair, equitable, and nondiscriminatory treatment. Under this treaty, the Parties also agree to international law standards for expropriation and compensation; free transfers of funds associated with investments; and the option of the investor to resolve disputes with the host government through international arbitration.

I recommend that the Senate consider this treaty as soon as possible, and give its advice and consent to ratification of the treaty, with protocol and related exchanges of letters, at an early date.

GEORGE BUSH

The White House,
June 2, 1992.

# Letter to Congressional Leaders Transmitting a Report on International Sanctions Against Iraq
*June 2, 1992*

*Dear Mr. Chairman:*

Enclosed is an unclassified report on sanctions taken by other nations against Iraq as required by section 586J(c) of the Foreign Operations, Export Financing, and Related Programs Appropriations Act, 1991 (Public Law 101–513).

Sincerely,

GEORGE BUSH

*Note: Identical letters were sent to Robert C. Byrd, chairman of the Senate Committee on Appropriations; Jamie L. Whitten, chairman of the House Committee on Appropriations; Dante B. Fascell, chairman of the House Committee on Foreign Affairs; and Claiborne Pell, chairman of the Senate Committee on Foreign Relations.*

# Statement by Press Secretary Fitzwater on Continuation of China's Most-Favored-Nation Trade Status
*June 2, 1992*

The President informed the Congress today that he plans to extend China's most-favored-nation (MFN) status for another year. In making this important decision, the President stressed that it is wrong to isolate China if we hope to influence China.

Section 402 of the Trade Act of 1974 explicitly links eligibility for MFN to the important human rights issue of free emigration. Continuation of the current Jackson-Vanik waiver (and thus MFN trade status) will substantially promote freedom of emigration from China, as it has since 1979. China continues to permit the departure of citizens who qualify for a U.S. immigrant visa.

Although we have seen positive, if limited, developments in our human rights dialog, the President has made clear to the Chinese that their respect for internationally recognized human rights is insufficient. We are deeply disappointed in China's limited actions with regard to internationally recognized human rights and cannot describe our relations as fully normal until the Chinese Government effectively addresses these concerns. We want to elicit a faster pace and a broader scope for human rights improvements in China. Withdrawal of MFN would achieve neither of these objectives.

Short of fully normal relations, maintaining a constructive policy of engagement with China has served U.S. interests. In our bilateral relationship, we have used the tools available to achieve the foreign policy goals shared by the administration and the Congress. This has been true of our targeted use of 301 and Special 301 trade investigations and our vigorous enforcement of the law against prison labor imports and textile fraud. Our nonproliferation dialog also has been successful: China has acknowledged international nonproliferation standards by acceding to the Nuclear Non-Proliferation Treaty and declaring adherence to Missile Technology Control Regime guidelines. We are monitoring these commitments closely.

We have generated positive results without withdrawing MFN from China. Withdrawal of MFN would inflict severe costs on American business people, investors, and consumers. It would mean lost jobs and failed businesses in the United States and a multibillion-dollar surcharge on American consumers' imports. Our direct engagement with the Chinese is on the whole a successful policy. We intend to maintain it in order vigorously to protect American interests while we promote positive change in China.

*Note: Presidential Determination No. 92–29 on trade with China was published in the Federal Register on June 10.*

## Appointment of the 1992–1993 White House Fellows
*June 2, 1992*

The President today announced the appointments of the 1992–93 White House fellows. This is the 28th class of fellows since the program was established in 1964. Fifteen fellows were chosen from nearly 700 applicants who were screened by 11 regional panels. The President's Commission on White House Fellowships, chaired by Ronna Romney, interviewed the 33 national finalists prior to recommending the 15 persons to the President. Their year of Government service will begin September 1, 1992.

Fellows serve for one year as members of the White House staff or as special assistants to members of the Cabinet. In addition to the work assignments, the fellowship includes an education program that parallels and broadens the unique experience of working at the highest levels of the Federal Government. The program is open to U.S. citizens in the early stages of their careers and from all occupations and professions. Federal Government employees are not eligible, with the exception of career Armed Forces personnel. Leadership, character, intellectual and professional ability, and commitment to community and national service are the principal criteria employed in the selection of fellows.

Applications for the 1993–94 program may be obtained by contacting the President's Commission on White House Fellowships, 712 Jackson Place, NW, Washington, DC 20503.

The 1992–93 White House fellows are:

*Belknap, Margaret H.,* of Shorewood, WI, a captain in the U.S. Army, is permanent associate professor in the department of systems engineering at the U.S. Military Academy. A 1981 graduate of the U.S. Military Academy, West Point, NY, Captain Belknap was commissioned in the Signal Corps and has served in a variety of tactical and strategic communications positions in the Pacific. She earned an M.S.E. in operations research from the University of Michigan in 1989. Captain Belknap was born May 23, 1959, in Shorewood, WI.

*Campbell, Kurt M.,* of Boston, MA, is associate professor of public policy and international relations and assistant director of the Center for Science and International Affairs at the John F. Kennedy School of Government. Dr. Campbell is a Navy Reserve officer currently serving in the Pentagon and was a distinguished Marshall scholar at Oxford University, England. He recently received a major grant from the Carnegie Corp. of New York to study military matters in the former Soviet Union. He received his B.A. in science, technology, and public affairs from the University of California, San Diego, in 1980; certificate of Soviet studies and music, University of Erevan, Soviet Armenia, in 1979; and received his Ph.D. in international relations from Oxford University in 1984. Dr. Campbell was born August 27, 1957, in Fresno, CA.

*Froman, Michael B.G.,* of San Anselmo, CA, is an international lawyer who has been directing the American Bar Association's pro bono legal assistance project in Albania. He received his juris doctorate from Harvard Law School in 1991 and graduated magna cum laude. Mr. Froman was a recipient of a Fulbright scholarship and a MacArthur Foundation fellowship which enabled him to complete a doctorate in international relations at Oxford University in 1988. He received a bachelor of arts, summa cum laude, from Princeton University in public and international affairs in 1985. Mr. Froman was born on August 20, 1962, in San Rafael,

CA.

*Gill, Steven L.*, of Nashville, TN, is a partner with the law firm of Boult, Cummings, Conners & Berry and a member of the adjunct faculty at Belmont University. He received his bachelor of arts degree, cum laude, in honors history at the University of Tennessee in 1979. He obtained his law degree at the University of Tennessee in 1982. After law school, he served as campaign coordinator for the reelection of Tennessee Governor Lamar Alexander. In 1988, Mr. Gill was selected to study in Tokyo as a guest of the Japanese Government. He has since been a leader in promoting Tennessee as a site for international trade and investment. Mr. Gill was born November 15, 1956, in Knoxville, TN.

*Golub, Lawrence E.*, of New York, NY, is a managing director of Wasserstein Perella Capital Markets, a division of the investment banking firm Wasserstein Perella & Co., Inc. He received his bachelor's degree in economics, magna cum laude, in 1980 from Harvard University and earned a law degree, magna cum laude, in 1984 from Harvard Law School, where he was elected to the *Harvard Law Review*. He earned an M.B.A. degree with high distinction from Harvard Business School in 1984, where he was selected as a Baker scholar. He is also a director of Bayou Steel Corp. Mr. Golub was born October 3, 1959, in New York, NY.

*Gordon, Robert L., III*, of Colorado Springs, CO, is a major in the U.S. Army and presently serves as the executive officer of the department of social sciences at the U.S. Military Academy, West Point. He graduated with a degree in engineering and additional concentration in public policy and national security from the U.S. Military Academy, West Point, in 1979. He was commissioned as an artillery officer and served in artillery units in the 4th Infantry Division, Fort Carson, CO. Major Gordon attended graduate school at Princeton University's Woodrow Wilson School for Public and International Affairs in 1989. He is a graduate of the Combined Armed Services Staff School at Fort Leavenworth. Major Gordon was born March 15, 1957, in Richmond, VA.

*Hooker, Richard D., Jr.*, of West Point, NY, is a career Army officer now serving as assistant professor of political science with the department of social sciences, U.S. Military Academy, West Point. A 1981 West Point graduate, Captain Hooker received master's and doctoral degrees in political science from the University of Virginia in 1989. Captain Hooker joined the Army in 1975, serving as a rifleman in the 82d Airborne Division before entering the U.S.

Military Academy. He has written widely for professional military journals. Captain Hooker was born January 6, 1957, in Fort Benning, GA.

*Jindra, Lawrence F.*, of Floral Park, NY, an ophthalmic surgeon, is a clinical assistant professor at the State University of New York and the director of the glaucoma consultation unit of the Northport Veterans Affairs Medical Center. A Phi Beta Kappa scholar, he was awarded a bachelor of arts, summa cum laude, in physics from Hofstra University in 1979 and received his ophthalmology residency at the Harkness Institute of Columbia University. As a Heed Foundation fellow he studied vision research at the Rockefeller University and served a glaucoma fellowship at Wills Eye Hospital. He earned a master of public administration degree with concentration in medicine, science, and technology from Harvard University's Kennedy School of Government in 1991 and was selected as a diplomacy fellow. He was awarded doctor of medicine with distinction in research from Down State Medical Center in 1983. He also serves as a battalion surgeon with the U.S. Marine Corps Reserve. Dr. Jindra was born September 10, 1958, in Mineola, NY.

*Kelley, Lloyd E.*, of Houston, TX, is currently an attorney with the firm of Fulbright & Jaworski, where he practices labor and employment law. Mr. Kelley served with the Houston Police Department for 11 years. While serving at the police department, he earned a bachelor's degree, cum laude, in economics from the University of Houston in 1983 and three master's degrees in criminal justice, public administration, and history from the University of Houston in 1987, Sam Houston State University in 1988, and Rice University in 1991, respectively. Mr. Kelley also received his law degree, cum laude, from the University of Houston in 1990. Mr. Kelley was born January 2, 1959, in Houston, TX.

*Murphy, Dennis J.*, of San Francisco, CA, is a lieutenant commander in the U.S. Navy. He is currently working in the Navy's Office of Legislative Affairs in Washington, DC, where he provides advice and congressional liaison for the Secretary of the Navy and Chief of Naval Operations for Navy Research, Development, Test and Evaluation. He received a bachelor's degree in economics from the U.S. Naval Academy in 1981. He served as the senior naval aide to the Chief of Naval Operations and the engineering officer of the U.S.S. *Nevada* (SSBN 733). He earned a master of science degree in engineering management from Catholic University in 1988. Lieutenant Commander

Murphy was born January 8, 1959, in Fresno, CA.

*Nelson, Thomas C.,* of Charlotte, NC, is a general partner and founder of Wakefield Group, a North Carolina-based venture capital firm. He also supports entrepreneurship through service as chairman of the Metrolina Entrepreneurial Council and as president of the North Carolina Venture Capital Association. Mr. Nelson graduated from Stanford University in 1984 with a bachelor of science degree in industrial engineering and later earned a master's degree in business administration from the Harvard Graduate School of Business in 1988. Mr. Nelson was born June 25, 1962, in Chicago, IL.

*Sampson, Rana S.,* of Brooklyn, NY, serves as a senior research associate with the Police Executive Research Forum in Washington, DC, a nonprofit research organization dedicated to improving the field of policing. Ms. Sampson earned her bachelor's degree, cum laude, from Columbia University in 1979 and her law degree, cum laude, from Harvard Law School in 1989. Ms. Sampson was born on January 10, 1958, in New York, NY.

*Warr, Dartanian,* of Cleveland, OH, a major in the U.S. Air Force, is currently a student at the Defense Systems Management College at Fort Belvoir, VA. Major Warr received his bachelor's degree from the U.S. Air Force Academy,

Colorado Springs, CO, in 1980. He was awarded a master's degree from Wright State University in Dayton, OH, in 1986 and a master's in business administration from Golden Gate University, San Francisco, CA, in 1988. Major Warr was born on June 25, 1958, in Cleveland, OH.

*Webster, William M., IV,* of Greenville, SC, is president of Carabo, Inc., the largest franchisee of Bojangles Famous Chicken 'n Biscuits restaurant chain. Webster received his bachelor's degree in English and German, summa cum laude, from Washington and Lee University in Lexington, VA, in 1979. He was awarded a Fulbright scholarship to attend the University of Regensburg in West Germany. He later earned a law degree from the University of Virginia School of Law in 1983. He was born November 7, 1957, in Greenville, SC.

*Wing, Michael J.,* of Tucson, AZ, is the president and chief executive officer of InfoPlan International, Inc., a market research firm that conducts operations nationwide and internationally. He earned a bachelor's degree in international affairs from the University of Colorado in 1981, an M.B.A. from Denver University in 1986, and a master's in public policy from Georgetown University in 1988. Wing has written several published articles including a forthcoming book. Mr. Wing was born July 1, 1959, in Tucson, AZ.

# Remarks Prior to a Meeting With Leaders of the House of Representatives
*June 3, 1992*

*Q.* Mr. President, why is it that so many people like Mr. Perot?

*The President.* Let me tell you what we're talking about today. We're talking about the balanced budget amendment. Going over a little history, the balanced budget amendment proposal is the first one as President that I sent up to the Congress, and it is time to pass it. I think here's something that we can do.

This is a bipartisan meeting, and I am grateful to the Members here who support this balanced budget amendment. We've got to stop spending more than we take in, and that's the theory behind this amendment. The time has come to pass it. I understand that some in the Congress are

starting to fight us on this, but I think the American people want it done.

What we're going to talk about here is how do we get something done for the taxpayer, and that is to stop spending more than we take in. It will discipline all branches of Government, and the time has come to pass it. I'm going to hear from Charles Stenholm, Bill Gradison, and others here as to how they feel that can be done.

So that's what we're talking about today. Thank you for your interest in this other——

*Q.* Aren't you only preaching to the choir, Mr. President? Day after day you only meet with people who agree with you.

*The President.* We're finished here. We're

going to try—thank you, Helen [Helen Thomas, United Press International], for your input on this. But we are going to keep on talking about this now in substance. We've got to get going because we only have, I'm told, 30 minutes. We've got stuff to do. Thank you for your interest, however.

*Note: The President spoke at 10:05 a.m. in the Cabinet Room at the White House. A tape was not available for verification of the content of these remarks.*

# Presidential Determination No. 92–30—Memorandum on Trade With Certain States of Eastern Europe and the Former Soviet Union
*June 3, 1992*

*Memorandum for the Secretary of State*

*Subject:* Determination Under Section 402(d)(1) of the Trade Act of 1974, as Amended—Continuation of Waiver Authority

Pursuant to the authority vested in me under the Trade Act of 1974, as amended, Public Law 93–618, 88 Stat. 1978 (hereinafter "the Act"), I determine, pursuant to section 402(d)(1) of the Act (19 U.S.C. 2432(d)(1)), that the further extension of the waiver authority granted by section 402(c) of the Act will substantially promote the objectives of section 402 of the Act. I further determine that the continuation of the waivers applicable to Albania, Armenia, Azerbaijan, Bulgaria, Byelarus, Georgia, Kazakhstan, Kyrgyzstan, Moldova, Mongolia, Romania, Russia, Ukraine, and Uzbekistan will substantially promote the objectives of section 402 of the Act.

You are authorized and directed to publish this determination in the *Federal Register.*

GEORGE BUSH

*[Filed with the Office of the Federal Register, 11:56 a.m., June 10, 1992]*

*Note: The Executive order is listed in Appendix E at the end of this volume.*

# Message to the Congress on Trade With Certain States of Eastern Europe and the Former Soviet Union
*June 3, 1992*

*To the Congress of the United States:*

I hereby transmit the documents referred to in section 402(d)(1) of the Trade Act of 1974, as amended (19 U.S.C. 2432(d)(1)) ("the Act"), with respect to a further extension of the authority to waive subsections (a) and (b) of section 402 of the Act. These documents continue in effect this waiver authority for a further 12-month period.

I include as part of these documents my determination that further extension of the waiver authority will substantially promote the objectives of section 402. I also include my determination that continuation of the waivers applicable to Albania, Armenia, Azerbaijan, Bulgaria, Byelarus, Georgia, Kazakhstan, Kyrgyzstan, Moldova, Mongolia, Romania, Russia, Ukraine, and Uzbekistan will substantially promote the objectives of section 402. The attached documents also include my reasons for recommending the extension of the waiver authority and for my determination that continuation of the waivers currently in effect for Albania, Armenia, Azerbaijan, Bulgaria, Byelarus, Georgia, Kazakhstan, Kyrgyzstan, Moldova, Mongolia, Romania, Russia, Ukraine, and Uzbekistan will substantially promote the objectives of section 402.

My determination with respect to the waiver applicable to the People's Republic of China and the reasons therefor is transmitted separately.

I intend to waive by Executive order application of sections 402(a) and 402(b) of the Act with respect to Tajikistan and Turkmenistan prior to July 3, 1992.

GEORGE BUSH

The White House,
June 3, 1992.

*Note: The Executive orders of June 3 and June 24 are listed in Appendix E at the end of this volume.*

# Presidential Determination No. 92–31—Memorandum on Trade With Tajikistan and Turkmenistan
*June 3, 1992*

*Memorandum for the Secretary of State*

*Subject:* Determination Under Section 402(c)(2)(A) of the Trade Act of 1974, as Amended—Tajikistan and Turkmenistan

Pursuant to section 402(c)(2)(A) of the Trade Act of 1974 (19 U.S.C. 2432(c)(2)(A)), as amended (the "Act"), I determine that a waiver by Executive order of the application of subsections (a) and (b) of section 402 of the Act with respect to Tajikistan and Turkmenistan will substantially promote the objectives of section 402.

You are authorized and directed to publish this determination in the *Federal Register.*

GEORGE BUSH

*[Filed with the Office of the Federal Register, 11:57 a.m., June 10, 1992]*

*Note: The Executive order of June 24 is listed in Appendix E at the end of this volume.*

# Message to the Congress on Trade With Tajikistan and Turkmenistan
*June 3, 1992*

*To the Congress of the United States:*

Pursuant to section 402(c)(2)(A) of the Trade Act of 1974 (the "Act") (19 U.S.C. 2432(c)(2)(A)), I have determined that a waiver of the application of subsections (a) and (b) of section 402 with respect to Tajikistan and Turkmenistan will substantially promote the objectives of section 402. A copy of that determination is enclosed. I have also received assurances with respect to the emigration practices of Tajikistan and Turkmenistan required by section 402(c)(2)(B) of the Act. This message constitutes the report to the Congress required by section 402(c)(2).

Pursuant to section 402(c)(2), I shall waive by Executive order the application of subsections (a) and (b) of section 402 of the Act with respect to Tajikistan and Turkmenistan.

GEORGE BUSH

The White House,
June 3, 1992.

*Note: The Executive order of June 24 is listed in Appendix E at the end of this volume.*

## Nomination of John Frank Bookout, Jr., To Be United States Ambassador to Saudi Arabia
*June 3, 1992*

The President today announced his intention to nominate John Frank Bookout, Jr., of Texas, to be Ambassador of the United States of America to the Kingdom of Saudi Arabia. He would succeed Chas.W. Freeman, Jr.

Currently Mr. Bookout serves as supervisory director of Royal Dutch Shell in The Hague, Netherlands. From 1976 to 1988, he served as president and chief executive officer of Shell Oil Co. in Houston, TX. From 1950 to 1976, Mr. Bookout served in several positions including: executive vice president for exploration and production in Houston, TX; president of Shell Canada, Ltd. in Toronto, Canada; and as vice president of New Orleans exploration and production.

Mr. Bookout graduated from the University of Texas at Austin (B.S. and M.A., 1950). He was born December 31, 1922, in Shreveport, LA. Mr. Bookout is married, has three children, and resides in Houston, TX.

## Presidential Determination No. 92–32—Memorandum on Trade With Angola
*June 3, 1992*

*Memorandum for the Secretary of State*

*Subject:* Determination Under Section 2(b)(2) of the Export-Import Bank Act of 1945, as Amended: People's Republic of Angola

Pursuant to the authority vested in me by section 2(b)(2)(C) of the Export-Import Bank Act of 1945, as amended (the Act), 12 U.S.C. 635(b)(2)(C), I hereby determine that the People's Republic of Angola has ceased to be a Marxist-Leninist country within the definition of such terms in subparagraph (B)(i) of such section.

You are authorized and directed to report this determination to the Congress and to publish it in the *Federal Register.*

GEORGE BUSH

[*Filed with the Office of the Federal Register, 11:58 a.m., June 10, 1992*]

*Note: This memorandum was released by the Office of the Press Secretary on June 4.*

## Remarks on Signing the Proclamation Commemorating the 50th Anniversary of World War II
*June 4, 1992*

May I salute Secretary Card and General Powell; the Deputy Secretary of Veterans Affairs, Mr. Principi; the Deputy Secretary of Defense with us, Don Atwood; Secretary Larry Garrett; Secretary Rice; and Michael Stone of the Army; General Mundy, who's right over here; and then the Members of Congress who are with us today. I believe Senator Cranston was going to be here. Here he is, right over here; see you, Alan. And of course, Congressmen Montgomery, Stump, Myers, and who am I missing—Senator, sorry. We have a distinguished group here to salute the occasion. And also Don

Wilson is with us, the Archivist, and Albert McCluskey, a veteran of the Battle of Midway, other veterans here today, and members of civic and veterans service organizations, and also some other members of the Joint Chiefs, I see. May I salute General Kicklighter, the Executive Director, and members of the Department of Defense's World War II Commemoration Committee.

Welcome, all, to the White House and to this special observance of the 50th anniversary of an event which linked Americans' hearts and minds, the monumental struggle known as the Second World War. Overnight, World War II literally transformed America from a people at peace to a nation at war that would define the course of history for the rest of this century.

The attack on Pearl Harbor forced America to abandon isolationism and take up the mantle of leadership. World War II was fought for American soil and sovereignty. It was also fought to defend people who, hating war, sought only peace, people everywhere who yearn for freedom, then and now.

The year 1942 was crucial to our history. Americans came together. Each citizen sought ways to do his or her part. And factories designed to build the tools of peace produced the tools of war: ships, planes, tanks, ammunition, all crucial to the Allied effort. It wasn't easy, but we did it. We did it fast. We did the hard work of freedom.

I was 17 on December 7, 1941, and like so many here, not so many in this room but like some—[*laughter*]—enlisted on my 18th birthday as a Seaman Second Class. I do remember vividly the news from the early days, how it was grim. Guam was overrun, and the reports from the Pacific were rather scary; Bataan and Corregidor fell. Yet the Battle of the Coral Sea foiled Japanese plans to invade Port Moresby and New Guinea. And 50 years ago this week our forces began what may have been the greatest naval battle of all time. Midway turned the tide of World War II. And the inevitable Allied victory, you could feel it. It began to take shape.

Winston Churchill once said of World War II, "There never was a war in all history easier to prevent." Today let us recall what the lion cried as a voice in the wilderness: "No one ever walks away from appeasing an aggressor. He only crawls."

Weakening our defenses during a time of peace is an open invitation to those with the potential to wage war. And as President, as long as I'm President, the military's commitment to defending freedom will be matched by our commitment to defending the military. Some say our victory in the cold war allows us to pull back to our own water's edge. And I say, just as America's vigilance helped us win that war, so a strong America can now help win the peace.

We seek a world where differences are solved peacefully, where the force of law really outlasts the use of force. Sacrifices made heroically 50 years ago have helped bring about a new and better world. And it's a world I thought of last December where, on the 50th anniversary of Pearl Harbor, Barbara and I looked at the sunken hull of the *Arizona* out there, the U.S.S. *Arizona*, tomb to more than a thousand great heroes, the greatest that any nation has ever known. There I thought of the wife whose best friend was her husband and the little boy whose brother, his idol, once vowed to take him fishing after the fighting stopped. I thought of the father whose son or daughter would now know him as a martyr but never as a dad. And I resolved once again we must never, ever let America's defenses down.

The men who died there in World War II would today, I am convinced, and I think I said it out there, be very, very proud of America: proud of what we have become as a Nation because of their service and sacrifice, proud of how their fate and faith still stir and shape us. So we honor them, and we remember them so that future generations will say of us what we do also: God bless this wondrous land, the United States of America.

World War II was a fight that we did not seek, against enemies that we didn't choose, for a cause that is first among all: the right of people everywhere to be free.

In that spirit, then, it is my honor to once again welcome all of you to the White House and to sign the proclamation designating the National Observance of the 50th

Anniversary of World War II. And thank you all for coming.

[*At this point, the President signed the proclamation.*]

Well, the deed is done. Thank you all very much for being with us.

*Note: The President spoke at 11:30 a.m. in the Roosevelt Room at the White House. The proclamation is listed in Appendix E at the end of this volume.*

# Nomination of Kenneth L. Brown To Be United States Ambassador to Ghana
## *June 4, 1992*

The President today announced his intention to nominate Kenneth L. Brown, of California, a career member of the Senior Foreign Service, class of Minister-Counselor, to be Ambassador of the United States of America to the Republic of Ghana. He would succeed Raymond Charles Ewing.

Currently Mr. Brown serves as Ambassador to Cote d'Ivoire in Abidjan, Cote d'Ivoire. From 1987 to 1989, he served as Deputy Assistant Secretary of State. Mr. Brown has served as consul general in Johannesburg, South Africa, 1984–87, and as Ambassador to the Congo, 1981–84. In addi-

tion, Mr. Brown has served in several positions at the State Department, including Director, Central African Affairs, 1980–81; Deputy Director, United Nations Political Affairs, 1979–80; and Deputy Director of the Press Office, 1977–79.

Mr. Brown graduated from Pomona College (B.A., 1959), Yale University (M.A., 1960), and New York University (M.A., 1975). He was born December 6, 1936, in Seminole, OK. Mr. Brown is married, has three children, and resides in Abidjan, Cote d'Ivoire.

# The President's News Conference
## *June 4, 1992*

*The President.* I have a brief statement, and then I'll be glad to take questions.

Two months ago, I asked the Congress to cut almost $8 billion in wasteful spending projects. Tonight I've just signed the cuts that Congress sent to me in response. It's not all that I asked for, but it is a start. Eight billion dollars sounds like a lot of money, and it is. But the fact remains: It isn't good enough, not by a long shot.

The American people know budget deficits threaten the long-term economic health of our country. Over the years, we've accumulated Federal debt totaling $65,000 for every family of four in America. This debt does not create more wealth; it merely helps pay for our current consumption. It reminds me of the old fellow who bragged

to his family that he'd finally borrowed enough money to pay off his debts.

Our political system, as it is now, has failed to meet its responsibility to address this problem. In the face of a several hundred billion dollar budget deficit, a piecemeal approach simply will not do the job. We need a constitutional amendment to balance the Federal budget, and we need it now.

Three years ago, in my first address to the Congress, I asked the Senate and the House to pass such an amendment. Every year since then, I have repeated the call. Like President Reagan before me, I have tried to get Congress to act responsibly and to restrain the growth of Federal spending. We've tried compromise. We've tried con-

889

frontation. We've tried quiet diplomacy with the congressional leaders. And none of this has been enough. Tonight I am more convinced than ever that a balanced budget amendment is the only way to force the Federal Government, both the Congress and the executive branch, to live within its means.

This month, both Houses of Congress will vote on a balanced budget amendment. It is impossible to underestimate the importance of this one decision. It will affect every other decision that the Government makes from that moment on, and it will bear directly on the quality of life that we leave the generations who follow us.

Victory will not come easily. The amendment requires a two-thirds majority from both the Senate and the House. I'm pleased to say that many serious-minded Members, Republicans and Democrats alike, support this measure. They understand this is not a partisan fight; it goes far beyond election-year politics. It is a fight for the economic security of the American people.

I realize that some in Washington consider a balanced budget amendment a rather radical step. Well, I strongly doubt that the American people consider a balanced budget amendment as radical. It's common sense, pure and simple. Each month millions of American families sit down to balance their checkbooks; 44 States, 44 States have their own constitutional balanced budget requirements. The Federal Government must now do the same.

The moment is at hand. In the coming days, we will face an extraordinary choice. We can choose either to accept the status quo, piling debt upon debt, or we can strike a bold new course, restoring fiscal sanity to the Federal Government. If we choose wrongly, our grandchildren and their grandchildren are going to bear the burden. I refuse to believe that we will make them pay the price for Washington's irresponsibility. For their sake, I urge every Congressman and every Senator to join me in supporting the swift approval of a balanced budget amendment.

Now I will be glad to respond to questions. I think, Terry [Terence Hunt, Associated Press], I think you have the first.

## Presidential Campaign

*Q.* Mr. President, I'd like to ask you about Ross Perot. People claim that you're hiding, and you're afraid to take him on directly. Will you commit yourself to debating Mr. Perot as well as Bill Clinton in the fall campaign?

*The President.* I'm sure there will be debates, and I will be ready to join the fray after the conventions. But as you know, I have not challenged directly either Perot or Clinton, Mr. Perot or Governor Clinton. I have no intention of changing that before the convention.

I am trying to get things done that will help this country. A balanced budget amendment is a good example of that. If I get too caught up in the political wars at this time, it will be even more difficult to get things through the Congress that will help: a crime bill, an education bill, balanced budget amendment, things that we really need. So I'm going to keep on this course that I've been. I've been faithful to it during the primary season, and I will continue to be until I make a decision to change.

*Q.* I mean in the fall campaign. I'm not talking about immediately, right now, but will you commit yourself to debating the two men——

*The President.* There will be debates.

*Q.* Mr. President, granting the legality, is it proper for a man, for a candidate with vast personal wealth and no spending limits to use that to obtain the Presidency? Since you've known Mr. Perot for so long, is he an insider, an outsider? Is he a man of principle, or does he go for the main——

*The President.* Helen [Helen Thomas, United Press International], I'd love to answer that question, and after the——

*Q.* Well, why don't you?

*The President.* Because I've vowed to keep my sights set on these legislative goals and on leading this country. If I get into characterizing one opponent or another, I diminish my effectiveness in doing that.

We've got a good chance now, and some of it's brought about by the primaries, I think, to pass this balanced budget amendment, for example. I'm a little disappointed that our education reform bill is languishing up there. I'd like to see us get a good energy bill soon. But if I start concentrating on the politics, I'm afraid I will waste an opportunity. I think we're in a real opportunity situation now.

*Q.* Do you think he's trying to buy the Presidency?

*The President.* Well, so far not. We'll wait and see.

Charles [Charles Bierbauer, Cable News Network].

*Q.* Mr. President, you've often said that you've not done so terrific a job of getting your message across. Tonight you've changed the venue. But I wanted to ask you if, indeed, what you've seen in the polls and the constant one-third or more of the electorate that's going other ways isn't a rejection of that message in and of itself?

*The President.* I don't think so because you ask in these deadly polls that I read all the time about, relating to issues, and it's vague out there. We've got a good program. Tonight maybe this is a more effective way to say we want a balanced budget amendment. We've got a good program on the Hill to achieve a balanced budget amendment or, after the balanced budget amendment is passed, to achieve a balanced budget.

So I think we've just got to keep hammering away on the issues because I believe the American people are with me. If they understand our total reform of education, they'll support it. Most Americans want a tougher crime bill. I heard people out on the West Coast, who don't vote for tougher crime legislation, all advertising in those 90-second bites they paid for, ads how tough they are on crime. Maybe we've got a better chance now to pass an administration crime bill.

So I'm going to keep focusing on those issues. Hopefully, the American people will say, "He has a sound program for domestic affairs, just as he does in foreign relations."

*Q.* But if I could follow, sir, hasn't the pattern through the primaries been such that the American people have been constantly looking for an alternative?

*The President.* Yes——

*Q.* You may have put Pat Buchanan behind, but now you've got Ross Perot. Is he the inheritor of that?

*The President.* No. Well, I don't think so. I'll tell you what, I think most people would concede that my problems stem from this sluggish, anemic economy. I think you can trace those problems to getting bigger with that. Now, I think the economy's improving. We still have some big problems there. For a person that's out of work, for him, that unemployment is 100 percent. For a woman that can't get a job that wants one, for her, unemployment is 100 percent.

So we've got to keep pushing ahead. I would make the appeal right now for our growth incentives to further stimulate an economy that is beginning to move and is beginning to move positively.

But no, I think my fortunes have been related to that. I think, if I'll take the blame, some of which I'll take, as the economy has been sick, I assume the American people are fair enough to give credit when there's recovery.

*Q.* Your spokesman today described Mr. Perot as a man whose entire history is to stomp into the group, demand to do things his way, and if he doesn't get it, to pick up his football and go home. The Vice President the other day questioned his judgment, saying he had been wrong on your most important decision of the Presidency, the Persian Gulf war. Do you share their assessments?

*The President.* I'm glad that they are putting their focus on these problems, but I'm not going to do it myself. I have a difference clearly as far as the Persian Gulf war goes, no question. I think the American people support the actions that I took. I believe it was correct. I believe we performed well. I believe we set back aggression. I believe there was a whole new pride in this country. The international community supported it overwhelmingly.

So as people point these things out, that's fair. As his supporters point out what they think might be foibles in me, that's fair, too. but I'm going to stay on the path that I've outlined.

*Balanced Budget*

*Q.* Mr. President, the amendment you're talking about would require a balanced budget within 2 years. If you're reelected, will you submit a balanced fiscal 1994 budget whether or not you're required to by a constitutional amendment?

*The President.* It won't be—of course, we have submitted a balanced—but it won't be in 2 years. We have submitted budgets that get in it; we've got one right up there now that does that. I think it's going to be 5 years.

### U.N. Conference on Environment

*Q.* Mr. President, if the experience of your EPA chief in Rio to date is any indication, there's quite a reception committee of harsh critics of this administration and of you, sir, waiting for you down there. Under the circumstances, if that's what the reception is going to be in Rio, why go?

*The President.* Well, because we've got a sound and sensible environmental record and we have a strong role of international leadership.

I wonder if the American taxpayer knows that we have spent something like $800 billion in the last 10 years on cleaning up things, the atmosphere, environment, in many, many ways? It is estimated that it will be $1.2 trillion spent by the United States taxpayers and businesses over the next 10 years.

We have a superb record to take to that convention. I am not going to go down there and forget about people that need jobs in the United States of America. I'm going to take a strong record, the leading record on science and technology, the leading record on oceans, the leading record on forests, the leading records on protecting the elephant, the leading records on CFC's. We've got a good record. But because I will not sign a treaty that, in my view, throws too many Americans out of work, I refuse to accept that kind of criticism from what I consider some of the extremes in the environmental movement, internationally or domestically.

So we've got a record to take there, Brit [Brit Hume, ABC News]. And I want to go down there. We're passing out booklets and little CD's, you know, little discs to show everything. I was out at Goddard the other day. The science that we have that can help the Third World is mind-boggling. We want to share it with these people.

But I want to keep this country growing, and I want to see us have the cleanest, best record in the world. Besides that, we have a Clean Air Act that others ought to take a look at and say, "You've done wonders in getting what you did through, President Bush." So I'm going to go on the offense, not defense.

*Q.* Well, I'm just wondering, sir, clearly, many of those who are there are aware of the elements of your record and have come to the conclusions which they so vocally express anyway. How do you think this can be a plus for you down there?

*The President.* Well, hey, listen, I'm used to a little criticism. I want to go on the offense and say what we've done and what we're prepared to do. I wouldn't go along with the extremes in many of these international negotiations. But I have some responsibility, responsibility for a cleaner environment and also responsibility to families in this country who want to work, some of whom can be thrown out of work if we go for too costly an answer to some of these problems. I'm not going to forget the American family.

If they don't understand it in Rio, too bad. I'm not going to be driven though, Brit, by the extremes of these movements. They started protesting before they even know what our position was. But I'm going there and take this record, and I'm convinced that it will be very productive.

### The Economy

*Q.* Mr. President, you say your problems in the primaries have been caused largely by the anemic economy. Yet the economy is improving, and the voters seem to be walking away from you in droves, sir. Don't you take it personally, and what are you going to do about it?

*The President.* I don't take it personally. As a guy that never looks at polls, as you know, I would like to cite a poll figure for you: 70 percent of the people in the most recent poll I saw that was done for our campaign said that they thought the economy was getting worse. And the economy is moving. There's still some problems. As I say, when a person's hurting for a job, that worries me. But gross national product,

GNP is moving. Industrial production is up. Payroll employment is up. Another thing that's up and then soon will be picked up in these broad polls is that Michigan survey on business confidence. So things are turning around, and yet, at this juncture, the American people haven't felt it. When they do, I expect to see some change.

But no, I don't take it personally. I honestly don't, Ellen [Ellen Warren, Knight-Ridder].

*Q.* Aren't the American people——

*The President.* I've been in tough times before.

*Q.* Well, sir, aren't the American people right in holding you personally responsible for the problems of this country?

*The President.* Well, I think they hold me responsible to some degree, and I think they hold the United States Congress responsible. I would remind the people that Congress appropriates every dime and tells me how to spend every dime. It's the Congress that does that. But sure, I'll accept my share of the responsibility for this long recession, and so will the Congress.

But the question isn't blame, the question is what you do about it. I've proposed tonight: Let's move on the balanced budget amendment. Let's move on my growth initiatives that would stimulate investment, like cutting the capital gains, moving on the investment allowance that speeds up depreciation, first-time credit for homebuyers. This is all good and valuable stuff that would speed this economy up.

So I don't think it's a question of blame. It's a question of staying in this nonpolitical mode for a while longer, challenging the Congress to help us help the American people.

*Q.* Well, sir, the Congress hasn't passed all these programs you talked about——

*The President.* It's not too late. They ought to try now.

*Q.* So why don't you tell us what you really think about Ross Perot?

*The President.* What's that have to do with it? Come on.

### Yugoslavia

*Q.* Sir, you say that you have a strong international leadership role. But the new world order that you are promoting is being challenged in Yugoslavia these days. It appears that the sanctions are not working against Serbia. When are you going to take the lead of an international coalition to force Milosevic out of Bosnia, the way you did with Saddam Hussein out of Kuwait?

*The President.* I think the sanctions—I'm not prepared to give up on the sanctions at all. They've only been in effect for a few days. As you know, first on this question of Yugoslavia, out in front was the United Nations. You had Cyrus Vance as a representative of the United Nations, did a superb job trying to negotiate, ably supplemented, I might say, by Peter Carrington. They tried to work that problem, had our full support.

The EC, which is right there in the neighborhood, tried to have an effective role. It now appears that a U.S. role, catalytic role, is important. Thus, we are moving forward. Secretary Baker made a very strong statement on this recently, has worked closely with the leaders of Europe. So we are united in this sanctions question. Let's see if it works. But I'm not prepared to say these sanctions will not work.

*Q.* Is the fact that the elections are approaching in the U.S. preventing a military action?

*The President.* I think prudence and caution prevents military actions. If I decide to change my mind on that, I will do it in an inclusive way. But at this juncture I want to stay with these sanctions.

Wait a minute. Gene [Gene Gibbons, Reuters], I'm sorry. I recognized him and did not follow through.

### Balanced Budget

*Q.* Mr. President, your Budget Director yesterday laid out a number of ways of bringing the deficit under control, even without a balanced budget amendment. But all of them would require taking on tough pressure groups. You have not often seemed to use the bully pulpit of the Presidency to do that, to take a direct head-on approach. Why not?

*The President.* We've got the program up there. There are some 30 pages of options. You don't have to touch Social Security to do this, and I'm not going to do that. We have made growth assumptions in there that can be easily met—4, 4, 3.2, 3.2, 3.2, those are the percentages of growth—can easily be met if we move with partial growth agenda that I've proposed.

So I will keep repeating, as I did in the State of the Union Message, as I did subsequently right here in this room: Get the Congress to pass this growth agenda.

But that's what's needed, plus some direct controls of spending. You can do it by controlling the growth of these spending programs, leave out Social Security, to the rate of inflation and population increase. It's not a gimmick; it works. It's not rosy scenario; it works. That is my detailed proposal.

I'd like to see some other detailed proposals, but that is a good one. It's sitting up there right now. It won't be done if we don't control the growth of mandatory programs. That's where, what, two-thirds or close to three-fourths of the budget is.

*Q.* But the limits on mandatory programs would involve pain and sacrifice. And yet, neither you nor Mr. Perot nor Mr. Clinton talks about that. Has Presidential politics become so sound-bite driven that it's politically suicidal to level with the American people?

*The President.* I don't think it's suicidal. And I think our program up there that gives many suggestions as to how to achieve this is good. And yes, it's not easy. Medicare, Medicaid growth is going through the roof. And yes, we're going to have to find ways to control it. But what we've done is detail the areas that need to be controlled. I think that is a sensible, sound, detailed program.

Kathy [Kathy Lewis, Dallas Morning News].

### Ross Perot and POW–MIA's

*Q.* Mr. President, a fair amount has been written about Ross Perot's role with the Reagan administration on the POW–MIA issue, and it relates directly to you. If one news report is correct, he's going to testify on the subject soon. You said you won't characterize him, but can't you tell us what your dealings were with him on this issue?

*The President.* I will be prepared to elaborate on that later on. My dealings were: I was a member of the Reagan ad-

ministration. For a while he was over being quite helpful, trying to do something about the prisoners. What happened beyond that—I saw a detailed story today that I simply cannot comment on. Marlin Fitzwater, then the Press Secretary for President Reagan, is on the record at a public press conference commenting on the Perot role, so I would refer you to that. That was back in, I believe in '87. I'd rather leave it right there. But if he's going to explain this to the Congress, that's good. I hadn't heard that.

### Presidential Campaign

*Q.* Mr. President, in the interest of party unity and since he has indicated that he is going to endorse you at the Houston convention, would you like Pat Buchanan to have the prime-time speech that he wants to have at the Republican Convention in August?

*The President.* Susan [Susan Spencer, CBS News], I'll be honest with you, I haven't focused on that at all. I welcome the support of all Republicans. Let's see how he handles this, and let the people handling the convention work it out. That is not on my agenda.

*Q.* With the benefit of hindsight, do you think his primary challenge was damaging to you or helpful or what?

*The President.* Well, I can't say it was particularly helpful. But he got into a long line of people criticizing me, five on the Democratic side and one there. But maybe I'm a little stronger for it. Maybe I'm a little better—be a little better candidate when it comes to the fall. I did not engage with Pat Buchanan. I don't plan to do that now. But I'll grope around to see if I can think of some reason it's helpful. [*Laughter*] But I have no hard feelings about that at all.

### Iraq

*Q.* Mr. President, critics of yours on Capitol Hill have said your policies toward Saddam Hussein before the Gulf war strengthened him and made him more likely to make an attack against one of his neighbors. How do you respond to that? I've got a followup.

*The President.* I respond that that's not

right. As I said at my last press conference, we tried, not through strengthening his nuclear or biological or chemical weapons has been alleged, not by giving him part of Kuwait has been alleged, but we tried to work with him on grain credits and things of this nature to avoid aggressive action. And it failed. It failed. That approach, holding out a hand, trying to get him to renounce terrorism and join the family of nations didn't work. And the minute he moved aggressively, we moved aggressively and set back aggression.

You've got a lot of people that opposed what happened on the war, stood there and didn't want to move, that are now trying to revise history. So I am not persuaded by the critics at all. I know what we did. There wasn't anything illegal. We tried hard, and I've said so. It didn't work, but we were not going to let aggression stand. When he moved into Kuwait, I decided this will not stand, and it didn't.

Yes, what's the followup?

*Q.* The followup: The House Judiciary Committee looks like they're going to recommend special prosecutors and counsel, investigators, and ask the Attorney General to——

*The President:* I wonder whether they're going to use the same prosecutors that are trying out there to see whether I was in Paris in 1980 and flew home in an SR–71 Blackbird? I mean, where are we going with the taxpayers' money in this political year? So let them look at it. It's no problem to me.

But I think at some point somebody ought to say, "Where is all this money going that goes to pay for these special prosecutors rummaging through files and proving nothing?" I was not in Paris. And we did nothing illegal or wrong here. We tried, and it didn't work. We moved, and that's the answer to it.

*Presidential Campaign*

*Q.* Mr. President, since you know Ross Perot, if you were to run into him while you're out campaigning for reelection, for example, what would you say to him to convince him to——

*The President.* Support me?

*Q.* ——support you and give up his quest

for the Presidency? What would you say?

*The President.* Well, I'd say "Ross, I think I've been a good President. I believe that a man of your ability and talent ought to support me. We've known each other a long time; in my view, it's been favorable." And just leave it there. I would admit it might be a little bit of a long shot in persuading him.

*Q.* But if he said, "Well, George, I hear what you're saying. You want me to follow you, but you've got to tell me where you're going," what would you say?

*The President.* Oh, I'd say, "Let me refresh you on our domestic agenda. Please give me your support for the balanced budget amendment that we're trying to pass right now, and bring along Bill Clinton if you've got any influence on him. We're talking about issues here. We've got a tough crime bill before the Congress. Help me pass it. We've got an education reform bill that literally revolutionizes education. Give me a hand with this one. If you know anybody in the Congress—it appears you may—give them a call." I'd take this approach, you see, to him. I'd try to enlist his help on support for our approach to the environment. I'd say, "Help me help these democratic countries around the world. Help me help them secure their democracy."

You see, I think we have a good agenda, and that's the approach I'd take, anyway.

Yes, Frank [Frank Murray, Washington Times].

*Two-Party System*

*Q.* Mr. President, you've spent much of your life as part of the two-party system. You've headed one of the major parties. In this unusual political year, how do you assess the viability of the two-party system in the future? And why would any candidate submit himself to grueling primaries if he could just announce and run?

*The President.* I think the two-party system has really given us the most stable political system in the world. And yes, we're going through an unusual period. But the two-party system has provided us fantastic historical stability. You look around the world and compare this system with any other democratic system, and I think that would avail. I'm sure the Brits take great pride in their parliamentary system, but I think our two-party system has provided us with the stability that heretofore we've simply taken for granted.

So my view, as this campaign unfolds, as all of us spell out our position on the issues, people are going to recognize that, and the two parties will be strong when this election is over.

### Primary Elections

*Q.* And the question of why any candidate would expose himself to the primaries and——

*The President.* That's what Barbara was asking me a few minutes ago.

*Q.* What's your answer?

*The President.* Say, hey, I want to continue this job to help this country. I want to help preserve world peace and strengthen it, and we've done pretty well there. I want to move forward on these issues that we're talking about here tonight, the balanced budget amendment. I won't repeat them all, but it's worth finishing the job.

Nobody likes the primary process. I had a call from a Senator, kind of asking how I was holding up because, he said, "Hey, you've been criticized a little in the newspapers and on the television." And I said, "Hey, that goes with the job. I'll do my best, and I think things are going to turn around in that regard." But to get out of the arena, to suggest that you're not going to run because it's not particularly pleasant, that's not the way I operate.

### Abortion

*Q.* Mr. President, there are many polls that now show that in California and elsewhere that most Republicans favor the pro-choice position on abortion. And I wonder, in view of that and in view of the clear feeling of pro-choice in the party, that you feel the platform needs to be changed, and what your own view is on the whole notion of whether the abortion debate is going to be prominent in the fall?

*The President.* Well, no, I hope the platform committee, in their wisdom, adopts the same language as we had before. Having said that, there is room in our party

for people that have different views on this issue. I am not persuaded that people all across this country vote on only one issue, abortion. I think they're interested in world peace. I think they're interested in education. I think they happen to be very supportive of the balanced budget amendment. So my position is well-known, and I'm going to stay with it. But as I say, we've got many good Republicans who disagree with me on that issue, and they may disagree with me on the balanced budget amendment or some of these other things I feel very passionately about.

Jim [Jim Miklaszewski, ABC News].

### Presidential Campaign

*Q.* You mentioned a moment ago the polls, the 70-percent figure about the economy. But you know, the cold war is over; Desert Storm has become pretty much a faded memory for many Americans. And people are turning inward and asking, "Well, Mr. President, what have you done for us lately?" More than 80 percent of the American people now feel that the United States is on the wrong track. How, between now and November, are you going to convince Americans that they are better off than they were 4 years ago?

*The President.* Most Americans are fundamentally optimistic, and they're going to see a recovering economy. It may not be as robust as we all like, but they're going to say as they feel that and as they see new opportunities and see a growth in this economy, they're going to say, "Hey, things are getting better."

Americans aren't pessimists. They're not down on the country. We've been through a long haul. Then I'm going to say to them, "Hey, do your kids go to bed at night with more worry or less worry about nuclear war?" I think that's a significant change. I think most every, every family in America is better off for those historic changes that my predecessor and I helped bring about. I use the word "helped."

So you've got to look at the whole picture. And then I think they're going to say, "Here's what the President has been trying to get through the Congress." And I come back to it: the balanced budget amendment, strong crime, whatever it is, good record on the environment. "What's he up against here?" They're going to have a clear choice to make.

Then they're going to say, "Does this President identify with my views on family, and does he share the leadership traits that I want to see in a leader?" and those kinds of things. Those aren't in focus now. They're not in focus because five Democrats were out there just hammering away on the President of the United States. I smile and say, "Look, we'll meet you in the fall." And one Republican was doing the same thing every single night. Had some assistance out here from time to time from one or the other in the room.

You know, I'm putting my confidence in the people saying, "We're going to get something done," and take the case to the American people on the issues. That's the way I think you ought to do it.

*Q.* But Mr. President, they aren't anywhere near that right now, and as a matter of fact, some of your advisers are pretty alarmed at the fact——

*The President.* No, they're not alarmed.

*Q.* Well, while the economic figures are improving, your own poll numbers are on the decline. They are not associating you, sir, with any improvement in the economy.

*The President.* But 70 percent of the people, as I told you, Jim, according to one, I thought it was one of your surveys, seem to think the economy's getting worse. I think it's getting better. It takes a while; there's a lag there. Unemployment's a lagging indicator, for example. So it takes a while to see the change.

I haven't been in the playing field on the primaries. I've been trying to get something done for the country. But when we go to the country and say, "Do you want a strong crime bill, or do you want this watered-down variety that's up in the Justice Department controlled by the Democrats that have been there forever; which do you want?" I think the American people will support me.

I'll say to them, "Do you want a balanced budget amendment that will make the executive branch and the legislative branch do something about the deficits, or do you want a lot of reasons from some entrenched politicians on Capitol Hill to tell you why it can't be done?" And see, I think when that is in focus, I think that the American people will support me. I've tried to keep the faith with the people, and I think one heartening point is people see the President is a strong leader. They may not like the direction things are going in, but that is something that I find rather comforting.

*Q.* So you haven't been tough enough, is that what you're saying?

*The President.* I need your assistance, Jim, in getting out the message now tonight, loud and clear, on what the President said about the balanced budget amendment. If you can put an editorial or two on there saying this is a good idea, it would help enormously. I don't think you can do that. But if you could I'd welcome that kind of support, because that's what the American people want, and we've got to get that message to the Congress.

*Justice Clarence Thomas*

*Q.* Mr. President, you said that your problems stem from the economy. In addition, are some of your problems also related to the Clarence Thomas-Anita Hill hearings?

*The President.* None. We forgot. Now we see a revision. We forget that the American people overwhelmingly supported Clarence Thomas. He is being a good Justice. And the fact that some candidates are out there trying to revise that part of history, I'm sorry, I don't agree with that. There may be some. Now, I can't say that everyone agrees with what I said. I support Clarence Thomas. I think he'll be an outstanding Justice. He passed a Senate that is controlled by the opposition party. He conducted himself with honor in those hearings. And that's my position. I'm proud to have stayed with him when the going got tough.

*Presidential Campaign*

*Q.* Mr. President, you say that the leadership qualities that are going to come up later are not in focus right now, but it would seem that leadership is the focus. That's the only thing that Ross Perot has been running on, is leadership. He has not addressed the issues; you are addressing the issues. How do you feel, what do you say to

Republicans who are going over and supporting him about your personal leadership qualities?

*The President.* I say take a look at what happened in Desert Storm where I didn't have to get anybody else's action. I moved. I saw a threat. I did what was required. I didn't have to get a Congress controlled by the opposition party to move. The people saw leadership and action there.

The people know that the House of Representatives and the Senate control all the legislation. My crime bill, my balanced budget quest, whatever it is, they control it all. So I think when this campaign gets really rolling, and it hasn't started from our standpoint, when that happens, I think these things will be in focus.

So I understand the quest for change and the appeal, "I can bring you the new answer here." I can understand all that. But I also think the American people are pretty smart. I think they're going to look at the overall record. I think they're going to analyze the proposals. I think they're going to look at a person's overall values. I think then I have the confidence that it won't be just the Republicans that will be supporting me; it will be the guy in the neighborhood who's wondering, "Who's going to be the best to take care of the criminal elements here? Who's going to support the incentives to improve the economy?" That's what I think.

*Q.* Mr. President, aren't we into a no-win situation here? Because even if you do win, even if you do defeat Ross Perot, there are going to be a lot of Republicans out there who supported him, and there's going to be a lot of reprisal and revenge.

*The President.* There's no reprisals. Look, Americans—as Helen says, we're through here, but let me tell you something. You're dealing in a little cocoon here. We're talking about something big: faith and confidence in the American people. This isn't done because there's something on the horizon right now and people are going to—you know, let them decide. Let them sort out this.

I can understand that appeal, "I'm from outside; I'll solve all the problems." And some day you guys are going start: How are you going to do it? How are you going to get this through the Congress? What do you believe? Do you think the President's right on the balanced budget amendment? Are you with him or against him? Do you think he's right as he tries to tighten down on crime legislation? How do you feel on the narcotic problem? How do you feel on world peace? Were you with him when he had to make a very tough call on setting back aggression, a move that was saluted all over the entire world and put this country together like it's never been together in the past, since World War II?

You see, I think we're dealing in a funny time here, a time warp. I think, come fall, when we're out there taking our case to the people, with an improved economy behind us, I still feel confident about the outcome of the political election. I feel confident about ability to heal any wounds that may have been opened along the way.

Thank you all very much. Thank you, Helen.

*Note: The President's 129th news conference began at 8:01 p.m. in the East Room at the White House. During the news conference, the following persons were referred to: Slobodan Milosevic, President of Serbia; Cyrus Vance, Special Negotiator for the United Nations on Yugoslavia; and Lord Peter Carrington, Special European Community Negotiator on Yugoslavia. H.R. 4990, approved June 4, was assigned Public Law No. 102–298.*

# Exchange With Reporters Prior to Discussions With Prime Minister Gro Harlem Brundtland of Norway
*June 5, 1992*

*U.N. Conference on Environment*

*Q.* Mr. President, are you trying to undercut Mr. Reilly at Rio? There's a problem there.

*The President.* Mr. Reilly, the top environmentalist, has my full support. He conducts himself the way he should, with great dignity and great decency. That a document that he prepared properly was leaked, I find terribly offensive. I saw him today on the television this morning, and I thought he was outstanding. In fact, I'm trying to call him to tell him that.

*Q.* Who leaked it?

*The President.* I have no idea, and I wish you'd help us on that one.

*Q.* Someone from the Vice President's office, perhaps?

*The President.* No, listen, I don't have any idea. But if we get a little more cooperation out of the press that thrives on leaks, why, maybe we could stop it. It's an insidious——

*Q.* Have you got any memos I can have?

*The President.* ——an insidious practice. And Bill Reilly is one of the top environmentalists in the world. He had some suggestions to make. He did it in the proper way. And that he was put in an embarrassing position by the leaking of a document and the printing of a confidential document, I find very offensive. I don't like it, and he has my full support.

*Q.* Well, beyond the leaks——

*The President.* And as soon as I get him, I'll tell him. So we have a good—after all of those questions last night, we have a good, sound environmental record. We have spent $800 billion in the last 10 years, cleaning up the environment. We're going to spend $1.2 trillion in the next 10 years, and we're sharing the world's best technology with the rest of the world.

So we're going to keep on this path, and the fact that some in the environmental movement have some difference with us has to be anticipated. That's to be expected. But we've got an outstanding record, and I must, as President, and will as a human

being keep in mind the needs of American families to have jobs. I·am the one that is burdened with finding the balance between sound environmental practice on the one hand and jobs for American families on the other.

We're walking a tight line there. We've found the proper formulation for America, and that is my responsibility. I'll go down to Rio and proclaim the solid points of a sound environmental record. We want to share this technology and this experience with the rest of the world.

*Q.* Sir, speaking——

*The President.* ——anything to be apologetic for, and now I want to get the views from a sound environmental Prime Minister who has been to Rio, with whom we have a lot in agreement and maybe some differences. And that's the way we learn, and that's the way things get better. So if you'll excuse us, we had a press conference last night. I don't think you were able to attend, but it was a good one. We answered most of the questions.

Thank you very much. This is the end of this. Thank you.

*[At this point, one group of reporters left the room, and another group entered.]*

*Prime Minister's Visit*

*The President.* May I say to the Norwegian journalists how very pleased I am to once again see your outstanding Prime Minister, our friend, a person that I admire and respect and with whom we have many, many things in common. When we have differences, we can always discuss them very frankly, but they've been few and far between since I've been President. But I'm anxious to hear from her now on Norway's priorities, what she found at Rio, where I'm sure she had a role of real leadership.

I just wanted to take this opportunity to welcome her back to the White House and let the people at home know the high regard the Americans have for her and for her government and certainly for her country.

### Environmental Policy

*Q.* Mr. President, what's your comment on the criticism of the American position in Rio?

*The President.* Hey, I get criticized at home. I don't have to go to Rio to get criticized. [*Laughter*] So we're used to it. We have a very sound and, I think, forward-looking environmental record. But as I just explained to the preceding wave, I feel a real obligation and part of my duty as President to do two things: One, formulate sound environmental policy, take the world's best environmental technology, and that's the United States', and share it with the world; and then, on the other hand, worry about American families, people that need jobs. You have to find the balance between economic growth and sound environmental practice. I'm convinced the two can go hand in hand.

So that's what we try to do, and I think some from the environmental movement don't understand this. Some from other countries have different priorities in terms of the unemployment numbers and all of this. So some in the Third World have differences in terms of how much resource can be given to them in terms of money.

So we've got all kinds of nuances of difference here, but I'm very proud of our record and of our environmental chief, Mr. Bill Reilly, who is down there. And I realize that in some areas people look at things differently than we do.

But I've got these two priorities: jobs and economic growth, the biggest economic engine in the world, and—it grows, it throws off much more funds to do it, to help other people with. Has to do that, and I'd have to be concerned about the families that are hurting when it's not growing properly.

Secondly, we spent $800 billion improving the environment in this country, $800 billion in the last 10 years. And it's going to be $1.2 trillion in the next decade. That's industry, government, everything. Out of all that, we learn a great deal technologically, and we're prepared to share that, our science and our technology, with the rest of the world. So we've got a good record. That's my answer, and we're so glad you all are here.

Now, we're going on to do a little business.

*Note: The exchange began at 10:40 a.m. in the Oval Office at the White House. A tape was not available for verification of the content of this exchange.*

# Statement by Press Secretary Fitzwater on the President's Meeting With Prime Minister Gro Harlem Brundtland of Norway
*June 5, 1992*

The President met for approximately 40 minutes this morning with Prime Minister Gro Harlem Brundtland of Norway. They discussed the Rio environmental conference, from which Prime Minister Brundtland had just come, and the roles of technology, alternate sources of fuel, and policies that are both environmentally and economically sound. The President stressed the strong leadership role the United States has played and his continuing commitment to improving the environment.

The two leaders also reviewed various issues of European security and agreed on the importance of U.S. global leadership and a continuing strong U.S. military presence in Europe as essential to peace and stability.

# White House Statement on the Ratification of the International Covenant on Civil and Political Rights
*June 5, 1992*

The President has signed the United States instrument of ratification of the International Covenant on Civil and Political Rights. A United Nations treaty, the Covenant articulates the principles inherent in a democracy, including freedom of expression and peaceful assembly, equal protection under the law, and the right to liberty and security.

By ratifying the Covenant, the United States is underscoring its commitment to these principles at home and abroad. We hope that our ratification of the Covenant will contribute to the fostering of democracy and human rights throughout the world.

# Message to the Congress on the National Emergency With Respect to Yugoslavia
*June 5, 1992*

*To the Congress of the United States:*

On June 1, 1992, pursuant to section 204(b) of the International Emergency Economic Powers Act (50 U.S.C. 1703(b)), and section 301 of the National Emergencies Act (50 U.S.C. 1631), I reported to the Congress by letters to the President of the Senate and the Speaker of the House, dated May 30, 1992, that I had exercised my statutory authority to issue Executive Order No. 12808 of May 30, 1992, that declared a national emergency and blocked "Yugoslav Government" property and property of the Governments of Serbia and Montenegro.

On May 30, 1992, the United Nations Security Council adopted Resolution No. 757 calling on member states to impose a comprehensive economic embargo against the Federal Republic of Yugoslavia (Serbia and Montenegro). Today I have taken additional steps to ensure that the economic measures we are taking with respect to the Federal Republic of Yugoslavia (Serbia and Montenegro) conform to United Nations Security Council Resolution No. 757 of May 30, 1992.

Specifically, pursuant to the International Emergency Economic Powers Act (50 U.S.C. 1701, *et seq.*), the National Emergencies Act (50 U.S.C. 1601, *et seq.*), section 1114 of the Federal Aviation Act of 1958, as amended (49 U.S.C. App. 1514), section 5 of the United Nations Participation Act of 1945, as amended (22 U.S.C. 287c), and section 301 of title 3 of the United States Code, I have issued a second Executive order, "Blocking Property of and Prohibiting Transactions with the Federal Republic of Yugoslavia (Serbia and Montenegro)," a copy of which is enclosed.

Among other things, the order that I have issued on this day:

- prohibits exports and imports of goods and services between the United States and the Federal Republic of Yugoslavia (Serbia and Montenegro), and any activity that promotes or is intended to promote such exportation and importation;

- prohibits any dealing by a U.S. person in connection with property originating in the Federal Republic of Yugoslavia (Serbia and Montenegro) exported from the Federal Republic of Yugoslavia (Serbia and Montenegro) after May 30, 1992, or intended for exportation to any country, and related activities;

- prohibits transactions related to transportation to or from the Federal Republic of Yugoslavia (Serbia and Montenegro), or the use of vessels or aircraft registered in the Federal Republic of Yugoslavia (Serbia and Montenegro), by U.S. persons or involving the use of U.S.-registered vessels and aircraft;

- prohibits the granting of permission to any aircraft to take off from, land in, or overfly the United States if that aircraft is destined to land in or take off from the territory of the Federal Republic of Yugoslavia (Serbia and Montenegro);
- prohibits the performance by any U.S. person of any contract in support of certain categories of projects in the Federal Republic of Yugoslavia (Serbia and Montenegro);
- continues to block all property of the Government of the Federal Republic of Yugoslavia (Serbia and Montenegro), as well as assets of the former Government of the Socialist Republic of Yugoslavia, located in the United States or in the possession or control of U.S. persons, including their foreign branches; and

- clarifies the definition of the Federal Republic of Yugoslavia (Serbia and Montenegro).

Today's order provides that the Secretary of the Treasury, in consultation with the Secretary of State, is authorized to take such actions, including the promulgation of rules and regulations, as may be necessary to carry out the purposes of the order.

The declaration of the national emergency made by Executive Order No. 12808 remains in force and is unaffected by today's order.

GEORGE BUSH

The White House,
June 5, 1992.

*Note: The Executive order is listed in Appendix E at the end of this volume.*

## Appointment of Laura M. Melillo as Special Assistant to the President and Deputy Press Secretary
*June 5, 1992*

The President today announced the appointment of Laura M. Melillo as Special Assistant to the President and Deputy Press Secretary. She would succeed Gary Foster.

Since 1987, Ms. Melillo has served in various capacities at the White House in the Office of the Press Secretary. She has served as Staff Assistant, 1987–89; Assistant Press Secretary and Television Coordinator, May 1989 to present; and Director of the Lower Press Office in overseeing the daily operations of the Press Office, August 1989 to present.

Ms. Melillo graduated from Miami University in Oxford, OH (B.S., 1987). She was born March 21, 1965, in Louisville, KY, and resides in Alexandria, VA.

## Statement by Press Secretary Fitzwater on Space-Based Global Change Observation
*June 5, 1992*

President Bush last week approved a National Space Policy Directive establishing a focused national effort to improve the world's ability to detect and document changes in the Earth, especially the global climate.

This policy directive, which was developed by the National Space Council chaired by Vice President Quayle:

- Establishes a comprehensive, multiagency effort to collect, analyze, and archive space-based observations on global change. This Space-Based Global Change Observation System (S–GCOS) will be led by NASA with participation from other Government Agencies.

• Directs that NASA's Earth Observing System (EOS) be developed using small and intermediate-sized satellites. Through the use of advanced technology and reduced design complexity, these satellites can be acquired more quickly and at less cost than previously planned. This will allow the timetable for obtaining critical data on global change to be accelerated.

• Assigns global change observation functions, including the development of technology, the collection of data, and the archiving of information, to NASA and the Departments of Energy, Commerce (NOAA), Interior, and Defense.

• Encourages international cooperation in global change observation from space and directs the Department of State to provide support to the implementing Agencies.

This directive augments previous Presidential directives and recognizes the recommendations of the Earth Observing System Engineering Review Panel.

# Radio Address to the Nation on the Balanced Budget Amendment
*June 6, 1992*

I want to talk to you today about a big idea, a big change in the way your Government works. For the past 12 years, President Reagan and I have tried to get Congress to act responsibly and restrain Federal spending. We've tried compromise. We've tried confrontation. And we've tried quiet diplomacy with the leaders of Congress. None of this has been enough. And so, my friends, the time has come to take some commonsense action. We must pass a constitutional amendment mandating a balanced budget.

For most of our Nation's history, there was an unwritten rule against deficit financing, against saddling future generations with a mountain of debt. But in recent times, we've moved away from that. Now, we're borrowing from the future to pay for indulgences of the present. Our future is at stake. To ensure long-term economic growth, we must get Federal spending under control.

I've called for big changes in many areas, reforms in how this Nation's gridlocked capital does business. Right now, we're coming out of tough times. The American people know that budget deficits threaten the long-term economic health of our country. Over the years, we've accumulated Federal debt totalling $65,000 for every family of

four. This doesn't create more wealth. It merely helps pay for our current consumption. And that's like taking out a car loan and never buying a car.

To make our economic future strong, the balanced budget is where we must start. Beginning well before I became your President, I have fought for a balanced budget amendment. As a matter of fact, on February 9th, 1989, the very first legislative proposal that I made as President was for Congress to adopt a balanced budget constitutional amendment. In each of the three budgets I've submitted since, I've repeated that plea.

Why am I so fiercely dedicated to this issue? Look at your own family. You know what happens when you spend more than you make. The devil's going to come demanding his due. Well, that's what our American family faces right now.

When you hear about a deficit measured in hundreds of billions of dollars, remember that's not "Monopoly" money. Some day, that debt must be paid with your money, as sure as your own personal debts will have to be paid with your money. It's unacceptable when this spending riptide has us drowning in debt, dragging us further out to sea.

This amendment will bring us back to

shore. Forty-four States already have some type of constitutional balanced budget requirement. Eighty percent of the American people want this amendment and the tougher scrutiny of Government spending which it will require.

We're fed up. We know it's time for partisan posturing to yield to responsibility to govern. It's time to stop treating our Federal Treasury like the corner cash machine.

Thomas Jefferson's words still ring true: "I place public debt as the greatest of the dangers to be feared." Today, we have within our grasp the power to conquer that fear. The key to this is twofold: We must control reckless Government spending, and we must encourage economic growth.

Last January, I proposed a solid, common-sense action plan to create jobs and stimu-late economic growth for the short term. Congress still needs to act on that plan and act now. A balanced budget amendment will help ensure economic security for the American people in the long term. Congress needs to act on that measure and act now.

We have a moral imperative to act on behalf of future generations. They are not yet here to represent themselves. It's time to protect our children and our children's children. And we're determined to enact this solemn bond between generations.

May God bless you and our great Nation.

*Note: This address was recorded at 10:03 a.m. on June 5 in the Cabinet Room at the White House for broadcast after 9 a.m. on June 6.*

## Remarks on the Arrival of Prime Minister John Major of the United Kingdom at Camp David, Maryland
*June 6, 1992*

Prime Minister and Mrs. Major, let me just give you a hearty welcome back to Camp David.

Forty-eight years ago today, Ike and Monty, Churchill and FDR, Allied soldiers, sailors, marines, and airmen, heroes all, forged the greatest armada in the history of man, the D-day invasion. Our goal was a legacy of peace. And to achieve it, we first had to win a war. June 6th, 1944, told the world that aggression will not stand. So it's fitting that the Prime Minister and I meet on this historic anniversary of a new beginning in Europe to talk about our countries' enduring special relationship and the future challenges that we face in this promising new world.

Already we've responded to each other not with just the formal handshake of two allies but with the embrace of two friends. And we meet as leaders of nations joined by a common culture and civilization, recalling how Dwight Eisenhower, beloved in Britain and America, once said of freedom, "To preserve it, the Londoner will fight, and so will the citizen of Abilene."

Over more than four decades of the cold war, we reaffirmed our relationship. Then came the Persian Gulf where, again, we stood fast so that liberty could prevail. Years from now, people will still marvel at British and American heroism in Operation Desert Storm. People will also note how the last year reaffirmed the strength of our alliance, the value of the rule of law, and that England will always be our friend.

Our Nation sprang from England's belief in the sanctity of the individual. Today, that belief has never been stronger, our alliance never firmer, our desire never deeper to build a free and peaceful world.

So Mr. Prime Minister, let me thank you, sir, for your determination and Britain's example to the world. Welcome back to the U.S.A., and I look forward to discussing a wide array of subjects with you in the couple of days ahead.

Thank you very much for coming our way again.

*Note: The President spoke at 4:05 p.m.*

# The President's News Conference With Prime Minister John Major of the United Kingdom at Camp David
*June 7, 1992*

*The President.* Let me just say that from our standpoint we've had a wonderful visit with the Prime Minister, covered a wide array of subjects, and managed to get in a couple of hours of relaxation after working some yesterday and then again this morning. So it's been a very good visit.

Mr. Prime Minister, a delight having you here, sir.

*The Prime Minister.* Well, Mr. President, thank you. I just want to thank you and Mrs. Bush for your hospitality. It's been a great weekend. We've had quite a few hours to talk as well as enjoy ourselves. A large number of subjects have been covered. I think perhaps it's best just to answer questions.

*The President.* Why don't we try to rotate them just so it might divide up the workload a little bit.

### Joint Session of Congress

*Q.* Newt Gingrich wants you to call a joint session of Congress, a special session to address the Nation's problems, to which Clinton and Perot would be invited as a symbol of unity. Do you go along with that? Do you think that's a good idea?

*The President.* Well, I hadn't heard the suggestion before, but let me think about it. I hadn't discussed—what would be the subject? I literally haven't had anything on this at all.

*Q.* Did you get the memorandum from him that——

*The President.* I haven't seen the memorandum from him. If it was part of that, then that's probably why.

### U.N. Conference on Environment

*Q.* Prime Minister, can I ask if you tried to persuade the President to change his mind about not signing the biodiversity treaty, and if you did, whether you met with any success?

*The Prime Minister.* We certainly had the opportunity of discussing Rio in all its aspects. And there are a number of areas where everyone is going to be able to sign

the conventions that are there in Rio. We have problems with the biodiversity convention as well as the United States. We have problems with some of the financial proposals and some other allied problems as well. I think we'll probably be able to solve them. But the difficulties that we instinctively see with them are a good deal less than those that the United States face.

### Presidential Campaign

*Q.* Mr. President, Prime Minister Major survived a challenge; he was an underdog in his campaign. Did he give you any advice on how to come from behind in your situation?

*The President.* Yes, a lot of good advice. Just stay with it.

*Q.* Just stay with it?

*The President.* Actually, he gave me—I don't know that he gave me specific advice on the campaign, but he set an example that I think bodes well for me. You've cited some of it. He was behind, had a lot of pundits out there suggesting he wouldn't win, and he won. So that's a pretty good example right there. It was a wonderful victory, and he was not discouraged when polls showed him not winning.

*Q.* If I may follow, sir, Senator Dole this morning on "Meet the Press" said that he thinks you need a different message. You're talking about change. He says that you should say, "Give me a Republican Congress or elect a Democrat President." Would you be willing to tell the voters that?

*The President.* Absolutely. But I'd like to say I would leave out the second part. [*Laughter*]

*Q.* That's the key part, though, sir.

*The President.* No, it's not, not as far as I'm concerned because, you see, I think our ideas and the ideas that Senator Dole believes in and I believe in are in accord with the thinking of the American people. I found that when I can take action as President that didn't require the Congress, that was seen as strong leadership, strong, incisive leadership. But when you get into a Congress that's divided, and particularly in this year when politics is the name of the game, then it's very different. So what I will be doing is taking that case to the American people in the fall.

Right now, I'm trying to get a few things through the Congress, and that requires bipartisan support, like the balanced budget amendment, trying to get that done; like educational reform, trying to get that done; anticrime legislation, trying to get that done.

So we have a little period in here where I will stay with that tack, will not get into going after either opponent and going after the Congress. But in the fall, I think Senator Dole is on to something for that.

*Q.* Mr. President, what——

*The President.* This is for the Prime Minister. Who has got one for——

*Q.* For you, sir, not for the Prime Minister.

*The Prime Minister.* I'm having an easy ride.

*Q.* It's actually a question for both of you.

*The Prime Minister.* I'll start then.

*The President.* That's good.

### U.N. Conference on Environment

*Q.* The question is, what is the difference between the United States and the rest of the G–7 over the biodiversity treaty?

*The Prime Minister.* Well, we all have different problems with the biodiversity treaty, with the biodiversity convention, on the levels of technology transfer, on the protection of intellectual property. Those are the areas of detail where particular problems arise. There's a great deal of difficulty for many of us in some of the financial proposals on biodiversity. They seem to call for very substantial commitments without, perhaps, some of the commitments as to how and where the money is going to be used. Now, I think we will be able to solve those, but our problems are different from those of the United States.

*The President.* And just to follow on, our problem is very much like the Prime Minister said, protection of intellectual property. And we do not have an open pocketbook. We cannot enter into something if we don't keep the commitment, and the financing arrangements are too open-ended for us on the biodiversity treaty.

Our answer on the positive side is to put much more emphasis on sound forestation. We've got a good record in that in the United States. We think that a good forestry program will take care of a lot of the needs, the biodiversity needs. So, though I will not sign that treaty as it sits on the table now, we will continue to be the leader, or a leader, a world leader in terms of forests and in terms of environmental technology.

So I have nothing to be apologetic for. I also have to be the one at this Conference that is responsible for jobs and people being at work in this country. I plan to fulfill my responsibilities in that regard while still taking a good, strong, forward-looking environmental message to Rio.

*Q.* Mr. President, on that point, sir, I know you said you have nothing to apologize for U.S. environmental policy at Rio, but how do you answer those who say that your objections to the biodiversity treaty and your watering down of the global warming treaty have more to do with American domestic politics than environmental policy?

*The President.* I say this on the climate change: We're not going to enter into commitments we don't keep. I will repeat: We have spent $800 billion cleaning up the air. We've got the Clean Air Act, which is the most forward-looking environmental legislation perhaps anywhere in the world. But I'm not going to make commitments that we simply cannot keep.

I think most people feel that the climate change treaty is a good one, and they're signing it. They wouldn't sign it if they didn't think it was good, and I think you're going to see the world sign on to it. But if your question is, do I have to also consider the working man and woman in this country and the families that could be thrown out of work by too many commitments, commitments we can't keep, or making our products noncompetitive in world markets, I do have to be worried about that. I am not going to sign—we didn't on global climate change go forward with something that we would not keep, commitments we wouldn't keep. So I think we're on a sound environmental wave here. Now, there are many groups and some countries that wish we'd gone further. But I've given you the reasons, and I'm not going to change.

### Trident Missile System

*Q.* Mr. Prime Minister, did you seek from the President any assurance that he would not share early warning technology with the former Soviet Union to the extent that the British deterrent no longer would be one? And could I ask the President what his response would be if Mr. Yeltsin presses him for the inclusion of the Trident missile system in any further arms reductions?

*The Prime Minister.* Well, let me answer since it's our missile system that's concerned, and I guess it's for us to include any missile system in any talks. And the Trident missile system is not going to be involved in any talks at this stage. It's absolutely central to our defense, it's crucial to our defense, is now, has been for some time, will be for some time in the future. And until the thresholds of nuclear weapons elsewhere are a good deal lower, there's no question of the British Government including Trident in any talks.

*The President.* And may I just add to that, it is not the policy of the United States to try to deal on the nuclear deterrent of the United Kingdom or France or anybody else. They know this; the Russian leader knows this. And so if he should raise it, which he won't, I would simply say I am not prepared to discuss this. This is a matter for discussion with the leaders of these various countries, not the United States.

*The Prime Minister.* And in any event, I had the opportunity of discussing that with President Yeltsin in London last year, so he knows the position.

### Ethnic Strife

*Q.* Mr. President, there's an arc of crisis from Kiev extending all the way through to the southern tier of Uzbekistan. Yugoslavia is involved in a hopeless civil war; the Czechs appear in danger of a political schism. Denmark's rejected the Common Market, and Saddam Hussein's still in power. Whatever happened to the new world order?

*The President.* The new world order is not facing one common objective, an aggressive international communism. That is gone, and out of the demise of that highly centralized philosophy and government in the Soviet Union comes some historic ethnic challenges and the kinds of struggling for sovereignty and democracy that you've just mentioned. These are growing pains, it seems to me. And what we want to do as the United States, and I know the United Kingdom feels the same way because we've talked about this today, we'd like to be catalysts for peace and catalysts to see this move towards democracy continue.

But nobody said that the emergence of freedom would be easy. What's different is we are not facing one aggressive international Communist force; that's what's entirely different. Democracy is on the move in these various countries you talk about. I don't know that any one of them wants to now turn its back on democracy, and some of those who have not been particularly democratic are saying they are.

So that's the positive side. But I am concerned about some of the ethnic strife, some of the struggles you mentioned. I am not as concerned on the Maastricht matter. I think that's a matter for the Europeans themselves to sort out. But when you have fighting and tensions based on ancient, sometimes ethnic animosity or ethnic pride, whatever, we'd like to be catalysts for peace; we'd like to find ways to help. And that's our role. But there's a tremendous difference than what it was a few years ago, tremendous.

*Q.* On that subject, there is a study——

*The President.* The next question is for the Prime Minister.

*Q.* There are conflicting reports in the British press about your plans to bail out or not bail out on pensions. Can you clear up the confusion?

*The Prime Minister.* There will be a statement made in the House early next week. I think it better wait for that.

### Disclosure of Confidential Information

*Q.* Mr. President, I know you're unhappy with leaks within your White House official family.

*The President.* So what's new? [*Laughter*]

*Q.* And some friends of Bill Reilly's are pointing a finger at the Vice President's office. Do you intend to try to find the source of that leak?

*The President.* John [John Cochran, NBC News], I find it extraordinarily difficult to find leakers. It is extraordinarily difficult. I'd like to find the leaker, and I'd like to see the leaker filed—fired. Filed would be all right. No, but the reason is it's very difficult to conduct government if somebody in his or her infinite wisdom can shape the decision by leaking documents. The debate and the discussion that should take place doesn't.

This was a very unhelpful leak. Bill Reilly was doing what he should, sending up here in confidence suggestions where we might be able to change the, I believe it was the biodiversity treaty, in order to have total harmony there. Some of the suggestions were, turns out, were not ones that we could accept. But he did it right; he put a confidential memo in. Then for someone, who may or may not have been opposed to the treaty or any changes, to leak it, it's insidious.

I know many people in the press thrive on this. This is good journalism to find it out. All I'm saying is I would go after the leaker if I could because it's bad government. It's very difficult to conduct sound and sensible policy when the lowest common denominator in some office in the vast bureaucracy can release a document. But how you find it, how you find a person that is that low and that determined to disrupt, I don't know. It's real bad. It does not help conduct sound policy.

And I can't say there's any national security at stake on this; there's not. But it was just mischievous and bad, and I told Bill Reilly that. I said, "You did it right." And I apologized for lack of discipline wherever it is, whatever Agency.

*Q.* Mr. Reilly said that he was not going to resign to give satisfaction to his enemies. This was leaked by somebody who is supposedly friendly to you.

*The President.* Well, help me find him, John. Help me find him. He'd be gainfully unemployed.

### Assistance for Russia

*Q.* Reverting to Russia, are you happy that the IMF package is on course for implementation? Are you worried that objections in Congress and perhaps delays in the Soviet, or in Russia in undergoing economic reform is going to hold it up?

*The Prime Minister.* Well, there are two components, aren't there? The IMF package and its implementation has to be dependent upon the Russians continuing with their reform program. That's what the IMF package is there for. So we want to see them continue with the reform program. Subject to that, we certainly want to see the package implemented as soon as possible.

### Haiti

*Q.* Mr. President, a question for both of you. First you, Mr. President. Are you prepared to send U.S. troops to Haiti in a peacekeeping force if that is to come about?

*The President.* No, not yet. And I'm hopeful we can find a way to have the OAS sanctions be effective, to have Aristide returned to power, and to have democracy reinstalled. Our major concern is the fact that democratic government has been overthrown. And it sets a bad example in a hemisphere that's moving inexorably towards full democracy. So I'm not thinking about force and troops at this point.

*Q.* I have a followup but on a different subject.

*The President.* In other words, two questions.

### Czechoslovakia

*Q.* But it's for both of you. Can you both respond—could you respond to the elections in Czechoslovakia, and what do you think that bodes for the country?

*The Prime Minister.* Well, I was in Czechoslovakia just last week. And there was a suggestion then that Mecair would do very well in Slovakia and that Klaus would do very well in the Czech lands. The last I saw of the way the results were coming out, that was pretty much the case.

I think the important question is the extent to which they're going to compromise to produce a satisfactory federal government. It seems to me it's very much in the interest of Czechoslovakia that there should be a federal government. They've recently reached an agreement with the European Community about an association agreement with the Community, which is of some importance to them and of value to the Community. We see it as a preparatory step to Czechoslovakia becoming a full member of the Community, though that is obviously quite a few years away. But that deal is with Czechoslovakia. It isn't with two separate parts of Czechoslovakia; it is with Czechoslovakia as a whole. So we want to see them form a satisfactory federal government. The discussions I had with Czech politicians from many parties just a week or so ago suggests to me that they will seek to achieve that.

*The President.* We had some discussion, and I have no differences, obviously, with the Prime Minister on this question. I talked to President Havel a long time ago about this, and this matter of separation has been widely debated and talked about. So I would stay with what Prime Minister Major said.

### Eastern Europe and Yugoslavia

*Q.* Mr. President, for both of you on the subject Eastern Europe and Yugoslavia, what did you discuss specifically with respect to Yugoslavia, the activities of NATO? You mentioned that you want the United States and European nations to be a catalyst. Did you discuss a more active role for NATO and NACC and anything that you're going to carry back, perhaps, to NATO and to the G–7?

*The President.* Well, we discussed a wide array of aspects of the problem. One we talked about a lot was the humanitarian aspects. We are very concerned, and we must be willing to find a way to help in a humanitarian sense.

Obviously, we talked about a wide array of options, but we didn't settle on any new course of action; it would be presumptuous for us to try to do that here. But we are going to stay with the sanctions and see where we go from the U.S. standpoint.

*Q.* Mr. Prime Minister, do you seek a more active role?

*The Prime Minister.* No. I think the President set out the position of our discussions this morning. We strongly supported the binding sanctions. We think we'll have to sit with the binding sanctions for a while. Clearly, we are concerned about what's happening in Sarajevo and elsewhere. We're obviously concerned about the humanitarian aspect of making sure there's food and medicine and other necessary help there. It's not immediately easy to see how that's going to be achieved, and we'll have to watch and see what can be done there. But on the substantive question, we stick with the sanctions, and we make them tough. I think that's clearly the way ahead in the short term.

*The President.* Marlin said we've got time for one each. Go ahead.

### The Economy

*Q.* Mr. President, were you surprised by the disappointing jobless figures on Friday? To what degree does that change your assessment on the economy, and will it hurt consumer confidence?

*The President.* One, I was a little surprised. Two, I noted with some reassurance that the total number of jobs went up by some 68,000. Secondly, employment, regrettably, is an historic lagging indicator in terms of recovery. Thirdly, no, I believe the recovery is at hand, and I think we're going to see a second quarter stronger than the first. But psychologically, it is certainly not good, and I would just say that I didn't think it would be 7.5 percent.

I'll say one other thing about that particular set of indicators. Normally, you go back and look in the history, punch out the Lexis or whatever, and you'll find that there's always a reappraisal one way or another of those particular figures. I don't know what will happen on those, but I still feel the economy is recovering, and I believe it's going to be a more robust of a recovery in the second quarter than it was in the first.

### British Royal Family

*Q.* Mr. Prime Minister, how worried are you about damage to the Royal Family from today's revelations in the Sunday Times?

*The Prime Minister.* Well, I'm not going to comment on the unsubstantiated rumors that I gather have been published today.

I've not had a chance to look at them in any depth. I would, I think, simply say this: The monarchy is very deeply rooted in the affections of the British, and so are the present Royal Family. And I see nothing that's going to change that.

### Presidential Campaign

*Q.* Did you discuss Ross Perot, either of you?

*The President.* I cannot tell a lie; his name came up.

*Q.* And what did you say about him?

*The President.* That's where I'll cut it off. We're not going to say what we said. Look, anybody looking at the American political scene is going to wonder about that. Without drawing the Prime Minister of the U.K. into the domestic politics of the United States, I would simply say I told him I feel confident of winning. I do better when I'm fighting. I do better when I'm coming from behind. I'm also one who remembers 4 years ago, maybe to this very minute, being 17 points back.

So this is a weird year, and I shared those sentiments with the Prime Minister. But he was enough of a leader and diplomat not to editorialize too much on that. He listened, I thought, with great fascination. It might have been with boredom; I don't know. But nevertheless, you know, of course that comes up. But let the American people sort all that out. For now, I'm going to try to keep on doing substantive things, both in the foreign policy area and domestic. Then we'll switch over when the time comes; then I'll be out there rolling shirt sleeves up and go to work in the political arena. And whoever's in there is going to be in for a good battle.

*Q.* But does it bother you that the public mood seems as sour now as it was in 1980 when the public voted Jimmy Carter out of office?

*The President.* I hadn't made that comparison.

*Q.* Any advice you'd offer in public, Prime Minister Major?

*The Prime Minister.* Not in public.

### Gulf War Friendly-Fire Victims

*Q.* Mr. Bush, a final question. Do you think there's anything you can do to reassure the British families of the friendly-fire victims who don't feel that you've lived up to your promises to them?

*The President.* I'll take that question, because I, the first place, saw what the Prime Minister said in the House, and I was very grateful for that. I talked to those families with a heavy heart; they had broken hearts. And we've looked into that matter. I hope we've provided all the information. But I am not going to go further than this. These are good young men. I was in combat myself, and I have seen, in front of my own eyes, the victim of friendly fire. So I know that these horrible things can happen.

What I tried to do is to console those grieving relatives when they were in the White House, and then to follow through to be sure that our Secretary of Defense provided his counterpart with whatever information would be required to get the facts out on this particular case.

But my heart goes out to the families. It did back then when I talked to them. It does now. But I see no reason to go beyond what we have already done in trying to fully account for this terrible tragedy, a tragedy of war.

*Note: The President's 130th news conference began at 4:05 p.m. at Camp David, MD. During the news conference, the following persons were referred to: Jean-Bertrand Aristide, ousted President of Haiti, and Czechoslovakian parliamentary candidates Vladimir Mecair of the Civic Democratic Party and Václav Klaus of the Movement for a Democratic Slovakia.*

## Remarks Prior to a Meeting With State Legislators
*June 8, 1992*

Welcome, all. Thank you very much for coming.

Let me just make a short statement here before we close the door and get into hearing from you all on this important amendment. But 44 States have constitutional provisions relating to a balanced budget. Passing a balanced budget amendment, in my view, is essential to the long-term economic health of this country. This is an idea whose time has come. We've been for it for a long, long time.

I want to hear from each of you as to how you think we can best get this done. But I appreciate your being here. It is priority. I think the country is sick and tired of deficits. This will help discipline the executive and the legislative branch, and we've got to get it done. So I appreciate your coming, and we'll see where we go here.

*Note: The President spoke at 11:15 a.m. in the Roosevelt Room at the White House.*

## Nomination of Mary Jo Jacobi To Be an Assistant Secretary of Commerce
*June 8, 1992*

The President today announced his intention to nominate Mary Jo Jacobi, of Mississippi, to be an Assistant Secretary of Commerce for Congressional and Intergovernmental Affairs. She would succeed Craig R. Helsing.

Since 1990, Ms. Jacobi has served as senior vice president at Group Public Affairs USA for the HSBC Group and all its U.S. operations, including Marine Midland Bank in New York, NY. Since 1985, she has served in several capacities with Drexel Burnham Lambert, Inc., in New York: senior vice president, 1990; member of the Board of Directors, 1989–90; first vice president, 1987–89; and corporate vice president, 1985–86. Ms. Jacobi has also served at the White House as Special Assistant to the President for Business Liaison, 1983–85, and as a member of the Presidential Advisory Committee on Trade Negotiations, 1986–88. She has also served at the Department of Commerce as Director of the Office of Business Liaison, 1982–83, and as executive assistant to the Associate Deputy Secretary, 1981–82.

Ms. Jacobi graduated from Loyola University in New Orleans (B.B.A., 1973) and from George Washington University (M.B.A., 1976). She was born December 7, 1951, in Bay St. Louis, MS. Ms. Jacobi currently resides in New York, NY.

## Appointment of Jeffrey W. Vogt as Special Assistant to the President for Public Liaison
*June 8, 1992*

The President announced today the appointment of Jeffrey W. Vogt as Special Assistant to the President for Public Liaison.

Since 1989, Mr. Vogt has served at the White House as Assistant Director (1989–90) and as Associate Director (1990–92) for the Office of Public Liaison. Mr. Vogt has served as the contact for the corporate, small business, and business association communities on economic and trade policy issues. Mr. Vogt previously served as a member of the President-elect's public affairs transition team; as finance director of Victory '88 at the Republican National Committee, 1988; and as national direct marketing coordinator for the George Bush for President campaign, 1987–88. Mr. Vogt is a former small business owner and has held other positions, which include: account

executive at the direct marketing firm of Stephen Winchell & Associates, 1985–86; sales representative for Coldwell Banker Real Estate, 1985–88; and finance director for the McMillan for Congress campaign in Bushnell, IL, 1984.

Mr. Vogt graduated from Colby College (B.A., 1984) in Waterville, ME. He was born June 18, 1962, in Grand Rapids, MI, and presently resides in Arlington, VA.

# Remarks Prior to a Meeting With Republican Congressional Leaders
*June 9, 1992*

*The President.* May I make just a comment while the cameras are here and first say that we are pushing from here, and I am grateful of the support around this table, for this balanced budget amendment, constitutional amendment. Now I'm told that the leadership on the Democratic side, trying to block the balanced budget amendment, are coming up with something they call the balanced budget act, which does not balance the budget. It does not require the adoption of a balanced budget, and it's kind of a stalking horse to give cover to Members who don't want to vote for the balanced budget amendment. And we've got to fight hard against it. I'm making phone calls.

The irony is that the Democratic leadership is fighting the balanced budget constitutional amendment, at the same time trying to ram through $2 billion in spending that's not required, all of which they declare an emergency so they can exempt it from the fiscal discipline of the budget act. And I think we've got to get that message out to the American people.

I will sign an emergency appropriation for areas that are affected by these recently declared Presidential disasters. I'd also support, as I know everybody here knows, money for summer jobs, additional money that could actually be spent if they agreed

to target it to the areas of actual need.

But I would just strongly urge our continuing opposition to these tactics up there and do something for the American people who are very much concerned about the deficit. And we're trying to get spending under control. And now we've got a real opportunity to show the American people we can do something.

I've approached this not in a partisan manner, working with many Democrats trying to get it through the House, the balanced budget amendment. And I'll keep doing that. But I really want to hear from you all in just a second as to how you feel we can get this one key job done, the same time making sure we're helping the cities in the sound way that we've proposed. They are not incompatible at all. So there we are.

*Q.* Do you think you're going to win?

*The President.* Well, we'll find that out from the leaders. I certainly hope so. The American people want it done. And here's a good, clear case to take to the Congress and say, look, the American people want this. Our troops are lined up solidly for it, advocating it, taking the case to the floor and elsewhere. But we've got to have some more bipartisan support for this.

Thank you all very much.

*Note: The President spoke at 9:50 a.m. in the Cabinet Room at the White House.*

## Remarks Prior to a Meeting With Business and Congressional Leaders
*June 9, 1992*

*Q.* Mr. President, you got a deal with the Russians today?

*The President.* We just had a chance to introduce Mr. Kozyrev to this distinguished group of Members of Congress, Senate and House, and to some of our outstanding business leaders. They're talking reform, and what we're talking here today on is reform. We want to see a balanced budget amendment passed; business leaders are joining Members of Congress and trying to get this done.

And so this is a rather unique meeting. We feel that creation of jobs and the economic prosperity of the American people are better served by the discipline on the budgeting process that would be brought to bear by a balanced budget amendment to the Constitution; discipline the executive branch, discipline the legislative branch. And so I'm hopeful that these business leaders and their colleagues will help us carry this message to the Hill. In their own baili-

wick, they've been out front strongly for this. And right around the table we have some of the leaders from the Congress, Democrat and Republican, who have been out front on this key question.

So we've got a lot of work to do, but I wanted it to resonate up on the Hill. This is a unique meeting to this Cabinet Room. And I'm very grateful to the business leaders that have taken the time to join these leaders in Congress who are out front on this key question.

So thank you all very much.

*Q.* Mr. President, is there——

*The President.* This is the end of the photo opportunity in which I prevailed with my speech. And no more questions. Thank you.

*Note: The President spoke at 11:05 a.m. in the Cabinet Room at the White House. In his remarks, he referred to Andrey Kozyrev, Foreign Minister of Russia.*

## Nomination of Frank G. Wisner To Be an Under Secretary of State
*June 9, 1992*

The President today announced his intention to nominate Frank G. Wisner, of the District of Columbia, a career member of the Senior Foreign Service, class of Career Minister, to be Under Secretary of State for Coordinating Security Assistance Programs. He would succeed Reginald Bartholomew.

From 1991 to the present, Ambassador Wisner has served as Ambassador to the Philippines in Manila. Prior to this he was Ambassador to the Arab Republic of Egypt, 1986–91. He was Deputy Assistant Secretary of State for African Affairs, 1982–86;

and Ambassador to the Republic of Zambia, 1979–82. He has also served in several positions at the Department of State: Deputy Executive Secretary, 1977–79; Director of the Office of Southern African Affairs, 1976–77; and Special Assistant to the Under Secretary, 1975–76.

Ambassador Wisner graduated from Princeton University (B.A., 1961). He was born July 2, 1938, in New York, NY. Ambassador Wisner is married, has four children, and resides in Manila, Philippines.

## Remarks at a Fundraising Dinner for Senator Arlen Specter in Bowmansdale, Pennsylvania
*June 9, 1992*

Thank you, Arlen, for that wonderfully warm introduction and, I might say at the top of these remarks, for being such a great United States Senator. It is essential that Arlen Specter be returned to office. May I just say that Barbara and I treasure our friendship with Joan and Arlen. We've known each other a long, long time. This isn't just kind of the normal political endorsement; I really mean it. There is a handful of United States Senators that really make things happen, that stand for principles, and that fight for his constituents. If you don't believe me, you ought to try riding in from the Philadelphia Airport, for example, into Philadelphia with Arlen. By the time you get there your arm is twisted out of its socket—*[laughter]*—he's brought up about eight proposals that will help Pennsylvania, and he never forgets how he got elected. He represents his constituents with honor and with principle. And you're very, very lucky to have him there.

May I thank Bob and Susan for this wonderful event. It's like being at the circus, and I'm not talking about all of you animals out there either. *[Laughter]* I'm just saying that it really is a wonderful way to campaign, and this beautiful countryside as we drove in made me want to count my blessings all over again. But thank you so much, to both of you, for hosting this wonderful dinner.

I know there are a lot of people to congratulate, but I congratulate Marilyn Ware Lewis and Alex Grass here who are the cochairmen of the dinner; salute my old friend and our State chairman, Elsie Hillman; another old friend who is with us tonight, a strong supporter of Arlen, the famous and wonderful Walter Annenberg who is here, right there. Barbara and I have been married 47 years, but every time she sees Walter, I worry a little bit about it. She re-falls in love with him. And I'm troubled by that. *[Laughter]* But we Bushes admire and respect him.

To Bob Jubelirer who is with us and Mi-

chael Ryan, it's good to see so many elected members of the Pennsylvania Legislature with us here; to Anne Anstine and Herb Barness, our national committee people. Barbara Hafer is with us; Ernie Preate. And I want to thank Tonia Tecce for the national anthem; the pledge, done well by those kids. I asked them if they were nervous; not at all. They did it well, not one glitch in the Pledge of Allegiance.

May I single out another old friend—I don't want to date him in terms of age, but we went to college around the same time. But I think he must have been behind me—Joe Paterno. What a wonderful representative. He remains an inspiration to me and to my boys and to our whole family. And I'm just delighted to be at his side once more.

Now, you all know why we're here tonight. We are here for Arlen Specter. Arlen spelled out the ground—they've got the craziest campaign rules, financing rules. Literally, I cannot talk to you, and I certainly will not, about why I want to be reelected President of the United States. However—*[laughter]*—I can talk to you tonight about why Arlen Specter should be reelected to the Senate and why our programs that we have before the United States Congress ought to be enacted. And that's exactly what I plan to do.

Arlen knows how hard and how frustrating it can be just to get things done, which is his motto, and he does it well. But in Washington, "Republican" has meant being outnumbered. I really believe if this economy keeps moving now, that we have an opportunity to do that which is absolutely essential to move this country forward: end divided Government and bring Republican leadership to both the Senate and the House of Representatives. There is a gridlock in Government, yes, because there are roadblocks in the United States Congress. And the American people deserve better than that right now. I believe we're going to see the changes.

Yes, the voters are calling for change. But they also know that there's a flip side to change. It's called trust: trust to make the right decisions; trust to block the wrong decisions; trust to make the tough calls and put the public's interest before the special interests; trust to cast the votes that aren't always popular, to take the stands that aren't always fashionable, and to be a leader and not just a servant.

Our leadership, as Arlen very generously said, has helped change the world. Today we had Mr. Kozyrev, the Foreign Minister of Russia, there. As I listened to this reformer talk, I couldn't help but think how far we have come in the last 3 years. It has been dramatic, the changes that have taken place around the world. The cold war is won, and our steadfast perseverance to the security needs of the country have changed the world.

Talk to any German, and they'll talk to you with pride about the U.S. role in the reunification of Germany. In the Middle East, ancient enemies talking to each other across the table, something that nobody would have dreamed possible a handful of years ago. There are plenty of problems out there as these new ethnic rivalries come to the surface, but Eastern Europe is free, and the former Soviet Union has now many, many independent countries all struggling to perfect democracy, struggling for freedom. It is an exciting thing that has taken place around the world. And in the Gulf, yes, freedom for a tiny country, but much more important than that, victory for a big idea, and that is that an aggressor bully cannot take over his neighbor without punishment.

They ask about it, and yes, there is a peace dividend. It's called peace, and we can take great pride in that. And one other point on this: When I saw some of the little kids here tonight, I thank God that our children go to bed at night far less worried about the specter of nuclear warfare. That is a major accomplishment in which we can all take pride.

And so I say we have, we have helped change the world. And I give my predecessor great credit. I give the Senators that have stood with us for strong defense and stood with us, say, on the Gulf, give them

lots of credit. We've helped change the world.

Now let me just talk for a minute about what we're trying to do to help change America. We're for free trade because Americans aren't afraid to meet and beat the competition. Protection is out; free and fair trade is in. And that means jobs for the American people.

Health care reform: I do not want to and I will not sign a socialized medicine nationalized plan. I have proposed the most comprehensive health care reform program. It makes insurance available to all, the poorest of the poor. But it preserves the quality of United States medicine, none better in the entire world.

We are for fundamental—I'm not talking about just transparent—we are for fundamental education reform. Our America 2000 is an innovative program that says to the Lehigh Valley, for example, where I was the other day, "You innovate. You figure out what's best for the people of Pennsylvania. And we will help you, but we will not dictate to you." We are going to revolutionize education in this country. If people have a choice of where their kids go to college, why shouldn't they have a choice as to where kids go to school? We are for school choice.

We are fighting hard for legal reform. When a guy can't coach Little League for fear of some silly suit; when a doctor can't deliver a baby for fear of some malpractice suit—[*applause*]. We are trying to have legal reform. We are blocked in the Senate today, as Arlen knows, by a very powerful lobby, but I will take this case to the American people. It is time we cared for each other a little more and sued each other a little less.

We are pushing for Government reform and so is Arlen because, you see, he and I believe that the Congress ought to abide by the same laws they make you and I live by.

While we're talking about Government reform, let me just expand on what our able Senator talked about. We have called for a balanced budget amendment. The very first piece of legislation that I took up to Capitol Hill when I was sworn in was a call for a balanced budget amendment. That was in

January of 1989, and we've done it each year. But the time has come now because, he is right, runaway spending threatens the future prosperity of our country. Every American family has to live within its means, and it's high time that the Federal Government did the same thing.

This balanced budget amendment is a top priority. Just today at the White House I met not only with the Republican leadership or some of the Democratic Congressmen, but we did something unique. We brought in some key business leaders who want to see this amendment passed and sat them down with this bipartisan congressional group that's spearheading this effort. We've had good sessions with other State legislators and other business groups. I've been working the phones to Capitol Hill, following up on the strong push that I tried to give it in last week's press conference, the press conference I gave at the White House that the networks didn't see fit to cover, incidentally. And I'm not too happy about that. But they can make their choices any way they want, but I'm going to take this message to the American people that we need a balanced budget amendment.

If the vote doesn't go our way and if the majority leaders on Capitol Hill get their way, the American people will then have it right in clear focus come fall, and they will decide on who wants to deal with this deficit or not.

Now, I've heard there's talk up there on Capitol Hill—Arlen, we didn't talk about this on the plane—about a balanced budget act. They say pass some legislation, a balanced budget act instead of an amendment. That act, incidentally, would not help balance the budget. But you and I know that Congress won't let a simple law get in the way of higher spending. No statute can substitute for the force of the Constitution of the United States. An amendment is the only answer.

Listen, I was with Arlen in Pittsburgh and with him in Philadelphia, and we both feel we ought to help the cities. Last month, I sent up a strong emergency package to assist the victims of violence in Los Angeles and other cities. Before the ink was dry, Congress had stuffed into that emergency bill an extra $1 billion, $1 billion spending.

In the meantime, people who desperately need help and need that emergency aid must wait. That's an iron-clad argument for a balanced budget amendment, and we need that amendment now.

So give us that amendment. And while we're at it, let me ask something else. Ask your legislators, demand of your legislators that they give the President what 43 Governors have, the line-item veto, and give us a chance.

Lastly, just let me say, Government alone, and everyone here knows this, simply cannot solve all the problems we face. Ask yourself what keeps a kid in school, what keeps a kid off the streets, what keeps a kid away from drugs? It's not Government. It is family. I will never forget when those mayors, from big cities and small, of the National League of Cities came to see me, including Tom Bradley of Los Angeles. And they said the underlying problem is the decline, the diminution of the American family. And they are absolutely correct about that. There's this feeling out there that we're in disarray and that we're off the track. The way to help correct that is to take the first step towards it, and that is put the family first.

Arlen has done that. My heavens, I don't know how closely you've followed his record. He coauthored the Missing Children Assistance Act. He increased the funding, took the leadership on it, for a worthy program called Healthy Start. He won Healthy Start grants for Pennsylvania, for Philadelphia and Pittsburgh. He's also been a leader in the fight against pornography, the dry rot that degrades women and exploits children and vandalizes our values. He's out front fighting for these things. So let the ultraliberals defend the vendors of pornography. He and I are going to protect the victims. And that's what we should be doing.

You know, Government can and must, as I said earlier, reform education. But parents, parents must read to their children, teach them a love of learning. And Government can and must fight crime. But families have got to instill in these kids the respect for the other guy, respect for property, respect for the value of the others' lives. Government can and must foster economic competitiveness. But the work ethic is learned at home. Barbara Bush is right when she says what happens in your house is more important than what happens in the White House. That is fundamentally correct.

So let us vow to do everything we can in our neighborhoods, in our communities to help strengthen the American family. You know, we've inherited a great country from those that came before. I don't believe this stuff that America's a declining Nation, not for one, single minute. We are a rising Nation. And we can overcome any kind of adversity that we have. We've always done it in our past, and we can do it now. But we must determine that we've also borrowed America from all those who are going to come afterward. And we know that America is great because America is good.

I am dedicated to work with Arlen Specter to demonstrate to the entire world what you and I know is so true: We are the

freest, we are the best, we are the fairest Nation on the face of the Earth. And give us the tools with which to work, and you watch this country move forward.

Thank you. And may God bless the United States. And be sure to reelect Arlen Specter to the United States Senate. Thank you very much.

*Note: The President spoke at 6:27 p.m. at Mumma Farm. In his remarks, he referred to Robert and Susan Mumma, owners of the farm; Elsie Hillman, Republican national committeewoman; publisher Walter H. Annenberg, president of the M.L. Annenberg Foundation; Robert C. Jubelirer, president pro tempore, Pennsylvania State Senate; Matthew J. Ryan, Republican leader, Pennsylvania State House of Representatives; Anne Anstine, chairman, Republican State Committee; Herbert Barness, Republican national committeeman; Barbara Hafer, State auditor general; Ernie Preate, State attorney general; and Joe Paterno, Pennsylvania State University football coach.*

# Address to the Nation on the Balanced Budget Amendment
*June 10, 1992*

Tomorrow the House of Representatives faces a critical vote on the balanced budget amendment, and right now is the time for some straight talk about our national deficit. With our Federal debt averaging $65,000 for the typical American family of four, I understand why the American people are fed up and why you are looking for change. I share your frustration, and I am determined to see things changed.

I am convinced that a balanced budget amendment is the only way to force the Federal Government, both the Congress and the executive branch, to live within its means. In fact, the very first address to Congress I made as President included a call for a balanced budget.

I confidently presented a balanced budget constitutional amendment to the Congress. I asked our Nation's elected leaders to put America's best interests first and

to join me in reaching a goal whose benefits will be measured in jobs and opportunity for ourselves and for our children.

Eighty percent of the American people agree: Government spending must be restrained and the budget balanced. Government is too big, and it spends too much. We are treating our national debt like the old fellow who borrowed money to pay off his loans. Inevitably, someone at some time must foot the bill. It is simply wrong to walk away from this mountain of debt and leave it to our kids.

Forty-four of our States have some kind of a constitutional requirement for a balanced budget. It's time for the Federal Government to follow their lead. We must balance the Federal budget without shifting the funding burden along to the States. We must pay our own way. Our future is at stake. Now is the time to pass a constitu-

917

tional amendment mandating a balanced budget.

Let me caution Americans not to be taken in by bold blustering. We can't wheel and deal the deficit away. There's no easy answer that we can jot out on a blank sheet of paper to wipe out a deficit of that magnitude. A balanced budget amendment is real action, and it will work. We should not be willing to risk our grandchildren's future on sound bites that merely sound real. The deficit is what's real. Congressional inaction is what's real. A constitutional amendment mandating a balanced budget is what's needed.

For that reason, I need your help to encourage your Congressman to do the right thing: Pass this balanced budget amendment. There is no single action that we can take that will be any more important than doing this for our Nation's future.

Thank you, and may God bless you, and may God bless the United States of America.

*Note: This address was recorded at 2:35 p.m. in Room 459 of the Old Executive Office Building for broadcast after 4 p.m.*

# Message to the Congress Transmitting the Annual Report of the Department of Energy
*June 10, 1992*

*To the Congress of the United States:*

In accordance with the requirements of section 657 of the Department of Energy Organization Act (Public Law 95–91; 42 U.S.C. 7267), I transmit herewith the 11th Annual Report of the Department of Energy, which covers the year 1990.

GEORGE BUSH

The White House,
June 10, 1992.

# Remarks and an Exchange With Reporters Prior to a Meeting With Congressional Leaders
*June 11, 1992*

*The President.* Let me just, first, thank the Members for coming here. And this is a critical and important vote. We must pass this balanced budget amendment. I thank those who are out front in the leadership role on this. And I would appeal to those that are still undecided to say that this is the way to discipline both branches of the United States Government, the Congress and the administration.

We've approached it—I hope Charlie would agree and others, Billy—in a nonpartisan way. We're going to continue to fight it on that basis. The people want this done. It will make all of us do what the people want, and that is to get this deficit under control once and for all.

So I thank you for coming at this very early hour. Charlie gave me my button, "Vote Yea on BBA," and that's the balanced budget amendment. And clearly, if I were in the House, where I started off, why, I would be voting yes. And we've talked about the arguments opposed to it, but I think the overwhelming evidence is that the people want this and that we ought to go ahead and take a role of leadership in getting this budget under control, this deficit under control.

So thank you so much for coming. As you know, I'm heading out in a couple of minutes. But I think this meeting is important, and I once again commend those who have been out front in a strong leadership role in the House of Representatives. It's been bipartisan, and it's been magnificent.

### Balanced Budget Amendment

*Q.* Mr. President, why do you think there's such a nasty, mean campaign against the balanced budget? Who's behind that?

*The President.* Well, I don't know because the people want it passed, Sarah [Sarah McClendon, McClendon News Service]. And I think it will be.

*Q.* They've got the Chamber of Commerce, and they've got the——

*The President.* The Chamber of Commerce will come around. They've got one particular amendment they want to pass first. But the business people across this country, the working people across this country realize that their future, their kids' future has been mortgaged. In other words, we're not passing out blame here; we're trying to do something about it.

And so I don't know, Sarah. But these people have stood up courageously, and they're fighting for it. That is not easy, and I support them, salute them.

### Panama

*Q.* Mr. President, are you worried about the situation in Panama?

*The President.* No.

*Q.* Violence where you're going speaking?

*The President.* No, no, not worried at all. We'll be received very well down there.

### Yugoslavia

*Q.* Mr. President, are you going to have them send troops over to Europe? The Balkans?

*The President.* We're concerned about the situation in Yugoslavia, but there's no commitment on that. We are going to safeguard human life. We're going to do what we can in a humanitarian way. We're working with the United Nations. But it's a little premature to be talking——

*Q.* You have to act quickly, don't you, though, to keep those people from starving?

*The President.* When the United States sees people that are hungry, we help. And again, that's bipartisan or nonpartisan. That's just been the hallmark of our country. So we will do what we should do. But I'm not going to go into the fact of using U.S. troops. We're not the world's policeman. It's a very complicated situation, but it's one that we're following very closely.

Thank you. Now I've got to get to work with these people.

### U.N. Conference on Environment

*Q.* Mr. President, do you expect the other countries to try to beat up on you in Rio?

*The President.* It doesn't matter. It doesn't matter. We are the United States. We are the leader in the environment. We've got a good record. Most of the groups that are criticizing are from the United States, I think. But that's all right; I've been there before. I'm going to represent the people on this visit and do it firmly in putting forward the best environmental record that any country has.

We've spent $800 billion in the last 10 years. We're going to spend $1.2 trillion in the next 10 years. And we share our technology with the world. We are way out front. And we're going to continue to stay out front, but we are not going to act like we have an open checkbook and that people are going to come in and tell us how much money to spend. We can't do it. We're trying to protect the taxpayer here through this balanced budget amendment, and I will protect the taxpayer down there in Rio. But I'm going to advocate a sound, strong environmental record.

Now, you all, thank you very much for interest in all of this. But I've got to get to work and see what I can do to help these people around this table at the waning hours of this debate.

*Note: The exchange began at 7:03 a.m. in the Cabinet Room at the White House. In the exchange, the President referred to Representatives Charles W. Stenholm and W.J. (Billy) Tauzin.*

## Remarks on Departure for the United Nations Conference on Environment and Development
*June 11, 1992*

Well, today I travel to Rio de Janeiro to join over 100 heads of state at the United Nations Conference on Environment and Development. Informally, the Rio meeting has been called the Earth summit. But I want to focus for just a minute on the official name. I think it's critical that we take both those words, environment and development, equally seriously. And we do.

On the environment, America's record is second to none. No other nation has done more, more rapidly to clean up the water, the air, or preserve public land. No other nation has done more to advance the state of technology that promises cleaner growth. We are proposing to double forest assistance. No other nation has put in place stricter standards to curb pollution in the future. We've done a great deal, and we are determined to do more.

But let me say up front: I am determined to protect the environment, and I'm also determined to protect the American taxpayer. The day of the open checkbook is over. I will go to Rio with a series of sound proposals designed to foster both environmental protection and economic growth. I'll sign a climate convention that calls for sound action, like increased energy efficiency and cleaner air. I'll offer technology cooperation because I believe American technology can help clean up the world's environment. I'll propose to share U.S. science, the most advanced in the world, to increase understanding of these complex issues. And I'll bring my Forests for the Future initiative, the most concrete and effective plan for dealing with the pressing problems of deforestation of all those that have been proposed at Rio.

Finally, I go to Rio with a firm conviction: Environmental protection and a growing economy are inseparable. No matter what some people may want to pretend, they are inseparable. It is counterproductive to promote one at the expense of the other.

For the past half-century, the United States has been a great engine of global economic growth, and it's going to stay that way. Every American knows what that means for us. What many may not know is that the world also has a stake in a strong American economy. Right now, one-half of the developing countries' exports of manufactured goods to all industrialized nations are sold, yes, in the United States of America. A weak economy in this country would harm workers in other nations and cut their export earnings to a trickle. Nations struggling to meet the most elemental needs of their people can spare little to protect the environment.

Many governments and many individuals from the U.S. and other nations have pressed us to sign a treaty on what's called biodiversity. I don't expect that pressure to let up when I reach Rio. The treaty's intent is noble, to ensure protection of natural habitat for the world's plants and animal life. The U.S. has better protections for species and habitat than any nation on Earth. No one disagrees with the goal of the treaty. But the truth is, it contains provisions that have nothing to do with biodiversity.

Take just one example: The private sector is proving it can help generate solutions to our environmental problems. The treaty includes provisions that discourage technological innovations, treat them as common property though they are developed at great cost by private companies and American workers. We know what will happen. Remove incentives, and we'll see fewer of the technological advances that help us protect our planet.

My Forests for the Future initiative will offer real assistance to protect habitats, a downpayment of $150 million in new U.S. assistance toward the goal of doubling worldwide funding for forests. It invites developing countries to propose their best plans for forest conservation, and it encourages innovation, like biotechnology, that will help us protect biodiversity worldwide.

I cannot speak for actions other nations

may take. But this I promise: I will stand up for American interests and the interests of a cleaner environment. And if the United States has to be the only nation to stand against the biodiversity treaty as now drawn, so be it.

I believe deeply in protecting our common environment, and I will proudly present in Rio the U.S. record that is second to none anywhere in the world.

*Note: The President spoke at 7:50 a.m. at Andrews Air Force Base in Camp Springs, MD.*

# Remarks at a Luncheon Hosted by President Guillermo Endara in Panama City, Panama
*June 11, 1992*

*The President.* Mr. President and Mr. Vice President and members of the Cabinet, Barbara and I are just delighted to be with you to witness firsthand the great progress that Panama has made since its liberation from that dictatorship and tyranny back in December 1989. Panama is once again free, democracy restored, and the rule of law prevails.

With your nation's return to democracy, Panama resumes its place in the world community. This country's path toward economic reform and also liberalization has rekindled economic enterprise. And maybe some don't realize it, but last year your nation's economic growth was the highest in the whole hemisphere. I salute your success and your efforts, which bring the prospect of a better future for all Panamanians.

Our countries have enjoyed a unique partnership since Panama gained its independence nearly 90 years ago. That partnership is embodied today in the 1977 Panama Canal treaties. Mr. President, let me just assure you the United States keeps its word: Those treaties will be fully implemented on schedule.

But what I really wanted to do to come here was to salute those of you in this room who stood up to the tyranny of Noriega and who dared to oppose him in the 1989 elections and who now have the responsibility for strengthening your democracy for future generations.

As we were riding in in the car I sensed a little nervousness on the part of my friend President Endara. I think he was worried that I might be offended by some show of protest. But what I saw and felt was that overwhelming welcome from the people along the streets. It expressed, I think, a genuine friendship between Panama and the United States. And for the tiny, tiny handful of people that are protesting, I said they ought to go up to San Francisco and get an idea what a real protest is like. [*Laughter*]

So we've been here, and we are very grateful to you. We salute you. And I would like to just propose a toast to the health of President and Mrs. Endara and to that lasting, strengthening friendship between Panama and the United States of America.

*Note: The President spoke at 1:15 p.m. at the Presidential Palace.*

# Remarks to the American Community in Panama City
*June 11, 1992*

Thank you so very, very much for that warm welcome. And General Joulwan, thank you for the introduction. And may I salute not only the general but also Ambassador Hinton, our distinguished Ambassador. He and Mrs. Hinton, Mrs. Joulwan, and you and the Embassy staff, Mr. Ambassador, are doing a first-rate job here in Panama. And I salute you for your work, your career, and your dedication in representing the United States of America.

I want to greet the graduates, seniors at Balboa and Cristobal High who are graduating today. Let me say hello to the Panama Canal Commission members, the Smithsonian Institute office people that are here. And to all of you serving the cause of freedom across the continents and oceans, my thanks for your service to our great country and for your dedication to the United States of America. And may God bless you all.

Now I want to say a few words to the Americans here, but before I do that, I want to say a word to the citizens of Panama. My Spanish isn't very good, so I'm going to ask for a little translation. But I first want to thank President Endara, Vice President Ford, Mayor Correa for the warm welcome they gave to us from the minute we arrived. I am grateful to each and every one of them.

May I say to the people of Panama, Barbara and I will never forget the warm welcome you gave us as we drove in from the airport and indeed as we drove to this base, thousands of people along the road expressing their appreciation for our great country. And let me say to them, we appreciate Panama. We appreciate Panama's move to democracy, and no tiny little left-wing demonstration is going to set your democracy back.

May I say in conclusion to the people in Panama, democracy takes a while to solidify it, to perfect it. Democracy doesn't come easy. But I could sense in that crowd today and amongst the leaders today the determination to perfect and see Panama's democracy come to total fulfillment. And let me say to the people of Panama, Barbara and I are grateful for the welcome. The day of the dictator is over, and you should take great pride in what your country has done.

All right, now, to all you Yankees out here—[*applause*]. In fact, I think I'll go to work here; it's hot out there. But a special hello to those from this base, from other bases here in Panama. I know that some of you came a long, long way, an hour-and-a-half drive across the Isthmus to come and

give us this tremendous welcome. And let me salute the seven from the Pacific side, Quarry Heights, Fort Clayton, Fort Kobbe, Howard, Albrook, Panama Canal-Rodman Naval Air Station, and Port Amador, and then the three on the Atlantic side, Fort Davis, Fort Sherman, and Galeta Island.

Working abroad, and Barbara and I have been there, is a learning experience in a way, managing diplomatic and domestic responsibilities. I just want you to know that we have tremendous respect, whether it's in the military, whether it's as civilians, for all who serve their country overseas. Your work, whether it was on the civilian side or on the military side, has helped give this wonderful country a chance for what we take for granted in the United States, that democratic experience and freedom. That's what your mission is about.

I know that a lot goes into planning a Presidential visit. I was on the receiving end of one of them over in China, and I thought I would never recover. But to all of those who worked with the arrangements on this visit, let me simply say we will do what we said: We will leave on schedule. And you can get back to normal.

But before I do, before I leave and before Barbara leaves, let me just say that you all should take pride in knowing that you serve at a time when Panama is reaching an entirely new status in the community of nations. Those of you who took part in Just Cause and those of you who have come since must take great satisfaction in Panama's accomplishments. Don't let this little ripple out there today that took place in the plaza, a handful of people trying to disrupt this wonderful welcome, don't let it discourage you. I'd say the same to the people. You can feel the heartbeat here, and you are partly responsible for that wonderful feeling between Panama and the United States of America.

Justice and freedom have been restored. With each sunrise the people of Panama wake to liberty's greatest gift: free elections, free press, and free worship. I must say that the plaza where we came from, there's a history there of protest and also vigil. But today that plaza is the people's park. And I wish every one of you could have seen the welcome we had before a handful of characters tried to disrupt it all. Each day you serve, you are visible reminders that freedom and democracy work. You're laying a foundation for cooperation between our nations that will last for generations to come.

As I know, as we saw tragically just yesterday, there are times when some of your comrades are called upon to make the ultimate sacrifice. I want you to know as Commander in Chief that we honor the memory of Corporal Hernandez here today, a veteran of Desert Storm, and the memories of all the proud, brave men and women in uniform who gave their all in the service of their country. The most fitting tribute to their memory and to their sacrifice is to complete the work they began. And therefore, we will continue to help the Panamanians build on their progress in strengthening democracy and developing their economic system so that future generations can share what you all have helped start, this new beginning.

We're going to work together to secure a future of free trade, a link to economic recovery, progress, and prosperity. Our countries are going to work together to bring an end to that dreadful narcotic trafficking that are poisoning the kids in Panama and poisoning the kids in the United States. We will not fail in crushing the narco-traffickers.

And so to each and every one of you, our profound thanks for your service. Once again, to President Endara and his colleagues, my sincere thanks for the warmth of the welcome and, much more important, for what Panama is doing as now a newly found proud member of the family of nations, moving down the path to democracy and freedom. It is a wonderful example.

Now we head off to the Environmental Conference down there in Rio. And I look forward to that because we're taking down there a sound, forward-looking message on the measure of the environment. And I believe that we're going to go just fine.

But thank you all for the service to the greatest, freest country on the face of the Earth, the United States of America. Thank you very much.

*Note: The President spoke at 3:25 p.m. at Albrook Air Force Base. In his remarks, he referred to Gen. George Joulwan, commander in chief, Southern Command, and U.S. Army Cpl. Zak A. Hernandez, who was killed June 10 by gunmen in Panama.*

# Statement on the Balanced Budget Amendment
*June 11, 1992*

Today's vote in the House shows that we are close to realizing a goal that the overwhelming majority of Americans support, adoption of a balanced budget constitutional amendment. The Democratic leadership's proposal was soundly defeated, and our bipartisan amendment came within just nine votes of getting the two-thirds needed to pass.

A balanced budget amendment is absolutely essential to the economic health of America. We cannot continue to burden our children and grandchildren with crippling Federal deficits.

I thank the 280 Members of the House, Republican and Democrat, who stood up to the special interests and voted for America's future. To the 153 Members who voted against balancing the Federal budget, I say this: The will of the American people could not be clearer. We must adopt a balanced budget amendment.

We are within striking distance of winning this fight. I will be discussing with key bipartisan supporters bringing the balanced budget amendment up again as soon as possible and finding those few extra votes needed to pass it.

## Appointment of Maria Solandros Eitel Sheehan as Special Assistant to the President and Deputy Director of Media Affairs
*June 11, 1992*

The President today announced the appointment of Maria Solandros Eitel Sheehan, of Washington State, as Special Assistant to the President and Deputy Director of Media Affairs.

Since 1989, Ms. Eitel Sheehan has served the President as Deputy Director of Media Affairs with responsibility for regional, specialty, and trade media. Before coming to the White House, Ms. Eitel Sheehan worked at the U.S. Information Agency as a program officer and producer for "Worldnet Dialogues" and as a correspondent for the television news program "America Today." In 1987, Ms. Eitel Sheehan worked at WETA–TV in Washington, DC, as an associ-ate producer for "World Beat," a foreign affairs television series. Prior to this, she served in the economics section of the U.S. Embassy in Cameroon. From 1983 to 1985, in Seattle, Ms. Eitel Sheehan worked in the news and documentary departments of NBC affiliate KING–TV and was a freelance reporter and producer for PBS station KCTS–TV.

Ms. Eitel Sheehan graduated from McGill University in Montreal, Canada (B.A., 1983) and Georgetown University School of Foreign Service (M.S.F.S., 1988). She was born June 26, 1962, in Everett, WA. She is married, has one child, and resides in Washington, DC.

## Address to the United Nations Conference on Environment and Development in Rio de Janeiro, Brazil
*June 12, 1992*

President Collor, Mr. Secretary-General, heads of delegation, may I first express my admiration to Secretary-General Boutros-Ghali and my gratitude to Secretary General Maurice Strong for his tireless work in bringing this Earth summit together. This is truly an historic gathering.

The Chinese have a proverb: If a man cheats the Earth, the Earth will cheat man. The idea of sustaining the planet so that it may sustain us is as old as life itself. We must leave this Earth in better condition than we found it.

Today this old truth must be applied to new threats facing the resources which sustain us all, the atmosphere and the ocean, the stratosphere and the biosphere. Our village is truly global. Some find the challenges ahead overwhelming. I believe that their pessimism is unfounded.

Twenty years ago, at the Stockholm conference, a chief concern of our predecessors was the horrible threat of nuclear war, the ultimate pollutant. No more. Upon my return from Rio, I will meet with Russian President Yeltsin in Washington, and the subject we will discuss is cooperation, not confrontation. Twenty years ago, some spoke of the limits to growth. Today we realize that growth is the engine of change and the friend of the environment.

Today, an unprecedented era of peace, freedom, and stability makes concerted action on the environment possible as never before. This summit is but one key step in the process of international cooperation on environment and development. The United States will work to carry forward the promise of Rio because as important as the road to Rio has been, what matters more is the road from Rio.

There are those who say that cooperation between developed and developing countries is impossible. Well, let them come to Latin America, where debt-for-nature swaps are protecting forests in Costa Rica and funding pollution control in Chile.

There are those who say that it takes state control to protect the environment. Well, let them go to Eastern Europe, where the poisoned bodies of children now pay for the sins of fallen dictators, and only the new breeze of freedom is allowing for cleanup.

There are those who say that change can never come because the interests of the status quo are too powerful. Well, let them come right here to Brazil, where President Collor is forging a new approach that recognizes the economic value of sustaining the rain forest.

There are those who say that economic growth and environmental protection cannot be compatible. Well, let them come to the United States, where, in the 20 years since Stockholm, our economy has grown by 57 percent, and yet we have cut the lead going into the air by 97 percent, the carbon monoxide by 41 percent, the particulates by 59 percent. We've cleaned up our water and preserved our parks, wilderness, and wildlife.

There are those who say that the leaders of the world do not care about the Earth and the environment. Well, let them all come here to Rio.

Mr. President, we have come to Rio. We've not only seen the concern, we share it. We not only care, we're taking action. We come to Rio with an action plan on climate change. It stresses energy efficiency, cleaner air, reforestation, new technology. I am happy to report that I have just signed the Framework Convention on Climate Change.

Today, I invite my colleagues from the industrialized world to join in a prompt start on the convention's implementation. I propose that our countries meet by January 1st to lay out our national plans for meeting the specific commitments in the Framework Convention. Let us join in translating the words spoken here into concrete action to protect the planet.

We come to Rio with a proposal to double global forest assistance. We stand ready to work together, respecting national sovereignty, on new strategies for forests for the future. As a downpayment, we will double U.S. forest bilateral assistance next year. And we will reform at home, phasing out clear-cutting as a standard practice on

U.S. national forests and working to plant one billion trees a year.

We come to Rio with an extensive program of technology cooperation. We stand ready, Government and private sector, to help spread green technology and launch a new generation of clean growth.

We come to Rio recognizing that the developing countries must play a role in protecting the global environment but will need assistance in pursuing these cleaner growths. So we stand ready to increase U.S. international environmental aid by 66 percent above the 1990 levels, on top of the more than $2.5 billion that we provide through the world's development banks for Agenda 21 projects.

We come to Rio with more scientific knowledge about the environment than ever before and with the wisdom that there is much, much we do that's not yet known. And we stand ready to share our science and to lead the world in a program of continued research.

We come to Rio prepared to continue ·America's unparalleled efforts to preserve species and habitat. And let me be clear. Our efforts to protect biodiversity itself will exceed, will exceed, the requirements of the treaty. But that proposed agreement threatens to retard biotechnology and undermine the protection of ideas. Unlike the climate agreement, its financing scheme will not work. And it is never easy, it is never easy to stand alone on principle, but sometimes leadership requires that you do. And now is such a time.

Let's face it, there has been some criticism of the United States. But I must tell you, we come to Rio proud of what we have accomplished and committed to extending the record on American leadership on the environment. In the United States, we have the world's tightest air quality standards on cars and factories, the most advanced laws for protecting lands and waters, and the most open processes for public participation.

Now for a simple truth: America's record on environmental protection is second to none. So I did not come here to apologize. We come to press on with deliberate purpose and forceful action. Such action will demonstrate our continuing commitment to leadership and to international cooperation on the environment.

We believe that the road to Rio must point toward both environmental protection and economic growth, environment and development. By now it's clear: To sustain development, we must protect the environment. And to protect the environment, we must sustain development.

It's been said that we don't inherit the Earth from our ancestors, we borrow it from our children. When our children look back on this time and this place, they will be grateful that we met at Rio, and they will certainly be pleased with the intentions stated and the commitments made. But they will judge us by the actions we take from this day forward. Let us not disappoint them.

Mr. President, once again, my congratulations to you, sir. Mr. Secretary-General, our sincere thanks. And thank you all very, very much.

*Note: The President spoke at 3:19 p.m. in the Assembly Hall at the Riocentro Conference Center.*

## Statement on Signing the Framework Convention on Climate Change
*June 12, 1992*

I have today signed the Framework Convention on Climate Change on behalf of the United States of America. This landmark agreement is a major step forward by the international community in taking action to address global climate change. It requires countries to formulate, implement, and publish national programs for mitigating climate change by limiting net emissions of greenhouse gases.

The Framework Convention is comprehensive, covering all sources and sinks of greenhouse gases. It provides the flexibility for national programs to be reviewed and updated as new scientific information becomes available. These are important and desirable features.

The United States already has been working to develop plans that are responsive to the requirements of the convention. In February of 1991, and again in the spring of this year, my administration published a detailed program of specific measures that the United States was prepared to undertake to address climate change. The administration also provided detailed estimates of the emissions effects of these measures. The U.S. plan stresses energy efficiency, cleaner air, new technology, and reforestation. It is estimated that our plan will reduce annual net greenhouse gas emissions by 125 to 200 million tons below projected levels in the year 2000.

Many of the items contained in the U.S. action agenda are already being implemented. Some were contained in the Clean Air Act of 1990. Some energy efficiency measures, such as EPA's Green Lights program, are being pursued under existing authority. Others, such as elements of the national energy strategy, have been proposed by the administration and are awaiting final action by the U.S. Congress.

No effort to address climate change can be successful without the participation of the developing countries. We have pledged support for country studies, for the Global Environmental Facility, and for various other programs to help these countries begin the process of developing action programs.

I have today invited the other industrialized nations who have signed the Framework Convention to join me in a prompt start on its implementation. I have proposed that our countries meet by January 1st to present and review our national action plans. We look forward to cooperating with the other developed nations in this regard and to seeing what specific measures they propose to undertake.

## Appointment of Shiree Sanchez as Special Assistant to the President for Public Liaison
*June 12, 1992*

The President today announced the appointment of Shiree Sanchez as Special Assistant to the President for Public Liaison.

Since 1989, Ms. Sanchez has served at the White House as Associate Director, Office of Public Liaison. Ms. Sanchez works on all issues related to Hispanic Americans and also is the liaison to Americans with disabilities.

Ms. Sanchez previously served as congressional liaison for the President-Elect's Inaugural Committee; as Texas director for Hispanic outreach for the George Bush for President campaign, 1987; and as executive director of the Republican National Committee Hispanic Auxiliary, 1988–89. Ms. Sanchez was appointed by the Governor of Texas to serve in the Texas department of commerce, 1986–87. Other positions Ms. Sanchez has held include: assistant director of the Republican Party of Texas, 1985–86; and sales manager for Micro-D International, Inc., of Huntington Beach, CA, 1982–86.

Ms. Sanchez attended the University of Texas and is a native of Austin, TX. She resides in Washington, DC.

## Nomination of Jose Antonio Villamil To Be an Under Secretary of Commerce
*June 12, 1992*

The President today announced his intention to nominate Jose Antonio Villamil, of Florida, to be Under Secretary of Commerce for Economic Affairs. He would succeed Michael Rucker Darby.

Since 1989, Mr. Villamil has served as Chief Economist for the Department of Commerce and was elevated to the position of Chief Economist and Special Adviser to the Secretary in 1991. From 1981 to 1989, he served as senior vice president and chief economist in the corporate planning and economics department in the office of the chairman of the board at the Southeast Bank in Miami, FL.

From 1978 to 1981, Mr. Villamil served as vice president and economist in the economics department with the Crocker National Bank in San Francisco, CA. He also served as financial economist in the economic research division with the Continental Illinois National Bank and Trust Company in Chicago, IL, 1975–78. In addition, Mr. Villamil has served as an economist in the Office of Developing Nations Finance at the Department of the Treasury, 1974–75. From 1973 to 1974, he served as an economic analyst in the international corporate banking division with the First National Bank of Miami in Miami, FL.

Mr. Villamil graduated from Louisiana State University (B.S. 1968; M.A. 1971). He is married, has four children, and resides in McLean, VA.

## The President's News Conference in Rio de Janeiro
*June 13, 1992*

*The President.* Well, let me first express my thanks and congratulations to President Collor and the Brazilian people and to all responsible for this Conference for their hospitality, for their tremendous success in hosting the Earth summit. It's obvious to all who came to Rio that the Brazilians made a special effort to accommodate so many heads of states and delegates and journalists and visitors. They managed it flawlessly, and they managed it with grace and good humor. We've had a very successful visit.

We've signed a climate convention. We've asked others to join us in presenting action plans for the implementation of the climate convention. We've won agreement on forest principles. We found a warm reception among the G–7 and many developing countries to our Forests for the Future initiative. Many U.S. proposals on oceans and public participation on the importance of economic instruments and free markets were included in this mammoth Agenda 21 document and the Rio Declaration.

Let me be clear on one fundamental point. The United States fully intends to be the world's preeminent leader in protecting the global environment. We have been that for many years. We will remain so. We believe that environment and development, the two subjects of this Conference, can and should go hand in hand. A growing economy creates the resources necessary for environmental protection, and environmental protection makes growth sustainable over the long term. I think that recognition of that fact by leaders from around the world is the central accomplishment of this important Rio Conference.

So with no further ado, I believe, Tom [Tom Raum, Associated Press], you have the first question, sir.

*Panama Demonstration and Environmental Policy*

*Q.* Mr. President, to what extent do the images Americans have seen back home of your being hustled off the stage in Panama and not being allowed to give your speech, and the isolation that the United States has had in Rio, to what extent does this erode into what Americans seem to still feel is your strong suit, your ability to conduct foreign policy?

*The President.* I think in both instances the reality will prevail. In Panama, Panama has made dramatic strides. They're a free country. They're a democratic country. I

think everybody who was there saw the warmth of the reception from the people of Panama along the streets, and it was tremendous.

What got the news, of course, was a handful of demonstrators in demonstration. The smoke blew the wrong way as the police tried to contain that small group, and that permitted the disruption of an outdoor rally. But that should not obscure the fact that Panama is democratic, Panama is free, Panama is growing at 9.6 percent, and the warmth from the Panamanian people was overwhelming. Can you let 300 people or 200, whichever it is, carry the day in terms of the reality? The answer is no. The hundreds of thousands of people were much more representative of the change.

Then I heard an interview from a prison today by Mr. Noriega, the discredited drug lord who's had a fair trial, as though his criticism means anything. I mean, come on.

Panama's doing well. And I was very proud to be there, and so I'd like to go back. What we did in helping in the first place to protect Americans' lives, secondly to restore democracy, it's good. It's very, very positive.

In terms of Rio, as I said yesterday, we are the leaders; we're not the followers. And the fact that we don't go along with every single covenant, I don't think that means a relinquishment of leadership. I think we are, and I think the record shows we are, the leading environmental nation in the world. So I would just reject the premise or say, no, this doesn't concern me.

*Q.* If I may do a followup, Mr. President. Along those lines, you set a January 1st target for another meeting of the Conference to discuss global warming. You've set a lot of deadlines for Congress that haven't been heeded. Your proposal yesterday wasn't particularly well-received by the other nations. Why do you think that that January 1st deadline will be heeded any more than your congressional deadlines?

*The President.* I don't think there's any comparison because I think the G–7 nations and the developed nations want to meet the commitments that they've signed up for. So I've not found that it wasn't received well at all. In fact, Bill Reilly told me it was well-received. And we will be there with specific plans.

Now, you want to talk about leadership? We will be there with specific plans, prepared to share, but more important, that others who have signed these documents ought to have specific plans. So I think this is a leadership role. We are challenging them to come forward. We will be there. I think the Third World and others are entitled to know that the commitments made are going to be commitments kept.

Brit [Brit Hume, ABC News].

*Q.* Mr. President, you and members of your administration feel that you came here with a good record on the environment and a good case to make for the positions you've taken. If that's so, sir, how is it that the words, remarks of your critics seem to so dominate the atmosphere?

*The President.* Well, I don't know. I guess it's because all the banks that weren't robbed today don't make news. When Americans criticize America outside of America, that seems to make news. The positive accomplishments I think should make the news, and I maintain that we have the best environmental record in the world. And I think the people I talked to yesterday certainly would concede that we have been world leaders.

But I can't answer that question for you, Brit, as to why the news is dominated by the critics. I have said that American environmental policy is not going to be dominated by the extremes, because I believe that the title of economic development as well as environmental protection is in order. I think both things count. Bill Reilly has made that point over and over again since he's been here.

But maybe it's the same as the Panama question. What dominates is the protest, not the fact that there was a great, warm reception along the way.

*Q.* Well, if I could follow up, sir——

*The President.* Yes.

*Q.* ——you, in one remark you made, and members of your administration have indicated that there are other nations here, some of whose officials were critical of your positions, who are in no position themselves, or their countries are in no position, to meet the terms of the climate change

treaty, for example, and yet they were privately critical of you. And you suggested that that was so. Would you care to elaborate on who they were and what they——

*The President.* No, I don't think I suggested that at all. What I'm saying is let's go forward.

*Q.* Do you think they're glad that you had taken the position that you have taken?

*The President.* Well, I think most are. I think most people are glad that we've taken this position to go forward. I was very pleased, incidentally, with the remarks by Chancellor Kohl, by Brian Mulroney; had a good talk with the Prime Minister of Japan before getting here; I'm most appreciative of John Major for what he said. So I think there's not only understanding but support for American positions.

Bill Reilly told me, and I don't want to get into a private conversation, but yesterday evening he talked to some of the developing nations' representatives, and they were rather supportive of what we said. So the fact that we didn't sign that one treaty does not diminish, in my view, the U.S. leadership role. Sometimes leadership is not going along with everybody else.

*'92 Elections*

*Q.* Mr. President, Mr. Quayle made a speech yesterday to the Federalist Society in which he called Ross Perot a temperamental person who has contempt for the Constitution and suggested that the country elect a Democratic President and a Democratic Congress if they couldn't elect a Republican President, a Republican Congress. How do you feel about these two suggestions?

*The President.* I feel they ought to elect a Republican President and a Republican Congress. I feel very unenthusiastic about the second one. [*Laughter*] And I feel that you better ask Mr. Quayle about what he said. I've vowed not to go after either of the opponents until after the convention, and I've also said that I'm getting kind of anxious to get after the convention.

*Q.* May I follow up, sir? This is your running mate echoing what Warren Rudman said, in which somebody's got to govern this country, and if it's going to be gridlocked between the White House and the Capitol, something has to be done. I realize it's hyperbole, but he's your running mate, and you disagree with those remarks?

*The President.* Well, I agree with him— listen, I say give me a Republican Congress, and we'll move on things. Let me give you an example. The American people want a balanced budget amendment to the Constitution. Seven cosponsors of that amendment were pulled off of the sponsorship and voted against their own amendment, their own resolution, because of the cracking of the whip by the Democratic leadership. The arrogance of the leadership to pull away people that had sponsored it, I'll tell you, the American people are not for that.

So I think in a wide array of issues, as I said at the press conference the other night, the American people back what we're standing for. They want revolutionary educational reform. They want tougher crime legislation. And I could just go through a whole litany of things that the American people want that I am advocating that have been blocked by a hostile, Democratic, politically leaning leadership in the United States Congress. So a lot can happen. There is gridlock. A lot can happen, however, if we have more Republicans in the Congress.

Look back to the early parts of the Reagan administration when we controlled the Senate. It was then that things moved forward, and that was only one house. I think the House, that's been in control by the Democrats so long, needs to be shaken up. And I think that's why I agree so strongly with that concept of give me a Republican Congress and watch this country change and move forward.

In foreign affairs, fortunately, I don't need a congressional acquiescence every step of the way.

Yes, Charles [Charles Bierbauer, Cable Network News].

### Environmental Policy

*Q.* Mr. President, some of the other leaders here, including some who say they know you well, feel that you might just, well, sign some of these agreements but not in an election year and that you are feeling pressured by the roller coaster nature of

policy. Can you comment on that, sir?

*The President.* Yes. I don't think that's true.

*Q.* Which one, there were several elements. Which, that you might sign these agreements?

*The President.* That I'm not pressured by domestic politics as to what our sound environmental practices are. We've got sound environmental practices. We are not going to sign up to things that we can't do. We're not going to sign up to do things we don't believe in. I happen to believe that in biodiversity it is important to protect our rights, our business rights. And I happen to think that when we do, whether it's in a biodiversity treaty or a GATT arrangement, we make things better for others. I believe that American biotechnology can help others. But it can't be if the product of that is taken away or if the incentive to innovate and the incentive to profit by your research is removed.

So, this isn't domestic politics '92 that determines whether I'm going to sign a biodiversity treaty or not, if that was the question.

*Q.* And their assertion that they sense in you an anxiety, a feeling of pressure?

*The President.* If they sense an anxiety, they may be right. I mean, this has been a tough, weird political year at home. But it has nothing to do with sound policy. It has nothing to do with whether I'm going to shape something as important as environmental policy based on an election that's, what, 4 or 5 months away.

Yes, Susan [Susan Spencer, CBS News].

### Presidential Campaign

*Q.* Mr. President, you have no assurance of getting a Republican Congress. And in light of that and the fact that you've now been in office for 4 years, why should the American people look to you as the agent of revolutionary change?

*The President.* Because they agree fundamentally with our ideas. When you see a group of Democrats can't run for office in California campaigning for tougher crime legislation and having voted against tougher crime legislation, I say there is a little bit of an indicator that the American people want tougher crime legislation, and they'd love to get it through. The way to get it through is put more people in Congress that agree with me.

Our ideas—when we talk about family values, or we talk about fiscal sanity, or when we talk about sound environmental practice, when we say that we're not going to throw people out of work needlessly—all of these things have support from the American people. And I would say that when you look around at this screwy year people do seem to be fingering Congress even more than the President.

*Q.* Sir, a lot of polls indicate that many of the American people say they don't know what it is you want to do in your second term.

*The President.* Well, maybe we need to make that a little clearer, and I think this Conference helps. I think the fact that somebody's going to take a focus on what's happened around the world, and they'll see the leadership we've brought to many things will be helpful. That's not in focus. You're dealing with polls all the time and some new trend. But the American people sort these things out. They'll sort it out, and I will win.

*Q.* Mr. Clinton has said that he will release a 100-day agenda of what he would do in the first 100 days, specifically. Will you do the same?

*The President.* I've already done it. But yes, I'll rephrase it and make it clearer because I think it is important that the American people know of my firm commitment to revolutionary educational change.

Here's a good example. We've got the best new education approach for the United States in history, the best. And we've had it up there—we've got the six goals. And it's hung up by the old thinkers in Congress. So I think maybe it would be a good idea. But I'm taking these ideas up there every single day with specificity to the Hill. It's a little different than when you're outside shooting in.

### Developing Nations

*Q.* Yes, Patricia Walsh, United Press International, a slightly little bit longer question for you, Mr. President. Some respected environmentalists here at the Earth summit say that poverty leads to many of the environmental problems and that poverty in developing nations is perpetuated by unending foreign debt and an unfair trade balance that funnels money from the south to the north. They criticize the Earth summit and wealthy nations like the United States for not focusing on these issues here. How would you respond to that criticism, please?

*The President.* I would take great credit for the fact that the United States has taken the leadership role, a unique one that's been well-received, in debt-for-equity swaps or forgiveness of debt or debt-for-environmental swaps. And I think that shows that we are sensitive to the problems of the Third World in terms of the economy.

I happen to believe that a successful conclusion to the GATT round, the Uruguay round of GATT, will do more than any foreign aid program of any country to help the Third World, because I believe their products will be able to flow more freely and they will be able to prosper by the market that they've been denied access to through various forms of protection. So both those areas I think would refute the allegation.

*Q.* As a followup, there are those who say that if the GATT is successful and these barriers are dropped, these developing nations will not be able to protect their own developing industries from the multilaterals coming in. How do you respond to that?

*The President.* Well, I say that the things they do best they'll be able to get into the world markets, and I just am convinced that free and fair trade is best for everybody. If you don't believe me, take a country that is now moving well along on the development path; talk to President Carlos Salinas of Mexico. He is convinced that the free trade agreement with Mexico will be good for him, Mexico, good for the United States, and good for the environment. And he's right. He believes that Mexico, and he's made this point over and over again, can do much more in environmental cleanup, environmental progress if this free trade agreement is met. Now, there's a very good refutation to the criticism you say some are making.

Yes, John [John Cochran, NBC News].

*Environmental Policy*

*Q.* A couple of questions about your wish back in the '88 campaign to be the environmental President. It would be difficult for a politician that got a parking ticket in a red-light district to campaign as a family values candidate, even though there may be a perfectly acceptable reason for his being there. Given the opposition of environmental groups, can you still campaign as the environmental President, and will you?

*The President.* Well, I think so—and for the very reasons that the man standing next to me, who has superb environmental credentials, has made over and over again here. You cannot go to the extreme. And yes, I do have to be concerned about the American worker, about taxes, about a lot of things like that; a President must be concerned. But I think we have an outstanding environmental record.

Let me just click off some of it for you: The Clean Air Act, and that was ours. We did it. We needed the Democrats' support, and we got it done. It is the most forward-looking piece of legislation that any country has in place.

We've got a national energy strategy that emphasizes alternate fuels and conservation and all of this part of it. We've got a forestation program that is second to none. I'd like to see the Congress move forward with my plan to plant a billion trees a year, and we're going to keep pushing on that.

We've done what's right environmentally on drilling, putting the sensitive, environmentally sensitive areas off bounds. We've done that in the Florida Keys, for example, and off of Big Sur.

We have over a billion dollars in new lands, and our parks, forests, wildlife refuges, have all been added to. So we have a good stewardship of the land.

We took the leadership in phasing out CFC's, and I think that is a very important environmental leadership role by the United States. Our budget for EPA is up considerably, our Environmental Protection Agency.

So I think along the lines we've done very, very well. And I think that's a case I will be proud to take to the American people.

*Q.* Can I follow up with one, sir?

*The President.* Yes, please.

*Q.* Sir, you talk about not wanting to jeopardize jobs by being overly conscious of environmental concerns, but you've never really been very specific about which jobs you would save with your policies, for example, on global warming and the biodiversity treaty.

*The President.* I will give you an example, and that was on the owl decision. There what was clearly at stake was some 30,000 jobs in the Northwest. That decision was met with some opposition by certain environmentalists, but it was a good decision. Some people regrettably will still be put out of work, but not near as many as if that arrangement had not been achieved.

*Russia-U.S. Relations*

*Q.* President Yeltsin fears the United States is trying to take strategic advantage in nuclear weapons. You'll be seeing him next week. Is this true, and are you optimistic you'll be able to reach an agreement with him?

*The President.* No, we are not trying to take strategic advantage of Russia. I hope that President Yeltsin knows that. Jim Baker is talking to Mr. Kozyrev; he's finished now, I believe. I talked to him yesterday. If Yeltsin still feels that way when he comes, President Yeltsin, I will make another effort to disabuse him of that.

I think we have a rare opportunity to move forward with Russia on many fronts, helping them solidify their reforms, helping the world get what it wants, which is more stability and progress in not only arms control but the whole nuclear proliferation field. These are very, very important things.

I might go back to Susan's [Susan Spencer, CBS News] question. I am very happy that we're talking now about these kinds of things when we weren't a few years ago to this degree. We've made dramatic progress, and our children, as somebody pointed out to me again yesterday, picking up on the theme that I have, go to bed at night far less worried about nuclear war. In the final analysis, the American people are going to say, well, this administration deserves some credit, not all but some credit for that.

So if President Yeltsin feels as you do, I will have no trouble disabusing him of this.

### Environmental Policy

*Q.* Mr. President, on the way back home today you will be flying for some two to three hours over the Amazon forests. Do you believe your 200-something U.S. million dollars of your Forests for the Future initiative will make a difference?

*The President.* Well, I certainly think it will, and most people here seem to think it will, yes. I salute President Collor for the steps he is taking in terms of preservation of that great forest.

You see, we've got a good record in terms of forest policy. We're doing something about below-cost timber sales in 10 national forests. We've signed this Tongass Timber Reform Act, which is in a very sensitive— below-cost timber sales in an extraordinarily sensitive American rain forest.

So I think we've got a good record. I'm very pleased with the way that forestry initiative has been received here. I noticed that it was singled out by several of the leaders in their speech yesterday. And it's those positive things that I think just emphasize once again the U.S. role of leadership in the environment.

### POW–MIA's

*Q.* Mr. President, what do you think, sir, of this revelation from Boris Yeltsin that the Soviet Union was holding 12 American POW's during the 1950's? And were you ever aware of this either in your role as once CIA Director or as President, and did you ever get a hint of this from your close relationship with Mikhail Gorbachev?

*The President.* No. In fact, I believe that Mr. Gorbachev denied it. And what do I think of it is, I think it's very, very credible and very good that President Yeltsin is coming forward with this kind of full disclosure. He's done it in other areas. He's done it in the field of biological and chemical weapons. It's one more reason why we want to work very closely with him, and I salute him for doing that.

### Presidential Campaign

*Q.* Mr. President, Mr. Perot has said that he would not raise taxes except in a nation-al emergency. And as someone who has had some experience on statements about no new taxes, I wonder if you feel that Mr. Perot is oversimplifying the situation and if you would agree with that on the other side? [*Laughter*]

*The President.* Well, you must have missed what I said earlier on, not wanting to engage Mr. Perot. So I'll respectfully not engage him on that.

### U.N. Conference on Environment

*Q.* Mr. President, in following up this Conference, what do you think you'll be doing in the way of supporting an international organization to oversee the work that has come out of this Conference?

*The President.* I think one of the main things we're going to do is go forward with this January 1st date in order to present detailed plans to meet the climate change commitments. We're pretty far along on that, and we're prepared to share with others. Bill Reilly will be actively involved in that. Any commitment we make here will be kept, and so we have a broad agenda to follow through on.

We forget that there are many, many commitments, some involving funds, some not, being made here at this Conference. And the EPA leadership will be extraordinarily busy in getting specific now to follow them up. I'm excited about that because I think our leadership is up to it, and I think others will welcome it.

### Iraq

*Q.* Mr. President, the House Judiciary Committee has now asked you to make your aides and documents available to provide further details about the assistance your administration gave to Iraq before the Gulf war. Do you intend to comply with that request?

*The President.* I don't know what——

*Q.* And what do you think of their efforts to create an independent counsel?

*The President.* I think it's political. I think it's purely political. We have had detailed testimony by Larry Eagleburger. I myself have discussed the policy. I sense a frustration on the part of the Democrats because of what we had to do and did in terms of the war. I think it is a pure political inquest, and we have complied fully. I know politics when I see it. I know political timing when I see it. So, we have disclosed, and we will continue to cooperate with Congress. But the determination on the special prosecutor, let's wait and see where that one goes.

But I must say that it smells political to me. I see these other hearings up there that have cost the taxpayers millions. And, incidentally, I will make one last appeal to the Congress: I would say, would you please say yes or no as to whether I was in Paris at any time, say nothing about the fall of 1980, because you're spending millions of the taxpayers' dollars trying to prove on the basis of a stupid book that I was there. Would you please certify to the American people whether this now-President and then-candidate was in Paris?

Why the Congress keeps spending the taxpayers' monies on these witch hunts, I do not know. I'm a little sick of it, but there's not a heck of a lot I can do about it except to express a continual and somewhat mounting frustration as I see now another attack. Our policy was well-known. We tried to bring Saddam Hussein into the family of nations. That policy was not successful. We did not enhance his nuclear, biological, or chemical weapon capability, a charge recklessly made in this political year. When we failed and when he took an aggression, the whole world joined with us in standing against it. Now some of the very people that opposed U.S. action are trying to redeem themselves by a lot of political inquiry. And I don't think the American people are going to stand for it.

Thank you all very much.

*Note: The President's 131st news conference began at 11 a.m. in the Sheraton Rio.*

# Remarks at the Groundbreaking Ceremony for the Korean War Veterans Memorial
*June 14, 1992*

Thank you very much, very much. May I say that it is an honor for me to be introduced by General Davis and to have just met with so many men that wear with pride the Congressional Medal of Honor, the highest award our country can give. And may I salute the Members of Congress who are with us today. I haven't seen them all, but over my shoulder is Senator Rudman, who fought in Korea; Senator Dole, a hero of World War II; Senator Chafee, who was in the Korean fight; and many others. I'm going to miss a few over here, but I got the ones I see. And Congressman Montgomery, a friend of all the veterans, holding up his hand so I wouldn't miss him. I'm going to get in trouble now. So there they are. Of course, I want to single out, as did others, General Stilwell. I was privileged to serve with him in the intelligence community. I respect him. I know of his record. I'm pleased that his beloved Alice is with us; his son, Dick, Jr.

His dream is now about to be fulfilled, his leadership rewarded.

Ambassador Hyun, may I ask you, sir, to pay our respects to President Roh Tae Woo. And you can tell him this: The United States is going to fulfill our obligations to peace on the Korean peninsula. The United States does not quit, and we will stay with the job. May I salute the members of the diplomatic corps.

We meet, you know, on a very special day. It is Flag Day. It is the 217th anniversary of the United States Army. It's a special occasion to break ground for a memorial to those veterans whose courage now lives as history, passed from one generation to another.

This is not a memorial to war, but a memorial to peace America has always fought for. I was Vice President when Ronald Reagan signed legislation authorizing the creation of a national Korean War Veterans Memorial. And today, as President, I'm proud to help honor America's peacemakers who served during the Korean war.

America's uniformed sons and daughters went to Korea not for themselves. Hating war, they sought only liberty. They fought so that the enslaved might be free. They fought in the Pusan Perimeter and at Inchon, on Heartbreak Ridge, and Pork Chop Hill, in the sea and the air and the gullies and the ridges. And to our 5.7 million Korean war veterans, a grateful Nation thanks you for what you did. For stopping totalitarianism, the entire free world still salutes you.

We remember first how America's finest took up arms and bore our burden for a cause larger than ourselves. Among them was Lieutenant Colonel John Page, then 46, at home in New Orleans with his wife and kids. He became one of the 54,246 Americans who gave their lives; the more than 103,000 that were wounded; the over 8,000 still missing or unaccounted for.

Let me put it plain: Though many MIA's have returned to America in the past years, no one can rest until all have been accounted for. I know our Secretary of Defense, our able Secretary of Defense, Dick Cheney, feels exactly that way and is doing everything he can to guarantee every single American is accounted for.

Men like John Page did the hard work of freedom. Seeking the enemy position, he asked to ride in a two-seat observer plane. Once in the air he told the pilot to fly low over their encampment. Speechless, the pilot watched as Page pulled pins from three grenades, leaned out of the cockpit, and dropped them on the enemy positions. Later he bombed foxholes with grenades, climbed aboard a tank and fired machine gun bursts which forced the enemy to flee, and then finally led a rush which destroyed an enemy roadblock and made three dozen of the enemy retreat.

John Page did all of this in his first 12 days in combat, which were his last 12 days on Earth. His last reported words were to a comrade, "Get back, that's an order. I'll cover you." And the Marine Corps named this Army man a recipient of the Navy Cross. America gave him the Medal of Honor. He showed how greatness touched all those who went to this unknown land

amid the shroud of darkness to illuminate the night.

Here in God's light amid the woods, we recall, as proved in Korea and again, as General Davis mentioned, in the Persian Gulf, that together allies could contain tyranny by combining strength. Fighting side by side under the flag of the United Nations, freedom-loving countries of the United States and the Republic of Korea and other allies strove to halt aggression.

And did we succeed? Did we ever. We built a stable peace that has lasted nearly 40 years, and together we held the line. And in the wake of North Korea's wanton aggression in June of 1950, America did not hesitate. The Eighth United States Army dispatched Task Force Smith as the lead element of what eventually—[*applause*]. And I saluted some of the veterans of that task force, a task force which eventually became a mighty United Nations effort to hold the line. Who can forget the epic battle of the First Marine Division at Chosin Reservoir. They held the line against overwhelming odds. And so did men named MacArthur and Ridgeway and Chesty Puller, veterans who serve in the Halls of Congress, some of whom are with us today, veterans like James Garner and Neil Armstrong.

These Americans sought the highest cause and the community of God and man, a world where the force of law outlasted the use of force. And so did other parties I want to thank, for instance, sponsors like the American Battle Monuments Commission, chaired by the great General P.X. Kelly behind me here, we owe him a vote of thanks; and the Korean War Veterans Memorial Advisory Board, with General Ray Davis as its chairman; and Chung Dul Ok, whose company donated over $1 million to this memorial.

Let me note this: Every penny, every penny of its funding has been privately financed. And thanks to the designers of this memorial's unforgettable silhouette, we salute them as well.

Finally, let me salute the foot soldiers you see in this memorial, whose memory we take with us, whose nobility enriches us. I mean the men and women who braved the heat and cold, lack of sleep and food, and the human hell of fire. They were rich and poor, black and white and red and brown and yellow. The soldiers I speak of were young, I'm sure afraid, and far from home. Yet in the foxholes, in the foothills, across the rugged snow-covered ridges, they were selfless. Most of all they were Americans.

At this wonderful site, just take a look at Ash Woods, a quiet grove of trees right near the majestic Lincoln Memorial. Recall how it endures as testimony to the living and the dead. When tyranny threatened, you were quick to answer your country's call. Sadly, your country wasn't quite as quick to answer your call for recognition of that sacrifice. And today we say, the length of time it has taken for this day to arrive only adds to the depth of our gratitude.

I believe that the Korean war showed that ours would not be the land of the free if it were not the home of the brave. And in that spirit, with eternal love for what you did and what you are, it is now my privilege to break the ground on behalf of every American for the Korean War Veterans Memorial.

May God bless those who served. And may God bless ours, the greatest, freest country on the face of the Earth, the United States of America. Thank you all very, very much.

*Note: The President spoke at 2:45 p.m. on the Mall. In his remarks, he referred to Gen. Richard Stilwell, who led the effort for the Korean War Veterans Memorial, and Hong-Choo Hyun, Ambassador of the Republic of Korea.*

## Remarks Prior to Discussions With President Sali Berisha of Albania
## *June 15, 1992*

*President Berisha.* I've been very pleased with the reception that Albanians felt to Mr. Baker, because on that occasion they showed that the propaganda against didn't work at all, and Albanians have had in their hearts and minds special feelings and very friendly feelings for the United States and United States Government and people.

*President Bush.* Well, that's good. You know, I just signed the agreement, sending it up to Capitol Hill to push forward now with these preferences. I just want you to know that I took great pleasure in doing that, and I want you to have a pen. You get a free pen there.

*President Berisha.* Thank you very much.

*President Bush.* That was the one I used to sign that paper. When you go up to see the Congress, I hope you'll encourage them to move swiftly now. We will do our best from here. But I don't think there will be any controversy at all on this. I think everybody salutes what you're doing.

*President Berisha.* It is for Albanian people a very historical signature.

*President Bush.* Well, it's important and——

*President Berisha.* Thank you very much. We appreciate also very much the attitude of United States adopted toward ex-Yugoslavia. And I could assure you that the heartiness of your attitude and the statesman that Mr. Baker did in London was very important to slow down the activity and to stop the shifting of the war to Kosovo and other regions.

*President Bush.* Well, we want to talk a little more about that when we have our private meeting, because we are very anxious to be helpful where we can. But you're so close to it; I want to get your views on Kosovo and see where we go.

*Note: The remarks began at 1:32 p.m. in the Oval Office at the White House. A tape was not available for verification of the content of these remarks. The proclamation on trade with Albania is listed in Appendix E at the end of this volume.*

# Letter to Congressional Leaders on Trade With Albania
*June 15, 1992*

*Dear Mr. Speaker: (Dear Mr. President:)*

In accordance with section 407 of the Trade Act of 1974 (Public Law 93–618, January 3, 1975; 88 Stat. 1978), as amended (the "Trade Act"), I am transmitting a copy of a proclamation that extends nondiscriminatory treatment to the products of Albania. I also enclose the text of the "Agreement on Trade Relations Between the United States of America and the Republic of Albania," including exchanges of letters that form an integral part of the Agreement, which was signed on May 14, 1992, and which is included as an annex to the proclamation.

The Agreement will provide a nondiscriminatory framework for our bilateral trade relations and thus strengthen both economic and political relations between the United States and Albania. Conclusion of this Agreement is an important step we can take to provide greater economic benefits to both countries. It will also give further impetus to the progress we have made in our overall diplomatic relations since last year and help to reinforce political and economic reform in Albania. In that context, the United States is encouraging Albania to continue to strive for a democratic, pluralistic society.

I believe that the Agreement is consistent with both the letter and the spirit of the Trade Act. It provides for mutual extension of nondiscriminatory tariff treatment while seeking to ensure overall reciprocity of economic benefits. It includes safeguard arrangements to ensure that our trade with Albania will grow without causing disruption to the U.S. market and consequent injury to domestic firms or loss of jobs for American workers.

The Agreement also confirms and expands for American businesses certain basic rights in conducting commercial transactions both within Albania and with Albanian nationals and business entities. Other provisions include those dealing with settlement of commercial disputes, financial transactions, and government commercial offices. Through this Agreement, Albania also undertakes obligations to modernize and upgrade very substantially its protection of intellectual property rights. Once fully implemented, the Albanian intellectual property regime will be on a par with that of our principal industrialized trading partners. This Agreement will not alter U.S. law or practice with respect to the protection of intellectual property.

On May 20, 1992, I waived application of subsections (a) and (b) of section 402 of the Trade Act to Albania. I determined that this waiver will substantially promote the objectives of section 402, and, pursuant to section 402(c)(2) of the Trade Act, notified the Congress that I have received assurances that the emigration practices of Albania will henceforth lead substantially to achievement of those objectives.

I urge that the Congress act as soon as possible to approve the "Agreement on Trade Relations Between the United States of America and the Republic of Albania" and the proclamation extending nondiscriminatory treatment to products of Albania by enactment of a joint resolution referred to in section 151 of the Trade Act.

Sincerely,

GEORGE BUSH

*Note: Identical letters were sent to Thomas S. Foley, Speaker of the House of Representatives, and Dan Quayle, President of the Senate. The proclamation and the agreement were published in the Federal Register on June 17.*

## Presidential Determination No. 92–33—Memorandum on Trade With Albania
*June 15, 1992*

*Memorandum for the Secretary of State*

*Subject:* Determination Under Section 405(a) of the Trade Act of 1974, as Amended—Albania

Pursuant to the authority vested in me under the Trade Act of 1974 (Public Law 93–618, January 3, 1975; 88 Stat. 1978), as amended (the "Trade Act"), I determine, pursuant to section 405(a) of the Trade Act (19 U.S.C. 2435(a)), that the "Agreement on Trade Relations Between the United States

of America and the Republic of Albania" will promote the purposes of the Trade Act and is in the national interest.

You are authorized and directed to transmit copies of this determination to the appropriate Members of Congress and to publish it in the *Federal Register.*

GEORGE BUSH

[*Filed with the Office of the Federal Register, 2:11 p.m., June 24, 1992*]

## Memorandum on the Generalized System of Preferences
*June 15, 1992*

*Memorandum for the United States Trade Representative*

*Subject:* Actions Concerning the Generalized System of Preferences

Pursuant to sections 502(b)(4), 502(b)(7), and 502(c)(5) and section 504 of the Trade Act of 1974, as amended (the 1974 Act) (19 U.S.C. 2462(b)(4), 2462(b)(7), 2462(c)(5), and 2464), I am authorized to make determinations concerning the alleged expropriation without compensation by a beneficiary developing country, to make findings concerning whether steps have been taken or are being taken by certain beneficiary developing countries to afford internationally recognized worker rights to workers in such countries, to take into account in determining the Generalized System of Preferences (GSP) eligibility of a beneficiary developing country the extent to which certain beneficiary developing countries are providing adequate and effective means under its laws for foreign nationals to secure, to exercise, and to enforce exclusive rights in intellectual property, including patents, trademarks, and copyrights, and to modify the application of duty-free treatment under the GSP currently being afforded to such

beneficiary developing countries as a result of my determinations.

Specifically, after considering a private sector request for a review concerning the alleged expropriation by Peru of property owned by a United States person allegedly without prompt, adequate, and effective compensation, without entering into good faith negotiations to provide such compensation or otherwise taking steps to discharge its obligations, and without submitting the expropriation claim to arbitration, I have decided to continue the review of the alleged expropriation by Peru.

Second, after considering various private sector requests for a review of whether or not certain beneficiary developing countries have taken or are taking steps to afford internationally recognized worker rights (as defined in section 502(a)(4) of the 1974 Act (19 U.S.C. 2462(a)(4)) to workers in such countries, and in accordance with section 502(b)(7) of the 1974 Act (19 U.S.C. 2462(b)(7)), I have determined that Bangladesh and Sri Lanka have taken or are taking steps to afford internationally recognized worker rights, and I have determined that Syria has not taken and is not taking steps to afford such internationally recognized rights. Therefore, I am notifying the Congress of my intention to suspend the GSP eligibility of Syria. Finally, I have determined to continue to review the status of such worker rights in El Salvador, Mauritania, Panama, and Thailand.

Third, after considering various private sector requests for a review of whether or not certain beneficiary developing countries are providing adequate and effective means under their laws for foreign nationals to secure, to exercise, and to enforce exclusive rights in intellectual property, including patents, trademarks, and copyrights, I have determined to continue the review of Guatemala and Malta.

Pursuant to section 504 of the 1974 Act, after considering various requests for a waiver of the application of section 504(c) of the 1974 Act (19 U.S.C. 2464(c)) with respect to certain eligible articles, I have determined that it is appropriate to modify the application of duty-free treatment under the GSP currently being afforded to certain articles and to certain beneficiary developing countries.

Specifically, pursuant to section 504(c)(3) of the 1974 Act (19 U.S.C. 2464(c)(3)), I have determined that it is appropriate to waive the application of section 504(c) of the 1974 Act with respect to certain eligible articles from certain beneficiary developing countries. I have received the advice of the United States International Trade Commission on whether any industries in the United States are likely to be adversely affected by such waivers, and I have determined, based on that advice and on the considerations described in sections 501 and 502(c) of the 1974 Act (19 U.S.C. 2461 and 2462(c)), that such waivers are in the national economic interest of the United States. The waivers of the application of section 504(c) of the 1974 Act apply to the eligible articles in the HTS subheadings and the beneficiary developing countries set opposite such HTS subheadings enumerated below.

These determinations shall be published in the *Federal Register.*

GEORGE BUSH

*[Filed with the Office of the Federal Register, 9:58 a.m., June 16, 1992]*

*Note: This memorandum and its annex were published in the Federal Register on June 17. The related proclamation is listed in Appendix E at the end of this volume.*

# Letter to Congressional Leaders on Trade With Syria
*June 15, 1992*

*Dear Mr. Speaker: (Dear Mr. President:)*

I am writing concerning the Generalized System of Preferences (GSP). The GSP program offers duty-free access to the U.S. market for products that are imported from developing countries. It is authorized by title V of the Trade Act of 1974.

Pursuant to title V, I have determined that Syria no longer meets the eligibility requirements set forth in the GSP law. In particular, I have determined that Syria has not taken and is not taking steps to afford internationally recognized worker rights. Accordingly, I intend to suspend Syria in-

definitely as a designated beneficiary developing country for purposes of the GSP.

This notice is submitted in accordance with section 502(a)(2) of the Trade Act of 1974.

Sincerely,

GEORGE BUSH

*Note: Identical letters were sent to Thomas S. Foley, Speaker of the House of Representatives, and Dan Quayle, President of the Senate. The related proclamation is listed in Appendix E at the end of this volume.*

## Memorandum on the Generalized System of Preferences
*June 15, 1992*

*Memorandum for the United States Trade
Representative*

*Subject:* Actions Concerning the
Generalized System of Preferences

Pursuant to section 504 of the 1974 Act, after considering various requests for a waiver of the application of section 504(c) of the 1974 Act (19 U.S.C. 2464(c)) with respect to certain eligible articles, I have determined that it is appropriate to modify the application of duty-free treatment under the Generalized System of Preferences (GSP) currently being afforded to certain articles and to certain beneficiary developing countries.

Specifically, pursuant to section 504(c)(3) of the 1974 Act (19 U.S.C. 2464(c)(3)), I have determined that it is appropriate to waive the application of section 504(c) of the 1974 Act with respect to Harmonized Tariff Schedule of the United States (HTS) subheading 2401.10.40 for Turkey. I have received the advice of the United States International Trade Commission on whether any industries in the United States are likely to be adversely affected by such waiver, and I have determined, based on that advice and on the considerations described in sections 501 and 502(c) of the 1974 Act (19 U.S.C. 2461 and 2462(c)), that such waiver is in the national economic interest of the United States.

Further, I have also determined, pursuant to section 504(d)(1) of the 1974 Act (19 U.S.C. 2464(d)(1)), that the limitation provided for in section 504(c)(1)(B) of the 1974 Act (19 U.S.C. 2464(c)(1)(B)) should not apply with respect to certain eligible articles because no like or directly competitive article was produced in the United States on January 3, 1985. Such articles are enumerated in the list below of HTS subheadings.

These determinations shall be published in the *Federal Register*.

GEORGE BUSH

*[Filed with the Office of the Federal Register, 5:07 p.m., June 15, 1992]*

*Note: This memorandum and its annex were published in the Federal Register on June 17. The related proclamation is listed in Appendix E at the end of this volume.*

## Statement by Press Secretary Fitzwater on the Supreme Court Decision on the *Alvarez-Machain* Case
*June 15, 1992*

With respect to the U.S. Supreme Court decision today on the *Alvarez-Machain* case: The United States understands that international cooperation is required to address effectively the threat posed by international criminal activity, particularly international terrorism and drug trafficking, to the world community. United States policy is to work cooperatively with foreign governments to combat that threat.

The United States also understands the importance to world peace and security of a system of international law. The United States strongly believes in fostering respect for international rules of law, including in particular the principles of respect for territorial integrity and sovereign equality of states.

U.S. policy is to cooperate with foreign states in achieving law enforcement objectives. Neither the arrest of Alvarez-Machain nor the recent U.S. Supreme Court decision reflects any change in this policy. Reflecting this policy, the United States has informed Mexico that following the arrest of Alvarez-Machain, the United States has taken additional steps to ensure that U.S. law enforcement activities overseas fully take into account foreign relations and international law.

## Appointment of Shirley M. Green as Deputy Assistant to the President for Presidential Messages and Correspondence
*June 15, 1992*

The President today announced the appointment of Shirley M. Green to be Deputy Assistant to the President for Presidential Messages and Correspondence.

Since February 1989, Mrs. Green has been Special Assistant to the President for Presidential Messages and Correspondence. From 1987 to 1989, Mrs. Green was Deputy Associate Administrator for Communications for the National Aeronautics and Space Administration. Prior to this she was Director of Public Affairs for NASA. From 1981 to 1985, Mrs. Green held the position of Deputy Press Secretary to Vice President George Bush.

Mrs. Green served previously as a member of the George Bush for President campaign staff in 1979–80, as public affairs director for the Texas Federation of Republican Women from 1969 to 1973, on the staff of Congressman Bob Price in 1967, and on the headquarters staff of the Texas Republican Party from 1965 to 1967. She was a local campaign chairman for numerous Republican candidates in Texas, including President Gerald Ford in 1976 and James A. Baker III in 1978.

Mrs. Green received a bachelor of business administration degree from the University of Texas in 1956. She has two daughters and resides in Washington, DC.

## Nomination of Robert S. Silberman To Be an Assistant Secretary of the Army
*June 15, 1992*

The President today announced his intention to nominate Robert S. Silberman, of Maryland, to be Assistant Secretary of the Army for Manpower and Reserve Affairs. He would succeed G. Kim Wincup.

Since 1990, Mr. Silberman has served as Principal Deputy Assistant Secretary of Defense for Force Management and Personnel. He served as Deputy Maritime Administrator with the U.S. Maritime Administration at the Department of Transportation, 1988–90. From 1986 to 1987, he served as senior project manager and special assistant to the president with the Ogden Corp. in New York, NY. He also served as a research and marketing specialist and project manager with the Henley Group-Signal Environmental Systems, Inc., in Hampton, NH, 1985–86.

Mr. Silberman graduated from Dartmouth College (B.A., 1980), and Johns Hopkins School of Advanced International Studies (M.A., 1990). He was born October 30, 1957, in Boston, MA. He is married, has three children, and resides in Bethesda, MD.

## Remarks at the Arrival Ceremony for President Boris Yeltsin of Russia
*June 16, 1992*

Mr. President and Mrs. Yeltsin, distinguished members of the Russian delegation, welcome to the United States of America. Also, a welcome to all of you who have come here to welcome President Yeltsin and Mrs. Yeltsin. Welcome to the White House.

Mr. President, today marks the beginning of a new era, a new kind of summit, not a meeting between two powers struggling for global supremacy but between two partners striving to build a democratic peace. From this summit we see a new horizon, a new world of peace and hope, a new world of cooperation and partnership between the American and Russian people. Our hope is that this partnership will end forever the old antagonisms that kept our people apart, that kept the world in confrontation and conflict.

Mr. President, your nation is embarked on a great experiment, a new Russian revolution with freedom as its goal. The progress that Russia has made and the promise of more to come owes much to the courage and vision of President Boris Yeltsin. Mr. President, like Peter the Great, you are redefining Russia's understanding of itself, redefining Russia's role in the world. But for the first time in modern Russian history, a leader claims as his authority not the dispensation of history but a democratic mandate. You come here as an elected leader, elected by the people in free and fair elections. And we salute you.

Already, Mr. President, together we're transforming our relations with benefits not simply to our two nations but to the entire world. Today the threat of a cataclysmic conventional war has vanished with the Warsaw Pact and the rise of democracy in Russia. Today the threat of a nuclear nightmare is more distant now than at any time since the dawn of the nuclear age.

Mr. President, I say this with a sense of pride, a sense of awe, and above all, a sense of history. There is no greater gift to the people of America, to the people of Russia, to the people all over the world than an end to the awful specter of global war. And think for just a minute about what that means not for presidents, not for heads of state or historians but for parents and for their children. It means a future free from fear.

This first U.S.-Russia summit gives us a chance to lay the foundation of a more peaceful and prosperous future for all of our citizens. We'll discuss Russia's historic transition to the free market, its integration into the world economy, and our commitment to support those reforms. We will seek new ways to expand trade between our two nations; to create wealth and growth and jobs; new levels of military cooperation to reduce further the risk of war; and finally, new agreements to reduce nuclear arms and to remove from our arsenals the most destructive weapons.

But this morning I want to focus on our ultimate goal, on the challenge we face to forge a new peace, a permanent peace between two nations who must never again be adversaries. Right now, the people of Russia are waging a valiant struggle for the very same rights and freedoms that we Americans prize so deeply. The fate of that revolution, the future of democracy in Russia and other new nations of the old Soviet empire is the most important foreign policy issue of our time. The United States and its democratic allies must play a key role in helping forge a democratic peace.

That is why I urge the Congress of the United States once again to pass the "FREEDOM Support Act" to strengthen democratic reform in Russia and the other new nations of the old Soviet Union. And yes, the aid that I've requested from the Congress is significant, but it is also a tiny fraction of the $4 trillion that this Nation spent to secure peace during the long cold war. The resources we devote now are an investment in a new century of peace with Russia.

History offers us a rare chance, a chance

to achieve what twice before this century has escaped our grasp. It is the vision that perished twice in the battlefields of Europe, the vision that gave us hope through the long cold war, the dream of a new world of freedom.

Mr. President, when we think of the world our children and theirs will inherit, no single factor will shape their future more than the fate of the revolution now unfold-ing in Russia. Your Russian revolution, like our American Revolution, simply must succeed.

Once again, my friend, welcome to the White House. And may God grant a peaceful future to the American and the Russian people. Welcome, sir. Glad you're here.

*Note: The President spoke at 10:11 a.m. on the South Lawn at the White House.*

# Exchange With Reporters Prior to Discussions With President Boris Yeltsin of Russia
*June 16, 1992*

## POW–MIA's

*Q.* Mr. President, do you think there are any POW's in the Soviet Union, Americans? This to President Bush first and then Yeltsin.

*President Yeltsin.* It is possible.

*Q.* Are they alive?

*President Yeltsin.* An investigating commission is working, led by Mr. Volkogonov. Many things have been revealed after the examination of the archives of the KGB and the Central Committee of the Communist Party. But that work is continuing both in the archives and in the places where the POW's were. We shall try to investigate each individual case. And all the information will be, of course, handed over to the American side. The initial information has been handed over to the Senate.

*Q.* Would you expect more information this week?

*President Bush.* Let me just thank President Yeltsin for this because this is a matter of grave concern to the American people. He has made these observations, pledged full cooperation and support. I think this really expresses as well as anything else this new era that we were both talking about on the lawn. And I have every confidence that what he says here is true, that they will get to the bottom of it. And if any single American is unaccounted for, they will go the extra mile to see that that person is accounted for. And I think that's what the American people need to know. I think

that's what President Yeltsin has clearly pledged to do. So we are grateful to him for that.

*Q.* Does it come as a complete surprise to you, Mr. President?

*President Bush.* Yes, it comes as a——

*Q.* You had no idea?

*President Bush.* Thank you all very much.

*Q.* Have you got an arms agreement yet?

*President Bush.* Out of here, Helen [Helen Thomas, United Press International].

[*At this point, one group of reporters left the room, and another group entered.*]

*Q.* ——additional information on the American POW's.

*President Yeltsin.* As I just answered that question.

*Q.* We were behind the doors.

*President Yeltsin.* The commission headed by Volkogonov was working and is continuing to work, and they're opening up all the data. If they said this issue doesn't exist, that there are no POW's there now, there are a lot of factors being opened up and discovered. And it's very possible that there are a few of them still left alive, even on our own territory perhaps. So the commission is continuing its work, and we are going to carry this all the way to the very ground to find out the fate of every single last American who might be on our territory.

*Q.* How much time will that require? What new ideas and projects were you talking about in your opening statement?

*President Yeltsin.* That's ahead. That's for our negotiations.

### Nuclear Arms Agreement

*Q.* Boris Nikolayevich, tell us please, and you, Mr. Bush, both agree that the program is very, very intense, a lot on the plate, 20 different issues. What are you going to be concentrating your attention on with Mr. Bush?

*President Yeltsin.* First of all, national security and deep cuts in nuclear arms. As a matter of fact, up until now we have not yet finalized this issue, but we have met with the President and with our delegations, of course, and the Secretaries of State and the Minister of Foreign Affairs, to sit

down and finalize this today. And I'm sure that we will find a solution, and we shall sign a balanced, equal agreement. I'm sure of that.

*Q.* Do you think you will be able to announce a new arms control agreement by the end of the day?

*President Bush.* As soon as you get out of here, we're going to talk about it.

Thank you all.

*Note: The exchange began at 10:35 a.m. in the Oval Office. President Yeltsin spoke in Russian, and his remarks were translated by an interpreter. A tape was not available for verification of the content of this exchange.*

## Remarks With President Boris Yeltsin of Russia Announcing Strategic Arms Reductions and an Exchange With Reporters
*June 16, 1992*

*President Bush.* Mr. President. Let me just say that I'm pleased to announce that President Yeltsin and I have just reached an extraordinary agreement on two areas of vital importance to our countries and to the world.

First, we have agreed on far-reaching new strategic arms reductions. Building on the agreement reached with Russia, Ukraine, Kazakhstan, and Byelarus, our two countries are now agreeing to even further dramatic strategic arms reductions, substantially below the levels determined by START. We've agreed to eliminate the world's most dangerous weapons, heavy ICBM's and all other multiple warhead ICBM's, and dramatically reduce our total strategic nuclear weapons.

Those dramatic reductions will take place in two phases. They will be completed no later than the year 2003 and may be completed as early as the year 2000 if the United States can assist Russia in the required destruction of ballistic missile systems. With this agreement the nuclear nightmare recedes more and more for ourselves, for our children, and for our grand-

children.

Just a few years ago, the United States was planning a strategic nuclear stockpile of about 13,000 warheads. Now President Yeltsin and I have agreed that both sides will go down to 3,000 to 3,500 warheads, with each nation determining its own force structure within that range.

I'd like to point out that this fundamental agreement, which in earlier years could not have been completed even in a decade, has been completed in only 5 months. Our ability to reach this agreement so quickly is a tribute to the new relationship between the United States and Russia and to the personal leadership of our guest, Boris Yeltsin.

In the near future, the United States and Russia will record our agreement in a brief treaty document that President Yeltsin and I will sign and submit for ratification in our countries. President Yeltsin and I have also agreed to work together, along with the allies and other interested states, to develop a concept for global protection systems against limited ballistic missile attack.

We will establish a senior group to explore practical steps towards that end, including the sharing of early warning and cooperation in developing ballistic missile defense capabilities and technologies. This group will also explore the development of a legal basis for cooperation, including new treaties and agreements and possible changes to existing treaties and agreements necessary to implement the global protection system. That group, headed by Dennis Ross for the United States, will first meet in Moscow within the next 30 days.

In conclusion, these are remarkable steps for our two countries, a departure from the tensions and the suspicions of the past and a tangible, important expression of our new relationship. They also hold major promise for a future world protected against the danger of limited ballistic missile attack.

Mr. President, all yours.

*President Yeltsin.* Mr. President, ladies and gentlemen. I would like to add a few words to what President Bush has just announced here. What we have achieved is an unparalleled and probably an unexpected thing for you and for the whole world. You are the first to hear about this historic decision, which has been reached today after just 5 months of negotiations. We are, in fact, meeting a sharp, dramatic reduction in the total number for the two sides of the amount of nuclear warheads from 21,000 to 6,000 to 7,000 for the United States of America and Russia.

Indeed, we have been able to cut, over those 5 months of negotiations, the total number of nuclear warheads to one-third, while it took 15 years under the START Treaty to make some reductions. This is an expression of the fundamental change in the political and economic relations between the United States of America and Russia. It is also an expression and proof of the personal trust and confidence that has been established between the Presidents of these countries, President Bush of the United States of America and the President of Russia.

These things have been achieved without deception, without anybody wishing to gain unilateral advantages. This is a result of the trust entertained by the President of the democratic Russia towards America and by the President of the United States towards the new Russia. This is the result of a care-

fully measured balance of security. We were not going in for numbers, for just 1,000, 2,000, 3,000 pieces. Rather, we have established a bracket for each country to elect the number they figure that it will consider appropriate for its own defense and security.

As I have told you, the total number will go down from 21,000 to 6,000 for two sides. Under the first phase, the reductions for the two sides will be down to 3,800 to 4,250 bracket; including ICBM's, 1,250; and heavy missiles, 650; SLBM's, 2,250. Under the second phase, we shall go down to respectively 3,000 and 3,500, including total reduction and destruction of heavy missiles. Land-based MIRV's will be reduced as well. SLBM's will go down to 1,750.

Each country will elect the figure that it will consider appropriate to ensure its defense and security. Thus, we are departing from the ominous parity where each country was exerting every effort to stay in line, which has led Russia, for instance, having half of its population living below the poverty line. We cannot afford it, and therefore, we must have minimum security level to deal with any possible eventuality which might arise anywhere in the world and threaten our security.

But we know one thing: We shall not fight against each other. This is a solemn undertaking that we are taking today, and it will be reflected as a matter of partnership and friendship in the charter that we are going to sign. Our proposal is to cut the process of destruction from the proposed 13 years down to 9 years. So the things that I have been mentioning before will be materialized by the year 2000.

I am happy to be involved here in this historic occasion, and I will also hope that I will be as happy when this thing is materialized, and President Bush and I will be celebrating together the implementation of that agreement in the year 2000. I thank you.

I want to add that these figures have been agreed with and ratified by the Secretary for Defense, Mr. Cheney, and the Defense Minister, Pavel Grachev, of the Russian Federation. I thank you.

*President Bush.* I would only add to that my gratitude to the Secretary of State; to

Mr. Kozyrev, his counterpart; and also to General Scowcroft and others that have worked on this and accomplished all this in record time.

We are going to have a press conference tomorrow and so maybe we'll just take one each here.

*Q.* Mr. President, just a few days ago, President Yeltsin was complaining you were trying to take advantage of him. How do you——

*President Bush.* I can't hear, there's too many questions.

*Q.* Vietnam POW's——

*President Bush.* Right here. I'm going to have a little statement on that in just a minute.

*Q.* Would you explain to people who might not understand why friends who trust each other and do not plan to attack would still need 7,000 nuclear warheads?

*President Bush.* What I am saying we've moved dramatically down from 13,000. This will be seen as an enormous move forward towards the relaxation of tension and towards the friendship that we feel for each other; the elimination of the most destabilizing of weapons is extraordinarily positive. The fact that each country, at this juncture in history, retains some nuclear weapons speaks for itself. Who knows what lies out there ahead? But certainly I agree with what President Yeltsin said, that there is no animosity. The cold war days are over. He came here in a spirit of forward movement on these arms control agreements, and that speaks for itself.

*President Yeltsin.* I would like to amplify on that. I would say that in response to your question, that the technical and financial resources that are required in order to destroy, dismantle, and reduce the total number of warheads and missiles from 21,000 to 6,000, 7,000 is enormous. This is the only thing that conditions this figure.

*POW–MIA's*

*President Bush.* With your permission, Mr. President, I would like to take the last question which relates to the POW–MIA discussions that we have had.

President Yeltsin and I discussed this morning that issue that is of the highest priority for our administration and, I know,

for every American: the fate of American POW's and MIA's from World War II, Korea, the cold war period, and Vietnam.

President Yeltsin informed me for the first time that Russia may have information about the fate of some of our servicemen from Vietnam. He said the Russian Government is pursuing this information vigorously, just as we speak. And with us today are President Yeltsin's adviser, Dmitri Volkogonov over here, Dmitri, and our able former Ambassador to the U.S.S.R., Ambassador Malcolm Toon. Now, they are the co-chairs of the joint U.S.-Russian Commission on POW–MIA's. They've met during the last few months along with the Members of the United States Congress who are also part of this bipartisan U.S. delegation to unearth information on American POW's and MIA's from 1945 on, and Russian POW's and MIA's from the Afghan war.

President Yeltsin and I have instructed both of these gentlemen to begin immediately a joint U.S.-Russian pursuit of the latest information that was given to me today. I have asked Ambassador Toon to return immediately to Moscow to work on this issue. And I want to assure all Americans and particularly those families of the American POW's and MIA's that we will spare no effort in working with our Russian colleagues to investigate all information in the Russian archives concerning our servicemen. While we do not have any specific information to make public today, I pledge to keep the American people informed of developments on this issue and as we find out more about these latest leads.

Let me just point out that the forthcoming comments by President Yeltsin is just one more sign of this improved new relationship between Russia and the United States of America. For him to go back and dig into these records without fear of embarrassment is an enormous consequence to the people of the United States of America. And I salute him for this. He has told me that he will go the last mile to find whatever it is exists about our possibility of American POW's and MIA's and to clear this record once and for all. And in so many other fields this demonstrates his leadership and the period of change that we are saluting and I saluted here today on the South Lawn of the White House.

So we're very grateful to you, Mr. President.

*Q.* Did he say that they're still alive?

*Q.* ——Americans are alive, Mr. President? Do you think——

*President Yeltsin.* I will only add a couple of words, Mr. President. Our commission, headed and chaired by Dmitri Volkogonov, has been meeting for several months now, and it has already met with some success. I can promise that the joint commission, which will be established following this press conference, will be working hard and will report to the American public all the information that will be found in the archives that we are going to open for it, including the archives in the KGB, in the Central Committee of the Communist Party regarding the fate of American POW's and MIA's.

*Q.* Mr. Bush, do you agree it's possible some of those Americans may still be alive?

*President Bush.* I would simply say that I have no evidence of that, but the cooperation that has been extended and again is being extended by the President of Russia will guarantee to the American people that if anyone's alive, that person, those people would be found. Equally as important to the loved ones is the accounting for any possible MIA. And so we have no evidence of anyone being alive, but I would simply say again that this is the best way to get to the bottom of it. This new approach by the President of Russia to go into these archives and to try to find missing records will be the best assurance that I can give the American people that the truth will be revealed finally.

*Q.* It there a danger of raising false hopes here, Mr. President?

*President Bush.* You've got to be careful of that, yes.

*Note: President Bush spoke at 2:47 p.m. in the Rose Garden at the White House. President Yeltsin spoke in Russian, and his remarks were translated by an interpreter.*

# Message to the Senate Returning Without Approval Legislation Amending the Mississippi Sioux Indian Judgment Fund Act
*June 16, 1992*

*To the Senate of the United States:*

I am returning herewith without my approval S. 2342. This bill would waive the 6-year statute of limitations, allowing three Sioux Indian tribes—the Sisseton-Wahpeton Sioux Tribe, the Devils Lake Sioux Tribe, and the Sisseton-Wahpeton Council of the Assiniboine and Sioux Tribes of the Fort Peck Indian Reservation—to bring an otherwise time-barred challenge to the 1972 Mississippi Sioux Indian Judgment Fund Act.

The 1972 Act apportioned to each of the three Tribes, and to a then-undetermined class of Sioux Indians who are not members of those Tribes, a percentage share of the proceeds from a 1967 judgment against the United States. The judgment rested on a finding that the United States had not paid adequate compensation to the Tribes in the 1860's for lands ceded to the United States.

The nonmember Indians are persons who are not now eligible for membership in any of the three Tribes, but who can trace their lineal ancestry to someone who was once a tribal member.

The Tribes were active participants in the administrative and legislative process leading to the 1972 Act, and they endorsed the Act and its distribution of the judgment. Nonetheless, in 1987, 15 years after enactment and 9 years after the statute of limitations had run, the Tribes sued the United States, challenging the Act's distribution to the nonmembers. The U.S. Court of Appeals for the Ninth Circuit affirmed a lower court's decision to dismiss the case, finding no excuse—legal, equitable, or otherwise—for the Tribes' failure to challenge the 1972 Act in a timely fashion, and the U.S. Supreme Court declined to review the Ninth

Circuit's decision. *Sisseton-Wahpeton Sioux Tribe, et al.* v. *United States,* 895 F.2d 588 (9th Cir. 1990), *cert. denied,* _____ U.S. _____ 11 S. Ct. 75 (1990).

I find no extraordinary circumstances or equities to justify an exception to the long-standing policy of the executive branch, which my Administration fully embraces, against *ad hoc* statute of limitations waivers and similar special relief bills. Also, there must be some definite, limited time during which the Government must be prepared to defend itself, and some finality to the pronouncements of the courts, the Congress, and the agencies.

Moreover, a waiver for the Tribes in this case would mean the waste of the considerable judicial and litigation resources that were expended in bringing the case to final resolution, and would require additional litigation that would otherwise be avoided. Thus, enactment of this bill would be inconsistent with Executive Order No. 12778 of October 23, 1991, which embodies my resolve to eliminate unnecessary, wasteful litigation.

In addition, I am concerned that enactment of this bill would be unfair to other tribes, and would serve as a highly undesirable and potentially expensive precedent.

Many other tribes were the recipients of settlement fund distributions, and many distributions, like the one challenged by the Tribes here, included payments to non-member Indians. Some of those tribes doubtless are dissatisfied with the terms of their distribution, but they are barred from a challenge by the statute of limitations. Numerous other Indian claims, totaling hundreds of millions of dollars, have been dismissed on statute of limitations or other jurisdictional grounds. In both categories of cases, tribes could rightfully claim that for purposes of fair treatment, they, too, should be allowed by the Congress to litigate the merits of their claims.

I note that S. 2342 received little, if any, consideration by the House of Representatives prior to its passage by that body. Instead, the bill was discharged from committee without hearings and brought immediately to the House floor. Had there been a full review of this proposal, I am confident that the outcome would have been different.

For these reasons, I cannot approve S. 2342.

GEORGE BUSH

The White House,
June 16, 1992.

# Message to the Congress Transmitting a Report on Federal Energy Activities
*June 16, 1992*

*To the Congress of the United States:*

I transmit herewith the annual report describing the activities of the Federal Government for fiscal year 1991 required by subtitle H, title V of the Energy Security Act (Public Law 96–264; 42 U.S.C. 8286, *et seq.*). These activities include the development of energy conservation and efficiency standards for new commercial and multi-family high-rise buildings and for new residential buildings.

GEORGE BUSH

The White House,
June 16, 1992.

## Memorandum on the Combined Federal Campaign
*June 16, 1992*

*Memorandum for the Heads of Executive Departments and Agencies*

The Combined Federal Campaign is an avenue through which thousands of Federal employees voluntarily express their concern for others.

I am delighted to inform you that Secretary of Education Lamar Alexander and Administrator of the Small Business Administration Patricia F. Saiki have agreed to serve as co-chairs of the 1992 Combined Federal Campaign of the National Capital Area. I ask that you support Administrator Saiki and Secretary Alexander by personally chairing the campaign in your agency and appointing a top official as your vice chairman.

Your commitment and visible support will help to guarantee a successful campaign this year. Together, we must do everything we can to encourage Federal employees everywhere to do their part in support of the 1992 Combined Federal Campaign.

GEORGE BUSH

## Nomination of Charles B. Salmon, Jr., To Be United States Ambassador to Laos
*June 16, 1992*

The President today announced his intention to nominate Charles B. Salmon, Jr., of New York, a career member of the Senior Foreign Service, class of Minister-Counselor, to be Ambassador of the United States to the Lao People's Democratic Republic.

Since 1989, Mr. Salmon has served as Chargé d'Affaires to the Lao People's Democratic Republic in Vientiane, Laos. He has served at the Department of State as Director of the Office of Philippine Affairs, 1986–89, and as Director of the Office of Thailand and Burma Affairs, 1985–86. Mr. Salmon served as Deputy Chief of Mission at the American Embassy in Rangoon, Burma, 1983–85, and as Deputy Chief of Mission at the American Embassy in Wellington, New Zealand, 1980–83.

Mr. Salmon graduated from Fordham University (A.B., 1959); Columbia University (M.A., 1960); and the National War College (1978). He was born January 3, 1938, in New York and presently resides in Vientiane, Laos.

## Nomination of Nicolas Miklos Salgo To Be United States Ambassador to Sweden
*June 16, 1992*

The President today announced his intention to nominate Nicolas Miklos Salgo, of Florida, to be Ambassador of the United States to Sweden. He would succeed Charles Edgar Redman.

Currently Ambassador Salgo serves as Ambassador on special bilateral property projects involving the Communist bloc at the Department of State. From 1983 to 1986, he served as U.S. Ambassador to Hungary. Ambassador Salgo founded the Watergate Improvement Associates in Washington, DC, 1960–77, and served as chairman of the Watergate Companies, 1977–83. He also served as vice chairman and chairman of Bangor Punta Corp. in Greenwich, CT, 1960–74, and founder and owner of Nicolas Salgo and Co. in New York, 1959–83.

Ambassador Salgo graduated from the University of Budapest (LL.D. and Ph.D., 1937). He was born August 17, 1914, in Budapest, Hungary. Ambassador Salgo is married, has two children, and resides in Washington, DC.

## Nomination of Irvin Hicks To Be Deputy Representative of the United States to the Security Council of the United Nations
*June 16, 1992*

The President today announced his intention to nominate Irvin Hicks, of Maryland, a career member of the Senior Foreign Service, class of Minister-Counselor, to be Deputy Representative of the United States of America to the Security Council in the United Nations, with the rank of Ambassador. He would succeed George Edward Moose.

From 1989 to 1991, Ambassador Hicks served as Deputy Assistant Secretary for African Affairs at the Department of State; his most recent assignment was Area Adviser for the 46th Session of the United Nations General Assembly. He also served as Deputy Assistant Secretary for Personnel from 1987 to 1989. From 1985 to 1987, he served as American Ambassador to the Republic of Seychelles. Ambassador Hicks has also served as Deputy Executive Director of the Bureau of African Affairs at the State Department, 1983–85; student at the U.S. Army War College in Carlisle, PA 1982–83; Chargé d'Affaires at the American Embassy in Lome, 1981–82; and Deputy Chief of Mission at the American Embassy in Lome, 1980–81.

Ambassador Hicks was born March 16, 1938, in Baltimore, MD. He presently resides in Camp Springs, MD.

## Remarks at the State Dinner for President Boris Yeltsin of Russia
*June 16, 1992*

Ladies and gentlemen, welcome to the White House. Mr. President and Mrs. Yeltsin, and distinguished guests all, Barbara and I are delighted to welcome you here tonight on a day that I think history will record as something very, very special. I am very pleased with the arrangements that we were able to work out with President Yeltsin today. I think it's good for mankind. I think it's good for the generations here and the generations to come. So you're here on an historic occasion, and we couldn't be more pleased.

Mr. President, tonight's dinner is a little bit more formal than the blue jeans and sweaters that we wore back up there at Camp David in February, but I believe the progress we made today would not have been possible without that private time we spent together and then without the hard work of our Secretary and your Foreign Minister, our Secretary of Defense, your Defense Minister, our Ambassador, your Ambassador. As I said this morning as I welcomed you to the White House, this meeting marks a new kind of summit, not a meeting between two powers that are struggling for global supremacy but between two partners striving to build a democratic peace.

This new relationship has its roots in the new Russian revolution, and that revolution owes so much to our guest here tonight. Just as crises show the mettle of a man, so too they show the strength of an idea. When, back in August of 1991, the old guard threatened to take Russia backward, Boris Yeltsin led the defense of democracy from the building the Russians call the White House. The coup plotters set out to destroy democracy, and instead, thanks to the courage of this man, they made it stronger.

Mr. President, you've been described many times as a maverick, a word coined in the American heartland to capture the independent streak that sets some individuals apart from the crowd. Well, I think our fellow Texans Jim Baker and Bob Strauss would agree you possess a certain spirit that you find on the plains of the West. And tonight we honor your courage and celebrate the new possibilities now open to us.

Think back to the cold war climate that marked earlier summits and how far we've come. How much safer, how much more hopeful to meet tonight as friends united by common ideals. More than 150 years ago de Tocqueville predicted that the United States and Russia would one day be the world's two great powers, rivals for world dominance. We must prove that prophecy was only true for a time and that our two nations can forge a new future in freedom.

Our governments will work to build stronger ties for the sake of peace and prosperity. We in this country must reach out, provide the assistance that can help Russia's democratic revolution succeed.

But the bonds that knit democracies together can never be created by government alone. Democracies grow together through the countless encounters that take place every day between private individuals—professionals, business and labor, artists and educators—in your country and ours. Gone are the days when vast parts of our countries were off-limits to foreign visitors. Under our new open lands agreement, for the first time Russian and American officials, and more important, Russian and American citizens, will be free to travel anywhere in each other's country to witness the customs and heritage that set us apart and the common humanity that draws us together.

So tonight, Mr. President, I offer this toast in the spirit of friendship to the new partnership between our people, to the success of the new Russian revolution, and to the health and happiness of Boris Yeltsin, the President of Russia.

*Note: The President spoke at 8:20 p.m. in the State Dining Room at the White House.*

# Remarks at the United States-Russia Business Summit
*June 17, 1992*

Thank you all very much. Mr. President. Thank you, Barbara. Please be seated. Let me just say what a joy it is to be here with Secretary Franklin, who's really taken off and doing a superb job for us at Commerce, and then, of course, giving me this opportunity in front of all our business leaders to salute President Yeltsin.

Yesterday was indeed an historic day, and I was proud to be at his side as we carved out a whole new approach to arms reduction; something big, something important, something that's going to benefit not only present generations but generations to come. And so you are most welcome here, sir.

Let me, before we hear from our special guest, President Yeltsin, let me just make a few comments on the business side of things. The U.S.-Russian Business Conference is important work. I will follow up in every way I can with the United States Congress to get them to pass the "FREEDOM Support Act." Let me be very clear to the American people: We are not supporting the "FREEDOM Support Act" simply because it benefits Russia. It is my view that the "FREEDOM Support Act" will benefit the United States of America and will benefit world peace and will benefit democracy and freedom.

So I ask the support of everyone in this

room, after yesterday's historic accomplishments, to join me in working that Hill up there, Congress, get them to go along and support the "FREEDOM Support Act." President Yeltsin will be talking about this, I'm sure, when he makes an historic address to the United States Congress, but I just wanted everyone here to know how committed we are. And yes, it's a tough political time and all of that, but it is in the interest of the United States of America to pass this act, and I need your help.

Later today we're going to conclude major treaties and agreements related to this new foundation between us: trade, bilateral investment and tax treaties, as well as the OPIC and Ex-Im agreements. Also effective today the United States will properly extend most-favored-nation status to Russia.

But my message to this conference is simple: Neither Government programs nor multilateral assistance is going to get this job done. Neither of those can do it. Private sector participation in the economies of Russia and the other states, especially involvement by American business, is critical to the success of Russia's bold venture into free markets. And that participation must be on a vast scale, measured in billions of dollars, for the challenge to be met.

To that end, I'm pleased to announce that OPIC, headed by Fred Zeder, who's so well-known to everybody here, OPIC is going to have an agreement between the U.S. and Russia, and that one enters into force today. This agreement's going to permit OPIC to provide investment insurance to American private investors. It's also going to provide additional financing and investor services for joint ventures in other products in the Federation. With OPIC and Ex-Im, everyone wins. Russia can tap into the ingenuity of American business in our capital goods, our know-how, and our technology, which are indeed the best in the entire world. In my view that help will enable Russia to develop its food and health sectors, recover its energy resources, privatize state industries, and convert military plants to civilian production.

Now Boris Yeltsin, President Boris Yeltsin, talked to us in great detail about this yesterday. I can just assure you from what

he told me then and from what our business-oriented and able Ambassador, Bob Strauss, has been telling me all along, he understands this. He understands their need for change. He understands the fact that they've got to do some streamlining themselves.

But what we want him to know while he's here is that we are interested in moving forward vigorously with private-sector participation to help not only Russia but certainly to help ourselves. That's the approach that I'll be taking as we encourage investment and as we encourage change in Russia to accommodate the needs of the business community. American businesses, by investing in trading with Russia, are going to create thousands of jobs here at home, and I think that's a point we ought to keep in mind.

With the OPIC in agreement, now in effect, Fred Zeder is going to be leading a group of 26 business representatives to Moscow and other Russian cities on one-on-one business meetings and site visits to develop private sector deals. This is just the beginning of what surely will become one of the largest two-way trading relationships in the entire world.

In '91, exports of American manufactured goods to Russia and other states have grown by almost 40 percent. We all know that the totals are not that large yet, but that's an enormous jump in just the one year. For the first time, Russia is participating in the community of free market international organizations. You know what they are: IMF and the World Bank and, at some point, the GATT. This would have been unthinkable just a few years ago. We will invite Russia and the other states to join with COCOM members in this new, informal, cooperative forum to provide significantly wider access to the high technology goods that previously were banned, previously denied.

So, as I said, the historic transformation of the Russian economy is one of the great challenges of our time. The hundreds of billions of dollars in capital and technologies that Russia will need will come, in large measure, not from governments but from private businesses. And as we all know, neither command economies nor any other government can produce wealth. Wealth is produced by the initiative and the energy of individual entrepreneurs.

So, let me conclude, but just signal once again the importance of business investment, business participation. I will do my level-best to make that climate, that business climate, good for investment abroad and to do what we can to facilitate the changes that are needed here to guarantee the utmost cooperation with the private sector here, with the cooperation with the private sector there.

I would be remiss if I didn't tell you of my high regard for President Yeltsin. He came in with that great show of courage that just excited every single American, standing on top of that tank standing up for democracy and freedom, standing against totalitarianism. The big thing—I will just stay standing because he's coming on in a minute—but the big thing is, Mr. President, we are going to support you. You've shown the way towards democracy and freedom in Russia, and it's in the interest of the United States of America to follow through. And we will. Thank you, sir.

*Note: The President spoke at 9:12 a.m. at the J.W. Marriott Hotel.*

# The President's News Conference With President Boris Yeltsin of Russia
*June 17, 1992*

*President Bush.* Well, Mr. President and distinguished members of the Russian delegation and distinguished guests, all. This has been an historic summit meeting. It brings us to the threshold of a new world, a world of hope and opportunity. The collapse of the U.S.S.R. and the emergence of a democratic Russia provides us with the greatest opportunity in our lifetime to win the permanent democratic peace that has eluded us through two world wars and the long cold war that followed.

President Yeltsin, as a result of this first-ever U.S.-Russia summit we've indeed formed a truly new relationship, one of peace, friendship, trust, and growing partnership. I am confident that this new relationship and our historic agreements at this summit will lead to a safer, more stable, and peaceful world into the next century.

Let me just say to the American people: Our support for Russia is unshakable because it is in our interest. Success for Russian democracy will enhance the security of every American. Think for just a minute about what that means, not for Presidents, nor for heads of state or historians, but for parents and their children. It means a future free from fear. And that is why I call upon the Congress to act quickly on the "FREEDOM Support Act," so that the American support reaches Russia when it is needed most, right now.

During the past 2 days the United States and Russia have defined a new military and security relationship. It is a new era. President Yeltsin and I have just signed a statement that will lead to the greatest arms reductions of the nuclear age, reductions far deeper than we could have hoped for even 6 months ago.

At this summit we've also opened a new chapter in our economic relationship. The economic agreements that we have signed today will pave the way for trade and investment in Russia, as will most-favored-nation status which takes effect today. We hope very much that Russia and the International Monetary Fund can reach a stand-by agreement soon in order to unlock the G–7's economic support package.

And finally, President Yeltsin and I signed the Washington Charter, which states formally our mutual commitment to a peaceful future together as democratic partners. This document, along with the many agreements we signed from open lands to Peace Corps, will help to put behind us for good the sad and too often tragic legacy of the cold war.

President Yeltsin's commitment to me to uncover all facts pertaining to American POW's and MIA's is yet another symbol of our changed relationship. His commitment to also investigate the KAL 007 tragedy in which 61 Americans lost their lives nearly 9 years ago speaks to our mutual willingness to face some of the unpleasant truths of the past together.

During these 2 days we embarked on a new partnership. It is now within our power to alter forever our relationship so that it becomes the greatest force for peace, a democratic peace, that the world has ever known.

Let that be our vision for the future. And today, Mr. President, I pledge to you to make my commitment to make that vision I've outlined a reality.

Once again, thank you, sir.

*President Yeltsin.* Honorable Mr. President, ladies and gentlemen. The time has come when we can now take stock of the short but fruitful period in our relationship when new principles of the cooperation between the United States and Russia have been made.

I value this as a very important period. We now have a basis for interaction. We now have something that we can fill with substantive content. I doubt if today's documents could have been signed if we had not been looking for points of contact and mutual interest that we have been looking for, for years.

But it was very important, also, to cast away negative traditions, the profound disgust to each other which was masked by charming manners and politeness. We have now begun in a very good tempo, and the documents that we have signed today are not designed to define what has already been established in context but to find new ways to go forward. And the treaties and agreements that we have signed today do not just pertain to the two countries of ours. They are a sketch for a future world. They are characteristic of the kind of features that we want to see in this world. This world is becoming more attractive, more humane, kinder than we see today.

We are not trying to think of some global problems of restructuring the world. We do not want to force or coerce all the nations

to join in this. We are looking for solving mutual problems based on mutual trust, including the personal trust between the two Presidents of Russia and the United States. We feel that it is on this basis primarily that we can get the best results.

Among the Russian-American relations, there are two things that are most important to my mind: strategic arms limitations and economic cooperation. The state of strategic arms has now been decided. Once the cold war was over, they turned out to be obsolete and unnecessary to mankind. And it is now simply a matter of calculating the best way and the best time schedule for destroying them and getting rid of them. Another important point is to defend the world from an accidental use of such arms in the world, and we have laid the basis for that, also.

Another very important area in our relationship is designing a good basis for fruitful economic cooperation and establishing all kinds of contacts in this economic sphere. We have concluded very important agreements that have removed obstacles in this way and to make it more attractive for businessmen to join in this effort, and this is very important for our country at this time. After 70 years of travesty as far as personal property was concerned, now private property is becoming ever more important and will become even more so in times to come.

In conclusion, I would like to draw your attention to the following. Less than anything else do we need to delude ourselves by what we have accomplished. We would like to strive to the maximum that we would like to see happen. And if we look at our dialog in this light, then there is only one conclusion. We have to intensely work and forge ahead, both in the United States and in Russia. For those who come after us, we have to leave a good heritage, and this is important for the peoples of both of our countries. I thank you, Mr. President, for creating wonderful conditions for our work, and I congratulate you for the wonderful result of this work.

*President Bush.* We'll take a few questions. Helen [Helen Thomas, United Press International].

## POW–MIA's

*Q.* President Yeltsin, in terms of the POW's and the MIA's, do you think that Mikhail Gorbachev or any of his predecessors, even going back to Stalin, Khrushchev, Brezhnev, knew about the possibility that Americans were being held? And why are you going to see Governor Clinton? Are you trying to touch all bases before November?

*President Yeltsin.* Well, that's just the point; they did know. That's the very point, that they kept it a secret. The point is that that era, when we kept the truth from each other, has come to an end, and we will now tell the truth to each other, person to person, and will never do a double-play.

## Meeting With Governor Clinton

*Q.* How about the Governor Clinton—Clinton?

*President Yeltsin.* Tomorrow morning I'm going to see Governor Clinton, and we will meet. And as for the future, Russia will respect the wishes of the American people.

## Korean Airliner Attack and POW–MIA's

*Q.* My name is Sonya, and I'm from the newspaper Izvestia. And Mr. Yeltsin, you have said that you would like to make public the facts connected with the Korean airliner. Our newspaper has already been doing this investigation for a number of years, and we have already found out a lot of things. Now we would like to know just exactly who was responsible for what happened, and what do you think we can expect?

*Q.* Mr. President, you referred—your presentation of your remarks to the KAL 007 shootdown, and you referred to the place by President Yeltsin that some facts would be revealed. And I wondered to which extent you think the American administration would be helpful in that regard as well. Is there anything you could say to us about the tragedy?

*President Yeltsin.* I will answer. You know that on the 20th of August at about 1800 hours of last year when it was clear that the coup leaders had lost, we seized the archives of the KGB and the former Central Committee of the Communist Party. We placed armed guards around the buildings. But several hours before that, one car from each place had time to remove some of the archives from those two buildings and destroy them. We do not know what was in those archives.

Now we are trying to check all of those archives, do a comprehensive check of all of them, and we stumbled upon one document which we feel might be the beginning of a chain that might help us to unravel the entire tragedy with the Korean Boeing. It was a memorandum from KGB to the Central Committee of the Communist Party where it says that such a tragedy had taken place, and so on and so forth and that there are documents which would clarify the entire picture. The next line then says these documents are so well concealed that it is doubtful that our children will be able to find them, those who come after us will be able to find them. So this is our task. So then we began to check all the archives of the KGB, and this is our challenge; we're trying to find those documents that were referred to. I still cherish the hope that we'll be able to find those documents, and if we do so we will immediately make them public. I will be the first to call President Bush personally and tell him about it. And I will call you, too. [*Laughter*]

*President Bush.* The gentleman asked me to follow on, and I would simply say, one, we have great respect for this approach. It will be most reassuring to the American people, not only as it relates to the airline, but also to the question that President Yeltsin handled so well before the Congress, the question of the POW's and MIA's. So I can't add anything to that except to say that we will pledge to him our full cooperation in terms of any inquiry or what we might have that they don't know at this time. It is essential for the families that we get to the bottom of this, and it's essential to strengthening further this very strong relationship. So that's all I could add.

Yes, Terry [Terence Hunt, Associated Press].

## Arms Agreements

*Q.* Mr. President, a two-part question: President Yeltsin today pledged to deactivate the heavy SS–18 missiles that he said are targeted on the United States. Is there a reciprocal move that the United States will make? And the second question is, you mentioned that these arms reductions are going to be the deepest of the nuclear age. Does this mean that the peace dividend will be even bigger than what was expected, and that will be more money for American cities and domestic problems?

*President Bush.* Well, let me say that we will live up to the agreement we entered into. I'm not prepared to say what we will do in regards to the question of defusing or targeting, but we will live up to the letter of the agreement that we have discussed.

What was the second part?

### Federal Budget

*Q.* It was peace dividend. Will the peace dividend be bigger?

*President Bush.* Well, a dividend is declared when you make a profit, and our Government is operating at an enormous, enormous deficit. And therefore, those who say take the money from this agreement and spend it on some Federal project have to understand that the American people want to get something done about this deficit and want to get something done so that we can get this economy growing. So I would not pledge that any savings that might accrue to us because of this far-reaching agreement would go to some Federal spending project.

On the other hand, I'm determined to help the cities. We've got some good proposals up there and for the Congress, and I believe they're working on them, and I hope that they'll pass them.

We're alternating between the visiting journalists and those familiar faces here at home.

### Russia–U.S. Agreements

*Q.* Thank you, Mr. President. Mr. Yeltsin, the reaction to your statement in Congress was overwhelming. What do you think the reaction of the Russian Parliament would be to the documents and the agreements that have been signed here today?

*President Yeltsin.* Yes, I believe that the Russian Parliament reflects, or should reflect, the opinion of the Russian people. The documents, the charters, the treaties that have been signed are promising. It is a promising step for improving the life of Russia, for progress in realizing reforms. Not to support them would be a crime towards one's own people. And I am certain that the Supreme Soviet will support what we signed.

### POW–MIA's

*Q.* President Yeltsin, there is still some confusion here in Washington over raising the issue of POW's and MIA's. Is there actual information that you have unearthed in these archives? It's a very sensitive issue in the United States, and people are asking whether there's actual evidence that there is some kind of chain or trail, as you termed it with the Korean incident, that gets people's hopes up that some of this information will come home.

*President Yeltsin.* I'm sorry, I'm not sure I understood the question. Are you talking about the Korean airliner or the POW's?

What we have on the POW's, I have written ten everything to and given it to the Senate, what we know today. But we have made a step forward even yesterday. President Bush has made the decision to create his own part of a commission, and it will be a joint commission then, and it will have cochairmen. On our part it will be General Volkogonov. He is the historian, and he is a very honest man. He has conducted this work for many years. From the American side the cochairman will be the former Ambassador to the Soviet Union, Mr. Toon. I think that when they join their efforts I think they will be able to move forward a lot faster in order to really clarify the entire picture.

### Global Defense System

*Q.* I am from the newspaper the Red Star. As we understood, you want to create a global defense system. What are the prospects or how do you intend to move forward with this system?

*President Bush.* Well, we've signed a broad, I would say, beginning agreement on that. I think President Yeltsin has touched on that in his public speeches, but I'd be glad to implement it. We want to guard against nuclear proliferation, reckless use of weapons of mass destruction. For a long time we've been doing research in this area, and it seems to us that this is a good area for cooperation with Russia. And so we've just begun on this from this agreement that we've entered into here today.

But it will develop, and there's good science, good technology on both sides. And we're determined to work together on this global defense area.

Yes, John [John Cochran, NBC News].

### POW–MIA's and Assistance for Russia

*Q.* Sir, a question to both of you regarding this question of American prisoners. We don't understand, sir, why former Soviet leaders would have wanted to keep these American prisoners quiet. In the case of Francis Gary Powers, Khrushchev used that as political propaganda to undermine President Eisenhower. Why would these prisoners have been kept alive and in camps without any publicity? Was it just meanness, cruelty? They just wanted to crush them, find out what they could? Do your archives reveal anything about that?

My question to you, sir, would be: Do you think that what Mr. Yeltsin had to say about the POW–MIA issue defused that issue completely today? What are your people telling you about the prospect of Russian aid now in Congress?

*President Yeltsin.* You have had a chance to ask this question of the former President of the former Soviet Union, why he kept this a secret. I'm not responsible for him. [*Laughter*]

*President Bush.* Good answer.

I think the way President Yeltsin handled that question was extraordinarily sensitive in the Congress today, was extraordinarily sensitive to American public opinion and to the anguish and grief of the families.

I would refer you to the various chairmen that are here with us today, representatives of both parties. But in my view he defused, by being so forthright and so forthcoming, the criticism that you say did exist. I think I know of one very honorable Senator who has probably as much at stake in this broad subject as any, Senator McCain, who was a prisoner himself in Vietnam for a long, long time. He was satisfied and pleased with the statement by President Yeltsin. So it is my hope that that matter has been disposed of.

We will go forward working cooperatively with Russia. I hope it's been disposed of.

I believe that the speech that he gave today, not just in this category but in all categories, helped assure the passage of the "FREEDOM Support Act." It is essential that we move forward and pass that. I know there's a lot of questions that will be asked up there, but it is in our interest. I know it's in the interest of both Russia and the United States, and we must not miss this opportunity. I'll say once again, we've spent literally trillions of dollars, trillions of dollars for defense. Here's an opportunity to take out an insurance policy for peace and democracy and to back a courageous leader and a courageous people. So I think it will pass. And I think his speech today, that I watched keenly, will help assure that passage. He was very well-received in the Congress, and maybe after this is over you can discuss this with some of the leaders of the Congress who are here.

### Russia–U.S. Agreements

*Q.* You were talking about the situation in which many Russians find themselves. What do you think the significance of this visit will be for the common people of Russia? What can you say about that?

*President Yeltsin.* I think that the negotiations themselves and the documents, and I might say that we will have signed about 39 documents, all in all. We have signed seven with President Bush and then the premiers, the deputy premiers, the deputy secretaries, the secretaries of state or foreign ministers are signing them, but each of these documents is profitable for Russians, for the Russian people.

Nowhere have we compromised our economic interests, our freedom, or the interests of the Russian people. We always kept in mind the interests of the people of Russia. I'm very grateful, by the way, to President Bush that he always took a position that if we do not take measures now to support Russia that this will not be a collapse of Russia only; it will also mean the collapse for the United States also, because it will mean new trillions of dollars for the arms race. And this is what we have to understand. This is inadmissible and impermissible. So each document is of direct import and direct benefit to Russian citizens.

### Assistance for Russia

*Q.* Mr. President, how serious do you think is the need for economic aid to Russia, and how soon do you think the United States will be able to make a contribution?

*President Bush.* I would simply say we think it's serious. We think that the changes that Russia has embarked on are absolutely essential. I know there are still some problems that remain with the IMF, but we had very frank discussions about that. We are prepared to help move this package forward as swiftly as possible. I think the President put it best when he talked about the urgency of this so I will let him add onto it. But we are viewing this as priority. We are viewing this as of prior consideration. We have many domestic issues here, and we're going to keep pushing forward on them, economic growth, help for the cities. We can do all of those and pass this "FREEDOM Support Act."

So we're going to keep pushing forward on the domestic front, but this is priority internationally. We are going to be prepared to be weighing in and talking in great depth about this when I go to the G–7 summit in Munich.

*Q.* This goes with it, Mr. President. What are the alternatives if Congress doesn't pass the aid to Russia?

*President Bush.* Well, I think they're going to pass it, and it's too hypothetical.

Do you want to comment on the urgency? No? Okay.

*President Yeltsin.* I think that, of course, these $24 billion are important, the $24 billion that would have come to us as credits from the IMF. It is an important thing for any civilized country, especially for Russia at this time, during this very difficult period of reforms. But these $24 billion will not save Russia; they will not even significantly help us. Perhaps they will help us to stabilize the ruble, they will help us to make the ruble convertible in July, once this question is decided.

But the most important thing is that once the IMF decides this issue, this will open the door for a powerful stream, influx of private capital. Those will not be credits. Those will be direct investments from private companies. We have talked to business people in the United States together with President Bush and the business people here understand that very well. And the same situation exists in other countries, and that will be a matter of hundreds of billions of dollars. And that will be very important aid. It will be direct aid. It will be civilized aid. It will support our private sector, which is what we want.

### Russia-U.S. Relations

*Q.* Russian Television, First Channel. This is a question to both Presidents. You have really had good results from this meeting. What is it that you have failed to accomplish or have not had time to accomplish? What do you think is your next point on the agenda? Should be for the next summit, perhaps?

*President Yeltsin.* You know, in addition to those issues which are reflected in the documents that have been signed, we discussed dozens and dozens of other issues which are not reflected in the documents, dozens of them. For example, there was a wonderful pleasure trip on a boat on the river which lasted an hour and 15 minutes. And even during that trip we worked, and we discussed a lot of issues that we will continue to talk about and will raise again at the next meeting. And I hope very much that the President of the United States will accept my invitation and will come and visit on an official visit to Moscow at the end of this year. And I am convinced that a very serious package of documents will be prepared by the time he comes for this visit.

*President Bush.* A summit of this nature is broken down into two general categories: one, agreements, where you sit down and you hammer out agreements. Many of them are precooked. The Arms Control Agreement was enhanced and was finalized because President Yeltsin came here with some new ideas and he and his Foreign Minister and Jim Baker and others here worked very hard on getting it finalized. So that's part of it; it's the agreements.

But I find that a lot of the benefit of a meeting of this nature is the kind of discussion that we had, not just on that boat where we talked for an hour about worldwide problems but the discussions that we had upstairs when I had some private time with the President, private time in the Oval Office with him, the Secretary, and Brent Scowcroft.

It is very important that Russia and the United States not pass in the dark; that we understand. He understands how we look at the Balkans, for example, and I understand how he does, or the Middle East or South America or Japan. It is very important that two very important countries like this discuss in detail without trying to hammer out agreements the world situation, and that's exactly what we did. I have a far better understanding of the problem he faces at home and perhaps he has a better understanding of the problems that we face here in this country.

### POW–MIA's

*Q.* Question for both Presidents, President Yeltsin first. I'd like to follow up on a question my colleague asked a few moments ago because of the sensitivity of the POW issues.

A few minutes ago you described to one of the Russian journalists a document that you'd found relating to the Korean airline shootdown. Can you describe to us any documents or details that you have found about the prisoner of war issue so that Americans might understand why you believe that prisoners might have been taken to Russia and why you believe there might be still some alive?

And President Bush, can you tell us if there are any documents you have found relating to this in the time since you have learned of this situation?

*President Bush.* I'll answer it—no—and then let him take the first part. There are none that have been brought to my attention.

*President Yeltsin.* What we know today and what I have informed the Senate about, we are prepared to submit all the documents on that score. As to what we find later, as we find it we will submit those documents. I assure you that there will be

no secrets; as we find them we will let them be known. It will be a joint commission, and they will be working together in the archives.

*Q.* Can you tell us, sir, what you have found already?

*President Yeltsin.* The most important thing is that we know the numerical picture. We know how many people there were on the territory, how many were left, what camps the POW's were held in, the citizens of the United States; which war they were from, whether it was World War II or the Korean war or any other incident. So that part of the picture is clear. We know who died, where they are buried. We know that, also.

What we still don't know, we don't know a certain number of people who really we can't find where they belong, and we don't know where they are, and we have simply no information about them. This is why we say that maybe some of them are still alive and are still in Russia. This is why we say we would like to find further documents on those people.

*President Bush.* May I say we are going to take two more questions, one from each side. But let me add something to this. This is not a one-sided question. We aren't holding anybody. I know of nobody ever having held people. But there's a lot of heartbreak in Russia. There's a lot of families that wonder what happened to their loved ones in Afghanistan. While we were having these frank talks, I told President Yeltsin we would do absolutely everything we can. We lack a lot of purchase in some of these areas, but we will do absolutely everything we can to cooperate with him to see that those young men, these Russians who are held, allegedly held in Afghanistan are returned.

So the heartbreak is on both sides. The agony is on both sides, different circumstances. But I just wanted you to know that we have pledged, and I want the people in Russia to know, that we have pledged to work cooperatively with President Yeltsin to try to get some information that might alleviate the suffering of families in Russia.

### Assistance for Russia

*Q.* I have a question for President Bush. Could you perhaps answer this somewhat delicate question? You talked about the preparedness of America to provide aid, but that there are difficulties. Could you tell us something about the possibilities that have arisen for helping Russia as a result of signing the kind of documents that you have signed? What is possible, and what makes it psychologically difficult? What should be changed in Russia to make it easier? What would be conducive to our being able to help?

*President Bush.* Change in Russia to make it easier would be going forward as briskly as possible with the reforms. That opens up not only cooperative support from the United States, but from the G–7 and other countries who want to help.

I think—just help me once again with the first part of that. I lost my train of thought.

*Q.* In order to formulate your answer——

*President Bush.* Okay, no, but what we can do—the first part of your question comes back to me—what we can do the most is to pass the "FREEDOM Support Act." Now, you say, what are the problems with that. Some of the big package relates to the reforms and the need to get it through the IMF. Very candidly, so the people of Russia will understand that, there is some sentiment here that we should concentrate all our efforts in terms of spending domestically.

It is my view—I don't think that's the will of the Congress, however. I believe the Congress will support the "FREEDOM Support Act." We are in an election year here. The people of Russia have to understand it's a little strange out there, and things work differently in an election year. But the case for this "FREEDOM Support Act" is so overriding that I am confident that we can lay the politics aside and get this passed. I don't know if the interpreter got this, but I think that President Yeltsin's speech today, and I notice the Senators all had to go vote, but I think that they would tell you that that speech today was so well-received that that will enhance passage of the "FREEDOM Support Act."

That is the answer to your question. What can the United States do? It can pass this. It can work with the international financial institutions to be sure to see if we can help eliminate some of the problems and work cooperatively with the G–7, who I'm convinced will want to help Russia. It's that kind of an approach.

We've got one more to go.

*Q.* I ask about what should be changed in Russia in order to make aid easier?

*President Bush.* Well, I just think accommodation as much as possible—and you've got Mr. Gaydar trying to very much do that, along with this President—to accommodate the requirements of the international financial institutions. We've made a commitment, here. We've made a commitment, and we're going to go forward with it.

The whole package needs to be passed by having these changes that the President's already started, go forward. There are certain requirements, there are some—I leave that to the financial experts that are here from Russia, but I can't say anything about the details except to say that what Russia can do is to try to iron out the requirements that lie ahead. I know that President Yeltsin's determined to do that, and I'm confident, with an able man like the Vice Premier here, if it can be done, he'll help get it done. So that's the only answer.

*President Yeltsin.* Just a moment, I also would like to give my evaluation, since I am a participant in these events. And on my part it is 9—in other words, 9 out of 10 is the probability of help of what we have decided upon. That's how I would evaluate it.

*President Bush.* I think so, too. Last question. Last question.

### Arms Agreements

*Q.* A question for both Presidents. President Yeltsin said that we don't want to force any other nations to join you. But now that you are so far down the road of disarmament, should some of the allies of the United States cut deeply their own nuclear weapons?

*President Yeltsin.* The thing is that when I was on an official visit in France or a working visit in the United Kingdom and when we discussed this issue in detail with the leaders of those countries, I personally came to the conclusion that, actually, we didn't really need to talk about these issues; it wasn't really necessary because the quantities are totally incommensurate.

Can you imagine 21,000 warheads, strategic warheads, that our two countries have in their possession and then take 100 that some other country has, is it really worth talking about? Is it worth arguing about? Especially once we began discussing it, they themselves come to the conclusion that the atmosphere in the world, once it changes, it will itself lead them to lower the level of the strategic armaments. Their own peoples will demand it. In France they have 5 submarines and we have hundreds; so how can we compare them?

*President Bush.* Let me just reiterate the policy of the United States. We do not negotiate somebody else's armaments; we talk about the United States. So I'm not going to go into that at all. Our policy is well-known, and I think that the President put this in very proper perspective here. We're dealing with something enormous in working down our own arsenals. We've got our plate pretty full there. But it is not for the President of the United States to start talking about the French or British deterrent, and that's not my role.

Thank you all very much. We're out of here.

*Note: The President's 132d news conference began at 4:47 p.m. in the East Room at the White House. During the news conference, the following persons were referred to: Gen. Dmitri Volkogonov, senior adviser to President Yeltsin, and Yegor Gaydar, First Deputy Prime Minister of Russia. President Yeltsin spoke in Russian, and his remarks were translated by an interpreter. The news conference followed a ceremony in which President Bush and President Yeltsin signed the Washington Charter for American-Russian Partnership and Friendship; Joint United States-Russian Statement on a Global Protection System; the Bilateral Investment Treaty; the Treaty for the Avoidance of Double Taxation; Joint Understanding on reductions in strategic offensive arms; Space Cooperation Agreement; and the Agreement on the Destruction and Safeguarding of Weapons and the Prevention of Weapons Proliferation.*

# Joint Understanding on Reductions in Strategic Offensive Arms
## June 17, 1992

The President of the United States of America and the President of the Russian Federation have agreed to substantial further reductions in strategic offensive arms. Specifically, the two sides have agreed upon and will promptly conclude a Treaty with the following provisions:

1. Within the seven-year period following entry into force of the START Treaty, they will reduce their strategic forces to no more than:

(a) an overall total number of warheads for each between 3800 and 4250 (as each nation shall determine) or such lower number as each nation shall decide.

(b) 1200 MIRVed ICBM warheads.

(c) 650 heavy ICBM warheads.

(d) 2160 SLBM warheads.

2. By the year 2003 (or by the end of the year 2000 if the United States can contribute to the financing of the destruction or elimination of strategic offensive arms in Russia), they will:

(a) reduce the overall total to no more than a number of warheads for each between 3000 and 3500 (as each nation shall determine) or such lower number as each nation shall decide.

(b) eliminate all MIRVed ICBMs.

(c) reduce SLBM warheads to between no more than 1700 to 1750 (as each nation shall determine).

3. For the purpose of calculating the overall totals described above:

(a) The number of warheads counted for heavy bombers with nuclear roles will be the number of nuclear weapons they are actually equipped to carry.

(b) Under agreed procedures, heavy bombers not to exceed 100 that were never equipped for long-range nuclear ALCMs and that are reoriented to conventional roles will not count against the overall total established by this agreement.

(i) Such heavy bombers will be based separately from heavy bombers with nuclear roles.

(ii) No nuclear weapons will be located at bases for heavy bombers with conventional roles.

(iii) Such aircraft and crews will not train or exercise for nuclear missions.

(iv) Current inspection procedures already agreed in the START Treaty will help affirm that these bombers have conventional roles. No new verification procedures are required.

(v) Except as otherwise agreed, these bombers will remain subject to the provisions of the START Treaty, including the inspection provisions.

4. The reductions required by this agreement will be carried out by eliminating missile launchers and heavy bombers using START procedures, and, in accordance with the plans of the two sides, by reducing the number of warheads on existing ballistic missiles other than the SS–18. Except as otherwise agreed, ballistic missile warheads will be calculated according to START counting rules.

5. The two Presidents directed that this agreement be promptly recorded in a brief Treaty document which they will sign and submit for ratification in their respective countries. Because this new agreement is separate from but builds upon the START Treaty, they continue to urge that the START Treaty be ratified and implemented as soon as possible.

DONE at Washington, this seventeenth day of June, 1992, in two copies, each in the English and Russian languages, both texts being equally authentic.

FOR THE UNITED STATES OF AMERICA

GEORGE BUSH

FOR THE RUSSIAN FEDERATION

BORIS YELTSIN

# Joint United States-Russian Statement on a Global Protection System
*June 17, 1992*

The Presidents continued their discussion of the potential benefits of a Global Protection System (GPS) against ballistic missiles, agreeing that it is important to explore the role for defenses in protecting against limited ballistic missile attacks. The two Presidents agreed that their two nations should work together with allies and other interested states in developing a concept for such a system as part of an overall strategy regarding the proliferation of ballistic missiles and weapons of mass destruction. Such cooperation would be a tangible expression of the new relationship that exists between Russia and the United States and would involve them in an important undertaking with other nations of the world community.

The two Presidents agreed it is necessary to start work without delay to develop the concept of the GPS. For this purpose they agreed to establish a high-level group to explore on a priority basis the following practical steps:

—The potential for sharing of early warning information through the establishment of an early warning center.

—The potential for cooperation with participating states in developing ballistic missile defense capabilities and technologies.

—The development of a legal basis for cooperation, including new treaties and agreements and possible changes to existing treaties and agreements necessary to implement a Global Protection System.

DONE at Washington, this seventeenth day of June, 1992, in two copies, each in the English and Russian languages, both texts being equally authentic.

FOR THE UNITED STATES OF AMERICA

GEORGE BUSH

FOR THE RUSSIAN FEDERATION

BORIS YELTSIN

# Joint Russian-American Declaration on Defense Conversion
## *June 17, 1992*

The United States of America and the Russian Federation recognize that defense conversion is a key challenge of the post Cold War era and essential for building a democratic peace. Both parties realize the hardships involved in defense conversion efforts. But the parties realize, too, that the successful conversion of resources no longer needed for defense is in the long-term economic and national security interests of their peoples. Therefore, the United States of America and the Russian Federation declare their intention to devote priority to cooperation in advancing defense conversion.

Recognizing the important role of the private sector and of practical participation by business communities in the complex task of defense conversion, the United States of America and the Russian Federation are establishing a U.S.-Russian Defense Conversion Committee to facilitate conversion through expanded trade and investment. The intergovernmental committee will be established within the framework of the U.S.-Russian Business Development Committee and will be designed to facilitate the exchange of information and the promotion of trade and investment, including through the development of contacts between interested groups, the expansion of information exchange on enterprises undergoing conversion, and, the improvement of conditions for commercial activities in both countries through the identification and removal of obstacles to expanded trade and investment. The Committee will inform the governments of both countries on a regular basis of the results of its activities, in order

that they may take timely and effective measures to eliminate impediments to bilateral cooperation in the area of conversion.

With the aim of promoting successful cooperation in conversion, each of the parties intends to take a number of practical steps in the near future.

The Russian Federation intends to establish on its territory a favorable political, economic, legal, and regulatory climate for American trade and investment, including the adoption of macroeconomic reforms necessary to institute convertibility of the ruble; the pursuit of complementary microeconomic reforms to support the privatization and demonopolization of industry; the enactment of laws to guarantee contract and property rights; and, the dissemination of internationally-accepted standards of basic business and financial information on enterprises undergoing conversion.

The United States intends to facilitate U.S. business engagement in commercially-viable conversion projects in Russia, including joint ventures, through the placement of long-term defense conversion resident advisers to serve as catalysts for U.S. business engagement and to provide expertise to local leaders and enterprise directors; the establishment in Russia of business centers with translation, education, and training facilities for U.S. businesses operating in Russia; the creation of a business information service ("BISNIS") in Washington to match businesses in Russia with potential investors in the United States; and, the involvement of the Trade and Development Program, the Overseas Private Investment

Corporation, and the Export-Import Bank to provide incentives to American private investment in commercially viable defense conversion projects.

The United States of America and the Russian Federation endorse the COCOM Cooperation Forum on Export Control as a means to heal Cold War divisions and advance conversion through helping to remove barriers to high technology trade, assisting in the establishment of COCOM-comparable export control regimes in Russia and the other new independent states, and establishing procedures to ensure the civil end-use of sensitive goods and technologies on matters of common concern. Both parties agree that this process is based on their mutual determination strictly to adhere to world standards of export controls in the area of the non-proliferation of weapons of mass destruction and related technologies, missiles and missile technology, destabilizing conventional armaments, and dual-use of goods and technologies.

The parties strongly encourage the expansion of bilateral defense and military contacts and the work of the North Atlantic Cooperation Council in addressing the full range of military issues that are critically linked to the success of conversion including civilian control of the military in a democracy; defense planning, budgeting, and procurement in a market economy; base closings and conversions; and demobilization and retraining as well as social protection.

# Joint Statement on Chemical Weapons
*June 17, 1992*

President Bush and President Yeltsin stressed their continuing commitment to the global elimination of chemical weapons. They expressed their conviction that the Geneva negotiations on a multilateral convention banning chemical weapons can be concluded by the end of August. They agreed to instruct their representatives accordingly, and called on all participants in the negotiations to do their utmost to achieve this goal. They expressed the hope that a ministerial meeting could be convened in that timeframe to approve the convention.

The two leaders underscored their support for the 1989 Wyoming Joint Memorandum on phased confidence-building measures in the area of chemical weapons destruction, and agreed to implement the new, cooperative provisions for detailed data exchanges and inspections included in the Joint Memorandum as soon as arrangements can be completed. They also agreed that the June 1990 bilateral chemical weapons Destruction Agreement would be updated and brought into force promptly.

# Nomination of Richard Monroe Miles To Be United States Ambassador to Azerbaijan
*June 17, 1992*

The President today announced his intention to nominate Richard Monroe Miles, of South Carolina, to be Ambassador of the United States of America to the Republic of Azerbaijan. This is a new position.

Since 1991, Mr. Miles has served as Principal Officer at the U.S. Embassy Office in Berlin. From 1988 to 1991, he served as Consul General in Leningrad. He was a fellow at the Center for International Affairs at Harvard University, 1987–88. From 1984 to 1987, Mr. Miles served as Counselor for Political Affairs at the American Embassy in Belgrade. From 1983 to 1984, he served as an assistant to Senator Ernest Hollings on an American Political Science Association fellowship. He has also served at the Department of State as Deputy Director and as Acting Director of the Office of Regional Security Affairs in the Bureau of Politico-Military Affairs, 1981–83; and as Yugoslav Desk Officer in the Office of East European Affairs in the Bureau of European Affairs, 1979–81.

Mr. Miles graduated from Bakersfield College (A.A., 1960); the University of California at Berkeley (A.B., 1962); and Indiana University (M.A., 1964). He was born January 8, 1937, in Little Rock, AR. Mr. Miles is married, has two children, and currently resides in Berlin.

# Nomination of Ruth A. Davis To Be United States Ambassador to Benin
*June 17, 1992*

The President today announced his intention to nominate Ruth A. Davis, of Georgia, a career member of the Senior Foreign Service, class of Minister-Counselor, to be Ambassador of the United States of America to the Republic of Benin. She would succeed Harriet Winsar Isom.

Currently Ms. Davis is serving as a member of the senior seminar at the Foreign Service Institute at the Department of State. From 1987 to 1991, she served as Consul General at the American Embassy in Barcelona, Spain. Ms. Davis has also served at the Department of State as Chief of Training and Liaison for the Bureau of Personnel, 1984–86; and Senior Watch Officer in the Operations Center, 1982–84. From 1980 to 1982, she served as special assistant for international affairs to the Mayor of Washington, DC. Ms. Davis also served as consular officer in Naples, Italy, 1976–80; Tokyo, Japan, 1973–76; Nairobi, Kenya, 1971–73; and Kinshasa, Zaire, 1969–71.

Ms. Davis graduated from the University of California at Berkeley (M.S.W., 1968) and Spelman College (B.A. 1966). She was born May 28, 1943, in Phoenix, AZ. Ms. Davis presently resides in Washington, DC.

# Appointment of Vernon B. Parker as Special Assistant to the President and Associate Director of Presidential Personnel
*June 17, 1992*

The President announced the appointment of Vernon B. Parker as Special Assistant to the President and Associate Director of Presidential Personnel. He will be responsible for boards and commissions.

Since January 1992, Mr. Parker has served as General Counsel of the Office of Personnel Management (OPM). Prior to this Mr. Parker served as Counselor to the Director of OPM and as Director of Policy. Prior to joining OPM, Mr. Parker was an attorney with Multinational Business Services, a private consulting firm in Washington, DC. He also worked as a financial analyst for Rockwell International in Los Angeles. Mr. Parker began his political career with the Fund for America's Future. During the 1988 Presidential primaries, he chaired a key research team, and he served as the GOP national director of Democrats for Bush-Quayle during the general election.

Mr. Parker graduated from Georgetown University Law Center, where he was editor-in-chief of the Georgetown American Criminal Law Journal and vice president of the Student Bar Association. He received his bachelor of science degree from California State University at Long Beach. Mr. Parker lives in McLean, VA, with his wife, Lisa, and daughter, Sonya.

# Nomination of Jon M. Huntsman, Jr., To Be United States Ambassador to Singapore
*June 17, 1992*

The President today announced his intention to nominate Jon M. Huntsman, Jr., of Utah, to be Ambassador of the United States of America to the Republic of Singapore. He would succeed Robert D. Orr.

From 1991 to the present, Mr. Huntsman has served as senior vice president and general manager of the international division of the Huntsman Chemical Corp. in Salt Lake City, UT. He served at the Department of Commerce as Deputy Assistant Secretary for East Asian and Pacific Affairs, 1990–91, and Deputy Assistant Secretary of the Trade Development Bureau at the International Trade Administration, 1989–90. Since 1984, Mr. Huntsman has held several positions at the Huntsman Chemical Corp., including vice president of international business and member of the board of directors, 1988–89; vice president and member of the board of directors of Huntsman Pacific Chemical Corp., 1987–89; and product manager, 1984–85.

Mr. Huntsman graduated from the University of Pennsylvania, receiving a bachelor of arts degree. He was born March 26, 1960, in Palo Alto, CA. Mr. Huntsman is married, has four children, and resides in Salt Lake City, UT.

# Nomination of Joseph S. Hulings III To Be United States Ambassador to Turkmenistan
*June 17, 1992*

The President today announced his intention to nominate Joseph S. Hulings III, of Virginia, to be Ambassador of the United States of America to the Republic of Turkmenistan. This is a new position.

Since 1990, Mr. Hulings has served as Minister-Counselor for Management at the American Embassy in Moscow. He has served at the Department of State as Special Coordinator for Moscow Projects, 1988–90; Deputy Special Coordinator for Moscow Projects, 1987–88; Special Program Officer for Schlesinger Study, 1987; and Deputy Director for the Office of Foreign Missions, 1985–87. Mr. Hulings has served as administrative counselor at the American Embassy in Moscow, 1982–85; administrative officer at the American Embassy in Belgrade, 1980–82; senior watch officer for the Operations Center at the State Department, 1978–80; administrative officer at the American Embassy in Moscow, 1976–78; administrative officer at the American Embassy in Helsinki, 1974–75; and budget officer and general services officer at the American Embassy in Vientiane, 1972–74.

Mr. Hulings graduated from the University of South Carolina (B.S., 1963; M.B.A., 1971). Mr. Hulings was born May 6, 1941, in Carlisle, PA. He served in the U.S. Navy, 1963–69. He is married, has two children, and currently resides at the American Embassy in Moscow.

## Remarks at a Dinner Hosted by President Boris Yeltsin of Russia
*June 17, 1992*

Mr. President, thank you for those very kind words. After what you did on Capitol Hill today, after that sensational speech—it brought the Members of Congress to their feet over and over again—there is absolutely no point in my giving a speech tonight. [*Laughter*]

What we Americans saw was a true democrat who understood the heartbeat of the American people. It came through over and over again, your sensitivity on the prisoners, for example, and many other ways.

I had a note from a very senior person in the communications business; I will give him or her plenty of cover by that definition. And that note said that in all the time that that person had been in Washington, and it's many, many years, there has never been a greater day for mankind than yesterday.

Some of it was clearly the historic agreement on arms control, arms reduction. Some of it was perhaps the agreements that we were to sign today. But I think much more of it was because that person saw a true democrat, a person committed to de-

mocracy and freedom, leading the great country of Russia. We could identify with that, as I say, and we salute you, sir. We know the problems at home are extraordinarily difficult, but I think you leave with all of us feeling that you're going to make it. Somehow, you and this wonderful group of young leaders you've brought with you here to Washington are going to make it.

Let me simply say in conclusion, we want to be at your side. We want to be at your side as you complete the democratic experiment and as you move your great country forward.

And so, may I propose a toast to President Boris Yeltsin and to his wonderful wife, to his team that taught us all a great deal about what commitment means, and to the friendship between Russia and the United States of America that has never, ever been stronger. May God bless your country, and may God bless the United States of America, too.

*Note: The President spoke at 8:05 p.m. at the Russian Embassy.*

## Remarks at a Ceremony Honoring Presidential Scholars
*June 18, 1992*

Please be seated, all of you. I know you've been waiting out here for a while. But let me first thank Governor Engler, one of the great Governors of our country out there in the State of Michigan, for his leadership, not simply for his being willing to lead in this field, Presidential scholars, but for what he's doing for our country. I'm also delighted to be with Lamar Alexander. He is literally trying to revolutionize the educational processes in this country. And we owe him a vote of gratitude, too—both of them.

When we were standing on that balcony a minute ago—I'm just sorry all of you weren't here then—with Boris Yeltsin, I

told him, but I want to just say again here today, that we are welcoming to the White House in this ceremony the best and the brightest of American students. We meet on the 28th anniversary of the highest scholastic award that a President can bestow, the Presidential Scholarship Program.

Earlier I was talking to Barbara about this, and she noted that if your scholastic brilliance continues into your career work, maybe you won't end up like I have, where your dog makes more money than you do as an author. [*Laughter*]

I've got to confess that things have changed since I was a student. Nowadays with computers, bringing an apple to the teacher has an entirely different meaning. [*Laughter*] But what really hasn't changed is the meaning of education. It can form the noblest character and lay the surest foundation of usefulness to mankind.

Take a look at this year's Presidential scholars, from all 50 States, from the District, U.S. territories, and families living abroad, and consider why you learn: not only for learning's sake, to help yourself, but also to help others. You know that scholarship can further service to Nation and certainly can further service to neighbor and community.

For instance, just to single out a few, here sits Cara Reichel of Rome, Georgia. She's written and illustrated this book. I want to thank her for the copy. Barbara and I are thrilled with the inscription; that's why we brought it along. Anarug Bansal of East Greenwich, Rhode Island. Where's Anarug? Right back here. In his experiments he found a chemical that blocks HIV activity in blood cells. One scholar's family emigrated from the former Soviet Union; another escaped from Hungary. All know how education stems from the human heart and the human mind.

Let me just tell you a little story. Once Albert Einstein and his wife, they visited California's Mount Wilson Observatory. Pointing to a very complex piece of equipment, Mrs. Einstein asked its purpose, and their guide said that it helped determine the shape of the universe. Mrs. Einstein was not impressed. "Oh," she said, "my husband uses the back of an envelope to work that out." [*Laughter*]

Well, Einstein used envelopes to ask questions and find solutions, and you may use typewriters and word processors or yellow legal pads. I'm told some of you are so intelligent you even know how to set the timer on a VCR. [*Laughter*] But the goal's the same: To become an educated person. Only then can you use this knowledge to lead humanity to the stars, becoming what we refer to as a Point of Light in the lives of your neighbors and your families and your friends.

That's what Lisa Kim of Minneapolis is doing. She formed a chamber ensemble to perform at local nursing homes and hospitals. And where is she now? Right here.

Congratulations on that. Joane Liu of Princeton Junction, where's Joane? Right over here. She teaches physically and mentally handicapped kids to sing and to read music. And in Davenport, Amy Symons, Amy? Right over here on the end. Amy is a peer tutor. And in Salt Lake City, Alexis Sentell spends hours at the Utah Food Bank. Alexis? Way back there. Across the country in Norwalk, Connecticut, Kendrew Witt coaches Special Olympic swimming. Kendrew, where is he? Right here in the front. Here's what he says, "I wanted to return to the community what it has given to me."

And it's principles like these—that's principles which explain why you've excelled inside and outside of the classroom. And for that we all ought to thank principals with an "al." We need, too, to thank your favorite teacher, your local minister, that close friend in your town or city who literally has inspired you to learn. That brings me to those who deserve the most thanks of all, your parents, giving of their time and of themselves. They truly showed the way.

This is your day, but it is also your parents' day. And Shannon Wallace is a Presidential scholar from Sewickley, Pennsylvania. Shannon? Right back here. And she asked, "How do you thank your parents for 18 years of a wonderful, solid upbringing?" And if I could suggest a way: Honor them. Remember always that learning and teaching is a lifelong enterprise.

Our pioneering program that I referred to earlier to literally revolutionize education, it's called America 2000, recognizes the fact that education is key to our economic survival. We know that education can help achieve America's three great legacies: family, jobs, and peace.

So our America 2000 program challenges students to stay involved in their schools and schools in their community. Our crusade seeks to make America number one in math and science by the year 2000, increasing our ability to learn and compete in the world, and making our great country more prosperous.

Education is our most enduring legacy, vital to everything we are and everything we can become. It's as young as you are, and it's as old as the Scriptures. And it can, indeed, make America a better Nation and ensure a more decent world.

To every Presidential scholar, my heartfelt congratulations. Barbara and I both congratulate you and honor you. And to all of you here, thank you parents for what you do. To the rest of you on the Commission, thank you for giving of yourselves to keep this wonderful program going forward.

Thank you all for coming to the White House on this very special low humidity day—[*laughter*]—on the South Lawn of the White House.

May God bless our great country. Thank you.

*Note: The President spoke at 9:10 a.m. on the South Lawn at the White House.*

# Question-and-Answer Session With Employees of Evergreen Oil in Newark, California
*June 18, 1992*

*Mr. Morgan.* It's my pleasure, Mr. President, to introduce to you some of our friends, our neighbors. Evergreen Oil is only possible because we have had some shareholders that have had a lot of foresight. The city of Newark has been very cooperative, a partnership. But most of all, our employees are the ones that made this possible.

So, now that I've got the mike, and I'm not going to have this chance again, I want to ask the first question. Is that all right?

*The President.* That's the way it is, give a guy a little power. [*Laughter*]

*Q.* I know there's been a lot of questions about the environment, but one of the things of our environment that has been in the press a lot lately, and I think as a father and a businessman and this sort of thing, I'd like to know how your historic treaty with President Yeltsin and the arms reductions is going to affect people like me and the rest of us here?

*The President.* Well, let me just say that this morning we said goodbye to President Yeltsin, a new kind of Russian leader. Democratically elected, he came to the United States with the vote of the people behind him. And what we worked out in the arms control field is literally historic. There will be no question that what happened as we move to eliminate now, have agreement to eliminate the most destabilizing missiles, in their case the big SS–18's, multiwarhead missiles that for years have

plagued everybody, that move is destined to make life better for our kids.

Curt and I were talking—he's got a big family and so do we—but for years the children in this country have been going to bed with the fear of nuclear weapons. What happened in the last 2 days is really historic. It has an effect not only on the psychology of all of this, but also it has an enormous effect on the jobs for the future. Because what we're doing now as we move down any military threat is to move forward with business exchanges, and the export potential in that country is enormous, which would mean jobs for the United States at home.

So it was historic. It's a joy doing business with this man. I wish all of you could have seen the way in which he was received, maybe you did see it on the tube, by the United States Congress.

The other point I'd make to those who are in service here, for years we've been dealing with the Soviets in the spirit of mistrust for plenty of reason. Anytime you're up against a totalitarian regime, you better keep your eyes open. Now we're moving away from that. And his offer to go in with the KGB file, go the extra miles to see if any information can be shed on Americans that are missing, this is very good. And we have a wide array of areas in which we're cooperating, including that one.

So it was a historic day, and I think it means a lot for generations to come. It doesn't mean that we don't need a strong defense. Who knows where the next trouble spot will be? We've got to be prepared, and we can't lay down our arms in hopes that everybody around the world is going to do that.

But this was a big meeting, and I think the historic agreement is going to mean an awful lot for the tranquility of our children. That's very important to me, and I know it is to Curt and everybody else here.

Now, who wants to shoot away, in a figurative sense here? [*Laughter*]

*Q.* Mr. President, I'd like to ask you—I'm sure you'll agree with me that the future of our country lies in educating our children. And 4 years ago you promised that you would be the education President. Since then, I've seen tuitions go out of the roof. I've seen classes be so limited in our State colleges, the students can't complete their degrees. I've seen our elementary schools get slashed to where there's not even a remedial reading instructor at our local elementary schools any longer. I'd like to know, if you're reelected in November, can you hold true to your promise to be the education President? And how are you going to do that?

*The President.* Let me tell you—the first place, a good question. Secondly, everything we do is affected by education. For the first time, since I've become President, for the first time in history we have six education goals.

Now, you might say, "Well, what does that accomplish?" It means that we've gotten all of the Governors of the States together, and they have agreed on the goals, the goals that we must strive for: better performance. Kids should start school ready to learn; that means much more emphasis on Head Start, which we've done. Nobody is too old to learn; that means more emphasis on adult education, which we've done. It means proficiency in math and science. It means voluntary testing. So we've got these goals.

Secondly, we have the most revolutionary program in education, called America 2000. I regret to report to you that America 2000's ingredients have been blocked in a hostile United States Congress that is thinking old thoughts. The problems you bring

up require new thinking. I would urge you to take a look at the America 2000. The way to achieve, not for my sake but for everybody's sake, better education is to pass our program America 2000.

It has things like school choice. You see, when I got out of the service and was on the GI bill, why, you could choose where you want to go to school. Pell Grants, you can choose where you want to go to school. But in elementary and secondary education, the parents have no choice. I believe the time has come for the parents to have choice in education. So we're stressing that.

The fundamentals, we've gotten too far away from them in many of our schools. We are stressing that.

So, first place, I think our schools are under constraints because of the economy. This, as you know, is the responsibility of the local government. I do not want the Federal Government to dictate curriculum to the cities. It's much better that Newark decides on its own and not have some bureaucrat in Washington setting the agenda. But we are spending more money by far on education. Head Start funding, which is to meet one of our national goals, is way up; Pell Grant funding is up. So the Federal Government, in spite of these enormous deficits that are ripping off everybody, is putting more money into education.

But the answer isn't more money; it is America 2000, our education program. We need the help in the United States Congress to get it passed.

Thank you.

*Q.* My question is, I saw you on CNN the other night, and the last question posed to you was, are you willing to open up an "Ask George Bush" line and meet with people, like Bill Clinton and Ross Perot had? I think that this is probably very good for your PR. But why don't you do this more?

*The President.* Well, I've been doing it, ever since I've been in politics. We had a thing called "Ask George Bush" when these other guys hadn't even started on this kind of an event, and we do do some of it. But I don't believe that the White House should have a—we have a comments line, but I just have a certain respect for the office, and I don't want to turn it into a call-in-show place. I mean I just think that I owe the people a certain respect for the office of the Presidency.

But this isn't the first time that we've done this. As a matter of fact, we did it not so long ago in an event not too far away in the valley, right here in California. I've been doing it. I did it up in the primaries up in New Hampshire, and I've been doing it ever since I've been running for office.

It's a good thing to do and you do learn. I learn from the questions and learn the anxieties of people. So we're going to keep on doing it. But I'm glad you think that it makes some sense. I'll be honest with you, though. I think in a campaign year you've got to draw the line somewhere. I am not going to be out there, kind of being a teenybopper at 68; I just can't do it. [*Laughter*]

Yes.

*Q.* Mr. President, in light of your goals for education, the environment, the rebuilding of the infrastructure, and the social problems, how are we going to make those goals come to pass in light of our financial situation, the deficit and such?

*The President.* We're not going to if we don't get this economy back. The national economy is recovering. Anemic growth: grew at two-point-some percent here in the first quarter; it will be, I think, a little bit stronger in the second quarter. So the national economy is recovering. Incidentally, 60 percent of the people in the poll I saw that same night I did that show think it's getting worse. In some areas like California it has been horrible, but we've got to get the economy recovering.

The other day we had a chance to discipline the executive branch and we had a chance to discipline the Congress by passing a balanced budget amendment to the Constitution. I was for it. We got well over a majority of the vote, but we did not get two-thirds because it was blocked by the entrenched liberal leadership in the United States Congress. Eighty percent of the American people want it. It would help. It wouldn't automatically do it, but it would force the tough decisions on the elected members of the Government.

And so that's one thing. I also would like to have what 43 Governors have, the line-item veto, and see if the President couldn't do a better job of cutting the spending than the United States Congress has done. But more important than just presiding over what we've got is to get this economy to grow. We have a growth program up there that would spur investment in small business. Included in it, also, is an incentive that would spur investment in homebuying. It is a $5,000 credit for the first-time home buyer. I believe that would not only offer the American dream to some young family but would stimulate jobs in our economy.

I believe that a capital gains tax reduction would stimulate risk-taking and stimulate investment. I believe that changing the IRA's in a way that would increase risk-taking would be very good. So we have a six—you know, everybody's got an eight-point or a ten-point program—we've got a six-point program to stimulate this economy, and it's been languishing in the Congress. In fact, to try to get it passed I ended up having to veto a tax bill because I just could not accept that, the fact that people are taxed too little in this country.

So we're going to keep pushing for economic growth, and as President the only weapon I've got now is to use that veto to keep bad things from happening. But I'm a little more optimistic because I think, one, things are beginning to move on the economy, and secondly, I think people want to see some of these incentives passed to stimulate economic growth. It is essential for California, I think, because we're suffering here with defense going down. In a way, that's good; in a way, that's not so good. Jobs way, it's tough. World peace, it's good. But we need to move with incentives in this economy, and I'm going to keep on fighting for them.

*Q.* Mr. President, I'd like to know how you're going to balance our immediate economic needs for growth with those of the long-term environmental needs. We didn't look real well in Rio, and I'm wondering how you want to balance those two things.

*The President.* Well, I'll tell you what, we may have a difference about Rio. I don't think leadership is going along with everybody else. We have the best environmental record in the whole world. Our technology is fantastic. What you're doing right here for conservation, what you're doing right here is an example of this.

So we've got a good record on the environment. We're the leaders in CFC's. We're the leaders in forestry. We're the leaders in ocean technology. We have the best programs for our parks and adding to wildernesses which, incidentally, a lot of that's happened since I've been President.

But what we've got to do is find a balance so we don't throw a lot of Americans out of work by going to the extreme. I could not sign that biodiversity treaty because, in my view, it would take technological innovation like this and hand it over to others and dry up our technology and dry up the labs. I stood up there against the whole world and said, "Look, we want to share our technology. We want to continue to lead on the environment, but I simply also, as President, must consider the working man and woman, the families of this country."

So we're trying to find the balance. We did come out of there in a lot of ways with what they call Agenda 21 and with the climate control agreement, all pretty good agreements. But I was singled out by many of the special interest groups as saying, "Hey, our President should have signed this." I didn't come in here to follow, to jump on the bandwagon. We're the United States, and we're going to continue to lead in environmental policy.

*Q.* Mr. President, I agree that we are leaders in the environment. But if reelected, what incentives would you devise to aid our country in reducing our overconsumption of the energy resources?

*The President.* We've got an energy bill before the Congress right now that does that, encourages alternative use of fuels. We have sound environmental practice on offshore. We've got—in this bill, I mean, all—from lighting, kinds of new light bulbs that really save an enormous amount of energy, to alternative uses of fuel. We've got a good program. It's hung up in the United States Congress right now. But I would press forward on that energy bill and try to move forward.

Let me say this as a word of caution, though. We are more and more dependent on foreign oil. It was about a year and a half ago, when the Persian Gulf situation got fired up, that it was predicted oil would go to $80 a barrel overseas. And I don't know if you saw what Saddam Hussein said the other day. He said the biggest mistake he made is when he first moved into Kuwait, that he didn't move into Saudi Arabia. You want to project something that would just shoot these gasoline prices right off the scoreboard, try that one on.

So what we've got to do, it seems to me, is to try to become less dependent on foreign oil for security reasons, and that means alternate sources. I may get into a big fight here, but I believe that nuclear power can be used safely. And it's clean-burning—I believe, clean. I believe that we ought to facilitate that rather than turn our back on that.

But it does concern me that we're becoming more dependent on foreign oil, and yet, I think the answer is conservation and alternative sources. That's in our energy bill.

*Q.* Mr. President—and I assume that you are—what do you think about the oil that we've got to send out for incineration?

*The President.* What you've got to send out for incineration? Help me, I'm not a technologist, but what I see here I like in terms—refining it.

*Q.* Well, the oil that fails our test that we do on the field, we send that out for incineration to Kansas, to a facility, the RCRA facility that burns it off.

*The President.* I'm sorry, I hate to say this. Yes, I'm President, but I don't know enough about the technology to know whether that's good or bad. [*Laughter*] But I assume this company, committed to environmental sanity, is not doing something that would—help me, though. Are you worried about it, or you think we need to do more of it, or what is it?

*Q.* Well, I think it should be recycled.

*The President.* Yes.

*Q.* And right now, some of the oil that fails, well, all the oil that fails the test is being burned off——

*The President.* I see.

*Q.* ——in the RCRA facility where they're licensed to do so.

*The President.* Well, let me check it. I'll just have to say I don't know. I think that's all right for a President, as along as you don't do it all the time. [*Laughter*]

*Q.* Mr. President?

*The President.* Shoot.

*Q.* With the recent close of many bases, military bases, do you have a plan for employment of our servicemen?

*The President.* Well, the answer is to get the economy moving so that the men and women coming out of the service get jobs in the private sector. I've addressed myself here to the things I think would help on that. The Defense Department is spending, it's either $6 billion or $7 billion in transformation as we move from defense to help people coming out of the military and also to help transfer some of our technology.

Our labs, for example, that have been devoted to some of this highest tech—and we spend $90 billion a year on everything in the Government on research—those that are now being—they're loosening up that technology to go into the private sector. That will mean jobs. We've extended the GI bill for veterans, for people coming out so that they can then use those benefits for their own education. And as I say, it's $6 billion or $7 billion out of the Defense Department for this transformation. So that's what we're doing about it.

*Q.* Hi, Mr. President. I noticed earlier you pretty much seem family oriented as far as the economy goes. But do you have any type of plan for the homeless? It seems like there's a growing number.

*The President.* Well, it does. And the plan for the homeless is to fully fund what's known as the McKinney Act, which we've done. The Federal Government has partial responsibility for that. But the responsibility the Federal Government has is to assist the States and municipalities as much as we can. I think we're spending more money as a result of that act on the homeless than we've had before. But it's a tough problem, and I don't believe the answer lies just at the Federal level.

I'll be honest with you: I continue to worry about a third of the homeless who have mental problems. We changed the laws somewhere back in the last couple of decades which permitted these people to

be free of care and attention, and that has exacerbated this problem. I'm not sure that it needs the Federal action on this, but it is an area of which I'm very much concerned, and without shifting responsibility.

I know when Barbara took Mrs. Yeltsin the other day to a soup kitchen there, it was to demonstrate that the Government can't do it all. The, what we call Points of Light, the volunteers that are helping all over the country, got to pitch in and do more. Federal level, the answer is fully funding of the McKinney bill, which we are trying to do and which we propose.

*Q.* Mr. President, I am a social worker, and I have been working with the Head Start program. I'm currently working in a skilled nursing facility, and I am very concerned about a lot of the senior citizens in our country. They live on fixed incomes. Many of them have inadequate economy, inadequate health care. What are your plans for the future?

*The President.* We've got a good health care program. Let me tell you how I feel about health care. I've noted that when people need specialized care, need quality care, they come to the United States. We have the best quality health care in the world. What we don't have is access for those that are in the poorer end of the economic scale. The proposal that we have up there guarantees access through pooling of insurance, guarantees access to every person.

It involves giving vouchers to these people that have no insurance. Those vouchers could only be used to get insurance. The insurance would be transferable, so when you left a company you couldn't be cut off and then not get it in the next place.

This is a very comprehensive bill. It includes in it, incidentally, trying to do something about malpractice reform. One of the reasons costs are so high is that all these doctors get sued, frivolously, a lot of the time. We're suing each other too much and caring for each other too little. So we're trying to get that under control.

But take a look. And I will say this: It is the only comprehensive health care reform proposal before the Congress right now. At first, they started off saying: Well, let's try the Canada plan. Let's try the "pay or play" plan that failed so miserably in Massachusetts that all the small companies started moving across the border to some other State. They're moving back now to our plan, which is expanded insurance coverage to guarantee against what you're talking about.

I still don't have an easy answer for you on how we get these health care costs under control. And we're never going to do what this gentleman is talking about, get this fiscal sanity going, until we control the mandatory programs that a President has no control over now. I'm talking about the increases in health care, and those kinds of programs that are just going right off the roof.

But I'd take a look at our program on health care reform in terms of making insurance available to all. It's expensive; I think it's long overdue, though.

*Q.* Mr. President, I represent 1,400 small-business people here in the State of California that perform the smog check program. We have the most proficient smog check program in the United States, in fact in the world. But yet, Mr. Reilly and EPA is stressing a centralized program. I know that you have supported a decentralized program, as it means jobs and income for small-business people. How will you help us in this situation if you're reelected?

*The President.* Well, what we're trying to do on a broad sense is to get Federal regulation under control. When you do that, you run into the special interests, but we have gotten to be too regulatory.

I headed a task force for President Reagan on deregulation, and we made some inroads. We have now frozen new regulations at the Federal level unless it can be shown that they're absolutely essential for somebody's health or something of that nature. So I think in a broad sense, the answer is, you've got to ask a person: Do you favor more regulation? Do you favor more control? Or, do you think that less regulation would mean more jobs? I am in the second camp. I believe less regulation means more jobs.

I have an obligation at the Federal level to protect worker safety, for example. But we can overdo it. We can pass frivolous regulations. I have an obligation to guarantee health as best one can, I believe. But we can overdo it by frivolous regulation. And sometimes, in the environmental area, we get too regulatory. I've had to rule very recently on a case that came down in the favor of less regulation.

I'll tell you when it gets to you as President, it's when you really have to sort out regulation and then the welfare of a family. I know there's a lot of spotted owl jokes around. But you go up to the Northwest; there are not many spotted owl jokes, because the question is: Do you protect this feathery little guy and go the extra mile if that means throwing 30,000 families out of work? I had to make a comedown the other day on a decision saying no. We've got to protect the environment. We've got to do better by the old growth forests. We've got to help preserve these species. But if you're asking me to choose between throwing 30,000 or 15,000 families out of work or the owl, I'm going to have to give an awful lot of emphasis to the families.

When we get this economy growing and things moving, then maybe you lean a little more towards protection. But I find in this job you're always balancing these interests. It isn't always black or white, and there was a decision I cite because it's a tough one. Some of the people out here with their signs I'm sure would be 100 percent on the other side. At least I have it in my conscience here and down in Rio: Hey, American family matters. And a lot of them are hurting, and as President I am not going to go down here, sign something away, and then have on my conscience that a family doesn't have a job.

*Q.* Mr. President, we've proved here that, using high technology, you could produce a product of the highest grade, emission-free. It seems like the big boys that have the money, like refineries and all that stuff, they tie things up with their money and their power in politics, if you will. Because we've proved here that you can produce a product by spending the money with no emissions, at what point in our history of mankind are we going to allow the big boys to continue to pollute just because they have the money and the power, if you will, to hold off when we've proved that it can be done now?

*The President.* My being here, I hope, identifies with your technology, identifies with the conservation ethic that I understand is prevalent here. You'd have to give me a specific to know where I would come on down on adjusting some differences between these interests. Again, I'm not a specialist; you could tell from my answer over here to this question on your industry.

But I do think that when you have this technology and when you have this commitment to the environment, what the Government should do is to be sure we're not standing in the way of your competing or of your being able to sell your service or sell your product. That gets back to this man's question on regulation, gets back to his on economic growth. So, I don't know again the issue of what major company is trying to cut down on what you're doing, but I want to be identified with those who are innovating and those who are conservation-oriented and those who are doing their part to clean up our environment and make us more efficient. And that's what I think you're doing.

*Q.* Mr. President, thank you. I'm also one of the people in that smog check program in California. And for some reason or other the EPA seems to think that they've been mandated by the Clean Air Act to inject a monopoly into the smog check system and force people to go to a centralized monopoly smog check deal. You commented on bureaucracy and the little guy and there are a lot of us out there that feel like we've been doing a hell of a job trying to clean up the air and now the EPA seems to think that their job is to put us out of business, and we don't understand.

*The President.* Well, I don't want any Government Agency to even have the reputation for trying to put people out of business; what we're trying to do is put them in business. Now, the Clean Air Act was historic environmental legislation. And yes, it's caused some burdens in some areas, but I still believe that it was proper.

I believe our use of market incentives to try to meet these pollution standards is very, very important. But again, in this case, please understand that if there's some

regional office or some area that is trying to act like they have the whole say and the local entrepreneurs or local agencies don't have any say, that is not what I want.

So in this case if there's some specifics I would be happy to take a look at it, because I don't believe any bureau in Washington or Department in Washington has a monopoly on how we do things.

The lady's question on education comes back to me, because for years we've had every mandate coming out of some subcommittee back there inflicted on local school boards. You want Federal money—it's your money—you want Federal money, you've got to comply with a bunch of standards out of Washington. Our whole approach to education is different. Our whole approach to deregulation is different.

So, it would distress me if local initiative on cleaning up smog, for example, was being overridden by needless, needless regulation. Now, if they'll argue, "Well, you're not doing enough," then we'd have to take a look at it and see that that's adjudicated.

*Q.* I brought a letter to the President. Maybe you can read it on the plane if you run out of——

*The President.* I'll read it. If I run out of light reading, I'll take a look at it. [*Laughter*] No, I'd be glad to, sir. You trying to get me out of here? [*Laughter*] This is fun.

*Q.* Thank you, Mr. President. How would you explain the current situation of so many people that voted for you 4 years ago are willing to vote for somebody like Ross Perot? Again, you've spent your whole life in the public service, and he hasn't. Why——

*The President.* Let me tell you this: Thank God, I have not spent my whole life—I computed it the other day: 50 percent since I got out of college in business, starting a business, running a small business, and doing stuff in business; and 50 percent in Government. I wear the business as a badge of honor because I think it gives me some feel for what it means to run something.

But look, I understand the discontent that's out there. This economy has been in the dregs. But I will end with this statement: I believe that when the whole record is looked at, the economy is coming back, and when people take a look at things like world peace, whether it's a good thing that their kids go to sleep at night without the fear of nuclear weapons, when they take a look at what we're talking about here and have done in terms of education goals, it will be fine. But right now, I think a lot of the problems that face me politically are saying, hey, everybody in ought to be out, and everybody out ought to be in.

But that's not the way it works. I mean, I will take the case to the American people that these ideas and many more that we haven't talked about are blocked by the Congress. I'll say this to the American people: You've got to work with Congress one way or another. We've tried it with Democrats controlling both Houses of the Congress, and that didn't work. When Jimmy Carter went out, inflation was right through the roof, interest rates were high, and the "misery index," they called it, was terrible.

What we haven't tried is where the Republicans have both, control. And the reason I say it ought to be tried is, I think what's on people's minds today, one of them, is safety in their neighborhoods, crime. I hear people coming out here on these little bites on television, saying, "Well, hey, we need a tough crime bill," the same people that vote against the tough crime bill that we want to get passed back in Washington. Right today, the American people want to back the law enforcement community and want strong anticrime, antinarcotic legislation. We have been trying to get it through the liberal leadership in the Congress for 3 years, and I'm going to take that case to the American people.

But right now I don't think it's in focus. I think what's in focus is kind of a discontent. But I believe it'll change, and I believe that our record will be—which it does include Clean Air Act, it does include child care legislation that gives the parents, rather than the Federal Government, the choice of where you have your children get cared for. It does include trying to get ahold of this Federal deficit. So I think what hap-

pens is we go through this period now, and then it gets in focus. I would remind some that 4 years ago to this very day I was 18 points behind the opponent. Got it on focus by November, and I'll be trying hard to do that.

But when it comes to who is doing something on this big painting, world peace, changes—right now you have a lot of revisionists on the Desert Storm. It was a proud moment. The reason it was a proud moment is, our country took the lead in an historic coalition and stood up against aggression. Now you've got a lot of people trying to tell us it was wrong, and it was right. So that one's not in focus, either.

So I think the record—I'm not satisfied that we've gotten enough done. But I'm going to say I want to be President for 4 years and here's why: I want to finish what we started on education. I want to do what I've said we're going to do here on health care, get that program through. I want to pass our anticrime, antinarcotics, pro-law-and-order crime package. That alone is enough reason to ask the people for their support for 4 years.

But right now, there's a hurricane blowing out there. And all I can do is try to run this country as best I can and then take this case forcefully.

I've been here for, what, 30 minutes sitting on this stool, and you haven't heard one negative comment against either of the two people that want my job. And you're not going to hear one until maybe the middle of August. [*Laughter*] But then you are, because I know how to fight. I'm not going to be their spear catcher for the rest of this year; I can tell you that.

I think Don's trying to get you guys back to work here.

Well, thank you very much for the opportunity and very good questions. You make Phil Donahue look like a piker out there.

*Note: The President spoke at 1:33 p.m. at the Evergreen Environmental Services Oil Refinery. Curt E. Morgan, chairman of the board, Evergreen Oil, Inc., introduced the President.*

## Statement by Press Secretary Fitzwater on Creation of the Monterey Bay National Marine Sanctuary
*June 18, 1992*

As outlined in his FY 1993 budget, the President authorized the creation of the Nation's largest marine sanctuary off Monterey, CA, and approved a strict management regime including a permanent ban on oil and gas development for the area, which includes a wide variety of pristine habitats.

The 5,312 square mile area proposed by the President was the largest option studied. With modifications only to exclude one minor area of lower resource value, Monterey Bay National Marine Sanctuary would be the Nation's largest, bigger than the State of Connecticut and larger than any of the national parks in the lower 48 States, including Yosemite and Yellowstone. It contains the largest underwater canyon in North America and is home to an expanding population of sea otters and a wide variety of whales, porpoises, seals, fish, and sea birds, including many endangered and threatened species.

The sanctuary will be overseen by the Commerce Department's National Oceanic and Atmospheric Administration (NOAA). The Notice of Availability for the Monterey Bay National Marine Sanctuary Final Environmental Impact Statement/Management Plan will appear in the *Federal Register* Friday, June 19, 1992. There is a 30-day public comment period, which closes July 20, 1992. After review of public comments received on the impact statement, the notice of designation and the final regulations will be published in the *Federal Register*.

The President requested $7.289 million for the national marine sanctuaries program in his fiscal year 1993 budget, an increase of nearly 50 percent from the FY 1992 appropriated level of $5 million for the 10 sanctuaries in existence; $510,600 was specifically identified in the budget increase for Monterey Bay Sanctuary's first year of operation.

The sanctuary is also home to the Nation's most expansive kelp forests, which provide food and shelter for the thousands of marine species which dwell there. The bay is the closest-to-shore deep ocean environment anywhere in the continental United States, straddles two major ecological regions, subtropical and temperate, and provides a unique area for extensive ocean research and education.

The Monterey Sanctuary will be the 11th in a network that spans from American Samoa to the Florida Keys and includes pristine coral reefs, the Civil War ironclad U.S.S. *Monitor*, the Channel Islands, and the Gulf of the Farallones, also off the coast of California. With the addition of Monterey Bay, President Bush will have designated three new sanctuaries, more than tripling the area protected under this program.

## Nomination of Richard H. Solomon To Be United States Ambassador to the Philippines
*June 18, 1992*

The President today announced his intention to nominate Richard H. Solomon, of Maryland, to be Ambassador of the United States of America to the Republic of the Philippines. He would succeed Frank G. Wisner.

Since 1989, Dr. Solomon has served as Assistant Secretary of State for East Asian and Pacific Affairs at the Department of State. He also served at the State Department as Director of the Policy Planning Staff, 1986–89. From 1976 to 1986, Dr. Solomon served as head of the political science department at the Rand Corp. in Santa

Monica, CA. He also served as a senior staff member for Asian Affairs with the National Security Council at the White House, 1971–76.

Dr. Solomon graduated from Massachu-setts Institute of Technology (S.B., 1960; Ph.D., 1966). He was born June 19, 1937, in Philadelphia, PA. Dr. Solomon is married, has three children, and resides in Bethesda, MD.

## Appointment of Mrs. Potter Stewart as United States Representative on the Executive Board of the United Nations Children's Fund
*June 18, 1992*

The President today announced his intention to appoint Mrs. Potter Stewart, of the District of Columbia, to be the Representative of the United States of America on the Executive Board of the United Nations Children's Fund. She would succeed Peter B. Teeley.

Mrs. Stewart has served as a volunteer with many organizations involved in youth, human needs, and international affairs. Mrs. Stewart has also served as a researcher for Time magazine and Life magazine, 1941–43.

Mrs. Stewart was born June 3, 1919. She currently resides in Washington, DC.

## Remarks and a Question-and-Answer Session With the Industrial League of Orange County in Irvine, California
*June 19, 1992*

*The President.* Thank you, Reed, very much. Please be seated. I was riding over here today with Senator John Seymour, our outstanding Senator in Washington who's fighting a good battle for everything those of us interested in business believe in, and he told me I was walking into the most influential group of people in Orange County. I want to just say to Reed Royalty, thank you, sir. To the Mayor, Sally Sheridan, I'm pleased to be back on her turf. I want to salute the other Orange County mayors.

And I would single out once again my good friend Senator Seymour, who's out here some place. And let me just say this is supposedly nonpolitical, but I want to see him return to the United States Senate; let's get it right up front. While we're at it, if we are going to move the growth and opportunity agenda forward, we must select Bruce Herschensohn, and so permit me yet another partisan plug. Both of them have earned it, deserve it, being in the United States Senate. And we need their leadership and support.

Now, Todd Nicholson and everyone from the Industrial League, the Orange County Forum, the many leaders of the local chambers of commerce who helped with this event, my sincere gratitude to you. You had one week, and look at this, it's unbelievable. I'm glad to be here with so many businessmen and businesswomen. Forty years ago I did start a business and that made me, I think, have some sensitivity and understanding what it means to take risks, to meet a payroll, and to add to the productivity of this great country.

I'm proud to work with three solid, strong leaders, not only for Orange County but for this country. Two of them are here, and I'm talking about Members of the House. My dear friend "B-1" Bob Dornan is not here, regrettably, but he's a good friend, and he's a champion of American values. But Chris Cox is with us, and he embodies the entrepreneurial spirit here today, and he's pushing great new ideas like turbo-enterprise zones. I salute him. And Dana Rohrabacher I'm told is here—I'm having a little trouble with the lights—but anyway, he is a stalwart advocate of reform, too, fresh off his surfboard. [*Laughter*]

All three of these Congressmen—the point I want to make is this: All three of them stood solidly with me in the fight to do what the American people want, to pass a balanced budget amendment to the Constitution. And we are not going to give up that fight. That will discipline the executive branch, and it will discipline the United States Congress. And it will facilitate the day when we can get done what the American people want and are properly demanding: the elimination of these deficits that are mortgaging the future of our children.

Today I want to talk about our Nation's transition into the post-cold-war era and what this means to a competitive economy. Three days ago I met there at the White House with Russia's freely elected President, Boris Yeltsin. It was indeed an historic meeting. We rejoiced at the new breeze of freedom that has swept the entire globe, scattering the last dust of that grim totalitarianism. And we spoke of the dreams that we share for our people, the American people, the people of Russia. It really was an extraordinary moment in history.

We stood next to each other in the Rose Garden and together announced the most sweeping nuclear arms cuts in history, reductions far deeper than we could have hoped for even 6 months ago. And in the process we will eliminate the most destabilizing weapons of all, those that terrify mankind the most, those multiple-warhead ICBM's. Russia will eliminate all 308 of those giant ICBM's, those SS–18's which alone carry more than 3,000 warheads. Each one of those warheads aimed at the United States, each one of them is more than 10 times more powerful than the bomb dropped on Hiroshima. That means that you and I will no longer fear for our children and grandchildren the threat of nuclear war that plagued us all for 40 years.

I know people in Orange County love politics, but I wish you could have seen Boris Yeltsin at work with the crowds and the people and the waving. We took him out on the Truman Balcony just before he left. I said, "I want you to see how a President spends some time," because we had the Presidential scholars out there on the lawn. No sooner do we get to the balcony and all of them were facing the other way. I really wanted him just to see the event. The next thing I know, he was waving so vigorously they all left the event, turned around, and came up, and he was greeting them like a long-lost brother. This guy really has a flair for public opinion, I'll tell you. But it says something. He was elected democratically. He came here as the first democratically elected leader of Russia, and the American people understood that and gave him a warm welcome.

But now with the cold war behind us, we have that freedom to focus more resources and more talent on the concerns that trouble us at home. And with the new partnership of peace we forged with Russia, we have the chance to expand trade, and that means then creating jobs and opportunities for Americans that will benefit both of our nations in the process.

While we look ahead to these exciting new horizons, there is one critical element that we must never forget: The cold war is over, but we still need a strong deterrent. Our requirements are changing, but the need will never disappear. Look at the threat posed by global instabilities, by terrorists, by renegade regimes looking to get control of sophisticated weapons. We must continue to invest in military R&D, and we will.

And in order to keep the peace, I make you this pledge: As long as I am President of the United States, I guarantee you that our country will remain the strongest country on the face of the Earth. We owe that to our children. Who knows where the next difficulties will crop up. And it's only the United States, only our country, that can lead for democracy and freedom.

The new challenges we face in the post-cold-war go beyond world security. There are still pioneer days ahead. At one point in the movie "Awakenings," a fellow who's been asleep for decades finally wakes up and has the whole world in front of him.

When his doctor asks him what he wants to do that day, his face breaks into a huge grin, and he shouts, "Everything!" That is the spirit that we need to call up right now, that purely American belief that America's future knows no limits.

I am tired of all the pessimists in this political year telling us what is wrong with the United States of America. I'm tired of it. The fact is we're entering a different economic world than the one we grew up in. William Jennings Bryan captured the bold spirit which will lead us to success when he said, "Destiny is not a matter of chance; it's a matter of choice. It's not a thing to be waited for; it's a thing to be achieved." The world economy of the 21st century will be a new age of American competition in a fiercely challenging global marketplace. And we simply have to make some changes if we expect to compete.

First, we have to realize the intensified need for sophisticated, well-educated workers. The worldwide high-tech explosion will leave us behind unless we literally reinvent American education, make our schools the best in the world, to turn out the best prepared workers in this world. To do this, let's borrow a page from business. I want to bring competition into our schools through ideas like school choice. Parents should have the right to choose their children's schools. And beyond that, I'll use every resource I can to pave our way into the future.

Our national technology initiative brings Government officials together with private businesses to let them know what Government can offer in technology. This moves new discoveries out of the Federal laboratories into the marketplace to save existing jobs and create new jobs.

Today, for example, I'm announcing an important regulatory change that will help many companies with defense-related businesses make the transition to the post-cold-war era. One unnecessary obstacle has been what they call the recoupment fee or tax, if you will, that DOD charges on military and commercial products sold to customers other than the U.S. Government. These fees hurt American workers by making it more difficult for them to compete for business here and abroad. Given the historic changes we've seen during the last year, this burden is no longer justified. And today, I am directing my Secretary of Defense to take what actions he can to eliminate these fees.

I will continue fighting for American jobs by encouraging trade and opening markets abroad. You know how vital that is since America is the world's leading exporting nation. And California leads America, accounting for one of every 8 U.S. export dollars, one out of every 8 to California. Just last year, a 13-percent increase over 1990, this State exported over $50 billion in goods, creating jobs up and down this golden coast. I will keep pushing for the North American free trade agreement. And some say NAFTA will cost jobs, and they are dead wrong. It will lower trade barriers, and it will establish one of the biggest and richest markets in the world with the potential of creating hundreds of thousands of jobs.

For the long term, Washington must have the courage to make hard choices. The Federal Government is too big, and it spends too much. It is time that the Congress woke up and listened to the American people. Most Americans believe as I do that the only way to discipline both the executive branch and the Congress is a constitutional amendment to balance the Federal budget. For years I've called for just such an amendment because to ensure long-term economic growth, we must get the Federal spending under control.

Now, I have a detailed plan before the Congress right now. It is up there. I brought along a copy just to show it to you. You might not have read much about it in this strange year out there. But the way it does it is the only way that the budget can be brought under control, and that is to control the growth of the mandatory programs. And it does it without raising taxes on the American people or on American business. Here it is in considerable detail. But we need, again, the discipline and the sense of urgency that the balanced budget amendment will bring. And while I'm at it, I would like to ask the American people this fall to give me what 43 Governors have, the line-item veto, and let the President have a shot at getting spending under control.

Nationally, our economy is recovering. Some good fundamentals are in place: low interest rates, low inflation, exports are strong. But in California, as everyone in this room knows, it is a challenging time. It's been a tough time. But you've risen to the challenge before. In particular, as the Defense Department downsizes, you face adapting from a military to a competitive civilian market. It's tough for companies and employees, but remember: Our Nation's economy is the most productive in the world. Together, we're going to use our strengths to bring back growth and opportunity right here to Orange County.

For 200 years, our prosperity has sprung from our ability to innovate, to create, to change as the world changes. And now is your time to shape your own identity in an evolving economy. That's the heart of what we call entrepreneurial capitalism, a heart that I still hear beating in Southern California. This area is like an R&D lab for the whole country.

All around us are marvelous examples of the technological transition from the cold war to the era of global economic competition. We will depend upon companies like many in Orange County who still develop and use technology that was begun for defense. I've seen examples here of some remarkably creative thinking. During the cold war, the military funded the development of many new manufacturing techniques. And now you're demonstrating astounding innovation by turning systems developed for national defense towards the commercial market, worldwide, I might add.

Right here, Hughes Aircraft is applying the military's global positioning satellite system to a new procedure controlling shipping traffic along our coastal waters. McDonnell Douglas, their SDIO-funded Delta Clipper program will dramatically reduce the costs of reaching into orbit. This will ensure that we lead the world's commercial aerospace industry. Rockwell is developing ways of using SDI's high-tech offshoots to give us smart cars and smart freeways and breaking gridlock on our highways. Now, that's got to be good news for Southern California. To them I say: Hurry up.

The more closely we look at these companies, the more we understand why they're thriving. It's because they are able to adapt and they're at the cutting edge of the postcold-war era, transforming this world into a productive peace. Defense conversion puts Orange County back in the business of job creation, a skill that you mastered in the eighties with the high-tech start-ups that made this area famous. And now you're redefining it for the nineties. Here, job creation doesn't mean job training. Your workers are already the most qualified in our labor force. What they need is opportunity. And if we give a budding entrepreneur a chance, he'll bring training, experience, and old-fashioned American hunger to his own business and create jobs for dozens, maybe even hundreds of fellow workers.

Venture capital regrettably has dried up. And so we must take action to get it flowing again. And so I am going to keep pushing Congress to slash the capital gains tax. They can call it a tax break for the rich, and I call it job opportunity for those that need jobs and need work. I'm going to keep pushing the Congress to make the research and experimentation tax credit permanent. As a Nation, this is how we must support our risk-takers, for their vision of today will be our future of tomorrow. We must bequeath to the next generation the legacies that define our future: strong families, good jobs, and world peace. As a Nation, we will chart a course to guide America into the new century where confidence and self-reliance produce greatness. I believe we're going to find that greatness.

I am delighted to be here. I appreciate this marvelous turnout and this warm welcome. Thank you all very much. And may God bless the United States of America. Thank you very much.

Be glad to take some questions out there.

*Moderator.* The President has graciously agreed to answer some of your questions for a few minutes. So what questions do you have?

*The President.* You've got to yell so I can hear you. Yes, ma'am?

*Multilateral Trade Negotiations*

*Q. [Inaudible]*

*The President.* The question is, how do we move forward the GATT, or what's the opportunity for it. As you know, the major stumbling block to a successful conclusion in the Uruguay round has been agriculture. We have had difficulties with the EC, particularly on agriculture. We are pushing to get this done, certainly to get it all but done before I go to Munich for the G–7 meetings.

This woman has put her finger on something that is vital, not just for the American economy but to Third World economies all over the world: the knocking down of these barriers. Because it is my belief that we can compete with anybody provided the playing field is level. So we're going to keep on. The stumbling block is agriculture. We still have some property rights differences. But I believe we'll get a deal.

The question is, how soon. We have pushed on it. We've had meetings recently with the EC ministers. I am now pressing for an EC ministerial before the Munich summit. I can't predict to you that GATT will be concluded before the G–7 meeting in Munich, but I am hopeful that then or shortly thereafter we will finally conclude a GATT deal. It is in our interest. There's a lot of special interest in various categories that are going to fight whatever agreement we get, but no longer should we be a protected society. We want to be the most competitive and the most productive society, and the way to do that, I think, is to knock down the barriers to our trade and just watch us move.

And so, we'll keep pushing on it. You want to put this in terms of benefiting the Third World, incidentally, I can't think of any action that would help them more than freer and fairer trade. The best answer is not these ever-increasing aid programs but trade. And that's all tied up in GATT. So we'll keep working on it. And we keep plugging away on knocking down the agricultural barriers that really have been holding up the GATT.

Yes, sir.

### Budget Rescissions

*Q.* [*Inaudible*]

*The President.* We've tried that on the rescission. And we've sent them up there.

The Justice Department advises me that the President does not have the power that I wish he had. So I also have to be somewhat—well, I have to be very diligent in safeguarding the Presidency. But I don't believe that that power exists, but if I can get an opinion from Justice, on whom I depend for these legal matters, to say, okay, it's all right on this particular piece of legislation for some reason, then I'd like to try it because I really believe the President should have it.

I am not told by our experts that that inherent power lies in the Presidency. I don't know that Bob Dole feels that it does, either. What I think he'd like to find is what I'd like to find, is a case to test it without doing violence to the protection of the office. So we're going to keep pushing.

In the meantime, though, we have tried the rescission route. What I'd like to see is a repeal of the impoundment bills that were put into effect in the seventies which really removes from the President the right to control spending. And I think we need that, particularly when we're operating at these big deficits. But that's the way I'm approaching it, and I hope like heck we can find a case to test this in the courts, one that my top attorney at Justice, Attorney General, says is okay to do.

Who's next? Yes, ma'am.

### Federal Industrial Policy

*Q.* I just returned from a study trip to Japan and Singapore, and we met with some of the top officials of companies and also the government. In both cases the government really plays an active role in helping technology-based companies focus their R&D, focus their technology directions and, as a result, position Japan and Singapore to be very, very strong players in the technology-based business. It seems to be—[*inaudible*]—somewhat in the United States in terms of that policy. What are you going to do?

*The President.* We spend $90 billion in the United States in the Government level on research and development, $90 billion. What we don't do—and you're correct, some of the Asian countries do do—is target. I do not believe in what is known as industrial policy where the Government decides which businesses are winners and which businesses are losers. I don't believe in that.

I came out of a business background. I believe that the market should set these goals and targets, not the Government. But we do have an enormous bunch of research that will benefit certain industries. And that is correct because what we've done is use that in terms of Government service, and now what we're saying is let's open up this lab technology and let it spill forth into the private sector. So some industries will benefit, but I am going to stop short of an industrial policy. I am going to stop short of the targeting that, for example, MITI—I think you're probably referring to the MITI minister, what those officials do in Japan. It has worked hardship on some of our businesses, but I don't think that makes the policy correct.

### Capital Gains Tax

*Q.* I'd like to see a lower capital gains tax rate, not across the board, that would benefit speculators in real estate and stocks; I'd like to see a lower capital gains tax only on securities newly issued by companies, large or small, equity or debt. This would reduce their need for bank loans, allow them to raise capital at a more advantageous rate, expand facilities, employ more people, and compete better in the world marketplace.

*The President.* I can understand that, and I'd rather have that than nothing. But I'd rather have the broader application to capital gains, and let me give you a good reason as it relates to Los Angeles. Peter Ueberroth is undertaking an assignment to try to bring private business into the heavily impacted urban areas. It is his belief, and I agree with him, that if we can get a broad elimination in these areas of capital gains that that would serve as a magnet to entrepreneurs to start new businesses.

So what you suggest may be the way that it evolves in the legislative process, but I would prefer to do what happened under the Steiger amendment in 1978, and that is have a broader across-the-board reduction of capital gains because I really believe that's what it's going to take to stimulate creation of new businesses. I understand

your point, but I would much prefer to see it broader.

### Russia and Yugoslavia

*Q.* Mr. President, when President Yeltsin was here, did you discuss with him the situation in Yugoslavia? Are there constructive acts that he can take to help that situation improve?

*The President.* We did discuss Yugoslavia at length. You may remember a boat trip out of Annapolis on the Severn that I took with him. That was billed as R&R, but I think it was probably the most fascinating session that I had with him in terms of a give-and-take on specific issues. I'll get to your question in a sec, but I just wanted to share with you what we were talking about out there because we started with what the French called a *tour d'horizon,* but we're talking about just a wide review of policies as it affects the new states in the former Soviet Union. It was fascinating hearing him discuss what's going to happen in Azerbaijan or Armenia or how they're going to treat the problems of Ukraine. It was just a marvelous experience, and I gave him the U.S. view on this thing.

We did talk about Yugoslavia. In answer to your question, I do not believe that the Soviets have any special role anymore. There was a time when Yugoslavia, and I think that's what you're referring to, really was almost a satellite to some degree, less so than some of Eastern Europe, but a satellite of the Soviet Union. That has been dissipated now, and Russia doesn't want the responsibility to deliver the Serbs, for example.

I think the role for them is in the United Nations. I think the role for Russia is as a veto-holding member of the United Nations family to go along with the common objectives of getting a cease-fire, of having the U.N. keep the peace, of helping with humanitarian aid which we simply have got to do. But I don't see them having a special assignment, although in fairness, he did say that they would like to be helpful. But I don't think that their history gives them, he doesn't feel, the special leverage that we might think just looking back a year or two.

### Aid to Russia

*Q.* Mr. President, what is your personal assessment of what is going on in Russia right now? We've heard a lot about the hardships there, and it seems that they are having a hard time. And, secondly, is the United States going to give Russia the support it needs to get its act together?

*The President.* What is going on there right now is indeed a manifestation of hardship. Yeltsin, I am convinced, really believes in democracy. I am convinced of that. It wasn't just the courage that he showed standing on the tank to put down the coup, but it was more than that. He has now put into effect some changes that really, really adversely impacts for the short run the lives of many of the people in Russia.

And so they're going through extraordinarily tough times. He warns things can get more difficult, things can get tougher. He is absolutely convinced that the path for prosperity lies through these fundamental reforms that lead to the convertibility of the ruble, for example; that leads to fairer trade; that invites investment in partnership. Therein lies tremendous potential for the United States, jobs and investment from America. Jobs in American investment and investment from America, it's there when you look at the tremendous potential of Russia.

But it is my view that we must not miss this opportunity to help them. We have spent trillions of dollars standing up against the Communist menace, and it was proper that we do that. We are now the undisputed leader of the world because we did it, and Russia is free and democratic, going through some of the darndest democratic gymnastics you've ever seen, challenging each other and fighting each other in the congress. Yeltsin's got problems worse than I do with the Congress. I mean, this guy's got real problems over there. But we want to help them. We want to pass the "FREEDOM Support Act" which unloosens tremendous amounts of money from the IFI's, international financial institutions, particularly the IMF and the World Bank. The U.S. contribution in cash is substantial but not all that substantial; it's in the hundreds of millions, not in the billions. But we are trying to get an increased quota for the IMF through our Congress. I am committed to the "FREEDOM Support Act," and I am challenging the Congress to move on this as an insurance policy for the people of the United States.

And yes, the demands are tough at home. A lot of people don't understand it, but once in a while a President has to be out front for what is right. I don't want to have on my conscience missing this chance to solidify the democratic experience, the move to a market economy. So I'm urging the Congress to move, hopefully as expeditiously as next week, to support the "FREEDOM Support Act" because I believe it's in our interest. This isn't in the interest just of Russia. I've got to see what's in the best interest of the United States of America. I believe that if we go forward with the "FREEDOM Support Act" we will be doing just that, doing what's best for our country and for the generations to come, not just in peace and prosperity and democracy but in markets and in opportunity, investment opportunity.

### Job Opportunities for Youth

*Q.* Mr. President, do you believe that starting a major program of work projects to put youth to work would be a good idea at this time?

*The President.* We think that we've designed a good program. I will sign soon legislation across the country to add to the summer job program $500 million. I believe that what we've done in terms of helping the cities and through our SBA and FEMA response to what happened in Los Angeles, coupled with our what is called a "Weed and Seed" initiative, weed out the criminals and then seed the urban areas with enterprise, is the approach we ought to take.

I would stop short of yet a new federally run bureaucracy to create jobs outside of the private sector. I really believe that jobs with dignity in the private sector is not only help short-run but is a longer run answer to the problems, whereas the Government programs start off well-intentioned and sometimes have pretty good short-run effects, but in the long run do not provide the kind of jobs that good job training and entrepreneurship and capital gains, bringing people to the cities, can provide. And so I am not in favor of a broad Government program, although I am strongly supporting aid that I have mentioned for the cities largely in terms of the summer job program.

Well, here's the last one, and then I promise to go peacefully and let you all eat or leave or whatever is next for you. I heard you were having broccoli, so I'm out of here. [*Laughter*] Now, what's next?

*Racial Harmony*

Q. Mr. President, Bob Johnson, from Washington, DC. What's your message to black and white Americans to help bring about racial harmony?

*The President.* That's a good question, Bob, and the answer is that the President must speak out at every opportunity, whether it relates to problems in the cities or whether it relates to the country in general, for racial harmony against discrimination of any kind. In addition to that, I point with considerable pride to legislation that some consider controversial.

I stood up against a civil rights bill that I felt would result in quotas. I don't believe in quotas. We passed a civil rights bill that I can say does not result in quotas and takes a step towards the elimination of discrimination in the workplace. We passed under our administration the ADA, which deals with people with disabilities. That is forward-looking legislation.

My point is, I'm not sure that more legislation is required. I do think more brotherhood is required; more compassion is required. I have tried very hard as President to speak out against discrimination, and I will continue to do so because we are one Nation. We're one Nation under God, and we ought never to forget it.

Thank you all very, very much. We're out of here.

*Note: The President spoke at 12:26 p.m. at the Hyatt Regency Irvine. In his remarks, he referred to Reed Royalty and Todd Nicholson, president and executive director of the league, and Peter Ueberroth, chairman of the Rebuild L.A. Committee.*

# Statement on Signing the Los Padres Condor Range and River Protection Act
*June 19, 1992*

I am pleased to sign into law H.R. 2556, the "Los Padres Condor Range and River Protection Act." This Act designates seven new wilderness areas, encompassing 400,450 acres, within the Los Padres National Forest in California as components of the National Wilderness Preservation System, more than doubling the wilderness acreage set aside within the Los Padres National Forest. The Act also designates segments of three rivers within the National Forest, totaling 84 miles, as components of the National Wild and Scenic Rivers System.

By signing this bill into law, we further the protection of unique and sensitive lands within the National Forest System. Our action here today is important for several reasons:

—Much of this area includes habitat for the nearly extinct California condor and preservation of this habitat is critical to condor recovery efforts.

—Nearly half of the Los Padres National Forest is now designated for permanent protection under the Wilderness Act, one of the highest percentages of any national forest in the country.

—It increases by 10 percent the amount of national forest lands in California that are protected under the Wilderness Act.

—It protects segments of Sespe Creek and the Sisquoc and Big Sur Rivers as wild, free-flowing rivers under the Wild and Scenic Rivers System.

—It provides for wild and scenic river studies on an additional 110 miles of rivers within the National Forest boundary, a few of the only free-flowing streams left in southern California.

Wilderness designation of these areas means that they will be managed to preserve their unique and natural character. By signing this bill into law, we enhance the diversity and beauty of the Nation's lands set aside for the enjoyment of both present and future generations of Americans as part of the National Wilderness Preservation and the National Wild and Scenic Rivers Systems.

As President I remain deeply committed to preserving our valuable natural resources. Since 1989, my budgets have doubled funding for parks, wildlife, and outdoor recreation and have tripled funds to States under the Land and Water Conservation Fund. Moreover, the length of rivers designated as wild and scenic has increased from 868 to 9,463 miles over the past 20 years. Finally, since 1982, the amount of lands protected as part of the National Wilderness Preservation System has averaged in excess of 1.5 million acres per year.

GEORGE BUSH

The White House,
June 19, 1992.

*Note: H.R. 2556, approved June 19, was assigned Public Law No. 102–301.*

## Message to the Senate Transmitting a Protocol to the Strategic Arms Reduction Treaty
*June 19, 1992*

*To the Senate of the United States:*

I am transmitting herewith, for the advice and consent of the Senate to ratification, the Protocol to the Treaty Between the United States of America and the Union of Soviet Socialist Republics on the Reduction and Limitation of Strategic Offensive Arms (the Protocol) signed at Lisbon, Portugal, on May 23, 1992. The Protocol is an integral part of the Treaty Between the United States of America and the Union of Soviet Socialist Republics on the Reduction and Limitation of Strategic Offensive Arms (the START Treaty), which I transmitted for the advice and consent of the Senate to ratification on November 25, 1991. The Protocol is designed to enable implementation of the START Treaty in the new international situation following the dissolution of the Soviet Union. The Protocol constitutes an amendment to the START Treaty, and I therefore request that it be considered along with the START Treaty for advice and consent to ratification.

I also transmit for the information of the Senate documents that are associated with, but not integral parts of, the Protocol or the START Treaty. These documents are letters containing legally binding commitments from the heads of state of the Republic of Byelarus, the Republic of Kazakhstan, and Ukraine concerning the removal of nuclear weapons and strategic offensive arms from their territories. Although not submitted for the advice and consent of the Senate to ratification, these documents are relevant to the consideration of the START Treaty by the Senate. No new U.S. security assurance or guarantees—beyond the assurances previously extended to all nonnuclear-weapon States Parties to the Non-Proliferation Treaty—are associated with any of these letters.

The START Treaty represents a nearly decade-long effort by the United States and the former Soviet Union to address the nature and magnitude of the threat that strategic nuclear weapons pose to both countries and to the world in general. As I indicated in transmitting that Treaty to the Senate, the United States had several objectives in the START negotiations. First, we consistently held the view that the START Treaty must enhance stability in times of crisis. Second, we sought an agreement that did not simply limit strategic arms, but that reduced them significantly below current levels. Third, we sought a treaty that would allow equality of U.S. strategic forces relative to those of the former Soviet Union. Fourth, we sought an agreement that would be effectively verifiable. And, finally, the United States placed great emphasis during the negotiations in seeking an agreement that would be supported by the American and allied publics.

I was fully convinced in 1991 and I remain fully convinced that the START Treaty achieves these objectives. In addition, the Protocol transmitted herewith has allowed us to achieve another important objective: ensuring that only one state emerging from the former Soviet Union will have nuclear weapons. To gain the benefits of START in the new international situation following the demise of the Soviet Union, it is necessary that Byelarus, Kazakhstan, Russia, and Ukraine—the four former Soviet republics within whose territory all strategic offensive arms are based and all declared START-related facilities are located—be legally bound by the START Treaty. The Protocol accomplishes this, while recognizing the sovereign and independent status of each of these four states.

Of equal importance, the Protocol obligates Byelarus, Kazakhstan, and Ukraine to adhere to the Nuclear Non-Proliferation Treaty as nonnuclear-weapon States Parties in the shortest possible time. In addition, the letters transmitted with the Protocol legally obligate these three states to eliminate all nuclear weapons and all strategic offensive arms located on their territories within 7 years following the date of entry into force of the START Treaty. The Protocol and the associated letters thus further one of our most fundamental non-proliferation objectives—that the number of nuclear-weapon states shall not be increased. Together with the START Treaty, the Protocol helps ensure that nuclear weapons will not be used in the future.

The START Treaty serves the interest of the United States and represents an important step in the stabilization of the strategic nuclear balance. With the addition of the Protocol, the START Treaty can be implemented in a manner consistent with the changed political circumstances following the demise of the Soviet Union and in a manner that achieves important non-proliferation goals. I therefore urge the Senate to give prompt and favorable consideration to the START Treaty, including its Annexes, Protocols, Memorandum of Understanding, and this new Protocol, and to give advice and consent to its ratification.

GEORGE BUSH

The White House
June 19, 1992.

# Nomination of William Harrison Courtney To Be United States Ambassador to Kazakhstan
*June 19, 1992*

The President today announced his intention to nominate William Harrison Courtney, of West Virginia, to be Ambassador of the United States of America to Kazakhstan. This is a new position.

Dr. Courtney currently serves as the Chargé d'Affaires in Kazakhstan. Prior to this he was Deputy United States Negotiator for the U.S.-Soviet Defense and Space Talks, United States Mission in Geneva, Switzerland. Dr. Courtney was Deputy Executive Secretary for the National Security Council, 1987. From 1984 to 1986, he was Special Assistant to the Under Secretary of State for Political Affairs at the Department of State, and Deputy Director of the Office of Strategic Nuclear Policy in the Bureau of Politico-Military Affairs, 1983–84.

Dr. Courtney graduated from West Virginia University (B.A., 1966) and Brown

University (Ph.D., 1980). He was born July 18, 1944, in Baltimore, MD. He is married and has two children.

# Nomination of Patricia Diaz Dennis To Be an Assistant Secretary of State
*June 19, 1992*

The President today announced his intention to nominate Patricia Diaz Dennis, of Virginia, to be Assistant Secretary of State for Human Rights and Humanitarian Affairs. She would succeed Richard Schifter.

Since 1991 Ms. Dennis has served as vice president for Government affairs for Sprint in Washington, DC. She has served as partner and chair of the communications section of the law firm of Jones, Day, Reavis & Pogue, 1989–91. From 1986 to 1989, she served as Commissioner of the Federal Communications Commission. She also served on the National Labor Relations Board from 1983 to 1986. Prior to that appointment Ms. Dennis served as an attorney with the American Broadcasting Company in Hollywood, CA, 1978–83.

Ms. Dennis graduated from the University of California in Los Angeles (A.B., 1970) and Loyola University of Los Angeles School of Law (J.D., 1973). She was born October 2, 1946, in Santa Rita, NM. Ms. Dennis is married, has three children, and resides in McLean, VA.

# Appointment of Edward J. Melanson, Jr., for the Personal Rank of Ambassador While Serving as Chief Negotiator for Defense and Space
*June 19, 1992*

The President today announced his intention to appoint Edward J. Melanson, Jr., of Virginia, to be accorded the personal rank of Ambassador in his capacity as Chief Negotiator for Defense and Space.

Since 1991 Mr. Melanson has served as Deputy Negotiator for Defense and Space for the U.S. Delegation to the Nuclear and Space Arms Negotiations in Geneva, Switzerland. From 1989 to 1991, he served as Assistant for National Security in the Office of Presidential Personnel at the White House. Mr. Melanson served as senior defense adviser for the United States Delegation for the Nuclear and Space Arms Negotiations with the Soviet Union in Geneva, 1985–88. He served at the Department of Defense as Assistant for International Space Policy, 1982–85; Assistant for International Intelligence Policy, 1979–82; Defense Representative to the U.S.–U.S.S.R. Anti-Satellite Negotiations, 1978–79; and Assistant for International Negotiations Policy, 1975–78.

Mr. Melanson graduated from Tufts University (B.A., 1967) and George Washington University (M.S., 1972). He served in the U.S. Navy, 1957–88. He was born December 14, 1935, in Stoneham, MA. Mr. Melanson is married, has two children, and resides in Springfield, VA.

## Nomination of John Stern Wolf To Be United States Ambassador to Malaysia
*June 19, 1992*

The President today announced his intention to nominate John Stern Wolf, of Maryland, a Minister-Counselor in the Senior Foreign Service, to be Ambassador of the United States of America to Malaysia. He would succeed Paul Matthews Cleveland.

Since 1989 Mr. Wolf has served as Principal Deputy Assistant Secretary of State for International Organization Affairs at the Department of State. He has also served at the Department of State as executive assistant to the Under Secretary of State for Political Affairs, 1988–89; and as Office Director of Regional and Multilateral Force and Observers Affairs in the Bureau of Near Eastern and South Asian Affairs, 1987–88.

Mr. Wolf has also served as Political Counselor at the American Embassy in Islamabad, Pakistan, 1984–87; special assistant to the Under Secretary of State for Science and Technology at the State Department, 1981–84; and financial economist in the Bureau of Economic and Business Affairs, 1979–81.

Mr. Wolf graduated from Dartmouth College (B.A., 1970) and Princeton University Woodrow Wilson School (mid-career fellow, 1978–79). He was born September 12, 1948, in Philadelphia, PA. Mr. Wolf is married, has two children, and resides in Bethesda, MD.

## Remarks to the Howard Jarvis Taxpayers Association in Universal City, California
*June 20, 1992*

Thank you very much. And Pete, thank you, Governor Wilson, for that introduction. And let me just say at the outset of these remarks how much I respect Pete Wilson. Here he is, with the economy obviously not doing well in California, but taking a tremendously courageous position, trying to whip that legislature in line and saying the way to solve our fiscal problems is by getting spending down, not taxes up. And we all deserve a big vote of thanks for him.

Let me also extend a thank you to our host—he and the directors and others here—but to our host today, Joel Fox, who is the president of the Howard Jarvis Taxpayers Association. If you want a good leader, get a strong man, get somebody in there that's going to take the positions he did and has taken. We respect him, and I thank him for this morning's hospitality.

And to each and every one of you, I apologize for being a little late. The weather got us, and we've been orbiting around out there. We've just landed, but we landed in an alternative air zone.

May I congratulate, on his primary win, one who really stands with you on principle, Bruce Herschensohn, who will make a great United States Senator. Speaking of Bruce and what he stands for, I will simply say it's a shame that I don't have time to tour the Universal Studio. But if I want to see behind-the-scenes tricks or outrageous fantasy, I don't have to visit Hollywood— [*laughter*]—I can watch the Congress try to deal with the budget of the United States of America.

And may I say, on a very sincere personal note, what a pleasure it is to see Estelle Jarvis. It's a special privilege to be with you and the members of the association. And Estelle, your late husband really was a true pioneer. In the Utah mining town where he grew up, he learned from his parents to love freedom, to take on responsibility, to dream dreams as big as the desert horizon. His political credo was simple and yet profound. He said, "Our freedom depends on four words: Government must be limited."

Here in California 14 years ago, Howard Jarvis won that famous victory, obviously assisted and helped by everybody here, that tax limitation plan called Proposition 13. He fired the first shot in what later became known as the Reagan revolution. And we're still feeling the reverberations today as we fight to expand freedom and hold back unnecessary burdens of Government. And it couldn't be more fitting that we meet this week, as Joel pointed out, just 2 days after the historic United States Supreme Court decision upholding Proposition 13. This was another tremendous victory for the rights of the taxpayer and the legacy of the late, great Howard Jarvis.

Our revolution isn't the work of a single Presidency; it's the mission for a whole generation of reform. Since President Reagan and I went to Washington in 1981, tax rates have been cut across the board. We made them flatter; we made them fairer. We've cut the top rate from 70 percent to 31 percent. We've raised the standard deduction. We've taken millions of low-to-moderate-income people off the tax rolls altogether. And we've made landmark reforms to get big Government regulation off the backs of our families and our businesses.

But we have much more to do. With the tax-and-spend liberals still in charge of the Congress, Government keeps growing. And Congress now spends nearly a quarter of what people in this country work to produce; that's right, almost 25 percent of the gross domestic product of the United States of America. The habit of deficit spending has brought us to the point that the national debt now equals about $65,000 for every family of four in the United States of America. And that is a mortgage on our kids' future. And it says we're not really as free a society as we should be. And why? Because Government is just too big, and it spends too much.

Again and again and again, the liberals in Congress have said no to spending reform. And it's no wonder that Americans keep clamoring for stricter limits on the power and the cost of Government. From coast to coast, people are mobilizing for change. The air is crackling with the feeling that

Howard Jarvis made his battle cry: I am mad as hell.

Maybe you're like millions of other Americans. You shop at K-Mart. You go to Carl's Jr. You work to get your kids through school and pay off a mortgage. And you know it's not only your right, it is your duty to your family to fight high taxes and Government waste. And when liberal elitists ridicule you and say we have social problems because of you, because you're greedy, well, naturally, you stand up and fight back.

Our fighting spirit has brought us to a turning point. We're on the threshold of something big. And already we're rolling back needless restrictions on innovation and job creation through my moratorium on new Federal regulations. Here's a small but symbolic example: A construction project, oddly enough an expansion—it's quite ironic here—an expansion of a homeless shelter, was being delayed by the bureaucracy because it was counter to a rule regarding wetlands. But what no one quite could understand was that this project was on a developed downtown city block, totally surrounded by concrete and pavement. Something was all wet all right, but it certainly wasn't the building site. The project is now underway. We're going to keep it up. For businesses, for charities, for homeowners, we're getting unreasonable regulation off of their backs. And I am pledged to continue that program of regulatory relief.

And I'm pushing hard to reform our civil justice system. We are simply suing each other too much and caring for each other too little. Americans want to stop nuisance lawsuits. Someone asked me the other day, if an apple a day keeps the doctor away, what works for lawyers? [*Laughter*] Let me add, parenthetically, I will continue to appoint well-qualified judges to our Federal courts, including the Supreme Court, who will interpret our Constitution and not legislate from the Federal Bench.

And I'm committed as strongly as ever to win more tax relief and reform. We need to lift the dead weight that punishes homeowners and prevents more investment and job creation, those sky-high taxes on capital gains. Get people back to work in this country. Frankly, I wish Congress would move on our other growth incentives. We need to enact another proposal to ease tax burdens on families and homeowners, like a $5,000 tax credit for that first-time homebuyer. I want those young families to participate in the American dream by owning their own homes.

As you may know, we are fighting for fundamental change in our education and welfare systems. It's time for parents to have the freedom to choose their kids' schools, public, private, and religious. That's how we'll give parents the muscle to change our schools and make them the best in the entire world.

And here, with Pete Wilson sitting here, we're preaching to the choir a little bit. But right now we have a welfare system designed by the liberal politicians and these social theorists. It's a burden on taxpayers, but that's not the worst of it. That's not my major concern, even. Much of the time, this system hurts the very people that it claims to help. The system discourages single mothers from getting married. It leaves too many young women and children without the stability of a home, two-parent home. And let's face it, the welfare state system traps too many people in a cycle of dependency, destroying dignity, telling the little guy who wants to pick himself up that he really doesn't have much of a chance. And I am determined to change that.

I'm working to transform this failed welfare system into something that makes sense, something that gives people a shot at dignity. Right now, I'm working with tough-minded, creative Governors like Pete Wilson, like Tommy Thompson—some of you may have read about his reforms, the Governor of Wisconsin—to give them flexibility under the Federal laws to try out new ideas and to turn around their State welfare programs. And with Governors in all 50 States like Pete and Tommy, we'd soon be making major progress fostering dignity and the rewards of work. We'll make more headway in connecting welfare with requirements for work, training, education. We'll get more deadbeat dads to pay the child support they owe. And we'd help a lot more families come together and stay together.

My proposal—another area—for health insurance reform is a model of the new way of thinking about social programs. You probably haven't heard much about it. It's before the Congress now. The liberal Democrats that hold control of Congress are too busy beating the drum for that stale idea of a Ted Kennedy-style system of nationalized health care. And I am going to veto anything that makes socialized medicine for America. We are not going to have that.

The plan I have makes good sense. It would help working people and needy people with vouchers and tax credits. It would provide access to insurance, make that available to everybody. And it would provide Americans like yourselves with quality care, care you can afford, while wringing out the excesses and the waste. That's because it uses old-fashioned American ideas: free markets and choice.

In the long run, reforming education and welfare could make a major contribution to increasing productivity and solving fiscal crisis. And health care reform can make a major contribution to improving and, put it this way, to getting rid of the worry that so many American families have. And we can make these reforms without raising taxes and without piling new burdens onto State and local taxpayers.

Hand-in-hand with these reforms goes the crusade to enforce fiscal discipline. This is absolutely essential to make these reforms work. Our burden of debt and uncontrolled spending results from almost four decades of liberal Democratic control of the United States House of Representatives. Time and again, Ronald Reagan and I have pushed for popular reforms. And I believe the American people want the President to have in law what 43 Governors have, that line-item veto. And I believe and I know the American people believe the only way to discipline both the Congress and the executive branch is through a constitutional amendment to balance the budget.

I hope you followed that debate. If you did, you'll know that standing in our way is the liberal hardcore of the Democratic Congress, barely more than one-third of the membership. Read the rollcall. Just take a look at it. Go back and look at the papers and read the rollcall from last week's vote in the House on the balanced budget amendment, and you'll see who I'm talking about. And pay attention to the Democrats who belong in a special Hall of Shame. I'm talking here about the 12 Democrats, two from California, who listed themselves as sponsors, as sponsors of the balanced budget amendment. They did that to look good and talk good to the people back home. And then these 12 switched sides and voted to kill the very amendment that they had sponsored. They did that to curry favor with those liberal party bosses that control the House of Representatives, and we'd better change that in this election coming up in the fall.

We know better than to expect these people to discipline themselves. This is the same crowd we've seen for decades, in charge, unchallenged, and out of control. Let me remind you: For the last 30 years, make that 35, I think, the Democrats have controlled the House of Representatives. For 24 out of the last 30 years, they've controlled the United States Senate. And the Congress appropriates—and people forget this, but let me say it—the Congress appropriates every single dime and tells the President how to spend every single dime.

Unlike one of my opponents for President, I don't believe the only way to confront a massive deficit is with a "massive tax increase," and that's in quotes because that's what he said. I know we can do it without raising taxes, and I have a detailed plan. This isn't just election year rhetoric. We have a detailed plan sitting up there before the United States Congress right now. It controls the growth of mandatory programs. It doesn't cut them; it permits the growth in inflation and in population. Doesn't touch Social Security. It doesn't raise taxes. And here it is.

So when the election rolls around, let's get some of these people who are saying they're going to change things to talk some specifics and to say how it's going to be done. Here it is. And we need again, though, the discipline and the sense of urgency that that balanced budget amendment will bring. And while I'm at it, I'd like the President to again have what 43 Governors have, let me repeat it, the line-item veto.

It is time for change. Somebody says, "You're for enterprise zones for the cities. That's not a new idea." I said, "Yes, it is; it has never been tried." And isn't it better to try something new, try what hasn't been tried: a Republican House, a Republican Senate, a Republican Congress. That has not been tried in 35 years, and it's time to make that kind of significant change.

In my introduction by our wonderful Governor and my friend, Pete mentioned something about international affairs. You listen to this debate for who should be President, and you might think foreign affairs don't exist, that we aren't really the only undisputed leader of the world today, which we are. So before I finish, I want to say a word about the summit meeting that Boris Yeltsin and I just completed in Washington, where we reached historic agreements for peace and for security. Thousands of visitors joined Barbara and me on the White House lawn to welcome the first democratically elected President of Russia. And I just wish, really, that each one of you could have been there with us to share in that very special moment. That's because it is patriotic people like you who helped make that moment possible.

Now the Russian people can worship freely. They can compete in free markets. They can choose their own government. And our children, our precious kids and grandkids, will no longer live in that same shadow of nuclear war that has haunted us for 40 years. And that is big, and that is important. And your support made that possible. And today, ordinary Russians thank God that ordinary Americans stood fast against the Communist dictatorship that threatened us and oppressed them.

I think what this shows is that if you have the will, the perseverance, there's always a chance to make a difference. Howard Jarvis spent 16 years fighting for tax limitation. He was 76 years old when at last he won, when he shook the establishment of this entire country. I've highlighted for you important proposals for the future, with a new Congress: Revolutionize our schools; put parents and kids ahead of bureaucrats. Reform our system of health care. Overhaul the welfare system; give needy people opportunity instead of dependency. Adopt a balanced budget amendment. And hold the line against excessive spending, taxes, and regulation. With a new Congress that shares our values, we can use the next 4 years to set our country on the right track for the next 40 years. And with your help, I know

we can.

Thank you all very, very much, and may God bless the United States of America. Thank you all.

*Note: The President spoke at 9:30 a.m. at the Universal City Hilton.*

## Remarks at the Texas State Republican Convention in Dallas, Texas
*June 20, 1992*

*The President.* Thank you so much for that warm welcome. Let me quickly say hello to a few of our dais guests: our elected officials Kay Bailey Hutchison and Rick Perry, doing a superb job for our State. May I salute the great Mayor of Dallas, Steve Bartlett, who served so well in Washington and now serving this city with such distinction.

And now, on to the political types like you and me: Ernie Angelo and Penny Butler, the Texas GOP National Committee members; Fred Meyer, our great chairman of this Texas State GOP. I want to thank Beverly Kaufman and all the women, all the members of the Texas Federation who came to meet me and who are doing a great job for us; single out our Bush-Quayle team, Jim Oberwetter, Barbara Patton; and of course, Rob Mosbacher, the chairman of Texas Victory '92. We have a great Republican congressional delegation from Texas, and I'm pleased so many members of that Texas congressional delegation could attend. I wish we had more like them in Washington, DC.

And last but not least, I'd like to single out the master of ceremonies with whom I served so closely in Washington as we battled to get some things past the Congress, as we stood up against many things that the Congress were trying to ram down the throats of the people, and I'm talking about Fred McClure, the emcee, my great friend and yours. Thank you, Fred.

Now, let me just say at the beginning I have never felt as strongly as I do now: I am proud to be a Texan. Barbara and I

raised our kids here. From 1948 on, we voted in every Presidential election here. I coached Little League here, built my business here, worked in the party here. My Presidential library will be here. My campaign started here. And when my work is over, I'll come back here. So it's great to be home. There is no place like Texas.

November 3d is but a few months away. And yes, the going's been rough for our country, but we're turning the corner. And I'll let the world in on a secret that you already know: I finish what I start. To finish the job the American people asked me to do, I need your help, Texas. Give me 4 more years as your leader, and let's get the job done.

*Audience members.* Four more years! Four more years! Four more years!

*The President.* A strange political year, yes. But snappy answers and glib talk will not get the job done. Let somebody else become the darling of the talking heads on television; I'm going to keep on fighting to get something done for this country. You wait until August, and we'll roll up our sleeves and get in that campaign mode. But there's too much at stake for America to forget about trust and judgment and values; too much at stake, as we say here, to buy a pig in a poke. And you can count on this: We will win in November. And I am convinced we are going to carry Texas, and we are going to win going away.

Just the the last 4 years, the world that we have known for the last 40 years has changed. And by our willingness to stand up for freedom and stand against aggression and fight for what's right, we changed the world. And our mission for the next 4 years is to shape our new world, not just abroad but right here at home. It's a big job to set the course for the next 40 years, and it means solving big problems with a level head, with tolerance and good judgment. Being President is a demanding job, and a President must be temperamentally suited for the job. I have been tested by fire, and I am the right man for that job.

You and I understand America and her problems, and we understand where we must go. And we all want families strong and united, good schools, safe neighborhoods, job-creating economy, and a world at peace. Since becoming your President, I have been to all 50 States in the country. I have felt the heartbeat of America. I felt it up close—farmers and ranchers and cities and city kids and teachers and truck drivers. I know the American people, and they are with us, but they're angry. They're angry at big Government, small results, and big excuses. And they are right: Government is too big, and it spends too much. And we've got to change that.

This election must be a referendum on some big ideas. And one of them is that Government works right without raising taxes. Unlike one of my opponents, I do not believe that the only way to ever balance the budget is, quote, a massive tax increase, unquote. The American people know that I proposed an amendment to balance the budget. They know I fought for it, the only Presidential candidate to support it. That's why in the fall, they will be with us. You send us more Congressmen from Texas who will do what the people want. And the people want a balanced budget amendment to the Constitution of the United States. And by the way, while you're still standing, the American people know that the President should have what 43 Governors have to control spending. They know I fought for it, and they will be with us. America wants the line-item veto. [*Applause*] Thank you.

Now, the taxpayers know how the budget gets busted. It's an arrogant, permanent, liberal, Democratic-controlled Congress, unaccountable to the people. The American people are with us, and it is time to limit the term for Members of Congress.

You and I know each other. And throughout my life in Texas you've seen me close up. When I sent our sons and daughters into battle in Panama and in Desert Storm, Texans anguished with me and overwhelmingly supported me. And when I agreed to pay a painful price for a spending controls deal on the budget, Lord knows you argued with me. And when I said I will not eat broccoli, every kid in Texas said, "Yes!" But through it all, you knew I wouldn't break with those Texas values that we hold most dear: freedom and faith, honor and decency, and, most of all, family.

History will record this: American leadership changed the world. Panama is a democratic country. Its democratically elected leaders, once beaten by those "dignity battalions," are now back in office, and its narco-trafficking dictator in jail where he belongs. And Eastern Europe is free. Germany is united. Imperial communism is dead and buried. And just this week, Boris Yeltsin and I stood in the Rose Garden to announce the most sweeping nuclear arms cuts in history, eliminating those enormous multiwarheaded ICBM's that have threatened the world. That is something big. That is something spectacular. Dreams come true for America. And these kids here will sleep at night without the same fear of nuclear war. I am proud of that record, and I will take that record to the American people.

But let me warn you, let me just put out this one word of warning. For all the great triumphs that freedom has made, the world still remains a dangerous place. That's why a big idea in this campaign is defending America's interests abroad. And the best way to keep America safe is to keep America strong. The Soviet bear might now be a creature of the past, but there are still plenty of wolves out there, and you know who they are. But as our actions in the Gulf proved, we will defend our interests. We will keep the wolves at bay. And we will never let aggression stand.

Yes, our successes abroad have laid the foundation for stepping up our attack on these domestic problems. And as I work to correct what's wrong, I will always remember: The people don't work for the Government; the Government works for the people.

No, to set things on a track right here at home we must start with a moral, even a spiritual revival across this country, particularly when it comes to instilling values in our kids. So here's another big idea. Fads may come and go, but in the Bush administration the family will always be in fashion. And that's how we put first things first. Families united, fathers and mothers staying together in spite of tough times because they love their kids and want them to grow up whole and strong. It all begins with the family. And we must find ways to strengthen the American family. The Commission I appointed will do just that. And all of us should make suggestions that will help.

You know, some of the ideas that I've put forth for changing America unnerved those who cling to the old thinking of the status quo. Not everyone is ready for new ideas, so it's going to take some time. And 4 years just haven't been enough to finish our mission. Some people say, why can't you bring the same kind of purpose and success to the domestic scene as you did in Desert Shield and Desert Storm? And the answer is: I didn't have to get permission from some old goat in the United States Congress to kick Saddam Hussein out of Kuwait. That's the reason.

*Audience members.* Four more years! Four more years! Four more years!

*The President.* Let me just add a word about that. Let me add a word about that decision. It is just plain irresponsible and out of touch with reality to suggest that a President should take a poll and get a tax increase before he leads the world against aggression. What the people want from their leaders is leadership, and that's exactly what the American people got in Desert Storm. I don't need to take a poll to know what's right when it comes to standing up against aggression. So you can write that one down, some of these opponents out there.

And would I like to see our domestic agenda off and running? You bet. And I understand the frustration that's out there, the same as you: family values under siege, second-rate schools, too much violence on too many streets. An old-thinking Congress can't get the job done. And for 35—now,

listen to this statistic—for 35 out of the last 35 years the Democrats, the liberal Democrats, have controlled the House of Representatives. And what do the people see as a result? A crooked post office and a lot of bounced checks. Let's change that. Let us change that. We must break this gridlock and recapture the trust of the American people. And the way to do that is Republican control of the House, Republican control of the Senate. You give me a Congress like that, and you watch this country move again.

Go, Aggies.

There's a right way and there's wrong way to set a new course. And the wrong way is to give up when things get tough, pick up your marbles and go home. And I will not give up on America, not now, not ever. We are going to get the job done. There has been too much pessimism, too many people trying to get elected by saying how bad things are, too many gloomy TV news stories about what's wrong with America. It is my view that America will always be a rising nation. And we can and we will make this country better. I am an optimist about the United States of America.

After a tough, tough recession, a tough recession where many families have been hurt, confidence is returning. Confidence is beginning to come back, to return to our economy. Some good fundamentals are in place: low interest rates, low inflation, stronger growth in the first quarter. The United States is still the largest, the most productive economy in the entire world, and don't ever forget that. The biggest mission, the biggest idea of this campaign is to accelerate economic growth to create hope and opportunity for everyone. And with our exports still climbing, there's solid proof that Americans can outcompete anyone, anytime, anywhere in the world.

Look right down a Texas road for examples: Texas beef on the market in Japan, Texas cotton to Europe, Texas oil and gas technology in demand everywhere. And I am going to fight to keep that technology state-of-the-art and to help keep our independent oil and gas producers competitive. I will keep pushing for a revised alternative minimum tax. And I'll keep pushing for cleaner fuels like natural gas. And I'll keep pushing to reduce our dangerous dependence on foreign oil, not by conservation alone, which is important, but by opening projects for domestic production like the ANWR in Alaska.

A rising nation educates her young people, and all across America a revolution in education, we call it America 2000, to bring back excellence to our schools. Well, we were the ones to start this revolution, and we are the ones that are leading it, and we will be the ones to complete it. And before we're done, whether it's public, private, or religious, parents are going to have the right to choose their children's schools.

And this audience knows it better than most, but there's another great and dynamic movement transforming our country. It's a volunteer movement of ordinary people solving problems right where they live, millions of courageous people taking direct and consequential action on their own. This is how we help create whole and good communities. And lest anyone forget, under my Presidency, this movement, this big idea is a national crusade. The real heroes of America, God bless them, are the ones we call the Points of Light, one American helping another solve these problems.

Despite the odds, we've had some successes on Capitol Hill. Legislation like the Child Care Act which said parents raise kids, not the Government; the Clean Air Act, linking a strong economy with a clean environment; the Americans with Disabilities Act, guaranteeing the disabled their rightful place in the mainstream. Give these people a chance, and that's what that legislation did. And sometimes my job up there, given the control of the Congress, is to keep bad things from happening. And when it comes to stopping bad legislation with my veto pen, it's Bush 26, the Congress 0. And it's going to stay that way.

I'm proud of our record. We've had to make the tough calls every day and every week. We proposed a better way for America, a new track for America. And like Texas, it is a big idea. And when Congress blocks the way, stuck in the muck of old thinking, we'll keep that heat on, keep pushing for change. One specific on that:

The Congress may have a vision problem on that, the Congress may have a vision problem, but don't for a minute think that we're going to give up on the superconducting super collider. It is forward-looking, and the country needs it, and the world needs it. It's good for Texas, and it's good for the United States of America.

And when the American people send me a Congress with a commitment to change, we'll pass the laws and do the work that the American people deserve. But let me say this: With or without the Congress, we are going to give the American people what they want. And that's not excuses; that is action.

This is an age of great change for America. And that's what makes November 3d so important. Change can seem to threaten the most valuable legacies that we hope to leave our children: good jobs, strong families, a Nation at peace. Change breeds uncertainty and skepticism, and I understand that. But, look, we are the United States of America, one Nation under God. And the genius of America is everywhere. It is in a society that places a premium on performance, not glitz; on service, not selfishness. A society that captures what Texas is all about. And let the skeptic say that it can't be done. The optimist will say, let's get to work. And I am ready. And, yes, we're in the fight of our lives, but it's worth the fight. And we are in it to win.

And I appreciate this sensationally warm Texas welcome. And may God bless you all. And may God bless the United States of America. Thank you very much. Thank you. Thank you all so much.

*Note: The President spoke at 4:06 p.m. at the Dallas Convention Center. In his remarks, he referred to Kay Bailey Hutchison, Texas State treasurer; Rick Perry, Texas commissioner of agriculture; Beverly Kaufman, president, Texas Federation of Republican Women; Jim Oberwetter, Bush-Quayle '92 Texas chairman; Barbara Patton, Bush-Quayle '92 Texas cochairman; and Frederick D. McClure, managing director, First Southwest Co., and former Assistant to the President for Legislative Affairs. The President also referred to the Texas A&M University Aggies.*

## Remarks on Signing Emergency Supplemental Appropriations Legislation
*June 22, 1992*

Welcome to the Rose Garden. I'm very pleased to welcome all of you on this short notice to the White House. But may I salute our Secretary of Labor, who's been very instrumental in all of this. Senator Seymour, Senator Hatch, Senator Stevens, Congressman Joe McDade, welcome, all. And all of them, along with some others that weren't able to be with us today, have been extraordinarily helpful in this legislation. May I salute Mayor Schmoke, Bob Neall.

It is a very special privilege to have some young Americans from right here in our Nation's Capital. They're the reason, kids like these are the reason why we produce this legislation. They're the reason we're fighting for far-reaching reforms to offer opportunity for a better future.

The supplemental appropriations bill that I am signing here today provides emergency funding for the nationwide disaster programs of the Federal Emergency Management Agency, FEMA, and for the Small Business Administration, SBA. This bill replenishes the resources of both Agencies for expenditures they're making to help the victims of this lawless violence in Los Angeles and the flood in Chicago. These funds are used to help shelter people that are affected by major disasters and to offer low-interest loans to individuals in businesses in the disaster areas.

The bill also will help finance more than 400,000 summer jobs through a program of the Department of Labor with a special focus on helping young people in America's largest urban areas. By providing for $1.45 billion in SBA-guaranteed loans, the bill will help small business across the country literally create thousands of new jobs.

I turned aside efforts by some in the Congress to spend more for the sake of spending more when the urgent need is for fundamental change to provide hope and opportunity for people in the inner cities. We've got to recognize these supplemental funds are a beginning, only a beginning, and that's the way it is. It's imperative that

we make a fundamental change, that we put in place the package of reforms that we call the New America Plan. There are several points to that plan:

First, it enhances Government's primary mission to ensure the personal safety of our people. Our neighborhoods, our streets must be free from crime. To strike a blow for our people's right to live free from fear, I am asking Congress now to act on my "Weed and Seed" program to fight urban crime, as well as enacting a tough new comprehensive crime bill.

People in our cities need more freedom and opportunity to achieve, to excel. The second part of this plan calls for enterprise zones to offer incentives for innovation and job creation in the greatest American tradition. It is high time we put this great idea into action. When I was in Los Angeles, support for enterprise zones were across the board, across party label, across age group label. It was an amazing amount of support. So we've got to get this put into action.

The third part, our HOPE initiative, will help turn public housing tenants into homeowners. There's no overestimating the dignity that that brings.

Fourth, our America 2000 education reforms will help extend to parents and kids right there in the inner cities the same choices that people in the suburbs already have.

Fifth, to give people new skills, we propose to reform job training.

Finally, the long-term well-being of neighborhoods that are now dangerous and depressed demands that we break with the culture of dependency. My agenda for welfare reform aims to reward work and learning, to insist that fathers take responsibility for their children, and to make families whole.

These are the keys to providing hope for this new generation. These are the only reliable means for making our cities the safe and prosperous places they ought to be. So again, I am urging the Congress to put an end to the delays and to take action on this New America Plan.

I thank you all for coming. Now I will invite the Senators and Congressman McDade to come up, and be glad to sign this important legislation.

[*At this point, the President signed the bill.*]

The deed is done. Thank you all very, very much.

*Note: The President spoke at 2 p.m. in the Rose Garden at the White House. In his remarks, he referred to Kurt Schmoke, Mayor of Baltimore, MD, and Robert R. Neall, county executive of Anne Arundel County, MD. H.R. 5132, the Dire Emergency Supplemental Appropriations Act, 1992, for Disaster Assistance To Meet Urgent Needs Because of Calamities Such as Those Which Occurred in Los Angeles and Chicago, approved June 22, was assigned Public Law No. 102–302.*

# Statement on Signing Emergency Supplemental Appropriations Legislation
*June 22, 1992*

Today I have signed into law H.R. 5132, an Act that provides supplemental appropriations for disaster assistance to meet urgent needs resulting from calamities such as those that occurred in Los Angeles and Chicago.

This Act provides emergency funding for disaster programs of the Federal Emergency Management Agency (FEMA) and the Small Business Administration (SBA). FEMA funds will be used to provide disaster-affected individuals and families with temporary housing assistance and to provide grants for the repair and replacement of property damaged as a result of major disasters. The SBA funds will be used to provide low-interest loans to individuals and businesses located in areas affected by recent disasters.

This funding will ensure that FEMA and SBA have sufficient resources to address the major disasters that have occurred this year, including the civil disturbance in Los Angeles and the flood in Chicago. I am pleased that the Congress provided these funds under terms and conditions that are acceptable to the Administration.

Funds provided by H.R. 5132 for the Department of Labor's summer youth jobs program represent a satisfactory compromise between the Congress and the Administration and will finance 414,000 summer jobs. I am particularly pleased that provisions of the Act give special weight to en-

suring that this funding is targeted to the areas of greatest need, particularly the country's largest urban areas.

In accordance with the applicable provisions of the Budget Enforcement Act of 1990, I am designating the following funding as emergency requirements:

* $300 million for FEMA disaster assistance;
* $500 million for the summer youth jobs program; and
* $143.8 million for SBA disaster loans.

The Act also provides nonemergency supplemental funding for SBA's business loan program, the cost of which is fully offset. These funds will provide up to $1.45 billion in loan guarantees for qualified small businesses. This additional funding will ensure that sufficient resources remain available for this program throughout the remainder of fiscal year 1992.

GEORGE BUSH

The White House,
June 22, 1992.

*Note: H.R. 5132, the Dire Emergency Supplemental Appropriations Act, 1992, for Disaster Assistance To Meet Urgent Needs Because of Calamities Such as Those Which Occurred in Los Angeles and Chicago, approved June 22, was assigned Public Law No. 102–302.*

## Remarks Prior to a Meeting With the House Republican Health Care Task Force
*June 22, 1992*

*The President.* Now, let me just say at the outset, what we are here to talk about is health care reform. We have some ideas up there that we feel make a great deal of sense. I know that some of you all have a program. I keep reading that the Democrats say they want to make a political statement before the convention. Far more important than a political statement, it seems to me, is getting something done that will allay the fears that people have and help in the health care reform area.

We've got a good program for insurance. We'll protect the quality of American health care. And what I'd like to get from everybody here today is how you feel we can get it done. The small market reforms are good; the increased tax deductions for the self-employed, very good; and we make some administrative statements. I'd like to hear if we could move forward on malpractice reform. But these are some of the ingredients of what we think is a very helpful, very practical, and forward-looking health care program. So I hope that we can move it.

*Perot Investigations*

*Q.* Mr. President, how do you feel about Ross Perot's private initiative to investigate you and your finances?

*The President.* Well, I better count to 10. [*Laughter*] I prefer not to take that question right now, frankly.

*Q.* Were you aware of the inquiry?

*The President.* No, there's something not very pleasant about all this. And let me tell you this: It's fine to investigate on one's own the Vice President of the United States; no evidence to support any investigation. But I feel a little tense about it when they—if the reports are true of investigating my children, my family. There's something—I don't think that's particularly right. But nevertheless, I've probably said too much here.

*Q.* No, you haven't.

*The President.* Put it this way: I've said all I'm going to say.

*Q.* Are you angry?

*The President.* I'm not sure that's the proper word. There will be plenty of time to find out what happened here, but I don't like what I see.

*Q.* You're going to call him up and ask him yourself what happened?

*Q.* Has he called you——

*The President.* Thank you very much. Thank you all.

*Q.* ——to apologize or complain?

*Note: The President spoke at 4:09 p.m. in the Cabinet Room at the White House. A tape was not available for verification of the content of these remarks.*

## Letter to Congressional Leaders on Trade With Romania
*June 22, 1992*

*Dear Mr. Speaker:*   *(Dear Mr. President:)*

In accordance with section 407 of the Trade Act of 1974 (Public Law 93–618, January 3, 1975; 88 Stat. 1978), as amended (the "Trade Act"), I am transmitting a copy of a proclamation that extends nondiscriminatory treatment to the products of Romania. I also enclose the text of the "Agree-ment on Trade Relations Between the Government of the United States of America and the Government of Romania," including exchanges of letters that form an integral part of the Agreement, which was signed on April 3, 1992, and which is included as an annex to the proclamation.

The Agreement will provide a nondiscriminatory framework for our bilateral trade relations and thus strengthen both economic and political relations between the United States and Romania. Conclusion of this Agreement is an important step we can take to provide greater economic benefits to both countries. It will also give further impetus to the progress we have made in our overall diplomatic relations since last year and help to reinforce political and economic reform in Romania. In that context, the United States is encouraging Romania to continue to strive for a democratic, pluralistic society, particularly through the conduct of early, free, and fair national elections.

I believe that the Agreement is consistent with both the letter and the spirit of the Trade Act. It provides for mutual extension of nondiscriminatory tariff treatment while seeking to ensure overall reciprocity of economic benefits. It includes safeguard arrangements to ensure that our trade with Romania will grow without causing disruption to the U.S. market and consequent injury to domestic firms or loss of jobs for American workers.

The Agreement also confirms and expands for American businesses certain basic rights in conducting commercial transactions both within Romania and with Romanian nationals and business entities. Other provisions include those dealing with settlement of commercial disputes, financial transactions, and government commercial offices. Through this Agreement, Romania also undertakes obligations to modernize and upgrade very substantially its protection of intellectual property rights. Once fully implemented, the Romanian intellectual property regime will be on a par with that of our principal industrialized trading partners. This Agreement will not alter U.S. law or practice with respect to the protection of intellectual property.

On August 17, 1991, I waived application of subsections (a) and (b) of section 402 of the Trade Act to Romania. I determined that this waiver will substantially promote the objectives of section 402, and, pursuant to section 402(c)(2) of the Trade Act, notified the Congress that I have received assurances that the emigration practices of Romania will henceforth lead substantially to achievement of those objectives.

I urge that the Congress act as soon as possible to approve the "Agreement on Trade Relations Between the Government of the United States of America and the Government of Romania" and the proclamation extending nondiscriminatory treatment to products of Romania by enactment of a joint resolution referred to in section 151 of the Trade Act.

Sincerely,

GEORGE BUSH

*Note: Identical letters were sent to Thomas S. Foley, Speaker of the House of Representatives, and Dan Quayle, President of the Senate. The proclamation is listed in Appendix E at the end of this volume. The agreement was published in the Federal Register on June 24.*

# Presidential Determination No. 92–34—Memorandum on Trade With Romania
*June 22, 1992*

*Memorandum for the Secretary of State*

*Subject:* Determination Under Section 405(a) of the Trade Act of 1974, as Amended—Romania

Pursuant to the authority vested in me under the Trade Act of 1974 (Public Law 93–618, January 3, 1975; 88 Stat. 1978), as amended (the "Trade Act"), I determine, pursuant to section 405(a) of the Trade Act (19 U.S.C. 2435(a)), that the "Agreement on Trade Relations Between the Government of the United States of America and the Government of Romania" will promote the purposes of the Trade Act and is in the national interest.

You are authorized and directed to transmit copies of this determination to the appropriate Members of Congress and to publish it in the *Federal Register.*

GEORGE BUSH

[*Filed with the Office of the Federal Register, 3:04 p.m., July 6, 1992*]

# Remarks and an Exchange With Reporters on a Possible Railroad Strike
*June 23, 1992*

*The President.* Well, let me just say I've had a first-class briefing from Secretary Card, doing a first-rate job over there at Transportation. I'm very much concerned. Let us hope that some last-minute breakthrough will avert a strike. But my message today, after listening to the Secretary and understanding how bad it would be for the people of this country, is that should a strike occur, Congress ought to do in this instance what they've done twice before, two preceding events like this, and that is to move promptly to protect the American people and to end the strike through legislation. I feel very strongly about it, and I think in this instance, should a strike occur, Congress has an obligation to move fast to protect the American people, whether it's a lockout or a strike.

*Q.* How would they——

*The President.* Legislation like happened the last two times.

*Q.* Mr. President, would you do anything before the possibility of a strike? Is there some kind of intervention or emergency declaration or anything?

*The President.* No. Andy can answer that.

*Secretary Card.* The President has exercised that responsibility when he created the Presidential Emergency Board. So——

*The President.* And you see, it's reported back. It's made sound recommendations, and the Secretary has been working diligently to try to get various parties to come along. But the unilateral action by the President does not apply. The only thing that could stop the strike, if one occurs, is to have legislation.

*Q.* What is the economic impact? Why is the economic impact so dire that Congress should move immediately?

*The President.* Well, first place, there's an enormous inconvenience to the American worker on the commuter side. And then as it begins to take a hold on moving freight and moving product, agricultural product for example, to market, it's terrible. So public good is not served by a prolonged strike. So it ought to end the day it begins.

*Q.* Mr. President, do you anticipate any downside in terms of political consequences for your reelection campaign with the rail strike?

*The President.* I have no idea of that. This is not a political matter. This is a matter of the national good and what's best for the American people. And what's best for the American people is to avoid a strike. But if a strike takes place, or a lockout, it could be ended and ended right away.

*Q.* Do you plan to call congressional leaders today, sir, to express your feelings?

*The President.* Well, they know our views; we've expressed it. But we were just talking about that. I might well do that. But if that would help, I'll do it.

*Q.* Have you been talking——

*Q.* If the legislation goes through, could it be passed?

*The President.* It could be done in a day. I mean yes, it's happened before. The last two times, I believe it was just one day.

*Secretary Card.* Seventeen hours.

*The President.* Yes, 17 hours, Andy is reminding me, was the last one.

*Q.* Have you been consulting with the automakers or the shippers or people that have urged you to take this action?

*The President.* The Secretary's talked to everybody, yes.

*Q.* Have you urged them not to do a lockout if there's a partial strike?

*The President.* Well, I'd leave the technical questions to the Secretary. He's tried to avoid shutdowns in every way, and he's gone the extra mile. A lot of people have been cooperative, he tells me. So it's not a one-sided picture here. But the bottom line is, the public are not served by a strike that lasts for any time at all. And so the Congress should do now, if that's the case and there is a strike tomorrow, it ought to do what it's done to incidents before this: move. The last one took 17 hours to legislate it, to solve it. It can be done that quick or quicker.

*Q.* Is there any reason——

*The President.* This is a challenge to the Congress to do what's best for the American people, should it get to that.

*Q.* Would a rail strike hurt the economic recovery, sir? Could it throw it back?

*The President.* Yes it could. It could adversely affect the workers in this country, and it could adversely affect a lot of things, depending, obviously, how long it goes on.

*Q.* Is there any reason for optimism in collective bargaining—will resolve this thing at this point?

*Secretary Card.* They're still at the table, which is a good sign; so the dialog is continuing.

*The President.* You've got several different entities, is a part of the problem here. Some seem to think that it can be avoided, and others think not.

*Q.* But it sounds like, from making the statement to us, that you feel pretty pessimistic.

*The President.* I feel I cannot tell the American people that I think it will be resolved through negotiation as it should be. So I just think it's important to get in focus the fact that if there is a strike, it ought to be quickly solved by legislation.

*Q.* Anything from Capitol Hill whether they would go along with that, sir?

*The President.* Different reaction from different Members of Congress, I'm told.

Thank you very much for your interest.

*Note: The President spoke at 11:54 a.m. in the Oval Office at the White House, following a meeting with Secretary of Transportation Andrew H. Card, Jr.*

# Remarks at the Presentation Ceremony for the National Medal of Science and the National Medal of Technology
*June 23, 1992*

Thank you, and welcome to the Rose Garden. Well, thank you very much. And what a beautiful day here in the Rose Garden. May I salute Dr. Bromley; Dr. Bernthal, the Deputy Director of the National Science Foundation; and of course, over my right shoulder here, Secretary Barbara Franklin, Secretary of Commerce; also Congressman Vander Jagt, who's so interested in all of this; and so many special guests here today, and then three generations of American scientists.

As I look out at the group here of the men and women that we honor, you may remember what Albert Einstein said to his fellow scientists: "Concern for man himself and his fate must always form the chief interest of all technical endeavors in order that the creations of our mind should be a blessing and not a curse to mankind." Today we honor men and women whose life's work answers Einstein's challenge. They bless mankind not only with the brilliance of their minds but with the integrity of their hearts.

I am very proud to present the National Medals of Science and Technology to our 16 recipients, to these men and women of persistent and, at times, clairvoyant determination. They've explained the frontiers of science on canvasses as infinitesimal as a single human cell and as infinite as space itself.

We honor them for their accomplishments. But we honor them, also, for having the courage to undertake the journey.

There's a church in Sussex, England which has a wonderful inscription that captures these recipients' pioneer spirit of innovation. The inscription says, "A vision without a task is but a dream; a task without a vision is drudgery; but a vision with a task is the hope of the world." The hope of our world lies in individuals who asked why and then followed wherever that question led. Scientists like Nobel Prize Laureate Howard Temin, a truly seminal thinker in the history of biology who reshaped our thoughts about RNA and DNA. Entrepreneurs like Bill Gates, who cofounded Microsoft and in the process literally led a revolution in the information industry. Visionaries like Eugene Shoemaker, who helped to transform our world, not only through the astounding breadth of his contributions to space explorations but also through the infectious enthusiasm of his imagination. Inventors like Norman Joseph Woodland, who developed a simple device of our daily lives: bar coding. You've seen first-hand how impressed I am—[*laughter*]—by how bar coding works. Amazing.

You all proved that America's greatest resource is the genius of our people. We must encourage, we must support it. That's why Congress must double the budget of the National Science Foundation by 1994 and keep funding on track in 1993 for the superconducting super collider. That's why I'm committed to increases in R&D funding, large increases in R&D funding, to let our most talented people push the limits of their imaginations to understand the universe and to use the results to create jobs in the future of others. And to support research I've also established a national technology initiative to bring Government officials together with private business to shape technology, to move the new discoveries out of the Federal labs into the marketplace.

In addition, I believe that we need to stimulate private sector investment, the engine obviously of any entrepreneurial economy. And that's why I'm going to continue to fight so hard to get Congress to slash the capital gains tax. This would create new businesses, encourage new innovation. I also want to make that R&E, that research and experimentation tax credit permanent.

The world economy of the 21st century will demand a new age of American competitiveness in a fiercely challenging global marketplace. In order to compete we must make immediate, drastic changes, beginning with the need for the best educated, the most well-educated workers. Many of you here today, I'm told, are teachers, influencing one dream at a time, and you know that education is the basis of our future. You know the terrible fact that in some math and science studies we rank almost last, almost last among the industrialized nations. Rest assured we will turn that around. I'm counting on you, and I pledge to you the support of this Government.

Technical competence is so vital that one of our six national education goals is to be the first in world math and science by the year 2000. In order to reach that goal our budget invests $768 million in precollege math and science education, an increase I believe it's about 18 percent over last year and 123 percent over the way things were just back in 1990.

We must open a new world of educational opportunity for America's children and give middle- and low-income families more of the same choice of all schools that wealthier families already have. So, later this week I'll announce a new proposal that will do just that. It's a "GI bill" for America's children.

Forty-eight years ago the original GI bill opened educational doors for our war vets by giving them dollars to spend at any school they chose, public, private, or religious. It created a competitive marketplace of colleges and universities and encouraged improvement through innovation. Now it's time that we give the families the same consumer power for choice in precollege schools. That's why I'm introducing this exciting and, I think, powerful bill for our future.

Our Nation can remain strong only by investing its resources and talents in science, technology, and education. And I want to recognize a group of special people who are dedicating their lives to that quest, our first class of Presidential faculty fellows, 30 young faculty members named for their excellence and promise in research and teaching. These scientists and engineers represent the best investment that we can make in our future. But I'd like to remind them of something. As you look at the distinguished medalists that we honor today, remember that whatever work you do, you will be standing on the shoulders of giants.

I want to tell you about something, in conclusion here, pretty unusual that I ran into—I want to say discovered—a few months ago up in New Hampshire. Dean Kamen is here. He is a very special individual. What I'm talking about, the discovery, was of something known as the Maize Craze competition. I'm not sure exactly how to describe it. Kids have to make a kind of a robot to fetch tennis balls out of a box filled with corn. Some of the best ideas sound pretty strange at first, but let me tell you, this is a terrific idea.

I was enormously impressed, Dean, by how this Maize Craze teams high school students with high-powered engineering teams from major universities and corporations, a great example of the private-public partnership that will lead us to excellence in the next century. I had forgotten what a salesman Dean is, but he just came into my office and he said, "Now, if these corporations can sponsor Olympic athletes, why isn't it a great idea that they encourage young scientists in the same way?" And he's absolutely right about that. Maize Craze is part of U.S. FIRST, a national alliance of business, education, and Government working to reverse declining student interest and performance in science and math.

I invited Dean to bring his winners here today, sponsors Xerox and NYPRO, and teams from Wilson Magnet and Clinton High Schools. We're honoring today a spectrum of achievers that goes then from high school to the pinnacle of research. In turn, we need to nurture every step on the educational ladder, for each depends on the soundness of the preceding one.

So I just came out here to say congratulations to all of you, especially, of course, to our distinguished medalists who show us the triumph of the human mind and the unfolding drama of the human imagination. May God bless all of you. And now, Dr. Bernthal will present the citations, and I will stand in awe as these geniuses come marching by.

Congratulations, and thank you all for coming.

[*At this point, Deputy Director Bernthal presented the medals.*]

Well, I believe that concludes our ceremony. Dean, are those young people with you here? Maybe we could ask them to stand up, all those that came down from the Maize group. Where are you, all of you scientists—tortured my mind up there.

Well, that concludes our ceremony. But we're just delighted you all were here, and thank you very much for coming. Thank you.

*Note: The President spoke at 1:38 p.m. in the Rose Garden at the White House. In his remarks, he referred to Dean L. Kamen, founder of U.S. FIRST, and D. Allan Bromley, Assistant to the President for Science and Technology and Director of the Office of Science and Technology Policy.*

# Message to the Congress Transmitting the Estonia-United States Fishery Agreement
*June 23, 1992*

*To the Congress of the United States:*

In accordance with the Magnuson Fishery Conservation and Management Act of 1976 (Public Law 94–265; 16 U.S.C. 1801, *et seq.*), I transmit herewith an Agreement between

the Government of the United States of America and the Government of the Republic of Estonia Concerning Fisheries off the Coasts of the United States, with annex, signed at Washington on June 1, 1992. The agreement constitutes a governing international fishery agreement within the requirements of section 201(c) of the Act.

Fishing industry interests of the United States have urged prompt implementation of this agreement to take advantage of opportunities for seasonal cooperative fishing ventures.

GEORGE BUSH

The White House,
June 23, 1992.

# Message to the House of Representatives Returning Without Approval the National Institutes of Health Revitalization Amendments of 1992
*June 23, 1992*

*To the House of Representatives:*

I am returning herewith without my approval H.R. 2507, the "National Institutes of Health Revitalization Amendments of 1992," which would extend and amend biomedical research authorities of the National Institutes of Health (NIH).

Before discussing the flaws of H.R. 2507, I must clarify two misperceptions. First, H.R. 2507 is not necessary to assure that Federal spending continue for biomedical research, or for research related to any disease, disorder, or condition. Second, H.R. 2507 is not necessary to increase support for research targeted at women's health needs. Great progress is being made in the area of women's health under the valued leadership of the first female director of the NIH.

H.R. 2507 is unacceptable to me on almost every ground: ethical, fiscal, administrative, philosophical, and legal. I repeatedly warned the Congress of this at each stage of the legislative process. The bill's provisions permitting the use of tissue from induced abortions for federally funded transplantation research involving human subjects are inconsistent with our Nation's deeply held beliefs. Moreover, it is clear that this legislation would be counterproductive to the attainment of our Nation's health research objectives.

H.R. 2507 is objectionable because it would lift the current moratorium on the use of Federal funds for fetal tissue transplantation research where the tissue is obtained from induced abortions. Let it be clear: this is not a moratorium on research. It is only a moratorium on the use of one source of tissue for that research. I believe this moratorium is important in order to prevent taxpayer funds from being used for research that many Americans find morally repugnant and because of its potential for promoting and legitimatizing abortion.

My Administration is strongly committed to pursuing research to find cures and treatments for such disorders as Parkinson's disease, diabetes, and Alzheimer's disease that have been held out as areas where fetal tissue research might be pursued. Fetal tissue transplantation research relating to these disorders can proceed without relying on tissue from induced abortions. Medical experts at the Department of Health and Human Services have assured me that ectopic pregnancies and spontaneous abortions provide sufficient and suitable tissue to meet anticipated research needs. Therefore, on May 19, 1992, I issued an Executive order establishing a fetal tissue bank that will collect tissue from these sources so as to meet the needs of the research community. The bank will provide tissue directly to scientists for their research. This approach truly represents the pro-research and ethical alternative that will allow this research to go forward without relying on a source of tissue that many find to be morally objectionable.

H.R. 2507 also contains fiscally irresponsible authorization levels. The total cost of the provisions in this legislation could exceed the FY 1993 Budget I presented to the Congress by $3.2 billion. It is exceedingly unlikely, if not impossible, that the Congress can fund the programs contained in H.R. 2507 while complying with the requirements of the Budget Enforcement Act. That being the case, the expectations that this bill will create are unreasonable. Those who suffer from the many diseases and disorders that are the subject of this unrealistic legislation will be sadly disappointed.

H.R. 2507 is also objectionable because its provisions regarding the appointment of "Ethics Advisory Boards" are inconsistent with the Appointments Clause of the Constitution. H.R. 2507 would effectively give these boards unilateral authority to make decisions concerning major research initiatives. As a policy matter, these decisions should be made by the President's chief officer on health issues: the Secretary of Health and Human Services. More fundamentally, however, the Appointments Clause requires that officers vested with this type of power be appointed by the President by and with the advice and consent of the Senate. Instead, H.R. 2507 provides that they are to be appointed by the Secretary of Health and Human Services and then purports to circumscribe the discretion of the appointing authority by imposing various requirements concerning the boards' composition. H.R. 2507's provisions regarding the Scientific and Technical Board on Biomedical and Behavioral Research Facilities and the Office of Research on Women's Health likewise raise Appointments Clause problems.

In addition, H.R. 2507 contains reporting requirements that impair the separation of powers. For example, the bill would require the Director of the National Cancer Institute to submit to specified committees of the Congress the original plan, and any revisions to that plan, regarding certain cancer research. This requirement to submit to the Congress what is in essence a draft plan without the prior review and approval of the executive branch clearly interferes with the deliberative process of the executive branch. The internal workings of the executive branch should be just that—internal. To require the executive branch to display each step in its deliberative process to the Congress would destroy my ability to speak as the single voice of a unitary executive.

I am also troubled by the increasingly frequent imposition of reporting requirements. H.R. 2507 imposes a significant number of new reporting requirements on an executive branch that already suffers under the burden of literally thousands of such requirements. Last October, I noted that "taken together such reports put a heavy burden on the reporting agencies at a time of scarce resources." Thus, I called for "an effort to minimize reporting requirements, both in terms of the number and frequency of reports that must be submitted, as well as the level of detail required." Bills such as H.R. 2507 move us in the opposite direction.

For these reasons, I am returning H.R. 2507 without my approval, and I ask the Congress to adopt a simple extension of those appropriations authorizations for the National Institutes of Health that need to be extended.

GEORGE BUSH

The White House,
June 23, 1992.

# Nomination of Christopher H. Phillips To Be a Member of the Board of Directors of the United States Institute of Peace
*June 23, 1992*

The President today announced his intention to nominate Christopher H. Phillips, of the District of Columbia, to be a member of the Board of Directors of the United States Institute of Peace for the remainder of the term expiring January 19, 1993. He would succeed Evron M. Kirkpatrick.

Since 1991 Ambassador Phillips has served as a consultant to the U.S. Department of State. From 1989 to 1991, he served as Ambassador to Brunei. Ambassador Phillips has also served as president of the U.S.-China Business Council, 1973–86; Deputy Permanent Representative of the United States to the United Nations, 1970–73; president of the U.S. Council of the International Chamber of Commerce and secretary-treasurer of the U.S. Business and Industry Advisory Committee to the Organization for Economic Cooperation and Development, 1965–69; and U.S. Representative on the United Nations Economic and Social Council, 1958–61.

Ambassador Phillips graduated from Harvard University (B.A., 1943). He was born December 6, 1920, in The Hague, The Netherlands. Ambassador Phillips is married, has three children, and resides in Washington, DC.

# Nomination of Nancy M. Dowdy To Be Special Representative for Arms Control Negotiations and Disarmament
*June 23, 1992*

The President today announced his intention to nominate Nancy M. Dowdy, of the District of Columbia, to be Special Representative for Arms Control Negotiations and Disarmament (Chief Science Adviser).

Since 1989 Dr. Dowdy has served at the Arms Control and Disarmament Agency as Representative to the Joint Compliance and Inspection Commission in Geneva, 1991–present, and Representative to the Strategic Arms Reduction Talks in Geneva, 1989–91.

She served at the University of Chicago in the office of the vice president as assistant vice president for research and for the Argonne National Laboratory, 1983–89.

Dr. Dowdy graduated from St. Louis University (B.S., 1960) and the University of Illinois (M.S., 1961; Ph.D., 1966). She was born October 25, 1938, in Jackson, MS. Dr. Dowdy currently resides in Washington, DC.

# Message to the Congress Transmitting Proposed Legislation on Credit Availability and Regulatory Relief
*June 24, 1992*

*To the Congress of the United States:*

I am pleased to transmit for your immediate consideration and enactment the "Credit Availability and Regulatory Relief Act of 1992." This proposed legislation will enhance the availability of credit in the economy by reducing regulatory burdens on depository institutions. Also transmitted is a section-by-section analysis.

The regulatory burden on the Nation's financial intermediaries has reached a level that imposes unacceptable costs on the economy as a whole. Needless regulations restrict credit, slowing economic growth and job creation. Excessive costs weaken financial institutions, exposing the taxpayer to the risk of loss. Rigid supervisory formulas distort business decisions and discourage banks, thrifts, and credit unions from pursuing their core lending activities. In 1991, the Nation's banks spent an estimated $10.7 billion on regulatory compliance, or over 59 percent of the system's entire annual profit. We cannot allow this unnecessary and oppressive burden to continue weighing down the consumer and business lending that will fuel economic recovery.

The Credit Availability and Regulatory Relief Act of 1992 reduces or eliminates a wide range of these unnecessary financial institution costs. Among the significant changes that would be made by the bill are:

1007

- Elimination of the requirement that banking agencies develop detailed "micromanagement" regulations for every aspect of an institution's managerial and operational conduct, from the compensation of employees to the ratio of market value to book value of an institution's stock;
- Enactment of a statutory requirement that the regulations of the various Federal banking agencies be as uniform as possible, to avoid the complexity, inconsistencies, and comparative distortions that result from widely varying regulatory practices;
- Reduction of audit costs, by returning auditors to their traditional function of investigating the accuracy of depository institution financial statements and eliminating the costly and misguided expansion of their role over legal and managerial matters;
- Alleviation of the significant paperwork burden imposed by the Community Reinvestment Act on small, rural depository institutions *without* exempting such institutions from the substantive requirements to satisfy the credit needs of their entire communities—coupled with creation of incentives for institutions to reach higher levels of compliance by streamlining expansion procedures for institutions with outstanding Community Reinvestment Act ratings; and
- Elimination of the requirement that the Federal Reserve write detailed "bright line" regulations on the amounts of credit that one depository

can extend to another, thus retaining the Federal Reserve's existing flexibility to supervise the payments system without unduly inhibiting correspondent banking relationships.

These changes, and the others made by the bill, will result in significant reductions to the administrative costs of depository institutions—costs that are currently passed on to borrowers in the form of restricted credit and higher priced loans.

I would like to emphasize that none of the bill's provisions will compromise in any way the safety and soundness of the financial system. The legislation makes no changes to those elements of the Administration's proposed supervisory reforms that the Congress did adopt last year. All existing capital standards will remain in force and will be neither weakened nor modified by the proposed legislation; the "prompt corrective action" framework mandating swift regulatory responses to developing institutional problems will remain unchanged; and bank regulators will continue to have exceptionally tough enforcement powers.

The legislation I am transmitting to you today is a broad and responsible solution to one of the major problems facing our financial system. The financial industry, the economy, and the public generally will benefit from enactment of this regulatory relief. I therefore urge the Congress to give high priority to the passage of the Administration's reforms.

GEORGE BUSH

The White House,
June 24, 1992.

## Statement on the Balanced Budget Amendment
*June 24, 1992*

This morning, I met with Members of the House of Representatives, Republicans and Democrats, who earlier this month voted in favor of a balanced budget constitutional amendment. I thanked them for the courage, vision, and responsibility they displayed supporting the balanced budget constitutional amendment. Their votes demonstrated their willingness to stand up to the special interests who perpetuate the status quo of deficit spending. Their votes show they take seriously the intolerable legacy of debt that future generations will inherit if we do not take prompt action to control

Federal spending.

The American people overwhelmingly support a balanced budget constitutional amendment. On June 10, we came within just nine votes of achieving the two-thirds majority needed to pass the amendment in the House of Representatives. We came very close to accomplishing our goal. At a minimum, we created an atmosphere in which the Federal Government is watching more carefully how it spends taxpayers' money.

Now we must act to lay the groundwork for the future. I can and will take the compelling case for a balanced budget constitutional amendment to the American people. I seek a permanent partnership for fiscal responsibility that bears no party label. I plan to work closely with Members of Congress from both parties who support the amendment to find the nine missing votes and then raise the issue again. In every way possible, we will press our fight to restrain Federal spending once and for all.

# Statement on the Supreme Court Decision on the *Lee* v. *Weisman* Case
*June 24, 1992*

I am very disappointed by the Supreme Court's decision in *Lee* v. *Weisman*. The Court said that a simple nondenominational prayer thanking God for the liberty of America at a public school graduation ceremony violates the first amendment. America is a land of religious pluralism, and this is one of our Nation's greatest strengths. While we must remain neutral toward par-ticular religions and protect freedom of conscience, we should not remain neutral toward religion itself. In this case, I believe that the Court has unnecessarily cast away the venerable and proper American tradition of nonsectarian prayer at public celebrations. I continue to believe that this type of prayer should be allowed in public schools.

# Nomination of David Heywood Swartz To Be United States Ambassador to Byelarus
*June 24, 1992*

The President today announced his intention to nominate David Heywood Swartz, of Virginia, to be Ambassador of the United States of America to the Republic of Byelarus. This is a new position.

Currently Mr. Swartz serves as Chargé d'Affaires in Minsk, Byelarus. Prior to this, he served at the Department of State as senior inspector in the Office of Inspector General, 1991–92; dean of the School of Language Studies at the Foreign Service Institute, 1989–91; and staff director at the Nuclear Risk Reduction Center, 1988–89. Mr. Swartz has also served as Deputy Chief of Mission at the American Embassy in Warsaw, Poland, 1984–88, and consul general at the U.S. consulate general in Calgary, Alberta, Canada, 1983–84. He attended the Canadian Defense College in Kingston, Ontario, Canada, 1982–83, and served as consul general at the U.S. consulate general in Zurich, Switzerland, 1980–82.

Mr. Swartz graduated from Southwestern College (B.A., 1964) and Florida State University (M.A., 1966). He was born March 3, 1942, in Chicago, IL. Mr. Swartz is married, has two children, and resides in Vienna, VA.

## Nomination of H. Douglas Barclay To Be a Member of the Board of Directors of the Overseas Private Investment Corporation
*June 24, 1992*

The President today announced his intention to nominate H. Douglas Barclay, of New York, to be a member of the Board of Directors of the Overseas Private Investment Corporation, U.S. International Development Cooperation Agency, for a term expiring December 17, 1994. This is a reappointment.

Since 1961, Mr. Barclay has served as a partner and associate with the law firm of Hiscock and Barclay in Syracuse, NY. Mr. Barclay has also served on the board of directors of KeyCorp and its subsidiaries and as an officer and general counsel to various other corporations. Mr. Barclay served in the New York State Senate from 1965 to 1984.

Mr. Barclay graduated from Yale College (B.A., 1955) and Syracuse University College of Law (J.D., 1961). He served as a commissioned officer in the U.S. Army Reserve. He was born July 5, 1932, in New York, NY. Mr. Barclay is married, has five children, and resides in Pulaski, NY.

## Appointment of James L. Pavitt as Special Assistant to the President for National Security Affairs
*June 24, 1992*

The President today announced the appointment of James L. Pavitt, of Virginia, to be Special Assistant to the President for National Security Affairs. He will also serve as Senior Director for Intelligence Programs.

Mr. Pavitt is currently Director for Intelligence Programs at the National Security Council, a position he has held since August 1990. Prior to joining the NSC staff, Mr. Pavitt, a career Central Intelligence Agency official, served in a variety of intelligence assignments in Europe, Asia, and Washington, DC. He also served as an intelligence officer with the U.S. Army, 1969–71.

Mr. Pavitt graduated from the University of Missouri (B.A., 1968) and was a National Defense Education Act fellow at Clark University (1969). He is a member of Phi Beta Kappa. Mr. Pavitt was born February 19, 1946, in St. Louis, MO. He has two children and resides in McLean, VA.

## Appointment of Douglas Alan Brook as Acting Director of the Office of Personnel Management
*June 24, 1992*

The President today announced that Douglas Alan Brook, of Virginia, will serve as Acting Director of the Office of Personnel Management, effective July 1, 1992.

Currently Mr. Brook serves as Assistant Secretary of the Army for Financial Management. From 1982 to 1990, he served as president of Brook Associates, Inc., in Washington, DC. Mr. Brook also served with Libbey-Owens-Ford Co. in Washington as vice president, 1979–82, and director of public affairs, 1976–79.

Mr. Brook graduated from the University of Michigan (B.A., 1965; M.A., 1967). He served in the U.S. Navy on active duty, 1968–70, and in the Naval Reserve, 1971 to present. He was born January 15, 1944, in Chicago, IL. Mr. Brook is married and re-

sides in Vienna, VA.

## Nomination of John H. Miller To Be a Member of the Board of Directors of the National Institute of Building Sciences
*June 24, 1992*

The President today announced his intention to nominate John H. Miller, of Connecticut, to be a member of the Board of Directors of the National Institute of Building Sciences for the term expiring September 7, 1992, and for a term expiring September 7, 1995. He would succeed Fred E. Hummel.

Since 1957, Mr. Miller has served with

the firm of Close, Jensen and Miller in Wethersfield, CT, as partner, 1957–75, and president, 1975–present.

Mr. Miller graduated from Trinity College (B.S., 1952) and Rensselaer Polytechnic Institute (B.S.C.E., 1953). He was born September 11, 1930, in New Britain, CT. Mr. Miller is married, has three children, and resides in Wethersfield, CT.

## Remarks at a Roundtable Discussion on Education Reform
*June 25, 1992*

*The President.* Good morning, everyone, and welcome. Excuse me for keeping you all waiting. But what we want to do here is talk about choice in education. I remember the GI bill working so well. It did nothing but make the colleges better. It's our theory that choice, at the level that we're going to talk about it today, can do nothing but make things better. But here's the firing line; here are people from the Governor on down right to the very most important level, Tommy, yours and mine, is the family level. So I've been interested in this since the first—one of the early meetings we had in 1989 was on school choice. I think it's an idea whose time has come.

But what I wanted to do today is, just before we go out and announce this "GI bill" for lower levels of education, perhaps the most important levels of education, is to hear from you all. Lamar Alexander has been our point man. This fits beautifully into a program we call America 2000, which encourages innovation at the local, the family, the State level. What I've heard about—and since I remember talking to some of you all about this when I was in

Milwaukee—but what I've heard about is the enormous success it's been. So what I wanted to do is to not put all of you on the spot with all this attention but literally, in an unstructured way, hear from the families.

Lamar, before I turn quickly to the Governor, do you want to say anything?

*Secretary Alexander.* Well, only this, Mr. President.

*The President.* Our Secretary of Education.

*Secretary Alexander.* I think Milwaukee has the opportunity to be the pioneer here because you have a bipartisan group in the State government who have used State funds to give middle- and low-income, or give low-income families more choices of the schools wealthier people have. Now you've got private business stepping up and expanding those choices to include religious schools. Then your "GI bill" for kids proposal would put the Federal Government into the action, and if Milwaukee wants to, give Milwaukee about $72 million. That would be a $1,000 scholarship for that many children, as long as they could spend it at any school. So all of that money could go to the public schools if the public schools can attract the children, or the families would have the absolute choice to take the money, tell private schools to meet the needs of children.

I think I'll stop there because I think the parents here and the teachers and the school principals and school leaders are the ones who know how this works, and I'd rather hear from them.

*Note: The President spoke at 9:20 a.m. in the Roosevelt Room at the White House. In his remarks, he referred to Gov. Tommy Thompson of Wisconsin.*

# Remarks Announcing Proposed Legislation To Establish a "GI Bill" for Children
## June 25, 1992

Welcome, all. Hey, we're glad you guys are here. Welcome, welcome, and please be seated. All you kids, welcome to the South Lawn of the White House. And to the Vice President and Mrs. Quayle and Secretary Alexander, a warm welcome. A particularly warm welcome to the Members of Congress, both House and Senate, that are with us today. Welcome to all of you, our very special guests, on this special occasion.

I have just come from a working session in the White House, working with some of the great experts on school choice. The parents, I think, made the most significant contribution to our working session because their dreams for their kids are the same dreams that all of us have. They want their kids to have a first-class education. They know from practical experience that a good education is absolutely essential to making a good living and to making a good life.

So let me just share a little from that meeting. Janette Williams told me about her son, Javon. The Williamses are here with us somewhere here today—whoops, here she is over here. Her kid starred on "60 Minutes," and that says something about the guy, if you go on that program and come off in one piece. [*Laughter*] He must be doing real well. But here's what she said, and this is serious. She said, "At his old school that was crowded, he used to get so bored that he would walk out. And thanks to the choice program in Milwaukee, he's at a new school. He's not doing those things anymore. He's doing his homework; he's even helping clean up the classroom

after school. They took the energy and turned it around."

Now, the Governor here, Tommy Thompson, the Governor of Wisconsin, is here with us today. I'm sorry that Polly Williams, who's been at the forefront of the school choice movement, couldn't be here, but she's at home looking after her mother. I would salute her values. But we miss her very, very much. Together, Polly and Tommy Thompson, the Governor, have taken the lead in helping parents like Janette Williams realize her dreams for her son Javon, creating scholarships for 1,000 Milwaukee children from low-income families so that they can attend private schools. Now, theirs is a bold experiment, to give low-income families more of the same choices of schools already available to wealthier families.

Mike Joyce of the Bradley Foundation was also in our meeting. And Bradley recently joined with other foundations and Milwaukee businesses to raise $3 million so that Milwaukee's low-income families will be able to choose their family's schools, including the religious schools. Mike told us this morning that parents picked up every one of the 4,500 scholarship applications the day after the scholarships were announced, 4,500, that fast. And don't let anybody tell you that the people of Milwaukee don't care about their kids' education.

No one should underestimate what's at stake here. A revolution is underway in Milwaukee and across this country, a revolution to make American schools the best in the world. I salute our Secretary of Education who is helping lead that revolution, Lamar Alexander.

Together with the Nation's Governors, we've set six ambitious national education goals. And I might say that this wasn't a partisan move; Democrats and Republicans alike of the Governors coming together to set six ambitious national education goals. In 44 States and 1,400 communities, we've already launched America 2000 to meet these goals.

Even earlier still, in January 1989, just before I was sworn in as President, we helped organize the White House Conference on Choice in Education. We believed then and we believe today a few fundamental truths. We believe that parents are their children's first teachers. Parents, not bureaucrats, know what's best for their kids.

At this point I would like to salute one of the two in purple, Barbara Bush—[*laughter*]—for her pointing this out to parents, that it's what they do, what happens in their home. Barbara's done a lot of that here and around the country. I might say that Marilyn Quayle's taking that same message of parental involvement all across our country, and we're very grateful to her.

So, it is our belief then that parents, not the Government, should choose their children's schools. So today I am proposing that we take another giant step forward in this revolution. I am sending to Congress legislation that would authorize an ambitious demonstration program, half a billion new Federal dollars to help communities all across America give $1,000 scholarships to children of middle- and low-income families so they can choose which schools their kids will attend.

This revolution is in the greatest American tradition. We've done it before, and it's worked. Forty-eight years ago this very week, President Roosevelt signed the GI bill, creating scholarships that veterans could use at any college, any college of their choice. The GI bill created opportunity for Americans who never would have had it, and in doing so it helped create the best system of colleges and universities in the world.

Now we can do that again, this time by helping State and local governments—and we're delighted the Mayor of Milwaukee is with us here today—this time by helping State and local governments create the best elementary and secondary schools in the world. The "GI bill" for children will help. It'll provide that help to these families. These dollars to spend at the schools of their choice will become the muscle that parents need to create the best schools for their kids.

Let me say to those who will attack our school choice initiative on the ground that it permits Government money to go to religious schools, you're wrong. I believe those critics are wrong. This is aid to the families, not aid to institutions. And again, if you set the clock back to the creation of that original GI bill, no one told the GI's that they couldn't go to S.M.U. or Notre Dame or Yeshiva or Howard. I haven't heard Members of Congress suggest that students stop using Pell grants and guaranteed student loans at Baptist colleges or Presbyterian seminaries. I don't hear an outcry because poor children at Catholic schools get their lunch paid for by Federal taxpayers. In the same way, parents must be free to use this money at the school they believe will best teach their child, whether the school is public, private, or religious. Let me try to be clear on this point: Accepting students with vouchers does not mean a school must sacrifice school prayer.

And let me say this to those who stand against extending school choice to low- and middle-income families: I simply do not buy the idea that someone cannot make a good decision just because that person is poor. We heard the same argument when we proposed child care vouchers for low-income families or when we proposed help for public housing tenants to own their own homes. So it's my belief that we ought to let families own their own home and choose their own schools regardless of their income level and give them help. Give them a shot at the American dream, if you will.

Finally, to those who claim that school choice will hurt the public schools, let me underscore this point: All of this new money can go to public schools if that's where the child chooses to go, where the family chooses to have the kid go. That decision will be in the hands of families, where it belongs.

There are several points to make about money. First, I want to make it clear that we're not talking here about a new Federal entitlement program. The Federal Government cannot afford one more entitlement, even for education. I've said many times that money alone isn't the answer. The United States already spends more per student for schools than any country in the world except Switzerland. I don't have to tell you where we stand in the international rankings of educational performance at the level we're talking about here today. Our universities and colleges are respected and have achieved the highest levels of achievement. But that, unfortunately, is not true as we talk about K through 12. So we need a revolution in American education, not more money to do it the same old way.

Investment in our schools will remain a primarily State and local responsibility. But Federal support for State and local scholarships can be a catalyst. For schools that attract choice students, it will give teachers and principals a welcome source of new funds. For our children, choice can help open up opportunities, create genuine change in our schools.

For too long, we've shielded schools from competition, allowed our schools a damaging monopoly power over our children. This monopoly turns students into statistics and turns parents into pawns. It is time we began thinking of a system of public education in which many providers offer a marketplace of opportunities, opportunities that give all of our children choices and access to the best education in the world. And so it is our firm belief, it is our firm belief that this "GI bill" for children will move America inevitably in that direction.

Abraham Lincoln once said, "Revolutions do not go backward." Milwaukee is not the only place in America that our revolution is underway. Last year in Indianapolis, Pat Rooney and the Educational CHOICE Charitable Trust began to offer tuition vouchers to Indianapolis students. I understand a bus-load of parents and students drove all night to be here today. If you're still awake, welcome, a special welcome to all of you. In San Antonio, the CEO Foundation has earmarked $1.5 million in vouchers for children in their community. California: Joe Alibrandi and thousands of supporters are pushing for a ballot initiative to provide voucher scholarships for every school-age child in the State. Overall in 1991, 10 States approved some form of new choice legislation, and 37 States had choice legislation pending in one form or another.

I've been told that there may just be a few folks here from Pennsylvania. [*Applause*] We're outnumbered. Well, it may take a few tries, but I never underestimate the persistence of parents: The children of Pennsylvania will have school choice.

From California to East Harlem, from coast to coast, the leaders of the school choice movement are sparking a revolution in American education. They're the true heroes of this education reform, and some of them are here with us today. They aren't afraid to stand up to the status quo, to say loud and clear that when it comes to educating our kids, business-as-usual simply isn't good enough. Let there be no mistake: Barbara and I and the Vice President and Marilyn, and certainly our Secretary, are very proud to stand with you.

You see, this revolution will succeed. It will succeed because it draws its strength from the very heart of the American creed. We have no truth more enduring than the idea that every American should have the opportunity for a first-class education. We have no principles more important than freedom, opportunity, and choice.

So thank you very, very much. And look at it this way, you're doing the Lord's work for our Nation's future, and you're doing it for the young people of this country. We are grateful to all of you. And may God bless the United States. And now I will sign this legislation.

*Note: The President spoke at 10:20 a.m. on the South Lawn at the White House. In his remarks, he referred to Polly Williams, Wisconsin State legislator.*

## Message to the Congress Transmitting Proposed Legislation To Establish a "GI Bill" for Children
*June 25, 1992*

*To the Congress of the United States:*

Forty-eight years ago this week, President Franklin Roosevelt signed the GI Bill. With the hope of duplicating the success of that historic legislation, I am pleased to transmit for your immediate consideration and enactment the "Federal Grants for State and Local 'GI Bills' for Children." This proposal is a crucial component of our efforts to help the country achieve the National Education Goals by the year 2000. Also transmitted is a section-by-section analysis.

This legislation would authorize half-a-billion new Federal dollars in fiscal year 1993, and additional amounts in later years, to help States and communities give $1,000 scholarships to middle- and low-income children. Families may spend these scholarships at any lawfully operating school of their choice—public, private, or religious. The result would be to give middle- and low-income families consumer power—dollars to spend at any school they choose. This is the muscle parents need to transform our education system and create the best schools in the world for all our children.

At the close of World War II, the Federal Government created the GI Bill giving veterans scholarships to use at any college of their choice—public, private, or religious. This consumer power gave veterans opportunity, helped to create the best system of colleges and universities in the world, and gave America a new generation of leaders. Now that the Cold War is over, the Federal Government should help State and local governments create GI Bills for children. Under this approach, scholarships would be available for middle- and low-income parents to use at the elementary or secondary school of their choice.

This bill will give middle- and low-income families more of the same choices available to wealthier families. Through families, it will provide new funds at the school site that teachers and principals can use to help all children achieve the high educational standards called for by the National Educa-

tion Goals. In addition, the legislation will create a marketplace of educational opportunities to help improve all schools; engage parents in their children's schooling; and encourage creation of other academic programs for children before and after school, on weekends, or during school vacations.

Once this proposal is enacted, any State or locality can apply for enough Federal funds to give each child of a middle- or low-income family a $1,000 annual scholarship. The governmental unit would have to take significant steps to provide a choice of schools to families with school children in the area and permit families to spend the $1,000 Federal scholarships at a wide variety of public and private schools. It would have to allow all lawfully operating schools in the area—public, private, and religious— to participate if they choose.

The Secretary of Education would select grantees on the basis of: (1) the number and variety of choices made available to families; (2) the extent to which the applicant has provided educational choices to all children, including children who are not eligible for scholarships; (3) the proportion of children who will participate who are from low-income families; and (4) the applicant's financial support (including private support) for the project.

The maximum family income for eligible children would be determined by the grantee, but it could not exceed the higher of the State or national median income, adjusted for family size. All eligible children in the project area would receive scholarships, as long as sufficient funds are available. If all eligible children cannot participate, the grantee would provide scholarships to those with the lowest family incomes. Students would continue to receive scholarships over the 4-year life of a project unless they leave school, move out of the area, or no longer meet the income criteria. Up to $500 of each scholarship may be used for other academic programs for children before and after school, on weekends, or during school

1015

vacations.

This bill provides aid to families, not institutions. However, as a condition of participating in this program, a school must comply with Federal anti-discrimination provisions of: section 601 of title VI of the Civil Rights Act of 1964 (race), section 901 of Title IX of the Education Amendments of 1972 (gender), and section 504 of the Rehabilitation Act of 1973 (disability).

Funding is authorized at $500 million in FY 1993, and "such sums as may be necessary" through FY 2000. The Department of Education would conduct a comprehensive evaluation of these demonstration projects. The evaluation would assess the impact of the program in such areas as educational achievement and parents' involvement in, and satisfaction with, their children's education.

I urge the Congress to take prompt and favorable action on this legislation.

GEORGE BUSH

The White House,
June 25, 1992.

# Remarks on the Railroad Strike and an Exchange With Reporters
*June 25, 1992*

*The President.* Let me just simply say that we're now in the second day of a national rail strike. And Secretary Card and his associates and others have worked all night, working with a bipartisan group on Capitol Hill to get the legislation to stop this strike. The trains are not moving as of this minute, however. Clearly the national interest is at stake here. We now face a complete halt of passenger and commuter rail lines. I urge the House and Senate to act to end this strike today; the national interest requires no less. There must be no further delay.

So I salute the Secretary and his people at the Department of Transportation, those Members that are working to end this strike. But it must happen, and it should happen today.

*Q.* What is the holdup?

*The President.* Well, Andy can give you more detail, but there's a difference of opinion amongst some of the Senators, I mean, some of the House Members and Senators. But the point is, no finger pointing here, I just want to use this office to encourage the Congress to move and move fast and settle this matter once and for all. I believe they can do it. In fact, I think they should do it.

*Q.* Well, is there something happening today that you know of?

*The President.* Well, talking's still going on on the legislation, yes.

*Q.* Mr. President, are you amenable to a 30-day cooling-off period and the appointment of——

*The President.* Look, we want that matter resolved once and for all. And that's what the administration position is——

*Q.* Mr. President, did you make a mistake the other day——

*The President.* ——that's in the best interest of the American people.

*Perot Investigations*

*Q.* Mr. President, did you make a mistake the other day when you criticized Ross Perot in an indirect fashion concerning the possible——

*The President.* I'm not taking any questions on that here, Jim [Jim Miklaszewski, NBC News]. Thank you very much. Nice try.

*Q.* Well, did you write a very amenable, friendly letter to him?

*The President.* Yes, I certainly did.

*Q.* Why, if he investigated your children?

*The President.* Well, go look at the dates, is the only thing I can suggest.

*Q.* But do you think he did investigate your kids?

*The President.* I don't know, Rita [Rita Beamish, Associated Press]. And I'm not going to take any more questions on it.

*Q.* Do you know anything abut Republican dirty tricks?

*The President.* I'm not going to take any more questions. Jim, you guys are getting a little hard of hearing here today. [*Laughter*]

*Note: The President spoke at 11:56 a.m. in* the Oval Office at the White House, prior to a meeting with Secretary of Transportation Andrew H. Card, Jr. A tape was not available for verification of the content of these remarks.

# Remarks to the College Republican Convention
## June 25, 1992

*The President.* Thank you all very much.

*Audience members.* Four more years! Four more years! Four more years! Bush-Quayle in '92! Bush-Quayle in '92! Bush-Quayle in '92!

*The President.* Thank you so very much. Let me start by thanking Tony. And lest some of you don't know it, he has done a first-class job in this centennial year as president of the College Republicans. It is the best party on campus. And thank you all for this warm and enthusiastic welcome.

Let me tell you something. Let me let you and the rest of the world in on a secret: I finish what I start. I am going to be re-elected for 4 more years. You know, we've heard the drumbeat for change; we've even heard the saxophone for change. I have news: You and I, we are the change. You give us 4 more years and give us, hopefully, a Republican House and a Republican Senate and then watch the change, Republican style.

You know, some have gotten so caught up in the moment that they've forgotten the hour, so caught up in changing course that they've forgotten where we're headed. I know where I'm headed, and I aim, with your help and with the help of the Congress, to lead America along to a future of good jobs, fueled by free trade, by low taxes. And I will keep on vetoing the Democratic tax bills that come down our way every day.

We will lead to a future where families stick together and fathers stick around and to another American century, a world of hard-won peace and growing freedom. Some would say, "Well, this is a tall order." They're right, and that's exactly because our vision doesn't ride on the next election,

though, it rests on the next generation. In just the last 4 years the world as we've known it before is gone. Our mission for the next 4 years is to shape the next 40 years, and we can do it.

I need your help in the fall elections. And the fall elections must be a referendum on some big ideas: what kind of economy we'll have in the future, what kind of families, and really it's this big, what kind of world. In America, blood, sweat, and tears have literally changed the face of the Earth, and American strength and determination have consequences. Look around the world. You don't hear one single thing about it in this strange campaign year, but it's your credit and ours and Ronald Reagan's and everybody that's gone before us.

Let me tell you what to remind the critics. Let me tell you what to remind the critics and those who would have hacked away at our defense spending. Eastern Europe is free. Germany is reunified. Ancient enemies are talking peace in the Middle East. And our own hemisphere, look south of our border, is almost totally democratic. Imperial communism is dead and buried. And just last week, standing in the Rose Garden, a democratically elected President of Russia stood with me in the Rose Garden as we announced the most sweeping nuclear arms cut in history. That is a sound record to take to the American people.

The doomsday clock and the bomb shelters and the nightmares of our children, they're folding out of the picture, and that's something to be proud of, that these kids tonight don't go to bed with the same kind of fear of nuclear war. Let's take credit for that change and take that case to the Amer-

1017

ican people.

Let me just add this on the foreign side of things. While the world has become more free, it is less certain. The Soviet bear may be a creature of the past, and it is, imperial Soviet communism. But there are plenty of wolves out there, and you know who they are. This is no fantasy of some cold warrior; these are the realities of the new world.

From where I sit as President, I can see, I can survey the situation. There are real differences here, and remember this one, real differences with our opponents. Come next November we're going to take it to the American people that America is safe but only as long as we remain strong. And as long as I'm President, we are going to stay strong.

*Audience members.* Four more years! Four more years! Four more years!

*The President.* You know, Ronald Reagan, speaking of being safe as long as we're strong, my predecessor knew this all along. President Reagan's picture of history has been vindicated. Now we've built on this legacy. And our actions in the Gulf—don't listen to these revisionists, those that sat on the sideline criticizing and now that are trying to turn history around. Our actions in the Gulf proved that America will stand up for its own interests. We will keep the wolves at bay. And as long as I am President, aggression will not stand.

Some say, how come the difference between domestic policy, the difficulty to move things that we need and want on the domestic scene compared to how things work abroad? The answer is, I did not have to get permission from some subcommittee controlled by the Democrats to kick Saddam Hussein out of Kuwait. When American lives are threatened, as they were in Panama, we took action. And we'd do it again to protect American lives.

On the domestic scene, we've had some successes up there on Capitol Hill—it's been tough—legislation like our Child Care Act which said that parents, parents should raise the kids, not the U.S. Government, the Clean Air Act that harnesses the market forces for a cleaner environment. And we've got a great record to take to the college campuses on the environment. We've spent $800 billion in the last 10

years, $1.2 trillion in the next, to clean up the environment and keep this world safe and sound, and we're going to do it. We passed the Americans with Disabilities Act, the most forward-looking piece of civil rights legislation in the last few years, and it says to the disabled, hey, you're going to be part of the mainstream, not kept out, not pushed aside. Take that one out there to the college campuses and to the American people.

Sometimes when you have a Congress controlled by politically active Democrat liberals, you've got to keep bad things from happening. And the record is, Bush 30, on these vetoes, Congress 0.

Let me just say a word on the veto. It's tough sometimes to stand up against what might be seemed and designated in the papers as a popular position. But principle demands that a President do what might not be popular, do what is principled, and I believe that Government should work for the people, not the other way around. The system is broken, and we're going to fix it.

Let me say this one: I think the executive branch could stand some disciplining, and I know very well the Democratic-controlled Congress could. So everybody in America knows that I've proposed an amendment to force a balanced Federal budget. They know I've fought for it, the only Presidential candidate to support it, and I am not going to give up that fight. I need your help.

It's just this simple: The Government is too big, and it spends too much. The American people know that, and the American people are with us when I call for what 43 Governors have in the States, 43 Governors, and I'm saying: Give me the line-item veto, and give us a chance to cut down on this spending.

The taxpayers know how the budget gets busted: an arrogant, permanent Congress, unaccountable. The American people are with us, and the time has come to limit the terms of the United States Congress.

Another one we've got going for us, and it's strong, and it's new, and it's good, and that is the total reform, a revolution in American education. Almost half a trillion dollars is spent at all levels on education each year. Does anyone think we are getting our money's worth?

*Audience members.* No!

*The President.* Of course not. So while the opposition stumbles along the beaten path with old ideas, we've come out with a brandnew trail. America 2000 is the program, and it is revolutionizing the way we'll educate our kids.

Today I sent up to the Congress the "GI bill" for children, a bill to help low- and middle-income parents choose what schools can best teach their kids. School choice can be a catalyst, the force behind a real revolution in our schools. The theory is this: Whether it's public, private, or religious, parents, not governments, will choose their children's schools.

Not everyone's going to like what we're doing. And frankly, I'd have to wonder if some people did. Not everyone is ready for these new ideas. We're not going to discover new horizons without the courage to lose sight of the shore, and we're halfway there.

Our journey's not done. I've found that sometimes in this job as President, you have to do something that's unpopular. The person that's there must have a steady hand, must have a proper temperament, must have an experienced eye, and must have some vision, some knowledge of the waters ahead. The American people know that there's a flip side to change, and that is called trust. I believe I have been a President to earn the trust of the American people.

*Audience members.* Four more years! Four more years! Four more years!

*The President.* The American people know this, too, that we've got to ground our drive for change in some things that do not or should not change, things like values and family and faith. Too many Americans now feel that the country's on the wrong track. And how do we get it back on? We take the first step when we put the American family first. I am going to keep on fighting to find ways to strengthen the American family.

A man who served as executive director of this organization once said, "Long before I was struck with cancer, I felt something stirring in American society. It was the sense among the people of this country that something was missing from their lives,

something crucial. And my illness helped me to see what was missing, a little heart, a lot of brotherhood." Lee Atwater always had a way of getting to the truth. There are millions of Americans, ordinary citizens who are guided by that truth. We call them Points of Light. If every life is a portrait of a person who lives it, they are signing theirs with charity and good will. They're the true heroes of this country.

Government must not get in the way of what de Tocqueville found, when he came to America, was unique about America: the propensity of one American to help another. When I talk about kinder and gentler Nation, that's what I mean. Many of you are actively involved, in some way trying to help your communities, your neighborhood, your colleges, or whatever it is. People who feel as we do on this, let me say the work is not finished, and neither is ours. And this is an age of great, great change for America.

Let me end this way: November 3d is so important. These issues, these values that you and I share are the values that most of the American people have. So what we will do now is wait for our convention to be over. I'll try to keep making decisions that affect the welfare of America by moving through some legislation that remains. But I can't wait for the day when that Republican Convention is over, and I am going to roll up my sleeves with you at my side, and we are going to go after those Democrats.

*Audience members.* Four more years! Four more years! Four more years!

*The President.* Let's see, I'm thinking back, for 6 months I've stood out there as a spear-catcher for five Democrats and now one independent. Let me tell you, I know how to take it, but I also know how to dish it out. We haven't even begun yet. We haven't even started. Five months, five months of pounding in that political arena, and I have not yet begun to fight. But when I do, with you at my side, we are going to win on November 3d.

Thank you all, and God bless you. And God bless the United States of America. Thank you very much.

*Note: The President spoke at 3:10 p.m. at*

*the Omni Shoreham Hotel. In his remarks, he referred to Tony Zagotta, chairman of* *the College Republican National Committee.*

## Message to the Congress Reporting Budget Deferrals
*June 25, 1992*

*To the Congress of the United States:*

In accordance with the Congressional Budget and Impoundment Control Act of 1974, I herewith report two revised deferrals, now totaling $2.2 billion in budgetary resources. Including the revised deferrals, funds withheld in FY 1992 now total $5.7 billion.

The deferrals affect Funds Appropriated to the President and the Department of Ag-

riculture. The details of the deferrals are contained in the attached reports.

GEORGE BUSH

The White House,
June 25, 1992.

*Note: The reports detailing the deferrals were published in the Federal Register on July 2.*

## Nomination of Kathryn D. Sullivan To Be Chief Scientist at the National Oceanic and Atmospheric Administration
*June 25, 1992*

The President today announced his intention to nominate Kathryn D. Sullivan, of California, to be Chief Scientist of the National Oceanic and Atmospheric Administration, Department of Commerce. She would succeed Sylvia Alice Earle.

Since 1990, Dr. Sullivan has served as NASA Mission Specialist at the Johnson

Space Center in Houston, TX. Dr. Sullivan graduated from the University of California at Santa Cruz (B.S., 1973) and Dalhousie University, Halifax, Nova Scotia (Ph.D., 1978). She serves in the U.S. Naval Reserve. Dr. Sullivan was born October 3, 1951, in Paterson, NJ, and currently resides in Houston, TX.

## Nomination of C.C. Hope, Jr., To Be a Member of the Board of Directors of the Federal Deposit Insurance Corporation
*June 25, 1992*

The President today announced his intention to nominate C.C. Hope, Jr., of North Carolina, to be a member of the Board of Directors of the Federal Deposit Insurance Corporation for a term expiring February 28, 1993. This is a reappointment.

Since 1986, Mr. Hope has served as a member of the Board of Directors of the Federal Deposit Insurance Corporation. He

served as vice chairman of the First Union National Bank in Charlotte, NC.

Mr. Hope graduated from Wake Forest University (B.S., 1943). He served in the U.S. Navy from 1943 to 1945. He was born February 5, 1920, in Charlotte, NC. Mr. Hope is married, has three children, and resides in Alexandria, VA.

## Nomination of Terrence B. Adamson To Be a Member of the Board of Directors of the State Justice Institute
*June 25, 1992*

The President today announced his intention to nominate Terrence B. Adamson, of Georgia, to be a member of the Board of Directors of the State Justice Institute for a term expiring September 17, 1994. This is a reappointment.

Since 1991, Mr. Adamson has served as a partner with the law firm of Donovan, Leisure, Rogovin, Huge, and Schiller in Washington, DC. He served as a partner with the law firm of Dow, Lohnes and Albertson in

Atlanta, GA, 1983–91, and as an associate with Hansell, Post, Brandon & Dorsey, 1974–77. Mr. Adamson also served as a fellow at the Institute of Politics at the Kennedy School of Government of Harvard University, 1979–80.

Mr. Adamson graduated from Emory University (B.A., 1968; J.D., 1973). He also served in the National Guard. Mr. Adamson is married, has three children, and resides in Washington, DC.

## Statement by Press Secretary Fitzwater on the President's Signing of Legislation To Resolve the Railroad Labor Dispute
*June 26, 1992*

The President is pleased that Congress, with bipartisan cooperation, has met its responsibility to end the rail crisis. The legislation the President has just signed will offer an opportunity for labor and management to settle the issues between themselves. If that proves impossible, the bill also

offers a fair way to resolve any impasse and keep the railroads and our economy moving.

*Note: H.J. Res. 517, approved June 26, was assigned Public Law No. 102–306.*

## Remarks at a Ceremony Marking the Return of the Remains of Ignacy Paderewski to Poland
*June 26, 1992*

Please be seated. This is a little much. But listen, I am so pleased to see so many distinguished Americans here and so many visitors here.

I first want to salute our Secretary, beautifully decked out for this occasion, but I have such confidence in Ed Derwinski and what he's doing for our country. I don't think there's anybody who is familiar with U.S.-Polish relations that does not credit Ed Derwinski for his commitment and his understanding. And I tell you, I've leaned on him for advice all along the way here. So

Ed, we're delighted you're here.

Ambassador Dziewanowski's here. President Walesa's Chief of Staff is here, Mr.— I've got to be sure I pronounce it right— Ziolkowski. Where are you, sir? Would you please stand up? We're just delighted that you're with us. You all know the Ambassador sitting out here. But anyway, we know him, and we consider him a great friend of the United States as well as a wonderful advocate for Poland.

So, welcome, all. Today we begin a series of ceremonies that are fulfilling the dream of one of the great men of our time, Ignacy Jan Paderewski. And I'm so pleased to see some kin here with us today. It's most appropriate.

This outstanding musical artist and, I would add, visionary statesman died in exile in America when the clouds of war and oppression loomed darkest over his native Poland. And by direction of President Franklin D. Roosevelt, Paderewski's remains were given a place of honor for temporary repose right across the river there at Arlington National Cemetery, temporary until Poland regained its freedom.

That day has come. Poland has thrown off the yoke of Soviet communism. The dream of Polish freedom and independence has really become a bright reality, and it's getting stronger every single day. Within a few days, the distinguished delegation here will escort Paderewski's remains home to Poland. On July 5th, and I'm really looking forward to this, Mr. Ambassador, Barbara and I will have the privilege of going back to Poland to attend the solemn requiem mass at St. John's Cathedral in Warsaw.

God gave Paderewski extraordinary talents, and he was generous in their use. He brought the beauty of classical music performances to hundreds of thousands of listeners around the globe. He shared his financial success with charities and with patriotic causes. He took a leading role in Poland's struggle for freedom. And indeed, more than anyone else, he was responsible for President Wilson's including Polish independence among his Fourteen Points for peace following the First World War. During the period of independence that followed, he put his talents for statesmanship into practice as Poland's Prime Minister. His life was truly a symphony.

The new birth of freedom in Poland, indeed in all of Europe, is in great part due to the perseverance of millions of people like yourselves here in the United States, people of the Polonia. Just as Paderewski had fought against dictatorship half a century earlier, people of Polish origin and culture in America played a critical role in razing the Iron Curtain and launching Europe into a new era of freedom and unity. We cannot name them all, but we should honor them just as we do such modern heroes as President Walesa and His Holiness Pope John Paul.

Barbara and I are looking forward to our return to Poland next week, to the warmth of that country, the warmth of its people. It will be one of the greatest honors of my Presidency to take part in the final rites for Ignacy Paderewski when, to paraphrase the stirring strain of the Polish anthem, he will be rejoined with the people of his nation.

As with my trip to Poland in July of 1989, we're making this visit also to demonstrate America's strong support for Poland's bold movement to democracy and free markets. It's going to be a different Poland from the country that I visited just 3 years ago. Alongside the great success of Poland's pioneering reforms are the hardships resulting from 40 years of Communist mismanagement. I want the Polish people to know that America stands resolutely with them in their heroic efforts today.

There is no way that I can adequately thank the many Polish Americans and others as well who have made this occasion possible. Your steadfast loyalty to America and to Poland is a great example to me as I conduct the affairs of this office in the office right behind us.

So may God bless you all. May God bless Poland and, of course, the United States of America.

Now turn the spotlight over here. Thank you all for coming.

*Note: The President spoke at 10:30 a.m. in the Rose Garden at the White House. In his remarks, he referred to Kazimierz Dziewanowski, Polish Ambassador to the United States, and Janusz Ziolkowski, Polish Secretary of State for Foreign Affairs.*

# Letter to Congressional Leaders Transmitting Proposed Legislation on Utah Public Lands Wilderness Designation
*June 26, 1992*

*Dear Mr. Speaker:   (Dear Mr. President:)*

I am pleased to submit for congressional consideration and passage the "Utah Public Lands Wilderness Act".

The Federal Land Policy and Management Act of 1976 (FLPMA), (43 U.S.C. 1701, *et seq.*), directs the Secretary of the Interior to review the wilderness potential of the public lands.

The review of the areas identified in Utah began immediately after the enactment of FLPMA and has now been completed. Approximately 3,258,250 acres of public lands in 95 areas in Utah met the minimum wilderness criteria and were designated as wilderness study areas (WSAs). These WSAs were studied and analyzed during the review process and the results documented in five environmental impact statements and five instant study area reports.

Based on the studies and reviews of the WSAs, the Secretary of the Interior recommends that all or part of 69 of the WSAs, totaling 1,958,339 acres of public lands, be designated as part of the National Wilderness Preservation System. From these 69 WSAs, the Secretary proposes to designate 70 wilderness areas by dividing one WSA into two wilderness areas.

I concur with the Secretary of the Interior's recommendations and am pleased to recommend designation of the 70 areas (totalling 1,958,339 acres) identified in the enclosed draft legislation as additions to the National Wilderness Preservation System.

The proposed additions represent the diversity of wilderness values in the State of Utah. These range from the block-faulted mountains of western Utah to the entrenched sandstone canyons of the Colorado Plateau in southern and eastern Utah. These areas span a wide variety of Utah landforms, ecosystems, and other natural systems and features. Their inclusion in the wilderness system will improve the geographic distribution of wilderness areas in Utah, and will complement existing areas of congressionally designated wilderness. They will provide new and outstanding opportunities for solitude and unconfined recreation.

The enclosed draft legislation provides that designation as wilderness shall not constitute a reservation of water or water rights for wilderness purposes. This is consistent with the fact that the Congress did not establish a Federal reserved water right for wilderness purposes. The Administration has established the policy that, where it is necessary to obtain water rights for wilderness purposes in a specific wilderness area, water rights would be sought from the State by filing under State water laws. Furthermore, it is the policy of the Administration that the designation of wilderness areas should not interfere with the use of water rights, State water administration, or the use of a State's interstate water allocation.

The draft legislation also provides for access to wilderness areas by Indian people for traditional cultural and religious purposes. Access by the general public may be limited in order to protect the privacy of religious cultural activities taking place in specific wilderness areas. In addition, to the fullest extent practicable, the Department of the Interior will coordinate with the Department of Defense to minimize the impact of any overflights during these religious cultural activities.

I further concur with the Secretary of the Interior that all or part of 63 of the WSAs encompassing 1,299,911 acres are not suitable for preservation as wilderness.

Also enclosed are a letter and report from the Secretary of the Interior concerning the WSAs discussed above and a section-by-section analysis of the draft legislation. I urge the Congress to act expeditiously and favorably on the proposed legislation so that the natural resources of these WSAs in Utah may be protected and preserved.

Sincerely,

GEORGE BUSH

*Note: Identical letters were sent to Thomas S. Foley, Speaker of the House of Representatives, and Dan Quayle, President of the Senate.*

## Designation of Marshall Jordan Breger as Acting Assistant Secretary of Labor
*June 26, 1992*

The President today directed Marshall Jordan Breger, of the District of Columbia, Solicitor for the Department of Labor, to perform the duties of the office of Assistant Secretary of Labor for Labor-Management Standards, effective June 29, 1992.

Since 1991, Mr. Breger has served as Solicitor at the Department of Labor. From 1985 to 1991, he served as Chairman of the Administrative Conference of the United States. He also served as Special Assistant to the President for Public Liaison at the White House, 1983–85.

Mr. Breger graduated from the University of Pennsylvania (B.A., 1967; M.A., 1967); Oriel College, Oxford University (B. Phil., 1970); and the University of Pennsylvania Law School (J.D., 1973). He was born August 14, 1946, in New York, NY. Mr. Breger is married, has two children, and resides in Silver Spring, MD.

## Nomination of Hugo Pomrehn To Be Under Secretary of Energy
*June 26, 1992*

The President today announced his intention to nominate Hugo Pomrehn, of California, to be Under Secretary of Energy. He would succeed John Chatfield Tuck.

Since 1967, Dr. Pomrehn has served in several positions with the Bechtel Corp., including vice president and manager of the Los Angeles Regional Office, 1990 to present; manager of special projects for quality management in San Francisco, 1989–90; and vice president and general manager of Bechtel-KWU Alliance in Gaithersburg, MD, 1988–89.

Dr. Pomrehn graduated from the University of Southern California (B.S., 1960); George Washington University (M.S., 1965); and the University of Southern California (M.S., 1969; Ph.D., 1975). He served as a Lieutenant in the U.S. Navy, 1960–64. He was born July 8, 1938, in Chicago Heights, IL. Dr. Pomrehn is married, has three children, and resides in Westminster, CA.

## Statement by Press Secretary Fitzwater on the Resignation of H. Lawrence Garrett III as Secretary of the Navy
*June 26, 1992*

President Bush accepts the resignation of Secretary of the Navy, H. Lawrence Garrett III. Secretary Garrett today submitted his letter of resignation to the President, accepting full responsibility for the Tailhook incident involving naval aviators.

President Bush today received a briefing by Secretary Cheney on the status of the Department of Defense investigations into the Tailhook incident. The Inspector General of the Navy has investigated the matter. A second investigation by the In- spector General of the Department of De- fense was ordered last week.

The President seeks a full, thorough, and expedited investigation that will result in actions to ensure the highest standards of equality and conduct among all members of the Navy. Sexual harassment will not be tol- erated.

## Statement by Press Secretary Fitzwater Announcing the Visit of Prime Minister Kiichi Miyazawa of Japan
*June 26, 1992*

The President will meet with Prime Min- ister Miyazawa of Japan for an official work- ing visit on Wednesday, July 1. The leaders will have an Oval Office meeting and then go to Camp David for private talks and dinner. Discussions are expected to include the upcoming G–7 summit in Munich as well as other international and bilateral issues.

## Radio Address to the Nation on a "GI Bill" for Children
*June 27, 1992*

Today I'd like to speak with you about a subject close to the heart of every Ameri- can: the education of our children. You might not know it to read the morning paper or watch the evening news, but there's a revolution going on in our coun- try, a revolution with a single aim: To make American schools the best in the world.

This week I proposed a giant step for- ward in that revolution. I sent to Congress legislation authorizing $500 million to help States and communities give children from middle- and low-income families a $1,000 scholarship. And here's the crucial part: Families will be allowed to spend this money at any school of their choice, wheth- er that school is public, private, or religious. This proposal is in the greatest American tradition.

Forty-eight years ago this week, President Roosevelt signed the GI bill creating schol- arships that veterans could use at any col- lege, any college of their choice. The GI bill created opportunity for Americans who never would have had it. And in so doing, it helped to create the best system of colleges and universities in the world. And we can do it again, this time with a "GI bill" for children, helping State and local govern- ments create the best elementary and sec- ondary schools in the world.

My proposal is based on a few fundamen- tal truths. I believe that parents are their children's first teachers. Parents, not bu- reaucrats, know what's best for their chil- dren. Parents, not the Government, should choose their children's schools. For too long we've shielded schools from competition, al- lowed them a damaging monopoly power over our children. This monopoly turns stu- dents into statistics and parents into pawns.

Let's be clear about who's hurt most by the present system. It's not the wealthy; they can already afford to send their chil- dren to whichever school they choose. The "GI bill" for children will give low- and middle-income families more of those choices. Whether it's the public school down the street or across town, whether it's a parochial or Yeshiva or Bible school, par- ents should be able to decide which school will provide the best education for their kids. By injecting competition into our edu- cation system, by allowing parents to choose their children's schools, we can break the monopoly, provide the catalyst to open up opportunities for our kids and create genuine change in our schools.

Abraham Lincoln said, "Revolutions do not go backward." And all across the country, from Pennsylvania to California, from San Antonio to Indianapolis, the school choice revolution is gaining steam.

I met with many leaders of that movement at the White House this week. They are the true heroes of school reform. They aren't afraid to stand up to the status quo, to say loud and clear that when it comes to educating our kids, business as usual just is not good enough. And I'm proud to stand at their side.

The protectors of the status quo should understand this revolution will succeed with or without their help. We will create the finest schools for our children and grandchildren. And we will do it by restoring to education the truest American principles: freedom and opportunity and choice.

Thank you for listening. And may God bless the United States of America.

*Note: This address was recorded at 8 a.m. on June 26 in the Cabinet Room at the White House for broadcast after 9 a.m. on June 27.*

## Remarks at the Dedication Ceremony for the Drug Enforcement Administration's New York Field Division Office in New York City
*June 29, 1992*

Thank you all very, very much. Thank you for the welcome back. And may I return those kind words by saying that I think we have an Attorney General, came in at a complicated time and is doing a superb job for law enforcement. And it's a joy working with Bill Barr. I want to salute another with us today, Bob Martinez, the former Governor. He and I started working when he was the Governor of the State of Florida. We interacted then mainly on the interdiction side of this drug war. And I have great confidence in the job he's doing as our drug czar.

I want to say to our friend Dave Dinkins, the illustrious Mayor of the city, that I am very grateful to you, sir, for being with us today, for the kind comments you made about our collective efforts to win this battle; to salute you for what our people tell me has been outstanding cooperation from the New York Police. You deserve a vote of thanks for that, and I am very proud once again to be at your side.

May I salute Rob Bonner, who is our head of DEA. I hope that most of you that work with DEA have had the opportunity to meet him. He is dedicated, and again, I'm grateful that he's heading this very, very important Agency. Mr. Austin is here, Dick

Austin of GSA. We're saluting a facility that I guess most of you have moved into a little before now. But it shows what can be done in these unique times, innovating from within and having the results be rather spectacular. Al DelliBovi is here. He's from HUD, our number two man there, doing a great job in the housing field. I thought I saw him. Oh, he's hiding way in the back over here.

May I salute, also, another man that I respect, Lee Brown. We trained him well in Houston, Texas, and look at him now. Here he is—[*laughter*]—here he is, doing a great job for New York and, I think, for all the people in the country. Monsignor O'Brien, I know of your work, sir, and thank you for putting it in focus with that wonderful invocation. To Bob Bryden, I got well-briefed coming up here on the effectiveness of this office, something that I'd learned from my own visit here a few years ago. But I salute you, sir, and I guess even more important, the day-in and day-out work of those people that work with you and for you here, a dedicated group. I guess there's no way that a President can adequately say thanks to those who put their lives on the line day-in and day-out for the young people and the families of this Nation. We are grateful to each and every one of you. And I'm pleased to be here.

You know, we meet at the end of a hectic month. Boris Yeltsin was in town just a week ago. He asked if I still thought that the day of the dictator was over, and I said I did. And he said, "Well, so who is this Steinbrenner that I keep hearing about up there?" [*Laughter*] It's good to be back in New York, I'll tell you.

But you know the message. I think it's a message that all of you can identify with. All Americans want families that are strong and united. All Americans want good schools and a job-creating economy and a world at peace. But all of this ties into your work because all Americans want neighborhoods that are safe, rejecting those who soft-pedal the need to be hard on crime. Some say that there are reasons that crime occur, and I'm sure that you can make a case for that. But I say there is never an excuse not to seek justice through the American system of law. And nowhere is this need clearer than this war that you all are engaged in, the war on drugs, a war this new office of DEA can help fight and win.

I was at that old DEA New York office in the spring of 1989, after the brutal murder of Agent Hatcher. And you know, in everybody's life there are events that make an impact on you. I'll never forget that one. It was brought home to me so clearly, the personal sacrifice and sometimes the personal suffering that goes with this fight against drugs. It was a sad occasion. And I tried to make clear then, and I repeat now, that we will win this war against drugs. As long as one American is hooked on drugs, that's one too many. And so we must stop drug use, not someplace, not sometime, but all across our country, now or as soon as possible.

And that's why—Bill Barr alluded to this—that's why the Federal budget for fiscal '93 calls for $12 billion for our national drug control strategy. That's $12 billion, nearly double the amount when we came into office in 1989. And the strategy does set ambitious goals. We hoped—and these goals were set with the advice of many people here, some previously in the DEA and others with it now and with Justice—to cut overall drug use by 10 percent. That's

what we set as a goal. Well, we surpassed that target. We wanted to slash occasional cocaine use by 10 percent; it went down 29. Adolescent cocaine use, the goal was 30-percent decrease, and I'm pleased to tell you that it's down by about 60 percent.

We've begun well, you might say; but we've only just begun. Look at Bedford Stuy or other communities across the country, the suburbs of any city, the broken canyons of Los Angeles, and there you'll see some of more than 12 million Americans who currently still use drugs and the 1.9 million of them who still use cocaine. We are not making the progress that we want to in this addictive group, younger than the teenagers, but certainly not old enough to be retired in any way. And we must make more progress there. Worse, more than 1.3 million of our kids do use drugs. And I grieve for these families and these kids.

While Federal funding can help, it certainly, it alone, is not enough. And that's why this antidrug campaign includes community action led by effective treatment, Federal, State, and local, to reduce drug use in our neighborhoods and schools. We also need prevention through widespread education. And we need business and labor and our families and schools to stop the drugs that lead to the death and bondage, drugs that really declare open season on the innocent.

Next comes perhaps the most crucial part of the crusade, law enforcement. The DEA New York Field Division seized more than $234 million in criminal assets in one year, in fiscal year 1991. And you know that a country that refused to allow totalitarians of the right and of the left to enslave the world will never allow the evil purveyors of drugs to enslave America.

And let me tell you something: Every time law enforcement officials come to the White House, I think: How can we better support them? And so by January 1st we will have 50 percent more Federal prosecutors than in 1988. We've also reauthorized the 1984 Victims of Crime Act and boosted its annual crime victims fund to $150 million. Now, these dollars did not come from taxpayers but from the criminals' fines and penalties. After all, crime shouldn't pay;

criminals should. And so we've moved to punish career criminals under the Federal Armed Career Criminal Act. No seasoned criminal should walk free because we didn't take the law and our law enforcement officers seriously.

Our administration has proposed $15.8 billion for anticrime policies for fiscal '93. And that's up 59 percent in 4 years. And yet, progress made is certainly not mission accomplished. Let's back up these law enforcement officials with laws that are fair, fast, and final.

You know what I'm talking about. Fair: When good cops act in good faith to nail criminals, those criminals should not go free because of some exclusionary rule technicality. Fast: We need habeas corpus reforms to stop the frivolous appeals choking our courts. Crime's victims must not suffer twice, once when they're victimized by the criminal and again when some liberal judge allows criminals to escape scot-free through some new loophole in the law. We also need laws that are final. I think my position is well-known on this, and I have no trouble defending it. For anyone who kills a law enforcement officer, no penalty is too tough. When drug kingpins inflict the ultimate evil on society, society demands that the ultimate penalty be inflicted on them.

Some say that legalization of drugs is the answer to drugs. And to that I say that we must never wave the white flag of surrender at the white scourge of cocaine.

So today I am again asking the United States Congress to pass crime legislation based on three principles: If criminals commit crimes, they'll be caught—more law enforcement support. If caught, they will be tried—more judges, more rapid going through the courts. And if convicted, they will be punished—not let them out on loopholes. We need a crime bill which strengthens, not weakens, our ability to uphold the laws, a crime bill like the "Crime Control Act of 1992." So let's pass this legislation and salute those who risk their lives to save ours.

And above all, let's remember this: To take back our streets we need to take criminals off the streets and put them behind bars for a long, long time. And in the past 4

years, over half a billion dollars in drug forfeiture money alone has been used to build prisons. And we need more, more prisons. In particular, our States need more prisons. Because for some career criminals, the iron bars of prison are the only bar against crime.

So, let me close with words from the heart about where and with whom I stand. I stand with those who fight criminals. Your work is not a 9-to-5 job with long lunches and friendly chats around some water cooler. It is filled with danger and fear. And I had two wonderful briefings on some of the complexities of this work when I arrived here this morning. It's not knowing whether you'll end your shift going home in a car or to the emergency room in an ambulance.

And let me just add something: I also stand against those who use films or records or television or video games to glorify killing law enforcement officers. It is sick. It is wrong for any company, I don't care how noble the name of the company, it is wrong for any company to issue records that approve of killing law enforcement officers.

And so I am delighted to be here to salute the greatest freedom fighters any nation could have, people who provide freedom from violence and freedom from drugs and freedom from fear. They're offering hope to every family across our country. And in that spirit, I am now truly honored to open the New York Field Division Office of the DEA. And again, especially to all who work out there on the front lines, may God bless you in your noble work.

Thank you very, very much.

*Note: The President spoke at 10:53 a.m. in the conference room at the DEA New York Field Division Office. In his remarks, he referred to Lee P. Brown, commissioner of the New York City Police Department; Msgr. William B. O'Brien, president of the Daytop Village drug treatment facility; Robert A. Bryden, Special Agent in Charge, DEA New York Field Division; and DEA Special Agent Everett E. Hatcher, who was killed in the line of duty on February 28, 1989.*

# Remarks at a Fundraising Luncheon for Senator Alfonse M. D'Amato in New York City
*June 29, 1992*

Thank you all so much. And Charlie, thank you, Ambassador, for that very, very generous introduction. And let me just thank all responsible for this highly successful lunch. I want to salute our two Members of Congress here today, Senator Pressler and Norm Lent; I'll get to the third in a minute. Chairman Rich Bond—if you want to get a guy to do a big national job, get someone from New York; and Rich is doing just that as chairman of the Republican National Committee.

I want to salute our new committeeman, Joe Mandello; glad Joe's family could make it out there. Bill Powers, our wonderful State chairman who's taking them on up there and winning more than his share, for all of us, I might add. And David Brewer, Doug Barclay, Jack Hennessy, heading up our campaign efforts and doing such a superb job in this fundraising. Another salute to Roy Goodman, an old friend down here, the State senator. And Michael Long, let me just say, Mike, how grateful I am to you and the others in the Conservative Party. What that means is that with your help and now with the help of everybody across this State, New York is not only in play as a key targeted State for the Republicans, it is a State we will win. And this is a very important endorsement.

May I thank Yung Soo Yoo and Rabbi Milton Balkany for their introduction as well and their saluting us at the beginning of this program.

And now I'm here today to salute a great leader, a force for good, a titan of politics, Mama D'Amato. I think Al's learned a thing or two from Mama, things like getting it done, making waves, taking them on, and winning. And that's exactly what he's going to do this fall. But I've seen it in Washington, and when Al takes them on, the rest of them take cover.

Voters are frustrated, and they're tired of the status quo, and they're calling for change. But they also know that there's a flip side to change, and it is called trust, trust to make the right decisions and to block the wrong ones. I believe that we have the values, I believe we have the record that entitles us to take our case to the American people and win 4 more years in the White House and 6 more for Al in the Senate.

Our values are right. When we talk about family values, I'm thinking of what those mayors came to tell me. Liberals and conservative, Democrats and Republicans from the mayors came to see me, and they said the biggest problem in the cities is the decline of the American family. And we are the party that's trying to strengthen the American family through choice and opportunity.

I appreciated what Al said about changing the world. And I do believe that thanks to my predecessor, thanks to our administration, there have been fundamental changes in the world. Eastern Europe is free; Germany is united; the international communism as we know it is dead. Ancient enemies are sitting talking to each other in the Middle East. Democracy is on the move south of our borders. And we have a fantastic record of standing up against aggression. And don't let the revisionists try to tell you that Desert Storm was bad; it was a tremendous success, and we are not going to let them alter the record.

I notice these signs, and let me simply say that, look, the Israeli elections underscore the dynamism of the Mideast's solitary democracy. They point out the dynamism of the process. And we are confident that we can work with that new Israeli government to deepen our partnership, to promote our common objective of peace with security for Israel. And I am dedicating myself to that.

There's another thing that we'll take to the American people, and you don't hear it from either of the opponents at this Presidential level, and I don't expect Al's going to hear much about it. But it was under our leadership that we can now turn to the

American people, particularly the children, and say, you can go to bed at night without that awful, deadly fear of nuclear war because of what we did in getting rid of these ICBM weapons. You listen to those pundits out there and listen to the opponents, you wouldn't think there was any responsibilities to the United States. We are the undisputed leader of the free world, and I don't care what the critics say. I am going to keep on leading for peace and democracy around the world.

And yes, yes, we're going to have some savings in defense, but I am not going to cut into the muscle of the defense. There are still many uncertainties out there, and the United States, in order to lead, must remain strong. Al has known that; Al has stood up against criticism on behalf of that principle. And I am convinced that we can keep our security strong so we can guarantee for the generations that come futures of peace and opportunity.

Some people say to me, "Hey, how come you can't bring the same kind of purpose and success to the domestic scene as you did in Desert Storm and Desert Shield?" And the fair answer to that is, we can. But when it came to going into Desert Storm, I didn't have to call one of the Senators entrenched on the Democratic side, one of the liberals, and get his permission. I did not have to stand up and watch everything I'm trying to do get blocked by the Senate. We moved, and then they came along. That is what we need in the Congress, and the way to get that is to give us more people like Al D'Amato and Terrence Pressler and Norman Lent and to get control of the Congress.

For 35 years, one party has controlled the House of Representatives. For 29 of the last 35, one party has controlled the United States Senate. We tried it with a Democratic President and a Democratic Congress, and we got the worst interest rates, the worst "misery index" in the history of this country. What hasn't been tried and what we're going to take to the people in the fall is this: Give us a Republican President, a Republican Senate, and a Republican House, and we can give you the values that you want.

We've gotten some things done early in the Presidency: A child care bill that says, isn't it better for the parents to choose how to have child care rather than have some Government bureaucracy. We've passed the foremost, far-looking, far forward-looking piece of civil rights legislation in the Americans for Disabilities Act that said, let's give these people a chance, let them fit in, give them an opportunity, not have some Government program out here to keep the people with disabilities isolated. We passed a Clean Air Act that used market forces, harnesses market forces for a cleaner environment.

But so much that we're trying to do, whether it's school choice or whether it's incentives for this economy, are being blocked by the United States Congress. And they control it; the Democrats control it. And I believe that the American people, in their quest for change, are going to say: Let's try something that hasn't been done in 35 years: Let's get a Republican Congress to back up this Republican President.

Sometimes the only time you can get something to happen down there is standing up against bad legislation. And I want to take this opportunity to thank our distinguished honoree, Al D'Amato, today for helping me with this veto record. The score is: Bush 30, Congress 0, on the veto. And we're going to keep on beating back bad legislation until we get good legislation.

Let me just click off a couple of our major initiatives. One of them is health care reform. It is not right that families go to bed wondering whether they're going to have any protection against illness. We have put forward on the Capitol Hill now, it's before the Congress, a new health care reform program that says we will make insurance available to everybody, the poorest of the poor, through a voucher system. We will revise and get rid of these awful malpractice suits by changing and getting some legal reform for this country. We're suing each other too much and caring for each other too little. So we've got a good, strong, health care proposal, and it doesn't do like some of these foreign countries or what some of the liberal Democrats want to do. It does not socialize medicine. It does not break every small business. It offers insurance to others, everybody. And it says we will maintain the quality of U.S. health care. It is the best in the world, and we are not going to diminish it by putting the Government in charge of our health care.

Another one is free trade. We stand proudly for free trade. And we're taking a hammering in some quarters. Election year is coming up; everybody is out pledging to this special interest, this protection or that protection. But let me tell you something: I am going to keep on fighting until we get a successful conclusion to the Uruguay round of GATT, and I am going to keep on fighting until we get a North American free trade agreement because that means jobs for the American worker. I am for free trade, not for protection, and we've got to keep fighting for those principles.

Another one is education reform. Mike talked about it, and Al D'Amato mentioned it. We've got a good program; it's not just another Government program. It's called America 2000. It literally revolutionizes the way we educate the kids from K to 12. We have the best university system in the world; we have the best quality education at that level. But what we don't have is the proper quality at those lower areas of education. And so our program says: Keep it close to the family, keep it close to the locality and the community, but literally revolutionize it. We've got a good, strong program to take, and Al is right. Our "GI bill" says this: Give the parents a choice. Give the family the same opportunity to choose those schools, religious, private, or public that we all got, the old guys here got when we got the GI bill right after World War II. It worked for the universities; it can work at the local level. What's wrong with letting the parents choose and giving them that opportunity?

We've got a great disagreement with the liberal Democrats on another one. I am fighting at every turn to do better on the deficit. The other day we had a vote in the Congress on a means to discipline the executive branch and discipline the United States Congress. Not a cure-all, but it was something that 80 percent of the American people want. It was victimized and brutalized and beaten back by that entrenched liberal Democrat leadership that wouldn't

stand up against the special interests. I will continue to fight for a balanced budget amendment to discipline us all in Washington, DC.

And while we're at it—and I heard a nice endorsement of this by the Democratic nominee, potential Democratic nominee for President—I think it's about time to give the President what 43 Governors have. If they can't do it up there with the liberals that control these committees, give the President a chance. Give me that line-item veto, and let's see if we can't do better on the spending side.

In conclusion, let me say this: This has been a weird political year—I'm talking strange. I've been in politics half my adult life, half of it in private business. It has been the strangest year I have ever seen. I think most people would agree with that. But in the final analysis, the American people are going to say this: Who has the temperament to lead this country? Who has the steadiness when the going gets really tough to make the proper decision? Who has the beliefs when it comes to the innate strength of American society, the family, the family values? Who has the will to fight for those values? Who has the demonstrated leadership to keep the peace and enhance it by helping democracy and freedom around the world? And who has the best program to stimulate the economy by getting jobs and opportunity moving by encouraging less regulation and by stimulating the investment tax credit and cutting the capital gains and changing the IRA's and doing all the things we should have done months ago to give the working man and woman an opportunity?

I believe we have not only the program, but I hope I have the integrity and that sense of honor about the United States to ask the American people: Give me 4 more years. Give Al D'Amato 6 more years. Give us more company on the House and in the Senate, and watch us get that job done. I cannot wait until the middle of August— right now I'm in a nonpolitical mode. [*Laughter*] But I cannot wait until the middle of August when I get unfettered and say, all right, now the time has come to take this case to the American people. Not just to go after the other guys—although I'm a little bit tired of hearing my name get criticized by five Democrats all spring long, and now some independent comes charging out with nothing but criticism. I'm ready to take them on when we get to August. And what happens here is this kind of arrangement will make us have a much better chance of taking them on, on our terms. Let them see if they can take the heat because I am going to dish it out and take the Republican record to the American people, and we are going to win in November.

Thank you very, very much.

*Note: The President spoke at 1:15 p.m. in the Grand Ballroom at the New York Hilton Hotel. In his remarks, he referred to Charles Gargano, former Ambassador to Trinidad and Tobago; Joe Mandello, chairman, Nassau County Republican Party; David Brewer, luncheon vice chairman; Douglas Barclay, New York State chairman, Bush-Quayle '92; Jack Hennessy, New York State finance chairman, Bush-Quayle '92; Michael Long, chairman, New York State Conservative Party; Yung Soo Yoo, luncheon general chairman; and Rabbi Yehoshua Balkany, dean of Yeshiva Bais Yaakov of Brooklyn, who gave the invocation.*

## Statement on the Supreme Court Decision on Abortion
*June 29, 1992*

I am pleased with the Supreme Court's decision upholding most of Pennsylvania's reasonable restrictions on abortion, such as the requirement that a teenager seek her parent's consent before obtaining an abortion. The Pennsylvania law supports family values in what is perhaps the most difficult question a family can confront.

My own position on abortion is well-known and remains unchanged. I oppose abortion in all cases except rape or incest or where the life of the mother is at stake.

## Question-and-Answer Session With the Michigan Law Enforcement Community in Detroit, Michigan
*June 29, 1992*

*Q.* Mr. President, I have the privilege of not only introducing you, but also to ask the first question. I would like, sir, as most of us have a feeling that drugs is the common denominator of most of the violent crime we have in our society, could you please comment on the relative success of your war on drugs?

*The President.* That's what we call a slow ball, in a way, in the trade. But first, let me just thank Brooks and thank all of you. I understand people have come from all across the State.

On the war on drugs: One, it's priority; two, it's not without major progress. The major progress lies in the reduction of the amount of cocaine being used by teenagers, and this is very good. We set the goal, I believe it was, at 20 percent. And it's down 60 percent. Where we're not making the progress we should—and I'm sure every one of you runs into it in one way or another—is in that age group of 35, these addicted users. It's extraordinarily difficult. And our war on drugs under Governor Bob Martinez, but working cooperatively with the local level, must do better in that area.

We're doing pretty well in interdiction. We've got a broader cooperation, broader use of our military, a stronger cooperation from the Presidents of the countries south of our border. Mexico is doing much better. There's been some differences, but mainly we're getting good cooperation there. The

Colombians have been very, very good in terms of cooperation. We're having some difficulties in Peru that have not been enhanced by the recent change down there. But generally speaking, cooperation is better. One of the things I'm trying to do with them, the leaders south of the border, is say, "Look, we know that you feel that if it weren't for us you wouldn't have the problems of the drug cartels, the narco-traffickers. But we also should tell you we are doing as much as we can and will do everything we can on the demand side of the equation."

So we've got to keep pushing to reduce demand in this country. Our educational programs are doing better. Incidentally, it will not be solved at the Federal level. You've got to have cooperation in all of what we call the Points of Light, but also the work that you all do with the kids in the communities.

So I'd say I'm proud of the record. The funding, Federal funding, is way up, way up. I think the last figure was $9 billion or something of that nature for the drug war. But I wish I could certify to the American people that the job was done. It's not, and we've just got to keep pushing.

One of the things we'd like to see passed, and maybe I'll get a question on it, is to get our crime bill, which is tough on the criminal, more compassionate for the victim of crime, get that through the Congress. And we simply have not been able to do it. It would be tougher on the death penalty, tougher on habeas corpus reform, tougher on the exclusionary rule reform. And we're hung up in the old thinkers in the Judiciary Committee, particularly of the House of Representatives. So we've got a ways to go there.

Who else?

*Q.* This past week I was with 35 other top police administrators in the country and spent the week discussing issues of violence in the country. Now, we all know in the profession that violence is not merely a law enforcement problem; it's a problem for society. The Governor in this State has proposed some sweeping changes in education and some changes that will improve the economy in this State. I know this is a question that's very difficult to answer, but

briefly, can you tell us what your prescription is for reducing violence in the country?

*The President.* One of the things that—and I guess politicians should be careful, but I don't think you need to be too careful—I am very much concerned with the content of some of the filth and some of the portrayals that go into the families, into the living rooms through the television. I don't think we can censor. They've got to be very careful about censorship. But this morning at a DEA opening of the new DEA building, I spoke out against some of these rap songs that speak out and talk about killing law enforcement officers. I mean, I just think that good taste and decent people ought to know better than to permit those things to be aired across our country. I think that's one area that we can be extraordinarily helpful.

Another, we've got to do better in the whole education front, and that ties in. I don't think you're going to legislate violence away.

Then the third answer I'd give is pass strong legislation at the Federal level that backs up the law enforcement officers. I think that will send as strong a message to criminals as you possibly can. But I know no better deterrent than tough sentencing and having the penalty fit the crime, and so we're working for that on our crime bill. But then it's got to be more than that. It's got to be common sense in programming. It's got to be families intervening to see that they give the kids the advantage of an education at home.

I know we talk about family values, and I am reminded that the mayors from the National League of Cities came to see me. The mayors, liberal mayors, conservatives, Republicans, Democrats, nonpartisan, and they said that the single biggest cause of the problems facing the urban area was the decline in the American family. And that gets to your question about violence. So we've now got a Commission, headed by the Governor of Missouri, to try to find ways through legislation to strengthen the family. It might be welfare reform. It might be examining every piece of legislation to see that there's no incentive for husband and wife to live apart. There's things that I think we can do legislatively there. But it's got to also get back to values that kids are taught, taught at home and taught in the school. So that's a combination of ways of looking at it.

*Q.* When you talk about family values, one of the things that we're really concerned about in the northwest portion of our State is not only the drug problem but more importantly the alcohol problem as probably the most abused drug. In 1968, we took cigarette advertising off the television airwaves of our country. And we have seen a drastic decline in the use of tobacco products until, virtually, they say by the year 2000 we may be almost a smokeless society. Is there any chance that we can get alcohol advertising off television nationally and stop brainwashing our children from the time they're old enough to comprehend?

*The President.* I think some alcohol is off the airwaves, and I think what the beer people have undertaken now are a lot of public service advertisements on alternate drivers, supporting Mothers Against Drunk Driving, these kinds of programs. Whether it will be ready for Federal legislation, I just don't know. I think right now it would be very difficult to pass that. And I'd like to see the success of the educational campaigns before we go to some total ban on all alcoholic beverage. I do believe that the media themselves have policed pretty well the hard liquor.

*Q.* What are you doing to have the Solicitor General get before the U.S. Supreme Court on impact decisions in criminal law?

*The President.* Not being a lawyer, you'll have to tell me what you mean by an impact decision. I'm blessed by not having been to law school—[*laughter*]—some would say it's an enormous handicap, but I don't know. Help. I don't know what an impact decision is, technically.

*Q.* The ones that—say, drugs—the one that was near and dear to my heart was where the Supreme Court allowed our officials to kidnap people in Mexico and bring them back to try here. How are we getting other cases like that before the Supreme Court?

*The President.* Our Solicitor General is very active in what he brings to the Court. I don't know if there's a formula on it, but

the whole emphasis of our administration is to support law enforcement. That one caused some big problems internationally, as you know. But I do think that we've got a good record of trying to get these, if that's an impact decision, an impact decision up for consideration by the Court.

But the big point I'd make, and I hope this doesn't sound too political at this nonpolitical event, is that we're trying to appoint judges to all levels in the court who will interpret, not legislate from the bench. And I think we've got a good record of appointing people who prove to be strong for law enforcement because we use that as a standard and do not use as a standard, kind of passing social legislation from the Federal bench.

I know that there's been some criticism of me in the press, but I'm going to continue to do that because I believe that's what a judge should do, whether it's at the district level or the circuit court level or certainly at the Supreme Court level.

*Q.* Regularly, I see the tragic consequences of young people and guns, especially handguns, but often Uzis. Is the Federal Government going to do anything to try to make an effort to slow down the proliferation of guns, which are apparently available to our children on the street for $25 to $100?

*The President.* I don't favor gun control. We did move, as you know, on clip size for automatic weapons. We've tried to do something about stopping the import of weapons come in here. There was a compromise that we had almost worked out last year relating to—I want to call it "instant identification," which I strongly favor. It's going to require some money. It's going to require use of computers. But I believe the need to do that transcends the other argument, which is you're violating individuals' rights.

So I think we can make progress on some areas. I just am reluctant to endorse something that would ban private ownership at a time when you see States that have very strong laws suffering from some of the highest levels of criminal activity with guns. So I've been more "go after the criminal" than it is the gun owner; and yet we have taken steps in those three areas I've mentioned to you.

*Q.* Mr. President, for the last few years we've been trying to get in Oakland County some surplus aircraft for the war on drugs and what have you. With the downsizing of some of the defense and with Desert Storm being over, do you see much in the way of Federal property going on the surplus list that perhaps local municipalities could pick up?

*The President.* There will be more. How much of it will be applicable to the kind of local law enforcement needs you spell out, I just don't know. But there will be more, obviously. What I'm doing on the defense side, I've made substantial cuts in the defense budget. I also should say to you, though, that though we've made dramatic strides towards world peace, and one of the things I take great pride in is that our team, following on my predecessor's record, have been able to do a lot for world peace, saying to the young people, for example, you have far less to worry about now from nuclear war than generations precedent. And that is something big, and that is something major.

And yes, our suggestions for cutting defense are out there being acted on, and defense spending is going down. The problem almost—and this is off your question, but I want to mention it here—is almost the other way. Some, recognizing that we've made some substantial progress toward world peace, are saying almost you don't need the muscle in the defense. And my view is we do. We've got to fight for reasonable levels and, I'd say, prudent levels of defense spending. So it won't be as big in the field you ask about as some might hope, but I have a responsibility as Commander in Chief and as President to implement my responsibilities for national security.

We think we've found a good formula, and we're going to stave off reckless cuts into the muscle of our defense. Who knows where the next big challenge will come from? I don't believe it will come from a Soviet Union back together again. The visit we had with Boris Yeltsin, incidentally, was very, very rewarding and substantive in that we reached agreement to eliminate these major ICBM's, you know, the biggest

of the missiles, the Soviet side the SS–18's. Nobody would have dreamed that was possible 4 years ago, and it is tremendous. And yet people go, "Ho-hum, what have you done lately?" So we've got to stay strong. I don't think a threat will come from there. I do worry about proliferation. I worry about some of the nuts around the world trying to acquire sophisticated weaponry, missile technology, nuclear technology, and all of that. And to guarantee all this as best we can, the peace, we've got to keep fairly high levels of defense spending. And I'm determined that we do just exactly that.

There's another one that may be controversial, but I am continuing to fight for the "FREEDOM Support Act," which supports, through the international financial institutions, the democracy and change in the Soviet Union. We've spent trillions of dollars, trillions, in defense standing up against the monolithic Communist threat, the aggressive Communist threat led by the Soviets. That's gone now. I think we have a stake at trying to help their democracy, and I think in the final analysis that will be very good for the American worker. That market is enormous. I have a responsibility to fight to get that through. And I think it's like buying an insurance policy for the future.

A long answer. You asked me what time it is, and I told you how to build a watch. But nevertheless.

*Q.* I'd like to start by saying we're very fortunate to have a President who is pro-law enforcement, a Governor who is pro-law enforcement. And we in the law enforcement community have a tendency to ask what you're going to do for us. I don't want to steal a Democrat saying, but let me ask once: You are having problems with your crime package. What can we do in the law enforcement community? As the sign says, "We're working together for safe communities." What can we do in the law enforcement community to better help you help us in terms of getting that legislation passed as well as other things?

*The President.* Well, the election can help, because I think it'll be very clear. We'll have big differences in terms of supporting crime legislation.

But I think the thing to do is, for those

who say they're for law enforcement in the Congress, come home and talk one way, to try to assure as law enforcement officials that they vote the same way in Washington. Now, the reason I say that is, I was out in California before the primary. I heard two or three Congress people running for Congress—notice the word "people" I used there, Congress people, so I leave out—finger what gender it was—campaigning as the great champions of strong law enforcement action, strong legislation. And yet I know, and they knew I knew, that they were voting against our strong crime package.

Now, I can see where you might want to change it. I can see where what the judge said, some people might want to have something in there on it. But you can tell from a voting record whether somebody is pro-law enforcement, backing up the cops, backing up the victims of crime—there's victims-of-crime legislation—or whether it's all rhetoric. And so I think you who are experts in the field and are laying your lives on the line for us—and that's the way I look at law enforcement—you ought to be darn sure that you pin down those who want to represent you on this all-important question. And let them be honest enough if they have a difference on handguns or something.

But nevertheless, there's a thrust to legislation: Is it pro-law enforcement and tougher on the criminal, or is it the other way around? The Senate, for example, watered down to a fare-thee-well a strong crime bill that we had in the Senate. They passed a better one last year, and then this year they've softened it up. And so I think you, more than most, will be in a position to get the various candidates on the record, and then hopefully, if they're elected, to see that they do what they said they'd do on it.

So, that's about all I know to do.

*Q.* Mr. President, one last question.

*The President.* I'm just getting warmed up here. Sir.

*Q.* Thanks, Mr. President. One thing I wanted to do is to possibly make a very short statement that the recent police-bashing that's going on in the media has been a very difficult thing for us. And I would just like to pass along that I know that with the

history in the media recently of brutality and what have you, I know that there's an important sensitivity that we have to have for the community and for the defendant. But yet, I'd like to not throw the baby out with the bath water. I ask that at every opportunity the politicos have, sir, to please stand up for us because the bashing really is making it difficult for our men and women to go out and do a good job day after day.

*The President.* Let me comment on what the lieutenant says, because he puts his finger on a very important point. When there's excess, when there's brutality, fix it, get it corrected right now—training, whatever it is. But I agree with you. And in Los Angeles, I made it a point to go talk to the LAPD, to go to the sheriff's headquarters there to make sure that they knew that I was supportive of law enforcement per se. And I do get a sense—there's a lot of programming of kind of the corrupt law enforcement person, and that has a way of subtly undermining people's confidence in this country.

So I have no hesitancy in speaking out, always, in favor of law enforcement. But you deserve more than that. You deserve to get backed up by the legislation as well. But it's a good warning and a good point you raise. I hope that nobody in our administration is overreacting to scenes of brutality that turn a lot of people off or painting with so broad a brush that the hundreds and thousands of people that are risking their lives for the American people get diminished in their service by something of that nature.

So we are going to continue to push for the public backing of our law enforcement community, the police, the sheriffs, whoever else it is; continue working with the courts by getting people on the bench who share this view that law enforcement is very important in the communities; try to do more emphasis on what we call the Points of Light, and that is putting the spotlight on the many things that police in their communities do to help others. I think of the D.A.R.E. program and the antidrugs as just one facet of your support for community activities, and it's thousands of fold where that takes place. So we've got to continue to support that, support that concept of voluntarism that I think the police in this country epitomize and demonstrate.

So I hear what you say. And I know the Governor—he and I have talked about this—he feels strongly about that here in the State of Michigan, and I can tell you I do nationally.

Now, since Brooks is throwing us out— and I was just getting warmed up.

*Q.* Maybe 5 more minutes.

*The President.* Five more minutes. All right. That's always what gets you in trouble. Got some back here? Go ahead, sir.

*Q.* Good evening. With the most recent events in Los Angeles and with the most recent attention in Congress, is there going to be more of a commitment of Federal dollars and resources to urban areas, such as not only Los Angeles but Detroit, of resources?

*The President.* That's a good question. And the answer is, I hope so. I went to Los Angeles, went to the community. Democrats, Republicans, liberals, conservative, men, women, all said that what was needed then—and let me add one other name, Peter Ueberroth who has taken on the job to bring private-sector jobs to the community in Los Angeles—all of them, every one of them, including the black mayors organization, said, "What do we need? We need enterprise zones in these communities with zero capital gains base to bring jobs immediately to the communities." That is hung up in a big, long debate now in the Congress.

We were able to get summer job money through, $500 million additional. We were able to get the SBA and the FEMA money replenished so we'll be able to take care of the small business loans and all of that in the various communities. But I am not satisfied. And our whole concept of enterprise zones, of homeownership we think would be of enormous benefit for the cities. And we're going to keep on pressing for this whole package—those aren't the only elements in it—that we think will help the cities.

I don't know, I can't make a prediction for you at this point as to what will happen. There's another program, and I would urge you to look at it if you're not familiar with

it, called "Weed and Seed." And the concept is weed out the criminal, back up the law enforcement people. And there's good, specific things in the "Weed and Seed" proposal that will help back law enforcement. And then the seeding aspect of it has some 20 areas that funding will go to, to help seeding hope and opportunity in the communities.

Now that one is hung up, too, in the Congress. We're not giving up and I hope we can get those proposals through the Congress. We're in a fight sometimes because I do have a responsibility to try to do something about these enormous Federal deficits. And once in a while, some say, "Hey, you think it's worth $500 million? Let me give you $2 billion." And that's where I get onto the side of having to say no.

But I think we can do better. And I think some of these ideas I mentioned have strong support, and that means they will get through, hopefully before the end of July. The bill we passed the other day and was signed will help. But it's not near as much as we should be doing for these cities. I think we still have a good chance.

*Q.* Mr. President, what precipitated the Rodney King incident was a police chase. And I think that's a question that we'd all like answered today, if there was something we could do—we're kind of at a quandary on police chases. Our policies and procedures, we definitely look into every one we can have. But however, lawsuits, it seems like is costing the cities, the townships, and villages millions of dollars in lawsuits in police chases. We can't, apparently, seem to get our legislators to make up their minds one way or the other, either tell us to chase or not to chase. But I'd like to know if there would be any Federal legislation at all that could put a possible cap on lawsuits?

*The President.* The answer is, if I had my way, yes. And I don't have my way yet. But we have legislation before the Congress to cap some of these suits, whether it's malpractice for doctors that are ramming the health care costs right through the roof or whether it's on these frivolous liability claims. And to be very, very candid and to call it as is, we are blocked by the trial lawyers lobby. And they're strong, and they're tough, and they control a handful, and we've got to keep fighting until we get this done. The frivolous lawsuit is running the cost of everything, insurance and everything else, right off the charts. The American people want it done, and we're having difficulty getting it done.

It's the same fight I had on the balanced budget amendment. It would have disciplined the executive branch, disciplined the legislative branch, and 80 percent of the people want it, and we got almost two-thirds of the vote. The leadership in the House of Representatives went to 12 Members who had sponsored the legislation and said, "Hey man, we need you. We need you to come on and just change it." And so 12 of the sponsors of the legislation, through strong-arm politics, were pulled off it. It's the same kind of pressure we're fighting in the Congress on trying to restrict liability and get it under control.

And this officer is so correct that the American people want this done. And again, it transcends party. This one powerful lobby has it stymied in the United States Congress. And that's one we've just got to get in focus, leave out party, take it to the American people and say, "Send us people that will at least get something done in terms of capping liability, restricting some of these frivolous liability suits."

*Q.* Mr. President, this really is the last question.

*The President.* All right.

*Q.* Mr. President, how do we get the criminal to do the time that he's sentenced to? Recently in Oakland County we buried several young women that were a victim of a man who still should have been in prison.

*The President.* Well, again, I'd have to defer to the Attorney General, to the legal experts. But we have mandatory sentencing in some Federal crimes. And Federal law, I believe, is a little tougher on this. I can get an argument with the judges or the lawyers around here. But I think we have tried to do that through the Federal Sentencing Commission. And again, it is not much help to law enforcement if a person is sentenced to fairly stiff terms and then walks out of there either on a technicality or after serving an abysmally short period of time.

I don't think I've been gender-fair; so can

we end with you, ma'am?

*Q.* I am chapter leader for southeastern Michigan for Parents of Murdered Children. My son was murdered in 1987. And I would like to know what this administration is doing or can do for the survivors of homicide victims?

*The President.* Well, we've passed one victims-of-crime legislation. We have some new provisions—I'm looking for Sam Skinner to help me—provisions in the new crime bill before the Congress for the victims of crime. And it is something that we've at least started moving forward on. The lady is right that we should be doing more. And that's in terms with the whole philosophy, more sympathy for the victims and less for the criminal.

So we've made some legislative headway. Don't pin me down on the details that are on it in the bill that we've got pending right now. But I believe you'll find that it is strongly supportive of the victims of crime. This is something that has been almost a national tragedy because for a long time there was literally very little that could be done or had been done.

The other thing, one of the things, and maybe this isn't directly on your point, but I know a lot of families feel this way, that when we talk about habeas corpus reform so you knock out frivolous appeals, it does bring certain comfort to the family that at least wants to know that justice is being done, that the person that murdered the family member is going to pay the price and not get frivolously appealed and appealed and appealed endlessly. And so part of our habeas corpus reform addresses itself to the victims of crime in that sense.

Well, listen, thank you all very, very much. I don't know who is in charge of the heat here, but I've lost about five pounds, and that wouldn't hurt me, as you can tell. But I just want to, once again, thank you all for taking the time. And I say this, you know, this is a strange political year. It's a strange political year. And I know anything you say is interpreted to be said for political gain. But I feel very, very strongly about what I've said here about backing law enforcement officials, and for me it does transcend politics. And for me, when a police officer—I keep in my desk the badge of a young police officer from New York as a reminder—gunned down. I go to the DEA when they honor the officers that are killed in fighting for us, for my family, fighting against narcotics.

So I hope it doesn't sound patronizing in this political year, but we strongly support the law enforcement community in this country. I will continue to fight for strong legislation, and I will continue to take the message out there against the kinds of things in the media that undermine the family or rejoice at those who stand up

against law enforcement, something like that. I think I have a moral obligation as President of the United States to take that kind of a message to the American people. And if you want to say "political," fine. But it's something I feel deeply in my heart.

So thank you all very much for what you're doing for your country and for your community. Thank you.

*Note: The President spoke at 5:14 p.m. at the Southfield Civic Center. In his remarks, he referred to Brooks Patterson, attorney and former Oakland County prosecutor.*

# Remarks at a Victory '92 Fundraising Dinner in Detroit
*June 29, 1992*

Let me thank the Governor for that warm introduction and all of you for this welcome and all of you for what you've done to help get out the vote, to help the party, to help this President, and to help all the Republicans standing for election next fall. This is truly a most successful occasion, I'm told. It seems to me I just left here having thanked all of you, but I'll do it one more time because I am delighted to have this fantastic support for all of us who are standing for election in the fall.

I was delighted to see so many members of the State legislature here. And, of course, I want to thank Randy Agley and Mike Timmis and Heinz Prechter and so many others—I'm going to get in trouble—everybody that had a hand in making this so successful. I want to single out Councilman Keith Butler and our Lieutenant Governor who I've known for a long, long time, Connie Binsfeld, and the Republican leadership that helped turn this great State around.

And I am looking forward to repeating the experience of Cobo Hall. Barbara and I when we came in here just about 12 years ago, across the street to another hotel, it was there that I was picked to be Vice President on the stand on the Republican ticket. And that has propelled us now into a fascinating experience. What I want to talk

to you tonight is I believe that we've got the record to take to the American people for 4 more years as President of the United States.

I like to finish what I start, and a lot of glib talk won't get the job done. I'm kind of holding back on going after the opponents until after the Republican Convention in the middle of August. But I'll tell you something: I am getting a little sick and tired of being on the receiving end of criticism day-in and day-out from all those sorry Democrats that were running for President, and now some independent. And when I am unleashed and when we get out of this mode, this nonpolitical mode we're in, I'll tell you, I'll be ready for the fray. I have never felt better, nor have I ever felt more eager to take my case to the American people.

Frankly, I don't care about those polls. Fortunately, when I was soaring around about 85 percent I said I didn't believe in the polls. Smartest thing I ever said. [*Laughter*] But they changed, and frankly, I don't think we're looking too bad. But let me tell you this: This election, when people get down to deciding who they want in the White House, they're going to say, "Who has the temperament, who has the experience, who has the record to lead this country for 4 years?" And I will be making the case, with your help, that we are the party that deserves a shot at controlling the United States Congress and, thus, facilitating our leadership.

Let me remind you: 35 years the Democrats have controlled the House of Representatives; 29 out of the last 35 years they've controlled the United States Senate. People are saying: Well, what about divided Government? Why don't you just say that you'll stand with whatever the people want, if they elect a Democratic Congress, a Democratic President? Let me tell you something. We tried that in the late seventies. We had a Democratic President. We had a Democratic House. We had a Democratic Senate. And we had the highest "misery rate" that this country has ever seen. It went right out through the roof. What we haven't tried is a Republican House, a Republican Senate, and a Republican President. And if you want to bring change to this country, help me elect a Republican Congress in the fall.

You know, this year, as I say, has been a little weird, a little peculiar. The other day Boris Yeltsin came to town, the President of Russia, a democratically elected in a free election, certifiably free election, came to Russia. We stood in the Rose Garden, made a deal, signed an agreement in the White House to banish from the face of the Earth these tremendous intercontinental ballistic missiles known as the SS–18. If any one of you has followed this and if you'd have said 4 years ago or 2 or even a few months ago that we could have worked out a deal to eliminate these most destabilizing weapons, people would have looked at you and said you're nuts.

We worked that deal out. Every child in America can sleep more securely without the fear of nuclear war that generations that preceded it had. And the country is totally focusing on something else. I am convinced that when we go to the people in the fall, we will say this: We have made the world safer because of our leadership in world affairs. And the American people are going to respond.

Heinz Prechter introduced me to a friend of his tonight who is here from East Germany. With tears in his eyes, he said, "Thank you, Mr. President, for being a catalyst in reunification of the Germanys." This is major.

Looking to the Middle East, you have ancient enemies talking to each other, the one thing the Arabs, the one thing the Israelis wanted—to sit down opposite the table. And it was your country that brought this about.

When Saddam Hussein invaded a neighbor, it was the United States that took the lead. Now you have a lot of revisionists running around Washington, DC, telling us that something was noble—that something was wrong. And they are crazy. What we did is set back aggression, put together a coalition to lead, and today the United States is the undisputed leader of the world. That's something we can take to the American people. And the Baltics are free, and South America is moving almost entirely democratic. We have a lot to be grateful for.

Let me say this parenthetically: I am going to keep pushing to a successful conclusion of the GATT round, a successful conclusion of the North American free trade agreement because that means not only jobs for the United States, it means opportunity for other countries. Build their economies, and that'll help the world economy. And we're going to be free traders, not protectionists. That's the case I'm going to take to the American people.

So, I believe the record for world peace and democracy and freedom is clear. Out of focus right now in terms of people's attention, but I think in the final analysis people are going to say: To whom do you trust the national security of our great country? Who best to enhance the peace? Who best to fight for democracy and freedom? And I believe that will conclude that I am that person to lead the country for 4 years.

Now, people say to me, "Well, you were successful on Desert Storm; why can't you bring that same kind of leadership to the domestic scene? Good question. And the answer is, we must make the changes in the United States Congress to move our program through because our values are in accord with the values of the American people.

Let me just give you one or two areas

where I think we have a fantastic case to take to the American people. I have just come from a law enforcement meeting where we had sheriffs and police chiefs from all across the State. And I told them: Look, what we need is a strong anticrime legislation. We need to vary the exclusionary rule so that we don't have cases frivolously thrown out. We need to change habeas corpus so that we don't have appeal after appeal that deny the swiftness of the law. We need to be tougher on those who commit crimes against other people in terms of taking their life. And that means tightening up on the death penalty laws. We have had strong anticrime legislation before the United States Congress. The Democrats talk a good game, and they haven't even given us a vote on our crime package. The American people want to back our law enforcement communities because they know that strengthens neighborhoods and strengthens families. And I think we have a good case to take on that.

On the economy, though I believe the economy is moving, I still feel that what we ought to do is put incentives into the tax system. And that means a capital gains cut; that means an investment tax allowance; that means changing the IRA's; that means a first-time credit for homebuyers so the young American family has a shot at the American dream. And that is stymied, all of it, by the Democratic Congress.

We had a fight the other day on the balanced budget amendment. That's not going to solve all the problems. It's going to discipline the executive branch. It'll darn sure discipline the spend-and-spend Congress. We got almost two-thirds of the vote. Twelve Democrats who sponsored the resolution, sponsored the amendment, were taken to the woodshed by that liberal leadership of the House of Representatives, beaten over the head until they were a pulp, and they voted against their own amendment, and the amendment went down. We need to change the leadership in the United States Congress and give the Republicans a chance.

The Government is too big, and it spends too much. And we're trying to do something about it. I'd like to ask the American people this fall: Give me what 43 Governors

have, give me that line-item veto, and give me a shot at cutting down on this Federal spending. You hear a lot now about these. Every candidate is supposed to get the budget in balance and get the deficit down. We have a concrete proposal before the United States Congress right now that makes some tough decisions. It controls the growth of mandatory spending programs. You can't do it just through the discretionary program. And it's languishing there as the Congress sends down bill after bill to me to raise people's taxes and to increase spending. We've got a good case to take to the American people, and says: Give me more Congressmen that will vote to control those mandatory programs, and then we can get this deficit down.

Speaking of Government reform, I think the time has come to limit the terms for the Members of Congress. The President's terms is limited; let's try to limit the terms of the Members of Congress and see if we can't keep them closer to the American people.

A major area where we've got outstanding proposals and a pretty darned good record is on education. We have a program called America 2000. It crosses party lines. The first thing I did as President was to get the Governors together, Democrat and Republican alike, to set the national education goals. Party was laid aside. The goals were set. And now we have a program to implement those goals called America 2000 that literally revolutionizes American education and brings to K through 12 the same kind of quality education that we're known for at the college and university level. And it is languishing. Parts of it are languishing in the House of Representatives because it has to go to some old subcommittee chairman that's been there for a thousand years and hasn't had a new thought since the day he arrived. We've got to change the United States Congress.

And while we're at it, I think we ought to have choice in education at K through 12. I was a beneficiary of the GI bill when I got out of the Navy in 1945. And they didn't say to me: Hey, you can't go to Holy Cross or you can't go to a private school. You went to wherever you wanted to go to; the family made that choice. In this instance, the sailor made that choice, the Navy man made the choice. And it's helped our colleges.

And the same thing can happen if they can pass our "GI bill" for children that we came up with the other day. It gives the families a little shot in the arm, gives them a little voucher so they can then choose where their children go to school. And it will help those schools that are bypassed because to stay alive they're going to have to compete. And it's not going to diminish the public education system. If you don't believe me, go up to Milwaukee and talk where it's been tried. Or go to Minnesota where they've been in the lead on choice in education. Choice in education is what we want. Choice in child care is what we now have because of Republican principles. And I want to take this case to the American people in the fall.

I want to thank some Members of Congress. I don't want to be down on all of them because one of the only tools the President has, when he is outnumbered in the Congress and when he is asked to pass things that the people who elected him oppose, is the veto. And the veto score: Bush 30, Congress 0. And I am going to keep on vetoing this tax-and-spend legislation as it comes to the White House until we can get enough people to pass sensible legislation.

Now, we've got a good record to take to the American people. The ideas and the values that I believe we all stand for are intact. What we need is to get it in focus now for the American people. I might say, parenthetically, when we talk about family values, this is not some demagogic exercise. When the mayors of some of the largest cities and some small ones too, the National League of Cities, came to see me—and I mentioned this to the law enforcement people this afternoon—they said that the biggest concern they had, the biggest single focus on the problem, the cause of the problems in urban America was the decline in the American family. And they are absolutely correct. I am convinced that we must find ways to strengthen the family. When I talk about reform of the welfare system, I have in mind a little girl who saved over

$1,000. And the welfare people came to her, her mother on welfare, and said your mother's going off of welfare if you save money like this because you're not allowed to accumulate over $1,000. Change the welfare reform, reform the welfare system so that you can eliminate this kind of stupidity, and in the process, strengthen the family. And that's what we're going to try to do.

I heard one of the candidates for President ridiculing the fact that I have a session each year reading to children. Symbolic, yes. But what is the symbol? It is the idea that adults ought to read to their kids or that parents ought to read to their kids. And let the cynics who think everything can be legislated miss the point. The point is that when Barbara Bush holds an AIDS baby in her arms, she's demonstrating compassion. And when she or I read to kids, we're saying parents ought to do this. They ought to hold their families together and love them. And every kid ought to have that kind of opportunity. And that isn't cynical politics, that's what this country wants.

I'm just getting warmed up on you guys, I'll tell you, because I've only mentioned about four issues here where I think we are just exactly where the heartbeat of America is. But you couldn't tell it because of all the noise and the fury out there of Politics '92: endless polls, weird talk shows, crazy groups every Sunday telling you what you think, ninety-two percent of the news on the economy being negative when the economy grew, admittedly slowly, but grew at 2.7 in the first quarter. Ninety-two percent negative. What kind of reporting is that?

But the American people are smart. They're going to sort it out. They're going to separate fiction from fact. They're going to know reality when they see it. And I'm going to say this to them: I have worked my heart out as President of the United States. Barb and I have tried to uphold the dignity and the decency and honor that belongs in the White House. I need 4 more years, with a Republican Congress this time, to finish the job for the American people. And I ask you for your support. I promise you I'll work my heart out to that end.

Thank you, and may God bless you all. Thank you.

Note: The President spoke at 7:15 p.m. in the Mackinac Ballroom at the Westin Hotel. In his remarks, he referred to Randolph J. Agley, chairman, Michigan Republican Finance Committee; and Michael T. Timmis and Heinz Prechter, dinner cochairmen.

## Designation of John B. Waters as Chairman of the Board of Directors of the Tennessee Valley Authority
*June 29, 1992*

The President today designated John B. Waters, of Tennessee, as Chairman of the Board of Directors of the Tennessee Valley Authority. He would succeed Marvin T. Runyon.

Since 1984, Mr. Waters has served as a member of the Tennessee Valley Authority Board. From 1961 to 1984, he served with the law firm of Hailey, Waters & Sykes in Sevierville, TN.

Mr. Waters graduated from the University of Tennessee (B.S., 1952), and the University of Tennessee Law School (J.D., 1961). He served in the U.S. Navy from 1952 to 1955. He was born July 15, 1929, in Sevierville, TN. Mr. Waters is married, has two children, and resides in Sevierville, TN.

## Remarks and a Question-and-Answer Session With the Agriculture Communicators Congress
*June 30, 1992*

*The President.* Thank you for that welcome. And to those of you from outside the beltway, as we say, welcome to Washington on this humid day. This Herb Plambeck memorial get-together—[*laughter*]—some of you may know the dean down there, but it's always a pleasure to see him and see so many of you.

Let me just say a word about our Secretary of Agriculture. He came into this job with considerable experience in agriculture, both out in the field and then in Congress. In my view, he has done an outstanding job for American agriculture. Not only has he worked hard here domestically, the concerns of the farmers very much on his mind, but I can tell you from watching him in action he has done a superb job in terms of negotiating to try to achieve a successful conclusion to the Uruguay round of GATT. And I am very, very grateful to him.

I'm delighted to see Sara Wyant and Marsha Mauzey and Dave King and Taylor Brown. And once again, let me say welcome to all of you.

Before I get into the agricultural topics, I'd like to make a short statement that I hope will be of interest to all of you, indeed, to all Americans. This morning Ambassador Malcolm Toon briefed me on his trip last week to Russia. He went there to determine whether the American POW's or MIA's could possibly be alive there; went there, the full cooperation pledged by Boris Yeltsin before he left. His report makes clear that Boris Yeltsin stands by his pledge, providing us access to Russian officials and opening up the KGB archives. But Ambassador Toon also reports that his search has yet to uncover any evidence that American POW's or MIA's are currently being held in Russia.

As President, I take it to be an article of faith, a solemn covenant with those who serve this country: The United States will always make every possible effort, take every possible action to learn the fate of those taken prisoner or missing in action. Our aim remains a full accounting for every

POW and MIA, nothing less. I'm grateful to Malcolm Toon for pursuing this important mission. He's home now. He's left some people there, and we are going to try to get to the bottom of this so we can allay the concerns of every family who might possibly be involved.

At my instruction, Ambassador Toon will continue his work with the full support of the Russian Government, including an exhaustive search of the Soviet archives. And the government, this may interest you, has promised to make a definitive statement on this issue within the next few weeks. They are taking their role very seriously. And we're going to pursue every credible account of American POW's or MIA's held by the Soviet regime.

Now to the issue at hand, the matrix of this wonderful get-together. First, my thanks to all of you for the great job you do in keeping the farmers and the ranchers and the agribusiness owners not just well-informed but the best informed in the entire world. I know you have their respect and gratitude and certainly mine, too.

Democracy works because at its heart is one fundamental principle, freedom. Freedom is about human rights, self-determination, peace among nations. It's also about the free flow of ideas and information, and that's where your job comes in. That's why your work is so important not only to democracy and free enterprise but also to agriculture.

Thanks, in part, to the job that you do every single day, agriculture is America's number one industry. There are still a lot of people in this country that don't understand this, so let me repeat it: Agriculture is America's number one industry.

The news lately has been taken up with urban issues. But I want you to know that rural issues are equally important. And my growth agenda that I'm trying to get through the Congress will benefit all Americans. With lower capital gains taxes, investment tax credits, we call them the investment tax allowances, and health care reform, farmers are major beneficiaries of our economic growth agenda.

Our policies have, I think we'd all agree, kept interest rates low. So farm debt has gone down, while income has gone up. And

with our commonsense agricultural policy, we can secure a more prosperous future for farmers by expanding and hopefully creating a lot of new markets, both at home and abroad.

With a fourth of our production sold abroad, the world looks to the American farmer for its food and fiber needs. This year, that adds up to an expected $41 billion in exports, the second highest in history, and an $18 billion positive trade balance. And that's not all. These farm exports generate hundreds of thousands of jobs right here at home. Exports are a key to agriculture's continued strength and economic growth. That's why our economic plan, the one I am pushing with Congress, includes programs to actively promote these agricultural sectors. And that's why we're working to expand markets, open new ones on several fronts.

We're going to knock down trade barriers and ensure fair competition for American farmers in the world marketplace. The GATT and the NAFTA agreements are critical, and I will not let up on my commitment to either of them. I will continue to press our trading partners. A GATT agreement is clearly in everyone's best interest because it will increase economic growth worldwide. But while we work for an agreement, we are not going to forget to defend the interests of American farmers.

America's agricultural prosperity is tied to exports. And 95 percent of the world's population lives outside the United States of America, and global population growth is outpacing ours by 70 percent each year. We want to make sure that our farmers and ranchers are in a position to take advantage of the trade opportunities this growth offers by freeing farmers to make decisions based on market demands.

Export credits to Russia and other new nations of the old U.S.S.R., we call them the C.I.S., are opening the door to a vast and important market for our agricultural goods, one that holds incredible potential for our producers. As you know, our able Secretary, Ed Madigan, announced earlier that we would make $150 million in export credit guarantees available to Russia around July 1st and another $150 million around

August 1st. However, in response to President Yeltsin's request, we announced that both credit guarantee packages, a total of $300 million, will be available on or about July 1st. This completes the $600 million credit guarantee offer that I made to Russia back on April 1st. And it brings to $4.85 billion the value of CCC credit guaranteed by my administration, those guarantees made available to assist U.S. agricultural exports to the former U.S.S.R. since January of '91.

Now, these and other export programs are keeping American ag products competitive, and they are boosting export sales. In addition to the expanding exports, regulatory reform has got to be a key priority. Our regulatory changes put the farmer back in charge. And as the old saying goes, the best way to solve farm problems is to consult the hardest hands.

I am very pleased with the job that Vice President Quayle and the Competitiveness Council are doing to cut back on excessive regulation. We're not talking here just about ag; we're talking about all across the industrial spectrum. But they're doing a superb job on limiting and restricting regulation and trying to eliminate the excessive regulations.

Since I announced a moratorium on new regulations in the State of the Union Address, we have saved $15 billion to $20 billion in the cost of excessive redtape. And this is just a downpayment on things to come. Our regulatory relief initiative is based on commonsense principles: putting the individual back in charge, creating jobs for Americans, and protecting property rights for all. That's guaranteed under the Constitution.

My commitment to developing alternative markets is equally strong. Technological advances have opened the way to create a new industrial feedstock for America, one derived from agricultural commodities that will give consumers products that are safer for the environment.

Ed Madigan shares my vision of tapping into this commercial potential, and we're seeing real success. In my home State of Texas, a group of imaginative entrepreneurs plan to make newsprint from a crop called kenaf. And in Nebraska, another group is making comforters and pillows out of milkweed floss, milkweed floss, you heard me correctly. In Illinois, Ed's home State, they plan to produce biodegradable plastics from farm products. Ed was over here, for all of you ardent golfers, showing me some golf tees made out of corn. I don't know that they'll help, but I'll try anything—[laughter]—so if I can get them back—

Then, of course, one subject that I know is on the minds of everybody, that's ethanol, a great American success story that is now the single largest industrial use of corn. And the Clean Air Act that I signed into law does provide new opportunities for ethanol. Let me say it straight out in plain English: I support ethanol. And I believe it must become a major player in the fuel market.

The oxygenated fuels program created by that clean air law will be up and running this fall. We want to make sure that ethanol is competitive in the reformulated gasoline program. To encourage ethanol use, I am today announcing my support for an amendment which makes the gas tax exemption for ethanol proportional to the amount of ethanol used in gasoline. This will allow ethanol blends to compete with other additives. The bottom line is less carbon monoxide for American citizens and more sales for American farmers.

You know, Americans are doers. With their hard work and determination to get the job done, they accomplish great things as long as the Government does not get in the way. I've said it before, and let me just say it here again today: It's America's entrepreneurs, men and women of faith and vision and imagination like our farmers, who create our Nation's wealth. So get Government out of their way and on their side, and you'll see that there's no limit to what they can do for this country.

I am convinced that one of the best things we can do for American agriculture is to bring these two trade agreements to a successful conclusion. If you want to see a growth in American agriculture, please do whatever you can when we get an agreement to help get it through the Congress. We're not going to take agreements up there that are bad. But I believe what I've said about American agriculture and about entrepreneurship. I just want you to know we're going to work right down to the wire to get these two agreements done.

Now, with no further ado, I understand it's in order to take a few questions. And I don't know how it's been arranged, but I'm sure Ed has thought out—maybe you just hold up your hand and yell. Oh, we've got a microphone over here.

*Q.* Mr. President, first of all, you may not be aware but we invited the other Presidential candidates to come and speak to us. You were the only one that could find time to do so, and we appreciate it very much.

*The President.* Hey.

*Q.* Having said that, I want to tell you that Farm Journal magazine is fortunate to have a number of editors located, we call it field editors, in different parts of the country. And they regularly attend many meetings with farmers and ranchers. And they report to us that farmers and ranchers really seem to identify with the un-candidate, Mr. Perot. Mr. President, can you tell us why farmers and ranchers should vote for you instead of Ross Perot or Governor Clinton?

*The President.* Well, I can tell you why I think they should vote for me, and let others sort out—because I'm not in what they call a campaign mode yet. I can't wait to get started actually—[*laughter*]—and that will be after the Republican Convention in the middle of August. What I've tried to do is get things done for this country. I've tried to stay out as much as possible, and I'll admit I'm not totally pure on this, of the political fray. And for about 6 months I've been pounded by both of them, plus several others that dropped out along the way. So I understand politics. I understand how the attack politics works. But I will be ready. I've never felt more fit, and I've never felt more up for a fight.

But what we're trying to do, and why I think farmers in the final analysis will be with me, is to put less emphasis on these government interventions into agriculture, trying to conclude successfully two trade agreements that will expand markets. I think we've handled the programs that are on the books now, I hope, with fairness. I am thinking of the export programs, things of that nature. I think the agricultural econ-

omy, though it could be better in certain sectors, is doing reasonably well, I think in some categories doing quite well. I think that farmers recognize that private sector initiatives are very important, and I hope they know that.

I don't think every farmer makes up his mind just on agricultural issues. I think minor details like world peace mean something to farmers and the fact that their kids go to bed at night with less fear of nuclear war. In the final analysis, I think that's something that will inure to the benefit of those I'm running with in the fall. I think we've done a good job in facilitating these dramatic changes around the world.

Where I feel a certain frustration is in my inability to get certain things passed through Congress. I happen to believe, as I said in my remarks, that a capital gains tax is very, very important for farmers. I think farmers identify with that. And the others are kind of all around on the field on this.

So I think things like that and the investment tax allowance, the first-time credit for homebuyers, that $5,000 credit, even though they're not just ag policy, are things that farmers' families can identify with.

Lastly, I'd like to take my case to the American people on what we call farmly values—family values—[*laughter*]—not in a contentious sense. But you see, Barbara and I both believe that family, the strength of the American family, is absolutely vital to where we're going to be as a country in the future. That means I am reviewing, as President, things like the welfare system to see how we can reform it to keep families together and not have some idiotic redtape keeping them apart.

So I would appeal to farmers not just on ag issues, where I think we've got a good record with good people managing the account, but on a broad array of philosophical questions that I think we agree with. I would again cite the world peace as something that is very important. You can't find it talked about. I see no media mention of it.

We entered into—you asked me what time it is, and I'm telling you how to build a watch here. [*Laughter*] But we had Boris Yeltsin here the other day. And I think of my times campaigning in Iowa years ago and how Iowa has kind of—I single out Iowa, but it's kind of an internationalist State in a sense, a great interest in all these things. We had Yeltsin standing here in the Rose Garden, and we entered into a deal to eliminate the biggest and the most threatening intercontinental ballistic missiles, the SS–18's of the Soviet Union. And it was almost "Ho-hum, what have you done for me recently?" This is major. This affects every family in agricultural or urban America, and it is significant.

I think that I will be taking the case to the American people, again, not just on these ag issues that I've talked about in my remarks but on a broad array of issues, and hoping, and I believe properly, that the economy, which has been stagnant and dull, will be vastly improved. And I point to the growth of the first quarter, 2.7 percent growth, and yet the American people feel, by over 60 percent, that things are getting worse in terms of the economy.

There is a gap between reality and perception. And part of my job when I do get into a campaign mode is to try to close that gap and be sure that we are judged on reality, not on these erroneous perceptions that are being portrayed in the political process. Did you get it?

*Q.* Thank you.

*The President.* All right. Who's next? I apologize for going on so long, but I'm practicing for when I do get in a political mode. [*Laughter*]

*Q.* You talked about rural activities a little bit, a while ago, and I would like to ask you to possibly elaborate, if you could. You know as well as I do in Texas, lots of rural area there in the farming and ranching industry, and it seems to be drying up, not only in Texas but in other parts of the United States. There's a lot of concerns, crop failures, environmental pressures, and health care needs in smaller communities. Can you kind of outline for us, if you can, what you plan on doing?

*The President.* Health care, we have the best, and I say this with appropriate modesty, the best health care reform proposal. It will have appeals in rural America because what it says is: We reject nationalized health care. We reject socialized medicine.

We are determined to preserve the quality of American health care. And the way to do it is to go through with this program that we now have defined up there that has a hallmark of it: Access for those people who do not have insurance.

It also has ways to revise and change the costs, the ever-escalating costs in health care. One of the things, a fundamental tenet, again, that I would like to see us get through Congress, but it is blocked by the trial lawyers, is this concept that we care for each other too little and sue each other too much. We want to change these liability, put some caps on some of this liability so we don't have these malicious lawsuits driving obstetricians out of business, for example. We've got a good health care program that I think will benefit rural America as well as urban America.

We're working very closely with Congressman Coleman on how we can better attract other jobs and opportunities to some areas in rural America that have been bypassed, more people in some concentrated areas leaving the farm.

I think the best thing that we can do is to guarantee that this overall economy recover. And as I say, it's growing. It's not growing near as robustly as I'd like to see it growing. But if we can pass the capital gains cut, the investment tax allowance, the first-time homebuyers tax credit—and that's something that would be good for rural America, I might add—I believe we can stimulate the economy without making the deficit worse.

I will take to the rural America as well as urban America my advocacy of and defense of a balanced budget amendment. It is time to discipline not just Congress; this will discipline every budgeteer in the executive branch, the branch I head. And we need it. And 80 percent of the American people want it. Twelve of the sponsors of the balanced budget amendment that favored it were beaten to their knees by the Democratic leadership who said, "Well, you've got to change your minds"—12 of the sponsors of it. And we lost by a handful of votes; almost got two-thirds in the Congress.

So I think there's some specific things that will appeal. But I also think there's some broader macroeconomic things that will appeal.

*Q.* We note that you held the line, although it was an unpopular line among some in the press, recently at the Earth summit in Rio on the balance between the environment and the business interests here in the United States. We wonder if this is something we may see more of in the future in your stance toward the wetlands and the endangered species policies here in the United States? And also, I wondered what will be your position in clarifying the roles of the agencies in coordinating wetlands policy?

*The President.* Well, first place, thank you for your comments about Rio. That's the first nice thing I've heard. My definition of leadership is not going out and just signing onto a piece of paper that—it doesn't matter how many other countries give it. We're the United States. We have the best record on the environment of any country, literally. You lay down the records, certainly the very best.

So I was not playing defense down there in Rio. I was simply saying, if you really want to help on medicines or if you really want to help on other aspects of biodiversity, don't enter into a treaty that fails to protect America's property rights, fails to protect those to whom the world is looking for scientific advancement and technological advancement.

So I'm quite sure that we were correct in that position. And we did not enter into a global climate change treaty that is going to increase the cost to this country. Let me tell you the figure: We have spent $800 billion on environment, $800 billion, this is private, obviously, as well as government, in the last 10 years. The estimate is $1.2 trillion in the next 10 years, and we are leading the world in this.

On terms of the wetlands, I had hoped that we could get the wetlands reserve program going fully forward. I believe it's a good answer. And I announced in California—I was just trying to get the date; anyway, it was last month sometime—the implementation of the wetlands reserve program. Now we've got to go and get it funded by the Congress. If funded, it will restore a million acres of wetlands without

imposing a burden on the farmers.

It is my view that on these decisions you ought to take in market force. I don't like takings. The recent Supreme Court decision, I think, was a decision the right way. Some guy goes and buys some property, and he's told he can't use it. Now, that isn't the American system.

I think we've got to move the manual out, and we're trying to move forward as quickly as possible on that. I think for a while it looked like we were too far over between the Corps and EPA on the regulatory side, and I hope that the steps we've taken recently have corrected that. But I guess the answer is to try to balance all of these interests.

You mentioned the endangered species. We had a decision coming out of the Interior Department the other day where I caught hell on both sides; therefore I figured we did something right. [*Laughter*] We got it from the extremes in the environmental movement, and then some developers thought we should have protected 30,000 logging jobs instead of 15,000. It is a very complicated problem. We've got to enforce the endangered species law. But when it comes to interpretation I also, and I told them this when we made this decision, I've got to have some responsibility for the American family, for people that are trying to make a living in a tough economic time.

I know that I will be—as we move into the political year, they will get on me because the extreme environmentalists are not happy. But I maintain in wetlands no net loss. It's a good policy. I think we can implement it so that it does not do damage to the American farmer. But we are going to be taking a strong environmental record to the American people; one that I'm proud of. And yet I recognize, hey, we're going to get it from both sides.

*Q.* Mr. President, I'm told——

*The President.* I forgot to tell you that I've got a radical view of wetlands. I think wetlands ought to be wet. [*Laughter*] I think you know what I mean. We had one example of a city block, I mean, they were trying to build a parking garage or something. Some guy came along and out of some weird interpretation claimed it was a wetland. So I think we've got to be wary of the extremes.

Yes, sir.

*Q.* Mr. President, I'm told that we only have time for one question. So before I ask it, I'd like to thank you, on behalf of the group, for coming today. The question is this: There's a perception in the country- side, reflected somewhat in Congress, that our wheat exports for the last few weeks or months have about ground to a halt because of the lack of EEP subsidy announcements and allocations by the Government; percep- tion that Secretary Madigan is doing his best, USDA is trying, but that Secretary Baker, Brent Scowcroft at the NSC are stop- ping it. My question to you, Mr. President: Is foreign policy going to dictate agricultur- al policy, or can you let Madigan be Mad- igan?

*The President.* Well, we can let Madigan be—almost be Madigan. [*Laughter*] The reason I say that is the farmer has no better friend. But what happens here when we get down into final negotiations on the GATT round, for example, I turn to Ed. And I said, "Now look, I have said I am not going to bring a GATT agreement to the Con- gress where the farmers can't support it." You know and I know that no matter what agreement we get, there may well be one farm group or another that says they don't like it. But I'm talking about an agreement that has broad support in agricultural Amer- ica. And so Ed will say, "Here's what we can do." We have not departed. We have not pushed him—and you can let him, after I'm out of here, he can correct me if he wants to—have not pushed him beyond what he thinks is in the best interest of the American farmer.

Now, in terms of emphasis, in terms of timing, as we come down to the wire on the NAFTA or on the Uruguay round, there are some times when you have to try through open and honest diplomacy to get the agreement. And if that means you don't slap somebody the first instance you have a chance with a fine or with some action that retaliates, okay, that's the way it is. I've got to keep in mind the big picture because I know that a successful conclusion to the GATT round is in the interest of the Ameri- can people.

I believe we have rather fully used the EEP.

*Secretary Madigan.* Eight hundred mil- lion dollars so far this year.

*The President.* Eight hundred million dol- lars so far this year. And I salute the Secre- tary for this. And obviously, I wish you had been with me, sir, when I was in Australia. They were on me about that—"How can you treat a friend"—I said, look, this is the law. This is what we should and must do, is to use those provisions of the law to en- hance our agricultural exports. And it's not aimed at you, Mr. Australian Foreign Minis- ter or whoever it was that was all over my case down there. It is the law of the land.

And incidentally, on EEP we are quite selective, and we don't try to bludgeon our friends. It wasn't passed for that end, as everybody here knows. So I think we've been fair in the application. I can't concede that sometimes timing is affected, a brand- new announcement of a protection or an encouragement to domestic agriculture item is held back for a few days. But I think we faithfully implemented the law.

I might add something on that. I hope it doesn't sound too defensive. I see a lot of revisionists talking about Iraq now. We did try through using agricultural credits to en- courage Saddam Hussein to join the family of nations. I remember a lot of support in agricultural America at the time. Now, a lot of people that opposed me on Desert Storm have a kind of revisionistic view of things, and they're trying to make it that this was wrong and that this gave him the funds to buy bombs or something of that nature. It isn't. The policy did not work, and we did what we had to do to stand up against ag- gression.

But here was a case where ag credits were caught up in a scene. Now people are trying to say those ag credits were the reason, you know, gave him the wherewith- al to take over a neighboring country, and I don't believe it. I don't believe it. I think we properly used these credits for what they were designed to do. I think it's been beneficial to American agriculture, and I'm going to continue to use them in a way that's beneficial to American agriculture with the national security interests of the

United States foremost in my mind.

So I can't say it's been perfect, but I do think that the Department and, I hope, the White House has done a good job in the implementation of the law and in the using of these credits. I can tell you that what I really would rejoice in, and what I will rejoice in, is when we get this GATT agreement closed and get it finalized and let the American farmer compete with others on a level playing field all around the world. And that is the final and best answer to your very penetrating question about the use of the EEP.

Thank you all very, very much.

*Note: The President spoke at 1:31 p.m. at the Department of Agriculture. In his remarks, he referred to Herb Plambeck and William Taylor Brown, former president and president, National Association of Farm Broadcasters; Sara Wyant Lutz, president, American Agricultural Editors Association; Marsha Mauzey, president, Agricultural Relations Council; and David King, president, Agricultural Communicators in Education.*

## Remarks on the Superconducting Super Collider
*June 30, 1992*

*The President.* Look, this meeting is about the super collider. And I just want to thank these most distinguished scientists for taking the strong scientific case up to Capitol Hill in support of this project. It is important not just for national pride; it's important to science generally that this be fully funded and that we stay out front, working, of course, with international partners the best we can, but that we remain out front. And I'm anxious to hear from you how you feel, sir, your testimony went. And thank you very much for going up there to the Senate. We've got to get in the Senate and get approved that which we failed to do in the House.

*Dr. Schwitters.* I think we had a chance to make the case for the SSC. We talked about the long-term value and need in the science and then the value of doing this kind of research for the country. We had a

few critical questions, but I think that the team answered them well because we do have good answers.

*The President.* Well, what we've got to do is get it restored in the conference and get this under control. We're fighting for it, and we are committed to it. We have a handful of these major scientific projects that need support, even though we've got tough budgetary conditions. This is no time to cut the funding for this project. We will fight with you for it.

*Dr. Schwitters.* Thank you very much. We really appreciate that.

*Note: The President spoke at 4:10 p.m. in the Roosevelt Room at the White House, during at a meeting with Government and private-sector scientists. Roy Schwitters was Director of the Superconducting Super Collider Laboratory in Waxahachie, TX.*

## Letter to Congressional Leaders Reporting on the Cyprus Conflict
*June 30, 1992*

*Dear Mr. Speaker:    (Dear Mr. Chairman:)*

In accordance with Public Law 95–384 (22 U.S.C. 2373(c)), I am submitting to you this bimonthly report on progress toward a

negotiated settlement of the Cyprus question. This report covers the last 21 days of March, all of April, and the first 15 days of May, 1992.

In mid-March, U.S. Special Cyprus Coordinator Nelson Ledsky traveled to the Eastern Mediterranean to see if he could clear up what Turkish officials had described as a "misunderstanding" on the part of U.N. negotiators, and thus get the U.N.-sponsored negotiating process restarted. He remained in the area for 10 days, during which time he consulted directly with President Vassiliou of Cyprus and Turkish Cypriot leader Mr. Rauf Denktash, as well as the Prime Ministers of Turkey and Greece. All of his conversation partners signalled their willingness—indeed, desire—to see a new round of U.N.-led negotiations begin.

On March 25, on the occasion of Greek National Day, I publicly restated the U.S. commitment to serve as a catalyst for the U.N. Cyprus effort. Two days later, President Vassiliou arrived in New York and met with the U.N. Secretary General. After additional meetings in New York, including consultations with the representatives of the permanent members of the U.N. Security Council, President Vassiliou visited several Greek- and Cypriot-American communities around the United States. I saw him in Washington on March 30 and reassured him of the commitment of the United States Government to do all it could to assist the U.N. to bring the Cyprus negotiations to an early, successful conclusion. On March 31 and April 1, the Cypriot leader had a number of meetings with individual Members of Congress and with congressional groups and committees and made a number of public appearances.

Mr. Denktash arrived in New York on March 30 for separate consultations with the U.N. Secretary General. Ambassador Ledsky also met with Mr. Denktash in New York on April 3.

Also on April 3, the U.N. Secretary General signed a lengthy report to the U.N. Security Council on his good offices mission in Cyprus (a copy attached). The Secretary General reported on the status of the negotiations and included some paragraphs describing the contents of the "set of ideas" on Cyprus as they then stood and on developments relating to the U.N. Force in Cyprus (UNFICYP). In the section on conclusions and recommendations, he decried the lack of progress since the summer of 1991 and asked the U.N. Security Council to actively support another determined effort on Cyprus that he was prepared to undertake, and to work directly with him and his representatives and all concerned to achieve a fair, permanent, and peaceful solution to the problem.

The Security Council responded on April 10 with Security Council Resolution 750 (a copy also attached), which commended the efforts of the Secretary General, reaffirmed the U.N.'s "good office mandate," endorsed the Secretary General's report of April 3, specifically his description of the "set of ideas," and asked the Secretary General to pursue intensive efforts during May and June to complete the "set of ideas" and submit a further report to the Security Council by July 1992. During this period, the Security Council also decided to "remain seized of the Cyprus question on an ongoing and direct basis."

During the 2 weeks that followed April 10, the Greek and Turkish Governments and the leadership of the Turkish Cypriot community in Cyprus accepted the Secretary General's "set of ideas" as the basis for further negotiations. After some internal debate, President Vassiliou sent a letter to the Secretary General outlining general Greek Cypriot agreement as well. On the basis of all these assurances, the U.N. Secretary General wrote to each of the parties again and sent his negotiators back to the area on May 8. Prior to their departure from New York, the U.N. negotiators briefed members of the Security Council on their plans.

In Cyprus, the negotiators met separately with Mr. Denktash and President Vassiliou from May 8 through May 12. The Nicosia meetings were followed by consultations in Ankara and Athens with the Prime Ministers and other officials of the Turkish and Greek Governments. These talks lasted through May 15. The U.N. negotiators briefed ambassadors of the permanent members of the Security Council at meetings hosted by Ambassador Lamb in Nicosia on May 11 and 18.

On the completion of this round of discussions, the negotiators, seemingly satisfied with the results, returned to New York to prepare a report for the Secretary General on the status of the negotiating effort. Based on this report the Secretary Géneral will decide on his next steps.

I remain convinced that the Secretary General's "set of ideas" provide a sound basis for further negotiations and eventual agreement. The United States Government and the U.N. Secretary General have received assurances from all parties that they also accept the "set of ideas" as the basis for

further work and that they will make a good faith effort to bring this process to a successful conclusion. I continue to believe that a negotiated solution can be reached.

Sincerely,

GEORGE BUSH

*Note: Identical letters were sent to Thomas S. Foley, Speaker of the House of Representatives, and Claiborne Pell, chairman of the Senate Committee on Foreign Relations.*

## Presidential Determination No. 92–35—Memorandum on the Extension of the Indonesia-U.S. Nuclear Energy Cooperation Agreement
*June 30, 1992*

*Memorandum for the Secretary of State, the Secretary of Energy*

*Subject:* Determination on Extending the Agreement for Cooperation Between the United States of America and the Republic of Indonesia Concerning Peaceful Uses of Nuclear Energy

I have considered the proposed agreement to extend for a period of 10 years the Agreement for Cooperation Between the United States of America and the Republic of Indonesia Concerning Peaceful Uses of Nuclear Energy, signed at Washington June 30, 1980, along with the views, recommen-

dations, and statements of the interested agencies.

I have determined that the performance of the agreement for an additional period of 10 years will promote, and will not constitute an unreasonable risk to, the common defense and security. Pursuant to section 123 b. of the Atomic Energy Act of 1954, as amended (42 U.S.C. 2153 (b)), I hereby approve the proposed agreement on extension and authorize its execution.

GEORGE BUSH

[*Filed with the Office of the Federal Register, 10:17 a.m., July 27, 1992*]

## Statement on Action Against Health Care Fraud
*June 30, 1992*

The Federal Government took another major step today to protect our citizens against a type of crime which victimizes all Americans, health care fraud.

More than 1,000 Federal agents and 120 other law enforcement officers carried out early morning raids in over 50 cities nationwide as part of Operation Goldpill, and we expect charges against some 200 individuals, corporations, and pharmacies. The tar-

gets of this unprecedented crackdown are pharmacists, other health care professionals, and prescription drug distributors who are charged with carrying out widespread fraud through excessive billings and the illegal diversion, repackaging, and distribution of prescription medicine.

These people are charged with betraying a sacred trust to their patients. These frauds result in the loss of billions from the pockets of every American who pays taxes and health insurance premiums. These crimes also pose potentially grave health hazards to patients.

The Government also has a sacred trust to protect all Americans. Health care and health care fraud have long been enforcement priorities for the Justice Department and Department of Health and Human Services. Let those medical professionals and others who prey on the public take heed: This is only phase one of Operation Goldpill. The FBI and other enforcement agencies working with them are using every law enforcement tool in our arsenal against these serious crimes, including undercover agents.

I wish to take this opportunity to congratulate Attorney General Barr, Health and Human Services Secretary Sullivan, the FBI, and the HHS Office of Inspector General for this outstanding example of the nationally coordinated effort. I look forward to the continued results of Operation Goldpill.

# Statement on the Balanced Budget Amendment
*June 30, 1992*

I call upon the Senate today to cut through the procedural obstacles and pass a balanced budget constitutional amendment.

Americans overwhelmingly support a constitutional amendment requiring a balanced Federal budget, and for good reason. The debt we accumulate today jeopardizes sustained economic growth and will burden our descendants for generations to come. A balanced budget amendment would help to provide the necessary discipline to our Government, both the legislative and executive branches, to make the difficult budget decisions.

Although the House of Representatives earlier this month voted overwhelmingly in favor of a balanced budget amendment, we fell just nine short of the necessary two-thirds majority of House Members voting. I strongly believe that that House vote should not be the end of the line. Senate passage now of the balanced budget amendment would provide an opportunity for the House to reconsider its earlier close vote and, once and for all, move to put in place the fiscal discipline the American people demand.

# Statement by Press Secretary Fitzwater on the President's Meeting With Foreign Minister Klaus Kinkel of Germany
*June 30, 1992*

The President met for approximately one-half hour in the Oval Office today with Klaus Kinkel, the Foreign Minister of Germany. This was the Foreign Minister's first meeting with the President. Their discussions were devoted mainly to U.S.-German relations, NATO, and the GATT round. The President underscored his belief in the importance of NATO and the U.S. presence in Europe to preserving our common security interests. He also expressed his hope for progress on the current round of the GATT negotiations.

## Appointment of Mark A. Guzzetta as Federal Representative to the Sabine River Compact Administration
*June 30, 1992*

The President today announced his intention to appoint Mark A. Guzzetta, of Florida, to be Federal Representative of the United States on the Sabine River Compact Administration. He would succeed James B. Furrh, Jr.

Since 1982, Mr. Guzzetta has served as founder and president of the Water Re-

sources Corp. in Boca Raton, FL. He has also served in several positions with the Hayward Tyler Pump Co. in Norwalk, CT, including contract manager, 1977–79, and southeast regional sales manager, 1979–81.

Mr. Guzzetta currently resides in Boca Raton, FL.

## Remarks Following Discussions With Prime Minister Kiichi Miyazawa of Japan
*July 1, 1992*

Mr. Prime Minister, to you and to the other members of the Japanese delegation, it is a real pleasure to have you back here at the White House.

We've had a very successful discussion inside, one that reaffirms the importance of the strong relationship between our two nations. We discussed, of course, our global partnership. We reviewed the prospects for the meeting that we're both attending, next week's G–7 summit in Munich.

First on our agenda was our mutual commitment to global peace and prosperity. I'm encouraged by what the Prime Minister told me about Japan's plans to stimulate economic growth. I had a chance to fill him in on ours. Both of us confirmed our desire for a strong and lasting recovery, and we also discussed the Uruguay round and the necessity of redoubling our efforts to increase global prosperity. This will directly benefit both the people of the United States and Japan, and we both want to see a successful conclusion of that round.

I also told the Prime Minister that I welcome the passage of Japan's peace cooperation bill. That will allow Japan to participate actively in building a lasting peace in Cambodia and in other world trouble spots. We agreed to cooperate on other regional threats and problems from nuclear and missile proliferation concerns in North Korea

to the resolution of the POW/MIA issue with Vietnam.

We talked about how at Munich we can assist in assuring the safety of nuclear power in the former Soviet Union. We reaffirmed full United States support for Japan's position on the Northern Territories.

Finally, I assured the Prime Minister of the importance of Asia to the United States, of our resolve to maintain our forward military presence in the Pacific and our appreciation for Japan's host nation support.

We've made progress in resolving some of the differences between us, particularly with regard to our trade relationship. Over the past 6 months, we've reached significant agreements to improve American industries' access to Japan's $9 billion computer market, to their $27 billion paper markets. These agreements are very good news to the American worker.

Still, I feel we have more to do. And, Mr. Prime Minister, I want to mention our continued interest in access to your markets for automobiles and auto parts, semiconductors, as well as cooperation on the super collider and striking down structural impediments to freer trade.

We'll track our progress on every item identified by our action plan. And sir, you can be assured we will do our part to improve our own competitiveness.

I've made it clear, and I'll continue to make it clear, that this administration and the American people are absolutely committed to trade that is both free and fair. Protectionism simply is not the answer. The record is clear. Our efforts the past 3 years have substantially increased American exports to Japan. And I will work to support the efforts of America's private sector to create an export vision to open foreign markets that mean more American jobs.

So we need to continue expanding, not closing, our trade relations. And whether it's protectionist measures in this country or in Japan, the result is the same thing. Protectionism punches a hole in a healthy economy.

So I'm confident that the Prime Minister and I depart here today knowing that we do not help our respective nations by hurting each other. He stood for that principle for a long, long time in various positions that he's held in Japan. I hope that I stand for that principle.

As important as our economic interaction is, I think it's also important for us to remember that America and Japan share three very important values: our support for the free market economic system, our love of political democracy, and our mutual interest in global peace and security. I am optimistic that our two nations can work closely to advance and protect these values in the Pacific Rim and elsewhere across the globe. And when these values are threatened, it's critical that our two nations unite. Our unity will be vital if these three key values are to survive and prosper in the new world that we see.

So let me say, Mr. Prime Minister, that I believe that this new period in world affairs holds great promise for the American-Japanese relationship. And once again, it is an honor to host you here in Washington to reaffirm our partnership, the respect and trust between our people, and to welcome you as a friend.

Thank you, sir.

*Note: The President spoke at 4:31 p.m. in the Rose Garden at the White House.*

# Message on the Observance of Independence Day
## *July 1, 1992*

As we Americans celebrate this 216th anniversary of our Nation's independence, we give thanks not only for our enduring heritage of liberty under law but also for the continuing expansion of democratic ideals around the globe. Blessed with an unbroken legacy of freedom and with unparalleled peace and prosperity, the United States stands today as a testament to the wisdom of its Founders—and as a model to all those peoples who aspire to systems of representative democracy and free enterprise. More than 200 years after our Declaration of Independence was signed, we know that no political creed his proved more just or powerful than the belief "that all men are created equal, that they are endowed by their Creator with certain unalienable Rights, that among these are Life, Liberty, and the Pursuit of Happiness."

On this occasion, however, we are also mindful that America's freedom and security were not always readily taken for granted. When our Nation's Founders sought "separate and equal station" for this country and proclaimed the American colonies free and independent States, they did so without the assurance of success. Ahead of them lay an uncertain future, and each understood the great risk that he and his compatriots were taking by signing the Declaration of Independence. Today, we can imagine the sense of trepidation that passed in the Signers' hearts as they pledged in support of that document their lives, their fortunes, and their sacred honor.

Yet, with a hope that was stronger than any fear and with a courage worthy of their great convictions, our ancestors launched a revolution of ideas that has continued to sweep the world. Independence Day is, therefore, a time of tremendous pride and inspiration for all Americans.

This year, we have added cause for celebration as Independence Day coincides with the 500th anniversary of Christopher Columbus's first journey to the Americas. The Columbus Quincentenary likewise recalls courage in the face of the unknown, and as we look to the future of the United States, we are heartened by the example and the achievements of the many pioneers and patriots who have gone before us. The continued preservation of our freedom will require no less industry and resolve on our part, and on this occasion, I offer a special salute to American service members everywhere, who are helping to chart they way to a safer, more peaceful world.

Barbara joins me in sending best wishes to our fellow Americans for a safe and enjoyable Independence Day.

GEORGE BUSH

## Message to the Congress Transmitting the Report of the Federal Labor Relations Authority
*July 1, 1992*

*To the Congress of the United States:*

In accordance with section 701 of the Civil Service Reform Act of 1978 (Public Law 95–454; 5 U.S.C. 7104(e)), I have the pleasure of transmitting to you the Thirteenth Annual Report of the Federal Labor Relations Authority for Fiscal Year 1991.

GEORGE BUSH

The White House,
July 1, 1992.

## Statement on Maryland Welfare Reform
*July 1, 1992*

I am pleased that my administration has approved Maryland's request for welfare waivers. This will allow Maryland to put in place a new system of incentives for welfare recipients to make sure their children receive necessary health care and attend school.

Pregnant women receiving welfare would be required to obtain regular prenatal care or not receive a special additional allowance. Families with young children receiving welfare would be required to obtain preventive health care for their children. This prenatal and preventive health care is available without cost to these families through the Medicaid program.

Maryland's reforms also create incentives for parents to make sure their children attend school. Welfare parents who behave responsibly and fulfill these requirements would receive higher payments than those who fail to see to the health care and education of their children.

While some are talking about welfare reform, we are helping to make it happen. Reform is taking place from the bottom up, with the States constructively serving as laboratories of democracy. My administration will continue to work with Maryland and other States in reforming our welfare system.

## Statement by Press Secretary Fitzwater on Congressional Findings on the President's Involvement in the Alleged Paris Meetings
*July 1, 1992*

We are glad that Congress, in a bipartisan report, concluded today what we knew all along: that President Bush had no involvement with any alleged meetings in Paris in October 1980, and in fact, he never left the country at that time.

*Note: The statement referred to the interim report, approved June 30, of the House Committee on Foreign Affairs Task Force To Investigate Certain Allegations Concerning the Holding of American Hostages by Iran in 1980.*

## Nomination of Robert E. Martinez To Be Associate Deputy Secretary of Transportation
*July 1, 1992*

The President today announced his intention to nominate Robert E. Martinez, of New Jersey, to be Associate Deputy Secretary of Transportation. He would succeed Robert L. Pettit.

Since 1990, Dr. Martinez has served as Deputy Administrator for the Maritime Administration at the Department of Transportation. He has also served as assistant executive director of the Business Roundtable in New York City, 1984–90; and as an associate consultant with Multinational Strategies, Inc., in New York City, 1983–84.

Dr. Martinez graduated from Columbia University (B.A., 1977) and Yale University (M.A., 1979; Ph.D., 1984). He was born May 22, 1955, in Havana, Cuba. Dr. Martinez is married, has one child, and resides in Arlington, VA.

## Appointment of Carroll E. Multz as Commissioner on the Upper Colorado River Commission
*July 1, 1992*

The President today announced his intention to appoint Carroll E. Multz, of Colorado, to be U.S. Commissioner on the Upper Colorado River Commission. He would succeed J.F. Ross.

Since 1985, Mr. Multz has served as a shareholder and member of the board of directors of the law firm of Carroll E. Multz, P.C., in Grand Junction, CO, and a partner with the law firm of McMichael, Benedict and Multz, 1987 to the present and served as a shareholder and member of the board of directors with the law firm of LaCroix, Achziger, Multz and Croker, P.C., 1981–85. He has also served as District Attorney for the Fourteenth Judicial District, CO, 1974–81, and a partner with the law firm of Multz, Riggs and Sandler, 1972–74.

Mr. Multz graduated from the University of Montana (B.S., 1958; J.D., 1961). He was born August 16, 1936, in Helena, MT. Mr. Multz is married, has two children, and resides in Grand Junction, CO.

## Remarks at a Meeting With the House Republican Conference on Health Care and an Exchange With Reporters
*July 2, 1992*

*The President.* Today I am sending to Congress the fourth piece of our comprehensive health care reform package, medical malpractice reform. Senate Republicans led by Bob Dole and John Chafee introduced a bill last November that includes many key elements similar to those in my plan. Here in the House, Republican Members led by Bob Michel and Newt Gingrich have recently finished months of work on a package that is very close to my own proposals, and we've been working intensively with the House Republican task force to hammer out differences.

We discussed the issue just now in our meeting, touched on it in our meeting with all House Republicans. And we now have legislation we can support and that represents a broad basis for agreement with all Republicans in the House and Senate. A Republican health care package is ready to be passed now. It should be passed now. And it will make a difference in the quality and in the availability of health care and in the growth of our economy. Our proposal: It helps small businesses pool together to offer their employees affordable health insurance. It lets the self-employed deduct 100 percent of their health insurance premiums from their taxes. It makes it possible for workers to change jobs without the fear of losing their health insurance. And it curbs the runaway costs of medical malpractice litigation.

Just as important, our proposal does not saddle our businesses and workers with costly new mandates or taxes or allow Federal bureaucracies to regulate prices and to ration services. All of us who have had any experience with bureaucracies know that trying to let the Government operate our health care system would be an absolute nightmare, and we are not going to permit that.

The proposals on which we've all come together today would correct the most important weaknesses in our system and control costs without sacrificing this quality that American medicine is known for, this high-quality health care that every American deserves and that really attracts people from overseas. Our Republicans are ready to move, and I urge the House to act swiftly.

Now I want to turn this over to our task force leader, Republican leader Bob Michel.

*Representative Michel.* Thank you, Mr. President. I certainly don't want to add or subtract to anything the President has said here other than, earlier in the year, when we recognized, obviously, that this would be one of the key issues in the country and we recruited members from significant committees that would be involved in health care on our side of the aisle, some of the best knowledgeable and informed people on our side worked the task force all year long.

Mr. President, we're most appreciative that you have seen fit to embrace the product of what our Members collectively have done in concert with the administration. Lou Sullivan is here and Gail Wilensky. And it's been a good team effort that we've put together.

I have something rather important, however, to give you. It's kind of a prescription of sorts to cure the gridlock around the Nation's health care system this year. The prescription, of course, is H.R. 5325, an action-now health care reform act. Congress should take this prescription as directed.

*The President.* Now, let's get this thing—this is a very important piece of paper here. Let's get it out here.

All right, well, thank you all. Well done. And thank all of you who had so much—including the Ways and Means leader, Bill Archer, for what they had to do with this, and Bill Gradison. Lou, thank you. Where's Gail? She needs a little—Gail Wilensky.

*Q.* Mr. President?

*The President.* Yes, this isn't a press conference, but maybe I've got time for one or two. What have you got?

## The Economy

*Q.* Mr. President, I'd like to know your reaction to the unemployment rate going up to the highest level in 8 years. And secondarily, you've been saying that the economy is improving but just that it seemed like the American people psychologically just weren't accepting it. What do you have to say to these people now who apparently did believe you and went out and looked for jobs, and they weren't there?

*The President.* Well, I say that, one, it's not good news. Two, unemployment has always been a lagging indicator. Three, the economy grew in the first quarter, and we're confident that it will grow in the second quarter. But the main message that I get out of this is that the Congress ought to pass the economic growth stimulant package that we have up here and that these people surrounding me have been trying to get through. If you really want to help America get back to work and make this indicator be less of a lagger and more of a leader, pass the things to stimulate the economy. That's exactly what's needed.

I would say it just shows that the recovery which we're in is not as robust as I'd like to see it. I will say the good news is the Federal Reserve Board has dropped the rates by 50 basis points, and I'm told that a couple of banks have already followed, lowering the prime rate. And I think that is a good way to stimulate growth. I think that will be very well-received by the markets and by the businesses, large and small, across the country. It's something that I'd indicated a few days ago I would like to see happen, and I think it's a very good thing. And I think we've got to get this money supply up, and this is a good step toward that end.

So I would offset the news that I don't like by saying I think this will be very, very well-received, and it's fundamentally important to the economy.

## Presidential Campaign

*Q.* Mr. President, Marlin Fitzwater this morning said that the opposition research, which is how the Democrats are describing it, was tantamount to a reliving of the plumbers' unit in the Nixon White House.

Do you think what they're doing is that scurrilous?

*The President.* Well, I'm not sure what they're doing. All I did was read one story saying they're investigating my family, and you know how I feel about that. But I almost would say: So what's new? I've been in public life a long time, and I think that kind of activity on their part has been going on for a long time. But that's not——

*Q.* But also on the Republicans' part, isn't it? Mr. Bond has said that there is opposition research.

*The President.* I thought you were asking about the story today.

*Q.* I am. But isn't this something both parties historically do?

*The President.* Opposition research? Absolutely. I think everybody does opposition research. I thought you were talking about investigating a personal side of one's family, which, of course, we're not doing. We're not doing that. We're not doing that.

*Q.* Are you opposed? You're not upset with it?

*The President.* Well, I'm not happy about it, Helen [Helen Thomas, United Press International]. But what can I do about what the Democratic National Committee does?

*Q.* Well, do you do it?

*The President.* I mean, they are not exactly the voice of the American people. Let them defend their own activities on that.

*Q.* Does this mean you feel free to do the same sort of research on the opposition?

*The President.* No, no. I have made very clear that we want to stay out of the sleaze business and stay on the issues. Now, we're going to continue to research on issues; of course we are. Maybe I misread the story, but I thought it was talking about investigating family and my sons and things of this nature which——

*Q.* They did mention personal finances in the morning Post——

*The President.* Well, look, let me tell you something. The personal finances—I've been in public life half my adult life, private life the other half, and I really believe that I have bent over backwards since the day I walked into that Chamber in terms of disclosure, trying to avoid conflict of interest. So I think they're going to drill a dry hole on that one because I have really tried my very, very best to keep the public trust. I told these friends who are in the Congress, I think I view as part of my responsibility keeping the public trust, the decency and honor of the Presidency. I've tried to do that, and I've tried to conduct myself that way in the Congress.

So, let them muck around in my garbage can, but they aren't going to find anything in terms of this, if you're asking now about a business connection.

I got to get out of here. I've been accused of having too many press conferences. I think it's 295 since I've been President.

*Unemployment Benefits*

*Q.* Let's get back on the point. Let's get back on the point, sir. The House today will be taking up a Democratic version of the unemployment extension, benefits extension bill. Many of the men up here say that there is a possibility of a veto.

*The President.* Well, our position is, I have supported unemployment extensions, guarantee extensions in the past. Every once in a while we've got to beat down ones that go so far that they just exacerbate the deficit that every American is concerned about. Let's hope that we can get a bill down there fast that I can sign.

But I have a certain custodianship for trying to support reasonable expenditures. If they send me something that we view and this leadership here views as too expensive, we'll have to send it back and urge them to get one down there that we can support.

But I hope that because people need help, we can get out and give it to them right quick. I do remember a time or two in the past where I had to veto legislation that just would have gone wild in terms of spending, and I'm prepared to do that again if we have to. I hope that's not what they send to me.

Last one, right here.

*The Economy*

*Q.* Mr. President, has the Federal Reserve now cut interest rates enough? Is that enough, the Federal Reserve cut today?

*The President.* I think it's pretty good. I think many of the market experts were saying it would be 25 basis points. I don't know. I mean, I am not an economist or a money supply expert. But all I know is, I think most people feel, and I certainly agree with this, that this would be stimulative and would be very well-received not just in the financial markets but by business, and particularly small business, that'll have a better shot now at creating something.

But it would be much better if we could pass these incentives that we have: the investment tax allowance, the first-time credit for homebuyers, $5000 we've proposed. I still feel that a capital gains reduction, a broad one, would create new businesses, new small businesses. We had some suggestions up here that Bill Archer and others have been very supportive of, and they have some of their own, on IRA's. So we need something that targets economic growth. My answer to the unemployment figures is: Please, now, Congress, do what you should have done some time ago in terms of stimulating the economy. It's growing, but I want to see the growth more robust.

The unemployment, there are too many people out of work. The way to get them back to work is to stimulate so that you'll have creation of new jobs. The interest rates, again, will help in this regard because I think it'll encourage existing businesses to more briskly go forward. But the reviews are mixed, the economy is still growing, and this figure, as I say, normally I think most experts would say a lagging indicator. But I've always said unemployment for one person, that's 100 percent, and that's too much. So we've got to keep moving until we get it back the way I'd like to see it in terms of economic growth.

I really do; I've got to go to work.

*Q.* This figure means the recovery is stalled.

*The President.* You've already had a question, madam.

*Q.* Following on the economy for a second. There are so many people, though, who really question whether or not you get it in terms of——

*The President.* I get it.

*Q.* ——these numbers are optimistic, and

yet, look at the numbers.

*The President.* I get it. I said these numbers are not good. But I've got an answer for it. The answer is that the Congress ought to pass these stimulants to the economy. And it is unarguable.

*Representatives.* Hear, hear!

*The President.* Everybody feels that it would help and get the economic growth more robust. The economy grew at 2.7 percent first quarter, and it's going to grow this time.

*Q.* So it's the Congress' fault?

*The President.* I'm not trying to assign blame. You asked me what I'd do about it, and I'm saying, stimulate the economy. It's the fault of the Democratic leadership that these economic growth provisions have not been enacted, yes, on that one. But hell, I'll take my share of the blame. Everybody should.

*Q.* Mr. President——

*The President.* ——report the things that are just kind of negative out there. This economy is growing. And yet, Mr. Lichter says that 92 percent and says everything's bad. I mean, see, I'd like it a little more balanced. I'd like to see this thing moving on reality, not on misperception.

*Q.* Do you always bring your—with you? [*Laughter*]

*The President.* I told them to keep this thing secret. Extraterrestrial who met with George Bush at Camp David—I told him, I said, if I'm going to meet with you—[*laughter*]—I told him it was for me all along. There he is. [*Laughter*]

*Q.* How do you stop blaming the media—every time you say people don't know that there is real recovery—I mean, they've seen it today.

*The President.* ——2.7 percent growth.

*Q.* Yes, but now you see what the unemployment is.

*The President.* Well, I never said unemployment was perfect. I've been saying too many people are out of work. Let's get them back to work by stimulating the economy.

*Q.* ——the deficit reduction bill that bipartisan House leaders——

*The President.* Deficit reduction? No, the first thing I'd like to see is have the Congress pass what I have just been proposing and have reproposed.

*Note: The President spoke at 10:23 a.m. in the House Chamber at the Capitol. The following persons were referred to: Gail R. Wilensky, Deputy Assistant to the President for Policy Development; Rich Bond, chairman, Republican National Committee; and S. Robert Lichter, codirector, Center for Media and Public Affairs. Part of this exchange could not be verified because the tape was incomplete.*

# Message to the Congress Transmitting Proposed Legislation on Health Care
## July 2, 1992

*To the Congress of the United States:*

I am pleased to transmit today for your immediate consideration and enactment the "Health Care Liability Reform and Quality of Care Improvement Act of 1992." Also transmitted is a section-by-section analysis.

This legislative proposal would assist in stemming the rising costs of health care caused by medical professional liability. During recent years, the costs of defensive medical practice and of litigation related to health care disputes have had a substantial impact on the affordability and availability of quality medical care. The bill attacks these very serious problems.

The bill would establish incentives for States to adopt within 3 years quality assurance measures and tort reforms. In addition, the health care reforms would apply to medical care and treatment funded through specific Federal programs pertaining to health care and employee benefits and to claims under the Federal Tort Claims Act. The tort reforms include: (1) a reasonable cap on noneconomic damages; (2) the elimination of joint and several liability for those damages; (3) prohibiting double recoveries by plaintiffs; and (4) permitting health care providers to pay damages for future costs periodically rather than in a lump sum.

Last year I recommended enactment of the "Health Care Liability Reform and Quality of Care Improvement Act of 1991." The enclosed bill includes the core provisions of that bill and expands its scope to ensure that treatment under federally funded health care and Federal employee benefit programs is subject to key reforms

regardless of State action. Claims arising from such health care would first be considered through a fair system of nonbinding arbitration, in an effort to resolve the claims without litigation.

I urge the prompt and favorable consideration of this proposal, which would complement the other initiatives the Administration is undertaking regarding malpractice and quality of care.

GEORGE BUSH

The White House,
July 2, 1992.

# Statement on the United States Nuclear Weapons Initiative
*July 2, 1992*

In the wake of the momentous changes in what was then the Soviet Union, last September 27 in an address to the Nation from the Oval Office I directed that the United States undertake dramatic changes and reductions in our nuclear arsenal and challenged the Soviet leadership to go down the same road with us. In that speech, I directed that the United States bring home from overseas and destroy our entire worldwide inventory of ground-launched theater nuclear weapons. At the same time, I announced that the United States would withdraw all tactical nuclear weapons from its surface ships, attack submarines, and those nuclear weapons associated with our land-based naval aircraft. Many of these are to be dismantled and destroyed.

Today I can tell you that all of the planned withdrawals are complete. All ground-launched tactical nuclear weapons have been returned to U.S. territory, as

have all naval tactical nuclear weapons. Those weapons designated to be destroyed are being retired and scheduled for destruction.

These historic measures would not have been possible without the full support of our allies around the world and without the farsighted and courageous leadership of Russian President Boris Yeltsin, Ukrainian President Leonid Kravchuk, Republic of Kazakhstan President Nursultan Nazarbayev, and Chairman of the Supreme Soviet of the Republic of Byelarus Stanislav Shushkevich. They pledged to honor Soviet commitments to take comparable steps reducing tactical nuclear weapons. It is important that the implementation of these commitments be successfully concluded.

Now I look forward to the prompt ratification of START and to concluding a treaty on the even more far-reaching reductions President Yeltsin and I announced at the recent summit in Washington.

# The President's News Conference With Foreign Journalists
*July 2, 1992*

*The President.* Thank you very much. And let me read a brief statement before responding to your questions.

Before I leave for Europe, I want to say just a few words about why I believe it is so important to the American people that I make this trip. Thanks to the courage and the sacrifice of millions of Americans, we've won the cold war, we and our allies standing shoulder-to-shoulder. Our task now is to secure the peace, to build an expanding world economy, one that opens new markets abroad and creates new jobs here at home. Our task will not be completed on one 5-day trip. But we can, at these meetings, advance the well-being of all of our countrymen, my countrymen.

In the new global economy now emerging, America's economic interests don't stop at the water's edge. And we will not prosper in a world stifled by trading blocs and tariff barriers. Seventy percent of our economic growth in the last 5 years has come from exports. And I will continue to fight for more economic growth, and that means free trade. Our progress so far has been substantial. Already the new democracies of the East are becoming attractive sites for U.S. investment, and nearly $2 billion committed this year alone. Those investments will help our allies secure democracy's great gains and create jobs for American workers. And that's my mission, to secure these benefits for America and the world.

In Warsaw, birthplace of the Revolution of '89, I will stand with the Polish people, show our support for their efforts to consolidate their hard-won freedom. In Munich, I will work with leaders of the world's great industrialized democracies to build a new world economy. I'll also meet with President Yeltsin to build on the historic steps that we took right here at the White House and to underscore our strong support for Russia's reforms. On this one there can be no doubt: An investment in Russian democracy is an investment in world peace. And finally, in Helsinki, I will meet for the first time with members of a CSCE not divided East from West but united in a democratic community of more than 50 nations.

So let me just add one point here on the eve of the Fourth of July: We must not forget, must never forget, that in Europe today rests 20 million American bodies— excuse me—20 American military cemeteries. I've been to a couple of them. And we must ensure that there will never be a 21st.

Look at how far we've already come. When I took office 3 years ago, adversaries faced us across a divided Europe. Today, the new democracies of Central and Eastern Europe are our partners. And the threat of nuclear war is more distant now than at any time since the advent of the nuclear age. And think of what that means, not for presidents or prime ministers, not for historians or heads of state but for parents and their children. It means a future free from fear.

For much of this century, it's been America's destiny to stand for liberty and against intolerance and to fight for freedom against oppression. And now at long last the moment has come for the lovers of freedom around the world to reap the rewards of our vigilance. The opportunity we face is historic, the first chance in more than a half century to build democratic peace and prosperity for America and for the world. This trip will, in my view, bring us just one step, but another step, closer to our goal.

Now I'd be glad to take some questions.

*Polish Reforms*

*Q.* Mr. President, Secretary Baker the other day said that you would be discussing with President Walesa some new ideas on advancement of Polish reforms. What will they be?

*The President.* I can't give you the exact detail. I think it would be inappropriate before meeting with the President. We have some ideas that would help stimulate investment. We salute President Walesa for what he's been able to do in reform already. It has not been easy. And there are serious questions that remain. But I'd prefer not to go into the details of what we might be discussing with him. As you know, the government's in transition, and I think it would be most appropriate to talk the specifics with him.

But let me just reaffirm the interest in the United States not only in reforms but the reforms that lead to further American investment. So it will be along the lines of what we can do to further stimulate trade but also U.S. investment in Poland. I think we've had a good start, but we need to go further. Stabilization is the subject that we'll be talking about, too.

*Aid to Russia and G-7 Membership*

*Q.* Mr. President, could you tell us, please, what will be your agenda for meeting with President Yeltsin? Will it be just an update of what you discussed here in Washington, sir, a month ago, or there will be new proposals, new initiatives? And secondly, this is the second time a Russian leader has been invited to a G-7 summit. The last time, it was back, of course, last year when Gorbachev was still the President of the Soviet Union. Do you think that Russia will be a permanent member of the G-7 sometime soon?

*The President.* On your first question, yes, there will be an update, because we've really spent a lot of time. The time we spent floating around on that boat on the Severn near Annapolis was total work time. In other words, we reviewed not just the things we talked about in our formal meetings, but we reviewed a wide array of other subjects. So there's some updating that needs to be done. One of the things I want to update him on is where we stand on what we call the "FREEDOM Support Act." And I hope there will be action on that before I leave, in the Senate. He is not expecting that the full Congress act on that before we meet in Munich.

So we'll talk about the "FREEDOM Support Act." And it'll really, I would say, be a followup on the discussions we had. He gave me a review of all the problems and the gains and the different crosscurrents in the former countries of the C.I.S., of the Soviet empire. We discussed a lot of these things. So I'm anxious to get updated from him on all of that.

And on the G-7, I will be prepared to discuss this, making it the G-8, if you will. These are, as we all know, meetings of the major economic powers. And certainly with Japan there and with the current members of the G-7, European members and Canada as well, that's what it's been up to date. Well, Russian economy is enormous. And they have big problems. But their size gives them a unique standing. So we'll have to see. I know other countries want to be in there. But Russia, because of its size and because of Yeltsin's coming at the invitation of Helmut Kohl, certainly we'll have that subject on the agenda. I can't say how I think it's going to work out because I just don't know.

*Q.* Do you support it?

*The President.* That's right.

*Multilateral Trade Negotiations*

*Q.* Mr. President, in the last summits in Houston and London, there were nice words and beautiful commitments on the GATT negotiations, but no results. Do you expect the same in Munich?

*The President.* Well, I don't think the Munich summit will be dominated by the GATT talks. In fact, I talked to Chancellor Kohl in the last couple of days, and it is neither his desires nor mine, nor the desire of any of the European leaders or indeed Brian Mulroney or indeed Prime Minister Miyazawa, to have that happen. I think it will be talked about, but it isn't going to be the major area of discussion. I am still not giving up on trying to get something done before then. But there's very little time left. And we are still in constant discussion with various European leaders about this.

I'd like to have seen it worked out before then. But definitely progress has been made in closing the gap since the last—I believe you put it in the timeframe of the last G-7 meeting. And a lot of the differences have been narrowed. But we still have some big ones, differences, and agriculture as you know remains the major stumbling block. But we're not going to give up on it. If we don't get something, some major breakthrough today or tomorrow, we're just going to keep on going because it is in the interest of the whole world. And I'll tell you the major beneficiaries of this would be the Third World. Trade for them offers them far better opportunities than just aid. So, we'll keep pushing on it.

### U.S. Nuclear Weapons

*Q.* Mr. President, with regard to your announcement this morning about the completion of the withdrawal of land and sea-based tactical nuclear weapons, what is its policy implication for the Asia and Pacific region, particularly in regard with your "neither confirm nor deny" nuclear weapons transfer principle?

*The President.* What announcement are you referring to, sir?

*Q.* It's a statement.

*Q.* Tactical weapons.

*The President.* What?

*Q.* It was out of NATO.

*Mr. Fitzwater.* That they completed the pull-out of the tactical nuclear weapons.

*Q.* It's a worldwide withdrawal.

*The President.* Oh. Well, I mean, that's just a progress report, and I don't think it has anything beyond what's on the face of it. We've said what we were going to do, and we've done it. And that's a good thing. But I don't think it has any implications for the old nuclear presence argument that affected many of our friends around the world. I mean, that's up for them to decide. I mean, we've made this statement; it seems to me that it might clear the way for resolution of differences we've had with some countries, but that's up for them to decide.

Our statement is still "neither confirm nor deny," but where we've said we don't have these weapons on board, we mean it. And they're not there. So, if that opens the doors for others, so much the better. I'm thinking of New Zealand and other countries where we've had, everyone knows, great differences on this.

### Korean Peninsula

*Q.* Do you think it will have a positive impact on the Korean Peninsula?

*The President.* Oh. Yes, I would hope it would. Excuse me, that's a very important point, and yes, I think it would. I think it should. I don't think there's anything new on them. In other words, I think that's been

discounted. But I think it's evidence of our good faith. I am convinced that the move should be up to North Korea to meet the international standards, to comply with IAEA and other rules. But the main thing is they've got to dispel the mistrust that exists regarding North Korea, and the way to do that is to be open, openness in terms of inspections.

This is an international press conference, and I'm trying to favor those who come from other countries or are accredited here from foreign journals of one kind or another. And I would only ask understanding and forbearance from the American White House press corps, championed by the front row here. They are very understanding as a rule, and in this time I would appeal to them to understand when I drift off and recognize others than the illustrious dean sitting in the front row.

### North American Free Trade Agreement

*Q.* Mr. President, will you be signing a North American free trade deal in San Diego in a couple of weeks, as reported today by the Journal of Commerce, with Prime Minister Mulroney and President Salinas? And can you comment on the negotiations?

*The President.* One, I don't know about what we'll be signing. That is not a scheduled event at this time. I'd love to think we can get the differences ironed out by then, but I don't want to set artificial timetables. We've had some differences with Mexico, but I'll tell you one thing: The negotiations have been serious. Again, I'll give the same answer I gave on the Uruguay round, the differences have been narrowed considerably. They know the areas that we're having difficulties with, and we know theirs, but I just don't know about any timetable of that nature. It has not come to me that we are going to be ready. What has come from me to our negotiators is to get politics out of the way, if any is in there, and sign a good agreement so I can sign or initial a good agreement as soon as possible.

So I want to take this opportunity to say there isn't any politics involved in this. I keep reading, "Well, the President may not want to take a deal up to the Hill or have it on the Hill," and that is not true. It is in the interest of the United States of America to get a good free trade agreement with North America, with Canada and Mexico. So that's all. So we have no timetable set, but again it's like GATT. I'd like to just keep pushing and get it done as soon as possible. I talked to President Salinas about 10 days ago and then subsequently talked to our negotiators. He's done the same thing. Jaime Serra, I believe, has been here. I know others have. And we're just going to keep on working on it.

## Yugoslavia

*Q.* Mr. President, after some months of effort by various European institutions including the European Community, the CSCE, there is still fighting and bloodshed in Yugoslavia and particularly in Bosnia. Are you disappointed with the performance of these European institutions so far, and how do you think this speaks of those who say it's time for a European security pillar to replace NATO?

*The President.* Well, I don't think it has anything to do with the replacement of NATO. I don't believe that. I believe that the United Nations and individual European countries have made strong efforts to bring about peace. We started by backing Cyrus Vance as the negotiator for the United Nations. Lord Carrington, in my view, has tried very, very hard. He started off against enormous odds. He's still engaged. And so I can't fault anybody for the fact that we do not have peace there. We have been, as you know, supportive of the peace efforts but not trying to have taken the lead in the peace process. But I would resist saying I think this shows a failure to utilize NATO earlier on or anything of that nature.

We remain committed to NATO. I think it is absolutely in the interest of the United States that a strong American presence be in NATO. As these different organizations are considered, I keep talking to our friends in Europe that NATO should be the prime organization there. And I think most of them, if not all, agree with that. So in this failure to bring tranquility to a troubled land or certainly failure to get in the humanitarian supplies that are necessary, I don't see any diminution of NATO's overall standing—if that was your question; I may have misunderstood it—at all. I salute the French President for what he did. That was not a multilateral approach; that was something that he tried to do on his own.

Some supplies are going in there now. I was very pleased to note, of all things, a private American venture went in there. The Americares, which is a wonderfully humane organization, had a plane land there at 9:05 this morning, or maybe it was 9:05 their time. But nevertheless, some supplies are getting in there.

The U.S. role has been to say, look, we want to help with the assistance, on a humanitarian basis. And that's the role we're in. We are not in a forward-leaning role as terms of saying our objectives is to bring lasting peace to this troubled land. That's what I'd like to see happen. But I think the immediate goal should be relief effort to the people that are suffering. And the environment one time looks benign, and then it looks a little more hazardous. So we've got to thread through it, and we'll do our part.

*Q.* To follow up, sir. You said that in the past we've supported and not tried taking the lead. Should we interpret Mr. Cheney's statement this week as the Americans are now prepared to start taking the lead?

*The President.* Well, no. I don't think it was so much as taking the lead but doing our part. As you know, we have a substantial military presence in the area. And my position, and I know it's Cheney's, is we're not ruling anything—or out. When I was talking about substantial presence, I'm talking primarily about the presence of our fleet there. I believe there's two carrier battle groups in the Med, one of them now up in the Adriatic. But nobody should interpret that as other than the fact that we're there. And beyond that, I can't say what we will or won't do. I don't think Cheney was signaling an increased, aggressive military presence there. And I think he'd answer the question the same way I do: that we're not going to rule anything in; we're not going to rule it out.

But I would say, we don't want to appear to be kind of, quote, taking the lead, unquote, when all this activity is going on.

The French have been active, the Italians at the EC were very forward leaning and active, and that's good. As far as we're concerned, that's fine.

### Japanese Constitution

*Q.* On the occasion of the Japanese Prime Minister's visit here, the Heritage Foundation issued a report recommending that to include Japan as a full and responsible, respected member of the international community, the Bush administration should privately urge Japan to start writing its own constitution. The report argues that the present Japanese Constitution, American-drafted one, particularly its renouncement of the use of force for even just and international and collective cause, makes Japan an exception to every other nation and somehow discourages responsible debate by the Japanese on international security issues. Some Japanese political leaders already advocate the constitutional revision for a similar reason. And I know this is a matter that only the Japanese can decide; but from the standpoint of Japan's ally and global partner, would you be inclined to discourage or encourage a movement towards such constitutional revision?

*The President.* I would be inclined to let Japan decide that by Japan's self, if you will. I wouldn't particularly like it if the Japanese Prime Minister told me what revisions we ought to have to the American Constitution. We're fighting that out all the time on the domestic scene. And I wouldn't like it. So I would butt out of that.

I will say we salute Japan for what they did in the Diet the other day, which moved a little more forward towards, I guess, the position that this foundation has advocated. But I'd leave it there. I've always been a little bit constrained when it comes to intervening in the internal matters of another country.

I can see why the question is addressed. Some have criticized Japan for not doing more, but they're coming along. They're feeling their way along, and, in my view, they were very supportive in terms of Desert Storm, not with troops but of fulfilling their obligations. They've been very supportive of host country matters when we have military presence over there. They've

taken this step in the Diet. And we support that, salute that. And I would leave the pace of change strictly up to the Japanese themselves. They have constitutional problems. They've got a keen sense of history. And they'll figure it out. And I'll stand at their side and be supportive.

### Canada-U.S. Trade

*Q.* Mr. President, did you give the steel case that was recently filed by the industry the top-level attention you promised Prime Minister Mulroney when it came to Canada before the case was filed? And as a follow-up, did you agree with the industry filing and including Canada?

*The President.* We give all these cases top-level consideration. We have laws in this country where people are allowed to bring their case to the various agencies. But, yes, I think that Prime Minister Mulroney had the distinct feeling that American politics were causing us to pull back into some kind of a protectionist mood vis-a-vis Canada. And I see enough of these cases to be able to say to myself that this is not the case. And when there's unfairness, the proper procedures will be followed. But I won't go into any specific case, but I owe him that kind of reassurance.

### Yugoslavia

*Q.* Mr. President, you said that you're not ruling anything in or out with regard to Yugoslavia. However, very senior people in your administration have made it clear that you do not intend to commit ground forces. You have many tens of thousands of troops in Europe. That is a very major crisis taking place in a new Europe. If the United States is not prepared to commit ground forces in such a context, would it not be reasonable for Europeans to say, why are the Americans here, and for American taxpayers to be saying, what are we doing there?

*The President.* I don't know what spokesman you're talking about, but I've said nothing here about what I will or won't do. And under our system, the President of the United States makes those decisions on the commitment of forces or not to commit forces. That's one of the decisions that rests with me, not with anybody else, not the

Congress, not anybody else.

So no decision has been taken on that. And I have had no pressure, to try to respond fully, from the United States Congress or any citizens here, to say why aren't we putting more troops into Sarajevo right now, for example. I haven't had any feeling that there's a great demand for that. What we want to do is play our part in the fulfillment of the mission to bring humanitarian relief in there. But I don't think there's a great eagerness to put American troops there on the ground or to send NATO in there. The United Nations has a role; they're fulfilling the role.

So I think you raise a good point. But I don't think it will diminish support for NATO on the part of the American people. Or even from the Europeans, I don't think it'll diminish support.

*NATO*

*Q.* The question is, sir, if you're not going to intervene or not prepared or not very much inclined to intervene in a conflict of that nature even in theory, then what are you doing in Europe?

*The President.* We're there to guarantee the peace. And we're there to say, we know history. And if we'd have stayed there in the past with some presence, maybe we could have averted some of the disaster that befell Europe. We're there because Europe wants us there, too. Not only do we want to be there in a presence in the most efficient organization of its kind, NATO, but I think the Europeans all want us there. In fact, I keep asking to be darned sure I'm right on that question. And they do.

And so NATO is there. But that doesn't mean when you have a humanitarian problem here or you have internal divisions in any countries, and there are many turmoils based on ancient ethnic rivalries and hatreds that are cropping up, that automatically NATO goes to general quarters. That's not NATO's mission. There's ways to decide whether NATO should be involved or not. And I tried to recite the history here of the United Nations role. And in this instance the United Nations has taken the lead. Some individual European leaders have taken the lead.

But I don't see it as diminishing NATO's

standing or certainly as diminishing NATO's commitment, the American people's wanting NATO to still have a strong U.S. presence. Because the fact that they're not in this crisis, you might turn to me after I finish answering that one and say, what about some of the other areas where there are trouble spots going on right now in what used to be the Soviet Union? There's a lot of trouble spots. And my answer would be to that question, that because NATO is there and it is the most efficient peacekeeping organization that exists, that doesn't mean that it's going to be injected into every single crisis area. So there's other mechanisms set up for this one, and it's a very complicated problem when I look at it.

Somebody asked me, how is it different from, say, Desert Storm or from the invasion of one country from another? And as these countries sort out these enormously complicated problems, I make the point that that is different. They're internal to a degree, and yet they're new countries. But I make a point that it is quite different than the overt invasion of one country by another. I'm sure some in Sarajevo might not agree with that, but I think the mission for NATO has to be looked at in terms of each crisis or each outbreak of hostilities. And in this one, we've had other organizations that are trying to solve the problem. And you've had other countries that have been, on their own, trying to solve the problem.

But I will do my level-best to see that this does not diminish NATO. I am absolutely convinced not only do we have a role there, but it's an insurance policy, if you will, against the kinds of conflagrations that we've seen in the past. And so it will stay strong. And there will be some bumps in the road, but NATO is going to be the major organization of its kind anywhere in the world, I think.

This is the last one, and then I really, according to Marlin, must be off. Twenty-three minutes, .47 seconds.

*Yugoslavia*

*Q.* Mr. President, but the impression is that United States are maybe too cautious, too uncertain on the Yugoslavia crisis; they don't exactly know what to do. Can you tell me if it's correct or wrong?

*The President.* Well, I don't think that it's that we don't know what to do. I can understand somebody saying, well, why doesn't the United States use its magnificent military power one way or another to end all this suffering? But it's not that we don't know what to do; it is that we were trying to work with others in the ways I've outlined here to try to bring about an environment in which we can bring relief to the area. So, that's the way I would answer the question. Did I get it?

*Q.* Yes.

*The President.* Yes, that's about it. I mean, the United States is not going to inject itself into every single crisis, no matter how heartrending, around the world. And where we try to work with the United Nations, for example, we have no apologies for that. There will be times when we have to take the lead, when we have to move forcefully, when we have a clear mission. I am not interested in seeing one single United States soldier pinned down in some kind of a guerrilla environment. We go in there, we're going to go in there and do what we said we're going to do and get out. And this environment is a little complicated so that I could certify to the American people that's what would happen.

*Q.* Sir, what have you told Prime Minister Mulroney about the Canadian troops? Have

you sent any special message to him as the Canadian troops went to——

*The President.* I gave him an 'atta boy. I saluted him for doing what they're doing with the United Nations.

*Q.* Have you offered U.N. air cover for the convoy or any further convoys?

*The President.* Well, we have not been asked to do that. But they're doing a wonderful job over there. And I think the Canadians who have stepped forward deserve a great vote of thanks from the entire world for what they're doing. And when you see those pictures on the television and you see those courageous people there, why, we salute them. But he has not asked for that.

Let me put it this way: Canadian forces get in trouble, they've got some friends right here, right here, strong friends that are grateful to them and who respect them and have stood at their side before, and we're not going to let a lot of Canadians get put into harm's way without support. Put it that way.

*Note: The President's 133d news conference began at 2:21 p.m. in Room 450 of the Old Executive Office Building. In his remarks, he referred to Jaime Serra, Secretary of Commerce and Industrial Development of Mexico; Cyrus Vance, Special Negotiator for the United Nations on Yugoslavia; and Lord Peter Carrington, Special European Community Negotiator on Yugoslavia.*

# Letter to Congressional Leaders on Trade With Colombia
*July 2, 1992*

*Dear Mr. Speaker: (Dear Mr. President:)*

Pursuant to section 203 of the Andean Trade Preference Act (ATPA) (19 U.S.C. 3202), I wish to inform you of my intent to designate Colombia as a beneficiary of the trade-liberalizing measures provided for in this Act. Designation will entitle the products of Colombia, except for products excluded statutorily, to duty-free treatment for a period ending on December 4, 2002.

Designation is an important step for Colombia in its effort to fight against narcotics

production and trafficking. The enhanced access to the U.S. market provided by the ATPA will encourage the production of and trade in legitimate products.

My decision to designate Colombia results from consultations concluded in April 1992 between this Administration and the Government of Colombia regarding the designation criteria set forth in section 203 of the ATPA. Colombia has demonstrated to my satisfaction that its laws, practices, and policies are in conformity with the designation criteria of the ATPA. The Government of Colombia has communicated on these matters by a letter to Ambassador Hills and in so doing has indicated its desire to be designated as a beneficiary.

On the basis of the statements and assurances in Colombia's letter, and taking into account information developed by the United States Embassy and through other sources, I have concluded that designation is appropriate at this time.

I am mindful that under section 203(e) of the ATPA, I retain the authority to suspend, withdraw, or limit the application of ATPA benefits from any designated country if a beneficiary's laws, policies, or practices are no longer in conformity with the designa-

tion criteria. The United States will keep abreast of developments in Colombia that are pertinent to the designation criteria.

This Administration looks forward to working closely with the Government of Colombia and with the private sectors of the United States and Colombia to ensure that the wide-ranging opportunities opened by the ATPA are fully utilized.

Sincerely,

GEORGE BUSH

*Note: Identical letters were sent to Thomas S. Foley, Speaker of the House of Representatives, and Dan Quayle, President of the Senate. The related proclamation is listed in Appendix E at the end of this volume.*

# Letter to Congressional Leaders on Trade With Bolivia
*July 2, 1992*

*Dear Mr. Speaker: (Dear Mr. President:)*
Pursuant to section 203 of the Andean Trade Preference Act (ATPA) (19 U.S.C. 3202), I wish to inform you of my intent to designate Bolivia as a beneficiary of the trade-liberalizing measures provided for in this Act. Designation will entitle the products of Bolivia, except for products excluded statutorily, to duty-free treatment for a period ending on December 4, 2002.

Designation is an important step for Bolivia in its effort to fight against narcotics production and trafficking. The enhanced access to the U.S. market provided by the ATPA will encourage the production of and trade in legitimate products.

My decision to designate Bolivia results from consultations concluded in April 1992 between this Administration and the Government of Bolivia regarding the designation criteria set forth in section 203 of the ATPA. Bolivia has demonstrated to my satisfaction that its laws, practices, and policies are in conformity with the designation criteria of the ATPA. The Government of Bolivia has communicated on these matters by a letter to Ambassador Hills and in so doing has indicated its desire to be designated as a

beneficiary.

On the basis of the statements and assurances in Bolivia's letter, and taking into account information developed by the United States Embassy and through other sources, I have concluded that designation is appropriate at this time.

I am mindful that under section 203(e) of the ATPA, I retain the authority to suspend, withdraw, or limit the application of ATPA benefits from any designated country if a beneficiary's laws, policies, or practices are no longer in conformity with the designation criteria. The United States will keep abreast of developments in Bolivia that are pertinent to the designation criteria.

This Administration looks forward to working closely with the Government of Bolivia and with the private sectors of the United States and Bolivia to ensure that the wide-ranging opportunities opened by the ATPA are fully utilized.

Sincerely,

GEORGE BUSH

*Note: Identical letters were sent to Thomas S. Foley, Speaker of the House of Represent-*

*atives, and Dan Quayle, President of the Senate. The related proclamation is listed in* *Appendix E at the end of this volume.*

# Letter to Congressional Leaders Transmitting a Report on Adherence to Arms Control Treaty Obligations
*July 2, 1992*

*Dear Mr. Speaker:    (Dear Mr. Chairman:)*

I am pleased to transmit a report on the adherence of the United States to arms control treaty obligations and on problems related to compliance by other nations with the provisions of arms control agreements to which the United States is a party. I am transmitting the classified and unclassified versions of the report.

This report was prepared by the United States Arms Control and Disarmament Agency in coordination with the Departments of State, Defense, and Energy, as well as the Joint Staff and the Intelligence Community.

The United States will continue to make clear that it expects scrupulous compliance from its arms control treaty partners and that full compliance is essential to a meaningful arms controls process. For its part, the United States will continue to take seriously its commitments to arms control agreements, to set rigid standards and detailed procedures for assuring that it meets these obligations, and to correct any errors in U.S. implementation that arise.

Sincerely,

GEORGE BUSH

*Note: Identical letters were sent to Thomas S. Foley, Speaker of the House of Representatives, and Claiborne Pell, Chairman of the Senate Foreign Relations Committee.*

# Message to the Congress Transmitting a Report on Nuclear Nonproliferation
*July 2, 1992*

*To the Congress of the United States:*

I have reviewed the activities of the United States Government departments and agencies during calendar year 1991 related to preventing nuclear proliferation, and I am pleased to submit my annual report pursuant to section 601(a) of the Nuclear Non-Proliferation Act of 1978 (Public Law 95–242, 22 U.S.C. 3281(a)).

As the report demonstrates, the United States continued its efforts during 1991 to prevent the spread of nuclear explosives to additional countries, one of my highest pri-orities. The events of the past year in Iraq and elsewhere underline the importance of these efforts to preserving our national security, by reducing the risk of war and increasing international stability. I am determined to build on the achievements discussed in this report and to work with the Congress toward our common goal: a safer and more secure future for all human kind.

GEORGE BUSH

The White House,
July 2, 1992.

## Message to the Senate Returning Without Approval the National Voter Registration Act of 1992
## *July 2, 1992*

*To the Senate of the United States:*

I am returning herewith without my approval S. 250, the "National Voter Registration Act of 1992."

This Administration strongly supports the goal of increasing participation in the electoral process. We have worked with leaders of both parties in an attempt to produce legislation that would accomplish that purpose. S. 250, however, would impose unnecessary, burdensome, expensive, and constitutionally questionable Federal regulation on the States in an area of traditional State authority. It would also expose the election process to an unacceptable risk of fraud and corruption without any reason to believe that it would increase electoral participation to any significant degree.

No justification has been demonstrated for the extensive procedural requirements—and significant related costs—imposed on the States by this bill. The proponents of S. 250 simply have not made the case that requiring the States to make voter registration easier will translate into increased voter participation at the polls. Indeed, a recent study by the Federal Election Commission suggests that registration requirements have no significant effect on participation rates. In addition, to the extent that State registration requirements discriminate against minority groups, the Voting Rights Act already provides an adequate remedy.

S. 250 would exempt from compliance with its requirements any State adopting an election day registration system. This exemption could create a compelling incentive for a State to adopt such a system, under which verification of voter eligibility is difficult. Thus, the bill would increase substantially the risk of voting fraud. It would not, however, provide sufficient authority for Federal law enforcement officials to respond to any resulting increases in election crime and public corruption.

It is critical that the States retain the authority to tailor voter registration procedures to unique local circumstances. S. 250 would prevent the States from doing this by forcing them to implement federally mandated and nationally standardized voter registration procedures. It would also restrict severely their ability to remove from the voter rolls the names of persons who have not voted in several years and who thus can be presumed fairly to have died or moved out of the jurisdiction. Enactment of S. 250 would deny the States their historic freedom to govern their own electoral processes and would contravene the important principles of federalism on which our country was founded.

S. 250 is constitutionally suspect. Although the Supreme Court has recognized that the Congress has general power to regulate Federal elections to the extent necessary to prevent fraud and preserve the integrity of the electoral process, there has been no suggestion that S. 250 would serve that goal. Nor has there been any showing that the bill is necessary to eliminate discriminatory practices. Accordingly, there is a serious constitutional question whether the Congress has the power to enact this legislation.

I support legislation that would assist the States in implementing appropriate reforms in order to make voter registration easier for the American public. I cannot, however, accept legislation that imposes an unnecessary and costly Federal regime on the States and that is, in addition, an open invitation to fraud and corruption.

For the reasons discussed above, I am returning S. 250 without my approval.

GEORGE BUSH

The White House,
July 2, 1992.

## Nomination of Mack F. Mattingly To Be United States Ambassador to the Seychelles
*July 2, 1992*

The President today announced his intention to nominate Mack F. Mattingly, of Georgia, to be Ambassador of the United States of America to the Republic of Seychelles. He would succeed Richard W. Carlson.

Since 1990, Senator Mattingly has served as a national and international speaker and writer on economic, defense, foreign policy, and political issues; a business adviser; and self-employed entrepreneur. From 1987 to 1990, he served as Assistant Secretary General for Defense Support for NATO in Brussels, Belgium. He served as a U.S. Senator from Georgia, 1981–87.

Senator Mattingly graduated from Indiana University (B.S., 1957). He served in the U.S. Air Force, 1951–55. He was born January 7, 1931, in Anderson, IN. Senator Mattingly is married, has two children, and resides in Saint Simons Island, GA.

## Nomination of Mary C. Pendleton To Be United States Ambassador to Moldova
*July 2, 1992*

The President today announced his intention to nominate Mary C. Pendleton, of Virginia, a career member of the Foreign Service, class one, to be Ambassador of the United States of America to the Republic of Moldova.

Since 1990, Ms. Pendleton has served as Director of the Administrative Training Division at the School of Professional Studies at the Foreign Service Institute. From 1989 to 1990, she was in senior training at the National Defense University Industrial College of the Armed Forces. Ms. Pendleton has served as a Foreign Service officer at the Department of State in several positions since 1975, including: administrative counselor at the American Embassy in Bucharest, Romania, 1987–89; post management officer in the Bureau of European and Canadian Affairs, 1984–87; administrative officer at the American Embassy in Lusaka, Zambia, 1982–84; a visa officer and staff aide at the American Embassy in Manila, Philippines, 1978–79; and a general services officer at the American Embassy in Khartoum, Sudan, 1976–77.

Ms. Pendleton graduated from Spalding University (B.A., 1962) and Indiana University (M.A., 1969). She was born June 15, 1940, in Jefferson County, KY. Ms. Pendleton currently resides in Arlington, VA.

## Nomination of Stanley Tuemler Escudero To Be United States Ambassador to Tajikistan
*July 2, 1992*

The President today announced his intention to nominate Stanley Tuemler Escudero, of Florida, a career member of the Senior Foreign Service, class of Counselor, to be Ambassador of the United States of America to the Republic of Tajikistan.

Currently, Mr. Escudero serves as Chargé d'Affaires and interim at the American Embassy in Dushanbe, Republic of Tajikistan. Mr. Escudero has also served as: Counselor for Political Affairs at the U.S. Embassy in Cairo, Egypt, 1990–92; member of the senior seminar at the Foreign Service Institute, 1989–90; political advisor to the commander-in-chief at Central Command in Tampa, FL, 1987–89; Counselor for Political Affairs at the American Embassy in New Delhi, India, 1984–87; legislative management officer in the Bureau of Congressional and Intergovernmental Affairs at the Department of State, 1981–84. Mr. Escudero has served in several other positions with the Department of State, including: Africa affairs officer in the Office of United Nations Political Affairs, Bureau of International Organization Affairs at the Department of State, 1977–80; Morocco desk officer, 1975–77; and staff aide to the Ambassador and political officer at the American Embassy in Tehran, Iran, 1971–75.

Mr. Escudero graduated from the University of Florida (B.A., 1965). He was born March 10, 1942, in Daytona Beach, FL Mr. Escudero is married, has two children, and resides in Dushanbe, Republic of Tajikistan.

# Nomination of John J. Easton, Jr., To Be an Assistant Secretary of Energy
*July 2, 1992*

The President today announced his intention to nominate John J. Easton, Jr., of Vermont, to be Assistant Secretary of Energy for Domestic and International Energy Policy. This is a new position.

Since 1989, Mr. Easton has served at the Department of Energy as General Counsel, 1991–present; and as Assistant Secretary for International Affairs and Energy Emergencies, 1989–91. Prior to joining the Department of Energy, Mr. Easton served with the law firm of Miller, Eggleston and Rosenberg, Ltd., 1987–89. Mr. Easton was twice elected attorney general of Vermont and served in that position from 1981 to 1985.

Mr. Easton graduated from the University of Colorado (B.S., 1964), and Georgetown University (J.D., 1970). He served in the U.S. Air Force from 1964 to 1968. He was born June 16, 1943, in San Francisco, CA. Mr. Easton currently resides in Arlington, VA.

# Nomination of Kent N. Brown To Be United States Ambassador to the Republic of Georgia
*July 2, 1992*

The President today announced his intention to nominate Kent N. Brown, of Virginia, a career member of the Senior Foreign Service, class of Counselor, to be Ambassador of the United States of America to the Republic of Georgia.

Since 1990, Mr. Brown has served as political adviser to the Supreme Allied Commander, Supreme Headquarters Allied Powers Europe in Casteau, Belgium. He has also served as: office director of the Bureau of Politico-Military Affairs at the Department of State, 1988–90; senior political adviser for the U.S. Mutual and Balanced Force Reductions and Conventional Forces in Europe Delegations in Vienna, 1984–88; a student at the North Atlantic Treaty Organization Defense College in Rome, 1983–84; Consular and political officer at the American Embassy in Moscow, 1980–83; and international affairs officer for the Bureau of European Affairs at the Department of State, 1975–79.

Mr. Brown graduated from the University of California, Davis, (B.A., 1964; M.A.,

1966). He has born May 7, 1944, in Oakland, CA. Mr. Brown is married, has two children, and resides in Casteau, Belgium.

# Remarks and an Exchange With Reporters on Departure for Camp David, Maryland
*July 2, 1992*

*The President.* I have two subjects I want to address very briefly before we leave here.

First, on the unemployment extension bill. This afternoon the House passed an unemployment bill, and the Senate is expected to act shortly; it may have already moved. But the bill that came out of the House-Senate conference is a good one. It took the best of the House and Senate positions. It's paid for, and it does not violate the budget agreement. And it preserves the fiscal discipline that is so vital to our economic recovery. There are no new taxes in the bill. It doesn't raise unemployment taxes or raise the unemployment wage-base. Most of the objectionable policies were dropped from it. The extra benefits will give unemployed Americans as much as 52 weeks of unemployment insurance. This is an important safeguard for workers who still can't find jobs as the economy continues to grow. And I'm glad that we were able to work it out with the Congress in the last couple of days.

The current program runs out on Saturday. I want to make sure that people keep getting these extended benefits. Therefore, I will sign this bill as soon as it reaches my desk. And I might say at the end of this statement, once again, I was very pleased to see the Fed move to reduce the rates because clearly that will have an economic stimulus that will help get this country back to work real fast.

The second subject: I have just concluded another meeting on AIDS. And with me is Bishop Swing, who ministers to many AIDS patients, is in the forefront of the struggle against AIDS. He comes from San Francisco, a friend to Barbara and to me. Also there was Dr. Burt Lee, my own personal

physician but who's had an active role in AIDS—he was on the AIDS Commission before he came here; Mary Fisher, who is personally involved with the disease; Dr. Fauci, one of our Nation's leading researchers out at NIH. And I mentioned, I think, Dr. Sullivan of HHS.

But we met in there, and I was asking them, how can I better convey the concern that I feel, and what can I do better to convey what we are doing? And I believe that I must have the Nation know that we're all enmeshed in the pain that people feel about this disease, whether they have the disease, afflicted by it, or whether they're people who just want to help.

I think it's important to emphasize that progress has been made. And we listened to Dr. Fauci talk about the progress that's been made, the hope that he and the other great researchers and scientists in this country have for progress on the vaccines, for example; the fact there are three different ways now to try to contain this disease.

And then the third point is the determination that we all feel that we must win this battle. And the bishop and Dr. Fauci pointed out to me something that I do know and perhaps have not articulated it, and that is that the United States has a key leadership role here. It's a worldwide problem. And our science is on the cutting edge. Our researchers aren't the only ones doing the job, but they are doing a superb job. I just want others around the world to know that we share their concerns, and we want to share our science with anyone we possibly can help. And so it was that area. We talked a little bit, Lou did, Lou Sullivan brought up the point he makes about the ADA bill where we are opposed to discrimination. And that bill, that forward civil rights legislation, addressed itself to that.

So it was a good meeting. And I will continue to find ways to take to the Nation the concern that I feel, that Barbara feels on this dreaded disease. It affects so many families. And we've got to make sure that we remain doing everything we can. As we all know, the funding for research is substantially up and the requests for next year very strong. But I wish there was more even. But we'll keep doing our job. And I have learned a lot from my dear friend Bishop Swing, again. And also, I'm grateful to those others that attended the meeting.

Thank you all very much.

### Proposed Family Life Executive Order

*Q.* Have you received the letter from the Baptists concerning the position that you've taken with—their objection to your position on "20/20" about hiring homosexuals? Not making a litmus test?

*The President.* I didn't hear anything about that. I didn't see anything.

*Q.* The Christian Life Commission has sent you a letter that said it's too late for meetings and that action is required on this policy. They're asking you——

*The President.* What is that?

*Q.* They're asking you to sign the proposed Executive order on family life—the definition, sir?

*The President.* Well, I'll have to take a look at what we're talking about here.

*Q.* What about Magic Johnson's concerns that he's raised?

*The President.* I think my position on family life is pretty well known to this country.

### AIDS Policy

*Q.* Have you had any more communication with Magic?

*The President.* No, and we've tried to get in touch with him. I asked Dr. Sullivan about that again. And I don't know that—I know I haven't been. But we have tried to get in touch with Magic Johnson. He's a part of the Commission. We know their reservations. But there's no hostility here. Anybody that has suggestions as to how I can do my job better in expressing the concerns that we feel as a Nation, so much the better. But I don't know what his latest

position is on this. But I'd be very anxious to hear from him and to understand more clearly what his concerns are.

*Q.* Are you open to a possible change in the immigration law, sir? That's been one of the major points of criticism.

*The President.* Well, we discussed it a little bit. And I know there's some concern on that. But I'd want to get some recommendations from our expert before I committed myself on that.

### The Economy

*Q.* Mr. President, since you've staked so much of your reelection on the economic recovery, doesn't the lagging unemployment, if it lags all the way to November, doesn't that decrease your chances for reelection?

*The President.* I don't know, Jim [Jim Miklaszewski, NBC News]. I hear so many things that decrease, or some that increase, my chances. I feel that we all have a stake, regardless of the politics, in an improved economy. All I know is that we would not have unemployment at this level if I could have gotten our investment incentives passed by the Congress. And I say that not to blame anybody, but what I've felt has been necessary all along is economic stimulus. That's why we had a specific program proposed, and most of it is languishing on Capitol Hill.

Having said that, the economy is growing. Having said that, I am very much concerned about the unemployment figures. I still maintain that unemployment is a lagging indicator because there are other things that are quite positive, including the fact that interest rates are even lower now than they've been. And that, inevitably, spurs investment and jobs.

So, there are mixed reports. One day we'll get a good statistic; another day we'll have one that isn't so good. But when it involves human life, when it involves somebody wanting to work that doesn't have a job, then of course we're concerned about that. I don't know about the political implications, but I am convinced that the economy is continuing to improve.

I've got to go.

*Note: The President spoke at 6:05 p.m. on the South Lawn at the White House. In his remarks, he referred to Rev. William E. Swing, Episcopal Bishop of the Diocese of San Francisco.*

# Radio Address to the Nation on Health Care Reform
*July 3, 1992*

Today, I'm asking all Americans to help me break a logjam holding up reform of our health care system. Health care in our country is too expensive, too complicated. And too many times, the system is downright unfair. I've proposed comprehensive reforms, including four pieces of legislation now waiting in Congress' in-box. Americans could begin enjoying the benefits of reform right away if only Congress would act.

Let me tell you about our plan, including my legislation and some initiatives by House and Senate Republicans. We would lower costs for patients and providers alike by keeping high taxes, costly litigation, and big bureaucracies off their backs. We're fighting to give self-employed Americans the same tax advantages that big corporations already have, and that is being able to take 100 percent of health insurance premiums off their income taxes.

Our legislation also would help small business and self-employed people get the same break as the big guys through new purchasing networks and broader risk pooling. That's good because it will help drive down health care costs for everyone. And House Republicans have a good idea to let both employers and employees contribute to new tax-free MediSave accounts for health care.

It's time to reform our antiquated system, move things into the electronic age. Our legislation would cut paperwork and redtape and put health insurance on a modern electronic billing system. Going to the doctor should involve no more paperwork than using a credit card. I've also asked that horse-and-buggy-era rules end and that practices for patient records and consumer health information be replaced with computerization. By the end of the decade, these two reforms alone would save Americans an estimated $24 billion a year.

Just this week I sent Congress a bill to curb the runaway costs of medical liability. Nearly every community in this country knows gifted medical people, conscientious men and women, who no longer use their talents and training because they're afraid of being wiped out by damage suits. That's wrong. And it hurts every one of us. Everywhere I travel in this country, people tell me Americans should make more effort helping each other instead of suing each other. And that's why I'm asking Congress to pass my plan to put caps on damages and encourage settling disputes out of court.

We need medical malpractice reform now. But there's a logjam, the old-time liberal leadership in the Senate and the House stalling my reforms. While I want to curb the excessive damage awards in medical malpractice cases, too many in that Capitol Hill crowd are too beholden to the trial lawyers lobby to act in the people's interest. Where I want the freedom and the proven efficiency of the modern market to work, the old-time leadership wants Federal bureaucrats to control prices and ration services.

The biggest story of our time is the failure of socialism and all its empty promises, including nationalized health care and government price-setting. But somehow this news that shook the world hasn't seeped through the doors of the Democratic cloakrooms on Capitol Hill.

And that's why I'm asking your help. Let's get them the message. Americans deserve a better health care system. And they support the principles of my plan. Let's get our Senators and Congressmen off the dime and make them bring my plan to a vote.

Thank you for listening. And may God bless the United States of America.

*Note: This address was recorded at 11:02 a.m. on July 2 in the Oval Office at the White House for broadcast after 6 a.m. on July 3.*

## Statement on Signing the Unemployment Compensation Amendments of 1992
*July 3, 1992*

Today I am pleased to sign into law H.R. 5260, the "Unemployment Compensation Amendments of 1992." This legislation would extend the Emergency Unemployment Compensation (EUC) program to March of next year. Without this extension, the EUC program would expire on July 4th.

Unemployment has a profound effect on people's lives. The extension of the EUC program is consistent with my strong and sustained commitment to providing needed assistance to the unemployed and their families while the economy recovers. These benefits will provide critical support to unemployed Americans until they can find jobs. I am pleased that the Administration and the Congress worked together successfully in the last few days to enact this important extension of benefits.

I call on the Congress to move rapidly on my economic growth package, with hopefully the same bipartisan spirit of cooperation. Enactment of these reforms and incentives is essential to creating the jobs that all Americans want. Action on them is long overdue. I urge the Congress now to turn to this unfinished business and to quickly enact my program for economic growth and job creation to ensure a strong, sustained recovery and long-term economic prosperity for our Nation.

GEORGE BUSH

The White House,
July 3, 1992

*Note: H.R. 5260, approved July 3, was assigned Public Law No. 102–318. An original was not available for verification of the content of this statement.*

## Statement by Press Secretary Fitzwater on the Andean Trade Preference Act
*July 3, 1992*

President Bush today proclaimed Bolivia and Colombia to be beneficiary countries under the Andean Trade Preference Act of 1991 (ATPA). These are the first two countries to be designated under the ATPA.

The ATPA is designed to help encourage a transition from the production of illicit drugs to legitimate products in the Andean countries. Under the Act, beneficiary countries may export a wide range of products to the United States on a duty-free or preferential tariff basis.

The President's action helps fulfill a commitment he made at the 1990 Cartagena drug summit to improve access to the U.S. market for exports from Andean countries. It is one element of the Bush administration's war against international drug trafficking. The administration is continuing its review of the status of other potential beneficiaries, Peru and Ecuador.

*Note: The proclamations of July 2 are listed in Appendix E at the end of this volume.*

## Statement by Press Secretary Fitzwater on the Macedonia Recognition Dispute
*July 3, 1992*

The President strongly supports early resolution of the dispute over recognition of the former Yugoslav Republic of Macedonia. In this connection, we welcome efforts of the European Community to find a solution, including those taken at the June 29 summit. The United States would support any solution that is acceptable to the parties themselves. The United States therefore stands ready to do what it can, in support of European Community efforts, to help the parties solve this problem so that they can get on with a normal relationship.

## Remarks to the Pepsi 400 Drivers and Owners in Daytona Beach, Florida
*July 4, 1992*

Thank you all very much. Thank you guys for the welcome, appreciate it. Thank you very, very much. First off, let me just pay my respects to the France family. Bill's late dad was a friend, and we mourn his passing, a great guy, great for racing, a great American, the values always intact. So I wanted to mention that at the beginning of these very brief remarks.

I salute the spirit of NASCAR, the spirit of racing. If there's ever a group of people that stood for what we call family values, American traditional values, it's this crowd I'm talking to right now. When I think of the Fourth of July, I count my blessings for our freedom. I know we've got some big problems in this country, but there's an awful lot right about the United States of America, too. And this spirit that you feel just the minute you get here expresses a lot about that.

So I really wanted to pop in here, just wish you well, tell you I'm glad to be back. This is my third visit to a race in Daytona.

Having been the grand marshal of the Daytona 500, why, I expect it's only downhill. But here I am as President of the United States; maybe that will help a little bit.

But keep up the great work for American sports, American values. We're very, very proud of you. And as for Richard Petty Day or Richard Petty, number 43—they're saluting him all the way around the track here— I'm proud to be at his side on this very special day, too.

Thank you all, and best of luck to all of you.

*Note: The President spoke at 9:52 a.m. in Garage 42C at Daytona International Speedway. In his remarks, he referred to William C. France, president of the National Association for Stock Car Auto Racing (NASCAR); the late William H.G. France, founder of NASCAR; and all-time champion driver Richard Petty, who was participating in his final race at Daytona International Speedway.*

## Remarks at the Richard Petty Tribute in Daytona Beach
*July 4, 1992*

Thank you all very much. I can think of no better place to wish our Nation happy Independence Day, happy Fourth of July, than standing right here with this patriotic, wonderful turnout of people, all-American crowd. Thank you very much.

This is the day when we celebrate our independence and count our blessings. The way I see it, yes, there are problems, but we are still the freest, fairest, and the greatest country on the face of the Earth.

I just met with the NASCAR drivers, a real thrill for a sports fan. They epitomize the best: the best in sportsmanship, the best in family, the best in patriotic values. So today, on the Fourth of July, this President comes not only to greet the American people and the fans here, but this President comes to greet a king, Richard Petty, one of the great Americans. Richard, I'm proud to be at your side.

*Note: The President spoke at 10:55 a.m. at Daytona International Speedway.*

## Remarks at an Independence Day Celebration in Faith, North Carolina
*July 4, 1992*

Thank you all very much. Mayor, thank you. Thank you very much, Mayor Hampton. And let me say to all of you, please be seated. [*Laughter*] Sorry about that. What a great day in Faith, and what a wonderful way to get here: play a couple of innings of ball, eat a little barbecue, drink a little of that wine or whatever they call it over there. [*Laughter*] Really, we're thrilled to be here, and thank you for that very, very warm welcome. I say warm, I use the term advisedly. [*Laughter*]

I'll tell you a little Trivial Pursuit: Fifty years ago almost to this day, I was a naval aviation cadet at Chapel Hill, North Carolina. That was my first taste of North Carolina hospitality, and this is my last and my very best up till now. So thank you all very, very much.

It's great to see our Governor here, doing a superb job for this State. You'll miss him in the governorship, but we've got to keep him active. He's done a great job for the State of North Carolina. May I pay my respects to another man I've been with shoulder to shoulder, Congressman Coble here, and just say to all of you, Daisy Bost and all that worked on this program, what a magnificent show this is. The Governor is right: We are proud to be in Faith, North Carolina, and proud to see this spirit alive and well.

I didn't hear the East Rowan High School Marching Band, but somebody—here they are right here. Fantastic.

But this is a very special American day. I just came from the races down there in Daytona, and we saluted the king, a son of North Carolina, Richard Petty. Dale Earnhardt, Dale showed us around and explained it, so it's been a great big high of a day for me here.

This one is a picture postcard holiday setting. You've got it all with the Little League and the softball games and the wheelbarrow races and the parade down Main Street. Now I'll be very short because I want to go over and try the bungee jumping. [*Laughter*] No, Barbara said it's okay to throw your hat in the ring, but not the whole body. [*Laughter*]

But we meet today in the State that gave birth to flight way back a thousand years ago, and on the day when the eagle soars proudest of all. We meet in smalltown America, in many ways, as I survey our great country, in many ways the spiritual heart of all America.

Several miles up the road is Salisbury, home to our friend Liddy Dole and home to Cheerwine—[*laughter*]—and a little east, Siler City, where television's Aunt Bea is buried. I've always wondered if Aunt Bea were with us today, if she'd be serving broccoli. I hope not. [*Laughter*]

Not every place in America is like these wonderful towns, but its values can and should be because the values that the

Mayor mentioned, the values the Governor talked about, the values that you hold dear are the values that hold our entire country together. And we never should forget that.

When I go back to Washington, Barbara and I, we have about an hour and a half, I believe it is, maybe a couple of hours at the airport. Then we fly to Poland, where I'll stand shoulder to shoulder Sunday morning with Lech Walesa, the President. Remember him? The guy that stood up for freedom when nobody else could do it in Poland? Stood up and took the heat, and now Poland is free. He looks to the United States, and he says, "Above all the countries, it was the United States of America that stood with me and offered me the hope for freedom."

You know what it means to be good neighbors. You know what it is to have families, strong and united; good schools; safe neighborhoods; job-creating economy; and a world at peace. Now, you go over to the Faith Soda Shop or the Hairport or R&I Variety, and you'll see the values that can achieve these goals. One is faith in self-reliance. You believe in equal rights for all Americans. Don't let anybody knock your town; you stand with me against bigotry and against racism. You believe in what is good and what is right.

Some regard principles as disposable, like TV dinners, but they couldn't be more wrong. Let others support some of this— films and the programs which mock small-town America. But I stand with the millions who support your America. And there's nothing wrong with a Nation more like Salisbury or Faith, North Carolina. And believe me, carry those principles with you.

It's not just the name of the town, but from this springs another smalltown virtue: We believe America is special because of fidelity to God. We have not forgotten that we are one Nation under God, and that's an important thing to point out on July 4th.

I heard from the Mayor that there are 553, technically, 553 residents. But she tells me that on Sunday more than 800 attend church services, and that's pretty good out of a town of 553. Think of that. You show why, according to a Gallup poll, America is the most religious nation on Earth.

Remember the small boy expressing that conviction: "God bless Mother and Daddy, my brother and sister." And he says, "Oh, and God, take care of yourself because if anything happens to you, we're all sunk." [*Laughter*] And that kid is right, just as right as he can be.

So, the American people really have mountains of faith. And I believe the God who gave us life also gave us liberty. So again, I'd like to use this wonderful occasion, this national holiday, perhaps our greatest, to call on the Congress to pass a constitutional amendment permitting voluntary prayer in the public schools.

Barbara and I were talking earlier to people for whom every day is the Fourth of July. They don't apologize for the choking up when you hear "The Star-Spangled Banner" or standing at attention when you say the Pledge of Allegiance. And they don't apologize for the lump in the throat when a few blocks away over here on Gantt Street in the American Legion building they visit a monument dedicated to the veterans, the living and the dead, of every American war.

Here in Faith, memories run long, just as principles run deep. And Jim touched on it, but you know how to answer those who say that the success of Desert Storm should be forgotten. But look, you had 76,000, as he said, troops in this one State, deployed from North Carolina. I don't think Saddam Hussein—who might by now have nuclear weapons, or if we hadn't challenged him we'd all be paying $10 for gas as he moved into Saudi Arabia—I don't think he doubts for a minute the will and the strength and the patriotism of the American people.

I know very well our veterans haven't forgotten it, those courageous, the best fighting forces we've ever put together. We stay together. I told Howard Coble—I sometimes risk being a little personal. But I was shot down in World War II, and I learned something. I learned something in combat: The wingman doesn't pull away from the flight leader. When I was shot down into the Pacific, it was my teammates, one located my raft, another shot down a boat that was put out from a Japanese island, and I learned this: We are a team. We're a united country. When the going gets tough, we get moving. We don't apologize, and we don't quit. We never quit. And we don't forget the POW's and the MIA's, I might add, either. We're with them.

Eisenhower spoke of "the great and priceless privilege of growing up in a small town." Well, Barbara and I are privileged to be in a small town that proves how right Ike was.

And ours is a nation, believe me, ours is a nation whose best days lie ahead. These kids here can go to bed at night with less fear of nuclear war because we've been here.

Now we've got to keep moving and bring that change to everybody in America that wants opportunity. And we can do it. Why?

Because on this special day of freedom we are still the United States of America: nothing to apologize for, everything to be proud of.

Thank you, and God bless each and every one of you.

*Note: The President spoke at 3:07 p.m. at Legion Park. In his remarks, he referred to Mayor Judy Hampton of Faith; Daisy Bost, program coordinator for the Independence Day celebration in Faith; Dale Earnhardt, NASCAR driver and Winston Cup champion; Elizabeth Hanford Dole, president of the American Red Cross; and the late Frances Bavier, actress.*

# Remarks Following Discussions With President Lech Walesa of Poland in Warsaw
## July 5, 1992

*President Walesa.* I'd like to state once again that we owe a great deal to America. We'd like to pay tribute to the President and try to do everything to retain the interest of the States and of Mr. President, and at the same time making it as good as possible for America.

American involvement in leading towards democracy was great. And in Poland, American involvement is necessary for Europe. We simply cannot envisage Europe without an American presence.

It is not safe at all here after the dismantling of the Soviet Union, only today the dangers are somewhat different. And I am convinced that without U.S. presence we won't make it at all. That is why I wish to thank the President and to thank America for everything that Central Europe has achieved, particularly in this very special moment, and hoping for the presence of the President and of America in order for us to be successful. It can be successful; it can be great business; however, only if we do it together.

Once more I wish to welcome you most cordially, Mr. President, and your delegation. And I would wish you less problems with this part of the world.

*President Bush.* And may I just respond and tell the Polish side here what I've just told President Walesa, and that is we have every intention of remaining involved. We appreciate the President's understanding of the importance of NATO. And we feel that a vigorous trade between Poland and the United States is in our interests as well as Poland's.

So I told the President we would do everything we can to keep the United States involved, to keep a strong NATO, to stay in touch on the security side of things, and then to figure out what we can do to go forward on the trade matters because we think he has properly assessed the security concerns and economic concerns in Europe, and we want to continue to be helpful. And we will be. We will be.

There is a great affection in the United States for Poland, as you know from your own visits there. And the fact that Poland wants us to do what we're doing, stay involved, try to be constructive partners, that's very helpful for the United States, too. So thank you for your hospitality.

*Note: The remarks began at 12:45 p.m. in the Green Room at the Royal Palace. President Walesa spoke in Polish, and his re-* *marks were translated by an interpreter. A tape was not available for verification of the content of these remarks.*

## Remarks to Polish Citizens in Warsaw
*July 5, 1992*

Thank you, Mr. President, for those very kind words. And good afternoon to Mrs. Walesa. It's a pleasure to be back here. I'm pleased that the U.S. Presidential delegation, headed by our own Secretary Derwinski, could be here today.

So hello, Warsaw, and hello, Poland. Thank you all for this warm welcome. Barbara and I are honored to be back once more, to come home once more to the birthplace of the Revolution of '89. And I'm especially pleased to come here from America's Fourth of July celebration of freedom and carry that same spirit to a free Poland.

This is truly a homecoming, the day Poland welcomes home a part of its proud history, a great patriot, a patron of freedom. You spoke eloquently of him. Through his long life, Ignacy Paderewski fought for a free and independent Poland. When independence came, Paderewski served as Prime Minister of your new nation. When occupation came, he joined the exiled government. And when he died, America gave this great friend of freedom a place alongside our honored dead in Arlington Cemetery to rest, in the words of our President Franklin Roosevelt, "until Poland would be free."

Few knew then how many dark days would come and go, how many lifetimes would pass until this day. When years passed without fanfare or ceremony, when a small, simple marker took the place of a larger stone, Poles understood. In 5 years or 50 years, Paderewski would one day come home to Polish soil.

Today, a patriot has come home. Today, Poland is free. And what a magnificent day this is. On this Sunday, from St. John's Cathedral to the village churches of Zakopane, the bells toll not simply the solemn requiem but a new beginning, a new birth of freedom for Poland and its people.

It's a new beginning not just for Poland but for all of Europe and the world. It is proper that we mark this new birth in your country. It was here in Poland that the Second World War began. It was here in Poland that the cold war first cast its shadow. And it was here in Poland that the people at long last brought the cold war to an end.

I've said many times that in the deepest sense, the cold war was a war of ideas, a contest between two ways of life. The rulers of the old regime claimed they saw the triumph of the totalitarian ideal written in the laws of history. They failed to see the love of freedom written in the human heart.

I recall my last visit to Poland: The fierce defiance and determination in the faces of the workers gathered in what was then called the Lenin Shipyard in Gdansk, the warmth and the welcome for America made plain to Barbara and me by you, the good people of Poland. We'll never forget it.

Just think of the new world that's emerged these past 3 years: Europe, whole and free; Russia, turning from dictatorship to democracy; Ukraine and the other nations of the old Soviet empire, free and independent. Look at this new world, and remember where that revolution began: right here in Poland.

Today, Poland stands transformed. Your bold economic reforms have earned the world's admiration and support. And what's more, they're working. Shelves that once stood empty are now stocked with goods. Gone is the old Communist Party headquarters, now home to the Warsaw Stock Exchange and the Polish-America Enterprise Fund, providing seed capital to help Poland's private sector growth and prosper.

Gone are the slogans and the sham reality; everywhere you hear new voices and new hope. Freedom has come home to Poland.

For all that is new, there are things that have not changed, things that sustained you through the darkest days: Polish strength, Polish spirit, Polish pride. Reaching your dreams will be difficult. I know the sheer volume of new voices can sometimes be deafening. But from the clamor of new voices must come democracy, a common vision of the common good.

Of course, in many places and for many people there is more pain than progress. But we must take care to separate cause from consequence. Poland's time of trial is not caused by private enterprise but by the stubborn legacy of four decades of Communist misrule. Make no mistake: The path you have chosen is the right path. And as you say, Mr. President, it is the path of pioneers. Free government and free enterprise have helped Poland overcome a crippling past. Free government and free markets will bring Poland a bright future.

Poland is no stranger to sacrifice. Many times before, you were asked to do without for the greater good of the state. But today is different. This time, yours is a sacrifice blessed by freedom, the sacrifice of a nation determined to make its destination democracy.

Poland has made great progress in its reforms, moving this country to a new stage in its economic revolution. As always, the United States of America stands ready to help. In 1989, the United States worked with Poland and others to establish a $1 billion fund to help support a free currency for a free Poland. Now we need to consider new uses for that fund, to help Poland as it faces today's challenges. That's why I am proposing that once Poland is back on track with the IMF that we make that fund available for other uses, perhaps to finance Polish exports or to help capitalize banks to support new businesses. The U.S. contribution alone will amount to $200 million.

This is a Polish and American idea that I will take to the economic summit at Munich. There I will urge the leaders of the world's great democracies to join with us to seek new ways to help Poland toward progress and prosperity. Let there be no doubt: America shares Poland's dream. America wants Poland to succeed. And we will stand at your side until success is guaranteed to everyone.

We mark today not simply the memory of a great Polish patriot, we celebrate the men of moral courage who sustain this nation: President Lech Walesa, Father Popieluszko, Pope John Paul II. But Poland could not have come this far, Poland could not have won its freedom if only a few had the courage to stand up against the state. Freedom was won by the everyday heroes of the underground, the men and women who kept faith when faith was forbidden, who spoke the truth against a wall of lies, the true heroes of democracy: the people of Poland.

Your strength of spirit drives away all doubt: Poland will succeed. Poland will succeed because Poles have made this journey before. In a strange new world called America, in the stockyards of Chicago, in the steelworks of Cleveland, in a thousand towns thousands of miles from this land they love, Poles worked and worshipped and built a better life—Polish hands building the American dream. Now at long last, Poles can build that dream right here at home.

As President of the United States of America, as a fellow democrat, as friend of a free Poland, I bring this message: America stands with you. America wants Poland to succeed and to prosper. America wants Poland, now and forever, to be free.

Thank you all for this warm welcome. May God bless the free people of Poland. And may God bless both our great countries, Poland and the United States of America. Thank you. Thank you very much.

*Note: The President spoke at approximately 2:30 p.m. at Castle Square. In his remarks, he referred to Father Jerzy Popieluszko, a Roman Catholic priest who was murdered in 1984.*

# Munich Economic Summit: Yugoslavia Communique
*July 7, 1992*

We, the leaders of our seven countries and representatives of the European Community, are deeply concerned about the ongoing Yugoslav crisis. We strongly condemn the use of violence in the former Yugoslavia and deplore the suffering inflicted upon its population. We particularly deplore those actions directed against civilian populations, as well as the forced expulsion of ethnic groups.

Although all parties have contributed to this state of affairs, the Serbian leadership and the Yugoslav army controlled by it bear the greatest share of the responsibility. We support the EC Conference on Yugoslavia chaired by Lord Carrington as the key forum for ensuring a durable and equitable political solution to the outstanding problems of the former Yugoslavia, including constitutional arrangements for Bosnia and Hercegovina.

We call on all parties to resume negotiations in that conference in good faith and without preconditions. We welcome the close consultations between the conference chaired by Lord Carrington, the EC, the U.N., and other parties concerned with the Yugoslav crisis.

These consultations could lead to the holding of a broader international conference to address unresolved questions, including issues related to minorities. We stress the absolute need for the parties in former Yugoslavia to show the will for peace which is indispensable to success and without which the peoples of former Yugoslavia will continue to suffer.

The tragic humanitarian situation, especially in Bosnia and Hercegovina, is unacceptable. We fully endorse as heads of state and government the efforts of the international community to provide relief. We welcome the efforts made in achieving the opening of the airport of Sarajevo, and we support actions taken by UNPROFOR to secure the airport.

The blockade of Sarajevo must be lifted and the shelling of the town stopped in order to sustain a comprehensive relief operation. We express our gratitude to all participants in the airlift to Sarajevo and the supply of its population. We appeal to all parties in Bosnia and Hercegovina not to imperil the humanitarian effort.

We firmly warn the parties concerned, including irregular forces, not to take any action that would endanger the lives of those engaged in the relief operation. Should these efforts fail due to an unwillingness of those concerned to fully cooperate with the United Nations, we believe the Security Council will have to consider other measures, not excluding military means, to achieve its humanitarian objectives.

The airlift to Sarajevo can only be the beginning of a larger humanitarian effort. Safe access by road to Sarajevo, as well as to other parts of Bosnia and Hercegovina in need, must be guaranteed. The needs of the hundreds of thousands of refugees and displaced persons require further significant financial support. We are willing to contribute and ask others also to make fair contributions.

We underline the need for Serbia and Croatia to respect the territorial integrity of Bosnia and Hercegovina and for all military forces not subject to the authority of the government of Bosnia and Hercegovina to either be withdrawn or disbanded and disarmed with their weapons placed under effective international monitoring.

We call on all parties to prevent the conflict from spreading to other parts of the former Yugoslavia.

We urge the Serbian leadership to respect minority rights in full, to refrain from further repression in Kosovo, and to engage in serious dialogue with representatives of Kosovo with a view to defining a status of autonomy according to the draft convention of the EC Conference on Yugoslavia.

Sanctions decided by the U.N. Security Council in Resolution 757, as well as all other provisions of relevant U.N. resolutions, must be fully implemented. We support the efforts of the U.N. peacekeeping forces in implementing the U.N. peace plan for Croatia and all its elements.

We demand that Serbs and Croats extend their full cooperation to the U.N. peace plan and make every effort to bring the bloodshed in Croatia to an end.

We do not accept Serbia and Montenegro as the sole successor state to the former Yugoslavia.

We call for the suspension of the delegation of Yugoslavia in the proceedings of the CSCE and other relevant international fora and organizations.

*Note: An original was not available for verification of the content of this communique.*

# Munich Economic Summit Political Declaration: Shaping the New Partnership
*July 7, 1992*

I. 1. We, the leaders of our seven countries and the representatives of the European Community, support the democratic revolution which has ended the East-West confrontation and has fundamentally changed the global political landscape. Since we last met, further dramatic changes have accelerated progress towards democracy, market-based economies, and social justice. The way has been opened for a new partnership of shared responsibilities, not only in Europe which at long last is reunited, but also in the Asia-Pacific region and elsewhere in the world. We are entering an era where confrontation has given way to cooperation.

2. This new partnership will take many forms. The former adversaries of East and West will cooperate extensively on economic, political and security issues. We look for the worldwide development of similar patterns of cooperation within regions and between regions. As developed countries, we offer continuing support and assistance to developing countries. We believe that transnational problems, in particular the proliferation of weapons of mass destruction, can be solved only through international cooperation. Partnership will flourish as common values take root, based on the principles of political and economic freedom, human rights, democracy, justice and the rule of law. We believe that political and economic freedom are closely linked and mutually reinforcing and that, to that end, good governance and respect for human rights are important criteria in providing economic assistance.

3. The countries of Central and Eastern Europe and the new states of the former Soviet Union can now seize unprecedented opportunities—but they also face enormous challenges. We will support them as they move toward the achievement of democratic societies and political and economic freedom. We encourage them to create a stable constitutional and legal framework for their reform programmes and commend their efforts to cut substantially the proportion of public spending devoted to the military sector.

4. The Treaty signed at Maastricht by the twelve members of the European Community is a historic step on the way to European Union. Its implementation will enhance political stability on the European continent and open up new opportunities for cooperation.

5. Since we last met, the creation of the North Atlantic Cooperation Council has enhanced the cooperative relationship of the North Atlantic Alliance with countries in Central and Eastern Europe and with the states of the former Soviet Union. WEU, too, is strengthening its relationship with countries in Central and Eastern Europe.

6. The need for international cooperation has also been underlined by new instabilities and conflicts due to resurgent nationalism and interethnic tensions. Communal and territorial disputes are being settled by force, causing death, destruction, and widespread dislocation of innocent people throughout the former Yugoslavia, in parts

of the former Soviet Union, and elsewhere in the world.

7. The full and immediate implementation of all CSCE commitments is essential in building security and stability in Europe. All CSCE states must solve their disputes by peaceful means and guarantee the equal treatment of all minorities. We call upon the Helsinki CSCE Summit to take decisions to strengthen the CSCE's capabilities for conflict prevention, crisis management and peaceful resolution of disputes. We also look forward to the establishment of a security cooperation forum at the Helsinki Summit. In this regard, we welcome the recent decisions by NATO foreign ministers and WEU ministers on support for peacekeeping operations carried out under the responsibility of the CSCE. We support the development of a regular and productive dialogue between Japan and the CSCE on matters of common concern.

8. In the Asia-Pacific region, existing regional frameworks, such as the ASEAN Post-Ministerial Conferences and the Asia-Pacific Economic Cooperation, have an important part to play in promoting peace and stability. We are seriously concerned at the present situation in Cambodia and urge all parties concerned to support UNTAC and uphold the still fragile peace process to bring it to a successful conclusion.

9. We welcome Russia's commitment to a foreign policy based on the principle of law and justice. We believe that this represents a basis for full normalization of the Russian-Japanese relationship through resolving the territorial issue.

II. 1. The end of the East-West confrontation provides a historic opportunity, but also underlines the urgent need to curb the proliferation of nuclear weapons, other weapons of mass destruction and missiles capable of delivering them. We are firmly of the view that the indefinite extension of the nuclear Non-Proliferation Treaty at the 1995 Review Conference will be a key step in this process and that the process of nuclear arms control and reduction must be continued. The motivation for nuclear proliferation will also be reduced through efforts to advance regional security.

2. We urge countries not yet parties to the NPT to join. We look forward to the early adherence to the NPT as non-nuclear weapons states of Ukraine, Kazakhstan and Belarus as well as the other non-Russian states of the former Soviet Union. We shall continue through bilateral contacts and the International Science and Technology Centres in Moscow and Kiev our efforts to inhibit the spread of expertise on weapons of mass destruction. We attach the highest importance to the establishment in the former Soviet Union of effective export controls on nuclear materials, weapons and other sensitive goods and technologies and will offer training and practical assistance to help achieve this.

3. The world needs the most effective possible action to safeguard nuclear materials and to detect and prevent the transfer or the illicit or clandestine production of nuclear weapons. Nuclear cooperation will in future be conditional on adherence to the NPT or an existing equivalent internationally binding agreement as well as on the adoption of full-scope International Atomic Energy Agency safeguards, as recently laid down by the Nuclear Suppliers Group. The IAEA must receive the resources necessary to strengthen the existing safeguards regime and to conduct effective special inspections of undeclared but suspect nuclear sites as one means of achieving this. We will support reference by the IAEA of unresolved cases of proliferation to the UN Security Council.

4. We reaffirm our willingness to share the benefits of peaceful nuclear technology with all other states, in accordance with our non-proliferation commitments.

5. We will continue to encourage all countries to adopt the guidelines of the Missile Technology Control Regime and welcome the recent decision by the plenary session of the MTCR to extend the scope of the guidelines to cover missiles capable of delivering all kinds of weapons of mass destruction. Each of us will continue our efforts to improve transparency and consultation in the transfer of conventional weapons and to encourage restraint in such transfers. Provision of full and timely information to the UN Arms Register is an important element in these efforts.

6. We will continue to intensify our coop-

eration in the area of export controls of sensitive items in the appropriate fora to reduce threats to international security. A major element of this effort is the informal exchange of information to improve and harmonize these export controls.

7. Arms control agreements which have been signed by the former Soviet Union, in particular the START and CFE treaties, must enter into force. The full implementation of the CFE Treaty will create the foundation for the new cooperative security framework in Europe. We welcome the far-reaching follow-on agreement on strategic nuclear weapons concluded by the US and Russia in June as another major step towards a safer, more stable world. Further measures, in particular the unilaterally announced elimination of ground-launched short-range nuclear weapons by the United States and the former Soviet Union, should be carried out as soon as possible. We support Russia in its efforts to secure the peaceful use of nuclear materials resulting from the elimination of nuclear weapons. The Geneva negotiations for a convention on the effective global ban on chemical weapons must be successfully concluded this year. We call on all nations to become original signatories to this convention.

III. 1. The new challenges underline the need for strengthening the UN, taking account of changing international circumstances. Since our last meeting in London the tasks and responsibilities of the UN have further increased in a dramatic way, especially in the area of crisis prevention, conflict management and the protection of minorities. The UN has played a central role in the international response to developments in the Gulf, in Cambodia, in the former Yugoslavia and in other regions of the world.

2. We support the UN's role in maintaining international peace and security. The accession to the UN of new states has reinforced the importance of this role. We call upon all these new member states to abide by their solemn undertakings to uphold the purposes and principles of the UN Charter.

3. We reaffirm our commitment to cooperate on existing refugee problems. We deplore action by any state or group against minorities that creates new flows of refugees and displaced persons.

4. We support moves undertaken so far by the Secretary-General to reform the Organization, including the appointment of a high-ranking emergency relief coordinator. The Secretary General's report "An Agenda for Peace" is a valuable contribution to the work of the United Nations on preventive diplomacy, peace-making and peace-keeping. We assure him of our readiness to provide the political support and resources needed to maintain international peace and security.

5. We strongly support improved cooperation between the UN and regional arrangements and agencies as envisaged in Chapter VIII of the UN Charter, which have an increasing role in solving conflicts.

6. In closing this Declaration, we reaffirm that recognition of the inherent dignity and of the equal and inalienable rights of all members of the human family is the foundation of freedom, justice and peace in the world. Human rights are not at the disposal of individual states or their governments. They cannot be subordinate to the rules of any political, ideological or religious system. The protection and the promotion of human rights remain one of the principal tasks of the community of nations.

*Note: This declaration was made available by the Office of the Press Secretary but was not issued as a White House press release.*

# Munich Economic Summit Declaration
*July 7, 1992*

1. We, the Heads of State and Government of seven major industrial nations and the President of the Commission of the European Community, have met in Munich

for our eighteenth annual Summit.

2. The international community is at the threshold of a new era, freed from the burden of the East-West conflict. Rarely have conditions been so favourable for shaping a permanent peace, guaranteeing respect for human rights, carrying through the principles of democracy, ensuring free markets, overcoming poverty and safeguarding the environment.

3. We are resolved, by taking action in a spirit of partnership, to seize the unique opportunities now available. While fundamental change entails risk, we place our trust in the creativity, effort and dedication of people as the true sources of economic and social progress. The global dimension of the challenges and the mutual dependencies call for world-wide cooperation. The close coordination of our policies as part of this cooperation is now more important than ever.

*World economy*

4. Strong world economic growth is the prerequisite for solving a variety of challenges we face in the post-Cold War world. Increasingly, there are signs of global economic recovery. But we will not take it for granted and will act together to assure the recovery gathers strength and growth picks up.

5. Too many people are out of work. The potential strength of people, factories and resources is not being fully employed. We are particularly concerned about the hardship unemployment creates.

6. Each of us faces somewhat different economic situations. But we all would gain greatly from stronger, sustainable non-inflationary growth.

7. Higher growth will help other countries, too. Growth generates trade. More trade will give a boost to developing nations and to the new democracies seeking to transform command economies into productive participants within the global marketplace. Their economic success is in our common interest.

8. A successful Uruguay Round will be a significant contribution to the future of the world economy. An early conclusion of the negotiations will reinforce our economies, promote the process of reform in Eastern Europe and give new opportunities for the well-being of other nations, including in particular the developing countries.

We regret the slow pace of the negotiations since we met in London last year. But there has been progress in recent months. Therefore we are convinced that a balanced agreement is within reach.

We welcome the reform of the European Community's Common Agricultural Policy which has just been adopted and which should facilitate the settlement of outstanding issues.

Progress has been made on the issue of internal support in a way which is consistent with the reform of the Common Agricultural Policy, on dealing with the volume of subsidized exports and on avoiding future disputes. These topics require further work. In addition, parties still have concerns in the areas of market access and trade in cereal substitutes that they seek to address.

We reaffirm that the negotiations should lead to a globally balanced result. An accord must create more open markets for goods and services and will require comparable efforts from all negotiating partners.

On this basis we expect that an agreement can be reached before the end of 1992.

9. We are committed, through coordinated and individual actions, to build confidence for investors, savers, and consumers: confidence that hard work will lead to a better quality of life; confidence that investments will be profitable; confidence that savings will be rewarded and that price stability will not be put at risk.

10. We pledge to adopt policies aimed at creating jobs and growth. We will seek to take the appropriate steps, recognizing our individual circumstances, to establish sound macroeconomic policies to spur stronger sustainable growth. With this in mind we have agreed on the following guidelines:

—to continue to pursue sound monetary and financial policies to support the upturn without rekindling inflation;

—to create the scope for lower interest rates through the reduction of excessive public deficits and the promotion of savings;

—to curb excessive public deficits above

all by limiting public spending. Taxpayers' money should be used more economically and more effectively.

—to integrate more closely our environmental and growth objectives, by encouraging market incentives and technological innovation to promote environmentally sound consumption and production.

As the risk of inflation recedes as a result of our policies, it will be increasingly possible for interest rates to come down. This will help promote new investment and therefore stronger growth and more jobs.

11. But good macroeconomic policies are not enough. All our economies are burdened by structural rigidities that constrain our potential growth rates. We need to encourage competition. We need to create a more hospitable environment for private initiative. We need to cut back excess regulation, which suppresses innovation, enterprise and creativity. We will strengthen employment opportunities through better training, education, and enhanced mobility. We will strengthen the basis for long-term growth through improvements in infrastructure and greater attention to research and development. We are urging these kinds of reforms for new democracies in the transition to market economies. We cannot demand less of ourselves.

12. The coordination of economic and financial policies is a central element in our common strategy for sustained, non-inflationary growth. We request our Finance Ministers to strengthen their cooperation on the basis of our agreed guidelines and to intensify their work to reduce obstacles to growth and therefore foster employment. We ask them to report to our meeting in Japan in 1993.

*United Nations Conference on Environment and Development (UNCED)*

13. The Earth Summit has been a landmark in heightening the consciousness of the global environmental challenges, and in giving new impetus to the process of creating a worldwide partnership on development and the environment. Rapid and concrete action is required to follow through on our commitments on climate change, to protect forests and oceans, to preserve

marine resources, and to maintain biodiversity. We therefore urge all countries, developed and developing, to direct their policies and resources towards sustainable development which safeguards the interest of both present and future generations.

14. To carry forward the momentum of the Rio Conference, we urge other countries to join us:

—in seeking to ratify the Climate Change Convention by the end of 1993,

—in drawing up and publishing national action plans, as foreseen at UNCED, by the end of 1993,

—in working to protect species and the habitats on which they depend,

—in giving additional financial and technical support to developing countries for sustainable development through official development assistance (ODA), in particular by replenishment of IDA, and for actions of global benefit through the Global Environment Facility (GEF) with a view to its being established as a permanent funding mechanism,

—in establishing at the 1992 UN General Assembly the Sustainable Development Commission which will have a vital role to play in monitoring the implementation of Agenda 21,

—in establishing an international review process for the forest principles, in an early dialogue, on the basis of the implementation of these principles, on possible appropriate internationally agreed arrangements, and in increased international assistance,

—in further improving monitoring of the global environment, including through better utilisation of data from satellite and other earth observation programmes,

—in the promotion of the development and diffusion of energy and environment technologies, including proposals for innovative technology programmes,

—by ensuring the international conference on straddling fish stocks and highly migratory fish stocks in the oceans is convened as soon as possible.

*Developing countries*

15. We welcome the economic and political progress which many developing countries have made, particularly in East and South-East Asia, but also in Latin America and in some parts of Africa. However, many countries throughout the world are still struggling against poverty. Sub-Sahara Africa, above all, gives cause for concern.

16. We are committed to dialogue and partnership founded on shared responsibility and a growing consensus on fundamental political and economic principles. Global challenges such as population growth and the environment can only be met through cooperative efforts by all countries. Reforming the economic and social sector of the UN system will be an important step to this end.

17. We welcome the growing acceptance of the principles of good governance. Economic and social progress can only be assured if countries mobilise their own potential, all segments of the population are involved and human rights are respected. Regional cooperation among developing countries enhances development and can contribute to stability, peaceful relations and reduced arms spending.

18. The industrial countries bear a special responsibility for a sound global economy. We shall pay regard to the effects of our policies on the developing countries. We will continue our best efforts to increase the quantity and quality of official development assistance in accordance with our commitments. We shall direct official development assistance more towards the poorest countries. Poverty, population policy, education, health, the role of women and the well-being of children merit special attention. We shall support in particular those countries that undertake credible efforts to help themselves. The more prosperous developing countries are invited to contribute to international assistance.

19. We underline the importance for developing countries of trade, foreign direct investment and an active private sector. Poor developing countries should be offered technical assistance to establish a more diversified export base especially in manufactured goods.

20. Negotiations on a substantial replenishment of IDA funds should be concluded before the end of 1992. The IMF should continue to provide concessional financing to support the reform programmes for the poorest countries. We call for an early decision by the IMF on the extension for one year of the Enhanced Structural Adjustment Facility and for the full examination of options for the subsequent period, including a renewal of the facility.

21. We are deeply concerned about the unprecedented drought in southern Africa. Two thirds of the Drought Appeal target has been met. But much remains to be done. We call on all countries to assist.

22. We welcome the progress achieved by many developing countries in overcoming the debt problems and regaining their creditworthiness. Initiatives of previous Summits have contributed to this. Nevertheless, many developing countries are still in a difficult situation.

23. We confirm the validity of the international debt strategy. We welcome the enhanced debt relief extended to the poorest countries by the Paris Club. We note that the Paris Club has agreed to consider the stock of debt approach, under certain conditions, after a period of three or four years, for the poorest countries that are prepared to adjust, and we encourage it to recognise the special situation of some highly indebted lower-middle-income countries on a case by case basis. We attach great importance to the enhanced use of voluntary debt conversions, including debt conversions for environmental protection.

*Central and eastern Europe*

24. We welcome the progress of the democracies in central and eastern Europe including the Baltic states (CEECs) towards political and economic reform and integration into the world economy. The reform must be pursued vigorously. Great efforts and even sacrifices are still required from their people. They have our continuing support.

25. We welcome the substantial multilateral and bilateral assistance in support of reform in the CEECs. Financing provided by the EBRD is playing a useful role. Since

1989, total assistance and commitments, in the form of grants, loans and credit guarantees by the Group of 24 and the international financial institutions, amounts to $52 billion. We call upon the Group of 24 to continue its coordination activity and to adapt it to the requirements of each reforming country. We reaffirm our readiness to make fair contributions.

26. We support the idea of working with Poland to reallocate, on the basis of existing arrangements, funds from the currency stabilization fund, upon agreement on an IMF programme, towards new uses in support of Poland's market reform effort, in particular by strengthening the competitiveness of Poland's business enterprises.

27. The industrial countries have granted substantial trade concessions to the CEECs in order to ensure that their reform efforts will succeed. But all countries should open their markets further. The agreements of the EC and EFTA countries aiming at the establishment of free trade areas with these countries are a significant contribution. We shall continue to offer the CEECs technical assistance in enhancing their export capacity.

28. We urge all CEECs to develop their economic relations with each other, with the new independent States of the former Soviet Union as well as more widely on a market-oriented basis and consistent with GATT principles. As a step in this direction we welcome the special cooperation among the CSFR, Poland and Hungary, and hope that free trade among them will soon be possible.

29. Investment from abroad should be welcomed. It is important for the development of the full economic potential of the CEECs. We urge the CEECs to focus their policies on the creation of attractive and reliable investment conditions for private capital. We are providing our bilateral credit insurance and guarantee instruments to promote foreign investment when these conditions, including servicing of debt, are met. We call upon enterprises in the industrial countries to avail themselves of investment opportunities in the CEECs.

### New independent States of the former Soviet Union

30. The far-reaching changes in the former Soviet Union offer an historic opportunity to make the world a better place: more secure, more democratic and more prosperous. Under President Yeltsin's leadership the Russian government has embarked on a difficult reform process. We look forward to our meeting with him to discuss our cooperation in support of these reforms. We are prepared to work with the leaders of all new States pursuing reforms. The success is in the interest of the international community.

31. We are aware that the transition will involve painful adjustments. We offer the new States our help for their self-help. Our cooperation will be comprehensive and will be tailored to their reform progress and internationally responsible behaviour, including further reductions in military spending and fulfilment of obligations already undertaken.

32. We encourage the new States to adopt sound economic policies, above all by bringing down budget deficits and inflation. Working with the IMF can bring experience to this task and lend credibility to the efforts being made. Macroeconomic stabilisation should not be delayed. It will only succeed if at the same time the building blocks of a market economy are also put into place, through privatisation, land reform, measures to promote investment and competition and appropriate social safeguards for the population.

33. Creditworthiness and the establishment of a dependable legal framework are essential if private investors are to be attracted. The creditworthiness of the new States will in particular be assessed by the way in which they discharge the financial obligations.

34. Private capital and entrepreneurial commitment must play a decisive and increasing part in economic reconstruction. We urge the new States to develop an efficient private business sector, in particular the body of small and medium-sized private companies which is indispensable for a market economy.

35. Rapid progress is particularly urgent

and attainable in two sectors: agriculture and energy. These sectors are of decisive importance in improving the supply situation and increasing foreign exchange revenue. Trade and industry in our countries are prepared to cooperate. Valuable time has already been lost because barriers to investment remain in place. For energy, we note the importance of the European Energy Charter for encouraging production and ensuring the security of supply. We urge rapid conclusion of the preparatory work.

36. All Summit participants have shown solidarity in a critical situation by providing extensive food aid, credits and medical assistance. They also have committed technical assistance. A broad inflow of know-how and experience to the new States is needed to help them realise their own potential. Both private and public sectors can contribute to this. What is needed most of all is concrete advice on the spot and practical assistance. The emphasis should be on projects selected for their value as a model or their strategic importance for the reform process. Partnerships and management assistance at corporate level can be particularly effective.

37. We stress the need for the further opening of international markets to products from the new States. Most-favoured-nation treatment should be applied to trade with the new States and consideration given to further preferential access. The new States should not impede reconstruction by setting up barriers to trade between themselves. It is in their own interest to cooperate on economic and monetary policy.

38. We want to help the new States to preserve their highly-developed scientific and technological skills and to make use of them in building up their economies. We call upon industry and science in the industrial countries to promote cooperation and exchange with the new States. By establishing International Science and Technology Centres we are helping to redirect the expertise of scientists and engineers who have sensitive knowledge in the manufacture of weapons of mass destruction towards peaceful purposes. We will continue our efforts to enable highly-qualified civil scientists to remain in the new States and to promote research cooperation with western industrial countries.

39. We welcome the membership of the new States in the international financial institutions. This will allow them to work out economic reform programmes in collaboration with these institutions and on this basis to make use of their substantial financial resources. Disbursements of these funds should be linked to progress in implementing reforms.

40. We support the phased strategy of cooperation between the Russian Government and the IMF. This will allow the IMF to disburse a first credit tranche in support of the most urgent stabilisation measures within the next few weeks while continuing to negotiate a comprehensive reform programme with Russia. This will pave the way for the full utilisation of the $ 24 bn support package announced in April. Out of this, $ 6 bn earmarked for a rouble stabilisation fund will be released when the necessary macroeconomic conditions are in place.

41. We suggest that country consultative groups should be set up for the new States, when appropriate, in order to foster close cooperation among the States concerned, international institutions and partners. The task of these groups would be to encourage structural reforms and to coordinate technical assistance.

*Safety of nuclear power plants in the new independent States of the former Soviet Union and in central and eastern Europe*

42. While we recognise the important role nuclear power plays in global energy supplies, the safety of Soviet-design nuclear power plants gives cause for great concern. Each State, through its safety authorities and plant operators, is itself responsible for the safety of its nuclear power plants. The new States concerned of the former Soviet Union and the countries of central and eastern Europe must give high priority to eliminating this danger. These efforts should be part of a market-oriented reform of energy policies encouraging commercial financing for the development of the energy sector.

43. A special effort should be made to improve the safety of these plants. We offer

the States concerned our support within the framework of a multilateral programme of action. We look to them to cooperate fully. We call upon other interested States to contribute as well.

44. The programme of action should comprise immediate measures in the following areas:
—operational safety improvements;
—near-term technical improvements to plants based on safety assessments;
—enhancing regulatory regimes.

Such measures can achieve early and significant safety gains.

45. In addition, the programme of action is to create the basis for longer-term safety improvements by the examination of
—the scope for replacing less safe plants by the development of alternative energy sources and the more efficient use of energy,
—the potential for upgrading plants of more recent design.

Complementary to this, we will pursue the early completion of a convention on nuclear safety.

46. The programme of action should develop clear priorities, provide coherence to the measures and ensure their earliest implementation. To implement the immediate measures, the existing G 24 coordination mandate on nuclear safety should be extended to the new States concerned of the former Soviet Union and at the same time made more effective. We all are prepared to strengthen our bilateral assistance.

In addition, we support the setting up of a supplementary multilateral mechanism, as appropriate, to address immediate operational safety and technical safety improvement measures not covered by bilateral programmes. We invite the international community to contribute to the funding. The fund would take account of bilateral funding, be administered by a steering body of donors on the basis of consensus, and be coordinated with and assisted by the G 24 and the EBRD.

47. Decisions on upgrading nuclear power plants of more recent design will require prior clarification of issues concerning plant safety, energy policy, alternative energy sources and financing. To establish a suitable basis on which such decisions can be made, we consider the following measures necessary:
—The necessary safety studies should be presented without delay.
—Together with the competent international organisations, in particular the IEA, the World Bank should prepare the required energy studies including replacement sources of energy and the cost implications. Based on these studies the World Bank and the EBRD should report as expeditiously as possible on potential financing requirements.

48. We shall review the progress made in this action programme at our meeting in 1993.

49. We take note of the representations that we received from various Heads of State or Government and organisations, and we will study them with interest.

*Next meeting*

50. We welcome and have accepted Prime Minister Miyazawa's invitation to Tokyo in July 1993.

*Note: This declaration was made available by the Office of the Press Secretary but was not issued as a White House press release.*

# Letter to Congressional Leaders Reporting on the National Emergency With Respect to Libya
## July 7, 1992

*Dear Mr. Speaker:   (Dear Mr. President:)*

I hereby report to the Congress on the developments since my last report of January 10, 1992, concerning the national emergency with respect to Libya that was declared in Executive Order No. 12543 of January 7, 1986. This report is submitted pursuant to section 401(c) of the National Emergencies Act, 50 U.S.C. 1641(c); section 204(c) of the International Emergency Economic Powers Act ("IEEPA"), 50 U.S.C. 1703(c); and section 505(c) of the International Security and Development Cooperation Act of 1985, 22 U.S.C. 2349aa–9(c).

1. Since my last report on January 10, 1992, the Libyan Sanctions Regulations (the "Regulations"), 31 C.F.R. Part 550, administered by the Office of Foreign Assets Control ("FAC") of the Department of the Treasury, have been amended. One amendment, published on January 14, 1992, 57 *Fed. Reg.* 1386, at 1389, amended the provisions of the Regulations relating to licensing and availability of information to reflect the closing of the Federal Reserve Bank of New York's Foreign Assets Control Division. A second amendment, published on March 30, 1992, 57 *Fed. Reg.* 10798, added the names of 46 companies to Appendix A of the Regulations, which contains a list of organizations determined to be within the definition of the term "Government of Libya" (Specially Designated Nationals of Libya).

2. During the current 6-month period, FAC made numerous decisions with respect to applications for licenses to engage in transactions under the Regulations, issuing nine new licenses. Three of the licenses authorize travel to Libya to discuss possible legal representation of the two indicated suspects in the bombing of Pan Am Flight 103. The remaining licenses authorize the correction of certain errors made by banks resulting in mistaken credits to blocked accounts. All of the licenses concern minor transactions of little or no economic benefit to Libya.

3. Various enforcement actions mentioned in previous reports continue to be pursued, and several new investigations of possibly significant violations of the Libyan sanctions were initiated. During the current reporting period, substantial monetary penalties were assessed against U.S. firms for engaging in prohibited transactions with Libya. In March 1992, FAC announced the collection of almost $550,000 in civil penalties from six companies for violations of U.S. sanctions against Libya, including almost

$350,000 from two "Yugoslav" entities with offices in the United States.

Due to aggressive enforcement efforts and increased public awareness, FAC has received numerous voluntary disclosures from U.S. firms concerning their sanctions violations. Many of these reports continue to be triggered by the periodic amendments to the Regulations listing additional organizations and individuals determined to be Specially Designated Nationals ("SDNs") of Libya. For purposes of the Regulations, all dealings with the organizations and individuals listed will be considered dealings with the Government of Libya. All unlicensed transactions with these persons, or in property in which they have an interest, are prohibited. The listing of Libyan SDNs is not a static list and will be augmented from time to time as additional organizations or individuals owned or controlled by, or acting on behalf of, the Government of Libya are identified.

In March 1992, FAC announced a new law enforcement initiative, Operation Roadblock, which targets U.S. travellers who violate the U.S. sanctions on Libya. Under this initiative, warning letters and requests for information are being sent to persons believed to have travelled to and worked in Libya, or made travel-related payments to Libya in violation of U.S. law. The investigation of suspected violations is being undertaken by FAC, assisted by an interagency task force including the Departments of State and Justice, the Treasury Department's Financial Crimes Enforcement Network (FinCEN), the Federal Bureau of Investigation, and the U.S. Customs Service.

4. The expenses incurred by the Federal Government in the 6-month period from December 15, 1991, through June 14, 1992, that are directly attributable to the exercise of powers and authorities conferred by the declaration of the Libyan national emergency are estimated at $590,000. Personnel costs were largely centered in the Department of the Treasury (particularly in the Office of Foreign Assets Control, the Office of the General Counsel, and the U.S. Customs Service), the Department of State, and the Department of Commerce.

5. The policies and actions of the Govern-

ment of Libya continue to pose an unusual and extraordinary threat to the national security and foreign policy of the United States. I shall continue to exercise the powers at my disposal to apply economic sanctions against Libya fully and effectively, as long as those measures are appropriate, and will continue to report periodically to the Congress on significant developments as

required by law.

Sincerely,

GEORGE BUSH

*Note: Identical letters were sent to Thomas S. Foley, Speaker of the House of Representatives, and Dan Quayle, President of the Senate.*

# Statement by Press Secretary Fitzwater on the Designation of Sean O'Keefe as Acting Secretary of the Navy
*July 7, 1992*

The President today named Sean O'Keefe Acting Secretary of the Navy, until such time as a successor is confirmed.

Since 1989, Mr. O'Keefe has served as Comptroller of the Department of Defense and in 1991 was also designated Chief Financial Officer of the Department. From 1981 to 1989, he served on the staff of the U.S. Senate Committee on Appropriations, serving as the minority counsel for the Defense Subcommittee. He served as the staff director for the Defense Subcommittee

until 1987. Mr. O'Keefe served in principal analyst positions on the staff for operations and maintenance, shipbuilding, and aircraft procurement appropriations. He also was a Presidential management intern in 1978.

Mr. O'Keefe graduated from Loyola University with a bachelor of arts degree in political science and received a master of public administration degree from Syracuse University. He was born January 27, 1956. He is married, has one daughter and one son, and resides in Arlington, VA.

# The President's News Conference in Munich, Germany
*July 8, 1992*

*The President.* I've spent the past 3 days discussing the responsibilities and opportunities that we have for encouraging stronger economic growth in our countries and, indeed, in the entire world. We've also discussed sustaining political reform in the emerging democracies as well as regional political issues, including Yugoslavia.

I would cite five key accomplishments at the Munich economic summit. We've succeeded in achieving a solid consensus on strengthening world growth. Recovery is underway in the United States. Japan, Germany, and Italy——

*Q.* [*Inaudible*]—the homeless. They mourn your decisions here. Repent. They mourn your decisions here. You're not

giving us your voice.

*The President.* I'm trying to give——

*Q.* [*Inaudible*]—us your voice in the U.S.

*The President.* I'm trying to give you my voice right now, and if you'd be quiet maybe you could hear it.

*Q.* But you're not giving it to us. We tried.

*The President.* Well, would you please sit down. We're in the middle of a press conference here.

*Q.* You're not giving us your voice there.

*The President.* Well, what's your question, sir?

*Q.* I'm under 25, and I want to know——

*The President.* Well, I can tell that. [*Laughter*] Now, what's your question?

*Q.* I want to know why Siemens gets more credit than the homeless in the United States?

*The President.* We'll get back to you on that. Now, if you'd please sit down, or I'll have to ask—because it's not fair to everybody else for you to be making a little political statement here. Who are you and who are you accredited to?

*Q.* My name is Charles Kane. I'm from the United States. I work with a magazine in The Netherlands. It's a youth magazine, and we want to know why we're not taken seriously. We're an environmental group.

*The President.* Well, maybe you're rude. People don't take rude people seriously. And if you interrupt a press conference like this, I'm sure that people would say that's why we don't take you seriously. Sit down, and I will take a question from you when we get in the question-and-answer period. Right now I would like to continue my statement, with your permission.

Now, where were we? We were talking about economic recovery. It's underway in the United States. Japan, Germany, and Italy have taken actions in the last few days to strengthen their growth. Also the United States has cut its interest rates. These actions will help our domestic economy continue its recovery. U.S. exports to a growing world economy will increase American jobs.

We'll work with Poland on new uses for its currency stabilization fund that will support market reform once Poland reaches agreement with the IMF on a program. I believe this is a very important encouragement for Poland and an expression of our faith in Poland's commitment to market reform.

We expressed strong support for President Yeltsin's reform efforts. This is a tribute to his leadership and vision in working to bring a great country firmly into the family of democratic, market-oriented countries.

We've demonstrated our commitment to the future of safe nuclear power by agreeing on a coordinated cooperative effort with Eastern Europe and the former Soviet Union to improve the safety of Soviet-designed power reactors.

And finally, we're taking a number of steps relating to Yugoslavia, both to relieve the horrible suffering in Bosnia and to contain the spread of ethnic violence.

With more growth, we will create new job opportunities at home. We will also be able to help emerging democracies establish the vibrant market economies so vital for their political and economic development.

We had a frank exchange of views on trade. We all recognize that completing the Uruguay round will give a major boost to world growth by expanding trade for all countries, developed as well as developing. I've worked hard over the past year to identify constructive solutions to tough issues. It's natural that as we get close to the end, the going gets tougher. But I will persevere because the benefits of success are tremendous. All summit leaders expect that an agreement can be reached by the end of the year.

Now, one thing stands out clearly from our discussions. The triumph of the ideals of democracy and free markets throughout the world means that distinctions between domestic and international economic policies are increasingly meaningless. This is particularly true for the U.S., where over 70 percent of our growth in the last 5 years has come from exports. Over 7 million American jobs are related to exports, and clearly, America's well-being is tied closely to the health of the world economy. What's happened here and how we all follow through on our commitments concerns every American.

And now I'll be glad to take some questions. I think Terry [Terence Hunt, Associated Press] has the first one.

*Russia*

*Q.* Mr. President, you said in Washington that you supported the idea of making the G–7 a G–8 with the addition of Russia. Is that going to fly or——

*The President.* I thought I said we were open-minded on it.

*Q.* Somebody said, "Do you support it?" and you said, "That's right."

*The President.* Well, I think you have to look at the whole statement. But look, this will be considered. Russia attended last year; Russia is attending this year. This matter has not yet come up. It will be discussed this afternoon. But clearly, I support President Yeltsin being here today. We have big differences in the world economies. And maybe it will be concluded that the seven plus one is the answer; that makes eight. But we'll just have to wait and see how the negotiations go.

*Q.* Are you concerned that Russia's backsliding on energy and inflation? Are you satisfied with the progress of their economic reform package?

*The President.* I don't think Russia is satisfied with the progress of their economic reform. And what we want to do is just encourage economic reform in every way. See, I feel that one of the quickest ways for that Russian economy to recover is to move forward on the energy front with private investment much more quickly.

What was the other part? Energy and what?

*Q.* They're printing many more rubles and adding——

*The President.* Inflation. I think there is a concern about inflation. But all of these matters will be discussed this afternoon. But we don't want to overlook the fact that President Yeltsin has come in; he's taken some courageous steps in terms of reform. He's made decisions at home that are quite unpopular. So as this big economy begins to move and begins to be much more market-oriented, there are bound to be problems. And yes, I'm sure they're concerned, as everybody is, about inflation.

*NATO*

*Q.* Mr. President, do you think that you have properly defined to the American people and to Congress the future role of NATO in terms of Europe in the post-cold-war world? That is, does it mean American troops will have to go into every ethnic struggle, every national civil war as they are assigned by NATO, and should we do that?

*The President.* No, it doesn't mean that American troops will go into every struggle. NATO, in our view, and I think in the view of most of the participants if not all, is the fundamental guarantor of European security. It is in the national interest of the United States in my view to keep a strong presence, a U.S. presence, in NATO. I don't

think anybody suggests that if there is a hiccup here or there or a conflict here or there that the United States is going to send troops.

Yugoslavia is a good example. What we're interested in doing is moving forward to help, but I've not committed to use U.S. troops there, and nobody has suggested that NATO troops are going to go into that arena.

*Q.* What did you mean by a guarantor of security? Someone said that you were waiting for the Red army to regroup. What is the meaning?

*The President.* The enemy at this juncture is unpredictability. A strong NATO that has kept the peace, helped keep the peace in Europe for 40-some years can keep it for the next 40 years. That's what we're talking about.

Now, let's go to this gentleman who is so agitated here.

*Nuclear Energy*

*Q.* I just want to know why there's no new nuclear power plants in the United States being built, but you're proposing for Siemens to build them in Eastern Europe.

*The President.* Well, I'd like some more to be built.

*Q.* Why are they so unsafe in our country and so safe in their country?

*The President.* I don't think——

*Q.* Why is it only the G–7——

*The President.* You've asked your question, sir, and let me try to answer it for you. I favor nuclear power. I believe that it can be safely used. I believe that it is environmentally sound. I have great confidence in U.S. technology. I notice that the French feel the same way. So I am not a President who is opposed to nuclear power. Indeed, our energy bill that we've got forward would facilitate ways for more safe use of nuclear power.

The debate here has been that we ought to try to help those areas that have nuclear facilities that might not have the latest technology and might not meet the same standards of safety that we use in our country.

Thank you very much. Now we'll go here.

*Q.* Do you respect the—

*The President.* You've had your question.

*Q.* Come on. Sit down.

*Q.* Think about it. Is the world going to be a better place——

*The President.* This is coming out of your time, gang, and we've got 20 minutes.

*Q.* Mr. President——

*Q.* Come on. This guy is not respecting us at all. You guys are all part of the system, too. Thanks a lot. Go ahead. We've given up.

*World Economic Growth and Domestic Jobs*

*Q.* Much has been said here by you and others about the benefits for the United States of accelerated growth in other economies of the world. You don't contend, do you, sir, that there will be any immediate benefits, such as on the unemployment rate in the United States, do you?

*The President.* Immediate benefit to world growth?

*Q.* From world growth on, for example, the unemployment rate in the United States.

*The President.* I think world growth is a guarantor of more employment in the United States because I think it will——

*Q.* But when?

*The President.* Well, it's very hard to put a particular date on it. You've got an economy now where, in our country, where you saw this investment from BMW, which is very good. But there's a delay before it will employ the 2,000 people or whatever that's predicted. But exports have saved our economy. They would be much more vigorous if the world was growing faster. So I think you just have to wait and see how fast countries grow. But as they grow, that is a much better market for American products.

*France and Trade Negotiations*

*Q.* Mr. President, every year, or at least for the last several years, we've come to these summits and been promised a trade agreement. You've done that again this year. Why should this year be different, particularly since you seem to have encountered such opposition from the French? Do you have promises from Mr. Mitterrand to deal with this once his referendum is over?

*The President.* I think there's a general feeling that the referendum is causing problems for the French. All I know is that we are going to keep pushing. We're ready to conclude one now. I have made very clear, some political comments to the contrary at home notwithstanding, that the politics does not interfere with the United States readiness to go forward. And we've made that point here. But I am disappointed.

We didn't come here, incidentally, Charles [Charles Bierbauer, Cable News Network], thinking that this was going to be the forum in which the GATT round would be solved. If I had felt that way, I think you would have seen our very able negotiators on the scene. But I think there's some political realities out there that make it more difficult for one country or another to conclude an agreement. All I know is we're going to keep pushing for it without regard to the U.S. election. It is in our interest. So that's the only way I know to answer.

*Q.* How far has President Mitterrand gone to give you assurances that he'll be prepared to deal after that referendum?

*The President.* I would not go into how far he's gone. I simply think that there will be more of a readiness on the part of the French after the referendum.

*The Global Economy*

*Q.* Mr. President, it seems to me that one could read this final communique and reasonably conclude that Poland and Russia got more out of the economic summit than the United States. Where's the beef for the U.S. economy?

*The President.* Where's what?

*Q.* Where's the beef for the U.S. economy?

*The President.* In the first place, these summits should not be looked at as coming out with an eight-point agenda or something like that. That's not what they're about. We have one global economy, and we're all involved in that global economy. And when we make commitments to growth, that benefits not just the G–7 plus one, but it benefits everybody else. And so I would simply say, as we move forward together with the Europeans, whether it's on Yugoslavia or whether it's on world growth, that is in the interest of the United States of

America. You can't separate out the international economy from the domestic economy.

### President Yeltsin

*Q.* I wanted to ask you about Boris Yeltsin, your latest opinion of him. He crashed in here, gate-crashed the dinner last night. He's complained about the $24 billion fund, that the IMF put more restrictions on him, that Russia's sovereignty would be insulted. Do you regard him as a really reliable partner or as a bit of a loose cannon?

*The President.* I regard him as a very courageous leader who is trying against some pretty tough odds to reform an authoritarian system, Communist system, and to make it into a market economy. And I can understand the frustration that he might feel and express from time to time about where's the beef, what's in this for us. But I think he also knows that when he gets advice on genuine reforms from the IMF that he must comply. So I think there may be frustration on his part. But on the other hand, I think all of us at this G–7 meeting support him and support what he's trying to do.

I would just take exception to the question, one part of it, where you say he crashed the dinner. A place was set; he got a warm welcome. [*Laughter*] So I don't think that's a very fair assessment to a courageous leader.

*Q.* Do you think the characterization that he's like a bull in a china shop is not accurate?

*The President.* Well, I've not heard that particular characterization. But the man is strong, and he's tough, and he's committed. And I have seen that in my various meetings with him, bilateral meetings. He's trying hard, and he has our respect. And he's up against big odds. We all know that. But he's got a good, young team around him, and you ought to give him great credit for that, Kozyrev and Gaydar, particularly on the financial side, the latter. And we're here to support him. I think he's conducted himself very, very well here.

### U.S. Economy and Leadership Role

*Q.* Mr. President, your aides said this week that they're having trouble getting your message out, in this case maybe on your international leadership and jobs creation through this global expansion on the economy. Who do you fault for that?

*The President.* I don't know what aides you're talking about. We'll keep getting it out. I think the way that we met here with these leaders and people see agreement on world growth, that's good. I think people feel that the world economy is growing, just as I feel the U.S. economy is growing. So if there's any blame, I guess I take the blame. But I don't buy into it that the message isn't getting out. I think people come to the recognition that we've got some problems, certainly problems when people are hurting and they don't have jobs. But on the other hand, as they begin to feel the economy moving, I think things will change.

I'm still interested in the statistic I saw—I forgot I don't read polls—that I read in a poll. What it said was that 60 percent of the people in the country still think the economy is getting worse. It's not. It is improving. Now, maybe not improving fast enough, but it is improving. There's a gap between perception and reality.

So on your question I think maybe the answer is: Just keep getting the truth out, getting the message out. Keep encouraging Congress to do that which I wish they had done long ago instead of about—I wish they would move forward now and stimulate the economy in some selective ways that we've been proposing since my State of the Union Message. They haven't done it. I'm going to keep encouraging them to do it because that would be the best thing we could do to help all Americans get back to work and to stimulate growth.

*Q.* Mr. President, there's been a good deal of speculation that the leadership role of the United States in the world and perhaps even that of the U.S. President is somewhat diminished with the end of the cold war, with the difficulties that all of the economies, including our own, are showing. Do you feel that at meetings like this, that the relationship between you and your peers and colleagues is different than it was before? And if so, how?

*The President.* No, I don't feel it.

*Q.* Do you feel that the economy of the United States, being in the shape it is, makes it more difficult for you to speak up and get your points across?

*The President.* No, because I think as you look around at world economies, a lot of the world economies are sharing the same problems. So I don't feel that at all. In fact, I feel since Desert Storm something quite different.

*Federal Budget Deficit*

*Q.* Mr. President, one of the key points of the communique is that the Government should curb excessive public deficits. At the same time, you've presided over the largest increase in the Federal deficit in the U.S. in history. My question is, we've heard you talk about the problems of the Great Society programs, the Carter administration, and the Democratic leadership. Have you given serious reflection to the thought of many economists that the deficit you are grappling with is in large part due to the policies of the Reagan administration, in which you served?

*The President.* No, I haven't given much thought to that, but I've given a lot of thought to how to get the deficit down. And the way to get the deficit down is to contain the growth of mandatory spending and is to keep the caps that we negotiated back in 1990 on discretionary spending and to stimulate economic growth. That is the way to get the U.S. deficits down. And some of that is reflected, incidentally, in the statement on growth that we made with the leaders here.

*Urban Policy*

*Q.* Just a followup. Just after the Los Angeles riots you were asked whether trickle-down economics had, in fact, worked to help the lower income people move up. And you said that you would consider everything, whether everything worked. Have you looked at that particular policy?

*The President.* Yes, and I've looked at what we ought to do for the cities. And we've proposed a good program, and I hope it will pass the Congress.

*Future U.S. Troop Deployment*

*Q.* The United States has supported a proposal at the summit that will be going to Helsinki for NATO to take part in peace-keeping in places like Yugoslavia. The United States will have 200,000 troops in NATO. Earlier you said that the United States would not be going to such places as Yugoslavia. How can we avoid taking part in peacekeeping with the use of American troops if NATO is going to undertake that role?

*The President.* Well, if NATO undertakes a role, of course, the United States of America is going to be involved in it. But in terms of Yugoslavia, our interest is in terms of trying to get humanitarian support in there. I have no plans to inject ourselves into a combat situation in Yugoslavia. We have naval power, we have air power, and we are a part of the security, obviously, a key and critical part of NATO. But nothing in that should be read that I would commit U.S. forces into combat. I'm just not saying what we're going to do on all that.

I thought Colin—I was looking at his statement today, and I think that he expresses administration policy very well on that, the purpose of providing humanitarian aid and not for trying to resolve the underlying political issue. So, Saul [Saul Friedman, Newsday], I think you've jumped out ahead of where consideration of the NATO role is for Yugoslavia at this point.

*Q.* I'm speaking of other such conflicts.

*The President.* Well, that's too hypothetical to go into. You saw the United States respond in the Middle East, and that wasn't a NATO operation. And yet, most of the countries in Europe in one way or other responded to be helpful.

*U.S. Leadership*

*Q.* A follow on Don's [Don Oberdorfer, Washington Post] earlier question. You've said several times at home that the U.S. is now the undisputed leader of the free world. I think a lot of people would agree. Yet, we're having difficulty exerting our national interest in areas like trade. And in these bloody conflicts in Yugoslavia and South Africa our leadership doesn't seem to be respected; our democratic values aren't being followed. I just wondered what do you make of this?

*The President.* I don't agree with your assessment of U.S. leadership, and I don't think anybody in this G–7 would agree with that. I just think that people still look to the United States. Now, we are working in concert with our allies. We've got a global economy. It's just not one country that solves a problem. I've believed since I've been President of working multilaterally when it's in our interest and when it can produce the most good, and I'm going to continue to do that.

So I don't accept the assessment. I think one thing that has been celebrated by everybody since we've been here is the significant reduction in nuclear arms. They look to that as a major leadership achievement of the United States of America and Russia. So I haven't encountered the kind of theme that you were asking about.

*Q.* I just wonder whether you feel that being a superpower isn't necessarily what it used to be cracked up to be.

*The President.* No, I think, in all candor—and I don't want to be offensive to others while I'm here in a multilateral environment—I think we are the sole remaining superpower. And that's when you consider economic and military and everything else. And I think others see it that way. But that doesn't mean that the way you lead is to dictate. That's not the way you try to do it.

*Yugoslavia*

*Q.* You've said that you went to war in the Persian Gulf for principle and that a new order came out of that. And now you're saying that you can't address the political problem in Yugoslavia. What does the new world order have to offer for the people of what used to be Yugoslavia, who need to have their political problems addressed, who have lost land and——

*The President.* I didn't say we couldn't address political problems. I said we're not going to use United States troops to solve the political problems. That's very different. We've got some vigorous diplomacy. We first work the humanitarian question, and then you do what you try to do in preconflict situations or conflict situations and try to use your best diplomatic effort. In this case, you work with the Europeans. You support Lord Carrington; you support Cyrus Vance when he was on the mission for the United Nations; you support these

G–7 neighbors of Yugoslavia. And so it's not a view of do you put force every time there is an occasion like this.

Take a look at the countries now free from the yoke of international communism and the former Soviet Union. If I followed your question to its logical conclusion, it would be suggesting the only way you're going to solve the problem of Azerbaijan and Armenia or the Crimea or wherever it is, is to inject U.S. force. And that's not the way we conduct our policy. That's not the way you keep the peace.

*Russia*

*Q.* Back to Mr. Yeltsin, sir. Economists are sounding increasingly alarmed that the $24 billion which are on offer to him overall is rather paltry given the enormous task and risks involved. For example, Germany has already spent more than $100 billion on transforming Eastern Germany just to maintain stability there. What's your view—I'm talking numbers here—what's your view, is $24 billion sufficient?

*The President.* I don't know that there's enough money in the world to instantly solve the problem of the Russian economy. I think it is a substantial commitment. But it's got to be accompanied with a continuation of this vigorous reform program in Russia. And that will do it more quickly than anything else.

We were talking before this meeting about the amount of capital that has flowed into South America since we've come into office and since the Brady plan and the Enterprise for the Americas have been put into effect. It is amazing the billions of dollars that have flowed into those countries as they have reformed—some are in the process of reforming—but as they have reformed their economies.

And therein lies the answer for Russia. It isn't going to be done simply through a grant from the IMF. But they've got to stay with the reform program that Yeltsin and Gaydar have very courageously put into effect, and they've got to build on it. They've got to move forward more quickly with energy investment. There's a lot of things that they'll be able to do and should do in order to get that dynamism of the private sector involved. And therein lies the ultimate answer. It isn't going to be through an injection of cash from one of the IFI's, the international financial institutions.

Time for two more.

*Multilateral Trade Negotiations*

*Q.* Mr. President, the interests of the European farmers seem to have been defended fairly effectively at this summit. Why is it that the interests of U.S. workers and farmers keep losing out at the trade talks?

*The President.* I don't think the U.S. farmers lost out at all. We are not going to enter into a deal that is detrimental to the U.S. agricultural economy. And I don't think anybody thinks we are.

What do you mean, "keeps losing out"? Maybe I missed something.

*Q.* Every year we're promised that there's going to be a GATT agreement by the end of the year, every year since you've been President. And every year it doesn't happen. Is there a reason to think it's going to happen——

*The President.* But that's not—making a bad deal is not something that the American farmer should be anything but grateful about. We're going to make a good deal, and it will benefit the agricultural economy because we can compete with anyone anywhere. So that's kind of the underpinning of the negotiation. So I don't think the U.S. farmer loses out when you don't rush to make an agreement that might not be a good one. You keep plodding until you get a good one, and that's what we're trying to do.

*Q.* Is the status quo acceptable to U.S. farmers?

*The President.* The status quo is better than a bad deal, but it's not as good as a good GATT agreement. And that's the answer. The way you asked the question, I don't think the American farmer keeps getting shafted. What he wants is access to markets because we know we can compete. That's the kind of agreement we're determined to get. It should be a fair agreement, and it will be a fair agreement.

*Economic Summit and Domestic Politics*

*Q.* Could you tell me a little bit about the atmospherics of this meeting and others?

With the exception of Prime Minister Major, everyone has their own domestic, political, electoral problems. Does that come up between you, and do you commiserate? How would you describe it?

*The President.* That's a very interesting question. And one thing you do get out of this summit is it's not just the United States that has this kind of mood of turmoil. It's very interesting when you talk to these leaders, not just strictly on the economic side but on the political side as well. And we do discuss it. Everyone, I think, shares the same confidence that I do that as the world growth takes place a lot of that discontent will go away. A lot of it is economic, not all of it; some of it's just antipolitical. But yes, we had some very interesting discussions on that.

*Q.* Do you ever come to the point of saying, "Look, I can't deal with that now; I'll have to deal with it 2 months from now"?

*The President.* No, I can't think of a single international question that I would address any differently if the election weren't right over the horizon. I made that very clear on the Uruguay round. So let me just clear the air on this. We want a deal. We think it's in everybody's interest to have a deal. And in no way is domestic election politics interfering with this.

I would cite the same thing here today in terms of the North American free trade agreement. It is in the interest of America to conclude a North American free trade agreement. And we're going to work to do just that. That will mean more jobs and more investment. Every time you get free trade, it does it. Look at the agreement with Canada. Trade's done nothing but go up, and that means jobs on both sides of the border.

So I can't think of anything that would be on the agenda that we have here or possible agenda where I would conduct myself differently because of an election coming up.

Thank you all very much.

*Note: The President's 134th news conference began at 11:58 a.m. at the Residenz. In his remarks, he referred to Andrey Kozyrev,*

*Russian Minister of Foreign Affairs; Yegor Gaydar, Russian Minister of Finance; Gen. Colin L. Powell, USA, Chairman, Joint Chiefs of Staff; Lord Peter Carrington, Spe-* *cial European Community Negotiator on Yugoslavia; and Cyrus Vance, Special Negotiator for the United Nations on Yugoslavia.*

# Remarks to the Conference on Security and Cooperation in Europe in Helsinki, Finland
*July 9, 1992*

May I first thank President Koivisto and the Government and the wonderful people of Finland for their hospitality.

It's fitting that we meet again in Helsinki, the city whose name came to symbolize hope and determination during the cold war. We declared the cold war over when we met in Paris in 1990. But even then we did not appreciate what awaited us. Since 1990, a vast empire has collapsed, a score of new states have been born, and a brutal war rages in the Balkans.

Our world has changed beyond recognition. But our principles have not changed. They have been proven right. With our principles as a compass, we must work as a community to challenge change toward the peaceful order that this century has thus far failed to deliver.

The United States has always supported CSCE as a vehicle for advancing human rights. During the cold war we saw the denial of human rights as a primary source of the confrontation that scarred Europe and threatened global war. And now a new ideology, intolerant nationalism, is spawning new divisions, new crimes, new conflicts. Because we believe that the key to security in the new age is to create a democratic peace, the United States sees an indispensable role for CSCE. Accordingly, I'd like to suggest a five-point agenda to make CSCE more effective.

First, let us commit ourselves to make democratic change irreversible. We must not be so paralyzed by the turmoil around us that we lose sight of our historic mission: completing the grand liberation of the past 3 years. We should use CSCE to nurture democratic ways in those societies where people have been oppressed for generations under the heel of the state. We should reject the notion that democracy has opened Pandora's box. Democracy is not the cause of these problems but rather the means by which people can resolve their differences and bring their aspirations into harmony. We have proof of this. In this room are leaders of nations for whom democracy has made both aggression and civil war unthinkable.

Second, let us all agree to be held accountable to the standards of conduct recorded in our solemn declarations. Those who violate CSCE norms must be singled out, criticized, isolated, even punished by sanctions. And let Serbia's absence today serve as a clear message to others.

Third, let us commit CSCE to attack the root causes of conflict. The Dutch initiative for a high commissioner for national minorities is an important step toward providing early warning. It will help us act before conflict erupts. My country has proposed a CSCE project on tolerance which can lead to practical cooperation in fighting discrimination and racial prejudice. We cannot fail to make this a top priority while the so-called ethnic cleansing of Muslims occurs in Bosnia even as we meet.

Fourth, let us strengthen our mechanisms for the settlement of disputes. CSCE should offer a flexible set of services for mediation, conciliation, arbitration so that conflicts can be averted. A prompt follow-on meeting should take up specific means for dispute settlement, including the U.S. idea whereby our community can insist that disputing parties submit to CSCE conciliation.

Fifth, let us decide right here and now to develop a credible Euro-Atlantic peacekeeping capability. This region remains heavily armed from cold war days. Ad hoc operations of hastily assembled units will not suffice, and this is why I consider NATO's offer to contribute to CSCE peacekeeping so vital. We've learned that Europe's problems are America's problems, her hopes and aspirations ours as well. Because of NATO, my country will keep substantial military capabilities in Europe that could contribute to peacekeeping under CSCE. But it is not for NATO alone to keep the peace in Europe. We welcome a WEU role, and we also invite every nation here to work directly with NATO in building a new Euro-Atlantic peacekeeping force.

I must conclude these remarks with another word on the nightmare in Bosnia. If our CSCE community is to have real meaning in this new world, let us be of one mind about our immediate aims. First, we should see to it that relief supplies get through no matter what it takes. Second, we should see

to it that the United Nations sanctions are respected no matter what it takes. Third, we should do all we can to prevent this conflict from spreading. And fourth, let us call with one voice for the guns to fall silent through a cease-fire on all fronts.

Let me close with this thought. We know more now than we did at our last gathering in Paris about this new era, its dangers, and yes, about its possibilities. There's still an abundance of uncertainty, and yet we cannot be daunted by the unknown. The steps we take here will be only first steps, but let them be determined first steps toward a true community of freedom and peace. To this end I came to Finland, to pledge the full support of the United States of America.

Thank you, Mr. Chairman.

*Note: The President spoke at 5:35 p.m. at the Helsinki Fair Center.*

# Statement on the New American Schools Design Competition
*July 9, 1992*

My education strategy, called America 2000, is based on the premise that if we are going to change our country we must change our schools, community by community. As part of that strategy, last year I invited leaders from the private sector to forge a path in designing new schools. They responded swiftly and generously, first by forming the New American Schools Development Corporation, then by initiating a nationwide competition for the best school designs imaginable. Their initiative generated an enormous response: Nearly 700 proposals were submitted.

Today, just over a year since its inception, the New American Schools Development Corporation has selected 11 design proposals to create the best schools in the world.

But every one of the design teams that competed to create the best schools in the world is also a winner. These New American School design teams are in the forefront of a movement that will, by the end of the 1990's, create revolutionary new schools. I know that America 2000 communities in every State will be anxious to study and to use these new school designs to help create their own new American schools.

The success of the New American Schools competition demonstrates that Americans welcome the opportunity for revolutionary change in the Nation's education system. That is why I am delighted by the announcement today and extend my hearty congratulations to the winning design teams.

## Exchange With Reporters Prior to Discussions With Prime Minister Jozsef Antall of Hungary in Helsinki, Finland
*July 10, 1992*

### Refugees

*Q.* ——give U.S. money for Bosnian refugees being in Hungary?

*The President.* Well, we're going to discuss a lot of questions here with my esteemed friend, and I'll have a better feeling for that after I discuss these matters. But it's a great honor and pleasure to see him. He has our full confidence, I can tell you that.

### Eastern Europe

*Q.* Do you think the changes in Eastern Europe are really irreversible?

*The President.* Well, I hope so and think so. I don't hear any word here other than trying to cement democracies and freedom. That's what this is all about, human rights as well.

### U.S. Naval Deployment and Czechoslovakia

*Q.* Mr. President, I'll try again—a question.

*The President.* Try it.

*Q.* Is the United States going to be part of the WEU's decision to send six ships in a monitoring mode?

*The President.* Well, there's been a lot of rumors about naval vessels. In fact, somebody was asking me earlier about new deployments. There have been no ships—since I've been here I've made no decisions of change. We have two task forces in the Mediterranean; one has been up and in and out of the Adriatic. But just to lay that to rest, there is no change, and no decisions have been made about further deployment of naval forces.

I look forward to seeing my dear friend here, who is doing a great job in terms of democracy and freedom. He's got a lot of refugee problems; we want to talk about that.

We had a meeting yesterday with President Havel. There's another problem. We talked about the emergence perhaps of two Republics, the splitting up of Czechoslovakia. We just strongly emphasized the need for that to be peaceful and to have it done by constitutional means. And it gave me a chance to express my appreciation to him, respect for President Havel, just as, again, I would say the same about Mr. Antall. The changes that these countries are undertaking are enormous, and they have the full respect and support of the United States.

### Yugoslavia

*Q.* Do you think this conference has achieved anything that's going to help stop the fighting in Yugoslavia?

*The President.* I think the more you talk about these problems, the concerted effort you saw taken between WEU and NATO, I think those things are very helpful. And everyone is determined to get humanitarian aid in there just as soon as possible and hopefully to stop the flow of refugees that are burdening many countries.

### Czechoslovakia

*Q.* Have you accepted it as a fait accompli, the breakup of Czechoslovakia?

*The President.* No. All I say is whatever happens ought to be constitutional, it ought to be within their rights to self-determination, and it ought to be peaceful. And I would take my guidance on that from the respected President Václav Havel.

*Q.* Mr. Antall, can we ask you a few questions?

*The Prime Minister.* There will be no second Yugoslavia out of Czechoslovakia.

### Refugees

*Q.* You might be wanting to comment about this notion of a high commissioner for refugees, you know, with the ethnic Hungarians and Romania and all, do you take hope from that? Is that a good thing?

*The Prime Minister.* We find it very important. On the basis of previous experience I can say it will be good not only for Hungarian minorities but other minorities, too. But, of course, you understand that we are very much involved and interested because this is going to be an alternative to recognize and respect the borders. And we hope that there will be no conflicts because of this.

## Bilateral Discussions

*The President.* I might add one thing on this question. One of the enormously productive byproducts for me in a multilateral meeting like this is a chance to have so many bilateral meetings. And I would cite Hungary as a good example. It is important to the United States that we stay in touch with the Hungarian leaders and see that we don't have any disconnects, see that we can help wherever help is wanted. And so we have these big communiques that come out of these meetings and all the pronouncements, but I find here, just as I did at the United Nations years ago, that you learn a lot and you can get a lot done in these bilateral meetings.

I don't know whether you agree with that.

## European Security

*The Prime Minister.* I completely agree with Mr. President. And at the same time I can also say that American presence in Europe is very important indeed from the point of the security of the European Continent. And as Prime Minister of Hungary, I can say NATO is one of the most important guarantees of European security. Therefore, apart from supporting European integration, we are committed as supporters of the transatlantic thought.

The role of NATO is seen even more important seeing the changes in the former Soviet Union and in the Eastern European region. I say so not only now and here; I said also the same in June 1990 when I was in Moscow. I was there as Prime Minister suggesting and proposing to dismantle the Warsaw Pact. I'm the only one being in office among those prior prime ministers now.

## U.S. Naval Deployment

*Q.* Mr. President, if we have two task forces in the Adriatic, why do you say there's no change?

*The President.* We don't have two task forces in the Adriatic; I said Mediterranean. If I didn't, I made a mistake.

*Q.* Well, are there any in the Adriatic?

*The President.* There might well be. There have been. They've been up and out, in and out of the Adriatic over the last few weeks. But I was trying to respond to a question. I have made no new decisions since being here on deployment of naval forces. Somebody had a story to that, and it is simply not true. But the fact that they've been in the Adriatic has been well-known.

*Note: The exchange began at 11:29 a.m. at the Helsinki Fair Center. Prime Minister Antall spoke in Hungarian, and his remarks were translated by an interpreter. A tape was not available for verification of the content of these remarks.*

# Remarks Prior to Discussions With President Václav Havel of Czechoslovakia in Helsinki
*July 10, 1992*

President Havel, I want to express my great admiration and respect for your courage and leadership. As negotiations move forward on the future of the federal state, I want to assure you that we respect the rights of the people of the two Republics to decide their future. We think it important that the process take place in accordance with democratic, constitutional procedures

and in a civil way so that good relations are maintained among all the peoples of the region.

*Note: The President spoke at approximately 4:30 p.m. at the Helsinki Fair Center. A tape was not available for verification of the content of these remarks.*

## Statement by Press Secretary Fitzwater on the Treaty on Conventional Armed Forces in Europe
*July 10, 1992*

Today at the Helsinki summit, President Bush, along with the leaders of 28 other European nations, agreed that the Treaty on Conventional Armed Forces in Europe (CFE) will be applied provisionally on July 17, 1992, to enter into force this fall with the full participation by the original signatories and the eight new states of the former Soviet Union with territory in CFE's zone of application.

The United States attaches great importance to this event because joining CFE is a key indication of the new states' commitment to achieving lower and more stable levels of conventional military forces in Europe. Along with our treaty partners, the United States has worked hard to make CFE a reality. In the end, it was achieved because all participants, East and West, recognized that CFE's unprecedented force reductions, information exchanges, and verification provisions are the cornerstone for efforts to further improve European security in the years ahead.

President Bush also signed the Concluding Act of the Negotiation on Personnel Strength of Conventional Armed Forces in Europe, otherwise known as the CFE–1A agreement. CFE–1A negotiations began shortly after the CFE Treaty was signed in 1990. The CFE–1A accord places politically binding limits on military manpower in Europe. Along with the equipment limits of the CFE Treaty, CFE–1A establishes comprehensive and stable levels of conventional military forces on the Continent.

## Statement on Signing the ADAMHA Reorganization Act
*July 10, 1992*

Today I am pleased to sign into law S. 1306, the "ADAMHA Reorganization Act," which amends certain alcohol, drug abuse, and mental health research and services programs.

S. 1306 reflects the Administration's continued commitment to help the victims of mental illness and substance abuse. It enhances mental health and substance abuse services and research designed to address the needs of the citizens of this Nation. S. 1306 will help us achieve the ambitious goals set forth in the Administration's National Drug Control Strategy.

Most important, this legislation sends a message of hope to the men, women, and children affected by substance abuse and mental illness in this country. Through programs such as residential treatment for substance-abusing pregnant women, S. 1306 will help reduce the number of newborn children exposed to drugs and alcohol. It will also help the estimated one-quarter of our population who, during the course of their lives, will suffer from a mental disorder. According to the Department of Health and Human Services (HHS), mental health and substance abuse disorders cost this Nation approximately $300 billion in health care costs, lost productivity, and other social costs, each and every year.

S. 1306 also has a number of other important provisions that were sought by the Administration. For example, it establishes a grant program to expand by approximately 38,400 the number of additional people who will receive substance abuse treatment in the coming year. This legislation requires the States to assess their efforts to reduce drug and alcohol abuse and to prepare a statewide treatment and prevention strategy. S. 1306 will also continue the prohibition on the use of Federal block grant funds for needle exchange programs. There is no evidence that such programs reduce the incidence of HIV infection, and distributing free needles to drug users only encourages more drug use.

S. 1306 will also reorganize the Alcohol, Drug Abuse, and Mental Health Administration (ADAMHA) within HHS. This reorganization, proposed by the Administration, will create for the first time an agency that is focused solely on providing services to those who suffer from, or are vulnerable to, mental illness and addictive disorders. The reorganization will allow us to develop more fully the ability to target services to people who need them. It will also enhance Federal leadership and help State and local organizations provide and improve services to address these important public health problems.

At the same time, the reorganization will strengthen the Nation's research agenda through the integration of ADAMHA's three research institutes—the National Institute on Alcohol Abuse and Alcoholism, the National Institute on Drug Abuse, and the National Institute of Mental Health— into the National Institutes of Health (NIH). Bringing research on mental illness and addictive disorders into the mainstream of biomedical and behavioral research at NIH will foster a greater exchange of information. It will also encourage the sharing of expertise in neuroscience and behavioral re-

search within the biomedical research community.

There are many positive features of S. 1306 that will help the victims of mental illness and substance abuse. I am, however, concerned about the cost of certain block grant mandates in the bill and the effect they will have on the ability of the States to provide substance abuse treatment services to those in need. Such mandates are inconsistent with the purpose of a block grant, which is to allow States the flexibility to design programs tailored to their specific needs. It is my intent that every effort be made to ensure that these mandates do not result in a reduction in the States' ability to provide treatment services to the greatest possible number of persons in need.

In signing this legislation today, I continue the Administration's commitment to address the immeasurable costs to our society and the suffering of our citizens that result from mental health illness and drug and alcohol abuse.

GEORGE BUSH

The White House,
July 10, 1992.

*Note: S. 1306, approved July 10, was assigned Public Law No. 102–321.*

## Statement on the Sentencing of Manuel Noriega
*July 10, 1992*

The sentence imposed today on Manuel Noriega is a fitting punishment for drug crimes that have harmed all Americans. It demonstrates that international drug felons are not above the law, no matter how great their wealth, their status, or their armed might.

Illegal drugs inflict great suffering throughout our Nation and the world.

Anyone who traffics in them should be brought to justice. Operation Just Cause freed the people of Panama from a brutal tyranny; the sentence handed down today demonstrates that it also led to the conviction and just punishment of an unrepentant drug criminal. For that, Americans and our allies abroad have reason to be proud.

## Letter to Congressional Leaders Transmitting a Report on United States Military Forces in Asia and the Pacific
*July 13, 1992*

*Dear Mr. Chairman:    (Dear Senator:)*
*(Dear Congressman:)*

Pursuant to section 1043(c) of the National Defense Authorization Act for Fiscal Years 1992 and 1993 (Public Law 102–190), I have the honor to transmit the enclosed report on the strategic posture and military force structure of the United States in Asia and the Pacific, including the forces in Hawaii.

Sincerely,

GEORGE BUSH

*Note: Identical letters were sent to Robert C. Byrd and Mark O. Hatfield, chairman and* *ranking Republican member, Senate Appropriations Committee; Sam Nunn and John W. Warner, chairman and ranking Republican member, Senate Armed Services Committee; Claiborne Pell and Jesse Helms, chairman and ranking Republican member, Senate Foreign Relations Committee; Jamie L. Whitten and Joseph M. McDade, chairman and ranking Republican member, House Appropriations Committee; Les Aspin and William L. Dickinson, chairman and ranking Republican member, House Armed Services Committee; and Dante B. Fascell and William S. Broomfield, chairman and ranking Republican member, House Foreign Affairs Committee.*

## Statement on Nuclear Nonproliferation Efforts
*July 13, 1992*

A few weeks ago, President Boris Yeltsin and I agreed to the most far-reaching reductions in nuclear weaponry since the dawn of the atomic age. Yet even as our own arsenals diminish, the spread of the capability to produce or acquire weapons of mass destruction and the means to deliver them constitutes a growing threat to U.S. national security interests and world peace. In a world in which regional tensions may unpredictably erupt into war, these weapons could have devastating consequences.

That is why this administration has fought so hard to stem the proliferation of these terrible weapons. We look back with pride on a solid record of accomplishment. Membership in the Nuclear Non-Proliferation Treaty has grown. The Missile Technology Control Regime and Australia Group have broadened their membership and expanded their controls against trade useful to the development of missiles and chemical and biological weapons. We have toughened our nonproliferation export controls, and other nations have followed suit. We have seen remarkable progress in building and strengthening regional arms control arrangements in Latin America, the Korean Peninsula, and the Middle East.

Yet we need to do more. The demand for these weapons persists, and new suppliers of key technologies are emerging. Export controls alone cannot create an airtight seal against proliferation. In an era of advancing technology and trade liberalization, we need to employ the full range of political, security, intelligence, and other tools at our disposal.

Therefore, I have set forth today a set of principles to guide our nonproliferation efforts in the years ahead and directed a number of steps to supplement our existing efforts. These steps include a decision not to produce plutonium and highly enriched uranium for nuclear explosive purposes and a number of proposals to strengthen international actions against those who contribute to the spread of weapons of mass destruction and the missiles that deliver them.

While these steps will strengthen the barriers against proliferation, success will require hard work and, at times, hard choices. The United States, however, is committed to take a leading role in the international effort to thwart the spread of technologies and weapons that cast a cloud over our future.

# Statement by Press Secretary Fitzwater on the President's Telephone Conversation With Prime Minister Yitzhak Rabin of Israel
*July 13, 1992*

Today, the President called Yitzhak Rabin to congratulate him on his victory and the formation of his government. The President told him how much he looked forward to working with him to deepen the U.S.-Israeli partnership and to promote the peace with security that the Israelis have rightly yearned for for so long.

The Prime Minister told the President about his desire to give the peace process new momentum, and they agreed that it would be good for Secretary Baker to visit Israel and its neighbors next week to get the ball rolling again. In addition, the President invited the Prime Minister to visit him in Kennebunkport early in August.

# Nomination of Walter Scott Light To Be United States Ambassador to Ecuador
*July 13, 1992*

The President today announced his intention to nominate Walter Scott Light, of Texas, to be Ambassador of the United States of America to the Republic of Ecuador. He would succeed Paul C. Lambert.

Since 1957, Mr. Light has served as president and chief executive officer of the Lighting Oil Co. in San Antonio, TX.

Mr. Light graduated from New Mexico Military Institute, Junior College Division (1951) and attended the University of Texas at Austin School of Business (1951–52) and Southern Methodist University School of Business (1953). Mr. Light served in the U.S. Air Force, 1953–55. He was born April 30, 1931, in Denton, TX. Mr. Light is married, has three children, and resides in San Antonio, TX.

# Nomination of Linton F. Brooks To Be Assistant Director of the United States Arms Control and Disarmament Agency
*July 13, 1992*

The President today announced his intention to nominate Linton F. Brooks, of Virginia, to be an Assistant Director of the United States Arms Control and Disarmament Agency at the Bureau of Strategic and Nuclear Affairs. He would succeed Susan Jane Koch.

Ambassador Brooks has served as head of the U.S. delegation on Nuclear and Space Talks and Chief Strategic Arms Reductions (START) Negotiator from 1991 to the present. From 1989 to 1991, Ambassador

Brooks served as deputy head of the delegation. He was confirmed by the U.S. Senate with the rank of Ambassador in 1990. From 1984 to 1989, he served as Director of Arms Control on the staff of the National Security Council. Ambassador Brooks has also served as special adviser to the Chief of Naval Operations, 1985, and Deputy Director of Strategic and Theater Nuclear Warfare Policy in the U.S. Navy, 1982–84.

Ambassador Brooks graduated from Duke University (B.S., 1959), the University of Maryland (M.A., 1972), and the U.S. War College (1979). He served for 30 years in the U.S. Navy. He was born August 15, 1938, in Boston, MA. Ambassador Brooks is married, has two children, and resides in Vienna, VA.

# Nomination of David P. Prosperi To Be a Member of the Board of Directors of the Corporation for Public Broadcasting
*July 13, 1992*

The President today announced his intention to nominate David P. Prosperi, of Illinois, to be a member of the Board of Directors of the Corporation for Public Broadcasting for a term expiring March 26, 1997. He would succeed Marshall Turner, Jr.

Since 1990, Mr. Prosperi has served as vice president of communications at the Chicago Board of Trade. He has also served as Assistant Secretary of Transportation at the Department of Transportation, 1989–90; deputy press secretary in the office of the President-elect, 1988–89; campaign press secretary for Vice Presidential nominee Dan Quayle, 1988; Assistant to the Secretary and Director of Public Affairs at the Department of the Interior, 1985–88; and press secretary to the Secretary at the Department of Energy, 1985.

Mr. Prosperi graduated from the University of Illinois (B.A., 1975) and George Washington University (M.B.A., 1983). He was born June 20, 1953, in Chicago, IL. Mr. Prosperi is married, has two children, and resides in Northbrook, IL.

# Nomination of Shirley W. Ryan To Be a Member of the National Council on Disability
*July 13, 1992*

The President today announced his intention to nominate Shirley W. Ryan, of Illinois, to be a member of the National Council on Disability for a term expiring September 17, 1994. She would succeed John Leopold.

Currently Ms. Ryan serves as president and cofounder of the Pathways Center for Children in Glenview, IL, founded in 1985. In addition, Ms. Ryan has served on the boards of several educational and philanthropic organizations.

Ms. Ryan graduated from Northwestern University (B.A., 1962). She was born January 5, 1939, in Gary, IN. Ms. Ryan is married, has three children, and currently resides in Kenilworth, IL.

## Exchange With Reporters in Sequoia National Forest, California
*July 14, 1992*

### Presidential Campaign

*Q.* Mr. President, can you lay the Baker rumors to rest, sir? Can you lay those Baker rumors to rest? Are you going to ask him to return?

*The President.* The truth is he and I are going fishing. It's pure fishing, pure fishing.

*Q.* But are you going to ask him to return to the White House or campaign——

*Q.* Mr. President, what's the most important domestic issue besides the economy?

*The President.* Well, there are so many of them, but education, crime; education, tranquility in the neighborhoods.

*Q.* Is America and the American economy better off than it was 4 years ago?

*The President.* Well, some parts of it are.

*Note: The exchange began at 11:15 a.m. A tape was not available for verification of the content of this exchange.*

## Remarks on Signing the Giant Sequoia in National Forests Proclamation in Sequoia National Forest
*July 14, 1992*

Dale Robertson, thank you, sir. As all of you know, Mr. Robertson is the Chief of the U.S. Forest Service. But I would like to take this opportunity not simply to thank him but to thank the other dedicated professionals that work in the Forest Service. And I'm just delighted to be here today and delighted that Bill Reilly, the head of EPA, is with us; that Congressman Bill Thomas, who claims this as part of his own congressional district—proudly proclaims it, brags about it, understandably so—is with us today; Forest Supervisor Sandra Key; and also an old friend, Derrick Crandall, could join us.

Let me begin by acknowledging the hard work and the valuable time being invested in our environment by the likes of Bruce Howard and the Save the Redwoods League, David Magney and the California Native Plant Society, the Audubon Society, the Nature Conservatory. They all do fantastic work in keeping this the way it ought to be.

I understand we have some special guests here. I met one group of them, and these are the kids from R.M. Pyles Boys Camp. They come out here away from it all to learn how to hike and fish and pitch a tent. They learn how to respect themselves and respect the land. I believe Teddy Roosevelt had these kids in mind when he spoke of the "beautiful gifts" that we've received from nature, gifts that we "ought to hand on as a precious heritage to our children and our children's children."

The fact is these forests, our lakes, and our lands, they are gifts, the commonwealth that we inherited from our parents, that we borrow from our kids. That's the spirit of this agreement that we'll salute here today. Different groups from Government agencies to private organizations have come together, bridging ideological divides in order to forge an agreement that protects our sequoia groves as part of our national legacy, our common heritage, if you will. Whatever name you put on it, our actions are going to speak louder than words. And when words are memories, when we are long gone, these trees will stand.

America has one of the oldest National Forest Systems in the world, the best National Park System in the world, and the best Wildlife Refuge System in the world. And yet, as President, I have said that the best simply is not good enough.

The Wallop-Breaux Trust Fund is a good example. It's helped us invest more than $200 million each year to improve our fishing waters and open them up to fishermen. Think of the Potomac River; go all the way across the country and think of the Potomac River in our Nation's Capital. Twenty years ago you literally couldn't even touch that water without being advised to get an inoculation. Now, on warm summer days the Potomac belongs to the windsurfers and the bass fishermen. Around the country, signs rimmed our lakes with the warning: Don't Touch the Water. In two decades, we have spent over $100 billion to clean up our waters. Today, more and more of our rivers and lakes are safer for the people who swim and fish in them, for the animals that live in and around them.

To help show off our clean rivers and lakes, last winter I signed ISTEA. Let me point out that is the Transportation Act, not the rap act. [*Laughter*] But that legislation will help bring America outdoors, revamping our scenic byways, blazing new trails, letting Americans become their own pioneers. That's what the pursuit of happiness is all about.

Some will look at the record and say that it isn't enough. I have a surprise for them. I couldn't agree more. Take a look at what I've asked for from Congress, and then take a look at what we've got.

We've proposed, lobbied, and signed the Clean Air Act, the most ambitious environmental law in history: Reduces acid rain by 50 percent, reduces air toxics by 90 percent, brings all cities into attainment with health standards. On this we had good congressional bipartisan cooperation, for which I'm grateful.

We've assessed more fines and penalties for violations of environmental law in 3 years than in the entire previous 18-year history of EPA. I don't see that record advertised in the political process or written about in the press, yet enforcement is traditionally one of the principal measures of an administration's environmental performance. We've convicted more people of environmental crimes in 3 years than in the previous 18 years of EPA. Think about that. A lot of people doing jail time, and those tempted to evade these very sound environmental laws, they're now reconsidering their actions.

We've doubled funding for national parks, wildlife, and outdoor recreation and tripled funds for States for parks and open spaces. We've proposed or added 20 new national parks. We've proposed or added 57 new national wildlife refuges. We've added 1.5 million new acres to national parks and then 6.4 million acres to the Wilderness System. We've added 2,700 miles of rivers to the Wild and Scenic Rivers System. We've increased funds for wetlands protection from $295 million in 1989 to $812 million in 1993.

Then we've also closed off the coastal oil development in California, in Oregon, in Washington, in Florida and New England until the year 2000. We've established three new national marine sanctuaries, including the largest ever, the one at Monterey Bay, that National Marine Sanctuary. We've increased funding for Federal fisheries management by $80 million and requested full funding for the Wallop-Breaux that I mentioned earlier for sport fish restoration.

Now, that is the record of our actions, of my actions. Now, let's turn our attention to Congress and its response to our proposals. In this year's budget, I requested increased funding for parks, recreation, and the outdoors. And here's what Congress said: Funding for parks, forests, and wildlife, $250 million cut; a Federal partnership with the States for parks and recreation, $32 million cut; park and forest acquisition, $73 million cut; resource recovery for Sequoia National Forest, cut; parks as classrooms, cut; tree planting, we've got a good new tree-planting initiative, cut. I could go on, but the very trees around us might get nervous. [*Laughter*]

But I cite this because I'm not sure the American people really understand this commitment and what we are trying to do. The fact is not just the trees but all of us ought to be a little nervous. Congress has met a fork in the road now, and they have a choice. On one hand they can gut these proposals, they can stuff them with pork and perks, and then turn around and complain about the environment. Or they can choose another path; they can look out for the voices that don't have a vote: the land, the children, the future generations. I'm asking Congress to do the right thing: full funding for our land, our trees, our waters, and our parks.

You see, we need more seasonal park rangers, not fewer. We need to acquire more land upstream, not less. Send a message to Congress: We need less papers, less posturing, less promises. And we really do need more action.

Now, we all want cleaner air and water. We all want a more beautiful America. Some flaunt their commitment with these sound bites, and I've proven mine through, I believe, sound policy proposals. Some have sent entire forests to their death to fill books with propaganda, short on facts and long on fiction. But our approach represents new thinking here, a new environmentalism that harnesses the power of the marketplace in the service of the environment.

The fact is only a growing economy can generate the resources that we need to take care of our natural assets. And our environmental policies are designed to give businesses new incentives to prevent pollution, to innovate and create new environmental technologies, and to save money by becoming more efficient. Our objective is to reconcile America's deep desire to improve our economic well-being, to have secure jobs and homes, to be able to educate our kids, and to have water we can drink and air that we can breathe. I believe this Nation can achieve both of these objectives. No other country in the world has come so far along this road. None will go farther

than the United States of America.

The steps we take here today can blaze a trail for others to follow. And in case anyone should miss the forest for the trees, so to speak, here's a reminder: They were here first. These trees have watched history go by. Some of these sequoias, I was reminded by Dale as we walked through the grove, were already seedlings by the time Christ walked the Earth.

I think back to Sequoyah himself. The first time he saw the Bible, he called it "talking leaves." I think those leaves have something to teach us today. In Revelations we learn that "the leaves of the tree were for the healing of the nations." We are healing our forests, our parks, and our lands. It's a beautiful country. And I want more and more of the American people to enjoy settings like we're in right here today. Let's remember to take time to come out, show our kids the land, to walk among the redwoods, to climb a mountain. Our land can heal us, too.

It is a joy for me to be out here with you all today in this beautiful setting. Thank you very much for coming. And may God bless our great country, the United States of America. Thank you very, very much.

*Note: The President spoke at 11:40 a.m. in the Sequoia Grove. In his remarks, he referred to Derrick Crandall, president of the American Recreation Coalition. The proclamation is listed in Appendix E at the end of this volume.*

# The President's News Conference With President Carlos Salinas of Mexico in San Diego, California
*July 14, 1992*

*President Bush.* President Salinas and I had a very good discussion. I think it was extremely constructive. We talked about the status of negotiation among our two countries and Canada to create this North American free trade area, NAFTA. We reaffirmed our commitment to reaching this sound NAFTA agreement just as soon as possible. Let me just say a word about the

importance of this historic undertaking.

We live in a global economy. The fastest growing sector of the American economy is our export sector. And Mexico is the fastest growing market for U.S. exports in the entire world. Over the last 5 years, U.S. merchandise exports to Mexico have increased an average of 17 percent per year, twice as fast as U.S. exports worldwide. And we've added some 400,000 new jobs to our economy just as a result. And now, over 600,000 U.S. jobs are built on our trade with Mexico. California alone, this State alone, exported $5.5 billion in goods to Mexico last year. And virtually every State has shared in that growth, not just States on the border. Michigan, Illinois, Ohio, New York, and Pennsylvania are among the top 10 exporters to Mexico along with California, Texas, and Arizona.

By building together the largest free trading region in the world, Mexico, the United States, and Canada are working to ensure that the future will bring increased prosperity, trade, and new jobs for the citizens of each of our countries. And because our trade ministers and their teams have made impressive progress in recent weeks, we agreed that our meeting today marks the beginning of the final stage of negotiations. A fitting analogy: We're in the ninth inning. In the spirit of this evening's All-Star Game, we are literally entering the top of the ninth. President Salinas and I have instructed our trade ministers to meet on July 25th to bring this final stage of negotiations to an early and successful conclusion. And we've consulted with our friend Canadian Prime Minister Brian Mulroney, and he has similarly instructed his trade minister.

We also agreed on the importance of pressing ahead with parallel efforts to ensure that the NAFTA enhances environmental quality and that labor issues are addressed effectively.

Mr. President, it's been a joy to see you again, sir, and thank you for coming back to the United States. The floor is yours.

*President Salinas.* We had a lot of issues on the agenda: trade, North American free trade agreement, the award rendered by the Supreme Court of Justice recently, the environment, fisheries, border crossings, amongst others. The dialog was open, frank, direct, respectful, a dialog which was held on the issues that have brought in certain tension in our relation and also on the issues that might enable us to have more beneficial relations for both nations.

Mr. President Bush, I'm very grateful for your hospitality.

*President Bush.* The President and I agreed we'd each take two questions. Then we want to get over to the ball game. And why don't we alternate them between— why don't we start right here.

*Trade Negotiations*

[*At this point, a reporter asked a question in Spanish, and a translation was not provided.*]

*President Bush.* Well, I'm embarrassed to say I don't have any late details on that. Financial institutions participating in Mexico have been on the agenda, and there have been discussions of that, but I don't get a feeling that that will be a stumbling block to any agreement.

*Alvarez-Machain Case*

[*At this point, a reporter asked a question in Spanish, and a translation was not provided.*]

*President Bush.* Is that addressed to me? Yes, that matter was discussed. The Supreme Court decrees the law of the land in our country. I know it's caused great hardship and great concern south of our border. I made very clear to President Salinas that we have no intention of doing anything of that nature again. I also repeated the heinous nature of the crime, and I'm sure the people of Mexico feel just as strongly as we do here about it.

So what we're trying to do is work this matter out in a way that will salve the understandable concern that President Salinas very frankly brought home to me. He told me this is a serious matter. He is a very frank man; that's one reason I have such respect for him. So we are going to try to resolve this, to lay every fear to rest, and I tried to do that with a very open letter, a letter that I wrote from the heart to the President. But yes, we had very frank discussions about it.

*Q.* President Bush, could you give us——

*President Bush.* We were going to just take two each, Randall [Randall Pinkston, CBS News]. But I'll come back to you. But we need two for President Salinas; then I'll take Randall. And then we're going to the ball game.

[*At this point, a question was asked and answered in Spanish, and a translation was* not provided.]

*President Bush.* Randall?

*Unauthorized Campaign Organization*

Q. President Bush, a two-parter, sir. Beyond filing a complaint with the FEC, what else can you do to stop Floyd Brown? And how do you respond to the family of Susan Coleman who believes that you have the power to stop him and his organization and their so-called dirty campaign tactics?

*President Bush.* The problem is we don't have the power. We will do whatever we can to stop any filthy campaign tactics. We have spoken out against it. We have written the contributors. Our record is clean on it, and for anyone to suggest differently is insidious. But we will do everything we can that's in the law to see that this man does not use my name in raising funds for these nefarious purposes. I've said it over and over again, and I'll keep saying it. And we're trying to file with the FEC or whatever else we can do. But the law is fairly complicated on this. We went through this once before with this person, and we're going to do whatever we can to stop it.

Q. Is a lawsuit possible, sir, beyond the FEC complaint?

*President Bush.* I don't know what—lawyers are talking about it now, and I think we've gone into the FEC to try to condemn it. But whether that has to be the first step, Randall, I'm sorry, I just rely on our lawyers to tell me that when I get back.

*Trade Negotiations*

[At this point, a question was asked and answered in Spanish, and a translation was not provided.]

*President Bush.* With your permission, may I add to that? The question, for those North American reporters who do not speak Spanish, related to the timing of NAFTA. And I concur with what President Salinas has said, but I would simply add for the gentleman that asked the question, not in an effort to slow things down but put things in perspective, to those that say you just haven't gone quick enough, the Canadian agreement with the United States took 39 months to negotiate. And we've been working this problem for 27.

Now, please do not take that as kind of a "Ho-hum, that gives us 12 more months." That's not the way we're looking at it. But I do think it's important to put it in perspective. We want to get it done as quick as possible. And I will repeat here what I told Mexico's distinguished President, and that is there is no American politics on my side, our administration's side, that suggests anything other than the promptest possible conclusion of a deal. And there isn't any politics. For those who, in the American scene, say, "Well, you shouldn't do it for politics," they're wrong. It is in the interest of the United States of America to conclude this deal tomorrow if we can get it done.

But I just wanted to add the dates, the time, so neither the Mexican negotiators nor the United States negotiators will be castigated by our silence on this. They're working hard. We've urged them to just go right down to the wire now as soon as possible. I gave you the dates in my statement. But I do think we need to look at it in perspective. Having said that, I want it done and done soon.

Thank you all very, very much.

*Note: President Bush's 135th news conference began at 4:10 p.m. in the California Room at the San Diego Mission. President Salinas spoke in Spanish, and his remarks were translated by an interpreter. During the news conference, President Bush referred to Floyd Brown, chairman, Presidential Victory Committee.*

# Statement on Meeting With President Carlos Salinas of Mexico
*July 14, 1992*

President Salinas and I had an extremely constructive discussion of the status of nego-tiations among our two countries and Canada to create a North American free trade area (NAFTA). We reaffirmed our commitment to reaching a sound NAFTA agreement as soon as possible. Let me just say a word about the importance of this historic undertaking.

We live in a global economy. The fastest growing sector of the American economy today is our export sector, and Mexico is the fastest growing market for U.S. exports in the world. U.S. merchandise exports to Mexico have increased 22 percent per year for each of the last 5 years, twice as fast as U.S. exports worldwide. Having added over 300,000 new jobs to our economy since 1986, we now have over 600,000 total U.S. jobs built on our exports to Mexico. California alone exported $5.5 billion in goods and services to Mexico last year. Virtually every State has shared in that growth, not just States on the border. Michigan, Illinois, Ohio, New York, and Pennsylvania are among the top 10 exporters to Mexico along with California, Texas, and Arizona.

By building together the largest free trading region in the world, Mexico, the United States, and Canada are working to ensure that the future will bring increased prosperity, trade, and new jobs for the citizens of each of our countries. Because our trade ministers and their teams have made impressive progress in recent weeks, we agreed that our meeting today marks the beginning of the final stage of negotiations. In the spirit of this evening's All-Star Game, we are entering the top of the ninth inning of negotiations. President Salinas and I have instructed our trade ministers to meet on July 25 to bring this final stage of negotiations to an early and successful conclusion. We have consulted with Canadian Prime Minister Mulroney, and he has similarly instructed his trade minister.

We also agreed on the importance of pressing ahead with parallel efforts to assure that the NAFTA enhances environmental quality and that labor issues are addressed effectively.

# Nomination of John Cameron Monjo To Be United States Ambassador to Pakistan
*July 14, 1992*

The President today announced his intention to nominate John Cameron Monjo, of Maryland, a career member of the Senior Foreign Service, class of Career Minister, to be Ambassador of the United States of America to the Islamic Republic of Pakistan. He would succeed Nicholas Platt.

Since 1989 Ambassador Monjo has served as Ambassador to Indonesia. Prior to this he served as Ambassador to Malaysia, 1987–89. He has held several positions at the Department of State, including Senior Deputy Assistant Secretary for East Asian and Pacific

Affairs, 1985–87; Deputy Assistant Secretary for East Asian and Pacific Affairs, 1983–85; Deputy Chief of Mission in Jakarta, Indonesia, 1982–83; Deputy Chief of Mission in Seoul, Korea, 1979–82; and country director for East Asian and Pacific Affairs in the Office of Philippine Affairs, 1978–79.

Ambassador Monjo graduated from the University of Pennsylvania (B.A., 1953). He served in the U.S. Navy from 1953 to 1956. He was born July 17, 1931, in Stamford, CT. Ambassador Monjo is married, has two children, and resides in Washington, DC.

## Nomination of Walter Scott Blackburn To Be a Member of the Board of Directors of the National Institute of Building Sciences
*July 14, 1992*

The President today announced his intention to nominate Walter Scott Blackburn, of Indiana, to be a member of the Board of Directors of the National Institute of Building Sciences for a term expiring September 7, 1993. He would succeed Kyle Clayton Boone.

Since 1974 Mr. Blackburn has served as president and owner of Blackburn Associates Architects, Inc., in Indianapolis, IN.

From 1967 to 1974, he served as principal with Snyder, Blackburn and Associates Architects, Inc.

Mr. Blackburn graduated from Howard University School of Architecture and Engineering (bachelor of architecture, 1963). He was born February 21, 1938, in Indianapolis, IN. Mr. Blackburn is married, has three children, and resides in Indianapolis, IN.

## Remarks in Boulder, Wyoming, on Ross Perot's Withdrawal From the Presidential Campaign
*July 16, 1992*

This is the President. I just called Ross Perot. On a very personal basis, I congratulated him. I told him I understood how difficult a decision it must have been. I told him that he had really and truly energized an awful lot of people.

Obviously, I told him I would welcome his support and the support of all those who have been out there working for him. I congratulated him on the excitement that he brought to the race, particularly the way he energized the volunteers. It is rather significant and certainly unique in these times what he was able to do, encouraging these volunteers.

Now we will make it clear to all those Perot supporters that we share many of their same principles and that we want their support and that we welcome them

warmly into our campaign. As I say, we share those principles. We need their help bringing about the implementation of these principles.

Many of the Perot supporters were basically conservative people. They were people that are worried about the values of family, that were worried about the economy and the need to get these deficits under control, the need to do something different about the neighborhoods. So I believe that we will have an opportunity to make clear to these people that they should feel at home with us as we start the campaign after the Republican Convention.

*Note: The President spoke at 11:10 a.m. to reporters by telephone from Secretary of State James A. Baker's ranch.*

## The President's News Conference in Pinedale, Wyoming
*July 16, 1992*

*The President.* Thank you all for coming over. And let me just say that I this morning, after receiving the news, called Ross

Perot; congratulated him on the way he has energized so many people in the political process; told him that, of course, I would welcome his support and the support of those who have gotten behind him. We share the same principles with many of those people. And we're going to work hard to win them over, get their support. But it was a good phone call, and I probably will be talking to Mr. Perot again before too long.

But I see this as a positive development in a sense because I am convinced that the conservatives who are supporting Ross Perot, the legions of conservative people, will end up being with me because I think they share the same values that I speak about, the same principles that we put forward, and the same desire to change this economy and get things moving again.

So it was a good conversation and a very interesting and fascinating development in a very turbulent political year.

*Presidential Campaign*

*Q.* Mr. President, did he indicate to you whether he would ever throw his support to either you or to Mr. Clinton? What did he say?

*The President.* No, there was no indication of that at all.

*Q.* Mr. President, even before Ross Perot appeared on the political scene, the "right track, wrong track" numbers in the polls were going in the wrong direction. The majority of the American people felt the country was headed in the wrong direction. How do you account for that, and what do you intend to do about it?

*The President.* I think the economy has been the main reason for that. The economy has been sluggish. There are obviously signs that the recovery is underway. Many people have not felt that recovery. And I am absolutely convinced that when you have a long, drawn-out recession, when people's family are hurting, this accounts for that.

*Q.* Mr. President, the Vice President criticized Ross Perot as a temperamental tycoon without respect for the Constitution. And other members of your administration and campaign have been critical of him. Don't you think his supporters are going to be a little bit mad at you when they think about who to turn to?

*The President.* No, I don't think so. No, I don't.

*Q.* Can you explain your optimism?

*The President.* Yes, because I think a lot of people that supported Ross want to see the kinds of changes that I want to see. They recognized in him a dynamic figure that could energize voters. But when it gets down to the issues, I think they're going to be much more on my side than on the side of the Democratic ticket.

*Q.* Mr. President, do you believe this development helps you in the long run?

*The President.* Yes, I think it does.

*Q.* Why exactly, because your aides have been saying that they thought he took votes away from Clinton. And now you're saying it helps you that he's out.

*The President.* Well, I don't know what my aides have been saying, but I can read the surveys like anybody else can. I think it helps us, and I think most people think so.

*Q.* You said you'd be talking to Perot again, Mr. President——

*The President.* What?

*Q.* You said you'd be talking to Mr. Perot again. What will that be about?

*The President.* We were sitting out, like on top of that mountain, although not that very mountain. It was a little hard to—we had a disconnect on the conversation.

*Q.* Also, Mr. President, there have been persistent speculations that at some point Secretary Baker would come over to your campaign.

*The President.* I've read those speculations, yes.

*Q.* Will you resolve that once and for all here today?

*The President.* No, I can't resolve it here today at all.

*Q.* Why not?

*The President.* I know nobody will believe this, but it is 3 o'clock in Wyoming, and honestly I have not talked about that with Jim Baker yet.

*Q.* So the option is open, Mr. President?

*The President.* Always when I'm talking to an old, trusted friend, all options are open about what I talk about. But what happens, that's pure speculation. That subject has not come up.

*Q.* Does the option remain that Mr. Baker would join the campaign——

*The President.* No, there's no options open or closed on it. I just haven't discussed it.

*Q.* In that case, why don't you foreclose it, stop all the speculation?

*The President.* Because I don't feel inclined to do that. I'm going to win this election, and I want the best possible team around me. Jim Baker's doing a superb job as Secretary of State, and he's off on a very important mission Saturday. So he's got a full portfolio right as it is. But who knows? I don't know.

*Q.* Can I follow up on that? The concerns about Secretary Baker coming back to the campaign, a lot of them come from a campaign that feels that they just haven't been able to get the job done. And now that you're moving past the Democratic Convention toward the Republican one, do you change tactics? Do you have a new strategy now? With that rally tomorrow in Wyoming, is that to begin the tougher candidacy?

*The President.* No, I've said that a lot of my own personal campaigning and how I campaign will be on hold until after the Republican Convention.

*Q.* Mr. President, how exactly did you hear about this announcement? Were you sitting fishing in a creek or what?

*The President.* I was fishing in a creek, and one of our aides came, I believe it was the military aide, and said that there was going to be a press conference in a few minutes and that it was widely reported in advance of the press conference that Mr. Perot intended to withdraw. I didn't hear the press conference. We've not listened to the television. I have not listened to the radio. I did, however, get a report, second-hand report, on the press conference and then after that placed a call to him.

*Q.* What exactly was your reaction when you heard it?

*The President.* I was surprised. I was surprised because Ross Perot has energized a lot of people in this country. He's gotten a lot of volunteers involved. You could feel it. And incidentally, there was some show of that out in San Diego. But I didn't detect any personal animosity from the people. I detect a great enthusiasm for Ross Perot. And that's one reason I think we have a

fertile field in which to hunt for more support.

*Q.* Mr. President, Ross Perot spoke of the revitalization of the Democratic Party as the reason that he was pulling out. You've obviously watched the convention and Clinton. Do you see that revitalization——

*The President.* I beg your pardon. I have not watched the convention.

*Q.* Have not seen any of the convention at all?

*The President.* Have not seen it at all, not seen it. I've read some clippings about it, but I've not listened to it nor watched it.

*Q.* You're just not interested?

*The President.* Same as I did 4 years ago. Just want a little respite.

*Q.* When he said revitalization of the Democratic Party, he indicated by saying that perhaps he would like to see these people go more toward Clinton than you, although he didn't say anything about you. When he talked to you——

*The President.* Well, I didn't hear that comment at all. What I thought he said, what I was told that he said for not continuing to run was that he wouldn't be able to get the votes that he would need if the race was thrown into the House, and he felt that it would be if he remained in the race.

*Q.* Did he indicate to you at all in his telephone call how he felt the voters should go?

*The President.* No. No indication whatsoever.

*Q.* Years ago, you and Ross Perot were friends, or at least just acquaintances. Are you going to put all this behind you, no hard feelings? Can you do that?

*The President.* Yes, I am.

*Q.* How can you do that?

*The President.* I always do that, Ann [Ann Compton, ABC News]. I always do that. I don't like to lose friends over politics. I never have. I've always turned the other cheek, and I've always tried to make new friends. And I don't think that's bad. I think that's a sign of character, not a sign of weakness.

*Q.* Mr. President, can you tell us anything about what Ross Perot said to you? Were you able to hear him at all?

*The President.* I heard fairly well. He had

a little difficulty. He told me it was breaking up. But no, he just said he appreciated the phone call and was very pleasant. But there was no substance discussed.

*Q.* What did he say when you said you'd be delighted to have his support?

*The President.* Well, didn't say anything. I didn't put it in the form that I was awaiting an answer at that very moment. It was more—I just mentioned it.

### President's Vacation

*Q.* Mr. President, you said that you hadn't discussed with Secretary Baker the possibility of him coming over to your campaign.

*The President.* That's true.

*Q.* What besides fishing have you been talking to him about up to——

*The President.* Family. I had a son up here. The joy of fishing with your son in a river in Wyoming, I'll tell you, it's hard to compare with anything. And he has his son Jamie here, and Susan Baker is here. Barbara's not here. She catches headaches at altitude, and so she didn't come. But we just fished, talking about fishing.

You know, when you're out in a river with a friend, it doesn't matter much what you talk about. And I've concluded, not just because of my own record, it doesn't matter whether you catch any fish or not. You're there, and you're in the outdoors, and you're away from all the hubbub of, I think, one of the ugliest political years I've ever seen. And I've been around the track a long time. You forget about your day-to-day cares. And it's been a total joy for me.

Now, all this development today has kind of changed this day a little bit from yesterday. But it's been most enjoyable. So I couldn't even tell you what we talked about. We joke. We have fun. We reminisce. Jim Baker and I go back a long, long time. And our families are interlocked. Our kids are friends.

### Presidential Campaign

*Q.* Do you think the campaign will be less ugly now?

*The President.* I hadn't felt that it's been hyper-ugly, the campaign itself.

*Q.* Did you discuss Ed Rollins' decision?

*The President.* Didn't come up. Didn't come up.

*Q.* You surprised by that?

*The President.* Yes, I was surprised. I was surprised.

*Q.* Mr. President, this campaign, with Mr. Perot out now, does seem to present perhaps a starker choice than it did in the past. Is that going to change the way in which you approach the next 3 months?

*The President.* Well, it's happened so soon that I haven't had a chance to talk to any strategists about that. But clearly a two-way race is more traditional in the sense of American politics. And I think in the final analysis that I'll win this race. I think people will look at the big picture, the whole picture, and I believe we'll win. I think our values are right. I think the fact that kids go to bed with a little less fear about nuclear war these days, I think that's extraordinarily positive. I think the economy's tough, but I think what we've proposed to correct it is going to prove to be better than the opponent's.

So I'm prepared to take my case to the American people in the fall with renewed confidence. And I believe that I'll win this race.

*Q.* Did you talk with Mr. Teeter, and what did he tell you?

*The President.* You mean after the Perot thing?

*Q.* That's right.

*The President.* Did not talk to him. Talked to him last night, but I didn't talk to him since the Perot matter.

*Q.* Mr. President, what do you think would have happened had he stayed in the race? If it had gone to the House, do you think you might have lost?

*The President.* I didn't ever think it would go to the House.

*Q.* Mr. President, one more. Now that Clinton is officially your opponent, what do you have to say about him?

*The President.* I'm reading the clips and listening all fall, all winter long. And I'll be prepared at the appropriate time to comment on that.

*Q.* Did you congratulate him on the telephone? Did you call him?

*The President.* Congratulate Clinton?

*Q.* Yes, sir.

*The President.* On what?

*Q.* On winning the nomination, I suppose.

*The President.* Oh no, I forgot to do that. [*Laughter*] But maybe I can do that now. He fought hard, and he won his party's nomination. Having been there before myself, I can say that's no mean achievement. But I'm perfectly glad to do that. And then we'll go to general quarters in the fall because we differ on almost everything on the issues, but we're going to keep it on the issues.

*Q.* Are you more optimistic now about the two-party system than you might have been when Perot hit a high point?

*The President.* I don't believe I ever lost confidence in the two-party system because when you look back at our country and then compare it to democracies around the world or other systems, we've had the most stable possible political system for 200 years. And for most of that you had a viable, strong two-party system. I think in the final analysis, the American people understand that. That has not been in focus up to this point. But I've not lost confidence in it. And I just think that it has served our country well for a long time. I do think that the question mark of going to the House having been removed, that clarifies things for the American electorate and makes it easier in a sense because I think in some people's minds there was some doubt about that.

I think Judy's [Judy A. Smith, Deputy Press Secretary] trying to get some——

*Q.* Is that a valid reason for dropping out, as Mr. Perot said, the fear of——

*The President.* I would leave that to him.

*Q.* Mr. President, will you debate Mr. Clinton, and would you favor a Vice Presidential debate in the fall campaign?

*The President.* I expect there will be both.

### Israel

*Q.* Any comment on the Israeli announcement on the settlements?

*The President.* No. If you'd help me with what announcement you're talking about.

*Q.* I believe they've announced they're freezing settlements.

*The President.* Well, the Israeli election was a lot about that. And I can't comment on the statement. I've not seen it. But I'm looking forward to receiving the Prime Minister of Israel and hopefully in the next couple of weeks, next 2 or 3 weeks. I've pledged to work to strengthen the very important relationship between the two countries. But I just can't comment on that particular because literally I'm—I've seen some clips, some summaries, what they call a White House News Summary. But I've not read the papers. I have not watched television. Sorry, Ann. And I have not listened to the radio on this. That's why I'm in such a wonderfully relaxed mood. And now I want to go back and catch a few more fish.

### President's Vacation

*Q.* How many fish did you catch, sir?

*The President.* It is an unimpressive record. However, here's my side of it. [*Laughter*] I would like you to—no, I caught two or three yesterday—three, and two today. But it's not—it's the hunt as well as catching the fish. It's trying to put the fly right where you think the action is and standing there in the beauty of this marvelous country of ours, standing in the middle of a stream. And it's very hard to describe. But for people that love the outdoors as I do, love this West as I do, why, they'll know what I mean. It's not catching the fish. It's being out there in nature with nature all around you.

*Q.* How's Jim Baker's cooking?

*The President.* Not near as good as his Secretary-of-State-ship. But his wife's cooking is superb.

Let me say hello to these guys. Thank you all for coming.

*Note: The President's 136th news conference began at 2:50 p.m. at the U.S. Air Force Pinedale Seismic Research Facility. In the news conference, the following persons were referred to: Robert Teeter, campaign chairman, Bush-Quayle '92; and Ed Rollins, former Perot campaign cochairman.*

## Letter to Congressional Leaders Reporting on Iraq's Compliance With United Nations Security Council Resolutions
*July 16, 1992*

*Dear Mr. Speaker: (Dear Mr. President:)*

Consistent with the Authorization for Use of Military Force Against Iraq Resolution (Public Law 102–1), and as part of my continuing effort to keep the Congress fully informed, I am again reporting on the status of efforts to obtain compliance by Iraq with the resolutions adopted by the U.N. Security Council.

Since the events described in my report of May 15, 1992, the Iraqi Government has provided what it terms a "full, final, and complete" disclosure of its programs for weapons of mass destruction (WMD). The Iraqi report, which reached the United Nations 2 months after it was originally promised, is now under review by the United Nations Special Commission on Iraq (UNSCOM) and the International Atomic Energy Agency (IAEA). The preliminary assessment of these organizations is that the Iraqis have provided little new information. The Iraqis also have provided the United Nations with a "Compliance and Monitoring Report," which aims to satisfy the requirement of U.N. Security Council Resolution 175 for a list of all sites subject to long-term monitoring. UNSCOM is assessing this report.

As of July 1, UNSCOM and IAEA have conducted 38 inspections in all four weapons categories. From May 26 to June 4, the 12th nuclear inspection team oversaw the destruction of three buildings at the al Atheer nuclear weapons fabrication facility. It also inspected uranium enrichment sites at Tarmiya and Ash Sharqat to prepare for the destruction and the rendering harmless of utilities and ventilation systems during the 13th inspection in July. The Iraqi Government continues to refuse IAEA requests for records detailing foreign suppliers of its nuclear weapons program.

A small Chemical Destruction Group entered Iraq on June 19. This team will spend several months in Iraq establishing a base and overseeing the long-term destruction of Iraqi chemical agents and weapons at the Muthanna Establishment. The operation will be run by a large multinational group, including two Americans. UNSCOM estimates the operation will take 12 to 18 months to complete. A second combined chemical and biological weapons team was in Iraq from June 26 to July 4 conducting inspections and destroying dual-use chemical production equipment.

From May 14 to 22, the 11th ballistic missile team inspected five sites, completed verification of Iraqi destruction of SCUD missile production and launcher components, and verified the destruction of missile production equipment. The 12th ballistic missile team is in Iraq from July 9 to 17 to inspect undeclared sites.

We view with particular concern the refusal by Iraqi authorities to grant immediate access by UNSCOM inspectors to the Agricultural Ministry in early July. The President of the U.N. Security Council has characterized this refusal as a material and unacceptable breach of Resolution 687. We are resolved that Iraq must not be allowed to defy the Security Council and evade its responsibilities under this resolution.

Continued Iraqi intransigence with respect to compliance with the relevant U.N. Security Council resolutions led UNSCOM to initiate a program of aerial surveillance of WMD activity in Iraq on June 21. Utilizing UNSCOM's German helicopters, two to three flights will be flown per week, with five to six sites covered on each flight; this program will provide more immediate and accurate information about Iraqi facilities. We strongly favor this aggressive approach by UNSCOM, which will broaden UNSCOM's ability to find suspect sites as well as conduct long-term monitoring.

UNSCOM continues to face a shortage of funds. U.S. efforts to alleviate this problem will result in payment of approximately $30 million for UNSCOM by the end of July. Discussions are ongoing with other nations regarding contributions by them to UNSCOM.

Since my last report, there has been further progress at the U.N. Compensation Commission concerning preparations for the processing of claims from individuals, corporations, other entities, governments, and international organizations that suffered direct loss or damage as a result of Iraq's unlawful invasion and occupation of Kuwait. The Governing Council of the Commission held its sixth session in Geneva from June 22 to 26 and has scheduled further meetings in September and December. (A meeting tentatively set for November has been cancelled.) At its June session, the Council approved the final part of the rules of procedure (the first three parts were approved in March). The entire set of rules was then issued as a Council decision. The rules provide a practical, nontechnical system for processing claims. The Council also decided that members of the Allied Coalition Armed Forces who were prisoners of war and mistreated in violation of international humanitarian law, including the 1949 Geneva Conventions, are eligible for compensation in accordance with the claims criteria previously adopted.

The Council continued its discussion of the "embargo loss" issue and agreed on a statement for the record promising that the issue of priority of payments would be considered. Also during the session of June 22 to 26, the Commission released to governments the form for corporate claims (Form E). The Council also reviewed the draft form for claims from governments and international organizations (Form F). The Executive Secretary reported that the $2 million loan from the Kuwaiti Government has been received, and the Commission has received another $1 million as a result of the U.S. contribution to the United Nations for activities under Resolution 687. The financial impasse of the past several months, however, has cost valuable time in developing computer software and other key projects. Now that operating funds have been received, the Secretariat will press ahead and try to recover as much lost time as possible. On June 26, the United States filed its first set of 200 claims with the Commission; altogether 10 governments filed claims by the end of the week. Meanwhile, the Department of State distributed to potential U.S. claimants the form for claims of individuals over $100,000 (Form D) and continued to collect and review small claims.

In accordance with paragraph 20 of Resolution 687, the Sanctions Committee continues to receive notice of shipments of foodstuffs to Iraq. The Sanctions Committee also continues to consider and, when appropriate, approve requests to send to Iraq materials and supplies for essential civilian needs. Iraq, in contrast, has for months maintained a full embargo against its northern provinces. Iraq has also refused to utilize the opportunity under Resolutions 706 and 712 to sell $1.6 billion in oil, most of the proceeds from which could be used by Iraq to purchase foodstuffs, medicines, materials, and supplies for essential civilian needs of its civilian population. The Iraqi authorities bear full responsibility for any suffering in Iraq that results from their refusal to implement Resolutions 706 and 712.

Through the International Committee of the Red Cross (ICRC), the United States, Kuwait, and our allies continue to press the Government of Iraq to comply with its obligations under Security Council resolutions to return all detained Kuwaiti and third-country nationals. Likewise, the United States and its allies continue to press the Government of Iraq to return to Kuwait all property and equipment removed from Kuwait by Iraq. Iraq continues to resist full cooperation on these issues and to resist unqualified ICRC access to detention facilities in Iraq.

Mindful of the finding of the U.N. Security Council in Resolution 688 that Iraq's repression of its civilian population threatens international peace and security in the region, we will continue to monitor carefully the treatment of Iraq's citizens in concert with our Coalition partners, and together we remain prepared to take appropriate steps if the situation requires. To this end, we will continue to maintain an appropriate level of forces in the region for as long as required by the situation in Iraq.

I remain grateful for the support of the Congress for these efforts, and I look forward to continued cooperation toward achieving our mutual objectives.

Sincerely,

GEORGE BUSH

*Note: Identical letters were sent to Thomas*

*S. Foley, Speaker of the House of Represent-*
*atives, and Dan Quayle, President of the*
*Senate.*

## Remarks to the Community in Jackson Hole, Wyoming
*July 17, 1992*

Thank you very very much for that warm welcome. Let me just say at the beginning of these remarks how grateful I am for the congressional delegation that I work with in Washington. If we had more men like the Congressman that just introduced me, Craig Thomas, if we had more like him in the House, I guarantee you this country would be moving forward faster with opportunity for all. I salute Malcolm Wallop, who I don't think is with us today, but also my dear friend Al Simpson, who stands tall, all right; we saw that. But he's out there for principle in the United States Senate. And he's a close personal friend, he and Ann, to Barbara and me. That disproves the theory that goes like this: Well, if you want a dog in Washington—I mean, want a friend in Washington, get a dog. [*Laughter*] My view is we've got the Simpsons and several others like them.

May I thank the Bar-J Wranglers down there, who did a great job, and the Jackson Hole Community Band and others who make this very, very special. I told the Mayor, Bill Westbrook, because I was sitting next to him here at barbecue, that for me this is a very special change of pace. I don't want to argue with my friend Al Simpson, but we're not quite into the one-on-one competitive mode yet. I'm going to hold back a little bit until after the Republican Convention. And then we're going after it. We're going to win this election because I'm going to take the case to the American people for sure.

I want to salute Senator Cliff Hanson, who is with us; his wife, Martha. Another Nebraska Senator is here, Senator Curtis, another good friend. And I'd be remiss if I didn't single out Estelle Stacy Carrier, with whom I worked when I was chairman of

the Republican National Committee, sitting over here. Someone told me that another man I was proud to have served with, Jim Watt, is here, a member of this community, and I salute him and wish him the best of everything.

Let me tell you this: With all the hue and cry of politics, I cannot think of a better way to spend a Friday noon, Friday afternoon—the big sky and the hot sun, this fantastic view, this marvelous helping of baked beans and coleslaw, not a single piece of broccoli anywhere on that whole table. [*Laughter*]

In the line over there somebody asked me if I wanted to comment on this week's big event, the one that captured the imagination of millions of TV viewers. And to be brutally honest, I thought the All-Star Game would be a lot closer than it was. [*Laughter*]

Let me just make a few comments because, seriously, it was an important week in American politics. And I salute the opposition. They ran a good show there, and I don't think there's any reason to be bitter or small about all of that.

But I want to say a word about yesterday's happening and about Ross Perot and that surprising announcement yesterday. I admit that as the incumbent President of the United States that it's tempting to quietly applaud the fact that this strange year, this strange political year, has suddenly become, quote, normal. But I can't do that. The grassroots fervor of the Perot supporters transcends what we call politics as usual.

You see, a vote was taken this spring and summer in America. No ballots were cast, but a vote was taken. No polls opened, but a referendum took place nonetheless. Nobody won this election, but politics lost. Politics lost because it's become increasingly irrelevant to many Americans. Its language is not understood around our kitchen tables. Politics for too many people has become synonymous with slogans, posturing, and it's come to mean the opposite of progress.

Today I have a message for anyone who supported Ross Perot and any American who identifies with that frustration that brought them together: I hear you. You've come through loud and clear. And Ross used to like to say two words more than any others, "you," meaning the people, "you" and "win." And today I can say to his supporters, while politics as usual may have lost, you have won. I hear the voices in so many accents say attention must be paid to our jobs, our schools, our families. Attention must be paid to our future. I hear that call, and more than that, I share that frustration.

In my first term in office I have learned that it is far easier to convince the leaders of diverse nations to mobilize to confront a tyrant than to convince the Congress to approve a relatively small tax incentive so that Americans, young Americans, can buy that first home. And we are going to keep fighting for those young Americans.

I say this not to bash the United States Congress but to tell you that the view from the White House looks the same as the view from your front porch. And the system needs repair. My message to the disillusioned and the disaffected is simple: Don't walk away from the system. Don't assume that without a protest vote there is no vote at all. The solution to our challenges today is the same that America has turned to so many times before, that mixture of values, experience, and ideas that we call leadership.

What kind of leadership do we need? I believe that our first priority is to provide more economic opportunity for more people. You see, too many people have worked for a company for 20 years only to worry that the next mail is going to bring in a pink slip. Too many parents have saved to send their kids to college only to find that once graduated, a kid can't get a good job.

The first order of business is to get the Federal deficit down by cutting Federal spending. And I need more help in that end. And yes, I believe that we should create incentives for the people in the businesses who create jobs and give them access to the new markets that are opening all around the world.

I also believe that we have to restore the traditional American values that have held our society together for 200 years. You know what they are. We're talking about respect. We're talking about knowing the difference between right and wrong. We're talking about helping our neighbors, putting the family, the American family, first, and putting our faith in something larger than ourselves. I happen to know a silver-haired philosopher who is not with us today named Barbara Bush. She says this, that what happens in your house is more important than what happens in the White House. It is far more important than what happens in the White House. That is true.

I believe Government can be a force to strengthen our families. And Government can reward work, not welfare dependency. Welfare can encourage families not to fall apart but to stick together. Government can give families in Wyoming and in every other State the option of deciding where our children should go to school, a church school, a private school, or a public school, wherever their parents choose. That is the American way.

I also believe that we must restore respect for the law. It is not enough to have peace in the world if people don't feel safe in their own backyards. What do you say to an elderly woman who watches the Berlin Wall fall on television but is afraid to walk to her grocery store? What do you say to a 10-year-old kid who hears of the Russians reducing nuclear weapons and then has to walk through a metal detector at school every morning? You say, "Enough is enough." Let's put an end to the lawlessness, and let's put an end to the drug use that results in so much of this illegal behavior.

So this is the kind of action I propose today, right now, to shake up the system and let America realize the opportunity before us. I am not pessimistic about the United States of America. We are the best and the finest, and we have lots to be proud of. Help me move this country forward.

I know it's not going to be easy. For 3

years now I've proposed dramatic changes in each of these areas that I mentioned today and run into roadblocks that Senator Simpson talked about. But as I said, politics as usual can be no more. You want action, and you want change. To anyone who wants to block that change, I say what you say, "Get out of our way and let America move forward once again."

For all our challenges, America's potential really has never been greater. If we can get our economy moving faster and restore our families and take back our streets, our potential is as tall as the mountains that surround us. And can we do it? You bet. I believe we can. I'm confident we can. If we can topple the Berlin Wall and if we can build a sturdy economy and if we can lift the Iron Curtain and if we can bring down the curtain on new-age values, if we can help people walk the streets free in Eastern Europe, we can take back the streets of America. And we must get that job done. If we can revive a world's faith in freedom, we can repair the American system. And this is our mission. It's to renew America, to complete the dream.

I have a feeling that I'm lecturing to the choir when it comes to family, comes to values, comes to faith. I'm lecturing to the choir with this group assembled. And I thank those with the civic clubs that have drawn this magnificent crowd together. But I am going to take this message of hope and opportunity all across the country. Four years from now, when I come back for a little more trout fishing, I look forward to standing before you to say, "Mission accomplished." We are America. We can get the job done. I need your help.

May I just simply say thank you for this fantastic Wyoming hospitality. And may God bless the United States of America, the greatest, freest, fairest country on the face of the Earth.

Thank you all, and good luck. Thank you very much. Thank you so much for a great welcome. What a wonderful way to come out of the mountains and see the real people that make this country great. Thank you so much.

*Note: The President spoke at 12:05 p.m. at Jackson Hole Airport. In his remarks, he referred to Senator Malcolm Wallop; Estelle Stacy Carrier, former secretary of the Republican National Committee; and James Watt, former Secretary of the Interior.*

# Nomination of Harriet Winsar Isom To Be United States Ambassador to Cameroon
*July 17, 1992*

The President today announced his intention to nominate Harriet Winsar Isom, of Oregon, a career member of the Senior Foreign Service, class of Minister-Counselor, to be Ambassador of the United States of America to the Republic of Cameroon. She would succeed Frances D. Cook.

Since 1989, Ambassador Isom has served as Ambassador to the Republic of Benin. She has also served as Chargé d'Affaires at the American Embassy in Vientiane, Laos, 1986–89; Director of Korean Affairs at the State Department, 1984–86; senior assignments officer with the Bureau of Personnel at the State Department, 1982–84; a participant in the senior seminar at the State Department, 1981–82; political counselor at the American Embassy in Jakarta, Indonesia, 1978–81; and consul of the American consulate in Medan, Sumatra, Indonesia, 1977–78.

Ambassador Isom graduated from Mills College (B.A., 1958) and Fletcher School of Law and Diplomacy (M.A.L.D., 1960). She was born November 4, 1936, in Heppner, OR. Ambassador Isom currently resides in Echo, OR.

# Remarks and a Question-and-Answer Session With Outdoor Groups in Salt Lake City, Utah
*July 18, 1992*

*The President.* Well, I came prepared with a few cheaters because on this beautiful day it is most fitting and appropriate that we talk about the environment, with the emphasis on those that like the outdoors and believe in multiple use and believe in fishing and believe in hunting and believe in camping. And I do, and my family does. I did want to try this morning, though, to put in perspective before taking questions what I think is a pretty good environmental record.

I don't pretend to be able to keep every organization happy. I can't do that because I also have a certain—not only do I feel a sense of obligation to stewardship of the parks and of the wilderness and of the great outdoors, but I also feel a sense of stewardship towards American families that are trying to work for a living. To achieve a balance between growth and the environment is something that I think every President ought to feel an obligation to achieve. And I've tried to do exactly that.

But before getting to the questions, and I hope it's not too self-serving, I thought I'd just click off some accomplishments that I think should make a difference to those who share my love of the outdoors.

We signed, I guess, the most forward-looking environmental legislation in modern times in a revival and renewal of the Clean Air Act, improvement of the Clean Air Act. I believe that it's going to have a major effect not just on the great outdoors as we all love it but on the cities and everything else.

We've assessed more fines for violations of environmental policy, environmental law, than any previous administration. And indeed, more people are incarcerated for actually violating the environmental laws of this country.

We've doubled the funding, doubled the funding for national parks, wildlife, and outdoor recreation, and tripled the funds, tripled the funds for States for parks and open space. I think that's a good record. We've

proposed or added 20 new national parks, proposed or added 57 new wildlife refuges, added 1.5 million new acres to the national parks, and added 6.4 million acres to the vast Wilderness System. Twenty-seven hundred miles of rivers to Wild and Scenic Rivers System have been added.

We've increased wetlands protection from 295 million to 812 million since I've been President. And I'd like to hear from some and maybe answer some questions on the controversy that surrounds the wetlands policy. But I believe our policy of no net loss is good. We've added to the wetlands to compensate for those areas where there has been loss.

We've closed off the oil development in certain environmentally sensitive areas of the California coast, the Florida coast, and in New England, isolating them until the year 2000 when we can look at technology and look at the environment. We've established three new national marine sanctuaries, including the most recent one in Monterey Bay, which is, I guess, the largest one ever; increased funding, and this comes as great interest to some here, for fishing, fisheries management, and $80 million added to that and requested full funding for Wallop-Breaux.

Let me just say here that when you get in Washington you might have some earmarked funds, but the propensity in the way it works with the Congress is they want to take those earmarked funds and use them for other purposes. I stood up against that because I believe in Wallop-Breaux; I believe that the money ought to be used for what we said it would be used for. And I'm going to keep on fighting for that principle. And we fought for a lot of projects, Superfund and all, where we've not gotten the funding we requested. But I'm going to keep on working to try to do that.

So I cite this because as you get into a political year and you get into a subject that has this many variations, environmental protection, you're bound to take some heat.

But I'm very proud of the record.

The last thing I'd mention is Rio de Janeiro. I do not consider it leadership to go and fall in line with a bunch of other countries who accept standards and don't live up to them. When the United States makes a commitment, we ought to keep our word. Great countries, like great men, should keep their word. That's what a former Justice of our Supreme Court said, and that's the way I feel. So I did not go down there to try to get in line, putting standards and prohibitions on the United States that we couldn't live up to or didn't want to.

So we did do well on forestry down there. We did do well on climate control. I have insisted that we don't make more regulations unless we know where the science is on these things. It's very inexact at this point. And yet, underlying it all was my commitment and our administration's commitment to a sound environment.

So that's where we stand. I don't know how this is all set up, Val, but I'll be glad to go for questions. Here's one right here.

*Q.* Our school last year built over 300 trees and——

*The President.* This one's not working. You come over here.

*Q.* Last year and every year our school built over 300 trees. And we did it in City Butte Canyon. Are they doing that all over the United States and the world?

*The President.* I think so. And every little bit helps. Every tree planted is part of a forestation initiative that is sound. We have a program to plant a billion trees a year, tiny little things, but Government can't do this. Schools, families, whoever have to get this job done. The United States is the leader in forestry. We are the leaders in trying to preserve the great rain forests. We've got a good record ourselves on it.

So what you say your school is doing, if everybody around the country at his or her school does the same thing, then we can achieve our goal. And it's very, very important. It's important to clean air. It's important to everything, including the sporting quality of the whole United States environment.

*Q.* President Bush, there is an abundant amount of wildlife in the United States today, and it's principally because hunters and fishermen have spent a lot of money, time, and resources to secure their habitat, to provide for their game management. There's a great deal of attack on this traditional wildlife management tool. Specifically, proposition 200 in Arizona is worded where they could ban hunting on public lands. What is your position on that issue?

*The President.* You know, I'm a hunter. I happen to be a quail hunter of only fair proportions, I might add. [*Laughter*] But when I go to hunt every year, and I try to do it, and I go down there, and I see these people standing out that oppose all hunting. They are inconsiderate of sound game management. They're inconsiderate of people who like to hunt and who recognize not only the fun of the sport but also the sound environmental practice of thinning out herds, for example, when it comes to deer or whatever else it is.

So I oppose what I consider extremists' tactics. I'd rather see sound management through sound sports practice than I would see some of these herds thinned out through famine and suffering of that kind.

So I will stand with the hunter. I don't think there's anything in sound hunting that is inconsistent with sound environmental policy. And I don't know about that proposition, but that's the way I feel.

Yes, sir.

*Q.* Mr. President, do we expect to see a reduction in spending abroad to fund these policies that you are proposing and trying to continue in the country now?

*The President.* Well, we've reduced defense spending tremendously. I mean, that's what overshadows all other spending that you might say abroad. Here's my position. We've won the cold war. What's happened, as I see these kids sitting here and I think about it, I think it's historic. They don't have little drills in their schools anymore like some of you all had about climbing under the desks for fear of nuclear warfare. The deal we hammered out with Yeltsin to eliminate these ICBM's, SS–18's, is major. It is a significant achievement for mankind, particularly for the young people in this country and elsewhere.

We still have an obligation to help people abroad. When there's famine in south

Africa, the southern part of Africa, I do think we have an obligation. I got a great lesson from the church the other day on how the mission of the church, actually in a private way, tries to help. The Government has an obligation to help.

So we're not going to be able to cut off all of our foreign aid or our defense because of the fact the world is a more calm, a more tranquil place. The spending has been reduced on defense particularly, and I think that we can probably reduce it more as we go along. But I don't think we should close our eyes to the fact that we're living in a place where you have terrorists, you have threats that crop up like the threat from the aggression of Saddam Hussein against Kuwait, where only the United States can stand and take action.

On foreign aid itself, you have to look at it, as I do, for an insurance policy, avoiding future catastrophe, and also the humanitarian side.

But to get back to your question, there will be a chance to redirect more of the funds from the security and foreign account to the domestic side. Whether it will be funneled into the environment and all I just can't say, because I think, as I've clicked off here at the beginning of this, the priorities that our administration has set—and frankly, some of them have been underfunded by the Congress. I'll continue to fight for full funding.

*Q.* As was alluded to earlier, wildlife populations are healthier and more numerous today than they have ever been. There are a few people who would stop hunting on our public lands, hunting and fishing on our public lands. And the wildlife has primarily benefited through funding by these wildlife organizations in property acquisition. Can you tell us what we can expect from your commitment to us as sportsmen as far as hunting and fishing on these public properties?

*The President.* I will resist any effort to stop hunting and fishing on these public lands. You know, I had a marvelous experience—not shared it with my friend the Lieutenant Governor, Johnny Morris, and others. But just the other day up in the Sequoia area in California, I met there with a group of kids that came from the inner

city of Los Angeles. We sat around in a little picnic area, and I started listening to these kids talk about their experience with gangs, being drummed in, beaten in, and then beaten out. If they go into the gang they have to be beaten up before they go into it; when they go out they get beaten up and then their families threatened.

Here were these kids sitting in the majesty of this sequoia grove, seeing the outdoors for the first time, understanding the joys of nature from which they've been sheltered because of their own underprivilege and because of their own backgrounds. They talked about the joy of camping out the night before and being with their—sitting around a little campfire talking to the other kids about their family problems. And that little incident brought home to me more clearly than anything I've done, except for a little bass fishing with some friends here, the need really to keep open, and still preserve, but to keep open these lands for sporting purposes, for fishing, for camping, for hunting.

So we are not going to permit in the name of environmental practice a shutting down of these areas to those who really need to experience the same joy those kids felt. I really feel strongly about it, and I pride myself on stewardship of our environmental resources, our environment. But I just don't think we can go to the extremes in the name of the environment, whether it's in this, trying to deny hunting or fishing to these areas, or whether it's to shut down businesses where families are needlessly thrown out of work.

I think of the endangered species. We're going through a very important debate and an important discussion of how do you preserve the endangered species and yet not say to a family, "Look, you all just aren't going to be able to make a living anymore." I feel as President a certain stewardship for that; I really do. We're trying to find a proper balance, and balance is a key word in all of this. But just to say you're going to preserve public lands by denying hunting and fishing, I'm strongly opposed to that.

*Q.* A number of groups here today are actively involved in habitat acquisition: Ducks Unlimited, Rocky Mountain Elk

Foundation. Will the Federal Government continue to support us in matching funds and help us develop a habitat for wildlife so we can continue to increase our herds and increase our duck populations?

*The President.* We should and will. And I don't know enough about the detail; Roger Porter is here and can answer the specifics. But yes, I mean, this is all of our common belief. I'm more familiar with Ducks Unlimited, but Ducks Unlimited I think offer sound environmental practice. They certainly don't oppose hunting, but they do propose and support programs for increasing the ducks and other fowl.

So I'm strongly in support of that. I'm just a little at a loss to give you any specifics in terms of numbers as to how the Federal Government might do a better job in working cooperatively here.

*Q.* President Bush, as past chairman of Ducks Unlimited for Utah, can you tell us a little bit how our no-net-loss program is working as far as the lands that have been taken, and what we're doing to replace those?

*The President.* Well, we're in a debate, and we're also in a struggle on wetlands. I think we're doing all right. We've added to the wetlands. We're continuing to purchase wetlands. I get into a fight with some—I think, some of the people on the extremes on wetland. I hear from a lot of farmers and a lot of agricultural people who have one little sump on the property for a short period of time, and then they're denied use of that land.

We had one extreme case of a downtown parking area where building couldn't take place because it was wet. So we're trying to stand against the extremes, and yet I'm trying to live up to this policy, which I believe is sound environmental practice, of no net loss of wetlands. We're trading, and we're buying. And I'm going to continue to support that concept.

I can't tell you that it's without a furor, because some of the groups are saying we're not doing enough. I think our record is pretty good in keeping the commitment I made several years ago to no net loss. But I would welcome from experts—and I'm surrounded by them here—criticism or suggestions as to what we could do to further

enhance the policy without going to the extreme.

Again, I think sometimes I get brought to my attention cases where one regulatory agency or another have overinterpreted the law and have kept reasonable development from taking place. So once again, I'll go back to the answer I gave over here to the question of hunting: We're trying to find a balanced policy, but the underpinning of it, in response to your question, no net loss. And that's why we're—[*inaudible*]—and purchasing wetlands.

Sir.

*Q.* Mr. President, as you probably know, the Central Utah Project is one of the most critical issues facing Utah outdoor interests. It's a project which has been repaired, in our view, through the mechanisms that have been established to meet the wildlife mitigation and environmental mitigation requirements. We understand that there is a problem with its passage now, and it's based upon, as I understand it, California Senator Seymour's efforts to get you to commit to veto the H.R. 429 omnibus water bill when it reaches your desk if it doesn't have the amendments he wants to serve the California agribusiness interests.

We're really interested, sir, in having you sign the bill when it gets to your desk, and even more, near term, we're interested, if you could, sir, in having you work with the Senate to get the Senate to assign some conferees so we can get that thing done during this Congress. Could you tell us where you are on that?

*The President.* Well, where we are is that I don't know what they're going to send me. And therefore, I can't commit to sign or veto until I know exactly what's in it. But in terms of the project itself, we have been and will continue to be supportive.

One of the great problems in this job—and that's why I strongly favor the line-item veto—is that you are sent under the name of, say, sound water practice or sound environmental practice a piece of legislation where then you always have to balance out does the good outweigh the bad.

But in terms of this project, we are supportive. I believe your Senators have been working diligently for it. I hope it comes in a way that I can strongly endorse that action.

*Q.* Mr. President, this is indeed a great pleasure. You have been in support of the free trade as evidenced by your support of the free trade agreement with Mexico and Canada. Therefore, I am sure that you are not aware of a U.S. Park Service-sponsored monopoly on Lake Powell, a national recreation area in southern Utah. All commerce in a 2,000-square-mile area, including five separate marinas in two States, is controlled by one company from Philadelphia, Pennsylvania. The lack of competition creates high prices and minimal level of quality service. This, I feel, is repressive and is rapidly driving many boaters away, thus hurting the marine business and restricting free enterprise in the State of Utah. Will your second administration address these inequities?

*The President.* The answer is, your predicate was correct; I'm not familiar with the details of Lake Powell. And thus I can honestly dodge having an opinion on this particular issue. But no, I believe there should be competition in these matters, if that's what the objection is. But I really don't want to speak on a subject that I should be perhaps familiar with but I'm not. But in principle, I can't argue with what I believe your question implied was a proper conclusion. But I just don't want to comment without knowing the facts.

*Q.* Good morning, Mr. President. I'm here representing Safari Club International. And we as hunters want to ask you as a hunter, and we as citizens: How can we deal with the people who want to deny us our second amendment rights, and how do we answer them properly and keep our amendment safe?

*The President.* I think a lot of it is, and this goes back to maybe a fundamental answer, but a lot is to who you elect to office. I think in the local level, in the State legislative level, Val's level, a lot of the decisions are made. A lot of them are made at the Federal level. But I think you just ought to find out and establish whatever candidate at whatever level's commitment to the environment, to hunting, to nonhunting, whatever it is. I know no other way to do it.

But the idea that we should, in the name of the environment, knuckle under to those who really want to tie up these assets and prohibit hunting and fishing is something that I would, will, and have stood up against. But I don't know any other way to do it other than to roll up your sleeve and be sure that those topics are covered in whatever election it is, every 2-year election or every 4-year election. And that's one good thing about it, because everybody has to put into focus his or her commitment on a question of that nature.

I am not persuaded that there's a big move against the hunter and against the fisherman. There's some groups that are strong, strongly vocal. But I do not believe they represent the mainstream. And I have had a hunting and fishing license as long as I've been old enough to, and I continue to enjoy sports. I'm mainly in the fishing end of things. But for fishing and hunting, I just think you have to take it to the legislative process. I know people are turned off from politics, but that doesn't mean that you withdraw and you pull away from it. If anybody should feel like withdrawing or pulling away from something, I could make a case for the Bush family. [*Laughter*] But I'm not about to do that because I do believe in some of the stuff that I—problems I'm faced to solve. And I'm going to keep on saying what I believe.

*Q.* You touched a little bit earlier on the situation—kids and the joy that you saw in the kids in getting maybe their first experience with the outdoors. Could you maybe carry that a little bit further and talk about your opinion on the—I broke them both. [*Laughter*] Throw them in the lake, put a hook on them. [*Laughter*] Talk about your opinion of the correlation between improved fishing and hunting and keeping the outdoors the way that we all want it, and these kids, taking these great kids and turning them into great adults, and the family values that perhaps are created out there, your thoughts on the family values.

*The President.* I could wax philosophical, but they asked me a pointed and understandably pointed question 2 days ago in Wyoming. And this one was put against a political backdrop of how come I didn't stay tuned into the convention that was going on in New York. I put it in terms of the joy that I felt fishing with my son in streams of Wyoming. He's grown; he's from Florida. But it's hard to describe unless you have done it. Ricky Clunn, that you guys know, talked about following in his underpants behind his father, fishing the streams of Oklahoma. I understand that. And I think most American family understand it. Some haven't had the opportunity to do it.

But it was very easy for me to give an honest answer that the joy of doing that with my son, albeit grown, really surpassed the politics of the moment. And I think if you feel it that strongly, you need to try to convey it to the parents and to the families that this really is a way that you can strengthen your family.

We talk about family values, and I hope not to the extreme on that. But anyone who has fished or hunted or hiked or camped with a child knows what I'm talking about. And what we have to do, I think, those of us that agree with this, is to make clear to the American people that's what we're talking about. We're not talking about something that's selfish. So when we talk about preserving the streams or the lakes for sound fishing practice, we're talking about something that has a way of strengthening families.

I know I'm not particularly articulate on this, but I really feel strongly when we talk about family that anything you do with your kids in the outdoors does nothing but strengthen the relationship between the parents and the kids at a time when—those kids that were coming out of that city in South Central, in L.A., they'd been denied that. And here, even though it wasn't with their parents, they were beginning to get that feeling of comradeship and of enjoyment and of really conversation, if you will, that strengthens, I think, the American family. So it's so hard to describe, but I feel it so strongly.

*Q.* Mr. President, as you travel across this beautiful Nation, a concern that we have is, I would like to know how you feel about it when there's a building that's sold to a foreign country, a public building, public lands? How do you feel, and what can we do about our lands and our buildings being sold to the Japanese and to foreign countries? We want to own our buildings. We want to own all of our ground here. How do you feel about that?

*The President.* I probably differ with you on it, because I think investment by the United States abroad is a sensible thing. I think it creates a tremendous amount of jobs in America. And I think you've got to look at each—I think you have to be sure that nobody takes over the United States of America. But in terms of the percentage of investment, much more is held by Britain and Holland, for example, than the Japanese.

So I am not one who worries about people investing in the United States, particularly if it means jobs. I'll tell you an example. The BMW people are opening a plant in South Carolina. They bought some land, and they're going to create something like 4,000 to 10,000 jobs building automobiles in the United States. Now, they have to have that land if they're going to put their plant there. And I think that's good for the United States.

What I don't think is good is if it gets into the security areas where our defenses and our legitimate security needs might be pulled——

*[At this point, the microphone failed.]*

Just as I was going to make a profound statement here. *[Laughter]*

I am not an isolationist. I don't believe we should pull back. I think we have too much to offer abroad, and I don't think we have to fear from people competing in this country.

So maybe you and I differ on it, but I don't—if you were going to say do you want to sell the great wilderness area of Utah to some foreign country, no, I don't want to do that. I think we've got to be very sure that we don't aimlessly get into something like that. But in terms of investment in this country, I think that means jobs in this country. I don't think it deters from the environment or the sporting ability to have the kinds of things we're talking about here today in terms of hunting, fishing, and outdoor recreation.

We probably differ, but I think I could

convince you. I don't think I have yet.

Listen, thank you all very, very much.

*Note: The President spoke at 9 a.m. at Red Butte Gardens. In his remarks, he referred to W. Val Oveson, Lieutenant Governor of* Utah; *John Morris, chairman, Bush-Quayle Outdoors Coalition; Roger Porter, Assistant to the President for Economic and Domestic Policy; and Rick Clunn, champion bass fisherman.*

## Remarks at Brigham Young University in Provo, Utah
*July 18, 1992*

Thank you very much. Thank you all for that warm welcome. And may I just single out your President. Mr. President—it sounds pretty good, doesn't it, for Rex—but to say to Rex Lee that I am delighted to have been introduced by him, a man who has served, first, his Government with such great distinction, integrity, and honor and now serves this wonderful university in a position of extraordinary leadership.

Allow me for a moment just to acknowledge Senator Hatch; Governor Norman Bangerter, my friend over here; Val Oveson, the Lieutenant Governor; Mayor Joseph Jenkins. And may I just suggest that it is appropriate that I pay and you all pay a special tribute to Senator Jake Garn, who's retiring this fall after years of dedicated service to Utah and to the entire Nation. And again, to President Lee and Provost Hafen and Ron Hyde and Dee Andersen, B.Y.U. Vice President, let me just say thank you for inviting me here today. More than that, I want to thank you for extending an invitation to all the Presidential candidates to come to B.Y.U. and share their views. And this is appropriate, the university not pulling back but permitting people to have a fair say in this important election year. I salute you for that.

I noticed that on your seal it says that the glory of God is intelligence. I would add that intelligence and education are absolutely necessary to fulfill your democratic obligation. So I salute you for your desire to learn more about all our candidates and where we want to lead this great Nation.

In this spirit of free speech let me register one strongly held view. I want to change things. And one thing I want to

change is the control of the House of Representatives in Washington. You talk about change, for 35 years, 36, one party has controlled that one institution, the House of Representatives. Enough of these bank scandals and post office scandals. We've got to change control, and that's why I want Richard Harrington in the United States Congress.

Let me say I agree with him on this, and with the Senators, that a strong America has led the world to change. We have not surrendered one single ounce of our sovereignty. We are the leader of the free world, undisputed, on our terms. We're the United States of America.

You know, B.Y.U. is a special place of physical beauty and spiritual strength, a place devoted to a simple creed: Enter to learn; go forth to serve. I happen to believe that there is no higher calling than serving humanity. So I say thank you for choosing B.Y.U. This home of the Cougars feels like my home. And thanks for that warm welcome.

I spent 2 days this past week far away from TV and radio, didn't listen—watch one or listen to the other—up in Wyoming, trout fishing with Secretary of State Jim Baker and our sons, Jamie and Jeb. But I'm aware that something else was going on in America this week, something real important. This is the week when all across America, crowds of panting, sweating people overran their neighborhood video stores. [*Laughter*] From Tallahassee to Tempe, Americans turned on their TV and decided they'd rather watch "Action Jackson" than listen to—well, never mind. Now, look, don't get the idea that this is some kind of partisan attack. Stop by Rich's Video down on Freedom Boulevard, and I'm sure Rich will tell you, give it to you straight. Sales aren't all that bad during the Republican Convention either. [*Laughter*] So I want to be fair about this.

I didn't get a chance, as I said, to see the other party on TV. But I couldn't help but notice one little comment made by one of the conventioneers. It was made by a man named McGovern. First name, same as mine, George. You remember him. Over the years Mr. McGovern hasn't always been my biggest fan. So I was kind of surprised by what he said in the newspaper. He called this year's Democratic ticket a Trojan horse. And he said, and I quote, "They're much more liberal underneath and will prove it when they're elected." Now, I know I've never said this publicly, but, one, they won't be elected, and George McGovern is an incredibly insightful man. [*Laughter*]

You may not believe this, but that's all I'm going to say about the other party. You didn't invite me here to talk about the other side. You want to know what I have to offer and what I believe and what's in my heart. Let me just start by explaining a little bit about where I see America today.

Here at B.Y.U. you like to say that the world is your campus, your president telling me about the numbers of foreign languages that are taught and spoken by the students on this campus. Well, that campus, internationally, has been through incredible change in 4 years. Because of our leadership, because of America's sacrifice and commitment, millions more people breathe free today. When you go to bed tonight, you can sleep knowing that we are safer from nuclear destruction: safer than we were a decade ago, safer than we were a year ago, safer than we were even a month ago, before I met with Boris Yeltsin in the White House to get rid of some of these nuclear weapons.

But this new world that we live in poses new challenges and new opportunities. The challenge is this: Can we compete now that so many other nations are playing our game? It's a tough question. But since the answer is, inevitably, yes, consider the opportunity we face: more of the world's people hungry for our products, more of the world's people eager for our services, more good jobs for you and all your classmates.

What do we need to take advantage of this opportunity? The same values, the same principles, the same ideas that we used to change the world. To start, I believe we need to get to work today to create more opportunity for more people. You can't build a home without a hammer, and you can't build a dream without a job. Work isn't just good for our wallets. Work elevates us. It teaches us values. It gives us purpose.

Some people tear down our economy. They say we're second-rate, second-class. But keep in mind just a few facts. We are still the world's largest and most vibrant economy. We've tamed the lion of inflation. And consider this: The last time interest rates stayed this low the "Brady Bunch" wasn't even on TV yet.

Our factories produce a higher percentage of the world's manufactured goods than we did 20 years ago. We've emerged as the world's export champion. Last year the Japanese Government asked who leads the world in 143 critical technology industries. Japanese firms led in 33 and the United States in 43. And I wouldn't be surprised to learn if that report was put together on software made right here in Utah.

But while our economy is growing today, it's not growing fast enough. Many of you are working your way through this great university. When you graduate, you don't want to get letters that say, "We'll keep your résumé on file." You want letters that say, "How fast can you get here and take the job?"

I used to run a business and meet a payroll. I learned the only way Government can create jobs is to help the people who create jobs. That means providing incentives so that businesses can create jobs. It means getting our own house in order by making like Paul Bunyan and taking an ax to the rotting tree that is the Federal budget deficit. Governor Norm Bangerter, just back from a trip to St. Petersburg, to Russia, came to have breakfast this morning. And this is his philosophy; it's the philosophy that Governor Bangerter follows and Utah follows. And we've got to bring some of that Utah attitude to Washington, DC. Like your Governor, we need a line-item veto. And we're going to get it. We're going to get the American people to insist we have it. Like you, we need a balanced budget amendment to the Constitution. And we're going to get that, too.

Thirty-one times in the past 3 years I've had to wield my veto pen, many times to cut away wasteful Government spending. With the help of Senator Orrin Hatch and then a new Congress coming in with him, we're going to continue to stand on principle and protect your pocketbooks. We're going to treat wasteful spending the way Carl Malone will treat another team's jump shot in Barcelona. We're going to swat it into the front row. [*Laughter*]

I also believe that we need to restore the special values that have carried this Nation for 200 years. Americans need to understand something that you all know very, very well and that your lives epitomize: "No other success can compensate for failure in the home." David O. McKay's words harken back to a different age. Today we can fly from Paris to New York and arrive earlier than we left, but do we too often leave behind the difference between right and wrong? We can explore a world beyond the stars, but do we too often ignore a neighbor down the street? We can turn natural ingredients into miracle medicines, but why do we feel the need to turn every argument into a lawsuit?

By the way, I am not going to give up; I'm going to continue to fight for legislation that puts a stop to all these frivolous lawsuits. We need to give doctors the chance to practice medicine, dads and moms to coach the Little League without worrying that they're going to end up in a courtroom every single week.

So where do we get our traditional values? Where do we get our traditional values? We learn them in our living rooms and in our churches. While religion and families help keep our lives together, Government can help keep our families together. Government can reward work, not welfare dependency. Welfare programs can and must encourage families not to fall

apart, but to stay together. Government can and must, in my view, give families in Utah and every other State the option of deciding where their kids are educated. Whether it's a public school, a private school, or a church school, it doesn't matter. Let the parents choose. That is the American way.

I also believe we need to restore respect for the law. Peace in the world, it's fine, but it's not enough. If people don't feel safe in their own backyard, it doesn't seem to matter. What do you say to an elderly woman who watches the Berlin Wall fall on television right before her eyes but is afraid to walk into her neighborhood grocery store? What do you say to kids in our cities who hear of the Russians reducing nuclear weapons but then have to walk through a metal detector at school every single morning? What do you say to these Americans? You say, "Enough is enough." Let's put an end to the lawlessness. Let's get rid of the drugs. And let's say *sayonara* to the crack dealers and the criminals. We can help with legislation. You can help in your neighborhoods and in your local institutions. But let's pledge to make America safe again.

As you know, this has been an important week in American politics for a couple of reasons. I met a guy in Wyoming yesterday who noted that the week I went fishing, one of my opponents dropped out of the race. And he wondered if I wanted to stay out West and bag another trophy hunting next week. [*Laughter*]

But let me just make a serious observation. It's easy for me to stand here as an incumbent President of the United States and quietly applaud Ross Perot's withdrawal from the campaign, to salute the fact that this strange political year is suddenly much more, quote, normal, unquote. But I can't do that. The fervor of the Perot supporters, of those sensational volunteers, transcends politics as usual.

There was an election in America this summer: no ballots cast, no polls open, but a referendum took place nonetheless. Nobody won, but politics lost. And politics lost because it is becoming irrelevant to more and more Americans. And for too many people, politics is now the opposite of progress. So my message to anyone dissatisfied with

America is this: Don't quit. Don't walk away from the system. Don't believe that because there's no protest voice you have no vote at all.

Ross Perot's supporters believe in the same principles in which I believe about cutting the size of Government, about letting parents choose their kids' day care and high schools. And most of all, we agree about the need to break the deadlock in Washington, DC.

It is time to say "So long" to politics as usual. More than that, it's high time to shake up the system. If you'll excuse just one more political observation, you give me a Congress that shares my values and your values, and you'd see this system not just shaken but rattled and even rolled. And you will see real progress in our great country.

I know that Provo is one of America's youngest cities. For years, more babies were born at Utah Valley Hospital than any other hospital in America, more than most hospitals in the world. I heard from some not-so-reliable sources that lately some hospitals way up in northern Europe are surpassing your birth rates. But I guess that in Utah babies are born because of hope. Well, way up in northern Europe they are born because of hope and weather. [*Laughter*]

Now, as I look out on this audience today,

my guess is you're probably asking the question that every young generation asks: Will the future be bright? Will the dream stay alive? And despite all our challenges, I am betting on America. And I know you are, too. I still believe in America's capacity to confront any challenge and seize any opportunity. If we can topple the Berlin Wall and if we can reduce the threat of nuclear weapons and if we can do those things, we can build a strong economy. And if we can lift that Iron Curtain, we can bring the curtain down on immorality and indifference. And if we can help people walk free in Eastern Europe, we can take back the streets in the United States of America.

So this then is our mission, and this is our crusade. And together I am absolutely confident that we can get the job done for the United States of America.

God bless you. And may God bless our great country. Thank you very, very much.

*Note: The President spoke at 11:20 a.m. at the Marriott Center. In his remarks, he referred to Ron Hyde, advancement vice president, and Dee Andersen, administrative vice president, Brigham Young University; and the late David O. McKay, president of the Church of Jesus Christ of Latter-day Saints during the 1950's.*

# Remarks and a Question-and-Answer Session With the American Legion Boys Nation
*July 20, 1992*

*The President.* Thanks for the welcome. Hey, listen, I came out here to welcome you guys to the White House. Well, thank you very much. Please be seated, and let's get underway here. But I want to salute the national commander of the American Legion, who's done a great job, Dom Di-Francesco, and an old friend. I am a legionnaire and have been for a long, long time, lifetime member. And I have great respect for what Dom and Bob Turner, the past national commander who is with us today and also now the assistant director for activities for Boys Nation, do.

The Legion does a lot of good works, and I can't think of any of them that's better than what brings us here today. So let me first congratulate all 96 of the outstanding young leaders that are here today, representing 48 States. And I understand that some of you come from as far away as Anchorage up in Alaska and as near as Falls Church across the river. And Reagan DeMas, you absolutely have to tell me what life is like in a place called Boring, Oregon. [*Laughter*] Where is he? We'll talk about that.

But anyway, for two of you, the journey

has taken you even further, all the way from Communist Vietnam. What a moving story is Won Lee's, Nhon Trong Nguyen's. They have a great story to tell, leaving culture and country behind to start over, to start afresh here in the United States of America. Your presence here today reminds us all of America's meaning, of America's magic.

We all know that Boys Nation's alumni often go on to do remarkable things. It's no secret that two of America's great political leaders got their start in this organization. I'm talking about a former Governor, now our Secretary of Education, Lamar Alexander, and I'm talking about a former Congressman, now our very able Secretary of Defense, Dick Cheney.

I've held Boys Nation in high regard for many years. I remember, maybe Dom does, as Vice President about 10 years ago I had the honor of greeting some of your predecessors right here in Washington. Many of you were young then, 6 or 7 years old. But it's good to see that our younger generation continues to come forward with what the whole country sees as model citizens. You've reason to be proud of your accomplishments, and I hope that you're going to continue to achieve great things for our country.

Right now the country is focusing on some big questions: how America can compete and win in the global economy; how we'll educate our citizens and do it better, do it different, but educate our citizens for a new century; and how we'll open opportunity to all Americans and then preserve one Nation under God. Big issues, every one of them. We've got to realize that the solution for every one of these challenges literally starts close to home.

The question is this—and I've heard this from the mayors of urban America; I've heard it from everyone: Can we stop the assault on the American family? Can we strengthen the family, help parents pass on the moral code and character that goes with it and sustain us as a nation? So today, when you're focusing on college and career, let me share a little advice from someone whose next experience with the teens won't come until I actually hold in my arms my 13th grandchild.

What will matter years from now won't be what you achieve or how much you earn or even what honors are showered on you along the way. What matters will be the kind of parent you've been, the kind of kids that you've raised. It all comes down to family. So today I want to salute the mothers and fathers who are here, every parent back home bursting with pride in you just because you're here, what you've achieved.

I also understand that while you're here in Washington you're going to be participating in your mock congress. I won't touch that one. [*Laughter*] But whether you end up in Congress or in front of the classroom or as leaders in business, your efforts and your skills will be absolutely vital to our country's continued success.

George Washington once challenged us to raise a standard to which the wise and honest can repair. And as a nation, our crusade is this: We must continue to defend our Nation's liberty and interest, and we must continually seek solutions to our country's ills, to refine this great democracy our forefathers created.

So let me urge you: Maintain your commitment to our country. Find ways to serve your neighbors and solve the problems of your communities. It cannot be done entirely from Washington, DC. Continue to spread the word about the benefits of our great system of democratic capitalism. And keep your eye on the greatest prize of all, ensuring that our country remains out there on the cutting edge, that America continues to be the example the whole world holds in awe. Believe me, the whole world still holds us in awe.

America is now and always will be the one nation that the entire world looks to for leadership. America is now and always will be a country whose purpose and values, whose global mission and economic success continues to be the success story of our time. And it's no secret why that's so. Throughout our history, individuals, achievers, people just like you have made it so.

America is now and always will be a rising nation. And we'll remain strong. We will succeed as long as young people like yourselves continue to support and advance the values upon which our success is based and, really, upon which this wonderful program, Dom, is based.

So keep up the great work. Congratulations on what you have already achieved. But there's a great challenge lying out there ahead of each and every one of you. So good luck, and may God bless you all. And may God bless our wonderful country.

Now, what I thought we'd do is take a few questions and then go—how we're going to do this—I never saw so many hands up.

Shoot.

### Voter Registration Bill Veto

*Q.* Mr. President, was the primary reason that you vetoed the motor voter bill the fact that it would increase the number of poor and young voters, groups in which you have little strength? If not, can we have a brief explanation?

*The President.* No, that had nothing to do with the veto of the bill. States have the right to set their own registration; everybody has a way to register. It has nothing to do with the poor and the young. Frankly, I think we're going to do very well with the young and, hopefully, with the poor. What it has to do, though, is with guarding against corruption of the voting process, and that's why I vetoed it.

### Urban Aid

*Q.* Mr. President, my question to you is, throughout your term previous to the Rodney King verdict and the L.A. riots in particular, your support for Secretary Jack Kemp's programs in the areas of housing and urban development appeared to come very reluctantly. Yet you approved generous emergency expenditures to help provide relief for the desperate situation at hand. If elected to a second term, do you plan to increase Government funding for the HUD programs?

*The President.* The answer is no, but the answer is I've been diligently for the program. The program is mine. I'm the President; I set the program. Kemp has been a superb advocate for homeownership, for enterprise zones, for the things that we believe really would have helped avoid some of the crisis in the cities. So I have been

advocating it and supporting it and introducing it in the Congress all along.

Even after the riots we had the Mayor of Los Angeles here, Tom Bradley; the Governor of the State; Peter Ueberroth, who is trying to bring jobs into the center city. They all supported strongly the enterprise zones. And it took weeks to get that passed even in the face of the riots.

So now, in terms of will I increase spending, I can't pledge that. I don't want to be in any false colors. I want these programs there to bring jobs in the private sectors into the city. I want our "Weed and Seed" program, which is weeding out the criminal elements and then seeding the areas with hope and opportunity, to pass. But there's another big problem facing this country, and it is the deficit. I know that this is the year when everybody promises, I'm going to do this for that, each little interest group, each big interest group being pledged and promised to, but I can't do that because I am determined to fight to get this deficit down.

So we've got good programs, and I think they'd make an enormous difference in the cities, and I hope you all can support them.

### Economic Plan

*Q.* The economic plan that Bill Clinton unveiled at the Democratic National Convention last week is rapidly gaining support. What flaws do you see in his plan as you compare it to your own?

*The President.* Well, I don't think it's rapidly gaining too much support. What I see is a program that does not address itself to the deficit, and I'll have a lot more to say about that later on. I think we've got to get the deficit down. I don't think you need to go raise taxes on people right now. I think that's a big mistake. I think it's counterproductive. When you analyze the program, they have this expression around here, smoke and mirrors. You're going to save it all by eliminating overhead, eliminating waste, and there's billions of dollars that is earmarked to do that. And I just don't think that's practical.

So when the campaign comes on, there's going to be a very serious comparative analysis on our part. I don't think the program is gaining strength. He had one that was quite different a few months ago, and now, just in time for the convention, out comes another one. But both of them result in taxing.

You see, I think the Government is spending too much, and that's why I had to answer this question here like that. I don't think people are taxed too little. I don't think that's the problem. So we're going to have a big difference on the economic approach. Our economic incentives are out there. They're strong, and they're good.

### North American Free Trade Agreement

*Q.* Regarding the United States and Mexico free trade agreement, don't you think that if it was passed that the standard of living in the Southwest United States will drop and it would also result in more unemployment? Also, what are the short- and long-term goals you hope to achieve by having this free trade agreement?

*The President.* I'm convinced that NAFTA, the North American free trade agreement, will increase the standard of living on both sides of the border. I am absolutely convinced that it will increase jobs for Americans. Look at what happened when we entered into the deal with Canada. Business is way up in both ways, trade going both ways. The same thing will happen in Mexico. And I am afraid that in the Mexican case in some of the opposition there is some discrimination against our southern neighbor.

I don't care whether it's good politics or bad politics, I'm going to work for free trade. I want to see the NAFTA agreement passed. And I am absolutely convinced that it will mean more jobs for Americans and good jobs. The argument is, well, all the companies will flee to Mexico. That's not true; they could do that now. There are many reasons that companies place investment where they do.

NAFTA is only going to increase Mexico's ability to import goods. It's going to increase their standard of living, which will bring relief to our borders out near San Diego where you have immigration going across the way. It will give them the wherewithal to have better environmental standards, and it will give more jobs to the

United States because our exports, which have already gone up substantially, will go up more.

So I'm for free trade. I'm not for protection. I'm not for promising one thing out in Detroit and then trying to deny that it was said some other part of the country.

### Education

*Q.* Mr. President, I would like to ask you with regard to education, do you think that a national standard achievement test at the lower grade levels would be a good way to gauge how well our education system is doing?

*The President.* Yes, and part of our program feels that a national system of volunteer testing would be good. That's part of our proposal. I emphasize the word "volunteer" because I still believe that your community should really control the curriculum and the hours and the teacher's pay and whatever it is. Most people forget that about 6 percent, I believe it is, of funding on education is at the Federal level, our level, and 90-some percent is where it belongs at the local and State level.

But this concept of testing is a good one. I think kids need to know where they stand with others across the country; parents have the right to have that information. But I emphasize it should be on a voluntary basis.

Let's get in the back rows, back here.

Oh, the man's bringing gifts. Come right up.

*Q.* I'd like to present this to you on behalf of Boys Nation.

*The President.* Thanks a lot. Now we're talking. This is great. Thank you very much, Steve.

*Q.* Mr. President, I'm a student of the middle class, and there's an ever-increasing problem with the students that I represent that we simply do not have the funds to attend the colleges of our choices to take the leadership roles in Government. What can you tell the students of the middle class to affirm the fact that the buck does stop here and you're taking a leadership position in our plight to have affordable college education?

*The President.* I can tell them that the best thing that we can do there is to get the whole economic system moving. I can tell them that we've increased funding for that kind of student loan program, and we've just got to keep doing it to support those that need scholarships. A big problem is when you're operating at these enormous deficits, you can't go out and promise to increase spending beyond which we've already increased it. I'm the guy that has the plan. The buck does stop here. We have increased programs for the funding for student loans, contrary to some of the political—I can't wait for this campaign to start to go after some of the things I'm hearing out there. But we've just got to keep going on it, and we will do our very best.

Way in back here. Yes.

*Foreign Aid*

*Q.* Mr. President, I'd just like to commend you on your fine foreign policy. But the question I pose to you is this: Do you feel the only way we can have a strong foreign policy is pumping the billions of dollars that we do into other countries' economy? Being a visitor to Washington, DC, we took a bus ride, and we drove through the Capital City, and I saw some of the most depressed and poverty-stricken areas I've ever seen. Why can't we bring some of that foreign policy money home to where it belongs in our Nation?

*The President.* Well, I'll tell you, maybe you've missed the fact that we've cut the defense budget substantially. We can't cut the muscle of defense. We're not going to do that. I stood here with Boris Yeltsin and did something that affected the lives of everybody here, everybody here. We worked out the most historic nuclear arms reduction package that's ever happened, thus reducing the fear of nuclear war that some of you guys may have grown up with when you were younger. The pressure has been bled off. We have to keep a strong defense. We have cut the defense budget by billions of dollars, and we'll continue to look at it as the world changes. But we can't cut into the muscle of it.

Secondly, in terms of foreign aid, it's always been unpopular. There's always a guy that says, "Don't do that abroad. Do it all at home." And that's a mood out there in this country. But it is in our interests, humanitarian interest, to help people abroad. It's the United States that always has taken the lead. As long as I'm President, we'll continue to take the lead. But we are going to have to try to do these things that will forestall our need to use military action.

That's the reason, rationale for it. But listen, I understand the desire to have more at home, and yet, again, I'm not going to please everybody by saying we're going to increase spending on one program or another. We've got a good budget. Spending has gone dramatically up. But we've got to hold the line on it now. We've got to get the deficit down.

*Presidential Campaign*

*Q.* Mr. President, I was wondering, isn't it disheartening that all of your actions are either maligned, belittled, or ignored by the national media?

*The President.* Now we're talking here. Those back here are not smiling, those beyond those with the red and white shirts. Look, you've got to take it in life. Nobody ever said it would be a bed of roses. I found that over the years in politics or in business or in whatever it is.

I have a very quiet confidence when I take my case to the American people that things will work out. But to be very honest, it's not pleasant. It's not pleasant. The one I don't like the most is when they go after your family, try to make corruption out of a family that's been honorable and decent. I don't like it when they do that kind of thing.

But they've got their job to do; I've got mine to do. I'm not going to be stampeded into anything by a lot of that kind of press. When we get into the campaign, I will try to draw the distinctions between myself and the opponents. I'll try to put out the positive aspects of our record: the war on crime; the fact that we've got a sound, revolutionary education program; what we're trying to do, in answer to your question, about bringing homeownership and hope into the cities; the fact that we've got the best health care reform of anybody up there, sitting right there, languishing, and the fact that we've got a program that if we could only get this Congress to work on it would do something for health care.

So we've got the programs. Now, the fact that that's not resonating and the press seems to be critical, that changes. I go back to '88, and I remember a great reporter for the New York Times—I don't know what he's doing now, but I think he's gone onto greater things—saying, "dogged by Iran-Contra, the President landed in Iowa today." They've always got some kind of sensationalist thing.

But the facts are the programs are sound. I hope that I will pass the test of commitment to country. I am proud, as I told Dom earlier, of having served my country. I believe that what we've accomplished around the world is substantial, major, the ending of the cold war. I think what we did with Yeltsin, getting rid of these ICBM's, I happen to think it's big, and you don't read a darn thing about it in the press.

I didn't listen, I've got to confess to you guys I did not listen to the Democratic National Convention. I was fishing. I suppose I could have turned on a radio, but I just didn't feel inclined to do it. But there was no mention, I am told retrospectively, of the major accomplishments that the American people and this administration has made in bringing peace to the world and standing up against aggression in the process, setting an example. So when I said in my remarks people look to the United States for leadership, they do, but that has no resonance. I think it will. I think every family in America in their hearts know that we are in a less-threatened position.

I loved it when I'm told that my opponent, one of them I guess, at the convention said, "Well we've changed the world. Now let's change America." Hey, a Democratic candidate dropped out of the race for plagiarism last year. This is a comment that I've been saying, and now we're trying to get it done. We have changed the world. Now let's change America. Use that same leadership.

And parenthetically, if you want to know what I think really needs to be changed, it is the control of the House of Representatives. We have had the same control of Congress, same control in the House since 1956, maybe earlier. They talk about institutions changing; Presidents have changed,

different parties; the Senate has changed. The one institution—those who know how to run the bank and the post office up there haven't changed for 36 years. We are going to take that case to the American people.

*The Economy*

*Q.* My question to you concerns us as young Americans. When we get out of college and university, how are we going to be assured as qualified Americans that there will be jobs for us to pursue our careers as citizens?

*The President.* One, the economy is improving. Not near enough. It is growing. You wouldn't hear that—I keep citing a statistic that 92 percent of the economic news has been negative as you analyze it. They've got this group that analyzes the news coverage. A tremendous percentage, 60 percent, think the economy's getting worse. A lot of people are hurting, but the overall national economy is growing, not near enough.

What I want to do is stimulate it to grow more. That was what was behind and still remains behind an incentive program that encourages buying homes; that encourages getting the deficit down; that encourages changing the—this is technical—but the IRA rules; that encourages an investment tax allowance to stimulate the investment in equipment that actually brings jobs. So jobs are being created, not fast enough.

If I can get the American people to give the strong support in Congress for the economic program, I believe that's the best guarantee of jobs for people. It is not going to be Government-created jobs, by the Government getting into the private sector. I oppose that. This idea of an industrial policy where the Government should pick the winners and losers is wrong. What we ought to do is increase the R&D credits so you stimulate the research that has made this country a job-creating country.

So that's the program that I'll be taking to the American people.

*AIDS*

*Q.* AIDS cases being so epidemic, do you have any national plans to inform the public and get the AIDS cases down so it doesn't keep rising?

*The President.* The question is on AIDS cases being so epidemic. Absolutely. We asked for $4.9 billion. We've been spending at the rate of about $4.3 billion on AIDS. That's about 10 times as much as on, say, cancer, per case. We have got to educate the American people, and I'm trying to do that. We've got to demonstrate compassion. We have got to go against behavior that causes AIDS. Education: AIDS is one disease that can't be totally controlled by behavior but some of it can, dirty needles, for example. So we've got to win that drug fight. We have got the biggest and best research, by far, program of any country in the world.

I had a couple of the top specialists in here the other day, Dr. Fauci at NIH. They are encouraged in what that research will bring. Some of you are—well, none of you were alive when they discovered the Salk vaccine for polio, but that's the line they're approaching it, our great research labs. I am somewhat optimistic about achieving a major breakthrough in that.

But in the meantime, we've got to speak with compassion. We've go to demonstrate the concern that we all feel in our hearts about this. We've got to be sure that we do the utmost we can in research. And then we've got to all speak out in terms of the behaviors that cause AIDS in some cases, not all, but in some cases. I plan to continue to do that.

But it's a national problem. It's one where we really—it's heartbreak hill. It's just everybody in one way or another has a friend that's touched with this. We just simply have to win this fight, and I'm optimistic we will.

Listen, I gather they're telling me we're out of here. But we only got about 4 percent of the questions, I think. But thank you very, very much. And I wish we didn't have to go. Thank you all. And good luck to all of you. We're very, very proud of you.

*Note: The President spoke at 9:32 a.m. in the Rose Garden at the White House. During the question-and-answer session, Steve Kennedy, Mississippi representative and secretary of the senate for Boys Nation, presented a polo shirt to the President.*

# Statement on the Resignation of Václav Havel as President of Czechoslovakia
*July 20, 1992*

Today President Václav Havel resigned from his post as the President of the Czech and Slovak Federal Republic. President Havel is one of the outstanding statesmen of our time, and we regret his departure. President Havel's courage has come to symbolize the determination of all the peoples of Eastern Europe to reject communism and to accept the challenges of the transition to democracy and a free market economy. He energized, as he once wrote, "the power of the powerless." President Havel has made a historic and heroic contribution to the cause of freedom. We are confident he will continue to do so whatever the future may bring.

The future of the Czech and Slovak Federal Republic is up to its people. We will respect their decision and are confident it will be peaceful, cooperative, and democratic. We look forward to sustaining our traditionally close relations with its people.

## Exchange With Reporters on Iraq
*July 21, 1992*

*Q.* Mr. President, have you heard anything about Saddam Hussein being assassinated?

*The President.* I only saw a wire service report. And they have no confirmation of that at all.

*Q.* Is the U.S. ready to turn up the heat on Iraq again, Mr. President?

*The President.* We want Iraq to comply with the United Nations resolution. And we are insisting that they comply with the U.N. resolution. But I know nothing about the other at all.

*Note: The exchange began at 10:20 a.m. on the South Lawn at the White House prior to the President's departure for Philadelphia, PA.*

## Remarks at the Presidential Open Forum on Educational Choice in Philadelphia, Pennsylvania
*July 21, 1992*

*The President.* Before taking your questions let me just make a few brief comments. The first, of course, is to say how very, very pleased I am to be here, and secondly, to thank Maria for that extraordinarily personal and generous and kind welcome and introduction; to say to Kelly Geiger, I'm glad he's not running for President this year—*[laughter]*—articulate guy that he is. But I was most moved, as I told His Eminence, by Kelly's presentation and by Maria's introduction.

I want to say how pleased I was to be here for the lovely grace, most appropriately said before our meeting here today. May I salute His Eminence Cardinal Bevilacqua and salute him for his leadership in working for the broad principle that kids ought to be able to choose the school that they attend. It is a sound principle, and I support it strongly.

Our "GI bill" for children is not conceived out of denigration for the public school system. Indeed, the way our proposal works, it would enhance and strengthen the public schools, as well as providing choice for the families that want to send their kids to parochial schools, to private schools, be they religious or not.

So we've got a good proposal. I support it all the way, and I will fight for it. I believe that it will make all schools better, not just those that are selected by the people who participate in this marvelous program.

I also want to salute Lamar Alexander, the former Governor of the State of Tennessee, an outstanding Secretary of Education who is not afraid to take on the educational establishment because he knows and I know that in the program we have, a program called America 2000, we are on the right track in terms of offering the best possible education to every kid in this country. We literally want to revolutionize education and bring the control and participation as close as possible to the families, as close as possible to the local communities. That's the rationale behind what I think is the best and boldest new education program that's been ever conceived for our country. Again, I want to take that case to the American people.

We've made some progress in education, but we've got to do more. We have six national education goals that we've set out, and it ranges all the way from Head Start, support for that, all the way up to the fact that no one's too old to learn. Lamar talked me into demonstrating that no one is too old to learn, and I've learned now how to turn on my computer, and I am making dramatic headway. *[Laughter]* I refuse to take on any of these kids, however, in computer science. But we've got a good program, and it fits nicely into the values that I believe the church here epitomizes.

One last conclusion, and then I'll take your questions. I met today with some mayors from various communities across the country, the Mayor of New Orleans, a large city, the Mayor of a tiny town of Herne, Texas, down in my part of the world. They got onto this subject of family values, something that Kelly talked about I thought in a most articulate way, something that obviously His Eminence stands for, and it's something we've been talking about at our table over here. I remembered not just this meeting but a meeting I had with the other mayors from the National League of Cities. They told me, as this group did today, that the major worry that they have in terms of cities, the major thing that contributes to crime in the cities or lack of discipline or disorder, is the decline of the American family. We have got to find ways to strengthen it.

In this audience, obviously, I'm preaching to the choir. I'm talking to people that live these values, in churches that stand for the values. But it is very, very important that we find ways to improve, to help families restore those great family values of discipline and respect and order, and respect for one's parents, and right from wrong, and the values that, I'll be honest, a lot of us, my generation, just took for granted simply. But now we've got to find ways as citizens, as people involved in politics, whether you're President of the United States or someone in the local spectrum here, to do what we can to strengthen the family values.

When Kelly spoke from his heart as he did, it made a tremendous impression on me. There's an awful lot of good out here in this country, an awful lot to be proud of, an awful lot to respect. We're in a funny time now where it's fashionable to tear down our country or to offer some theory that we've been wrong in the past. But when it comes to values, when it comes to education, I think that we must turn to where our strength is, and that is helping improve the family, but it is also in our faith. I won't ever forget as long as I'm President, Lincoln talked about going to his knees in prayer. I'll also not forget that we are one

Nation under God, and that's something we must never forget.

We have these wandering microphone holders here. I don't know how they were selected for this awesome responsibility. But nevertheless, somebody stick their hand up, and we'll just take a few questions before I have to go on to New Jersey.

All right, don't be shy. Kelly, come on, you ask—let me just—we're encouraging this. Here we are, right here, sir.

*[A participant expressed concern about the affordability of parochial school for his grandchildren and supported the President's proposal.]*

*The President.* Well, we're going to continue to support it, Officer. I'll tell you, I am not pessimistic about the economic future. One of the things we must do—and set aside for a minute this question of educational choice—one of the things we must do is succeed in our overall approach to quality education. The way we are going to guarantee the future for your kids and those that follow is going to be to have an economic environment, an economic environment in this country where people can get jobs.

We've been through this long, slow recession. We're growing a little bit now as a country. In my view, we are poised for a good recovery. Our interest rates are down; inflation is down, and all of this. But to succeed, to really compete in the world, we are going to have to succeed in achieving by the end of this decade our six educational goals. I think we can do it. If we do, we're going to be able to compete. We'll have better jobs, and we're going to be able to sell more abroad. Exports have saved us, incidentally, in this slow, anemic time, a time of anemic economic growth.

So as I look at how to answer the questions to your kids coming along, one of them has got to be success in achieving these six national educational goals. Then, of course, a part of that is school choice; a part of that is encouraging, every way we can, excellence in education.

We've got good programs to increase the math and science. I was only half kidding when I mentioned the computer. We are not going to succeed and compete abroad if we don't do better in math and science. Lamar has pushed through some very strong support for those who are studying and teaching in math and science. So we can make it, but we've got to go along and succeed in our goals here.

Yes, sir.

*[A participant asked about the funding for the President's proposal.]*

*The President.* The money is coming from a regular appropriation, if we can get it passed. It will start as a $500 million demonstration program, and it's figured into our budget so it will not increase the deficit. It will come through the regular appropriations process in the Congress if we can get the United States Congress to think new thoughts. The problem is many that control the educational establishment in Washington are in the grips of a very powerful union, the NEA. If you'll excuse me one political comment, it seems to be an arm of the opposition party. They are not thinking anew. They are fighting us on school choice, and many of the Congressmen just don't want to stand up against that.

But it doesn't matter what party you're in, we've got to get the programs through. Then, if it gets passed, it is already covered under our budget, so it won't add to the deficit. That's the way it will come, regular appropriations.

*[A participant asked about educational assistance for middle-income families.]*

*The President.* You're right. And this program that we're talking about here today, there is no means testing. A family like yours would be covered, a family like yours who, you know, hard-working people and want to have this question of choice. That $1,000 would go to the family. As His Eminence said, it isn't a question of church and state being involved here; we're talking about to the family.

Let me give you an example of how this would work, and this goes back into history. When I got out of the Navy a thousand years ago, I participated in what was called the GI bill. They didn't say to me, you can have this money to go to a certain kind of school, a public university or a parochial or private university. You can go wherever you want. That has benefited the public universities. Most people that look back and analyze participation in the GI bill will tell you that the competition that came from this benefited the public university.

That same principle of choice and no means testing will apply to this program that we're talking about now. So you would get some relief. That doesn't answer how you cope with the other costs, but in terms of this educational "GI bill" for children, the middle class that you're talking about would be covered.

Yes, way back there, Father.

*[A participant expressed concern that lower income and minority students could not afford Catholic schools and asked if the President's proposal could really be passed.]*

*The President.* I'm not sure I can answer in the affirmative. I can tell you we are totally committed. I can't guarantee you that this Congress, sitting there as it is, will pass it. We all need to get behind it. But I can guarantee you I am going to clearly take this case to the American people this fall, get it in focus, and have that a part of the ingredient upon which people vote.

I am determined not to bring into this lovely school arena, gymnasium, or whatever wonderful auditorium we're in a lot of partisan politics. But here is an issue upon which I have a distinct difference with my opponent. I will be making that case, not in a negative way but saying, here's what I am for; here's what I am going to fight for. If you believe in this, you ought to vote not only for me but for Members of the United States Congress whose support is going to be necessary to pass this legislation.

But the reason I have to hedge a little on the question is, I'll be honest with you, we're moving into a very political environment in Washington, and I don't know whether this Congress is going to take up and support this legislation now or not. I'm going to challenge them to do that, but we'll see if they do it. But that's the one good thing about an ugly election year; you get it in focus. Right now it's not. I don't think every American is thinking, am I for the "GI bill" or not? I've got to do a better job making them know that this is an issue.

But the good thing is that will be clearly a distinction between candidates for Presidency, for Congress. And the American people will decide. Then you move early; you move quick with that mandate ringing in the ears of the Congress to get it passed. I think it will be held over. I hope we can get it done soon.

*[A participant asked about funding for education of handicapped children.]*

*The President.* Presidents are never supposed to say "I don't know." That's a very bad form. And Presidents are supposed to know absolutely everything and not be quite as omnipotent as the Cardinal but nevertheless—*[laughter]*—know a lot. I would ask Lamar to address the question of what kind of funding we're doing. But I will say this, one of the great, the most forward-looking pieces of civil rights legislation that has been passed in history was the Americans for Disabilities Act. I take great pride in being the steward of that legislation. In fairness, I've got to say it wasn't Republican; it wasn't just Democrat. It was a case where we could get together with the Congress and do something that was right for people, so that people that were born with disabilities would not be shoved off to the side but find a way to get instrumentally involved in the system itself to the best of their abilities.

Lamar, do you know the answer on funding, what we're doing on special ed? Maybe you could grab the mike. And if you don't, pass it over to the Cardinal. *[Laughter]*

*Secretary Alexander.* Two quick points, Mr. President; I'll be glad to sit down with the lady afterwards and talk a little more. One is the funding for special education has been increased, but not as much as it takes to fully fund the law that you've mentioned. The President's top budget priority: more new money into Education this year than any other Department in the Federal budget.

Second, there have been big increases in Head Start over the last 4 years, 127 percent while the Federal budget only went up 25 percent. That helps with the early intervention for young children.

*The President.* In fact, we have fully funded, I think it's every 4-year-old, isn't it, eligible 4-year-old.

Back again? Shoot, Doctor.

*[The participant also suggested better dissemination of information to local groups to enable them to work for congressional support of the national education goals.]*

*The President.* It's a very broad and difficult question to answer. Clearly, citizen participation is going to make a difference. It doesn't hurt to start with your own Congressman, regardless of party. It doesn't hurt to start with your own Senators. But I think that we do need to do a better job, and I would accept full responsibility for this, in getting the American people informed.

Because, you're right, a lot of this has been languishing in the Congress. I have a great big battle with the Congress on many, many issues. I'm not saying I'm always right, but the result has been, as we try to move these kind of things through, and the American people are saying there's gridlock, nothing can happen. The way to change that is to look at the electoral process. Do not get turned off for politics. If you believe in this "GI bill" or if you believe in strengthening the family or whatever it is, then vote for people that agree with you. Then you can dramatically change things.

So that is the fundamental way to get it done. But how we can disseminate information better, that's something that I've got to find out because I don't think a lot of people know of the conviction I feel on education, on excellence, on choice, and on these very, some would say, revolutionary concepts but concepts that ought to be tried.

So don't give up on the political process is what I'd say.

*[A participant urged others to vote for candidates who support educational choice.]*

*The President.* Thank you, sir, very much. I'll make a broad comment on that; certainly grateful for what this gentleman said. There's disenchantment. But the worst thing to do is to give up: "So, I'm not going to vote. I'm going to sit on the sidelines. Nobody can get anything done." You look around the world today, and the United States is still the envy of the entire world. For us to give up on our system because of a frustration, we ought not to do that. We have got to do exactly what you've said.

I am not going to give up on fighting for this. The election offers us a great opportunity. I'm not just talking about me; as you said, I'm talking about Congress where we must change things. I won't give you my political speech about one party controlling the United States Congress since 1956. They don't know how to run a post office, and they don't know how to run a bank. We need to change that while we're at it.

*[A participant said that without financial assistance, her younger siblings would be unable to attend Catholic high school.]*

*The President.* Was there a question, or are you just explaining? If there was a question, I am embarrassed to say I couldn't hear it. But I did get your statement. Thank you.

*[A participant speculated that the collapse of the private school system would place a burden on public education.]*

*The President.* You know how to complicate my life; don't do that. You ask a good question. You know, I love the pride that obviously you feel in the education you're getting. I love the family feeling around here about the importance of providing this kind of education with family and faith and all of that as a centerpiece. I mean, that's good.

As President I've got to look at that, and then I've got to look beyond it: What can we do to strengthen all the education in this country? They aren't going to crater; these schools are not going to crater. The private schools are not going to crater and fall down. You've got too much going for you in terms of excellence. And yes, it's a strain on the Catholic Church. I was told by a leading businessman in Philadelphia coming out here that business people in Philadelphia put up something like $75 million, I believe was the fee—not Catholic; others put it up there—to support the parochial schools, the private schools and parochial schools, because they believed in offering the best possible quality education.

So don't worry that the whole system is going to collapse.

But as President, and I'm sure everyone here would agree with this, it isn't a question of just making these schools better and then denying the great public school system in this country. We want to make that better. We want to bring change to those marvelous institutions that can do a better job. We think this whole concept of choice will improve everybody else as well as helping the families.

So I don't look at it in a catastrophic sense. I look at it in the sense of real opportunity to help families here, to help kids here achieve what they want to achieve, but not at the expense of the public schools. That's the point we've got to make.

The NEA, that national union, is fighting me on this. They are fighting hard, but they are not willing to look at the big picture. They're not willing to look at the establishment. Art, sitting at our table, was telling me about that. He's a teacher in the public schools, and this NEA crowd is fighting any kind of change because they just like it the way it's been. I don't like it the way it's been. I want to help those public schools get better. I want to see families have their choice to send their kids to the schools they want. And that's the message. That's the underlying message. So when you hear the big assault on us in the fall about this question, please do not be taken in by that rhetoric. This is going to enhance education all across the board, in my view.

All right. Are we out of here? Okay, I'm going to violate a rule. I've been in politics a long time, half my life in politics, half in private life. This lesson I learned in politics: If you take one more question, you always get in trouble. But go ahead, what is it? Question, not a speech, please, sir. *[Laughter]*

*[A participant stated his support for the President's reelection as the best way to address the Nation's problems.]*

*The President.* That is the exception that proves the rule I was talking about. *[Laughter]*

Let me say, first of all, thank you. I think I know where you're coming from. Even

Presidents get moved by anecdotes and talk of family like that.

We do have to win this war against drugs and crime. This gentleman's a police officer. We have anticrime legislation—again, I don't want to be placing blame, but it is languishing in the House of Representatives—that would support the police officers that are laying their lives on the line for you and me every single day: more support for them, tougher sentencing, a little more respect for the victims of crime, and a little less concern about the criminal himself.

We have got legislation up there that really needs to go now to the American people. I'll be doing this in the fall after we get out of this funny period we're in now, and say: Do you want to be tougher on this crime? Do you want to have, yes, rehabilitation and all of that? Do you want to strengthen the families that are threatened when some mother's coming home at night on a subway or a bus and the kids waiting there, doesn't even know if she's going to make it back there? The answer is we do have to be hardnosed and tough against the criminal element and then support those and try to rehabilitate some of these kids that are caught up in this drug fight.

We've got a good program called "Weed and Seed" that I went over with the police chief here before he moved out to California. It weeds out of the neighborhoods the criminal elements and then seeds them with jobs and hope and opportunity and homeownership and a lot of other things.

So, no Federal program is going to solve it. What's going to solve it is what you feel surrounded by family, love, and faith in this room. I really mean this. Don't take my word for it; talk to these mayors. How do we restructure and strengthen the American family?

But I will do my level-best to take to the American people the case that your comments brought to my mind: Strengthen the family and the neighborhoods by protection; do it by education; do it by changing the welfare system to have respect for learning and work and not just dependency. Then do it in a Christian way, as I would say here in a Christian setting, but do it in a way of faith because you've got to recognize that a lot of people have had it very, very rough.

I will end with this, and I hope you understand. Barbara Bush says what happens in your house is what's more important than in the White House. In a way she's right because what she's talking about there is the need to hold these families together, lift these kids up and give them the love. Every kid has to have somebody that knows his name. Sometimes, in this hopelessness and despair, that doesn't take place.

So, I really want to help you try to get to the bottom of what you've talking about here. It is an odd year. It has not been particularly pleasant for me or my family, but I'm a fighter, and I'm going to take this case to the American people.

May God bless all of you. Thank you very, very much.

*Note: The President spoke at 12:36 p.m. at Archbishop Ryan High School. In his remarks, he referred to students Maria Manzoni, a junior at St. Maria Goretti High School, and Kelly Geiger, a senior at Roman Catholic High School; and Anthony Cardinal Bevilacqua, Archbishop of Philadelphia.*

# Remarks to Religious and Ethnic Groups in Garfield, New Jersey
*July 21, 1992*

May I thank you, Governor Kean, for that warm welcome back. May I salute our assemblyman, Chuck Haytaian, our senate president, Don DiFrancesco, and our House candidate, Pat Roma. I'm delighted to see you all. May I ask that we pay our respects to His Beatitude, Metropolitan Theodosius, the Archbishop of Washington, the Primate of the Church; and Archbishop Peter, Bishop Paul, Father Alex, and members of the Three Saints parish. Thank you for welcoming me and so many thousands of your neighbors in New Jersey. Good afternoon to Congresswoman Marge Roukema, that's out there somewhere, and the wonderful people in this audience that represent the rich diversity of New Jersey.

Your heritage is Cuban and Vietnamese and Jewish and Christian and Irish and African and Polish and Chinese and Armenian and so many, many others, and you're Americans all. You are Americans. Your spirit enriches our country, and it fuels the flame of freedom all over the world.

These gleaming church domes remind me of the skyline of a great city. Since my last trip to Moscow, the Russian people have toppled the idols of Soviet communism. They have begun renewing the Russian nation. And just consider the signs of the times: In Red Square this Easter, the gigantic picture of Lenin was gone, and in its place was a massive icon of the Risen Lord, a powerful symbol of the new birth of freedom for believers all around the world.

Today Germany is free and united. Ukraine is free and democratic. Poland is free. And the rollcall of freedom includes Hungary and Armenia, the Czech and Slovak Republic, Bulgaria, Byelarus, Lithuania, Estonia, Latvia, and many, many more. At long last, the captive nations of the old Soviet empire are free.

But our work is not finished. In Asia, in Latin America, in other regions, some nations still suffer oppression. Some people are still struggling to be free. That's why, one of the reasons, I want your support to serve 4 more years as President, to complete the job of freedom around the world. We've got to use our energy, we've got to use our experience to solidify the historic changes that have given birth to these new democracies abroad and made us secure at home.

These events benefit every American. The free world's triumph in the cold war, brought about by the steadfast efforts of America, of the American people, of her allies, gives us a chance to establish for these kids here a lasting peace. The momentous arms agreement that I reached last month with President Yeltsin, this reduction with its sweeping cuts in nuclear weapons, will make us more secure than at any time since the dawn of the nuclear age. These kids can go to sleep without worrying about nuclear war because of the changes we have brought to this country.

Little more than 2 years ago, I welcomed to the White House Poland's then—the first non-Communist prime minister since Stalin's conquest of Eastern Europe. This brave man, Tadeusz Mazowiecki, spoke some of the clearest and wisest words about the times we live in. He said, "History is accelerating." And with those words, he foretold the fall of the Soviet empire.

This wave of history, this surge of hope is not confined to Europe. The Afghan people have won back their homeland. In Angola and in other African countries, people are digging out from under the rubble of tyranny. Mark my words: During my second term as President, the probability is high, it is very high that greater freedom will come to more than a billion people in Vietnam, in North Korea, and in China.

Closer to home, we also have more victories for freedom. The Castro dictatorship is on its last legs. Here's what I envision: Within the next 4 years, I will be the first President of the United States to set foot on the soil of a free and democratic Cuba, and that's good for all of us. I am determined to keep America the leader in the struggle for world freedom.

I am every bit as determined to protect the sources of our strength right here at home in the good old U.S.A. During the next 4 years, I'll keep helping American workers and entrepreneurs carry us to new heights of achievement. I will fight for the rights of American parents and American families. We must restore respect for the American family. The family is under siege. The choices in this election are clear: On one side, the advocates of the liberal agenda; on the other side are you and I and those values of family that we share.

They want to tighten the monopoly on our kids' education. I am fighting on your side, as Tom said, for parents' rights to choose their children's schools, public, private, or religious. And our "GI bill" for children gives middle- and low-income families more of the same choices of all schools that people with a lot of money already have. Two years ago, they tried to create a new bureaucracy, this one for child care. I won my fight to let parents choose their children's care, including church-based care. I will keep on fighting for that kind of choice for the American family.

They want public schools to hand out birth control pills and devices to teenaged kids. They believe it's no business of the parents and that it's strictly a matter between our children and the Government. They even encourage kids to hire lawyers and haul their parents into court. I believe kids need mothers and fathers, not Big Brother bureaucracy. The bond between the parent and the child is sacred, and it is fundamental.

The big government, liberal approach to welfare has failed. That's why, just yesterday, I enthusiastically approved New Jersey's request to try a new approach to make parents in the welfare system more responsible, to put parents back to work.

And I'm ready to fight 4 more years to protect the traditional rights of parents and families. Families are central to any civilization. More than a century ago, Dostoyevsky imagined a nightmare world, a place where an all-powerful state crushed the natural rights of individuals and families. "And if God is dead," he wrote, "then everything is permitted."

Well, looking out over this magnificent audience, I can feel it: I know that your faith is alive, and family is the most important thing we have here on this Earth. And we take to heart the words of "America the Beautiful": "Confirm thy soul in self-control..." We know that the America we love, the America that's such a powerful beacon to the entire world, will not stay strong if the culture and the Government teach our kids that anything goes.

Think about it. If we can tear down the Berlin Wall, we can build a strong economy. If we can lift that Iron Curtain, we can bring the curtain down on immorality and indifference and lawlessness. If we can help people walk free through the streets of Europe, there's no reason we cannot take back our streets right here in our neighborhoods in the United States of America.

You know, being here reminds me that next month marks the first anniversary of that attempted coup in Moscow, of those fateful days in August when Russia's democratic future was laid on the line, when world peace hung in the balance. I'm sure each one of us has indelible memories of those days. I certainly do, and I am proud that we had the courage and the leadership to stand by Russia's democrats in their hour of need. I am grateful for what Boris Yeltsin said about American leadership and making it possible for democracy to come to Russia.

You know, earlier this year, I had the privilege of hearing Slava Rostropovich recount his memories at the National Prayer Breakfast in Washington. He'd flown to Moscow at the first news of the coup, and he stood 3 days and nights with President Yeltsin and the defenders of freedom and democracy, protecting what the Russians call their White House. He told us that deep in the night the only sound was from the movement of the tank treads. And he said, "The aura of faith was almost palpable. In that moment the salvation of us all and of the future of the country came only from God."

My fellow Americans, we have the good fortune not to live in the shadow of machine guns and tanks. America will be safe so long as the United States of America stays strong, so long as we continue to lead around the world.

Let me repeat it: Barbara and I count it a great blessing that when your kids and our grandchildren go to bed at night they don't have the fear, that same kind of fear, that fear of nuclear threat that we faced until just a few months ago. This is momentous. This is important to the entire world. I am proud that our leadership brought it about.

Of course, we've got hard work ahead. We've got to keep our national security second to none. We've got to prove the pessimists wrong about America's ability to compete and to create jobs and to expand America, to expand opportunity for all. We must protect and renew our most precious resource, America's families.

Now, to meet these challenges, to lead the Nation, to fight on your side of the values we share—put party politics aside— but to fight on your share for these values, on your side, that's why I'm asking you to help me win another 4 years as President of the United States of America. I will not let you down. I will fight for the faith. I will fight for the American families. We are one Nation under God, and never forget it. We can overcome any problems we face.

Thank you. And may God bless this great country, the freest, the fairest, the greatest country on the face of the Earth. Thank you all. Thank you very, very much.

*Note: The President spoke at 3:22 p.m. at*

*Three Saints Russian Orthodox Church. In his remarks, he referred to Metropolitan Theodosius (Lazor), Primate, Orthodox Church in America; Archbishop Peter (L'Huiller), Orthodox Diocese of New York and New Jersey; Bishop Paul (Ponomarev), Vicar Bishop of the Patriarch of Moscow and administrator of the U.S. patriarchal parishes; the Very Reverend Alexander Golubov, rector, Three Saints Church; and Mstislav Rostropovich, National Symphony Orchestra director.*

## Statement on New Jersey Welfare Reform
*July 21, 1992*

In my State of the Union Address, I pledged to help any State to reform its welfare system by making it easier to obtain waivers of Federal law and regulation. I am pleased that we have approved Federal waivers that will allow New Jersey to implement its welfare reforms. These waivers will allow New Jersey to try a new approach to helping welfare dependent families become independent.

New Jersey's approach, called the Family Development Program, will encourage responsible behavior by parents receiving welfare. It will also offer incentives for such parents to work.

New ideas for reforming welfare abound in the States. I am pleased New Jersey will be one of the "laboratories of democracy" for welfare reform. Careful efforts to try new ideas and evaluate how well they work can help us create a better welfare system. New Jersey's efforts today will make for smarter policy tomorrow.

## Message to the Congress Transmitting the Luxembourg-United States Social Security Agreement
*July 21, 1992*

*To the Congress of the United States:*

Pursuant to section 233(e)(1) of the Social Security Act, as amended by the Social Security Amendments of 1977 (Public Law 95–216, 42 U.S.C. 433(e)(1)), I transmit herewith the Agreement between the United States of America and the Grand Duchy of Luxembourg on Social Security, which consists of two separate instruments—a principal agreement and an administrative arrangement. The agreement was signed at Luxembourg on February 12, 1992.

The United States-Luxembourg agreement is similar in objective to the social security agreements already in force with Austria, Belgium, Canada, France, Germany, Italy, The Netherlands, Norway, Portugal, Spain, Sweden, Switzerland, and the United Kingdom. Such bilateral agreements provide for limited coordination between the United States and foreign social security systems to eliminate dual social security coverage and taxation, and to help prevent the loss of benefit protection that can occur when workers divide their careers between two countries.

I also transmit for the information of the Congress a report prepared by the Department of Health and Human Services, explaining the key points of the agreement, along with a paragraph-by-paragraph explanation of the provisions of the principal agreement and the related administrative arrangement. In addition, as required by section 233(e)(1) of the Social Security Act, a report on the effect of the agreement on income and expenditures of the U.S. Social Security program and the number of individuals affected by the agreement is also enclosed. I note that the Department of State and the Department of Health and Human Services have recommended the agreement and related documents to me.

I commend the Agreement between the United States of America and the Grand Duchy of Luxembourg on Social Security and related documents.

GEORGE BUSH

The White House,
July 21, 1992.

# Message to the Congress Transmitting the Report on Federal Conservation and Use of Petroleum and Natural Gas
*July 21, 1992*

*To the Congress of the United States:*

As required by section 403(c) of the Powerplant and Industrial Fuel Use Act of 1978, as amended (42 U.S.C. 8373(c)), I hereby transmit the 13th annual report describing Federal actions with respect to the conservation and use of petroleum and natural gas in Federal facilities, which covers calendar year 1991.

GEORGE BUSH

The White House,
July 21, 1992.

# Notice on Continuation of Iraqi Emergency
*July 21, 1992*

On August 2, 1990, by Executive Order No. 12722, I declared a national emergency to deal with the unusual and extraordinary threat to the national security and foreign policy of the United States constituted by the actions and policies of the Government of Iraq. By Executive Orders Nos. 12722 of August 2 and 12724 of August 9, 1990, I imposed trade sanctions on Iraq and blocked Iraqi government assets. Because the Government of Iraq has continued its activities hostile to U.S. interests in the Middle East, the national emergency declared on August 2, 1990, and the measures adopted on August 2 and August 9, 1990, to deal with that emergency must continue in effect beyond August 2, 1992. Therefore, in accordance with section 202(d) of the National Emergencies Act (50 U.S.C. 1622(d)), I am continuing the national emergency with respect to Iraq.

This notice shall be published in the *Federal Register* and transmitted to the Congress.

GEORGE BUSH

The White House,
July 21, 1992.

[*Filed with the Office of the Federal Register, 4:07 p.m., July 21, 1992*]

*Note: This notice was published in the Federal Register on July 23.*

# Message to the Congress on Continuation of the National Emergency With Respect to Iraq
## *July 21, 1992*

*To the Congress of the United States:*

Section 202(d) of the National Emergencies Act (50 U.S.C. 1622(d)) provides for the automatic termination of a national emergency unless, prior to the anniversary date of its declaration, the President publishes in the *Federal Register* and transmits to the Congress a notice stating that the emergency is to continue in effect beyond the anniversary date. In accordance with this provision, I have sent the enclosed notice, stating that the Iraqi emergency is to continue in effect beyond August 2, 1992, to the *Federal Register* for publication.

The crisis between the United States and Iraq that led to the declaration on August 2, 1990, of a national emergency has not been resolved. The Government of Iraq continues to engage in activities inimical to stability in the Middle East and hostile to U.S. interests in the region. Such Iraqi actions pose a continuing unusual and extraordinary threat to the national security and vital foreign policy interests of the United States. For these reasons, I have determined that it is necessary to maintain in force the broad authorities necessary to apply economic pressure to the Government of Iraq.

GEORGE BUSH

The White House,
July 21, 1992.

# Presidential Determination No. 92–36—Memorandum on Refugee Assistance to Burma
## *July 21, 1992*

*Memorandum for the Secretary of State*

*Subject:* Determination Pursuant to Section 2(c)(1) of the Migration and Refugee Assistance Act of 1962, as Amended—Burma

Pursuant to section 2(c)(1) of the Migration and Refugee Assistance Act of 1962, as amended, 22 U.S.C. 2601(c)(1), I hereby determine that it is important to the national interest that $3 million be made available from the U.S. Emergency Refugee and Migration Assistance Fund (the ERMA Fund) to meet the unexpected and urgent refugee needs of Burmese refugees and displaced persons. These funds may be contributed on a multilateral or bilateral basis as appropriate to international organizations, private voluntary organizations, and other governmental and nongovernmental organizations engaged in this relief effort.

You are authorized and directed to inform the appropriate committees of the Congress of this determination and the obligation of funds under this authority, and to publish this memorandum in the *Federal Register*.

GEORGE BUSH

*[Filed with the Office of the Federal Register, 2:40 p.m., July 28, 1992]*

## Nomination of Lou E. Dantzler To Be a Member of the National Commission on America's Urban Families
*July 21, 1992*

The President today appointed Lou E. Dantzler, of California, to be a member of the National Commission on America's Urban Families. This is a new position.

Currently Mr. Dantzler serves as executive director of the Challengers Boys and Girls Club in south central Los Angeles. He founded the Challengers Club in 1968 in the aftermath of the Watts riots. The club provides activities, including arts and crafts, sports, health instruction, and field trips to nearly 2,200 members, ages 6 through 17. The success of the Challengers is due in large part to a commitment to strong families and parental involvement. On May 8, 1992, President Bush recognized the Challengers Club as the 766th Daily Point of Light. Mr. Dantzler has received numerous awards for his dedicated work with children, including an NAACP Image Award in 1990, and he was the recipient of the 1991 L.A. Sentinel Outstanding Organization of the Year.

Mr. Dantzler served in the Air Force from 1956 to 1960. He is married, has two children, and resides in Los Angeles, CA.

## Remarks to the President's Drug Advisory Council
*July 22, 1992*

Please be seated, and thank you very, very much. I don't know why they get such a distinguished group here so early. I would like the record to show that Jim and I are almost on time. I saw some nervous looks up at the sky. But here we are in the Rose Garden. I look around this audience, and I am very grateful not just for your being here but for this wonderful level of participation in the fight against drugs.

Obviously, I remain not only grateful to but most impressed with the work that Jim Burke is doing. Bill Moss is with us today, Michael Walsh, and then other members of the President's Drug Advisory Council. Alvah Chapman, my heavens, what he's done not only on the national scene but in the community there in Florida is remarkable. And so many other business and community leaders, I salute you all.

I would say this: I would like to salute people who have helped achieve the improbable. You ask anyone with a teenager or a grandchild, and drugs are no longer cool. When we presented this bipartisan— and we want to keep it that way—bipartisan drug strategy almost 3 years ago, we put great emphasis on the role of prevention in the private sector. Today, I just want to thank all of you for what you've done to help curb the drug use that declares open season on the innocent.

The administration had hoped to cut the overall drug use by 10 percent, and you all helped surpass that goal. We wanted to slash occasional cocaine use by 15 percent; it went down 22. Three separate studies confirm that adolescents' use of cocaine dropped 63 percent from 1988 to 1991. And America, a lot of America, put it this way, is clearly giving up drugs, and especially the young. Therein lies an awful lot of hope.

This is an important start, and I emphasize that word "start," in a difficult fight. Today, according to the national drug control policy, there are still up to 12 million users of illegal drugs. That's why in November of 1989, we created the President's Drug Advisory Council to further mobilize the private sector in our antidrug strategy. And thus began a great crusade of citizen-formed community coalitions against drugs.

In January I saw it firsthand when I met with more than 700 coalition leaders attending your national leadership forum. I am told there are more than 900 of these community organizations, with more being formed daily.

I look forward to this October when they will be helped by a new organization growing out of the President's Drug Advisory Council, the Community Antidrug Coalitions of America. Now, this group is going to work with business, with labor, with community leaders to eliminate drugs.

So will another major initiative of our Council, which I'm pleased to announce today. Eight months ago, I met with the Council's Workplace Committee, and from that has come a program which seeks to make every workplace in America drug-free, and its title, a very simple one: Drugs Don't Work.

Today the good news is that close to 90 percent of large companies do have antidrug programs, and we know that they do work. The bad news is that we don't have programs where now they are needed the most, in small and medium-sized businesses. Here you'll find many of the more than 2 million Americans who use cocaine and the 12 million overall who use drugs. It's for them that you and Council members like Frank Tasco and Al Casey and David Clare, George Dillon have teamed to provide freedom from drugs in the marketplace.

Last year I went down to the Tropicana plant, to Tropicana Products in Florida and heard about their employee assistance program. One day an employee called this program's toll-free line for help in battling addiction and alcoholism, and then very recently he wrote the local newspaper saying, and here's his quote, "The substance abuse treatment program was a godsend." Well, there's stories like this all over the country.

It's also true of the employee of New England Telephone who sent a thank-you note to Paul O'Brien. The letter described how the company's tough stand forced the woman to confront her alcohol and drug problem. Today she's back at work, healthy and productive.

From coast to coast, business and labor are working to drive drugs out of the workplace. Let me salute these beginnings, and let me also challenge you to build upon them.

Today drugs cost the economy more than $60 billion annually in lost productivity, health care, and other expenses. This harms the ability of our businesses to succeed and compete. By defeating drugs we will help America win in the global economy, we'll help educate our citizens for a new century, and we'll open more opportunity than ever for all Americans, preserving one Nation under God.

Stopping drug abuse will help put America back to work, instill pride, increase productivity, improve quality, and then again heighten our competitiveness. Stopping drugs will also strengthen the family, reaffirming values like discipline and self-reliance, courtesy, and belief in God.

If you ever want to understand the importance of your work, do as I did yesterday when I met with the black mayors association, or do what I did a couple of months before that when I met with the mayors from the National League of Cities. They talked about the decline of the American family as the major source of urban decay. They went on to emphasize the need to win this battle against drugs as the way not just to whip the drug problem but to reunite and strengthen the American family. They know that drug abuse costs incomes and jobs, hurts the children, destroys marriages. We've got to end it, and we will.

We must all just pledge renewal that we're going to get this job done. And that's why we have worked with the private sector to expand and improve workplace programs. It's why our antidrug budget for '93, fiscal '93, is up by 93 percent since I took office.

Today I would urge the Congress once again, call on the United States Congress to fund this request to spur effective treatment and prevention. Above all, I call on the Congress to pass crime legislation now up on the Hill. I still strongly favor a death penalty for drug kingpins who kill our police officers. Let those who sow the wind of crime reap the whirlwind of punishment.

As business and community leaders, each of you is helping with a crusade. It really is as historic as Normandy and as deadly as Pork Chop Hill, as monumental as the fall of imperial communism. It's a crusade to take drugs off the streets so that Americans can take back the streets. We've got our work cut out for us, but I know that we're going to triumph.

I am very grateful to all of you for what we've already done. I'm not sure the American—maybe this is something I can help with—I'm not sure the American people know that we have had some dramatic successes, thanks to the work of the private sector and dedicated individuals sitting right here. We've got our work cut out for us, but we've done a lot. With this new initiative, I'm confident that what you'll do

in the future will get the job done.

So thank you all very, very much. Thanks for coming. And may God bless our great country. Thank you.

*Note: The President spoke at 9:15 a.m. in the Rose Garden at the White House. In his remarks, he referred to PDAC officials James Burke, Chairman, J. Michael Walsh, Executive Director, and William Moss, former Chairman; PDAC member Alvah H. Chapman, Jr.; and Paul O'Brien, chairman, New England Telephone.*

# Exchange with Reporters on the Presidential Campaign
*July 22, 1992*

*Q.* Mr. President, is the Vice President's chair a little uncertain these days?

*The President.* No, it's very certain. I'm not going to take any questions here because we've got an awful lot of work to do. I hope you'll understand, Charles [Charles Bierbauer, Cable News Network], but we're not going to take any more questions now.

*Q.* What about Secretary Baker?

*The President.* A lot of crazy rumors floating around, aren't there? But I'm not going to——

*Q.* Would you like to stop the rumors, sir?

*The President.* ——say anything about it. No. I'm just going to let——

*Q.* Where do you think these rumors are coming from, sir?

*The President.* ——you guys get in that feeding frenzy that you love. And keep working on it, and be sure you get good sources, though, because I read some that don't look pretty good—don't look very good.

*Q.* Which ones are they, Mr. President?

*The President.* Source is you guys writing.

*Q.* Why do you think all these rumors are out there, sir?

*The President.* I don't know, Charles, I don't know. My health is pretty good, though, and I want to challenge the press corps, everybody who's 67 and over, to a

race around the Oval here. [*Laughter*] You'll maybe run into a few of the younger crowd—sorry, that's not a direct assault on you cameramen. I want to be careful. [*Laughter*]

But seriously, it's a crazy time on rumors. We get phone calls: Barbara's sick; Marilyn Quayle's sick; I'm not feeling well. I don't know what's going on out there. But I don't believe in repeating them or encouraging the printing of them.

Thank you all very much.

*Q.* Are there any others you would like to put to rest?

*The President.* Yes, like I'm feeling good; I am. Put to rest the health rumors. It is weird. Maybe this is the normal procedure every 4 years, but I don't remember it quite on such funny things like whether I'm in good health or not. Charles' associate asked me the question, and I thought she was criticizing the amount of food I was eating going through the barbecue line. She said to me, "What about your health?" I said, "Well, I'm not eating too much," or something. It turned out it was the rumors.

*Q.* We don't make them up, we just pass them on. [*Laughter*]

*Note: The President spoke at 11:12 a.m. in the Cabinet Room at the White House prior to a Cabinet meeting.*

# Remarks at the Presentation Ceremony for the National Medal of the Arts
*July 22, 1992*

Welcome, everybody. Sorry for holding you up for a few minutes here. Welcome to the White House. May I salute Dr. Radice. I don't see Lamar. He was to be here, Lamar Alexander, our Secretary of Education. I think I just left him, and he'll be along. Dr. Lynne Cheney, Members of the Congress, and so many distinguished guests, welcome.

Barbara and I are both delighted to be here and proud to be part of an America which values arts as well as business or science or politics. President Kennedy expressed so well the importance of this ideal when he said, "Roosevelt and Lincoln understood that the life of the arts is very close to the center of a nation's purpose and is a test of the quality of a nation's civilization."

Well, we're here today to pay tribute to some extraordinary men and women, men and women of genius and passion who enrich that quality of life in our America. "Made in U.S.A." has a new meaning today, for almost all these artists were born in small American towns, trained here in their own country, then turned this uniquely American vision to a wide range of artistic fields. Because of their vision, today we celebrate the sheer and priceless pleasure of being American.

For some, being American means being born into a certain regional tradition with the talent to preserve that legacy and carry it to a wider audience. Earl Scruggs brought the fast and furious banjo-pickin' licks of his bluegrass revolution from Flint Hill, North Carolina, to Carnegie Hall. Down the road in Nashville, for over a half a century, a sprightly cracker-barrel philosopher named Minnie Pearl has been dispensing down-home wisdom and a whole lot of down-deep laughter. Jazz pianist Billy Taylor's music, including Jazzmobile Outreach, "makes a joyful noise" and gives a special streetwise swing to this most American form of expression.

For some, being American means striving to brand the bold spirit of this land onto work that is universal and timeless. American-born and -trained Marilyn Horne not only sings with the passion and precision that embody opera at its grandest, but she also introduced composers such as Handel to audiences here at home. By elevating American choral music to the highest levels of excellence, the sweep of Robert Shaw's work has proclaimed the majesty of God throughout this Nation.

For some, being American means reaching from their roots to touch the Nation on a larger-than-life canvas. Robert Wise brings the perspective of his Indiana childhood to the crafting of movies of imagination and humanity from "The Sound of Music" to "West Side Story." And with the courage and sheer power of his fierce talent, Mississippi's James Earl Jones has stamped his purely American mark on classical roles and created new characters who explore a man's quest for dignity.

I might say on a very personal note, when I saw "The Hunt for Red October" and "Patriot Games," I enjoyed his performance as Director of the CIA, a role that I played briefly myself. [*Laughter*]

For some, being American means flourishing this country's impatient exuberance in the face of dusty tradition. Out of Robert Venturi's genius sprang the post-modern movement of architecture, forever altering the way we see the cities around us. The writings of Denise Scott Brown, his wife and partner, have stimulated the American awareness of architecture as public art.

For some, being American means passionate stewards of the arts, committed to bringing theater, painting, dance, music, and so much more to all kinds of Americans across this country. Millions have been stirred and moved by cultural programming like "Omnibus," part of the video trails blazed by Robert Saudek, now caretaker to television's legacy at the Museum of Broadcasting.

Two special companies have set the standard in corporate philanthropy. They give hundreds of grants and millions of dollars, but most importantly, they give the example of believing in the importance of arts for America. The AT&T Foundation supports innovative projects all across the country, ranging from tours by dance companies and ethnic artists to original drama and music composition. The Lila Wallace-Reader's Digest Fund aids American performing, visual, and literary artists who have a real dream, and it also cares for the future, generously funding arts education.

I want to take a moment for a special salute to someone whose work has intrigued me since I first met him here at the White House a couple of years ago. When you talk about being American, nothing can capture the richness and depth of that experience quite like native American art. Not only is it our oldest and proudest tradition, but in native American society, art and life are strands of the same cloth. The ancient patterns on blankets and the dances and the colors: Art is an integral and time-honored part of daily life. So I'm very proud to salute Allan Houser. His hands transform bronze and stone to capture the true meaning of this country's unbroken spirit. His sculptures eloquently echo this Nation's heritage of proud Apache chiefs and speak

for the essential humanity of all Americans.

I firmly believe that our number one goal for the 21st century must be education. The high-tech challenges of this global marketplace we're living in will be absolutely overwhelming. But as we equip our kids with the skills to compete, we also must help them develop as complete human beings. One way to do this is through the arts. For without knowledge of the beauty and depth of the human spirit, our successes are hollow and our lives lacking.

President John Adams wrote this: "I must study politics that my sons may have liberty to study mathematics and philosophy in order to give their children a right to study painting, poetry, and music." That is why we celebrate these men and women today.

Congratulations to all. Thank you for your contributions to the great tapestry that is American art. Now I'd like to ask Dr. Radice to assist me in presenting these medals, if you would.

*Note: The President spoke at 12:04 p.m. in the East Room at the White House. In his remarks, he referred to Anne Radice, Acting Chairman, National Endowment for the Arts, and Lynne V. Cheney, Chairman, National Endowment for the Humanities.*

# Remarks at an Antidrug Rally in Arlington, Virginia
*July 22, 1992*

Reverend, thank you, sir. It is most fitting that a ceremony like this, where we celebrate what a community has done, open its meeting with prayer. I'm proud to be here. My dear friend the Congressman from here, Frank Wolf, he and I came over together, and he was ecstatic in trying to give me the heartbeat of this community and tell me what you all have achieved.

I've read about it, I've seen stories from time to time, but there's nothing like being on the scene to get a real feel. All I will say is that we have got to find various ways with which to win the battle against drugs, and this community is setting an example really for the rest of the Nation.

So what I wanted to do here today was simply turn it over to you all and hear what you've done. This morning I met at the White House with some business leaders, and they're working in the business community to make the business places free of drugs, workplaces drug-free. And they're making progress.

The reduction in cocaine, casual use by teenagers is down by 63 percent in the last 3 years. So you all are making some progress.

But I really came over to not only congratulate you on this, what is it, the second anniversary of the initiation of this project, but to say that the Government couldn't possibly have done it, it couldn't possibly have happened without this community involvement, dedicated women, dedicated men saying, "Look, we're going to safeguard these kids, these precious kids, against the use of drugs." So what I want to do is hear from you as to how it went.

*Note: The President spoke at 1:58 p.m. at Drew Elementary School. In his remarks, he referred to Richard Green, associate pastor of Mount Salvation Baptist Church, who gave the invocation.*

# Letter to Congressional Leaders Transmitting Proposed Legislation on Oregon Public Lands Wilderness Designation
*July 22, 1992*

*Dear Mr. Speaker: (Dear Mr. President:)*

I am pleased to submit for congressional consideration and passage the "Oregon Public Lands Wilderness Act".

The Federal Land Policy and Management Act of 1976 (FLPMA), (43 U.S.C. 1701, *et seq.*), directs the Secretary of the Interior to review the wilderness potential of the public lands.

The review of the areas identified in Oregon began immediately after the enactment of FLPMA and has now been completed. Approximately 2,806,598 acres of public lands in 92 areas in Oregon met the minimum wilderness criteria and were designated as wilderness study areas (WSAs). These WSAs were studied and analyzed during the review process and the results documented in three environmental impact statements and five instant study area reports.

Based on the studies and reviews of the WSAs, the Secretary of the Interior recommends that all or part of 49 of the WSAs, totaling 1,278,073 acres of public lands, be designated as part of the National Wilderness Preservation System.

I concur with the Secretary of the Interior's recommendations and am pleased to recommend designation of the 49 areas (totaling 1,278,073 acres) identified in the enclosed draft legislation as additions to the National Wilderness Preservation System.

The proposed additions represent the diversity of wilderness values in the State of Oregon. These range from the 9,730-foot Steens Mountain peak, to the deep canyons of the Owyhee River and the John Day River, to the small islands off the Oregon coast. These areas span a wide variety of Oregon landforms, ecosystems, and other natural systems and features. Their inclusion in the wilderness system will improve the geographic distribution of wilderness areas in Oregon, and will complement existing areas of congressionally designated wilderness. They will provide new and outstanding opportunities for solitude and unconfined recreation.

The enclosed draft legislation provides that designation as wilderness shall not constitute a reservation of water or water rights for wilderness purposes. This is consistent with the fact that the Congress did not establish a Federal reserved water right for wilderness purposes. The Administration has established the policy that, where it is necessary to obtain water rights for wilderness purposes in a specific wilderness area, water rights would be sought from the State by filing under State water laws. Furthermore, it is the policy of the Administration that the designation of wilderness areas should not interfere with the use of water rights, State water administration, or the use of a State's interstate water allocation.

The draft legislation also provides for access to wilderness areas by Indian people for traditional cultural and religious purposes. Access by the general public may be limited in order to protect the privacy of religious cultural activities taking place in specific wilderness areas. In addition, to the fullest extent practicable, the Department of the Interior will coordinate with the Department of Defense to minimize the impact of any overflights during these religious cultural activities.

I further concur with the Secretary of the Interior that all or part of 76 of the WSAs encompassing 1,528,525 acres are not suitable for preservation as wilderness.

Also enclosed are a letter and report from the Secretary of the Interior concerning the WSAs discussed above and a section-by-section analysis of the draft legislation. I urge the Congress to act expeditiously and favor-

ably on the proposed legislation so that the natural resources of these WSAs in Oregon may be protected and preserved.

Sincerely,

GEORGE BUSH

*Note: Identical letters were sent to Thomas S. Foley, Speaker of the House of Representatives, and Dan Quayle, President of the Senate.*

# Nomination of Alan Greenspan To Be United States Alternate Governor of the International Monetary Fund
*July 22, 1992*

The President today announced his intention to nominate Alan Greenspan, of New York, to be U.S. Alternate Governor of the International Monetary Fund for a term of 5 years. This is a reappointment.

Dr. Greenspan currently serves as Chairman and Member of the Board of Governors of the Federal Reserve System. Prior to this, he served as chairman of Townsend-Greenspan Co. & Inc., 1954–74 and 1977–

87. Dr. Greenspan served on the Council of Economic Advisers, 1970–74; as Chairman of the Council of Economic Advisers, 1974–77; and was a member of the President's Economic Policy Advisory Board, 1981.

Dr. Greenspan graduated from New York University (B.S., 1948; M.A., 1950; and Ph.D., 1977). He was born March 6, 1926, in New York, NY, and currently resides in Washington, DC.

# Nomination of Genta Hawkins Holmes To Be Director General of the Foreign Service
*July 22, 1992*

The President today announced his intention to nominate Genta Hawkins Holmes, of California, a career member of the Senior Foreign Service, class of Minister-Counselor, to be Director General of the Foreign Service. She would succeed Edward J. Perkins.

Ambassador Holmes currently serves as U.S. Ambassador to Namibia, 1990–present. She has also served as Deputy Chief of Mission in Pretoria, South Africa, 1988–89; Port-Au-Prince, Haiti, 1986–88; and Lilongwe, Malawi, 1984–86. Ambassador Holmes has also served at the State Department in several other positions, including

international affairs officer at the Bureau of African Affairs, 1983; participant in the Senior Seminar at the State Department, 1982; and at the Agency for International Development as Assistant Administrator for Legislative Affairs and as Acting Administrator, 1979–81.

Ambassador Holmes graduated from the University of Southern California (A.B., 1962). She was born September 3, 1940, in Anadarko, OK. Ambassador Holmes is married and currently resides in San Francisco, CA.

## Statement on Signing the Higher Education Amendments of 1992
*July 23, 1992*

Today I am signing into law S. 1150, the "Higher Education Amendments of 1992." It reauthorizes the many programs in the Higher Education Act of 1965. The legislation is broad in scope and significance, encompassing both the Pell Grant and Guaranteed Student Loan programs as well as a variety of other programs to assist students and institutions of higher education. I hope that many middle- and low-income families who dream of a college education for their children will find that this legislation helps to make their dreams reality.

Educator Robert Maynard Hutchins once said: "The object of education is to prepare the young to educate themselves throughout their lives." I think the key phrase here is "throughout their lives." Our intention is to make it easier for all Americans to pursue postsecondary education and training throughout their lifetimes—whether they are just out of high school or returning to school later in life. The world has changed, and a solid education is critical for all of us to compete effectively in today's global economy and function as responsible citizens in our American democracy.

In pursuing the reauthorization of the Higher Education Act of 1965, my Administration was guided by three major principles: improving access to postsecondary education—especially for middle- and low-income students and families; enhancing accountability of all who play a role in postsecondary education programs; and promoting educational excellence. This legislation is not perfect, but it moves in the direction of these principles. It contains a number of valuable program integrity and loan default prevention provisions. In particular, these provisions will crack down on sham schools that have defrauded students and the American taxpayer in the past. The legislation also will take the first steps toward establishing the principle of rewarding academic achievement through the establishment of Presidential Access Scholarships. This is an important first step, and I will work to raise further the academic achieve-

ment standards for this program.

I am particularly gratified that segments of my AMERICA 2000 strategy are part of this legislation. It provides for an alternative certification program by which States will develop new routes to teacher certification. In addition, the legislation authorizes academies for teachers and school leaders to provide these educators with in-service training in academic and other educational areas.

I am also pleased that eligibility for Pell Grants has been provided to students studying for degrees on a less than half-time basis. This provision was part of my "Lifelong Learning Act." Providing grants to individuals taking as little as one course at a time toward their degree offers American men and women some of the flexibility they need to improve their employment skills while recognizing their commitments to jobs and families. This provision enables a working mother in a low-wage job to receive financial assistance for courses that would qualify her for a better paying, high-skilled job. It allows education to become the mechanism by which those at the back of the line can move to the front of the line—and realize the American dream.

In addition to the laudable aspects of S. 1150, the legislation unfortunately includes certain constitutionally troublesome provisions relating to reports to the Congress containing legislative recommendations and the use of audit standards established by the Comptroller General. I will construe these provisions to avoid constitutional difficulties and preserve the separation of powers required by the Constitution.

We now have the best system of colleges and universities in the world. As a next step, I would like to see the same excellence at the elementary and secondary school level. To change our country, we must change our schools, and I am pleased that the revolution has started and is spreading. There are 1,500 communities and 44 States committed to the AMERICA 2000 strategy.

My AMERICA 2000 legislation calls for four transforming ideas: (1) a new generation of break-the-mold New American Schools; (2) world class standards and a system of voluntary national exams that measure progress that schools make toward meeting those standards; (3) broad flexibility for teachers and principals to help children achieve greater learning; and (4) parental choice of schools so that middle- and low-income families have more of the same choices of schools for their children that are now the preserve of wealthier families. We cannot afford to accept business-as-usual here in Washington while the country demands change and improvement.

Yesterday, Senator Danforth and Congressman Gradison introduced my "Federal Grants for State and Local 'GI Bills' for Children." It will give middle- and low-income families consumer power—dollars to spend at any lawfully operating school of their choice—public, private, or religious. Just as the original GI Bill and Pell Grants transformed higher education, the "GI Bills" for Children will help transform elementary and secondary education.

I am pleased to sign the "Higher Education Amendments of 1992." I look forward to signing the "Federal Grants for State and Local 'GI Bills' for Children" in the near future, and I am hopeful we can work together to produce an AMERICA 2000 bill just as we worked together on the bill I am signing today.

GEORGE BUSH

The White House,
July 23, 1992.

*Note: S. 1150, approved July 23, was assigned Public Law No. 102–325.*

## Remarks on Signing the Higher Education Amendments of 1992 in Annandale, Virginia
*July 23, 1992*

Please be seated, and thank you very, very much. Dr. Ernst, thank you, sir, for that very nice explanation and that wonderful introduction. Let me say how pleased I am to be here on this campus, be here at this marvelous community college about which I've heard so many good things.

I'm delighted to be with Lamar Alexander. I know the Members of Congress here have met him and worked with him, but some of the students here and some of the faculty may not have. In my view, nonpartisan view, a purely objective view, Lamar Alexander is really doing a superb job for the Nation's education, and I'm delighted he's here.

I want to salute the Members of Congress that came all the way over. Lamar was telling me and our own people in the White House have told me that this was truly a bipartisan effort. The leaders out here today reflect that, and they have stood by education for a long, long time. So I welcome them, salute them, particularly the members of the Senate Labor and Human Resources Committee, the House Committee, the House Education and Labor Committee.

I also want to salute the members of the NOVA community. It's a pleasure, as I say, to be here in Virginia, the cradle of American education, and then to sign into law this higher education bill, the Higher Education Amendments of 1992, and help thereby move our schools into the 21st century.

After this is over, we're going to pass these out to everybody, and then tonight we will have a quiz—[*laughter*]—on the ingredients therein. But I told Dr. Ernst that I'm impressed with NOVA's mission, curriculum, and most especially your choice of last year's commencement speaker—[*laughter*]—a silver-haired philosopher named Barbara Bush, who still feels honored and delighted.

But there are a couple of things I don't like to do. You know one, eating broccoli.

But the other is speaking where Barbara has already spoken. It's sort of like being asked to play guitar after Garth Brooks. [*Laughter*] So I want to break my rule one time because this occasion is important and the hospitality that she received was so memorable.

We do gather at a momentous time in our country's history. Over the past 4 years, we've seen changes of almost Biblical proportions in the world. I think we rejoice that the cold war is over. What does that mean for you and your families? Well, I think when children go to bed at night, they'll be safer from the specter of nuclear war and safer than they were a decade ago, safer than they were a year ago, and safer, I think, than just a month or so ago when we had that rather historic agreement with Boris Yeltsin. So I think that's good news. It's good news for the young people that are with us today. It's good news for our country. I happen to feel it's good news for the whole world.

But this new world does pose enormous challenges; big opportunities, though. From Poland to Paraguay, other nations are trying to copy our system of free enterprise. And here's the question: How do we win when more of the world's nations are playing our game? The opportunity is huge. The economists say when we win, we will share in a maximized proportion of ever-increasing global prosperity. I had that translated into English, and that means good, steady jobs for you and your families. So then you've got to ask, how do you win those jobs? I believe we cannot renew America without renewing our schools.

Consider a couple of facts. In 1980, a man with a college education made on an average $11,000 more per year than a man with only a high school education. By 1990, that gap had increased to more than $16,000, and the exact same pattern happened with women's income. Those facts shout a simple truth: Education makes the difference. Every American deserves the chance to get on the ladder of opportunity and climb up.

I want to tell you about a woman I admire. She's not someone you'll read about in the paper, won't see her on television. She is someone who might be your neighbor or the mother of one of your kids'

friends. She has two disabled children and a life that's had many good breaks and then a couple of bad ones. But she also has a dream that she won't let go: She wants to be a nurse. Now she will get the financial help that she needs to fulfill that dream. Some day this courageous lady's children will sit in the audience and watch Mom receive her nursing degree. This woman who's done so much for so many will now be able to serve even more people. The president of Phi Theta Kappa, Frances McIntire. When I heard her story and saw her determination, I was mighty proud, proud of Frances, proud that we're giving thousands of men and women like her a better chance to get the education they desire and deserve.

This act that I'm signing today gives a hand up to lower income students who need help the most. But it also reaches out into the middle-income families, the ones who skipped a vacation and drove the old clunker so that their kids could go to college. Too often, the funding cracks have been so big that these solid, decent families have slipped on through, and their children's dreams have been in danger of slipping away. Well, no longer. It's a matter of fairness. It's a matter of our future.

This act also reflects an important new phenomenon. We used to think of education like measles vaccines, like first dates, or like learning to drive, something we only did when we were young. Today, education never ends. Although our temples may be graying and our jogging routes a little shorter, we always have to learn. And this act recognizes that simple fact, just as this great community college has recognized that fact, making Federal aid available for part-time students who are taking a class or two toward their degree while still holding down a job.

How much richer our Nation's future will be. Each year, millions of families will be able to get more Federal assistance and then pass on to their kids the legacy of education. But this higher education act does more than open up Federal funding to middle-income and to part-time students. It also sets tough standards to rid Federal aid programs of fraud and abuse both by sham schools and by students who default on their loans. In addition, some student aid will now be contingent on academic performance. The act includes parts of what we call proudly our America 2000 program, including academies for teachers and school leaders and something called alternative certification.

Now, that's a program near and dear to my heart, so let me try to explain it. When I lived out in Odessa, Texas, in 1948, I'd just graduated from college, and I went out there and had a little extra time on my hands. I tried to volunteer to teach night courses. My college economics degree was not good enough because I didn't have the required courses, mandatory courses then, in education, and that bothered me. Then I learned that without a teaching degree, even Albert Einstein couldn't teach high school science. Now, I might understand keeping me out of there. I might get embarrassed around the computer or something. But Albert Einstein? Come on.

In my first months in office, I proposed legislation to allow the "Einsteins" to teach without traditional certification. After 3 years and 3 tries, now the Congress has agreed to this. This helps, in my view, open up huge talent pools to bring into our classrooms. Now we can find a way, for example, to encourage more of our men and women who are leaving the armed services to put their skills to work leading future generations in the classroom.

By the way, I'm pleased to note that this past spring I did receive my alternative teaching certificate from the State of Texas. The woman who sent me my certificate, Delia Stafford, is with us today. She's a champion of change, willing to try something different because our children deserve nothing less. I think it's good to give her a round of applause for her innovative approach.

Our system of higher education is indeed the best in the entire world because it's rooted in the American ideals that make it excellent, accessible, and accountable. America 2000 is the revolution that believes those ideals must be transferred to our elementary and secondary schools. Just yesterday Senator Danforth and Senator Gradison introduced my State and local "GI bill" for

children which will transform precollege education by giving middle- and low-income families $1,000 scholarships to send their kids to their choice of schools. I don't know about you, but that gives me 1,000 reasons to cheer. Higher education thrives on competition, thrives on choice. We must bring those incentives to elementary and secondary schools. It's time we let parents, not the Government, choose their kids' schools, public, private, or religious.

I mentioned earlier how I believe that education is now a lifelong endeavor. So I feel it is only appropriate to conclude with a quote I remember from my own school days, a quote from Longfellow, something about great heights not being achieved by "sudden flight" but by "toiling upward in the night." Longfellow's advice could apply to the task of renewing our schools. It won't be done with headlines; it won't be done with slogans, or even money alone. What it takes is innovation, courage, a willingness in every community to roll up our sleeves and reform this vital American institution.

We are toiling upward in the night, and today we climb a little bit higher. And when we've reached our plateau, we will look out upon a new generation of American schools and a stronger foundation for our Nation.

So now, on behalf of Frances McIntire and the legions of students at NOVA and across the country who will benefit, it is with great pride and great gratitude to the Congress, particularly the Members here today, that I sign into law the Higher Education Amendments of 1992. As I sign I would like to ask Secretary Alexander, Dr. Ernst, and Delia Stafford to come forward, and Frances, you too. Then I'd love to invite the Members of Congress to come up and say hello and turn around to demonstrate at least the nonpartisan or the bipartisan spirit of this occasion.

Again, my thanks to you ladies and gentlemen for being with us today.

*Note: The President spoke at 1:48 p.m. at Northern Virginia Community College. In his remarks, he referred to Richard J. Ernst, president of the college; Senator John C. Danforth of Missouri; and Representative Willis D. Gradison, Jr., of Ohio.*

# Memorandum on the President's Tree Planting Initiative
*July 23, 1992*

*Memorandum for the Heads of Certain Departments and Agencies*

*Subject:* President's Tree Planting Initiative

I am writing to remind you of this Administration's continuing commitment to increase tree planting across America. The national tree planting program, a component of the America the Beautiful initiative, calls for public/private partnerships involving communities and volunteers throughout the Nation. Our goal is to plant and maintain in our cities and countryside an additional one billion trees per year through the year 2000. This is an ambitious goal that will significantly enhance the environment and boost economic activity. Federal agency leadership will contribute greatly to the achievement of this goal.

During this last year, a representative of your organization has been asked to participate in a coordinating committee to promote, inform, and participate in tree planting activities in your agency nationwide. I urge you to energetically support the committee and its activities in order to ensure that the Federal Government does its part for tree planting.

Americans are enthusiastically joining this effort. Urban tree planting increased by 25 percent last year. In rural America, our cost-sharing program with private nonindustrial private landowners is now underway and should result in the planting of an additional 200 million trees this year—a 10 percent increase over past years but a long way from our goal due to insufficient funding from the Congress.

My FY 1993 budget seeks to double the level of funding for the tree planting initiative to $138 million. Reforestation remains a cornerstone of my commitment to protecting and enhancing America's natural resources and environment in a way that is consistent with our efforts to promote economic growth.

On June 1, at the United Nations Conference on Environment and Development in Rio de Janeiro, I announced the Forests for the Future Initiative to conserve and sustain the Earth's forests. Appropriate models for worldwide commitment and action to save the forests may well stem from the public/private partnerships developed in your agency. With your help, we can reach our goal.

GEORGE BUSH

*The Secretary of State, the Secretary of the Treasury, the Secretary of Defense, the Secretary of the Army, the Acting Secretary of the Navy, the Secretary of the Air Force, the Attorney General, the Secretary of the Interior, the Secretary of Agriculture, the Secretary of Commerce, the Secretary of Labor, the Secretary of Health and Human Services, the Secretary of Housing and Urban Development, the Secretary of Transportation, the Secretary of Energy, the Secretary of Education, the Secretary of Veterans Affairs, the Administrator of the Environmental Protection Agency, the Administrator of General Services, the Administrator of the National Aeronautics and Space Administration, the Administrator of the Small Business Administration, the Director of the United States Information Agency, the Chairman of the Postal Rate Commission, the Director of the Institute of Museum Services, the Chairman of the Council on Environmental Quality, the Acting Director of the Office of Policy Development, the Director of the Office of Management and Budget, the Director of the Office of Science and Technology Policy*

## Statement by Press Secretary Fitzwater on the Escape of Pablo Escobar
*July 23, 1992*

Pablo Escobar escaped from prison when Colombian authorities attempted to move him to a more secure facility. This is unfortunate at a time when President Gaviria was trying to control the prison and put an end to Escobar's criminal activities. Escobar and his ilk represent a threat to law-abiding, civilized societies throughout the hemisphere, and they must be brought to justice.

This incident underlines the difficulties legitimate governments have in halting drug trafficking and placing drug traffickers before the bar of justice. We have strongly supported President Gaviria and the people of Colombia in their valiant fight against these violent international criminal organizations. We will continue that support and cooperation, especially to strengthen the Colombian judicial system.

## Remarks to the National League of Families of American Prisoners and Missing in Southeast Asia in Arlington, Virginia
*July 24, 1992*

*The President.* Thank you all. Well, Sue, thank you very much. And Ann, glad to be back with you and this organization. To the members of the board, my respects; to the family, friends.

Let me first start off by saluting two former NSC hands, Bud McFarland and Dick Childress over here who have worked very hard on all of this, and also the chairman emeritus, George Brooks.

Let me begin by thanking you for the opportunity to speak again to what has got to be one of the bravest and most dedicated groups of Americans in this country.

We live in a marvelous time, a time of tremendous opportunity. We've seen the end of the cold war and the collapse of imperial communism and a new birth of freedom from Moscow to Managua. America's courage, America's vision, America's values have indeed changed the world. And yes, the cold war may be over, but the noble cause that took your fathers, your sons, and your husbands away from home is with us still. Our work must not end and will not end until you have answers about your loved ones.

Over the past 20 years, the National League of Families has seen the issue of your missing swept up in international or domestic politics, manipulated by foreign governments, exploited by con men, sensationalized by the media. All that time, you never lost sight of what you were looking for: good faith, an honest effort to resolve your uncertainty, to find answers to the agonizing question that you live with every day.

Sometimes you may have wondered whether your Government had forgotten you. When President Reagan and I took office in '81, we made your ordeal our top priority. We knew that with all the uncertainties you live with, the one thing you should be sure of is that your Government really cares.

You're talking to a person that was shot down himself in combat. Fortunately, I wasn't taken prisoner, but I was shot down in combat. I understand a little bit what that means. I understand what it means. And so we set out to meet with you to ask your advice.

When we took office, no policy-level negotiations with Vietnam, Laos, or Cambodia had been held for several years. Despite the fears of some that negotiating with Vietnam implied recognition, despite the fears of others that the POW-MIA issue was a cold war fantasy, we took your advice and entered into high-level negotiations.

When we took office, some saw this issue as a matter between this Nation and Vietnam, not part of the broader relations between the U.S. and the Soviets, China, and our friends in Asia, the ASEAN countries. We took your advice and urged our friends as well as our adversaries to help us find the answers.

Let me add that I am gratified to hear the ASEAN ambassadors are here today. I salute them over there. They are cooperating with us. Their countries deserve great credit for their understanding, for their help, and for their fellowship with you, the families.

Most important of all, when we took office, we came up against a string of official statements——

*[At this point, audience members interrupted the President's remarks.]*

*The President.* Here, would you come over a minute? Is that the——

*Audience member.* This is symptomatic of the issue, President. This is our 23d meeting. Gosh darn it, why can't you—[*inaudible*]—and negotiate. The Vietnamese have everything we want. We have everything they want.

*Moderator.* Excuse me, do the majority of the families here want to hear the President? The majority of them would like to hear the President.

*[At this point, audience members again interrupted.]*

*Moderator.* We are so embarrassed.
*The President.* It's an election year.
*Moderator.* That's no excuse.
*Audience members.* We won't budge! Tell the truth! We won't budge! Tell the truth!
*Moderator.* I think it might be very important—if those who wish to hear the President will simply ask others to sit down, possibly we can hear what the President wants to say. And maybe if the media will stop taking pictures of the minority, they'll go away.

*[At this point, league officers made efforts to restore order in the audience.]*

*The President.* What's happening?

*Audience member.* We want you to continue your——[*applause*]
*The President.* Where were we? [*Laughter*]
*Audience member.* Down in front!
*The President.* Yes, let's get these guys down in front, that's right.

No, no, no, this is very emotional, understandably emotional. The thing that I would say to you, however, as a veteran and one who still wears my Navy wings from time to time, is I hope you understand how I feel about patriotism, about service to my country. And I will put my record up against anybody here.

*[At this point, audience members again interrupted the President's remarks.]*

*Moderator.* Sit down!
*The President.* And I just—would you please be quiet and let me finish. Would you please shut up and sit down.

I would say this: To suggest that a Commander in Chief that led this country into its most successful recent effort would condone for one single day the personal knowledge of a person held against his will, whether it's here or anyplace else, is simply totally unfair.

Now, to say I understand the agony that I've reheard here today is true. I do. But I do not like the suggestion that any American anywhere would know of a live American being held somewhere against his will, whether it's here or the allegation being over in the other part of the world. Iran, the suggestion was made that we left people being prisoner in Iran so to win an election. Now, what kind of an allegation is that to make against a patriot? What kind to make against—it is not.

So I would simply say to you: I care about it. We are trying, and we're going to continue to try. And I understand the divisions here. I understand the divisions we hear in these hearings. I understand the agony that people feel. But I would also like to ask that you understand where I'm coming from on this issue. I think most of you do. I'm going to continue to try.

We talked about Presidential commissions and congressional committees indicating that they felt Vietnam had done all it could, and once again, we took your advice. We refused to accept the fact that the book was closed. It's no secret to any of you that for many years now, significant lobbying has taken place in opposition to this policy. Some of it comes from those same voices we've heard since the seventies, people who want us to pretend Vietnam never happened. Some comes from people who seek to smooth over sticking points that stand in the way of commercial opportunities. Others say, "Look, the war is over. Let's move on." And that is something we can and will never say.

Now, for us, the POW–MIA issue is not a sticking point, not some bad dream we shake off, not a footnote from a forgotten time we can simply ignore. The POW–MIA issue is something entirely different, something more. This I want you to understand: It is a question of justice, of oaths sworn, of commitments kept, and a nation's test of its own worth measured in the life of one, lone individual. This we know: The wounds won't heal, the American family will not be whole, as I said earlier, so long as the brave men remain missing.

In my Inaugural Address as President, I did say that good will begets good will. In the spirit of that statement, we developed a detailed road map for Vietnam, a road map that addresses our objectives as well as that Government's desire in terms of diplomatic and economic relations with the United States. Let me be very clear: Without further positive movement on the POW's and MIA's, we cannot and will not continue to move forward with Hanoi.

Now, the other side of this is, where they have moved, we've responded. When the Government of Vietnam pledged greater cooperation, including field operations, we greatly increased our manpower, even opened a permanent office in Hanoi. While we've seen an unprecedented level of joint investigations, these activities have not provided the concrete results that we seek. Make no mistake, we want to continue and expand our joint efforts. And I'll never accept joint activities as a substitute for real results. Your long years of uncertainty must end, and I am pledged to end them in any way I can.

Now as a measure of simple human de-cency, I call on the Government of Vietnam again to repatriate all recovered and readily recoverable remains. I call on the Government of Vietnam to act without delay. I can say in return the United States stands ready to move forward on the road map that we've laid out.

My message is the same to the other nations of Indochina. In Laos, our joint field operations have produced definitive answers, but the process remains painfully slow and cumbersome. We recognize the reality that most of our men unaccounted for in Laos were lost in areas under Viet-namese control. Our relations with Laos have grown from wary distrust in those early eighties to a broader, more open relationship. We cannot let this momentum wane. I address the Lao leaders when I say our relationship can grow further and will, if and when they provide the cooperation we now seek.

Our years of trying to seek cooperation from Cambodia and the Soviets were not rewarded until just recently. The U.N.-sponsored settlement plan in Cambodia, the historic changes in the lands that used to be the Soviet Union have opened the way for unprecedented access. We will push hard to translate this access into answers.

I know you've lived through hopes and then hopes dashed before. Unfortunately, and it breaks my heart to see this happen, we have seen false reporting. I think we would all agree there have been some scam operations that divert manpower and sap our resources. I simply cannot fathom the cruelty of those who would exploit that issue for personal gain.

Nevertheless, we are determined not to allow such incidents to discourage us. We're going to continue to pursue and openly re-ceive information from all sources and con-tinue to treat each report, every report, as the breakthrough that just might end the ordeal of one single American family.

I think our efforts have produced some results. For 241 families, the uncertainty has ended. For others, too many others, the questions linger. Every day now, it seems, the news purports to unearth some great new revelation of fact, facts that you've known for 20 years and facts we've shared with you for a decade.

Well, the key fact is one we all agree on: There are Americans who did not return home at the end of hostilities and Americans last known to be alive. Accounting for these men remains this highest priority. Although there's not proof that any Americans are now alive, in the absence of firm answers, our assumption will always be: Let facts direct our policy, and let hope be our guide.

So the policy remains: full disclosure, full disclosure of all relevant information to families. And we're going to continue to cooperate fully with congressional committees to ensure the access they must have to perform their oversight role.

But there are some things we're not going to do, however loud the critics may complain. We will not publicly release any information that would jeopardize ongoing intelligence or negotiating efforts to account for your missing loved ones.

Let the critics complain. We have got to get this job done. As President, I take it to be an article of faith, a solemn covenant with those who serve this country: The United States will make every possible effort always, take every possible action to account for those taken prisoner or missing in action. Our aim remains the fullest possible accounting for POW's and MIA's and nothing less. And I want you to know that comes to you with conviction.

Let me just say something about this gentleman sitting here. Tell me your name again—Jeff. I can't pretend to know the grief that you carry in your heart. My experience in combat was a little different. My wingman was shot down the first—disappeared the first mission I was on. We had maybe something like 7 out of our squadron of 15 killed.

I understand what combat is, but because of the way Barbara and I feel about our family, I can't try to say that I understand the grief that you carry with you every day,

the anguish of uncertainty. So I don't want to try to put myself with everybody here who has suffered for a long time on an equal plane in that sense. That's not what I'm trying to do.

But I can remember that day that I mentioned to you 50 years ago, when I was a scared kid, 20 years old, I think, floating around just a couple of miles off a Japanese-held island. I remember the uncertainty at that moment. I can remember, when I wasn't wondering if anyone would find me at all, my worry was, who's going to find me.

So what I'm trying to say is I can identify with those who served, and I can identify with their sacrifice. I can identify as a father who lost a child with the family implications, but again I'm not trying to put myself on the same plane with those who have suffered a lot.

But what I want to tell you is: I mean what I tell you, in terms of priority. I know there's doubt here, and I know people are saying, as this gentleman said right from the heart, "Go over there and bring them back." Do you think if I knew of one single person and where he is and how it was, that I wouldn't do that? Of course, I'd do that.

So all I'm asking, all I'm here to say is I am the President, and I am the Commander in Chief. Some of you believe it and some of you may not, but we are going to get this job done, and we are going to account for every single person who is missing. I'm going to keep on it. I don't care how long it takes.

Thank you very, very much. Thank you.

*Note: The President spoke at 9:35 a.m. at the Stouffer Concourse Hotel. In his remarks, he referred to Sue Scott, chairman of the board, and Ann Mills Griffiths, executive director, National League of Families of American Prisoners and Missing in Southeast Asia, who served as moderators.*

## Remarks at a Community Picnic in Brookville, Ohio
*July 24, 1992*

Thank you very, very much. Hey, listen, thanks for that warm Brookville welcome, and thanks for inviting me to this great picnic. My thanks to the Brookville High School Band, pressed into service out of school but playing well.

May I salute Ohio's Governor, Governor Voinovich, an old friend doing a great job for this State, and our Lieutenant Governor, Mike DeWine, an old friend of mine and of Barbara's, he and his Fran. We want to see him win this year. Mayor Duncan, may I thank you, sir, and your wonderful family for making us feel so welcome and salute all the present and future legislators.

I see a sign back here that I agree with: "Let's Change Control of the United States Congress." Let's change that Congress.

May I salute a man I just threw a horseshoe with, Cloyce Copley, 97 years old. Boy, I hope I'm like that when I'm 97, and I bet the rest of you do, too.

Let me just start by a comment about the world we live in, particularly seeing these children here. We have changed, literally since I have become President, we have changed the world. Now we want to use that leadership to make things better in the United States of America. Just think of it: The Soviet Union and Soviet communism are no more. The Berlin Wall is down. Ancient enemies are talking to each other in the Middle East, and we're going to move peace forward in that area. Democracy is on the move in Latin America. And these young kids go to sleep at night without the same fear of nuclear weapons that their parents had. That is fantastic for the United States of America.

It's a new world, and it's a fantastic challenge in it. When we kicked, with the help of many young men and women here, kicked Saddam Hussein out of Kuwait, we said, "Aggression will not stand." That is an important principle.

So you couldn't tell it from listening to the Democratic Convention, which I was spared because I was fishing in Wyoming, but I might say, foreign affairs and the national security of this country are still important. We still don't know what's going to crop up in the terrorist field or some unpredictable enemy. As long as I am President I will keep the United States of America strong and number one. We cannot forget that.

So the question now comes: With the help of the American people we have changed the world; it is a more peaceful world. Now let us take that involvement with the world to make us the most competitive nation on the face of the Earth. Let's change things.

That's why I am running for reelection. We've changed the world; now help me change America for the better. Education, winning the battle against drugs, driving criminals out of our communities: We can do it if we pull together.

But I think it's particularly appropriate here at this marvelous community celebration to think about another threat, another threat facing us more dangerous than a missile. I'm talking about the breakdown of the American family. Here today we see it strong, and I want to protect it and help strengthen it.

The opposition would have you believe that family values is merely a slogan. I don't look at it that way at all. I don't believe that. Here's what Ruth Ditmer Ream of Brookville said, here's her poem: "Describe a world short on hope where there is so much pain, how can we mend the golden thread to weave our dreams again?" We can mend that thread, but we have got to find ways to strengthen the traditional American family.

You see, I have a different approach than the opponents. I believe the family can do things no Government program can do. Let's take a look at Brookville and share it with the rest of this great country of ours. Where would you find a Government program that would guarantee that Brookville High School would have a 95-percent attendance record? Government cannot do that. Family can. Where would you find a

Government program that motivates six of your best and brightest to earn perfect grade scores, and the class of '92 right here in Brookville to earn more than a quarter of a million dollars in college scholarships? Now, Government cannot do that, but the family can if they help those kids.

Let me give you an example. Where would you find a Government program to teach and shape a good, solid young man like Derek Brown, who can become a national merit scholar? Government alone can't. They can help, but they cannot do it. His family can. Your families can.

So let the other side ridicule family values. I'm talking about work, responsibility, loving thy neighbor, respect for the Creator. Family teaches us right from wrong and discipline, and it teaches us kindness, too. So let me tell you how I want to see the Government help in strengthening the traditional American family.

Here we are. It's expensive to raise a family today. I believe the Government can help ease that burden. Yesterday I signed a law expanding financial aid to students, young and old, not just the poor but also the middle class who are desperately strapped by economic times. We did this so that your son and daughter can go to college and chase a dream. Parents who want to go back to college and finish the degree, even if it has to be one course at a time, you all deserve our support. This legislation will help give you that support.

Let me tell you another area. What about the young children of working parents who need quality day care? I have fought for an important new effort to help assist the working parents, and I stood for principle against those who said that only government-sponsored day care will do. It will not. I ask what's wrong with day care in an aunt's house or even in a church? Today I am pleased to announce that we are issuing the first regulations implementing historic child care legislation guaranteeing that parents who get Federal help in paying for child care will get the kind of care they choose. It is not the Government to tell them. You see, it is my belief that the fathers and mothers know best how to care for these kids and should have a choice in how child care works when it comes to the kids.

I also believe that same principle of choice ought to apply to our schools. When I got out of the service they had the GI bill. It didn't say what school you had to go to. It said you could go to any one, religious, private, or public school. I now have the "GI bill" for children that permits just that, giving the parents choice in where their kids go to school.

There are other ideas. This economy has been sluggish. I have had incentives to get this economy moving, and the Congress, thinking those same old thoughts, refused to think new ones. I'd like to see a $5,000 tax credit to help young families share in the American dream and buy their first home. Get the Congress to pass that.

I want the families to be able to use their IRA's without penalty for unexpected health care costs. Get the Congress to get off its—get the job done.

We know that in recent years the number of single-parent families have exploded. Half the kids in single-parent homes live in poverty, 5 times the rate of others. Well, the Berlin Wall crumbled. Russians trooped to the polls. The Poles opened a new stock exchange. We got all these things going, but we need to help these children and help these families. That's what this program is all about.

One last point, and then we'll let you get back to having some fun, one last point. When I talk about change, take a look at one institution that has not changed in the last few years. Presidents come and go; different parties have come and gone. But look at the United States Congress. One party has controlled the House of Representatives for 36 years. The result: They can't run a little tiny post office, and they can't do anything but screw up a bank. So if you want to get done what I know you do, getting this balanced budget amendment, if you want that line-item veto, if you want to help me move this economy forward, change the control of the United States Congress.

There's another point. Terms of Presidents are limited. What's wrong with limiting the terms of some of these old geezers that have been there forever?

Let that new ticket talk about change, and I'll lay my record up against them any single day for constructive change for the United States. We have changed the world; now help me constructively change the United States of America.

Thank you all, and God bless you. Thank you very much.

*Note: The President spoke at 1 p.m. in Golden Gate Park. In his remarks, he referred to Mayor Michael A. Duncan of Brookville.*

# Remarks in a Roundtable Discussion on Families in Columbia, Missouri
*July 24, 1992*

*The President.* Well, Governor, all yours, sir.

*Governor John Ashcroft.* Well, President Bush, the members of the National Commission on Urban American Families and these Missouri families, we're all pleased to be here with you this afternoon. I'm delighted to welcome you back to Missouri, to welcome the Commission to Missouri. I'm pleased that these families are here to share their unique stories of work, their commitment, the kind of intensity and industry that's needed to build strong families and hold them together.

We thank you for making families a priority, Mr. President. Until you became the spokesperson who was emphasizing families, I think families were becoming America's forgotten people. But thanks to your care and concern, Americans are turning towards home, and we think that's very important.

Your Commission is working aggressively to fulfill our mission as outlined in your Executive order. In the 77 days since we received our charter, we've worked hard to find out what can be done to strengthen families. We've been in Oakland and San Francisco in California, and Minneapolis in Minnesota, in Dallas in Texas, and Washington, DC. And just yesterday, we visited a place that, well, you're very concerned about; we were in south central Los Angeles. In the coming months, we'll also be hearing from families and experts in New York and Chicago and Knoxville. Mr. President, your Commission is a hard-working one.

*The President.* I might interrupt to say thank you to the Commission members. Some of them came a long, long way, the Governor was telling me, and others have a long way to go in returning home. But thank you for what you're doing. And please tell the others I'm very, very grateful, anxious to hear. But excuse the interruption.

*Governor Ashcroft.* No, that's quite all right. We've heard from a wide variety of people from the academic, public officials, policy analysts, activists, but most of all, we've heard from families in every area. In city after city, we've heard them tell us that the troubling concerns about the condition of family life in America are broadly held. They're shared concerns. People understand that families indeed are in trouble, and when we have troubled families, that makes for troubled neighborhoods. Families are telling us that society is somehow polluting or contaminating the family atmosphere. Analysts see the trend of family decline as part of a cultural shift in our society away from valuing family and community in favor of emphasizing self-indulgence.

Our statistics that we're developing indicate that family decline is a problem that's common to all Americans, black, white, rich, as well as poor. Family breakdown shatters lives whether it's in the affluent suburbs or in—hurts the children in small towns as well as large cities.

But we're also hearing that people have hope. Many are filled with optimism and are relearning the value and strength that can be found in support of American families. We're discovering that America is blessed with good volunteers, people who have great spirit and tremendous heart and are tremendously committed to sharing. There are professionals who are dedicated to helping as well.

So, Mr. President, we thank you for meeting with us, and we thank you for caring deeply about America's families. We'd invite you to speak with us about your sense of these matters. And then I'd like to introduce you to some of these Missouri families who've come——

*The President.* I would only add that, in the first place, I'm very grateful to Governor Ashcroft and former Mayor Strauss for heading up this important effort. It's nonpartisan. It is national in scope. It simply says we must explore ways to strengthen the family. Some of that, I expect, might be recommendations changing laws so that it will encourage people who now make a little more dough who live apart to stay together. I'm sure it will get into other items that are affected by legislation.

The main thing is we've got the emphasis here on the right thing. I will simply repeat to the Commissioners and to these families what I've heard from two recent groups of mayors, both of them: one, the National League of Cities; the other, the black mayors association I met with the other day. Both of them said that the major cause for concern and cause for the problems in urban America was the decline of the family. So they're saying, "Hey, help us find ways to strengthen family."

That's what motivated—actually, it was the National League of Cities that suggested that we do this, make this a national Commission, make this something national. Of course, I was proud to announce it back in the State of the Union meeting. And I'm just anxious to hear from you or from some of these families what their experience has been.

I also have a little grandparently advice. And that is that all kids, everybody under 12, ought to be released to sit in the shade of that tree over there or go inside if they want to. That's my position as President, but you don't have to do it. [*Laughter*] But otherwise, I think you might enjoy it. Because I know if I were a kid, I'd be a little

restless out there, especially if I was all dressed up like you are. [*Laughter*] So you ought to feel free to go sit under a nice, cool tree over there, but don't forget to come back to your parents because they love you very much. Maybe there's a place inside, I don't know. You can explore around there, but don't get lost.

All right. Now who's going to—John, what's going to happen?

*Governor Ashcroft.* Well, we have a number of Missouri families with us today who are examples of how public, how private, how religious programs can work to strengthen families. Of course, we expect you to ask questions. But I want to invite Commission members also to make remarks.

[*At this point, participants described the operation and beneficial effects of various programs.*]

*The President.* That's great.

*Governor Ashcroft.* The Cochair of this Commission is Mayor Strauss of Dallas, Texas, and she's been a great Commission member in every respect. Go right ahead.

*Mayor Strauss.* Thank you, Governor. Have we heard from everybody? The families?

*Governor Ashcroft.* I think we have, yes.

*Mayor Strauss.* Because I feel moved as a member of this Commission, as Cochair, to say to you, Mr. President, how much we appreciate the fact that you have put this at the top of your agenda. It's not that it's anything new to you because we know that there are many, many programs, Federal programs and encouragement of the private sector, to help those who need help: families, the poor, the ill, the elderly.

But this new thrust is going to do so much good. I thank you for the opportunity to be a member of this Commission and to travel all over America and hear the voice of America telling us that problems that are so threatening to all of us, teenage pregnancy and gangs and crime and drugs, school dropout, so many are the result of the breakdown of the family and, in turn, perpetuate the breakdown of the family.

*The President.* Yes.

*Mayor Strauss.* So we want you to know

we have heard you. We know what your goal is, and we will do everything in our power to meet that goal and provide for a better future for the people of this country. And we thank you.

*The President.* Thanks for those kind words.

But is it too early to ask the Commissioners, are you beginning—of course, the Commission's been, what, in effect 70 days or something like that, 77 days, traveled to many States, which I think is very important. Because I think it's important that when the report comes in, it has a national concept to it, that it isn't regional in any sense. I think that's important.

But is it too early for the Commissioners to indicate, or do you think the final report will have more in the way of legislative suggestions as to how we'd change things or what new things we can do legislatively to strengthen the family? Or is it going to be more apt to be along the lines of some of the things we've heard here today, community programs, perhaps sponsored and keyed at the State and local level?

*Mayor Strauss.* It's going to be a combination.

*The President.* Combination.

*Commissioner Alphonso Jackson.* In traveling around the country, I think that what we're finding is there are a combination of both. There's going to have to be some legislative changes. But I think more than anything else, it's going to have to come directly from community involvement. As [*inaudible*] said yesterday, each individual community is going to have to make a commitment.

I think what we're finding in traveling around this country—that's been often said that the President's not in touch. I think you're very much in touch. I think the people in this community sense that the family is the key core to change what is happening in our country.

We were in Los Angeles yesterday, and I think it was reinforced again when we had major discussions with producers and directors of major television and movie shows yesterday. It seems in some way that they might be out of touch, but the families were in touch. I think they reiterated that to them. And I think we got something

very, very deep out of that. I think we've traveled to four or five cities, and the more we travel, the more we find out that the families sense that they're in crisis. But there is hope, and the hope is creating community organizations to bring the family back as a basic unit.

So I would say that it's going to take a combination of both.

*The President.* Right. I didn't know, the Governor did not tell me that you'd met with the media. And I think properly so because I think they need to change some of these things that they're engaged in under the name of entertainment. What we don't hear about are some of the things that they have been able to do, are willing to do. Then I should think that the Commission would look at the great potential if they could be mobilized to do more.

Why I say that is, I went out some time ago now, a long time ago, and they had a meeting of a lot of the leading executives in the media business. They decided that they would dedicate, I think it was one Saturday, maybe more, every cartoon that the kids watch on Saturday to have an antidrug message. That's not necessarily directly family, but clearly, every family would agree use of drugs make it tough on family.

They did it. They did it all. There were no pricetags on it. They just shifted the content of those programs. And I'm wondering if you ought to take, I'm sure you will, but maybe take a look at some positive suggestions along that line of what some of these media outlets and innovation entertainment can do, to do what that one group of people did on that one Saturday. I mean, I think there's tremendous potential there.

I think they'd be open-minded about it. One of the things we've got going, it's not exactly family, but is this partnership, media partnership headed by Jim Burke, remember that ran—you may know him; I think John knows him—ran Johnson & Johnson. He took on a commitment to get a billion dollars of pro bono advertising on the antidrug scene, and he's up to around $500 million or $600 million now. And you see these—I don't know if you remember the one with the fried egg cracking and all that. Well, that was one that they did, totally pro bono, not Government. And they just went and persuaded the networks and others to do this.

David, you were going to say something. But maybe in this whole area of recommending to some of these very powerful media outlets, they can do what you ask of them.

I interrupted you, I know.

*Commissioner David Blankenhorn.* That's your right. I was going to say that one of the things we're hearing a lot is that—and I believe very strongly—we have to look for ways to bring fathers back into the home. This is really a big issue, as you know. A lot of the indicators we have tell us that child well-being is declining in the country. The biggest reason it's declining is the family breakup, the erosion of marriage. A lot of this is a cultural issue; it can't be legislated. But there are some things in the area of tax policy, welfare law reform, child support payments, and so on that can be done to send good signals and incentives about the importance of fatherhood. To me, that's kind of the core issue out there as regards child well-being that we are hearing as we listen to people.

*The President.* That's interesting. There's also a kind of disciplinary component of that where a person, a father who takes off and does have a financial obligation set by the court, that that person fulfill that obligation. He can't go off living alone and leave the mother with the kids and leave them hung out there to dry without fulfilling that obligation. So that's already in the mill, people trying to figure out how to do it. But you're right about that.

*Governor Ashcroft.* Before we leave, I want to call on Irene Johnson from Chicago. She's been a very important member, a valuable member of the Commission. She has the perspective that, well, has resonated with the people who have come to testify in virtually every city to which we've come. Irene, thank you for being here today.

*Commissioner Irene Johnson.* Thank you very much. Mr. President, it's an honor to meet you in person, and I want to thank you personally for this assignment that you've given us. In reference to your statement about the things that we have found as we go around America, we think that

there will need to be some policy changes also. The communities do have to play a very important part, but the other part that we've heard is that we have to deal with the spiritual aspect, that people have to go back to what America was built on, and that was faith in God. So we hear a lot of families saying that that kind of thread has led them to do community services and the kinds of things that we see families are dealing with, particularly the Jones family and many other families that we have met.

I'm just pleased to know that we believe that you have that spirit of God in you, the reason why you are concerned about the families and gave us this assignment. So we appreciate that, and we are going to do our best in all of that.

*The President.* You know, it would be very interesting, I don't know how the Commission would determine this, to see, of the families who are having difficulties in the sense, both combination of economic difficulties, remembering what Dave talked about single-parent families, how faith—I don't know how you could; it's so private in one way—but how faith matters, whether they still have the seeds of faith to sustain them or whether they just lost that and perhaps through some ministry could reacquire it. I don't know. I mean, I'd be interested.

What do you think?

*Commissioner Josephine Velazquez.* In all the programs that we have been viewing, wherever we see that there is a religious factor built into it, a spiritual factor build into the program, you can see that the results you get are so much more positive. So it is a very positive aspect and something that we should look into. We have lost that. And we have been shown—a lot of these families come up to say, and a lot of the children, "Why don't we have our prayer back in schools?"—things that they're missing. We lost it somewhere along the line, and the American people are asking for it to be back.

*Commissioner Jackson.* I'd like to give you a comment. I think yesterday, Mr. President, in Los Angeles, we had a story told by a young man who is today 27 years old. His mother left under unusual circumstances. They lived in Nicholson Gardens, which is a public housing development in Los Angeles. At 17 he had to become the father, the mother of the family. His youngest brother was 2 months old when she left the home. He has raised every one of them.

But he said yesterday the most important thing was his faith and commitment in God and that he had to fight through a court system to keep his sisters and brothers. And now he has become an assistant manager at Nicholas Gardens. But he specifically said to us yesterday that without his deep abiding belief in God, that he could not have made it, and that was the driving force keeping him going every day.

*The President.* Isn't that fascinating? Gosh.

*Governor Ashcroft.* Mr. President, we thank you very much for coming and just hearing a little bit of the reflection of what we've been hearing around America from the Commission and also hearing from individuals in Missouri. And these are the type of people, individuals who we've been hearing from in a variety of stops from one coast to the other. And they're inspiring to me in a lot of ways. They've fought through tough odds. Sometimes they've had bad starts. But the possibility of rescuing situations is coming on strong, putting families back together that had been apart, bringing children back into the home that had been in foster care.

We're inspired. You've given us a challenging but inspiring job. And we just want to thank you for letting us report to you on a little bit of an interim basis and letting us feel again the intensity of your personal concern on this issue.

*The President.* Well, I'm delighted. And thanks to the Commission members and also to the witnesses, or whatever we call them, these four families that shared this with us. I sit back there in Washington, and it really brings it home much more personally when you hear what individual families have done and are still doing.

As for you kids, next time we do this, it's going to be nice and cool. [*Laughter*] Next time that's the way it's going to be.

Thank you all so much.

*Governor Ashcroft.* We deliver the report in December. It will be cooler then.

*The President.* All right. That sounds far off now. [*Laughter*]

*Note: The President spoke at 3:25 p.m. in Shelter Gardens Park.*

## Remarks at the Show Me State Games in Columbia
*July 24, 1992*

May I salute our great Governor and thank him and all of you for that warm welcome. And to Mary Ann McCollum, our Mayor, thank you, ma'am, for welcoming us to your city, making us feel so at home. May I also salute Gary Filbert, the executive director of these wonderful games; Dr. Jerry Brouder, the chancellor of the university, from whom we've heard. I thought Stephanie, Miss Missouri, did a fantastic job singing "The Star-Spangled Banner" over there. And while we're passing out tributes, I thought that Jordan and Greg did okay on the Pledge of Allegiance, too. Never missed a beat. So thank you very, very much.

For me it's a great pleasure to be back here, several times I've been here, but back in Columbia. This is the one Tigers den that I'm always happy to walk into. And everybody involved should take great pride in this fantastic Show Me Games. It's marvelous, and our congratulations go out, of course, to all the competitors. I have only one regret, not that I can't compete with you all but that I won't get to see you in action.

The Governor has told me what a marvelous event this is. The games now are, what, in their 7th year, but the spirit really is as old as America itself. And you're all here to do your best in a tough competition. The Olympic creed, I'm sure some of you are familiar with it, it really says it the best: "The most important thing is not to win but to take part; not to have conquered but to have fought well."

You come from all over this State, from all walks of life, from every age group. And your youngest competitor, from right here in Columbia, is 4 years old. He's out there somewhere, I guess. It might be hard to see him. He's a swimmer. We heard about the oldest competitor: Vernon Kennedy of Mendin is 85 years young, and I understand he specializes in throwing javelins. Maybe I will ask him to join me in the political wars that lie ahead. [*Laughter*]

This Show Me Games takes place at a momentous moment in our history. While you're warming up and working out, the Olympic athletes will be doing the same over there in Barcelona. I told the Governor that the head of our delegation, the national delegation, not the Olympic competitors themselves but the head of it, is a man who's been here to Columbia, Arnold Schwarzenegger, who is taking the message of fitness for America all the way across to those games.

They're going to be competing there against the long jumpers from marvelous new countries: Croatia, Slovenia boxers, Lithuanian basketball players, pole vaulters from what they call the Unified Team. And these places really didn't even breathe free just 4 years ago. And the simple fact is—it's reflected in these games for the very first time—is that the cold war that has obsessed the free world for so long is over. We won that cold war. The nations of the world said, "Show me." The nations of the world said, "Show me what democracy and freedom means. Show me a way of life I can aspire to." And guess what, we showed them. America showed them.

I believe now that we have changed the world, we can change and renew America. And you see, the new world brings both challenges and opportunities. The question is whether we can compete now that more and more nations are playing our game. Once we win this competition, and we will, our children will enjoy a prosperity that we can't imagine. And I really believe that.

Competing in this new world isn't going to be easy. It's going to require that we change our way of doing business. One priority is to strengthen and restore, and John referred to this, strengthen and restore the building block of our Nation, represented here by so many today, the American family.

I think these Show Me Games might well be called the family games. I know of the Beaumonts, for example, who have come from Sparta to join in the games. It's the middle of the haying season, so dad Terry couldn't make it. But Cindy is here with four of her kids to participate in the shooting competition. And listen to what she says: "It's so easy these days for family members to be doing their own things. We work hard to do things as a family. We work hard, and we play hard." And that sounds like a Missouri family to me.

On a personal basis, I can relate to that. Family sports have always been a big part of our family life. I remember way back on the plains of west Texas back in 1948 and on in through the early fifties, coaching a team there on the Little League team, and Barbara remembers too, maybe not quite so fondly. She spent so much time carpooling our kids from one game to another that we get thank-you notes from the president of Texaco. Keep it up, he'd say. [*Laughter*] Of course, it didn't stop with Little League. There were hunting trips and swimming meets and tennis lessons and lots of fishing. And there's one great drawback to fishing with your kids: They keep you honest.

I'm reminded of a story about that great Missourian, Mark Twain. One time Mark Twain snuck off to do some fishing. It was off-season, which is why he had to kind of sneak around. But on the train back home, he couldn't resist bragging to the fellow next to him. And after he was done describing all the fish that he'd caught, Twain asked the guy what he did for a living. And the reply, "I am the State game warden. Who are you?" Twain almost swallowed his cigar, and he said, "Sir, I am the biggest darned liar in the entire United States of America." [*Laughter*]

He was stretching it a little bit, but there's no stretching how much these games mean to the fans and the competitors alike. And I love the motto. I love the motto, "Show me what you're made of." Sports are about character, about shaping character, about nourishing it. When you take the time to teach your son to shoot a bull's-eye or teach your daughter to throw a strike, you're teaching more than a skill. You're teaching values, values like perseverance, sportsmanship, motivation, effort: priceless gifts that your kids will use long after you're gone.

Of course, the American family is under siege today from so many forces. But I have a plan to use Government to help keep these families together. And last year, we signed a new law that helps parents choose the quality of day care. Whether it's a school or relative's house or whether it's a local church, working parents ought to be able to choose where their children will be cared for. That keeps the family strong.

Similarly, you might ask about older kids who want to go to college but can't afford tuition. Well, yesterday we signed a new law expanding college financial aid, especially for middle class families who are squeezed by rising costs.

I think we'd all agree that it's pretty simple; you ought to be able to climb the ladder of education and reach your dream. And that's what we're trying to do. We're advancing ideas to make buying homes more affordable, to increase the tax exemptions for children. And for families on welfare, we want to create incentives for them not to fall apart but to hang in there, to stay together.

This morning, or just this afternoon, John, I met with Governor Ashcroft. You know, he is heading a very important Presidential Commission, a National Commission on America's Urban Families. And to get more ideas, we met to discuss what we can do to put the family back in the winner's circle.

Now, I've gone on a little longer, but I'm worried that Vernon Kennedy of Mendin might pick up his javelin and show me that I've been talking too long. So let me end.

And let me just say that the family remains our most potent weapon as a nation. America will always be first so long as we put the American family first.

Here in Columbia, and I'm sure the people from the rest of the State know about this, I think one of the favorite sons of Columbia is a graduate of Hickman High. He went on to make quite a name for himself, Sam Walton. He was a great achiever; we all know that. But he always knew that his greatest legacy would be the children he gave to the world. And that's why he made sure, in his own words, that his kids "received your everyday heartland upbringing based on the bedrock values, a belief in the importance of hard work, honesty, neighborliness, and thrift."

I know that in this sophisticated age, some people might find those home truths a little corny. But I don't, and I know you don't, either. We know what Sam Walton knew: Fashions come and go, but the old bedrock values never go out of style.

Let me say as I end this speech, I salute the mentors, the coaches, the mothers, the dads who bring out the best in these kids. Thank you from the bottom of my heart and the Nation's heart for what you are doing, not just to inculcate into these kids this competitive spirit but to hold together the American family in the process.

Now it is my pleasure to lead the athletes in the Olympic oath. And I leave here inspired. And let me just say, may God bless the United States of America, our great country. Thank you very, very much.

*Note: The President spoke at 4:38 p.m. in Hearnes Center at the University of Missouri. In his remarks, he referred to Stephanie Patterson, Miss Missouri, 1992; Jordan Rentschler, Girl Scout Troop #382; Greg Mees, Boy Scout Troop #4; and the late Samuel M. Walton, founder of Wal-Mart Stores, Inc.*

# Nominations to the National Institute Board for the National Institute for Literacy
*July 24, 1992*

On the eve of the anniversary of his historic legislation for literacy, the President today announced his nominees for the National Institute Board for the National Institute for Literacy.

The National Institute for Literacy is the centerpiece of the National Literacy Act, signed into law by the President on July 25 of last year. The Institute will catalyze the national effort to achieve full literacy by the year 2000 by providing a focal point for research, technical assistance, dissemination, policy analysis, and program evaluation in the field of literacy.

The National Institute Board is being established to provide independent advice on the operation of the Institute, make recommendations concerning the appointment of the Director and staff, and receive reports from the interagency group of the Secretaries of Education, Labor, and Health and Human Services, as well as from the Institute's Director.

The President intends to nominate the following individuals for terms of 3 years:

*John Corcoran,* of California. Currently Mr. Corcoran is the founder and CEO of the Brehon Co., a commercial and residential real estate building, development, and investment firm. He also serves as a member of the board of directors of the San Diego Literacy Council and leads "Students at Risk" in-service workshops for professional educators. Mr. Corcoran's story of overcoming a 48-year literacy handicap has appeared on "Phil Donahue," "Larry King Live," and "20/20."

*Helen B. Crouch,* of New York. Currently Ms. Crouch serves as the executive director and president of the Literacy Volunteers of America, Inc. (LVA). Ms. Crouch began her work with LVA as a volunteer tutor in 1969. Since that time she has served on the national board of directors and as chairperson until her appointment as president in 1981. Ms. Crouch is the past chairperson and founder of the National Coalition for Literacy.

*Sharon Darling,* of Kentucky. Ms. Darling is the current president of the National Center for Family Literacy, Inc. Ms. Darling served as the executive director of Literacy Concepts, Inc.,

in 1987–88 where she served as a consultant to the National Governors' Association and the U.S. Department of Education. As director of the division of adult community education for the Kentucky Department of Education from 1984 to 1987, Ms. Darling directed the adult literacy, community education, and GED programs for the State.

*Jon Deveaux,* of New York. Currently Mr. Deveaux serves as the executive director of the Bronx Educational Services (BES) which he founded in 1973. In 1990 a BES National Training Center for Literacy Teachers was established. Mr. Deveaux and the staff have trained hundreds of literacy teachers from around the Nation. Mr. Deveaux served as the chairperson of the New York State Literacy Council from 1988 to 1990.

*Gov. Jim Edgar,* of Illinois. Jim Edgar was inaugurated as the 38th Governor of Illinois in 1991. Prior to his election, Governor Edgar served as the secretary of state from 1981 to 1990. As secretary of state and State librarian, Governor Edgar created and oversaw a strong statewide network of programs and support for literacy. Governor Edgar's adult literacy program became a model for the Nation, and he was presented a literacy award by the American Library Trustee Association in 1986, given annually to an individual who has made an outstanding contribution in addressing the problem of adult illiteracy.

*Badi G. Foster,* of Illinois. Mr. Foster currently serves as vice president of targeted selection and development for Aetna Life and Casualty Corp. He is the former president of the Aetna Institute for Corporate Education since its inception in 1981. Prior to his work with Aetna, Mr. Foster was the director of field experience programs for the Graduate School of Education at Harvard University.

*Ronald M. Gillum,* of Michigan. Dr. Gillum is the State director of adult extended learning services for the Michigan Department of Education. Dr. Gillum has been with the Michigan Department of Education for 19 years, during which time he served as the director of the adult occupational educational programs. Dr. Gillum was the recipient of the U.S. Department of Education's Outstanding Leadership Award in Literacy in 1985.

*Benita C. Somerfield,* of New York. Ms. Somerfield currently serves as the president of Simon & Schuster Workplace Resources which publishes material for low-literate adults in public and private sector job-related programs. Since 1988 she has also served as executive director (volunteer) of the Barbara Bush Foundation for Family Literacy. From 1986 to 1988 Ms. Somerfield was Special Adviser for Adult Literacy at the U.S. Department of Education.

*Susan Vogel*, of Illinois. Currently Dr. Vogel is chair and professor of the department of educational psychology, counseling, and special education at Northern Illinois University. From 1988 to 1989, Dr. Vogel served as the director of research for the National Institute of Dyslexia, following which she was the head of the department of special education at Eastern Michigan University. Dr. Vogel received a Ph.D. in learning disabilities and communicative disorders from Northwestern University.

# Remarks and an Exchange With Reporters on Arrival From Camp David, Maryland
*July 26, 1992*

## War on Drugs

*The President.* I have two brief statements. In addition to yesterday's meeting with our national security advisers on the situation in Iraq, which has been widely reported, I spent considerable time today reviewing the antidrug fight in our communities.

Jim Burke, who heads the Partnership for a Drug-Free America, gave me a very thorough and encouraging report at Camp David about the progress that our Nation is making in turning away from the drug culture. It's happening; America is turning off drugs. Problems remain, to be sure, but impressive progress is being made on the demand side of the equation, particularly among our youth.

So he and I today reviewed the data that shows a cultural change is taking place. Kids are rejecting drugs. There's been a 56 percent drop in use by 13- to 17-year-olds in one study, a drop of 48 percent among this group in another. So these are very important trends. In our workplace programs, people are really putting out the effort. Virtually 90 percent of our major companies have highly effective programs, and companies are expanding a program called Drugs Don't Work. Our country's getting the message. At least 900 communities across the country have organized antidrug coalitions, and more of them are being formed every day.

Now, we still have a serious drug problem in the United States, with an estimated 6 million addicts. This drug problem is embedded in every other social issue that we're dealing with as a Nation. So we've got to do more. But I was very pleased with Mr. Burke's report on behalf of the Partnership for a Drug-Free America.

## Iraq

Now, on Iraq: Iraq's belated announcement that it will allow the United Nations Special Commission to carry out an inspection of the Agricultural Ministry in Baghdad does not alter the fact that for some 3 weeks Saddam Hussein flagrantly violated U.N. Security Council Resolution 687. Nor does this announcement change the fact that Iraq deliberately and callously harassed and abused the U.N. inspectors seeking to carry out their mandate. That mandate: Immediate, unimpeded, unconditional, unrestricted access to any site the U.N. deems warranted for inspection.

And yes, now, once again, Saddam Hussein has caved in. While Saddam has bent to the will of the U.N., the question remains whether after this delay a truly effective inspection of the Ministry is still possible. The real test of his behavior will be in future U.N. inspections. Behavior along the lines we've just witnessed will not be tolerated.

Saddam has long pursued a pattern of willful noncompliance and obstruction of the United Nations Special Commission. For over a year he has lied about the extent of Iraq's weapons of mass destruction programs and sought to conceal them from the United Nations and the International Atomic Energy Agency. Now, this is unacceptable. Iraq must and will be held to the standard of full compliance with Security Council Resolution 687.

Saddam's violation of the will of the international community, as expressed in the United Nations Security Council resolutions, continues in other important areas. Iraq has refused to participate in the work of the Iraq-Kuwait Border Commission. Iraq has refused to account for Kuwaiti citizens seized during the occupation of the emirate and to return property that was stolen by the occupiers. Iraq has not renewed the memorandum of understanding with the U.N. and has stepped up its harassment of U.N. officials and humanitarian agencies operating in the country.

Saddam has stepped up his persecution of the Iraqi people in flagrant violation of U.N. Security Council Resolution 688, including recent use of jet fighters against the Shia and maintaining a blockade of the Kurds. Iraq has refused to accept U.N. Security Council Resolutions 706 and 712, which would allow for that sale of oil for food and medicine, choosing instead to have the Iraqi people suffer unnecessarily, denying them food.

The international community cannot tolerate continued Iraqi defiance of the United Nations and the rule of law. There is too much at stake for the region, for the United Nations, and for the world.

I'll just take a couple of questions, just a couple of questions here.

*Q.* Does this mean that you find unsatisfactory the settlement that was made at the U.N. and are rejecting it, or is this a temporary settlement of the——

*The President.* No, we support Dr. Ekeus. He has our full respect and confidence. So that inspection will go forward, belatedly so, but it will go forward.

*Q.* Do you feel, Mr. President, that there is a need now for some kind of ultimatum, some kind of deadline given them, some kind of threat of military aid?

*The President.* Some kind of threat?

*Q.* I mean military action. Pardon me.

*The President.* I don't know that any more is required right at this minute. I

think everyone knows that we are determined to see these resolutions complied with. We are in very close touch with our allies. This standoff now has been resolved by his caving in, by his backing down in spite of bluster and threats to the contrary. But there are many other inspections to come.

*Q.* Mr. President, does that mean then that the crisis in general is not over, that there will be continuing incidents with Saddam Hussein?

*The President.* Well, the way to end the crisis is for him to fully comply with these resolutions I outlined. Until then there will be a lot of tension because the whole world is now more determined than ever to see that he does comply. So I can't say there's no reason for concern anymore at all. There's plenty of reason.

*Q.* Mr. President, some U.S. military forces are en route to the region. In view of the agreement that has been worked out, will you order those forces to stand down, to be pulled back, or is that military option still open?

*The President.* Well, normally I don't discuss the deployment of military forces, and I'm inclined to stay with that right now. I don't think there will be any drastic changes in existing plans.

*Q.* Mr. President, you seem to be saying that the next time there won't be any time for warning, you're not going to let one of these crises build up like this. Is that what you're telling us?

*The President.* You can interpret it any way you want. All I'm trying to do is express the unanimous determination of the Security Council.

*Q.* Mr. President, Deputy Secretary Eagleburger said today he expects Secretary Baker to stay at the State Department for a long, long time. Is that your view as well, or is he going to move to the campaign shortly?

*The President.* I have no comments on that subject.

*Q.* Mr. President, Saddam Hussein said today that "the mother of all battles" is not over. What do you say to him?

*The President.* I say to him, if it's not over, he better hope it is.

*Q.* Is he still a threat to his neighbors in the Middle East?

*The President.* No, Saddam Hussein is a threat to the Iraqi people. He's a threat to his own people. He's brutalizing his own people in failing to comply. He is a threat to peace and security in the area. There's no question about all of that. Our argument is not with the Iraqi people. I've said that since day one of all of this. I will repeat it here today: Our argument is with Saddam Hussein, the bully, the dictator, the brutal merchant of death. And that's it. It is not with the Iraqi people. And once again, he has caved in after a lot of bluster.

But all I want to do here is express for the United States our determination to see him comply with these resolutions. We haven't forgotten, and nor have the other members of the Security Council. So against a solid wall, he once again caved in. I guess there's a certain humiliation factor for him with his own people. But I would simply say we've just got to look ahead now and see that other inspections go forward and that he complies with these resolutions, the subject of which I discussed here a few minutes ago.

Last one here.

*Q.* Can I just clarify, is the threat of force not over until full compliance begins?

*The President.* I haven't threatened or changed anything. The options that the United States and our partners have available to us are well-known. Let's just see that he complies with the resolutions. I'm not here to threaten. I'm simply here to say that I'm glad that he cratered once again on this threatening, but to reiterate our determination to see these resolutions complied with. That's all that this is about, and it's got to be done in timely fashion.

I salute Mr. Ekeus. He's a courageous man. And he worked hard to get access to this Ministry, which he should have had given to him automatically, by very competent professionals, very competent inspectors.

There will be another occasion along the line here because there are other inspections that will take place. So we just have to keep plugging ahead to be sure this man does what international law calls for him to do.

Thank you all very much.

*Note: The President spoke at 4:35 p.m. on the South Lawn at the White House. In his remarks, he referred to Rolf Ekeus, Executive Director, United Nations Special Commission on Iraq.*

## Remarks to Holland American Wafer Employees in Wyoming, Michigan
*July 27, 1992*

Thank you very, very much. Governor, John, thank you, sir. The problem with Governor Engler is you're never quite sure where he stands. [*Laughter*] Thank you so much for that warm introduction, my friend, and let me just say I am very, very proud to be at Governor Engler's side.

I want to say to John and Stuart Vander Heide, I am very pleased to be here, and I've had a good day. And I appreciate those who ended up having to go through sitting with us under the arcs at lunch. But they made me understand the heartbeat of this wonderful company. I want to thank all of you at our table and everybody else that's made us feel so welcome here.

I'm pleased that Congressman Henry and Mayor Voorhees could be with us today. And I want to single out another one who is from this area, but who has served our country with great distinction. He shed—nobody thought this was possible—his partisan politics, where he's helped me enormously over the years, to go over to Italy and serve with great distinction as our Ambassador: Pete Secchia over here, from Grand Rapids.

Let me just kind of put a Surgeon General's note on this speech. I have not shifted gears yet from trying to make some good things happen for this country, including yesterday making some decisions about standing up to be sure that Saddam Hussein lives up to these U.N. resolutions. He's going to do it. He may not know it, but he is going to live up to those resolutions.

But the warning label is that I haven't quite shifted gears yet to get into this mode that I'm looking forward to, which is the 4-year dance that American politicians go through where you really take your case strongly, not only about yourself and why you want to be reelected but about the others, to the American people. That will happen right after our convention, Republican Convention, in August of this year. But for now I want to talk to you on some broader principles.

Americans may not realize it when they reach for the cereal on the shelves, but this industry, our food industry, provides more food for less than any other nation in the entire world. The company, this one, is one reason we are the world's leader. So I'm pleased to announce that Stu and John have recruited me for a national crusade. Starting today, I will not only argue passionately that broccoli's benefits are overblown—[*laughter*]—but that sugar wafers should be one of the four essential ingredients in a healthy diet.

I'm told that this company was the originator of something called the survival biscuit. Well, it was one of the tokens of the cold war, a bit of nourishment to fill your stomach as you huddled somewhere in a bomb shelter in case the unthinkable became tragically real. While it may not be great for survival biscuit sales, the cold war is, thankfully, over. Survival biscuits have gone the way of the doomsday clock, "Fail-Safe" movies, duck-and-cover drills.

Today, America is safer than ever before, safer than we were a decade ago, safer than we were a year ago, and safer than we were just a few weeks ago, when I sat down with Boris Yeltsin and agreed to eliminate the world's most dangerous and destabilizing nuclear weapons, those great big ICBM's. This is good for your kids, and it's good for my grandkids. We all should take great pride in it.

Now that we have changed the world, the taxpayers and the leaders working together, it's time, high time, that we change America, time to turn our attention to pressing challenges like how to give a pink slip to our slow-growth economy—it's growing but far too slow—how to make our families more like the Waltons and a little bit less like the Simpsons, and how to take back our streets from the crack dealers and the criminals.

This election year, we're told, is about how we can change to meet these challenges. But this election is not just about change because change has a flip side. That flip side is called trust. When you get down to it, this election will be like every other. When you go into that voting booth and pull the curtain behind you, trust matters.

That's the way it should be. Many times in the White House late at night, the phone rings. Usually it's some young aide double-checking on the next day's schedule. But occasionally it's another voice, more serious, more solemn, carrying news of a coup in a powerful country or asking how we should stand up to a bully halfway around the world. The American people need to know that the man who answers that phone has the experience, the seasoning, the guts to do the right thing.

That's trust in the traditional sense. But people who've spent their lives in government forget that trust is more even than that. I'm a Texan. I raised my children there. I built my businesses there. I voted there in every Presidential election since my first, including that one, that 1948 election, the year the press and the pundits counted Harry Truman out before the fight began. We remember that one, and I remember it. So wait until August.

I believe our heartbeat can be felt in places like Wyoming, Michigan, not Washington, DC. So I stake my claim in a simple philosophy: To lead a great Nation, you must first trust the people you lead. If you look at almost every important issue we face, you see a clearer choice, a choice between those who put their faith in average Americans and those who put their faith in Government. Let me explain what I mean, starting with the basics, home and family.

The most difficult question many parents face is, who will care for the kids while we're working? A few years ago, Washington wanted to help, but their idea was to rock the cradle with the heavy hand of bureaucracy. All the plans boiled down to creating some new kind of Government apparatus, like a "Pentagon" for child care.

I fought for a different approach and won. Our landmark legislation allows parents, not the Government, to decide whether your children are cared for in a school, a relative's home, or a church. When it comes to raising our children, I say, why not trust the people? It is better than having the Government try to do something like child care out of Washington, DC.

What about our education system? To renew America we must renew our schools. We all know this. But money alone won't do it. We already spend more money per student than almost any other country, and our kids still rank near the bottom in crucial subjects like math and science. Again, a lot of ideas floating around, most of them to pump more tax money, that's your money, into the system, the same old system. I say, try something different: Open up schools to competition, and trust you to decide whether your kids, whether you want them to learn in a public school, a private school, or a religious school.

When it comes to education I say, why not trust the people? Why not give the people the same choice that I had when I had the GI bill coming out of World War II—they didn't say you can only go to one kind of school—public, private, religious. And we ought to try that, and then watch these schools improve. I believe it's the time to put the trust in the people.

What about Government regulation? Sure, some of it is absolutely necessary, even essential. If you believe that there is a Government solution to every problem, an alphabet agency for every issue, then you look at regulation not as a necessary evil but as a necessary way to rein in people's evil tendencies. Well, the result can be crazy, as this story proves.

The time had come recently for a Government agency to update its rules on hardhats. That's right, hardhats. Someone in that agency stumbled upon a potential national

crisis, workers being infected from putting someone else's hardhat on their head. The alarms went off. The bureaucratic blood boiled. One small fact was overlooked. There wasn't a single documented case anywhere in the United States of anyone getting infected from wearing someone else's hardhat. That didn't deter the bureaucrat. So with the best of intentions, the rule was written: Every hardhat must be disinfected before one worker passed it on to another. Estimated cost to the business: $13 million a year. Measurable benefit: slightly less than zero.

Luckily, this story has a happy ending, but only because we were there to give it one. We found the regulation before it hit the books and said America can survive without this particular hardhat regulation. We may have done you hairnetters a great service by beating back the hardhat regulation; try to pass one of those along and say that germs are being passed. But anyway, can you imagine what might have happened if these enterprising regulators had made their way into the vast, unregulated territory of lunch pails and thermos bottles?

Some believe the solution to our problems is more Government regulation. I take a very different view. I've put a moratorium on new Federal regulation, to give businesses like this one room to breathe and grow and create jobs. It's a matter of trust, of putting people ahead of Government. When it comes to the most pressing issue of the election year, revving up our economy, forgetting this idea is not just a nuisance; it can be downright dangerous.

The revolutions of the past few years herald a new era of global economic competition, with free markets from Siberia to Santiago. Can the U.S. compete now that everyone is playing our game? Despite all the criticism you've heard lately, keep in mind a few facts. We are the largest, most envied economy in the entire world.

Inflation, that Jesse James who robs the middle class of dreams, as John has said, as our Governor has said, has been put safely behind bars. The last time interest rates stayed this low, "The Brady Bunch" wasn't even in reruns yet. Despite all the stories about our problems, our workers are still the most productive in the entire world, more productive than the English, the Germans, the Japanese, much more productive.

So there are some good, sound things out there. But while our economy is growing, it's growing too slow; it's got to grow faster. The question is how. The other side suggests a simple two-part solution, Governor Engler talked about that: First, raise Government spending, and then, raise taxes.

Now, as you evaluate their idea, keep this in mind. Here in Michigan, you already work 128 days just to pay your taxes before you earn a single dime to spend on your family. Now, I don't think anyone wants to go for 129 days. All this talk of spending and taxes causes me to wonder if the other side is a little hard of hearing. Abraham Lincoln spoke of government "of the people, by the people, for the people." But they seem to keep saying, "of the Government, by the Government, for the Government."

They're hard to dissuade. I'll give you a great example. In January I proposed a commonsense, comprehensive plan to get this economy moving faster, right now. The plan includes tax incentives to encourage businesses to hire new workers, breaks for young families who want to buy that first home, a tax break for them so they can participate in the American dream. Half a million jobs would have been created if the Congress had acted right away.

But they didn't. Instead Congress sent back what you might call an anti-trust program: new Government spending and new taxes. And I vetoed it and said, "I am not going to increase taxes on the American people at this time." We're not going to do that. So I sent their plan back, and I'm still waiting almost 200 days later. This economic recovery plan is being held hostage, and the ransom note reads, "Wait till after the election." Today I say to the Congress, House of Representatives and the Senate, especially: Release the economy. Approve this jobs program, and put America back to work, now.

So you see, it all does come down to a question of trust. I trust you to spend and save your money more wisely than a budget planner in Washington.

You'll say this is common sense, and I agree. But there's a certain type of person attracted to Government for whom the word "trust" has strange meaning. Most of them have spent their lives in Government and don't have much experience in the real world. They say they want to put people first. But if you look real close at what they're proposing, the people they put first are all on the Government payroll.

A leader of a free people must understand that Government can not only help, it can hinder. He must have the confidence to say, "I trust you. I trust the people." Ultimately you must decide who you trust, who has the experience, the ideals, and the ideas to find the appropriate balance.

Of course, America will change, just as we've changed the world. The question now is who will change America for the better? It won't be people whose only enthusiasm is for Government, who measure progress by programs enacted and special interests satisfied.

If you want to know who's going to change America, look at who is sitting right next to you. Look around you. It's going to be the guy who works an extra shift every week so his son can go to the school of his choice. It's going to be the small businessman who takes a risk on a new product, the computer hacker working in a lonely garage, that merit scholar from south central L.A., the entrepreneur with a future as big as his dreams.

There's your answer: The American people are going to change America. But only if they have a Government, particularly a Congress, with the wisdom to know its own limits and with a leadership who knows where the true American imagination lies. Countries around the world have at long last understood the power of trusting the people. America will change by reaffirming the lesson it has taught the world, by trusting a leader who trusts you.

I am delighted to have been here. Thank you very, very much. May God bless you, and may God bless our great, free, wonderful country, the United States of America. Thank you very, very much.

*Note: The President spoke at 12:13 p.m. at the plant. In his remarks, he referred to*

John S. Vander Heide, chairman of the board, and Stuart Vander Heide, president, Holland American Wafer Co.

# Remarks on Arrival in Appleton, Wisconsin
*July 27, 1992*

Thank you all for this marvelous turnout. I do have an official announcement I want to make today. I first want to salute Governor Thompson, Senator Kasten, and our distinguished Members of the United States House of Representatives. Great to be back in this State that's built on faith and family and freedom. Wisconsin is a great example to the rest of America, just as America is to the entire world. And today I'm very proud to be in a place where programs like Learnfare and Workfare and the Parental Responsibility Act all tell America: Watch Wisconsin because Wisconsin works.

Governor Thompson wants Wisconsin to work even better, and that's why he's joined my crusade to reform our welfare system. Let's face it, we know the system has failed the people. It doesn't lift families from poverty; it traps them there. Welfare discourages families from staying together. And when the system rips families apart, it's time to rip apart that system.

Now, Americans yearn to keep families whole and give our kids the learning skills and, yes, track down parents who run out on their kids. They know that if America doesn't change the welfare system for the better, the welfare system is going to change America for the worse. That means trying, therefore, new plans, new ideas, a new kind of reform. Only then can we break the cycle of dependency.

In my State of the Union Address last January, I made a commitment to far-reaching reform. I acted because I believe we can no longer afford the existing welfare system. Our recipients can't afford to be dependent on government for their livelihood, and our taxpayers can't afford to pay the welfare bill, and our economy can't afford the lost productivity.

I also acted because I trust the American people and because I believe that those on welfare, what they really want is a piece of the American dream: homeownership, a good job, opportunities for their children, and strong, loving families. And therefore, I am determined to make it quicker and easier for States who choose to reform their welfare systems to get the Federal waivers that they need to help the people help themselves.

Last April my administration signed a first waiver for Wisconsin. And today it will sign a second giving Governor Thompson the freedom to further reform this State's welfare program. Governor Thompson's ultimate goal is to break the cycle of dependency that traps so many people and create incentives for recipients to work and learn. He understands that more important than having an America that helps people in need is building an America where fewer people need to be helped.

Today I want to challenge other States in our country to follow Wisconsin's lead in bringing new ideas to our welfare system. Last week we approved New Jersey's Family Development Program, whose reforms in the State welfare program reward work and unite families. And I am confident other States will now do what America does best, bring local genius to local needs.

In coming months, we are going to watch Wisconsin to see how Wisconsin works. Together, we can help change that welfare system and, in doing so, change America. I'm proud to sign this waiver. I congratulate Governor Thompson and the people of Wisconsin.

Thank you all very, very much.

*Note: The President spoke at 1:19 p.m. at the Outagamie County Airport.*

## Remarks to Outlook Graphics Employees in Neenah, Wisconsin
*July 27, 1992*

Thank you all very, very much. Please be seated. Thank you and good afternoon, everyone. Let me just say thank you to the Governor for that very kind introduction. But let me tell you this: I know these Governors, all of them, and you've got one of the very best, if not the very best, in the entire United States. I really mean that, a solid friend, a strong leader and innovator. You're lucky, and I'm lucky, too, because he sets an example. He brings new ideas to these Governors meetings. He sets a high example for everybody including the President of the United States, and I am very, very pleased to be with him.

Of course, I'm very pleased to see my great friend, your Senator Bob Kasten; and these two Congressmen, Toby Roth and Tom Petri, who are doing a first-class job. If we had more like them, you talk about change, we could change America and change it fast for the better. I am glad they could join us today, as well as Mr. Herbert Grover, the superintendent of public instruction for the State of Wisconsin. He's doing a first-class job for education statewide. And David Erdmann, thank you, sir, for your hospitality. I'm just delighted to be here.

Now, it is a pleasure to be here. For any sports fan, it's a thrill to be at the birthplace of America's sports trading cards, and for me, it's a little humbling. I don't dare ask how many hundreds of George Bush cards you have to trade to get one Michael Jordan. [*Laughter*]

I've come here to talk a little bit about our future, about the kind of nation we want for ourselves and our children. The world has undergone remarkable changes in the past few years. And today our kids worry about the usual things, about school friends, about such earth-shattering questions as "Where can I get an Olympic Dream Team card?" But I can tell you one thing they don't worry about anymore, the specter of nuclear war.

Today, America is safer than ever before, safer than we were a decade ago, safer than we were a year ago, and safer than we were just a few weeks ago, when I sat down with Boris Yeltsin, the President of Russia, to eliminate some of the most dangerous nuclear weapons on the face of the Earth, getting rid of those great big SS–18 ICBM's. That's good change. That is positive, and it's great for these young people here today.

Now that we've changed the world, it is time to change America and time to turn our attention to pressing challenges like how to give a pink slip to our slow-growth economy, and how to make America's families more like the Waltons and a little bit less like the Simpsons—[*laughter*]—how to take back our streets from the crack dealers and the criminals. Progress has been made, as I announced yesterday at the White House, in the casual use of cocaine by these teenagers, dramatic improvement, almost 60 percent down in the last 3 years. But we've still got a long way to go. We've got to win that battle.

This election year, we're told, is about how we can change to meet these challenges. But this election is not just about change because change has a flip side. It's called trust. When you get down to it, this election will be like every other. When you go into that voting booth and pull the curtain behind you, trust matters.

That's the way it should be. Many times in the White House late at night, the phone rings. Usually it's some young aide calling in about doublechecking the next day's schedule. But occasionally it's another voice, more serious, more solemn, carrying news of a coup in a powerful country or asking how we should stand up to the "Baghdad bully" halfway around the world. The American people need to know that the man who answers that phone has the experience, the seasoning, to do the right thing. I believe I have proved I am that man.

That is trust in the traditional sense. But people who've spent their lives in government forget that trust is even more than that. I'm a Texan, raised my children there, built my business there, voted there in every Presidential election since my first, the 1948 election, the year, if you'll go back and remember, some of you older types here, the year the press and the pundits counted out Harry Truman before the fight even began.

I believe our country's heartbeat can be felt in places like Neenah, Wisconsin, not Washington, DC. So I stake my claim in a simple philosophy: To lead a great nation, you must first trust the people that you lead. If you look at almost every important issue we face, you see a clear choice, a choice between those who put their faith in average Americans and those who put their faith solely in the Government. Let me explain what I mean, starting with the basics, home and family.

The most difficult question that many parents face is, who will care for the kids while we're working? A few years ago, Washington wanted to help, but the idea back there was to rock the cradle with the heavy hand of the bureaucracy. All the plans boiled down to creating some new kind of Government apparatus, like a "Pentagon" for child care.

I fought for a different approach, with the support of these Members of the United States Congress, and we won. Our landmark legislation allows parents, not the Government, to decide whether your children are cared for in a school, a relative's home, or a church. When it comes to raising children, I say, don't put your faith in the Government bureaucracy. Why not trust the parents, the ones who are responsible for bringing these kids up?

Now, what about our educational system? To renew America we must renew our schools. We all know this. Money alone is not going to do it. We already spend more money—this is a little scary—we already spend more money per student than almost any other country in the world, and our children still rank near the bottom in crucial subjects like math and science. Again, a lot of ideas floating around, most of them to pump more tax money into the same old system, the same old programs that have failed the American family. I say, try something different: Open up schools to competition, and trust you, trust you to decide whether you want your kids to learn in a

public school, a private school, or a religious school. School choice is the answer.

When it comes to education to give our kids a better chance, isn't it time to try something different? The old way has failed, has not worked. Why not trust the people?

What about Government regulation? Sure, some of it's necessary; some of it even essential. But if you believe that there is a Government solution to every problem, an alphabet agency for every issue, then you look at regulation not as a necessary evil but as a necessary way to rein in people's evil tendencies. It can lead to the same crazy behavior. Let me tell you a story about one crazy regulation affecting hardhats. Hardhats, that's right.

Here's what happened. Back in Washington, someone in an agency stumbled upon a potential national crisis, workers being infected from putting on someone else's hardhat. The alarms went off. The bureaucratic blood boiled. One small fact was overlooked. There wasn't a single documented case anywhere in the United States of America of anyone getting infected from wearing someone else's hardhat. That didn't deter the bureaucrat. So with the best of intentions, the rule was written: Every hardhat must be disinfected before one worker passed it on to another. Estimated cost to business: $13 million a year. Measurable benefit: slightly less than zero.

Now, there is a happy ending to this story, but only because we were there to give it one. We found the regulation before it hit the books and said America can survive without that particular hardhat regulation. But can you imagine what might have happened if these enterprising regulators had made their way into the vast, unregulated territory of lunch pails or thermos bottles? Think of the threat to the Nation. [*Laughter*]

Some believe the solution to our problems is more Government regulation. I take a very different view. I've put a moratorium on new Federal regulations, to give businesses like this one, growing enterprise business, giving it room to breathe and grow and create jobs for these young people here today. On child care, education, regulation, it is a matter of trust, trusting Americans to make their own choices.

The point is not to let people fend entirely for themselves. Americans are a generous people, and Government must never shirk its responsibilities. But programs have to give people a hand up and trust human ingenuity to take it from there.

You'll find a good example of what Government can do right here at Outlook. Last April I challenged the Nation's Governors to join me in a new national job training effort. I introduced a program called the "Youth Apprenticeship Act" in Congress. The program is geared especially to teenagers who want to work, who want to learn a skill, but may be tempted to drop out of school, true to form.

Then comes along Governor Thompson, Tommy Thompson. He's already reaching out to these young people. The youth apprenticeship program will encourage young people to complete a sound high school education while getting on-the-job training at great companies like Outlook. I salute Outlook and Governor Thompson for helping me create a work force that's ready for the challenges of the 21st century.

So I believe we can give Americans the tools. And then it's a matter of trust, trusting Americans to make their own choices. When it comes to the most pressing issue of the election year, revving up our economy, forgetting this idea of trust is not just a nuisance, it can be downright dangerous.

The revolutions of the past few years herald a new era of global economic competition, with free markets from Siberia to Santiago. Can the United States compete now that everyone is playing our game of free markets? Well, I know we can. Despite all the criticism you've heard lately, keep in mind just a few facts. Who is the largest, most envied economy in the entire world? The good ol' U.S.A.

Look at inflation, the Jesse James who robs the middle class of dreams. We have locked that crook in a maximum security cell, so he can't steal the paycheck of the working men and women of this country. The last time interest rates were this low, "The Brady Bunch" wasn't even in reruns yet. Despite all the stories about our problems, and we've got plenty, but despite all the stories, you are still the most productive workers in the entire world. You put these workers up against the English, the Germans, the Japanese, and you, you American taxpayers, you win; you American entrepreneurs and business people, you win; and the work force itself wins.

But while our economy is growing, it clearly has got to grow faster. The question is how. The other side suggests a simple two-part solution: First, raise Government spending, and second, raise taxes.

Now, as you evaluate their idea, keep this in mind. Here in Wisconsin, you already work 126 days just to pay your taxes before you earn a single dime to spend on the family. I don't know about you, but I don't want you to have to pay 127 days.

Let me just describe for you what I'm up against. In January I proposed a commonsense plan in the State of the Union Message, commonsense plan to get this economy moving faster, right now. The plan included tax incentives to encourage businesses to hire new workers, tax breaks for young families who want to buy that first home. If Congress had acted right away, half a million jobs would have been created for your neighbors, your family, and your friends.

But they didn't. Instead Congress sent back what you might call an anti-trust program: new Government spending and new taxes. So I vetoed their plan and sent it right back to them. And thanks to these Congressmen, that veto was upheld. I am still waiting, pressing for these incentives to get passed by the Senate and the House. I am still waiting almost 200 days later. This economic recovery plan is being held hostage, held hostage, and the ransom note reads, "Wait till after the election." Today I say to the Congress and the Senate, especially: Release the economy. Approve this jobs program, and put America back to work right now.

Speaking of numbers, this is a great place to speak about numbers, right here at Outlook: number 16 means Joe Montana; number 9, my dear friend with whom I attended the All-Star Game in San Diego, number 9, Ted Williams; number 15, a Packer named Starr. Here's a number for you, 38. Think hard now, 38. That's how many years the Democrats have controlled the House of Representatives. Get rid of number 38, and we can make America number one for sure for many years to come. If you want to change something, the one institution that hasn't changed, if you want to change something, change control of the United States House of Representatives, and watch what we can do for America.

I'm getting fired up for after our convention in August. [*Laughter*] You'll notice this has been relatively nonpartisan up until now. [*Laughter*] Relatively.

No, but you see, it all comes down to a question of trust. I trust you to spend and save your money more wisely than a budget planner in Washington.

You say this is all common sense, and I agree. But there's a certain type of person attracted to Government for whom the word "trust" has a strange meaning. Most of them have spent all their lives in Government and don't have much experience in the real world. Half my adult life spent in service and the other half trying to work for a living and make a paycheck and build a business, I think that's a good qualification for President of the United States of America. They say they want to put people first. But if you look real close, the people that they put first are all on a Government payroll.

I stand with the flag-waving, yes, and the God-fearing, yes, and the tax-paying, hardworking people of America. A leader of a free people must understand that Government can not only help, it can hinder. He must have the confidence to say, "I trust you. I trust the people." Ultimately you must decide who you trust, who has the experience, the ideals, and the ideas to find the appropriate balance.

Yes, America will change, just as we have changed the entire world. The question now is who will change America for the better? It won't be people whose only enthusiasm is for Government, who measure progress by programs created and special interests satisfied.

If you want to know who's going to change America, look around you. Look around. It's going to be the guy who works an extra shift every week so his son can go to the school of his choice. It's going to be the small-business woman who takes a risk on a new product, the computer hacker working in a lonely garage, the merit scholar from south central L.A., the entrepreneur with a crazy idea of putting players' faces on cards and turning us all into wonderful kids once again.

There's your answer, some of it, I might say, sitting right back here: These apprentices, wanting to work, wanting to learn. There's your answer: The American people are going to change America. But only if they have a Government, particularly a Congress, with the wisdom to know its own limits, with a leadership who knows where the true American imagination lies. Countries around the world have at long last understood the power of trusting the people. America will change by reaffirming the lesson that we have taught the entire world, by trusting a leader who trusts you.

It is a great pleasure to be back in the wonderful State of Wisconsin. Thank you all. May God bless the United States of America, the greatest, freest country on the face of the Earth. Thank you very, very much.

*Note: The President spoke at 2:09 p.m. at Outlook Graphics Corp. In his remarks, he referred to David Erdmann, president of the corporation.*

## Letter to Congressional Leaders Transmitting Proposed Legislation on Wyoming Public Lands Wilderness Designation
*July 27, 1992*

*Dear Mr. Speaker:  (Dear Mr. President:)*

I am pleased to submit for congressional consideration and passage the "Wyoming Public Lands Wilderness Act".

The Federal Land Policy and Management Act of 1976 (FLPMA), (43 U.S.C. 1701, *et seq.*), directs the Secretary of the Interior to review the wilderness potential of the public lands.

The review of the areas identified in Wyoming began immediately after the enactment of FLPMA and has now been completed. Approximately 577,504 acres of public lands in 42 areas in Wyoming met the minimum wilderness criteria and were designated as wilderness study areas (WSAs). These WSAs were studied and analyzed during the review process and the results documented in nine environmental impact statements and one instant study area report.

Based on the studies and reviews of the WSAs, the Secretary of the Interior is recommending that all or part of 21 of the WSAs, totaling 240,364 acres of public lands, be designated as part of the National Wilderness Preservation System. From these 21 WSAs, the Secretary proposes to designate 20 wilderness areas by consolidating two WSAs into one wilderness area.

I concur with the Secretary of the Interior's recommendations and am pleased to recommend designation of the 20 areas (totalling 240,364 acres) identified in the enclosed draft legislation as additions to the National Wilderness Preservation System.

The proposed additions represent the diversity of wilderness values in the State of Wyoming. These range from the badlands of Adobetown and the Honeycomb Buttes, to the canyon of the Sweetwater River, to the subalpine regions of the Ferris Mountains and Raymond Mountain. These areas span a wide variety of Wyoming landforms, ecosystems, and other natural systems and features. Their inclusion in the wilderness system will improve the geographic distribution of wilderness areas in Wyoming, and will complement existing areas of congressionally designated wilderness. They will provide new and outstanding opportunities for solitude and unconfined recreation.

The enclosed draft legislation provides that designation as wilderness shall not constitute a reservation of water or water rights for wilderness purposes. This is consistent with the fact that the Congress did not establish a Federal reserved water right for wilderness purposes. The Administration has established the policy that, where it is necessary to obtain water rights for wilderness purposes in a specific wilderness area, water rights would be sought from the State by filing under State water laws. Furthermore, it is the policy of the Administration that the designation of wilderness areas should not interfere with the use of water rights, State water administration, or the use of a State's interstate water allocation.

The draft legislation also provides for access to wilderness areas by Indian people for traditional cultural and religious purposes. Access by the general public may be limited in order to protect the privacy of religious cultural activities taking place in specific wilderness areas. In addition, to the fullest extent practicable, the Department of the Interior will coordinate with the Department of Defense to minimize the impact of any overflights during these religious cultural activities.

I further concur with the Secretary of the Interior that all or part of 30 of the WSAs encompassing 337,140 acres are not suitable for preservation as wilderness.

Also enclosed are a letter and report from the Secretary of the Interior concerning the WSAs discussed above and a section-by-section analysis of the draft legislation. I urge the Congress to act expeditiously and favorably on the proposed legislation so that the natural resources of these WSAs in Wyoming may be protected and preserved.

Sincerely,

GEORGE BUSH

*Note: Identical letters were sent to Thomas S. Foley, Speaker of the House of Represent-* atives, and Dan Quayle, President of the Senate.

# Message to the Congress Transmitting the Report of the National Science Foundation
*July 27, 1992*

*To the Congress of the United States:*

In accordance with 42 U.S.C. 1863(j)(1), I transmit herewith the annual report of the National Science Foundation for Fiscal Year 1991.

The White House,
July 27, 1992.

GEORGE BUSH

# Statement by Press Secretary Fitzwater on the Situation in Somalia
*July 27, 1992*

The tragedy in Somalia, where vast numbers of people are suffering and dying from famine caused by a senseless civil war, requires the urgent attention of the international community. We strongly support the proposals of U.N. Secretary-General Boutros Boutros-Ghali to mobilize the international community to meet these urgent humanitarian needs and to convince the warring Somali factions to end the fighting. We urge the Security Council at its meeting today to take the actions needed to accelerate the delivery of food and medicine and to promote a peaceful settlement of this dispute.

The United States stands ready to do its part to support these efforts. We have committed $63 million over the past 2 years for humanitarian relief including airlifts of food and medical supplies. We will commit additional resources as needed. However, more must be done to create conditions where this vital assistance can reach the people who so desperately need it.

First and foremost, it is imperative that the leaders of the Somali factions themselves put the needs of their own people first and allow the food to reach all Somalis in need. We urge the United Nations to move as quickly as possible to deploy an effective number of security guards to permit relief supplies to move into and within Somalia. We are prepared to contribute generously to fund such an effort.

# White House Fact Sheet: The State of Wisconsin's Two-Tier Welfare Demonstration Project
*July 27, 1992*

The President today announced approval of a second Federal waiver for the State of Wisconsin's welfare reform effort. The waivers will enable Wisconsin to implement a two-tier welfare benefit. Recipients of Aid to Families with Dependent Children welfare benefits who are new arrivals to Wisconsin would receive the benefit level paid in that person's State of origin, regardless of whether the State of origin's rate is higher or lower than Wisconsin's.

### The Problem

Wisconsin's survey of new welfare recipients in Milwaukee County for June 1992 found 16 percent had moved to Wisconsin, applied for welfare benefits within 90 days of arriving in the State, and had never previously lived in Wisconsin. Of this group, 28 percent had moved from Illinois.

In explaining why it seeks waivers, Wisconsin notes that, except for Minnesota, welfare benefits in all adjoining and nearby States are lower than in Wisconsin. Wisconsin's welfare benefit for a family of three is $517 per month. The level in Illinois, the most populous adjoining State, is $367 per month for a family of three. Payments are $288 per month in Indiana, $426 in Iowa, and $532 in Minnesota for families of three.

### The President's Proposal

In his State of the Union Address, the President pledged to help any State attempting to reform its welfare system to promote individual responsibility by making it easier to obtain quickly any waiver of Federal regulations that may be required.

Today's is the sixth such waiver to be approved since the State of the Union. It is the second for Wisconsin; Wisconsin received its first waiver on April 17. Other waivers have been approved for California, Maryland, New Jersey, and Oregon.

### Wisconsin's Two-Tier Welfare Demonstration Project

The project will run for 3 years in up to six Wisconsin counties. The two-tier benefit will be in effect in Milwaukee, Kenosha, Racine, and up to three other counties. In those counties, AFDC benefits for a new arrival in the State would be paid at the level in that person's State of origin, regardless of whether the State of origin's rate is higher or lower than Wisconsin's. A person arriving in the State to take a job who is employed for at least 90 days and subsequently seeks AFDC will be paid at the Wisconsin rate. A person who is a former Wisconsin resident for at least 6 months will also be paid at the Wisconsin rate.

Results in the counties where the two-tier benefit is in effect will be compared to three other counties and the balance of the State where the two-tier benefit will not be in effect. The project will operate for 3 years, after which its effects will be evaluated to assess whether AFDC recipients move to the State for the purposes of obtaining higher AFDC benefits.

## White House Fact Sheet: The Wisconsin Youth Apprenticeship Program
*July 27, 1992*

Today the President commended Wisconsin Governor Tommy Thompson for his efforts in developing a statewide youth apprenticeship program. The Wisconsin youth apprenticeship program, undertaken in partnership with the U.S. Department of Labor, which provided $200,000 in seed money to the State, will provide an integrated statewide approach to the education and job training needs of students throughout the State.

### The Problem

Upwards of one-fifth of American students drop out of high school. Most experience difficulty in securing permanent employment. Few have the skills that will enable them to succeed in today's work force. The rapid pace of technical innovation demands not only higher skills but also higher levels of educational achievement.

Many of those students who drop out view high school as primarily preparation for college. They do not consider high school relevant to what they intend to do in the future. Apprenticeship programs, which in many countries serve as a bridge between school and work, are not generally available as an option to U.S. high school students.

### The President's Proposal

The President's proposed "Youth Apprenticeship Act of 1992," submitted to Congress on May 13, 1992, would facilitate developing youth apprenticeship programs. The Federal role includes program certifi-

cation and seed money. A description of this proposed legislation is outlined in an April 14, 1992, White House fact sheet.

In response to the President's directive to Secretary of Labor Lynn Martin to work with States to encourage apprenticeship initiatives, youth apprenticeship research and demonstration projects have been initiated in six States including Wisconsin.

*Note: The fact sheet issued by the Office of the Press Secretary also contained a detailed description of the Wisconsin program.*

# Remarks to Hispanic Business Leaders
## *July 28, 1992*

Nice to see you all. Thank you, and welcome to the Rose Garden. May I just say a word at the beginning of the great confidence I have in Secretary Barbara Franklin, our new Secretary of Commerce, and in our very able Ambassador, Carla Hills, who is doing a superb job hammering out the details, trying to achieve this NAFTA agreement; also continuing to work, both of them, on the need to get a worldwide agreement on successful conclusion to the Uruguay round of GATT. But we are very, very fortunate in this country to have this kind of leadership in these two terribly important jobs.

May I say to Jesus Chavarria, the editor and publisher of Hispanic Business, thank you for your leadership in bringing together so many dynamic men and women from the Hispanic-owned businesses. Frankly—you want to hear it for him? Okay, let's do it. [*Applause*] Why don't you stand up?

But it's a wonderful thing that you do, and I'm sure everybody here would agree with that. But people across the country ought to know of this and ought to agree because, really, you enliven this country. You're keeping America great, all these businesspeople here. And we salute you.

We do believe in the future, and we know how to get there. Obviously, our future depends on freedom. Freedom works, and freedom is right. And as I see this free economic system working with you

at the helms, you are the heroes of the economy because you create jobs, you meet a payroll. The only people with a tougher challenge might be either one of two people: the coach of the Angolan basketball team—[*laughter*]—or maybe, really, the guy that shot the arrow to light the torch. You talk about courage. Brent Scowcroft said, "I think somebody was up there with a cigarette lighter just in case it missed." [*Laughter*] But nevertheless—hey, wait a minute, we've got to be serious here.

You have come to Washington at a tough time, too late for the cherry blossoms, just in time for the humidity. And today I'd like to add a little heat because I really have something that's on my mind.

The economy is growing, albeit too slowly. Hispanic-owned businesses are in the vanguard of this growth, in the forefront of creating new, good jobs for Americans. And we need to grow faster. And we know what's holding us back. Let me sum it up in a simple sentence: Government is too big. The Government side is too big, and it spends too much. An old guard of tax-and-spend politicians has controlled Congress for most of 40 years. And believe me, that is a fact. Already this year I've given Congress a choice between economic growth and big Government. And Congress sided with the big Government.

Here's what happened. And I recite this

history because I think it's important you have it in mind when you go up to Capitol Hill. In January I proposed a commonsense, comprehensive plan to get this economy moving faster, right then. The plan includes tax incentives to encourage businesses to hire new workers and breaks for young families who want to buy a first home. Half a million jobs would have been created if the Congress had acted right away.

That didn't happen. Instead Congress passed a package of new Government spending and new taxes. They knew I would have to veto that package. And so I did. I sent the plan back, and I'm still waiting almost 200 days later. This economic recovery plan is being held hostage, and the ransom note reads, I think we all know this, "Wait until after the election."

We need that first-time credit. We need the investment tax allowance. We need to change these IRA's. We need to move on capital gains to create more small businesses. The party that controls Congress is holding jobs and free enterprise hostage. They talk about class warfare, about squeezing more from the rich. What they don't say is that more than half of those affected by the proposed hike in individual tax rates are family farmers, small-business men and women, people just like yourselves. So you are out there trying to create jobs, and you need a pat on the back, not $100 billion in new taxes and Federal mandates on your shoulders.

I do understand that you're going up to Capitol Hill later, and I'd ask you to take a message up there with you: Tell the Members we need quicker growth now, and tell them to approve these growth initiatives that are still up there without delay. Tell them to release the economy and approve the jobs program and put America back to work right now.

We're together today because we also share a vision for the long term. We want to build a solid future, a future for our country in the world economy. And one of the most exciting developments in our Nation's history is coming now to fruition. You've heard about it here this morning. I'm talking, obviously, about the North American free trade agreement. Our negotiators reported solid progress from meet-

ings in Mexico last weekend. And they're going to meet again, I think, in just a few days. We're very close to completing an agreement. And that agreement will mean more jobs, more growth, more opportunity for American workers.

Look at the numbers. During the recent partial opening of the Mexican market since 1986, U.S. exports to Mexico have almost tripled. They have almost tripled. More than 600,000 American workers now owe their jobs to trade with Mexico. We enjoy a robust trade surplus with Mexico, $2.1 billion last year. And it's estimated that we'll achieve a surplus of more than $8 billion this year. The new jobs created by trade with Mexico are to be found not only in the border States but all across the country. Our top 10 States exporting to Mexico, let me just click off some, include Michigan, Illinois, New York, Pennsylvania, and Florida. They don't exactly border the Rio Grande.

When the trade agreement goes to Congress, not if but when, we are going to need the utmost help from each and every one of you. Please don't have any illusions that this is going to be an easy fight. The leadership of Hispanic business men and women was crucial, crucial in winning that Fast Track effort that I heard Carla discussing just before I came out here. This new round of the battle will make Fast Track seem easy by comparison; we know that. But we are ready, and we've got to be sure we keep— the battle itself for this must be nonpartisan or bipartisan or however you want to look at it. We need support from everybody to get this done.

We've consulted closely with the Congress and with business leaders every step of the way in these negotiations. Again, I just can't tell you the number of hours that Carla Hills and her team has spent, properly so, in my view, but with the various business and labor and environmental interests all across our country, keeping them informed, getting their suggestions, bringing them along. We made commitments to Congress last year, and we are going to meet each and every one of them. And when we wrap up the agreement, it's going to be a good deal for American consumers and businesses and especially for American workers.

To me, ideas like free trade are worth fighting for because, really, you've got to put it in the broad context. We're fighting for our children's futures. I know that's not politically popular in all places. I know there's an awful lot of special interests that are lined up against a potential free trade agreement; we understand that.

Too many of us in national politics often act like an old South Carolina Senator some of you may remember, Olin Johnston. He didn't like to cover anything controversial in these newsletters that he sent out to his constituents. He told his aide, "Just put in a column about communism." The aide complied, writing a crackerjack column exposing the evils of communism, putting the good Senator squarely on the side of America. The Senator read the draft, and he said, "Son, how many Communists do you think we have in South Carolina?" The aide answered, "Well, I suppose maybe five or six." And the Senator replied, "Well, just make sure they don't get this newsletter." [*Laughter*]

Well, I guess Carla knows and Barbara knows and I know that more than five or six people are going to stand against free trade. But I'm not going to back down. You know it's right, and I know it's right. And just on this one, trust me to do what is right for America and to do what's right for the future.

So I hope you'll agree with me. And inasmuch as NAFTA—we're talking about mainly Mexico today, I might peripherally say I am very proud that we have such a good bilateral relationship with that important republic to our south. It's never been better. And once again, I'd like to salute President Carlos Salinas, the President of Mexico, who's working very closely with us to bring this agreement to fulfillment.

And one last point I want to make. There isn't any political timing on this. Carla explained to you the timing, the realities of the law and what we must comply with and how we must do it. But in spite of opposition, nobody is going to turn this one into a political football because we're going forward to do something what is right for the United States.

So thank you all very much for what the Hispanic businessmen and businesswomen are doing to build a very solid foundation for the future. And on this very beautiful day, may God bless you all and the United States of America.

Thank you very, very much.

*Note: The President spoke at 9:35 a.m. in the Rose Garden at the White House.*

# Message to the Senate Transmitting the Russia-United States Investment Treaty
*July 28, 1992*

*To the Senate of the United States:*

With a view to receiving the advice and consent of the Senate to ratification, I transmit herewith the Treaty Between the United States of America and the Russian Federation Concerning the Encouragement and Reciprocal Protection of Investment, with Protocol and related exchanges of letters, signed at Washington on June 17, 1992. I transmit also, for the information of the Senate, the report of the Department of State with respect to this treaty.

This treaty creates a favorable legal framework for U.S. investment in Russia. By adopting the treaty's high standards for protection of U.S. investment, Russia seeks to encourage the U.S. private sector to invest in Russia. For the United States Government, the treaty serves the goals of aiding Russia's transition to a market economy and of strengthening our bilateral economic ties.

In addition, the treaty is fully consistent with U.S. policy toward international investment. A specific tenet, reflected in this treaty, is that U.S. investment abroad and foreign investment in the United States should receive fair, equitable, and nondiscriminatory treatment. Under this treaty, the Parties also agree to international law standards for expropriation and expropriation compensation; free transfers of funds associated with investments; and the option of the investor to resolve disputes with the host government through international arbitration.

I recommend that the Senate consider this treaty as soon as possible, and give its advice and consent to ratification of the treaty, with protocol and related exchanges of letters, at an early date.

GEORGE BUSH

The White House,
July 28, 1992.

## Statement by Press Secretary Fitzwater on the President's Meeting With President-Elect Sixto Duran-Ballen of Ecuador
*July 28, 1992*

The President met this afternoon with President-elect Sixto Duran of Ecuador. The President congratulated President-elect Duran on his election to the Presidency of Ecuador and commended the people of Ecuador for the peaceful, democratic way they have chosen their leaders in three Presidential elections since 1979. The President assured Mr. Duran that the United States wants to maintain excellent relations with his country and support Ecuador's ef-

forts at economic reform and regional narcotics cooperation.

President-elect Duran will be inaugurated on August 10, 1992. The United States will be represented by a special Presidential mission.

President Bush last met President-elect Duran in March of 1987, when he visited Ecuador in the aftermath of a major earthquake.

## Statement on Senate Action on the Alternative Minimum Tax
*July 29, 1992*

My national energy strategy was designed to increase domestic energy production, reduce our dependence on imports, promote conservation and efficiency, and create American jobs. Today, the Senate took a major step towards these important goals.

I am pleased the Senate overwhelmingly rejected an attempt to kill alternative mini-

mum tax (AMT) relief for independent oil and gas producers. AMT relief removes a disincentive to the production of American oil and gas at a time when we desperately need more domestically produced energy. It will free up more than $1 billion of capital over the next 5 years, capital that will enable us to make needed investments in America's future.

## Remarks at the Superconducting Super Collider Laboratory in Waxahachie, Texas
*July 30, 1992*

Thank you all so much for that introduction. Thanks for that welcome back home. Thank you so very much, and good morning everyone. Please be seated—never mind. [*Laughter*]

Joe Barton, thank you sir, for your kind introduction, your generous comments. And let me just say to you, some of whom are constituents, many friends, the confidence I have in this man knows no bounds. He's an outstanding Representative for this area of Texas in the United States Congress.

May I also acknowledge our dais companions: the Deputy Secretary for Energy that Joe talked to you about, Linda Stuntz; Jack Martin; Joe Cipriano; and of course, Dr. Roy Schwitters. Joe and Roy were kind enough to lead Linda and me on a tour of this impressive facility. And out there in the audience someplace, another I'm grateful to is Waxahachie's Mayor, Joe Grubbs. We salute him and thank him for his city's hospitality.

Now, the super collider. The super collider is one of the greatest scientific projects in the entire world. This place attracts scientific genius the way our U.S. basketball players attract autograph seekers over there in Barcelona. So for me it is an incredible honor to be among you and to hear of your dreams and accomplishments.

As much as any State, Texas is a land of old and new, a place where "boot" means something you wear on your feet and what you do to turn on your computer each morning. And so I come here to talk just a little bit about what we need to do to prepare for the economy of the 21st century.

I'd like to start with a story not about the economy but football, a story about a freshman who walked out onto the field over at S.M.U. for his first football practice. He told the coach, "Look, I can throw the ball 60 yards in a perfect spiral. I can run the 40 in 4.4. My punts usually carry 75 yards into the wind." The coach looked at this guy; he said, "Kid, everybody has a weakness. What's yours?" And this freshman said, "Well, some people might tell you I have a

tendency to exaggerate a little bit."

Well, when we look at our economy, we should resist the urge to exaggerate our problems. Sure we face some very stiff challenges, but let's not forget a few facts. We're the world's largest economy. No other nation sells more products outside its borders; exports tremendously high. Inflation is the lowest in two decades. And if you want to talk to the world's most productive workers, you don't have to brush up on your Japanese or your German. The "Dream Team" of workers can be found right here in the United States of America.

So the question today is not can America compete; we know we can do that. The question is how do we stay number one and share our prosperity with more Americans and create more jobs for the American worker.

First, we face some short-term challenges. This morning the new economic numbers came out; they were released, telling you something you probably can pick up from conversations down at the local hardware store. The economy is growing, but it's got to grow faster. The economy grew at, what, 2.9 percent in the first quarter, and now—that was stronger than originally reported—but only 1.4 percent in the second. Housing sales, though, were much stronger than expected, up 8 percent in June. But overall, while the national economy is still growing, it is not growing fast enough.

Now, economists are going to tell you that this kind of uneven growth is not unusual. Since World War II, the first year of every recovery has shown the same pattern, with one quarter up and the next quarter down a little bit. Most of the economists, blue chip economists, predict that the economy is going to get stronger the rest of the year, and I believe that they're right. But we have got to act now to guarantee that.

On January 29th, I put forward a specific program to create new jobs with incentives to encourage businesses to hire new workers and help Americans who want to buy a new home. If that plan was in place, it would have been creating almost 15,000 new jobs a day, over a half a million jobs since February. For 183 days, in spite of the efforts of Joe Barton and a handful of others, the Congress has dillied and dallied while too many Americans are looking for work. They have made some progress, but we need this program of growth incentives passed right now. I hope you and all of these people will join me. I hope you'll join me in reminding Congress that we can't wait another 183 days. This sign is right: We the people need jobs. And we need to stimulate this economy and get those jobs. So help me pass that growth program. No more holding the American economy hostage to politics. Vote for this economic recovery program, and put more Americans to work now.

Now, that's the short-term program, but the real question on Americans' minds is: What about 5 years from now? What about 10 years, 20? Will America still be the world's leading economy? That's the question that I want to just focus on in this very special place this morning.

You know, our economy has changed in many ways since Barbara and I moved to Odessa 44 years ago, back in 1948. Back then, everybody was talking about new developments in television, atomic energy. This was just after World War II, and everyone in the neighborhood would turn out when somebody drove home in a brandnew car.

Today the new industries are computers, biotech, material science. You not only can get a new car; you can get a car with a new fax machine inside it. I can't quite understand for the life of me why anyone wants to get faxed something while they are going along at 65 miles an hour or 60.

Back when I started out in business, you could get a job based on what you could lift with your shoulders. Today a good job depends on what you can fit inside your head. Back then, America reigned supreme in steel and emerging industries like electronics, and today we're competing for the lead in emerging basic industries of the 21st century: computers, biotech, and material science.

It's fashionable this year for people to talk about change, about preparing for the future. But for the past 3 years, without a lot of hype or fanfare, we've put forward a series of dramatic ideas to change America so that we will win in the new economic olympics. From our unprecedented effort to open up new markets to our products to our program to make our grade and elementary schools as great as our colleges, from proposed record increases in basic laboratory research to new ways to help our companies get ideas from the laboratory to the marketplace, from new incentives for American business men and women to new efforts to rip away the regulations that hinder innovation, from top to bottom our entire program is designed to build America for the 21st century.

Now, some advocate a very different, different approach. They want to erect protectionist walls around our economy. They suggest that Government should invest directly in industry and that maybe it's time we try having some guy in Washington pick economic winners and losers.

I don't trust that approach. I trust our business men and women to create and innovate. I trust our workers to perform. I trust you, our best researchers and scientists, to lead America to a bigger and brighter future. All you need is some tools, and that's what our programs provide.

First, in an age when knowledge is king, we want Americans to wear the crown. I admit I am very proud of our young people's domination in swimming and basketball. But by the year 2000 I want our kids to be champions not just in the pool and on the court, I want them to be number one in the math class and in the science lab.

Our second priority is to extend America's heritage as the world's leader in technology. The new industries that I've mentioned this morning will potentially create millions of new jobs. We don't want them nurtured in Germany or Japan. We want them built here in Texas, here in America.

The programs that we've put forward to build America are all prejudiced, yes. They are prejudiced to the future, loyal only to our children. But we can make this investment without new taxes or budget-busting spending today.

The Federal Government already spends, here it is, $1.4 trillion of your money every year. So I have proposed to do what you do with your family budget every weekend: set priorities. Cut back on mandatory spending today, and do away with almost 250 Government programs that simply don't work anymore.

I've got a friend that many of you know, Randy Travis, and he sings something about love going on "forever and ever." Well, I'm not sure Randy would sing the same tune about a taxpayer-supported research program on the mating habits of minks. We've got to get rid of those needless programs.

But then we come to priorities. The super collider is big priority, a big part of our investment in America's future. When you talk basic research, this is the Louvre, the pyramids, Niagara Falls, all rolled into one.

Where once we reached for the Moon above to explore new frontiers of our universe, soon we'll begin to tunnel below to learn about the fundamental question of science, how our universe began.

A couple of weeks ago, I hosted a meeting on this project in the White House with seven preeminent scientists, including four Nobel prize winners, four Nobel laureates. They started talking about quarks and quenches, and I wondered for a minute if they had all spent the weekend bird hunting. But nevertheless—[*laughter*]—but beneath all the discussion about matter and antimatter was real talk about what matters to our kids' future: maintaining America's technological supremacy.

History has shown again and again that by pushing technology to ever-higher levels of accomplishment, we can achieve immensely practical consequences. To give you just one example, at Argonne Laboratories years ago, scientists were trying to purify liquid hydrogen for use with what was then the world's largest accelerator. They ended up figuring out a way to make artificial kidneys for just $15 apiece. That resulted from this fundamental science. The same kind of developments will occur right here, on a scale never before imagined. Here, for example, is where a new electronics industry is going to be born.

Some in Congress don't see it this way. They talk a good game about investment.

While they proclaim to be "future's friend" they have repeatedly blocked programs I have put forward in education and research. And now, they've set their sights on the super collider.

The House last month voted to shut down this project, the House of Representatives, in spite of the heroic efforts of this scientist, this Congressman with me here today, and this Deputy Secretary of Energy with me here today. Now, the Senate will consider it soon. And no one should be under any illusion: Savings from killing the super collider will not be used to reduce the deficit, as some said.

Some Members of Congress want to use this money to support organized interests whose backing they need in an election year. They will squander the taxpayer's money today rather than invest in our economy with tomorrow in sight. Make no mistake: This is a battle being waged right now in the Congress between the patrons of the past, and the architects of the future. And that is every one of you standing here today.

It may not be popular in all places, but I am determined, election year or not, to do what is right for America. Today I say: I stand with our young people who want the jobs of tomorrow. I stand with our future. And I will fight hard and continue to fight hard for the super collider, and call everybody necessary to get them to do what is right by science and technology.

Five hundred years ago this Monday, a man named Columbus set sail on a journey that brought him to the shores of this great land. But in many respects, America's voyage is never-ending. Centuries after Columbus set sail, our forebears tread this soil in wagon trains, and two centuries after that, scientists at Johnson Space Center watched as brave Americans set sail for the stars.

Today, new frontiers beckon; new discoveries await; new progress lies before us. Our adventure is not to sail the open ocean but rather to go to the edge of the universe and see the birth of space and of time. Our vessel is not called *Santa Maria*, it is the super collider. But human imagination is still our compass and human ingenuity and yearning for progress our only power. To those who would sacrifice tomorrow for today, I say: Trust in America's future. Trust in America's incredible capacity for renewal and innovation. Trust in the spirit that is here today, for ours is an eternal voyage to greatness. And each and every one of you is a part of that voyage.

Thank you for listening. May God bless Texas, and God bless the United States of America. Thank you very much.

*Note: The President spoke at 10:32 a.m. in the String Test Building. In his remarks, he referred to Jack Martin, chairman, Texas National Research Commission; Joseph Cipriano, director of the Superconducting Super Collider Project, Department of Energy; and Roy Schwitters, Director, Superconducting Super Collider Laboratory.*

## Remarks to Odetics, Inc., Associates in Anaheim, California
*July 30, 1992*

Thank you very much for that wonderfully warm Odetics welcome. Joel, let me tell you why Odetics was selected: its innovation, achievement, and attitude. May I thank your fellow founders, Mr. Gudmundson, Mr. Muensch, Daly, Schulz, and Jim Welch for the hospitality, and all of you most of all for this hospitality.

On board every American space shuttle is Odetics. You're everywhere I'm told, in the security camera, in the convenience store, and the corner ATM machine. I've always wondered where all this stuff came from. I think you've done for robotics what the guy at that Olympics ceremony has done for the under fire archery, if you remember that fellow. [*Laughter*]

As Joel pointed out to me early on, the credit goes to the people behind the technology, the Odetics associates, the workers here who have done such a great job.

Barbara was especially thrilled when she heard I was coming out here. She said, "If everything you tell me about Odetics is true, then maybe you can find someone out there who can teach you how to set the time on our VCR." We need help. I don't know how you all handle it; we just leave ours flashing—[*laughter*]—12:00, 12:00. That way you're right two times every 24 hours. [*Laughter*]

I think you all have played a significant part in what I believe is the central triumph of our time, the free world's great victory in the cold war. But as you know, that triumph means changes in the very

industry that helped us carry the day. Many defense-related firms are grappling with the new realities, and not all are doing it with the success that you're having right here.

We know we can reduce defense spending, cut it substantially and responsibly. The victory in the cold war makes it mandatory for a President to do just that. And I have proposed a sensible defense build-down, a blueprint that recognizes, post-cold-war realities but still gives this country the muscle that we need to meet whatever danger comes our way.

We also know that we need to help defense firms and defense workers make the adjustment, to help technology-intensive companies like yours compete and win in the economic olympics, where the prizes aren't medals, but they're good jobs, and they're bigger paychecks.

I happen to believe that the best defense conversion program is a strong national economy, and that is my first and overriding priority. And this morning there were some economic numbers out showing that— you can probably pick this up from conversations with your neighbors—the American economy is growing nationally, but not fast enough. Most economists predict the economy's going to get stronger the rest of the year nationally. That's true, I believe. But your friends and neighbors do not want to wait for new jobs to be created; they want them now.

On January 29th, I put forward a specific program to spur the economic economy, would not have increased this deficit, but to spur the economic economy with incentives to encourage businesses to hire new workers and help Americans who want to buy a home. If that plan was in place, it would have created 15,000 jobs a day, over half a million jobs since February. For 183 days, the Congress has dillydallied with this plan while we could be creating new jobs for Americans.

So do me a favor, help me send the United States Congress a message, the one institution that hasn't changed control for 38 years: Don't hold the American economy hostage to politics. Tell them to vote for a recovery program and get this country back to work right now.

A stronger economy is going to help a lot of your associates in related companies who might be looking for work these days. But we also need to help the defense firms and the workers make the adjustment and transfer your technological expertise to other parts of our economy.

That's the idea behind what we call a national technology initiative to help bring new technologies, those that have been developed at taxpayers' expense in our labs, out of the Federal labs and into the marketplace. And that's why we're pioneering a new program to help members of the defense community, civilian and military, find new careers in America's classrooms.

It's why we're doing away with something called—this is technical—but called the recoupment fee. This is a tax charged against military and commercial products sold to customers other than the U.S. Government. These fees hurt American companies, American workers by making it more difficult for them to compete for business here and abroad. I've told the Secretary of Defense to eliminate these fees. If the Government unties the hands of businesses, I know that we can beat the pants off foreign competition. I think we can help through this transition.

But, you know, as another Californian used to say, "Peace through strength never goes out of style." And we cannot lose sight of the fact that for all the great gains that we've made for freedom and for all the peace of mind we've secured for our children because of the elimination or certainly

the reduction, significant reduction of the threat of nuclear war, the world still is a dangerous place.

I think back to the oath that I took on the Capitol steps there when I first became President, to preserve, to protect, and to defend the Constitution of the United States, and of the trust placed in me, the trust I've done my best to repay to keep this Nation safe and secure. I am proud of these accomplishments here and thankful that we've been able to give the order that so many Presidents long to give, for many of our nuclear forces to stand down from alert.

Yet in many ways, I know that our world today is more uncertain, far more unpredictable than the world we left behind. The Soviet bear, that unified international Communist Soviet bear, may be extinct, but there are still plenty of wolves out there in the world, renegade rulers, outlaw regimes, terrorist regimes, Baghdad bullies. I won't allow them to get a finger on the nuclear trigger. This President, will never allow a lone wolf to endanger American security. We owe that to these kids right here today. Yes, the world is a safer place, but we've got to keep it safe.

I've been told about a certain political speech not too many weeks ago. I missed it; I was fishing in Wyoming. [*Laughter*] It went on about the future of the country, I'm told, for about an hour. Out of all that time, that speech spent about one minute on the national security of this Nation, one minute, 141 words to be exact. If you blinked or had to do something else or even heated up a ham and cheese sandwich in the microwave, you missed the entire part about the national security and world peace.

Well, I guess it's all part of the change thing. But when it comes to national defense, I am worried that the other side is for change. They want to change the subject, and their silence speaks volumes. I don't believe that foreign policy and national security is a footnote, a loose end we wrap up and then safely forget. The defense budget is more than a piggy bank for folks who want to get busy beating swords into pork barrels. We've got to fight to keep this country sufficiently strong.

So someone has to set the record straight and has to speak up for the muscle—not the waste, not that we can't cut—but has to speak up for the needed muscle that gives meaning to American leadership. Someone has to say, even now that we've won the cold war: America is safe, but just so long as America stays strong.

If we took the course that some recommend, we literally wouldn't know what we're missing until we found it out in the heat of battle. But the truth is that Odetics and other frontline firms around California, you'd feel it first. The other side proposes to cut nearly $60 billion in defense cuts beyond and below the level we see as the minimum necessary for national security, and we cannot let that happen: almost 4 times more cuts than what we believe is responsible so that I can certify to these young people here that your future is going to be safe.

Cuts of that magnitude would jeopardize America's ability to defend our citizens, our interests, and our ideals. Let me bring it very close to home. Cuts of that magnitude would cost workers in the defense industry as many as one million jobs. So we've got two reasons. The first and most important, we've got to do what my oath committed me to do: guarantee the national security of this country. Then we've got to also think about the American worker and not needlessly push him out of work.

I know that the California economy is struggling these days, and that some of it comes, and I'll accept the blame for this, from what I think are the responsible cuts that we've approved. As the cold war ended, it was appropriate that we make some defense cuts.

But think of the shockwaves that reckless defense cuts would touch off in construction and electronics and aerospace. Think of what those layoffs will do to housing prices. Think of the workers, think of the families,

from die cutters and welders to design teams and engineers thrown out of work and then over onto the welfare.

You know, when a ship is decommissioned, it's said to be put in mothballs. Well, if we follow that plan, the opposition's plan, the only industry hiring would be the mothball industry. We cannot let that happen to our country.

As long as I am President, I make this pledge: I will not let our economy be wrecked and our security threatened by the politically appealing idea of gutting our national defense. They want to gut the defense, and we cannot let that happen.

So in conclusion let me just say, this year you're going to hear a lot of talk about change. But to me this election, like every other one, is also about trust. Who do you trust to change America? Who do you trust, not to do what's easy or sounds good, might be responding to some poll out there, but to do what is right for you and for your children and for the families of this country and for America?

I make this pledge to you, not to do what is unwise or politically expedient, but I pledge to fulfill the trust that you have placed in me by doing what is right for this country.

I am very, very pleased to be here. Now I will end with the word that I know will get me a nice standing ovation: Odetics! Go for it!

Thank you very much.

*Note: The President spoke at 1:53 p.m. at the automated tape library division of Odetics, Inc. In his remarks, he referred to company officers Joel Slutzky, chairman of the board and chief executive officer; Crandall L. Gudmundson, president; Gerry Muensch, vice president of marketing; Kevin C. Daly, vice president and chief technical officer; Gordon Schulz, vice president of mechanical engineering; and James P. Welch, vice president of electrical engineering.*

## Message to the Senate Transmitting the Protocol to the Ireland-United States Friendship, Commerce, and Navigation Treaty
*July 30, 1992*

*To the Senate of the United States:*

With a view to receiving the advice and consent of the Senate to ratification, I transmit herewith the Protocol to the Treaty of Friendship, Commerce and Navigation between the United States of America and Ireland of January 21, 1950, signed at Washington on June 24, 1992. I transmit also, for the information of the Senate, the report of the Department of State with respect to this protocol.

This protocol will establish the legal basis by which the United States may issue investor (E–2) visas to qualified nationals of Ireland. The protocol modifies the U.S.-Ireland friendship, commerce, and navigation (FCN) treaty to allow for entry and sojourn of investors. This is a benefit provided in the large majority of U.S. FCN treaties. It is also a benefit already accorded to U.S. investors in Ireland who are eligible for visas that offer comparable benefits to those that would be accorded nationals of Ireland under E–2 visa status.

As I reaffirmed in my December 1991 policy statement, the United States has long championed the benefits of an open investment climate, both at home and abroad. U.S. policy is to welcome market-driven foreign investment and to permit capital to flow freely to seek its highest return. Ireland also provides an open investment climate. Visas for investors facilitate investment activity and thus directly support our mutual policy objectives of an open investment climate.

I recommend that the Senate consider this protocol as soon as possible and give its advice and consent to ratification of the protocol at an early date.

GEORGE BUSH

The White House,
July 30, 1992.

## Message to the Senate Transmitting the Protocol to the Finland-United States Friendship, Commerce, and Consular Rights Treaty
*July 30, 1992*

*To the Senate of the United States:*

With a view to receiving the advice and consent of the Senate to ratification, I transmit herewith the Protocol to the Treaty of Friendship, Commerce, and Consular Rights Between the United States of America and the Republic of Finland of February 13, 1934, as modified by the Protocol of December 4, 1952, signed at Washington on July 1, 1991. I transmit also, for the information of the Senate, the report of the Department of State with respect to this protocol.

This protocol will establish the legal basis by which the United States may issue investor (E–2) visas to qualified nationals of Finland. The protocol modifies the U.S.-Finland friendship, commerce, and navigation (FCN) treaty to allow for entry and sojourn of investors. This is a benefit provided in the large majority of U.S. FCN treaties. It is also a benefit already accorded to U.S. investors in Finland who are eligible for visas that offer comparable benefits to those that would be accorded nationals of Finland under E–2 visa status.

As I reaffirmed in my December 1991 policy statement, the United States has long championed the benefits of an open investment climate, both at home and abroad. U.S. policy is to welcome market-driven foreign investment and to permit capital to flow freely to seek its highest return. Finland also provides an open investment climate. Visas for investors facilitate invest-ment activity and thus directly support our mutual policy objectives of an open invest-ment climate.

I recommend that the Senate consider this protocol as soon as possible and give its advice and consent to ratification of the protocol at an early date.

GEORGE BUSH

The White House,
July 30, 1992.

## Statement by Deputy Press Secretary Smith on Deployment of C–130 Aircraft to Angola
*July 30, 1992*

In response to requests by Angolan Presi-dent dos Santos, UNITA President Savimbi, and U.N. Secretary-General Boutros-Ghali, the President has instructed the Depart-ment of Defense to deploy three U.S. C–130 aircraft to Angola for approximately 6 weeks. The aircraft will be used to support transportation of troops demobilized in ac-cordance with the peace accords between UNITA and the Angolan Government and to support the elections that will take place September 29–30.

Since assuming office, the Bush adminis-tration has worked to achieve a peaceful resolution of the civil conflict in Angola in a fashion that would permit that war-torn country to move into an era of peace and multiparty democracy. The fighting has ended, and Angola is now firmly embarked on the first free elections in its history. Ap-proximately 4 million citizens have already registered to vote for the first time in their lives. President Bush attaches high priority to ensuring that free and fair elections take place as scheduled and that all parties re-spect the outcome of the elections.

## White House Fact Sheet: The Bush Administration's Policies for an American Technological Revolution
*July 30, 1992*

The President today met with the scien-tists, management, and workers at the world's largest science and engineering project, the superconducting super collider (SSC). He reaffirmed his continuing strong support of the Federal investment in this unprecedented scientific undertaking which will provide broad societal benefits.

*The Problem*

Technological innovation is essential to sustained economic growth. Those nations that innovate most successfully will com-pete best in an increasingly integrated global economy.

International competitiveness requires needed investments in basic research and efficiently commercializing the results of that research. It involves a technology policy that recognizes the important role of entrepreneurs and the need for flexibility in deploying resources to their most efficient uses.

*The Bush Administration Principles*

Since 1989, President Bush has aggres-sively pushed a strong science and technolo-gy agenda, and he has proposed devoting an unprecedented level of resources to R&D.

The President's science and technology agenda relies on six basic principles:

The private sector must be free to deter-mine its own research priorities;

The Federal Government must promote sound tax policies that stimulate private sector investment in R&D and technological innovation;

The Federal Government must assure that its regulations do not impede firms from developing products or from bringing safe, new products to market;

The Federal Government must support a strong program of basic and applied R&D which provides broad societal benefits;

The Federal Government must work cooperatively with the private sector in the development of generic or enabling technologies;

Federally funded technology must be transferred swiftly and effectively to the private sector for commercialization.

The President has taken these six principles and developed a comprehensive strategy for enhancing America's technology prowess and competitiveness. It includes:

Opening up foreign markets to U.S. goods;

Accelerating technology transfer;

Investing in the future: Strengthening our knowledge base and increasing Federal support for emerging technologies;

Educating our students for a world of technology;

Coordinating with the private sector in consortia and other arrangements to develop generic or enabling technologies;

Stimulating private sector R&D through sound tax policies; and

Promoting technology through a sound regulatory system.

OPENING UP FOREIGN MARKETS TO U.S. GOODS

The U.S. remains the world leader in the export of scientific and technological knowledge. Our high-tech exports have increased by two-thirds since 1987, and we enjoy a $37 billion trade surplus of high-tech exports with the rest of the world. The President is determined to maintain this position by opening new foreign markets and by protecting the intellectual property rights of those on the leading edge of scientific and technological innovation.

1. *Bilateral Agreements With Japan.* The administration has opened Japanese markets to U.S. high-tech goods through trade agreements covering supercomputers, satellites, semiconductors, and amorphous metals.

2. *Intellectual Property Rights in the Uruguay Round.* The administration is currently negotiating to ensure that the U.S. science and engineering base is protected from foreign pirating of technology.

3. *North American Free Trade Agreement (NAFTA).* The administration is completing the negotiations on the NAFTA which will open new opportunities for American exporters and the free flow of investment capital into the technologically intensive fields of the environment, medicine, agriculture, electronics, and telecommunications.

4. *U.S./Asia Environmental Partnership.* This unprecedented coalition of U.S. and Asian government units, businesses, and community groups is working together to enhance Asia's environment. This will result in the greater export of American technological know-how and equipment.

ACCELERATING TECHNOLOGY TRANSFER

The Federal Government has invested billions of dollars in creating the world's finest, most advanced research laboratories. This valuable national resource can assist civilian research efforts to investigate and develop commercially viable technologies.

*Technology Transfer.* The FY 1993 budget proposes a significant increase in technology transfer activities, including almost 1,500 cooperative research and development agreements (CRADA's) between Government laboratories and private industry, an increase of 60 percent over the past 2 years; approximately 4,500 new invention disclosures; 2,000 patent applications; and almost 300 technology licenses awarded.

*The Administration's National Technology Initiative.* Ten conferences have been held across the country, and five more are scheduled between now and December 1, 1992. These conferences act as catalysts for creating new partnerships among Government, universities, and American companies to better translate new technologies into marketable goods and services. A list of the conferences is attached.

*Expanding the Role of the National Laboratories.* The FY 1993 budget proposes that national laboratories play a greater role in high priority areas of civilian applied

R&D by helping to form R&D consortia and other collaborative arrangements led by industry and academia.

## Remarks at a Breakfast With Community Service Clubs in Riverside, California
*July 31, 1992*

Thank you very, very much for that warm welcome. And Governor, my friend Pete Wilson, thank you for that kind and generous introduction. You stole most of what I had planned to say—[*laughter*]—but I don't want to take up too much of your Friday morning here. Let me just, before getting going, quickly thank some of our hosts: Jim Milam, who I met on the way in; Bill Bonnett; your able emcee, Bob Wolf, of the Lincoln Club, a man who also gave a fine introduction; Ken Calvert, a man who really can and will make a difference in Washington, DC; Paul Rout of the California Department of Social Services. And a quick hello to all you political types on the dais: Dave Kelly, Bill Leonard, Dan Hollingsworth, Ethel Silver. And I want to be sure to mention the various service clubs, particularly the Rotary, who I understand this is a routine breakfast meeting for Rotary here, but the other service clubs that joined in to make me feel so welcome.

This has been a big week for America, especially with Olympic games going on. I admit to being a special fan of Pablo Morales. He's a swimmer who missed out in '84. He didn't make the team in 1988, and then he came back this year to earn a gold medal at the ripe old age of 27. Now, I don't know why, but I kind of like a guy who proves that youth and inexperience are no match for maturity and determination. [*Laughter*]

We gather today at a moment of great change around the world; Pete touched on this. The past 4 years have been a rough time for Robert Ludlum and other fiction writers. With all that's been happening in the world, is there any more room left for imaginative scenarios? They said the Germans would never tear down the Berlin Wall. I remember the ridicule that President Reagan got when he stood and he said, "Take down that wall." A lot of people thought he was out of touch with reality, and he wasn't. They said Russians would never troop to the polls, but they are. They said the world would never come together to say "enough" to a Baghdad bully, but we did, and we will again if we have to. He is going to mind and match every one of those U.N. resolutions and live up to them. You believe me.

Now that we've changed the world, it is high time to change America. I believe our first priority must be to build an economy for the 21st century, a strong, vibrant economy that provides a good job for every American who wants one.

I wanted to come here and give a political speech. But out of total respect for the service clubs and recognizing the nonpolitical nature of these service clubs, I'm going to hold back.

But let me just tell those of you who are interested in politics, you wait 2 years from now—I mean 2 weeks from now—[*laughter*]—you wait, because I've been going through a little javelin catching for about 10 months from the political opposition. And I cannot wait for our convention to roll up my sleeves and go after them and tell the American people what's really going on. They've been dishing it out for about 10 months, helped by some on the editorial pages. Let's see if they can take it, starting 2 weeks from now. That's the way I feel about it.

Now, back to my nonpolitical self here. [*Laughter*] Today I want to spend a few minutes really talking about a big part of my strategy for America's future. It's something you all are interested in, and it sometimes transcends politics. I'm talking about reforming our welfare system. We can't afford the welfare system that we have today. The taxpayers know it; the recipients know it; the economists know it. Welfare is a system that literally wastes millions of tax dollars a year, and we can't afford that.

Welfare was designed to be temporary. Temporary. But today, more than half of all recipients receive a check for at least 8 years, and we can't afford that. Economic competitors are able to call on the ingenuity and industry of their entire society, and yet, welfare deprives our economy of millions of citizens who never learned the simple values of hard work and responsibility. We can't afford that system anymore.

Welfare punches a hole in the heart of the American dream. So let's fix the hole so we can fulfill the dream. This is not a new complaint, of course. We've known of welfare shortcomings for years, even decades. So today I invoke what you might call "the Willis Carrier principle." Willis Carrier is the guy who was responsible for your being here in Riverside this morning. Here's why: For centuries men and women have complained about hot, sticky weather, or in some cases, hot, dry weather, and never did anything about it. Then in 1914 Willis Carrier decided to do something about it, and he invented air conditioning. Here's the real interesting part: Carrier invented air conditioning in Buffalo, New York—[*laughter*]—which is like someone inventing a tanning bed out here in California.

But the Carrier principle is this: Talk doesn't matter; action counts. The good news about our welfare system is that today, without a lot of hype or fanfare, real action is taking place. Today my administration is releasing a paper that describes the changes, the progress, and yes, the opportunity. All our reforms are based on the simple belief that the principles that guide change are the principles that should never change.

One of those principles is an old idea called trust. I put my trust in people. I put my trust in people, not in the Federal Government. I believe that with the right incentives, people can be trusted to do the right thing.

The old welfare system failed because when a recipient wanted to get a job and earn money, welfare said no. And when you wanted to keep your family together, welfare said no. And when you saved to go to college, if your family was on welfare, welfare said no. I want a system that rewards responsibility, and I want a system that says yes.

Now, in making these changes, I've put my trust in the States more than Washington. That's the philosophical underpinning of our approach to welfare. So a big part of our effort is to give States the freedom to make the changes they want, new ideas, new opportunities, new flexibility.

I asked Gail Wilensky, my very able welfare reform specialist who works with me in the White House, asked her this: What is the basic problem? She said that key old thinkers in the United States Congress and old thinkers in the bureaucracy really believe—it's a conviction with them—really believe that welfare policy should be controlled and dictated from Washington, DC. They are 100 percent wrong. We must put the trust in the States and in the communities and thus in the people.

Our initiatives come in many forms, and they take many shapes. From job training programs right here in Riverside to our successful effort to make sure that every eligible 4-year-old gets a head start before kindergarten. That's why we've increased funding and requests for funding in Head Start so much.

Our first priority is remarkable in its simplicity: Welfare should be a force to keep families together. And as I've traveled across America the past 3 years to every single State, I've come to agree more and more with a certain silver-haired philosopher named Barbara Bush, who I wish were here today. She puts it this way: What happens in your house is far more important than what happens in the White House. The family is the foundation of our Nation. But it's crumbling in places, and we must strengthen the family. That means changing the way welfare works.

Welfare was originally designed to help widows and is still oriented toward single parents. So if two parents stay together and one works even part-time, they can lose their check. Fathers faced an awful Hobson's choice: the kids or the weekly payment. And far too many chose the payment.

We've given States like Wisconsin the freedom to experiment with allowing moms or dads to work without losing payments. I believe it's time we encourage families to stick together and fathers to stick around. But when dads do take off, we don't forget. And last year, we collected a record $6 billion in payments from these deadbeat fathers. If you're a dad and you're not around, my message is simple: There is nowhere for you to hide. You must do what's right by your family, by those children.

Keeping families together is a start, just a start. But we have to go even farther. We have to reward hard work, and we have to reward saving. You can't build a home without a hammer, and you can't build a dream without a job. Work isn't just good for our wallets. Work lifts us up. It elevates us. It teaches us values. It gives us a purpose.

But too often welfare has treated work as an afterthought or literally discouraged work altogether. So we've made a major commitment to job training, and we're pushing an idea that will allow recipients to pay for training and education and not have it cut from their benefits check. Training can't be an option, a thing I'll get around to later. We've given States like Oregon the authority to cut welfare checks if recipients don't learn a skill and get a job. And the point is this: 8 years is too long for someone to go without a skill or a purpose, for people who take welfare with no regard for self-improvement. We need to say, "Get a job, or get off the dole." Some recipients shop from State to State looking for the highest payments. We shouldn't encourage that practice; our system should not encourage that practice. States should be able to say, "You come here, you get a fair deal, not a free bonus."

Our third priority, perhaps the most important, is to promote personal responsibility. I hope you know how much I value children. One way to provide real relief from the craziness of Washington is sit down with a grandchild and read a book. But too many Americans, many on welfare, are having children they can't afford, can't support, just aren't ready for, and we have to do something about it. The system has to find a way to do something about that.

We're allowing States to decide if it's time to say, "No more money if you have another child." Let some try that. I know this is a tough call, a tough decision, but so is a system in which poverty is handed down from generation to generation.

These ideas are happening in Wisconsin, in New Jersey, in Oregon, in Maryland, and yes, right here in California. Pete Wilson is fighting hard against an entrenched bureaucracy there in Sacramento to end the practice of welfare shopping, to reward work, not welfare, to keep families together, to encourage learning, and to encourage responsibility.

So today I say to the people of California: Help your Governor make welfare work in California. It will encourage work. It will strengthen the family. And it will help save the most endangered species in California, the taxpayer.

Americans today lack faith in welfare. Recipients lack faith in welfare. But that's not welfare's greatest failing. Far greater is that welfare makes Americans lack faith in themselves.

The single mother riding the early bus in east L.A., the fearful teenager hiding from the gang in Chicago, the 6-year-old throwing rocks against the wall in Bed-Stuy back in New York, they all want what we want: a chance, hope, and opportunity. Giving them that chance is not just right for them; it is what is right for all of us. It is what is right for America. So let's work hard now to make these changes that will give dignity to those who have been stripped of their dignity.

Thank you very, very much for listening. Thanks for the welcome. And may God bless the United States of America.

*Note: The President spoke at 8:15 a.m. at the Riverside Convention Center. In his remarks, he referred to James R. Milam, president, Riverside Rotary Club; William H. Bonnett III, lieutenant governor, Riverside Kiwanis; Robert Wolf, chairman, Riverside County Lincoln Club; Kenneth S. Calvert, Republican candidate for Congress in the 43d district of California; Paul Rout, assistant director, social services division of Riverside County; State legislators David Kelly and Bill Leonard; Dan Hollingsworth, chair, Riverside County Republican Party;* *and Ethel Silver, chair, Victory '92 in Riverside County.*

## White House Fact Sheet: The President's Welfare Reform Strategy
*July 31, 1992*

In his State of the Union Address, President Bush said his administration would help States that wanted to reform their welfare systems by granting a quick review of their welfare waiver requests. The President today called for additional welfare reform demonstrations and legislative changes that would create more flexibility for States and localities. The President's plan is detailed in an administration paper on welfare reform released today.

### The Problem: Welfare Dependency

Currently there are more than 13 million recipients of Aid to Families with Dependent Children (AFDC) benefits, more than 25.5 million food stamps recipients, and more than 30 million people on Medicaid. The problem addressed by the administration's proposals and paper released today is not welfare receipt but welfare dependency. Half of all new public assistance recipients will be off the rolls in less than 2 years. But too many others will be trapped in the system. At any point in time, about two-thirds of those on welfare will be on for 8 or more years.

Important determinants of dependency are: teen motherhood; dropping out of school; no prior work experience.

The consequences of dependency can be severe: long-term poverty; entrapment in crime ridden neighborhoods; and higher chances that one's children will themselves become dependent on welfare.

These and other facts about welfare receipt and dependency are reviewed in a data appendix to the paper released today.

### The President's Principles

The President's fundamental goal for welfare reform is to create incentives that will enable welfare recipients to leave the system at the earliest possible time, as economically self-sufficient and responsible participants in their community.

At the same time, we have begun to open the doors of opportunity to one of the larger groups that has been relegated to welfare dependency, individuals with disabilities. The Americans with Disabilities Act, which took effect recently, gives these individuals the opportunity to gain control over their own lives and compete for jobs on a level playing field.

Federal programs that serve welfare recipients must instill responsibility and serve as a ladder of opportunity.

### Accomplishments

The paper released today reviews the administration's accomplishments, which include:

*Expanding the Earned Income Tax Credit (EITC),* which will provide an additional $18 billion in assistance to low-income working families over the next 5 years.

*Implementing the Job Opportunities and Basic Skills Training (JOBS) program.* Over $1 billion is available this year for job search, training, and education services, child care, and more than 500,000 welfare recipients are participating each month.

*Increasing child support enforcement* resulting in over $6 billion collected in fiscal year (FY) 1992.

*Expanding the Head Start program* to $2.8 billion in FY 1993 for all eligible 4-year-old children whose parents want them to participate, an increase of 127 percent since the President took office.

### Pending Proposals

The President's welfare reform proposals that have been pending before the Congress include:

*The Community Opportunity Act,* proposed in May 1991. This proposal would create broad authority to permit testing of innovative programs. It would allow proposals to come forward from State and local governments as well as grass roots groups.

*Increasing the AFDC assets limit.* States would be allowed to raise the amount of assets a family could accumulate and still stay on welfare from $1,000 to $10,000. Presently, individuals saving for college or to start a business may get thrown off welfare. The family's choice: spend any savings or lose your welfare benefits.

*Escrow Savings Accounts.* A demonstration would test whether long-term AFDC recipients would be more likely to work their way off welfare if, when they did, they received a bonus payment based on foregone AFDC benefits.

*Plan for Achieving Self-Support (PASS).* States would have the option of excluding income used by an AFDC family head to become self-employed when assessing whether a recipient qualifies for AFDC benefits.

### The President's Proposal

The President's proposal affirms his commitment to State innovation. Welfare waiver requests are being processed rapidly, and promising areas of innovation are identified.

### Review of welfare waiver requests

The President promised a quick review of welfare waiver applications in his State of the Union Address. Requests from Wisconsin, Oregon, Maryland, California, and New Jersey have been approved; requests from Utah and Michigan are under review.

The ideas included in those waivers include incentives for work and family formation, for immunization and obtaining preventive health services, and for responsible childbearing and school attendance.

### Areas in need of innovation

The administration today identified three areas where further innovation is important. Those areas are: (1) Providing comprehensive services for teen parents; (2) Promoting parental responsibility; and (3) Encouraging self-sufficiency.

Interventions for unmarried teen parents were identified as the highest priority. These individuals are the most likely to become welfare recipients, especially long-term recipients.

### Legislative changes

The President called for legislative changes to expand waiver authority, provide greater program flexibility, and strengthen programs.

1. Expanded waiver authority: Waiver authority comparable to the broad authority that today applies to AFDC will be proposed for food stamps and Federal housing programs. For example, current law does not allow for coordinated incentives and rules across cash, food, and housing assistance programs.

Waiver authority will also be proposed to allow the Davis-Bacon Act to be waived to allow the homeless and public housing residents to work in housing improvement projects. Those homeless and public housing residents who are gaining skills while working may not have the productivity needed to earn the wages required under Davis-Bacon.

2. Greater program flexibility: The administration will propose a targeted version of the Community Opportunity Act (COA) proposal it offered last year. The COA would allow States and communities to undertake broad reform programs that cut across multiple program lines. The new proposal, the Community Opportunity Pilot Project Act (COPPA), would make the authority initially available for projects in five sites. For example, the Atlanta Project, a community effort to address the problem of Atlanta's most troubled neighborhoods that former President Carter has discussed with President Bush, could redesign the operation of Federal programs in Atlanta under COPPA.

Legislation will be proposed to allow greater flexibility to State and local officials. The greatest additional flexibility will affect work requirements for welfare recipients. The legislative changes will:

Allow inclusion of food stamps and the value of having Medicaid in determining the amount a welfare recipient must "work off" as part of a workfare program;

Remove limitations on positions to which welfare recipients can be assigned to fulfill a workfare obligation;

Remove prohibitions on extended job search and requirements for intake assessment in JOBS, enabling State and local officials to give job search higher priority; and

Allow States to move from a "cash up front" to a "pay for performance" approach for welfare payments, with payment made after the performance of assigned program activities such as schooling or job search.

3. Stronger values: The requirement that AFDC recipients cooperate in establishing who is the father of their children would be expanded to include all relevant information and cooperation with followup efforts.

Separate and often unnecessarily stricter Federal requirements for evicting convicted felons from public housing would be repealed. This proposal would defer to local law instead of providing a separate Federal requirement for eviction.

# Appointment of Constance Horner as a Member of the Council of the Administrative Conference of the United States
*July 31, 1992*

The President today announced his intention to appoint Constance Horner, Assistant to the President and Director of Presidential Personnel, of the District of Columbia, as a member of the Council of the Administrative Conference of the United States for a term of 3 years. She would succeed James W. Cicconi.

Since 1991, Mrs. Horner has served as Assistant to the President and Director of Presidential Personnel. Prior to this, Mrs. Horner served as Deputy Secretary of the Department of Health and Human Services, 1989–91; Director of the Office of Personnel Management, 1985–90; Associate Director of the Office of Management and Budget, 1983–85; Director of VISTA and Acting Associate Director of ACTION, VISTA's parent agency; and Deputy Assistant Director of ACTION for policy and planning. She has also served on the President's Commission on White House Fellowships and the President's Commission on Executive Exchange.

Mrs. Horner graduated from the University of Pennsylvania (B.A., 1964) and the University of Chicago (M.A., 1967). She is also a fellow of the National Academy of Public Administration. Mrs. Horner was born February 24, 1942, in New Jersey. She is married, has two children, and resides in Washington, DC.

# *Appendix A*—Digest of Other White House Announcements

*The following list includes the President's public schedule and other items of general interest announced by the Office of the Press Secretary and not included elsewhere in this book.*

### January 1

In the morning, the President and Mrs. Bush greeted the American consulate community at the Ritz-Carlton Hotel, their residence during their stay in Sydney, Australia, which began on December 31, 1991. President Bush then went to Kirribilli House where he met with Prime Minister Paul Keating.

In the afternoon, the President and Mrs. Bush traveled to Canberra, Australia. Following an arrival ceremony at RAAF Base Fairbairn, they greeted the U.S. Embassy community at the residence of U.S. Ambassador to Australia Melvin Sembler, which was their residence during their stay in Canberra.

In the evening, the President and Mrs. Bush attended a reception and dinner hosted by the Governor-General and Mrs. Bill Hayden at Government House.

### January 2

In the morning, the President met at Parliament House with:
—Prime Minister Paul J. Keating;
—the Australian Cabinet;
—John Hewson, Leader of the Opposition;
—representatives of rural organizations;
—the Presidential business delegation.

In the afternoon, the President attended a working luncheon hosted by Prime Minister Keating at Parliament House. Later in the afternoon, the President and Mrs. Bush visited with Australian schoolchildren in Mural Hall at Parliament House.

That evening, the President and Mrs. Bush received a courtesy call by former Prime Minister and Mrs. Robert Hawke at the U.S. Ambassador's residence.

### January 3

In the morning, the President and Mrs. Bush participated in a wreath-laying ceremony at the Australian War Memorial. Following the ceremony, they traveled to Melbourne, Australia.

Upon their arrival in Melbourne, they went to the World Congress Centre, where the President met with U.S. and Australian business leaders. Following the meeting, the President and Mrs.

Bush attended a reception with the Coral Sea Commemorative Council and later greeted the American consulate community.

In the afternoon, the President and Mrs. Bush traveled to Singapore.

In the evening, following their arrival, they went to the Shangri-La Hotel, their residence during their stay in Singapore.

### January 4

In the morning, after an arrival ceremony at Istana Palace, the President and Mrs. Bush paid a courtesy call on President and Mrs. Wee Kim Wee. The President later met at the palace with Prime Minister Goh Chok Tong and with the Presidential business delegation.

In the afternoon, the President went to the Westin Stamford Hotel where he attended a meeting of the Association of South East Asian Nations (ASEAN) Business Council. He later attended a luncheon hosted by Prime Minister Goh at the Compass Rose Restaurant. The President and Mrs. Bush then greeted the American Embassy community at the Singapore American School. Later, the President met with Senior Minister Lee Kuan Yew at the Raffles Hotel.

In the evening, the President and Mrs. Bush attended a dinner hosted by President Wee at the Westin Plaza Hotel.

The President announced his intention to nominate Albert V. Casey, of Texas, to be chief executive officer of the Resolution Trust Corporation, a new position. From 1988 to 1991, Mr. Casey served as chairman and chief executive officer of First Republic Bank Corp. in Dallas, TX.

### January 5

In the morning, the President hosted a coffee in his suite for the ASEAN Ambassadors.

The President and Mrs. Bush then traveled to Seoul, South Korea. Following their arrival, they went to the National Cemetery for a wreath-laying ceremony. After the ceremony, they went to Ambassador Donald P. Gregg's residence, where they stayed during their visit to Seoul.

In the evening, the President and Mrs. Bush dined with President and Mrs. Roh Tae Woo and their respective national security advisers and ambassadors at the Blue House, President Roh's residence.

*January 6*

In the morning, the President and Mrs. Bush participated in the official arrival ceremony at the Blue House. The President then met with President Roh.

In the afternoon, the President greeted the leadership of the Korean National Assembly. Later, the President and Mrs. Bush greeted the American Embassy community at Collier Field House.

*January 7*

Following a morning departure ceremony, the President and Mrs. Bush traveled to Kyoto, Japan, where they toured the Imperial Palace.

In the afternoon, the President and Mrs. Bush had lunch at the Tsuruya Restaurant with former Prime Minister and Mrs. Toshiki Kaifu. Later, they traveled to Kashihara and then to Tokyo.

Following their evening arrival in Tokyo, the President and Mrs. Bush went to the Akasaka Palace, their residence during their visit to Tokyo.

*January 8*

In the morning, the President gave an interview to the NBC "Today" show and to Detroit television stations. Later, the President and Mrs. Bush attended an arrival ceremony with Emperor Akihito and Empress Michiko at the Akasaka Palace and then accompanied them to the Imperial Palace for a courtesy call. After returning to the Akasaka Palace, the President met with Prime Minister Kiichi Miyazawa.

In the afternoon, the President met and had a working luncheon with Prime Minister Miyazawa in the Akasaka Palace Annex. Later, the President gave an interview to the CBS "This Morning" show.

*January 9*

In the afternoon, the President met with Prime Minister Miyazawa at the Akasaka Palace.

*January 10*

In the morning, the President and Mrs. Bush paid a farewell call on the Emperor and Empress at the Akasaka Palace. Later in the morning, the President and Mrs. Bush returned to Washington, DC.

In the afternoon, the President and Mrs. Bush went to Camp David, MD.

The President announced recess appointments of the following individuals to be members of the Board of Directors of the Legal Services Corporation:

*J. Blakeley Hall*, of Texas.
*William Lee Kirk, Jr.*, of Florida.
*Jo Betts Love*, of Mississippi.
*Guy Vincent Molinari*, of New York.

*Jeanine E. Wolbeck*, of Minnesota.
*Howard H. Dana, Jr.*, of Maine.
*Penny L. Pullen*, of Illinois.
*Thomas D. Rath*, of New Hampshire.
*Basile J. Uddo*, of Louisiana.
*George W. Wittgraf*, of Iowa.

The White House announced that the President will meet with Prime Minister Carl Bildt of Sweden at the White House on February 20.

*January 12*

In the afternoon, the President and Mrs. Bush returned to the White House from Camp David, MD.

*January 13*

In the morning, the President traveled to Kansas City, MO, where he attended a reception hosted by the board of directors of the American Farm Bureau Federation and met with the Federal Executive Board of Kansas City.

In the afternoon, the President returned to Washington, DC.

*January 14*

The President met at the White House with the Vice President; Samuel K. Skinner, Chief of Staff to the President; Brent Scowcroft, Assistant to the President for National Security Affairs; and members of the CIA briefing staff.

The President attended a White House meeting of the leadership of the Health Care Equity Action League and then went to the J.W. Marriott Hotel for the first meeting of the Bush-Quayle '92 National Finance Committee.

After returning to the White House, the President met with:

—Samuel K. Skinner;
—the Vice President, for lunch;
—Secretary of State James A. Baker III;
—Secretary of Defense Dick Cheney.

The President announced his intention to appoint James A. McClure, of Idaho, to be a member of the Board of Trustees of the John F. Kennedy Center for the Performing Arts for a term expiring September 1, 2000. He would succeed Joan Mondale. Currently Senator McClure serves as a partner with the law firm of Givens, Pursley, Webb & Huntley in Boise, ID.

The President announced his intention to appoint the following individuals to be members of the International Cultural and Trade Center Commission:

*Jonathan W. Sloat*, of the District of Columbia, for a term expiring August 20, 1997. He would succeed Michael R. Gardner. Currently Mr. Sloat serves as a legislative and financial consultant in Washington, DC.
*Fritz Alan Korth*, of Texas, for a term expiring August 20, 1997. He would succeed Donald A. Brown. Cur-

rently Mr. Korth serves as a partner with the law firm of Korth & Korth in Washington, DC.

*January 15*

In the morning, the President traveled to New Hampshire.

In the evening, the President returned to Washington, DC.

The President announced the recess appointment of Albert V. Casey, of Texas, to be Chief Executive Officer, Resolution Trust Corporation. This is a new position.

The President announced recess appointments of the following individuals to be directors of the Federal Housing Finance Board:

*Daniel F. Evans, Jr.*, of Indiana. He will be designated Chairperson.

*Marilyn R. Seymann*, of Arizona.

*Lawrence U. Costiglio*, of New York.

*William C. Perkins*, of Wisconsin.

*January 16*

The President met at the White House with:
—the Vice President; Samuel K. Skinner, Chief of Staff to the President; Brent Scowcroft, Assistant to the President for National Security Affairs; and members of the CIA briefing staff;
—Samuel K. Skinner;
—a delegation of mayors and other locally elected officials.

The President had lunch with the Joint Chiefs of Staff. He then gave an interview to New England television stations.

Later in the afternoon, the President met with:
—Samuel K. Skinner;
—Secretary of Defense Dick Cheney.

The President announced his intention to appoint the following individuals to be members of the Advisory Commission on Intergovernmental Relations:

*Debra Rae Anderson*, of South Dakota, for a term of 2 years. This is a reappointment. Currently Ms. Anderson serves as a Deputy Assistant to the President and Director of the Office of Intergovernmental Affairs at the White House.

*Mary Ellen Joyce*, of Virginia, for a term of 2 years. This is a reappointment. Currently Ms. Joyce serves as a senior regulatory analyst for the American Petroleum Institute in Washington, DC.

The President announced his intention to nominate the following individuals to be members of the Peace Corps National Advisory Council:

*Eugene C. Johnson*, of Maryland, for a term expiring October 6, 1992. He would succeed Gary Dale Robinson. Currently Mr. Johnson serves as president of Business Mail Express in Falls Church, VA.

*Tahlman Krumm, Jr.*, of Ohio, for a term expiring October 6, 1993. This is a reappointment. Currently Mr.

Krumm serves as director of US Healthstar in Columbus, OH.

The President announced his intention to appoint Frederick F. Jenny, of Pennsylvania, to be a member of the President's National Security Telecommunications Advisory Committee. He would succeed Paul G. Stern. Currently Mr. Jenny serves as senior vice president of Unisys and president of the defense systems unit in McLean, VA.

The President announced his intention to nominate Salvador Lew, of Florida, to be a member of the Advisory Board for Cuba Broadcasting for a term of 2 years. This is a new position. From 1973 to 1988, Mr. Lew served as president and general manager of WRHC radio station in Miami, FL.

The President announced his intention to appoint Russell E. Train, of the District of Columbia, to be a member of the Advisory Committee for Trade Policy and Negotiations for a term of 2 years. He would succeed Lawrence R. Pugh. Currently Mr. Train serves as the chairman of the World Wildlife Fund in Washington, DC.

*January 17*

In the morning, the President traveled to Atlanta, GA. Upon arrival, he toured the exhibition hall at the Dr. Martin Luther King, Jr. Center, accompanied by Coretta Scott King. Later, the President and Mrs. King went to the courtyard for a wreath-laying ceremony at the tomb of Dr. King.

In the afternoon, the President returned to Andrews Air Force Base, MD, where he was joined by Mrs. Bush. They then went to Camp David, MD, for the weekend.

The President announced his intention to appoint Raymond P. Shafer, of Pennsylvania, to be a member of the National Advisory Council on the Public Service. Upon appointment, he will be designated Chairman. This is a new position. From 1967 to 1971, Governor Shafer served as the Governor of the State of Pennsylvania.

*January 20*

In the afternoon, the President and Mrs. Bush returned to the White House from a weekend stay at Camp David, MD.

*January 21*

The President met at the White House with the Vice President; Samuel K. Skinner, Chief of Staff to the President; Brent Scowcroft, Assistant to the President for National Security Affairs; and members of the CIA briefing staff.

Following the meetings, the President traveled to Catonsville, MD. Later in the morning, he returned to Washington, DC.

In the afternoon, the President met with Samuel K. Skinner.

The President declared a major disaster existed in the Commonwealth of Puerto Rico and ordered Federal aid to supplement Commonwealth and local recovery efforts in the area struck by severe storms and flooding on January 5–6.

*January 22*

The President met at the White House with:
—the Vice President; Samuel K. Skinner, Chief of Staff to the President; Brent Scowcroft, Assistant to the President for National Security Affairs; and members of the CIA briefing staff;
—heads of regulatory agencies;
—Samuel K. Skinner.

The President announced his intention to designate Rita DiMartino, of New York, as a member of the Board of Governors of the United Service Organizations, Inc., for a term of 3 years. She would succeed Lucille G. Murchison. Currently Ms. DiMartino serves as director of Federal Government affairs for AT&T in Washington, DC.

The President announced his intention to appoint Carol Iannone, of New York, to be a member of the Board of Trustees of the Woodrow Wilson International Center for Scholars for a term expiring October 23, 1996. She would succeed Theodore C. Barreaux. Currently Dr. Iannone serves as a professor with the Gallatin Division of New York University in New York, NY.

*January 23*

The President met at the White House with:
—the Vice President; Samuel K. Skinner, Chief of Staff to the President; Brent Scowcroft, Assistant to the President for National Security Affairs; and members of the CIA briefing staff;
—Samuel K. Skinner.

The President announced his intention to nominate the following individuals to be members of the Board of Directors of the State Justice Institute:

*Carlos R. Garza*, of Texas, for a term expiring September 17, 1994. He would succeed Daniel John Meador. Currently Mr. Garza serves as a consultant in Vienna, VA.
*Vivi L. Dilweg*, of Wisconsin, for a term expiring September 17, 1994. This is a reappointment. Since 1982, Judge Dilweg has served as a Brown County circuit judge in Green Bay, WI.
*David Brock*, of New Hampshire, for a term expiring September 17, 1994. He would succeed Clement Clay Torbert, Jr. Currently Justice Brock serves as chief justice of the Supreme Court of New Hampshire in Concord, NH.

*January 24*

The President met at the White House with:
—the Vice President; Samuel K. Skinner, Chief of Staff to the President; Brent Scowcroft, Assistant to the President for National Security Affairs; and members of the CIA briefing staff;
—Samuel K. Skinner;
—Secretary of State James A. Baker III;
—Desmond Howard, winner of the 1991 Heisman trophy;
—NASA astronauts.

The President announced his intention to nominate the following individuals to be members of the Board of Regents of the Uniformed Services University of the Health Sciences:

*John E. Connolly*, of California, for a term expiring June 20, 1997. He would succeed Sam A. Nixon. Currently Dr. Connolly serves as an attending surgeon and professor in the department of surgery at the University of California in Irvine, CA.
*William D. Skelton*, of Georgia, for a term expiring June 20, 1997. He would succeed Mario Efrain Ramirez. Currently Dr. Skelton serves as a professor and dean of psychiatry with Mercer University School of Medicine in Macon, GA.

The following individual will be designated chairman:

*Everett Alvarez, Jr.*, of Maryland. Mr. Alvarez has been serving as a member of the Board since 1988. Currently Mr. Alvarez serves as president of CONWAL, Inc., in Falls Church, VA.

*January 27*

The President met at the White House with:
—the Vice President; Samuel K. Skinner, Chief of Staff to the President; Brent Scowcroft, Assistant to the President for National Security Affairs; and members of the CIA briefing staff;
—Samuel K. Skinner;
—Republican congressional leaders;
—Secretary of the Treasury Nicholas F. Brady.

The President selected the following individuals to represent the United States at the 48th session of the United Nations Human Rights Commission in Geneva, Switzerland, January 27–March 6:

*Head of Delegation:*

*John Kenneth Blackwell*. Since 1991, Ambassador Blackwell has served as Chief Delegate of the United States to the United Nations Human Rights Commission. In addition, he serves as a senior fellow at the Urban Morgan Institute for Human Rights at the University of Cincinnati, having served as Mayor of Cincinnati.

*Alternate Heads of Delegation:*

*Otto J. Reich*. Currently Ambassador Reich serves as a partner and director with the Brock Group in Washington, DC, having served as U.S. Ambassador to Venezuela.

*Ambassador Morris Abram.* Currently Ambassador Abram serves as the U.S. Representative to the European office of the United Nations in Geneva, Switzerland. He has served as a former chairman of the National Conference on Soviet Jewry and Vice Chairman of the U.S. Commission on Civil Rights.

*Public Delegates:*

*John F. Burgess.* Currently Mr. Burgess serves as associate vice president for alumni relations of Georgetown University in Washington, DC.

*Michael L. Davis.* Currently Mr. Davis serves as president of Metropolitan Immigration Centers of America, Inc., in Los Angeles, CA.

*Clyde Collins Snow.* Currently Dr. Snow serves as a consultant in forensic anthropology and as a member of the graduate faculty and an adjunct professor of anthropology at the University of Oklahoma. He also serves as an adjunct professor of forensic sciences at Central State University in Edmond, OK.

### January 28

The President met at the White House with:
—the Vice President; Samuel K. Skinner, Chief of Staff to the President; Brent Scowcroft, Assistant to the President for National Security Affairs; and members of the CIA briefing staff;
—Samuel K. Skinner;
—Republican Members of Congress;
—Cabinet members.

In the evening, the President and Mrs. Bush went to the Capitol, where the President attended a reception hosted by the congressional leadership in the Speaker's Conference Room prior to his address to a joint session of the Congress.

The White House announced that President Bush will travel to Orlando, FL, on February 4 to address the annual convention of the National Grocers Association at the Orange County Convention Center.

### January 29

In the morning, the President met at the White House with:
—the Vice President; Samuel K. Skinner, Chief of Staff to the President; Brent Scowcroft, Assistant to the President for National Security Affairs; and members of the CIA briefing staff;
—Samuel K. Skinner.

Later, he went to the Capitol, where he met with congressional leaders.

In the afternoon, the President met at the White House with Samuel K. Skinner.

The President announced his intention to appoint the following individuals to be members of the Commission for the Preservation of America's Heritage Abroad:

*Warren L. Miller,* of the District of Columbia, for a term expiring February 27, 1992, succeeding A. Morgan Mason; and an additional term expiring February 27, 1995, as a reappointment. Currently Mr. Miller serves as Of Counsel with the law firm of Reed, Smith, Shaw & McClay in Washington, DC.

*Gary J. Lavine,* of New York, for a term expiring February 27, 1992, succeeding Dalia Debennis Bobelis; and an additional term expiring February 27, 1995, as a reappointment. Currently Mr. Lavine serves as senior vice president and general counsel for the Niagara Power Corp. in Syracuse, NY.

*Levi Goldberger,* of New York, for a term expiring July 13, 1992, and an additional term expiring July 13, 1995. These are reappointments. Since 1966, Mr. Goldberger has served as a field underwriter for Mutual of New York.

*Edgar Gluck,* of New York, for a term expiring June 24, 1992, and an additional term expiring June 24, 1995. These are reappointments. Currently Mr. Gluck serves as a special assistant to the superintendent for community affairs for the New York State Police in New York, NY.

*Abraham Friedlander,* of New York, for a term expiring June 24, 1992, and an additional term expiring June 24, 1995. These are reappointments. Currently Rabbi Friedlander serves as rabbi of the Congregation Ateres Tzvi in Brooklyn, NY.

*Chaskel Besser,* of New York, for a term expiring August 9, 1992, and an additional term expiring August 9, 1995. These are reappointments. Currently Rabbi Besser serves as rabbi of the Congregation B'nai Israel in New York, NY.

### January 30

In the morning, the President and Mrs. Bush traveled to Philadelphia, PA, and in the afternoon they traveled to New York City. There the President met at the Waldorf Astoria Hotel with:
—President Rodrigo Borja of Ecuador;
—Prime Minister Carlos Veiga of Cape Verde;
—Chancellor Franz Vranitzky of Austria;
—Prime Minister Wilfried Martens of Belgium;
—King Hassan II of Morocco.

In the evening, the President had a working dinner with Prime Minister John Major of the United Kingdom at the hotel.

The President transmitted to the Congress the fourth biennial report of the Interagency Arctic Research Policy Committee (February 1, 1990, to January 31, 1992).

### January 31

In the morning, the President met at the Waldorf Astoria Hotel with:
—President Carlos Andrés Pérez of Venezuela;
—Prime Minister P.V. Narasimha Rao of India;
—President François Mitterrand of France.

In the afternoon, the President attended a luncheon at the United Nations and a session of the Security Council.

In the evening, the President met with Premier Li Peng of China at the United Nations. Following the meeting, the President and Mrs. Bush returned to Washington, DC, where they attended the Republican National Committee winter meeting at the Capital Hilton Hotel.

The President appointed the following individuals to be members of the Advisory Committee on the Arts, John F. Kennedy Center for the Performing Arts:

*Michael R. Farley,* of Arizona. He would succeed Leota Hays. Currently Mr. Farley serves as president of Farley & Associates in Tucson, AZ.

*Joan S. Bradley,* of Nevada. She would succeed Lillian Nicolosi Nall. Since 1979, Ms. Bradley has served as a member of the board of trustees for KNPB–TV in Nevada.

*February 1*

In the morning, the President had a meeting followed by a working luncheon with President Boris Yeltsin of Russia at Camp David, MD.

*February 2*

In the afternoon, the President and Mrs. Bush returned to the White House from a weekend stay at Camp David, MD.

In the evening, the President and Mrs. Bush hosted a dinner for the National Governors' Association on the State Floor.

*February 3*

The President met at the White House with:
—the Vice President; Samuel K. Skinner, Chief of Staff to the President; Brent Scowcroft, Assistant to the President for National Security Affairs; and members of the CIA briefing staff;
—Samuel K. Skinner;
—the Vice President, for lunch.

In the afternoon, the President and Mrs. Bush hosted an inaugural anniversary gala reception on the State Floor.

In the evening, the President and Mrs. Bush attended the inaugural anniversary gala at the Kennedy Center.

The President selected the following individuals to represent him at the opening ceremonies of the winter Olympic games in Albertville, France, February 8:

*Head of Delegation:*
*Dorothy LeBlond*

*Delegates:*
*Nancy Ellis*
*Osborne Day*
*Melanie Griffith*
*Don Johnson*

*February 4*

In the morning, the President traveled to Orlando, FL. Following his arrival, he went to the Orange County Convention/Civic Center where he had roundtable discussions with Florida business leaders and then toured the exhibit area.

In the afternoon, the President returned to Washington, DC, and later met with Samuel K. Skinner, Chief of Staff to the President.

*February 5*

The President met at the White House with:
—the Vice President; Samuel K. Skinner, Chief of Staff to the President; Brent Scowcroft, Assistant to the President for National Security Affairs; and members of the CIA briefing staff;
—Samuel K. Skinner;
—Republican congressional leaders;
—Secretary of State James A. Baker III, for lunch.

In the afternoon, the President met with the President's Commission on Environmental Quality in the Roosevelt Room. Following the meeting, he signed the Economic Report of the President in the Oval Office.

The President announced his intention to appoint John J. McKetta, Jr., of Texas, to be a member of the Nuclear Waste Technical Review Board for a term expiring April 19, 1992, as a new position, and an additional term expiring April 19, 1996, as a reappointment. Currently Dr. McKetta serves as a professor in the department of chemical engineering at the University of Texas at Austin.

The President announced his intention to appoint Anna Sparks, of California, to be the Federal Representative on the Klamath River Compact Commission. She would succeed Nell Kuonen. She will also serve as chairman. Currently Ms. Sparks serves as the 5th district supervisor for Humboldt County, CA.

The President declared a major disaster existed in the State of Delaware and ordered Federal aid to supplement State and local recovery efforts in the area struck by a severe coastal storm and flooding on January 4–5.

*February 6*

The President met at the White House with the Vice President; Samuel K. Skinner, Chief of Staff to the President; Brent Scowcroft, Assistant to the President for National Security Affairs; and members of the CIA briefing staff.

Following a morning meeting with Samuel K. Skinner, the President traveled to Cleveland, OH, where he toured University Hospitals of Cleveland.

In the afternoon, the President traveled to Las Vegas, NV, where he toured Opportunity Village and the University Medical Center of Southern Nevada.

In the evening, the President traveled to San Diego, CA.

*February 7*

In the morning, the President toured Logan Heights Family Health Center in San Diego, CA. Following his address to the Rotary Club, the President returned to Andrews Air Force Base, MD, and then went to Camp David, MD.

The President announced his intention to appoint the following individuals to be members of the Commission on Broadcasting to the People's Republic of China. These are new positions:

*Robert John Hughes,* of Utah. Currently Mr. Hughes is a syndicated columnist and director of the international media studies program at Brigham Young University in Provo, UT.

*Donald M. Anderson,* of the District of Columbia. Currently Mr. Anderson serves as president of the United States-China Business Council in Washington, DC.

The President declared a major disaster existed in the Republic of the Marshall Islands and ordered Federal aid to supplement State and local recovery efforts in the area struck by Tropical Storm Axel on January 6.

The President declared a major disaster existed in the Federated States of Micronesia and ordered Federal aid to supplement State and local recovery efforts in the area struck by Typhoon Axel on January 8–10.

*February 9*

In the afternoon, the President and Mrs. Bush returned to the White House from a weekend stay at Camp David, MD.

*February 10*

The President met at the White House with:
—the Vice President; Samuel K. Skinner, Chief of Staff to the President; Brent Scowcroft, Assistant to the President for National Security Affairs; and members of the CIA briefing staff;
—Samuel K. Skinner;
—Secretary of the Treasury Nicholas F. Brady;
—President Rene Felber of Switzerland.

*February 11*

The President met at the White House with:
—the Vice President; Samuel K. Skinner, Chief of Staff to the President; Brent Scowcroft, Assistant to the President for National Security Affairs; and members of the CIA briefing staff;
—Samuel K. Skinner;

—Rajendra Saboo, president of Rotary International;
—Prime Minister Suleyman Demirel of Turkey, for lunch.

In the afternoon, the President had a telephone conversation with Governor Jim Edgar of Illinois to discuss the America 2000 education initiative.

Later in the afternoon, the President and Mrs. Bush hosted a reception for the Bush-Quayle '92 campaign leadership on the State Floor.

*February 12*

The President met at the White House with:
—the Vice President; Samuel K. Skinner, Chief of Staff to the President; Brent Scowcroft, Assistant to the President for National Security Affairs; and members of the CIA briefing staff;
—Cabinet members.

Later in the morning, the President and Mrs. Bush traveled to Concord, NH.

In the afternoon, the President toured the General Electric plant in Hooksett, NH, and then visited Bedford Mall in Bedford, NH.

In the evening, the President and Mrs. Bush returned to Washington, DC.

*February 13*

The President met at the White House with:
—the Vice President; Samuel K. Skinner, Chief of Staff to the President; Brent Scowcroft, Assistant to the President for National Security Affairs; and members of the CIA briefing staff;
—Samuel K. Skinner;
—the Vice President, for lunch.

The President announced his intention to appoint the following individuals to be members of the Cultural Property Advisory Committee:

*Allan S. Chait,* of New York, for a term expiring April 25, 1993. He would succeed Alfred E. Stendahl. Currently Mr. Chait serves as president of the Ralph M. Chait Galleries, Inc., in New York, NY.

*Edward R. Hudson, Jr.,* of Texas, for a term expiring April 25, 1994. He would succeed James William Alsdorf. Mr. Hudson is an independent oil producer in Fort Worth, TX.

*William E. Martin,* of California, for a term expiring April 25, 1993. He would succeed Michael Kelly. Currently Mr. Martin is a detective for the Los Angeles Police Department in Los Angeles, CA.

The President appointed Salvador Bonilla-Mathe, of Florida, to be a member of the Board of Directors of the Federal National Mortgage Association for a term expiring on the date of the annual meeting of the stockholders in 1992. He would succeed Al Cardenas. Since 1988, Mr. Bonilla-Mathe has served as president and chief executive officer of the Gulf Bank in Miami, FL.

The President selected Representative William L. Dickinson, of Alabama, to represent him at the Asian Aerospace '92 exhibition, a conference and airshow to be held in Singapore, February 25–March 1.

*February 14*

The President met at the White House with:
—the Vice President; Samuel K. Skinner, Chief of Staff to the President; Brent Scowcroft, Assistant to the President for National Security Affairs; and members of the CIA briefing staff;
—Samuel K. Skinner;
—Jean Chretien, leader of the Liberal Party of Canada;
—Easter Seal poster child Mandi Rutherford and adult representative Daniel Giuliano.

Later in the morning, the President signed the American Heart Month proclamation at a ceremony in the Oval Office.

The President announced his intention to nominate Kenneth C. Rogers, of New Jersey, to be a member of the Nuclear Regulatory Commission for the term of 5 years expiring June 30, 1997. This is a reappointment. Currently Dr. Rogers serves as Commissioner of the Nuclear Regulatory Commission in Rockville, MD.

The President appointed Gloria E.A. Toote, of New York, to be a member of the Board of Directors of the Federal National Mortgage Association for a term expiring on the date of the annual meeting of the stockholders in 1992. She would succeed Henry C. Cashen II. Currently Dr. Toote serves as president of Trea Estates in New York, NY.

*February 15*

In the morning, the President and Mrs. Bush traveled to Nashua, NH, where they visited Nashua Mall.

In the afternoon, the President and Mrs. Bush traveled to Manchester, NH, where they met with Bishop Leo O'Neil of the archdiocese of Manchester and toured a fishing and outdoor show at the National Guard Armory.

In the evening, the President and Mrs. Bush visited Temple Adath Yeshurun.

*February 16*

In the morning, the President and Mrs. Bush attended services at First Congregational Church. Following the service, they greeted Sunday school students and parents.

In the afternoon, they returned to Washington, DC.

*February 17*

In the morning, the President gave interviews to New Hampshire radio stations.

In the evening, the President gave an interview to New England television stations.

*February 18*

The President met at the White House with:
—the Vice President; Samuel K. Skinner, Chief of Staff to the President; Brent Scowcroft, Assistant to the President for National Security Affairs; and members of the CIA briefing staff;
—Samuel K. Skinner;
—Republican congressional leaders;
—Attorney General William P. Barr, for lunch;
—Secretary of Veterans Affairs Edward J. Derwinski.

*February 19*

In the morning, the President traveled to Knoxville, TN.

In the afternoon, the President returned to Washington, DC, and met with:
—Samuel K. Skinner, Chief of Staff to the President;
—Secretary of State James A. Baker III.

*February 20*

The President met at the White House with:
—the Vice President; Samuel K. Skinner, Chief of Staff to the President; Brent Scowcroft, Assistant to the President for National Security Affairs; and members of the CIA briefing staff;
—Samuel K. Skinner;
—Prime Minister Carl Bildt of Sweden, for lunch;
—Episcopal Church Foundation officers;
—Secretary of State James A. Baker III.

In the afternoon, the President hosted the National Republican Senatorial Trust reception on the State Floor.

The President announced his intention to designate Robert John Hughes, of Utah, as Chairperson of the Commission on Broadcasting to the People's Republic of China. Currently Mr. Hughes is a syndicated columnist for the Christian Science Monitor in Provo, UT. He served as Director of the U.S. Information Agency in 1981 and Director of the Voice of America in 1982.

The President announced his intention to appoint the following individuals to be members of the Commission for the Preservation of America's Heritage Abroad:

*Judy Baar Topinka*, of Illinois, for a term expiring February 27, 1995. This is a reappointment. Since 1984, Senator Topinka has served in the Illinois State Senate.

*Sigmund Strochlitz,* of Connecticut, for a term expiring August 9, 1992, succeeding Lawrence J. Majewski, and an additional term expiring August 9, 1995, as a reappointment. Currently Mr. Strochlitz serves as president of Whaling City Ford in New London, CT.

*Morris A. Shmidman,* of New York, for a term expiring June 24, 1992, and an additional term expiring June 24, 1995. These are reappointments. Currently Rabbi Shmidman serves as executive director of the Council of Jewish Organizations of Borough Park in Brooklyn, NY.

*Israel Rubin,* of Maryland, for a term expiring August 9, 1993. This is a reappointment. Since 1980, Mr. Rubin has served as a financial consultant in Potomac, MD.

*Stan Rose,* of Kansas, for a term expiring June 24, 1992, succeeding Norman H. Stahl, and an additional term expiring June 24, 1995, as a reappointment. Mr. Rose has served as chairman and publisher of Sun Publications, Inc., in Overland Park, KS.

*Leslie Keller,* of New York, for a term expiring August 2, 1993. This is a reappointment. Currently Mr. Keller serves as president of the Emanuel Foundation for Hungarian Culture in Rego Park, NY.

*Eugene Huppin,* of Washington, for a term expiring June 24, 1992, succeeding Arthur Berney, and an additional term expiring June 24, 1995, as a reappointment. Currently Mr. Huppin is an attorney with the law firm of Huppin, Ewing, Anderson & Paul, P.S., in Spokane, WA.

*Joseph Halfon,* of New York, for a term expiring February 27, 1995. He would succeed Mary Lou O'Brien. Since 1976, Mr. Halfon has served as principal of Joseph Halfon Realty in Spring Valley, NY.

The President announced his intention to nominate William Bailey, of Connecticut, to be a member of the National Council on the Arts, National Foundation on the Arts and the Humanities, for a term expiring September 3, 1996. He would succeed Helen Frankenthaler. Currently Mr. Bailey is an art professor at the Yale School of Art in New Haven, CT, and is also a painter.

*February 21*

The President met at the White House with:
—the Vice President; Samuel K. Skinner, Chief of Staff to the President; Brent Scowcroft, Assistant to the President for National Security Affairs; and members of the CIA briefing staff;
—Samuel K. Skinner;
—Secretary of State James A. Baker III.

In the afternoon, the President traveled to Charleston, SC, and met with southern leaders for the Bush-Quayle campaign. He later returned to Andrews Air Force Base, MD, and then went to Camp David, MD, for the weekend.

The White House announced that the President will meet with Chancellor Kohl of Germany at Camp David during the weekend of March 21–22.

*February 23*

In the afternoon, the President and Mrs. Bush returned to the White House from a weekend stay at Camp David, MD.

*February 24*

The President met at the White House with:
—the Vice President; Samuel K. Skinner, Chief of Staff to the President; Brent Scowcroft, Assistant to the President for National Security Affairs; and members of the CIA briefing staff;
—Samuel K. Skinner;
—the Vice President, for lunch;
—Secretary of the Treasury Nicholas F. Brady.

*February 25*

In the morning, the President and Mrs. Bush traveled to San Francisco, CA, and in the afternoon, they traveled to Los Angeles, CA, where they attended the U.S./Mexico Environmental Border Plan Agreement meeting.

The President announced his intention to appoint James B. Furrh, Jr., of Mississippi, to be the Representative of the United States to the Southern States Energy Board. He would succeed Richard Offutt Doub. Currently Mr. Furrh is an independent oil producer with James Furrh, Jr., Inc., Oil & Gas in Jackson, MS.

The President announced his intention to appoint Bernard Cardinal Law, of Massachusetts, to be a member and Chairman of the Commission on Legal Immigration Reform for the term expiring January 20, 1993. This is a new position. Since 1984, His Eminence Bernard Cardinal Law has served as the Archbishop of Boston.

The President announced his intention to appoint Rear Adm. James E. Miller to be the Department of the Navy member of the Committee for Purchase from the Blind and Other Severely Handicapped. He would succeed Daniel W. McKinnon, Jr. Currently Rear Admiral Miller serves as Commander of the Naval Supply Systems Command and Chief of Supply Corps.

The President declared a major disaster existed in the State of California and ordered Federal aid to supplement State and local recovery efforts in the area struck by severe rainstorms, snowstorms, wind, flooding, and mudslides beginning February 10–18.

*February 26*

In the morning, the President and Mrs. Bush traveled to San Antonio, TX, for the second regional drug summit. The President met at the Marriott Rivercenter Hotel with:
—President Alberto Fujimori of Peru;
—President César Gaviria of Colombia;
—President Rodrigo Borja of Ecuador;
—President Jaime Paz Zamora of Bolivia.

The President announced his intention to appoint Asher J. Scharf, of New York, to be a member of the Commission for the Preservation of America's Heritage Abroad for a term expiring July 13, 1992, and an additional term expiring July 13, 1995. This is a reappointment. Currently Mr. Scharf is a builder and developer in Brooklyn, NY.

The President announced his intention to appoint Walter Gellhorn, of New York, to be a member of the Council of the Administrative Conference of the United States for a term of 3 years. This is a reappointment. Currently Mr. Gellhorn is a professor emeritus at Columbia University in New York, NY.

The President announced his intention to appoint the following individuals to be members of the Arctic Research Commission:

*George B. Newton*, of Virginia, for a term of 4 years. This is a new position. Currently Mr. Newton serves as director of the Center for Signature Warfare, Systems Analysis Group, Systems Planning Corp. in Arlington, VA.

*Charles H. Johnson*, of Alaska, for a term expiring February 26, 1993. He would succeed Oliver Leavitt. Currently Mr. Johnson serves as president of Denali Financial Services in Nome, AK.

### February 27

In the morning, the President had a working breakfast at the Marriott Rivercenter Hotel with President Carlos Salinas of Mexico.

In the afternoon, the President attended a working luncheon with the summit participants at the McNay Art Museum.

Later, the President and Mrs. Bush traveled to Houston, TX. Upon arrival, they went to their residence at the Houstonian Hotel.

The President transmitted to the Congress the 1992 Trade Policy Agenda and 1991 Annual Report on the Trade Agreements Program.

### February 28

In the afternoon, the President gave interviews to Dallas television stations at the Houstonian Hotel.

### February 29

In the morning, the President and Mrs. Bush traveled to Dallas, TX, and to Atlanta, GA.

In the afternoon, the President attended a Bush-Quayle Georgia leadership meeting and reception at the Marriott Marquis Hotel.

### March 1

In the morning, the President and Mrs. Bush attended services at First Baptist Church in Atlanta, GA. Later, the President gave interviews to Atlanta television stations at the Hyatt Regency Hotel. Following the interviews, the President

and Mrs. Bush traveled to Savannah, GA. In the afternoon, they returned to Washington, DC.

### March 2

The President met at the White House with:
—the Vice President; Samuel K. Skinner, Chief of Staff to the President; Brent Scowcroft, Assistant to the President for National Security Affairs; and members of the CIA briefing staff;
—Samuel K. Skinner.

Later in the morning, the President had an economic briefing in the Oval Office. Following the briefing, he met with:
—the Vice President, for lunch;
—Secretary of Defense Richard B. Cheney.

### March 3

The President met at the White House with:
—the Vice President; Samuel K. Skinner, Chief of Staff to the President; Brent Scowcroft, Assistant to the President for National Security Affairs; and members of the CIA briefing staff;
—Samuel K. Skinner.

Later, the President traveled to Chicago, IL, where he gave interviews to Chicago television stations at the Hyatt Regency O'Hare Hotel. In the afternoon, the President returned to Washington, DC.

The President declared a major disaster existed in the State of New Jersey and ordered Federal aid to supplement State and local recovery efforts in the area struck by a severe northeast coastal storm on January 4, 1992.

### March 4

In the morning, the President traveled to Tampa, FL, where he attended the annual Florida State Strawberry Festival. The President then traveled to Miami, FL.

### March 5

In the morning, the President traveled to Columbia, SC. In the afternoon, he traveled to Memphis, TN, and then to Oklahoma City, OK.

The President announced his intention to appoint the following individuals to be members of the National Advisory Council on the Public Service. These are new positions:

*John Brademas*, of New York. Currently Dr. Brademas serves as president of New York University in New York, NY.

*Hal Daub*, of Nebraska. Currently Mr. Daub serves as principal and director of Federal Government affairs of Deloitte & Touche, an international accounting firm in Washington, DC. From 1980 to 1988, Mr. Daub served as a U.S. Congressman from the Second District of Nebraska.

*Samuel T. Mok*, of Maryland. Since 1986, Mr. Mok has served as Comptroller and Chief Financial Officer of the U.S. Department of the Treasury in Washington, DC.

*Antonia Coello Novello*, of the District of Columbia. Currently Dr. Novello serves as the U.S. Surgeon General in Washington, DC.

*Edward Joseph Perkins*, of the District of Columbia. Currently Director Perkins serves as Director General of the Foreign Service at the U.S. Department of State in Washington, DC.

*Jesse M. Rios*, of Illinois. Currently Mr. Rios serves as president of the National Council of Field Labor Locals in Chicago, IL.

*Shirin R. Tahir-Kheli*, of Pennsylvania. Currently Dr. Tahir-Kheli serves as Alternate Representative of the United States for Special Political Affairs at the United Nations in New York, NY.

*Charles Graves Untermeyer*, of Texas. Currently Director Untermeyer serves as Associate Director for Broadcasting and Director of the Voice of America in Washington, DC.

## March 6

In the morning, the President traveled to Baton Rouge, LA, where he was joined by Mrs. Bush. In the afternoon, they traveled to Jackson, MS, and then to Pensacola, FL.

## March 7

In the morning, the President and Mrs. Bush traveled from Pensacola, FL, to Montgomery, AL, where they attended a bass fishing tournament. They then returned to Andrews Air Force Base, MD, and went on to Camp David, MD.

## March 9

In the morning, the President and Mrs. Bush returned to the White House from Camp David, MD.

The President met at the White House with:
—the Vice President; Samuel K. Skinner, Chief of Staff to the President; Brent Scowcroft, Assistant to the President for National Security Affairs; and members of the CIA briefing staff;
—Samuel K. Skinner.

Later, the President had a domestic briefing in the Oval Office. Following the briefing, he met with:
—leaders of Veterans of Foreign Wars, Disabled American Veterans, and the American Legion;
—Secretary of the Treasury Nicholas F. Brady.

In the afternoon, the President had a telephone conversation with Gov. Bob Miller of Nevada to kick off the Nevada 2000 education initiative.

In the afternoon, the President met in the Roosevelt Room with members of the National Republican Senatorial and Congressional Committees to discuss the President's Dinner, a joint fundraising event.

The President announced his intention to designate the following individuals to the Arkansas-Oklahoma Arkansas River Compact Commission:

*United States Commissioner:*

*Ronald N. Fuller*, of Arkansas. He would succeed J.J. Vigneault III. He will serve as Chairman. Currently Mr. Fuller serves as president of Fuller Enterprises in Little Rock, AR.

*United States Alternate Commissioner:*

*Joe M. Allbaugh*, of Oklahoma. He would succeed Baren Healey. Currently Mr. Allbaugh serves as deputy secretary of transportation with the Oklahoma Department of Transportation in Oklahoma City, OK.

The President announced his intention to appoint the following individuals to be members of the Cultural Property Advisory Committee for terms expiring April 25, 1994:

*Michael Ward*, of New York. He would succeed Glenn C. Randall. Since 1983, Dr. Ward has served as founder and director of Michael Ward, Inc., in New York, NY.

*James McCredie*, of New Jersey. He would succeed Thomas K. Seligman. Currently Dr. McCredie serves as director of the Institute of Fine Arts in New York, NY.

The President announced his intention to appoint the following individuals to be members of the United States Holocaust Memorial Council:

*Steven E. Some*, of Maryland, for a term expiring January 15, 1995. He would succeed Laurence A. Tisch. Currently Mr. Some serves as president of Steven E. Some Associates in Washington, DC.

*Dalck Feith*, of Pennsylvania, for a term expiring January 15, 1996. This is a reappointment. Dr. Feith is the owner of Dalco Manufacturing Co. and Lansdale Fisheries, Inc., in Lansdale, PA.

## March 10

The President met at the White House with:
—the Vice President; Samuel K. Skinner, Chief of Staff to the President; Brent Scowcroft, Assistant to the President for National Security Affairs; and members of the CIA briefing staff;
—Samuel K. Skinner;
—Rabbi Abraham Shapiro of Israel;
—the Vice President, for lunch;
—select Members of Congress.

The President selected the following individuals to represent him at the Mauritian Republic Day ceremonies in Mauritius, March 12:

*Head of Delegation:*
*Laurie Firestone*

*Delegates:*
*Ambassador Penne Korth*
*Margaret Bush*

The President announced his intention to appoint Nien Yuan Yao Cheng, of the District of Columbia, to be a member of the Commission on Broadcasting to the People's Republic of China. This is a new position. Currently Ms. Cheng is an author.

The President announced his intention to appoint the following individuals to be members of the Commission on the Assignment of Women in the Armed Forces. These are new positions:

*Robert T. Herres,* of Texas. Upon appointment, he will be designated Chairman. Currently General Herres serves as vice chairman and chief operating officer for insurance and information services for USAA Insurance in San Antonio, TX.

*Mary E. Clarke,* of Alabama. Currently Major General Clarke serves as Chairman of the Advisory Committee on Women Veterans at the Veterans Administration.

*Samuel G. Cockerham,* of Virginia. Currently Brigadier General Cockerham serves as a consultant for defense, aviation, and strategic mobility systems in Alexandria, VA.

*Elaine Donnelly,* of Michigan. Currently Ms. Donnelly serves as executive director of the Coalition of Military Readiness in Livonia, MI.

*Thomas V. Draude,* of Illinois. Currently Brigadier General Draude serves as Director of Public Affairs at the Marine Corps Headquarters in Washington, DC.

*Mary M. Finch,* of Arizona. Currently Captain Finch is a tactical officer at the U.S. Military Academy, West Point, NY.

*William Darryl Henderson,* of California. Dr. Henderson most recently served as Commander of the U.S. Army Research Institute in Washington, DC.

*James R. Hogg,* of Virginia. Currently Mr. Hogg serves as president and chief executive officer of the National Security Industrial Association in Washington, DC.

*Newton Minow,* of Illinois. Currently Mr. Minow serves as a counsel with the law firm of Sidley and Austin in Chicago, IL.

*Charles C. Moskos,* of Illinois. Currently Dr. Moskos serves as a professor of sociology at Northwestern University in Evanston, IL.

*Meredith Ann Neizer,* of Texas. Currently Ms. Neizer serves as systems development trainer at Sealand Services, Inc., in Farmers Branch, TX.

*Kate Walsh O'Beirne,* of Virginia. Currently Ms. O'Beirne serves as vice president of government relations for the Heritage Foundation in Washington, DC.

*Ronald D. Ray,* of Kentucky. Currently Mr. Ray is an attorney at law for the firm of Ronald D. Ray, Counsellors at Law in Louisville, KY.

*Maxwell R. Thurman,* of Virginia. From 1989 to 1990, General Thurman served as Commander in Chief of the U.S. Southern Command in Quarry Heights, Panama.

*Sarah F. White,* of Virginia. Currently Ms. White serves as executive assistant to the Science Applications International Corp. in McLean, VA.

*March 11*

The President met at the White House with:

—the Vice President; Samuel K. Skinner, Chief of Staff to the President; Brent Scowcroft, Assistant to the President for National Security Affairs; and members of the CIA briefing staff;

—select Members of Congress;

—Samuel K. Skinner.

In the afternoon, in a ceremony on the State Floor, the President received diplomatic credentials from Ambassadors Syeda Abida Hussain of Pakistan, Anatol Dinbergs of Latvia, Stasys Lozoraitis of Lithuania, Pita Kewa Nacuva of Fiji, Noureddine Yazid Zerhouni of Algeria, and Vladimir Petrovich Lukin of Russia.

The White House announced that President Bush has invited President Richard von Weizsäcker of the Federal Republic of Germany to visit the United States from April 28 to May 3. President von Weizsäcker will visit the White House on April 29.

The President announced that the following individuals will represent him at the 36th session of the Commission on the Status of Women in Vienna, Austria, March 11–20:

*Head of Delegation:*

*Ambassador Judy McLennan.* Currently Ambassador McLennan is the United States Representative to the United Nations Commission on the Status of Women.

*Delegates:*

*Gwendolyn Boeke.* Currently Ms. Boeke serves as a Republican national committeewoman from Iowa.

*Patricia Harrison.* Currently Ms. Harrison serves as a partner with the E. Bruce Harrison Co. and as president of the National Women's Economic Alliance.

*Elsie Vartanian.* Currently Ms. Vartanian serves as Director of the Women's Bureau at the U.S. Department of Labor in Washington, DC.

*Gwendolyn King.* Currently Ms. King serves as Administrator of the Social Security Administration.

The President announced his intention to appoint William R. Neale, of Indiana, to be a member of the Council of the Administrative Conference of the United States for a term of 3 years. He would succeed Edward L. Weidenfeld. Currently Mr. Neale serves as a partner with the law firm of Krieg Devault Alexander & Capehart in Indianapolis, IN.

The President announced his intention to appoint George H. Walker IV, of Missouri, to be a member of the Commission on Presidential Scholars. He would succeed Betty S. Holmes. Currently Mr. Walker serves as an associate with the Palmer Group in Philadelphia, PA.

The President appointed David R. Clare, of Florida, to be a member of the President's Drug Advisory Council. He would succeed Albert Vincent Casey. From 1976 to 1989, Mr. Clare served as president and chairman of the executive committee of Johnson & Johnson.

### March 12

In the morning, the President met at the White House with:

—the Vice President; Samuel K. Skinner, Chief of Staff to the President; Brent Scowcroft, Assistant to the President for National Security Affairs; and members of the CIA briefing staff;

—Samuel K. Skinner.

Later, the President had a domestic briefing in the Oval Office. Following the briefing, he met with:

—select Members of Congress;

—Secretary of State James A. Baker III.

In the afternoon, the President went to the Israeli Embassy to sign the book of condolences for former Prime Minister Menachem Begin.

In the evening, the President and Mrs. Bush attended the National Republican Senatorial Committee dinner at the Pension Building.

The President announced his intention to appoint the following individuals to be members of the National Commission on America's Urban Families, to serve for the life of the Commission. These are new positions:

*John David Ashcroft*, of Missouri. He will be appointed Chairman. Currently Governor Ashcroft serves as the Governor of Missouri.

*Annette Strauss*, of Texas. She will be appointed Co-chairman. From 1987 to 1991, Ms. Strauss served as the Mayor of Dallas, TX.

*Victor Ashe*, of Tennessee. Currently Mr. Ashe serves as the Mayor of the city of Knoxville, TN.

*David Blankenhorn*, of New York. Currently Mr. Blankenhorn serves as president of the Institute for American Values in New York, NY.

*Alphonso Jackson*, of Texas. Currently Mr. Jackson serves as the executive director of the housing authority of the city of Dallas, TX.

*Irene Johnson*, of Illinois. Currently Ms. Johnson serves as president of LeClaire Courts Resident Management Corp. in Chicago, IL.

*Josephine Velazquez*, of Florida. Currently Ms. Velazquez is involved with the Florida Guardian Ad Litem Program and is actively involved as chairman of various fundraising projects to benefit the Children's Home Society in Miami, FL.

*Bill Wilson*, of New York. Currently Mr. Wilson is pastor of the Metro Assembly of God in Brooklyn, NY.

The President announced his intention to designate J. Michael Farrell, of the District of Columbia, to be Chairman of the National Commission on Libraries and Information Science. Mr. Farrell has been a member of the Commission since October 17, 1990. Currently he serves as a partner with the law firm of Manatt, Phelps, Rothenberg & Phillips in Washington, DC.

### March 13

In the morning, the President traveled to Kalamazoo, MI, where he toured the Stryker Corp. medical manufacturing facility. Later, he traveled to Detroit, MI. In the afternoon, the President returned to Andrews Air Force Base, MD, and then went to Camp David, MD, for the weekend.

### March 15

The President and Mrs. Bush returned to the White House from a weekend stay at Camp David, MD.

### March 16

In the morning, the President met at the White House with the Vice President; Samuel K. Skinner, Chief of Staff to the President; Brent Scowcroft, Assistant to the President for National Security Affairs; and members of the CIA briefing staff.

The President traveled to Milwaukee, WI, where he toured the assembly line at Steeltech Manufacturing, Inc. He then traveled to Chicago, IL, where he was joined by Mrs. Bush. In the evening, they returned to Washington, DC.

### March 17

In the morning, the President and Mrs. Bush traveled to Bentonville, AR, and returned to Washington, DC, later in the day.

### March 18

In the morning, the President met at the White House with:

—the Vice President; Samuel K. Skinner, Chief of Staff to the President; Brent Scowcroft, Assistant to the President for National Security Affairs; and members of the CIA briefing staff;

—Samuel K. Skinner;

—economic advisers;

—Secretary of State James A. Baker III.

The President presented the Presidential Citizen's Medal to the families of deceased hostages William Buckley and William R. Higgins in the Oval Office.

The President hosted a reception for the National Republican Congressional Campaign leadership on the State Floor.

The President transmitted to the Congress the annual report of the ACTION Agency for fiscal year 1991.

The President announced his intention to appoint the following individuals to the United

States Holocaust Memorial Council for the terms indicated:

*Chairman:*

*Harvey M. Meyerhoff,* of Maryland, for a term of 5 years. This is a reappointment. He has served as a member of the Council since 1986. Currently Mr. Meyerhoff serves as chairman of the board of Magna Properties in Baltimore, MD.

*Member:*

*Theodore N. Lerner,* of Maryland, for a term expiring January 15, 1996. This is a reappointment. Currently Mr. Lerner serves as president of the Lerner Co. in Bethesda, MD.

The President declared a major disaster existed in the State of Vermont. He ordered Federal aid to supplement State and local recovery efforts in the area struck by heavy rains, ice jams, and flooding on March 11.

*March 19*

The President met in the morning at the White House with:

—the Vice President; Samuel K. Skinner, Chief of Staff to the President; Brent Scowcroft, Assistant to the President for National Security Affairs; and members of the CIA briefing staff;
—Samuel K. Skinner;
—the Cabinet;
—the Executive Committee of the Asian American Voters' Coalition;
—muscular dystrophy poster child, Drew Johnson;
—the Vice President, for lunch.

In the afternoon, the President and Mrs. Bush hosted a reception for the National Newspaper Association on the State Floor. In the evening, the President and Mrs. Bush attended the Radio and Television Correspondents Association dinner at the Washington Hilton Hotel.

The President announced his intention to appoint the following individuals to serve as members of the United States Commission on Improving the Effectiveness of the United Nations. These are new positions:

*Gary E. MacDougal,* of Illinois. Since 1969, Mr. MacDougal has served as chairman and chief executive officer of Mark Control Corp. in Chicago, IL.

*Richard John Neuhaus,* of New York. Currently Mr. Neuhaus serves as director of the Institute of Religion and Public Life in New York, NY.

*Harris O. Schoenberg,* of New York. Currently Mr. Schoenberg serves as director of United Nations Affairs for B'nai B'rith International in New York, NY.

*Jose S. Sorzano,* of Virginia. Currently Mr. Sorzano serves as chairman of the Austin Group, Inc., in Arlington, VA. In addition, he has served as Ambassador and U.S. Representative to the United Nations, 1981–85.

*March 20*

The President held morning meetings at the White House with:

—the Vice President; Samuel K. Skinner, Chief of Staff to the President; Brent Scowcroft, Assistant to the President for National Security Affairs; and members of the CIA briefing staff;
—Samuel K. Skinner;
—Secretary of State James A. Baker III.

In the afternoon, the President presented the Commander in Chief Trophy to Air Force Academy representatives in the Roosevelt Room. He then addressed the National Federation of Republican Women in the Old Executive Office Building. Later, the President and Mrs. Bush traveled to Camp David, MD, for the weekend.

The White House announced that the President has invited Prime Minister Michael Manley of Jamaica to the White House for a private dinner on Tuesday, March 24.

The President declared a major disaster existed in the State of Texas. He ordered Federal aid to supplement State and local recovery efforts in the area struck by severe storms and flooding since March 4.

The President also declared a major disaster existed in the State of Mississippi. He ordered Federal aid to supplement State and local recovery efforts in the areas struck by severe storms and tornadoes on March 9–10.

*March 21*

The President had a morning meeting and a working luncheon with Chancellor Helmut Kohl of Germany at Camp David, MD.

*March 22*

The President and Mrs. Bush, accompanied by Chancellor and Mrs. Kohl, returned to the White House from Camp David, MD, in the afternoon.

*March 23*

In the morning, the President met at the White House with the Vice President; Samuel K. Skinner, Chief of Staff to the President; Brent Scowcroft, Assistant to the President for National Security Affairs; and members of the CIA briefing staff. The President also had a domestic briefing in the Oval Office.

The President had afternoon meetings with:
—Samuel K. Skinner;
—Secretary of Defense Richard B. Cheney.

*March 24*

The President met at the White House with:
—the Vice President; Samuel K. Skinner, Chief of Staff to the President; Brent Scowcroft, Assistant to the President for National Securi-

ty Affairs; and members of the CIA briefing
staff;

—Samuel K. Skinner;

—the Vice President, for lunch;

—March of Dimes poster child Edward Michael Eissey;

—White House news photographers.

In the evening, the President and Mrs. Bush
hosted a private dinner in the Residence for
Prime Minister Michael Manley of Jamaica.

Press Secretary Fitzwater issued a release stating that the President's only medication is a daily
Synthroid pill for his thyroid condition.

The President announced his intention to appoint the following individuals to be members of
the National Advisory Council on Indian Education:

*Josephus D. Jacobs,* of North Carolina, for a term expiring September 29, 1993. He would succeed Helen M.
Scheirbeck. From 1970 to 1984, Mr. Jacobs served as a
county supervisor for the Farmers Home Administration in Raleigh, NC.

*Eddie L. Tullis,* of Alabama, for a term expiring September 29, 1994. This is a reappointment. Since 1976, Mr.
Tullis has served as chairman of the Poarch Band of
Creek Indians in Atmore, AL.

*Francis G. Whitebird,* of South Dakota, for a term expiring September 29, 1993. He would succeed Ronald P.
Andrade. Currently Mr. Whitebird serves as a coordinator for the South Dakota State Indian Affairs Office
in Pierre, SD.

*Albert A. Yazzie,* of Arizona, for a term expiring September 29, 1993. He would succeed Gloria Ann Duus.
Since 1980, Mr. Yazzie has served as superintendent
for the Ganado Unified Schools, District 20, in
Ganado, AZ.

*Sergio A. Maldonado,* of Arizona, for a term expiring
September 29, 1992. He would succeed Omar J. Lane.
Since 1985, Mr. Maldonado has served as an Indian
education supervisor for the Federal programs of the
Tempe Elementary District 3 in Tempe, AZ.

*William D. Edmo, Sr.,* of Idaho, for a term expiring
September 29, 1992. He would succeed Andrea L.
Barlow. From 1989 to 1990, Dr. Edmo served as a
grantsmanship specialist with Shoshone-Bannock
Tribes, Inc., in Fort Hall, ID.

*Sacajawea Ramona Tecumseh,* of Iowa, for a term expiring September 29, 1992. She would succeed Robert
Keams Chiago. Currently Ms. Tecumseh is a doctoral
student at Arizona State University in Tempe, AZ.

*Theresa Farley Neese,* of Oklahoma, for a term expiring
September 29, 1992. She would succeed Marie Cox.
Ms. Neese has served as director of small business and
chief lobbyist for the Oklahoma State Chamber of
Commerce and Industry in Oklahoma City, OK.

The President announced his intention to
nominate the following individuals to be mem-

bers of the National Science Board, National Science Foundation:

*For terms expiring May 10, 1998:*

*F. Albert Cotton,* of Texas. This is a reappointment. Currently Dr. Cotton serves as a Robert A. Welch distinguished professor of chemistry and director of the
laboratory for molecular structure and bonding at the
department of chemistry of Texas A&M University in
College Station, TX.

*James L. Powell,* of Pennsylvania. This is a reappointment. Currently Dr. Powell serves as president and
chief executive officer of the Franklin Institute in
Philadelphia, PA.

*Charles Edward Hess,* of California. He would succeed
John C. Hancock. Currently Dr. Hess serves as a professor of agriculture and environmental science at the
University of California at Davis.

*John Hopcroft,* of New York. He would succeed Frederick Phillips Brooks. Currently Dr. Hopcroft serves as a
professor in the department of computer science at
Cornell University in Ithaca, NY.

*Frank H.T. Rhodes,* of New York. Currently Dr. Rhodes
serves as president of Cornell University in Ithaca, NY.

*For the remainder of the term expiring May 10,
1992, succeeding Mary Lowe Good, and an
additional term expiring May 10, 1998, as a
reappointment:*

*Richard Neil Zare,* of California. Currently Dr. Zare
serves as a Marguerite Blake Wilbur professor of
chemistry at Stanford University in Stanford, CA.

*March 25*

The President met in the morning at the
White House with:

—the Vice President; Samuel K. Skinner, Chief
of Staff to the President; Brent Scowcroft,
Assistant to the President for National Security Affairs; and members of the CIA briefing
staff.

The President had afternoon meetings with:

—Samuel K. Skinner;

—Secretary of State James A. Baker III.

*March 26*

In the afternoon, the President had a domestic
briefing in the Oval Office and then met with
Samuel K. Skinner, Chief of Staff to the President. Later, the President hosted a reception for
Republican Senators on the State Floor.

The President announced his intention to appoint the following individuals to be members of
the Commission for the Preservation of America's
Heritage Abroad:

*Julius Berman,* of New York, for a term expiring August
17, 1992, and an additional term expiring August 17,
1995. This is a reappointment. Currently Mr. Berman
serves as executive vice president and chief legal officer of the Olympia and York Companies in New York,
NY.

*Hertz Frankel,* of New York, for a term expiring July 13, 1993. He would succeed Gerald E. Rosen. Currently Mr. Frankel serves as director of Bedford-Harrison Day Care in Brooklyn, NY.

The President announced his intention to nominate Bruce D. Goodman, of Pennsylvania, to be a Commissioner of the Copyright Royalty Tribunal, for a term of 7 years. He would succeed Mario F. Aguero. Currently Mr. Goodman serves as president of FYI Network, Inc., a cable television programming channel in Washington, DC.

*March 27*
The President met in the morning at the White House with:
—the Vice President; Samuel K. Skinner, Chief of Staff to the President; Brent Scowcroft, Assistant to the President for National Security Affairs; and members of the CIA briefing staff;
—Secretary of State James A. Baker III.

Later, the President taped a radio address for broadcast on March 28.

In the afternoon, the President met with the Latin Builders Association.

The White House announced that the President will meet with President Francesco Cossiga of Italy on April 7.

The President announced his intention to nominate the following individuals to be members of the National Council on the Humanities for terms expiring January 26, 1998:

*Paul A. Cantor,* of Virginia. He would succeed Aram Bakshian, Jr. Currently Dr. Cantor serves as a professor of English at the University of Virginia in Charlottesville, VA.

*Bruce Cole,* of Indiana. He would succeed Alvin H. Bernstein. Currently Dr. Cole serves as a distinguished professor of fine arts with the Hope School of Fine Arts at Indiana University in Bloomington, IN.

*Joseph H. Hagan,* of Massachusetts. He would succeed Paul J. Olscamp. Currently Dr. Hagan serves as president of Assumption College in Worcester, MA.

*Theodore S. Hamerow,* of Wisconsin. He would succeed John Shelton Reed, Jr. Dr. Hamerow has served as professor emeritus and chairman of the department of history at the University of Wisconsin in Madison, WI.

*Alicia Juarrero,* of Maryland. She would succeed Robert Hollander. Since 1975, Dr. Juarrero has served as a professor of philosophy at Prince George's Community College in Largo, MD.

*Alan Charles Kors,* of Pennsylvania. He would succeed Carolynn Reid-Wallace. Currently Dr. Kors serves as a professor of history at the University of Pennsylvania in Philadelphia, PA.

*Condoleezza Rice,* of California. She would succeed David Lowenthal. Currently Dr. Rice serves as a professor of political science at Stanford University in Stanford, CA.

*John R. Searle,* of California. He would succeed Robert B. Stevens. Since 1967, Dr. Searle has served as a professor of philosophy at the University of California in Berkeley, CA.

*March 28*
In the evening, the President and Mrs. Bush attended the Gridiron Dinner at the Capital Hilton Hotel.

*March 30*
The President met at the White House with:
—the Vice President; Samuel K. Skinner, Chief of Staff to the President; Brent Scowcroft, Assistant to the President for National Security Affairs; and members of the CIA briefing staff;
—Samuel K. Skinner;
—domestic advisers;
—the Vice President, for lunch;
—Secretary of the Treasury Nicholas F. Brady.

In the evening, the President and Mrs. Bush attended the Youth for Tomorrow gala at the Kennedy Center.

*March 31*
The President met at the White House with:
—the Vice President; Samuel K. Skinner, Chief of Staff to the President; Brent Scowcroft, Assistant to the President for National Security Affairs; and members of the CIA briefing staff;
—Samuel K. Skinner;
—Secretary of State James A. Baker III.

The President transmitted to Congress the 26th annual report of the Department of Housing and Urban Development for calendar year 1990.

The President announced his intention to appoint the following individuals to be members of Emergency Boards Nos. 220, 221, 222, to investigate railroad labor disputes:

*Benjamin Aaron,* of Santa Monica, CA. Mr. Aaron will serve as the Chairman of all three Boards. Currently he is a professor of law at the University of California at Los Angeles School of Law and an arbitrator in numerous industries.

*David Twomey,* of Quincy, MA. Mr. Twomey will be a member of all three Boards. He currently is an arbitrator and a professor at the Boston College School of Management.

*Eric J. Schmertz,* of Riverdale, NY. Mr. Schmertz will be a member of all three Boards. Currently he is a professor of law at the Hofstra School of Law and an arbitrator in numerous industries.

*Arnold M. Zack,* of Boston, MA. Mr. Zack will be a member of the two Boards handling the Conrail and Amtrak disputes. He currently serves as arbitrator and mediator in numerous industries.

*Preston Jay Moore,* of Oklahoma City, OK. Mr. Moore will be a member of the two Boards handling the Conrail and Amtrak disputes. He currently serves as an arbitrator in numerous industries.

*April 1*

The President met at the White House with:
—former President Jimmy Carter;
—the Vice President; Samuel K. Skinner, Chief of Staff to the President; Brent Scowcroft, Assistant to the President for National Security Affairs; and members of the CIA briefing staff;
—congressional leaders;
—economic advisers.

In the evening, the President and Mrs. Bush attended the National Republican Senatorial Committee Roundtable dinner at the National Museum of Women in the Arts.

*April 2*

The President met at the White House with:
—the Vice President; Samuel K. Skinner, Chief of Staff to the President; Brent Scowcroft, Assistant to the President for National Security Affairs; and members of the CIA briefing staff;
—Samuel K. Skinner;
—domestic advisers;
—Secretary of State James A. Baker III;
—Hispanic leaders.

In an afternoon ceremony in the Oval Office, the President received diplomatic credentials from Ambassadors Mohamed Fall Ainina of Mauritania, Berhane Gebre-Christos of Ethiopia, Takakazu Kuriyama of Japan, and Acheikh Ibn Oumar Said of Chad.

*April 3*

In the morning, the President met at the White House with the Vice President; Samuel K. Skinner, Chief of Staff to the President; Brent Scowcroft, Assistant to the President for National Security Affairs; and members of the CIA briefing staff. He then taped a radio address for broadcast on April 4.

Later, the President traveled to Philadelphia, PA, and then to Camp David, MD, where he was joined by Mrs. Bush.

The President announced his intention to designate Susan M. Coughlin, of Pennsylvania, to be Vice Chairman of the National Transportation Safety Board for a term of 2 years. She has served as Vice Chairman since June 21, 1990. From 1987 to 1990, Ms. Coughlin served as Deputy Federal Railroad Administrator at the U.S. Department of Transportation in Washington, DC.

The President announced his intention to nominate Carl W. Vogt, of Maryland, to be a member of the National Transportation Safety Board for the term expiring December 31, 1996. He would succeed James L. Kolstad. He will also be nominated to be Chairman for a term of 2 years. Currently Mr. Vogt serves as partner-in-

charge with the law firm of Fulbright & Jaworski in Washington, DC.

*April 6*

In the morning, the President and Mrs. Bush returned to the White House from a weekend stay at Camp David, MD.

In the afternoon, the President traveled to Baltimore, MD, where he attended the opening day baseball game at the new Oriole Park at Camden Yards. Following the game, the President returned to Washington, DC.

*April 7*

The President met at the White House with:
—the Vice President; Samuel K. Skinner, Chief of Staff to the President; Brent Scowcroft, Assistant to the President for National Security Affairs; and members of the CIA briefing staff;
—Samuel K. Skinner.

*April 8*

In the morning, the President participated in Great American Read-Aloud Day by reading to students from St. Peter's School, Washington, DC, in the Diplomatic Reception Room at the White House.

Later, the President met with:
—the Vice President; Samuel K. Skinner, Chief of Staff to the President; Brent Scowcroft, Assistant to the President for National Security Affairs; and members of the CIA briefing staff;
—Samuel K. Skinner;
—Postmaster General Anthony Frank;
—Secretary of State James A. Baker III.

In the evening, the President and Mrs. Bush hosted a reception for the Republican National Committee Eagles on the State Floor.

The President announced his intention to appoint Victor H. Ashe, Mayor of Knoxville, TN, to be a member of the Advisory Commission on Intergovernmental Relations for a term of 2 years. This is a reappointment.

The President announced his intention to appoint Jeannine Smith Clark, of the District of Columbia, to be a member of the Commission of Fine Arts for a term of 4 years. She would succeed Pascal Regan. Currently Ms. Clark serves as a member of the Board of Regents at the Smithsonian Institution in Washington, DC.

The President has selected the following individuals to represent him at the 50th anniversary observance of the fall of Bataan in the Philippines, April 9:

*Head of Delegation:*

*Ambassador Frank Wisner*, of the District of Columbia. Currently Ambassador Wisner serves as the U.S. Ambassador to the Philippines.

*Delegates:*

*Paul Blanco*, of California. Currently Dr. Blanco serves as chairman of the National Organization of Filipino-American Republicans.

*William Edwards*, of Mississippi. Commander Edwards is a World War II veteran and retired naval commander.

*April 9*

The President met at the White House with:
—the Vice President; Samuel K. Skinner, Chief of Staff to the President; Brent Scowcroft, Assistant to the President for National Security Affairs; and members of the CIA briefing staff;
—Samuel K. Skinner;
—domestic advisers;
—McDonald's Capitol Classic all-star high school basketball teams;
—the Vice President, for lunch;
—Secretary of Health and Human Services Louis Sullivan and FDA Commissioner David Kessler.

In the evening, the President and Mrs. Bush hosted a reception for the Republican National Committee Eagles on the State Floor.

*April 10*

The President held morning meetings at the White House with:
—the Vice President; Samuel K. Skinner, Chief of Staff to the President; Brent Scowcroft, Assistant to the President for National Security Affairs; and members of the CIA briefing staff;
—Samuel K. Skinner;
—State Lieutenant Governors;
—Secretary of State James A. Baker III.

Later, the President taped a radio address for broadcast on April 11.

In the afternoon, the President met with Prime Minister Marián Čalfa of Czechoslovakia. The President and Mrs. Bush then went to Camp David, MD, for the weekend.

*April 12*

In the afternoon, the President and Mrs. Bush returned to the White House from a weekend stay at Camp David, MD.

*April 13*

The President met at the White House with:

—the Vice President; Samuel K. Skinner, Chief of Staff to the President; Brent Scowcroft, Assistant to the President for National Security Affairs; and members of the CIA briefing staff;
—Samuel K. Skinner;
—domestic advisers;
—select Cabinet members, for lunch;
—representatives of the law enforcement community;
—Secretary of Defense Dick Cheney.

The President announced his intention to nominate Philip Brunelle, of Minnesota, to be a member of the National Council on the Arts for the remainder of the term expiring September 3, 1994. He would succeed Phyllis Curtain. Currently Mr. Brunelle serves as artistic director and founder of the Plymouth Music Series of Minnesota in Minneapolis, MN.

*April 14*

The President held morning meetings at the White House with:
—the Vice President; Samuel K. Skinner, Chief of Staff to the President; Brent Scowcroft, Assistant to the President for National Security Affairs; and members of the CIA briefing staff;
—Samuel K. Skinner.

In the afternoon, the President traveled to Fraser, MI, where he toured the assembly line of Giddings & Lewis, Inc. Following the tour, the President traveled to Dearborn, MI. In the evening, he returned to Washington, DC.

The President announced his intention to nominate Thomas Grady, of Massachusetts, to be a member of the Board of Directors of the Overseas Private Investment Corporation for a term expiring December 17, 1994. This is a reappointment. Currently Mr. Grady serves as a partner with the law firm of Grady & Dwyer in Washington, DC.

The President announced his intention to appoint the following individuals to be members of the National Commission for Employment Policy for the terms indicated. These are reappointments:

*Roger J. Whyte*, of Maryland, for a term expiring March 20, 1995. Currently Mr. Whyte serves as vice president of A.T. Kearney Executive Search in Washington, DC.

*Henri S. Rauschenbach*, of Massachusetts, for a term expiring February 19, 1995. Currently Senator Rauschenbach serves as a Massachusetts State senator.

*April 15*

The President met at the White House with:
—the Vice President; Samuel K. Skinner, Chief of Staff to the President; Brent Scowcroft,

Assistant to the President for National Security Affairs; and members of the CIA briefing staff;

—Samuel K. Skinner;

—economic advisers;

—the Vice President, for lunch;

—Secretary of State James A. Baker III.

The President named Secretary of Defense Dick Cheney and Secretary of Education Lamar Alexander to be his personal representatives to the celebration of Australian-American Friendship Week and the commemoration of the 50th anniversary of the Battle of the Coral Sea.

The President declared a major disaster existed in the State of Illinois and ordered Federal aid to supplement State and local recovery efforts in the area struck by flooding beginning on April 13.

*April 16*

In the morning, the President taped a radio address at the White House for broadcast on April 18. He then met with:

—the Vice President; Samuel K. Skinner, Chief of Staff to the President; Brent Scowcroft, Assistant to the President for National Security Affairs; and members of the CIA briefing staff;

—Samuel K. Skinner;

—members of the Satmar community.

Later, the President traveled to Allentown, PA, where he met with the leadership of the Lehigh Valley 2000 education initiative. Following his remarks to the Lehigh Valley 2000 community, the President traveled to Kennebunkport, ME, for the Easter weekend. He was joined by Mrs. Bush at their home on Walker's Point.

The President announced his intention to appoint the following individuals:

*Charles C. Krueger*, of New York, to be a Commissioner of the United States section of the Great Lakes Fishery Commission for a term of 6 years. This is a reappointment. Currently Dr. Krueger serves as an associate professor in the department of natural resources at Cornell University in Ithaca, NY.

*Harry H. Whiteley*, of Michigan, to be Alternate Commissioner of the United States section of the Great Lakes Fishery Commission. He would succeed Robert L. Athey. Currently Mr. Whiteley owns Harry H. Whiteley Associates in Rogers City, MI.

*April 20*

In the morning, the President and Mrs. Bush traveled from their home in Kennebunkport, ME, to Columbus, OH. Following the opening of the AmeriFlora '92 Exposition, they returned to Washington, DC.

The President held afternoon meetings with:

—Secretary of the Treasury Nicholas F. Brady;

—Samuel K. Skinner, Chief of Staff to the President.

The President announced his intention to nominate Steven Manaster, of Utah, to be a Commissioner of the Commodity Futures Trading Commission for the term expiring April 13, 1997. He would succeed Fowler C. West. Currently Dr. Manaster serves in the University of Utah department of finance as a professor and as a Wasatch advisors distinguished faculty scholar in Salt Lake City, UT.

The President announced his intention to nominate Pamela J. Turner, of the District of Columbia, to be a member of the U.S. Advisory Commission on Public Diplomacy for a term expiring July 1, 1995. This is a reappointment. Currently Ms. Turner serves as vice president of government relations for the National Cable Television Association in Washington, DC.

*April 21*

The President met at the White House with:

—the Vice President; Samuel K. Skinner, Chief of Staff to the President; Brent Scowcroft, Assistant to the President for National Security Affairs; and members of the CIA briefing staff;

—national evangelical leaders;

—the Vice President, for lunch;

—Samuel K. Skinner.

The President announced his intention to nominate Tony Armendariz, of Texas, to be a member of the Federal Labor Relations Authority for a term of 5 years expiring July 29, 1997. This is a reappointment. Since 1989, Mr. Armendariz has served as a member of the Federal Labor Relations Authority in Washington, DC.

*April 22*

The President met at the White House with:

—the Vice President; Samuel K. Skinner, Chief of Staff to the President; Brent Scowcroft, Assistant to the President for National Security Affairs; and members of the CIA briefing staff;

—Samuel K. Skinner;

—Secretary of State James A. Baker III.

*April 23*

The President held morning meetings at the White House with:

—the Vice President; Samuel K. Skinner, Chief of Staff to the President; Brent Scowcroft, Assistant to the President for National Security Affairs; and members of the CIA briefing staff;

—Samuel K. Skinner;

—domestic advisers.

In the evening, the President and Mrs. Bush hosted a reception for the 60th anniversary of the Folger Shakespeare Library on the State Floor.

*April 24*

The President held morning meetings at the White House with:

—the Vice President; Samuel K. Skinner, Chief of Staff to the President; Brent Scowcroft, Assistant to the President for National Security Affairs; and members of the CIA briefing staff;

—Samuel K. Skinner;

—Secretary of State James A. Baker III.

In the afternoon, the President met with the AMVETS leadership. Later he and Mrs. Bush traveled to Camp David, MD, for the weekend.

The White House announced that Prime Minister Brian Mulroney of Canada will meet with the President on May 20 in Washington, DC.

The President announced his intention to appoint Charles G. Palm, of California, to be a member of the National Historical Publications and Records Commission for a term expiring December 26, 1995. This is a reappointment. Currently Mr. Palm serves as archivist and deputy director of the Hoover Institution at Stanford University in Stanford, CA.

The President announced his intention to appoint the following individuals to be Commissioners of the Franklin Delano Roosevelt Memorial Commission:

*Irving Berlin,* of Illinois. He would succeed Calvin M. Whitesell. Currently Mr. Berlin owns Irving Berlin, Ltd., in Chicago, IL.

*Doris H. McClory,* of Illinois. She would succeed Jennings Randolph. From 1960 to 1969, Ms. McClory served as an associate producer with Goodson-Todman Productions.

*Carol M. Palmer,* of Maryland. She would succeed Eugene J. Keogh. Since 1984, Ms. Palmer has served as a legal administrator with the law firm of Preston, Thorgrimson, Ellis & Holman in Washington, DC.

*David B. Roosevelt,* of Texas. He would succeed Edmund J. "Pat" Brown. Currently Mr. Roosevelt serves as executive vice president and chief executive officer of Morse, Williams & Co. in New York, NY.

The President announced his intention to appoint the following individuals to be members of the Advisory Committee on the Arts, John F. Kennedy Center for the Performing Arts:

*Abbey J. Butler,* of New York. He would succeed Martha B. Zeder. Currently Mr. Butler serves as president of C.B. Equities Capital Corp. and cochairman of the FoxMeyer Corp. in New York, NY.

*Herbert F. Collins,* of Massachusetts. He would succeed Naomi Zeavin. Currently Mr. Collins serves as chairman of the board and cofounder of Boston Capital Partners, Inc., in Boston, MA.

*Robert E. Gable,* of Kentucky. He would succeed James Thompson. Currently Mr. Gable serves as chairman of the board of the Stearns Co. in Lexington, KY.

The White House announced that the President accorded Frederick Morris Bush, of Maryland, the personal rank of Ambassador during his tenure as Commissioner General of the U.S. exhibition at the Universal Exposition in Seville, Spain.

*April 26*

In the afternoon, the President and Mrs. Bush returned to the White House from a weekend stay at Camp David, MD.

*April 27*

In the morning, the President met at the White House with the Vice President; Samuel K. Skinner, Chief of Staff to the President; Brent Scowcroft, Assistant to the President for National Security Affairs; and members of the CIA briefing staff.

The President then traveled to Miami, FL, and Charlotte, NC. In the evening, he returned to Washington, DC.

The President announced his intention to appoint the following individuals to be members of the Advisory Committee to the Pension Benefit Guaranty Corporation:

*W. Gordon Binns, Jr.,* of New York, for a term expiring February 19, 1995. This is a reappointment. Currently Mr. Binns serves as vice president and chief investment funds officer for the General Motors Corp. in New York, NY.

*Kenneth Keene,* of Connecticut, for a term expiring February 19, 1995. This is a reappointment. From 1972 to 1984, Mr. Keene served as a member of the board of directors of Johnson & Higgins.

*Stephen F. Keller,* of California, for a term expiring February 19, 1995. This is a reappointment. Currently Mr. Keller serves as an attorney with the law firm of Fulbright & Jaworski in Los Angeles, CA.

*April 28*

The President met at the White House with:

—the Vice President; Samuel K. Skinner, Chief of Staff to the President; Brent Scowcroft, Assistant to the President for National Security Affairs; and members of the CIA briefing staff;

—Samuel K. Skinner;

—Republican congressional leaders;

—National Science Bowl winners;

—the 1992 Big Brother and Big Sister;

—select Cabinet members, for lunch.

*April 29*

In the morning, the President met at the White House with:

—the Vice President; Samuel K. Skinner, Chief of Staff to the President; Brent Scowcroft,

Assistant to the President for National Security Affairs; and members of the CIA briefing staff;

—Samuel K. Skinner.

He met in the afternoon with Secretary of State James A. Baker III.

*April 30*
In the morning, the President signed the Executive order on infrastructure privatization in a ceremony in the Oval Office. He then met with:
—the Vice President, Samuel K. Skinner, Chief of Staff to the President; Brent Scowcroft, Assistant to the President for National Security Affairs; and members of the CIA briefing staff;
—Samuel K. Skinner;
—Senator and Mrs. Connie Mack, Cancer Courage Award recipients.

In the afternoon, the President traveled to Columbus, OH, and returned to Washington, DC, in the evening.

The President announced his intention to appoint the following individuals to be members of the Commission for the Preservation of America's Heritage Abroad:

*Arthur Schneier,* of New York, for a term expiring February 27, 1995. This is a reappointment. Upon appointment, he will be designated Chairman. Currently Rabbi Schneier serves as senior rabbi of the Park East Synagogue in New York, NY.

*Dov S. Zakheim,* of Maryland, for a term expiring February 27, 1995. This is a reappointment. Currently Dr. Zakheim serves as chief executive officer with the System Planning Corp. in Arlington, VA.

*May 1*
The President met in the morning at the White House with:
—the Vice President; Samuel K. Skinner, Chief of Staff to the President; Brent Scowcroft, Assistant to the President for National Security Affairs; and members of the CIA briefing staff;
—Samuel K. Skinner;
—civil rights community leaders;
—Secretary of State James A. Baker III.

In the afternoon, the President signed the Law Day proclamation in a ceremony in the Roosevelt Room. He then met with Goldman Environmental Prize winners in the Oval Office.

The President appointed the following individuals to be members of the Board of Visitors to the United States Naval Academy:

*Catherine C. Colgan,* of Virginia, for a term expiring December 30, 1994. She would succeed Arthur B. Culvahouse, Jr. Currently Ms. Colgan serves as president of Colgan Communications in Virginia Beach, VA.

*Frederick D. McClure,* of Texas, for a term expiring December 30, 1994. He would succeed John Chatfield Tuck. Currently Mr. McClure serves as managing director of the First Southwest Co. in Dallas, TX.

In the evening, the President and Mrs. Bush traveled to Camp David, MD, for the weekend.

*May 2*
The President declared a major disaster existed in the county and the city of Los Angeles, CA, and ordered Federal aid to supplement State and local recovery efforts in Los Angeles County, affected by fires during a period of civil disturbances beginning on April 29.

*May 3*
The President and Mrs. Bush, accompanied by several family members, attended morning church services at the Camp David Evergreen Chapel, where Lt. John Frusti, Camp David chaplain, offered a prayer of reconciliation.

In the afternoon, the President and Mrs. Bush returned to the White House from a weekend stay at Camp David, MD.

*May 4*
The President held morning meetings at the White House with:
—the Vice President; Samuel K. Skinner, Chief of Staff to the President; Brent Scowcroft, Assistant to the President for National Security Affairs; and members of the CIA briefing staff;
—Samuel K. Skinner;
—senior domestic advisers;
—North American members of the Council for Sustainable Development;
—the asthma and allergy poster child.

In the afternoon, the President met with Secretary of the Treasury Nicholas F. Brady. Later, he attended the National Rehabilitation Hospital fundraiser at the Avenel Club in Potomac, MD.

The President declared a major disaster existed in the State of California and ordered Federal aid to supplement State and local recovery efforts in the area struck by earthquakes and aftershocks beginning on April 25.

The President announced his intention to appoint Paul A. Vander Myde, of Virginia, to be a member of the Council of the Administrative Conference of the United States for a term of 3 years. He would succeed R. Carter Sanders, Jr. Currently Mr. Vander Myde serves as vice president for corporate affairs of the VSE Corp. of Alexandria, VA.

The President announced his intention to designate Harold P. Freeman, of New York, as Chairman of the President's Cancer Panel for a term of one year. This is a reappointment. Currently Dr. Freeman serves as director of surgery at the Harlem Hospital in New York, NY.

The President announced his intention to appoint Charles B. Wilson, of California, to be a member of the National Cancer Advisory Board for a term expiring March 9, 1998. He would succeed Kenneth Olden. Currently Dr. Wilson serves as director of the Brain Tumor Research Center at the University of California in San Francisco, CA.

The President announced his intention to appoint Amoretta M. Hoeber, of Virginia, to be a Representative of the United States of America on the Joint Commission on the Environment, established by the Panama Canal Treaty of 1977, for a term of 3 years. She would succeed Norman C. Roberts. Currently Ms. Hoeber serves as senior staff member of TRW Environmental Safety System, Inc., in Fairfax, VA.

*May 5*

The President met at the White House with:
—the Vice President; Samuel K. Skinner, Chief of Staff to the President; Brent Scowcroft, Assistant to the President for National Security Affairs; and members of the CIA briefing staff;
—Secretary of Housing and Urban Development Jack Kemp, Secretary of Labor Lynn M. Martin, Secretary of Health and Human Services Louis W. Sullivan, and Attorney General William P. Barr.

The President also met with the Senate Republican Conference at the Capitol and then returned to the White House for lunch with the Vice President.

In an afternoon ceremony on the State Floor, the President received diplomatic credentials from Ambassadors Aurel-Dragos Munteanu of Romania, Juan Esteban Aguirre of Paraguay, and Oleh Bilorus of Ukraine.

*May 6*

The President met at the White House with:
—Secretary of State James A. Baker III;
—the Vice President; Samuel K. Skinner, Chief of Staff to the President; Brent Scowcroft, Assistant to the President for National Security Affairs; and members of the CIA briefing staff.

In the afternoon, President Bush and President Leonid Kravchuk of Ukraine went to Camp David, MD, for a brief visit.

In the evening, the President traveled to Los Angeles, CA.

*May 7*

In the morning, the President toured the area damaged by the civil disturbances in south central Los Angeles.

The President held meetings with:
—State and local officials;
—Hispanic economic development leaders;
—the Presidential task force on civil disturbances in Los Angeles.

The President accorded Jay Van Andel, of Michigan, the personal rank of Ambassador during his tenure as Commissioner General of the United States pavilion at the International Exposition in Genoa, Italy. Currently Mr. Van Andel serves as chairman of the board of Amway Corp. in Ada, MI.

*May 8*

Following his morning address to Los Angeles community groups, the President returned to Washington, DC.

The President announced his intention to appoint Henry Clement Pitot III, of New York, to be a member of the President's Cancer Panel for a term expiring February 20, 1995. He would succeed Geza J. Jako. Currently Dr. Pitot serves as professor of oncology and pathology at the McArdle Laboratory for Cancer Research at the University of Wisconsin Medical School in Madison, WI.

*May 9*

In the evening, the President and Mrs. Bush attended the White House Correspondents Association dinner at the Washington Hilton Hotel.

*May 11*

The President held morning meetings at the White House with:
—Secretary of Defense Dick Cheney;
—the Vice President; Samuel K. Skinner, Chief of Staff to the President; Brent Scowcroft, Assistant to the President for National Security Affairs; and members of the CIA briefing staff;
—Samuel K. Skinner.

In the afternoon, the President traveled to Philadelphia, PA, where he attended a briefing with members of the Violent Traffickers Project and met with residents of the Spring Garden neighborhood. In the evening, he returned to Washington, DC.

*May 12*

In the morning, the President met at the White House with:
—the Vice President; Samuel K. Skinner, Chief of Staff to the President; Brent Scowcroft, Assistant to the President for National Security Affairs; and members of the CIA briefing staff;
—Samuel K. Skinner;
—congressional leaders.

*May 13*

The President held morning meetings at the White House with:

—Secretary of State James A. Baker III;
—the Vice President; Samuel K. Skinner, Chief of Staff to the President; Brent Scowcroft, Assistant to the President for National Security Affairs; and members of the CIA briefing staff;
—Samuel K. Skinner.

In the afternoon, the President met with Prime Minister Esko Aho of Finland. The President then traveled to Baltimore, MD, where he toured the East Baltimore Medical Center, and returned to Washington, DC, in the late afternoon.

The President announced his intention to appoint Andrew H. Card, Jr., Secretary of Transportation, to be a member of the Advisory Commission on Intergovernmental Relations for a term of 2 years. He would succeed Samuel K. Skinner.

The President announced his intention to appoint the following individuals to be members of the National Commission for Employment Policy:

*Robert O. Snelling, Sr.*, of Texas, for a term expiring September 30, 1994. He would succeed A. Wayne Roberts. Mr. Snelling is currently chairman of the board and president of Snelling and Snelling, Inc., in Dallas, TX.

*Charles G. Bakaly, Jr.*, of California, for a term expiring September 30, 1994. He would succeed James W. Winchester. Mr. Bakaly is currently a senior partner with the firm of O'Melveny & Myers in Los Angeles, CA.

*James J. Lack*, of New York, for a term expiring September 30, 1994. He would succeed Jerry J. Naylor. Since 1979, Mr. Lack has been a New York State senator.

The President announced his intention to appoint the following individuals to be members of the Federal Service Impasses Panel for terms expiring on January 10, 1997. These are reappointments:

*N. Victor Goodman*, of Ohio. Currently Mr. Goodman serves as a partner with the law firm of Benesch, Friedlander, Coplan and Aronoff in Columbus, OH.

*Daniel H. Kruger*, of Michigan. Currently Dr. Kruger serves as a professor of industrial relations at Michigan State University in East Lansing, MI.

The President announced his intention to appoint the following individuals to be members of the U.S. Nuclear Waste Technical Review Board:

*John E. Cantlon*, of Michigan, for a term expiring April 19, 1996. This is a reappointment. Upon appointment, he will be designated Chairman. From 1975 to 1991, Dr. Cantlon served as vice president for research and graduate studies at Michigan State University in East Lansing, MI.

*Clarence R. Allen*, of California, for a term expiring April 19, 1996. This is a reappointment. Currently Dr. Allen serves as a professor of geology and geophysics

at the California Institute of Technology in Pasadena, CA.

*Gary Brewer*, of Michigan, for a term expiring April 19, 1996. He would succeed Melvin W. Carter. Currently Dr. Brewer serves as professor of resource policy and management and dean of the School of Natural Resources at the University of Michigan in Ann Arbor, MI.

The President today announced his intention to appoint the following individuals to be members of the President's National Security Telecommunications Advisory Committee:

*John N. McMahon*, of California. He would succeed R. A. Fuhrman. Currently Mr. McMahon serves as president of Lockheed Missiles and Space Systems Group and president of Lockheed Missiles & Space Co. in Calabasas, CA.

*D. Travis Engen*, of Connecticut. He would succeed Rand V. Araskog. Currently Mr. Engen serves as executive vice president of the ITT Corp. in New York, NY.

*May 14*

The President met at the White House with:
—the Vice President; Samuel K. Skinner, Chief of Staff to the President; Brent Scowcroft, Assistant to the President for National Security Affairs; and members of the CIA briefing staff;
—economic advisers;
—Samuel K. Skinner;
—the multiple sclerosis Mother and Father of the Year;
—select Cabinet members, for lunch.

*May 15*

The President held a morning meeting at the White House with the Vice President; Samuel K. Skinner, Chief of Staff to the President; Brent Scowcroft, Assistant to the President for National Security Affairs; and members of the CIA briefing staff. Later, the President traveled to Pittsburgh, PA, where he met with community leaders.

In the afternoon, the President traveled to Houston, TX.

*May 17*

In the morning, the President traveled from Houston, TX, to South Bend, IN, and returned to Washington, DC, in the evening .

*May 18*

The President met at the White House with the Vice President; Samuel K. Skinner, Chief of Staff to the President; Brent Scowcroft, Assistant to the President for National Security Affairs; and members of the CIA briefing staff. Later, he signed the Older Americans Month proclamation at a ceremony in the Oval Office.

The President held afternoon meetings with:

—Cabinet members;
—Secretary of the Treasury Nicholas F. Brady;
—Samuel K. Skinner.

*May 19*
The President met at the White House with:
—the Vice President; Samuel K. Skinner, Chief of Staff to the President; Brent Scowcroft, Assistant to the President for National Security Affairs; and members of the CIA briefing staff;
—Samuel K. Skinner.

The President declared a major disaster existed in the Commonwealth of Virginia and ordered Federal aid to supplement State and local recovery efforts in the area struck by severe storms and flooding on April 21–22.

*May 20*
The President met at the White House with:
—the Vice President; Samuel K. Skinner, Chief of Staff to the President; Brent Scowcroft, Assistant to the President for National Security Affairs; and members of the CIA briefing staff;
—Samuel K. Skinner;
—Secretary of State James A. Baker III.

The President appointed the following individuals to be members of the Board of Directors of the Federal National Mortgage Association for terms ending on the date of the annual meeting of the stockholders in 1993. These are reappointments:

*Christine M. Diemer*, of California. Currently Ms. Diemer serves as executive director of the Building Industry Association in Santa Ana, CA.
*Gloria E.A. Toote*, of New York. Currently Ms. Toote serves as president of Trea Estates in New York, NY.
*George L. Clark, Jr.*, of New York. Currently Mr. Clark serves as president of George L. Clark, Inc., in Brooklyn, NY.
*Salvador Bonilla-Mathe*, of Florida. Currently Mr. Bonilla-Mathe serves as president and chief executive officer of the Gulf Bank in Miami, FL.
*J. Brian Gaffney*, of Connecticut. Currently Mr. Gaffney serves as a partner with the law firm of Gaffney, Pease & DiFabio in New Britain, CT.

The President declared an emergency existed in the Federated States of Micronesia and ordered Federal aid to supplement State and local recovery efforts in the area struck by drought beginning March 30.

*May 21*
The President held a morning meeting at the White House with the Vice President; Samuel K. Skinner, Chief of Staff to the President; Brent Scowcroft, Assistant to the President for National Security Affairs; and members of the CIA briefing staff.

In the afternoon, the President traveled to Cleveland, OH, where he met with community leaders, and then to Westchester, NY.

In the evening, the President traveled to Kennebunkport, ME, where he was joined by Mrs. Bush for the Memorial Day holiday weekend.

The President announced that David J. Beightol has been named Executive Director of the Presidential Task Force on Los Angeles Recovery. On Monday, May 4, 1992, the President established a task force of Cabinet deputies and other key Federal officials to assist the recovery of Los Angeles. The President appointed David T. Kearns, Deputy Secretary, Department of Education, and Alfred A. DelliBovi, Deputy Secretary, Department of Housing and Urban Development as cochairmen of the task force.

The President announced his intention to appoint Lee J. Weddig, of Maryland, to be a U.S. Commissioner on the International Commission for the Conservation of Atlantic Tunas for a term of 3 years. This is a reappointment. Currently Mr. Weddig serves as executive vice president of the National Fisheries Institute in Arlington, VA.

The President appointed the following individuals to be members of the Board of Directors of the Federal Home Loan Mortgage Corporation for the terms expiring on the date of the next annual meeting of the common stockholders in 1993:

*George L. Argyros*, of California. This is a reappointment. Currently Mr. Argyros serves as president and chief executive officer of the Arnel Development Co. in Costa Mesa, CA.
*Thomas Ludlow Ashley*, of the District of Columbia. This is a reappointment. Currently Mr. Ashley serves as president of the Association of Bank Holding Companies in Washington, DC.
*Armando J. Bucelo, Jr.*, of Florida. This is a reappointment. Currently Mr. Bucelo serves as an attorney with the law offices of Armando J. Bucelo, Jr., in Miami, FL.
*Shannon Fairbanks*, of the District of Columbia. This is a reappointment. Currently Ms. Fairbanks serves as executive vice president of the American Real Estate Group in Washington, DC.

*May 25*
In the morning, the President and Mrs. Bush participated in a Memorial Day ceremony at the American Legion post in Kennebunkport, ME.

In the afternoon, they returned to Washington, DC, from a holiday weekend stay at their home in Kennebunkport.

*May 26*
The President met at the White House with:
—the Vice President; Samuel K. Skinner, Chief of Staff to the President; Brent Scowcroft, Assistant to the President for National Securi-

ty Affairs; and members of the CIA briefing staff;
—Samuel K. Skinner;
—domestic advisers;
—the Vice President, for lunch;
—Blue Angels pilots.

*May 27*
In the morning, the President met at the White House with:
—the Vice President; Samuel K. Skinner, Chief of Staff to the President; Brent Scowcroft, Assistant to the President for National Security Affairs; and members of the CIA briefing staff;
—Samuel K. Skinner.

The President traveled to Annapolis, MD, and returned to Washington, DC, in the afternoon. He then met with Mayor Teddy Kollek of Jerusalem.

Later, the President traveled to Atlanta, GA, and returned to Washington, DC, in the evening.

*May 28*
The President held morning meetings at the White House with:
—the Vice President; Samuel K. Skinner, Chief of Staff to the President; Brent Scowcroft, Assistant to the President for National Security Affairs; and members of the CIA briefing staff;
—Samuel K. Skinner;
—Secretary of State James A. Baker III.

In the afternoon, the President traveled to Phoenix, AZ, where he addressed Arizona delegates to the Republican Party Convention. In the evening, the President traveled to Los Angeles, CA.

The President announced his intention to nominate Marshall Lee Miller, of Virginia, to be a member of the U.S. Advisory Commission on Public Diplomacy for a term expiring July 1, 1994. He would succeed Edwin J. Feulner, Jr. Currently Mr. Miller serves as a partner with the law firm of Baker and Hostetler in Washington, DC.

The President announced his intention to nominate Max M. Kampelman, of the District of Columbia, to be a member of the Board of Directors of the United States Institute of Peace for a term expiring January 19, 1995. He would succeed Morris I. Leibman. Currently Dr. Kampelman serves as a partner with the law firm of Fried, Frank, Harris, Shriver and Jacobson in Washington, DC.

*May 29*
In the morning, the President met with State and local officials in Los Angeles, CA.

In the afternoon the President met with former President Ronald Reagan.

The President announced his intention to appoint James Robert Beall, of Virginia, to be a member of the Interstate Commission on the Potomac River Basin. He would succeed Frank J. Donatelli. Currently Mr. Beall serves as an associate and project manager of William H. Gordon and Associates in Woodbridge, VA.

The President announced his intention to appoint Norman R. Augustine, of Maryland, to be Governor on the Board of Governors of the American National Red Cross, for a term of 3 years. He would succeed George F. Moody. He will also be designated as principal officer of the Corporation. Currently Mr. Augustine serves as chairman and chief executive officer of the Martin Marietta Corp. in Bethesda, MD.

*May 30*
In the morning, the President traveled from Los Angeles to Fresno, CA, where he held a roundtable discussion with agricultural leaders at Fresno Airport. He then toured the Simpson Vineyard and was briefed on vineyard water technology.

In the afternoon, the President traveled to Dallas, TX. In the evening, he returned to Andrews Air Force Base, MD, and then went to Camp David, MD, for the remainder of the weekend.

*June 1*
In the afternoon, the President traveled from Camp David, MD, to the Goddard Space Flight Center in Greenbelt, MD, where he participated in a tour and briefing. He then returned to Washington, DC.

*June 2*
The President held morning meetings at the White House with:
—the Vice President; Samuel K. Skinner, Chief of Staff to the President; Brent Scowcroft, Assistant to the President for National Security Affairs; and members of the CIA briefing staff;
—Samuel K. Skinner;
— bipartisan congressional leaders.

In the evening, the President and Mrs. Bush hosted a barbecue for members of Congress on the South Lawn.

The President announced his intention to appoint the following individuals to be members of the Federal Council on the Aging for a term of 3 years:

*Max L. Friedersdorf*, of Florida. He would succeed Normen E. Wymbs. Upon appointment, he will be designated chairman. Currently Mr. Friedersdorf serves as chairman of the advisory board of the Association of Retired Americans.

*Charles W. Kane,* of Florida. He would succeed June Allyson. Currently Mr. Kane serves as a member of the advisory council of the department of elder affairs for the State of Florida.

The President announced his intention to appoint the following individuals to be Governors of the Board of the Governors, American National Red Cross, for terms of 3 years. These are reappointments:

*James Addison Baker III,* Secretary of State

*Dick Cheney,* Secretary of Defense

*Louis W. Sullivan,* Secretary of Health and Human Services

## June 3

The President met at the White House with:
—the Vice President; Samuel K. Skinner, Chief of Staff to the President; Brent Scowcroft, Assistant to the President for National Security Affairs; and members of the CIA briefing staff;
—Samuel K. Skinner;
—Secretary of State James A. Baker III;
—Balanced Budget Amendment Coalition members;
—former Finance Minister Edouard Balladur of France.

## June 4

The President held morning meetings at the White House with:
—the Vice President; Samuel K. Skinner, Chief of Staff to the President; Brent Scowcroft, Assistant to the President for National Security Affairs; and members of the CIA briefing staff;
—Samuel K. Skinner;
—Eastern Caribbean leaders.

The President and Mrs. Bush had lunch with the Vice President and Mrs. Quayle at the Naval Observatory.

Later in the afternoon, the President met with Special Emissary Shin Kanemaru of Japan.

The President has selected the following individuals to represent him at the inauguration of the new President of Mali, June 8:

*Head of Delegation:*

*Louis W.Sullivan,* Secretary of Health and Human Services

*Delegate:*

*Frank Royal,* of Virginia.

The President appointed the following individuals to be members of the J. William Fulbright Foreign Scholarship Board for the terms indicated:

*George Stuart Heyer, Jr.,* of Texas, for a term expiring September 22, 1994. He would succeed James Robert Whelan. Currently Dr. Heyer serves as a professor of history of doctrine at the Austin Presbyterian Theological Seminary in Austin, TX.

*Daniel Pipes,* of Pennsylvania, for a term expiring September 22, 1994. He would succeed Nelson V. Nee. Currently Dr. Pipes serves as director of the Foreign Policy Research Institute in Philadelphia, PA.

*Esther Lee Yao,* of Texas, for a term expiring September 22, 1993. She would succeed Philip N. Marcus. Currently Dr. Yao serves as an associate professor at the University of Houston at Clear Lake in Houston, TX.

The President announced his intention to nominate Mary Mohs, of Wisconsin, to be a member of the National Museum Services Board for a term expiring December 6, 1994. She would succeed Marilyn Logsdon Mennello. Currently Ms. Mohs serves as vice chairman of the Henry Vilas 200 Commission and chairman of the Madison Landmarks Commission in Madison, WI.

The President announced his intention to appoint Pat M. Stevens IV, Brigadier General, U.S. Army, to be a United States Commissioner to the Red River Compact Commission. He would succeed Thomas Allen Sands. Currently Mr. Stevens serves as Commanding General of the Army Engineer Division for the Lower Mississippi Valley in Vicksburg, MS.

The President announced his intention to appoint Edward J. Cording, of Illinois, to be a member of the Nuclear Waste Technical Review Board for a term expiring April 19, 1996. He would succeed Don U. Deere. Currently Dr. Cording serves as a professor of civil engineering at the University of Illinois at Urbana in Urbana, IL.

The President announced his intention to appoint Bobbie Greene Kilberg, Deputy Assistant to the President and Director of the Office of Intergovernmental Affairs, to be a member of the Advisory Commission on Intergovernmental Relations for a term of 2 years. She would succeed Debra Rae Anderson.

## June 5

The President met at the White House with:
—the Vice President; Samuel K. Skinner, Chief of Staff to the President; Brent Scowcroft, Assistant to the President for National Security Affairs; and members of the CIA briefing staff;
—Samuel K. Skinner.

In the afternoon, the President and Mrs. Bush traveled to Camp David, MD, for the weekend.

## June 7

In the afternoon, President and Mrs. Bush, accompanied by Prime Minister and Mrs. Major of the United Kingdom, returned to the White House from a weekend stay at Camp David, MD.

*June 8*

The President met at the White House with:
—the Vice President; Samuel K. Skinner, Chief of Staff to the President; Brent Scowcroft, Assistant to the President for National Security Affairs; and members of the CIA briefing staff;
—Samuel K. Skinner;
—Attorney General William P. Barr;
—Secretary of Defense Dick Cheney.

The President announced that John Joseph Murphy, of Texas, has agreed to serve as the chairman of the Citizens Democracy Corps. He would succeed Drew Lewis. Mr. Murphy serves as chairman of the board and chief executive officer of Dresser Industries, Inc., in Dallas, TX.

The President announced his intention to appoint Zvi Kestenbaum, of New York, to be a member of the Commission for the Preservation of America's Heritage Abroad for a term expiring February 27, 1995. This is a reappointment. Currently Rabbi Kestenbaum serves as executive director of the Opportunity Development Association in Brooklyn, NY.

The President announced his intention to appoint the following individuals to be Commissioners on the United States Section of the Pacific Salmon Commission:

*David A. Colson*, of Maryland, for a term expiring January 5, 1994. This is a reappointment. Currently Mr. Colson serves as Deputy Assistant Secretary of State for Oceans and Fisheries Affairs at the State Department in Washington, DC.

*Gerald I. James*, of Washington, for a term expiring January 5, 1996. He would succeed Guy R. McMinds. Currently Mr. James serves as program manager for the Lummi Tribe and has served as a member and vice chairman of the Lummi Indian Business Council.

*Charles P. Meacham*, of Alaska, for the remainder of the term expiring January 5, 1994. He would succeed Don W. Collinsworth. Currently Mr. Meacham serves as deputy commissioner of the Alaska Department of Fish and Game in Juneau, AK.

*June 9*

The President held morning meetings at the White House with:
—the Vice President; Samuel K. Skinner, Chief of Staff to the President; Brent Scowcroft, Assistant to the President for National Security Affairs; and members of the CIA briefing staff;
—Samuel K. Skinner;
—Foreign Minister Andrey Kozyrev of Russia.

In the afternoon, the President traveled to Bowmansdale, PA, and returned to Washington, DC, in the evening.

The White House announced that the President transmitted to the Congress the annual report on the administration of the Federal Railroad Safety Act of 1970 for calendar year 1990.

*June 10*

The President met at the White House with:
—the Vice President; Samuel K. Skinner, Chief of Staff to the President; Brent Scowcroft, Assistant to the President for National Security Affairs; and members of the CIA briefing staff;
—select House Democrats;
—select Senate Republicans;
—Secretary of State James A. Baker III;
—Samuel K. Skinner.

The President announced his intention to appoint Luis M. Proenza, of Alaska, to be a member of the Arctic Research Commission for a term expiring February 26, 1996. He would succeed John H. Steele. Currently Dr. Proenza serves as vice chancellor for research and dean of the graduate school at the University of Alaska, Fairbanks.

The President announced his intention to nominate Barbara Hackman Franklin, Secretary of Commerce, to be a member of the Competitiveness Policy Council for the remainder of a term expiring October 16, 1992. She would succeed Robert Adam Mosbacher.

The President announced his intention to appoint the following individuals to be members of the U.S. Holocaust Memorial Council for the terms indicated:

*Albert Abramson*, of Maryland, for a term expiring January 15, 1997. This is a reappointment. Currently Mr. Abramson serves as founder of Tower Construction Co. in Bethesda, MD.

*Joseph A. Cannon*, of Utah, for the remainder of the term expiring January 15, 1994. He would succeed Marshall Ezralow. Mr. Cannon has served as chairman of the board of directors, president, and chief executive officer of Geneva Steel in Provo, UT.

*Mimi Weyforth Dawson*, of the District of Columbia, for a term expiring January 15, 1997. She would succeed Bobbie Greene Kilberg. Currently Ms. Dawson serves as a consultant with Wiley, Rein & Fielding.

*George Deukmejian*, of California, for a term expiring January 15, 1997. This is a reappointment. Currently Governor Deukmejian serves as partner with the law firm of Sidley and Austin in Los Angeles, CA.

*William Anthony Duna*, of Minnesota, for a term expiring January 15, 1997. This is a reappointment. Currently Mr. Duna serves as the owner of Bill Duna Productions in Minneapolis, MN.

*Abraham H. Foxman*, of New Jersey, for a term expiring January 15, 1997. This is a reappointment. Currently Mr. Foxman serves as national director of the Anti-Defamation League of B'nai B'rith.

*Harold Gershowitz*, of Illinois, for the remainder of the term expiring January 15, 1994. He would succeed

Michael H. Moskow. Currently Mr. Gershowitz serves as senior vice president of Waste Management, Inc., in Oak Brook, IL.

*Barbara George Gold*, of Illinois, for a term expiring January 15, 1997. She would succeed Philip Abrams. Currently Ms. Gold serves as midwestern director of the American ORT Federation in Chicago, IL.

*Steven H. Goldberg*, of New York, for a term expiring January 15, 1997. He would succeed Matthew Brown. Currently Mr. Goldberg serves as president and founder of Campaign Telecommunications, Inc., in New York, NY.

*Robert J. Horn*, of Maryland, for a term expiring January 15, 1997. This is a reappointment. Currently Mr. Horn serves as assistant vice president and manager of Federal affairs for the Detroit Edison Co. in Washington, DC.

*Richard M. Rosenbaum*, of New York, for a term expiring January 15, 1997. This is a reappointment. Currently Mr. Rosenbaum serves as a partner with the law firm of Nixon, Hargrave, Devans and Doyle in Rochester, NY.

*Sheila Rabb Weidenfeld*, of the District of Columbia, for a term expiring January 15, 1997. This is a reappointment. Since 1978, Ms. Weidenfeld has served as president and chief executive officer of D.C. Productions, Ltd., in Washington, DC.

## June 11

In the morning, the President and Mrs. Bush traveled to Panama City, Panama. Following an arrival ceremony at Paitilla International Airport, the President met with President Guillermo Endara at the Presidential Palace.

In the afternoon, the President and Mrs. Bush went to Plaza Belisario Porras, where demonstrations prevented a scheduled ceremony from taking place.

Late in the afternoon, the President and Mrs. Bush traveled to Rio de Janeiro, Brazil, to attend the United Nations Conference on Environment and Development.

## June 12

In the morning, the President held a meeting at the Sheraton Hotel and Towers with U.S. nongovernmental observers of the United Nations Conference on Environment and Development. He then attended a session of the Conference at the Riocentro Conference Center and a luncheon with environmental leaders.

In the evening, the President and Mrs. Bush attended a dinner with President Fernando Collor of Brazil and Mrs. Collor at Palacio Laranjeiras.

## June 13

In the afternoon, the President attended a reception and luncheon for heads of state and government at the Riocentro Conference Center in Rio de Janeiro, Brazil. Later in the afternoon, the President and Mrs. Bush departed for Washington, DC, and arrived very early the next morning.

## June 15

The President met at the White House with:
—the Vice President; Samuel K. Skinner, Chief of Staff to the President; Brent Scowcroft, Assistant to the President for National Security Affairs; and members of the CIA briefing staff;
—Samuel K. Skinner.

In the evening, President and Mrs. Bush attended a Republican National Committee Presidential Trust fundraising dinner in Potomac, MD.

The President announced his intention to nominate Joshua M. Javits, of the District of Columbia, to be a member of the National Mediation Board for a term expiring July 1, 1995. This is a reappointment. Currently Mr. Javits serves as a member of the National Mediation Board in Washington, DC. From 1985 to 1988, Mr. Javits served on several permanent arbitration panels. He has also served as an attorney with the law firm of Cades, Schutte, Fleming & Wright in Washington, DC, 1985–87.

The President today announced his intention to appoint the following individuals to be members of the Advisory Council on Historic Preservation:

*Andrew H. Card, Jr.*, Secretary of Transportation. He would succeed Samuel K. Skinner.

*Jane L.S. Davidson*, of Pennsylvania, for a term expiring June 10, 1995. She would succeed Dennis F. Mullins. Currently Ms. Davidson serves as Chester County Historic Preservation officer in Westchester, PA.

*Barnabas McHenry*, of New York, for a term expiring June 10, 1996. He would succeed Lucille Clarke Dumbrill. Currently Mr. McHenry serves as chairman and member of various preservation and conservation as well as cultural organizations in New York, NY.

*Margaret Zuehlke Robson*, of the District of Columbia, for a term expiring June 10, 1996. She would succeed Lynn Kartavich. Ms. Robson is actively involved in civic and community programs in Washington, DC.

## June 16

The President met at the White House with:
—the Vice President; Samuel K. Skinner, Chief of Staff to the President; Brent Scowcroft, Assistant to the President for National Security Affairs; and members of the CIA briefing staff;
—Samuel K. Skinner;
—Secretary of the Treasury Nicholas F. Brady.

The President today announced his intention to appoint:

*Don E. Newquist*, of Texas, to be Chairman of the United States International Trade Commission for the term expiring June 16, 1994. This is a reappointment.

Mr. Newquist has served as a member of the International Trade Commission since 1988.

*Peter S. Watson,* of California, to be Vice Chairman of the United States International Trade Commission for the term expiring June 16, 1994. He would succeed Anne E. Brunsdale. Since 1991, Mr. Watson has served as a member of the International Trade Commission. Prior to this he served as Director of Asian Affairs at the National Security Council, 1989–91.

*June 17*

The President met at the White House with:
—the Vice President; Samuel K. Skinner, Chief of Staff to the President; Brent Scowcroft, Assistant to the President for National Security Affairs; and members of the CIA briefing staff;
—Samuel K. Skinner;
—Secretary of State James A. Baker III.

In the afternoon, President Bush and President Boris Yeltsin of Russia traveled to Annapolis, MD, where they cruised the Severn River.

*June 18*

In the morning, the President and Mrs. Bush hosted a coffee at the White House for President and Mrs. Yeltsin. President Bush then met with the Vice President; Samuel K. Skinner, Chief of Staff to the President; Brent Scowcroft, Assistant to the President for National Security Affairs; and members of the CIA briefing staff.

Later in the morning, the President traveled to Newark, CA.

In the afternoon, the President met with northern California Republican leaders at the Newark Hilton Hotel. Following a Republican fundraising dinner in Orinda, the President traveled to Newport Beach, CA.

The President has selected the following individuals to represent him at the closing ceremonies of the summer Olympics in Barcelona, Spain:

*Head of Delegation:*
*Arnold Schwarzenegger*

*Delegates:*
*Marvin Bush,* of Virginia.
*Margaret Bush,* of Virginia.
*Willard Heminway,* of Connecticut.
*Mary Lou Retton,* of Texas.
*Kristi Yamaguchi,* of California.
*Greg Anthony,* of Nevada.

*June 19*

In the morning, the President held roundtable discussions with Asian media representatives and Hispanic media representatives at the Four Seasons Hotel in Newport Beach, CA.

In the afternoon, the President attended a southern California Republican leadership meeting at the Four Seasons Hotel.

The President declared a major disaster existed in the State of New Mexico and ordered Federal aid to supplement State and local recovery efforts in the area struck by severe thunderstorms, hail, and flooding on May 22, 1992, through May 25, 1992.

The President announced his intention to nominate Malcolm S. Forbes, Jr., of New Jersey, to be a member of the Board for International Broadcasting for a term expiring April 28, 1995. This is a reappointment. Since 1985, Mr. Forbes has served as Chairman of the Board for International Broadcasting. Currently Mr. Forbes serves as editor-in-chief, president, and chief executive officer of Forbes, Inc., and Forbes magazine.

*June 20*

In the morning, the President traveled from Newport Beach, CA, to Universal City, CA, where he participated in a roundtable discussion with leaders of taxpayers organizations. He then traveled to Dallas, TX, where he was joined by Mrs. Bush.

In the afternoon, the President and Mrs. Bush returned to Andrews Air Force Base, MD, and then went to Camp David, MD, for the remainder of the weekend.

*June 22*

In the morning, President and Mrs. Bush returned to the White House from Camp David, MD. The President then met at the White House with the Vice President; Samuel K. Skinner, Chief of Staff to the President; Brent Scowcroft, Assistant to the President for National Security Affairs; and members of the CIA briefing staff. The President then met separately with Samuel K. Skinner.

The President announced his intention to designate Gary A. Glaser, of Ohio, to be Chairperson of the Credit Standards Advisory Committee. Mr. Glaser was appointed to the Committee on January 1, 1991.

The President announced his intention to appoint the following individuals to be members of the Risk Assessment and Management Commission:

*Barbara A. Bankoff,* of the District of Columbia. This is a new position. Since 1989, Ms. Bankoff has served as president of Bankoff Associates in Washington, DC.

*Thorne G. Auchter,* of Florida. This is a new position. Currently Mr. Auchter serves as director and chief executive officer of the Institute for Regulatory Policy in Washington, DC.

*Anthony J. Thompson,* of Maryland. This is a new position. Since 1987, Mr. Thompson has served as a partner with the firm of Perkin Coie in Washington, DC.

## June 23

The President met in the morning at the White House with the Vice President; Samuel K. Skinner, Chief of Staff to the President; Brent Scowcroft, Assistant to the President for National Security Affairs; and members of the CIA briefing staff; and in the afternoon with Samuel K. Skinner.

In the evening, President and Mrs. Bush hosted a barbecue for White House news photographers on the South Lawn.

## June 24

The President met in the morning at the White House with:

—Secretary of Transportation Andrew H. Card, Jr.;
—the Vice President; Samuel K. Skinner, Chief of Staff to the President; Brent Scowcroft, Assistant to the President for National Security Affairs; and members of the CIA briefing staff;
—Samuel K. Skinner.

In the afternoon, the President met with Secretary of State James A. Baker III.

The President announced his intention to appoint the following individuals to be members of the Martin Luther King, Jr., Federal Holiday Commission for terms of 1 year:

*Bob Martinez*, Director of the Office of National Drug Control Policy. This is a reappointment.
*Jack Kemp*, Secretary of Housing and Urban Development. This is a reappointment.
*William S. Sessions*, Director of the Federal Bureau of Investigation. This is a reappointment.

## June 25

The President met at the White House with:

—the Vice President; Samuel K. Skinner, Chief of Staff to the President; Brent Scowcroft, Assistant to the President for National Security Affairs; and members of the CIA briefing staff;
—the Vice President, for lunch;
—Samuel K. Skinner;
—White House fellows;
—Dr. Donald W. Ingwerson, National School Superintendent of the Year.

In the late afternoon, the President hosted a reception for the New American Schools Development Corp. on the State Floor.

The President announced his intention to appoint the following individuals as members of the Operating Committee of the Critical Technologies Institute. These are new positions:

*Nicholas F. Brady*, Secretary of the Treasury, for a term of 2 years.
*Michael J. Boskin*, Chairman of the Council of Economic Advisers, for a term of 3 years.

*Richard G. Darman*, Director of the Office of Management and Budget, for a term of 1 year.
*Adm. Jonathan T. Howe*, United States Navy, Deputy Assistant to the President for National Security Affairs, for a term of 4 years.

The President announced his intention to designate D. Allan Bromley, Director of the Office of Science and Technology Policy, to be Chairman of the Operating Committee of the Critical Technologies Institute. Currently Dr. Bromley serves as Assistant to the President and Director of the Office of Science and Technology Policy at the White House.

## June 26

The President held morning meetings at the White House with:

—the Vice President; Samuel K. Skinner, Chief of Staff to the President; Brent Scowcroft, Assistant to the President for National Security Affairs; and members of the CIA briefing staff;
—Samuel K. Skinner;
—heads of Polish-American organizations;
—Secretary of State James A. Baker III.

In the evening, the President met with Lt. Paula Coughlin, USN. Later in the evening, the President and Mrs. Bush traveled to Camp David, MD, for the weekend.

The President declared a major disaster existed in the State of Minnesota and ordered Federal aid to supplement State and local recovery efforts in the area struck by severe storms, flooding, and tornadoes on June 16–20.

The President has selected the following individuals to represent him at the inauguration of Philippine President Fidel Ramos, June 30:

*Head of Delegation:*

*Elaine Chao*, of California. Currently Ms. Chao serves as Director of the Peace Corps.

*Delegates:*

*Elliot Richardson*, of Massachusetts. Mr. Richardson currently serves as Special Representative of the President for the Multilateral Assistance Initiative.
*Oscar Domodon*, of California. Currently Dr. Domodon is a dentist in Long Beach, CA, and is State chairman of the Filipino-American Republican Council of California.

## June 28

In the afternoon, the President and Mrs. Bush returned to the White House from a weekend stay at Camp David, MD.

## June 29

In the morning, the President met at the White House with the Vice President; Samuel K. Skinner, Chief of Staff to the President; Brent Scowcroft, Assistant to the President for National

Security Affairs; and members of the CIA briefing staff. The President then traveled to New York City where he attended a briefing at the Drug Enforcement Administration and held a roundtable discussion with New York State Conservative Party members at the New York Hilton Hotel.

In the afternoon, the President traveled to Detroit, MI, where he attended an early evening reception with the Michigan Team 100 at the Westin Hotel.

In the evening, the President returned to Washington, DC.

*June 30*

The President held morning meetings at the White House with:

—Gen. John Galvin, USA;

—the Vice President; Samuel K. Skinner, Chief of Staff to the President; Brent Scowcroft, Assistant to the President for National Security Affairs; and members of the CIA briefing staff;

—William J. Althouse of the U.S. Conference of Mayors;

—Ambassador Malcolm Toon.

In the afternoon, the President met with Samuel K. Skinner.

In the evening, the President and Mrs. Bush hosted a picnic for the Diplomatic Corps on the South Lawn.

The President announced that in keeping with his America 2000 education initiative, two historically black colleges, Clark-Atlanta University and Morris Brown College, have been selected to perform information science and training research under the Army's Centers of Excellence program.

*July 1*

The President held morning meetings at the White House with:

—the Vice President; Samuel K. Skinner, Chief of Staff to the President; Brent Scowcroft, Assistant to the President for National Security Affairs; and members of the CIA briefing staff;

—domestic advisers;

—Samuel K. Skinner.

Following their afternoon meeting, the President and Prime Minister Kiichi Miyazawa of Japan went to Camp David, MD, for private talks and dinner.

In the evening, the President and Prime Minister Miyazawa traveled from Camp David, MD, to the Capital Center in Landover, MD, where they were joined by Mrs. Bush and attended a concert by Luciano Pavarotti. Following the concert, the President and Mrs. Bush returned to the White House.

*July 2*

The President held morning meetings at the White House with the Vice President; Samuel K. Skinner, Chief of Staff to the President; Brent Scowcroft, Assistant to the President for National Security Affairs; and members of the CIA briefing staff.

In the afternoon, the President made a conference call from the Oval Office to Bush-Quayle campaign and Republican Party leaders.

In the evening, the President went to Camp David, MD.

The President declared a major disaster existed in the State of California and ordered Federal aid to supplement State and local recovery efforts in the area struck by earthquakes and continuing aftershocks that began on June 28.

The President also declared a major disaster existed in the State of South Dakota and ordered Federal aid to supplement State and local recovery efforts in the area struck by severe storms, tornadoes, and flooding on June 13–23.

The White House announced that President Bush will meet with President Carlos Salinas of Mexico in San Diego on July 14.

*July 4*

In the morning, the President traveled from Camp David, MD, to Andrews Air Force Base, MD, and then on to Daytona Beach, FL.

In the afternoon, the President traveled to Faith, NC.

In the evening, after returning to Andrews Air Force Base, MD, the President was joined by Mrs. Bush, and they traveled to Warsaw, Poland.

*July 5*

After their morning arrival in Warsaw, the President and Mrs. Bush attended an arrival ceremony at the Royal Castle. Following a meeting with President Lech Walesa, President Bush met with other Polish officials.

In the early afternoon, the President and Mrs. Bush attended a memorial service for Ignacy Paderewski at St. John's Basilica Church. After the service, the President and Mrs. Bush met with Cardinal Josef Glemp. Later, the President and Mrs. Bush participated in a departure ceremony in the courtyard of the Royal Castle. In the mid-afternoon, the President and Mrs. Bush traveled to Munich, Germany.

In the evening, President Bush had dinner with President François Mitterrand of France at the Sheraton Hotel in Munich.

*July 6*

In the morning, the President met at the Munich Sheraton Hotel with Prime Minister Giuliano Amato of Italy. He later attended a working breakfast with Chancellor Helmut Kohl of Germany at the Vier Jahreszeiten Hotel. After returning to the Sheraton Hotel, the President attended a signing ceremony at which Gov. Carroll A. Campbell of South Carolina and Eberhard von Kuenheim, chairman of the board of BMW, signed a declaration regarding the construction of a BMW plant in South Carolina. Following an arrival ceremony at the Residenz, the President attended a luncheon hosted by Chancellor Kohl at the Spatenhaus Restaurant.

In the afternoon, the President attended the opening session of the economic summit at the Residenz.

In the evening, the President attended a reception and dinner hosted by Chancellor Kohl at Nymphenburg Castle.

The President appointed James O. Campbell, of Alaska, to be a member of the Arctic Research Commission for a term expiring February 26, 1996. He would succeed Elmer E. Rasmuson. Currently Mr. Campbell serves as president and chief executive officer of the Alaska Commercial Corp.

*July 7*

After meeting at the Munich Sheraton Hotel with President Jacques Delors of the European Community, President Bush attended morning sessions of the economic summit at the Residenz. After a luncheon meeting with heads of delegations, the President attended another session of the economic summit.

In the evening, the President and Mrs. Bush attended a reception and ballet hosted by the Chancellor and Mrs. Kohl and a dinner hosted by Minister President Max Streibl of Bavaria and Mrs. Streibl at the Residenz.

*July 8*

The President attended the morning session of the economic summit at the Residenz in Munich.

After a luncheon hosted by President and Mrs. Richard von Weizsäcker of Germany, President Bush and other heads of delegations to the economic summit met with President Boris Yeltsin of Russia.

In the evening, the President and Mrs. Bush traveled to Helsinki, Finland.

*July 9*

In the morning, the President met at the Guest House in Helsinki with Prime Minister Constantine Mitsotakis of Greece and Chairman Eduard Shevardnadze of the Republic of Georgia.

The President later attended the opening ceremony and morning session of the Conference on Security and Cooperation in Europe (CSCE) at the Helsinki Fair Center. He then met with:
—NATO Secretary General Manfred Woerner;
—President Alija Izetbegovic of Bosnia;
—Prime Minister Suleyman Demirel of Turkey.

After a working luncheon, the President attended the second session of the CSCE. He then met with President Leonid Kravchuk of Ukraine and President Stanislav Shushkevich of Byelarus.

In the evening, the President and Mrs. Bush attended a state dinner at the Presidential Palace hosted by President and Mrs. Mauno Koivisto of Finland.

The President announced his intention to appoint Bruce M. Todd, Mayor of Austin, TX, to be a member of the Advisory Commission on Intergovernmental Relations for a term of 2 years. He would succeed Donald M. Fraser.

The President announced his intention to appoint J. Alfred Rider, of California, to be a member of the President's Committee on Mental Retardation for a term expiring May 11, 1994. This is a reappointment.

The White House announced that the President has directed Marion Clifton Blakey, of Mississippi, Assistant Secretary of Transportation for Public Affairs, to perform the duties of the Office of Administrator of the National Highway Traffic Safety Administration.

The White House announced that the President has submitted to the Congress requests for FY 1992 appropriations for the Departments of Defense, Housing and Urban Development, Justice, Labor, and Veterans Affairs; the Commission on Civil Rights; the Equal Employment Opportunity Commission; and the National Commission on Libraries and Information Science. The President also submitted amendments to FY 1993 requests for the Departments of Defense, Energy, Health and Human Services, and the Treasury; the Office of Personnel Management; the Commission on Civil Rights; and the Equal Employment Opportunity Commission. In addition, the President transmitted three FY 1993 requests for the legislative and judicial branches.

*July 10*

In the morning, after meeting with President Koivisto at the Presidential Palace in Helsinki, President Bush went to the Helsinki Fair Center for the CFE–1A agreement signing and the final CSCE sessions. Between the sessions, President Bush met with President Arnold Ruutel of Estonia, President Anatolijs Gorbunovs of Latvia, and President Vytautas Landsbergis of Lithuania. The President and Mrs. Bush then traveled to Kennebunkport, ME, for the weekend.

*July 13*

The President appointed the following individuals to be members of the Advisory Committee for Trade Policy and Negotiations for terms of 2 years:

*Georgette Mosbacher,* of Texas. She would succeed Barbara Hackman Franklin. Currently Ms. Mosbacher serves as president and chief executive officer of Georgette Mosbacher Enterprises.

*George M.C. Fisher,* of Illinois. He would succeed Robert Galvin. Since 1990, Mr. Fisher has served as chairman of the board and chief executive officer of Motorola, Inc.

*P. Roy Vagelos,* of New Jersey. He would succeed Edward T. Pratt. Since 1985, Dr. Vagelos has served as chairman, president, and chief executive officer of Merck & Co., Inc.

*Walter Y. Elisha,* of North Carolina. He would succeed Richard M. Morrow. Currently Mr. Elisha serves as chairman, chief executive officer, and a director of Springs Industries.

*Michael A. Miles,* of New York. He would succeed Allen F. Jacobson. Currently Mr. Miles serves as chairman of the board and chief executive officer of Philip Morris Co., Inc.

*Ralph S. Larsen,* of New Jersey. He would succeed Philip E. Lippincott. Currently Mr. Larsen serves as chairman of the board and chief executive officer of Johnson & Johnson.

*Thomas G. Labrecque,* of New Jersey. He would succeed A.W. Clausen. Currently Mr. Labrecque serves as chairman and chief executive officer and member of the board of directors of the Chase Manhattan Corp.

*July 14*

In the morning, the President traveled from Kennebunkport, ME, to Bakersfield, CA, and on to Sequoia National Forest. While there, the President hiked, held a roundtable discussion with outdoor magazine editors, and had lunch with youth from R.M. Pyles Boys Camp.

In the afternoon, the President traveled to San Diego, CA, where he met with President Carlos Salinas of Mexico. The two Presidents then attended the Major League All-Star Baseball Game at Jack Murphy Stadium.

In the evening, the President traveled to Boulder, WY, to Secretary of State James A. Baker's ranch.

The White House announced that President Bush ordered the general counsel of his campaign to file a complaint with the Federal Election Commission against Floyd Brown and his Presidential Victory Campaign.

The President nominated the following individuals to be members of the Advisory Board of the Saint Lawrence Seaway Development Corporation:

*Sterling G. Sechrist,* of Ohio. He would succeed Virgil E. Brown. Since 1950, Mr. Sechrist has served with Bank One of Medina County in Wadsworth, OH, as vice-president and trust officer, 1952; executive vice-presi-

dent and director, 1962; chairman of the board, 1970; and chairman emeritus after his retirement in 1979.

*Edward Morgan Paluso,* of Pennsylvania. He would succeed Steven Reimers. Since 1972, Mr. Paluso has served as County Commissioner of Washington County, PA.

The President announced his intention to appoint Jack Steel, of Texas, to be a member of the Commission on Presidential Scholars. He would succeed Fran Chiles.

*July 16*

The President announced his intention to appoint the following individuals to be members of the President's Committee on the National Medal of Science:

*Edward A. Frieman,* of California, for a term expiring December 31, 1993. He would succeed David R. Challoner. He will be designated Chairman. Since 1986, Dr. Frieman has served as director of the Scripps Institute of Oceanography in La Jolla, CA.

*Edward C. Stone, Jr.,* of California, for a term expiring December 31, 1994. He would succeed Roland H. Carlson. Currently Dr. Stone serves as Director of the Jet Propulsion Laboratory in Pasadena, CA.

*George H. Heilmeier,* of New Jersey, for a term expiring December 31, 1994. He would succeed Carl O. Bostrom. Currently Dr. Heilmeier serves as president and chief executive officer of Bellcore (Bell Communications Research) in Livingston, NJ.

*July 17*

In the morning, the President traveled from Boulder, WY, to Jackson, WY.

In the afternoon, the President traveled to Salt Lake City, UT, where he met with Mormon Church leaders at the Latter-day Saints headquarters and with Utah Republican leaders at the Marriott Hotel.

*July 18*

In the morning, the President traveled from Salt Lake City, UT, to Provo, UT. In the afternoon, he traveled from Utah to Hagerstown, MD, and then on to Camp David, MD, for the remainder of the weekend.

*July 19*

In the evening, the President returned to the White House from Camp David, MD.

*July 20*

The President held meetings at the White House with:

—the Vice President; Samuel K. Skinner, Chief of Staff to the President; Brent Scowcroft, Assistant to the President for National Security Affairs; and members of the CIA briefing staff.

—the Vice President, for lunch;

—domestic advisers;

—economic advisers;
—Secretary of the Treasury Nicholas F. Brady;
—Samuel K. Skinner.

In the evening, the President spoke by satellite from a video services studio in Washington, DC, to Bush-Quayle national campaign volunteers, leaders, and supporters.

*July 21*

The President held morning meetings at the White House with:
—the Vice President; Samuel K. Skinner, Chief of Staff to the President; Brent Scowcroft, Assistant to the President for National Security Affairs; and members of the CIA briefing staff;
—the leadership of the National Conference of Black Mayors.

Later in the morning, the President traveled to Philadelphia, PA. In the afternoon, the President traveled to Garfield, NJ, and then returned to Washington, DC.

*July 22*

The President held morning meetings at the White House with:
—domestic advisers;
—the Vice President; Samuel K. Skinner, Chief of Staff to the President; Brent Scowcroft, Assistant to the President for National Security Affairs; and members of the CIA briefing staff.

In the afternoon, the President again met with domestic advisers.

The President announced his intention to appoint Leo Melamed, of Illinois, to be a member of the United States Holocaust Memorial Council for the remainder of the term expiring January 15, 1995. He would succeed William Alexander Scott III. Since 1965, Mr. Melamed has served as chairman of Dellsher Investment Co., Inc., in Chicago, IL. From 1976 to 1990, he served as special counsel to the board of the Chicago Mercantile Exchange as well as chairman of the executive committee from 1985 to 1990.

*July 23*

The President held morning meetings at the White House with:
—domestic advisers;
—the Vice President; Samuel K. Skinner, Chief of Staff to the President; Brent Scowcroft, Assistant to the President for National Security Affairs; and members of the CIA briefing staff.

In the afternoon, the President met with Samuel K. Skinner.

*July 24*

The President held morning meetings at the White House with:
—domestic advisers;
—the Vice President; Samuel K. Skinner, Chief of Staff to the President; Brent Scowcroft, Assistant to the President for National Security Affairs; and members of the CIA briefing staff.

Later in the morning, the President traveled to Brookville, OH.

In the afternoon, the President traveled to Dayton, OH, where he attended a Republican leadership meeting. He then went to Columbia, MO.

In the evening, the President traveled to Hagerstown, MD, and then on to Camp David, MD, for the weekend.

*July 26*

In the afternoon, the President returned to the White House from a weekend stay at Camp David, MD.

*July 27*

The President held morning meetings at the White House with:
—domestic advisers;
—the Vice President; Samuel K. Skinner, Chief of Staff to the President; Brent Scowcroft, Assistant to the President for National Security Affairs; and members of the CIA briefing staff.

Later in the morning, the President traveled to Wyoming, MI, where he toured the Holland American Wafer Co. plant and had lunch with the employees.

In the afternoon, the President traveled to Neenah, WI, where he toured the Outlook Graphics Corp. plant with students of the youth apprenticeship program.

Later in the afternoon, the President returned to Washington, DC.

In the evening, the President met at the White House with national security advisers.

The President announced his intention to appoint the following individuals as members of the Cultural Property Advisory Committee:

*Jack A. Josephson*, of New York, for a term expiring April 25, 1995. This is a reappointment. Mr. Josephson will be designated Chairman. From 1979 to 1986, Mr. Josephson served as president of Sellers and Josephson, Inc.

*Harold Mark Keshishian*, of Maryland, for a term expiring April 25, 1995. This is a reappointment. Since 1985, Mr. Keshishian has served as president of Mark Keshishian & Sons.

*Frederick William Lange*, of Colorado, for a term expiring April 25, 1995. This is a reappointment. Since

1986, Dr. Lange has served as curator of anthropology and director of the Center for Central American Art and Archaeology at the University of Colorado.

*Richard Stockton MacNeish*, of Massachusetts, for a term expiring April 25, 1993. He would succeed Leslie Elizabeth Wildesen. Since 1986, Dr. MacNeish has served as director of the Andover Foundation for Archaeological Research.

## July 28

The President met at the White House with:
—domestic advisers;
—congressional leaders;
—the Vice President; Samuel K. Skinner, Chief of Staff to the President; Brent Scowcroft, Assistant to the President for National Security Affairs; and members of the CIA briefing staff;
—Samuel K. Skinner.

In the afternoon, the President attended a Presidential lecture series presentation in the East Room.

The President declared a major disaster existed in the State of Arkansas and ordered Federal aid to supplement State and local recovery efforts in the area struck by severe thunderstorms and high winds on June 14–19.

## July 29

In the morning, the President met at the White House with:
—domestic advisers;
—the Vice President; Samuel K. Skinner, Chief of Staff to the President; Brent Scowcroft, Assistant to the President for National Security Affairs; and members of the CIA briefing staff;
—Gov. Carroll A. Campbell of South Carolina;
—Attorney General William P. Barr;
—the Vice President, for lunch.

In the afternoon, the President met at the White House with:
—Secretary of State James A. Baker III;
—domestic advisers;
—economic advisers;
—Samuel K. Skinner.

## July 30

In the morning, the President traveled to Waxahachie, TX, where he toured the superconduct-

ing super collider facility. He then traveled to Orange County, CA.

In the evening, the President attended a Presidential Trust reception and dinner in private residences in Los Angeles.

The President received a report of the Presidential Task Force on Los Angeles Recovery. The Task Force was set up by the President after the Los Angeles riots to help speed the delivery of services to Los Angeles. The report contained a six-point action plan designed to help the people of Los Angeles rebuild their neighborhoods and address the problems of crime, lack of educational opportunities, welfare dependency, and lack of jobs.

The President has selected the following individuals to represent him at the inauguration ceremony for President-elect Sixto Duran-Ballen of Ecuador, August 10:

### Head of Delegation:

*Governor Bob Martinez*, of Florida. Currently Governor Martinez serves as Director of the Office of National Drug Control Policy.

### Delegates:

*Kim Flower*, of New York. Currently Ms. Flower serves as executive vice president of the Americas Society and Managing Director of the Council of the Americas. Prior to this, she served as Director of Latin American Affairs at the National Security Council, 1987–88.

*Tirso Del Junco*, of California. Dr. Del Junco is vice chairman of the California Republican Party.

*Dr. and Mrs. Walter F. Abendschein*, of Maryland.

## July 31

In the morning, the President visited the Greater Avenues of Independence Headquarters in Los Angeles for a briefing and tour.

In midmorning, the President traveled to Andrews Air Force Base, MD, and then went to Camp David, MD.

The President announced his intention to appoint Wayne Allard, of Colorado, to serve in an advisory capacity on the Board of Trustees of the James Madison Memorial Fellowship Foundation for a term expiring December 12, 1996. He would succeed Paul B. Henry.

## Appendix B—Nominations Submitted to the Senate

*The following list does not include promotions of members of the Uniformed Services, nominations to the Service Academies, or nominations of Foreign Service officers.*

### Submitted January 22

The following named persons to be Associate Judges of the Superior Court of the District of Columbia for the term of 15 years:

Stephanie Duncan-Peters, of the District of Columbia, vice Warren Roger King, elevated.

Ann O'Regan Keary, of the District of Columbia, vice George H. Goodrich, retired.

Judith E. Retchin, of the District of Columbia, vice Bruce S. Mencher, retired.

William M. Jackson, of the District of Columbia, vice William Courtleigh Gardner, retired.

The following named persons to be members of the Peace Corps National Advisory Council for the terms indicated:

Eugene C. Johnson, of Maryland, for a term expiring October 6, 1992, vice Gary Dale Robinson.

Tahlman Krumm, Jr., of Ohio, for a term expiring October 6, 1993 (reappointment).

Salvador Lew,
of Florida, to be a member of the Advisory Board for Cuba Broadcasting for a term of 2 years (new position).

### Submitted January 23

The following named persons to be members of the General Advisory Committee of the U.S. Arms Control and Disarmament Agency:

Anne Armstrong, of Texas, vice Harriet Fast Scott, resigned.

James Alan Abrahamson, of California, vice Robert B. Hotz, resigned.

Harold M. Agnew, of California, vice John P. Roche, resigned.

Juan A. Benitez, of Idaho, vice Jaime Oaxaca, resigned.

James H. Binns, Jr., of Pennsylvania, vice Francis P. Hoeber, resigned.

George A. Carver, Jr., of Virginia, vice Charles Burton Marshall, resigned.

Marjorie S. Holt, of Maryland (reappointment).

### Submitted January 27

Barbara Hackman Franklin,
of Pennsylvania, to be Secretary of Commerce.

Edward E. Carnes,
of Alabama, to be U.S. Circuit Judge for the Eleventh Circuit, vice Frank M. Johnson, Jr., retired.

Sidney A. Fitzwater,
of Texas, to be U.S. Circuit Judge for the Fifth Circuit, vice Thomas Gibbs Gee, retired.

John G. Roberts, Jr.,
of Maryland, to be U.S. Circuit Judge for the District of Columbia Circuit, vice Clarence Thomas, elevated.

John A. Smietanka,
of Michigan, to be U.S. Circuit Judge for the Sixth Circuit (new position).

Karen J. Williams,
of South Carolina, to be U.S. Circuit Judge for the Fourth Circuit, vice Robert F. Chapman, retired.

Kenneth R. Carr,
of Texas, to be U.S. District Judge for the Western District of Texas (new position).

James W. Jackson,
of Ohio, to be U.S. District Judge for the Northern District of Ohio, vice Richard B. McQuade, Jr., resigned.

Terral R. Smith,
of Texas, to be U.S. District Judge for the Western District of Texas (new position).

Jack W. Selden,
of Alabama, to be U.S. Attorney for the Northern District of Alabama for the term of 4 years, vice Frank W. Donaldson, term expired.

Shirley D. Peterson,
of Maryland, to be Commissioner of Internal Revenue, vice Fred T. Goldberg, Jr., resigned.

Fred T. Goldberg, Jr.,
of Missouri, to be an Assistant Secretary of the Treasury, vice Kenneth W. Gideon, resigned.

The following named persons to be members of the Board of Directors of the State Justice Institute for terms expiring September 17, 1994:

David Brock, of New Hampshire, vice Clement Clay Torbert, Jr., term expired.

Vivi L. Dilweg, of Wisconsin (reappointment).

Carlos R. Garza, of Texas, vice Daniel John Meador, term expired.

The following named persons to be members of the Board of Regents of the Uniformed Services University of the Health Sciences for terms expiring June 20, 1997:

John E. Connolly, of California, vice Sam A. Nixon, term expired.

William D. Skelton, of Georgia, vice Mario Efrain Ramirez, resigned.

*Submitted January 30*

Andrew H. Card, Jr.,
of Massachusetts, to be Secretary of Transportation.

Shirley Gray Adamovich,
of New Hampshire, to be a member of the National Commission on Libraries and Information Science for a term expiring July 19, 1996, vice Raymond J. Petersen, term expired.

John Agresto,
of New Mexico, to be a member of the National Advisory Council on Educational Research and Improvement for a term expiring September 30, 1992, vice Max Charles Graeber, term expired.

Shirley Chilton-O'Dell,
of California, to be a member of the Federal Retirement Thrift Investment Board for a term expiring September 25, 1994, vice Richard H. Headlee, term expired.

Hugh Hardy,
of New York, to be a member of the National Council on the Arts for a term expiring September 3, 1996, vice M. Ray Kingston, term expired.

Wells B. McCurdy,
of Washington, to be a member of the Board of Directors of the Overseas Private Investment Corporation for a term expiring December 17, 1993, vice Evan Griffith Galbraith, term expired.

Ian M. Ross,
of New Jersey, to be a member of the National Science Board, National Science Foundation, for a term expiring May 10, 1998 (reappointment).

*Submitted February 14*

Robert C. Frasure,
of West Virginia, a career member of the Senior Foreign Service, class of Counselor, to be Ambassador Extraordinary and Plenipotentiary of the United States of America to Estonia.

Darryl Norman Johnson,
of Washington, a career member of the Senior Foreign Service, class of Minister-Counselor, to be Ambassador Extraordinary and Plenipotentiary of the United States of America to Lithuania.

Ints M. Silins,
of Virginia, a career member of the Senior Foreign Service, class of Counselor, to be Ambassador Extraordinary and Plenipotentiary of the United States of America to Latvia.

Herman Jay Cohen,
an Assistant Secretary of State, to be a member of the Board of Directors of the African Development Foundation for a term expiring September 22, 1997 (reappointment).

*Submitted February 18*

George J. Terwilliger III,
of Vermont, to be Deputy Attorney General, vice William Pelham Barr.

Marc Allen Baas,
of Florida, a career member of the Senior Foreign Service, class of Minister-Counselor, to be Ambassador Extraordinary and Plenipotentiary of the United States of America to Ethiopia.

Kenneth C. Rogers,
of New Jersey, to be a member of the Nuclear Regulatory Commission for the term of 5 years expiring June 30, 1997 (reappointment).

*Submitted February 21*

Vice Admiral William O. Studeman,
U.S. Navy, to be Deputy Director of Central Intelligence, and to have the rank of Admiral while so serving.

*Submitted February 25*

William Bailey,
of Connecticut, to be a member of the National Council on the Arts for a term expiring September 3, 1996, vice Helen Frankenthaler, term expired.

*Submitted February 27*

Joseph Gerard Sullivan,
of Virginia, a career member of the Senior Foreign Service, class of Minister-Counselor, to be Ambassador Extraordinary and Plenipotentiary of the United States of America to the Republic of Nicaragua.

Stephen Norris,
of Virginia, to be a member of the Federal Retirement Thrift Investment Board for a term ex-

piring October 11, 1994, vice Stephen E. Bell, term expired.

*Submitted March 3*

Wayne A. Budd,
of Massachusetts, to be Associate Attorney General, vice Francis Anthony Keating II, resigned.

Alvin A. Schall,
of Maryland, to be U.S. Circuit Judge for the Federal Circuit, vice Edward S. Smith, retired.

*Submitted March 4*

Carl J. Kunasek,
of Arizona, to be Commissioner on Navajo and Hopi Relocation, Office of Navajo and Hopi Indian Relocation, for a term of 2 years (reappointment).

Roger L. Wollman,
of South Dakota, to be a member of the United States Sentencing Commission for a term expiring October 31, 1997, vice George E. MacKinnon, term expired.

*Submitted March 10*

Federico A. Moreno,
of Florida, to be U.S. Circuit Judge for the Eleventh Circuit, vice Paul H. Roney, retired.

Susan H. Black,
of Florida, to be U.S. Circuit Judge for the Eleventh Circuit, vice Thomas A. Clark, retired.

I. Lewis Libby, Jr.,
of the District of Columbia, to be Deputy Under Secretary of Defense for Policy (new position).

James B. Huff, Sr.,
of Mississippi, to be Administrator of the Rural Electrification Administration for a term of 10 years, vice Gary C. Byrne, resigned.

*Submitted March 12*

Gregori Lebedev,
of Virginia, to be Inspector General, Department of Defense, vice Susan J. Crawford.

*Submitted March 13*

Vicki Ann O'Meara,
of Illinois, to be an Assistant Attorney General, vice Richard Burleson Stewart, resigned.

Edward J. Damich,
of Virginia, to be a Commissioner of the Copyright Royalty Tribunal for a term of 7 years, vice J.C. Argetsinger, term expired.

*Submitted March 20*

Michael Boudin,
of Massachusetts, to be U.S. Circuit Judge for the First Circuit, vice Levin H. Campbell, retired.

Dennis G. Jacobs,
of New York, to be U.S. Circuit Judge for the Second Circuit, vice Wilfred Feinberg, retired.

Justin P. Wilson,
of Tennessee, to be U.S. Circuit Judge for the Sixth Circuit, vice Robert B. Krupansky, retired.

Richard H. Kyle,
of Minnesota, to be U.S. District Judge for the District of Minnesota, vice Robert G. Renner, retired.

C. LeRoy Hansen,
of New Mexico, to be U.S. District Judge for the District of New Mexico (new position).

John G. Heyburn II,
of Kentucky, to be U.S. District Judge for the Western District of Kentucky, vice Thomas A. Ballantine, Jr., deceased.

Gordon J. Quist,
of Michigan, to be U.S. District Judge for the Western District of Michigan (new position).

Paul L. Shechtman,
of New York, to be U.S. District Judge for the Southern District of New York, vice Richard Owen, retired.

Percy Anderson,
of California, to be U.S. District Judge for the Central District of California, vice Robert C. Bonner, resigned.

Lawrence O. Davis,
of Missouri, to be U.S. District Judge for the Eastern District of Missouri (new position).

Andrew S. Hanen,
of Texas, to be U.S. District Judge for the Southern District of Texas (new position).

Joe Kendall,
of Texas, to be U.S. District Judge for the Northern District of Texas (new position).

Russell T. Lloyd,
of Texas, to be U.S. District Judge for the Southern District of Texas (new position).

Linda H. McLaughlin,
of California, to be U.S. District Judge for the Central District of California (new position).

Lee H. Rosenthal,
of Texas, to be U.S. District Judge for the Southern District of Texas (new position).

John F. Walter,
of California, to be U.S. District Judge for the Central District of California (new position).

Daniel S. Goldin,
of California, to be Administrator of the National Aeronautics and Space Administration, vice Richard Harrison Truly, resigned.

*Submitted March 24*

Thomas R. Pickering,
of New Jersey, a career member of the Senior Foreign Service, with the personal rank of Career Ambassador, to be Ambassador Extraordinary and Plenipotentiary of the United States of America to India.

Gene E. Voigts,
of Missouri, to be U.S. District Judge for the Western District of Missouri, vice Scott O. Wright, retired.

David Spears Addington,
of Virginia, to be General Counsel of the Department of Defense, vice Terrence O'Donnell, resigned.

Duane Acker,
of Virginia, to be an Assistant Secretary of Agriculture, vice Charles E. Hess, resigned.

Bruno Victor Manno,
of Ohio, to be Assistant Secretary of Education for Policy and Planning, vice Charles E.M. Kolb, resigned.

Thomas P. Kerester,
of Virginia, to be Chief Counsel for Advocacy, Small Business Administration, vice Frank S. Swain, resigned.

*Submitted March 26*

Manuel H. Quintana,
of New York, to be U.S. District Judge for the Southern District of New York, a new position created by P.L. 101–650, approved December 1, 1990.

Richard Neil Zare,
of California, to be a member of the National Science Board, National Science Foundation, for the remainder of the term expiring May 10, 1992, vice Mary Lowe Good, resigned.

The following named persons to be members of the National Science Board, National Science Foundation, for terms expiring May 10, 1998:

F. Albert Cotton, of Texas (reappointment).

Charles Edward Hess, of California, vice John C. Hancock, term expiring.

John Hopcroft, of New York, vice Frederick Phillips Brooks, Jr., term expiring.

James L. Powell, of Pennsylvania (reappointment).

Frank H.T. Rhodes, of New York (reappointment).

Richard Neil Zare, of California (reappointment).

*Submitted April 1*

Wade F. Horn,
of Maryland, to be Deputy Director for Demand Reduction, Office of National Drug Control Policy, vice Herbert D. Kleber, resigned.

Charles A. Banks,
of Arkansas, to be U.S. District Judge for the Eastern District of Arkansas, vice G. Thomas Eisele, retired.

Alfred V. Covello,
of Connecticut, to be U.S. District Judge for the District of Connecticut (new position).

Carol E. Jackson,
of Missouri, to be U.S. District Judge for the Eastern District of Missouri, vice William L. Hungate, retired.

Irene M. Keeley,
of West Virginia, to be U.S. District Judge for the Northern District of West Virginia (new position).

Jerome B. Simandle,
of New Jersey, to be U.S. District Judge for the District of New Jersey (new position).

*Submitted April 2*

Lauralee M. Peters,
of Virginia, a career member of the Senior Foreign Service, class of Minister-Counselor, to be Ambassador Extraordinary and Plenipotentiary of the United States of America to the Republic of Sierra Leone.

Lourdes G. Baird,
of California, to be U.S. District Judge for the Central District of California (new position).

Robert D. Hunter,
of Alabama, to be U.S. District Judge for the Northern District of Alabama, vice E. B. Haltom, Jr., retired.

Maureen E. Mahoney,
of Virginia, to be U.S. District Judge for the Eastern District of Virginia, vice Albert V. Bryan, Jr., retired.

Joan M. McEntee,
of New York, to be Under Secretary of Commerce for Export Administration, vice Dennis Edward Kloske, resigned.

*Submitted April 7*

Richard G. Kopf,
of Nebraska, to be U.S. District Judge for the District of Nebraska, vice Warren K. Urbom, retired.

James S. Mitchell,
of Nebraska, to be U.S. District Judge for the District of Nebraska (new position).

Marvin H. Kosters,
of Virginia, to be Commissioner of Labor Statistics, U.S. Department of Labor, for a term of 4 years, vice Janet L. Norwood, term expired.

Carl W. Vogt,
of Maryland, to be a member of the National Transportation Safety Board for the term expiring December 31, 1996, vice James L. Kolstad, term expired.

Carl W. Vogt,
of Maryland, to be Chairman of the National Transportation Safety Board for a term of 2 years, vice James L. Kolstad, term expired.

Brig. Gen. Pat M. Stevens IV,
U.S. Army, to be a member and President of the Mississippi River Commission, vice Arthur E. Williams.

Brig. Gen. Albert J. Genetti, Jr.,
U.S. Army, to be a member of the Mississippi River Commission, vice Paul Y. Chinen.

*Submitted April 8*

William Dean Hansen,
of Idaho, to be Chief Financial Officer, Department of Education, vice John Theodore Sanders, resigned.

Emerson J. Elliott,
of Virginia, to be Commissioner of Education Statistics, Department of Education, for a term expiring June 20, 1995 (new position).

*Submitted April 9*

Irma E. Gonzalez,
of California, to be U.S. District Judge for the Southern District of California, vice J. Lawrence Irving, resigned.

Hume Alexander Horan,
of the District of Columbia, a career member of the Senior Foreign Service, class of Career Minister, to be Ambassador Extraordinary and Plenipotentiary of the United States of America to the Republic of Cote d'Ivoire.

Kenton Wesley Keith,
of Missouri, a career member of the Senior Foreign Service, class of Minister-Counselor, to be Ambassador Extraordinary and Plenipotentiary of the United States of America to the State of Qatar.

Donald K. Petterson,
of California, a career member of the Senior Foreign Service, class of Minister-Counselor, to be Ambassador Extraordinary and Plenipotentiary of the United States of America to the Republic of the Sudan.

Christian R. Holmes IV,
of California, to be an Assistant Administrator of the Environmental Protection Agency, vice Charles L. Grizzle, resigned.

Christian R. Holmes IV,
of California, to be Chief Financial Officer, Environmental Protection Agency (new position).

Daniel A. Sumner,
of North Carolina, to be an Assistant Secretary of Agriculture, vice Bruce L. Gardner, resigned.

Daniel A. Sumner,
of North Carolina, to be a member of the Board of Directors of the Commodity Credit Corporation, vice Bruce L. Gardner.

Carol Johnson Johns,
of Maryland, to be a member of the Board of Regents of the Uniformed Services University of the Health Sciences for a term expiring June 20, 1997 (reappointment).

Virginia Stanley Douglas,
of California, to be a member of the Board of Directors of the National Institute of Building Sciences for a term expiring September 7, 1993, vice MacDonald G. Becket, term expired.

Norman H. Stahl,
of New Hampshire, to be U.S. Circuit Judge for the First Circuit, vice David H. Souter, elevated.

Joseph A. DiClerico, Jr.,
of New Hampshire, to be U.S. District Judge for
the District of New Hampshire (new position).

Michael J. Melloy,
of Iowa, to be U.S. District Judge for the Northern District of Iowa, vice David R. Hansen, elevated.

Rudolph T. Randa,
of Wisconsin, to be U.S. District Judge for the
Eastern District of Wisconsin, vice Robert W.
Warren, retired.

Jerome H. Powell,
of New York, to be an Under Secretary of the
Treasury, vice Robert R. Glauber, resigned.

Timothy E. Flanigan,
of Virginia, to be an Assistant Attorney General,
vice J. Michael Luttig.

John Cunningham Dugan,
of the District of Columbia, to be an Assistant
Secretary of the Treasury, vice Jerome H. Powell.

*Withdrawn April 9*

Jerry Ralph Curry,
of Virginia, to be Administrator of the Federal
Aviation Administration, vice James Buchanan
Busey IV, which was sent to the Senate November 22, 1991.

*Submitted April 28*

Dennis P. Barrett,
of Washington, a career member of the Senior
Foreign Service, class of Minister-Counselor, to
be Ambassador Extraordinary and Plenipotentiary of the United States of America to the Democratic Republic of Madagascar.

Richard Goodwin Capen, Jr.,
of Florida, to be Ambassador Extraordinary and
Plenipotentiary of the United States of America
to Spain.

Roger A. McGuire,
of Ohio, a career member of the Senior Foreign
Service, class of Counselor, to be Ambassador Ex-
traordinary and Plenipotentiary of the United
States of America to the Republic of Guinea-
Bissau.

William Lacy Swing,
of North Carolina, a career member of the Senior
Foreign Service, class of Career Minister, to be
Ambassador Extraordinary and Plenipotentiary of
the United States of America to the Federal Republic of Nigeria.

Linda Gillespie Stuntz,
of Virginia, to be Deputy Secretary of Energy,
vice W. Henson Moore.

Nathaniel M. Gorton,
of Massachusetts, to be U.S. District Judge for the
District of Massachusetts (new position).

William Clark, Jr.,
of the District of Columbia, a career member of
the Senior Foreign Service, class of Career Minister, to be an Assistant Secretary of State, vice
Richard H. Solomon.

James P. Covey,
of the District of Columbia, a career member of
the Senior Foreign Service, class of Minister-
Counselor, to be Assistant Secretary of State for
South Asian Affairs (new position).

James D. Jameson,
of California, to be an Assistant Secretary of
Commerce, vice Timothy John McBride, resigned.

Clarence H. Albright, Jr.,
of Virginia, to be General Counsel of the Department of Housing and Urban Development, vice
Francis Anthony Keating II.

G. Kim Wincup,
of Maryland, to be an Assistant Secretary of the
Air Force, vice John J. Welch, Jr.

James Thomas Grady,
of Massachusetts, to be a member of the Board of
Directors of the Overseas Private Investment
Corporation for a term expiring December 17,
1994 (reappointment).

Steven Manaster,
of Utah, to be a Commissioner of the Commodity
Futures Trading Commission for the term expiring April 13, 1997, vice Fowler C. West, term
expiring.

Tony Armendariz,
of Texas, to be a member of the Federal Labor
Relations Authority for a term of 5 years expiring
July 29, 1997 (reappointment).

Pamela J. Turner,
of the District of Columbia, to be a member of
the United States Advisory Commission on Public
Diplomacy for a term expiring July 1, 1995 (reappointment).

Philip Brunelle,
of Minnesota, to be a member of the National
Council on the Arts for the remainder of the

term expiring September 3, 1994, vice Phyllis Curtain, resigned.

*Submitted April 30*

Ronald B. Leighton,
of Washington, to be U.S. District Judge for the Western District of Washington, vice Jack E. Tanner, retired.

*Submitted May 5*

Robert L. Barry,
of New Hampshire, a career member of the Senior Foreign Service, class of Career Minister, to be Ambassador Extraordinary and Plenipotentiary of the United States of America to the Republic of Indonesia.

Reginald Bartholomew,
of the District of Columbia, a career member of the Senior Foreign Service, class of Career Minister, to be the United States Permanent Representative on the Council of the North Atlantic Treaty Organization, with the rank and status of Ambassador Extraordinary and Plenipotentiary.

Adrian A. Basora,
of New Hampshire, a career member of the Senior Foreign Service, class of Minister-Counselor, to be Ambassador Extraordinary and Plenipotentiary of the United States of America to the Czech and Slovak Federal Republic.

Arthur J. Rothkopf,
of the District of Columbia, to be Deputy Secretary of Transportation, vice James Buchanan Busey IV, resigned.

Thomas C. Richards,
of Texas, to be Administrator of the Federal Aviation Administration, vice James Buchanan Busey IV.

Michael James Toohey,
of Virginia, to be an Assistant Secretary of Transportation, vice Galen Joseph Reser, resigned.

Joseph J. DiNunno,
of Maryland, to be a member of the Defense Nuclear Facilities Safety Board for the remainder of the term expiring October 18, 1995, vice Edson G. Case.

Barry Zorthian,
of the District of Columbia, to be a member of the Board for International Broadcasting for a term expiring May 20, 1995 (reappointment).

*Submitted May 6*

Peter Barry Teeley,
of Virginia, to be Ambassador Extraordinary and Plenipotentiary of the United States of America to Canada.

Peter Jon deVos,
of Florida, a career member of the Senior Foreign Service, class of Minister-Counselor, to be Ambassador Extraordinary and Plenipotentiary of the United States of America to the United Republic of Tanzania.

Robert E. Gribbin III,
of Alabama, a career member of the Senior Foreign Service, class of Counselor, to be Ambassador Extraordinary and Plenipotentiary of the United States of America to the Central African Republic.

*Submitted May 7*

David C. Fields,
of California, a career member of the Senior Foreign Service, class of Minister-Counselor, to be Ambassador Extraordinary and Plenipotentiary of the United States of America to the Republic of the Marshall Islands.

William Henry Gerald FitzGerald,
of the District of Columbia, to be Ambassador Extraordinary and Plenipotentiary of the United States of America to Ireland.

Princeton Nathan Lyman,
of Maryland, a career member of the Senior Foreign Service, class of Career Minister, to be Ambassador Extraordinary and Plenipotentiary of the United States of America to the Republic of South Africa.

William Thornton Pryce,
of Pennsylvania, a career member of the Senior Foreign Service, class of Minister-Counselor, to be Ambassador Extraordinary and Plenipotentiary of the United States of America to the Republic of Honduras.

Teresita Currie Schaffer,
of New York, a career member of the Senior Foreign Service, class of Minister-Counselor, to be Ambassador Extraordinary and Plenipotentiary of the United States of America to the Democratic Socialist Republic of Sri Lanka and to serve concurrently and without additional compensation as Ambassador Extraordinary and Plenipotentiary of the United States of America to the Republic of Maldives.

*Submitted May 12*

William Graham Walker,
of California, a career member of the Senior Foreign Service, class of Minister-Counselor, to be Ambassador Extraordinary and Plenipotentiary of the United States of America to Argentina.

Alexander Fletcher Watson,
of Massachusetts, a career member of the Senior Foreign Service, class of Career Minister, to be Ambassador Extraordinary and Plenipotentiary of the United States of America to the Federative Republic of Brazil.

*Submitted May 13*

Marilyn McAfee,
of Florida, a career member of the Senior Foreign Service, class of Minister-Counselor, to be Ambassador Extraordinary and Plenipotentiary of the United States of America to the Republic of Guatemala.

Robert F. Goodwin,
of Maryland, to be Ambassador Extraordinary and Plenipotentiary of the United States of America to New Zealand, and to serve concurrently and without additional compensation as Ambassador Extraordinary and Plenipotentiary of the United States of America to Western Samoa.

David J. Dunford,
of Arizona, a career member of the Senior Foreign Service, class of Minister-Counselor, to be Ambassador Extraordinary and Plenipotentiary of the United States of America to the Sultanate of Oman.

*Submitted May 14*

Donald Herman Alexander,
of Missouri, to be Ambassador Extraordinary and Plenipotentiary of the United States of America to the Kingdom of The Netherlands.

Joyce A. Doyle,
of New York, to be a member of the Federal Mine Safety and Health Review Commission for a term of 6 years expiring August 30, 1998 (reappointment).

Joseph Charles Wilson IV,
of California, a career member of the Senior Foreign Service, class of Counselor, to be Ambassador Extraordinary and Plenipotentiary of the United States of America to the Gabonese Republic, and to serve concurrently without additional compensation as Ambassador Extraordinary and Plenipotentiary of the United States of America to the Democratic Republic of Sao Tome and Principe.

Thomas E. Harvey,
of the District of Columbia, to be a member of the Board of Directors of the U.S. Institute of Peace for the remainder of the term expiring January 19, 1993, vice John Norton Moore, resigned.

John F. Daffron, Jr.,
of Virginia, to be a member of the Board of Directors of the State Justice Institute for a term expiring September 17, 1994 (reappointment).

*Submitted May 19*

William Arthur Rugh,
of Maryland, a career member of the Senior Foreign Service, class of Career Minister, to be Ambassador Extraordinary and Plenipotentiary of the United States of America to the United Arab Emirates.

Gregory F. Chapados,
of Alaska, to be Assistant Secretary of Commerce for Communications and Information, vice Janice Obuchowski, resigned.

Evan J. Kemp, Jr.,
of the District of Columbia, to be a member of the Equal Employment Opportunity Commission for a term expiring July 1, 1997 (reappointment).

Roberto Martinez,
of Florida, to be U.S. Attorney for the Southern District of Florida for the term of 4 years, vice Leon B. Kellner, resigned.

The following named persons to be members of the Federal Energy Regulatory Commission for the terms indicated:

Jerry Jay Langdon, of Texas, for the term expiring June 30, 1996 (reappointment).
William C. Liedtke III, of Oklahoma, for the term expiring June 30, 1997, vice Charles A. Trabandt, term expiring.

*Submitted May 21*

James E. Gilleran,
of California, to be Comptroller of the Currency for a term of 5 years, vice Robert Logan Clarke, term expired.

Don J. Svet,
of New Mexico, to be U.S. Attorney for the District of New Mexico for the term of 4 years, vice William L. Lutz, resigned.

The following named persons to be members of the Civil Liberties Public Education Fund Board of Directors for the terms indicated:

*For terms of 2 years:*

Bruce T. Kaji, of California
Tomio Moriguchi, of Washington

*For terms of 3 years:*

Edwin C. Hiroto, of California
William H. Marumoto, of Virginia
S. Stephen Nakashima, of California
George Shoichi Oki, Sr., of California
Grant Masashi Ujifusa, of New York

*Submitted June 2*

Ritajean Hartung Butterworth,
of Washington, to be a member of the Board of
Directors of the Corporation for Public Broadcasting for a term expiring March 26, 1997, vice
William Lee Hanley, Jr., resigned.

William D. Quarles,
of Maryland, to be U.S. District Judge for the
District of Maryland, vice Alexander Harvey II,
retired.

James A. McIntyre,
of California, to be U.S. District Judge for the
Southern District of California (new position).

Henry Lee Clarke,
of California, a career member of the Senior Foreign Service, class of Minister-Counselor, to be
Ambassador Extraordinary and Plenipotentiary of
the United States of America to the Republic of
Uzbekistan.

Donald Burnham Ensenat,
of Louisiana, to be Ambassador Extraordinary
and Plenipotentiary of the United States of
America to Brunei.

Edward Hurwitz,
of the District of Columbia, a career member of
the Senior Foreign Service, class of Minister-
Counselor, to be Ambassador Extraordinary and
Plenipotentiary of the United States of America
to the Republic of Kyrgyzstan.

Joseph Monroe Segars,
of Pennsylvania, a career member of the Senior
Foreign Service, class of Counselor, to be Ambas-
sador Extraordinary and Plenipotentiary of the
United States of America to the Republic of Cape
Verde.

Anthony Cecil Eden Quainton,
of the District of Columbia, a career member of
the Senior Foreign Service, class of Career Minister, to be Assistant Secretary of State for Diplomatic Security, vice Sheldon J. Krys.

Robert L. Gallucci,
of Virginia, to be an Assistant Secretary of State,
vice Richard A. Clarke.

Walter B. McCormick, Jr.,
of Missouri, to be General Counsel of the Department of Transportation, vice Arthur J. Rothkopf.

Alison Podell Rosenberg,
of Virginia, to be an Assistant Administrator of
the Agency for International Development, vice
Scott M. Spangler.

Max M. Kampelman,
of the District of Columbia, to be a member of
the Board of Directors of the U.S. Institute of
Peace for a term expiring January 19, 1995, vice
Morris I. Leibman, term expired.

The following named persons to be members of
the U.S. Advisory Commission on Public Diplomacy for terms expiring July 1, 1994:

Jay I. Kislak, of Florida, vice Richard B. Stone.
Marshall Lee Miller, of Virginia, vice Edwin J.
Feulner, Jr., term expired.

*Submitted June 3*

John Frank Bookout, Jr.,
of Texas, to be Ambassador Extraordinary and
Plenipotentiary of the United States of America
to the Kingdom of Saudi Arabia.

Kenneth R. Mancuso,
of Rhode Island, to be U.S. Marshal for the District of Rhode Island for the term of 4 years, vice
Donald W. Wyatt, resigned.

*Submitted June 4*

Donald M. Kendall,
of Connecticut, to be a member of the Board of
Directors of the Overseas Private Investment
Corporation for the remainder of the term expiring December 17, 1992, vice J. Carter Beese, Jr.,
resigned; and for an additional term expiring December 17, 1995, reappointment.

*Submitted June 9*

Kenneth L. Brown,
of California, a career member of the Senior Foreign Service, class of Minister-Counselor, to be
Ambassador Extraordinary and Plenipotentiary of
the United States of America to the Republic of
Ghana.

Mary Jo Jacobi,
of Mississippi, to be an Assistant Secretary of
Commerce, vice Craig R. Helsing, resigned.

Mary Mohs,
of Wisconsin, to be a member of the National Museum Services Board for a term expiring December 6, 1994, vice Marilyn Logsdon Mennello, term expired.

J. Michael Farrell,
of the District of Columbia, to be a member of the National Commission on Libraries and Information Science for a term expiring July 19, 1997 (reappointment).

*Submitted June 10*

Frank G. Wisner,
of the District of Columbia, a career member of the Senior Foreign Service, class of Career Minister, to be Under Secretary of State for Coordinating Security Assistance Programs, vice Reginald Bartholomew.

*Submitted June 11*

Norman D. Shumway,
of California, to be a member of the Board of Directors of the Legal Services Corporation for the remainder of the term expiring July 13, 1993, vice Luis Guinot, Jr., resigned, to which position he was appointed during the recess of the Senate from August 2, 1991, to September 10, 1991.

*Submitted June 16*

Ruth A. Davis,
of Georgia, a career member of the Senior Foreign Service, class of Minister-Counselor, to be Ambassador Extraordinary and Plenipotentiary of the United States of America to the Republic of Benin.

Charles B. Salmon, Jr.,
of New York, a career member of the Senior Foreign Service, class of Minister-Counselor, to be Ambassador Extraordinary and Plenipotentiary of the United States of America to the Lao People's Democratic Republic.

Jon M. Huntsman, Jr.,
of Utah, to be Ambassador Extraordinary and Plenipotentiary of the United States of America to the Republic of Singapore.

Nicolas Miklos Salgo,
of Florida, to be Ambassador Extraordinary and Plenipotentiary of the United States of America to Sweden.

Irvin Hicks,
of Maryland, a career member of the Senior Foreign Service, class of Minister-Counselor, to be Deputy Representative of the United States of America in the Security Council of the United Nations, with the rank of Ambassador.

*Submitted June 17*

Richard Monroe Miles,
of South Carolina, a career member of the Senior Foreign Service, class of Minister-Counselor, to be Ambassador Extraordinary and Plenipotentiary of the United States of America to the Republic of Azerbaijan.

Joseph S. Hulings III,
of Virginia, a career member of the Senior Foreign Service, class of Minister-Counselor, to be Ambassador Extraordinary and Plenipotentiary of the United States of America to the Republic of Turkmenistan.

*Submitted June 19*

Richard H. Solomon,
of Maryland, to be Ambassador Extraordinary and Plenipotentiary of the United States of America to the Republic of the Philippines.

Raymond L. Finch,
of the Virgin Islands, to be a Judge for the District Court of the Virgin Islands for a term of 10 years, vice David V. O'Brien, deceased.

John Stern Wolf,
of Maryland, a career member of the Senior Foreign Service, class of Minister-Counselor, to be Ambassador Extraordinary and Plenipotentiary of the United States of America to Malaysia.

The following named individuals to be Associate Judges of the Superior Court of the District of Columbia for terms of 15 years:

> Brook Hedge, of the District of Columbia, vice Emmet G. Sullivan, elevated.
>
> Lee F. Satterfield, of the District of Columbia, vice Robert McCance Scott.

*Submitted June 23*

William Harrison Courtney,
of West Virginia, a career member of the Senior Foreign Service, class of Counselor, to be Ambassador Extraordinary and Plenipotentiary of the United States of America to the Republic of Kazakhstan.

Patricia Diaz Dennis,
of Virginia, to be Assistant Secretary of State for Human Rights and Humanitarian Affairs, vice Richard Schifter, resigned.

Malcolm S. Forbes, Jr.,
of New Jersey, to be a member of the Board for International Broadcasting for a term expiring April 28, 1995 (reappointment).

*Submitted June 25*

David Heywood Swartz,
of Virginia, a career member of the Senior Foreign Service, class of Minister-Counselor, to be Ambassador Extraordinary and Plenipotentiary of the United States of America to the Republic of Byelarus.

H. Douglas Barclay,
of New York, to be a member of the Board of Directors of the Overseas Private Investment Corporation for a term expiring December 17, 1994 (reappointment).

John H. Miller,
of Connecticut, to be a member of the Board of Directors of the National Institute of Building Sciences for a term expiring September 7, 1992, vice Fred E. Hummel, resigned.

John H. Miller,
of Connecticut, to be a member of the Board of Directors of the National Institute of Building Sciences for a term expiring September 7, 1995 (reappointment).

*Submitted June 26*

Hugo Pomrehn,
of California, to be Under Secretary of Energy, vice John Chatfield Tuck, resigned.

John A. Mendez,
of California, to be U.S. Attorney for the Northern District of California for the term of 4 years, vice Joseph P. Russoniello, resigned.

Kathryn D. Sullivan,
of California, to be Chief Scientist of the National Oceanic and Atmospheric Administration, vice Sylvia Alice Earle, resigned.

C.C. Hope, Jr.,
of North Carolina, to be a member of the Board of Directors of the Federal Deposit Insurance Corporation for a term expiring February 28, 1993 (reappointment).

Terrence B. Adamson,
of Georgia, to be a member of the Board of Directors of the State Justice Institute for a term expiring September 17, 1994 (reappointment).

*Submitted July 1*

Robert E. Martinez,
of New Jersey, to be Associate Deputy Secretary of Transportation, vice Robert L. Pettit, resigned.

John S. Simmons,
of South Carolina, to be U.S. Attorney for the District of South Carolina for a term of 4 years, vice E. Bart Daniel, resigned.

*Submitted July 2*

Richard Conway Casey,
of New York, to be U.S. District Judge for the Southern District of New York, vice Robert W. Sweet, retired.

John J. Easton, Jr.,
of Vermont, to be an Assistant Secretary of Energy (Domestic and International Energy Policy).

Stanley Tuemler Escudero,
of Florida, a career member of the Senior Foreign Service, class of Counselor, to be Ambassador Extraordinary and Plenipotentiary of the United States of America to the Republic of Tajikistan.

Kent N. Brown,
of Virginia, a career member of the Senior Foreign Service, class of Counselor, to be Ambassador Extraordinary and Plenipotentiary of the United States of America to the Republic of Georgia.

Ilana Diamond Rovner,
of Illinois, to be U.S. Circuit Judge for the Seventh Circuit, vice Harlington Wood, Jr., retired.

John Phil Gilbert,
of Illinois, to be U.S. District Judge for the Southern District of Illinois, vice James L. Foreman, retired.

Mary C. Pendleton,
of Virginia, a career member of the Foreign Service, class one, to be Ambassador Extraordinary and Plenipotentiary of the United States of America to the Republic of Moldova.

Mack F. Mattingly,
of Georgia, to be Ambassador Extraordinary and Plenipotentiary of the United States of America to the Republic of Seychelles.

Larry R. Hicks,
of Nevada, to be U.S. District Judge for the District of Nevada, vice Edward C. Reed, Jr., retired.

John W. Sedwick,
of Alaska, to be U.S. District Judge for the District of Alaska, vice Andrew J. Kleinfeld, position elevated.

*Submitted July 20*

John Cameron Monjo,
of Maryland, a career member of the Senior Foreign Service, class of Career Minister, to be Ambassador Extraordinary and Plenipotentiary of the United States of America to the Islamic Republic of Pakistan.

Harriet Winsar Isom,
of Oregon, a career member of the Senior Foreign Service, class of Minister-Counselor, to be Ambassador Extraordinary and Plenipotentiary of the United States of America to the Republic of Cameroon.

Linton F. Brooks,
of Virginia, to be an Assistant Director of the U.S. Arms Control and Disarmament Agency, vice Susan Jane Koch, resigned.

David P. Prosperi,
of Illinois, to be a member of the Board of Directors of the Corporation for Public Broadcasting for a term expiring March 26, 1997, vice Marshall Turner, Jr., term expired.

Shirley W. Ryan,
of Illinois, to be a member of the National Council on Disability for a term expiring September 17, 1994, vice John Leopold, term expired.

Walter Scott Blackburn,
of Indiana, to be a member of the Board of Directors of the National Institute of Building Sciences for a term expiring September 7, 1993, vice Kyle Clayton Boone, term expired.

The following named persons to be Members of the Advisory Board of the Saint Lawrence Seaway Development Corporation:

Edward Morgan Paluso, of Pennsylvania, vice L. Steven Reimers.
Sterling G. Sechrist, of Ohio, vice Virgil E. Brown, resigned.

*Submitted July 22*

Genta Hawkins Holmes,
of California, a career member of the Senior Foreign Service, class of Minister-Counselor, to be Director General of the Foreign Service, vice Edward Joseph Perkins.

Alan Greenspan,
of New York, to be U.S. Alternate Governor of the International Monetary Fund for a term of 5 years (reappointment).

John S. Unpingco,
of Guam, to be Judge for the District Court of Guam for the term of 10 years, vice Christobal C. Duenas, resigned.

*Withdrawn July 22*

Donald Herman Alexander,
of Missouri, to be Ambassador Extraordinary and Plenipotentiary of the United States of America to the Kingdom of the Netherlands, which was sent to the Senate on May 14, 1992.

*Submitted July 27*

R. Edgar Campbell,
of Georgia, to be U.S. District Judge for the Middle District of Georgia (new position).

Joanna Seybert,
of New York, to be U.S. District Judge for the Eastern District of New York (new position).

The following named persons to be members of the National Institute Board for the National Institute for Literacy for terms of 3 years (new positions):

John Corcoran, of California
Helen B. Crouch, of New York
Sharon Darling, of Kentucky
Jim Edgar, of Illinois
Jon Deveaux, of New York
Ronald M. Gillum, of Michigan
Benita C. Somerfield, of New York
Susan Ann Vogel, of Illinois

*Submitted July 28*

Walter Scott Light,
of Texas, to be Ambassador Extraordinary and Plenipotentiary of the United States of America to the Republic of Ecuador.

Kathryn H. Vratil,
of Kansas, to be U.S. District Judge for the District of Kansas, vice Earl E. O'Connor, retired.

The following named persons to be Judges of the U.S. Tax Court for terms expiring 15 years after they take office:

Carolyn P. Chiechi, of Maryland, vice Arthur L. Nims III, retired.
David Laro, of Michigan, vice Jules G. Korner III.

# Appendix C—Checklist of White House Press Releases

*The following list contains releases of the Office of the Press Secretary which are not included in this book.*

*Released January 4*

Fact sheet:
U.S.-Asia environmental partnership

*Released January 6*

Advance text:
Remarks at the American and Korean Chambers of Commerce luncheon in Seoul

*Released January 8*

Transcript:
Press briefing on the President's meetings in Japan—by Brent Scowcroft, Assistant to the President for National Security Affairs

Fact sheet:
A Strategy for World Growth

Fact sheet:
The Japanese economy in 1991 and the FY 1992 budget

Fact sheet:
Japan corporate program

Fact sheet:
Government procurement

Advance text:
Remarks at the state dinner hosted by Prime Minister Kiichi Miyazawa of Japan in Tokyo

*Released January 9*

Fact sheet:
Major projects agreement

Fact sheet:
Paper

Fact sheet:
Telecommunications

Fact sheet:
Computer procurement

Fact sheet:
Standards, certification, and testing

Fact sheet:
Glass

Fact sheet:
U.S.-Japan achievements on economic issues

Fact sheet:
Joint trade expansion program

Fact sheet:
U.S.-Japan economic relations

Fact sheet:
U.S.-Japan achievements on autos and auto parts

*Released January 10*

Advance text:
Remarks to the President's Drug Advisory Council

Announcement:
Nomination of Jack W. Selden to be U.S. Attorney for the Northern District of Alabama

*Released January 13*

Advance text:
Excerpts from remarks to the American Farm Bureau Federation in Kansas City, MO

*Released January 14*

Fact sheet:
Action to promote alternative fuel vehicles

*Released January 17*

Fact sheet:
Creating job opportunities by improving the Federal job training system

*Released January 21*

Announcement:
White House Conference on Indian Education participants

Announcement:
Nomination of new and continuing members of the General Advisory Committee of the U.S. Arms Control and Disarmament Agency

Fact sheet:
Meeting the national education goals: the President's Head Start initiative

Fact sheet:
U.S. Assistance to the former Soviet Union

*Released January 22*

Fact sheet:
U.S.-Japan computer agreement

Transcript:
Press briefing on trade policy—by Carla A. Hills, U.S. Trade Representative

*Released January 23*

Fact sheet:
Highlights of the President's environmental budget for fiscal year 1993

Transcript:
Press briefing on environmental policy—by William K. Reilly, Administrator, Environmental Protection Agency

*Released January 24*

Announcement:
Nomination of Sidney A. Fitzwater to be U.S. Circuit Judge for the Fifth Circuit

Announcement:
Nomination of John A. Smietanka to be U.S. Circuit Judge for the Sixth Circuit

Announcement:
Nomination of Edward E. Carnes to be U.S. Circuit Judge for the Eleventh Circuit

Announcement:
Nomination of John G. Roberts, Jr., to be U.S. Circuit Judge for the District of Columbia

Announcement:
Nomination of Terral R. Smith to be U.S. District Judge for the Western District of Texas

Announcement:
Nomination of Kenneth R. Carr to be U.S. District Judge for the Western District of Texas

Announcement:
Nomination of Karen J. Williams to be U.S. Circuit Judge for the Fourth Circuit

Announcement:
Nomination of James W. Jackson to be U.S. District Judge for the Northern District of Ohio

*Released January 27*

Fact sheet:
Highlights of the President's crime and drug control budget for fiscal year 1993

Transcript:
Press briefing on the war on drugs—by George Terwiliger, Acting Deputy Attorney General; James O. Mason, Assistant Secretary of Health and Human Services; Frank Kalder, Director of Budget and Legislative Affairs, Office of National Drug Control Policy; Terry Pell, Acting Chief of Staff, Office of National Drug Control Policy; and Dr. Lloyd Johnston, University of Michigan

*Released January 28*

White House statement:
Highlights of the President's growth agenda

Fact sheet:
The President's State of the Union Address

*Released January 29*

Transcript:
Press briefing on the fiscal year 1993 budget—by Secretary of the Treasury Nicholas F. Brady; Richard G. Darman, Director, Office of Management and Budget; and Michael J. Boskin, Chairman, Council of Economic Advisers

Fact sheet:
The President's budget for FY 1993

*Released January 30*

Fact sheet:
The President's plan for reducing the burdens of regulation through administrative action

*Released January 31*

Transcript:
Press briefing on the President's visit to the United Nations—by Secretary of State James A. Baker III

*Released February 4*

Fact sheet:
"Access to Justice Act of 1992"

*Released February 5*

Transcript:
Press briefing on the economic report—by Michael J. Boskin, Chairman, Council of Economic Advisers

*Released February 6*

Fact sheet:
The President's comprehensive health reform program

*Released February 7*

Advance text:
Remarks to the San Diego Rotary Club in San Diego, CA

*Released February 11*

Fact sheet:
Accelerated phaseout of ozone-depleting substances

Fact sheet:
The Enterprise for the Americas Initiative's Multilateral Investment Fund

Transcript
Press briefing on the visit of Prime Minister Suleyman Demirel of Turkey—by David Gompert, National Security Council Senior Director for European and Eurasian Affairs

*Released February 19*

Fact sheet:
Investing in research, development, and technological innovation

Advance text:
Remarks to community and business leaders in Knoxville, TN

*Released February 24*

Transcript:
Press briefing on the drug summit in San Antonio, TX—by Bob Martinez, Director, Office of National Drug Control Policy, and Bernard W. Aronson, Assistant Secretary of State for Inter-American Affairs

Advance text:
Remarks at the Bush-Quayle campaign kickoff in Bethesda, MD

*Released February 25*

Advance text:
Remarks at a Bush-Quayle fundraising luncheon in San Francisco, CA

Advance text:
Remarks on trade and environmental cooperation with Mexico

Fact sheet:
Integrated environmental plan for the Mexico-U.S. border area

Fact sheet:
Review of environmental effects of free trade with Mexico

*Released February 27*

Transcript:
Press briefing on the drug summit in San Antonio, TX—by Bernard W. Aronson, Assistant Secretary of State for Inter-American Affairs, and Thomas E. McNamara, National Security Council Senior Director for International Programs

*Released February 28*

Announcement:
Nomination of Alvin A. Schall to be U.S. Circuit Judge for the Federal Circuit

*Released February 29*

Advance text:
Remarks to the Associated General Contractors of America in Dallas, TX

*Released March 3*

Advance text:
Remarks to the National Association of Evangelicals in Chicago, IL

Fact sheet:
Assistance to Bulgaria

*Released March 6*

Fact sheet:
Economic improvement steps for the natural gas industry

*Released March 7*

Fact sheet:
Bush administration proposals concerning outdoor recreation and wildlife

*Released March 9*

Announcement:
Nomination of Federico A. Moreno to be U.S. Circuit Judge for the Eleventh Circuit

Announcement:
Nomination of Susan H. Black to be U.S. Circuit Judge for the Eleventh Circuit

Advance text:
Remarks to the National League of Cities

*Released March 11*

Remarks at the Richard Nixon Library dinner

*Released March 13*

Fact sheet:
Onboard refueling vapor recovery systems for new cars

*Released March 16*

Advance text:
Remarks to Steeltech employees in Milwaukee, WI

Advance text:
Remarks at a Bush-Quayle fundraising luncheon in Milwaukee

Advance text:
Remarks at a Bush-Quayle fundraising dinner in Chicago, IL

*Released March 18*

Fact sheet:
Transportation reforms

Announcement:
Nomination of Lawrence O. Davis to be U.S. District Judge for the Eastern District of Missouri

Announcement:
Nomination of John F. Walter to be U.S. District Judge for the Central District of California

Announcement:
Nomination of Joe Kendall to be U.S. District Judge for the Northern District of Texas

Announcement:
Nomination of Percy Anderson to be U.S. District Judge for the Central District of California

Announcement:
Nomination of Lee H. Rosenthal to be U.S. District Judge for the Southern District of Texas

Announcement:
Nomination of Russell T. Lloyd to be U.S. District Judge for the Southern District of Texas

Announcement:
Nomination of Andrew S. Hanen to be U.S. District Judge for the Southern District of Texas

Announcement:
Nomination of Linda H. McLaughlin to be U.S. District Judge for the Central District of California

*Released March 20*

Advance text:
Remarks to Republican Members of Congress and Presidential appointees

Fact sheet:
Address to Republican Members of Congress and Presidential appointees

Fact sheet:
Implementing the *Beck* decision

Announcement:
Transmittal of 67 messages to Congress containing 68 rescission proposals

Announcement:
Nomination of Paul L. Shechtman to be U.S. District Judge for the Southern District of New York

Announcement:
Nomination of John G. Heyburn II to be U.S. District Judge for the Western District of Kentucky

Announcement:
Nomination of Richard H. Kyle to be U.S. District Judge for the District of Minnesota

Announcement:
Nomination of Justin P. Wilson to be U.S. Circuit Judge for the Sixth Circuit

Announcement:
Nomination of Gordon J. Quist to be U.S. District Judge for the Western District of Michigan

Announcement:
Nomination of C. LeRoy Hansen to be U.S. District Judge for the District of New Mexico

Announcement:
Nomination of Michael Boudin to be U.S. Circuit Judge for the First Circuit

Announcement:
Nomination of Dennis G. Jacobs to be U.S. Circuit Judge for the Second Circuit

*Released March 24*

Fact sheet:
Environmental quality report

Advance text:
Remarks to the National American Wholesale Grocers Association

Statement:
President's medication

*Released March 25*

Statement:
White House medical care

*Released March 26*

Announcement:
Nomination of Manuel H. Quintana to be U.S. District Judge for Southern District of New York

*Released March 27*

Announcement:
Nomination of Scott J. Poe to be U.S. Marshal for the Eastern District of Kentucky

Fact sheet:
Trade with the former Soviet Union

*Released March 30*

Announcement:
Nomination of Charles W. Larson to be U.S. Attorney for the Northern District of Iowa

Announcement:
Nomination of Jay D. Gardner to be U.S. Attorney for the Southern District of Georgia

Announcement:
Nomination of Loretta A. Preska to be U.S. District Judge for the Southern District of New York

*Released March 31*

Announcement:
Second annual President's Environment and Conservation Challenge Awards program

*Released April 1*

Fact sheet:
Multilateral financial assistance package for Russia

Fact sheet:
"FREEDOM Support Act of 1992"

Fact sheet:
Agricultural assistance for the NIS

Announcement:
Nomination of Irene M. Keeley to be U.S. District Judge for the Northern District of West Virginia

Announcement:
Nomination of Alfred V. Covello to be U.S. District Judge for the District of Connecticut

Announcement:
Nomination of Jerome B. Simandle to be U.S. District Judge for the District of New Jersey

Announcement:
Nomination of Carol E. Jackson to be U.S. District Judge for the Eastern District of Missouri

Announcement:
Nomination of Charles A. Banks to be U.S. District Judge for the Eastern District of Arkansas

*Released April 2*

Announcement:
Nomination of Maureen E. Mahoney to be U.S. District Judge for the Eastern District of Virginia

Announcement:
Nomination of Robert D. Hunter to be U.S. District Judge for the Northern District of Alabama

Announcement:
Nomination of Lourdes G. Baird to be U.S. District Judge for the Central district of California

Fact sheet:
Financial services reforms

Transcript:
Press briefing on the visit of Prime Minister Felipe González of Spain—by Thomas Niles, Assistant Secretary of State for European and Canadian Affairs

*Released April 3*

Advance text:
Remarks to the Federalist Society of Philadelphia in Philadelphia, PA

Fact sheet:
President's address on governmental reform

Announcement:
Nomination of James S. Mitchell to be U.S. District Judge for the District of Nebraska

Announcement:
Nomination of Richard G. Kopf to be U.S. District Judge for the District of Nebraska

*Released April 7*

Statement:
Foreign access to United States ports

Announcement:
Office of Government Ethics report on former Chief of Staff John Sununu's travel on military aircraft

Announcement:
Nomination of Emerson J. Elliot to be Commissioner of Education Statistics, Department of Education

*Released April 8*

Announcement:
Nomination of Irma E. Gonzalez to be U.S. District Judge for the Southern District of California

Announcement:
Nomination of Carol Johnson Johns to be a member of the Board of Regents of the Uniformed Services University of the Health Sciences

Announcement:
Nomination of Virginia Stanley Douglas to be a member of the Board of Directors of the National Institute of Building Sciences

*Released April 9*

Fact sheet:
Reforms to the drug approval process

Fact sheet:
"The Accountability in Government Act of 1992"

Announcement:
Nomination of Michael J. Melloy to be U.S. District Judge for the Northern District of Iowa

Announcement:
Nomination of Norman H. Stahl to be U.S. Circuit Judge for the First Circuit

Announcement:
Nomination of Joseph A. DiClerico, Jr., to be U.S. District Judge for the District of New Hampshire

Announcement:
Nomination of Rudolph T. Randa to be U.S. District Judge for the Eastern District of Wisconsin

Announcement:
Transmittal of 28 special messages to Congress containing budget rescissions

Announcement:
Travel policy: the new policy on the use of military aircraft by the Chief of Staff and National Security Adviser

*Released April 10*

Transcript:
Press briefing on Wisconsin welfare reform—by Secretary of Health and Human Services Louis W. Sullivan and Gov. Tommy Thompson of Wisconsin

Fact sheet:
The State of Wisconsin's parental and family responsibility demonstration project

*Released April 13*

Fact sheet:
Executive action protecting workers' rights

*Released April 14*

Advance text:
Remarks to Giddings & Lewis employees and local chambers of commerce in Fraser, MI

Fact sheet:
Job Training 2000: creating a comprehensive and unified Federal job training system

Fact sheet:
"The Youth Apprenticeship Act of 1992"

Advance text:
Remarks at a Bush-Quayle fundraising dinner in Dearborn, MI

*Released April 16*

Fact sheet:
"The Lifelong Learning Act of 1992"

Advance text:
Remarks to the Lehigh Valley 2000 community in Allentown, PA

Fact sheet:
America 2000: first-year accomplishments

Transcript:
Press briefing on proposed education and job training legislation—by Secretary of Education Lamar Alexander

*Released April 20*

Fact sheet:
AmeriFlora '92

*Released April 22*

Announcement:
Nomination of Nathaniel M. Gorton to be U.S. District Judge for the District of Massachusetts

Transcript:
Press briefing on the President's meeting with European Council President Anibal Cavaco Silva and European Commission President Jacques Delors—by Thomas Niles, Assistant Secretary of State for European and Canadian Affairs

*Released April 23*

Advance text:
Remarks to the Forum of the Americas

Fact sheet:
The U.S.-Japan paper agreement

*Released April 24*

Transcript:
Press briefing on banking and finance regulatory reform—by Michael J. Boskin, Chairman, Council of Economic Advisers; C. Boyden Gray, Counsel to the President; John E. Robson, Deputy Secretary of the Treasury; Timothy Ryan, Director, Office of Thrift Supervision; Stephen Steinbrink, Acting Comptroller of the Currency; Susan Phillips, Board of Governors, Federal Reserve Board; William Taylor, Chairman, Federal Deposit Insurance Corp.; and F. Henry Habicht, Deputy Administrator, Environmental Protection Agency.

Fact sheet:
Financial services reforms

Announcement:
Winners of the 1992 President's Annual Points of Light Awards

*Released April 27*

Advance text:
Remarks at the Florida International University commencement ceremony in Miami Beach, FL

Advance text:
Remarks at a Bush-Quayle fundraising dinner in Charlotte, NC

*Released April 28*

Transcript:
Press briefing on financial services regulatory reform—by Michael J. Boskin, Chairman, Council of Economic Advisers; John E. Robson, Deputy Secretary of the Treasury; Richard Breeden, Chairman, Securities and Exchange Commission; and Wendy Gramm, Chairman, Commodity Futures Trading Commission

*Released April 29*

Advance text:
Remarks on regulatory reform

Transcript:
Press briefing on regulatory reform—by Michael J. Boskin, Chairman, Council of Economic Advisers, and C. Boyden Gray, Counsel to the President

Fact sheet:
Regulatory Reform Initiative

*Released April 30*

Announcement:
Nomination of Ronald B. Leighton to be U.S. District Judge for the Western District of Washington

Fact sheet:
Executive order on infrastructure privatization

*Released May 1*

Fact sheet:
Michael Jackson recognized as Points of Light ambassador

*Released May 3*

Statement:
National Day of Prayer

*Released May 4*

Announcement:
Nomination of Barry Zorthian to be a member of the Board for International Broadcasting

*Released May 5*

Fact sheet:
Truck, rail, and ocean shipping reforms

Transcript:
Press briefing on truck, rail, and ocean shipping reforms—by C. Boyden Gray, Counsel to the President; Ed Philbin, Chairman, Interstate Commerce Commission; Ming Hsu, Chairman, Federal Maritime Commission; and James Rill, Assistant Attorney General for the Antitrust Division

Announcement:
Nomination of Joseph J. DiNunno to be a member of the Defense Nuclear Facilities Safety Board

*Released May 6*

Fact sheet:
Agreement on trade relations between the United States and Ukraine

Fact sheet:
U.S.-Ukraine OPIC agreement

Fact sheet:
Agreement on establishing a Peace Corps program between the United States and Ukraine

Fact sheet:
Science and Technology Center in Ukraine

Fact sheet:
Technical assistance for Ukraine

Fact sheet:
Federal relief assistance to individuals, families, communities, and businesses in Los Angeles

Fact sheet:
"Weed and Seed" program to aid needy Los Angeles communities

*Released May 12*

Fact sheet:
President Bush's initiatives for strengthening urban areas

Fact sheet:
The administration's program for reducing tax compliance burdens for small employers

Transcript:
Press briefing on the President's urban aid initiatives—by Jack Kemp, Secretary of Housing and Urban Development; William P. Barr, Attorney General; Lamar Alexander, Secretary of Education; Pat Saiki, Small Business Administrator; and Richard G. Darman, Director, Office of Management and Budget

*Released May 13*

Advance text:
Remarks to the health care and business community in Baltimore, MD

Transcript:
Press briefing on the President's meeting with President Patricio Aylwin of Chile—by Bernard W. Aronson, Assistant Secretary of State for Inter-American Affairs

Announcement:
Nomination of Thomas E. Harvey to be a member of the Board of Directors of the U.S. Institute of Peace

*Released May 14*

Announcement:
Nomination of Joyce A. Doyle to be a member of the Federal Mine Safety and Health Review Commission

*Released May 15*

Announcement:
Presidential Faculty Fellows Program award recipients

*Released May 18*

Announcement:
Nomination of Roberto Martinez to be U.S. Attorney for the Southern District of Florida

*Released May 19*

Fact sheet:
Report of the Presidential Task Force on Los Angeles Recovery

Fact sheet:
American technical assistance programs to Kazakhstan

Fact sheet:
Agreement on trade relations between the United States and Kazakhstan

Fact sheet:
Bilateral investment treaty between the United States and the Republic of Kazakhstan

Fact sheet:
U.S.-Kazakhstan OPIC agreement

Fact sheet:
American humanitarian assistance to Kazakhstan

Transcript:
Press briefing on establishment of the fetal tissue bank—by James O. Mason, Assistant Secretary for Health

Transcript:
Press briefing on the President's meeting with President Nursultan Nazarbayev of Kazakhstan—by Thomas Niles, Assistant Secretary of State for European and Canadian Affairs

*Released May 20*

Announcement:
Nomination of Don J. Svet to be U.S. Attorney for the District of New Mexico

Announcement:
Nomination of members of the Civil Liberties Public Education Fund Board of Directors

*Released May 21*

Announcement:
Appointment of David J. Beightol as Executive Director of the Presidential Task Force on Los Angeles Recovery

*Released May 22*

Fact sheet:
"New Mexico Public Lands Wilderness Act"

*Released May 26*

Fact sheet:
FDA biotechnology food policy

Press briefing on biotechnology food policy—by Louis W. Sullivan, Secretary of Health and Human Services; David Kessler, Commissioner of Food and Drugs; Michael J. Boskin, Chairman, Council of Economic Advisers; and C. Boyden Gray, Counsel to the President

*Released May 27*

Announcement:
Nomination of James A. McIntyre to be U.S. District Judge for the Southern District of California

Statement:
President's meeting with Mayor Teddy Kollek of Jerusalem

*Released May 28*

Advance text:
Excerpt of remarks prepared for delivery to the Veterans Coalition

Fact sheet:
Defense adjustment assistance

Statement:
Presidential Emergency Boards Nos. 220, 221, and 222

*Released May 29*

Fact sheet:
Federal relief assistance to individuals, families, communities, and businesses in Los Angeles, CA

*Released May 30*

Fact sheet:
Wetlands reserve program

*Released June 1*

Announcement:
Nomination of Ritajean Hartung Butterworth to be a member of the Board of Directors of the Corporation for Public Broadcasting

Announcement:
Nomination of Jay I. Kislak to be a member of U.S. Advisory Commission on Public Diplomacy

Fact sheet:
Forests for the Future initiative

Fact sheet:
Bush administration environmental accomplishments in support of UNCED

*Released June 2*

Announcement:
Nomination of C. Christopher Hagy to be U.S. District Judge for the Northern District of Georgia

Announcement:
Nomination of Louis J. Leonatti to be U.S. District Judge for the Eastern District of Missouri

Announcement:
Nomination of J. Douglas Drushal to be U.S. District Judge for the Northern District of Ohio

Announcement:
Nomination of Leonard E. Davis to be U.S. District Judge for the Eastern District of Texas

*Released June 3*

Transcript:
Press briefing on the balanced budget amendment—by Richard G. Darman, Director, Office of Management and Budget

*Released June 4:*

Announcement:
Nomination of Donald M. Kendall to be a member of the Board of Directors of the Overseas Private Investment Corporation

*Released June 5*

Fact sheet:
Space-based global change observation

*Released June 8*

Announcement:
Nomination of J. Michael Farrell to be a member of the National Commission of Libraries and Information Science

*Released June 9*

Transcript:
Excerpt of press briefing on nuclear weapons reductions—by Secretary of State James A. Baker III and Foreign Minister Andrey Kozyrev of Russia

Advance text:
Excerpt of remarks at a fundraising dinner for Senator Arlen Specter in Bowmansdale, PA

*Released June 11*

Advance text:
Remarks on departure for the United Nations Conference on Environment and Development

Advance text:
Remarks at Plaza Belisario Porras in Panama City, Panama

Advance text:
Remarks to the American community in Panama City

Transcript:
Excerpt of press briefing on the demonstrations in Panama City—by Press Secretary Fitzwater

*Released June 12*

Transcript:
Press briefing on the U.N. Conference on Environment and Development—by William K. Reilly, Administrator, Environmental Protection Agency

*Released June 15*

Transcript:
Press briefing on Russian-U.S. relations and the President's meeting with President Boris Yeltsin of Russia—by Secretary of State James A. Baker III

*Released June 16*

Advance text:
Remarks at the state dinner for President Boris Yeltsin of Russia

Fact sheet:
Joint U.S.-Russian Commission on POW/MIA's

*Released June 17*

Announcement:
U.S.-Russian agreements

Text:
Charter for American-Russian Partnership and Friendship

Fact sheet:
Charter for American-Russian Partnership and Friendship

Background:
U.S. assistance to Russia

Background:
Treaty for the avoidance of double taxation

Background:
Agreement on trade relations between the United States and Russia

Background:
Bilateral investment treaty between the United States and the Russian Federation

Background:
Eximbank operations in Russia

Fact sheet:
Fuels and energy agreement

Text:
Joint Statement on bilateral issues

Background:
Open Lands memorandum of understanding between the United States and Russia

Background:
OPIC investment incentive agreement between the United States and the Russian Federation

Background:
Opening new U.S. and Russian consulates

Fact sheet:
Removal of ceilings on U.S. and Russian personnel

Text:
Joint Statement on Bosnia-Hercegovina

Fact sheet:
Chemical weapons issues

Background:
COCOM issues

Text:
Joint Statement on Cooperation in Space

Background:
Agreement on the destruction and safeguarding of weapons and the prevention of weapons proliferation between the United States and Russia

Background:
Agreement on establishing a Peace Corps program between the United States and the Russian Federation

Text:
Joint Statement on Korean Nuclear Non-Proliferation

Fact sheet:
Nuclear reactor safety assistance for Russia

Background:
U.S.-Russian civil aviation M.O.U.

Background:
Technical migration assistance for Russia

Text:
Joint Statement on Beringia International Park

Text:
Joint Statement on Conservation of Lake Baikal

Text:
Joint Statement on the Need for Voluntary Suspension of Fishing in the Central Bering Sea

Text:
Joint Statement on Research and Conservation of the Bering Sea Ecosystem

Text:
Joint Statement on Science and Technology Cooperation

*Released June 18*

Announcement:
Nomination of Raymond L. Finch to be U.S. District Judge for the District Court of the Virgin Islands

*Released June 19*

Fact sheet:
Defense procurement reforms

Announcement:
Nomination of Brook Hedge to be an Associate Judge of the Superior Court of the District of Columbia

Announcement:
Nomination of Lee F. Satterfield to be an Associate Judge of the Superior Court of the District of Columbia

*Released June 20*

Advance text:
Remarks to the Howard Jarvis Taxpayers Association in Universal City, CA

*Released June 23*

Announcement:
Nomination of Katharine J. Armentrout to be U.S. District Judge for the District of Maryland

Announcement:
Nomination of James J. McMonagle to be U.S. District Judge for the Northern District of Ohio

*Released June 24*

Statement:
Rail strike

Transcript:
Press briefing on the budget—by Richard G. Darman, Director, Office of Management and Budget

*Released June 25*

Fact sheet:
Federal grants for State and local "GI bills" for children

Transcript:
Press briefing on legislation proposing a "GI bill" for children—by Secretary of Education Lamar Alexander

*Released June 26*

Fact sheet:
"Utah Public Lands Wilderness Act"

Announcement:
Nomination of John A. Mendez to be U.S. Attorney for the Northern District of California

*Released June 30*

Transcript:
Press briefing on the Munich economic summit—by Secretary of the Treasury Nicholas F. Brady

Statement:
Designation of two historically black colleges for information science and training research under the U.S. Army's Centers of Excellence program

*Released July 1*

Fact sheet:
Recent U.S.-Japan achievements on economic issues

Transcript:
Press briefing on the President's visits to Warsaw, Munich, and Helsinki—by Secretary of State James A. Baker III

Transcript:
Press briefing on the President's meeting with Prime Minister Kiichi Miyazawa of Japan—by Douglas Paal, National Security Council Senior Director for Asian Affairs

*Released July 2*

Transcript:
Press briefing on the President's health care reform proposal—by Louis W. Sullivan, Secretary of Health and Human Services; Gail R. Wilensky, Deputy Assistant to the President for Policy Development; and Stuart Gerson, Assistant Attorney General

Announcement:
Nomination of Richard Conway Casey to be U.S. District Judge for the Southern District of New York

Announcement:
Nomination of John Phil Gilbert to be U.S. District Judge for the Southern District of Illinois

Announcement:
Nomination of Ilana Diamond Rovner to be U.S. Circuit Judge for the Seventh Circuit

Fact sheet:
Medical liability legislation

*Released July 5*

Advance text:
Remarks on Polish independence in Warsaw

Fact sheet:
Enterprise funds

Fact sheet:
Polish stabilization fund

Fact sheet:
New housing assistance for Poland

*Released July 6*

Transcript:
Press briefing on the agreement on construction of a BMW plant in South Carolina—by Gov. Carroll A. Campbell

Transcript:
Press briefing on the meeting of finance ministers at the Munich economic summit—by Nicholas F. Brady, Secretary of the Treasury, and David Mulford, Under Secretary of the Treasury

Transcript:
Press briefing on the meeting of heads of government at the Munich economic summit—by Brent Scowcroft, Assistant to the President for National Security Affairs

Announcement:
Nomination of Larry R. Hicks to be U.S. District Judge for the District of Nevada

Announcement:
Nomination of John W. Sedwick to be U.S. District Judge for the District of Alaska

*Released July 7*

Transcript:
Press briefing on the Munich economic summit—by Secretary of State James A. Baker III

*Released July 9*

Advance text:
Remarks to the Conference on Security and Cooperation in Europe in Helsinki, Finland

Statement:
Announcement of requests for fiscal year 1992 appropriations

Transcript:
Press briefing on the CSCE summit—by Secretary of State James A. Baker III

*Released July 10*

Transcript:
Press briefing on the situation in the former Republic of Yugoslavia—by Secretary of State James A. Baker III

Fact sheet:
The CFE Treaty and the CFE–1A agreement

Fact sheet:
CSCE Forum for Security Cooperation

*Released July 13*

Fact sheet:
Nonproliferation initiative

Fact sheet:
Existing nonproliferation efforts

*Released July 14*

Fact sheet:
Protecting and enhancing forests and the outdoors

Fact sheet:
North American free trade agreement (NAFTA) negotiations

Statement:
Floyd Brown and the Citizens for Bush Organization

Announcement:
Appointment of Jack Steel to be a member of the Commission on Presidential Scholars

*Released July 21*

Announcement:
Nomination of John S. Unpingco to be District Judge for Guam

Fact sheet:
National Medal of Arts

*Released July 22*

Announcement:
National Medal of Arts recipients

Fact sheet:
"Oregon Public Lands Wilderness Act"

*Released July 23*

Transcript:
Press briefing on the Higher Education Amendments of 1992—by Carolynn Reid-Wallace, Assistant Secretary for Postsecondary Education

Transcript:
Press briefing on the midsession review of the budget—by Richard G. Darman, Director, Office of Management and Budget, and Michael J. Boskin, Chairman, Council of Economic Advisers

*Released July 24*

Announcement:
Nomination of Joanna Seybert to be U.S. District Judge for the Eastern District of New York

Announcement:
Nomination of R. Edgar Campbell to be U.S. District Judge for the Middle District of Georgia

*Released July 27*

Announcement:
Nomination of Kathryn H. Vratil to be U.S. District Judge for the District of Kansas

Fact sheet:
"Wyoming Public Lands Wilderness Act"

*Released July 28*

Transcript:
Press briefing on the North American free trade agreement—by Carla A. Hills, U.S. Trade Representative

Transcript:
Press briefing on Operation Triggerlock—by Attorney General William P. Barr

*Released July 30*

Announcement:
Presidential Task Force on Los Angeles Recovery report

*Released July 31*

Announcement:
Nomination of Wayne Allard to serve in an advisory capacity on the Board of Trustees of the James Madison Memorial Fellowship Foundation

Transcript:
Press briefing on welfare reform—by Gail R. Wilensky, Deputy Assistant to the President for Policy Development

# Appendix D—Acts Approved by the President

*Approved February 7*

H.R. 4095 / Public Law 102–244
To increase the number of weeks for which benefits are payable under the Emergency Unemployment Compensation Act of 1991, and for other purposes

*Approved February 14*

H.R. 1989 / Public Law 102–245
American Technology Preeminence Act of 1991

*Approved February 18*

S. 1415 / Public Law 102–246
To provide for additional membership on the Library of Congress Trust Fund Board, and for other purposes

*Approved February 24*

H.R. 2927 / Public Law 102–247
Omnibus Insular Areas Act of 1992

*Approved March 3*

H.R. 543 / Public Law 102–248
To establish the Manzanar National Historic Site in the State of California, and for other purposes

H.R. 476 / Public Law 102–249
Michigan Scenic Rivers Act of 1991

*Approved March 5*

H.R. 355 / Public Law 102–250
Reclamation States Emergency Drought Relief Act of 1991

*Approved March 9*

H.R. 3866 / Public Law 102–251
To provide for the designation of the Flower Garden Banks National Marine Sanctuary

*Approved March 10*

H.J. Res. 395 / Public Law 102–252
Designating February 6, 1992, as "National Women and Girls in Sports Day"

H.J. Res. 350 / Public Law 102–253
Designating March 1992 as "Irish-American Heritage Month"

*Approved March 11*

H.J. Res. 343 / Public Law 102–254
To designate March 12, 1992, as "Girl Scouts of the United States of America 80th Anniversary Day"

*Approved March 12*

H.R. 4113 / Public Law 102–255
To permit the transfer before the expiration of the otherwise applicable 60-day congressional review period of the obsolete training aircraft carrier U.S.S. *Lexington* to the Corpus Christi Area Convention and Visitors Bureau, Corpus Christi, Texas, for use as a naval museum and memorial

H.R. 2092 / Public Law 102–256
Torture Victim Protection Act of 1991

*Approved March 17*

S.J. Res. 176 / Public Law 102–257
To designate March 19, 1992, as "National Women in Agriculture Day"

*Approved March 19*

S. 996 / Public Law 102–258
To authorize and direct the Secretary of the Interior to terminate a reservation of use and occupancy at the Buffalo National River; and for other purposes

S. 2184 / Public Law 102–259
Morris K. Udall Scholarship and Excellence in National Environmental and Native American Public Policy Act of 1992

*Approved March 20*

H.J. Res. 446 / Public Law 102–260
Waiving certain enrollment requirements with respect to H.R. 4210 of the 102d Congress

S. 1467 / Public Law 102–261
To designate the Federal Building and the United States Courthouse located at 15 Lee Street in Montgomery, Alabama, as the "Frank M. Johnson, Jr. Federal Building and United States Courthouse"

S. 1889 / Public Law 102–262
To designate the Federal Building and the
United States Courthouse located at 111 South
Wolcott Street in Casper, Wyoming, as the
"Ewing T. Kerr Federal Building and United
States Courthouse"

S.J. Res. 240 / Public Law 102–263
Designating March 25, 1992, as "Greek Inde-
pendence Day: A National Day of Celebration of
Greek and American Democracy"

*Approved March 26*

H.J. Res. 284 / Public Law 102–264
To designate the week beginning April 12, 1992,
as "National Public Safety Telecommunicators
Week"

S. 2324 / Public Law 102–265
To amend the Food Stamp Act of 1977 to make a
technical correction relating to exclusions from
income under the food stamp program, and for
other purposes

*Approved April 1*

H.J. Res. 456 / Public Law 102–266
Making further continuing appropriations for the
fiscal year 1992, and for other purposes

*Approved April 2*

H.J. Res. 272 / Public Law 102–267
To proclaim March 20, 1992, as "National Agriculture Day"

*Approved April 13*

H.J. Res. 410 / Public Law 102–268
Designating April 14, 1992, as "Education and
Sharing Day, U.S.A."

*Approved April 15*

S.J. Res. 246 / Public Law 102–269
To designate April 15, 1992 as "National Recy-
cling Day"

*Approved April 16*

S.J. Res. 271 / Public Law 102–270
Expressing the sense of the Congress regarding
the peace process in Liberia and authorizing limited assistance to support this process

*Approved April 20*

S. 606 / Public Law 102–271
To amend the Wild and Scenic Rivers Act by
designating certain segments of the Allegheny
River in the Commonwealth of Pennsylvania as a

component of the National Wild and Scenic
Rivers System, and for other purposes

*Approved April 21*

H.R. 3686 / Public Law 102–272
To amend title 28, United States Code, to make
changes in the places of holding court in the
Eastern District of North Carolina

H.R. 4449 / Public Law 102–273
To authorize jurisdictions receiving funds for
fiscal year 1992 under the HOME Investment
Partnerships Act that are allocated for new construction to use the funds, at the discretion of the
jurisdiction, for other eligible activities under
such Act and to amend the Stewart B. McKinney
Homeless Assistance Amendments Act of 1988 to
authorize local governments that have financed
housing projects that have been provided a section 8 financial adjustment factor to use recap-
tured amounts available from refinancing of the
projects for housing activities

S. 985 / Public Law 102–274
Horn of Africa Recovery and Food Security Act

*Approved April 22*

S. 1743 / Public Law 102–275
Arkansas Wild and Scenic Rivers Act of 1992

*Approved April 28*

H.R. 4572 / Public Law 102–276
To direct the Secretary of Health and Human
Services to grant a waiver of the requirement
limiting the maximum number of individuals enrolled with a health maintenance organization
who may be beneficiaries under the medicare or
medicaid programs in order to enable the
Dayton Area Health Plan, Inc., to continue to
provide services through January 1994 to individuals residing in Montgomery County, Ohio, who
are enrolled under a State plan for medical assistance under title XIX of the Social Security Act

H.J. Res. 402 / Public Law 102–277
Approving the location of a memorial to George
Mason

*Approved May 9*

S.J. Res. 174 / Public Law 102–278
Designating the month of May 1992, as "National
Amyotrophic Lateral Sclerosis Awareness Month"

S.J. Res. 222 / Public Law 102–279
To designate 1992 as the "Year of Reconciliation
Between American Indians and non-Indians"

*Approved May 11*

H.J. Res. 430 / Public Law 102–280
To designate May 4, 1992, through May 10, 1992,
as "Public Service Recognition Week"

*Approved May 13*

H.R. 3337 / Public Law 102–281
To require the Secretary of the Treasury to mint
coins in commemoration of the 200th anniversary
of the White House, and for other purposes

H.R. 2454 / Public Law 102–282
Generic Drug Enforcement Act of 1992

*Approved May 14*

H.J. Res. 425 / Public Law 102–283
Designating May 10, 1992, as "Infant Mortality
Awareness Day"

S.J. Res. 251 / Public Law 102–284
To designate the month of May 1992 as "National
Huntington's Disease Awareness Month"

*Approved May 18*

H.R. 2763 / Public Law 102–285
National Geologic Mapping Act of 1992

H.R. 4184 / Public Law 102–286
To designate the Department of Veterans Affairs
Medical Center located in Northampton, Massachusetts, as the "Edward P. Boland Department
of Veterans Affairs Medical Center"

H.J. Res. 466 / Public Law 102–287
Designating April 26, 1992, through May 2, 1992,
as "National Crime Victims' Rights Week"

*Approved May 19*

H.J. Res. 388 / Public Law 102–288
Designating the month of May 1992, as "National
Foster Care Month"

*Approved May 20*

H.R. 4774 / Public Law 102–289
To provide flexibility to the Secretary of Agriculture to carry out food assistance programs in certain countries

H.J. Res. 371 / Public Law 102–290
Designating May 31, 1992, through June 6, 1992,
as a "Week for the National Observance of the
Fiftieth Anniversary of World War II"

S. 2378 / Public Law 102–291
To amend title 38, United States Code, to extend
certain authorities relating to the administration
of veterans laws, and for other purposes

*Approved May 26*

S. 1182 / Public Law 102–292
Fishlake National Forest Enlargement Act

*Approved May 27*

S. 452 / Public Law 102–293
To authorize a transfer of administrative jurisdic-
tion over certain land to the Secretary of the
Interior, and for other purposes

S. 749 / Public Law 102–294
To rename and expand the boundaries of the
Mound City Group National Monument in Ohio

*Approved May 28*

S. 838 / Public Law 102–295
Child Abuse, Domestic Violence, Adoption and
Family Services Act of 1992

S.J. Res. 254 / Public Law 102–296
Commending the New York Stock Exchange on
the occasion of its bicentennial

*Approved June 2*

S. 2569 / Public Law 102–297
To provide for the temporary continuation in
office of the current Deputy Security Advisor in
a flag officer grade in the Navy

*Approved June 4*

H.R. 4990 / Public Law 102–298
Rescinding certain budget authority

*Approved June 9*

S. 870 / Public Law 102–299
Golden Gate National Recreation Area Addition
Act of 1992

*Approved June 15*

H.R. 1917 / Private Law 102–3
For the relief of Michael Wu

*Approved June 16*

S. 2783 / Public Law 102–300
Medical Device Amendments of 1992

*Approved June 19*

H.R. 2556 / Public Law 102–301
Los Padres Condor Range and River Protection
Act

*Approved June 22*

H.R. 5132 / Public Law 102–302
Dire Emergency Supplemental Appropriations Act, 1992, for Disaster Assistance To Meet Urgent Needs Because of Calamities Such as Those Which Occurred in Los Angeles and Chicago

*Approved June 23*

H.J. Res. 445 / Public Law 102–303
Designating June 1992 as "National Scleroderma Awareness Month"

H.R. 1642 / Public Law 102–304
Palo Alto Battlefield National Historic Site Act of 1991

H.J. Res. 442 / Public Law 102–305
To designate July 5, 1992, through July 11, 1992, as "National Awareness Week for Life-Saving Techniques"

*Approved June 26*

H.J. Res. 517 / Public Law 102–306
To provide for a settlement of the railroad labor-management disputes between certain railroads and certain of their employees

S. 756 / Public Law 102–307
Copyright Amendments Act of 1992

S. 2703 / Public Law 102–308
To authorize the President to appoint General Thomas C. Richards to the Office of Administrator of the Federal Aviation Administration

*Approved June 30*

H.J. Res. 470 / Public Law 102–309
To designate the month of September 1992 as "National Spina Bifida Awareness Month"

*Approved July 1*

S. 2905 / Public Law 102–310
To provide a 4-month extension of the transition rule for separate capitalization of savings associations' subsidiaries

*Approved July 2*

H.R. 4548 / Public Law 102–311
International Peacekeeping Act of 1992

H.R. 3041 / Public Law 102–312
To designate the Federal building located at 1520 Market Street, St. Louis, Missouri, as the "L. Douglas Abram Federal Building"

H.R. 2818 / Public Law 102–313
To designate the Federal building located at 78 Center Street in Pittsfield, Massachusetts, as the "Silvio O. Conte Federal Building", and for other purposes

H.R. 3711 / Public Law 102–314
WIC Farmers' Market Nutrition Act of 1992

H.J. Res. 499 / Public Law 102–315
Designating July 2, 1992, as "National Literacy Day"

H.J. Res. 509 / Public 102–316
To extend through September 30, 1992, the period in which there remains available for obligation certain amounts appropriated for the Bureau of Indian Affairs for the school operations costs of Bureau-funded schools

S. 2901 / Public Law 102–317
To direct the Secretary of Health and Human Services to extend the waiver granted to the Tennessee Primary Care Network of the enrollment mix requirement under the medicaid program

*Approved July 3*

H.R. 5260 / Public Law 102–318
Unemployment Compensation Amendments of 1992

*Approved July 8*

H.J. Res. 459 / Public Law 102–319
Designating the week beginning July 26, 1992 as "Lyme Disease Awareness Week"

*Approved July 10*

S. 1254 / Public Law 102–320
To increase the authorized acreage limit for the Assateague Island National Seashore on the Maryland mainland, and for other purposes

S. 1306 / Public Law 102–321
ADAMHA Reorganization Act

*Approved July 19*

H.R. 5412 / Public Law 102–322
To authorize the transfer of certain naval vessels to Greece and Taiwan

*Approved July 20*

S.J. Res. 324 / Public Law 102–323
To commend the NASA Langley Research Center on the celebration of its 75th anniversary on July 17, 1992

*Approved July 22*

S. 2780 / Public Law 102–324
To amend the Food Security Act of 1985 to remove certain easement requirements under the conservation reserve program, and for other purposes

*Approved July 23*

S. 1150 / Public Law 102–325
Higher Education Amendments of 1992

H.R. 158 / Public Law 102–326
To designate the building in Hiddenite, North Carolina, which houses the primary operations of the United States Postal Service as the "Zora Leah S. Thomas Post Office Building"

H.R. 4505 / Public Law 102–327
To designate the facility of the United States Postal Service located at 20 South Montgomery Street in Trenton, New Jersey, as the "Arthur J. Holland United States Post Office Building"

# Appendix E—Proclamations and Executive Orders

*The texts of the proclamations and Executive orders are printed in the Federal Register (F.R.) at the citations listed below. The documents are also printed in title 3 of the Code of Federal Regulations and in the Weekly Compilation of Presidential Documents.*

## PROCLAMATIONS

## EXECUTIVE ORDERS

## Appendix F—Points of Light Recognition Program

The President named the following individuals and institutions as exemplars of his commitment to making community service central to the life and work of every American. The daily recognition program, which began on November 22, 1989, was a national tribute to voluntarism. The recipients for the period covered by this volume are listed in chronological order.

Susan and Terry Brimmer, of St. Petersburg, FL

Annie Smith, of West Hempfield, PA

Hartford School Volunteer Program, of Hartford, CT

Volunteers of the 50th Flying Training Squad, of Columbus, MS

Qadir Aware, of Sioux Falls, SD

Timothy Wolf, of North Canton, OH

Volunteers of the Parent Assistance Center, of Santa Fe, NM

Volunteers of the Age to Age program at Arkansas Tech University, of Russellville, AR

Sun Sounds Radio Reading Service, of Phoenix, AZ

The Community Stewpot, Inc., of Jackson, MS

Hugh Larkins, Jr., of Nashville, TN

Pinellas County Schools Volunteer Program, of Pinellas County, FL

Community Harvest Food Bank, of Fort Wayne, IN

El Centro de la Raza, of Seattle, WA

Volunteers of Fresh Start Surgical Gifts, Inc., of Encinitas, CA

Ricky Lee Reel, of Fort Dodge, IA

Philadelphia Anti-Graffiti Network, of Philadelphia, PA

Volunteers of Project Love, of Bartow, FL

Suzanne Bergen, of Chattanooga, TN

Leroy Shingoitewa, of Moenkopi, AZ

Volunteers of the Arc of Benton County, of Corvallis, OR

Volunteers of Community Friends of Addison County, of Middlebury, VT

James Joseph, of New Orleans, LA

Chris Vig, of Eau Claire, WI

Seniors Helping Others (SHO), of Kingston, RI

John and Donna Steer, of Charlotte, AR

Volunteers of the 24 Hour Crisis Response Team, of Irvine, CA

Betsy Stites, of Longview, TX

Volunteers of Orchard Manor Tenants' Association, of Charleston, WV

Volunteers of Habitat for Humanity, of Harrisburg, PA

Patrick Hughes, of Evanston, IL

Julius C. Mitchell, of Greenville, NC

Thora Shaw, of Webb City, MO

Volunteers of the Minority and Women Chambers' Coalition, of Denver, CO

Volunteers of Health Care Access, Inc., of Lawrence, KS

Volunteers of SUCCESS NOW!, of Wilmington, DE

Kathy Heiple, of Norman, OK

Lillian Smith, of Provo, UT

Bea Gaddy, of Baltimore, MD

Volunteers of Specialink, of Covington, KY

Fred Stavinoha, of Rosenberg, TX

Nicole Bagley, of Alma, GA

Volunteers of the Fort Smith Community Dental Clinic, of Fort Smith, AR

Volunteers of the Lend-A-Hand program, of Boulder City, NV

Volunteers of the Children's Advocacy Center of Sullivan County, of Blountville, TN

Volunteers Services Program of the International Institute of Boston, of Boston, MA

Alice Harris, of Los Angeles, CA

Ron Watson, of Pittsboro, NC

San Antonio Spurs Drug-Free Youth Basketball League, of San Antonio, TX

Donnalee Velvick, of Nampa, ID

Volunteers of Operation: DIGNITY, of Decatur, GA

Volunteers of the Pilot Parent Program, of Omaha, NE

Volunteers of the ServiceMASTER Co. Limited Partnership, of Downers Grove, IL

Volunteers of Samaritan Ministries, of Winston-Salem, NC

Volunteers of the Louisville Chapter of the Elfun Society, of Louisville, KY

*Volunteers of TreeUtah*, of Salt Lake City, UT

*Volunteers of Sojourners' Place, Inc.*, of Wilmington, DE

*Barbara Tschetter*, of Huron, SD

*Volunteers of Parents Anonymous*, of Buffalo and Erie County, NY

*Penny and Chuck Hauer*, of Conner, MT

*Volunteers of the Desert Chapter of the Brandeis University National Women's Committee*, of Palm Springs, CA

*Jenny Richardson*, of Portland, OR

*Volunteers of the Education and Employment Ministry*, of Oklahoma City, OK

*Volunteers and staff of Health Care Network, Inc.*, of Racine, WI

*Jhoon Rhee*, of Arlington, VA

*Volunteers of the R.M. Pyles Boys Camp*, of Valencia, CA

*Tara Holland*, of Tallahassee, FL

*Volunteers of My Guardian Angel*, of Dallas, TX

*Volunteers of Love Outreach*, of Richmond, VA

*Volunteers of the Medical Van Project of the Travelers Aid Society*, of Rhode Island

*Mary Ellen Heron*, of Spokane, WA

*George Milton Bird*, of Shelby, AL

*Keith Sackett*, of Towanda, PA

*Volunteers of the Science & Math Achiever Teams (SMArTeams)*, of New Haven, CT

*Tom Cooper*, of Albuquerque, NM

*Richard Hassell*, of Norfolk, VA

*Volunteers of the Cuban American Bar Association*, of Miami, FL

*Volunteers of St. Mary's Interfaith Dining Room*, of Stockton, CA

*Volunteers of Any Baby Can (ABC), Inc.*, of San Antonio, TX

*Volunteers of the Lunch Buddy Program*, of Olympia, WA

*Joe Sloan*, of Louisville, KY

*Doris Tate*, of Rancho Palos Verdes, CA

*Patricia Mascolo*, of Akron, OH

*Volunteers of the Rotary Reader Program*, of Hilton Head Island, SC

*Volunteers of the Wyoming Colony of Delta Chi Fraternity*, of Laramie, WY

*Anne Johnson*, of Shreveport, LA

*Jerry Thomasson*, of Arvada, CO

*Volunteers of Coakley Proud*, of Harlingen, TX

*Thomas Cooney, Sr.*, of Palm Harbor, FL

*Volunteers of Teen Connections*, of Rapid City, SD

*Volunteers of Kroger Company—Daniel Webster School Partners-in-Education*, of Indianapolis, IN

*Volunteer Victim Advocates*, of Mobile, AL

*Kristin Wunderlie*, of Parma, OH

*Anisa Kintz*, of Conway, SC

*Volunteers of the Mount Rainier Volunteer Network*, of Des Moines, WA

*Vicki Davis*, of Little Rock, AR

*Volunteers of the Vietnam Veterans Leadership Program*, of Pittsburgh, PA

*Volunteers of the Survivors of Crime, Inc.*, of Essex, VT

*Bobby J. Trimble*, of Midland, TX

*Volunteers of the Youth and Elderly Against Crime Project*, of Miami, FL

*Jeff Gower*, of Schenectady, NY

*Volunteers of the Chi Chi Rodriguez Youth Foundation, Inc.*, of Clearwater, FL

*Volunteers of New York City Relief*, of New York, NY

*Employee volunteers of the Community Involvement Team of Trustmark National Bank*, of Hattiesburg, MS

*Rosemarie Williams*, of Riverside, CA

*Volunteers of the Green Mountain Teen Institute Spaulding High School*, of Barre, VT

*Volunteers of Community Outreach of Taylor University*, of Upland, IN

*Maria Santos de Blay*, of Rio Piedras, PR

*Volunteers of Adopt-A-Cub*, of Central, SC

*Challengers Boys and Girls Club*, of Los Angeles, CA

*Ursula Velasquez-Eidschun*, of Tulsa, OK

*Volunteers of Mom's House*, of Johnstown, PA

*Almon Madigan*, of West Granby, CT

*Isabel Peters McMahel*, of Phoenix, AZ

*Girls Inc.*, of St. Louis, MO

*Wes Schollander*, of Winston-Salem, NC

*Volunteers of the Lord's Place*, of West Palm Beach, FL

*Walter Bush*, of Eyota, MN

*Youth Exchanging With Seniors (Y.E.S.)*, of Lubbock, TX

*Rosemary Smith*, of Spartanburg, SC

*Volunteers of Car Care for Elders*, of Spokane, WA

*Volunteers of St. Joseph's Home*, of Cincinnati, OH

*Isis Johnson*, of New Orleans, LA

*Volunteers of the Senior Companion Program*, of Racine, WI

Bruce Mayville, of Rochester, NY

*Volunteers of PPG/Langley Partnership in Education*, of Pittsburgh, PA

*Volunteers of STRIVE, Inc.*, of Newton, NC

*Volunteers of Shepherd Ministries, Inc.*, of Cincinnati, OH

Stephanie Rivard-Lucas, of Houston, TX

*Volunteers of Students and Tutors for the Advancement of Reading Skills (STARS)*, of Ogden, UT

Kay Reibold, of Raleigh, NC

*Volunteers of Ventures in Partnership*, of Lincoln, NE

Marjorie Ward, of Port Huron, MI

Pedro (Pete) Delgadillo, of Corpus Christi, TX

Winifred McKenzie, of Nashville, TN

*Volunteers of the New Life Style Program*, of St. Louis, MO

Irene Dixon-Darnell, of Reno, NV

James Meador, of Shreveport, LA

Jean Marie Davis, of Lemoyne, PA

*Volunteers of the Family Friends Program*, of Hartford, CT

Mehmet Fatin (Fred) Baki, of Mount Dora, FL

*Volunteers of the Wonderland Day Care*, of West Plains, MO

*Volunteers of the Mended Hearts, Inc.*, of Pawtucket, RI

*Volunteers and staff of the Wind River Youth Center*, of Pinedale, WY

Gloria Dessart, of Knoxville, TN

*Volunteers of the Principle Achievers Program*, of Baltimore, MD

*Volunteers of Chrysalis, A Center for Women*, of Minneapolis, MN

*Volunteers of the Alemany Tutorial Project*, of San Francisco, CA

*Volunteers of Religious Community Services, Inc.*, of New Bern, NC

*The Fleenor Family*, of Beckley, WV

*Volunteers of Project SPARK and Project Kindle*, of Rochester, NY

Leanne Rean, of Dover, NH

*Volunteers of the Hahnemann Homeless Clinic*, of Philadelphia, PA

Clara Green, of Carmel, IN

Staci L. Wietrecki, of Mundelein, IL

*Volunteers of the Minority Youth Appreciation Society, Inc.*, of Richmond, VA

*Volunteers of the Center for Group Counseling*, of Boca Raton, FL

*Volunteers of the Elbow Learning Lab*, of Griffin, GA

Larry and Joanne Murphy, of Oneida, WI

Walter "Dean" Adams, of Abilene, TX

Barbara Stark, of Sacramento, CA

*Volunteers of Washington Women's Education and Employment*, of Takoma, WA

Rene and Nancy Bergeron, of Springfield, MO

Beatriz Martinez Salazar, of Carrollton, TX

Gerald Wiley, of Dillingham, AK

Darien Emergency Medical Services, of Darien, CT

Sun Lakes Volunteers, of Sun Lakes, AZ

Susan Dee Sims, of Evansville, IN

*Volunteers of the Central Wyoming Rescue Mission*, Casper, WY

*Volunteers of ACCESS*, of Dearborn, MI

Diane Ulvang, of Fort Collins, CO

*Volunteers of the Community Based Training Program*, of Dubuque, IA

*The Men of ADOBE*, of Benicia, CA

*Phyllis Chunn-Duncan and the Volunteers of Communi-Care*, of Statesville, NC

William Paul Fetzer, of Lebanon, PA

Derrick Thomas, of Independence, MO

*Volunteers of Urban Concern, Inc.*, of Columbus, OH

Thomas Floyd, of Spartanburg, SC

Joseph Thompson, of Topeka, KS

*Volunteers of Reaching the Youth of San Antonio, Inc.*, of San Antonio, TX

Barbara Catherine Connelly, of Shirley, NY

*Volunteers of Ginghamsburg United Methodist Church*, of Tipp City, OH

*Volunteers of Frontline Outreach, Inc.*, of Orlando, FL

Don Davidson, of Lupton, MI

Mary Lemen, of Escondido, CA

*Sun City Center Emergency Squad #1*, of Sun City Center, FL

*Volunteers of Compeer Program*, of Grand Haven, MI

*Volunteers of Haven House Family Services*, of Wayne, NE

*Cicely Ratcliff and volunteers of the Live Now Ministries, Inc.*, of Brownsville, TX

Marc Peretzman, of Bridgeport, CT

Maria Ana Alvarez-Reyes, of Miami, FL

# Subject Index

Abortion—132, 270, 368, 570, 670, 707, 803, 830, 896, 1005, 1032
Academic Decathlon, U.S.—628
ACTION—1227
Administration. *See* other part of subject
Administrative Conference of the U.S.—1214, 1224, 1226, 1235
Advertising Council—738
Advisory. *See* other part of subject
Aeronautics and Space Administration, National—241, 417, 873, 903
Afghanistan, conflict resolution—580
Africa. *See* specific country
African-American (Black) History Month, National—163, 281
African Americans. *See* specific subject; Civil rights
Agency. *See* other part of subject
Aging, Federal Council on the—658, 1239
Agriculture
    Environmental impact—862
    Farming—75, 1043
    International government subsidies—6, 10, 13, 19, 77, 497
    Pesticides—866
    Trade negotiations and agreements. *See* Commerce, international
Agriculture, Department of
    Assistant Secretaries—463, 483, 563
    Budget—1020
    Commodity Credit Corporation—524, 538, 694, 1045
    Deputy Secretary—860, 862, 866
    Drought assistance—389
    Food assistance—705
    Rural Electrification Administration—403
    Secretary—189, 190, 1044, 1049
AID. *See* Development Cooperation Agency, U.S. International
AIDS. *See* Health and medical care
Air Force, Department of the
    Air Force Academy, U.S.—1228
    Assistant Secretary—607
Aircraft. *See* Aviation
Alaska
    Arctic National Wildlife Refuge—191
    Mineral resources, report—314
Albania
    President—936
    Trade with U.S.—807, 885, 936-938
Algeria, Ambassador to U.S.—1226
Ambassadors. *See* specific country
America 2000. *See* Education, quality
American. *See* other part of subject
Angola
    Economic assistance—273

Angola—Continued
    President—1207
    Trade with U.S.—887
    U.S. assistance—1207
Arctic National Wildlife Refuge. *See* Alaska
Arctic Research Commission—1224, 1241, 1246
Arctic Research Policy Committee, Interagency—1219
Argentina, U.S. Ambassador—735
Arizona
    President's visit—841, 843, 1239
    Republican Party events—843, 1239
Arkansas
    Governor—584, 586
    President's visit—464
    Thunderstorms—1249
Arkansas-Oklahoma Arkansas River Compact Commission—1225
Armed Forces, U.S.
    *See also* specific military department; Defense and national security
    Base closings—101, 104, 107, 973
    International role. *See* specific country or region
    Los Angeles civil disturbances—685, 702, 728
    POW-MIA's—482, 933, 935, 943, 946, 957, 1043, 1168
Armenia
    Refugees—839
    Trade with U.S.—540, 885
Arms and munitions
    *See also* Defense and national security; Nuclear weapons
    Arms control negotiations and agreements—134, 158, 243, 346, 575, 963, 1071, 1088, 1108
    Chemical and biological weapons—84, 176, 462, 806, 964, 1124
    Export controls—519
    Missile systems—493
Arms Control and Disarmament Agency, U.S.—798, 1071, 1111
Army, Department of the
    *See also* Armed Forces, U.S.
    Assistant Secretaries—390, 941
    Centers for Excellence programs—1245
    Corps of Engineers—273
Arts and the Humanities, National Foundation on the
    Arts, National Council on the—1223, 1232
    Arts, National Endowment for the—290
    Humanities, National Council on the—1230
    Humanities, National Endowment for the—659
Arts, National Council on the. *See* Arts and the Humanities, National Foundation on the

# Name Index

# Document Categories List